Geometric Formulas

Conversion Between Radians and Degrees: π radians $= 180°$

Triangle	**Circle**	**Sector of Circle**
$A = \frac{1}{2}bh$	$A = \pi r^2$	$A = \frac{1}{2}r^2\theta$ (θ in radians)
$= \frac{1}{2}ab\sin\theta$	$C = 2\pi r$	$s = r\theta$ (θ in radians)

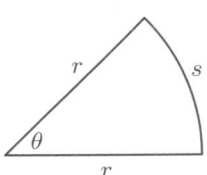

Sphere	**Cylinder**	**Cone**
$V = \frac{4}{3}\pi r^3$ $A = 4\pi r^2$	$V = \pi r^2 h$	$V = \frac{1}{3}\pi r^2 h$

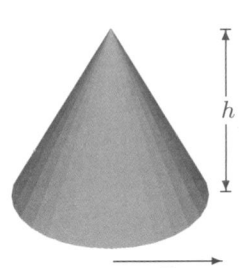

Trigonometric Functions

$$\sin\theta = \frac{y}{r}$$

$$\cos\theta = \frac{x}{r}$$

$$\tan\theta = \frac{y}{x}$$

$$\tan\theta = \frac{\sin\theta}{\cos\theta}$$

$$\cos^2\theta + \sin^2\theta = 1$$

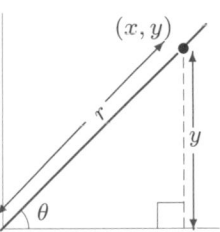

$$\sin(A\pm B) = \sin A\cos B\pm\cos A\sin B$$

$$\cos(A\pm B) = \cos A\cos B\mp\sin A\sin B$$

$$\sin(2A) = 2\sin A\cos A$$

$$\cos(2A) = 2\cos^2 A-1 = 1-2\sin^2 A$$

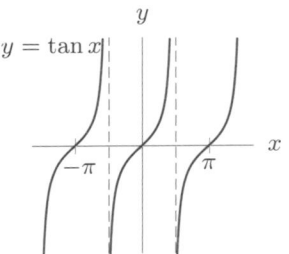

The Binomial Theorem

$$(x + y)^n = x^n + nx^{n-1}y + \frac{n(n-1)}{1\cdot 2}x^{n-2}y^2 + \frac{n(n-1)(n-2)}{1\cdot 2\cdot 3}x^{n-3}y^3 + \cdots + nxy^{n-1} + y^n$$

$$(x - y)^n = x^n - nx^{n-1}y + \frac{n(n-1)}{1\cdot 2}x^{n-2}y^2 - \frac{n(n-1)(n-2)}{1\cdot 2\cdot 3}x^{n-3}y^3 + \cdots \pm nxy^{n-1} \mp y^n$$

CALCULUS

Sixth Edition

CALCULUS

Sixth Edition

Produced by the Calculus Consortium and initially funded by a National Science Foundation Grant.

Deborah Hughes-Hallett
University of Arizona

William G. McCallum
University of Arizona

Andrew M. Gleason
Harvard University

Eric Connally
Harvard University Extension

David Lovelock
University of Arizona

Cody L. Patterson
University of Arizona

Daniel E. Flath
Macalester College

Guadalupe I. Lozano
University of Arizona

Douglas Quinney
University of Keele

Selin Kalaycıoğlu
New York University

Jerry Morris
Sonoma State University

Karen Rhea
University of Michigan

Brigitte Lahme
Sonoma State University

David Mumford
Brown University

Adam H. Spiegler
Loyola University Chicago

Patti Frazer Lock
St. Lawrence University

Brad G. Osgood
Stanford University

Jeff Tecosky-Feldman
Haverford College

David O. Lomen
University of Arizona

Thomas W. Tucker
Colgate University

with the assistance of

Otto K. Bretscher
Colby College

Adrian Iovita
University of Washington

David E. Sloane, MD
Harvard Medical School

Coordinated by

Elliot J. Marks

WILEY

ACQUISITIONS EDITOR	Shannon Corliss
PUBLISHER	Laurie Rosatone
SENIOR EDITORIAL ASSISTANT	Jacqueline Sinacori
DEVELOPMENTAL EDITOR	Anne Scanlan-Rohrer/Two Ravens Editorial
MARKETING MANAGER	Melanie Kurkjian
SENIOR PRODUCT DESIGNER	Tom Kulesa
OPERATIONS MANAGER	Melissa Edwards
ASSOCIATE CONTENT EDITOR	Beth Pearson
SENIOR PRODUCTION EDITOR	Ken Santor
COVER DESIGNER	Madelyn Lesure
COVER AND CHAPTER OPENING PHOTO	©Patrick Zephyr/Patrick Zephyr Nature Photography

Problems from Calculus: The Analysis of Functions, by Peter D. Taylor (Toronto: Wall & Emerson, Inc., 1992). Reprinted with permission of the publisher.

This book was set in Times Roman by the Consortium using TEX, Mathematica, and the package ASTEX, which was written by Alex Kasman. It was printed and bound by R.R. Donnelley / Jefferson City. The cover was printed by R.R. Donnelley.

This book is printed on acid-free paper.

Founded in 1807, John Wiley & Sons, Inc. has been a valued source of knowledge and understanding for more than 200 years, helping people around the world meet their needs and fulfill their aspirations. Our company is built on a foundation of principles that include responsibility to the communities we serve and where we live and work. In 2008, we launched a Corporate Citizenship Initiative, a global effort to address the environmental, social, economic, and ethical challenges we face in our business. Among the issues we are addressing are carbon impact, paper specifications and procurement, ethical conduct within our business and among our vendors, and community and charitable support. For more information, please visit our website: www.wiley.com/go/citizenship.

This material is based upon work supported by the National Science Foundation under Grant No. DUE-9352905. Opinions expressed are those of the authors and not necessarily those of the Foundation.

ISBN-13 cloth 978-0470-88861-2
ISBN-13 binder-ready 978-1118-23114-2

PREFACE

Calculus is one of the greatest achievements of the human intellect. Inspired by problems in astronomy, Newton and Leibniz developed the ideas of calculus 300 years ago. Since then, each century has demonstrated the power of calculus to illuminate questions in mathematics, the physical sciences, engineering, and the social and biological sciences.

Calculus has been so successful both because its central theme—change—is pivotal to an analysis of the natural world and because of its extraordinary power to reduce complicated problems to simple procedures. Therein lies the danger in teaching calculus: it is possible to teach the subject as nothing but procedures—thereby losing sight of both the mathematics and of its practical value. This edition of *Calculus* continues our effort to promote courses in which understanding and computation reinforce each other.

Mathematical Thinking Supported by Theory and Modeling

The first stage in the development of mathematical thinking is the acquisition of a clear intuitive picture of the central ideas. In the next stage, the student learns to reason with the intuitive ideas in plain English. After this foundation has been laid, there is a choice of direction. All students benefit from both theory and modeling, but the balance may differ for different groups. Some students, such as mathematics majors, may prefer more theory, while others may prefer more modeling. For instructors wishing to emphasize the connection between calculus and other fields, the text includes:

- A variety of problems from the **physical sciences** and **engineering**.
- Examples from the **biological sciences** and **economics**.
- Models from the **health sciences** and of **population growth**.
- New problems on **sustainability**.
- New case studies on **medicine** by David E. Sloane, MD.

Origin of the Text

From the beginning, this textbook grew out of a community of mathematics instructors eager to find effective ways for students to learn calculus. This Sixth Edition of *Calculus* reflects the many voices of users at research universities, four-year colleges, community colleges, and secondary schools. Their input and that of our partner disciplines, engineering and the natural and social sciences, continue to shape our work.

Active Learning: Good Problems

As instructors ourselves, we know that interactive classrooms and well-crafted problems promote student learning. Since its inception, the hallmark of our text has been its innovative and engaging problems. These problems probe student understanding in ways often taken for granted. Praised for their creativity and variety, the influence of these problems has extended far beyond the users of our textbook.

The Sixth Edition continues this tradition. Under our approach, which we called the "Rule of Four," ideas are presented graphically, numerically, symbolically, and verbally, thereby encouraging students with a variety of learning styles to expand their knowledge. This edition expands the types of problems available:

- New **Strengthen Your Understanding** problems at the end of every section. These problems ask students to reflect on what they have learned by deciding "What is wrong?" with a statement and to "Give an example" of an idea.
- **ConcepTests** promote active learning in the classroom. These can be used with or without clickers (personal response systems), and have been shown to dramatically improve student learning. Available in a book or on the web at www.wiley.com/college/hughes-hallett.

- **Class Worksheets** allow instructors to engage students in individual or group class-work. Samples are available in the Instructor's Manual, and all are on the web at www.wiley.com/college/hughes-hallett.

- Updated **Data and Models**. For example, Section 11.7 follows the current debate on *Peak Oil Production*, underscoring the importance of mathematics in understanding the world's economic and social problems.

- **Projects** at the end of each chapter provide opportunities for a sustained investigation, often using skills from different parts of the course.

- **Drill Exercises** build student skill and confidence.

- **Online Problems** available in WileyPLUS or WeBWorK, for example. Many problems are randomized, providing students with expanded opportunities for practice with immediate feedback.

Symbolic Manipulation and Technology

To use calculus effectively, students need skill in both symbolic manipulation and the use of technology. The balance between the two may vary, depending on the needs of the students and the wishes of the instructor. The book is adaptable to many different combinations.

The book does not require any specific software or technology. It has been used with graphing calculators, graphing software, and computer algebra systems. Any technology with the ability to graph functions and perform numerical integration will suffice. Students are expected to use their own judgment to determine where technology is useful.

Content

This content represents our vision of how calculus can be taught. It is flexible enough to accommodate individual course needs and requirements. Topics can easily be added or deleted, or the order changed.

Changes to the text in the Sixth Edition are in italics. In all chapters, many new problems were added and others were updated.

Chapter 1: A Library of Functions

This chapter introduces all the elementary functions to be used in the book. Although the functions are probably familiar, the graphical, numerical, verbal, and modeling approach to them may be new. We introduce exponential functions at the earliest possible stage, since they are fundamental to the understanding of real-world processes. The chapter concludes with a section on limits, allowing for a discussion of continuity at a point and on an interval. The section on limits is flexible enough to allow for a brief introduction before derivatives or for a more extensive treatment.

Chapter 2: Key Concept: The Derivative

The purpose of this chapter is to give the student a practical understanding of the definition of the derivative and its interpretation as an instantaneous rate of change. The power rule is introduced; other rules are introduced in Chapter 3.

Chapter 3: Short-Cuts to Differentiation

The derivatives of all the functions in Chapter 1 are introduced, as well as the rules for differentiating products; quotients; and composite, inverse, hyperbolic, and implicitly defined functions.

Chapter 4: Using the Derivative

The aim of this chapter is to enable the student to use the derivative in solving problems, including optimization, graphing, rates, parametric equations, and indeterminate forms. It is not necessary to cover all the sections in this chapter.

To increase access to optimization, many sections of this chapter have been streamlined. Optimization and Modeling are now in Section 4.3, followed by Families of Functions and Modeling in Section 4.4. Upper and lower bounds have been moved to Section 4.2, and geometric optimization is now combined with Optimization and Modeling. Section 4.8 on Parametric Equations is linked to Appendix D, allowing discussion of velocity as a vector.

Chapter 5: Key Concept: The Definite Integral

The purpose of this chapter is to give the student a practical understanding of the definite integral as a limit of Riemann sums and to bring out the connection between the derivative and the definite integral in the Fundamental Theorem of Calculus.

Section 5.3 now includes the application of the Fundamental Theorem of Calculus to the computation of definite integrals. The use of integrals to find averages is now in Section 5.4.

Chapter 6: Constructing Antiderivatives

This chapter focuses on going backward from a derivative to the original function, first graphically and numerically, then analytically. It introduces the Second Fundamental Theorem of Calculus and the concept of a differential equation.

Section 6.3 on Differential Equations and Motion contains the material from the former Section 6.5.

Chapter 7: Integration

This chapter includes several techniques of integration, including substitution, parts, partial fractions, and trigonometric substitutions; others are included in the table of integrals. There are discussions of numerical methods and of improper integrals.

Section 7.4 now includes the use of triangles to help students visualize a trigonometric substitution. The two former sections on numerical methods have been combined into Section 7.5.

Chapter 8: Using the Definite Integral

This chapter emphasizes the idea of subdividing a quantity to produce Riemann sums which, in the limit, yield a definite integral. It shows how the integral is used in geometry, physics, economics, and probability; polar coordinates are introduced. It is not necessary to cover all the sections in this chapter.

Chapter 9: Sequences and Series

This chapter focuses on sequences, series of constants, and convergence. It includes the integral, ratio, comparison, limit comparison, and alternating series tests. It also introduces geometric series and general power series, including their intervals of convergence.

Chapter 10: Approximating Functions

This chapter introduces Taylor Series and Fourier Series using the idea of approximating functions by simpler functions.

Chapter 11: Differential Equations

This chapter introduces differential equations. The emphasis is on qualitative solutions, modeling, and interpretation.

Section 11.7 on Logistic Models (formerly on population models) has been rewritten around the thought-provoking predictions of peak oil production. This section encourages students to use the skills learned earlier in the course to analyze a problem of global importance. Sections 11.10 and 11.11 on Second Order Differential Equations are now on the web at www.wiley.com/college/hughes-hallett.

Chapter 12: Functions of Several Variables

This chapter introduces functions of many variables from several points of view, using surface graphs, contour diagrams, and tables. We assume throughout that functions of two or more variables are defined on regions with piecewise smooth boundaries. We conclude with a section on continuity.

Chapter 13: A Fundamental Tool: Vectors

This chapter introduces vectors geometrically and algebraically and discusses the dot and cross product.

Chapter 14: Differentiating Functions of Several Variables

Partial derivatives, directional derivatives, gradients, and local linearity are introduced. The chapter also discusses higher order partial derivatives, quadratic Taylor approximations, and differentiability.

Chapter 15: Optimization

The ideas of the previous chapter are applied to optimization problems, both constrained and unconstrained.

Chapter 16: Integrating Functions of Several Variables

This chapter discusses double and triple integrals in Cartesian, polar, cylindrical, and spherical coordinates.
The former Section 16.7 has been moved to the new Chapter 21.

Chapter 17: Parameterization and Vector Fields

This chapter discusses parameterized curves and motion, vector fields and flowlines.
The former Section 17.5 has been moved to the new Chapter 21.

Chapter 18: Line Integrals

This chapter introduces line integrals and shows how to calculate them using parameterizations. Conservative fields, gradient fields, the Fundamental Theorem of Calculus for Line Integrals, and Green's Theorem are discussed.

Chapter 19: Flux Integrals and Divergence

This chapter introduces flux integrals and shows how to calculate them over surface graphs, portions of cylinders, and portions of spheres. The divergence is introduced and its relationship to flux integrals discussed in the Divergence Theorem.
This new chapter combines Sections 19.1 and 19.2 with Sections 20.1 and 20.2 from the fifth edition

Chapter 20: The Curl and Stokes' Theorem

The purpose of this chapter is to give students a practical understanding of the curl and of Stokes' Theorem and to lay out the relationship between the theorems of vector calculus.
This chapter consists of Sections 20.3–20.5 from the fifth edition.

Chapter 21: Parameters, Coordinates, and Integrals

This new chapter covers parameterized surfaces, the change of variable formula in a double or triple integral, and flux though a parameterized surface.

Appendices

There are appendices on roots, accuracy, and bounds; complex numbers; Newton's Method; and determinants.

Projects

There are new projects in Chapter 12: "Heathrow"; Chapter 19: "Solid Angle"; and Chapter 20: "Magnetic field generated by a current in a wire".

Choice of Paths: Lean or Expanded

For those who prefer the lean topic list of earlier editions, we have kept clear the main conceptual paths. For example,

- The Key Concept chapters on the derivative and the definite integral (Chapters 2 and 5) can be covered at the outset of the course, right after Chapter 1.

- Limits and Continuity (Sections 1.7 and 1.8) can be covered in depth before the introduction of the derivative (Sections 2.1 and 2.2), or after.
- Approximating Functions Using Series (Chapter 10) can be covered before, or without, Chapter 9.
- In Chapter 4 (Using the Derivative), instructors can select freely from Sections 4.3–4.8.
- Chapter 8 (Using the Definite Integral) contains a wide range of applications. Instructors can select one or two to do in detail.

Supplementary Materials and Additional Resources

Supplements for the instructor can be obtained online at the book companion site or by contacting your Wiley representative. The following supplementary materials are available for this edition:

- **Instructor's Manual** containing teaching tips, calculator programs, overhead transparency masters, sample worksheets, and sample syllabi.
- **Computerized Test Bank**, comprised of nearly 7,000 questions, mostly algorithmically-generated, which allows for multiple versions of a single test or quiz.
- **Instructor's Solution Manual** with complete solutions to all problems.
- **Student Solution Manual** with complete solutions to half the odd-numbered problems.
- **Additional Material**, elaborating specially marked points in the text and password-protected electronic versions of the instructor ancillaries, can be found on the web at www.wiley.com/college/hughes-hallett.

ConcepTests

ConcepTests, modeled on the pioneering work of Harvard physicist Eric Mazur, are questions designed to promote active learning during class, particularly (but not exclusively) in large lectures. Our evaluation data show students taught with ConcepTests outperformed students taught by traditional lecture methods 73% versus 17% on conceptual questions, and 63% versus 54% on computational problems.

Faculty Resource Network

A peer-to-peer network of academic faculty dedicated to the effective use of technology in the classroom, this group can help you apply innovative classroom techniques and implement specific software packages. Visit www.facultyresourcenetwork.com or speak to your Wiley representative.

WileyPLUS

WileyPLUS, Wiley's digital learning environment, is loaded with all of the supplements above, and also features:

- Online version of the text, featuring hyperlinks to referenced content, applets, and supplements.
- Homework management tools, which enable the instructor to assign questions easily and grade them automatically, using a rich set of options and controls.
- QuickStart pre-designed reading and homework assignments. Use them as-is or customize them to fit the needs of your classroom.
- Guided Online (GO) Exercises, which prompt students to build solutions step by step. Rather than simply grading an exercise answer as wrong, GO problems show students precisely where they are making a mistake.
- Animated applets, which can be used in class to present and explore key ideas graphically and dynamically—especially useful for display of three-dimensional graphs in multivariable calculus.
- Algebra & Trigonometry Refresher material, which provide students with an opportunity to brush up on material necessary to master Calculus, as well as to determine areas that require further review.
- Graphing Calculator Manual, to help students get the most out of their graphing calculators, and to show how they can apply the numerical and graphing functions of their calculators to their study of calculus.

AP Teacher's Guide

The AP Guide, written by experienced AP teachers, provides day-by-day syllabi for AB and BC Calculus, sample multiple choice questions, a listing of the past 25 years of AP free-response questions by chapter of the text, teaching tips, and labs to encourage student exploration of concepts.

Acknowledgements

First and foremost, we want to express our appreciation to the National Science Foundation for their faith in our ability to produce a revitalized calculus curriculum and, in particular, to our program officers, Louise Raphael, John Kenelly, John Bradley, and James Lightbourne. We also want to thank the members of our Advisory Board, Benita Albert, Lida Barrett, Simon Bernau, Robert Davis, M. Lavinia DeConge-Watson, John Dossey, Ron Douglas, Eli Fromm, William Haver, Seymour Parter, John Prados, and Stephen Rodi.

In addition, a host of other people around the country and abroad deserve our thanks for their contributions to shaping this edition. They include: Huriye Arikan, Ruth Baruth, Paul Blanchard, Lewis Blake, David Bressoud, Stephen Boyd, Lucille Buonocore, Jo Cannon, Ray Cannon, Phil Cheifetz, Scott Clark, Jailing Dai, Ann Davidian, Tom Dick, Srdjan Divac, Tevian Dray, Steven Dunbar, David Durlach, John Eggers, Wade Ellis, Johann Engelbrecht, Brad Ernst, Sunny Fawcett, Paul Feehan, Sol Friedberg, Melanie Fulton, Tom Gearhart, David Glickenstein, Chris Goff, Sheldon P. Gordon, Salim Haïdar, Elizabeth Hentges, Rob Indik, Adrian Iovita, David Jackson, Sue Jensen, Alex Kasman, Matthias Kawski, Mike Klucznik, Donna Krawczyk, Stephane Lafortune, Andrew Lawrence, Carl Leinert, Andrew Looms, Bin Lu, Alex Mallozzi, Corinne Manogue, Jay Martin, Eric Mazur, Abby McCallum, Dan McGee, Ansie Meiring, Lang Moore, Jerry Morris, Hideo Nagahashi, Kartikeya Nagendra, Alan Newell, Steve Olson, John Orr, Arnie Ostebee, Andrew Pasquale, Wayne Raskind, Maria Robinson, Laurie Rosatone, Ayse Sahin, Nataliya Sandler, Ken Santor, Anne Scanlan-Rohrer, Ellen Schmierer, Michael Sherman, Pat Shure, Scott Pilzer, David Smith, Ernie Solheid, Misha Stepanov, Steve Strogatz, Peter Taylor, Dinesh Thakur, Sally Thomas, Joe Thrash, Alan Tucker, Doug Ulmer, Ignatios Vakalis, Bill Vélez, Joe Vignolini, Stan Wagon, Hannah Winkler, Debra Wood, Aaron Wootton, Deane Yang, Bruce Yoshiwara, Kathy Yoshiwara, and Paul Zorn.

Reports from the following reviewers were most helpful for the fifth edition:
Lewis Blake, Patrice Conrath, Christopher Ennis, John Eggers, Paul DeLand, Dana Fine, Dave Folk, Elizabeth Hodes, Richard Jenson, Emelie Kenney, Michael Kinter, Douglas Lapp, Glenn Ledder, Eric Marland, Cindy Moss, Michael Naylor, Genevra Neumann, Dennis Piontkowski, Robert Reed, Laurence Small, Ed Soares, Diana Staats, Kurt Verdeber, Elizabeth Wilcox, and Deborah Yoklic.

Reports from the following reviewers were most helpful for the sixth edition:
Barbara Armenta, James Baglama, Jon Clauss, Ann Darke, Marcel Finan, Dana Fine, Michael Huber, Greg Marks, Wes Ostertag, Ben Smith, Mark Turner, Aaron Weinberg, and Jianying Zhang.

Deborah Hughes-Hallett	Brigitte Lahme	Cody L. Patterson
Andrew M. Gleason	Patti Frazer Lock	Douglas Quinney
William G. McCallum	David O. Lomen	Karen Rhea
Eric Connally	David Lovelock	Adam Spiegler
Daniel E. Flath	Guadalupe I. Lozano	Jeff Tecosky-Feldman
Selin Kalaycıoğlu	Brad G. Osgood	Thomas W. Tucker

To Students: How to Learn from this Book

- This book may be different from other math textbooks that you have used, so it may be helpful to know about some of the differences in advance. This book emphasizes at every stage the *meaning* (in practical, graphical or numerical terms) of the symbols you are using. There is much less emphasis on "plug-and-chug" and using formulas, and much more emphasis on the interpretation of these formulas than you may expect. You will often be asked to explain your ideas in words or to explain an answer using graphs.

- The book contains the main ideas of calculus in plain English. Your success in using this book will depend on your reading, questioning, and thinking hard about the ideas presented. Although you may not have done this with other books, you should plan on reading the text in detail, not just the worked examples.

- There are very few examples in the text that are exactly like the homework problems. This means that you can't just look at a homework problem and search for a similar–looking "worked out" example. Success with the homework will come by grappling with the ideas of calculus.

- Many of the problems that we have included in the book are open-ended. This means that there may be more than one approach and more than one solution, depending on your analysis. Many times, solving a problem relies on common sense ideas that are not stated in the problem but which you will know from everyday life.

- Some problems in this book assume that you have access to a graphing calculator or computer. There are many situations where you may not be able to find an exact solution to a problem, but you can use a calculator or computer to get a reasonable approximation.

- This book attempts to give equal weight to four methods for describing functions: graphical (a picture), numerical (a table of values) algebraic (a formula), and verbal. Sometimes you may find it easier to translate a problem given in one form into another. The best idea is to be flexible about your approach: if one way of looking at a problem doesn't work, try another.

- Students using this book have found discussing these problems in small groups very helpful. There are a great many problems which are not cut-and-dried; it can help to attack them with the other perspectives your colleagues can provide. If group work is not feasible, see if your instructor can organize a discussion session in which additional problems can be worked on.

- You are probably wondering what you'll get from the book. The answer is, if you put in a solid effort, you will get a real understanding of one of the most important accomplishments of the millennium—calculus—as well as a real sense of the power of mathematics in the age of technology.

CONTENTS

4 USING THE DERIVATIVE   185

5 KEY CONCEPT: THE DEFINITE INTEGRAL   271

6 CONSTRUCTING ANTIDERIVATIVES   319

11 DIFFERENTIAL EQUATIONS   585

12 FUNCTIONS OF SEVERAL VARIABLES   665

13 A FUNDAMENTAL TOOL: VECTORS   717

14 DIFFERENTIATING FUNCTIONS OF SEVERAL VARIABLES 757

15 OPTIMIZATION: LOCAL AND GLOBAL EXTREMA 829

16 INTEGRATING FUNCTIONS OF SEVERAL VARIABLES 867

21 PARAMETERS, COORDINATES, AND INTEGRALS   1073

APPENDIX   1095

READY REFERENCE   1123

ANSWERS TO ODD-NUMBERED PROBLEMS   1141

INDEX   1205

Chapter One

A LIBRARY OF FUNCTIONS

Contents

1.1 FUNCTIONS AND CHANGE

In mathematics, a *function* is used to represent the dependence of one quantity upon another.

Let's look at an example. Syracuse, New York has the highest annual snowfall of any US city because of the "lake effect" snow coming from cold Northwest winds blowing over nearby Lake Erie. Lake effect snowfall has been heavier over the last few decades; some have suggested this is due to the warming of Lake Erie by climate change. In December 2010, Syracuse got 66.9 inches of snow in one 12 day period, all of it from lake effect snow. See Table 1.1.

Table 1.1 *Daily snowfall in Syracuse, December 5–16, 2010*

Date (December 2010)	5	6	7	8	9	10	11	12	13	14	15	16
Snowfall in inches	6.8	12.2	9.3	14.9	1.9	0.1	0.0	0.0	1.4	5.0	11.9	3.4

You may not have thought of something so unpredictable as daily snowfall as being a function, but it *is* a function of date, because each day gives rise to one snowfall total. There is no formula for the daily snowfall (otherwise we would not need a weather bureau), but nevertheless the daily snowfall in Syracuse does satisfy the definition of a function: Each date, t, has a unique snowfall, S, associated with it.

We define a function as follows:

> A **function** is a rule that takes certain numbers as inputs and assigns to each a definite output number. The set of all input numbers is called the **domain** of the function and the set of resulting output numbers is called the **range** of the function.

The input is called the *independent variable* and the output is called the *dependent variable*. In the snowfall example, the domain is the set of December dates $\{5, 6, 7, 8, 9, 10, 11, 12, 13, 14, 15, 16\}$ and the range is the set of daily snowfalls $\{0.0, 0.1, 1.4, 1.9, 3.4, 5.0, 6.8, 9.3, 11.9, 12.2, 14.9\}$. We call the function f and write $S = f(t)$. Notice that a function may have identical outputs for different inputs (December 11 and 12, for example).

Some quantities, such as date, are *discrete*, meaning they take only certain isolated values (dates must be integers). Other quantities, such as time, are *continuous* as they can be any number. For a continuous variable, domains and ranges are often written using interval notation:

The set of numbers t such that $a \leq t \leq b$ is called a *closed interval* and written $[a, b]$.

The set of numbers t such that $a < t < b$ is called an *open interval* and written (a, b).

The Rule of Four: Tables, Graphs, Formulas, and Words

Functions can be represented by tables, graphs, formulas, and descriptions in words. For example, the function giving the daily snowfall in Syracuse can be represented by the graph in Figure 1.1, as well as by Table 1.1.

Figure 1.1: Syracuse snowfall, December, 2010

As another example of a function, consider the snow tree cricket. Surprisingly enough, all such crickets chirp at essentially the same rate if they are at the same temperature. That means that the chirp rate is a function of temperature. In other words, if we know the temperature, we can determine the chirp rate. Even more surprisingly, the chirp rate, C, in chirps per minute, increases steadily with the temperature, T, in degrees Fahrenheit, and can be computed by the formula

$$C = 4T - 160$$

to a fair degree of accuracy. We write $C = f(T)$ to express the fact that we think of C as a function of T and that we have named this function f. The graph of this function is in Figure 1.2.

Figure 1.2: Cricket chirp rate versus temperature

Examples of Domain and Range

If the domain of a function is not specified, we usually take it to be the largest possible set of real numbers. For example, we usually think of the domain of the function $f(x) = x^2$ as all real numbers. However, the domain of the function $g(x) = 1/x$ is all real numbers except zero, since we cannot divide by zero.

Sometimes we restrict the domain to be smaller than the largest possible set of real numbers. For example, if the function $f(x) = x^2$ is used to represent the area of a square of side x, we restrict the domain to nonnegative values of x.

Example 1   The function $C = f(T)$ gives chirp rate as a function of temperature. We restrict this function to temperatures for which the predicted chirp rate is positive, and up to the highest temperature ever recorded at a weather station, 136°F. What is the domain of this function f?

Solution   If we consider the equation

$$C = 4T - 160$$

simply as a mathematical relationship between two variables C and T, any T value is possible. However, if we think of it as a relationship between cricket chirps and temperature, then C cannot be less than 0. Since $C = 0$ leads to $0 = 4T - 160$, and so $T = 40°F$, we see that T cannot be less than 40°F. (See Figure 1.2.) In addition, we are told that the function is not defined for temperatures above 136°. Thus, for the function $C = f(T)$ we have

$$\text{Domain} = \text{All } T \text{ values between } 40°F \text{ and } 136°F$$
$$= \text{All } T \text{ values with } 40 \leq T \leq 136$$
$$= [40, 136].$$

Example 2   Find the range of the function f, given the domain from Example 1. In other words, find all possible values of the chirp rate, C, in the equation $C = f(T)$.

Solution   Again, if we consider $C = 4T - 160$ simply as a mathematical relationship, its range is all real C values. However, when thinking of the meaning of $C = f(T)$ for crickets, we see that the function predicts cricket chirps per minute between 0 (at $T = 40°F$) and 384 (at $T = 136°F$). Hence,

$$\text{Range} = \text{All } C \text{ values from 0 to 384}$$
$$= \text{All } C \text{ values with } 0 \leq C \leq 384$$
$$= [0, 384].$$

In using the temperature to predict the chirp rate, we thought of the temperature as the *independent variable* and the chirp rate as the *dependent variable*. However, we could do this backward, and calculate the temperature from the chirp rate. From this point of view, the temperature is dependent on the chirp rate. Thus, which variable is dependent and which is independent may depend on your viewpoint.

Linear Functions

The chirp-rate function, $C = f(T)$, is an example of a *linear function*. A function is linear if its slope, or rate of change, is the same at every point. The rate of change of a function that is not linear may vary from point to point.

Olympic and World Records

During the early years of the Olympics, the height of the men's winning pole vault increased approximately 8 inches every four years. Table 1.2 shows that the height started at 130 inches in 1900, and increased by the equivalent of 2 inches a year. So the height was a linear function of time from 1900 to 1912. If y is the winning height in inches and t is the number of years since 1900, we can write

$$y = f(t) = 130 + 2t.$$

Since $y = f(t)$ increases with t, we say that f is an *increasing function*. The coefficient 2 tells us the rate, in inches per year, at which the height increases.

Table 1.2 *Men's Olympic pole vault winning height (approximate)*

Year	1900	1904	1908	1912
Height (inches)	130	138	146	154

This rate of increase is the *slope* of the line in Figure 1.3. The slope is given by the ratio

$$\text{Slope} = \frac{\text{Rise}}{\text{Run}} = \frac{146 - 138}{8 - 4} = \frac{8}{4} = 2 \text{ inches/year.}$$

Calculating the slope (rise/run) using any other two points on the line gives the same value.

What about the constant 130? This represents the initial height in 1900, when $t = 0$. Geometrically, 130 is the *intercept* on the vertical axis.

Figure 1.3: Olympic pole vault records

You may wonder whether the linear trend continues beyond 1912. Not surprisingly, it doesn't exactly. The formula $y = 130 + 2t$ predicts that the height in the 2008 Olympics would be 346 inches or 28 feet 10 inches, which is considerably higher than the actual value of 19 feet 6.65 inches. There is clearly a danger in *extrapolating* too far from the given data. You should also observe that the data in Table 1.2 is discrete, because it is given only at specific points (every four years). However, we have treated the variable t as though it were continuous, because the function $y = 130 + 2t$ makes sense for all values of t. The graph in Figure 1.3 is of the continuous function because it is a solid line, rather than four separate points representing the years in which the Olympics were held.

As the pole vault heights have increased over the years, the time to run the mile has decreased. If y is the world record time to run the mile, in seconds, and t is the number of years since 1900, then records show that, approximately,

$$y = g(t) = 260 - 0.39t.$$

The 260 tells us that the world record was 260 seconds in 1900 (at $t = 0$). The slope, -0.39, tells us that the world record decreased by about 0.39 seconds per year. We say that g is a *decreasing function*.

Difference Quotients and Delta Notation

We use the symbol Δ (the Greek letter capital delta) to mean "change in," so Δx means change in x and Δy means change in y.

The slope of a linear function $y = f(x)$ can be calculated from values of the function at two points, given by x_1 and x_2, using the formula

$$m = \frac{\text{Rise}}{\text{Run}} = \frac{\Delta y}{\Delta x} = \frac{f(x_2) - f(x_1)}{x_2 - x_1}.$$

The quantity $(f(x_2) - f(x_1))/(x_2 - x_1)$ is called a *difference quotient* because it is the quotient of two differences. (See Figure 1.4.) Since $m = \Delta y/\Delta x$, the units of m are y-units over x-units.

Figure 1.4: Difference quotient $= \dfrac{f(x_2) - f(x_1)}{x_2 - x_1}$

Families of Linear Functions

A **linear function** has the form

$$y = f(x) = b + mx.$$

Its graph is a line such that
- m is the **slope**, or rate of change of y with respect to x.
- b is the **vertical intercept**, or value of y when x is zero.

Notice that if the slope, m, is zero, we have $y = b$, a horizontal line.

To recognize that a table of x and y values comes from a linear function, $y = b + mx$, look for differences in y-values that are constant for equally spaced x-values.

Formulas such as $f(x) = b + mx$, in which the constants m and b can take on various values, give a *family of functions*. All the functions in a family share certain properties—in this case, all the graphs are straight lines. The constants m and b are called *parameters*; their meaning is shown in Figures 1.5 and 1.6. Notice that the greater the magnitude of m, the steeper the line.

Figure 1.5: The family $y = mx$ (with $b = 0$)   **Figure 1.6**: The family $y = b + x$ (with $m = 1$)

Increasing versus Decreasing Functions

The terms increasing and decreasing can be applied to other functions, not just linear ones. See Figure 1.7. In general,

> A function f is **increasing** if the values of $f(x)$ increase as x increases.
> A function f is **decreasing** if the values of $f(x)$ decrease as x increases.
>
> The graph of an *increasing* function *climbs* as we move from left to right.
> The graph of a *decreasing* function *falls* as we move from left to right.
>
> A function $f(x)$ is **monotonic** if it increases for all x or decreases for all x.

Increasing   Decreasing

Figure 1.7: Increasing and decreasing functions

Proportionality

A common functional relationship occurs when one quantity is *proportional* to another. For example, the area, A, of a circle is proportional to the square of the radius, r, because

$$A = f(r) = \pi r^2.$$

> We say y is (directly) **proportional** to x if there is a nonzero constant k such that
>
> $$y = kx.$$
> This k is called the constant of proportionality.

We also say that one quantity is *inversely proportional* to another if one is proportional to the reciprocal of the other. For example, the speed, v, at which you make a 50-mile trip is inversely proportional to the time, t, taken, because v is proportional to $1/t$:

$$v = 50 \left(\frac{1}{t} \right) = \frac{50}{t}.$$

Exercises and Problems for Section 1.1

Exercises

1. The population of a city, P, in millions, is a function of t, the number of years since 1970, so $P = f(t)$. Explain the meaning of the statement $f(35) = 12$ in terms of the population of this city.

2. The pollutant PCB (polychlorinated biphenyl) affects the thickness of pelican eggs. Thinking of the thickness, T, of the eggs, in mm, as a function of the concentration, P, of PCBs in ppm (parts per million), we have $T = f(P)$. Explain the meaning of $f(200)$ in terms of thickness of pelican eggs and concentration of PCBs.

3. Describe what Figure 1.8 tells you about an assembly line whose productivity is represented as a function of the number of workers on the line.

Figure 1.8

For Exercises 4–7, find an equation for the line that passes through the given points.

4. $(0, 0)$ and $(1, 1)$ 5. $(0, 2)$ and $(2, 3)$

6. $(-2, 1)$ and $(2, 3)$ 7. $(-1, 0)$ and $(2, 6)$

For Exercises 8–11, determine the slope and the y-intercept of the line whose equation is given.

8. $2y + 5x - 8 = 0$ 9. $7y + 12x - 2 = 0$

10. $-4y + 2x + 8 = 0$ 11. $12x = 6y + 4$

12. Match the graphs in Figure 1.9 with the following equations. (Note that the x and y scales may be unequal.)

    (a) $y = x - 5$ (b) $-3x + 4 = y$
    (c) $5 = y$ (d) $y = -4x - 5$
    (e) $y = x + 6$ (f) $y = x/2$

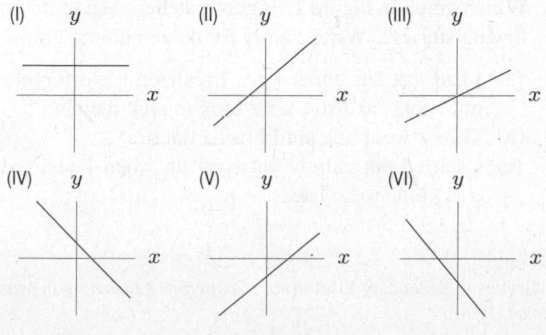

Figure 1.9

13. Match the graphs in Figure 1.10 with the following equations. (Note that the x and y scales may be unequal.)

    (a) $y = -2.72x$ (b) $y = 0.01 + 0.001x$
    (c) $y = 27.9 - 0.1x$ (d) $y = 0.1x - 27.9$
    (e) $y = -5.7 - 200x$ (f) $y = x/3.14$

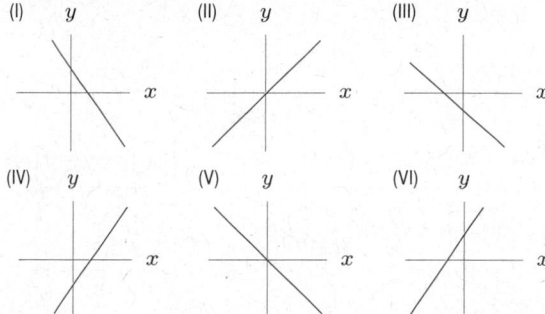

Figure 1.10

14. Estimate the slope and the equation of the line in Figure 1.11.

Figure 1.11

15. Find an equation for the line with slope m through the point (a, c).

16. Find a linear function that generates the values in Table 1.3.

Table 1.3

x	5.2	5.3	5.4	5.5	5.6
y	27.8	29.2	30.6	32.0	33.4

For Exercises 17–19, use the facts that parallel lines have equal slopes and that the slopes of perpendicular lines are negative reciprocals of one another.

17. Find an equation for the line through the point $(2, 1)$ which is perpendicular to the line $y = 5x - 3$.

18. Find equations for the lines through the point $(1, 5)$ that are parallel to and perpendicular to the line with equation $y + 4x = 7$.

19. Find equations for the lines through the point (a, b) that are parallel and perpendicular to the line $y = mx + c$, assuming $m \neq 0$.

For Exercises 20–23, give the approximate domain and range of each function. Assume the entire graph is shown.

20.

21.

22.

23.

Find domain and range in Exercises 24–25.

24. $y = x^2 + 2$

25. $y = \dfrac{1}{x^2 + 2}$

26. If $f(t) = \sqrt{t^2 - 16}$, find all values of t for which $f(t)$ is a real number. Solve $f(t) = 3$.

In Exercises 27–31, write a formula representing the function.

27. The volume of a sphere is proportional to the cube of its radius, r.

28. The average velocity, v, for a trip over a fixed distance, d, is inversely proportional to the time of travel, t.

29. The strength, S, of a beam is proportional to the square of its thickness, h.

30. The energy, E, expended by a swimming dolphin is proportional to the cube of the speed, v, of the dolphin.

31. The number of animal species, N, of a certain body length, l, is inversely proportional to the square of l.

Problems

In Problems 32–35 the function $S = f(t)$ gives the average annual sea level, S, in meters, in Aberdeen, Scotland,[1] as a function of t, the number of years before 2008. Write a mathematical expression that represents the given statement.

32. In 1983 the average annual sea level in Aberdeen was 7.019 meters.

33. The average annual sea level in Aberdeen in 2008.

34. The average annual sea level in Aberdeen was the same in 1865 and 1911.

35. The average annual sea level in Aberdeen increased by 1 millimeter from 2007 to 2008.

36. In December 2010, the snowfall in Minneapolis was unusually high,[2] leading to the collapse of the roof of the Metrodome. Figure 1.12 gives the snowfall, S, in Minneapolis for December 6–15, 2010.

(a) How do you know that the snowfall data represents a function of date?

(b) Estimate the snowfall on December 12.

(c) On which day was the snowfall more than 10 inches?

(d) During which consecutive two-day interval was the increase in snowfall largest?

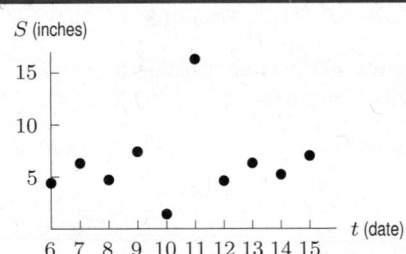

Figure 1.12

37. The value of a car, $V = f(a)$, in thousands of dollars, is a function of the age of the car, a, in years.

(a) Interpret the statement $f(5) = 6$

(b) Sketch a possible graph of V against a. Is f an increasing or decreasing function? Explain.

(c) Explain the significance of the horizontal and vertical intercepts in terms of the value of the car.

38. Which graph in Figure 1.13 best matches each of the following stories?[3] Write a story for the remaining graph.

(a) I had just left home when I realized I had forgotten my books, and so I went back to pick them up.

(b) Things went fine until I had a flat tire.

(c) I started out calmly but sped up when I realized I was going to be late.

[1] www.decc.gov.uk, accessed June 2011

[2] http://www.crh.noaa.gov/mpx/Climate/DisplayRecords.php

[3] Adapted from Jan Terwel, "Real Math in Cooperative Groups in Secondary Education." *Cooperative Learning in Mathematics*, ed. Neal Davidson, p. 234 (Reading: Addison Wesley, 1990).

Figure 1.13

39. An object is put outside on a cold day at time $t = 0$. Its temperature, $H = f(t)$, in °C, is graphed in Figure 1.14.

   (a) What does the statement $f(30) = 10$ mean in terms of temperature? Include units for 30 and for 10 in your answer.
   (b) Explain what the vertical intercept, a, and the horizontal intercept, b, represent in terms of temperature of the object and time outside.

Figure 1.14

40. A rock is dropped from a window and falls to the ground below. The height, s (in meters), of the rock above ground is a function of the time, t (in seconds), since the rock was dropped, so $s = f(t)$.

   (a) Sketch a possible graph of s as a function of t.
   (b) Explain what the statement $f(7) = 12$ tells us about the rock's fall.
   (c) The graph drawn as the answer for part (a) should have a horizontal and vertical intercept. Interpret each intercept in terms of the rock's fall.

41. In a California town, the monthly charge for waste collection is $8 for 32 gallons of waste and $12.32 for 68 gallons of waste.

   (a) Find a linear formula for the cost, C, of waste collection as a function of the number of gallons of waste, w.
   (b) What is the slope of the line found in part (a)? Give units and interpret your answer in terms of the cost of waste collection.
   (c) What is the vertical intercept of the line found in part (a)? Give units and interpret your answer in terms of the cost of waste collection.

42. For tax purposes, you may have to report the value of your assets, such as cars or refrigerators. The value you report drops with time. "Straight-line depreciation" assumes that the value is a linear function of time. If a $950 refrigerator depreciates completely in seven years, find a formula for its value as a function of time.

43. A company rents cars at $40 a day and 15 cents a mile. Its competitor's cars are $50 a day and 10 cents a mile.

   (a) For each company, give a formula for the cost of renting a car for a day as a function of the distance traveled.
   (b) On the same axes, graph both functions.
   (c) How should you decide which company is cheaper?

44. Residents of the town of Maple Grove who are connected to the municipal water supply are billed a fixed amount monthly plus a charge for each cubic foot of water used. A household using 1000 cubic feet was billed $40, while one using 1600 cubic feet was billed $55.

   (a) What is the charge per cubic foot?
   (b) Write an equation for the total cost of a resident's water as a function of cubic feet of water used.
   (c) How many cubic feet of water used would lead to a bill of $100?

Problems 45–48 ask you to plot graphs based on the following story: "As I drove down the highway this morning, at first traffic was fast and uncongested, then it crept nearly bumper-to-bumper until we passed an accident, after which traffic flow went back to normal until I exited."

45. Driving speed against time on the highway

46. Distance driven against time on the highway

47. Distance from my exit vs time on the highway

48. Distance between cars vs distance driven on the highway

49. Let $f(t)$ be the number of US billionaires in the US in year t.

   (a) Express the following statements[4] in terms of f.

      (i) In 1985 there were 13 US billionaires.

      (ii) In 1990 there were 99 US billionaires.

   (b) Find the average yearly increase in the number of US billionaires between 1985 and 1990. Express this using f.
   (c) Assuming the yearly increase remains constant, find a formula predicting the number of US billionaires in year t.

---

[4]//hypertextbook.com/facts/2005/MichelleLee.shtml

50. An alternative to petroleum-based diesel fuel, biodiesel, is derived from renewable resources such as food crops, algae, and animal oils. The table shows the recent annual percent growth in US biodiesel consumption.[5]

Year	2005	2006	2007	2008	2009
% growth over previous yr	237	186.6	37.2	−11.7	7.3

(a) Find the largest time interval over which the percentage growth in the US consumption of biodiesel was an increasing function of time. Interpret what increasing means, practically speaking, in this case.

(b) Find the largest time interval over which the actual US consumption of biodiesel was an increasing function of time. Interpret what increasing means, practically speaking, in this case.

51. Hydroelectric power is electric power generated by the force of moving water. Figure 1.15 shows[6] the annual percent growth in hydroelectric power consumption by the US industrial sector between 2004 and 2009.

(a) Find the largest time interval over which the percentage growth in the US consumption of hydroelectric power was a decreasing function of time. Interpret what decreasing means, practically speaking, in this case.

(b) Find the largest time interval over which the actual US consumption of hydroelectric power was a decreasing function of time. Interpret what decreasing means, practically speaking, in this case.

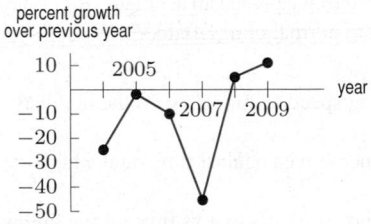

Figure 1.15

52. Solar panels are arrays of photovoltaic cells that convert solar radiation into electricity. The table shows the annual percent change in the US price per watt of a solar panel.[7]

Year	2004	2005	2006	2007	2008
% growth over previous yr	−5.7	6.7	9.7	−3.7	3.6

(a) Find the largest time interval over which the percentage growth in the US price per watt of a solar panel was an increasing function of time. Interpret what increasing means, practically speaking, in this case.

(b) Find the largest time interval over which the actual price per watt of a solar panel was an increasing function of time. Interpret what increasing means, practically speaking, in this case.

53. Table 1.4 shows the average annual sea level, S, in meters, in Aberdeen, Scotland,[8] as a function of time, t, measured in years before 2008.

Table 1.4

t	0	25	50	75	100	125
S	7.094	7.019	6.992	6.965	6.938	6.957

(a) What was the average sea level in Aberdeen in 2008?

(b) In what year was the average sea level 7.019 meters? 6.957 meters?

(c) Table 1.5 gives the average sea level, S, in Aberdeen as a function of the year, x. Complete the missing values.

Table 1.5

x	1883	?	1933	1958	1983	2008
S	?	6.938	?	6.992	?	?

54. A controversial 1992 Danish study[9] reported that men's average sperm count has decreased from 113 million per milliliter in 1940 to 66 million per milliliter in 1990.

(a) Express the average sperm count, S, as a linear function of the number of years, t, since 1940.

(b) A man's fertility is affected if his sperm count drops below about 20 million per milliliter. If the linear model found in part (a) is accurate, in what year will the average male sperm count fall below this level?

55. The table gives the average weight, w, in pounds, of American men in their sixties for height, h, in inches.[10]

(a) How do you know that the data in this table could represent a linear function?

(b) Find weight, w, as a linear function of height, h. What is the slope of the line? What are the units for the slope?

---

[5]http://www.eia.doe.gov/aer/renew.html. Accessed February 2011.

[6]Yearly values have been joined with segments to highlight trends in the data, however values in between years should not be inferred from the segments. From http://www.eia.doe.gov/aer/renew.html. Accessed February 2011.

[7]We use the official price per peak watt, which uses the maximum number of watts a solar panel can produce under ideal conditions. From http://www.eia.doe.gov/aer/renew.html. Accessed February 2011.

[8]www.decc.gov.uk, accessed June 2011.

[9]"Investigating the Next Silent Spring," *US News and World Report*, pp. 50–52 (March 11, 1996).

[10]Adapted from "Average Weight of Americans by Height and Age," *The World Almanac* (New Jersey: Funk and Wagnalls, 1992), p. 956.

(c) Find height, h, as a linear function of weight, w. What is the slope of the line? What are the units for the slope?

h (inches)	68	69	70	71	72	73	74	75
w (pounds)	166	171	176	181	186	191	196	201

56. An airplane uses a fixed amount of fuel for takeoff, a (different) fixed amount for landing, and a third fixed amount per mile when it is in the air. How does the total quantity of fuel required depend on the length of the trip? Write a formula for the function involved. Explain the meaning of the constants in your formula.

57. The cost of planting seed is usually a function of the number of acres sown. The cost of the equipment is a *fixed cost* because it must be paid regardless of the number of acres planted. The costs of supplies and labor vary with the number of acres planted and are called *variable costs*. Suppose the fixed costs are $10,000 and the variable costs are $200 per acre. Let C be the total cost, measured in thousands of dollars, and let x be the number of acres planted.

(a) Find a formula for C as a function of x.
(b) Graph C against x.
(c) Which feature of the graph represents the fixed costs? Which represents the variable costs?

58. You drive at a constant speed from Chicago to Detroit, a distance of 275 miles. About 120 miles from Chicago you pass through Kalamazoo, Michigan. Sketch a graph of your distance from Kalamazoo as a function of time.

59. (a) Consider the functions graphed in Figure 1.16(a). Find the coordinates of C.

(b) Consider the functions in Figure 1.16(b). Find the coordinates of C in terms of b.

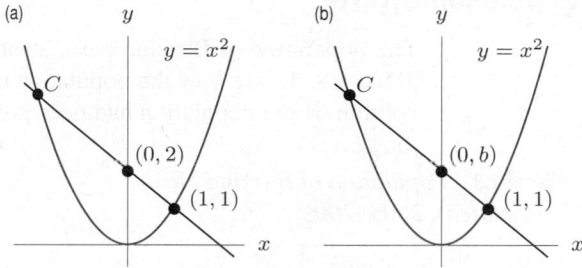

Figure 1.16

60. When Galileo was formulating the laws of motion, he considered the motion of a body starting from rest and falling under gravity. He originally thought that the velocity of such a falling body was proportional to the distance it had fallen. What do the experimental data in Table 1.6 tell you about Galileo's hypothesis? What alternative hypothesis is suggested by the two sets of data in Table 1.6 and Table 1.7?

Table 1.6

Distance (ft)	0	1	2	3	4
Velocity (ft/sec)	0	8	11.3	13.9	16

Table 1.7

Time (sec)	0	1	2	3	4
Velocity (ft/sec)	0	32	64	96	128

Strengthen Your Understanding

In Problems 61–62, explain what is wrong with the statement.

61. Values of y on the graph of $y = 0.5x - 3$ increase more slowly than values of y on the graph of $y = 0.5 - 3x$.

62. The equation $y = 2x + 1$ indicates that y is directly proportional to x with a constant of proportionality 2.

In Problems 63–64, give an example of:

63. A linear function with a positive slope and a negative x-intercept.

64. A formula representing the statement "q is inversely proportional to the cube root of p and has a positive constant of proportionality."

Are the statements in Problems 65–68 true or false? Give an explanation for your answer.

65. For any two points in the plane, there is a linear function whose graph passes through them.

66. If $y = f(x)$ is a linear function, then increasing x by 1 unit changes the corresponding y by m units, where m is the slope.

67. If y is a linear function of x, then the ratio y/x is constant for all points on the graph at which $x \neq 0$.

68. If $y = f(x)$ is a linear function, then increasing x by 2 units adds $m + 2$ units to the corresponding y, where m is the slope.

69. Which of the following functions has its domain identical with its range?

(a) $f(x) = x^2$ (b) $g(x) = \sqrt{x}$
(c) $h(x) = x^3$ (d) $i(x) = |x|$

1.2 EXPONENTIAL FUNCTIONS

Population Growth

The population of Burkina Faso, a sub-Saharan African country,[11] from 2003 to 2009 is given in Table 1.8. To see how the population is growing, we look at the increase in population in the third column. If the population had been growing linearly, all the numbers in the third column would be the same.

Table 1.8 *Population of Burkina Faso (estimated), 2003–2009*

Year	Population (millions)	Change in population (millions)
2003	12.853	
		0.437
2004	13.290	
		0.457
2005	13.747	
		0.478
2006	14.225	
		0.496
2007	14.721	
		0.513
2008	15.234	
		0.523
2009	15.757	

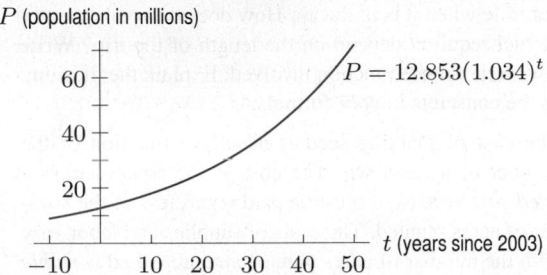

Figure 1.17: Population of Burkina Faso (estimated): Exponential growth

Suppose we divide each year's population by the previous year's population. For example,

$$\frac{\text{Population in 2004}}{\text{Population in 2003}} = \frac{13.290 \text{ million}}{12.853 \text{ million}} = 1.034$$

$$\frac{\text{Population in 2005}}{\text{Population in 2004}} = \frac{13.747 \text{ million}}{13.290 \text{ million}} = 1.034.$$

The fact that both calculations give 1.034 shows the population grew by about 3.4% between 2003 and 2004 *and* between 2004 and 2005. Similar calculations for other years show that the population grew by a factor of about 1.034, or 3.4%, every year. Whenever we have a constant growth factor (here 1.034), we have exponential growth. The population t years after 2003 is given by the *exponential* function

$$P = 12.853(1.034)^t.$$

If we assume that the formula holds for 50 years, the population graph has the shape shown in Figure 1.17. Since the population is growing faster and faster as time goes on, the graph is bending upward; we say it is *concave up*. Even exponential functions which climb slowly at first, such as this one, eventually climb extremely quickly.

> To recognize that a table of t and P values comes from an exponential function, look for ratios of P values that are constant for equally spaced t values.

Concavity

We have used the term concave up[12] to describe the graph in Figure 1.17. In words:

> The graph of a function is **concave up** if it bends upward as we move left to right; it is **concave down** if it bends downward. (See Figure 1.18 for four possible shapes.) A line is neither concave up nor concave down.

---

[11] dataworldbank.org, accessed January 12, 2011.
[12] In Chapter 2 we consider concavity in more depth.

Figure 1.18: Concavity of a graph

Elimination of a Drug from the Body

Now we look at a quantity which is decreasing exponentially instead of increasing. When a patient is given medication, the drug enters the bloodstream. As the drug passes through the liver and kidneys, it is metabolized and eliminated at a rate that depends on the particular drug. For the antibiotic ampicillin, approximately 40% of the drug is eliminated every hour. A typical dose of ampicillin is 250 mg. Suppose $Q = f(t)$, where Q is the quantity of ampicillin, in mg, in the bloodstream at time t hours since the drug was given. At $t = 0$, we have $Q = 250$. Since every hour the amount remaining is 60% of the previous amount, we have

$$f(0) = 250$$
$$f(1) = 250(0.6)$$
$$f(2) = (250(0.6))(0.6) = 250(0.6)^2,$$

and after t hours,

$$Q = f(t) = 250(0.6)^t.$$

This is an *exponential decay function*. Some values of the function are in Table 1.9; its graph is in Figure 1.19.

Notice the way in which the function in Figure 1.19 is decreasing. Each hour a smaller quantity of the drug is removed than in the previous hour. This is because as time passes, there is less of the drug in the body to be removed. Compare this to the exponential growth in Figure 1.17, where each step upward is larger than the previous one. Notice, however, that both graphs are concave up.

Table 1.9 *Drug elimination*

t (hours)	Q (mg)
0	250
1	150
2	90
3	54
4	32.4
5	19.4

Figure 1.19: Drug elimination: Exponential decay

The General Exponential Function

We say P is an **exponential function** of t with base a if

$$P = P_0 a^t,$$

where P_0 is the initial quantity (when $t = 0$) and a is the factor by which P changes when t increases by 1.
If $a > 1$, we have exponential growth; if $0 < a < 1$, we have exponential decay.

Provided $a > 0$, the largest possible domain for the exponential function is all real numbers. The reason we do not want $a \leq 0$ is that, for example, we cannot define $a^{1/2}$ if $a < 0$. Also, we do not usually have $a = 1$, since $P = P_0 1^t = P_0$ is then a constant function.

The value of a is closely related to the percent growth (or decay) rate. For example, if $a = 1.03$, then P is growing at 3%; if $a = 0.94$, then P is decaying at 6%.

Example 1   Suppose that $Q = f(t)$ is an exponential function of t. If $f(20) = 88.2$ and $f(23) = 91.4$:

(a)   Find the base.   (b)   Find the growth rate.   (c)   Evaluate $f(25)$.

Solution   (a)   Let
$$Q = Q_0 a^t.$$

Substituting $t = 20, Q = 88.2$ and $t = 23, Q = 91.4$ gives two equations for Q_0 and a:

$$88.2 = Q_0 a^{20} \quad \text{and} \quad 91.4 = Q_0 a^{23}.$$

Dividing the two equations enables us to eliminate Q_0:

$$\frac{91.4}{88.2} = \frac{Q_0 a^{23}}{Q_0 a^{20}} = a^3.$$

Solving for the base, a, gives

$$a = \left(\frac{91.4}{88.2}\right)^{1/3} = 1.012.$$

(b)   Since $a = 1.012$, the growth rate is $0.012 = 1.2\%$.

(c)   We want to evaluate $f(25) = Q_0 a^{25} = Q_0 (1.012)^{25}$. First we find Q_0 from the equation

$$88.2 = Q_0 (1.012)^{20}.$$

Solving gives $Q_0 = 69.5$. Thus,

$$f(25) = 69.5(1.012)^{25} = 93.6.$$

Half-Life and Doubling Time

Radioactive substances, such as uranium, decay exponentially. A certain percentage of the mass disintegrates in a given unit of time; the time it takes for half the mass to decay is called the *half-life* of the substance.

A well-known radioactive substance is carbon-14, which is used to date organic objects. When a piece of wood or bone was part of a living organism, it accumulated small amounts of radioactive carbon-14. Once the organism dies, it no longer picks up carbon-14. Using the half-life of carbon-14 (about 5730 years), we can estimate the age of the object. We use the following definitions:

> The **half-life** of an exponentially decaying quantity is the time required for the quantity to be reduced by a factor of one half.
>
> The **doubling time** of an exponentially increasing quantity is the time required for the quantity to double.

The Family of Exponential Functions

The formula $P = P_0 a^t$ gives a family of exponential functions with positive parameters P_0 (the initial quantity) and a (the base, or growth/decay factor). The base tells us whether the function is increasing ($a > 1$) or decreasing ($0 < a < 1$). Since a is the factor by which P changes when t is increased by 1, large values of a mean fast growth; values of a near 0 mean fast decay. (See Figures 1.20 and 1.21.) All members of the family $P = P_0 a^t$ are concave up.

Figure 1.20: Exponential growth: $P = a^t$, for $a > 1$

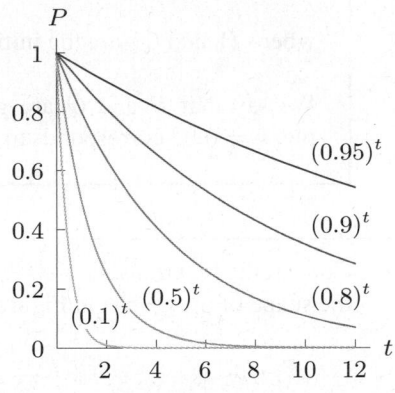

Figure 1.21: Exponential decay: $P = a^t$, for $0 < a < 1$

Example 2   Figure 1.22 is the graph of three exponential functions. What can you say about the values of the six constants, a, b, c, d, p, q?

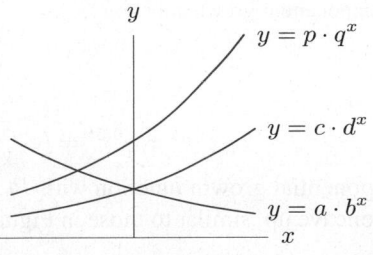

Figure 1.22

Solution   All the constants are positive. Since a, c, p represent y-intercepts, we see that $a = c$ because these graphs intersect on the y-axis. In addition, $a = c < p$, since $y = p \cdot q^x$ crosses the y-axis above the other two.

Since $y = a \cdot b^x$ is decreasing, we have $0 < b < 1$. The other functions are increasing, so $1 < d$ and $1 < q$.

Exponential Functions with Base e

The most frequently used base for an exponential function is the famous number $e = 2.71828\ldots$. This base is used so often that you will find an e^x button on most scientific calculators. At first glance, this is all somewhat mysterious. Why is it convenient to use the base $2.71828\ldots$? The full answer to that question must wait until Chapter 3, where we show that many calculus formulas come out neatly when e is used as the base. We often use the following result:

Any **exponential growth** function can be written, for some $a > 1$ and $k > 0$, in the form

$$P = P_0a^t \quad \text{or} \quad P = P_0e^{kt}$$

and any **exponential decay** function can be written, for some $0 < a < 1$ and $-k < 0$, as

$$Q = Q_0a^t \quad \text{or} \quad Q = Q_0e^{-kt},$$

where P_0 and Q_0 are the initial quantities.

We say that P and Q are growing or decaying at a *continuous*[13] *rate* of k. (For example, $k = 0.02$ corresponds to a continuous rate of 2%.)

Example 3 Convert the functions $P = e^{0.5t}$ and $Q = 5e^{-0.2t}$ into the form $y = y_0a^t$. Use the results to explain the shape of the graphs in Figures 1.23 and 1.24.

Figure 1.23: An exponential growth function

Figure 1.24: An exponential decay function

Solution We have

$$P = e^{0.5t} = (e^{0.5})^t = (1.65)^t.$$

Thus, P is an exponential growth function with $P_0 = 1$ and $a = 1.65$. The function is increasing and its graph is concave up, similar to those in Figure 1.20. Also,

$$Q = 5e^{-0.2t} = 5(e^{-0.2})^t = 5(0.819)^t,$$

so Q is an exponential decay function with $Q_0 = 5$ and $a = 0.819$. The function is decreasing and its graph is concave up, similar to those in Figure 1.21.

Example 4 The quantity, Q, of a drug in a patient's body at time t is represented for positive constants S and k by the function $Q = S(1 - e^{-kt})$. For $t \geq 0$, describe how Q changes with time. What does S represent?

Solution The graph of Q is shown in Figure 1.25. Initially none of the drug is present, but the quantity increases with time. Since the graph is concave down, the quantity increases at a decreasing rate. This is realistic because as the quantity of the drug in the body increases, so does the rate at which the body excretes the drug. Thus, we expect the quantity to level off. Figure 1.25 shows that S is the saturation level. The line $Q = S$ is called a *horizontal asymptote*.

[13]The reason that k is called the continuous rate is explored in detail in Chapter 11.

Figure 1.25: Buildup of the quantity of a drug in body

Exercises and Problems for Section 1.2

Exercises

In Exercises 1–4, decide whether the graph is concave up, concave down, or neither.

1.

2.

3.

4.

The functions in Exercises 5–8 represent exponential growth or decay. What is the initial quantity? What is the growth rate? State if the growth rate is continuous.

5. $P = 5(1.07)^t$

6. $P = 7.7(0.92)^t$

7. $P = 3.2e^{0.03t}$

8. $P = 15e^{-0.06t}$

Write the functions in Exercises 9–12 in the form $P = P_0a^t$. Which represent exponential growth and which represent exponential decay?

9. $P = 15e^{0.25t}$

10. $P = 2e^{-0.5t}$

11. $P = P_0e^{0.2t}$

12. $P = 7e^{-\pi t}$

In Exercises 13–14, let $f(t) = Q_0a^t = Q_0(1 + r)^t$.
(a) Find the base, a.
(b) Find the percentage growth rate, r.

13. $f(5) = 75.94$ and $f(7) = 170.86$

14. $f(0.02) = 25.02$ and $f(0.05) = 25.06$

15. A town has a population of 1000 people at time $t = 0$. In each of the following cases, write a formula for the population, P, of the town as a function of year t.

(a) The population increases by 50 people a year.
(b) The population increases by 5% a year.

16. An air-freshener starts with 30 grams and evaporates. In each of the following cases, write a formula for the quantity, Q grams, of air-freshener remaining t days after the start and sketch a graph of the function. The decrease is:

(a) 2 grams a day
(b) 12% a day

17. For which pairs of consecutive points in Figure 1.26 is the function graphed:

(a) Increasing and concave up?
(b) Increasing and concave down?
(c) Decreasing and concave up?
(d) Decreasing and concave down?

Figure 1.26

18. The table gives the average temperature in Wallingford, Connecticut, for the first 10 days in March.

(a) Over which intervals was the average temperature increasing? Decreasing?
(b) Find a pair of consecutive intervals over which the average temperature was increasing at a decreasing rate. Find another pair of consecutive intervals over which the average temperature was increasing at an increasing rate.

Day	1	2	3	4	5	6	7	8	9	10
°F	42°	42°	34°	25°	22°	34°	38°	40°	49°	49°

Problems

19. (a) Which (if any) of the functions in the following table could be linear? Find formulas for those functions.
(b) Which (if any) of these functions could be exponential? Find formulas for those functions.

x	$f(x)$	$g(x)$	$h(x)$
-2	12	16	37
-1	17	24	34
0	20	36	31
1	21	54	28
2	18	81	25

In Problems 20–21, find all the tables that have the given characteristic.

(A)
x	0	40	80	160
y	2.2	2.2	2.2	2.2

(B)
x	-8	-4	0	8
y	51	62	73	95

(C)
x	-4	-3	4	6
y	18	0	4.5	-2.25

(D)
x	3	4	5	6
y	18	9	4.5	2.25

20. y could be a linear function of x.

21. y could be an exponential function of x.

22. In 2010, the world's population reached 6.91 billion and was increasing at a rate of 1.1% per year. Assume that this growth rate remains constant. (In fact, the growth rate has decreased since 1987.)

(a) Write a formula for the world population (in billions) as a function of the number of years since 2010.
(b) Estimate the population of the world in the year 2020.
(c) Sketch world population as a function of years since 2010. Use the graph to estimate the doubling time of the population of the world.

23. (a) A population, P, grows at a continuous rate of 2% a year and starts at 1 million. Write P in the form $P = P_0 e^{kt}$, with P_0, k constants.
(b) Plot the population in part (a) against time.

24. A certain region has a population of 10,000,000 and an annual growth rate of 2%. Estimate the doubling time by guessing and checking.

25. A photocopy machine can reduce copies to 80% of their original size. By copying an already reduced copy, further reductions can be made.

(a) If a page is reduced to 80%, what percent enlargement is needed to return it to its original size?
(b) Estimate the number of times in succession that a page must be copied to make the final copy less than 15% of the size of the original.

26. When a new product is advertised, more and more people try it. However, the rate at which new people try it slows as time goes on.

(a) Graph the total number of people who have tried such a product against time.
(b) What do you know about the concavity of the graph?

27. Sketch reasonable graphs for the following. Pay particular attention to the concavity of the graphs.

(a) The total revenue generated by a car rental business, plotted against the amount spent on advertising.
(b) The temperature of a cup of hot coffee standing in a room, plotted as a function of time.

28. Each of the functions g, h, k in Table 1.10 is increasing, but each increases in a different way. Which of the graphs in Figure 1.27 best fits each function?

Table 1.10

t	$g(t)$	$h(t)$	$k(t)$
1	23	10	2.2
2	24	20	2.5
3	26	29	2.8
4	29	37	3.1
5	33	44	3.4
6	38	50	3.7

Figure 1.27

29. Each of the functions in Table 1.11 decreases, but each decreases in a different way. Which of the graphs in Figure 1.28 best fits each function?

Table 1.11

x	$f(x)$	$g(x)$	$h(x)$
1	100	22.0	9.3
2	90	21.4	9.1
3	81	20.8	8.8
4	73	20.2	8.4
5	66	19.6	7.9
6	60	19.0	7.3

Figure 1.28

30. One of the main contaminants of a nuclear accident, such as that at Chernobyl, is strontium-90, which decays exponentially at a continuous rate of approximately 2.47% per year. After the Chernobyl disaster, it was suggested that it would be about 100 years before the region would again be safe for human habitation. What percent of the original strontium-90 would still remain then?

Give a possible formula for the functions in Problems 31–34.

31.

$(2, 12)$
3

32.

$(-1, 8)$ $(1, 2)$

33.

$(2, 18)$
$(1, 6)$

34.

4
$(1, 2)$

35. Table 1.12 shows some values of a linear function f and an exponential function g. Find exact values (not decimal approximations) for each of the missing entries.

Table 1.12

x	0	1	2	3	4
$f(x)$	10	?	20	?	?
$g(x)$	10	?	20	?	?

36. Match the functions $h(s)$, $f(s)$, and $g(s)$, whose values are in Table 1.13, with the formulas

$$y = a(1.1)^s, \quad y = b(1.05)^s, \quad y = c(1.03)^s,$$

assuming a, b, and c are constants. Note that the function values have been rounded to two decimal places.

Table 1.13

s	$h(s)$	s	$f(s)$	s	$g(s)$
2	1.06	1	2.20	3	3.47
3	1.09	2	2.42	4	3.65
4	1.13	3	2.66	5	3.83
5	1.16	4	2.93	6	4.02
6	1.19	5	3.22	7	4.22

37. (a) Estimate graphically the doubling time of the exponentially growing population shown in Figure 1.29. Check that the doubling time is independent of where you start on the graph.

(b) Show algebraically that if $P = P_0 a^t$ doubles between time t and time $t + d$, then d is the same number for any t.

population

Figure 1.29

38. A deposit of P_0 into a bank account has a doubling time of 50 years. No other deposits or withdrawals are made.

(a) How much money is in the bank account after 50 years? 100 years? 150 years? (Your answer will involve P_0.)

(b) How many times does the amount of money double in t years? Use this to write a formula for P, the amount of money in the account after t years.

39. A 325 mg aspirin has a half-life of H hours in a patient's body.

(a) How long does it take for the quantity of aspirin in the patient's body to be reduced to 162.5 mg? To 81.25 mg? To 40.625 mg? (Note that $162.5 = 325/2$, etc. Your answers will involve H.)

(b) How many times does the quantity of aspirin, A mg, in the body halve in t hours? Use this to give a formula for A after t hours.

40. (a) The half-life of radium-226 is 1620 years. If the initial quantity of radium is Q_0, explain why the quantity, Q, of radium left after t years, is given by

$$Q = Q_0 \left(\frac{1}{2}\right)^{t/1620}.$$

(b) What percentage of the original amount of radium is left after 500 years?

41. In the early 1960s, radioactive strontium-90 was released during atmospheric testing of nuclear weapons and got into the bones of people alive at the time. If the half-life of strontium-90 is 29 years, what fraction of the strontium-90 absorbed in 1960 remained in people's bones in 2010? [Hint: Write the function in the form $Q = Q_0(1/2)^{t/29}$.]

42. Aircraft require longer takeoff distances, called takeoff rolls, at high altitude airports because of diminished air density. The table shows how the takeoff roll for a certain light airplane depends on the airport elevation. (Takeoff rolls are also strongly influenced by air temperature; the data shown assume a temperature of $0°$ C.) Determine a formula for this particular aircraft that gives the takeoff roll as an exponential function of airport elevation.

Elevation (ft)	Sea level	1000	2000	3000	4000
Takeoff roll (ft)	670	734	805	882	967

Problems 43–44 concern biodiesel, a fuel derived from renewable resources such as food crops, algae, and animal oils. The table shows the percent growth over the previous year in US biodiesel consumption.[14]

Year	2003	2004	2005	2006	2007	2008	2009
% growth	−12.5	92.9	237	186.6	37.2	−11.7	7.3

43. (a) According to the US Department of Energy, the US consumed 91 million gallons of biodiesel in 2005. Approximately how much biodiesel (in millions of gallons) did the US consume in 2006? In 2007?

(b) Graph the points showing the annual US consumption of biodiesel, in millions of gallons of biodiesel, for the years 2005 to 2009. Label the scales on the horizontal and vertical axes.

44. (a) True or false: The annual US consumption of biodiesel grew exponentially from 2003 to 2005. Justify your answer without doing any calculations.

(b) According to this data, during what single year(s), if any, did the US consumption of biodiesel at least double?

(c) According to this data, during what single year(s), if any, did the US consumption of biodiesel at least triple?

45. Hydroelectric power is electric power generated by the force of moving water. The table shows the annual percent change in hydroelectric power consumption by the US industrial sector.[15]

Year	2005	2006	2007	2008	2009
% growth over previous yr	−1.9	−10	−45.4	5.1	11

(a) According to the US Department of Energy, the US industrial sector consumed about 29 trillion BTUs of hydroelectric power in 2006. Approximately how much hydroelectric power (in trillion BTUs) did the US consume in 2007? In 2005?

(b) Graph the points showing the annual US consumption of hydroelectric power, in trillion BTUs, for the years 2004 to 2009. Label the scales on the horizontal and vertical axes.

(c) According to this data, when did the largest yearly decrease, in trillion BTUs, in the US consumption of hydroelectric power occur? What was this decrease?

Problems 46–47 concern wind power, which has been used for centuries to propel ships and mill grain. Modern wind power is obtained from windmills which convert wind energy into electricity. Figure 1.30 shows the annual percent growth in US wind power consumption[16] between 2005 and 2009.

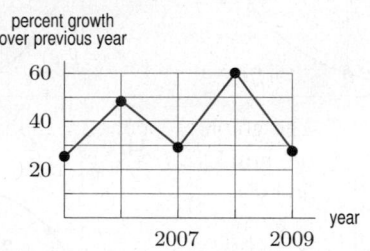

Figure 1.30

46. (a) According to the US Department of Energy, the US consumption of wind power was 341 trillion BTUs in 2007. How much wind power did the US consume in 2006? In 2008?

(b) Graph the points showing the annual US consumption of wind power, in trillion BTUs, for the years 2005 to 2009. Label the scales on the horizontal and vertical axes.

(c) Based on this data, in what year did the largest yearly increase, in trillion BTUs, in the US consumption of wind power occur? What was this increase?

47. (a) According to Figure 1.30, during what single year(s), if any, did the US consumption of wind power energy increase by at least 40%? Decrease by at least 40%?

(b) Did the US consumption of wind power energy double from 2006 to 2008?

Strengthen Your Understanding

In Problems 48–49, explain what is wrong with the statement.

48. The function $y = e^{-0.25x}$ is decreasing and its graph is concave down.

49. The function $y = 2x$ is increasing, and its graph is concave up.

In Problems 50–52, give an example of:

50. A formula representing the statement "q decreases at a constant percent rate, and $q = 2.2$ when $t = 0$."

51. A function that is increasing at a constant percent rate and that has the same vertical intercept as $f(x) = 0.3x + 2$.

52. A function with a horizontal asymptote at $y = -5$ and range $y > -5$.

---

[14]http://www.eia.doe.gov/aer/renew.html. Accessed February 2011.

[15]From http://www.eia.doe.gov/aer/renew.html. Accessed February 2011.

[16]Yearly values have been joined with segments to highlight trends in the data. Actual values in between years should not be inferred from the segments. From http://www.eia.doe.gov/aer/renew.html. Accessed February 2011.

Are the statements in Problems 53–59 true or false? Give an explanation for your answer.

53. The function $y = 2 + 3e^{-t}$ has a y-intercept of $y = 3$.

54. The function $y = 5 - 3e^{-4t}$ has a horizontal asymptote of $y = 5$.

55. If $y = f(x)$ is an exponential function and if increasing x by 1 increases y by a factor of 5, then increasing x by 2 increases y by a factor of 10.

56. If $y = Ab^x$ and increasing x by 1 increases y by a factor of 3, then increasing x by 2 increases y by a factor of 9.

57. An exponential function can be decreasing.

58. If a and b are positive constants, $b \neq 1$, then $y = a + ab^x$ has a horizontal asymptote.

59. The function $y = 20/(1 + 2e^{-kt})$ with $k > 0$, has a horizontal asymptote at $y = 20$.

1.3 NEW FUNCTIONS FROM OLD

Shifts and Stretches

The graph of a constant multiple of a given function is easy to visualize: each y-value is stretched or shrunk by that multiple. For example, consider the function $f(x)$ and its multiples $y = 3f(x)$ and $y = -2f(x)$. Their graphs are shown in Figure 1.31. The factor 3 in the function $y = 3f(x)$ stretches each $f(x)$ value by multiplying it by 3; the factor -2 in the function $y = -2f(x)$ stretches $f(x)$ by multiplying by 2 and reflects it about the x-axis. You can think of the multiples of a given function as a family of functions.

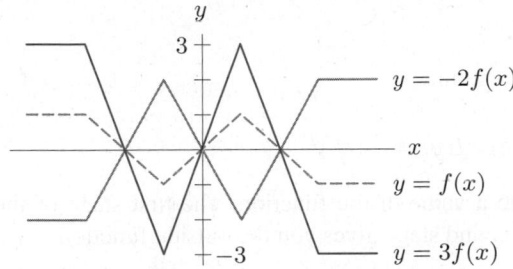

Figure 1.31: Multiples of the function $f(x)$

Figure 1.32: Graphs of $y = x^2$ with $y = x^2 + 4$ and $y = (x - 2)^2$

It is also easy to create families of functions by shifting graphs. For example, $y - 4 = x^2$ is the same as $y = x^2 + 4$, which is the graph of $y = x^2$ shifted up by 4. Similarly, $y = (x - 2)^2$ is the graph of $y = x^2$ shifted right by 2. (See Figure 1.32.)

- Multiplying a function by a constant, c, stretches the graph vertically (if $c > 1$) or shrinks the graph vertically (if $0 < c < 1$). A negative sign (if $c < 0$) reflects the graph about the x-axis, in addition to shrinking or stretching.
- Replacing y by $(y - k)$ moves a graph up by k (down if k is negative).
- Replacing x by $(x - h)$ moves a graph to the right by h (to the left if h is negative).

Composite Functions

If oil is spilled from a tanker, the area of the oil slick grows with time. Suppose that the oil slick is always a perfect circle. Then the area, A, of the oil slick is a function of its radius, r:

$$A = f(r) = \pi r^2.$$

The radius is also a function of time, because the radius increases as more oil spills. Thus, the area, being a function of the radius, is also a function of time. If, for example, the radius is given by

$$r = g(t) = 1 + t,$$

then the area is given as a function of time by substitution:

$$A = \pi r^2 = \pi(1+t)^2.$$

We are thinking of A as a *composite function* or a "function of a function," which is written

$$A = \underbrace{f(g(t))}_{\substack{\text{Composite function;} \\ f \text{ is outside function,} \\ g \text{ is inside function}}} = \pi(g(t))^2 = \pi(1+t)^2.$$

To calculate A using the formula $\pi(1+t)^2$, the first step is to find $1+t$, and the second step is to square and multiply by π. The first step corresponds to the inside function $g(t) = 1 + t$, and the second step corresponds to the outside function $f(r) = \pi r^2$.

Example 1   If $f(x) = x^2$ and $g(x) = x - 2$, find each of the following:
(a) $f(g(3))$ (b) $g(f(3))$ (c) $f(g(x))$ (d) $g(f(x))$

Solution   (a) Since $g(3) = 1$, we have $f(g(3)) = f(1) = 1$.
(b) Since $f(3) = 9$, we have $g(f(3)) = g(9) = 7$. Notice that $f(g(3)) \neq g(f(3))$.
(c) $f(g(x)) = f(x - 2) = (x - 2)^2$.
(d) $g(f(x)) = g(x^2) = x^2 - 2$. Again, notice that $f(g(x)) \neq g(f(x))$.
Notice that the horizontal shift in Figure 1.32 can be thought of as a composition $f(g(x)) = (x-2)^2$.

Example 2   Express each of the following functions as a composition:

(a) $h(t) = (1 + t^3)^{27}$ (b) $k(y) = e^{-y^2}$ (c) $l(y) = -(e^y)^2$

Solution   In each case think about how you would calculate a value of the function. The first stage of the calculation gives you the inside function, and the second stage gives you the outside function.

(a) For $(1 + t^3)^{27}$, the first stage is cubing and adding 1, so an inside function is $g(t) = 1 + t^3$. The second stage is taking the 27th power, so an outside function is $f(y) = y^{27}$. Then

$$f(g(t)) = f(1 + t^3) = (1 + t^3)^{27}.$$

In fact, there are lots of different answers: $g(t) = t^3$ and $f(y) = (1 + y)^{27}$ is another possibility.
(b) To calculate e^{-y^2} we square y, take its negative, and then take e to that power. So if $g(y) = -y^2$ and $f(z) = e^z$, then we have

$$f(g(y)) = e^{-y^2}.$$

(c) To calculate $-(e^y)^2$, we find e^y, square it, and take the negative. Using the same definitions of f and g as in part (b), the composition is

$$g(f(y)) = -(e^y)^2.$$

Since parts (b) and (c) give different answers, we see the order in which functions are composed is important.

Odd and Even Functions: Symmetry

There is a certain symmetry apparent in the graphs of $f(x) = x^2$ and $g(x) = x^3$ in Figure 1.33. For each point (x, x^2) on the graph of f, the point $(-x, x^2)$ is also on the graph; for each point (x, x^3) on the graph of g, the point $(-x, -x^3)$ is also on the graph. The graph of $f(x) = x^2$ is symmetric about the y-axis, whereas the graph of $g(x) = x^3$ is symmetric about the origin. The graph of any polynomial involving only even powers of x has symmetry about the y-axis, while polynomials with only odd powers of x are symmetric about the origin. Consequently, any functions with these symmetry properties are called *even* and *odd*, respectively.

Figure 1.33: Symmetry of even and odd functions

For any function f,
f is an **even** function if $f(-x) = f(x)$ for all x.
f is an **odd** function if $f(-x) = -f(x)$ for all x.

For example, $g(x) = e^{x^2}$ is even and $h(x) = x^{1/3}$ is odd. However, many functions do not have any symmetry and are neither even nor odd.

Inverse Functions

On August 26, 2005, the runner Kenenisa Bekele[17] of Ethiopia set a world record for the 10,000-meter race. His times, in seconds, at 2000-meter intervals are recorded in Table 1.14, where $t = f(d)$ is the number of seconds Bekele took to complete the first d meters of the race. For example, Bekele ran the first 4000 meters in 629.98 seconds, so $f(4000) = 629.98$. The function f was useful to athletes planning to compete with Bekele.

Let us now change our point of view and ask for distances rather than times. If we ask how far Bekele ran during the first 629.98 seconds of his race, the answer is clearly 4000 meters. Going backward in this way from numbers of seconds to numbers of meters gives f^{-1}, the *inverse function*[18] of f. We write $f^{-1}(629.98) = 4000$. Thus, $f^{-1}(t)$ is the number of meters that Bekele ran during the first t seconds of his race. See Table 1.15, which contains values of f^{-1}.

The independent variable for f is the dependent variable for f^{-1}, and vice versa. The domains and ranges of f and f^{-1} are also interchanged. The domain of f is all distances d such that $0 \le d \le 10000$, which is the range of f^{-1}. The range of f is all times t, such that $0 \le t \le 1577.53$, which is the domain of f^{-1}.

Table 1.14   *Bekele's running time*

d (meters)	$t = f(d)$ (seconds)
0	0.00
2000	315.63
4000	629.98
6000	944.66
8000	1264.63
10000	1577.53

Table 1.15   *Distance run by Bekele*

t (seconds)	$d = f^{-1}(t)$ (meters)
0.00	0
315.63	2000
629.98	4000
944.66	6000
1264.63	8000
1577.53	10000

Which Functions Have Inverses?

If a function has an inverse, we say it is *invertible*. Let's look at a function which is not invertible. Consider the flight of the Mercury spacecraft *Freedom 7*, which carried Alan Shepard, Jr. into space

---

[17]kenenisabekelle.com/, accessed January 11, 2011.
[18]The notation f^{-1} represents the inverse function, which is not the same as the reciprocal, $1/f$.

in May 1961. Shepard was the first American to journey into space. After launch, his spacecraft rose to an altitude of 116 miles, and then came down into the sea. The function $f(t)$ giving the altitude in miles t minutes after lift-off does not have an inverse. To see why not, try to decide on a value for $f^{-1}(100)$, which should be the time when the altitude of the spacecraft was 100 miles. However, there are two such times, one when the spacecraft was ascending and one when it was descending. (See Figure 1.34.)

The reason the altitude function does not have an inverse is that the altitude has the same value for two different times. The reason the Bekele time function did have an inverse is that each running time, t, corresponds to a unique distance, d.

Figure 1.34: Two times, t_1 and t_2, at which altitude of spacecraft is 100 miles

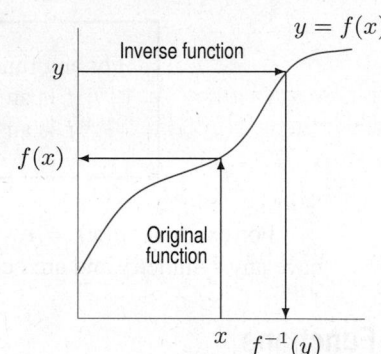

Figure 1.35: A function which has an inverse

Figure 1.35 suggests when an inverse exists. The original function, f, takes us from an x-value to a y-value, as shown in Figure 1.35. Since having an inverse means there is a function going from a y-value to an x-value, the crucial question is whether we can get back. In other words, does each y-value correspond to a unique x-value? If so, there's an inverse; if not, there is not. This principle may be stated geometrically, as follows:

> A function has an inverse if (and only if) its graph intersects any horizontal line at most once.

For example, the function $f(x) = x^2$ does not have an inverse because many horizontal lines intersect the parabola twice.

Definition of an Inverse Function

If the function f is invertible, its inverse is defined as follows:

$$f^{-1}(y) = x \quad \text{means} \quad y = f(x).$$

Formulas for Inverse Functions

If a function is defined by a formula, it is sometimes possible to find a formula for the inverse function. In Section 1.1, we looked at the snow tree cricket, whose chirp rate, C, in chirps per minute, is approximated at the temperature, T, in degrees Fahrenheit, by the formula

$$C = f(T) = 4T - 160.$$

So far we have used this formula to predict the chirp rate from the temperature. But it is also possible to use this formula backward to calculate the temperature from the chirp rate.

Example 3   Find the formula for the function giving temperature in terms of the number of cricket chirps per minute; that is, find the inverse function f^{-1} such that

$$T = f^{-1}(C).$$

Solution   Since C is an increasing function, f is invertible. We know $C = 4T - 160$. We solve for T, giving

$$T = \frac{C}{4} + 40,$$

so

$$f^{-1}(C) = \frac{C}{4} + 40.$$

Graphs of Inverse Functions

The function $f(x) = x^3$ is increasing everywhere and so has an inverse. To find the inverse, we solve

$$y = x^3$$

for x, giving

$$x = y^{1/3}.$$

The inverse function is

$$f^{-1}(y) = y^{1/3}$$

or, if we want to call the independent variable x,

$$f^{-1}(x) = x^{1/3}.$$

The graphs of $y = x^3$ and $y = x^{1/3}$ are shown in Figure 1.36. Notice that these graphs are the reflections of one another about the line $y = x$. For example, $(8, 2)$ is on the graph of $y = x^{1/3}$ because $2 = 8^{1/3}$, and $(2, 8)$ is on the graph of $y = x^3$ because $8 = 2^3$. The points $(8, 2)$ and $(2, 8)$ are reflections of one another about the line $y = x$.

In general, we have the following result.

If the x- and y-axes have the same scales, the graph of f^{-1} is the reflection of the graph of f about the line $y = x$.

Figure 1.36: Graphs of inverse functions, $y = x^3$ and $y = x^{1/3}$, are reflections about the line $y = x$

Exercises and Problems for Section 1.3

Exercises

For the functions f in Exercises 1–3, graph:

(a) $f(x+2)$ (b) $f(x-1)$ (c) $f(x)-4$
(d) $f(x+1)+3$ (e) $3f(x)$ (f) $-f(x)+1$

1.

2.

3.

In Exercises 4–7, use Figure 1.37 to graph the functions.

Figure 1.37

4. $n(t) = m(t) + 2$ **5.** $p(t) = m(t-1)$

6. $k(t) = m(t+1.5)$

7. $w(t) = m(t-0.5) - 2.5$

For the functions f and g in Exercises 8–11, find

(a) $f(g(1))$ (b) $g(f(1))$ (c) $f(g(x))$
(d) $g(f(x))$ (e) $f(t)g(t)$

8. $f(x) = x^2, g(x) = x + 1$

9. $f(x) = \sqrt{x+4}, g(x) = x^2$

10. $f(x) = e^x, g(x) = x^2$

11. $f(x) = 1/x, g(x) = 3x + 4$

12. For $g(x) = x^2 + 2x + 3$, find and simplify:

(a) $g(2+h)$ (b) $g(2)$
(c) $g(2+h) - g(2)$

13. If $f(x) = x^2 + 1$, find and simplify:

(a) $f(t+1)$ (b) $f(t^2+1)$ (c) $f(2)$
(d) $2f(t)$ (e) $(f(t))^2 + 1$

Simplify the quantities in Exercises 14–17 using $m(z) = z^2$.

14. $m(z+1) - m(z)$ **15.** $m(z+h) - m(z)$

16. $m(z) - m(z-h)$ **17.** $m(z+h) - m(z-h)$

18. Let p be the price of an item and q be the number of items sold at that price, where $q = f(p)$. What do the following quantities mean in terms of prices and quantities sold?

(a) $f(25)$ (b) $f^{-1}(30)$

19. Let $C = f(A)$ be the cost, in dollars, of building a store of area A square feet. In terms of cost and square feet, what do the following quantities represent?

(a) $f(10{,}000)$ (b) $f^{-1}(20{,}000)$

20. Let $f(x)$ be the temperature (°F) when the column of mercury in a particular thermometer is x inches long. What is the meaning of $f^{-1}(75)$ in practical terms?

21. (a) Write an equation for a graph obtained by vertically stretching the graph of $y = x^2$ by a factor of 2, followed by a vertical upward shift of 1 unit. Sketch it.
(b) What is the equation if the order of the transformations (stretching and shifting) in part (a) is interchanged?
(c) Are the two graphs the same? Explain the effect of reversing the order of transformations.

22. Use Figure 1.38 to graph each of the following. Label any intercepts or asymptotes that can be determined.

(a) $y = f(x) + 3$ (b) $y = 2f(x)$
(c) $y = f(x+4)$ (d) $y = 4 - f(x)$

Figure 1.38

For Exercises 23–24, decide if the function $y = f(x)$ is invertible.

23.

24.

For Exercises 25–27, use a graph of the function to decide whether or not it is invertible.

25. $f(x) = x^2 + 3x + 2$ **26.** $f(x) = x^3 - 5x + 10$

27. $f(x) = x^3 + 5x + 10$

Are the functions in Exercises 28–35 even, odd, or neither?

28. $f(x) = x^6 + x^3 + 1$ **29.** $f(x) = x^3 + x^2 + x$

30. $f(x) = x^4 - x^2 + 3$ **31.** $f(x) = x^3 + 1$

32. $f(x) = 2x$ **33.** $f(x) = e^{x^2 - 1}$

34. $f(x) = x(x^2 - 1)$ **35.** $f(x) = e^x - x$

Problems

For Problems 36–39, determine functions f and g such that $h(x) = f(g(x))$. [Note: There is more than one correct answer. Do not choose $f(x) = x$ or $g(x) = x$.]

36. $h(x) = (x + 1)^3$ **37.** $h(x) = x^3 + 1$

38. $h(x) = \sqrt{x^2 + 4}$ **39.** $h(x) = e^{2x}$

Find possible formulas for the graphs in Problems 40–41 using shifts of x^2 or x^3.

40.

41.

42. **(a)** Use Figure 1.39 to estimate $f^{-1}(2)$.
  (b) Sketch a graph of f^{-1} on the same axes.

Figure 1.39

43. Write a table of values for f^{-1}, where f is as given below. The domain of f is the integers from 1 to 7. State the domain of f^{-1}.

x	1	2	3	4	5	6	7
$f(x)$	3	−7	19	4	178	2	1

For Problems 44–47, decide if the function f is invertible.

44. $f(d)$ is the total number of gallons of fuel an airplane has used by the end of d minutes of a particular flight.

45. $f(t)$ is the number of customers in Macy's department store at t minutes past noon on December 18, 2008.

46. $f(n)$ is the number of students in your calculus class whose birthday is on the nth day of the year.

47. $f(w)$ is the cost of mailing a letter weighing w grams.

In Problems 48–51 the functions $r = f(t)$ and $V = g(r)$ give the radius and the volume of a commercial hot air balloon being inflated for testing. The variable t is in minutes, r is in feet, and V is in cubic feet. The inflation begins at $t = 0$. In each case, give a mathematical expression that represents the given statement.

48. The volume of the balloon t minutes after inflation began.

49. The volume of the balloon if its radius were twice as big.

50. The time that has elapsed when the radius of the balloon is 30 feet.

51. The time that has elapsed when the volume of the balloon is 10,000 cubic feet.

In Problems 52–55, use Figure 1.40 to estimate the function value or explain why it cannot be done.

Figure 1.40

52. $u(v(10))$ **53.** $u(v(40))$

54. $v(u(10))$ **55.** $v(u(40))$

56. Figure 1.41 shows $f(t)$, the number (in millions) of motor vehicles registered[19] in the world in the year t.

  (a) Is f invertible? Explain.

  (b) What is the meaning of $f^{-1}(400)$ in practical terms? Evaluate $f^{-1}(400)$.

  (c) Sketch the graph of f^{-1}.

Figure 1.41

For Problems 57–62, use the graphs in Figure 1.42.

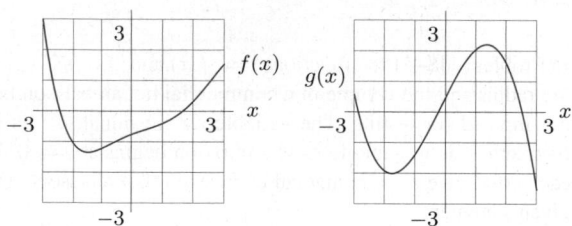

Figure 1.42

57. Estimate $f(g(1))$.

58. Estimate $g(f(2))$.

59. Estimate $f(f(1))$.

60. Graph $f(g(x))$.

61. Graph $g(f(x))$.

62. Graph $f(f(x))$.

63. Figure 1.43 is a graph of the function $f(t)$. Here $f(t)$ is the depth in meters below the Atlantic Ocean floor where t million-year-old rock can be found.[20]

  (a) Evaluate $f(15)$, and say what it means in practical terms.

  (b) Is f invertible? Explain.

  (c) Evaluate $f^{-1}(120)$, and say what it means in practical terms.

  (d) Sketch a graph of f^{-1}.

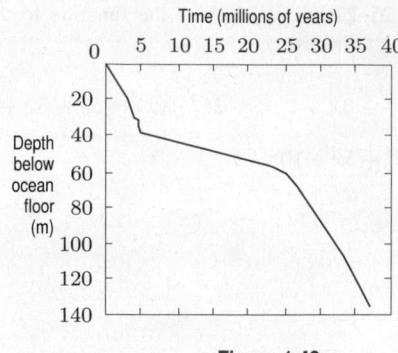

Figure 1.43

64. A tree of height y meters has, on average, B branches, where $B = y - 1$. Each branch has, on average, n leaves, where $n = 2B^2 - B$. Find the average number of leaves of a tree as a function of height.

65. A spherical balloon is growing with radius $r = 3t + 1$, in centimeters, for time t in seconds. Find the volume of the balloon at 3 seconds.

66. The cost of producing q articles is given by the function $C = f(q) = 100 + 2q$.

  (a) Find a formula for the inverse function.

  (b) Explain in practical terms what the inverse function tells you.

67. How does the graph of $Q = S(1 - e^{-kt})$ in Example 4 on page 16 relate to the graph of the exponential decay function, $y = Se^{-kt}$?

68. Complete the following table with values for the functions f, g, and h, given that:

  (a) f is an even function.

  (b) g is an odd function.

  (c) h is the composition $h(x) = g(f(x))$.

x	$f(x)$	$g(x)$	$h(x)$
-3	0	0	
-2	2	2	
-1	2	2	
0	0	0	
1			
2			
3			

---

[19]www.earth-policy.org, accessed June 5, 2011. In 2000, about 30% of the registered vehicles were in the US.

[20]Data of Dr. Murlene Clark based on core samples drilled by the research ship *Glomar Challenger*, taken from *Initial Reports of the Deep Sea Drilling Project.*

Strengthen Your Understanding

In Problems 69–71, explain what is wrong with the statement.

69. The graph of $f(x) = -(x+1)^3$ is the graph of $g(x) = -x^3$ shifted right by 1 unit.

70. $f(x) = 3x+5$ and $g(x) = -3x-5$ are inverse functions of each other.

71. The inverse of $f(x) = x$ is $f^{-1}(x) = 1/x$.

In Problems 72–75, give an example of:

72. An invertible function whose graph contains the point $(0, 3)$.

73. An even function whose graph does not contain the point $(0, 0)$.

74. An increasing function $f(x)$ whose values are greater than those of its inverse function $f^{-1}(x)$ for $x > 0$.

75. Two functions $f(x)$ and $g(x)$ such that moving the graph of f to the left 2 units gives the graph of g and moving the graph of f up 3 also gives the graph of g.

Are the statements in Problems 76–83 true or false? Give an explanation for your answer.

76. The graph of $f(x) = 100(10^x)$ is a horizontal shift of the graph of $g(x) = 10^x$.

77. If f is an increasing function, then f^{-1} is an increasing function.

78. If a function is even, then it does not have an inverse.

79. If a function is odd, then it does not have an inverse.

80. The function $f(x) = e^{-x^2}$ is decreasing for all x.

81. If $g(x)$ is an even function then $f(g(x))$ is even for every function $f(x)$.

82. If $f(x)$ is an even function then $f(g(x))$ is even for every function $g(x)$.

83. There is a function which is both even and odd.

Suppose f is an increasing function and g is a decreasing function. In Problems 84–87, give an example for f and g for which the statement is true, or say why such an example is impossible.

84. $f(x) + g(x)$ is decreasing for all x.

85. $f(x) - g(x)$ is decreasing for all x.

86. $f(x)g(x)$ is decreasing for all x.

87. $f(g(x))$ is increasing for all x.

1.4 LOGARITHMIC FUNCTIONS

In Section 1.2, we approximated the population of Burkina Faso (in millions) by the function

$$P = f(t) = 12.853(1.034)^t,$$

where t is the number of years since 2003. Now suppose that instead of calculating the population at time t, we ask when the population will reach 20 million. We want to find the value of t for which

$$20 = f(t) = 12.853(1.034)^t.$$

We use logarithms to solve for a variable in an exponent.

Logarithms to Base 10 and to Base e

We define the *logarithm* function, $\log_{10} x$, to be the inverse of the exponential function, 10^x, as follows:

> The **logarithm** to base 10 of x, written $\log_{10} x$, is the power of 10 we need to get x. In other words,
>
> $$\log_{10} x = c \quad \text{means} \quad 10^c = x.$$
>
> We often write $\log x$ in place of $\log_{10} x$.

The other frequently used base is e. The logarithm to base e is called the *natural logarithm* of x, written $\ln x$ and defined to be the inverse function of e^x, as follows:

> The **natural logarithm** of x, written $\ln x$, is the power of e needed to get x. In other words,
>
> $$\ln x = c \quad \text{means} \quad e^c = x.$$

Values of $\log x$ are in Table 1.16. Because no power of 10 gives 0, $\log 0$ is undefined. The graph of $y = \log x$ is shown in Figure 1.44. The domain of $y = \log x$ is positive real numbers; the range is all real numbers. In contrast, the inverse function $y = 10^x$ has domain all real numbers and range all positive real numbers. The graph of $y = \log x$ has a vertical asymptote at $x = 0$, whereas $y = 10^x$ has a horizontal asymptote at $y = 0$.

One big difference between $y = 10^x$ and $y = \log x$ is that the exponential function grows extremely quickly whereas the log function grows extremely slowly. However, $\log x$ does go to infinity, albeit slowly, as x increases. Since $y = \log x$ and $y = 10^x$ are inverse functions, the graphs of the two functions are reflections of one another about the line $y = x$, provided the scales along the x- and y-axes are equal.

Table 1.16 *Values for* $\log x$ *and* 10^x

x	$\log x$		x	10^x
0	undefined		0	1
1	0		1	10
2	0.3		2	100
3	0.5		3	10^3
4	0.6		4	10^4
$\vdots$	$\vdots$		$\vdots$	$\vdots$
10	1		10	10^{10}

Figure 1.44: Graphs of $\log x$ and 10^x

The graph of $y = \ln x$ in Figure 1.45 has roughly the same shape as the graph of $y = \log x$. The x-intercept is $x = 1$, since $\ln 1 = 0$. The graph of $y = \ln x$ also climbs very slowly as x increases. Both graphs, $y = \log x$ and $y = \ln x$, have *vertical asymptotes* at $x = 0$.

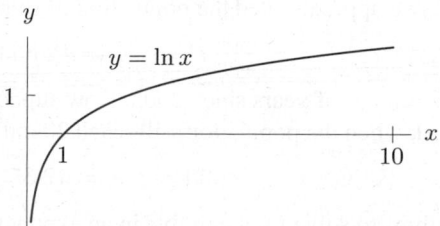

Figure 1.45: Graph of the natural logarithm

The following properties of logarithms may be deduced from the properties of exponents:

Properties of Logarithms

Note that $\log x$ and $\ln x$ are not defined when x is negative or 0.

1. $\log(AB) = \log A + \log B$
2. $\log\left(\dfrac{A}{B}\right) = \log A - \log B$
3. $\log(A^p) = p\log A$
4. $\log(10^x) = x$
5. $10^{\log x} = x$

1. $\ln(AB) = \ln A + \ln B$
2. $\ln\left(\dfrac{A}{B}\right) = \ln A - \ln B$
3. $\ln(A^p) = p\ln A$
4. $\ln e^x = x$
5. $e^{\ln x} = x$

In addition, $\log 1 = 0$ because $10^0 = 1$, and $\ln 1 = 0$ because $e^0 = 1$.

Solving Equations Using Logarithms

Logs are frequently useful when we have to solve for unknown exponents, as in the next examples.

Example 1   Find t such that $2^t = 7$.

Solution   First, notice that we expect t to be between 2 and 3 (because $2^2 = 4$ and $2^3 = 8$). To calculate t, we take logs to base 10 of both sides. (Natural logs could also be used.)

$$\log(2^t) = \log 7.$$

Then use the third property of logs, which says $\log(2^t) = t \log 2$, and get:

$$t \log 2 = \log 7.$$

Using a calculator to find the logs gives

$$t = \frac{\log 7}{\log 2} \approx 2.81.$$

Example 2   Find when the population of Burkina Faso reaches 20 million by solving $20 = 12.853(1.034)^t$.

Solution   Dividing both sides of the equation by 12.853, we get

$$\frac{20}{12.853} = (1.034)^t.$$

Now take logs of both sides:

$$\log\left(\frac{20}{12.853}\right) = \log(1.034^t).$$

Using the fact that $\log(A^t) = t \log A$, we get

$$\log\left(\frac{20}{12.853}\right) = t \log(1.034).$$

Solving this equation using a calculator to find the logs, we get

$$t = \frac{\log(20/12.853)}{\log(1.034)} = 13.22 \text{ years}$$

which is between $t = 13$ and $t = 14$. This value of t corresponds to the year 2016.

Example 3   Traffic pollution is harmful to school-age children. The concentration of carbon monoxide, CO, in the air near a busy road is a function of distance from the road. The concentration decays exponentially at a continuous rate of 3.3% per meter.[21] At what distance from the road is the concentration of CO half what it is on the road?

Solution   If C_0 is the concentration of CO on the road, then the concentration x meters from the road is

$$C = C_0 e^{-0.033x}.$$

We want to find the value of x making $C = C_0/2$, that is,

$$C_0 e^{-0.033x} = \frac{C_0}{2}.$$

Dividing by C_0 and then taking natural logs yields

$$\ln\left(e^{-0.033x}\right) = -0.033x = \ln\left(\frac{1}{2}\right) = -0.6931,$$

so

$$x = 21 \text{ meters.}$$

At 21 meters from the road the concentration of CO in the air is half the concentration on the road.

---

[21]Rickwood, P. and Knight, D. (2009). "The health impacts of local traffic pollution on primary school age children." *State of Australian Cities 2009 Conference Proceedings.*

In Example 3 the decay rate was given. However, in many situations where we expect to find exponential growth or decay, the rate is not given. To find it, we must know the quantity at two different times and then solve for the growth or decay rate, as in the next example.

Example 4   The population of Mexico was 99.9 million in 2000 and 113.4 million in 2010.[22] Assuming it increases exponentially, find a formula for the population of Mexico as a function of time.

Solution   If we measure the population, P, in millions and time, t, in years since 2000, we can say

$$P = P_0 e^{kt} = 99.9 e^{kt},$$

where $P_0 = 99.9$ is the initial value of P. We find k by using the fact that $P = 113.4$ when $t = 10$, so

$$113.4 = 99.9 e^{k \cdot 10}.$$

To find k, we divide both sides by 99.9, giving

$$\frac{113.4}{99.9} = 1.135 = e^{10k}.$$

Now take natural logs of both sides:

$$\ln(1.135) = \ln(e^{10k}).$$

Using a calculator and the fact that $\ln(e^{10k}) = 10k$, this becomes

$$0.127 = 10k.$$

So

$$k = 0.0127,$$

and therefore

$$P = 99.9 e^{0.0127t}.$$

Since $k = 0.0127 = 1.27\%$, the population of Mexico was growing at a continuous rate of 1.27% per year.

In Example 4 we chose to use e for the base of the exponential function representing Mexico's population, making clear that the continuous growth rate was 1.27%. If we had wanted to emphasize the annual growth rate, we could have expressed the exponential function in the form $P = P_0 a^t$.

Example 5   Give a formula for the inverse of the following function (that is, solve for t in terms of P):

$$P = f(t) = 12.853(1.034)^t.$$

Solution   We want a formula expressing t as a function of P. Take logs:

$$\log P = \log(12.853(1.034)^t).$$

Since $\log(AB) = \log A + \log B$, we have

$$\log P = \log 12.853 + \log((1.034)^t).$$

Now use $\log(A^t) = t \log A$:

$$\log P = \log 12.853 + t \log 1.034.$$

Solve for t in two steps, using a calculator at the final stage:

$$t \log 1.034 = \log P - \log 12.853$$

$$t = \frac{\log P}{\log 1.034} - \frac{\log 12.853}{\log 1.034} = 68.868 \log P - 76.375.$$

---

[22]http://data.worldbank.org/country/mexico. Accessed January 14, 2012.

Thus,

$$f^{-1}(P) = 68.868 \log P - 76.375.$$

Note that

$$f^{-1}(20) = 68.868(\log 20) - 76.375 = 13.22,$$

which agrees with the result of Example 2.

Exercises and Problems for Section 1.4

Exercises

Simplify the expressions in Exercises 1–6 completely.

1. $e^{\ln(1/2)}$

2. $10^{\log(AB)}$

3. $5e^{\ln(A^2)}$

4. $\ln(e^{2AB})$

5. $\ln(1/e) + \ln(AB)$

6. $2\ln(e^A) + 3\ln B^e$

For Exercises 7–18, solve for x using logs.

7. $3^x = 11$

8. $17^x = 2$

9. $20 = 50(1.04)^x$

10. $4 \cdot 3^x = 7 \cdot 5^x$

11. $7 = 5e^{0.2x}$

12. $2^x = e^{x+1}$

13. $50 = 600e^{-0.4x}$

14. $2e^{3x} = 4e^{5x}$

15. $7^{x+2} = e^{17x}$

16. $10^{x+3} = 5e^{7-x}$

17. $2x - 1 = e^{\ln x^2}$

18. $4e^{2x-3} - 5 = e$

For Exercises 19–24, solve for t. Assume a and b are positive constants and k is nonzero.

19. $a = b^t$

20. $P = P_0 a^t$

21. $Q = Q_0 a^{nt}$

22. $P_0 a^t = Q_0 b^t$

23. $a = be^t$

24. $P = P_0 e^{kt}$

In Exercises 25–28, put the functions in the form $P = P_0 e^{kt}$.

25. $P = 15(1.5)^t$

26. $P = 10(1.7)^t$

27. $P = 174(0.9)^t$

28. $P = 4(0.55)^t$

Find the inverse function in Exercises 29–31.

29. $p(t) = (1.04)^t$

30. $f(t) = 50e^{0.1t}$

31. $f(t) = 1 + \ln t$

Problems

32. The population of a region is growing exponentially. There were 40,000,000 people in 2000 ($t = 0$) and 48,000,000 in 2010. Find an expression for the population at any time t, in years. What population would you predict for the year 2020? What is the doubling time?

33. One hundred kilograms of a radioactive substance decay to 40 kg in 10 years. How much remains after 20 years?

34. A culture of bacteria originally numbers 500. After 2 hours there are 1500 bacteria in the culture. Assuming exponential growth, how many are there after 6 hours?

35. The population of the US was 281.4 million in 2000 and 308.7 million in 2010.[23] Assuming exponential growth,

  (a) In what year is the population expected to go over 350 million?

  (b) What population is predicted for the 2020 census?

36. The concentration of the car exhaust fume nitrous oxide, NO_2, in the air near a busy road is a function of distance from the road. The concentration decays exponentially at a continuous rate of 2.54% per meter.[24] At what distance from the road is the concentration of NO_2 half what it is on the road?

37. For children and adults with diseases such as asthma, the number of respiratory deaths per year increases by 0.33% when pollution particles increase by a microgram per cubic meter of air.[25]

  (a) Write a formula for the number of respiratory deaths per year as a function of quantity of pollution in the air. (Let Q_0 be the number of deaths per year with no pollution.)

  (b) What quantity of air pollution results in twice as many respiratory deaths per year as there would be without pollution?

---

[23]http://2010.census.gov/2010census/. Accessed April 17, 2011.

[24]Rickwood, P. and Knight, D. (2009). "The health impacts of local traffic pollution on primary school age children." *State of Australian Cities 2009 Conference Proceedings*.

[25]Brook, R. D., Franklin, B., Cascio, W., Hong, Y., Howard, G., Lipsett, M., Luepker, R., Mittleman, M., Samet, J., and Smith, S. C. (2004). "Air pollution and cardiovascular disease." *Circulation,* 109(21):2655267.

38. The number of alternative fuel vehicles[26] running on E85, fuel that is up to 85% plant-derived ethanol, increased exponentially in the US between 2003 and 2008.

    (a) Use this information to complete the missing table values.

    (b) How many E85-powered vehicles were there in the US in 2003?

    (c) By what percent did the number of E85-powered vehicles grow from 2004 to 2008?

Year	2004	2005	2006	2007	2008
Number of E85 vehicles	211,800	?	?	?	450,327

39. At time t hours after taking the cough suppressant hydrocodone bitartrate, the amount, A, in mg, remaining in the body is given by $A = 10(0.82)^t$.

    (a) What was the initial amount taken?

    (b) What percent of the drug leaves the body each hour?

    (c) How much of the drug is left in the body 6 hours after the dose is administered?

    (d) How long is it until only 1 mg of the drug remains in the body?

40. A cup of coffee contains 100 mg of caffeine, which leaves the body at a continuous rate of 17% per hour.

    (a) Write a formula for the amount, A mg, of caffeine in the body t hours after drinking a cup of coffee.

    (b) Graph the function from part (a). Use the graph to estimate the half-life of caffeine.

    (c) Use logarithms to find the half-life of caffeine.

41. The exponential function $y(x) = Ce^{\alpha x}$ satisfies the conditions $y(0) = 2$ and $y(1) = 1$. Find the constants C and α. What is $y(2)$?

42. Without a calculator or computer, match the functions e^x, $\ln x$, x^2, and $x^{1/2}$ to their graphs in Figure 1.46.

Figure 1.46

43. With time, t, in years since the start of 1980, textbook prices have increased at 6.7% per year while inflation has been 3.3% per year.[27] Assume both rates are continuous growth rates.

    (a) Find a formula for $B(t)$, the price of a textbook in year t if it cost $\$B_0$ in 1980.

    (b) Find a formula for $P(t)$, the price of an item in year t if it cost $\$P_0$ in 1980 and its price rose according to inflation.

    (c) A textbook cost $50 in 1980. When is its price predicted to be double the price that would have resulted from inflation alone?

44. In November 2010, a "tiger summit" was held in St. Petersburg, Russia.[28] In 1900, there were 100,000 wild tigers worldwide; in 2010 the number was 3200.

    (a) Assuming the tiger population has decreased exponentially, find a formula for $f(t)$, the number of wild tigers t years since 1900.

    (b) Between 2000 and 2010, the number of wild tigers decreased by 40%. Is this percentage larger or smaller than the decrease in the tiger population predicted by your answer to part (a)?

45. In 2011, the populations of China and India were approximately 1.34 and 1.19 billion people[29], respectively. However, due to central control the annual population growth rate of China was 0.4% while the population of India was growing by 1.37% each year. If these growth rates remain constant, when will the population of India exceed that of China?

46. The third-quarter revenue of Apple® went from $3.68 billion[30] in 2005 to $15.68 billion[31] in 2010. Find an exponential function to model the revenue as a function of years since 2005. What is the continuous percent growth rate, per year, of sales?

47. The world population was 6.9 billion at the end of 2010 and is predicted to reach 9 billion by the end of 2050.[32]

    (a) Assuming the population is growing exponentially, what is the continuous growth rate per year?

    (b) The United Nations celebrated the "Day of 5 Billion" on July 11, 1987, and the "Day of 6 Billion" on October 12, 1999. Using the growth rate in part (a), when is the "Day of 7 Billion" predicted to be?

---

[26]http://www.eia.doe.gov/aer/renew.html

[27]Data from "Textbooks headed for ash heap of history", http://educationtechnews.com, Vol 5, 2010.

[28]"Tigers would be extinct in Russia if unprotected," Yahoo! News, Nov. 21, 2010.

[29]http://www.indexmundi.com/. Accessed April 17, 2011.

[30]http://www.apple.com/pr/library/2005/oct/11results.html. Accessed April 27, 2011.

[31]http://www.apple.com/pr/library/2010/01/25results.html. Accessed April 27, 2011.

[32]"Reviewing the Bidding on the Climate Files", in About Dot Earth, *New York Times*, Nov. 19, 2010.

48. In the early 1920s, Germany had tremendously high inflation, called hyperinflation. Photographs of the time show people going to the store with wheelbarrows full of money. If a loaf of bread cost $1/4$ marks in 1919 and 2,400,000 marks in 1922, what was the average yearly inflation rate between 1919 and 1922?

49. Different isotopes (versions) of the same element can have very different half-lives. With t in years, the decay of plutonium-240 is described by the formula

$$Q = Q_0 e^{-0.00011t},$$

whereas the decay of plutonium-242 is described by

$$Q = Q_0 e^{-0.0000018t}.$$

Find the half-lives of plutonium-240 and plutonium-242.

50. The size of an exponentially growing bacteria colony doubles in 5 hours. How long will it take for the number of bacteria to triple?

51. Air pressure, P, decreases exponentially with height, h, above sea level. If P_0 is the air pressure at sea level and h is in meters, then

$$P = P_0 e^{-0.00012h}.$$

  (a) At the top of Mount McKinley, height 6194 meters (about 20,320 feet), what is the air pressure, as a percent of the pressure at sea level?
  (b) The maximum cruising altitude of an ordinary commercial jet is around 12,000 meters (about 39,000 feet). At that height, what is the air pressure, as a percent of the sea level value?

52. Find the equation of the line l in Figure 1.47.

Figure 1.47

53. In 2010, there were about 246 million vehicles (cars and trucks) and about 308.7 million people in the US.[33] The number of vehicles grew 15.5% over the previous decade, while the population has been growing at 9.7% per decade. If the growth rates remain constant, when will there be, on average, one vehicle per person?

54. A picture supposedly painted by Vermeer (1632–1675) contains 99.5% of its carbon-14 (half-life 5730 years). From this information decide whether the picture is a fake. Explain your reasoning.

55. Is there a difference between $\ln[\ln(x)]$ and $\ln^2(x)$? [Note: $\ln^2(x)$ is another way of writing $(\ln x)^2$.]

56. If $h(x) = \ln(x + a)$, where $a > 0$, what is the effect of increasing a on
  (a) The y-intercept?   **(b)** The x-intercept?

57. If $h(x) = \ln(x + a)$, where $a > 0$, what is the effect of increasing a on the vertical asymptote?

58. If $g(x) = \ln(ax + 2)$, where $a \neq 0$, what is the effect of increasing a on
  (a) The y-intercept?   **(b)** The x-intercept?

59. If $f(x) = a \ln(x + 2)$, what is the effect of increasing a on the vertical asymptote?

60. If $g(x) = \ln(ax + 2)$, where $a \neq 0$, what is the effect of increasing a on the vertical asymptote?

Strengthen Your Understanding

In Problems 61–62, explain what is wrong with the statement.

61. The function $-\log|x|$ is odd.

62. For all $x > 0$, the value of $\ln(100x)$ is 100 times larger than $\ln x$.

In Problems 63–64, give an example of:

63. A function $f(x)$ such that $\ln(f(x))$ is only defined for $x < 0$.

64. A function with a vertical asymptote at $x = 3$ and defined only for $x > 3$.

Are the statements in Problems 65–68 true or false? Give an explanation for your answer.

65. The graph of $f(x) = \ln x$ is concave down.

66. The graph of $g(x) = \log(x - 1)$ crosses the x-axis at $x = 1$.

67. The inverse function of $y = \log x$ is $y = 1/\log x$.

68. If a and b are positive constants, then $y = \ln(ax + b)$ has no vertical asymptote.

[33]http://www.autoblog.com/2010/01/04/report-number-of-cars-in-the-u-s-dropped-by-four-million-in-20/   and http://2010.census.gov/news/releases/operations/cb10-cn93.html. Accessed February 2012.

1.5 TRIGONOMETRIC FUNCTIONS

Trigonometry originated as part of the study of triangles. The name *tri-gon-o-metry* means the measurement of three-cornered figures, and the first definitions of the trigonometric functions were in terms of triangles. However, the trigonometric functions can also be defined using the unit circle, a definition that makes them periodic, or repeating. Many naturally occurring processes are also periodic. The water level in a tidal basin, the blood pressure in a heart, an alternating current, and the position of the air molecules transmitting a musical note all fluctuate regularly. Such phenomena can be represented by trigonometric functions.

Radians

There are two commonly used ways to represent the input of the trigonometric functions: radians and degrees. The formulas of calculus, as you will see, are neater in radians than in degrees.

> An angle of 1 **radian** is defined to be the angle at the center of a unit circle which cuts off an arc of length 1, measured counterclockwise. (See Figure 1.48(a).) A unit circle has radius 1.

An angle of 2 radians cuts off an arc of length 2 on a unit circle. A negative angle, such as $-1/2$ radians, cuts off an arc of length $1/2$, but measured clockwise. (See Figure 1.48(b).)

Figure 1.48: Radians defined using unit circle

It is useful to think of angles as rotations, since then we can make sense of angles larger than $360°$; for example, an angle of $720°$ represents two complete rotations counterclockwise. Since one full rotation of $360°$ cuts off an arc of length 2π, the circumference of the unit circle, it follows that

$$360° = 2\pi \text{ radians}, \quad \text{so} \quad 180° = \pi \text{ radians}.$$

In other words, 1 radian $= 180°/\pi$, so one radian is about $60°$. The word radians is often dropped, so if an angle or rotation is referred to without units, it is understood to be in radians.

Radians are useful for computing the length of an arc in any circle. If the circle has radius r and the arc cuts off an angle θ, as in Figure 1.49, then we have the following relation:

> Arc length $= s = r\theta$.

Figure 1.49: Arc length of a sector of a circle

The Sine and Cosine Functions

The two basic trigonometric functions—the sine and cosine—are defined using a unit circle. In Figure 1.50, an angle of t radians is measured counterclockwise around the circle from the point $(1, 0)$. If P has coordinates (x, y), we define

$$\cos t = x \quad \text{and} \quad \sin t = y.$$

We assume that the angles are *always* in radians unless specified otherwise.

Since the equation of the unit circle is $x^2 + y^2 = 1$, writing $\cos^2 t$ for $(\cos t)^2$, we have the identity

$$\cos^2 t + \sin^2 t = 1.$$

As t increases and P moves around the circle, the values of $\sin t$ and $\cos t$ oscillate between 1 and -1, and eventually repeat as P moves through points where it has been before. If t is negative, the angle is measured clockwise around the circle.

Amplitude, Period, and Phase

The graphs of sine and cosine are shown in Figure 1.51. Notice that sine is an odd function, and cosine is even. The maximum and minimum values of sine and cosine are $+1$ and -1, because those are the maximum and minimum values of y and x on the unit circle. After the point P has moved around the complete circle once, the values of $\cos t$ and $\sin t$ start to repeat; we say the functions are *periodic*.

> For any periodic function of time, the
> - **Amplitude** is half the distance between the maximum and minimum values (if it exists).
> - **Period** is the smallest time needed for the function to execute one complete cycle.

The amplitude of $\cos t$ and $\sin t$ is 1, and the period is 2π. Why 2π? Because that's the value of t when the point P has gone exactly once around the circle. (Remember that $360° = 2\pi$ radians.)

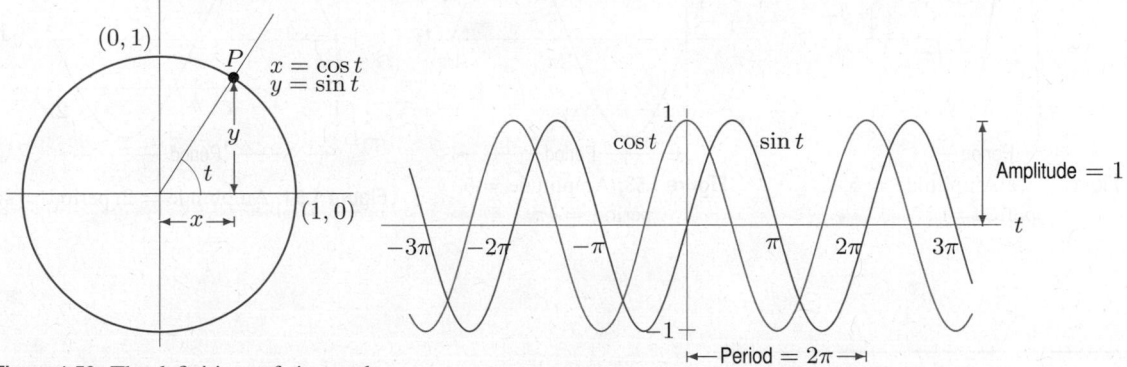

Figure 1.50: The definitions of $\sin t$ and $\cos t$

Figure 1.51: Graphs of $\cos t$ and $\sin t$

In Figure 1.51, we see that the sine and cosine graphs are exactly the same shape, only shifted horizontally. Since the cosine graph is the sine graph shifted $\pi/2$ to the left,

$$\cos t = \sin(t + \pi/2).$$

Equivalently, the sine graph is the cosine graph shifted $\pi/2$ to the right, so

$$\sin t = \cos(t - \pi/2).$$

We say that the *phase difference* or *phase shift* between $\sin t$ and $\cos t$ is $\pi/2$.

Functions whose graphs are the shape of a sine or cosine curve are called *sinusoidal* functions.

To describe arbitrary amplitudes and periods of sinusoidal functions, we use functions of the form

$$f(t) = A\sin(Bt) \qquad \text{and} \qquad g(t) = A\cos(Bt),$$

where $|A|$ is the amplitude and $2\pi/|B|$ is the period.

The graph of a sinusoidal function is shifted horizontally by a distance $|h|$ when t is replaced by $t - h$ or $t + h$.

Functions of the form $f(t) = A\sin(Bt) + C$ and $g(t) = A\cos(Bt) + C$ have graphs which are shifted vertically by C and oscillate about this value.

Example 1   Find and show on a graph the amplitude and period of the functions

(a) $y = 5\sin(2t)$
(b) $y = -5\sin\left(\dfrac{t}{2}\right)$
(c) $y = 1 + 2\sin t$

Solution

(a) From Figure 1.52, you can see that the amplitude of $y = 5\sin(2t)$ is 5 because the factor of 5 stretches the oscillations up to 5 and down to -5. The period of $y = \sin(2t)$ is π, because when t changes from 0 to π, the quantity $2t$ changes from 0 to 2π, so the sine function goes through one complete oscillation.

(b) Figure 1.53 shows that the amplitude of $y = -5\sin(t/2)$ is again 5, because the negative sign reflects the oscillations in the t-axis, but does not change how far up or down they go. The period of $y = -5\sin(t/2)$ is 4π because when t changes from 0 to 4π, the quantity $t/2$ changes from 0 to 2π, so the sine function goes through one complete oscillation.

(c) The 1 shifts the graph $y = 2\sin t$ up by 1. Since $y = 2\sin t$ has an amplitude of 2 and a period of 2π, the graph of $y = 1 + 2\sin t$ goes up to 3 and down to -1, and has a period of 2π. (See Figure 1.54.) Thus, $y = 1 + 2\sin t$ also has amplitude 2.

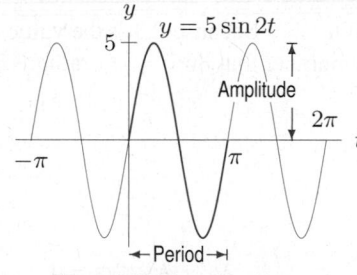

Figure 1.52: Amplitude = 5, period = π

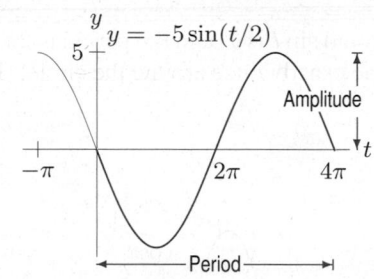

Figure 1.53: Amplitude = 5, period = 4π

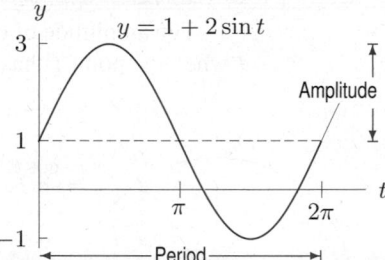

Figure 1.54: Amplitude = 2, period = 2π

Example 2   Find possible formulas for the following sinusoidal functions.

Solution   (a) This function looks like a sine function with amplitude 3, so $g(t) = 3\sin(Bt)$. Since the function executes one full oscillation between $t = 0$ and $t = 12\pi$, when t changes by 12π, the quantity Bt changes by 2π. This means $B \cdot 12\pi = 2\pi$, so $B = 1/6$. Therefore, $g(t) = 3\sin(t/6)$ has the graph shown.

(b) This function looks like an upside-down cosine function with amplitude 2, so $f(t) = -2\cos(Bt)$. The function completes one oscillation between $t = 0$ and $t = 4$. Thus, when t changes by 4, the quantity Bt changes by 2π, so $B \cdot 4 = 2\pi$, or $B = \pi/2$. Therefore, $f(t) = -2\cos(\pi t/2)$ has the graph shown.

(c) This function looks like the function $g(t)$ in part (a), but shifted a distance of π to the right. Since $g(t) = 3\sin(t/6)$, we replace t by $(t - \pi)$ to obtain $h(t) = 3\sin[(t - \pi)/6]$.

Example 3   On July 1, 2007, high tide in Boston was at midnight. The water level at high tide was 9.9 feet; later, at low tide, it was 0.1 feet. Assuming the next high tide is at exactly 12 noon and that the height of the water is given by a sine or cosine curve, find a formula for the water level in Boston as a function of time.

Solution   Let y be the water level in feet, and let t be the time measured in hours from midnight. The oscillations have amplitude 4.9 feet ($= (9.9 - 0.1)/2$) and period 12, so $12B = 2\pi$ and $B = \pi/6$. Since the water is highest at midnight, when $t = 0$, the oscillations are best represented by a cosine function. (See Figure 1.55.) We can say

$$\text{Height above average} = 4.9\cos\left(\frac{\pi}{6}t\right).$$

Since the average water level was 5 feet ($= (9.9 + 0.1)/2$), we shift the cosine up by adding 5:

$$y = 5 + 4.9\cos\left(\frac{\pi}{6}t\right).$$

Figure 1.55: Function approximating the tide in Boston on July 1, 2007

Example 4   Of course, there's something wrong with the assumption in Example 3 that the next high tide is at noon. If so, the high tide would always be at noon or midnight, instead of progressing slowly through the day, as in fact it does. The interval between successive high tides actually averages about 12 hours 24 minutes. Using this, give a more accurate formula for the height of the water as a function of time.

Solution   The period is 12 hours 24 minutes $= 12.4$ hours, so $B = 2\pi/12.4$, giving

$$y = 5 + 4.9\cos\left(\frac{2\pi}{12.4}t\right) = 5 + 4.9\cos(0.507t).$$

Example 5   Use the information from Example 4 to write a formula for the water level in Boston on a day when the high tide is at 2 pm.

Solution When the high tide is at midnight,

$$y = 5 + 4.9 \cos(0.507t).$$

Since 2 pm is 14 hours after midnight, we replace t by $(t - 14)$. Therefore, on a day when the high tide is at 2 pm,

$$y = 5 + 4.9 \cos(0.507(t - 14)).$$

The Tangent Function

If t is any number with $\cos t \neq 0$, we define the tangent function as follows

$$\tan t = \frac{\sin t}{\cos t}.$$

Figure 1.50 on page 37 shows the geometrical meaning of the tangent function: $\tan t$ is the slope of the line through the origin $(0, 0)$ and the point $P = (\cos t, \sin t)$ on the unit circle.

The tangent function is undefined wherever $\cos t = 0$, namely, at $t = \pm\pi/2, \pm3\pi/2, \ldots$, and it has a vertical asymptote at each of these points. The function $\tan t$ is positive where $\sin t$ and $\cos t$ have the same sign. The graph of the tangent is shown in Figure 1.56.

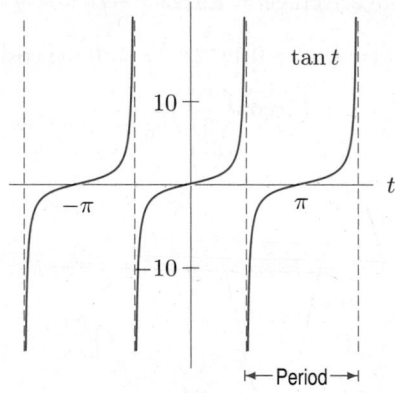

Figure 1.56: The tangent function

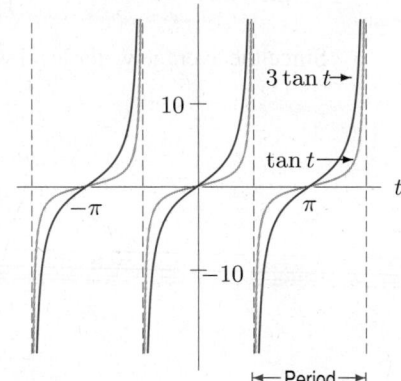

Figure 1.57: Multiple of tangent

The tangent function has period π, because it repeats every π units. Does it make sense to talk about the amplitude of the tangent function? Not if we're thinking of the amplitude as a measure of the size of the oscillation, because the tangent becomes infinitely large near each vertical asymptote. We can still multiply the tangent by a constant, but that constant no longer represents an amplitude. (See Figure 1.57.)

The Inverse Trigonometric Functions

On occasion, you may need to find a number with a given sine. For example, you might want to find x such that

$$\sin x = 0$$

or such that

$$\sin x = 0.3.$$

The first of these equations has solutions $x = 0, \pm\pi, \pm2\pi, \ldots$. The second equation also has infinitely many solutions. Using a calculator and a graph, we get

$$x \approx 0.305, 2.84, 0.305 \pm 2\pi, 2.84 \pm 2\pi, \ldots.$$

For each equation, we pick out the solution between $-\pi/2$ and $\pi/2$ as the preferred solution. For example, the preferred solution to $\sin x = 0$ is $x = 0$, and the preferred solution to $\sin x = 0.3$ is $x = 0.305$. We define the inverse sine, written "arcsin" or "$\sin^{-1}$," as the function which gives the preferred solution.

> For $-1 \leq y \leq 1$,
> $$\arcsin y = x$$
> means
> $$\sin x = y \quad \text{with} \quad -\frac{\pi}{2} \leq x \leq \frac{\pi}{2}.$$

Thus the arcsine is the inverse function to the piece of the sine function having domain $[-\pi/2, \pi/2]$. (See Table 1.17 and Figure 1.58.) On a calculator, the arcsine function[34] is usually denoted by $\boxed{\sin^{-1}}$.

Table 1.17 *Values of* $\sin x$ *and* $\sin^{-1} x$

x	$\sin x$		x	$\sin^{-1} x$
$-\frac{\pi}{2}$	-1.000		-1.000	$-\frac{\pi}{2}$
-1.0	-0.841		-0.841	-1.0
-0.5	-0.479		-0.479	-0.5
0.0	0.000		0.000	0.0
0.5	0.479		0.479	0.5
1.0	0.841		0.841	1.0
$\frac{\pi}{2}$	1.000		1.000	$\frac{\pi}{2}$

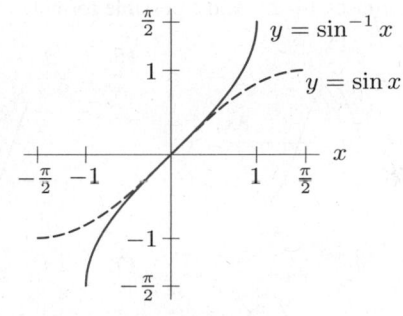

Figure 1.58: The arcsine function

The inverse tangent, written "arctan" or "$\tan^{-1}$," is the inverse function for the piece of the tangent function having the domain $-\pi/2 < x < \pi/2$. On a calculator, the inverse tangent is usually denoted by $\boxed{\tan^{-1}}$. The graph of the arctangent is shown in Figure 1.60.

> For any y,
> $$\arctan y = x$$
> means
> $$\tan x = y \quad \text{with} \quad -\frac{\pi}{2} < x < \frac{\pi}{2}.$$

The inverse cosine function, written "arccos" or "$\cos^{-1}$," is discussed in Problem 55. The range of the arccosine function is $0 \leq x \leq \pi$.

Figure 1.59: The tangent function   **Figure 1.60:** The arctangent function

[34] Note that $\sin^{-1} x = \arcsin x$ is not the same as $(\sin x)^{-1} = 1/\sin x$.

Exercises and Problems for Section 1.5

Exercises

For Exercises 1–9, draw the angle using a ray through the origin, and determine whether the sine, cosine, and tangent of that angle are positive, negative, zero, or undefined.

1. $\frac{3\pi}{2}$ **2.** 2π **3.** $\frac{\pi}{4}$

4. 3π **5.** $\frac{\pi}{6}$ **6.** $\frac{4\pi}{3}$

7. $\frac{-4\pi}{3}$ **8.** 4 **9.** -1

Find the period and amplitude in Exercises 10–13.

10. $y = 7\sin(3t)$ **11.** $z = 3\cos(u/4) + 5$

12. $w = 8 - 4\sin(2x + \pi)$ **13.** $r = 0.1\sin(\pi t) + 2$

For Exercises 14–23, find a possible formula for each graph.

14.

15.

16.

17.

18.

19.

20.

21.

22.

23.

In Exercises 24–26, calculate the quantity without using the the trigonometric functions on your calculator. You are given that $\sin(\pi/12) = 0.259$ and $\cos(\pi/5) = 0.809$. You may want to draw a picture showing the angles involved and check your answer on a calculator.

24. $\cos\left(-\frac{\pi}{5}\right)$ **25.** $\sin\frac{\pi}{5}$ **26.** $\cos\frac{\pi}{12}$

In Exercises 27–31, find a solution to the equation if possible. Give the answer in exact form and in decimal form.

27. $2 = 5\sin(3x)$ **28.** $1 = 8\cos(2x + 1) - 3$

29. $8 = 4\tan(5x)$ **30.** $1 = 8\tan(2x + 1) - 3$

31. $8 = 4\sin(5x)$

Problems

32. Without a calculator or computer, match the formulas with the graphs in Figure 1.61.

(a) $y = 2\cos(t - \pi/2)$ (b) $y = 2\cos t$

(c) $y = 2\cos(t + \pi/2)$

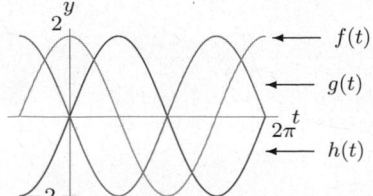

Figure 1.61

33. What is the difference between $\sin x^2$, $\sin^2 x$, and $\sin(\sin x)$? Express each of the three as a composition. (Note: $\sin^2 x$ is another way of writing $(\sin x)^2$.)

34. On the graph of $y = \sin x$, points P and Q are at consecutive lowest and highest points. Find the slope of the line through P and Q.

35. A population of animals oscillates sinusoidally between a low of 700 on January 1 and a high of 900 on July 1.

(a) Graph the population against time.
(b) Find a formula for the population as a function of time, t, in months since the start of the year.

36. The desert temperature, H, oscillates daily between $40°$F at 5 am and $80°$F at 5 pm. Write a possible formula for H in terms of t, measured in hours from 5 am.

37. (a) Match the functions $\omega = f(t), \omega = g(t), \omega = h(t),$ $\omega = k(t)$, whose values are in the table, with the functions with formulas:

(i) $\omega = 1.5 + \sin t$ (ii) $\omega = 0.5 + \sin t$
(iii) $\omega = -0.5 + \sin t$ (iv) $\omega = -1.5 + \sin t$

(b) Based on the table, what is the relationship between the values of $g(t)$ and $k(t)$? Explain this relationship using the formulas you chose for g and k.

(c) Using the formulas you chose for g and h, explain why all the values of g are positive, whereas all the values of h are negative.

t	$f(t)$	t	$g(t)$	t	$h(t)$	t	$k(t)$
6.0	−0.78	3.0	1.64	5.0	−2.46	3.0	0.64
6.5	−0.28	3.5	1.15	5.1	−2.43	3.5	0.15
7.0	0.16	4.0	0.74	5.2	−2.38	4.0	−0.26
7.5	0.44	4.5	0.52	5.3	−2.33	4.5	−0.48
8.0	0.49	5.0	0.54	5.4	−2.27	5.0	−0.46

38. The depth of water in a tank oscillates sinusoidally once every 6 hours. If the smallest depth is 5.5 feet and the largest depth is 8.5 feet, find a possible formula for the depth in terms of time in hours.

39. The voltage, V, of an electrical outlet in a home as a function of time, t (in seconds), is $V = V_0 \cos(120\pi t)$.

(a) What is the period of the oscillation?
(b) What does V_0 represent?
(c) Sketch the graph of V against t. Label the axes.

40. The power output, P, of a solar panel varies with the position of the sun. Let $P = 10 \sin \theta$ watts, where θ is the angle between the sun's rays and the panel, $0 \le \theta \le \pi$. On a typical summer day in Ann Arbor, Michigan, the sun rises at 6 am and sets at 8 pm and the angle is $\theta = \pi t/14$, where t is time in hours since 6 am and $0 \le t \le 14$.

(a) Write a formula for a function, $f(t)$, giving the power output of the solar panel (in watts) t hours after 6 am on a typical summer day in Ann Arbor.
(b) Graph the function $f(t)$ in part (a) for $0 \le t \le 14$.
(c) At what time is the power output greatest? What is the power output at this time?
(d) On a typical winter day in Ann Arbor, the sun rises at 8 am and sets at 5 pm. Write a formula for a function, $g(t)$, giving the power output of the solar panel (in watts) t hours after 8 am on a typical winter day.

41. A baseball hit at an angle of θ to the horizontal with initial velocity v_0 has horizontal range, R, given by

$$R = \frac{v_0^2}{g} \sin(2\theta).$$

Here g is the acceleration due to gravity. Sketch R as a function of θ for $0 \le \theta \le \pi/2$. What angle gives the maximum range? What is the maximum range?

42. The visitors' guide to St. Petersburg, Florida, contains the chart shown in Figure 1.62 to advertise their good weather. Fit a trigonometric function approximately to the data, where H is temperature in degrees Fahrenheit, and the independent variable is time in months. In order to do this, you will need to estimate the amplitude and period of the data, and when the maximum occurs. (There are many possible answers to this problem, depending on how you read the graph.)

Figure 1.62: "St. Petersburg...where we're famous for our wonderful weather and year-round sunshine." (Reprinted with permission)

43. The Bay of Fundy in Canada has the largest tides in the world. The difference between low and high water levels is 15 meters (nearly 50 feet). At a particular point the depth of the water, y meters, is given as a function of time, t, in hours since midnight by

$$y = D + A \cos(B(t - C)).$$

(a) What is the physical meaning of D?
(b) What is the value of A?
(c) What is the value of B? Assume the time between successive high tides is 12.4 hours.
(d) What is the physical meaning of C?

44. A compact disc spins at a rate of 200 to 500 revolutions per minute. What are the equivalent rates measured in radians per second?

45. When a car's engine makes less than about 200 revolutions per minute, it stalls. What is the period of the rotation of the engine when it is about to stall?

46. What is the period of the earth's revolution around the sun?

47. What is the approximate period of the moon's revolution around the earth?

48. For a boat to float in a tidal bay, the water must be at least 2.5 meters deep. The depth of water around the boat, $d(t)$, in meters, where t is measured in hours since midnight, is

$$d(t) = 5 + 4.6 \sin(0.5t).$$

(a) What is the period of the tides in hours?
(b) If the boat leaves the bay at midday, what is the latest time it can return before the water becomes too shallow?

49. Match graphs A-D in Figure 1.63 with the functions below. Assume a, b, c and d are positive constants.

$$f(t) = \sin t + b \qquad\qquad h(t) = \sin t + e^{ct} + d$$
$$g(t) = \sin t + at + b \qquad\quad r(t) = \sin t - e^{ct} + b$$

Figure 1.63

50. In Figure 1.64, the blue curve shows monthly mean carbon dioxide (CO_2) concentration, in parts per million (ppm) at Mauna Loa Observatory, Hawaii, as a function of t, in months, since December 2005. The black curve shows the monthly mean concentration adjusted for seasonal CO_2 variation.[35]

(a) Approximately how much did the monthly mean CO_2 increase between December 2005 and December 2010?

(b) Find the average monthly rate of increase of the monthly mean CO_2 between December 2005 and December 2010. Use this information to find a linear function that approximates the black curve.

(c) The seasonal CO_2 variation between December 2005 and December 2010 can be approximated by a sinusoidal function. What is the approximate period of the function? What is its amplitude? Give a formula for the function.

(d) The blue curve may be approximated by a function of the form $h(t) = f(t) + g(t)$, where $f(t)$ is sinusoidal and $g(t)$ is linear. Using your work in parts (b) and (c), find a possible formula for $h(t)$. Graph $h(t)$ using the scale in Figure 1.64.

Figure 1.64

51. (a) Use a graphing calculator or computer to estimate the period of $2 \sin \theta + 3 \cos(2\theta)$.

(b) Explain your answer, given that the period of $\sin \theta$ is 2π and the period of $\cos(2\theta)$ is π.

52. Find the area of the trapezoidal cross-section of the irrigation canal shown in Figure 1.65.

Figure 1.65

53. Graph $y = \sin x$, $y = 0.4$, and $y = -0.4$.

(a) From the graph, estimate to one decimal place all the solutions of $\sin x = 0.4$ with $-\pi \le x \le \pi$.

(b) Use a calculator to find $\arcsin(0.4)$. What is the relation between $\arcsin(0.4)$ and each of the solutions you found in part (a)?

(c) Estimate all the solutions to $\sin x = -0.4$ with $-\pi \le x \le \pi$ (again, to one decimal place).

(d) What is the relation between $\arcsin(0.4)$ and each of the solutions you found in part (c)?

54. Find the angle, in degrees, that a wheelchair ramp makes with the ground if the ramp rises 1 foot over a horizontal distance of

(a) 12 ft, the normal requirement[36]

(b) 8 ft, the steepest ramp legally permitted

(c) 20 ft, the recommendation if snow can be expected on the ramp

55. This problem introduces the arccosine function, or inverse cosine, denoted by $\boxed{\cos^{-1}}$ on most calculators.

(a) Using a calculator set in radians, make a table of values, to two decimal places, of $g(x) = \arccos x$, for $x = -1, -0.8, -0.6, \dots, 0, \dots, 0.6, 0.8, 1$.

(b) Sketch the graph of $g(x) = \arccos x$.

(c) Why is the domain of the arccosine the same as the domain of the arcsine?

(d) What is the range of the arccosine?

(e) Why is the range of the arccosine *not* the same as the range of the arcsine?

---

[35]http://www.esrl.noaa.gov/gmd/ccgg/trends/. Accessed March 2011. Monthly means joined by segments to highlight trends.

[36]http://www.access-board.gov/adaag/html/adaag.htm#4.1.6(3)a, accessed June 6, 2011.

Strengthen Your Understanding

In Problems 56–57, explain what is wrong with the statement.

56. For the function $f(x) = \sin(Bx)$ with $B > 0$, increasing the value of B increases the period.

57. For positive A, B, C, the maximum value of the function $y = A\sin(Bx) + C$ is $y = A$.

In Problems 58–59, give an example of:

58. A sine function with period 23.

59. A cosine function which oscillates between values of 1200 and 2000.

Are the statements in Problems 60–72 true or false? Give an explanation for your answer.

60. The function $f(\theta) = \cos\theta - \sin\theta$ is increasing on $0 \le \theta \le \pi/2$.

61. The function $f(t) = \sin(0.05\pi t)$ has period 0.05.

62. If t is in seconds, $g(t) = \cos(200\pi t)$ executes 100 cycles in one second.

63. The function $f(\theta) = \tan(\theta - \pi/2)$ is not defined at $\theta = \pi/2, 3\pi/2, 5\pi/2 \ldots$.

64. $\sin|x| = \sin x$ for $-2\pi < x < 2\pi$

65. $\sin|x| = |\sin x|$ for $-2\pi < x < 2\pi$

66. $\cos|x| = |\cos x|$ for $-2\pi < x < 2\pi$

67. $\cos|x| = \cos x$ for $-2\pi < x < 2\pi$

68. The function $f(x) = \sin(x^2)$ is periodic, with period 2π.

69. The function $g(\theta) = e^{\sin\theta}$ is periodic.

70. If $f(x)$ is a periodic function with period k, then $f(g(x))$ is periodic with period k for every function $g(x)$.

71. If $g(x)$ is a periodic function, then $f(g(x))$ is periodic for every function $f(x)$.

72. The function $f(x) = |\sin x|$ is even.

1.6 POWERS, POLYNOMIALS, AND RATIONAL FUNCTIONS

Power Functions

A *power function* is a function in which the dependent variable is proportional to a power of the independent variable:

> A **power function** has the form
> $$f(x) = kx^p, \qquad \text{where } k \text{ and } p \text{ are constant.}$$

For example, the volume, V, of a sphere of radius r is given by

$$V = g(r) = \frac{4}{3}\pi r^3.$$

As another example, the gravitational force, F, on a unit mass at a distance r from the center of the earth is given by Newton's Law of Gravitation, which says that, for some positive constant k,

$$F = \frac{k}{r^2} \quad \text{or} \quad F = kr^{-2}.$$

We consider the graphs of the power functions x^n, with n a positive integer. Figures 1.66 and 1.67 show that the graphs fall into two groups: odd and even powers. For n greater than 1, the odd powers have a "seat" at the origin and are increasing everywhere else. The even powers are first decreasing and then increasing. For large x, the higher the power of x, the faster the function climbs.

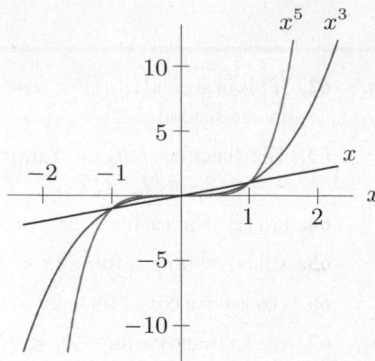

Figure 1.66: Odd powers of x: "Seat" shaped for $n > 1$

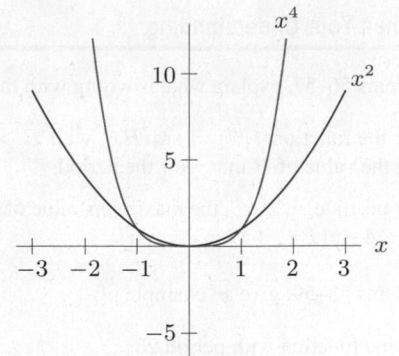

Figure 1.67: Even powers of x: $\bigcup$-shaped

Exponentials and Power Functions: Which Dominate?

In everyday language, the word exponential is often used to imply very fast growth. But do exponential functions always grow faster than power functions? To determine what happens "in the long run," we often want to know which functions *dominate* as x gets arbitrarily large.

Let's consider $y = 2^x$ and $y = x^3$. The close-up view in Figure 1.68(a) shows that between $x = 2$ and $x = 4$, the graph of $y = 2^x$ lies below the graph of $y = x^3$. The far-away view in Figure 1.68(b) shows that the exponential function $y = 2^x$ eventually overtakes $y = x^3$. Figure 1.68(c), which gives a very far-away view, shows that, for large x, the value of x^3 is insignificant compared to 2^x. Indeed, 2^x is growing so much faster than x^3 that the graph of 2^x appears almost vertical in comparison to the more leisurely climb of x^3.

We say that Figure 1.68(a) gives a *local* view of the functions' behavior, whereas Figure 1.68(c) gives a *global* view.

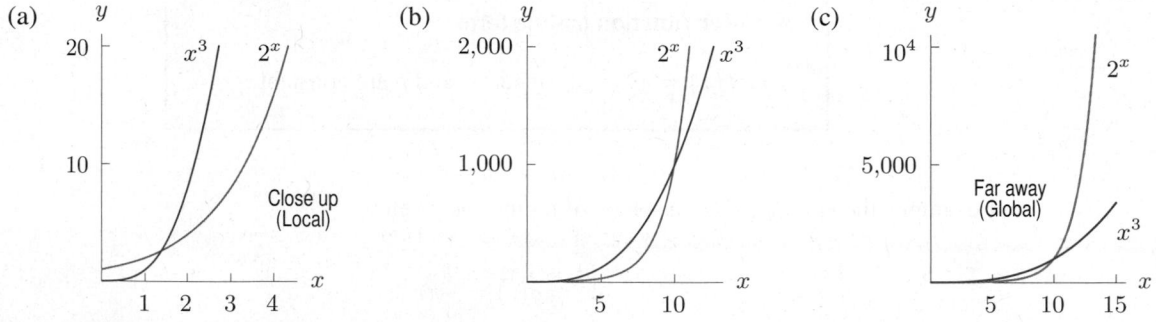

Figure 1.68: Comparison of $y = 2^x$ and $y = x^3$: Notice that $y = 2^x$ eventually dominates $y = x^3$

In fact, *every* exponential growth function eventually dominates *every* power function. Although an exponential function may be below a power function for some values of x, if we look at large enough x-values, a^x (with $a > 1$) will eventually dominate x^n, no matter what n is.

Polynomials

Polynomials are the sums of power functions with nonnegative integer exponents:

$$y = p(x) = a_n x^n + a_{n-1} x^{n-1} + \cdots + a_1 x + a_0.$$

Quadratic ($n = 2$)   Cubic ($n = 3$)   Quartic ($n = 4$)   Quintic ($n = 5$)

Figure 1.69: Graphs of typical polynomials of degree n

Here n is a nonnegative integer called the *degree* of the polynomial, and $a_n, a_{n-1}, \ldots, a_1, a_0$ are constants, with leading coefficient $a_n \neq 0$. An example of a polynomial of degree $n = 3$ is

$$y = p(x) = 2x^3 - x^2 - 5x - 7.$$

In this case $a_3 = 2, a_2 = -1, a_1 = -5$, and $a_0 = -7$. The shape of the graph of a polynomial depends on its degree; typical graphs are shown in Figure 1.69. These graphs correspond to a positive coefficient for x^n; a negative leading coefficient turns the graph upside down. Notice that the quadratic "turns around" once, the cubic "turns around" twice, and the quartic (fourth degree) "turns around" three times. An nth degree polynomial "turns around" at most $n - 1$ times (where n is a positive integer), but there may be fewer turns.

Example 1   Find possible formulas for the polynomials whose graphs are in Figure 1.70.

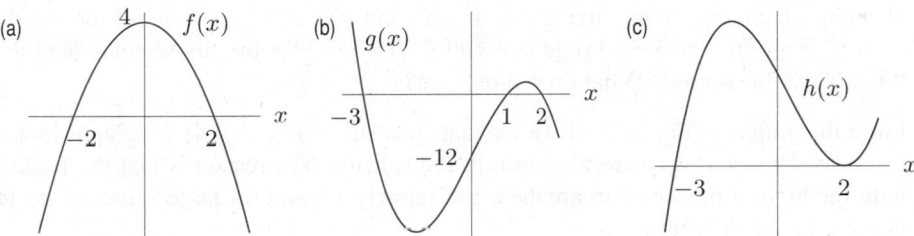

(a)   (b)   (c)

Figure 1.70: Graphs of polynomials

Solution   (a) This graph appears to be a parabola, turned upside down, and moved up by 4, so

$$f(x) = -x^2 + 4.$$

The negative sign turns the parabola upside down and the $+4$ moves it up by 4. Notice that this formula does give the correct x-intercepts since $0 = -x^2 + 4$ has solutions $x = \pm 2$. These values of x are called *zeros* of f.

We can also solve this problem by looking at the x-intercepts first, which tell us that $f(x)$ has factors of $(x + 2)$ and $(x - 2)$. So

$$f(x) = k(x + 2)(x - 2).$$

To find k, use the fact that the graph has a y-intercept of 4, so $f(0) = 4$, giving

$$4 = k(0 + 2)(0 - 2),$$

or $k = -1$. Therefore, $f(x) = -(x + 2)(x - 2)$, which multiplies out to $-x^2 + 4$.

Note that $f(x) = 4 - x^4/4$ also has the same basic shape, but is flatter near $x = 0$. There are many possible answers to these questions.

(b) This looks like a cubic with factors $(x + 3)$, $(x - 1)$, and $(x - 2)$, one for each intercept:

$$g(x) = k(x + 3)(x - 1)(x - 2).$$

Since the y-intercept is -12, we have

$$-12 = k(0 + 3)(0 - 1)(0 - 2).$$

So $k = -2$, and we get the cubic polynomial

$$g(x) = -2(x+3)(x-1)(x-2).$$

(c) This also looks like a cubic with zeros at $x = 2$ and $x = -3$. Notice that at $x = 2$ the graph of $h(x)$ touches the x-axis but does not cross it, whereas at $x = -3$ the graph crosses the x-axis. We say that $x = 2$ is a *double zero*, but that $x = -3$ is a single zero.

To find a formula for $h(x)$, imagine the graph of $h(x)$ to be slightly lower down, so that the graph has one x-intercept near $x = -3$ and two near $x = 2$, say at $x = 1.9$ and $x = 2.1$. Then a formula would be

$$h(x) \approx k(x+3)(x-1.9)(x-2.1).$$

Now move the graph back to its original position. The zeros at $x = 1.9$ and $x = 2.1$ move toward $x = 2$, giving

$$h(x) = k(x+3)(x-2)(x-2) = k(x+3)(x-2)^2.$$

The double zero leads to a repeated factor, $(x-2)^2$. Notice that when $x > 2$, the factor $(x-2)^2$ is positive, and when $x < 2$, the factor $(x-2)^2$ is still positive. This reflects the fact that $h(x)$ does not change sign near $x = 2$. Compare this with the behavior near the single zero at $x = -3$, where h does change sign.

We cannot find k, as no coordinates are given for points off of the x-axis. Any positive value of k stretches the graph vertically but does not change the zeros, so any positive k works.

Example 2   Using a calculator or computer, graph $y = x^4$ and $y = x^4 - 15x^2 - 15x$ for $-4 \leq x \leq 4$ and for $-20 \leq x \leq 20$. Set the y range to $-100 \leq y \leq 100$ for the first domain, and to $-100 \leq y \leq 200{,}000$ for the second. What do you observe?

Solution   From the graphs in Figure 1.71 we see that close up ($-4 \leq x \leq 4$) the graphs look different; from far away, however, they are almost indistinguishable. The reason is that the leading terms (those with the highest power of x) are the same, namely x^4, and for large values of x, the leading term dominates the other terms.

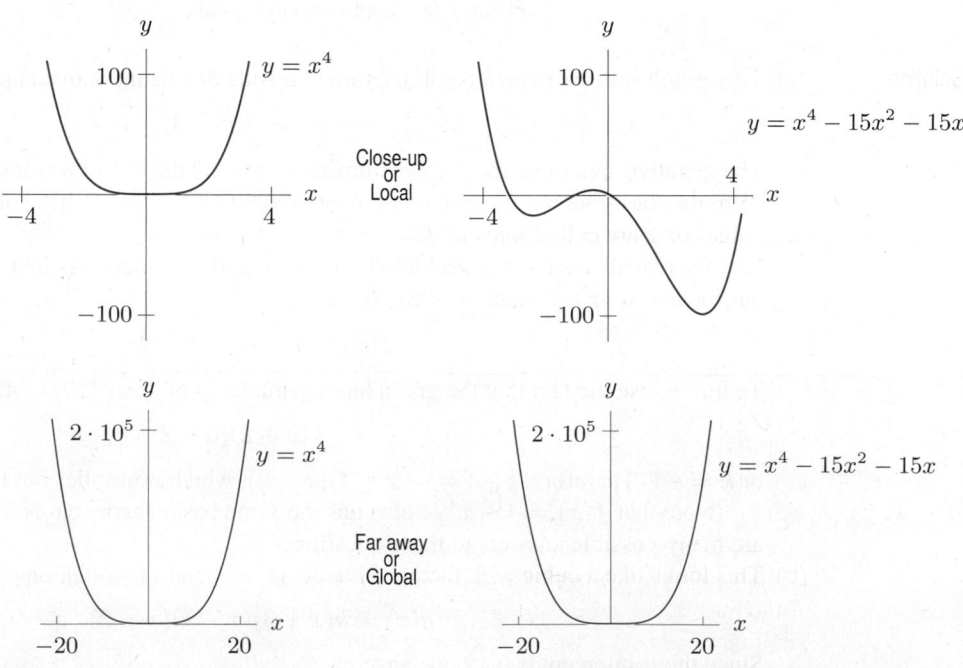

Figure 1.71: Local and global views of $y = x^4$ and $y = x^4 - 15x^2 - 15x$

Rational Functions

Rational functions are ratios of polynomials, p and q:

$$f(x) = \frac{p(x)}{q(x)}.$$

Example 3   Look at a graph and explain the behavior of $y = \dfrac{1}{x^2 + 4}$.

Solution   The function is even, so the graph is symmetric about the y-axis. As x gets larger, the denominator gets larger, making the value of the function closer to 0. Thus the graph gets arbitrarily close to the x-axis as x increases without bound. See Figure 1.72.

Figure 1.72: Graph of $y = \frac{1}{x^2+4}$

In the previous example, we say that $y = 0$ (i.e. the x-axis) is a *horizontal asymptote*. Writing "$\rightarrow$" to mean "tends to," we have $y \rightarrow 0$ as $x \rightarrow \infty$ and $y \rightarrow 0$ as $x \rightarrow -\infty$.

> If the graph of $y = f(x)$ approaches a horizontal line $y = L$ as $x \rightarrow \infty$ or $x \rightarrow -\infty$, then the line $y = L$ is called a **horizontal asymptote**.[37] This occurs when
>
> $$f(x) \rightarrow L \quad \text{as} \quad x \rightarrow \infty \qquad \text{or} \qquad f(x) \rightarrow L \quad \text{as} \quad x \rightarrow -\infty.$$
>
> If the graph of $y = f(x)$ approaches the vertical line $x = K$ as $x \rightarrow K$ from one side or the other, that is, if
>
> $$y \rightarrow \infty \quad \text{or} \quad y \rightarrow -\infty \quad \text{when} \quad x \rightarrow K,$$
>
> then the line $x = K$ is called a **vertical asymptote**.

The graphs of rational functions may have vertical asymptotes where the denominator is zero. For example, the function in Example 3 has no vertical asymptotes as the denominator is never zero. The function in Example 4 has two vertical asymptotes corresponding to the two zeros in the denominator.

Rational functions have horizontal asymptotes if $f(x)$ approaches a finite number as $x \rightarrow \infty$ or $x \rightarrow -\infty$. We call the behavior of a function as $x \rightarrow \pm\infty$ its *end behavior*.

Example 4   Look at a graph and explain the behavior of $y = \dfrac{3x^2 - 12}{x^2 - 1}$, including end behavior.

Solution   Factoring gives

$$y = \frac{3x^2 - 12}{x^2 - 1} = \frac{3(x + 2)(x - 2)}{(x + 1)(x - 1)}$$

so $x = \pm 1$ are vertical asymptotes. If $y = 0$, then $3(x + 2)(x - 2) = 0$ or $x = \pm 2$; these are the x-intercepts. Note that zeros of the denominator give rise to the vertical asymptotes, whereas zeros of the numerator give rise to x-intercepts. Substituting $x = 0$ gives $y = 12$; this is the y-intercept. The function is even, so the graph is symmetric about the y-axis.

---

[37] We are assuming that $f(x)$ gets arbitrarily close to L as $x \rightarrow \infty$.

Table 1.18   *Values of*
$y = \frac{3x^2 - 12}{x^2 - 1}$

x	$y = \frac{3x^2 - 12}{x^2 - 1}$
± 10	2.909091
± 100	2.999100
± 1000	2.999991

Figure 1.73: Graph of the function $y = \frac{3x^2 - 12}{x^2 - 1}$

To see what happens as $x \to \pm\infty$, look at the y-values in Table 1.18. Clearly y is getting closer to 3 as x gets large positively or negatively. Alternatively, realize that as $x \to \pm\infty$, only the highest powers of x matter. For large x, the 12 and the 1 are insignificant compared to x^2, so

$$y = \frac{3x^2 - 12}{x^2 - 1} \approx \frac{3x^2}{x^2} = 3 \quad \text{for large } x.$$

So $y \to 3$ as $x \to \pm\infty$, and therefore the horizontal asymptote is $y = 3$. See Figure 1.73. Since, for $x > 1$, the value of $(3x^2 - 12)/(x^2 - 1)$ is less than 3, the graph lies *below* its asymptote. (Why doesn't the graph lie below $y = 3$ when $-1 < x < 1$?)

Exercises and Problems for Section 1.6

Exercises

For Exercises 1–2, what happens to the value of the function as $x \to \infty$ and as $x \to -\infty$?

1. $y = 0.25x^3 + 3$

2. $y = 2 \cdot 10^{4x}$

In Exercises 3–10, determine the end behavior of each function as $x \to +\infty$ and as $x \to -\infty$.

3. $f(x) = -10x^4$

4. $f(x) = 3x^5$

5. $f(x) = 5x^4 - 25x^3 - 62x^2 + 5x + 300$

6. $f(x) = 1000 - 38x + 50x^2 - 5x^3$

7. $f(x) = \dfrac{3x^2 + 5x + 6}{x^2 - 4}$

8. $f(x) = \dfrac{10 + 5x^2 - 3x^3}{2x^3 - 4x + 12}$

9. $f(x) = 3x^{-4}$

10. $f(x) = e^x$

In Exercises 11–16, which function dominates as $x \to \infty$?

11. $1000x^4$ or $0.2x^5$

12. $10e^{0.1x}$ or $5000x^2$

13. $100x^5$ or 1.05^x

14. $2x^4$ or $10x^3 + 25x^2 + 50x + 100$

15. $20x^4 + 100x^2 + 5x$ or $25 - 40x^2 + x^3 + 3x^5$

16. $\sqrt{x}$ or $\ln x$

17. Each of the graphs in Figure 1.74 is of a polynomial. The windows are large enough to show end behavior.

(a) What is the minimum possible degree of the polynomial?

(b) Is the leading coefficient of the polynomial positive or negative?

Figure 1.74

Find cubic polynomials for the graphs in Exercises 18–19.

18.

19.

Find possible formulas for the graphs in Exercises 20–23.

20.

21.

22.

23.

In Exercises 24–26, choose the functions that are in the given family, assuming a, b, and c are constants.

$$f(x) = \sqrt{x^4 + 16} \qquad g(x) = ax^{23}$$

$$h(x) = -\frac{1}{5^{x-2}} \qquad p(x) = \frac{a^3 b^x}{c}$$

$$q(x) = \frac{ab^2}{c} \qquad r(x) = -x + b - \sqrt{cx^4}$$

24. Exponential   **25.** Quadratic   **26.** Linear

Problems

27. How many distinct roots can a polynomial of degree 5 have? (List all possibilities.) Sketch a possible graph for each case.

28. A rational function $y = f(x)$ is graphed in Figure 1.75. If $f(x) = g(x)/h(x)$ with $g(x)$ and $h(x)$ both quadratic functions, give possible formulas for $g(x)$ and $h(x)$.

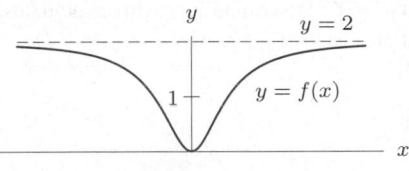

Figure 1.75

29. Find a calculator window in which the graphs of $f(x) = x^3 + 1000x^2 + 1000$ and $g(x) = x^3 - 1000x^2 - 1000$ appear indistinguishable.

30. For each function, fill in the blanks in the statements:

$f(x) \to$ _____ as $x \to -\infty$,

$f(x) \to$ _____ as $x \to +\infty$.

(a) $f(x) = 17 + 5x^2 - 12x^3 - 5x^4$

(b) $f(x) = \dfrac{3x^2 - 5x + 2}{2x^2 - 8}$

(c) $f(x) = e^x$

31. The DuBois formula relates a person's surface area s, in m², to weight w, in kg, and height h, in cm, by

$$s = 0.01 w^{0.25} h^{0.75}.$$

(a) What is the surface area of a person who weighs 65 kg and is 160 cm tall?

(b) What is the weight of a person whose height is 180 cm and who has a surface area of 1.5 m²?

(c) For people of fixed weight 70 kg, solve for h as a function of s. Simplify your answer.

32. According to *Car and Driver*, an Alfa Romeo going at 70 mph requires 177 feet to stop. Assuming that the stopping distance is proportional to the square of velocity, find the stopping distances required by an Alfa Romeo going at 35 mph and at 140 mph (its top speed).

33. Poiseuille's Law gives the rate of flow, R, of a gas through a cylindrical pipe in terms of the radius of the pipe, r, for a fixed drop in pressure between the two ends of the pipe.

(a) Find a formula for Poiseuille's Law, given that the rate of flow is proportional to the fourth power of the radius.

(b) If $R = 400$ cm³/sec in a pipe of radius 3 cm for a certain gas, find a formula for the rate of flow of that gas through a pipe of radius r cm.

(c) What is the rate of flow of the same gas through a pipe with a 5 cm radius?

34. A box of fixed volume V has a square base with side length x. Write a formula for the height, h, of the box in terms of x and V. Sketch a graph of h versus x.

35. A closed cylindrical can of fixed volume V has radius r.

(a) Find the surface area, S, as a function of r.

(b) What happens to the value of S as $r \to \infty$?

(c) Sketch a graph of S against r, if $V = 10$ cm³.

In Problems 36–38, find all horizontal and vertical asymptotes for each rational function.

36. $f(x) = \dfrac{5x - 2}{2x + 3}$

37. $f(x) = \dfrac{x^2 + 5x + 4}{x^2 - 4}$

38. $f(x) = \dfrac{5x^3 + 7x - 1}{x^3 - 27}$

39. The height of an object above the ground at time t is given by

$$s = v_0 t - \frac{g}{2}t^2,$$

where v_0 is the initial velocity and g is the acceleration due to gravity.

   (a) At what height is the object initially?
   (b) How long is the object in the air before it hits the ground?
   (c) When will the object reach its maximum height?
   (d) What is that maximum height?

40. A pomegranate is thrown from ground level straight up into the air at time $t = 0$ with velocity 64 feet per second. Its height at time t seconds is $f(t) = -16t^2 + 64t$. Find the time it hits the ground and the time it reaches its highest point. What is the maximum height?

41. (a) If $f(x) = ax^2 + bx + c$, what can you say about the values of a, b, and c if:

   (i) $(1, 1)$ is on the graph of $f(x)$?
   (ii) $(1, 1)$ is the vertex of the graph of $f(x)$? [Hint: The axis of symmetry is $x = -b/(2a)$.]
   (iii) The y-intercept of the graph is $(0, 6)$?

   (b) Find a quadratic function satisfying all three conditions.

42. A cubic polynomial with positive leading coefficient is shown in Figure 1.76 for $-10 \le x \le 10$ and $-10 \le y \le 10$. What can be concluded about the total number of zeros of this function? What can you say about the location of each of the zeros? Explain.

Figure 1.76

43. After running 3 miles at a speed of x mph, a man walked the next 6 miles at a speed that was 2 mph slower. Express the total time spent on the trip as a function of x. What horizontal and vertical asymptotes does the graph of this function have?

44. Which of the functions I–III meet each of the following descriptions? There may be more than one function for each description, or none at all.

   (a) Horizontal asymptote of $y = 1$.
   (b) The x-axis is a horizontal asymptote.

   (c) Symmetric about the y-axis.
   (d) An odd function.
   (e) Vertical asymptotes at $x = \pm 1$.

   I. $y = \dfrac{x - 1}{x^2 + 1}$ II. $y = \dfrac{x^2 - 1}{x^2 + 1}$ III. $y = \dfrac{x^2 + 1}{x^2 - 1}$

45. Values of three functions are given in Table 1.19, rounded to two decimal places. One function is of the form $y = ab^t$, one is of the form $y = ct^2$, and one is of the form $y = kt^3$. Which function is which?

Table 1.19

t	$f(t)$	t	$g(t)$	t	$h(t)$
2.0	4.40	1.0	3.00	0.0	2.04
2.2	5.32	1.2	5.18	1.0	3.06
2.4	6.34	1.4	8.23	2.0	4.59
2.6	7.44	1.6	12.29	3.0	6.89
2.8	8.62	1.8	17.50	4.0	10.33
3.0	9.90	2.0	24.00	5.0	15.49

46. Use a graphing calculator or a computer to graph $y = x^4$ and $y = 3^x$. Determine approximate domains and ranges that give each of the graphs in Figure 1.77.

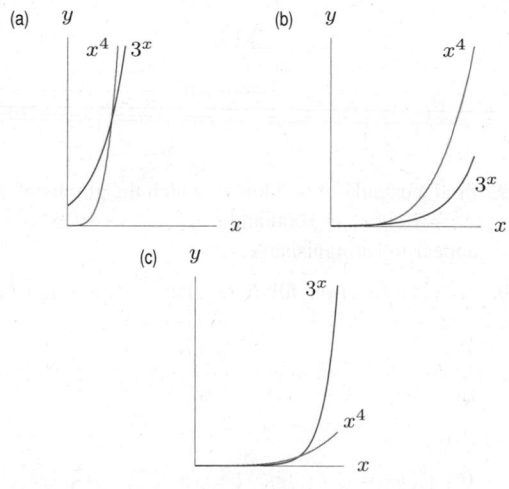

Figure 1.77

47. The rate, R, at which a population in a confined space increases is proportional to the product of the current population, P, and the difference between the carrying capacity, L, and the current population. (The carrying capacity is the maximum population the environment can sustain.)

   (a) Write R as a function of P.
   (b) Sketch R as a function of P.

48. Consider the point P at the intersection of the circle $x^2 + y^2 = 2a^2$ and the parabola $y = x^2/a$ in Figure 1.78. If a is increased, the point P traces out a curve. For $a > 0$, find the equation of this curve.

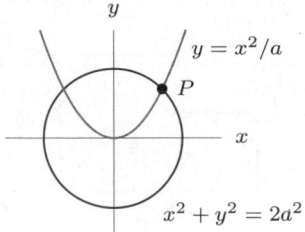

Figure 1.78

49. When an object of mass m moves with a velocity v that is small compared to the velocity of light, c, its energy is given approximately by

$$E \approx \frac{1}{2}mv^2.$$

If v is comparable in size to c, then the energy must be computed by the exact formula

$$E = mc^2 \left(\frac{1}{\sqrt{1 - v^2/c^2}} - 1 \right).$$

(a) Plot a graph of both functions for E against v for $0 \le v \le 5 \cdot 10^8$ and $0 \le E \le 5 \cdot 10^{17}$. Take $m = 1$ kg and $c = 3 \cdot 10^8$ m/sec. Explain how you can predict from the exact formula the position of the vertical asymptote.

(b) What do the graphs tell you about the approximation? For what values of v does the first formula give a good approximation to E?

Strengthen Your Understanding

In Problems 50–51, explain what is wrong with the statement.

50. The graph of a polynomial of degree 5 cuts the horizontal axis five times.

51. Every rational function has a horizontal asymptote.

In Problems 52–57, give an example of:

52. A polynomial of degree 3 whose graph cuts the horizontal axis three times to the right of the origin.

53. A rational function with horizontal asymptote $y = 3$.

54. A rational function that is not a polynomial and that has no vertical asymptote.

55. A function that has a vertical asymptote at $x = -7\pi$.

56. A function that has exactly 17 vertical asymptotes.

57. A function that has a vertical asymptote which is crossed by a horizontal asymptote.

Are the statements in Problems 58–59 true or false? Give an explanation for your answer.

58. Every polynomial of even degree has a least one real zero.

59. Every polynomial of odd degree has a least one real zero.

60. List the following functions in order from smallest to largest as $x \to \infty$ (that is, as x increases without bound).

(a) $f(x) = -5x$ **(b)** $g(x) = 10^x$

(c) $h(x) = 0.9^x$ **(d)** $k(x) = x^5$

(e) $l(x) = \pi^x$

1.7 INTRODUCTION TO CONTINUITY

This section gives an intuitive introduction to the idea of *continuity*. This leads to the concept of limit and a definition of continuity in Section 1.8.

Continuity of a Function on an Interval: Graphical Viewpoint

Roughly speaking, a function is said to be *continuous* on an interval if its graph has no breaks, jumps, or holes in that interval. Continuity is important because, as we shall see, continuous functions have many desirable properties.

For example, to locate the zeros of a function, we often look for intervals where the function changes sign. In the case of the function $f(x) = 3x^3 - x^2 + 2x - 1$, for instance, we expect[38] to find a zero between 0 and 1 because $f(0) = -1$ and $f(1) = 3$. (See Figure 1.79.) To be sure that $f(x)$ has a zero there, we need to know that the graph of the function has no breaks or jumps in it. Otherwise the graph could jump across the x-axis, changing sign but not creating a zero. For example, $f(x) = 1/x$ has opposite signs at $x = -1$ and $x = 1$, but no zeros for $-1 \le x \le 1$

---

[38] This is due to the Intermediate Value Theorem, which is discussed on page 55.

because of the break at $x = 0$. (See Figure 1.80.) To be certain that a function has a zero in an interval on which it changes sign, we need to know that the function is defined and continuous in that interval.

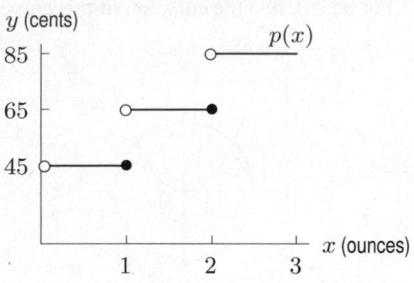

Figure 1.79: The graph of $f(x) = 3x^3 - x^2 + 2x - 1$

Figure 1.80: No zero although $f(-1)$ and $f(1)$ have opposite signs

Figure 1.81: Cost of mailing a letter

A continuous function has a graph which can be drawn without lifting the pencil from the paper.

Example: The function $f(x) = 3x^3 - x^2 + 2x - 1$ is continuous on any interval. (See Figure 1.79.)

Example: The function $f(x) = 1/x$ is not defined at $x = 0$. It is continuous on any interval not containing the origin. (See Figure 1.80.)

Example: Suppose $p(x)$ is the price of mailing a first-class letter weighing x ounces. It costs 45¢ for one ounce or less, 65¢ between one and two ounces, and so on. So the graph (in Figure 1.81) is a series of steps. This function is not continuous on any open interval containing a positive integer because the graph jumps at these points.

Which Functions Are Continuous?

Requiring a function to be continuous on an interval is not asking very much, as any function whose graph is an unbroken curve over the interval is continuous. For example, exponential functions, polynomials, and the sine and cosine are continuous on every interval. Rational functions are continuous on any interval in which their denominators are not zero. Functions created by adding, multiplying, or composing continuous functions are also continuous.

The Intermediate Value Theorem

Continuity tells us about the values taken by a function. In particular, a continuous function cannot skip values. For example, the function in the next example must have a zero because its graph cannot skip over the x-axis.

Example 1   What do the values in Table 1.20 tell you about the zeros of $f(x) = \cos x - 2x^2$?

Table 1.20

x	$f(x)$
0	1.00
0.2	0.90
0.4	0.60
0.6	0.11
0.8	−0.58
1.0	−1.46

Figure 1.82: Zeros occur where the graph of a continuous function crosses the horizontal axis

Solution   Since $f(x)$ is the difference of two continuous functions, it is continuous. We conclude that $f(x)$ has at least one zero in the interval $0.6 < x < 0.8$, since $f(x)$ changes from positive to negative on that interval. The graph of $f(x)$ in Figure 1.82 suggests that there is only one zero in the interval $0 \le x \le 1$, but we cannot be sure of this from the graph or the table of values.

In the previous example, we concluded that $f(x) = \cos x - 2x^2$ has a zero between $x = 0$ and $x = 1$ because $f(x)$ is positive at $x = 0$ and negative at $x = 1$. More generally, an intuitive notion of continuity tells us that, as we follow the graph of a continuous function f from some point $(a, f(a))$ to another point $(b, f(b))$, then f takes on all intermediate values between $f(a)$ and $f(b)$. (See Figure 1.83.) This is:

Theorem 1.1: Intermediate Value Theorem

Suppose f is continuous on a closed interval $[a, b]$. If k is any number between $f(a)$ and $f(b)$, then there is at least one number c in $[a, b]$ such that $f(c) = k$.

The Intermediate Value Theorem depends on the formal definition of continuity given in Section 1.8. See also www.wiley.com/college/hughes-hallett. The key idea is to find successively smaller subintervals of $[a, b]$ on which f changes from less than k to more than k. These subintervals converge on the number c.

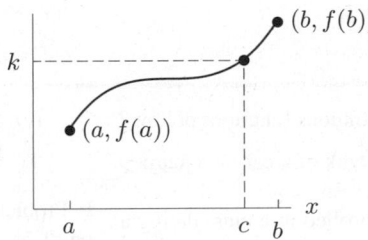

Figure 1.83: The Intermediate Value Theorem

Continuity of a Function at a Point: Numerical Viewpoint

A function is continuous if nearby values of the independent variable give nearby values of the function. In practical work, continuity is important because it means that small errors in the independent variable lead to small errors in the value of the function.

Example: Suppose that $f(x) = x^2$ and that we want to compute $f(\pi)$. Knowing f is continuous tells us that taking $x = 3.14$ should give a good approximation to $f(\pi)$, and that we can get as accurate an approximation to $f(\pi)$ as we want by using enough decimals of π.

Example: If $p(x)$ is the cost of mailing a letter weighing x ounces, then $p(0.99) = p(1) = 45¢$, whereas $p(1.01) = 65¢$, because as soon as we get over 1 ounce, the price jumps up to 65¢. So a small difference in the weight of a letter can lead to a significant difference in its mailing cost. Hence p is not continuous at $x = 1$.

In other words, if $f(x)$ is continuous at $x = c$, the values of $f(x)$ approach $f(c)$ as x approaches c. Using the concept of a limit introduced in Section 1.8, we can define more precisely what it means for the values of $f(x)$ to approach $f(c)$ as x approaches c.

Example 2   Investigate the continuity of $f(x) = x^2$ at $x = 2$.

Solution   From Table 1.21, it appears that the values of $f(x) = x^2$ approach $f(2) = 4$ as x approaches 2. Thus f appears to be continuous at $x = 2$. Continuity at a point describes behavior of a function *near* a point, as well as *at* the point.

Table 1.21   *Values of x^2 near $x = 2$*

x	1.9	1.99	1.999	2.001	2.01	2.1
x^2	3.61	3.96	3.996	4.004	4.04	4.41

Exercises and Problems for Section 1.7

Exercises

In Exercises 1–10, is the function continuous on the interval?

1. $\dfrac{1}{x-2}$ on $[-1,1]$

2. $\dfrac{1}{x-2}$ on $[0,3]$

3. $\dfrac{1}{\sqrt{2x-5}}$ on $[3,4]$

4. $\dfrac{x}{x^2+2}$ on $[-2,2]$

5. $2x + x^{2/3}$ on $[-1,1]$

6. $2x + x^{-1}$ on $[-1,1]$

7. $\dfrac{1}{\cos x}$ on $[0,\pi]$

8. $\dfrac{1}{\sin x}$ on $[-\frac{\pi}{2},\frac{\pi}{2}]$

9. $\dfrac{e^x}{e^x-1}$ on $[-1,1]$

10. $\dfrac{e^{\sin\theta}}{\cos\theta}$ on $[-\frac{\pi}{4},\frac{\pi}{4}]$

In Exercises 11–14, show that there is a number c, with $0 \le c \le 1$, such that $f(c) = 0$.

11. $f(x) = x^3 + x^2 - 1$

12. $f(x) = e^x - 3x$

13. $f(x) = x - \cos x$

14. $f(x) = 2^x - 1/x$

15. Are the following functions continuous? Explain.

(a) $f(x) = \begin{cases} x & x \le 1 \\ x^2 & 1 < x \end{cases}$

(b) $g(x) = \begin{cases} x & x \le 3 \\ x^2 & 3 < x \end{cases}$

Problems

16. Which of the following are continuous functions of time?

(a) The quantity of gas in the tank of a car on a journey between New York and Boston.

(b) The number of students enrolled in a class during a semester.

(c) The age of the oldest person alive.

17. A car is coasting down a hill at a constant speed. A truck collides with the rear of the car, causing it to lurch ahead. Graph the car's speed from a time shortly before impact to a time shortly after impact. Graph the distance from the top of the hill for this time period. What can you say about the continuity of each of these functions?

18. An electrical circuit switches instantaneously from a 6 volt battery to a 12 volt battery 7 seconds after being turned on. Graph the battery voltage against time. Give formulas for the function represented by your graph. What can you say about the continuity of this function?

In Problems 19–22 find k so that the function is continuous on any interval.

19. $f(x) = \begin{cases} kx & x \le 3 \\ 5 & 3 < x \end{cases}$

20. $f(x) = \begin{cases} kx & 0 \le x < 2 \\ 3x^2 & 2 \le x \end{cases}$

21. $g(t) = \begin{cases} t + k & t \le 5 \\ kt & 5 < t \end{cases}$

22. $h(x) = \begin{cases} k\cos x & 0 \le x \le \pi \\ 12 - x & \pi < x \end{cases}$

23. (a) For $k = 1$, sketch

$$f(x) = \begin{cases} kx & 0 \le x \le 2 \\ (x-2)^2 + 3 & 2 < x \le 4. \end{cases}$$

(b) Find the value of k so that $f(x)$ is continuous at $x = 2$.

(c) Sketch $f(x)$ using the value of k you found in part (a).

In Problems 24–29, find a value of k making $h(x)$ continuous on $[0,5]$.

24. $h(x) = \begin{cases} kx & 0 \le x < 1 \\ x + 3 & 1 \le x \le 5. \end{cases}$

25. $h(x) = \begin{cases} kx & 0 \le x \le 1 \\ 2kx + 3 & 1 < x \le 5. \end{cases}$

26. $h(x) = \begin{cases} k\sin x & 0 \le x \le \pi \\ x + 4 & \pi < x \le 5. \end{cases}$

27. $h(x) = \begin{cases} e^{kx} & 0 \le x < 2 \\ x + 1 & 2 \le x \le 5. \end{cases}$

28. $h(x) = \begin{cases} 0.5x & 0 \le x < 1 \\ \sin(kx) & 1 \le x \le 5. \end{cases}$

29. $h(x) = \begin{cases} \ln(kx + 1) & 0 \le x \le 2 \\ x + 4 & 2 < x \le 5. \end{cases}$

30. For t in months, a population, in thousands, is approximated by a continuous function

$$P(t) = \begin{cases} e^{kt} & 0 \le t \le 12 \\ 100 & t > 12. \end{cases}$$

(a) What is the initial value of the population?

(b) What must be the value of k?

(c) Describe in words how the population is changing.

31. Is the following function continuous on $[-1,1]$?

$$f(x) = \begin{cases} \dfrac{x}{|x|} & x \ne 0 \\ 0 & x = 0 \end{cases}$$

32. Discuss the continuity of the function g graphed in Figure 1.84 and defined as follows:

$$g(\theta) = \begin{cases} \dfrac{\sin\theta}{\theta} & \text{for } \theta \neq 0 \\ 1/2 & \text{for } \theta = 0. \end{cases}$$

Figure 1.84

33. A 0.6 ml dose of a drug is injected into a patient steadily for half a second. At the end of this time, the quantity, Q, of the drug in the body starts to decay exponentially at a continuous rate of 0.2% per second. Using formulas, express Q as a continuous function of time, t in seconds.

34. Sketch the graphs of three different functions that are continuous on $0 \leq x \leq 1$ and that have the values given in the table. The first function is to have exactly one zero in $[0, 1]$, the second is to have at least two zeros in the interval $[0.6, 0.8]$, and the third is to have at least two zeros in the interval $[0, 0.6]$.

x	0	0.2	0.4	0.6	0.8	1.0
$f(x)$	1.00	0.90	0.60	0.11	−0.58	−1.46

35. Let $p(x)$ be a cubic polynomial with $p(5) < 0$, $p(10) > 0$, and $p(12) < 0$. What can you say about the number and location of zeros of $p(x)$?

36. (a) What does a graph of $y = e^x$ and $y = 4 - x^2$ tell you about the solutions to the equation $e^x = 4 - x^2$?
(b) Evaluate $f(x) = e^x + x^2 - 4$ at $x = -4, -3, -2, -1, 0, 1, 2, 3, 4$. In which intervals do the solutions to $e^x = 4 - x^2$ lie?

37. (a) Sketch the graph of a continuous function f with *all* of the following properties:

    (i) $f(0) = 2$

    (ii) $f(x)$ is decreasing for $0 \leq x \leq 3$

    (iii) $f(x)$ is increasing for $3 < x \leq 5$

    (iv) $f(x)$ is decreasing for $x > 5$

    (v) $f(x) \to 9$ as $x \to \infty$

(b) Is it possible that the graph of f is concave down for all $x > 6$? Explain.

38. (a) Does $f(x)$ satisfy the conditions for the Intermediate Value Theorem on $0 \leq x \leq 2$ if

$$f(x) = \begin{cases} e^x & 0 \leq x \leq 1 \\ 4 + (x-1)^2 & 1 < x \leq 2? \end{cases}$$

(b) What are $f(0)$ and $f(2)$? Can you find a value of k between $f(0)$ and $f(2)$ such that the equation $f(x) = k$ has no solution? If so, what is it?

Strengthen Your Understanding

In Problems 39–40, explain what is wrong with the statement.

39. For any function $f(x)$, if $f(a) = 2$ and $f(b) = 4$, the Intermediate Value Theorem says that f takes on the value 3 for some x between a and b.

40. If $f(x)$ is continuous on $0 \leq x \leq 2$ and if $f(0) = 0$ and $f(2) = 10$, the Intermediate Value Theorem says that $f(1) = 5$.

In Problems 41–44, give an example of:

41. A function which is defined for all x and continuous everywhere except at $x = 15$.

42. A function to which the Intermediate Value Theorem does not apply on the interval $-1 \leq x \leq 1$.

43. A function that is continuous on $[0, 1]$ but not continuous on $[1, 3]$.

44. A function that is increasing but not continuous on $[0, 10]$.

Are the statements in Problems 45–47 true or false? Give an explanation for your answer.

45. If a function is not continuous at a point, then it is not defined at that point.

46. If f is continuous on the interval $[0, 10]$ and $f(0) = 0$ and $f(10) = 100$, then $f(c)$ cannot be negative for c in $[0, 10]$.

47. If $f(x)$ is not continuous on the interval $[a, b]$, then $f(x)$ must omit at least one value between $f(a)$ and $f(b)$.

1.8 LIMITS

The concept of *limit* is the underpinning of calculus. In Section 1.7, we said that a function f is continuous at $x = c$ if the values of $f(x)$ approach $f(c)$ as x approaches c. In this section, we define a limit, which makes precise what we mean by approaching.

The Idea of a Limit

We first introduce some notation:

> We write $\lim_{x \to c} f(x) = L$ if the values of $f(x)$ approach L as x approaches c.

How should we find L, or even know whether such a number exists? We will look for trends in the values of $f(x)$ as x gets closer to c, but $x \neq c$. A graph from a calculator or computer often helps.

Example 1   Use a graph to estimate $\lim_{\theta \to 0} \left(\dfrac{\sin \theta}{\theta} \right)$. (Use radians.)

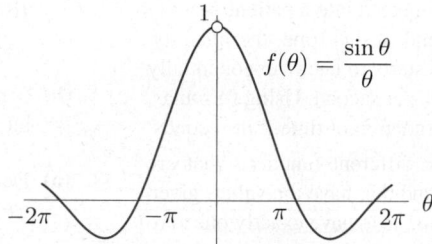

Figure 1.85: Find the limit as $\theta \to 0$

Solution   Figure 1.85 shows that as θ approaches 0 from either side, the value of $\sin \theta / \theta$ appears to approach 1, suggesting that $\lim_{\theta \to 0}(\sin \theta / \theta) = 1$. Zooming in on the graph near $\theta = 0$ provides further support for this conclusion. Notice that $\sin \theta / \theta$ is undefined at $\theta = 0$.

Figure 1.85 strongly suggests that $\lim_{\theta \to 0}(\sin \theta / \theta) = 1$, but to be sure we need to be more precise about words like "approach" and "close."

Definition of Limit

By the beginning of the 19th century, calculus had proved its worth, and there was no doubt about the correctness of its answers. However, it was not until the work of the French mathematician Augustin Cauchy (1789–1857) that calculus was put on a rigorous footing. Cauchy gave a formal definition of the limit, similar to the following:

> A function f is defined on an interval around c, except perhaps at the point $x = c$. We define the **limit** of the function $f(x)$ as x approaches c, written $\lim_{x \to c} f(x)$, to be a number L (if one exists) such that $f(x)$ is as close to L as we want whenever x is sufficiently close to c (but $x \neq c$). If L exists, we write
> $$\lim_{x \to c} f(x) = L.$$

Shortly, we see how "as close as we want" and "sufficiently close" are expressed using inequalities. First, we look at $\lim_{\theta \to 0}(\sin \theta / \theta)$ more closely (see Example 1).

Example 2   By graphing $y = (\sin\theta)/\theta$ in an appropriate window, find how close θ should be to 0 in order to make $(\sin\theta)/\theta$ within 0.01 of 1.

Solution   Since we want $(\sin\theta)/\theta$ to be within 0.01 of 1, we set the y-range on the graphing window to go from 0.99 to 1.01. Our first attempt with $-0.5 \le \theta \le 0.5$ yields the graph in Figure 1.86. Since we want the y-values to stay within the range $0.99 < y < 1.01$, we do not want the graph to leave the window through the top or bottom. By trial and error, we find that changing the θ-range to $-0.2 \le \theta \le 0.2$ gives the graph in Figure 1.87. Thus, the graph suggests that $(\sin\theta)/\theta$ is within 0.01 of 1 whenever θ is within 0.2 of 0. Proving this requires an analytical argument, not just graphs from a calculator.

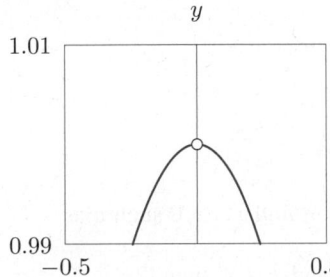

Figure 1.86: $(\sin\theta)/\theta$ with $-0.5 \le \theta \le 0.5$

Figure 1.87: $(\sin\theta)/\theta$ with $-0.2 \le \theta \le 0.2$

When we say "$f(x)$ is close to L," we measure closeness by the distance between $f(x)$ and L, expressed using absolute values:

$$|f(x) - L| = \text{Distance between } f(x) \text{ and } L.$$

When we say "as close to L as we want," we use ϵ (the Greek letter epsilon) to specify how close. We write

$$|f(x) - L| < \epsilon$$

to indicate that we want the distance between $f(x)$ and L to be less than ϵ. In Example 2 we used $\epsilon = 0.01$. Similarly, we interpret "x is sufficiently close to c" as specifying a distance between x and c:

$$|x - c| < \delta,$$

where δ (the Greek letter delta) tells us how close x should be to c. In Example 2 we found $\delta = 0.2$.

If $\lim_{x \to c} f(x) = L$, we know that no matter how narrow the horizontal band determined by ϵ in Figure 1.88, there is always a δ which makes the graph stay within that band, for $c - \delta < x < c + \delta$.

Thus we restate the definition of a limit, using symbols:

Definition of Limit

We define $\lim_{x \to c} f(x)$ to be the number L (if one exists) such that for every $\epsilon > 0$ (as small as we want), there is a $\delta > 0$ (sufficiently small) such that if $|x - c| < \delta$ and $x \ne c$, then $|f(x) - L| < \epsilon$.

We have arrived at a formal definition of limit. Let's see if it agrees with our intuition.

Figure 1.88: What the definition of the limit means graphically

---

Example 3   Use the definition of limit to show that $\lim_{x \to 3} 2x = 6$.

Solution   We must show how, given any $\epsilon > 0$, we can find a $\delta > 0$ such that

$$\text{If } |x - 3| < \delta \text{ and } x \neq 3, \text{ then } |2x - 6| < \epsilon.$$

Since $|2x - 6| = 2|x - 3|$, to get $|2x - 6| < \epsilon$ we require that $|x - 3| < \epsilon/2$. Thus we take $\delta = \epsilon/2$.

It is important to understand that the ϵ, δ definition does not make it easier to calculate limits; rather, the ϵ, δ definition makes it possible to put calculus on a rigorous foundation. From this foundation, we can prove the following properties. See Problems 78–80.

Theorem 1.2: Properties of Limits

Assuming all the limits on the right-hand side exist:

1. If b is a constant, then $\lim_{x \to c} (bf(x)) = b \left(\lim_{x \to c} f(x) \right)$.

2. $\lim_{x \to c} (f(x) + g(x)) = \lim_{x \to c} f(x) + \lim_{x \to c} g(x)$.

3. $\lim_{x \to c} (f(x)g(x)) = \left(\lim_{x \to c} f(x) \right) \left(\lim_{x \to c} g(x) \right)$.

4. $\lim_{x \to c} \dfrac{f(x)}{g(x)} = \dfrac{\lim_{x \to c} f(x)}{\lim_{x \to c} g(x)}$, provided $\lim_{x \to c} g(x) \neq 0$.

5. For any constant k, $\lim_{x \to c} k = k$.

6. $\lim_{x \to c} x = c$.

These properties underlie many limit calculations, though we may not acknowledge them explicitly.

Example 4   Explain how the limit properties are used in the following calculation:

$$\lim_{x \to 3} \frac{x^2 + 5x}{x + 9} = \frac{3^2 + 5 \cdot 3}{3 + 9} = 2.$$

Solution   We calculate this limit in stages, using the limit properties to justify each step:

$$\lim_{x \to 3} \frac{x^2 + 5x}{x + 9} = \frac{\lim_{x \to 3}(x^2 + 5x)}{\lim_{x \to 3}(x + 9)} \qquad \text{(Property 4, since } \lim_{x \to 3}(x + 9) \neq 0)$$

$$= \frac{\lim_{x \to 3}(x^2) + \lim_{x \to 3}(5x)}{\lim_{x \to 3} x + \lim_{x \to 3} 9} \qquad \text{(Property 2)}$$

$$= \frac{\left(\lim_{x \to 3} x\right)^2 + 5\left(\lim_{x \to 3} x\right)}{\lim_{x \to 3} x + \lim_{x \to 3} 9} \qquad \text{(Properties 1 and 3)}$$

$$= \frac{3^2 + 5 \cdot 3}{3 + 9} = 2. \qquad \text{(Properties 5 and 6)}$$

One- and Two-Sided Limits

When we write

$$\lim_{x \to 2} f(x),$$

we mean the number that $f(x)$ approaches as x approaches 2 *from both sides*. We examine values of $f(x)$ as x approaches 2 through values greater than 2 (such as 2.1, 2.01, 2.003) and values less than 2 (such as 1.9, 1.99, 1.994). If we want x to approach 2 only through values greater than 2, we write

$$\lim_{x \to 2^+} f(x)$$

for the number that $f(x)$ approaches (assuming such a number exists). Similarly,

$$\lim_{x \to 2^-} f(x)$$

denotes the number (if it exists) obtained by letting x approach 2 through values less than 2. We call $\lim_{x \to 2^+} f(x)$ a *right-hand limit* and $\lim_{x \to 2^-} f(x)$ a *left-hand limit*. Problems 43 and 44 ask for formal definitions of left- and right-hand limits.

Figure 1.89: Left- and right-hand limits at $x = 2$

For the function graphed in Figure 1.89, we have

$$\lim_{x \to 2^-} f(x) = L_1 \qquad \lim_{x \to 2^+} f(x) = L_2.$$

If the left- and right-hand limits were equal, that is, if $L_1 = L_2$, then it can be proved that $\lim_{x \to 2} f(x)$ exists and $\lim_{x \to 2} f(x) = L_1 = L_2$. Since $L_1 \neq L_2$ in Figure 1.89, we see that $\lim_{x \to 2} f(x)$ does not exist in this case.

When Limits Do Not Exist

Whenever there is no number L such that $\lim_{x \to c} f(x) = L$, we say $\lim_{x \to c} f(x)$ does not exist. Here are three examples in which limits fail to exist.

Example 5   Explain why $\lim\limits_{x \to 2} \dfrac{|x - 2|}{x - 2}$ does not exist.

Solution   Figure 1.90 shows the problem: The right-hand limit and the left-hand limit are different. For $x > 2$, we have $|x - 2| = x - 2$, so as x approaches 2 from the right,

$$\lim_{x \to 2^+} \frac{|x - 2|}{x - 2} = \lim_{x \to 2^+} \frac{x - 2}{x - 2} = \lim_{x \to 2^+} 1 = 1.$$

Similarly, if $x < 2$, then $|x - 2| = 2 - x$ so

$$\lim_{x \to 2^-} \frac{|x - 2|}{x - 2} = \lim_{x \to 2^-} \frac{2 - x}{x - 2} = \lim_{x \to 2^-} (-1) = -1.$$

So if $\lim\limits_{x \to 2} \dfrac{|x - 2|}{x - 2} = L$ then L would have to be both 1 and -1. Since L cannot have two different values, the limit does not exist.

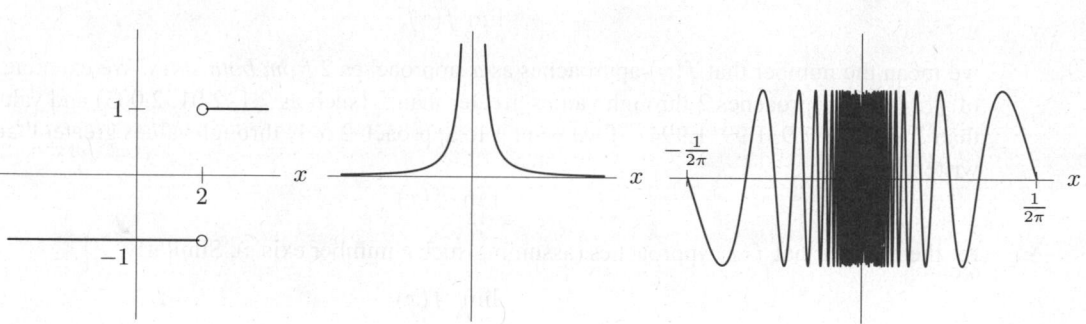

Figure 1.90: Graph of $|x - 2|/(x - 2)$

Figure 1.91: Graph of $1/x^2$

Figure 1.92: Graph of $\sin(1/x)$

Example 6   Explain why $\lim\limits_{x \to 0} \dfrac{1}{x^2}$ does not exist.

Solution   As x approaches zero, $1/x^2$ becomes arbitrarily large, so it cannot approach any finite number L. See Figure 1.91. Therefore we say $1/x^2$ has no limit as $x \to 0$.

If $\lim\limits_{x \to a} f(x)$ does not exist because $f(x)$ gets arbitrarily large on both sides of a, we also say $\lim\limits_{x \to a} f(x) = \infty$. So in Example 6 we could say $\lim\limits_{x \to 0} 1/x^2 = \infty$. This behavior may also be described as "diverging to infinity."

Example 7   Explain why $\lim\limits_{x \to 0} \sin\left(\dfrac{1}{x}\right)$ does not exist.

Solution   The sine function has values between -1 and 1. The graph in Figure 1.92 oscillates more and more rapidly as $x \to 0$. There are x-values approaching 0 where $\sin(1/x) = -1$. There are also x-values approaching 0 where $\sin(1/x) = 1$. So if the limit existed, it would have to be both -1 and 1. Thus, the limit does not exist.

Limits at Infinity

Sometimes we want to know what happens to $f(x)$ as x gets large, that is, the end behavior of f.

> If $f(x)$ gets as close to a number L as we please when x gets sufficiently large, then we write
>
> $$\lim_{x \to \infty} f(x) = L.$$
>
> Similarly, if $f(x)$ approaches L when x is negative and has a sufficiently large absolute value, then we write
>
> $$\lim_{x \to -\infty} f(x) = L.$$

The symbol ∞ does not represent a number. Writing $x \to \infty$ means that we consider arbitrarily large values of x. If the limit of $f(x)$ as $x \to \infty$ or $x \to -\infty$ is L, we say that the graph of f has $y = L$ as a *horizontal asymptote*. Problem 45 asks for a formal definition of $\lim_{x \to \infty} f(x)$.

Example 8   Investigate $\lim_{x \to \infty} \dfrac{1}{x}$ and $\lim_{x \to -\infty} \dfrac{1}{x}$.

Solution   A graph of $f(x) = 1/x$ in a large window shows $1/x$ approaching zero as x increases in either the positive or the negative direction (see Figure 1.93). This is as we would expect, since dividing 1 by larger and larger numbers yields answers which are closer and closer to zero. This suggests that

$$\lim_{x \to \infty} \frac{1}{x} = \lim_{x \to -\infty} \frac{1}{x} = 0,$$

and that $f(x) = 1/x$ has $y = 0$ as a horizontal asymptote as $x \to \pm\infty$.

Figure 1.93: The end behavior of $f(x) = 1/x$

Definition of Continuity

We can now give a precise definition of continuity using limits.

> The function f is **continuous** at $x = c$ if f is defined at $x = c$ and if
>
> $$\lim_{x \to c} f(x) = f(c).$$
>
> In other words, $f(x)$ is as close as we want to $f(c)$ provided x is close enough to c. The function is **continuous on an interval** $[a, b]$ if it is continuous at every point in the interval.[39]

Constant functions and $f(x) = x$ are continuous for all x. Using the continuity of sums and products, we can show that any polynomial is continuous. Proving that $\sin x$, $\cos x$, and e^x are

---

[39]If c is an endpoint of the interval, we define continuity at $x = c$ using one-sided limits at c.

continuous is more difficult. The following theorem, based on the properties of limits on page 60, makes it easier to decide whether certain combinations of functions are continuous.

Theorem 1.3: Continuity of Sums, Products, and Quotients of Functions

Suppose that f and g are continuous on an interval and that b is a constant. Then, on that same interval,

1. $bf(x)$ is continuous.
2. $f(x) + g(x)$ is continuous.
3. $f(x)g(x)$ is continuous.
4. $f(x)/g(x)$ is continuous, provided $g(x) \neq 0$ on the interval.

We prove the third of these properties.

Proof Let c be any point in the interval. We must show that $\lim_{x \to c}(f(x)g(x)) = f(c)g(c)$. Since $f(x)$ and $g(x)$ are continuous, we know that $\lim_{x \to c} f(x) = f(c)$ and $\lim_{x \to c} g(x) = g(c)$. So, by the third property of limits in Theorem 1.2,

$$\lim_{x \to c}(f(x)g(x)) = \left(\lim_{x \to c} f(x)\right)\left(\lim_{x \to c} g(x)\right) = f(c)g(c).$$

Since c was chosen arbitrarily, we have shown that $f(x)g(x)$ is continuous at every point in the interval.

Theorem 1.4: Continuity of Composite Functions

If f and g are continuous, and if the composite function $f(g(x))$ is defined on an interval, then $f(g(x))$ is continuous on that interval.

Assuming the continuity of $\sin x$ and e^x, Theorem 1.4 shows us, for example, that $\sin(e^x)$ and $e^{\sin x}$ are both continuous.

Although we now have a formal definition of continuity, some properties of continuous functions, such as the Intermediate Value Theorem, can be difficult to prove. For a further treatment of limits and continuity, see www.wiley.com/college/hughes-hallett.

Exercises and Problems for Section 1.8

Exercises

1. Use Figure 1.94 to give approximate values for the following limits (if they exist).

  (a) $\lim_{x \to -2} f(x)$ **(b)** $\lim_{x \to 0} f(x)$

  (c) $\lim_{x \to 2} f(x)$ **(d)** $\lim_{x \to 4} f(x)$

2. Use Figure 1.95 to estimate the following limits, if they exist.

  (a) $\lim_{x \to 1^-} f(x)$ **(b)** $\lim_{x \to 1^+} f(x)$ **(c)** $\lim_{x \to 1} f(x)$

  (d) $\lim_{x \to 2^-} f(x)$ **(e)** $\lim_{x \to 2^+} f(x)$ **(f)** $\lim_{x \to 2} f(x)$

Figure 1.94

Figure 1.95

3. Using Figures 1.96 and 1.97, estimate

(a) $\lim_{x \to 1^-} (f(x) + g(x))$ (b) $\lim_{x \to 1^+} (f(x) + 2g(x))$

(c) $\lim_{x \to 1^-} f(x)g(x)$ (d) $\lim_{x \to 1^+} \dfrac{f(x)}{g(x)}$

Figure 1.96

Figure 1.97

In Exercises 4–9, draw a possible graph of $f(x)$. Assume $f(x)$ is defined and continuous for all real x.

4. $\lim_{x \to \infty} f(x) = -\infty$ and $\lim_{x \to -\infty} f(x) = -\infty$

5. $\lim_{x \to \infty} f(x) = -\infty$ and $\lim_{x \to -\infty} f(x) = +\infty$

6. $\lim_{x \to \infty} f(x) = 1$ and $\lim_{x \to -\infty} f(x) = +\infty$

7. $\lim_{x \to \infty} f(x) = -\infty$ and $\lim_{x \to -\infty} f(x) = 3$

8. $\lim_{x \to \infty} f(x) = +\infty$ and $\lim_{x \to -1} f(x) = 2$

9. $\lim_{x \to 3} f(x) = 5$ and $\lim_{x \to -\infty} f(x) = +\infty$

In Exercises 10–15, give $\lim_{x \to -\infty} f(x)$ and $\lim_{x \to +\infty} f(x)$.

10. $f(x) = -x^4$

11. $f(x) = 5 + 21x - 2x^3$

12. $f(x) = x^5 + 25x^4 - 37x^3 - 200x^2 + 48x + 10$

13. $f(x) = \dfrac{3x^3 + 6x^2 + 45}{5x^3 + 25x + 12}$

14. $f(x) = 8x^{-3}$

15. $f(x) = 25e^{0.08x}$

Estimate the limits in Exercises 16–17 graphically.

16. $\lim_{x \to 0} \dfrac{|x|}{x}$

17. $\lim_{x \to 0} x \ln |x|$

18. Does $f(x) = \dfrac{|x|}{x}$ have right or left limits at 0? Is $f(x)$ continuous?

Use a graph to estimate each of the limits in Exercises 19–28. Use radians unless degrees are indicated by θ°.

19. $\lim_{\theta \to 0} \dfrac{\sin(2\theta)}{\theta}$

20. $\lim_{\theta \to 0} \dfrac{\cos\theta - 1}{\theta}$

21. $\lim_{\theta \to 0} \dfrac{\sin\theta^\circ}{\theta^\circ}$

22. $\lim_{\theta \to 0} \dfrac{\theta}{\tan(3\theta)}$

23. $\lim_{h \to 0} \dfrac{e^h - 1}{h}$

24. $\lim_{h \to 0} \dfrac{e^{5h} - 1}{h}$

25. $\lim_{h \to 0} \dfrac{2^h - 1}{h}$

26. $\lim_{h \to 0} \dfrac{3^h - 1}{h}$

27. $\lim_{h \to 0} \dfrac{\cos(3h) - 1}{h}$

28. $\lim_{h \to 0} \dfrac{\sin(3h)}{h}$

For the functions in Exercises 29–31, use algebra to evaluate the limits $\lim_{x \to a+} f(x)$, $\lim_{x \to a-} f(x)$, and $\lim_{x \to a} f(x)$ if they exist. Sketch a graph to confirm your answers.

29. $a = 4$, $f(x) = \dfrac{|x - 4|}{x - 4}$

30. $a = 2$, $f(x) = \dfrac{|x - 2|}{x}$

31. $a = 3$, $f(x) = \begin{cases} x^2 - 2, & 0 < x < 3 \\ 2, & x = 3 \\ 2x + 1, & 3 < x \end{cases}$

32. Estimate how close θ should be to 0 to make $(\sin\theta)/\theta$ stay within 0.001 of 1.

33. Write the definition of the following statement both in words and in symbols:

$$\lim_{h \to a} g(h) = K.$$

Problems

In Problems 34–37, is the function continuous for all x? If not, say where it is not continuous and explain in what way the definition of continuity is not satisfied.

34. $f(x) = 1/x$

35. $f(x) = \begin{cases} |x|/x & x \neq 0 \\ 0 & x = 0 \end{cases}$

36. $f(x) = \begin{cases} x/x & x \neq 0 \\ 1 & x = 0 \end{cases}$

37. $f(x) = \begin{cases} 2x/x & x \neq 0 \\ 3 & x = 0 \end{cases}$

38. By graphing $y = (1 + x)^{1/x}$, estimate $\lim_{x \to 0} (1 + x)^{1/x}$. You should recognize the answer you get. What does the limit appear to be?

39. Investigate $\lim_{h \to 0} (1 + h)^{1/h}$ numerically.

40. What does a calculator suggest about $\lim_{x \to 0^+} xe^{1/x}$? Does the limit appear to exist? Explain.

41. If $p(x)$ is the function on page 54 giving the price of mailing a first-class letter, explain why $\lim_{x \to 1} p(x)$ does not exist.

42. The notation $\lim_{x \to 0+}$ means that we only consider values of x greater than 0. Estimate the limit

$$\lim_{x \to 0+} x^x,$$

either by evaluating x^x for smaller and smaller positive values of x (say $x = 0.1, 0.01, 0.001, \ldots$) or by zooming in on the graph of $y = x^x$ near $x = 0$.

In Problems 43–45, modify the definition of limit on page 59 to give a definition of each of the following.

43. A right-hand limit **44.** A left-hand limit

45. $\lim_{x \to \infty} f(x) = L$

For the functions in Problems 46–53, do the following:

(a) Make a table of values of $f(x)$ for $x = 0.1, 0.01, 0.001, 0.0001, -0.1, -0.01, -0.001,$ and -0.0001.

(b) Make a conjecture about the value of $\lim_{x \to 0} f(x)$.

(c) Graph the function to see if it is consistent with your answers to parts (a) and (b).

(d) Find an interval for x near 0 such that the difference between your conjectured limit and the value of the function is less than 0.01. (In other words, find a window of height 0.02 such that the graph exits the sides of the window and not the top or bottom of the window.)

46. $f(x) = 3x + 1$ **47.** $f(x) = x^2 - 1$

48. $f(x) = \sin 2x$ **49.** $f(x) = \sin 3x$

50. $f(x) = \dfrac{\sin 2x}{x}$ **51.** $f(x) = \dfrac{\sin 3x}{x}$

52. $f(x) = \dfrac{e^x - 1}{x}$ **53.** $f(x) = \dfrac{e^{2x} - 1}{x}$

Assuming that limits as $x \to \infty$ have the properties listed for limits as $x \to c$ on page 60, use algebraic manipulations to evaluate $\lim_{x \to \infty}$ for the functions in Problems 54–63.

54. $f(x) = \dfrac{x + 3}{2 - x}$ **55.** $f(x) = \dfrac{\pi + 3x}{\pi x - 3}$

56. $f(x) = \dfrac{x - 5}{5 + 2x^2}$ **57.** $f(x) = \dfrac{x^2 + 2x - 1}{3 + 3x^2}$

58. $f(x) = \dfrac{x^2 + 4}{x + 3}$ **59.** $f(x) = \dfrac{2x^3 - 16x^2}{4x^2 + 3x^3}$

60. $f(x) = \dfrac{x^4 + 3x}{x^4 + 2x^5}$ **61.** $f(x) = \dfrac{3e^x + 2}{2e^x + 3}$

62. $f(x) = \dfrac{2^{-x} + 5}{3^{-x} + 7}$ **63.** $f(x) = \dfrac{2e^{-x} + 3}{3e^{-x} + 2}$

In Problems 64–71, find a value of the constant k such that the limit exists.

64. $\lim_{x \to 4} \dfrac{x^2 - k^2}{x - 4}$ **65.** $\lim_{x \to 1} \dfrac{x^2 - kx + 4}{x - 1}$

66. $\lim_{x \to -2} \dfrac{x^2 + 4x + k}{x + 2}$ **67.** $\lim_{x \to \infty} \dfrac{x^2 + 3x + 5}{4x + 1 + x^k}$

68. $\lim_{x \to -\infty} \dfrac{e^{2x} - 5}{e^{kx} + 3}$ **69.** $\lim_{x \to \infty} \dfrac{x^3 - 6}{x^k + 3}$

70. $\lim_{x \to \infty} \dfrac{3^{kx} + 6}{3^{2x} + 4}$ **71.** $\lim_{x \to -\infty} \dfrac{3^{kx} + 6}{3^{2x} + 4}$

For each value of ϵ in Problems 72–73, find a positive value of δ such that the graph of the function leaves the window $a - \delta < x < a + \delta, b - \epsilon < y < b + \epsilon$ by the sides and not through the top or bottom.

72. $f(x) = -2x + 3$; $a = 0$; $b = 3$; $\epsilon = 0.2, 0.1, 0.02, 0.01, 0.002, 0.001$.

73. $g(x) = -x^3 + 2$; $a = 0$; $b = 2$; $\epsilon = 0.1, 0.01, 0.001$.

74. Show that $\lim_{x \to 0} (-2x + 3) = 3$. [Hint: Use Problem 72.]

75. Consider the function $f(x) = \sin(1/x)$.

(a) Find a sequence of x-values that approach 0 such that $\sin(1/x) = 0$.
[Hint: Use the fact that $\sin(\pi) = \sin(2\pi) = \sin(3\pi) = \ldots = \sin(n\pi) = 0$.]

(b) Find a sequence of x-values that approach 0 such that $\sin(1/x) = 1$.
[Hint: Use the fact that $\sin(n\pi/2) = 1$ if $n = 1, 5, 9, \ldots$.]

(c) Find a sequence of x-values that approach 0 such that $\sin(1/x) = -1$.

(d) Explain why your answers to any two of parts (a)–(c) show that $\lim_{x \to 0} \sin(1/x)$ does not exist.

For the functions in Problems 76–77, do the following:

(a) Make a table of values of $f(x)$ for $x = a + 0.1, a + 0.01, a + 0.001, a + 0.0001, a - 0.1, a - 0.01, a - 0.001,$ and $a - 0.0001$.

(b) Make a conjecture about the value of $\lim_{x \to a} f(x)$.

(c) Graph the function to see if it is consistent with your answers to parts (a) and (b).

(d) Find an interval for x containing a such that the difference between your conjectured limit and the value of the function is less than 0.01 on that interval. (In other words, find a window of height 0.02 such that the graph exits the sides of the window and not the top or bottom of the window.)

76. $f(x) = \dfrac{\cos 2x - 1 + 2x^2}{x^3}, \quad a = 0$

77. $f(x) = \dfrac{\cos 3x - 1 + 4.5x^2}{x^3}, \quad a = 0$

78. This problem suggests a proof of the first property of limits on page 60: $\lim\limits_{x \to c} bf(x) = b \lim\limits_{x \to c} f(x)$.

    (a) First, prove the property in the case $b = 0$.

    (b) Now suppose that $b \neq 0$. Let $\epsilon > 0$. Show that if $|f(x) - L| < \epsilon/|b|$, then $|bf(x) - bL| < \epsilon$.

    (c) Finally, prove that if $\lim\limits_{x \to c} f(x) = L$ then $\lim\limits_{x \to c} bf(x) = bL$. [Hint: Choose δ so that if $|x-c| < \delta$, then $|f(x) - L| < \epsilon/|b|$.]

79. Prove the second property of limits: $\lim\limits_{x \to c} (f(x) + g(x)) = \lim\limits_{x \to c} f(x) + \lim\limits_{x \to c} g(x)$. Assume that the limits on the right exist.

80. This problem suggests a proof of the third property of limits (assuming the limits on the right exist):

$$\lim\limits_{x \to c} (f(x)g(x)) = \left(\lim\limits_{x \to c} f(x) \right) \left(\lim\limits_{x \to c} g(x) \right)$$

Let $L_1 = \lim\limits_{x \to c} f(x)$ and $L_2 = \lim\limits_{x \to c} g(x)$.

    (a) First, show that if $\lim\limits_{x \to c} f(x) = \lim\limits_{x \to c} g(x) = 0$, then $\lim\limits_{x \to c} (f(x)g(x)) = 0$.

    (b) Show algebraically that $f(x)g(x) = (f(x) - L_1)(g(x) - L_2) + L_1 g(x) + L_2 f(x) - L_1 L_2$.

    (c) Use the second limit property (see Problem 79) to explain why $\lim\limits_{x \to c} (f(x) - L_1) = \lim\limits_{x \to c} (g(x) - L_2) = 0$.

    (d) Use parts (a) and (c) to explain why $\lim\limits_{x \to c} (f(x) - L_1)(g(x) - L_2) = 0$.

    (e) Finally, use parts (b) and (d) and the first and second limit properties to show that $$\lim\limits_{x \to c} (f(x)g(x)) = \left(\lim\limits_{x \to c} f(x) \right) \left(\lim\limits_{x \to c} g(x) \right).$$

81. Show $f(x) = x$ is continuous everywhere.

82. Use Problem 81 to show that for any positive integer n, the function x^n is continuous everywhere.

83. Use Theorem 1.2 on page 60 to explain why if f and g are continuous on an interval, then so are $f + g$, fg, and f/g (assuming $g(x) \neq 0$ on the interval).

Strengthen Your Understanding

In Problems 84–86, explain what is wrong with the statement.

84. If $P(x)$ and $Q(x)$ are polynomials, $P(x)/Q(x)$ must be continuous for all x.

85. $\lim\limits_{x \to 1} \dfrac{x - 1}{|x - 1|} = 1$

86. If $\lim\limits_{x \to c} f(x)$ exists, then $f(x)$ is continuous at $x = c$.

In Problems 87–88, give an example of:

87. A rational function that has a limit at $x = 1$ but is not continuous at $x = 1$.

88. A function $f(x)$ where $\lim\limits_{x \to \infty} f(x) = 2$ and $\lim\limits_{x \to -\infty} f(x) = -2$.

Suppose that $\lim\limits_{x \to 3} f(x) = 7$. Are the statements in Problems 89–95 true or false? If a statement is true, explain how you know. If a statement is false, give a counterexample.

89. $\lim\limits_{x \to 3} (xf(x)) = 21$.

90. If $g(3) = 4$, then $\lim\limits_{x \to 3} (f(x)g(x)) = 28$.

91. If $\lim\limits_{x \to 3} g(x) = 5$, then $\lim\limits_{x \to 3} (f(x) + g(x)) = 12$.

92. If $\lim\limits_{x \to 3} (f(x) + g(x)) = 12$, then $\lim\limits_{x \to 3} g(x) = 5$.

93. $f(2.99)$ is closer to 7 than $f(2.9)$ is.

94. If $f(3.1) > 0$, then $f(3.01) > 0$.

95. If $\lim\limits_{x \to 3} g(x)$ does not exist, then $\lim\limits_{x \to 3} (f(x)g(x))$ does not exist.

Which of the statements in Problems 96–100 are true about every function $f(x)$ such that $\lim\limits_{x \to c} f(x) = L$? Give a reason for your answer.

96. If $f(x)$ is within 10^{-3} of L, then x is within 10^{-3} of c.

97. There is a positive ϵ such that, provided x is within 10^{-3} of c, and $x \neq c$, we can be sure $f(x)$ is within ϵ of L.

98. For any positive ϵ, we can find a positive δ such that, provided x is within δ of c, and $x \neq c$, we can be sure that $f(x)$ is within ϵ of L.

99. For each $\epsilon > 0$, there is a $\delta > 0$ such that if x is not within δ of c, then $f(x)$ is not within ϵ of L.

100. For each $\epsilon > 0$, there is some $\delta > 0$ such that if $f(x)$ is within ϵ of L, then we can be sure that x is within δ of c.

101. Which of the following statements is a direct consequence of the statement: "If f and g are continuous at $x = a$ and $g(a) \neq 0$ then f/g is continuous at $x = a$?"

    (a) If f and g are continuous at $x = a$ and $f(a) \neq 0$ then g/f is continuous at $x = a$.

    (b) If f and g are continuous at $x = a$ and $g(a) = 0$, then f/g is not continuous at $x = a$.

    (c) If f, g, are continuous at $x = a$, but f/g is not continuous at $x = a$, then $g(a) = 0$.

    (d) If f and f/g are continuous at $x = a$ and $g(a) \neq 0$, then g is continuous at $x = a$.

CHAPTER SUMMARY (see also Ready Reference at the end of the book)

- **Function terminology**
  Domain/range, increasing/decreasing, concavity, zeros (roots), even/odd, end behavior, asymptotes.

- **Linear functions**
  Slope, vertical intercept. Grow by equal amounts in equal times.

- **Exponential functions**
  Exponential growth and decay, with base e, growth rate, continuous growth rate, doubling time, half life. Grow by equal percentages in equal times.

- **Logarithmic functions**
  Log base 10, natural logarithm.

- **Trigonometric functions**
  Sine and cosine, tangent, amplitude, period, arcsine, arctangent.

- **Power functions**

- **Polynomials and rational functions**

- **New functions from old**
  Inverse functions, composition of functions, shifting, stretching, shrinking.

- **Working with functions**
  Find a formula for a linear, exponential, power, logarithmic, or trigonometric function, given graph, table of values, or verbal description. Find vertical and horizontal asymptotes. End behavior. Proportional relationships.

- **Comparisons between functions**
  Exponential functions dominate power and linear functions.

- **Continuity**
  Interpret graphically and numerically. Intermediate Value Theorem.

- **Limits**
  Graphical interpretation, ϵ-δ definition, properties, one-sided limits, limits to infinity.

REVIEW EXERCISES AND PROBLEMS FOR CHAPTER ONE

Exercises

Find formulas for the functions described in Exercises 1–8.

1. A line with slope 2 and x-intercept 5.

2. A parabola opening downward with its vertex at $(2, 5)$.

3. A parabola with x-intercepts ± 1 and y-intercept 3.

4. The bottom half of a circle centered at the origin and with radius $\sqrt{2}$.

5. The top half of a circle with center $(-1, 2)$ and radius 3.

6. A cubic polynomial having x-intercepts at 1, 5, 7.

7. A rational function of the form $y = ax/(x + b)$ with a vertical asymptote at $x = 2$ and a horizontal asymptote of $y = -5$.

8. A cosine curve with a maximum at $(0, 5)$, a minimum at $(\pi, -5)$, and no maxima or minima in between.

9. When a patient with a rapid heart rate takes a drug, the heart rate plunges dramatically and then slowly rises again as the drug wears off. Sketch the heart rate against time from the moment the drug is administered.

10. If $g(x) = (4 - x^2)/(x^2 + x)$, find the domain of $g(x)$. Solve $g(x) = 0$.

11. The entire graph of $f(x)$ is shown in Figure 1.98.

  (a) What is the domain of $f(x)$?
  (b) What is the range of $f(x)$?
  (c) List all zeros of $f(x)$.
  (d) List all intervals on which $f(x)$ is decreasing.

  (e) Is $f(x)$ concave up or concave down at $x = 6$?
  (f) What is $f(4)$?
  (g) Is this function invertible? Explain.

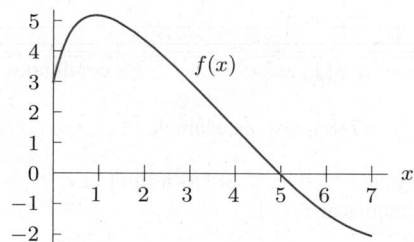

Figure 1.98

12. For $f(n) = 3n^2 - 2$ and $g(n) = n + 1$, find and simplify:

  (a) $f(n) + g(n)$
  (b) $f(n)g(n)$
  (c) The domain of $f(n)/g(n)$
  (d) $f(g(n))$
  (e) $g(f(n))$

13. Let $m = f(A)$ be the minimum annual gross income, in thousands of dollars, needed to obtain a 30-year home mortgage loan of A thousand dollars at an interest rate of 6%. What do the following quantities represent in terms of the income needed for a loan?

  (a) $f(100)$ **(b)** $f^{-1}(75)$

For Exercises 14–17, solve for t using logs.

14. $5^t = 7$ **15.** $2 = (1.02)^t$ **16.** $7 \cdot 3^t = 5 \cdot 2^t$

17. $5.02(1.04)^t = 12.01(1.03)^t$

In Exercises 18–19, put the functions in the form $P = P_0 e^{kt}$.

18. $P = P_0 2^t$ **19.** $P = 5.23(0.2)^t$

For Exercises 20–21, find functions f and g such that $h(x) = f(g(x))$. [Note: Do not choose $f(x) = x$ or $g(x) = x$.]

20. $h(x) = \ln(x^3)$ **21.** $h(x) = (\ln x)^3$

Find the amplitudes and periods in Exercises 22–23.

22. $y = 5\sin(x/3)$ **23.** $y = 4 - 2\cos(5x)$

24. Consider the function $y = 5 + \cos(3x)$.

   (a) What is its amplitude?
   (b) What is its period?
   (c) Sketch its graph.

25. Determine the end behavior of each function as $x \to +\infty$ and as $x \to -\infty$.

   (a) $f(x) = x^7$ (b) $f(x) = 3x + 7x^3 - 12x^4$

   (c) $f(x) = x^{-4}$ (d) $f(x) = \dfrac{6x^3 - 5x^2 + 2}{x^3 - 8}$

In Exercises 26–27, which function dominates as $x \to \infty$?

26. $10 \cdot 2^x$ or $72{,}000x^{12}$ **27.** $0.25\sqrt{x}$ or $25{,}000x^{-3}$

Find possible formulas for the graphs in Exercises 28–41.

28.

29.

30.

31.

32.

33.

34.

35.

36.

37.

38.

39.

40.

41.

Are the functions in Exercises 42–43 continuous on $[-1, 1]$?

42. $g(x) = \dfrac{1}{x^2 + 1}$ **43.** $h(x) = \dfrac{1}{1 - x^2}$

44. Use Figure 1.99 to estimate the limits if they exist:

   (a) $\lim\limits_{x \to 0} f(x)$ (b) $\lim\limits_{x \to 1} f(x)$

   (c) $\lim\limits_{x \to 2} f(x)$ (d) $\lim\limits_{x \to 3^-} f(x)$

Figure 1.99

For the functions in Exercises 45–46, use algebra to evaluate the limits $\lim\limits_{x \to a+} f(x)$, $\lim\limits_{x \to a-} f(x)$, and $\lim\limits_{x \to a} f(x)$ if they exist. Sketch a graph to confirm your answers.

45. $a = 3$, $f(x) = \dfrac{x^3 |2x - 6|}{x - 3}$

46. $a = 0$, $f(x) = \begin{cases} e^x & -1 < x < 0 \\ 1 & x = 0 \\ \cos x & 0 < x < 1 \end{cases}$

Problems

47. The yield, Y, of an apple orchard (in bushels) as a function of the amount, a, of fertilizer (in pounds) used on the orchard is shown in Figure 1.100.

  (a) Describe the effect of the amount of fertilizer on the yield of the orchard.
  (b) What is the vertical intercept? Explain what it means in terms of apples and fertilizer.
  (c) What is the horizontal intercept? Explain what it means in terms of apples and fertilizer.
  (d) What is the range of this function for $0 \le a \le 80$?
  (e) Is the function increasing or decreasing at $a = 60$?
  (f) Is the graph concave up or down near $a = 40$?

Figure 1.100

48. The graph of Fahrenheit temperature, °F, as a function of Celsius temperature, °C, is a line. You know that 212°F and 100°C both represent the temperature at which water boils. Similarly, 32°F and 0°C both represent water's freezing point.

  (a) What is the slope of the graph?
  (b) What is the equation of the line?
  (c) Use the equation to find what Fahrenheit temperature corresponds to 20°C.
  (d) What temperature is the same number of degrees in both Celsius and Fahrenheit?

49. The demand function for a certain product, $q = D(p)$, is linear, where p is the price per item in dollars and q is the quantity demanded. If p increases by \$5, market research

shows that q drops by two items. In addition, 100 items are purchased if the price is \$550.

  (a) Find a formula for
    (i) q as a linear function of p
    (ii) p as a linear function of q
  (b) Draw a graph with q on the horizontal axis.

50. A flight from Dulles Airport in Washington, DC, to La-Guardia Airport in New York City has to circle La-Guardia several times before being allowed to land. Plot a graph of the distance of the plane from Washington, DC, against time, from the moment of takeoff until landing.

51. The force, F, between two atoms depends on the distance r separating them. See Figure 1.101. A positive F represents a repulsive force; a negative F represents an attractive force.

  (a) What happens to the force if the atoms start with $r = a$ and are
    (i) Pulled slightly further apart?
    (ii) Pushed slightly closer together?
  (b) The atoms are said to be in *stable equilibrium* if the force between them is zero and the atoms tend to return to the equilibrium after a minor disturbance. Does $r = a$ represent a stable equilibrium? Explain.

Figure 1.101

52. When the Olympic Games were held outside Mexico City in 1968, there was much discussion about the effect the high altitude (7340 feet) would have on the athletes. Assuming air pressure decays exponentially by 0.4% every 100 feet, by what percentage is air pressure reduced by moving from sea level to Mexico City?

---

[40]http://www.indexmundi.com/ukraine/population.html. Accessed April 17, 2011.

53. The population of the Ukraine fell from 45.7 million in 2009 to 45.42 million in 2010.[40] Assuming exponential decline, in what year is the population predicted to be 45 million?

54. During April 2006, Zimbabwe's inflation rate averaged 0.67% a day. This means that, on average, prices went up by 0.67% from one day to the next.

   (a) By what percentage did prices in Zimbabwe increase in April of 2006?

   (b) Assuming the same rate all year, what was Zimbabwe's annual inflation rate during 2006?

55. Hydroelectric power is electric power generated by the force of moving water. The table shows the annual percent change in hydroelectric power consumption by the US industrial sector.[41]

   (a) According to the table, during what single year(s), if any, did the US consumption of hydroelectric power energy increase by at least 10%? Decrease by 10% or more?

   (b) True or False: The hydroelectric power consumption nearly doubled from 2008 to 2009.

   (c) True or False: The hydroelectric power consumption decreased by about 36% from 2006 to 2009.

Year	2005	2006	2007	2008	2009
% growth over previous yr	−1.9	−10	−45.4	5.1	11

56. A kilogram weighs about 2.2 pounds.

   (a) Write a formula for the function, f, which gives an object's mass in kilograms, k, as a function of its weight in pounds, p.

   (b) Find a formula for the inverse function of f. What does this inverse function tell you, in practical terms?

57. The graph of $f(x)$ is a parabola that opens upward and the graph of $g(x)$ is a line with negative slope. Describe the graph of $g(f(x))$ in words.

58. Each of the functions in the table is increasing over its domain, but each increases in a different way. Match the functions f, g, h to the graphs in Figure 1.102.

x	$f(x)$	x	$g(x)$	x	$h(x)$
1	1	3.0	1	10	1
2	2	3.2	2	20	2
4	3	3.4	3	28	3
7	4	3.6	4	34	4
11	5	3.8	5	39	5
16	6	4.0	6	43	6
22	7	4.2	7	46.5	7
29	8	4.4	8	49	8
37	9	4.6	9	51	9
47	10	4.8	10	52	10

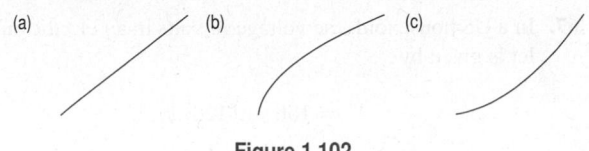

Figure 1.102

59. A culture of 100 bacteria doubles after 2 hours. How long will it take for the number of bacteria to reach 3,200?

60. If $f(x) = a \ln(x + 2)$, how does increasing a affect

   (a) The y-intercept?   (b) The x-intercept?

61. What is the doubling time of prices which are increasing by 5% a year?

62. Find the half-life of a radioactive substance that is reduced by 30% in 20 hours.

63. The air in a factory is being filtered so that the quantity of a pollutant, P (in mg/liter), is decreasing according to the function $P = P_0 e^{-kt}$, where t is time in hours. If 10% of the pollution is removed in the first five hours:

   (a) What percentage of the pollution is left after 10 hours?

   (b) How long is it before the pollution is reduced by 50%?

   (c) Plot a graph of pollution against time. Show the results of your calculations on the graph.

   (d) Explain why the quantity of pollutant might decrease in this way.

64. The half-life of radioactive strontium-90 is 29 years. In 1960, radioactive strontium-90 was released into the atmosphere during testing of nuclear weapons, and was absorbed into people's bones. How many years does it take until only 10% of the original amount absorbed remains?

65. What is the period of the motion of the minute hand of a clock?

66. In an electrical outlet, the voltage, V, in volts, is given as a function of time, t, in seconds, by the formula

$$V = V_0 \sin(120\pi t).$$

   (a) What does V_0 represent in terms of voltage?

   (b) What is the period of this function?

   (c) How many oscillations are completed in 1 second?

[41]http://www.eia.doe.gov/aer/renew.html. Accessed February 2011.

67. In a US household, the voltage in volts in an electric outlet is given by

$$V = 156 \sin(120\pi t),$$

where t is in seconds. However, in a European house, the voltage is given (in the same units) by

$$V = 339 \sin(100\pi t).$$

Compare the voltages in the two regions, considering the maximum voltage and number of cycles (oscillations) per second.

68. (a) How does the parameter A affect the graph of $y = A \sin(Bx)$? (Plot for $A = 1, 2, 3$ with $B = 1$.)
(b) How does the parameter B affect the graph of $y = A \sin(Bx)$? (Plot for $B = 1, 2, 3$ with $A = 1$.)

69. Water is flowing down a cylindrical pipe of radius r.

(a) Write a formula for the volume, V, of water that emerges from the end of the pipe in one second if the water is flowing at a rate of

(i) 3 cm/sec   (ii) k cm/sec

(b) Graph your answer to part (a)(ii) as a function of

(i) r, assuming k is constant

(ii) k, assuming r is constant

70. Values of three functions are given in Table 1.22, rounded to two decimal places. Two are power functions and one is an exponential. One of the power functions is a quadratic and one a cubic. Which one is exponential? Which one is quadratic? Which one is cubic?

Table 1.22

x	$f(x)$	x	$g(x)$	x	$k(x)$
8.4	5.93	5.0	3.12	0.6	3.24
9.0	7.29	5.5	3.74	1.0	9.01
9.6	8.85	6.0	4.49	1.4	17.66
10.2	10.61	6.5	5.39	1.8	29.19
10.8	12.60	7.0	6.47	2.2	43.61
11.4	14.82	7.5	7.76	2.6	60.91

71. Figure 1.103 shows the *hat function*

$$h_N(x) = \begin{cases} 0 & \text{if } x < N-1 \\ 1 + x - N & \text{if } N-1 \le x < N \\ 1 + N - x & \text{if } N \le x < N+1 \\ 0 & \text{if } N+1 \le x \end{cases}.$$

(a) Graph the function $f(x) = 3h_1(x) + 2h_2(x) + 4h_3(x)$.
(b) Describe the graph of $g(x) = ah_1(x) + bh_2(x) + ch_3(x)$.

Figure 1.103: Graph of $h_N(x)$

72. The point P moves around the circle of radius 5 shown in Figure 1.104. The angle θ, in radians, is given as a function of time, t, by the graph in Figure 1.105.

(a) Estimate the coordinates of P when $t = 1.5$.
(b) Describe in words the motion of the point P on the circle.

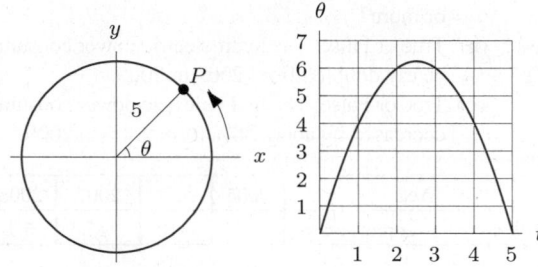

Figure 1.104   **Figure 1.105**

73. Match the following functions with the graphs in Figure 1.106. Assume $0 < b < a$.

(a) $y = \dfrac{a}{x} - x$ (b) $y = \dfrac{(x-a)(x+a)}{x}$

(c) $y = \dfrac{(x-a)(x^2+a)}{x^2}$ (d) $y = \dfrac{(x-a)(x+a)}{(x-b)(x+b)}$

Figure 1.106

74. Use a computer or calculator to sketch the functions

$$y(x) = \sin x \quad \text{and} \quad z_k(x) = ke^{-x}$$

for $k = 1, 2, 4, 6, 8, 10$. In each case find the smallest positive solution of the equation $y(x) = z_k(x)$. Now define a new function f by

$$f(k) = \{\text{Smallest positive solution of } y(x) = z_k(x)\}.$$

Explain why the function $f(k)$ is not continuous on the interval $0 \le k \le 10$.

For each value of ϵ in Problems 75–76, find a positive value of δ such that the graph of the function leaves the window $a - \delta < x < a + \delta, b - \epsilon < y < b + \epsilon$ by the sides and not through the top or bottom.

75. $h(x) = \sin x, a = b = 0, \epsilon = 0.1, 0.05, 0.0007.$

76. $k(x) = \cos x, a = 0, b = 1, \epsilon = 0.1, 0.001, 0.00001.$

77. If possible, choose k so that the following function is continuous on any interval:

$$f(x) = \begin{cases} \dfrac{5x^3 - 10x^2}{x - 2} & x \ne 2 \\ k & x = 2 \end{cases}$$

78. Find k so that the following function is continuous on any interval:

$$j(x) = \begin{cases} k \cos x & x \le 0 \\ e^x - k & x > 0 \end{cases}$$

CAS Challenge Problems

79. (a) Factor $f(x) = x^4 + bx^3 - cx^3 - a^2x^2 - bcx^2 - a^2bx + a^2cx + a^2bc$ using a computer algebra system.
(b) Assuming a, b, c are constants with $0 < a < b < c$, use your answer to part (a) to make a hand sketch of the graph of f. Explain how you know its shape.

80. (a) Using a computer algebra system, factor $f(x) = -x^5 + 11x^4 - 46x^3 + 90x^2 - 81x + 27.$
(b) Use your answer to part (a) to make a hand sketch of the graph of f. Explain how you know its shape.

81. Let $f(x) = e^{6x} + e^{5x} - 2e^{4x} - 10e^{3x} - 8e^{2x} + 16e^x + 16.$

(a) What happens to the value of $f(x)$ as $x \to \infty$? As $x \to -\infty$? Explain your answer.
(b) Using a computer algebra system, factor $f(x)$ and predict the number of zeros of the function $f(x)$.
(c) What are the exact values of the zeros? What is the relationship between successive zeros?

82. Let $f(x) = x^2 - x.$

(a) Find the polynomials $f(f(x))$ and $f(f(f(x)))$ in expanded form.
(b) What do you expect to be the degree of the polynomial $f(f(f(f(f(f(x))))))$? Explain.

83. (a) Use a computer algebra system to rewrite the rational function

$$f(x) = \frac{x^3 - 30}{x - 3}$$

in the form

$$f(x) = p(x) + \frac{r(x)}{q(x)},$$

where $p(x), q(x), r(x)$ are polynomials and the degree of $r(x)$ is less than the degree of $q(x)$.
(b) What is the vertical asymptote of f? Use your answer to part (a) to write the formula for a function whose graph looks like the graph of f for x near the vertical asymptote.
(c) Use your answer to part (a) to write the formula for a function whose graph looks like the graph of f for $x \to \infty$ and $x \to -\infty$.
(d) Using graphs, confirm the asymptote you found in part (b) and the formula you found in part (c).

For Problems 84–85, we note that a function can be written as a polynomial in $\sin x$ (or $\cos x$) if it is of the form $p(\sin x)$ (or $p(\cos x)$) for some polynomial $p(x)$. For example, $\cos 2x$ can be written as a polynomial in $\sin x$ because $\cos(2x) = 1 - 2\sin^2 x = p(\sin x)$, where $p(x) = 1 - 2x^2$.

84. Use the trigonometric capabilities of your computer algebra system to express $\sin(5x)$ as a polynomial in $\sin x$.

85. Use the trigonometric capabilities of your computer algebra system to express $\cos(4x)$ as a polynomial in

(a) $\sin x$
(b) $\cos x$.

PROJECTS FOR CHAPTER ONE

1. Matching Functions to Data

From the data in Table 1.23, determine a possible formula for each function.[42] Write an explanation of your reasoning.

---

[42]Based on a problem by Lee Zia.

Table 1.23

x	$f(x)$	$g(x)$	$h(x)$	$F(x)$	$G(x)$	$H(x)$
-5	-10	20	25	0.958924	0.544021	2.958924
-4.5	-9	19	20.25	0.97753	-0.412118	2.97753
-4	-8	18	16	0.756802	-0.989358	2.756802
-3.5	-7	17	12.25	0.350783	-0.656987	2.350783
-3	-6	16	9	-0.14112	0.279415	1.85888
-2.5	-5	15	6.25	-0.598472	0.958924	1.401528
-2	-4	14	4	-0.909297	0.756802	1.090703
-1.5	-3	13	2.25	-0.997495	-0.14112	1.002505
-1	-2	12	1	-0.841471	-0.909297	1.158529
-0.5	-1	11	0.25	-0.479426	-0.841471	1.520574
0	0	10	0	0	0	2
0.5	1	9	0.25	0.479426	0.841471	2.479426
1	2	8	1	0.841471	0.909297	2.841471
1.5	3	7	2.25	0.997495	0.14112	2.997495
2	4	6	4	0.909297	-0.756802	2.909297
2.5	5	5	6.25	0.598472	-0.958924	2.598472
3	6	4	9	0.14112	-0.279415	2.14112
3.5	7	3	12.25	-0.350783	0.656987	1.649217
4	8	2	16	-0.756802	0.989358	1.243198
4.5	9	1	20.25	-0.97753	0.412118	1.02247
5	10	0	25	-0.958924	-0.544021	1.041076

2. Which Way is the Wind Blowing?

Mathematicians name a wind by giving the angle *toward* which it is blowing measured counterclockwise from east. Meteorologists give the angle *from* which it is blowing measured clockwise from north. Both use values from $0°$ to $360°$. Figure 1.107 shows the two angles for a wind blowing from the northeast.

(a) Graph the mathematicians' angle θ_{math} as a function of the meteorologists' angle θ_{met}.

(b) Find a piecewise formula that gives θ_{math} in terms of θ_{met}.

Figure 1.107

Chapter Two

KEY CONCEPT: THE DERIVATIVE

Contents

2.1 HOW DO WE MEASURE SPEED?

The speed of an object at an instant in time is surprisingly difficult to define precisely. Consider the statement: "At the instant it crossed the finish line, the horse was traveling at 42 mph." How can such a claim be substantiated? A photograph taken at that instant will show the horse motionless—it is no help at all. There is some paradox in trying to study the horse's motion at a particular instant in time, since by focusing on a single instant we stop the motion!

Problems of motion were of central concern to Zeno and other philosophers as early as the fifth century B.C. The modern approach, made famous by Newton's calculus, is to stop looking for a simple notion of speed at an instant, and instead to look at speed over small time intervals containing the instant. This method sidesteps the philosophical problems mentioned earlier but introduces new ones of its own.

We illustrate the ideas discussed above by an idealized example, called a thought experiment. It is idealized in the sense that we assume that we can make measurements of distance and time as accurately as we wish.

A Thought Experiment: Average and Instantaneous Velocity

We look at the speed of a small object (say, a grapefruit) that is thrown straight upward into the air at $t = 0$ seconds. The grapefruit leaves the thrower's hand at high speed, slows down until it reaches its maximum height, and then speeds up in the downward direction and finally, "Splat!" (See Figure 2.1.)

Suppose that we want to determine the speed, say, at $t = 1$ second. Table 2.1 gives the height, y, of the grapefruit above the ground as a function of time. During the first second the grapefruit travels $90 - 6 = 84$ feet, and during the second second it travels only $142 - 90 = 52$ feet. Hence the grapefruit traveled faster over the first interval, $0 \leq t \leq 1$, than the second interval, $1 \leq t \leq 2$.

Figure 2.1: The grapefruit's path is straight up and down

Table 2.1   *Height of the grapefruit above the ground*

t (sec)	0	1	2	3	4	5	6
y (feet)	6	90	142	162	150	106	30

Velocity versus Speed

From now on, we will distinguish between velocity and speed. Suppose an object moves along a line. We pick one direction to be positive and say that the *velocity* is positive if it is in the same direction, and negative if it is in the opposite direction. For the grapefruit, upward is positive and downward is negative. (See Figure 2.1.) *Speed* is the magnitude of the velocity and so is always positive or zero.

> If $s(t)$ is the position of an object at time t, then the **average velocity** of the object over the interval $a \leq t \leq b$ is
>
> $$\text{Average velocity} = \frac{\text{Change in position}}{\text{Change in time}} = \frac{s(b) - s(a)}{b - a}.$$
>
> In words, the **average velocity** of an object over an interval is the net change in position during the interval divided by the change in time.

Example 1   Compute the average velocity of the grapefruit over the interval $4 \leq t \leq 5$. What is the significance of the sign of your answer?

Solution   During this one-second interval, the grapefruit moves $(106 - 150) = -44$ feet. Therefore the average velocity is $-44/(5 - 4) = -44$ ft/sec. The negative sign means the height is decreasing and the grapefruit is moving downward.

Example 2   Compute the average velocity of the grapefruit over the interval $1 \leq t \leq 3$.

Solution   Average velocity $= (162 - 90)/(3 - 1) = 72/2 = 36$ ft/sec.

The average velocity is a useful concept since it gives a rough idea of the behavior of the grapefruit: If two grapefruits are hurled into the air, and one has an average velocity of 10 ft/sec over the interval $0 \leq t \leq 1$ while the second has an average velocity of 100 ft/sec over the same interval, the second one is moving faster.

But average velocity over an interval does not solve the problem of measuring the velocity of the grapefruit at *exactly* $t = 1$ second. To get closer to an answer to that question, we have to look at what happens near $t = 1$ in more detail. The data[1] in Figure 2.2 shows the average velocity over small intervals on either side of $t = 1$.

Notice that the average velocity before $t = 1$ is slightly more than the average velocity after $t = 1$. We expect to define the velocity *at* $t = 1$ to be between these two average velocities. As the size of the interval shrinks, the values of the velocity before $t = 1$ and the velocity after $t = 1$ get closer together. In the smallest interval in Figure 2.2, both velocities are 68.0 ft/sec (to one decimal place), so we define the velocity at $t = 1$ to be 68.0 ft/sec (to one decimal place).

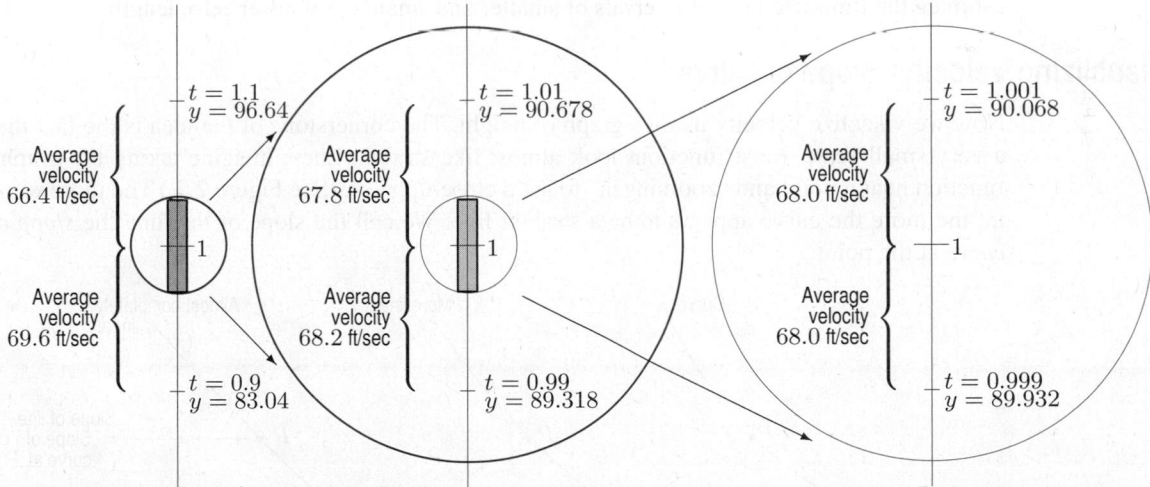

Figure 2.2: Average velocities over intervals on either side of $t = 1$: showing successively smaller intervals

Of course, if we calculate to more decimal places, the average velocities before and after $t = 1$ would no longer agree. To calculate the velocity at $t = 1$ to more decimal places of accuracy, we take smaller and smaller intervals on either side of $t = 1$ until the average velocities agree to the number of decimal places we want. In this way, we can estimate the velocity at $t = 1$ to any accuracy.

[1]The data is in fact calculated from the formula $y = 6 + 100t - 16t^2$.

Defining Instantaneous Velocity Using Limit Notation

When we take smaller and smaller intervals, it turns out that the average velocities get closer and closer to 68 ft/sec. It seems natural, then, to define *instantaneous velocity* at the instant $t = 1$ to be 68 ft/sec. Its definition depends on our being convinced that smaller and smaller intervals give averages that come arbitrarily close to 68; that is, the average speed approaches 68 ft/sec as a limit.

Notice how we have replaced the original difficulty of computing velocity at a point by a search for an argument to convince ourselves that the average velocities approach a limit as the time intervals shrink in size. Showing that the limit is exactly 68 requires the precise definition of limit given in Section 1.8.

To define instantaneous velocity at an arbitrary point $t = a$, we use the same method as for $t = 1$. On small intervals of size h around $t = a$, we calculate

$$\text{Average velocity} = \frac{s(a + h) - s(a)}{h}.$$

The instantaneous velocity is the number that the average velocities approach as the intervals decrease in size, that is, as h becomes smaller. So we make the following definition:

Let $s(t)$ be the position at time t. Then the **instantaneous velocity** at $t = a$ is defined as

$$\text{Instantaneous velocity} \atop \text{at } t = a \quad = \quad \lim_{h \to 0} \frac{s(a + h) - s(a)}{h}.$$

In words, the **instantaneous velocity** of an object at time $t = a$ is given by the limit of the average velocity over an interval, as the interval shrinks around a.

This limit refers to the number that the average velocities approach as the intervals shrink. To estimate the limit, we look at intervals of smaller and smaller, but never zero, length.

Visualizing Velocity: Slope of Curve

Now we visualize velocity using a graph of height. The cornerstone of the idea is the fact that, on a very small scale, most functions look almost like straight lines. Imagine taking the graph of a function near a point and "zooming in" to get a close-up view. (See Figure 2.3.) The more we zoom in, the more the curve appears to be a straight line. We call the slope of this line the *slope of the curve* at the point.

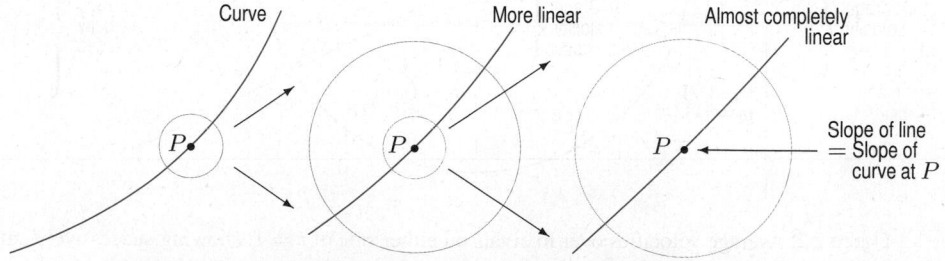

Figure 2.3: Estimating the slope of the curve at the point by "zooming in"

To visualize the instantaneous velocity, we think about how we calculated it. We took average velocities over small intervals containing $t = 1$. Two such velocities are represented by the slopes of the lines in Figure 2.4. As the length of the interval shrinks, the slope of the line gets closer to the slope of the curve at $t = 1$.

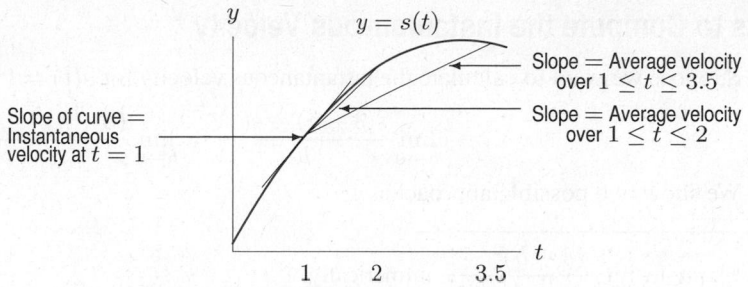

Figure 2.4: Average velocities over small intervals

The **instantaneous velocity** is the slope of the curve at a point.

Let's go back to the grapefruit. Figure 2.5 shows the height of the grapefruit plotted against time. (Note that this is not a picture of the grapefruit's path, which is straight up and down.)

How can we visualize the average velocity on this graph? Suppose $y = s(t)$. We consider the interval $1 \leq t \leq 2$ and the expression

$$\text{Average velocity} = \frac{\text{Change in position}}{\text{Change in time}} = \frac{s(2) - s(1)}{2 - 1} = \frac{142 - 90}{1} = 52 \text{ ft/sec.}$$

Now $s(2) - s(1)$ is the change in position over the interval, and it is marked vertically in Figure 2.5. The 1 in the denominator is the time elapsed and is marked horizontally in Figure 2.5. Therefore,

$$\text{Average velocity} = \frac{\text{Change in position}}{\text{Change in time}} = \text{Slope of line joining } B \text{ and } C.$$

(See Figure 2.5.) A similar argument shows the following:

The **average velocity** over any time interval $a \leq t \leq b$ is the slope of the line joining the points on the graph of $s(t)$ corresponding to $t = a$ and $t = b$.

Figure 2.5 shows how the grapefruit's velocity varies during its journey. At points A and B the curve has a large positive slope, indicating that the grapefruit is traveling up rapidly. Point D is almost at the top: the grapefruit is slowing down. At the peak, the slope of the curve is zero: the fruit has slowed to zero velocity for an instant in preparation for its return to earth. At point E the curve has a small negative slope, indicating a slow velocity of descent. Finally, the slope of the curve at point G is large and negative, indicating a large downward velocity that is responsible for the "Splat."

Figure 2.5: The height, y, of the grapefruit at time t

Using Limits to Compute the Instantaneous Velocity

Suppose we want to calculate the instantaneous velocity for $s(t) = t^2$ at $t = 3$. We must find:

$$\lim_{h \to 0} \frac{s(3+h) - s(3)}{h} = \lim_{h \to 0} \frac{(3+h)^2 - 9}{h}.$$

We show two possible approaches.

Example 3   Estimate $\lim_{h \to 0} \dfrac{(3+h)^2 - 9}{h}$ numerically.

Solution   The limit is the value approached by this expression as h approaches 0. The values in Table 2.2 seem to be converging to 6 as $h \to 0$. So it is a reasonable guess that

$$\lim_{h \to 0} \frac{(3+h)^2 - 9}{h} = 6.$$

However, we cannot be sure that the limit is *exactly* 6 by looking at the table. To calculate the limit exactly requires algebra.

Table 2.2   *Values of* $\left((3+h)^2 - 9\right)/h$ *near* $h = 0$

h	-0.1	-0.01	-0.001	0.001	0.01	0.1
$\left((3+h)^2 - 9\right)/h$	5.9	5.99	5.999	6.001	6.01	6.1

Example 4   Use algebra to find $\lim_{h \to 0} \dfrac{(3+h)^2 - 9}{h}$.

Solution   Expanding the numerator gives

$$\frac{(3+h)^2 - 9}{h} = \frac{9 + 6h + h^2 - 9}{h} = \frac{6h + h^2}{h}.$$

Since taking the limit as $h \to 0$ means looking at values of h near, but not equal, to 0, we can cancel h, giving

$$\lim_{h \to 0} \frac{(3+h)^2 - 9}{h} = \lim_{h \to 0} (6+h).$$

As h approaches 0, the values of $(6+h)$ approach 6, so

$$\lim_{h \to 0} \frac{(3+h)^2 - 9}{h} = \lim_{h \to 0} (6+h) = 6.$$

Exercises and Problems for Section 2.1

Exercises

1. The distance, s, a car has traveled on a trip is shown in the table as a function of the time, t, since the trip started. Find the average velocity between $t = 2$ and $t = 5$.

t (hours)	0	1	2	3	4	5
s (km)	0	45	135	220	300	400

2. The table gives the position of a particle moving along the x-axis as a function of time in seconds, where x is in meters. What is the average velocity of the particle from $t = 0$ to $t = 4$?

t	0	2	4	6	8
$x(t)$	-2	4	-6	-18	-14

3. The table gives the position of a particle moving along the x-axis as a function of time in seconds, where x is in angstroms. What is the average velocity of the particle from $t = 2$ to $t = 8$?

t	0	2	4	6	8
$x(t)$	0	14	-6	-18	-4

4. Figure 2.6 shows a particle's distance from a point. What is the particle's average velocity from $t = 0$ to $t = 3$?

Figure 2.6

Figure 2.7

5. Figure 2.7 shows a particle's distance from a point. What is the particle's average velocity from $t = 1$ to $t = 3$?

6. At time t in seconds, a particle's distance $s(t)$, in micrometers (μm), from a point is given by $s(t) = e^t - 1$. What is the average velocity of the particle from $t = 2$ to $t = 4$?

7. At time t in seconds, a particle's distance $s(t)$, in centimeters, from a point is given by $s(t) = 4 + 3\sin t$. What is the average velocity of the particle from $t = \pi/3$ to $t = 7\pi/3$?

8. In a time of t seconds, a particle moves a distance of s meters from its starting point, where $s = 3t^2$.

   (a) Find the average velocity between $t = 1$ and $t = 1 + h$ if:

      (i) $h = 0.1$,   (ii) $h = 0.01$,   (iii) $h = 0.001$.

(b) Use your answers to part (a) to estimate the instantaneous velocity of the particle at time $t = 1$.

9. In a time of t seconds, a particle moves a distance of s meters from its starting point, where $s = 4t^3$.

   (a) Find the average velocity between $t = 0$ and $t = h$ if:

      (i) $h = 0.1$,   (ii) $h = 0.01$,   (iii) $h = 0.001$.

   (b) Use your answers to part (a) to estimate the instantaneous velocity of the particle at time $t = 0$.

10. In a time of t seconds, a particle moves a distance of s meters from its starting point, where $s = \sin(2t)$.

   (a) Find the average velocity between $t = 1$ and $t = 1 + h$ if:

      (i) $h = 0.1$,   (ii) $h = 0.01$,   (iii) $h = 0.001$.

   (b) Use your answers to part (a) to estimate the instantaneous velocity of the particle at time $t = 1$.

11. A car is driven at a constant speed. Sketch a graph of the distance the car has traveled as a function of time.

12. A car is driven at an increasing speed. Sketch a graph of the distance the car has traveled as a function of time.

13. A car starts at a high speed, and its speed then decreases slowly. Sketch a graph of the distance the car has traveled as a function of time.

Problems

Estimate the limits in Problems 14–17 by substituting smaller and smaller values of h. For trigonometric functions, use radians. Give answers to one decimal place.

14. $\lim\limits_{h \to 0} \dfrac{(3+h)^3 - 27}{h}$ 15. $\lim\limits_{h \to 0} \dfrac{\cos h - 1}{h}$

16. $\lim\limits_{h \to 0} \dfrac{7^h - 1}{h}$ 17. $\lim\limits_{h \to 0} \dfrac{e^{1+h} - e}{h}$

18. Match the points labeled on the curve in Figure 2.8 with the given slopes.

Slope	Point
-3	
-1	
0	
$1/2$	
1	
2	

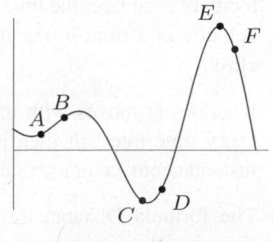

Figure 2.8

19. For the function shown in Figure 2.9, at what labeled points is the slope of the graph positive? Negative? At which labeled point does the graph have the greatest (i.e., most positive) slope? The least slope (i.e., negative and with the largest magnitude)?

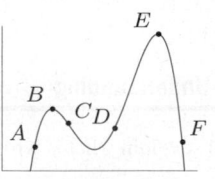

Figure 2.9

20. For the graph $y = f(x)$ in Figure 2.10, arrange the following numbers from smallest to largest:

- The slope of the graph at A.
- The slope of the graph at B.
- The slope of the graph at C.
- The slope of the line AB.
- The number 0.
- The number 1.

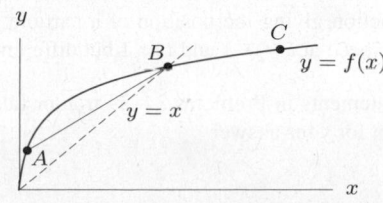

Figure 2.10

21. The graph of $f(t)$ in Figure 2.11 gives the position of a particle at time t. List the following quantities in order, smallest to largest.

- A, average velocity between $t = 1$ and $t = 3$,
- B, average velocity between $t = 5$ and $t = 6$,
- C, instantaneous velocity at $t = 1$,
- D, instantaneous velocity at $t = 3$,
- E, instantaneous velocity at $t = 5$,
- F, instantaneous velocity at $t = 6$.

Figure 2.11

22. Find the average velocity over the interval $0 \le t \le 0.2$, and estimate the velocity at $t = 0.2$ of a car whose position, s, is given by the following table.

t (sec)	0	0.2	0.4	0.6	0.8	1.0
s (ft)	0	0.5	1.8	3.8	6.5	9.6

23. A particle moves at varying velocity along a line and $s = f(t)$ represents the particle's distance from a point as a function of time, t. Sketch a possible graph for f if the average velocity of the particle between $t = 2$ and $t = 6$ is the same as the instantaneous velocity at $t = 5$.

24. A ball is tossed into the air from a bridge, and its height, y (in feet), above the ground t seconds after it is thrown is given by

$$y = f(t) = -16t^2 + 50t + 36.$$

(a) How high above the ground is the bridge?
(b) What is the average velocity of the ball for the first second?
(c) Approximate the velocity of the ball at $t = 1$ second.
(d) Graph f, and determine the maximum height the ball reaches. What is the velocity at the time the ball is at the peak?
(e) Use the graph to decide at what time, t, the ball reaches its maximum height.

Use algebra to evaluate the limits in Problems 25–28.

25. $\lim\limits_{h \to 0} \dfrac{(2+h)^2 - 4}{h}$

26. $\lim\limits_{h \to 0} \dfrac{(1+h)^3 - 1}{h}$

27. $\lim\limits_{h \to 0} \dfrac{3(2+h)^2 - 12}{h}$

28. $\lim\limits_{h \to 0} \dfrac{(3+h)^2 - (3-h)^2}{2h}$

Strengthen Your Understanding

In Problems 29–31, explain what is wrong with the statement.

29. Velocity and speed are the same.

30. Since $\lim_{h \to 0}(2+h)^2 = 4$, we have

$$\lim_{h \to 0} \frac{(2+h)^2 - 2^2}{h} = 0.$$

31. The particle whose position is shown in Figure 2.11 has velocity at time $t = 4$ greater than the velocity at $t = 2$.

In Problems 32–33, give an example of:

32. A function which has a negative instantaneous velocity for $t < 0$ and a positive instantaneous velocity for $t > 0$.

33. A function giving the position of a particle that has the same speed at $t = -1$ and $t = 1$ but different velocities.

Are the statements in Problems 34–39 true or false? Give an explanation for your answer.

34. If a car is going 50 miles per hour at 2 pm and 60 miles per hour at 3 pm then it travels between 50 and 60 miles during the hour between 2 pm and 3 pm.

35. If a car travels 80 miles between 2 and 4 pm, then its velocity is close to 40 mph at 2 pm.

36. If the time interval is short enough, then the average velocity of a car over the time interval and the instantaneous velocity at a time in the interval can be expected to be close.

37. If an object moves with the same average velocity over every time interval, then its average velocity equals its instantaneous velocity at any time.

38. The formula Distance traveled = Average velocity × Time is valid for every moving object for every time interval.

39. By definition, the instantaneous velocity of an object equals a difference quotient.

2.2 THE DERIVATIVE AT A POINT

Average Rate of Change

In Section 2.1, we looked at the change in height divided by the change in time; this ratio is called the *difference quotient*. Now we define the rate of change of a function f that depends on a variable other than time. We say:

$$\text{Average rate of change of } f \atop \text{over the interval from } a \text{ to } a + h = \frac{f(a + h) - f(a)}{h}.$$

The numerator, $f(a + h) - f(a)$, measures the change in the value of f over the interval from a to $a + h$. The difference quotient is the change in f divided by the change in the independent variable, which we call x. Although the interval is no longer necessarily a time interval, we still talk about the *average rate of change* of f over the interval. If we want to emphasize the independent variable, we talk about the average rate of change of f *with respect to x*.

Instantaneous Rate of Change: The Derivative

We define the *instantaneous rate of change* of a function at a point in the same way that we defined instantaneous velocity: we look at the average rate of change over smaller and smaller intervals. This instantaneous rate of change is called the *derivative of f at a*, denoted by $f'(a)$.

> The **derivative of f at a**, written $f'(a)$, is defined as
>
> $$\text{Rate of change} \atop \text{of } f \text{ at } a = f'(a) = \lim_{h \to 0} \frac{f(a + h) - f(a)}{h}.$$
>
> If the limit exists, then f is said to be **differentiable at a**.

To emphasize that $f'(a)$ is the rate of change of $f(x)$ as the variable x changes, we call $f'(a)$ the derivative of f *with respect to x* at $x = a$. When the function $y = s(t)$ represents the position of an object, the derivative $s'(t)$ is the velocity.

Example 1   Eucalyptus trees, common in California and the Pacific Northwest, grow better with more water. Scientists in North Africa, analyzing where to plant trees, found that the volume of wood that grows on a square kilometer, in meters^3, is approximated by[2]

$$V(r) = 0.2r^2 - 20r + 600,$$

where r is rainfall in cm per year, and $60 \leq r \leq 120$.

(a) Calculate the average rate of change of V with respect to r over the intervals $90 \leq r \leq 100$ and $100 \leq r \leq 110$.

(b) By choosing small values for h, estimate the instantaneous rate of change of V with respect to r at $r = 100$ cm.

Solution   (a) Using the formula for the average rate of change gives

$$\text{Average rate of change of volume} \atop \text{for } 90 \leq r \leq 100 = \frac{V(100) - V(90)}{10} = \frac{600 - 420}{10} = 18 \text{ meter}^3/\text{cm}.$$

---

[2]"Is urban forestry a solution to the energy crises of Sahelian cities?" by Cornelia Sepp, www.nzdl.org, accessed Feb 11, 2012.

$$\text{Average rate of change of volume} \atop \text{for } 100 \le r \le 110 \quad = \frac{V(110) - V(100)}{10} = \frac{820 - 600}{10} = 22 \text{ meter}^3/\text{cm}.$$

So we see that the average rate of change of the volume of wood grown on a square kilometer increases as the rainfall increases.

(b) With $h = 0.1$ and $h = -0.1$, we have the difference quotients

$$\frac{V(100.1) - V(100)}{0.1} = 20.02 \text{ m}^3/\text{cm} \quad \text{and} \quad \frac{V(99.9) - V(100)}{-0.1} = 19.98 \text{ m}^3/\text{cm}.$$

With $h = 0.01$ and $h = -0.01$,

$$\frac{V(100.01) - V(100)}{0.01} = 20.002 \text{ m}^3/\text{cm} \quad \text{and} \quad \frac{V(99.99) - V(100)}{-0.01} = 19.998 \text{ m}^3/\text{cm}.$$

These difference quotients suggest that when the yearly rainfall is 100 cm, the instantaneous rate of change of the volume of wood grown on a square kilometer is about 20 meter³ per cm of rainfall. To confirm that the instantaneous rate of change of the function is exactly 20, that is, $V'(100) = 20$, we would need to take the limit as $h \to 0$.

Visualizing the Derivative: Slope of Curve and Slope of Tangent

As with velocity, we can visualize the derivative $f'(a)$ as the slope of the graph of f at $x = a$. In addition, there is another way to think of $f'(a)$. Consider the difference quotient $(f(a + h) - f(a))/h$. The numerator, $f(a + h) - f(a)$, is the vertical distance marked in Figure 2.12 and h is the horizontal distance, so

$$\text{Average rate of change of } f = \frac{f(a + h) - f(a)}{h} = \text{Slope of line } AB.$$

As h becomes smaller, the line AB approaches the tangent line to the curve at A. (See Figure 2.13.) We say

$$\text{Instantaneous rate of change} \atop \text{of } f \text{ at } a \quad = \lim_{h \to 0} \frac{f(a + h) - f(a)}{h} = \text{Slope of tangent at } A.$$

Figure 2.12: Visualizing the average rate of change of f

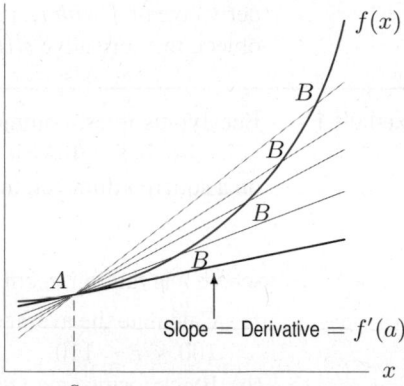

Figure 2.13: Visualizing the instantaneous rate of change of f

---

The derivative at point A can be interpreted as:
- The slope of the curve at A.
- The slope of the tangent line to the curve at A.

The slope interpretation is often useful in gaining rough information about the derivative, as the following examples show.

Example 2   Is the derivative of $\sin x$ at $x = \pi$ positive or negative?

Solution   Looking at a graph of $\sin x$ in Figure 2.14 (remember, x is in radians), we see that a tangent line drawn at $x = \pi$ has negative slope. So the derivative at this point is negative.

Figure 2.14: Tangent line to $\sin x$ at $x = \pi$

Recall that if we zoom in on the graph of a function $y = f(x)$ at the point $x = a$, we usually find that the graph looks like a straight line with slope $f'(a)$.

Example 3   By zooming in on the point $(0,0)$ on the graph of the sine function, estimate the value of the derivative of $\sin x$ at $x = 0$, with x in radians.

Solution   Figure 2.15 shows graphs of $\sin x$ with smaller and smaller scales. On the interval $-0.1 \leq x \leq 0.1$, the graph looks like a straight line of slope 1. Thus, the derivative of $\sin x$ at $x = 0$ is about 1.

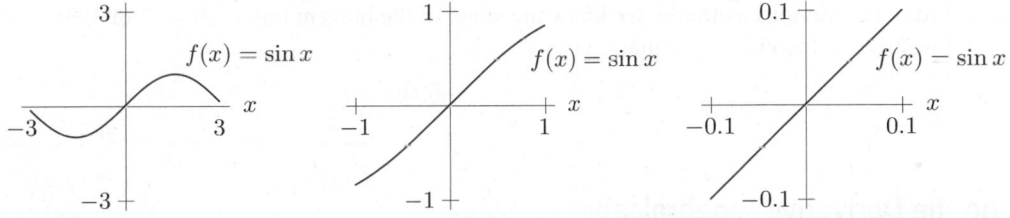

Figure 2.15: Zooming in on the graph of $\sin x$ near $x = 0$ shows the derivative is about 1 at $x = 0$

Later we will show that the derivative of $\sin x$ at $x = 0$ is exactly 1. (See page 152 in Section 3.5.) From now on we will assume that this is so. This simple result is one of the reasons we choose to use radians when doing calculus with trigonometric functions. If we had done Example 3 in degrees, the derivative of $\sin x$ would have turned out to be a much messier number. (See Problem 24, page 89.)

Estimating the Derivative

Example 4   Estimate the value of the derivative of $f(x) = 2^x$ at $x = 0$ graphically and numerically.

Solution   Graphically: Figure 2.16 indicates that the graph is concave up. Assuming this, the slope at A is between the slope of BA and the slope of AC. Since

$$\text{Slope of line } BA = \frac{(2^0 - 2^{-1})}{(0 - (-1))} = \frac{1}{2} \quad \text{and} \quad \text{Slope of line } AC = \frac{(2^1 - 2^0)}{(1 - 0)} = 1,$$

we know that at $x = 0$ the derivative of 2^x is between $1/2$ and 1.

Numerically: To estimate the derivative at $x = 0$, we look at values of the difference quotient

$$\frac{f(0 + h) - f(0)}{h} = \frac{2^h - 2^0}{h} = \frac{2^h - 1}{h}$$

for small h. Table 2.3 shows some values of 2^h together with values of the difference quotients. (See Problem 33 on page 89 for what happens for very small values of h.)

$f(x) = 2^x$

Slope $= 1$

Slope $= \frac{1}{2}$

Tangent line
Slope $= f'(0)$

Figure 2.16: Graph of $y = 2^x$ showing the derivative at $x = 0$

Table 2.3   *Numerical values for difference quotient of 2^x at $x = 0$*

h	2^h	Difference quotient: $\frac{2^h - 1}{h}$
-0.0003	0.999792078	0.693075
-0.0002	0.999861380	0.693099
-0.0001	0.999930688	0.693123
0	1	
0.0001	1.00006932	0.693171
0.0002	1.00013864	0.693195
0.0003	1.00020797	0.693219

The concavity of the curve tells us that difference quotients calculated with negative h's are smaller than the derivative, and those calculated with positive h's are larger. From Table 2.3 we see that the derivative is between 0.693123 and 0.693171. To three decimal places, $f'(0) = 0.693$.

Example 5   Find an approximate equation for the tangent line to $f(x) = 2^x$ at $x = 0$.

Solution   From the previous example, we know the slope of the tangent line is about 0.693. Since the tangent line has y-intercept 1, its equation is

$$y = 0.693x + 1.$$

Computing the Derivative Algebraically

The graph of $f(x) = 1/x$ in Figure 2.17 leads us to expect that $f'(2)$ is negative. To compute $f'(2)$ exactly, we use algebra.

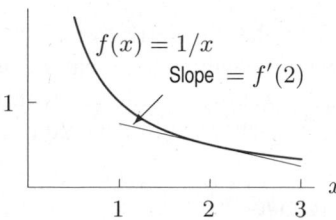

$f(x) = 1/x$

Slope $= f'(2)$

Figure 2.17: Tangent line to $f(x) = 1/x$ at $x = 2$

Example 6   Find the derivative of $f(x) = 1/x$ at the point $x = 2$.

Solution   The derivative is the limit of the difference quotient, so we look at

$$f'(2) = \lim_{h \to 0} \frac{f(2+h) - f(2)}{h}.$$

Using the formula for f and simplifying gives

$$f'(2) = \lim_{h \to 0} \frac{1}{h} \left(\frac{1}{2+h} - \frac{1}{2} \right) = \lim_{h \to 0} \left(\frac{2 - (2+h)}{2h(2+h)} \right) = \lim_{h \to 0} \frac{-h}{2h(2+h)}.$$

Since the limit only examines values of h close to, but not equal to, zero, we can cancel h. We get

$$f'(2) = \lim_{h \to 0} \frac{-1}{2(2+h)} = -\frac{1}{4}.$$

Thus, $f'(2) = -1/4$. The slope of the tangent line in Figure 2.17 is $-1/4$.

Exercises and Problems for Section 2.2

Exercises

1. The table shows values of $f(x) = x^3$ near $x = 2$ (to three decimal places). Use it to estimate $f'(2)$.

x	1.998	1.999	2.000	2.001	2.002
x^3	7.976	7.988	8.000	8.012	8.024

2. By choosing small values for h, estimate the instantaneous rate of change of the function $f(x) - x^3$ with respect to x at $x = 1$.

3. The income that a company receives from selling an item is called the revenue. Production decisions are based, in part, on how revenue changes if the quantity sold changes; that is, on the rate of change of revenue with respect to quantity sold. Suppose a company's revenue, in dollars, is given by $R(q) = 100q - 10q^2$, where q is the quantity sold in kilograms.

   (a) Calculate the average rate of change of R with respect to q over the intervals $1 \leq q \leq 2$ and $2 \leq q \leq 3$.
   (b) By choosing small values for h, estimate the instantaneous rate of change of revenue with respect to change in quantity at $q = 2$ kilograms.

4. (a) Make a table of values rounded to two decimal places for the function $f(x) = e^x$ for $x = 1, 1.5, 2, 2.5,$ and 3. Then use the table to answer parts (b) and (c).
   (b) Find the average rate of change of $f(x)$ between $x = 1$ and $x = 3$.
   (c) Use average rates of change to approximate the instantaneous rate of change of $f(x)$ at $x = 2$.

5. (a) Make a table of values, rounded to two decimal places, for $f(x) = \log x$ (that is, log base 10) with $x = 1, 1.5, 2, 2.5, 3$. Then use this table to answer parts (b) and (c).
   (b) Find the average rate of change of $f(x)$ between $x = 1$ and $x = 3$.
   (c) Use average rates of change to approximate the instantaneous rate of change of $f(x)$ at $x = 2$.

6. If $f(x) = x^3 + 4x$, estimate $f'(3)$ using a table with values of x near 3, spaced by 0.001.

7. Graph $f(x) = \sin x$, and use the graph to decide whether the derivative of $f(x)$ at $x = 3\pi$ is positive or negative.

8. For the function $f(x) = \log x$, estimate $f'(1)$. From the graph of $f(x)$, would you expect your estimate to be greater than or less than $f'(1)$?

9. Estimate $f'(2)$ for $f(x) = 3^x$. Explain your reasoning.

10. The graph of $y = f(x)$ is shown in Figure 2.18. Which is larger in each of the following pairs?

    (a) Average rate of change: Between $x = 1$ and $x = 3$? Or between $x = 3$ and $x = 5$?
    (b) $f(2)$ or $f(5)$?
    (c) $f'(1)$ or $f'(4)$?

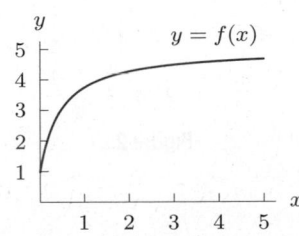

Figure 2.18

11. Figure 2.19 shows the graph of f. Match the derivatives in the table with the points a, b, c, d, e.

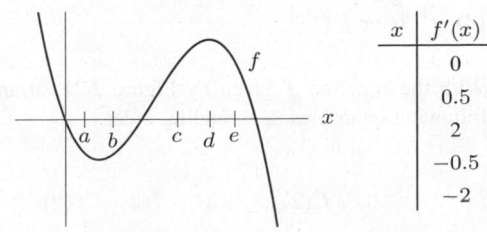

x	$f'(x)$
	0
	0.5
	2
	-0.5
	-2

Figure 2.19

12. Label points $A, B, C, D, E,$ and F on the graph of $y = f(x)$ in Figure 2.20.

(a) Point A is a point on the curve where the derivative is negative.

(b) Point B is a point on the curve where the value of the function is negative.

(c) Point C is a point on the curve where the derivative is largest.

(d) Point D is a point on the curve where the derivative is zero.

(e) Points E and F are different points on the curve where the derivative is about the same.

Figure 2.20

Problems

13. Suppose that $f(x)$ is a function with $f(100) = 35$ and $f'(100) = 3$. Estimate $f(102)$.

14. Show how to represent the following on Figure 2.21.

(a) $f(4)$

(b) $f(4) - f(2)$

(c) $\dfrac{f(5) - f(2)}{5 - 2}$

(d) $f'(3)$

Figure 2.21

15. For each of the following pairs of numbers, use Figure 2.21 to decide which is larger. Explain your answer.

(a) $f(3)$ or $f(4)$?

(b) $f(3) - f(2)$ or $f(2) - f(1)$?

(c) $\dfrac{f(2) - f(1)}{2 - 1}$ or $\dfrac{f(3) - f(1)}{3 - 1}$?

(d) $f'(1)$ or $f'(4)$?

16. With the function f given by Figure 2.21, arrange the following quantities in ascending order:

$$0, \quad f'(2), \quad f'(3), \quad f(3) - f(2)$$

17. The function in Figure 2.22 has $f(4) = 25$ and $f'(4) = 1.5$. Find the coordinates of the points A, B, C.

Tangent line

$f(x)$

Figure 2.22

18. Use Figure 2.23 to fill in the blanks in the following statements about the function g at point B.

(a) $g(\_\_) = \_\_$

(b) $g'(\_\_) = \_\_$

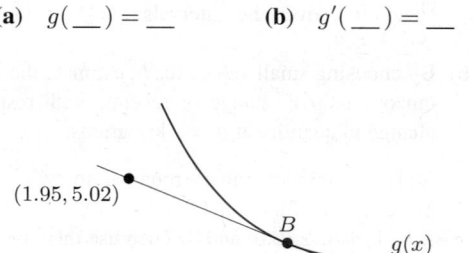

Figure 2.23

19. On a copy of Figure 2.24, mark lengths that represent the quantities in parts (a)–(d). (Pick any positive x and h.)

(a) $f(x)$

(b) $f(x + h)$

(c) $f(x + h) - f(x)$

(d) h

(e) Using your answers to parts (a)–(d), show how the quantity $\dfrac{f(x + h) - f(x)}{h}$ can be represented as the slope of a line in Figure 2.24.

Figure 2.24 **Figure 2.25**

20. On a copy of Figure 2.25, mark lengths that represent the quantities in parts (a)–(d). (Pick any convenient x, and assume $h > 0$.)

    (a) $f(x)$ **(b)** $f(x+h)$ **(c)** $f(x+h) - f(x)$ **(d)** h

    (e) Using your answers to parts (a)–(d), show how the quantity $\dfrac{f(x+h) - f(x)}{h}$ can be represented as the slope of a line on the graph.

21. Consider the function shown in Figure 2.26.

    (a) Write an expression involving f for the slope of the line joining A and B.

    (b) Draw the tangent line at C. Compare its slope to the slope of the line in part (a).

    (c) Are there any other points on the curve at which the slope of the tangent line is the same as the slope of the tangent line at C? If so, mark them on the graph. If not, why not?

Figure 2.26

22. **(a)** If f is even and $f'(10) = 6$, what is $f'(-10)$?

    (b) If f is any even function and $f'(0)$ exists, what is $f'(0)$?

23. If g is an odd function and $g'(4) = 5$, what is $g'(-4)$?

24. **(a)** Estimate $f'(0)$ if $f(x) = \sin x$, with x in degrees.

    (b) In Example 3 on page 85, we found that the derivative of $\sin x$ at $x = 0$ was 1. Why do we get a different result here? (This problem shows why radians are almost always used in calculus.)

25. Find the equation of the tangent line to $f(x) = x^2 + x$ at $x = 3$. Sketch the function and this tangent line.

26. Estimate the instantaneous rate of change of the function $f(x) = x \ln x$ at $x = 1$ and at $x = 2$. What do these values suggest about the concavity of the graph between 1 and 2?

27. Estimate the derivative of $f(x) = x^x$ at $x = 2$.

28. For $y = f(x) = 3x^{3/2} - x$, use your calculator to construct a graph of $y = f(x)$, for $0 \le x \le 2$. From your graph, estimate $f'(0)$ and $f'(1)$.

29. Let $f(x) = \ln(\cos x)$. Use your calculator to approximate the instantaneous rate of change of f at the point $x = 1$. Do the same thing for $x = \pi/4$. (Note: Be sure that your calculator is set in radians.)

30. On October 17, 2006, in an article called "US Population Reaches 300 Million," the BBC reported that the US gains 1 person every 11 seconds. If $f(t)$ is the US population in millions t years after October 17, 2006, find $f(0)$ and $f'(0)$.

31. The population, $P(t)$, of China,[3] in billions, can be approximated by

$$P(t) = 1.267(1.007)^t,$$

where t is the number of years since the start of 2000. According to this model, how fast was the population growing at the start of 2000 and at the start of 2007? Give your answers in millions of people per year.

32. **(a)** Graph $f(x) = \frac{1}{2}x^2$ and $g(x) = f(x) + 3$ on the same set of axes. What can you say about the slopes of the tangent lines to the two graphs at the point $x = 0$? $x = 2$? Any point $x = x_0$?

    (b) Explain why adding a constant value, C, to any function does not change the value of the slope of its graph at any point. [Hint: Let $g(x) = f(x) + C$, and calculate the difference quotients for f and g.]

33. Suppose Table 2.3 on page 86 is continued with smaller values of h. A particular calculator gives the results in Table 2.4. (Your calculator may give slightly different results.) Comment on the values of the difference quotient in Table 2.4. In particular, why is the last value of $(2^h - 1)/h$ zero? What do you expect the calculated value of $(2^h - 1)/h$ to be when $h = 10^{-20}$?

Table 2.4 *Questionable values of difference quotients of 2^x near $x = 0$*

h	Difference quotient: $(2^h - 1)/h$
10^{-4}	0.6931712
10^{-6}	0.693147
10^{-8}	0.6931
10^{-10}	0.69
10^{-12}	0

[3] www.unescap.org/stat/data/apif/index.asp, accessed May 1, 2007.

34. (a) Let $f(x) = x^2$. Explain what Table 2.5 tells us about $f'(1)$.
   (b) Find $f'(1)$ exactly.
   (c) If x changes by 0.1 near $x = 1$, what does $f'(1)$ tell us about how $f(x)$ changes? Illustrate your answer with a sketch.

Table 2.5

x	x^2	Difference in successive x^2 values
0.998	0.996004	
		0.001997
0.999	0.998001	
		0.001999
1.000	1.000000	
		0.002001
1.001	1.002001	
		0.002003
1.002	1.004004	

Use algebra to evaluate the limits in Problems 35–40.

35. $\lim\limits_{h \to 0} \dfrac{(-3 + h)^2 - 9}{h}$

36. $\lim\limits_{h \to 0} \dfrac{(2 - h)^3 - 8}{h}$

37. $\lim\limits_{h \to 0} \dfrac{1/(1 + h) - 1}{h}$

38. $\lim\limits_{h \to 0} \dfrac{1/(1 + h)^2 - 1}{h}$

39. $\lim\limits_{h \to 0} \dfrac{\sqrt{4 + h} - 2}{h}$ [Hint: Multiply by $\sqrt{4 + h} + 2$ in numerator and denominator.]

40. $\lim\limits_{h \to 0} \dfrac{1/\sqrt{4 + h} - 1/2}{h}$

Find the derivatives in Problems 41–46 algebraically.

41. $f(x) = 5x^2$ at $x = 10$ **42.** $f(x) = x^3$ at $x = -2$

43. $g(t) = t^2 + t$ at $t = -1$ **44.** $f(x) = x^3 + 5$ at $x = 1$

45. $g(x) = 1/x$ at $x = 2$ **46.** $g(z) = z^{-2}$, find $g'(2)$

For Problems 47–50, find the equation of the line tangent to the function at the given point.

47. $f(x) = 5x^2$ at $x = 10$ **48.** $f(x) = x^3$ at $x = -2$

49. $f(x) = x$ at $x = 20$ **50.** $f(x) = 1/x^2$ at $(1, 1)$

Strengthen Your Understanding

In Problems 51–52, explain what is wrong with the statement.

51. For the function $f(x) = \log x$ we have $f'(0.5) < 0$.

52. The derivative of a function $f(x)$ at $x = a$ is the tangent line to the graph of $f(x)$ at $x = a$.

In Problems 53–54, give an example of:

53. A continuous function which is always increasing and positive.

54. A linear function with derivative 2 at $x = 0$.

Are the statements in Problems 55–57 true or false? Give an explanation for your answer.

55. You cannot be sure of the exact value of a derivative of a function at a point using only the information in a table of values of the function. The best you can do is find an approximation.

56. If you zoom in (with your calculator) on the graph of $y = f(x)$ in a small interval around $x = 10$ and see a straight line, then the slope of that line equals the derivative $f'(10)$.

57. If $f(x)$ is concave up, then $f'(a) < (f(b) - f(a))/(b - a)$ for $a < b$.

58. Assume that f is an odd function and that $f'(2) = 3$, then $f'(-2) =$

   (a) 3 **(b)** -3
   (c) 1/3 **(d)** $-1/3$

2.3 THE DERIVATIVE FUNCTION

In the previous section we looked at the derivative of a function at a fixed point. Now we consider what happens at a variety of points. The derivative generally takes on different values at different points and is itself a function.

First, remember that the derivative of a function at a point tells us the rate at which the value of the function is changing at that point. Geometrically, we can think of the derivative as the slope of the curve or of the tangent line at the point.

Example 1   Estimate the derivative of the function $f(x)$ graphed in Figure 2.27 at $x = -2, -1, 0, 1, 2, 3, 4, 5$.

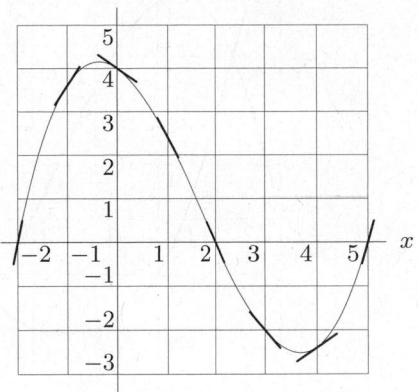

Figure 2.27: Estimating the derivative graphically as the slope of the tangent line

Solution   From the graph we estimate the derivative at any point by placing a straightedge so that it forms the tangent line at that point, and then using the grid squares to estimate the slope of the straightedge. For example, the tangent at $x = -1$ is drawn in Figure 2.27, and has a slope of about 2, so $f'(-1) \approx 2$. Notice that the slope at $x = -2$ is positive and fairly large; the slope at $x = -1$ is positive but smaller. At $x = 0$, the slope is negative, by $x = 1$ it has become more negative, and so on. Some estimates of the derivative are listed in Table 2.6. You should check these values. Are they reasonable? Is the derivative positive where you expect? Negative?

Table 2.6   *Estimated values of derivative of function in Figure 2.27*

x	-2	-1	0	1	2	3	4	5
$f'(x)$	6	2	-1	-2	-2	-1	1	4

Notice that for every x-value, there's a corresponding value of the derivative. Therefore, the derivative is itself a function of x.

For any function f, we define the **derivative function**, f', by

$$f'(x) = \text{ Rate of change of } f \text{ at } x = \lim_{h \to 0} \frac{f(x+h) - f(x)}{h}.$$

For every x-value for which this limit exists, we say f is *differentiable at* that x-value. If the limit exists for all x in the domain of f, we say f is *differentiable everywhere*. Most functions we meet are differentiable at every point in their domain, except perhaps for a few isolated points.

The Derivative Function: Graphically

Example 2   Sketch the graph of the derivative of the function shown in Figure 2.27.

Solution   We plot the values of the derivative in Table 2.6 and connect them with a smooth curve to obtain the estimate of the derivative function in Figure 2.28. Values of the derivative function give slopes of the original graph.

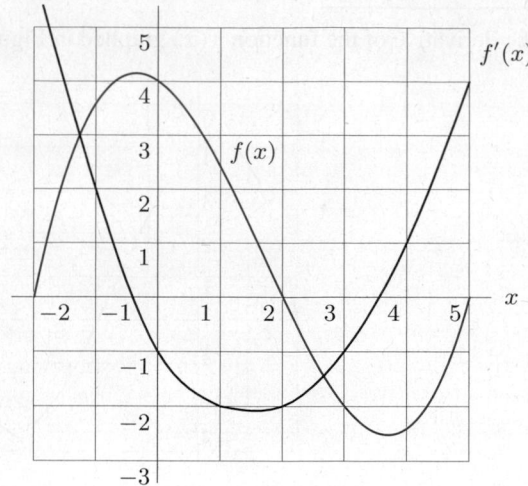

Figure 2.28: Function (colored) and derivative (black) from Example 1

Check that this graph of f' makes sense: Where the values of f' are positive, f is increasing ($x < -0.3$ or $x > 3.8$) and where f' is negative, f is decreasing. Notice that at the points where f has large positive slope, such as $x = -2$, the graph of the derivative is far above the x-axis, as it should be, since the value of the derivative is large there. At points where the slope is gentler, such as $x = -1$, the graph of f' is closer to the x-axis, since the derivative is smaller.

What Does the Derivative Tell Us Graphically?

Where f' is positive, the tangent line to f is sloping up; where f' is negative, the tangent line to f is sloping down. If $f' = 0$ everywhere, then the tangent line to f is horizontal everywhere, and f is constant. We see that the sign of f' tells us whether f is increasing or decreasing.

> If $f' > 0$ on an interval, then f is *increasing* over that interval.
> If $f' < 0$ on an interval, then f is *decreasing* over that interval.

Moreover, the magnitude of the derivative gives us the magnitude of the rate of change; so if f' is large (positive or negative), then the graph of f is steep (up or down), whereas if f' is small the graph of f slopes gently. With this in mind, we can learn about the behavior of a function from the behavior of its derivative.

The Derivative Function: Numerically

If we are given values of a function instead of its graph, we can estimate values of the derivative.

Example 3   Table 2.7 gives values of $c(t)$, the concentration (μg/cm^3) of a drug in the bloodstream at time t (min). Construct a table of estimated values for $c'(t)$, the rate of change of $c(t)$ with respect to time.

Table 2.7   *Concentration as a function of time*

t (min)	0	0.1	0.2	0.3	0.4	0.5	0.6	0.7	0.8	0.9	1.0
$c(t)$ (μg/cm^3)	0.84	0.89	0.94	0.98	1.00	1.00	0.97	0.90	0.79	0.63	0.41

Solution   We estimate values of c' using the values in the table. To do this, we have to assume that the data points are close enough together that the concentration does not change wildly between them. From the table, we see that the concentration is increasing between $t = 0$ and $t = 0.4$, so we expect a positive derivative there. However, the increase is quite slow, so we expect the derivative to be small. The concentration does not change between 0.4 and 0.5, so we expect the derivative to be roughly 0 there. From $t = 0.5$ to $t = 1.0$, the concentration starts to decrease, and the rate of decrease gets larger and larger, so we expect the derivative to be negative and of greater and greater magnitude.

Using the data in the table, we estimate the derivative using the difference quotient:

$$c'(t) \approx \frac{c(t + h) - c(t)}{h}.$$

Since the data points are 0.1 apart, we use $h = 0.1$, giving, for example,

$$c'(0) \approx \frac{c(0.1) - c(0)}{0.1} = \frac{0.89 - 0.84}{0.1} = 0.5 \ \mu\text{g/cm}^3\text{/min}$$

$$c'(0.1) \approx \frac{c(0.2) - c(0.1)}{0.1} = \frac{0.94 - 0.89}{0.1} = 0.5 \ \mu\text{g/cm}^3\text{/min}.$$

See Table 2.8. Notice that the derivative has small positive values until $t = 0.4$, where it is roughly 0, and then it gets more and more negative, as we expected. The slopes are graphed in Figure 2.29.

Table 2.8 *Estimated derivative of concentration*

t	$c'(t)$
0	0.5
0.1	0.5
0.2	0.4
0.3	0.2
0.4	0.0
0.5	−0.3
0.6	−0.7
0.7	−1.1
0.8	−1.6
0.9	−2.2

Figure 2.29: Graph of concentration as a function of time

Improving Numerical Estimates for the Derivative

In the previous example, the estimate for the derivative at 0.2 used the interval to the right; we found the average rate of change between $t = 0.2$ and $t = 0.3$. However, we could equally well have gone to the left and used the rate of change between $t = 0.1$ and $t = 0.2$ to approximate the derivative at 0.2. For a more accurate result, we could average these slopes and say

$$c'(0.2) \approx \frac{1}{2} \left(\begin{array}{c} \text{Slope to left} \\ \text{of } 0.2 \end{array} + \begin{array}{c} \text{Slope to right} \\ \text{of } 0.2 \end{array} \right) = \frac{0.5 + 0.4}{2} = 0.45.$$

In general, averaging the slopes leads to a more accurate answer.

Derivative Function: From a Formula

If we are given a formula for f, can we come up with a formula for f'? We often can, as shown in the next example. Indeed, much of the power of calculus depends on our ability to find formulas for the derivatives of all the functions we described earlier. This is done systematically in Chapter 3.

Derivative of a Constant Function

The graph of a constant function $f(x) = k$ is a horizontal line, with a slope of 0 everywhere. Therefore, its derivative is 0 everywhere. (See Figure 2.30.)

$$\text{If } f(x) = k, \text{ then } f'(x) = 0.$$

Figure 2.30: A constant function

Derivative of a Linear Function

We already know that the slope of a straight line is constant. This tells us that the derivative of a linear function is constant.

$$\text{If } f(x) = b + mx, \text{ then } f'(x) = \text{Slope} = m.$$

Derivative of a Power Function

Example 4   Find a formula for the derivative of $f(x) = x^2$.

Solution   Before computing the formula for $f'(x)$ algebraically, let's try to guess the formula by looking for a pattern in the values of $f'(x)$. Table 2.9 contains values of $f(x) = x^2$ (rounded to three decimals), which we can use to estimate the values of $f'(1)$, $f'(2)$, and $f'(3)$.

Table 2.9   *Values of $f(x) = x^2$ near $x = 1$, $x = 2$, $x = 3$ (rounded to three decimals)*

x	x^2	x	x^2	x	x^2
0.999	0.998	1.999	3.996	2.999	8.994
1.000	1.000	2.000	4.000	3.000	9.000
1.001	1.002	2.001	4.004	3.001	9.006
1.002	1.004	2.002	4.008	3.002	9.012

Near $x = 1$, the value of x^2 increases by about 0.002 each time x increases by 0.001, so

$$f'(1) \approx \frac{0.002}{0.001} = 2.$$

Similarly, near $x = 2$ and $x = 3$, the value of x^2 increases by about 0.004 and 0.006, respectively, when x increases by 0.001. So

$$f'(2) \approx \frac{0.004}{0.001} = 4 \quad \text{and} \quad f'(3) \approx \frac{0.006}{0.001} = 6.$$

Knowing the value of f' at specific points can never tell us the formula for f', but it certainly can be suggestive: Knowing $f'(1) \approx 2$, $f'(2) \approx 4$, $f'(3) \approx 6$ suggests that $f'(x) = 2x$.

The derivative is calculated by forming the difference quotient and taking the limit as h goes to zero. The difference quotient is

$$\frac{f(x+h) - f(x)}{h} = \frac{(x+h)^2 - x^2}{h} = \frac{x^2 + 2xh + h^2 - x^2}{h} = \frac{2xh + h^2}{h}.$$

Since h never actually reaches zero, we can cancel it in the last expression to get $2x + h$. The limit of this as h goes to zero is $2x$, so

$$f'(x) = \lim_{h \to 0} (2x + h) = 2x.$$

Example 5   Calculate $f'(x)$ if $f(x) = x^3$.

Solution   We look at the difference quotient

$$\frac{f(x+h) - f(x)}{h} = \frac{(x+h)^3 - x^3}{h}.$$

Multiplying out gives $(x + h)^3 = x^3 + 3x^2 h + 3xh^2 + h^3$, so

$$f'(x) = \lim_{h \to 0} \frac{x^3 + 3x^2 h + 3xh^2 + h^3 - x^3}{h} = \lim_{h \to 0} \frac{3x^2 h + 3xh^2 + h^3}{h}.$$

Since in taking the limit as $h \to 0$, we consider values of h near, but not equal to, zero, we can cancel h, giving

$$f'(x) = \lim_{h \to 0} \frac{3x^2 h + 3xh^2 + h^3}{h} = \lim_{h \to 0} (3x^2 + 3xh + h^2).$$

As $h \to 0$, the value of $(3xh + h^2) \to 0$, so

$$f'(x) = \lim_{h \to 0} (3x^2 + 3xh + h^2) = 3x^2.$$

The previous two examples show how to compute the derivatives of power functions of the form $f(x) = x^n$, when n is 2 or 3. We can use the Binomial Theorem to show the *power rule* for a positive integer n:

If $f(x) = x^n$ then $f'(x) = nx^{n-1}$.

This result is in fact valid for any real value of n.

Exercises and Problems for Section 2.3

Exercises

1. (a) Estimate $f'(2)$ using the values of f in the table.
   (b) For what values of x does $f'(x)$ appear to be positive? Negative?

x	0	2	4	6	8	10	12
$f(x)$	10	18	24	21	20	18	15

2. Find approximate values for $f'(x)$ at each of the x-values given in the following table.

x	0	5	10	15	20
$f(x)$	100	70	55	46	40

For Exercises 3–12, graph the derivative of the given functions.

3.

4.

5.

6.

7.

8.

9.

10.

11.

12.

For Exercises 13–18, sketch the graph of $f(x)$, and use this graph to sketch the graph of $f'(x)$.

13. $f(x) = 5x$

14. $f(x) = x^2$

15. $f(x) = x(x-1)$

16. $f(x) = e^x$

17. $f(x) = \cos x$

18. $f(x) = \ln x$

In Exercises 19–20, find a formula for the derivative using the power rule. Confirm it using difference quotients.

19. $k(x) = 1/x$

20. $l(x) = 1/x^2$

Find a formula for the derivatives of the functions in Exercises 21–22 using difference quotients.

21. $g(x) = 2x^2 - 3$

22. $m(x) = 1/(x+1)$

Problems

23. In each case, graph a smooth curve whose slope meets the condition.

   (a) Everywhere positive and increasing gradually.
   (b) Everywhere positive and decreasing gradually.
   (c) Everywhere negative and increasing gradually (becoming less negative).
   (d) Everywhere negative and decreasing gradually (becoming more negative).

24. Draw a possible graph of $y = f(x)$ given the following information about its derivative.

   • $f'(x) > 0$ for $x < -1$
   • $f'(x) < 0$ for $x > -1$
   • $f'(x) = 0$ at $x = -1$

25. For $f(x) = \ln x$, construct tables, rounded to four decimals, near $x = 1$, $x = 2$, $x = 5$, and $x = 10$. Use the tables to estimate $f'(1)$, $f'(2)$, $f'(5)$, and $f'(10)$. Then guess a general formula for $f'(x)$.

26. Given the numerical values shown, find approximate values for the derivative of $f(x)$ at each of the x-values given. Where is the rate of change of $f(x)$ positive? Where is it negative? Where does the rate of change of $f(x)$ seem to be greatest?

x	0	1	2	3	4	5	6	7	8
$f(x)$	18	13	10	9	9	11	15	21	30

27. Values of x and $g(x)$ are given in the table. For what value of x does $g'(x)$ appear to be closest to 3?

x	2.7	3.2	3.7	4.2	4.7	5.2	5.7	6.2
$g(x)$	3.4	4.4	5.0	5.4	6.0	7.4	9.0	11.0

28. In the graph of f in Figure 2.31, at which of the labeled x-values is

   (a) $f(x)$ greatest?   **(b)** $f(x)$ least?
   (c) $f'(x)$ greatest?   **(d)** $f'(x)$ least?

Figure 2.31

For Problems 29–38, sketch the graph of $f'(x)$.

29.

30.

31.

32.

33.

34.

35.

36.

37.

38.

39. Roughly sketch the shape of the graph of a quadratic polynomial, f, if it is known that:

• $(1, 3)$ is on the graph of f.
• $f'(0) = 3$, $f'(2) = 1$, $f'(3) = 0$.

40. A vehicle moving along a straight road has distance $f(t)$ from its starting point at time t. Which of the graphs in Figure 2.32 could be $f'(t)$ for the following scenarios? (Assume the scales on the vertical axes are all the same.)

(a) A bus on a popular route, with no traffic
(b) A car with no traffic and all green lights
(c) A car in heavy traffic conditions

Figure 2.32

41. A child inflates a balloon, admires it for a while and then lets the air out at a constant rate. If $V(t)$ gives the volume of the balloon at time t, then Figure 2.33 shows $V'(t)$ as a function of t. At what time does the child:

(a) Begin to inflate the balloon?
(b) Finish inflating the balloon?
(c) Begin to let the air out?
(d) What would the graph of $V'(t)$ look like if the child had alternated between pinching and releasing the open end of the balloon, instead of letting the air out at a constant rate?

Figure 2.33

42. Figure 2.34 shows a graph of voltage across an electrical capacitor as a function of time. The current is proportional to the derivative of the voltage; the constant of proportionality is positive. Sketch a graph of the current as a function of time.

Figure 2.34

43. Figure 2.35 is the graph of f', the derivative of a function f. On what interval(s) is the function f

(a) Increasing? **(b)** Decreasing?

Figure 2.35: Graph of f', not f

44. The derivative of f is the spike function in Figure 2.36. What can you say about the graph of f?

Figure 2.36

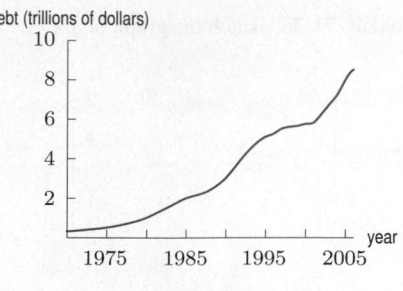

Figure 2.37

45. The population of a herd of deer is modeled by

$$P(t) = 4000 + 500 \sin\left(2\pi t - \frac{\pi}{2}\right)$$

where t is measured in years from January 1.

(a) How does this population vary with time? Sketch a graph of $P(t)$ for one year.
(b) Use the graph to decide when in the year the population is a maximum. What is that maximum? Is there a minimum? If so, when?
(c) Use the graph to decide when the population is growing fastest. When is it decreasing fastest?
(d) Estimate roughly how fast the population is changing on the first of July.

46. The graph in Figure 2.37 shows the accumulated federal debt since 1970. Sketch the derivative of this function. What does it represent?

47. Draw the graph of a continuous function $y = f(x)$ that satisfies the following three conditions:

- $f'(x) > 0$ for $x < -2$,
- $f'(x) < 0$ for $-2 < x < 2$,
- $f'(x) = 0$ for $x > 2$.

48. Draw the graph of a continuous function $y = f(x)$ that satisfies the following three conditions:

- $f'(x) > 0$ for $1 < x < 3$
- $f'(x) < 0$ for $x < 1$ and $x > 3$
- $f'(x) = 0$ at $x = 1$ and $x = 3$

49. If $\lim_{x \to \infty} f(x) = 50$ and $f'(x)$ is positive for all x, what is $\lim_{x \to \infty} f'(x)$? (Assume this limit exists.) Explain your answer with a picture.

50. Using a graph, explain why if $f(x)$ is an even function, then $f'(x)$ is odd.

51. Using a graph, explain why if $g(x)$ is an odd function, then $g'(x)$ is even.

Strengthen Your Understanding

In Problems 52–54, explain what is wrong with the statement.

52. The graph of the derivative of the function $f(x) = \cos x$ is always above the x-axis.

53. A function, f, whose graph is above the x-axis for all x has a positive derivative for all x.

54. If $f'(x) = g'(x)$ then $f(x) = g(x)$.

In Problems 55–56, give an example of:

55. A function representing the position of a particle which has positive velocity for $0 < t < 0.5$ and negative velocity for $0.5 < t < 1$.

56. A family of linear functions all with the same derivative.

Are the statements in Problems 57–60 true or false? Give an explanation for your answer.

57. The derivative of a linear function is constant.

58. If $g(x)$ is a vertical shift of $f(x)$, then $f'(x) = g'(x)$.

59. If $f'(x)$ is increasing, then $f(x)$ is also increasing.

60. If $f(a) \neq g(a)$, then $f'(a) \neq g'(a)$.

2.4 INTERPRETATIONS OF THE DERIVATIVE

We have seen the derivative interpreted as a slope and as a rate of change. In this section, we see other interpretations. The purpose of these examples is not to make a catalog of interpretations but to illustrate the process of obtaining them.

An Alternative Notation for the Derivative

So far we have used the notation f' to stand for the derivative of the function f. An alternative notation for derivatives was introduced by the German mathematician Wilhelm Gottfried Leibniz (1646–1716). If the variable y depends on the variable x, that is, if

$$y = f(x),$$

then he wrote dy/dx for the derivative, so

$$\frac{dy}{dx} = f'(x).$$

Leibniz's notation is quite suggestive if we think of the letter d in dy/dx as standing for "small difference in . . . ." The notation dy/dx reminds us that the derivative is a limit of ratios of the form

$$\frac{\text{Difference in } y\text{-values}}{\text{Difference in } x\text{-values}}.$$

The notation dy/dx suggests the units for the derivative: the units for y divided by the units for x. The separate entities dy and dx officially have no independent meaning: they are all part of one notation. In fact, a good way to view the notation dy/dx is to think of d/dx as a single symbol meaning "the derivative with respect to x of . . .." So dy/dx can be viewed as

$$\frac{d}{dx}(y), \quad \text{meaning "the derivative with respect to } x \text{ of } y\text{."}$$

On the other hand, many scientists and mathematicians think of dy and dx as separate entities representing "infinitesimally" small differences in y and x, even though it is difficult to say exactly how small "infinitesimal" is. Although not formally correct, it can be helpful to think of dy/dx as a small change in y divided by a small change in x.

For example, recall that if $s = f(t)$ is the position of a moving object at time t, then $v = f'(t)$ is the velocity of the object at time t. Writing

$$v = \frac{ds}{dt}$$

reminds us that v is a velocity, since the notation suggests a distance, ds, over a time, dt, and we know that distance over time is velocity. Similarly, we recognize

$$\frac{dy}{dx} = f'(x)$$

as the slope of the graph of $y = f(x)$ since slope is vertical rise, dy, over horizontal run, dx.

The disadvantage of Leibniz's notation is that it is awkward to specify the x-value at which we are evaluating the derivative. To specify $f'(2)$, for example, we have to write

$$\left.\frac{dy}{dx}\right|_{x=2}.$$

Using Units to Interpret the Derivative

The following examples illustrate how useful units can be in suggesting interpretations of the derivative. We use the fact that the units of the instantaneous and the average rate of change are the same.

For example, suppose $s = f(t)$ gives the distance, in meters, of a body from a fixed point as a function of time, t, in seconds. Then knowing that

$$\left.\frac{ds}{dt}\right|_{t=2} = f'(2) = 10 \text{ meters/sec}$$

tells us that when $t = 2$ seconds, the body is moving at an instantaneous velocity of 10 meters/sec. This means that if the body continued to move at this speed for a whole second, it would move 10 meters. In practice, however, the velocity of the body may not remain 10 meters/sec for long. Notice that the units of instantaneous velocity and of average velocity are the same.

Example 1   The cost C (in dollars) of building a house A square feet in area is given by the function $C = f(A)$. What is the practical interpretation of the function $f'(A)$?

Solution   In the alternative notation,

$$f'(A) = \frac{dC}{dA}.$$

This is a cost divided by an area, so it is measured in dollars per square foot. You can think of dC as the extra cost of building an extra dA square feet of house. Then you can think of dC/dA as the additional cost per square foot. So if you are planning to build a house roughly A square feet in area, $f'(A)$ is the cost per square foot of the *extra* area involved in building a slightly larger house, and is called the *marginal cost*. The marginal cost is probably smaller than the average cost per square foot for the entire house, since once you are already set up to build a large house, the cost of adding a few square feet is likely to be small.

Example 2   The cost of extracting T tons of ore from a copper mine is $C = f(T)$ dollars. What does it mean to say that $f'(2000) = 100$?

Solution   In the alternative notation,

$$f'(2000) = \left.\frac{dC}{dT}\right|_{T=2000} = 100.$$

Since C is measured in dollars and T is measured in tons, dC/dT must be measured in dollars per ton. So the statement $f'(2000) = 100$ says that when 2000 tons of ore have already been extracted from the mine, the cost of extracting the next ton is approximately \$100.

Example 3   If $q = f(p)$ gives the number of pounds of sugar produced when the price per pound is p dollars, then what are the units and the meaning of the statement $f'(3) = 50$?

Solution   Since $f'(3)$ is the limit as $h \to 0$ of the difference quotient

$$\frac{f(3+h) - f(3)}{h},$$

the units of $f'(3)$ and the difference quotient are the same. Since $f(3+h) - f(3)$ is in pounds and h is in dollars, the units of the difference quotient and $f'(3)$ are pounds/dollar. The statement

$$f'(3) = 50 \text{ pounds/dollar}$$

tells us that the instantaneous rate of change of q with respect to p is 50 when $p = 3$. In other words, when the price is \$3, the quantity produced is increasing at 50 pounds/dollar. Thus, if the price increased by a dollar, the quantity produced would increase by approximately 50 pounds.

Example 4   Water is flowing through a pipe at a constant rate of 10 cubic feet per second. Interpret this rate as the derivative of some function.

Solution   You might think at first that the statement has something to do with the velocity of the water, but in fact a flow rate of 10 cubic feet per second could be achieved either with very slowly moving water through a large pipe, or with very rapidly moving water through a narrow pipe. If we look at the units—cubic feet per second—we realize that we are being given the rate of change of a quantity measured in cubic feet. But a cubic foot is a measure of volume, so we are being told the rate of change of a volume. One way to visualize this is to imagine all the water that is flowing through the pipe ending up in a tank somewhere. Let $V(t)$ be the volume of water in the tank at time t. Then we are being told that the rate of change of $V(t)$ is 10, or

$$V'(t) = \frac{dV}{dt} = 10.$$

Example 5   Let $N = g(t)$ be the estimated number of alternative-fueled vehicles[4] in use in the US, in thousands, where t is the number of years since 1995. Explain the meaning of the statements:

(a) $g'(6) = 38$ (b) $g^{-1}(696) = 12$ (c) $(g^{-1})'(696) = 0.0145$

Solution   (a) The units of N are thousands of vehicles, the units of t are years, so the units of $g'(t)$ are thousand vehicles per year. Thus, the statement $g'(6) = 38$ tells us that in the year 2001, the use of alternative-fueled vehicles was increasing at 38,000 per year. Thus, in the year between 2001 and 2002, we would have expected the number of alternative-fueled vehicles in use in the US to increase by about 38,000 vehicles.

(b) The statement $g^{-1}(696) = 12$, which is equivalent to $g(12) = 696$, tells us that the year in which the number of alternative-fueled vehicles was 696,000 was 2007.

(c) The units of $(g^{-1})'(V)$ are years per thousand vehicles. The statement $(g^{-1})'(696) = 0.0145$ tells us that when the number of alternative-fueled vehicles was 696,000, it took about 0.0145 years, or between 5 and 6 days, for the number of alternative-fueled vehicles to grow by a thousand vehicles.

Exercises and Problems for Section 2.4

Exercises

1. The cost, C (in dollars), to produce g gallons of a chemical can be expressed as $C = f(g)$. Using units, explain the meaning of the following statements in terms of the chemical:

(a) $f(200) = 1300$ (b) $f'(200) = 6$

2. The time for a chemical reaction, T (in minutes), is a function of the amount of catalyst present, a (in milliliters), so $T = f(a)$.

(a) If $f(5) = 18$, what are the units of 5? What are the units of 18? What does this statement tell us about the reaction?

(b) If $f'(5) = -3$, what are the units of 5? What are the units of -3? What does this statement tell us?

3. The temperature, T, in degrees Fahrenheit, of a cold yam placed in a hot oven is given by $T = f(t)$, where t is the time in minutes since the yam was put in the oven.

(a) What is the sign of $f'(t)$? Why?

(b) What are the units of $f'(20)$? What is the practical meaning of the statement $f'(20) = 2$?

4. The temperature, H, in degrees Celsius, of a cup of coffee placed on the kitchen counter is given by $H = f(t)$, where t is in minutes since the coffee was put on the counter.

(a) Is $f'(t)$ positive or negative? Give a reason for your answer.

(b) What are the units of $f'(20)$? What is its practical meaning in terms of the temperature of the coffee?

5. The cost, C (in dollars), to produce q quarts of ice cream is $C = f(q)$. In each of the following statements, what are the units of the two numbers? In words, what does each statement tell us?

(a) $f(200) = 600$ (b) $f'(200) = 2$

6. An economist is interested in how the price of a certain item affects its sales. At a price of $\$p$, a quantity, q, of the item is sold. If $q = f(p)$, explain the meaning of each of the following statements:

(a) $f(150) = 2000$ (b) $f'(150) = -25$

7. Suppose $C(r)$ is the total cost of paying off a car loan borrowed at an annual interest rate of $r\%$. What are the units of $C'(r)$? What is the practical meaning of $C'(r)$? What is its sign?

8. Let $f(x)$ be the elevation in feet of the Mississippi River x miles from its source. What are the units of $f'(x)$? What can you say about the sign of $f'(x)$?

9. Suppose $P(t)$ is the monthly payment, in dollars, on a mortgage which will take t years to pay off. What are the units of $P'(t)$? What is the practical meaning of $P'(t)$? What is its sign?

10. After investing $\$1000$ at an annual interest rate of 7% compounded continuously for t years, your balance is $\$B$, where $B = f(t)$. What are the units of dB/dt? What is the financial interpretation of dB/dt?

[4]http://www.eia.doe.gov/aer/renew.html, accessed January 12, 2011.

11. Investing $1000 at an annual interest rate of $r\%$, compounded continuously, for 10 years gives you a balance of B, where $B = g(r)$. Give a financial interpretation of the statements:

    (a) $g(5) \approx 1649$.
    (b) $g'(5) \approx 165$. What are the units of $g'(5)$?

12. Meteorologists define the temperature lapse rate to be $-dT/dz$ where T is the air temperature in Celsius at altitude z kilometers above the ground.

    (a) What are the units of the lapse rate?
    (b) What is the practical meaning of a lapse rate of 6.5?

Problems

13. A laboratory study investigating the relationship between diet and weight in adult humans found that the weight of a subject, W, in pounds, was a function, $W = f(c)$, of the average number of Calories per day, c, consumed by the subject.

    (a) In terms of diet and weight, interpret the statements $f(1800) = 155$, $f'(2000) = 0$, and $f^{-1}(162) = 2200$.
    (b) What are the units of $f'(c) = dW/dc$?

14. In 2011, the Greenland Ice Sheet was melting at a rate between 82 and 224 cubic km per year.[5]

    (a) What derivative does this tell us about? Define the function and give units for each variable.
    (b) What numerical statement can you make about the derivative? Give units.

15. A city grew in population throughout the 1980s and into the early 1990s. The population was at its largest in 1995, and then shrank until 2010. Let $P = f(t)$ represent the population of the city t years since 1980. Sketch graphs of $f(t)$ and $f'(t)$, labeling the units on the axes.

16. If t is the number of years since 2011, the population, P, of China, in billions, can be approximated by the function

$$P = f(t) = 1.34(1.004)^t.$$

Estimate $f(9)$ and $f'(9)$, giving units. What do these two numbers tell you about the population of China?

17. An economist is interested in how the price of a certain commodity affects its sales. Suppose that at a price of $\$p$, a quantity q of the commodity is sold. If $q = f(p)$, explain in economic terms the meaning of the statements $f(10) = 240,000$ and $f'(10) = -29,000$.

18. On May 9, 2007, CBS Evening News had a 4.3 point rating. (Ratings measure the number of viewers.) News executives estimated that a 0.1 drop in the ratings for the CBS Evening News corresponds to a $5.5 million drop in revenue.[6] Express this information as a derivative. Specify the function, the variables, the units, and the point at which the derivative is evaluated.

19. The population of Mexico in millions is $P = f(t)$, where t is the number of years since 1980. Explain the meaning of the statements:

    (a) $f'(6) = 2$ **(b)** $f^{-1}(95.5) = 16$
    (c) $(f^{-1})'(95.5) = 0.46$

20. Let $f(t)$ be the number of centimeters of rainfall that has fallen since midnight, where t is the time in hours. Interpret the following in practical terms, giving units.

    (a) $f(10) = 3.1$ **(b)** $f^{-1}(5) = 16$
    (c) $f'(10) = 0.4$ **(d)** $(f^{-1})'(5) = 2$

21. Water is flowing into a tank; the depth, in feet, of the water at time t in hours is $h(t)$. Interpret, with units, the following statements.

    (a) $h(5) = 3$ **(b)** $h'(5) = 0.7$
    (c) $h^{-1}(5) = 7$ **(d)** $(h^{-1})'(5) = 1.2$

22. Let $p(h)$ be the pressure in dynes per cm^2 on a diver at a depth of h meters below the surface of the ocean. What do each of the following quantities mean to the diver? Give units for the quantities.

    (a) $p(100)$ **(b)** h such that $p(h) = 1.2 \cdot 10^6$
    (c) $p(h) + 20$ **(d)** $p(h + 20)$
    (e) $p'(100)$ **(f)** h such that $p'(h) = 100,000$

23. Let $g(t)$ be the height, in inches, of Amelia Earhart (one of the first woman airplane pilots) t years after her birth. What are the units of $g'(t)$? What can you say about the signs of $g'(10)$ and $g'(30)$? (Assume that $0 \le t < 39$, the age at which Amelia Earhart's plane disappeared.)

24. If $g(v)$ is the fuel efficiency, in miles per gallon, of a car going at v miles per hour, what are the units of $g'(90)$? What is the practical meaning of the statement $g'(55) = -0.54$?

25. Let P be the total petroleum reservoir on Earth in the year t. (In other words, P represents the total quantity of petroleum, including what's not yet discovered, on Earth at time t.) Assume that no new petroleum is being made and that P is measured in barrels. What are the units of dP/dt? What is the meaning of dP/dt? What is its sign? How would you set about estimating this derivative in practice? What would you need to know to make such an estimate?

26. **(a)** If you jump out of an airplane without a parachute, you fall faster and faster until air resistance causes you to approach a steady velocity, called the *terminal* velocity. Sketch a graph of your velocity against time.
    (b) Explain the concavity of your graph.
    (c) Assuming air resistance to be negligible at $t = 0$, what natural phenomenon is represented by the slope of the graph at $t = 0$?

---

[5]www.climate.org/topics/sea-level, accessed June 5, 2011.
[6]OC Register, May 9, 2007; *The New York Times*, May 14, 2007.

27. Let W be the amount of water, in gallons, in a bathtub at time t, in minutes.

   (a) What are the meaning and units of dW/dt?

   (b) Suppose the bathtub is full of water at time t_0, so that $W(t_0) > 0$. Subsequently, at time $t_p > t_0$, the plug is pulled. Is dW/dt positive, negative, or zero:

     (i) For $t_0 < t < t_p$?

     (ii) After the plug is pulled, but before the tub is empty?

     (iii) When all the water has drained from the tub?

28. A company's revenue from car sales, C (in thousands of dollars), is a function of advertising expenditure, a, in thousands of dollars, so $C = f(a)$.

   (a) What does the company hope is true about the sign of f'?

   (b) What does the statement $f'(100) = 2$ mean in practical terms? How about $f'(100) = 0.5$?

   (c) Suppose the company plans to spend about $100,000 on advertising. If $f'(100) = 2$, should the company spend more or less than $100,000 on advertising? What if $f'(100) = 0.5$?

29. In May 2007 in the US, there was one birth every 8 seconds, one death every 13 seconds, and one new international migrant every 27 seconds.[7]

   (a) Let $f(t)$ be the population of the US, where t is time in seconds measured from the start of May 2007. Find $f'(0)$. Give units.

   (b) To the nearest second, how long did it take for the US population to add one person in May 2007?

30. During the 1970s and 1980s, the build up of chlorofluorocarbons (CFCs) created a hole in the ozone layer over Antarctica. After the 1987 Montreal Protocol, an agreement to phase out CFC production, the ozone hole has shrunk. The ODGI (ozone depleting gas index) shows the level of CFCs present.[8] Let $O(t)$ be the ODGI for Antarctica in year t; then $O(2000) = 95$ and $O'(2000) = -1.25$. Assuming that the ODGI decreases at a constant rate, estimate when the ozone hole will have recovered, which occurs when ODGI $= 0$.

31. Let $P(x)$ be the number of people of height $\leq x$ inches in the US. What is the meaning of $P'(66)$? What are its units? Estimate $P'(66)$ (using common sense). Is $P'(x)$ ever negative? [Hint: You may want to approximate $P'(66)$ by a difference quotient, using $h = 1$. Also, you may assume the US population is about 300 million, and note that 66 inches = 5 feet 6 inches.]

32. When you breathe, a muscle (called the diaphragm) reduces the pressure around your lungs and they expand to fill with air. The table shows the volume of a lung as a function of the reduction in pressure from the diaphragm.

Pulmonologists (lung doctors) define the *compliance* of the lung as the derivative of this function.[9]

   (a) What are the units of compliance?

   (b) Estimate the maximum compliance of the lung.

   (c) Explain why the compliance gets small when the lung is nearly full (around 1 liter).

Pressure reduction (cm of water)	Volume (liters)
0	0.20
5	0.29
10	0.49
15	0.70
20	0.86
25	0.95
30	1.00

33. The compressibility index, γ, of cold matter (in a neutron star or black hole) is given by

$$\gamma = \frac{\delta + (p/c^2)}{p} \frac{dp}{d\delta},$$

where p is the pressure (in dynes/cm^2), δ is the density (in g/cm^3), and $c \approx 3 \cdot 10^{10}$ is the speed of light (in cm/sec). Figure 2.38 shows the relationship between δ, γ, and p. Values of $\log p$ are marked along the graph.[10]

   (a) Estimate $dp/d\delta$ for cold iron, which has a density of about 10 g/cm^3. What does the magnitude of your answer tell you about cold iron?

   (b) Estimate $dp/d\delta$ for the matter inside a white dwarf star, which has a density of about 10^6 g/cm^3. What does your answer tell you about matter inside a white dwarf?

Figure 2.38

---

[7]www.census.gov, accessed May 14, 2007.

[8]www.esrl.noaa.gov/gmd/odgi

[9]Adapted from John B. West, *Respiratory Physiology*, 4th Ed. (New York: Williams and Wilkins, 1990).

[10]From C. W. Misner, K. S. Thorne, and J. A. Wheeler, *Gravitation* (San Francisco: W. H. Freeman and Company, 1973).

Strengthen Your Understanding

In Problems 34–36, explain what is wrong with the statement.

34. If the position of a car at time t is given by $s(t)$ then the velocity of the car is $s'(t)$ and the units of s' are meters per second.

35. A spherical balloon originally contains 3 liters of air and it is leaking 1% of its volume per hour. If $r(t)$ is the radius of the balloon at time t then $r'(t) > 0$.

36. A laser printer takes $T(P)$ minutes to produce P pages, so the derivative $\dfrac{dT}{dP}$ is measured in pages per minute.

In Problems 37–38, give an example of:

37. A function whose derivative is measured in years/dollar.

38. A function whose derivative is measured in miles/day.

Are the statements in Problems 39–41 true or false? Give an explanation for your answer.

39. If $y = f(x)$, then $\left.\dfrac{dy}{dx}\right|_{x=a} = f'(a)$.

40. If $f(t)$ is the quantity in grams of a chemical produced after t minutes and $g(t)$ is the same quantity in kilograms, then $f'(t) = 1000g'(t)$.

41. If $f(t)$ is the quantity in kilograms of a chemical produced after t minutes and $g(t)$ is the quantity in kilograms produced after t seconds, then $f'(t) = 60g'(t)$.

For Problems 42–43, assume $g(v)$ is the fuel efficiency, in miles per gallon, of a car going at a speed of v miles per hour.

42. What are the units of $g'(v) = \dfrac{dg}{dv}$? There may be more than one option.

(a) $(\text{miles})^2/(\text{gal})(\text{hour})$
(b) hour/gal
(c) gal/hour
(d) $(\text{gal})(\text{hour})/(\text{miles})^2$
(e) $(\text{miles/gallon})/(\text{miles/hour})$

43. What is the practical meaning of $g'(55) = -0.54$? There may be more than one option.

(a) When the car is going 55 mph, the rate of change of the fuel efficiency decreases *to* approximately 0.54 miles/gal.
(b) When the car is going 55 mph, the rate of change of the fuel efficiency decreases *by* approximately 0.54 miles/gal.
(c) If the car speeds up from 55 mph to 56 mph, then the fuel efficiency is approximately -0.54 miles per gallon.
(d) If the car speeds up from 55 mph to 56 mph, then the car becomes less fuel efficient by approximately 0.54 miles per gallon.

2.5 THE SECOND DERIVATIVE

Since the derivative is itself a function, we can consider its derivative. For a function f, the derivative of its derivative is called the *second derivative*, and written f'' (read "f double-prime"). If $y = f(x)$, the second derivative can also be written as $\dfrac{d^2y}{dx^2}$, which means $\dfrac{d}{dx}\left(\dfrac{dy}{dx}\right)$, the derivative of $\dfrac{dy}{dx}$.

What Do Derivatives Tell Us?

Recall that the derivative of a function tells you whether a function is increasing or decreasing:

- If $f' > 0$ on an interval, then f is *increasing* over that interval.
- If $f' < 0$ on an interval, then f is *decreasing* over that interval.

If f' is always positive on an interval or always negative on an interval, then f is monotonic over that interval.

Since f'' is the derivative of f',

- If $f'' > 0$ on an interval, then f' is *increasing* over that interval.
- If $f'' < 0$ on an interval, then f' is *decreasing* over that interval.

What does it mean for f' to be increasing or decreasing? An example in which f' is increasing is shown in Figure 2.39, where the curve is bending upward, or is *concave up*. In the example shown in Figure 2.40, in which f' is decreasing, the graph is bending downward, or is *concave down*. These figures suggest the following result:

If $f'' > 0$ on an interval, then f' is increasing, so the graph of f is concave up there.

If $f'' < 0$ on an interval, then f' is decreasing, so the graph of f is concave down there.

Figure 2.39: Meaning of f'': The slope of f increases from left to right, f'' is positive, and f is concave up

Figure 2.40: Meaning of f'': The slope of f decreases from left to right, f'' is negative, and f is concave down

Warning! The graph of a function f can be concave up everywhere and yet have $f'' = 0$ at some point. For instance, the graph of $f(x) = x^4$ in Figure 2.41 is concave up, but it can be shown that $f''(0) = 0$. If we are told that the graph of a function f is concave up, we can be sure that f'' is not negative, that is $f'' \geq 0$, but not that f'' is positive, $f'' > 0$.

Figure 2.41: Graph of $f(x) = x^4$

If the graph of f is concave up and f'' exists on an interval, then $f'' \geq 0$ there.
If the graph of f is concave down and f'' exists on an interval, then $f'' \leq 0$ there.

Example 1   For the functions graphed in Figure 2.42, what can be said about the sign of the second derivative?

Figure 2.42: What signs do the second derivatives have?

Solution
(a) The graph of f is concave up everywhere, so $f'' \geq 0$ everywhere.
(b) The graph of g is concave down everywhere, so $g'' \leq 0$ everywhere.
(c) For $t < 0$, the graph of h is concave down, so $h'' \leq 0$ there. For $t > 0$, the graph of h is concave up, so $h'' \geq 0$ there.

Example 2   Sketch the second derivative f'' for the function f of Example 1 on page 91, graphed with its derivative, f', in Figure 2.43. Relate the resulting graph of f'' to the graphs of f and f'.

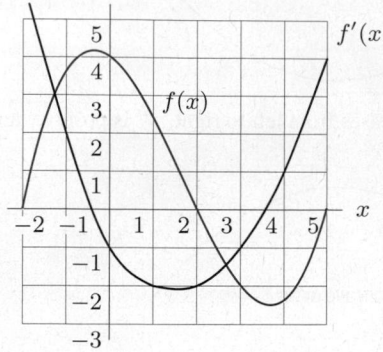

Figure 2.43: Function, f in color; derivative, f', in black

Figure 2.44: Graph of f''

Solution   We want to sketch the derivative of f'. We do this by estimating the slopes of f' and plotting them, obtaining Figure 2.44.

We observe that where $f'' > 0$, the graph of f is concave up and f' is increasing, and that where $f'' < 0$, the graph of f is concave down and f' is decreasing. Where $f''(x) = 0$, the graph of f changes from concave up to concave down, and f' changes from decreasing to increasing.

Interpretation of the Second Derivative as a Rate of Change

If we think of the derivative as a rate of change, then the second derivative is a rate of change of a rate of change. If the second derivative is positive, the rate of change of f is increasing; if the second derivative is negative, the rate of change of f is decreasing.

The second derivative can be a matter of practical concern. A 2009 article[11] reported that although the US economy was shrinking, the rate of decrease had slowed. (The derivative of the size of the economy was negative and the second derivative was positive). The article continued "although the economy is spiralling down, it is doing so more slowly."

Example 3   A population, P, growing in a confined environment often follows a *logistic* growth curve, like that shown in Figure 2.45. Relate the sign of d^2P/dt^2 to how the rate of growth, dP/dt, changes over time. What are practical interpretations of t_0 and L?

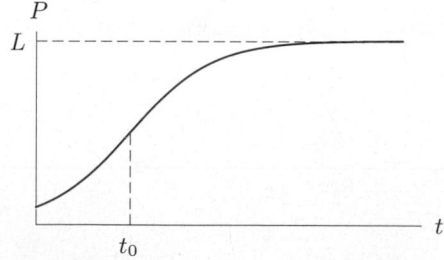

Figure 2.45: Logistic growth curve

Solution   For $t < t_0$, the rate of growth, dP/dt, is increasing and $d^2P/dt^2 \geq 0$. At t_0, the rate dP/dt is a maximum. In other words, at time t_0 the population is growing fastest. For $t > t_0$, the rate of growth, dP/dt, is decreasing and $dP^2/dt^2 \leq 0$. At t_0, the curve changes from concave up to concave down, and $d^2P/dt^2 = 0$ there.

[11]*The Economist,* February 19, 2009, Washington, DC, "The second derivative may be turning positive," www.economist.com/node/13145616

The quantity L represents the limiting value of the population as $t \to \infty$. Biologists call L the *carrying capacity* of the environment.

Example 4   Tests on the 2011 Chevy Corvette ZR1 sports car gave the results[12] in Table 2.10.
(a) Estimate dv/dt for the time intervals shown.
(b) What can you say about the sign of d^2v/dt^2 over the period shown?

Table 2.10   *Velocity of 2011 Chevy Corvette ZR1*

Time, t (sec)	0	3	6	9	12
Velocity, v (meters/sec)	0	23	42	59	72

Solution   (a) For each time interval we can calculate the average rate of change of velocity. For example, from $t = 0$ to $t = 3$ we have

$$\frac{dv}{dt} \approx \text{Average rate of change of velocity} = \frac{23 - 0}{3 - 0} = 7.67 \; \frac{\text{m/sec}}{\text{sec}}.$$

Estimated values of dv/dt are in Table 2.11.

(b) Since the values of dv/dt are decreasing between the points shown, we expect $d^2v/dt^2 \leq 0$. The graph of v against t in Figure 2.46 supports this; it is concave down. The fact that $dv/dt > 0$ tells us that the car is speeding up; the fact that $d^2v/dt^2 \leq 0$ tells us that the rate of increase decreased (actually, did not increase) over this time period.

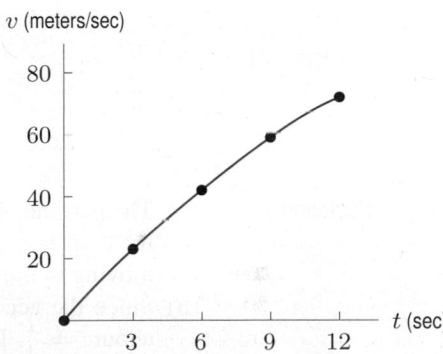

Table 2.11   *Estimates for dv/dt (meters/sec/sec)*

Time interval (sec)	$0 - 3$	$3 - 6$	$6 - 9$	$9 - 12$
Average rate of change (dv/dt)	7.67	6.33	5.67	4.33

Figure 2.46: Velocity of 2011 Chevy Corvette ZR1

Velocity and Acceleration

When a car is speeding up, we say that it is accelerating. We define *acceleration* as the rate of change of velocity with respect to time. If $v(t)$ is the velocity of an object at time t, we have

$$\begin{array}{ll} \text{Average acceleration} \\ \text{from } t \text{ to } t + h \end{array} = \frac{v(t + h) - v(t)}{h},$$

$$\text{Instantaneous acceleration} = v'(t) = \lim_{h \to 0} \frac{v(t + h) - v(t)}{h}.$$

If the term velocity or acceleration is used alone, it is assumed to be instantaneous. Since velocity is the derivative of position, acceleration is the second derivative of position. Summarizing:

[12]Adapted from data in http://www.corvette-web-central.com/Corvettetopspeed.html

If $y = s(t)$ is the position of an object at time t, then

- Velocity: $v(t) = \dfrac{dy}{dt} = s'(t)$.

- Acceleration: $a(t) = \dfrac{d^2y}{dt^2} = s''(t) = v'(t)$.

Example 5   A particle is moving along a straight line; its acceleration is zero only once. Its distance, s, to the right of a fixed point is given by Figure 2.47. Estimate:

(a) When the particle is moving to the right and when it is moving to the left.

(b) When the acceleration of the particle is zero, when it is negative, and when it is positive.

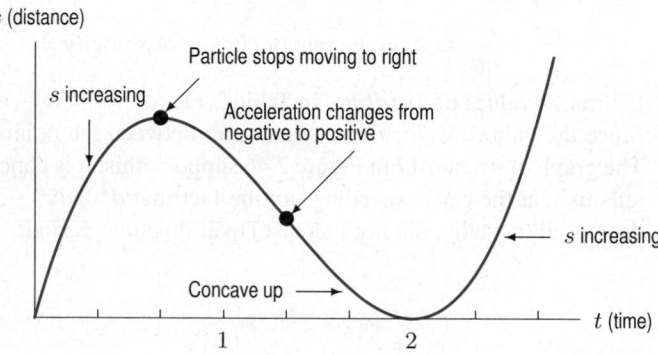

Figure 2.47: Distance of particle to right of a fixed point

Solution   (a) The particle is moving to the right whenever s is increasing. From the graph, this appears to be for $0 < t < \frac{2}{3}$ and for $t > 2$. For $\frac{2}{3} < t < 2$, the value of s is decreasing, so the particle is moving to the left.

(b) Since the acceleration is zero only once, this must be when the curve changes concavity, at about $t = \frac{4}{3}$. Then the acceleration is negative for $t < \frac{4}{3}$, since the graph is concave down there, and the acceleration is positive for $t > \frac{4}{3}$, since the graph is concave up there.

Exercises and Problems for Section 2.5

Exercises

1. Fill in the blanks:

    (a) If f'' is positive on an interval, then f' is _____ on that interval, and f is _____ on that interval.

    (b) If f'' is negative on an interval, then f' is _____ on that interval, and f is _____ on that interval.

Figure 2.48

2. For the function graphed in Figure 2.48, are the following nonzero quantities positive or negative?

    (a) $f(2)$ (b) $f'(2)$ (c) $f''(2)$

3. At one of the labeled points on the graph in Figure 2.49 both dy/dx and d^2y/dx^2 are positive. Which is it?

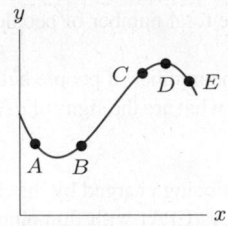

Figure 2.49

4. At exactly two of the labeled points in Figure 2.50, the derivative f' is 0; the second derivative f'' is not zero at any of the labeled points. On a copy of the table, give the signs of f, f', f'' at each marked point.

Point	f	f'	f''
A			
B			
C			
D			

Figure 2.50

5. Graph the functions described in parts (a)–(d).

(a) First and second derivatives everywhere positive.

(b) Second derivative everywhere negative; first derivative everywhere positive.

(c) Second derivative everywhere positive; first derivative everywhere negative.

(d) First and second derivatives everywhere negative.

6. Sketch the graph of a function whose first derivative is everywhere negative and whose second derivative is positive for some x-values and negative for other x-values.

7. Sketch the graph of the height of a particle against time if velocity is positive and acceleration is negative.

For Exercises 8–13, give the signs of the first and second derivatives for the following functions. Each derivative is either positive everywhere, zero everywhere, or negative everywhere.

8.

9.

10.

11.

12.

13.

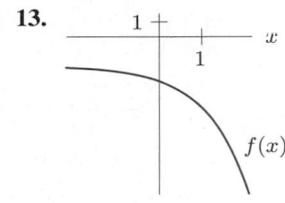

14. The position of a particle moving along the x-axis is given by $s(t) = 5t^2 + 3$. Use difference quotients to find the velocity $v(t)$ and acceleration $a(t)$.

Problems

15. The table gives the number of passenger cars, $C = f(t)$, in millions,[13] in the US in the year t.

(a) Do $f'(t)$ and $f''(t)$ appear to be positive or negative during the period 1975–1990?

(b) Do $f'(t)$ and $f''(t)$ appear to be positive or negative during the period 1990-2000?

(c) Estimate $f'(2005)$. Using units, interpret your answer in terms of passenger cars.

t	1975	1980	1985	1990	1995	2000	2005
C	106.7	121.6	127.9	133.7	128.4	133.6	136.6

16. An accelerating sports car goes from 0 mph to 60 mph in five seconds. Its velocity is given in the following table, converted from miles per hour to feet per second, so that all time measurements are in seconds. (Note: 1 mph

is 22/15 ft/sec.) Find the average acceleration of the car over each of the first two seconds.

Time, t (sec)	0	1	2	3	4	5
Velocity, $v(t)$ (ft/sec)	0	30	52	68	80	88

17. Sketch the curves described in (a)–(c):

(a) Slope is positive and increasing at first but then is positive and decreasing.

(b) The first derivative of the function whose graph is in part (a).

(c) The second derivative of the function whose graph is in part (a).

[13]www.bts.gov/publications/national_transportation_statistics/html/table_01_11.html. Accessed April 27, 2011.

In Problems 18–23, graph the second derivative of the function.

18.

19.

20.

21.

22.

23.

24. Let $P(t)$ represent the price of a share of stock of a corporation at time t. What does each of the following statements tell us about the signs of the first and second derivatives of $P(t)$?

(a) "The price of the stock is rising faster and faster."
(b) "The price of the stock is close to bottoming out."

25. In economics, *total utility* refers to the total satisfaction from consuming some commodity. According to the economist Samuelson:[14]

> As you consume more of the same good, the total (psychological) utility increases. However, …with successive new units of the good, your total utility will grow at a slower and slower rate because of a fundamental tendency for your psychological ability to appreciate more of the good to become less keen.

(a) Sketch the total utility as a function of the number of units consumed.
(b) In terms of derivatives, what is Samuelson saying?

26. "Winning the war on poverty" has been described cynically as slowing the rate at which people are slipping below the poverty line. Assuming that this is happening:

(a) Graph the total number of people in poverty against time.
(b) If N is the number of people below the poverty line at time t, what are the signs of dN/dt and d^2N/dt^2? Explain.

27. An industry is being charged by the Environmental Protection Agency (EPA) with dumping unacceptable levels of toxic pollutants in a lake. Over a period of several months, an engineering firm makes daily measurements of the rate at which pollutants are being discharged into the lake. The engineers produce a graph similar to either Figure 2.51(a) or Figure 2.51(b). For each case, give an idea of what argument the EPA might make in court against the industry and of the industry's defense.

Figure 2.51

28. At which of the marked x-values in Figure 2.52 can the following statements be true?

(a) $f(x) < 0$
(b) $f'(x) < 0$
(c) $f(x)$ is decreasing
(d) $f'(x)$ is decreasing
(e) Slope of $f(x)$ is positive
(f) Slope of $f(x)$ is increasing

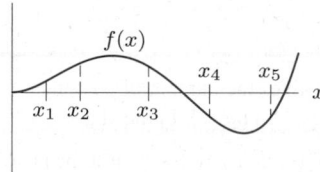

Figure 2.52

29. Figure 2.53 gives the position, $f(t)$, of a particle at time t. At which of the marked values of t can the following statements be true?

(a) The position is positive
(b) The velocity is positive
(c) The acceleration is positive
(d) The position is decreasing
(e) The velocity is decreasing

---

[14]From Paul A. Samuelson, *Economics*, 11th edition (New York: McGraw-Hill, 1981).

Figure 2.53

30. The graph of f' (not f) is given in Figure 2.54. At which of the marked values of x is

(a) $f(x)$ greatest?   (b) $f(x)$ least?
(c) $f'(x)$ greatest?   (d) $f'(x)$ least?
(e) $f''(x)$ greatest?   (f) $f''(x)$ least?

Figure 2.54: Graph of f', not f

31. A function f has $f(5) = 20$, $f'(5) = 2$, and $f''(x) < 0$, for $x \geq 5$. Which of the following are possible values for $f(7)$ and which are impossible?

(a) 26   (b) 24   (c) 22

32. Chlorofluorocarbons (CFCs) were used as propellants in spray cans until their build up in the atmosphere started destroying the ozone, which protects us from ultraviolet rays. Since the 1987 Montreal Protocol (an agreement to curb CFCs), the CFCs in the atmosphere above the US have been reduced from a high of 3200 parts per trillion (ppt) in 1994 to 2750 ppt in 2010.[15] The reduction has been approximately linear. Let $C(t)$ be the concentration of CFCs in ppt in year t.

(a) Find $C(1994)$ and $C(2010)$.
(b) Estimate $C'(1994)$ and $C'(2010)$.
(c) Assuming $C(t)$ is linear, find a formula for $C(t)$.
(d) When is $C(t)$ expected to reach 1850 ppt, the level before CFCs were introduced?
(e) If you were told that in the future, $C(t)$ would not be exactly linear, and that $C''(t) > 0$, would your answer to part (d) be too early or too late?

Strengthen Your Understanding

In Problems 33–34, explain what is wrong with the statement.

33. A function that is not concave up is concave down.

34. When the acceleration of a car is zero, the car is not moving.

In Problems 35–36, give an example of:

35. A function that has a non-zero first derivative but zero second derivative.

36. A function for which $f'(0) = 0$ but $f''(0) \neq 0$.

Are the statements in Problems 37–41 true or false? Give an explanation for your answer.

37. If $f''(x) > 0$ then $f'(x)$ is increasing.

38. The instantaneous acceleration of a moving particle at time t is the limit of difference quotients.

39. A function which is monotonic on an interval is either increasing or decreasing on the interval.

40. The function $f(x) = x^3$ is monotonic on any interval.

41. The function $f(x) = x^2$ is monotonic on any interval.

2.6 DIFFERENTIABILITY

What Does It Mean for a Function to Be Differentiable?

A function is differentiable at a point if it has a derivative there. In other words:

> The function f is **differentiable** at x if
> $$\lim_{h \to 0} \frac{f(x+h) - f(x)}{h} \qquad \text{exists.}$$
>
> Thus, the graph of f has a nonvertical tangent line at x. The value of the limit and the slope of the tangent line are the derivative of f at x.

[15]www.esrl.noaa.gov/gmd/odgi

Occasionally we meet a function which fails to have a derivative at a few points. A function fails to be differentiable at a point if:

- The function is not continuous at the point.

- The graph has a sharp corner at that point.

- The graph has a vertical tangent line.

Figure 2.55 shows a function which appears to be differentiable at all points except $x = a$ and $x = b$. There is no tangent at A because the graph has a corner there. As x approaches a from the left, the slope of the line joining P to A converges to some positive number. As x approaches a from the right, the slope of the line joining P to A converges to some negative number. Thus the slopes approach different numbers as we approach $x = a$ from different sides. Therefore the function is not differentiable at $x = a$. At B, the graph has a vertical tangent. As x approaches b, the slope of the line joining B to Q does not approach a limit; it just keeps growing larger and larger. Again, the limit defining the derivative does not exist and the function is not differentiable at $x = b$.

Figure 2.55: A function which is not differentiable at A or B

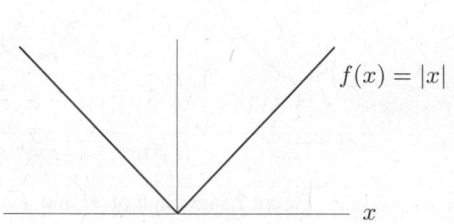

Figure 2.56: Graph of absolute value function, showing point of non-differentiability at $x = 0$

Examples of Nondifferentiable Functions

An example of a function whose graph has a corner is the *absolute value* function defined as follows:

$$f(x) = |x| = \begin{cases} x & \text{if } x \geq 0, \\ -x & \text{if } x < 0. \end{cases}$$

This function is called *piecewise linear* because each part of it is linear. Its graph is in Figure 2.56. Near $x = 0$, even close-up views of the graph of $f(x)$ look the same, so this is a corner which can't be straightened out by zooming in.

Example 1   Try to compute the derivative of the function $f(x) = |x|$ at $x = 0$. Is f differentiable there?

Solution   To find the derivative at $x = 0$, we want to look at

$$\lim_{h \to 0} \frac{f(h) - f(0)}{h} = \lim_{h \to 0} \frac{|h| - 0}{h} = \lim_{h \to 0} \frac{|h|}{h}.$$

As h approaches 0 from the right, h is positive, so $|h| = h$, and the ratio is always 1. As h approaches 0 from the left, h is negative, so $|h| = -h$, and the ratio is -1. Since the limits are different from each side, the limit of the difference quotient does not exist. Thus, the absolute value function is not differentiable at $x = 0$. The limits of 1 and -1 correspond to the fact that the slope of the right-hand part of the graph is 1, and the slope of the left-hand part is -1.

Example 2   Investigate the differentiability of $f(x) = x^{1/3}$ at $x = 0$.

Solution   This function is smooth at $x = 0$ (no sharp corners) but appears to have a vertical tangent there. (See Figure 2.57.) Looking at the difference quotient at $x = 0$, we see

$$\lim_{h \to 0} \frac{(0 + h)^{1/3} - 0^{1/3}}{h} = \lim_{h \to 0} \frac{h^{1/3}}{h} = \lim_{h \to 0} \frac{1}{h^{2/3}}.$$

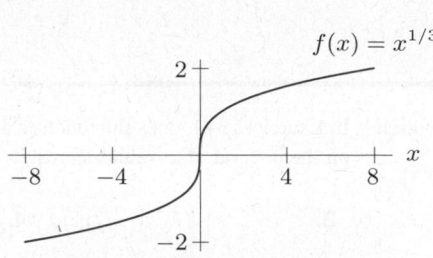

Figure 2.57: Continuous function not differentiable at $x = 0$: Vertical tangent

Figure 2.58: Continuous function not differentiable at $x = 1$

As $h \to 0$ the denominator becomes small, so the fraction grows without bound. Hence, the function fails to have a derivative at $x = 0$.

Example 3   Consider the function given by the formulas

$$g(x) = \begin{cases} x + 1 & \text{if} \quad x \leq 1 \\ 3x - 1 & \text{if} \quad x > 1. \end{cases}$$

Draw the graph of g. Is g continuous? Is g differentiable at $x = 1$?

Solution   The graph in Figure 2.58 has no breaks in it, so the function is continuous. However, the graph has a corner at $x = 1$ which no amount of magnification will remove. To the left of $x = 1$, the slope is 1; to the right of $x = 1$, the slope is 3. Thus, the difference quotient at $x = 1$ has no limit, so the function g is not differentiable at $x = 1$.

The Relationship Between Differentiability and Continuity

The fact that a function which is differentiable at a point has a tangent line suggests that the function is continuous there, as the next theorem shows.

> ### Theorem 2.1: A Differentiable Function Is Continuous
>
> If $f(x)$ is differentiable at a point $x = a$, then $f(x)$ is continuous at $x = a$.

Proof   We assume f is differentiable at $x = a$. Then we know that $f'(a)$ exists where

$$f'(a) = \lim_{x \to a} \frac{f(x) - f(a)}{x - a}.$$

To show that f is continuous at $x = a$, we want to show that $\lim_{x \to a} f(x) = f(a)$. We calculate $\lim_{x \to a}(f(x) - f(a))$, hoping to get 0. By algebra, we know that for $x \neq a$,

$$f(x) - f(a) = (x - a) \cdot \frac{f(x) - f(a)}{x - a}.$$

Taking the limits, we have

$$\lim_{x \to a}(f(x) - f(a)) = \lim_{x \to a}\left((x - a)\frac{f(x) - f(a)}{x - a}\right)$$

$$= \left(\lim_{x \to a}(x - a)\right) \cdot \left(\lim_{x \to a}\frac{f(x) - f(a)}{x - a}\right) \qquad \text{(By Theorem 1.2, Property 3)}$$

$$= 0 \cdot f'(a) = 0. \qquad \text{(Since } f'(a) \text{ exists)}$$

Thus we know that $\lim_{x \to a} f(x) = f(a)$, which means $f(x)$ is continuous at $x = a$.

Exercises and Problems for Section 2.6

Exercises

For the graphs in Exercises 1–2, list the x-values for which the function appears to be

(a) Not continuous. (b) Not differentiable.

In Exercises 3–4, does the function appear to be differentiable on the interval of x-values shown?

1.

2.

3.

4.

Problems

Decide if the functions in Problems 5–7 are differentiable at $x = 0$. Try zooming in on a graphing calculator, or calculating the derivative $f'(0)$ from the definition.

5. $f(x) = (x + |x|)^2 + 1$

6. $f(x) = \begin{cases} x \sin(1/x) + x & \text{for } x \neq 0 \\ 0 & \text{for } x = 0 \end{cases}$

7. $f(x) = \begin{cases} x^2 \sin(1/x) & \text{for } x \neq 0 \\ 0 & \text{for } x = 0 \end{cases}$

8. In each of the following cases, sketch the graph of a continuous function $f(x)$ with the given properties.

(a) $f''(x) > 0$ for $x < 2$ and for $x > 2$ and $f'(2)$ is undefined.

(b) $f''(x) > 0$ for $x < 2$ and $f''(x) < 0$ for $x > 2$ and $f'(2)$ is undefined.

9. Look at the graph of $f(x) = (x^2 + 0.0001)^{1/2}$ shown in Figure 2.59. The graph of f appears to have a sharp corner at $x = 0$. Do you think f has a derivative at $x = 0$?

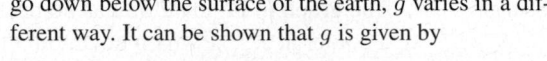

Figure 2.59

10. The acceleration due to gravity, g, varies with height above the surface of the earth, in a certain way. If you go down below the surface of the earth, g varies in a different way. It can be shown that g is given by

$$g = \begin{cases} \dfrac{GMr}{R^3} & \text{for } r < R \\[3mm] \dfrac{GM}{r^2} & \text{for } r \geq R \end{cases}$$

where R is the radius of the earth, M is the mass of the earth, G is the gravitational constant, and r is the distance to the center of the earth.

(a) Sketch a graph of g against r.

(b) Is g a continuous function of r? Explain your answer.

(c) Is g a differentiable function of r? Explain your answer.

11. An electric charge, Q, in a circuit is given as a function of time, t, by

$$Q = \begin{cases} C & \text{for } t \leq 0 \\ Ce^{-t/RC} & \text{for } t > 0, \end{cases}$$

where C and R are positive constants. The electric current, I, is the rate of change of charge, so

$$I = \frac{dQ}{dt}.$$

(a) Is the charge, Q, a continuous function of time?

(b) Do you think the current, I, is defined for all times, t? [Hint: To graph this function, take, for example, $C = 1$ and $R = 1$.]

12. A magnetic field, B, is given as a function of the distance, r, from the center of a wire as follows:

$$B = \begin{cases} \dfrac{r}{r_0}B_0 & \text{for } r \le r_0 \\[2ex] \dfrac{r_0}{r}B_0 & \text{for } r > r_0. \end{cases}$$

   (a) Sketch a graph of B against r. What is the meaning of the constant B_0?
   (b) Is B continuous at $r = r_0$? Give reasons.
   (c) Is B differentiable at $r = r_0$? Give reasons.

13. A cable is made of an insulating material in the shape of a long, thin cylinder of radius r_0. It has electric charge distributed evenly throughout it. The electric field, E, at a distance r from the center of the cable is given by

$$E = \begin{cases} kr & \text{for } r \le r_0 \\[2ex] k\dfrac{r_0^2}{r} & \text{for } r > r_0. \end{cases}$$

   (a) Is E continuous at $r = r_0$?
   (b) Is E differentiable at $r = r_0$?
   (c) Sketch a graph of E as a function of r.

14. Graph the function defined by

$$g(r) = \begin{cases} 1 + \cos(\pi r/2) & \text{for } -2 \le r \le 2 \\ 0 & \text{for } r < -2 \text{ or } r > 2. \end{cases}$$

   (a) Is g continuous at $r = 2$? Explain your answer.
   (b) Do you think g is differentiable at $r = 2$? Explain your answer.

15. The potential, ϕ, of a charge distribution at a point on the y-axis is given by

$$\phi = \begin{cases} 2\pi\sigma\left(\sqrt{y^2 + a^2} - y\right) & \text{for } y \ge 0 \\[2ex] 2\pi\sigma\left(\sqrt{y^2 + a^2} + y\right) & \text{for } y < 0 \end{cases}$$

where σ and a are positive constants. [Hint: To graph this function, take, for example, $2\pi\sigma = 1$ and $a = 1$.]

   (a) Is ϕ continuous at $y = 0$?
   (b) Do you think ϕ is differentiable at $y = 0$?

16. Sometimes, odd behavior can be hidden beneath the surface of a rather normal-looking function. Consider the following function:

$$f(x) = \begin{cases} 0 & \text{if } x < 0 \\ x^2 & \text{if } x \ge 0. \end{cases}$$

   (a) Sketch a graph of this function. Does it have any vertical segments or corners? Is it differentiable everywhere? If so, sketch the derivative f' of this function. [Hint: You may want to use the result of Example 4 on page 94.]
   (b) Is the derivative function, $f'(x)$, differentiable everywhere? If not, at what point(s) is it not differentiable? Draw the second derivative of $f(x)$ wherever it exists. Is the second derivative function, $f''(x)$, differentiable? Continuous?

Strengthen Your Understanding

In Problems 17–18, explain what is wrong with the statement.

17. A function f that is not differentiable at $x = 0$ has a graph with a sharp corner at $x = 0$.

18. If f is not differentiable at a point then it is not continuous at that point.

In Problems 19–21, give an example of:

19. A continuous function that is not differentiable at $x = 2$.

20. An invertible function that is not differentiable at $x = 0$.

21. A rational function that has zeros at $x = \pm 1$ and is not differentiable at $x = \pm 2$.

Are the statements in Problems 22–26 true or false? If a statement is true, give an example illustrating it. If a statement is false, give a counterexample.

22. There is a function which is continuous on $[1, 5]$ but not differentiable at $x = 3$.

23. If a function is differentiable, then it is continuous.

24. If a function is continuous, then it is differentiable.

25. If a function is not continuous, then it is not differentiable.

26. If a function is not differentiable, then it is not continuous.

27. Which of the following would be a counterexample to the statement: "If f is differentiable at $x = a$ then f is continuous at $x = a$"?

   (a) A function which is not differentiable at $x = a$ but is continuous at $x = a$.
   (b) A function which is not continuous at $x = a$ but is differentiable at $x = a$.
   (c) A function which is both continuous and differentiable at $x = a$.
   (d) A function which is neither continuous nor differentiable at $x = a$.

CHAPTER SUMMARY (see also Ready Reference at the end of the book)

- **Rate of change**
  Average, instantaneous.

- **Definition of derivative**
  Difference quotient, limit.

- **Estimating and computing derivatives**
  Estimate derivatives from a graph, table of values, or formula. Use definition to find derivatives of simple functions algebraically. Know derivatives of constant, linear, and power functions.

- **Interpretation of derivatives**
  Rate of change, instantaneous velocity, slope, using units.

- **Second derivative**
  Concavity, acceleration.

- **Working with derivatives**
  Understand relation between sign of f' and whether f is increasing or decreasing. Sketch graph of f' from graph of f.

- **Differentiability**

REVIEW EXERCISES AND PROBLEMS FOR CHAPTER TWO

Exercises

1. At time t in seconds, a particle's distance $s(t)$, in cm, from a point is given in the table. What is the average velocity of the particle from $t = 3$ to $t = 10$?

t	0	3	6	10	13
$s(t)$	0	72	92	144	180

In Exercises 2–7, find the average velocity for the position function $s(t)$, in mm, over the interval $1 \leq t \leq 3$, where t is in seconds.

2. $s(t) = 12t - t^2$

3. $s(t) = \ln(t)$

4.

t	0	1	2	3
$s(t)$	7	3	7	11

5.

t	0	1	2	3
$s(t)$	8	4	2	4

6.

7.

8. In a time of t seconds, a particle moves a distance of s meters from its starting point, where $s = 4t^2 + 3$.

   (a) Find the average velocity between $t = 1$ and $t = 1 + h$ if:

   (i) $h = 0.1$,   (ii) $h = 0.01$,   (iii) $h = 0.001$.

   (b) Use your answers to part (a) to estimate the instantaneous velocity of the particle at time $t = 1$.

9. A bicyclist pedals at a fairly constant rate, with evenly spaced intervals of coasting. Sketch a graph of the distance she has traveled as a function of time.

10. As you drive away from home, your speed is fast, then slow, then fast again. Draw a graph of your distance from home as a function of time.

11. **(a)** Graph $f(x) = x \sin x$ for $-10 \leq x \leq 10$.

   (b) How many zeros does $f(x)$ have on this interval?

   (c) Is f increasing or decreasing at $x = 1$? At $x = 4$?

   (d) On which interval is the average rate of change greater: $0 \leq x \leq 2$ or $6 \leq x \leq 8$?

   (e) Is the instantaneous rate of change greater at $x = -9$ or $x = 1$?

12. **(a)** Using the data in the table, estimate an equation for the tangent line to the graph of $f(x)$ at $x = 0.6$.

   (b) Using this equation, estimate $f(0.7)$, $f(1.2)$, and $f(1.4)$. Which of these estimates is most likely to be reliable? Why?

x	0	0.2	0.4	0.6	0.8	1.0
$f(x)$	3.7	3.5	3.5	3.9	4.0	3.9

Sketch the graphs of the derivatives of the functions shown in Exercises 13–18. Be sure your sketches are consistent with the important features of the graphs of the original functions.

13.

14.

15.

16.

17.

18.

19. Roughly sketch the shape of the graph of a cubic polynomial, f, if it is known that:

- $(0, 3)$ is on the graph of f.
- $f'(0) = 4$, $f'(1) = 0$, $f'(2) = -\frac{4}{3}$, $f'(4) = 4$.

In Exercises 20–21, graph the second derivative of the function.

20.

21.

In Exercises 22–23, find a formula for the derivative of the function algebraically.

22. $f(x) = 5x^2 + x$ **23.** $n(x) = (1/x) + 1$

24. Find the derivative of $f(x) = x^2 + 1$ at $x = 3$ algebraically. Find the equation of the tangent line to f at $x = 3$.

25. **(a)** Between which pair of consecutive points in Figure 2.60 is the average rate of change of k

    (a) Greatest?   **(b)** Closest to zero?

  (b) Between which two pairs of consecutive points are the average rates of change of k closest?

Figure 2.60

In Exercises 26–30, use the difference quotient definition of the derivative to find a formula for the derivative of the function.

26. $f(x) = 3x - 1$ **27.** $f(x) = 5x^2$

28. $f(x) = x^2 + 4$ **29.** $f(x) = 3x^2 - 7$

30. $f(x) = x^3$

In Exercises 31–35, evaluate the limit algebraically for $a > 0$.

31. $\lim\limits_{h \to 0} \dfrac{(a+h)^2 - a^2}{h}$ **32.** $\lim\limits_{h \to 0} \dfrac{1/(a+h) - 1/a}{h}$

33. $\lim\limits_{h \to 0} \dfrac{1/(a+h)^2 - 1/a^2}{h}$

34. $\lim\limits_{h \to 0} \dfrac{\sqrt{a+h} - \sqrt{a}}{h}$ [Hint: Multiply by $\sqrt{a+h} + \sqrt{a}$ in numerator and denominator.]

35. $\lim\limits_{h \to 0} \dfrac{1/\sqrt{a+h} - 1/\sqrt{a}}{h}$

Problems

36. Sketch the graph of a function whose first and second derivatives are everywhere positive.

37. Figure 2.61 gives the position, $y = s(t)$, of a particle at time t. Arrange the following numbers from smallest to largest:

- The instantaneous velocity at A.
- The instantaneous velocity at B.
- The instantaneous velocity at C.
- The average velocity between A and B.
- The number 0.
- The number 1.

Figure 2.61

38. Match each property (a)–(d) with one or more of graphs (I)–(IV) of functions.

  (a) $f'(x) = 1$ for all $0 \le x \le 4$.
  (b) $f'(x) > 0$ for all $0 \le x \le 4$
  (c) $f'(2) = 1$
  (d) $f'(1) = 2$

39. **(a)** In Figure 2.62, if $f(t)$ gives the position of a particle at time t, list the labeled points at which the particle has zero velocity.

(b) If we now suppose instead that $f(t)$ is the *velocity* of a particle at time t, what is the significance of the points listed in your answer to part (a)?

Figure 2.62

40. The table[16] gives the number of passenger cars, $C = f(t)$, in millions, in the US in the year t.

(a) During the period 2003–2007, when is $f'(t)$ positive? Negative?

(b) Estimate $f'(2006)$. Using units, interpret your answer in terms of passenger cars.

t (year)	2003	2004	2005	2006	2007
C (cars, in millions)	135.7	136.4	136.6	135.4	135.9

41. Let $f(t)$ be the depth, in centimeters, of water in a tank at time t, in minutes.

(a) What does the sign of $f'(t)$ tell us?

(b) Explain the meaning of $f'(30) = 20$. Include units.

(c) Using the information in part (b), at time $t = 30$ minutes, find the rate of change of depth, in meters, with respect to time in hours. Give units.

42. If t is the number of years since 2009, the population, P, of Ukraine,[17] in millions, can be approximated by the function
$$P = f(t) = 45.7e^{-0.0061t}$$
Estimate $f(6)$ and $f'(6)$, giving units. What do these two numbers tell you about the population of Ukraine?

43. The revenue, in thousands of dollars, earned by a gas station when the price of gas is $\$p$ per gallon is $R(p)$.

(a) What are the units of $R'(3)$? Interpret this quantity.

(b) What are the units of $(R^{-1})'(5)$? Interpret this quantity.

44. **(a)** Give an example of a function with $\lim_{x \to 2} f(x) = \infty$.

(b) Give an example of a function with $\lim_{x \to 2} f(x) = -\infty$.

45. Draw a possible graph of $y = f(x)$ given the following information about its derivative:

- For $x < -2$, $f'(x) > 0$ and the derivative is increasing.
- For $-2 < x < 1$, $f'(x) > 0$ and the derivative is decreasing.
- At $x = 1$, $f'(x) = 0$.
- For $x > 1$, $f'(x) < 0$ and the derivative is decreasing (getting more and more negative).

46. Suppose $f(2) = 3$ and $f'(2) = 1$. Find $f(-2)$ and $f'(-2)$, assuming that $f(x)$ is

(a) Even   **(b)** Odd.

47. Do the values for the function $y = k(x)$ in the table suggest that the graph of $k(x)$ is concave up or concave down for $1 \le x \le 3.3$? Write a sentence in support of your conclusion.

x	1.0	1.2	1.5	1.9	2.5	3.3
$k(x)$	4.0	3.8	3.6	3.4	3.2	3.0

48. Suppose that $f(x)$ is a function with $f(20) = 345$ and $f'(20) = 6$. Estimate $f(22)$.

49. Students were asked to evaluate $f'(4)$ from the following table which shows values of the function f:

x	1	2	3	4	5	6
$f(x)$	4.2	4.1	4.2	4.5	5.0	5.7

- Student A estimated the derivative as $f'(4) \approx \dfrac{f(5) - f(4)}{5 - 4} = 0.5$.
- Student B estimated the derivative as $f'(4) \approx \dfrac{f(4) - f(3)}{4 - 3} = 0.3$.
- Student C suggested that they should split the difference and estimate the average of these two results, that is, $f'(4) \approx \frac{1}{2}(0.5 + 0.3) = 0.4$.

[16]www.bts.gov. Accessed April 27, 2011.

[17]http://www.indexmundi.com/ukraine/population.html. Accessed April 27, 2011.

(a) Sketch the graph of f, and indicate how the three estimates are represented on the graph.

(b) Explain which answer is likely to be best.

(c) Use Student C's method to find an algebraic formula to approximate $f'(x)$ using increments of size h.

50. Use Figure 2.63 to fill in the blanks in the following statements about the function f at point A.

(a) $f(\underline{}) = \underline{}$ (b) $f'(\underline{}) = \underline{}$

$(7.2, 3.8)$ • Tangent line

$f(x)$

$(7, 3)$ • A

Figure 2.63

51. Use Figure 2.64. At point A, we are told that $x = 1$. In addition, $f(1) = 3$, $f'(1) = 2$, and $h = 0.1$. What are the values of $x_1, x_2, x_3, y_1, y_2, y_3$?

Figure 2.64

52. Given all of the following information about a function f, sketch its graph.

- $f(x) = 0$ at $x = -5, x = 0$, and $x = 5$
- $\lim_{x \to -\infty} f(x) = \infty$
- $\lim_{x \to \infty} f(x) = -3$
- $f'(x) = 0$ at $x = -3, x = 2.5$, and $x = 7$

53. Suppose w is the weight of a stack of papers in an open container, and t is time. A lighted match is thrown into the stack at time $t = 0$.

(a) What is the sign of dw/dt for t while the stack of paper is burning?

(b) What behavior of dw/dt indicates that the fire is no longer burning?

(c) If the fire starts small but increases in vigor over a certain time interval, then does dw/dt increase or decrease over that interval? What about $|dw/dt|$?

54. A yam has just been taken out of the oven and is cooling off before being eaten. The temperature, T, of the yam (measured in degrees Fahrenheit) is a function of how long it has been out of the oven, t (measured in minutes). Thus, we have $T = f(t)$.

(a) Is $f'(t)$ positive or negative? Why?

(b) What are the units for $f'(t)$?

55. For some painkillers, the size of the dose, D, given depends on the weight of the patient, W. Thus, $D = f(W)$, where D is in milligrams and W is in pounds.

(a) Interpret the statements $f(140) = 120$ and $f'(140) = 3$ in terms of this painkiller.

(b) Use the information in the statements in part (a) to estimate $f(145)$.

56. In April 1991, the *Economist* carried an article[18] which said:

> Suddenly, everywhere, it is not the rate of change of things that matters, it is the rate of change of rates of change. Nobody cares much about inflation; only whether it is going up or down. Or rather, whether it is going up fast or down fast. "Inflation drops by disappointing two points," cries the billboard. Which roughly translated means that prices are still rising, but less fast than they were, though not quite as much less fast as everybody had hoped.

In the last sentence, there are three statements about prices. Rewrite these as statements about derivatives.

57. At time, t, in years, the US population is growing at 0.8% per year times its size, $P(t)$, at that moment. Using the derivative, write an equation representing this statement.

---

[18]From "The Tyranny of Differential Calculus: $d^2P/dt^2 > 0 =$ misery." *The Economist* (London: April 6, 1991).

58. A continuous function defined for all x has the following properties:

- f is increasing
- f is concave down
- $f(5) = 2$
- $f'(5) = \frac{1}{2}$

(a) Sketch a possible graph for f.
(b) How many zeros does f have?
(c) What can you say about the location of the zeros?
(d) What is $\lim\limits_{x \to -\infty} f(x)$?
(e) Is it possible that $f'(1) = 1$?
(f) Is it possible that $f'(1) = \frac{1}{4}$?

59. (a) Using the table, estimate $f'(0.6)$ and $f'(0.5)$.
(b) Estimate $f''(0.6)$.
(c) Where do you think the maximum and minimum values of f occur in the interval $0 \le x \le 1$?

x	0	0.2	0.4	0.6	0.8	1.0
$f(x)$	3.7	3.5	3.5	3.9	4.0	3.9

60. Let $g(x) = \sqrt{x}$ and $f(x) = kx^2$, where k is a constant.

(a) Find the slope of the tangent line to the graph of g at the point $(4, 2)$.
(b) Find the equation of this tangent line.
(c) If the graph of f contains the point $(4, 2)$, find k.
(d) Where does the graph of f intersect the tangent line found in part (b)?

61. A circle with center at the origin and radius of length $\sqrt{19}$ has equation $x^2 + y^2 = 19$. Graph the circle.

(a) Just from looking at the graph, what can you say about the slope of the line tangent to the circle at the point $(0, \sqrt{19})$? What about the slope of the tangent at $(\sqrt{19}, 0)$?
(b) Estimate the slope of the tangent to the circle at the point $(2, -\sqrt{15})$ by graphing the tangent carefully at that point.
(c) Use the result of part (b) and the symmetry of the circle to find slopes of the tangents drawn to the circle at $(-2, \sqrt{15})$, $(-2, -\sqrt{15})$, and $(2, \sqrt{15})$.

62. Each of the graphs in Figure 2.65 shows the position of a particle moving along the x-axis as a function of time, $0 \le t \le 5$. The vertical scales of the graphs are the same. During this time interval, which particle has

(a) Constant velocity?
(b) The greatest initial velocity?
(c) The greatest average velocity?
(d) Zero average velocity?
(e) Zero acceleration?
(f) Positive acceleration throughout?

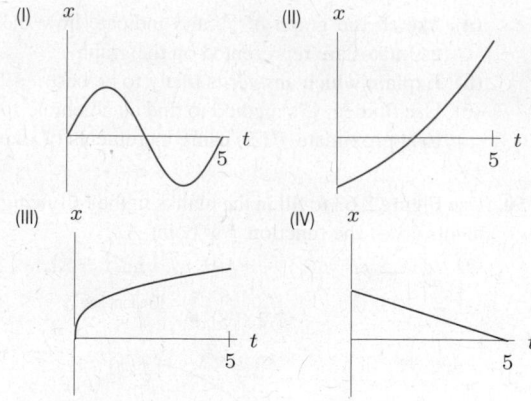

Figure 2.65

63. The population of a herd of deer is modeled by

$$P(t) = 4000 + 400 \sin\left(\frac{\pi}{6}t\right) + 180 \sin\left(\frac{\pi}{3}t\right)$$

where t is measured in months from the first of April.

(a) Use a calculator or computer to sketch a graph showing how this population varies with time.

Use the graph to answer the following questions.

(b) When is the herd largest? How many deer are in it at that time?
(c) When is the herd smallest? How many deer are in it then?
(d) When is the herd growing the fastest? When is it shrinking the fastest?
(e) How fast is the herd growing on April 1?

64. The number of hours, H, of daylight in Madrid is a function of t, the number of days since the start of the year. Figure 2.66 shows a one-month portion of the graph of H.

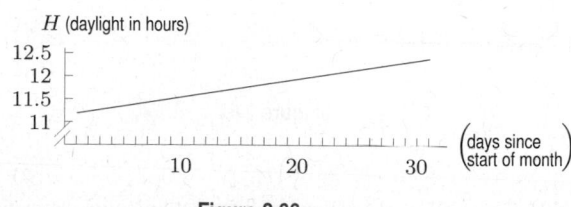

Figure 2.66

(a) Comment on the shape of the graph. Why does it look like a straight line?
(b) What month does this graph show? How do you know?
(c) What is the approximate slope of this line? What does the slope represent in practical terms?

65. You put a yam in a hot oven, maintained at a constant temperature of $200°C$. As the yam picks up heat from the oven, its temperature rises.[19]

   (a) Draw a possible graph of the temperature T of the yam against time t (minutes) since it is put into the oven. Explain any interesting features of the graph, and in particular explain its concavity.

   (b) At $t = 30$, the temperature T of the yam is $120°$ and increasing at the (instantaneous) rate of $2°/min$. Using this information and the shape of the graph, estimate the temperature at time $t = 40$.

   (c) In addition, you are told that at $t = 60$, the temperature of the yam is $165°$. Can you improve your estimate of the temperature at $t = 40$?

   (d) Assuming all the data given so far, estimate the time at which the temperature of the yam is $150°$.

66. You are given the following values for the error function, $\text{erf}(x)$.

$$\text{erf}(0) = 0 \quad \text{erf}(1) = 0.84270079$$
$$\text{erf}(0.1) = 0.11246292 \quad \text{erf}(0.01) = 0.01128342.$$

   (a) Use all this information to determine your best estimate for $\text{erf}'(0)$. (Give only those digits of which you feel reasonably certain.)

   (b) You find that $\text{erf}(0.001) = 0.00112838$. How does this extra information change your answer to part (a)?

67. **(a)** Use your calculator to approximate the derivative of the hyperbolic sine function (written $\sinh x$) at the points 0, 0.3, 0.7, and 1.

   (b) Can you find a relation between the values of this derivative and the values of the hyperbolic cosine (written $\cosh x$)?

68. In 2009, a study was done on the impact of sea level rise in the mid-Atlantic states.[20] Let $a(t)$ be the depth of the sea in millimeters (mm) at a typical point on the Atlantic Coast, and let $m(t)$ be the depth of the sea in mm at a typical point on the Gulf of Mexico, with time t in years since data collection started.

   (a) The study reports "Sea level is rising and there is evidence that the rate is accelerating." What does this statement tell us about $a(t)$ and $m(t)$?

   (b) The study also reports "The Atlantic Coast and the Gulf of Mexico experience higher rates of sea-level rise (2 to 4 mm per year and 2 to 10 mm per year, respectively) than the current global average (1.7 mm per year)." What does this tell us about $a(t)$ and $m(t)$?

   (c) Assume the rate at which the sea level rises on the Atlantic Coast and the Gulf of Mexico are constant for a century and within the ranges given in the report.

      (i) What is the largest amount the sea could rise on the Atlantic Coast during a century? Your answer should be a range of values.

      (ii) What is the shortest amount of time in which the sea level in the Gulf of Mexico could rise 1 meter?

CAS Challenge Problems

69. Use a computer algebra system to find the derivative of $f(x) = \sin^2 x + \cos^2 x$ and simplify your answer. Explain your result.

70. **(a)** Use a computer algebra system to find the derivative of $f(x) = 2 \sin x \cos x$.

   (b) Simplify $f(x)$ and $f'(x)$ using double angle formulas. Write down the derivative formula that you get after doing this simplification.

71. **(a)** Use a computer algebra system to find the second derivative of $g(x) = e^{-ax^2}$ with respect to x.

   (b) Graph $g(x)$ and $g''(x)$ on the same axes for $a = 1, 2, 3$ and describe the relation between the two graphs.

   (c) Explain your answer to part (b) in terms of concavity.

72. **(a)** Use a computer algebra system to find the derivative of $f(x) = \ln(x)$, $g(x) = \ln(2x)$, and $h(x) = \ln(3x)$. What is the relationship between the answers?

   (b) Use the properties of logarithms to explain what you see in part (a).

73. **(a)** Use a computer algebra system to find the derivative of $(x^2 + 1)^2$, $(x^2 + 1)^3$, and $(x^2 + 1)^4$.

   (b) Conjecture a formula for the derivative of $(x^2 + 1)^n$ that works for any integer n. Check your formula using the computer algebra system.

74. **(a)** Use a computer algebra system to find the derivatives of $\sin x$, $\cos x$ and $\sin x \cos x$.

   (b) Is the derivative of a product of two functions always equal to the product of their derivatives?

---

[19]From Peter D. Taylor, *Calculus: The Analysis of Functions* (Toronto: Wall & Emerson, Inc., 1992).
[20]www.epa.gov/climatechange/effects/coastal/sap4-1.html, *Coastal Sensitivity to Sea-Level Rise: A Focus on the Mid-Atlantic Region,* US Climate Change Science Program, January 2009.

PROJECTS FOR CHAPTER TWO

1. **Hours of Daylight as a Function of Latitude**

    Let $S(x)$ be the number of sunlight hours on a cloudless June 21, as a function of latitude, x, measured in degrees.

    (a) What is $S(0)$?

    (b) Let x_0 be the latitude of the Arctic Circle ($x_0 \approx 66°30'$). In the northern hemisphere, $S(x)$ is given, for some constants a and b, by the formula:

    $$S(x) = \begin{cases} a + b \arcsin\left(\dfrac{\tan x}{\tan x_0}\right) & \text{for } 0 \leq x < x_0 \\ 24 & \text{for } x_0 \leq x \leq 90. \end{cases}$$

    Find a and b so that $S(x)$ is continuous.

    (c) Calculate $S(x)$ for Tucson, Arizona ($x = 32°13'$) and Walla Walla, Washington ($46°4'$).

    (d) Graph $S(x)$, for $0 \leq x \leq 90$.

    (e) Does $S(x)$ appear to be differentiable?

2. **US Population**

    Census figures for the US population (in millions) are listed in Table 2.12. Let f be the function such that $P = f(t)$ is the population (in millions) in year t.

Table 2.12 *US population (in millions), 1790–2000*

Year	Population	Year	Population	Year	Population	Year	Population
1790	3.9	1850	23.1	1910	92.0	1970	205.0
1800	5.3	1860	31.4	1920	105.7	1980	226.5
1810	7.2	1870	38.6	1930	122.8	1990	248.7
1820	9.6	1880	50.2	1940	131.7	2000	281.4
1830	12.9	1890	62.9	1950	150.7		
1840	17.1	1900	76.0	1960	179.0		

(a) **(i)** Estimate the rate of change of the population for the years 1900, 1945, and 2000.

   (ii) When, approximately, was the rate of change of the population greatest?

   (iii) Estimate the US population in 1956.

   (iv) Based on the data from the table, what would you predict for the census in the year 2010?

(b) Assume that f is increasing (as the values in the table suggest). Then f is invertible.

   (i) What is the meaning of $f^{-1}(100)$?

   (ii) What does the derivative of $f^{-1}(P)$ at $P = 100$ represent? What are its units?

   (iii) Estimate $f^{-1}(100)$.

   (iv) Estimate the derivative of $f^{-1}(P)$ at $P = 100$.

(c) **(i)** Usually we think the US population $P = f(t)$ as a smooth function of time. To what extent is this justified? What happens if we zoom in at a point of the graph? What about events such as the Louisiana Purchase? Or the moment of your birth?

   (ii) What do we in fact mean by the rate of change of the population at a particular time t?

   (iii) Give another example of a real-world function which is not smooth but is usually treated as such.

Chapter Three

SHORT-CUTS TO DIFFERENTIATION

Contents

3.1 POWERS AND POLYNOMIALS

Derivative of a Constant Times a Function

Figure 3.1 shows the graph of $y = f(x)$ and of three multiples: $y = 3f(x)$, $y = \frac{1}{2}f(x)$, and $y = -2f(x)$. What is the relationship between the derivatives of these functions? In other words, for a particular x-value, how are the slopes of these graphs related?

Figure 3.1: A function and its multiples: Derivative of multiple is multiple of derivative

Multiplying the value of a function by a constant stretches or shrinks the original graph (and reflects it across the x-axis if the constant is negative). This changes the slope of the curve at each point. If the graph has been stretched, the "rises" have all been increased by the same factor, whereas the "runs" remain the same. Thus, the slopes are all steeper by the same factor. If the graph has been shrunk, the slopes are all smaller by the same factor. If the graph has been reflected across the x-axis, the slopes will all have their signs reversed. In other words, if a function is multiplied by a constant, c, so is its derivative:

Theorem 3.1: Derivative of a Constant Multiple

If f is differentiable and c is a constant, then

$$\frac{d}{dx}[cf(x)] = cf'(x).$$

Proof Although the graphical argument makes the theorem plausible, to prove it we must use the definition of the derivative:

$$\frac{d}{dx}[cf(x)] = \lim_{h \to 0} \frac{cf(x+h) - cf(x)}{h} = \lim_{h \to 0} c \frac{f(x+h) - f(x)}{h}$$

$$= c \lim_{h \to 0} \frac{f(x+h) - f(x)}{h} = cf'(x).$$

We can take c across the limit sign by the properties of limits (part 1 of Theorem 1.2 on page 60).

Derivatives of Sums and Differences

Suppose we have two functions, $f(x)$ and $g(x)$, with the values listed in Table 3.1. Values of the sum $f(x) + g(x)$ are given in the same table.

Table 3.1 *Sum of Functions*

x	$f(x)$	$g(x)$	$f(x) + g(x)$
0	100	0	100
1	110	0.2	110.2
2	130	0.4	130.4
3	160	0.6	160.6
4	200	0.8	200.8

We see that adding the increments of $f(x)$ and the increments of $g(x)$ gives the increments of $f(x) + g(x)$. For example, as x increases from 0 to 1, $f(x)$ increases by 10 and $g(x)$ increases by 0.2, while $f(x) + g(x)$ increases by $110.2 - 100 = 10.2$. Similarly, as x increases from 3 to 4, $f(x)$ increases by 40 and $g(x)$ by 0.2, while $f(x) + g(x)$ increases by $200.8 - 160.6 = 40.2$.

From this example, we see that the rate at which $f(x) + g(x)$ is increasing is the sum of the rates at which $f(x)$ and $g(x)$ are increasing. Similar reasoning applies to the difference, $f(x) - g(x)$. In terms of derivatives:

Theorem 3.2: Derivative of Sum and Difference

If f and g are differentiable, then

$$\frac{d}{dx}[f(x) + g(x)] = f'(x) + g'(x) \quad \text{and} \quad \frac{d}{dx}[f(x) - g(x)] = f'(x) - g'(x).$$

Proof Using the definition of the derivative:

$$\frac{d}{dx}[f(x) + g(x)] = \lim_{h \to 0} \frac{[f(x+h) + g(x+h)] - [f(x) + g(x)]}{h}$$

$$= \lim_{h \to 0} \left[\underbrace{\frac{f(x+h) - f(x)}{h}}_{\text{Limit of this is } f'(x)} + \underbrace{\frac{g(x+h) - g(x)}{h}}_{\text{Limit of this is } g'(x)} \right]$$

$$= f'(x) + g'(x).$$

We have used the fact that the limit of a sum is the sum of the limits, part 2 of Theorem 1.2 on page 60. The proof for $f(x) - g(x)$ is similar.

Powers of x

In Chapter 2 we showed that

$$f'(x) = \frac{d}{dx}(x^2) = 2x \quad \text{and} \quad g'(x) = \frac{d}{dx}(x^3) = 3x^2.$$

The graphs of $f(x) = x^2$ and $g(x) = x^3$ and their derivatives are shown in Figures 3.2 and 3.3. Notice $f'(x) = 2x$ has the behavior we expect. It is negative for $x < 0$ (when f is decreasing), zero for $x = 0$, and positive for $x > 0$ (when f is increasing). Similarly, $g'(x) = 3x^2$ is zero when $x = 0$, but positive everywhere else, as g is increasing everywhere else.

Figure 3.2: Graphs of $f(x) = x^2$ and its derivative $f'(x) = 2x$

Figure 3.3: Graphs of $g(x) = x^3$ and its derivative $g'(x) = 3x^2$

These examples are special cases of the power rule, which we justify for any positive integer n on page 127:

The Power Rule

For any constant real number n,

$$\frac{d}{dx}(x^n) = nx^{n-1}.$$

Problem 80 asks you to show that this rule holds for negative integral powers; such powers can also be differentiated using the quotient rule (Section 3.3). In Section 3.6 we indicate how to justify the power rule for powers of the form $1/n$.

Example 1   Use the power rule to differentiate (a) $\dfrac{1}{x^3}$,   (b) $x^{1/2}$,   (c) $\dfrac{1}{\sqrt[3]{x}}$.

Solution   (a) For $n = -3$: $\dfrac{d}{dx}\left(\dfrac{1}{x^3}\right) = \dfrac{d}{dx}(x^{-3}) = -3x^{-3-1} = -3x^{-4} = -\dfrac{3}{x^4}.$

(b) For $n = 1/2$: $\dfrac{d}{dx}\left(x^{1/2}\right) = \dfrac{1}{2}x^{(1/2)-1} = \dfrac{1}{2}x^{-1/2} = \dfrac{1}{2\sqrt{x}}.$

(c) For $n = -1/3$: $\dfrac{d}{dx}\left(\dfrac{1}{\sqrt[3]{x}}\right) = \dfrac{d}{dx}\left(x^{-1/3}\right) = -\dfrac{1}{3}x^{(-1/3)-1} = -\dfrac{1}{3}x^{-4/3} = -\dfrac{1}{3x^{4/3}}.$

Example 2   Use the definition of the derivative to justify the power rule for $n = -2$: Show $\dfrac{d}{dx}(x^{-2}) = -2x^{-3}$.

Solution   Provided $x \neq 0$, we have

$$\frac{d}{dx}\left(x^{-2}\right) = \frac{d}{dx}\left(\frac{1}{x^2}\right) = \lim_{h \to 0}\left(\frac{\frac{1}{(x+h)^2} - \frac{1}{x^2}}{h}\right) = \lim_{h \to 0}\frac{1}{h}\left[\frac{x^2 - (x+h)^2}{(x+h)^2 x^2}\right] \quad \text{(Combining fractions over a common denominator)}$$

$$= \lim_{h \to 0}\frac{1}{h}\left[\frac{x^2 - (x^2 + 2xh + h^2)}{(x+h)^2 x^2}\right] \quad \text{(Multiplying out)}$$

$$= \lim_{h \to 0}\frac{-2xh - h^2}{h(x+h)^2 x^2} \quad \text{(Simplifying numerator)}$$

$$= \lim_{h \to 0}\frac{-2x - h}{(x+h)^2 x^2} \quad \text{(Dividing numerator and denominator by } h\text{)}$$

$$= \frac{-2x}{x^4} \quad \text{(Letting } h \to 0\text{)}$$

$$= -2x^{-3}.$$

The graphs of x^{-2} and its derivative, $-2x^{-3}$, are shown in Figure 3.4. Does the graph of the derivative have the features you expect?

Figure 3.4: Graphs of x^{-2} and its derivative, $-2x^{-3}$

Justification of $\dfrac{d}{dx}\left(x^n\right) = nx^{n-1}$, for n a Positive Integer

To calculate the derivatives of x^2 and x^3, we had to expand $(x+h)^2$ and $(x+h)^3$. To calculate the derivative of x^n, we must expand $(x+h)^n$. Let's look back at the previous expansions:

$$(x+h)^2 = x^2 + 2xh + h^2, \qquad (x+h)^3 = x^3 + 3x^2h + 3xh^2 + h^3,$$

and multiply out a few more examples:

$$(x+h)^4 = x^4 + 4x^3h + 6x^2h^2 + 4xh^3 + h^4,$$
$$(x+h)^5 = x^5 + 5x^4h + \underbrace{10x^3h^2 + 10x^2h^3 + 5xh^4 + h^5}.$$

Terms involving h^2 and higher powers of h

In general, we can say

$$(x+h)^n = x^n + nx^{n-1}h + \underbrace{\cdots + h^n}.$$

Terms involving h^2 and higher powers of h

We have just seen this is true for $n = 2, 3, 4, 5$. It can be proved in general using the Binomial Theorem (see www.wiley.com/college/hughes-hallett). Now to find the derivative,

$$\frac{d}{dx}(x^n) = \lim_{h \to 0} \frac{(x+h)^n - x^n}{h}$$

$$= \lim_{h \to 0} \frac{(x^n + nx^{n-1}h + \cdots + h^n) - x^n}{h}$$

Terms involving h^2 and higher powers of h

$$= \lim_{h \to 0} \frac{nx^{n-1}h + \overbrace{\cdots + h^n}}{h}.$$

When we factor out h from terms involving h^2 and higher powers of h, each term will still have an h in it. Factoring and dividing, we get:

Terms involving h and higher powers of h

$$\frac{d}{dx}(x^n) = \lim_{h \to 0} \frac{h(nx^{n-1} + \cdots + h^{n-1})}{h} = \lim_{h \to 0}(nx^{n-1} + \overbrace{\cdots + h^{n-1}}).$$

But as $h \to 0$, all terms involving an h will go to 0, so

$$\frac{d}{dx}(x^n) = \lim_{h \to 0}(nx^{n-1} + \underbrace{\cdots + h^{n-1}}) = nx^{n-1}.$$

These terms go to 0

Derivatives of Polynomials

Now that we know how to differentiate powers, constant multiples, and sums, we can differentiate any polynomial.

Example 3 Find the derivatives of (a) $5x^2 + 3x + 2$, (b) $\sqrt{3}x^7 - \dfrac{x^5}{5} + \pi$.

Solution (a)

$$\frac{d}{dx}(5x^2 + 3x + 2) = 5\frac{d}{dx}(x^2) + 3\frac{d}{dx}(x) + \frac{d}{dx}(2)$$

$$= 5 \cdot 2x + 3 \cdot 1 + 0 \qquad \text{(Since the derivative of a constant, $\frac{d}{dx}(2)$, is zero.)}$$

$$= 10x + 3.$$

(b)

$$\frac{d}{dx}\left(\sqrt{3}x^7 - \frac{x^5}{5} + \pi\right) = \sqrt{3}\frac{d}{dx}(x^7) - \frac{1}{5}\frac{d}{dx}(x^5) + \frac{d}{dx}(\pi)$$

$$= \sqrt{3} \cdot 7x^6 - \frac{1}{5} \cdot 5x^4 + 0 \qquad \text{(Since } \pi \text{ is a constant, } d\pi/dx = 0.\text{)}$$

$$= 7\sqrt{3}x^6 - x^4.$$

We can also use the rules we have seen so far to differentiate expressions that are not polynomials.

Example 4 Differentiate (a) $5\sqrt{x} - \dfrac{10}{x^2} + \dfrac{1}{2\sqrt{x}}$.   (b) $0.1x^3 + 2x^{\sqrt{2}}$.

Solution (a) $\dfrac{d}{dx}\left(5\sqrt{x} - \dfrac{10}{x^2} + \dfrac{1}{2\sqrt{x}}\right) = \dfrac{d}{dx}\left(5x^{1/2} - 10x^{-2} + \dfrac{1}{2}x^{-1/2}\right)$

$$= 5 \cdot \frac{1}{2}x^{-1/2} - 10(-2)x^{-3} + \frac{1}{2}\left(-\frac{1}{2}\right)x^{-3/2}$$

$$= \frac{5}{2\sqrt{x}} + \frac{20}{x^3} - \frac{1}{4x^{3/2}}.$$

(b) $\dfrac{d}{dx}(0.1x^3 + 2x^{\sqrt{2}}) = 0.1\dfrac{d}{dx}(x^3) + 2\dfrac{d}{dx}(x^{\sqrt{2}}) = 0.3x^2 + 2\sqrt{2}x^{\sqrt{2}-1}.$

Example 5 Find the second derivative and interpret its sign for
(a) $f(x) = x^2$,   (b) $g(x) = x^3$,   (c) $k(x) = x^{1/2}$.

Solution (a) If $f(x) = x^2$, then $f'(x) = 2x$, so $f''(x) = \dfrac{d}{dx}(2x) = 2$. Since f'' is always positive, f is concave up, as expected for a parabola opening upward. (See Figure 3.5.)

(b) If $g(x) = x^3$, then $g'(x) = 3x^2$, so $g''(x) = \dfrac{d}{dx}(3x^2) = 3\dfrac{d}{dx}(x^2) = 3 \cdot 2x = 6x$. This is positive for $x > 0$ and negative for $x < 0$, which means x^3 is concave up for $x > 0$ and concave down for $x < 0$. (See Figure 3.6.)

(c) If $k(x) = x^{1/2}$, then $k'(x) = \frac{1}{2}x^{(1/2)-1} = \frac{1}{2}x^{-1/2}$, so

$$k''(x) = \frac{d}{dx}\left(\frac{1}{2}x^{-1/2}\right) = \frac{1}{2} \cdot \left(-\frac{1}{2}\right)x^{-(1/2)-1} = -\frac{1}{4}x^{-3/2}.$$

Now k' and k'' are only defined on the domain of k, that is, $x \geq 0$. When $x > 0$, we see that $k''(x)$ is negative, so k is concave down. (See Figure 3.7.)

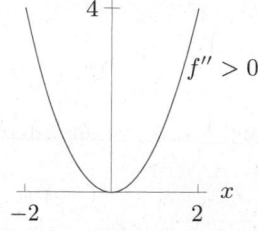

Figure 3.5: $f(x) = x^2$ has $f''(x) = 2$

Figure 3.6: $g(x) = x^3$ has $g''(x) = 6x$

Figure 3.7: $k(x) = x^{1/2}$ has $k''(x) = -\frac{1}{4}x^{-3/2}$

Example 6 If the position of a body, in meters, is given as a function of time t, in seconds, by

$$s = -4.9t^2 + 5t + 6,$$

find the velocity and acceleration of the body at time t.

Solution   The velocity, v, is the derivative of the position:

$$v = \frac{ds}{dt} = \frac{d}{dt}(-4.9t^2 + 5t + 6) = -9.8t + 5,$$

and the acceleration, a, is the derivative of the velocity:

$$a = \frac{dv}{dt} = \frac{d}{dt}(-9.8t + 5) = -9.8.$$

Note that v is in meters/second and a is in meters/second^2.

Example 7   Figure 3.8 shows the graph of a cubic polynomial. Both graphically and algebraically, describe the behavior of the derivative of this cubic.

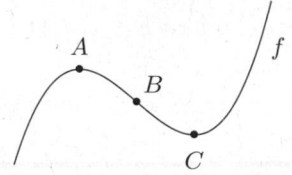

Figure 3.8: The cubic of Example 7   **Figure 3.9**: Derivative of the cubic of Example 7

Solution   Graphical approach: Suppose we move along the curve from left to right. To the left of A, the slope is positive; it starts very positive and decreases until the curve reaches A, where the slope is 0. Between A and C the slope is negative. Between A and B the slope is decreasing (getting more negative); it is most negative at B. Between B and C the slope is negative but increasing; at C the slope is zero. From C to the right, the slope is positive and increasing. The graph of the derivative function is shown in Figure 3.9.

Algebraic approach: f is a cubic that goes to $+\infty$ as $x \to +\infty$, so

$$f(x) = ax^3 + bx^2 + cx + d$$

with $a > 0$. Hence,

$$f'(x) = 3ax^2 + 2bx + c,$$

whose graph is a parabola opening upward, as in Figure 3.9.

Exercises and Problems for Section 3.1

Exercises

1. Let $f(x) = 7$. Using the definition of the derivative, show that $f'(x) = 0$ for all values of x.

2. Let $f(x) = 17x + 11$. Use the definition of the derivative to calculate $f'(x)$.

For Exercises 3–5, determine if the derivative rules from this section apply. If they do, find the derivative. If they don't apply, indicate why.

3. $y = 3^x$ **4.** $y = x^3$ **5.** $y = x^\pi$

For Exercises 6–49, find the derivatives of the given functions. Assume that a, b, c, and k are constants.

6. $y = x^{12}$ **7.** $y = x^{11}$

8. $y = -x^{-11}$ **9.** $y = x^{-12}$

10. $y = x^{3.2}$ **11.** $y = x^{-3/4}$

12. $y = x^{4/3}$ **13.** $y = x^{3/4}$

14. $y = x^2 + 5x + 7$ **15.** $f(t) = t^3 - 3t^2 + 8t - 4$

16. $f(x) = \dfrac{1}{x^4}$ **17.** $g(t) = \dfrac{1}{t^5}$

18. $f(z) = -\dfrac{1}{z^{6.1}}$ **19.** $y = \dfrac{1}{r^{7/2}}$

20. $y = \sqrt{x}$ **21.** $f(x) = \sqrt[4]{x}$

22. $h(\theta) = \dfrac{1}{\sqrt[3]{\theta}}$ **23.** $f(x) = \sqrt{\dfrac{1}{x^3}}$

24. $h(x) = \ln e^{ax}$ **25.** $y = 4x^{3/2} - 5x^{1/2}$

26. $f(t) = 3t^2 - 4t + 1$ **27.** $y = 17x + 24x^{1/2}$

28. $y = z^2 + \dfrac{1}{2z}$ **29.** $f(x) = 5x^4 + \dfrac{1}{x^2}$

30. $h(w) = -2w^{-3} + 3\sqrt{w}$ **31.** $y = -3x^4 - 4x^3 - 6x$

32. $y = 3t^5 - 5\sqrt{t} + \dfrac{7}{t}$ **33.** $y = 3t^2 + \dfrac{12}{\sqrt{t}} - \dfrac{1}{t^2}$

34. $y = \sqrt{x}(x + 1)$ **35.** $y = t^{3/2}(2 + \sqrt{t})$

36. $h(t) = \dfrac{3}{t} + \dfrac{4}{t^2}$ **37.** $h(\theta) = \theta(\theta^{-1/2} - \theta^{-2})$

38. $y = \dfrac{x^2 + 1}{x}$ **39.** $f(z) = \dfrac{z^2 + 1}{3z}$

40. $g(x) = \dfrac{x^2 + \sqrt{x} + 1}{x^{3/2}}$ **41.** $y = \dfrac{\theta - 1}{\sqrt{\theta}}$

42. $g(t) = \dfrac{\sqrt{t}(1 + t)}{t^2}$ **43.** $j(x) = \dfrac{x^3}{a} + \dfrac{a}{b}x^2 - cx$

44. $f(x) = \dfrac{ax + b}{x}$ **45.** $h(x) = \dfrac{ax + b}{c}$

46. $V = \frac{4}{3}\pi r^2 b$ **47.** $w = 3ab^2 q$

48. $y = ax^2 + bx + c$ **49.** $P = a + b\sqrt{t}$

Problems

For Problems 50–55, determine if the derivative rules from this section apply. If they do, find the derivative. If they don't apply, indicate why.

50. $y = (x + 3)^{1/2}$ **51.** $y = \pi^x$

52. $g(x) = x^\pi - x^{-\pi}$ **53.** $y = 3x^2 + 4$

54. $y = \dfrac{1}{3x^2 + 4}$ **55.** $y = \dfrac{1}{3z^2} + \dfrac{1}{4}$

56. The graph of $y = x^3 - 9x^2 - .16x + 1$ has a slope of 5 at two points. Find the coordinates of the points.

57. Find the equation of the line tangent to the graph of f at $(1, 1)$, where f is given by $f(x) = 2x^3 - 2x^2 + 1$.

58. (a) Find the equation of the tangent line to $f(x) = x^3$ at the point where $x = 2$.
 (b) Graph the tangent line and the function on the same axes. If the tangent line is used to estimate values of the function, will the estimates be overestimates or underestimates?

59. Find the equation of the line tangent to $y = x^2 + 3x - 5$ at $x = 2$.

60. Find the equation of the line tangent to $f(x)$ at $x = 2$, if

$$f(x) = \frac{x^3}{2} - \frac{4}{3x}.$$

61. Using a graph to help you, find the equations of all lines through the origin tangent to the parabola

$$y = x^2 - 2x + 4.$$

Sketch the lines on the graph.

62. On what intervals is the graph of $f(x) = x^4 - 4x^3$ both decreasing and concave up?

63. For what values of x is the function $y = x^5 - 5x$ both increasing and concave up?

64. If $f(x) = 4x^3 + 6x^2 - 23x + 7$, find the intervals on which $f'(x) \geq 1$.

65. If $f(x) = (3x + 8)(2x - 5)$, find $f'(x)$ and $f''(x)$.

66. Given $p(x) = x^n - x$, find the intervals over which p is a decreasing function when:

 (a) $n = 2$ (b) $n = \frac{1}{2}$ (c) $n = -1$

67. Suppose W is proportional to r^3. The derivative dW/dr is proportional to what power of r?

68. The height of a sand dune (in centimeters) is represented by $f(t) = 700 - 3t^2$, where t is measured in years since 2005. Find $f(5)$ and $f'(5)$. Using units, explain what each means in terms of the sand dune.

69. A ball is dropped from the top of the Empire State building to the ground below. The height, y, of the ball above the ground (in feet) is given as a function of time, t, (in seconds) by

$$y = 1250 - 16t^2.$$

 (a) Find the velocity of the ball at time t. What is the sign of the velocity? Why is this to be expected?
 (b) Show that the acceleration of the ball is a constant. What are the value and sign of this constant?
 (c) When does the ball hit the ground, and how fast is it going at that time? Give your answer in feet per second and in miles per hour (1 ft/sec = 15/22 mph).

70. At a time t seconds after it is thrown up in the air, a tomato is at a height of $f(t) = -4.9t^2 + 25t + 3$ meters.

 (a) What is the average velocity of the tomato during the first 2 seconds? Give units.
 (b) Find (exactly) the instantaneous velocity of the tomato at $t = 2$. Give units.
 (c) What is the acceleration at $t = 2$?
 (d) How high does the tomato go?
 (e) How long is the tomato in the air?

71. A particle is moving on the x-axis, where x is in centimeters. Its velocity, v, in cm/sec, when it is at the point with coordinate x is given by

$$v = x^2 + 3x - 2.$$

Find the acceleration of the particle when it is at the point $x = 2$. Give units in your answer.

72. Let $f(t)$ and $g(t)$ give, respectively, the amount of water (in acre-feet) in two different reservoirs on day t. Suppose that $f(0) = 2000, g(0) = 1500$ and that $f'(0) = 11, g'(0) = 13.5$. Let $h(t) = f(t) - g(t)$.

   (a) Evaluate $h(0)$ and $h'(0)$. What do these quantities tell you about the reservoir?
   (b) Assume h' is constant for $0 \leq t \leq 250$. Does h have any zeros? What does this tell you about the reservoirs?

73. If M is the mass of the earth and G is a constant, the acceleration due to gravity, g, at a distance r from the center of the earth is given by

$$g = \frac{GM}{r^2}.$$

   (a) Find dg/dr.
   (b) What is the practical interpretation (in terms of acceleration) of dg/dr? Why would you expect it to be negative?
   (c) You are told that $M = 6 \cdot 10^{24}$ and $G = 6.67 \cdot 10^{-20}$ where M is in kilograms and r in kilometers. What is the value of dg/dr at the surface of the earth ($r = 6400$ km)?
   (d) What does this tell you about whether or not it is reasonable to assume g is constant near the surface of the earth?

74. The period, T, of a pendulum is given in terms of its length, l, by

$$T = 2\pi\sqrt{\frac{l}{g}},$$

where g is the acceleration due to gravity (a constant).

   (a) Find dT/dl.
   (b) What is the sign of dT/dl? What does this tell you about the period of pendulums?

75. (a) Use the formula for the area of a circle of radius r, $A = \pi r^2$, to find dA/dr.
   (b) The result from part (a) should look familiar. What does dA/dr represent geometrically?
   (c) Use the difference quotient to explain the observation you made in part (b).

76. What is the formula for V, the volume of a sphere of radius r? Find dV/dr. What is the geometrical meaning of dV/dr?

77. Show that for any power function $f(x) = x^n$, we have $f'(1) = n$.

78. Given a power function of the form $f(x) = ax^n$, with $f'(2) = 3$ and $f'(4) = 24$, find n and a.

79. Is there a value of n which makes $y = x^n$ a solution to the equation $13x(dy/dx) = y$? If so, what value?

80. Using the definition of derivative, justify the formula $d(x^n)/dx = nx^{n-1}$.

   (a) For $n = -1$; for $n = -3$.
   (b) For any negative integer n.

81. (a) Find the value of a making $f(x)$ continuous at $x = 1$:

$$f(x) = \begin{cases} ax & 0 \leq x \leq 1 \\ x^2 + 3 & 1 < x \leq 2. \end{cases}$$

   (b) With the value of a you found in part (a), does $f(x)$ have a derivative at every point in $0 \leq x \leq 2$? Explain.

82. Find values of a and b making $f(x)$ continuous and differentiable on $0 < x < 2$:

$$f(x) = \begin{cases} ax + b & 0 \leq x \leq 1 \\ x^2 + 3 & 1 < x \leq 2. \end{cases}$$

Strengthen Your Understanding

In Problems 83–84, explain what is wrong with the statement.

83. The only function that has derivative $2x$ is x^2.

84. The derivative of $f(x) = 1/x^2$ is $f'(x) = 1/(2x)$.

In Problems 85–87, give an example of:

85. Two functions $f(x)$ and $g(x)$ such that

$$\frac{d}{dx}(f(x) + g(x)) = 2x + 3.$$

86. A function whose derivative is $g'(x) = 2x$ and whose graph has no x-intercepts.

87. A function which has second derivative equal to 6 everywhere.

Are the statements in Problems 88–90 true or false? Give an explanation for your answer.

88. The derivative of a polynomial is always a polynomial.

89. The derivative of π/x^2 is $-\pi/x$.

90. If $f'(2) = 3.1$ and $g'(2) = 7.3$, then the graph of $f(x) + g(x)$ has slope 10.4 at $x = 2$.

Suppose that f'' and g'' exist and that f and g are concave up for all x. Are the statements in Problems 91–92 true or false for all such f and g? If a statement is true, explain how you know. If a statement is false, give a counterexample.

91. $f(x) + g(x)$ is concave up for all x.

92. $f(x) - g(x)$ cannot be concave up for all x.

3.2 THE EXPONENTIAL FUNCTION

What do we expect the graph of the derivative of the exponential function $f(x) = a^x$ to look like? The exponential function in Figure 3.10 increases slowly for $x < 0$ and more rapidly for $x > 0$, so the values of f' are small for $x < 0$ and larger for $x > 0$. Since the function is increasing for all values of x, the graph of the derivative must lie above the x-axis. It appears that the graph of f' may resemble the graph of f itself.

Figure 3.10: $f(x) = a^x$, with $a > 1$

In this section we see that $f'(x) = k \cdot a^x$, where k is a constant, so in fact $f'(x)$ is proportional to $f(x)$. This property of exponential functions makes them particularly useful in modeling because many quantities have rates of change which are proportional to themselves. For example, the simplest model of population growth has this property.

Derivatives of Exponential Functions and the Number e

We start by calculating the derivative of $g(x) = 2^x$, which is given by

$$g'(x) = \lim_{h \to 0} \left(\frac{2^{x+h} - 2^x}{h} \right) = \lim_{h \to 0} \left(\frac{2^x 2^h - 2^x}{h} \right) = \lim_{h \to 0} 2^x \left(\frac{2^h - 1}{h} \right)$$

$$= \lim_{h \to 0} \left(\frac{2^h - 1}{h} \right) \cdot 2^x. \qquad \text{(Since x and 2^x are fixed during this calculation).}$$

To find $\lim_{h \to 0} (2^h - 1)/h$, see Table 3.2 where we have substituted values of h near 0. The table suggests that the limit exists and has value 0.693. Let us call the limit k, so $k = 0.693$. Then

$$\frac{d}{dx}(2^x) = k \cdot 2^x = 0.693 \cdot 2^x.$$

So the derivative of 2^x is proportional to 2^x with constant of proportionality 0.693. A similar calculation shows that the derivative of $f(x) = a^x$ is

$$f'(x) = \lim_{h \to 0} \left(\frac{a^{x+h} - a^x}{h} \right) = \lim_{h \to 0} \left(\frac{a^h - 1}{h} \right) \cdot a^x.$$

Table 3.2

h	$(2^h - 1)/h$
-0.1	0.6697
-0.01	0.6908
-0.001	0.6929
0.001	0.6934
0.01	0.6956
0.1	0.7177

Table 3.3

a	$k = \lim_{h \to 0} \frac{a^h - 1}{h}$
2	0.693
3	1.099
4	1.386
5	1.609
6	1.792
7	1.946

Table 3.4

h	$(1 + h)^{1/h}$
-0.001	2.7196422
-0.0001	2.7184178
-0.00001	2.7182954
0.00001	2.7182682
0.0001	2.7181459
0.001	2.7169239

The quantity $\lim_{h \to 0}(a^h - 1)/h$ is also a constant, although the value of the constant depends on a. Writing $k = \lim_{h \to 0}(a^h - 1)/h$, we see that the derivative of $f(x) = a^x$ is proportional to a^x:

$$\frac{d}{dx}(a^x) = k \cdot a^x.$$

For particular values of a, we can estimate k by substituting values of h near 0 into the expression $(a^h - 1)/h$. Table 3.3 shows the results. Notice that for $a = 2$, the value of k is less than 1, while for $a = 3, 4, 5, \ldots$, the values of k are greater than 1. The values of k appear to be increasing, so we guess that there is a value of a between 2 and 3 for which $k = 1$. If so, we have found a value of a with the remarkable property that the function a^x is equal to its own derivative.

So let us look for such an a. This means we want to find a such that

$$\lim_{h \to 0} \frac{a^h - 1}{h} = 1, \qquad \text{or, for small } h, \qquad \frac{a^h - 1}{h} \approx 1.$$

Solving for a, we can estimate a as follows:

$$a^h - 1 \approx h, \qquad \text{or} \qquad a^h \approx 1 + h, \qquad \text{so} \qquad a \approx (1 + h)^{1/h}.$$

Taking small values of h, as in Table 3.4, we see $a \approx 2.718 \ldots$. This is the number e introduced in Chapter 1. In fact, it can be shown that if

$$e = \lim_{h \to 0}(1 + h)^{1/h} = 2.718 \ldots \quad \text{then} \quad \lim_{h \to 0} \frac{e^h - 1}{h} = 1.$$

This means that e^x is its own derivative:

$$\boxed{\frac{d}{dx}(e^x) - e^x.}$$

Figure 3.11 shows the graphs 2^x, 3^x, and e^x together with their derivatives. Notice that the derivative of 2^x is below the graph of 2^x, since $k < 1$ there, and the graph of the derivative of 3^x is above the graph of 3^x, since $k > 1$ there. With $e \approx 2.718$, the function e^x and its derivative are identical.

Note on Round-Off Error and Limits

If we try to evaluate $(1 + h)^{1/h}$ on a calculator by taking smaller and smaller values of h, the values of $(1 + h)^{1/h}$ at first get closer to $2.718 \ldots$. However, they will eventually move away again because of the *round-off error* (that is, errors introduced by the fact that the calculator can only hold a certain number of digits).

As we try smaller and smaller values of h, how do we know when to stop? Unfortunately, there is no fixed rule. A calculator can only suggest the value of a limit, but can never confirm that this value is correct. In this case, it looks like the limit is $2.718 \ldots$ because the values of $(1 + h)^{1/h}$ approach this number for a while. To be sure this is correct, we have to find the limit analytically.

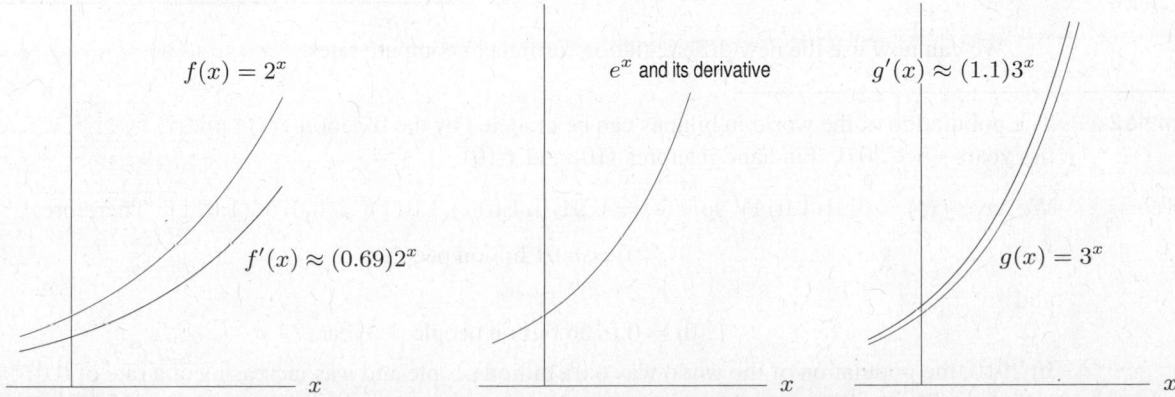

Figure 3.11: Graphs of the functions 2^x, e^x, and 3^x and their derivatives

A Formula for the Derivative of a^x

To get a formula for the derivative of a^x, we must calculate

$$f'(x) = \lim_{h \to 0} \frac{a^{x+h} - a^x}{h} = \underbrace{\left(\lim_{h \to 0} \frac{a^h - 1}{h} \right)}_{k} a^x.$$

However, without knowing the value of a, we can't use a calculator to estimate k. We take a different approach, rewriting $a = e^{\ln a}$, so

$$\lim_{h \to 0} \frac{a^h - 1}{h} = \lim_{h \to 0} \frac{(e^{\ln a})^h - 1}{h} = \lim_{h \to 0} \frac{e^{(\ln a)h} - 1}{h}.$$

To evaluate this limit, we use a limit that we already know:

$$\lim_{h \to 0} \frac{e^h - 1}{h} = 1.$$

In order to use this limit, we substitute $t = (\ln a)h$. Since t approaches 0 as h approaches 0, we have

$$\lim_{h \to 0} \frac{e^{(\ln a)h} - 1}{h} = \lim_{t \to 0} \frac{e^t - 1}{(t/\ln a)} = \lim_{t \to 0} \left(\ln a \cdot \frac{e^t - 1}{t} \right) = \ln a \left(\lim_{t \to 0} \frac{e^t - 1}{t} \right) = (\ln a) \cdot 1 = \ln a.$$

Thus, we have

$$f'(x) = \lim_{h \to 0} \frac{a^{x+h} - a^x}{h} = \left(\lim_{h \to 0} \frac{a^h - 1}{h} \right) a^x = (\ln a) a^x.$$

In Section 3.6 we obtain the same result by another method. We conclude that:

$$\boxed{\frac{d}{dx}(a^x) = (\ln a) a^x.}$$

Thus, for any a, the derivative of a^x is proportional to a^x. The constant of proportionality is $\ln a$. The derivative of a^x is equal to a^x if the constant of proportionality is 1, that is, if $\ln a = 1$, then $a = e$. The fact that the constant of proportionality is 1 when $a = e$ makes e a particularly convenient base for exponential functions.

Example 1   Differentiate $2 \cdot 3^x + 5e^x$.

Solution

$$\frac{d}{dx}(2 \cdot 3^x + 5e^x) = 2\frac{d}{dx}(3^x) + 5\frac{d}{dx}(e^x) = 2\ln 3 \cdot 3^x + 5e^x \approx (2.1972)3^x + 5e^x.$$

We can now use the new differentiation formula to compute rates.

Example 2   The population of the world in billions can be modeled by the function $f(t) = 6.91(1.011)^t$, where t is years since 2010. Find and interpret $f(0)$ and $f'(0)$.

Solution   We have $f(t) = 6.91(1.011)^t$ so $f'(t) = 6.91(\ln 1.011)(1.011)^t = 0.0756(1.011)^t$. Therefore,

$$f(0) = 6.91 \text{ billion people}$$

and

$$f'(0) = 0.0756 \text{ billion people per year.}$$

In 2010, the population of the world was 6.91 billion people and was increasing at a rate of 0.0756 billion, or 75.6 million, people per year.

Exercises and Problems for Section 3.2

Exercises

In Exercises 1–26, find the derivatives of the functions . Assume that a, b, c, and k are constants.

1. $f(x) = 2e^x + x^2$

2. $y = 5t^2 + 4e^t$

3. $f(x) = a^{5x}$

4. $f(x) = 12e^x + 11^x$

5. $y = 5x^2 + 2^x + 3$

6. $f(x) = 2^x + 2 \cdot 3^x$

7. $y = 4 \cdot 10^x - x^3$

8. $z = (\ln 4)e^x$

9. $y = \dfrac{3^x}{3} + \dfrac{33}{\sqrt{x}}$

10. $y = 2^x + \dfrac{2}{x^3}$

11. $z = (\ln 4)4^x$

12. $f(t) = (\ln 3)^t$

13. $y = 5 \cdot 5^t + 6 \cdot 6^t$

14. $h(z) = (\ln 2)^z$

15. $f(x) = e^2 + x^e$

16. $y = \pi^2 + \pi^x$

17. $f(x) = e^\pi + \pi^x$

18. $f(x) = \pi^x + x^\pi$

19. $f(x) = e^k + k^x$

20. $f(x) = e^{1+x}$

21. $f(t) = e^{t+2}$

22. $f(\theta) = e^{k\theta} - 1$

23. $y(x) = a^x + x^a$

24. $f(x) = x^{\pi^2} + (\pi^2)^x$

25. $g(x) = 2x - \dfrac{1}{\sqrt[3]{x}} + 3^x - e$

26. $f(x) = (3x^2 + \pi)(e^x - 4)$

Problems

In Problems 27–37, can the functions be differentiated using the rules developed so far? Differentiate if you can; otherwise, indicate why the rules discussed so far do not apply.

27. $y - x^2 + 2^\pi$

28. $y = \sqrt{x} - \left(\frac{1}{2}\right)^x$

29. $y = x^2 \cdot 2^x$

30. $f(s) = 5^s e^s$

31. $y = e^{x+5}$

32. $y = e^{5x}$

33. $y = 4^{(x^2)}$

34. $f(z) = (\sqrt{4})^z$

35. $f(\theta) - 4^{\sqrt{\theta}}$

36. $f(x) = 4^{(3^x)}$

37. $y = \dfrac{2^x}{x}$

38. An animal population is given by $P(t) = 300(1.044)^t$ where t is the number of years since the study of the population began. Find $P'(5)$ and interpret your result.

39. With a yearly inflation rate of 5%, prices are given by

$$P = P_0(1.05)^t,$$

where P_0 is the price in dollars when $t = 0$ and t is time in years. Suppose $P_0 = 1$. How fast (in cents/year) are prices rising when $t = 10$?

40. The value of an automobile purchased in 2009 can be approximated by the function $V(t) = 25(0.85)^t$, where t is the time, in years, from the date of purchase, and $V(t)$ is the value, in thousands of dollars.

    (a) Evaluate and interpret $V(4)$, including units.

    (b) Find an expression for $V'(t)$, including units.

    (c) Evaluate and interpret $V'(4)$, including units.

    (d) Use $V(t)$, $V'(t)$, and any other considerations you think are relevant to write a paragraph in support of or in opposition to the following statement: "From a monetary point of view, it is best to keep this vehicle as long as possible."

41. In 2009, the population of Mexico was 111 million and growing 1.13% annually, while the population of the US was 307 million and growing 0.975% annually.[1] If we measure growth rates in people/year, which population was growing faster in 2009?

42. Some antique furniture increased very rapidly in price over the past decade. For example, the price of a particular rocking chair is well approximated by

$$V = 75(1.35)^t,$$

where V is in dollars and t is in years since 2000. Find the rate, in dollars per year, at which the price is increasing at time t.

43. (a) Find the slope of the graph of $f(x) = 1 - e^x$ at the point where it crosses the x-axis.

    (b) Find the equation of the tangent line to the curve at this point.

    (c) Find the equation of the line perpendicular to the tangent line at this point. (This is the *normal* line.)

44. Find the value of c in Figure 3.12, where the line l tangent to the graph of $y = 2^x$ at $(0, 1)$ intersects the x-axis.

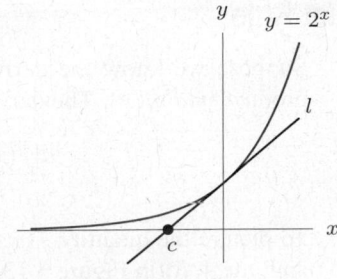

Figure 3.12

[1]https://www.cia.gov/library/publications/the-world-factbook/print/ms.html and https://www.cia.gov/library/publications/the-world-factbook/print/us.html, accessed 4/14/09.

45. Find the quadratic polynomial $g(x) = ax^2 + bx + c$ which best fits the function $f(x) = e^x$ at $x = 0$, in the sense that

$$g(0) = f(0), \text{ and } g'(0) = f'(0), \text{ and } g''(0) = f''(0).$$

Using a computer or calculator, sketch graphs of f and g on the same axes. What do you notice?

46. Using the equation of the tangent line to the graph of e^x at $x = 0$, show that

$$e^x \geq 1 + x$$

for all values of x. A sketch may be helpful.

47. For what value(s) of a are $y = a^x$ and $y = 1 + x$ tangent at $x = 0$? Explain.

48. Explain for which values of a the function a^x is increasing and for which values it is decreasing. Use the fact that, for $a > 0$,

$$\frac{d}{dx}(a^x) = (\ln a)a^x.$$

Strengthen Your Understanding

In Problems 49–50, explain what is wrong with the statement.

49. The derivative of $f(x) = 2^x$ is $f'(x) = x2^{x-1}$.

50. The derivative of $f(x) = \pi^e$ is $f'(x) = e\pi^{e-1}$.

In Problems 51–52, give an example of:

51. An exponential function for which the derivative is always negative.

52. A function f such that $f'''(x) = f(x)$.

Are the statements in Problems 53–55 true or false? Give an explanation for your answer.

53. If $f(x)$ is increasing, then $f'(x)$ is increasing.

54. There is no function such that $f'(x) = f(x)$ for all x.

55. If $f(x)$ is defined for all x, then $f'(x)$ is defined for all x.

3.3 THE PRODUCT AND QUOTIENT RULES

We now know how to find derivatives of powers and exponentials, and of sums and constant multiples of functions. This section shows how to find the derivatives of products and quotients.

Using Δ Notation

To express the difference quotients of general functions, some additional notation is helpful. We write Δf, read "delta f," for a small change in the value of f at the point x,

$$\Delta f = f(x + h) - f(x).$$

In this notation, the derivative is the limit of the ratio $\Delta f / h$:

$$f'(x) = \lim_{h \to 0} \frac{\Delta f}{h}.$$

The Product Rule

Suppose we know the derivatives of $f(x)$ and $g(x)$ and want to calculate the derivative of the product, $f(x)g(x)$. The derivative of the product is calculated by taking the limit, namely,

$$\frac{d[f(x)g(x)]}{dx} = \lim_{h \to 0} \frac{f(x+h)g(x+h) - f(x)g(x)}{h}.$$

To picture the quantity $f(x + h)g(x + h) - f(x)g(x)$, imagine the rectangle with sides $f(x + h)$ and $g(x + h)$ in Figure 3.13, where $\Delta f = f(x + h) - f(x)$ and $\Delta g = g(x + h) - g(x)$. Then

$$f(x + h)g(x + h) - f(x)g(x) = (\text{Area of whole rectangle}) - (\text{Unshaded area})$$

$$= \text{Area of the three shaded rectangles}$$

$$= \Delta f \cdot g(x) + f(x) \cdot \Delta g + \Delta f \cdot \Delta g.$$

Now divide by h:

$$\frac{f(x+h)g(x+h) - f(x)g(x)}{h} = \frac{\Delta f}{h} \cdot g(x) + f(x) \cdot \frac{\Delta g}{h} + \frac{\Delta f \cdot \Delta g}{h}.$$

Figure 3.13: Illustration for the product rule (with Δf, Δg positive)

To evaluate the limit as $h \to 0$, we examine the three terms on the right separately. Notice that

$$\lim_{h \to 0} \frac{\Delta f}{h} \cdot g(x) = f'(x)g(x) \quad \text{and} \quad \lim_{h \to 0} f(x) \cdot \frac{\Delta g}{h} = f(x)g'(x).$$

In the third term we multiply the top and bottom by h to get $\dfrac{\Delta f}{h} \cdot \dfrac{\Delta g}{h} \cdot h$. Then,

$$\lim_{h \to 0} \frac{\Delta f \cdot \Delta g}{h} = \lim_{h \to 0} \frac{\Delta f}{h} \cdot \frac{\Delta g}{h} \cdot h = \lim_{h \to 0} \frac{\Delta f}{h} \cdot \lim_{h \to 0} \frac{\Delta g}{h} \cdot \lim_{h \to 0} h = f'(x) \cdot g'(x) \cdot 0 = 0.$$

Therefore, we conclude that

$$\lim_{h \to 0} \frac{f(x+h)g(x+h) - f(x)g(x)}{h} = \lim_{h \to 0} \left(\frac{\Delta f}{h} \cdot g(x) + f(x) \cdot \frac{\Delta g}{h} + \frac{\Delta f \cdot \Delta g}{h} \right)$$

$$= \lim_{h \to 0} \frac{\Delta f}{h} \cdot g(x) + \lim_{h \to 0} f(x) \cdot \frac{\Delta g}{h} + \lim_{h \to 0} \frac{\Delta f \cdot \Delta g}{h}$$

$$= f'(x)g(x) + f(x)g'(x).$$

Thus we have proved the following rule:

Theorem 3.3: The Product Rule

If $u = f(x)$ and $v = g(x)$ are differentiable, then

$$(fg)' = f'g + fg'.$$

The product rule can also be written

$$\frac{d(uv)}{dx} = \frac{du}{dx} \cdot v + u \cdot \frac{dv}{dx}.$$

In words:

> The derivative of a product is the derivative of the first times the second plus the first times the derivative of the second.

Another justification of the product rule is given in Problem 41 on page 174.

Example 1   Differentiate (a) $x^2 e^x$,   (b) $(3x^2 + 5x)e^x$,   (c) $\dfrac{e^x}{x^2}$.

Solution   (a)

$$\frac{d(x^2 e^x)}{dx} = \left(\frac{d(x^2)}{dx}\right)e^x + x^2\frac{d(e^x)}{dx} = 2xe^x + x^2 e^x = (2x + x^2)e^x.$$

(b)

$$\frac{d((3x^2 + 5x)e^x)}{dx} = \left(\frac{d(3x^2 + 5x)}{dx}\right)e^x + (3x^2 + 5x)\frac{d(e^x)}{dx}$$

$$= (6x + 5)e^x + (3x^2 + 5x)e^x = (3x^2 + 11x + 5)e^x.$$

(c) First we must write $\dfrac{e^x}{x^2}$ as the product $x^{-2}e^x$:

$$\frac{d}{dx}\left(\frac{e^x}{x^2}\right) = \frac{d(x^{-2}e^x)}{dx} = \left(\frac{d(x^{-2})}{dx}\right)e^x + x^{-2}\frac{d(e^x)}{dx}$$

$$= -2x^{-3}e^x + x^{-2}e^x = (-2x^{-3} + x^{-2})e^x.$$

The Quotient Rule

Suppose we want to differentiate a function of the form $Q(x) = f(x)/g(x)$. (Of course, we have to avoid points where $g(x) = 0$.) We want a formula for Q' in terms of f' and g'.

Assuming that $Q(x)$ is differentiable, we can use the product rule on $f(x) = Q(x)g(x)$:

$$f'(x) = Q'(x)g(x) + Q(x)g'(x)$$

$$= Q'(x)g(x) + \frac{f(x)}{g(x)}g'(x).$$

Solving for $Q'(x)$ gives

$$Q'(x) = \frac{f'(x) - \dfrac{f(x)}{g(x)}g'(x)}{g(x)}.$$

Multiplying the top and bottom by $g(x)$ to simplify gives

$$\frac{d}{dx}\left(\frac{f(x)}{g(x)}\right) = \frac{f'(x)g(x) - f(x)g'(x)}{(g(x))^2}.$$

So we have the following rule:

Theorem 3.4: The Quotient Rule

If $u = f(x)$ and $v = g(x)$ are differentiable, then

$$\left(\frac{f}{g}\right)' = \frac{f'g - fg'}{g^2},$$

or equivalently,

$$\frac{d}{dx}\left(\frac{u}{v}\right) = \frac{\dfrac{du}{dx}\cdot v - u\cdot\dfrac{dv}{dx}}{v^2}.$$

In words:

The derivative of a quotient is the derivative of the numerator times the denominator minus the numerator times the derivative of the denominator, all over the denominator squared.

Example 2   Differentiate (a) $\dfrac{5x^2}{x^3 + 1}$,   (b) $\dfrac{1}{1 + e^x}$,   (c) $\dfrac{e^x}{x^2}$.

Solution   (a)

$$\frac{d}{dx}\left(\frac{5x^2}{x^3 + 1}\right) = \frac{\left(\dfrac{d}{dx}(5x^2)\right)(x^3 + 1) - 5x^2\dfrac{d}{dx}(x^3 + 1)}{(x^3 + 1)^2} = \frac{10x(x^3 + 1) - 5x^2(3x^2)}{(x^3 + 1)^2}$$

$$= \frac{-5x^4 + 10x}{(x^3 + 1)^2}.$$

(b)

$$\frac{d}{dx}\left(\frac{1}{1 + e^x}\right) = \frac{\left(\dfrac{d}{dx}(1)\right)(1 + e^x) - 1\dfrac{d}{dx}(1 + e^x)}{(1 + e^x)^2} = \frac{0(1 + e^x) - 1(0 + e^x)}{(1 + e^x)^2}$$

$$= \frac{-e^x}{(1 + e^x)^2}.$$

(c) This is the same as part (c) of Example 1, but this time we do it by the quotient rule.

$$\frac{d}{dx}\left(\frac{e^x}{x^2}\right) = \frac{\left(\dfrac{d(e^x)}{dx}\right)x^2 - e^x\left(\dfrac{d(x^2)}{dx}\right)}{(x^2)^2} = \frac{e^x x^2 - e^x(2x)}{x^4}$$

$$= e^x\left(\frac{x^2 - 2x}{x^4}\right) = e^x\left(\frac{x - 2}{x^3}\right).$$

This is, in fact, the same answer as before, although it looks different. Can you show that it is the same?

Exercises and Problems for Section 3.3

Exercises

1. If $f(x) = x^2(x^3 + 5)$, find $f'(x)$ two ways: by using the product rule and by multiplying out before taking the derivative. Do you get the same result? Should you?

2. If $f(x) = 2^x \cdot 3^x$, find $f'(x)$ two ways: by using the product rule and by using the fact that $2^x \cdot 3^x = 6^x$. Do you get the same result?

For Exercises 3–30, find the derivative. It may be to your advantage to simplify first. Assume that a, b, c, and k are constants.

3. $f(x) = xe^x$

4. $y = x \cdot 2^x$

5. $y = \sqrt{x} \cdot 2^x$

6. $y = (t^2 + 3)e^t$

7. $f(x) = (x^2 - \sqrt{x})3^x$

8. $y = (t^3 - 7t^2 + 1)e^t$

9. $f(x) = \dfrac{x}{e^x}$

10. $g(x) = \dfrac{25x^2}{e^x}$

11. $y = \dfrac{t + 1}{2^t}$

12. $g(w) = \dfrac{w^{3.2}}{5^w}$

13. $q(r) = \dfrac{3r}{5r + 2}$

14. $g(t) = \dfrac{t - 4}{t + 4}$

15. $z = \dfrac{3t + 1}{5t + 2}$

16. $z = \dfrac{t^2 + 5t + 2}{t + 3}$

17. $f(t) = 2te^t - \dfrac{1}{\sqrt{t}}$

18. $f(x) = \dfrac{x^2 + 3}{x}$

19. $w = \dfrac{y^3 - 6y^2 + 7y}{y}$

20. $g(t) = \dfrac{4}{3 + \sqrt{t}}$

21. $f(z) = \dfrac{z^2 + 1}{\sqrt{z}}$

22. $w = \dfrac{5 - 3z}{5 + 3z}$

23. $h(r) = \dfrac{r^2}{2r + 1}$

24. $f(z) = \dfrac{3z^2}{5z^2 + 7z}$

25. $w(x) = \dfrac{17e^x}{2^x}$

26. $h(p) = \dfrac{1 + p^2}{3 + 2p^2}$

27. $f(x) = \dfrac{x^2 + 3x + 2}{x + 1}$

28. $f(x) = \dfrac{ax + b}{cx + k}$

29. $y = \left(x^2 + 5\right)^3 \left(3x^3 - 2\right)^2$

30. $f(x) = (2 - 4x - 3x^2)(6x^e - 3\pi)$

Problems

In Problems 31–33, use Figure 3.14 and the product or quotient rule to estimate the derivative, or state why the rules of this section do not apply. The graph of $f(x)$ has a sharp corner at $x = 2$.

Figure 3.14

31. Let $h(x) = f(x) \cdot g(x)$. Find:

    (a) $h'(1)$ **(b)** $h'(2)$ **(c)** $h'(3)$

32. Let $k(x) = (f(x))/(g(x))$. Find:

    (a) $k'(1)$ **(b)** $k'(2)$ **(c)** $k'(3)$

33. Let $j(x) = (g(x))/(f(x))$. Find:

    (a) $j'(1)$ **(b)** $j'(2)$ **(c)** $j'(3)$

For Problems 34–39, let $h(x) = f(x) \cdot g(x)$, and $k(x) = f(x)/g(x)$, and $l(x) = g(x)/f(x)$. Use Figure 3.15 to estimate the derivatives.

Figure 3.15

34. $h'(1)$ **35.** $k'(1)$ **36.** $h'(2)$

37. $k'(2)$ **38.** $l'(1)$ **39.** $l'(2)$

40. Differentiate $f(t) = e^{-t}$ by writing it as $f(t) = \dfrac{1}{e^t}$.

41. Differentiate $f(x) = e^{2x}$ by writing it as $f(x) = e^x \cdot e^x$.

42. Differentiate $f(x) = e^{3x}$ by writing it as $f(x) = e^x \cdot e^{2x}$ and using the result of Problem 41.

43. For what intervals is $f(x) = xe^x$ concave up?

44. For what intervals is $g(x) = \dfrac{1}{x^2 + 1}$ concave down?

45. Find the equation of the tangent line to the graph of $f(x) = \dfrac{2x - 5}{x + 1}$ at the point at which $x = 0$.

46. Find the equation of the tangent line at $x = 1$ to $y = f(x)$ where $f(x) = \dfrac{3x^2}{5x^2 + 7x}$.

47. **(a)** Differentiate $y = \dfrac{e^x}{x}$, $y = \dfrac{e^x}{x^2}$, and $y = \dfrac{e^x}{x^3}$.

    (b) What do you anticipate the derivative of $y = \dfrac{e^x}{x^n}$ will be? Confirm your guess.

In Problems 48–51, the functions $f(x)$, $g(x)$, and $h(x)$ are differentiable for all values of x. Find the derivative of each of the following functions, using symbols such as $f(x)$ and $f'(x)$ in your answers as necessary.

48. $x^2 f(x)$ **49.** $4^x (f(x) + g(x))$

50. $\dfrac{f(x)}{g(x) + 1}$ **51.** $\dfrac{f(x)g(x)}{h(x)}$

52. Suppose f and g are differentiable functions with the values shown in the following table. For each of the following functions h, find $h'(2)$.

    (a) $h(x) = f(x) + g(x)$ **(b)** $h(x) = f(x)g(x)$

    (c) $h(x) = \dfrac{f(x)}{g(x)}$

x	$f(x)$	$g(x)$	$f'(x)$	$g'(x)$
2	3	4	5	-2

53. If $H(3) = 1, H'(3) = 3, F(3) = 5, F'(3) = 4$, find:

    (a) $G'(3)$ if $G(z) = F(z) \cdot H(z)$
    (b) $G'(3)$ if $G(w) = F(w)/H(w)$

54. Let $f(3) = 6$, $g(3) = 12$, $f'(3) = \frac{1}{2}$, and $g'(3) = \frac{4}{3}$. Evaluate the following when $x = 3$.

$$(f(x)g(x))' - (g(x) - 4f'(x))$$

55. Find a possible formula for a function $y = f(x)$ such that $f'(x) = 10x^9 e^x + x^{10} e^x$.

56. The quantity, q, of a certain skateboard sold depends on the selling price, p, in dollars, so we write $q = f(p)$. You are given that $f(140) = 15{,}000$ and $f'(140) = -100$.

    (a) What do $f(140) = 15{,}000$ and $f'(140) = -100$ tell you about the sales of skateboards?

    (b) The total revenue, R, earned by the sale of skateboards is given by $R = pq$. Find $\left.\dfrac{dR}{dp}\right|_{p=140}$.

    (c) What is the sign of $\left.\dfrac{dR}{dp}\right|_{p=140}$? If the skateboards are currently selling for \$140, what happens to revenue if the price is increased to \$141?

57. When an electric current passes through two resistors with resistance r_1 and r_2, connected in parallel, the combined resistance, R, can be calculated from the equation

$$\frac{1}{R} = \frac{1}{r_1} + \frac{1}{r_2}.$$

Find the rate at which the combined resistance changes with respect to changes in r_1. Assume that r_2 is constant.

58. A museum has decided to sell one of its paintings and to invest the proceeds. If the picture is sold between the years 2000 and 2020 and the money from the sale is invested in a bank account earning 5% interest per year compounded annually, then $B(t)$, the balance in the year 2020, depends on the year, t, in which the painting is sold and the sale price $P(t)$. If t is measured from the year 2000 so that $0 < t < 20$ then

$$B(t) = P(t)(1.05)^{20-t}.$$

(a) Explain why $B(t)$ is given by this formula.
(b) Show that the formula for $B(t)$ is equivalent to

$$B(t) = (1.05)^{20}\frac{P(t)}{(1.05)^t}.$$

(c) Find $B'(10)$, given that $P(10) = 150{,}000$ and $P'(10) = 5000$.

59. Let $f(v)$ be the gas consumption (in liters/km) of a car going at velocity v (in km/hr). In other words, $f(v)$ tells you how many liters of gas the car uses to go one kilometer, if it is going at velocity v. You are told that

$$f(80) = 0.05 \text{ and } f'(80) = 0.0005.$$

(a) Let $g(v)$ be the distance the same car goes on one liter of gas at velocity v. What is the relationship between $f(v)$ and $g(v)$? Find $g(80)$ and $g'(80)$.
(b) Let $h(v)$ be the gas consumption in liters per hour. In other words, $h(v)$ tells you how many liters of gas the car uses in one hour if it is going at velocity v. What is the relationship between $h(v)$ and $f(v)$? Find $h(80)$ and $h'(80)$.
(c) How would you explain the practical meaning of the values of these functions and their derivatives to a driver who knows no calculus?

60. The function $f(x) = e^x$ has the properties

$$f'(x) = f(x) \text{ and } f(0) = 1.$$

Explain why $f(x)$ is the only function with both these properties. [Hint: Assume $g'(x) = g(x)$, and $g(0) = 1$, for some function $g(x)$. Define $h(x) = g(x)/e^x$, and compute $h'(x)$. Then use the fact that a function with a derivative of 0 must be a constant function.]

61. Find $f'(x)$ for the following functions with the product rule, rather than by multiplying out.

(a) $f(x) = (x-1)(x-2)$.
(b) $f(x) = (x-1)(x-2)(x-3)$.
(c) $f(x) = (x-1)(x-2)(x-3)(x-4)$.

62. Use the answer from Problem 61 to guess $f'(x)$ for the following function:

$$f(x) = (x-r_1)(x-r_2)(x-r_3)\cdots(x-r_n)$$

where $r_1, r_2, \ldots, r_n$ are any real numbers.

63. (a) Provide a three-dimensional analogue for the geometrical demonstration of the formula for the derivative of a product, given in Figure 3.13 on page 137. In other words, find a formula for the derivative of $F(x) \cdot G(x) \cdot H(x)$ using Figure 3.16.
(b) Confirm your results by writing $F(x) \cdot G(x) \cdot H(x)$ as $[F(x) \cdot G(x)] \cdot H(x)$ and using the product rule twice.
(c) Generalize your result to n functions: what is the derivative of

$$f_1(x) \cdot f_2(x) \cdot f_3(x) \cdots f_n(x)?$$

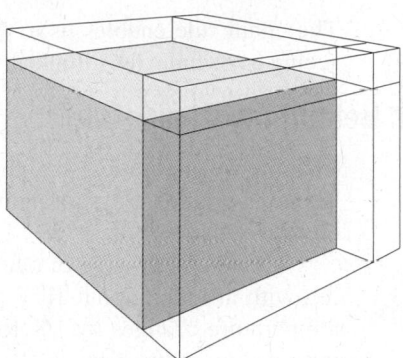

Figure 3.16: A graphical representation of the three-dimensional product rule

64. If $P(x) = (x-a)^2 Q(x)$, where $Q(x)$ is a polynomial and $Q(a) \neq 0$, we call $x = a$ a double zero of the polynomial $P(x)$.

(a) If $x = a$ is a double zero of a polynomial $P(x)$, show that $P(a) = P'(a) = 0$.
(b) If $P(x)$ is a polynomial and $P(a) = P'(a) = 0$, show that $x = a$ is a double zero of $P(x)$.

65. Find and simplify $\dfrac{d^2}{dx^2}\left(f(x)g(x)\right)$.

Strengthen Your Understanding

In Problems 66–68, explain what is wrong with the statement.

66. The derivative of $f(x) = x^2 e^x$ is $f'(x) = 2xe^x$.

67. Differentiating $f(x) = x/(x+1)$ by the quotient rule

gives

$$f'(x) = \frac{x\frac{d}{dx}(x+1) - (x+1)\frac{d}{dx}(x)}{(x+1)^2}.$$

68. The quotient $f(x) = (x+1)/e^{-x}$ cannot be differentiated using the product rule.

In Problems 69–70, give an example of:

69. A function involving a sine and an exponential that can be differentiated using the product rule or the quotient rule.

70. A function $f(x)$ that can be differentiated both using the product rule and in some other way.

Are the statements in Problems 71–73 true or false? Give an explanation for your answer.

71. Let f and g be two functions whose second derivatives are defined. Then

$$(fg)'' = fg'' + f''g.$$

72. If the function $f(x)/g(x)$ is defined but not differentiable at $x = 1$, then either $f(x)$ or $g(x)$ is not differentiable at $x = 1$.

73. Suppose that f'' and g'' exist and f and g are concave up for all x, then $f(x)g(x)$ is concave up for all x.

74. Which of the following would be a counterexample to the product rule?

(a) Two differentiable functions f and g satisfying $(fg)' = f'g'$.

(b) A differentiable function f such that $(xf(x))' = xf'(x) + f(x)$.

(c) A differentiable function f such that $(f(x)^2)' = 2f(x)$.

(d) Two differentiable functions f and g such that $f'(a) = 0$ and $g'(a) = 0$ and fg has positive slope at $x = a$.

3.4 THE CHAIN RULE

The chain rule enables us to differentiate composite functions such as $\sqrt{x^2 + 1}$ or e^{-x^2}. Before seeing a formula, let's think about the derivative of a composite function in a practical situation.

Intuition Behind the Chain Rule

Imagine we are moving straight upward in a hot air balloon. Let y be our distance from the ground. The temperature, H, is changing as a function of altitude, so $H = f(y)$. How does our temperature change with time?

The rate of change of our temperature is affected both by how fast the temperature is changing with altitude (about $16°F$ per mile), and by how fast we are climbing (say 2 mph). Then our temperature changes by $16°$ for every mile we climb, and since we move 2 miles in an hour, our temperature changes by $16 \cdot 2 = 32$ degrees in an hour.

Since temperature is a function of height, $H = f(y)$, and height is a function of time, $y = g(t)$, we can think of temperature as a composite function of time, $H = f(g(t))$, with f as the outside function and g as the inside function. The example suggests the following result, which turns out to be true:

$$\boxed{\begin{array}{ccc} \text{Rate of change} & & \text{Rate of change} & & \text{Rate of change} \\ \text{of composite function} & = & \text{of outside function} & \times & \text{of inside function} \end{array}}$$

The Derivative of a Composition of Functions

We now obtain a formula for the chain rule. Suppose $f(g(x))$ is a composite function, with f being the outside function and g being the inside. Let us write

$$z = g(x) \quad \text{and} \quad y = f(z), \quad \text{so} \quad y = f(g(x)).$$

Then a small change in x, called Δx, generates a small change in z, called Δz. In turn, Δz generates a small change in y called Δy. Provided Δx and Δz are not zero, we can say:

$$\frac{\Delta y}{\Delta x} = \frac{\Delta y}{\Delta z} \cdot \frac{\Delta z}{\Delta x}.$$

Since $\dfrac{dy}{dx} = \lim\limits_{\Delta x \to 0} \dfrac{\Delta y}{\Delta x}$, this suggests that in the limit as Δx, Δy, and Δz get smaller and smaller, we have:

The Chain Rule

$$\frac{dy}{dx} = \frac{dy}{dz} \cdot \frac{dz}{dx}.$$

In other words:

> The rate of change of a composite function is the product of the rates of change of the outside and inside functions.

Since $\frac{dy}{dz} = f'(z)$ and $\frac{dz}{dx} = g'(x)$, we can also write

$$\frac{d}{dx} f(g(x)) = f'(z) \cdot g'(x).$$

Substituting $z = g(x)$, we can rewrite this as follows:

Theorem 3.5: The Chain Rule

If f and g are differentiable functions, then

$$\frac{d}{dx} f(g(x)) = f'(g(x)) \cdot g'(x).$$

In words:

> The derivative of a composite function is the product of the derivatives of the outside and inside functions. The derivative of the outside function must be evaluated at the inside function.

A justification of the chain rule is given in Problem 42 on page 175. The following example shows how units confirm that the rate of change of a composite function is the product of the rates of change of the outside and inside functions.

Example 1   The length, L, in micrometers (μm), of steel depends on the air temperature, $H°$C, and the temperature H depends on time, t, measured in hours. If the length of a steel bridge increases by $0.2\ \mu$m for every degree increase in temperature, and the temperature is increasing at $3°$C per hour, how fast is the length of the bridge increasing? What are the units for your answer?

Solution   We want to know how much the length of the bridge changes in one hour; this rate is in μm/hr. We are told that the length of the bridge changes by $0.2\ \mu$m for each degree that the temperature changes, and that the temperature changes by $3°$C each hour. Thus, in one hour, the length of the bridge changes by $0.2 \cdot 3 = 0.6\ \mu$m.

Now we do the same calculation using derivative notation and the chain rule. We know that

$$\text{Rate length increasing with respect to temperature} = \frac{dL}{dH} = 0.2\ \mu\text{m/}°\text{C}$$

$$\text{Rate temperature increasing with respect to time} = \frac{dH}{dt} = 3°\text{C/hr}.$$

We want to calculate the rate at which the length is increasing with respect to time, or dL/dt. We think of L as a function of H, and H as a function of t. The chain rule tells us that

$$\frac{dL}{dt} = \frac{dL}{dH} \cdot \frac{dH}{dt} = \left(0.2 \frac{\mu\text{m}}{°\text{C}} \right) \cdot \left(3 \frac{°\text{C}}{\text{hr}} \right) = 0.6\ \mu\text{m/hr}.$$

Thus, the length is increasing at $0.6\ \mu$m/hr. Notice that the units work out as we expect.

Example 1 shows us how to interpret the chain rule in practical terms. The next examples show how the chain rule is used to compute derivatives of functions given by formulas.

Example 2 Find the derivatives of the following functions:

(a) $(x^2 + 1)^{100}$ (b) $\sqrt{3x^2 + 5x - 2}$ (c) $\dfrac{1}{x^2 + x^4}$ (d) e^{3x} (e) e^{x^2}

Solution

(a) Here $z = g(x) = x^2 + 1$ is the inside function; $f(z) = z^{100}$ is the outside function. Now $g'(x) = 2x$ and $f'(z) = 100z^{99}$, so

$$\frac{d}{dx}((x^2 + 1)^{100}) = 100z^{99} \cdot 2x = 100(x^2 + 1)^{99} \cdot 2x = 200x(x^2 + 1)^{99}.$$

(b) Here $z = g(x) = 3x^2 + 5x - 2$ and $f(z) = \sqrt{z}$, so $g'(x) = 6x + 5$ and $f'(z) = \dfrac{1}{2\sqrt{z}}$. Hence

$$\frac{d}{dx}(\sqrt{3x^2 + 5x - 2}) = \frac{1}{2\sqrt{z}} \cdot (6x + 5) = \frac{1}{2\sqrt{3x^2 + 5x - 2}} \cdot (6x + 5).$$

(c) Let $z = g(x) = x^2 + x^4$ and $f(z) = 1/z$, so $g'(x) = 2x + 4x^3$ and $f'(z) = -z^{-2} = -\dfrac{1}{z^2}$. Then

$$\frac{d}{dx}\left(\frac{1}{x^2 + x^4}\right) = -\frac{1}{z^2}(2x + 4x^3) = -\frac{2x + 4x^3}{(x^2 + x^4)^2}.$$

We could have done this problem using the quotient rule. Try it and see that you get the same answer!

(d) Let $z = g(x) = 3x$ and $f(z) = e^z$. Then $g'(x) = 3$ and $f'(z) = e^z$, so

$$\frac{d}{dx}\left(e^{3x}\right) = e^z \cdot 3 = 3e^{3x}.$$

(e) To figure out which is the inside function and which is the outside, notice that to evaluate e^{x^2} we first evaluate x^2 and then take e to that power. This tells us that the inside function is $z = g(x) = x^2$ and the outside function is $f(z) = e^z$. Therefore, $g'(x) = 2x$, and $f'(z) = e^z$, giving

$$\frac{d}{dx}(e^{x^2}) = e^z \cdot 2x = e^{x^2} \cdot 2x = 2xe^{x^2}.$$

To differentiate a complicated function, we may have to use the chain rule more than once, as in the following example.

Example 3 Differentiate: (a) $\sqrt{e^{-x/7} + 5}$ (b) $(1 - e^{2\sqrt{t}})^{19}$

Solution

(a) Let $z = g(x) = e^{-x/7} + 5$ be the inside function; let $f(z) = \sqrt{z}$ be the outside function. Now $f'(z) = \dfrac{1}{2\sqrt{z}}$, but we need the chain rule to find $g'(x)$.

We choose inside and outside functions whose composition is $g(x)$. Let $u = h(x) = -x/7$ and $k(u) = e^u + 5$ so $g(x) = k(h(x)) = e^{-x/7} + 5$. Then $h'(x) = -1/7$ and $k'(u) = e^u$, so

$$g'(x) = e^u \cdot \left(-\frac{1}{7}\right) = -\frac{1}{7}e^{-x/7}.$$

Using the chain rule to combine the derivatives of $f(z)$ and $g(x)$, we have

$$\frac{d}{dx}(\sqrt{e^{-x/7} + 5}) = \frac{1}{2\sqrt{z}}\left(-\frac{1}{7}e^{-x/7}\right) = -\frac{e^{-x/7}}{14\sqrt{e^{-x/7} + 5}}.$$

(b) Let $z = g(t) = 1 - e^{2\sqrt{t}}$ be the inside function and $f(z) = z^{19}$ be the outside function. Then $f'(z) = 19z^{18}$ but we need the chain rule to differentiate $g(t)$.

Now we choose $u = h(t) = 2\sqrt{t}$ and $k(u) = 1 - e^u$, so $g(t) = k(h(t))$. Then $h'(t) = 2 \cdot \frac{1}{2} t^{-1/2} = \frac{1}{\sqrt{t}}$ and $k'(u) = -e^u$, so

$$g'(t) = -e^u \cdot \frac{1}{\sqrt{t}} = -\frac{e^{2\sqrt{t}}}{\sqrt{t}}.$$

Using the chain rule to combine the derivatives of $f(z)$ and $g(t)$, we have

$$\frac{d}{dx}(1 - e^{2\sqrt{t}})^{19} = 19z^{18}\left(-\frac{e^{2\sqrt{t}}}{\sqrt{t}}\right) = -19\frac{e^{2\sqrt{t}}}{\sqrt{t}}\left(1 - e^{2\sqrt{t}}\right)^{18}.$$

It is often faster to use the chain rule without introducing new variables, as in the following examples.

Example 4   Differentiate $\sqrt{1 + e^{\sqrt{3+x^2}}}$.

Solution   The chain rule is needed four times:

$$\frac{d}{dx}\left(\sqrt{1 + e^{\sqrt{3+x^2}}}\right) = \frac{1}{2}\left(1 + e^{\sqrt{3+x^2}}\right)^{-1/2} \cdot \frac{d}{dx}\left(1 + e^{\sqrt{3+x^2}}\right)$$

$$= \frac{1}{2}\left(1 + e^{\sqrt{3+x^2}}\right)^{-1/2} \cdot e^{\sqrt{3+x^2}} \cdot \frac{d}{dx}\left(\sqrt{3+x^2}\right)$$

$$= \frac{1}{2}\left(1 + e^{\sqrt{3+x^2}}\right)^{-1/2} \cdot e^{\sqrt{3+x^2}} \cdot \frac{1}{2}\left(3+x^2\right)^{-1/2} \cdot \frac{d}{dx}\left(3+x^2\right)$$

$$= \frac{1}{2}\left(1 + e^{\sqrt{3+x^2}}\right)^{-1/2} \cdot e^{\sqrt{3+x^2}} \cdot \frac{1}{2}\left(3+x^2\right)^{-1/2} \cdot 2x.$$

Example 5   Find the derivative of e^{2x} by the chain rule and by the product rule.

Solution   Using the chain rule, we have

$$\frac{d}{dx}(e^{2x}) = e^{2x} \cdot \frac{d}{dx}(2x) = e^{2x} \cdot 2 = 2e^{2x}.$$

Using the product rule, we write $e^{2x} = e^x \cdot e^x$. Then

$$\frac{d}{dx}(e^{2x}) = \frac{d}{dx}(e^x e^x) = \left(\frac{d}{dx}(e^x)\right)e^x + e^x\left(\frac{d}{dx}(e^x)\right) = e^x \cdot e^x + e^x \cdot e^x = 2e^{2x}.$$

Using the Product and Chain Rules to Differentiate a Quotient

If you prefer, you can differentiate a quotient by the product and chain rules, instead of by the quotient rule. The resulting formulas may look different, but they will be equivalent.

Example 6   Find $k'(x)$ if $k(x) = \dfrac{x}{x^2 + 1}$.

Solution   One way is to use the quotient rule:

$$k'(x) = \frac{1 \cdot (x^2 + 1) - x \cdot (2x)}{(x^2 + 1)^2}$$

$$= \frac{1 - x^2}{(x^2 + 1)^2}.$$

Alternatively, we can write the original function as a product,

$$k(x) = x\frac{1}{x^2 + 1} = x \cdot (x^2 + 1)^{-1},$$

and use the product rule:

$$k'(x) = 1 \cdot (x^2 + 1)^{-1} + x \cdot \frac{d}{dx}\left[(x^2 + 1)^{-1}\right].$$

Now use the chain rule to differentiate $(x^2 + 1)^{-1}$, giving

$$\frac{d}{dx}\left[(x^2 + 1)^{-1}\right] = -(x^2 + 1)^{-2} \cdot 2x = \frac{-2x}{(x^2 + 1)^2}.$$

Therefore,

$$k'(x) = \frac{1}{x^2 + 1} + x \cdot \frac{-2x}{(x^2 + 1)^2} = \frac{1}{x^2 + 1} - \frac{2x^2}{(x^2 + 1)^2}.$$

Putting these two fractions over a common denominator gives the same answer as the quotient rule.

Exercises and Problems for Section 3.4

Exercises

In Exercises 1–56, find the derivatives. Assume that a and b are constants.

1. $f(x) = (x + 1)^{99}$

2. $w = (t^3 + 1)^{100}$

3. $g(x) = (4x^2 + 1)^7$

4. $f(x) = \sqrt{1 - x^2}$

5. $y = \sqrt{e^x + 1}$

6. $w = (\sqrt{t} + 1)^{100}$

7. $h(w) = (w^4 - 2w)^5$

8. $s(t) = (3t^2 + 4t + 1)^3$

9. $w(r) = \sqrt{r^4 + 1}$

10. $k(x) = (x^3 + e^x)^4$

11. $f(x) = e^{2x}\left(x^2 + 5^x\right)$

12. $y = e^{3w/2}$

13. $g(x) = e^{\pi x}$

14. $B = 15e^{0.20t}$

15. $w = 100e^{-x^2}$

16. $f(\theta) = 2^{-\theta}$

17. $y = \pi^{(x+2)}$

18. $g(x) = 3^{(2x+7)}$

19. $f(t) = te^{5-2t}$

20. $p(t) = e^{4t+2}$

21. $v(t) = t^2 e^{-ct}$

22. $g(t) = e^{(1+3t)^2}$

23. $w = e^{\sqrt{s}}$

24. $y = e^{-4t}$

25. $y = \sqrt{s^3 + 1}$

26. $y = te^{-t^2}$

27. $f(z) = \sqrt{z}e^{-z}$

28. $z(x) = \sqrt[3]{2^x + 5}$

29. $z = 2^{5t-3}$

30. $w = \sqrt{(x^2 \cdot 5^x)^3}$

31. $f(y) = \sqrt{10^{(5-y)}}$

32. $f(z) = \frac{\sqrt{z}}{e^z}$

33. $y = \frac{\sqrt{z}}{2^z}$

34. $y = \left(\frac{x^2 + 2}{3}\right)^2$

35. $h(x) = \sqrt{\frac{x^2 + 9}{x + 3}}$

36. $y = \frac{e^x - e^{-x}}{e^x + e^{-x}}$

37. $y = \frac{1}{e^{3x} + x^2}$

38. $h(z) = \left(\frac{b}{a + z^2}\right)^4$

39. $f(x) = \frac{1}{\sqrt{x^3 + 1}}$

40. $f(z) = \frac{1}{(e^z + 1)^2}$

41. $w = (t^2 + 3t)(1 - e^{-2t})$

42. $h(x) = 2e^{3x}$

43. $f(x) = 6e^{5x} + e^{-x^2}$

44. $f(x) = e^{-(x-1)^2}$

45. $f(w) = (5w^2 + 3)e^{w^2}$

46. $f(\theta) = (e^\theta + e^{-\theta})^{-1}$

47. $y = \sqrt{e^{-3t^2} + 5}$

48. $z = (te^{3t} + e^{5t})^9$

49. $f(y) = e^{e^{(y^2)}}$

50. $f(t) = 2e^{-2e^{2t}}$

51. $f(x) = (ax^2 + b)^3$

52. $f(t) = ae^{bt}$

53. $f(x) = axe^{-bx}$

54. $g(\alpha) = e^{\alpha e^{-2\alpha}}$

55. $y = ae^{-be^{-cx}}$

56. $y = \left(e^x - e^{-x}\right)^2$

Problems

In Problems 57–60, use Figure 3.17 and the chain rule to estimate the derivative, or state why the chain rule does not apply. The graph of $f(x)$ has a sharp corner at $x = 2$.

Figure 3.17

57. Let $h(x) = f(g(x))$. Find:

   (a) $h'(1)$ **(b)** $h'(2)$ **(c)** $h'(3)$

58. Let $u(x) = g(f(x))$. Find:

   (a) $u'(1)$ **(b)** $u'(2)$ **(c)** $u'(3)$

59. Let $v(x) = f(f(x))$. Find:

   (a) $v'(1)$ **(b)** $v'(2)$ **(c)** $v'(3)$

60. Let $w(x) = g(g(x))$. Find:

   (a) $w'(1)$ **(b)** $w'(2)$ **(c)** $w'(3)$

In Problems 61–64, use Figure 3.18 to evaluate the derivative.

Figure 3.18

61. $\frac{d}{dx} f(g(x))|_{x=30}$ **62.** $\frac{d}{dx} f(g(x))|_{x=70}$

63. $\frac{d}{dx} g(f(x))|_{x=30}$ **64.** $\frac{d}{dx} g(f(x))|_{x=70}$

65. Find the equation of the tangent line to $f(x) = (x-1)^3$ at the point where $x = 2$.

66. Find the equation of the line tangent to $y = f(x)$ at $x = 1$, where $f(x)$ is the function in Exercise 43.

67. Find the equation of the line tangent to $f(t) = 100e^{-0.3t}$ at $t = 2$.

68. For what values of x is the graph of $y = e^{-x^2}$ concave down?

69. For what intervals is $f(x) = xe^{-x}$ concave down?

70. Suppose $f(x) = (2x+1)^{10}(3x-1)^7$. Find a formula for $f'(x)$. Decide on a reasonable way to simplify your result, and find a formula for $f''(x)$.

71. A fish population is approximated by $P(t) = 10e^{0.6t}$, where t is in months. Calculate and use units to explain what each of the following tells us about the population:

   (a) $P(12)$ **(b)** $P'(12)$

72. Find the mean and variance of the normal distribution of statistics using parts (a) and (b) with $m(t) = e^{\mu t + \sigma^2 t^2 / 2}$.

   (a) Mean $= m'(0)$
   (b) Variance $= m''(0) - (m'(0))^2$

73. If the derivative of $y = k(x)$ equals 2 when $x = 1$, what is the derivative of

   (a) $k(2x)$ when $x = \frac{1}{2}$?
   (b) $k(x+1)$ when $x = 0$?
   (c) $k\left(\frac{1}{4}x\right)$ when $x = 4$?

74. Is $x = \sqrt[3]{2t+5}$ a solution to the equation $3x^2 \frac{dx}{dt} = 2$? Why or why not?

75. Find a possible formula for a function $m(x)$ such that $m'(x) = x^5 \cdot e^{(x^6)}$.

76. Given $F(2) = 1, F'(2) = 5, F(4) = 3, F'(4) = 7$ and $G(4) = 2, G'(4) = 6, G(3) = 4, G'(3) = 8$, find:

   (a) $H(4)$ if $H(x) = F(G(x))$
   (b) $H'(4)$ if $H(x) = F(G(x))$
   (c) $H(4)$ if $H(x) = G(F(x))$
   (d) $H'(4)$ if $H(x) = G(F(x))$
   (e) $H'(4)$ if $H(x) = F(x)/G(x)$

77. Given $y = f(x)$ with $f(1) = 4$ and $f'(1) = 3$, find

   (a) $g'(1)$ if $g(x) = \sqrt{f(x)}$.
   (b) $h'(1)$ if $h(x) = f(\sqrt{x})$.

78. Figure 3.19 is the graph of $f(x)$. Let $h(x) = e^{f(x)}$ and $p(x) = f(e^x)$. Estimate the solution(s) to the equations

   (a) $h'(x) = 0$ **(b)** $p'(x) = 0$

Figure 3.19

In Problems 79–83, use Figures 3.20 and 3.21 and $h(x) = f(g(x))$.

Figure 3.20

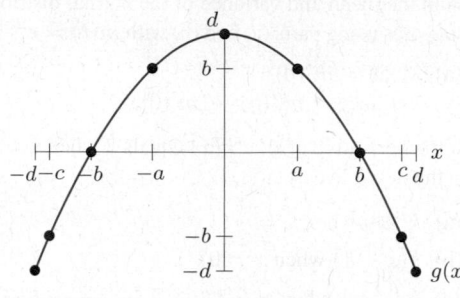

Figure 3.21

79. Evaluate $h(0)$ and $h'(0)$.

80. At $x = -c$, is h positive, negative, or zero? Increasing or decreasing?

81. At $x = a$, is h increasing or decreasing?

82. What are the signs of $h(d)$ and $h'(d)$?

83. How does the value of $h(x)$ change on the interval $-d < x < -b$?

84. The world's population[2] is about $f(t) = 6.91e^{0.011t}$ billion, where t is time in years since 2010. Find $f(0)$, $f'(0)$, $f(10)$, and $f'(10)$. Using units, interpret your answers in terms of population.

85. The 2010 Census[3] determined the population of the US was 308.75 million on April 1, 2010. If the population was increasing exponentially at a rate of 2.85 million per year on that date, find a formula for the population as a function of time, t, in years since that date.

86. Since the 1950s, the carbon dioxide concentration in the air has been recorded at the Mauna Loa Observatory in Hawaii.[4] A graph of this data is called the Keeling Curve, after Charles Keeling, who started recording the data. With t in years since 1950, fitting functions to the data gives three models for the carbon dioxide concentration in parts per million (ppm):

$$f(t) = 303 + 1.3t$$
$$g(t) = 304e^{0.0038t}$$
$$h(t) = 0.0135t^2 + 0.5133t + 310.5.$$

(a) What family of function is used in each model?

(b) Find the rate of change of carbon dioxide in 2010 in each of the three models. Give units.

(c) Arrange the three models in increasing order of the rates of change they give for 2010. (Which model predicts the largest rate of change in 2010? Which predicts the smallest?)

(d) Consider the same three models for all positive time t. Will the ordering in part (c) remain the same for all t? If not, how will it change?

87. Annual net sales for the Hershey Company, in billion dollars, in t years from 2008 can be approximated by $f(t) = 5.1e^{0.043t}$. Find $f(5)$ and $f'(5)$. Give units and interpret in terms of Hershey sales.

88. A yam is put in a hot oven, maintained at a constant temperature 200°C. At time $t = 30$ minutes, the temperature T of the yam is 120° and is increasing at an (instantaneous) rate of 2°/min. Newton's law of cooling (or, in our case, warming) implies that the temperature at time t is given by

$$T(t) = 200 - ae^{-bt}.$$

Find a and b.

89. If you invest P dollars in a bank account at an annual interest rate of $r\%$, then after t years you will have B dollars, where

$$B = P\left(1 + \frac{r}{100}\right)^t.$$

(a) Find dB/dt, assuming P and r are constant. In terms of money, what does dB/dt represent?

(b) Find dB/dr, assuming P and t are constant. In terms of money, what does dB/dr represent?

90. The balance in a bank account t years after money is deposited is given by $f(t) = 1000e^{0.08t}$ dollars.

(a) How much money was deposited? What is the interest rate earned by the account?

(b) Find $f(10)$ and $f'(10)$. Give units and interpret in terms of balance in the account.

91. The theory of relativity predicts that an object whose mass is m_0 when it is at rest will appear heavier when moving at speeds near the speed of light. When the object is moving at speed v, its mass m is given by

$$m = \frac{m_0}{\sqrt{1 - (v^2/c^2)}}, \qquad \text{where } c \text{ is the speed of light.}$$

(a) Find dm/dv.

(b) In terms of physics, what does dm/dv tell you?

---

[2] http://www.indexmundi.com/world/. Accessed April 27, 2011.

[3] http://2010.census.gov/2010census/

[4] www.esrl.hoaa.gov/gmd/ccgg

92. The charge, Q, on a capacitor which starts discharging at time $t = 0$ is given by

$$Q = \begin{cases} Q_0 & \text{for } t \leq 0 \\ Q_0 e^{-t/RC} & \text{for } t > 0, \end{cases}$$

where R and C are positive constants depending on the circuit and Q_0 is the charge at $t = 0$, where $Q_0 \neq 0$. The current, I, flowing in the circuit is given by $I = dQ/dt$.

(a) Find the current I for $t < 0$ and for $t > 0$.
(b) Is it possible to define I at $t = 0$?
(c) Is the function Q differentiable at $t = 0$?

93. A polynomial f is said to have a *zero of multiplicity* m at $x = a$ if

$$f(x) = (x - a)^m h(x),$$

with h a polynomial such that $h(a) \neq 0$. Explain why a polynomial having a zero of multiplicity m at $x = a$ satisfies $f^{(p)}(a) = 0$, for $p = 1, 2, \ldots m - 1$.
[Note: $f^{(p)}$ is the pth derivative.]

94. Find and simplify $\dfrac{d^2}{dx^2}(f(g(x)))$.

95. Find and simplify $\dfrac{d^2}{dx^2}\left(\dfrac{f(x)}{g(x)}\right)$ using the product and chain rules.

Strengthen Your Understanding

In Problems 96–97, explain what is wrong with the statement.

96. The derivative of $g(x) = (e^x + 2)^5$ is $g'(x) = 5(e^x + 2)^4$.

97. The derivative of $w(x) = e^{x^2}$ is $w'(x) = e^{x^2}$.

In Problems 98–99, give an example of:

98. A function involving a sine and an exponential that requires the chain rule to differentite.

99. A function that can be differentiated both using the chain rule and by another method.

Are the statements in Problems 100–102 true or false? If a statement is true, explain how you know. If a statement is false, give a counterexample.

100. $(fg)'(x)$ is never equal to $f'(x)g'(x)$.

101. If the derivative of $f(g(x))$ is equal to the derivative of $f(x)$ for all x, then $g(x) = x$ for all x.

102. Suppose that f'' and g'' exist and that f and g are concave up for all x, then $f(g(x))$ is concave up for all x.

3.5 THE TRIGONOMETRIC FUNCTIONS

Derivatives of the Sine and Cosine

Since the sine and cosine functions are periodic, their derivatives must be periodic also. (Why?) Let's look at the graph of $f(x) = \sin x$ in Figure 3.22 and estimate the derivative function graphically.

$$f(x) = \sin x$$

Figure 3.22: The sine function

First we might ask where the derivative is zero. (At $x = \pm\pi/2, \pm3\pi/2, \pm5\pi/2$, etc.) Then ask where the derivative is positive and where it is negative. (Positive for $-\pi/2 < x < \pi/2$, negative for $\pi/2 < x < 3\pi/2$, etc.) Since the largest positive slopes are at $x = 0, 2\pi$, and so on, and the largest negative slopes are at $x = \pi, 3\pi$, and so on, we get something like the graph in Figure 3.23.

$$f'(x)$$

Figure 3.23: Derivative of $f(x) = \sin x$

The graph of the derivative in Figure 3.23 looks suspiciously like the graph of the cosine function. This might lead us to conjecture, quite correctly, that the derivative of the sine is the cosine.

Of course, we cannot be sure, just from the graphs, that the derivative of the sine really is the cosine. However, for now we'll assume that the derivative of the sine *is* the cosine and confirm the result at the end of the section.

One thing we can do now is to check that the derivative function in Figure 3.23 has amplitude 1 (as it ought to if it is the cosine). That means we have to convince ourselves that the derivative of $f(x) = \sin x$ is 1 when $x = 0$. The next example suggests that this is true when x is in radians.

Example 1   Using a calculator set in radians, estimate the derivative of $f(x) = \sin x$ at $x = 0$.

Solution   Since $f(x) = \sin x$,

$$f'(0) = \lim_{h \to 0} \frac{\sin(0 + h) - \sin 0}{h} = \lim_{h \to 0} \frac{\sin h}{h}.$$

Table 3.5 contains values of $(\sin h)/h$ which suggest that this limit is 1, so we estimate

$$f'(0) = \lim_{h \to 0} \frac{\sin h}{h} = 1.$$

Table 3.5

h (radians)	-0.1	-0.01	-0.001	-0.0001	0.0001	0.001	0.01	0.1
$(\sin h)/h$	0.99833	0.99998	1.0000	1.0000	1.0000	1.0000	0.99998	0.99833

Warning: It is important to notice that in the previous example h was in *radians*; any conclusions we have drawn about the derivative of $\sin x$ are valid *only* when x is in radians. If you find the derivative with h in degrees, you get a different result.

Example 2   Starting with the graph of the cosine function, sketch a graph of its derivative.

Solution   The graph of $g(x) = \cos x$ is in Figure 3.24(a). Its derivative is 0 at $x = 0, \pm\pi, \pm2\pi$, and so on; it is positive for $-\pi < x < 0$, $\pi < x < 2\pi$, and so on; and it is negative for $0 < x < \pi$, $2\pi < x < 3\pi$, and so on. The derivative is in Figure 3.24(b).

Figure 3.24: $g(x) = \cos x$ and its derivative, $g'(x)$

As we did with the sine, we use the graphs to make a conjecture. The derivative of the cosine in Figure 3.24(b) looks exactly like the graph of sine, except reflected across the x-axis. But how can we be sure that the derivative is $-\sin x$?

Example 3   Use the relation $\dfrac{d}{dx}(\sin x) = \cos x$ to show that $\dfrac{d}{dx}(\cos x) = -\sin x$.

Solution   Since the cosine function is the sine function shifted to the left by $\pi/2$ (that is, $\cos x = \sin(x + \pi/2)$), we expect the derivative of the cosine to be the derivative of the sine, shifted to the left by $\pi/2$. Differentiating using the chain rule:

$$\frac{d}{dx}(\cos x) = \frac{d}{dx}\left(\sin\left(x + \frac{\pi}{2}\right)\right) = \cos\left(x + \frac{\pi}{2}\right).$$

But $\cos(x + \pi/2)$ is the cosine shifted to the left by $\pi/2$, which gives a sine curve reflected across the x-axis. So we have

$$\frac{d}{dx}(\cos x) = \cos\left(x + \frac{\pi}{2}\right) = -\sin x.$$

At the end of this section and in Problems 66 and 67, we show that our conjectures for the derivatives of $\sin x$ and $\cos x$ are correct. Thus, we have:

$$\boxed{\text{For } x \text{ in radians,} \qquad \frac{d}{dx}(\sin x) = \cos x \quad \text{and} \quad \frac{d}{dx}(\cos x) = -\sin x.}$$

Example 4 Differentiate (a) $\ 2\sin(3\theta)$, (b) $\ \cos^2 x$, (c) $\ \cos(x^2)$, (d) $\ e^{-\sin t}$.

Solution Use the chain rule:

(a) $\dfrac{d}{d\theta}(2\sin(3\theta)) = 2\dfrac{d}{d\theta}(\sin(3\theta)) = 2(\cos(3\theta))\dfrac{d}{d\theta}(3\theta) = 2(\cos(3\theta))3 = 6\cos(3\theta).$

(b) $\dfrac{d}{dx}(\cos^2 x) = \dfrac{d}{dx}\left((\cos x)^2\right) = 2(\cos x)\cdot\dfrac{d}{dx}(\cos x) = 2(\cos x)(-\sin x) = -2\cos x \sin x.$

(c) $\dfrac{d}{dx}\left(\cos(x^2)\right) = -\sin(x^2)\cdot\dfrac{d}{dx}(x^2) = -2x\sin(x^2).$

(d) $\dfrac{d}{dt}(e^{-\sin t}) = e^{-\sin t}\dfrac{d}{dt}(-\sin t) = -(\cos t)e^{-\sin t}.$

Derivative of the Tangent Function

Since $\tan x = \sin x/\cos x$, we differentiate $\tan x$ using the quotient rule. Writing $(\sin x)'$ for $d(\sin x)/dx$, we have:

$$\frac{d}{dx}(\tan x) = \frac{d}{dx}\left(\frac{\sin x}{\cos x}\right) = \frac{(\sin x)'(\cos x) - (\sin x)(\cos x)'}{\cos^2 x} = \frac{\cos^2 x + \sin^2 x}{\cos^2 x} = \frac{1}{\cos^2 x}.$$

$$\boxed{\text{For } x \text{ in radians,} \qquad \frac{d}{dx}(\tan x) = \frac{1}{\cos^2 x}.}$$

The graphs of $f(x) = \tan x$ and $f'(x) = 1/\cos^2 x$ are in Figure 3.25. Is it reasonable that f' is always positive? Are the asymptotes of f' where we expect?

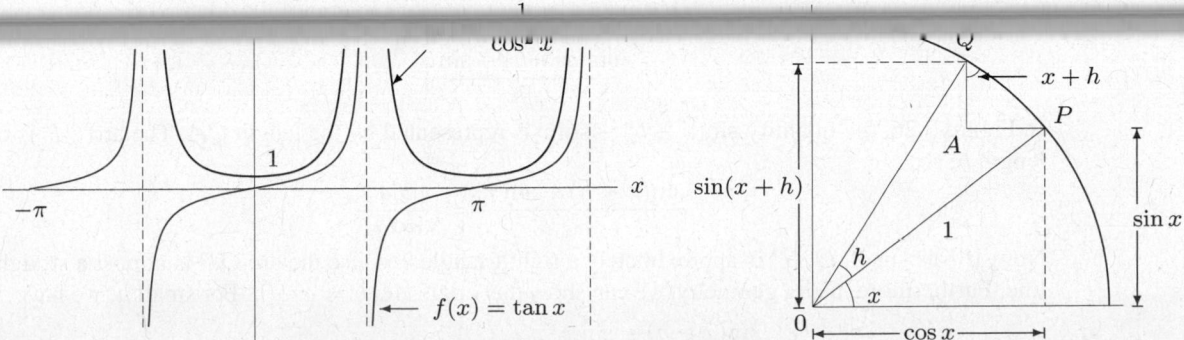

Figure 3.25: The function $\tan x$ and its derivative

Figure 3.26: Unit circle showing $\sin(x + h)$ and $\sin x$

Example 5   Differentiate (a) $2\tan(3t)$,   (b) $\tan(1-\theta)$,   (c) $\dfrac{1+\tan t}{1-\tan t}$.

Solution   (a) Use the chain rule:

$$\frac{d}{dt}(2\tan(3t)) = 2\frac{1}{\cos^2(3t)}\frac{d}{dt}(3t) = \frac{6}{\cos^2(3t)}.$$

(b) Use the chain rule:

$$\frac{d}{d\theta}(\tan(1-\theta)) = \frac{1}{\cos^2(1-\theta)} \cdot \frac{d}{d\theta}(1-\theta) = -\frac{1}{\cos^2(1-\theta)}.$$

(c) Use the quotient rule:

$$\frac{d}{dt}\left(\frac{1+\tan t}{1-\tan t}\right) = \frac{\frac{d}{dt}(1+\tan t)(1-\tan t) - (1+\tan t)\frac{d}{dt}(1-\tan t)}{(1-\tan t)^2}$$

$$= \frac{\frac{1}{\cos^2 t}(1-\tan t) - (1+\tan t)\left(-\frac{1}{\cos^2 t}\right)}{(1-\tan t)^2}$$

$$= \frac{2}{\cos^2 t \cdot (1-\tan t)^2}.$$

Example 6   The Bay of Fundy in Canada is known for extreme tides. The depth of the water, y, in meters can be modeled as a function of time, t, in hours after midnight, by

$$y = 10 + 7.5\cos(0.507t).$$

How quickly is the depth of the water rising or falling at 6:00 am and at 9:00 am?

Solution   To find how fast the water depth is changing, we compute the derivative of y, using the chain rule:

$$\frac{dy}{dt} = -7.5(0.507)\sin(0.507t) = -3.8025\sin(0.507t).$$

When $t = 6$, we have $\dfrac{dy}{dt} = -3.8025\sin(0.507 \cdot 6) = -0.378$ meters/hour. So the tide is falling at 0.378 meters/hour.

When $t = 9$, we have $\dfrac{dy}{dt} = -3.8025\sin(0.507 \cdot 9) = 3.760$ meters/hour. So the tide is rising at 3.760 meters/hour.

Informal Justification of $\frac{d}{dx}(\sin x) = \cos x$

Consider the unit circle in Figure 3.26. To find the derivative of $\sin x$, we need to estimate

$$\frac{\sin(x+h) - \sin x}{h}.$$

In Figure 3.26, the quantity $\sin(x+h) - \sin x$ is represented by the length QA. The arc QP is of length h, so

$$\frac{\sin(x+h) - \sin x}{h} = \frac{QA}{\text{Arc } QP}.$$

Now, if h is small, QAP is approximately a right triangle because the arc QP is almost a straight line. Furthermore, using geometry, we can show that angle $AQP = x + h$. For small h, we have

$$\frac{\sin(x+h) - \sin x}{h} = \frac{QA}{\text{Arc } QP} \approx \cos(x+h).$$

As $h \to 0$, the approximation gets better, so

$$\frac{d}{dx}(\sin x) = \lim_{h \to 0} \frac{\sin(x+h) - \sin x}{h} = \cos x.$$

Other derivations of this result are given in Problems 66 and 67 on pages 154–155.

Exercises and Problems for Section 3.5

Exercises

1. Construct a table of values for $\cos x$, $x = 0, 0.1, 0.2, \ldots, 0.6$. Using the difference quotient, estimate the derivative at these points (use $h = 0.001$), and compare it with $-\sin x$.

In Exercises 2–47, find the derivatives of the functions. Assume a, b, and c are constants.

2. $r(\theta) = \sin \theta + \cos \theta$

3. $s(\theta) = \cos \theta \sin \theta$

4. $z = \cos(4\theta)$

5. $f(x) = \sin(3x)$

6. $y = 5 \sin(3t)$

7. $P = 4 \cos(2t)$

8. $g(x) = \sin(2 - 3x)$

9. $R(x) = 10 - 3\cos(\pi x)$

10. $g(\theta) = \sin^2(2\theta) - \pi\theta$

11. $g(t) = (2 + \sin(\pi t))^3$

12. $f(x) = x^2 \cos x$

13. $w = \sin(e^t)$

14. $f(x) = e^{\cos x}$

15. $f(y) = e^{\sin y}$

16. $z = \theta e^{\cos \theta}$

17. $R(\theta) = e^{\sin(3\theta)}$

18. $g(\theta) = \sin(\tan \theta)$

19. $w(x) = \tan(x^2)$

20. $f(x) = \sqrt{1 - \cos x}$

21. $f(x) = \sqrt{3 + \sin(8x)}$

22. $f(x) = \cos(\sin x)$

23. $f(x) = \tan(\sin x)$

24. $k(x) = \sqrt{(\sin(2x))^3}$

25. $f(x) = 2x \sin(3x)$

26. $y = e^\theta \sin(2\theta)$

27. $f(x) = e^{-2x} \cdot \sin x$

28. $z = \sqrt{\sin t}$

29. $y = \sin^5 \theta$

30. $g(z) = \tan(e^z)$

31. $z = \tan(e^{-3\theta})$

32. $w = e^{-\sin \theta}$

33. $Q = \cos(e^{2x})$

34. $h(t) = t \cos t + \tan t$

35. $f(\alpha) = \cos \alpha + 3 \sin \alpha$

36. $k(\alpha) = \sin^5 \alpha \cos^3 \alpha$

37. $f(\theta) = \theta^3 \cos \theta$

38. $y = \cos^2 w + \cos(w^2)$

39. $y = \sin(\sin x + \cos x)$

40. $y = \sin(2x) \cdot \sin(3x)$

41. $P = \frac{\cos t}{t^3}$

42. $t(\theta) = \frac{\cos \theta}{\sin \theta}$

43. $f(x) = \sqrt{\frac{1 - \sin x}{1 - \cos x}}$

44. $r(y) = \frac{y}{\cos y + a}$

45. $G(x) = \frac{\sin^2 x + 1}{\cos^2 x + 1}$

46. $y = a \sin(bt) + c$

47. $P = a \cos(bt + c)$

Problems

48. Is the graph of $y = \sin(x^4)$ increasing or decreasing when $x = 10$? Is it concave up or concave down?

49. Find the line tangent to $f(t) = 3 \sin(2t) + 5$ at the point where $t = \pi$.

50. Find the 50th derivative of $y = \cos x$.

51. Find $d^2 w / dt^2$ as a function of x if $dx/dt = x \sin x$.

52. Find a possible formula for the function $q(x)$ such that

$$q'(x) = \frac{e^x \cdot \sin x - e^x \cdot \cos x}{(\sin x)^2}.$$

53. Find a function $F(x)$ satisfying $F'(x) = \sin(4x)$.

54. Let $f(x) = \sin^2 x + \cos^2 x$.

    (a) Find $f'(x)$ using the formula for $f(x)$ and derivative formulas from this section. Simplify your answer.

(b) Use a trigonometric identity to check your answer to part (a). Explain.

55. Let $f'(x) = \sin\left(x^2\right)$, Find $h''(x)$ if $h(x) = f\left(x^2\right)$.

56. On page 39 the depth, y, in feet, of water in Boston harbor is given in terms of t, the number of hours since midnight, by

$$y = 5 + 4.9 \cos\left(\frac{\pi}{6}t\right).$$

    (a) Find dy/dt. What does dy/dt represent, in terms of water level?

    (b) For $0 \le t \le 24$, when is dy/dt zero? (Figure 1.55 on page 39 may be helpful.) Explain what it means (in terms of water level) for dy/dt to be zero.

57. A boat at anchor is bobbing up and down in the sea. The vertical distance, y, in feet, between the sea floor and the boat is given as a function of time, t, in minutes, by

$$y = 15 + \sin(2\pi t).$$

(a) Find the vertical velocity, v, of the boat at time t.

(b) Make rough sketches of y and v against t.

58. The voltage, V, in volts, in an electrical outlet is given as a function of time, t, in seconds, by the function $V = 156 \cos(120\pi t)$.

(a) Give an expression for the rate of change of voltage with respect to time.

(b) Is the rate of change ever zero? Explain.

(c) What is the maximum value of the rate of change?

59. An oscillating mass at the end of a spring is at a distance y from its equilibrium position given by

$$y = A\sin\left(\left(\sqrt{\frac{k}{m}}\right)t\right).$$

The constant k measures the stiffness of the spring.

(a) Find a time at which the mass is farthest from its equilibrium position. Find a time at which the mass is moving fastest. Find a time at which the mass is accelerating fastest.

(b) What is the period, T, of the oscillation?

(c) Find dT/dm. What does the sign of dT/dm tell you?

60. With t in years, the population of a herd of deer is represented by

$$P(t) = 4000 + 500\sin\left(2\pi t - \frac{\pi}{2}\right).$$

(a) How does this population vary with time? Graph $P(t)$ for one year.

(b) When in the year the population is a maximum? What is that maximum? Is there a minimum? If so, when?

(c) When is the population growing fastest? When is it decreasing fastest?

(d) How fast is the population changing on July 1?

61. An environmentalist reports that the depth of the water in a new reservoir is approximated by

$$h = d(t) = \begin{cases} kt & 0 \le t \le 2 \\ 50 + \sin(0.1t) & t > 2, \end{cases}$$

where t is in weeks since the date the reservoir was completed and h is in meters.

(a) During what period was the reservoir filling at a constant rate? What was that rate?

(b) In this model, is the rate at which the water level is changing defined for all times $t > 0$? Explain.

62. The metal bar of length l in Figure 3.27 has one end attached at the point P to a circle of radius a. Point Q at the other end can slide back and forth along the x-axis.

(a) Find x as a function of θ.

(b) Assume lengths are in centimeters and the angular speed ($d\theta/dt$) is 2 radians/second counterclockwise. Find the speed at which the point Q is moving when

(i) $\theta = \pi/2$,   (ii) $\theta = \pi/4$.

Figure 3.27

63. Find the equations of the tangent lines to the graph of $f(x) = \sin x$ at $x = 0$ and at $x = \pi/3$. Use each tangent line to approximate $\sin(\pi/6)$. Would you expect these results to be equally accurate, since they are taken equally far away from $x = \pi/6$ but on opposite sides? If the accuracy is different, can you account for the difference?

64. If $k \ge 1$, the graphs of $y = \sin x$ and $y = ke^{-x}$ intersect for $x \ge 0$. Find the smallest value of k for which the graphs are tangent. What are the coordinates of the point of tangency?

65. A wave travels along a string that is joined to a thicker rope. The wave both reflects back along the string and is transmitted to the rope. For positive constants k_1, k_2, w and time t, the wave along the string, given by $x < 0$, is

$$f(x) = \cos(k_1 x - wt) + R\cos(-k_1 x - wt)$$

and the wave along the rope, given by $x > 0$, is

$$g(x) = T\cos(k_2 x - wt).$$

For every value of t, the two waves have the same tangent line at $x = 0$, so they have the same value and same slope at $x = 0$. Use this fact to show that

$$R = \frac{k_1 - k_2}{k_1 + k_2} \quad \text{and} \quad T = \frac{2k_1}{k_1 + k_2}.$$

These amplitudes are called the *reflection coefficient*, R, and the *transmission coefficient*, T.

66. We will use the following identities to calculate the derivatives of $\sin x$ and $\cos x$:

$$\sin(a + b) = \sin a \cos b + \cos a \sin b$$
$$\cos(a + b) = \cos a \cos b - \sin a \sin b.$$

(a) Use the definition of the derivative to show that if $f(x) = \sin x$,

$$f'(x) = \sin x \lim_{h \to 0} \frac{\cos h - 1}{h} + \cos x \lim_{h \to 0} \frac{\sin h}{h}.$$

(b) Estimate the limits in part (a) with your calculator to explain why $f'(x) = \cos x$.

(c) If $g(x) = \cos x$, use the definition of the derivative to show that $g'(x) = -\sin x$.

67. In this problem you will calculate the derivative of $\tan \theta$ rigorously (and without using the derivatives of $\sin \theta$ or $\cos \theta$). You will then use your result for $\tan \theta$ to calculate the derivatives of $\sin \theta$ and $\cos \theta$. Figure 3.28 shows $\tan \theta$ and $\Delta(\tan \theta)$, which is the change in $\tan \theta$, namely $\tan(\theta + \Delta \theta) - \tan \theta$.

(a) By paying particular attention to how the two figures relate and using the fact that

$$\frac{\text{Area of}}{\text{Sector OAQ}} \leq \frac{\text{Area of}}{\text{Triangle OQR}} \leq \frac{\text{Area of}}{\text{Sector OBR}}$$

explain why

$$\frac{\Delta\theta}{2\pi} \cdot \frac{\pi}{(\cos\theta)^2} \leq \frac{\Delta(\tan\theta)}{2} \leq \frac{\Delta\theta}{2\pi} \cdot \frac{\pi}{(\cos(\theta + \Delta\theta))^2}.$$

[Hint: A sector of a circle with angle α at the center has area $\alpha/(2\pi)$ times the area of the whole circle.]

(b) Use part (a) to show as $\Delta\theta \to 0$ that

$$\frac{\Delta \tan \theta}{\Delta \theta} \to \left(\frac{1}{\cos \theta}\right)^2,$$

and hence that $\dfrac{d(\tan\theta)}{d\theta} = \left(\dfrac{1}{\cos\theta}\right)^2.$

(c) Derive the identity $(\tan\theta)^2 + 1 = \left(\dfrac{1}{\cos\theta}\right)^2.$ Then differentiate both sides of this identity with respect to θ, using the chain rule and the result of part (b) to show that $\dfrac{d}{d\theta}(\cos\theta) = -\sin\theta.$

(d) Differentiate both sides of the identity $(\sin\theta)^2 + (\cos\theta)^2 = 1$ and use the result of part (c) to show that $\dfrac{d}{d\theta}(\sin\theta) = \cos\theta.$

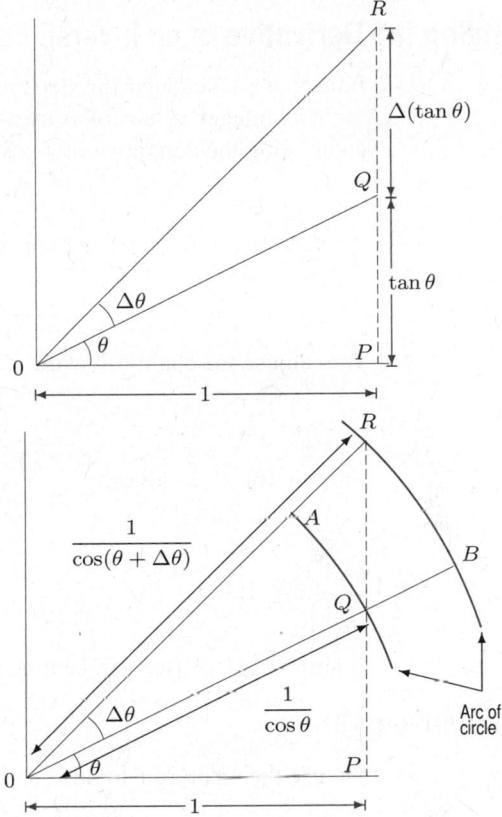

Figure 3.28: $\tan\theta$ and $\Delta(\tan\theta)$

Strengthen Your Understanding

In Problems 68–69, explain what is wrong with the statement.

68. The derivative of $n(x) = \sin(\cos x)$ is $n'(x) = \cos(-\sin x)$.

69. The derivative of $f(x) = \sin(\sin x)$ is $f'(x) = (\cos x)(\sin x) + (\sin x)(\cos x)$.

In Problems 70–71, give an example of:

70. A trigonometric function whose derivative must be calculated using the chain rule.

71. A function $f(x)$ such that $f''(x) = -f(x)$.

Are the statements in Problems 72–74 true or false? Give an explanation for your answer.

72. The derivative of $\tan\theta$ is periodic.

73. If a function is periodic, with period c, then so is its derivative.

74. The only functions whose fourth derivatives are equal to $\cos t$ are of the form $\cos t + C$, where C is any constant.

3.6 THE CHAIN RULE AND INVERSE FUNCTIONS

In this section we will use the chain rule to calculate the derivatives of fractional powers, logarithms, exponentials, and the inverse trigonometric functions.[5] The same method is used to obtain a formula for the derivative of a general inverse function.

Finding the Derivative of an Inverse Function: Derivative of $x^{1/2}$

Earlier we calculated the derivative of x^n with n an integer, but we have been using the result for non-integer values of n as well. We now confirm that the power rule holds for $n = 1/2$ by calculating the derivative of $f(x) = x^{1/2}$ using the chain rule. Since

$$(f(x))^2 = x,$$

the derivative of $(f(x))^2$ and the derivative of x must be equal, so

$$\frac{d}{dx}(f(x))^2 = \frac{d}{dx}(x).$$

We can use the chain rule with $f(x)$ as the inside function to obtain:

$$\frac{d}{dx}(f(x))^2 = 2f(x) \cdot f'(x) = 1.$$

Solving for $f'(x)$ gives

$$f'(x) = \frac{1}{2f(x)} = \frac{1}{2x^{1/2}},$$

or

$$\frac{d}{dx}(x^{1/2}) = \frac{1}{2x^{1/2}} = \frac{1}{2}x^{-1/2}.$$

A similar calculation can be used to obtain the derivative of $x^{1/n}$ where n is a positive integer.

Derivative of $\ln x$

We use the chain rule to differentiate an identity involving $\ln x$. Since $e^{\ln x} = x$, we have

$$\frac{d}{dx}(e^{\ln x}) = \frac{d}{dx}(x),$$

$$e^{\ln x} \cdot \frac{d}{dx}(\ln x) = 1. \qquad \text{(Since } e^x \text{ is outside function and } \ln x \text{ is inside function)}$$

Solving for $d(\ln x)/dx$ gives

$$\frac{d}{dx}(\ln x) = \frac{1}{e^{\ln x}} = \frac{1}{x},$$

so

$$\boxed{\frac{d}{dx}(\ln x) = \frac{1}{x}.}$$

Example 1   Differentiate (a) $\ln(x^2 + 1)$ (b) $t^2 \ln t$ (c) $\sqrt{1 + \ln(1 - y)}$.

Solution   (a) Using the chain rule:

$$\frac{d}{dx}\left(\ln(x^2 + 1)\right) = \frac{1}{x^2 + 1}\frac{d}{dx}(x^2 + 1) = \frac{2x}{x^2 + 1}.$$

(b) Using the product rule:

$$\frac{d}{dt}(t^2 \ln t) = \frac{d}{dt}(t^2) \cdot \ln t + t^2 \frac{d}{dt}(\ln t) = 2t \ln t + t^2 \cdot \frac{1}{t} = 2t \ln t + t.$$

---

[5]It requires a separate justification, not given here, that these functions are differentiable.

(c) Using the chain rule:

$$\frac{d}{dy}\left(\sqrt{1+\ln(1-y)}\right) = \frac{d}{dy}\left(1+\ln(1-y)\right)^{1/2}$$

$$= \frac{1}{2}\left(1+\ln(1-y)\right)^{-1/2} \cdot \frac{d}{dy}\left(1+\ln(1-y)\right) \qquad \text{(Using the chain rule)}$$

$$= \frac{1}{2\sqrt{1+\ln(1-y)}} \cdot \frac{1}{1-y} \cdot \frac{d}{dy}(1-y) \qquad \text{(Using the chain rule again)}$$

$$= \frac{-1}{2(1-y)\sqrt{1+\ln(1-y)}}.$$

Derivative of a^x

In Section 3.2, we saw that the derivative of a^x is proportional to a^x. Now we see another way of calculating the constant of proportionality. We use the identity

$$\ln(a^x) = x\ln a.$$

Differentiating both sides, using $\dfrac{d}{dx}(\ln x) = \dfrac{1}{x}$ and the chain rule, and remembering that $\ln a$ is a constant, we obtain:

$$\frac{d}{dx}(\ln a^x) = \frac{1}{a^x} \cdot \frac{d}{dx}(a^x) = \ln a.$$

Solving gives the result we obtained earlier:

$$\boxed{\frac{d}{dx}(a^x) = (\ln a)a^x.}$$

Derivatives of Inverse Trigonometric Functions

In Section 1.5 we defined $\arcsin x$ as the angle between $-\pi/2$ and $\pi/2$ (inclusive) whose sine is x. Similarly, $\arctan x$ as the angle strictly between $-\pi/2$ and $\pi/2$ whose tangent is x. To find $\dfrac{d}{dx}(\arctan x)$ we use the identity $\tan(\arctan x) = x$. Differentiating using the chain rule gives

$$\frac{1}{\cos^2(\arctan x)} \cdot \frac{d}{dx}(\arctan x) = 1,$$

so

$$\frac{d}{dx}(\arctan x) = \cos^2(\arctan x).$$

Using the identity $1 + \tan^2\theta = \dfrac{1}{\cos^2\theta}$, and replacing θ by $\arctan x$, we have

$$\cos^2(\arctan x) = \frac{1}{1+\tan^2(\arctan x)} = \frac{1}{1+x^2}.$$

Thus we have

$$\boxed{\frac{d}{dx}(\arctan x) = \frac{1}{1+x^2}.}$$

By a similar argument, we obtain the result:

$$\frac{d}{dx}(\arcsin x) = \frac{1}{\sqrt{1-x^2}}.$$

Example 2   Differentiate (a) $\arctan(t^2)$ (b) $\arcsin(\tan\theta)$.

Solution   Use the chain rule:

(a) $\dfrac{d}{dt}\left(\arctan(t^2)\right) = \dfrac{1}{1+(t^2)^2}\cdot\dfrac{d}{dt}(t^2) = \dfrac{2t}{1+t^4}.$

(b) $\dfrac{d}{dt}\left(\arcsin(\tan\theta)\right) = \dfrac{1}{\sqrt{1-(\tan\theta)^2}}\cdot\dfrac{d}{d\theta}(\tan\theta) = \dfrac{1}{\sqrt{1-\tan^2\theta}}\cdot\dfrac{1}{\cos^2\theta}.$

Derivative of a General Inverse Function

Each of the previous results gives the derivative of an inverse function. In general, if a function f has a differentiable inverse, f^{-1}, we find its derivative by differentiating $f(f^{-1}(x)) = x$ by the chain rule:

$$\frac{d}{dx}\left(f\left(f^{-1}(x)\right)\right) = 1$$

$$f'\left(f^{-1}(x)\right)\cdot\frac{d}{dx}\left(f^{-1}(x)\right) = 1$$

so

$$\frac{d}{dx}\left(f^{-1}(x)\right) = \frac{1}{f'(f^{-1}(x))}.$$

Thus, the derivative of the inverse is the reciprocal of the derivative of the original function, but evaluated at the point $f^{-1}(x)$ instead of the point x.

Example 3   Figure 3.29 shows $f(x)$ and $f^{-1}(x)$. Using Table 3.6, find

(a) (i) $f(2)$ (ii) $f^{-1}(2)$ (iii) $f'(2)$ (iv) $(f^{-1})'(2)$

(b) The equation of the tangent lines at the points P and Q.

(c) What is the relationship between the two tangent lines?

Table 3.6

x	$f(x)$	$f'(x)$
0	1	0.7
1	2	1.4
2	4	2.8
3	8	5.5

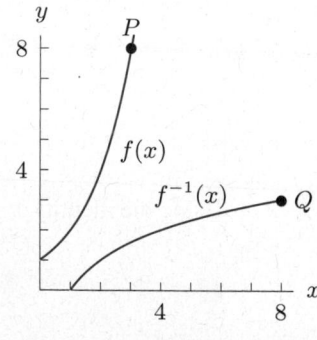

Figure 3.29

Solution   (a) Reading from the table, we have

(i) $f(2) = 4$.

(ii) $f^{-1}(2) = 1$.

(iii) $f'(2) = 2.8$.

(iv) To find the derivative of the inverse function, we use

$$(f^{-1})'(2) = \frac{1}{f'(f^{-1}(2))} = \frac{1}{f'(1)} = \frac{1}{1.4} = 0.714.$$

Notice that the derivative of f^{-1} is the reciprocal of the derivative of f. However, the derivative of f^{-1} is evaluated at 2, while the derivative of f is evaluated at 1, where $f^{-1}(2) = 1$ and $f(1) = 2$.

(b) At the point P, we have $f(3) = 8$ and $f'(3) = 5.5$, so the equation of the tangent line at P is

$$y - 8 = 5.5(x - 3).$$

At the point Q, we have $f^{-1}(8) = 3$, so the slope at Q is

$$(f^{-1})'(8) = \frac{1}{f'(f^{-1}(8))} = \frac{1}{f'(3)} = \frac{1}{5.5}.$$

Thus, the equation of the tangent line at Q is

$$y - 3 = \frac{1}{5.5}(x - 8).$$

(c) The two tangent lines have reciprocal slopes, and the points $(3, 8)$ and $(8, 3)$ are reflections of one another in the line $y = x$. Thus, the two tangent lines are reflections of one another in the line $y = x$.

Exercises and Problems for Section 3.6

Exercises

For Exercises 1–41, find the derivative. It may be to your advantage to simplify before differentiating. Assume a, b, c, and k are constants.

1. $f(t) = \ln(t^2 + 1)$

2. $f(x) = \ln(1 - x)$

3. $f(x) = \ln(5x^2 + 3)$

4. $y = 2x^2 + 3\ln x$

5. $y = \arcsin(x + 1)$

6. $f(x) = \arctan(3x)$

7. $P = 3\ln(x^2 + 5x + 3)$

8. $Q = a\ln(bx + c)$

9. $f(x) = \ln(e^{2x})$

10. $f(x) = e^{\ln(e^{2x^2 + 3})}$

11. $f(x) = \ln(1 - e^{-x})$

12. $f(\alpha) = \ln(\sin \alpha)$

13. $f(x) = \ln(e^x + 1)$

14. $y = x\ln x - x + 2$

15. $j(x) = \ln(e^{ax} + b)$

16. $y = x^3 \ln x$

17. $h(w) = w^3 \ln(10w)$

18. $f(x) = \ln(e^{7x})$

19. $f(x) = e^{(\ln x) + 1}$

20. $f(\theta) = \ln(\cos \theta)$

21. $f(t) = \ln(e^{\ln t})$

22. $f(y) = \arcsin(y^2)$

23. $s(x) = \arctan(2 - x)$

24. $g(\alpha) = \sin(\arcsin \alpha)$

25. $g(t) = e^{\arctan(3t^2)}$

26. $g(t) = \cos(\ln t)$

27. $h(z) = z^{\ln 2}$

28. $h(w) = w \arcsin w$

29. $f(x) = e^{\ln(kx)}$

30. $r(t) = \arcsin(2t)$

31. $j(x) = \cos\left(\sin^{-1} x\right)$

32. $f(x) = \cos(\arctan 3x)$

33. $f(z) = \dfrac{1}{\ln z}$

34. $g(t) = \dfrac{\ln(kt) + t}{\ln(kt) - t}$

35. $f(w) = 6\sqrt{w} + \dfrac{1}{w^2} + 5\ln w$

36. $y = 2x(\ln x + \ln 2) - 2x + e$

37. $f(x) = \ln(\sin x + \cos x)$

38. $f(t) = \ln(\ln t) + \ln(\ln 2)$

39. $T(u) = \arctan\left(\dfrac{u}{1 + u}\right)$

40. $a(t) = \ln\left(\dfrac{1 - \cos t}{1 + \cos t}\right)^4$

41. $f(x) = \cos(\arcsin(x + 1))$

Problems

42. Let $f(x) = \ln(3x)$.

   (a) Find $f'(x)$ and simplify your answer.

   (b) Use properties of logs to rewrite $f(x)$ as a sum of logs.

   (c) Differentiate the result of part (b). Compare with the result in part (a).

43. On what intervals is $\ln(x^2 + 1)$ concave up?

44. Use the chain rule to obtain the formula for $\dfrac{d}{dx}(\arcsin x)$.

45. Using the chain rule, find $\dfrac{d}{dx}(\log x)$.
(Recall $\log x = \log_{10} x$.)

46. To compare the acidity of different solutions, chemists use the pH (which is a single number, not the product of p and H). The pH is defined in terms of the concentration, x, of hydrogen ions in the solution as

$$\text{pH} = -\log x.$$

Find the rate of change of pH with respect to hydrogen ion concentration when the pH is 2. [Hint: Use the result of Problem 45.]

47. The number of years, T, it takes an investment of $1000 to grow to F in an account which pays 5% interest compounded continuously is given by

$$T = g(F) = 20 \ln(0.001F).$$

Find $g(5000)$ and $g'(5000)$. Give units with your answers and interpret them in terms of money in the account.

48. A firm estimates that the total revenue, R, in dollars, received from the sale of q goods is given by

$$R = \ln(1 + 1000q^2).$$

The marginal revenue, MR, is the rate of change of the total revenue as a function of quantity. Calculate the marginal revenue when $q = 10$.

49. **(a)** Find the equation of the tangent line to $y = \ln x$ at $x = 1$.

   (b) Use it to calculate approximate values for $\ln(1.1)$ and $\ln(2)$.

   (c) Using a graph, explain whether the approximate values are smaller or larger than the true values. Would the same result have held if you had used the tangent line to estimate $\ln(0.9)$ and $\ln(0.5)$? Why?

50. **(a)** Find the equation of the best quadratic approximation to $y = \ln x$ at $x = 1$. The best quadratic approximation has the same first and second derivatives as $y = \ln x$ at $x = 1$.

   (b) Use a computer or calculator to graph the approximation and $y = \ln x$ on the same set of axes. What do you notice?

   (c) Use your quadratic approximation to calculate approximate values for $\ln(1.1)$ and $\ln(2)$.

51. **(a)** For $x > 0$, find and simplify the derivative of $f(x) = \arctan x + \arctan(1/x)$.

   (b) What does your result tell you about f?

52. Imagine you are zooming in on the graph of each of the following functions near the origin:

$$y = x \qquad\qquad y = \sqrt{x}$$
$$y = x^2 \qquad\qquad y = \sin x$$
$$y = x \sin x \qquad\quad y = \tan x$$
$$y = \sqrt{x/(x+1)} \;\; y = x^3$$
$$y = \ln(x+1) \qquad y = \tfrac{1}{2}\ln(x^2 + 1)$$
$$y = 1 - \cos x \qquad y = \sqrt{2x - x^2}$$

Which of them look the same? Group together those functions which become indistinguishable, and give the equations of the lines they look like.

In Problems 53–56, use Figure 3.30 to find a point x where $h(x) = n(m(x))$ has the given derivative.

Figure 3.30

53. $h'(x) = -2$

54. $h'(x) = 2$

55. $h'(x) = 1$

56. $h'(x) = -1$

In Problems 57–59, use Figure 3.31 to estimate the derivatives.

Figure 3.31

57. $(f^{-1})'(5)$ **58.** $(f^{-1})'(10)$ **59.** $(f^{-1})'(15)$

In Problems 60–62, use Figure 3.32 to calculate the derivative.

$(2.1, 5.3)$

$f(x)$

$(2, 5)$

Figure 3.32

60. $h'(2)$ if $h(x) = (f(x))^3$

61. $k'(2)$ if $k(x) = (f(x))^{-1}$

62. $g'(5)$ if $g(x) = f^{-1}(x)$

63. (a) Given that $f(x) = x^3$, find $f'(2)$.
   (b) Find $f^{-1}(x)$.
   (c) Use your answer from part (b) to find $(f^{-1})'(8)$.
   (d) How could you have used your answer from part (a) to find $(f^{-1})'(8)$?

64. (a) For $f(x) = 2x^5 + 3x^3 + x$, find $f'(x)$.
   (b) How can you use your answer to part (a) to determine if $f(x)$ is invertible?
   (c) Find $f(1)$.
   (d) Find $f'(1)$.
   (e) Find $(f^{-1})'(6)$.

65. Use the table and the fact that $f(x)$ is invertible and differentiable everywhere to find $(f^{-1})'(3)$.

x	$f(x)$	$f'(x)$
3	1	7
6	2	10
9	3	5

66. At a particular location, $f(p)$ is the number of gallons of gas sold when the price is p dollars per gallon.

   (a) What does the statement $f(2) = 4023$ tell you about gas sales?
   (b) Find and interpret $f^{-1}(4023)$.
   (c) What does the statement $f'(2) = -1250$ tell you about gas sales?
   (d) Find and interpret $(f^{-1})'(4023)$

67. Let $P = f(t)$ give the US population[6] in millions in year t.

   (a) What does the statement $f(2005) = 296$ tell you about the US population?
   (b) Find and interpret $f^{-1}(296)$. Give units.
   (c) What does the statement $f'(2005) = 2.65$ tell you about the population? Give units.
   (d) Evaluate and interpret $(f^{-1})'(296)$. Give units.

68. Figure 3.33 shows the number of motor vehicles,[7] $f(t)$, in millions, registered in the world t years after 1965. With units, estimate and interpret

   (a) $f(20)$
   (b) $f'(20)$
   (c) $f^{-1}(500)$
   (d) $(f^{-1})'(500)$

(millions)

Figure 3.33

69. Using Figure 3.34, where $f'(2) = 2.1$, $f'(4) = 3.0$, $f'(6) = 3.7$, $f'(8) = 4.2$, find $(f^{-1})'(8)$.

Figure 3.34

70. If f is increasing and $f(20) = 10$, which of the two options, (a) or (b), must be wrong?

   (a) $f'(10)(f^{-1})'(20) = 1$.
   (b) $f'(20)(f^{-1})'(10) = 2$.

71. An invertible function $f(x)$ has values in the table. Evaluate

   (a) $f'(a) \cdot (f^{-1})'(A)$
   (b) $f'(b) \cdot (f^{-1})'(B)$
   (c) $f'(c) \cdot (f^{-1})'(C)$

x	a	b	c	d
$f(x)$	A	B	C	D

72. If f is continuous, invertible, and defined for all x, why must at least one of the statements $(f^{-1})'(10) = 8$, $(f^{-1})'(20) = -6$ be wrong?

73. (a) Calculate $\lim_{h\to 0}(\ln(1 + h)/h)$ by identifying the limit as the derivative of $\ln(1 + x)$ at $x = 0$.
   (b) Use the result of part (a) to show that $\lim_{h\to 0}(1 + h)^{1/h} = e$.
   (c) Use the result of part (b) to calculate the related limit, $\lim_{n\to\infty}(1 + 1/n)^n$.

---

[6]Data from www.census.gov/Press-Release/www/releases/archives/population/006142.html, accessed May 27, 2007.

[7]www.earth-policy.org, accessed May 18, 2007.

Strengthen Your Understanding

In Problems 74–76, explain what is wrong with the statement.

74. If $w(x) = \ln(1 + x^4)$ then $w'(x) = 1/(1 + x^4)$.

75. The derivative of $f(x) = \ln(\ln x)$ is

$$f'(x) = \frac{1}{x} \ln x + \ln x \frac{1}{x} = \frac{2 \ln x}{x}.$$

76. Given $f(2) = 6, f'(2) = 3$, and $f^{-1}(3) = 4$, we have

$$(f^{-1})'(2) = \frac{1}{f^{-1}(f'(2))} = \frac{1}{f^{-1}(3)} = \frac{1}{4}.$$

In Problems 77–80, give an example of:

77. A function that is equal to a constant multiple of its derivative but that is not equal to its derivative.

78. A function whose derivative is c/x, where c is a constant.

79. A function $f(x)$ for which $f'(x) = f'(cx)$, where c is a constant.

80. A function f such that $\frac{d}{dx}\left(f^{-1}(x)\right) = \frac{1}{f'(x)} = 1$.

Are the statements in Problems 81–82 true or false? Give an explanation for your answer.

81. The graph of $\ln(x^2)$ is concave up for $x > 0$.

82. If $f(x)$ has an inverse function, $g(x)$, then the derivative of $g(x)$ is $1/f'(x)$.

3.7 IMPLICIT FUNCTIONS

In earlier chapters, most functions were written in the form $y = f(x)$; here y is said to be an *explicit* function of x. An equation such as

$$x^2 + y^2 = 4$$

is said to give y as an *implicit* function of x. Its graph is the circle in Figure 3.35. Since there are x-values which correspond to two y-values, y is not a function of x on the whole circle. Solving gives

$$y = \pm\sqrt{4 - x^2},$$

where $y = \sqrt{4 - x^2}$ represents the top half of the circle and $y = -\sqrt{4 - x^2}$ represents the bottom half. So y is a function of x on the top half, and y is a different function of x on the bottom half.

But let's consider the circle as a whole. The equation does represent a curve which has a tangent line at each point. The slope of this tangent can be found by differentiating the equation of the circle with respect to x:

$$\frac{d}{dx}(x^2) + \frac{d}{dx}(y^2) = \frac{d}{dx}(4).$$

If we think of y as a function of x and use the chain rule, we get

$$2x + 2y\frac{dy}{dx} = 0.$$

Solving gives

$$\frac{dy}{dx} = -\frac{x}{y}.$$

Top half:
$y = \sqrt{4 - x^2}$

Negative slope $= -x/y$

Bottom half:
$y = -\sqrt{4 - x^2}$

Positive slope $= -x/y$

Figure 3.35: Graph of $x^2 + y^2 = 4$

Curve has slope 2/5 here

Figure 3.36: Graph of $y^3 - xy = -6$ and its tangent line at $(7, 2)$

The derivative here depends on both x and y (instead of just on x). This is because for many x-values there are two y-values, and the curve has a different slope at each one. Figure 3.35 shows that for x and y both positive, we are on the top right quarter of the curve and the slope is negative (as the formula predicts). For x positive and y negative, we are on the bottom right quarter of the curve and the slope is positive (as the formula predicts).

Differentiating the equation of the circle has given us the slope of the curve at all points except $(2, 0)$ and $(-2, 0)$, where the tangent is vertical. In general, this process of *implicit differentiation* leads to a derivative whenever the expression for the derivative does not have a zero in the denominator.

Example 1   Make a table of x and approximate y-values for the equation $y^3 - xy = -6$ near $x = 7, y = 2$. Your table should include the x-values $6.8, 6.9, 7.0, 7.1$, and 7.2.

Solution   We would like to solve for y in terms of x, but we cannot isolate y by factoring. There is a formula for solving cubics, somewhat like the quadratic formula, but it is too complicated to be useful here. Instead, first observe that $x = 7$, $y = 2$ does satisfy the equation. (Check this!) Now find dy/dx by implicit differentiation:

$$\frac{d}{dx}(y^3) - \frac{d}{dx}(xy) = \frac{d}{dx}(-6)$$

$$3y^2\frac{dy}{dx} - 1 \cdot y - x\frac{dy}{dx} = 0 \quad \text{(Differentiating with respect to x)}$$

$$3y^2\frac{dy}{dx} - x\frac{dy}{dx} = y$$

$$(3y^2 - x)\frac{dy}{dx} = y \quad \text{(Factoring out $\frac{dy}{dx}$)}$$

$$\frac{dy}{dx} = \frac{y}{3y^2 - x}.$$

When $x = 7$ and $y = 2$, we have

$$\frac{dy}{dx} = \frac{2}{12 - 7} = \frac{2}{5}.$$

(See Figure 3.36.) The equation of the tangent line at $(7, 2)$ is

$$y - 2 = \frac{2}{5}(x - 7)$$

or

$$y = 0.4x - 0.8.$$

Since the tangent lies very close to the curve near the point $(7, 2)$, we use the equation of the tangent line to calculate the following approximate y-values:

x	6.8	6.9	7.0	7.1	7.2
Approximate y	1.92	1.96	2.00	2.04	2.08

Notice that although the equation $y^3 - xy = -6$ leads to a curve which is difficult to deal with algebraically, it still looks like a straight line locally.

Example 2   Find all points where the tangent line to $y^3 - xy = -6$ is either horizontal or vertical.

Solution   From the previous example, $\dfrac{dy}{dx} = \dfrac{y}{3y^2 - x}$. The tangent is horizontal when the numerator of dy/dx equals 0, so $y = 0$. Since we also must satisfy $y^3 - xy = -6$, we get $0^3 - x \cdot 0 = -6$, which is impossible. We conclude that there are no points on the curve where the tangent line is horizontal.

The tangent is vertical when the denominator of dy/dx is 0, giving $3y^2 - x = 0$. Thus, $x = 3y^2$ at any point with a vertical tangent line. Again, we must also satisfy $y^3 - xy = -6$, so

$$y^3 - (3y^2)y = -6,$$

$$-2y^3 = -6,$$

$$y = \sqrt[3]{3} \approx 1.442.$$

We can then find x by substituting $y = \sqrt[3]{3}$ in $y^3 - xy = -6$. We get $3 - x(\sqrt[3]{3}) = -6$, so $x = 9/(\sqrt[3]{3}) \approx 6.240$. So the tangent line is vertical at $(6.240, 1.442)$.

Using implicit differentiation and the expression for dy/dx to locate the points where the tangent is vertical or horizontal, as in the previous example, is a first step in obtaining an overall picture of the curve $y^3 - xy = -6$. However, filling in the rest of the graph, even roughly, by using the sign of dy/dx to tell us where the curve is increasing or decreasing can be difficult.

Exercises and Problems for Section 3.7

Exercises

For Exercises 1–21, find dy/dx. Assume a, b, c are constants.

1. $x^2 + y^2 = \sqrt{7}$

2. $x^2 + y^3 = 8$

3. $x^2 + xy - y^3 = xy^2$

4. $x^2 + y^2 + 3x - 5y = 25$

5. $xy + x + y = 5$

6. $x^2y - 2y + 5 = 0$

7. $x^2y^3 - xy = 6$

8. $\sqrt{x} = 5\sqrt{y}$

9. $\sqrt{x} + \sqrt{y} = 25$

10. $xy - x - 3y - 4 = 0$

11. $6x^2 + 4y^2 = 36$

12. $ax^2 - by^2 = c^2$

13. $\ln x + \ln(y^2) = 3$

14. $x \ln y + y^3 = \ln x$

15. $\sin(xy) = 2x + 5$

16. $e^{\cos y} = x^3 \arctan y$

17. $\arctan(x^2y) = xy^2$

18. $e^{x^2} + \ln y = 0$

19. $(x - a)^2 + y^2 = a^2$

20. $x^{2/3} + y^{2/3} = a^{2/3}$

21. $\sin(ay) + \cos(bx) = xy$

In Exercises 22–25, find the slope of the tangent to the curve at the point specified.

22. $x^2 + y^2 = 1$ at $(0, 1)$

23. $\sin(xy) = x$ at $(1, \pi/2)$

24. $x^3 + 2xy + y^2 = 4$ at $(1, 1)$

25. $x^3 + 5x^2y + 2y^2 = 4y + 11$ at $(1, 2)$

For Exercises 26–30, find the equations of the tangent lines to the following curves at the indicated points.

26. $xy^2 = 1$ at $(1, -1)$

27. $\ln(xy) = 2x$ at $(1, e^2)$

28. $y^2 = \dfrac{x^2}{xy - 4}$ at $(4, 2)$

29. $y = \dfrac{x}{y + a}$ at $(0, 0)$

30. $x^{2/3} + y^{2/3} = a^{2/3}$ at $(a, 0)$

Problems

31. (a) Find dy/dx given that $x^2 + y^2 - 4x + 7y = 15$.
    (b) Under what conditions on x and/or y is the tangent line to this curve horizontal? Vertical?

32. (a) Find the slope of the tangent line to the ellipse $\dfrac{x^2}{25} + \dfrac{y^2}{9} = 1$ at the point (x, y).
    (b) Are there any points where the slope is not defined?

33. Find the equations of the tangent lines at $x = 2$ to the ellipse
$$\frac{(x - 2)^2}{16} + \frac{y^2}{4} = 1.$$

34. (a) Find the equations of the tangent lines to the circle $x^2 + y^2 = 25$ at the points where $x = 4$.
    (b) Find the equations of the normal lines to this circle at the same points. (The normal line is perpendicular to the tangent line at that point.)
    (c) At what point do the two normal lines intersect?

35. (a) If $x^3 + y^3 - xy^2 = 5$, find dy/dx.
    (b) Using your answer to part (a), make a table of approximate y-values of points on the curve near $x =$

1, $y = 2$. Include $x = 0.96, 0.98, 1, 1.02, 1.04$.
    (c) Find the y-value for $x = 0.96$ by substituting $x = 0.96$ in the original equation and solving for y using a computer or calculator. Compare with your answer in part (b).
    (d) Find all points where the tangent line is horizontal or vertical.

36. Find the equation of the tangent line to the curve $y = x^2$ at $x = 1$. Show that this line is also a tangent to a circle centered at $(8, 0)$ and find the equation of this circle.

37. At pressure P atmospheres, a certain fraction f of a gas decomposes. The quantities P and f are related, for some positive constant K, by the equation
$$\frac{4f^2P}{1 - f^2} = K.$$
    (a) Find df/dP.
    (b) Show that $df/dP < 0$ always. What does this mean in practical terms?

38. Sketch the circles $y^2 + x^2 = 1$ and $y^2 + (x-3)^2 = 4$. There is a line with positive slope that is tangent to both circles. Determine the points at which this tangent line touches each circle.

39. If $y = \arcsin x$ then $x = \sin y$. Use implicit differentiation on $x = \sin y$ to show that

$$\frac{d}{dx}\arcsin x = \frac{1}{\sqrt{1-x^2}}.$$

40. Show that the power rule for derivatives applies to rational powers of the form $y = x^{m/n}$ by raising both sides to the nth power and using implicit differentiation.

41. For constants a, b, n, R, Van der Waal's equation relates the pressure, P, to the volume, V, of a fixed quantity of a gas at constant temperature T:

$$\left(P + \frac{n^2 a}{V^2}\right)(V - nb) = nRT.$$

Find the rate of change of volume with pressure, dV/dP.

Strengthen Your Understanding

In Problems 42–43, explain what is wrong with the statement.

42. If $y = \sin(xy)$ then $dy/dx = y\cos(xy)$.

43. The formula $dy/dx = -x/y$ gives the slope of the circle $x^2 + y^2 = 10$ at every point in the plane except where $y = 0$.

In Problems 44–45, give an example of:

44. A formula for dy/dx leading to a vertical tangent at $y = 2$ and a horizontal tangent at $x = \pm 2$.

45. A curve that has two horizontal tangents at the same x-value, but no vertical tangents.

46. True or false? Explain your answer: If y satisfies the equation $y^2 + xy - 1 = 0$, then dy/dx exists everywhere.

3.8 HYPERBOLIC FUNCTIONS

There are two combinations of e^x and e^{-x} which are used so often in engineering that they are given their own name. They are the *hyperbolic sine*, abbreviated sinh, and the *hyperbolic cosine*, abbreviated cosh. They are defined as follows:

Hyperbolic Functions

$$\cosh x = \frac{e^x + e^{-x}}{2} \qquad \sinh x = \frac{e^x - e^{-x}}{2}$$

Properties of Hyperbolic Functions

The graphs of $\cosh x$ and $\sinh x$ are given in Figures 3.37 and 3.38 together with the graphs of multiples of e^x and e^{-x}. The graph of $\cosh x$ is called a *catenary*; it is the shape of a hanging cable.

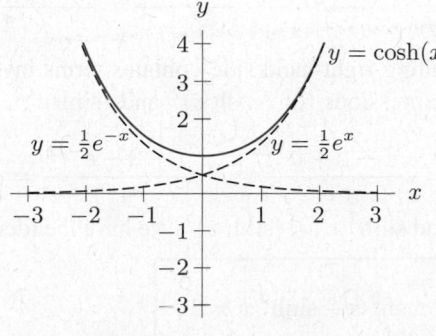

Figure 3.37: Graph of $y = \cosh x$

Figure 3.38: Graph of $y = \sinh x$

The graphs suggest that the following results hold:

$$\cosh 0 = 1 \qquad \sinh 0 = 0$$

$$\cosh(-x) = \cosh x \qquad \sinh(-x) = -\sinh x$$

To show that the hyperbolic functions really do have these properties, we use their formulas.

Example 1 Show that (a) $\cosh(0) = 1$ (b) $\cosh(-x) = \cosh x$

Solution   (a) Substituting $x = 0$ into the formula for $\cosh x$ gives

$$\cosh 0 = \frac{e^0 + e^{-0}}{2} = \frac{1+1}{2} = 1.$$

(b) Substituting $-x$ for x gives

$$\cosh(-x) = \frac{e^{-x} + e^{-(-x)}}{2} = \frac{e^{-x} + e^x}{2} = \cosh x.$$

Thus, we know that $\cosh x$ is an even function.

Example 2 Describe and explain the behavior of $\cosh x$ as $x \to \infty$ and $x \to -\infty$.

Solution   From Figure 3.37, it appears that as $x \to \infty$, the graph of $\cosh x$ resembles the graph of $\frac{1}{2}e^x$. Similarly, as $x \to -\infty$, the graph of $\cosh x$ resembles the graph of $\frac{1}{2}e^{-x}$. This behavior is explained by using the formula for $\cosh x$ and the facts that $e^{-x} \to 0$ as $x \to \infty$ and $e^x \to 0$ as $x \to -\infty$:

$$\text{As } x \to \infty, \qquad \cosh x = \frac{e^x + e^{-x}}{2} \to \frac{1}{2}e^x.$$

$$\text{As } x \to -\infty, \qquad \cosh x = \frac{e^x + e^{-x}}{2} \to \frac{1}{2}e^{-x}.$$

Identities Involving cosh x and sinh x

The reason the hyperbolic functions have names that remind us of the trigonometric functions is that they share similar properties. A familiar identity for trigonometric functions is

$$(\cos x)^2 + (\sin x)^2 = 1.$$

To discover an analogous identity relating $(\cosh x)^2$ and $(\sinh x)^2$, we first calculate

$$(\cosh x)^2 = \left(\frac{e^x + e^{-x}}{2} \right)^2 = \frac{e^{2x} + 2e^x e^{-x} + e^{-2x}}{4} = \frac{e^{2x} + 2 + e^{-2x}}{4}$$

$$(\sinh x)^2 = \left(\frac{e^x - e^{-x}}{2} \right)^2 = \frac{e^{2x} - 2e^x e^{-x} + e^{-2x}}{4} = \frac{e^{2x} - 2 + e^{-2x}}{4}.$$

If we add these expressions, the resulting right-hand side contains terms involving both e^{2x} and e^{-2x}. If, however, we subtract the expressions for $(\cosh x)^2$ and $(\sinh x)^2$, we obtain a simple result:

$$(\cosh x)^2 - (\sinh x)^2 = \frac{e^{2x} + 2 + e^{-2x}}{4} - \frac{e^{2x} - 2 + e^{-2x}}{4} = \frac{4}{4} = 1.$$

Thus, writing $\cosh^2 x$ for $(\cosh x)^2$ and $\sinh^2 x$ for $(\sinh x)^2$, we have the identity

$$\cosh^2 x - \sinh^2 x = 1$$

This identity shows us how the hyperbolic functions got their name. Suppose (x, y) is a point in the plane and $x = \cosh t$ and $y = \sinh t$ for some t. Then the point (x, y) lies on the hyperbola $x^2 - y^2 = 1$.

The Hyperbolic Tangent

Extending the analogy to the trigonometric functions, we define

$$\tanh x = \frac{\sinh x}{\cosh x} = \frac{e^x - e^{-x}}{e^x + e^{-x}}$$

Derivatives of Hyperbolic Functions

We calculate the derivatives using the fact that $\frac{d}{dx}(e^x) = e^x$. The results are again reminiscent of the trigonometric functions. For example,

$$\frac{d}{dx}(\cosh x) = \frac{d}{dx}\left(\frac{e^x + e^{-x}}{2}\right) = \frac{e^x - e^{-x}}{2} = \sinh x.$$

We find $\frac{d}{dx}(\sinh x)$ similarly, giving the following results:

$$\frac{d}{dx}(\cosh x) = \sinh x \qquad \frac{d}{dx}(\sinh x) = \cosh x$$

Example 3   Compute the derivative of $\tanh x$.

Solution   Using the quotient rule gives

$$\frac{d}{dx}(\tanh x) = \frac{d}{dx}\left(\frac{\sinh x}{\cosh x}\right) = \frac{(\cosh x)^2 - (\sinh x)^2}{(\cosh x)^2} = \frac{1}{\cosh^2 x}.$$

Exercises and Problems for Section 3.8

Exercises

In Exercises 1–11, find the derivative of the function.

1. $y = \sinh(3z + 5)$

2. $y = \cosh(2x)$

3. $g(t) = \cosh^2 t$

4. $f(t) = \cosh(\sinh t)$

5. $f(t) = t^3 \sinh t$

6. $y = \cosh(3t)\sinh(4t)$

7. $y = \tanh(3 + \sinh x)$

8. $f(t) = \cosh(e^{t^2})$

9. $g(\theta) = \ln(\cosh(1 + \theta))$

10. $f(y) = \sinh(\sinh(3y))$

11. $f(t) = \cosh^2 t - \sinh^2 t$

12. Show that $d(\sinh x)/dx = \cosh x$.

13. Show that $\sinh 0 = 0$.

14. Show that $\sinh(-x) = -\sinh(x)$.

In Exercises 15–16, simplify the expressions.

15. $\cosh(\ln t)$

16. $\sinh(\ln t)$

Problems

17. Describe and explain the behavior of $\sinh x$ as $x \to \infty$ and as $x \to -\infty$.

18. If $x = \cosh t$ and $y = \sinh t$, explain why the point (x, y) always lies on the curve $x^2 - y^2 = 1$. (This curve is called a hyperbola and gave this family of functions its name.)

19. Is there an identity analogous to $\sin(2x) = 2\sin x \cos x$ for the hyperbolic functions? Explain.

20. Is there an identity analogous to $\cos(2x) = \cos^2 x - \sin^2 x$ for the hyperbolic functions? Explain.

Prove the identities in Problems 21–22.

21. $\cosh(A + B) = \cosh A \cosh B + \sinh A \sinh B$

22. $\sinh(A + B) = \sinh A \cosh B + \cosh A \sinh B$

In Problems 23–26, find the limit of the function as $x \to \infty$.

23. $\dfrac{\sinh(2x)}{\cosh(3x)}$

24. $\dfrac{e^{2x}}{\sinh(2x)}$

25. $\dfrac{\sinh(x^2)}{\cosh(x^2)}$

26. $\dfrac{\cosh(2x)}{\sinh(3x)}$

27. For what values of k is $\lim\limits_{x \to \infty} e^{-3x} \cosh kx$ finite?

28. For what values of k is $\lim\limits_{x \to \infty} \dfrac{\sinh kx}{\cosh 2x}$ finite?

29. The cable between the two towers of a power line hangs in the shape of the curve

$$y = \frac{T}{w} \cosh\left(\frac{wx}{T}\right),$$

where T is the tension in the cable at its lowest point and w is the weight of the cable per unit length. This curve is called a *catenary*.

(a) Suppose the cable stretches between the points $x = -T/w$ and $x = T/w$. Find an expression for the "sag" in the cable. (That is, find the difference between the height of the cable at the highest and lowest points.)

(b) Show that the shape of the cable satisfies the equation

$$\frac{d^2 y}{dx^2} = \frac{w}{T}\sqrt{1 + \left(\frac{dy}{dx}\right)^2}.$$

30. The Saint Louis Arch can be approximated by using a function of the form $y = b - a \cosh(x/a)$. Putting the origin on the ground in the center of the arch and the y-axis upward, find an approximate equation for the arch given the dimensions shown in Figure 3.39. (In other words, find a and b.)

615 ft

530 ft

Figure 3.39

31. (a) Using a calculator or computer, sketch the graph of $y = 2e^x + 5e^{-x}$ for $-3 \le x \le 3, 0 \le y \le 20$. Observe that it looks like the graph of $y = \cosh x$. Approximately where is its minimum?

(b) Show algebraically that $y = 2e^x + 5e^{-x}$ can be written in the form $y = A \cosh(x - c)$. Calculate the values of A and c. Explain what this tells you about the graph in part (a).

32. The following problem is a generalization of Problem 31. Show that any function of the form

$$y = Ae^x + Be^{-x}, \quad A > 0, \ B > 0,$$

can be written, for some K and c, in the form

$$y = K \cosh(x - c).$$

What does this tell you about the graph of $y = Ae^x + Be^{-x}$?

33. (a) Find $\tanh 0$.

(b) For what values of x is $\tanh x$ positive? Negative? Explain your answer algebraically.

(c) On what intervals is $\tanh x$ increasing? Decreasing? Use derivatives to explain your answer.

(d) Find $\lim_{x \to \infty} \tanh x$ and $\lim_{x \to -\infty} \tanh x$. Show this information on a graph.

(e) Does $\tanh x$ have an inverse? Justify your answer using derivatives.

Strengthen Your Understanding

In Problems 34–37, explain what is wrong with the statement.

34. The function $f(x) = \cosh x$ is periodic.

35. The derivative of the function $f(x) = \cosh x$ is $f'(x) = -\sinh x$.

36. $\cosh^2 x + \sinh^2 x = 1$.

37. $\tanh x \to \infty$ as $x \to \infty$.

In Problems 38–40, give an example of:

38. A hyperbolic function which is concave up.

39. A value of k such that $\lim\limits_{x \to \infty} e^{kx} \cosh x$ does not exist.

40. A function involving the hyperbolic cosine that passes through the point $(1, 3)$.

Are the statements in Problems 41–45 true or false? Give an explanation for your answer.

41. The function $\tanh x$ is odd, that is, $\tanh(-x) = -\tanh x$.

42. The 100th derivative of $\sinh x$ is $\cosh x$.

43. $\sinh x + \cosh x = e^x$.

44. The function $\sinh x$ is periodic.

45. The function $\sinh^2 x$ is concave down everywhere.

3.9 LINEAR APPROXIMATION AND THE DERIVATIVE

The Tangent Line Approximation

When we zoom in on the graph of a differentiable function, it looks like a straight line. In fact, the graph is not exactly a straight line when we zoom in; however, its deviation from straightness is so small that it can't be detected by the naked eye. Let's examine what this means. The straight line that we think we see when we zoom in on the graph of $f(x)$ at $x = a$ has slope equal to the derivative, $f'(a)$, so the equation is

$$y = f(a) + f'(a)(x - a).$$

The fact that the graph looks like a line means that y is a good approximation to $f(x)$. (See Figure 3.40.) This suggests the following definition:

The Tangent Line Approximation

Suppose f is differentiable at a. Then, for values of x near a, the tangent line approximation to $f(x)$ is

$$f(x) \approx f(a) + f'(a)(x - a).$$

The expression $f(a) + f'(a)(x - a)$ is called the *local linearization* of f near $x = a$. We are thinking of a as fixed, so that $f(a)$ and $f'(a)$ are constant.
The **error**, $E(x)$, in the approximation is defined by

$$E(x) = f(x) - f(a) - f'(a)(x - a).$$

It can be shown that the tangent line approximation is the best linear approximation to f near a. See Problem 43.

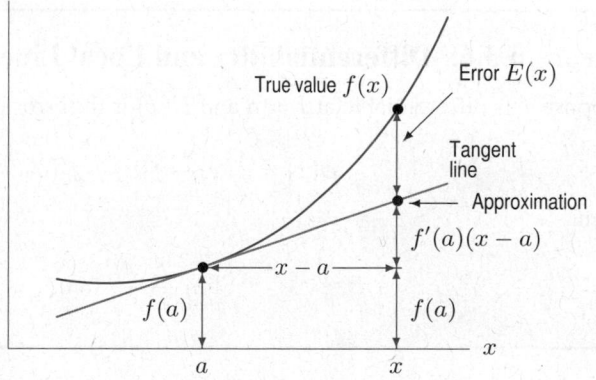

Figure 3.40: The tangent line approximation and its error

Example 1   What is the tangent line approximation for $f(x) = \sin x$ near $x = 0$?

Solution   The tangent line approximation of f near $x = 0$ is

$$f(x) \approx f(0) + f'(0)(x - 0).$$

If $f(x) = \sin x$, then $f'(x) = \cos x$, so $f(0) = \sin 0 = 0$ and $f'(0) = \cos 0 = 1$, and the approximation is

$$\sin x \approx x.$$

This means that, near $x = 0$, the function $f(x) = \sin x$ is well approximated by the function $y = x$. If we zoom in on the graphs of the functions $\sin x$ and x near the origin, we won't be able to tell them apart. (See Figure 3.41.)

Figure 3.41: Tangent line approximation to $y = \sin x$

Example 2   What is the local linearization of e^{kx} near $x = 0$?

Solution   If $f(x) = e^{kx}$, then $f(0) = 1$ and, by the chain rule, $f'(x) = ke^{kx}$, so $f'(0) = ke^{k \cdot 0} = k$. Thus

$$f(x) \approx f(0) + f'(0)(x - 0)$$

becomes

$$e^{kx} \approx 1 + kx.$$

This is the tangent line approximation to e^{kx} near $x = 0$. In other words, if we zoom in on the functions $f(x) = e^{kx}$ and $y = 1 + kx$ near the origin, we won't be able to tell them apart.

Estimating the Error in the Approximation

Let us look at the error, $E(x)$, which is the difference between $f(x)$ and the local linearization. (Look back at Figure 3.40.) The fact that the graph of f looks like a line as we zoom in means that not only is $E(x)$ small for x near a, but also that $E(x)$ is small relative to $(x - a)$. To demonstrate this, we prove the following theorem about the ratio $E(x)/(x - a)$.

> ### Theorem 3.6: Differentiability and Local Linearity
>
> Suppose f is differentiable at $x = a$ and $E(x)$ is the error in the tangent line approximation, that is:
> $$E(x) = f(x) - f(a) - f'(a)(x - a).$$
> Then
> $$\lim_{x \to a} \frac{E(x)}{x - a} = 0.$$

Proof Using the definition of $E(x)$, we have

$$\frac{E(x)}{x - a} = \frac{f(x) - f(a) - f'(a)(x - a)}{x - a} = \frac{f(x) - f(a)}{x - a} - f'(a).$$

Taking the limit as $x \to a$ and using the definition of the derivative, we see that

$$\lim_{x \to a} \frac{E(x)}{x - a} = \lim_{x \to a} \left(\frac{f(x) - f(a)}{x - a} - f'(a) \right) = f'(a) - f'(a) = 0.$$

Theorem 3.6 says that $E(x)$ approaches 0 faster than $(x - a)$. For the function in Example 3, we see that $E(x) \approx k(x - a)^2$ for constant k if x is near a.

Example 3   Let $E(x)$ be the error in the tangent line approximation to $f(x) = x^3 - 5x + 3$ for x near 2.

(a) What does a table of values for $E(x)/(x - 2)$ suggest about $\lim_{x \to 2} E(x)/(x - 2)$?

(b) Make another table to see that $E(x) \approx k(x-2)^2$. Estimate the value of k. Check that a possible value is $k = f''(2)/2$.

Solution

(a) Since $f(x) = x^3 - 5x + 3$, we have $f'(x) = 3x^2 - 5$, and $f''(x) = 6x$. Thus, $f(2) = 1$ and $f'(2) = 3 \cdot 2^2 - 5 = 7$, so the tangent line approximation for x near 2 is

$$f(x) \approx f(2) + f'(2)(x-2)$$
$$f(x) \approx 1 + 7(x-2).$$

Thus,

$$E(x) = \text{True value} - \text{Approximation} = (x^3 - 5x + 3) - (1 + 7(x-2)).$$

The values of $E(x)/(x-2)$ in Table 3.7 suggest that $E(x)/(x-2)$ approaches 0 as $x \to 2$.

(b) Notice that if $E(x) \approx k(x-2)^2$, then $E(x)/(x-2)^2 \approx k$. Thus we make Table 3.8 showing values of $E(x)/(x-2)^2$. Since the values are all approximately 6, we guess that $k = 6$ and $E(x) \approx 6(x-2)^2$.

Since $f''(2) = 12$, our value of k satisfies $k = f''(2)/2$.

Table 3.7

x	$E(x)/(x-2)$
2.1	0.61
2.01	0.0601
2.001	0.006001
2.0001	0.00060001

Table 3.8

x	$E(x)/(x-2)^2$
2.1	6.1
2.01	6.01
2.001	6.001
2.0001	6.0001

The relationship between $E(x)$ and $f''(x)$ that appears in Example 3 holds more generally. If $f(x)$ satisfies certain conditions, it can be shown that the error in the tangent line approximation behaves near $x = a$ as

$$E(x) \approx \frac{f''(a)}{2}(x-a)^2.$$

This is part of a general pattern for obtaining higher-order approximations called Taylor polynomials, which are studied in Chapter 10.

Why Differentiability Makes a Graph Look Straight

We use the properties of the error $E(x)$ to understand why differentiability makes a graph look straight when we zoom in.

Example 4

Consider the graph of $f(x) = \sin x$ near $x = 0$, and its linear approximation computed in Example 1. Show that there is an interval around 0 with the property that the distance from $f(x) = \sin x$ to the linear approximation is less than $0.1|x|$ for all x in the interval.

Solution

The linear approximation of $f(x) = \sin x$ near 0 is $y = x$, so we write

$$\sin x = x + E(x).$$

Since $\sin x$ is differentiable at $x = 0$, Theorem 3.6 tells us that

$$\lim_{x \to 0} \frac{E(x)}{x} = 0.$$

If we take $\epsilon = 1/10$, then the definition of limit guarantees that there is a $\delta > 0$ such that

$$\left|\frac{E(x)}{x}\right| < 0.1 \quad \text{for all} \quad |x| < \delta.$$

In other words, for x in the interval $(-\delta, \delta)$, we have $|x| < \delta$, so

$$|E(x)| < 0.1|x|.$$

(See Figure 3.42.)

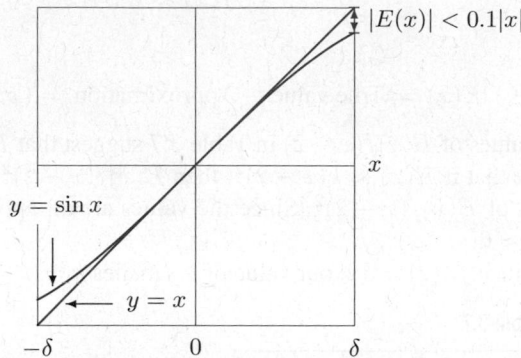

Figure 3.42: Graph of $y = \sin x$ and its linear approximation $y = x$, showing a window in which the magnitude of the error, $|E(x)|$, is less than $0.1|x|$ for all x in the window

We can generalize from this example to explain why differentiability makes the graph of f look straight when viewed over a small graphing window. Suppose f is differentiable at $x = a$. Then we know $\lim\limits_{x \to a} \left|\frac{E(x)}{x - a}\right| = 0$. So, for any $\epsilon > 0$, we can find a δ small enough so that

$$\left|\frac{E(x)}{x - a}\right| < \epsilon, \qquad \text{for} \quad a - \delta < x < a + \delta.$$

So, for any x in the interval $(a - \delta, a + \delta)$, we have

$$|E(x)| < \epsilon|x - a|.$$

Thus, the error, $E(x)$, is less than ϵ times $|x - a|$, the distance between x and a. So, as we zoom in on the graph by choosing smaller ϵ, the deviation, $|E(x)|$, of f from its tangent line shrinks, even relative to the scale on the x-axis. So, zooming makes a differentiable function look straight.

Exercises and Problems for Section 3.9

Exercises

1. Find the tangent line approximation for $\sqrt{1 + x}$ near $x = 0$.

2. What is the tangent line approximation to e^x near $x = 0$?

3. Find the tangent line approximation to $1/x$ near $x = 1$.

4. Find the local linearization of $f(x) = x^2$ near $x = 1$.

5. What is the local linearization of e^{x^2} near $x = 1$?

6. Show that $1 - x/2$ is the tangent line approximation to $1/\sqrt{1 + x}$ near $x = 0$.

7. Show that $e^{-x} \approx 1 - x$ near $x = 0$.

8. Local linearization gives values too small for the function x^2 and too large for the function $\sqrt{x}$. Draw pictures to explain why.

9. Using a graph like Figure 3.41, estimate to one decimal place the magnitude of the error in approximating $\sin x$ by x for $-1 \leq x \leq 1$. Is the approximation an over- or an underestimate?

10. For x near 0, local linearization gives

$$e^x \approx 1 + x.$$

Using a graph, decide if the approximation is an over- or underestimate, and estimate to one decimal place the magnitude of the error for $-1 \leq x \leq 1$.

Problems

11. (a) Find the best linear approximation, $L(x)$, to $f(x) = e^x$ near $x = 0$.
   (b) What is the sign of the error, $E(x) = f(x) - L(x)$ for x near 0?
   (c) Find the true value of the function at $x = 1$. What is the error? (Give decimal answers.) Illustrate with a graph.
   (d) Before doing any calculations, explain which you expect to be larger, $E(0.1)$ or $E(1)$, and why.
   (e) Find $E(0.1)$.

12. (a) Find the tangent line approximation to $\cos x$ at $x = \pi/4$.
   (b) Use a graph to explain how you know whether the tangent line approximation is an under- or overestimate for $0 \le x \le \pi/2$.
   (c) To one decimal place, estimate the error in the approximation for $0 \le x \le \pi/2$.

13. (a) Graph $f(x) = x^3 - 3x^2 + 3x + 1$.
   (b) Find and add to your sketch the local linearization to $f(x)$ at $x = 2$.
   (c) Mark on your sketch the true value of $f(1.5)$, the tangent line approximation to $f(1.5)$ and the error in the approximation.

14. (a) Show that $1 + kx$ is the local linearization of $(1+x)^k$ near $x = 0$.
   (b) Someone claims that the square root of 1.1 is about 1.05. Without using a calculator, do you think that this estimate is about right?
   (c) Is the actual number above or below 1.05?

15. Figure 3.43 shows $f(x)$ and its local linearization at $x = a$. What is the value of a? Of $f(a)$? Is the approximation an under- or overestimate? Use the linearization to approximate the value of $f(1.2)$.

Figure 3.43

In Problems 16–17, the equation has a solution near $x = 0$. By replacing the left side of the equation by its linearization, find an approximate value for the solution.

16. $e^x + x = 2$

17. $x + \ln(1 + x) = 0.2$

18. (a) Given that $f(7) = 13$ and $f'(7) = -0.38$, estimate $f(7.1)$.
   (b) Suppose also $f''(x) < 0$ for all x. Does this make your answer to part (a) an under- or overestimate?

19. (a) Explain why the following equation has a solution near 0:
   $$e^t = 0.02t + 1.098.$$
   (b) Replace e^t by its linearization near 0. Solve the new equation to get an approximate solution to the original equation.

20. The speed of sound in dry air is
   $$f(T) = 331.3\sqrt{1 + \frac{T}{273.15}} \text{ meters/second}$$
   where T is the temperature in degrees Celsius. Find a linear function that approximates the speed of sound for temperatures near $0°$C.

21. Air pressure at sea level is 30 inches of mercury. At an altitude of h feet above sea level, the air pressure, P, in inches of mercury, is given by
   $$P = 30e^{-3.23 \times 10^{-5} h}$$
   (a) Sketch a graph of P against h.
   (b) Find the equation of the tangent line at $h = 0$.
   (c) A rule of thumb used by travelers is that air pressure drops about 1 inch for every 1000-foot increase in height above sea level. Write a formula for the air pressure given by this rule of thumb.
   (d) What is the relation between your answers to parts (b) and (c)? Explain why the rule of thumb works.
   (e) Are the predictions made by the rule of thumb too large or too small? Why?

22. On October 7, 2010, the *Wall Street Journal*[8] reported that Android cell phone users had increased to 10.9 million by the end of August 2010 from 866,000 a year earlier. During the same period, iPhone users increased to 13.5 million, up from 7.8 million a year earlier. Let $A(t)$ be the number of Android users, in millions, at time t in years since the end of August 2009. Let $P(t)$ be the number of iPhone users in millions.
   (a) Estimate $A'(0)$. Give units.
   (b) Estimate $P'(0)$. Give units.
   (c) Using the tangent line approximation, when are the numbers of Android and iPhone users predicted to be the same?
   (d) What assumptions did you make in part (c)?

[8]"Apple Readies Verizon iPhone", WSJ, Oct 7, 2010.

23. Writing g for the acceleration due to gravity, the period, T, of a pendulum of length l is given by

$$T = 2\pi\sqrt{\frac{l}{g}}.$$

   (a) Show that if the length of the pendulum changes by Δl, the change in the period, ΔT, is given by

$$\Delta T \approx \frac{T}{2l}\Delta l.$$

   (b) If the length of the pendulum increases by 2%, by what percent does the period change?

24. Suppose now the length of the pendulum in Problem 23 remains constant, but that the acceleration due to gravity changes.

   (a) Use the method of the preceding problem to relate ΔT approximately to Δg, the change in g.
   (b) If g increases by 1%, find the percent change in T.

25. Suppose f has a continuous positive second derivative for all x. Which is larger, $f(1+\Delta x)$ or $f(1)+f'(1)\Delta x$? Explain.

26. Suppose $f'(x)$ is a differentiable decreasing function for all x. In each of the following pairs, which number is the larger? Give a reason for your answer.

   (a) $f'(5)$ and $f'(6)$
   (b) $f''(5)$ and 0
   (c) $f(5 + \Delta x)$ and $f(5) + f'(5)\Delta x$

Problems 27–29 investigate the motion of a projectile shot from a cannon. The fixed parameters are the acceleration of gravity, $g = 9.8$ m/sec^2, and the muzzle velocity, $v_0 = 500$ m/sec, at which the projectile leaves the cannon. The angle θ, in degrees, between the muzzle of the cannon and the ground can vary.

27. The range of the projectile is

$$f(\theta) = \frac{v_0^2}{g}\sin\frac{\pi\theta}{90}wq = 25510\sin\frac{\pi\theta}{90}\text{ meters.}$$

   (a) Find the range with $\theta = 20°$.
   (b) Find a linear function of θ that approximates the range for angles near $20°$.
   (c) Find the range and its approximation from part (b) for $21°$.

28. The time that the projectile stays in the air is

$$t(\theta) = \frac{2v_0}{g}\sin\frac{\pi\theta}{180} = 102\sin\frac{\pi\theta}{180}\text{ seconds.}$$

   (a) Find the time in the air for $\theta = 20°$.
   (b) Find a linear function of θ that approximates the time in the air for angles near $20°$.
   (c) Find the time in air and its approximation from part (b) for $21°$.

29. At its highest point the projectile reaches a peak altitude given by

$$h(\theta) = \frac{v_0^2}{2g}\sin^2\frac{\pi\theta}{180} = 12755\sin^2\frac{\pi\theta}{180}\text{ meters.}$$

   (a) Find the peak altitude for $\theta = 20°$.
   (b) Find a linear function of θ that approximates the peak altitude for angles near $20°$.
   (c) Find the peak altitude and its approximation from part (b) for $21°$.

In Problems 30–32, find the local linearization of $f(x)$ near 0 and use this to approximate the value of a.

30. $f(x) = (1 + x)^r,\quad a = (1.2)^{3/5}$
31. $f(x) = e^{kx},\quad a = e^{0:3}$
32. $f(x) = \sqrt{b^2 + x},\quad a = \sqrt{26}$

In Problems 33–37, find a formula for the error $E(x)$ in the tangent line approximation to the function near $x = a$. Using a table of values for $E(x)/(x-a)$ near $x = a$, find a value of k such that $E(x)/(x-a) \approx k(x-a)$. Check that, approximately, $k = f''(a)/2$ and that $E(x) \approx (f''(a)/2)(x-a)^2$.

33. $f(x) = x^4,\ a = 1$
34. $f(x) = \cos x,\ a = 0$
35. $f(x) = e^x,\ a = 0$
36. $f(x) = \sqrt{x},\ a = 1$
37. $f(x) = \ln x,\ a = 1$

38. Multiply the local linearization of e^x near $x = 0$ by itself to obtain an approximation for e^{2x}. Compare this with the actual local linearization of e^{2x}. Explain why these two approximations are consistent, and discuss which one is more accurate.

39. (a) Show that $1 - x$ is the local linearization of $\dfrac{1}{1 + x}$ near $x = 0$.
   (b) From your answer to part (a), show that near $x = 0$,

$$\frac{1}{1 + x^2} \approx 1 - x^2.$$

   (c) Without differentiating, what do you think the derivative of $\dfrac{1}{1 + x^2}$ is at $x = 0$?

40. From the local linearizations of e^x and $\sin x$ near $x = 0$, write down the local linearization of the function $e^x \sin x$. From this result, write down the derivative of $e^x \sin x$ at $x = 0$. Using this technique, write down the derivative of $e^x \sin x/(1 + x)$ at $x = 0$.

41. Use local linearization to derive the product rule,

$$[f(x)g(x)]' = f'(x)g(x) + f(x)g'(x).$$

[Hint: Use the definition of the derivative and the local linearizations $f(x+h) \approx f(x)+f'(x)h$ and $g(x+h) \approx g(x) + g'(x)h$.]

42. Derive the chain rule using local linearization. [Hint: In other words, differentiate $f(g(x))$, using $g(x + h) \approx g(x) + g'(x)h$ and $f(z + k) \approx f(z) + f'(z)k$.]

43. Consider a function f and a point a. Suppose there is a number L such that the linear function g

$$g(x) = f(a) + L(x - a)$$

is a good approximation to f. By good approximation, we mean that

$$\lim_{x \to a} \frac{E_L(x)}{x - a} = 0,$$

where $E_L(x)$ is the approximation error defined by

$$f(x) = g(x) + E_L(x) = f(a) + L(x - a) + E_L(x).$$

Show that f is differentiable at $x = a$ and that $f'(a) = L$. Thus the tangent line approximation is the only good linear approximation.

44. Consider the graph of $f(x) = x^2$ near $x = 1$. Find an interval around $x = 1$ with the property that throughout any smaller interval, the graph of $f(x) = x^2$ never differs from its local linearization at $x = 1$ by more than $0.1|x - 1|$.

Strengthen Your Understanding

In Problems 45–46, explain what is wrong with the statement.

45. To approximate $f(x) = e^x$, we can always use the linear approximation $f(x) = e^x \approx x + 1$.

46. The linear approximation for $F(x) = x^3 + 1$ near $x = 0$ is an underestimate for the function F for all x, $x \neq 0$.

In Problems 47–49, give an example of:

47. Two different functions that have the same linear approximation near $x = 0$.

48. A non-polynomial function that has the tangent line approximation $f(x) \approx 1$ near $x = 0$.

49. A function that does not have a linear approximation at $x = -1$.

50. Let f be a differentiable function and let L be the linear function $L(x) = f(a) + k(x - a)$ for some constant a. Decide whether the following statements are true or false for all constants k. Explain your answer.

   (a) L is the local linearization for f near $x = a$,

   (b) If $\lim_{x \to a} (f(x) - L(x)) = 0$, then L is the local linearization for f near $x = a$.

3.10 THEOREMS ABOUT DIFFERENTIABLE FUNCTIONS

A Relationship Between Local and Global: The Mean Value Theorem

We often want to infer a global conclusion (for example, f is increasing on an interval) from local information (for example, f' is positive at each point on an interval). The following theorem relates the average rate of change of a function on an interval (global information) to the instantaneous rate of change at a point in the interval (local information).

Theorem 3.7: The Mean Value Theorem

If f is continuous on $a \leq x \leq b$ and differentiable on $a < x < b$, then there exists a number c, with $a < c < b$, such that

$$f'(c) = \frac{f(b) - f(a)}{b - a}.$$

In other words, $f(b) - f(a) = f'(c)(b - a)$.

To understand this theorem geometrically, look at Figure 3.44. Join the points on the curve where $x = a$ and $x = b$ with a secant line and observe that

$$\text{Slope of secant line} = \frac{f(b) - f(a)}{b - a}.$$

Now consider the tangent lines drawn to the curve at each point between $x = a$ and $x = b$. In general, these lines have different slopes. For the curve shown in Figure 3.44, the tangent line at

$x = a$ is flatter than the secant line. Similarly, the tangent line at $x = b$ is steeper than the secant line. However, there appears to be at least one point between a and b where the slope of the tangent line to the curve is precisely the same as the slope of the secant line. Suppose this occurs at $x = c$. Then

$$\text{Slope of tangent line} = f'(c) = \frac{f(b) - f(a)}{b - a}.$$

The Mean Value Theorem tells us that the point $x = c$ exists, but it does not tell us how to find c. Problems 44 and 45 in Section 4.2 show how the Mean Value Theorem can be derived.

Figure 3.44: The point c with $f'(c) = \frac{f(b) - f(a)}{b - a}$

If f satisfies the conditions of the Mean Value Theorem on $a < x < b$ and $f(a) = f(b) = 0$, the Mean Value Theorem tells us that there is a point c, with $a < c < b$, such that $f'(c) = 0$. This result is called **Rolle's Theorem**.

The Increasing Function Theorem

We say that a function f is *increasing* on an interval if, for any two numbers x_1 and x_2 in the interval such that $x_1 < x_2$, we have $f(x_1) < f(x_2)$. If instead we have $f(x_1) \leq f(x_2)$, we say f is *nondecreasing*.

Theorem 3.8: The Increasing Function Theorem

Suppose that f is continuous on $a \leq x \leq b$ and differentiable on $a < x < b$.
- If $f'(x) > 0$ on $a < x < b$, then f is increasing on $a \leq x \leq b$.
- If $f'(x) \geq 0$ on $a < x < b$, then f is nondecreasing on $a \leq x \leq b$.

Proof   Suppose $a \leq x_1 < x_2 \leq b$. By the Mean Value Theorem, there is a number c, with $x_1 < c < x_2$, such that

$$f(x_2) - f(x_1) = f'(c)(x_2 - x_1).$$

If $f'(c) > 0$, this says $f(x_2) - f(x_1) > 0$, which means f is increasing. If $f'(c) \geq 0$, this says $f(x_2) - f(x_1) \geq 0$, which means f is nondecreasing.

It may seem that something as simple as the Increasing Function Theorem should follow immediately from the definition of the derivative, and you may be surprised that the Mean Value Theorem is needed.

The Constant Function Theorem

If f is constant on an interval, then we know that $f'(x) = 0$ on the interval. The following theorem is the converse.

Theorem 3.9: The Constant Function Theorem

Suppose that f is continuous on $a \leq x \leq b$ and differentiable on $a < x < b$. If $f'(x) = 0$ on $a < x < b$, then f is constant on $a \leq x \leq b$.

Proof   The proof is the same as for the Increasing Function Theorem, only in this case $f'(c) = 0$ so $f(x_2) - f(x_1) = 0$. Thus $f(x_2) = f(x_1)$ for $a \leq x_1 < x_2 \leq b$, so f is constant.

A proof of the Constant Function Theorem using the Increasing Function Theorem is given in Problems 17 and 25.

The Racetrack Principle

Theorem 3.10: The Racetrack Principle[9]

Suppose that g and h are continuous on $a \leq x \leq b$ and differentiable on $a < x < b$, and that $g'(x) \leq h'(x)$ for $a < x < b$.
- If $g(a) = h(a)$, then $g(x) \leq h(x)$ for $a \leq x \leq b$.
- If $g(b) = h(b)$, then $g(x) \geq h(x)$ for $a \leq x \leq b$.

The Racetrack Principle has the following interpretation. We can think of $g(x)$ and $h(x)$ as the positions of two racehorses at time x, with horse h always moving faster than horse g. If they start together, horse h is ahead during the whole race. If they finish together, horse g was ahead during the whole race.

Proof   Consider the function $f(x) = h(x) - g(x)$. Since $f'(x) = h'(x) - g'(x) \geq 0$, we know that f is nondecreasing by the Increasing Function Theorem. So $f(x) \geq f(a) = h(a) - g(a) = 0$. Thus $g(x) \leq h(x)$ for $a \leq x \leq b$. This proves the first part of the Racetrack Principle. Problem 24 asks for a proof of the second part.

Example 1   Explain graphically why $e^x \geq 1 + x$ for all values of x. Then use the Racetrack Principle to prove the inequality.

Solution   The graph of the function $y = e^x$ is concave up everywhere and the equation of its tangent line at the point $(0, 1)$ is $y = x + 1$. (See Figure 3.45.) Since the graph always lies above its tangent, we have the inequality

$$e^x \geq 1 + x.$$

Figure 3.45: Graph showing that $e^x \geq 1 + x$

[9]Based on the Racetrack Principle in *Calculus & Mathematica*, by William Davis, Horacio Porta, Jerry Uhl (Reading: Addison Wesley, 1994).

Now we prove the inequality using the Racetrack Principle. Let $g(x) = 1 + x$ and $h(x) = e^x$. Then $g(0) = h(0) = 1$. Furthermore, $g'(x) = 1$ and $h'(x) = e^x$. Hence $g'(x) \leq h'(x)$ for $x \geq 0$. So by the Racetrack Principle, with $a = 0$, we have $g(x) \leq h(x)$, that is, $1 + x \leq e^x$.

For $x \leq 0$ we have $h'(x) \leq g'(x)$. So by the Racetrack Principle, with $b = 0$, we have $g(x) \leq h(x)$, that is, $1 + x \leq e^x$.

Exercises and Problems for Section 3.10

Exercises

In Exercises 1–5, decide if the statements are true or false. Give an explanation for your answer.

1. Let $f(x) = [x]$, the greatest integer less than or equal to x. Then $f'(x) = 0$, so $f(x)$ is constant by the Constant Function Theorem.

2. If $a < b$ and $f'(x)$ is positive on $[a, b]$ then $f(a) < f(b)$.

3. If $f(x)$ is increasing and differentiable on the interval $[a, b]$, then $f'(x) > 0$ on $[a, b]$.

4. The Racetrack Principle can be used to justify the statement that if two horses start a race at the same time, the horse that wins must have been moving faster than the other throughout the race.

5. Two horses start a race at the same time and one runs slower than the other throughout the race. The Racetrack Principle can be used to justify the fact that the slower horse loses the race.

Do the functions graphed in Exercises 6–9 appear to satisfy the hypotheses of the Mean Value Theorem on the interval $[a, b]$? Do they satisfy the conclusion?

6.

7.

8.

9.

Problems

10. Applying the Mean Value Theorem with $a = 2$, $b = 7$ to the function in Figure 3.46 leads to $c = 4$. What is the equation of the tangent line at 4?

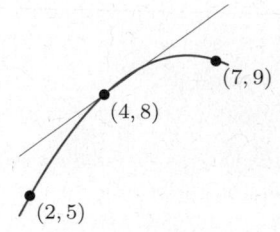

Figure 3.46

11. Applying the Mean Value Theorem with $a = 3$, $b = 13$ to the function in Figure 3.47 leads to the point c shown. What is the value of $f'(c)$? What can you say about the values of $f'(x_1)$ and $f'(x_2)$?

Figure 3.47

12. Let $p(x) = x^5 + 8x^4 - 30x^3 + 30x^2 - 31x + 22$. What is the relationship between $p(x)$ and $f(x) = 5x^4 + 32x^3 - 90x^2 + 60x - 31$? What do the values of $p(1)$ and $p(2)$ tell you about the values of $f(x)$?

13. Let $p(x)$ be a seventh-degree polynomial with 7 distinct zeros. How many zeros does $p'(x)$ have?

14. Use the Racetrack Principle and the fact that $\sin 0 = 0$ to show that $\sin x \leq x$ for all $x \geq 0$.

15. Use the Racetrack Principle to show that $\ln x \leq x - 1$.

16. Use the fact that $\ln x$ and e^x are inverse functions to show that the inequalities $e^x \geq 1 + x$ and $\ln x \leq x - 1$ are equivalent for $x > 0$.

17. State a Decreasing Function Theorem, analogous to the Increasing Function Theorem. Deduce your theorem from the Increasing Function Theorem. [Hint: Apply the Increasing Function Theorem to $-f$.]

18. Dominic drove from Phoenix to Tucson on Interstate 10, a distance of 116 miles. The speed limit on this highway varies between 55 and 75 miles per hour. He started his trip at 11:44 pm and arrived in Tucson at 1:12 am. Prove that Dominic was speeding at some point during his trip.

In Problems 19–22, use one of the theorems in this section to prove the statements .

19. If $f'(x) \leq 1$ for all x and $f(0) = 0$, then $f(x) \leq x$ for all $x \geq 0$.

20. If $f''(t) \leq 3$ for all t and $f(0) = f'(0) = 0$, then $f(t) \leq \frac{3}{2}t^2$ for all $t \geq 0$.

21. If $f'(x) = g'(x)$ for all x and $f(5) = g(5)$, then $f(x) = g(x)$ for all x.

22. If f is differentiable and $f(0) < f(1)$, then there is a number c, with $0 < c < 1$, such that $f'(c) > 0$.

23. The position of a particle on the x-axis is given by $s = f(t)$; its initial position and velocity are $f(0) = 3$ and

$f'(0) = 4$. The acceleration is bounded by $5 \leq f''(t) \leq 7$ for $0 \leq t \leq 2$. What can we say about the position $f(2)$ of the particle at $t = 2$?

24. Suppose that g and h are continuous on $[a, b]$ and differentiable on (a, b). Prove that if $g'(x) \leq h'(x)$ for $a < x < b$ and $g(b) = h(b)$, then $h(x) \leq g(x)$ for $a \leq x \leq b$.

25. Deduce the Constant Function Theorem from the Increasing Function Theorem and the Decreasing Function Theorem. (See Problem 17.)

26. Prove that if $f'(x) = g'(x)$ for all x in (a, b), then there is a constant C such that $f(x) = g(x) + C$ on (a, b). [Hint: Apply the Constant Function Theorem to $h(x) = f(x) - g(x)$.]

27. Suppose that $f'(x) = f(x)$ for all x. Prove that $f(x) = Ce^x$ for some constant C. [Hint: Consider $f(x)/e^x$.]

28. Suppose that f is continuous on $[a, b]$ and differentiable on (a, b) and that $m \leq f'(x) \leq M$ on (a, b). Use the Racetrack Principle to prove that $f(x) - f(a) \leq M(x - a)$ for all x in $[a, b]$, and that $m(x - a) \leq f(x) - f(a)$ for all x in $[a, b]$. Conclude that $m \leq (f(b) - f(a))/(b - a) \leq M$. This is called the Mean Value Inequality. In words: If the instantaneous rate of change of f is between m and M on an interval, so is the average rate of change of f over the interval.

29. Suppose that $f''(x) \geq 0$ for all x in (a, b). We will show the graph of f lies above the tangent line at $(c, f(c))$ for any c with $a < c < b$.

(a) Use the Increasing Function Theorem to prove that $f'(c) \leq f'(x)$ for $c \leq x < b$ and that $f'(x) \leq f'(c)$ for $a < x \leq c$.

(b) Use (a) and the Racetrack Principle to conclude that $f(c) + f'(c)(x - c) \leq f(x)$, for $a < x < b$.

Strengthen Your Understanding

In Problems 30–32, explain what is wrong with the statement.

30. The Mean Value Theorem applies to $f(x) = |x|$, for $-2 < x < 2$.

31. The following function satisfies the conditions of the Mean Value Theorem on the interval $[0, 1]$:

$$f(x) = \begin{cases} x & \text{if } 0 < x \leq 1 \\ 1 & \text{if } x = 0. \end{cases}$$

32. If $f'(x) = 0$ on $a < x < b$, then by the Constant Function Theorem f is constant on $a \leq x \leq b$.

In Problems 33–37, give an example of:

33. An interval where the Mean Value Theorem applies when $f(x) = \ln x$.

34. An interval where the Mean Value Theorem does not apply when $f(x) = 1/x$.

35. A continuous function f on the interval $[-1, 1]$ that does not satisfy the conclusion of the Mean Value Theorem.

36. A function f that is differentiable on the interval $(0, 2)$, but does not satisfy the conclusion of the Mean Value Theorem on the interval $[0, 2]$.

37. A function that is differentiable on $(0, 1)$ and not continuous on $[0, 1]$, but which satisfies the conclusion of the Mean Value Theorem.

Are the statements in Problems 38–41 true or false for a function f whose domain is all real numbers? If a statement is true, explain how you know. If a statement is false, give a counterexample.

38. If $f'(x) \geq 0$ for all x, then $f(a) \leq f(b)$ whenever $a \leq b$.

39. If $f'(x) \leq g'(x)$ for all x, then $f(x) \leq g(x)$ for all x.

40. If $f'(x) = g'(x)$ for all x, then $f(x) = g(x)$ for all x.

41. If $f'(x) \leq 1$ for all x and $f(0) = 0$, then $f(x) \leq x$ for all x.

CHAPTER SUMMARY (see also Ready Reference at the end of the book)

- **Derivatives of elementary functions**
  Power, polynomial, rational, exponential, logarithmic, trigonometric, inverse trigonometric, and hyperbolic functions.

- **Derivatives of sums, differences, and constant multiples**

- **Product and quotient rules**

- **Chain rule**

- **Differentiation of implicitly defined functions and inverse functions**

- **Hyperbolic functions**

- **Tangent line approximation, local linearity**

- **Theorems about differentiable functions**
  Mean value theorem, increasing function theorem, constant function theorem, Racetrack Principle.

REVIEW EXERCISES AND PROBLEMS FOR CHAPTER THREE

Exercises

Find derivatives for the functions in Exercises 1–73. Assume a, b, c, and k are constants.

1. $w = (t^2 + 1)^{100}$

2. $f(t) = e^{3t}$

3. $z = \dfrac{t^2 + 3t + 1}{t + 1}$

4. $y = \dfrac{\sqrt{t}}{t^2 + 1}$

5. $h(t) = \dfrac{4 - t}{4 + t}$

6. $f(x) = x^e$

7. $f(x) = \dfrac{x^3}{9}(3 \ln x - 1)$

8. $f(x) = \dfrac{1 + x}{2 + 3x + 4x^2}$

9. $g(\theta) = e^{\sin \theta}$

10. $y = \sqrt{\theta}\left(\sqrt{\theta} + \dfrac{1}{\sqrt{\theta}}\right)$

11. $f(w) = \ln(\cos(w - 1))$

12. $f(y) = \ln\left(\ln(2y^3)\right)$

13. $g(x) = x^k + k^x$

14. $y = e^{-\pi} + \pi^{-e}$

15. $z = \sin^3 \theta$

16. $f(t) = \cos^2(3t + 5)$

17. $M(\alpha) = \tan^2(2 + 3\alpha)$

18. $s(\theta) = \sin^2(3\theta - \pi)$

19. $h(t) = \ln\left(e^{-t} - t\right)$

20. $p(\theta) = \dfrac{\sin(5 - \theta)}{\theta^2}$

21. $w(\theta) = \dfrac{\theta}{\sin^2 \theta}$

22. $f(\theta) = \dfrac{1}{1 + e^{-\theta}}$

23. $g(w) = \dfrac{1}{2^w + e^w}$

24. $f(t) = \dfrac{t^2 + t^3 - 1}{t^4}$

25. $h(z) = \sqrt{\dfrac{\sin(2z)}{\cos(2z)}}$

26. $q(\theta) = \sqrt{4\theta^2 - \sin^2(2\theta)}$

27. $w = 2^{-4z} \sin(\pi z)$

28. $g(t) = \arctan(3t - 4)$

29. $r(\theta) = e^{(e^\theta + e^{-\theta})}$

30. $m(n) = \sin(e^n)$

31. $G(\alpha) = e^{\tan(\sin \alpha)}$

32. $g(t) = t \cos(\sqrt{t}e^t)$

33. $f(r) = (\tan 2 + \tan r)^e$

34. $h(x) = xe^{\tan x}$

35. $y = e^{2x} \sin^2(3x)$

36. $g(x) = \tan^{-1}(3x^2 + 1)$

37. $y = 2^{\sin x} \cos x$

38. $F(x) = \ln(e^{ax}) + \ln b$

39. $y = e^{\theta - 1}$

40. $f(t) = e^{-4kt} \sin t$

41. $H(t) = (at^2 + b)e^{-ct}$

42. $g(\theta) = \sqrt{a^2 - \sin^2 \theta}$

43. $y = 5^x + 2$

44. $f(x) = \dfrac{a^2 - x^2}{a^2 + x^2}$

45. $w(r) = \dfrac{ar^2}{b + r^3}$

46. $f(s) = \dfrac{a^2 - s^2}{\sqrt{a^2 + s^2}}$

47. $y = \arctan\left(\dfrac{2}{x}\right)$

48. $r(t) = \ln\left(\sin\left(\dfrac{t}{k}\right)\right)$

49. $g(w) = \dfrac{5}{(a^2 - w^2)^2}$

50. $y = \dfrac{e^{2x}}{x^2 + 1}$

51. $g(u) = \dfrac{e^{au}}{a^2 + b^2}$ **52.** $y = \dfrac{e^{ax} - e^{-ax}}{e^{ax} + e^{-ax}}$

53. $f(x) = \dfrac{x}{1 + \ln x}$ **54.** $z = \dfrac{e^{t^2} + t}{\sin(2t)}$

55. $f(t) = \sin \sqrt{e^t + 1}$ **56.** $g(y) = e^{2e^{(y^3)}}$

57. $y = 6x^3 + 4x^2 - 2x$

58. $g(z) = \dfrac{z^7 + 5z^6 - z^3}{z^2}$

59. $f(z) = (\ln 3)z^2 + (\ln 4)e^z$

60. $y = 3x - 2 \cdot 4^x$

61. $f(x) = x^3 + 3^x$

62. $f(\theta) = \theta^2 \sin \theta + 2\theta \cos \theta - 2 \sin \theta$

63. $y = \sqrt{\cos(5\theta) + \sin^2(6\theta)}$

64. $r(\theta) = \sin\left((3\theta - \pi)^2\right)$

65. $z = (s^2 - \sqrt{s})(s^2 + \sqrt{s})$

66. $N(\theta) = \tan(\arctan(k\theta))$

67. $h(t) = e^{kt}(\sin at + \cos bt)$

68. $f(y) = 4^y(2 - y^2)$

69. $f(t) = (\sin(2t) - \cos(3t))^4$

70. $s(y) = \sqrt[3]{(\cos^2 y + 3 + \sin^2 y)}$

71. $f(x) = (4 - x^2 + 2x^3)(6 - 4x + x^7)$

72. $h(x) = \left(\dfrac{1}{x} - \dfrac{1}{x^2}\right)(2x^3 + 4)$

73. $f(z) = \sqrt{5z} + 5\sqrt{z} + \dfrac{5}{\sqrt{z}} - \sqrt{\dfrac{5}{z}} + \sqrt{5}$

For Exercises 74–75, assume that y is a differentiable function of x and find dy/dx.

74. $x^3 + y^3 - 4x^2y = 0$

75. $\cos^2 y + \sin^2 y = y + 2$

76. Find the slope of the curve $x^2 + 3y^2 = 7$ at $(2, -1)$.

77. Assume y is a differentiable function of x and that $y + \sin y + x^2 = 9$. Find dy/dx at the point $x = 3, y = 0$.

78. Find the equations for the lines tangent to the graph of $xy + y^2 = 4$ where $x = 3$.

Problems

79. If $f(t) = 2t^3 - 4t^2 + 3t - 1$, find $f'(t)$ and $f''(t)$.

80. If $f(x) = 13 - 8x + \sqrt{2}x^2$ and $f'(r) = 4$, find r.

81. If $f(x) = x^3 - 6x^2 - 15x + 20$, find analytically all values of x for which $f'(x) = 0$. Show your answers on a graph of f.

82. (a) Find the *eighth* derivative of $f(x) = x^7 + 5x^5 - 4x^3 + 6x - 7$. Think ahead!
    (The nth derivative, $f^{(n)}(x)$, is the result of differentiating $f(x)$ n times.)
    (b) Find the seventh derivative of $f(x)$.

For Problems 83–88, use Figure 3.48.

85. Let $h(x) = s(s(x))$. Estimate:

   (a) $h'(1)$ (b) $h'(2)$

86. Estimate all values of x for which the tangent line to $y = s(s(x))$ is horizontal.

87. Let $h(x) = x^2 t(x)$ and $p(x) = t(x^2)$. Estimate:

   (a) $h'(-1)$ (b) $p'(-1)$

88. Find an approximate equation for the tangent line to $r(x) = s(t(x))$ at $x = 1$.

For Problems 89–92, let $h(x) = f(g(x))$ and $k(x) = g(f(x))$. Use Figure 3.49 to estimate the derivatives.

Figure 3.48

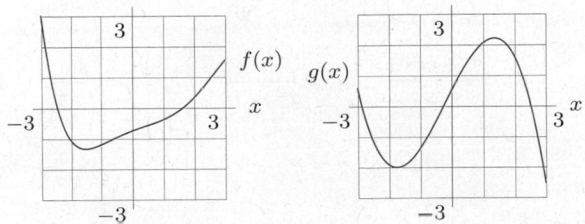

Figure 3.49

83. Let $h(x) = t(x)s(x)$ and $p(x) = t(x)/s(x)$. Estimate:

   (a) $h'(1)$ (b) $h'(0)$ (c) $p'(0)$

84. Let $r(x) = s(t(x))$. Estimate $r'(0)$.

89. $h'(1)$ **90.** $k'(1)$ **91.** $h'(2)$ **92.** $k'(2)$

93. Using the information in the table about f and g, find:

(a) $h(4)$ if $h(x) = f(g(x))$
(b) $h'(4)$ if $h(x) = f(g(x))$
(c) $h(4)$ if $h(x) = g(f(x))$
(d) $h'(4)$ if $h(x) = g(f(x))$
(e) $h'(4)$ if $h(x) = g(x)/f(x)$
(f) $h'(4)$ if $h(x) = f(x)g(x)$

x	1	2	3	4
$f(x)$	3	2	1	4
$f'(x)$	1	4	2	3
$g(x)$	2	1	4	3
$g'(x)$	4	2	3	1

94. Given: $r(2) = 4$, $s(2) = 1$, $s(4) = 2$, $r'(2) = -1$, $s'(2) = 3$, $s'(4) = 3$. Compute the following derivatives, or state what additional information you would need to be able to do so.

(a) $H'(2)$ if $H(x) = r(x) \cdot s(x)$
(b) $H'(2)$ if $H(x) = \sqrt{r(x)}$
(c) $H'(2)$ if $H(x) = r(s(x))$
(d) $H'(2)$ if $H(x) = s(r(x))$

95. If $g(2) = 3$ and $g'(2) = -4$, find $f'(2)$ for the following:

(a) $f(x) = x^2 - 4g(x)$ (b) $f(x) = \dfrac{x}{g(x)}$

(c) $f(x) = x^2 g(x)$ (d) $f(x) = (g(x))^2$

(e) $f(x) = x \sin(g(x))$ (f) $f(x) = x^2 \ln(g(x))$

96. For parts (a)–(f) of Problem 95, determine the equation of the line tangent to f at $x = 2$.

97. Imagine you are zooming in on the graphs of the following functions near the origin:

$y = \arcsin x$ $y = \sin x - \tan x$ $y = x - \sin x$

$y = \arctan x$ $y = \dfrac{\sin x}{1 + \sin x}$ $y = \dfrac{x^2}{x^2 + 1}$

$y = \dfrac{1 - \cos x}{\cos x}$ $y = \dfrac{x}{x^2 + 1}$ $y = \dfrac{\sin x}{x} - 1$

$y = -x \ln x$ $y = e^x - 1$ $y = x^{10} + \sqrt[10]{x}$

$y = \dfrac{x}{x + 1}$

Which of them look the same? Group together those functions which become indistinguishable, and give the equation of the line they look like. [Note: $(\sin x)/x - 1$ and $-x \ln x$ never quite make it to the origin.]

---

98. The graphs of $\sin x$ and $\cos x$ intersect once between 0 and $\pi/2$. What is the angle between the two curves at the point where they intersect? (You need to think about how the angle between two curves should be defined.)

In Problems 99–100, show that the curves meet at least once and determine whether the curves are perpendicular at the point of intersection.

99. $y = 1 + x - x^2$ and $y = 1 - x + x^2$
100. $y = 1 - x^3/3$ and $y = x - 1$
101. For some constant b and $x > 0$, let $y = x \ln x - bx$. Find the equation of the tangent line to this graph at the point at which the graph crosses the x-axis.

In Problems 102–104, find the limit as $x \to -\infty$.

102. $\dfrac{\cosh(2x)}{\sinh(3x)}$ **103.** $\dfrac{e^{-2x}}{\sinh(2x)}$ **104.** $\dfrac{\sinh(x^2)}{\cosh(x^2)}$

105. Consider the function $f(x) = \sqrt{x}$.

(a) Find and sketch $f(x)$ and the tangent line approximation to $f(x)$ near $x = 4$.
(b) Compare the true value of $f(4.1)$ with the value obtained by using the tangent line approximation.
(c) Compare the true and approximate values of $f(16)$.
(d) Using a graph, explain why the tangent line approximation is a good one when $x = 4.1$ but not when $x = 16$.

106. Figure 3.50 shows the tangent line approximation to $f(x)$ near $x = a$.

(a) Find a, $f(a)$, $f'(a)$.
(b) Estimate $f(2.1)$ and $f(1.98)$. Are these under- or overestimates? Which estimate would you expect to be more accurate and why?

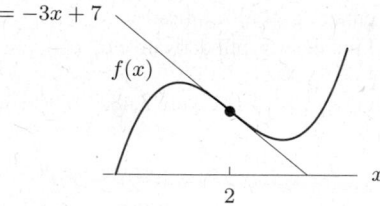

Figure 3.50

107. Global temperatures have been rising, on average, for more than a century, sparking concern that the polar ice will melt and sea levels will rise. With t in years since 1880, fitting functions to the data[10] gives three models for the average global temperature in Celsius:

$$f(t) = 13.625 + 0.006t$$
$$g(t) = 0.00006t^2 - 0.0017t + 13.788$$
$$h(t) = 13.63e^{0.0004t}.$$

(a) What family of functions is used in each model?

---

[10]From data.giss.nasa.gov/gistemp/tabledate/GLB.Ts.txt

(b) Find the rate of change of temperature in 2010 in each of the three models. Give units.

(c) For each model, find the change in temperature over a 130-year period if the temperature had been changing at the rate you found in part (b) for that model.

(d) For each model, find the predicted change in temperature for the 130 years from 1880 to 2010.

(e) For which model, if any, are the answers equal in parts (c) and (d)?

(f) For which model is the discrepancy largest between the answers in parts (c) and (d)?

108. In 2009, the population of Hungary[11] was approximated by

$$P = 9.906(0.997)^t,$$

where P is in millions and t is in years since 2009. Assume the trend continues.

(a) What does this model predict for the population of Hungary in the year 2020?

(b) How fast (in people/year) does this model predict Hungary's population will be decreasing in 2020?

109. The gravitational attraction, F, between the earth and a satellite of mass m at a distance r from the center of the earth is given by

$$F = \frac{GMm}{r^2},$$

where M is the mass of the earth, and G is a constant. Find the rate of change of force with respect to distance.

110. The distance, s, of a moving body from a fixed point is given as a function of time, t, by $s = 20e^{t/2}$.

(a) Find the velocity, v, of the body as a function of t.

(b) Find a relationship between v and s, then show that s satisfies the differential equation $s' = \frac{1}{2}s$.

111. At any time, t, a population, $P(t)$, is growing at a rate proportional to the population at that moment.

(a) Using derivatives, write an equation representing the growth of the population. Let k be the constant of proportionality.

(b) Show that the function $P(t) = Ae^{kt}$ satisfies the equation in part (a) for any constant A.

112. An object is oscillating at the end of a spring. Its position, in centimeters, relative to a fixed point, is given as a function of time, t, in seconds, by

$$y = y_0 \cos(2\pi\omega t), \quad \text{with } \omega \text{ a constant.}$$

(a) Find an expression for the velocity and acceleration of the object.

(b) How do the amplitudes of the position, velocity, and acceleration functions compare? How do the periods of these functions compare?

(c) Show that the function y satisfies the differential equation

$$\frac{d^2y}{dt^2} + 4\pi^2\omega^2 y = 0.$$

113. The total number of people, N, who have contracted a disease by a time t days after its outbreak is given by

$$N = \frac{1,000,000}{1 + 5,000e^{-0.1t}}.$$

(a) In the long run, how many people get the disease?

(b) Is there any day on which more than a million people fall sick? Half a million? Quarter of a million? (Note: You do not have to find on what days these things happen.)

114. The world population was 6.7 billion at the beginning of 2008. An exponential model predicts the population to be $P(t) = 6.7e^{kt}$ billion t years after 2008, where k is the continuous annual growth rate.

(a) How long does the model predict it will take for the population to reach 10 billion, as a function $f(k)$?

(b) One current estimate is $k = 0.012 = 1.2\%$. How long will it take for the population to reach 10 billion if k has this value?

(c) For continuous growth rates near 1.2%, find a linear function of k that approximates the time for the world population to reach 10 billion.

(d) Find the time to reach 10 billion and its approximation from part (c) if the continuous growth rate is 1.0%.

115. The acceleration due to gravity, g, is given by

$$g = \frac{GM}{r^2},$$

where M is the mass of the earth, r is the distance from the center of the earth, and G is the universal gravitational constant.

(a) Show that when r changes by Δr, the change in the acceleration due to gravity, Δg, is given by

$$\Delta g \approx -2g\frac{\Delta r}{r}.$$

(b) What is the significance of the negative sign?

(c) What is the percent change in g when moving from sea level to the top of Pike's Peak (4.315 km)? Assume the radius of the earth is 6400 km.

116. Given that f and g are differentiable everywhere, g is the inverse of f, and that $f(3) = 4$, $f'(3) = 6$, $f'(4) = 7$, find $g'(4)$.

117. An increasing function $f(x)$ has the value $f(10) = 5$. Explain how you know that the calculations $f'(10) = 8$ and $(f^{-1})'(5) = 8$ cannot both be correct.

118. A particle is moving on the x-axis. It has velocity $v(x)$ when it is at the point with coordinate x. Show that its acceleration at that point is $v(x)v'(x)$.

---

[11]https://www.cia.gov/library/publications/the-world-factbook/print/hu.html, accessed 4/14/09.

119. If f is decreasing and $f(20) = 10$, which of the following must be incorrect?

(a) $(f^{-1})'(20) = -3$.   (b) $(f^{-1})'(10) = 12$.

120. Find the nth derivative of the following functions:

(a) $\ln x$ (b) xe^x (c) $e^x \cos x$

121. The derivative f' gives the (absolute) rate of change of a quantity f, and f'/f gives the relative rate of change of the quantity. In this problem, we show that the product rule is equivalent to an additive rule for relative rates of change. Assume $h = f \cdot g$ with $f \neq 0$ and $g \neq 0$.

(a) Show that the additive rule

$$\frac{f'}{f} + \frac{g'}{g} = \frac{h'}{h}$$

implies the product rule, by multiplying through by h and using the fact that $h = f \cdot g$.

(b) Show that the product rule implies the additive rule in part (a), by starting with the product rule and dividing through by $h = f \cdot g$.

122. The relative rate of change of a function f is defined to be f'/f. Find an expression for the relative rate of change of a quotient f/g in terms of the relative rates of change of the functions f and g.

CAS Challenge Problems

123. (a) Use a computer algebra system to differentiate $(x + 1)^x$ and $(\sin x)^x$.

(b) Conjecture a rule for differentiating $(f(x))^x$, where f is any differentiable function.

(c) Apply your rule to $g(x) = (\ln x)^x$. Does your answer agree with the answer given by the computer algebra system?

(d) Prove your conjecture by rewriting $(f(x))^x$ in the form $e^{h(x)}$.

For Problems 124–126,

(a) Use a computer algebra system to find and simplify the derivative of the given function.

(b) Without a computer algebra system, use differentiation rules to calculate the derivative. Make sure that the answer simplifies to the same answer as in part (a).

(c) Explain how you could have predicted the derivative by using algebra before taking the derivative.

124. $f(x) = \sin(\arcsin x)$

125. $g(r) = 2^{-2r} 4^r$

126. $h(t) = \ln(1 - 1/t) + \ln(t/(t - 1))$

PROJECTS FOR CHAPTER THREE

1. Rule of 70

The "Rule of 70" is a rule of thumb to estimate how long it takes money in a bank to double. Suppose the money is in an account earning $i\%$ annual interest, compounded yearly. The Rule of 70 says that the time it takes the amount of money to double is approximately $70/i$ years, assuming i is small. Find the local linearization of $\ln(1 + x)$ near $x = 0$, and use it to explain why this rule works.

2. Newton's Method

Read about how to find roots using bisection and Newton's method in Appendices A and C.

(a) What is the smallest positive zero of the function $f(x) = \sin x$? Apply Newton's method, with initial guess $x_0 = 3$, to see how fast it converges to $\pi = 3.1415926536\ldots$.

   (i) Compute the first two approximations, x_1 and x_2; compare x_2 with π.

   (ii) Newton's method works very well here. Explain why. To do this, you will have to outline the basic idea behind Newton's method.

   (iii) Estimate the location of the zero using bisection, starting with the interval $[3, 4]$. How does bisection compare to Newton's method in terms of accuracy?

(b) Newton's method can be very sensitive to your initial estimate, x_0. For example, consider finding a zero of $f(x) = \sin x - \frac{2}{3}x$.

   (i) Use Newton's method with the following initial estimates to find a zero:

$$x_0 = 0.904, \quad x_0 = 0.905, \quad x_0 = 0.906.$$

   (ii) What happens?

© Patrick Zephyr/Patrick Zephyr Nature Photography

Chapter Four

USING THE DERIVATIVE

Contents

4.1   USING FIRST AND SECOND DERIVATIVES

What Derivatives Tell Us About a Function and Its Graph

As we saw in Chapter 2, the connection between derivatives of a function and the function itself is given by the following:

- If $f' > 0$ on an interval, then f is increasing on that interval.
- If $f' < 0$ on an interval, then f is decreasing on that interval.

If f' is always positive on an interval or always negative on an interval, then f is monotonic over that interval.

- If $f'' > 0$ on an interval, then the graph of f is concave up on that interval.
- If $f'' < 0$ on an interval, then the graph of f is concave down on that interval.

We can do more with these principles now than we could in Chapter 2 because we now have formulas for the derivatives of the elementary functions.

When we graph a function on a computer or calculator, we often see only part of the picture, and we may miss some significant features. Information given by the first and second derivatives can help identify regions with interesting behavior.

Example 1   Use the first and second derivatives to analyze the function $f(x) = x^3 - 9x^2 - 48x + 52$.

Solution   Since f is a cubic polynomial, we expect a graph that is roughly S-shaped. We can use the derivative to determine where the function is increasing and where it is decreasing. The derivative of f is

$$f'(x) = 3x^2 - 18x - 48.$$

To find where $f' > 0$ or $f' < 0$, we first find where $f' = 0$, that is, where $3x^2 - 18x - 48 = 0$. Factoring, we get $3(x + 2)(x - 8) = 0$, so $x = -2$ or $x = 8$. Since $f' = 0$ *only* at $x = -2$ and $x = 8$, and since f' is continuous, f' cannot change sign on any of the three intervals $x < -2$, or $-2 < x < 8$, or $8 < x$. How can we tell the sign of f' on each of these intervals? One way is to pick a point and substitute into f'. For example, since $f'(-3) = 33 > 0$, we know f' is positive for $x < -2$, so f is increasing for $x < -2$. Similarly, since $f'(0) = -48$ and $f'(10) = 72$, we know that f decreases between $x = -2$ and $x = 8$ and increases for $x > 8$. Summarizing:

	$x = -2$		$x = 8$	
f increasing $\nearrow$		f decreasing $\searrow$		f increasing $\nearrow$	→ x
$f' > 0$	$f' = 0$	$f' < 0$	$f' = 0$	$f' > 0$

We find that $f(-2) = 104$ and $f(8) = -396$. Hence on the interval $-2 < x < 8$ the function decreases from a high of 104 to a low of -396. One more point on the graph is easy to get: the y intercept, $f(0) = 52$. With just these three points we can get a graph. See Figure 4.1.

In Figure 4.1, we see that part of the graph is concave up and part is concave down. We can use the second derivative to analyze concavity. We have

$$f''(x) = 6x - 18.$$

Thus, $f''(x) < 0$ when $x < 3$ and $f''(x) > 0$ when $x > 3$, so the graph of f is concave down for $x < 3$ and concave up for $x > 3$. At $x = 3$, we have $f''(x) = 0$. See Figure 4.1. Summarizing:

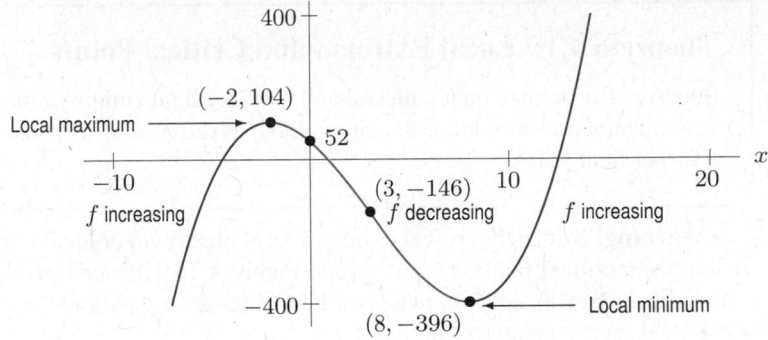

Figure 4.1: Useful graph of $f(x) = x^3 - 9x^2 - 48x + 52$

Local Maxima and Minima

We are often interested in points such as those marked local maximum and local minimum in Figure 4.1. We have the following definition:

> Suppose p is a point in the domain of f:
> - f has a **local minimum** at p if $f(p)$ is less than or equal to the values of f for points near p.
> - f has a **local maximum** at p if $f(p)$ is greater than or equal to the values of f for points near p.

We use the adjective "local" because we are describing only what happens near p. Local maxima and minima are sometimes called *local extrema*.

How Do We Detect a Local Maximum or Minimum?

In the preceding example, the points $x = -2$ and $x = 8$, where $f'(x) = 0$, played a key role in leading us to local maxima and minima. We give a name to such points:

> For any function f, a point p in the domain of f where $f'(p) = 0$ or $f'(p)$ is undefined is called a **critical point** of the function. In addition, the point $(p, f(p))$ on the graph of f is also called a critical point. A **critical value** of f is the value, $f(p)$, at a critical point, p.

Notice that "critical point of f" can refer either to points in the domain of f or to points on the graph of f. You will know which meaning is intended from the context.

Geometrically, at a critical point where $f'(p) = 0$, the line tangent to the graph of f at p is horizontal. At a critical point where $f'(p)$ is undefined, there is no horizontal tangent to the graph—there's either a vertical tangent or no tangent at all. (For example, $x = 0$ is a critical point for the absolute value function $f(x) = |x|$.) However, most of the functions we work with are differentiable everywhere, and therefore most of our critical points are of the $f'(p) = 0$ variety.

The critical points divide the domain of f into intervals within which the sign of the derivative remains the same, either positive or negative. Therefore, if f is defined on the interval between two successive critical points, its graph cannot change direction on that interval; it is either increasing or decreasing. The following result, which is proved on page 192, tells us that all local maxima and minima which are not at endpoints occur at critical points.

Theorem 4.1: Local Extrema and Critical Points

Suppose f is defined on an interval and has a local maximum or minimum at the point $x = a$, which is not an endpoint of the interval. If f is differentiable at $x = a$, then $f'(a) = 0$. Thus, a is a critical point.

Warning! Not every critical point is a local maximum or local minimum. Consider $f(x) = x^3$, which has a critical point at $x = 0$. (See Figure 4.2.) The derivative, $f'(x) = 3x^2$, is positive on both sides of $x = 0$, so f increases on both sides of $x = 0$, and there is neither a local maximum nor a local minimum at $x = 0$.

Figure 4.2: Critical point which is not a local maximum or minimum

Testing for Local Maxima and Minima at a Critical Point

If f' has different signs on either side of a critical point p, with $f'(p) = 0$, then the graph changes direction at p and looks like one of those in Figure 4.3. So we have the following criterion:

The First-Derivative Test for Local Maxima and Minima

Suppose p is a critical point of a continuous function f. Moving from left to right:
- If f' changes from negative to positive at p, then f has a local minimum at p.
- If f' changes from positive to negative at p, then f has a local maximum at p.

Figure 4.3: Changes in direction at a critical point, p: Local maxima and minima

Example 2   Use a graph of the function $f(x) = \dfrac{1}{x(x-1)}$ to observe its local maxima and minima. Confirm your observation analytically.

Solution   The graph in Figure 4.4 suggests that this function has no local minima but that there is a local maximum at about $x = \frac{1}{2}$. Confirming this analytically means using the formula for the derivative to show that what we expect is true. Since $f(x) = (x^2 - x)^{-1}$, we have

$$f'(x) = -1(x^2 - x)^{-2}(2x - 1) = -\frac{2x - 1}{(x^2 - x)^2}.$$

So $f'(x) = 0$ where $2x - 1 = 0$. Thus, the only critical point in the domain of f is $x = \frac{1}{2}$.

Furthermore, $f'(x) > 0$ where $0 < x < 1/2$, and $f'(x) < 0$ where $1/2 < x < 1$. Thus, f increases for $0 < x < 1/2$ and decreases for $1/2 < x < 1$. According to the first derivative test, the critical point $x = 1/2$ is a local maximum.

For $-\infty < x < 0$ or $1 < x < \infty$, there are no critical points and no local maxima or minima. Although $1/(x(x-1)) \to 0$ both as $x \to \infty$ and as $x \to -\infty$, we don't say 0 is a local minimum because $1/(x(x-1))$ never actually *equals* 0.

Notice that although $f' > 0$ everywhere that it is defined for $x < 1/2$, the function f is not increasing throughout this interval. The problem is that f and f' are not defined at $x = 0$, so we cannot conclude that f is increasing when $x < 1/2$.

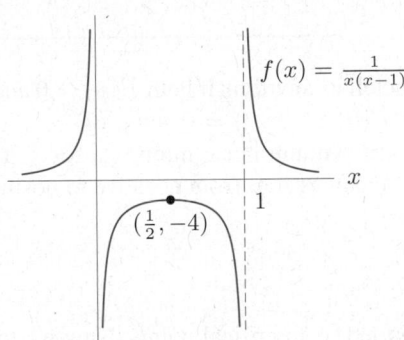

Figure 4.4: Find local maxima and minima

Figure 4.5: Explain the absence of local maxima and minima for $x \geq 0$

Example 3   The graph of $f(x) = \sin x + 2e^x$ is in Figure 4.5. Using the derivative, explain why there are no local maxima or minima for $x \geq 0$.

Solution   Local maxima and minima can occur only at critical points. Now $f'(x) = \cos x + 2e^x$, which is defined for all x. We know $\cos x$ is always between -1 and 1, and $2e^x \geq 2$ for $x \geq 0$, so $f'(x)$ cannot be 0 for any $x \geq 0$. Therefore there are no local maxima or minima there.

The Second-Derivative Test for Local Maxima and Minima

Knowing the concavity of a function can also be useful in testing if a critical point is a local maximum or a local minimum. Suppose p is a critical point of f, with $f'(p) = 0$, so that the graph of f has a horizontal tangent line at p. If the graph is concave up at p, then f has a local minimum at p. Likewise, if the graph is concave down, f has a local maximum. (See Figure 4.6.) This suggests:

The Second-Derivative Test for Local Maxima and Minima

- If $f'(p) = 0$ and $f''(p) > 0$ then f has a local minimum at p.
- If $f'(p) = 0$ and $f''(p) < 0$ then f has a local maximum at p.
- If $f'(p) = 0$ and $f''(p) = 0$ then the test tells us nothing.

Figure 4.6: Local maxima and minima and concavity

Example 4   Classify as local maxima or local minima the critical points of $f(x) = x^3 - 9x^2 - 48x + 52$.

Solution   As we saw in Example 1 on page 186,

$$f'(x) = 3x^2 - 18x - 48$$

and the critical points of f are $x = -2$ and $x = 8$. We have

$$f''(x) = 6x - 18.$$

Thus $f''(8) = 30 > 0$, so f has a local minimum at $x = 8$. Since $f''(-2) = -30 < 0$, f has a local maximum at $x = -2$.

Warning! The second-derivative test does not tell us anything if both $f'(p) = 0$ and $f''(p) = 0$. For example, if $f(x) = x^3$ and $g(x) = x^4$, both $f'(0) = f''(0) = 0$ and $g'(0) = g''(0) = 0$. The point $x = 0$ is a minimum for g but is neither a maximum nor a minimum for f. However, the first-derivative test is still useful. For example, g' changes sign from negative to positive at $x = 0$, so we know g has a local minimum there.

Concavity and Inflection Points

Investigating points where the slope changes sign led us to critical points. Now we look at points where the concavity changes.

> A point, p, at which the graph of a continuous function, f, changes concavity is called an **inflection point** of f.

The words "inflection point of f" can refer either to a point in the domain of f or to a point on the graph of f. The context of the problem will tell you which is meant.

How Do We Detect an Inflection Point?

To identify candidates for an inflection point of a continuous function, we often use the second derivative.

> Suppose f'' is defined on both sides of a point p:
> - If f'' is zero or undefined at p, then p is a possible inflection point.
> - To test whether p is an inflection point, check whether f'' changes sign at p.

The following example illustrates how local maxima and minima and inflection points are found.

Example 5   For $x \geq 0$, find the local maxima and minima and inflection points for $g(x) = xe^{-x}$ and sketch the graph of g.

Solution   Taking derivatives and simplifying, we have

$$g'(x) = (1 - x)e^{-x} \quad \text{and} \quad g''(x) = (x - 2)e^{-x}.$$

So $x = 1$ is a critical point, and $g' > 0$ for $x < 1$ and $g' < 0$ for $x > 1$. Hence g increases to a local maximum at $x = 1$ and then decreases. Since $g(0) = 0$ and $g(x) > 0$ for $x > 0$, there is a local minimum at $x = 0$. Also, $g(x) \to 0$ as $x \to \infty$. There is an inflection point at $x = 2$ since $g'' < 0$ for $x < 2$ and $g'' > 0$ for $x > 2$. The graph is sketched in Figure 4.7.

Figure 4.7: Graph of $g(x) = xe^{-x}$

Warning! Not every point x where $f''(x) = 0$ (or f'' is undefined) is an inflection point (just as not every point where $f' = 0$ is a local maximum or minimum). For instance $f(x) = x^4$ has $f''(x) = 12x^2$ so $f''(0) = 0$, but $f'' > 0$ when $x < 0$ and when $x > 0$, so there is *no* change in concavity at $x = 0$. See Figure 4.8.

Figure 4.8: Graph of $f(x) = x^4$

Inflection Points and Local Maxima and Minima of the Derivative

Inflection points can also be interpreted in terms of first derivatives. Applying the First Derivative Test for local maxima and minima to f', we obtain the following result:

Suppose a function f has a continuous derivative. If f'' changes sign at p, then f has an inflection point at p, and f' has a local minimum or a local maximum at p.

Figure 4.9 shows two inflection points. Notice that the curve crosses the tangent line at these points and that the slope of the curve is a maximum or a minimum there.

Figure 4.9: Change in concavity at p: Points of inflection

Example 6   Water is being poured into the vase in Figure 4.10 at a constant rate, measured in volume per unit time. Graph $y = f(t)$, the depth of the water against time, t. Explain the concavity and indicate the inflection points.

Solution   At first the water level, y, rises slowly because the base of the vase is wide, and it takes a lot of water to make the depth increase. However, as the vase narrows, the rate at which the water is rising increases. Thus, y is increasing at an increasing rate and the graph is concave up. The rate of increase in the water level is at a maximum when the water reaches the middle of the vase, where the diameter is smallest; this is an inflection point. After that, the rate at which y increases decreases again, so the graph is concave down. (See Figure 4.11.)

Figure 4.10: A vase

Figure 4.11: Graph of depth of water in the vase, y, against time, t

Showing Local Extrema Are at Critical Points

We now prove Theorem 4.1, which says that inside an interval, local maxima and minima can only occur at critical points. Suppose that f has a local maximum at $x = a$. Assuming that $f'(a)$ is defined, the definition of the derivative gives

$$f'(a) = \lim_{h \to 0} \frac{f(a+h) - f(a)}{h}.$$

Since this is a two-sided limit, we have

$$f'(a) = \lim_{h \to 0^-} \frac{f(a+h) - f(a)}{h} = \lim_{h \to 0^+} \frac{f(a+h) - f(a)}{h}.$$

By the definition of local maximum, $f(a+h) \le f(a)$ for all sufficiently small h. Thus $f(a+h) - f(a) \le 0$ for sufficiently small h. The denominator, h, is negative when we take the limit from the left and positive when we take the limit from the right. Thus

$$\lim_{h \to 0^-} \frac{f(a+h) - f(a)}{h} \ge 0 \quad \text{and} \quad \lim_{h \to 0^+} \frac{f(a+h) - f(a)}{h} \le 0.$$

Since both these limits are equal to $f'(a)$, we have $f'(a) \ge 0$ and $f'(a) \le 0$, so we must have $f'(a) = 0$. The proof for a local minimum at $x = a$ is similar.

Exercises and Problems for Section 4.1

Exercises

1. Indicate all critical points on the graph of f in Figure 4.12 and determine which correspond to local maxima of f, which to local minima, and which to neither.

Figure 4.12

2. Graph a function which has exactly one critical point, at $x = 2$, and exactly one inflection point, at $x = 4$.

3. Graph a function with exactly two critical points, one of which is a local minimum and the other is neither a local maximum nor a local minimum.

In Exercises 4–8, use derivatives to find the critical points and inflection points.

4. $f(x) = x^3 - 9x^2 + 24x + 5$

5. $f(x) = x^5 - 10x^3 - 8$

6. $f(x) = x^5 + 15x^4 + 25$

7. $f(x) = 5x - 3\ln x$

8. $f(x) = 4xe^{3x}$

In Exercises 9–12, find all critical points and then use the first-derivative test to determine local maxima and minima. Check your answer by graphing.

9. $f(x) = 3x^4 - 4x^3 + 6$ **10.** $f(x) = (x^2 - 4)^7$

11. $f(x) = (x^3 - 8)^4$ **12.** $f(x) = \dfrac{x}{x^2 + 1}$

In Exercises 13–14, find the critical points of the function and classify them as local maxima or local minima or neither.

13. $g(x) = xe^{-3x}$ **14.** $h(x) = x + 1/x$

15. (a) Use a graph to estimate the x-values of any critical points and inflection points of $f(x) = e^{-x^2}$.
   (b) Use derivatives to find the x-values of any critical points and inflection points exactly.

In Exercises 16–19, the function f is defined for all x. Use the graph of f' to decide:
   (a) Over what intervals is f increasing? Decreasing?
   (b) Does f have local maxima or minima? If so, which, and where?

16.

17.

18.

19.

Problems

20. (a) Show that if a is a positive constant, then $x = 0$ is the only critical point of $f(x) = x + a\sqrt{x}$.
   (b) Use derivatives to show that f is increasing and its graph is concave down for all $x > 0$.

21. (a) If b is a positive constant and $x > 0$, find all critical points of $f(x) = x - b\ln x$.
   (b) Use the second-derivative test to determine whether the function has a local maximum or local minimum at each critical point.

22. (a) If a is a nonzero constant, find all critical points of
$$f(x) = \frac{a}{x^2} + x.$$
   (b) Use the second-derivative test to show that if a is positive then the graph has a local minimum, and if a is negative then the graph has a local maximum.

23. If U and V are positive constants, find all critical points of
$$F(t) = Ue^t + Ve^{-t}.$$

24. Indicate on the graph of the derivative function f' in Figure 4.13 the x-values that are critical points of the function f itself. At which critical points does f have local maxima, local minima, or neither?

Figure 4.13

25. Indicate on the graph of the derivative f' in Figure 4.14 the x-values that are inflection points of the function f.

Figure 4.14

26. Indicate on the graph of the second derivative f'' in Figure 4.15 the x-values that are inflection points of the function f.

Figure 4.15

For Problems 27–30, sketch a possible graph of $y = f(x)$, using the given information about the derivatives $y' = f'(x)$ and $y'' = f''(x)$. Assume that the function is defined and continuous for all real x.

27.

28.

29.

30.

31. Suppose f has a continuous derivative whose values are given in the following table.

   (a) Estimate the x-coordinates of critical points of f for $0 \leq x \leq 10$.

   (b) For each critical point, indicate if it is a local maximum of f, local minimum, or neither.

x	0	1	2	3	4	5	6	7	8	9	10
$f'(x)$	5	2	1	-2	-5	-3	-1	2	3	1	-1

32. **(a)** The following table gives values of the differentiable function $y = f(x)$. Estimate the x-values of critical points of $f(x)$ on the interval $0 < x < 10$. Classify each critical point as a local maximum, local minimum, or neither.

   (b) Now assume that the table gives values of the continuous function $y = f'(x)$ (instead of $f(x)$). Estimate and classify critical points of the function $f(x)$.

x	0	1	2	3	4	5	6	7	8	9	10
y	1	2	1	-2	-5	-3	-1	2	3	1	-1

33. If water is flowing at a constant rate (i.e., constant volume per unit time) into the vase in Figure 4.16, sketch a graph of the depth of the water against time. Mark on the graph the time at which the water reaches the corner of the vase.

Figure 4.16

Figure 4.17

34. If water is flowing at a constant rate (i.e., constant volume per unit time) into the Grecian urn in Figure 4.17, sketch a graph of the depth of the water against time. Mark on the graph the time at which the water reaches the widest point of the urn.

35. Find and classify the critical points of $f(x) = x^3(1-x)^4$ as local maxima and minima.

36. If $m, n \geq 2$ are integers, find and classify the critical points of $f(x) = x^m(1 - x)^n$.

37. The rabbit population on a small Pacific island is approximated by

$$P = \frac{2000}{1 + e^{5.3 - 0.4t}}$$

with t measured in years since 1774, when Captain James Cook left 10 rabbits on the island.

   (a) Graph P. Does the population level off?
   (b) Estimate when the rabbit population grew most rapidly. How large was the population at that time?
   (c) What natural causes could lead to the shape of the graph of P?

38. Find values of a and b so that the function $f(x) = x^2 + ax + b$ has a local minimum at the point $(6, -5)$.

39. Find the value of a so that the function $f(x) = xe^{ax}$ has a critical point at $x = 3$.

40. Find constants a and b in the function $f(x) = axe^{bx}$ such that $f(\frac{1}{3}) = 1$ and the function has a local maximum at $x = \frac{1}{3}$.

41. Graph $f(x) = x + \sin x$, and determine where f is increasing most rapidly and least rapidly.

42. You might think the graph of $f(x) = x^2 + \cos x$ should look like a parabola with some waves on it. Sketch the actual graph of $f(x)$ using a calculator or computer. Explain what you see using $f''(x)$.

Problems 43–44 show graphs of the three functions f, f', f''. Identify which is which.

43.

44.

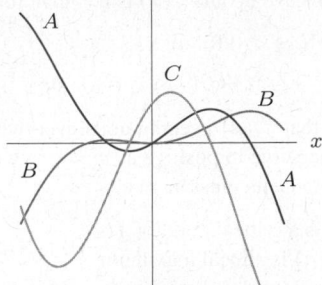

Problems 45–46 show graphs of f, f', f''. Each of these three functions is either odd or even. Decide which functions are odd and which are even. Use this information to identify which graph corresponds to f, which to f', and which to f''.

45.

46.

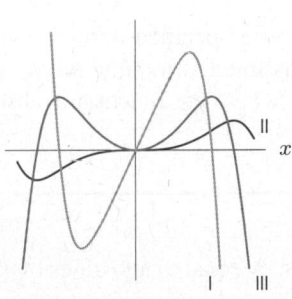

47. Use the derivative formulas and algebra to find the intervals where $f(x) = (x + 50)/(x^2 + 525)$ is increasing and the intervals where it is decreasing. It is possible, but difficult, to solve this problem by graphing f; describe the difficulty.

48. Let f be a function with $f(x) > 0$ for all x. Set $g = 1/f$.

   (a) If f is increasing in an interval around x_0, what about g?

   (b) If f has a local maximum at x_1, what about g?

   (c) If f is concave down at x_2, what about g?

In Problems 49–50, the differentiable function f has $x = 1$ as its only zero and $x = 2$ as its only critical point. For the given functions, find all

(a) Zeros   **(b)** Critical points.

49. $y = f\left(x^2 - 3\right)$ **50.** $y = (f(x))^2 + 3$

In Problems 51–52, the graph of f lies entirely above the x-axis and $f'(x) < 0$ for all x.

   (a) Give the critical point(s) of the function, or explain how you know there are none.

   (b) Say where the function increases and where it decreases.

51. $y = (f(x))^2$ **52.** $y = f\left(x^2\right)$

Strengthen Your Understanding

In Problems 53–54, explain what is wrong with the statement.

53. An increasing function has no inflection points.

54. For any function f, if $f''(0) = 0$, there is an inflection point at $x = 0$.

In Problems 55–57, give an example of:

55. A function which has no critical points on the interval between 0 and 1.

56. A function, f, which has a critical point at $x = 1$ but for which $f'(1) \neq 0$.

57. A function with local maxima and minima at an infinite number of points.

Are the statements in Problems 58–66 true or false for a function f whose domain is all real numbers? If a statement is true, explain how you know. If a statement is false, give a counterexample.

58. A local minimum of f occurs at a critical point of f.

59. If $x = p$ is not a critical point of f, then $x = p$ is not a local maximum of f.

60. A local maximum of f occurs at a point where

$$f'(x) = 0.$$

61. If $x = p$ is not a local maximum of f, then $x = p$ is not a critical point of f.

62. If $f'(p) = 0$, then $f(x)$ has a local minimum or local maximum at $x = p$.

63. If $f'(x)$ is continuous and $f(x)$ has no critical points, then f is everywhere increasing or everywhere decreasing.

64. If $f''(x)$ is continuous and the graph of f has an inflection point at $x = p$, then $f''(p) = 0$.

65. A critical point of f must be a local maximum or minimum of f.

66. Every cubic polynomial has an inflection point.

In Problems 67–72, give an example of a function f that makes the statement true, or say why such an example is impossible. Assume that f'' exists everywhere.

67. f is concave up and $f(x)$ is positive for all x.

68. f is concave down and $f(x)$ is positive for all x.

69. f is concave down and $f(x)$ is negative for all x.

70. f is concave up and $f(x)$ is negative for all x.

71. $f(x)f''(x) < 0$ for all x.

72. $f(x)f'(x)f''(x)f'''(x) < 0$ for all x.[1]

73. Given that $f'(x)$ is continuous everywhere and changes from negative to positive at $x = a$, which of the following statements must be true?

   (a) a is a critical point of $f(x)$
   (b) $f(a)$ is a local maximum
   (c) $f(a)$ is a local minimum
   (d) $f'(a)$ is a local maximum
   (e) $f'(a)$ is a local minimum

4.2 OPTIMIZATION

The largest and smallest values of a quantity often have practical importance. For example, automobile engineers want to construct a car that uses the least amount of fuel, scientists want to calculate which wavelength carries the maximum radiation at a given temperature, and urban planners want to design traffic patterns to minimize delays. Such problems belong to the field of mathematics called *optimization*. The next three sections show how the derivative provides an efficient way of solving many optimization problems.

Global Maxima and Minima

The single greatest (or least) value of a function f over a specified domain is called the *global maximum* (or *minimum*) of f. Recall that the local maxima and minima tell us where a function is locally largest or smallest. Now we are interested in where the function is absolutely largest or smallest in a given domain. We say

Suppose p is a point in the domain of f:
- f has a **global minimum** at p if $f(p)$ is less than or equal to all values of f.
- f has a **global maximum** at p if $f(p)$ is greater than or equal to all values of f.

Global maxima and minima are sometimes called *extrema* or *optimal values*.

Existence of Global Extrema

The following theorem describes when global extrema are guaranteed to exist:

Theorem 4.2: The Extreme Value Theorem

If f is continuous on the closed interval $a \leq x \leq b$, then f has a global maximum and a global minimum on that interval.

For a proof of Theorem 4.2, see www.wiley.com/college/hughes-hallett.

---

[1] From the 1998 William Lowell Putnam Mathematical Competition, by permission of the Mathematical Association of America.

How Do We Find Global Maxima and Minima?

If f is a continuous function defined on a closed interval $a \leq x \leq b$ (that is, an interval containing its endpoints), then Theorem 4.2 guarantees that global maxima and minima exist. Figure 4.18 illustrates that the global maximum or minimum of f occurs either at a critical point or at an endpoint of the interval, $x = a$ or $x = b$. These points are the candidates for global extrema.

Figure 4.18: Global maximum and minimum on a closed interval $a \leq x \leq b$

Global Maxima and Minima on a Closed Interval: Test the Candidates

For a continuous function f on a closed interval $a \leq x \leq b$:
- Find the critical points of f in the interval.
- Evaluate the function at the critical points and at the endpoints, a and b. The largest value of the function is the global maximum; the smallest value is the global minimum.

If the function is defined on an open interval $a < x < b$ (that is, an interval not including its endpoints) or on all real numbers, there may or may not be a global maximum or minimum. For example, there is no global maximum in Figure 4.19 because the function has no actual largest value. The global minimum in Figure 4.19 coincides with the local minimum. There is a global minimum but no global maximum in Figure 4.20.

Global Maxima and Minima on an Open Interval or on All Real Numbers

For a continuous function, f, find the value of f at all the critical points and sketch a graph. Look at values of f when x approaches the endpoints of the interval, or approaches $\pm\infty$, as appropriate. If there is only one critical point, look at the sign of f' on either side of the critical point.

Figure 4.19: Global minimum on
$a < x < b$

Figure 4.20: Global minimum when the
domain is all real numbers

Example 1   Find the global maxima and minima of $f(x) = x^3 - 9x^2 - 48x + 52$ on the following intervals:

(a) $-5 \leq x \leq 12$ (b) $-5 \leq x \leq 14$ (c) $-5 \leq x < \infty.$

Solution   (a) We have previously obtained the critical points $x = -2$ and $x = 8$ using

$$f'(x) = 3x^2 - 18x - 48 = 3(x+2)(x-8).$$

We evaluate f at the critical points and the endpoints of the interval:

$$f(-5) = (-5)^3 - 9(-5)^2 - 48(-5) + 52 = -58$$
$$f(-2) = 104$$
$$f(8) = -396$$
$$f(12) = -92.$$

Comparing these function values, we see that the global maximum on $[-5, 12]$ is 104 and occurs at $x = -2$, and the global minimum on $[-5, 12]$ is -396 and occurs at $x = 8$.

(b) For the interval $[-5, 14]$, we compare

$$f(-5) = -58, \quad f(-2) = 104, \quad f(8) = -396, \quad f(14) = 360.$$

The global maximum is now 360 and occurs at $x = 14$, and the global minimum is still -396 and occurs at $x = 8$. Since the function is increasing for $x > 8$, changing the right-hand end of the interval from $x = 12$ to $x = 14$ alters the global maximum but not the global minimum. See Figure 4.21.

(c) Figure 4.21 shows that for $-5 \leq x < \infty$ there is no global maximum, because we can make $f(x)$ as large as we please by choosing x large enough. The global minimum remains -396 at $x = 8$.

Figure 4.21: Graph of $f(x) = x^3 - 9x^2 - 48x + 52$

Figure 4.22: Graph of $g(x) = x - \sin(2x)$

Example 2   Find the global maximum and minimum of $g(x) = x - \sin(2x)$ on the interval $0 \leq x \leq \pi/2$.

Solution   Since $g(x) = x - \sin(2x)$ is continuous and the interval $0 \leq x \leq \pi/2$ is closed, there must be a global maximum and minimum. The possible candidates are critical points in the interval and endpoints. Since there are no points where $g'(x)$ is undefined, we solve $g'(x) = 0$ to find all the critical points:

$$g'(x) = 1 - 2\cos(2x) = 0,$$

so $\cos(2x) = 1/2$. Therefore $2x = \pi/3, 5\pi/3, \ldots$. Thus the only critical point in the interval is $x = \pi/6$. We compare values of g at the critical points and the endpoints:

$$g(0) = 0, \quad g(\pi/6) = \pi/6 - \sqrt{3}/2 = -0.342, \quad g(\pi/2) = \pi/2 = 1.571.$$

Thus the global maximum is 1.571 at $x = \pi/2$ and the global minimum is -0.342 at $x = \pi/6$. See Figure 4.22.

Example 3   Jared is coughing. The speed in m/sec, $v(r)$, with which he expels air depends on the radius, r, of his windpipe, given for $0 \leq r \leq 9$ in mm by

$$v(r) = 0.1(9 - r)r^2.$$

What value of r maximizes the speed? For what value is the speed minimized?

Solution   Notice that $v(0) = v(9) = 0$, and that $v(r)$ is positive for $0 < r < 9$. Therefore the maximum occurs somewhere between $r = 0$ and $r = 9$. Since

$$v(r) = 0.1(9 - r)r^2 = 0.9r^2 - 0.1r^3,$$

the derivative is

$$v'(r) = 1.8r - 0.3r^2 = 0.3r(6 - r).$$

The derivative is zero if $r = 0$ or $r = 6$. These are the critical points of v. We already know $v(0) = v(9) = 0$, and

$$v(6) = 0.1(9 - 6)6^2 = 10.8 \text{ m/sec.}$$

Thus, v has a global maximum at $r = 6$ mm. The global minimum of $v = 0$ m/sec occurs at both endpoints $r = 0$ mm and $r = 9$ mm.

In applications of optimization, the function being optimized often contains a parameter whose value depends on the situation, and the maximum or minimum depends on the parameter.

Example 4   (a) For a positive constant b, the surge function $f(t) = te^{-bt}$ gives the quantity of a drug in the body for time $t \geq 0$. Find the global maximum and minimum of $f(t)$ for $t \geq 0$.
(b) Find the value of b making $t = 10$ the global maximum.

Solution   (a) Differentiating and factoring gives

$$f'(t) = 1 \cdot e^{-bt} - bte^{-bt} = (1 - bt)e^{-bt},$$

so there is a critical point at $t = 1/b$.

The sign of f' is determined by the sign of $(1 - bt)$, so f' is positive to the left of $t = 1/b$ and negative to the right of $t = 1/b$. Since f increases to the left of $t = 1/b$ and decreases to the right of $t = 1/b$, the global maximum occurs at $t = 1/b$. In addition, $f(0) = 0$ and $f(t) \geq 0$ for all $t \geq 0$, so the global minimum occurs at $t = 0$. Thus

The global maximum value is $f\left(\dfrac{1}{b}\right) = \dfrac{1}{b}e^{-b(1/b)} = \dfrac{e^{-1}}{b}$.

The global minimum value is $f(0) = 0$.
(b) Since $t = 10$ gives the global maximum, we have $1/b = 10$, so $b = 0.1$. See Figure 4.23.

Figure 4.23: Graph of $f(t) = te^{-bt}$ for $b = 0.1$

Example 5   When an arrow is shot into the air, its range, R, is defined as the horizontal distance from the archer to the point where the arrow hits the ground. If the ground is horizontal and we neglect air resistance, it can be shown that

$$R = \frac{v_0{}^2 \sin(2\theta)}{g},$$

where v_0 is the initial velocity of the arrow, g is the (constant) acceleration due to gravity, and θ is the angle above horizontal, so $0 \leq \theta \leq \pi/2$. (See Figure 4.24.) What angle θ maximizes R?

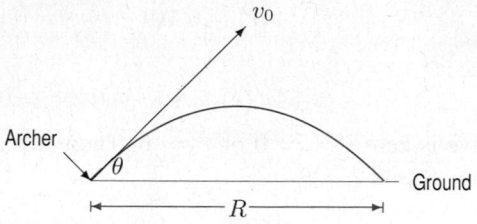

Figure 4.24: Arrow's path

Solution   We can find the maximum of this function without using calculus. The maximum value of R occurs when $\sin(2\theta) = 1$, so $\theta = \arcsin(1)/2 = \pi/4$, giving $R = v_0^2/g$.

Let's see how we can do the same problem with calculus. We want to find the global maximum of R for $0 \leq \theta \leq \pi/2$. First we look for critical points:

$$\frac{dR}{d\theta} = 2\frac{v_0^2 \cos(2\theta)}{g}.$$

Setting $dR/d\theta$ equal to 0, we get

$$0 = \cos(2\theta), \quad \text{or} \quad 2\theta = \pm\frac{\pi}{2}, \pm\frac{3\pi}{2}, \pm\frac{5\pi}{2}, \ldots$$

so $\pi/4$ is the only critical point in the interval $0 \leq \theta \leq \pi/2$. The range at $\theta = \pi/4$ is $R = v_0{}^2/g$.

Now we must check the value of R at the endpoints $\theta = 0$ and $\theta = \pi/2$. Since $R = 0$ at each endpoint (the arrow is shot horizontally or vertically), the critical point $\theta = \pi/4$ gives both a local and a global maximum on $0 \leq \theta \leq \pi/2$. Therefore, the arrow goes farthest if shot at an angle of $\pi/4$, or $45°$.

Finding Upper and Lower Bounds

A problem which is closely related to finding maxima and minima is finding the *bounds* of a function. In Example 1 on page 198, the value of $f(x)$ on the interval $[-5, 12]$ ranges from -396 to 104. Thus

$$-396 \leq f(x) \leq 104,$$

and we say that -396 is a *lower bound* for f and 104 is an *upper bound* for f on $[-5, 12]$. (See Appendix A for more on bounds.) Of course, we could also say that

$$-400 \leq f(x) \leq 150,$$

so that f is also bounded below by -400 and above by 150 on $[-5, 12]$. However, we consider the -396 and 104 to be the *best possible bounds* because they describe more accurately how the function $f(x)$ behaves on $[-5, 12]$.

Example 6   An object on a spring oscillates about its equilibrium position at $y = 0$. See Figure 4.25. Its displacement, y, from equilibrium is given as a function of time, t, by

$$y = e^{-t} \cos t.$$

Find the greatest distance the object goes above and below the equilibrium for $t \geq 0$.

Solution   We are looking for bounds for y as a function of t. What does the graph look like? We can think of it as a cosine curve with a decreasing amplitude of e^{-t}; in other words, it is a cosine curve squashed between the graphs of $y = e^{-t}$ and $y = -e^{-t}$, forming a wave with lower and lower crests and shallower and shallower troughs. (See Figure 4.26.)

Figure 4.25: Object on spring
($y < 0$ below equilibrium)

Figure 4.26: $f(t) = e^{-t} \cos t$ for $t \geq 0$

From the graph, we see that for $t \geq 0$, the curve lies between the horizontal lines $y = -1$ and $y = 1$. This means that -1 and 1 are bounds:

$$-1 \leq e^{-t} \cos t \leq 1.$$

The line $y = 1$ is the best possible upper bound because the graph does come up that high (at $t = 0$). However, we can find a better lower bound if we find the global minimum value of y for $t \geq 0$; this minimum occurs in the first trough between $t = \pi/2$ and $t = 3\pi/2$ because later troughs are squashed closer to the t-axis. At the minimum, $dy/dt = 0$. The product rule gives

$$\frac{dy}{dt} = (-e^{-t}) \cos t + e^{-t}(-\sin t) = -e^{-t}(\cos t + \sin t) = 0.$$

Since e^{-t} is never 0, we must have

$$\cos t + \sin t = 0, \quad \text{so} \quad \frac{\sin t}{\cos t} = -1.$$

The smallest positive solution of

$$\tan t = -1 \quad \text{is} \quad t = \frac{3\pi}{4}.$$

Thus, the global minimum we see on the graph occurs at $t = 3\pi/4$. The value of y there is

$$y = e^{-3\pi/4} \cos\left(\frac{3\pi}{4}\right) \approx -0.07.$$

The greatest distance the object goes below equilibrium is 0.07. Thus, for all $t \geq 0$,

$$-0.07 \leq e^{-t} \cos t \leq 1.$$

Notice how much smaller in magnitude the lower bound is than the upper. This is a reflection of how quickly the factor e^{-t} causes the oscillation to die out.

Exercises and Problems for Section 4.2

Exercises

For Exercises 1–2, indicate all critical points on the given graphs. Determine which correspond to local minima, local maxima, global minima, global maxima, or none of these. (Note that the graphs are on closed intervals.)

1.

2.

3. For $x > 0$, find the x-value and the corresponding y-value that maximizes $y = 25 + 6x^2 - x^3$, by

   (a) Estimating the values from a graph of y.
   (b) Finding the values using calculus.

In Exercises 4–10, find the global maximum and minimum for the function on the closed interval.

4. $f(x) = x^3 - 3x^2 + 20, \quad -1 \le x \le 3$

5. $f(x) = x^4 - 8x^2, \quad -3 \le x \le 1$

6. $f(x) = xe^{-x^2/2}, \quad -2 \le x \le 2$

7. $f(x) = 3x^{1/3} - x, \quad -1 \le x \le 8$

8. $f(x) = x - 2\ln(x + 1), \quad 0 \le x \le 2$

9. $f(x) = x^2 - 2|x|, \quad -3 \le x \le 4$

10. $f(x) = \dfrac{x+1}{x^2+3}, \quad -1 \le x \le 2$

In Exercises 11–13, find the value(s) of x for which:

   (a) $f(x)$ has a local maximum or local minimum. Indicate which ones are maxima and which are minima.

   (b) $f(x)$ has a global maximum or global minimum.

11. $f(x) = x^{10} - 10x$, and $0 \le x \le 2$

12. $f(x) = x - \ln x$, and $0.1 \le x \le 2$

13. $f(x) = \sin^2 x - \cos x$, and $0 \le x \le \pi$

In Exercises 14–19, find the exact global maximum and minimum values of the function. The domain is all real numbers unless otherwise specified.

14. $g(x) = 4x - x^2 - 5$

15. $f(x) = x + 1/x$ for $x > 0$

16. $g(t) = te^{-t}$ for $t > 0$

17. $f(x) = x - \ln x$ for $x > 0$

18. $f(t) = \dfrac{t}{1+t^2}$

19. $f(t) = (\sin^2 t + 2)\cos t$

In Exercises 20–25, find the best possible bounds for the function.

20. $x^3 - 4x^2 + 4x, \quad$ for $\quad 0 \le x \le 4$

21. $e^{-x^2}, \quad$ for $|x| \le 0.3$

22. $x^3 e^{-x}, \quad$ for $x \ge 0$

23. $x + \sin x, \quad$ for $0 \le x \le 2\pi$

24. $\ln(1 + x), \quad$ for $x \ge 0$

25. $\ln(1 + x^2), \quad$ for $-1 \le x \le 2$

Problems

26. A grapefruit is tossed straight up with an initial velocity of 50 ft/sec. The grapefruit is 5 feet above the ground when it is released. Its height, in feet, at time t seconds is given by

$$y = -16t^2 + 50t + 5.$$

How high does it go before returning to the ground?

27. Find the value(s) of x that give critical points of $y = ax^2 + bx + c$, where a, b, c are constants. Under what conditions on a, b, c is the critical value a maximum? A minimum?

28. What value of w minimizes S if $S - 5pw = 3qw^2 - 6pq$ and p and q are positive constants?

29. Let $y = at^2 e^{-bt}$ with a and b positive constants. For $t \ge 0$, what value of t maximizes y? Sketch the curve if $a = 1$ and $b = 1$.

30. For some positive constant C, a patient's temperature change, T, due to a dose, D, of a drug is given by

$$T = \left(\frac{C}{2} - \frac{D}{3}\right) D^2.$$

   (a) What dosage maximizes the temperature change?
   (b) The sensitivity of the body to the drug is defined as dT/dD. What dosage maximizes sensitivity?

31. A warehouse selling cement has to decide how often and in what quantities to reorder. It is cheaper, on average, to place large orders, because this reduces the ordering cost per unit. On the other hand, larger orders mean higher storage costs. The warehouse always reorders cement in the same quantity, q. The total weekly cost, C, of ordering and storage is given by

$$C = \frac{a}{q} + bq, \quad \text{where } a, b \text{ are positive constants.}$$

(a) Which of the terms, a/q and bq, represents the ordering cost and which represents the storage cost?

(b) What value of q gives the minimum total cost?

32. The bending moment M of a beam, supported at one end, at a distance x from the support is given by

$$M = \tfrac{1}{2}wLx - \tfrac{1}{2}wx^2,$$

where L is the length of the beam, and w is the uniform load per unit length. Find the point on the beam where the moment is greatest.

33. A chemical reaction converts substance A to substance Y. At the start of the reaction, the quantity of A present is a grams. At time t seconds later, the quantity of Y present is y grams. The rate of the reaction, in grams/sec, is given by

$$\text{Rate} = ky(a - y), \quad k \text{ is a positive constant.}$$

(a) For what values of y is the rate nonnegative? Graph the rate against y.

(b) For what values of y is the rate a maximum?

34. The potential energy, U, of a particle moving along the x-axis is given by

$$U = b\left(\frac{a^2}{x^2} - \frac{a}{x}\right),$$

where a and b are positive constants and $x > 0$. What value of x minimizes the potential energy?

35. For positive constants A and B, the force between two atoms in a molecule is given by

$$f(r) = -\frac{A}{r^2} + \frac{B}{r^3},$$

where $r > 0$ is the distance between the atoms. What value of r minimizes the force between the atoms?

36. When an electric current passes through two resistors with resistance r_1 and r_2, connected in parallel, the combined resistance, R, can be calculated from the equation

$$\frac{1}{R} = \frac{1}{r_1} + \frac{1}{r_2},$$

where R, r_1, and r_2 are positive. Assume that r_2 is constant.

(a) Show that R is an increasing function of r_1.

(b) Where on the interval $a \leq r_1 \leq b$ does R take its maximum value?

37. As an epidemic spreads through a population, the number of infected people, I, is expressed as a function of the number of susceptible people, S, by

$$I = k\ln\left(\frac{S}{S_0}\right) - S + S_0 + I_0, \quad \text{for } k, S_0, I_0 > 0.$$

(a) Find the maximum number of infected people.

(b) The constant k is a characteristic of the particular disease; the constants S_0 and I_0 are the values of S and I when the disease starts. Which of the following affects the maximum possible value of I? Explain.

- The particular disease, but not how it starts.
- How the disease starts, but not the particular disease.
- Both the particular disease and how it starts.

38. Two points on the curve $y = \dfrac{x^3}{1 + x^4}$ have opposite x-values, x and $-x$. Find the points making the slope of the line joining them greatest.

39. The function $y = t(x)$ is positive and continuous with a global maximum at the point $(3, 3)$. Graph $t(x)$ if $t'(x)$ and $t''(x)$ have the same sign for $x < 3$, but opposite signs for $x > 3$.

40. Figure 4.27 gives the derivative of $g(x)$ on $-2 \leq x \leq 2$.

(a) Write a few sentences describing the behavior of $g(x)$ on this interval.

(b) Does the graph of $g(x)$ have any inflection points? If so, give the approximate x-coordinates of their locations. Explain your reasoning.

(c) What are the global maxima and minima of g on $[-2, 2]$?

(d) If $g(-2) = 5$, what do you know about $g(0)$ and $g(2)$? Explain.

Figure 4.27

41. Figure 4.28 shows the second derivative of $h(x)$ for $-2 \leq x \leq 1$. If $h'(-1) = 0$ and $h(-1) = 2$,

(a) Explain why $h'(x)$ is never negative on this interval.

(b) Explain why $h(x)$ has a global maximum at $x = 1$.

(c) Sketch a possible graph of $h(x)$ for $-2 \leq x \leq 1$.

Figure 4.28

42. Show that if $f''(x)$ is continuous and $f(x)$ has exactly two critical points, then $f'(x)$ has a local maximum or local minimum between the two critical points.

43. You are given the n numbers $a_1, a_2, a_3, \cdots, a_n$. For a variable x, consider the expression

$$D = (x-a_1)^2 + (x-a_2)^2 + (x-a_3)^2 + \cdots + (x-a_n)^2.$$

Show that D is a minimum when x is the average of $a_1, a_2, a_3, \cdots, a_n$.

44. In this problem we prove a special case of the Mean Value Theorem where $f(a) = f(b) = 0$. This special case is called Rolle's Theorem: If f is continuous on $[a, b]$ and differentiable on (a, b), and if $f(a) = f(b) = 0$, then there is a number c, with $a < c < b$, such that

$$f'(c) = 0.$$

By the Extreme Value Theorem, f has a global maximum and a global minimum on $[a, b]$.

(a) Prove Rolle's Theorem in the case that both the global maximum and the global minimum are at endpoints of $[a, b]$. [Hint: $f(x)$ must be a very simple function in this case.]

(b) Prove Rolle's Theorem in the case that either the global maximum or the global minimum is not at an endpoint. [Hint: Think about local maxima and minima.]

45. Use Rolle's Theorem to prove the Mean Value Theorem. Suppose that $f(x)$ is continuous on $[a, b]$ and differentiable on (a, b). Let $g(x)$ be the difference between $f(x)$ and the y-value on the secant line joining $(a, f(a))$ to $(b, f(b))$, so

$$g(x) = f(x) - f(a) - \frac{f(b) - f(a)}{b - a}(x - a).$$

(a) Show $g(x)$ on a sketch of $f(x)$.

(b) Use Rolle's Theorem (Problem 44) to show that there must be a point c in (a, b) such that $g'(c) = 0$.

(c) Show that if c is the point in part (b), then

$$f'(c) = \frac{f(b) - f(a)}{b - a}.$$

Strengthen Your Understanding

In Problems 46–48, explain what is wrong with the statement.

46. The function $f(x) = (x-1)^2(x-2)$, $0 \le x \le 3$ has a global maximum at $x = 1$.

47. The global minimum of $f(x) = x^4$ on any closed interval $a \le x \le b$ occurs at $x = 0$.

48. The best possible bounds for $f(x) = 1/(1-x)$ on the interval $0 \le x \le 2$ are $f(0) \le f(x) \le f(2)$.

In Problems 49–52, give an example of:

49. A function which has a global maximum at $x = 0$ and a global minimum at $x = 1$ on the interval $0 \le x \le 1$ but no critical points in between $x = 0$ and $x = 1$.

50. A function for which the global maximum is equal to the global minimum.

51. An interval where the best possible bounds for $f(x) = x^2$ are $2 \le f(x) \le 5$.

52. A differentiable function f with best possible bounds $-1 \le f(x) \le 1$ on the interval $-4 \le x \le 4$.

In Problems 53–57, let $f(x) = x^2$. Decide if the following statements are true or false. Explain your answer.

53. f has an upper bound on the interval $(0, 2)$.

54. f has a global maximum on the interval $(0, 2)$.

55. f does not have a global minimum on the interval $(0, 2)$.

56. f does not have a global minimum on any interval (a, b).

57. f has a global minimum on any interval $[a, b]$.

58. Which of the following statements is implied by the statement "If f is continuous on $[a, b]$ then f has a global maximum on $[a, b]$?"

(a) If f has a global maximum on $[a, b]$ then f must be continuous on $[a, b]$.

(b) If f is not continuous on $[a, b]$ then f does not have a global maximum on $[a, b]$.

(c) If f does not have a global maximum on $[a, b]$ then f is not continuous on $[a, b]$.

Are the statements in Problems 59–63 true of false? Give an explanation for your answer.

59. Since the function $f(x) = 1/x$ is continuous for $x > 0$ and the interval $(0, 1)$ is bounded, f has a maximum on the interval $(0, 1)$.

60. The Extreme Value Theorem says that only continuous functions have global maxima and minima on every closed, bounded interval.

61. The global maximum of $f(x) = x^2$ on every closed interval is at one of the endpoints of the interval.

62. A function can have two different upper bounds.

63. If a differentiable function $f(x)$ has a global maximum on the interval $0 \le x \le 10$ at $x = 0$, then $f'(0) \le 0$.

4.3 OPTIMIZATION AND MODELING

Finding global maxima and minima is often made possible by having a formula for the function to be maximized or minimized. The process of translating a problem into a function with a known formula is called *mathematical modeling*. The examples that follow give the flavor of modeling.

Example 1 What are the dimensions of an aluminum can that holds 40 in^3 of juice and that uses the least material? Assume that the can is cylindrical, and is capped on both ends.

Solution It is often a good idea to think about a problem in general terms before trying to solve it. Since we're trying to use as little material as possible, why not make the can very small, say, the size of a peanut? We can't, since the can must hold 40 in^3. If we make the can short, to try to use less material in the sides, we'll have to make it fat as well, so that it can hold 40 in^3. See Figure 4.29(a).

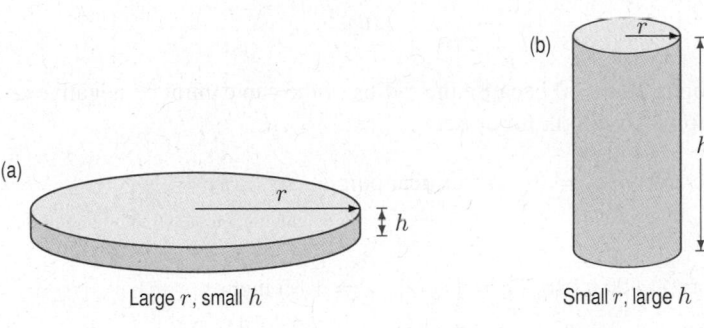

Figure 4.29: Various cylindrical-shaped cans

Table 4.1 *Height, h, and material, M, used in can for various choices of radius, r*

r (in)	h (in)	M (in^2)
0.2	318.31	400.25
1	12.73	86.28
2	3.18	65.13
3	1.41	83.22
4	0.80	120.53
10	0.13	636.32

If we try to save material by making the top and bottom small, the can has to be tall to accommodate the 40 in^3 of juice. So any savings we get by using a small top and bottom may be outweighed by the height of the sides. See Figure 4.29(b).

Table 4.1 gives the height h and amount of material M used in the can for some choices of the radius, r. You can see that r and h change in opposite directions, and that more material is used at the extremes (very large or very small r) than in the middle. It appears that the radius needing the smallest amount of material, M, is somewhere between 1 and 3 inches. Thinking of M as a function of the radius, r, we get the graph in Figure 4.30. The graph shows that the global minimum we want is at a critical point.

Figure 4.30: Total material used in can, M, as a function of radius, r

Both the table and the graph were obtained from a mathematical model, which in this case is a formula for the material used in making the can. Finding such a formula depends on knowing the geometry of a cylinder, in particular its area and volume. We have

$$M = \text{Material used in the can} = \text{Material in ends} + \text{Material in the side}$$

where

Material in ends $= 2 \cdot$ Area of a circle with radius $r = 2 \cdot \pi r^2$,

Material in the side $=$ Area of curved side of cylinder with height h and radius $r = 2\pi rh$.

We have
$$M = 2\pi r^2 + 2\pi rh.$$

However, h is not independent of r: if r grows, h shrinks, and vice-versa. To find the relationship, we use the fact that the volume of the cylinder, $\pi r^2 h$, is equal to the constant 40 in^3:

$$\text{Volume of can} = \pi r^2 h = 40, \quad \text{giving} \quad h = \frac{40}{\pi r^2}.$$

This means
$$\text{Material in the side} = 2\pi rh = 2\pi r \frac{40}{\pi r^2} = \frac{80}{r}.$$

Thus we obtain the formula for the total material, M, used in a can of radius r if the volume is 40 in^3:

$$M = 2\pi r^2 + \frac{80}{r}.$$

The domain of this function is all $r > 0$ because the radius of the can cannot be negative or zero.

To find the minimum of M, we look for critical points:

$$\frac{dM}{dr} = 4\pi r - \frac{80}{r^2} = 0 \quad \text{at a critical point,} \quad \text{so} \quad 4\pi r = \frac{80}{r^2}.$$

Therefore,

$$\pi r^3 = 20, \quad \text{so} \quad r = \left(\frac{20}{\pi}\right)^{1/3} = 1.85 \text{ inches,}$$

which agrees with the graph in Figure 4.30. We also have

$$h = \frac{40}{\pi r^2} = \frac{40}{\pi (1.85)^2} = 3.7 \text{ inches.}$$

The material used is $M = 2\pi(1.85)^2 + 80/1.85 = 64.7$ in^2.

To confirm that we have found the global minimum, we look at the formula for dM/dr. For small r, the $-80/r^2$ term dominates and for large r, the $4\pi r$ term dominates, so dM/dr is negative for $r < 1.85$ and positive for $r > 1.85$. Thus, M is decreasing for $r < 1.85$ and increasing for $r > 1.85$, so the global minimum occurs at $r = 1.85$.

Practical Tips for Modeling Optimization Problems

1. Make sure that you know what quantity or function is to be optimized.

2. If possible, make several sketches showing how the elements that vary are related. Label your sketches clearly by assigning variables to quantities which change.

3. Try to obtain a formula for the function to be optimized in terms of the variables that you identified in the previous step. If necessary, eliminate from this formula all but one variable. Identify the domain over which this variable varies.

4. Find the critical points and evaluate the function at these points and the endpoints (if relevant) to find the global maxima and/or minima.

The next example, another problem in geometry, illustrates this approach.

Example 2   Alaina wants to get to the bus stop as quickly as possible. The bus stop is across a grassy park, 2000 feet west and 600 feet north of her starting position. Alaina can walk west along the edge of the park on the sidewalk at a speed of 6 ft/sec. She can also travel through the grass in the park, but only at a rate of 4 ft/sec. What path gets her to the bus stop the fastest?

Solution

Figure 4.31: Three possible paths to the bus stop

We might first think that she should take a path that is the shortest distance. Unfortunately, the path that follows the shortest distance to the bus stop is entirely in the park, where her speed is slow. (See Figure 4.31(a).) That distance is $\sqrt{2000^2 + 600^2} = 2088$ feet, which takes her about 522 seconds to traverse. She could instead walk quickly the entire 2000 feet along the sidewalk, which leaves her just the 600-foot northward journey through the park. (See Figure 4.31(b).) This method would take $2000/6 + 600/4 \approx 483$ seconds total walking time.

But can she do even better? Perhaps another combination of sidewalk and park gives a shorter travel time. For example, what is the travel time if she walks 1000 feet west along the sidewalk and the rest of the way through the park? (See Figure 4.31(c).) The answer is about 458 seconds.

We make a model for this problem. We label the distance that Alaina walks west along the sidewalk x and the distance she walks through the park y, as in Figure 4.32. Then the total time, t, is

$$t = t_{\text{sidewalk}} + t_{\text{park}}.$$

Since

$$\text{Time} = \text{Distance}/\text{Speed},$$

and she can walk 6 ft/sec on the sidewalk and 4 ft/sec in the park, we have

$$t = \frac{x}{6} + \frac{y}{4}.$$

Now, by the Pythagorean Theorem, $y = \sqrt{(2000 - x)^2 + 600^2}$. Therefore

$$t = \frac{x}{6} + \frac{\sqrt{(2000 - x)^2 + 600^2}}{4} \qquad \text{for } 0 \le x \le 2000.$$

We can find the critical points of this function analytically. (See Problem 15 on page 211.) Alternatively, we can graph the function on a calculator and estimate the critical point, which is $x \approx 1463$ feet. This gives a minimum total time of about 445 seconds.

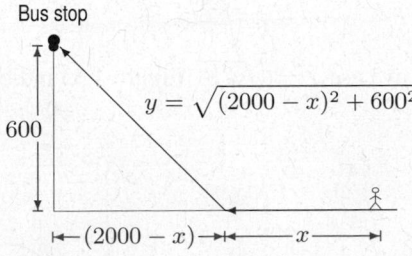

Figure 4.32: Modeling time to bus stop

Figure 4.33: Find the rectangle of maximum area with one corner on $y = \sqrt{x}$

Example 3   Figure 4.33 shows the curves $y = \sqrt{x}$, $x = 9$, $y = 0$, and a rectangle with vertical sides at $x = a$ and $x = 9$. Find the dimensions of the rectangle having the maximum possible area.

Solution   We want to choose a to maximize the area of the rectangle with corners at $(a, \sqrt{a})$ and $(9, \sqrt{a})$. The area of this rectangle is given by

$$R = \text{Height} \cdot \text{Length} = \sqrt{a}(9 - a) = 9a^{1/2} - a^{3/2}.$$

We are restricted to $0 \leq a \leq 9$. To maximize this area, we first set $dR/da = 0$ to find critical points:

$$\frac{dR}{da} = \frac{9}{2}a^{-1/2} - \frac{3}{2}a^{1/2} = 0$$

$$\frac{9}{2\sqrt{a}} = \frac{3\sqrt{a}}{2},$$

$$18 = 6a$$

$$a = 3.$$

Notice that $R = 0$ at the endpoints $a = 0$ and $a = 9$, and R is positive between these values. Since $a = 3$ is the only critical point, the rectangle with the maximum area has length $9 - 3 = 6$ and height $\sqrt{3}$.

Example 4   A closed box has a fixed surface area A and a square base with side x.

(a) Find a formula for the volume, V, of the box as a function of x. What is the domain of V?
(b) Graph V as a function of x.
(c) Find the maximum value of V.

Solution   (a) The height of the box is h, as shown in Figure 4.34. The box has six sides, four with area xh and two, the top and bottom, with area x^2. Thus,

$$4xh + 2x^2 = A.$$

So

$$h = \frac{A - 2x^2}{4x}.$$

Then, the volume, V, is given by

$$V = x^2 h = x^2 \left(\frac{A - 2x^2}{4x} \right) = \frac{x}{4}\left(A - 2x^2\right) = \frac{A}{4}x - \frac{1}{2}x^3.$$

Since the area of the top and bottom combined must be less than A, we have $2x^2 \leq A$. Thus, the domain of V is $0 \leq x \leq \sqrt{A/2}$.

(b) Figure 4.35 shows the graph for $x \geq 0$. (Note that A is a positive constant.)
(c) To find the maximum, we differentiate, regarding A as a constant:

$$\frac{dV}{dx} = \frac{A}{4} - \frac{3}{2}x^2 = 0$$

so

$$x = \pm\sqrt{\frac{A}{6}}.$$

Since $x \geq 0$ in the domain of V, we use $x = \sqrt{A/6}$. Figure 4.35 indicates that at this value of x, the volume is a maximum.

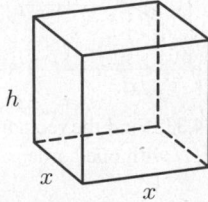

Figure 4.34: Box with base of side x, height h, surface area A, and volume V

$$V = \frac{A}{4}x - \frac{1}{2}x^3$$

Figure 4.35: Volume, V, against length of side of base, x

From the formula, we see that $dV/dx > 0$ for $x < \sqrt{A/6}$, so V is increasing, and that $dV/dx < 0$ for $x > \sqrt{A/6}$, so V is decreasing. Thus, $x = \sqrt{A/6}$ gives the global maximum. Evaluating V at $x = \sqrt{A/6}$ and simplifying, we get

$$V = \frac{A}{4}\sqrt{\frac{A}{6}} - \frac{1}{2}\left(\sqrt{\frac{A}{6}}\right)^3 = \left(\frac{A}{6}\right)^{3/2}.$$

Example 5   A light is suspended at a height h above the floor. (See Figure 4.36.) The illumination at the point P is inversely proportional to the square of the distance from the point P to the light and directly proportional to the cosine of the angle θ. How far from the floor should the light be to maximize the illumination at the point P?

Figure 4.36: How high should the light be?

Solution   If the illumination is represented by I and r is the distance from the light to the point P, then we know that for some $k \geq 0$,

$$I = \frac{k\cos\theta}{r^2}.$$

Since $r^2 = h^2 + 10^2$ and $\cos\theta = h/r = h/\sqrt{h^2 + 10^2}$, we have, for $h \geq 0$,

$$I = \frac{kh}{(h^2 + 10^2)^{3/2}}.$$

To find the height at which I is maximized, we differentiate using the quotient rule:

$$\begin{aligned}
\frac{dI}{dh} &= \frac{k(h^2 + 10^2)^{3/2} - kh(\frac{3}{2}(h^2 + 10^2)^{1/2}(2h))}{[(h^2 + 10^2)^{3/2}]^2} \\
&= \frac{(h^2 + 10^2)^{1/2}[k(h^2 + 10^2) - 3kh^2]}{(h^2 + 10^2)^3} \\
&= \frac{k(h^2 + 10^2) - 3kh^2}{(h^2 + 10^2)^{5/2}} \\
&= \frac{k(10^2 - 2h^2)}{(h^2 + 10^2)^{5/2}}.
\end{aligned}$$

Setting $dI/dh = 0$ for $h \geq 0$ gives

$$10^2 - 2h^2 = 0$$
$$h = \sqrt{50} \text{ meters.}$$

Since $dI/dh > 0$ for $h < \sqrt{50}$ and $dI/dh < 0$ for $h > \sqrt{50}$, there is a local maximum at $h = \sqrt{50}$ meters. There is only one critical point, so the global maximum of I occurs at that point. Thus, the illumination is greatest if the light is suspended at a height of $\sqrt{50} \approx 7$ meters above the floor.

A Graphical Example: Minimizing Gas Consumption

Next we look at an example in which a function is given graphically and the optimum values are read from a graph. We already know how to estimate the optimum values of $f(x)$ from a graph of $f(x)$—read off the highest and lowest values. In this example, we see how to estimate the optimum value of the quantity $f(x)/x$ from a graph of $f(x)$ against x. The question we investigate is how to set driving speeds to maximize fuel efficiency.[2]

Example 6   Gas consumption, g (in gallons/hour), as a function of velocity, v (in mph), is given in Figure 4.37. What velocity minimizes the gas consumption per mile, represented by g/v?

Figure 4.37: Gas consumption versus velocity

Solution   Figure 4.38 shows that g/v is the slope of the line from the origin to the point P. Where on the curve should P be to make the slope a minimum? From the possible positions of the line shown in Figure 4.38, we see that the slope of the line is both a local and global minimum when the line is tangent to the curve. From Figure 4.39, we can see that the velocity at this point is about 50 mph. Thus to minimize gas consumption per mile, we should drive about 50 mph.

Figure 4.38: Graphical representation of gas consumption per mile, g/v

Figure 4.39: Velocity for maximum fuel efficiency

Exercises and Problems for Section 4.3

Exercises

1. The sum of two nonnegative numbers is 100. What is the maximum value of the product of these two numbers?

2. The product of two positive numbers is 784. What is the minimum value of their sum?

3. The sum of three nonnegative numbers is 36, and one of the numbers is twice one of the other numbers. What is the maximum value of the product of these three numbers?

4. The perimeter of a rectangle is 64 cm. Find the lengths of the sides of the rectangle giving the maximum area.

5. If you have 100 feet of fencing and want to enclose a rectangular area up against a long, straight wall, what is the largest area you can enclose?

For the solids in Exercises 6–9, find the dimensions giving the minimum surface area, given that the volume is 8 cm^3.

6. A closed rectangular box, with a square base x by x cm and height h cm.

7. An open-topped rectangular box, with a square base x by x cm and height h cm.

8. A closed cylinder with radius r cm and height h cm.

9. A cylinder open at one end with radius r cm and height h cm.

[2]Adapted from Peter D. Taylor, *Calculus: The Analysis of Functions* (Toronto: Wall & Emerson, 1992).

In Exercises 10–11, find the x-value maximizing the shaded area. One vertex is on the graph of $f(x) = x^2/3 - 50x + 1000$, where $0 \le x \le 20$.

10.

11.

12. A rectangle has one side on the x-axis and two vertices on the curve

$$y = \frac{1}{1 + x^2}.$$

Find the vertices of the rectangle with maximum area.

13. A right triangle has one vertex at the origin and one vertex on the curve $y = e^{-x/3}$ for $1 \le x \le 5$. One of the two perpendicular sides is along the x-axis; the other is parallel to the y-axis. Find the maximum and minimum areas for such a triangle.

14. A rectangle has one side on the x-axis, one side on the y-axis, one vertex at the origin and one on the curve $y = e^{-2x}$ for $x \ge 0$. Find the

(a) Maximum area   (b) Minimum perimeter

Problems

15. Find analytically the exact critical point of the function which represents the time, t, to walk to the bus stop in Example 2. Recall that t is given by

$$t = \frac{x}{6} + \frac{\sqrt{(2000 - x)^2 + 600^2}}{4}.$$

16. Of all rectangles with given area, A, which has the shortest diagonals?

17. A rectangular beam is cut from a cylindrical log of radius 30 cm. The strength of a beam of width w and height h is proportional to wh^2. (See Figure 4.40.) Find the width and height of the beam of maximum strength.

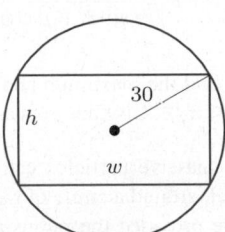

Figure 4.40

In Problems 18–19 a vertical line divides a region into two pieces. Find the value of the coordinate x that maximizes the product of the two areas.

18.

19.

In Problems 20–22 the figures are made of rectangles and semicircles.

(a) Find a formula for the area.

(b) Find a formula for the perimeter.

(c) Find the dimensions x and y that maximize the area given that the perimeter is 100.

20.

21.

22.
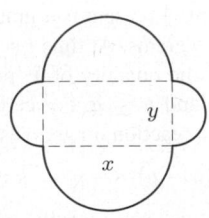

23. A piece of wire of length L cm is cut into two pieces. One piece, of length x cm, is made into a circle; the rest is made into a square.

(a) Find the value of x that makes the sum of the areas of the circle and square a minimum. Find the value of x giving a maximum.

(b) For the values of x found in part (a), show that the ratio of the length of wire in the square to the length of wire in the circle is equal to the ratio of the area of the square to the area of the circle.[3]

(c) Are the values of x found in part (a) the only values of x for which the ratios in part (b) are equal?

---

[3]From Sally Thomas.

In Problems 24–27, find the minimum and maximum values of the expression where x and y are lengths in Figure 4.41 and $0 \leq x \leq 10$.

Figure 4.41

24. x **25.** y **26.** $x + 2y$ **27.** $2x + y$

28. Which point on the curve $y = \sqrt{1 - x}$ is closest to the origin?

29. Find the point(s) on the ellipse

$$\frac{x^2}{9} + y^2 = 1$$

(a) Closest to the point $(2, 0)$.
(b) Closest to the focus $(\sqrt{8}, 0)$.

[Hint: Minimize the square of the distance—this avoids square roots.]

30. What are the dimensions of the closed cylindrical can that has surface area 280 square centimeters and contains the maximum volume?

31. A hemisphere of radius 1 sits on a horizontal plane. A cylinder stands with its axis vertical, the center of its base at the center of the sphere, and its top circular rim touching the hemisphere. Find the radius and height of the cylinder of maximum volume.

32. In a chemical reaction, substance A combines with substance B to form substance Y. At the start of the reaction, the quantity of A present is a grams, and the quantity of B present is b grams. At time t seconds after the start of the reaction, the quantity of Y present is y grams. Assume $a < b$ and $y \leq a$. For certain types of reactions, the rate of the reaction, in grams/sec, is given by

   Rate $= k(a - y)(b - y)$, k is a positive constant.

(a) For what values of y is the rate nonnegative? Graph the rate against y.
(b) Use your graph to find the value of y at which the rate of the reaction is fastest.

33. A smokestack deposits soot on the ground with a concentration inversely proportional to the square of the distance from the stack. With two smokestacks 20 miles apart, the concentration of the combined deposits on the line joining them, at a distance x from one stack, is given by

$$S = \frac{k_1}{x^2} + \frac{k_2}{(20 - x)^2}$$

where k_1 and k_2 are positive constants which depend on the quantity of smoke each stack is emitting. If $k_1 = 7k_2$, find the point on the line joining the stacks where the concentration of the deposit is a minimum.

34. A wave of wavelength λ traveling in deep water has speed, v, given for positive constants c and k, by

$$v = k\sqrt{\frac{\lambda}{c} + \frac{c}{\lambda}}$$

As λ varies, does such a wave have a maximum or minimum velocity? If so, what is it? Explain.

35. A circular ring of wire of radius r_0 lies in a plane perpendicular to the x-axis and is centered at the origin. The ring has a positive electric charge spread uniformly over it. The electric field in the x-direction, E, at the point x on the axis is given by

$$E = \frac{kx}{(x^2 + r_0^2)^{3/2}} \quad \text{for} \quad k > 0.$$

At what point on the x-axis is the field greatest? Least?

36. A woman pulls a sled which, together with its load, has a mass of m kg. If her arm makes an angle of θ with her body (assumed vertical) and the coefficient of friction (a positive constant) is μ, the least force, F, she must exert to move the sled is given by

$$F = \frac{mg\mu}{\sin \theta + \mu \cos \theta}.$$

If $\mu = 0.15$, find the maximum and minimum values of F for $0 \leq \theta \leq \pi/2$. Give answers as multiples of mg.

37. Four equally massive particles can be made to rotate, equally spaced, around a circle of radius r. This is physically possible provided the radius and period T of the rotation are chosen so that the following *action* function is at its global minimum:

$$A(r) = \frac{r^2}{T} + \frac{T}{r}, \quad r > 0.$$

(a) Find the radius r at which $A(r)$ has a global minimum.
(b) If the period of the rotation is doubled, determine whether the radius of the rotation increases or decreases, and by approximately what percentage.

38. You run a small furniture business. You sign a deal with a customer to deliver up to 400 chairs, the exact number to be determined by the customer later. The price will be $90 per chair up to 300 chairs, and above 300, the price will be reduced by $0.25 per chair (on the whole order) for every additional chair over 300 ordered. What are the largest and smallest revenues your company can make under this deal?

39. The cost of fuel to propel a boat through the water (in dollars per hour) is proportional to the cube of the speed. A certain ferry boat uses $100 worth of fuel per hour when cruising at 10 miles per hour. Apart from fuel, the cost of running this ferry (labor, maintenance, and so on) is $675 per hour. At what speed should it travel so as to minimize the cost *per mile* traveled?

40. A business sells an item at a constant rate of r units per month. It reorders in batches of q units, at a cost of $a + bq$ dollars per order. Storage costs are k dollars per item per month, and, on average, $q/2$ items are in storage, waiting to be sold. [Assume r, a, b, k are positive constants.]

   (a) How often does the business reorder?
   (b) What is the average monthly cost of reordering?
   (c) What is the total monthly cost, C of ordering and storage?
   (d) Obtain Wilson's lot size formula, the optimal batch size which minimizes cost.

41. A bird such as a starling feeds worms to its young. To collect worms, the bird flies to a site where worms are to be found, picks up several in its beak, and flies back to its nest. The *loading curve* in Figure 4.42 shows how the number of worms (the load) a starling collects depends on the time it has been searching for them.[4] The curve is concave down because the bird can pick up worms more efficiently when its beak is empty; when its beak is partly full, the bird becomes much less efficient. The traveling time (from nest to site and back) is represented by the distance PO in Figure 4.42. The bird wants to maximize the rate at which it brings worms to the nest, where

$$\text{Rate worms arrive} = \frac{\text{Load}}{\text{Traveling time} + \text{Searching time}}$$

   (a) Draw a line in Figure 4.42 whose slope is this rate.
   (b) Using the graph, estimate the load which maximizes this rate.
   (c) If the traveling time is increased, does the optimal load increase or decrease? Why?

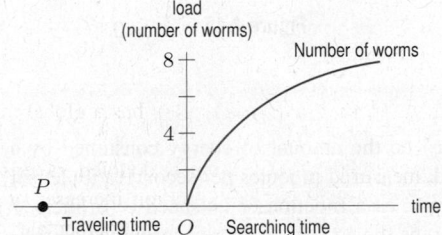

Figure 4.42

42. On the same side of a straight river are two towns, and the townspeople want to build a pumping station, S. See Figure 4.43. The pumping station is to be at the river's edge with pipes extending straight to the two towns. Where

should the pumping station be located to minimize the total length of pipe?

Figure 4.43

43. A pigeon is released from a boat (point B in Figure 4.44) floating on a lake. Because of falling air over the cool water, the energy required to fly one meter over the lake is twice the corresponding energy e required for flying over the bank ($e = 3$ joule/meter). To minimize the energy required to fly from B to the loft, L, the pigeon heads to a point P on the bank and then flies along the bank to L. The distance $\overline{AL}$ is 2000 m, and $\overline{AB}$ is 500 m.

   (a) Express the energy required to fly from B to L via P as a function of the angle θ (the angle BPA).
   (b) What is the optimal angle θ?
   (c) Does your answer change if $\overline{AL}$, $\overline{AB}$, and e have different numerical values?

Figure 4.44

44. To get the best view of the Statue of Liberty in Figure 4.45, you should be at the position where θ is a maximum. If the statue stands 92 meters high, including the pedestal, which is 46 meters high, how far from the base should you be? [Hint: Find a formula for θ in terms of your distance from the base. Use this function to maximize θ, noting that $0 \leq \theta \leq \pi/2$.]

©Wesley Hitt/Getty Images

Figure 4.45

---

[4]Alex Kacelnick (1984). Reported by J. R. Krebs and N. B. Davis, *An Introduction to Behavioural Ecology* (Oxford: Blackwell, 1987).

45. A light ray starts at the origin and is reflected off a mirror along the line $y = 1$ to the point $(2, 0)$. See Figure 4.46. Fermat's Principle says that light's path minimizes the time of travel.[5] The speed of light is a constant.

(a) Using Fermat's Principle, find the optimal position of P.

(b) Using your answer to part (a), derive the Law of Reflection, that $\theta_1 = \theta_2$.

Figure 4.46

46. (a) For which positive number x is $x^{1/x}$ largest? Justify your answer.

[Hint: You may want to write $x^{1/x} = e^{\ln(x^{1/x})}$.]

(b) For which positive integer n is $n^{1/n}$ largest? Justify your answer.

(c) Use your answer to parts (a) and (b) to decide which is larger: $3^{1/3}$ or $\pi^{1/\pi}$.

47. The *arithmetic mean* of two numbers a and b is defined as $(a+b)/2$; the *geometric mean* of two positive numbers a and b is defined as $\sqrt{ab}$.

(a) For two positive numbers, which of the two means is larger? Justify your answer.

[Hint: Define $f(x) = (a+x)/2 - \sqrt{ax}$ for fixed a.]

(b) For three positive numbers a, b, c, the arithmetic and geometric mean are $(a+b+c)/3$ and $\sqrt[3]{abc}$, respectively. Which of the two means of three numbers is larger? [Hint: Redefine $f(x)$ for fixed a *and* b.]

48. A line goes through the origin and a point on the curve $y = x^2 e^{-3x}$, for $x \geq 0$. Find the maximum slope of such a line. At what x-value does it occur?

49. The distance, s, traveled by a cyclist, who starts at 1 pm, is given in Figure 4.47. Time, t, is in hours since noon.

(a) Explain why the quantity s/t is represented by the slope of a line from the origin to the point (t, s) on the graph.

(b) Estimate the time at which the quantity s/t is a maximum.

(c) What is the relationship between the quantity s/t and the instantaneous speed of the cyclist at the time you found in part (b)?

Figure 4.47

50. When birds lay eggs, they do so in clutches of several at a time. When the eggs hatch, each clutch gives rise to a brood of baby birds. We want to determine the clutch size which maximizes the number of birds surviving to adulthood per brood. If the clutch is small, there are few baby birds in the brood; if the clutch is large, there are so many baby birds to feed that most die of starvation. The number of surviving birds per brood as a function of clutch size is shown by the benefit curve in Figure 4.48.[6]

(a) Estimate the clutch size which maximizes the number of survivors per brood.

(b) Suppose also that there is a biological cost to having a larger clutch: the female survival rate is reduced by large clutches. This cost is represented by the dotted line in Figure 4.48. If we take cost into account by assuming that the optimal clutch size in fact maximizes the vertical distance between the curves, what is the new optimal clutch size?

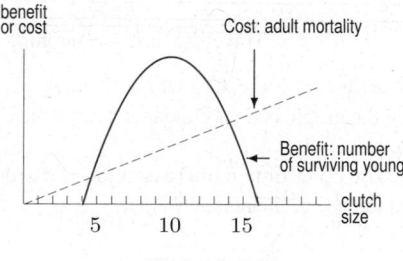

Figure 4.48

51. Let $f(v)$ be the amount of energy consumed by a flying bird, measured in joules per second (a joule is a unit of energy), as a function of its speed v (in meters/sec). Let $a(v)$ be the amount of energy consumed by the same bird, measured in joules per meter.

(a) Suggest a reason in terms of the way birds fly for the shape of the graph of $f(v)$ in Figure 4.49.

(b) What is the relationship between $f(v)$ and $a(v)$?

(c) Where on the graph is $a(v)$ a minimum?

---

[5]See, for example, D. Halliday, R. Resnik, K. Kane, *Physics*, Vol 2, 4th ed, (New York: Wiley, 1992), p. 909.

[6]Data from C. M. Perrins and D. Lack, reported by J. R. Krebs and N. B. Davies in *An Introduction to Behavioural Ecology* (Oxford: Blackwell, 1987).

(d) Should the bird try to minimize $f(v)$ or $a(v)$ when it is flying? Why?

Figure 4.49

52. The forward motion of an aircraft in level flight is reduced by two kinds of forces, known as *induced drag* and *parasite drag*. Induced drag is a consequence of the downward deflection of air as the wings produce lift. Parasite drag results from friction between the air and the entire surface of the aircraft. Induced drag is inversely proportional to the square of speed and parasite drag is directly proportional to the square of speed. The sum of induced drag and parasite drag is called total drag. The graph in Figure 4.50 shows a certain aircraft's induced drag and parasite drag functions.

(a) Sketch the total drag as a function of air speed.
(b) Estimate two different air speeds which each result in a total drag of 1000 pounds. Does the total drag function have an inverse? What about the induced and parasite drag functions?
(c) Fuel consumption (in gallons per hour) is roughly proportional to total drag. Suppose you are low on fuel and the control tower has instructed you to enter a circular holding pattern of indefinite duration to await the passage of a storm at your landing field. At what air speed should you fly the holding pattern? Why?

Figure 4.50

53. Let $f(v)$ be the fuel consumption, in gallons per hour, of a certain aircraft as a function of its airspeed, v, in miles per hour. A graph of $f(v)$ is given in Figure 4.51.

(a) Let $g(v)$ be the fuel consumption of the same aircraft, but measured in gallons per mile instead of gallons per hour. What is the relationship between $f(v)$ and $g(v)$?
(b) For what value of v is $f(v)$ minimized?
(c) For what value of v is $g(v)$ minimized?
(d) Should a pilot try to minimize $f(v)$ or $g(v)$?

Figure 4.51

Strengthen Your Understanding

In Problems 54–56, explain what is wrong with the statement.

54. If A is the area of a rectangle of sides x and $2x$, for $0 \leq x \leq 10$, the maximum value of A occurs where $dA/dx = 0$.

55. An open box is made from a 20-inch square piece of cardboard by cutting squares of side h from the corners and folding up the edges, giving the box in Figure 4.52. To find the maximum volume of such a box, we work on the domain $h \geq 0$.

56. The solution of an optimization problem modeled by a quadratic function occurs at the vertex of the quadratic.

In Problems 57–59, give an example of:

57. The sides of a rectangle with perimeter 20 cm and area smaller than 10 cm^2.

58. A context for a modeling problem where you are given that $xy = 120$ and you are minimizing the quantity $2x + 6y$.

59. A modeling problem where you are minimizing the cost of the material in a cylindrical can of volume 250 cubic centimeters.

Figure 4.52: Box of volume $V = h(20 - 2h)^2$

4.4 FAMILIES OF FUNCTIONS AND MODELING

We saw in Chapter 1 that knowledge of one function can provide knowledge of the graphs of many others. The shape of the graph of $y = x^2$ also tells us, indirectly, about the graphs of $y = x^2 + 2$, $y = (x + 2)^2$, $y = 2x^2$, and countless other functions. We say that all functions of the form $y = a(x + b)^2 + c$ form a *family of functions*; their graphs are like that of $y = x^2$, except for shifts and stretches determined by the values of a, b, and c. The constants a, b, c are called *parameters*. Different values of the parameters give different members of the family.

The Bell-Shaped Curve: $y = e^{-(x-a)^2/b}$

The family of bell-shaped curves includes the family of *normal density* functions, used in probability and statistics.[7] We assume that $b > 0$. See Section 8.8 for applications of the normal distribution.
    First we let $b = 1$ and examine the role of a.

Example 1   Graph $y = e^{-(x-a)^2}$ for $a = -2, 0, 2$ and explain the role of a in the shape of the graph.

Solution   See Figure 4.53. The role of the parameter a is to shift the graph of $y = e^{-x^2}$ to the right or left. Notice that the value of y is always positive. Since $y \to 0$ as $x \to \pm\infty$, the x-axis is a horizontal asymptote. Thus $y = e^{-(x-a)^2}$ is the family of horizontal shifts of the bell-shaped curve $y = e^{-x^2}$.

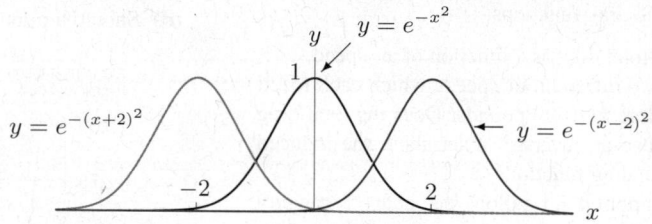

Figure 4.53: The family $y = e^{-(x-a)^2}$

We now consider the role of the parameter b by studying the family with $a = 0$.

Example 2   Find the critical points and points of inflection of $y = e^{-x^2/b}$.

Solution   To investigate the critical points and points of inflection, we calculate

$$\frac{dy}{dx} = -\frac{2x}{b} e^{-x^2/b}$$

and, using the product rule, we get

$$\frac{d^2y}{dx^2} = -\frac{2}{b} e^{-x^2/b} - \frac{2x}{b}\left(-\frac{2x}{b} e^{-x^2/b}\right) = \frac{2}{b}\left(\frac{2x^2}{b} - 1\right) e^{-x^2/b}.$$

Critical points occur where $dy/dx = 0$, that is, where

$$\frac{dy}{dx} = -\frac{2x}{b} e^{-x^2/b} = 0.$$

Since $e^{-x^2/b}$ is never zero, the only critical point is $x = 0$. At that point, $y = 1$ and $d^2y/dx^2 < 0$. Hence, by the second derivative test, there is a local maximum at $x = 0$, and this is also a global maximum.
    Inflection points occur where the second derivative changes sign; thus, we start by finding values of x for which $d^2y/dx^2 = 0$. Since $e^{-x^2/b}$ is never zero, $d^2y/dx^2 = 0$ when

$$\frac{2x^2}{b} - 1 = 0.$$

[7]Probabilists divide our function by a constant, $\sqrt{\pi b}$, to get the normal density.

Solving for x gives

$$x = \pm\sqrt{\frac{b}{2}}.$$

Looking at the expression for d^2y/dx^2, we see that d^2y/dx^2 is negative for $x = 0$, and positive as $x \to \pm\infty$. Therefore the concavity changes at $x = -\sqrt{b/2}$ and at $x = \sqrt{b/2}$, so we have inflection points at $x = \pm\sqrt{b/2}$.

Returning to the two-parameter family $y = e^{-(x-a)^2/b}$, we conclude that there is a maximum at $x = a$, obtained by horizontally shifting the maximum at $x = 0$ of $y = e^{-x^2/b}$ by a units. There are inflection points at $x = a \pm \sqrt{b/2}$ obtained by shifting the inflection points $x = \pm\sqrt{b/2}$ of $y = e^{-x^2/b}$ by a units. (See Figure 4.54.) At the inflection points $y = e^{-1/2} \approx 0.6$.

With this information we can see the effect of the parameters. The parameter a determines the location of the center of the bell and the parameter b determines how narrow or wide the bell is. (See Figure 4.55.) If b is small, then the inflection points are close to a and the bell is sharply peaked near a; if b is large, the inflection points are farther away from a and the bell is spread out.

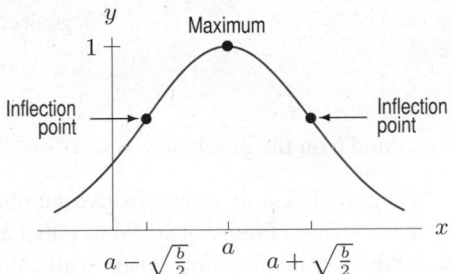

Figure 4.54: Graph of $y = e^{-(x-a)^2/b}$: bell-shaped curve with peak at $x = a$

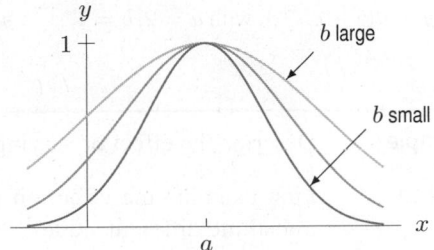

Figure 4.55: Graph of $y = e^{-(x-a)^2/b}$ for fixed a and various b

Modeling with Families of Functions

One reason for studying families of functions is their use in mathematical modeling. Confronted with the problem of modeling some phenomenon, a crucial first step involves recognizing families of functions which might fit the available data.

Motion Under Gravity: $y = -4.9t^2 + v_0 t + y_0$

The position of an object moving vertically under the influence of gravity can be described by a function in the two-parameter family

$$y = -4.9t^2 + v_0 t + y_0$$

where t is time in seconds and y is the distance in meters above the ground. Why do we need the parameters v_0 and y_0? Notice that at time $t = 0$ we have $y = y_0$. Thus the parameter y_0 gives the height above ground of the object at time $t = 0$. Since $dy/dt = -9.8t + v_0$, the parameter v_0 gives the velocity of the object at time $t = 0$. From this equation we see that $dy/dt = 0$ when $t = v_0/9.8$. This is the time when the object reaches its maximum height.

Example 3   Give a function describing the position of a projectile launched upward from ground level with an initial velocity of 50 m/sec. How high does the projectile rise?

Solution   We have $y_0 = 0$ and $v_0 = 50$, so the height of the projectile after t seconds is $y = -4.9t^2 + 50t$. It reaches its maximum height when $t = 50/9.8 = 5.1$ seconds, and its height at that time is $-4.9(5.1)^2 + 50(5.1) = 127.5$, or about 128 meters.

Exponential Model with a Limit: $y = a(1 - e^{-bx})$

We consider $a, b > 0$. The graph of one member, with $a = 2$ and $b = 1$, is in Figure 4.56. Such a graph represents a quantity which is increasing but leveling off. For example, a body dropped in a thick fluid speeds up initially, but its velocity levels off as it approaches a terminal velocity. Similarly, if a pollutant pouring into a lake builds up toward a saturation level, its concentration may be described in this way. The graph also represents the temperature of an object in an oven.

Figure 4.56: One member of the family $y = a(1 - e^{-bx})$, with $a = 2, b = 1$

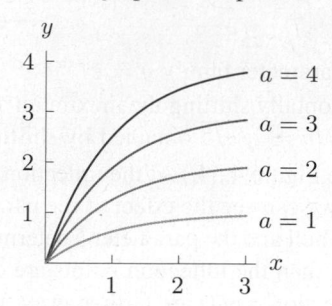

Figure 4.57: Fixing $b = 1$ gives $y = a(1 - e^{-x})$, graphed for various a

Figure 4.58: Fixing $a = 2$ gives $y = 2(1 - e^{-bx})$, graphed for various b

Example 4   Describe the effect of varying the parameters a and b on the graph of $y = a(1 - e^{-bx})$.

Solution   First examine the effect on the graph of varying a. Fix b at some positive number, say $b = 1$. Substitute different values for a and look at the graphs in Figure 4.57. We see that as x gets larger, y approaches a from below, so a is an upper bound for this function. Analytically, this follows from the fact that $e^{-bx} \to 0$ as $x \to \infty$. Physically, the value of a represents the terminal velocity of a falling body or the saturation level of the pollutant in the lake.

Now examine the effect of varying b on the graph. Fix a at some positive number, say $a = 2$. Substitute different values for b and look at the graphs in Figure 4.58. The parameter b determines how sharply the curve rises and how quickly it gets close to the line $y = a$.

Let's confirm the last observation in Example 4 analytically. For $y = a(1 - e^{-bx})$, we have $dy/dx = abe^{-bx}$, so the slope of the tangent to the curve at $x = 0$ is ab. For larger b, the curve rises more rapidly at $x = 0$. How long does it take the curve to climb halfway up from $y = 0$ to $y = a$? When $y = a/2$, we have

$$a(1 - e^{-bx}) = \frac{a}{2}, \qquad \text{which leads to} \qquad x = \frac{\ln 2}{b}.$$

If b is large then $(\ln 2)/b$ is small, so in a short distance the curve is already half way up to a. If b is small, then $(\ln 2)/b$ is large and we have to go a long way out to get up to $a/2$. See Figure 4.59.

Figure 4.59: Tangent at $x = 0$ to $y = a(1 - e^{-bx})$, with fixed a, and large and small b

The following example illustrates an application of this family.

Example 5 The number, N, of people who have heard a rumor spread by mass media by time t is modeled by

$$N(t) = a(1 - e^{-bt}).$$

There are 200,000 people in the population who hear the rumor eventually. If 10% of them heard it the first day, find a and b, assuming t is measured in days.

Solution Since $\lim\limits_{t \to \infty} N(t) = a$, we have $a = 200{,}000$. When $t = 1$, we have $N = 0.1(200{,}000) = 20{,}000$ people, so substituting into the formula gives

$$N(1) = 20{,}000 = 200{,}000\left(1 - e^{-b(1)}\right).$$

Solving for b gives

$$0.1 = 1 - e^{-b}$$
$$e^{-b} = 0.9$$
$$b = -\ln 0.9 = 0.105.$$

The Logistic Model: $y = L/(1 + Ae^{-kt})$

The *logistic* family is often used to model population growth when it is limited by the environment. (See Section 11.7.) We assume that $L, A, k > 0$ and we look at the roles of each of the three parameters in turn.

Figure 4.60: Graph of $y = L/(1 + Ae^{-kt})$ varying L with $A = 50$, $k = 1$

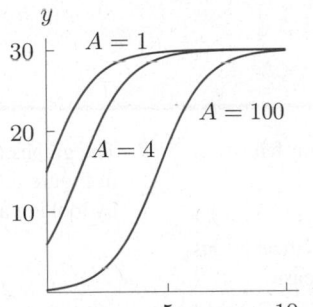

Figure 4.61: Graph of $y = L/(1 + Ae^{-kt})$ varying A with $L = 30$, $k = 1$

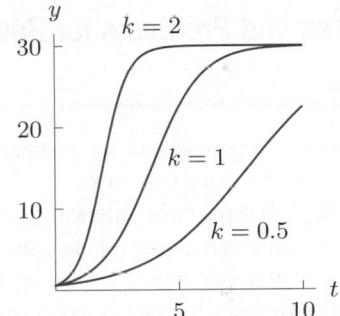

Figure 4.62: Graph of $y = L/(1 + Ae^{-kt})$ varying k, with $L = 30$, $A = 50$

Logistic curves with varying values of L are shown in Figure 4.60. The values of y level off as $t \to \infty$ because $Ae^{-kt} \to 0$ as $t \to \infty$. Thus, as t increases, the values of y approach L. The line $y = L$ is a horizontal asymptote, called the *limiting value* or *carrying capacity*, and representing the maximum sustainable population. The parameter L stretches or shrinks the graph vertically.

In Figure 4.61 we investigate the effect of the parameter A, with k and L fixed. The parameter A alters the point at which the curve cuts the y-axis—larger values of A move the y-intercept closer to the origin. At $t = 0$ we have $y = L/(1 + A)$, confirming that increasing A decreases the value of y at $t = 0$.

Figure 4.62 shows the effect of the parameter k. With L and A fixed, we see that varying k affects the rate at which the function approaches the limiting value L. If k is small, the graph rises slowly; if k is large, the graph rises steeply. At $t = 0$, we have $dy/dt = LAk/(1 + A)^2$, so the initial slope of a logistic curve is proportional to k.

The graphs suggest that none of the curves has a critical point for $t > 0$. Some curves appear to have a point of inflection; others have none. To investigate, we take derivatives:

$$\frac{dy}{dt} = \frac{LAke^{-kt}}{(1 + Ae^{-kt})^2}.$$

Since every factor of dy/dt is positive, the first derivative is always positive. Thus, there are no critical points and the function is always increasing.

Using a computer algebra system or the quotient rule, we find

$$\frac{d^2y}{dt^2} = \frac{LAk^2e^{-kt}(-1 + Ae^{-kt})}{(1 + Ae^{-kt})^3}.$$

Since L, A, k, e^{-kt}, and the denominator are always positive, the sign of d^2y/dt^2 is determined by the sign of $(-1 + Ae^{-kt})$. Points of inflection may occur where $d^2y/dt^2 = 0$. This is where $-1 + Ae^{-kt} = 0$, or

$$Ae^{-kt} = 1.$$

At this value of t,

$$y = \frac{L}{1 + Ae^{-kt}} = \frac{L}{1 + 1} = \frac{L}{2}.$$

In Problem 22 on page 221, we see that d^2y/dt^2 changes sign at $y = L/2$. Since the concavity changes at $y = L/2$, there is a point of inflection when the population is half the carrying capacity. If the initial population is $L/2$ or above, there is no inflection point. (See the top graph in Figure 4.61.)

To find the value of t at the inflection point, we solve for t in the equation

$$Ae^{-kt} = 1$$
$$t = \frac{\ln(1/A)}{-k} = \frac{\ln A}{k}.$$

Thus, increasing the value of A moves the inflection point to the right. (See the bottom two graphs in Figure 4.61.)

Exercises and Problems for Section 4.4

Exercises

In Exercises 1–6, investigate the one-parameter family of functions. Assume that a is positive.

(a) Graph $f(x)$ using three different values for a.

(b) Using your graph in part (a), describe the critical points of f and how they appear to move as a increases.

(c) Find a formula for the x-coordinates of the critical point(s) of f in terms of a.

1. $f(x) = (x - a)^2$

2. $f(x) = x^3 - ax$

3. $f(x) = ax^3 - x$

4. $f(x) = x - a\sqrt{x}$

5. $f(x) = x^2e^{-ax}$

6. $f(x) = \dfrac{a}{x^2} + x$ for $x > 0$

7. Consider the family

$$y = \frac{A}{x + B}.$$

(a) If $B = 0$, what is the effect of varying A on the graph?

(b) If $A = 1$, what is the effect of varying B?

(c) On one set of axes, graph the function for several values of A and B.

8. If A and B are positive constants, find all critical points of

$$f(w) = \frac{A}{w^2} - \frac{B}{w}.$$

9. The graphs of $f(x) = 1 + e^{-ax}$ for $a = 1, 2$, and 5, are in Figure 4.63. Without a calculator, identify the graphs by looking at $f'(0)$.

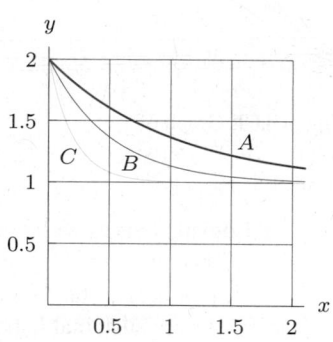

Figure 4.63

10. The graphs of $f(x) = xe^{-ax}$ for $a = 1, 2$, and 3, are in Figure 4.64. Without a calculator, identify the graphs by locating the critical points of $f(x)$.

Figure 4.64

In Exercises 11–16, investigate the given two parameter family of functions. Assume that a and b are positive.

(a) Graph $f(x)$ using $b = 1$ and three different values for a.

(b) Graph $f(x)$ using $a = 1$ and three different values for b.

(c) In the graphs in parts (a) and (b), how do the critical points of f appear to move as a increases? As b increases?

(d) Find a formula for the x-coordinates of the critical point(s) of f in terms of a and b.

11. $f(x) = (x - a)^2 + b$

12. $f(x) = x^3 - ax^2 + b$

13. $f(x) = ax(x - b)^2$

14. $f(x) = \dfrac{ax}{x^2 + b}$

15. $f(x) = \sqrt{b - (x - a)^2}$

16. $f(x) = \dfrac{a}{x} + bx$ for $x > 0$

Problems

17. The graphs of the function $f(x) = x + a^2/x$ for $a = 1$ and 2, and a third integer value of a, are shown in Figure 4.65. Without a calculator, identify the graphs, and estimate the third value of a.

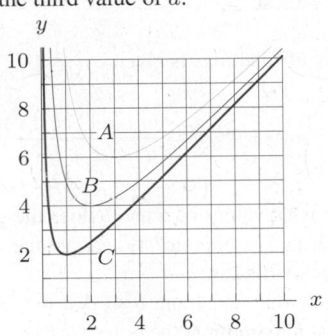

Figure 4.65

18. The graphs of the function $f(x) = x + a \sin x$ for various values of $a > 0$ are shown in Figure 4.66. Explain why, no matter what the positive value of a, the curves intersect in the same points.

Figure 4.66

19. (a) Sketch graphs of $y = xe^{-bx}$ for $b = 1, 2, 3, 4$. Describe the graphical significance of b.

(b) Find the coordinates of the critical point of $y = xe^{-bx}$ and use it to confirm your answer to part (a).

20. Consider the surge function $y = axe^{-bx}$ for $a, b > 0$.

(a) Find the local maxima, local minima, and points of inflection.

(b) How does varying a and b affect the shape of the graph?

(c) On one set of axes, graph this function for several values of a and b.

21. Find a formula for the family of cubic polynomials with an inflection point at the origin. How many parameters are there?

22. (a) Derive formulas for the first and second derivatives of the logistic function:

$$y = \frac{L}{1 + Ae^{-kt}} \quad \text{for } L, A, \text{ and } k \text{ positive constants.}$$

(b) Derive a formula for the t value of any inflection point(s).

(c) Use the second derivative to determine the concavity on either side of any inflection points.

23. (a) Graph $f(x) = x + a \sin x$ for $a = 0.5$ and $a = 3$.

(b) For what values of a is $f(x)$ increasing for all x?

24. (a) Graph $f(x) = x^2 + a \sin x$ for $a = 1$ and $a = 20$.

(b) For what values of a is $f(x)$ concave up for all x?

25. Consider the family of functions $y = a \cosh(x/a)$ for $a > 0$. Sketch graphs for $a = 1, 2, 3$. Describe in words the effect of increasing a.

26. Sketch several members of the family $y = e^{-ax} \sin bx$ for $b = 1$, and describe the graphical significance of the parameter a.

27. Sketch several members of the family $e^{-ax} \sin bx$ for $a = 1$, and describe the graphical significance of the parameter b.

28. If $a > 0$, $b > 0$, show that $f(x) = a(1 - e^{-bx})$ is everywhere increasing and everywhere concave down.

29. Let $f(x) = bxe^{1+bx}$, where b is constant and $b > 0$.

(a) What is the x-coordinate of the critical point of f?

(b) Is the critical point a local maximum or a local minimum?

(c) Show that the y-coordinate of the critical point does not depend on the value of b.

30. Let $h(x) = e^{-x} + kx$, where k is any constant. For what value(s) of k does h have

(a) No critical points?
(b) One critical point?
(c) A horizontal asymptote?

31. Let $g(x) = x - ke^x$, where k is any constant. For what value(s) of k does the function g have a critical point?

Find formulas for the functions described in Problems 32–43.

32. A function of the form $y = a(1 - e^{-bx})$ with $a, b > 0$ and a horizontal asymptote of $y = 5$.

33. A function of the form $y = be^{-(x-a)^2/2}$ with its maximum at the point $(0, 3)$.

34. A curve of the form $y = e^{-(x-a)^2/b}$ for $b > 0$ with a local maximum at $x = 2$ and points of inflection at $x = 1$ and $x = 3$.

35. A logistic curve with carrying capacity of 12, y-intercept of 4, and point of inflection at $(0.5, 6)$.

36. A function of the form $y = \dfrac{a}{1 + be^{-t}}$ with y-intercept 2 and an inflection point at $t = 1$.

37. A cubic polynomial with a critical point at $x = 2$, an inflection point at $(1, 4)$, and a leading coefficient of 1.

38. A fourth-degree polynomial whose graph is symmetric about the y-axis, has a y-intercept of 0, and global maxima at $(1, 2)$ and $(-1, 2)$.

39. A function of the form $y = a \sin(bt^2)$ whose first critical point for positive t occurs at $t = 1$ and whose derivative is 3 when $t = 2$.

40. A function of the form $y = a \cos(bt^2)$ whose first critical point for positive t occurs at $t = 1$ and whose derivative is -2 when $t = 1/\sqrt{2}$.

41. A function of the form $y = ae^{-x} + bx$ with the global minimum at $(1, 2)$.

42. A function of the form $y = bxe^{-ax}$ with a local maximum at $(3, 6)$.

43. A function of the form $y = at + b/t$, with a local minimum $(3, 12)$ and a local maximum at $(-3, -12)$.

44. Consider the family of functions $y = f(x) = x - k\sqrt{x}$, with k a positive constant and $x \geq 0$. Show that the graph of $f(x)$ has a local minimum at a point whose x-coordinate is $1/4$ of the way between its x-intercepts.

45. For any constant a, let $f(x) = ax - x \ln x$ for $x > 0$.

(a) What is the x-intercept of the graph of $f(x)$?
(b) Graph $f(x)$ for $a = -1$ and $a = 1$.
(c) For what values of a does $f(x)$ have a critical point for $x > 0$? Find the coordinates of the critical point and decide if it is a local maximum, a local minimum, or neither.

46. Let $f(x) = x^2 + \cos(kx)$, for $k > 0$.

(a) Graph f for $k = 0.5, 1, 3, 5$. Find the smallest number k at which you see points of inflection in the graph of f.
(b) Explain why the graph of f has no points of inflection if $k \leq \sqrt{2}$, and infinitely many points of inflection if $k > \sqrt{2}$.
(c) Explain why f has only a finite number of critical points, no matter what the value of k.

47. Let $f(x) = e^x - kx$, for $k > 0$.

(a) Graph f for $k = 1/4, 1/2, 1, 2, 4$. Describe what happens as k changes.
(b) Show that f has a local minimum at $x = \ln k$.
(c) Find the value of k for which the local minimum is the largest.

48. A family of functions is given by

$$r(x) = \frac{1}{a + (x - b)^2}.$$

(a) For what values of a and b does the graph of r have a vertical asymptote? Where are the vertical asymptotes in this case?
(b) Find values of a and b so that the function r has a local maximum at the point $(3, 5)$.

49. (a) Find all critical points of $f(x) = x^4 + ax^2 + b$.
(b) Under what conditions on a and b does this function have exactly one critical point? What is the one critical point, and is it a local maximum, a local minimum, or neither?
(c) Under what conditions on a and b does this function have exactly three critical points? What are they? Which are local maxima and which are local minima?
(d) Is it ever possible for this function to have two critical points? No critical points? More than three critical points? Give an explanation in each case.

50. Let $y = Ae^x + Be^{-x}$ for any constants A, B.

(a) Sketch the graph of the function for

(i) $A = 1, B = 1$ (ii) $A = 1, B = -1$
(iii) $A = 2, B = 1$ (iv) $A = 2, B = -1$
(v) $A = -2, B = -1$ (vi) $A = -2, B = 1$

(b) Describe in words the general shape of the graph if A and B have the same sign. What effect does the sign of A have on the graph?
(c) Describe in words the general shape of the graph if A and B have different signs. What effect does the sign of A have on the graph?
(d) For what values of A and B does the function have a local maximum? A local minimum? Justify your answer using derivatives.

51. The temperature, T, in $^\circ$ C, of a yam put into a 200°C oven is given as a function of time, t, in minutes, by

$$T = a(1 - e^{-kt}) + b.$$

(a) If the yam starts at 20°C, find a and b.
(b) If the temperature of the yam is initially increasing at 2°C per minute, find k.

52. For positive a, b, the potential energy, U, of a particle is

$$U = b\left(\frac{a^2}{x^2} - \frac{a}{x}\right) \quad \text{for } x > 0.$$

(a) Find the intercepts and asymptotes.
(b) Compute the local maxima and minima.
(c) Sketch the graph.

53. The force, F, on a particle with potential energy U is given by

$$F = -\frac{dU}{dx}.$$

Using the expression for U in Problem 52, graph F and U on the same axes, labeling intercepts and local maxima and minima.

54. The Lennard-Jones model predicts the potential energy $V(r)$ of a two-atom molecule as a function of the distance r between the atoms to be

$$V(r) = \frac{A}{r^{12}} - \frac{B}{r^6}, \quad r > 0,$$

where A and B are positive constants.

(a) Evaluate $\lim_{r \to 0^+} V(r)$, and interpret your answer.

(b) Find the critical point of $V(r)$. Is it a local maximum or local minimum?
(c) The inter-atomic force is given by $F(r) = -V'(r)$. At what distance r is the inter-atomic force zero? (This is called the equilibrium size of the molecule.)
(d) Describe how the parameters A and B affect the equilibrium size of the molecule.

55. For positive A, B, the force between two atoms is a function of the distance, r, between them:

$$f(r) = -\frac{A}{r^2} + \frac{B}{r^3} \quad r > 0.$$

(a) What are the zeros and asymptotes of f?
(b) Find the coordinates of the critical points and inflection points of f.
(c) Graph f.
(d) Illustrating your answers with a sketch, describe the effect on the graph of f of:

   (i) Increasing B, holding A fixed
   (ii) Increasing A, holding B fixed

56. An organism has size W at time t. For positive constants A, b, and c, the Gompertz growth function gives

$$W = Ae^{-e^{b-ct}}, \quad t \geq 0.$$

(a) Find the intercepts and asymptotes.
(b) Find the critical points and inflection points.
(c) Graph W for various values of A, b, and c.
(d) A certain organism grows fastest when it is about 1/3 of its final size. Would the Gompertz growth function be useful in modeling its growth? Explain.

Strengthen Your Understanding

In Problems 57–58, explain what is wrong with the statement.

57. Every function of the form $f(x) = x^2 + bx + c$, where b and c are constants, has two zeros.

58. Every function of the form $f(x) = a/x + bx$, where a and b are non-zero constants, has two critical points.

In Problems 59–62, give an example of:

59. A family of quadratic functions which has zeros at $x = 0$ and $x = b$.

60. A member of the family $f(x) = ax^3 - bx$ that has no critical points.

61. A family of functions, $f(x)$, depending on a parameter a, such that each member of the family has exactly one critical point.

62. A family of functions, $g(x)$, depending on two parameters, a and b, such that each member of the family has

exactly two critical points and one inflection point. You may want to restrict a and b.

63. Let $f(x) = ax + b/x$. Suppose a and b are positive. What happens to $f(x)$ as b increases?

(a) The critical points move further apart.
(b) The critical points move closer together.
(c) The critical values move further apart.
(d) The critical values move closer together.

64. Let $f(x) = ax + b/x$. Suppose a and b are positive. What happens to $f(x)$ as a increases?

(a) The critical points move further apart.
(b) The critical points move closer together.
(c) The critical values move further apart.
(d) The critical values move closer together.

4.5   APPLICATIONS TO MARGINALITY

Management decisions within a particular business usually aim at maximizing profit for the company. In this section we see how the derivative can be used to maximize profit. Profit depends on both production cost and revenue (or income) from sales. We begin by looking at the cost and revenue functions.

> The **cost function**, $C(q)$, gives the total cost of producing a quantity q of some good.

What sort of function do we expect C to be? The more goods that are made, the higher the total cost, so C is an increasing function. In fact, cost functions usually have the general shape shown in Figure 4.67. The intercept on the C-axis represents the *fixed costs*, which are incurred even if nothing is produced. (This includes, for instance, the machinery needed to begin production.) The cost function increases quickly at first and then more slowly because producing larger quantities of a good is usually more efficient than producing smaller quantities—this is called *economy of scale*. At still higher production levels, the cost function starts to increase faster again as resources become scarce, and sharp increases may occur when new factories have to be built. Thus, the graph of $C(q)$ may start out concave down and become concave up later on.

Figure 4.67: Cost as a function of quantity

> The **revenue function**, $R(q)$, gives the total revenue received by a firm from selling a quantity q of some good.

Revenue is income obtained from sales. If the price per item is p, and the quantity sold is q, then

$$\text{Revenue} = \text{Price} \times \text{Quantity}, \quad \text{so} \quad R = pq.$$

If the price per item does not depend on the quantity sold, then the graph of $R(q)$ is a straight line through the origin with slope equal to the price p. See Figure 4.68. In practice, for large values of q, the market may become glutted, causing the price to drop, giving $R(q)$ the shape in Figure 4.69.

Figure 4.68: Revenue: Constant price

Figure 4.69: Revenue: Decreasing price

The profit is usually written as π. (Economists use π to distinguish it from the price, p; this π has nothing to do with the area of a circle, and merely stands for the Greek equivalent of the letter "p.") The profit resulting from producing and selling q items is defined by

$$\text{Profit} = \text{Revenue} - \text{Cost}, \quad \text{so} \quad \pi(q) = R(q) - C(q).$$

Example 1   If cost, C, and revenue, R, are given by the graph in Figure 4.70, for what production quantities, q, does the firm make a profit? Approximately what production level maximizes profit?

Figure 4.70: Costs and revenues for Example 1

Solution   The firm makes a profit whenever revenues are greater than costs, that is, when $R > C$. The graph of R is above the graph of C approximately when $130 < q < 215$. Production between $q = 130$ units and $q = 215$ units generates a profit. The vertical distance between the cost and revenue curves is largest at q_0, so q_0 units gives maximum profit.

Marginal Analysis

Many economic decisions are based on an analysis of the costs and revenues "at the margin." Let's look at this idea through an example.

Suppose we are running an airline and we are trying to decide whether to offer an additional flight. How should we decide? We'll assume that the decision is to be made purely on financial grounds: if the flight will make money for the company, it should be added. Obviously we need to consider the costs and revenues involved. Since the choice is between adding this flight and leaving things the way they are, the crucial question is whether the *additional costs* incurred are greater or smaller than the *additional revenues* generated by the flight. These additional costs and revenues are called the *marginal costs* and *marginal revenues*.

Suppose $C(q)$ is the function giving the total cost of running q flights. If the airline had originally planned to run 100 flights, its costs would be $C(100)$. With the additional flight, its costs would be $C(101)$. Therefore,

$$\text{Additional cost "at the margin"} = C(101) - C(100).$$

Now

$$C(101) - C(100) = \frac{C(101) - C(100)}{101 - 100},$$

and this quantity is the average rate of change of cost between 100 and 101 flights. In Figure 4.71 the average rate of change is the slope of the line joining the $C(100)$ and $C(101)$ points on the graph. If the graph of the cost function is not curving fast near the point, the slope of this line is close to the slope of the tangent line there. Therefore, the average rate of change is close to the instantaneous rate of change. Since these rates of change are not very different, many economists choose to define marginal cost, MC, as the instantaneous rate of change of cost with respect to quantity:

Figure 4.71: Marginal cost: Slope of one of these lines

> Marginal cost = $MC = C'(q)$ so   Marginal cost $\approx C(q+1) - C(q)$.

Similarly, if the revenue generated by q flights is $R(q)$ and the number of flights increases from 100 to 101, then

$$\text{Additional revenue "at the margin"} = R(101) - R(100).$$

Now $R(101) - R(100)$ is the average rate of change of revenue between 100 and 101 flights. As before, the average rate of change is usually almost equal to the instantaneous rate of change, so economists often define:

> Marginal revenue = $MR = R'(q)$ so   Marginal revenue $\approx R(q+1) - R(q)$.

We often refer to total cost, C, and total revenue, R, to distinguish them from marginal cost, MC, and marginal revenue, MR. If the words cost and revenue are used alone, they are understood to mean total cost and total revenue.

Example 2   If $C(q)$ and $R(q)$ for the airline are given in Figure 4.72, should the company add the 101st flight?

Solution   The marginal revenue is the slope of the revenue curve, and the marginal cost is the slope of the cost curve at the point 100. From Figure 4.72, you can see that the slope at the point A is smaller than the slope at B, so $MC < MR$. This means that the airline will make more in extra revenue than it will spend in extra costs if it runs another flight, so it should go ahead and run the 101st flight.

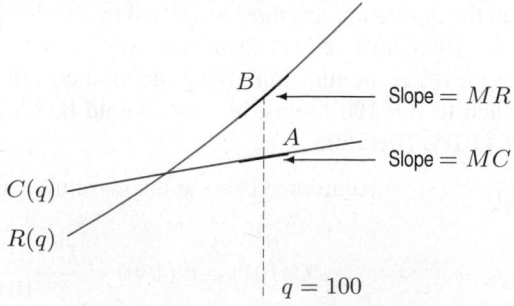

Figure 4.72: Should the company add the 101st flight?

Since MC and MR are derivative functions, they can be estimated from the graphs of total cost and total revenue.

Example 3   If R and C are given by the graphs in Figure 4.73, sketch graphs of $MR = R'(q)$ and $MC = C'(q)$.

Figure 4.73: Total revenue and total cost for Example 3

Solution   The revenue graph is a line through the origin, with equation

$$R = pq$$

where p is the price, which is a constant. The slope is p and

$$MR = R'(q) = p.$$

The total cost is increasing, so the marginal cost is always positive (above the q-axis). For small q values, the total cost curve is concave down, so the marginal cost is decreasing. For larger q, say $q > 100$, the total cost curve is concave up and the marginal cost is increasing. Thus the marginal cost has a minimum at about $q = 100$. (See Figure 4.74.)

Figure 4.74: Marginal revenue and costs for Example 3

Maximizing Profit

Now let's look at how to maximize profit, given functions for total revenue and total cost.

Example 4   Find the maximum profit if the total revenue and total cost are given, for $0 \leq q \leq 200$, by the curves R and C in Figure 4.75.

Figure 4.75: Maximum profit at $q = 140$

Solution   The profit is represented by the vertical difference between the curves and is marked by the vertical arrows on the graph. When revenue is below cost, the company is taking a loss; when revenue is above cost, the company is making a profit. We can see that the profit is largest at about $q = 140$, so this is the production level we're looking for. To be sure that the local maximum is a global maximum, we need to check the endpoints. At $q = 0$ and $q = 200$, the profit is negative, so the global maximum is indeed at $q = 140$.

To find the actual maximum profit, we estimate the vertical distance between the curves at $q = 140$. This gives a maximum profit of $\$80,000 - \$60,000 = \$20,000$.

Suppose we wanted to find the minimum profit. In this example, we must look at the endpoints, when $q = 0$ or $q = 200$. We see the minimum profit is negative (a loss), and it occurs at $q = 0$.

Maximum Profit Occurs Where $MR = MC$

In Example 4, observe that at $q = 140$ the slopes of the two curves in Figure 4.75 are equal. To the left of $q = 140$, the revenue curve has a larger slope than the cost curve, and the profit increases as q increases. The company will make more money by producing more units, so production should increase toward $q = 140$. To the right of $q = 140$, the slope of the revenue curve is less than the slope of the cost curve, and the profit is decreasing. The company will make more money by producing fewer units so production should decrease toward $q = 140$. At the point where the slopes are equal, the profit has a local maximum; otherwise the profit could be increased by moving toward that point. Since the slopes are equal at $q = 140$, we have $MR = MC$ there.

Now let's look at the general situation. To maximize or minimize profit over an interval, we optimize the profit, π, where

$$\pi(q) = R(q) - C(q).$$

We know that global maxima and minima can only occur at critical points or at endpoints of an interval. To find critical points of π, look for zeros of the derivative:

$$\pi'(q) = R'(q) - C'(q) = 0.$$

So

$$R'(q) = C'(q),$$

that is, the slopes of the revenue and cost curves are equal. This is the same observation that we made in the previous example. In economic language,

> The maximum (or minimum) profit can occur where
>
> Marginal cost = Marginal revenue.

Of course, maximal or minimal profit does not *have* to occur where $MR = MC$; there are also the endpoints to consider.

Example 5   Find the quantity q which maximizes profit if the total revenue, $R(q)$, and total cost, $C(q)$, are given in dollars by

$$R(q) = 5q - 0.003q^2$$
$$C(q) = 300 + 1.1q,$$

where $0 \leq q \leq 800$ units. What production level gives the minimum profit?

Solution   We look for production levels that give marginal revenue = marginal cost:

$$MR = R'(q) = 5 - 0.006q$$
$$MC = C'(q) = 1.1.$$

So $5 - 0.006q = 1.1$, giving

$$q = 3.9/0.006 = 650 \text{ units.}$$

Does this value of q represent a local maximum or minimum of π? We can tell by looking at production levels of 649 units and 651 units. When $q = 649$ we have $MR = \$1.106$, which is greater than the (constant) marginal cost of $\$1.10$. This means that producing one more unit will bring in more revenue than its cost, so profit will increase. When $q = 651$, $MR = \$1.094$, which is *less* than MC, so it is not profitable to produce the 651st unit. We conclude that $q = 650$ is a local maximum for the profit function π. The profit earned by producing and selling this quantity is $\pi(650) = R(650) - C(650) = \$967.50$.

To check for global maxima we need to look at the endpoints. If $q = 0$, the only cost is $\$300$ (the fixed costs) and there is no revenue, so $\pi(0) = -\$300$. At the upper limit of $q = 800$, we have $\pi(800) = \$900$. Therefore, the maximum profit is at the production level of 650 units, where $MR = MC$. The minimum profit (a loss) occurs when $q = 0$ and there is no production at all.

Exercises and Problems for Section 4.5

Exercises

1. Figure 4.76 shows cost and revenue. For what production levels is the profit function positive? Negative? Estimate the production at which profit is maximized.

Figure 4.76

2. Figure 4.77 gives cost and revenue. What are fixed costs? What quantity maximizes profit, and what is the maximum profit earned?

Figure 4.77

3. Total cost and revenue are approximated by the functions $C = 5000 + 2.4q$ and $R = 4q$, both in dollars. Identify the fixed cost, marginal cost per item, and the price at which this commodity is sold.

In Exercises 4–7, give the cost, revenue, and profit functions.

4. An online seller of T-shirts pays $500 to start up the website and $6 per T-shirt, then sells the T-shirts for $12 each.

5. A car wash operator pays $35,000 for a franchise, then spends $10 per car wash, which costs the consumer $15.

6. A couple running a house-cleaning business invests $5000 in equipment, and they spend $15 in supplies to clean a house, for which they charge $60.

7. A lemonade stand operator sets up the stand for free in front of the neighbor's house, makes 5 quarts of lemonade for $4, then sells each 8 oz cup for 25 cents.

8. The revenue from selling q items is $R(q) = 500q - q^2$, and the total cost is $C(q) = 150 + 10q$. Write a function that gives the total profit earned, and find the quantity which maximizes the profit.

9. Revenue is given by $R(q) = 450q$ and cost is given by $C(q) = 10,000 + 3q^2$. At what quantity is profit maximized? What is the total profit at this production level?

10. A company estimates that the total revenue, R, in dollars, received from the sale of q items is $R = \ln(1 + 1000q^2)$. Calculate and interpret the marginal revenue if $q = 10$.

11. Table 4.2 shows cost, $C(q)$, and revenue, $R(q)$.

    (a) At approximately what production level, q, is profit maximized? Explain your reasoning.

    (b) What is the price of the product?

    (c) What are the fixed costs?

Table 4.2

q	0	500	1000	1500	2000	2500	3000
$R(q)$	0	1500	3000	4500	6000	7500	9000
$C(q)$	3000	3800	4200	4500	4800	5500	7400

12. Table 4.3 shows marginal cost, MC, and marginal revenue, MR.

    (a) Use the marginal cost and marginal revenue at a production of $q = 5000$ to determine whether production should be increased or decreased from 5000.

    (b) Estimate the production level that maximizes profit.

Table 4.3

q	5000	6000	7000	8000	9000	10000
MR	60	58	56	55	54	53
MC	48	52	54	55	58	63

Problems

13. Let $C(q)$ be the total cost of producing a quantity q of a certain product. See Figure 4.78.

    (a) What is the meaning of $C(0)$?

    (b) Describe in words how the marginal cost changes as the quantity produced increases.

    (c) Explain the concavity of the graph (in terms of economics).

    (d) Explain the economic significance (in terms of marginal cost) of the point at which the concavity changes.

    (e) Do you expect the graph of $C(q)$ to look like this for all types of products?

Figure 4.78

14. When production is 2000, marginal revenue is \$4 per unit and marginal cost is \$3.25 per unit. Do you expect maximum profit to occur at a production level above or below 2000? Explain.

15. If $C'(500) = 75$ and $R'(500) = 100$, should the quantity produced be increased or decreased from $q = 500$ in order to increase profits?

16. An online seller of knitted sweaters finds that it costs \$35 to make her first sweater. Her cost for each additional sweater goes down until it reaches \$25 for her 100th sweater, and after that it starts to rise again. If she can sell each sweater for \$35, is the quantity sold that maximizes her profit less than 100? Greater than 100?

17. The marginal revenue and marginal cost for a certain item are graphed in Figure 4.79. Do the following quantities maximize profit for the company? Explain your answer.

    (a) $q = a$ **(b)** $q = b$

Figure 4.79

18. The total cost $C(q)$ of producing q goods is given by:

$$C(q) = 0.01q^3 - 0.6q^2 + 13q.$$

    (a) What is the fixed cost?

    (b) What is the maximum profit if each item is sold for \$7? (Assume you sell everything you produce.)

    (c) Suppose exactly 34 goods are produced. They all sell when the price is \$7 each, but for each \$1 increase in price, 2 fewer goods are sold. Should the price be raised, and if so by how much?

19. A company manufactures only one product. The quantity, q, of this product produced per month depends on the amount of capital, K, invested (i.e., the number of machines the company owns, the size of its building, and so on) and the amount of labor, L, available each month. We assume that q can be expressed as a *Cobb-Douglas production function*:

$$q = cK^\alpha L^\beta,$$

where c, α, β are positive constants, with $0 < \alpha < 1$ and $0 < \beta < 1$. In this problem we will see how the Russian government could use a Cobb-Douglas function to estimate how many people a newly privatized industry might employ. A company in such an industry has only a small amount of capital available to it and needs to use all of it, so K is fixed. Suppose L is measured in man-hours per month, and that each man-hour costs the company w rubles (a ruble is the unit of Russian currency). Suppose the company has no other costs besides labor, and that each unit of the good can be sold for a fixed price of p rubles. How many man-hours of labor per month should the company use in order to maximize its profit?

20. An agricultural worker in Uganda is planting clover to increase the number of bees making their home in the region. There are 100 bees in the region naturally, and for every acre put under clover, 20 more bees are found in the region.

    (a) Draw a graph of the total number, $N(x)$, of bees as a function of x, the number of acres devoted to clover.
    (b) Explain, both geometrically and algebraically, the shape of the graph of:
        (i) The marginal rate of increase of the number of bees with acres of clover, $N'(x)$.
        (ii) The average number of bees per acre of clover, $N(x)/x$.

21. If you invest x dollars in a certain project, your return is $R(x)$. You want to choose x to maximize your return per dollar invested,[8] which is

$$r(x) = \frac{R(x)}{x}.$$

    (a) The graph of $R(x)$ is in Figure 4.80, with $R(0) = 0$. Illustrate on the graph that the maximum value of $r(x)$ is reached at a point at which the line from the origin to the point is tangent to the graph of $R(x)$.
    (b) Also, the maximum of $r(x)$ occurs at a point at which the slope of the graph of $r(x)$ is zero. On the same axes as part (a), sketch $r(x)$. Illustrate that the maximum of $r(x)$ occurs where its slope is 0.
    (c) Show, by taking the derivative of the formula for $r(x)$, that the conditions in part (a) and (b) are equivalent: the x-value at which the line from the origin is tangent to the graph of R is the same as the x-value at which the graph of r has zero slope.

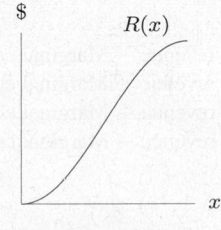

Figure 4.80

Problems 22–23 involve the *average cost* of manufacturing a quantity q of a good, which is defined to be

$$a(q) = \frac{C(q)}{q}.$$

22. Figure 4.81 shows the cost of production, $C(q)$, as a function of quantity produced, q.

    (a) For some q_0, sketch a line whose slope is the marginal cost, MC, at that point.
    (b) For the same q_0, explain why the average cost $a(q_0)$ can be represented by the slope of the line from that point on the curve to the origin.
    (c) Use the method of Example 6 on page 210 to explain why at the value of q which minimizes $a(q)$, the average and marginal costs are equal.

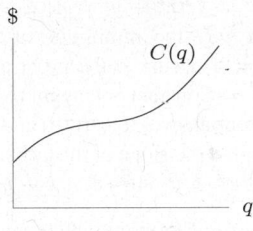

Figure 4.81

23. The average cost per item to produce q items is given by

$$a(q) = 0.01q^2 - 0.6q + 13, \quad \text{for} \quad q > 0.$$

    (a) What is the total cost, $C(q)$, of producing q goods?
    (b) What is the minimum marginal cost? What is the practical interpretation of this result?
    (c) At what production level is the average cost a minimum? What is the lowest average cost?
    (d) Compute the marginal cost at $q = 30$. How does this relate to your answer to part (c)? Explain this relationship both analytically and in words.

24. The production function $f(x)$ gives the number of units of an item that a manufacturing company can produce from x units of raw material. The company buys the raw material at price w dollars per unit and sells all it produces at a price of p dollars per unit. The quantity of raw material that maximizes profit is denoted by x^*.

    (a) Do you expect the derivative $f'(x)$ to be positive or negative? Justify your answer.
    (b) Explain why the formula $\pi(x) = pf(x) - wx$ gives the profit $\pi(x)$ that the company earns as a function of the quantity x of raw materials that it uses.

---

[8]From Peter D. Taylor, *Calculus: The Analysis of Functions* (Toronto: Wall & Emerson, 1992).

(c) Evaluate $f'(x^*)$.

(d) Assuming it is nonzero, is $f''(x^*)$ positive or negative?

(e) If the supplier of the raw materials is likely to change the price w, then it is appropriate to treat x^* as a function of w. Find a formula for the derivative dx^*/dw and decide whether it is positive or negative.

(f) If the price w goes up, should the manufacturing company buy more or less of the raw material?

In many applications, we want to maximize or minimize some quantity subject to a condition. Such constrained optimization problems are solved using Lagrange multipliers in multivariable calculus; Problems 25–27 show an alternate method.[9]

25. Minimize $x^2 + y^2$ while satisfying $x + y = 4$ using the following steps.

(a) Graph $x + y = 4$. On the same axes, graph $x^2 + y^2 = 1$, $x^2 + y^2 = 4$, $x^2 + y^2 = 9$.

(b) Explain why the minimum value of $x^2 + y^2$ on $x + y = 4$ occurs at the point at which a graph of $x^2 + y^2 =$ Constant is tangent to the line $x + y = 4$.

(c) Using your answer to part (b) and implicit differentiation to find the slope of the circle, find the minimum value of $x^2 + y^2$ such that $x + y = 4$.

26. The quantity Q of an item which can be produced from quantities x and y of two raw materials is given by $Q = 10xy$ at a cost of $C = x + 2y$ thousand dollars. If the budget for raw materials is 10 thousand dollars, find the maximum production using the following steps.

(a) Graph $x + 2y = 10$ in the first quadrant. On the same axes, graph $Q = 10xy = 100$, $Q = 10xy = 200$, and $Q = 10xy = 300$.

(b) Explain why the maximum production occurs at a point at which a production curve is tangent to the cost line $C = 10$.

(c) Using your answer to part (b) and implicit differentiation to find the slope of the curve, find the maximum production under this budget.

27. With quantities x and y of two raw materials available, $Q = x^{1/2}y^{1/2}$ thousand items can be produced at a cost of $C = 2x + y$ thousand dollars. Using the following steps, find the minimum cost to produce 1 thousand items.

(a) Graph $x^{1/2}y^{1/2} = 1$. On the same axes, graph $2x + y = 2$, $2x + y = 3$, and $2x + y = 4$.

(b) Explain why the minimum cost occurs at a point at which a cost line is tangent to the production curve $Q = 1$.

(c) Using your answer to part (b) and implicit differentiation to find the slope of the curve, find the minimum cost to meet this production level.

Strengthen Your Understanding

In Problems 28–29, explain what is wrong with the statement.

28. If $C(100) = 90$ and $R(100) = 150$, increasing the quantity produced from 100 increases profit.

29. For the cost, C, and revenue, R, in Figure 4.82, profit is maximized when the quantity produced is about 3,500 units.

$ (thousands)

300

200

100

5   10   15 q (thousands)

Figure 4.82

In Problems 30–31, give an example of:

30. A quantity, q, in Figure 4.82 where $MC > MR$.

31. Cost and revenue curves such that the item can never be sold for a profit.

32. Which is correct? A company generally wants to

(a) Maximize revenue
(b) Maximize marginal revenue
(c) Minimize cost
(d) Minimize marginal cost
(e) None of the above

33. Which is correct? A company can increase its profit by increasing production if, at its current level of production,

(a) Marginal revenue − Marginal cost > 0
(b) Marginal revenue − Marginal cost $= 0$
(c) Marginal revenue − Marginal cost < 0
(d) Marginal revenue − Marginal cost is increasing

[9]Kelly Black, "Putting Constraints in Optimization for First-Year Calculus Students," pp. 310–312, *SIAM Review*, Vol. 39, No. 2, June 1997.

4.6 RATES AND RELATED RATES

Derivatives represent rates of change. In this section, we see how to calculate rates in a variety of situations.

Example 1   A spherical snowball is melting. Its radius decreases at a constant rate of 2 cm per minute from an initial value of 70 cm. How fast is the volume decreasing half an hour later?

Solution   The radius, r, starts at 70 cm and decreases at 2 cm/min. At time t minutes since the start,

$$r = 70 - 2t \text{ cm.}$$

The volume of the snowball is given by

$$V = \frac{4}{3}\pi r^3 = \frac{4}{3}\pi(70 - 2t)^3 \text{ cm}^3.$$

The rate at which the volume is changing at time t is

$$\frac{dV}{dt} = \frac{4}{3}\pi \cdot 3(70 - 2t)^2(-2) = -8\pi(70 - 2t)^2 \text{ cm}^3/\text{min.}$$

The volume is measured in cm^3, and time is in minutes, so after half an hour $t = 30$, and

$$\left.\frac{dV}{dt}\right|_{t=30} = -8\pi(70 - 2 \cdot 30)^2 = -800\pi \text{ cm}^3/\text{min.}$$

Thus, the rate at which the volume is increasing is $-800\pi \approx -2500 \text{ cm}^3/\text{min}$; the rate at which the volume is decreasing is about 2500 cm^3/min.

Example 2   A skydiver of mass m jumps from a plane at time $t = 0$. Under certain assumptions, the distance, $s(t)$, he has fallen in time t is given by

$$s(t) = \frac{m^2 g}{k^2}\left(\frac{kt}{m} + e^{-kt/m} - 1\right) \quad \text{for some positive constant } k.$$

(a) Find $s'(0)$ and $s''(0)$ and interpret in terms of the skydiver.
(b) Relate the units of $s'(t)$ and $s''(t)$ to the units of t and $s(t)$.

Solution   (a) Differentiating using the chain rule gives

$$s'(t) = \frac{m^2 g}{k^2}\left(\frac{k}{m} + e^{-kt/m}\left(-\frac{k}{m}\right)\right) = \frac{mg}{k}\left(1 - e^{-kt/m}\right)$$

$$s''(t) = \frac{mg}{k}(-e^{kt/m})\left(-\frac{k}{m}\right) = ge^{-kt/m}.$$

Since $e^{-k \cdot 0/m} = 1$, evaluating at $t = 0$ gives

$$s'(0) = \frac{mg}{k}(1 - 1) = 0 \quad \text{and} \quad s''(0) = g.$$

The first derivative of distance is velocity, so the fact that $s'(0) = 0$ tells us that the skydiver starts with zero velocity. The second derivative of distance is acceleration, so the fact that $s''(0) = g$ tells us that the skydiver's initial acceleration is g, the acceleration due to gravity.

(b) The units of velocity, $s'(t)$, and acceleration, $s''(t)$, are given by

$$\text{Units of } s'(t) \text{ are } \frac{\text{Units of } s(t)}{\text{Units of } t} = \frac{\text{Units of distance}}{\text{Units of time}}; \quad \text{for example, meters/sec.}$$

$$\text{Units of } s''(t) \text{ are } \frac{\text{Units of } s'(t)}{\text{Units of } t} = \frac{\text{Units of distance}}{(\text{Units of time})^2}; \quad \text{for example, meters/sec}^2.$$

Related Rates

In Example 1, the radius of the snowball decreased at a constant rate. A more realistic scenario is that the radius decreases at a varying rate. In this case, we may not be able to write a formula for V as a function of t. However, we may still be able to calculate dV/dt, as in the following example.

Example 3   A spherical snowball melts in such a way that the instant at which its radius is 20 cm, its radius is decreasing at 3 cm/min. At what rate is the volume of the ball of snow changing at that instant?

Solution   Since the snowball is spherical, we again have that

$$V = \frac{4}{3}\pi r^3.$$

We can no longer write a formula for r in terms of t, but we know that

$$\frac{dr}{dt} = -3 \quad \text{when} \quad r = 20.$$

We want to know dV/dt when $r = 20$. Think of r as an (unknown) function of t and differentiate the expression for V with respect to t using the chain rule:

$$\frac{dV}{dt} = \frac{4}{3}\pi \cdot 3r^2 \frac{dr}{dt} = 4\pi r^2 \frac{dr}{dt}.$$

At the instant at which $r = 20$ and $dr/dt = -3$, we have

$$\frac{dV}{dt} = 4\pi \cdot 20^2 \cdot (-3) = -4800\pi \approx -15{,}080 \text{ cm}^3/\text{min}.$$

So the volume of the ball is decreasing at a rate of 15,080 cm^3 per minute at the moment when $r = 20$ cm. Notice that we have sidestepped the problem of not knowing r as a function of t by calculating the derivatives only at the moment we are interested in.

Example 4   Figure 4.83 shows the fuel consumption, g, in miles per gallon (mpg), of a car traveling at v mph. At one moment, the car was going 70 mph and its deceleration was 8000 miles/hour^2. How fast was the fuel consumption changing at that moment? Include units.

Figure 4.83: Fuel consumption versus velocity

Solution   Acceleration is rate of change of velocity, dv/dt, and we are told that the deceleration is 8000 miles/hour^2, so we know $dv/dt = -8000$ when $v = 70$. We want dg/dt. The chain rule gives

$$\frac{dg}{dt} = \frac{dg}{dv} \cdot \frac{dv}{dt}.$$

The value of dg/dv is the slope of the curve in Figure 4.83 at $v = 70$. Since the points $(30, 40)$ and $(100, 20)$ lie approximately on the tangent to the curve at $v = 70$, we can estimate the derivative

$$\frac{dg}{dv} \approx \frac{20 - 40}{100 - 30} = -\frac{2}{7} \text{ mpg/mph.}$$

Thus,

$$\frac{dg}{dt} = \frac{dg}{dv} \cdot \frac{dv}{dt} \approx -\frac{2}{7}(-8000) \approx 2300 \text{ mpg/hr.}$$

In other words, fuel consumption is increasing at about $2300/60 \approx 38$ mpg per minute. Since we approximated dg/dv, we can only get a rough estimate for dg/dt.

A famous problem involves the rate at which the top of a ladder slips down a wall as the foot of the ladder moves.

Example 5   (a) A 3-meter ladder stands against a high wall. The foot of the ladder moves outward at a constant speed of 0.1 meter/sec. When the foot is 1 meter from the wall, how fast is the top of the ladder falling? What about when the foot is 2 meters from the wall?

(b) If the foot of the ladder moves out at a constant speed, how does the speed at which the top falls change as the foot gets farther out?

Solution   (a) Let the foot be x meters from the base of the wall and let the top be y meters from the base. See Figure 4.84. Then, since the ladder is 3 meters long, by Pythagoras' Theorem,

$$x^2 + y^2 = 3^2 = 9.$$

Thinking of x and y as functions of t, we differentiate with respect to t using the chain rule:

$$2x\frac{dx}{dt} + 2y\frac{dy}{dt} = 0.$$

We are interested in the moment at which $dx/dt = 0.1$ and $x = 1$. We want to know dy/dt, so we solve, giving

$$\frac{dy}{dt} = -\frac{x}{y}\frac{dx}{dt}.$$

When the foot of the ladder is 1 meter from the wall, $x = 1$ and $y = \sqrt{9 - 1^2} = \sqrt{8}$, so

$$\frac{dy}{dt} = -\frac{1}{\sqrt{8}}0.1 = -0.035 \text{ meter/sec.}$$

Thus, the top falls at 0.035 meter/sec.
When the foot is 2 meters from the wall, $x = 2$ and $y = \sqrt{9 - 2^2} = \sqrt{5}$, so

$$\frac{dy}{dt} = -\frac{2}{\sqrt{5}}0.1 = -0.089 \text{ meter/sec.}$$

Thus, the top falls at 0.089 meter/sec. Notice that the top falls faster when the base of the ladder is farther from the wall.

(b) As the foot of the ladder moves out, x increases and y decreases. Looking at the expression

$$\frac{dy}{dt} = -\frac{x}{y}\frac{dx}{dt},$$

we see that if dx/dt is constant, the magnitude of dy/dt increases as the foot gets farther out. Thus, the top falls faster and faster.

Wall

Ladder
3 meters

y

Ground

x

Figure 4.84: Side view of ladder standing against wall (x, y in meters)

Example 6   An airplane, flying at 450 km/hr at a constant altitude of 5 km, is approaching a camera mounted on the ground. Let θ be the angle of elevation above the ground at which the camera is pointed. See Figure 4.85. When $\theta = \pi/3$, how fast does the camera have to rotate in order to keep the plane in view?

Solution   Suppose the camera is at point C and the plane is vertically above point B. Let x km be the distance between B and C. The fact that the plane is moving horizontally toward C at 450 km/hr means that x is decreasing and $dx/dt = -450$ km/hr. From Figure 4.85, we see that $\tan \theta = 5/x$.

Differentiating $\tan \theta = 5/x$ with respect to t and using the chain rule gives

$$\frac{1}{\cos^2 \theta} \frac{d\theta}{dt} = -5x^{-2} \frac{dx}{dt}.$$

Plane

5 km

Camera

θ

Ground

C x B

Figure 4.85: Plane approaching a camera at C (side view; x in km)

We want to calculate $d\theta/dt$ when $\theta = \pi/3$. At that moment, $\cos \theta = 1/2$ and $\tan \theta = \sqrt{3}$, so $x = 5/\sqrt{3}$. Substituting gives

$$\frac{1}{(1/2)^2} \frac{d\theta}{dt} = -5 \left(\frac{5}{\sqrt{3}} \right)^{-2} \cdot (-450)$$

$$\frac{d\theta}{dt} = 67.5 \text{ radians/hour.}$$

Since there are 60 minutes in an hour, the camera must turn at roughly 1 radian per minute if it is to remain pointed at the plane. With 1 radian $\approx 60°$, this is a rotation of about one degree per second.

Exercises and Problems for Section 4.6

Exercises

1. With time, t, in minutes, the temperature, H, in degrees Celsius, of a bottle of water put in the refrigerator at $t = 0$ is given by

$$H = 4 + 16e^{-0.02t}.$$

How fast is the water cooling initially? After 10 minutes? Give units.

2. According to the US Census, the world population P, in billions, was approximately

$$P = 6.7e^{0.011t},$$

where t is in years since January 1, 2007. At what rate was the world's population increasing on that date? Give your answer in millions of people per year. [The world population growth rate has actually decreased since 2007.]

3. The power, P, dissipated when a 9-volt battery is put across a resistance of R ohms is given by

$$P = \frac{81}{R}.$$

What is the rate of change of power with respect to resistance?

4. With length, l, in meters, the period T, in seconds, of a pendulum is given by

$$T = 2\pi\sqrt{\frac{l}{9.8}}.$$

   (a) How fast does the period increase as l increases?
   (b) Does this rate of change increase or decrease as l increases?

5. A plane is climbing at 500 feet per minute, and the air temperature outside the plane is falling at $2°C$ per 1000 feet. What is the rate of change (as a function of time) of the air temperature just outside the plane?

6. Atmospheric pressure decays exponentially as altitude increases. With pressure, P, in inches of mercury and altitude, h, in feet above sea level, we have

$$P = 30e^{-3.23 \times 10^{-5}h}.$$

   (a) At what altitude is the atmospheric pressure 25 inches of mercury?
   (b) A glider measures the pressure to be 25 inches of mercury and experiences a pressure increase of 0.1 inches of mercury per minute. At what rate is it changing altitude?

7. The gravitational force, F, on a rocket at a distance, r, from the center of the earth is given by

$$F = \frac{k}{r^2},$$

where $k = 10^{13}$ newton $\cdot$ km^2. When the rocket is 10^4 km from the center of the earth, it is moving away at 0.2 km/sec. How fast is the gravitational force changing at that moment? Give units. (A newton is a unit of force.)

8. A voltage V across a resistance R generates a current

$$I = \frac{V}{R}.$$

A constant voltage of 9 volts is put across a resistance that is increasing at a rate of 0.2 ohms per second when the resistance is 5 ohms. At what rate is the current changing?

9. If θ is the angle between a line through the origin and the positive x-axis, the area, in cm^2, of part of a rose petal is

$$A = \frac{9}{16}(4\theta - \sin(4\theta)).$$

If the angle θ is increasing at a rate of 0.2 radians per minute, at what rate is the area changing when $\theta = \pi/4$?

10. The potential, ϕ, of a charge distribution at a point on the positive x-axis is given, for x in centimeters, by

$$\phi = 2\pi\left(\sqrt{x^2 + 4} - x\right).$$

A particle at $x = 3$ is moving to the left at a rate of 0.2 cm/sec. At what rate is its potential changing?

11. The average cost per item, C, in dollars, of manufacturing a quantity q of cell phones is given by

$$C = \frac{a}{q} + b \qquad \text{where } a, b \text{ are positive constants.}$$

   (a) Find the rate of change of C as q increases. What are its units?
   (b) If production increases at a rate of 100 cell phones per week, how fast is the average cost changing? Is the average cost increasing or decreasing?

12. If $x^2 + y^2 = 25$ and $dx/dt = 6$, find dy/dt when y is positive and

   (a) $x = 0$ (b) $x = 3$ (c) $x = 4$

13. A pyramid has height h and a square base with side x. The volume of a pyramid is $V = \frac{1}{3}x^2h$. If the height remains fixed and the side of the base is decreasing by 0.002 meter/yr, what rate is the volume decreasing when the height is 120 meters and the width is 150 meters?

14. A thin uniform rod of length l cm and a small particle lie on a line separated by a distance of a cm. If K is a positive constant and F is measured in newtons, the gravitational force between them is

$$F = \frac{K}{a(a+l)}.$$

(a) If a is increasing at the rate 2 cm/min when $a = 15$ and $l = 5$, how fast is F decreasing?

(b) If l is decreasing at the rate 2 cm/min when $a = 15$ and $l = 5$, how fast is F increasing?

15. The Dubois formula relates a person's surface area, s, in meters^2, to weight, w, in kg, and height, h, in cm, by

$$s = 0.01w^{0.25}h^{0.75}.$$

(a) What is the surface area of a person who weighs 60 kg and is 150 cm tall?

(b) The person in part (a) stays constant height but increases in weight by 0.5 kg/year. At what rate is his surface area increasing when his weight is 62 kg?

Problems

16. A rectangle has one side of 10 cm. How fast is the area of the rectangle changing at the instant when the other side is 12 cm and increasing at 3 cm per minute?

17. A rectangle has one side of 8 cm. How fast is the diagonal of the rectangle changing at the instant when the other side is 6 cm and increasing at 3 cm per minute?

18. A right triangle has one leg of 7 cm. How fast is its area changing at the instant that the other leg has length 10 cm and is decreasing at 2 cm per second?

19. The area, A, of a square is increasing at 3 cm^2 per minute. How fast is the side length of the square changing when $A = 576$ cm^2?

20. If two electrical resistances, R_1 and R_2, are connected in parallel, their combined resistance, R, is given by

$$\frac{1}{R} = \frac{1}{R_1} + \frac{1}{R_2}.$$

Suppose R_1 is held constant at 10 ohms, and that R_2 is increasing at 2 ohms per minute when R_2 is 20 ohms. How fast is R changing at that moment?

21. A dose, D, of a drug causes a temperature change, T, in a patient. For C a positive constant, T is given by

$$T = \left(\frac{C}{2} - \frac{D}{3}\right) D^2.$$

(a) What is the rate of change of temperature change with respect to dose?

(b) For what doses does the temperature change increase as the dose increases?

22. An item costs $500 at time $t = 0$ and costs \$P in year t. When inflation is $r\%$ per year, the price is given by

$$P = 500e^{rt/100}.$$

(a) If r is a constant, at what rate is the price rising (in dollars per year)

(i) Initially?   (ii) After 2 years?

(b) Now suppose that r is increasing by 0.3 per year when $r = 4$ and $t = 2$. At what rate (dollars per year) is the price increasing at that time?

23. For positive constants A and B, the force, F, between two atoms in a molecule at a distance r apart is given by

$$F = -\frac{A}{r^2} + \frac{B}{r^3}.$$

(a) How fast does force change as r increases? What type of units does it have?

(b) If at some time t the distance is changing at a rate k, at what rate is the force changing with time? What type of units does this rate of change have?

24. For positive constants k and g, the velocity, v, of a particle of mass m at time t is given by

$$v = \frac{mg}{k}\left(1 - e^{-kt/m}\right).$$

At what rate is the velocity changing at time 0? At $t = 1$? What do your answers tell you about the motion?

25. A 10 m ladder leans against a vertical wall and the bottom of the ladder slides away from the wall at a rate of 0.5 m/sec. How fast is the top of the ladder sliding down the wall when the bottom of the ladder is

(a) 4 m from the wall?   (b) 8 m from the wall?

26. Gasoline is pouring into a vertical cylindrical tank of radius 3 feet. When the depth of the gasoline is 4 feet, the depth is increasing at 0.2 ft/sec. How fast is the volume of gasoline changing at that instant?

27. Water is being pumped into a vertical cylinder of radius 5 meters and height 20 meters at a rate of 3 meters^3/min. How fast is the water level rising when the cylinder is half full?

28. A spherical snowball is melting. Its radius is decreasing at 0.2 cm per hour when the radius is 15 cm. How fast is its volume decreasing at that time?

29. The radius of a spherical balloon is increasing by 2 cm/sec. At what rate is air being blown into the balloon at the moment when the radius is 10 cm? Give units in your answer.

30. The circulation time of a mammal (that is, the average time it takes for all the blood in the body to circulate once and return to the heart) is proportional to the fourth root of the body mass of the mammal. The constant of proportionality is 17.40 if circulation time is in seconds and body mass is in kilograms. The body mass of a growing child is 45 kg and is increasing at a rate of 0.1 kg/month. What is the rate of change of the circulation time of the child?

31. A certain quantity of gas occupies a volume of $20 \, \text{cm}^3$ at a pressure of 1 atmosphere. The gas expands without the addition of heat, so, for some constant k, its pressure, P, and volume, V, satisfy the relation

$$PV^{1.4} = k.$$

(a) Find the rate of change of pressure with volume. Give units.
(b) The volume is increasing at $2 \, \text{cm}^3/\text{min}$ when the volume is $30 \, \text{cm}^3$. At that moment, is the pressure increasing or decreasing? How fast? Give units.

32. The metal frame of a rectangular box has a square base. The horizontal rods in the base are made out of one metal and the vertical rods out of a different metal. If the horizontal rods expand at a rate of 0.001 cm/hr and the vertical rods expand at a rate of 0.002 cm/hr, at what rate is the volume of the box expanding when the base has an area of $9 \, \text{cm}^2$ and the volume is $180 \, \text{cm}^3$?

33. A ruptured oil tanker causes a circular oil slick on the surface of the ocean. When its radius is 150 meters, the radius of the slick is expanding by 0.1 meter/minute and its thickness is 0.02 meter. At that moment:

(a) How fast is the area of the slick expanding?
(b) The circular slick has the same thickness everywhere, and the volume of oil spilled remains fixed. How fast is the thickness of the slick decreasing?

34. A potter forms a piece of clay into a cylinder. As he rolls it, the length, L, of the cylinder increases and the radius, r, decreases. If the length of the cylinder is increasing at 0.1 cm per second, find the rate at which the radius is changing when the radius is 1 cm and the length is 5 cm.

35. A cone-shaped coffee filter of radius 6 cm and depth 10 cm contains water, which drips out through a hole at the bottom at a constant rate of 1.5 cm^3 per second.

(a) If the filter starts out full, how long does it take to empty?
(b) Find the volume of water in the filter when the depth of the water is h cm.
(c) How fast is the water level falling when the depth is 8 cm?

36. Water is being poured into the cone-shaped container in Figure 4.86. When the depth of the water is 2.5 in, it is

increasing at 3 in/min. At that time, how fast is the surface area, A, that is covered by water increasing? [Hint: $A = \pi r s$, where r, s are as shown.]

Figure 4.86: Cone and cross section

37. Grit, which is spread on roads in winter, is stored in mounds which are the shape of a cone. As grit is added to the top of a mound at 2 cubic meters per minute, the angle between the slant side of the cone and the vertical remains $45°$. How fast is the height of the mound increasing when it is half a meter high? [Hint: Volume $V = \pi r^2 h/3$, where r is radius and h is height.]

38. A gas station stands at the intersection of a north-south road and an east-west road. A police car is traveling toward the gas station from the east, chasing a stolen truck which is traveling north away from the gas station. The speed of the police car is 100 mph at the moment it is 3 miles from the gas station. At the same time, the truck is 4 miles from the gas station going 80 mph. At this moment:

(a) Is the distance between the car and truck increasing or decreasing? How fast? (Distance is measured along a straight line joining the car and the truck.)
(b) How does your answer change if the truck is going 70 mph instead of 80 mph?

39. The London Eye is a large Ferris wheel that has diameter 135 meters and revolves continuously. Passengers enter the cabins at the bottom of the wheel and complete one revolution in about 27 minutes. One minute into the ride a passenger is rising at 0.06 meters per second. How fast is the horizontal motion of the passenger at that moment?

40. Point P moves around the unit circle.[10] (See Figure 4.87.) The angle θ, in radians, changes with time as shown in Figure 4.88.

(a) Estimate the coordinates of P when $t = 2$.
(b) When $t = 2$, approximately how fast is the point P moving in the x-direction? In the y-direction?

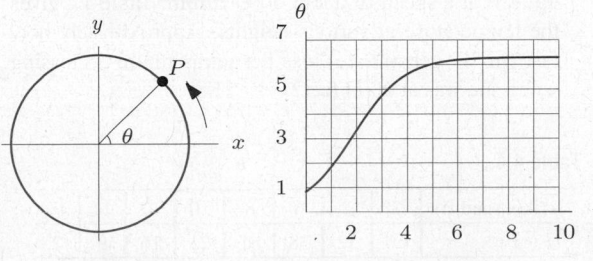

Figure 4.87   **Figure 4.88**

---

[10]Based on an idea from Caspar Curjel.

41. Figure 4.89 shows the number of gallons, G, of gasoline used on a trip of M miles.

    (a) The function f is linear on each of the intervals $0 < M < 70$ and $70 < M < 100$. What is the slope of these lines? What are the units of these slopes?

    (b) What is gas consumption (in miles per gallon) during the first 70 miles of this trip? During the next 30 miles?

    (c) Figure 4.90 shows distance traveled, M (in miles), as a function of time t, in hours since the start of the trip. Describe this trip in words. Give a possible explanation for what happens one hour into the trip. What do your answers to part (b) tell you about the trip?

    (d) If we let $G = k(t) = f(h(t))$, estimate $k(0.5)$ and interpret your answer in terms of the trip.

    (e) Find $k'(0.5)$ and $k'(1.5)$. Give units and interpret your answers.

Figure 4.89

Figure 4.90:

42. On February 16, 2007, paraglider Eva Wisnierska[11] was caught in a freak thunderstorm over Australia and carried upward at a speed of about 3000 ft/min. Table 4.4 gives the temperature at various heights. Approximately how fast (in °F/ per minute) was her temperature decreasing when she was at 4000 feet?

Table 4.4

y (thousand ft)	2	4	6	8	10	12	14	16
H (°F)	60	52	38	31	23	16	9	2

43. Coroners estimate time of death using the rule of thumb that a body cools about 2°F during the first hour after death and about 1°F for each additional hour. Assuming an air temperature of 68°F and a living body temperature of 98.6°F, the temperature $T(t)$ in °F of a body at a time t hours since death is given by

$$T(t) = 68 + 30.6e^{-kt}.$$

    (a) For what value of k will the body cool by 2°F in the first hour?

    (b) Using the value of k found in part (a), after how many hours will the temperature of the body be decreasing at a rate of 1°F per hour?

    (c) Using the value of k found in part (a), show that, 24 hours after death, the coroner's rule of thumb gives approximately the same temperature as the formula.

44. A train is traveling at 0.8 km/min along a long straight track, moving in the direction shown in Figure 4.91. A movie camera, 0.5 km away from the track, is focused on the train.

    (a) Express z, the distance between the camera and the train, as a function of x.

    (b) How fast is the distance from the camera to the train changing when the train is 1 km from the camera? Give units.

    (c) How fast is the camera rotating (in radians/min) at the moment when the train is 1 km from the camera?

Figure 4.91

45. A lighthouse is 2 km from the long, straight coastline shown in Figure 4.92. Find the rate of change of the distance of the spot of light from the point O with respect to the angle θ.

Figure 4.92

[11]www.sciencedaily.com, accessed May 15, 2007.

46. When the growth of a spherical cell depends on the flow of nutrients through the surface, it is reasonable to assume that the growth rate, dV/dt, is proportional to the surface area, S. Assume that for a particular cell $dV/dt = \frac{1}{3}S$. At what rate is its radius r increasing?

47. The length of each side of a cube is increased at a constant rate. Which is greater, the relative rate of change of the volume of the cube, $\frac{1}{V}\frac{dV}{dt}$, or the relative change of the surface area of the cube, $\frac{1}{A}\frac{dA}{dt}$?

48. A circular region is irrigated by a 20 meter long pipe, fixed at one end and rotating horizontally, spraying water. One rotation takes 5 minutes. A road passes 30 meters from the edge of the circular area. See Figure 4.93.

(a) How fast is the end of the pipe, P, moving?

(b) How fast is the distance PQ changing when θ is $\pi/2$? When θ is 0?

Figure 4.93

49. A water tank is in the shape of an inverted cone with depth 10 meters and top radius 8 meters. Water is flowing into the tank at 0.1 cubic meters/min but leaking out at a rate of $0.004h^2$ cubic meters/min, where h is the depth of the water in meters. Can the tank ever overflow?

50. For the amusement of the guests, some hotels have elevators on the outside of the building. One such hotel is 300 feet high. You are standing by a window 100 feet above the ground and 150 feet away from the hotel, and the elevator descends at a constant speed of 30 ft/sec, starting at time $t = 0$, where t is time in seconds. Let θ be the angle between the line of your horizon and your line of sight to the elevator. (See Figure 4.94.)

(a) Find a formula for $h(t)$, the elevator's height above the ground as it descends from the top of the hotel.

(b) Using your answer to part (a), express θ as a function of time t and find the rate of change of θ with respect to t.

(c) The rate of change of θ is a measure of how fast the elevator appears to you to be moving. At what height is the elevator when it appears to be moving fastest?

Figure 4.94

51. In a romantic relationship between Angela and Brian, who are unsuited for each other, $a(t)$ represents the affection Angela has for Brian at time t days after they meet, while $b(t)$ represents the affection Brian has for Angela at time t. If $a(t) > 0$ then Angela likes Brian; if $a(t) < 0$ then Angela dislikes Brian; if $a(t) = 0$ then Angela neither likes nor dislikes Brian. Their affection for each other is given by the relation $(a(t))^2 + (b(t))^2 = c$, where c is a constant.

(a) Show that $a(t) \cdot a'(t) = -b(t) \cdot b'(t)$.

(b) At any time during their relationship, the rate per day at which Brian's affection for Angela changes is $b'(t) = -a(t)$. Explain what this means if Angela

    (i) Likes Brian,   (ii) Dislikes Brian.

(c) Use parts (a) and (b) to show that $a'(t) = b(t)$. Explain what this means if Brian

    (i) Likes Angela,   (ii) Dislikes Angela.

(d) If $a(0) = 1$ and $b(0) = 1$ who first dislikes the other?

52. In a 19th century sea-battle, the number of ships on each side remaining t hours after the start are given by $x(t)$ and $y(t)$. If the ships are equally equipped, the relation between them is $(x(t))^2 - (y(t))^2 = c$, where c is a positive constant. The battle ends when one side has no ships remaining.

(a) If, at the start of the battle, 50 ships on one side oppose 40 ships on the other, what is the value of c?

(b) If $y(3) = 16$, what is $x(3)$? What does this represent in terms of the battle?

(c) There is a time T when $y(T) = 0$. What does this T represent in terms of the battle?

(d) At the end of the battle, how many ships remain on the victorious side?

(e) At any time during the battle, the rate per hour at which y loses ships is directly proportional to the number of x ships, with constant of proportionality k. Write an equation that represents this. Is k positive or negative?

(f) Show that the rate per hour at which x loses ships is directly proportional to the number of y ships, with constant of proportionality k.

(g) Three hours after the start of the battle, x is losing ships at the rate of 32 ships per hour. What is k? At what rate is y losing ships at this time?

Strengthen Your Understanding

In Problems 53–54, explain what is wrong with the statement.

53. If the radius, R, of a circle increases at a constant rate, its diameter, D, increases at the same constant rate.

54. If two variables x and y are functions of t and are related by the equation $y = 1 - x^2$ then $dy/dt = -2x$.

In Problems 55–56, give an example of:

55. Two functions f and g where $y = f(x)$ and $x = g(t)$ such that dy/dt and dx/dt are both constant.

56. Two functions g and f where $x = g(t)$ and $y = f(x)$ such that dx/dt is constant and dy/dt is not constant.

Are the statements in Problems 57–58 true of false? Give an explanation for your answer.

57. If the radius of a circle is increasing at a constant rate, then so is the circumference.

58. If the radius of a circle is increasing at a constant rate, then so is the area.

59. The light in the lighthouse in Figure 4.95 rotates at 2 revolutions per minute. To calculate the speed at which the spot of light moves along the shore, it is best to differentiate:

(a) $r^2 = 5^2 + x^2$
(b) $x = r \sin \theta$
(c) $x = 5 \tan \theta$
(d) $r^2 = 2^2 + x^2$

Figure 4.95

4.7 L'HOPITAL'S RULE, GROWTH, AND DOMINANCE

Suppose we want to calculate the exact value of the limit

$$\lim_{x \to 0} \frac{e^{2x} - 1}{x}.$$

Substituting $x = 0$ gives us $0/0$, which is undefined:

$$\frac{e^{2(0)} - 1}{0} = \frac{1 - 1}{0} = \frac{0}{0}.$$

Substituting values of x near 0 gives us an approximate value for the limit.

However, the limit can be calculated exactly using local linearity. Suppose we let $f(x)$ be the numerator, so $f(x) = e^{2x} - 1$, and $g(x)$ be the denominator, so $g(x) = x$. Then $f(0) = 0$ and $f'(x) = 2e^{2x}$, so $f'(0) = 2$. When we zoom in on the graph of $f(x) = e^{2x} - 1$ near the origin, we see its tangent line $y = 2x$ shown in Figure 4.96. We are interested in the ratio $f(x)/g(x)$, which is approximately the ratio of the y-values in Figure 4.96. So, for x near 0,

$$\frac{f(x)}{g(x)} = \frac{e^{2x} - 1}{x} \approx \frac{2x}{x} = \frac{2}{1} = \frac{f'(0)}{g'(0)}.$$

As $x \to 0$, this approximation gets better, and we have

$$\lim_{x \to 0} \frac{e^{2x} - 1}{x} = 2.$$

Figure 4.96: Ratio $(e^{2x} - 1)/x$ is approximated by ratio of slopes as we zoom in near the origin

Figure 4.97: Ratio $f(x)/g(x)$ is approximated by ratio of slopes, $f'(a)/g'(a)$, as we zoom in at a

L'Hopital's Rule

If $f(a) = g(a) = 0$, we can use the same method to investigate limits of the form

$$\lim_{x \to a} \frac{f(x)}{g(x)}.$$

As in the previous case, we zoom in on the graphs of $f(x)$ and $g(x)$. Figure 4.97 shows that both graphs cross the x-axis at $x = a$. This suggests that the limit of $f(x)/g(x)$ as $x \to a$ is the ratio of slopes, giving the following result:

L'Hopital's rule:[12] If f and g are differentiable, $f(a) = g(a) = 0$, and $g'(a) \neq 0$, then

$$\lim_{x \to a} \frac{f(x)}{g(x)} = \frac{f'(a)}{g'(a)}.$$

Example 1 Use l'Hopital's rule to confirm that $\lim\limits_{x \to 0} \dfrac{\sin x}{x} = 1$.

Solution Let $f(x) = \sin x$ and $g(x) = x$. Then $f(0) = g(0) = 0$ and $f'(x) = \cos x$ and $g'(x) = 1$. Thus,

$$\lim_{x \to 0} \frac{\sin x}{x} = \frac{\cos 0}{1} = 1.$$

If we also have $f'(a) = g'(a) = 0$, then we can use the following result:

More general form of l'Hopital's rule: If f and g are differentiable and $f(a) = g(a) = 0$, then

$$\lim_{x \to a} \frac{f(x)}{g(x)} = \lim_{x \to a} \frac{f'(x)}{g'(x)},$$

provided the limit on the right exists.

Example 2 Calculate $\lim\limits_{t \to 0} \dfrac{e^t - 1 - t}{t^2}$.

Solution Let $f(t) = e^t - 1 - t$ and $g(t) = t^2$. Then $f(0) = e^0 - 1 - 0 = 0$ and $g(0) = 0$, and $f'(t) = e^t - 1$ and $g'(t) = 2t$. So

$$\lim_{t \to 0} \frac{e^t - 1 - t}{t^2} = \lim_{t \to 0} \frac{e^t - 1}{2t}.$$

---

[12]Marquis de l'Hopital (1661–1704) was a French nobleman who wrote the first calculus text.

Since $f'(0) = g'(0) = 0$, the ratio $f'(0)/g'(0)$ is not defined. So we use l'Hopital's rule again:

$$\lim_{t \to 0} \frac{e^t - 1 - t}{t^2} = \lim_{t \to 0} \frac{e^t - 1}{2t} = \lim_{t \to 0} \frac{e^t}{2} = \frac{1}{2}.$$

We can also use l'Hopital's rule in cases involving infinity.

L'Hopital's rule applies to limits involving infinity, provided f and g are differentiable. For a any real number or $\pm\infty$:

- When $\lim_{x \to a} f(x) = \pm\infty$ and $\lim_{x \to a} g(x) = \pm\infty$,

or

- When $\lim_{x \to \infty} f(x) = \lim_{x \to \infty} g(x) = 0$.

it can be shown that:

$$\lim_{x \to a} \frac{f(x)}{g(x)} = \lim_{x \to a} \frac{f'(x)}{g'(x)},$$

provided the limit on the right-hand side exists.

The next example shows how this version of l'Hopital's rule is used.

Example 3   Calculate $\lim_{x \to \infty} \dfrac{5x + e^{-x}}{7x}$.

Solution   Let $f(x) = 5x + e^{-x}$ and $g(x) = 7x$. Then $\lim_{x \to \infty} f(x) = \lim_{x \to \infty} g(x) = \infty$, and $f'(x) = 5 - e^{-x}$ and $g'(x) = 7$, so

$$\lim_{x \to \infty} \frac{5x + e^{-x}}{7x} = \lim_{x \to \infty} \frac{(5 - e^{-x})}{7} = \frac{5}{7}.$$

Dominance: Powers, Polynomials, Exponentials, and Logarithms

In Chapter 1, we see that some functions are much larger than others as $x \to \infty$. For positive functions f and g, we say that g *dominates* f as $x \to \infty$ if $\lim_{x \to \infty} \dfrac{f(x)}{g(x)} = 0$. L'Hopital's rule gives us an easy way of checking this.

Example 4   Check that $x^{1/2}$ dominates $\ln x$ as $x \to \infty$.

Solution   We apply l'Hopital's rule to $(\ln x)/x^{1/2}$:

$$\lim_{x \to \infty} \frac{\ln x}{x^{1/2}} = \lim_{x \to \infty} \frac{1/x}{\frac{1}{2}x^{-1/2}}.$$

To evaluate this limit, we simplify and get

$$\lim_{x \to \infty} \frac{1/x}{\frac{1}{2}x^{-1/2}} = \lim_{x \to \infty} \frac{2x^{1/2}}{x} = \lim_{x \to \infty} \frac{2}{x^{1/2}} = 0.$$

Therefore we have

$$\lim_{x \to \infty} \frac{\ln x}{x^{1/2}} = 0,$$

which tells us that $x^{1/2}$ dominates $\ln x$ as $x \to \infty$.

Example 5   Check that any exponential function of the form e^{kx} (with $k > 0$) dominates any power function of the form Ax^p (with A and p positive) as $x \to \infty$.

Solution   We apply l'Hopital's rule repeatedly to Ax^p/e^{kx}:

$$\lim_{x\to\infty} \frac{Ax^p}{e^{kx}} = \lim_{x\to\infty} \frac{Apx^{p-1}}{ke^{kx}} = \lim_{x\to\infty} \frac{Ap(p-1)x^{p-2}}{k^2 e^{kx}} = \cdots$$

Keep applying l'Hopital's rule until the power of x is no longer positive. Then the limit of the numerator must be a finite number, while the limit of the denominator must be ∞. Therefore we have

$$\lim_{x\to\infty} \frac{Ax^p}{e^{kx}} = 0,$$

so e^{kx} dominates Ax^p.

Recognizing the Form of a Limit

Although expressions like $0/0$ and ∞/∞ have no numerical value, they are useful in describing the form of a limit. We can also use l'Hopital's rule to calculate some limits of the form $0 \cdot \infty$, $\infty - \infty$, 1^∞, 0^0, and ∞^0.

Example 6   Calculate $\lim_{x\to\infty} xe^{-x}$.

Solution   Since $\lim_{x\to\infty} x = \infty$ and $\lim_{x\to\infty} e^{-x} = 0$, we see that

$$xe^{-x} \to \infty \cdot 0 \qquad \text{as } x \to \infty.$$

Rewriting

$$\infty \cdot 0 \quad \text{as} \quad \frac{\infty}{\frac{1}{0}} = \frac{\infty}{\infty}$$

gives a form whose value can be determined using l'Hopital's rule, so we rewrite the function xe^{-x} as

$$xe^{-x} = \frac{x}{e^x} \to \frac{\infty}{\infty} \qquad \text{as } x \to \infty.$$

Taking $f(x) = x$ and $g(x) = e^x$ gives $f'(x) = 1$ and $g'(x) = e^x$, so

$$\lim_{x\to\infty} xe^{-x} = \lim_{x\to\infty} \frac{x}{e^x} = \lim_{x\to\infty} \frac{1}{e^x} = 0.$$

A Famous Limit

In the following example, l'Hopital's rule is applied to calculate a limit that can be used to define e.

Example 7   Evaluate $\lim_{x\to\infty} \left(1 + \frac{1}{x}\right)^x$.

Solution   As $x \to \infty$, we see that $\left(1 + \frac{1}{x}\right)^x \to 1^\infty$, a form whose value in this context is to be determined. Since $\ln 1^\infty = \infty \cdot \ln 1 = \infty \cdot 0$, we write

$$y = \left(1 + \frac{1}{x}\right)^x$$

and find the limit of $\ln y$:

$$\lim_{x\to\infty} \ln y = \lim_{x\to\infty} \ln\left(1 + \frac{1}{x}\right)^x = \lim_{x\to\infty} x\ln\left(1 + \frac{1}{x}\right) = \infty \cdot 0.$$

As in the previous example, we rewrite

$$\infty \cdot 0 \quad \text{as} \quad \frac{0}{\frac{1}{\infty}} = \frac{0}{0},$$

which suggests rewriting

$$\lim_{x\to\infty} x\ln\left(1+\frac{1}{x}\right) \quad \text{as} \quad \lim_{x\to\infty} \frac{\ln(1+1/x)}{1/x}.$$

Since $\lim_{x\to\infty} \ln(1+1/x) = 0$ and $\lim_{x\to\infty} (1/x) = 0$, we can use l'Hopital's rule with $f(x) = \ln(1+1/x)$ and $g(x) = 1/x$. We have

$$f'(x) = \frac{1}{1+1/x}\left(-\frac{1}{x^2}\right) \quad \text{and} \quad g'(x) = -\frac{1}{x^2},$$

so

$$\lim_{x\to\infty} \ln y = \lim_{x\to\infty} \frac{\ln(1+1/x)}{1/x} = \lim_{x\to\infty} \frac{1}{1+1/x}\left(-\frac{1}{x^2}\right)\Big/\left(-\frac{1}{x^2}\right)$$

$$= \lim_{x\to\infty} \frac{1}{1+1/x} = 1.$$

Since $\lim_{x\to\infty} \ln y = 1$, we have

$$\lim_{x\to\infty} y = e^1 = e.$$

Example 8   Put the following limits in a form that can be evaluated using l'Hopital's rule:

(a) $\lim_{x\to 0^+} x\ln x$ (b) $\lim_{x\to\infty} x^{1/x}$ (c) $\lim_{x\to 0^+} x^x$ (d) $\lim_{x\to 0} \frac{1}{x} - \frac{1}{\sin x}$

Solution   (a) We have

$$\lim_{x\to 0^+} x\ln x = 0\cdot\infty.$$

We can rewrite

$$0\cdot\infty \quad \text{as} \quad \frac{\infty}{1/0} = \frac{\infty}{\infty}.$$

This corresponds to rewriting

$$\lim_{x\to 0^+} x\ln x \quad \text{as} \quad \lim_{x\to 0^+} \frac{\ln x}{1/x}.$$

This is an ∞/∞ form that can be evaluated using l'Hopital's rule. (Note that we could also have written

$$0\cdot\infty \quad \text{as} \quad \frac{0}{1/\infty} = \frac{0}{0},$$

but this leads to rewriting

$$\lim_{x\to 0^+} x\ln x \quad \text{as} \quad \lim_{x\to 0^+} \frac{x}{1/\ln x}.$$

It turns out that l'Hopital's rule fails to simplify this limit.)

(b) In this case we have a ∞^0 form, so we take the logarithm and get a $0\cdot\infty$ form:

$$\lim_{x\to\infty} \ln(x^{1/x}) = \lim_{x\to\infty} \frac{1}{x}\ln x = \lim_{x\to\infty} \frac{\ln x}{x}.$$

This is an ∞/∞ form that can be evaluated using l'Hopital's rule. Once we get the answer, we exponentiate it to get the original limit.

(c) Since $\lim_{x\to 0^+} x = 0$, this is a 0^0 form. If we take the logarithm, we get

$$\ln 0^0 = 0\cdot\ln 0 = 0\cdot\infty.$$

This corresponds to the limit

$$\lim_{x\to 0^+} \ln x^x = \lim_{x\to 0^+} x\ln x,$$

which is considered in part (a).

(d) We have
$$\lim_{x \to 0} \frac{1}{x} - \frac{1}{\sin x} = \frac{1}{0} - \frac{1}{0} = \infty - \infty.$$

Limits like this can often be calculated by adding the fractions:
$$\lim_{x \to 0} \frac{1}{x} - \frac{1}{\sin x} = \lim_{x \to 0} \frac{\sin x - x}{x \sin x},$$

giving a $0/0$ form that can be evaluated using l'Hopital's rule twice.

Exercises and Problems for Section 4.7

Exercises

In Exercises 1–11, find the limit. Use l'Hopital's rule if it applies.

1. $\displaystyle\lim_{x \to 2} \frac{x - 2}{x^2 - 4}$

2. $\displaystyle\lim_{x \to 1} \frac{x^2 + 3x - 4}{x - 1}$

3. $\displaystyle\lim_{x \to 1} \frac{x^6 - 1}{x^4 - 1}$

4. $\displaystyle\lim_{x \to 0} \frac{e^x - 1}{\sin x}$

5. $\displaystyle\lim_{x \to 0} \frac{\sin x}{e^x}$

6. $\displaystyle\lim_{x \to 1} \frac{\ln x}{x - 1}$

7. $\displaystyle\lim_{x \to \infty} \frac{\ln x}{x}$

8. $\displaystyle\lim_{x \to \infty} \frac{(\ln x)^3}{x^2}$

9. $\displaystyle\lim_{x \to 0} \frac{e^{4x} - 1}{\cos x}$

10. $\displaystyle\lim_{x \to 1} \frac{x^a - 1}{x^b - 1}, b \neq 0$

11. $\displaystyle\lim_{x \to a} \frac{\sqrt[3]{x} - \sqrt[3]{a}}{x - a}, a \neq 0$

In Exercises 12–15, which function dominates as $x \to \infty$?

12. x^5 and $0.1x^7$

13. $0.01x^3$ and $50x^2$

14. $\ln(x + 3)$ and $x^{0.2}$

15. x^{10} and $e^{0.1x}$

Problems

16. The functions f and g and their tangent lines at $(4, 0)$ are shown in Figure 4.98. Find $\displaystyle\lim_{x \to 4} \frac{f(x)}{g(x)}$.

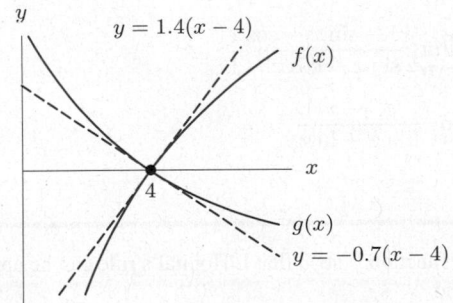

Figure 4.98

For Problems 17–20, find the sign of $\displaystyle\lim_{x \to a} \frac{f(x)}{g(x)}$ from the figure.

17.

18.

19. **20.**

Assume $f''(a) \neq 0, g''(a) \neq 0$ Assume $f'''(a) \neq 0, g'''(a) \neq 0$

Based on your knowledge of the behavior of the numerator and denominator, predict the value of the limits in Problems 21–24. Then find each limit using l'Hopital's rule.

21. $\displaystyle\lim_{x \to 0} \frac{x^2}{\sin x}$

22. $\displaystyle\lim_{x \to 0} \frac{\sin^2 x}{x}$

23. $\displaystyle\lim_{x \to 0} \frac{\sin x}{x^{1/3}}$

24. $\displaystyle\lim_{x \to 0} \frac{x}{(\sin x)^{1/3}}$

In Problems 25–30, describe the form of the limit ($0/0$, ∞/∞, $\infty \cdot 0$, $\infty - \infty$, 1^∞, 0^0, or ∞^0, or none of these). Does l'Hopital's rule apply? If so, explain how.

25. $\displaystyle\lim_{x \to \infty} \frac{x}{e^x}$

26. $\displaystyle\lim_{x \to 1} \frac{x}{x - 1}$

27. $\displaystyle\lim_{t \to \infty} \left(\frac{1}{t} - \frac{2}{t^2} \right)$

28. $\displaystyle\lim_{t \to 0^+} \frac{1}{t} - \frac{1}{e^t - 1}$

29. $\displaystyle\lim_{x \to 0} (1 + x)^x$

30. $\displaystyle\lim_{x \to \infty} (1 + x)^{1/x}$

In Problems 31–44 determine whether the limit exists, and where possible evaluate it.

31. $\lim\limits_{x \to 1} \dfrac{\ln x}{x^2 - 1}$

32. $\lim\limits_{t \to \pi} \dfrac{\sin^2 t}{t - \pi}$

33. $\lim\limits_{n \to \infty} \sqrt[n]{n}$

34. $\lim\limits_{x \to 0^+} x \ln x$

35. $\lim\limits_{x \to 0} \dfrac{\sinh(2x)}{x}$

36. $\lim\limits_{x \to 0} \dfrac{1 - \cosh(3x)}{x}$

37. $\lim\limits_{x \to 1^-} \dfrac{\cos^{-1} x}{x - 1}$

38. $\lim\limits_{x \to 0} \left(\dfrac{1}{x} - \dfrac{1}{\sin x} \right)$

39. $\lim\limits_{t \to 0^+} \left(\dfrac{2}{t} - \dfrac{1}{e^t - 1} \right)$

40. $\lim\limits_{t \to 0} \left(\dfrac{1}{t} - \dfrac{1}{e^t - 1} \right)$

41. $\lim\limits_{x \to \infty} \left(1 + \sin \left(\dfrac{3}{x} \right) \right)^x$

42. $\lim\limits_{t \to 0} \dfrac{\sin^2 At}{\cos At - 1}, A \neq 0$

43. $\lim\limits_{t \to \infty} e^t - t^n$, where n is a positive integer

44. $\lim\limits_{x \to 0^+} x^a \ln x$, where a is a positive constant.

In Problems 45–47, explain why l'Hopital's rule cannot be used to calculate the limit. Then evaluate the limit if it exists.

45. $\lim\limits_{x \to 1} \dfrac{\sin(2x)}{x}$

46. $\lim\limits_{x \to 0} \dfrac{\cos x}{x}$

47. $\lim\limits_{x \to \infty} \dfrac{e^{-x}}{\sin x}$

In Problems 48–50, evaluate the limit using the fact that

$$\lim\limits_{n \to \infty} \left(1 + \dfrac{1}{n} \right)^n = e.$$

48. $\lim\limits_{x \to 0^+} (1 + x)^{1/x}$

49. $\lim\limits_{n \to \infty} \left(1 + \dfrac{2}{n} \right)^n$

50. $\lim\limits_{x \to 0^+} (1 + kx)^{t/x}; k > 0$

51. Show that $\lim\limits_{n \to \infty} \left(1 - \dfrac{1}{n} \right)^n = e^{-1}$.

52. Use the result of Problem 51 to evaluate

$$\lim\limits_{n \to \infty} \left(1 - \dfrac{\lambda}{n} \right)^n.$$

Evaluate the limits in Problems 53–55 where

$$f(t) = \left(\dfrac{3^t + 5^t}{2} \right)^{1/t} \quad \text{for } t \neq 0.$$

53. $\lim\limits_{t \to -\infty} f(t)$

54. $\lim\limits_{t \to +\infty} f(t)$

55. $\lim\limits_{t \to 0} f(t)$

In Problems 56–59, evaluate the limits as x approaches 0.

56. $\dfrac{\sinh(2x)}{x}$

57. $\dfrac{1 - \cosh(3x)}{x}$

58. $\dfrac{1 - \cosh(5x)}{x^2}$

59. $\dfrac{x - \sinh(x)}{x^3}$

Problems 60–62 are examples Euler used to illustrate l'Hopital's rule. Find the limit.

60. $\lim\limits_{x \to 0} \dfrac{e^x - 1 - \ln(1 + x)}{x^2}$

61. $\lim\limits_{x \to \pi/2} \dfrac{1 - \sin x + \cos x}{\sin x + \cos x - 1}$

62. $\lim\limits_{x \to 1} \dfrac{x^x - x}{1 - x + \ln x}$

Strengthen Your Understanding

In Problems 63–64, explain what is wrong with the statement.

63. There is a positive integer n such that function x^n dominates e^x as $x \to \infty$.

64. L'Hopital's rule shows that

$$\lim\limits_{x \to \infty} \dfrac{5x + \cos x}{x} = 5.$$

In Problems 65–66, give an example of:

65. A limit of a rational function for which l'Hopital's rule cannot be applied.

66. A function f such that L'Hopital's rule can be applied to find

$$\lim\limits_{x \to \infty} \dfrac{f(x)}{\ln x}.$$

67. Is the following statement true of false? If $g'(a) \neq 0$, then $\lim\limits_{x \to a} \dfrac{f(x)}{g(x)} = \dfrac{f'(a)}{g'(a)}$. Give an explanation for your answer.

68. Which of the limits cannot be computed with l'Hopital's rule?

(a) $\lim\limits_{x \to 0} \dfrac{\sin x}{x}$

(b) $\lim\limits_{x \to 0} \dfrac{\cos x}{x}$

(c) $\lim\limits_{x \to 0} \dfrac{x}{\sin x}$

(d) $\lim\limits_{x \to \infty} \dfrac{x}{e^x}$

4.8 PARAMETRIC EQUATIONS

Representing Motion in the Plane

To represent the motion of a particle in the xy-plane we use two equations, one for the x-coordinate of the particle, $x = f(t)$, and another for the y-coordinate, $y = g(t)$. Thus at time t the particle is at the point $(f(t), g(t))$. The equation for x describes the right-left motion; the equation for y describes the up-down motion. The two equations for x and y are called *parametric equations* with *parameter t*.

Example 1   Describe the motion of the particle whose coordinates at time t are $x = \cos t$ and $y = \sin t$.

Solution   Since $(\cos t)^2 + (\sin t)^2 = 1$, we have $x^2 + y^2 = 1$. That is, at any time t the particle is at a point (x, y) on the unit circle $x^2 + y^2 = 1$. We plot points at different times to see how the particle moves on the circle. (See Figure 4.99 and Table 4.5.) The particle completes one full trip counterclockwise around the circle every 2π units of time. Notice how the x-coordinate goes repeatedly back and forth from -1 to 1 while the y-coordinate goes repeatedly up and down from -1 to 1. The two motions combine to trace out a circle.

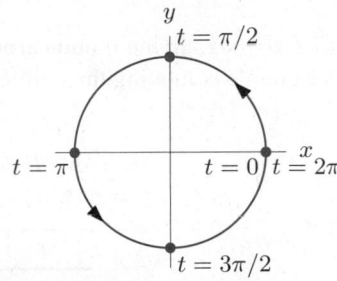

Figure 4.99: The circle parameterized by $x = \cos t, y = \sin t$

Table 4.5 *Points on the circle with $x = \cos t$, $y = \sin t$*

t	x	y
0	1	0
$\pi/2$	0	1
π	-1	0
$3\pi/2$	0	-1
2π	1	0

Example 2   Figure 4.100 shows the graphs of two functions, $f(t)$ and $g(t)$. Describe the motion of the particle whose coordinates at time t are $x = f(t)$ and $y = g(t)$.

Figure 4.100: Graphs of $x = f(t)$ and $y = g(t)$ used to trace out the path $(f(t), g(t))$ in Figure 4.101

Solution   Between times $t = 0$ and $t = 1$, the x-coordinate goes from 0 to 1, while the y-coordinate stays fixed at 0. So the particle moves along the x-axis from $(0, 0)$ to $(1, 0)$. Then, between times $t = 1$ and $t = 2$, the x-coordinate stays fixed at $x = 1$, while the y-coordinate goes from 0 to 1. Thus, the particle moves along the vertical line from $(1, 0)$ to $(1, 1)$. Similarly, between times $t = 2$ and $t = 3$, it moves horizontally back to $(0, 1)$, and between times $t = 3$ and $t = 4$ it moves down the y-axis to $(0, 0)$. Thus, it traces out the square in Figure 4.101.

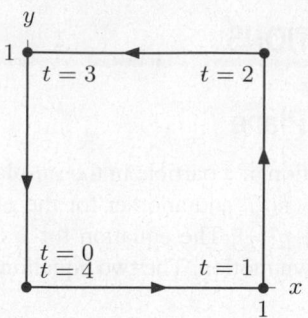

Figure 4.101: The square parameterized by $(f(t), g(t))$

Different Motions Along the Same Path

Example 3   Describe the motion of the particle whose x and y coordinates at time t are given by the equations

$$x = \cos(3t), \quad y = \sin(3t).$$

Solution   Since $(\cos(3t))^2 + (\sin(3t))^2 = 1$, we have $x^2 + y^2 = 1$, giving motion around the unit circle. But from Table 4.6, we see that the particle in this example is moving three times as fast as the particle in Example 1. (See Figure 4.102.)

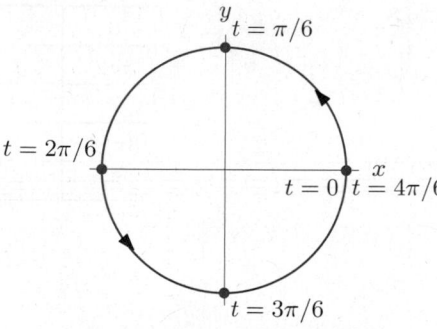

Figure 4.102: The circle parameterized by $x = \cos(3t)$, $y = \sin(3t)$

Table 4.6   *Points on circle with* $x = \cos(3t)$, $y = \sin(3t)$

t	x	y
0	1	0
$\pi/6$	0	1
$2\pi/6$	-1	0
$3\pi/6$	0	-1
$4\pi/6$	1	0

Example 3 is obtained from Example 1 by replacing t by $3t$; this is called a *change in parameter*. If we make a change in parameter, the particle traces out the same curve (or a part of it) but at a different speed or in a different direction.

Example 4   Describe the motion of the particle whose x and y coordinates at time t are given by

$$x = \cos(e^{-t^2}), \quad y = \sin(e^{-t^2}).$$

Solution   As in Examples 1 and 3, we have $x^2 + y^2 = 1$ so the motion lies on the unit circle. As time t goes from $-\infty$ (way back in the past) to 0 (the present) to ∞ (way off in the future), e^{-t^2} goes from near 0 to 1 back to near 0. So $(x, y) = (\cos(e^{-t^2}), \sin(e^{-t^2}))$ goes from near $(1, 0)$ to $(\cos 1, \sin 1)$ and back to near $(1, 0)$. The particle does not actually reach the point $(1, 0)$. (See Figure 4.103 and Table 4.7.)

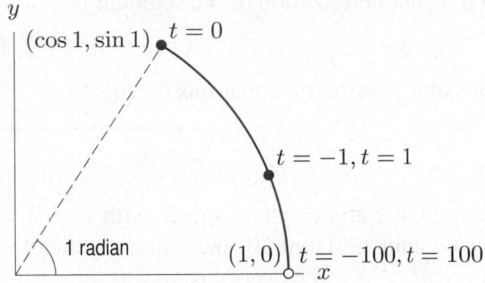

Figure 4.103: The circle parameterized by
$x = \cos(e^{-t^2}), y = \sin(e^{-t^2})$

Table 4.7 *Points on circle with* $x = \cos(e^{-t^2})$, $y = \sin(e^{-t^2})$

t	x	y
-100	~ 1	~ 0
-1	0.93	0.36
0	0.54	0.84
1	0.93	0.36
100	~ 1	~ 0

Motion in a Straight Line

An object moves with constant speed along a straight line through the point (x_0, y_0). Both the x- and y-coordinates have a constant rate of change. Let $a = dx/dt$ and $b = dy/dt$. Then at time t the object has coordinates $x = x_0 + at$, $y = y_0 + bt$. (See Figure 4.104.) Notice that a represents the change in x in one unit of time, and b represents the change in y. Thus the line has slope $m = b/a$.

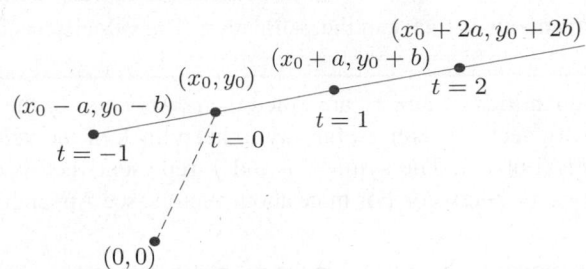

Figure 4.104: The line $x = x_0 + at$, $y = y_0 + bt$

This yields the following:

Parametric Equations for a Straight Line

An object moving along a line through the point (x_0, y_0), with $dx/dt = a$ and $dy/dt = b$, has parametric equations
$$x = x_0 + at, \quad y = y_0 + bt.$$
The slope of the line is $m = b/a$.

Example 5 Find parametric equations for:

(a) The line passing through the points $(2, -1)$ and $(-1, 5)$.
(b) The line segment from $(2, -1)$ to $(-1, 5)$.

Solution (a) Imagine an object moving with constant speed along a straight line from $(2, -1)$ to $(-1, 5)$, making the journey from the first point to the second in one unit of time. Then $dx/dt = ((-1) - 2)/1 = -3$ and $dy/dt = (5 - (-1))/1 = 6$. Thus the parametric equations are
$$x = 2 - 3t, \quad y = -1 + 6t.$$

(b) In the parameterization in part (a), $t = 0$ corresponds to the point $(2, -1)$ and $t = 1$ corresponds to the point $(-1, 5)$. So the parameterization of the segment is

$$x = 2 - 3t, \quad y = -1 + 6t, \qquad 0 \leq t \leq 1.$$

There are many other possible parametric equations for this line.

Speed and Velocity

An object moves along a straight line at a constant speed, with $dx/dt = a$ and $dy/dt = b$. In one unit of time, the object moves a units horizontally and b units vertically. Thus, by the Pythagorean Theorem, it travels a distance $\sqrt{a^2 + b^2}$. So its speed is

$$\text{Speed} = \frac{\text{Distance traveled}}{\text{Time taken}} = \frac{\sqrt{a^2 + b^2}}{1} = \sqrt{a^2 + b^2}.$$

For general motion along a curve with varying speed, we make the following definition:

> The **instantaneous speed** of a moving object is defined to be
>
> $$v = \sqrt{\left(\frac{dx}{dt}\right)^2 + \left(\frac{dy}{dt}\right)^2}.$$
>
> The quantity $v_x = dx/dt$ is the **instantaneous velocity** in the x-direction; $v_y = dy/dt$ is the **instantaneous velocity** in the y-direction. The **velocity vector** $\vec{v}$ is written $\vec{v} = v_x\vec{i} + v_y\vec{j}$.

The quantities v_x and v_y are called the *components* of the velocity in the x- and y-directions. The velocity vector $\vec{v}$ is a useful way to keep track of the velocities in both directions using one mathematical object. The symbols $\vec{i}$ and $\vec{j}$ represent vectors of length one in the positive x and y-directions, respectively. For more about vectors, see Appendix D.

Example 6   A particle moves along a curve in the xy-plane with $x(t) = 2t + e^t$ and $y(t) = 3t - 4$, where t is time. Find the velocity vector and speed of the particle when $t = 1$.

Solution   Differentiating gives

$$\frac{dx}{dt} = 2 + e^t, \quad \frac{dy}{dt} = 3.$$

When $t = 1$ we have $v_x = 2 + e, v_y = 3$. So the velocity vector is $\vec{v} = (2 + e)\vec{i} + 3\vec{j}$ and the speed is $\sqrt{(2 + e)^2 + 3^2} = \sqrt{13 + 4e + e^2} = 5.591$.

Example 7   A particle moves in the xy-plane with $x = 2t^3 - 9t^2 + 12t$ and $y = 3t^4 - 16t^3 + 18t^2$, where t is time.

(a) At what times is the particle

  (i) Stopped   (ii) Moving parallel to the x- or y- axis?

(b) Find the speed of the particle at time t.

Solution   (a) Differentiating gives

$$\frac{dx}{dt} = 6t^2 - 18t + 12, \quad \frac{dy}{dt} = 12t^3 - 48t^2 + 36t.$$

We are interested in the points at which $dx/dt = 0$ or $dy/dt = 0$. Solving gives

$$\frac{dx}{dt} = 6(t^2 - 3t + 2) = 6(t - 1)(t - 2) \quad \text{so} \quad \frac{dx}{dt} = 0 \quad \text{if } t = 1 \text{ or } t = 2.$$

$$\frac{dy}{dt} = 12t(t^2 - 4t + 3) = 12t(t - 1)(t - 3) \quad \text{so} \quad \frac{dy}{dt} = 0 \quad \text{if } t = 0, t = 1, \text{ or } t = 3.$$

(i) The particle is stopped if both dx/dt and dy/dt are 0, which occurs at $t = 1$.

(ii) The particle is moving parallel to the x-axis if $dy/dt = 0$ but $dx/dt \neq 0$. This occurs at $t = 0$ and $t = 3$. The particle is moving parallel to the y-axis if $dx/dt = 0$ but $dy/dt \neq 0$. This occurs at $t = 2$.

(b) We have

$$\text{Speed} = \sqrt{\left(\frac{dx}{dt}\right)^2 + \left(\frac{dy}{dt}\right)^2} = \sqrt{(6t^2 - 18t + 12)^2 + (12t^3 - 48t^2 + 36t)^2}.$$

Example 8   A child is sitting on a Ferris wheel of diameter 10 meters, making one revolution every 2 minutes. Find the speed of the child

(a) Using geometry.   (b) Using a parameterization of the motion.

Solution   (a) The child moves at a constant speed around a circle of radius 5 meters, completing one revolution every 2 minutes. One revolution around a circle of radius 5 is a distance of 10π, so the child's speed is $10\pi/2 = 5\pi \approx 15.7$ m/min. See Figure 4.105.

Figure 4.105: Motion of a child on a Ferris wheel at two different times is represented by the arrows. The direction of each arrow is the direction of motion at that time.

(b) The Ferris wheel has radius 5 meters and completes 1 revolution counterclockwise every 2 minutes. If the origin is at the center of the circle and we measure x and y in meters, the motion is parameterized by equations of the form

$$x = 5\cos(\omega t), \quad y = 5\sin(\omega t),$$

where ω is chosen to make the period 2 minutes. Since the period of $\cos(\omega t)$ and $\sin(\omega t)$ is $2\pi/\omega$, we must have

$$\frac{2\pi}{\omega} = 2, \quad \text{so} \quad \omega = \pi.$$

Thus, for t in minutes, the motion is described by the equations

$$x = 5\cos(\pi t), \quad y = 5\sin(\pi t).$$

So the speed is given by

$$v = \sqrt{\left(\frac{dx}{dt}\right)^2 + \left(\frac{dy}{dt}\right)^2}$$

$$= \sqrt{(-5\pi)^2 \sin^2(\pi t) + (5\pi)^2 \cos^2(\pi t)} = 5\pi\sqrt{\sin^2(\pi t) + \cos^2(\pi t)} = 5\pi \approx 15.7 \text{ m/min},$$

which agrees with the speed we calculated in part (a).

Tangent Lines

To find the tangent line at a point (x_0, y_0) to a curve given parametrically, we find the straight line motion through (x_0, y_0) with the same velocity in the x and y directions as a particle moving along the curve.

Example 9   Find the tangent line at the point $(1, 2)$ to the curve defined by the parametric equations

$$x = t^3, \quad y = 2t.$$

Solution   At time $t = 1$ the particle is at the point $(1, 2)$. The velocity in the x-direction at time t is $v_x = dx/dt = 3t^2$, and the velocity in the y-direction is $v_y = dy/dt = 2$. So at $t = 1$ the velocity in the x-direction is 3 and the velocity in the y-direction is 2. Thus the tangent line has parametric equations

$$x = 1 + 3t, \quad y = 2 + 2t.$$

Parametric Representations of Curves in the Plane

Sometimes we are more interested in the curve traced out by the particle than we are in the motion itself. In that case we call the parametric equations a *parameterization* of the curve. As we can see by comparing Examples 1 and 3, two different parameterizations can describe the same curve in the xy-plane. Though the parameter, which we usually denote by t, may not have physical meaning, it is often helpful to think of it as time.

Example 10   Give a parameterization of the semicircle of radius 1 shown in Figure 4.106.

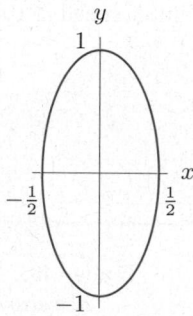

Figure 4.106: Parameterization of   Figure 4.107: Parameterization of the
semicircle for Example 10   ellipse $4x^2 + y^2 = 1$ for Example 11

Solution   We can use the equations $x = \cos t$ and $y = \sin t$ for counterclockwise motion in a circle, from Example 1 on page 249. The particle passes $(0, 1)$ at $t = \pi/2$, moves counterclockwise around the circle, and reaches $(0, -1)$ at $t = 3\pi/2$. So a parameterization is

$$x = \cos t, \; y = \sin t, \quad \frac{\pi}{2} \le t \le \frac{3\pi}{2}.$$

To find the xy-equation of a curve given parametrically, we eliminate the parameter t in the parametric equations. In the previous example, we use the Pythagorean identity, so

$$\cos^2 t + \sin^2 t = 1 \quad \text{gives} \quad x^2 + y^2 = 1.$$

Example 11   Give a parameterization of the ellipse $4x^2 + y^2 = 1$ shown in Figure 4.107.

Solution   Since $(2x)^2 + y^2 = 1$, we adapt the parameterization of the circle in Example 1. Replacing x by $2x$ gives the equations $2x = \cos t, y = \sin t$. A parameterization of the ellipse is thus

$$x = \tfrac{1}{2} \cos t, \qquad y = \sin t, \qquad 0 \le t \le 2\pi.$$

We usually require that the parameterization of a curve go from one end of the curve to the other without retracing any portion of the curve. This is different from parameterizing the motion of a particle, where, for example, a particle may move around the same circle many times.

Parameterizing the Graph of a Function

The graph of any function $y = f(x)$ can be parameterized by letting the parameter t be x:

$$x = t, \quad y = f(t).$$

Example 12 Give parametric equations for the curve $y = x^3 - x$. In which direction does this parameterization trace out the curve?

Solution Let $x = t$, $y = t^3 - t$. Thus, $y = t^3 - t = x^3 - x$. Since $x = t$, as time increases the x-coordinate moves from left to right, so the particle traces out the curve $y = x^3 - x$ from left to right.

Curves Given Parametrically

Some complicated curves can be graphed more easily using parametric equations; the next example shows such a curve.

Example 13 Assume t is time in seconds. Sketch the curve traced out by the particle whose motion is given by

$$x = \cos(3t), \quad y = \sin(5t).$$

Solution The x-coordinate oscillates back and forth between 1 and -1, completing 3 oscillations every 2π seconds. The y-coordinate oscillates up and down between 1 and -1, completing 5 oscillations every 2π seconds. Since both the x- and y-coordinates return to their original values every 2π seconds, the curve is retraced every 2π seconds. The result is a pattern called a Lissajous figure. (See Figure 4.108.) Problems 57–60 concern Lissajous figures $x = \cos(at)$, $y = \sin(bt)$ for other values of a and b.

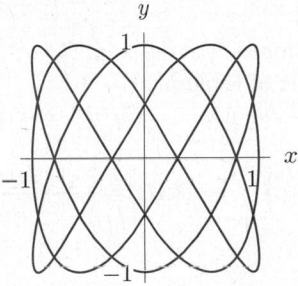

Figure 4.108: A Lissajous figure: $x = \cos(3t), y = \sin(5t)$

Slope and Concavity of Parametric Curves

Suppose we have a curve traced out by the parametric equations $x = f(t)$, $y = g(t)$. To find the slope at a point on the curve, we could, in theory, eliminate the parameter t and then differentiate the function we obtain. However, the chain rule gives us an easier way.

Suppose the curve traced out by the parametric equations is represented by $y = h(x)$. (It may be represented by an implicit function.) Thinking of x and y as functions of t, the chain rule gives

$$\frac{dy}{dt} = \frac{dy}{dx} \cdot \frac{dx}{dt},$$

so we obtain the slope of the curve as a function of t:

$$\boxed{\text{Slope of curve} = \frac{dy}{dx} = \frac{dy/dt}{dx/dt}.}$$

We can find the second derivative, d^2y/dx^2, by a similar method and use it to investigate the concavity of the curve. The chain rule tells us that if w is any differentiable function of x, then

$$\frac{dw}{dx} = \frac{dw/dt}{dx/dt}.$$

For $w = dy/dx$, we have

$$\frac{dw}{dx} = \frac{d}{dx}\left(\frac{dy}{dx}\right) = \frac{d^2y}{dx^2},$$

so the chain rule gives the second derivative at any point on a parametric curve:

$$\frac{d^2y}{dx^2} = \frac{d}{dt}\left(\frac{dy}{dx}\right) \bigg/ \frac{dx}{dt}.$$

Example 14   If $x = \cos t$, $y = \sin t$, find the point corresponding to $t = \pi/4$, the slope of the curve at the point, and d^2y/dx^2 at the point.

Solution   The point corresponding to $t = \pi/4$ is $(\cos(\pi/4), \sin(\pi/4)) = (1/\sqrt{2}, 1/\sqrt{2})$.
To find the slope, we use

$$\frac{dy}{dx} = \frac{dy/dt}{dx/dt} = \frac{\cos t}{-\sin t},$$

so when $t = \pi/4$,

$$\text{Slope} = \frac{\cos(\pi/4)}{-\sin(\pi/4)} = -1.$$

Thus, the curve has slope -1 at the point $(1/\sqrt{2}, 1/\sqrt{2})$. This is as we would expect, since the curve traced out is the circle of Example 1.
To find d^2y/dx^2, we use $w = dy/dx = -(\cos t)/(\sin t)$, so

$$\frac{d^2y}{dx^2} = \frac{d}{dt}\left(-\frac{\cos t}{\sin t}\right)\bigg/(-\sin t) = -\frac{(-\sin t)(\sin t) - (\cos t)(\cos t)}{\sin^2 t} \cdot \left(-\frac{1}{\sin t}\right) = -\frac{1}{\sin^3 t}.$$

Thus, at $t = \pi/4$

$$\left.\frac{d^2y}{dx^2}\right|_{t=\pi/4} = -\frac{1}{(\sin(\pi/4))^3} = -2\sqrt{2}.$$

Since the second derivative is negative, the concavity is negative. This is as expected, since the point is on the top half of the circle where the graph is bending downward.

Exercises and Problems for Section 4.8

Exercises

For Exercises 1–4, use the graphs of f and g to describe the motion of a particle whose position at time t is given by $x = f(t), y = g(t)$.

1.

2.

3.

4.

In Exercises 5–11, write a parameterization for the curves in the xy-plane.

5. A circle of radius 3 centered at the origin and traced out clockwise.

6. A vertical line through the point $(-2, -3)$.

7. A circle of radius 5 centered at the point $(2, 1)$ and traced out counterclockwise.

8. A circle of radius 2 centered at the origin traced clockwise starting from $(-2, 0)$ when $t = 0$.

9. The line through the points $(2, -1)$ and $(1, 3)$.

10. An ellipse centered at the origin and crossing the x-axis at ± 5 and the y-axis at ± 7.

11. An ellipse centered at the origin, crossing the x-axis at ± 3 and the y-axis at ± 7. Start at the point $(-3, 0)$ and trace out the ellipse counterclockwise.

Exercises 12–17 give parameterizations of the unit circle or a part of it. Describe in words how the circle is traced out, including when and where the particle is moving clockwise and when and where the particle is moving counterclockwise.

12. $x = \sin t, \quad y = \cos t$

13. $x = \cos t, \quad y = -\sin t$

14. $x = \cos(t^2), \quad y = \sin(t^2)$

15. $x = \cos(t^3 - t), \quad y = \sin(t^3 - t)$

16. $x = \cos(\ln t), \quad y = \sin(\ln t)$

17. $x = \cos(\cos t), \quad y = \sin(\cos t)$

In Exercises 18–20, what curves do the parametric equations trace out? Find the equation for each curve.

18. $x = 2 + \cos t, \ y = 2 - \sin t$

19. $x = 2 + \cos t, \ y = 2 - \cos t$

20. $x = 2 + \cos t, \ y = \cos^2 t$

In Exercises 21–26, the parametric equations describe the motion of a particle. Find an equation of the curve along which the particle moves.

21. $x = 3t + 1$
$y = t - 4$

22. $x = t^2 + 3$
$y = t^2 - 2$

23. $x = t + 4$
$y = t^2 - 3$

24. $x = \cos 3t$
$y = \sin 3t$

25. $x = 3\cos t$
$y = 3\sin t$

26. $x = 2 + 5\cos t$
$y = 7 + 5\sin t$

In Exercises 27–29, find an equation of the tangent line to the curve for the given value of t.

27. $x = t^3 - t, \quad y = t^2 \quad$ when $t = 2$

28. $x = t^2 - 2t, \quad y = t^2 + 2t \quad$ when $t = 1$

29. $x = \sin(3t), \quad y = \sin(4t) \quad$ when $t = \pi$

For Exercises 30–33, find the speed for the given motion of a particle. Find any times when the particle comes to a stop.

30. $x = t^2, \quad y = t^3$

31. $x = \cos(t^2), \quad y = \sin(t^2)$

32. $x = \cos 2t, \quad y = \sin t$

33. $x = t^2 - 4t, \ y = t^3 - 12t$

34. Find parametric equations for the tangent line at $t = 2$ for Problem 30.

Problems

Problems 35–36 show motion twice around a square, beginning at the origin at time $t = 0$ and parameterized by $x = f(t), y = g(t)$. Sketch possible graphs of f and g consisting of line segments.

35.

36.

37. A line is parameterized by $x = 10 + t$ and $y = 2t$.

(a) What part of the line do we get by restricting t to $t < 0$?

(b) What part of the line do we get by restricting t to $0 \le t \le 1$?

38. A line is parameterized by $x = 2 + 3t$ and $y = 4 + 7t$.

(a) What part of the line is obtained by restricting t to nonnegative numbers?

(b) What part of the line is obtained if t is restricted to $-1 \le t \le 0$?

(c) How should t be restricted to give the part of the line to the left of the y-axis?

39. (a) Explain how you know that the following two pairs of equations parameterize the same line:

$$x = 2 + t, y = 4 + 3t \text{ and } x = 1 - 2t, y = 1 - 6t.$$

(b) What are the slope and y intercept of this line?

40. Describe the similarities and differences among the motions in the plane given by the following three pairs of parametric equations:
(a) $x = t$, $y = t^2$ (b) $x = t^2$, $y = t^4$
(c) $x = t^3$, $y = t^6$.

41. What can you say about the values of a, b and k if the equations

$$x = a + k\cos t, \quad y = b + k\sin t, \qquad 0 \leq t \leq 2\pi,$$

trace out the following circles in Figure 4.109?
(a) C_1 (b) C_2 (c) C_3

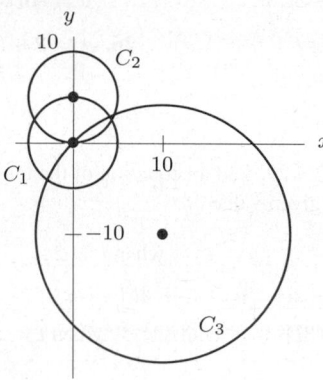

Figure 4.109

42. Suppose $a, b, c, d, m, n, p, q > 0$. Match each pair of parametric equations with one of the lines l_1, l_2, l_3, l_4 in Figure 4.110.

I. $\begin{cases} x = a + ct, \\ y = -b + dt. \end{cases}$ II. $\begin{cases} x = m + pt, \\ y = n - qt. \end{cases}$

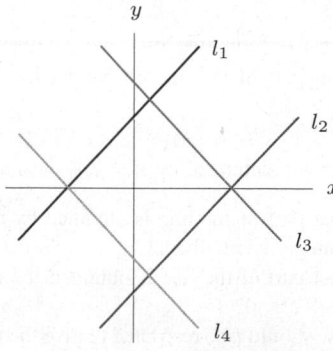

Figure 4.110

43. Describe in words the curve represented by the parametric equations

$$x = 3 + t^3, \quad y = 5 - t^3.$$

44. (a) Sketch the parameterized curve $x = t\cos t$, $y = t\sin t$ for $0 \leq t \leq 4\pi$.
(b) By calculating the position at $t = 2$ and $t = 2.01$, estimate the speed at $t = 2$.
(c) Use derivatives to calculate the speed at $t = 2$ and compare your answer to part (b).

45. The position of a particle at time t is given by $x = e^t$ and $y = 2e^{2t}$.
(a) Find dy/dx in terms of t.
(b) Eliminate the parameter and write y in terms of x.
(c) Using your answer to part (b), find dy/dx in terms of x.

46. For x and y in meters, the motion of the particle given by

$$x = t^3 - 3t, \quad y = t^2 - 2t,$$

where the y-axis is vertical and the x-axis is horizontal.
(a) Does the particle ever come to a stop? If so, when and where?
(b) Is the particle ever moving straight up or down? If so, when and where?
(c) Is the particle ever moving straight horizontally right or left? If so, when and where?

47. At time t, the position of a particle moving on a curve is given by $x = e^{2t} - e^{-2t}$ and $y = 3e^{2t} + e^{-2t}$.
(a) Find all values of t at which the curve has
  (i) A horizontal tangent.
  (ii) A vertical tangent.
(b) Find dy/dx in terms of t.
(c) Find $\lim_{t\to\infty} dy/dx$.

48. Figure 4.111 shows the graph of a parameterized curve $x = f(t)$, $y = f'(t)$ for a function $f(t)$.
(a) Is $f(t)$ an increasing or decreasing function?
(b) As t increases, is the curve traced from P to Q or from Q to P?
(c) Is $f(t)$ concave up or concave down?

Figure 4.111

49. At time t, the position of a particle is $x(t) = 5\sin(2t)$ and $y(t) = 4\cos(2t)$, with $0 \le t < 2\pi$.

(a) Graph the path of the particle for $0 \le t < 2\pi$, indicating the direction of motion.

(b) Find the position and velocity of the particle when $t = \pi/4$.

(c) How many times does the particle pass through the point found in part (b)?

(d) What does your answer to part (b) tell you about the direction of the motion relative to the coordinate axes when $t = \pi/4$?

(e) What is the speed of the particle at time $t = \pi$?

50. At time t, a projectile launched with angle of elevation α and initial velocity v_0 has position $x(t) = (v_0\cos\alpha)t$ and $y(t) = (v_0\sin\alpha)t - \frac{1}{2}gt^2$, where g is the acceleration due to gravity.

(a) A football player kicks a ball at an angle of $36°$ above the ground with an initial velocity of 60 feet per second. Write the parametric equations for the position of the football at time t seconds. Use $g = 32$ ft/sec^2.

(b) Graph the path that the football follows.

(c) How long does it take for the football to hit the ground? How far is it from the spot where the football player kicked it?

(d) What is the maximum height the football reaches during its flight?

(e) At what speed is the football traveling 1 second after it was kicked?

51. Two particles move in the xy-plane. At time t, the position of particle A is given by $x(t) = 4t - 4$ and $y(t) = 2t - k$, and the position of particle B is given by $x(t) = 3t$ and $y(t) = t^2 - 2t - 1$.

(a) If $k = 5$, do the particles ever collide? Explain.

(b) Find k so that the two particles do collide.

(c) At the time that the particles collide in part (b), which particle is moving faster?

52. (a) Find d^2y/dx^2 for $x = t^3 + t, y = t^2$.

(b) Is the curve concave up or down at $t = 1$?

53. (a) An object moves along the path $x = 3t$ and $y = \cos(2t)$, where t is time. Write the equation for the line tangent to this path at $t = \pi/3$.

(b) Find the smallest positive value of t for which the y-coordinate is a local maximum.

(c) Find d^2y/dx^2 when $t = 2$. What does this tell you about the concavity of the graph at $t = 2$?

54. The position of a particle at time t is given by $x = e^t + 3$ and $y = e^{2t} + 6e^t + 9$.

(a) Find dy/dx in terms of t.

(b) Find d^2y/dx^2. What does this tell you about the concavity of the graph?

(c) Eliminate the parameter and write y in terms of x.

(d) Using your answer from part (c), find dy/dx and d^2y/dx^2 in terms of x. Show that these answers are the same as the answers to parts (a) and (b).

55. A particle moves in the xy-plane so that its position at time t is given by $x = \sin t$ and $y = \cos(2t)$ for $0 \le t < 2\pi$.

(a) At what time does the particle first touch the x-axis? What is the speed of the particle at that time?

(b) Is the particle ever at rest?

(c) Discuss the concavity of the graph.

56. Derive the general formula for the second derivative d^2y/dx^2 of a parametrically defined curve:

$$\frac{d^2y}{dx^2} = \frac{(dx/dt)(d^2y/dt^2) - (dy/dt)(d^2x/dt^2)}{(dx/dt)^3}.$$

Graph the Lissajous figures in Problems 57–60 using a calculator or computer.

57. $x = \cos 2t, \quad y = \sin 5t$

58. $x = \cos 3t, \quad y = \sin 7t$

59. $x = \cos 2t, \quad y = \sin 4t$

60. $x = \cos 2t, \quad y = \sin \sqrt{3}t$

61. A hypothetical moon orbits a planet which in turn orbits a star. Suppose that the orbits are circular and that the moon orbits the planet 12 times in the time it takes for the planet to orbit the star once. In this problem we will investigate whether the moon could come to a stop at some instant. (See Figure 4.112.)

(a) Suppose the radius of the moon's orbit around the planet is 1 unit and the radius of the planet's orbit around the star is R units. Explain why the motion of the moon relative to the star can be described by the parametric equations

$$x = R\cos t + \cos(12t), \quad y = R\sin t + \sin(12t).$$

(b) Find values for R and t such that the moon stops relative to the star at time t.

(c) On a graphing calculator, plot the path of the moon for the value of R you obtained in part (b). Experiment with other values for R.

Figure 4.112

Strengthen Your Understanding

In Problems 62–63, explain what is wrong with the statement.

62. The line segment from $(2, 2)$ to $(0, 0)$ is parameterized by $x = 2t$, $y = 2t$, $0 \le t \le 1$.

63. A circle of radius 2 centered at $(0, 1)$ is parameterized by $x = 2\cos \pi t$, $y = 2\sin \pi t$, $0 \le t \le 2$.

In Problems 64–65, give an example of:

64. A parameterization of a quarter circle centered at the origin of radius 2 in the first quadrant.

65. A parameterization of the line segment between $(0, 0)$ and $(1, 2)$.

Are the statements in Problems 66–67 true of false? Give an explanation for your answer.

66. The curve given parametrically by $x = f(t)$ and $y = g(t)$ has no sharp corners if f and g are differentiable.

67. If a curve is given parametrically by $x = \cos(t^2)$, $y = \sin(t^2)$, then its slope is $\tan(t^2)$.

CHAPTER SUMMARY (see also Ready Reference at the end of the book)

- **Local extrema**
  Maximum, minimum, critical point, tests for local maxima/minima.

- **Using the second derivative**
  Concavity, inflection point.

- **Families of curves**
  Role of parameters

- **Optimization**
  Global extremum, modeling problems, graphical optimization, upper and lower bounds, extreme value theorem.

- **Marginality**
  Cost/revenue functions, marginal cost/marginal revenue functions.

- **Rates and Related Rates**

- **L'Hopital's Rule**
  Limits, growth, dominance

- **Parametric equations**
  Motion of a particle in the plane, parametric equations for lines and other curves, velocity, tangent lines, slope, concavity.

REVIEW EXERCISES AND PROBLEMS FOR CHAPTER FOUR

Exercises

For Exercises 1–2, indicate all critical points on the given graphs. Which correspond to local minima, local maxima, global maxima, global minima, or none of these? (Note that the graphs are on closed intervals.)

1.

2.

In Exercises 3–6, do the following:
(a) Find f' and f''.
(b) Find the critical points of f.
(c) Find any inflection points.
(d) Evaluate f at the critical points and the endpoints. Identify the global maxima and minima of f.
(e) Sketch f. Indicate clearly where f is increasing or decreasing, and its concavity.

3. $f(x) = x^3 - 3x^2$ $(-1 \le x \le 3)$

4. $f(x) = x + \sin x$ $(0 \le x \le 2\pi)$

5. $f(x) = e^{-x} \sin x$ $(0 \le x \le 2\pi)$

6. $f(x) = x^{-2/3} + x^{1/3}$ $(1.2 \le x \le 3.5)$

In Exercises 7–9, find the limits as x tends to $+\infty$ and $-\infty$, and then proceed as in Exercises 3–6. (That is, find f', etc.).

7. $f(x) = 2x^3 - 9x^2 + 12x + 1$

8. $f(x) = \dfrac{4x^2}{x^2 + 1}$

9. $f(x) = xe^{-x}$

In Exercises 10–13, find the global maximum and minimum for the function on the closed interval.

10. $f(x) = e^{-x} \sin x$, $0 \le x \le 2\pi$

11. $f(x) = e^x + \cos x$, $0 \le x \le \pi$

12. $f(x) = x^2 + 2x + 1$, $0 \le x \le 3$

13. $f(x) = e^{-x^2}$, $0 \le x \le 10$

In Exercises 14–16, find the exact global maximum and minimum values of the function.

14. $h(z) = \dfrac{1}{z} + 4z^2$ for $z > 0$

15. $g(t) = \dfrac{1}{t^3 + 1}$ for $t \ge 0$

16. $f(x) = \dfrac{1}{(x-1)^2 + 2}$

In Exercises 17–23, use derivatives to identify local maxima and minima and points of inflection. Graph the function.

17. $f(x) = x^3 + 3x^2 - 9x - 15$

18. $f(x) = x^5 - 15x^3 + 10$

19. $f(x) = x - 2\ln x$ for $x > 0$

20. $f(x) = e^{-x^2}$

21. $f(x) = x^2 e^{5x}$

22. $f(x) = \dfrac{x^2}{x^2 + 1}$

23. When you cough, your windpipe contracts. The speed, $v(r)$, with which you expel air depends on the radius, r, of your windpipe. If a is the normal (rest) radius of your windpipe, then for $0 \le r \le a$, the speed is given by:

$$v(r) = k(a - r)r^2 \quad \text{where } k \text{ is a positive constant.}$$

What value of r maximizes the speed? For what value is the speed minimized?

24. Find the point where the following curve is steepest:

$$y = \frac{50}{1 + 6e^{-2t}} \qquad \text{for } t \ge 0.$$

25. The graphs of the function $f(x) = x/(x^2 + a^2)$ for $a = 1, 2$, and 3, are shown in Figure 4.113. Without a calculator, identify the graphs by locating the critical points of $f(x)$.

Figure 4.113

26. The graphs of the function $f(x) = 1 - e^{-ax}$ for $a = 1, 2$, and 3, are shown in Figure 4.114. Without a calculator, identify the graphs.

Figure 4.114

27. **(a)** Find all critical points and all inflection points of the function $f(x) = x^4 - 2ax^2 + b$. Assume a and b are positive constants.
  (b) Find values of the parameters a and b if f has a critical point at the point $(2, 5)$.
  (c) If there is a critical point at $(2, 5)$, where are the inflection points?

28. **(a)** For a a positive constant, find all critical points of $f(x) = x - a\sqrt{x}$.
  (b) What value of a gives a critical point at $x = 5$? Does $f(x)$ have a local maximum or a local minimum at this critical point?

29. If a and b are nonzero constants, find the domain and all critical points of

$$f(x) = \frac{ax^2}{x - b}.$$

30. The average of two nonnegative numbers is 180. What is the largest possible product of these two numbers?

31. The product of three positive numbers is 192, and one of the numbers is twice one of the other numbers. What is the minimum value of their sum?

32. The difference between two numbers is 24. If both numbers are 100 or greater, what is the minimum value of their product?

33. **(a)** Fixed costs are \$3 million; variable costs are \$0.4 million per item. Write a formula for total cost as a function of quantity, q.
  (b) The item in part (a) is sold for \$0.5 million each. Write a formula for revenue as a function of q.
  (c) Write a formula for the profit function for this item.

34. A number x is increasing. When $x = 10$, the square of x is increasing at 5 units per second. How fast is x increasing at that time?

35. The mass of a cube in grams is $M = x^3 + 0.1x^4$, where x is the length of one side in centimeters. If the length is increasing at a rate of 0.02 cm/hr, at what rate is the mass of the cube increasing when its length is 5 cm?

36. If θ is the angle between a line through the origin and the positive x-axis, the area, in cm^2, of part of a cardioid is

$$A = 3\theta + 4\sin\theta + \frac{1}{2}\sin(2\theta).$$

If the angle θ is increasing at a rate of 0.3 radians per minute, at what rate is the area changing when $\theta = \pi/2$?

In Exercises 37–38, describe the motion of a particle moving according to the parametric equations. Find an equation of the curve along which the particle moves.

37. $x = 4 - 2t$
    $y = 4t + 1$

38. $x = 2\sin t$
    $y = 2\cos t$

Problems

39. Figure 4.115 is the graph of f', the derivative of a function f. At which of the points $0, x_1, x_2, x_3, x_4, x_5$, is the function f:

   (a) At a local maximum value?
   (b) At a local minimum value?
   (c) Climbing fastest?
   (d) Falling most steeply?

Figure 4.115: Graph of f' not f

40. Figure 4.116 is a graph of f'. For what values of x does f have a local maximum? A local minimum?

Figure 4.116: Graph of f' (not f)

41. On the graph of f' in Figure 4.117, indicate the x-values that are critical points of the function f itself. Are they local maxima, local minima, or neither?

Figure 4.117: Graph of f' (not f)

42. Graph f given that:

- $f'(x) = 0$ at $x = 2$, $f'(x) < 0$ for $x < 2$, $f'(x) > 0$ for $x > 2$,
- $f''(x) = 0$ at $x = 4$, $f''(x) > 0$ for $x < 4$, $f''(x) < 0$ for $x > 4$.

In Problems 43–47, find formulas for the functions.

43. A cubic polynomial with a local maximum at $x = 1$, a local minimum at $x = 3$, a y-intercept of 5, and an x^3 term whose coefficient is 1.

44. A quartic polynomial whose graph is symmetric about the y-axis and has local maxima at $(-1, 4)$ and $(1, 4)$ and a y-intercept of 3.

45. A function of the form $y = ax^b \ln x$, where a and b are nonzero constants, which has a local maximum at the point $(e^2, 6e^{-1})$.

46. A function of the form $y = A\sin(Bx) + C$ with a maximum at $(5, 2)$, a minimum at $(15, 1.5)$, and no critical points between these two points.

47. A function of the form $y = axe^{-bx^2}$ with a global maximum at $(1, 2)$ and a global minimum at $(-1, -2)$.

In Problems 48–51, find the dimensions of the solid giving the maximum volume, given that the surface area is 8 cm^2.

48. A closed rectangular box, with a square base x by x cm and height h cm.

49. A open-topped rectangular box, with a square base x by x cm and height h cm.

50. A closed cylinder with radius r cm and height h cm.

51. A cylinder open at one end with radius r cm and height h cm.

In Problems 52–54, find the best possible bounds for the functions.

52. $e^{-x} \sin x$,   for $x \geq 0$

53. $x \sin x$,   for $0 \leq x \leq 2\pi$

54. $x^3 - 6x^2 + 9x + 5$ for $0 \leq x \leq 5$

55. Find the value(s) of m, if any, that give the global maximum and minimum of P as a function of m where

$$6jm^2 + P = 4jk - 5km, \quad \text{for positive constants } j \text{ and } k.$$

56. Find values of a and b so that the function $y = axe^{-bx}$ has a local maximum at the point $(2, 10)$.

57. **(a)** Find all critical points of $f(t) = at^2 e^{-bt}$, assuming a and b are nonzero constants.
   (b) Find values of the parameters a and b so that f has a critical point at the point $(5, 12)$.
   (c) Identify each critical point as a local maximum or local minimum of the function f in part (b).

58. What effect does increasing the value of a have on the graph of $f(x) = x^2 + 2ax$? Consider roots, maxima and minima, and both positive and negative values of a.

59. Sketch several members of the family $y = x^3 - ax^2$ on the same axes. Show that the critical points lie on the curve $y = -\frac{1}{2}x^3$.

60. A drug is injected into a patient at a rate given by $r(t) = ate^{-bt}$ ml/sec, where t is in seconds since the injection started, $0 \leq t \leq 5$, and a and b are constants. The maximum rate of 0.3 ml/sec occurs half a second after the injection starts. Find a formula for a and b.

61. An object at a distance p from a thin glass lens produces an image at a distance q from the lens, where

$$\frac{1}{p} + \frac{1}{q} = \frac{1}{f}.$$

The constant f is called the focal length of the lens. Suppose an object is moving at 3 mm per second toward a lens of focal length 15 mm. How fast and in what direction is the image moving at the moment at which the object is 35 mm from the lens?

62. Any body radiates energy at various wavelengths. Figure 4.118 shows the intensity of the radiation of a black body at a temperature $T = 3000$ kelvins as a function of the wavelength. The intensity of the radiation is highest in the infrared range, that is, at wavelengths longer than that of visible light (0.4–0.7μm). Max Planck's radiation law, announced to the Berlin Physical Society on October 19, 1900, states that

$$r(\lambda) = \frac{a}{\lambda^5(e^{b/\lambda} - 1)}.$$

Find constants a and b so that the formula fits the graph. (Later in 1900 Planck showed from theory that $a = 2\pi c^2 h$ and $b = \frac{hc}{Tk}$ where $c =$ speed of light, $h =$ Planck's constant, and $k =$ Boltzmann's constant.)

intensity of radiation
$r(\lambda)$ (MW/m^2/μm)

(0.96, 3.13)

wavelength
λ (μm)
4

Figure 4.118

63. An electric current, I, in amps, is given by

$$I = \cos(wt) + \sqrt{3}\sin(wt),$$

where $w \neq 0$ is a constant. What are the maximum and minimum values of I?

64. The efficiency of a screw, E, is given by

$$E = \frac{(\theta - \mu\theta^2)}{\mu + \theta}, \quad \theta > 0,$$

where θ is the angle of pitch of the thread and μ is the coefficient of friction of the material, a (positive) constant. What value of θ maximizes E?

65. A rectangle has one side on the x-axis and two corners on the top half of the circle of radius 1 centered at the origin. Find the maximum area of such a rectangle. What are the coordinates of its vertices?

66. The hypotenuse of a right triangle has one end at the origin and one end on the curve $y = x^2 e^{-3x}$, with $x \geq 0$. One of the other two sides is on the x-axis, the other side is parallel to the y-axis. Find the maximum area of such a triangle. At what x-value does it occur?

67. Which point on the parabola $y = x^2$ is nearest to $(1, 0)$? Find the coordinates to two decimals. [Hint: Minimize the square of the distance—this avoids square roots.]

68. Find the coordinates of the point on the parabola $y = x^2$ which is closest to the point $(3, 0)$.

69. The cross-section of a tunnel is a rectangle of height h surmounted by a semicircular roof section of radius r (See Figure 4.119). If the cross-sectional area is A, determine the dimensions of the cross section which minimize the perimeter.

r

h

Figure 4.119

70. A landscape architect plans to enclose a 3000 square-foot rectangular region in a botanical garden. She will use shrubs costing \$45 per foot along three sides and fencing costing \$20 per foot along the fourth side. Find the minimum total cost.

71. A rectangular swimming pool is to be built with an area of 1800 square feet. The owner wants 5-foot wide decks along either side and 10-foot wide decks at the two ends. Find the dimensions of the smallest piece of property on which the pool can be built satisfying these conditions.

72. (a) A cruise line offers a trip for \$2000 per passenger. If at least 100 passengers sign up, the price is reduced for *all* the passengers by \$10 for every additional passenger (beyond 100) who goes on the trip. The boat can accommodate 250 passengers. What number of passengers maximizes the cruise line's total revenue? What price does each passenger pay then?

   (b) The cost to the cruise line for n passengers is $80,000 + 400n$. What is the maximum profit that the cruise line can make on one trip? How many passengers must sign up for the maximum to be reached and what price will each pay?

73. A manufacturer's cost of producing a product is given in Figure 4.120. The manufacturer can sell the product for a price p each (regardless of the quantity sold), so that the total revenue from selling a quantity q is $R(q) = pq$.

   (a) The difference $\pi(q) = R(q) - C(q)$ is the total profit. For which quantity q_0 is the profit a maximum? Mark your answer on a sketch of the graph.

   (b) What is the relationship between p and $C'(q_0)$? Explain your result both graphically and analytically. What does this mean in terms of economics? (Note that p is the slope of the line $R(q) = pq$. Note also that $\pi(q)$ has a maximum at $q = q_0$, so $\pi'(q_0) = 0$.)

   (c) Graph $C'(q)$ and p (as a horizontal line) on the same axes. Mark q_0 on the q-axis.

74. Using the cost and revenue graphs in Figure 4.120, sketch the following functions. Label the points q_1 and q_2.

   (a) Total profit   **(b)** Marginal cost

   (c) Marginal revenue

Figure 4.120

75. A ship is steaming due north at 12 knots (1 knot = 1.85 kilometers/hour) and sights a large tanker 3 kilometers away northwest steaming at 15 knots due east. For reasons of safety, the ships want to maintain a distance of at least 100 meters between them. Use a calculator or computer to determine the shortest distance between them if they remain on their current headings, and hence decide if they need to change course.

76. A polystyrene cup is in the shape of a frustum (the part of a cone between two parallel planes cutting the cone), has top radius $2r$, base radius r and height h. The surface area S of such a cup is given by $S = 3\pi r\sqrt{r^2 + h^2}$ and its volume V by $V = 7\pi r^2 h/3$. If the cup is to hold 200 ml, use a calculator or a computer to estimate the value of r that minimizes its surface area.

77. Suppose $g(t) = (\ln t)/t$ for $t > 0$.

   (a) Does g have either a global maximum or a global minimum on $0 < t < \infty$? If so, where, and what are their values?

   (b) What does your answer to part (a) tell you about the number of solutions to the equation

$$\frac{\ln x}{x} = \frac{\ln 5}{5}?$$

(Note: There are many ways to investigate the number of solutions to this equation. We are asking you to draw a conclusion from your answer to part (a).)

   (c) Estimate the solution(s).

78. For $a > 0$, the following line forms a triangle in the first quadrant with the x- and y-axes:

$$a(a^2 + 1)y = a - x.$$

   (a) In terms of a, find the x- and y-intercepts of the line.

   (b) Find the area of the triangle, as a function of a.

   (c) Find the value of a making the area a maximum.

   (d) What is this greatest area?

   (e) If you want the triangle to have area $1/5$, what choices do you have for a?

79. **(a)** Water is flowing at a constant rate (i.e., constant volume per unit time) into a cylindrical container standing vertically. Sketch a graph showing the depth of water against time.

   (b) Water is flowing at a constant rate into a cone-shaped container standing on its point. Sketch a graph showing the depth of the water against time.

80. The vase in Figure 4.121 is filled with water at a constant rate (i.e., constant volume per unit time).

   (a) Graph $y = f(t)$, the depth of the water, against time, t. Show on your graph the points at which the concavity changes.

   (b) At what depth is $y = f(t)$ growing most quickly? Most slowly? Estimate the ratio between the growth rates at these two depths.

Figure 4.121

81. A chemical storage tank is in the shape of an inverted cone with depth 12 meters and top radius 5 meters. When the depth of the chemical in the tank is 1 meter, the level is falling at 0.1 meters per minute. How fast is the volume of chemical changing?

In Problems 82–83, describe the form of the limit ($0/0$, ∞/∞, $\infty \cdot 0$, $\infty - \infty$, 1^∞, 0^0, ∞^0, or none of these). Does l'Hopital's rule apply? If so, explain how.

82. $\lim\limits_{x\to 0} \dfrac{x}{e^x}$

83. $\lim\limits_{x\to 1} \dfrac{\sin \pi x}{x - 1}$

In Problems 84–87, determine whether the limit exists, and where possible evaluate it.

84. $\lim\limits_{t\to 0} \dfrac{e^t - 1 - t}{t^2}$

85. $\lim\limits_{t\to 0+} \dfrac{3\sin t - \sin 3t}{3\tan t - \tan 3t}$

86. $\lim\limits_{x\to 0} \dfrac{1 - \cosh(5x)}{x^2}$

87. $\lim\limits_{x\to 0} \dfrac{x - \sinh(x)}{x^3}$

88. The rate of change of a population depends on the current population, P, and is given by

$$\frac{dP}{dt} = kP(L - P) \qquad \text{for positive constants } k, L.$$

(a) For what nonnegative values of P is the population increasing? Decreasing? For what values of P does the population remain constant?

(b) Find d^2P/dt^2 as a function of P.

89. A spherical cell is growing at a constant rate of $400 \ \mu m^3/day$ ($1 \ \mu m = 10^{-6}$ m). At what rate is its radius increasing when the radius is $10 \ \mu m$?

90. A raindrop is a perfect sphere with radius r cm and surface area S cm^2. Condensation accumulates on the raindrop at a rate equal to kS, where $k = 2$ cm/sec. Show that the radius of the raindrop increases at a constant rate and find that rate.

91. A horizontal disk of radius a centered at the origin in the xy-plane is rotating about a vertical axis through the center. The angle between the positive x-axis and a radial line painted on the disk is θ radians.

(a) What does $d\theta/dt$ represent?

(b) What is the relationship between $d\theta/dt$ and the speed v of a point on the rim?

92. The depth of soot deposited from a smokestack is given by $D = K(r + 1)e^{-r}$, where r is the distance from the smokestack. What is the relationship between the rate of change of r with respect to time and the rate of change of D with respect to time?

93. The mass of a circular oil slick of radius r is $M = K\left(r - \ln(1 + r)\right)$, where K is a positive constant. What is the relationship between the rate of change of the radius with respect to t and the rate of change of the mass with respect to time?

94. Ice is being formed in the shape of a circular cylinder with inner radius 1 cm and height 3 cm. The outer radius of the ice is increasing at 0.03 cm per hour when the outer radius is 1.5 cm. How fast is the volume of the ice increasing at this time?

95. Sand falls from a hopper at a rate of 0.1 cubic meters per hour and forms a conical pile beneath. If the side of the cone makes an angle of $\pi/6$ radians with the vertical, find the rate at which the height of the cone increases. At what rate does the radius of the base increase? Give both answers in terms of h, the height of the pile in meters.

96. (a) A hemispherical bowl of radius 10 cm contains water to a depth of h cm. Find the radius of the surface of the water as a function of h.

(b) The water level drops at a rate of 0.1 cm per hour. At what rate is the radius of the water decreasing when the depth is 5 cm?

97. A particle lies on a line perpendicular to a thin circular ring and through its center. The radius of the ring is a, and the distance from the point to the center of the ring is y. For a positive constant K, the gravitational force exerted by the ring on the particle is given by

$$F = \frac{Ky}{(a^2 + y^2)^{3/2}},$$

If y is increasing, how is F changing with respect to time, t, when

(a) $y = 0$ (b) $y = a/\sqrt{2}$ (c) $y = 2a$

98. A voltage, V volts, applied to a resistor of R ohms produces an electric current of I amps where $V = IR$. As the current flows the resistor heats up and its resistance falls. If 100 volts is applied to a resistor of 1000 ohms the current is initially 0.1 amps but rises by 0.001 amps/minute. At what rate is the resistance falling if the voltage remains constant?

99. A train is heading due west from St. Louis. At noon, a plane flying horizontally due north at a fixed altitude of 4 miles passes directly over the train. When the train has traveled another mile, it is going 80 mph, and the plane has traveled another 5 miles and is going 500 mph. At that moment, how fast is the distance between the train and the plane increasing?

Problems 100–101 involve Boyle's Law, which states that for a fixed quantity of gas at a constant temperature, the pressure, P, and the volume, V, are inversely related. Thus, for some constant k

$$PV = k.$$

100. A fixed quantity of gas is allowed to expand at constant temperature. Find the rate of change of pressure with respect to volume.

101. A certain quantity of gas occupies 10 cm^3 at a pressure of 2 atmospheres. The pressure is increased, while keeping the temperature constant.

(a) Does the volume increase or decrease?

(b) If the pressure is increasing at a rate of 0.05 atmospheres/minute when the pressure is 2 atmospheres, find the rate at which the volume is changing at that moment. What are the units of your answer?

CAS Challenge Problems

102. A population, P, in a restricted environment may grow with time, t, according to the *logistic function*

$$P = \frac{L}{1 + Ce^{-kt}}$$

where L is called the carrying capacity and L, C and k are positive constants.

  (a) Find $\lim_{t \to \infty} P$. Explain why L is called the carrying capacity.

  (b) Using a computer algebra system, show that the graph of P has an inflection point at $P = L/2$.

103. For positive a, consider the family of functions

$$y = \arctan\left(\frac{\sqrt{x} + \sqrt{a}}{1 - \sqrt{ax}}\right), \qquad x > 0.$$

  (a) Graph several curves in the family and describe how the graph changes as a varies.

  (b) Use a computer algebra system to find dy/dx, and graph the derivative for several values of a. What do you notice?

  (c) Do your observations in part (b) agree with the answer to part (a)? Explain. [Hint: Use the fact that $\sqrt{ax} = \sqrt{a}\sqrt{x}$ for $a > 0$, $x > 0$.]

104. The function arcsinh x is the inverse function of $\sinh x$.

  (a) Use a computer algebra system to find a formula for the derivative of arcsinh x.

  (b) Derive the formula by hand by differentiating both sides of the equation

$$\sinh(\text{arcsinh } x) = x.$$

[Hint: Use the identity $\cosh^2 x - \sinh^2 x = 1$.]

105. The function arccosh x, for $x \geq 0$, is the inverse function of $\cosh x$, for $x \geq 0$.

  (a) Use a computer algebra system to find the derivative of arccosh x.

  (b) Derive the formula by hand by differentiating both sides of the equation

$$\cosh(\text{arccosh } x) = x, \quad x \geq 1.$$

[Hint: Use the identity $\cosh^2 x - \sinh^2 x = 1$.]

106. Consider the family of functions

$$f(x) = \frac{\sqrt{a + x}}{\sqrt{a} + \sqrt{x}}, \quad x \geq 0, \quad \text{for positive } a.$$

  (a) Using a computer algebra system, find the local maxima and minima of f.

  (b) On one set of axes, graph this function for several values of a. How does varying a affect the shape of the graph? Explain your answer in terms of the answer to part (a).

  (c) Use your computer algebra system to find the inflection points of f when $a = 2$.

107. **(a)** Use a computer algebra system to find the derivative of

$$y = \arctan\left(\sqrt{\frac{1 - \cos x}{1 + \cos x}}\right).$$

  (b) Graph the derivative. Does the graph agree with the answer you got in part (a)? Explain using the identity $\cos(x) = \cos^2(x/2) - \sin^2(x/2)$.

108. In 1696, the first calculus textbook was published by the Marquis de l'Hopital. The following problem is a simplified version of a problem from this text.

    In Figure 4.122, two ropes are attached to the ceiling at points $\sqrt{3}$ meters apart. The rope on the left is 1 meter long and has a pulley attached at its end. The rope on the right is 3 meters long; it passes through the pulley and has a weight tied to its end. When the weight is released, the ropes and pulley arrange themselves so that the distance from the weight to the ceiling is maximized.

  (a) Show that the maximum distance occurs when the weight is exactly halfway between the the points where the ropes are attached to the ceiling. [Hint: Write the vertical distance from the weight to the ceiling in terms of its horizontal distance to the point at which the left rope is tied to the ceiling. A computer algebra system will be useful.]

  (b) Does the weight always end up halfway between the ceiling anchor points no matter how long the left-hand rope is? Explain.

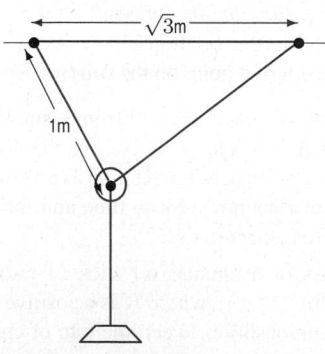

Figure 4.122

PROJECTS FOR CHAPTER FOUR

1. **Medical Case Study: Impact of Asthma on Breathing**[13]

   Asthma is a common breathing disease in which inflammation in the airways of the lungs causes episodes of shortness of breath, coughing, and chest tightness. Patients with asthma often have wheezing, an abnormal sound heard on exhalation due to turbulent airflow. Turbulent airflow is caused by swelling, mucus secretion, and constriction of muscle in the walls of the airways, shrinking the radius of the air passages leading to increased resistance to airflow and making it harder for patients to exhale.

   An important breathing test for asthma is called *spirometry*. In this test, a patient takes in as deep a breath as he or she can, and then exhales as rapidly, forcefully, and for as long as possible through a tube connected to an analyzer. The analyzer measures a number of parameters and generates two graphs.

   (a) Figure 4.123 is a volume-time curve for an asthma-free patient, showing the volume of air exhaled, V, as a function of time, t, since the test began.[14]

   (i) What is the physical interpretation of the slope of the volume-time curve?

   (ii) The volume VC shown on the volume-time graph is called the (forced) vital capacity (FVC or simply VC). Describe the physical meaning of VC.

   (b) Figure 4.124 is the flow-volume curve for the same patient.[15] The flow-volume curve shows the flow rate, dV/dt, of air as a function of V, the volume of air exhaled.

   (i) What is the physical interpretation of the slope of the flow-volume curve?

   (ii) Describe how the slope of the flow-volume curve changes as V increases from 0 to 5.5 liters. Explain what this means for the patient's breath.

   (iii) Sketch the slope of the flow-volume curve.

   (iv) What is the volume of air that has been exhaled when the flow rate is a maximum, and what is that maximal rate, the *peak expiratory flow*? Explain how this maximal rate is identified on the flow-volume curve and how the volume at which the maximal rate occurs is identified on the slope curve in part (b)(iii).

   (c) How do you imagine the volume-time curve and the flow-volume curve would be different for a patient with acute asthma? Draw curves to illustrate your thinking.

   Figure 4.123: Volume-time curve   **Figure 4.124:** Flow-volume curve

2. **Building a Greenhouse**

   Your parents are going to knock out the bottom of the entire length of the south wall of their house and turn it into a greenhouse by replacing the bottom portion of the wall with a huge sloped piece of glass (which is expensive). They have already decided they are going to spend a certain fixed amount. The triangular ends of the greenhouse will be made of various materials they already have lying around.[16]

---

[13]From David E. Sloane, M.D.

[14]Image based on www.aafp.org/afp/2004/0301/p1107.html, accessed July 9, 2011.

[15]Image from http://www.aafp.org/afp/2004/0301/p1107.html, accessed July 9, 2011.

[16]Adapted from M. Cohen, E. Gaughan, A. Knoebel, D. Kurtz, D. Pengelley, *Student Research Projects in Calculus* (Washington DC: Mathematical Association of America, 1992).

The floor space in the greenhouse is only considered usable if they can both stand up in it, so part of it will be unusable. They want to choose the dimensions of the greenhouse to get the most usable floor space. What should the dimensions of the greenhouse be and how much usable space will your parents get?

3. Fitting a Line to Data

(a) The line which best fits the data points $(x_1, y_1), (x_2, y_2) \ldots (x_n, y_n)$ is the one which minimizes the sum of the squares of the vertical distances from the points to the line. These are the distances marked in Figure 4.125. Find the best fitting line of the form $y = mx$ for the points $(2, 3.5), (3, 6.8), (5, 9.1)$.

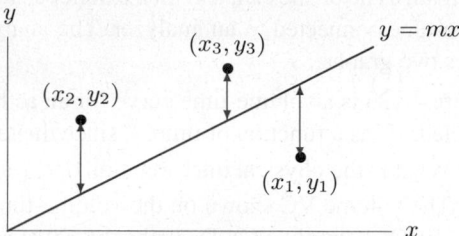

Figure 4.125

(b) A cone with height and radius both equal to r has volume, V, proportional to r^3; that is, $V = kr^3$ for some constant k. A lab experiment is done to measure the volume of several cones; the results are in the following table. Using the method of part (a), determine the best value of k. [Note: Since the volumes were determined experimentally, the values may not be accurate. Assume that the radii were measured accurately.]

Radius (cm)	2	5	7	8
Volume (cm^3)	8.7	140.3	355.8	539.2

(c) Using the method of part (a), show that the best fitting line of the form $y = mx$ for the points $(x_1, y_1), (x_2, y_2) \ldots (x_n, y_n)$ has

$$m = \frac{x_1 y_1 + x_2 y_2 + \cdots + x_n y_n}{x_1^2 + x_2^2 + \cdots + x_n^2}.$$

4. Firebreaks

The summer of 2000 was devastating for forests in the western US: over 3.5 million acres of trees were lost to fires, making this the worst fire season in 30 years. This project studies a fire management technique called *firebreaks*, which reduce the damage done by forest fires. A firebreak is a strip where trees have been removed in a forest so that a fire started on one side of the strip will not spread to the other side. Having many firebreaks helps confine a fire to a small area. On the other hand, having too many firebreaks involves removing large swaths of trees.[17]

(a) A forest in the shape of a 50 km by 50 km square has firebreaks in rectangular strips 50 km by 0.01 km. The trees between two firebreaks are called a stand of trees. All firebreaks in this forest are parallel to each other and to one edge of the forest, with the first firebreak at the edge of the forest. The firebreaks are evenly spaced throughout the forest. (For example, Figure 4.126 shows four firebreaks.) The total area lost in the case of a fire is the area of the stand of trees in which the fire started plus the area of all the firebreaks.

---

[17]Adapted from D. Quinney and R. Harding, *Calculus Connections* (New York: John Wiley & Sons, 1996).

Figure 4.126

(i) Find the number of firebreaks that minimizes the total area lost to the forest in the case of a fire.

(ii) If a firebreak is 50 km by b km, find the optimal number of firebreaks as a function of b. If the width, b, of a firebreak is quadrupled, how does the optimal number of firebreaks change?

(b) Now suppose firebreaks are arranged in two equally spaced sets of parallel lines, as shown in Figure 4.127. The forest is a 50 km by 50 km square, and each firebreak is a rectangular strip 50 km by 0.01 km. Find the number of firebreaks in each direction that minimizes the total area lost to the forest in the case of a fire.

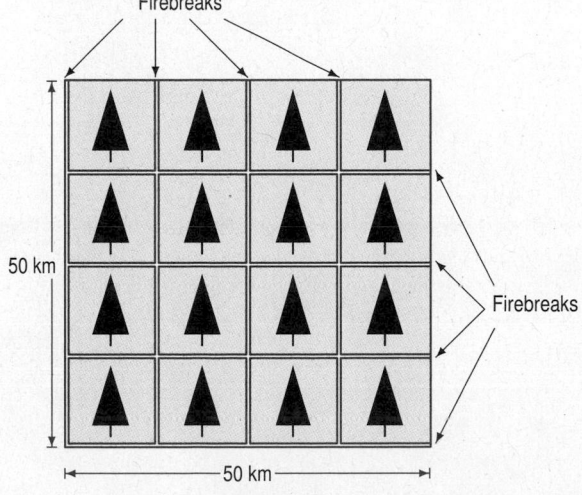

Figure 4.127

Chapter Five

KEY CONCEPT: THE DEFINITE INTEGRAL

Contents

5.1 HOW DO WE MEASURE DISTANCE TRAVELED?

For positive constant velocities, we can find the distance a moving object travels using the formula

$$\text{Distance} = \text{Velocity} \times \text{Time}.$$

In this section we see how to estimate the distance when the velocity is not a constant.

A Thought Experiment: How Far Did the Car Go?

Velocity Data Every Two Seconds

A car is moving with increasing velocity. Table 5.1 shows the velocity every two seconds:

Table 5.1 *Velocity of car every two seconds*

Time (sec)	0	2	4	6	8	10
Velocity (ft/sec)	20	30	38	44	48	50

How far has the car traveled? Since we don't know how fast the car is moving at every moment, we can't calculate the distance exactly, but we can make an estimate. The velocity is increasing, so the car is going at least 20 ft/sec for the first two seconds. Since Distance = Velocity × Time, the car goes at least $20 \cdot 2 = 40$ feet during the first two seconds. Likewise, it goes at least $30 \cdot 2 = 60$ feet during the next two seconds, and so on. During the ten-second period it goes at least

$$20 \cdot 2 + 30 \cdot 2 + 38 \cdot 2 + 44 \cdot 2 + 48 \cdot 2 = 360 \text{ feet.}$$

Thus, 360 feet is an underestimate of the total distance traveled during the ten seconds.

To get an overestimate, we can reason this way: During the first two seconds, the car's velocity is at most 30 ft/sec, so it moved at most $30 \cdot 2 = 60$ feet. In the next two seconds it moved at most $38 \cdot 2 = 76$ feet, and so on. Therefore, over the ten-second period it moved at most

$$30 \cdot 2 + 38 \cdot 2 + 44 \cdot 2 + 48 \cdot 2 + 50 \cdot 2 = 420 \text{ feet.}$$

Therefore,

$$360 \text{ feet} \leq \text{Total distance traveled} \leq 420 \text{ feet.}$$

There is a difference of 60 feet between the upper and lower estimates.

Velocity Data Every One Second

What if we want a more accurate estimate? Then we make more frequent velocity measurements, say every second, as in Table 5.2.

As before, we get a lower estimate for each second by using the velocity at the beginning of that second. During the first second the velocity is at least 20 ft/sec, so the car travels at least $20 \cdot 1 = 20$ feet. During the next second the car moves at least 26 feet, and so on. We have

$$\begin{aligned}
\text{New lower estimate} &= 20 \cdot 1 + 26 \cdot 1 + 30 \cdot 1 + 34 \cdot 1 + 38 \cdot 1 \\
&\quad + 41 \cdot 1 + 44 \cdot 1 + 46 \cdot 1 + 48 \cdot 1 + 49 \cdot 1 \\
&= 376 \text{ feet.}
\end{aligned}$$

Table 5.2 *Velocity of car every second*

Time (sec)	0	1	2	3	4	5	6	7	8	9	10
Velocity (ft/sec)	20	26	30	34	38	41	44	46	48	49	50

Notice that this lower estimate is greater than the old lower estimate of 360 feet.

We get a new upper estimate by considering the velocity at the end of each second. During the first second the velocity is at most 26 ft/sec, so the car moves at most $26 \cdot 1 = 26$ feet; in the next second it moves at most 30 feet, and so on.

$$\text{New upper estimate} = 26 \cdot 1 + 30 \cdot 1 + 34 \cdot 1 + 38 \cdot 1 + 41 \cdot 1$$
$$+ 44 \cdot 1 + 46 \cdot 1 + 48 \cdot 1 + 49 \cdot 1 + 50 \cdot 1$$
$$= 406 \text{ feet}.$$

This is less than the old upper estimate of 420 feet. Now we know that

$$376 \text{ feet} \leq \text{Total distance traveled} \leq 406 \text{ feet}.$$

The difference between upper and lower estimates is now 30 feet, half of what it was before. By halving the interval of measurement, we have halved the difference between the upper and lower estimates.

Visualizing Distance on the Velocity Graph: Two-Second Data

We can represent both upper and lower estimates on a graph of the velocity. The graph also shows how changing the time interval between velocity measurements changes the accuracy of our estimates.

The velocity can be graphed by plotting the two-second data in Table 5.1 and drawing a curve through the data points. (See Figure 5.1.) The area of the first dark rectangle is $20 \cdot 2 = 40$, the lower estimate of the distance moved during the first two seconds. The area of the second dark rectangle is $30 \cdot 2 = 60$, the lower estimate for the distance moved in the next two seconds. The total area of the dark rectangles represents the lower estimate for the total distance moved during the ten seconds.

If the dark and light rectangles are considered together, the first area is $30 \cdot 2 = 60$, the upper estimate for the distance moved in the first two seconds. The second area is $38 \cdot 2 = 76$, the upper estimate for the next two seconds. The upper estimate for the total distance is represented by the sum of the areas of the dark and light rectangles. Therefore, the area of the light rectangles alone represents the difference between the two estimates.

To visualize the difference between the two estimates, look at Figure 5.1 and imagine the light rectangles all pushed to the right and stacked on top of each other. This gives a rectangle of width 2 and height 30. The height, 30, is the difference between the initial and final values of the velocity: $30 = 50 - 20$. The width, 2, is the time interval between velocity measurements.

Figure 5.1: Velocity measured every 2 seconds

Figure 5.2: Velocity measured every second

Visualizing Distance on the Velocity Graph: One-Second Data

Figure 5.2 shows the velocities measured every second. The area of the dark rectangles again represents the lower estimate, and the area of the dark and light rectangles together represent the upper estimate. As before, the difference between the two estimates is represented by the area of the light rectangles. This difference can be calculated by stacking the light rectangles vertically, giving a rectangle of the same height as before but of half the width. Its area is therefore half what it was before. Again, the height of this stack is $50 - 20 = 30$, but its width is now 1.

Example 1   What would be the difference between the upper and lower estimates if the velocity were given every tenth of a second? Every hundredth of a second? Every thousandth of a second?

Solution   Every tenth of a second: Difference between estimates $= (50 - 20)(1/10) = 3$ feet.
Every hundredth of a second: Difference between estimates $= (50 - 20)(1/100) = 0.3$ feet.
Every thousandth of a second: Difference between estimates $= (50 - 20)(1/1000) = 0.03$ feet.

Example 2   How frequently must the velocity be recorded in order to estimate the total distance traveled to within 0.1 feet?

Solution   The difference between the velocity at the beginning and end of the observation period is $50 - 20 = 30$. If the time between successive measurements is Δt, then the difference between the upper and lower estimates is $(30)\Delta t$. We want

$$(30)\Delta t < 0.1,$$

or

$$\Delta t < \frac{0.1}{30} = 0.0033.$$

So if the measurements are made less than 0.0033 seconds apart, the distance estimate is accurate to within 0.1 feet.

Visualizing Distance on the Velocity Graph: Area Under Curve

As we make more frequent velocity measurements, the rectangles used to estimate the distance traveled fit the curve more closely. See Figures 5.3 and 5.4. In the limit, as the number of subdivisions increases, we see that the distance traveled is given by the area between the velocity curve and the horizontal axis. See Figure 5.5. In general:

> If the velocity is positive, the total distance traveled is the area under the velocity curve.

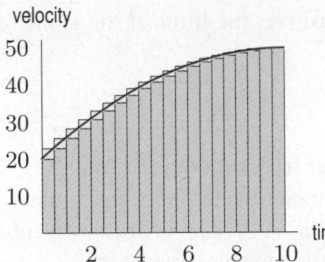

Figure 5.3: Velocity measured every 1/2 second

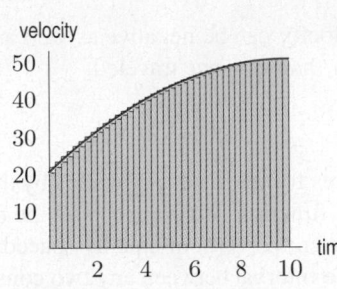

Figure 5.4: Velocity measured every 1/4 second

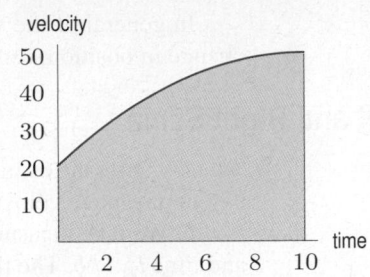

Figure 5.5: Distance traveled is area under curve

Example 3 With time t in seconds, the velocity of a bicycle, in feet per second, is given by $v(t) = 5t$. How far does the bicycle travel in 3 seconds?

Solution The velocity is linear. See Figure 5.6. The distance traveled is the area between the line $v(t) = 5t$ and the t-axis. Since this region is a triangle of height 15 and base 3,

$$\text{Distance traveled} = \text{Area of triangle} = \frac{1}{2} \cdot 15 \cdot 3 = 22.5 \text{ feet.}$$

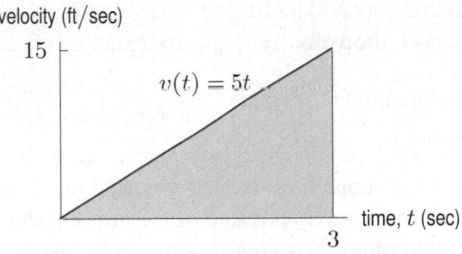

Figure 5.6: Shaded area represents distance traveled

Negative Velocity and Change in Position

In the thought experiment, the velocity is positive and our sums represent distance traveled. What if the velocity is sometimes negative?

Example 4 A particle moves along the y-axis with velocity 30 cm/sec for 5 seconds and velocity -10 cm/sec for the next 5 seconds. Positive velocity indicates upward motion; negative velocity represents downward motion. What is represented by the sum

$$30 \cdot 5 + (-10) \cdot 5?$$

Solution The first term in the sum represents an upward motion of $30 \cdot 5 = 150$ centimeters. The second term represents a motion of $(-10) \cdot 5 = -50$ centimeters, that is, 50 centimeters downward. Thus, the sum represents a change in position of $150 - 50 = 100$ centimeters upward.

Figure 5.7 shows velocity versus time. The area of the rectangle above the t-axis represents upward distance, while the area of the rectangle below the t-axis represents downward distance.

Figure 5.7: Difference in areas gives change in position

In general, if the velocity can be negative as well as positive, the limit of the sums represents change in position, rather than distance traveled.

Left and Right Sums

We now write the estimates for the distance traveled by the car in new notation. Let $v = f(t)$ denote any nonnegative velocity function. We want to find the distance traveled between times $t = a$ and $t = b$. We take measurements of $f(t)$ at equally spaced times $t_0, t_1, t_2, \ldots, t_n$, with time $t_0 = a$ and time $t_n = b$. The time interval between any two consecutive measurements is

$$\Delta t = \frac{b-a}{n},$$

where Δt means the change, or increment, in t.

During the first time interval, from t_0 and t_1, the velocity can be approximated by $f(t_0)$, so the distance traveled is approximately

$$f(t_0)\Delta t.$$

During the second time interval, the velocity is about $f(t_1)$, so the distance traveled is about

$$f(t_1)\Delta t.$$

Continuing in this way and adding all the estimates, we get an estimate for the total distance traveled. In the last interval, the velocity is approximately $f(t_{n-1})$, so the last term is $f(t_{n-1})\Delta t$:

Total distance traveled
between $t = a$ and $t = b$ $\approx f(t_0)\Delta t + f(t_1)\Delta t + f(t_2)\Delta t + \cdots + f(t_{n-1})\Delta t.$

This is called a *left-hand sum* because we used the value of velocity from the left end of each time interval. It is represented by the sum of the areas of the rectangles in Figure 5.8.

We can also calculate a *right-hand sum* by using the value of the velocity at the right end of each time interval. In that case the estimate for the first interval is $f(t_1)\Delta t$, for the second interval it is $f(t_2)\Delta t$, and so on. The estimate for the last interval is now $f(t_n)\Delta t$, so

Total distance traveled
between $t = a$ and $t = b$ $\approx f(t_1)\Delta t + f(t_2)\Delta t + f(t_3)\Delta t + \cdots + f(t_n)\Delta t.$

The right-hand sum is represented by the area of the rectangles in Figure 5.9.

If f is an increasing function, as in Figures 5.8 and 5.9, the left-hand sum is an underestimate and the right-hand sum is an overestimate of the total distance traveled. If f is decreasing, as in Figure 5.10, then the roles of the two sums are reversed.

Figure 5.8: Left-hand sums

Figure 5.9: Right-hand sums

Figure 5.10: Left and right sums if f is decreasing

Accuracy of Estimates

For either increasing or decreasing velocity functions, the exact value of the distance traveled lies somewhere between the two estimates. Thus, the accuracy of our estimate depends on how close these two sums are. For a function which is increasing throughout or decreasing throughout the interval $[a, b]$:

$$\left| \begin{array}{c} \text{Difference between} \\ \text{upper and lower estimates} \end{array} \right| = \left| \begin{array}{c} \text{Difference between} \\ f(a) \text{ and } f(b) \end{array} \right| \cdot \Delta t = |f(b) - f(a)| \cdot \Delta t.$$

(Absolute values make the differences nonnegative.) In Figure 5.10, the area of the light rectangles is the difference between estimates. By making the time interval, Δt, between measurements small enough, we can make this difference between lower and upper estimates as small as we like.

Exercises and Problems for Section 5.1

Exercises

1. Figure 5.11 shows the velocity of a car for $0 \leq t \leq 12$ and the rectangles used to estimate of the distance traveled.

   (a) Do the rectangles represent a left or a right sum?
   (b) Do the rectangles lead to an upper or a lower estimate?
   (c) What is the value of n?
   (d) What is the value of Δt?
   (e) Give an approximate value for the estimate.

Figure 5.11

2. The velocity $v(t)$ in Table 5.3 is increasing, $0 \leq t \leq 12$.

   (a) Find an upper estimate for the total distance traveled using

   (i) $n = 4$ (ii) $n = 2$

   (b) Which of the two answers in part (a) is more accurate? Why?
   (c) Find a lower estimate of the total distance traveled using $n = 4$.

Table 5.3

t	0	3	6	9	12
$v(t)$	34	37	38	40	45

3. The velocity $v(t)$ in Table 5.4 is decreasing, $2 \leq t \leq 12$. Using $n = 5$ subdivisions to approximate the total distance traveled, find

   (a)   An upper estimate   **(b)**   A lower estimate

Table 5.4

t	2	4	6	8	10	12
$v(t)$	44	42	41	40	37	35

4. A car comes to a stop five seconds after the driver applies the brakes. While the brakes are on, the velocities in the table are recorded.

(a) Give lower and upper estimates of the distance the car traveled after the brakes were applied.

(b) On a sketch of velocity against time, show the lower and upper estimates of part (a).

(c) Find the difference between the estimates. Explain how this difference can be visualized on the graph in part (b).

Time since brakes applied (sec)	0	1	2	3	4	5
Velocity (ft/sec)	88	60	40	25	10	0

5. Figure 5.12 shows the velocity, v, of an object (in meters/sec). Estimate the total distance the object traveled between $t = 0$ and $t = 6$.

Figure 5.12

6. At time, t, in seconds, your velocity, v, in meters/second, is given by

$$v(t) = 1 + t^2 \quad \text{for} \quad 0 \le t \le 6.$$

Use $\Delta t = 2$ to estimate the distance traveled during this time. Find the upper and lower estimates, and then average the two.

7. Figure 5.13 shows the velocity of a particle, in cm/sec, along a number line for time $-3 \le t \le 3$.

(a) Describe the motion in words: Is the particle changing direction or always moving in the same direction? Is the particle speeding up or slowing down?

(b) Make over and underestimates of the distance traveled for $-3 \le t \le 3$.

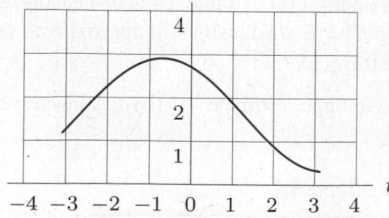

Figure 5.13

8. For time, t, in hours, $0 \le t \le 1$, a bug is crawling at a velocity, v, in meters/hour given by

$$v = \frac{1}{1 + t}.$$

Use $\Delta t = 0.2$ to estimate the distance that the bug crawls during this hour. Find an overestimate and an underestimate. Then average the two to get a new estimate.

Exercises 9–12 show the velocity, in cm/sec, of a particle moving along a number line. (Positive velocities represent movement to the right; negative velocities to the left.) Compute the change in position between times $t = 0$ and $t = 5$ seconds.

9.

10.

11.

12.

13. Use the expressions for left and right sums on page 276 and Table 5.5.

(a) If $n = 4$, what is Δt? What are t_0, t_1, t_2, t_3, t_4? What are $f(t_0), f(t_1), f(t_2), f(t_3), f(t_4)$?

(b) Find the left and right sums using $n = 4$.

(c) If $n = 2$, what is Δt? What are t_0, t_1, t_2? What are $f(t_0), f(t_1), f(t_2)$?

(d) Find the left and right sums using $n = 2$.

Table 5.5

t	15	17	19	21	23
$f(t)$	10	13	18	20	30

14. Use the expressions for left and right sums on page 276 and Table 5.6.

(a) If $n = 4$, what is Δt? What are t_0, t_1, t_2, t_3, t_4? What are $f(t_0), f(t_1), f(t_2), f(t_3), f(t_4)$?

(b) Find the left and right sums using $n = 4$.

(c) If $n = 2$, what is Δt? What are t_0, t_1, t_2? What are $f(t_0), f(t_1), f(t_2)$?

(d) Find the left and right sums using $n = 2$.

Table 5.6

t	0	4	8	12	16
$f(t)$	25	23	22	20	17

Problems

15. Roger runs a marathon. His friend Jeff rides behind him on a bicycle and clocks his speed every 15 minutes. Roger starts out strong, but after an hour and a half he is so exhausted that he has to stop. Jeff's data follow:

Time since start (min)	0	15	30	45	60	75	90
Speed (mph)	12	11	10	10	8	7	0

(a) Assuming that Roger's speed is never increasing, give upper and lower estimates for the distance Roger ran during the first half hour.

(b) Give upper and lower estimates for the distance Roger ran in total during the entire hour and a half.

(c) How often would Jeff have needed to measure Roger's speed in order to find lower and upper estimates within 0.1 mile of the actual distance he ran?

16. The velocity of a particle moving along the x-axis is given by $f(t) = 6 - 2t$ cm/sec. Use a graph of $f(t)$ to find the exact change in position of the particle from time $t = 0$ to $t = 4$ seconds.

In Problems 17–20, find the difference between the upper and lower estimates of the distance traveled at velocity $f(t)$ on the interval $a \leq t \leq b$ for n subdivisions.

17. $f(t) = 5t + 8, a = 1, b = 3, n = 100$

18. $f(t) = 25 - t^2, a = 1, b = 4, n = 500$

19. $f(t) = \sin t, a = 0, b = \pi/2, n = 100$

20. $f(t) = e^{-t^2/2}, a = 0, b = 2, n = 20$

21. A baseball thrown directly upward at 96 ft/sec has velocity $v(t) = 96 - 32t$ ft/sec at time t seconds.

(a) Graph the velocity from $t = 0$ to $t = 6$.

(b) When does the baseball reach the peak of its flight? How high does it go?

(c) How high is the baseball at time $t = 5$?

22. Figure 5.14 gives your velocity during a trip starting from home. Positive velocities take you away from home and negative velocities take you toward home. Where are you at the end of the 5 hours? When are you farthest from home? How far away are you at that time?

Figure 5.14

23. When an aircraft attempts to climb as rapidly as possible, its climb rate decreases with altitude. (This occurs because the air is less dense at higher altitudes.) The table shows performance data for a single-engine aircraft.

Altitude (1000 ft)	0	1	2	3	4	5
Climb rate (ft/min)	925	875	830	780	730	685
Altitude (1000 ft)	6	7	8	9	10	
Climb rate (ft/min)	635	585	535	490	440	

(a) Calculate upper and lower estimates for the time required for this aircraft to climb from sea level to 10,000 ft.

(b) If climb rate data were available in increments of 500 ft, what would be the difference between a lower and upper estimate of climb time based on 20 subdivisions?

24. A bicyclist is pedaling along a straight road for one hour with a velocity v shown in Figure 5.15. She starts out five kilometers from the lake and positive velocities take her toward the lake. [Note: The vertical lines on the graph are at 10 minute (1/6 hour) intervals.]

(a) Does the cyclist ever turn around? If so, at what time(s)?

(b) When is she going the fastest? How fast is she going then? Toward the lake or away?

(c) When is she closest to the lake? Approximately how close to the lake does she get?

(d) When is she farthest from the lake? Approximately how far from the lake is she then?

Figure 5.15

25. Two cars travel in the same direction along a straight road. Figure 5.16 shows the velocity, v, of each car at time t. Car B starts 2 hours after car A and car B reaches a maximum velocity of 50 km/hr.

(a) For approximately how long does each car travel?

(b) Estimate car A's maximum velocity.

(c) Approximately how far does each car travel?

Figure 5.16

26. Two cars start at the same time and travel in the same direction along a straight road. Figure 5.17 gives the velocity, v, of each car as a function of time, t. Which car:

   (a) Attains the larger maximum velocity?
   (b) Stops first?
   (c) Travels farther?

Figure 5.17

27. A car initially going 50 ft/sec brakes at a constant rate (constant negative acceleration), coming to a stop in 5 seconds.

   (a) Graph the velocity from $t = 0$ to $t = 5$.
   (b) How far does the car travel?
   (c) How far does the car travel if its initial velocity is doubled, but it brakes at the same constant rate?

28. A woman drives 10 miles, accelerating uniformly from rest to 60 mph. Graph her velocity versus time. How long does it take for her to reach 60 mph?

29. An object has zero initial velocity and a constant acceleration of 32 ft/sec^2. Find a formula for its velocity as a function of time. Use left and right sums with $\Delta t = 1$ to find upper and lower bounds on the distance that the object travels in four seconds. Find the precise distance using the area under the curve.

Problems 30–31 concern hybrid cars such as the Toyota Prius that are powered by a gas-engine, electric-motor combination, but can also function in Electric-Vehicle (EV) only mode. Figure 5.18 shows the velocity, v, of a 2010 Prius Plug-in Hybrid Prototype operating in normal hybrid mode and EV-only mode, respectively, while accelerating from a stoplight.[1]

Figure 5.18

30. Could the car travel half a mile in EV-only mode during the first 25 seconds of movement?

31. Assume two identical cars, one running in normal hybrid mode and one running in EV-only mode, accelerate together in a straight path from a stoplight. Approximately how far apart are the cars after 15 seconds?

Strengthen Your Understanding

In Problems 32–33, explain what is wrong with the statement.

32. If a car accelerates from 0 to 50 ft/sec in 10 seconds, then it travels 250 ft.

33. For any acceleration, you can estimate the total distance traveled by a car in 1 second to within 0.1 feet by recording its velocity every 0.1 second.

In Problems 34–35, give an example of:

34. A velocity function f and an interval $[a, b]$ such that the distance denoted by the right-hand sum for f on $[a, b]$ is less than the distance denoted by the left-hand sum, no matter what the number of subdivisions.

35. A velocity $f(t)$ and an interval $[a, b]$ such that at least 100 subdivisions are needed in order for the difference between the upper and lower estimates to be less than or equal to 0.1.

Are the statements in Problems 36–38 true or false? Give an explanation for your answer.

36. For an increasing velocity function on a fixed time interval, the left-hand sum with a given number of subdivisions is always less than the corresponding right-hand sum.

37. For a decreasing velocity function on a fixed time interval, the difference between the left-hand sum and right-hand sum is halved when the number of subdivisions is doubled.

38. For a given velocity function on a given interval, the difference between the left-hand sum and right-hand sum gets smaller as the number of subdivisions gets larger.

39. A bicyclist starts from home and rides back and forth along a straight east/west highway. Her velocity is given

---

[1]www.motortrend.com/, accessed May 2011.

in Figure 5.19 (positive velocities indicate travel toward the east, negative toward the west).

(a) On what time intervals is she stopped?

(b) How far from home is she the first time she stops, and in what direction?

(c) At what time does she bike past her house?

(d) If she maintains her velocity at $t = 11$, how long will it take her to get back home?

Figure 5.19

5.2   THE DEFINITE INTEGRAL

In Section 5.1, we saw how distance traveled can be approximated by a sum of areas of rectangles. We also saw how the approximation improves as the width of the rectangles gets smaller. In this section, we construct these sums for any function f, whether or not it represents a velocity.

Sigma Notation

Suppose $f(t)$ is a continuous function for $a \leq t \leq b$. We divide the interval from a to b into n equal subdivisions, and we call the width of an individual subdivision Δt, so

$$\Delta t = \frac{b - a}{n}.$$

Let $t_0, t_1, t_2, \ldots, t_n$ be endpoints of the subdivisions. Both the left-hand and right-hand sums can be written more compactly using *sigma*, or summation, notation. The symbol $\sum$ is a capital sigma, or Greek letter "S." We write

$$\text{Right-hand sum} = f(t_1)\Delta t + f(t_2)\Delta t + \cdots + f(t_n)\Delta t = \sum_{i=1}^{n} f(t_i)\Delta t.$$

The $\sum$ tells us to add terms of the form $f(t_i)\Delta t$. The "$i = 1$" at the base of the sigma sign tells us to start at $i = 1$, and the "n" at the top tells us to stop at $i = n$.

In the left-hand sum we start at $i = 0$ and stop at $i = n - 1$, so we write

$$\text{Left-hand sum} = f(t_0)\Delta t + f(t_1)\Delta t + \cdots + f(t_{n-1})\Delta t = \sum_{i=0}^{n-1} f(t_i)\Delta t.$$

Taking the Limit to Obtain the Definite Integral

Now we take the limit of these sums as n goes to infinity. If f is continuous for $a \leq t \leq b$, the limits of the left- and right-hand sums exist and are equal. The *definite integral* is the limit of these sums. A formal definition of the definite integral is given in the online supplement to the text at www.wiley.com/college/hughes-hallett.

Suppose f is continuous for $a \leq t \leq b$. The **definite integral** of f from a to b, written

$$\int_a^b f(t)\, dt,$$

is the limit of the left-hand or right-hand sums with n subdivisions of $a \leq t \leq b$ as n gets arbitrarily large. In other words,

$$\int_a^b f(t)\, dt = \lim_{n \to \infty} (\text{Left-hand sum}) = \lim_{n \to \infty} \left(\sum_{i=0}^{n-1} f(t_i)\Delta t \right)$$

and

$$\int_a^b f(t)\, dt = \lim_{n \to \infty} (\text{Right-hand sum}) = \lim_{n \to \infty} \left(\sum_{i=1}^{n} f(t_i)\Delta t \right).$$

Each of these sums is called a *Riemann sum*, f is called the *integrand*, and a and b are called the *limits of integration*.

The "$\int$" notation comes from an old-fashioned "S," which stands for "sum" in the same way that $\sum$ does. The "dt" in the integral comes from the factor Δt. Notice that the limits on the $\sum$ symbol are 0 and $n-1$ for the left-hand sum, and 1 and n for the right-hand sum, whereas the limits on the $\int$ sign are a and b.

Computing a Definite Integral

In practice, we often approximate definite integrals numerically using a calculator or computer. They use programs which compute sums for larger and larger values of n, and eventually give a value for the integral. Some (but not all) definite integrals can be computed exactly. However, any definite integral can be approximated numerically.

In the next example, we see how numerical approximation works. For each value of n, we show an over- and an under-estimate for the integral $\int_1^2 (1/t)\, dt$. As we increase the value of n, the over- and under-estimates get closer together, trapping the value of the integral between them. By increasing the value of n sufficiently, we can calculate the integral to any desired accuracy.

Example 1   Calculate the left-hand and right-hand sums with $n = 2$ for $\int_1^2 \dfrac{1}{t}\, dt$. What is the relation between the left- and right-hand sums for $n = 10$ and $n = 250$ and the integral?

Solution   Here $a = 1$ and $b = 2$, so for $n = 2$, $\Delta t = (2 - 1)/2 = 0.5$. Therefore, $t_0 = 1$, $t_1 = 1.5$ and $t_2 = 2$. (See Figure 5.20.) We have

$$\text{Left-hand sum} = f(1)\Delta t + f(1.5)\Delta t = 1(0.5) + \frac{1}{1.5}(0.5) = 0.8333,$$

$$\text{Right-hand sum} = f(1.5)\Delta t + f(2)\Delta t = \frac{1}{1.5}(0.5) + \frac{1}{2}(0.5) = 0.5833.$$

In Figure 5.20 we see that the left-hand sum is bigger than the area under the curve and the right-hand sum is smaller. So the area under the curve $f(t) = 1/t$ from $t = 1$ to $t = 2$ is between them:

$$0.5833 < \int_1^2 \frac{1}{t}\, dt < 0.8333.$$

Since $1/t$ is decreasing, when $n = 10$ in Figure 5.21 we again see that the left-hand sum is larger than the area under the curve, and the right-hand sum smaller. A calculator or computer gives

$$0.6688 < \int_1^2 \frac{1}{t}\, dt < 0.7188.$$

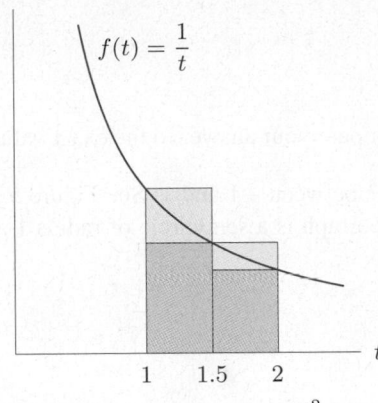

Figure 5.20: Approximating $\int_1^2 \frac{1}{t}\, dt$ with $n = 2$

Figure 5.21: Approximating $\int_1^2 \frac{1}{t}\, dt$ with $n = 10$

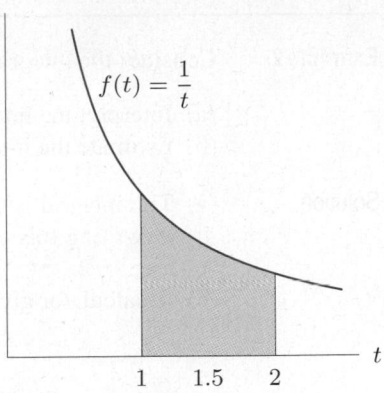

Figure 5.22: Shaded area is exact value of $\int_1^2 \frac{1}{t}\, dt$

The left- and right-hand sums trap the exact value of the integral between them. As the subdivisions become finer, the left- and right-hand sums get closer together.

When $n = 250$, a calculator or computer gives

$$0.6921 < \int_1^2 \frac{1}{t}\, dt < 0.6941.$$

So, to two decimal places, we can say that

$$\int_1^2 \frac{1}{t}\, dt \approx 0.69.$$

The exact value is known to be $\int_1^2 \frac{1}{t}\, dt = \ln 2 = 0.693147\ldots$. See Figure 5.22.

The Definite Integral as an Area

If $f(x)$ is positive we can interpret each term $f(x_0)\Delta x$, $f(x_1)\Delta x, \ldots$ in a left- or right-hand Riemann sum as the area of a rectangle. See Figure 5.23. As the width Δx of the rectangles approaches zero, the rectangles fit the curve of the graph more exactly, and the sum of their areas gets closer and closer to the area under the curve shaded in Figure 5.24. This suggests that:

> When $f(x) \geq 0$ and $a < b$:
>
> $$\text{Area under graph of } f \text{ and above } x\text{-axis between } a \text{ and } b = \int_a^b f(x)\, dx.$$

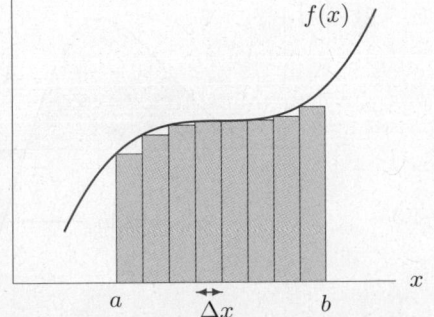

Figure 5.23: Area of rectangles approximating the area under the curve

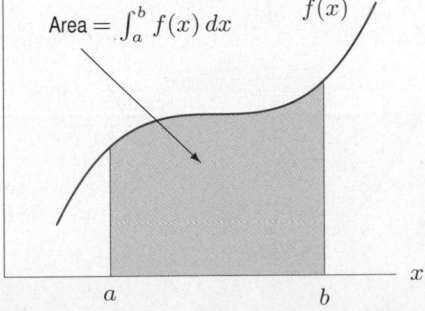

Figure 5.24: The definite integral $\int_a^b f(x)\, dx$

Example 2   Consider the integral $\int_{-1}^{1} \sqrt{1 - x^2}\, dx$.

(a) Interpret the integral as an area, and find its exact value.

(b) Estimate the integral using a calculator or computer. Compare your answer to the exact value.

Solution   (a) The integral is the area under the graph of $y = \sqrt{1 - x^2}$ between -1 and 1. See Figure 5.25. Rewriting this equation as $x^2 + y^2 = 1$, we see that the graph is a semicircle of radius 1 and area $\pi/2$.

(b) A calculator gives the value of the integral as $1.5707963\ldots$.

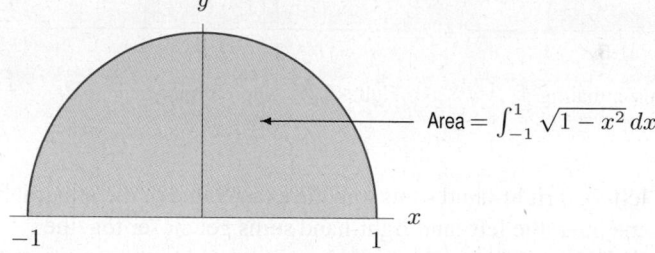

Figure 5.25: Area interpretation of $\int_{-1}^{1} \sqrt{1 - x^2}\, dx$

When $f(x)$ Is Not Positive

We have assumed in drawing Figure 5.24 that the graph of $f(x)$ lies above the x-axis. If the graph lies below the x-axis, then each value of $f(x)$ is negative, so each $f(x)\Delta x$ is negative, and the area gets counted negatively. In that case, the definite integral is the negative of the area.

> When $f(x)$ is positive for some x values and negative for others, and $a < b$:
>
> $\int_{a}^{b} f(x)\, dx$ is the sum of areas above the x-axis, counted positively, and areas below the x-axis, counted negatively.

Example 3   How does the definite integral $\int_{-1}^{1} (x^2 - 1)\, dx$ relate to the area between the parabola $y = x^2 - 1$ and the x-axis?

Solution   A calculator gives $\int_{-1}^{1} (x^2 - 1)\, dx = -1.33$. Since the parabola lies below the axis between $x = -1$ and $x = 1$ (see Figure 5.26), the area between the parabola and the x-axis is approximately 1.33.

Figure 5.26: Integral $\int_{-1}^{1} (x^2 - 1)\, dx$ is negative of shaded area

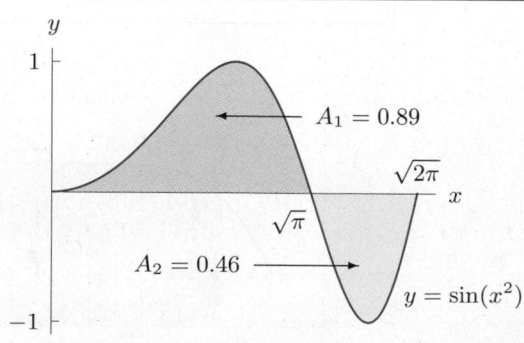

Figure 5.27: Integral $\int_{0}^{\sqrt{2\pi}} \sin(x^2)\, dx = A_1 - A_2$

Example 4   Interpret the definite integral $\int_0^{\sqrt{2\pi}} \sin(x^2)\, dx$ in terms of areas.

Solution   The integral is the area above the x-axis, A_1, minus the area below the x-axis, A_2. See Figure 5.27. Estimating the integral with a calculator gives

$$\int_0^{\sqrt{2\pi}} \sin(x^2)\, dx = 0.43.$$

The graph of $y = \sin(x^2)$ crosses the x-axis where $x^2 = \pi$, that is, at $x = \sqrt{\pi}$. The next crossing is at $x = \sqrt{2\pi}$. Breaking the integral into two parts and calculating each one separately gives

$$\int_0^{\sqrt{\pi}} \sin(x^2)\, dx = 0.89 \quad \text{and} \quad \int_{\sqrt{\pi}}^{\sqrt{2\pi}} \sin(x^2)\, dx = -0.46.$$

So $A_1 = 0.89$ and $A_2 = 0.46$. Then, as we would expect,

$$\int_0^{\sqrt{2\pi}} \sin(x^2)\, dx = A_1 - A_2 = 0.89 - 0.46 = 0.43.$$

More General Riemann Sums

Left- and right-hand sums are special cases of Riemann sums. For a general Riemann sum we allow subdivisions to have different lengths. Also, instead of evaluating f only at the left or right endpoint of each subdivision, we allow it to be evaluated anywhere in the subdivision. Thus, a general Riemann sum has the form

$$\sum_{i=1}^{n} \text{Value of } f(t) \text{ at some point in } i^{\text{th}} \text{ subdivision} \times \text{Length of } i^{\text{th}} \text{ subdivision}.$$

(See Figure 5.28.) As before, we let $t_0, t_1, \ldots, t_n$ be the endpoints of the subdivisions, so the length of the ith subdivision is $\Delta t_i = t_i - t_{i-1}$. For each i we choose a point c_i in the ith subinterval at which to evaluate f, leading to the following definition:

A general Riemann sum for f on the interval $[a, b]$ is a sum of the form

$$\sum_{i=1}^{n} f(c_i)\Delta t_i,$$

where $a = t_0 < t_1 < \cdots < t_n = b$, and, for $i = 1, \ldots, n$, $\Delta t_i = t_i - t_{i-1}$, and $t_{i-1} \leq c_i \leq t_i$.

If f is continuous, we can make a general Riemann sum as close as we like to the value of the definite integral by making the interval lengths small enough. Thus, in approximating definite integrals or in proving theorems about them, we can use general Riemann sums rather than left- or right-hand sums. Generalized Riemann sums are especially useful in establishing properties of the definite integral; see www.wiley.com/college/hughes-hallett.

Figure 5.28: A general Riemann sum approximating $\int_a^b f(t)\, dt$

Exercises and Problems for Section 5.2

Exercises

In Exercises 1–2, rectangles have been drawn to approximate $\int_0^6 g(x)\,dx$.

  (a) Do the rectangles represent a left or a right sum?

  (b) Do the rectangles lead to an upper or a lower estimate?

  (c) What is the value of n?

  (d) What is the value of Δx?

1.   **2.**

3. Figure 5.29 shows a Riemann sum approximation with n subdivisions to $\int_a^b f(x)\,dx$.

  (a) Is it a left- or right-hand approximation? Would the other one be larger or smaller?

  (b) What are a, b, n and Δx?

Figure 5.29

4. Using Figure 5.30, draw rectangles representing each of the following Riemann sums for the function f on the interval $0 \le t \le 8$. Calculate the value of each sum.

  (a) Left-hand sum with $\Delta t = 4$

  (b) Right-hand sum with $\Delta t = 4$

  (c) Left-hand sum with $\Delta t = 2$

  (d) Right-hand sum with $\Delta t = 2$

Figure 5.30

In Exercises 5–10, use a calculator or a computer to find the value of the definite integral.

5. $\displaystyle\int_1^4 (x^2 + x)\,dx$ **6.** $\displaystyle\int_0^3 2^x\,dx$

7. $\displaystyle\int_{-1}^1 e^{-x^2}\,dx$ **8.** $\displaystyle\int_0^3 \ln(y^2 + 1)\,dy$

9. $\displaystyle\int_0^1 \sin(t^2)\,dt$ **10.** $\displaystyle\int_3^4 \sqrt{e^z + z}\,dz$

11. Use the table to estimate $\int_0^{40} f(x)\,dx$. What values of n and Δx did you use?

x	0	10	20	30	40
$f(x)$	350	410	435	450	460

12. Use the table to estimate $\int_0^{12} f(x)\,dx$.

x	0	3	6	9	12
$f(x)$	32	22	15	11	9

13. Use the table to estimate $\int_0^{15} f(x)\,dx$.

x	0	3	6	9	12	15
$f(x)$	50	48	44	36	24	8

14. Write out the terms of the right-hand sum with $n = 5$ that could be used to approximate $\displaystyle\int_3^7 \frac{1}{1+x}\,dx$. Do not evaluate the terms or the sum.

15. Use Figure 5.31 to estimate $\int_0^{20} f(x)\,dx$.

Figure 5.31

16. Use Figure 5.32 to estimate $\int_{-10}^{15} f(x)dx$.

Figure 5.32

17. Using Figure 5.33, estimate $\int_{-3}^{5} f(x)dx$.

Figure 5.33

Problems

18. The graph of $f(t)$ is in Figure 5.34. Which of the following four numbers could be an estimate of $\int_{0}^{1} f(t)dt$ accurate to two decimal places? Explain your choice.

    I. -98.35 II. 71.84   III. 100.12 IV. 93.47

Figure 5.34

19. (a) What is the area between the graph of $f(x)$ in Figure 5.35 and the x-axis, between $x = 0$ and $x = 5$?
    (b) What is $\int_{0}^{5} f(x)\,dx$?

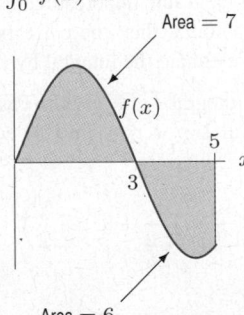

Figure 5.35

20. Find the total area between $y = 4 - x^2$ and the x-axis for $0 \leq x \leq 3$.

21. (a) Find the total area between $f(x) = x^3 - x$ and the x-axis for $0 \leq x \leq 3$.
    (b) Find $\int_{0}^{3} f(x)dx$.
    (c) Are the answers to parts (a) and (b) the same? Explain.

In Problems 22–28, find the area of the regions between the curve and the horizontal axis

22. Under $y = 6x^3 - 2$ for $5 \leq x \leq 10$.

23. Under the curve $y = \cos t$ for $0 \leq t \leq \pi/2$.

24. Under $y = \ln x$ for $1 \leq x \leq 4$.

25. Under $y = 2\cos(t/10)$ for $1 \leq t \leq 2$.

26. Under the curve $y = \cos \sqrt{x}$ for $0 \leq x \leq 2$.

27. Under the curve $y = 7 - x^2$ and above the x-axis.

28. Above the curve $y = x^4 - 8$ and below the x-axis.

29. Use Figure 5.36 to find the values of
    (a) $\int_{a}^{b} f(x)\,dx$ **(b)** $\int_{b}^{c} f(x)\,dx$
    (c) $\int_{a}^{c} f(x)\,dx$ **(d)** $\int_{a}^{c} |f(x)|\,dx$

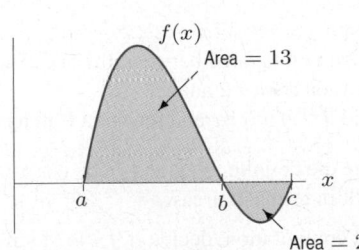

Figure 5.36

30. Given $\int_{-2}^{0} f(x)dx = 4$ and Figure 5.37, estimate:
    (a) $\int_{0}^{2} f(x)dx$ **(b)** $\int_{-2}^{2} f(x)dx$
    (c) The total shaded area.

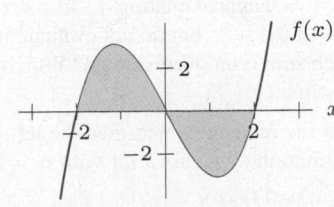

Figure 5.37

31. **(a)** Using Figure 5.38, find $\int_{-3}^{0} f(x)\,dx$.

(b) If the area of the shaded region is A, estimate $\int_{-3}^{4} f(x)\,dx$.

Figure 5.38

32. Use Figure 5.39 to find the values of

(a) $\int_{0}^{2} f(x)\,dx$ **(b)** $\int_{3}^{7} f(x)\,dx$

(c) $\int_{2}^{7} f(x)\,dx$ **(d)** $\int_{5}^{8} f(x)\,dx$

Figure 5.39: Graph consists of a semicircle and line segments

33. **(a)** Graph $f(x) = x(x+2)(x-1)$.

(b) Find the total area between the graph and the x-axis between $x = -2$ and $x = 1$.

(c) Find $\int_{-2}^{1} f(x)\,dx$ and interpret it in terms of areas.

34. Compute the definite integral $\int_{0}^{4} \cos\sqrt{x}\,dx$ and interpret the result in terms of areas.

35. Without computation, decide if $\int_{0}^{2\pi} e^{-x}\sin x\,dx$ is positive or negative. [Hint: Sketch $e^{-x}\sin x$.]

36. Estimate $\int_{0}^{1} e^{-x^2}\,dx$ using $n = 5$ rectangles to form a

(a) Left-hand sum   **(b)** Right-hand sum

37. **(a)** On a sketch of $y = \ln x$, represent the left Riemann sum with $n = 2$ approximating $\int_{1}^{2} \ln x\,dx$. Write out the terms in the sum, but do not evaluate it.

(b) On another sketch, represent the right Riemann sum with $n = 2$ approximating $\int_{1}^{2} \ln x\,dx$. Write out the terms in the sum, but do not evaluate it.

(c) Which sum is an overestimate? Which sum is an underestimate?

38. **(a)** Draw the rectangles that give the left-hand sum approximation to $\int_{0}^{\pi} \sin x\,dx$ with $n = 2$.

(b) Repeat part (a) for $\int_{-\pi}^{0} \sin x\,dx$.

(c) From your answers to parts (a) and (b), what is the value of the left-hand sum approximation to $\int_{-\pi}^{\pi} \sin x\,dx$ with $n = 4$?

39. **(a)** Use a calculator or computer to find $\int_{0}^{6} (x^2 + 1)\,dx$. Represent this value as the area under a curve.

(b) Estimate $\int_{0}^{6} (x^2 + 1)\,dx$ using a left-hand sum with $n = 3$. Represent this sum graphically on a sketch of $f(x) = x^2 + 1$. Is this sum an overestimate or underestimate of the true value found in part (a)?

(c) Estimate $\int_{0}^{6} (x^2 + 1)\,dx$ using a right-hand sum with $n = 3$. Represent this sum on your sketch. Is this sum an overestimate or underestimate?

40. **(a)** Graph $f(x) = \begin{cases} 1 - x & 0 \le x \le 1 \\ x - 1 & 1 < x \le 2. \end{cases}$

(b) Find $\int_{0}^{2} f(x)\,dx$.

(c) Calculate the 4-term left Riemann sum approximation to the definite integral. How does the approximation compare to the exact value?

41. Estimate $\int_{1}^{2} x^2\,dx$ using left- and right-hand sums with four subdivisions. How far from the true value of the integral could your estimate be?

42. Without computing the sums, find the difference between the right- and left-hand Riemann sums if we use $n = 500$ subintervals to approximate $\int_{-1}^{1} (2x^3 + 4)\,dx$.

43. Sketch the graph of a function f (you do not need to give a formula for f) on an interval $[a, b]$ with the property that with $n = 2$ subdivisions,

$$\int_{a}^{b} f(x)\,dx < \text{Left-hand sum } < \text{Right-hand sum.}$$

44. Write a few sentences in support of or in opposition to the following statement:

"If a left-hand sum underestimates a definite integral by a certain amount, then the corresponding right-hand sum will overestimate the integral by the same amount."

45. Consider the integral $\int_{1}^{2} (1/t)\,dt$ in Example 1. By dividing the interval $1 \le t \le 2$ into 10 equal parts, we can show that

$$0.1\left(\frac{1}{1.1} + \frac{1}{1.2} + \ldots + \frac{1}{2}\right) \le \int_{1}^{2} \frac{1}{t}\,dt$$

and

$$\int_{1}^{2} \frac{1}{t}\,dt \le 0.1\left(\frac{1}{1} + \frac{1}{1.1} + \ldots + \frac{1}{1.9}\right).$$

(a) Now divide the interval $1 \le t \le 2$ into n equal parts to show that

$$\sum_{r=1}^{n} \frac{1}{n+r} < \int_{1}^{2} \frac{1}{t}\,dt < \sum_{r=0}^{n-1} \frac{1}{n+r}.$$

(b) Show that the difference between the upper and lower sums in part (a) is $1/(2n)$.

(c) The exact value of $\int_{1}^{2} (1/t)\,dt$ is $\ln 2$. How large should n be to approximate $\ln 2$ with an error of at most $5 \cdot 10^{-6}$, using one of the sums in part (a)?

Strengthen Your Understanding

In Problems 46–47, explain what is wrong with the statement.

46. For any function, $\int_1^3 f(x)\,dx$ is the area between the the graph of f and the x-axis on $1 \le x \le 3$.

47. The left-hand sum with 10 subdivisions for the integral $\int_1^2 \sin(x)\,dx$ is

$$0.1\left(\sin(1) + \sin(1.1) + \cdots + \sin(2)\right).$$

In Problems 48–49, give an example of:

48. A function f and an interval $[a, b]$ such that $\int_a^b f(x)\,dx$ is negative.

49. A function f such that $\int_1^3 f(x)\,dx < \int_1^2 f(x)\,dx$.

In Problems 50–52 decide whether the statement is true or false. Justify your answer.

50. On the interval $a \le t \le b$, the integral of the velocity is the total distance traveled from $t - a$ to $t - b$.

51. A 4-term left-hand Riemann sum approximation cannot give the exact value of a definite integral.

52. If $f(x)$ is decreasing and $g(x)$ is increasing, then $\int_a^b f(x)\,dx \ne \int_a^b g(x)\,dx$.

In Problems 53–55, is the statement true for all continuous functions $f(x)$ and $g(x)$? Explain your answer.

53. $\int_0^2 f(x)\,dx \le \int_0^3 f(x)\,dx$.

54. $\int_0^2 f(x)\,dx = \int_0^2 f(t)\,dt$.

55. If $\int_2^6 f(x)\,dx \le \int_2^6 g(x)\,dx$, then $f(x) \le g(x)$ for $2 \le x \le 6$.

In Problems 56–57, graph a continuous function $f(x) \ge 0$ on $[0, 10]$ with the given properties.

56. The maximum value taken on by $f(x)$ for $0 \le x \le 10$ is 1. In addition $\int_0^{10} f(x)\,dx = 5$.

57. The maximum value taken on by $f(x)$ for $0 \le x \le 10$ is 5. In addition $\int_0^{10} f(x)\,dx = 1$.

5.3 THE FUNDAMENTAL THEOREM AND INTERPRETATIONS

The Notation and Units for the Definite Integral

Just as the Leibniz notation dy/dx for the derivative reminds us that the derivative is the limit of a ratio of differences, the notation for the definite integral helps us recall the meaning of the integral. The symbol

$$\int_a^b f(x)\,dx$$

reminds us that an integral is a limit of sums of terms of the form "$f(x)$ times a small difference of x." Officially, dx is not a separate entity, but a part of the whole integral symbol. Just as one thinks of d/dx as a single symbol meaning "the derivative with respect to x of... ," one can think of $\int_a^b \ldots dx$ as a single symbol meaning "the integral of ... with respect to x."

However, many scientists and mathematicians informally think of dx as an "infinitesimally" small bit of x multiplied by $f(x)$. This viewpoint is often the key to interpreting the meaning of a definite integral. For example, if $f(t)$ is the velocity of a moving particle at time t, then $f(t)\,dt$ may by thought of informally as velocity $\times$ time, giving the distance traveled by the particle during a small bit of time dt. The integral $\int_a^b f(t)\,dt$ may then be thought of as the sum of all these small distances, giving us the net change in position of the particle between $t = a$ and $t = b$. The notation for the integral suggests units for the value of the integral. Since the terms being added up are products of the form "$f(x)$ times a difference in x," the unit of measurement for $\int_a^b f(x)\,dx$ is the product of the units for $f(x)$ and the units for x. For example, if $f(t)$ is velocity measured in meters/second and t is time measured in seconds, then

$$\int_a^b f(t)\,dt$$

has units of (meters/sec)$\times$(sec) = meters. This is what we expect, since the value of this integral represents change in position.

As another example, graph $y = f(x)$ with the same units of measurement of length along the x- and y-axes, say cm. Then $f(x)$ and x are measured in the same units, so

$$\int_a^b f(x)\,dx$$

is measured in square units of cm $\times$ cm $=$ cm^2. Again, this is what we would expect since in this context the integral represents an area.

The Fundamental Theorem of Calculus

We have seen that change in position can be calculated as the limit of Riemann sums of the velocity function $v = f(t)$. Thus, change in position is given by the definite integral $\int_a^b f(t)\,dt$. If we let $F(t)$ denote the position function, then the change in position can also be written as $F(b) - F(a)$. Thus we have:

$$\int_a^b f(t)\,dt = \begin{array}{c} \text{Change in position from} \\ t = a \text{ to } t = b \end{array} = F(b) - F(a)$$

We also know that the position F and velocity f are related using derivatives: $F'(t) = f(t)$. Thus, we have uncovered a connection between the integral and derivative, which is so important it is called the Fundamental Theorem of Calculus. It applies to any function F with a continuous derivative $f = F'$.

Theorem 5.1: The Fundamental Theorem of Calculus[2]

If f is continuous on the interval $[a, b]$ and $f(t) = F'(t)$, then

$$\int_a^b f(t)\,dt = F(b) - F(a).$$

To understand the Fundamental Theorem of Calculus, think of $f(t) = F'(t)$ as the rate of change of the quantity $F(t)$. To calculate the total change in $F(t)$ between times $t = a$ and $t = b$, we divide the interval $a \le t \le b$ into n subintervals, each of length Δt. For each small interval, we estimate the change in $F(t)$, written ΔF, and add these. In each subinterval we assume the rate of change of $F(t)$ is approximately constant, so that we can say

$$\Delta F \approx \text{Rate of change of } F \times \text{Time elapsed.}$$

For the first subinterval, from t_0 to t_1, the rate of change of $F(t)$ is approximately $F'(t_0)$, so

$$\Delta F \approx F'(t_0)\,\Delta t.$$

Similarly, for the second interval

$$\Delta F \approx F'(t_1)\,\Delta t.$$

Summing over all the subintervals, we get

$$\begin{array}{c} \text{Total change in } F(t) \\ \text{between } t = a \text{ and } t = b \end{array} = \sum_{i=0}^{n-1} \Delta F \approx \sum_{i=0}^{n-1} F'(t_i)\,\Delta t.$$

We have approximated the change in $F(t)$ as a left-hand sum.

However, the total change in $F(t)$ between the times $t = a$ and $t = b$ is simply $F(b) - F(a)$. Taking the limit as n goes to infinity converts the Riemann sum to a definite integral and suggests the following interpretation of the Fundamental Theorem of Calculus:[3]

---

[2]This result is sometimes called the First Fundamental Theorem of Calculus, to distinguish it from the Second Fundamental Theorem of Calculus discussed in Section 6.4.

[3]We could equally well have used a right-hand sum, since the definite integral is their common limit.

$$F(b) - F(a) = \begin{array}{c} \text{Total change in } F(t) \\ \text{between } t = a \text{ and } t = b \end{array} = \int_a^b F'(t)\, dt.$$

In words, the definite integral of a rate of change gives the total change.

This argument does not, however, constitute a proof of the Fundamental Theorem. The errors in the various approximations must be investigated using the definition of limit. A proof is given in Section 6.4 where we learn how to construct antiderivatives using the Second Fundamental Theorem of Calculus.

Example 1   If $F'(t) = f(t)$ and $f(t)$ is velocity in miles/hour, with t in hours, what are the units of $\int_a^b f(t)\, dt$ and $F(b) - F(a)$?

Solution   Since the units of $f(t)$ are miles/hour and the units of t are hours, the units of $\int_a^b f(t)\, dt$ are (miles/hour) $\times$ hours $=$ miles. Since F measures change in position, the units of $F(b) - F(a)$ are miles. As expected, the units of $\int_a^b f(t)\, dt$ and $F(b) - F(a)$ are the same.

The Definite Integral of a Rate of Change: Applications of the Fundamental Theorem

Many applications are based on the Fundamental Theorem, which tells us that the definite integral of a rate of change gives the total change.

Example 2   Let $F(t)$ represent a bacteria population which is 5 million at time $t = 0$. After t hours, the population is growing at an instantaneous rate of 2^t million bacteria per hour. Estimate the total increase in the bacteria population during the first hour, and the population at $t = 1$.

Solution   Since the rate at which the population is growing is $F'(t) = 2^t$, we have

$$\text{Change in population} = F(1) - F(0) = \int_0^1 2^t\, dt.$$

Using a calculator to evaluate the integral,

$$\text{Change in population} = \int_0^1 2^t\, dt = 1.44 \text{ million bacteria}.$$

Since $F(0) = 5$, the population at $t = 1$ is given by

$$\text{Population} = F(1) = F(0) + \int_0^1 2^t\, dt = 5 + 1.44 = 6.44 \text{ million}.$$

The following example shows how representing a quantity as a definite integral, and thereby as an area, can be helpful even if we don't evaluate the integral.

Example 3   Two cars start from rest at a traffic light and accelerate for several minutes. Figure 5.40 shows their velocities as a function of time.

(a)   Which car is ahead after one minute?   (b)   Which car is ahead after two minutes?

Figure 5.40: Velocities of two cars in Example 3.
Which is ahead when?

Solution
(a) For the first minute car 1 goes faster than car 2, and therefore car 1 must be ahead at the end of one minute.

(b) At the end of two minutes the situation is less clear, since car 1 was going faster for the first minute and car 2 for the second. However, if $v = f(t)$ is the velocity of a car after t minutes, then we know that

$$\text{Distance traveled in two minutes} = \int_0^2 f(t)\, dt,$$

since the integral of velocity is distance traveled. This definite integral may also be interpreted as the area under the graph of f between 0 and 2. Since the area representing the distance traveled by car 2 is clearly larger than the area for car 1 (see Figure 5.40), we know that car 2 has traveled farther than car 1.

Example 4
Biological activity in water is reflected in the rate at which carbon dioxide, CO_2, is added or removed. Plants take CO_2 out of the water during the day for photosynthesis and put CO_2 into the water at night. Animals put CO_2 into the water all the time as they breathe. Figure 5.41 shows the rate of change of the CO_2 level in a pond.[4] At dawn, there were 2.600 mmol of CO_2 per liter of water.

(a) At what time was the CO_2 level lowest? Highest?

(b) Estimate how much CO_2 enters the pond during the night ($t = 12$ to $t = 24$).

(c) Estimate the CO_2 level at dusk (twelve hours after dawn).

(d) Does the CO_2 level appear to be approximately in equilibrium?

Figure 5.41: Rate at which CO_2 enters a pond over a 24-hour period

[4]Data from R. J. Beyers, *The Pattern of Photosynthesis and Respiration in Laboratory Microsystems* (Mem. 1st. Ital. Idrobiol., 1965).

Solution   Let $f(t)$ be the rate at which CO_2 is entering the water at time t and let $F(t)$ be the concentration of CO_2 in the water at time t, so $F'(t) = f(t)$.

(a) From Figure 5.41, we see $f(t)$ is negative for $0 \leq t \leq 12$, so the CO_2 level is decreasing during this interval (daytime). Since $f(t)$ is positive for $12 < t < 24$, the CO_2 level is increasing during this interval (night). The CO_2 is lowest at $t = 12$ (dusk) and highest at $t = 0$ and $t = 24$ (dawn).

(b) We want to calculate the total change in the CO_2 level in the pond, $F(24) - F(12)$. By the Fundamental Theorem of Calculus,

$$F(24) - F(12) = \int_{12}^{24} f(t) \, dt.$$

We use values of $f(t)$ from the graph (displayed in Table 5.7) to construct a left Riemann sum approximation to this integral with $n = 6$, $\Delta t = 2$:

$$\int_{12}^{24} f(t) \, dt \approx f(12) \cdot 2 + f(14) \cdot 2 + f(16) \cdot 2 + \cdots + f(22) \cdot 2$$

$$\approx (0.000)2 + (0.045)2 + (0.035)2 + \cdots + (0.012)2 = 0.278.$$

Thus, between $t = 12$ and $t = 24$,

$$\text{Change in } CO_2 \text{ level} = F(24) - F(12) = \int_{12}^{24} f(t) \, dt \approx 0.278 \text{ mmol/liter.}$$

(c) To find the CO_2 level at $t = 12$, we use the Fundamental Theorem to estimate the change in CO_2 level during the day:

$$F(12) - F(0) = \int_0^{12} f(t) \, dt$$

Using a left Riemann sum as in part (b), we have

$$F(12) - F(0) = \int_0^{12} f(t) \, dt \approx -0.328.$$

Since initially there were $F(0) = 2.600$ mmol/liter, we have

$$F(12) = F(0) - 0.328 = 2.272 \text{ mmol/liter.}$$

(d) The amount of CO_2 removed during the day is represented by the area of the region below the t-axis; the amount of CO_2 added during the night is represented by the area above the t-axis. These areas look approximately equal, so the CO_2 level is approximately in equilibrium.

Using Riemann sums to estimate these areas, we find that about 0.278 mmol/l of CO_2 was released into the pond during the night and about 0.328 mmol/l of CO_2 was absorbed from the pond during the day. These quantities are sufficiently close that the difference could be due to measurement error, or to errors from the Riemann sum approximation.

Table 5.7   *Rate, $f(t)$, at which CO_2 is entering or leaving water (read from Figure 5.41)*

t	$f(t)$	t	$f(t)$	t	$f(t)$	t	$f(t)$	t	$f(t)$	t	$f(t)$
0	0.000	4	−0.039	8	−0.026	12	0.000	16	0.035	20	0.020
2	−0.044	6	−0.035	10	−0.020	14	0.045	18	0.027	22	0.012

Calculating Definite Integrals: Computational Use of the Fundamental Theorem

The Fundamental Theorem of Calculus owes its name to its central role in linking rates of change (derivatives) to total change. However, the Fundamental Theorem also provides an exact way of computing certain definite integrals.

Example 5   Compute $\int_1^3 2x\,dx$ by two different methods.

Solution   Using left- and right-hand sums, we can approximate this integral as accurately as we want. With $n = 100$, for example, the left-sum is 7.96 and the right sum is 8.04. Using $n = 500$ we learn

$$7.992 < \int_1^3 2x\,dx < 8.008.$$

The Fundamental Theorem, on the other hand, allows us to compute the integral exactly. We take $f(x) = 2x$. We know that if $F(x) = x^2$, then $F'(x) = 2x$. So we use $f(x) = 2x$ and $F(x) = x^2$ and obtain

$$\int_1^3 2x\,dx = F(3) - F(1) = 3^2 - 1^2 = 8.$$

Notice that to use the Fundamental Theorem to calculate a definite integral, we need to know the antiderivative, F. Chapter 6 discusses how antiderivatives are computed.

Exercises and Problems for Section 5.3

Exercises

1. If $f(t)$ is measured in dollars per year and t is measured in years, what are the units of $\int_a^b f(t)\,dt$?

2. If $f(t)$ is measured in meters/second^2 and t is measured in seconds, what are the units of $\int_a^b f(t)\,dt$?

3. If $f(x)$ is measured in pounds and x is measured in feet, what are the units of $\int_a^b f(x)\,dx$?

In Exercises 4–7, explain in words what the integral represents and give units.

4. $\int_1^3 v(t)\,dt$, where $v(t)$ is velocity in meters/sec and t is time in seconds.

5. $\int_0^6 a(t)\,dt$, where $a(t)$ is acceleration in km/hr^2 and t is time in hours.

6. $\int_{2005}^{2011} f(t)\,dt$, where $f(t)$ is the rate at which the world's population is growing in year t, in billion people per year.

7. $\int_0^5 s(x)\,dx$, where $s(x)$ is rate of change of salinity (salt concentration) in gm/liter per cm in sea water, and where x is depth below the surface of the water in cm.

8. For the two cars in Example 3, page 291, estimate:
   (a) The distances moved by car 1 and car 2 during the first minute.
   (b) The time at which the two cars have gone the same distance.

In Exercises 9–14, let $f(t) = F'(t)$. Write the integral $\int_a^b f(t)\,dt$ and evaluate it using the Fundamental Theorem of Calculus.

9. $F(t) = t^2$; $a = 1, b = 3$

10. $F(t) = 3t^2 + 4t$; $a = 2, b = 5$

11. $F(t) = \ln t$; $a = 1, b = 5$

12. $F(t) = \sin t$; $a = 0, b = \pi/2$

13. $F(t) = 7 \cdot 4^t$; $a = 2, b = 3$

14. $F(t) = \tan t$; $a = 0, b = \pi$

Problems

15. (a) Differentiate $x^3 + x$.
    (b) Use the Fundamental Theorem of Calculus to find
    $$\int_0^2 (3x^2 + 1)\,dx.$$

16. (a) What is the derivative of $\sin t$?
    (b) The velocity of a particle at time t is $v(t) = \cos t$. Use the Fundamental Theorem of Calculus to find the total distance traveled by the particle between $t = 0$ and $t = \pi/2$.

17. (a) If $F(t) = \frac{1}{2}\sin^2 t$, find $F'(t)$.

    (b) Find $\int_{0.2}^{0.4} \sin t \cos t \, dt$ two ways:

        (i) Numerically.

        (ii) Using the Fundamental Theorem of Calculus.

18. (a) If $F(x) = e^{x^2}$, find $F'(x)$.

    (b) Find $\int_0^1 2xe^{x^2} \, dx$ two ways:

        (i) Numerically.

        (ii) Using the Fundamental Theorem of Calculus.

19. Pollution is removed from a lake on day t at a rate of $f(t)$ kg/day.

    (a) Explain the meaning of the statement $f(12) = 500$.

    (b) If $\int_5^{15} f(t) \, dt = 4000$, give the units of the 5, the 15, and the 4000.

    (c) Give the meaning of $\int_5^{15} f(t) \, dt = 4000$.

20. Oil leaks out of a tanker at a rate of $r = f(t)$ gallons per minute, where t is in minutes. Write a definite integral expressing the total quantity of oil which leaks out of the tanker in the first hour.

21. Water is leaking out of a tank at a rate of $R(t)$ gallons/hour, where t is measured in hours.

    (a) Write a definite integral that expresses the total amount of water that leaks out in the first two hours.

    (b) In Figure 5.42, shade the region whose area represents the total amount of water that leaks out in the first two hours.

    (c) Give an upper and lower estimate of the total amount of water that leaks out in the first two hours.

Figure 5.42

22. As coal deposits are depleted, it becomes necessary to strip-mine larger areas for each ton of coal. Figure 5.43 shows the number of acres of land per million tons of coal that will be defaced during strip-mining as a function of the number of million tons removed, starting from the present day.

    (a) Estimate the total number of acres defaced in extracting the next 4 million tons of coal (measured from the present day). Draw four rectangles under the curve, and compute their area.

    (b) Re-estimate the number of acres defaced using rectangles above the curve.

    (c) Use your answers to parts (a) and (b) to get a better estimate of the actual number of acres defaced.

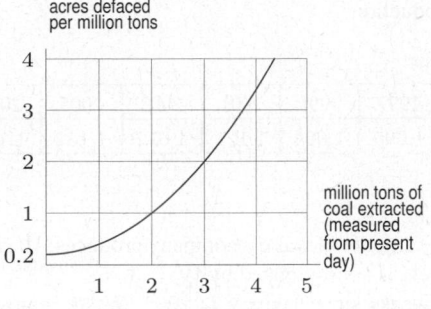

Figure 5.43

23. The rate at which the world's oil is consumed (in billions of barrels per year) is given by $r = f(t)$, where t is in years and $t = 0$ is the start of 2004.

    (a) Write a definite integral representing the total quantity of oil consumed between the start of 2004 and the start of 2009.

    (b) Between 2004 and 2009, the rate was modeled by $r = 32e^{0.05t}$. Using a left-hand sum with five subdivisions, find an approximate value for the total quantity of oil consumed between the start of 2004 and the start of 2009.

    (c) Interpret each of the five terms in the sum from part (b) in terms of oil consumption.

24. A bungee jumper leaps off the starting platform at time $t = 0$ and rebounds once during the first 5 seconds. With velocity measured downward, for t in seconds and $0 \leq t \leq 5$, the jumper's velocity is approximated[5] by $v(t) = -4t^2 + 16t$ meters/sec.

    (a) How many meters does the jumper travel during the first five seconds?

    (b) Where is the jumper relative to the starting position at the end of the five seconds?

    (c) What does $\int_0^5 v(t) \, dt$ represent in terms of the jump?

25. An old rowboat has sprung a leak. Water is flowing into the boat at a rate, $r(t)$, given in the table.

    (a) Compute upper and lower estimates for the volume of water that has flowed into the boat during the 15 minutes.

    (b) Draw a graph to illustrate the lower estimate.

t minutes	0	5	10	15
$r(t)$ liters/min	12	20	24	16

[5]Based on www.itforus.oeiizk.waw.pl/tresc/activ//modules/bj.pdf. Accessed Feb 12, 2012.

26. Annual coal production in the US (in billion tons per year) is given in the table.[6] Estimate the total amount of coal produced in the US between 1997 and 2009. If $r = f(t)$ is the rate of coal production t years since 1997, write an integral to represent the 1997–2009 coal production.

Year	1997	1999	2001	2003	2005	2007	2009
Rate	1.090	1.094	1.121	1.072	1.132	1.147	1.073

27. The amount of waste a company produces, W, in tons per week, is approximated by $W = 3.75e^{-0.008t}$, where t is in weeks since January 1, 2005. Waste removal for the company costs \$15/ton. How much does the company pay for waste removal during the year 2005?

28. A two-day environmental cleanup started at 9 am on the first day. The number of workers fluctuated as shown in Figure 5.44. If the workers were paid \$10 per hour, how much was the total personnel cost of the cleanup?

Figure 5.44

29. Suppose in Problem 28 that the workers were paid \$10 per hour for work during the time period 9 am to 5 pm and were paid \$15 per hour for work during the rest of the day. What would the total personnel costs of the cleanup have been under these conditions?

30. A warehouse charges its customers \$5 per day for every 10 cubic feet of space used for storage. Figure 5.45 records the storage used by one company over a month. How much will the company have to pay?

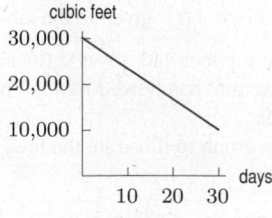

Figure 5.45

31. A cup of coffee at $90°C$ is put into a $20°C$ room when $t = 0$. The coffee's temperature is changing at a rate of $r(t) = -7e^{-0.1t}$ °C per minute, with t in minutes. Estimate the coffee's temperature when $t = 10$.

32. Water is pumped out of a holding tank at a rate of $5 - 5e^{-0.12t}$ liters/minute, where t is in minutes since the pump is started. If the holding tank contains 1000 liters of water when the pump is started, how much water does it hold one hour later?

Problems 33–34 concern the graph of f' in Figure 5.46.

Figure 5.46: Graph of f', not f

33. Which is greater, $f(0)$ or $f(1)$?

34. List the following in increasing order:
$$\frac{f(4) - f(2)}{2}, \quad f(3) - f(2), \quad f(4) - f(3).$$

35. A force F parallel to the x-axis is given by the graph in Figure 5.47. Estimate the work, W, done by the force, where $W = \int_0^{16} F(x)\, dx$.

Figure 5.47

36. Let $f(1) = 7, f'(t) = e^{-t^2}$. Use left- and right-hand sums of 5 rectangles each to estimate $f(2)$.

37. The graph of a continuous function f is given in Figure 5.48. Rank the following integrals in ascending numerical order. Explain your reasons.

(i) $\int_0^2 f(x)\, dx$ (ii) $\int_0^1 f(x)\, dx$

(iii) $\int_0^2 (f(x))^{1/2}\, dx$ (iv) $\int_0^2 (f(x))^2\, dx$.

Figure 5.48

[6]http://www.eia.doe.gov/cneaf/coal/page/special/tbl1.html. Accessed May 2011.

38. The graphs in Figure 5.49 represent the velocity, v, of a particle moving along the x-axis for time $0 \leq t \leq 5$. The vertical scales of all graphs are the same. Identify the graph showing which particle:

(a) Has a constant acceleration.
(b) Ends up farthest to the left of where it started.
(c) Ends up the farthest from its starting point.
(d) Experiences the greatest initial acceleration.
(e) Has the greatest average velocity.
(f) Has the greatest average acceleration.

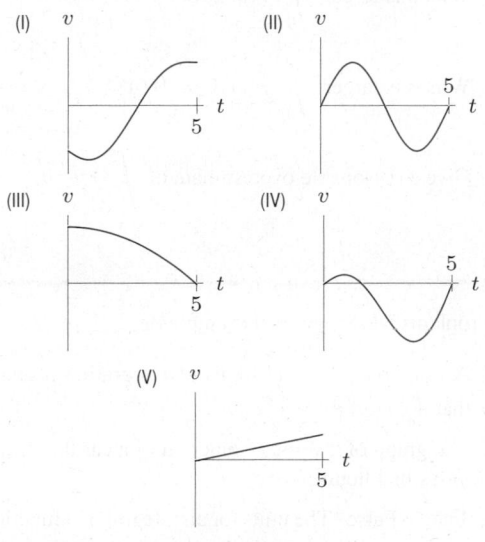

Figure 5.49

39. A car speeds up at a constant rate from 10 to 70 mph over a period of half an hour. Its fuel efficiency (in miles per gallon) increases with speed; values are in the table. Make lower and upper estimates of the quantity of fuel used during the half hour.

Speed (mph)	10	20	30	40	50	60	70
Fuel efficiency (mpg)	15	18	21	23	24	25	26

In Problems 40–41, oil is pumped from a well at a rate of $r(t)$ barrels per day. Assume that t is in days, $r'(t) < 0$ and $t_0 > 0$.

40. What does the value of $\int_0^{t_0} r(t)\, dt$ tells us about the oil well?

41. Rank in order from least to greatest:

$$\int_0^{2t_0} r(t)\, dt, \int_{t_0}^{2t_0} r(t)\, dt, \int_{2t_0}^{3t_0} r(t)\, dt.$$

42. Height velocity graphs are used by endocrinologists to follow the progress of children with growth deficiencies. Figure 5.50 shows the height velocity curves of an average boy and an average girl between ages 3 and 18.

(a) Which curve is for girls and which is for boys? Explain how you can tell.
(b) About how much does the average boy grow between ages 3 and 10?
(c) The growth spurt associated with adolescence and the onset of puberty occurs between ages 12 and 15 for the average boy and between ages 10 and 12.5 for the average girl. Estimate the height gained by each average child during this growth spurt.
(d) When fully grown, about how much taller is the average man than the average woman? (The average boy and girl are about the same height at age 3.)

Figure 5.50

In Problems 43–45, evaluate the expressions using Table 5.8. Give exact values if possible; otherwise, make the best possible estimates using left-hand Riemann sums.

Table 5.8

t	0.0	0.1	0.2	0.3	0.4	0.5
$f(t)$	0.3	0.2	0.2	0.3	0.4	0.5
$g(t)$	2.0	2.9	5.1	5.1	3.9	0.8

43. $\displaystyle\int_0^{0.5} f(t)\, dt$

44. $\displaystyle\int_{0.2}^{0.5} g'(t)\, dt$

45. $\displaystyle\int_0^{0.3} g\left(f(t)\right)\, dt$

In Problems 46–48, let $C(n)$ be a city's cost, in millions of dollars, for plowing the roads, when n inches of snow have fallen. Let $c(n) = C'(n)$. Evaluate the expressions and interpret your answers in terms of the cost of plowing snow, given

$$c'(n) < 0, \qquad \int_0^{15} c(n)\, dn = 7.5, \qquad c(15) = 0.7,$$

$$c(24) = 0.4, \qquad\qquad C(15) = 8, \qquad C(24) = 13.$$

46. $\displaystyle\int_{15}^{24} c(n)\, dn$

47. $C(0)$

48. $\displaystyle c(15) + \int_{15}^{24} c'(n)\, dn$

Problems 49–51 refer to a May 2, 2010, article:[7]

"The crisis began around 10 am yesterday when a 10-foot wide pipe in Weston sprang a leak, which worsened throughout the afternoon and eventually cut off Greater Boston from the Quabbin Reservoir, where most of its water supply is stored…Before water was shut off to the ruptured pipe [at 6:40 pm], brown water had been roaring from a massive crater [at a rate of] 8 million gallons an hour rushing into the nearby Charles River."

Let $r(t)$ be the rate in gallons/hr that water flowed from the pipe t hours after it sprang its leak.

49. Which is larger: $\displaystyle\int_0^2 r(t)\, dt$ or $\displaystyle\int_2^4 r(t)\, dt$?

50. Which is larger: $\displaystyle\int_0^4 r(t)\, dt$ or $4r(4)$?

51. Give a reasonable overestimate of $\displaystyle\int_0^8 r(t)\, dt$.

Strengthen Your Understanding

In Problems 52–53, explain what is wrong with the statement.

52. If $f(t)$ represents the rate, in lbs per year, at which a dog gains weight t years after it is born, then $\int_0^4 f(t)dt$ represents the weight of the dog when the dog is four years old.

53. If $f(x) = \sqrt{x}$ the Fundamental Theorem of Calculus states that $\int_4^9 \sqrt{x}\, dx = \sqrt{9} - \sqrt{4}$.

In Problems 54–55, give an example of:

54. A function $f(x)$ and limits of integration a and b such that $\int_a^b f(x)\, dx = e^4 - e^2$.

55. The graph of a velocity function of a car that travels 200 miles in 4 hours.

56. True or False? The units for an integral of a function $f(x)$ are the same as the units for $f(x)$.

5.4 THEOREMS ABOUT DEFINITE INTEGRALS

Properties of the Definite Integral

For the definite integral $\int_a^b f(x)\, dx$, we have so far only considered the case $a < b$. We now allow $a \geq b$. We still set $x_0 = a$, $x_n = b$, and $\Delta x = (b-a)/n$. As before, we have $\int_a^b f(x)dx = \lim_{n \to \infty} \sum_{i=1}^n f(x_i)\Delta x$.

Theorem 5.2: Properties of Limits of Integration

If a, b, and c are any numbers and f is a continuous function, then

1. $\displaystyle\int_b^a f(x)\, dx = -\int_a^b f(x)\, dx.$

2. $\displaystyle\int_a^c f(x)\, dx + \int_c^b f(x)\, dx = \int_a^b f(x)\, dx.$

In words:
   1. The integral from b to a is the negative of the integral from a to b.
   2. The integral from a to c plus the integral from c to b is the integral from a to b.

---

[7]"A catastrophic rupture hits region's water system," *The Boston Globe*, May 2, 2010.

By interpreting the integrals as areas, we can justify these results for $f \geq 0$. In fact, they are true for all functions for which the integrals make sense.

Why is $\int_b^a f(x)\,dx = -\int_a^b f(x)\,dx$?

By definition, both integrals are approximated by sums of the form $\sum f(x_i)\Delta x$. The only difference in the sums for $\int_b^a f(x)\,dx$ and $\int_a^b f(x)\,dx$ is that in the first $\Delta x = (a-b)/n = -(b-a)/n$ and in the second $\Delta x = (b-a)/n$. Since everything else about the sums is the same, we must have $\int_b^a f(x)\,dx = -\int_a^b f(x)\,dx$.

Why is $\int_a^c f(x)\,dx + \int_c^b f(x)\,dx = \int_a^b f(x)\,dx$?

Suppose $a < c < b$. Figure 5.51 suggests that $\int_a^c f(x)\,dx + \int_c^b f(x)\,dx = \int_a^b f(x)\,dx$ since the area under f from a to c plus the area under f from c to b together make up the whole area under f from a to b.

This property holds for all numbers a, b, and c, not just those satisfying $a < c < b$. (See Figure 5.52.) For example, the area under f from 3 to 6 is equal to the area from 3 to 8 *minus* the area from 6 to 8, so

$$\int_3^6 f(x)\,dx = \int_3^8 f(x)\,dx - \int_6^8 f(x)\,dx = \int_3^8 f(x)\,dx + \int_8^6 f(x)\,dx.$$

Figure 5.51: Additivity of the definite integral $(a < c < b)$

Figure 5.52: Additivity of the definite integral $(a < b < c)$

Example 1   Given that $\int_0^{1.25} \cos(x^2)\,dx = 0.98$ and $\int_0^1 \cos(x^2)\,dx = 0.90$, what are the values of the following integrals? (See Figure 5.53.)

(a) $\displaystyle\int_1^{1.25} \cos(x^2)\,dx$ (b) $\displaystyle\int_{-1}^1 \cos(x^2)\,dx$ (c) $\displaystyle\int_{1.25}^{-1} \cos(x^2)\,dx$

Figure 5.53: Graph of $f(x) = \cos(x^2)$

Solution   (a) Since, by the additivity property,

$$\int_0^{1.25} \cos(x^2)\,dx = \int_0^1 \cos(x^2)\,dx + \int_1^{1.25} \cos(x^2)\,dx,$$

we get

$$0.98 = 0.90 + \int_1^{1.25} \cos(x^2)\,dx,$$

so

$$\int_1^{1.25} \cos(x^2)\,dx = 0.08.$$

(b) By the additivity property, we have

$$\int_{-1}^{1} \cos(x^2)\, dx = \int_{-1}^{0} \cos(x^2)\, dx + \int_{0}^{1} \cos(x^2)\, dx.$$

By the symmetry of $\cos(x^2)$ about the y-axis,

$$\int_{-1}^{0} \cos(x^2)\, dx = \int_{0}^{1} \cos(x^2)\, dx = 0.90.$$

So

$$\int_{-1}^{1} \cos(x^2)\, dx = 0.90 + 0.90 = 1.80.$$

(c) Using both properties in Theorem 5.2, we have

$$\int_{1.25}^{-1} \cos(x^2)\, dx = -\int_{-1}^{1.25} \cos(x^2)\, dx = -\left(\int_{-1}^{0} \cos(x^2)\, dx + \int_{0}^{1.25} \cos(x^2)\, dx \right)$$
$$= -(0.90 + 0.98) = -1.88.$$

Theorem 5.3: Properties of Sums and Constant Multiples of the Integrand

Let f and g be continuous functions and let c be a constant.

1. $\displaystyle\int_{a}^{b} (f(x) \pm g(x))\, dx = \int_{a}^{b} f(x)\, dx \pm \int_{a}^{b} g(x)\, dx.$

2. $\displaystyle\int_{a}^{b} cf(x)\, dx = c \int_{a}^{b} f(x)\, dx.$

In words:

1. The integral of the sum (or difference) of two functions is the sum (or difference) of their integrals.

2. The integral of a constant times a function is that constant times the integral of the function.

Why Do These Properties Hold?

Both can be visualized by thinking of the definite integral as the limit of a sum of areas of rectangles.

For property 1, suppose that f and g are positive on the interval $[a, b]$ so that the area under $f(x) + g(x)$ is approximated by the sum of the areas of rectangles like the one shaded in Figure 5.54. The area of this rectangle is

$$(f(x_i) + g(x_i))\Delta x = f(x_i)\Delta x + g(x_i)\Delta x.$$

Since $f(x_i)\Delta x$ is the area of a rectangle under the graph of f, and $g(x_i)\Delta x$ is the area of a rectangle under the graph of g, the area under $f(x) + g(x)$ is the sum of the areas under $f(x)$ and $g(x)$. For property 2, notice that multiplying a function by c stretches or shrinks the graph in the vertical direction by a factor of c. Thus, it stretches or shrinks the height of each approximating rectangle by c, and hence multiplies the area by c.

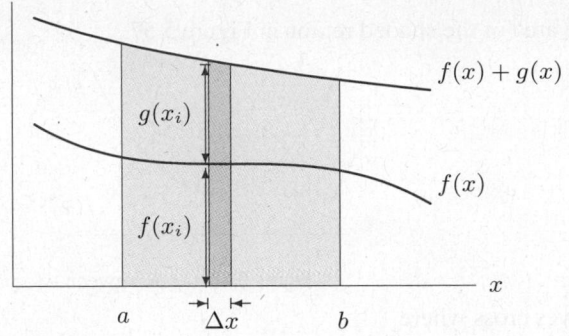

Figure 5.54: Area $= \int_a^b [f(x) + g(x)] \, dx = \int_a^b f(x) \, dx + \int_a^b g(x) \, dx$

Example 2   Evaluate the definite integral $\int_0^2 (1 + 3x) \, dx$ exactly.

Solution   We can break this integral up as follows:

$$\int_0^2 (1 + 3x) \, dx = \int_0^2 1 \, dx \; + \; \int_0^2 3x \, dx = \int_0^2 1 \, dx \; + \; 3 \int_0^2 x \, dx.$$

From Figures 5.55 and 5.56 and the area interpretation of the integral, we see that

$$\int_0^2 1 \, dx = \begin{array}{c} \text{Area of} \\ \text{rectangle} \end{array} = 2 \quad \text{and} \quad \int_0^2 x \, dx = \begin{array}{c} \text{Area of} \\ \text{triangle} \end{array} = \frac{1}{2} \cdot 2 \cdot 2 = 2.$$

Therefore,

$$\int_0^2 (1 + 3x) \, dx = \int_0^2 1 \, dx + 3 \int_0^2 x \, dx - 2 + 3 \cdot 2 = 8.$$

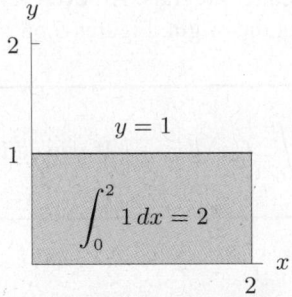

Figure 5.55: Area representing $\int_0^2 1 \, dx$

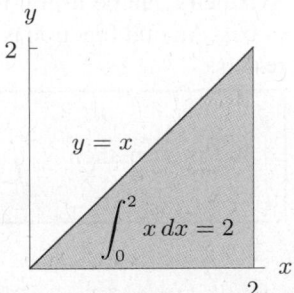

Figure 5.56: Area representing $\int_0^2 x \, dx$

Area Between Curves

Theorem 5.3 enables us to find the area of a region between curves. We have the following result:

If the graph of $f(x)$ lies above the graph of $g(x)$ for $a \le x \le b$, then

$$\begin{array}{c} \text{Area between } f \text{ and } g \\ \text{for } a \le x \le b \end{array} = \int_a^b \big(f(x) - g(x)\big) \, dx.$$

Example 3   Find the area of the shaded region in Figure 5.57.

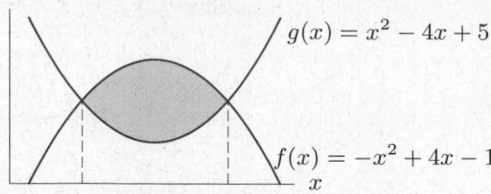

Figure 5.57: Area between two parabolas

Solution   The curves cross where

$$x^2 - 4x + 5 = -x^2 + 4x - 1$$
$$2x^2 - 8x + 6 = 0$$
$$2(x-1)(x-3) = 0$$
$$x = 1, 3.$$

Since $f(x) = -x^2 + 4x - 1$ is above $g(x) = x^2 - 4x + 5$ for x between 1 and 3, we find the shaded area by subtraction:

$$\text{Area} = \int_1^3 f(x)\,dx - \int_1^3 g(x)\,dx = \int_1^3 (f(x) - g(x))\,dx$$

$$= \int_1^3 ((-x^2 + 4x - 1) - (x^2 - 4x + 5))\,dx$$

$$= \int_1^3 (-2x^2 + 8x - 6)\,dx = 2.667.$$

Using Symmetry to Evaluate Integrals

Symmetry can be useful in evaluating definite integrals. An even function is symmetric about the y-axis. An odd function is symmetric about the origin. Figures 5.58 and 5.59 suggest the following results:

> If f is even, then $\displaystyle\int_{-a}^a f(x)\,dx = 2\int_0^a f(x)\,dx.$ If g is odd, then $\displaystyle\int_{-a}^a g(x)\,dx = 0.$

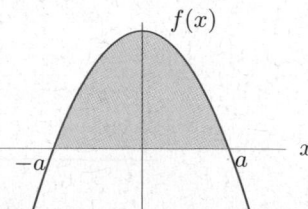

Figure 5.58: For an even function,
$\int_{-a}^a f(x)\,dx = 2\int_0^a f(x)\,dx$

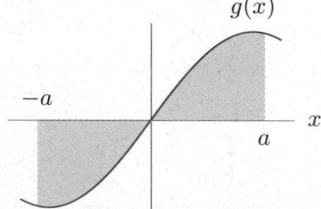

Figure 5.59: For an odd function,
$\int_{-a}^a g(x)\,dx = 0$

Example 4   Given that $\int_0^\pi \sin t\,dt = 2$, find (a) $\displaystyle\int_{-\pi}^\pi \sin t\,dt$ (b) $\displaystyle\int_{-\pi}^\pi |\sin t|\,dt$

Solution   Graphs of $\sin t$ and $|\sin t|$ are in Figures 5.60 and 5.61.

(a) Since $\sin t$ is an odd function

$$\int_{-\pi}^\pi \sin t\,dt = 0.$$

(b) Since $|\sin t|$ is an even function

$$\int_{-\pi}^{\pi} |\sin t|\, dt = 2\int_{0}^{\pi} |\sin t|\, dt = 4.$$

Figure 5.60

Figure 5.61

Comparing Integrals

Suppose we have constants m and M such that $m \le f(x) \le M$ for $a \le x \le b$. We say f is *bounded above* by M and *bounded below* by m. Then the graph of f lies between the horizontal lines $y = m$ and $y = M$. So the definite integral lies between $m(b-a)$ and $M(b-a)$. See Figure 5.62.

Suppose $f(x) \le g(x)$ for $a \le x \le b$, as in Figure 5.63. Then the definite integral of f is less than or equal to the definite integral of g. This leads us to the following results:

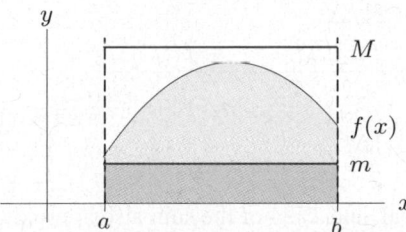

Figure 5.62: The area under the graph of f lies between the areas of the rectangles

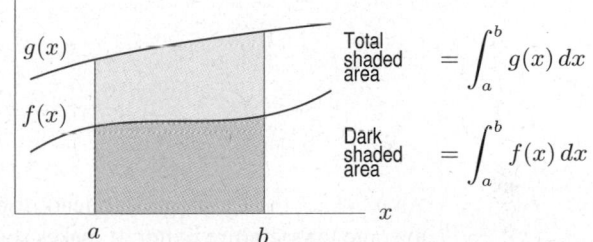

Figure 5.63: If $f(x) \le g(x)$ then $\int_a^b f(x)\, dx \le \int_a^b g(x)\, dx$

Theorem 5.4: Comparison of Definite Integrals

Let f and g be continuous functions.

1. If $m \le f(x) \le M$ for $a \le x \le b$, then $\quad m(b-a) \le \displaystyle\int_a^b f(x)\, dx \le M(b-a)$.

2. If $f(x) \le g(x)$ for $a \le x \le b$, then $\quad \displaystyle\int_a^b f(x)\, dx \le \int_a^b g(x)\, dx$.

Example 5   Explain why $\displaystyle\int_0^{\sqrt{\pi}} \sin(x^2)\, dx \le \sqrt{\pi}$.

Solution   Since $\sin(x^2) \le 1$ for all x (see Figure 5.64), part 2 of Theorem 5.4 gives

$$\int_0^{\sqrt{\pi}} \sin(x^2)\, dx \le \int_0^{\sqrt{\pi}} 1\, dx = \sqrt{\pi}.$$

Figure 5.64: Graph showing that $\int_0^{\sqrt{\pi}} \sin(x^2)\, dx < \sqrt{\pi}$

The Definite Integral as an Average

We know how to find the average of n numbers: Add them and divide by n. But how do we find the average value of a continuously varying function? Let us consider an example. Suppose $f(t)$ is the temperature at time t, measured in hours since midnight, and that we want to calculate the average temperature over a 24-hour period. One way to start is to average the temperatures at n equally spaced times, $t_1, t_2, \ldots, t_n$, during the day.

$$\text{Average temperature} \approx \frac{f(t_1) + f(t_2) + \cdots + f(t_n)}{n}.$$

The larger we make n, the better the approximation. We can rewrite this expression as a Riemann sum over the interval $0 \leq t \leq 24$ if we use the fact that $\Delta t = 24/n$, so $n = 24/\Delta t$:

$$\text{Average temperature} \approx \frac{f(t_1) + f(t_2) + \cdots + f(t_n)}{24/\Delta t}$$
$$= \frac{f(t_1)\Delta t + f(t_2)\Delta t + \cdots + f(t_n)\Delta t}{24}$$
$$= \frac{1}{24} \sum_{i=1}^{n} f(t_i)\Delta t.$$

As $n \to \infty$, the Riemann sum tends toward an integral, and $1/24$ of the sum also approximates the average temperature better. It makes sense, then, to write

$$\text{Average temperature} = \lim_{n \to \infty} \frac{1}{24} \sum_{i=1}^{n} f(t_i)\Delta t = \frac{1}{24} \int_0^{24} f(t)\, dt.$$

We have found a way of expressing the average temperature over an interval in terms of an integral. Generalizing for any function f, if $a < b$, we define

$$\begin{array}{cc} \text{Average value of } f \\ \text{from } a \text{ to } b \end{array} = \frac{1}{b-a} \int_a^b f(x)\, dx.$$

How to Visualize the Average on a Graph

The definition of average value tells us that

$$(\text{Average value of } f) \cdot (b - a) = \int_a^b f(x)\, dx.$$

Let's interpret the integral as the area under the graph of f. Then the average value of f is the height of a rectangle whose base is $(b - a)$ and whose area is the same as the area under the graph of f. (See Figure 5.65.)

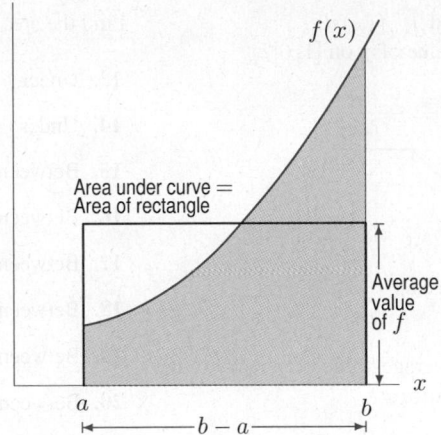

Figure 5.65: Area and average value

Example 6   Suppose that $C(t)$ represents the daily cost of heating your house, measured in dollars per day, where t is time measured in days and $t = 0$ corresponds to January 1, 2008. Interpret $\int_0^{90} C(t)\,dt$

and $\dfrac{1}{90 - 0}\int_0^{90} C(t)\,dt.$

Solution   The units for the integral $\int_0^{90} C(t)\,dt$ are (dollars/day) $\times$ (days) = dollars. The integral represents the total cost in dollars to heat your house for the first 90 days of 2008, namely the months of January, February, and March. The second expression is measured in (1/days)(dollars) or dollars per day, the same units as $C(t)$. It represents the average cost per day to heat your house during the first 90 days of 2008.

Example 7   In the year 2000, the population of Nevada was modeled by the function

$$P = f(t) = 2.020(1.036)^t,$$

where P is in millions of people and t is in years since 2000. Use this function to predict the average population of Nevada between the years 2000 and 2020.

Solution   We want the average value of $f(t)$ between $t = 0$ and $t = 20$. This is given by

$$\text{Average population} = \frac{1}{20 - 0}\int_0^{20} f(t)\,dt = \frac{1}{20}(58.748) = 2.937.$$

We used a calculator to evaluate the integral. The average population of Nevada between 2000 and 2020 is predicted to be about 2.9 million people.

Exercises and Problems for Section 5.4

Exercises

In Exercises 1–6, find the integral, given that $\int_a^b f(x)\,dx = 8$, $\int_a^b (f(x))^2\,dx = 12$, $\int_a^b g(t)\,dt = 2$, and $\int_a^b (g(t))^2\,dt = 3$.

1. $\int_a^b (f(x) + g(x))\,dx$

2. $\int_a^b cf(z)\,dz$

3. $\int_a^b \left((f(x))^2 - (g(x))^2\right)\,dx$

4. $\int_a^b (f(x))^2\,dx - \left(\int_a^b f(x)\,dx\right)^2$

5. $\int_a^b \left(c_1 g(x) + (c_2 f(x))^2\right)\,dx$

6. $\int_{a+5}^{b+5} f(x - 5)\,dx$

In Exercises 7–10, find the average value of the function over the given interval.

7. $g(t) = 1 + t$ over $[0, 2]$

8. $g(t) = e^t$ over $[0, 10]$

9. $f(x) = 2$ over $[a, b]$

10. $f(x) = 4x + 7$ over $[1, 3]$

11. (a) Using Figure 5.66, find $\int_1^6 f(x)\,dx$.
    (b) What is the average value of f on $[1, 6]$?

Figure 5.66

12. How do the units for the average value of f relate to the units for $f(x)$ and the units for x?

Find the area of the regions in Exercises 13–20.

13. Under $y = e^x$ and above $y = 1$ for $0 \le x \le 2$.

14. Under $y = 5\ln(2x)$ and above $y = 3$ for $3 \le x \le 5$.

15. Between $y = x^2$ and $y = x^3$ for $0 \le x \le 1$.

16. Between $y = x^{1/2}$ and $y = x^{1/3}$ for $0 \le x \le 1$.

17. Between $y = \sin x + 2$ and $y = 0.5$ for $6 \le x \le 10$.

18. Between $y = \cos t$ and $y = \sin t$ for $0 \le t \le \pi$.

19. Between $y = e^{-x}$ and $y = 4(x - x^2)$.

20. Between $y = e^{-x}$ and $y = \ln x$ for $1 \le x \le 2$.

Problems

21. (a) Let $\int_0^3 f(x)dx = 6$. What is the average value of $f(x)$ on the interval $x = 0$ to $x = 3$?
    (b) If $f(x)$ is even, what is $\int_{-3}^3 f(x)dx$? What is the average value of $f(x)$ on the interval $x = -3$ to $x = 3$?
    (c) If $f(x)$ is odd, what is $\int_{-3}^3 f(x)dx$? What is the average value of $f(x)$ on the interval $x = -3$ to $x = 3$?

22. Using Figure 5.67, write $\int_0^3 f(x)\,dx$ in terms of $\int_{-1}^1 f(x)\,dx$ and $\int_1^3 f(x)\,dx$.

Figure 5.67

23. (a) Assume $a \le b$. Use geometry to construct a formula in terms of a and b for
$$\int_a^b 1\,dx.$$
    (b) Use the result of part (a) to find:
    (i) $\int_2^5 1\,dx$　(ii) $\int_{-3}^8 1\,dx$　(iii) $\int_1^3 23\,dx$

24. If $\int_2^5 (2f(x) + 3)\,dx = 17$, find $\int_2^5 f(x)\,dx$.

25. The value, V, of a Tiffany lamp, worth \$225 in 1975, increases at 15% per year. Its value in dollars t years after 1975 is given by
$$V = 225(1.15)^t.$$
Find the average value of the lamp over the period 1975–2010.

26. (a) Assume that $0 \le a \le b$. Use geometry to construct a formula in terms of a and b for
$$\int_a^b x\,dx.$$
    (b) Use the result of part (a) to find:
    (i) $\int_2^5 x\,dx$　(ii) $\int_{-3}^8 x\,dx$　(iii) $\int_1^3 5x\,dx$

27. If $f(x)$ is odd and $\int_{-2}^3 f(x)\,dx = 30$, find $\int_2^3 f(x)\,dx$.

28. If $f(x)$ is even and $\int_{-2}^2 (f(x) - 3)\,dx = 8$, find $\int_0^2 f(x)\,dx$.

29. Without any computation, find $\int_{-\pi/4}^{\pi/4} x^3 \cos x^2\,dx$.

30. If the average value of f on the interval $2 \le x \le 5$ is 4, find $\int_2^5 (3f(x) + 2)\,dx$.

31. Suppose $\int_1^3 3x^2\,dx = 26$ and $\int_1^3 2x\,dx = 8$. What is $\int_1^3 (x^2 - x)\,dx$?

32. Figure 5.68 shows the rate, $f(x)$, in thousands of algae per hour, at which a population of algae is growing, where x is in hours.
    (a) Estimate the average value of the rate over the interval $x = -1$ to $x = 3$.
    (b) Estimate the total change in the population over the interval $x = -3$ to $x = 3$.

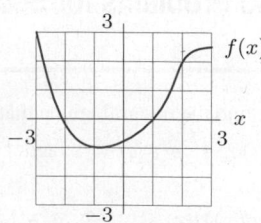

Figure 5.68

33. (a) Using Figure 5.69, estimate $\int_{-3}^{3} f(x)\, dx$.

   (b) Which of the following average values of $f(x)$ is larger?

     (i) Between $x = -3$ and $x = 3$

     (ii) Between $x = 0$ and $x = 3$

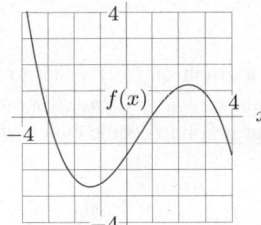

Figure 5.69

34. A bar of metal is cooling from $1000°$C to room temperature, $20°$C. The temperature, H, of the bar t minutes after it starts cooling is given, in $°$C, by

$$H = 20 + 980e^{-0.1t}.$$

   (a) Find the temperature of the bar at the end of one hour.

   (b) Find the average value of the temperature over the first hour.

   (c) Is your answer to part (b) greater or smaller than the average of the temperatures at the beginning and the end of the hour? Explain this in terms of the concavity of the graph of H.

35. In 2010, the population of Mexico[8] was growing at 1.1% a year. Assuming that this growth rate continues into the future and that t is in years since 2010, the Mexican population, P, in millions, is given by

$$P = 112(1.011)^{t}.$$

   (a) Predict the average population of Mexico between 2010 and 2050.

   (b) Find the average of the population in 2010 and the predicted population in 2050.

   (c) Explain, in terms of the concavity of the graph of P, why your answer to part (b) is larger or smaller than your answer to part (a).

36. (a) Using a graph, decide if the area under $y = e^{-x^2/2}$ between 0 and 1 is more or less than 1.

   (b) Find the area.

37. Without computation, show that $2 \le \int_{0}^{2} \sqrt{1 + x^3}\, dx \le 6$.

38. Without calculating the integral, explain why the following statements are false.

   (a) $\int_{-2}^{-1} e^{x^2}\, dx = -3$ (b) $\int_{-1}^{1} \left| \dfrac{\cos(x+2)}{1 + \tan^2 x} \right| dx = 0$

For Problems 39–42, mark the quantity on a copy of the graph of f in Figure 5.70.

Figure 5.70

39. A length representing $f(b) - f(a)$.

40. A slope representing $\dfrac{f(b) - f(a)}{b - a}$.

41. An area representing $F(b) - F(a)$, where $F' = f$.

42. A length roughly approximating

$$\frac{F(b) - F(a)}{b - a}, \text{ where } F' = f.$$

43. Using the graph of f in Figure 5.71, arrange the following quantities in increasing order, from least to greatest.

   (i) $\int_{0}^{1} f(x)\, dx$ (ii) $\int_{1}^{2} f(x)\, dx$

   (iii) $\int_{0}^{2} f(x)\, dx$ (iv) $\int_{2}^{3} f(x)\, dx$

   (v) $-\int_{1}^{2} f(x)\, dx$ (vi) The number 0

   (vii) The number 20   (viii) The number -10

Figure 5.71

44. (a) Using Figures 5.72 and 5.73, find the average value on $0 \le x \le 2$ of

     (i) $f(x)$ (ii) $g(x)$ (iii) $f(x) \cdot g(x)$

   (b) Is the following statement true? Explain your answer.

$$\text{Average}(f) \cdot \text{Average}(g) = \text{Average}(f \cdot g)$$

Figure 5.72   **Figure 5.73**

---

[8]http://www.indexmundi.com/mexico/population_growth_rate.html. Accessed April 29, 2011.

45. **(a)** Without computing any integrals, explain why the average value of $f(x) = \sin x$ on $[0, \pi]$ must be between 0.5 and 1.

(b) Compute this average.

46. Figure 5.74 shows the *standard normal distribution* from statistics, which is given by

$$\frac{1}{\sqrt{2\pi}} e^{-x^2/2}.$$

Statistics books often contain tables such as the following, which show the area under the curve from 0 to b for various values of b.

Figure 5.74

b	$\frac{1}{\sqrt{2\pi}} \int_0^b e^{-x^2/2}\, dx$
1	0.3413
2	0.4772
3	0.4987
4	0.5000

Use the information given in the table and the symmetry of the curve about the y-axis to find:

(a) $\dfrac{1}{\sqrt{2\pi}} \displaystyle\int_1^3 e^{-x^2/2}\, dx$ **(b)** $\dfrac{1}{\sqrt{2\pi}} \displaystyle\int_{-2}^3 e^{-x^2/2}\, dx$

In Problems 47–48, evaluate the expression, if possible, or say what additional information is needed, given that $\int_{-4}^4 g(x)\, dx = 12$.

47. $\displaystyle\int_0^4 g(x)\, dx$ **48.** $\displaystyle\int_{-4}^4 g(-x)\, dx$

In Problems 49–52, evaluate the expression if possible, or say what extra information is needed, given $\int_0^7 f(x)\, dx = 25$.

49. $\sqrt{\displaystyle\int_0^7 f(x)\, dx}$ **50.** $\displaystyle\int_0^{3.5} f(x)\, dx$

51. $\displaystyle\int_{-2}^5 f(x+2)\, dx$ **52.** $\displaystyle\int_0^7 (f(x)+2)\, dx$

53. **(a)** Sketch a graph of $f(x) = \sin(x^2)$ and mark on it the points $x = \sqrt{\pi}, \sqrt{2\pi}, \sqrt{3\pi}, \sqrt{4\pi}$.

(b) Use your graph to decide which of the four numbers

$$\int_0^{\sqrt{n\pi}} \sin(x^2)\, dx \quad n = 1, 2, 3, 4$$

is largest. Which is smallest? How many of the numbers are positive?

For Problems 54–56, assuming $F' = f$, mark the quantity on a copy of Figure 5.75.

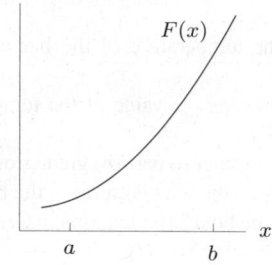

Figure 5.75

54. A slope representing $f(a)$.

55. A length representing $\displaystyle\int_a^b f(x)\, dx$.

56. A slope representing $\dfrac{1}{b-a} \displaystyle\int_a^b f(x)\, dx$.

57. In Chapter 2, the average velocity over the time interval $a \leq t \leq b$ was defined to be $(s(b) - s(a))/(b - a)$, where $s(t)$ is the position function. Use the Fundamental Theorem of Calculus to show that the average value of the velocity function $v(t)$, on the interval $a \leq t \leq b$, is also $(s(b) - s(a))/(b - a)$.

Strengthen Your Understanding

In Problems 58–60, explain what is wrong with the statement.

58. If $f(x)$ is a continuous function on $[a, b]$ such that $\int_a^b f(x)\, dx \geq 0$, then $f(x) \geq 0$ for all x in $[a, b]$.

59. If $f(x)$ is a continuous function on the interval $[a, b]$, then $\int_a^b (5 + 3f(x))\, dx = 5 + 3\int_a^b f(x)\, dx$.

60. If $f(t)$ is the population of fish in a lake on day t, then the average population over a 6-month period is given by

$$\frac{1}{6} \int_0^6 f(t)\, dt.$$

In Problems 61–63, give an example of:

61. A continuous function $f(x)$ on the interval $[0, 1]$ such that $\int_0^1 2f(x)\,dx < \int_0^1 f(x)\,dx$.

62. A continuous function $f(x)$ on the interval $[0, 4]$ such that $\int_0^4 f(x)\,dx = 0$, but $f(x)$ is not equal to 0 everywhere on $[0, 4]$.

63. An expression involving a definite integral that can be interpreted as the average speed for a car over a 5-hour journey.

In Problems 64–78, are the statements true for all continuous functions $f(x)$ and $g(x)$? Give an explanation for your answer.

64. If $\int_0^2 (f(x) + g(x))\,dx = 10$ and $\int_0^2 f(x)\,dx = 3$, then $\int_0^2 g(x)\,dx - 7$.

65. If $\int_0^2 (f(x) + g(x))\,dx = 10$, then $\int_0^2 f(x)\,dx = 3$ and $\int_0^2 g(x)\,dx = 7$.

66. If $\int_0^2 f(x)\,dx = 6$, then $\int_0^4 f(x)\,dx = 12$.

67. If $\int_0^2 f(x)\,dx = 6$ and $g(x) = 2f(x)$, then $\int_0^2 g(x)\,dx = 12$.

68. If $\int_0^2 f(x)\,dx = 6$ and $h(x) = f(5x)$, then $\int_0^2 h(x)\,dx = 30$.

69. If $a = b$, then $\int_a^b f(x)\,dx = 0$.

70. If $a \neq b$, then $\int_a^b f(x)\,dx \neq 0$.

71. $\int_1^2 f(x)\,dx + \int_2^3 g(x)\,dx = \int_1^3 (f(x) + g(x))\,dx$.

72. $\int_{-1}^1 f(x)\,dx = 2\int_0^1 f(x)\,dx$.

73. If $f(x) \leq g(x)$ on the interval $[a, b]$, then the average value of f is less than or equal to the average value of g on the interval $[a, b]$.

74. The average value of f on the interval $[0, 10]$ is the average of the average value of f on $[0, 5]$ and the average value of f on $[5, 10]$.

75. If $a < c < d < b$, then the average value of f on the interval $[c, d]$ is less than the average value of f on the interval $[a, b]$.

76. Suppose that A is the average value of f on the interval $[1, 4]$ and B is the average value of f on the interval $[4, 9]$. Then the average value of f on $[1, 9]$ is the weighted average $(3/8)A + (5/8)B$.

77. On the interval $[a, b]$, the average value of $f(x) + g(x)$ is the average value of $f(x)$ plus the average value of $g(x)$.

78. The average value of the product, $f(x)g(x)$, of two functions on an interval equals the product of the average values of $f(x)$ and $g(x)$ on the interval.

79. Which of the following statements follow directly from the rule

$$\int_a^b (f(x) + g(x))\,dx = \int_a^b f(x)\,dx + \int_a^b g(x)\,dx?$$

(a) If $\int_a^b (f(x) + g(x))\,dx = 5 + 7$, then $\int_a^b f(x)\,dx = 5$ and $\int_a^b g(x)\,dx = 7$.

(b) If $\int_a^b f(x)\,dx = \int_a^b g(x)\,dx = 7$, then $\int_a^b (f(x) + g(x))\,dx = 14$.

(c) If $h(x) = f(x) + g(x)$, then $\int_a^b (h(x) - g(x))\,dx = \int_a^b h(x)\,dx - \int_a^b g(x)\,dx$.

CHAPTER SUMMARY (see also Ready Reference at the end of the book)

- **Definite integral as limit of right or left sums**
- **Fundamental Theorem of Calculus**
- **Interpretations of the definite integral**
  Area, total change from rate of change, change in position given velocity, $(b - a) \cdot$ average value.
- **Properties of the definite integral**

Properties involving integrand, properties involving limits, comparison between integrals.

- **Working with the definite integral**
  Estimate definite integral from graph, table of values, or formula. Units of the definite integral.
- **Theorems about definite integrals**

REVIEW EXERCISES AND PROBLEMS FOR CHAPTER FIVE

Exercises

1. A car comes to a stop six seconds after the driver applies the brakes. While the brakes are on, the velocities recorded are in Table 5.9.

Table 5.9

Time since brakes applied (sec)	0	2	4	6
Velocity (ft/sec)	88	45	16	0

(a) Give lower and upper estimates for the distance the car traveled after the brakes were applied.

(b) On a sketch of velocity against time, show the lower and upper estimates of part (a).

2. A student is speeding down Route 11 in his fancy red Porsche when his radar system warns him of an obstacle 400 feet ahead. He immediately applies the brakes, starts to slow down, and spots a skunk in the road directly ahead of him. The "black box" in the Porsche records the car's speed every two seconds, producing the following table. The speed decreases throughout the 10 seconds it takes to stop, although not necessarily at a constant rate.

Time since brakes applied (sec)	0	2	4	6	8	10
Speed (ft/sec)	100	80	50	25	10	0

(a) What is your best estimate of the total distance the student's car traveled before coming to rest?

(b) Which one of the following statements can you justify from the information given?

(i) The car stopped before getting to the skunk.

(ii) The "black box" data is inconclusive. The skunk may or may not have been hit.

(iii) The skunk was hit by the car.

3. Use Figure 5.76 to estimate $\int_0^3 f(x)\,dx$.

Figure 5.76   **Figure 5.77**

4. Use Figure 5.77 to estimate $\int_{-15}^{20} f(x)\,dx$.

5. Using the table, estimate $\int_0^{100} f(t)\,dt$.

t	0	20	40	60	80	100
$f(t)$	1.2	2.8	4.0	4.7	5.1	5.2

6. A village wishes to measure the quantity of water that is piped to a factory during a typical morning. A gauge on the water line gives the flow rate (in cubic meters per hour) at any instant. The flow rate is about 100 m³/hr at 6 am and increases steadily to about 280 m³/hr at 9 am.

(a) Using only this information, give your best estimate of the total volume of water used by the factory between 6 am and 9 am.

(b) How often should the flow rate gauge be read to obtain an estimate of this volume to within 6 m³?

7. You jump out of an airplane. Before your parachute opens you fall faster and faster, but your acceleration decreases as you fall because of air resistance. The table gives your acceleration, a (in m/sec²), after t seconds.

t	0	1	2	3	4	5
a	9.81	8.03	6.53	5.38	4.41	3.61

(a) Give upper and lower estimates of your speed at $t = 5$.

(b) Get a new estimate by taking the average of your upper and lower estimates. What does the concavity of the graph of acceleration tell you about your new estimate?

In Exercises 8–9, let $f(t) = F'(t)$. Write the integral $\int_a^b f(t)\,dt$ and evaluate it using the Fundamental Theorem of Calculus.

8. $F(t) = t^4$, $a = -1$, $b = 1$

9. $F(t) = 3t^4 - 5t^3 + 5t$; $a = -2$, $b = 1$

Find the area of the regions in Exercises 10–16.

10. Between the parabola $y = 4 - x^2$ and the x-axis.

11. Between $y = x^2 - 9$ and the x-axis.

12. Under one arch of $y = \sin x$ and above the x-axis.

13. Between the line $y = 1$ and one arch of $y = \sin \theta$.

14. Between $y = -x^2 + 5x - 4$ and the x-axis, $0 \le x \le 3$.

15. Between $y = \cos x + 7$ and $y = \ln(x - 3)$, $5 \le x \le 7$.

16. Above the curve $y = -e^x + e^{2(x-1)}$ and below the x-axis, for $x \ge 0$.

Problems

17. Find $\int_{-1}^1 |x|\,dx$ geometrically.

18. A car accelerates smoothly from 0 to 60 mph in 10 seconds with the velocity given in Figure 5.78. Estimate how far the car travels during the 10-second period.

Figure 5.78

19. A car going 80 ft/sec (about 55 mph) brakes to a stop in 8 seconds. Its velocity is recorded every 2 seconds and is given in the following table.

(a) Give your best estimate of the distance traveled by the car during the 8 seconds.

(b) To estimate the distance traveled accurate to within 20 feet, how often should you record the velocity?

t (seconds)	0	2	4	6	8
$v(t)$ (ft/sec)	80	52	28	10	0

20. Using the graph of $2 + \cos x$, for $0 \leq x \leq 4\pi$, list the following quantities in increasing order: the value of the integral $\int_0^{4\pi} (2 + \cos x)\, dx$, the left sum with $n = 2$ subdivisions, and the right sum with $n = 2$ subdivisions.

21. Your velocity is $v(t) = \sin(t^2)$ mph for t in hours, $0 \leq t \leq 1.1$. Find the distance traveled during this time.

22. Your velocity is $v(t) = \ln(t^2 + 1)$ ft/sec for t in seconds, $0 \leq t \leq 3$. Find the distance traveled during this time.

23. The following table gives the emissions, E, of nitrogen oxides in millions of metric tons per year in the US.[9] Let t be the number of years since 1970 and $E = f(t)$.

   (a) What are the units and meaning of $\int_0^{30} f(t)\,dt$?
   (b) Estimate $\int_0^{30} f(t)\,dt$.

Year	1970	1975	1980	1985	1990	1995	2000
E	26.9	26.4	27.1	25.8	25.5	25.0	22.6

24. After a spill of radioactive iodine, measurements showed the ambient radiation levels at the site of the spill to be four times the maximum acceptable limit. The level of radiation from an iodine source decreases according to the formula
$$R(t) = R_0 e^{-0.004t}$$
where R is the radiation level (in millirems/hour) at time t in hours and R_0 is the initial radiation level (at $t = 0$).

   (a) How long will it take for the site to reach an acceptable level of radiation?
   (b) How much total radiation (in millirems) will have been emitted by that time, assuming the maximum acceptable limit is 0.6 millirems/hour?

25. Coal gas is produced at a gasworks. Pollutants in the gas are removed by scrubbers, which become less and less efficient as time goes on. The following measurements, made at the start of each month, show the rate at which pollutants are escaping (in tons/month) in the gas:

Time (months)	0	1	2	3	4	5	6
Rate pollutants escape	5	7	8	10	13	16	20

   (a) Make an overestimate and an underestimate of the total quantity of pollutants that escape during the first month.
   (b) Make an overestimate and an underestimate of the total quantity of pollutants that escape during the six months.
   (c) How often would measurements have to be made to find overestimates and underestimates which differ by less than 1 ton from the exact quantity of pollutants that escaped during the first six months?

26. Figure 5.79 shows the rate of change of the quantity of water in a water tower, in liters per day, during the month of April. If the tower had 12,000 liters of water in it on April 1, estimate the quantity of water in the tower on April 30.

rate (liters/day)

Figure 5.79

27. For the function f in Figure 5.80, write an expression involving one or more definite integrals of f that denote:

   (a) The average value of f for $0 \leq x \leq 5$.
   (b) The average value of $|f|$ for $0 \leq x \leq 5$.

Figure 5.80

28. For the even function f in Figure 5.80, consider the average value of f over the following intervals:

   I. $0 \leq x \leq 1$ II. $0 \leq x \leq 2$
   III. $0 \leq x \leq 5$ IV. $-2 \leq x \leq 2$

   (a) For which interval is the average value of f least?
   (b) For which interval is the average value of f greatest?
   (c) For which pair of intervals are the average values equal?

29. (a) Suppose $f'(x) = \sin(x^2)$ and $f(0) = 2$. Use a graph of $f'(x)$ to decide which is larger:
   (i) $f(0)$ or $f(1)$ (ii) $f(2)$ or $f(2.5)$

   (b) Estimate $f(b)$ for $b = 0, 1, 2, 3$.

30. (a) If $F(t) = t(\ln t) - t$, find $F'(t)$.

   (b) Find $\int_{10}^{12} \ln t \, dt$ two ways:
   (i) Numerically.
   (ii) Using the Fundamental Theorem of Calculus.

---

[9]*The World Almanac and Book of Facts 2005*, p. 177 (New York: World Almanac Books).

31. Statisticians sometimes use values of the function

$$F(b) = \int_0^b e^{-x^2}\, dx.$$

(a) What is $F(0)$?

(b) Does the value of F increase or decrease as b increases? (Assume $b \geq 0$.)

(c) Find $F(1)$, $F(2)$, and $F(3)$.

In Problems 32–35, find $\int_2^5 f(x)\, dx$.

32. $f(x)$ is odd and $\int_{-2}^5 f(x)\, dx = 8$

33. $f(x)$ is even, $\int_{-2}^2 f(x)\, dx = 6$, and $\int_{-5}^5 f(x)\, dx = 14$

34. $\int_2^5 (3f(x) + 4)\, dx = 18$

35. $\int_2^4 2f(x)\, dx = 8$ and $\int_5^4 f(x)\, dx = 1$

36. Without any computation, find the values of

(a) $\displaystyle\int_{-2}^2 \sin x\, dx$,   (b) $\displaystyle\int_{-\pi}^\pi x^{113}\, dx$.

37. Suppose f is periodic, its graph repeating every p units. Given that $\int_0^p f(x)\, dx > 0$, evaluate and simplify

$$\frac{\displaystyle\int_0^{2p} f(x)\, dx + \int_p^{5p} f(x)\, dx}{\displaystyle\int_{5p}^{7p} f(x)\, dx}.$$

38. The function f is even (that is, its graph is symmetric about the y-axis). Use this fact to evaluate and simplify

$$\frac{\displaystyle\int_{-r}^r f(x)\, dx + \int_0^r f(x)\, dx}{\displaystyle\int_{-r}^0 f(x)\, dx}, \quad \text{for } r > 0.$$

[Hint: Use the area interpretation of the integral.]

39. (a) Use Figure 5.81 to explain why $\int_{-3}^3 xe^{-x^2}\, dx = 0$.

(b) Find the left-hand sum approximation with $n = 3$ to $\int_0^3 xe^{-x^2}\, dx$. Give your answer to four decimal places.

(c) Repeat part (b) for $\int_{-3}^0 xe^{-x^2}\, dx$.

(d) Do your answers to parts (b) and (c) add to 0? Explain.

Figure 5.81

40. Two trains travel along parallel tracks. The velocity, v, of the trains as functions of time t are shown in Figure 5.82.

(a) Describe in words the trips taken by each train.

(b) Estimate the ratio of the following quantities for Train A to Train B:

(i) Maximum velocity   (ii) Time traveled

(iii) Distance traveled

Figure 5.82

41. Worldwide, wind energy generating capacity, W megawatts, t years after 2000, can be modeled[10] by $W = 21{,}000e^{0.22t}$.

(a) What was wind energy generating capacity in 2000? in 2010?

(b) What annual continuous percent increase is indicated by the model?

(c) Estimate average wind energy generating capacity between 2000 and 2010.

In Problems 42–45, let $r(t)$ be the rate, in kg/sec, at which a spaceship burns fuel at time t sec. Assume that $r(t) > 0$ and $r'(t) < 0$ for $0 \leq t \leq T$, where T is the time at which all the fuel has burned. Let T_h be the time at which half the fuel has burned and Q be the initial amount of fuel in kg. State which of the following two expressions is larger, or that they are equal, or that there is not enough information to decide.

42. $\displaystyle\int_0^T r(t)\, dt$ and Q

43. $\displaystyle\int_0^{0.5T} r(t)\, dt$ and $\displaystyle\int_{0.5T}^T r(t)\, dt$

44. $\displaystyle\int_0^{T/3} r(t)\, dt$ and $Q/3$

45. $\displaystyle\int_0^{T_h} r(t)\, dt$ and $\displaystyle\int_0^{0.5T} r(t)\, dt$

46. Use the property $\int_b^a f(x)\, dx = -\int_a^b f(x)\, dx$ to show that $\int_a^a f(x)\, dx = 0$.

47. The average value of $y = v(x)$ equals 4 for $1 \leq x \leq 6$, and equals 5 for $6 \leq x \leq 8$. What is the average value of $v(x)$ for $1 \leq x \leq 8$?

[10]Global Wind Energy Council - Global Trends, www.gwec.net, accessed October 2010.

48. **(a)** For any continuous function f, is
$$\int_1^2 f(x)\, dx + \int_2^3 f(x)\, dx = \int_1^3 f(x)\, dx?$$
(b) For any function f, add the left-hand sum approximation with 10 subdivisions to $\int_1^2 f(x)\, dx$ to the left-hand sum approximation with 10 subdivisions to $\int_2^3 f(x)\, dx$. Do you get the left-sum approximations with 10 subdivisions to $\int_1^3 f(x)\, dx$? If not, interpret the result as a different Riemann Sum.

49. Using Figure 5.83, list the following integrals in increasing order (from smallest to largest). Which integrals are negative, which are positive? Give reasons.

I. $\int_a^b f(x)\, dx$ II. $\int_a^c f(x)\, dx$ III. $\int_a^e f(x)\, dx$
IV. $\int_b^e f(x)\, dx$ V. $\int_b^c f(x)\, dx$

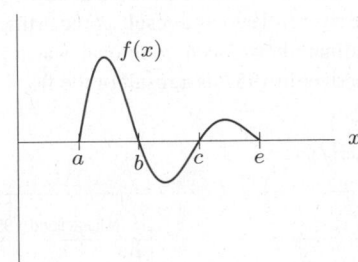

Figure 5.83

In Problems 50–52, the function $F(t)$ gives the thickness, in inches, of ice on a roof t hours after midnight, where $f(t) = F'(t)$, $f(2) = 0.5$, $F(7) = 4$, $F(9) = 5$, and

$$\int_2^{3.5} f'(t)\, dt = 0.75 \quad \text{and} \quad \int_4^7 f(t)\, dt = 1.5.$$

Evaluate the expressions and explain what your answers tell you about the ice on the roof.

50. $\int_7^9 f(t)\, dt$ **51.** $F(4)$ **52.** $F'(3.5)$

53. For the even function f graphed in Figure 5.84:

(a) Suppose you know $\int_0^2 f(x)\, dx$. What is $\int_{-2}^2 f(x)\, dx$?

(b) Suppose you know $\int_0^5 f(x)\, dx$ and $\int_2^5 f(x)\, dx$. What is $\int_0^2 f(x)\, dx$?

(c) Suppose you know $\int_{-2}^5 f(x)\, dx$ and $\int_{-2}^2 f(x)\, dx$. What is $\int_0^5 f(x)\, dx$?

Figure 5.84

54. For the even function f graphed in Figure 5.84:

(a) Suppose you know $\int_{-2}^2 f(x)\, dx$ and $\int_0^5 f(x)\, dx$. What is $\int_2^5 f(x)\, dx$?

(b) Suppose you know $\int_{-2}^5 f(x)\, dx$ and $\int_{-2}^0 f(x)\, dx$. What is $\int_2^5 f(x)\, dx$?

(c) Suppose you know $\int_2^5 f(x)\, dx$ and $\int_{-2}^5 f(x)\, dx$. What is $\int_0^2 f(x)\, dx$?

55. A mouse moves back and forth in a straight tunnel, attracted to bits of cheddar cheese alternately introduced to and removed from the ends (right and left) of the tunnel. The graph of the mouse's velocity, v, is given in Figure 5.85, with positive velocity corresponding to motion toward the right end. Assuming that the mouse starts ($t = 0$) at the center of the tunnel, use the graph to estimate the time(s) at which:

(a) The mouse changes direction.
(b) The mouse is moving most rapidly to the right; to the left.
(c) The mouse is farthest to the right of center; farthest to the left.
(d) The mouse's speed (i.e., the magnitude of its velocity) is decreasing.
(e) The mouse is at the center of the tunnel.

Figure 5.85

Problems 56–57 concern hybrid cars such as the Toyota Prius that are powered by a gas-engine, electric-motor combination, but can also function in Electric-Vehicle (EV) only mode, without power from the engine. Figure 5.86[11] shows the velocity, v, of a 2010 Prius Plug-in Hybrid Prototype operating in normal hybrid mode and EV-only mode, respectively, while accelerating from a stoplight.

Figure 5.86

56. About how far, in feet, does the 2010 Prius Prototype travel in EV-only mode during the first 15 seconds of movement?

57. Assume two identical cars, one running in normal hybrid mode and one running in EV-only mode, accelerate together in a straight path from a stoplight. Approximately how far apart are the cars after 5 seconds?

58. The Montgolfier brothers (Joseph and Etienne) were eighteenth-century pioneers in the field of hot-air ballooning. Had they had the appropriate instruments, they might have left us a record, like that shown in Figure 5.87, of one of their early experiments. The graph shows their vertical velocity, v, with upward as positive.

(a) Over what intervals was the acceleration positive? Negative?

(b) What was the greatest altitude achieved, and at what time?

(c) At what time was the upward acceleration greatest?

(d) At what time was the deceleration greatest?

(e) What might have happened during this flight to explain the answer to part (d)?

(f) This particular flight ended on top of a hill. How do you know that it did, and what was the height of the hill above the starting point?

Figure 5.87

59. The Glen Canyon Dam at the top of the Grand Canyon prevents natural flooding. In 1996, scientists decided an artificial flood was necessary to restore the environmental balance. Water was released through the dam at a controlled rate[12] shown in Figure 5.88. The figure also shows the rate of flow of the last natural flood in 1957.

(a) At what rate was water passing through the dam in 1996 before the artificial flood?

(b) At what rate was water passing down the river in the pre-flood season in 1957?

(c) Estimate the maximum rates of discharge for the 1996 and 1957 floods.

(d) Approximately how long did the 1996 flood last? How long did the 1957 flood last?

(e) Estimate how much additional water passed down the river in 1996 as a result of the artificial flood.

(f) Estimate how much additional water passed down the river in 1957 as a result of the flood.

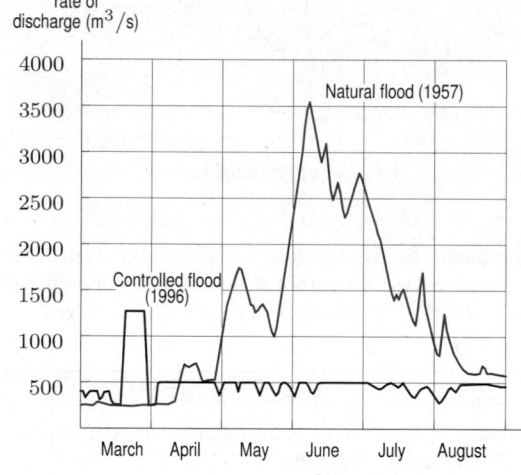

Figure 5.88

60. Using Figure 5.89, list from least to greatest,

(a) $f'(1)$.

(b) The average value of $f(x)$ on $0 \le x \le a$.

(c) The average value of the rate of change of $f(x)$, for $0 \le x \le a$.

(d) $\int_0^a f(x)\, dx$.

Figure 5.89

---

[11]www.motortrend.com/. Retrieved May 2011.
[12]Adapted from M. Collier, R. Webb, E. Andrews, "Experimental Flooding in Grand Canyon," *Scientific American* (January 1997).

In Problems 61–64, let $f(x) = F'(x)$ where, for all x,

$$f'(x) > 0 \quad \text{and} \quad f''(x) < 0.$$

Explain whether the expression gives the exact value of $f(3.1)$, an underestimate of $f(3.1)$, or an overestimate of $f(3.1)$, or if there is not enough information to decide.

61. $f(3) + 0.1f'(3)$

62. $f(3) + \displaystyle\int_3^{3.1} f'(t)\,dt$

63. $\dfrac{F(3.11) - F(3.1)}{0.01}$

64. $f(3) + \displaystyle\sum_{i=1}^{n} f'(x_i)\,\Delta x$, where $n > 0, \Delta x = 0.1/n, x_0 = 3, x_n = 3.1$, with $x_0, x_1, \ldots, x_n$ evenly spaced.

65. The number of days a cold-blooded organism, such as an insect, takes to mature depends on the surrounding temperature, H. Each organism has a minimum temperature $H_{\min}$ below which no development takes place.[13] For an interval of time, Δt, on which the temperature is constant, the increase in maturity of the organism can be measured by the number of degree-days, ΔS, where t is in days and

$$\Delta S = (H - H_{\min})\Delta t.$$

(a) If H varies with time, so $H = f(t)$, write an integral that represents the total number of degree-days, S, required if development to maturity takes T days.

(b) An organism which has $H_{\min} = 15°\text{C}$ requires 125 degree-days to develop to maturity. Estimate the development time if the temperature, $H°\text{C}$, at time t days is in Table 5.10.

Table 5.10

t	1	2	3	4	5	6	7	8	9	10	11	12
H	20	22	27	28	27	31	29	30	28	25	24	26

66. Let $\theta(x)$ be the angle of the tangent line at x of the graph of f with the horizontal, as in Figure 5.90. Show that

(a) $\tan\theta = f'(x)$

(b) $1 + (f'(x))^2 = \dfrac{1}{\cos^2\theta}$

(c) $\dfrac{d\theta}{dx} = \cos^2\theta\dfrac{d}{dx}(\tan\theta) = \dfrac{f''(x)}{1 + (f'(x))^2}$

(d) $\theta(b) - \theta(a) = \displaystyle\int_a^b \dfrac{f''(x)}{1 + (f'(x))^2}\,dx$

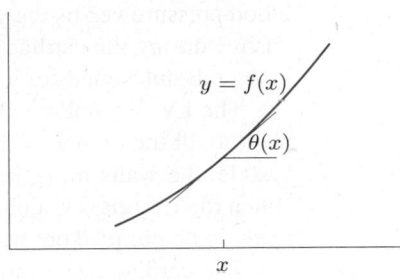

Figure 5.90

CAS Challenge Problems

67. Consider the definite integral $\int_0^1 x^4\,dx$.

(a) Write an expression for a right-hand Riemann sum approximation for this integral using n subdivisions. Express each x_i, $i = 1, 2, \ldots, n$, in terms of i.

(b) Use a computer algebra system to obtain a formula for the sum you wrote in part (a) in terms of n.

(c) Take the limit of this expression for the sum as $n \to \infty$, thereby finding the exact value of this integral.

68. Repeat Problem 67, using the definite integral $\int_0^1 x^5\,dx$.

For Problems 69–71, you will write a Riemann sum approximating a definite integral and use a computer algebra system to find a formula for the Riemann sum. By evaluating the limit of this sum as the number of subdivisions approaches infinity, you will obtain the definite integral.

69. (a) Using summation notation, write the left-hand Rie-

mann sum with n subdivisions for $\int_1^2 t\,dt$.

(b) Use a computer algebra system to find a formula for the Riemann sum.

(c) Evaluate the limit of the sum as n approaches infinity.

(d) Calculate directly the area under the graph of $y = t$ between $t = 1$ and $t = 2$, and compare it with your answer to part (c).

70. (a) Using summation notation, write the left-hand Riemann sum with n subdivisions for $\int_1^2 t^2\,dt$.

(b) Use a computer algebra system to find a formula for the Riemann sum.

(c) Evaluate the limit of the sum as n approaches infinity.

(d) What is the area under the graph of $y = t^2$ between $t = 1$ and $t = 2$?

71. (a) Using summation notation, write the right-hand Riemann sum with n subdivisions for $\int_0^\pi \sin x\,dx$.

---

[13]Information from http://www.ento.vt.edu/~sharov/PopEcol/popecol.html (Accessed Nov. 18, 2003).

(b) Use a computer algebra system to find a formula for the Riemann sum. [Note: Not all computer algebra systems can evaluate this sum.]

(c) Use a computer algebra system to evaluate the limit of the sum as n approaches infinity.

(d) Confirm your answer to part (c) by calculating the definite integral with the computer algebra system.

In Problems 72–73:

(a) Use a computer algebra system to compute the given definite integral.

(b) From your answer to part (a) and the Fundamental Theorem of Calculus, guess a function whose derivative is the integrand. Check your guess using the computer algebra system.

[Hint: Make sure that the constants a, b, and c do not have previously assigned values in your computer algebra system.]

72. $\int_a^b \sin(cx)\,dx$

73. $\int_a^c \frac{x}{1 + bx^2}\,dx, \quad b > 0$

PROJECTS FOR CHAPTER FIVE

1. **Medical Case Study: Cardiac Cycle**[14]

Physiologists who study the heart measure and plot quantities that reflect many aspects of cardiac function. One of the most famous plots is the pressure-volume loop, which shows the blood pressure versus the volume of blood in the left ventricle (LV). Both pressure and volume change during the cardiac cycle, the periodic relaxation and contraction of the heart, reflected in the lub-dub sounds of a heartbeat.

The LV is a hollow chamber with walls made of muscle. The LV pumps blood from the heart to all the organs of the body. When the LV contracts, a phase of the cardiac cycle called systole, the walls move in and blood is expelled from the heart and flows out to the organs. When the LV relaxes, a phase called diastole, its walls move out and it fills up with new blood, ready to be pumped out with the next LV contraction.

The cardiac cycle for the LV can be simplified into four phases. Points on the pressure-volume loop in Figure 5.91 represent the pressure and volume at different times during the cycle, and the arrows show the direction of change. When the LV has just finished contracting (so systole ends, and diastole begins), the volume of blood is at a minimum ($D1$). In Phase 1, isometric relaxation, the LV relaxes, causing a drop in the LV pressure, while the volume stays the same, as no new blood can flow into the LV yet. At $D2$, isometric relaxation ends and Phase 2 begins: the LV starts to fill up with new blood, causing an increase in LV volume and a small increase in pressure. At $S1$, diastole ends and the muscular walls of the LV start to contract, initiating systole. In Phase 3, isometric contraction pressure rises rapidly, but no blood is ejected yet, so LV volume remains constant. Phase 4 starts at $S2$, and blood is rapidly expelled from the LV, so the volume decreases, and there is a mild decrease in pressure. This brings the cycle back to $D1$ as systole ends and diastole is ready to begin again.

(a) For each of the four phases of the cardiac cycle, decide whether the work done by the LV wall on the blood is positive, negative, or zero.

(b) Using the units of pressure and volume, find the units of area of regions in the pressure-volume plane.

(c) Suppose Phases 2 and 4 are the graphs of two functions, $g(V)$ and $f(V)$, respectively. Explain why the integral represents the work done by the LV wall on the blood in each phase.

  (i) Phase 4, $\int_a^b f(V)\,dV$

  (ii) Phase 2, $-\int_a^b g(V)\,dV$

(d) Express the area enclosed by the pressure-volume loop as an integral. Using part (c), give the physical meaning of this area.

---

[14]From David E. Sloane, M.D.

Figure 5.91: Pressure-volume loop

2. The Car and the Truck

A car starts at noon and travels along a straight road with the velocity shown in Figure 5.92. A truck starts at 1 pm from the same place and travels along the same road at a constant velocity of 50 mph.

(a) How far away is the car when the truck starts?

(b) How fast is the distance between the car and the truck increasing or decreasing at 3 pm? What is the practical significance (in terms of the distance between the car and the truck) of the fact that the car's velocity is maximized at about 2 pm?

(c) During the period when the car is ahead of the truck, when is the distance between them greatest, and what is that greatest distance?

(d) When does the truck overtake the car, and how far have both traveled then?

(e) Suppose the truck starts at noon. (Everything else remains the same.) Sketch a new graph showing the velocities of both car and truck against time.

(f) How many times do the two graphs in part (e) intersect? What does each intersection mean in terms of the distance between the two?

Figure 5.92: Velocity of car starting at noon

3. An Orbiting Satellite

A NASA satellite orbits the earth every 90 minutes. During an orbit, the satellite's electric power comes either from solar array wings, when these are illuminated by the sun, or from batteries. The batteries discharge whenever the satellite uses more electricity than the solar array can provide or whenever the satellite is in the shadow of the earth (where the solar array cannot be used). If the batteries are overused, however, they can be damaged.[15]

---

[15]Adapted from Amy C. R. Gerson, "Electrical Engineering: Space Systems," in *She Does Math! Real Life Problems from Women on the Job*, ed. Marla Parker, p. 61 (Washington, DC: Mathematical Association of America, 1995).

You are to determine whether the batteries could be damaged in either of the following operations. You are told that the battery capacity is 50 ampere-hours. If the total battery discharge does not exceed 40% of battery capacity, the batteries will not be damaged.

(a) Operation 1 is performed by the satellite while orbiting the earth. At the beginning of a given 90-minute orbit, the satellite performs a 15-minute maneuver which requires more current than the solar array can deliver, causing the batteries to discharge. The maneuver causes a sinusoidally varying battery discharge of period 30 minutes with a maximum discharge of ten amperes at 7.5 minutes. For the next 45 minutes the solar array meets the total satellite current demand, and the batteries do not discharge. During the last 30 minutes, the satellite is in the shadow of the earth and the batteries supply the total current demand of 30 amperes.

   (i) The battery current in amperes is a function of time. Plot the function, showing the current in amperes as a function of time for the 90-minute orbit. Write a formula (or formulas) for the battery current function.

   (ii) Calculate the total battery discharge (in units of ampere-hours) for the 90-minute orbit for Operation 1.

   (iii) What is your recommendation regarding the advisability of Operation 1?

(b) Operation 2 is simulated at NASA's laboratory in Houston. The following graph was produced by the laboratory simulation of the current demands on the battery during the 90-minute orbit required for Operation 2.

Figure 5.93: Battery discharge simulation graph for Operation 2

   (i) Calculate the total battery discharge (in units of ampere-hours) for the 90-minute orbit for Operation 2.

   (ii) What is your recommendation regarding the advisability of Operation 2?

Chapter Six

CONSTRUCTING ANTIDERIVATIVES

Contents

6.1 ANTIDERIVATIVES GRAPHICALLY AND NUMERICALLY

The Family of Antiderivatives

If the derivative of F is f, we call F an *antiderivative* of f. For example, since the derivative of x^2 is $2x$, we say that

$$x^2 \text{ is an antiderivative of } 2x.$$

Notice that $2x$ has many antiderivatives, since $x^2 + 1$, $x^2 + 2$, and $x^2 + 3$, all have derivative $2x$. In fact, if C is any constant, we have

$$\frac{d}{dx}(x^2 + C) = 2x + 0 = 2x,$$

so any function of the form $x^2 + C$ is an antiderivative of $2x$. The function $f(x) = 2x$ has a *family of antiderivatives*.

Let us look at another example. If v is the velocity of a car and s is its position, then $v = ds/dt$ and s is an antiderivative of v. As before, $s + C$ is an antiderivative of v for any constant C. In terms of the car, adding C to s is equivalent to adding C to the odometer reading. Adding a constant to the odometer reading simply means measuring distance from a different point, which does not alter the car's velocity.

Visualizing Antiderivatives Using Slopes

Suppose we have the graph of f', and we want to sketch an approximate graph of f. We are looking for the graph of f whose slope at any point is equal to the value of f' there. Where f' is above the x-axis, f is increasing; where f' is below the x-axis, f is decreasing. If f' is increasing, f is concave up; if f' is decreasing, f is concave down.

Example 1   The graph of f' is given in Figure 6.1. Sketch a graph of f in the cases when $f(0) = 0$ and $f(0) = 1$.

Figure 6.1: Graph of f'

Figure 6.2: Two different f's which have the same derivative f'

Solution   For $0 \leq x \leq 2$, the function f has a constant slope of 1, so the graph of f is a straight line. For $2 \leq x \leq 4$, the function f is increasing but more and more slowly; it has a maximum at $x = 4$ and decreases thereafter. (See Figure 6.2.) The solutions with $f(0) = 0$ and $f(0) = 1$ start at different points on the vertical axis but have the same shape.

Example 2   Sketch a graph of the antiderivative F of $f(x) = e^{-x^2}$ satisfying $F(0) = 0$.

Solution   The graph of $f(x) = e^{-x^2}$ is shown in Figure 6.3. The slope of the antiderivative $F(x)$ is given by $f(x)$. Since $f(x)$ is always positive, the antiderivative $F(x)$ is always increasing. Since $f(x)$ is increasing for negative x, we know that $F(x)$ is concave up for negative x. Since $f(x)$ is decreasing for positive x, we know that $F(x)$ is concave down for positive x. Since $f(x) \to 0$ as $x \to \pm\infty$, the graph of $F(x)$ levels off at both ends. See Figure 6.4.

Figure 6.3: Graph of $f(x) = e^{-x^2}$

Figure 6.4: An antiderivative $F(x)$ of
$f(x) = e^{-x^2}$

Example 3   For the function f' given in Figure 6.5, sketch a graph of three antiderivative functions f, one with $f(0) = 0$, one with $f(0) = 1$, and one with $f(0) = 2$.

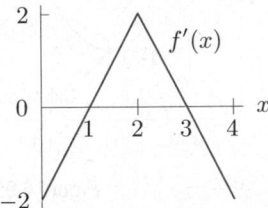

Figure 6.5: Slope function, f'

Figure 6.6: Antiderivatives f

Solution   To graph f, start at the point on the vertical axis specified by the initial condition and move with slope given by the value of f' in Figure 6.5. Different initial conditions lead to different graphs for f, but for a given x-value they all have the same slope (because the value of f' is the same for each). Thus, the different f curves are obtained from one another by a vertical shift. See Figure 6.6.

- Where f' is positive ($1 < x < 3$), we see f is increasing; where f' is negative ($0 < x < 1$ or $3 < x < 4$), we see f is decreasing.
- Where f' is increasing ($0 < x < 2$), we see f is concave up; where f' is decreasing ($2 < x < 4$), we see f is concave down.
- Where $f' = 0$, we see f has a local maximum at $x - 3$ and a local minimum at $x = 1$.
- Where f' has a maximum ($x = 2$), we see f has a point of inflection.

Computing Values of an Antiderivative Using Definite Integrals

A graph of f' shows where f is increasing and where f is decreasing. We can calculate the actual value of the function f using the Fundamental Theorem of Calculus (Theorem 5.1 on page 290): If f' is continuous, then

$$\int_a^b f'(x)\,dx = f(b) - f(a).$$

If we know $f(a)$, we can estimate $f(b)$ by computing the definite integral using area or Riemann sums.

Example 4   Figure 6.7 is the graph of the derivative $f'(x)$ of a function $f(x)$. It is given that $f(0) = 100$. Sketch the graph of $f(x)$, showing all critical points and inflection points of f and giving their coordinates.

Figure 6.7: Graph of derivative

Solution   The critical points of f occur at $x = 0$, $x = 20$, and $x = 30$, where $f'(x) = 0$. The inflection points of f occur at $x = 10$ and $x = 25$, where $f'(x)$ has a maximum or minimum. To find the coordinates of the critical points and inflection points of f, we evaluate $f(x)$ for $x = 0, 10, 20, 25, 30$. Using the Fundamental Theorem, we can express the values of $f(x)$ in terms of definite integrals. We evaluate the definite integrals using the areas of triangular regions under the graph of $f'(x)$, remembering that areas below the x-axis are subtracted. (See Figure 6.8.)

Figure 6.8: Finding $f(10) = f(0) + \int_0^{10} f'(x)\,dx$

Figure 6.9: Graph of $f(x)$

Since $f(0) = 100$, the Fundamental Theorem gives us the following values of f, which are marked in Figure 6.9.

$$f(10) = f(0) + \int_0^{10} f'(x)\,dx = 100 + (\text{Shaded area in Figure 6.8}) = 100 + \frac{1}{2}(10)(20) = 200,$$

$$f(20) = f(10) + \int_{10}^{20} f'(x)\,dx = 200 + \frac{1}{2}(10)(20) = 300,$$

$$f(25) = f(20) + \int_{20}^{25} f'(x)\,dx = 300 - \frac{1}{2}(5)(10) = 275,$$

$$f(30) = f(25) + \int_{25}^{30} f'(x)\,dx = 275 - \frac{1}{2}(5)(10) = 250.$$

Example 5   Suppose $F'(t) = t \cos t$ and $F(0) = 2$. Find $F(b)$ at the points $b = 0, 0.1, 0.2, \ldots, 1.0$.

Solution   We apply the Fundamental Theorem with $f(t) = t \cos t$ and $a = 0$ to get values for $F(b)$:

$$F(b) - F(0) = \int_0^b F'(t)\,dt = \int_0^b t \cos t\,dt.$$

Since $F(0) = 2$, we have

$$F(b) = 2 + \int_0^b t \cos t\,dt.$$

Calculating the definite integral $\int_0^b t \cos t\,dt$ numerically for $b = 0, 0.1, 0.2, \ldots, 1.0$ gives the values for F in Table 6.1:

Table 6.1 *Approximate values for F*

b	0	0.1	0.2	0.3	0.4	0.5	0.6	0.7	0.8	0.9	1.0
$F(b)$	2.000	2.005	2.020	2.044	2.077	2.117	2.164	2.216	2.271	2.327	2.382

Notice that $F(b)$ appears to be increasing between $b = 0$ and $b = 1$. This could have been predicted from the fact that $t \cos t$, the derivative of $F(t)$, is positive for t between 0 and 1.

Exercises and Problems for Section 6.1

Exercises

1. Fill in the blanks in the following statements, assuming that $F(x)$ is an antiderivative of $f(x)$:

   (a) If $f(x)$ is positive over an interval, then $F(x)$ is _____ over the interval.

   (b) If $f(x)$ is increasing over an interval, then $F(x)$ is _____ over the interval.

2. Use Figure 6.10 and the fact that $P = 0$ when $t = 0$ to find values of P when $t = 1, 2, 3, 4$ and 5.

Figure 6.10

3. Use Figure 6.11 and the fact that $P = 2$ when $t = 0$ to find values of P when $t = 1, 2, 3, 4$ and 5.

Figure 6.11

In Exercises 4–11, sketch two functions F such that $F' = f$. In one case let $F(0) = 0$ and in the other, let $F(0) = 1$.

4.

5.

6.

7.

8.

9.

10.

11.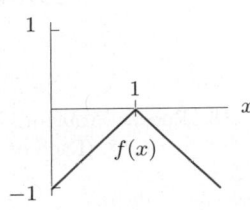

Problems

12. Let $F(x)$ be an antiderivative of $f(x)$.

    (a) If $\int_2^5 f(x)\,dx = 4$ and $F(5) = 10$, find $F(2)$.

    (b) If $\int_0^{100} f(x)\,dx = 0$, what is the relationship between $F(100)$ and $F(0)$?

13. Estimate $f(x)$ for $x = 2, 4, 6$, using the given values of $f'(x)$ and the fact that $f(0) = 100$.

x	0	2	4	6
$f'(x)$	10	18	23	25

14. Estimate $f(x)$ for $x = 2, 4, 6$, using the given values of $f'(x)$ and the fact that $f(0) = 50$.

x	0	2	4	6
$f'(x)$	17	15	10	2

15. A particle moves back and forth along the x-axis. Figure 6.12 approximates the velocity of the particle as a function of time. Positive velocities represent movement to the right and negative velocities represent movement to the left. The particle starts at the point $x = 5$. Graph the distance of the particle from the origin, with distance measured in kilometers and time in hours.

Figure 6.12

16. Assume f' is given by the graph in Figure 6.13. Suppose f is continuous and that $f(0) = 0$.

 (a) Find $f(3)$ and $f(7)$.
 (b) Find all x with $f(x) = 0$.
 (c) Sketch a graph of f over the interval $0 \le x \le 7$.

Figure 6.13

17. The graph of dy/dt against t is in Figure 6.14. The three shaded regions each have area 2. If $y = 0$ when $t = 0$, draw the graph of y as a function of t, labeling the known y-values, maxima and minima, and inflection points. Mark $t_1, t_2, \ldots, t_5$ on the t axis.[1]

Figure 6.14

18. Repeat Problem 17 for the graph of dy/dt given in Figure 6.15. (Each of the three shaded regions has area 2.)

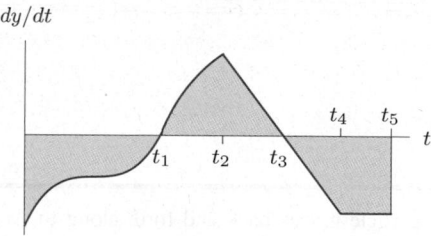

Figure 6.15

19. Using Figure 6.16, sketch a graph of an antiderivative $G(t)$ of $g(t)$ satisfying $G(0) = 5$. Label each critical point of $G(t)$ with its coordinates.

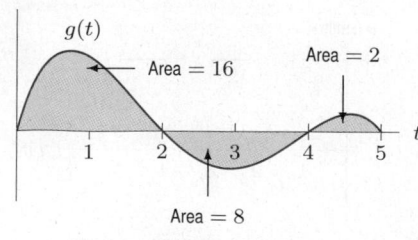

Figure 6.16

20. Using the graph of g' in Figure 6.17 and the fact that $g(0) = 50$, sketch the graph of $g(x)$. Give the coordinates of all critical points and inflection points of g.

Figure 6.17

21. Figure 6.18 shows the rate of change of the concentration of adrenaline, in micrograms per milliliter per minute, in a person's body. Sketch a graph of the concentration of adrenaline, in micrograms per milliliter, in the body as a function of time, in minutes.

Figure 6.18

22. Urologists are physicians who specialize in the health of the bladder. In a common diagnostic test, urologists monitor the emptying of the bladder using a device that produces two graphs. In one of the graphs the flow rate (in milliliters per second) is measured as a function of time (in seconds). In the other graph, the volume emptied from the bladder is measured (in milliliters) as a function of time (in seconds). See Figure 6.19.

 (a) Which graph is the flow rate and which is the volume?
 (b) Which one of these graphs is an antiderivative of the other?

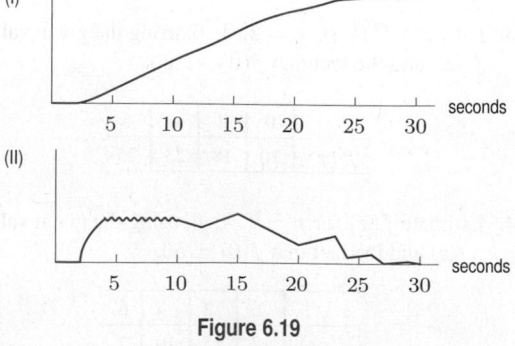

Figure 6.19

---

[1]From *Calculus: The Analysis of Functions*, by Peter D. Taylor (Toronto: Wall & Emerson, Inc., 1992).

In Problems 23–26, sketch two functions F with $F'(x) = f(x)$. In one, let $F(0) = 0$; in the other, let $F(0) = 1$. Mark x_1, x_2, and x_3 on the x-axis of your graph. Identify local maxima, minima, and inflection points of $F(x)$.

23.

24.

25.

26.

27. Use a graph of $f(x) = 2\sin(x^2)$ to determine where an antiderivative, F, of this function reaches its maximum on $0 \leq x \leq 3$. If $F(1) = 5$, find the maximum value attained by F.

28. Two functions, $f(x)$ and $g(x)$, are shown in Figure 6.20. Let F and G be antiderivatives of f and g, respectively. On the same axes, sketch graphs of the antiderivatives $F(x)$ and $G(x)$ satisfying $F(0) = 0$ and $G(0) = 0$. Compare F and G, including a discussion of zeros and x- and y-coordinates of critical points.

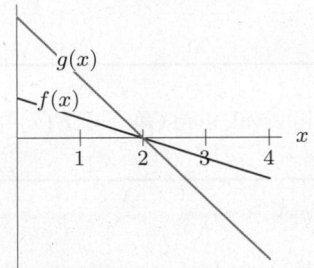

Figure 6.20

29. The graph in Figure 6.21 records the spillage rate at a toxic waste treatment plant over the 50 minutes it took to plug the leak.

    (a) Complete the table for the total quantity spilled in liters in time t minutes since the spill started.

Time t (min)	0	10	20	30	40	50
Quantity (liters)	0					

    (b) Graph the total quantity leaked against time for the entire fifty minutes. Label axes and include units.

Figure 6.21

30. The Quabbin Reservoir in the western part of Massachusetts provides most of Boston's water. The graph in Figure 6.22 represents the flow of water in and out of the Quabbin Reservoir throughout 2007.

    (a) Sketch a graph of the quantity of water in the reservoir, as a function of time.

    (b) When, in the course of 2007, was the quantity of water in the reservoir largest? Smallest? Mark and label these points on the graph you drew in part (a).

    (c) When was the quantity of water increasing most rapidly? Decreasing most rapidly? Mark and label these times on both graphs.

    (d) By July 2008 the quantity of water in the reservoir was about the same as in January 2007. Draw plausible graphs for the flow into and the flow out of the reservoir for the first half of 2008.

Figure 6.22

Strengthen Your Understanding

In Problems 31–32, explain what is wrong with the statement.

31. Let $F(x)$ be an antiderivative of $f(x)$. If $f(x)$ is everywhere increasing, then $F(x) \geq 0$.

32. If $F(x)$ and $G(x)$ are both antiderivatives of $f(x)$, then $H(x) = F(x) + G(x)$ must also be an antiderivative of $f(x)$.

In Problems 33–34, give an example of:

33. A graph of a function $f(x)$ such that $\int_0^2 f(x)\,dx = 0$.

34. A graph of a function $f(x)$ whose antiderivative is increasing everywhere.

Are the statements in Problems 35–36 true or false? Give an explanation for your answer.

35. A function $f(x)$ has at most one derivative.

36. If $f(t)$ is a linear function with positive slope, then an antiderivative, F, is a linear function.

6.2 CONSTRUCTING ANTIDERIVATIVES ANALYTICALLY

What Is an Antiderivative of $f(x) = 0$?

A function whose derivative is zero everywhere on an interval must have a horizontal tangent line at every point of its graph, and the only way this can happen is if the function is constant. Alternatively, if we think of the derivative as a velocity, and if the velocity is always zero, then the object is standing still; the position function is constant. A rigorous proof of this result using the definition of the derivative is surprisingly subtle. (See the Constant Function Theorem on page 177.)

> If $F'(x) = 0$ on an interval, then $F(x) = C$ on this interval, for some constant C.

What Is the Most General Antiderivative of f?

We know that if a function f has an antiderivative F, then it has a family of antiderivatives of the form $F(x) + C$, where C is any constant. You might wonder if there are any others. To decide, suppose that we have two functions F and G with $F' = f$ and $G' = f$: that is, F and G are both antiderivatives of the same function f. Since $F' = G'$ we have $(G - F)' = 0$. But this means that we must have $G - F = C$, so $G(x) = F(x) + C$, where C is a constant. Thus, any two antiderivatives of the same function differ only by a constant.

> If F and G are both antiderivatives of f on an interval, then $G(x) = F(x) + C$.

The Indefinite Integral

All antiderivatives of $f(x)$ are of the form $F(x) + C$. We introduce a notation for the general antiderivative that looks like the definite integral without the limits and is called the *indefinite integral*:

$$\int f(x)\,dx = F(x) + C.$$

It is important to understand the difference between

$$\int_a^b f(x)\,dx \qquad \text{and} \qquad \int f(x)\,dx.$$

The first is a number and the second is a family of *functions*. The word "integration" is frequently used for the process of finding the antiderivative as well as of finding the definite integral. The context usually makes clear which is intended.

What Is an Antiderivative of $f(x) = k$?

If k is a constant, the derivative of kx is k, so we have

An antiderivative of k is kx.

Using the indefinite integral notation, we have

If k is constant,

$$\int k\,dx = kx + C.$$

Finding Antiderivatives

Finding antiderivatives of functions is like taking square roots of numbers: if we pick a number at random, such as 7 or 493, we may have trouble finding its square root without a calculator. But if we happen to pick a number such as 25 or 64, which we know is a perfect square, then we can find its square root exactly. Similarly, if we pick a function which we recognize as a derivative, then we can find its antiderivative easily.

For example, to find an antiderivative of $f(x) = x$, notice that $2x$ is the derivative of x^2; this tells us that x^2 is an antiderivative of $2x$. If we divide by 2, then we guess that

An antiderivative of x is $\dfrac{x^2}{2}$.

To check this statement, take the derivative of $x^2/2$:

$$\frac{d}{dx}\left(\frac{x^2}{2}\right) = \frac{1}{2}\cdot\frac{d}{dx}\,x^2 = \frac{1}{2}\cdot 2x = x.$$

What about an antiderivative of x^2? The derivative of x^3 is $3x^2$, so the derivative of $x^3/3$ is $3x^2/3 = x^2$. Thus,

An antiderivative of x^2 is $\dfrac{x^3}{3}$.

The pattern looks like

An antiderivative of x^n is $\dfrac{x^{n+1}}{n+1}$.

(We assume $n \neq -1$, or we would have $x^0/0$, which does not make sense.) It is easy to check this formula by differentiation:

$$\frac{d}{dx}\left(\frac{x^{n+1}}{n+1}\right) = \frac{(n+1)x^n}{n+1} = x^n.$$

In indefinite integral notation, we have shown that

$$\int x^n\,dx = \frac{x^{n+1}}{n+1} + C, \quad n \neq -1.$$

What about when $n = -1$? In other words, what is an antiderivative of $1/x$? Fortunately, we know a function whose derivative is $1/x$, namely, the natural logarithm. Thus, since

$$\frac{d}{dx}(\ln x) = \frac{1}{x},$$

we know that

$$\int \frac{1}{x}\,dx = \ln x + C, \quad \text{for } x > 0.$$

If $x < 0$, then $\ln x$ is not defined, so it can't be an antiderivative of $1/x$. In this case, we can try $\ln(-x)$:

$$\frac{d}{dx}\ln(-x) = (-1)\frac{1}{-x} = \frac{1}{x}$$

so

$$\int \frac{1}{x}\,dx = \ln(-x) + C, \quad \text{for } x < 0.$$

This means $\ln x$ is an antiderivative of $1/x$ if $x > 0$, and $\ln(-x)$ is an antiderivative of $1/x$ if $x < 0$. Since $|x| = x$ when $x > 0$ and $|x| = -x$ when $x < 0$, we can collapse these two formulas into:

An antiderivative of $\dfrac{1}{x}$ is $\ln|x|$.

Therefore

$$\int \frac{1}{x}\,dx = \ln|x| + C.$$

Since the exponential function is its own derivative, it is also its own antiderivative; thus

$$\int e^x\,dx = e^x + C.$$

Also, antiderivatives of the sine and cosine are easy to guess. Since

$$\frac{d}{dx}\sin x = \cos x \quad \text{and} \quad \frac{d}{dx}\cos x = -\sin x,$$

we get

$$\int \cos x\,dx = \sin x + C \quad \text{and} \quad \int \sin x\,dx = -\cos x + C.$$

Example 1   Find $\int (3x + x^2)\,dx$.

Solution   We know that $x^2/2$ is an antiderivative of x and that $x^3/3$ is an antiderivative of x^2, so we expect

$$\int (3x + x^2)\,dx = 3\left(\frac{x^2}{2}\right) + \frac{x^3}{3} + C.$$

You should always check your antiderivatives by differentiation—it's easy to do. Here

$$\frac{d}{dx}\left(\frac{3}{2}x^2 + \frac{x^3}{3} + C\right) = \frac{3}{2}\cdot 2x + \frac{3x^2}{3} = 3x + x^2.$$

The preceding example illustrates that the sum and constant multiplication rules of differentiation work in reverse:

Theorem 6.1: Properties of Antiderivatives: Sums and Constant Multiples

In indefinite integral notation,

1. $\int (f(x) \pm g(x))\, dx = \int f(x)\, dx \pm \int g(x)\, dx$

2. $\int cf(x)\, dx = c \int f(x)\, dx.$

In words,

1. An antiderivative of the sum (or difference) of two functions is the sum (or difference) of their antiderivatives.

2. An antiderivative of a constant times a function is the constant times an antiderivative of the function.

These properties are analogous to the properties for definite integrals given on page 300 in Section 5.4, even though definite integrals are numbers and antiderivatives are functions.

Example 2   Find $\int (\sin x + 3 \cos x)\, dx$.

Solution   We break the antiderivative into two terms:

$$\int (\sin x + 3 \cos x)\, dx = \int \sin x\, dx + 3 \int \cos x\, dx = -\cos x + 3 \sin x + C.$$

Check by differentiating:

$$\frac{d}{dx}(-\cos x + 3 \sin x + C) = \sin x + 3 \cos x.$$

Using Antiderivatives to Compute Definite Integrals

As we saw in Section 5.3, the Fundamental Theorem of Calculus gives us a way of calculating definite integrals. Denoting $F(b) - F(a)$ by $F(x)\big|_a^b$, the theorem says that if $F' = f$ and f is continuous, then

$$\int_a^b f(x)\, dx = F(x)\Big|_a^b = F(b) - F(a).$$

To find $\int_a^b f(x)\, dx$, we first find F, and then calculate $F(b) - F(a)$. This method of computing definite integrals gives an exact answer. However, the method only works in situations where we can find the antiderivative $F(x)$. This is not always easy; for example, none of the functions we have encountered so far is an antiderivative of $\sin(x^2)$.

Example 3   Compute $\int_1^2 3x^2\, dx$ using the Fundamental Theorem.

Solution   Since $F(x) = x^3$ is an antiderivative of $f(x) = 3x^2$,

$$\int_1^2 3x^2\, dx = F(x)\Big|_1^2 = F(2) - F(1),$$

gives

$$\int_1^2 3x^2\, dx = x^3\Big|_1^2 = 2^3 - 1^3 = 7.$$

Notice in this example we used the antiderivative x^3, but $x^3 + C$ works just as well because the constant C cancels out:

$$\int_1^2 3x^2 \, dx = (x^3 + C)\Big|_1^2 = (2^3 + C) - (1^3 + C) = 7.$$

Example 4   Compute $\int_0^{\pi/4} \dfrac{1}{\cos^2 \theta} \, d\theta$ exactly.

Solution   We use the Fundamental Theorem. Since $F(\theta) = \tan \theta$ is an antiderivative of $f(\theta) = 1/\cos^2 \theta$, we get

$$\int_0^{\pi/4} \frac{1}{\cos^2 \theta} \, d\theta = \tan \theta \Big|_0^{\pi/4} = \tan\left(\frac{\pi}{4}\right) - \tan(0) = 1.$$

Exercises and Problems for Section 6.2

Exercises

In Exercises 1–16, find an antiderivative.

1. $f(x) = 5$

2. $f(t) = 5t$

3. $f(x) = x^2$

4. $g(t) = t^2 + t$

5. $g(z) = \sqrt{z}$

6. $h(z) = \dfrac{1}{z}$

7. $r(t) = \dfrac{1}{t^2}$

8. $h(t) = \cos t$

9. $g(z) = \dfrac{1}{z^3}$

10. $q(y) = y^4 + \dfrac{1}{y}$

11. $f(z) = e^z$

12. $g(t) = \sin t$

13. $f(t) = 2t^2 + 3t^3 + 4t^4$

14. $p(t) = t^3 - \dfrac{t^2}{2} - t$

15. $f(t) = \dfrac{t^2 + 1}{t}$

16. $f(x) = 5x - \sqrt{x}$

In Exercises 17–28, find the general antiderivative.

17. $f(t) = 6t$

18. $h(x) = x^3 - x$

19. $f(x) = x^2 - 4x + 7$

20. $g(t) = \sqrt{t}$

21. $r(t) = t^3 + 5t - 1$

22. $f(z) = z + e^z$

23. $g(x) = \sin x + \cos x$

24. $h(x) = 4x^3 - 7$

25. $p(t) = \dfrac{1}{\sqrt{t}}$

26. $p(t) = 2 + \sin t$

27. $g(x) = \dfrac{5}{x^3}$

28. $h(t) = \dfrac{7}{\cos^2 t}$

In Exercises 29–36, find an antiderivative $F(x)$ with $F'(x) = f(x)$ and $F(0) = 0$. Is there only one possible solution?

29. $f(x) = 3$

30. $f(x) = 2x$

31. $f(x) = -7x$

32. $f(x) = 2 + 4x + 5x^2$

33. $f(x) = \dfrac{1}{4}x$

34. $f(x) = x^2$

35. $f(x) = \sqrt{x}$

36. $f(x) = \sin x$

In Exercises 37–50, find the indefinite integrals.

37. $\displaystyle\int (5x + 7) \, dx$

38. $\displaystyle\int \left(4t + \dfrac{1}{t}\right) dt$

39. $\displaystyle\int (2 + \cos t) \, dt$

40. $\displaystyle\int 7e^x \, dx$

41. $\displaystyle\int (3e^x + 2\sin x) \, dx$

42. $\displaystyle\int (4e^x - 3\sin x) \, dx$

43. $\displaystyle\int \left(5x^2 + 2\sqrt{x}\right) dx$

44. $\displaystyle\int (x + 3)^2 \, dx$

45. $\displaystyle\int \dfrac{8}{\sqrt{x}} \, dx$

46. $\displaystyle\int \left(\dfrac{3}{t} - \dfrac{2}{t^2}\right) dt$

47. $\displaystyle\int (e^x + 5) \, dx$

48. $\displaystyle\int t^3(t^2 + 1) \, dt$

49. $\displaystyle\int \left(\sqrt{x^3} - \dfrac{2}{x}\right) dx$

50. $\displaystyle\int \left(\dfrac{x + 1}{x}\right) dx$

In Exercises 51–60, evaluate the definite integrals exactly [as in $\ln(3\pi)$], using the Fundamental Theorem, and numerically [$\ln(3\pi) \approx 2.243$]:

51. $\int_0^3 (x^2 + 4x + 3)\, dx$ **52.** $\int_1^3 \frac{1}{t}\, dt$

53. $\int_0^{\pi/4} \sin x\, dx$ **54.** $\int_0^1 2e^x\, dx$

55. $\int_0^2 3e^x\, dx$

56. $\int_2^5 (x^3 - \pi x^2)\, dx$

57. $\int_0^1 \sin\theta\, d\theta$

58. $\int_1^2 \frac{1 + y^2}{y}\, dy$

59. $\int_0^2 \left(\frac{x^3}{3} + 2x\right) dx$

60. $\int_0^{\pi/4} (\sin t + \cos t)\, dt$

Problems

61. Water is pumped into a cylindrical tank, standing vertically, at a decreasing rate given at time t minutes by

$$r(t) = 120 - 6t \text{ ft}^3/\text{min} \quad \text{for } 0 \le t \le 10.$$

The tank has radius 5 ft and is empty when $t = 0$. Find the depth of water in the tank at $t = 4$.

62. A car moves along a straight line with velocity, in feet/second, given by

$$v(t) = 6 - 2t \quad \text{for } t \ge 0.$$

(a) Describe the car's motion in words. (When is it moving forward, backward, and so on?)

(b) The car's position is measured from its starting point. When is it farthest forward? Backward?

(c) Find s, the car's position measured from its starting point, as a function of time.

63. A helicopter rotor slows down at a constant rate from 350 revs/min to 260 revs/min in 1.5 minutes.

(a) Find the angular acceleration during this time interval. What are the units of this acceleration?

(b) Assuming the angular acceleration remains constant, how long does it take for the rotor to stop? (Measure time from the moment when speed was 350 revs/min.)

(c) How many revolutions does the rotor make between the time the angular speed was 350 revs/min and stopping?

64. In drilling an oil well, the total cost, C, consists of fixed costs (independent of the depth of the well) and marginal costs, which depend on depth; drilling becomes more expensive, per meter, deeper into the earth. Suppose the fixed costs are 1,000,000 riyals (the riyal is the unit of currency of Saudi Arabia), and the marginal costs are

$$C'(x) = 4000 + 10x \text{ riyals/meter,}$$

where x is the depth in meters. Find the total cost of drilling a well x meters deep.

65. Use the Fundamental Theorem to find the area under $f(x) = x^2$ between $x = 0$ and $x = 3$.

66. Find the exact area of the region bounded by the x-axis and the graph of $y = x^3 - x$.

67. Calculate the exact area above the graph of $y = \frac{1}{2}\left(\frac{3}{\pi}x\right)^2$ and below the graph of $y = \cos x$. The curves intersect at $x = \pm\pi/3$.

68. Find the exact area of the shaded region in Figure 6.23 between $y = 3x^2 - 3$ and the x-axis.

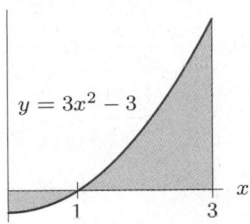

$y = 3x^2 - 3$

Figure 6.23

69. (a) Find the exact area between $f(x) = x^3 - 7x^2 + 10x$, the x-axis, $x = 0$, and $x = 5$.

(b) Find $\int_0^5 (x^3 - 7x^2 + 10x)\, dx$ exactly and interpret this integral in terms of areas.

70. Find the exact area between the curve $y = e^x - 2$ and the x-axis for $0 \le x \le 2$.

71. Find the exact area between the curves $y = x^2$ and $y = 2 - x^2$.

72. Find the exact area between the x-axis and the graph of $f(x) = (x - 1)(x - 2)(x - 3)$.

73. Consider the area between the curve $y = e^x - 2$ and the x-axis, between $x = 0$ and $x = c$ for $c > 0$. Find the value of c making the area above the axis equal to the area below the axis.

74. The area under $1/\sqrt{x}$ on the interval $1 \le x \le b$ is equal to 6. Find the value of b using the Fundamental Theorem.

75. Find the exact positive value of c which makes the area under the graph of $y = c(1 - x^2)$ and above the x-axis equal to 1.

76. Sketch the parabola $y = x(x - \pi)$ and the curve $y = \sin x$, showing their points of intersection. Find the exact area between the two graphs.

77. Find the exact average value of $f(x) = \sqrt{x}$ on the interval $0 \le x \le 9$. Illustrate your answer on a graph of $f(x) = \sqrt{x}$.

In Problems 78–79, evaluate the integral using $f(x) = 4x^{-3}$.

78. $\displaystyle\int_1^3 f\left(x^{-1}\right) \, dx$

79. $\displaystyle\int_1^3 f'\left(x\right) \, dx$

80. If A_n is the area between the curves $y = x$ and $y = x^n$, show that $A_n \to \frac{1}{2}$ as $n \to \infty$ and explain this result graphically.

81. (a) Explain why you can rewrite x^x as $x^x = e^{x \ln x}$ for $x > 0$.
   (b) Use your answer to part (a) to find $\dfrac{d}{dx}(x^x)$.
   (c) Find $\displaystyle\int x^x(1 + \ln x)dx$.
   (d) Find $\displaystyle\int_1^2 x^x(1 + \ln x)dx$ exactly using part (c). Check your answer numerically.

82. (a) What is the average value of $f(t) = \sin t$ over $0 \le t \le 2\pi$? Why is this a reasonable answer?
   (b) Find the average of $f(t) = \sin t$ over $0 \le t \le \pi$.

83. The origin and the point (a, a) are at opposite corners of a square. Calculate the ratio of the areas of the two parts into which the curve $\sqrt{x} + \sqrt{y} = \sqrt{a}$ divides the square.

Strengthen Your Understanding

In Problems 84–85, explain what is wrong with the statement.

84. $\displaystyle\int \frac{3x^2 + 1}{2x} \, dx = \frac{x^3 + x}{x^2} + C$

85. For all n, $\displaystyle\int x^n \, dx = \frac{x^{n+1}}{n + 1} + C$.

In Problems 86–87, give an example of:

86. Two different functions $F(x)$ and $G(x)$ that have the same derivative.

87. A function $f(x)$ whose antiderivative $F(x)$ has a graph which is a line with negative slope.

Are the statements in Problems 88–96 true or false? Give an explanation for your answer.

88. An antiderivative of $3\sqrt{x + 1}$ is $2(x + 1)^{3/2}$.

89. An antiderivative of $3x^2$ is $x^3 + \pi$.

90. An antiderivative of $1/x$ is $\ln|x| + \ln 2$.

91. An antiderivative of e^{-x^2} is $-e^{-x^2}/2x$.

92. $\int f(x) \, dx = (1/x) \int x f(x) \, dx$.

93. If $F(x)$ is an antiderivative of $f(x)$ and $G(x) = F(x) + 2$, then $G(x)$ is an antiderivative of $f(x)$.

94. If $F(x)$ and $G(x)$ are two antiderivatives of $f(x)$ for $-\infty < x < \infty$ and $F(5) > G(5)$, then $F(10) > G(10)$.

95. If $F(x)$ is an antiderivative of $f(x)$ and $G(x)$ is an antiderivative of $g(x)$, then $F(x) \cdot G(x)$ is an antiderivative of $f(x) \cdot g(x)$.

96. If $F(x)$ and $G(x)$ are both antiderivatives of $f(x)$ on an interval, then $F(x) - G(x)$ is a constant function.

6.3 DIFFERENTIAL EQUATIONS AND MOTION

An equation of the form

$$\frac{dy}{dx} = f(x)$$

is an example of a *differential equation*. Finding the *general solution* to the differential equation means finding the general antiderivative $y = F(x) + C$ with $F'(x) = f(x)$. Chapter 11 gives more details.

Example 1 Find and graph the general solution of the differential equation

$$\frac{dy}{dx} = 2x.$$

Solution We are asking for a function whose derivative is $2x$. One antiderivative of $2x$ is

$$y = x^2.$$

The general solution is therefore

$$y = x^2 + C,$$

where C is any constant. Figure 6.24 shows several curves in this family.

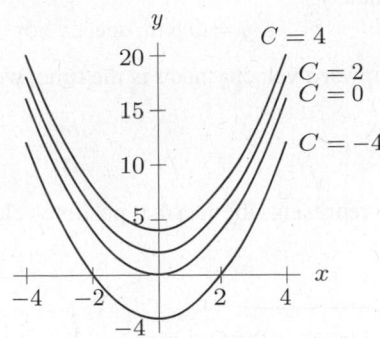

Figure 6.24: Solution curves of
$dy/dx = 2x$

How Can We Pick One Solution to the Differential Equation $\dfrac{dy}{dx} = f(x)$?

Picking one antiderivative is equivalent to selecting a value of C. To do this, we need an extra piece of information, usually that the solution curve passes through a particular point (x_0, y_0). The differential equation plus the extra condition

$$\frac{dy}{dx} = f(x), \qquad y(x_0) = y_0$$

is called an *initial value problem*. (The *initial condition* $y(x_0) = y_0$ is shorthand for $y = y_0$ when $x = x_0$.) An initial value problem usually has a unique solution, called the *particular solution*.

Example 2   Find the solution of the initial value problem

$$\frac{dy}{dx} = 2x, \quad y(3) = 5.$$

Solution   We have already seen that the general solution to the differential equation is $y = x^2 + C$. The initial condition allows us to determine the constant C. Substituting $y(3) = 5$ gives

$$5 = y(3) = 3^2 + C,$$

so C is given by

$$C = -4.$$

Thus, the (unique) solution is

$$y = x^2 - 4$$

Figure 6.24 shows this particular solution, marked $C = -4$.

Equations of Motion

We now use differential equations to analyze the motion of an object falling freely under the influence of gravity. It has been known since Galileo's time that an object moving under the influence of gravity (ignoring air resistance) has constant acceleration, g. In the most frequently used units, its value is approximately

$$g = 9.8 \text{ m/sec}^2, \quad \text{or} \quad g = 32 \text{ ft/sec}^2.$$

Thus, if v is the upward velocity and t is the time, we have the differential equation

$$\frac{dv}{dt} = -g.$$

The negative sign represents the fact that positive velocity is measured upward, whereas gravity acts downward.

Example 3   A stone is dropped from a 100-foot-high building. Find, as functions of time, its position and velocity. When does it hit the ground, and how fast is it going at that time?

Solution   Suppose t is measured in seconds from the time when the stone was dropped. If we measure distance, s, in feet above the ground, then the velocity, v, is in ft/sec upward, and the acceleration due to gravity is 32 ft/sec^2 downward, so we have the differential equation

$$\frac{dv}{dt} = -32.$$

From what we know about antiderivatives, the general solution is

$$v = -32t + C,$$

where C is some constant. Since $v = C$ when $t = 0$, the constant C represents the initial velocity, v_0. The fact that the stone is dropped rather than thrown tells us that the initial velocity is zero, so the initial condition is $v_0 = 0$. Substituting gives

$$0 = -32(0) + C \quad \text{so} \quad C = 0.$$

Thus,

$$v = -32t.$$

But now we can write a second differential equation:

$$v = \frac{ds}{dt} = -32t.$$

The general solution is

$$s = -16t^2 + K,$$

where K is another constant.

Since the stone starts at the top of the building, we have the initial condition $s = 100$ when $t = 0$. Substituting gives

$$100 = -16(0^2) + K, \quad \text{so} \quad K = 100,$$

and therefore

$$s = -16t^2 + 100.$$

Thus, we have found both v and s as functions of time.

The stone hits the ground when $s = 0$, so we must solve

$$0 = -16t^2 + 100$$

giving $t^2 = 100/16$ or $t = \pm 10/4 = \pm 2.5$ sec. Since t must be positive, $t = 2.5$ sec. At that time, $v = -32(2.5) = -80$ ft/sec. (The velocity is negative because we are considering moving up as positive and down as negative.) After the stone hits the ground, the differential equation no longer applies.

Example 4   An object is thrown vertically upward with a speed of 10 m/sec from a height of 2 meters above the ground. Find the highest point it reaches and the time when it hits the ground.

Solution   We must find the position as a function of time. In this example, the velocity is in m/sec, so we use $g = 9.8$ m/sec^2. Measuring distance in meters upward from the ground, we have the differential equation

$$\frac{dv}{dt} = -9.8.$$

As before, v is a function whose derivative is constant, so

$$v = -9.8t + C.$$

Since the initial velocity is 10 m/sec upward, we know that $v = 10$ when $t = 0$. Substituting gives

$$10 = -9.8(0) + C \quad \text{so} \quad C = 10.$$

Thus,

$$v = -9.8t + 10.$$

To find s, we use

$$v = \frac{ds}{dt} = -9.8t + 10$$

and look for a function that has $-9.8t + 10$ as its derivative. The general solution is

$$s = -4.9t^2 + 10t + K,$$

where K is any constant. To find K, we use the fact that the object starts at a height of 2 meters above the ground, so $s = 2$ when $t = 0$. Substituting gives

$$2 = -4.9(0)^2 + 10(0) + K, \quad \text{so} \quad K = 2,$$

and therefore

$$s = -4.9t^2 + 10t + 2.$$

The object reaches its highest point when the velocity is 0, so at that time

$$v = -9.8t + 10 = 0.$$

This occurs when

$$t = \frac{10}{9.8} \approx 1.02 \text{ sec.}$$

When $t = 1.02$ seconds,

$$s = -4.9(1.02)^2 + 10(1.02) + 2 \approx 7.10 \text{ meters.}$$

So the maximum height reached is 7.10 meters. The object reaches the ground when $s = 0$:

$$0 = -4.9t^2 + 10t + 2.$$

Solving this using the quadratic formula gives

$$t \approx -0.18 \quad \text{and} \quad t \approx 2.22 \text{ sec.}$$

Since the time at which the object hits the ground must be positive, $t \approx 2.22$ seconds.

History of the Equations of Motion

The problem of a body moving freely under the influence of gravity near the surface of the earth intrigued mathematicians and philosophers from Greek times onward and was finally solved by Galileo and Newton. The question to be answered was: How do the velocity and the position of the body vary with time? We define s to be the position, or height, of the body above a fixed point (often ground level), v is the velocity of the body measured upward, and a is the acceleration. The velocity and position at time $t = 0$ are represented by v_0 and s_0 respectively. We assume that the acceleration of the body is a constant, $-g$ (the negative sign means that the acceleration is downward), so

$$\frac{dv}{dt} = a = -g.$$

Problem 35 asks you to show that the motion satisfies

$$v = -gt + v_0,$$
$$s = -\frac{g}{2}t^2 + v_0 t + s_0.$$

Our derivation of the formulas for the velocity and the position of the body hides an almost 2000-year struggle to understand the mechanics of falling bodies, from Aristotle's *Physics* to Galileo's *Dialogues Concerning Two New Sciences*.

Though it is an oversimplification of his ideas, we can say that Aristotle's conception of motion was primarily in terms of *change of position*. This seems entirely reasonable; it is what we commonly observe, and this view dominated discussions of motion for centuries. But it misses a subtlety that was brought to light by Descartes, Galileo, and, with a different emphasis, by Newton. That subtlety is now usually referred to as the *principle of inertia*.

This principle holds that a body traveling undisturbed at constant velocity in a straight line will continue in this motion indefinitely. Stated another way, it says that one cannot distinguish in any absolute sense (that is, by performing an experiment), between being at rest and moving with constant velocity in a straight line. If you are reading this book in a closed room and have no external reference points, there is no experiment that will tell you, one way or the other, whether you are at rest or whether you, the room, and everything in it are moving with constant velocity in a straight line. Therefore, as Newton saw, an understanding of motion should be based on *change of velocity* rather than change of position. Since acceleration is the rate of change of velocity, it is acceleration that must play a central role in the description of motion.

Newton placed a new emphasis on the importance of *forces*. Newton's laws of motion do not say what a force *is*, they say how it *acts*. His first law is the principle of inertia, which says what happens in the *absence* of a force—there is no change in velocity. His second law says that a force acts to produce a change in velocity, that is, an acceleration. It states that $F = ma$, where m is the mass of the object, F is the net force, and a is the acceleration produced by this force.

Galileo demonstrated that a body falling under the influence of gravity does so with constant acceleration. Assuming we can neglect air resistance, this constant acceleration is independent of the mass of the body. This last fact was the outcome of Galileo's famous observation around 1600 that a heavy ball and a light ball dropped off the Leaning Tower of Pisa hit the ground at the same time. Whether or not he actually performed this experiment, Galileo presented a very clear thought experiment in the *Dialogues* to prove the same point. (This point was counter to Aristotle's more common-sense notion that the heavier ball would reach the ground first.) Galileo showed that the mass of the object did not appear as a variable in the equation of motion. Thus, the same constant-acceleration equation applies to all bodies falling under the influence of gravity.

Nearly a hundred years after Galileo's experiment, Newton formulated his laws of motion and gravity, which gave a theoretical explanation of Galileo's experimental observation that the acceleration due to gravity is independent of the mass of the body. According to Newton, acceleration is caused by force, and in the case of falling bodies, that force is the force of gravity.

Exercises and Problems for Section 6.3

Exercises

1. Show that $y = xe^{-x} + 2$ is a solution of the initial value problem

$$\frac{dy}{dx} = (1-x)e^{-x}, \quad y(0) = 2.$$

2. Show that $y = \sin(2t)$, for $0 \le t < \pi/4$, is a solution to the initial value problem

$$\frac{dy}{dt} = 2\sqrt{1-y^2}, \quad y(0) = 0.$$

In Exercises 3–8, find the general solution to the differential equation.

3. $\dfrac{dy}{dx} = 2x$

4. $\dfrac{dy}{dt} = t^2$

5. $\dfrac{dy}{dx} = x^3 + 5x^4$

6. $\dfrac{dy}{dt} = e^t$

7. $\dfrac{dy}{dx} = \cos x$

8. $\dfrac{dy}{dx} = \dfrac{1}{x}$, where $x > 0$

In Exercises 9–12, find the solution of the initial value problem.

9. $\dfrac{dy}{dx} = 3x^2, \quad y(0) = 5$

10. $\dfrac{dy}{dx} = x^5 + x^6, \quad y(1) = 2$

11. $\dfrac{dy}{dx} = e^x, \quad y(0) = 7$

12. $\dfrac{dy}{dx} = \sin x, \quad y(0) = 3$

Problems

13. A rock is thrown downward with velocity 10 ft/sec from a bridge 100 ft above the water. How fast is the rock going when it hits the water?

14. A water balloon launched from the roof of a building at time $t = 0$ has vertical velocity $v(t) = -32t + 40$ feet/sec at time t seconds, with $v > 0$ corresponding to upward motion.

  (a) If the roof of the building is 30 feet above the ground, find an expression for the height of the water balloon above the ground at time t.
  (b) What is the average velocity of the balloon between $t = 1.5$ and $t = 3$ seconds?
  (c) A 6-foot person is standing on the ground. How fast is the water balloon falling when it strikes the person on the top of the head?

15. A car starts from rest at time $t = 0$ and accelerates at $-0.6t + 4$ meters/sec^2 for $0 \le t \le 12$. How long does it take for the car to go 100 meters?

16. Ice is forming on a pond at a rate given by

$$\frac{dy}{dt} = k\sqrt{t},$$

where y is the thickness of the ice in inches at time t measured in hours since the ice started forming, and k is a positive constant. Find y as a function of t.

17. A revenue $R(p)$ is obtained by a farmer from selling grain at price p dollars/unit. The marginal revenue is given by $R'(p) = 25 - 2p$.

  (a) Find $R(p)$. Assume the revenue is zero when the price is zero.

  (b) For what prices does the revenue increase as the price increases? For what prices does the revenue decrease as price increases?

18. A firm's marginal cost function is $MC = 3q^2 + 6q + 9$.

  (a) Write a differential equation for the total cost, $C(q)$.
  (b) Find the total cost function if the fixed costs are 400.

19. A tomato is thrown upward from a bridge 25 m above the ground at 40 m/sec.

  (a) Give formulas for the acceleration, velocity, and height of the tomato at time t.
  (b) How high does the tomato go, and when does it reach its highest point?
  (c) How long is it in the air?

20. A car going 80 ft/sec (about 55 mph) brakes to a stop in five seconds. Assume the deceleration is constant.

  (a) Graph the velocity against time, t, for $0 \le t \le 5$ seconds.
  (b) Represent, as an area on the graph, the total distance traveled from the time the brakes are applied until the car comes to a stop.
  (c) Find this area and hence the distance traveled.
  (d) Now find the total distance traveled using antidifferentiation.

21. An object is shot vertically upward from the ground with an initial velocity of 160 ft/sec.

(a) At what rate is the velocity decreasing? Give units.

(b) Explain why the graph of velocity of the object against time (with upward positive) is a line.

(c) Using the starting velocity and your answer to part (b), find the time at which the object reaches the highest point.

(d) Use your answer to part (c) to decide when the object hits the ground.

(e) Graph the velocity against time. Mark on the graph when the object reaches its highest point and when it lands.

(f) Find the maximum height reached by the object by considering an area on the graph.

(g) Now express velocity as a function of time, and find the greatest height by antidifferentiation.

22. A stone thrown upward from the top of a 320-foot cliff at 128 ft/sec eventually falls to the beach below.

(a) How long does the stone take to reach its highest point?

(b) What is its maximum height?

(c) How long before the stone hits the beach?

(d) What is the velocity of the stone on impact?

23. A 727 jet needs to attain a speed of 200 mph to take off. If it can accelerate from 0 to 200 mph in 30 seconds, how long must the runway be? (Assume constant acceleration.)

24. A cat, walking along the window ledge of a New York apartment, knocks off a flower pot, which falls to the street 200 feet below. How fast is the flower pot traveling when it hits the street? (Give your answer in ft/sec and in mph, given that 1 ft/sec = 15/22 mph.)

25. An Acura NSX going at 70 mph stops in 157 feet. Find the acceleration, assuming it is constant.

26. **(a)** Find the general solution of the differential equation $dy/dx = 2x + 1$.

(b) Sketch a graph of at least three solutions.

(c) Find the solution satisfying $y(1) = 5$. Graph this solution with the others from part (b).

27. **(a)** Find and graph the general solution of the differential equation

$$\frac{dy}{dx} = \sin x + 2.$$

(b) Find the solution of the initial value problem

$$\frac{dy}{dx} = \sin x + 2, \quad y(3) = 5.$$

28. On the moon, the acceleration due to gravity is about 1.6 m/sec^2 (compared to $g \approx 9.8$ m/sec^2 on earth). If you drop a rock on the moon (with initial velocity 0), find formulas for:

(a) Its velocity, $v(t)$, at time t.

(b) The distance, $s(t)$, it falls in time t.

29. **(a)** Imagine throwing a rock straight up in the air. What is its initial velocity if the rock reaches a maximum height of 100 feet above its starting point?

(b) Now imagine being transplanted to the moon and throwing a moon rock vertically upward with the same velocity as in part (a). How high will it go? (On the moon, $g = 5$ ft/sec^2.)

30. An object is dropped from a 400-foot tower. When does it hit the ground and how fast is it going at the time of the impact?

31. The object in Problem 30 falls off the same 400-foot tower. What would the acceleration due to gravity have to be to make it reach the ground in half the time?

32. A ball that is dropped from a window hits the ground in five seconds. How high is the window? (Give your answer in feet.)

33. On the moon the acceleration due to gravity is 5 ft/sec^2. An astronaut jumps into the air with an initial upward velocity of 10 ft/sec. How high does he go? How long is the astronaut off the ground?

34. A particle of mass, m, acted on by a force, F, moves in a straight line. Its acceleration, a, is given by Newton's Law:

$$F = ma.$$

The work, W, done by a constant force when the particle moves through a displacement, d, is

$$W = Fd.$$

The velocity, v, of the particle as a function of time, t, is given in Figure 6.25. What is the sign of the work done during each of the time intervals: $[0, t_1]$, $[t_1, t_2]$, $[t_2, t_3]$, $[t_3, t_4], [t_2, t_4]$?

Figure 6.25

35. Assume the acceleration of a moving body is $-g$ and its initial velocity and position are v_0 and s_0 respectively. Find velocity, v, and position, s, as a function of t.

36. Galileo was the first person to show that the distance traveled by a body falling from rest is proportional to the square of the time it has traveled, and independent of the mass of the body. Derive this result from the fact that the acceleration due to gravity is a constant.

37. While attempting to understand the motion of bodies under gravity, Galileo stated that:

> The time in which any space is traversed by a body starting at rest and uniformly accelerated is equal to the time in which that same space would be traversed by the same body moving at a uniform speed whose value is the mean of the highest velocity and the velocity just before acceleration began.

(a) Write Galileo's statement in symbols, defining all the symbols you use.

(b) Check Galileo's statement for a body dropped off a 100-foot building accelerating from rest under gravity until it hits the ground.

(c) Show why Galileo's statement is true in general.

38. Newton's law of gravity says that the gravitational force between two bodies is attractive and given by

$$F = \frac{GMm}{r^2},$$

where G is the gravitational constant, m and M are the masses of the two bodies, and r is the distance between them. This is the famous *inverse square law*. For a falling body, we take M to be the mass of the earth and r to be the distance from the body to the center of the earth. So, actually, r changes as the body falls, but for anything we can easily observe (say, a ball dropped from the Tower of Pisa), it won't change significantly over the course of the motion. Hence, as an approximation, it is reasonable to assume that the force is constant. According to Newton's second law, acceleration is caused by a force and

$$\text{Force} = \text{Mass} \times \text{Acceleration.}$$

(a) Find the differential equation for the position, s of a moving body as a function of time.

(b) Explain how the differential equation shows the acceleration of the body is independent of its mass.

39. In his *Dialogues Concerning Two New Sciences*, Galileo wrote:

> The distances traversed during equal intervals of time by a body falling from rest stand to one another in the same ratio as the odd numbers beginning with unity.

Assume, as is now believed, that $s = -(gt^2)/2$, where s is the total distance traveled in time t, and g is the acceleration due to gravity.

(a) How far does a falling body travel in the first second (between $t = 0$ and $t = 1$)? During the second second (between $t = 1$ and $t = 2$)? The third second? The fourth second?

(b) What do your answers tell you about the truth of Galileo's statement?

Strengthen Your Understanding

In Problems 40–43, explain what is wrong with the statement.

40. A rock dropped from a 400-foot cliff takes twice as long to hit the ground as it would if it were dropped from a 200-foot cliff.

41. The function $y = \cos(t^2)$ is a solution to the initial value problem

$$\frac{dy}{dt} = -\sin(t^2), \quad y(0) = 1.$$

42. Two solutions to a differential equation $dy/dx = f(x)$ have graphs which cross at the initial value.

43. A differential equation cannot have a constant solution.

In Problems 44–45, give an example of:

44. Two different solutions to the differential equation

$$\frac{dy}{dt} = t + 3.$$

45. A differential equation that has solution $y = \cos(5x)$.

Are the statements in Problems 46–54 true or false? Give an explanation for your answer.

46. If $F(x)$ is an antiderivative of $f(x)$, then $y = F(x)$ is a solution to the differential equation $dy/dx = f(x)$.

47. If $y = F(x)$ is a solution to the differential equation $dy/dx = f(x)$, then $F(x)$ is an antiderivative of $f(x)$.

48. If an object has constant nonzero acceleration, then the position of the object as a function of time is a quadratic polynomial.

49. In an initial value problem for the differential equation $dy/dx = f(x)$, the value of y at $x = 0$ is always specified.

50. If $f(x)$ is positive for all x, then there is a solution of the differential equation $dy/dx = f(x)$ where $y(x)$ is positive for all x.

51. If $f(x) > 0$ for all x then every solution of the differential equation $dy/dx = f(x)$ is an increasing function.

52. If two solutions of a differential equation $dy/dx = f(x)$ have different values at $x = 3$ then they have different values at every x.

53. If the function $y = f(x)$ is a solution of the differential equation $dy/dx = \sin x/x$, then the function $y = f(x) + 5$ is also a solution.

54. There is only one solution $y(t)$ to the initial value problem $dy/dt = 3t^2$, $y(1) = \pi$.

6.4 SECOND FUNDAMENTAL THEOREM OF CALCULUS

Suppose f is an elementary function, that is, a combination of constants, powers of x, $\sin x$, $\cos x$, e^x, and $\ln x$. Then we have to be lucky to find an antiderivative F which is also an elementary function. But if we can't find F as an elementary function, how can we be sure that F exists at all? In this section we use the definite integral to construct antiderivatives.

Construction of Antiderivatives Using the Definite Integral

Consider the function $f(x) = e^{-x^2}$. We would like to find a way of calculating values of its antiderivative, F, which is not an elementary function. However, assuming F exists, we know from the Fundamental Theorem of Calculus that

$$F(b) - F(a) = \int_a^b e^{-t^2}\, dt.$$

Setting $a = 0$ and replacing b by x, we have

$$F(x) - F(0) = \int_0^x e^{-t^2}\, dt.$$

Suppose we want the antiderivative that satisfies $F(0) = 0$. Then we get

$$F(x) = \int_0^x e^{-t^2}\, dt.$$

This is a formula for F. For any value of x, there is a unique value for $F(x)$, so F is a function. For any fixed x, we can calculate $F(x)$ numerically. For example,

$$F(2) = \int_0^2 e^{-t^2}\, dt = 0.88208\ldots.$$

Notice that our expression for F is not an elementary function; we have *created* a new function using the definite integral. The next theorem says that this method of constructing antiderivatives works in general. This means that if we define F by

$$F(x) = \int_a^x f(t)\, dt,$$

then F must be an antiderivative of f.

Theorem 6.2: Construction Theorem for Antiderivatives

(Second Fundamental Theorem of Calculus) If f is a continuous function on an interval, and if a is any number in that interval, then the function F defined on the interval as follows is an antiderivative of f:

$$F(x) = \int_a^x f(t)\, dt.$$

Proof   Our task is to show that F, defined by this integral, is an antiderivative of f. We want to show that $F'(x) = f(x)$. By the definition of the derivative,

$$F'(x) = \lim_{h \to 0} \frac{F(x+h) - F(x)}{h}.$$

To gain some geometric insight, let's suppose f is positive and h is positive. Then we can visualize

$$F(x) = \int_a^x f(t)\, dt \quad \text{and} \quad F(x+h) = \int_a^{x+h} f(t)\, dt$$

as areas, which leads to representing

$$F(x+h) - F(x) = \int_x^{x+h} f(t)\, dt$$

as a difference of two areas. From Figure 6.26, we see that $F(x+h) - F(x)$ is roughly the area of a rectangle of height $f(x)$ and width h (shaded darker in Figure 6.26), so we have

$$F(x+h) - F(x) \approx f(x)h,$$

hence

$$\frac{F(x+h) - F(x)}{h} \approx f(x).$$

More precisely, we can use Theorem 5.4 on comparing integrals on page 303 to conclude that

$$mh \le \int_x^{x+h} f(t)\, dt \le Mh,$$

where m is the greatest lower bound for f on the interval from x to $x + h$ and M is the least upper bound on that interval. (See Figure 6.27.) Hence

$$mh \le F(x+h) - F(x) \le Mh,$$

so

$$m \le \frac{F(x+h) - F(x)}{h} \le M.$$

Since f is continuous, both m and M approach $f(x)$ as h approaches zero. Thus

$$f(x) \le \lim_{h \to 0} \frac{F(x+h) - F(x)}{h} \le f(x).$$

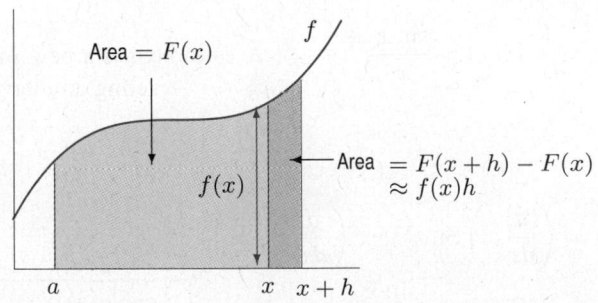

Figure 6.26: $F(x+h) - F(x)$ is area of roughly rectangular region

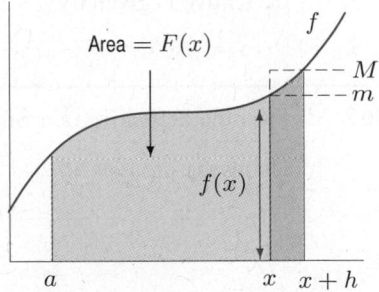

Figure 6.27: Upper and lower bounds for $F(x+h) - F(x)$

Thus both inequalities must actually be equalities, so we have the result we want:

$$f(x) = \lim_{h \to 0} \frac{F(x+h) - F(x)}{h} = F'(x).$$

Relationship Between the Construction Theorem and the Fundamental Theorem of Calculus

If F is constructed as in Theorem 6.2, then we have just shown that $F' = f$. Suppose G is any other antiderivative of f, so $G' = f$, and therefore $F' = G'$. Since the derivative of $F - G$ is zero, the Constant Function Theorem on page 177 tells us that $F - G$ is a constant, so $F(x) = G(x) + C$.

Since we know $F(a) = 0$ (by the definition of F), we can write

$$\int_a^b f(t)\, dt = F(b) = F(b) - F(a) = (G(b) + C) - (G(a) + C) = G(b) - G(a).$$

This result, that the definite integral $\int_a^b f(t)\,dt$ can be evaluated using any antiderivative of f, is the (First) Fundamental Theorem of Calculus. Thus, we have shown that the First Fundamental Theorem of Calculus can be obtained from the Construction Theorem (the Second Fundamental Theorem of Calculus).

Using the Construction Theorem for Antiderivatives

The construction theorem enables us to write down antiderivatives of functions that do not have elementary antiderivatives. For example, an antiderivative of $(\sin x)/x$ is

$$F(x) = \int_0^x \frac{\sin t}{t}\,dt.$$

Notice that F is a function; we can calculate its values to any degree of accuracy.[2] This function already has a name: it is called the *sine-integral*, and it is denoted $\mathrm{Si}(x)$.

Example 1   Construct a table of values of $\mathrm{Si}(x)$ for $x = 0, 1, 2, 3$.

Solution   Using numerical methods, we calculate the values of $\mathrm{Si}(x) = \int_0^x (\sin t)/t\,dt$ given in Table 6.2. Since the integrand is undefined at $t = 0$, we took the lower limit as 0.00001 instead of 0.

Table 6.2 *A table of values of Si(x)*

x	0	1	2	3
$\mathrm{Si}(x)$	0	0.95	1.61	1.85

The reason the sine-integral has a name is that some scientists and engineers use it all the time (for example, in optics). For them, it is just another common function like sine or cosine. Its derivative is given by

$$\frac{d}{dx}\,\mathrm{Si}(x) = \frac{\sin x}{x}.$$

Example 2   Find the derivative of $x\,\mathrm{Si}(x)$.

Solution   Using the product rule,

$$\frac{d}{dx}\,(x\,\mathrm{Si}(x)) = \left(\frac{d}{dx}\,x\right)\mathrm{Si}(x) + x\left(\frac{d}{dx}\,\mathrm{Si}(x)\right)$$

$$= 1 \cdot \mathrm{Si}(x) + x\frac{\sin x}{x}$$

$$= \mathrm{Si}(x) + \sin x.$$

Exercises and Problems for Section 6.4

Exercises

1. For $x = 0, 0.5, 1.0, 1.5$, and 2.0, make a table of values for $I(x) = \int_0^x \sqrt{t^4 + 1}\,dt$.

2. Assume that $F'(t) = \sin t \cos t$ and $F(0) = 1$. Find $F(b)$ for $b = 0,\ 0.5,\ 1,\ 1.5,\ 2,\ 2.5$, and 3.

3. (a) Continue the table of values for $\mathrm{Si}(x) = \int_0^x (\sin t/t)\,dt$ on page 342 for $x = 4$ and $x = 5$.
   (b) Why is $\mathrm{Si}(x)$ decreasing between $x = 4$ and $x = 5$?

In Exercises 4–6, write an expression for the function, $f(x)$, with the given properties.

4. $f'(x) = \sin(x^2)$ and $f(0) = 7$

5. $f'(x) = (\sin x)/x$ and $f(1) = 5$

6. $f'(x) = \mathrm{Si}(x)$ and $f(0) = 2$

---

[2]You may notice that the integrand, $(\sin t)/t$, is undefined at $t = 0$; such improper integrals are treated in more detail in Chapter 7.

In Exercises 7–10, let $F(x) = \int_0^x f(t)\,dt$. Graph $F(x)$ as a function of x.

7.

8.

9.

10.

Find the derivatives in Exercises 11–16.

11. $\dfrac{d}{dx} \int_0^x \cos(t^2)\,dt$

12. $\dfrac{d}{dt} \int_4^t \sin(\sqrt{x})\,dx$

13. $\dfrac{d}{dx} \int_1^x (1+t)^{200}\,dt$

14. $\dfrac{d}{dx} \int_2^x \ln(t^2+1)\,dt$

15. $\dfrac{d}{dx} \int_{0.5}^x \arctan(t^2)\,dt$

16. $\dfrac{d}{dx} \left[\mathrm{Si}(x^2)\right]$

Problems

17. Find intervals where the graph of $F(x) = \int_0^x e^{-t^2}\,dt$ is concave up and concave down.

18. Use properties of the function $f(x) = xe^{-x}$ to determine the number of values x that make $F(x) = 0$, given $F(x) = \int_1^x f(t)\,dt$.

For Problems 19–21, let $F(x) = \int_0^x \sin(t^2)\,dt$.

19. Approximate $F(x)$ for $x = 0,\ 0.5,\ 1,\ 1.5,\ 2,\ 2.5$.

20. Using a graph of $F'(x)$, decide where $F(x)$ is increasing and where $F(x)$ is decreasing for $0 \le x \le 2.5$.

21. Does $F(x)$ have a maximum value for $0 \le x \le 2.5$? If so, at what value of x does it occur, and approximately what is that maximum value?

22. Use Figure 6.28 to sketch a graph of $F(x) = \int_0^x f(t)\,dt$. Label the points x_1, x_2, x_3.

Figure 6.28

23. The graph of the derivative F' of some function F is given in Figure 6.29. If $F(20) = 150$, estimate the maximum value attained by F.

Figure 6.29

24. Let $g(x) = \int_0^x f(t)\,dt$. Using Figure 6.30, find

(a) $g(0)$ (b) $g'(1)$

(c) The interval where g is concave up.

(d) The value of x where g takes its maximum on the interval $0 \le x \le 8$.

Figure 6.30

25. Let $F(x) = \int_0^x \sin(2t)\,dt$.

(a) Evaluate $F(\pi)$.

(b) Draw a sketch to explain geometrically why the answer to part (a) is correct.

(c) For what values of x is $F(x)$ positive? negative?

26. Let $F(x) = \int_2^x (1/\ln t)\,dt$ for $x \ge 2$.

(a) Find $F'(x)$.

(b) Is F increasing or decreasing? What can you say about the concavity of its graph?

(c) Sketch a graph of $F(x)$.

27. Let $R(x) = \int_0^x \sqrt{1+t^2}\,dt$

(a) Evaluate $R(0)$ and determine if R is an even or an odd function.

(b) Is R increasing or decreasing?

(c) What can you say about concavity?

(d) Sketch a graph of $R(x)$.

(e) Show that $\lim_{x\to\infty}(R(x)/x^2)$ exists and find its value.

28. Suppose that $f(x)$ is a continuous function and $\int_a^b f(t)\,dt = 0$ for all a and b.

(a) Show that $F(x) = \int_a^x f(t)\,dt = 0$ for all x.

(b) Show that $f(x) = 0$ for all x.

In Problems 29–30, find the value of the function with the given properties.

29. $F(1)$, where $F'(x) = e^{-x^2}$ and $F(0) = 2$

30. $G(-1)$, where $G'(x) = \cos(x^2)$ and $G(0) = -3$

In Problems 31–34, estimate the value of each expression, given $w(t) = \int_0^t q(x)\,dx$ and $v(t) = \int_0^t q'(x)\,dx$. Table 6.3 gives values for $q(x)$, a function with negative first and second derivatives. Are your answers under- or overestimates?

Table 6.3

x	0.0	0.1	0.2	0.3	0.4	0.5
$q(x)$	5.3	5.2	4.9	4.5	3.9	3.1

31. $w(0.4)$

32. $v(0.4)$

33. $w'(0.4)$

34. $v'(0.4)$

In Problems 35–38, use the chain rule to calculate the derivative.

35. $\dfrac{d}{dx}\displaystyle\int_0^{x^2} \ln(1+t^2)\,dt$

36. $\dfrac{d}{dt}\displaystyle\int_1^{\sin t} \cos(x^2)\,dx$

37. $\dfrac{d}{dt}\displaystyle\int_{2t}^4 \sin(\sqrt{x})\,dx$

38. $\dfrac{d}{dx}\displaystyle\int_{-x^2}^{x^2} e^{t^2}\,dt$

In Problems 39–42, find the given quantities. The *error function*, $\mathrm{erf}(x)$, is defined by

$$\mathrm{erf}(x) = \frac{2}{\sqrt{\pi}} \int_0^x e^{-t^2}\,dt.$$

39. $\dfrac{d}{dx}(x\,\mathrm{erf}(x))$

40. $\dfrac{d}{dx}(\mathrm{erf}(\sqrt{x}))$

41. $\dfrac{d}{dx}\left(\displaystyle\int_0^{x^3} e^{-t^2}\,dt\right)$

42. $\dfrac{d}{dx}\left(\displaystyle\int_x^{x^3} e^{-t^2}\,dt\right)$

Strengthen Your Understanding

In Problems 43–45, explain what is wrong with the statement.

43. $\dfrac{d}{dx}\displaystyle\int_0^5 t^2\,dt = x^2$.

44. $F(x) = \displaystyle\int_{-2}^x t^2\,dt$ has a local minimum at $x = 0$.

45. For the function $f(x)$ shown in Figure 6.31, $F(x) = \int_0^x f(t)\,dt$ has a local minimum at $x = 2$.

Figure 6.31:

In Problems 46–47, give an example of:

46. A function, $F(x)$, constructed using the Second Fundamental Theorem of Calculus such that F is a nondecreasing function and $F(0) = 0$.

47. A function $G(x)$, constructed using the Second Fundamental Theorem of Calculus such that G is concave up and $G(7) = 0$.

Are the statements in Problems 48–53 true or false? Give an explanation for your answer.

48. Every continuous function has an antiderivative.

49. $\int_0^x \sin(t^2)\,dt$ is an antiderivative of $\sin(x^2)$.

50. If $F(x) = \int_0^x f(t)\,dt$, then $F(5) - F(3) = \int_3^5 f(t)\,dt$.

51. If $F(x) = \int_0^x f(t)\,dt$, then $F(x)$ must be increasing.

52. If $F(x) = \int_0^x f(t)\,dt$ and $G(x) = \int_2^x f(t)\,dt$, then $F(x) = G(x) + C$.

53. If $F(x) = \int_0^x f(t)\,dt$ and $G(x) = \int_0^x g(t)\,dt$, then $F(x) + G(x) = \int_0^x (f(t) + g(t))\,dt$.

CHAPTER SUMMARY (see also Ready Reference at the end of the book)

- **Constructing antiderivatives**
  Graphically, numerically, analytically.
- **The family of antiderivatives**
  The indefinite integral.
- **Differential equations**

Initial value problems, uniform motion.
- **Construction theorem (Second Fundamental Theorem of Calculus)**
  Constructing antiderivatives using definite integrals.
- **Equations of motion**

REVIEW EXERCISES AND PROBLEMS FOR CHAPTER SIX

Exercises

1. The graph of a derivative $f'(x)$ is shown in Figure 6.32. Fill in the table of values for $f(x)$ given that $f(0) = 2$.

x	0	1	2	3	4	5	6
$f(x)$	2						

Figure 6.32: Graph of f', not f

2. Figure 6.33 shows f. If $F' = f$ and $F(0) = 0$, find $F(b)$ for $b = 1, 2, 3, 4, 5, 6$.

Figure 6.33

In Exercises 3–4, graph $F(x)$ such that $F'(x) = f(x)$ and $F(0) = 0$.

3.

4.

5. (a) Using Figure 6.34, estimate $\int_0^7 f(x)dx$.
   (b) If F is an antiderivative of the same function f and $F(0) = 25$, estimate $F(7)$.

Figure 6.34

In Exercises 6–27, find the indefinite integrals.

6. $\displaystyle\int 5x \, dx$

7. $\displaystyle\int x^3 \, dx$

8. $\displaystyle\int \sin\theta \, d\theta$

9. $\displaystyle\int (x^3 - 2) \, dx$

10. $\displaystyle\int \left(t^2 + \frac{1}{t^2}\right) dt$

11. $\displaystyle\int \frac{4}{t^2} \, dt$

12. $\displaystyle\int (x^2 + 5x + 8) \, dx$

13. $\displaystyle\int 4\sqrt{w} \, dw$

14. $\displaystyle\int (4t + 7) \, dt$

15. $\displaystyle\int \cos\theta \, d\theta$

16. $\displaystyle\int \left(t\sqrt{t} + \frac{1}{t\sqrt{t}}\right) dt$

17. $\displaystyle\int \left(x + \frac{1}{\sqrt{x}}\right) dx$

18. $\displaystyle\int (\pi + x^{11}) \, dx$

19. $\displaystyle\int \left(3\cos t + 3\sqrt{t}\right) dt$

20. $\displaystyle\int \left(\frac{y^2 - 1}{y}\right)^2 dy$

21. $\displaystyle\int \frac{1}{\cos^2 x} \, dx$

22. $\displaystyle\int \left(\frac{2}{x} + \pi\sin x\right) dx$

23. $\displaystyle\int \left(\frac{x^2 + x + 1}{x}\right) dx$

24. $\displaystyle\int 5e^z \, dz$

25. $\displaystyle\int 2^x \, dx$

26. $\displaystyle\int (3\cos x - 7\sin x) \, dx$

27. $\displaystyle\int (2e^x - 8\cos x) \, dx$

In Exercises 28–29, evaluate the definite integral exactly [as in $\ln(3\pi)$], using the Fundamental Theorem, and numerically [$\ln(3\pi) \approx 2.243$]:

28. $\int_{-3}^{-1} \frac{2}{r^3}\, dr$

29. $\int_{-\pi/2}^{\pi/2} 2\cos\phi\, d\phi$

For Exercises 30–35, find an antiderivative $F(x)$ with $F'(x) = f(x)$ and $F(0) = 4$.

30. $f(x) = x^2$

31. $f(x) = x^3 + 6x^2 - 4$

32. $f(x) = \sqrt{x}$

33. $f(x) = e^x$

34. $f(x) = \sin x$

35. $f(x) = \cos x$

36. Use the fact that $(x^x)' = x^x(1 + \ln x)$ to evaluate exactly: $\int_1^3 x^x(1 + \ln x)\, dx$.

37. Show that $y = x + \sin x - \pi$ satisfies the initial value problem

$$\frac{dy}{dx} = 1 + \cos x, \quad y(\pi) = 0.$$

38. Show that $y = x^n + A$ is a solution of the differential equation $y' = nx^{n-1}$ for any value of A.

In Exercises 39–42, find the general solution of the differential equation.

39. $\frac{dy}{dx} = x^3 + 5$

40. $\frac{dy}{dx} = 8x + \frac{1}{x}$

41. $\frac{dW}{dt} = 4\sqrt{t}$

42. $\frac{dr}{dp} = 3\sin p$

In Exercises 43–46, find the solution of the initial value problem.

43. $\frac{dy}{dx} = 6x^2 + 4x, \quad y(2) = 10$

44. $\frac{dP}{dt} = 10e^t, \quad P(0) = 25$

45. $\frac{ds}{dt} = -32t + 100, \quad s = 50$ when $t = 0$

46. $\frac{dq}{dz} = 2 + \sin z, \quad q = 5$ when $z = 0$

Find the derivatives in Exercises 47–48.

47. $\frac{d}{dt} \int_t^\pi \cos(z^3)\, dz$

48. $\frac{d}{dx} \int_x^1 \ln t\, dt$

Problems

49. Use Figure 6.35 and the fact that $F(2) = 3$ to sketch the graph of $F(x)$. Label the values of at least four points.

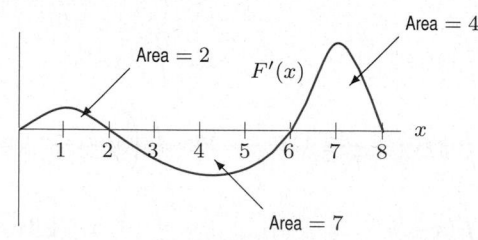

Figure 6.35

50. The vertical velocity of a cork bobbing up and down on the waves in the sea is given by Figure 6.36. Upward is considered positive. Describe the motion of the cork at each of the labeled points. At which point(s), if any, is the acceleration zero? Sketch a graph of the height of the cork above the sea floor as a function of time.

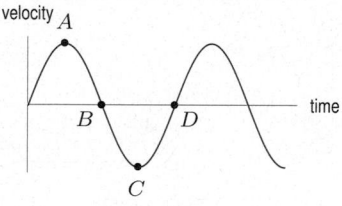

Figure 6.36

In Problems 51–52, a graph of f is given. Let $F'(x) = f(x)$.

(a) What are the x-coordinates of the critical points of $F(x)$?

(b) Which critical points are local maxima, which are local minima, and which are neither?

(c) Sketch a possible graph of $F(x)$.

51.

52.

53. The graph of f'' is given in Figure 6.37. Draw graphs of f and f', assuming both go through the origin, and use them to decide at which of the labeled x-values:

(a) $f(x)$ is greatest.
(b) $f(x)$ is least.
(c) $f'(x)$ is greatest.
(d) $f'(x)$ is least.
(e) $f''(x)$ is greatest.
(f) $f''(x)$ is least.

Figure 6.37: Graph of f''

54. Assume f' is given by the graph in Figure 6.38. Suppose f is continuous and that $f(3) = 0$.

(a) Sketch a graph of f.
(b) Find $f(0)$ and $f(7)$.
(c) Find $\int_0^7 f'(x)\,dx$ in two different ways.

Figure 6.38

55. Use the Fundamental Theorem to find the area under $f(x) = x^2$ between $x = 1$ and $x = 4$.

56. Calculate the exact area between the x-axis and the graph of $y = 7 - 8x + x^2$.

57. Find the exact area below the curve $y = x^3(1 - x)$ and above the x-axis.

58. Find the exact area enclosed by the curve $y = x^2(1-x)^2$ and the x-axis.

59. Find the exact area between the curves $y = x^2$ and $x = y^2$.

60. Calculate the exact area above the graph of $y = \sin\theta$ and below the graph of $y = \cos\theta$ for $0 \le \theta \le \pi/4$.

61. Find the exact area between $f(\theta) = \sin\theta$ and $g(\theta) = \cos\theta$ for $0 \le \theta \le 2\pi$.

62. Find the exact value of the area between the graphs of $y = \cos x$ and $y = e^x$ for $0 \le x \le 1$.

63. Find the exact value of the area between the graphs of $y = \sinh x$, $y = \cosh x$, for $-1 \le x \le 1$.

64. Use the Fundamental Theorem to determine the value of b if the area under the graph of $f(x) = 8x$ between $x = 1$ and $x = b$ is equal to 192. Assume $b > 1$.

65. Find the exact positive value of c if the area between the graph of $y = x^2 - c^2$ and the x-axis is 36.

66. Use the Fundamental Theorem to find the average value of $f(x) = x^2 + 1$ on the interval $x = 0$ to $x = 10$. Illustrate your answer on a graph of $f(x)$.

67. The average value of the function $v(x) = 6/x^2$ on the interval $[1, c]$ is equal to 1. Find the value of c.

In Problems 68–70, evaluate the expression using $f(x) = 5\sqrt{x}$.

68. $\displaystyle\int_1^4 f^{-1}(x)\,dx$

69. $\displaystyle\int_1^4 (f(x))^{-1}\,dx$

70. $\displaystyle\left(\int_1^4 f(x)\,dx\right)^{-1}$

In Problems 71–72, evaluate and simplify the expressions given that $f(t) = \displaystyle\int_0^t tx^2\,dx$.

71. $f(2)$

72. $f(n)$

Calculate the derivatives in Problems 73–76.

73. $\displaystyle\frac{d}{dx}\int_2^{x^3} \sin(t^2)\,dt$

74. $\displaystyle\frac{d}{dx}\int_{\cos x}^3 e^{t^2}\,dt$

75. $\displaystyle\frac{d}{dx}\int_{-x}^x e^{-t^4}\,dt$

76. $\displaystyle\frac{d}{dt}\int_{e^t}^{t^3} \sqrt{1 + x^2}\,dx$

77. A store has an inventory of Q units of a product at time $t = 0$. The store sells the product at the steady rate of Q/A units per week, and it exhausts the inventory in A weeks.

(a) Find a formula $f(t)$ for the amount of product in inventory at time t. Graph $f(t)$.
(b) Find the average inventory level during the period $0 \le t \le A$. Explain why your answer is reasonable.

78. For $0 \leq t \leq 10$ seconds, a car moves along a straight line with velocity

$$v(t) = 2 + 10t \text{ ft/sec.}$$

(a) Graph $v(t)$ and find the total distance the car has traveled between $t = 0$ and $t = 10$ seconds using the formula for the area of a trapezoid.

(b) Find the function $s(t)$ that gives the position of the car as a function of time. Explain the meaning of any new constants.

(c) Use your function $s(t)$ to find the total distance traveled by the car between $t = 0$ and $t = 10$ seconds. Compare with your answer in part (a).

(d) Explain how your answers to parts (a) and (c) relate to the Fundamental Theorem of Calculus.

79. For a function f, you are given the graph of the derivative f' in Figure 6.39 and that $f(0) = 50$.

(a) On the interval $0 \leq t \leq 5$, at what value of t does f appear to reach its maximum value? Its minimum value?

(b) Estimate these maximum and minimum values.

(c) Estimate $f(5) - f(0)$.

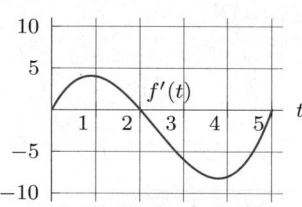

Figure 6.39

80. The acceleration, a, of a particle as a function of time is shown in Figure 6.40. Sketch graphs of velocity and position against time. The particle starts at rest at the origin.

Figure 6.40

81. The angular speed of a car engine increases from 1100 revs/min to 2500 revs/min in 6 sec.

(a) Assuming that it is constant, find the angular acceleration in revs/min^2.

(b) How many revolutions does the engine make in this time?

82. Figure 6.41 is a graph of

$$f(x) = \begin{cases} -x + 1, & \text{for } 0 \leq x \leq 1; \\ x - 1, & \text{for } 1 < x \leq 2. \end{cases}$$

(a) Find a function F such that $F' = f$ and $F(1) = 1$.

(b) Use geometry to show the area under the graph of f above the x-axis between $x = 0$ and $x = 2$ is equal to $F(2) - F(0)$.

(c) Use parts (a) and (b) to check the Fundamental Theorem of Calculus.

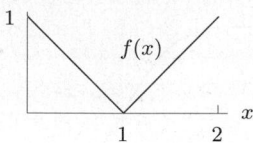

Figure 6.41

83. If a car goes from 0 to 80 mph in six seconds with constant acceleration, what is that acceleration?

84. A car going at 30 ft/sec decelerates at a constant 5 ft/sec^2.

(a) Draw up a table showing the velocity of the car every half second. When does the car come to rest?

(b) Using your table, find left and right sums which estimate the total distance traveled before the car comes to rest. Which is an overestimate, and which is an underestimate?

(c) Sketch a graph of velocity against time. On the graph, show an area representing the distance traveled before the car comes to rest. Use the graph to calculate this distance.

(d) Now find a formula for the velocity of the car as a function of time, and then find the total distance traveled by antidifferentiation. What is the relationship between your answer to parts (c) and (d) and your estimates in part (b)?

85. An object is thrown vertically upward with a velocity of 80 ft/sec.

(a) Make a table showing its velocity every second.

(b) When does it reach its highest point? When does it hit the ground?

(c) Using your table, write left and right sums which under- and overestimate the height the object attains.

(d) Use antidifferentiation to find the greatest height it reaches.

86. If $A(r)$ represents the area of a circle of radius r and $C(r)$ represents its circumference, it can be shown that $A'(r) = C(r)$. Use the fact that $C(r) = 2\pi r$ to obtain the formula for $A(r)$.

87. If $V(r)$ represents the volume of a sphere of radius r and $S(r)$ represents its surface area, it can be shown that $V'(r) = S(r)$. Use the fact that $S(r) = 4\pi r^2$ to obtain the formula for $V(r)$.

88. A car, initially moving at 60 mph, has a constant deceleration and stops in a distance of 200 feet. What is its deceleration? (Give your answer in ft/sec². Note that 1 mph = 22/15 ft/sec.)

89. The birth rate, B, in births per hour, of a bacteria population is given in Figure 6.42. The curve marked D gives the death rate, in deaths per hour, of the same population.

    (a) Explain what the shape of each of these graphs tells you about the population.

    (b) Use the graphs to find the time at which the net rate of increase of the population is at a maximum.

    (c) At time $t = 0$ the population has size N. Sketch the graph of the total number born by time t. Also sketch the graph of the number alive at time t. Estimate the time at which the population is a maximum.

Figure 6.42

90. Water flows at a constant rate into the left side of the W-shaped container in Figure 6.43. Sketch a graph of the height, H, of the water in the left side of the container as a function of time, t. The container starts empty.

Figure 6.43

In Problems 91–92, the quantity, $N(t)$ in kg, of pollutant that has leeched from a toxic waste site after t days, is given by

$$N(t) = \int_0^t r(x)\, dx, \quad \text{where } r(x) > 0,\ r'(x) < 0.$$

91. If there is enough information to decide, determine whether $N(t)$ is an increasing or a decreasing function and whether its graph concave up or concave down.

92. Rank in order from least to greatest:

$$N(20),\, N(10),\, N(20) - N(10),\, N(15) - N(5).$$

93. Let $f(x)$ have one zero, at $x = 3$, and suppose $f'(x) < 0$ for all x and that

$$\int_0^3 f(t)\, dt = -\int_3^5 f(t)\, dt.$$

Define $F(x) = \int_0^x f(t)\, dt$ and $G(x) = \int_1^x F(t)\, dt$.

    (a) Find the zeros and critical points of F.

    (b) Find the zeros and critical points of G.

94. Let $P(x) = \int_0^x \arctan(t^2)\, dt$.

    (a) Evaluate $P(0)$ and determine if P is an even or an odd function.

    (b) Is P increasing or decreasing?

    (c) What can you say about concavity?

    (d) Sketch a graph of $P(x)$.

CAS Challenge Problems

95. **(a)** Set up a right-hand Riemann sum for $\int_a^b x^3 dx$ using n subdivisions. What is Δx? Express each x_i, for $i = 1, 2, \ldots, n$, in terms of i.

    (b) Use a computer algebra system to find an expression for the Riemann sum in part (a); then find the limit of this expression as $n \to \infty$.

    (c) Simplify the final expression and compare the result to that obtained using the Fundamental Theorem of Calculus.

96. **(a)** Use a computer algebra system to find $\int e^{2x}\, dx$, $\int e^{3x}\, dx$, and $\int e^{3x+5}\, dx$.

    (b) Using your answers to part (a), conjecture a formula for $\int e^{ax+b}\, dx$, where a and b are constants.

    (c) Check your formula by differentiation. Explain which differentiation rules you are using.

97. **(a)** Use a computer algebra system to find $\int \sin(3x)\, dx$,
$\int \sin(4x)\, dx$, and $\int \sin(3x - 2)\, dx$.

    (b) Using your answers to part (a), conjecture a formula for $\int \sin(ax + b)\, dx$, where a and b are constants.

    (c) Check your formula by differentiation. Explain which differentiation rules you are using.

98. **(a)** Use a computer algebra system to find

$$\int \frac{x-2}{x-1}\, dx, \quad \int \frac{x-3}{x-1}\, dx, \quad \text{and} \quad \int \frac{x-1}{x-2}\, dx.$$

    (b) If a and b are constants, use your answers to part (a) to conjecture a formula for

$$\int \frac{x-a}{x-b}\, dx.$$

    (c) Check your formula by differentiation. Explain which rules of differentiation you are using.

99. (a) Use a computer algebra system to find

$$\int \frac{1}{(x-1)(x-3)}\,dx, \quad \int \frac{1}{(x-1)(x-4)}\,dx$$

and

$$\int \frac{1}{(x-1)(x+3)}\,dx.$$

(b) If a and b are constants, use your answers to part (a) to conjecture a formula for

$$\int \frac{1}{(x-a)(x-b)}\,dx.$$

(c) Check your formula by differentiation. Explain which rules of differentiation you are using.

PROJECTS FOR CHAPTER SIX

1. Distribution of Resources

Whether a resource is distributed evenly among members of a population is often an important political or economic question. How can we measure this? How can we decide if the distribution of wealth in this country is becoming more or less equitable over time? How can we measure which country has the most equitable income distribution? This problem describes a way of making such measurements. Suppose the resource is distributed evenly. Then any 20% of the population will have 20% of the resource. Similarly, any 30% will have 30% of the resource and so on. If, however, the resource is not distributed evenly, the poorest $p\%$ of the population (in terms of this resource) will not have $p\%$ of the goods. Suppose $F(x)$ represents the fraction of the resource owned by the poorest fraction x of the population. Thus $F(0.4) = 0.1$ means that the poorest 40% of the population owns 10% of the resource.

(a) What would F be if the resource were distributed evenly?

(b) What must be true of any such F? What must $F(0)$ and $F(1)$ equal? Is F increasing or decreasing? Is the graph of F concave up or concave down?

(c) Gini's index of inequality, G, is one way to measure how evenly the resource is distributed. It is defined by

$$G = 2 \int_0^1 (x - F(x))\,dx.$$

Show graphically what G represents.

2. Yield from an Apple Orchard

Figure 6.44 is a graph of the annual yield, $y(t)$, in bushels per year, from an orchard t years after planting. The trees take about 10 years to get established, but for the next 20 years they give a substantial yield. After about 30 years, however, age and disease start to take their toll, and the annual yield falls off.[3]

(a) Represent on a sketch of Figure 6.44 the total yield, $F(M)$, up to M years, with $0 \leq M \leq 60$. Write an expression for $F(M)$ in terms of $y(t)$.

(b) Sketch a graph of $F(M)$ against M for $0 \leq M \leq 60$.

(c) Write an expression for the average annual yield, $a(M)$, up to M years.

(d) When should the orchard be cut down and replanted? Assume that we want to maximize average revenue per year, and that fruit prices remain constant, so that this is achieved by maximizing average annual yield. Use the graph of $y(t)$ to estimate the time at which the average annual yield is a maximum. Explain your answer geometrically and symbolically.

---

[3]From Peter D. Taylor, *Calculus: The Analysis of Functions* (Toronto: Wall & Emerson, Inc., 1992).

y (annual yield)

t (time in years)

Figure 6.44

3. Slope Fields

Suppose we want to sketch the antiderivative, F, of the function f. To get an accurate graph of F, we must be careful about making F have the right slope at every point. The slope of F at any point (x, y) on its graph should be $f(x)$, since $F'(x) = f(x)$. We arrange this as follows: at the point (x, y) in the plane, draw a small line segment with slope $f(x)$. Do this at many points. We call such a diagram a *slope field*. If $f(x) = x$, we get the slope field in Figure 6.45.

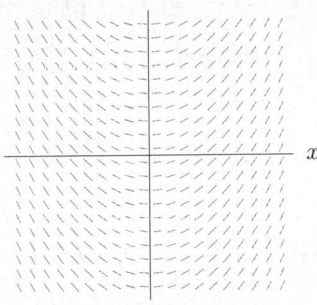

Figure 6.45: Slope field of $f(x) = x$

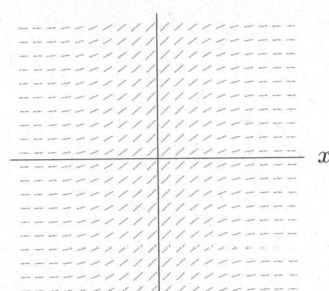

Figure 6.46: Slope field of $f(x) = e^{-x^2}$

Notice how the lines in Figure 6.45 seem to be arranged in a parabolic pattern. This is because the general antiderivative of x is $x^2/2 + C$, so the lines are all the tangent lines to the family of parabolas $y = x^2/2 + C$. This suggests a way of finding antiderivatives graphically even if we can't write down a formula for them: plot the slopes, and see if they suggest the graph of an antiderivative. For example, if you do this with $f(x) = e^{-x^2}$, which is one of the functions that does not have an elementary antiderivative, you get Figure 6.46.

You can see the ghost of the graph of a function lurking behind the slopes in Figure 6.46; in fact there is a whole stack of them. If you move across the plane in the direction suggested by the slope field at every point, you will trace out a curve. The slope field is tangent to the curve everywhere, so this is the graph of an antiderivative of e^{-x^2}.

(a) (i) Sketch a graph of $f(t) = \dfrac{\sin t}{t}$.

(ii) What does your graph tell you about the behavior of

$$\text{Si}(x) = \int_0^x \frac{\sin(t)}{t} dt$$

for $x > 0$? Is $\text{Si}(x)$ always increasing or always decreasing? Does $\text{Si}(x)$ cross the x-axis for $x > 0$?

(iii) By drawing the slope field for $f(t) = \dfrac{\sin t}{t}$, decide whether $\lim\limits_{x \to \infty} \text{Si}(x)$ exists.

(b)   (i) Use your calculator or computer to sketch a graph of $y = x^{\sin x}$ for $0 < x \leq 20$.

(ii) Using your answer to part (i), sketch by hand a graph of the function F, where

$$F(x) = \int_0^x t^{\sin t}\, dt.$$

(iii) Use a slope field program to check your answer to part (ii).

(c) Let $F(x)$ be the antiderivative of $\sin(x^2)$ satisfying $F(0) = 0$.

(i) Describe any general features of the graph of F that you can deduce by looking at the graph of $\sin(x^2)$ in Figure 6.47.

(ii) By drawing a slope field (using a calculator or computer), sketch a graph of F. Does F ever cross the x-axis in the region $x > 0$? Does $\lim\limits_{x \to \infty} F(x)$ exist?

Figure 6.47

Chapter Seven

INTEGRATION

Contents

7.1 INTEGRATION BY SUBSTITUTION

In Chapter 3, we learned rules to differentiate any function obtained by combining constants, powers of x, $\sin x$, $\cos x$, e^x, and $\ln x$, using addition, multiplication, division, or composition of functions. Such functions are called *elementary*.

In this chapter, we introduce several methods of antidifferentiation. However, there is a great difference between looking for derivatives and looking for antiderivatives. Every elementary function has elementary derivatives, but most elementary functions—such as $\sqrt{x^3 + 1}$, $(\sin x)/x$, and e^{-x^2}—do not have elementary antiderivatives.

All commonly occurring antiderivatives can be found with a computer algebra system (CAS). However, just as it is useful to be able to calculate $3 + 4$ without a calculator, we usually calculate some antiderivatives by hand.

The Guess-and-Check Method

A good strategy for finding simple antiderivatives is to *guess* an answer (using knowledge of differentiation rules) and then *check* the answer by differentiating it. If we get the expected result, then we're done; otherwise, we revise the guess and check again.

The method of guess-and-check is useful in reversing the chain rule. According to the chain rule,

$$\frac{d}{dx}(f(g(x))) = \underbrace{f'}_{\text{Derivative of outside}} \overbrace{(g(x))}^{\text{Inside}} \cdot \underbrace{g'(x)}_{\text{Derivative of inside}}.$$

Thus, any function which is the result of applying the chain rule is the product of two factors: the "derivative of the outside" and the "derivative of the inside." If a function has this form, its antiderivative is $f(g(x))$.

Example 1   Find $\displaystyle\int 3x^2 \cos(x^3)\, dx$.

Solution   The function $3x^2 \cos(x^3)$ looks like the result of applying the chain rule: there is an "inside" function x^3 and its derivative $3x^2$ appears as a factor. Since the outside function is a cosine which has a sine as an antiderivative, we guess $\sin(x^3)$ for the antiderivative. Differentiating to check gives

$$\frac{d}{dx}(\sin(x^3)) = \cos(x^3) \cdot (3x^2).$$

Since this is what we began with, we know that

$$\int 3x^2 \cos(x^3)\, dx = \sin(x^3) + C.$$

The basic idea of this method is to try to find an inside function whose derivative appears as a factor. This works even when the derivative is missing a constant factor, as in the next example.

Example 2   Find $\displaystyle\int x^3 \sqrt{x^4 + 5}\, dx$.

Solution   Here the inside function is $x^4 + 5$, and its derivative appears as a factor, with the exception of a missing 4. Thus, the integrand we have is more or less of the form

$$g'(x)\sqrt{g(x)},$$

with $g(x) = x^4 + 5$. Since $x^{3/2}/(3/2)$ is an antiderivative of the outside function $\sqrt{x}$, we might guess that an antiderivative is

$$\frac{(g(x))^{3/2}}{3/2} = \frac{(x^4 + 5)^{3/2}}{3/2}.$$

Let's check and see:

$$\frac{d}{dx}\left(\frac{(x^4+5)^{3/2}}{3/2}\right) = \frac{3}{2}\frac{(x^4+5)^{1/2}}{3/2} \cdot 4x^3 = 4x^3(x^4+5)^{1/2},$$

so $\dfrac{(x^4+5)^{3/2}}{3/2}$ is too big by a factor of 4. The correct antiderivative is

$$\frac{1}{4}\frac{(x^4+5)^{3/2}}{3/2} = \frac{1}{6}(x^4+5)^{3/2}.$$

Thus

$$\int x^3\sqrt{x^4+5}\,dx = \frac{1}{6}(x^4+5)^{3/2} + C.$$

As a final check:

$$\frac{d}{dx}\left(\frac{1}{6}(x^4+5)^{3/2}\right) = \frac{1}{6}\cdot\frac{3}{2}(x^4+5)^{1/2}\cdot 4x^3 = x^3(x^4+5)^{1/2}.$$

As we see in the preceding example, antidifferentiating a function often involves "correcting for" constant factors: if differentiation produces an extra factor of 2, antidifferentiation will require a factor of $\frac{1}{2}$.

The Method of Substitution

When the integrand is complicated, it helps to formalize this guess-and-check method as follows:

> ### To Make a Substitution
>
> Let w be the "inside function" and $dw = w'(x)\,dx = \dfrac{dw}{dx}dx.$

Let's redo the first example using a substitution.

Example 3   Find $\displaystyle\int 3x^2\cos(x^3)\,dx.$

Solution   As before, we look for an inside function whose derivative appears—in this case x^3. We let $w = x^3$. Then $dw = w'(x)\,dx = 3x^2\,dx$. The original integrand can now be completely rewritten in terms of the new variable w:

$$\int 3x^2\cos(x^3)\,dx = \int \cos\underbrace{(x^3)}_{w}\cdot\underbrace{3x^2\,dx}_{dw} = \int\cos w\,dw = \sin w + C = \sin(x^3) + C.$$

By changing the variable to w, we can simplify the integrand. We now have $\cos w$, which can be antidifferentiated more easily. The final step, after antidifferentiating, is to convert back to the original variable, x.

Why Does Substitution Work?

The substitution method makes it look as if we can treat dw and dx as separate entities, even canceling them in the equation $dw = (dw/dx)dx$. Let's see why this works. Suppose we have an integral of the form $\int f(g(x))g'(x)\,dx$, where $g(x)$ is the inside function and $f(x)$ is the outside function. If F is an antiderivative of f, then $F' = f$, and by the chain rule $\frac{d}{dx}(F(g(x))) = f(g(x))g'(x)$. Therefore,

$$\int f(g(x))g'(x)\,dx = F(g(x)) + C.$$

Now write $w = g(x)$ and $dw/dx = g'(x)$ on both sides of this equation:

$$\int f(w) \frac{dw}{dx} \, dx = F(w) + C.$$

On the other hand, knowing that $F' = f$ tells us that

$$\int f(w) \, dw = F(w) + C.$$

Thus, the following two integrals are equal:

$$\int f(w) \frac{dw}{dx} \, dx = \int f(w) \, dw.$$

Substituting w for the inside function and writing $dw = w'(x)dx$ leaves the indefinite integral unchanged.

Let's revisit the second example that we did by guess-and-check.

Example 4   Find $\displaystyle\int x^3 \sqrt{x^4 + 5} \, dx$.

Solution   The inside function is $x^4 + 5$, with derivative $4x^3$. The integrand has a factor of x^3, and since the only thing missing is a constant factor, we try

$$w = x^4 + 5.$$

Then

$$dw = w'(x) \, dx = 4x^3 \, dx,$$

giving

$$\frac{1}{4} dw = x^3 \, dx.$$

Thus,

$$\int x^3 \sqrt{x^4 + 5} \, dx = \int \sqrt{w} \, \frac{1}{4} dw = \frac{1}{4} \int w^{1/2} \, dw = \frac{1}{4} \cdot \frac{w^{3/2}}{3/2} + C = \frac{1}{6}(x^4 + 5)^{3/2} + C.$$

Once again, we get the same result as with guess-and-check.

Warning

We saw in the preceding example that we can apply the substitution method when a *constant* factor is missing from the derivative of the inside function. However, we may not be able to use substitution if anything other than a constant factor is missing. For example, setting $w = x^4 + 5$ to find

$$\int x^2 \sqrt{x^4 + 5} \, dx$$

does us no good because $x^2 \, dx$ is not a constant multiple of $dw = 4x^3 \, dx$. Substitution works if the integrand contains the derivative of the inside function, *to within a constant factor.*

Some people prefer the substitution method over guess-and-check since it is more systematic, but both methods achieve the same result. For simple problems, guess-and-check can be faster.

Example 5   Find $\displaystyle\int e^{\cos \theta} \sin \theta \, d\theta$.

Solution   We let $w = \cos \theta$ since its derivative is $-\sin \theta$ and there is a factor of $\sin \theta$ in the integrand. This gives

$$dw = w'(\theta) \, d\theta = -\sin \theta \, d\theta,$$

so

$$-dw = \sin\theta\,d\theta.$$

Thus

$$\int e^{\cos\theta}\sin\theta\,d\theta = \int e^{w}(-dw) = (-1)\int e^{w}\,dw = -e^{w} + C = -e^{\cos\theta} + C.$$

Example 6   Find $\displaystyle\int \frac{e^{t}}{1 + e^{t}}\,dt$.

Solution   Observing that the derivative of $1 + e^{t}$ is e^{t}, we see $w = 1 + e^{t}$ is a good choice. Then $dw = e^{t}\,dt$, so that

$$\int \frac{e^{t}}{1 + e^{t}}\,dt = \int \frac{1}{1 + e^{t}}\,e^{t}\,dt = \int \frac{1}{w}\,dw = \ln|w| + C$$
$$= \ln|1 + e^{t}| + C$$
$$= \ln(1 + e^{t}) + C. \qquad \text{(Since } (1 + e^{t}) \text{ is always positive.)}$$

Since the numerator is $e^{t}\,dt$, we might also have tried $w = e^{t}$. This substitution leads to the integral $\int (1/(1 + w))dw$, which is better than the original integral but requires another substitution, $u = 1 + w$, to finish. There are often several different ways of doing an integral by substitution.

Notice the pattern in the previous example: having a function in the denominator and its derivative in the numerator leads to a natural logarithm. The next example follows the same pattern.

Example 7   Find $\displaystyle\int \tan\theta\,d\theta$.

Solution   Recall that $\tan\theta = (\sin\theta)/(\cos\theta)$. If $w = \cos\theta$, then $dw = -\sin\theta\,d\theta$, so

$$\int \tan\theta\,d\theta = \int \frac{\sin\theta}{\cos\theta}\,d\theta = \int \frac{-dw}{w} = -\ln|w| + C = -\ln|\cos\theta| + C.$$

One way to think of integration is in terms of standard forms, whose antiderivatives are known. Substitution is useful for putting a complicated integral in a standard form.

Example 8   Give a substitution w and constants k, n so that the following integral has the form $\int kw^{n}\,dw$:

$$\int e^{x}\cos^{3}(e^{x})\sin(e^{x})\,dx.$$

Solution   We notice that one of the factors in the integrand is $(\cos(e^{x}))^{3}$, so if we let $w = \cos(e^{x})$, this factor is w^{3}. Then $dw = (-\sin(e^{x}))e^{x}\,dx$, so

$$\int e^{x}\cos^{3}(e^{x})\sin(e^{x})\,dx = \int \cos^{3}(e^{x})(\sin(e^{x}))e^{x}\,dx = \int w^{3}(-dw).$$

Therefore, we choose $w = \cos(e^{x})$ and then $k = -1, n = 3$.

Definite Integrals by Substitution

Example 9   Compute $\int_0^2 xe^{x^2}\, dx$.

Solution   To evaluate this definite integral using the Fundamental Theorem of Calculus, we first need to find an antiderivative of $f(x) = xe^{x^2}$. The inside function is x^2, so we let $w = x^2$. Then $dw = 2x\, dx$, so $\frac{1}{2}\, dw = x\, dx$. Thus,

$$\int xe^{x^2}\, dx = \int e^w \frac{1}{2}\, dw = \frac{1}{2}e^w + C = \frac{1}{2}e^{x^2} + C.$$

Now we find the definite integral

$$\int_0^2 xe^{x^2}\, dx = \frac{1}{2}e^{x^2}\Big|_0^2 = \frac{1}{2}(e^4 - e^0) = \frac{1}{2}(e^4 - 1).$$

There is another way to look at the same problem. After we established that

$$\int xe^{x^2}\, dx = \frac{1}{2}e^w + C,$$

our next two steps were to replace w by x^2, and then x by 2 and 0. We could have directly replaced the original limits of integration, $x = 0$ and $x = 2$, by the corresponding w limits. Since $w = x^2$, the w limits are $w = 0^2 = 0$ (when $x = 0$) and $w = 2^2 = 4$ (when $x = 2$), so we get

$$\int_{x=0}^{x=2} xe^{x^2}\, dx = \frac{1}{2}\int_{w=0}^{w=4} e^w\, dw = \frac{1}{2}e^w\Big|_0^4 = \frac{1}{2}\left(e^4 - e^0\right) = \frac{1}{2}(e^4 - 1).$$

As we would expect, both methods give the same answer.

To Use Substitution to Find Definite Integrals

Either
- Compute the indefinite integral, expressing an antiderivative in terms of the original variable, and then evaluate the result at the original limits,

or
- Convert the original limits to new limits in terms of the new variable and do not convert the antiderivative back to the original variable.

Example 10   Evaluate $\int_0^{\pi/4} \dfrac{\tan^3 \theta}{\cos^2 \theta}\, d\theta$.

Solution   To use substitution, we must decide what w should be. There are two possible inside functions, $\tan \theta$ and $\cos \theta$. Now

$$\frac{d}{d\theta}(\tan \theta) = \frac{1}{\cos^2 \theta} \quad \text{and} \quad \frac{d}{d\theta}(\cos \theta) = -\sin \theta,$$

and since the integral contains a factor of $1/\cos^2 \theta$ but not of $\sin \theta$, we try $w = \tan \theta$. Then $dw = (1/\cos^2 \theta)d\theta$. When $\theta = 0$, $w = \tan 0 = 0$, and when $\theta = \pi/4$, $w = \tan(\pi/4) = 1$, so

$$\int_0^{\pi/4} \frac{\tan^3 \theta}{\cos^2 \theta}\, d\theta = \int_0^{\pi/4} (\tan \theta)^3 \cdot \frac{1}{\cos^2 \theta}\, d\theta = \int_0^1 w^3\, dw = \frac{1}{4}w^4\Big|_0^1 = \frac{1}{4}.$$

Example 11   Evaluate $\int_1^3 \dfrac{dx}{5 - x}$.

Solution   Let $w = 5 - x$, so $dw = -dx$. When $x = 1$, $w = 4$, and when $x = 3$, $w = 2$, so

$$\int_1^3 \frac{dx}{5-x} = \int_4^2 \frac{-dw}{w} = -\ln|w| \Big|_4^2 = -(\ln 2 - \ln 4) = \ln\left(\frac{4}{2}\right) = \ln 2 = 0.693.$$

Notice that we write the limit $w = 4$ at the bottom, even though it is larger than $w = 2$, because $w = 4$ corresponds to the lower limit $x = 1$.

More Complex Substitutions

In the examples of substitution presented so far, we guessed an expression for w and hoped to find dw (or some constant multiple of it) in the integrand. What if we are not so lucky? It turns out that it often works to let w be some messy expression contained inside, say, a cosine or under a root, even if we cannot see immediately how such a substitution helps.

Example 12   Find $\int \sqrt{1 + \sqrt{x}}\, dx$.

Solution   This time, the derivative of the inside function is nowhere to be seen. Nevertheless, we try $w = 1 + \sqrt{x}$. Then $w - 1 = \sqrt{x}$, so $(w - 1)^2 = x$. Therefore $2(w - 1)\, dw = dx$. We have

$$\int \sqrt{1 + \sqrt{x}}\, dx = \int \sqrt{w}\, 2(w - 1)\, dw = 2\int w^{1/2}(w - 1)\, dw$$

$$= 2\int (w^{3/2} - w^{1/2})\, dw = 2\left(\frac{2}{5}w^{5/2} - \frac{2}{3}w^{3/2}\right) + C$$

$$= 2\left(\frac{2}{5}(1 + \sqrt{x})^{5/2} - \frac{2}{3}(1 + \sqrt{x})^{3/2}\right) + C.$$

Notice that the substitution in the preceding example again converts the inside of the messiest function into something simple. In addition, since the derivative of the inside function is not waiting for us, we have to solve for x so that we can get dx entirely in terms of w and dw.

Example 13   Find $\int (x + 7)\sqrt[3]{3 - 2x}\, dx$.

Solution   Here, instead of the derivative of the inside function (which is -2), we have the factor $(x + 7)$. However, substituting $w = 3 - 2x$ turns out to help anyway. Then $dw = -2\, dx$, so $(-1/2)\, dw = dx$. Now we must convert everything to w, including $x + 7$. If $w = 3 - 2x$, then $2x = 3 - w$, so $x = 3/2 - w/2$, and therefore we can write $x + 7$ in terms of w. Thus

$$\int (x + 7)\sqrt[3]{3 - 2x}\, dx = \int \left(\frac{3}{2} - \frac{w}{2} + 7\right)\sqrt[3]{w}\left(-\frac{1}{2}\right) dw$$

$$= -\frac{1}{2}\int \left(\frac{17}{2} - \frac{w}{2}\right) w^{1/3}\, dw$$

$$= -\frac{1}{4}\int (17 - w)w^{1/3}\, dw$$

$$= -\frac{1}{4}\int (17w^{1/3} - w^{4/3})\, dw$$

$$= -\frac{1}{4}\left(17\frac{w^{4/3}}{4/3} - \frac{w^{7/3}}{7/3}\right) + C$$

$$= -\frac{1}{4}\left(\frac{51}{4}(3 - 2x)^{4/3} - \frac{3}{7}(3 - 2x)^{7/3}\right) + C.$$

Looking back over the solution, the reason this substitution works is that it converts $\sqrt[3]{3 - 2x}$, the messiest part of the integrand, to $\sqrt[3]{w}$, which can be combined with the other factor and then integrated.

Exercises and Problems for Section 7.1

Exercises

1. Use substitution to express each of the following integrals as a multiple of $\int_a^b (1/w)\, dw$ for some a and b. Then evaluate the integrals.

(a) $\displaystyle\int_0^1 \frac{x}{1+x^2}\, dx$ **(b)** $\displaystyle\int_0^{\pi/4} \frac{\sin x}{\cos x}\, dx$

2. (a) Find the derivatives of $\sin(x^2+1)$ and $\sin(x^3+1)$.

(b) Use your answer to part (a) to find antiderivatives of:

(i) $x\cos(x^2+1)$ (ii) $x^2\cos(x^3+1)$

(c) Find the general antiderivatives of:

(i) $x\sin(x^2+1)$ (ii) $x^2\sin(x^3+1)$

Find the integrals in Exercises 3–48. Check your answers by differentiation.

3. $\displaystyle\int e^{3x}\, dx$

4. $\displaystyle\int te^{t^2}\, dt$

5. $\displaystyle\int e^{-x}\, dx$

6. $\displaystyle\int 25e^{-0.2t}\, dt$

7. $\displaystyle\int \sin(2x)\, dx$

8. $\displaystyle\int t\cos(t^2)\, dt$

9. $\displaystyle\int \sin(3-t)\, dt$

10. $\displaystyle\int xe^{-x^2}\, dx$

11. $\displaystyle\int (r+1)^3\, dr$

12. $\displaystyle\int y(y^2+5)^8\, dy$

13. $\displaystyle\int x^2(1+2x^3)^2\, dx$

14. $\displaystyle\int t^2(t^3-3)^{10}\, dt$

15. $\displaystyle\int x(x^2+3)^2\, dx$

16. $\displaystyle\int x(x^2-4)^{7/2}\, dx$

17. $\displaystyle\int y^2(1+y)^2\, dy$

18. $\displaystyle\int (2t-7)^{73}\, dt$

19. $\displaystyle\int x^2 e^{x^3+1}\, dx$

20. $\displaystyle\int \frac{dy}{y+5}$

21. $\displaystyle\int \frac{1}{\sqrt{4-x}}\, dx$

22. $\displaystyle\int (x^2+3)^2\, dx$

23. $\displaystyle\int \sin\theta(\cos\theta+5)^7\, d\theta$

24. $\displaystyle\int \sqrt{\cos 3t}\,\sin 3t\, dt$

25. $\displaystyle\int \sin^6\theta\cos\theta\, d\theta$

26. $\displaystyle\int \sin^3\alpha\cos\alpha\, d\alpha$

27. $\displaystyle\int \sin^6(5\theta)\cos(5\theta)\, d\theta$

28. $\displaystyle\int \tan(2x)\, dx$

29. $\displaystyle\int \frac{(\ln z)^2}{z}\, dz$

30. $\displaystyle\int \frac{e^t+1}{e^t+t}\, dt$

31. $\displaystyle\int \frac{(t+1)^2}{t^2}\, dt$

32. $\displaystyle\int \frac{y}{y^2+4}\, dy$

33. $\displaystyle\int \frac{dx}{1+2x^2}$

34. $\displaystyle\int \frac{dx}{\sqrt{1-4x^2}}$

35. $\displaystyle\int \frac{\cos\sqrt{x}}{\sqrt{x}}\, dx$

36. $\displaystyle\int \frac{e^{\sqrt{y}}}{\sqrt{y}}\, dy$

37. $\displaystyle\int \frac{1+e^x}{\sqrt{x+e^x}}\, dx$

38. $\displaystyle\int \frac{e^x}{2+e^x}\, dx$

39. $\displaystyle\int \frac{x+1}{x^2+2x+19}\, dx$

40. $\displaystyle\int \frac{t}{1+3t^2}\, dt$

41. $\displaystyle\int \frac{e^x-e^{-x}}{e^x+e^{-x}}\, dx$

42. $\displaystyle\int \frac{x\cos(x^2)}{\sqrt{\sin(x^2)}}\, dx$

43. $\displaystyle\int \sinh 3t\, dt$

44. $\displaystyle\int \cosh x\, dx$

45. $\displaystyle\int \cosh(2w+1)\, dw$

46. $\displaystyle\int (\sinh z)e^{\cosh z}\, dz$

47. $\displaystyle\int \cosh^2 x\sinh x\, dx$

48. $\displaystyle\int x\cosh x^2\, dx$

For the functions in Exercises 49–56, find the general antiderivative. Check your answers by differentiation.

49. $p(t) = \pi t^3 + 4t$

50. $f(x) = \sin 3x$

51. $f(x) = 2x\cos(x^2)$

52. $r(t) = 12t^2\cos(t^3)$

53. $f(x) = \sin(2-5x)$

54. $f(x) = e^{\sin x}\cos x$

55. $f(x) = \dfrac{x}{x^2+1}$

56. $f(x) = \dfrac{1}{3\cos^2(2x)}$

For Exercises 57–64, use the Fundamental Theorem to calculate the definite integrals.

57. $\displaystyle\int_0^\pi \cos(x+\pi)\, dx$

58. $\displaystyle\int_0^{1/2} \cos(\pi x)\, dx$

59. $\displaystyle\int_0^{\pi/2} e^{-\cos\theta}\sin\theta\, d\theta$

60. $\displaystyle\int_1^2 2xe^{x^2}\, dx$

61. $\displaystyle\int_1^4 \frac{e^{\sqrt{x}}}{\sqrt{x}}\, dx$

62. $\displaystyle\int_{-1}^{e-2} \frac{1}{t+2}\, dt$

63. $\displaystyle\int_1^4 \frac{\cos\sqrt{x}}{\sqrt{x}}\, dx$

64. $\displaystyle\int_0^2 \frac{x}{(1+x^2)^2}\, dx$

For Exercises 65–70, evaluate the definite integrals. Whenever possible, use the Fundamental Theorem of Calculus, perhaps after a substitution. Otherwise, use numerical methods.

65. $\int_{-1}^{3} (x^3 + 5x)\, dx$

66. $\int_{-1}^{1} \frac{1}{1 + y^2}\, dy$

67. $\int_{1}^{3} \frac{1}{x}\, dx$

68. $\int_{1}^{3} \frac{dt}{(t + 7)^2}$

69. $\int_{-1}^{2} \sqrt{x + 2}\, dx$

70. $\int_{1}^{2} \frac{\sin t}{t}\, dt$

Find the integrals in Exercises 71–78.

71. $\int y\sqrt{y + 1}\, dy$

72. $\int z(z + 1)^{1/3}\, dz$

73. $\int \frac{t^2 + t}{\sqrt{t + 1}}\, dt$

74. $\int \frac{dx}{2 + 2\sqrt{x}}$

75. $\int x^2\sqrt{x - 2}\, dx$

76. $\int (z + 2)\sqrt{1 - z}\, dz$

77. $\int \frac{t}{\sqrt{t + 1}}\, dt$

78. $\int \frac{3x - 2}{\sqrt{2x + 1}}\, dx$

Problems

In Problems 79–82, show the two integrals are equal using a substitution.

79. $\int_{0}^{\pi/3} 3\sin^2(3x)\, dx = \int_{0}^{\pi} \sin^2(y)\, dy$

80. $\int_{1}^{2} 2\ln(s^2 + 1)\, ds = \int_{1}^{4} \frac{\ln(t + 1)}{\sqrt{t}}\, dt$

81. $\int_{1}^{e} (\ln w)^3\, dw = \int_{0}^{1} z^3 e^z\, dz$

82. $\int_{0}^{\pi} x\cos(\pi - x)\, dx = \int_{0}^{\pi} (\pi - t)\cos t\, dt$

83. Using the substitution $w = x^2$, find a function $g(w)$ such that $\int_{\sqrt{a}}^{\sqrt{b}} dx = \int_{a}^{b} g(w)\, dw$ for all $0 < a < b$.

84. Using the substitution $w = e^x$, find a function $g(w)$ such that $\int_{a}^{b} e^{-x}\, dx = \int_{e^a}^{e^b} g(w)\, dw$ for all $a < b$.

In Problems 85–89, explain why the two antiderivatives are really, despite their apparent dissimilarity, different expressions of the same problem. You do not need to evaluate the integrals.

85. $\int \frac{e^x\, dx}{1 + e^{2x}}$ and $\int \frac{\cos x\, dx}{1 + \sin^2 x}$

86. $\int \frac{\ln x}{x}\, dx$ and $\int x\, dx$

87. $\int e^{\sin x}\cos x\, dx$ and $\int \frac{e^{\arcsin x}}{\sqrt{1 - x^2}}\, dx$

88. $\int (\sin x)^3 \cos x\, dx$ and $\int (x^3 + 1)^3 x^2\, dx$

89. $\int \sqrt{x + 1}\, dx$ and $\int \frac{\sqrt{1 + \sqrt{x}}}{\sqrt{x}}\, dx$

In Problems 90–96, evaluate the integral. Your answer should not contain f, which is a differentiable function with the following values:

x	0	1	$\pi/2$	e	3
$f(x)$	5	7	8	10	11
$f'(x)$	2	4	6	9	12

90. $\int_{0}^{1} f'(x)\sin f(x)\, dx$

91. $\int_{1}^{3} f'(x)e^{f(x)}\, dx$

92. $\int_{1}^{3} \frac{f'(x)}{f(x)}\, dx$

93. $\int_{0}^{1} e^x f'(e^x)\, dx$

94. $\int_{1}^{e} \frac{f'(\ln x)}{x}\, dx$

95. $\int_{0}^{1} f'(x)(f(x))^2\, dx$

96. $\int_{0}^{\pi/2} \sin x \cdot f'(\cos x)\, dx$

In Problems 97–100, find an expression for the integral which contains g but no integral sign.

97. $\int g'(x)(g(x))^4\, dx$

98. $\int g'(x)e^{g(x)}\, dx$

99. $\int g'(x)\sin g(x)\, dx$

100. $\int g'(x)\sqrt{1 + g(x)}\, dx$

In Problems 101–103, find a substitution w and constants k, n so that the integral has the form $\int kw^n\, dw$.

101. $\int x^2\sqrt{1 - 4x^3}\, dx$

102. $\int \frac{\cos t}{\sin t}\, dt$

103. $\int \frac{2x\, dx}{(x^2 - 3)^2}$

In Problems 104–106, find constants k, n, w_0, w_1 so the the integral has the form $\int_{w_0}^{w_1} kw^n\, dw$.

104. $\int_{1}^{5} \frac{3x\, dx}{\sqrt{5x^2 + 7}}$, $\quad w = 5x^2 + 7$

105. $\int_{0}^{5} \frac{2^x\, dx}{2^x + 3}$, $\quad w = 2^x + 3$

106. $\int_{\pi/12}^{\pi/4} \sin^7(2x)\cos(2x)\, dx$, $\quad w = \sin 2x$

In Problems 107–111, find a substitution w and a constant k so that the integral has the form $\int k e^w \, dw$.

107. $\int x e^{-x^2} \, dx$

108. $\int e^{\sin \phi} \cos \phi \, d\phi$

109. $\int \sqrt{e^r} \, dr$

110. $\int \dfrac{z^2 \, dz}{e^{-z^3}}$

111. $\int e^{2t} e^{3t-4} \, dt$

In Problems 112–113, find a substitution w and constants a, b, A so that the integral has the form $\int_a^b A e^w \, dw$.

112. $\int_3^7 e^{2t-3} \, dt$

113. $\int_0^1 e^{\cos(\pi t)} \sin(\pi t) \, dt$

114. Integrate:

(a) $\int \dfrac{1}{\sqrt{x}} \, dx$

(b) $\int \dfrac{1}{\sqrt{x+1}} \, dx$

(c) $\int \dfrac{1}{\sqrt{x}+1} \, dx$

115. If appropriate, evaluate the following integrals by substitution. If substitution is not appropriate, say so, and do not evaluate.

(a) $\int x \sin(x^2) \, dx$

(b) $\int x^2 \sin x \, dx$

(c) $\int \dfrac{x^2}{1+x^2} \, dx$

(d) $\int \dfrac{x}{(1+x^2)^2} \, dx$

(e) $\int x^3 e^{x^2} \, dx$

(f) $\int \dfrac{\sin x}{2 + \cos x} \, dx$

In Problems 116–122, find the exact area.

116. Under $f(x) = x e^{x^2}$ between $x = 0$ and $x = 2$.

117. Under $f(x) = 1/(x+1)$ between $x = 0$ and $x = 2$.

118. Under $f(x) = \sinh(x/2)$ between $x = 0$ and $x = 2$.

119. Under $f(\theta) = (e^{\theta+1})^3$ for $0 \le \theta \le 2$.

120. Between e^t and e^{t+1} for $0 \le t \le 2$.

121. Between $y = e^x$, $y = 3$, and the y-axis.

122. Under one arch of the curve $V(t) = V_0 \sin(\omega t)$, where $V_0 > 0$ and $\omega > 0$.

123. Find the exact average value of $f(x) = 1/(x+1)$ on the interval $x = 0$ to $x = 2$. Sketch a graph showing the function and the average value.

124. Let $g(x) = f(2x)$. Show that the average value of f on the interval $[0, 2b]$ is the same as the average value of g on the interval $[0, b]$.

125. Suppose $\int_0^2 g(t) \, dt = 5$. Calculate the following:

(a) $\int_0^4 g(t/2) \, dt$

(b) $\int_0^2 g(2-t) \, dt$

126. Suppose $\int_0^1 f(t) \, dt = 3$. Calculate the following:

(a) $\int_0^{0.5} f(2t) \, dt$

(b) $\int_0^1 f(1-t) \, dt$

(c) $\int_1^{1.5} f(3 - 2t) \, dt$

127. (a) Calculate exactly: $\int_{-\pi}^{\pi} \cos^2 \theta \sin \theta \, d\theta$.

(b) Calculate the exact area under the curve $y = \cos^2 \theta \sin \theta$ between $\theta = 0$ and $\theta = \pi$.

128. Find $\int 4x(x^2 + 1) \, dx$ using two methods:

(a) Do the multiplication first, and then antidifferentiate.

(b) Use the substitution $w = x^2 + 1$.

(c) Explain how the expressions from parts (a) and (b) are different. Are they both correct?

129. (a) Find $\int \sin \theta \cos \theta \, d\theta$.

(b) You probably solved part (a) by making the substitution $w = \sin \theta$ or $w = \cos \theta$. (If not, go back and do it that way.) Now find $\int \sin \theta \cos \theta \, d\theta$ by making the *other* substitution.

(c) There is yet another way of finding this integral which involves the trigonometric identities

$$\sin(2\theta) = 2 \sin \theta \cos \theta$$
$$\cos(2\theta) = \cos^2 \theta - \sin^2 \theta.$$

Find $\int \sin \theta \cos \theta \, d\theta$ using one of these identities and then the substitution $w = 2\theta$.

(d) You should now have three different expressions for the indefinite integral $\int \sin \theta \cos \theta \, d\theta$. Are they really different? Are they all correct? Explain.

For Problems 130–131, find a substitution w and constants a, b, k so that the integral has the form $\int_a^b k f(w) \, dw$.

130. $\int_1^9 f\left(6x\sqrt{x}\right) \sqrt{x} \, dx$

131. $\int_2^5 \dfrac{f\left(\ln\left(x^2 + 1\right)\right) x \, dx}{x^2 + 1}$

132. Find the solution of the initial value problem

$$y' = \tan x + 1, \quad y(0) = 1.$$

133. Let $I_{m,n} = \int_0^1 x^m (1-x)^n \, dx$ for constant m, n. Show that $I_{m,n} = I_{n,m}$.

134. Let $f(t)$ be the velocity in meters/second of a car at time t in seconds. Give an integral for the change of position of the car

(a) For the time interval $0 \le t \le 60$.

(b) In terms of T in minutes, for the same time interval.

135. Over the past fifty years the carbon dioxide level in the atmosphere has increased. Carbon dioxide is believed to drive temperature, so predictions of future carbon dioxide levels are important. If $C(t)$ is carbon dioxide level in parts per million (ppm) and t is time in years since 1950, three possible models are:[1]

I $C'(t) = 1.3$
II $C'(t) = 0.5 + 0.03t$
III $C'(t) = 0.5e^{0.02t}$

(a) Given that the carbon dioxide level was 311 ppm in 1950, find $C(t)$ for each model.
(b) Find the carbon dioxide level in 2020 predicted by each model.

136. Let $f(t)$ be the rate of flow, in cubic meters per hour, of a flooding river at time t in hours. Give an integral for the total flow of the river

(a) Over the 3-day period $0 \le t \le 72$.
(b) In terms of time T in days over the same 3-day period.

137. With t in years since 2000, the population, P, of the world in billions can be modeled by $P = 6.1e^{0.012t}$.

(a) What does this model predict for the world population in 2010? In 2020?
(b) Use the Fundamental Theorem to predict the average population of the world between 2000 and 2010.

138. Oil is leaking out of a ruptured tanker at the rate of $r(t) = 50e^{-0.02t}$ thousand liters per minute.

(a) At what rate, in liters per minute, is oil leaking out at $t - 0$? At $t - 60$?
(b) How many liters leak out during the first hour?

139. Throughout much of the 20th century, the yearly consumption of electricity in the US increased exponentially at a continuous rate of 7% per year. Assume this trend continues and that the electrical energy consumed in 1900 was 1.4 million megawatt-hours.

(a) Write an expression for yearly electricity consumption as a function of time, t, in years since 1900.
(b) Find the average yearly electrical consumption throughout the 20th century.
(c) During what year was electrical consumption closest to the average for the century?
(d) Without doing the calculation for part (c), how could you have predicted which half of the century the answer would be in?

140. An electric current, $I(t)$, flowing out of a capacitor, decays according to $I(t) = I_0e^{-t}$, where t is time. Find the charge, $Q(t)$, remaining in the capacitor at time t. The initial charge is Q_0 and $Q(t)$ is related to $I(t)$ by

$$Q'(t) = -I(t).$$

141. If we assume that wind resistance is proportional to velocity, then the downward velocity, v, of a body of mass m falling vertically is given by

$$v = \frac{mg}{k}\left(1 - e^{-kt/m}\right),$$

where g is the acceleration due to gravity and k is a constant. Find the height, h, above the surface of the earth as a function of time. Assume the body starts at height h_0.

142. If we assume that wind resistance is proportional to the square of velocity, then the downward velocity, v, of a falling body is given by

$$v = \sqrt{\frac{g}{k}}\left(\frac{e^{t\sqrt{gk}} - e^{-t\sqrt{gk}}}{e^{t\sqrt{gk}} + e^{-t\sqrt{gk}}}\right).$$

Use the substitution $w = e^{t\sqrt{gk}} + e^{-t\sqrt{gk}}$ to find the height, h, of the body above the surface of the earth as a function of time. Assume the body starts at a height h_0.

143. (a) Between 2000 and 2010, ACME Widgets sold widgets at a continuous rate of $R = R_0e^{0.125t}$ widgets per year, where t is time in years since January 1, 2000. Suppose they were selling widgets at a rate of 1000 per year on January 1, 2000. How many widgets did they sell between 2000 and 2010? How many did they sell if the rate on January 1, 2000 was 1,000,000 widgets per year?
(b) In the first case (1000 widgets per year on January 1, 2000), how long did it take for half the widgets in the ten-year period to be sold? In the second case (1,000,000 widgets per year on January 1, 2000), when had half the widgets in the ten-year period been sold?
(c) In 2010, ACME advertised that half the widgets it had sold in the previous ten years were still in use. Based on your answer to part (b), how long must a widget last in order to justify this claim?

144. The rate at which water is flowing into a tank is $r(t)$ gallons/minute, with t in minutes.

(a) Write an expression approximating the amount of water entering the tank during the interval from time t to time $t + \Delta t$, where Δt is small.
(b) Write a Riemann sum approximating the total amount of water entering the tank between $t = 0$ and $t = 5$. Write an exact expression for this amount.
(c) By how much has the amount of water in the tank changed between $t = 0$ and $t = 5$ if $r(t) = 20e^{0.02t}$?
(d) If $r(t)$ is as in part (c), and if the tank contains 3000 gallons initially, find a formula for $Q(t)$, the amount of water in the tank at time t.

[1] Based on data from www.esrl.noaa.gov/gmd/ccgg.

Strengthen Your Understanding

In Problems 145–147, explain what is wrong with the statement.

145. $\int (f(x))^2 \, dx = (f(x))^3/3 + C$.

146. $\int \cos(x^2) \, dx = \sin(x^2)/(2x) + C$.

147. $\int_0^{\pi/2} \cos(3x) \, dx = (1/3) \int_0^{\pi/2} \cos w \, dw$.

In Problems 148–149, give an example of:

148. A possible $f(\theta)$ so that the following integral can be integrated by substitution:

$$\int f(\theta) e^{\cos \theta} \, d\theta.$$

149. An indefinite integral involving $\sin(x^3 - 3x)$ that can be evaluated by substitution.

In Problems 150–152, decide whether the statements are true or false. Give an explanation for your answer.

150. $\int f'(x) \cos(f(x)) \, dx = \sin(f(x)) + C$.

151. $\int (1/f(x)) \, dx = \ln |f(x)| + C$.

152. $\int t \sin(5 - t^2) \, dt$ can be evaluated using substitution.

7.2 INTEGRATION BY PARTS

The method of substitution reverses the chain rule. Now we introduce *integration by parts*, which is based on the product rule.

Example 1 Find $\int x e^x \, dx$.

Solution We are looking for a function whose derivative is xe^x. The product rule might lead us to guess xe^x, because we know that the derivative has two terms, one of which is xe^x:

$$\frac{d}{dx}(xe^x) = \frac{d}{dx}(x)e^x + x\frac{d}{dx}(e^x) = e^x + xe^x.$$

Of course, our guess is wrong because of the extra e^x. But we can adjust our guess by subtracting e^x; this leads us to try $xe^x - e^x$. Let's check it:

$$\frac{d}{dx}(xe^x - e^x) = \frac{d}{dx}(xe^x) - \frac{d}{dx}(e^x) = e^x + xe^x - e^x = xe^x.$$

It works, so $\int x e^x \, dx = xe^x - e^x + C$.

Example 2 Find $\int \theta \cos \theta \, d\theta$.

Solution We guess the antiderivative is $\theta \sin \theta$ and use the product rule to check:

$$\frac{d}{d\theta}(\theta \sin \theta) = \frac{d(\theta)}{d\theta} \sin \theta + \theta \frac{d}{d\theta}(\sin \theta) = \sin \theta + \theta \cos \theta.$$

To correct for the extra $\sin \theta$ term, we must subtract from our original guess something whose derivative is $\sin \theta$. Since $\frac{d}{d\theta}(\cos \theta) = -\sin \theta$, we try:

$$\frac{d}{d\theta}(\theta \sin \theta + \cos \theta) = \frac{d}{d\theta}(\theta \sin \theta) + \frac{d}{d\theta}(\cos \theta) = \sin \theta + \theta \cos \theta - \sin \theta = \theta \cos \theta.$$

Thus, $\int \theta \cos \theta \, d\theta = \theta \sin \theta + \cos \theta + C$.

The General Formula for Integration by Parts

We can formalize the process illustrated in the last two examples in the following way. We begin with the product rule:

$$\frac{d}{dx}(uv) = u'v + uv'$$

where u and v are functions of x with derivatives u' and v', respectively. We rewrite this as:

$$uv' = \frac{d}{dx}(uv) - u'v$$

and then integrate both sides:

$$\int uv' \, dx = \int \frac{d}{dx}(uv) \, dx - \int u'v \, dx.$$

Since an antiderivative of $\frac{d}{dx}(uv)$ is just uv, we get the following formula:

Integration by Parts

$$\int uv' \, dx = uv - \int u'v \, dx.$$

This formula is useful when the integrand can be viewed as a product and when the integral on the right-hand side is simpler than that on the left. In effect, we were using integration by parts in the previous two examples. In Example 1, we let $xe^x = (x) \cdot (e^x) = uv'$, and choose $u = x$ and $v' = e^x$. Thus, $u' = 1$ and $v = e^x$, so

$$\int \underbrace{(x)}_{u} \underbrace{(e^x)}_{v'} \, dx = \underbrace{(x)}_{u} \underbrace{(e^x)}_{v} - \int \underbrace{(1)}_{u'} \underbrace{(e^x)}_{v} \, dx = xe^x - e^x + C.$$

So uv represents our first guess, and $\int u'v \, dx$ represents the correction to our guess.

Notice what would have happened if, instead of $v = e^x$, we took $v = e^x + C_1$. Then

$$\int xe^x \, dx = x(e^x + C_1) - \int (e^x + C_1) \, dx$$
$$= xe^x + C_1 x - e^x - C_1 x + C$$
$$= xe^x - e^x + C,$$

as before. Thus, it is not necessary to include an arbitrary constant in the antiderivative for v; any antiderivative will do.

What would have happened if we had picked u and v' the other way around? If $u = e^x$ and $v' = x$, then $u' = e^x$ and $v = x^2/2$. The formula for integration by parts then gives

$$\int xe^x \, dx = \frac{x^2}{2}e^x - \int \frac{x^2}{2} \cdot e^x \, dx,$$

which is true but not helpful since the integral on the right is worse than the one on the left. To use this method, we must choose u and v' to make the integral on the right easier to find than the integral on the left.

How to Choose u and v'

- Whatever you let v' be, you need to be able to find v.
- It helps if u' is simpler than u (or at least no more complicated than u).
- It helps if v is simpler than v' (or at least no more complicated than v').

If we pick $v' = x$ in Example 1, then $v = x^2/2$, which is certainly "worse" than v'.

There are some examples which don't look like good candidates for integration by parts because they don't appear to involve products, but for which the method works well. Such examples often involve $\ln x$ or the inverse trigonometric functions. Here is one:

Example 3   Find $\displaystyle\int_2^3 \ln x \, dx$.

Solution   This does not look like a product unless we write $\ln x = (1)(\ln x)$. Then we might say $u = 1$ so $u' = 0$, which certainly makes things simpler. But if $v' = \ln x$, what is v? If we knew, we would not need integration by parts. Let's try the other way: if $u = \ln x$, $u' = 1/x$ and if $v' = 1$, $v = x$, so

$$\int_2^3 \underbrace{(\ln x)}_{u} \underbrace{(1)}_{v'} \, dx = \underbrace{(\ln x)}_{u} \underbrace{(x)}_{v} \bigg|_2^3 - \int_2^3 \underbrace{\left(\frac{1}{x}\right)}_{u'} \cdot \underbrace{(x)}_{v} \, dx$$

$$= x \ln x \bigg|_2^3 - \int_2^3 1 \, dx = (x \ln x - x) \bigg|_2^3$$

$$= 3 \ln 3 - 3 - 2 \ln 2 + 2 = 3 \ln 3 - 2 \ln 2 - 1.$$

Notice that when doing a definite integral by parts, we must remember to put the limits of integration (here 2 and 3) on the uv term (in this case $x \ln x$) as well as on the integral $\int u'v \, dx$.

Example 4   Find $\displaystyle\int x^6 \ln x \, dx$.

Solution   View $x^6 \ln x$ as uv' where $u = \ln x$ and $v' = x^6$. Then $v = \frac{1}{7}x^7$ and $u' = 1/x$, so integration by parts gives us:

$$\int x^6 \ln x \, dx = \int (\ln x) x^6 \, dx = (\ln x)\left(\frac{1}{7}x^7\right) - \int \frac{1}{7}x^7 \cdot \frac{1}{x} \, dx$$

$$= \frac{1}{7}x^7 \ln x - \frac{1}{7}\int x^6 \, dx$$

$$= \frac{1}{7}x^7 \ln x - \frac{1}{49}x^7 + C.$$

In Example 4 we did not choose $v' = \ln x$, because it is not immediately clear what v would be. In fact, we used integration by parts in Example 3 to find the antiderivative of $\ln x$. Also, using $u = \ln x$, as we have done, gives $u' = 1/x$, which can be considered simpler than $u = \ln x$. This shows that u does not have to be the first factor in the integrand (here x^6).

Example 5   Find $\displaystyle\int x^2 \sin 4x \, dx$.

Solution   If we let $v' = \sin 4x$, then $v = -\frac{1}{4}\cos 4x$, which is no worse than v'. Also letting $u = x^2$, we get $u' = 2x$, which is simpler than $u = x^2$. Using integration by parts:

$$\int x^2 \sin 4x \, dx = x^2 \left(-\frac{1}{4}\cos 4x\right) - \int 2x \left(-\frac{1}{4}\cos 4x\right) \, dx$$

$$= -\frac{1}{4}x^2 \cos 4x + \frac{1}{2}\int x \cos 4x \, dx.$$

The trouble is we still have to grapple with $\int x \cos 4x \, dx$. This can be done by using integration by parts again with a new u and v, namely $u = x$ and $v' = \cos 4x$:

$$\int x \cos 4x \, dx = x \left(\frac{1}{4} \sin 4x \right) - \int 1 \cdot \frac{1}{4} \sin 4x \, dx$$

$$= \frac{1}{4} x \sin 4x - \frac{1}{4} \cdot \left(-\frac{1}{4} \cos 4x \right) + C$$

$$= \frac{1}{4} x \sin 4x + \frac{1}{16} \cos 4x + C.$$

Thus,

$$\int x^2 \sin 4x \, dx = -\frac{1}{4} x^2 \cos 4x + \frac{1}{2} \int x \cos 4x \, dx$$

$$= -\frac{1}{4} x^2 \cos 4x + \frac{1}{2} \left(\frac{1}{4} x \sin 4x + \frac{1}{16} \cos 4x + C \right)$$

$$= -\frac{1}{4} x^2 \cos 4x + \frac{1}{8} x \sin 4x + \frac{1}{32} \cos 4x + C.$$

Notice that, in this example, each time we used integration by parts, the exponent of x went down by 1. In addition, when the arbitrary constant C is multiplied by $\frac{1}{2}$, it is still represented by C.

Example 6   Find $\int \cos^2 \theta \, d\theta$.

Solution   Using integration by parts with $u = \cos \theta$, $v' = \cos \theta$ gives $u' = -\sin \theta$, $v = \sin \theta$, so we get

$$\int \cos^2 \theta \, d\theta = \cos \theta \sin \theta + \int \sin^2 \theta \, d\theta.$$

Substituting $\sin^2 \theta = 1 - \cos^2 \theta$ leads to

$$\int \cos^2 \theta \, d\theta = \cos \theta \sin \theta + \int (1 - \cos^2 \theta) \, d\theta$$

$$= \cos \theta \sin \theta + \int 1 \, d\theta - \int \cos^2 \theta \, d\theta.$$

Looking at the right side, we see that the original integral has reappeared. If we move it to the left, we get

$$2 \int \cos^2 \theta \, d\theta = \cos \theta \sin \theta + \int 1 \, d\theta = \cos \theta \sin \theta + \theta + C.$$

Dividing by 2 gives

$$\int \cos^2 \theta \, d\theta = \frac{1}{2} \cos \theta \sin \theta + \frac{1}{2} \theta + C.$$

Problem 53 asks you to do this integral by another method.

The previous example illustrates a useful technique: Use integration by parts to transform the integral into an expression containing another copy of the same integral, possibly multiplied by a coefficient, then solve for the original integral.

Example 7   Use integration by parts twice to find $\int e^{2x} \sin(3x) \, dx$.

Solution   Using integration by parts with $u = e^{2x}$ and $v' = \sin(3x)$ gives $u' = 2e^{2x}$, $v = -\frac{1}{3} \cos(3x)$, so we get

$$\int e^{2x} \sin(3x) \, dx = -\frac{1}{3} e^{2x} \cos(3x) + \frac{2}{3} \int e^{2x} \cos(3x) \, dx.$$

On the right side we have an integral similar to the original one, with the sine replaced by a cosine. Using integration by parts on that integral in the same way gives

$$\int e^{2x}\cos(3x)\,dx = \frac{1}{3}e^{2x}\sin(3x) - \frac{2}{3}\int e^{2x}\sin(3x)\,dx.$$

Substituting this into the expression we obtained for the original integral gives

$$\int e^{2x}\sin(3x)\,dx = -\frac{1}{3}e^{2x}\cos(3x) + \frac{2}{3}\left(\frac{1}{3}e^{2x}\sin(3x) - \frac{2}{3}\int e^{2x}\sin(3x)\,dx\right)$$

$$= -\frac{1}{3}e^{2x}\cos(3x) + \frac{2}{9}e^{2x}\sin(3x) - \frac{4}{9}\int e^{2x}\sin(3x)\,dx.$$

The right side now has a copy of the original integral, multiplied by $-4/9$. Moving it to the left, we get

$$\left(1 + \frac{4}{9}\right)\int e^{2x}\sin(3x)\,dx = -\frac{1}{3}e^{2x}\cos(3x) + \frac{2}{9}e^{2x}\sin(3x).$$

Dividing through by the coefficient on the left, $(1+4/9) = 13/9$ and adding a constant of integration C, we get

$$\int e^{2x}\sin(3x)\,dx = \frac{9}{13}\left(-\frac{1}{3}e^{2x}\cos(3x) + \frac{2}{9}e^{2x}\sin(3x)\right) + C$$

$$= \frac{1}{13}e^{2x}\left(2\sin(3x) - 3\cos(3x)\right) + C.$$

Example 8   Use a computer algebra system to investigate $\int \sin(x^2)\,dx$.

Solution   It can be shown that $\sin(x^2)$ has no elementary antiderivative. A computer algebra system gives an antiderivative involving a non-elementary function, the Fresnel Integral, which you may not recognize.

Exercises and Problems for Section 7.2

Exercises

1. Use integration by parts to express $\int x^2 e^x\,dx$ in terms of

    (a) $\displaystyle\int x^3 e^x\,dx$ (b) $\displaystyle\int xe^x\,dx$

2. Write $\arctan x = 1\cdot\arctan x$ to find $\int \arctan x\,dx$.

Find the integrals in Exercises 3–32.

3. $\displaystyle\int t\sin t\,dt$ 4. $\displaystyle\int t^2\sin t\,dt$

5. $\displaystyle\int te^{5t}\,dt$ 6. $\displaystyle\int t^2 e^{5t}\,dt$

7. $\displaystyle\int pe^{-0.1p}\,dp$ 8. $\displaystyle\int (z+1)e^{2z}\,dz$

9. $\displaystyle\int x\ln x\,dx$ 10. $\displaystyle\int x^3\ln x\,dx$

11. $\displaystyle\int q^5\ln 5q\,dq$ 12. $\displaystyle\int \theta^2\cos 3\theta\,d\theta$

13. $\displaystyle\int \sin^2\theta\,d\theta$ 14. $\displaystyle\int \cos^2(3\alpha+1)\,d\alpha$

15. $\displaystyle\int (\ln t)^2\,dt$ 16. $\displaystyle\int \ln(x^2)\,dx$

17. $\displaystyle\int y\sqrt{y+3}\,dy$ 18. $\displaystyle\int (t+2)\sqrt{2+3t}\,dt$

19. $\displaystyle\int (\theta+1)\sin(\theta+1)\,d\theta$ 20. $\displaystyle\int \frac{z}{e^z}\,dz$

21. $\displaystyle\int \frac{\ln x}{x^2}\,dx$ 22. $\displaystyle\int \frac{y}{\sqrt{5-y}}\,dy$

23. $\displaystyle\int \frac{t+7}{\sqrt{5-t}}\,dt$ 24. $\displaystyle\int x(\ln x)^4\,dx$

25. $\int r(\ln r)^2\,dr$ **26.** $\int \arcsin w\,dw$

27. $\int \arctan 7z\,dz$ **28.** $\int x\arctan x^2\,dx$

29. $\int x^3 e^{x^2}\,dx$ **30.** $\int x^5 \cos x^3\,dx$

31. $\int x\sinh x\,dx$ **32.** $\int (x-1)\cosh x\,dx$

Evaluate the integrals in Exercises 33–40 both exactly [e.g. $\ln(3\pi)$] and numerically [e.g. $\ln(3\pi) \approx 2.243$].

33. $\int_1^5 \ln t\,dt$ **34.** $\int_3^5 x\cos x\,dx$

35. $\int_0^{10} ze^{-z}\,dz$ **36.** $\int_1^3 t\ln t\,dt$

37. $\int_0^1 \arctan y\,dy$ **38.** $\int_0^5 \ln(1+t)\,dt$

39. $\int_0^1 \arcsin z\,dz$ **40.** $\int_0^1 u\arcsin u^2\,du$

41. For each of the following integrals, indicate whether integration by substitution or integration by parts is more appropriate. Do not evaluate the integrals.

(a) $\int x\sin x\,dx$ **(b)** $\int \dfrac{x^2}{1+x^3}\,dx$

(c) $\int xe^{x^2}\,dx$ **(d)** $\int x^2\cos(x^3)\,dx$

(e) $\int \dfrac{1}{\sqrt{3x+1}}\,dx$ **(f)** $\int x^2\sin x\,dx$

(g) $\int \ln x\,dx$

42. Find $\int_1^2 \ln x\,dx$ numerically. Find $\int_1^2 \ln x\,dx$ using antiderivatives. Check that your answers agree.

Problems

In Problems 43–45, using properties of ln, find a substitution w and constant k so that the integral has the form $\int k\ln w\,dw$.

43. $\int \ln\left((5-3x)^2\right)\,dx$ **44.** $\int \ln\left(\dfrac{1}{\sqrt{4-5x}}\right)\,dx$

45. $\int \dfrac{\ln\left((\ln x)^3\right)}{x}\,dx$

In Problems 46–51, find the exact area.

46. Under $y = te^{-t}$ for $0 \le t \le 2$.

47. Under $f(z) = \arctan z$ for $0 \le z \le 2$.

48. Under $f(y) = \arcsin y$ for $0 \le y \le 1$.

49. Between $y = \ln x$ and $y = \ln(x^2)$ for $1 \le x \le 2$.

50. Between $f(t) = \ln(t^2-1)$ and $g(t) = \ln(t-1)$ for $2 \le t \le 3$.

51. Under the first arch of $f(x) = x\sin x$.

52. In Exercise 13, you evaluated $\int \sin^2\theta\,d\theta$ using integration by parts. (If you did not do it by parts, do so now!) Redo this integral using the identity $\sin^2\theta = (1-\cos 2\theta)/2$. Explain any differences in the form of the answer obtained by the two methods.

53. Compute $\int \cos^2\theta\,d\theta$ in two different ways and explain any differences in the form of your answers. (The identity $\cos^2\theta = (1+\cos 2\theta)/2$ may be useful.)

54. Use integration by parts twice to find $\int e^x\sin x\,dx$.

55. Use integration by parts twice to find $\int e^\theta\cos\theta\,d\theta$.

56. Use the results from Problems 54 and 55 and integration by parts to find $\int xe^x\sin x\,dx$.

57. Use the results from Problems 54 and 55 and integration by parts to find $\int \theta e^\theta\cos\theta\,d\theta$.

58. If f is a twice differentiable function, find
$$\int f''(x)\ln x\,dx + \int \frac{f(x)}{x^2}\,dx$$
(Your answer should contain f, but no integrals.)

59. If f is a twice differentiable function, find $\int xf''(x)\,dx$. (Your answer should contain f, but no integrals.)

60. Use the table with $f(x) = F'(x)$ to find $\int_0^5 xf'(x)\,dx$.

x	0	1	2	3	4	5
$f(x)$	2	-5	-6	-1	10	27
$F(x)$	10	8	2	-2	2	20

In Problems 61–64, derive the given formulas.

61. $\int x^n e^x\,dx = x^n e^x - n\int x^{n-1}e^x\,dx$

62. $\int x^n\cos ax\,dx = \dfrac{1}{a}x^n\sin ax - \dfrac{n}{a}\int x^{n-1}\sin ax\,dx$

63. $\int x^n\sin ax\,dx = -\dfrac{1}{a}x^n\cos ax + \dfrac{n}{a}\int x^{n-1}\cos ax\,dx$

64. $\int \cos^n x\,dx = \dfrac{1}{n}\cos^{n-1}x\sin x + \dfrac{n-1}{n}\int \cos^{n-2}x\,dx$

65. Integrating $e^{ax}\sin bx$ by parts twice gives
$$\int e^{ax}\sin bx\,dx = e^{ax}(A\sin bx + B\cos bx) + C.$$
(a) Find the constants A and B in terms of a and b. [Hint: Don't actually perform the integration.]
(b) Evaluate $\int e^{ax}\cos bx\,dx$ by modifying the method in part (a). [Again, do not perform the integration.]

66. Estimate $\int_0^{10} f(x)g'(x)\,dx$ if $f(x) = x^2$ and g has the values in the following table.

x	0	2	4	6	8	10
$g(x)$	2.3	3.1	4.1	5.5	5.9	6.1

67. Let f be a function with $f(0) = 6$, $f(1) = 5$, and $f'(1) = 2$. Evaluate the integral $\int_0^1 xf''(x)\,dx$.

68. Given $h(x) = f(x)\sqrt{x}$ and $g'(x) = f(x)/\sqrt{x}$, rewrite in terms of $h(x)$ and $g(x)$:

$$\int f'(x)\sqrt{x}\,dx.$$

Your answer should not include integrals, $f(x)$, $h'(x)$, or $g'(x)$.

69. Given that $f(7) = 0$ and $\int_0^7 f(x)\,dx = 5$, evaluate

$$\int_0^7 xf'(x)\,dx.$$

70. Let $F(a)$ be the area under the graph of $y = x^2 e^{-x}$ between $x = 0$ and $x = a$, for $a > 0$.

(a) Find a formula for $F(a)$.
(b) Is F an increasing or decreasing function?
(c) Is F concave up or concave down for $0 < a < 2$?

71. The concentration, C, in ng/ml, of a drug in the blood as a function of the time, t, in hours since the drug was administered is given by $C = 15te^{-0.2t}$. The area under the concentration curve is a measure of the overall effect of the drug on the body, called the bioavailability. Find the bioavailability of the drug between $t = 0$ and $t = 3$.

72. The voltage, V, in an electric circuit is given as a function of time, t, by

$$V = V_0 \cos(\omega t + \phi).$$

Each of the positive constants, V_0, ω, ϕ is increased (while the other two are held constant). What is the effect of each increase on the following quantities:

(a) The maximum value of V?

(b) The maximum value of dV/dt?
(c) The average value of V^2 over one period of V?

73. During a surge in the demand for electricity, the rate, r, at which energy is used can be approximated by

$$r = te^{-at},$$

where t is the time in hours and a is a positive constant.

(a) Find the total energy, E, used in the first T hours. Give your answer as a function of a.
(b) What happens to E as $T \to \infty$?

74. Given $h(x) = f(x) \ln |x|$ and $g'(x) = \dfrac{f(x)}{x}$, rewrite

$$\int f'(x) \ln |x|\,dx. \text{ in terms of } h(x) \text{ and } g(x).$$

75. The *error function*, $\mathrm{erf}(x)$, is defined by

$$\mathrm{erf}(x) = \frac{2}{\sqrt{\pi}} \int_0^x e^{-t^2}\,dt.$$

(a) Let $u = \mathrm{erf}(x)$. Use integration by parts to write $\int \mathrm{erf}(x)\,dx = uv - \int v\,u'\,dx.$ Give u' and v'.

(b) Evaluate the integral $\int v\,u'\,dx$ from part (a) by making a substitution w. Give the values of w and dw.

(c) Use your answers to parts (a) and (b) to find $\int \mathrm{erf}(x)\,dx$. Your answer may involve $\mathrm{erf}(x)$.

76. The *Eulerian logarithmic integral* $\mathrm{Li}(x)$ is defined[2] as $\mathrm{Li}(x) = \displaystyle\int_2^x \frac{1}{\ln t}\,dt$. Letting $u = \mathrm{Li}(x)$ and $v = \ln x$, use integration by parts to evaluate $\int \mathrm{Li}(x)x^{-1}\,dx$. Your answer will involve $\mathrm{Li}(x)$.

Strengthen Your Understanding

In Problems 77–79, explain what is wrong with the statement.

77. To integrate $\int t \ln t\,dt$ by parts, use $u = t$, $v' = \ln t$.

78. The integral $\int \arctan x\,dx$ cannot be evaluated using integration by parts since the integrand is not a product of two functions.

79. Using integration by parts, we can show that

$$\int f(x)\,dx = xf'(x) - \int xf'(x)\,dx.$$

In Problems 80–82, give an example of:

80. An integral using only powers of θ and $\sin \theta$ which can be evaluated using integration by parts twice.

81. An integral that requires three applications of integration by parts.

82. An integral of the form $\int f(x)g(x)\,dx$ that can be evaluated using integration by parts either with $u = f(x)$ or with $u = g(x)$.

---

[2]http://en.wikipedia.org/wiki/Logarithmic_integral_function#Offset_logarithmic_integral, accessed February 17, 2011.

In Problems 83–85, decide whether the statements are true or false. Give an explanation for your answer.

83. $\int t \sin(5 - t) \, dt$ can be evaluated by parts.

84. The integral $\int t^2 e^{3-t} \, dt$ can be done by parts.

85. When integrating by parts, it does not matter which factor we choose for u.

7.3 TABLES OF INTEGRALS

Today, many integrals are done using a CAS. Traditionally, the antiderivatives of commonly used functions were compiled in a table, such as the one in the back of this book. Other tables include *CRC Standard Mathematical Tables* (Boca Raton, Fl: CRC Press). The key to using these tables is being able to recognize the general class of function that you are trying to integrate, so you can know in what section of the table to look.

Warning: This section involves long division of polynomials and completing the square. You may want to review these topics!

Using the Table of Integrals

Part I of the table inside the back cover gives the antiderivatives of the basic functions x^n, a^x, $\ln x$, $\sin x$, $\cos x$, and $\tan x$. (The antiderivative for $\ln x$ is found using integration by parts and is a special case of the more general formula III-13.) Most of these are already familiar.

Part II of the table contains antiderivatives of functions involving products of e^x, $\sin x$, and $\cos x$. All of these antiderivatives were obtained using integration by parts.

Example 1   Find $\displaystyle\int \sin 7z \sin 3z \, dz$.

Solution   Since the integrand is the product of two sines, we should use II-10 in the table,

$$\int \sin 7z \sin 3z \, dz = -\frac{1}{40}(7 \cos 7z \sin 3z - 3 \cos 3z \sin 7z) + C.$$

Part III of the table contains antiderivatives for products of a polynomial and e^x, $\sin x$, or $\cos x$. It also has an antiderivative for $x^n \ln x$, which can easily be used to find the antiderivatives of the product of a general polynomial and $\ln x$. Each *reduction formula* is used repeatedly to reduce the degree of the polynomial until a zero-degree polynomial is obtained.

Example 2   Find $\displaystyle\int (x^5 + 2x^3 - 8)e^{3x} \, dx$.

Solution   Since $p(x) = x^5 + 2x^3 - 8$ is a polynomial multiplied by e^{3x}, this is of the form in III-14. Now $p'(x) = 5x^4 + 6x^2$ and $p''(x) = 20x^3 + 12x$, and so on, giving

$$\int (x^5 + 2x^3 - 8)e^{3x} \, dx = e^{3x} \left(\frac{1}{3}(x^5 + 2x^3 - 8) - \frac{1}{9}(5x^4 + 6x^2) + \frac{1}{27}(20x^3 + 12x) \right.$$
$$\left. - \frac{1}{81}(60x^2 + 12) + \frac{1}{243}(120x) - \frac{1}{729} \cdot 120 \right) + C.$$

Here we have the successive derivatives of the original polynomial $x^5 + 2x^3 - 8$, occurring with alternating signs and multiplied by successive powers of 1/3.

Part IV of the table contains reduction formulas for the antiderivatives of $\cos^n x$ and $\sin^n x$, which can be obtained by integration by parts. When n is a positive integer, formulas IV-17 and IV-18 can be used repeatedly to reduce the power n until it is 0 or 1.

Example 3   Find $\int \sin^6 \theta \, d\theta$.

Solution   Use IV-17 repeatedly:

$$\int \sin^6 \theta \, d\theta = -\frac{1}{6} \sin^5 \theta \cos \theta + \frac{5}{6} \int \sin^4 \theta \, d\theta$$

$$\int \sin^4 \theta \, d\theta = -\frac{1}{4} \sin^3 \theta \cos \theta + \frac{3}{4} \int \sin^2 \theta \, d\theta$$

$$\int \sin^2 \theta \, d\theta = -\frac{1}{2} \sin \theta \cos \theta + \frac{1}{2} \int 1 \, d\theta.$$

Calculate $\int \sin^2 \theta \, d\theta$ first, and use this to find $\int \sin^4 \theta \, d\theta$; then calculate $\int \sin^6 \theta \, d\theta$. Putting this all together, we get

$$\int \sin^6 \theta \, d\theta = -\frac{1}{6} \sin^5 \theta \cos \theta - \frac{5}{24} \sin^3 \theta \cos \theta - \frac{15}{48} \sin \theta \cos \theta + \frac{15}{48} \theta + C.$$

The last item in **Part IV** of the table is not a formula: it is advice on how to antidifferentiate products of integer powers of $\sin x$ and $\cos x$. There are various techniques to choose from, depending on the nature (odd or even, positive or negative) of the exponents.

Example 4   Find $\int \cos^3 t \sin^4 t \, dt$.

Solution   Here the exponent of $\cos t$ is odd, so IV-23 recommends making the substitution $w = \sin t$. Then $dw = \cos t \, dt$. To make this work, we'll have to separate off one of the cosines to be part of dw. Also, the remaining even power of $\cos t$ can be rewritten in terms of $\sin t$ by using $\cos^2 t = 1 - \sin^2 t = 1 - w^2$, so that

$$\int \cos^3 t \sin^4 t \, dt = \int \cos^2 t \sin^4 t \cos t \, dt$$

$$= \int (1 - w^2) w^4 \, dw = \int (w^4 - w^6) \, dw$$

$$= \frac{1}{5} w^5 - \frac{1}{7} w^7 + C = \frac{1}{5} \sin^5 t - \frac{1}{7} \sin^7 t + C.$$

Example 5   Find $\int \cos^2 x \sin^4 x \, dx$.

Solution   In this example, both exponents are even. The advice given in IV-23 is to convert to all sines or all cosines. We'll convert to all sines by substituting $\cos^2 x = 1 - \sin^2 x$, and then we'll multiply out the integrand:

$$\int \cos^2 x \sin^4 x \, dx = \int (1 - \sin^2 x) \sin^4 x \, dx = \int \sin^4 x \, dx - \int \sin^6 x \, dx.$$

In Example 3 we found $\int \sin^4 x \, dx$ and $\int \sin^6 x \, dx$. Put them together to get

$$\int \cos^2 x \sin^4 x \, dx = -\frac{1}{4} \sin^3 x \cos x - \frac{3}{8} \sin x \cos x + \frac{3}{8} x$$

$$- \left(-\frac{1}{6} \sin^5 x \cos x - \frac{5}{24} \sin^3 x \cos x - \frac{15}{48} \sin x \cos x + \frac{15}{48} x \right) + C$$

$$= \frac{1}{6} \sin^5 x \cos x - \frac{1}{24} \sin^3 x \cos x - \frac{3}{48} \sin x \cos x + \frac{3}{48} x + C.$$

The last two parts of the table are concerned with quadratic functions: **Part V** has expressions with quadratic denominators; **Part VI** contains square roots of quadratics. The quadratics that appear in these formulas are of the form $x^2 \pm a^2$ or $a^2 - x^2$, or in factored form $(x-a)(x-b)$, where a and b are different constants. Quadratics can be converted to these forms by factoring or completing the square.

Preparing to Use the Table: Transforming the Integrand

To use the integral table, we often need to manipulate or reshape integrands to fit entries in the table. The manipulations that tend to be useful are factoring, long division, completing the square, and substitution.

Using Factoring

Example 6 Find $\int \dfrac{3x+7}{x^2+6x+8}\,dx$.

Solution In this case we factor the denominator to get it into a form in the table:

$$x^2 + 6x + 8 = (x+2)(x+4).$$

Now in V-27 we let $a = -2$, $b = -4$, $c = 3$, and $d = 7$, to obtain

$$\int \frac{3x+7}{x^2+6x+8}\,dx = \frac{1}{2}\left(\ln|x+2| - (-5)\ln|x+4|\right) + C.$$

Long Division

Example 7 Find $\int \dfrac{x^2}{x^2+4}\,dx$.

Solution A good rule of thumb when integrating a rational function whose numerator has a degree greater than or equal to that of the denominator is to start by doing *long division*. This results in a polynomial plus a simpler rational function as a remainder. Performing long division here, we obtain:

$$\frac{x^2}{x^2+4} = 1 - \frac{4}{x^2+4}.$$

Then, by V-24 with $a = 2$, we obtain:

$$\int \frac{x^2}{x^2+4}\,dx = \int 1\,dx - 4\int \frac{1}{x^2+4}\,dx = x - 4\cdot\frac{1}{2}\arctan\frac{x}{2} + C.$$

Completing the Square to Rewrite the Quadratic in the Form $w^2 + a^2$

Example 8 Find $\int \dfrac{1}{x^2+6x+14}\,dx$.

Solution By completing the square, we can get this integrand into a form in the table:

$$x^2 + 6x + 14 = (x^2 + 6x + 9) - 9 + 14$$
$$= (x+3)^2 + 5.$$

Let $w = x + 3$. Then $dw = dx$ and so the substitution gives

$$\int \frac{1}{x^2+6x+14}\,dx = \int \frac{1}{w^2+5}\,dw = \frac{1}{\sqrt{5}}\arctan\frac{w}{\sqrt{5}} + C = \frac{1}{\sqrt{5}}\arctan\frac{x+3}{\sqrt{5}} + C,$$

where the antidifferentiation uses V-24 with $a^2 = 5$.

Substitution

Getting an integrand into the right form to use a table of integrals involves substitution and a variety of algebraic techniques.

Example 9   Find $\int e^t \sin(5t + 7)\, dt$.

Solution   This looks similar to II-8. To make the correspondence more complete, let's try the substitution $w = 5t + 7$. Then $dw = 5\, dt$, so $dt = \frac{1}{5}\, dw$. Also, $t = (w - 7)/5$. Then the integral becomes

$$\int e^t \sin(5t + 7)\, dt = \int e^{(w-7)/5} \sin w\, \frac{dw}{5}$$

$$= \frac{e^{-7/5}}{5} \int e^{w/5} \sin w\, dw. \qquad \text{(Since } e^{(w-7)/5} = e^{w/5}e^{-7/5} \text{ and } e^{-7/5} \text{ is a constant)}$$

Now we can use II-8 with $a = \frac{1}{5}$ and $b = 1$ to write

$$\int e^{w/5} \sin w\, dw = \frac{1}{(\frac{1}{5})^2 + 1^2} e^{w/5} \left(\frac{\sin w}{5} - \cos w \right) + C,$$

so

$$\int e^t \sin(5t + 7)\, dt = \frac{e^{-7/5}}{5} \left(\frac{25}{26} e^{(5t+7)/5} \left(\frac{\sin(5t + 7)}{5} - \cos(5t + 7) \right) \right) + C$$

$$= \frac{5e^t}{26} \left(\frac{\sin(5t + 7)}{5} - \cos(5t + 7) \right) + C.$$

Example 10   Find a substitution w and constants k, n so that the following integral has the form $\int kw^n \ln w\, dw$, found in III-15:

$$\int \frac{\ln(x + 1) + \ln(x - 1)}{\sqrt{x^2 - 1}} x\, dx$$

Solution   First we use properties of ln to simplify the integral:

$$\int \frac{\ln(x + 1) + \ln(x - 1)}{\sqrt{x^2 - 1}} x\, dx = \int \frac{\ln((x + 1)(x - 1))}{\sqrt{x^2 - 1}} x\, dx = \int \frac{\ln(x^2 - 1)}{\sqrt{x^2 - 1}} x\, dx.$$

Let $w = x^2 - 1$, $dw = 2x\, dx$, so that $x\, dx = (1/2)\, dw$. Then

$$\int \frac{\ln(x^2 - 1)}{\sqrt{x^2 - 1}} x\, dx = \int w^{-1/2} \ln w\, \frac{1}{2} dw = \int \frac{1}{2} w^{-1/2} \ln w\, dw,$$

so $k = 1/2$, $n = -1/2$.

Exercises and Problems for Section 7.3

Exercises

For Exercises 1–40, antidifferentiate using the table of integrals. You may need to transform the integrand first.

1. $\int x^5 \ln x\, dx$

2. $\int e^{-3\theta} \cos \theta\, d\theta$

3. $\int x^3 \sin 5x\, dx.$

4. $\int (x^2 + 3) \ln x\, dx.$

5. $\int (x^3 + 5)^2\, dx.$

6. $\int \sin w \cos^4 w\, dw$

7. $\int \sin^4 x\, dx$

8. $\int x^3 e^{2x}\, dx$

9. $\int x^2 e^{3x}\, dx$

10. $\int x^2 e^{x^3}\, dx$

11. $\int x^4 e^{3x}\, dx$

12. $\int u^5 \ln(5u)\, du$

13. $\int \frac{1}{3 + y^2}\, dy$

14. $\int \frac{dx}{9x^2 + 16}$

15. $\int \dfrac{dx}{\sqrt{25 - 16x^2}}$ **16.** $\int \dfrac{dx}{\sqrt{9x^2 + 25}}$

17. $\int \sin 3\theta \cos 5\theta \, d\theta$ **18.** $\int \sin 3\theta \sin 5\theta \, d\theta$

19. $\int \dfrac{1}{\cos^3 x} \, dx$ **20.** $\int \dfrac{t^2 + 1}{t^2 - 1} \, dt$

21. $\int e^{5x} \sin 3x \, dx$ **22.** $\int \cos 2y \cos 7y \, dy$

23. $\int y^2 \sin 2y \, dy$ **24.** $\int x^3 \sin x^2 \, dx$

25. $\int \dfrac{1}{\cos^4 7x} \, dx$ **26.** $\int \dfrac{1}{\sin^3 3\theta} \, d\theta$

27. $\int \dfrac{1}{\sin^2 2\theta} \, d\theta$ **28.** $\int \dfrac{1}{\cos^5 x} \, dx.$

29. $\int \dfrac{1}{x^2 + 4x + 3} \, dx$ **30.** $\int \dfrac{1}{x^2 + 4x + 4} \, dx$

31. $\int \dfrac{dz}{z(z - 3)}$ **32.** $\int \dfrac{dy}{4 - y^2}$

33. $\int \dfrac{1}{1 + (z + 2)^2} \, dz$ **34.** $\int \dfrac{1}{y^2 + 4y + 5} \, dy$

35. $\int \sin^3 x \, dx$ **36.** $\int \tan^4 x \, dx$

37. $\int \sinh^3 x \cosh^2 x \, dx$ **38.** $\int \sinh^2 x \cosh^3 x \, dx$

39. $\int \sin^3 3\theta \cos^2 3\theta \, d\theta$ **40.** $\int z e^{2z^2} \cos(2z^2) \, dz$

For Exercises 41–50, evaluate the definite integrals. Whenever possible, use the Fundamental Theorem of Calculus, perhaps after a substitution. Otherwise, use numerical methods.

41. $\int_0^{\pi/12} \sin(3\alpha) \, d\alpha$ **42.** $\int_{-\pi}^{\pi} \sin 5x \cos 6x \, dx$

43. $\int_1^2 (x - 2x^3) \ln x \, dx$ **44.** $\int_0^1 \sqrt{3 - x^2} \, dx$

45. $\int_0^1 \dfrac{1}{x^2 + 2x + 1} \, dx$ **46.** $\int_0^1 \dfrac{dx}{x^2 + 2x + 5}$

47. $\int_0^{1/\sqrt{2}} \dfrac{x}{\sqrt{1 - x^4}} \, dx$ **48.** $\int_0^1 \dfrac{(x + 2)}{(x + 2)^2 + 1} \, dx$

49. $\int_{\pi/4}^{\pi/3} \dfrac{dx}{\sin^3 x}$ **50.** $\int_{-3}^{-1} \dfrac{dx}{\sqrt{x^2 + 6x + 10}}$

Problems

In Problems 51–52, using properties of ln, find a substitution w and constants k, n so that the integral has the form

$$\int k w^n \ln w \, dw.$$

51. $\int (2x + 1)^3 \ln(2x + 1) \, dx$

52. $\int (2x + 1)^3 \ln \dfrac{1}{\sqrt{2x + 1}} \, dx$

In Problems 53–55, find constants a, b, c, m, n so that the integral is in one of the following forms from a table of integrals.[3] Give the form (i)–(iii) you use.

(i) $\int \dfrac{dx}{ax^2 + bx + c}$ (ii) $\int \dfrac{mx + n}{ax^2 + bx + c} \, dx$

(iii) $\int \dfrac{dx}{(ax^2 + bx + c)^n}, \; n > 0$

53. $\int \dfrac{dx}{5 - \dfrac{x}{4} - \dfrac{x^2}{6}}$ **54.** $\int \dfrac{dx}{2x + \dfrac{5}{7 + 3x}}$

55. $\int \dfrac{dx}{(x^2 - 5x + 6)^3(x^2 - 4x + 4)^2(x^2 - 6x + 9)^2}$

In Problems 56–57, find constants a, b, λ so that the integral has the form found in some tables of integrals:[4]

$$\int \dfrac{e^{2\lambda x}}{a e^{\lambda x} + b} \, dx.$$

56. $\int \dfrac{e^{6x}}{4 + e^{3x+1}} \, dx$ **57.** $\int \dfrac{e^{8x}}{4 e^{4x} + 5 e^{6x}} \, dx$

58. According to a table of integrals,[5]

$$\int x^2 e^{bx} \, dx = e^{bx} \left(\dfrac{x^2}{b} - \dfrac{2x}{b^2} + \dfrac{2}{b^3} \right) + C.$$

(a) Find a substitution w and constant k so that the integral $\int x^5 e^{bx^2} \, dx$ can be rewritten in the form

$$\int k w^2 e^{bw} \, dw.$$

(b) Evaluate the integral in terms of x. Your answer may involve the constant b.

59. Show that for all integers m and n, with $m \neq \pm n$, $\int_{-\pi}^{\pi} \sin m\theta \sin n\theta \, d\theta = 0$.

60. Show that for all integers m and n, with $m \neq \pm n$, $\int_{-\pi}^{\pi} \cos m\theta \cos n\theta \, d\theta = 0$.

---

[3] http://en.wikipedia.org/wiki/List_of_integrals_of_rational_functions, page accessed February 24, 2010.
[4] http://en.wikipedia.org/wiki/List_of_integrals_of_exponential_functions, page accessed May 5, 2010.
[5] http://en.wikipedia.org/wiki/List_of_integrals_of_exponential_functions, page accessed February 17, 2011.

61. The voltage, V, in an electrical outlet is given as a function of time, t, by the function $V = V_0 \cos(120\pi t)$, where V is in volts and t is in seconds, and V_0 is a positive constant representing the maximum voltage.

   (a) What is the average value of the voltage over 1 second?

   (b) Engineers do not use the average voltage. They use the root mean square voltage defined by $\overline{V} = \sqrt{\text{average of } (V^2)}$. Find $\overline{V}$ in terms of V_0. (Take the average over 1 second.)

   (c) The standard voltage in an American house is 110 volts, meaning that $\overline{V} = 110$. What is V_0?

62. For some constants A and B, the rate of production, $R(t)$, of oil in a new oil well is modeled by:

$$R(t) = A + Be^{-t}\sin(2\pi t)$$

where t is the time in years, A is the equilibrium rate, and B is the "variability" coefficient.

   (a) Find the total amount of oil produced in the first N years of operation. (Take N to be an integer.)

   (b) Find the average amount of oil produced per year over the first N years (where N is an integer).

   (c) From your answer to part (b), find the average amount of oil produced per year as $N \to \infty$.

   (d) Looking at the function $R(t)$, explain how you might have predicted your answer to part (c) without doing any calculations.

   (e) Do you think it is reasonable to expect this model to hold over a very long period? Why or why not?

Strengthen Your Understanding

In Problems 63–67, explain what is wrong with the statement.

63. The table of integrals cannot be used to find $\displaystyle\int \frac{dt}{7 - t^2}$.

64. If $a > 0$, then $\int 1/(x^2 + 4x + a)\, dx$ always involves arctan.

65. By Formula II-8 of the table with $a = 1, b = 1$,

$$\int e^x \sin x\, dx = \frac{1}{2}e^x(\sin x - \cos x) + C.$$

Therefore

$$\int e^{2x+1}\sin(2x+1)\, dx =$$

$$\frac{1}{2}e^{2x+1}(\sin(2x+1) - \cos(2x+1)) + C.$$

66. The integral $\int \sin x \cos x\, dx$ with $a = 1, b = 1$ is undefined according to Table Formula II-12 since, for $a \neq b$,

$$\int \sin(ax)\cos(bx)\, dx =$$

$$\frac{1}{b^2 - a^2}(b\sin(ax)\sin(bx) + a\cos(ax)\cos(bx)) + C.$$

67. The table can be used to evaluate $\int \sin x/x\, dx$.

In Problems 68–69, give an example of:

68. An indefinite integral involving a square root that can be evaluated by first completing a square.

69. An indefinite integral involving $\sin x$ that can be evaluated with a reduction formula

In Problems 70–73, decide whether the statements are true or false. Give an explanation for your answer.

70. $\int \sin^7 \theta \cos^6 \theta\, d\theta$ can be written as a polynomial with $\cos \theta$ as the variable.

71. $\int 1/(x^2 + 4x + 5)\, dx$ involves a natural logarithm.

72. $\int 1/(x^2 + 4x - 5)\, dx$ involves an arctangent.

73. $\int x^{-1}((\ln x)^2 + (\ln x)^3)\, dx$ is a polynomial with $\ln x$ as the variable.

7.4 ALGEBRAIC IDENTITIES AND TRIGONOMETRIC SUBSTITUTIONS

Although not all functions have elementary antiderivatives, many do. In this section we introduce two powerful methods of integration which show that large classes of functions have elementary antiderivatives. The first is the method of partial fractions, which depends on an algebraic identity, and allows us to integrate rational functions. The second is the method of trigonometric substitutions, which allows us to handle expressions involving the square root of a quadratic polynomial. Some of the formulas in the table of integrals can be derived using the techniques of this section.

Method of Partial Fractions

The integral of some rational functions can be obtained by splitting the integrand into *partial fractions*. For example, to find

$$\int \frac{1}{(x-2)(x-5)}\, dx,$$

the integrand is split into partial fractions with denominators $(x-2)$ and $(x-5)$. We write

$$\frac{1}{(x-2)(x-5)} = \frac{A}{x-2} + \frac{B}{x-5},$$

where A and B are constants that need to be found. Multiplying by $(x-2)(x-5)$ gives the identity

$$1 = A(x-5) + B(x-2)$$

so

$$1 = (A+B)x - 5A - 2B.$$

Since this equation holds for all x, the constant terms on both sides must be equal.[6] Similarly, the coefficients of x on both sides must be equal. So

$$-5A - 2B = 1$$
$$A + B = 0.$$

Solving these equations gives $A = -1/3$, $B = 1/3$. Thus,

$$\frac{1}{(x-2)(x-5)} = \frac{-1/3}{x-2} + \frac{1/3}{x-5}.$$

(Check the answer by writing the right-hand side over the common denominator $(x-2)(x-5)$.)

Example 1 Use partial fractions to integrate $\displaystyle\int \frac{1}{(x-2)(x-5)}\, dx$.

Solution We split the integrand into partial fractions, each of which can be integrated:

$$\int \frac{1}{(x-2)(x-5)}\, dx = \int \left(\frac{-1/3}{x-2} + \frac{1/3}{x-5}\right)\, dx = -\frac{1}{3}\ln|x-2| + \frac{1}{3}\ln|x-5| + C.$$

You can check that using formula V-26 in the integral table gives the same result.

This method can be used to derive formulas V-26 and V-27 in the integral table. A similar method works whenever the denominator of the integrand factors into distinct linear factors and the numerator has degree less than the denominator.

Example 2 Find $\displaystyle\int \frac{x+2}{x^2+x}\, dx$.

Solution We factor the denominator and split the integrand into partial fractions:

$$\frac{x+2}{x^2+x} = \frac{x+2}{x(x+1)} = \frac{A}{x} + \frac{B}{x+1}.$$

Multiplying by $x(x+1)$ gives the identity

$$x+2 = A(x+1) + Bx$$
$$= (A+B)x + A.$$

Equating constant terms and coefficients of x gives $A = 2$ and $A + B = 1$, so $B = -1$. Then we split the integrand into two parts and integrate:

$$\int \frac{x+2}{x^2+x}\, dx = \int \left(\frac{2}{x} - \frac{1}{x+1}\right)\, dx = 2\ln|x| - \ln|x+1| + C.$$

The next example illustrates what to do if there is a repeated factor in the denominator.

Example 3 Calculate $\displaystyle\int \frac{10x - 2x^2}{(x-1)^2(x+3)}\, dx$ using partial fractions of the form $\dfrac{A}{x-1}$, $\dfrac{B}{(x-1)^2}$, $\dfrac{C}{x+3}$.

---

[6]We have not shown that the equation holds for $x=2$ and $x=5$, but these values do not affect the argument.

Solution   We are given that the squared factor, $(x - 1)^2$, leads to partial fractions of the form:

$$\frac{10x - 2x^2}{(x - 1)^2(x + 3)} = \frac{A}{x - 1} + \frac{B}{(x - 1)^2} + \frac{C}{x + 3}.$$

Multiplying through by $(x - 1)^2(x + 3)$ gives

$$10x - 2x^2 = A(x - 1)(x + 3) + B(x + 3) + C(x - 1)^2$$
$$= (A + C)x^2 + (2A + B - 2C)x - 3A + 3B + C.$$

Equating the coefficients of x^2 and x and the constant terms, we get the simultaneous equations:

$$A + C = -2$$
$$2A + B - 2C = 10$$
$$-3A + 3B + C = 0.$$

Solving gives $A = 1, B = 2, C = -3$. Thus, we obtain three integrals which can be evaluated:

$$\int \frac{10x - 2x^2}{(x - 1)^2(x + 3)} \, dx = \int \left(\frac{1}{x - 1} + \frac{2}{(x - 1)^2} - \frac{3}{x + 3} \right) dx$$
$$= \ln|x - 1| - \frac{2}{(x - 1)} - 3\ln|x + 3| + K.$$

For the second integral, we use the fact that $\int 2/(x-1)^2 dx = 2 \int (x-1)^{-2} dx = -2(x-1)^{-1} + K$.

If there is a quadratic in the denominator which cannot be factored, we need an expression of the form $Ax + B$ in the numerator, as the next example shows.

Example 4   Find $\int \dfrac{2x^2 - x - 1}{(x^2 + 1)(x - 2)} \, dx$ using partial fractions of the form $\dfrac{Ax + B}{x^2 + 1}$ and $\dfrac{C}{x - 2}$.

Solution   We are given that the quadratic denominator, $(x^2 + 1)$, which cannot be factored further, has a numerator of the form $Ax + B$, so we have

$$\frac{2x^2 - x - 1}{(x^2 + 1)(x - 2)} = \frac{Ax + B}{x^2 + 1} + \frac{C}{x - 2}.$$

Multiplying by $(x^2 + 1)(x - 2)$ gives

$$2x^2 - x - 1 = (Ax + B)(x - 2) + C(x^2 + 1)$$
$$= (A + C)x^2 + (B - 2A)x + C - 2B.$$

Equating the coefficients of x^2 and x and the constant terms gives the simultaneous equations

$$A + C = 2$$
$$B - 2A = -1$$
$$C - 2B = -1.$$

Solving gives $A = B = C = 1$, so we rewrite the integral as follows:

$$\int \frac{2x^2 - x - 1}{(x^2 + 1)(x - 2)} \, dx = \int \left(\frac{x + 1}{x^2 + 1} + \frac{1}{x - 2} \right) dx.$$

This identity is useful provided we can perform the integration on the right-hand side. The first integral can be done if it is split into two; the second integral is similar to those in the previous examples. We have

$$\int \frac{2x^2 - x - 1}{(x^2 + 1)(x - 2)} \, dx = \int \frac{x}{x^2 + 1} \, dx + \int \frac{1}{x^2 + 1} \, dx + \int \frac{1}{x - 2} \, dx.$$

To calculate $\int (x/(x^2 + 1)) \, dx$, substitute $w = x^2 + 1$, or guess and check. The final result is

$$\int \frac{2x^2 - x - 1}{(x^2 + 1)(x - 2)} \, dx = \frac{1}{2} \ln|x^2 + 1| + \arctan x + \ln|x - 2| + K.$$

The next example shows what to do if the numerator has degree larger than the denominator.

Example 5   Calculate $\displaystyle\int \frac{x^3 - 7x^2 + 10x + 1}{x^2 - 7x + 10} \, dx$ using long division before integrating.

Solution   The degree of the numerator is greater than the degree of the denominator, so we divide first:

$$\frac{x^3 - 7x^2 + 10x + 1}{x^2 - 7x + 10} = \frac{x(x^2 - 7x + 10) + 1}{x^2 - 7x + 10} = x + \frac{1}{x^2 - 7x + 10}.$$

The remainder, in this case $1/(x^2 - 7x + 10)$, is a rational function on which we try to use partial fractions. We have

$$\frac{1}{x^2 - 7x + 10} = \frac{1}{(x - 2)(x - 5)}$$

so in this case we use the result of Example 1 to obtain

$$\int \frac{x^3 - 7x^2 + 10x + 1}{x^2 - 7x + 10} \, dx = \int \left(x + \frac{1}{(x - 2)(x - 5)} \right) dx = \frac{x^2}{2} - \frac{1}{3} \ln|x-2| + \frac{1}{3} \ln|x-5| + C.$$

Many, though not all, rational functions can be integrated by the strategy suggested by the previous examples.

Strategy for Integrating a Rational Function, $\dfrac{P(x)}{Q(x)}$

- If degree of $P(x) \geq$ degree of $Q(x)$, try long division and the method of partial fractions on the remainder.

- If $Q(x)$ is the product of distinct linear factors, use partial fractions of the form

$$\frac{A}{(x - c)}.$$

- If $Q(x)$ contains a repeated linear factor, $(x - c)^n$, use partial fractions of the form

$$\frac{A_1}{(x - c)} + \frac{A_2}{(x - c)^2} + \cdots + \frac{A_n}{(x - c)^n}.$$

- If $Q(x)$ contains an unfactorable quadratic $q(x)$, try a partial fraction of the form

$$\frac{Ax + B}{q(x)}.$$

To use this method, we must be able to integrate each partial fraction. We can integrate terms of the form $A/(x-c)^n$ using the power rule (if $n > 1$) and logarithms (if $n = 1$). Next we see how to integrate terms of the form $(Ax + B)/q(x)$, where $q(x)$ is an unfactorable quadratic.

Trigonometric Substitutions

Section 7.1 showed how substitutions could be used to transform complex integrands. Now we see how substitution of $\sin\theta$ or $\tan\theta$ can be used for integrands involving square roots of quadratics or unfactorable quadratics.

Sine Substitutions

Substitutions involving $\sin\theta$ make use of the Pythagorean identity, $\cos^2\theta + \sin^2\theta = 1$, to simplify an integrand involving $\sqrt{a^2 - x^2}$.

Example 6   Find $\displaystyle\int \frac{1}{\sqrt{1-x^2}}\,dx$ using the substitution $x = \sin\theta$.

Solution   If $x = \sin\theta$, then $dx = \cos\theta\,d\theta$, and substitution converts $1 - x^2$ to a perfect square:

$$\int \frac{1}{\sqrt{1-x^2}}\,dx = \int \frac{1}{\sqrt{1-\sin^2\theta}}\cos\theta\,d\theta = \int \frac{\cos\theta}{\sqrt{\cos^2\theta}}\,d\theta.$$

Now either $\sqrt{\cos^2\theta} = \cos\theta$ or $\sqrt{\cos^2\theta} = -\cos\theta$ depending on the values taken by θ. If we choose $-\pi/2 \le \theta \le \pi/2$, then $\cos\theta \ge 0$, so $\sqrt{\cos^2\theta} = \cos\theta$. Then

$$\int \frac{\cos\theta}{\sqrt{\cos^2\theta}}\,d\theta = \int \frac{\cos\theta}{\cos\theta}\,d\theta = \int 1\,d\theta = \theta + C = \arcsin x + C.$$

The last step uses the fact that $\theta = \arcsin x$ if $x = \sin\theta$ and $-\pi/2 \le \theta \le \pi/2$.

From now on, when we substitute $\sin\theta$, we assume that the interval $-\pi/2 \le \theta \le \pi/2$ has been chosen. Notice that the previous example is the case $a = 1$ of VI-28 in the table of integrals. The next example illustrates how to choose the substitution when $a \ne 1$.

Example 7   Use a trigonometric substitution to find $\displaystyle\int \frac{1}{\sqrt{4-x^2}}\,dx$.

Solution   This time we choose $x = 2\sin\theta$, with $-\pi/2 \le \theta \le \pi/2$, so that $4 - x^2$ becomes a perfect square:

$$\sqrt{4-x^2} = \sqrt{4 - 4\sin^2\theta} = 2\sqrt{1-\sin^2\theta} = 2\sqrt{\cos^2\theta} = 2\cos\theta.$$

Then $dx = 2\cos\theta\,d\theta$, so substitution gives

$$\int \frac{1}{\sqrt{4-x^2}}\,dx = \int \frac{1}{2\cos\theta}2\cos\theta\,d\theta = \int 1\,d\theta = \theta + C = \arcsin\left(\frac{x}{2}\right) + C.$$

The general rule for choosing a sine substitution is:

> To simplify $\sqrt{a^2 - x^2}$, for constant a, try $x = a\sin\theta$, with $-\pi/2 \le \theta \le \pi/2$.

Notice $\sqrt{a^2 - x^2}$ is only defined on the interval $[-a, a]$. Assuming that the domain of the integrand is $[-a, a]$, the substitution $x = a\sin\theta$, with $-\pi/2 \le \theta \le \pi/2$, is valid for all x in the domain, because its range is $[-a, a]$ and it has an inverse $\theta = \arcsin(x/a)$ on $[-a, a]$.

Example 8   Find the area of the ellipse $4x^2 + y^2 = 9$.

Solution   Solving for y shows that $y = \sqrt{9 - 4x^2}$ gives the upper half of the ellipse. From Figure 7.1, we see that

$$\text{Area} = 4 \int_0^{3/2} \sqrt{9 - 4x^2}\, dx.$$

To decide which trigonometric substitution to use, we write the integrand as

$$\sqrt{9 - 4x^2} = 2\sqrt{\frac{9}{4} - x^2} = 2\sqrt{\left(\frac{3}{2}\right)^2 - x^2}.$$

This suggests that we should choose $x = (3/2)\sin\theta$, so that $dx = (3/2)\cos\theta\, d\theta$ and

$$\sqrt{9 - 4x^2} = 2\sqrt{\left(\frac{3}{2}\right)^2 - \left(\frac{3}{2}\right)^2 \sin^2\theta} = 2\left(\frac{3}{2}\right)\sqrt{1 - \sin^2\theta} = 3\cos\theta.$$

When $x = 0$, $\theta = 0$, and when $x = 3/2$, $\theta = \pi/2$, so

$$4\int_0^{3/2} \sqrt{9 - 4x^2}\, dx = 4\int_0^{\pi/2} 3\cos\theta\left(\frac{3}{2}\right)\cos\theta\, d\theta = 18\int_0^{\pi/2} \cos^2\theta\, d\theta.$$

Using Example 6 on page 367 or table of integrals IV-18, we find

$$\int \cos^2\theta\, d\theta = \frac{1}{2}\cos\theta\sin\theta + \frac{1}{2}\theta + C.$$

So we have

$$\text{Area} = 4\int_0^{3/2} \sqrt{9 - 4x^2}\, dx = \frac{18}{2}\left(\cos\theta\sin\theta + \theta\right)\Big|_0^{\pi/2} = 9\left(0 + \frac{\pi}{2}\right) = \frac{9\pi}{2}.$$

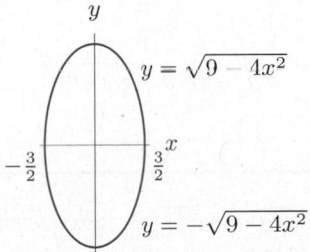

Figure 7.1: The ellipse $4x^2 + y^2 = 9$

In Example 8, we did not return to the original variable x after making the substitution because we had also converted the limits of the definite integral. However, if we are calculating an indefinite integral, we have to return to the original variable. In the next example, we see how a triangle representing the substitution can be useful.

Example 9   Find the indefinite integral $\int \sqrt{9 - 4x^2}\, dx$ corresponding to Example 8.

Solution   From Example 8, we know if $x = (3/2)\sin\theta$, then

$$\int \sqrt{9 - 4x^2}\, dx = \frac{1}{2}\cos\theta\sin\theta + \frac{1}{2}\theta + C.$$

To rewrite the antiderivative in terms of the original variable x, we use the fact that $\sin\theta = 2x/3$ to write $\theta = \arcsin(2x/3)$. To express $\cos\theta$ in terms of x, we draw the right triangle in Figure 7.2

with opposite side $2x$ and hypotenuse 3, so $\sin\theta = 2x/3$. Then we use the Pythagorean Theorem to see that $\cos\theta = \sqrt{9 - 4x^2}/3$, so

$$\int \sqrt{9 - 4x^2}\,dx = \frac{1}{2}\cos\theta\sin\theta + \frac{1}{2}\theta + C$$

$$= \frac{1}{2}\cdot\frac{2x}{3}\cdot\frac{\sqrt{9 - 4x^2}}{3} + \frac{1}{2}\arcsin\frac{2x}{3} + C = \frac{x\sqrt{9 - 4x^2}}{9} + \frac{1}{2}\arcsin\frac{2x}{3} + C.$$

Figure 7.2: Triangle with $\sin\theta = 2x/3$

Tangent Substitutions

Integrals involving $a^2 + x^2$ may be simplified by a substitution involving $\tan\theta$ and the trigonometric identities $\tan\theta = \sin\theta/\cos\theta$ and $\cos^2\theta + \sin^2\theta = 1$.

Example 10 Find $\displaystyle\int \frac{1}{x^2 + 9}\,dx$ using the substitution $x = 3\tan\theta$.

Solution If $x = 3\tan\theta$, then $dx = (3/\cos^2\theta)\,d\theta$, so

$$\int \frac{1}{x^2 + 9}\,dx = \int\left(\frac{1}{9\tan^2\theta + 9}\right)\left(\frac{3}{\cos^2\theta}\right)d\theta = \frac{1}{3}\int\frac{1}{\left(\frac{\sin^2\theta}{\cos^2\theta} + 1\right)\cos^2\theta}\,d\theta$$

$$= \frac{1}{3}\int\frac{1}{\sin^2\theta + \cos^2\theta}\,d\theta = \frac{1}{3}\int 1\,d\theta = \frac{1}{3}\theta + C = \frac{1}{3}\arctan\left(\frac{x}{3}\right) + C.$$

> To simplify $a^2 + x^2$ or $\sqrt{a^2 + x^2}$, for constant a, try $x = a\tan\theta$, with $-\pi/2 < \theta < \pi/2$.

Note that $a^2 + x^2$ and $\sqrt{a^2 + x^2}$ are defined on $(-\infty, \infty)$. Assuming that the domain of the integrand is $(-\infty, \infty)$, the substitution $x = a\tan\theta$, with $-\pi/2 < \theta < \pi/2$, is valid for all x in the domain, because its range is $(-\infty, \infty)$ and it has an inverse $\theta = \arctan(x/a)$ on $(-\infty, \infty)$.

Example 11 Use a tangent substitution to show that the following two integrals are equal:

$$\int_0^1 \sqrt{1 + x^2}\,dx = \int_0^{\pi/4}\frac{1}{\cos^3\theta}\,d\theta.$$

What area do these integrals represent?

Solution We put $x = \tan\theta$, with $-\pi/2 < \theta < \pi/2$, so that $dx = (1/\cos^2\theta)\,d\theta$, and

$$\sqrt{1 + x^2} = \sqrt{1 + \frac{\sin^2\theta}{\cos^2\theta}} = \sqrt{\frac{\cos^2\theta + \sin^2\theta}{\cos^2\theta}} = \frac{1}{\cos\theta}.$$

When $x = 0$, $\theta = 0$, and when $x = 1$, $\theta = \pi/4$, so

$$\int_0^1 \sqrt{1 + x^2}\,dx = \int_0^{\pi/4}\left(\frac{1}{\cos\theta}\right)\left(\frac{1}{\cos^2\theta}\right)d\theta = \int_0^{\pi/4}\frac{1}{\cos^3\theta}\,d\theta.$$

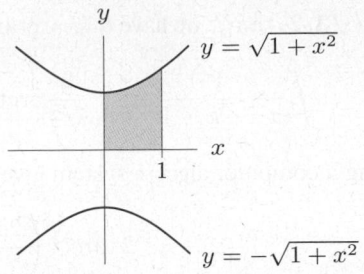

Figure 7.3: The hyperbola $y^2 - x^2 = 1$

The integral $\int_0^1 \sqrt{1 + x^2}\, dx$ represents the area under the hyperbola $y^2 - x^2 = 1$ in Figure 7.3.

Completing the Square to Use a Trigonometric Substitution

To make a trigonometric substitution, we may first need to complete the square.

Example 12   Find $\displaystyle\int \frac{3}{\sqrt{2x - x^2}}\, dx$.

Solution   To use a sine or tangent substitution, the expression under the square root sign should be in the form $a^2 + x^2$ or $a^2 - x^2$. Completing the square, we get

$$2x - x^2 = 1 - (x - 1)^2.$$

This suggests we substitute $x - 1 = \sin\theta$, or $x = \sin\theta + 1$. Then $dx = \cos\theta\, d\theta$, and

$$\int \frac{3}{\sqrt{2x - x^2}}\, dx = \int \frac{3}{\sqrt{1 - (x - 1)^2}}\, dx = \int \frac{3}{\sqrt{1 - \sin^2\theta}} \cos\theta\, d\theta$$

$$= \int \frac{3}{\cos\theta} \cos\theta\, d\theta = \int 3\, d\theta = 3\theta + C.$$

Since $x - 1 = \sin\theta$, we have $\theta = \arcsin(x - 1)$, so

$$\int \frac{3}{\sqrt{2x - x^2}}\, dx = 3\arcsin(x - 1) + C.$$

Example 13   Find $\displaystyle\int \frac{1}{x^2 + x + 1}\, dx$.

Solution   Completing the square, we get

$$x^2 + x + 1 = \left(x + \frac{1}{2}\right)^2 + \frac{3}{4} = \left(x + \frac{1}{2}\right)^2 + \left(\frac{\sqrt{3}}{2}\right)^2.$$

This suggests we substitute $x + 1/2 = (\sqrt{3}/2)\tan\theta$, or $x = -1/2 + (\sqrt{3}/2)\tan\theta$. Then $dx = (\sqrt{3}/2)(1/\cos^2\theta)\, d\theta$, so

$$\int \frac{1}{x^2 + x + 1}\, dx = \int \left(\frac{1}{(x + \frac{1}{2})^2 + \frac{3}{4}}\right)\left(\frac{\sqrt{3}}{2}\frac{1}{\cos^2\theta}\right) d\theta$$

$$= \frac{\sqrt{3}}{2} \int \left(\frac{1}{\frac{3}{4}\tan^2\theta + \frac{3}{4}}\right)\left(\frac{1}{\cos^2\theta}\right) d\theta = \frac{2}{\sqrt{3}} \int \frac{1}{(\tan^2\theta + 1)\cos^2\theta}\, d\theta$$

$$= \frac{2}{\sqrt{3}} \int \frac{1}{\sin^2\theta + \cos^2\theta}\, d\theta = \frac{2}{\sqrt{3}} \int 1\, d\theta = \frac{2}{\sqrt{3}}\theta + C.$$

Since $x + 1/2 = (\sqrt{3}/2)\tan\theta$, we have $\theta = \arctan((2/\sqrt{3})x + 1/\sqrt{3})$, so

$$\int \frac{1}{x^2 + x + 1}\, dx = \frac{2}{\sqrt{3}} \arctan\left(\frac{2}{\sqrt{3}}x + \frac{1}{\sqrt{3}}\right) + C.$$

Alternatively, using a computer algebra system gives[7]

$$\frac{2\tan^{-1}\left(\dfrac{2x + 1}{\sqrt{3}}\right)}{\sqrt{3}},$$

essentially the same as we obtained by hand. You can check either answer by differentiation.

Exercises and Problems for Section 7.4

Exercises

Split the functions in Exercises 1–7 into partial fractions.

1. $\dfrac{x + 1}{6x + x^2}$

2. $\dfrac{20}{25 - x^2}$

3. $\dfrac{1}{w^4 - w^3}$

4. $\dfrac{2y}{y^3 - y^2 + y - 1}$

5. $\dfrac{8}{y^3 - 4y}$

6. $\dfrac{2(1 + s)}{s(s^2 + 3s + 2)}$

7. $\dfrac{2}{s^4 - 1}$

In Exercises 8–14, find the antiderivative of the function in the given exercise.

8. Exercise 1

9. Exercise 2

10. Exercise 3

11. Exercise 4

12. Exercise 5

13. Exercise 6

14. Exercise 7

In Exercises 15–19, evaluate the integral.

15. $\displaystyle\int \frac{3x^2 - 8x + 1}{x^3 - 4x^2 + x + 6}\, dx$; use $\dfrac{A}{x - 2} + \dfrac{B}{x + 1} + \dfrac{C}{x - 3}$.

16. $\displaystyle\int \frac{dx}{x^3 - x^2}$; use $\dfrac{A}{x} + \dfrac{B}{x^2} + \dfrac{C}{x - 1}$.

17. $\displaystyle\int \frac{10x + 2}{x^3 - 5x^2 + x - 5}\, dx$; use $\dfrac{A}{x - 5} + \dfrac{Bx + C}{x^2 + 1}$.

18. $\displaystyle\int \frac{x^4 + 12x^3 + 15x^2 + 25x + 11}{x^3 + 12x^2 + 11x}\, dx$;

use division and $\dfrac{A}{x} + \dfrac{B}{x + 1} + \dfrac{C}{x + 11}$.

19. $\displaystyle\int \frac{x^4 + 3x^3 + 2x^2 + 1}{x^2 + 3x + 2}\, dx$; use division.

In Exercises 20–22, use the substitution to find the integral.

20. $\displaystyle\int \frac{1}{\sqrt{9 - 4x^2}}\, dx, \quad x = \frac{3}{2}\sin t$

21. $\displaystyle\int \frac{1}{\sqrt{4x - 3 - x^2}}\, dx, \quad x = \sin t + 2$

22. $\displaystyle\int \frac{1}{x^2 + 4x + 5}\, dx, \quad x = \tan t - 2$

23. Which of the following integrals are best done by a trigonometric substitution, and what substitution?

(a) $\displaystyle\int \sqrt{9 - x^2}\, dx$

(b) $\displaystyle\int x\sqrt{9 - x^2}\, dx$

24. Give a substitution (not necessarily trigonometric) which could be used to compute the following integrals:

(a) $\displaystyle\int \frac{x}{\sqrt{x^2 + 10}}\, dx$

(b) $\displaystyle\int \frac{1}{\sqrt{x^2 + 10}}\, dx$

Problems

25. Find a value of k and a substitution w such that

$$\int \frac{12x - 2}{(3x + 2)(x - 1)}\, dx = k \int \frac{dw}{w}.$$

26. Find values of A and B such that

$$\int \frac{12x - 2}{(3x + 2)(x - 1)}\, dx = \int \frac{A\, dx}{3x + 2} + \int \frac{B\, dx}{x - 1}.$$

---

[7]wolframalpha.com, January 11, 2011.

27. Write the integral $\displaystyle\int \frac{2x+9}{(3x+5)(4-5x)}\,dx$ in the form $\displaystyle\int \frac{cx+d}{(x-a)(x-b)}\,dx$. Give the values of a, b, c, d. You need not evaluate the integral.

28. Write the integral $\displaystyle\int \frac{dx}{\sqrt{12-4x^2}}$ in the form $\displaystyle\int \frac{k\,dx}{\sqrt{a^2-x^2}}$. Give the values of the positive constants a and k. You need not evaluate the integral.

29. Using the fact that $e^{2x}=(e^x)^2$, write the integral

$$\int_0^{\ln 7} \frac{2e^x+1}{e^{2x}-4e^x+3}\cdot e^x\,dx$$

in the form

$$\int_r^s \left(\frac{A}{w-3}+\frac{B}{w-1}\right)dw.$$

State the values of A, B, w, dw, r, s. (Note that r and s are values of w, not x.) You need not evaluate the integral.

30. (a) Evaluate $\displaystyle\int \frac{3x+6}{x^2+3x}\,dx$ by partial fractions.

(b) Show that your answer to part (a) agrees with the answer you get by using the integral tables.

Complete the square and give a substitution (not necessarily trigonometric) which could be used to compute the integrals in Problems 31–38.

31. $\displaystyle\int \frac{1}{x^2+2x+2}\,dx$

32. $\displaystyle\int \frac{1}{x^2+6x+25}\,dx$

33. $\displaystyle\int \frac{dy}{y^2+3y+3}$

34. $\displaystyle\int \frac{x+1}{x^2+2x+2}\,dx$

35. $\displaystyle\int \frac{4}{\sqrt{2z-z^2}}\,dz$

36. $\displaystyle\int \frac{z-1}{\sqrt{2z-z^2}}\,dz$

37. $\displaystyle\int (t+2)\sin(t^2+4t+7)\,dt$

38. $\displaystyle\int (2-\theta)\cos(\theta^2-4\theta)\,d\theta$

Calculate the integrals in Problems 39–54.

39. $\displaystyle\int \frac{1}{(x-5)(x-3)}\,dx$

40. $\displaystyle\int \frac{1}{(x+2)(x+3)}\,dx$

41. $\displaystyle\int \frac{1}{(x+7)(x-2)}\,dx$

42. $\displaystyle\int \frac{x}{x^2-3x+2}\,dx$

43. $\displaystyle\int \frac{dz}{z^2+z}$

44. $\displaystyle\int \frac{dx}{x^2+5x+4}$

45. $\displaystyle\int \frac{dP}{3P-3P^2}$

46. $\displaystyle\int \frac{3x+1}{x^2-3x+2}\,dx$

47. $\displaystyle\int \frac{y+2}{2y^2+3y+1}\,dy$

48. $\displaystyle\int \frac{x+1}{x^3+x}\,dx$

49. $\displaystyle\int \frac{x-2}{x^2+x^4}\,dx$

50. $\displaystyle\int \frac{y^2}{25+y^2}\,dy$

51. $\displaystyle\int \frac{dz}{(4-z^2)^{3/2}}$

52. $\displaystyle\int \frac{10}{(s+2)(s^2+1)}\,ds$

53. $\displaystyle\int \frac{1}{x^2+4x+13}\,dx$

54. $\displaystyle\int \frac{e^x\,dx}{(e^x-1)(e^x+2)}$

In Problems 55–64, evaluate the indefinite integral, using a trigonometric substitution and a triangle to express the answer in terms of x. Assume $-\pi/2\le\theta\le\pi/2$.

55. $\displaystyle\int \frac{1}{x^2\sqrt{1+x^2}}\,dx$

56. $\displaystyle\int \frac{x^2}{\sqrt{9-x^2}}\,dx$

57. $\displaystyle\int \frac{\sqrt{1-4x^2}}{x^2}\,dx$

58. $\displaystyle\int \frac{\sqrt{25-9x^2}}{x}\,dx$

59. $\displaystyle\int \frac{1}{x\sqrt{9-4x^2}}\,dx$

60. $\displaystyle\int \frac{1}{x\sqrt{1+16x^2}}\,dx$

61. $\displaystyle\int \frac{1}{x^2\sqrt{4-x^2}}\,dx$

62. $\displaystyle\int \frac{1}{(25+4x^2)^{3/2}}\,dx$

63. $\displaystyle\int \frac{1}{(16-x^2)^{3/2}}\,dx$

64. $\displaystyle\int \frac{x^2}{(1+9x^2)^{3/2}}\,dx$

Find the exact area of the regions in Problems 65–70.

65. Bounded by $y=3x/((x-1)(x-4)), y=0, x=2, x=3$.

66. Bounded by $y=(3x^2+x)/((x^2+1)(x+1)), y=0, x=0, x=1$.

67. Bounded by $y=x^2/\sqrt{1-x^2}, y=0, x=0, x=1/2$.

68. Bounded by $y=x^3/\sqrt{4-x^2}, y=0, x=0, x=\sqrt{2}$.

69. Bounded by $y=1/\sqrt{x^2+9}, y=0, x=0, x=3$.

70. Bounded by $y=1/(x\sqrt{x^2+9}), y=0, x=\sqrt{3}, x=3$.

Calculate the integrals in Problems 71–73 by partial fractions and then by using the indicated substitution. Show that the results you get are the same.

71. $\displaystyle\int \frac{dx}{1-x^2}$; substitution $x=\sin\theta$.

72. $\displaystyle\int \frac{2x}{x^2-1}\,dx$; substitution $w=x^2-1$.

73. $\int \dfrac{3x^2+1}{x^3+x}\, dx$; substitution $w = x^3 + x$.

74. (a) Show $\int \dfrac{1}{\sin^2 \theta}\, d\theta = -\dfrac{1}{\tan \theta} + C.$

    (b) Calculate $\int \dfrac{dy}{y^2 \sqrt{5 - y^2}}.$

Solve Problems 75–77 without using integral tables.

75. Calculate the integral $\int \dfrac{1}{(x-a)(x-b)}\, dx$ for

    (a) $a \neq b$ (b) $a = b$

76. Calculate the integral $\int \dfrac{x}{(x-a)(x-b)}\, dx$ for

    (a) $a \neq b$ (b) $a = b$

77. Calculate the integral $\int \dfrac{1}{x^2 - a}\, dx$ for

    (a) $a > 0$ (b) $a = 0$ (c) $a < 0$

78. A rumor is spread in a school. For $0 < a < 1$ and $b > 0$, the time t at which a fraction p of the school population has heard the rumor is given by

$$t(p) = \int_a^p \dfrac{b}{x(1-x)}\, dx.$$

    (a) Evaluate the integral to find an explicit formula for $t(p)$. Write your answer so it has only one ln term.

    (b) At time $t = 0$ one percent of the school population ($p = 0.01$) has heard the rumor. What is a?

(c) At time $t = 1$ half the school population ($p = 0.5$) has heard the rumor. What is b?

(d) At what time has 90% of the school population ($p = 0.9$) heard the rumor?

79. The Law of Mass Action tells us that the time, T, taken by a chemical to create a quantity x_0 of the product (in molecules) is given by

$$T = \int_0^{x_0} \dfrac{k\, dx}{(a-x)(b-x)}$$

where a and b are initial quantities of the two ingredients used to make the product, and k is a positive constant. Suppose $0 < a < b$.

    (a) Find the time taken to make a quantity $x_0 = a/2$ of the product.

    (b) What happens to T as $x_0 \to a$?

80. The moment-generating function, $m(t)$, which gives useful information about the normal distribution of statistics, is defined by

$$m(t) = \int_{-\infty}^{\infty} e^{tx} \dfrac{e^{-x^2/2}}{\sqrt{2\pi}}\, dx.$$

Find a formula for $m(t)$. [Hint: Complete the square and use the fact that $\int_{-\infty}^{\infty} e^{-x^2/2}\, dx = \sqrt{2\pi}$.]

Strengthen Your Understanding

In Problems 81–82, explain what is wrong with the statement.

81. To integrate

$$\int \dfrac{1}{(x-1)^2(x-2)}\, dx$$

using a partial fraction decomposition, let

$$\dfrac{1}{(x-1)^2(x-2)} = \dfrac{A}{(x-1)^2} + \dfrac{B}{x-2}.$$

82. Use the substitution $x = 2\sin\theta$ to integrate the following integral:

$$\int \dfrac{1}{(x^2 + 4)^{3/2}}\, dx.$$

In Problems 83–86, give an example of:

83. A rational function whose antiderivative is not a rational function.

84. An integral whose evaluation requires factoring a cubic.

85. A linear polynomial $P(x)$ and a quadratic polynomial $Q(x)$ such that the rational function $P(x)/Q(x)$ does not have a partial fraction decomposition of the form

$$\dfrac{P(x)}{Q(x)} = \dfrac{A}{x-r} + \dfrac{B}{x-s}$$

for some constants A, B, r, and s.

86. An integral that can be made easier to evaluate by using the trigonometric substitution $x = \frac{3}{2}\sin\theta$.

In Problems 87–88, decide whether the statements are true or false. Give an explanation for your answer.

87. The integral $\int \dfrac{1}{\sqrt{9 - t^2}}\, dt$ can be made easier to evaluate by using the substitution $t = 3\tan\theta$.

88. To calculate $\int \dfrac{1}{x^3 + x^2}\, dx$, we can split the integrand into

$$\int \left(\dfrac{A}{x} + \dfrac{B}{x^2} + \dfrac{C}{x+1} \right) dx$$

For Problems 89–90, which technique is useful in evaluating the integral?

(a) Integration by parts   (b) Partial fractions
(c) Long division   (d) Completing the square
(e) A trig substitution   (f) Other substitutions

89. $\int \dfrac{x^2}{\sqrt{1 - x^2}}\, dx$ 90. $\int \dfrac{x^2}{1 - x^2}\, dx$

7.5 NUMERICAL METHODS FOR DEFINITE INTEGRALS

Many functions do not have elementary antiderivatives. To evaluate the definite integrals of such functions, we cannot use the Fundamental Theorem; we must use numerical methods. We know how to approximate a definite integral numerically using left- and right-hand Riemann sums; in this section, we introduce more accurate methods.

The Midpoint Rule

In the left- and right-hand Riemann sums, the heights of the rectangles are found using the left-hand or right-hand endpoints, respectively, of the subintervals. For the *midpoint rule*, we use the midpoint of each of the subintervals.

For example, in approximating $\int_1^2 f(x)\,dx$ by a Riemann sum with two subdivisions, we first divide the interval $1 \leq x \leq 2$ into two pieces. The midpoint of the first subinterval is 1.25 and the midpoint of the second is 1.75. The heights of the two rectangles are $f(1.25)$ and $f(1.75)$, respectively. (See Figure 7.4.) The Riemann sum is

$$f(1.25)0.5 + f(1.75)0.5.$$

Figure 7.4 shows that evaluating f at the midpoint of each subdivision often gives a better approximation to the area under the curve than evaluating f at either end.

Figure 7.4: Midpoint rule with two subdivisions

Thus, we have three ways of estimating an integral using a Riemann sum:

1. The **left rule** uses the left endpoint of each subinterval.
2. The **right rule** uses the right endpoint of each subinterval.
3. The **midpoint rule** uses the midpoint of each subinterval.

We write $\text{LEFT}(n)$, $\text{RIGHT}(n)$, and $\text{MID}(n)$ to denote the results obtained by using these rules with n subdivisions.

Example 1   For $\displaystyle\int_1^2 \frac{1}{x}\,dx$, compute $\text{LEFT}(2)$, $\text{RIGHT}(2)$ and $\text{MID}(2)$, and compare your answers with the exact value of the integral.

Solution   For $n = 2$ subdivisions of the interval $[1, 2]$, we use $\Delta x = 0.5$. Then, to four decimal places,

$$\text{LEFT}(2) = f(1)(0.5) + f(1.5)(0.5) = \frac{1}{1}(0.5) + \frac{1}{1.5}(0.5) = 0.8333$$

$$\text{RIGHT}(2) = f(1.5)(0.5) + f(2)(0.5) = \frac{1}{1.5}(0.5) + \frac{1}{2}(0.5) = 0.5833$$

$$\text{MID}(2) = f(1.25)(0.5) + f(1.75)(0.5) = \frac{1}{1.25}(0.5) + \frac{1}{1.75}(0.5) = 0.6857.$$

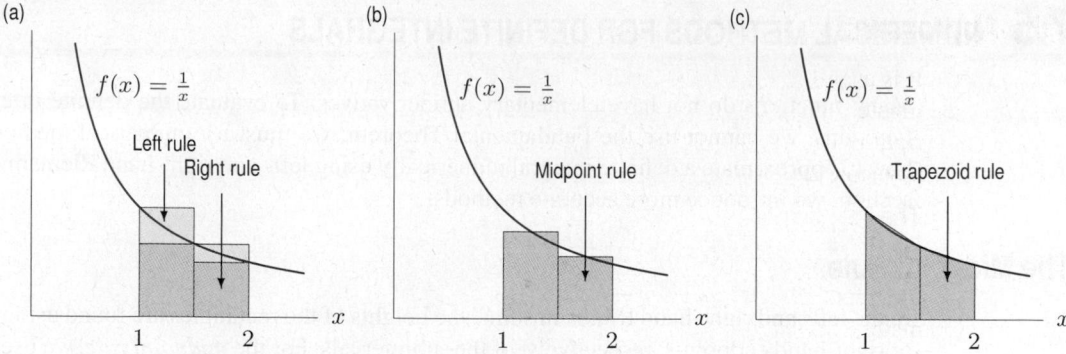

Figure 7.5: Left, right, midpoint, and trapezoid approximations to $\int_1^2 \frac{1}{x}\,dx$

All three Riemann sums in this example are approximating

$$\int_1^2 \frac{1}{x}\,dx = \ln x\Big|_1^2 = \ln 2 - \ln 1 = \ln 2 = 0.6931.$$

With only two subdivisions, the left and right rules give quite poor approximations but the midpoint rule is already fairly close to the exact answer. Figures 7.5(a) and (b) show that the midpoint rule is more accurate than the left and right rules because the error to the left of the midpoint tends to cancel the error to the right of the midpoint.

The Trapezoid Rule

We have just seen how the midpoint rule can have the effect of balancing out the errors of the left and right rules. Another way of balancing these errors is to average the results from the left and right rules. This approximation is called the *trapezoid rule*:

$$\text{TRAP}(n) = \frac{\text{LEFT}(n) + \text{RIGHT}(n)}{2}.$$

The trapezoid rule averages the values of f at the left and right endpoints of each subinterval and multiplies by Δx. This is the same as approximating the area under the graph of f in each subinterval by a trapezoid (see Figure 7.6).

Figure 7.6: Area used in the trapezoid rule

Example 2   For $\int_1^2 \frac{1}{x}\,dx$, compare the trapezoid rule with two subdivisions with the left, right, and midpoint rules.

Solution   In the previous example we got $\text{LEFT}(2) = 0.8333$ and $\text{RIGHT}(2) = 0.5833$. The trapezoid rule is the average of these, so $\text{TRAP}(2) = 0.7083$. (See Figure 7.5(c).) The exact value of the integral is 0.6931, so the trapezoid rule is better than the left or right rules. The midpoint rule is still the best, however, since $\text{MID}(2) = 0.6857$.

Is the Approximation an Over- or Underestimate?

It is useful to know when a rule is producing an overestimate and when it is producing an underestimate. In Chapter 5 we saw that if the integrand is increasing, the left rule underestimates and the right rule overestimates the integral. If the integrand is decreasing, the roles reverse. Now we see how concavity relates to the errors in the trapezoid and midpoint rules.

The Trapezoid Rule

If the graph of the function is concave down on $[a, b]$, then each trapezoid lies below the graph and the trapezoid rule underestimates. If the graph is concave up on $[a, b]$, the trapezoid rule overestimates. (See Figure 7.7.)

f concave down:
Trapezoid underestimates

f concave up:
Trapezoid overestimates

Figure 7.7: Error in the trapezoid rule

The Midpoint Rule

To understand the relationship between the midpoint rule and concavity, take a rectangle whose top intersects the curve at the midpoint of a subinterval. Draw a tangent to the curve at the midpoint; this gives a trapezoid. See Figure 7.8. (This is *not* the same trapezoid as in the trapezoid rule.) The midpoint rectangle and the new trapezoid have the same area, because the shaded triangles in Figure 7.8 are congruent. Hence, if the graph of the function is concave down, the midpoint rule overestimates; if the graph is concave up, the midpoint rule underestimates. (See Figure 7.9.)

If the graph of f is concave down on $[a, b]$, then

$$\text{TRAP}(n) \leq \int_a^b f(x)\, dx \leq \text{MID}(n).$$

If the graph of f is concave up on $[a, b]$, then

$$\text{MID}(n) \leq \int_a^b f(x)\, dx \leq \text{TRAP}(n).$$

Figure 7.8: Midpoint rectangle and
trapezoid with same area

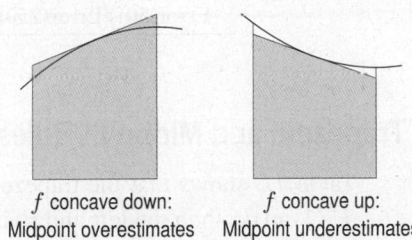

f concave down: f concave up:
Midpoint overestimates   Midpoint underestimates

Figure 7.9: Error in the midpoint rule

When we compute an approximation, we are always concerned about the error, namely the difference between the exact answer and the approximation. We usually do not know the exact error; if we did, we would also know the exact answer. We take

Error = Actual value − Approximate value.

The errors for some methods are much smaller than those for others. In general, the midpoint and trapezoid rules are more accurate than the left or right rules. Comparing the errors in the midpoint and trapezoid rules suggests an even better method, called Simpson's rule.

Error in Left and Right Rules

We work with the example $\int_1^2 (1/x) \, dx$ because we know the exact value of this integral ($\ln 2$) and we can investigate the behavior of the errors.

Let us see what happens to the error in the left and right rules as we increase n. The results are in Table 7.1. A positive error indicates that the Riemann sum is less than the exact value, $\ln 2$. Notice that the errors for the left and right rules have opposite signs but are approximately equal in magnitude. (See Figure 7.10.) This leads us to want to average the left and right rules; this average is the trapezoid rule.

Table 7.1 *Errors for the left and right rule approximation to $\int_1^2 \frac{1}{x} \, dx = \ln 2 \approx 0.6931471806$*

n	Error in left rule	Error in right rule
2	−0.1402	0.1098
10	−0.0256	0.0244
50	−0.0050	0.0050
250	−0.0010	0.0010

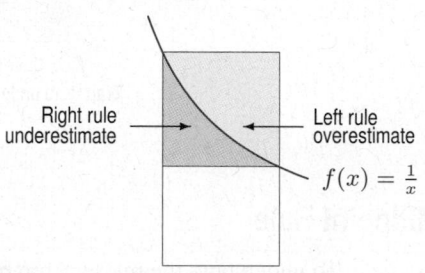

Figure 7.10: Errors in left and right sums

There is another pattern to the errors in Table 7.1. If we compute the *ratio* of the errors in Table 7.2, we see that the error[8] in both the left and right rules decreases by a factor of about 5 as n increases by a factor of 5.

There is nothing special about the number 5; the same holds for any factor. To get one extra digit of accuracy in any calculation, we must make the error $1/10$ as big, so we must increase n by a factor of 10. In fact, *for the left or right rules, each extra digit of accuracy requires about 10 times the work.*

Table 7.2 *Ratio of the errors as n increases for $\int_1^2 \frac{1}{x} \, dx$*

	Ratio of errors in left rule	Ratio of errors in right rule
Error(2)/Error(10)	5.47	4.51
Error(10)/Error(50)	5.10	4.90
Error(50)/Error(250)	5.02	4.98

Error in Trapezoid and Midpoint Rules

Table 7.3 shows that the trapezoid and midpoint rules generally produce better approximations to $\int_1^2 (1/x) \, dx$ than the left and right rules.

Again there is a pattern to the errors. For each n, the midpoint rule is noticeably better than the trapezoid rule; the error for the midpoint rule, in absolute value, seems to be about half the error of the trapezoid rule. To see why, compare the shaded areas in Figure 7.11. Also, notice in Table 7.3 that the errors for the two rules have opposite signs; this is due to concavity.

---

[8]The values in Table 7.1 are rounded to 4 decimal places; those in Table 7.2 were computed using more decimal places and then rounded.

Table 7.3 *The errors for the trapezoid and midpoint rules for $\int_1^2 \frac{1}{x}\,dx$*

n	Error in trapezoid rule	Error in midpoint rule
2	−0.0152	0.0074
10	−0.00062	0.00031
50	−0.0000250	0.0000125
250	−0.0000010	0.0000005

Figure 7.11: Errors in the midpoint and trapezoid rules

We are interested in how the errors behave as n increases. Table 7.4 gives the ratios of the errors for each rule. For each rule, we see that as n increases by a factor of 5, the error decreases by a factor of about $25 = 5^2$. In fact, it can be shown that this squaring relationship holds for any factor, so increasing n by a factor of 10 will decrease the error by a factor of about $100 = 10^2$. Reducing the error by a factor of 100 is equivalent to adding two more decimal places of accuracy to the result. In other words: *In the trapezoid or midpoint rules, each extra 2 digits of accuracy requires about 10 times the work.*

Table 7.4 *Ratios of the errors as n increases for $\int_1^2 \frac{1}{x}\,dx$*

	Ratio of errors in trapezoid rule	Ratio of errors in midpoint rule
Error(2)/Error(10)	24.33	23.84
Error(10)/Error(50)	24.97	24.95
Error(50)/Error(250)	25.00	25.00

Simpson's Rule

Observing that the trapezoid error has the opposite sign and about twice the magnitude of the midpoint error, we may guess that a weighted average of the two rules, with the midpoint rule weighted twice the trapezoid rule, has a smaller error. This approximation is called *Simpson's rule*[9]:

$$\text{SIMP}(n) = \frac{2 \cdot \text{MID}(n) + \text{TRAP}(n)}{3}.$$

Table 7.5 gives the errors for Simpson's rule. Notice how much smaller the errors are than the previous errors. Of course, it is a little unfair to compare Simpson's rule at $n = 50$, say, with the previous rules, because Simpson's rule must compute the value of f at both the midpoint and the endpoints of each subinterval and hence involves evaluating the function at twice as many points.

We see in Table 7.5 that as n increases by a factor of 5, the errors decrease by a factor of about 600, or about 5^4. Again this behavior holds for any factor, so increasing n by a factor of 10 decreases the error by a factor of about 10^4. In other words: *In Simpson's rule, each extra 4 digits of accuracy requires about 10 times the work.*

Table 7.5 *The errors for Simpson's rule and the ratios of the errors*

n	Error	Ratio
2	−0.0001067877	550.15
10	−0.0000001940	632.27
50	−0.0000000003	

---

[9]Some books and computer programs use slightly different terminology for Simpson's rule; what we call $n = 50$, they call $n = 100$.

Alternate Approach to Numerical Integration: Approximating by Lines and Parabolas

These rules for numerical integration can be obtained by approximating $f(x)$ on subintervals by a function:
- The left and right rules use constant functions.
- The trapezoid and midpoint rules use linear functions.
- Simpson's rule uses quadratic functions.

Problems 36 and 37 on page 394 show how a quadratic approximation leads to Simpson's rule.

Exercises and Problems for Section 7.5

Exercises

In Exercises 1–6, sketch the area given by the following approximations to $\int_a^b f(x)dx$. Identify each approximation as an overestimate or an underestimate.

(a) LEFT(2)   (b) RIGHT(2)
(c) TRAP(2)   (d) MID(2)

1.
2.

3.
4.

5.
6.

7. Calculate the following approximations to $\int_0^6 x^2 dx$.

(a) LEFT(2)   (b) RIGHT(2)
(c) TRAP(2)   (d) MID(2)

8. (a) Find LEFT(2) and RIGHT(2) for $\int_0^4 (x^2 + 1)\, dx$.
   (b) Illustrate your answers to part (a) graphically. Is each approximation an underestimate or overestimate?

9. (a) Find MID(2) and TRAP(2) for $\int_0^4 (x^2 + 1)\, dx$.
   (b) Illustrate your answers to part (a) graphically. Is each approximation an underestimate or overestimate?

10. Calculate the following approximations to $\int_0^\pi \sin \theta\, d\theta$.

(a) LEFT(2)   (b) RIGHT(2)
(c) TRAP(2)   (d) MID(2)

Problems

11. Use Table 7.6 to estimate $\int_1^2 g(t)\, dt$ by MID(5).

Table 7.6

t	1.0	1.1	1.2	1.3	1.4	1.5
$g(t)$	−2.1	−2.9	−3.4	−3.7	−3.6	−3.2
t	1.6	1.7	1.8	1.9	2.0	2.1
$g(t)$	−2.5	−1.7	−0.7	0.5	2.1	4.1

12. Compute MID(4) for the integral $\int_0^2 f(x)\, dx$ using the values in Table 7.7.

Table 7.7

x	0	0.25	0.50	0.75	1.00	1.25
$f(x)$	2.3	5.8	7.8	9.3	10.3	10.8
x	1.50	1.75	2.00	2.25	2.50	2.75
$f(x)$	10.8	10.3	9.3	7.8	5.8	3.3

In Problems 13–14, compute approximations to $\int_2^3 (1/x^2)\, dx$.

13. TRAP(2)   **14.** MID(2)

15. (a) Estimate $\int_0^1 1/(1 + x^2)\, dx$ by subdividing the interval into eight parts using:
   (i) the left Riemann sum
   (ii) the right Riemann sum
   (iii) the trapezoidal rule
   (b) Since the exact value of the integral is $\pi/4$, you can estimate the value of π using part (a). Explain why your first estimate is too large and your second estimate too small.

16. Using the table, estimate the total distance traveled from time $t = 0$ to time $t = 6$ using LEFT, RIGHT, and TRAP.

Time, t	0	1	2	3	4	5	6
Velocity, v	3	4	5	4	7	8	11

17. Using Figure 7.12, order the following approximations to the integral $\int_0^3 f(x)\,dx$ and its exact value from smallest to largest:

LEFT(n), RIGHT(n), MID(n), TRAP(n), Exact value.

Figure 7.12

18. The results from the left, right, trapezoid, and midpoint rules used to approximate $\int_0^1 g(t)\,dt$, with the same number of subdivisions for each rule, are as follows: 0.601, 0.632, 0.633, 0.664.

   (a) Using Figure 7.13, match each rule with its approximation.
   (b) Between which two consecutive approximations does the true value of the integral lie?

Figure 7.13

In Problems 19–22, decide which approximation—left, right, trapezoid, or midpoint—is guaranteed to give an overestimate for $\int_0^5 f(x)\,dx$, and which is guaranteed to give an underestimate. (There may be more than one.)

19.

20.

21.

22.

23. Consider the integral $\int_0^4 3\sqrt{x}\,dx$.

   (a) Estimate the value of the integral using MID(2).
   (b) Use the Fundamental Theorem of Calculus to find the exact value of the definite integral.
   (c) What is the error for MID(2)?
   (d) Use your knowledge of how errors change and your answer to part (c) to estimate the error for MID(20).
   (e) Use your answer to part (d) to estimate the approximation MID(20).

24. Using a fixed number of subdivisions, we approximate the integrals of f and g on the interval in Figure 7.14.

   (a) For which function, f or g, is LEFT more accurate? RIGHT? Explain.
   (b) For which function, f or g, is TRAP more accurate? MID? Explain.

Figure 7.14

25. (a) Values for $f(x)$ are in the table. Which of the four approximation methods in this section is most likely to give the best estimate of $\int_0^{12} f(x)\,dx$? Estimate the integral using this method.
   (b) Assume $f(x)$ is continuous with no critical points or points of inflection on the interval $0 \le x \le 12$. Is the estimate found in part (a) an over- or underestimate? Explain.

x	0	3	6	9	12
$f(x)$	100	97	90	78	55

26. (a) Find the exact value of $\int_0^{2\pi} \sin\theta\,d\theta$.
   (b) Explain, using pictures, why the MID(1) and MID(2) approximations to this integral give the exact value.
   (c) Does MID(3) give the exact value of this integral? How about MID(n)? Explain.

27. To investigate the relationship between the integrand and the errors in the left and right rules, imagine integrating a linear function. For one subinterval of integration, sketch lines with small f' and large f'. How do the errors compare?

28. To investigate the relationship between the integrand and the errors in the midpoint and trapezoid rules, imagine an integrand whose graph is concave down over one subinterval of integration. Sketch graphs where f'' has small magnitude and where f'' has large magnitude. How do the errors compare?

29. (a) Show geometrically why $\int_0^1 \sqrt{2 - x^2}\, dx = \frac{\pi}{4} + \frac{1}{2}$.
[Hint: Break up the area under $y = \sqrt{2 - x^2}$ from $x = 0$ to $x = 1$ into two pieces: a sector of a circle and a right triangle.]

   (b) Approximate $\int_0^1 \sqrt{2 - x^2}\, dx$ for $n = 5$ using the left, right, trapezoid, and midpoint rules. Compute the error in each case using the answer to part (a), and compare the errors.

30. The width, in feet, at various points along the fairway of a hole on a golf course is given in Figure 7.15. If one pound of fertilizer covers 200 square feet, estimate the amount of fertilizer needed to fertilize the fairway.

0   100   200   300   400   500   600   700   800   900   1000

Figure 7.15

Problems 31–35 involve approximating $\int_a^b f(x)\, dx$.

31. Show $\text{RIGHT}(n) = \text{LEFT}(n) + f(b)\Delta x - f(a)\Delta x$.

32. Show $\text{TRAP}(n) = \text{LEFT}(n) + \frac{1}{2}\left(f(b) - f(a)\right)\Delta x$.

33. Show $\text{LEFT}(2n) = \frac{1}{2}\left(\text{LEFT}(n) + \text{MID}(n)\right)$.

34. Check that the equations in Problems 31 and 32 hold for $\int_1^2 (1/x)\, dx$ when $n = 10$.

35. Suppose that $a = 2$, $b = 5$, $f(2) = 13$, $f(5) = 21$ and that $\text{LEFT}(10) = 3.156$ and $\text{MID}(10) = 3.242$. Use Problems 31–33 to compute $\text{RIGHT}(10)$, $\text{TRAP}(10)$, $\text{LEFT}(20)$, $\text{RIGHT}(20)$, and $\text{TRAP}(20)$.

Problems 36–37 show how Simpson's rule can be obtained by approximating the integrand, f, by quadratic functions.

36. Suppose that $a < b$ and that m is the midpoint $m = (a + b)/2$. Let $h = b - a$. The purpose of this problem is to show that if f is a quadratic function, then

$$\int_a^b f(x)\, dx = \frac{h}{3}\left(\frac{f(a)}{2} + 2f(m) + \frac{f(b)}{2}\right).$$

   (a) Show that this equation holds for the functions $f(x) = 1$, $f(x) = x$, and $f(x) = x^2$.

   (b) Use part (a) and the properties of the integral on page 300 to show that the equation holds for any quadratic function, $f(x) = Ax^2 + Bx + C$.

37. Consider the following method for approximating $\int_a^b f(x)\, dx$. Divide the interval $[a, b]$ into n equal subintervals. On each subinterval approximate f by a quadratic function that agrees with f at both endpoints and at the midpoint of the subinterval.

   (a) Explain why the integral of f on the subinterval $[x_i, x_{i+1}]$ is approximately equal to the expression

   $$\frac{h}{3}\left(\frac{f(x_i)}{2} + 2f(m_i) + \frac{f(x_{i+1})}{2}\right),$$

   where m_i is the midpoint of the subinterval, $m_i = (x_i + x_{i+1})/2$. (See Problem 36.)

   (b) Show that if we add up these approximations for each subinterval, we get Simpson's rule:

   $$\int_a^b f(x)\, dx \approx \frac{2 \cdot \text{MID}(n) + \text{TRAP}(n)}{3}.$$

Strengthen Your Understanding

In Problems 38–41, explain what is wrong with the statement.

38. The midpoint rule never gives the exact value of a definite integral.

39. $\text{TRAP}(n) \to 0$ as $n \to \infty$.

40. For any integral, $\text{TRAP}(n) \geq \text{MID}(n)$.

41. If, for a certain integral, it takes 3 nanoseconds to improve the accuracy of TRAP from one digit to three digits, then it also takes 3 nanoseconds to improve the accuracy from 8 digits to 10 digits.

In Problems 42–43, give an example of:

42. A continuous function $f(x)$ on the interval $[0, 1]$ such that $\text{RIGHT}(10) < \int_0^1 f(x)\, dx < \text{MID}(10)$.

43. A continuous function $f(x)$ on the interval $[0, 10]$ such that $\text{TRAP}(40) > \text{TRAP}(80)$.

In Problems 44–45, decide whether the statements are true or false. Give an explanation for your answer.

44. The midpoint rule approximation to $\int_0^1 (y^2 - 1)\, dy$ is always smaller than the exact value of the integral.

45. The trapezoid rule approximation is never exact.

The left and right Riemann sums of a function f on the interval $[2, 6]$ are denoted by $\text{LEFT}(n)$ and $\text{RIGHT}(n)$, respectively, when the interval is divided into n equal parts. In Problems 46–56, decide whether the statements are true for all continuous functions, f. Give an explanation for your answer.

46. If $n = 10$, then the subdivision size is $\Delta x = 1/10$.

47. If we double the value of n, we make Δx half as large.

48. $\text{LEFT}(10) \leq \text{RIGHT}(10)$

49. As n approaches infinity, LEFT(n) approaches 0.

50. LEFT(n) $-$ RIGHT(n) $= (f(2) - f(6))\Delta x$.

51. Doubling n decreases the difference LEFT(n) $-$ RIGHT(n) by exactly the factor $1/2$.

52. If LEFT(n) $=$ RIGHT(n) for all n, then f is a constant function.

53. The trapezoid estimate TRAP(n) $=$ (LEFT(n) $+$ RIGHT(n))$/2$ is always closer to $\int_2^6 f(x)dx$ than LEFT(n) or RIGHT(n).

54. $\int_2^6 f(x)\,dx$ lies between LEFT(n) and RIGHT(n).

55. If LEFT(2) $< \int_a^b f(x)\,dx$, then LEFT(4) $< \int_a^b f(x)\,dx$.

56. If $0 < f' < g'$ everywhere, then the error in approximating $\int_a^b f(x)\,dx$ by LEFT(n) is less than the error in approximating $\int_a^b g(x)\,dx$ by LEFT(n).

7.6 IMPROPER INTEGRALS

Our original discussion of the definite integral $\int_a^b f(x)\,dx$ assumed that the interval $a \le x \le b$ was of finite length and that f was continuous. Integrals that arise in applications do not necessarily have these nice properties. In this section we investigate a class of integrals, called *improper* integrals, in which one limit of integration is infinite or the integrand is unbounded. As an example, to estimate the mass of the earth's atmosphere, we might calculate an integral which sums the mass of the air up to different heights. In order to represent the fact that the atmosphere does not end at a specific height, we let the upper limit of integration get larger and larger, or tend to infinity.

We consider improper integrals with positive integrands since they are the most common.

One Type of Improper Integral: When the Limit of Integration Is Infinite

Here is an example of an improper integral:

$$\int_1^\infty \frac{1}{x^2}\,dx.$$

To evaluate this integral, we first compute the definite integral $\int_1^b (1/x^2)\,dx$:

$$\int_1^b \frac{1}{x^2}\,dx = -x^{-1}\Big|_1^b = -\frac{1}{b} + \frac{1}{1}.$$

Now take the limit as $b \to \infty$. Since

$$\lim_{b\to\infty} \int_1^b \frac{1}{x^2}\,dx = \lim_{b\to\infty}\left(-\frac{1}{b} + 1\right) = 1,$$

we say that the improper integral $\int_1^\infty (1/x^2)\,dx$ *converges* to 1.

If we think in terms of areas, the integral $\int_1^\infty (1/x^2)\,dx$ represents the area under $f(x) = 1/x^2$ from $x = 1$ extending infinitely far to the right. (See Figure 7.16(a).) It may seem strange that this region has finite area. What our limit computations are saying is that

$$\text{When } b = 10: \qquad \int_1^{10} \frac{1}{x^2}\,dx = -\frac{1}{x}\Big|_1^{10} = -\frac{1}{10} + 1 = 0.9$$

$$\text{When } b = 100: \qquad \int_1^{100} \frac{1}{x^2}\,dx = -\frac{1}{100} + 1 = 0.99$$

$$\text{When } b = 1000: \qquad \int_1^{1000} \frac{1}{x^2}\,dx = -\frac{1}{1000} + 1 = 0.999$$

and so on. In other words, as b gets larger and larger, the area between $x = 1$ and $x = b$ tends to 1. See Figure 7.16(b). Thus, it does make sense to declare that $\int_1^\infty (1/x^2)\,dx = 1$.

Figure 7.16: Area representation of improper integral

Of course, in another example, we might not get a finite limit as b gets larger and larger. In that case we say the improper integral *diverges*.

Suppose $f(x)$ is positive for $x \geq a$.

If $\displaystyle\lim_{b \to \infty} \int_a^b f(x)\, dx$ is a finite number, we say that $\displaystyle\int_a^\infty f(x)\, dx$ **converges** and define

$$\int_a^\infty f(x)\, dx = \lim_{b \to \infty} \int_a^b f(x)\, dx.$$

Otherwise, we say that $\displaystyle\int_a^\infty f(x)\, dx$ **diverges**. We define $\displaystyle\int_{-\infty}^b f(x)\, dx$ similarly.

Similar definitions apply if $f(x)$ is negative.

Example 1   Does the improper integral $\displaystyle\int_1^\infty \frac{1}{\sqrt{x}}\, dx$ converge or diverge?

Solution   We consider

$$\int_1^b \frac{1}{\sqrt{x}}\, dx = \int_1^b x^{-1/2}\, dx = 2x^{1/2} \Big|_1^b = 2b^{1/2} - 2.$$

We see that $\int_1^b (1/\sqrt{x})\, dx$ grows without bound as $b \to \infty$. We have shown that the area under the curve in Figure 7.17 is not finite. Thus we say the integral $\int_1^\infty (1/\sqrt{x})\, dx$ *diverges*. We could also say $\int_1^\infty (1/\sqrt{x})\, dx = \infty$.

Notice that $f(x) \to 0$ as $x \to \infty$ does not guarantee convergence of $\int_a^\infty f(x)\, dx$.

Figure 7.17: $\int_1^\infty \frac{1}{\sqrt{x}}\, dx$ diverges

---

What is the difference between the functions $1/x^2$ and $1/\sqrt{x}$ that makes the area under the graph of $1/x^2$ approach 1 as $x \to \infty$, whereas the area under $1/\sqrt{x}$ grows very large? Both functions approach 0 as x grows, so as b grows larger, smaller bits of area are being added to the definite integral. The difference between the functions is subtle: the values of the function $1/\sqrt{x}$ *don't shrink fast enough* for the integral to have a finite value. Of the two functions, $1/x^2$ drops to 0 much faster than $1/\sqrt{x}$, and this feature keeps the area under $1/x^2$ from growing beyond 1.

Example 2   Find $\int_0^\infty e^{-5x}\,dx$.

Solution   First we consider $\int_0^b e^{-5x}\,dx$:

$$\int_0^b e^{-5x}\,dx = -\frac{1}{5}e^{-5x}\Big|_0^b = -\frac{1}{5}e^{-5b} + \frac{1}{5}.$$

Since $e^{-5b} = \dfrac{1}{e^{5b}}$, this term tends to 0 as b approaches infinity, so $\int_0^\infty e^{-5x}\,dx$ converges. Its value is

$$\int_0^\infty e^{-5x}\,dx = \lim_{b\to\infty}\int_0^b e^{-5x}\,dx = \lim_{b\to\infty}\left(-\frac{1}{5}e^{-5b} + \frac{1}{5}\right) = 0 + \frac{1}{5} = \frac{1}{5}.$$

Since e^{5x} grows very rapidly, we expect that e^{-5x} will approach 0 rapidly. The fact that the area approaches $1/5$ instead of growing without bound is a consequence of the speed with which the integrand e^{-5x} approaches 0.

Example 3   Determine for which values of the exponent, p, the improper integral $\int_1^\infty \dfrac{1}{x^p}\,dx$ diverges.

Solution   For $p \neq 1$,

$$\int_1^b x^{-p}\,dx = \frac{1}{-p+1}x^{-p+1}\Big|_1^b = \left(\frac{1}{-p+1}b^{-p+1} - \frac{1}{-p+1}\right).$$

The important question is whether the exponent of b is positive or negative. If it is negative, then as b approaches infinity, b^{-p+1} approaches 0. If the exponent is positive, then b^{-p+1} grows without bound as b approaches infinity. What happens if $p = 1$? In this case we get

$$\int_1^\infty \frac{1}{x}\,dx = \lim_{b\to\infty}\ln x\Big|_1^b = \lim_{b\to\infty}\ln b - \ln 1.$$

Since $\ln b$ becomes arbitrarily large as b approaches infinity, the integral grows without bound. We conclude that $\int_1^\infty (1/x^p)\,dx$ diverges precisely when $p \leq 1$. For $p > 1$ the integral has the value

$$\int_1^\infty \frac{1}{x^p}\,dx = \lim_{b\to\infty}\int_1^b \frac{1}{x^p}\,dx = \lim_{b\to\infty}\left(\frac{1}{-p+1}b^{-p+1} - \frac{1}{-p+1}\right) = -\left(\frac{1}{-p+1}\right) = \frac{1}{p-1}.$$

Application of Improper Integrals to Energy

The energy, E, required to separate two charged particles, originally a distance a apart, to a distance b, is given by the integral

$$E = \int_a^b \frac{kq_1q_2}{r^2}\,dr$$

where q_1 and q_2 are the magnitudes of the charges and k is a constant. If q_1 and q_2 are in coulombs, a and b are in meters, and E is in joules, the value of the constant k is $9 \cdot 10^9$.

Example 4   A hydrogen atom consists of a proton and an electron, with opposite charges of magnitude $1.6\cdot10^{-19}$ coulombs. Find the energy required to take a hydrogen atom apart (that is, to move the electron from its orbit to an infinite distance from the proton). Assume that the initial distance between the electron and the proton is the Bohr radius, $R_B = 5.3 \cdot 10^{-11}$ meter.

Solution   Since we are moving from an initial distance of R_B to a final distance of ∞, the energy is represented by the improper integral

$$E = \int_{R_B}^{\infty} k\frac{q_1 q_2}{r^2}\, dr = kq_1q_2 \lim_{b\to\infty} \int_{R_B}^{b} \frac{1}{r^2}\, dr$$

$$= kq_1q_2 \lim_{b\to\infty} \left. -\frac{1}{r} \right|_{R_B}^{b} = kq_1q_2 \lim_{b\to\infty} \left(-\frac{1}{b} + \frac{1}{R_B} \right) = \frac{kq_1q_2}{R_B}.$$

Substituting numerical values, we get

$$E = \frac{(9\cdot 10^9)(1.6\cdot 10^{-19})^2}{5.3\cdot 10^{-11}} \approx 4.35\cdot 10^{-18} \text{ joules.}$$

This is about the amount of energy needed to lift a speck of dust 0.000000025 inch off the ground. (In other words, not much!)

What happens if the limits of integration are $-\infty$ and ∞? In this case, we break the integral at any point and write the original integral as a sum of two new improper integrals.

> For a positive function $f(x)$, we can use any (finite) number c to define
>
> $$\int_{-\infty}^{\infty} f(x)\, dx = \int_{-\infty}^{c} f(x)\, dx + \int_{c}^{\infty} f(x)\, dx.$$
>
> If *either* of the two new improper integrals diverges, we say the original integral diverges. Only if both of the new integrals have a finite value do we add the values to get a finite value for the original integral.

It is not hard to show that the preceding definition does not depend on the choice for c.

Another Type of Improper Integral: When the Integrand Becomes Infinite

There is another way for an integral to be improper. The interval may be finite but the function may be unbounded near some points in the interval. For example, consider $\int_0^1 (1/\sqrt{x})\, dx$. Since the graph of $y = 1/\sqrt{x}$ has a vertical asymptote at $x = 0$, the region between the graph, the x-axis, and the lines $x = 0$ and $x = 1$ is unbounded. Instead of extending to infinity in the horizontal direction as in the previous improper integrals, this region extends to infinity in the vertical direction. See Figure 7.18(a). We handle this improper integral in a similar way as before: we compute $\int_a^1 (1/\sqrt{x})\, dx$ for values of a slightly larger than 0 and look at what happens as a approaches 0 from the positive side. (This is written as $a \to 0^+$.)

First we compute the integral:

$$\int_a^1 \frac{1}{\sqrt{x}}\, dx = \left. 2x^{1/2} \right|_a^1 = 2 - 2a^{1/2}.$$

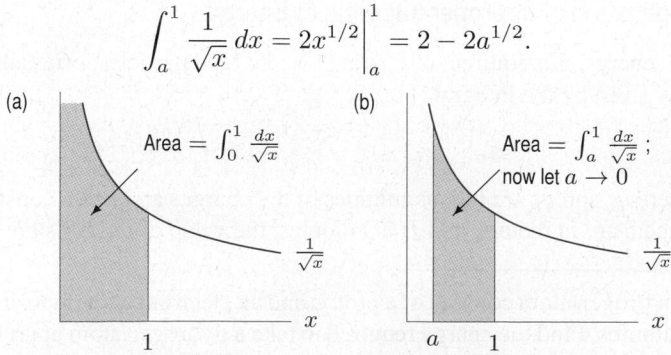

Figure 7.18: Area representation of improper integral

Now we take the limit:

$$\lim_{a \to 0^+} \int_a^1 \frac{1}{\sqrt{x}} \, dx = \lim_{a \to 0^+} (2 - 2a^{1/2}) = 2.$$

Since the limit is finite, we say the improper integral converges, and that

$$\int_0^1 \frac{1}{\sqrt{x}} \, dx = 2.$$

Geometrically, what we have done is to calculate the finite area between $x = a$ and $x = 1$ and take the limit as a tends to 0 from the right. See Figure 7.18(b). Since the limit exists, the integral converges to 2. If the limit did not exist, we would say the improper integral diverges.

Example 5   Investigate the convergence of $\int_0^2 \frac{1}{(x-2)^2} \, dx$.

Solution   This is an improper integral since the integrand tends to infinity as x approaches 2 and is undefined at $x = 2$. Since the trouble is at the right endpoint, we replace the upper limit by b, and let b tend to 2 from the left. This is written $b \to 2^-$, with the "$-$" signifying that 2 is approached from below. See Figure 7.19.

$$\int_0^2 \frac{1}{(x-2)^2} \, dx = \lim_{b \to 2^-} \int_0^b \frac{1}{(x-2)^2} \, dx = \lim_{b \to 2^-} (-1)(x-2)^{-1} \Big|_0^b = \lim_{b \to 2^-} \left(-\frac{1}{(b-2)} - \frac{1}{2}\right).$$

Therefore, since $\lim\limits_{b \to 2^-} \left(-\dfrac{1}{b-2}\right)$ does not exist, the integral diverges.

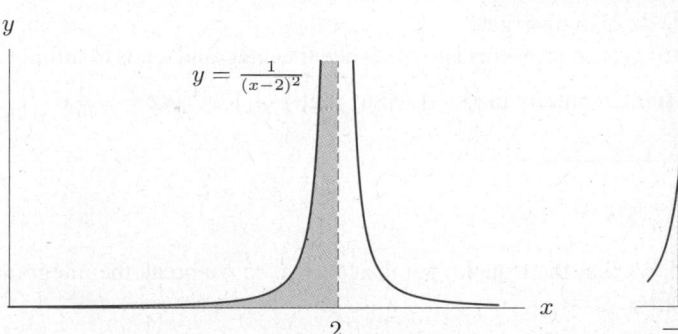

Figure 7.19: Shaded area represents $\int_0^2 \frac{1}{(x-2)^2} \, dx$

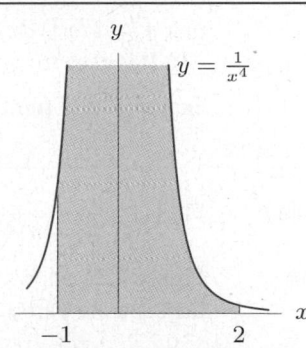

Figure 7.20: Shaded area represents $\int_{-1}^2 \frac{1}{x^4} \, dx$

Suppose $f(x)$ is positive and continuous on $a \le x < b$ and tends to infinity as $x \to b$.

If $\lim\limits_{c \to b^-} \int_a^c f(x) \, dx$ is a finite number, we say that $\int_a^b f(x) \, dx$ **converges** and define

$$\int_a^b f(x) \, dx = \lim_{c \to b^-} \int_a^c f(x) \, dx.$$

Otherwise, we say that $\int_a^b f(x) \, dx$ **diverges**.

When $f(x)$ tends to infinity as x approaches a, we define convergence in a similar way. In addition, an integral can be improper because the integrand tends to infinity *inside* the interval of integration rather than at an endpoint. In this case, we break the given integral into two (or more) improper integrals so that the integrand tends to infinity only at endpoints.

Suppose that $f(x)$ is positive and continuous on $[a, b]$ except at the point c. If $f(x)$ tends to infinity as $x \to c$, then we define

$$\int_a^b f(x)\, dx = \int_a^c f(x)\, dx + \int_c^b f(x)\, dx.$$

If *either* of the two new improper integrals diverges, we say the original integral diverges. Only if *both* of the new integrals have a finite value do we add the values to get a finite value for the original integral.

Example 6   Investigate the convergence of $\int_{-1}^2 \dfrac{1}{x^4}\, dx$.

Solution   See Figure 7.20. The trouble spot is $x = 0$, rather than $x = -1$ or $x = 2$. We break the given improper integral into two improper integrals each of which has $x = 0$ as an endpoint:

$$\int_{-1}^2 \frac{1}{x^4}\, dx = \int_{-1}^0 \frac{1}{x^4}\, dx + \int_0^2 \frac{1}{x^4}\, dx.$$

We can now use the previous technique to evaluate the new integrals, if they converge. Since

$$\int_0^2 \frac{1}{x^4}\, dx = \lim_{a \to 0^+} -\frac{1}{3}x^{-3}\Big|_a^2 = \lim_{a \to 0^+} \left(-\frac{1}{3}\right)\left(\frac{1}{8} - \frac{1}{a^3}\right)$$

the integral $\int_0^2 (1/x^4)\, dx$ diverges. Thus, the original integral diverges. A similar computation shows that $\int_{-1}^0 (1/x^4)\, dx$ also diverges.

It is easy to miss an improper integral when the integrand tends to infinity inside the interval. For example, it is fundamentally incorrect to say that $\int_{-1}^2 (1/x^4)\, dx = -\frac{1}{3}x^{-3}\Big|_{-1}^2 = -\frac{1}{24} - \frac{1}{3} = -\frac{3}{8}$.

Example 7   Find $\int_0^6 \dfrac{1}{(x-4)^{2/3}}\, dx$.

Solution   Figure 7.21 shows that the trouble spot is at $x = 4$, so we break the integral at $x = 4$ and consider the separate parts.

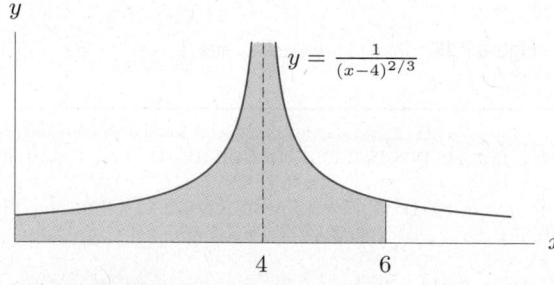

Figure 7.21: Shaded area represents $\int_0^6 \frac{1}{(x-4)^{2/3}}\, dx$

We have

$$\int_0^4 \frac{1}{(x-4)^{2/3}}\, dx = \lim_{b \to 4^-} 3(x-4)^{1/3}\Big|_0^b = \lim_{b \to 4^-}\left(3(b-4)^{1/3} - 3(-4)^{1/3}\right) = 3(4)^{1/3}.$$

Similarly,

$$\int_4^6 \frac{1}{(x-4)^{2/3}}\, dx = \lim_{a \to 4^+} 3(x-4)^{1/3}\Big|_a^6 = \lim_{a \to 4^+}\left(3 \cdot 2^{1/3} - 3(a-4)^{1/3}\right) = 3(2)^{1/3}.$$

Since both of these integrals converge, the original integral converges:

$$\int_0^6 \frac{1}{(x-4)^{2/3}}\,dx = 3(4)^{1/3} + 3(2)^{1/3} = 8.542.$$

Finally, there is a question of what to do when an integral is improper at both endpoints. In this case, we just break the integral at any interior point of the interval. The original integral diverges if either or both of the new integrals diverge.

Example 8 Investigate the convergence of $\int_0^\infty \frac{1}{x^2}\,dx$.

Solution This integral is improper both because the upper limit is ∞ and because the function is undefined at $x = 0$. We break the integral into two parts at, say, $x = 1$. We know by Example 3 that $\int_1^\infty (1/x^2)\,dx$ has a finite value. However, the other part, $\int_0^1 (1/x^2)\,dx$, diverges since:

$$\int_0^1 \frac{1}{x^2}\,dx = \lim_{a\to 0^+} -x^{-1}\Big|_a^1 = \lim_{a\to 0^+}\left(\frac{1}{a} - 1\right).$$

Therefore $\int_0^\infty \frac{1}{x^2}\,dx$ diverges as well.

Exercises and Problems for Section 7.6

Exercises

1. Shade the area represented by:
   (a) $\int_1^\infty (1/x^2)\,dx$ (b) $\int_0^1 (1/\sqrt{x})\,dx$

2. Evaluate the improper integral $\int_0^\infty e^{-0.4x}\,dx$ and sketch the area it represents.

3. (a) Use a calculator or computer to estimate $\int_0^b xe^{-x}dx$ for $b = 5, 10, 20$.
   (b) Use your answers to part (a) to estimate the value of $\int_0^\infty xe^{-x}dx$, assuming it is finite.

4. (a) Sketch the the area represented by the improper integral $\int_{-\infty}^\infty e^{-x^2}dx$.
   (b) Use a calculator or computer to estimate $\int_{-a}^a e^{-x^2}dx$ for $a = 1,2,3,4,5$.
   (c) Use the answers to part (b) to estimate the value of $\int_{-\infty}^\infty e^{-x^2}dx$, assuming it is finite.

Calculate the integrals in Exercises 5–33, if they converge. You may calculate the limits by appealing to the dominance of one function over another, or by l'Hopital's rule.

5. $\int_1^\infty \frac{1}{5x+2}\,dx$

6. $\int_1^\infty \frac{1}{(x+2)^2}\,dx$

7. $\int_0^1 \ln x\,dx$

8. $\int_0^\infty e^{-\sqrt{x}}\,dx$

9. $\int_0^\infty xe^{-x^2}\,dx$

10. $\int_1^\infty e^{-2x}\,dx$

11. $\int_0^\infty \frac{x}{e^x}\,dx$

12. $\int_1^\infty \frac{x}{4+x^2}\,dx$

13. $\int_{-\infty}^0 \frac{e^x}{1+e^x}\,dx$

14. $\int_{-\infty}^\infty \frac{dz}{z^2+25}$

15. $\int_0^4 \frac{1}{\sqrt{x}}\,dx$

16. $\int_{\pi/4}^{\pi/2} \frac{\sin x}{\sqrt{\cos x}}\,dx$

17. $\int_0^1 \frac{1}{v}\,dv$

18. $\int_0^1 \frac{x^4+1}{x}\,dx$

19. $\int_1^\infty \frac{1}{x^2+1}\,dx$

20. $\int_1^\infty \frac{1}{\sqrt{x^2+1}}\,dx$

21. $\int_0^4 \frac{-1}{u^2-16}\,du$

22. $\int_1^\infty \frac{y}{y^4+1}\,dy$

23. $\int_2^\infty \frac{dx}{x\ln x}$

24. $\int_0^1 \frac{\ln x}{x}\,dx$

25. $\int_{16}^{20} \frac{1}{y^2-16}\,dy$

26. $\int_0^\pi \frac{1}{\sqrt{x}}e^{-\sqrt{x}}\,dx$

27. $\int_3^\infty \frac{dx}{x(\ln x)^2}$

28. $\int_0^2 \frac{1}{\sqrt{4-x^2}}\,dx$

29. $\int_4^\infty \frac{dx}{(x-1)^2}$

30. $\int_4^\infty \frac{dx}{x^2-1}$

31. $\int_7^\infty \frac{dy}{\sqrt{y-5}}$

32. $\int_0^3 \frac{y\,dy}{\sqrt{9-y^2}}$

33. $\int_3^6 \frac{d\theta}{(4-\theta)^2}$

Problems

34. Find a formula (not involving integrals) for

$$f(x) = \int_{-\infty}^{x} e^t \, dt.$$

35. In statistics we encounter $P(x)$, a function defined by

$$P(x) = \frac{1}{\sqrt{\pi}} \int_0^x e^{-t^2} \, dt.$$

Use a calculator or computer to evaluate

   (a) $P(1)$ **(b)** $P(\infty)$

36. Find the area under the curve $y = xe^{-x}$ for $x \geq 0$.

37. Find the area under the curve $y = 1/\cos^2 t$ between $t = 0$ and $t = \pi/2$.

In Problems 38–41, evaluate $f(3)$.

38. $f(x) = \displaystyle\int_0^{\infty} x^{-t} dt$ **39.** $f(x) = \displaystyle\int_1^{\infty} t^{-x} dt$

40. $f(x) = \displaystyle\int_0^{\infty} xe^{-xt} \, dt$ **41.** $f(x) = \displaystyle\int_0^{\infty} 2txe^{-tx^2} dt$

42. For $\alpha > 0$, calculate

   (a) $\displaystyle\int_0^{\infty} \frac{e^{-y/\alpha}}{\alpha} \, dy$ **(b)** $\displaystyle\int_0^{\infty} \frac{ye^{-y/\alpha}}{\alpha} \, dy$

   (c) $\displaystyle\int_0^{\infty} \frac{y^2 e^{-y/\alpha}}{\alpha} \, dy$

43. The rate, r, at which people get sick during an epidemic of the flu can be approximated by $r = 1000te^{-0.5t}$, where r is measured in people/day and t is measured in days since the start of the epidemic.

   (a) Sketch a graph of r as a function of t.
   (b) When are people getting sick fastest?
   (c) How many people get sick altogether?

44. Find the energy required to separate opposite electric charges of magnitude 1 coulomb. The charges are initially 1 meter apart and one is moved infinitely far from the other. (The definition of energy is on page 397.)

45. Given that $\int_{-\infty}^{\infty} e^{-x^2} dx = \sqrt{\pi}$, calculate the exact value of

$$\int_{-\infty}^{\infty} e^{-(x-a)^2/b} \, dx.$$

46. Assuming $g(x)$ is a differentiable function whose values are bounded for all x, derive Stein's identity, which is used in statistics:

$$\int_{-\infty}^{\infty} g'(x)e^{-x^2/2} \, dx = \int_{-\infty}^{\infty} xg(x)e^{-x^2/2} \, dx.$$

47. Given that

$$\int_0^{\infty} \frac{x^4 e^x}{(e^x - 1)^2} \, dx = \frac{4\pi^4}{15}$$

evaluate

$$\int_0^{\infty} \frac{x^4 e^{2x}}{(e^{2x} - 1)^2} \, dx.$$

48. The gamma function is defined for all $x > 0$ by the rule

$$\Gamma(x) = \int_0^{\infty} t^{x-1} e^{-t} \, dt.$$

   (a) Find $\Gamma(1)$ and $\Gamma(2)$.
   (b) Integrate by parts with respect to t to show that, for positive n,

$$\Gamma(n+1) = n\Gamma(n).$$

   (c) Find a simple expression for $\Gamma(n)$ for positive integers n.

Strengthen Your Understanding

In Problems 49–50, explain what is wrong with the statement.

49. If both $\int_1^{\infty} f(x) \, dx$ and $\int_1^{\infty} g(x) \, dx$ diverge, then so does $\int_1^{\infty} f(x)g(x) \, dx$.

50. If $\int_1^{\infty} f(x) \, dx$ diverges, then $\lim_{x\to\infty} f(x) \neq 0$.

In Problems 51–52, give an example of:

51. A function $f(x)$, continuous for $x \geq 1$, such that $\lim_{x\to\infty} f(x) = 0$, but $\int_1^{\infty} f(x)dx$ diverges.

52. A function $f(x)$, continuous at $x = 2$ and $x = 5$, such that the integral $\int_2^5 f(x) \, dx$ is improper and divergent.

In Problems 53–58, decide whether the statements are true or false. Give an explanation for your answer.

53. If f is continuous for all x and $\int_0^{\infty} f(x) \, dx$ converges, then so does $\int_a^{\infty} f(x) \, dx$ for all positive a.

54. If $f(x)$ is a positive periodic function, then $\int_0^{\infty} f(x) \, dx$ diverges.

55. If $f(x)$ is continuous and positive for $x > 0$ and if $\lim_{x\to\infty} f(x) = 0$, then $\int_0^{\infty} f(x) \, dx$ converges.

56. If $f(x)$ is continuous and positive for $x > 0$ and if $\lim_{x\to\infty} f(x) = \infty$, then $\int_0^{\infty} (1/f(x)) \, dx$ converges.

57. If $\int_0^{\infty} f(x) \, dx$ and $\int_0^{\infty} g(x) \, dx$ both converge, then $\int_0^{\infty} (f(x) + g(x)) \, dx$ converges.

58. If $\int_0^\infty f(x)\,dx$ and $\int_0^\infty g(x)\,dx$ both diverge, then $\int_0^\infty (f(x)+g(x))\,dx$ diverges.

Suppose that f is continuous for all real numbers and that $\int_0^\infty f(x)\,dx$ converges. Let a be any positive number. Decide which of the statements in Problems 59–62 are true and which are false. Give an explanation for your answer.

59. $\int_0^\infty a f(x)\,dx$ converges.

60. $\int_0^\infty f(ax)\,dx$ converges.

61. $\int_0^\infty f(a+x)\,dx$ converges.

62. $\int_0^\infty (a+f(x))\,dx$ converges.

7.7 COMPARISON OF IMPROPER INTEGRALS

Making Comparisons

Sometimes it is difficult to find the exact value of an improper integral by antidifferentiation, but it may be possible to determine whether an integral converges or diverges. The key is to *compare* the given integral to one whose behavior we already know. Let's look at an example.

Example 1 Determine whether $\displaystyle\int_1^\infty \frac{1}{\sqrt{x^3+5}}\,dx$ converges.

Solution First, let's see what this integrand does as $x \to \infty$. For large x, the 5 becomes insignificant compared with the x^3, so

$$\frac{1}{\sqrt{x^3+5}} \approx \frac{1}{\sqrt{x^3}} = \frac{1}{x^{3/2}}.$$

Since

$$\int_1^\infty \frac{1}{\sqrt{x^3}}\,dx = \int_1^\infty \frac{1}{x^{3/2}}\,dx = \lim_{b\to\infty} \int_1^b \frac{1}{x^{3/2}}\,dx = \lim_{b\to\infty} -2x^{-1/2}\Big|_1^b = \lim_{b\to\infty}\left(2 - 2b^{-1/2}\right) = 2,$$

the integral $\int_1^\infty (1/x^{3/2})\,dx$ converges. So we expect our integral to converge as well.

In order to confirm this, we observe that for $0 \le x^3 \le x^3 + 5$, we have

$$\frac{1}{\sqrt{x^3+5}} \le \frac{1}{\sqrt{x^3}}.$$

and so for $b \ge 1$,

$$\int_1^b \frac{1}{\sqrt{x^3+5}}\,dx \le \int_1^b \frac{1}{\sqrt{x^3}}\,dx.$$

(See Figure 7.22.) Since $\int_1^b (1/\sqrt{x^3+5})\,dx$ increases as b approaches infinity but is always smaller than $\int_1^b (1/x^{3/2})\,dx < \int_1^\infty (1/x^{3/2})\,dx = 2$, we know $\int_1^\infty (1/\sqrt{x^3+5})\,dx$ must have a finite value less than 2. Thus,

$$\int_1^\infty \frac{dx}{\sqrt{x^3+5}} \quad \text{converges to a value less than 2.}$$

Total shaded area $= \int_1^\infty \dfrac{dx}{\sqrt{x^3}}$

Dark shaded area $= \int_1^\infty \dfrac{1}{\sqrt{x^3+5}}\,dx$

$y = \dfrac{1}{\sqrt{x^3}}$

$y = \dfrac{1}{\sqrt{x^3+5}}$

Figure 7.22: Graph showing $\int_1^\infty \frac{1}{\sqrt{x^3+5}}\,dx \le \int_1^\infty \frac{dx}{\sqrt{x^3}}$

Notice that we first looked at the behavior of the integrand as $x \to \infty$. This is useful because the convergence or divergence of the integral is determined by what happens as $x \to \infty$.

The Comparison Test for $\displaystyle\int_a^\infty f(x)\, dx$

Assume $f(x)$ is positive. Making a comparison involves two stages:

1. Guess, by looking at the behavior of the integrand for large x, whether the integral converges or not. (This is the "behaves like" principle.)

2. Confirm the guess by comparison with a positive function $g(x)$:

   - If $f(x) \leq g(x)$ and $\int_a^\infty g(x)\, dx$ converges, then $\int_a^\infty f(x)\, dx$ converges.
   - If $g(x) \leq f(x)$ and $\int_a^\infty g(x)\, dx$ diverges, then $\int_a^\infty f(x)\, dx$ diverges.

Example 2   Decide whether $\displaystyle\int_4^\infty \frac{dt}{(\ln t) - 1}$ converges or diverges.

Solution   Since $\ln t$ grows without bound as $t \to \infty$, the -1 is eventually going to be insignificant in comparison to $\ln t$. Thus, as far as convergence is concerned,

$$\int_4^\infty \frac{1}{(\ln t) - 1}\, dt \quad \text{behaves like} \quad \int_4^\infty \frac{1}{\ln t}\, dt.$$

Does $\int_4^\infty (1/\ln t)\, dt$ converge or diverge? Since $\ln t$ grows very slowly, $1/\ln t$ goes to zero very slowly, and so the integral probably does not converge. We know that $(\ln t) - 1 < \ln t < t$ for all positive t. So, provided $t > e$, we take reciprocals:

$$\frac{1}{(\ln t) - 1} > \frac{1}{\ln t} > \frac{1}{t}.$$

Since $\int_4^\infty (1/t)\, dt$ diverges, we conclude that

$$\int_4^\infty \frac{1}{(\ln t) - 1}\, dt \quad \text{diverges.}$$

How Do We Know What to Compare With?

In Examples 1 and 2, we investigated the convergence of an integral by comparing it with an easier integral. How did we pick the easier integral? This is a matter of trial and error, guided by any information we get by looking at the original integrand as $x \to \infty$. We want the comparison integrand to be easy and, in particular, to have a simple antiderivative.

Useful Integrals for Comparison

- $\displaystyle\int_1^\infty \frac{1}{x^p}\, dx$ converges for $p > 1$ and diverges for $p \leq 1$.

- $\displaystyle\int_0^1 \frac{1}{x^p}\, dx$ converges for $p < 1$ and diverges for $p \geq 1$.

- $\displaystyle\int_0^\infty e^{-ax}\, dx$ converges for $a > 0$.

Of course, we can use any function for comparison, provided we can determine its behavior.

Example 3   Investigate the convergence of $\displaystyle\int_1^\infty \frac{(\sin x) + 3}{\sqrt{x}}\, dx$.

Solution   Since it looks difficult to find an antiderivative of this function, we try comparison. What happens to this integrand as $x \to \infty$? Since $\sin x$ oscillates between -1 and 1,

$$\frac{2}{\sqrt{x}} = \frac{-1+3}{\sqrt{x}} \leq \frac{(\sin x)+3}{\sqrt{x}} \leq \frac{1+3}{\sqrt{x}} = \frac{4}{\sqrt{x}},$$

the integrand oscillates between $2/\sqrt{x}$ and $4/\sqrt{x}$. (See Figure 7.23.)

What do $\int_1^\infty (2/\sqrt{x})\,dx$ and $\int_1^\infty (4/\sqrt{x})\,dx$ do? As far as convergence is concerned, they certainly do the same thing, and whatever that is, the original integral does it too. It is important to notice that $\sqrt{x}$ grows very slowly. This means that $1/\sqrt{x}$ gets small slowly, which means that convergence is unlikely. Since $\sqrt{x} = x^{1/2}$, the result in the preceding box (with $p = \frac{1}{2}$) tells us that $\int_1^\infty (1/\sqrt{x})\,dx$ diverges. So the comparison test tells us that the original integral diverges.

Total shaded area $= \int_1^b \frac{(\sin x)+3}{\sqrt{x}}\,dx$

Dark shaded area $= \int_1^b \frac{2}{\sqrt{x}}\,dx$

$y = \frac{4}{\sqrt{x}}$

$y = \frac{(\sin x)+3}{\sqrt{x}}$

$y = \frac{2}{\sqrt{x}}$

Figure 7.23: Graph showing $\int_1^b \frac{2}{\sqrt{x}}\,dx \leq \int_1^b \frac{(\sin x)+3}{\sqrt{x}}\,dx$, for $b \geq 1$

Notice that there are two possible comparisons we could have made in Example 3:

$$\frac{2}{\sqrt{x}} \leq \frac{(\sin x)+3}{\sqrt{x}} \qquad \text{or} \qquad \frac{(\sin x)+3}{\sqrt{x}} \leq \frac{4}{\sqrt{x}}.$$

Since both $\int_1^\infty (2/\sqrt{x})\,dx$ and $\int_1^\infty (4/\sqrt{x})\,dx$ diverge, only the first comparison is useful. Knowing that an integral is *smaller* than a divergent integral is of no help whatsoever!

The next example shows what to do if the comparison does not hold throughout the interval of integration.

Example 4   Show $\displaystyle\int_1^\infty e^{-x^2/2}\,dx$ converges.

Solution   We know that $e^{-x^2/2}$ goes very rapidly to zero as $x \to \infty$, so we expect this integral to converge. Hence we look for some larger integrand which has a convergent integral. One possibility is $\int_1^\infty e^{-x}\,dx$, because e^{-x} has an elementary antiderivative and $\int_1^\infty e^{-x}\,dx$ converges. What is the relationship between $e^{-x^2/2}$ and e^{-x}? We know that for $x \geq 2$,

$$x \leq \frac{x^2}{2} \quad \text{so} \quad -\frac{x^2}{2} \leq -x,$$

and so, for $x \geq 2$

$$e^{-x^2/2} \leq e^{-x}.$$

Since this inequality holds only for $x \geq 2$, we split the interval of integration into two pieces:

$$\int_1^\infty e^{-x^2/2}\,dx = \int_1^2 e^{-x^2/2}\,dx + \int_2^\infty e^{-x^2/2}\,dx.$$

Now $\int_1^2 e^{-x^2/2}\,dx$ is finite (it is not improper) and $\int_2^\infty e^{-x^2/2}\,dx$ is finite by comparison with $\int_2^\infty e^{-x}\,dx$. Therefore, $\int_1^\infty e^{-x^2/2}\,dx$ is the sum of two finite pieces and therefore must be finite.

The previous example illustrates the following general principle:

If f is positive and continuous on $[a, b]$,

$$\int_a^\infty f(x)\, dx \text{ and } \int_b^\infty f(x)\, dx$$

either both converge or both diverge.

In particular, when the comparison test is applied to $\int_a^\infty f(x)\, dx$, the inequalities for $f(x)$ and $g(x)$ do not need to hold for all $x \geq a$ but only for x greater than some value, say b.

Exercises and Problems for Section 7.7

Exercises

In Exercises 1–9, use the box on page 404 and the behavior of rational and exponential functions as $x \to \infty$ to predict whether the integrals converge or diverge.

1. $\displaystyle\int_1^\infty \frac{x^2}{x^4 + 1}\, dx$

2. $\displaystyle\int_2^\infty \frac{x^3}{x^4 - 1}\, dx$

3. $\displaystyle\int_1^\infty \frac{x^2 + 1}{x^3 + 3x + 2}\, dx$

4. $\displaystyle\int_1^\infty \frac{1}{x^2 + 5x + 1}\, dx$

5. $\displaystyle\int_1^\infty \frac{x}{x^2 + 2x + 4}\, dx$

6. $\displaystyle\int_1^\infty \frac{x^2 - 6x + 1}{x^2 + 4}\, dx$

7. $\displaystyle\int_1^\infty \frac{5x + 2}{x^4 + 8x^2 + 4}\, dx$

8. $\displaystyle\int_1^\infty \frac{1}{e^{5t} + 2}\, dt$

9. $\displaystyle\int_1^\infty \frac{x^2 + 4}{x^4 + 3x^2 + 11}\, dx$

In Exercises 10–25, decide if the improper integral converges or diverges.

10. $\displaystyle\int_{50}^\infty \frac{dz}{z^3}$

11. $\displaystyle\int_1^\infty \frac{dx}{1 + x}$

12. $\displaystyle\int_1^\infty \frac{dx}{x^3 + 1}$

13. $\displaystyle\int_5^8 \frac{6}{\sqrt{t - 5}}\, dt$

14. $\displaystyle\int_0^1 \frac{1}{x^{19/20}}\, dx$

15. $\displaystyle\int_{-1}^5 \frac{dt}{(t + 1)^2}$

16. $\displaystyle\int_{-\infty}^\infty \frac{du}{1 + u^2}$

17. $\displaystyle\int_1^\infty \frac{du}{u + u^2}$

18. $\displaystyle\int_1^\infty \frac{d\theta}{\sqrt{\theta^2 + 1}}$

19. $\displaystyle\int_2^\infty \frac{d\theta}{\sqrt{\theta^3 + 1}}$

20. $\displaystyle\int_0^1 \frac{d\theta}{\sqrt{\theta^3 + \theta}}$

21. $\displaystyle\int_0^\infty \frac{dy}{1 + e^y}$

22. $\displaystyle\int_1^\infty \frac{2 + \cos \phi}{\phi^2}\, d\phi$

23. $\displaystyle\int_0^\infty \frac{dz}{e^z + 2^z}$

24. $\displaystyle\int_0^\pi \frac{2 - \sin \phi}{\phi^2}\, d\phi$

25. $\displaystyle\int_4^\infty \frac{3 + \sin \alpha}{\alpha}\, d\alpha$

Problems

26. The graphs of $y = 1/x$, $y = 1/x^2$ and the functions $f(x)$, $g(x)$, $h(x)$, and $k(x)$ are shown in Figure 7.24.

(a) Is the area between $y = 1/x$ and $y = 1/x^2$ on the interval from $x = 1$ to ∞ finite or infinite? Explain.

(b) Using the graph, decide whether the integral of each of the functions $f(x)$, $g(x)$, $h(x)$ and $k(x)$ on the interval from $x = 1$ to ∞ converges, diverges, or whether it is impossible to tell.

Figure 7.24

27. Suppose $\int_a^\infty f(x)\,dx$ converges. What does Figure 7.25 suggest about the convergence of $\int_a^\infty g(x)\,dx$?

Figure 7.25

For what values of p do the integrals in Problems 28–29 converge or diverge?

28. $\displaystyle\int_2^\infty \frac{dx}{x(\ln x)^p}$

29. $\displaystyle\int_1^2 \frac{dx}{x(\ln x)^p}$

30. (a) Find an upper bound for

$$\int_3^\infty e^{-x^2}\,dx.$$

[Hint: $e^{-x^2} \le e^{-3x}$ for $x \ge 3$.]

(b) For any positive n, generalize the result of part (a) to find an upper bound for

$$\int_n^\infty e^{-x^2}\,dx$$

by noting that $nx \le x^2$ for $x \ge n$.

31. In Planck's Radiation Law, we encounter the integral

$$\int_1^\infty \frac{dx}{x^5(e^{1/x} - 1)}.$$

(a) Explain why a graph of the tangent line to e^t at $t = 0$ tells us that for all t

$$1 + t \le e^t.$$

(b) Substituting $t = 1/x$, show that for all $x \ne 0$

$$e^{1/x} - 1 > \frac{1}{x}.$$

(c) Use the comparison test to show that the original integral converges.

Strengthen Your Understanding

In Problems 32–35, explain what is wrong with the statement.

32. $\int_1^\infty 1/(x^3 + \sin x)\,dx$ converges by comparison with $\int_1^\infty 1/x^3\,dx$.

33. $\int_1^\infty 1/(x^{\sqrt{2}} + 1)\,dx$ is divergent.

34. If $0 \le f(x) \le g(x)$ and $\int_0^\infty g(x)\,dx$ diverges then by the comparison test $\int_0^\infty f(x)\,dx$ diverges.

35. Let $f(x) > 0$. If $\int_1^\infty f(x)\,dx$ is convergent then so is $\int_1^\infty 1/f(x)\,dx$.

In Problems 36–37, give an example of:

36. A continuous function $f(x)$ for $x \ge 1$ such that the improper integral $\int_1^\infty f(x)dx$ can be shown to converge by comparison with the integral $\int_1^\infty 3/(2x^2)\,dx$.

37. A positive, continuous function $f(x)$ such that $\int_1^\infty f(x)dx$ diverges and

$$f(x) \le \frac{3}{7x - 2\sin x}, \quad \text{for } x \ge 1.$$

In Problems 38–39, decide whether the statements are true or false. Give an explanation for your answer.

38. The integral $\displaystyle\int_0^\infty \frac{1}{e^x + x}\,dx$ converges.

39. The integral $\displaystyle\int_0^1 \frac{1}{x^2 - 3}\,dx$ diverges.

CHAPTER SUMMARY (see also Ready Reference at the end of the book)

- **Integration techniques**
  Substitution, parts, partial fractions, trigonometric substitution, using tables.
- **Numerical approximations**

  Riemann sums (left, right, midpoint), trapezoid rule, Simpson's rule, approximation errors.
- **Improper integrals**
  Convergence/divergence, comparison test for integrals.

REVIEW EXERCISES AND PROBLEMS FOR CHAPTER SEVEN

Exercises

For Exercises 1–4, find an antiderivative.

1. $q(t) = (t+1)^2$

2. $p(\theta) = 2\sin(2\theta)$

3. $f(x) = 5^x$

4. $r(t) = e^t + 5e^{5t}$

For Exercises 5–110, evaluate the following integrals. Assume $a, b, c,$ and k are constants. Exercises 7–69 can be done without an integral table, as can some of the later problems.

5. $\displaystyle\int (3w+7)\,dw$

6. $\displaystyle\int e^{2r}\,dr$

7. $\displaystyle\int \sin t\,dt$

8. $\displaystyle\int \cos 2t\,dt$

9. $\displaystyle\int e^{5z}\,dz$

10. $\displaystyle\int \cos(x+1)\,dx$

11. $\displaystyle\int \sin 2\theta\,d\theta$

12. $\displaystyle\int (x^3-1)^4 x^2\,dx$

13. $\displaystyle\int \left(x^{3/2} + x^{2/3}\right)\,dx$

14. $\displaystyle\int (e^x + 3^x)\,dx$

15. $\displaystyle\int \frac{1}{e^z}\,dz$

16. $\displaystyle\int \left(\frac{4}{x^2} - \frac{3}{x^3}\right)\,dx$

17. $\displaystyle\int \frac{x^3+x+1}{x^2}\,dx$

18. $\displaystyle\int \frac{(1+\ln x)^2}{x}\,dx$

19. $\displaystyle\int te^{t^2}\,dt$

20. $\displaystyle\int x\cos x\,dx$

21. $\displaystyle\int x^2 e^{2x}\,dx$

22. $\displaystyle\int x\sqrt{1-x}\,dx$

23. $\displaystyle\int y\ln y\,dy$

24. $\displaystyle\int y\sin y\,dy$

25. $\displaystyle\int (\ln x)^2\,dx$

26. $\displaystyle\int e^{0.5-0.3t}\,dt$

27. $\displaystyle\int \sin^2\theta\cos\theta\,d\theta$

28. $\displaystyle\int x\sqrt{4-x^2}\,dx$

29. $\displaystyle\int \frac{(u+1)^3}{u^2}\,du$

30. $\displaystyle\int \frac{\cos\sqrt{y}}{\sqrt{y}}\,dy$

31. $\displaystyle\int \frac{1}{\cos^2 z}\,dz$

32. $\displaystyle\int \cos^2\theta\,d\theta$

33. $\displaystyle\int t^{10}(t-10)\,dt$

34. $\displaystyle\int \tan(2x-6)\,dx$

35. $\displaystyle\int \frac{(\ln x)^2}{x}\,dx$

36. $\displaystyle\int \frac{(t+2)^2}{t^3}\,dt$

37. $\displaystyle\int \left(x^2+2x+\frac{1}{x}\right)\,dx$

38. $\displaystyle\int \frac{t+1}{t^2}\,dt$

39. $\displaystyle\int te^{t^2+1}\,dt$

40. $\displaystyle\int \tan\theta\,d\theta$

41. $\displaystyle\int \sin(5\theta)\cos(5\theta)\,d\theta$

42. $\displaystyle\int \frac{x}{x^2+1}\,dx$

43. $\displaystyle\int \frac{dz}{1+z^2}$

44. $\displaystyle\int \frac{dz}{1+4z^2}$

45. $\displaystyle\int \cos^3 2\theta\sin 2\theta\,d\theta$

46. $\displaystyle\int \sin 5\theta\cos^3 5\theta\,d\theta$

47. $\displaystyle\int \sin^3 z\cos^3 z\,dz$

48. $\displaystyle\int t(t-10)^{10}\,dt$

49. $\displaystyle\int \cos\theta\sqrt{1+\sin\theta}\,d\theta$

50. $\displaystyle\int xe^x\,dx$

51. $\displaystyle\int t^3 e^t\,dt$

52. $\displaystyle\int_1^3 x(x^2+1)^{70}\,dx$

53. $\displaystyle\int (3z+5)^3\,dz$

54. $\displaystyle\int \frac{du}{9+u^2}$

55. $\displaystyle\int \frac{\cos w}{1+\sin^2 w}\,dw$

56. $\displaystyle\int \frac{1}{x}\tan(\ln x)\,dx$

57. $\displaystyle\int \frac{1}{x}\sin(\ln x)\,dx$

58. $\displaystyle\int \frac{w\,dw}{\sqrt{16-w^2}}$

59. $\displaystyle\int \frac{e^{2y}+1}{e^{2y}}\,dy$

60. $\displaystyle\int \frac{\sin w\,dw}{\sqrt{1-\cos w}}$

61. $\displaystyle\int \frac{dx}{x\ln x}$

62. $\displaystyle\int \frac{du}{3u+8}$

63. $\displaystyle\int \frac{x\cos\sqrt{x^2+1}}{\sqrt{x^2+1}}\,dx$

64. $\displaystyle\int \frac{t^3}{\sqrt{1+t^2}}\,dt$

65. $\displaystyle\int ue^{ku}\,du$

66. $\displaystyle\int (w+5)^4 w\,dw$

67. $\displaystyle\int e^{\sqrt{2x+3}}\,dx$

68. $\displaystyle\int (e^x+x)^2\,dx$

69. $\displaystyle\int u^2\ln u\,du$

70. $\displaystyle\int \frac{5x+6}{x^2+4}\,dx$

71. $\int \dfrac{1}{\sin^3(2x)}\, dx$

72. $\int \dfrac{dr}{r^2 - 100}$

73. $\int y^2 \sin(cy)\, dy$

74. $\int e^{-ct} \sin kt\, dt$

75. $\int e^{5x} \cos(3x)\, dx$

76. $\int \left(x^{\sqrt{k}} + \sqrt{k^x} \right) dx$

77. $\int \sqrt{3 + 12x^2}\, dx.$

78. $\int \dfrac{1}{\sqrt{x^2 - 3x + 2}}\, dx$

79. $\int \dfrac{x^3}{x^2 + 3x + 2}\, dx$

80. $\int \dfrac{x^2 + 1}{x^2 - 3x + 2}\, dx$

81. $\int \dfrac{dx}{ax^2 + bx}$

82. $\int \dfrac{ax + b}{ax^2 + 2bx + c}\, dx$

83. $\int \left(\dfrac{x}{3} + \dfrac{3}{x} \right)^2 dx$

84. $\int \dfrac{2^t}{2^t + 1}\, dt$

85. $\int 10^{1-x}\, dx$

86. $\int (x^2 + 5)^3\, dx$

87. $\int v \arcsin v\, dv$

88. $\int \sqrt{4 - x^2}\, dx$

89. $\int \dfrac{z^3}{z - 5}\, dz$

90. $\int \dfrac{\sin w \cos w}{1 + \cos^2 w}\, dw$

91. $\int \dfrac{1}{\tan(3\theta)}\, d\theta$

92. $\int \dfrac{x}{\cos^2 x}\, dx$

93. $\int \dfrac{x + 1}{\sqrt{x}}\, dx$

94. $\int \dfrac{x}{\sqrt{x + 1}}\, dx$

95. $\int \dfrac{\sqrt{\sqrt{x} + 1}}{\sqrt{x}}\, dx$

96. $\int \dfrac{e^{2y}}{e^{2y} + 1}\, dy$

97. $\int \dfrac{z}{(z^2 - 5)^3}\, dz$

98. $\int \dfrac{z}{(z - 5)^3}\, dz$

99. $\int \dfrac{(1 + \tan x)^3}{\cos^2 x}\, dx$

100. $\int \dfrac{(2x - 1)e^{x^2}}{e^x}\, dx$

101. $\int (2x + 1)e^{x^2} e^x\, dx$

102. $\int \sqrt{y^2 - 2y + 1}\,(y - 1)\, dy$

103. $\int \sin x(\sqrt{2 + 3\cos x})\, dx$

104. $\int (x^2 - 3x + 2)e^{-4x}\, dx$

105. $\int \sin^2(2\theta) \cos^3(2\theta)\, d\theta$

106. $\int \cos(2\sin x) \cos x\, dx$

107. $\int (x + \sin x)^3 (1 + \cos x)\, dx$

108. $\int \left(2x^3 + 3x + 4 \right) \cos(2x)\, dx$

109. $\int \sinh^2 x \cosh x\, dx$

110. $\int (x + 1) \sinh(x^2 + 2x)\, dx$

For Exercises 111–124, evaluate the definite integrals using the Fundamental Theorem of Calculus and check your answers numerically.

111. $\int_0^1 x(1 + x^2)^{20}\, dx$

112. $\int_4^1 x\sqrt{x^2 + 4}\, dx$

113. $\int_0^\pi \sin\theta(\cos\theta + 5)^7\, d\theta$

114. $\int_0^1 \dfrac{x}{1 + 5x^2}\, dx$

115. $\int_1^2 \dfrac{x^2 + 1}{x}\, dx$

116. $\int_1^3 \ln(x^3)\, dx$

117. $\int_1^e (\ln x)^2\, dx$

118. $\int_{-\pi}^\pi e^{2x} \sin 2x\, dx$

119. $\int_0^{10} ze^{-z}\, dz$

120. $\int_{-\pi/3}^{\pi/4} \sin^3\theta \cos\theta\, d\theta$

121. $\int_1^8 \dfrac{e^{\sqrt[3]{x}}}{\sqrt[3]{x^2}}\, dx$

122. $\int_0^1 \dfrac{dx}{x^2 + 1}$

123. $\int_{-\pi/4}^{\pi/4} \cos^2\theta \sin^5\theta\, d\theta$

124. $\int_{-2}^0 \dfrac{2x + 4}{x^2 + 4x + 5}\, dx$

125. Use partial fractions on $\dfrac{1}{x^2 - 1}$ to find $\int \dfrac{1}{x^2 - 1}\, dx.$

126. **(a)** Use partial fractions to find $\int \dfrac{1}{x^2 - x}\, dx.$
  (b) Show that your answer to part (a) agrees with the answer you get by using the integral tables.

127. Use partial fractions to find $\int \dfrac{1}{x(L - x)}\, dx$, where L is constant.

Evaluate the integrals in Exercises 128–139 using partial fractions or a trigonometric substitution (a and b are positive constants).

128. $\int \dfrac{1}{(x - 2)(x + 2)}\, dx$

129. $\int \dfrac{1}{\sqrt{25 - x^2}}\, dx,$

130. $\int \dfrac{1}{x(x + 5)}\, dx$

131. $\int \dfrac{1}{\sqrt{1 - 9x^2}}\, dx$

132. $\int \dfrac{2x+3}{x(x+2)(x-1)}dx$ **133.** $\int \dfrac{3x+1}{x(x^2-1)}dx$

on its value.

134. $\int \dfrac{1+x^2}{x(1+x)^2}dx$ **135.** $\int \dfrac{1}{x^2+2x+2}dx$

144. $\int_4^\infty \dfrac{dt}{t^{3/2}}$ **145.** $\int_{10}^\infty \dfrac{dx}{x\ln x}$

136. $\int \dfrac{1}{x^2+4x+5}dx$ **137.** $\int \dfrac{1}{\sqrt{a^2-(bx)^2}}dx$

146. $\int_0^\infty we^{-w}\,dw$ **147.** $\int_{-1}^1 \dfrac{1}{x^4}dx$

138. $\int \dfrac{\cos x}{\sin^3 x+\sin x}dx$ **139.** $\int \dfrac{e^x}{e^{2x}-1}dx$

148. $\int_{-\pi/4}^{\pi/4}\tan\theta\,d\theta$ **149.** $\int_2^\infty \dfrac{1}{4+z^2}dz$

Calculate the integrals in Exercises 140–143, if they converge. You may calculate the limits by appealing to the dominance of one function over another, or by l'Hopital's rule.

150. $\int_{10}^\infty \dfrac{1}{z^2-4}dz$ **151.** $\int_{-5}^{10}\dfrac{dt}{\sqrt{t+5}}$

152. $\int_0^{\pi/2}\dfrac{1}{\sin\phi}d\phi$ **153.** $\int_0^{\pi/4}\tan 2\theta\,d\theta$

140. $\int_0^4 \dfrac{dx}{\sqrt{16-x^2}}$ **141.** $\int_0^3 \dfrac{5}{x^2}dx$

142. $\int_0^2 \dfrac{1}{x-2}dx$ **143.** $\int_0^8 \dfrac{1}{\sqrt[3]{8-x}}dx$

154. $\int_1^\infty \dfrac{x}{x+1}dx$ **155.** $\int_0^\infty \dfrac{\sin^2\theta}{\theta^2+1}d\theta$

156. $\int_0^\pi \tan^2\theta d\theta$ **157.** $\int_0^1 (\sin x)^{-3/2}dx$

For Exercises 144–157 decide if the integral converges or diverges. If the integral converges, find its value or give a bound

Problems

In Problems 158–160, find the exact area.

158. Under $y=(e^x)^2$ for $0\le x\le 1$.

159. Between $y=(e^x)^3$ and $y=(e^x)^2$ for $0\le x\le 3$.

160. Between $y=e^x$ and $y=5e^{-x}$ and the y-axis.

161. The curves $y=\sin x$ and $y=\cos x$ cross each other infinitely often. What is the area of the region bounded by these two curves between two consecutive crossings?

162. Evaluate $\int_0^2 \sqrt{4-x^2}\,dx$ using its geometric interpretation.

In Problems 163–164, find a substitution w and constants k,p so that the integral has the form $\int kw^p\,dw$.

163. $\int 3x^4\sqrt{3x^5+2}\,dx$ **164.** $\int \dfrac{5\sin(3\theta)\,d\theta}{\cos^3(3\theta)}$

In Problems 165–168, give the substitution and the values of any constants to rewrite the integral in the desired form.

165. $\int \dfrac{dx}{(2x-3)(3x-2)}$ as $\int\left(\dfrac{A}{2x-3}+\dfrac{B}{3x-2}\right)dx$

166. $\int (x^2+x)\cos(0.5x-1)\,dx$ as $\int p(u)\cos(u)\,du$, where $p(u)$ is a polynomial

167. $\int x^3 e^{-x^2}\,dx$ as $\int kue^u\,du$

168. $\int \dfrac{\cos^4\left(\sqrt{x}\right)\sin\sqrt{x}\,dx}{\sqrt{x}}$ as $\int ku^n\,du$

In Problems 169–172, explain why the following pairs of antiderivatives are really, despite their apparent dissimilarity, different expressions of the same problem. You do not need to evaluate the integrals.

169. $\int \dfrac{1}{\sqrt{1-x^2}}dx$ and $\int \dfrac{x\,dx}{\sqrt{1-x^4}}$

170. $\int \dfrac{dx}{x^2+4x+4}$ and $\int \dfrac{x}{(x^2+1)^2}dx$

171. $\int \dfrac{x}{1-x^2}dx$ and $\int \dfrac{1}{x\ln x}dx$

172. $\int \dfrac{x}{x+1}dx$ and $\int \dfrac{1}{x+1}dx$

In Problems 173–174, show the two integrals are equal using a substitution.

173. $\int_0^2 e^{-w^2}\,dw = \int_0^1 2e^{-4x^2}\,dx$

174. $\int_0^3 \dfrac{\sin t}{t}dt = \int_0^1 \dfrac{\sin 3t}{t}dt$

175. A function is defined by $f(t)=t^2$ for $0\le t\le 1$ and $f(t)=2-t$ for $1<t\le 2$. Compute $\int_0^2 f(t)\,dt$.

176. (a) Find $\int (x+5)^2 \, dx$ in two ways:
   (i) By multiplying out
   (ii) By substituting $w = x + 5$
(b) Are the results the same? Explain.

177. Suppose $\int_{-1}^{1} h(z) \, dz = 7$, and that $h(z)$ is even. Calculate the following:

(a) $\int_{0}^{1} h(z) \, dz$ **(b)** $\int_{-4}^{-2} 5h(z+3) \, dz$

178. Find the average (vertical) height of the shaded area in Figure 7.26.

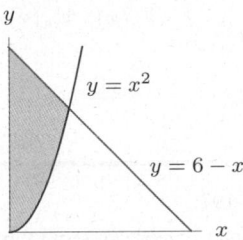

$y = x^2$

$y = 6 - x$

Figure 7.26

179. Find the average (horizontal) width of the shaded area in Figure 7.26.

180. (a) Find the average value of the following functions over one cycle:
   (i) $f(t) = \cos t$
   (ii) $g(t) = |\cos t|$
   (iii) $k(t) = (\cos t)^2$
(b) Write the averages you have just found in ascending order. Using words and graphs, explain why the averages come out in the order they do.

181. What, if anything, is wrong with the following calculation?

$$\int_{-2}^{2} \frac{1}{x^2} \, dx = -\frac{1}{x} \Big|_{-2}^{2} = -\frac{1}{2} - \left(-\frac{1}{-2}\right) = -1.$$

182. Let

$$E(x) = \int \frac{e^x}{e^x + e^{-x}} \, dx \text{ and } F(x) = \int \frac{e^{-x}}{e^x + e^{-x}} \, dx.$$

(a) Calculate $E(x) + F(x)$.
(b) Calculate $E(x) - F(x)$.
(c) Use your results from parts (a) and (b) to calculate $E(x)$ and $F(x)$.

183. Using Figure 7.27, put the following approximations to the integral $\int_{a}^{b} f(x) \, dx$ and its exact value in order from smallest to largest: LEFT(5), LEFT(10), RIGHT(5), RIGHT(10), MID(10), TRAP(10), Exact value

a b x

Figure 7.27

184. You estimate $\int_{0}^{0.5} f(x) dx$ by the trapezoid and midpoint rules with 100 steps. Which of the two estimates is an overestimate, and which is an underestimate, of the true value of the integral if

(a) $f(x) = 1 + e^{-x}$ **(b)** $f(x) = e^{-x^2}$
(c) $f(x)$ is a line

185. (a) Using the left rectangle rule, a computer takes two seconds to compute a particular definite integral accurate to 4 digits to the right of the decimal point. How long (in years) does it take to get 8 digits correct using the left rectangle rule? How about 12 digits? 20 digits?
(b) Repeat part (a) but this time assume that the trapezoidal rule is being used throughout.

186. Given that $\int_{0}^{\infty} e^{-x^2} \, dx = \frac{\sqrt{\pi}}{2}$, find $\int_{0}^{\infty} x^2 e^{-x^2} \, dx$.

187. A population, P, is said to be growing logistically if the time, T, taken for it to increase from P_1 to P_2 is given by

$$T = \int_{P_1}^{P_2} \frac{k \, dP}{P(L - P)},$$

where k and L are positive constants and $P_1 < P_2 < L$.

(a) Calculate the time taken for the population to grow from $P_1 = L/4$ to $P_2 = L/2$.
(b) What happens to T as $P_2 \to L$?

188. In 2005, the average per-capita income in the US was \$34,586 and increasing at a rate of $r(t) = 1556.37e^{0.045t}$ dollars per year, where t is the number of years since 2005.

(a) Estimate the average per-capita income in 2015.
(b) Find a formula for the average per-capita income as a function of time after 2005.

189. A patient is given an injection of Imitrex, a migraine medicine, at a rate of $r(t) = 2te^{-2t}$ ml/sec, where t is the number of seconds since the injection started.

(a) By letting $t \to \infty$, estimate the total quantity of Imitrex injected.
(b) What fraction of this dose has the patient received at the end of 5 seconds?

190. In 1990 humans generated $1.4 \cdot 10^{20}$ joules of energy from petroleum. At the time, it was estimated that all of the earth's petroleum would generate approximately 10^{22} joules. Assuming the use of energy generated by petroleum increases by 2% each year, how long will it be before all of our petroleum resources are used up?

191. An organism has a development time of T days at a temperature $H = f(t)°C$. The total the number of degree-days S required for development to maturity is a constant defined by

$$S = \int_0^T (f(t) - H_{\min})dt.$$

(a) Evaluate this integral for $T = 18$, $f(t) = 30°C$, and $H_{\min} = 10°C$. What are the units of S?

(b) Illustrate this definite integral on a graph. Label the features corresponding to T, $f(t)$, $H_{\min}$, and S.

(c) Now suppose $H = g(t) = 20 + 10\cos(2\pi t/6)°C$. Assuming that S remains constant, write a definite integral which determines the new development time, T_2. Sketch a graph illustrating this new integral. Judging from the graph, how does T_2 compare to T? Find T_2.

192. For a positive integer n, let $\Psi_n(x) = C_n \sin(n\pi x)$ be the wave function used in describing the behavior of an electron. If n and m are different positive integers, find

$$\int_0^1 \Psi_n(x) \cdot \Psi_m(x)\,dx.$$

CAS Challenge Problems

193. (a) Use a computer algebra system to find $\int \dfrac{\ln x}{x}\,dx$, $\int \dfrac{(\ln x)^2}{x}\,dx$, and $\int \dfrac{(\ln x)^3}{x}\,dx$.

(b) Guess a formula for $\int \dfrac{(\ln x)^n}{x}\,dx$ that works for any positive integer n.

(c) Use a substitution to check your formula.

194. (a) Using a computer algebra system, find $\int (\ln x)^n\,dx$ for $n = 1, 2, 3, 4$.

(b) There is a formula relating $\int (\ln x)^n\,dx$ to $\int (\ln x)^{n-1}\,dx$ for any positive integer n. Guess this formula using your answer to part (a). Check your guess using integration by parts.

In Problems 195–197:

(a) Use a computer algebra system to find the indefinite integral of the given function.

(b) Use the computer algebra system again to differentiate the result of part (a). Do not simplify.

(c) Use algebra to show that the result of part (b) is the same as the original function. Show all the steps in your calculation.

195. $\sin^3 x$

196. $\sin x \cos x \cos(2x)$

197. $\dfrac{x^4}{(1 + x^2)^2}$

PROJECTS FOR CHAPTER SEVEN

1. Taylor Polynomial Inequalities

(a) Use the fact that $e^x \geq 1 + x$ for all values of x and the formula

$$e^x = 1 + \int_0^x e^t\,dt$$

to show that

$$e^x \geq 1 + x + \frac{x^2}{2}$$

for all positive values of x. Generalize this idea to get inequalities involving higher-degree polynomials.

(b) Use the fact that $\cos x \leq 1$ for all x and repeated integration to show that

$$\cos x \leq 1 - \frac{x^2}{2!} + \frac{x^4}{4!}.$$

Chapter Eight

USING THE DEFINITE INTEGRAL

Contents

8.1   AREAS AND VOLUMES

In Chapter 5, we calculated areas under graphs using definite integrals. We obtained the integral by slicing up the region, constructing a Riemann sum, and then taking a limit. In this section, we calculate areas of other regions, as well as volumes, using definite integrals. To obtain the integral, we again slice up the region and construct a Riemann sum.

Finding Areas by Slicing

Example 1   Use horizontal slices to set up a definite integral to calculate the area of the isosceles triangle in Figure 8.1.

Figure 8.1: Isosceles triangle

Figure 8.2: Horizontal slices of isosceles triangle

Solution   Notice that we can find the area of a triangle without using an integral; we will use this to check the result from integration:

$$\text{Area} = \frac{1}{2} \text{ Base} \cdot \text{ Height} = 25 \text{ cm}^2.$$

To calculate the area using horizontal slices we divide the region into strips; see Figure 8.2. A typical strip is approximately a rectangle of length w_i and width Δh, so

$$\text{Area of strip} \approx w_i \Delta h \text{ cm}^2.$$

To get w_i in terms of h_i, the height above the base, use the similar triangles in Figure 8.2:

$$\frac{w_i}{10} = \frac{5 - h_i}{5}$$
$$w_i = 2(5 - h_i) = 10 - 2h_i.$$

Summing the areas of the strips gives the Riemann sum approximation:

$$\text{Area of triangle} \approx \sum_{i=1}^{n} w_i \Delta h = \sum_{i=1}^{n} (10 - 2h_i) \Delta h \text{ cm}^2.$$

Taking the limit as $n \to \infty$, the change in h shrinks and we get the integral:

$$\text{Area of triangle} = \lim_{n \to \infty} \sum_{i=1}^{n} (10 - 2h_i) \Delta h = \int_0^5 (10 - 2h) \, dh \text{ cm}^2.$$

Evaluating the integral gives

$$\text{Area of triangle} = \int_0^5 (10 - 2h) \, dh = (10h - h^2) \Big|_0^5 = 25 \text{ cm}^2.$$

Notice that the limits in the definite integral are the limits for the variable h. Once we decide to slice the triangle horizontally, we know that a typical slice has thickness Δh, so h is the variable in our definite integral, and the limits must be values of h.

Example 2   Use horizontal slices to set up a definite integral representing the area of the semicircle of radius 7 cm in Figure 8.3.

Figure 8.3: Semicircle

Figure 8.4: Horizontal slices of semicircle

Solution   As in Example 1, to calculate the area using horizontal slices, we divide the region into strips; see Figure 8.4. A typical strip at height h_i above the base has width w_i and thickness Δh, so

$$\text{Area of strip} \approx w_i \Delta h \text{ cm}^2.$$

To get w_i in terms of h_i, we use the Pythagorean Theorem in Figure 8.4:

$$h_i^2 + \left(\frac{w_i}{2}\right)^2 = 7^2,$$

so

$$w_i = \sqrt{4(7^2 - h_i^2)} = 2\sqrt{49 - h_i^2}.$$

Summing the areas of the strips gives the Riemann sum approximation:

$$\text{Area of semicircle} \approx \sum_{i=1}^{n} w_i \Delta h = \sum_{i=1}^{n} 2\sqrt{49 - h_i^2} \Delta h \text{ cm}^2.$$

Taking the limit as $n \to \infty$, the change in h shrinks and we get the integral:

$$\text{Area of semicircle} = \lim_{n \to \infty} \sum_{i=1}^{n} 2\sqrt{49 - h_i^2} \Delta h = 2\int_0^7 \sqrt{49 - h^2}\, dh \text{ cm}^2.$$

Using the table of integrals VI-30 and VI-28, or a calculator or computer, gives

$$\text{Area of semicircle} = 2 \cdot \frac{1}{2}\left(h\sqrt{49 - h^2} + 49\arcsin\left(\frac{h}{7}\right)\right)\Bigg|_0^7 - 49\arcsin 1 - \frac{49}{2}\pi - 76.97 \text{ cm}^2.$$

As a check, notice that the area of the whole circle of radius 7 is $\pi \cdot 7^2 = 49\pi \text{ cm}^2$.

Finding Volumes by Slicing

To calculate the volume of a solid using Riemann sums, we chop the solid into slices whose volumes we can estimate.

Figure 8.5: Cone cut into vertical slices

Figure 8.6: Cone cut into horizontal slices

Let's see how we might slice a cone standing with the vertex uppermost. We could divide the cone vertically into arch-shaped slices; see Figure 8.5. We could also divide the cone horizontally, giving coin-shaped slices; see Figure 8.6.

To calculate the volume of the cone, we choose the circular slices because it is easier to estimate the volumes of the coin-shaped slices.

Example 3   Use horizontal slicing to find the volume of the cone in Figure 8.7.

Figure 8.7: Cone

Figure 8.8: Vertical cross-section of cone in Figure 8.7

Solution   Each slice is a circular disk of thickness Δh. See Figure 8.7. The disk at height h_i above the base has radius $r_i = \frac{1}{2} w_i$. From Figure 8.8 and the previous example, we have

$$w_i = 10 - 2h_i \quad \text{so} \quad r_i = 5 - h_i.$$

Each slice is approximately a cylinder of radius r_i and thickness Δh, so

$$\text{Volume of slice} \approx \pi r_i^2 \Delta h = \pi (5 - h_i)^2 \Delta h \text{ cm}^3.$$

Summing over all slices, we have

$$\text{Volume of cone} \approx \sum_{i=1}^{n} \pi (5 - h_i)^2 \Delta h \text{ cm}^3.$$

Taking the limit as $n \to \infty$, so $\Delta h \to 0$, gives

$$\text{Volume of cone} = \lim_{n \to \infty} \sum_{i=1}^{n} \pi (5 - h_i)^2 \Delta h = \int_0^5 \pi (5 - h)^2 \, dh \text{ cm}^3.$$

The integral can be evaluated using the substitution $u = 5 - h$ or by multiplying out $(5 - h)^2$. Using the substitution, we have

$$\text{Volume of cone} = \int_0^5 \pi (5 - h)^2 dh = -\frac{\pi}{3} (5 - h)^3 \Big|_0^5 = \frac{125}{3} \pi \text{ cm}^3.$$

Note that the sum represented by the $\sum$ sign is over all the strips. To simplify the notation, in the future, we will not write limits for $\sum$ or subscripts on the variable, since all we want is the final expression for the definite integral. We now calculate the volume of a hemisphere by slicing.

Example 4   Set up and evaluate an integral giving the volume of the hemisphere of radius 7 cm in Figure 8.9.

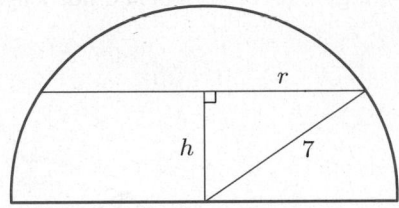

Figure 8.9: Slicing to find the volume of a hemisphere

Figure 8.10: Vertical cut through center of hemisphere showing relation between r_i and h_i

Solution   We will not use the formula $\frac{4}{3}\pi r^3$ for the volume of a sphere. However, our approach can be used to derive that formula.

Divide the hemisphere into horizontal slices of thickness Δh cm. (See Figure 8.9.) Each slice is circular. Let r be the radius of the slice at height h, so

$$\text{Volume of slice} \approx \pi r^2 \Delta h \ \text{cm}^3.$$

We express r in terms of h using the Pythagorean Theorem as in Example 2. From Figure 8.10, we have

$$h^2 + r^2 = 7^2,$$

so

$$r = \sqrt{7^2 - h^2} = \sqrt{49 - h^2}.$$

Thus,

$$\text{Volume of slice} \approx \pi r^2 \, \Delta h = \pi(7^2 - h^2) \, \Delta h \ \text{cm}^3.$$

Summing the volumes of all slices gives:

$$\text{Volume} \approx \sum \pi r^2 \, \Delta h = \sum \pi(7^2 - h^2) \, \Delta h \ \text{cm}^3.$$

As the thickness of each slice tends to zero, the sum becomes a definite integral. Since the radius of the hemisphere is 7, we know that h varies from 0 to 7, so these are the limits of integration:

$$\text{Volume} = \int_0^7 \pi(7^2 - h^2) \, dh = \pi \left(7^2 h - \frac{1}{3}h^3 \right) \Big|_0^7 = \frac{2}{3}\pi 7^3 = 718.4 \ \text{cm}^3.$$

Notice that the volume of the hemisphere is half of $\frac{4}{3}\pi 7^3$ cm^3, as we expected.

We now use slicing to find the volume of a pyramid. We do not use the formula, $V = \frac{1}{3}b^2 \cdot h$, for the volume of a pyramid of height h and square base of side length b, but our approach can be used to derive that formula.

Example 5   Compute the volume, in cubic feet, of the Great Pyramid of Egypt, whose base is a square 755 feet by 755 feet and whose height is 410 feet.

Solution   We slice the pyramid horizontally, creating square slices with thickness Δh. The bottom layer is a square slice 755 feet by 755 feet and volume about $(755)^2 \Delta h$ ft^3. As we move up the pyramid, the layers have shorter side lengths. We divide the height into n subintervals of length Δh. See Figure 8.11. Let s be the side length of the slice at height h; then

$$\text{Volume of slice} \approx s^2 \, \Delta h \text{ ft}^3.$$

Figure 8.11: The Great Pyramid   **Figure 8.12**: Cross-section relating s and h

We express s as a function of h using the vertical cross-section in Figure 8.12. By similar triangles, we get

$$\frac{s}{755} = \frac{(410 - h)}{410}.$$

Thus,

$$s = \left(\frac{755}{410}\right)(410 - h),$$

and the total volume, V, is approximated by adding the volumes of the n layers:

$$V \approx \sum s^2 \, \Delta h = \sum \left(\left(\frac{755}{410}\right)(410 - h)\right)^2 \Delta h \text{ ft}^3.$$

As the thickness of each slice tends to zero, the sum becomes a definite integral. Finally, since h varies from 0 to 410, the height of the pyramid, we have

$$V = \int_0^{410} \left(\left(\frac{755}{410}\right)(410 - h)\right)^2 dh = \left(\frac{755}{410}\right)^2 \int_0^{410} (410 - h)^2 \, dh$$

$$= \left(\frac{755}{410}\right)^2 \left(-\frac{(410 - h)^3}{3}\right)\Bigg|_0^{410} = \left(\frac{755}{410}\right)^2 \frac{(410)^3}{3} = \frac{1}{3}(755)^2(410) \approx 78 \text{ million ft}^3.$$

Note that $V = \frac{1}{3}(755)^2(410) = \frac{1}{3}b^2 \cdot h$, as expected.

Exercises and Problems for Section 8.1

Exercises

1. (a) Write a Riemann sum approximating the area of the region in Figure 8.13, using vertical strips as shown.
   (b) Evaluate the corresponding integral.

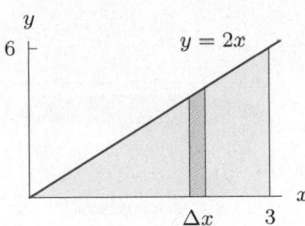

Figure 8.13

2. (a) Write a Riemann sum approximating the area of the region in Figure 8.14, using vertical strips as shown.
   (b) Evaluate the corresponding integral.

Figure 8.14

3. (a) Write a Riemann sum approximating the area of the region in Figure 8.15, using horizontal strips as shown.
   (b) Evaluate the corresponding integral.

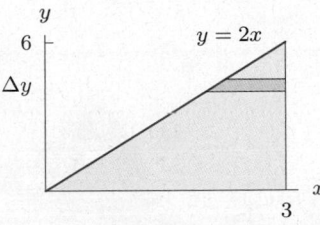

Figure 8.15

4. (a) Write a Riemann sum approximating the area of the region in Figure 8.16, using horizontal strips as shown.
   (b) Evaluate the corresponding integral.

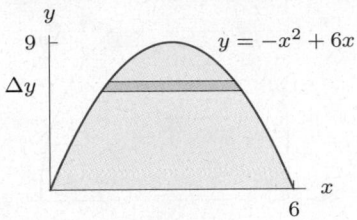

Figure 8.16

In Exercises 5–12, write a Riemann sum and then a definite integral representing the area of the region, using the strip shown. Evaluate the integral exactly.

5.

6.

7.

8.

9.

10.

11.

12.

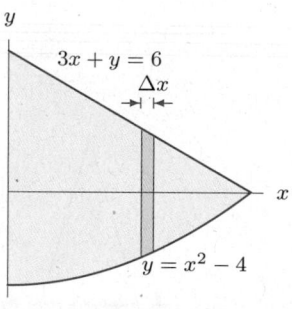

In Exercises 13–18, write a Riemann sum and then a definite integral representing the volume of the region, using the slice shown. Evaluate the integral exactly. (Regions are parts of cones, cylinders, spheres, and pyramids.)

13.

14.

15.

16.

17.

18.

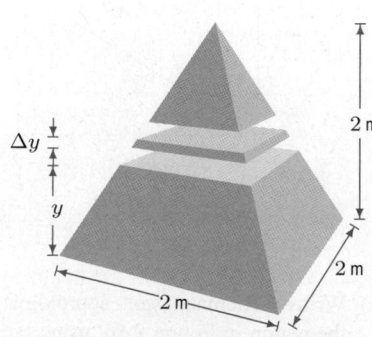

Problems

The integrals in Problems 19–22 represent the area of either a triangle or part of a circle, and the variable of integration measures a distance. In each case, say which shape is represented, and give the radius of the circle or the base and height of the triangle. Make a sketch to support your answer showing the variable and all other relevant quantities.

19. $\int_0^1 3x\,dx$

20. $\int_{-9}^9 \sqrt{81 - x^2}\,dx$

21. $\int_0^{\sqrt{15}} \sqrt{15 - h^2}\,dh$

22. $\int_0^7 5\left(1 - \frac{h}{7}\right)dh$

23. The integral $\int_0^1 (x - x^2)\,dx$ represents the area of a region between two curves in the plane. Make a sketch of this region.

In Problems 24–27, construct and evaluate definite integral(s) representing the area of the region described, using:
(a) Vertical slices   **(b)** Horizontal slices

24. Enclosed by $y = x^2$ and $y = 3x$.

25. Enclosed by $y = 2x$ and $y = 12 - x$ and the y-axis.

26. Enclosed by $y = x^2$ and $y = 6 - x$ and the x-axis.

27. Enclosed by $y = 2x$ and $x = 5$ and $y = 6$ and the x-axis.

The integrals in Problems 28–31 represent the volume of either a hemisphere or a cone, and the variable of integration measures a length. In each case, say which shape is represented, and give the radius of the hemisphere or the radius and height of the cone. Make a sketch to support your answer showing the variable and all other relevant quantities.

28. $\int_0^{12} \pi(144 - h^2)\,dh$

29. $\int_0^{12} \pi(x/3)^2\,dx$

30. $\int_0^6 \pi(3 - y/2)^2\,dy$

31. $\int_0^2 \pi(2^2 - (2-y)^2)\,dy$

32. Find the volume of a sphere of radius r by slicing.

33. Set up and evaluate an integral to find the volume of a cone of height 12 m and base radius 3 m.

34. Find, by slicing, a formula for the volume of a cone of height h and base radius r.

35. Figure 8.17 shows a solid with both rectangular and triangular cross sections.

(a) Slice the solid parallel to the triangular faces. Sketch one slice and calculate its volume in terms of x, the distance of the slice from one end. Then write and evaluate an integral giving the volume of the solid.
(b) Repeat part (a) for horizontal slices. Instead of x, use h, the distance of a slice from the top.

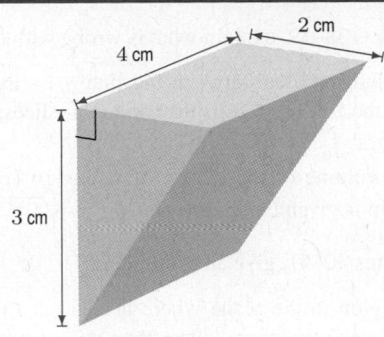
Figure 8.17

36. A rectangular lake is 150 km long and 3 km wide. The vertical cross-section through the lake in Figure 8.18 shows that the lake is 0.2 km deep at the center. (These are the approximate dimensions of Lake Mead, the largest reservoir in the US, which provides water to California, Nevada, and Arizona.) Set up and evaluate a definite integral giving the total volume of water in the lake.

Figure 8.18: Not to scale

37. A dam has a rectangular base 1400 meters long and 160 meters wide. Its cross-section is shown in Figure 8.19. (The Grand Coulee Dam in Washington state is roughly this size.) By slicing horizontally, set up and evaluate a definite integral giving the volume of material used to build this dam.

Figure 8.19: Not to scale

Strengthen Your Understanding

In Problems 38–39, explain what is wrong with the statement.

38. To find the area between the line $y = 2x$, the y-axis, and the line $y = 8$ using horizontal slices, evaluate the integral $\int_0^8 2y \, dy$.

39. The volume of the sphere of radius 10 centered at the origin is given by the integral $\int_{-10}^{10} \pi \sqrt{10^2 - x^2} \, dx$.

In Problems 40–41, give an example of:

40. A region in the plane where it is easier to compute the area using horizontal slices than it is with vertical slices. Sketch the region.

41. A triangular region in the plane for which both horizontal and vertical slices work just as easily.

In Problems 42–45, are the statements true or false? Give an explanation for your answer.

42. The integral $\int_{-3}^3 \pi(9 - x^2) \, dx$ represents the volume of a sphere of radius 3.

43. The integral $\int_0^h \pi(r - y) \, dy$ gives the volume of a cone of radius r and height h.

44. The integral $\int_0^r \pi \sqrt{r^2 - y^2} \, dy$ gives the volume of a hemisphere of radius r.

45. A cylinder of radius r and length l is lying on its side. Horizontal slicing tells us that the volume is given by $\int_{-r}^r 2l \sqrt{r^2 - y^2} \, dy$.

8.2 APPLICATIONS TO GEOMETRY

In Section 8.1, we calculated volumes using slicing and definite integrals. In this section, we use the same method to calculate the volumes of more complicated regions as well as the length of a curve. The method is summarized in the following steps:

To Compute a Volume or Length Using an Integral

- Divide the solid (or curve) into small pieces whose volume (or length) we can easily approximate;

- Add the contributions of all the pieces, obtaining a Riemann sum that approximates the total volume (or length);

- Take the limit as the number of terms in the sum tends to infinity, giving a definite integral for the total volume (or total length).

In the previous section, all the slices we created were disks or rectangles. We now look at different ways of generating volumes whose cross-sections include circles, rectangles, and also rings.

Volumes of Revolution

One way to create a solid having circular cross-sections is to revolve a region in the plane around a line, giving a *solid of revolution,* as in the following examples.

Example 1
The region bounded by the curve $y = e^{-x}$ and the x-axis between $x = 0$ and $x = 1$ is revolved around the x-axis. Find the volume of this solid of revolution.

Solution
We slice the region perpendicular to the x-axis, giving circular disks of thickness Δx. See Figure 8.20. The radius of the disk is $y = e^{-x}$, so:

$$\text{Volume of the slice} \approx \pi y^2 \, \Delta x = \pi (e^{-x})^2 \, \Delta x,$$

$$\text{Total volume} \approx \sum \pi y^2 \, \Delta x = \sum \pi \left(e^{-x} \right)^2 \, \Delta x.$$

As the thickness of each slice tends to zero, we get:

$$\text{Total volume } = \int_0^1 \pi(e^{-x})^2\, dx = \pi \int_0^1 e^{-2x}\, dx = \pi \left(-\frac{1}{2}\right) e^{-2x}\Big|_0^1$$

$$= \pi \left(-\frac{1}{2}\right)(e^{-2} - e^0) = \frac{\pi}{2}(1 - e^{-2}) \approx 1.36.$$

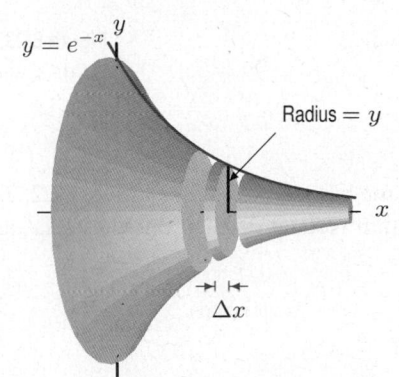

Figure 8.20: A thin strip rotated around the x-axis to form a circular slice

Figure 8.21: A table leg

Example 2   A table leg in Figure 8.21 has a circular cross section with radius r cm at a height of y cm above the ground given by $r = 3 + \cos(\pi y/25)$. Find the volume of the table leg.

Solution   The table leg is formed by rotating the curve $r = 3 + \cos(\pi y/25)$ around the y-axis. Slicing the table leg horizontally gives circular disks of thickness Δy and radius $r = 3 + \cos(\pi y/25)$.

To set up a definite integral for the volume, we find the volume of a typical slice:

$$\text{Volume of slice } \approx \pi r^2 \Delta y = \pi \left(3 + \cos\left(\frac{\pi}{25}y\right)\right)^2 \Delta y.$$

Summing over all slices gives the Riemann sum approximation:

$$\text{Total volume } = \sum \pi \left(3 + \cos\left(\frac{\pi}{25}y\right)\right)^2 \Delta y.$$

Taking the limit as $\Delta y \to 0$ gives the definite integral:

$$\text{Total volume } = \lim_{\Delta y \to 0} \sum \pi \left(3 + \cos\left(\frac{\pi}{25}y\right)\right)^2 \Delta y = \int_0^{100} \pi \left(3 + \cos\left(\frac{\pi}{25}y\right)\right)^2 dy.$$

Evaluating the integral numerically gives:

$$\text{Total volume } = \int_0^{100} \pi \left(3 + \cos\left(\frac{\pi}{25}y\right)\right)^2 dy = 2984.5 \text{ cm}^3.$$

Example 3   The region bounded by the curves $y = x$ and $y = x^2$ is rotated about the line $y = 3$. Compute the volume of the resulting solid.

Figure 8.22: Cutaway view of volume showing inner and outer radii

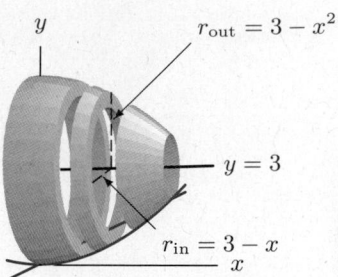

Figure 8.23: One slice (a disk-with-a-hole)

Solution   The solid is shaped like a bowl with the base removed. See Figure 8.22. To compute the volume, we divide the area in the xy-plane into thin vertical strips of thickness Δx, as in Figure 8.24.

Figure 8.24: The region for Example 3

As each strip is rotated around the line $y = 3$, it sweeps out a slice shaped like a circular disk with a hole in it. See Figure 8.23. This disk-with-a-hole has an inner radius of $r_{\text{in}} = 3 - x$ and an outer radius of $r_{\text{out}} = 3 - x^2$. Think of the slice as a circular disk of radius r_{out} from which has been removed a smaller disk of radius r_{in}. Then:

$$\text{Volume of slice} \approx \pi r_{\text{out}}^2 \, \Delta x - \pi r_{\text{in}}^2 \, \Delta x = \pi (3 - x^2)^2 \, \Delta x - \pi (3 - x)^2 \, \Delta x.$$

Adding the volumes of all the slices, we have:

$$\text{Total volume} = V \approx \sum \left(\pi r_{\text{out}}^2 - \pi r_{\text{in}}^2 \right) \Delta x = \sum \left(\pi (3 - x^2)^2 - \pi (3 - x)^2 \right) \Delta x.$$

We let Δx, the thickness of each slice, tend to zero to obtain a definite integral. Since the curves $y = x$ and $y = x^2$ intersect at $x = 0$ and $x = 1$, these are the limits of integration:

$$V = \int_0^1 \left(\pi (3 - x^2)^2 - \pi (3 - x)^2 \right) dx = \pi \int_0^1 \left((9 - 6x^2 + x^4) - (9 - 6x + x^2) \right) dx$$

$$= \pi \int_0^1 (6x - 7x^2 + x^4) \, dx = \pi \left(3x^2 - \frac{7x^3}{3} + \frac{x^5}{5} \right) \Big|_0^1 \approx 2.72.$$

Volumes of Regions of Known Cross-Section

We now calculate the volume of a solid constructed by a different method. Starting with a region in the xy-plane as a base, the solid is built by standing squares, semicircles, or triangles vertically on edge in this region.

Example 4   Find the volume of the solid whose base is the region in the xy-plane bounded by the curves $y = x^2$ and $y = 8 - x^2$ and whose cross-sections perpendicular to the x-axis are squares with one side in the xy-plane. (See Figure 8.25.)

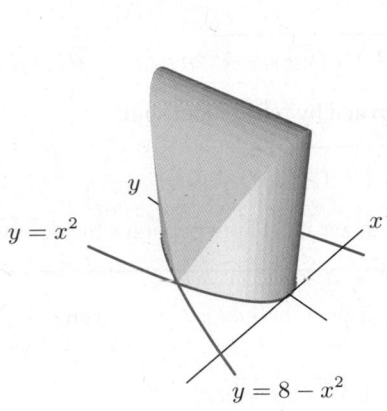

Figure 8.25: The solid for Example 4

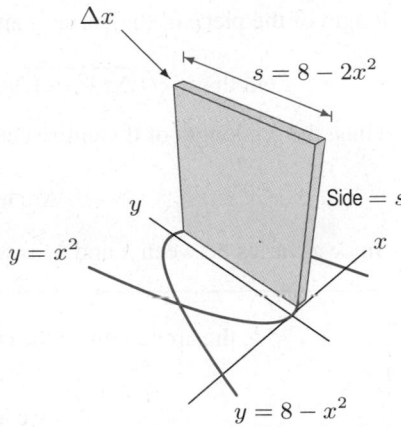

Figure 8.26: A slice of the solid for Example 4

Solution   We view the solid as a loaf of bread sitting on the xy-plane and made up of square slices. A typical slice of thickness Δx is shown in Figure 8.26. The side length, s, of the square is the distance (in the y direction) between the two curves, so $s = (8 - x^2) - x^2 = 8 - 2x^2$, giving

$$\text{Volume of slice} \approx s^2 \, \Delta x = (8 - 2x^2)^2 \, \Delta x.$$

Thus

$$\text{Total volume} = V \approx \sum s^2 \, \Delta x = \sum (8 - 2x^2)^2 \, \Delta x.$$

As the thickness Δx of each slice tends to zero, the sum becomes a definite integral. Since the curves $y = x^2$ and $y = 8 - x^2$ intersect at $x = -2$ and $x = 2$, these are the limits of integration. We have

$$V = \int_{-2}^{2} (8 - 2x^2)^2 \, dx = \int_{-2}^{2} (64 - 32x^2 + 4x^4) \, dx$$

$$= \left(64x - \frac{32}{3}x^3 + \frac{4}{5}x^5 \right) \Big|_{-2}^{2} = \frac{2048}{15} \approx 136.5.$$

Arc Length

A definite integral can be used to compute the *arc length*, or length, of a curve. To compute the length of the curve $y = f(x)$ from $x = a$ to $x = b$, where $a < b$, we divide the curve into small pieces, each one approximately straight.

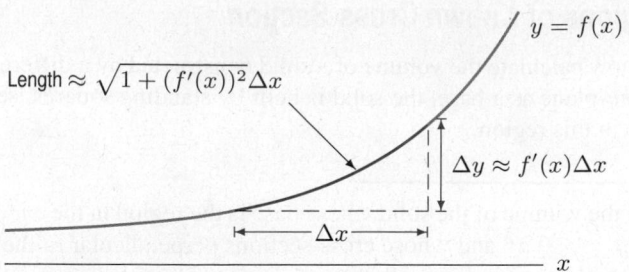

Figure 8.27: Length of a small piece of curve approximated using Pythagoras' theorem

Figure 8.27 shows that a small change Δx corresponds to a small change $\Delta y \approx f'(x)\,\Delta x$. The length of the piece of the curve is approximated by

$$\text{Length} \approx \sqrt{(\Delta x)^2 + (\Delta y)^2} \approx \sqrt{(\Delta x)^2 + (f'(x)\,\Delta x)^2} = \sqrt{1 + (f'(x))^2}\,\Delta x.$$

Thus, the arc length of the entire curve is approximated by a Riemann sum:

$$\text{Arc length} \approx \sum \sqrt{1 + (f'(x))^2}\,\Delta x.$$

Since x varies between a and b, as we let Δx tend to zero, the sum becomes the definite integral:

For $a < b$, the arc length of the curve $y = f(x)$ from $x = a$ to $x = b$ is given by

$$\text{Arc length} = \int_a^b \sqrt{1 + (f'(x))^2}\,dx.$$

Example 5   Set up and evaluate an integral to compute the length of the curve $y = x^3$ from $x = 0$ to $x = 5$.

Solution   If $f(x) = x^3$, then $f'(x) = 3x^2$, so

$$\text{Arc length} = \int_0^5 \sqrt{1 + (3x^2)^2}\,dx.$$

Although the formula for the arc length of a curve is easy to apply, the integrands it generates often do not have elementary antiderivatives. Evaluating the integral numerically, we find the arc length to be 125.68. To check that the answer is reasonable, notice that the curve starts at $(0, 0)$ and goes to $(5, 125)$, so its length must be at least the length of a straight line between these points, or $\sqrt{5^2 + 125^2} = 125.10$. (See Figure 8.28.)

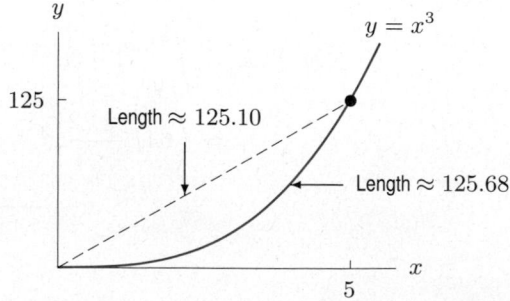

Figure 8.28: Arc length of $y = x^3$ (Note: The picture is distorted because the scales on the two axes are quite different.)

Arc Length of a Parametric Curve

A particle moving along a curve in the plane given by the parametric equations $x = f(t)$, $y = g(t)$, where t is time, has speed given by:

$$v(t) = \sqrt{\left(\frac{dx}{dt}\right)^2 + \left(\frac{dy}{dt}\right)^2}.$$

We can find the distance traveled by a particle along a curve between $t = a$ and $t = b$ by integrating its speed. Thus,

$$\text{Distance traveled} = \int_a^b v(t)\, dt.$$

If the particle never stops or reverses its direction as it moves along the curve, the distance it travels is the same as the length of the curve. This suggests the following formula:

If a curve is given parametrically for $a \leq t \leq b$ by differentiable functions and if the velocity $v(t)$ is not 0 for $a < t < b$, then

$$\text{Arc length of curve} = \int_a^b v(t)\, dt = \int_a^b \sqrt{\left(\frac{dx}{dt}\right)^2 + \left(\frac{dy}{dt}\right)^2}\, dt.$$

Example 6   Find the circumference of the ellipse given by the parametric equations

$$x = 2\cos t, \quad y = \sin t, \quad 0 \leq t \leq 2\pi.$$

Solution   The circumference of this curve is given by an integral which must be calculated numerically:

$$\text{Circumference} = \int_0^{2\pi} \sqrt{\left(\frac{dx}{dt}\right)^2 + \left(\frac{dy}{dt}\right)^2}\, dt = \int_0^{2\pi} \sqrt{(-2\sin t)^2 + (\cos t)^2}\, dt$$

$$= \int_0^{2\pi} \sqrt{4\sin^2 t + \cos^2 t}\, dt = 9.69.$$

Since the ellipse is inscribed in a circle of radius 2 and circumscribes a circle of radius 1, we expect the length of the ellipse to be between $2\pi(2) \approx 12.57$ and $2\pi(1) \approx 6.28$, so the value of 9.69 is reasonable.

Exercises and Problems for Section 8.2

Exercises

1. **(a)** The region in Figure 8.29 is rotated around the x-axis. Using the strip shown, write an integral giving the volume.
   (b) Evaluate the integral.

2. **(a)** The region in Figure 8.30 is rotated around the x-axis. Using the strip shown, write an integral giving the volume.
   (b) Evaluate the integral.

Figure 8.29

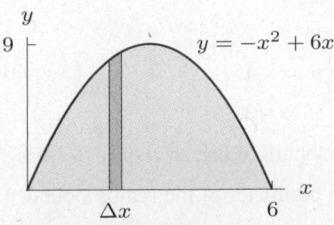

Figure 8.30

3. **(a)** The region in Figure 8.31 is rotated around the y-axis. Write an integral giving the volume.
   (b) Evaluate the integral.

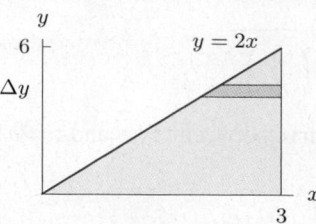

Figure 8.31

4. **(a)** The region in Figure 8.32 is rotated around the y-axis. Using the strip shown, write an integral giving the volume.
   (b) Evaluate the integral.

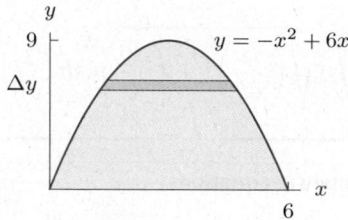

Figure 8.32

In Exercises 5–14, the region is rotated around the x-axis. Find the volume.

5. Bounded by $y = x^2, y = 0, x = 0, x = 1$.

6. Bounded by $y = (x+1)^2, y = 0, x = 1, x = 2$.

7. Bounded by $y = 4 - x^2, y = 0, x = -2, x = 0$.

8. Bounded by $y = \sqrt{x+1}, y = 0, x = -1, x = 1$.

9. Bounded by $y = e^x, y = 0, x = -1, x = 1$.

10. Bounded by $y = \cos x, y = 0, x = 0, x = \pi/2$.

11. Bounded by $y = 1/(x+1), y = 0, x = 0, x = 1$.

12. Bounded by $y = \sqrt{\cosh 2x}, y = 0, x = 0, x = 1$.

13. Bounded by $y = x^2, y = x, x = 0, x = 1$.

14. Bounded by $y = e^{3x}, y = e^x, x = 0, x = 1$.

For Exercises 15–20, find the arc length of the graph of the function from $x = 0$ to $x = 2$.

15. $f(x) = x^2/2$

16. $f(x) = \cos x$

17. $f(x) = \ln(x + 1)$

18. $f(x) = \sqrt{x^3}$

19. $f(x) = \sqrt{4 - x^2}$

20. $f(x) = \cosh x$

Find the length of the parametric curves in Exercises 21–24.

21. $x = 3 + 5t, y = 1 + 4t$ for $1 \le t \le 2$. Explain why your answer is reasonable.

22. $x = \cos(e^t), y = \sin(e^t)$ for $0 \le t \le 1$. Explain why your answer is reasonable.

23. $x = \cos(3t), y = \sin(5t)$ for $0 \le t \le 2\pi$.

24. $x = \cos^3 t, y = \sin^3 t$, for $0 \le t \le 2\pi$.

Problems

In Problems 25–28 set up, but do not evaluate, an integral that represents the volume obtained when the region in the first quadrant is rotated about the given axis.

25. Bounded by $y = \sqrt[3]{x}, x = 4y$. Axis $x = 9$.

26. Bounded by $y = \sqrt[3]{x}, x = 4y$. Axis $y = 3$.

27. Bounded by $y = 0, x = 9, y = \frac{1}{3}x$. Axis $y = -2$.

28. Bounded by $y = 0, x = 9, y = \frac{1}{3}x$. Axis $x = -1$.

In Problems 29–32, set up definite integral(s) to find the volume obtained when the region between $y = x^2$ and $y = 5x$ is rotated about the given axis. Do not evaluate the integral(s).

29. The x-axis

30. The y-axis

31. The line $y = -4$

32. The line $x = -3$

33. Find the length of one arch of $y = \sin x$.

34. Find the perimeter of the region bounded by $y = x$ and $y = x^2$.

35. Consider the hyperbola $x^2 - y^2 = 1$ in Figure 8.33.
    (a) The shaded region $2 \le x \le 3$ is rotated around the x-axis. What is the volume generated?
    (b) What is the arc length with $y \ge 0$ from $x = 2$ to $x = 3$?

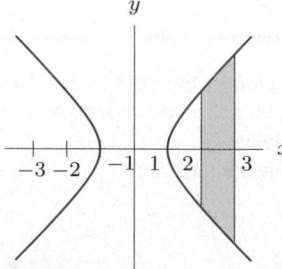

Figure 8.33

36. Rotating the ellipse $x^2/a^2 + y^2/b^2 = 1$ about the x-axis generates an ellipsoid. Compute its volume.

For Problems 37–39, sketch the solid obtained by rotating each region around the indicated axis. Using the sketch, show how to approximate the volume of the solid by a Riemann sum, and hence find the volume.

37. Bounded by $y = x^3$, $x = 1$, $y = -1$. Axis: $y = -1$.

38. Bounded by $y = \sqrt{x}$, $x = 1$, $y = 0$. Axis: $x = 1$.

39. Bounded by the first arch of $y = \sin x$, $y = 0$. Axis: x axis.

Problems 40–45 concern the region bounded by $y = x^2$, $y = 1$, and the y-axis, for $x \geq 0$. Find the volume of the following solids.

40. The solid obtained by rotating the region around the y-axis.

41. The solid obtained by rotating the region about the x-axis.

42. The solid obtained by rotating the region about the line $y = -2$.

43. The solid whose base is the region and whose cross-sections perpendicular to the x-axis are squares.

44. The solid whose base is the region and whose cross-sections perpendicular to the x-axis are semicircles.

45. The solid whose base is the region and whose cross-sections perpendicular to the y-axis are equilateral triangles.

For Problems 46–50 consider the region bounded by $y = e^x$, the x-axis, and the lines $x = 0$ and $x = 1$. Find the volume of the following solids.

46. The solid obtained by rotating the region about the x-axis.

47. The solid obtained by rotating the region about the horizontal line $y = -3$.

48. The solid obtained by rotating the region about the horizontal line $y = 7$.

49. The solid whose base is the given region and whose cross-sections perpendicular to the x-axis are squares.

50. The solid whose base is the given region and whose cross-sections perpendicular to the x-axis are semicircles.

51. Find a curve $y = g(x)$, such that when the region between the curve and the x-axis for $0 \leq x \leq \pi$ is revolved around the x-axis, it forms a solid with volume given by

$$\int_0^\pi \pi(4 - 4\cos^2 x)\, dx.$$

[Hint: Use the identity $\sin^2 x = 1 - \cos^2 x$.]

52. A particle starts at the origin and moves along the curve $y = 2x^{3/2}/3$ in the positive x-direction at a speed of 3 cm/sec, where x, y are in cm. Find the position of the particle at $t = 6$.

53. A tree trunk has a circular cross section at every height; its circumference is given in the following table. Estimate the volume of the tree trunk using the trapezoid rule.

Height (feet)	0	20	40	60	80	100	120
Circumference (feet)	26	22	19	14	6	3	1

54. Rotate the bell-shaped curve $y = e^{-x^2/2}$ shown in Figure 8.34 around the y-axis, forming a hill-shaped solid of revolution. By slicing horizontally, find the volume of this hill.

Figure 8.34

55. (a) A pie dish is 9 inches across the top, 7 inches across the bottom, and 3 inches deep. See Figure 8.35. Compute the volume of this dish.

(b) Make a rough estimate of the volume in cubic inches of a single cut-up apple, and estimate the number of apples needed to make an apple pie that fills this dish.

Figure 8.35

56. A 100 cm long gutter is made of three strips of metal, each 5 cm wide; Figure 8.36 shows a cross-section.

(a) Find the volume of water in the gutter when the depth is h cm.

(b) What is the maximum value of h?

(c) What is the maximum volume of water that the gutter can hold?

(d) If the gutter is filled with half the maximum volume of water, is the depth larger or smaller than half of the answer to part (b)? Explain how you can answer without any calculation.

(e) Find the depth of the water when the gutter contains half the maximum possible volume.

Figure 8.36

57. The design of boats is based on Archimedes' Principle, which states that the buoyant force on an object in water is equal to the weight of the water displaced. Suppose you want to build a sailboat whose hull is parabolic with cross section $y = ax^2$, where a is a constant. Your boat will have length L and its maximum draft (the maximum vertical depth of any point of the boat beneath the water line) will be H. See Figure 8.37. Every cubic meter of water weighs 10,000 newtons. What is the maximum possible weight for your boat and cargo?

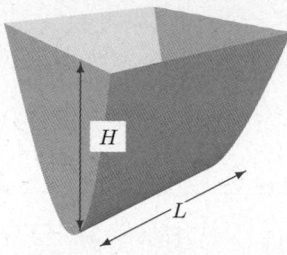

Figure 8.37

58. The circumference of a tree at different heights above the ground is given in the table below. Assume that all horizontal cross-sections of the tree are circles. Estimate the volume of the tree.

Height (inches)	0	20	40	60	80	100	120
Circumference (inches)	31	28	21	17	12	8	2

59. A bowl has the shape of the graph of $y = x^4$ between the points $(1, 1)$ and $(-1, 1)$ rotated about the y-axis. When the bowl contains water to a depth of h units, it flows out through a hole in the bottom at a rate (volume/time) proportional to $\sqrt{h}$, with constant of proportionality 6.

 (a) Show that the water level falls at a constant rate.
 (b) Find how long it takes to empty the bowl if it is originally full to the brim.

60. The hull of a boat has widths given by the following table. Reading across a row of the table gives widths at points 0, 10, ..., 60 feet from the front to the back at a certain level below waterline. Reading down a column of the table gives widths at levels 0, 2, 4, 6, 8 feet below waterline at a certain distance from the front. Use the trapezoidal rule to estimate the volume of the hull below waterline.

		Front of boat $\longrightarrow$ Back of boat						
		0	10	20	30	40	50	60
	0	2	8	13	16	17	16	10
Depth	2	1	4	8	10	11	10	8
below	4	0	3	4	6	7	6	4
waterline	6	0	1	2	3	4	3	2
(in feet)	8	0	0	1	1	1	1	1

61. (a) Write an integral which represents the circumference of a circle of radius r.
 (b) Evaluate the integral, and show that you get the answer you expect.

62. Compute the perimeter of the region used for the base of the solids in Problems 46–50.

63. Write an integral that represents the arc length of the portion of the graph of $f(x) = -x(x - 4)$ that lies above the x-axis. Do not evaluate the integral.

64. Find a curve $y = f(x)$ whose arc length from $x = 1$ to $x = 4$ is given by

$$\int_1^4 \sqrt{1 + \sqrt{x}}\, dx.$$

65. Write a simplified expression that represents the arc length of the concave-down portion of the graph of $f(x) = e^{-x^2}$. Do not evaluate your answer.

66. Write an expression that represents the arc length of the concave-down portion of the graph of $f(x) = x^4 - 8x^3 + 18x^2 + 3x + 7$. Do not simplify or evaluate the answer.

67. With x and b in meters, a chain hangs in the shape of the catenary $\cosh x = \frac{1}{2}(e^x + e^{-x})$ for $-b \le x \le b$. If the chain is 10 meters long, how far apart are its ends?

68. There are very few elementary functions $y = f(x)$ for which arc length can be computed in elementary terms using the formula

$$\int_a^b \sqrt{1 + \left(\frac{dy}{dx}\right)^2}\, dx.$$

You have seen some such functions f in Problems 18, 19, and 67, namely, $f(x) = \sqrt{x^3}$, $f(x) = \sqrt{4 - x^2}$, and $f(x) = \frac{1}{2}(e^x + e^{-x})$. Try to find some other function that "works," that is, a function whose arc length you can find using this formula and antidifferentiation.

69. After doing Problem 68, you may wonder what sort of functions can represent arc length. If $g(0) = 0$ and g is differentiable and increasing, then can $g(x)$, $x \ge 0$, represent arc length? That is, can we find a function $f(t)$ such that

$$\int_0^x \sqrt{1 + (f'(t))^2}\, dt = g(x)?$$

 (a) Show that $f(x) = \int_0^x \sqrt{(g'(t))^2 - 1}\, dt$ works as long as $g'(x) \ge 1$. In other words, show that the arc length of the graph of f from 0 to x is $g(x)$.
 (b) Show that if $g'(x) < 1$ for some x, then $g(x)$ cannot represent the arc length of the graph of any function.
 (c) Find a function f whose arc length from 0 to x is $2x$.

70. Consider the graph of the equation

$$|x|^k + |y|^k = 1, \quad k \text{ constant.}$$

For k an even integer, the absolute values are unnecessary. For example, for $k = 2$, we see the equation gives

the circle

$$x^2 + y^2 = 1.$$

(a) Sketch the graph of the equation for $k = 1, 2, 4$.
(b) Find the arc length of the three graphs in part (a). [Note: $k = 4$ may require a computer.]

Strengthen Your Understanding

In Problems 71–73, explain what is wrong with the statement.

71. The solid obtained by rotating the region bounded by the curves $y = 2x$ and $y = 3x$ between $x = 0$ and $x = 5$ around the x-axis has volume $\int_0^5 \pi(3x - 2x)^2 \, dx$.

72. The arc length of the curve $y = \sin x$ from $x = 0$ to $x = \pi/4$ is $\int_0^{\pi/4} \sqrt{1 + \sin^2 x} \, dx$.

73. The arc length of the curve $y = x^5$ between $x = 0$ and $x = 2$ is less than 32.

In Problems 74–77, give an example of:

74. A region in the plane which gives the same volume whether rotated about the x-axis or the y-axis.

75. A region where the solid obtained by rotating the region around the x-axis has greater volume than the solid obtained by revolving the region around the y-axis.

76. Two different curves from $(0, 0)$ to $(10, 0)$ that have the same arc length.

77. A function $f(x)$ whose graph passes through the points $(0, 0)$ and $(1, 1)$ and whose arc length between $x = 0$ and $x = 1$ is greater than $\sqrt{2}$.

Are the statements in Problems 78–81 true or false? If a statement is true, explain how you know. If a statement is false, give a counterexample.

78. Of two solids of revolution, the one with the greater volume is obtained by revolving the region in the plane with the greater area.

79. If f is differentiable on the interval $[0, 10]$, then the arc length of the graph of f on the interval $[0, 1]$ is less than the arc length of the graph of f on the interval $[1, 10]$.

80. If f is concave up for all x and $f'(0) = 3/4$, then the arc length of the graph of f on the interval $[0, 4]$ is at least 5.

81. If f is concave down for all x and $f'(0) = 3/4$, then the arc length of the graph of f on the interval $[0, 4]$ is at most 5.

8.3 AREA AND ARC LENGTH IN POLAR COORDINATES

Many curves and regions in the plane are easier to describe in polar coordinates than in Cartesian coordinates. Thus their areas and arc lengths are best found using integrals in polar coordinates.

A point, P, in the plane is often identified by its *Cartesian coordinates* (x, y), where x is the horizontal distance to the point from the origin and y is the vertical distance.[1] Alternatively, we can identify the point, P, by specifying its distance, r, from the origin and the angle, θ, shown in Figure 8.38. The angle θ is measured counterclockwise from the positive x-axis to the line joining P to the origin. The labels r and θ are called the *polar coordinates* of point P.

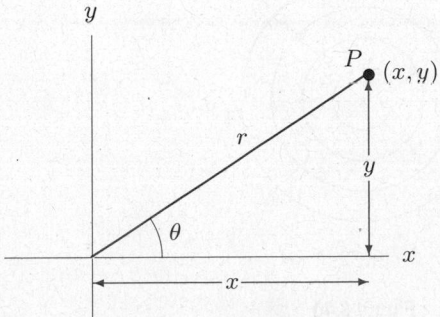

Figure 8.38: Cartesian and polar coordinates for the point P

Figure 8.39: Points on the plane for Example 1

---

[1] Cartesian coordinates can also be called rectangular coordinates.

Relation Between Cartesian and Polar Coordinates

From the right triangle in Figure 8.38, we see that

- $x = r \cos \theta$ and $y = r \sin \theta$
- $r = \sqrt{x^2 + y^2}$ and $\tan \theta = \dfrac{y}{x}$, $x \neq 0$

The angle θ is determined by the equations $\cos \theta = x/\sqrt{x^2 + y^2}$ and $\sin \theta = y/\sqrt{x^2 + y^2}$.

Warning: In general $\theta \neq \tan^{-1}(y/x)$. It is not possible to determine which quadrant θ is in from the value of $\tan \theta$ alone.

Example 1   (a) Give Cartesian coordinates for the points with polar coordinates (r, θ) given by $P = (7, \pi/3)$, $Q = (5, 0)$, $R = (5, \pi)$.

(b) Give polar coordinates for the points with Cartesian coordinates (x, y) given by $U = (3, 4)$ and $V = (0, -5)$.

Solution   (a) See Figure 8.39 on page 431. Point P is a distance of 7 from the origin. The angle θ is $\pi/3$ radians (60°). The Cartesian coordinates of P are

$$x = r \cos \theta = 7 \cos \frac{\pi}{3} = \frac{7}{2} \quad \text{and} \quad y = r \sin \theta = 7 \sin \frac{\pi}{3} = \frac{7\sqrt{3}}{2}.$$

Point Q is located a distance of 5 units along the positive x-axis with Cartesian coordinates

$$x = r \cos \theta = 5 \cos 0 = 5 \quad \text{and} \quad y = r \sin \theta = 5 \sin 0 = 0.$$

For point R, which is on the negative x-axis,

$$x = r \cos \theta = 5 \cos \pi = -5 \quad \text{and} \quad y = r \sin \theta = 5 \sin \pi = 0.$$

(b) For $U = (3, 4)$, we have $r = \sqrt{3^2 + 4^2} = 5$ and $\tan \theta = 4/3$. A possible value for θ is $\theta = \arctan 4/3 = 0.927$ radians, or about 53°. The polar coordinates of U are $(5, 0.927)$. The point V falls on the negative y-axis, so we can choose $r = 5$, $\theta = 3\pi/2$ for its polar coordinates. In this case, we cannot use $\tan \theta = y/x$ to find θ, because $\tan \theta = y/x = -5/0$ is undefined.

Because the angle θ can be allowed to wrap around the origin more than once, there are many possibilities for the polar coordinates of a point. For the point V in Example 1, we can also choose $\theta = -\pi/2$ or $\theta = 7\pi/2$, so that $(5, -\pi/2)$, $(5, 7\pi/2)$, and $(5, 3\pi/2)$ are all polar coordinates for V. However, we often choose θ between 0 and 2π.

Example 2   Give three possible sets of polar coordinates for the point P in Figure 8.40.

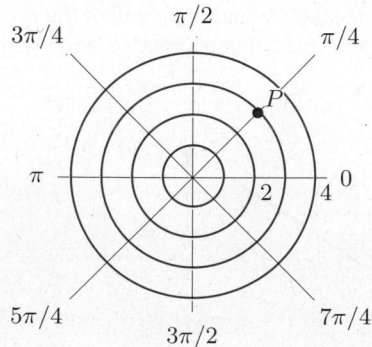

Figure 8.40

Solution   Because $r = 3$ and $\theta = \pi/4$, one set of polar coordinates for P is $(3, \pi/4)$. We can also use $\theta = \pi/4 + 2\pi = 9\pi/4$ and $\theta = \pi/4 - 2\pi = -7\pi/4$, to get $(3, 9\pi/4)$ and $(3, -7\pi/4)$.

Graphing Equations in Polar Coordinates

The equations for certain graphs are much simpler when expressed in polar coordinates than in Cartesian coordinates. On the other hand, some graphs that have simple equations in Cartesian coordinates have complicated equations in polar coordinates.

Example 3   (a) Describe in words the graphs of the equation $y = 1$ (in Cartesian coordinates) and the equation $r = 1$ (in polar coordinates).

(b) Write the equation $r = 1$ using Cartesian coordinates. Write the equation $y = 1$ using polar coordinates.

Solution   (a) The equation $y = 1$ describes a horizontal line. Since the equation $y = 1$ places no restrictions on the value of x, it describes every point having a y-value of 1, no matter what the value of its x-coordinate. Similarly, the equation $r = 1$ places no restrictions on the value of θ. Thus, it describes every point having an r-value of 1, that is, having a distance of 1 from the origin. This set of points is the unit circle. See Figure 8.41.

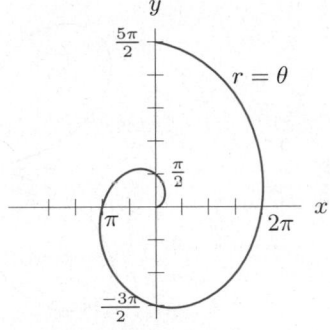

Figure 8.41: The graph of the equation $r = 1$ is the unit circle because $r = 1$ for every point regardless of the value of θ. The graph of $y = 1$ is a horizontal line since $y = 1$ for any x

Figure 8.42: A graph of the Archimedean spiral $r = \theta$

(b) Since $r = \sqrt{x^2 + y^2}$, we rewrite the equation $r = 1$ using Cartesian coordinates as $\sqrt{x^2 + y^2} = 1$, or, squaring both sides, as $x^2 + y^2 = 1$. We see that the equation for the unit circle is simpler in polar coordinates than it is in Cartesian coordinates.

On the other hand, since $y = r \sin \theta$, we can rewrite the equation $y = 1$ in polar coordinates as $r \sin \theta = 1$, or, dividing both sides by $\sin \theta$, as $r = 1/\sin \theta$. We see that the equation for this horizontal line is simpler in Cartesian coordinates than in polar coordinates.

Example 4   Graph the equation $r = \theta$. The graph is called an *Archimedean spiral* after the Greek mathematician Archimedes who described its properties (although not by using polar coordinates).

Solution   To construct this graph, use the values in Table 8.1. To help us visualize the shape of the spiral, we convert the angles in Table 8.1 to degrees and the r-values to decimals. See Table 8.2.

Table 8.1   *Points on the Archimedean spiral $r = \theta$, with θ in radians*

θ	0	$\frac{\pi}{6}$	$\frac{\pi}{3}$	$\frac{\pi}{2}$	$\frac{2\pi}{3}$	$\frac{5\pi}{6}$	π	$\frac{7\pi}{6}$	$\frac{4\pi}{3}$	$\frac{3\pi}{2}$
r	0	$\frac{\pi}{6}$	$\frac{\pi}{3}$	$\frac{\pi}{2}$	$\frac{2\pi}{3}$	$\frac{5\pi}{6}$	π	$\frac{7\pi}{6}$	$\frac{4\pi}{3}$	$\frac{3\pi}{2}$

Table 8.2   *Points on the Archimedean spiral $r = \theta$, with θ in degrees*

θ	0	30°	60°	90°	120°	150°	180°	210°	240°	270°
r	0.00	0.52	1.05	1.57	2.09	2.62	3.14	3.67	4.19	4.71

Notice that as the angle θ increases, points on the curve move farther from the origin. At 0°, the point is at the origin. At 30°, it is 0.52 units away from the origin, at 60° it is 1.05 units away, and at 90° it is 1.57 units away. As the angle winds around, the point traces out a curve that moves away from the origin, giving a spiral. (See Figure 8.42.)

In our definition, r is positive. However, graphs of curves in polar coordinates are traditionally drawn using negative values of r as well, because this makes the graphs symmetric. If an equation $r = f(\theta)$ gives a negative r-value, it is plotted in the opposite direction to θ. See Examples 5 and 6 and Figures 8.43 and 8.45.

Example 5   For $a > 0$ and n a positive integer, curves of the form $r = a \sin n\theta$ or $r = a \cos n\theta$ are called *roses*. Graph the roses

(a) $r = 3 \sin 2\theta$

(b) $r = 4 \cos 3\theta$

Solution   (a) Using a calculator or making a table of values, we see that the graph is a rose with four petals, each extending a distance of 3 from base to tip. See Figure 8.43. Negative values of r for $\pi/2 < \theta < \pi$ and $3\pi/2 < \theta < 2\pi$ give the petals in Quadrants II and IV. For example, $\theta = 3\pi/4$ gives $r = -3$, which is plotted 3 units from the origin in the direction opposite to $\theta = 3\pi/4$, namely in Quadrant IV.

(b) The graph is a rose with three petals, each extending 4 from base to tip. See Figure 8.44.

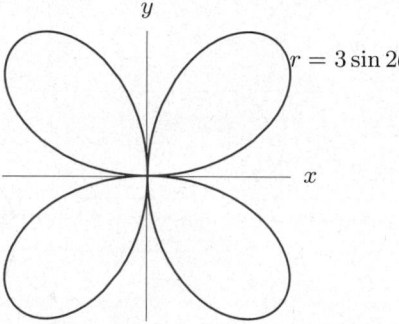

Figure 8.43: Graph of $r = 3 \sin 2\theta$
(petals in Quadrants II and IV have $r < 0$)

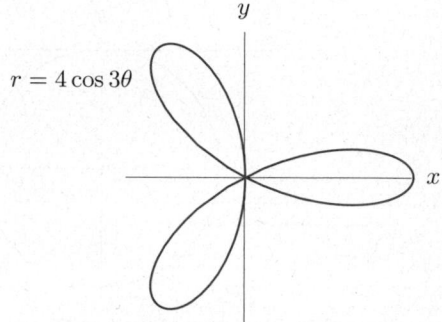

Figure 8.44: Graph of $r = 4 \cos 3\theta$

Example 6   Curves of the form $r = a + b \sin \theta$ or $r = a + b \cos \theta$ are called *limaçons*. Graph $r = 1 + 2 \cos \theta$ and $r = 3 + 2 \cos \theta$.

Solution   See Figures 8.45 and 8.46. The equation $r = 1 + 2 \cos \theta$ leads to negative r values for some θ values between $\pi/2$ and $3\pi/2$; these values give the inner loop in Figure 8.45. For example, $\theta = \pi$ gives $r = -1$, which is plotted 1 unit from the origin in the direction opposite to $\theta = \pi$, namely on the positive x-axis. The equation $r = 3 + 2 \cos \theta$ does not lead to negative r-values.

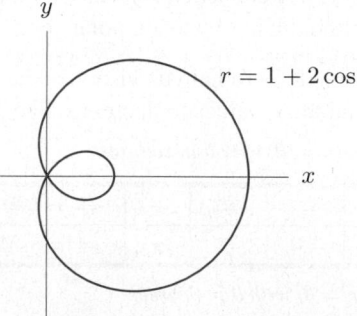

Figure 8.45: Graph of $r = 1 + 2 \cos \theta$
(inner loop has $r < 0$)

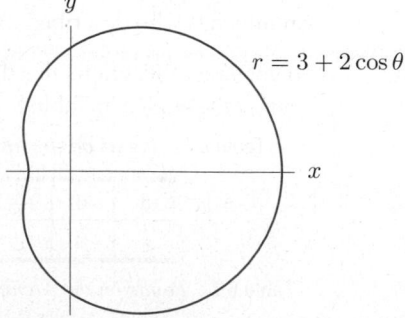

Figure 8.46: Graph of $r = 3 + 2 \cos \theta$

Polar coordinates can be used with inequalities to describe regions that are obtained from circles. Such regions are often much harder to represent in Cartesian coordinates.

Example 7   Using inequalities, describe a compact disc with outer diameter 120 mm and inner diameter 15 mm.

Solution   The compact disc lies between two circles of radius 7.5 mm and 60 mm. See Figure 8.47. Thus, if the origin is at the center, the disc is represented by

$$7.5 \leq r \leq 60 \quad \text{and} \quad 0 \leq \theta \leq 2\pi.$$

Figure 8.47: Compact disc

Figure 8.48: Pizza slice

Example 8   An 18 inch pizza is cut into 12 slices. Use inequalities to describe one of the slices.

Solution   The pizza has radius 9 inches; the angle at the center is $2\pi/12 = \pi/6$. See Figure 8.48. Thus, if the origin is at the center of the original pizza, the slice is represented by

$$0 \leq r \leq 9 \quad \text{and} \quad 0 \leq \theta \leq \frac{\pi}{6}.$$

Area in Polar Coordinates

We can use a definite integral to find the area of a region described in polar coordinates. As previously, we slice the region into small pieces, construct a Riemann sum, and take a limit to obtain the definite integral. In this case, the slices are approximately circular sectors.

To calculate the area of the sector in Figure 8.49, we think of the area of the sector as a fraction $\theta/2\pi$ of the area of the entire circle (for θ in radians). Then

$$\text{Area of sector } = \frac{\theta}{2\pi} \cdot \pi r^2 = \frac{1}{2} r^2 \theta.$$

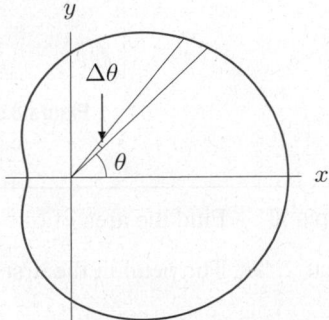

Figure 8.49: Area of shaded sector
$= \frac{1}{2} r^2 \theta$ (for θ in radians)

Figure 8.50: Finding the area of
the limaçon $r = 3 + 2\cos\theta$

Example 9   Use circular sectors to set up a definite integral to calculate the area of the region bounded by the limaçon $r = 3 + 2\cos\theta$, for $0 \leq \theta \leq 2\pi$. See Figure 8.50.

Solution   The slices are not exactly circular sectors because the radius r depends on θ. However,

$$\text{Area of sector } \approx \frac{1}{2} r^2 \Delta\theta = \frac{1}{2}(3 + 2\cos\theta)^2 \Delta\theta.$$

Thus, for the whole area,

$$\text{Area of region} \approx \sum \frac{1}{2}(3 + 2\cos\theta)^2 \, \Delta\theta.$$

Taking the limit as $n \to \infty$ and $\Delta\theta \to 0$ gives the integral

$$\text{Area} = \int_0^{2\pi} \frac{1}{2}(3 + 2\cos\theta)^2 \, d\theta.$$

To compute this integral, we expand the integrand and use integration by parts or formula IV-18 from the table of integrals:

$$\text{Area} = \frac{1}{2}\int_0^{2\pi}(9 + 12\cos\theta + 4\cos^2\theta)\,d\theta$$

$$= \frac{1}{2}\left(9\theta + 12\sin\theta + \frac{4}{2}(\cos\theta\sin\theta + \theta)\right)\Bigg|_0^{2\pi}$$

$$= \frac{1}{2}(18\pi + 0 + 4\pi) = 11\pi.$$

The reasoning in Example 9 suggests a general area formula.

For a curve $r = f(\theta)$, with $f(\theta) \geq 0$, the area in Figure 8.51 is given by

$$\text{Area of region enclosed} = \frac{1}{2}\int_\alpha^\beta f(\theta)^2 \, d\theta.$$

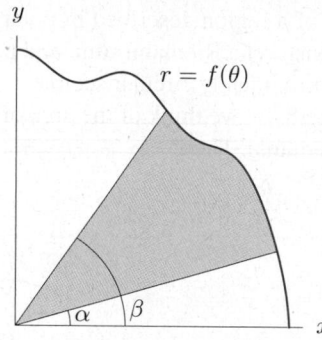

Figure 8.51: Area in polar coordinates

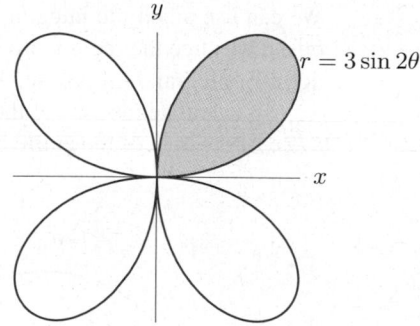

Figure 8.52: One petal of the rose $r = 3\sin 2\theta$ with $0 \leq \theta \leq \pi/2$

Example 10   Find the area of one petal of the four-petal rose $r = 3\sin 2\theta$ in Figure 8.52.

Solution   The petal in the first quadrant is described by $r = 3\sin 2\theta$ for $0 \leq \theta \leq \pi/2$, so

$$\text{Area of shaded region} = \frac{1}{2}\int_0^{\pi/2}(3\sin 2\theta)^2 \, d\theta = \frac{9}{2}\int_0^{\pi/2}\sin^2 2\theta \, d\theta.$$

Using the substitution $w = 2\theta$, we rewrite the integral and use integration by parts or formula IV-17 from the table of integrals:

$$\text{Area} = \frac{9}{2}\int_0^{\pi/2}\sin^2 2\theta \, d\theta = \frac{9}{4}\int_0^{\pi}\sin^2 w \, dw$$

$$= \frac{9}{4}\left(-\frac{1}{2}\cos w \sin w + \frac{1}{2}w\right)\Bigg|_0^{\pi} = \frac{9}{4}\cdot\frac{\pi}{2} = \frac{9\pi}{8}.$$

Slope in Polar Coordinates

For a curve $r = f(\theta)$, we can express x and y in terms of θ as a parameter, giving

$$x = r\cos\theta = f(\theta)\cos\theta \quad \text{and} \quad y = r\sin\theta = f(\theta)\sin\theta.$$

To find the slope of the curve, we use the formula for the slope of a parametric curve

$$\frac{dy}{dx} = \frac{dy/d\theta}{dx/d\theta}.$$

Example 11 Find the slope of the curve $r = 3\sin 2\theta$ at $\theta = \pi/3$.

Solution Expressing x and y in terms of θ, we have

$$x = 3\sin(2\theta)\cos\theta \quad \text{and} \quad y = 3\sin(2\theta)\sin\theta.$$

The slope is given by

$$\frac{dy}{dx} = \frac{6\cos(2\theta)\sin\theta + 3\sin(2\theta)\cos\theta}{6\cos(2\theta)\cos\theta - 3\sin(2\theta)\sin\theta}.$$

At $\theta = \pi/3$, we have

$$\left.\frac{dy}{dx}\right|_{\theta=\pi/3} = \frac{6(-1/2)(\sqrt{3}/2) + 3(\sqrt{3}/2)(1/2)}{6(-1/2)(1/2) - 3(\sqrt{3}/2)(\sqrt{3}/2)} = \frac{\sqrt{3}}{5}.$$

Arc Length in Polar Coordinates

We can calculate the arc length of the curve $r = f(\theta)$ by expressing x and y in terms of θ as a parameter

$$x = f(\theta)\cos\theta \quad y = f(\theta)\sin\theta$$

and using the formula for the arc length of a parametric curve:

$$\text{Arc length} = \int_{\alpha}^{\beta} \sqrt{\left(\frac{dx}{d\theta}\right)^2 + \left(\frac{dy}{d\theta}\right)^2}\, d\theta.$$

The calculations may be simplified by using the alternate form of the arc length integral in Problem 45.

Example 12 Find the arc length of one petal of the rose $r = 3\sin 2\theta$ for $0 \leq \theta \leq \pi/2$. See Figure 8.52.

Solution The curve is given parametrically by

$$x = 3\sin(2\theta)\cos\theta \quad \text{and} \quad y = 3\sin(2\theta)\sin\theta.$$

Thus, calculating $dx/d\theta$ and $dy/d\theta$ and evaluating the integral on a calculator, we have:

$$\text{Arc length} = \int_{0}^{\pi/2} \sqrt{(6\cos(2\theta)\cos\theta - 3\sin(2\theta)\sin\theta)^2 + (6\cos(2\theta)\sin\theta + 3\sin(2\theta)\cos\theta)^2}\, d\theta$$
$$= 7.266.$$

Exercises and Problems for Section 8.3

Exercises

Convert the polar coordinates in Exercises 1–4 to Cartesian coordinates. Give exact answers.

1. $(1, 2\pi/3)$

2. $(\sqrt{3}, -3\pi/4)$

3. $(2\sqrt{3}, -\pi/6)$

4. $(2, 5\pi/6)$

Convert the Cartesian coordinates in Exercises 5–8 to polar coordinates.

5. $(1, 1)$

6. $(-1, 0)$

7. $(\sqrt{6}, -\sqrt{2})$

8. $(-\sqrt{3}, 1)$

9. (a) Make a table of values for the equation $r = 1 - \sin\theta$. Include $\theta = 0, \pi/3, \pi/2, 2\pi/3, \pi, \cdots$.
(b) Use the table to graph the equation $r = 1 - \sin\theta$ in the xy-plane. This curve is called a *cardioid*.
(c) At what point(s) does the cardioid $r = 1 - \sin\theta$ intersect a circle of radius 1/2 centered at the origin?
(d) Graph the curve $r = 1 - \sin 2\theta$ in the xy-plane. Compare this graph to the cardioid $r = 1 - \sin\theta$.

10. Graph the equation $r = 1 - \sin(n\theta)$, for $n = 1, 2, 3, 4$. What is the relationship between the value of n and the shape of the graph?

11. Graph the equation $r = 1 - \sin\theta$, with $0 \le \theta \le n\pi$, for $n = 2, 3, 4$. What is the relationship between the value of n and the shape of the graph?

12. Graph the equation $r = 1 - n\sin\theta$, for $n = 2, 3, 4$. What is the relationship between the value of n and the shape of the graph?

13. Graph the equation $r = 1 - \cos\theta$. Describe its relationship to $r = 1 - \sin\theta$.

14. Give inequalities that describe the flat surface of a washer that is one inch in diameter and has an inner hole with a diameter of 3/8 inch.

15. Graph the equation $r = 1 - \sin(2\theta)$ for $0 \le \theta \le 2\pi$. There are two loops. For each loop, give a restriction on θ that shows all of that loop and none of the other loop.

16. A slice of pizza is one eighth of a circle of radius 1 foot. The slice is in the first quadrant, with one edge along the x-axis, and the center of the pizza at the origin. Give inequalities describing this region using:

(a) Polar coordinates   (b) Rectangular coordinates

In Exercises 17–19, give inequalities for r and θ which describe the following regions in polar coordinates.

17.

18.

19.

Note: Region extends indefinitely in the y-direction.

20. Find the slope of the curve $r = 2$ at $\theta = \pi/4$.

21. Find the slope of the curve $r = e^\theta$ at $\theta = \pi/2$.

22. Find the slope of the curve $r = 1 - \cos\theta$ at $\theta = \pi/2$.

23. Find the arc length of the curve $r = e^\theta$ from $\theta = \pi/2$ to $\theta = \pi$.

24. Find the arc length of the curve $r = \theta^2$ from $\theta = 0$ to $\theta = 2\pi$.

Problems

25. Sketch the polar region described by the following integral expression for area:

$$\frac{1}{2} \int_0^{\pi/3} \sin^2(3\theta)\, d\theta.$$

26. Find the area inside the spiral $r = \theta$ for $0 \le \theta \le 2\pi$.

27. Find the area between the two spirals $r = \theta$ and $r = 2\theta$ for $0 \le \theta \le 2\pi$.

28. Find the area inside the cardioid $r = 1 + \cos\theta$ for $0 \le \theta \le 2\pi$.

29. (a) In polar coordinates, write equations for the line $x = 1$ and the circle of radius 2 centered at the origin.
   (b) Write an integral in polar coordinates representing the area of the region to the right of $x = 1$ and inside the circle.
   (c) Evaluate the integral.

30. Show that the area formula for polar coordinates gives the expected answer for the area of the circle $r = a$ for $0 \le \theta \le 2\pi$.

31. Show that the arc length formula for polar coordinates gives the expected answer for the circumference of the circle $r = a$ for $0 \le \theta \le 2\pi$.

32. Find the area inside the circle $r = 1$ and outside the cardioid $r = 1 + \sin\theta$.

33. Find the area inside the cardioid $r = 1 - \sin\theta$ and outside the circle $r = 1/2$.

34. Find the area lying outside $r = 2\cos\theta$ and inside $r = 1 + \cos\theta$.

35. (a) Graph $r = 2\cos\theta$ and $r = 2\sin\theta$ on the same axes.
   (b) Using polar coordinates, find the area of the region shared by both curves.

36. For what value of a is the area enclosed by $r = \theta, \theta = 0$, and $\theta = a$ equal to 1?

37. (a) Sketch the bounded region inside the lemniscate $r^2 = 4\cos 2\theta$ and outside the circle $r = \sqrt{2}$.
   (b) Compute the area of the region described in part (a).

38. Using Example 11 on page 437, find the equation of the tangent line to the curve $r = 3\sin 2\theta$ at $\theta = \pi/3$.

39. Using Example 11 on page 437 and Figure 8.43, find the points where the curve $r = 3\sin 2\theta$ has horizontal and vertical tangents.

40. For what values of θ on the polar curve $r = \theta$, with $0 \le \theta \le 2\pi$, are the tangent lines horizontal? Vertical?

41. (a) In Cartesian coordinates, write an equation for the tangent line to $r = 1/\theta$ at $\theta = \pi/2$.
   (b) The graph of $r = 1/\theta$ has a horizontal asymptote as θ approaches 0. Find the equation of this asymptote.

42. Find the maximum value of the y-coordinate of points on the limaçon $r = 1 + 2\cos\theta$.

Find the arc length of the curves in Problems 43–44.

43. $r = \theta, 0 \le \theta \le 2\pi$

44. $r = 1/\theta, \pi \le \theta \le 2\pi$

45. For the curve $r = f(\theta)$ from $\theta = \alpha$ to $\theta = \beta$, show that

$$\text{Arc length} = \int_\alpha^\beta \sqrt{(f'(\theta))^2 + (f(\theta))^2} \, d\theta.$$

46. Find the arc length of the spiral $r = \theta$ where $0 \le \theta \le \pi$.

47. Find the arc length of part of the cardioid $r = 1 + \cos\theta$ where $0 \le \theta \le \pi/2$.

Strengthen Your Understanding

In Problems 48–51, explain what is wrong with the statement.

48. The point with Cartesian coordinates (x, y) has polar coordinates $r = \sqrt{x^2 + y^2}, \theta = \tan^{-1}(y/x)$.

49. All points of the curve $r = \sin(2\theta)$ for $\pi/2 < \theta < \pi$ are in quadrant II.

50. If the slope of the curve $r = f(\theta)$ is positive, then $dr/d\theta$ is positive.

51. Any polar curve that is symmetric about both the x and y axes must be a circle, centered at the origin.

In Problems 52–55, give an example of:

52. Two different pairs of polar coordinates (r, θ) that correspond to the same point in the plane.

53. The equation of a circle in polar coordinates.

54. A polar curve $r = f(\theta)$ that is symmetric about neither the x-axis nor the y-axis.

55. A polar curve $r = f(\theta)$ other than a circle that is symmetric about the x-axis.

8.4 DENSITY AND CENTER OF MASS

Density and How to Slice a Region

The examples in this section involve the idea of *density*. For example,

- A population density is measured in, say, people per mile (along the edge of a road), or people per unit area (in a city), or bacteria per cubic centimeter (in a test tube).

- The density of a substance (e.g. air, wood, or metal) is the mass of a unit volume of the substance and is measured in, say, grams per cubic centimeter.

Suppose we want to calculate the total mass or total population, but the density is not constant over a region.

> **To find total quantity from density:** Divide the region into small pieces in such a way that the density is approximately constant on each piece, and add the contributions of the pieces.

Example 1   The Massachusetts Turnpike ("the Pike") starts in the middle of Boston and heads west. The number of people living next to it varies as it gets farther from the city. Suppose that, x miles out of town, the population density adjacent to the Pike is $P = f(x)$ people/mile. Express the total population living next to the Pike within 5 miles of Boston as a definite integral.

Solution   Divide the Pike up into segments of length Δx. The population density at the center of Boston is $f(0)$; let's use that density for the first segment. This gives an estimate of

People living in first segment $\approx f(0)$ people/ mile $\cdot \Delta x$ mile $= f(0)\Delta x$ people.

Figure 8.53: Population along the Massachusetts Turnpike

Similarly, the population in a typical segment x miles from the center of Boston is the population density times the length of the interval, or roughly $f(x)\,\Delta x$. (See Figure 8.53.) The sum of all these estimates gives the estimate

$$\text{Total population} \approx \sum f(x)\,\Delta x.$$

Letting $\Delta x \to 0$ gives

$$\text{Total population} = \lim_{\Delta x \to 0} \sum f(x)\,\Delta x = \int_0^5 f(x)\,dx.$$

The 5 and 0 in the limits of the integral are the upper and lower limits of the interval over which we are integrating.

Example 2   The air density h meters above the earth's surface is $f(h)$ kg/m^3. Find the mass of a cylindrical column of air 2 meters in diameter and 25 kilometers high, with base on the surface of the earth.

Solution   The column of air is a circular cylinder 2 meters in diameter and 25 kilometers, or 25,000 meters, high. First we must decide how we are going to slice this column. Since the air density varies with altitude but remains constant horizontally, we take horizontal slices of air. That way, the density will be more or less constant over the whole slice, being close to its value at the bottom of the slice. (See Figure 8.54.)

Figure 8.54: Slicing a column of air horizontally

A slice is a cylinder of height Δh and diameter 2 m, so its radius is 1 m. We find the approximate mass of the slice by multiplying its volume by its density. If the thickness of the slice is Δh, then its volume is $\pi r^2 \cdot \Delta h = \pi 1^2 \cdot \Delta h = \pi \Delta h$ m^3. The density of the slice is given by $f(h)$. Thus,

$$\text{Mass of slice} \approx \text{Volume} \cdot \text{Density} = (\pi \Delta h \text{ m}^3)(f(h) \text{ kg/m}^3) = \pi \Delta h \cdot f(h) \text{ kg}.$$

Adding these slices up yields a Riemann sum:

$$\text{Total mass} \approx \sum \pi f(h) \, \Delta h \text{ kg}.$$

As $\Delta h \to 0$, this sum approximates the definite integral:

$$\text{Total mass} = \int_0^{25,000} \pi f(h) \, dh \text{ kg}.$$

In order to get a numerical value for the mass of air, we need an explicit formula for the density as a function of height, as in the next example.

Example 3   Find the mass of the column of air in Example 2 if the density of air at height h is given by

$$P = f(h) = 1.28 e^{-0.000124h} \text{ kg/m}^3.$$

Solution   Using the result of the previous example, we have

$$\text{Mass} = \int_0^{25,000} \pi 1.28 e^{-0.000124h} \, dh = \frac{-1.28\pi}{0.000124} \left(e^{-0.000124h} \Big|_0^{25,000} \right)$$

$$= \frac{1.28\pi}{0.000124} \left(e^0 - e^{-0.000124(25,000)} \right) \approx 31,000 \text{ kg}.$$

It requires some thought to figure out how to slice a region. The key point is that you want the density to be nearly constant within each piece.

Example 4   The population density in Ringsburg is a function of the distance from the city center. At r miles from the center, the density is $P = f(r)$ people per square mile. Ringsburg is circular with radius 5 miles. Write a definite integral that expresses the total population of Ringsburg.

Solution   We want to slice Ringsburg up and estimate the population of each slice. If we were to take straight-line slices, the population density would vary on each slice, since it depends on the distance from the city center. We want the population density to be pretty close to constant on each slice. We therefore take slices that are thin rings around the center. (See Figure 8.55.) Since the ring is very thin, we can approximate its area by straightening it into a thin rectangle. (See Figure 8.56.) The width of the rectangle is Δr miles, and its length is approximately equal to the circumference of the ring, $2\pi r$ miles, so its area is about $2\pi r \, \Delta r$ mi^2. Since

$$\text{Population on ring} \approx \text{Density} \cdot \text{Area},$$

we get

$$\text{Population on ring} \approx (f(r) \text{ people/mi}^2)(2\pi r \Delta r \text{ mi}^2) = f(r) \cdot 2\pi r \, \Delta r \text{ people}.$$

Adding the contributions from each ring, we get

$$\text{Total population} \approx \sum 2\pi r f(r) \, \Delta r \text{ people}.$$

So

$$\text{Total population} = \int_0^5 2\pi r f(r) \, dr \text{ people}.$$

Figure 8.55: Ringsburg

Figure 8.56: Ring from Ringsburg (straightened out)

Note: You may wonder what happens if we calculate the area of the ring by subtracting the area of the inner circle (πr^2) from the area of the outer circle ($\pi(r + \Delta r)^2$), giving

$$\text{Area} = \pi(r + \Delta r)^2 - \pi r^2.$$

Multiplying out and subtracting, we get

$$\text{Area} = \pi(r^2 + 2r\,\Delta r + (\Delta r)^2) - \pi r^2$$
$$= 2\pi r\,\Delta r + \pi(\Delta r)^2.$$

This expression differs from the one we used before by the $\pi(\Delta r)^2$ term. However, as Δr becomes very small, $\pi(\Delta r)^2$ becomes much, much smaller. We say its smallness is of *second order*, since the power of the small factor, Δr, is 2. In the limit as $\Delta r \to 0$, we can ignore $\pi(\Delta r)^2$.

Center of Mass

The center of mass of a mechanical system is important for studying its behavior when in motion. For example, some sport utility vehicles and light trucks tend to tip over in accidents, because of their high centers of mass.

In this section, we first define the center of mass for a system of point masses on a line. Then we use the definite integral to extend this definition.

Point Masses

Two children on a seesaw, one twice the weight of the other, will balance if the lighter child is twice as far from the pivot as the heavier child. Thus, the balance point is 2/3 of the way from the lighter child and 1/3 of the way from the heavier child. This balance point is the *center of mass* of the mechanical system consisting of the masses of the two children (we ignore the mass of the seesaw itself). See Figure 8.57.

To find the balance point, we use the *displacement* (signed distance) of each child from the pivot to calculate the *moment*, where

$$\text{Moment of mass about pivot} = \text{Mass} \times \text{Displacement from pivot}.$$

A moment represents the tendency of a child to turn the system about the pivot point; the seesaw balances if the total moment is zero. Thus, the center of mass is the point about which the total moment is zero.

Figure 8.57: Children on seesaw

Figure 8.58: Center of mass of point masses

Example 5   Calculate the position of the center of mass of the children in Figure 8.57 using moments.

Solution   Suppose the center of mass in Figure 8.58 is at a distance of $\bar{x}$ from the left end. The moment of the left mass about the center of mass is $-2m\bar{x}$ (it is negative since it is to the left of the center of mass); the moment of the right mass about the center of mass is $m(l - \bar{x})$. The system balances if

$$-2m\bar{x} + m(l - \bar{x}) = 0 \quad \text{or} \quad ml - 3m\bar{x} = 0 \quad \text{so} \quad \bar{x} = \frac{1}{3}l.$$

Thus, the center of mass is $l/3$ from the left end.

We use the same method to calculate the center of mass, $\bar{x}$, of the system in Figure 8.59. The sum of the moments of the three masses about $\bar{x}$ is 0, so

$$m_1(x_1 - \bar{x}) + m_2(x_2 - \bar{x}) + m_3(x_3 - \bar{x}) = 0.$$

Solving for $\bar{x}$, we get

$$m_1\bar{x} + m_2\bar{x} + m_3\bar{x} = m_1x_1 + m_2x_2 + m_3x_3$$

$$\bar{x} = \frac{m_1x_1 + m_2x_2 + m_3x_3}{m_1 + m_2 + m_3} = \frac{\sum_{i=1}^{3} m_ix_i}{\sum_{i=1}^{3} m_i}.$$

Generalizing leads to the following formula:

> The **center of mass** of a system of n point masses $m_1, m_2, \ldots, m_n$ located at positions $x_1, x_2, \ldots, x_n$ along the x-axis is given by
>
> $$\bar{x} = \frac{\sum x_i m_i}{\sum m_i}.$$

The numerator is the sum of the moments of the masses about the origin; the denominator is the total mass of the system.

Figure 8.59: Discrete masses m_1, m_2, m_3

Example 6   Show that the definition of $\bar{x}$ gives the same answer as we found in Example 5.

Solution   Suppose the origin is at the left end of the seesaw in Figure 8.57. The total mass of the system is $2m + m = 3m$. We compute

$$\bar{x} = \frac{\sum x_i m_i}{\sum m_i} = \frac{1}{3m}(2m \cdot 0 + m \cdot l) = \frac{ml}{3m} = \frac{l}{3}.$$

Continuous Mass Density

Instead of discrete masses arranged along the x-axis, suppose we have an object lying on the x-axis between $x = a$ and $x = b$. At point x, suppose the object has mass density (mass per unit length) of $\delta(x)$. To calculate the center of mass of such an object, divide it into n pieces, each of length

Δx Mass $m_i \approx \delta(x_i)\Delta x$

Figure 8.60: Calculating the center of mass of an object of variable density, $\delta(x)$

Δx. On each piece, the density is nearly constant, so the mass of the piece is given by density times length. See Figure 8.60. Thus, if x_i is a point in the ith piece,

$$\text{Mass of the } i^{\text{th}} \text{ piece, } m_i \approx \delta(x_i)\Delta x.$$

Then the formula for the center of mass, $\bar{x} = \sum x_i m_i / \sum m_i$, applied to the n pieces of the object gives

$$\bar{x} = \frac{\sum x_i \delta(x_i)\Delta x}{\sum \delta(x_i)\Delta x}.$$

In the limit as $n \to \infty$ we have the following formula:

> The **center of mass** $\bar{x}$ of an object lying along the x-axis between $x = a$ and $x = b$ is
>
> $$\bar{x} = \frac{\int_a^b x\delta(x)\,dx}{\int_a^b \delta(x)\,dx},$$
>
> where $\delta(x)$ is the density (mass per unit length) of the object.

As in the discrete case, the denominator is the total mass of the object.

Example 7   Find the center of mass of a 2-meter rod lying on the x-axis with its left end at the origin if:
(a) The density is constant and the total mass is 5 kg.   (b) The density is $\delta(x) = 15x^2$ kg/m.

Solution   (a) Since the density is constant along the rod, we expect the balance point to be in the middle, that is, $\bar{x} = 1$. To check this, we compute $\bar{x}$. The density is the total mass divided by the length, so $\delta(x) = 5/2$ kg/m. Then

$$\bar{x} = \frac{\text{Moment}}{\text{Mass}} = \frac{\int_0^2 x \cdot \frac{5}{2}\,dx}{5} = \frac{1}{5} \cdot \frac{5}{2} \cdot \frac{x^2}{2}\Big|_0^2 = 1 \text{ meter.}$$

(b) Since more of the mass of the rod is closer to its right end (the density is greatest there), we expect the center of mass to be in the right half of the rod, that is, between $x = 1$ and $x = 2$. We have

$$\text{Total mass} = \int_0^2 15x^2\,dx = 5x^3\Big|_0^2 = 40 \text{ kg.}$$

Thus,

$$\bar{x} = \frac{\text{Moment}}{\text{Mass}} = \frac{\int_0^2 x \cdot 15x^2\,dx}{40} = \frac{15}{40} \cdot \frac{x^4}{4}\Big|_0^2 = 1.5 \text{ meter.}$$

Two- and Three-Dimensional Regions

For a system of masses that lies in the plane, the center of mass is a point with coordinates $(\bar{x}, \bar{y})$. In three dimensions, the center of mass is a point with coordinates $(\bar{x}, \bar{y}, \bar{z})$. To compute the center of mass in three dimensions, we use the following formulas in which $A_x(x)$ is the area of a slice perpendicular to the x-axis at x, and $A_y(y)$ and $A_z(z)$ are defined similarly. In two dimensions, we use the same formulas for $\bar{x}$ and $\bar{y}$, but we interpret $A_x(x)$ and $A_y(y)$ as the lengths of strips perpendicular to the x- and y-axes, respectively.

For a region of constant density δ, the center of mass is given by

$$\bar{x} = \frac{\int x\delta A_x(x)\,dx}{\text{Mass}} \qquad \bar{y} = \frac{\int y\delta A_y(y)\,dy}{\text{Mass}} \qquad \bar{z} = \frac{\int z\delta A_z(z)\,dz}{\text{Mass}}.$$

The expression $\delta A_x(x)\Delta x$ is the moment of a slice perpendicular to the x-axis. Thus, these formulas are extensions of that on page 444. In the two- and three-dimensional case, we are assuming that the density δ is constant. If the density is not constant, finding the center of mass may require a double or triple integral from multivariable calculus.

Example 8 Find the coordinates of the center of mass of the isosceles triangle in Figure 8.61. The triangle has constant density and mass m.

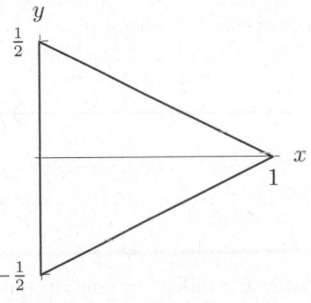

Figure 8.61: Find center of mass of this triangle

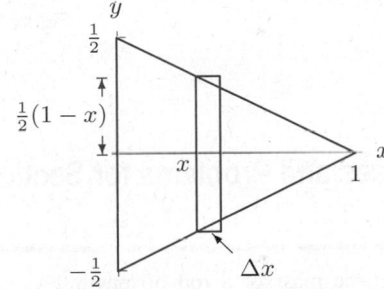

Figure 8.62: Sliced triangle

Solution Because the mass of the triangle is symmetrically distributed with respect to the x-axis, $\bar{y} = 0$. We expect $\bar{x}$ to be closer to $x = 0$ than to $x = 1$, since the triangle is wider near the origin.

The area of the triangle is $\frac{1}{2} \cdot 1 \cdot 1 = \frac{1}{2}$. Thus, Density = Mass/Area = $2m$. If we slice the triangle into strips of width Δx, then the strip at position x has length $A_x(x) = 2 \cdot \frac{1}{2}(1-x) = (1-x)$. (See Figure 8.62.) So

$$\text{Area of strip } = A_x(x)\Delta x \approx (1-x)\Delta x.$$

Since the density is $2m$, the center of mass is given by

$$\bar{x} = \frac{\int x\delta A_x(x)\,dx}{\text{Mass}} = \frac{\int_0^1 2mx(1-x)\,dx}{m} = 2\left(\frac{x^2}{2} - \frac{x^3}{3}\right)\bigg|_0^1 = \frac{1}{3}.$$

So the center of mass of this triangle is at the point $(\bar{x}, \bar{y}) = (1/3, 0)$.

Example 9 Find the center of mass of a hemisphere of radius 7 cm and constant density δ.

Solution Stand the hemisphere with its base horizontal in the xy-plane, with the center at the origin. Symmetry tells us that its center of mass lies directly above the center of the base, so $\bar{x} = \bar{y} = 0$. Since the hemisphere is wider near its base, we expect the center of mass to be nearer to the base than the top.

To calculate the center of mass, slice the hemisphere into horizontal disks, as in Figure 8.63. A disk of thickness Δz at height z above the base has

$$\text{Volume of disk } = A_z(z)\Delta z \approx \pi(7^2 - z^2)\Delta z \text{ cm}^3.$$

So, since the density is δ,

$$\overline{z} = \frac{\int z\delta A_z(z)\,dz}{\text{Mass}} = \frac{\int_0^7 z\delta\pi(7^2 - z^2)\,dz}{\text{Mass}}.$$

Since the total mass of the hemisphere is $\left(\frac{2}{3}\pi 7^3\right)\delta$, we get

$$\overline{z} = \frac{\delta\pi\int_0^7(7^2 z - z^3)\,dz}{\text{Mass}} = \frac{\delta\pi\left(7^2 z^2/2 - z^4/4\right)\big|_0^7}{\text{Mass}} = \frac{\frac{7^4}{4}\delta\pi}{\frac{2}{3}\pi 7^3\delta} = \frac{21}{8} = 2.625 \text{ cm}.$$

The center of mass of the hemisphere is 2.625 cm above the center of its base. As expected, it is closer to the base of the hemisphere than its top.

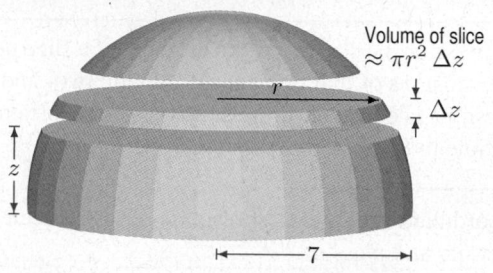

Figure 8.63: Slicing to find the center of mass of a hemisphere

Exercises and Problems for Section 8.4

Exercises

1. Find the mass of a rod of length 10 cm with density $\delta(x) = e^{-x}$ gm/cm at a distance of x cm from the left end.

2. A plate occupying the region $0 \le x \le 2, 0 \le y \le 3$ has density $\delta = 5$ gm/cm^2. Set up two integrals giving the mass of the plate, one corresponding to strips in the x-direction and one corresponding to strips in the y-direction.

3. A rod has length 2 meters. At a distance x meters from its left end, the density of the rod is given by

$$\delta(x) = 2 + 6x \text{ gm/m}.$$

(a) Write a Riemann sum approximating the total mass of the rod.

(b) Find the exact mass by converting the sum into an integral.

4. If a rod lies along the x-axis between a and b, the moment of the rod is $\int_a^b x\delta(x)\,dx$, where $\delta(x)$ is its density in grams/meter at a position x meters. Find the moment and center of mass of the rod in Problem 3.

5. The density of cars (in cars per mile) down a 20-mile stretch of the Pennsylvania Turnpike is approximated by

$$\delta(x) = 300\left(2 + \sin\left(4\sqrt{x + 0.15}\right)\right),$$

at a distance x miles from the Breezewood toll plaza.

(a) Sketch a graph of this function for $0 \le x \le 20$.

(b) Write a Riemann sum that approximates the total number of cars on this 20-mile stretch.

(c) Find the total number of cars on the 20-mile stretch.

6. **(a)** Find a Riemann sum which approximates the total mass of a 3×5 rectangular sheet, whose density per unit area at a distance x from one of the sides of length 5 is $1/(1 + x^4)$.

(b) Calculate the mass.

7. A point mass of 2 grams located 3 centimeters to the left of the origin and a point mass of 5 grams located 4 centimeters to the right of the origin are connected by a thin, light rod. Find the center of mass of the system.

8. Find the center of mass of a system containing three point masses of 5 gm, 3 gm, and 1 gm located respectively at $x = -10, x = 1$, and $x = 2$.

9. Find the mass of the block $0 \le x \le 10, 0 \le y \le 3$, $0 \le z \le 1$, whose density δ, is given by

$$\delta = 2 - z \quad \text{for } 0 \le z \le 1.$$

Problems

Problems 10–12 refer to a colony of bats which flies out of a cave each night to eat insects. To estimate the colony's size, a naturalist counts samples of bats at different distances from the cave. Table 8.3 gives n, her count per hectare, at a distance r km from the cave. For instance, she counts 300 bats in one hectare at the cave's mouth, and 219 bats in one hectare one kilometer from the cave. The bat count r km from the cave is the same in all directions. [Note that 1 km^2 = 100 hectares, written 100 ha.]

Table 8.3

r	0	1	2	3	4	5
n	300	219	160	117	85	62

10. Give an overestimate of the number of bats between 3 and 4 km from the cave.

11. Give an underestimate of the number of bats between 3 and 4 km from the cave.

12. Letting $n = f(r)$, write an integral in terms of f representing the number of bats in the cave. Assume that bats fly no farther away than 5 km from the cave. Do not evaluate the integral.

13. Find the total mass of the triangular region in Figure 8.64, which has density $\delta(x) = 1 + x$ grams/cm^2.

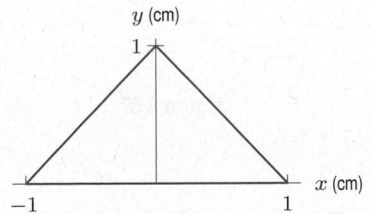

Figure 8.64

14. A rectangular plate is located with vertices at points $(0,0), (2,0), (2,3)$ and $(0,3)$ in the xy-plane. The density of the plate at point (x, y) is $\delta(y) = 2 + y^2$ gm/cm^2 and x and y are in cm. Find the total mass of the plate.

15. Circle City, a typical metropolis, is densely populated near its center, and its population gradually thins out toward the city limits. In fact, its population density is $10,000(3 - r)$ people/square mile at distance r miles from the center.

    (a) Assuming that the population density at the city limits is zero, find the radius of the city.

    (b) What is the total population of the city?

16. The density of oil in a circular oil slick on the surface of the ocean at a distance r meters from the center of the slick is given by $\delta(r) = 50/(1 + r)$ kg/m^2.

    (a) If the slick extends from $r = 0$ to $r = 10,000$ m, find a Riemann sum approximating the total mass of oil in the slick.

    (b) Find the exact value of the mass of oil in the slick by turning your sum into an integral and evaluating it.

    (c) Within what distance r is half the oil of the slick contained?

17. The soot produced by a garbage incinerator spreads out in a circular pattern. The depth, $H(r)$, in millimeters, of the soot deposited each month at a distance r kilometers from the incinerator is given by $H(r) = 0.115e^{-2r}$.

    (a) Write a definite integral giving the total volume of soot deposited within 5 kilometers of the incinerator each month.

    (b) Evaluate the integral you found in part (a), giving your answer in cubic meters.

18. A cardboard figure has the shape shown in Figure 8.65. The region is bounded on the left by the line $x = a$, on the right by the line $x = b$, above by $f(x)$, and below by $g(x)$. If the density $\delta(x)$ gm/cm^2 varies only with x, find an expression for the total mass of the figure, in terms of $f(x), g(x)$, and $\delta(x)$.

Figure 8.65

19. The storage shed in Figure 8.66 is the shape of a half-cylinder of radius r and length l.

    (a) What is the volume of the shed?

    (b) The shed is filled with sawdust whose density (mass/unit volume) at any point is proportional to the distance of that point from the floor. The constant of proportionality is k. Calculate the total mass of sawdust in the shed.

Figure 8.66

20. The following table gives the density D (in gm/cm^3) of the earth at a depth x km below the earth's surface. The radius of the earth is about 6370 km. Find an upper and a lower bound for the earth's mass such that the upper bound is less than twice the lower bound. Explain your reasoning; in particular, what assumptions have you made about the density?

x	0	1000	2000	2900	3000	4000	5000	6000	6370
D	3.3	4.5	5.1	5.6	10.1	11.4	12.6	13.0	13.0

21. Water leaks out of a tank through a square hole with 1-inch sides. At time t (in seconds) the velocity of water flowing through the hole is $v = g(t)$ ft/sec. Write a definite integral that represents the total amount of water lost in the first minute.

22. An exponential model for the density of the earth's atmosphere says that if the temperature of the atmosphere were constant, then the density of the atmosphere as a function of height, h (in meters), above the surface of the earth would be given by

$$\delta(h) = 1.28e^{-0.000124h} \text{ kg/m}^3.$$

(a) Write (but do not evaluate) a sum that approximates the mass of the portion of the atmosphere from $h = 0$ to $h = 100$ m (i.e., the first 100 meters above sea level). Assume the radius of the earth is 6400 km.

(b) Find the exact answer by turning your sum in part (a) into an integral. Evaluate the integral.

23. Three point masses of 4 gm each are placed at $x = -6, 1$ and 3. Where should a fourth point mass of 4 gm be placed to make the center of mass at the origin?

24. A rod of length 3 meters with density $\delta(x) = 1 + x^2$ grams/meter is positioned along the positive x-axis, with its left end at the origin. Find the total mass and the center of mass of the rod.

25. A rod with density $\delta(x) = 2 + \sin x$ lies on the x-axis between $x = 0$ and $x = \pi$. Find the center of mass of the rod.

26. A rod of length 1 meter has density $\delta(x) = 1 + kx^2$ grams/meter, where k is a positive constant. The rod is lying on the positive x-axis with one end at the origin.

(a) Find the center of mass as a function of k.

(b) Show that the center of mass of the rod satisfies $0.5 < \bar{x} < 0.75$.

27. A rod of length 2 meters and density $\delta(x) = 3 - e^{-x}$ kilograms per meter is placed on the x-axis with its ends at $x = \pm 1$.

(a) Will the center of mass of the rod be on the left or right of the origin? Explain.

(b) Find the coordinate of the center of mass.

28. One half of a uniform circular disk of radius 1 meter lies in the xy-plane with its diameter along the y-axis, its center at the origin, and $x > 0$. The mass of the half-disk is 3 kg. Find $(\bar{x}, \bar{y})$.

29. A metal plate, with constant density 2 gm/cm^2, has a shape bounded by the curve $y = x^2$ and the x-axis, with $0 \le x \le 1$ and x, y in cm.

(a) Find the total mass of the plate.

(b) Sketch the plate, and decide, on the basis of the shape, whether $\bar{x}$ is less than or greater than $1/2$.

(c) Find $\bar{x}$.

30. A metal plate, with constant density 5 gm/cm^2, has a shape bounded by the curve $y = \sqrt{x}$ and the x-axis, with $0 \le x \le 1$ and x, y in cm.

(a) Find the total mass of the plate.

(b) Find $\bar{x}$ and $\bar{y}$.

31. An isosceles triangle with uniform density, altitude a, and base b is placed in the xy-plane as in Figure 8.67. Show that the center of mass is at $\bar{x} = a/3, \bar{y} = 0$. Hence show that the center of mass is independent of the triangle's base.

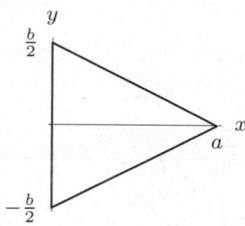

Figure 8.67

32. Find the center of mass of a cone of height 5 cm and base diameter 10 cm with constant density δ gm/cm^3.

33. A solid is formed by rotating the region bounded by the curve $y = e^{-x}$ and the x-axis between $x = 0$ and $x = 1$, around the x-axis. It was shown in Example 1 on page 422 that the volume of this solid is $\pi(1 - e^{-2})/2$. Assuming the solid has constant density δ, find $\bar{x}$ and $\bar{y}$.

34. (a) Find the mass of a pyramid of constant density δ gm/cm^3 with a square base of side 40 cm and height 10 cm. [That is, the vertex is 10 cm above the center of the base.]

(b) Find the center of mass of the pyramid.

Strengthen Your Understanding

In Problems 35–38, explain what is wrong with the statement.

35. A 10 cm rod can have mass density given by $f(x) = x^2 - 5x$ gm/cm, at a point x cm from one end.

36. The center of mass of a rod with density x^2 gm/cm for $0 \le x \le 10$ is given by $\int_0^{10} x^3 \, dx$.

37. If the center of mass of a rod is in the center of the rod, then the density of the rod is constant.

38. A disk with radius 3 cm and density $\delta(r) = 3 - r$ gm/cm^2, where r is in centimeters from the center of the disk, has total mass 27π gm.

In Problems 39–41, give an example of:

39. A mass density on a rod such that the rod is most dense at one end but the center of mass is nearer the other end.

40. A rod of length 2 cm, whose density $\delta(x)$ makes the center of mass not at the center of the rod.

41. A rod of length 2 cm, whose density $\delta(x)$ makes the center of mass at the center of the rod.

In Problems 42–48, are the statements true or false? Give an explanation for your answer.

42. To find the total population in a circular city, we always slice it into concentric rings, no matter what the population density function.

43. A city occupies a region in the xy-plane, with population density $\delta(y) = 1 + y$. To set up an integral representing the total population in the city, we should slice the region parallel to the y-axis.

44. The population density in a circular city of radius 2 depends on the distance r from the center by $f(r) = 10 - 3r$, so that the density is greatest at the center. Then the population of the inner city, $0 \le r \le 1$, is greater than the population of the suburbs, $1 \le r \le 2$.

45. The location of the center of mass of a system of three masses on the x-axis does not change if all the three masses are doubled.

46. The center of mass of a region in the plane cannot be outside the region.

47. Particles are shot at a circular target. The density of particles hitting the target decreases with the distance from the center. To set up a definite integral to calculate the total number of particles hitting the target, we should slice the region into concentric rings.

48. A metal rod of density $f(x)$ lying along the x-axis from $x = 0$ to $x = 4$ has its center of mass at $x = 2$. Then the two halves of the rod on either side of $x = 2$ have equal mass.

8.5 APPLICATIONS TO PHYSICS

Although geometric problems were a driving force for the development of the calculus in the seventeenth century, it was Newton's spectacularly successful applications of the calculus to physics that most clearly demonstrated the power of this new mathematics.

Work

In physics the word "work" has a technical meaning which is different from its everyday meaning. Physicists say that if a constant force, F, is applied to some object to move it a distance, d, then the force has done work on the object. The force must be parallel to the motion (in the same or the opposite direction). We make the following definition:

$$\text{Work done} = \text{Force} \cdot \text{Distance} \qquad \text{or} \qquad W = F \cdot d.$$

Notice that if we walk across a room holding a book, we do no work on the book, since the force we exert on the book is vertical, but the motion of the book is horizontal. On the other hand, if we lift the book from the floor to a table, we accomplish work.

There are several sets of units in common use. To measure work, we will generally use the two sets of units, International (SI) and British, in the following table.

	Force	Distance	Work	Conversions
International (SI) units	newton (nt)	meter (m)	joule (j)	1 lb = 4.45 nt
British units	pound (lb)	foot (ft)	foot-pound (ft-lb)	1 ft = 0.305 m
				1 ft-lb = 1.36 joules

One joule of work is done when a force of 1 newton moves an object through 1 meter, so 1 joule $=$ 1 newton-meter.

Example 1   Calculate the work done on an object when

    (a)   A force of 2 newtons moves it 12 meters.   (b)   A 3-lb force moves it 4 feet.

Solution   (a)   Work done $=$ 2 nt $\cdot$ 12 m $=$ 24 joules.   (b)   Work done $=$ 3 lb $\cdot$ 4 ft $=$ 12 ft-lb.

In the previous example, the force was constant and we calculated the work by multiplication. In the next example, the force varies, so we need an integral. We divide up the distance moved and sum to get a definite integral representing the work.

Example 2   Hooke's Law says that the force, F, required to compress the spring in Figure 8.68 by a distance x, in meters, is given by $F = kx$, for some constant k. Find the work done in compressing the spring by 0.1 m if $k = 8$ nt/m.

Figure 8.68: Compression of spring: Force   **Figure 8.69**: Work done in compressing
is kx spring a small distance Δx is $kx\Delta x$

Solution   Since k is in newtons/meter and x is in meters, we have $F = 8x$ newtons. Since the force varies with x, we divide the distance moved into small increments, Δx, as in Figure 8.69. Then

$$\text{Work done in moving through an increment} \approx F\Delta x = 8x\Delta x \text{ joules.}$$

So, summing over all increments gives the Riemann sum approximation

$$\text{Total work done} \approx \sum 8x\Delta x.$$

Taking the limit as $\Delta x \to 0$ gives

$$\text{Total work done} = \int_0^{0.1} 8x\,dx = 4x^2 \Big|_0^{0.1} = 0.04 \text{ joules.}$$

In general, if force is a function $F(x)$ of position x, then in moving from $x = a$ to $x = b$,

$$\boxed{\text{Work done} = \int_a^b F(x)\,dx.}$$

The Force Due to Gravity: Mass versus Weight

When an object is lifted, work is done against the force exerted by gravity on the object. By Newton's Second Law, the downward gravitational force acting on a mass m is mg, where g is the acceleration due to gravity. To lift the object, we need to exert a force equal to the gravitational force but in the opposite direction.

In International units, $g = 9.8$ m/sec^2, and we usually measure mass, m, in *kilograms*. In British units, mass is seldom used. Instead, we usually talk about the *weight* of an object, which is the force exerted by gravity on the object. Roughly speaking, the mass represents the quantity of matter in an object, whereas the weight represents the force of gravity on it. The mass of an object is the same everywhere, whereas the weight can vary if, for example, the object is moved to outer space where gravitational forces are smaller.

When we are given the weight of an object, we do not multiply by g to find the gravitational force as it has already been done. In British units, a *pound* is a unit of weight. In International units, a kilogram is a unit of mass, and the unit of weight is a newton, where 1 newton $= 1$ kg $\cdot$ m/sec^2.

Example 3   How much work is done in lifting

(a)   A 5-pound book 3 feet off the floor?   (b)   A 1.5-kilogram book 2 meters off the floor?

Solution   (a) The force due to gravity is 5 lb, so $W = F \cdot d = (5 \text{ lb})(3 \text{ ft}) = 15$ foot-pounds.
(b) The force due to gravity is $mg = (1.5 \text{ kg})(g \text{ m/sec}^2)$, so

$$W = F \cdot d = [(1.5 \text{ kg})(9.8 \text{ m/sec}^2)] \cdot (2 \text{ m}) = 29.4 \text{ joules.}$$

In the previous example, work is found by multiplication. In the next example, different parts of the object move different distances, so an integral is needed.

Example 4   A 28-meter uniform chain with a mass density of 2 kilograms per meter is dangling from the roof of a building. How much work is needed to pull the chain up onto the top of the building?

Solution   Since 1 meter of the chain has mass density 2 kg, the gravitational force per meter of chain is $(2 \text{ kg})(9.8 \text{ m/sec}^2) = 19.6$ newtons. Let's divide the chain into small sections of length Δy, each requiring a force of $19.6 \, \Delta y$ newtons to move it against gravity. See Figure 8.70. If Δy is small, all of this piece is hauled up approximately the same distance, namely y, so

$$\text{Work done on the small piece} \approx (19.6 \, \Delta y \text{ newtons})(y \text{ meters}) = 19.6y \, \Delta y \text{ joules.}$$

The work done on the entire chain is given by the total of the work done on each piece:

$$\text{Work done} \approx \sum 19.6y \, \Delta y \text{ joules.}$$

As $\Delta y \to 0$, we obtain a definite integral. Since y varies from 0 to 28 meters, the total work is

$$\text{Work done} = \int_0^{28} (19.6y) \, dy = 9.8y^2 \Big|_0^{28} = 7683.2 \text{ joules.}$$

Top of building

y

Δy

Figure 8.70: Chain for Example 4

Example 5   Calculate the work done in pumping oil from the cone-shaped tank in Figure 8.71 to the rim. The oil has density 800 kg/m³ and its vertical depth is 10 m.

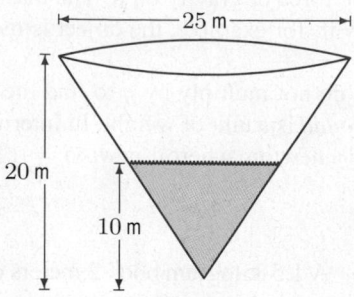

Figure 8.71: Cone-shaped tank containing oil

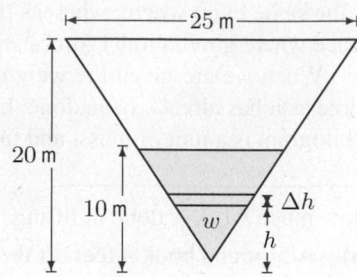

Figure 8.72: Slicing the oil horizontally to compute work

Solution   We slice the oil horizontally because each part of such a slice moves the same vertical distance. Each slice is approximately a circular disk with radius $w/2$ m, so, with h in meters,

$$\text{Volume of slice} \approx \pi \left(\frac{w}{2}\right)^2 \Delta h = \frac{\pi}{4} w^2 \Delta h \text{ m}^3.$$

$$\text{Force of gravity on slice } = \text{ Density } \cdot g \cdot \text{ Volume } = 800 g \frac{\pi}{4} w^2 \Delta h = 200\pi g w^2 \Delta h \text{ nt.}$$

Since each part of the slice has to move a vertical distance of $(20 - h)$ m, we have

$$\text{Work done on slice} \approx \text{ Force } \cdot \text{ Distance} = 200\pi g w^2 \Delta h \text{ nt } \cdot (20 - h) \text{ m}$$
$$= 200\pi g w^2 (20 - h) \Delta h \text{ joules.}$$

To find w in terms of h, we use the similar triangles in Figure 8.72:

$$\frac{w}{h} = \frac{25}{20} \quad \text{so} \quad w = \frac{5}{4} h = 1.25 h.$$

Thus,

$$\text{Work done on strip} \approx 200\pi g (1.25h)^2 (20 - h) \Delta h = 312.5\pi g h^2 (20 - h) \Delta h \text{ joules.}$$

Summing and taking the limit as $\Delta h \to 0$ gives an integral with upper limit $h = 10$, the depth of the oil.

$$\text{Total work } = \lim_{\Delta h \to 0} \sum 312.5\pi g h^2 (20 - h) \Delta h = \int_0^{10} 312.5\pi g h^2 (20 - h) \, dh \text{ joules.}$$

Evaluating the integral using $g = 9.8$ m/sec² gives

$$\text{Total work } = 312.5\pi g \left(20\frac{h^3}{3} - \frac{h^4}{4}\right)\Bigg|_0^{10} = 1,302,083\pi g \approx 4.0 \cdot 10^7 \text{ joules.}$$

In the following example, information is given in British units about the weight of the pyramid, so we do not need to multiply by g to find the gravitational force.

Example 6   It is reported that the Great Pyramid of Egypt was built in 20 years. If the stone making up the pyramid has a density of 200 pounds per cubic foot, find the total amount of work done in building the pyramid. The pyramid is 410 feet high and has a square base 755 feet by 755 feet. Estimate how many workers were needed to build the pyramid.

Figure 8.73: Pyramid for Example 6

Solution   We assume that the stones were originally located at the approximate height of the construction site. Imagine the pyramid built in layers as we did in Example 5 on page 418.

By similar triangles, the layer at height h has a side length $s = 755(410 - h)/410$ ft. (See Figure 8.73.) The layer at height h has a volume of $s^2 \, \Delta h$ ft^3, so its weight is $200 s^2 \, \Delta h$ lb. This layer is lifted through a height of h, so

$$\text{Work to lift layer} = (200 s^2 \, \Delta h \text{ lb})(h \text{ ft}) = 200 s^2 h \, \Delta h \text{ ft-lb}.$$

Summing over all layers gives

$$\text{Total work} \approx \sum 200 s^2 \, h \Delta h = \sum 200 \left(\frac{755}{410}\right)^2 (410 - h)^2 h \, \Delta h \text{ ft-lb}.$$

Since h varies from 0 to 410, as $\Delta h \to 0$, we obtain

$$\text{Total work} = \int_0^{410} 200 \left(\frac{755}{410}\right)^2 (410 - h)^2 h \, dh \approx 1.6 \cdot 10^{12} \text{ foot-pounds}.$$

We have calculated the total work done in building the pyramid; now we want to estimate the total number of workers needed. Let's assume every laborer worked 10 hours a day, 300 days a year, for 20 years. Assume that a typical worker lifted ten 50 pound blocks a distance of 4 feet every hour, thus performing 2000 foot-pounds of work per hour (this is a very rough estimate). Then each laborer performed $(10)(300)(20)(2000) = 1.2 \cdot 10^8$ foot-pounds of work over a twenty-year period. Thus, the number of workers needed was about $(1.6 \cdot 10^{12})/(1.2 \cdot 10^8)$, or about 13,000.

Force and Pressure

We can use the definite integral to compute the force exerted by a liquid on a surface, for example, the force of water on a dam. The idea is to get the force from the *pressure*. The pressure in a liquid is the force per unit area exerted by the liquid. Two things you need to know about pressure are:

- At any point, pressure is exerted equally in all directions—up, down, sideways.
- Pressure increases with depth. (That is one of the reasons why deep sea divers have to take much greater precautions than scuba divers.)

At a depth of h meters, the pressure, p, exerted by the liquid, measured in newtons per square meter, is given by computing the total weight of a column of liquid h meters high with a base of 1 square meter. The volume of such a column of liquid is just h cubic meters. If the liquid has density δ (mass per unit volume), then its weight per unit volume is δg, where g is the acceleration due to gravity. The weight of the column of liquid is $\delta g h$, so

$$\boxed{\text{Pressure} = \text{Mass density} \cdot g \cdot \text{Depth} \quad \text{or} \quad p = \delta g h.}$$

Provided the pressure is constant over a given area, we also have the following relation:

$$\boxed{\text{Force} = \text{Pressure} \cdot \text{Area.}}$$

The units and data we will generally use are given in the following table:

	Density of water	Force	Area	Pressure	Conversions
SI units	1000 kg/m^3 (mass)	newton (nt)	meter^2	pascal (nt/m^2)	1 lb = 4.45 nt
British units	62.4 lb/ft^3 (weight)	pound (lb)	foot^2	lb/ft^2	1ft^2 = 0.093 m^2
					1 lb/ft^2 = 47.9 pa

In International units, the mass density of water is 1000 kg/m^3, so the pressure at a depth of h meters is $\delta g h = 1000 \cdot 9.8 h = 9800 h$ nt/m^2. See Figure 8.74.

In British units, the density of the liquid is usually given as a weight per unit volume, rather than a mass per unit volume. In that case, we do not need to multiply by g because it has already been done. For example, water weighs 62.4 lb/ft^3, so the pressure at depth h feet is $62.4h$ lb/ft^2. See Figure 8.75.

Figure 8.74: Pressure exerted by column of water (International units)

Figure 8.75: Pressure exerted by a column of water (British units)

If the pressure is constant over a surface, we calculate the force on the surface by multiplying the pressure by the area of the surface. If the pressure is not constant, we divide the surface into small pieces *in such a way that the pressure is nearly constant on each one* to obtain a definite integral for the force on the surface. Since the pressure varies with depth, we divide the surface into horizontal strips, each of which is at an approximately constant depth.

Example 7   In 1912, the ocean liner Titanic sank to the bottom of the Atlantic, 12,500 feet (nearly 2.5 miles) below the surface. Find the force on one side of a 100-foot square plate at the depth of the Titanic if the plate is: (a) Lying horizontally   (b) Standing vertically.

Solution   (a) When the plate is horizontal, the pressure is the same at every point on the plate, so

$$\text{Pressure } = 62.4 \text{ lb/ft}^3 \cdot 12{,}500 \text{ ft } = 780{,}000 \text{ lb/ft}^2.$$

To imagine this pressure, convert to pounds per square inch, giving $780{,}000/144 \approx 5400$ lb/in^2. For the horizontal plate

$$\text{Force } = 780{,}000 \text{ lb/ft}^2 \cdot 100^2 \text{ ft}^2 = 7.8 \cdot 10^9 \text{ pounds.}$$

(b) When the plate is vertical, only the bottom is at 12,500 feet; the top is at 12,400 feet. Dividing into horizontal strips of width Δh, as in Figure 8.76, we have

$$\text{Area of strip} = 100\Delta h \text{ ft}^2.$$

Since the pressure on a strip at a depth of h feet is $62.4h$ lb/ft^2,

$$\text{Force on strip} \approx 62.4h \cdot 100\Delta h = 6240h\Delta h \text{ pounds}.$$

Summing over all strips and taking the limit as $\Delta h \to 0$ gives a definite integral. The strips vary in depth from 12,400 to 12,500 feet, so

$$\text{Total force} = \lim_{\Delta h \to 0} \sum 6240h\Delta h = \int_{12,400}^{12,500} 6240h \, dh \text{ pounds}.$$

Evaluating the integral gives

$$\text{Total force} = 6240\frac{h^2}{2}\Big|_{12,400}^{12,500} = 3120(12,500^2 - 12,400^2) = 7.77 \cdot 10^9 \text{ pounds}.$$

Notice that the answer to part (b) is smaller than the answer to part (a). This is because part of the plate is at a smaller depth in part (b) than in part (a).

Figure 8.76: Square plate at bottom of ocean; h measured from the surface of water

Example 8   Figure 8.77 shows a dam approximately the size of Hoover Dam, which stores water for California, Nevada, and Arizona. Calculate:

(a)   The water pressure at the base of the dam.   (b)   The total force of the water on the dam.

Figure 8.77: Trapezoid-shaped dam

Figure 8.78: Dividing dam into horizontal strips

Solution   (a) Since the density of water is $\delta = 1000$ kg/m^3, at the base of the dam,

$$\text{Water pressure} = \delta gh = 1000 \cdot 9.8 \cdot 220 = 2.156 \cdot 10^6 \text{ nt/m}^2.$$

(b) To calculate the force on the dam, we divide the dam into horizontal strips because the pressure along each strip is approximately constant. See Figure 8.78. Since each strip is approximately rectangular,

$$\text{Area of strip} \approx w\Delta h \text{ m}^2.$$

The pressure at a depth of h meters is $\delta gh = 9800h$ nt/m². Thus,

$$\text{Force on strip} \approx \text{Pressure} \cdot \text{Area} = 9800hw\Delta h \text{ nt.}$$

To find w in terms of h, we use the fact that w decreases linearly from $w = 400$ when $h = 0$ to $w = 200$ when $h = 220$. Thus w is a linear function of h, with slope $(200 - 400)/220 = -10/11$, so

$$w = 400 - \frac{10}{11}h.$$

Thus

$$\text{Force on strip} \approx 9800h\left(400 - \frac{10}{11}h\right)\Delta h \text{ nt.}$$

Summing over all strips and taking the limit as $\Delta h \to 0$ gives

$$\text{Total force on dam} = \lim_{\Delta h \to 0} \sum 9800h\left(400 - \frac{10}{11}h\right)\Delta h$$
$$= \int_0^{220} 9800h\left(400 - \frac{10}{11}h\right) dh \text{ newtons.}$$

Evaluating the integral gives

$$\text{Total force} = 9800\left(200h^2 - \frac{10}{33}h^3\right)\Big|_0^{220} = 6.32 \cdot 10^{10} \text{ newtons.}$$

In fact, Hoover Dam is not flat, as the problem assumed, but arched, to better withstand the pressure.

Exercises and Problems for Section 8.5

Exercises

1. Find the work done on a 40 lb suitcase when it is raised 9 inches.

2. Find the work done on a 20 kg suitcase when it is raised 30 centimeters.

3. A particle x feet from the origin has a force of $x^2 + 2x$ pounds acting on it. What is the work done in moving the object from the origin a distance of 1 foot?

In Exercises 4–6, the force, F, required to compress a spring by a distance x meters is given by $F = 3x$ newtons.

4. Find the work done in compressing the spring from $x = 1$ to $x = 2$.

5. Find the work done to compress the spring to $x = 3$, starting at the equilibrium position, $x = 0$.

6. (a) Find the work done in compressing the spring from $x = 0$ to $x = 1$ and in compressing the spring from $x = 4$ to $x = 5$.

(b) Which of the two answers is larger? Why?

7. A circular steel plate of radius 20 ft lies flat on the bottom of a lake, at a depth of 150 ft. Find the force on the plate due to the water pressure.

8. A fish tank is 2 feet long and 1 foot wide, and the depth of the water is 1 foot. What is the force on the bottom of the fish tank?

9. A child fills a bucket with sand so that the bucket and sand together weigh 10 lbs, lifts it 2 feet up and then walks along the beach, holding the bucket at a constant height of 2 ft above the ground. How much work is done on the bucket after the child has walked 100 ft?

10. The gravitational force on a 1 kg object at a distance r meters from the center of the earth is $F = 4 \cdot 10^{14}/r^2$ newtons. Find the work done in moving the object from the surface of the earth to a height of 10^6 meters above the surface. The radius of the earth is $6.4 \cdot 10^6$ meters.

Problems

11. How much work is required to lift a 1000-kg satellite from the surface of the earth to an altitude of $2 \cdot 10^6$ m? The gravitational force is $F = GMm/r^2$, where M is the mass of the earth, m is the mass of the satellite, and r is the distance between them. The radius of the earth is $6.4 \cdot 10^6$ m, its mass is $6 \cdot 10^{24}$ kg, and in these units the gravitational constant, G, is $6.67 \cdot 10^{-11}$.

12. A worker on a scaffolding 75 ft above the ground needs to lift a 500 lb bucket of cement from the ground to a point 30 ft above the ground by pulling on a rope weighing 0.5 lb/ft. How much work is required?

13. An anchor weighing 100 lb in water is attached to a chain weighing 3 lb/ft in water. Find the work done to haul the anchor and chain to the surface of the water from a depth of 25 ft.

14. A 1000-lb weight is being lifted to a height 10 feet off the ground. It is lifted using a rope which weighs 4 lb per foot and which is being pulled up by construction workers standing on a roof 30 feet off the ground. Find the work done to lift the weight.

15. A bucket of water of mass 20 kg is pulled at constant velocity up to a platform 40 meters above the ground. This takes 10 minutes, during which time 5 kg of water drips out at a steady rate through a hole in the bottom. Find the work needed to raise the bucket to the platform.

16. A 2000-lb cube of ice must be lifted 100 ft, and it is melting at a rate of 4 lb per minute. If it can be lifted at a rate of one foot every minute, find the work needed to get the block of ice to the desired height.

17. A cylindrical garbage can of depth 3 ft and radius 1 ft fills with rainwater up to a depth of 2 ft. How much work would be done in pumping the water up to the top edge of the can? (Water weighs 62.4 lb/ft^3.)

18. A rectangular swimming pool 50 ft long, 20 ft wide, and 10 ft deep is filled with water to a depth of 9 ft. Use an integral to find the work required to pump all the water out over the top.

19. A water tank is in the form of a right circular cylinder with height 20 ft and radius 6 ft. If the tank is half full of water, find the work required to pump all of it over the top rim.

20. Suppose the tank in Problem 19 is full of water. Find the work required to pump all of it to a point 10 ft above the top of the tank.

21. Water in a cylinder of height 10 ft and radius 4 ft is to be pumped out. Find the work required if

   (a) The tank is full of water and the water is to pumped over the top of the tank.
   (b) The tank is full of water and the water must be pumped to a height 5 ft above the top of the tank.
   (c) The depth of water in the tank is 8 ft and the water must be pumped over the top of the tank.

22. A water tank is in the shape of a right circular cone with height 18 ft and radius 12 ft at the top. If it is filled with water to a depth of 15 ft, find the work done in pumping all of the water over the top of the tank. (The density of water is $\delta = 62.4$ lb/ft^3.)

23. A cone with height 12 ft and radius 4 ft, pointing downward, is filled with water to a depth of 9 ft. Find the work required to pump all the water out over the top.

24. A gas station stores its gasoline in a tank under the ground. The tank is a cylinder lying horizontally on its side. (In other words, the tank is not standing vertically on one of its flat ends.) If the radius of the cylinder is 4 feet, its length is 12 feet, and its top is 10 feet under the ground, find the total amount of work needed to pump the gasoline out of the tank. (Gasoline weighs 42 lb/ft^3.)

25. A cylindrical barrel, standing upright on its circular end, contains muddy water. The top of the barrel, which has diameter 1 meter, is open. The height of the barrel is 1.8 meter and it is filled to a depth of 1.5 meter. The density of the water at a depth of h meters below the surface is given by $\delta(h) = 1 + kh$ kg/m^3, where k is a positive constant. Find the total work done to pump the muddy water to the top rim of the barrel. (You can leave π, k, and g in your answer.)

26. (a) The trough in Figure 8.79 is full of water. Find the force of the water on a triangular end.
    (b) Find the work to pump all the water over the top.

Figure 8.79

27. (a) A reservoir has a dam at one end. The dam is a rectangular wall, 1000 feet long and 50 feet high. Approximate the total force of the water on the dam by a Riemann sum.
    (b) Write an integral which represents the force, and evaluate it.

28. What is the total force on the bottom and each side of a full rectangular water tank that has length 20 ft, width 10 ft, and depth 15 ft?

29. A rectangular dam is 100 ft long and 50 ft high. If the water is 40 ft deep, find the force of the water on the dam.

30. A lobster tank in a restaurant is 4 ft long by 3 ft wide by 2 ft deep. Find the water force on the bottom and on each of the four sides.

31. The Three Gorges Dam started operation in China in 2008. With the largest electrical generating capacity in the world, the dam is about 2000 m long and 180 m high, and has created a lake longer than Lake Superior.[2] Assume the dam is rectangular in shape.

(a) Estimate the water pressure at the base of the dam.
(b) Set up and evaluate a definite integral giving the total force of the water on the dam.

32. On August 12, 2000, the Russian submarine Kursk sank to the bottom of the sea, 350 feet below the surface. Find the following at the depth of the Kursk.

(a) The water pressure in pounds per square foot and pounds per square inch.
(b) The force on a 5-foot square metal sheet held

(i) Horizontally.   (ii) Vertically.

33. The ocean liner Titanic lies under 12,500 feet of water at the bottom of the Atlantic Ocean.

(a) What is the water pressure at the Titanic? Give your answer in pounds per square foot and pounds per square inch.
(b) Set up and calculate an integral giving the total force on a circular porthole (window) of diameter 6 feet standing vertically with its center at the depth of the Titanic.

34. Set up and calculate a definite integral giving the total force on the dam shown in Figure 8.80, which is about the size of the Aswan Dam in Egypt.

Figure 8.80

35. We define the electric potential at a distance r from an electric charge q by q/r. The electric potential of a charge distribution is obtained by adding up the potential from each point. Electric charge is sprayed (with constant density σ in units of charge/unit area) on to a circular disk of radius a. Consider the axis perpendicular to the disk and through its center. Find the electric potential at the point P on this axis at a distance R from the center. (See Figure 8.81.)

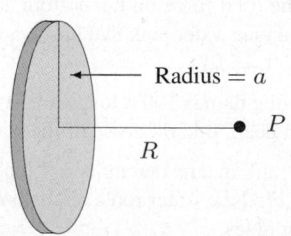

Figure 8.81

For Problems 36–37, find the kinetic energy of the rotating body. Use the fact that the kinetic energy of a particle of mass m moving at a speed v is $\frac{1}{2}mv^2$. Slice the object into pieces in such a way that the velocity is approximately constant on each piece.

36. Find the kinetic energy of a rod of mass 10 kg and length 6 m rotating about an axis perpendicular to the rod at its midpoint, with an angular velocity of 2 radians per second. (Imagine a helicopter blade of uniform thickness.)

37. Find the kinetic energy of a phonograph record of uniform density, mass 50 gm and radius 10 cm rotating at $33\frac{1}{3}$ revolutions per minute.

For Problems 38–40, find the gravitational force between two objects. Use the fact that the gravitational attraction between particles of mass m_1 and m_2 at a distance r apart is Gm_1m_2/r^2. Slice the objects into pieces, use this formula for the pieces, and sum using a definite integral.

38. What is the force of gravitational attraction between a thin uniform rod of mass M and length l and a particle of mass m lying in the same line as the rod at a distance a from one end?

39. Two long, thin, uniform rods of lengths l_1 and l_2 lie on a straight line with a gap between them of length a. Suppose their masses are M_1 and M_2, respectively, and the constant of the gravitation is G. What is the force of attraction between the rods? (Use the result of Problem 38.)

40. Find the gravitational force exerted by a thin uniform ring of mass M and radius a on a particle of mass m lying on a line perpendicular to the ring through its center. Assume m is at a distance y from the center of the ring.

41. A uniform, thin, circular disk of radius a and mass M lies on a horizontal plane. The point P lies a distance y directly above O, the center of the disk. Calculate the gravitational force on a mass m at the point P. (See Figure 8.82.) Use the fact that the gravitational force exerted on the mass m by a thin horizontal ring of radius r, mass μ, and center O is toward O and given by

$$F = \frac{G\mu my}{(r^2 + y^2)^{3/2}}, \quad \text{where } G \text{ is constant.}$$

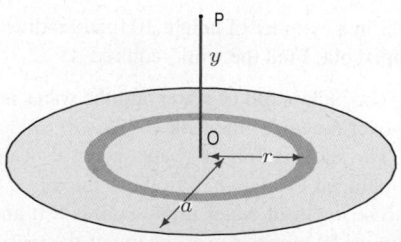

Figure 8.82

Strengthen Your Understanding

In Problems 42–44, explain what is wrong with the statement.

42. A 20 meter rope with a mass of 30 kg dangles over the edge of a cliff. Ignoring friction, the work required to pull the rope to the top of the cliff is

$$\text{Work} = (30 \text{ kg}) \left(9.8 \ \frac{\text{m}}{\text{sec}^2} \right) (20 \text{ m}).$$

43. A cylindrical tank is 10 meters deep. It takes twice as much work to pump all the oil out through the top of the tank when the tank is full as when the tank is half full.

44. Lifting a 10 kg rock 2 meters off the ground requires 20 joules of work.

In Problems 45–46, give an example of:

45. A situation where work can be computed as Force × Distance without doing an integral.

46. Two cylindrical tanks A and B such that it takes less work to pump the water from tank A to a height of 10 meters than from tank B. Both tanks contain the same volume of water and are less than 10 meters high.

In Problems 47–52, are the statements true or false? Give an explanation for your answer.

47. It takes more work to lift a 20 lb weight 10 ft slowly than to lift it the same distance quickly.

48. Work can be negative or positive.

49. The force on a rectangular dam is doubled if its length stays the same and its depth is doubled.

50. To find the force of water on a vertical wall, we always slice the wall horizontally, no matter what the shape of the wall.

51. The force of a liquid on a wall can be negative or positive.

52. If the average value of the force $F(x)$ is 7 on the interval $1 \le x \le 4$, then the work done by the force in moving from $x = 1$ to $x = 4$ is 21.

8.6 APPLICATIONS TO ECONOMICS

Present and Future Value

Many business deals involve payments in the future. If you buy a car or furniture, for example, you may buy it on credit and pay over a period of time. If you are going to accept payment in the future under such a deal, you obviously need to know how much you should be paid. Being paid $100 in the future is clearly worse than being paid $100 today for many reasons. If you are given the money today, you can do something else with it—for example, put it in the bank, invest it somewhere, or spend it. Thus, even without considering inflation, if you are to accept payment in the future, you would expect to be paid more to compensate for this loss of potential earnings. The question we will consider now is, how much more?

To simplify matters, we consider only what we would lose by not earning interest; we will not consider the effect of inflation. Let's look at some specific numbers. Suppose you deposit $100 in an account which earns 3% interest compounded annually, so that in a year's time you will have $103. Thus, $100 today will be worth $103 a year from now. We say that the $103 is the *future value* of the $100, and that the $100 is the *present value* of the $103. Observe that the present value is smaller than the future value. In general, we say the following:

> • The **future value**, B, of a payment, P, is the amount to which the P would have grown if deposited in an interest-bearing bank account.
>
> • The **present value**, P, of a future payment, B, is the amount which would have to be deposited in a bank account today to produce exactly B in the account at the relevant time in the future.

With an interest rate of r, compounded annually, and a time period of t years, a deposit of P grows to a future balance of B, where

$$B = P(1+r)^t, \quad \text{or equivalently,} \quad P = \frac{B}{(1+r)^t}.$$

Note that for a 3% interest rate, $r = 0.03$. If instead of annual compounding, we have continuous compounding, we get the following result:

$$B = Pe^{rt}, \quad \text{or equivalently,} \quad P = \frac{B}{e^{rt}} = Be^{-rt}.$$

Example 1   You win the lottery and are offered the choice between $1 million in four yearly installments of $250,000 each, starting now, and a lump-sum payment of $920,000 now. Assuming a 6% interest rate, compounded continuously, and ignoring taxes, which should you choose?

Solution   We will do the problem in two ways. First, we assume that you pick the option with the largest present value. The first of the four $250,000 payments is made now, so

$$\text{Present value of first payment} = \$250,000.$$

The second payment is made one year from now, so

$$\text{Present value of second payment} = \$250,000e^{-0.06(1)}.$$

Calculating the present value of the third and fourth payments similarly, we find:

$$\text{Total present value} = \$250,000 + \$250,000e^{-0.06(1)} + \$250,000e^{-0.06(2)} + \$250,000e^{-0.06(3)}$$
$$\approx \$250,000 + \$235,441 + \$221,730 + \$208,818$$
$$= \$915,989.$$

Since the present value of the four payments is less than $920,000, you are better off taking the $920,000 right now.

Alternatively, we can compare the future values of the two pay schemes. The scheme with the highest future value is the best from a purely financial point of view. We calculate the future value of both schemes three years from now, on the date of the last $250,000 payment. At that time,

$$\text{Future value of the lump sum payment} = \$920,000e^{0.06(3)} \approx \$1,101,440.$$

Now we calculate the future value of the first $250,000 payment:

$$\text{Future value of the first payment} = \$250,000e^{0.06(3)}.$$

Calculating the future value of the other payments similarly, we find:

$$\text{Total future value} = \$250,000e^{0.06(3)} + \$250,000e^{0.06(2)} + \$250,000e^{0.06(1)} + \$250,000$$
$$\approx \$299,304 + \$281,874 + \$265,459 + \$250,000$$
$$= \$1,096,637.$$

The future value of the $920,000 payment is greater, so you are better off taking the $920,000 right now. Of course, since the present value of the $920,000 payment is greater than the present value of the four separate payments, you would expect the future value of the $920,000 payment to be greater than the future value of the four separate payments.

(Note: If you read the fine print, you will find that many lotteries do not make their payments right away, but often spread them out, sometimes far into the future. This is to reduce the present value of the payments made, so that the value of the prizes is much less than it might first appear!)

Income Stream

When we consider payments made to or by an individual, we usually think of *discrete* payments, that is, payments made at specific moments in time. However, we may think of payments made by a company as being *continuous*. The revenues earned by a huge corporation, for example, come in essentially all the time and can be represented by a continuous *income stream*, written

$$P(t) \text{ dollars/year.}$$

Notice that $P(t)$ is the *rate* at which deposits are made (its units are dollars per year, for example) and that this rate may vary with time, t.

Present and Future Values of an Income Stream

Just as we can find the present and future values of a single payment, so we can find the present and future values of a stream of payments. We will assume that interest is compounded continuously.

Suppose that we want to calculate the present value of the income stream described by a rate of $P(t)$ dollars per year, and that we are interested in the period from now until M years in the future. We divide the stream into many small deposits, each of which is made at approximately one instant. We divide the interval $0 \le t \le M$ into subintervals, each of length Δt:

Assuming Δt is small, the rate, $P(t)$, at which deposits are being made will not vary much within one subinterval. Thus, between t and $t + \Delta t$:

$$\text{Amount deposited} \approx \text{Rate of deposits} \times \text{Time}$$
$$\approx (P(t) \text{ dollars/year})(\Delta t \text{ years})$$
$$= P(t)\Delta t \text{ dollars.}$$

Measured from the present, the deposit of $P(t)\Delta t$ is made t years in the future. Thus,

$$\begin{array}{c} \text{Present value of money deposited} \\ \text{in interval } t \text{ to } t + \Delta t \end{array} \approx P(t)\Delta t e^{-rt}.$$

Summing over all subintervals gives

$$\text{Total present value} \approx \sum P(t)e^{-rt}\Delta t \text{ dollars.}$$

In the limit as $\Delta t \to 0$, we get the following integral:

$$\boxed{\text{Present value} = \int_0^M P(t)e^{-rt}dt \text{ dollars.}}$$

In computing future value, the deposit of $P(t)\Delta t$ has a period of $(M - t)$ years to earn interest, and therefore

$$\begin{array}{c} \text{Future value of money deposited} \\ \text{in interval } t \text{ to } t + \Delta t \end{array} \approx (P(t)\Delta t)\, e^{r(M-t)}.$$

Summing over all subintervals, we get:

$$\text{Total future value} \approx \sum P(t)\Delta t e^{r(M-t)} \text{ dollars.}$$

As the length of the subdivisions tends toward zero, the sum becomes an integral:

$$\text{Future value} = \int_0^M P(t)e^{r(M-t)}dt \text{ dollars.}$$

In addition, by writing $e^{r(M-t)} = e^{rM} \cdot e^{-rt}$ and factoring out e^{rM}, we see that

$$\text{Future value} = e^{rM} \cdot \text{Present value.}$$

Example 2   Find the present and future values of a constant income stream of $1000 per year over a period of 20 years, assuming an interest rate of 10% compounded continuously.

Solution   Using $P(t) = 1000$ and $r = 0.1$, we have

$$\text{Present value} = \int_0^{20} 1000e^{-0.1t}dt = 1000\left(-\frac{e^{-0.1t}}{0.1}\right)\Bigg|_0^{20} = 10{,}000(1-e^{-2}) \approx 8646.65 \text{ dollars.}$$

There are two ways to compute the future value. Using the present value of $8646.65, we have

$$\text{Future value} = 8646.65e^{0.1(20)} = 63{,}890.58 \text{ dollars.}$$

Alternatively, we can use the integral formula:

$$\text{Future value} = \int_0^{20} 1000e^{0.1(20-t)}dt = \int_0^{20} 1000e^2 e^{-0.1t}dt$$

$$= 1000e^2\left(-\frac{e^{-0.1t}}{0.1}\right)\Bigg|_0^{20} = 10{,}000e^2(1-e^{-2}) \approx 63{,}890.58 \text{ dollars.}$$

Notice that the total amount deposited is $1000 per year for 20 years, or $20,000. The additional $43,895.58 of the future value comes from interest earned.

Supply and Demand Curves

In a free market, the quantity of a certain item produced and sold can be described by the supply and demand curves of the item. The *supply curve* shows the quantity of the item the producers will supply at different price levels. It is usually assumed that as the price increases, the quantity supplied will increase. The consumers' behavior is reflected in the *demand curve*, which shows what quantity of goods are bought at various prices. An increase in price is usually assumed to cause a decrease in the quantity purchased. See Figure 8.83.

Figure 8.83: Supply and demand curves

It is assumed that the market settles to the *equilibrium price* and *quantity*, p^* and q^*, where the graphs cross. At equilibrium, a quantity q^* of an item is produced and sold for a price of p^* each.

Consumer and Producer Surplus

Notice that at equilibrium, a number of consumers have bought the item at a lower price than they would have been willing to pay. (For example, there are some consumers who would have been willing to pay prices up to p_1.) Similarly, there are some suppliers who would have been willing to produce the item at a lower price (down to p_0, in fact). We define the following terms:

> • The **consumer surplus** measures the consumers' gain from trade. It is the total amount gained by consumers by buying the item at the current price rather than at the price they would have been willing to pay.
>
> • The **producer surplus** measures the suppliers' gain from trade. It is the total amount gained by producers by selling at the current price, rather than at the price they would have been willing to accept.
>
> In the absence of price controls, the current price is assumed to be the equilibrium price.

Both consumers and producers are richer for having traded. The consumer and producer surplus measure how much richer they are.

Suppose that all consumers buy the good at the maximum price they are willing to pay. Divide the interval from 0 to q^* into subintervals of length Δq. Figure 8.84 shows that a quantity Δq of items are sold at a price of about p_1, another Δq are sold for a slightly lower price of about p_2, the next Δq for a price of about p_3, and so on. Thus,

$$\text{Consumers' total expenditure} \approx p_1\Delta q + p_2\Delta q + p_3\Delta q + \cdots = \sum p_i \Delta q.$$

If D is the demand function given by $p = D(q)$, and if all consumers who were willing to pay more than p^* paid as much as they were willing, then as $\Delta q \to 0$, we would have

$$\text{Consumer expenditure} = \int_0^{q^*} D(q)\,dq = \begin{array}{l}\text{Area under demand}\\ \text{curve from 0 to } q^*.\end{array}$$

Now if all goods are sold at the equilibrium price, the consumers' actual expenditure is p^*q^*, the area of the rectangle between the axes and the lines $q = q^*$ and $p = p^*$. Thus, if p^* and q^* are equilibrium price and quantity, the consumer surplus is calculated as follows:

$$\text{Consumer surplus} = \left(\int_0^{q^*} D(q)\,dq\right) - p^*q^* = \begin{array}{l}\text{Area under demand}\\ \text{curve above } p = p^*.\end{array}$$

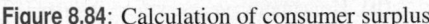

Figure 8.84: Calculation of consumer surplus

Figure 8.85: Consumer and producer surplus

See Figure 8.85. Similarly, if the supply curve is given by the function $p = S(q)$ and p^* and q^* are equilibrium price and quantity, the producer surplus is calculated as follows:

$$\text{Producer surplus} = p^*q^* - \left(\int_0^{q^*} S(q)\,dq\right) = \begin{array}{l}\text{Area between supply}\\ \text{curve and line } p = p^*.\end{array}$$

Exercises and Problems for Section 8.6

Exercises

In Exercises 1–7 give an expression that represents the statement. Do not simplify your expression.

1. The future value of single C deposit, after 25 years, at a 3% interest rate compounded annually.

2. The present value of C deposited 25 years from now, at a 3% interest rate compounded annually.

3. The present value of a deposit of C, made 5 years from now, with a 3% interest rate compounded continuously.

4. The present value of an income stream paying C dollars/year for a period of 15 years, at a 2% interest rate compounded continuously.

5. The future value at the end of 15 years of an income stream paying C dollars/year throughout the 15 years, at a 2% interest rate compounded continuously.

6. The future value, at the end of C years, of a series of three $500 deposits, where the first deposit is made now, the second a year from now, and the third two years from now. Assume a 2% interest rate compounded continuously.

7. The continuous interest rate for a deposit C that will grow to $25,000 in 30 years.

8. Find the future value of an income stream of $1000 per year, deposited into an account paying 8% interest, compounded continuously, over a 10-year period.

9. (a) Find the present and future values of a constant income stream of $100 per year over a period of 20 years, assuming a 10% annual interest rate compounded continuously.

(b) How many years will it take for the balance to reach $5000?

10. Find the present and future values of an income stream of $2000 a year, for a period of 5 years, if the continuous interest rate is 8%.

11. A person deposits money into a retirement account, which pays 7% interest compounded continuously, at a rate of $1000 per year for 20 years. Calculate:

(a) The balance in the account at the end of the 20 years.

(b) The amount of money actually deposited into the account.

(c) The interest earned during the 20 years.

Exercises 12–14 concern a single deposit of $10,000. Find the continuous interest rate yielding a future value of $20,000 in the given time period.

12. 60 years   **13.** 15 years   **14.** 5 years

Exercises 15–17 concern a constant income stream that pays a total of $20,000 over a certain time period with an interest rate of 2% compounded continuously. Find the rate at which money is paid, in dollars/year, and the future value of the stream at the end of the given time period.

15. 5 years   **16.** 10 years   **17.** 20 years

Problems

18. Find a constant income stream (in dollars per year) which after 10 years has a future value of $20,000, assuming a continuous interest rate of 3%.

19. Draw a graph, with time in years on the horizontal axis, of what an income stream might look like for a company that sells sunscreen in the northeast United States.

20. On March 6, 2007, the Associated Press reported that Ed Nabors had won half of a $390 million jackpot, the largest lottery prize in US history at the time. Suppose he was given the choice of receiving his $195 million share paid out continuously over 20 years or one lump sum of $120 million paid immediately.

(a) Which option is better if the interest rate is 6%, compounded continuously? An interest rate of 3%?

(b) If Mr. Nabors chose the lump-sum option, what assumption was he making about interest rates?

21. (a) A bank account earns 10% interest compounded continuously. At what (constant, continuous) rate

must a parent deposit money into such an account in order to save $100,000 in 10 years for a child's college expenses?

(b) If the parent decides instead to deposit a lump sum now in order to attain the goal of $100,000 in 10 years, how much must be deposited now?

22. (a) If you deposit money continuously at a constant rate of $1000 per year into a bank account that earns 5% interest, how many years will it take for the balance to reach $10,000?

(b) How many years would it take if the account had $2000 in it initially?

23. A business associate who owes you $3000 offers to pay you $2800 now, or else pay you three yearly installments of $1000 each, with the first installment paid now. If you use only financial reasons to make your decision, which option should you choose? Justify your answer, assuming a 6% interest rate per year, compounded continuously.

In Problems 24–27 find the continuous interest rate that yields a future value of $18,000 in 20 years for each $9000 investment.

24. A single $9000 deposit.

25. An initial $6000 deposit plus a second $3000 deposit made three years after the first.

26. An initial $3000 deposit plus a second $6000 deposit made three years after the first.

27. An income stream of $300 per year.

28. A family wants to save for college tuition for their daughter. What continuous yearly interest rate $r\%$ is needed in their savings account if their deposits of $4800 per year are to grow to $100,000 in 15 years? Assume that they make deposits continuously throughout the year.

29. Big Tree McGee is negotiating his rookie contract with a professional basketball team. They have agreed to a three-year deal which will pay Big Tree a fixed amount at the end of each of the three years, plus a signing bonus at the beginning of his first year. They are still haggling about the amounts and Big Tree must decide between a big signing bonus and fixed payments per year, or a smaller bonus with payments increasing each year. The two options are summarized in the table. All values are payments in millions of dollars.

	Signing bonus	Year 1	Year 2	Year 3
Option #1	6.0	2.0	2.0	2.0
Option #2	1.0	2.0	4.0	6.0

(a) Big Tree decides to invest all income in stock funds which he expects to grow at a rate of 10% per year, compounded continuously. He would like to choose the contract option which gives him the greater future value at the end of the three years when the last payment is made. Which option should he choose?

(b) Calculate the present value of each contract offer.

30. Sales of Version 6.0 of a computer software package start out high and decrease exponentially. At time t, in years, the sales are $s(t) = 50e^{-t}$ thousands of dollars per year. After two years, Version 7.0 of the software is released and replaces Version 6.0. Assuming that all income from software sales is immediately invested in government bonds which pay interest at a 6% rate compounded continuously, calculate the total value of sales of Version 6.0 over the two-year period.

31. The value of good wine increases with age. Thus, if you are a wine dealer, you have the problem of deciding whether to sell your wine now, at a price of $\$P$ a bottle, or to sell it later at a higher price. Suppose you know that the amount a wine-drinker is willing to pay for a bottle of this wine t years from now is $\$P(1 + 20\sqrt{t})$. Assuming continuous compounding and a prevailing interest rate of 5% per year, when is the best time to sell your wine?

32. An oil company discovered an oil reserve of 100 million barrels. For time $t > 0$, in years, the company's extraction plan is a linear declining function of time as follows:

$$q(t) = a - bt,$$

where $q(t)$ is the rate of extraction of oil in millions of barrels per year at time t and $b = 0.1$ and $a = 10$.

(a) How long does it take to exhaust the entire reserve?

(b) The oil price is a constant $20 per barrel, the extraction cost per barrel is a constant $10, and the market interest rate is 10% per year, compounded continuously. What is the present value of the company's profit?

33. You are manufacturing a particular item. After t years, the rate at which you earn a profit on the item is $(2-0.1t)$ thousand dollars per year. (A negative profit represents a loss.) Interest is 10%, compounded continuously,

(a) Write a Riemann sum approximating the present value of the total profit earned up to a time M years in the future.

(b) Write an integral representing the present value in part (a). (You need not evaluate this integral.)

(c) For what M is the present value of the stream of profits on this item maximized? What is the present value of the total profit earned up to that time?

34. In 1980, before the unification of Germany in 1990 and the introduction of the Euro, West Germany made a loan of 20 billion Deutsche Marks to the Soviet Union, to be used for the construction of a natural gas pipeline connecting Siberia to Western Russia, and continuing to West Germany (Urengoi–Uschgorod–Berlin). Assume that the deal was as follows: In 1985, upon completion of the pipeline, the Soviet Union would deliver natural gas to West Germany, at a constant rate, for all future times. Assuming a constant price of natural gas of 0.10 Deutsche Mark per cubic meter, and assuming West Germany expects 10% annual interest on its investment (compounded continuously), at what rate does the Soviet Union have to deliver the gas, in billions of cubic meters per year? Keep in mind that delivery of gas could not begin until the pipeline was completed. Thus, West Germany received no return on its investment until after five years had passed. (Note: A more complex deal of this type was actually made between the two countries.)

35. In May 1991, *Car and Driver* described a Jaguar that sold for $980,000. At that price only 50 have been sold. It is estimated that 350 could have been sold if the price had been $560,000. Assuming that the demand curve is a straight line, and that $560,000 and 350 are the equilibrium price and quantity, find the consumer surplus at the equilibrium price.

36. Using Riemann sums, explain the economic significance of $\int_0^{q^*} S(q)\,dq$ to the producers.

37. Using Riemann sums, give an interpretation of producer surplus, $\int_0^{q^*}(p^* - S(q))\,dq$ analogous to the interpretation of consumer surplus.

38. In Figure 8.85, page 463, mark the regions representing the following quantities and explain their economic meaning:

   (a) p^*q^* **(b)** $\int_0^{q^*} D(q)\,dq$

   (c) $\int_0^{q^*} S(q)\,dq$ **(d)** $\int_0^{q^*} D(q)\,dq - p^*q^*$

   (e) $p^*q^* - \int_0^{q^*} S(q)\,dq$ **(f)** $\int_0^{q^*}(D(q)-S(q))\,dq$

39. The dairy industry is an example of cartel pricing: the government has set milk prices artificially high. On a supply and demand graph, label p^+, a price above the equilibrium price. Using the graph, describe the effect of forcing the price up to p^+ on:

   (a) The consumer surplus.
   (b) The producer surplus.
   (c) The total gains from trade (Consumer surplus + Producer surplus).

40. Rent controls on apartments are an example of price controls on a commodity. They keep the price artificially low (below the equilibrium price). Sketch a graph of supply and demand curves, and label on it a price p^- below the equilibrium price. What effect does forcing the price down to p^- have on:

   (a) The producer surplus?
   (b) The consumer surplus?
   (c) The total gains from trade (Consumer surplus + Producer surplus)?

Strengthen Your Understanding

In Problems 41–44, explain what is wrong with the statement.

41. The future value of an income stream of $2000 per year after 10 years is $15,000, assuming a 3% continuous interest rate per year.

42. The present value of a lump-sum payment S dollars one year from now is greater with an annual interest rate of 4% than with an annual interest rate of 3%.

43. Payments are made at a constant rate of P dollars per year over a two-year period. The present value of these payments is $2Pe^{-2r}$, where r is the continuous interest rate per year.

44. Producer surplus is measured in the same units as the quantity, q.

In Problems 45–48, give an example of:

45. Supply and demand curves where producer surplus is smaller than consumer surplus.

46. A continuous interest rate such that a $10,000 payment in 10 years' time has a present value of less than $5000.

47. An interest rate, compounded annually, and a present value that correspond to a future value of $5000 one year from now.

48. An interest rate, compounded annually, and a table of values that shows how much money you would have to put down in a single deposit t years from now, at $t = 0, 1, 2, 3$, or 4, if you want to have $10,000 ten years from now (ignoring inflation).

8.7 DISTRIBUTION FUNCTIONS

Understanding the distribution of various quantities through the population is important to decision makers. For example, the income distribution gives useful information about the economic structure of a society. In this section we will look at the distribution of ages in the US. To allocate funding for education, health care, and social security, the government needs to know how many people are in each age group. We will see how to represent such information by a density function.

US Age Distribution

The data in Table 8.4 shows how the ages of the US population were distributed in 1995. To represent this information graphically we use a type[3] of *histogram*, putting a vertical bar above each age group in such a way that the *area* of each bar represents the fraction of the population in that age group. The total area of all the rectangles is $100\% = 1$. We only consider people who are less than 100 years old.[4] For the 0–20 age group, the base of the rectangle is 20, and we want the area to be 0.29, so the height must be $0.29/20 = 0.0145$. We treat ages as though they were continuously distributed. The category 0–20, for example, contains people who are just one day short of their twentieth birthday. (See Figure 8.86.)

---

[3]There are other types of histogram which have frequency on the vertical axis.

[4]In fact, 0.02% of the population is over 100, but this is too small to be visible on the histogram.

Table 8.4 *Distribution of ages in the US in 1995*

Age group	Fraction of total population
0–20	29% = 0.29
20–40	31% = 0.31
40–60	24% = 0.24
60–80	13% = 0.13
80–100	3% = 0.03

Figure 8.86: How ages were distributed in the US in 1995

Example 1   In 1995, estimate what fraction of the US population was:

(a)   Between 20 and 60 years old.
(b)   Less than 10 years old.
(c)   Between 75 and 80 years old.
(d)   Between 80 and 85 years old.

Solution

(a) We add the fractions, so $0.31 + 0.24 = 0.55$; that is, 55% of the US population was in this age group.

(b) To find the fraction less than 10 years old, we could assume, for example, that the population was distributed evenly over the 0–20 group. (This means we are assuming that babies were born at a fairly constant rate over the last 20 years, which is probably reasonable.) If we make this assumption, then we can say that the population less than 10 years old was about half that in the 0–20 group, that is, 0.145 of the total population. Notice that we get the same result by computing the area of the rectangle from 0 to 10. (See Figure 8.87.)

(c) To find the population between 75 and 80 years old, since 0.13 of Americans in 1995 were in the 60-80 group, we might apply the same reasoning and say that $\frac{1}{4}(0.13) = 0.0325$ of the population was in this age group. This result is represented as an area in Figure 8.87. The assumption that the population was evenly distributed is not a good one here; certainly there were more people between the ages of 60 and 65 than between 75 and 80. Thus, the estimate of 0.0325 is certainly too high.

(d) Again using the (faulty) assumption that ages in each group were distributed uniformly, we would find that the fraction between 80 and 85 was $\frac{1}{4}(0.03) = 0.0075$. (See Figure 8.87.) This estimate is also poor—there were certainly more people in the 80–85 group than, say, the 95–100 group, and so the 0.0075 estimate is too low.

Figure 8.87: Ages in the US in 1995 — various subgroups (for Example 1)

Table 8.5 *Ages in the US in 1995 (more detailed)*

Age group	Fraction of total population
0–10	$15\% = 0.15$
10–20	$14\% = 0.14$
20–30	$14\% = 0.14$
30–40	$17\% = 0.17$
40–50	$14\% = 0.14$
50–60	$10\% = 0.10$
60–70	$8\% = 0.08$
70–80	$5\% = 0.05$
80–90	$2\% = 0.02$
90–100	$1\% = 0.01$

Figure 8.88: Smoothing out the age histogram

Smoothing Out the Histogram

We could get better estimates if we had smaller age groups (each age group in Figure 8.86 is 20 years, which is quite large). The more detailed data in Table 8.5 leads to the new histogram in Figure 8.88. As we get more detailed information, the upper silhouette of the histogram becomes smoother, but the area of any of the bars still represents the percentage of the population in that age group. Imagine, in the limit, replacing the upper silhouette of the histogram by a smooth curve in such a way that area under the curve above one age group is the same as the area in the corresponding rectangle. The total area under the whole curve is again $100\% = 1$. (See Figure 8.88.)

The Age Density Function

If t is age in years, we define $p(t)$, the age *density function*, to be a function which "smooths out" the age histogram. This function has the property that

$$\begin{array}{c}\text{Fraction of population} \\ \text{between ages } a \text{ and } b\end{array} = \begin{array}{c}\text{Area under graph of } p \\ \text{between } a \text{ and } b\end{array} = \int_a^b p(t)dt.$$

If a and b are the smallest and largest possible ages (say, $a = 0$ and $b = 100$), so that the ages of all of the population are between a and b, then

$$\int_a^b p(t)dt = \int_0^{100} p(t)dt = 1.$$

What does the age density function p tell us? Notice that we have not talked about the meaning of $p(t)$ itself, but *only* of the integral $\int_a^b p(t)\,dt$. Let's look at this in a bit more detail. Suppose, for example, that $p(10) = 0.015$ per year. This is *not* telling us that 0.015 of the population is precisely 10 years old (where 10 years old means exactly 10, not $10\frac{1}{2}$, not $10\frac{1}{4}$, not 10.1). However, $p(10) = 0.015$ does tell us that for some small interval Δt around 10, the fraction of the population with ages in this interval is approximately $p(10)\,\Delta t = 0.015\,\Delta t$.

The Probability Density Function

Suppose we are interested in how a certain characteristic, x, is distributed through a population. For example, x might be height or age if the population is people, or might be wattage for a population of light bulbs. Then we define a general density function with the following properties:

The function, $p(x)$, is a **probability density function**, or pdf, if

$$\begin{array}{ccc} \text{Fraction of population for which} \\ x \text{ is between } a \text{ and } b \end{array} = \begin{array}{c} \text{Area under graph of } p \\ \text{between } a \text{ and } b \end{array} = \int_a^b p(x)dx.$$

$$\int_{-\infty}^{\infty} p(x)\,dx = 1 \quad \text{and} \quad p(x) \geq 0 \quad \text{for all } x.$$

The density function must be nonnegative because its integral always gives a fraction of the population. Also, the fraction of the population with x between $-\infty$ and ∞ is 1 because the entire population has the characteristic x between $-\infty$ and ∞. The function p that was used to smooth out the age histogram satisfies this definition of a density function. We do not assign a meaning to the value $p(x)$ directly, but rather interpret $p(x)\,\Delta x$ as the fraction of the population with the characteristic in a short interval of length Δx around x.

The density function is often approximated by formulas, as in the next example.

Example 2   Find formulas to approximate the density function, p, for the US age distribution. To reflect Figure 8.88, use a continuous function, constant at 0.015 up to age 40 and then dropping linearly.

Solution   We have $p(t) = 0.015$ for $0 \leq t < 40$. For $t \geq 40$, we need a linear function sloping downward. Because p is continuous, we have $p(40) = 0.015$. Because p is a density function we have $\int_0^{100} p(t)dt = 1$. Suppose b is as in Figure 8.89; then

$$\int_0^{100} p(t)dt = \int_0^{40} p(t)dt + \int_{40}^{100} \cdot p(t)dt = 40(0.015) + \frac{1}{2}(0.015)b = 1,$$

where $\int_{40}^{100} p(t)dt$ is given by the area of the triangle. This gives

$$\frac{0.015}{2}b = 0.4, \quad \text{and so} \quad b \approx 53.3.$$

Thus the slope of the line is $-0.015/53.3 \approx -0.00028$, so for $40 \leq t \leq 40 + 53.3 = 93.3$, we have

$$p(t) - 0.015 = -0.00028(t - 40),$$
$$p(t) = 0.0262 - 0.00028t.$$

According to this way of smoothing the data, there is no one over 93.3 years old, so $p(t) = 0$ for $t > 93.3$.

Figure 8.89: Age density function

Cumulative Distribution Function for Ages

Another way of showing how ages are distributed in the US is by using the *cumulative distribution function* $P(t)$, defined by

$$P(t) = \begin{array}{c} \text{Fraction of population} \\ \text{of age less than } t \end{array} = \int_0^t p(x)dx.$$

Thus, P is the antiderivative of p with $P(0) = 0$, and $P(t)$ gives the area under the density curve between 0 and t.

Notice that the cumulative distribution function is nonnegative and increasing (or at least non-decreasing), since the number of people younger than age t increases as t increases. Another way of seeing this is to notice that $P' = p$, and p is positive (or nonnegative). Thus the cumulative age distribution is a function which starts with $P(0) = 0$ and increases as t increases. $P(t) = 0$ for $t < 0$ because, when $t < 0$, there is no one whose age is less than t. The limiting value of P, as $t \to \infty$, is 1 since as t becomes very large (100 say), everyone is younger than age t, so the fraction of people with age less than t tends toward 1. (See Figure 8.90.) For t less than 40, the graph of P is a straight line, because p is constant there. For $t > 40$, the graph of P levels off as p tends to 0.

Figure 8.90: $P(t)$, the cumulative age distribution function, and its relation to $p(x)$, the age density function

Cumulative Distribution Function

A **cumulative distribution function**, or cdf, $P(t)$, of a density function p, is defined by

$$P(t) = \int_{-\infty}^{t} p(x)\, dx = \quad \begin{array}{l} \text{Fraction of population having} \\ \text{values of } x \text{ below } t. \end{array}$$

Thus, P is an antiderivative of p, that is, $P' = p$.
Any cumulative distribution has the following properties:
- P is increasing (or nondecreasing).
- $\displaystyle\lim_{t \to \infty} P(t) = 1$ and $\displaystyle\lim_{t \to -\infty} P(t) = 0.$
- $\begin{array}{l} \text{Fraction of population having} \\ \text{values of } x \text{ between } a \text{ and } b \end{array} = \int_{a}^{b} p(x)\, dx = P(b) - P(a).$

Exercises and Problems for Section 8.7

Exercises

1. Match the graphs of the density functions (a), (b), and (c) with the graphs of the cumulative distribution functions I, II, and III.

In Exercises 2–4, graph a density function and a cumulative distribution function which could represent the distribution of income through a population with the given characteristics.

2. A large middle class.

3. Small middle and upper classes and many poor people.

4. Small middle class, many poor and many rich people.

Decide if the function graphed in Exercises 5–10 is a probability density function (pdf) or a cumulative distribution function (cdf). Give reasons. Find the value of c. Sketch and label the other function. (That is, sketch and label the cdf if the problem shows a pdf, and the pdf if the problem shows a cdf.)

9.

10.

5.

6.

7.

8.

11. Let $p(x)$ be the density function for annual family income, where x is in thousands of dollars. What is the meaning of the statement $p(70) = 0.05$?

12. Find a density function $p(x)$ such that $p(x) = 0$ when $x \geq 5$ and when $x < 0$, and is decreasing when $0 \leq x \leq 5$.

Problems

13. Figure 8.91 shows the distribution of kinetic energy of molecules in a gas at temperatures 300 kelvins and 500 kelvins. At higher temperatures, more of the molecules in a gas have higher kinetic energies. Which graph corresponds to which temperature?

Figure 8.91

14. A large number of people take a standardized test, receiving scores described by the density function p graphed in Figure 8.92. Does the density function imply that most people receive a score near 50? Explain why or why not.

Figure 8.92

15. An experiment is done to determine the effect of two new fertilizers A and B on the growth of a species of peas.

The cumulative distribution functions of the heights of the mature peas without treatment and treated with each of A and B are graphed in Figure 8.93.

(a) About what height are most of the unfertilized plants?

(b) Explain in words the effect of the fertilizers A and B on the mature height of the plants.

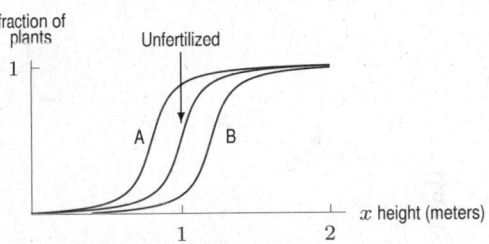

Figure 8.93

16. Suppose $F(x)$ is the cumulative distribution function for heights (in meters) of trees in a forest.

(a) Explain in terms of trees the meaning of the statement $F(7) = 0.6$.

(b) Which is greater, $F(6)$ or $F(7)$? Justify your answer in terms of trees.

17. Suppose that $p(x)$ is the density function for heights of American men, in inches. What is the meaning of the statement $p(68) = 0.2$?

18. Suppose $P(t)$ is the fraction of the US population of age less than t. Using Table 8.5 on page 468, make a table of values for $P(t)$.

19. Figure 8.94 shows a density function and the corresponding cumulative distribution function.[5]

(a) Which curve represents the density function and which represents the cumulative distribution function? Give a reason for your choice.

[5]Adapted from *Calculus*, by David A. Smith and Lawrence C. Moore (Lexington, D.C. Heath, 1994).

(b) Put reasonable values on the tick marks on each of the axes.

Figure 8.94

20. The density function and cumulative distribution function of heights of grass plants in a meadow are in Figures 8.95 and 8.96, respectively.

(a) There are two species of grass in the meadow, a short grass and a tall grass. Explain how the graph of the density function reflects this fact.

(b) Explain how the graph of the cumulative distribution function reflects the fact that there are two species of grass in the meadow.

(c) About what percentage of the grasses in the meadow belong to the short grass species?

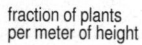

fraction of plants
per meter of height

Figure 8.95

Figure 8.96

21. After measuring the duration of many telephone calls, the telephone company found their data was well approximated by the density function $p(x) = 0.4e^{-0.4x}$, where x is the duration of a call, in minutes.

(a) What percentage of calls last between 1 and 2 minutes?

(b) What percentage of calls last 1 minute or less?

(c) What percentage of calls last 3 minutes or more?

(d) Find the cumulative distribution function.

22. Students at the University of California were surveyed and asked their grade point average. (The GPA ranges from 0 to 4, where 2 is just passing.) The distribution of GPAs is shown in Figure 8.97.[6]

(a) Roughly what fraction of students are passing?

(b) Roughly what fraction of the students have honor grades (GPAs above 3)?

(c) Why do you think there is a peak around 2?

(d) Sketch the cumulative distribution function.

fraction of students
per GPA

Figure 8.97

23. Figure 8.98[6] shows the distribution of elevation, in miles, across the earth's surface. Positive elevation denotes land above sea level; negative elevation shows land below sea level (i.e., the ocean floor).

(a) Describe in words the elevation of most of the earth's surface.

(b) Approximately what fraction of the earth's surface is below sea level?

fraction of earth's surface
per mile of elevation

Figure 8.98

24. Consider a population of individuals with a disease. Suppose that t is the number of years since the onset of the disease. The death density function, $f(t) = cte^{-kt}$, approximates the fraction of the sick individuals who die in the time interval $[t, t + \Delta t]$ as follows:

$$\text{Fraction who die } \approx f(t)\Delta t = cte^{-kt}\Delta t$$

where c and k are positive constants whose values depend on the particular disease.

(a) Find the value of c in terms of k.

(b) If 40% of the population dies within 5 years, find c and k.

(c) Find the cumulative death distribution function, $C(t)$. Give your answer in terms of k.

---

[6]Adapted from *Statistics*, by Freedman, Pisani, Purves, and Adikhari (New York: Norton, 1991).

Strengthen Your Understanding

In Problems 25–31, explain what is wrong with the statement.

25. If $p(x)$ is a probability density function with $p(1) = 0.02$, then the probability that x takes the value 1 is 0.02.

26. If $P(x)$ is a cumulative distribution function with $P(5) = 0.4$, then the probability that $x = 5$ is 0.4.

27. The function $p(t) = t^2$ is a density function.

28. The function $p(x) = x^2 e^x$ is a density function.

29. The function $P(x) = x^2 e^x$ is a cumulative distribution function.

30. The function $P(t) = e^{-t^2}$ is a cumulative distribution function.

31. A probability density function is always increasing.

In Problems 32–35, give an example of:

32. A density function that is greater than zero on $0 \leq x \leq 20$ and zero everywhere else.

33. A cumulative distribution function that is piecewise linear.

34. A probability density function which is nonzero only between $x = 2$ and $x = 7$.

35. A cumulative distribution function with $P(3) = 0$ and $P(7) = 1$.

In Problems 36–37, are the statements true or false? Give an explanation for your answer.

36. If $p(x) = xe^{-x^2}$ for all x, then $p(x)$ is a probability density function.

37. If $p(x) = xe^{-x^2}$ for all $x > 0$ and $p(x) = 0$ for $x \leq 0$, then $p(x)$ is a probability density function.

8.8 PROBABILITY, MEAN, AND MEDIAN

Probability

Suppose we pick a member of the US population at random and ask what is the probability that the person is between, say, the ages of 70 and 80. We saw in Table 8.5 on page 468 that $5\% = 0.05$ of the population is in this age group. We say that the probability, or chance, that the person is between 70 and 80 is 0.05. Using any age density function $p(t)$, we can define probabilities as follows:

$$\begin{array}{l} \text{Probability that a person is} \\ \text{between ages } a \text{ and } b \end{array} = \begin{array}{l} \text{Fraction of population} \\ \text{between ages } a \text{ and } b \end{array} = \int_a^b p(t)\, dt.$$

Since the cumulative distribution function gives the fraction of the population younger than age t, the cumulative distribution can also be used to calculate the probability that a randomly selected person is in a given age group.

$$\begin{array}{l} \text{Probability that a person is} \\ \text{younger than age } t \end{array} = \begin{array}{l} \text{Fraction of population} \\ \text{younger than age } t \end{array} = P(t) = \int_0^t p(x)\, dx.$$

In the next example, both a density function and a cumulative distribution function are used to describe the same situation.

Example 1   Suppose you want to analyze the fishing industry in a small town. Each day, the boats bring back at least 2 tons of fish, and never more than 8 tons.

(a) Using the density function describing the daily catch in Figure 8.99, find and graph the corresponding cumulative distribution function and explain its meaning.

(b) What is the probability that the catch will be between 5 and 7 tons?

Figure 8.99: Density function of daily catch

Solution   (a) The cumulative distribution function $P(t)$ is equal to the fraction of days on which the catch is less than t tons of fish. Since the catch is never less than 2 tons, we have $P(t) = 0$ for $t \leq 2$. Since the catch is always less than 8 tons, we have $P(t) = 1$ for $t \geq 8$. For t in the range $2 < t < 8$, we must evaluate the integral

$$P(t) = \int_{-\infty}^{t} p(x)dx = \int_{2}^{t} p(x)dx.$$

This integral equals the area under the graph of $p(x)$ between $x = 2$ and $x = t$. It can be calculated by noting that $p(x)$ is given by the formula

$$p(x) = \begin{cases} 0.04x & \text{for } 2 \leq x \leq 6 \\ -0.06x + 0.6 & \text{for } 6 < x \leq 8 \end{cases}$$

and $p(x) = 0$ for $x < 2$ or $x > 8$. Thus, for $2 \leq t \leq 6$,

$$P(t) = \int_{2}^{t} 0.04x \, dx = 0.04 \frac{x^2}{2} \Big|_{2}^{t} = 0.02t^2 - 0.08.$$

And for $6 \leq t \leq 8$,

$$P(t) = \int_{2}^{t} p(x) \, dx = \int_{2}^{6} p(x) \, dx + \int_{6}^{t} p(x) \, dx$$

$$= 0.64 + \int_{6}^{t} (-0.06x + 0.6) \, dx = 0.64 + \left(-0.06 \frac{x^2}{2} + 0.6x \right) \Big|_{6}^{t}$$

$$= -0.03t^2 + 0.6t - 1.88.$$

Thus

$$P(t) = \begin{cases} 0.02t^2 - 0.08 & \text{for } 2 \leq t \leq 6 \\ -0.03t^2 + 0.6t - 1.88 & \text{for } 6 < t \leq 8. \end{cases}$$

In addition $P(t) = 0$ for $t < 2$ and $P(t) = 1$ for $8 < t$. (See Figure 8.100.)

Figure 8.100: Cumulative distribution of daily catch

Figure 8.101: Shaded area represents the probability that the catch is between 5 and 7 tons

(b) The probability that the catch is between 5 and 7 tons can be found using either the density function, p, or the cumulative distribution function, P. If we use the density function, this probability can be represented by the shaded area in Figure 8.101, which is about 0.43:

$$\text{Probability catch is between 5 and 7 tons} = \int_5^7 p(x)\,dx = 0.43.$$

The probability can be found from the cumulative distribution as follows:

$$\text{Probability catch is between 5 and 7 tons} = P(7) - P(5) = 0.85 - 0.42 = 0.43.$$

The Median and Mean

It is often useful to be able to give an "average" value for a distribution. Two measures that are in common use are the *median* and the *mean*.

The Median

A **median** of a quantity x distributed through a population is a value T such that half the population has values of x less than (or equal to) T, and half the population has values of x greater than (or equal to) T. Thus, a median T satisfies

$$\int_{-\infty}^{T} p(x)\,dx = 0.5,$$

where p is the density function. In other words, half the area under the graph of p lies to the left of T.

Example 2 Find the median age in the US in 1995, using the age density function given by

$$p(t) = \begin{cases} 0.015 & \text{for } 0 \le t \le 40 \\ 0.0262 - 0.00028t & \text{for } 40 < t \le 93.3. \end{cases}$$

Solution We want to find the value of T such that

$$\int_{-\infty}^{T} p(t)\,dt = \int_0^T p(t)\,dt = 0.5.$$

Since $p(t) = 0.015$ up to age 40, we have

$$\text{Median} = T = \frac{0.5}{0.015} \approx 33 \text{ years.}$$

(See Figure 8.102.)

Figure 8.102: Median of age distribution

Figure 8.103: Shaded area is percentage of population with age between t and $t + \Delta t$

The Mean

Another commonly used average value is the *mean*. To find the mean of N numbers, you add the numbers and divide the sum by N. For example, the mean of the numbers 1, 2, 7, and 10 is $(1 + 2 + 7 + 10)/4 = 5$. The mean age of the entire US population is therefore defined as

$$\text{Mean age} = \frac{\sum \text{Ages of all people in the US}}{\text{Total number of people in the US}}.$$

Calculating the sum of all the ages directly would be an enormous task; we will approximate the sum by an integral. The idea is to "slice up" the age axis and consider the people whose age is between t and $t + \Delta t$. How many are there?

The fraction of the population between t and $t + \Delta t$ is the area under the graph of p between these points, which is well approximated by the area of the rectangle, $p(t)\Delta t$. (See Figure 8.103.) If the total number of people in the population is N, then

$$\text{Number of people with age between } t \text{ and } t + \Delta t \approx p(t)\Delta t N.$$

The age of all of these people is approximately t:

$$\text{Sum of ages of people between age } t \text{ and } t + \Delta t \approx tp(t)\Delta t N.$$

Therefore, adding and factoring out an N gives us

$$\text{Sum of ages of all people} \approx \left(\sum tp(t)\Delta t \right) N.$$

In the limit, as we allow Δt to shrink to 0, the sum becomes an integral, so

$$\text{Sum of ages of all people} = \left(\int_0^{100} tp(t)dt \right) N.$$

Therefore, with N equal to the total number of people in the US, and assuming no person is over 100 years old,

$$\text{Mean age} = \frac{\text{Sum of ages of all people in US}}{N} = \int_0^{100} tp(t)dt.$$

We can give the same argument for any[7] density function $p(x)$.

---

[7]Provided all the relevant improper integrals converge.

If a quantity has density function $p(x)$,

$$\textbf{Mean value} \text{ of the quantity} = \int_{-\infty}^{\infty} xp(x)\,dx.$$

It can be shown that the mean is the point on the horizontal axis where the region under the graph of the density function, if it were made out of cardboard, would balance.

Example 3 Find the mean age of the US population, using the density function of Example 2.

Solution The formula for p is

$$p(t) = \begin{cases} 0 & \text{for } t < 0 \\ 0.015 & \text{for } 0 \le t \le 40 \\ 0.0262 - 0.00028t & \text{for } 40 < t \le 93.3 \\ 0 & \text{for } t > 93.3. \end{cases}$$

Using these formulas, we compute

$$\text{Mean age} = \int_0^{100} tp(t)dt = \int_0^{40} t(0.015)dt + \int_{40}^{93.3} t(0.0262 - 0.00028t)dt$$

$$= 0.015\frac{t^2}{2}\Big|_0^{40} + 0.0262\frac{t^2}{2}\Big|_{40}^{93.3} - 0.00028\frac{t^3}{3}\Big|_{40}^{93.3} \approx 35 \text{ years.}$$

The mean is shown is Figure 8.104.

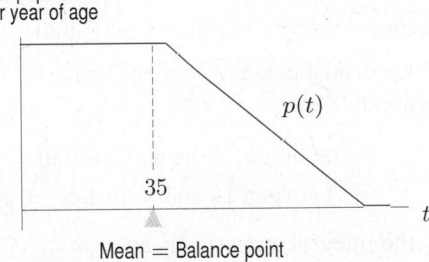

fraction of population
per year of age

35

Mean = Balance point

Figure 8.104: Mean of age distribution

Normal Distributions

How much rain do you expect to fall in your home town this year? If you live in Anchorage, Alaska, the answer is something close to 15 inches (including the snow). Of course, you don't expect exactly 15 inches. Some years have more than 15 inches, and some years have less. Most years, however, the amount of rainfall is close to 15 inches; only rarely is it well above or well below 15 inches. What does the density function for the rainfall look like? To answer this question, we look at rainfall data over many years. Records show that the distribution of rainfall is well-approximated by a *normal distribution*. The graph of its density function is a bell-shaped curve which peaks at 15 inches and slopes downward approximately symmetrically on either side.

Normal distributions are frequently used to model real phenomena, from grades on an exam to the number of airline passengers on a particular flight. A normal distribution is characterized by its *mean*, μ, and its *standard deviation*, σ. The mean tells us the location of the central peak. The standard deviation tells us how closely the data is clustered around the mean. A small value of σ tells us that the data is close to the mean; a large σ tells us the data is spread out. In the following formula for a normal distribution, the factor of $1/(\sigma\sqrt{2\pi})$ makes the area under the graph equal to 1.

A **normal distribution** has a density function of the form

$$p(x) = \frac{1}{\sigma\sqrt{2\pi}}e^{-(x-\mu)^2/(2\sigma^2)},$$

where μ is the mean of the distribution and σ is the standard deviation, with $\sigma > 0$.

To model the rainfall in Anchorage, we use a normal distribution with $\mu = 15$ and $\sigma = 1$. (See Figure 8.105.)

$\left(15, \frac{1}{\sqrt{2\pi}}\right)$ $p(x) = \frac{1}{\sqrt{2\pi}}e^{-(x-15)^2/2}$

Figure 8.105: Normal distribution with $\mu = 15$ and $\sigma = 1$

Example 4   For Anchorage's rainfall, use the normal distribution with the density function with $\mu = 15$ and $\sigma = 1$ to compute the fraction of the years with rainfall between
(a)   14 and 16 inches,   (b)   13 and 17 inches,   (c)   12 and 18 inches.

Solution   (a) The fraction of the years with annual rainfall between 14 and 16 inches is $\int_{14}^{16}\frac{1}{\sqrt{2\pi}}e^{-(x-15)^2/2}\,dx$.
Since there is no elementary antiderivative for $e^{-(x-15)^2/2}$, we find the integral numerically. Its value is about 0.68.

$$\begin{array}{c}\text{Fraction of years with rainfall}\\\text{between 14 and 16 inches}\end{array} = \int_{14}^{16}\frac{1}{\sqrt{2\pi}}e^{-(x-15)^2/2}\,dx \approx 0.68.$$

(b) Finding the integral numerically again:

$$\begin{array}{c}\text{Fraction of years with rainfall}\\\text{between 13 and 17 inches}\end{array} = \int_{13}^{17}\frac{1}{\sqrt{2\pi}}e^{-(x-15)^2/2}\,dx \approx 0.95.$$

(c)

$$\begin{array}{c}\text{Fraction of years with rainfall}\\\text{between 12 and 18 inches}\end{array} = \int_{12}^{18}\frac{1}{\sqrt{2\pi}}e^{-(x-15)^2/2}\,dx \approx 0.997.$$

Since 0.95 is so close to 1, we expect that most of the time the rainfall will be between 13 and 17 inches a year.

Among the normal distributions, the one having $\mu = 0$, $\sigma = 1$ is called the *standard normal distribution*. Values of the corresponding cumulative distribution function are published in tables.

Exercises and Problems for Section 8.8

Exercises

1. Show that the area under the fishing density function in Figure 8.99 on page 474 is 1. Why is this to be expected?

2. Find the mean daily catch for the fishing data in Figure 8.99, page 474.

3. **(a)** Using a calculator or computer, sketch graphs of the density function of the normal distribution

$$p(x) = \frac{1}{\sigma\sqrt{2\pi}}e^{-(x-\mu)^2/(2\sigma^2)}.$$

    (i) For fixed μ (say, $\mu = 5$) and varying σ (say, $\sigma = 1, 2, 3$).

    (ii) For varying μ (say, $\mu = 4, 5, 6$) and fixed σ (say, $\sigma = 1$).

  (b) Explain how the graphs confirm that μ is the mean of the distribution and that σ is a measure of how closely the data is clustered around the mean.

Problems

4. A quantity x is distributed with density function $p(x) = 0.5(2 - x)$ for $0 \leq x \leq 2$ and $p(x) = 0$ otherwise. Find the mean and median of x.

5. A quantity x has cumulative distribution function $P(x) = x - x^2/4$ for $0 \leq x \leq 2$ and $P(x) = 0$ for $x < 0$ and $P(x) = 1$ for $x > 2$. Find the mean and median of x.

6. The probability of a transistor failing between $t = a$ months and $t = b$ months is given by $c\int_a^b e^{-ct}dt$, for some constant c.

  (a) If the probability of failure within the first six months is 10%, what is c?

  (b) Given the value of c in part (a), what is the probability the transistor fails within the second six months?

7. Suppose that x measures the time (in hours) it takes for a student to complete an exam. All students are done within two hours and the density function for x is

$$p(x) = \begin{cases} x^3/4 & \text{if } 0 < x < 2 \\ 0 & \text{otherwise.} \end{cases}$$

  (a) What proportion of students take between 1.5 and 2.0 hours to finish the exam?

  (b) What is the mean time for students to complete the exam?

  (c) Compute the median of this distribution.

8. In 1950 an experiment was done observing the time gaps between successive cars on the Arroyo Seco Freeway.[8] The data show that the density function of these time gaps was given approximately by

$$p(x) = ae^{-0.122x}$$

where x is the time in seconds and a is a constant.

  (a) Find a.

  (b) Find P, the cumulative distribution function.

  (c) Find the median and mean time gap.

  (d) Sketch rough graphs of p and P.

9. Consider a group of people who have received treatment for a disease such as cancer. Let t be the *survival time*, the number of years a person lives after receiving treatment. The density function giving the distribution of t is $p(t) = Ce^{-Ct}$ for some positive constant C.

  (a) What is the practical meaning for the cumulative distribution function $P(t) = \int_0^t p(x)\, dx$?

  (b) The survival function, $S(t)$, is the probability that a randomly selected person survives for at least t years. Find $S(t)$.

  (c) Suppose a patient has a 70% probability of surviving at least two years. Find C.

10. While taking a walk along the road where you live, you accidentally drop your glove, but you don't know where. The probability density $p(x)$ for having dropped the glove x kilometers from home (along the road) is

$$p(x) = 2e^{-2x} \quad \text{for } x \geq 0.$$

  (a) What is the probability that you dropped it within 1 kilometer of home?

  (b) At what distance y from home is the probability that you dropped it within y km of home equal to 0.95?

11. The distribution of IQ scores can be modeled by a normal distribution with mean 100 and standard deviation 15.

  (a) Write the formula for the density function of IQ scores.

  (b) Estimate the fraction of the population with IQ between 115 and 120.

12. The speeds of cars on a road are approximately normally distributed with a mean $\mu = 58$ km/hr and standard deviation $\sigma = 4$ km/hr.

  (a) What is the probability that a randomly selected car is going between 60 and 65 km/hr?

  (b) What fraction of all cars are going slower than 52 km/hr?

13. Consider the normal distribution, $p(x)$.

  (a) Show that $p(x)$ is a maximum when $x = \mu$. What is that maximum value?

  (b) Show that $p(x)$ has points of inflection where $x = \mu + \sigma$ and $x = \mu - \sigma$.

  (c) Describe in your own words what μ and σ tell you about the distribution.

14. For a normal population of mean 0, show that the fraction of the population within one standard deviation of the mean does not depend on the standard deviation.

[Hint: Use the substitution $w = x/\sigma$.]

---

[8]Reported by Daniel Furlough and Frank Barnes.

15. Which of the following functions makes the most sense as a model for the probability density representing the time (in minutes, starting from $t = 0$) that the next customer walks into a store?

(a) $p(t) = \begin{cases} \cos t & 0 \le t \le 2\pi \\ e^{t-2\pi} & t \ge 2\pi \end{cases}$

(b) $p(t) = 3e^{-3t}$ for $t \ge 0$

(c) $p(t) = e^{-3t}$ for $t \ge 0$

(d) $p(t) = 1/4$ for $0 \le t \le 4$

16. Let $P(x)$ be the cumulative distribution function for the household income distribution in the US in 2009.[9] Values of $P(x)$ are in the following table:

Income x (thousand \$)	20	40	60	75	100
$P(x)$ (%)	29.5	50.1	66.8	76.2	87.1

(a) What percent of the households made between \$40,000 and \$60,000? More than \$100,000?

(b) Approximately what was the median income?

(c) Is the statement "More than one-third of households made between \$40,000 and \$75,000" true or false?

17. If we think of an electron as a particle, the function

$$P(r) = 1 - (2r^2 + 2r + 1)e^{-2r}$$

is the cumulative distribution function of the distance, r, of the electron in a hydrogen atom from the center of the atom. The distance is measured in Bohr radii. (1 Bohr radius = 5.29×10^{-11} m. Niels Bohr (1885–1962) was a Danish physicist.)

For example, $P(1) = 1 - 5e^{-2} \approx 0.32$ means that the electron is within 1 Bohr radius from the center of the atom 32% of the time.

(a) Find a formula for the density function of this distribution. Sketch the density function and the cumulative distribution function.

(b) Find the median distance and the mean distance. Near what value of r is an electron most likely to be found?

(c) The Bohr radius is sometimes called the "radius of the hydrogen atom." Why?

Strengthen Your Understanding

In Problems 18–19, explain what is wrong with the statement.

18. A median T of a quantity distributed through a population satisfies $p(T) = 0.5$ where p is the density function.

19. The following density function has median 1:

$$p(x) = \begin{cases} 0 & \text{for } x < 0 \\ 2(1-x) & \text{for } 0 \le x \le 1 \\ 0 & \text{for } x > 1. \end{cases}$$

In Problems 20–21, give an example of:

20. A distribution with a mean of $1/2$ and standard deviation $1/2$.

21. A distribution with a mean of $1/2$ and median $1/2$.

In Problems 22–26, a quantity x is distributed through a population with probability density function $p(x)$ and cumulative distribution function $P(x)$. Decide if each statement is true or false. Give an explanation for your answer.

22. If $p(10) = 1/2$, then half the population has $x < 10$.

23. If $P(10) = 1/2$, then half the population has $x < 10$.

24. If $p(10) = 1/2$, then the fraction of the population lying between $x = 9.98$ and $x = 10.04$ is about 0.03.

25. If $p(10) = p(20)$, then none of the population has x values lying between 10 and 20.

26. If $P(10) = P(20)$, then none of the population has x values lying between 10 and 20.

CHAPTER SUMMARY (see also Ready Reference at the end of the book)

- **Geometry**
  Area, volume, arc length.

- **Density**
  Finding total quantity from density, center of mass.

- **Physics**
  Work, force and pressure.

- **Economics**

  Present and future value of income stream, consumer and producer surplus.

- **Probability**
  Density function, cumulative distribution function, mean, median, normal distribution.

- **Polar coordinates**
  Area, slope, arc length.

---

[9]http://www.census.gov/hhes/www/income/income.html, accessed on January 7, 2012.

REVIEW EXERCISES AND PROBLEMS FOR CHAPTER EIGHT

Exercises

1. Imagine a hard-boiled egg lying on its side cut into thin slices. First think about vertical slices and then horizontal ones. What would these slices look like? Sketch them.

For each region in Exercises 2–4, write a definite integral which represents its area. Evaluate the integral to derive a formula for the area.

2. A rectangle with base b and height h:

3. A circle of radius r:

4. A right triangle of base b and height h:

In Exercises 5–9, the region is rotated about the x-axis. Find the volume

5. Bounded by $y = x^2 + 1$, the x-axis, $x = 0$, $x = 4$.

6. Bounded by $y = \sqrt{x}$, x-axis, $x = 1$, $x = 2$.

7. Bounded by $y = e^{-2x}$, the x-axis, $x = 0$, $x = 1$.

8. Bounded by $y = 4 - x^2$ and the x-axis.

9. Bounded by $y = 2x$, $y = x$, $x = 0$, $x = 3$.

Exercises 10–15 refer to the regions marked in Figure 8.106. Set up, but do not evaluate, an integral that represents the volume obtained when the region is rotated about the given axis.

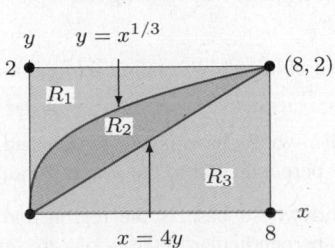

Figure 8.106

10. R_2 about the x-axis

11. R_1 about the y-axis

12. R_1 about the line $y = -2$

13. R_3 about the line $x = 10$

14. R_3 about the line $y = 3$

15. R_2 about the line $x = -3$

16. Find the volume of the region in Figure 8.107, given that the radius, r of the circular slice at h is $r = \sqrt{h}$.

Figure 8.107

17. Find, by slicing, the volume of a cone whose height is 3 cm and whose base radius is 1 cm. Slice the cone as shown in Figure 8.6 on page 416.

18. (a) Set up and evaluate an integral giving the volume of a pyramid of height 10 m and square base 8 m by 8 m.

    (b) The pyramid in part (a) is cut off at a height of 6 m. See Figure 8.108. Find the volume.

Figure 8.108

19. The exterior of a holding tank is a cylinder with radius 3 m and height 6 m; the interior is cone-shaped; Figure 8.109 shows its cross-section. Using an integral, find the volume of material needed to make the tank.

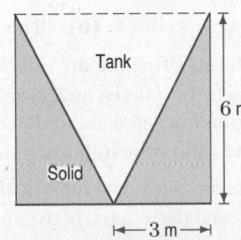

Figure 8.109

For the curves described in Exercises 20–21, write the integral that gives the exact length of the curve; do not evaluate it.

20. One arch of the sine curve, from $x = 0$ to $x = \pi$.

21. The ellipse with equation $(x^2/a^2) + (y^2/b^2) = 1$.

In Exercises 22–23, find the arc length of the function from $x = 0$ to $x = 3$. Use a graph to explain why your answer is reasonable.

22. $f(x) = \sin x$

23. $f(x) = 5x^2$

For Exercises 24–26, find the arc lengths.

24. $f(x) = \sqrt{1 - x^2}$ from $x = 0$ to $x = 1$

25. $f(x) = e^x$ from $x = 1$ to $x = 2$

26. $f(x) = \dfrac{1}{3}x^3 + \dfrac{1}{4x}$ from $x = 1$ to $x = 2$.

In Exercises 27–28, find the length of the parametric curves. Give exact answers if possible.

27. $x = 3 \cos t$, $y = 2 \sin t$, for $0 \le t \le 2\pi$.

28. $x = 1 + \cos(2t)$, $y = 3 + \sin(2t)$, for $0 \le t \le \pi$.

In Exercises 29–33, let $f(x) = x^p$, for $x \ge 0$ and $p > 1$. Note that $f(0) = 0$, $f(1) = 1$, and f is increasing with a concave-up graph. Use geometrical arguments to order the given quantities.

29. $\displaystyle\int_0^1 f(x)\, dx$ and $\dfrac{1}{2}$

30. $\displaystyle\int_0^{0.5} f'(x)\, dx$ and $\dfrac{1}{2}$

31. $\displaystyle\int_0^1 f^{-1}(x)\, dx$ and $\dfrac{1}{2}$

32. $\displaystyle\int_0^1 \pi\, (f(x))^2\, dx$ and $\dfrac{\pi}{3}$

33. $\displaystyle\int_0^1 \sqrt{1 + (f'(x))^2}\, dx$ and $\sqrt{2}$

Problems

34. (a) Find the area of the region between $y = x^2$ and $y = 2x$.
   (b) Find the volume of the solid of revolution if this region is rotated about the x-axis.
   (c) Find the length of the perimeter of this region.

35. The integral $\displaystyle\int_0^2 \left(\sqrt{4 - x^2} - (-\sqrt{4 - x^2})\right) dx$ represents the area of a region in the plane. Sketch this region.

In Problems 36–37, set up definite integral(s) to find the volume obtained when the region between $y = x^2$ and $y = 5x$ is rotated about the given axis. Do not evaluate the integral(s).

36. The line $y = 30$ **37.** The line $x = 8$

38. (a) Sketch the solid obtained by rotating the region bounded by $y = \sqrt{x}$, $x = 1$, and $y = 0$ around the line $y = 0$.
   (b) Approximate its volume by Riemann sums, showing the volume represented by each term in your sum on the sketch.
   (c) Now find the volume of this solid using an integral.

39. Using the region of Problem 38, find the volume when it is rotated around
   (a) The line $y = 1$.   (b) The y-axis.

40. (a) Find (in terms of a) the area of the region bounded by $y = ax^2$, the x-axis, and $x = 2$. Assume $a > 0$.
   (b) If this region is rotated about the x-axis, find the volume of the solid of revolution in terms of a.

41. (a) Find (in terms of b) the area of the region between $y = e^{-bx}$ and the x-axis, between $x = 0$ and $x = 1$. Assume $b > 0$.
   (b) If this region is rotated about the x-axis, find the volume of the solid of revolution in terms of b.

For Problems 42–44, set up and compute an integral giving the volume of the solid of revolution.

42. Bounded by $y = \sin x$, $y = 0.5x$, $x = 0$, $x = 1.9$;
   (a) Rotated about the x-axis.
   (b) Rotated about $y = 5$.

43. Bounded by $y = 2x$, the x-axis, $x = 0$, $x = 4$. Axis: $y = -5$.

44. Bounded by $y = x^2$, the x-axis, $x = 0$, $x = 3$;
   (a) Rotated about $y = -2$.
   (b) Rotated about $y = 10$.

Problems 45–50 concern the region bounded by the quarter circle $x^2 + y^2 = 1$, with $x \ge 0$, $y \ge 0$. Find the volume of the following solids.

45. The solid obtained by rotating the region about the x-axis.

46. The solid obtained by rotating the region about the line $x = -2$.

47. The solid obtained by rotating the region about the line $x = 1$.

48. The solid whose base is the region and whose cross-sections perpendicular to the x-axis are squares.

49. The solid whose base is the region and whose cross-sections perpendicular to the y-axis are semicircles.

50. The solid whose base is the region and whose cross-section perpendicular to the y-axis is an isosceles right triangle with one leg in the region.

In Problems 51–52, what does the expression represent geometrically in terms of the function $f(x) = x(x-3)^2$? Do not evaluate the expressions.

51. $\displaystyle\int_0^3 x(x-3)^2\, dx$

52. $\displaystyle\int_0^3 \pi x^2(x-3)^4\, dx$

53. The catenary $\cosh x = \frac{1}{2}(e^x + e^{-x})$ represents the shape of a hanging cable. Find the exact length of this catenary between $x = -1$ and $x = 1$.

54. The reflector behind a car headlight is made in the shape of the parabola $x = \frac{4}{9}y^2$, with a circular cross-section, as shown in Figure 8.110.

    (a) Find a Riemann sum approximating the volume contained by this headlight.

    (b) Find the volume exactly.

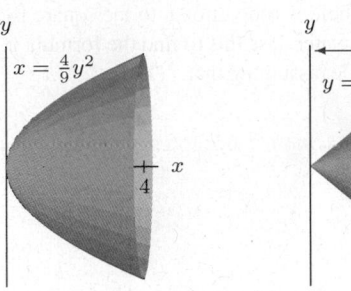

Figure 8.110   Figure 8.111

55. In this problem, you will derive the formula for the volume of a right circular cone with height l and base radius b by rotating the line $y = ax$ from $x = 0$ to $x = l$ around the x-axis. See Figure 8.111.

    (a) What value should you choose for a such that the cone will have height l and base radius b?

    (b) Given this value of a, find the volume of the cone.

56. Figure 8.112 shows a cross section through an apple. (Scale: One division = 1/2 inch.)

    (a) Give a rough estimate for the volume of this apple (in cubic inches).

    (b) The density of these apples is about 0.03 lb/in^3 (a little less than the density of water—as you might expect, since apples float). Estimate how much this apple would cost. (They go for 80 cents a pound.)

Figure 8.112

57. The circle $x^2 + y^2 = 1$ is rotated about the line $y = 3$ forming a torus (a doughnut-shaped figure). Find the volume of this torus.

58. Find a curve whose arc length is $\displaystyle\int_3^8 \sqrt{1 + e^{6t}}\, dt$.

59. Water is flowing in a cylindrical pipe of radius 1 inch. Because water is viscous and sticks to the pipe, the rate of flow varies with the distance from the center. The speed of the water at a distance r inches from the center is $10(1 - r^2)$ inches per second. What is the rate (in cubic inches per second) at which water is flowing through the pipe?

Problems 60–64 concern C, the circle $r = 2a\cos\theta$, for $-\pi/2 \le \theta \le \pi/2$, of radius $a > 0$ centered at the point $(x, y) = (a, 0)$ on the x-axis.

60. By converting to Cartesian coordinates, show that $r = 2a\cos\theta$ gives the circle described.

61. Find the area of the circle C by integrating in polar coordinates.

62. Find the area of the region enclosed by C and outside the circle of radius a centered at the origin. What percent is this of the area of C?

63. **(a)** Find the slope of C at the angle θ.
    (b) At what value of θ does the maximum y-value occur?

64. Calculate the arc length of C using polar coordinates.

65. Write a definite integral for the volume of the bounded region formed by rotating the graph of $y = (x-1)^2(x+2)$ around the x-axis. You need not evaluate this integral.

66. Find the center of mass of a system containing four identical point masses of 3 gm, located at $x = -5, -3, 2, 7$.

67. A metal plate, with constant density 2 gm/cm^2, has a shape bounded by the two curves $y = x^2$ and $y = \sqrt{x}$, with $0 \le x \le 1$, and x, y in cm.

    (a) Find the total mass of the plate.

    (b) Because of the symmetry of the plate about the line $y = x$, we have $\bar{x} = \bar{y}$. Sketch the plate and decide, on the basis of the shape, whether $\bar{x}$ is less than or greater than 1/2.

    (c) Find $\bar{x}$ and $\bar{y}$.

68. A 200-lb weight is attached to a 20-foot rope and dangling from the roof of a building. The rope weighs 2 lb/ft. Find the work done in lifting the weight to the roof.

69. A 10 ft pole weighing 20 lbs lies flat on the ground. Keeping one end of the pole braced on the ground, the other end is lifted until the pole stands vertically. Once the pole is upright, the segment of length Δx at height x has been raised a vertical distance of x ft. How much work is done to raise the pole vertically?

70. Water is raised from a well 40 ft deep by a bucket attached to a rope. When the bucket is full, it weighs 30 lb. However, a leak in the bucket causes it to lose water at a rate of 1/4 lb for each foot that the bucket is raised. Neglecting the weight of the rope, find the work done in raising the bucket to the top.

71. A rectangular water tank has length 20 ft, width 10 ft, and depth 15 ft. If the tank is full, how much work does it take to pump all the water out?

72. A fuel oil tank is an upright cylinder, buried so that its circular top is 10 feet beneath ground level. The tank has a radius of 5 feet and is 15 feet high, although the current oil level is only 6 feet deep. Calculate the work required to pump all of the oil to the surface. Oil weighs 50 lb/ft^3.

73. An underground tank filled with gasoline of density 42 lb/ft^3 is a hemisphere of radius 5 ft, as in Figure 8.113. Use an integral to find the work to pump the gasoline over the top of the tank.

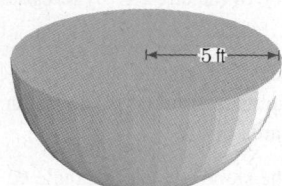

Figure 8.113

74. The dam in Hannawa Falls, NY, on the Raquette River is approximately 60 feet across and 25 feet high. Find the water force on the dam.

75. A crane lifts a 1000 lb object to a height of 20 ft using chain that weighs 2 lb/ft. If the crane arm is at a height of 50 ft, find the work required.

76. Find the present and future values of an income stream of $3000 per year over a 15-year period, assuming a 6% annual interest rate compounded continuously.

77. A nuclear power plant produces strontium-90 at a rate of 3 kg/yr. How much of the strontium produced since 1971 (when the plant opened) was still around in 1992? (The half-life of strontium-90 is 28 years.)

78. Mt. Shasta is a cone-like volcano whose radius at an elevation of h feet above sea level is approximately $(3.5 \cdot 10^5)/\sqrt{h + 600}$ feet. Its bottom is 400 feet above sea level, and its top is 14,400 feet above sea level. See Figure 8.114. (Note: Mt. Shasta is in northern California, and for some time was thought to be the highest point in the US outside Alaska.)

(a) Give a Riemann sum approximating the volume of Mt. Shasta.

(b) Find the volume in cubic feet.

Figure 8.114: Mt. Shasta

79. Figure 8.115 shows an ancient Greek water clock called a clepsydra, which is designed so that the depth of the water decreases at a constant rate as the water runs out a hole in the bottom. This design allows the hours to be marked by a uniform scale. The tank of the clepsydra is a volume of revolution about a vertical axis. According to Torricelli's law, the exit speed of the water flowing through the hole is proportional to the square root of the depth of the water. Use this to find the formula $y = f(x)$ for this profile, assuming that $f(1) = 1$.

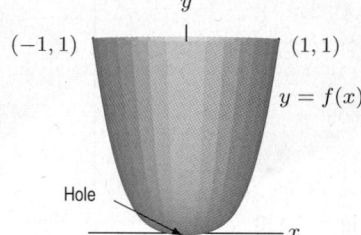

Figure 8.115

80. Suppose that $P(t)$ is the cumulative distribution function for age in the US, where x is measured in years. What is the meaning of the statement $P(70) = 0.76$?

81. Figure 8.116 shows the distribution of the velocity of molecules in two gases. In which gas is the average velocity larger?

Figure 8.116

82. A radiation detector is a circular disk which registers photons hitting it. The probability that a photon hitting the disk at a distance r from the center is actually detected is given by $S(r)$. A radiation detector of radius R is bombarded by constant radiation of N photons per second per unit area. Write an integral representing the number of photons per second registered by the detector.

83. Housing prices depend on the distance in miles r from a city center according to

$$p(r) = 400e^{-0.2r^2}, \quad \text{price in \$1000s.}$$

Assuming 1000 houses per square mile, what is the total value of the houses within 7 miles of the city center?

84. A blood vessel is cylindrical with radius R and length l. The blood near the boundary moves slowly; blood at the center moves the fastest. The velocity, v, of the blood at a distance r from the center of the artery is given by

$$v = \frac{P}{4\eta l}(R^2 - r^2)$$

where P is the pressure difference between the ends of the blood vessel and η is the viscosity of blood.

(a) Find the rate at which the blood is flowing down the blood vessel. (Give your answer as a volume per unit time.)

(b) Show that your result agrees with Poiseuille's Law, which says that the rate at which blood is flowing down the blood vessel is proportional to the radius of the blood vessel to the fourth power.

85. A car moving at a speed of v mph achieves $25 + 0.1v$ mpg (miles per gallon) for v between 20 and 60 mph. Your speed as a function of time, t, in hours, is given by

$$v = 50\frac{t}{t+1} \text{ mph.}$$

How many gallons of gas do you consume between $t = 2$ and $t = 3$?

86. A bowl is made by rotating the curve $y = ax^2$ around the y-axis (a is a constant).

(a) The bowl is filled with water to depth h. What is the volume of water in the bowl? (Your answer will contain a and h.)

(b) What is the area of the surface of the water if the bowl is filled to depth h? (Your answer will contain a and h.)

(c) Water is evaporating from the surface of the bowl at a rate proportional to the surface area, with proportionality constant k. Find a differential equation satisfied by h as a function of time, t. (That is, find an equation for dh/dt.)

(d) If the water starts at depth h_0, find the time taken for all the water to evaporate.

87. A cylindrical centrifuge of radius 1 m and height 2 m is filled with water to a depth of 1 meter (see Figure 8.117(I)). As the centrifuge accelerates, the water level rises along the wall and drops in the center; the cross-section will be a parabola. (See Figure 8.117(II).)

(a) Find the equation of the parabola in Figure 8.117(II) in terms of h, the depth of the water at its lowest point.

(b) As the centrifuge rotates faster and faster, either water will be spilled out the top, as in Figure 8.117(III), or the bottom of the centrifuge will be exposed, as in Figure 8.117(IV). Which happens first?

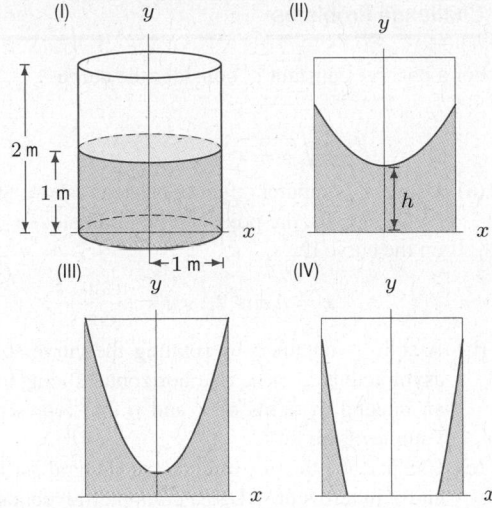

Figure 8.117

In Problems 88–89, you are given two objects that have the same mass M, the same radius R, and the same angular velocity about the indicated axes (say, one revolution per minute). Use reasoning (not computation) to determine which of the two objects has the greater kinetic energy. (The kinetic energy of a particle of mass m with speed v is $\frac{1}{2}mv^2$.)

88.

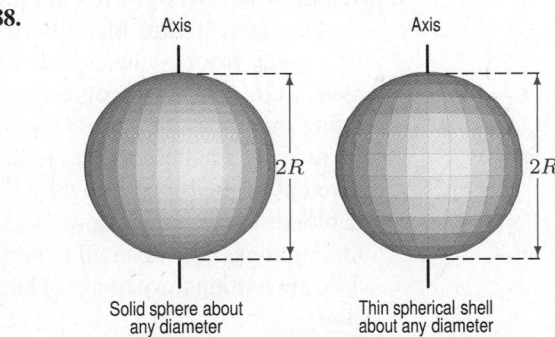

Solid sphere about any diameter

Thin spherical shell about any diameter

89.

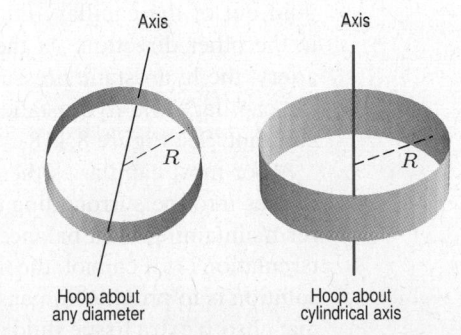

Hoop about any diameter

Hoop about cylindrical axis

CAS Challenge Problems

90. For a positive constant a, consider the curve

$$y = \sqrt{\frac{x^3}{a - x}}, \qquad 0 \le x < a.$$

(a) Using a computer algebra system, show that for $0 \le t < \pi/2$, the point with coordinates (x, y) lies on the curve if:

$$x = a \sin^2 t, \quad y = \frac{a \sin^3 t}{\cos t}.$$

(b) A solid is obtained by rotating the curve about its asymptote at $x = a$. Use horizontal slicing to write an integral in terms of x and y that represents the volume of this solid.

(c) Use part (a) to substitute in the integral for both x and y in terms of t. Use a computer algebra system or trigonometric identities to calculate the volume of the solid.

For Problems 91–92, define $A(t)$ to be the arc length of the graph of $y = f(x)$ from $x = 0$ to $x = t$, for $t \ge 0$.

(a) Use the integral expression for arc length and a computer algebra system to obtain a formula for $A(t)$.

(b) Graph $A(t)$ for $0 \le t \le 10$. What simple function does $A(t)$ look like? What does this tell you about the approximate value of $A(t)$ for large t?

(c) In order to estimate arc length visually, you need the same scales on both axes, so that the lengths are not distorted in one direction. Draw a graph of $f(x)$ with viewing window $0 \le x \le 100$, $0 \le y \le 100$. Explain what you noticed in part (b) in terms of this graph.

91. $f(x) = x^2$

92. $f(x) = \sqrt{x}$

93. A bead is formed by drilling a cylindrical hole of circular cross section and radius a through a sphere of radius $r > a$, the axis of the hole passing through the center of the sphere.

(a) Write a definite integral expressing the volume of the bead.

(b) Find a formula for the bead by evaluating the definite integral in part (a).

PROJECTS FOR CHAPTER EIGHT

1. Medical Case Study: Flux of Fluid from a Capillary[10]

The heart pumps blood throughout the body, the arteries are the blood vessels carrying blood away from the heart, and the veins return blood to the heart. Close to the heart, arteries are very large. As they progress toward tissues (such as the brain), the arteries branch repeatedly, getting smaller as they do. The smallest blood vessels are capillaries—microscopic, living tubes that link the smallest arteries to the smallest veins. The capillary is where nutrients and fluids move out of the blood into the adjacent tissues and waste products from the tissues move into the blood. The key to this process is the capillary wall, which is only one cell thick, allowing the unfettered passage of small molecules, such as water, ions, oxygen, glucose, and amino acids, while preventing the passage of large components of the blood (such as large proteins and blood cells).

Precise measurements demonstrate that the flux (rate of flow) of fluid through the capillary wall is not constant over the length of the capillary. Fluids in and around the capillary are subjected to two forces. The *hydrostatic pressure*, resulting from the heart's pumping, pushes fluid out of the capillary into the surrounding tissue. The *oncotic pressure* drives absorption in the other direction. At the start of a capillary, where the capillary branches off the small artery, the hydrostatic pressure is high while the oncotic pressure is low. Along the length of the capillary, the hydrostatic pressure decreases while the oncotic pressure is approximately constant. See Figure 8.118.

For most capillaries there is a net positive value for flow: more fluid flows from the capillaries into the surrounding tissue than the other way around. This presents a major problem for maintaining fluid balance in the body. How is the fluid left in the tissues to get back into circulation? If it cannot, the tissues progressively swell (a condition called edema). Evolution's solution is to provide humans and other mammals with a second set of vessels, the lymphatics, that absorb extra tissue fluid and provide one way routes back to the bloodstream.

---

[10]From David E. Sloane, M.D.

Along a cylindrical capillary of length $L = 0.1$ cm and radius $r = 0.0004$ cm, the hydrostatic pressure, p_h, varies from 35 mm Hg at the artery end to 15 mm Hg at the vein end. (mm Hg, millimeters of mercury, is a unit of pressure.) The oncotic pressure, p_o, is approximately 23 mm Hg throughout the length of the capillary.

(a) Find a formula for p_h as a function of x, the distance in centimeters from the artery end of the capillary, assuming that p_h is a linear function of x.

(b) Find a formula for p, the net outward pressure, as a function of x.

(c) The rate of movement, j, of fluid volume per capillary wall area across the capillary wall is proportional to the net pressure. We have $j = k \cdot p$ where k, the hydraulic conductivity, has value

$$k = 10^{-7} \frac{\text{cm}}{\text{sec} \cdot \text{mm Hg}}.$$

Check that j has units of volume per time per area.

(d) Write and evaluate an integral for the net volume flow rate (volume per unit time) through the wall of the entire capillary.

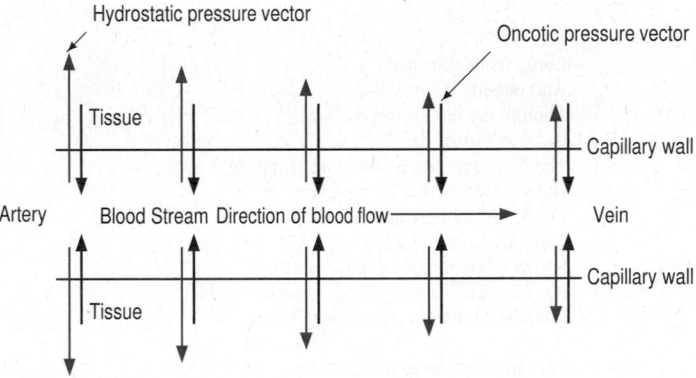

Figure 8.118: Vectors representing pressure in and out of capillary

2. Medical Case Study: Testing for Kidney Disease[11]

Patients with kidney disease often have protein in their urine. While small amounts of protein are not very worrisome, more than 1 gram of protein excreted in 24 hours warrants active treatment. The most accurate method for measuring urine protein is to have the patient collect all his or her urine in a container for a full 24 hour period. The total mass of protein can then be found by measuring the volume and protein concentration of the urine.

However, this process is not as straightforward as it sounds. Since the urine is collected intermittently throughout the 24 hour period, the first urine voided sits in the container longer than the last urine voided. During this time, the proteins slowly fall to the bottom of the container. Thus, at the end of a 24 hour collection period, there is a higher concentration of protein on the bottom of the container than at the top.

One could try to mix the urine so that the protein concentration is more uniform, but this forms bubbles that trap the protein, leading to an underestimate of the total amount excreted. A better way to determine the total protein is to measure the concentration at the top and at the bottom, and then calculate the total protein.

(a) Suppose a patient voids 2 litres (2000 ml) of urine in 24 hours and collects it in a cylindrical container of diameter 10 cm (note that 1 cm^3 = 1 ml). A technician determines that the protein concentration at the top is 0.14 mg/ml, and at the bottom is 0.96 mg/ml. Assume that the concentration of protein varies linearly from the top to the bottom.

(i) Find a formula for c, the protein concentration in mg/ml, as a function of y, the distance in centimeters from the base of the cylinder.

---

[11]From David E. Sloane, M.D.

(ii) Determine the quantity of protein in a slice of the cylinder extending from height y to $y + \Delta y$.

(iii) Write an integral that gives the total quantity of protein in the urine sample. Does this patient require active treatment?

(b) Assuming that concentration changes linearly with height, another way to estimate the quantity of protein in the sample is to multiply the average of the top and bottom protein concentrations by the volume of urine collected. Show that this procedure gives the same answer as integration, no matter what the radius of the cylindrical container, the volume collected, and the top and bottom protein concentrations.

3. Volume Enclosed by Two Cylinders

Two cylinders are inscribed in a cube of side length 2, as shown in Figure 8.119. What is the volume of the solid that the two cylinders enclose? [Hint: Use horizontal slices.] Note: The solution was known to Archimedes. The Chinese mathematician Liu Hui (third century A.D.) tried to find this volume, but he failed; he wrote a poem about his efforts calling the enclosed volume a "box-lid:"

Look inside the cube
And outside the box-lid;
Though the dimension increases,
It doesn't quite fit.
The marriage preparations are complete;
But square and circle wrangle,
Thick and thin are treacherous plots,
They are incompatible.
I wish to give my humble reflections,
But fear that I will miss the correct principle;
I dare to let the doubtful points stand,
Waiting
For one who can expound them.

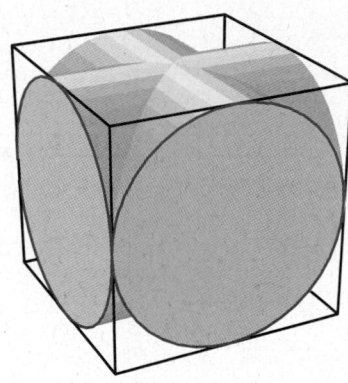

Figure 8.119

4. Length of a Hanging Cable

The distance between the towers of the main span of the Golden Gate Bridge is about 1280 m; the sag of the cable halfway between the towers on a cold winter day is about 143 m. See Figure 8.120.

Figure 8.120

(a) How long is the cable, assuming it has an approximately parabolic shape? (Represent the cable as a parabola of the form $y = kx^2$ and determine k to at least 1 decimal place.)

(b) On a hot summer day the cable is about 0.05% longer, due to thermal expansion. By how much does the sag increase? Assume no movement of the towers.

5. Surface Area of an Unpaintable Can of Paint

This project introduces the formula for the surface area of a volume of revolution and shows that it is possible to have a solid with finite volume but infinite surface area.

We know that the arclength of the curve $y = f(x)$ from a to b can be found using the integral

$$\text{Arc length} = \int_a^b \sqrt{1 + (f'(x))^2}\, dx.$$

Figure 8.121 shows the corresponding arc length of a small piece of the curve. Similarly, it can be shown that the surface area from a to b of the solid obtained by revolving $y = f(x)$ around the x-axis is given by

$$\text{Surface area} = 2\pi \int_a^b f(x)\sqrt{1 + (f'(x))^2}\, dx.$$

We can see this why this might be true by looking at Figure 8.122. We approximate the small piece of the surface by a slanted cylinder of radius y and "height" equal to the arclength of the curve, so that

$$\text{Surface area of edge of slice} \approx 2\pi y \sqrt{1 + (f'(x))^2}\, \Delta x.$$

Integrating this expression from $x = a$ to $x = b$ gives the surface area of the solid.

Figure 8.121

Figure 8.122

(a) Calculate the surface area of a sphere of radius r.

(b) Calculate the surface area of a cone of radius r and height h.

(c) Rotate the curve $y = 1/x$ for $x \geq 1$ around the x-axis. Find the volume of this solid.

(d) Show that the surface area of the solid in part (c) is infinite. [Hint: You might not be able to find an antiderivative of the integrand in the surface area formula; can you get a lower bound on the integral?]

(e) (Optional. Requires Chapter 11.) Find a curve such that when the portion of the curve from $x = a$ to $x = b$ is rotated around the x-axis (for any a and b), the volume of the solid of revolution is equal to its surface area. You may assume $dy/dx \geq 0$.

6. **Maxwell's Distribution of Molecular Velocities**

Let v be the speed, in meters/second, of an oxygen molecule, and let $p(v)$ be the density function of the speed distribution of oxygen molecules at room temperature. Maxwell showed that

$$p(v) = av^2 e^{-mv^2/(2kT)},$$

where $k = 1.4 \times 10^{-23}$ is the Boltzmann constant, T is the temperature in Kelvin (at room temperature, $T = 293$), and $m = 5 \times 10^{-26}$ is the mass of the oxygen molecule in kilograms.

(a) Find the value of a.

(b) Estimate the median and the mean speed. Find the maximum of $p(v)$.

(c) How do your answers in part (b) for the mean and the maximum of $p(v)$ change as T changes?

Chapter Nine

SEQUENCES AND SERIES

Contents

9.1 SEQUENCES

A sequence[1] is an infinite list of numbers $s_1, s_2, s_3, \ldots, s_n, \ldots$. We call s_1 the first term, s_2 the second term; s_n is the general term. For example, the sequence of squares, $1, 4, 9, \ldots, n^2, \ldots$ can be denoted by the general term $s_n = n^2$. Thus, a sequence is a function whose domain is the positive integers, but it is traditional to denote the terms of a sequence using subscripts, s_n, rather than function notation, $s(n)$. In addition, we may talk about sequences whose general term has no simple formula, such as the sequence $3, \; 3.1, \; 3.14, \; 3.141, \; 3.1415, \ldots$, in which s_n gives the first n digits of π.

The Numerical, Algebraic, and Graphical Viewpoint

Just as we can view a function algebraically, numerically, graphically, or verbally, we can view sequences in different ways. We may give an algebraic formula for the general term. We may give the numerical values of the first few terms of the sequence, suggesting a pattern for the later terms.

Example 1   Give the first six terms of the following sequences:

(a) $s_n = \dfrac{n(n+1)}{2}$

(b) $s_n = \dfrac{n + (-1)^n}{n}$

Solution   (a) Substituting $n = 1, 2, 3, 4, 5, 6$ into the formula for the general term, we get

$$\frac{1 \cdot 2}{2}, \frac{2 \cdot 3}{2}, \frac{3 \cdot 4}{2}, \frac{4 \cdot 5}{2}, \frac{5 \cdot 6}{2}, \frac{6 \cdot 7}{2} = 1, 3, 6, 10, 15, 21.$$

(b) Substituting $n = 1, 2, 3, 4, 5, 6$ into the formula for the general term, we get

$$\frac{1-1}{1}, \frac{2+1}{2}, \frac{3-1}{3}, \frac{4+1}{4}, \frac{5-1}{5}, \frac{6+1}{6} = 0, \frac{3}{2}, \frac{2}{3}, \frac{5}{4}, \frac{4}{5}, \frac{7}{6}.$$

Example 2   Give a general term for the following sequences:

(a) $1, 2, 4, 8, 16, 32, \ldots$

(b) $\dfrac{7}{2}, \dfrac{7}{5}, \dfrac{7}{8}, \dfrac{7}{11}, \dfrac{1}{2}, \dfrac{7}{17}, \ldots$

Solution   Although the first six terms do not determine the sequence, we can sometimes use them to guess a possible formula for the general term.

(a) We have powers of 2, so we guess $s_n = 2^n$. When we check by substituting in $n = 1, 2, 3, 4, 5, 6$, we get $2, 4, 8, 16, 32, 64$, instead of $1, 2, 4, 8, 16, 32$. We fix our guess by subtracting 1 from the exponent, so the general term is

$$s_n = 2^{n-1}.$$

Substituting the first six values of n shows that the formula checks.

(b) In this sequence, the fifth term looks different from the others, whose numerators are all 7. We can fix this by rewriting $1/2 = 7/14$. The sequence of denominators is then $2, 5, 8, 11, 14, 17$. This looks like a linear function with slope 3, so we expect the denominator has formula $3n + k$ for some k. When $n = 1$, the denominator is 2, so

$$2 = 3 \cdot 1 + k \quad \text{giving} \quad k = -1$$

and the denominator of s_n is $3n - 1$. Our general term is then

$$s_n = \frac{7}{3n - 1}.$$

To check this, evaluate s_n for $n = 1, \ldots, 6$.

There are two ways to visualize a sequence. One is to plot points with n on the horizontal axis and s_n on the vertical axis. The other is to label points on a number line $s_1, s_2, s_3, \ldots$. See Figure 9.1 for the sequence $s_n = 1 + (-1)^n/n$.

---

[1]In everyday English, the words "sequence" and "series" are used interchangeably. In mathematics, they have different meanings and cannot be interchanged.

Figure 9.1: The sequence $s_n = 1 + (-1)^n/n$

Defining Sequences Recursively

Sequences can also be defined *recursively*, by giving an equation relating the nth term to the previous terms and as many of the first few terms as are needed to get started.

Example 3   Give the first six terms of the recursively defined sequences.

(a) $s_n = s_{n-1} + 3$ for $n > 1$ and $s_1 = 4$
(b) $s_n = -3s_{n-1}$ for $n > 1$ and $s_1 = 2$
(c) $s_n = \frac{1}{2}(s_{n-1} + s_{n-2})$ for $n > 2$ and $s_1 = 0, s_2 = 1$
(d) $s_n = ns_{n-1}$ for $n > 1$ and $s_1 = 1$

Solution   (a) When $n = 2$, we obtain $s_2 = s_1 + 3 = 4 + 3 = 7$. When $n = 3$, we obtain $s_3 = s_2 + 3 = 7 + 3 = 10$. In words, we obtain each term by adding 3 to the previous term. The first six terms are
$$4, \ 7, \ 10, \ 13, \ 16, \ 19.$$

(b) Each term is -3 times the previous term, starting with $s_1 = 2$. We have $s_2 = -3s_1 = -3 \cdot 2 = -6$ and $s_3 = -3s_2 = -3(-6) = 18$. Continuing, we get
$$2, \ -6, \ 18, \ -54, \ 162, \ -486.$$

(c) Each term is the average of the previous two terms, starting with $s_1 = 0$ and $s_2 = 1$. We get $s_3 = (s_2 + s_1)/2 = (1 + 0)/2 = 1/2$. Then $s_4 = (s_3 + s_2)/2 = ((1/2) + 1)/2 = 3/4$. Continuing, we get
$$0, 1, \frac{1}{2}, \frac{3}{4}, \frac{5}{8}, \frac{11}{16}.$$

(d) Here $s_2 = 2s_1 = 2 \cdot 1 = 2$ so $s_3 = 3s_2 = 3 \cdot 2 = 6$ and $s_4 = 4s_3 = 4 \cdot 6 = 24$. Continuing gives
$$1, \ 2, \ 6, \ 24, \ 120, \ 720.$$

The general term of part (d) of the previous example is given by $s_n = n(n-1)(n-2)\ldots 3 \cdot 2 \cdot 1$, which is denoted $s_n = n!$ and is called n factorial. We define $0! = 1$.

We can also look at the first few terms of a sequence and try to guess a recursive definition by looking for a pattern.

Example 4   Give a recursive definition of the following sequences.

(a) $1, 3, 7, 15, 31, 63, \ldots$ (b) $1, 4, 9, 16, 25, 36, \ldots$

Solution   (a) Each term is twice the previous term plus one; for example $7 = 2 \cdot 3 + 1$ and $63 = 2 \cdot 31 + 1$. Thus, a recursive definition is
$$s_n = 2s_{n-1} + 1 \text{ for } n > 1 \text{ and } s_1 = 1.$$

There are other ways to define the sequence recursively. We might notice, for example, that the differences of consecutive terms are powers of 2. Thus, we could also use
$$s_n = s_{n-1} + 2^{n-1} \quad \text{for } n > 1 \text{ and } s_1 = 1.$$

(b) We recognize the terms as the squares of the positive integers, but we are looking for a recursive definition which relates consecutive terms. We see that

$$s_2 = s_1 + 3$$
$$s_3 = s_2 + 5$$
$$s_4 = s_3 + 7$$
$$s_5 = s_4 + 9,$$

so the differences between consecutive terms are consecutive odd integers. The difference between s_n and s_{n-1} is $2n - 1$, so a recursive definition is

$$s_n = s_{n-1} + 2n - 1, \text{ for } n > 1 \text{ and } s_1 = 1.$$

Recursively defined sequences, sometimes called recurrence relations, are powerful tools used frequently in computer science, as well as in differential equations. Finding a formula for the general term can be surprisingly difficult.

Convergence of Sequences

The limit of a sequence s_n as $n \to \infty$ is defined the same way as the limit of a function $f(x)$ as $x \to \infty$; see also Problem 61.

> The sequence $s_1, s_2, s_3, \ldots, s_n, \ldots$ has a **limit** L, written $\lim_{n \to \infty} s_n = L$, if s_n is as close to L as we please whenever n is sufficiently large. If a limit, L, exists, we say the sequence **converges** to its limit L. If no limit exists, we say the sequence **diverges**.

To calculate the limit of a sequence, we use what we know about the limits of functions, including the properties in Theorem 1.2 and the following facts:

- The sequence $s_n = x^n$ converges to 0 if $|x| < 1$ and diverges if $|x| > 1$
- The sequence $s_n = 1/n^p$ converges to 0 if $p > 0$

Example 5   Do the following sequences converge or diverge? If a sequence converges, find its limit.

(a) $s_n = (0.8)^n$ (b) $s_n = \dfrac{1 - e^{-n}}{1 + e^{-n}}$ (c) $s_n = \dfrac{n^2 + 1}{n}$ (d) $s_n = 1 + (-1)^n$

Solution   (a) Since $0.8 < 1$, the sequence converges by the first fact and the limit is 0.

(b) Since $e^{-1} < 1$, we have $\lim_{n \to \infty} e^{-n} = \lim_{n \to \infty} (e^{-1})^n = 0$ by the first fact. Thus, using the properties of limits from Section 1.8, we have

$$\lim_{n \to \infty} \frac{1 - e^{-n}}{1 + e^{-n}} = \frac{1 - 0}{1 + 0} = 1.$$

(c) Since $(n^2 + 1)/n$ grows without bound as $n \to \infty$, the sequence s_n diverges.

(d) Since $(-1)^n$ alternates in sign, the sequence alternates between 0 and 2. Thus the sequence s_n diverges, since it does not get close to any fixed value.

Convergence and Bounded Sequences

A sequence s_n is *bounded* if there are numbers K and M such that $K \le s_n \le M$ for all terms. If $\lim_{n \to \infty} s_n = L$, then from some point on, the terms are bounded between $L - 1$ and $L + 1$. Thus we have the following fact:

> A convergent sequence is bounded.

On the other hand, a bounded sequence need not be convergent. In Example 5, we saw that $1+(-1)^n$ diverges, but it is bounded between 0 and 2. To ensure that a bounded sequence converges we need to rule out this sort of oscillation. The following theorem gives a condition that ensures convergence for a bounded sequence. A sequence s_n is called *monotone* if it is either increasing, that is $s_n < s_{n+1}$ for all n, or decreasing, that is $s_n > s_{n+1}$ for all n.

Theorem 9.1: Convergence of a Monotone, Bounded Sequence

If a sequence s_n is bounded and monotone, it converges.

To understand this theorem graphically, see Figure 9.2. The sequence s_n is increasing and bounded above by M, so the values of s_n must "pile up" at some number less than or equal to M. This number is the limit.[2]

Figure 9.2: Values of s_n for $n = 1, 2, \cdots, 10$

Example 6   The sequence $s_n = (1/2)^n$ is decreasing and bounded below by 0, so it converges. We have already seen that it converges to 0.

Example 7   The sequence $s_n = (1 + 1/n)^n$ can be shown to be increasing and bounded (see Project 2 on page 534). Theorem 9.1 then guarantees that this sequence has a limit, which turns out to be e. (In fact, the sequence can be used to define e.)

Example 8   If $s_n = (1 + 1/n)^n$, find s_{100} and s_{1000}. How many decimal places agree with e?

Solution   We have $s_{100} = (1.01)^{100} = 2.7048$ and $s_{1000} = (1.001)^{1000} = 2.7169$. Since $e = 2.7183\ldots$, we see that s_{100} agrees with e to one decimal place and s_{1000} agrees with e to two decimal places.

Exercises and Problems for Section 9.1

Exercises

For Exercises 1–6, find the first five terms of the sequence from the formula for $s_n, n \geq 1$.

1. $2^n + 1$

2. $n + (-1)^n$

3. $\dfrac{2n}{2n + 1}$

4. $(-1)^n \left(\dfrac{1}{2}\right)^n$

5. $(-1)^{n+1} \left(\dfrac{1}{2}\right)^{n-1}$

6. $\left(1 - \dfrac{1}{n+1}\right)^{n+1}$

In Exercises 7–12, find a formula for $s_n, n \geq 1$.

7. $4, 8, 16, 32, 64, \ldots$

8. $1, 3, 7, 15, 31, \ldots$

9. $2, 5, 10, 17, 26, \ldots$

10. $1, -3, 5, -7, 9, \ldots$

11. $1/3, 2/5, 3/7, 4/9, 5/11, \ldots$

12. $1/2, -1/4, 1/6, -1/8, 1/10, \ldots$

Problems

Do the sequences in Problems 13–24 converge or diverge? If a sequence converges, find its limit.

13. 2^n

14. $(0.2)^n$

15. $3 + e^{-2n}$

16. $(-0.3)^n$

17. $\dfrac{n}{10} + \dfrac{10}{n}$

18. $\dfrac{2^n}{3^n}$

19. $\dfrac{2n + 1}{n}$

20. $\dfrac{(-1)^n}{n}$

21. $\dfrac{1}{n} + \ln n$

22. $\dfrac{2n + (-1)^n 5}{4n - (-1)^n 3}$

23. $\dfrac{\sin n}{n}$

24. $\cos(\pi n)$

---

[2]See the online supplement for a proof.

25. Match formulas (a)–(d) with graphs (I)–(IV).

   (a) $s_n = 1 - 1/n$ **(b)** $s_n = 1 + (-1)^n/n$

   (c) $s_n = 1/n$ **(d)** $s_n = 1 + 1/n$

26. Match formulas (a)–(e) with descriptions (I)–(V) of the behavior of the sequence as $n \to \infty$.

   (a) $s_n = n(n + 1) - 1$

   (b) $s_n = 1/(n + 1)$

   (c) $s_n = 1 - n^2$

   (d) $s_n = \cos(1/n)$

   (e) $s_n = (\sin n)/n$

   (I) Diverges to $-\infty$

   (II) Diverges to $+\infty$

   (III) Converges to 0 through positive numbers

   (IV) Converges to 1

   (V) Converges to 0 through positive and negative numbers

27. Match formulas (a)–(e) with graphs (I)–(V).

   (a) $s_n = 2 - 1/n$

   (b) $s_n = (-1)^n 2 + 1/n$

   (c) $s_n = 2 + (-1)^n/n$

   (d) $s_n = 2 + 1/n$

   (e) $s_n = (-1)^n 2 + (-1)^n/n$

In Problems 28–31, find the first six terms of the recursively defined sequence.

28. $s_n = 2s_{n-1} + 3$ for $n > 1$ and $s_1 = 1$

29. $s_n = s_{n-1} + n$ for $n > 1$ and $s_1 = 1$

30. $s_n = s_{n-1} + \left(\frac{1}{2}\right)^{n-1}$ for $n > 1$ and $s_1 = 0$

31. $s_n = s_{n-1} + 2s_{n-2}$ for $n > 2$ and $s_1 = 1$, $s_2 = 5$

In Problems 32–33, let $a_1 = 8, b_1 = 5$, and, for $n > 1$,

$$a_n = a_{n-1} + 3n$$
$$b_n = b_{n-1} + a_{n-1}.$$

32. Give the values of a_2, a_3, a_4.

33. Give the values of b_2, b_3, b_4, b_5.

34. Suppose $s_1 = 0, s_2 = 0, s_3 = 1$, and that $s_n = s_{n-1} + s_{n-2} + s_{n-3}$ for $n \geq 4$. The members of the resulting sequence are called *tribonacci numbers*.[3] Find $s_4, s_5, \ldots, s_{10}$.

Problems 35–37 concern analog signals in electrical engineering, which are continuous functions $f(t)$, where t is time. To digitize the signal, we sample $f(t)$ every Δt to form the sequence $s_n = f(n\Delta t)$. For example, if $f(t) = \sin t$ with t in seconds, sampling f every $1/10$ second produces the sequence $\sin(1/10)$, $\sin(2/10)$, $\sin(3/10)$, ... Give the first 6 terms of a sampling of the signal every Δt seconds.

35. $f(t) = (t - 1)^2, \Delta t = 0.5$

36. $f(t) = \cos 5t, \Delta t = 0.1$

37. $f(t) = \dfrac{\sin t}{t}, \Delta t = 1$

In Problems 38–40, we smooth a sequence, $s_1, s_2, s_3, \ldots$, by replacing each term s_n by t_n, the average of s_n with its neighboring terms

$$t_n = \frac{(s_{n-1} + s_n + s_{n+1})}{3} \text{ for } n > 1.$$

Start with $t_1 = (s_1 + s_2)/2$, since s_1 has only one neighbor. Smooth the given sequence once and then smooth the resulting sequence. What do you notice?

38. $18, -18, 18, -18, 18, -18, 18 \ldots$

39. $0, 0, 0, 18, 0, 0, 0, 0 \ldots$

40. $1, 2, 3, 4, 5, 6, 7, 8 \ldots$

In Problems 41–46, find a recursive definition for the sequence.

41. $1, 3, 5, 7, 9, \ldots$ **42.** $2, 4, 6, 8, 10, \ldots$

43. $3, 5, 9, 17, 33, \ldots$ **44.** $1, 5, 14, 30, 55, \ldots$

45. $1, 3, 6, 10, 15, \ldots$ **46.** $1, 2, \dfrac{3}{2}, \dfrac{5}{3}, \dfrac{8}{5}, \dfrac{13}{8}, \ldots$

---

[3]http://en.wikipedia.org/wiki/Tribonacci_numbers, page accessed March 16, 2011.

In Problems 47–49, show that the sequence s_n satisfies the recurrence relation.

47. $s_n = 3n - 2$
$s_n = s_{n-1} + 3$ for $n > 1$ and $s_1 = 1$

48. $s_n = n(n+1)/2$
$s_n = s_{n-1} + n$ for $n > 1$ and $s_1 = 1$

49. $s_n = 2n^2 - n$
$s_n = s_{n-1} + 4n - 3$ for $n > 1$ and $s_1 = 1$

In Problems 50–53, for the function f define a sequence recursively by $x_n = f(x_{n-1})$ for $n > 1$ and $x_1 = a$. Depending on f and the starting value a, this sequence may converge to a limit L. If L exists, it has the property that $f(L) = L$. For the functions and starting values given, use a calculator to see if the sequence converges. [To obtain the terms of the sequence, repeatedly push the function button.]

50. $f(x) = \cos x, a = 0$ **51.** $f(x) = e^{-x}, a = 0$

52. $f(x) = \sin x, a = 1$ **53.** $f(x) = \sqrt{x}, a = 0.5$

54. Let V_n be the number of new SUVs sold in the US in month n, where $n = 1$ is January 2004. In terms of SUVs, what do the following represent?

(a) V_{10}
(b) $V_n - V_{n-1}$
(c) $\sum_{i=1}^{12} V_i$ and $\sum_{i=1}^{n} V_i$

55. (a) Let s_n be the number of ancestors a person has n generations ago. (Your ancestors are your parents, grandparents, great-grandparents, etc.) What is s_1? s_2? Find a formula for s_n.
(b) For which n is s_n greater than 6 billion, the current world population? What does this tell you about your ancestors?

56. For $1 \le n \le 10$, find a formula for p_n, the payment in year n on a loan of \$100,000. Interest is 5% per year, compounded annually, and payments are made at the end of each year for ten years. Each payment is \$10,000 plus the interest on the amount of money outstanding.

57. (a) Cans are stacked in a triangle on a shelf. The bottom row contains k cans, the row above contains one can fewer, and so on, until the top row, which has one can. How many rows are there? Find a_n, the number of cans in the nth row, $1 \le n \le k$ (where the top row is $n = 1$).
(b) Let T_n be the total number of cans in the top n rows. Find a recurrence relation for T_n in terms of T_{n-1}.
(c) Show that $T_n = \frac{1}{2}n(n+1)$ satisfies the recurrence relation.

58. You are deciding whether to buy a new or a two-year-old car (of the same make) based on which will have cost you less when you resell it at the end of three years. Your cost consists of two parts: the loss in value of the car and the repairs. A new car costs \$20,000 and loses 12% of its value each year. Repairs are \$400 the first year and increase by 18% each subsequent year.

(a) For a new car, find the first three terms of the sequence d_n giving the depreciation (loss of value) in dollars in year n. Give a formula for d_n.
(b) Find the first three terms of the sequence r_n, the repair cost in dollars for a new car in year n. Give a formula for r_n.
(c) Find the total cost of owning a new car for three years.
(d) Find the total cost of owning the two-year-old car for three years. Which should you buy?

59. The Fibonacci sequence, first studied by the thirteenth century Italian mathematician Leonardo di Pisa, also known as Fibonacci, is defined recursively by

$$F_n = F_{n-1} + F_{n-2} \text{ for } n > 2 \text{ and } F_1 = 1, F_2 = 1.$$

The Fibonacci sequence occurs in many branches of mathematics and can be found in patterns of plant growth (phyllotaxis).

(a) Find the first 12 terms.
(b) Show that the sequence of successive ratios F_{n+1}/F_n appears to converge to a number r satisfying the equation $r^2 = r + 1$. (The number r was known as the golden ratio to the ancient Greeks.)
(c) Let r satisfy $r^2 = r + 1$. Show that the sequence $s_n = Ar^n$, where A is constant, satisfies the Fibonacci equation $s_n = s_{n-1} + s_{n-2}$ for $n > 2$.

60. This problem defines the Calkin-Wilf-Newman sequence of positive rational numbers. The sequence is remarkable because every positive rational number appears as one of its terms and none appears more than once. Every real number x can be written as an integer A plus a number B where $0 \le B < 1$. For example, for $x = 12/5 = 2+2/5$ we have $A = 2$ and $B = 2/5$. For $x = 3 = 3 + 0$ we have $A = 3$ and $B = 0$. Define the function $f(x)$ by

$$f(x) = A + (1 - B).$$

For example, $f(12/5) = 2 + (1 - 2/5) = 13/5$ and $f(3) = 3 + (1 - 0) = 4$.

(a) Evaluate $f(x)$ for $x = 25/8, 13/9$, and π.
(b) Find the first six terms of the recursively defined Calkin-Wilf-Newman sequence: $s_n = 1/f(s_{n-1})$ for $n > 1$ and $s_1 = 1$.

61. Write a definition for $\lim_{n \to \infty} s_n = L$ similar to the ϵ, δ definition for $\lim_{x \to a} f(x) = L$ in Section 1.8. Instead of δ, you will need N, a value of n.

62. The sequence s_n is increasing, the sequence t_n converges, and $s_n \le t_n$ for all n. Show that s_n converges.

Strengthen Your Understanding

In Problems 63–64, explain what is wrong with the statement.

63. The sequence $s_n = \dfrac{3n + 10}{7n + 3}$, which begins with the terms $\dfrac{13}{10}, \dfrac{16}{17}, \dfrac{19}{24}, \dfrac{22}{31}, \ldots$ converges to 0 because the terms of the sequence get smaller and smaller.

64. If a convergent sequence consists entirely of terms greater than 2, then the limit of the sequence must be greater than 2.

In Problems 65–66, give an example of:

65. An increasing sequence that converges to 0.

66. A monotone sequence that does not converge.

Decide if the statements in Problems 67–74 are true or false. Give an explanation for your answer.

67. You can tell if a sequence converges by looking at the first 1000 terms.

68. If the terms s_n of a convergent sequence are all positive then $\lim\limits_{n \to \infty} s_n$ is positive.

69. If the sequence s_n of positive terms is unbounded, then the sequence has a term greater than a million.

70. If the sequence s_n of positive terms is unbounded, then the sequence has an infinite number of terms greater than a million.

71. If a sequence s_n is convergent, then the terms s_n tend to zero as n increases.

72. A monotone sequence cannot have both positive and negative terms.

73. If a monotone sequence of positive terms does not converge, then it has a term greater than a million.

74. If all terms s_n of a sequence are less than a million, then the sequence is bounded.

75. Which of the sequences I–IV is monotone and bounded for $n \geq 1$?

$$\text{I. } s_n = 10 - \frac{1}{n}$$
$$\text{II. } s_n = \frac{10n + 1}{n}$$
$$\text{III. } s_n = \cos n$$
$$\text{IV. } s_n = \ln n$$

(a) I
(b) I and II
(c) II and IV
(d) I, II, and III

9.2 GEOMETRIC SERIES

Adding the terms of a sequence produces a *series*. For example, we have the sequence $1, 2, 3, 4, 5, 6, \ldots$ and the series $1 + 2 + 3 + 4 + 5 + 6 + \cdots$. This section introduces infinite series of constants, which are sums of the form

$$1 + \tfrac{1}{2} + \tfrac{1}{3} + \tfrac{1}{4} + \cdots$$
$$0.4 + 0.04 + 0.004 + 0.0004 + \cdots.$$

The individual numbers, $1, \tfrac{1}{2}, \tfrac{1}{3}, \ldots$, or $0.4, 0.04, \ldots$, etc., are called *terms* in the series. To talk about the *sum* of the series, we must first explain how to add infinitely many numbers.

Let us look at the repeated administration of a drug. In this example, the terms in the series represent each dose; the sum of the series represents the drug level in the body in the long run.

Repeated Drug Dosage

A person with an ear infection is told to take antibiotic tablets regularly for several days. Since the drug is being excreted by the body between doses, how can we calculate the quantity of the drug remaining in the body at any particular time?

To be specific, let's suppose the drug is ampicillin (a common antibiotic) taken in 250 mg doses four times a day (that is, every six hours). It is known that at the end of six hours, about 4% of the drug is still in the body. What quantity of the drug is in the body right after the tenth tablet? The fortieth?

Let Q_n represent the quantity, in milligrams, of ampicillin in the blood right after the nth tablet.

Then

$$Q_1 = 250 \qquad\qquad\qquad\qquad\qquad\qquad\qquad\qquad = 250 \text{ mg}$$

$$Q_2 = \underbrace{250(0.04)}_{\text{Remnants of first tablet}} + \underbrace{250}_{\text{New tablet}} \qquad\qquad\qquad\qquad = 260 \text{ mg}$$

$$Q_3 = Q_2(0.04) + 250 = (250(0.04) + 250)(0.04) + 250$$
$$= \underbrace{250(0.04)^2 + 250(0.04)}_{\text{Remnants of first and second tablets}} + \underbrace{250}_{\text{New tablet}} \qquad\qquad = 260.4 \text{ mg}$$

$$Q_4 = Q_3(0.04) + 250 = \left(250(0.04)^2 + 250(0.04) + 250\right)(0.04) + 250$$
$$= \underbrace{250(0.04)^3 + 250(0.04)^2 + 250(0.04)}_{\text{Remnants of first, second, and third tablets}} + \underbrace{250}_{\text{New tablet}} \qquad = 260.416 \text{ mg.}$$

Looking at the pattern that is emerging, we guess that

$$Q_{10} = 250(0.04)^9 + 250(0.04)^8 + 250(0.04)^7 + \cdots + 250(0.04)^2 + 250(0.04) + 250.$$

Notice that there are 10 terms in this sum—one for every tablet—but that the highest power of 0.04 is the ninth, because no tablet has been in the body for more than 9 six-hour time periods. Now suppose we actually want to find the numerical value of Q_{10}. It seems that we have to add 10 terms—fortunately, there's a better way. Notice the remarkable fact that if you subtract $(0.04)Q_{10}$ from Q_{10}, all but two terms drop out. First, multiplying by 0.04, we get

$$(0.04)Q_{10} = 250(0.04)^{10} + 250(0.04)^9 + 250(0.04)^8 + \cdots + 250(0.04)^3 + 250(0.04)^2 + 250(0.04).$$

Subtracting gives
$$Q_{10} - (0.04)Q_{10} = 250 - 250(0.04)^{10}.$$

Factoring Q_{10} on the left and solving for Q_{10} gives

$$Q_{10}(1 - 0.04) = 250\left(1 - (0.04)^{10}\right)$$
$$Q_{10} = \frac{250\left(1 - (0.04)^{10}\right)}{1 - 0.04}.$$

This is called the *closed-form* expression for Q_{10}. It is easy to evaluate on a calculator, giving $Q_{10} = 260.42$ (to two decimal places). Similarly, Q_{40} is given in closed form by

$$Q_{40} = \frac{250\left(1 - (0.04)^{40}\right)}{1 - 0.04}.$$

Evaluating this on a calculator shows $Q_{40} = 260.42$, which is the same (to two decimal places) as Q_{10}. Thus after ten tablets, the value of Q_n appears to have stabilized at just over 260 mg.

Looking at the closed forms for Q_{10} and Q_{40}, we can see that, in general, Q_n must be given by

$$Q_n = \frac{250\left(1 - (0.04)^n\right)}{1 - 0.04}.$$

What Happens as $n \to \infty$?

What does this closed form for Q_n predict about the long-run level of ampicillin in the body? As $n \to \infty$, the quantity $(0.04)^n \to 0$. In the long run, assuming that 250 mg continue to be taken every six hours, the level right after a tablet is taken is given by

$$Q_n = \frac{250\left(1 - (0.04)^n\right)}{1 - 0.04} \to \frac{250(1 - 0)}{1 - 0.04} = 260.42.$$

The Geometric Series in General

In the previous example we encountered sums of the form $a + ax + ax^2 + \cdots + ax^8 + ax^9$ (with $a = 250$ and $x = 0.04$). Such a sum is called a finite *geometric series*. A geometric series is one in which each term is a constant multiple of the one before. The first term is a, and the constant multiplier, or *common ratio* of successive terms, is x.

A **finite geometric series** has the form

$$a + ax + ax^2 + \cdots + ax^{n-2} + ax^{n-1}.$$

An **infinite geometric series** has the form

$$a + ax + ax^2 + \cdots + ax^{n-2} + ax^{n-1} + ax^n + \cdots.$$

The "$\cdots$" at the end of the second series tells us that the series is going on forever—in other words, that it is infinite.

Sum of a Finite Geometric Series

The same procedure that enabled us to find the closed form for Q_{10} can be used to find the sum of any finite geometric series. Suppose we write S_n for the sum of the first n terms, which means up to the term containing x^{n-1}:

$$S_n = a + ax + ax^2 + \cdots + ax^{n-2} + ax^{n-1}.$$

Multiply S_n by x:

$$xS_n = ax + ax^2 + ax^3 + \cdots + ax^{n-1} + ax^n.$$

Now subtract xS_n from S_n, which cancels out all terms except for two, giving

$$S_n - xS_n = a - ax^n$$
$$(1 - x)S_n = a(1 - x^n).$$

Provided $x \neq 1$, we can solve to find a closed form for S_n as follows:

The **sum of a finite geometric series** is given by

$$S_n = a + ax + ax^2 + \cdots + ax^{n-1} = \frac{a(1 - x^n)}{1 - x}, \qquad \text{provided } x \neq 1.$$

Note that the value of n in the formula for S_n is the number of terms in the sum S_n.

Sum of an Infinite Geometric Series

In the ampicillin example, we found the sum Q_n and then let $n \to \infty$. We do the same here. The sum Q_n, which shows the effect of the first n doses, is an example of a *partial sum*. The first three partial sums of the series $a + ax + ax^2 + \cdots + ax^{n-1} + ax^n + \cdots$ are

$$S_1 = a$$
$$S_2 = a + ax$$
$$S_3 = a + ax + ax^2.$$

To find the sum of this infinite series, we consider the partial sum, S_n, of the first n terms. The formula for the sum of a finite geometric series gives

$$S_n = a + ax + ax^2 + \cdots + ax^{n-1} = \frac{a(1 - x^n)}{1 - x}.$$

What happens to S_n as $n \to \infty$? It depends on the value of x. If $|x| < 1$, then $x^n \to 0$ as $n \to \infty$, so

$$\lim_{n\to\infty} S_n = \lim_{n\to\infty} \frac{a(1-x^n)}{1-x} = \frac{a(1-0)}{1-x} = \frac{a}{1-x}.$$

Thus, provided $|x| < 1$, as $n \to \infty$ the partial sums S_n approach a limit of $a/(1-x)$. When this happens, we define the sum S of the infinite geometric series to be that limit and say the series *converges* to $a/(1-x)$.

For $|x| < 1$, the **sum of the infinite geometric series** is given by

$$S = a + ax + ax^2 + \cdots + ax^{n-1} + ax^n + \cdots = \frac{a}{1-x}.$$

If, on the other hand, $|x| > 1$, then x^n and the partial sums have no limit as $n \to \infty$ (if $a \neq 0$). In this case, we say the series *diverges*. If $x > 1$, the terms in the series become larger and larger in magnitude, and the partial sums diverge to $+\infty$ (if $a > 0$) or $-\infty$ (if $a < 0$). When $x < -1$, the terms become larger in magnitude, the partial sums oscillate as $n \to \infty$, and the series diverges.

What happens when $x = 1$? The series is

$$a + a + a + a + \cdots,$$

and if $a \neq 0$, the partial sums grow without bound, and the series does not converge. When $x = -1$, the series is

$$a - a + a - a + a - \cdots,$$

and, if $a \neq 0$, the partial sums oscillate between a and 0, and the series does not converge.

Example 1   For each of the following infinite geometric series, find several partial sums and the sum (if it exists).

(a) $1 + \dfrac{1}{2} + \dfrac{1}{4} + \dfrac{1}{8} + \cdots$ (b) $1 + 2 + 4 + 8 + \cdots$ (c) $6 - 2 + \dfrac{2}{3} - \dfrac{2}{9} + \dfrac{2}{27} - \cdots$

Solution   (a) This series may be written

$$1 + \frac{1}{2} + \left(\frac{1}{2}\right)^2 + \left(\frac{1}{2}\right)^3 + \cdots$$

which we can identify as a geometric series with $a = 1$ and $x = \frac{1}{2}$, so $S = \dfrac{1}{1 - (1/2)} = 2$.

Let's check this by finding the partial sums:

$$S_1 = 1$$
$$S_2 = 1 + \frac{1}{2} = \frac{3}{2} = 2 - \frac{1}{2}$$
$$S_3 = 1 + \frac{1}{2} + \frac{1}{4} = \frac{7}{4} = 2 - \frac{1}{4}$$
$$S_4 = 1 + \frac{1}{2} + \frac{1}{4} + \frac{1}{8} = \frac{15}{8} = 2 - \frac{1}{8}.$$

The sequence of partial sums begins

$$1, 2 - \frac{1}{2}, 2 - \frac{1}{4}, 2 - \frac{1}{8}, \ldots.$$

The formula for S_n gives

$$S_n = \frac{1 - (\frac{1}{2})^n}{1 - \frac{1}{2}} = 2 - \left(\frac{1}{2}\right)^{n-1}.$$

Thus, the partial sums are creeping up to the value $S = 2$, so $S_n \to 2$ as $n \to \infty$.

(b) The partial sums of this geometric series (with $a = 1$ and $x = 2$) grow without bound, so the series has no sum:

$$S_1 = 1$$
$$S_2 = 1 + 2 = 3$$
$$S_3 = 1 + 2 + 4 = 7$$
$$S_4 = 1 + 2 + 4 + 8 = 15.$$

The sequence of partial sums begins

$$1, 3, 7, 15, \ldots.$$

The formula for S_n gives

$$S_n = \frac{1 - 2^n}{1 - 2} = 2^n - 1.$$

(c) This is an infinite geometric series with $a = 6$ and $x = -\frac{1}{3}$. The partial sums,

$$S_1 = 6.00, \quad S_2 = 4.00, \quad S_3 \approx 4.67, \quad S_4 \approx 4.44, \quad S_5 \approx 4.52, \quad S_6 \approx 4.49,$$

appear to be converging to 4.5. This turns out to be correct because the sum is

$$S = \frac{6}{1 - (-1/3)} = 4.5.$$

Regular Deposits into a Savings Account

People who save money often do so by putting some fixed amount aside regularly. To be specific, suppose $1000 is deposited every year in a savings account earning 5% a year, compounded annually. What is the balance, B_n, in dollars, in the savings account right after the nth deposit?

As before, let's start by looking at the first few years:

$$B_1 = 1000$$
$$B_2 = B_1(1.05) + 1000 = \underbrace{1000(1.05)}_{\text{Original deposit}} + \underbrace{1000}_{\text{New deposit}}$$
$$B_3 = B_2(1.05) + 1000 = \underbrace{1000(1.05)^2 + 1000(1.05)}_{\text{First two deposits}} + \underbrace{1000}_{\text{New deposit}}$$

Observing the pattern, we see

$$B_n = 1000(1.05)^{n-1} + 1000(1.05)^{n-2} + \cdots + 1000(1.05) + 1000.$$

So B_n is a finite geometric series with $a = 1000$ and $x = 1.05$. Thus we have

$$B_n = \frac{1000\left(1 - (1.05)^n\right)}{1 - 1.05}.$$

We can rewrite this so that both the numerator and denominator of the fraction are positive:

$$B_n = \frac{1000\left((1.05)^n - 1\right)}{1.05 - 1}.$$

What Happens as $n \to \infty$?

Common sense tells you that if you keep depositing $1000 in an account and it keeps earning interest, your balance grows without bound. This is what the formula for B_n shows also: $(1.05)^n \to \infty$ as $n \to \infty$, so B_n has no limit. (Alternatively, observe that the infinite geometric series of which B_n is a partial sum has $x = 1.05$, which is greater than 1, so the series does not converge.)

Exercises and Problems for Section 9.2

Exercises

In Exercises 1–7, is a sequence or a series given?

1. $2^2, 4^2, 6^2, 8^2, \ldots$

2. $2^2 + 4^2 + 6^2 + 8^2 + \cdots$

3. $1 + 2, 3 + 4, 5 + 6, 7 + 8, \ldots$

4. $1, -2, 3, -4, 5, \ldots$

5. $1 - 2 + 3 - 4 + 5 - \cdots$

6. $1 + 2 + 3 + 4 + 5 + 6 + 7 + 8 + \cdots$

7. $-S_1 + S_2 - S_3 + S_4 - S_5 + \cdots$

In Exercises 8–18, decide which of the following are geometric series. For those which are, give the first term and the ratio between successive terms. For those which are not, explain why not.

8. $5 - 10 + 20 - 40 + 80 - \cdots$

9. $1 + \dfrac{1}{2} + \dfrac{1}{3} + \dfrac{1}{4} + \dfrac{1}{5} + \cdots$

10. $2 + 1 + \dfrac{1}{2} + \dfrac{1}{4} + \dfrac{1}{8} + \cdots$

11. $1 - \dfrac{1}{2} + \dfrac{1}{4} - \dfrac{1}{8} + \dfrac{1}{16} + \cdots$

12. $1 + x + 2x^2 + 3x^3 + 4x^4 + \cdots$

13. $1 + 2z + (2z)^2 + (2z)^3 + \cdots$

14. $3 + 3z + 6z^2 + 9z^3 + 12z^4 + \cdots$

15. $1 - x + x^2 - x^3 + x^4 - \cdots$

16. $1 - y^2 + y^4 - y^6 + \cdots$

17. $y^2 + y^3 + y^4 + y^5 + \cdots$

18. $z^2 - z^4 + z^8 - z^{16} + \cdots$

In Exercises 19–22, say how many terms are in the finite geometric series and find its sum.

19. $2 + 2(0.1) + 2(0.1)^2 + \cdots + 2(0.1)^{25}$

20. $2(0.1) + 2(0.1)^2 + \cdots + 2(0.1)^{10}$

21. $2(0.1)^5 + 2(0.1)^6 + \cdots + 2(0.1)^{13}$

22. $8 + 4 + 2 + 1 + \dfrac{1}{2} + \cdots + \dfrac{1}{2^{10}}$

In Exercises 23–25, find the sum of the infinite geometric series.

23. $36 + 12 + 4 + \dfrac{4}{3} + \dfrac{4}{9} + \cdots$

24. $-810 + 540 - 360 + 240 - 160 + \cdots$

25. $80 + \dfrac{80}{\sqrt{2}} + 40 + \dfrac{40}{\sqrt{2}} + 20 + \dfrac{20}{\sqrt{2}} + \cdots$

In Exercises 26–31, find the sum of the series. For what values of the variable does the series converge to this sum?

26. $1 + z/2 + z^2/4 + z^3/8 + \cdots$

27. $1 + 3x + 9x^2 + 27x^3 + \cdots$

28. $y - y^2 + y^3 - y^4 + \cdots$

29. $2 - 4z + 8z^2 - 16z^3 + \cdots$

30. $3 + x + x^2 + x^3 + \cdots$

31. $4 + y + y^2/3 + y^3/9 + \cdots$

Problems

32. This problem shows another way of deriving the long-run ampicillin level. (See page 498.) In the long run the ampicillin levels off to Q mg right after each tablet is taken. Six hours later, right before the next dose, there will be less ampicillin in the body. However, if stability has been reached, the amount of ampicillin that has been excreted is exactly 250 mg because taking one more tablet raises the level back to Q mg. Use this to solve for Q.

33. On page 499, you saw how to compute the quantity Q_n mg of ampicillin in the body right after the nth tablet of 250 mg, taken once every six hours.

   (a) Do a similar calculation for P_n, the quantity of ampicillin (in mg) in the body right *before* the nth tablet is taken.

   (b) Express P_n in closed form.

   (c) What is $\lim_{n \to \infty} P_n$? Is this limit the same as $\lim_{n \to \infty} Q_n$? Explain in practical terms why your answer makes sense.

34. Figure 9.3 shows the quantity of the drug atenolol in the blood as a function of time, with the first dose at time $t = 0$. Atenolol is taken in 50 mg doses once a day to lower blood pressure.

   (a) If the half-life of atenolol in the blood is 6.3 hours, what percentage of the atenolol present at the start of a 24-hour period is still there at the end?

   (b) Find expressions for the quantities $Q_0, Q_1, Q_2, Q_3, \ldots$, and Q_n shown in Figure 9.3. Write the expres-

sion for Q_n in closed form.

   (c) Find expressions for the quantities $P_1, P_2, P_3, \ldots$, and P_n shown in Figure 9.3. Write the expression for P_n in closed form.

Figure 9.3

35. Draw a graph like that in Figure 9.3 for 250 mg of ampicillin taken every 6 hours, starting at time $t = 0$. Put on the graph the values of $Q_1, Q_2, Q_3, \ldots$ introduced in the text on page 499 and the values of $P_1, P_2, P_3, \ldots$ calculated in Problem 33.

36. Once a day, eight tons of pollutants are dumped into a bay. Of this, 25% is removed by natural processes each day. What happens to the quantity of pollutants in the bay over time? Give the long-run quantity right after a dump.

37. **(a)** The total reserves of a non-renewable resource are 400 million tons. Annual consumption, currently 25 million tons per year, is expected to rise by 1% each year. After how many years will the reserves be exhausted?

(b) Instead of increasing by 1% per year, suppose consumption was decreasing by a constant percentage per year. If existing reserves are never to be exhausted, what annual percentage reduction in consumption is required?

38. One way of valuing a company is to calculate the present value of all its future earnings. A farm expects to sell $1000 worth of Christmas trees once a year forever, with the first sale in the immediate future. What is the present value of this Christmas tree business? The interest rate is 1% per year, compounded continuously.

39. Around January 1, 1993, Barbra Streisand signed a contract with Sony Corporation for $2 million a year for 10 years. Suppose the first payment was made on the day of signing and that all other payments were made on the first day of the year. Suppose also that all payments were made into a bank account earning 4% a year, compounded annually.

(a) How much money was in the account
  (i) On the night of December 31, 1999?
  (ii) On the day the last payment was made?
(b) What was the present value of the contract on the day it was signed?

40. Bill invests $200 at the start of each month for 24 months, starting now. If the investment yields 0.5% per month, compounded monthly, what is its value at the end of 24 months?

41. Peter wishes to create a retirement fund from which he can draw $20,000 when he retires and the same amount at each anniversary of his retirement for 10 years. He plans to retire 20 years from now. What investment need he make today if he can get a return of 5% per year, compounded annually?

42. In theory, drugs that decay exponentially always leave a residue in the body. However, in practice, once the drug has been in the body for 5 half-lives, it is regarded as being eliminated.[4] If a patient takes a tablet of the same drug every 5 half-lives forever, what is the upper limit to the amount of drug that can be in the body?

43. This problem shows how to estimate the cumulative effect of a tax cut on a country's economy. Suppose the government proposes a tax cut totaling $100 million. We assume that all the people who have extra money spend 80% of it and save 20%. Thus, of the extra income generated by the tax cut, $100(0.8) million = $80 million is spent and becomes extra income to someone else. These people also spend 80% of their additional income, or $80(0.8) million, and so on. Calculate the total additional spending created by such a tax cut.

44. (a) What is the present value of a $1000 bond which pays $50 a year for 10 years, starting one year from now? Assume the interest rate is 5% per year, compounded annually.
(b) Since $50 is 5% of $1000, this bond is called a 5% bond. What does your answer to part (a) tell you about the relationship between the principal and the present value of this bond if the interest rate is 5%?
(c) If the interest rate is more than 5% per year, compounded annually, which is larger: the principal or the present value of the bond? Why is the bond then described as *trading at a discount*?
(d) If the interest rate is less than 5% per year, compounded annually, why is the bond described as *trading at a premium*?

45. The government proposes a tax cut of $100 million as in Problem 43, but that economists now predict that people will spend 90% of their extra income and save only 10%. How much additional spending would be generated by the tax cut under these assumptions?

46. A ball is dropped from a height of 10 feet and bounces. Each bounce is $\frac{3}{4}$ of the height of the bounce before. Thus, after the ball hits the floor for the first time, the ball rises to a height of $10(\frac{3}{4}) = 7.5$ feet, and after it hits the floor for the second time, it rises to a height of $7.5(\frac{3}{4}) = 10(\frac{3}{4})^2 = 5.625$ feet. (Assume that there is no air resistance.)

(a) Find an expression for the height to which the ball rises after it hits the floor for the nth time.
(b) Find an expression for the total vertical distance the ball has traveled when it hits the floor for the first, second, third, and fourth times.
(c) Find an expression for the total vertical distance the ball has traveled when it hits the floor for the nth time. Express your answer in closed form.

47. You might think that the ball in Problem 46 keeps bouncing forever since it takes infinitely many bounces. This is not true!

(a) Show that a ball dropped from a height of h feet reaches the ground in $\frac{1}{4}\sqrt{h}$ seconds. (Assume $g = 32$ ft/sec^2)
(b) Show that the ball in Problem 46 stops bouncing after

$$\frac{1}{4}\sqrt{10} + \frac{1}{2}\sqrt{10}\sqrt{\frac{3}{4}}\left(\frac{1}{1-\sqrt{3/4}}\right) \approx 11 \text{ seconds.}$$

---

[4]http://dr.pierce1.net/PDF/half_life.pdf, accessed on May 10, 2003.

Strengthen Your Understanding

In Problems 48–49, explain what is wrong with the statement.

48. The sequence $4, 1, \frac{1}{4}, \frac{1}{16}, \ldots$ converges to $\dfrac{4}{1 - 1/4} = \dfrac{16}{3}$.

49. The sum of the infinite geometric series $1 - \frac{3}{2} + \frac{9}{4} - \frac{27}{8} + \cdots$ is $\dfrac{1}{1 + 3/2} = \dfrac{2}{5}$.

In Problems 50–53, give an example of:

50. A geometric series that does not converge.

51. A geometric series in which a term appears more than once.

52. A finite geometric series with four distinct terms whose sum is 10.

53. An infinite geometric series that converges to 10.

54. Which of the following geometric series converge?

   (I) $20 - 10 + 5 - 2.5 + \cdots$
   (II) $1 - 1.1 + 1.21 - 1.331 + \cdots$
   (III) $1 + 1.1 + 1.21 + 1.331 + \cdots$
   (IV) $1 + y^2 + y^4 + y^6 + \cdots$, for $-1 < y < 1$

   (a) (I) only
   (b) (IV) only
   (c) (I) and (IV)
   (d) (II) and (IV)
   (e) None of the other choices is correct.

9.3 CONVERGENCE OF SERIES

We now consider general series in which each term a_n is a number. The series can be written compactly using a $\sum$ sign as follows:

$$\sum_{n=1}^{\infty} a_n = a_1 + a_2 + a_3 + \cdots + a_n + \cdots.$$

For any values of a and x, the geometric series is such a series, with general term $a_n = ax^{n-1}$.

Partial Sums and Convergence of Series

As in Section 9.2, we define the *partial sum*, S_n, of the first n terms of a series as

$$S_n = \sum_{i=1}^{n} a_i = a_1 + a_2 + \cdots + a_n.$$

To investigate the convergence of the series, we consider the sequence of partial sums

$$S_1, S_2, S_3, \ldots, S_n, \ldots.$$

If S_n has a limit as $n \to \infty$, then we define the sum of the series to be that limit.

> If the sequence S_n of partial sums converges to S, so $\lim_{n \to \infty} S_n = S$, then we say the series $\sum_{n=1}^{\infty} a_n$ **converges** and that its sum is S. We write $\sum_{n=1}^{\infty} a_n = S$. If $\lim_{n \to \infty} S_n$ does not exist, we say that the series **diverges**.

The following example shows how a series leads to sequence of partial sums and how we use them to determine convergence.

Example 1   Investigate the convergence of the series with $a_n = 1/(n(n+1))$:

$$\sum_{n=1}^{\infty} a_n = \frac{1}{2} + \frac{1}{6} + \frac{1}{12} + \frac{1}{20} + \cdots.$$

Solution   In order to determine whether the series converges, we first find the partial sums:

$$S_1 = \frac{1}{2}$$

$$S_2 = \frac{1}{2} + \frac{1}{6} = \frac{2}{3}$$

$$S_3 = \frac{1}{2} + \frac{1}{6} + \frac{1}{12} = \frac{3}{4}$$

$$S_4 = \frac{1}{2} + \frac{1}{6} + \frac{1}{12} + \frac{1}{20} = \frac{4}{5}$$

$$\vdots$$

It appears that $S_n = n/(n+1)$ for each positive integer n. We check that this pattern continues by assuming that $S_n = n/(n+1)$ for a given integer n, adding a_{n+1}, and simplifying

$$S_{n+1} = S_n + a_{n+1} = \frac{n}{n+1} + \frac{1}{(n+1)(n+2)} = \frac{n^2 + 2n + 1}{(n+1)(n+2)} = \frac{n+1}{n+2}.$$

Thus the sequence of partial sums has formula $S_n = n/(n+1)$, which converges to 1, so the series $\sum_{n=1}^{\infty} a_n$ converges to 1. That is, we can say that

$$\frac{1}{2} + \frac{1}{6} + \frac{1}{12} + \frac{1}{20} + \cdots = 1.$$

Visualizing Series

We can visualize the terms of the series in Example 1 as the heights of the bars in Figure 9.4. The partial sums of the series are illustrated by stacking the bars on top of each other in Figure 9.5.

Figure 9.4: Terms of the series with $a_n = 1/(n(n+1))$

Figure 9.5: Partial sums of the series with $a_n = 1/(n(n+1))$

Here are some properties that are useful in determining whether or not a series converges.

Theorem 9.2: Convergence Properties of Series

1. If $\displaystyle\sum_{n=1}^{\infty} a_n$ and $\displaystyle\sum_{n=1}^{\infty} b_n$ converge and if k is a constant, then

   - $\displaystyle\sum_{n=1}^{\infty} (a_n + b_n)$ converges to $\displaystyle\sum_{n=1}^{\infty} a_n + \sum_{n=1}^{\infty} b_n$.

   - $\displaystyle\sum_{n=1}^{\infty} k a_n$ converges to $k \displaystyle\sum_{n=1}^{\infty} a_n$.

2. Changing a finite number of terms in a series does not change whether or not it converges, although it may change the value of its sum if it does converge.

3. If $\displaystyle\lim_{n \to \infty} a_n \neq 0$ or $\displaystyle\lim_{n \to \infty} a_n$ does not exist, then $\displaystyle\sum_{n=1}^{\infty} a_n$ diverges.

4. If $\displaystyle\sum_{n=1}^{\infty} a_n$ diverges, then $\displaystyle\sum_{n=1}^{\infty} k a_n$ diverges if $k \neq 0$.

For proofs of these properties, see Problems 39–42. As for improper integrals, the convergence of a series is determined by its behavior for large n. (See the "behaves like" principle on page 404.) From Property 2 we see that, if N is a positive integer, then $\sum_{n=1}^{\infty} a_n$ and $\sum_{n=N}^{\infty} a_n$ either both converge or both diverge. Thus, if all we care about is the convergence of a series, we can omit the limits and write $\sum a_n$.

Example 2   Does the series $\sum (1 - e^{-n})$ converge?

Solution   Since the terms in the series $a_n = 1 - e^{-n}$ tend to 1, not 0, as $n \to \infty$, the series diverges by Property 3 of Theorem 9.2.

Comparison of Series and Integrals

We investigate the convergence of some series by comparison with an improper integral. The *harmonic series* is the infinite series

$$\sum_{n=1}^{\infty} \frac{1}{n} = 1 + \frac{1}{2} + \frac{1}{3} + \frac{1}{4} + \cdots + \frac{1}{n} + \cdots.$$

Convergence of this sum would mean that the sequence of partial sums

$$S_1 = 1, \quad S_2 = 1 + \frac{1}{2}, \quad S_3 = 1 + \frac{1}{2} + \frac{1}{3}, \quad \cdots, \quad S_n = 1 + \frac{1}{2} + \frac{1}{3} + \cdots + \frac{1}{n}, \quad \cdots$$

tends to a limit as $n \to \infty$. Let's look at some values:

$$S_1 = 1, \quad S_{10} \approx 2.93, \quad S_{100} \approx 5.19, \quad S_{1000} \approx 7.49, \quad S_{10000} \approx 9.79.$$

The growth of these partial sums is slow, but they do in fact grow without bound, so the harmonic series diverges. This is justified in the following example and in Problem 46.

Example 3   Show that the harmonic series $1 + 1/2 + 1/3 + 1/4 + \cdots$ diverges.

Solution   The idea is to approximate $\int_1^{\infty} (1/x)\, dx$ by a left-hand sum, where the terms $1, 1/2, 1/3, \ldots$ are heights of rectangles of base 1. In Figure 9.6, the sum of the areas of the 3 rectangles is larger than the area under the curve between $x = 1$ and $x = 4$, and the same kind of relationship holds for the first n rectangles. Thus, we have

$$S_n = 1 + \frac{1}{2} + \frac{1}{3} + \cdots + \frac{1}{n} > \int_1^{n+1} \frac{1}{x} \, dx = \ln(n+1).$$

Since $\ln(n+1)$ gets arbitrarily large as $n \to \infty$, so do the partial sums, S_n. Thus, the partial sums have no limit, so the series diverges.

Figure 9.6: Comparing the harmonic series to $\int_1^\infty (1/x) \, dx$

Notice that the harmonic series diverges, even though $\displaystyle\lim_{n \to \infty} a_n = \lim_{n \to \infty} (1/n) = 0$. Although Property 3 of Theorem 9.2 guarantees $\sum a_n$ diverges if $\displaystyle\lim_{n \to \infty} a_n \neq 0$, it is possible for $\sum a_n$ to either converge or diverge if $\displaystyle\lim_{n \to \infty} a_n = 0$. When we have $\displaystyle\lim_{n \to \infty} a_n = 0$, we must investigate the series further to determine whether it converges or diverges.

Example 4   By comparison with the improper integral $\int_1^\infty (1/x^2) \, dx$, show that the following series converges:

$$\sum_{n=1}^\infty \frac{1}{n^2} = 1 + \frac{1}{4} + \frac{1}{9} + \cdots.$$

Solution   Since we want to show that $\displaystyle\sum_{n=1}^\infty 1/n^2$ converges, we want to show that the partial sums of this series tend to a limit. We do this by showing that the sequence of partial sums increases and is bounded above, so Theorem 9.1 applies.

Each successive partial sum is obtained from the previous one by adding one more term in the series. Since all the terms are positive, the sequence of partial sums is increasing.

To show that the partial sums of $\displaystyle\sum_{n=1}^\infty 1/n^2$ are bounded, we consider the right-hand sum represented by the area of the rectangles in Figure 9.7. We start at $x = 1$, since the area under the curve is infinite for $0 \leq x \leq 1$. The shaded rectangles in Figure 9.7 suggest that:

$$\frac{1}{4} + \frac{1}{9} + \frac{1}{16} + \cdots + \frac{1}{n^2} \leq \int_1^\infty \frac{1}{x^2} \, dx.$$

Figure 9.7: Comparing $\sum_{n=1}^\infty 1/n^2$ to $\int_1^\infty (1/x^2) \, dx$

The area under the graph is finite, since

$$\int_1^\infty \frac{1}{x^2}\, dx = \lim_{b\to\infty} \int_1^b \frac{1}{x^2}\, dx = \lim_{b\to\infty} \left(-\frac{1}{b} + 1\right) = 1.$$

To get S_n, we add 1 to both sides, giving

$$S_n = 1 + \frac{1}{4} + \frac{1}{9} + \frac{1}{16} + \cdots + \frac{1}{n^2} \le 1 + \int_1^\infty \frac{1}{x^2}\, dx = 2.$$

Thus, the sequence of partial sums is bounded above by 2. Hence, by Theorem 9.1 the sequence of partial sums converges, so the series converges.

Notice that we have shown that the series in the Example 4 converges, but we have not found its sum. The integral gives us a bound on the partial sums, but it does not give us the limit of the partial sums. Euler proved the remarkable fact that the sum is $\pi^2/6$.

The method of Examples 3 and 4 can be used to prove the following theorem. See Problem 45.

Theorem 9.3: The Integral Test

Suppose $a_n = f(n)$, where $f(x)$ is decreasing and positive.

- If $\displaystyle\int_1^\infty f(x)\, dx$ converges, then $\sum a_n$ converges.

- If $\displaystyle\int_1^\infty f(x)\, dx$ diverges, then $\sum a_n$ diverges.

Suppose $f(x)$ is continuous. Then if $f(x)$ is positive and decreasing for all x beyond some point, say c, the integral test can be used.

The integral test allows us to analyze a family of series, the p-series, and see how convergence depends on the parameter p.

Example 5   For what values of p does the series $\displaystyle\sum_{n=1}^{\infty} 1/n^p$ converge?

Solution   If $p \le 0$, the terms in the series $a_n = 1/n^p$ do not tend to 0 as $n \to \infty$. Thus the series diverges for $p \le 0$.

If $p > 0$, we compare $\displaystyle\sum_{n=1}^{\infty} 1/n^p$ to the integral $\int_1^\infty 1/x^p\, dx$. In Example 3 of Section 7.6 we saw that the integral converges if $p > 1$ and diverges if $p \le 1$. By the integral test, we conclude that $\sum 1/n^p$ converges if $p > 1$ and diverges if $p \le 1$.

We can summarize Example 5 as follows:

The p-**series** $\displaystyle\sum_{n=1}^{\infty} 1/n^p$ converges if $p > 1$ and diverges if $p \le 1$.

Exercises and Problems for Section 9.3

Exercises

In Exercises 1–3, find the first five terms of the sequence of partial sums.

1. $\displaystyle\sum_{n=1}^{\infty} n$ **2.** $\displaystyle\sum_{n=1}^{\infty} \frac{(-1)^n}{n}$ **3.** $\displaystyle\sum_{n=1}^{\infty} \frac{1}{n(n+1)}$

In Exercises 4–7, use the integral test to decide whether the series converges or diverges.

4. $\displaystyle\sum_{n=1}^{\infty} \frac{1}{(n+2)^2}$ **5.** $\displaystyle\sum_{n=1}^{\infty} \frac{n}{n^2+1}$

6. $\displaystyle\sum_{n=1}^{\infty} \frac{1}{e^n}$ **7.** $\displaystyle\sum_{n=2}^{\infty} \frac{1}{n(\ln n)^2}$

8. Use comparison with $\int_1^{\infty} x^{-3}\,dx$ to show that $\sum_{n=2}^{\infty} 1/n^3$ converges to a number less than or equal to $1/2$.

9. Use comparison with $\int_0^{\infty} 1/(x^2+1)\,dx$ to show that $\sum_{n=1}^{\infty} 1/(n^2+1)$ converges to a number less than or equal to $\pi/2$.

In Exercises 10–12, explain why the integral test cannot be used to decide if the series converges or diverges.

10. $\displaystyle\sum_{n=1}^{\infty} n^2$ **11.** $\displaystyle\sum_{n=1}^{\infty} \frac{(-1)^n}{n}$ **12.** $\displaystyle\sum_{n=1}^{\infty} e^{-n}\sin n$

Problems

In Problems 13–32, does the series converge or diverge?

13. $\displaystyle\sum_{n=0}^{\infty} \frac{3}{n+2}$ **14.** $\displaystyle\sum_{n=0}^{\infty} \frac{4}{2n+1}$

15. $\displaystyle\sum_{n=0}^{\infty} \frac{2}{\sqrt{2+n}}$ **16.** $\displaystyle\sum_{n=0}^{\infty} \frac{2n}{1+n^4}$

17. $\displaystyle\sum_{n=0}^{\infty} \frac{2n}{(1+n^2)^2}$ **18.** $\displaystyle\sum_{n=0}^{\infty} \frac{2n}{\sqrt{4+n^2}}$

19. $\displaystyle\sum_{n=1}^{\infty} \frac{3}{(2n-1)^2}$ **20.** $\displaystyle\sum_{n=1}^{\infty} \frac{4}{(2n+1)^3}$

21. $\displaystyle\sum_{n=0}^{\infty} \frac{3}{n^2+4}$ **22.** $\displaystyle\sum_{n=0}^{\infty} \frac{2}{1+4n^2}$

23. $\displaystyle\sum_{n=1}^{\infty} \frac{n}{n+1}$ **24.** $\displaystyle\sum_{n=0}^{\infty} \frac{n+1}{2n+3}$

25. $\displaystyle\sum_{n=1}^{\infty} \left(\frac{1}{2}\right)^n + \left(\frac{2}{3}\right)^n$ **26.** $\displaystyle\sum_{n=1}^{\infty} \left(\left(\frac{3}{4}\right)^n + \frac{1}{n}\right)$

27. $\displaystyle\sum_{n=1}^{\infty} \frac{n+2^n}{n2^n}$ **28.** $\displaystyle\sum_{n=1}^{\infty} \frac{\ln n}{n}$

29. $\displaystyle\sum_{n=1}^{\infty} \frac{1}{n(1+\ln n)}$ **30.** $\displaystyle\sum_{n=3}^{\infty} \frac{n+1}{n^2+2n+2}$

31. $\displaystyle\sum_{n=0}^{\infty} \frac{1}{n^2+2n+2}$ **32.** $\displaystyle\sum_{n=2}^{\infty} \frac{n\ln n+4}{n^2}$

33. Show that $\displaystyle\sum_{n=1}^{\infty} \frac{1}{\ln(2^n)}$ diverges.

34. Show that $\displaystyle\sum_{n=1}^{\infty} \frac{1}{(\ln(2^n))^2}$ converges.

35. (a) Find the partial sum, S_n, of $\displaystyle\sum_{n=1}^{\infty} \ln\left(\frac{n+1}{n}\right)$.
(b) Does the series in part (a) converge or diverge?

36. (a) Show $r^{\ln n} = n^{\ln r}$ for positive numbers n and r.
(b) For what values $r > 0$ does $\sum_{n=1}^{\infty} r^{\ln n}$ converge?

37. Consider the series $\displaystyle\sum_{k=1}^{\infty} \frac{1}{k(k+1)} = \frac{1}{1\cdot 2} + \frac{1}{2\cdot 3} + \cdots$.

(a) Show that $\dfrac{1}{k} - \dfrac{1}{k+1} = \dfrac{1}{k(k+1)}$.
(b) Use part (a) to find the partial sums S_3, S_{10}, and S_n.
(c) Use part (b) to show that the sequence of partial sums S_n, and therefore the series, converges to 1.

38. Consider the series

$$\sum_{k=1}^{\infty} \ln\left(\frac{k(k+2)}{(k+1)^2}\right) = \ln\left(\frac{1\cdot 3}{2\cdot 2}\right) + \ln\left(\frac{2\cdot 4}{3\cdot 3}\right) + \cdots.$$

(a) Show that the partial sum of the first three nonzero terms $S_3 = \ln(5/8)$.
(b) Show that the partial sum $S_n = \ln\left(\dfrac{n+2}{2(n+1)}\right)$.
(c) Use part (b) to show that the partial sums S_n, and therefore the series, converge to $\ln(1/2)$.

39. Show that if $\sum a_n$ and $\sum b_n$ converge and if k is a constant, then $\sum (a_n + b_n)$, $\sum (a_n - b_n)$, and $\sum k a_n$ converge.

40. Let N be a positive integer. Show that if $a_n = b_n$ for $n \geq N$, then $\sum a_n$ and $\sum b_n$ either both converge, or both diverge.

41. Show that if $\sum a_n$ converges, then $\lim_{n \to \infty} a_n = 0$. [Hint: Consider $\lim_{n \to \infty} (S_n - S_{n-1})$, where S_n is the nth partial sum.]

42. Show that if $\sum a_n$ diverges and $k \neq 0$, then $\sum k a_n$ diverges.

43. The series $\sum a_n$ converges. Explain, by looking at partial sums, why the series $\sum (a_{n+1} - a_n)$ also converges.

44. The series $\sum a_n$ diverges. Give examples that show the series $\sum (a_{n+1} - a_n)$ could converge or diverge.

45. In this problem, you will justify the integral test. Suppose $c \geq 0$ and $f(x)$ is a decreasing positive function, defined for all numbers $x \geq c$, with $f(n) = a_n$ for all integers $n \geq c$.

  (a) Suppose that $\int_c^\infty f(x)\,dx$ diverges. By considering rectangles above the graph of f, show that $\sum a_n$ diverges. [Hint: See Example 3 on page 507.]

  (b) Suppose $\int_c^\infty f(x)\,dx$ converges. By considering rectangles under the graph of f, show that $\sum a_n$ converges. [Hint: See Example 4 on page 508.]

46. Consider the following grouping of terms in the harmonic series:

$$1 + \left(\frac{1}{2}\right) + \left(\frac{1}{3} + \frac{1}{4}\right) + \left(\frac{1}{5} + \frac{1}{6} + \frac{1}{7} + \frac{1}{8}\right) +$$
$$\left(\frac{1}{9} + \frac{1}{10} + \cdots + \frac{1}{16}\right) + \cdots$$

  (a) Show that the sum of each group of fractions is more than $1/2$.

  (b) Explain why this shows that the harmonic series does not converge.

47. Show that $\displaystyle\sum_{n=2}^{\infty} \frac{1}{n \ln n}$ diverges.

  (a) Using the integral test.

  (b) By considering the grouping of terms

$$\left(\frac{1}{2\ln 2}\right) + \left(\frac{1}{3\ln 3} + \frac{1}{4\ln 4}\right)$$
$$+ \left(\frac{1}{5\ln 5} + \frac{1}{6\ln 6} + \frac{1}{7\ln 7} + \frac{1}{8\ln 8}\right) + \cdots.$$

48. Consider the sequence given by

$$a_n = \left(1 + \frac{1}{2} + \frac{1}{3} + \cdots \frac{1}{n}\right) - \ln(n+1).$$

  (a) Show that $a_n < a_{n+1}$ for all n. [Use a left-sum approximation to $\int_1^{n+1} (1/x)\,dx$ with $\Delta x = 1$.]

  (b) Show that $a_n < 1$ for all n.

  (c) Explain why $\lim_{n \to \infty} a_n$ exists.

  (d) The number $\gamma = \lim_{n \to \infty} a_n$ is called *Euler's constant*. Estimate γ to two decimal places by computing a_{200}.

49. On page 509, we gave Euler's result

$$\sum_{n=1}^{\infty} \frac{1}{n^2} = \frac{\pi^2}{6}.$$

  (a) Find the sum of the first 20 terms of this series. Give your answer to three decimal places.

  (b) Use your answer to estimate π. Give your answer to two decimal places.

  (c) Repeat parts (a) and (b) with 100 terms.

  (d) Use a right sum approximation to bound the error in approximating $\pi^2/6$ by $\sum_{n=1}^{20} (1/n^2)$ and by $\sum_{n=1}^{100} (1/n^2)$.

50. This problem approximates e using

$$e = \sum_{n=0}^{\infty} \frac{1}{n!}.$$

  (a) Find a lower bound for e by evaluating the first five terms of the series.

  (b) Show that $1/n! \leq 1/2^{n-1}$ for $n \geq 1$.

  (c) Find an upper bound for e using part (b).

51. In this problem we investigate how fast the partial sums $S_N = 1^5 + 2^5 + 3^5 + \cdots + N^5$ of the divergent series $\sum_{n=1}^{\infty} n^5$ grow as N gets larger and larger. Show that

  (a) $S_N > N^6/6$ by considering the right-hand Riemann sum for $\int_0^N x^5 dx$ with $\Delta x = 1$.

  (b) $S_N < ((N+1)^6 - 1)/6$ by considering the left-hand Riemann sum for $\int_1^{N+1} x^5 dx$ with $\Delta x = 1$.

  (c) $\lim_{N \to \infty} S_N/(N^6/6) = 1$. We say that S_N is asymptotic to $N^6/6$ as N goes to infinity.

52. In 1913, the English mathematician G. H. Hardy received a letter from the then-unknown Indian mathematical genius Srinivasa Ramanujan, and was astounded by the results it contained.[5] In particular, Hardy was interested in Ramanujan's results involving infinite series, such as:

$$\frac{2}{\pi} = 1 - 5\left(\frac{1}{2}\right)^3 + 9\left(\frac{1 \times 3}{2 \times 4}\right)^3 - 13\left(\frac{1 \times 3 \times 5}{2 \times 4 \times 6}\right)^3 + \cdots.$$

In this problem you will find a formula for the general term a_n of this series.

  (a) Write a formula in terms of n for c_n where $c_1 = 1, c_2 = -5, c_3 = 9, c_4 = -13, \ldots$.

[5]http://en.wikipedia.org/wiki/Srinivasa_Ramanujan, page accessed April 2, 2011.

(b) For products of all odd or even values up to n, we use the so-called *double factorial* notation $n!!$. For instance, we write $7!! = 1 \times 3 \times 5 \times 7$ and $8!! = 2 \times 4 \times 6 \times 8$. By definition,[6] we assume that $(-1)!! = 0!! = 1!! = 1$ and that $2!! = 2$. With this notation, write a formula in terms of n for b_n where

$$b_2 = \left(\frac{1}{2}\right)^3, b_3 = \left(\frac{1 \times 3}{2 \times 4}\right)^3, b_4 = \left(\frac{1 \times 3 \times 5}{2 \times 4 \times 6}\right)^3, \ldots$$

(c) Use your answers to parts (a) and (b), write a formula in terms of n for a_n where

$$a_1 = 1, a_2 = -5\left(\frac{1}{2}\right)^3, a_3 = 9\left(\frac{1 \times 3}{2 \times 4}\right)^3,$$

$$a_4 = -13\left(\frac{1 \times 3 \times 5}{2 \times 4 \times 6}\right)^3, \ldots.$$

Strengthen Your Understanding

In Problems 53–54, explain what is wrong with the statement.

53. The series $\sum (1/n)^2$ converges because the terms approach zero as $n \to \infty$.

54. The integral $\int_1^\infty (1/x^3)\,dx$ and the series $\sum_{n=1}^\infty 1/n^3$ both converge to the same value, $\frac{1}{2}$.

In Problems 55–56, give an example of:

55. A series $\sum_{n=1}^\infty a_n$ with $\lim_{n\to\infty} a_n = 0$, but such that $\sum_{n=1}^\infty a_n$ diverges.

56. A convergent series $\sum_{n=1}^\infty a_n$, whose terms are all positive, such that the series $\sum_{n=1}^\infty \sqrt{a_n}$ is not convergent.

Decide if the statements in Problems 57–64 are true or false. Give an explanation for your answer.

57. $\displaystyle\sum_{n=1}^\infty (1 + (-1)^n)$ is a series of nonnegative terms.

58. If a series converges, then the sequence of partial sums of the series also converges.

59. If $\sum |a_n + b_n|$ converges, then $\sum |a_n|$ and $\sum |b_n|$ converge.

60. The series $\displaystyle\sum_{n=1}^\infty 2^{(-1)^n}$ converges.

61. If a series $\sum a_n$ converges, then the terms, a_n, tend to zero as n increases.

62. If the terms, a_n, of a series tend to zero as n increases, then the series $\sum a_n$ converges.

63. If $\sum a_n$ does not converge and $\sum b_n$ does not converge, then $\sum a_n b_n$ does not converge.

64. If $\sum a_n b_n$ converges, then $\sum a_n$ and $\sum b_n$ converge.

65. Which of the following defines a convergent sequence of partial sums?

(a) Each term in the sequence is closer to the last term than any two prior consecutive terms.

(b) Assume that the sequence of partial sums converges to a number, L. Regardless of how small a number you give me, say ϵ, I can find a value of N such that the Nth term of the sequence is within ϵ of L.

(c) Assume that the sequence of partial sums converges to a number, L. I can find a value of N such that all the terms in the sequence, past the Nth term, are less than L.

(d) Assume that the sequence of partial sums converges to a number, L. Regardless of how small a number you give me, say ϵ, I can find a value of N such that all the terms in the sequence, past the Nth term, are within ϵ of L.

9.4 TESTS FOR CONVERGENCE

Comparison of Series

In Section 7.7, we compared two integrals to decide whether an improper integral converged. In Theorem 9.3 we compared an integral and a series. Now we compare two series.

Theorem 9.4: Comparison Test

Suppose $0 \leq a_n \leq b_n$ for all n beyond a certain value.

- If $\sum b_n$ converges, then $\sum a_n$ converges.
- If $\sum a_n$ diverges, then $\sum b_n$ diverges.

Since $a_n \leq b_n$, the plot of the a_n terms lies under the plot of the b_n terms. (See Figure 9.8.) The comparison test says that if the total area for $\sum b_n$ is finite, then the total area for $\sum a_n$ is finite also. If the total area for $\sum a_n$ is not finite, then neither is the total area for $\sum b_n$.

---

[6]http://mathworld.wolfram.com/DoubleFactorial.html, page accessed April 2, 2011.

Figure 9.8: Each a_n is represented by the area of a dark rectangle, and each b_n by a dark plus a light rectangle

---

Example 1   Use the comparison test to determine whether the series $\displaystyle\sum_{n=1}^{\infty} \frac{1}{n^3 + 1}$ converges.

Solution   For $n \geq 1$, we know that $n^3 \leq n^3 + 1$, so

$$0 \leq \frac{1}{n^3 + 1} \leq \frac{1}{n^3}.$$

Thus, every term in the series $\sum_{n=1}^{\infty} 1/(n^3 + 1)$ is less than or equal to the corresponding term in $\sum_{n=1}^{\infty} 1/n^3$. Since we saw that $\sum_{n=1}^{\infty} 1/n^3$ converges as a p-series with $p > 1$, we know that $\sum_{n=1}^{\infty} 1/(n^3 + 1)$ converges.

Example 2   Decide whether the following series converge: (a) $\displaystyle\sum_{n=1}^{\infty} \frac{n-1}{n^3 + 3}$ (b) $\displaystyle\sum_{n=1}^{\infty} \frac{6n^2 + 1}{2n^3 - 1}$.

Solution   (a) Since the convergence is determined by the behavior of the terms for large n, we observe that

$$\frac{n-1}{n^3 + 3} \quad \text{behaves like} \quad \frac{n}{n^3} = \frac{1}{n^2} \quad \text{as} \quad n \to \infty.$$

Since $\sum 1/n^2$ converges, we guess that $\sum (n-1)/(n^3 + 3)$ converges. To confirm this, we use the comparison test. Since a fraction increases if its numerator is made larger or its denominator is made smaller, we have

$$0 \leq \frac{n-1}{n^3 + 3} \leq \frac{n}{n^3} = \frac{1}{n^2} \quad \text{for all} \quad n \geq 1.$$

Thus, the series $\sum (n-1)/(n^3 + 3)$ converges by comparison with $\sum 1/n^2$.

(b) First, we observe that

$$\frac{6n^2 + 1}{2n^3 - 1} \quad \text{behaves like} \quad \frac{6n^2}{2n^3} = \frac{3}{n} \quad \text{as} \quad n \to \infty.$$

Since $\sum 1/n$ diverges, so does $\sum 3/n$, and we guess that $\sum (6n^2 + 1)/(2n^3 - 1)$ diverges. To confirm this, we use the comparison test. Since a fraction decreases if its numerator is made smaller or its denominator is made larger, we have

$$0 \leq \frac{6n^2}{2n^3} \leq \frac{6n^2 + 1}{2n^3 - 1},$$

so

$$0 \leq \frac{3}{n} \leq \frac{6n^2 + 1}{2n^3 - 1}.$$

Thus, the series $\sum (6n^2 + 1)/(2n^3 - 1)$ diverges by comparison with $\sum 3/n$.

Limit Comparison Test

The comparison test uses the relationship between the terms of two series, $a_n \leq b_n$, which can be difficult to establish. However, the convergence or divergence of a series depends only on the long-run behavior of the terms as $n \to \infty$; this idea leads to the *limit comparison test*.

Example 3   Predict the convergence or divergence of

$$\sum \frac{n^2 - 5}{n^3 + n + 2}.$$

Solution   As $n \to \infty$, the highest power terms in the numerator and denominator, n^2 and n^3, dominate. Thus the term

$$a_n = \frac{n^2 - 5}{n^3 + n + 2}$$

behaves, as $n \to \infty$, like

$$\frac{n^2}{n^3} = \frac{1}{n}.$$

Since the harmonic series $\sum 1/n$ diverges, we guess that $\sum a_n$ also diverges. However, the inequality

$$\frac{n^2 - 5}{n^3 + n + 2} \leq \frac{1}{n}$$

is in the wrong direction to use with the comparison test to confirm divergence, since we need the given series to be greater than a known divergent series.

The following test can be used to confirm a prediction of convergence or divergence, as in Example 3, without inequalities.

Theorem 9.5: Limit Comparison Test

Suppose $a_n > 0$ and $b_n > 0$ for all n. If

$$\lim_{n \to \infty} \frac{a_n}{b_n} = c \qquad \text{where } c > 0,$$

then the two series $\sum a_n$ and $\sum b_n$ either both converge or both diverge.

The limit $\lim_{n \to \infty} a_n/b_n = c$ captures the idea that a_n "behaves like" cb_n as $n \to \infty$.

Example 4   Use the limit comparison test to determine if the following series converge or diverge.

(a) $\sum \dfrac{n^2 - 5}{n^3 + n + 2}$

(b) $\sum \sin\left(\dfrac{1}{n}\right)$

Solution   (a) We take $a_n = \dfrac{n^2 - 5}{n^3 + n + 2}$. Because a_n behaves like $\dfrac{n^2}{n^3} = \dfrac{1}{n}$ as $n \to \infty$ we take $b_n = 1/n$. We have

$$\lim_{n \to \infty} \frac{a_n}{b_n} = \lim_{n \to \infty} \frac{1}{1/n} \cdot \frac{n^2 - 5}{n^3 + n + 2} = \lim_{n \to \infty} \frac{n^3 - 5n}{n^3 + n + 2} = 1.$$

The limit comparison test applies with $c = 1$. Since $\sum 1/n$ diverges, the limit comparison test shows that $\sum \dfrac{n^2 - 5}{n^3 + n + 2}$ also diverges.

(b) Since $\sin x \approx x$ for x near 0, we know that $\sin(1/n)$ behaves like $1/n$ as $n \to \infty$. We apply the limit comparison test with $a_n = \sin(1/n)$ and $b_n = 1/n$. We have

$$\lim_{n \to \infty} \frac{a_n}{b_n} = \lim_{n \to \infty} \frac{\sin(1/n)}{1/n} = 1.$$

Thus $c = 1$ and since $\sum 1/n$ diverges, the series $\sum \sin(1/n)$ also diverges.

Series of Both Positive and Negative Terms

If $\sum a_n$ has both positive and negative terms, then its plot has rectangles lying both above and below the horizontal axis. See Figure 9.9. The total area of the rectangles is no longer equal to $\sum a_n$. However, it is still true that if the total area of the rectangles above and below the axis is finite, then the series converges. The area of the nth rectangle is $|a_n|$, so we have:

Theorem 9.6: Convergence of Absolute Values Implies Convergence

If $\sum |a_n|$ converges, then so does $\sum a_n$.

Problem 93 shows how to prove this result.

Figure 9.9: Representing a series with positive and negative terms

---

Example 5   Explain how we know that the following series converges:

$$\sum_{n=1}^{\infty} \frac{(-1)^{n-1}}{n^2} = 1 - \frac{1}{4} + \frac{1}{9} - \cdots.$$

Solution   Writing $a_n = (-1)^{n-1}/n^2$, we have

$$|a_n| = \left| \frac{(-1)^{n-1}}{n^2} \right| = \frac{1}{n^2}.$$

The p-series $\sum 1/n^2$ converges, since $p > 1$, so $\sum (-1)^{n-1}/n^2$ converges.

Comparison with a Geometric Series: The Ratio Test

A geometric series $\sum a_n$ has the property that the ratio a_{n+1}/a_n is constant for all n. For many other series, this ratio, although not constant, tends to a constant as n increases. In some ways, such series behave like geometric series. In particular, a geometric series converges if the ratio $|a_{n+1}/a_n| < 1$. A non-geometric series also converges if the ratio $|a_{n+1}/a_n|$ tends to a limit which is less than 1. This idea leads to the following test.

Theorem 9.7: The Ratio Test

For a series $\sum a_n$, suppose the sequence of ratios $|a_{n+1}|/|a_n|$ has a limit:

$$\lim_{n \to \infty} \frac{|a_{n+1}|}{|a_n|} = L.$$

- If $L < 1$, then $\sum a_n$ converges.
- If $L > 1$, or if L is infinite,[7] then $\sum a_n$ diverges.
- If $L = 1$, the test does not tell us anything about the convergence of $\sum a_n$.

---

[7]That is, the sequence $|a_{n+1}|/|a_n|$ grows without bound.

Proof Here are the main steps in the proof. Suppose $\lim\limits_{n \to \infty} \dfrac{|a_{n+1}|}{|a_n|} = L < 1$. Let x be a number between L and 1. Then for all sufficiently large n, say for all $n \geq k$, we have

$$\frac{|a_{n+1}|}{|a_n|} < x.$$

Then,

$$|a_{k+1}| < |a_k|x,$$
$$|a_{k+2}| < |a_{k+1}|x < |a_k|x^2,$$
$$|a_{k+3}| < |a_{k+2}|x < |a_k|x^3,$$

and so on. Thus, writing $a = |a_k|$, we have for $i = 1, 2, 3, \ldots,$

$$|a_{k+i}| < ax^i.$$

Now we can use the comparison test: $\sum |a_{k+i}|$ converges by comparison with the geometric series $\sum ax^i$. Since $\sum |a_{k+i}|$ converges, Theorem 9.6 tells us that $\sum a_{k+i}$ converges. So, by property 2 of Theorem 9.2, we see that $\sum a_n$ converges too.

If $L > 1$, then for sufficiently large n, say $n \geq m$,

$$|a_{n+1}| > |a_n|,$$

so the sequence $|a_m|, |a_{m+1}|, |a_{m+2}|, \ldots,$ is increasing. Thus, $\lim\limits_{n \to \infty} a_n \neq 0$, so $\sum a_n$ diverges (by Theorem 9.2, property 3). The argument in the case that $|a_{n+1}|/|a_n|$ is unbounded is similar.

Example 6   Show that the following series converges:

$$\sum_{n=1}^{\infty} \frac{1}{n!} = 1 + \frac{1}{2!} + \frac{1}{3!} + \cdots.$$

Solution   Since $a_n = 1/n!$ and $a_{n+1} = 1/(n+1)!$, we have

$$\frac{|a_{n+1}|}{|a_n|} = \frac{1/(n+1)!}{1/n!} = \frac{n!}{(n+1)!} = \frac{n(n-1)(n-2)\cdots 2 \cdot 1}{(n+1)n(n-1)\cdots 2 \cdot 1}.$$

We cancel $n(n-1)(n-2) \cdot \cdots \cdot 2 \cdot 1$, giving

$$\lim_{n \to \infty} \frac{|a_{n+1}|}{|a_n|} = \lim_{n \to \infty} \frac{n!}{(n+1)!} = \lim_{n \to \infty} \frac{1}{n+1} = 0.$$

Because the limit is 0, which is less than 1, the ratio test tells us that $\sum\limits_{n=1}^{\infty} 1/n!$ converges. In Chapter 10, we see that the sum is $e - 1$.

Example 7   What does the ratio test tell us about the convergence of the following two series?

$$\sum_{n=1}^{\infty} \frac{1}{n} \quad \text{and} \quad \sum_{n=1}^{\infty} \frac{(-1)^{n-1}}{n}.$$

Solution   Because $|(-1)^n| = 1$, in both cases we have $\lim_{n \to \infty} |a_{n+1}/a_n| = \lim_{n \to \infty} n/(n+1) = 1$. The first series is the harmonic series, which diverges. However, Example 8 will show that the second series converges. Thus, if the ratio test gives a limit of 1, the ratio test does not tell us anything about the convergence of a series.

Alternating Series

A series is called an *alternating series* if the terms alternate in sign. For example,

$$\sum_{n=1}^{\infty} \frac{(-1)^{n-1}}{n} = 1 - \frac{1}{2} + \frac{1}{3} - \frac{1}{4} + \cdots + \frac{(-1)^{n-1}}{n} + \cdots.$$

The convergence of an alternating series can often be determined using the following test:

Theorem 9.8: Alternating Series Test

An alternating series of the form

$$\sum_{n=1}^{\infty} (-1)^{n-1} a_n = a_1 - a_2 + a_3 - a_4 + \cdots + (-1)^{n-1} a_n + \cdots$$

converges if

$$0 < a_{n+1} < a_n \quad \text{for all } n \qquad \text{and} \qquad \lim_{n \to \infty} a_n = 0.$$

Although we do not prove this result, we can see why it is reasonable. The first partial sum, $S_1 = a_1$, is positive. The second, $S_2 = a_1 - a_2$, is still positive, since $a_2 < a_1$, but S_2 is smaller than S_1. (See Figure 9.10.) The next sum, $S_3 = a_1 - a_2 + a_3$, is greater than S_2 but smaller than S_1. The partial sums oscillate back and forth, and since the distance between them tends to 0, they eventually converge.

Figure 9.10: Partial sums, S_1, S_2, S_3, S_4 of an alternating series

---

Example 8   Show that the following alternating harmonic series converges:

$$\sum_{n=1}^{\infty} \frac{(-1)^{n-1}}{n}.$$

Solution   We have $a_n = 1/n$ and $a_{n+1} = 1/(n+1)$. Thus,

$$a_{n+1} = \frac{1}{n+1} < \frac{1}{n} = a_n \quad \text{for all } n, \quad \text{and} \quad \lim_{n \to \infty} 1/n = 0.$$

Thus, the hypothesis of Theorem 9.8 is satisfied, so the alternating harmonic series converges.

Suppose S is the sum of an alternating series, so $S = \lim_{n \to \infty} S_n$. Then S is trapped between any two consecutive partial sums, say S_3 and S_4 or S_4 and S_5, so

$$S_2 < S_4 < \cdots < S < \cdots < S_3 < S_1.$$

Thus, the error in using S_n to approximate the true sum S is less than the distance from S_n to S_{n+1}, which is a_{n+1}. Stated symbolically, we have the following result:

> ## Theorem 9.9: Error Bounds for Alternating Series
>
> Let $S_n = \sum_{i=1}^{n} (-1)^{i-1} a_i$ be the nth partial sum of an alternating series and let $S = \lim_{n \to \infty} S_n$. Suppose that $0 < a_{n+1} < a_n$ for all n and $\lim_{n\to\infty} a_n = 0$. Then
>
> $$|S - S_n| < a_{n+1}.$$

Thus, provided S_n converges to S by the alternating series test, the error in using S_n to approximate S is less than the magnitude of the first term of the series which is omitted in the approximation.

Example 9   Estimate the error in approximating the sum of the alternating harmonic series $\sum_{n=1}^{\infty} (-1)^{n-1}/n$ by the sum of the first nine terms.

Solution   The ninth partial sum is given by

$$S_9 = 1 - \frac{1}{2} + \frac{1}{3} - \cdots + \frac{1}{9} = 0.7456\ldots.$$

The first term omitted is $-1/10$, with magnitude 0.1. By Theorem 9.9, we know that the true value of the sum differs from $0.7456\ldots$ by less than 0.1.

Absolute and Conditional Convergence

> We say that the series $\sum a_n$ is
> - **Absolutely convergent** if $\sum a_n$ and $\sum |a_n|$ both converge.
> - **Conditionally convergent** if $\sum a_n$ converges but $\sum |a_n|$ diverges.

Conditionally convergent series rely on cancellation between positive and negative terms for their convergence.

Example: The series $\sum_{n=1}^{\infty} \frac{(-1)^{n-1}}{n^2}$ is absolutely convergent because the series converges and the p-series $\sum 1/n^2$ also converges.

Example: The series $\sum_{n=1}^{\infty} \frac{(-1)^{n-1}}{n}$ is conditionally convergent because the series converges but the harmonic series $\sum 1/n$ diverges.

Exercises and Problems for Section 9.4

Exercises

Use the comparison test to confirm the statements in Exercises 1–3.

1. $\sum_{n=4}^{\infty} \frac{1}{n}$ diverges, so $\sum_{n=4}^{\infty} \frac{1}{n-3}$ diverges.

2. $\sum_{n=1}^{\infty} \frac{1}{n^2}$ converges, so $\sum_{n=1}^{\infty} \frac{1}{n^2+2}$ converges.

3. $\sum_{n=1}^{\infty} \frac{1}{n^2}$ converges, so $\sum_{n=1}^{\infty} \frac{e^{-n}}{n^2}$ converges.

In Exercises 4–7, use end behavior to compare the series to a p-series and predict whether the series converges or diverges.

4. $\sum_{n=1}^{\infty} \frac{n^3+1}{n^4+2n^3+2n}$

5. $\sum_{n=1}^{\infty} \frac{n+4}{n^3+5n-3}$

6. $\sum_{n=1}^{\infty} \frac{1}{n^4+3n^3+7}$

7. $\sum_{n=1}^{\infty} \frac{n-4}{\sqrt{n^3+n^2+8}}$

In Exercises 8–13, use the comparison test to determine whether the series converges.

8. $\displaystyle\sum_{n=1}^{\infty} \frac{1}{3^n + 1}$

9. $\displaystyle\sum_{n=1}^{\infty} \frac{1}{n^4 + e^n}$

10. $\displaystyle\sum_{n=2}^{\infty} \frac{1}{\ln n}$

11. $\displaystyle\sum_{n=1}^{\infty} \frac{n^2}{n^4 + 1}$

12. $\displaystyle\sum_{n=1}^{\infty} \frac{n \sin^2 n}{n^3 + 1}$

13. $\displaystyle\sum_{n=1}^{\infty} \frac{2^n + 1}{n2^n - 1}$

In Exercises 14–20, use the ratio test to decide whether the series converges or diverges.

14. $\displaystyle\sum_{n=1}^{\infty} \frac{n}{2^n}$

15. $\displaystyle\sum_{n=1}^{\infty} \frac{1}{(2n)!}$

16. $\displaystyle\sum_{n=1}^{\infty} \frac{(n!)^2}{(2n)!}$

17. $\displaystyle\sum_{n=1}^{\infty} \frac{n!(n+1)!}{(2n)!}$

18. $\displaystyle\sum_{n=1}^{\infty} \frac{1}{r^n n!}, r > 0$

19. $\displaystyle\sum_{n=1}^{\infty} \frac{1}{ne^n}$

20. $\displaystyle\sum_{n=0}^{\infty} \frac{2^n}{n^3 + 1}$

Which of the series in Exercises 21–24 are alternating?

21. $\displaystyle\sum_{n=1}^{\infty} (-1)^n \left(2 - \frac{1}{n}\right)$

22. $\displaystyle\sum_{n=1}^{\infty} \cos(n\pi)$

23. $\displaystyle\sum_{n=1}^{\infty} (-1)^n \cos(n\pi)$

24. $\displaystyle\sum_{n=1}^{\infty} (-1)^n \cos n$

Use the alternating series test to show that the series in Exercises 25–28 converge.

25. $\displaystyle\sum_{n=1}^{\infty} \frac{(-1)^{n-1}}{\sqrt{n}}$

26. $\displaystyle\sum_{n=1}^{\infty} \frac{(-1)^{n-1}}{2n + 1}$

27. $\displaystyle\sum_{n=1}^{\infty} \frac{(-1)^{n-1}}{n^2 + 2n + 1}$

28. $\displaystyle\sum_{n=1}^{\infty} \frac{(-1)^{n-1}}{e^n}$

In Exercises 29–37, determine whether the series is absolutely convergent, conditionally convergent, or divergent.

29. $\displaystyle\sum \frac{(-1)^n}{2^n}$

30. $\displaystyle\sum \frac{(-1)^n}{2n}$

31. $\displaystyle\sum (-1)^n \frac{n}{n+1}$

32. $\displaystyle\sum \frac{(-1)^n}{n^4 + 7}$

33. $\displaystyle\sum \frac{(-1)^{n-1}}{n \ln n}$

34. $\displaystyle\sum_{n=1}^{\infty} \frac{\cos n}{n^2}$

35. $\displaystyle\sum_{n=1}^{\infty} \frac{(-1)^{n-1}}{\sqrt{n}}$

36. $\displaystyle\sum (-1)^{n-1} \arcsin\left(\frac{1}{n}\right)$

37. $\displaystyle\sum \frac{(-1)^{n-1} \arctan(1/n)}{n^2}$

In Exercises 38–48, use the limit comparison test to determine whether the series converges or diverges.

38. $\displaystyle\sum_{n=1}^{\infty} \frac{5n + 1}{3n^2}$, by comparing to $\displaystyle\sum_{n=1}^{\infty} \frac{1}{n}$

39. $\displaystyle\sum_{n=1}^{\infty} \left(\frac{1+n}{3n}\right)^n$, by comparing to $\displaystyle\sum_{n=1}^{\infty} \left(\frac{1}{3}\right)^n$

[Hint: $\lim_{n\to\infty} (1 + 1/n)^n = e$.]

40. $\displaystyle\sum \left(1 - \cos\frac{1}{n}\right)$, by comparing to $\displaystyle\sum 1/n^2$

41. $\displaystyle\sum \frac{1}{n^4 - 7}$

42. $\displaystyle\sum \frac{n+1}{n^2 + 2}$

43. $\displaystyle\sum \frac{n^3 - 2n^2 + n + 1}{n^4 - 2}$

44. $\displaystyle\sum \frac{2^n}{3^n - 1}$

45. $\displaystyle\sum \frac{1}{2\sqrt{n} + \sqrt{n+2}}$

46. $\displaystyle\sum \left(\frac{1}{2n - 1} - \frac{1}{2n}\right)$

47. $\displaystyle\sum \frac{n}{\cos n + e^n}$

48. $\displaystyle\sum \frac{4\sin n + n}{n^2}$

Problems

In Problems 49–50, explain why the comparison test cannot be used to decide if the series converges or diverges.

In Problems 51–52, explain why the ratio test cannot be used to decide if the series converges or diverges.

49. $\displaystyle\sum_{n=1}^{\infty} \frac{(-1)^n}{n^2}$

50. $\displaystyle\sum_{n=1}^{\infty} \sin n$

51. $\displaystyle\sum_{n=1}^{\infty} (-1)^n$

52. $\displaystyle\sum_{n=1}^{\infty} \sin n$

In Problems 53–56, explain why the alternating series test cannot be used to decide if the series converges or diverges.

53. $\displaystyle\sum_{n=1}^{\infty}(-1)^{n-1}n$

54. $\displaystyle\sum_{n=1}^{\infty}(-1)^{n-1}\sin n$

55. $\displaystyle\sum_{n=1}^{\infty}(-1)^{n-1}\left(2-\frac{1}{n}\right)$

56. $\dfrac{2}{1}-\dfrac{1}{1}+\dfrac{2}{2}-\dfrac{1}{2}+\dfrac{2}{3}-\dfrac{1}{3}+\cdots$

In Problems 57–59, use a computer or calculator to investigate the behavior of the partial sums of the alternating series. Which appear to converge? Confirm convergence using the alternating series test. If a series converges, estimate its sum.

57. $1-2+3-4+5+\cdots+(-1)^{n}(n+1)+\cdots$

58. $1-0.1+0.01-0.001+\cdots+(-1)^{n}10^{-n}+\cdots$

59. $1-\dfrac{1}{1!}+\dfrac{1}{2!}-\dfrac{1}{3!}+\cdots+(-1)^{n}\dfrac{1}{n!}+\cdots$

In Problems 60–78, determine whether the series converges.

60. $\displaystyle\sum_{n=1}^{\infty}\frac{8^{n}}{n!}$

61. $\displaystyle\sum_{n=1}^{\infty}\frac{n2^{n}}{3^{n}}$

62. $\displaystyle\sum_{n=0}^{\infty}\frac{(0.1)^{n}}{n!}$

63. $\displaystyle\sum_{n=1}^{\infty}\frac{(n-1)!}{n^{2}}$

64. $\displaystyle\sum_{n=0}^{\infty}e^{-n}$

65. $\displaystyle\sum_{n=1}^{\infty}e^{n}$

66. $\displaystyle\sum_{n=1}^{\infty}\frac{(2n)!}{(n!)^{2}}$

67. $\displaystyle\sum_{n=1}^{\infty}\frac{1}{n^{2}}\tan\left(\frac{1}{n}\right)$

68. $\displaystyle\sum_{n=1}^{\infty}\frac{n+1}{n^{3}+6}$

69. $\displaystyle\sum_{n=1}^{\infty}\frac{5n+2}{2n^{2}+3n+7}$

70. $\displaystyle\sum_{n=1}^{\infty}\frac{(-1)^{n-1}}{\sqrt{3n-1}}$

71. $\displaystyle\sum_{n=1}^{\infty}\frac{(-1)^{n-1}2^{n}}{n^{2}}$

72. $\displaystyle\sum_{n=1}^{\infty}\frac{\sin n}{n^{2}}$

73. $\displaystyle\sum_{n=1}^{\infty}\frac{\sin n^{2}}{n^{2}}$

74. $\displaystyle\sum_{n=1}^{\infty}\frac{\cos(n\pi)}{n}$

75. $\displaystyle\sum_{n=2}^{\infty}\frac{n+2}{n^{2}-1}$

76. $\displaystyle\sum_{n=2}^{\infty}\frac{3}{\ln n^{2}}$

77. $\displaystyle\sum_{n=1}^{\infty}\frac{1}{\sqrt{n^{2}(n+2)}}$

78. $\displaystyle\sum_{n=1}^{\infty}\frac{n(n+1)}{\sqrt{n^{3}+2n^{2}}}$

In Problems 79–83, for what values of a does the series converge?

79. $\displaystyle\sum_{n=1}^{\infty}\left(\frac{2}{n}\right)^{a}$

80. $\displaystyle\sum_{n=1}^{\infty}\left(\frac{2}{a}\right)^{n}, a>0$

81. $\displaystyle\sum_{n=1}^{\infty}(\ln a)^{n}, a>0$

82. $\displaystyle\sum_{n=1}^{\infty}\frac{\ln n}{n^{a}}$

83. $\displaystyle\sum_{n=1}^{\infty}(-1)^{n}\arctan\left(\frac{a}{n}\right), a>0$

The series in Problems 84–86 converge by the alternating series test. Use Theorem 9.9 to find how many terms give a partial sum, S_{n}, within 0.01 of the sum, S, of the series.

84. $\displaystyle\sum_{n=1}^{\infty}\frac{(-1)^{n-1}}{n}$

85. $\displaystyle\sum_{n=1}^{\infty}\left(-\frac{2}{3}\right)^{n-1}$

86. $\displaystyle\sum_{n=1}^{\infty}\frac{(-1)^{n-1}}{(2n)!}$

87. Suppose $0\leq b_{n}\leq 2^{n}\leq a_{n}$ and $0\leq c_{n}\leq 2^{-n}\leq d_{n}$ for all n. Which of the series $\sum a_{n}, \sum b_{n}, \sum c_{n}$, and $\sum d_{n}$ definitely converge and which definitely diverge?

88. Given two convergent series $\sum a_{n}$ and $\sum b_{n}$, we know that the term-by-term sum $\sum(a_{b}+b_{n})$ converges. What about the series formed by taking the products of the terms $\sum a_{n}\cdot b_{n}$? This problem shows that it may or may not converge.

    (a) Show that if $\sum a_{n}=\sum 1/n^{2}$ and $\sum b_{n}=\sum 1/n^{3}$, then $\sum a_{n}\cdot b_{n}$ converges.

    (b) Explain why $\sum(-1)^{n}/\sqrt{n}$ converges.

    (c) Show that if $a_{n}=b_{n}=(-1)^{n}/\sqrt{n}$, then $\sum a_{n}\cdot b_{n}$ does not converge.

89. Suppose that $b_{n}>0$ for all n and $\sum b_{n}$ converges. Show that if $\lim_{n\to\infty}a_{n}/b_{n}=0$ then $\sum a_{n}$ converges.

90. Suppose that $b_{n}>0$ for all n and $\sum b_{n}$ diverges. Show that if $\lim_{n\to\infty}a_{n}/b_{n}=\infty$ then $\sum a_{n}$ diverges.

91. A series $\sum a_{n}$ of positive terms (that is, $a_{n}>0$) can be used to form another series $\sum b_{n}$ where each term b_{n} is the average of the first n terms of the original series, that is, $b_{n}=(a_{1}+a_{2}+\cdots+a_{n})/n$. Show that $\sum b_{n}$ does not converge (even if $\sum a_{n}$ does). [Hint: Compare $\sum b_{n}$ to a multiple of the harmonic series.]

92. Show that if $\sum|a_{n}|$ converges, then $\sum(-1)^{n}a_{n}$ converges.

93. **(a)** For a series $\sum a_{n}$, show that $0\leq a_{n}+|a_{n}|\leq 2|a_{n}|$.

    (b) Use part (a) to show that if $\sum|a_{n}|$ converges, then $\sum a_{n}$ converges.

Problems 94–95 introduce the *root test* for convergence. Given a series $\sum a_{n}$ of positive terms (that is, $a_{n}>0$) such that the root $\sqrt[n]{a_{n}}$ has a limit r as $n\to\infty$,

    • if $r<1$, then $\sum a_{n}$ converges

- if $r > 1$, then $\sum a_n$ diverges
- if $r = 1$, then $\sum a_n$ could converge or diverge.

(This test works since $\lim_{n \to \infty} \sqrt[n]{a_n} = r$ tells us that the series is comparable to a geometric series with ratio r.) Use this test to determine the behavior of the series.

94. $\displaystyle\sum_{n=1}^{\infty} \left(\frac{2}{n}\right)^n$

95. $\displaystyle\sum_{n=1}^{\infty} \left(\frac{5n+1}{3n^2}\right)^n$

Strengthen Your Understanding

In Problems 96–98, explain what is wrong with the statement.

96. The series $\sum (-1)^{2n}/n^2$ converges by the alternating series test.

97. The series $\sum 1/(n^2 + 1)$ converges by the ratio test.

98. The series $\sum 1/n^{3/2}$ converges by comparison with $\sum 1/n^2$.

In Problems 99–101, give an example of:

99. A series $\sum_{n=1}^{\infty} a_n$ that converges but $\sum_{n=1}^{\infty} |a_n|$ diverges.

100. An alternating series that does not converge.

101. A series $\sum a_n$ such that

$$\lim_{n \to \infty} \frac{|a_{n+1}|}{|a_n|} = 3.$$

Decide if the statements in Problems 102–117 are true or false. Give an explanation for your answer.

102. If the terms s_n of a sequence alternate in sign, then the sequence converges.

103. If $0 \le a_n \le b_n$ for all n and $\sum a_n$ converges, then $\sum b_n$ converges.

104. If $0 \le a_n \le b_n$ for all n and $\sum a_n$ diverges, then $\sum b_n$ diverges.

105. If $b_n \le a_n \le 0$ for all n and $\sum b_n$ converges, then $\sum a_n$ converges.

106. If $\sum a_n$ converges, then $\sum |a_n|$ converges.

107. If $\sum a_n$ converges, then $\lim_{n \to \infty} |a_{n+1}|/|a_n| \neq 1$.

108. $\displaystyle\sum_{n=0}^{\infty} (-1)^n \cos(2\pi n)$ is an alternating series.

109. The series $\displaystyle\sum_{n=0}^{\infty} (-1)^n 2^n$ converges.

110. If $\sum a_n$ converges, then $\sum (-1)^n a_n$ converges.

111. If an alternating series converges by the alternating series test, then the error in using the first n terms of the series to approximate the entire series is less in magnitude than the first term omitted.

112. If an alternating series converges, then the error in using the first n terms of the series to approximate the entire series is less in magnitude than the first term omitted.

113. If $\sum |a_n|$ converges, then $\sum (-1)^n |a_n|$ converges.

114. To find the sum of the alternating harmonic series $\sum (-1)^{n-1}/n$ to within 0.01 of the true value, we can sum the first 100 terms.

115. If $\sum a_n$ is absolutely convergent, then it is convergent.

116. If $\sum a_n$ is conditionally convergent, then it is absolutely convergent.

117. If $a_n > 0.5b_n > 0$ for all n and $\sum b_n$ diverges, then $\sum a_n$ diverges.

118. Which test will help you determine if the series converges or diverges?

$$\sum_{k=1}^{\infty} \frac{1}{k^3 + 1}$$

(a) Integral test
(b) Comparison test
(c) Ratio test

9.5 POWER SERIES AND INTERVAL OF CONVERGENCE

In Section 9.2 we saw that the geometric series $\sum ax^n$ converges for $-1 < x < 1$ and diverges otherwise. This section studies the convergence of more general series constructed from powers. Chapter 10 shows how such power series are used to approximate functions such as e^x, $\sin x$, $\cos x$, and $\ln x$.

A **power series** about $x = a$ is a sum of constants times powers of $(x - a)$:

$$C_0 + C_1(x - a) + C_2(x - a)^2 + \cdots + C_n(x - a)^n + \cdots = \sum_{n=0}^{\infty} C_n(x - a)^n.$$

We think of a as a constant. For any fixed x, the power series $\sum C_n(x - a)^n$ is a series of numbers like those considered in Section 9.3. To investigate the convergence of a power series, we consider the partial sums, which in this case are the polynomials $S_n(x) = C_0 + C_1(x-a) + C_2(x-a)^2 + \cdots + C_n(x - a)^n$. As before, we consider the sequence[8]

$$S_0(x),\ S_1(x),\ S_2(x),\ \ldots, S_n(x), \ldots.$$

> For a fixed value of x, if this sequence of partial sums converges to a limit S, that is, if $\lim_{n\to\infty} S_n(x) = S$, then we say that the power series **converges** to S for this value of x.

A power series may converge for some values of x and not for others.

Example 1   Find an expression for the general term of the series and use it to write the series using $\sum$ notation:

$$\frac{(x-2)^4}{4} - \frac{(x-2)^6}{9} + \frac{(x-2)^8}{16} - \frac{(x-2)^{10}}{25} + \cdots.$$

Solution   The series is about $x = 2$ and the odd terms are zero. We use $(x-2)^{2n}$ and begin with $n = 2$. Since the series alternates and is positive for $n = 2$, we multiply by $(-1)^n$. For $n = 2$, we divide by 4, for $n = 3$ we divide by 9, and in general, we divide by n^2. One way to write this series is

$$\sum_{n=2}^{\infty} \frac{(-1)^n(x-2)^{2n}}{n^2}.$$

Example 2   Determine whether the power series $\displaystyle\sum_{n=0}^{\infty} \frac{x^n}{2^n}$ converges or diverges for

(a) $x = -1$ (b) $x = 3$

Solution   (a) Substituting $x = -1$, we have

$$\sum_{n=0}^{\infty} \frac{x^n}{2^n} = \sum_{n=0}^{\infty} \frac{(-1)^n}{2^n} = \sum_{n=0}^{\infty} \left(-\frac{1}{2}\right)^n.$$

This is a geometric series with ratio $-1/2$, so the series converges to $1/(1 - (-\frac{1}{2})) = 2/3$.
(b) Substituting $x = 3$, we have

$$\sum_{n=0}^{\infty} \frac{x^n}{2^n} = \sum_{n=0}^{\infty} \frac{3^n}{2^n} = \sum_{n=0}^{\infty} \left(\frac{3}{2}\right)^n.$$

This is a geometric series with ratio greater than 1, so it diverges.

Numerical and Graphical View of Convergence

Consider the series

$$(x-1) - \frac{(x-1)^2}{2} + \frac{(x-1)^3}{3} - \frac{(x-1)^4}{4} + \cdots + (-1)^{n-1}\frac{(x-1)^n}{n} + \cdots.$$

To investigate the convergence of this series, we look at the sequence of partial sums graphed in

---

[8]Here we call the first term in the sequence $S_0(x)$ rather than $S_1(x)$ so that the last term of $S_n(x)$ is $C_n(x - a)^n$.

Figure 9.11. The graph suggests that the partial sums converge for x in the interval $(0, 2)$. In Examples 4 and 5, we show that the series converges for $0 < x \leq 2$. This is called the *interval of convergence* of this series.

At $x = 1.4$, which is inside the interval, the series appears to converge quite rapidly:

$$S_5(1.4) = 0.33698\ldots \qquad S_7(1.4) = 0.33653\ldots$$
$$S_6(1.4) = 0.33630\ldots \qquad S_8(1.4) = 0.33645\ldots$$

Table 9.1 shows the results of using $x = 1.9$ and $x = 2.3$ in the power series. For $x = 1.9$, which is inside the interval of convergence but close to an endpoint, the series converges, though rather slowly. For $x = 2.3$, which is outside the interval of convergence, the series diverges: the larger the value of n, the more wildly the series oscillates. In fact, the contribution of the twenty-fifth term is about 28; the contribution of the hundredth term is about $-2,500,000,000$. Figure 9.11 shows the interval of convergence and the partial sums.

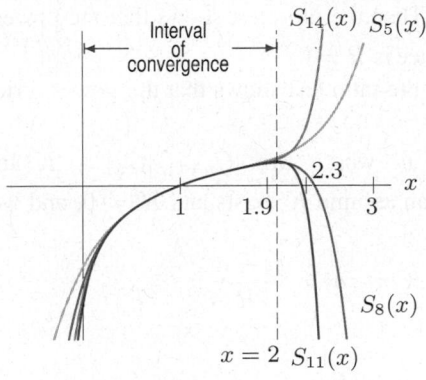

Figure 9.11: Partial sums for series in Example 4 converge for $0 < x < 2$

Table 9.1 *Partial sums for series in Example 4 with $x = 1.9$ inside interval of convergence and $x = 2.3$ outside*

n	$S_n(1.9)$	n	$S_n(2.3)$
2	0.495	2	0.455
5	0.69207	5	1.21589
8	0.61802	8	0.28817
11	0.65473	11	1.71710
14	0.63440	14	-0.70701

Notice that the interval of convergence, $0 < x \leq 2$, is centered on $x = 1$. Since the interval extends one unit on either side, we say the *radius of convergence* of this series is 1.

Intervals of Convergence

Each power series falls into one of three cases, characterized by its *radius of convergence*, R. This radius gives an *interval of convergence*.

- The series converges only for $x = a$; the **radius of convergence** is defined to be $R = 0$.
- The series converges for all values of x; the **radius of convergence** is defined to be $R = \infty$.
- There is a positive number R, called the **radius of convergence**, such that the series converges for $|x - a| < R$ and diverges for $|x - a| > R$. See Figure 9.12.

Using the radius of convergence, we make the following definition:

- The **interval of convergence** is the interval between $a - R$ and $a + R$, including any endpoint where the series converges.

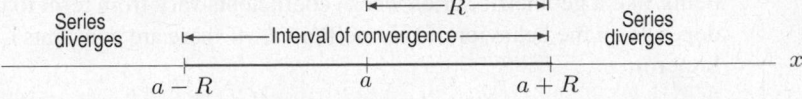

Figure 9.12: Radius of convergence, R, determines an interval, centered at $x = a$, in which the series converges

There are some series whose radius of convergence we already know. For example, the geometric series

$$1 + x + x^2 + \cdots + x^n + \cdots$$

converges for $|x| < 1$ and diverges for $|x| \geq 1$, so its radius of convergence is 1. Similarly, the series

$$1 + \frac{x}{3} + \left(\frac{x}{3}\right)^2 + \cdots + \left(\frac{x}{3}\right)^n + \cdots$$

converges for $|x/3| < 1$ and diverges for $|x/3| \geq 1$, so its radius of convergence is 3.

The next theorem gives a method of computing the radius of convergence for many series. To find the values of x for which the power series $\sum_{n=0}^{\infty} C_n(x-a)^n$ converges, we use the ratio test. Writing $a_n = C_n(x-a)^n$ and assuming $C_n \neq 0$ and $x \neq a$, we have

$$\lim_{n\to\infty} \frac{|a_{n+1}|}{|a_n|} = \lim_{n\to\infty} \frac{|C_{n+1}(x-a)^{n+1}|}{|C_n(x-a)^n|} = \lim_{n\to\infty} \frac{|C_{n+1}||x-a|}{|C_n|} = |x-a| \lim_{n\to\infty} \frac{|C_{n+1}|}{|C_n|}.$$

Case 1. Suppose $\lim_{n\to\infty} |a_{n+1}|/|a_n|$ is infinite. Then the ratio test shows that the power series converges only for $x = a$. The radius of convergence is $R = 0$.

Case 2. Suppose $\lim_{n\to\infty} |a_{n+1}|/|a_n| = 0$. Then the ratio test shows that the power series converges for all x. The radius of convergence is $R = \infty$.

Case 3. Suppose $\lim_{n\to\infty} |a_{n+1}|/|a_n| = K|x-a|$, where $\lim_{n\to\infty} |C_{n+1}|/|C_n| = K$. In Case 1, K does not exist; in Case 2, $K = 0$. Thus, we can assume K exists and $K \neq 0$, and we can define $R = 1/K$. Then we have

$$\lim_{n\to\infty} \frac{|a_{n+1}|}{|a_n|} = K|x-a| = \frac{|x-a|}{R},$$

so the ratio test tells us that the power series:

- Converges for $\dfrac{|x-a|}{R} < 1$; that is, for $|x-a| < R$

- Diverges for $\dfrac{|x-a|}{R} > 1$; that is, for $|x-a| > R$.

The results are summarized in the following theorem.

Theorem 9.10: Method for Computing Radius of Convergence

To calculate the radius of convergence, R, for the power series $\sum_{n=0}^{\infty} C_n(x-a)^n$, use the ratio test with $a_n = C_n(x-a)^n$.

- If $\lim_{n\to\infty} |a_{n+1}|/|a_n|$ is infinite, then $R = 0$.

- If $\lim_{n\to\infty} |a_{n+1}|/|a_n| = 0$, then $R = \infty$.

- If $\lim_{n\to\infty} |a_{n+1}|/|a_n| = K|x-a|$, where K is finite and nonzero, then $R = 1/K$.

Note that the ratio test does not tell us anything if $\lim_{n\to\infty} |a_{n+1}|/|a_n|$ fails to exist, which can occur, for example, if some of the C_ns are zero.

A proof that a power series has a radius of convergence and of Theorem 9.10 is given in the online theory supplement. To understand these facts informally, we can think of a power series as being like a geometric series whose coefficients vary from term to term. The radius of convergence depends on the behavior of the coefficients: if there are constants C and K such that for larger and larger n,

$$|C_n| \approx CK^n,$$

then it is plausible that $\sum C_n x^n$ and $\sum CK^n x^n = \sum C(Kx)^n$ converge or diverge together. The geometric series $\sum C(Kx)^n$ converges for $|Kx| < 1$, that is, for $|x| < 1/K$. We can find K using the ratio test, because

$$\frac{|a_{n+1}|}{|a_n|} = \frac{|C_{n+1}||(x-a)^{n+1}|}{|C_n||(x-a)^n|} \approx \frac{CK^{n+1}|(x-a)^{n+1}|}{CK^n|(x-a)^n|} = K|x-a|.$$

Example 3   Show that the following power series converges for all x:

$$1 + x + \frac{x^2}{2!} + \frac{x^3}{3!} + \cdots + \frac{x^n}{n!} + \cdots .$$

Solution   Because $C_n = 1/n!$, none of the C_ns are zero and we can use the ratio test:

$$\lim_{n\to\infty} \frac{|a_{n+1}|}{|a_n|} = |x| \lim_{n\to\infty} \frac{|C_{n+1}|}{|C_n|} = |x| \lim_{n\to\infty} \frac{1/(n+1)!}{1/n!} = |x| \lim_{n\to\infty} \frac{n!}{(n+1)!} = |x| \lim_{n\to\infty} \frac{1}{n+1} = 0.$$

This gives $R = \infty$, so the series converges for all x. We see in Chapter 10 that it converges to e^x.

Example 4   Determine the radius of convergence of the series

$$\frac{(x-1)}{3} - \frac{(x-1)^2}{2\cdot 3^2} + \frac{(x-1)^3}{3\cdot 3^3} - \frac{(x-1)^4}{4\cdot 3^4} + \cdots + (-1)^{n-1}\frac{(x-1)^n}{n\cdot 3^n} + \cdots .$$

What does this tell us about the interval of convergence of this series?

Solution   Because $C_n = (-1)^{n-1}/(n\cdot 3^n)$ is never zero we can use the ratio test. We have

$$\lim_{n\to\infty} \frac{|a_{n+1}|}{|a_n|} = |x-1| \lim_{n\to\infty} \frac{|C_{n+1}|}{|C_n|} = |x-1| \lim_{n\to\infty} \frac{\left|\frac{(-1)^n}{(n+1)\cdot 3^{n+1}}\right|}{\left|\frac{(-1)^{n-1}}{n\cdot 3^n}\right|} = |x-1| \lim_{n\to\infty} \frac{n}{3(n+1)} = \frac{|x-1|}{3}.$$

Thus, $K = 1/3$ in Theorem 9.10, so the radius of convergence is $R = 1/K = 3$. The power series converges for $|x-1| < 3$ and diverges for $|x-1| > 3$, so the series converges for $-2 < x < 4$. Notice that the radius of convergence does not tell us what happens at the endpoints, $x = -2$ and $x = 4$. The endpoints are investigated in Example 5.

What Happens at the Endpoints of the Interval of Convergence?

The ratio test does not tell us whether a power series converges at the endpoints of its interval of convergence, $x = a \pm R$. There is no simple theorem that answers this question. Since substituting $x = a \pm R$ converts the power series to a series of numbers, the tests in Sections 9.3 and 9.4 are often useful.

Example 5   Determine the interval of convergence of the series

$$\frac{(x-1)}{3} - \frac{(x-1)^2}{2\cdot 3^2} + \frac{(x-1)^3}{3\cdot 3^3} - \frac{(x-1)^4}{4\cdot 3^4} + \cdots + (-1)^{n-1}\frac{(x-1)^n}{n\cdot 3^n} + \cdots .$$

Solution   In Example 4 we showed that this series has $R = 3$; it converges for $-2 < x < 4$ and diverges for $x < -2$ or $x > 4$. We need to determine whether it converges at the endpoints of the interval of convergence, $x = -2$ and $x = 4$. At $x = 4$, we have the series

$$1 - \frac{1}{2} + \frac{1}{3} - \frac{1}{4} + \cdots + \frac{(-1)^{n-1}}{n} + \cdots .$$

This is an alternating series with $a_n = 1/(n+1)$, so by the alternating series test (Theorem 9.8), it converges. At $x = -2$, we have the series

$$-1 - \frac{1}{2} - \frac{1}{3} - \frac{1}{4} - \cdots - \frac{1}{n} - \cdots .$$

This is the negative of the harmonic series, so it diverges. Therefore, the interval of convergence is $-2 < x \le 4$. The right endpoint is included and the left endpoint is not.

Series with All Odd, or All Even, Terms

The ratio test requires $\lim\limits_{n\to\infty} |a_{n+1}|/|a_n|$ to exist for $a_n = C_n(x-a)^n$. What happens if the power series has only even or odd powers, so some of the coefficients C_n are zero? Then we use the fact that an infinite series can be written in several ways and pick one in which the terms are nonzero.

Example 6   Find the radius and interval of convergence of the series

$$1 + 2^2 x^2 + 2^4 x^4 + 2^6 x^6 + \cdots.$$

Solution   If we take $a_n = 2^n x^n$ for n even and $a_n = 0$ for n odd, $\lim\limits_{n\to\infty} |a_{n+1}|/|a_n|$ does not exist. Therefore, for this series we take

$$a_n = 2^{2n} x^{2n},$$

so that, replacing n by $n+1$, we have

$$a_{n+1} = 2^{2(n+1)} x^{2(n+1)} = 2^{2n+2} x^{2n+2}.$$

Thus,

$$\frac{|a_{n+1}|}{|a_n|} = \frac{|2^{2n+2} x^{2n+2}|}{|2^{2n} x^{2n}|} = |2^2 x^2| = 4x^2.$$

We have

$$\lim_{n\to\infty} \frac{|a_{n+1}|}{|a_n|} = 4x^2.$$

The ratio test guarantees that the power series converges if $4x^2 < 1$, that is, if $|x| < \frac{1}{2}$. The radius of convergence is $\frac{1}{2}$. The series converges for $-\frac{1}{2} < x < \frac{1}{2}$ and diverges for $x > \frac{1}{2}$ or $x < -\frac{1}{2}$. At $x = \pm\frac{1}{2}$, all the terms in the series are 1, so the series diverges (by Theorem 9.2, Property 3). Thus, the interval of convergence is $-\frac{1}{2} < x < \frac{1}{2}$.

Example 7   Write the general term a_n of the following series so that none of the terms are zero:

$$x - \frac{x^3}{3!} + \frac{x^5}{5!} - \frac{x^7}{7!} + \frac{x^9}{9!} - \cdots.$$

Solution   This series has only odd powers. We can get odd integers using $2n-1$ for $n \geq 1$, since

$$2 \cdot 1 - 1 = 1, \qquad 2 \cdot 2 - 1 = 3, \qquad 2 \cdot 3 - 1 = 5, \text{ etc.}$$

Also, the signs of the terms alternate, with the first (that is, $n = 1$) term positive, so we include a factor of $(-1)^{n-1}$. Thus we get

$$a_n = (-1)^{n-1} \frac{x^{2n-1}}{(2n-1)!}.$$

We see in Chapter 10 that the series converges to $\sin x$. Exercise 24 shows that the radius of convergence of this series is infinite, so that it converges for all values of x.

Exercises and Problems for Section 9.5

Exercises

Which of the series in Exercises 1–4 are power series?

1. $x - x^3 + x^6 - x^{10} + x^{15} - \cdots$

2. $\dfrac{1}{x} + \dfrac{1}{x^2} + \dfrac{1}{x^3} + \dfrac{1}{x^4} + \cdots$

3. $1 + x + (x-1)^2 + (x-2)^3 + (x-3)^4 + \cdots$

4. $x^7 + x + 2$

In Exercises 5–10, find an expression for the general term of the series. Give the starting value of the index (n or k, for example).

5. $\dfrac{1}{2}x + \dfrac{1\cdot 3}{2^2 \cdot 2!}x^2 + \dfrac{1\cdot 3\cdot 5}{2^3 \cdot 3!}x^3 + \cdots$

6. $px + \dfrac{p(p-1)}{2!}x^2 + \dfrac{p(p-1)(p-2)}{3!}x^3 + \cdots$

7. $1 - \dfrac{(x-1)^2}{2!} + \dfrac{(x-1)^4}{4!} - \dfrac{(x-1)^6}{6!} + \cdots$

8. $(x-1)^3 - \dfrac{(x-1)^5}{2!} + \dfrac{(x-1)^7}{4!} - \dfrac{(x-1)^9}{6!} + \cdots$

9. $\dfrac{x-a}{1} + \dfrac{(x-a)^2}{2\cdot 2!} + \dfrac{(x-a)^3}{4\cdot 3!} + \dfrac{(x-a)^4}{8\cdot 4!} + \cdots$

10. $2(x+5)^3 + 3(x+5)^5 + \dfrac{4(x+5)^7}{2!} + \dfrac{5(x+5)^9}{3!} + \cdots$

In Exercises 11–23, find the radius of convergence.

11. $\displaystyle\sum_{n=0}^{\infty} nx^n$

12. $\displaystyle\sum_{n=0}^{\infty} (5x)^n$

13. $\displaystyle\sum_{n=0}^{\infty} n^3 x^n$

14. $\displaystyle\sum_{n=0}^{\infty} (2^n + n^2)x^n$

15. $\displaystyle\sum_{n=0}^{\infty} \dfrac{(n+1)x^n}{2^n + n}$

16. $\displaystyle\sum_{n=1}^{\infty} \dfrac{2^n(x-1)^n}{n}$

17. $\displaystyle\sum_{n=1}^{\infty} \dfrac{(x-3)^n}{n2^n}$

18. $\displaystyle\sum_{n=0}^{\infty} (-1)^n \dfrac{x^{2n}}{(2n)!}$

19. $x - \dfrac{x^2}{4} + \dfrac{x^3}{9} - \dfrac{x^4}{16} + \dfrac{x^5}{25} - \cdots$

20. $1 + 2x + \dfrac{4x^2}{2!} + \dfrac{8x^3}{3!} + \dfrac{16x^4}{4!} + \dfrac{32x^5}{5!} + \cdots$

21. $1 + 2x + \dfrac{4!x^2}{(2!)^2} + \dfrac{6!x^3}{(3!)^2} + \dfrac{8!x^4}{(4!)^2} + \dfrac{10!x^5}{(5!)^2} + \cdots$

22. $3x + \dfrac{5}{2}x^2 + \dfrac{7}{3}x^3 + \dfrac{9}{4}x^4 + \dfrac{11}{5}x^5 + \cdots$

23. $x - \dfrac{x^3}{3} + \dfrac{x^5}{5} - \dfrac{x^7}{7} + \cdots$

24. Show that the radius of convergence of the power series
$$x - \dfrac{x^3}{3!} + \dfrac{x^5}{5!} - \dfrac{x^7}{7!} + \cdots \text{ in Example 7 is infinite.}$$

Problems

25. (a) Determine the radius of convergence of the series
$$x - \dfrac{x^2}{2} + \dfrac{x^3}{3} - \dfrac{x^4}{4} + \cdots + (-1)^{n-1}\dfrac{x^n}{n} + \cdots.$$
What does this tell us about the interval of convergence of this series?

(b) Investigate convergence at the end points of the interval of convergence of this series.

26. Show that the series $\displaystyle\sum_{n-1}^{\infty} \dfrac{(2x)^n}{n}$ converges for $|x| < 1/2$. Investigate whether the series converges for $x = 1/2$ and $x = -1/2$.

In Problems 27–34, find the interval of convergence.

27. $\displaystyle\sum_{n=0}^{\infty} \dfrac{x^n}{3^n}$

28. $\displaystyle\sum_{n=2}^{\infty} \dfrac{(x-3)^n}{n}$

29. $\displaystyle\sum_{n=1}^{\infty} \dfrac{n^2 x^{2n}}{2^{2n}}$

30. $\displaystyle\sum_{n=1}^{\infty} \dfrac{(-1)^n (x-5)^n}{2^n n^2}$

31. $\displaystyle\sum_{n=1}^{\infty} \dfrac{x^{2n+1}}{n!}$

32. $\displaystyle\sum_{n=0}^{\infty} n!x^n$

33. $\displaystyle\sum_{n=1}^{\infty} \dfrac{(5x)^n}{\sqrt{n}}$

34. $\displaystyle\sum_{n=1}^{\infty} \dfrac{(5x)^{2n}}{\sqrt{n}}$

In Problems 35–38, use the formula for the sum of a geometric series to find a power series centered at the origin that converges to the expression. For what values does the series converge?

35. $\dfrac{1}{1+2z}$

36. $\dfrac{2}{1+y^2}$

37. $\dfrac{3}{1-z/2}$

38. $\dfrac{8}{4+y}$

39. For constant p, find the radius of convergence of the binomial power series:[9]
$$1 + px + \dfrac{p(p-1)x^2}{2!} + \dfrac{p(p-1)(p-2)x^3}{3!} + \cdots.$$

---

[9]For an explanation of the name, see Section 10.2.

40. Show that if $C_0 + C_1x + C_2x^2 + C_3x^3 + \cdots$ converges for $|x| < R$ with R given by the ratio test, then so does $C_1 + 2C_2x + 3C_3x^2 + \cdots$. Assume $C_i \neq 0$ for all i.

41. The series $\sum C_nx^n$ converges at $x = -5$ and diverges at $x = 7$. What can you say about its radius of convergence?

42. The series $\sum C_n(x + 7)^n$ converges at $x = 0$ and diverges at $x = -17$. What can you say about its radius of convergence?

43. The series $\sum C_nx^n$ converges when $x = -4$ and diverges when $x = 7$. Decide whether each of the following statements is true or false, or whether this cannot be determined.

    (a) The power series converges when $x = 10$.
    (b) The power series converges when $x = 3$.
    (c) The power series diverges when $x = 1$.
    (d) The power series diverges when $x = 6$.

44. If $\sum C_n(x - 3)^n$ converges at $x = 7$ and diverges at $x = 10$, what can you say about the convergence at $x = 11$? At $x = 5$? At $x = 0$?

45. Bessel functions are important in such diverse areas as describing planetary motion and the shape of a vibrating drumhead. The Bessel function of order 0 is defined by

$$J(x) = \sum_{n=0}^{\infty} \frac{(-1)^n x^{2n}}{2^{2n}(n!)^2}.$$

    (a) Find the domain of $J(x)$ by finding the interval of convergence for this power series.
    (b) Find $J(0)$.
    (c) Find the partial sum polynomials S_0, S_1, S_2, S_3, S_4.
    (d) Estimate $J(1)$ to three decimal places.
    (e) Use your answer to part (d) to estimate $J(-1)$.

46. For all x-values for which it converges, the function f is defined by the series

$$f(x) = \sum_{n=0}^{\infty} \frac{x^n}{n!}.$$

    (a) What is $f(0)$?
    (b) What is the domain of f?
    (c) Assuming that f' can be calculated by differentiating the series term-by-term, find the series for $f'(x)$. What do you notice?
    (d) Guess what well-known function f is.

47. From Exercise 24 we know the following series converges for all x. We define $g(x)$ to be its sum:

$$g(x) = \sum_{n=1}^{\infty}(-1)^{n-1}\frac{x^{2n-1}}{(2n-1)!}.$$

    (a) Is $g(x)$ odd, even, or neither? What is $g(0)$?
    (b) Assuming that derivatives can be computed term by term, show that $g''(x) = -g(x)$.
    (c) Guess what well-known function g might be. Check your guess using $g(0)$ and $g'(0)$.

48. The functions $p(x)$ and $q(x)$ are defined by the series

$$p(x) = \sum_{n=0}^{\infty}(-1)^n\frac{x^{2n}}{(2n)!}, \quad q(x) = \sum_{n=1}^{\infty}(-1)^{n-1}\frac{x^{2n-1}}{(2n-1)!}.$$

Assuming that these series converge for all x and that multiplication can be done term by term:

    (a) Find the series for $(p(x))^2 + (q(x))^2$ up to the term in x^6.
    (b) Guess what well-known functions p and q could be.

Strengthen Your Understanding

In Problems 49–50, explain what is wrong with the statement.

49. If $\lim_{n\to\infty}|C_{n+1}/C_n| = 0$, then the radius of convergence for $\sum C_nx^n$ is 0.

50. The series $\sum C_nx^n$ diverges at $x = 2$ and converges at $x = 3$.

In Problems 51–53, give an example of:

51. A power series that is divergent at $x = 0$.

52. A power series that converges at $x = 5$ but nowhere else.

53. A series $\sum C_nx^n$ with radius of convergence 1 and that converges at $x = 1$ and $x = -1$.

Decide if the statements in Problems 54–66 are true or false. Give an explanation for your answer.

54. $\sum_{n=1}^{\infty}(x - n)^n$ is a power series.

55. If the power series $\sum C_nx^n$ converges for $x = 2$, then it converges for $x = 1$.

56. If the power series $\sum C_nx^n$ converges for $x = 1$, then the power series converges for $x = 2$.

57. If the power series $\sum C_nx^n$ does not converge for $x = 1$, then the power series does not converge for $x = 2$.

58. $\sum C_n(x - 1)^n$ and $\sum C_nx^n$ have the same radius of convergence.

59. If $\sum C_nx^n$ and $\sum B_nx^n$ have the same radius of convergence, then the coefficients, C_n and B_n, must be equal.

60. If a power series converges at one endpoint of its interval of convergence, then it converges at the other.

61. A power series always converges at at least one point.

62. If the power series $\sum C_n x^n$ converges at $x = 10$, then it converges at $x = -9$.

63. If the power series $\sum C_n x^n$ converges at $x = 10$, then it converges at $x = -10$.

64. $-5 < x \leq 7$ is a possible interval of convergence of a power series.

65. $-3 < x < 2$ could be the interval of convergence of $\sum C_n x^n$.

66. If $-11 < x < 1$ is the interval of convergence of $\sum C_n (x - a)^n$, then $a = -5$.

67. The power series $\sum C_n x^n$ diverges at $x = 7$ and converges at $x = -3$. At $x = -9$, the series is

(a) Conditionally convergent
(b) Absolutely convergent
(c) Alternating
(d) Divergent
(e) Cannot be determined.

CHAPTER SUMMARY (see also Ready Reference at the end of the book)

- **Sequences**
  Recursive definition, monotone, bounded, convergence.
- **Geometric series**
  Finite sum, infinite sum.
- **Harmonic series**
- **Alternating series**

- **Tests for convergence of series**
  Integral test, p-series, comparison test, limit comparison test, ratio test, alternating series test.
  Absolute and conditional convergence.

- **Power series**
  Ratio test for radius of convergence, interval of convergence.

REVIEW EXERCISES AND PROBLEMS FOR CHAPTER NINE

Exercises

In Exercises 1–8, find the sum of the series.

1. $3 + \dfrac{3}{2} + \dfrac{3}{4} + \dfrac{3}{8} + \cdots + \dfrac{3}{2^{10}}$

2. $-2 + 1 - \dfrac{1}{2} + \dfrac{1}{4} - \dfrac{1}{8} + \dfrac{1}{16} - \cdots$

3. $125 + 100 + 80 + \cdots + 125(0.8)^{20}$

4. $(0.5)^3 + (0.5)^4 + \cdots + (0.5)^k$

5. $b^5 + b^6 + b^7 + b^8 + b^9 + b^{10}$

6. $\displaystyle\sum_{n=4}^{\infty} \left(\dfrac{1}{3}\right)^n$ **7.** $\displaystyle\sum_{n=4}^{20} \left(\dfrac{1}{3}\right)^n$ **8.** $\displaystyle\sum_{n=0}^{\infty} \dfrac{3^n + 5}{4^n}$

In Exercises 9–12, find the the first four partial sums of the geometric series, a formula for the nth partial sum, and the sum of the series, if it exists.

9. $36 + 12 + 4 + \dfrac{4}{3} + \dfrac{4}{9} + \cdots$

10. $1280 - 960 + 720 - 540 + 405 - \cdots$

11. $-810 + 540 - 360 + 240 - 160 + \cdots$

12. $2 + 6z + 18z^2 + 54z^3 + \cdots$

In Exercises 13–16, does the sequence converge or diverge? If a sequence converges, find its limit.

13. $\dfrac{3 + 4n}{5 + 7n}$

14. $(-1)^n \dfrac{(n + 1)}{n}$

15. $\sin\left(\dfrac{\pi}{4} n\right)$

16. $\dfrac{2^n}{n^3}$

In Exercises 17–20, use the integral test to decide whether the series converges or diverges.

17. $\displaystyle\sum_{n=1}^{\infty} \dfrac{1}{n^3}$ **18.** $\displaystyle\sum_{n=1}^{\infty} \dfrac{3n^2 + 2n}{n^3 + n^2 + 1}$

19. $\displaystyle\sum_{n=0}^{\infty} n e^{-n^2}$ **20.** $\displaystyle\sum_{n=2}^{\infty} \dfrac{2}{n^2 - 1}$

In Exercises 21–23, use the ratio test to decide if the series converges or diverges.

21. $\displaystyle\sum_{n=1}^{\infty} \dfrac{1}{2^n n!}$ **22.** $\displaystyle\sum_{n=1}^{\infty} \dfrac{(n - 1)!}{5^n}$

23. $\displaystyle\sum_{n=1}^{\infty} \dfrac{(2n)!}{n!(n + 1)!}$

In Exercises 24–25, use the alternating series test to decide whether the series converges.

24. $\displaystyle\sum_{n=1}^{\infty} \dfrac{(-1)^n}{n^2 + 1}$ **25.** $\displaystyle\sum_{n=1}^{\infty} \dfrac{(-1)^{n-1}}{\sqrt{n^2 + 1}}$

In Exercises 26–29, determine whether the series is absolutely convergent, conditionally convergent, or divergent.

26. $\sum \dfrac{(-1)^n}{n^{1/2}}$

27. $\sum (-1)^n \left(1 + \dfrac{1}{n^2}\right)$

28. $\sum \dfrac{(-1)^{n-1} \ln n}{n}$

29. $\sum \dfrac{(-1)^{n-1}}{\arctan n}$

In Exercises 30–31, use the comparison test to confirm the statement.

30. $\displaystyle\sum_{n=1}^{\infty} \left(\dfrac{1}{3}\right)^n$ converges, so $\displaystyle\sum_{n=1}^{\infty} \left(\dfrac{n^2}{3n^2 + 4}\right)^n$ converges.

31. $\displaystyle\sum_{n=1}^{\infty} \dfrac{1}{n}$ diverges, so $\displaystyle\sum_{n=1}^{\infty} \dfrac{1}{n \sin^2 n}$ diverges.

In Exercises 32–35, use the limit comparison test to determine whether the series converges or diverges.

32. $\sum \dfrac{\sqrt{n-1}}{n^2 + 3}$

33. $\sum \dfrac{n^3 - 2n^2 + n + 1}{n^5 - 2}$

34. $\sum \sin \dfrac{1}{n^2}$

35. $\sum \dfrac{1}{\sqrt{n^3 - 1}}$

In Exercises 36–57, determine whether the series converges.

36. $\displaystyle\sum_{n=1}^{\infty} \dfrac{1}{n+1}$

37. $\displaystyle\sum_{n=1}^{\infty} \dfrac{1}{n^3}$

38. $\displaystyle\sum_{n=3}^{\infty} \dfrac{2}{\sqrt{n-2}}$

39. $\displaystyle\sum_{n=1}^{\infty} \dfrac{(-1)^{n-1}}{\sqrt{n}+1}$

40. $\displaystyle\sum_{n=1}^{\infty} \dfrac{n^2}{n^2 + 1}$

41. $\displaystyle\sum_{n=1}^{\infty} \dfrac{n^2}{n^3 + 1}$

42. $\displaystyle\sum_{n=1}^{\infty} \dfrac{3^n}{(2n)!}$

43. $\displaystyle\sum_{n=1}^{\infty} \dfrac{(2n)!}{(n!)^2}$

44. $\displaystyle\sum_{n=1}^{\infty} \dfrac{n^2 + 2^n}{n^2 2^n}$

45. $\displaystyle\sum_{n=1}^{\infty} \dfrac{3^{2n}}{(2n)!}$

46. $\displaystyle\sum_{n=1}^{\infty} 2^{-n} \dfrac{(n+1)}{(n+2)}$

47. $\displaystyle\sum_{n=1}^{\infty} (-1)^n \dfrac{2^n}{(2n+1)!}$

48. $\displaystyle\sum_{n=1}^{\infty} (-1)^n \dfrac{n+1}{\sqrt{n}}$

49. $\displaystyle\sum_{n=0}^{\infty} \dfrac{2 + 3^n}{5^n}$

50. $\displaystyle\sum_{n=1}^{\infty} \left(\dfrac{1 + 5n}{4n}\right)^n$

51. $\displaystyle\sum_{n=1}^{\infty} \dfrac{1}{2 + \sin n}$

52. $\displaystyle\sum_{n=3}^{\infty} \dfrac{1}{(2n-5)^3}$

53. $\displaystyle\sum_{n=2}^{\infty} \dfrac{1}{n^3 - 3}$

54. $\displaystyle\sum_{n=1}^{\infty} \dfrac{\sin(n\pi/2)}{n^3}$

55. $\displaystyle\sum_{k=1}^{\infty} \ln\left(1 + \dfrac{1}{k}\right)$

56. $\displaystyle\sum_{n=1}^{\infty} \dfrac{n}{2^n}$

57. $\displaystyle\sum_{n=2}^{\infty} \dfrac{1}{(\ln n)^2}$

In Exercises 58–61, find the radius of convergence.

58. $\displaystyle\sum_{n=1}^{\infty} \dfrac{(2n)! x^n}{(n!)^2}$

59. $\displaystyle\sum_{n=0}^{\infty} \dfrac{x^n}{n! + 1}$

60. $x + 4x^2 + 9x^3 + 16x^4 + 25x^5 + \cdots$

61. $\dfrac{x}{3} + \dfrac{2x^2}{5} + \dfrac{3x^3}{7} + \dfrac{4x^4}{9} + \dfrac{5x^5}{11} + \cdots$

In Exercises 62–65, find the interval of convergence.

62. $\displaystyle\sum_{n=1}^{\infty} \dfrac{x^n}{3^n n^2}$

63. $\displaystyle\sum_{n=0}^{\infty} \dfrac{(-1)^n (x-2)^n}{5^n}$

64. $\displaystyle\sum_{n=1}^{\infty} \dfrac{(-1)^n x^n}{n}$

65. $\displaystyle\sum_{n=1}^{\infty} \dfrac{x^n}{n!}$

Problems

66. Write the first four terms of the sequence given by

$$s_n = \dfrac{(-1)^n (2n+1)^2}{2^{2n-1} + (-1)^{n+1}}, \quad n \geq 1.$$

In Problems 67–68, find a possible formula for the general term of the sequence.

67. $s_1, s_2, s_3, s_4, s_5, \ldots = 5, 7, 9, 11, 13, \ldots$

68. $t_1, t_2, t_3, t_4, t_5, \ldots = 9, 25, 49, 81, 121, \ldots$

In Problems 69–70, let $a_1 = 5, b_1 = 10$ and, for $n > 1$,

$$a_n = a_{n-1} + 2n \quad \text{and} \quad b_n = b_{n-1} + a_{n-1}.$$

69. Give the values of a_2, a_3, a_4.

70. Give the values of b_2, b_3, b_4, b_5.

71. For $r > 0$, how does the convergence of the following series depend on r?

$$\sum_{n=1}^{\infty} \frac{n^r + r^n}{n^r r^n}$$

72. The series $\sum C_n (x - 2)^n$ converges when $x = 4$ and diverges when $x = 6$. Decide whether each of the following statements is true or false, or whether this cannot be determined.

  (a) The power series converges when $x = 7$.
  (b) The power series diverges when $x = 1$.
  (c) The power series converges when $x = 0.5$.
  (d) The power series diverges when $x = 5$.
  (e) The power series converges when $x = -3$.

73. For all the t-values for which it converges, the function h is defined by the series

$$h(t) = \sum_{n=0}^{\infty} (-1)^n \frac{t^{2n}}{(2n)!}.$$

  (a) What is the domain of h?
  (b) Is h odd, even, or neither?
  (c) Assuming that derivatives can be computed term by term, show that

$$h''(t) = -h(t).$$

74. A \$200,000 loan is to be repaid over 20 years in equal monthly installments of \$$M$, beginning at the end of the first month. Find the monthly payment if the loan is at an annual rate of 9%, compounded monthly. [Hint: Find an expression for the present value of the sum of all of the monthly payments, set it equal to \$200,000, and solve for M.]

75. The extraction rate of a mineral is currently 12 million tons a year, but this rate is expected to fall by 5% each year. What minimum level of world reserves would allow extraction to continue indefinitely?

76. A new car costs \$30,000; it loses 10% of its value each year. Maintenance is \$500 the first year and increases by 20% annually.

  (a) Find a formula for l_n, the value lost by the car in year n.
  (b) Find a formula for m_n, the maintenance expenses in year n.
  (c) In what year do maintenance expenses first exceed the value lost by the car?

Problems 77–79 are about *bonds*, which are issued by a government to raise money. An individual who buys a \$1000 bond gives the government \$1000 and in return receives a fixed sum of money, called the *coupon*, every six months or every year for the life of the bond. At the time of the last coupon, the individual also gets back the \$1000, or *principal*.

77. What is the present value of a \$1000 bond which pays \$50 a year for 10 years, starting one year from now? Assume the interest rate is 6% per year, compounded annually.

78. What is the present value of a \$1000 bond which pays \$50 a year for 10 years, starting one year from now? Assume the interest rate is 4% per year, compounded annually.

79. In the nineteenth century, the railroads issued 100-year bonds. Consider a \$100 bond which paid \$5 a year, starting a year after it was sold. Assume interest rates are 4% per year, compounded annually.

  (a) Find the present value of the bond.
  (b) Suppose that instead of maturing in 100 years, the bond was to have paid \$5 a year forever. This time the principal, \$100, is never repaid. What is the present value of the bond?

80. Cephalexin is an antibiotic with a half-life in the body of 0.9 hours, taken in tablets of 250 mg every six hours.

  (a) What percentage of the cephalexin in the body at the start of a six-hour period is still there at the end (assuming no tablets are taken during that time)?
  (b) Write an expression for Q_1, Q_2, Q_3, Q_4, where Q_n mg is the amount of cephalexin in the body right after the nth tablet is taken.
  (c) Express Q_3, Q_4 in closed form and evaluate them.
  (d) Write an expression for Q_n and put it in closed form.
  (e) If the patient keeps taking the tablets, use your answer to part (d) to find the quantity of cephalexin in the body in the long run, right after taking a tablet.

81. Before World War I, the British government issued what are called *consols*, which pay the owner or his heirs a fixed amount of money every year forever. (Cartoonists of the time described aristocrats living off such payments as "pickled in consols.") What should a person expect to pay for consols which pay £10 a year forever? Assume the first payment is one year from the date of purchase and that interest remains 4% per year, compounded annually. (£ denotes pounds, the British unit of currency.)

82. This problem illustrates how banks create credit and can thereby lend out more money than has been deposited. Suppose that initially \$100 is deposited in a bank. Experience has shown bankers that on average only 8% of the money deposited is withdrawn by the owner at any time. Consequently, bankers feel free to lend out 92% of their deposits. Thus \$92 of the original \$100 is loaned out to other customers (to start a business, for example). This \$92 becomes someone else's income and, sooner or later, is redeposited in the bank. Thus 92% of \$92, or \$92(0.92) = \$84.64, is loaned out again and eventually redeposited. Of the \$84.64, the bank again loans out 92%, and so on.

  (a) Find the total amount of money deposited in the bank as a result of these transactions.

(b) The total amount of money deposited divided by the original deposit is called the *credit multiplier*. Calculate the credit multiplier for this example and explain what this number tells us.

83. Baby formula can contain bacteria which double in number every half hour at room temperature and every 10 hours in the refrigerator.[10] There are B_0 bacteria initially.

    (a) Write formulas for
       (i) R_n, the number of bacteria n hours later if the baby formula is kept at room temperature.
       (ii) F_n, the number of bacteria n hours later if the baby formula is kept in the refrigerator.
       (iii) Y_n, the ratio of the number of bacteria at room temperature to the number of bacteria in the refrigerator.
    (b) How many hours does it take before there are a million times as many bacteria in baby formula kept at room temperature as there are in baby formula kept in the refrigerator?

84. The sequence $1, 5/8, 14/27, 15/32, \ldots$ is defined by:

$$s_1 = 1$$
$$s_2 = \frac{1}{2}\left(\left(\frac{1}{2}\right)^2 + \left(\frac{2}{2}\right)^2\right) = \frac{5}{8}$$
$$s_3 = \frac{1}{3}\left(\left(\frac{1}{3}\right)^2 + \left(\frac{2}{3}\right)^2 + \left(\frac{3}{3}\right)^2\right) = \frac{14}{27}.$$

    (a) Extend the pattern and find s_5.
    (b) Write an expression for s_n using sigma notation.
    (c) Use Riemann sums to evaluate $\lim_{n \to \infty} s_n$.

85. Estimate $\sum_{n=1}^{\infty} \frac{(-1)^{n-1}}{(2n-1)!}$ to within 0.01 of the actual sum of the series.

86. Is it possible to construct a convergent alternating series $\sum_{n=1}^{\infty}(-1)^{n-1}a_n$ for which $0 < a_{n+1} < a_n$ but $\lim_{n \to \infty} a_n \neq 0$?

87. Suppose that $0 \leq b_n \leq 2^n$ for all n. Give two examples of series $\sum b_n$ that satisfy this condition, one that diverges and one that converges.

88. Show that if $\sum a_n$ converges and $\sum b_n$ diverges, then $\sum(a_n + b_n)$ diverges. [Hint: Assume that $\sum(a_n + b_n)$ converges and consider $\sum(a_n + b_n) - \sum a_n$.]

In Problems 89–93, the series $\sum a_n$ converges with $a_n > 0$ for all n. Does the series converge or diverge or is there not enough information to tell?

89. $\sum a_n/n$ 90. $\sum 1/a_n$ 91. $\sum na_n$

92. $\sum(a_n + a_n/2)$ 93. $\sum a_n^2$

94. Does $\sum_{n=1}^{\infty}\left(\frac{1}{n} + \frac{1}{n}\right)$ converge or diverge? Does $\sum_{n=1}^{\infty}\left(\frac{1}{n} - \frac{1}{n}\right)$ converge or diverge? Is the statement "If $\sum a_n$ and $\sum b_n$ diverge, then $\sum(a_n + b_n)$ may or may not diverge" true?

95. This problem shows how you can create a fractal called a *Cantor Set*. Take a line segment of length 1, divide it into three equal pieces and remove the middle piece. We are left with two smaller line segments. At the second stage, remove the middle third of each of the two segments. We now have four smaller line segments left. At the third stage, remove the middle third of each of the remaining segments. Continue in this manner.

    (a) Draw a picture that illustrates this process.
    (b) Find a series that gives the total length of the pieces we have removed after the nth stage.
    (c) If we continue the process indefinitely, what is the total length of the pieces that we remove?

96. Although the harmonic series does not converge, the partial sums grow very, very slowly. Take a right-hand sum approximating the integral of $f(x) = 1/x$ on the interval $[1, n]$, with $\Delta x = 1$, to show that

$$\frac{1}{2} + \frac{1}{3} + \frac{1}{4} + \cdots + \frac{1}{n} < \ln n.$$

If a computer could add a million terms of the harmonic series each second, estimate the sum after one year.

97. Estimate the sum of the first 100,000 terms of the harmonic series,

$$\sum_{k=1}^{100,000} \frac{1}{k},$$

to the closest integer. [Hint: Use left- and right-hand sums of the function $f(x) = 1/x$ on the interval from 1 to 100,000 with $\Delta x = 1$.]

98. Is the following argument true or false? Give reasons for your answer.

Consider the infinite series $\sum_{n=2}^{\infty} \frac{1}{n(n-1)}$. Since $\frac{1}{n(n-1)} = \frac{1}{n-1} - \frac{1}{n}$ we can write this series as

$$\sum_{n=2}^{\infty} \frac{1}{n-1} - \sum_{n=2}^{\infty} \frac{1}{n}.$$

For the first series $a_n = 1/(n-1)$. Since $n - 1 < n$ we have $1/(n-1) > 1/n$ and so this series diverges by comparison with the divergent harmonic series $\sum_{n=2}^{\infty} \frac{1}{n}$. The second series is the divergent harmonic series. Since both series diverge, their difference also diverges.

---

[10]Iverson, C. and Forsythe, F., reported in "Baby Food Could Trigger Meningitis," www.newscientist.com, June 3, 2004.

PROJECTS FOR CHAPTER NINE

1. **Medical Case Study: Drug Desensitization Schedule**[11]

   Some patients have allergic reactions to critical medications for which there are no effective alternatives. In some such cases, the drug can be given safely by a process known as drug desensitization. Desensitization starts by administering a very small amount of the needed medication intravenously, and then progressively increasing the concentration or the rate that the drug is infused until the full dose is achieved.

   An example of a drug desensitization regimen is shown in Table 9.2. Three solutions of the drug at different concentrations (full strength, 10-fold diluted, and 100-fold diluted) are prepared. The procedure starts with a low rate of infusion of the most dilute solution and progresses in 15 minute steps until the highest infusion rate of the most concentrated solution is reached. At the last stage, the infusion runs until the target dose is reached.

   (a) For a target dose of 500 mg of a drug and a full strength solution of 2 mg/ml, make a spreadsheet that enables you to fill out the first 11 steps in Table 9.2, each of which runs for 15 minutes.

   (b) How much of the drug is administered in the 12th step? How long does this step last? Fill in the last row of the table.

   (c) Show how a geometric series can be used to calculate the total drug administered in the first 11 steps.

   (d) How long does it take from the beginning of step 1 for the patient to receive the target dose?

Table 9.2

Step	Solution	Concentration (mg/ml)	Rate (ml/hr)	Time (min)	Volume infused per step (ml)	Dose administered per step (mg)	Cumulative dose (mg)	Ratio of dose administered in this step to dose administered in previous step
1	100-fold dilution		2.5					
2	100-fold dilution		5.0					
3	100-fold dilution		10.0					
4	100-fold dilution		20.0					
5	10-fold dilution		4.0					
6	10-fold dilution		8.0					
7	10-fold dilution		16.0					
8	10-fold dilution		32.0					
9	undiluted		6.4					
10	undiluted		12.8					
11	undiluted		25.6					
12	undiluted		51.2					

2. **A Definition of** e

   We show that the sequence $s_n = \left(1 + \dfrac{1}{n}\right)^n$ converges; its limit can be used to define e.

   (a) For a fixed integer $n > 0$, let $f(x) = (n+1)x^n - nx^{n+1}$. For $x > 1$, show f is decreasing and that $f(x) < 1$. Hence, for $x > 1$,

   $$x^n(n+1-nx) < 1.$$

   (b) Substitute the following x-value into the inequality from part (a):

   $$x = \frac{1+1/n}{1+1/(n+1)},$$

---

[11]From David E. Sloane, M.D.

and show that

$$x^n \left(\frac{n+1}{n+2} \right) < 1.$$

(c) Use the inequality from part (b) to show that $s_n < s_{n+1}$ for all $n > 0$. Conclude that the sequence is increasing.

(d) Substitute $x = 1 + 1/2n$ into the inequality from part (a) to show that

$$\left(1 + \frac{1}{2n} \right)^n < 2.$$

(e) Use the inequality from part (d) to show $s_{2n} < 4$. Conclude that the sequence is bounded.

(f) Use parts (c) and (e) to show that the sequence has a limit.

3. **Probability of Winning in Sports**

In certain sports, winning a game requires a lead of two points. That is, if the score is tied you have to score two points in a row to win.

(a) For some sports (e.g. tennis), a point is scored every play. Suppose your probability of scoring the next point is always p. Then, your opponent's probability of scoring the next point is always $1 - p$.

  (i) What is the probability that you win the next two points?

  (ii) What is the probability that you and your opponent split the next two points, that is, that neither of you wins both points?

  (iii) What is the probability that you split the next two points but you win the two after that?

  (iv) What is the probability that you either win the next two points or split the next two and then win the next two after that?

  (v) Give a formula for your probability w of winning a tied game.

  (vi) Compute your probability of winning a tied game when $p = 0.5$; when $p = 0.6$; when $p = 0.7$; when $p = 0.4$. Comment on your answers.

(b) In other sports (e.g. volleyball prior to 1999), you can score a point only if it is your turn, with turns alternating until a point is scored. Suppose your probability of scoring a point when it is your turn is p, and your opponent's probability of scoring a point when it is her turn is q.

  (i) Find a formula for the probability S that you are the first to score the next point, assuming it is currently your turn.

  (ii) Suppose that if you score a point, the next turn is yours. Using your answers to part (a) and your formula for S, compute the probability of winning a tied game (if you need two points in a row to win).

    • Assume $p = 0.5$ and $q = 0.5$ and it is your turn.
    • Assume $p = 0.6$ and $q = 0.5$ and it is your turn.

4. **Prednisone**

Prednisone is often prescribed for acute asthma attacks. For 5 mg tablets, typical instructions are: "Take 8 tablets the first day, 7 the second, and decrease by one tablet each day until all tablets are gone." Prednisone decays exponentially in the body, and 24 hours after taking k mg, there are kx mg in the body.

(a) Write formulas involving x for the amount of prednisone in the body

  (i) 24 hours after taking the first dose (of 8 tablets), right before taking the second dose (of 7 tablets).

  (ii) Immediately after taking the second dose (of 7 tablets).

  (iii) Immediately after taking the third dose (of 6 tablets).

   (iv) Immediately after taking the eighth dose (of 1 tablet).

   (v) 24 hours after taking the eighth dose.

   (vi) n days after taking the eighth dose.

(b) Find a closed form for the sum $T = 8x^7 + 7x^6 + 6x^5 + \cdots + 2x + 1$, which is the number of prednisone tablets in the body immediately after taking the eighth dose.

(c) If a patient takes all the prednisone tablets as prescribed, how many days after taking the eighth dose is there less than 3% of a prednisone tablet in the patient's body? The half-life of prednisone is about 24 hours.

(d) A patient is prescribed n tablets of prednisone the first day, $n - 1$ the second, and one tablet fewer each day until all tablets are gone. Write a formula that represents T_n, the number of prednisone tablets in the body immediately after taking all tablets. Find a closed-form sum for T_n.

Chapter Ten

APPROXIMATING FUNCTIONS USING SERIES

Contents

10.1 TAYLOR POLYNOMIALS

In this section, we see how to approximate a function by polynomials.

Linear Approximations

We already know how to approximate a function using a degree-1 polynomial, namely the tangent line approximation given in Section 3.9 :

$$f(x) \approx f(a) + f'(a)(x - a).$$

The tangent line and the curve have the same slope at $x = a$. As Figure 10.1 suggests, the tangent line approximation to the function is generally more accurate for values of x close to a.

Figure 10.1: Tangent line approximation of $f(x)$ for x near a

We first focus on $a = 0$. The tangent line approximation at $x = 0$ is referred to as the *first Taylor approximation* at $x = 0$, or as follows:

Taylor Polynomial of Degree 1 Approximating $f(x)$ for x near 0

$$f(x) \approx P_1(x) = f(0) + f'(0)x$$

Example 1   Find the Taylor polynomial of degree 1 for $g(x) = \cos x$, with x in radians, for x near 0.

Solution   The tangent line at $x = 0$ is just the horizontal line $y = 1$, as shown in Figure 10.2, so $P_1(x) = 1$. We have

$$g(x) = \cos x \approx 1, \quad \text{for } x \text{ near 0.}$$

If we take $x = 0.05$, then

$$g(0.05) = \cos(0.05) = 0.998\ldots,$$

which is quite close to the approximation $\cos x \approx 1$. Similarly, if $x = -0.1$, then

$$g(-0.1) = \cos(-0.1) = 0.995\ldots$$

is close to the approximation $\cos x \approx 1$. However, if $x = 0.4$, then

$$g(0.4) = \cos(0.4) = 0.921\ldots,$$

so the approximation $\cos x \approx 1$ is less accurate. For x near 0, the graph suggests that the farther x is from 0, the worse the approximation, $\cos x \approx 1$, is likely to be.

Figure 10.2: Graph of $\cos x$ and its tangent line at $x = 0$

The previous example shows that the Taylor polynomial of degree 1 might actually have degree less than 1.

Quadratic Approximations

To get a more accurate approximation, we use a quadratic function instead of a linear function.

Example 2   Find the quadratic approximation to $g(x) = \cos x$ for x near 0.

Solution   To ensure that the quadratic, $P_2(x)$, is a good approximation to $g(x) = \cos x$ at $x = 0$, we require that $\cos x$ and the quadratic have the same value, the same slope, and the same second derivative at $x = 0$. That is, we require $P_2(0) = g(0)$, $P_2'(0) = g'(0)$, and $P_2''(0) = g''(0)$. We take the quadratic polynomial

$$P_2(x) = C_0 + C_1 x + C_2 x^2$$

and determine C_0, C_1, and C_2. Since

$$P_2(x) = C_0 + C_1 x + C_2 x^2 \quad \text{and} \quad g(x) = \cos x$$
$$P_2'(x) = C_1 + 2C_2 x \qquad\qquad g'(x) = -\sin x$$
$$P_2''(x) = 2C_2 \qquad\qquad g''(x) = -\cos x,$$

we have

$$C_0 = P_2(0) = g(0) = \cos 0 = 1 \qquad \text{so} \quad C_0 = 1$$
$$C_1 = P_2'(0) = g'(0) = -\sin 0 = 0 \qquad\qquad C_1 = 0$$
$$2C_2 = P_2''(0) = g''(0) = -\cos 0 = -1, \qquad C_2 = -\tfrac{1}{2}.$$

Consequently, the quadratic approximation is

$$\cos x \approx P_2(x) = 1 + 0 \cdot x - \frac{1}{2}x^2 = 1 - \frac{x^2}{2}, \quad \text{for } x \text{ near } 0.$$

Figure 10.3 suggests that the quadratic approximation $\cos x \approx P_2(x)$ is better than the linear approximation $\cos x \approx P_1(x)$ for x near 0. Let's compare the accuracy of the two approximations. Recall that $P_1(x) = 1$ for all x. At $x = 0.4$, we have $\cos(0.4) = 0.921\ldots$ and $P_2(0.4) = 0.920$, so the quadratic approximation is a significant improvement over the linear approximation. The magnitude of the error is about 0.001 instead of 0.08.

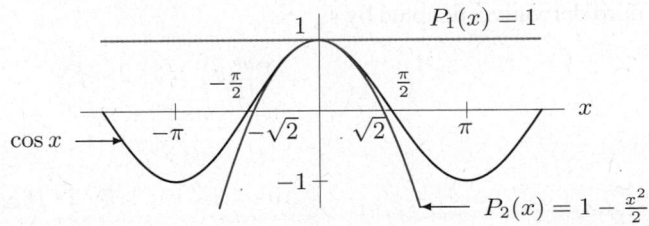

Figure 10.3: Graph of $\cos x$ and its linear, $P_1(x)$, and quadratic, $P_2(x)$, approximations for x near 0

Generalizing the computations in Example 2, we define the *second Taylor approximation* at $x = 0$.

Taylor Polynomial of Degree 2 Approximating $f(x)$ for x near 0

$$f(x) \approx P_2(x) = f(0) + f'(0)x + \frac{f''(0)}{2}x^2$$

Higher-Degree Polynomials

In a small interval around $x = 0$, the quadratic approximation to a function is usually a better approximation than the linear (tangent line) approximation. However, Figure 10.3 shows that the quadratic can still bend away from the original function for large x. We can attempt to fix this by using an approximating polynomial of higher degree. Suppose that we approximate a function $f(x)$ for x near 0 by a polynomial of degree n:

$$f(x) \approx P_n(x) = C_0 + C_1 x + C_2 x^2 + \cdots + C_{n-1} x^{n-1} + C_n x^n.$$

We need to find the values of the constants: C_0, C_1, $C_2, \ldots, C_n$. To do this, we require that the function $f(x)$ and each of its first n derivatives agree with those of the polynomial $P_n(x)$ at the point $x = 0$. In general, the higher the degree of a Taylor polynomial, the larger the interval on which the function and the polynomial remain close to each other.

To see how to find the constants, let's take $n = 3$ as an example:

$$f(x) \approx P_3(x) = C_0 + C_1 x + C_2 x^2 + C_3 x^3.$$

Substituting $x = 0$ gives

$$f(0) = P_3(0) = C_0.$$

Differentiating $P_3(x)$ yields

$$P_3'(x) = C_1 + 2C_2 x + 3C_3 x^2,$$

so substituting $x = 0$ shows that

$$f'(0) = P_3'(0) = C_1.$$

Differentiating and substituting again, we get

$$P_3''(x) = 2 \cdot 1 C_2 + 3 \cdot 2 \cdot 1 C_3 x,$$

which gives

$$f''(0) = P_3''(0) = 2 \cdot 1 C_2,$$

so that

$$C_2 = \frac{f''(0)}{2 \cdot 1}.$$

The third derivative, denoted by P_3''', is

$$P_3'''(x) = 3 \cdot 2 \cdot 1 C_3,$$

so

$$f'''(0) = P_3'''(0) = 3 \cdot 2 \cdot 1 C_3,$$

and then

$$C_3 = \frac{f'''(0)}{3 \cdot 2 \cdot 1}.$$

You can imagine a similar calculation starting with $P_4(x)$ and using the fourth derivative $f^{(4)}$, which would give

$$C_4 = \frac{f^{(4)}(0)}{4 \cdot 3 \cdot 2 \cdot 1},$$

and so on. Using factorial notation,[1] we write these expressions as

$$C_3 = \frac{f'''(0)}{3!}, \quad C_4 = \frac{f^{(4)}(0)}{4!}.$$

---

[1] Recall that $k! = k(k-1) \cdots 2 \cdot 1$. In addition, $1! = 1$, and $0! = 1$.

Writing $f^{(n)}$ for the nth derivative of f, we have, for any positive integer n,

$$C_n = \frac{f^{(n)}(0)}{n!}.$$

So we define the nth *Taylor approximation* at $x = 0$:

Taylor Polynomial of Degree n Approximating $f(x)$ for x near 0

$$f(x) \approx P_n(x)$$

$$= f(0) + f'(0)x + \frac{f''(0)}{2!}x^2 + \frac{f'''(0)}{3!}x^3 + \frac{f^{(4)}(0)}{4!}x^4 + \cdots + \frac{f^{(n)}(0)}{n!}x^n$$

We call $P_n(x)$ the Taylor polynomial of degree n centered at $x = 0$ or the Taylor polynomial about (or around) $x = 0$.

Example 3   Construct the Taylor polynomial of degree 7 approximating the function $f(x) = \sin x$ for x near 0. Compare the value of the Taylor approximation with the true value of f at $x = \pi/3$.

Solution   We have

$$
\begin{aligned}
f(x) &= & \sin x & \quad \text{giving} & f(0) &= & 0 \\
f'(x) &= & \cos x & & f'(0) &= & 1 \\
f''(x) &= & -\sin x & & f''(0) &= & 0 \\
f'''(x) &= & -\cos x & & f'''(0) &= & -1 \\
f^{(4)}(x) &= & \sin x & & f^{(4)}(0) &= & 0 \\
f^{(5)}(x) &= & \cos x & & f^{(5)}(0) &= & 1 \\
f^{(6)}(x) &= & -\sin x & & f^{(6)}(0) &= & 0 \\
f^{(7)}(x) &= & -\cos x & & f^{(7)}(0) &= & -1.
\end{aligned}
$$

Using these values, we see that the Taylor polynomial approximation of degree 7 is

$$\sin x \approx P_7(x) = 0 + 1 \cdot x + \frac{0}{2!} \cdot x^2 - \frac{1}{3!} \cdot x^3 + \frac{0}{4!} \cdot x^4 + \frac{1}{5!} \cdot x^5 + \frac{0}{6!} \cdot x^6 - \frac{1}{7!} \cdot x^7$$

$$= x - \frac{x^3}{3!} + \frac{x^5}{5!} - \frac{x^7}{7!}, \quad \text{for } x \text{ near } 0.$$

Notice that since $f^{(8)}(0) = 0$, the seventh and eighth Taylor approximations to $\sin x$ are the same.

In Figure 10.4 we show the graphs of the sine function and the approximating polynomial of degree 7 for x near 0. They are indistinguishable where x is close to 0. However, as we look at values of x farther away from 0 in either direction, the two graphs move apart. To check the accuracy of this approximation numerically, we see how well it approximates $\sin(\pi/3) = \sqrt{3}/2 = 0.8660254\ldots$.

Figure 10.4: Graph of $\sin x$ and its seventh-degree Taylor polynomial, $P_7(x)$, for x near 0

When we substitute $\pi/3 = 1.0471976\ldots$ into the polynomial approximation, we obtain $P_7(\pi/3) = 0.8660213\ldots$, which is extremely accurate—to about four parts in a million.

Example 4   Graph the Taylor polynomial of degree 8 approximating $g(x) = \cos x$ for x near 0.

Solution　We find the coefficients of the Taylor polynomial by the method of the preceding example, giving

$$\cos x \approx P_8(x) = 1 - \frac{x^2}{2!} + \frac{x^4}{4!} - \frac{x^6}{6!} + \frac{x^8}{8!}.$$

Figure 10.5 shows that $P_8(x)$ is close to the cosine function for a larger interval of x-values than the quadratic approximation $P_2(x) = 1 - x^2/2$ in Example 2 on page 539.

Figure 10.5: $P_8(x)$ approximates $\cos x$ better than $P_2(x)$ for x near 0

Example 5　Construct the Taylor polynomial of degree 10 about $x = 0$ for the function $f(x) = e^x$.

Solution　We have $f(0) = 1$. Since the derivative of e^x is equal to e^x, all the higher-order derivatives are equal to e^x. Consequently, for any $k = 1, 2, \ldots, 10$, $f^{(k)}(x) = e^x$ and $f^{(k)}(0) = e^0 = 1$. Therefore, the Taylor polynomial approximation of degree 10 is given by

$$e^x \approx P_{10}(x) = 1 + x + \frac{x^2}{2!} + \frac{x^3}{3!} + \frac{x^4}{4!} + \cdots + \frac{x^{10}}{10!}, \quad \text{for } x \text{ near } 0.$$

To check the accuracy of this approximation, we use it to approximate $e = e^1 = 2.718281828\ldots$. Substituting $x = 1$ gives $P_{10}(1) = 2.718281801$. Thus, P_{10} yields the first seven decimal places for e. For large values of x, however, the accuracy diminishes because e^x grows faster than any polynomial as $x \to \infty$. Figure 10.6 shows graphs of $f(x) = e^x$ and the Taylor polynomials of degree $n = 0, 1, 2, 3, 4$. Notice that each successive approximation remains close to the exponential curve for a larger interval of x-values.

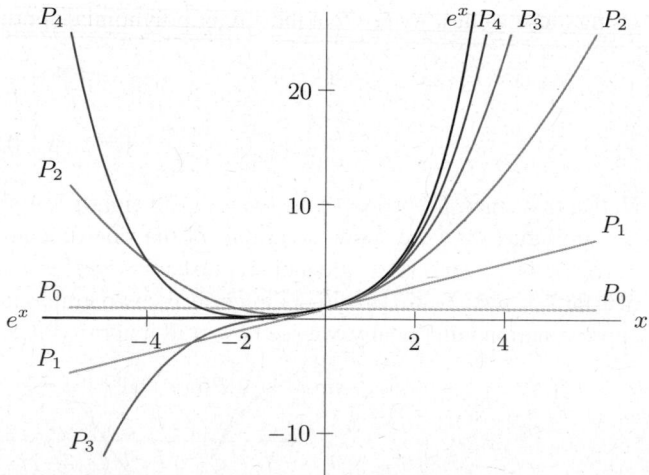

Figure 10.6: For x near 0, the value of e^x is more closely approximated by higher-degree Taylor polynomials

Example 6　Construct the Taylor polynomial of degree n approximating $f(x) = \dfrac{1}{1 - x}$ for x near 0.

Solution　Differentiating gives $f(0) = 1$, $f'(0) = 1$, $f''(0) = 2$, $f'''(0) = 3!$, $f^{(4)}(0) = 4!$, and so on. This means

$$\frac{1}{1 - x} \approx P_n(x) = 1 + x + x^2 + x^3 + x^4 + \cdots + x^n, \quad \text{for } x \text{ near } 0.$$

Let us compare the Taylor polynomial with the formula obtained from the sum of a finite geometric series on page 500:

$$\frac{1 - x^{n+1}}{1 - x} = 1 + x + x^2 + x^3 + x^4 + \cdots + x^n.$$

If x is close to 0 and x^{n+1} is small enough to neglect, the formula for the sum of a finite geometric series gives us the Taylor approximation of degree n:

$$\frac{1}{1 - x} \approx 1 + x + x^2 + x^3 + x^4 + \cdots + x^n.$$

Taylor Polynomials Around $x = a$

Suppose we want to approximate $f(x) = \ln x$ by a Taylor polynomial. This function has no Taylor polynomial about $x = 0$ because the function is not defined for $x \leq 0$. However, it turns out that we can construct a polynomial centered about some other point, $x = a$.

First, let's look at the equation of the tangent line at $x = a$:

$$y = f(a) + f'(a)(x - a).$$

This gives the first Taylor approximation

$$f(x) \approx f(a) + f'(a)(x - a) \quad \text{for } x \text{ near } a.$$

The $f'(a)(x - a)$ term is a correction term that approximates the change in f as x moves away from a.

Similarly, the Taylor polynomial $P_n(x)$ centered at $x = a$ is set up as $f(a)$ plus correction terms that are zero for $x = a$. This is achieved by writing the polynomial in powers of $(x - a)$ instead of powers of x:

$$f(x) \approx P_n(x) = C_0 + C_1(x - a) + C_2(x - a)^2 + \cdots + C_n(x - a)^n.$$

If we require n derivatives of the approximating polynomial $P_n(x)$ and the original function $f(x)$ to agree at $x = a$, we get the following result for the nth Taylor approximation at $x = a$:

Taylor Polynomial of Degree n Approximating $f(x)$ for x near a

$$f(x) \approx P_n(x)$$
$$= f(a) + f'(a)(x - a) + \frac{f''(a)}{2!}(x - a)^2 + \cdots + \frac{f^{(n)}(a)}{n!}(x - a)^n$$

We call $P_n(x)$ the Taylor polynomial of degree n centered at $x = a$ or the Taylor polynomial about $x = a$.

You can derive the formula for these coefficients in the same way that we did for $a = 0$. (See Problem 34, page 545.)

Example 7   Construct the Taylor polynomial of degree 4 approximating the function $f(x) = \ln x$ for x near 1.

Solution   We have

$$
\begin{aligned}
f(x) &= \ln x & \text{so} \quad f(1) &= \ln(1) = 0 \\
f'(x) &= 1/x & f'(1) &= 1 \\
f''(x) &= -1/x^2 & f''(1) &= -1 \\
f'''(x) &= 2/x^3 & f'''(1) &= 2 \\
f^{(4)}(x) &= -6/x^4, & f^{(4)}(1) &= -6.
\end{aligned}
$$

The Taylor polynomial is therefore

$$\ln x \approx P_4(x) = 0 + (x - 1) - \frac{(x - 1)^2}{2!} + 2\frac{(x - 1)^3}{3!} - 6\frac{(x - 1)^4}{4!}$$

$$= (x - 1) - \frac{(x - 1)^2}{2} + \frac{(x - 1)^3}{3} - \frac{(x - 1)^4}{4}, \quad \text{for } x \text{ near } 1.$$

Figure 10.7: Taylor polynomials approximate $\ln x$ closely for x near 1, but not necessarily farther away

Graphs of $\ln x$ and several of its Taylor polynomials are shown in Figure 10.7. Notice that $P_4(x)$ stays reasonably close to $\ln x$ for x near 1, but bends away as x gets farther from 1. Also, note that the Taylor polynomials are defined for $x \leq 0$, but $\ln x$ is not.

The examples in this section suggest that the following results are true for common functions:
- Taylor polynomials centered at $x = a$ give good approximations to $f(x)$ for x near a. Farther away, they may or may not be good.
- The higher the degree of the Taylor polynomial, the larger the interval over which it fits the function closely.

Exercises and Problems for Section 10.1

Exercises

For Exercises 1–10, find the Taylor polynomials of degree n approximating the functions for x near 0. (Assume p is a constant.)

1. $\dfrac{1}{1-x}$, $n = 3, 5, 7$ **2.** $\dfrac{1}{1+x}$, $n = 4, 6, 8$

3. $\sqrt{1+x}$, $n = 2, 3, 4$ **4.** $\sqrt[3]{1-x}$, $n = 2, 3, 4$

5. $\cos x$, $n = 2, 4, 6$ **6.** $\ln(1+x)$, $n = 5, 7, 9$

7. $\arctan x$, $n = 3, 4$ **8.** $\tan x$, $n = 3, 4$

9. $\dfrac{1}{\sqrt{1+x}}$, $n = 2, 3, 4$ **10.** $(1+x)^p$, $n = 2, 3, 4$

For Exercises 11–16, find the Taylor polynomial of degree n for x near the given point a.

11. $\sqrt{1-x}$, $a = 0$, $n = 3$

12. e^x, $a = 1$, $n = 4$

13. $\dfrac{1}{1+x}$, $a = 2$, $n = 4$

14. $\cos x$, $a = \pi/2$, $n = 4$

15. $\sin x$, $a = -\pi/4$, $n = 3$

16. $\ln(x^2)$, $a = 1$, $n = 4$

Problems

17. The Taylor polynomial of degree 7 of $f(x)$ is given by

$$P_7(x) = 1 - \frac{x}{3} + \frac{5x^2}{7} + 8x^3 - \frac{x^5}{11} + 8x^7.$$

Find the Taylor polynomial of degree 3 of $f(x)$.

18. The function $f(x)$ is approximated near $x = 0$ by the third-degree Taylor polynomial

$$P_3(x) = 2 - x - x^2/3 + 2x^3.$$

Give the value of

(a) $f(0)$ (b) $f'(0)$

(c) $f''(0)$ (d) $f'''(0)$

19. Find the second-degree Taylor polynomial for $f(x) = 4x^2 - 7x + 2$ about $x = 0$. What do you notice?

20. Find the third-degree Taylor polynomial for $f(x) = x^3 + 7x^2 - 5x + 1$ about $x = 0$. What do you notice?

21. (a) Based on your observations in Problems 19–20, make a conjecture about Taylor approximations in the case when f is itself a polynomial.

(b) Show that your conjecture is true.

22. Find the value of $f^{(5)}(1)$ if $f(x)$ is approximated near $x = 1$ by the Taylor polynomial

$$p(x) = \sum_{n=0}^{10} \frac{(x-1)^n}{n!}.$$

In Problems 23–24, find a simplified formula for $P_5(x)$, the fifth-degree Taylor polynomial approximating f near $x = 0$.

23. Use the values in the table.

$f(0)$	$f'(0)$	$f''(0)$	$f'''(0)$	$f^{(4)}(0)$	$f^{(5)}(0)$
-3	5	-2	0	-1	4

24. Let $f(0) = -1$ and, for $n > 0$, $f^{(n)}(0) = -(-2)^n$.

For Problems 25–28, suppose $P_2(x) = a + bx + cx^2$ is the second-degree Taylor polynomial for the function f about $x = 0$. What can you say about the signs of a, b, and c if f has the graph given below?

25.

26.

27.

28.

29. Use the Taylor approximation for x near 0,
$$\sin x \approx x - \frac{x^3}{3!},$$
to explain why $\lim\limits_{x \to 0} \frac{\sin x}{x} = 1$.

30. Use the fourth-degree Taylor approximation for x near 0,
$$\cos x \approx 1 - \frac{x^2}{2!} + \frac{x^4}{4!},$$
to explain why $\lim\limits_{x \to 0} \frac{1 - \cos x}{x^2} = \frac{1}{2}$.

31. Use a fourth-degree Taylor approximation for e^h, for h near 0, to evaluate the following limits. Would your answer be different if you used a Taylor polynomial of higher degree?

(a) $\lim\limits_{h \to 0} \dfrac{e^h - 1 - h}{h^2}$

(b) $\lim\limits_{h \to 0} \dfrac{e^h - 1 - h - \frac{h^2}{2}}{h^3}$

32. If $f(2) = g(2) = h(2) = 0$, and $f'(2) = h'(2) = 0$, $g'(2) = 22$, and $f''(2) = 3$, $g''(2) = 5$, $h''(2) = 7$, calculate the following limits. Explain your reasoning.

(a) $\lim\limits_{x \to 2} \dfrac{f(x)}{h(x)}$

(b) $\lim\limits_{x \to 2} \dfrac{f(x)}{g(x)}$

33. One of the two sets of functions, f_1, f_2, f_3, or g_1, g_2, g_3, is graphed in Figure 10.8; the other set is graphed in Figure 10.9. Points A and B each have $x = 0$. Taylor polynomials of degree 2 approximating these functions near $x = 0$ are as follows:

$$f_1(x) \approx 2 + x + 2x^2 \qquad g_1(x) \approx 1 + x + 2x^2$$
$$f_2(x) \approx 2 + x - x^2 \qquad g_2(x) \approx 1 + x + x^2$$
$$f_3(x) \approx 2 + x + x^2 \qquad g_3(x) \approx 1 - x + x^2.$$

(a) Which group of functions, the fs or the gs, is represented by each figure?

(b) What are the coordinates of the points A and B?

(c) Match each function with the graphs (I)–(III) in the appropriate figure.

Figure 10.8   Figure 10.9

34. Derive the formulas given in the box on page 543 for the coefficients of the Taylor polynomial approximating a function f for x near a.

35. **(a)** Find and multiply the Taylor polynomials of degree 1 near $x = 0$ for the two functions $f(x) = 1/(1-x)$ and $g(x) = 1/(1 - 2x)$.

(b) Find the Taylor polynomial of degree 2 near $x = 0$ for the function $h(x) = f(x)g(x)$.

(c) Is the product of the Taylor polynomials for $f(x)$ and $g(x)$ equal to the Taylor polynomial for the function $h(x)$?

36. **(a)** Find and multiply the Taylor polynomials of degree 1 near $x = 0$ for the two functions $f(x)$ and $g(x)$.

(b) Find the Taylor polynomial of degree 2 near $x = 0$ for the function $h(x) = f(x)g(x)$.

(c) Show that the product of the Taylor polynomials for $f(x)$ and $g(x)$ and the Taylor polynomial for the function $h(x)$ are the same if $f''(0)g(0) + f(0)g''(0) = 0$.

37. **(a)** Find the Taylor polynomial approximation of degree 4 about $x = 0$ for the function $f(x) = e^{x^2}$.

(b) Compare this result to the Taylor polynomial approximation of degree 2 for the function $f(x) = e^x$ about $x = 0$. What do you notice?

(c) Use your observation in part (b) to write out the Taylor polynomial approximation of degree 20 for the function in part (a).

(d) What is the Taylor polynomial approximation of degree 5 for the function $f(x) = e^{-2x}$?

38. The integral $\int_0^1 (\sin t/t)\, dt$ is difficult to approximate using, for example, left Riemann sums or the trapezoid rule because the integrand $(\sin t)/t$ is not defined at $t = 0$. However, this integral converges; its value is $0.94608\ldots$. Estimate the integral using Taylor polynomials for $\sin t$ about $t = 0$ of

(a) Degree 3   (b) Degree 5

39. Consider the equations $\sin x = 0.2$ and $x - \dfrac{x^3}{3!} = 0.2$.

(a) How many solutions does each equation have?

(b) Which of the solutions of the two equations are approximately equal? Explain.

40. When we model the motion of a pendulum, we replace the differential equation

$$\frac{d^2\theta}{dt^2} = -\frac{g}{l}\sin\theta \quad \text{by} \quad \frac{d^2\theta}{dt^2} = -\frac{g}{l}\theta,$$

where θ is the angle between the pendulum and the vertical. Explain why, and under what circumstances, it is reasonable to make this replacement.

41. (a) Using a graph, explain why the following equation has a solution at $x = 0$ and another just to the right of $x = 0$:

$$\cos x = 1 - 0.1x.$$

(b) Replace $\cos x$ by its second-degree Taylor polynomial near 0 and solve the equation. Your answers are approximations to the solutions to the original equation at or near 0.

Strengthen Your Understanding

In Problems 42–43, explain what is wrong with the statement.

42. If $f(x) = \ln(2+x)$, then the second-degree Taylor polynomial approximating $f(x)$ near $x = 0$ has a negative constant term.

43. Let $f(x) = \dfrac{1}{1-x}$. The coefficient of the x term of the Taylor polynomial of degree 3 approximating $f(x)$ near $x = 0$ is -1.

In Problems 44–45, give an example of:

44. A function $f(x)$ for which every Taylor polynomial approximation near $x = 0$ involves only odd powers of x.

45. A third-degree Taylor polynomial near $x = 1$ approximating a function $f(x)$ with $f'(1) = 3$.

Decide if the statements in Problems 46–53 are true or false. Give an explanation for your answer.

46. If $f(x)$ and $g(x)$ have the same Taylor polynomial of degree 2 near $x = 0$, then $f(x) = g(x)$.

47. Using $\sin\theta \approx \theta - \theta^3/3!$ with $\theta = 1°$, we have $\sin(1°) \approx 1 - 1^3/6 = 5/6$.

48. The Taylor polynomial of degree 2 for e^x near $x = 5$ is $1 + (x-5) + (x-5)^2/2$.

49. If the Taylor polynomial of degree 2 for $f(x)$ near $x = 0$ is $P_2(x) = 1 + x - x^2$, then $f(x)$ is concave up near $x = 0$.

50. The quadratic approximation to $f(x)$ for x near 0 is better than the linear approximation for all values of x.

51. A Taylor polynomial for f near $x = a$ touches the graph of f only at $x = a$.

52. The linear approximation to $f(x)$ near $x = -1$ shows that if $f(-1) = g(-1)$ and $f'(-1) < g'(-1)$, then $f(x) < g(x)$ for all x sufficiently close to -1 (but not equal to -1).

53. The quadratic approximation to $f(x)$ near $x = -1$ shows that if $f(-1) = g(-1)$, $f'(-1) = g'(-1)$, and $f''(-1) < g''(-1)$, then $f(x) < g(x)$ for all x sufficiently close to -1 (but not equal to -1).

10.2 TAYLOR SERIES

In the previous section we saw how to approximate a function near a point by Taylor polynomials. Now we define a Taylor series, which is a power series that can be thought of as a Taylor polynomial that goes on forever.

Taylor Series for $\cos x$, $\sin x$, e^x

We have the following Taylor polynomials centered at $x = 0$ for $\cos x$:

$$\cos x \approx P_0(x) = 1$$

$$\cos x \approx P_2(x) = 1 - \frac{x^2}{2!}$$

$$\cos x \approx P_4(x) = 1 - \frac{x^2}{2!} + \frac{x^4}{4!}$$

$$\cos x \approx P_6(x) = 1 - \frac{x^2}{2!} + \frac{x^4}{4!} - \frac{x^6}{6!}$$

$$\cos x \approx P_8(x) = 1 - \frac{x^2}{2!} + \frac{x^4}{4!} - \frac{x^6}{6!} + \frac{x^8}{8!}.$$

Here we have a sequence of polynomials, $P_0(x)$, $P_2(x)$, $P_4(x)$, $P_6(x)$, $P_8(x)$, ..., each of which is a better approximation to $\cos x$ than the last, for x near 0. When we go to a higher-degree polynomial (say from P_6 to P_8), we add more terms ($x^8/8!$, for example), but the terms of lower degree don't change. Thus, each polynomial includes the information from all the previous ones. We represent the whole sequence of Taylor polynomials by writing the *Taylor series* for $\cos x$:

$$1 - \frac{x^2}{2!} + \frac{x^4}{4!} - \frac{x^6}{6!} + \frac{x^8}{8!} - \cdots.$$

Notice that the partial sums of this series are the Taylor polynomials, $P_n(x)$.

We define the Taylor series for $\sin x$ and e^x similarly. It turns out that, for these functions, the Taylor series converges to the function for all x, so we can write the following:

$$\sin x = x - \frac{x^3}{3!} + \frac{x^5}{5!} - \frac{x^7}{7!} + \frac{x^9}{9!} - \cdots$$

$$\cos x = 1 - \frac{x^2}{2!} + \frac{x^4}{4!} - \frac{x^6}{6!} + \frac{x^8}{8!} - \cdots$$

$$e^x = 1 + x + \frac{x^2}{2!} + \frac{x^3}{3!} + \frac{x^4}{4!} + \cdots$$

These series are also called *Taylor expansions* of the functions $\sin x$, $\cos x$, and e^x about $x = 0$. The *general term* of a Taylor series is a formula which gives any term in the series. For example, $x^n/n!$ is the general term in the Taylor expansion for e^x, and $(-1)^k x^{2k}/(2k)!$ is the general term in the expansion for $\cos x$. We call n or k the *index*.

Taylor Series in General

Any function f, all of whose derivatives exist at 0, has a Taylor series. However, the Taylor series for f does not necessarily converge to $f(x)$ for all values of x. For the values of x for which the series does converge to $f(x)$, we have the following formula:

Taylor Series for $f(x)$ About $x = 0$

$$f(x) = f(0) + f'(0)x + \frac{f''(0)}{2!}x^2 + \frac{f'''(0)}{3!}x^3 + \cdots + \frac{f^{(n)}(0)}{n!}x^n + \cdots$$

In addition, just as we have Taylor polynomials centered at points other than 0, we can also have a Taylor series centered at $x = a$ (provided all the derivatives of f exist at $x = a$). For the values of x for which the series converges to $f(x)$, we have the following formula:

Taylor Series for $f(x)$ About $x = a$

$$f(x) = f(a) + f'(a)(x - a) + \frac{f''(a)}{2!}(x - a)^2 + \frac{f'''(a)}{3!}(x - a)^3 + \cdots + \frac{f^{(n)}(a)}{n!}(x - a)^n + \cdots$$

The Taylor series is a power series whose partial sums are the Taylor polynomials. As we saw in Section 9.5, power series generally converge on an interval centered at $x = a$.

For a given function f and a given x, even if the Taylor series converges, it might not converge to $f(x)$. However, the Taylor series for most common functions, including e^x, $\cos x$, and $\sin x$, do converge to the original function for all x. See Section 10.4.

Convergence of Taylor Series

Let us look again at the Taylor polynomial for $\ln x$ about $x = 1$ that we derived in Example 7 on page 543. A similar calculation gives the Taylor series

$$\ln x = (x - 1) - \frac{(x - 1)^2}{2} + \frac{(x - 1)^3}{3} - \frac{(x - 1)^4}{4} + \cdots + (-1)^{n-1}\frac{(x - 1)^n}{n} + \cdots.$$

Example 4 on page 525 and Example 5 on page 525 show that this power series has interval of convergence $0 < x \leq 2$. However, although we know that the series converges in this interval, we do not yet know that its sum is $\ln x$. The fact that in Figure 10.10 the polynomials fit the curve well for $0 < x < 2$ suggests that the Taylor series does converge to $\ln x$ for $0 < x \leq 2$. For such x-values, a higher-degree polynomial gives, in general, a better approximation.

However, when $x > 2$, the polynomials move away from the curve and the approximations get worse as the degree of the polynomial increases. Thus, the Taylor polynomials are effective only as approximations to $\ln x$ for values of x between 0 and 2; outside that interval, they should not be used. Inside the interval, but near the ends, 0 or 2, the polynomials converge very slowly. This means we might have to take a polynomial of very high degree to get an accurate value for $\ln x$.

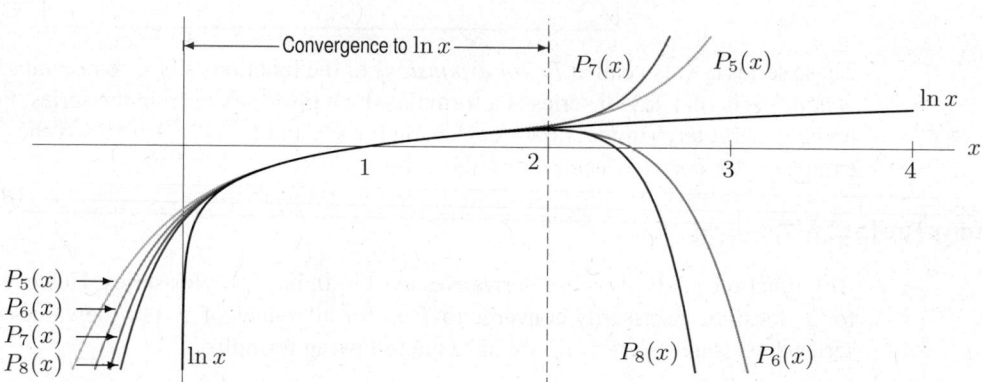

Figure 10.10: Taylor polynomials $P_5(x), P_6(x), P_7(x), P_8(x), \ldots$ converge to $\ln x$ for $0 < x \leq 2$ and diverge outside that interval

Proving that the Taylor series converges to $\ln x$ between 0 and 2, as Figure 10.10 suggests, requires the error term introduced in Section 10.4.

Example 1   Find the Taylor series for $\ln(1 + x)$ about $x = 0$, and investigate its convergence to $\ln(1 + x)$.

Solution   Taking derivatives of $\ln(1 + x)$ and substituting $x = 0$ leads to the Taylor series

$$\ln(1 + x) = x - \frac{x^2}{2} + \frac{x^3}{3} - \frac{x^4}{4} + \cdots.$$

Notice that this is the same series that we get by substituting $(1 + x)$ for x in the series for $\ln x$:

$$\ln x = (x - 1) - \frac{(x - 1)^2}{2} + \frac{(x - 1)^3}{3} - \frac{(x - 1)^4}{4} + \cdots \qquad \text{for } 0 < x \leq 2.$$

Since the series for $\ln x$ about $x = 1$ converges to $\ln x$ for x between 0 and 2, the Taylor series for $\ln(1 + x)$ about $x = 0$ converges to $\ln(1 + x)$ for x between -1 and 1. Notice that the series could not possibly converge to $\ln(1 + x)$ for $x \leq -1$ since $\ln(1 + x)$ is not defined there.

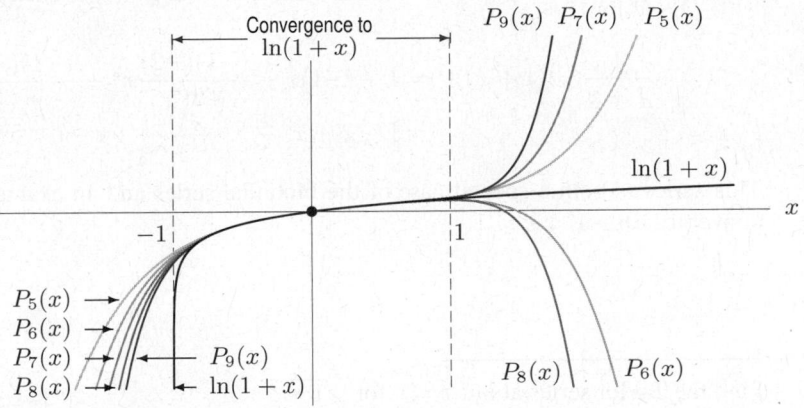

Figure 10.11: Convergence of the Taylor series for $\ln(1 + x)$

The Binomial Series Expansion

We now find the Taylor series about $x = 0$ for the function $f(x) = (1 + x)^p$, with p a constant, but not necessarily a positive integer. Taking derivatives:

$$f(x) = (1 + x)^p \qquad\qquad \text{so} \quad f(0) = 1$$
$$f'(x) = p(1 + x)^{p-1} \qquad\qquad f'(0) = p$$
$$f''(x) = p(p - 1)(1 + x)^{p-2} \qquad\qquad f''(0) = p(p - 1)$$
$$f'''(x) = p(p - 1)(p - 2)(1 + x)^{p-3}, \qquad\qquad f'''(0) = p(p - 1)(p - 2).$$

Thus, the third-degree Taylor polynomial for x near 0 is

$$(1 + x)^p \approx P_3(x) = 1 + px + \frac{p(p - 1)}{2!}x^2 + \frac{p(p - 1)(p - 2)}{3!}x^3.$$

Graphing $P_3(x), P_4(x), \ldots$ for various specific values of p suggests that the Taylor polynomials converge to $f(x)$ for $-1 < x < 1$. (See Problems 26–27, page 551.) The Taylor series for $f(x) = (1 + x)^p$ about $x = 0$ is as follows:

The Binomial Series

$$(1 + x)^p = 1 + px + \frac{p(p - 1)}{2!}x^2 + \frac{p(p - 1)(p - 2)}{3!}x^3 + \cdots \qquad \text{for } -1 < x < 1.$$

In fact, when p is a positive integer, the binomial series gives the same result as multiplying $(1 + x)^p$ out. (Newton discovered that the binomial series can be used for noninteger exponents.)

Example 2   Find the Taylor series about $x = 0$ for $\dfrac{1}{1+x}$.

Solution   Since $\dfrac{1}{1+x} = (1+x)^{-1}$, use the binomial series with $p = -1$. Then

$$\frac{1}{1+x} = (1+x)^{-1} = 1 + (-1)x + \frac{(-1)(-2)}{2!}x^2 + \frac{(-1)(-2)(-3)}{3!}x^3 + \cdots$$

$$= 1 - x + x^2 - x^3 + \cdots \quad \text{for } -1 < x < 1.$$

This series is both a special case of the binomial series and an example of a geometric series. It converges for $-1 < x < 1$.

Example 3   Find the Taylor series about $x = 0$ for $\sqrt{1+x}$.

Solution   Since $\sqrt{1+x} = (1+x)^{1/2}$, we use the binomial series with $p = 1/2$. Then

$$f(x) = \sqrt{1+x} = 1 + \frac{1}{2}x + \frac{(\frac{1}{2})(-\frac{1}{2})x^2}{2!} + \frac{(\frac{1}{2})(-\frac{1}{2})(-\frac{3}{2})x^3}{3!} + \cdots$$

$$= 1 + \frac{1}{2}x + \frac{(-\frac{1}{4})x^2}{2!} + \frac{(\frac{3}{8})x^3}{3!} + \cdots$$

$$= 1 + \frac{x}{2} - \frac{x^2}{8} + \frac{x^3}{16} + \cdots.$$

Exercises and Problems for Section 10.2

Exercises

For Exercises 1–7, find the first four nonzero terms of the Taylor series for the function about 0.

1. $(1+x)^{3/2}$ **2.** $\sqrt[4]{x+1}$

3. $\sin(-x)$ **4.** $\ln(1-x)$

5. $\dfrac{1}{1-x}$ **6.** $\dfrac{1}{\sqrt{1+x}}$

7. $\sqrt[3]{1-y}$

For Exercises 8–15, find the first four terms of the Taylor series for the function about the point a.

8. $\sin x$, $a = \pi/4$ **9.** $\cos \theta$, $a = \pi/4$

10. $\cos t$, $a = \pi/6$ **11.** $\sin \theta$, $a = -\pi/4$

12. $\tan x$, $a = \pi/4$ **13.** $1/x$, $a = 1$

14. $1/x$, $a = 2$ **15.** $1/x$, $a = -1$

In Exercises 16–23, find an expression for the general term of the series and give the range of values for the index (n or k, for example).

16. $\dfrac{1}{1-x} = 1 + x + x^2 + x^3 + x^4 + \cdots$

17. $\dfrac{1}{1+x} = 1 - x + x^2 - x^3 + x^4 - \cdots$

18. $\ln(1-x) = -x - \dfrac{x^2}{2} - \dfrac{x^3}{3} - \dfrac{x^4}{4} - \cdots$

19. $\ln(1+x) = x - \dfrac{x^2}{2} + \dfrac{x^3}{3} - \dfrac{x^4}{4} + \dfrac{x^5}{5} - \cdots$

20. $\sin x = x - \dfrac{x^3}{3!} + \dfrac{x^5}{5!} - \dfrac{x^7}{7!} + \cdots$

21. $\arctan x = x - \dfrac{x^3}{3} + \dfrac{x^5}{5} - \dfrac{x^7}{7} + \cdots$

22. $e^{x^2} = 1 + x^2 + \dfrac{x^4}{2!} + \dfrac{x^6}{3!} + \dfrac{x^8}{4!} + \cdots$

23. $x^2 \cos x^2 = x^2 - \dfrac{x^6}{2!} + \dfrac{x^{10}}{4!} - \dfrac{x^{14}}{6!} + \cdots$

24. Compute the binomial series expansion for $(1+x)^3$. What do you notice?

Problems

25. By graphing the function $f(x) = \dfrac{1}{\sqrt{1+x}}$ and several of its Taylor polynomials, estimate the interval of convergence of the series you found in Exercise 6.

26. By graphing the function $f(x) = \sqrt{1+x}$ and several of its Taylor polynomials, estimate where the series we found in Example 3 converges to $\sqrt{1+x}$.

27. **(a)** By graphing the function $f(x) = \dfrac{1}{1-x}$ and several of its Taylor polynomials, estimate where the series you found in Exercise 5 converges to $1/(1-x)$.
(b) Compute the radius of convergence analytically.

28. Find the radius of convergence of the Taylor series around $x = 0$ for e^x.

29. Find the radius of convergence of the Taylor series around $x = 0$ for $\ln(1-x)$.

30. **(a)** Write the general term of the binomial series for $(1+x)^p$ about $x = 0$.
(b) Find the radius of convergence of this series.

31. Using the Taylor series for $f(x) = e^x$ around 0, compute the following limit:

$$\lim_{x\to 0} \frac{e^x - 1}{x}.$$

32. Use the fact that the Taylor series of $g(x) = \sin(x^2)$ is

$$x^2 - \frac{x^6}{3!} + \frac{x^{10}}{5!} - \frac{x^{14}}{7!} + \cdots$$

to find $g''(0)$, $g'''(0)$, and $g^{(10)}(0)$. (There is an easy way and a hard way to do this!)

33. The Taylor series of $f(x) = x^2 e^{x^2}$ about $x = 0$ is

$$x^2 + x^4 + \frac{x^6}{2!} + \frac{x^8}{3!} + \frac{x^{10}}{4!} + \cdots.$$

Find $\left.\dfrac{d}{dx}\left(x^2 e^{x^2}\right)\right|_{x=0}$ and $\left.\dfrac{d^6}{dx^6}\left(x^2 e^{x^2}\right)\right|_{x=0}$.

34. One of the two sets of functions, f_1, f_2, f_3, or g_1, g_2, g_3 is graphed in Figure 10.12; the other set is graphed in Figure 10.13. Taylor series for the functions about a point corresponding to either A or B are as follows:

$$f_1(x) = 3 + (x - 1) - (x - 1)^2 + \cdots$$
$$f_2(x) = 3 - (x - 1) + (x - 1)^2 + \cdots$$
$$f_3(x) = 3 - 2(x - 1) + (x - 1)^2 + \cdots$$
$$g_1(x) = 5 - (x - 4) - (x - 4)^2 + \cdots$$
$$g_2(x) = 5 - (x - 4) + (x - 4)^2 + \cdots$$
$$g_3(x) = 5 + (x - 4) + (x - 4)^2 + \cdots.$$

(a) Which group of functions is represented in each figure?

(b) What are the coordinates of the points A and B?
(c) Match each function with the graphs (I)–(III) in the appropriate figure.

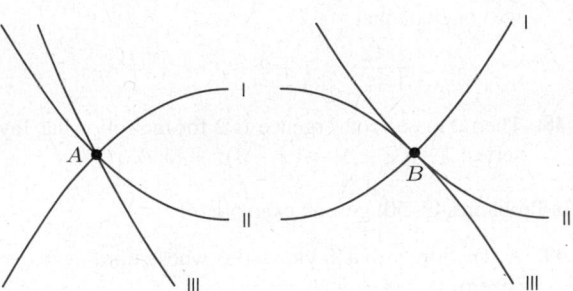

Figure 10.12   **Figure 10.13**

By recognizing each series in Problems 35–43 as a Taylor series evaluated at a particular value of x, find the sum of each of the following convergent series.

35. $1 + \dfrac{2}{1!} + \dfrac{4}{2!} + \dfrac{8}{3!} + \cdots + \dfrac{2^n}{n!} + \cdots$

36. $1 - \dfrac{1}{3!} + \dfrac{1}{5!} - \dfrac{1}{7!} + \cdots + \dfrac{(-1)^n}{(2n+1)!} + \cdots$

37. $1 + \dfrac{1}{4} + \left(\dfrac{1}{4}\right)^2 + \left(\dfrac{1}{4}\right)^3 + \cdots + \left(\dfrac{1}{4}\right)^n + \cdots$

38. $1 - \dfrac{100}{2!} + \dfrac{10000}{4!} + \cdots + \dfrac{(-1)^n \cdot 10^{2n}}{(2n)!} + \cdots$

39. $\dfrac{1}{2} - \dfrac{\left(\frac{1}{2}\right)^2}{2} + \dfrac{\left(\frac{1}{2}\right)^3}{3} - \dfrac{\left(\frac{1}{2}\right)^4}{4} + \cdots + \dfrac{(-1)^n \cdot \left(\frac{1}{2}\right)^{n+1}}{(n+1)} + \cdots$

40. $1 - 0.1 + 0.1^2 - 0.1^3 + \cdots$

41. $1 + 3 + \dfrac{9}{2!} + \dfrac{27}{3!} + \dfrac{81}{4!} + \cdots$

42. $1 - \dfrac{1}{2!} + \dfrac{1}{4!} - \dfrac{1}{6!} + \cdots$

43. $1 - 0.1 + \dfrac{0.01}{2!} - \dfrac{0.001}{3!} + \cdots$

In Problems 44–45 solve exactly for the variable.

44. $1 + x + x^2 + x^3 + \cdots = 5$

45. $x - \dfrac{1}{2}x^2 + \dfrac{1}{3}x^3 + \cdots = 0.2$

46. Let $i = \sqrt{-1}$. We define $e^{i\theta}$ by substituting $i\theta$ in the Taylor series for e^x. Use this definition[2] to explain Euler's formula

$$e^{i\theta} = \cos\theta + i\sin\theta.$$

---

[2]Complex numbers are discussed in Appendix B.

Strengthen Your Understanding

In Problems 47–48, explain what is wrong with the statement.

47. Since
$$\frac{1}{1-x} = 1 + x + x^2 + x^3 + \cdots,$$
we conclude that
$$\frac{1}{1-2} = 1 + 2 + 2^2 + 2^3 + \cdots.$$

48. The radius of convergence is 2 for the following Taylor series: $1 + (x-3) + (x-3)^2 + (x-3)^3 + \cdots$.

In Problems 49–50, give an example of:

49. A function with a Taylor series whose third-degree term is zero.

50. A Taylor series that is convergent at $x = -1$.

Decide if the statements in Problems 51–55 are true or false. Assume that the Taylor series for a function converges to that function. Give an explanation for your answer.

51. The Taylor series for $\sin x$ about $x = \pi$ is
$$(x - \pi) - \frac{(x-\pi)^3}{3!} + \frac{(x-\pi)^5}{5!} - \cdots.$$

52. If f is an even function, then the Taylor series for f near $x = 0$ has only terms with even exponents.

53. If f has the following Taylor series about $x = 0$, then $f^{(7)}(0) = -8$:
$$f(x) = 1 - 2x + \frac{3}{2!}x^2 - \frac{4}{3!}x^3 + \cdots.$$
(Assume the pattern of the coefficients continues.)

54. The Taylor series for f converges everywhere f is defined.

55. The graphs of e^x and its Taylor polynomial $P_{10}(x)$ get further and further apart as $x \to \infty$.

10.3 FINDING AND USING TAYLOR SERIES

Finding a Taylor series for a function means finding the coefficients. Assuming the function has all its derivatives defined, finding the coefficients can always be done, in theory at least, by differentiation. That is how we derived the four most important Taylor series, those for the functions e^x, $\sin x$, $\cos x$, and $(1+x)^p$.

For many functions, however, computing Taylor series coefficients by differentiation can be a very laborious business. We now introduce easier ways of finding Taylor series, if the series we want is closely related to a series that we already know.

New Series by Substitution

Suppose we want to find the Taylor series for e^{-x^2} about $x = 0$. We could find the coefficients by differentiation. Differentiating e^{-x^2} by the chain rule gives $-2xe^{-x^2}$, and differentiating again gives $-2e^{-x^2} + 4x^2e^{-x^2}$. Each time we differentiate we use the product rule, and the number of terms grows. Finding the tenth or twentieth derivative of e^{-x^2}, and thus the series for e^{-x^2} up to the x^{10} or x^{20} terms, by this method is tiresome (at least without a computer or calculator that can differentiate).

Fortunately, there's a quicker way. Recall that
$$e^y = 1 + y + \frac{y^2}{2!} + \frac{y^3}{3!} + \frac{y^4}{4!} + \cdots \quad \text{for all } y.$$

Substituting $y = -x^2$ tells us that
$$e^{-x^2} = 1 + (-x^2) + \frac{(-x^2)^2}{2!} + \frac{(-x^2)^3}{3!} + \frac{(-x^2)^4}{4!} + \cdots$$
$$= 1 - x^2 + \frac{x^4}{2!} - \frac{x^6}{3!} + \frac{x^8}{4!} - \cdots \quad \text{for all } x.$$

Using this method, it is easy to find the series up to the x^{10} or x^{20} terms. It can be shown that this is the Taylor series for e^{-x^2}.

Example 1   Find the Taylor series about $x = 0$ for $f(x) = \dfrac{1}{1+x^2}$.

Solution   The binomial series tells us that

$$\frac{1}{1+y} = (1+y)^{-1} = 1 - y + y^2 - y^3 + y^4 - \cdots \quad \text{for } -1 < y < 1.$$

Substituting $y = x^2$ gives

$$\frac{1}{1+x^2} = 1 - x^2 + x^4 - x^6 + x^8 - \cdots \quad \text{for } -1 < x < 1,$$

which is the Taylor series for $\dfrac{1}{1+x^2}$.

New Series by Differentiation and Integration

Just as we can get new series by substitution, we can also get new series by differentiation and integration. Term-by-term differentiation of a Taylor series for $f(x)$ gives a Taylor series for $f'(x)$; antidifferentiation works similarly.

Example 2   Find the Taylor Series about $x = 0$ for $\dfrac{1}{(1-x)^2}$ from the series for $\dfrac{1}{1-x}$.

Solution   We know that $\dfrac{d}{dx}\left(\dfrac{1}{1-x}\right) = \dfrac{1}{(1-x)^2}$, so we start with the geometric series

$$\frac{1}{1-x} = 1 + x + x^2 + x^3 + x^4 + \cdots \text{ for } -1 < x < 1.$$

Differentiation term by term gives the binomial series

$$\frac{1}{(1-x)^2} = \frac{d}{dx}\left(\frac{1}{1-x}\right) = 1 + 2x + 3x^2 + 4x^3 + \cdots \text{ for } -1 < x < 1.$$

Example 3   Find the Taylor series[3] about $x = 0$ for $\arctan x$ from the series for $\dfrac{1}{1+x^2}$.

Solution   We know that $\dfrac{d}{dx}(\arctan x) = \dfrac{1}{1+x^2}$, so we use the series from Example 1:

$$\frac{d}{dx}(\arctan x) = \frac{1}{1+x^2} = 1 - x^2 + x^4 - x^6 + x^8 - \cdots \quad \text{for } -1 < x < 1.$$

Antidifferentiating term by term gives

$$\arctan x = \int \frac{1}{1+x^2}\, dx = C + x - \frac{x^3}{3} + \frac{x^5}{5} - \frac{x^7}{7} + \frac{x^9}{9} - \cdots \quad \text{for } -1 < x < 1,$$

where C is the constant of integration. Since $\arctan 0 = 0$, we have $C = 0$, so

$$\arctan x = x - \frac{x^3}{3} + \frac{x^5}{5} - \frac{x^7}{7} + \frac{x^9}{9} - \cdots \quad \text{for } -1 < x < 1.$$

Multiplying and Substituting Taylor Series

We can also form a Taylor series for a product of two functions. In some cases, this is easy; for example, if we want to find the Taylor series about $x = 0$ for the function $f(x) = x^2 \sin x$, we can start with the Taylor series for $\sin x$,

$$\sin x = x - \frac{x^3}{3!} + \frac{x^5}{5!} - \frac{x^7}{7!} + \cdots,$$

---

[3]The series for $\arctan x$ was discovered by James Gregory (1638–1675).

and multiply the series by x^2:

$$x^2 \sin x = x^2 \left(x - \frac{x^3}{3!} + \frac{x^5}{5!} - \frac{x^7}{7!} + \cdots \right)$$

$$= x^3 - \frac{x^5}{3!} + \frac{x^7}{5!} - \frac{x^9}{7!} + \cdots.$$

However, in some cases, finding a Taylor series for a product of two functions requires more work.

Example 4   Find the Taylor series about $x = 0$ for $g(x) = \sin x \cos x$.

Solution   The Taylor series about $x = 0$ for $\sin x$ and $\cos x$ are

$$\sin x = x - \frac{x^3}{3!} + \frac{x^5}{5!} - \cdots$$

$$\cos x = 1 - \frac{x^2}{2!} + \frac{x^4}{4!} - \cdots.$$

So we have

$$g(x) = \sin x \cos x = \left(x - \frac{x^3}{3!} + \frac{x^5}{5!} - \cdots \right) \left(1 - \frac{x^2}{2!} + \frac{x^4}{4!} - \cdots \right).$$

To multiply these two series, we must multiply each term of the series for $\sin x$ by each term of the series for $\cos x$. Because each series has infinitely many terms, we organize the process by first determining the constant term of the product, then the linear term, and so on.

The constant term of this product is zero because there is no combination of a term from the first series and a term from the second that yields a constant. The linear term of the product is x; we obtain this term by multiplying the x from the first series by the 1 from the second. The degree-2 term of the product is also zero; more generally, we notice that every even-degree term of the product is zero because every combination of a term from the first series and a term from the second yields an odd-degree term. To find the degree-3 term, observe that the combinations of terms that yield degree-3 terms are $x \cdot -\frac{x^2}{2!} = -\frac{1}{2}x^3$ and $-\frac{x^3}{3!} \cdot 1 = -\frac{1}{6}x^3$, and thus the degree-3 term is $-\frac{1}{2}x^3 - \frac{1}{6}x^3 = -\frac{2}{3}x^3$. Continuing in this manner, we find that

$$g(x) = x - \frac{2}{3}x^3 + \frac{2}{15}x^5 - \cdots.$$

There is another way to find this series. Notice that $\sin x \cos x = \frac{1}{2}\sin(2x)$. Substituting $2x$ into the Taylor series about $x = 0$ for the sine function, we get

$$\sin(2x) = 2x - \frac{(2x)^3}{3!} + \frac{(2x)^5}{5!} - \cdots$$

$$= 2x - \frac{4}{3}x^3 + \frac{4}{15}x^5 - \cdots.$$

Therefore, we have

$$g(x) = \frac{1}{2}\sin(2x) = x - \frac{2}{3}x^3 + \frac{2}{15}x^5 - \cdots.$$

We can also obtain a Taylor series for a composite function by substituting a Taylor series into another one, as in the next example.

Example 5   Find the Taylor series about $\theta = 0$ for $g(\theta) = e^{\sin \theta}$.

Solution   For all y and θ, we know that

$$e^y = 1 + y + \frac{y^2}{2!} + \frac{y^3}{3!} + \frac{y^4}{4!} + \cdots$$

and

$$\sin\theta = \theta - \frac{\theta^3}{3!} + \frac{\theta^5}{5!} - \cdots.$$

Let's substitute the series for $\sin\theta$ for y:

$$e^{\sin\theta} = 1 + \left(\theta - \frac{\theta^3}{3!} + \frac{\theta^5}{5!} - \cdots\right) + \frac{1}{2!}\left(\theta - \frac{\theta^3}{3!} + \frac{\theta^5}{5!} - \cdots\right)^2 + \frac{1}{3!}\left(\theta - \frac{\theta^3}{3!} + \frac{\theta^5}{5!} - \cdots\right)^3 + \cdots.$$

To simplify, we multiply out and collect terms. The only constant term is the 1, and there's only one θ term. The only θ^2 term is the first term we get by multiplying out the square, namely $\theta^2/2!$. There are two contributors to the θ^3 term: the $-\theta^3/3!$ from within the first parentheses and the first term we get from multiplying out the cube, which is $\theta^3/3!$. Thus the series starts

$$e^{\sin\theta} = 1 + \theta + \frac{\theta^2}{2!} + \left(-\frac{\theta^3}{3!} + \frac{\theta^3}{3!}\right) + \cdots$$

$$= 1 + \theta + \frac{\theta^2}{2!} + 0 \cdot \theta^3 + \cdots \qquad \text{for all } \theta.$$

Applications of Taylor Series

Example 6   Use the series for $\arctan x$ to estimate the numerical value of π.

Solution   Since $\arctan 1 = \pi/4$, we use the series for $\arctan x$ from Example 3. We assume—as is the case—that the series does converge to $\pi/4$ at $x = 1$. Substituting $x = 1$ into the series for $\arctan x$ gives

$$\pi = 4\arctan 1 = 4\left(1 - \frac{1}{3} + \frac{1}{5} - \frac{1}{7} + \frac{1}{9} - \cdots\right).$$

Table 10.1   *Approximating π using the series for $\arctan x$*

n	4	5	25	100	500	1000	10,000
S_n	2.895	3.340	3.182	3.132	3.140	3.141	3.141

Table 10.1 shows the value of the nth partial sum, S_n, obtained by summing the nonzero terms from 1 through n. The values of S_n do seem to converge to $\pi = 3.141\ldots$. However, this series converges very slowly, meaning that we have to take a large number of terms to get an accurate estimate for π. So this way of calculating π is not particularly practical. (A better one is given in Project 2, page 583.) However, the expression for π given by this series is surprising and elegant.

A basic question we can ask about two functions is which one gives larger values. Taylor series can often be used to answer this question over a small interval. If the constant terms of the series for two functions are the same, compare the linear terms; if the linear terms are the same, compare the quadratic terms, and so on.

Example 7   By looking at their Taylor series, decide which of the following functions is largest for t near 0.
(a) e^t (b) $\dfrac{1}{1-t}$

Solution   The Taylor expansion about $t = 0$ for e^t is

$$e^t = 1 + t + \frac{t^2}{2!} + \frac{t^3}{3!} + \cdots.$$

Viewing $1/(1-t)$ as the sum of a geometric series with initial term 1 and common ratio t, we have

$$\frac{1}{1-t} = 1 + t + t^2 + t^3 + \cdots \text{for } -1 < t < 1.$$

Notice that these two series have the same constant term and the same linear term. However, their remaining terms are different. For values of t near zero, the quadratic terms dominate all of the subsequent terms,[4] so we can use the approximations

$$e^t \approx 1 + t + \frac{t^2}{2}$$

$$\frac{1}{1-t} \approx 1 + t + t^2.$$

Since

$$1 + t + \frac{1}{2}t^2 < 1 + t + t^2,$$

and since the approximations are valid for t near 0, we conclude that, for t near 0,

$$e^t < \frac{1}{1-t}.$$

See Figure 10.14.

Figure 10.14: Comparing two functions near $t = 0$

Example 8

Two electrical charges of equal magnitude and opposite signs located near one another are called an electrical dipole. The charges Q and $-Q$ are a distance r apart. (See Figure 10.15.) The electric field, E, at the point P, at a distance R from the dipole is given by

$$E = \frac{Q}{R^2} - \frac{Q}{(R+r)^2}.$$

Use series to investigate the behavior of the electric field far to the left along the line through the dipole. Show that when R is large in comparison to r, the electric field is approximately proportional to $1/R^3$.

Figure 10.15: Approximating the electric field at P due to a dipole consisting of charges Q and $-Q$ a distance r apart

Solution

In order to use a series approximation, we need a variable whose value is small. Although we know that r is much smaller than R, we do not know that r itself is small. The quantity r/R is, however, very small. Hence we expand $1/(R+r)^2$ in powers of r/R so that we can safely use only the first few terms of the Taylor series. First we rewrite using algebra:

$$\frac{1}{(R+r)^2} = \frac{1}{R^2(1+r/R)^2} = \frac{1}{R^2}\left(1 + \frac{r}{R}\right)^{-2}.$$

---

[4]To make this argument rigorous, we need the Lagrange error bound given in the next section.

Now we use the binomial expansion for $(1+x)^p$ with $x = r/R$ and $p = -2$:

$$\frac{1}{R^2}\left(1 + \frac{r}{R}\right)^{-2} = \frac{1}{R^2}\left(1 + (-2)\left(\frac{r}{R}\right) + \frac{(-2)(-3)}{2!}\left(\frac{r}{R}\right)^2 + \frac{(-2)(-3)(-4)}{3!}\left(\frac{r}{R}\right)^3 + \cdots\right)$$

$$= \frac{1}{R^2}\left(1 - 2\frac{r}{R} + 3\frac{r^2}{R^2} - 4\frac{r^3}{R^3} + \cdots\right).$$

So, substituting the series into the expression for E, we have

$$E = \frac{Q}{R^2} - \frac{Q}{(R+r)^2} = Q\left(\frac{1}{R^2} - \frac{1}{R^2}\left(1 - 2\frac{r}{R} + 3\frac{r^2}{R^2} - 4\frac{r^3}{R^3} + \cdots\right)\right)$$

$$= \frac{Q}{R^2}\left(2\frac{r}{R} - 3\frac{r^2}{R^2} + 4\frac{r^3}{R^3} - \cdots\right).$$

Since r/R is smaller than 1, the binomial expansion for $(1+r/R)^{-2}$ converges. We are interested in the electric field far away from the dipole. The quantity r/R is small there, and $(r/R)^2$ and higher powers are smaller still. Thus, we approximate by disregarding all terms except the first, giving

$$E \approx \frac{Q}{R^2}\left(\frac{2r}{R}\right), \quad \text{so} \quad E \approx \frac{2Qr}{R^3}.$$

Since Q and r are constants, this means that E is approximately proportional to $1/R^3$.

In the previous example, we say that E is *expanded in terms of* r/R, meaning that the variable in the expansion is r/R.

Exercises and Problems for Section 10.3

Exercises

In Exercises 1–10, using known Taylor series, find the first four nonzero terms of the Taylor series about 0 for the function.

1. e^{-x}

2. $\sqrt{1-2x}$

3. $\cos(\theta^2)$

4. $\ln(1-2y)$

5. $\arcsin x$

6. $t\sin(3t)$

7. $\dfrac{1}{\sqrt{1-z^2}}$

8. $\dfrac{z}{e^{z^2}}$

9. $\phi^3\cos(\phi^2)$

10. $\arctan(r^2)$

Find the Taylor series about 0 for the functions in Exercises 11–13, including the general term.

11. $(1+x)^3$

12. $t\sin(t^2) - t^3$

13. $\dfrac{1}{\sqrt{1-y^2}}$

For Exercises 14–19, expand the quantity about 0 in terms of the variable given. Give four nonzero terms.

14. $\dfrac{1}{2+x}$ in terms of $\dfrac{x}{2}$

15. $\sqrt{T+h}$ in terms of $\dfrac{h}{T}$

16. $\dfrac{1}{a-r}$ in terms of $\dfrac{r}{a}$

17. $\dfrac{1}{(a+r)^2}$ in terms of $\dfrac{r}{a}$

18. $\sqrt[3]{P+t}$ in terms of $\dfrac{t}{P}$

19. $\dfrac{a}{\sqrt{a^2+x^2}}$ in terms of $\dfrac{x}{a}$, where $a > 0$

Problems

In Problems 20–23, using known Taylor series, find the first four nonzero terms of the Taylor series about 0 for the function.

20. $\sqrt{(1+t)}\sin t$

21. $e^t\cos t$

22. $\sqrt{1+\sin\theta}$

23. $\dfrac{1}{1 - \ln(1+t)}$

24. (a) Find the first three nonzero terms of the Taylor series for $e^x + e^{-x}$.
  (b) Explain why the graph of $e^x + e^{-x}$ looks like a parabola near $x = 0$. What is the equation of this parabola?

25. (a) Find the first three nonzero terms of the Taylor series for $e^x - e^{-x}$.

(b) Explain why the graph of $e^x - e^{-x}$ near $x = 0$ looks like the graph of a cubic polynomial symmetric about the origin. What is the equation for this cubic?

26. Find the first three terms of the Taylor series for $f(x) = e^{x^2}$ around 0. Use this information to approximate the integral

$$\int_0^1 e^{x^2}\,dx.$$

27. Find the sum of $\displaystyle\sum_{p=1}^{\infty} px^{p-1}$ for $|x| < 1$.

28. For values of y near 0, put the following functions in increasing order, using their Taylor expansions.

(a) $\ln(1 + y^2)$ **(b)** $\sin(y^2)$ **(c)** $1 - \cos y$

29. For values of θ near 0, put the following functions in increasing order, using their Taylor expansions.

(a) $1 + \sin\theta$ **(b)** e^θ **(c)** $\dfrac{1}{\sqrt{1 - 2\theta}}$

30. A function has the following Taylor series about $x = 0$:

$$f(x) = \sum_{n=0}^{\infty} \frac{x^{2n+1}}{2n+1}.$$

Find the ninth-degree Taylor polynomial for $f(2x)$.

31. Figure 10.16 shows the graphs of the four functions below for values of x near 0. Use Taylor series to match graphs and formulas.

(a) $\dfrac{1}{1 - x^2}$ **(b)** $(1 + x)^{1/4}$

(c) $\sqrt{1 + \dfrac{x}{2}}$ **(d)** $\dfrac{1}{\sqrt{1 - x}}$

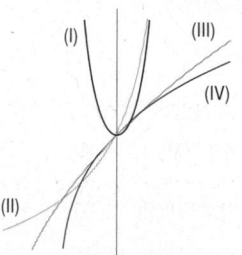

Figure 10.16

32. The *sine integral* function is defined by the improper integral $\text{Si}(x) = \displaystyle\int_0^x \frac{\sin t}{t}\,dt$. Use the Taylor polynomial, $P_7(x)$, of degree 7 about $x = 0$ for the sine function to estimate $\text{Si}(2)$.

33. Write out the first four nonzero terms of the Taylor series about $x = 0$ for $f(x) = \displaystyle\int_0^x \sin\left(t^2\right)\,dt$.

34. (a) Find the Taylor series for $f(t) = te^t$ about $t = 0$.

(b) Using your answer to part (a), find a Taylor series expansion about $x = 0$ for

$$\int_0^x te^t\,dt.$$

(c) Using your answer to part (b), show that

$$\frac{1}{2} + \frac{1}{3} + \frac{1}{4(2!)} + \frac{1}{5(3!)} + \frac{1}{6(4!)} + \cdots = 1.$$

35. Find the sum of $\displaystyle\sum_{n=1}^{\infty} \frac{k^{n-1}}{(n-1)!}e^{-k}$.

36. The hyperbolic sine and cosine are differentiable and satisfy the conditions $\cosh 0 = 1$ and $\sinh 0 = 0$, and

$$\frac{d}{dx}(\cosh x) = \sinh x \qquad \frac{d}{dx}(\sinh x) = \cosh x.$$

(a) Using only this information, find the Taylor approximation of degree $n = 8$ about $x = 0$ for $f(x) = \cosh x$.

(b) Estimate the value of $\cosh 1$.

(c) Use the result from part (a) to find a Taylor polynomial approximation of degree $n = 7$ about $x = 0$ for $g(x) = \sinh x$.

37. Use the series for e^x to find the Taylor series for $\sinh 2x$ and $\cosh 2x$.

38. Use Taylor series to explain the patterns in the digits in the following expansions:

(a) $\dfrac{1}{0.98} = 1.02040816\ldots$

(b) $\left(\dfrac{1}{0.99}\right)^2 = 1.020304050607\ldots$

39. Padé approximants are rational functions used to approximate more complicated functions. In this problem, you will derive the Padé approximant to the exponential function.

(a) Let $f(x) = (1 + ax)/(1 + bx)$, where a and b are constants. Write down the first three terms of the Taylor series for $f(x)$ about $x = 0$.

(b) By equating the first three terms of the Taylor series about $x = 0$ for $f(x)$ and for e^x, find a and b so that $f(x)$ approximates e^x as closely as possible near $x = 0$.

40. One of Einstein's most amazing predictions was that light traveling from distant stars would bend around the sun on the way to earth. His calculations involved solving for ϕ in the equation

$$\sin\phi + b(1 + \cos^2\phi + \cos\phi) = 0,$$

where b is a very small positive constant.

(a) Explain why the equation could have a solution for ϕ which is near 0.

(b) Expand the left-hand side of the equation in Taylor series about $\phi = 0$, disregarding terms of order ϕ^2 and higher. Solve for ϕ. (Your answer will involve b.)

41. A hydrogen atom consists of an electron, of mass m, orbiting a proton, of mass M, where m is much smaller than M. The *reduced mass*, μ, of the hydrogen atom is defined by

$$\mu = \frac{mM}{m+M}.$$

(a) Show that $\mu \approx m$.

(b) To get a more accurate approximation for μ, express μ as m times a series in m/M.

(c) The approximation $\mu \approx m$ is obtained by disregarding all but the constant term in the series. The first-order correction is obtained by including the linear term but no higher terms. If $m \approx M/1836$, by what percentage does including the linear term change the estimate $\mu \approx m$?

42. Resonance in electric circuits leads to the expression

$$\left(\omega L - \frac{1}{\omega C}\right)^2,$$

where ω is the variable and L and C are constants.

(a) Find ω_0, the value of ω making the expression zero.

(b) In practice, ω fluctuates about ω_0, so we are interested in the behavior of this expression for values of ω near ω_0. Let $\omega = \omega_0 + \Delta\omega$ and expand the expression in terms of $\Delta\omega$ up to the first nonzero term. Give your answer in terms of $\Delta\omega$ and L but not C.

43. The Michelson-Morley experiment, which contributed to the formulation of the theory of relativity, involved the difference between the two times t_1 and t_2 that light took to travel between two points. If v is velocity; l_1, l_2, and c are constants; and $v < c$, then t_1 and t_2 are given by

$$t_1 = \frac{2l_2}{c(1 - v^2/c^2)} - \frac{2l_1}{c\sqrt{1 - v^2/c^2}}$$

$$t_2 = \frac{2l_2}{c\sqrt{1 - v^2/c^2}} - \frac{2l_1}{c(1 - v^2/c^2)}.$$

(a) Find an expression for $\Delta t = t_1 - t_2$, and give its Taylor expansion in terms of v^2/c^2 up to the second nonzero term.

(b) For small v, to what power of v is Δt proportional? What is the constant of proportionality?

44. The theory of relativity predicts that when an object moves at speeds close to the speed of light, the object appears heavier. The apparent, or relativistic, mass, m, of the object when it is moving at speed v is given by the formula

$$m = \frac{m_0}{\sqrt{1 - v^2/c^2}},$$

where c is the speed of light and m_0 is the mass of the object when it is at rest.

(a) Use the formula for m to decide what values of v are possible.

(b) Sketch a rough graph of m against v, labeling intercepts and asymptotes.

(c) Write the first three nonzero terms of the Taylor series for m in terms of v.

(d) For what values of v do you expect the series to converge?

45. The potential energy, V, of two gas molecules separated by a distance r is given by

$$V = -V_0\left(2\left(\frac{r_0}{r}\right)^6 - \left(\frac{r_0}{r}\right)^{12}\right),$$

where V_0 and r_0 are positive constants.

(a) Show that if $r = r_0$, then V takes on its minimum value, $-V_0$.

(b) Write V as a series in $(r - r_0)$ up through the quadratic term.

(c) For r near r_0, show that the difference between V and its minimum value is approximately proportional to $(r - r_0)^2$. In other words, show that $V - (-V_0) = V + V_0$ is approximately proportional to $(r - r_0)^2$.

(d) The force, F, between the molecules is given by $F = -dV/dr$. What is F when $r = r_0$? For r near r_0, show that F is approximately proportional to $(r - r_0)$.

46. Van der Waal's equation relates the pressure, P, and the volume, V, of a fixed quantity of a gas at constant temperature T:

$$\left(P + \frac{n^2 a}{V^2}\right)(V - nb) = nRT,$$

where a, b, n, R are constants. Find the first two nonzero terms of the Taylor series of P in terms for $1/V$.

Strengthen Your Understanding

In Problems 47–48, explain what is wrong with the statement.

47. Within its radius of convergence, $\dfrac{1}{2+x} = 1 - \dfrac{x}{2} + \left(\dfrac{x}{2}\right)^2 - \left(\dfrac{x}{2}\right)^3 + \cdots$.

48. Using the Taylor series for $e^x = 1 + x + \frac{x^2}{2!} + \frac{x^3}{3!} + \cdots$, we find that $e^{-x} = 1 - x - \frac{x^2}{2!} - \frac{x^3}{3!} - \cdots$.

In Problems 49–50, give an example of:

49. A function with no Taylor series around 0.

50. A function $f(x)$ that does not have a Taylor series around 0 even though $f(0)$ is defined.

Decide if the statements in Problems 51–55 are true or false. Assume that the Taylor series for a function converges to that function. Give an explanation for your answer.

51. To find the Taylor series for $\sin x + \cos x$ about any point, add the Taylor series for $\sin x$ and $\cos x$ about that point.

52. The Taylor series for $x^3 \cos x$ about $x = 0$ has only odd powers.

53. The Taylor series for $f(x)g(x)$ about $x = 0$ is

$$f(0)g(0) + f'(0)g'(0)x + \frac{f''(0)g''(0)}{2!}x^2 + \cdots.$$

54. If $L_1(x)$ is the linear approximation to $f_1(x)$ near $x = 0$ and $L_2(x)$ is the linear approximation to $f_2(x)$ near $x = 0$, then $L_1(x) + L_2(x)$ is the linear approximation to $f_1(x) + f_2(x)$ near $x = 0$.

55. If $L_1(x)$ is the linear approximation to $f_1(x)$ near $x = 0$ and $L_2(x)$ is the linear approximation to $f_2(x)$ near $x = 0$, then $L_1(x)L_2(x)$ is the quadratic approximation to $f_1(x)f_2(x)$ near $x = 0$.

56. Given that the radius of convergence of the Taylor series for $\ln(1 - x)$ about $x = 0$ is 1, what is the radius of convergence of the Taylor series about $x = 0$ for the following functions ?

   (a) $\ln(4 - x)$
   (b) $\ln(4 + x)$
   (c) $\ln(1 + 4x^2)$

57. Given that the Taylor series for $\tan x = x + x^3/3 + 21x^5/120 + \cdots$, then that of $3 \tan(x/3)$ is

   (a) $3x + x^3 + 21x^5/120 + \cdots$
   (b) $3x + x^3 + 21x^5/40 + \cdots$
   (c) $x + x^3/27 + 7x^5/3240 + \cdots$
   (d) $x + x^3/3 + 21x^5/120 + \cdots$

10.4   THE ERROR IN TAYLOR POLYNOMIAL APPROXIMATIONS

In order to use an approximation with confidence, we need to know how big the error could be. The error is the difference between the exact answer and the approximate value. When we use $P_n(x)$, the nth-degree Taylor polynomial, to approximate $f(x)$, the error is the difference

$$E_n(x) = f(x) - P_n(x).$$

We want to find a *bound* on the magnitude of the error, $|E_n|$; that is, we want a number that we are sure is bigger than $|E_n|$. In practice, we want a bound which is reasonably close to the maximum value of $|E_n|$.

Lagrange found an expression for the error bound whose form is similar to a term in the Taylor series:

Theorem 10.1: The Lagrange Error Bound for $P_n(x)$

Suppose f and all its derivatives are continuous. If $P_n(x)$ is the nth Taylor polynomial for $f(x)$ about a, then

$$|E_n(x)| = |f(x) - P_n(x)| \leq \frac{M}{(n+1)!}|x - a|^{n+1},$$

where $\left|f^{(n+1)}\right| \leq M$ on the interval between a and x.

To find M in practice, we often find the maximum of $|f^{(n+1)}|$ on the interval and pick any larger value for M. See page 563 for a justification of Theorem 10.1.

Using the Lagrange Error Bound for Taylor Polynomials

Example 1   Give a bound on the error, E_4, when e^x is approximated by its fourth-degree Taylor polynomial about 0 for $-0.5 \leq x \leq 0.5$.

Solution   Let $f(x) = e^x$. We need to find a bound for the fifth derivative, $f^{(5)}(x) = e^x$. Since e^x is increasing, its largest value is at the endpoint of the interval:

$$|f^{(5)}(x)| \leq e^{0.5} = \sqrt{e} \quad \text{for } -0.5 \leq x \leq 0.5.$$

Since $\sqrt{e} < 2$, we can take $M = 2$ (or any larger value). Then

$$|E_4| = |f(x) - P_4(x)| \leq \frac{2}{5!}|x|^5.$$

This means, for example, that on $-0.5 \leq x \leq 0.5$, the approximation

$$e^x \approx 1 + x + \frac{x^2}{2!} + \frac{x^3}{3!} + \frac{x^4}{4!}$$

has an error of at most $\frac{2}{120}(0.5)^5 < 0.0006$.

The Lagrange error bound for Taylor polynomials can be used to see how the accuracy of the approximation depends on the value of x and the value of n. Observe that the error bound for a Taylor polynomial of degree n is proportional to $|x - a|^{n+1}$. That means, for example, with a Taylor polynomial of degree n centered at 0, if we decrease x by a factor of 2, the error bound decreases by a factor of 2^{n+1}.

Example 2   Compare the errors in the approximations

$$e^{0.1} \approx 1 + 0.1 + \frac{1}{2!}(0.1)^2 \quad \text{and} \quad e^{0.05} \approx 1 + (0.05) + \frac{1}{2!}(0.05)^2.$$

Solution   We are approximating e^x by its second-degree Taylor polynomial about 0. We evaluate the polynomial first at $x = 0.1$, and then at $x = 0.05$. Since we have decreased x by a factor of 2, the error bound decreases by a factor of about $2^3 = 8$. To see what actually happens to the errors, we compute them:

$$e^{0.1} - \left(1 + 0.1 + \frac{1}{2!}(0.1)^2\right) = 1.105171 - 1.105000 = 0.000171$$

$$e^{0.05} - \left(1 + 0.05 + \frac{1}{2!}(0.05)^2\right) = 1.051271 - 1.051250 = 0.000021$$

Since $(0.000171)/(0.000021) = 8.1$, the error has also decreased by a factor of about 8.

Convergence of the Taylor Series for $\cos x$

We have already seen that the Taylor polynomials centered at $x = 0$ for $\cos x$ are good approximations for x near 0. (See Figure 10.17.) In fact, for any value of x, if we take a Taylor polynomial centered at $x = 0$ of high enough degree, its graph is nearly indistinguishable from the graph of the cosine function near that point.

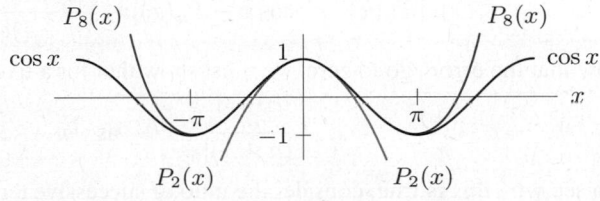

Figure 10.17: Graph of $\cos x$ and two Taylor polynomials for x near 0

Let's see what happens numerically. Let $x = \pi/2$. The successive Taylor polynomial approximations to $\cos(\pi/2) = 0$ about $x = 0$ are

$$
\begin{aligned}
P_2(\pi/2) &= & 1 - (\pi/2)^2/2! & & = -0.23370\ldots \\
P_4(\pi/2) &= 1 - (\pi/2)^2/2! + (\pi/2)^4/4! = & & & 0.01997\ldots \\
P_6(\pi/2) &= & \cdots & & = -0.00089\ldots \\
P_8(\pi/2) &= & \cdots & & = 0.00002\ldots.
\end{aligned}
$$

It appears that the approximations converge to the true value, $\cos(\pi/2) = 0$, very rapidly. Now take a value of x somewhat farther away from 0, say $x = \pi$; then $\cos \pi = -1$ and

$$
\begin{aligned}
P_2(\pi) &= 1 - (\pi)^2/2! = & -3.93480\ldots \\
P_4(\pi) &= \quad\cdots\quad = & 0.12391\ldots \\
P_6(\pi) &= \quad\cdots\quad = & -1.21135\ldots \\
P_8(\pi) &= \quad\cdots\quad = & -0.97602\ldots \\
P_{10}(\pi) &= \quad\cdots\quad = & -1.00183\ldots \\
P_{12}(\pi) &= \quad\cdots\quad = & -0.99990\ldots \\
P_{14}(\pi) &= \quad\cdots\quad = & -1.000004\ldots.
\end{aligned}
$$

We see that the rate of convergence is somewhat slower; it takes a 14th-degree polynomial to approximate $\cos \pi$ as accurately as an 8th-degree polynomial approximates $\cos(\pi/2)$. If x were taken still farther away from 0, then we would need still more terms to obtain as accurate an approximation of $\cos x$.

Exercise 18 on page 527 uses the ratio test to show that the Taylor series for $\cos x$ converges for all values of x. In addition, we will prove that it converges to $\cos x$ using Theorem 10.1. Thus, we are justified in writing the equality:

$$
\cos x = 1 - \frac{x^2}{2!} + \frac{x^4}{4!} - \frac{x^6}{6!} + \frac{x^8}{8!} - \cdots \qquad \text{for all } x.
$$

Showing that the Taylor Series for cos x Converges to cos x

The Lagrange error bound in Theorem 10.1 allows us to see if the Taylor series for a function converges to that function. In the series for $\cos x$, the odd powers are missing, so we assume n is even and write

$$
E_n(x) = \cos x - P_n(x) = \cos x - \left(1 - \frac{x^2}{2!} + \cdots + (-1)^{n/2}\frac{x^n}{n!} \right),
$$

giving

$$
\cos x = 1 - \frac{x^2}{2!} + \cdots + (-1)^{n/2}\frac{x^n}{n!} + E_n(x).
$$

Thus, for the Taylor series to converge to $\cos x$, we must have $E_n(x) \to 0$ as $n \to \infty$.

Showing $E_n(x) \to 0$ as $n \to \infty$

Proof   Since $f(x) = \cos x$, the $(n+1)^{\text{st}}$ derivative, $f^{(n+1)}(x)$, is $\pm \cos x$ or $\pm \sin x$, no matter what n is. So for all n, we have $|f^{(n+1)}(x)| \leq 1$ on the interval between 0 and x.

By the Lagrange error bound with $M = 1$, we have

$$
|E_n(x)| = |\cos x - P_n(x)| \leq \frac{|x|^{n+1}}{(n+1)!} \qquad \text{for every } n.
$$

To show that the errors go to zero, we must show that for a fixed x,

$$
\frac{|x|^{n+1}}{(n+1)!} \to 0 \quad \text{as} \quad n \to \infty.
$$

To see why this is true, consider the ratio of successive terms of this sequence. We have

$$
\frac{|x|^{n+2}/(n+2)!}{|x|^{n+1}/(n+1)!} = \frac{|x|}{n+2}.
$$

Therefore, we obtain the $(n+1)^{\text{st}}$ term of this sequence, $|x|^{n+2}/(n+2)!$, by multiplying the previous term, $|x|^{n+1}/(n+1)!$, by $|x|/(n+2)$. Since $|x|$ is fixed and $n+2$ is increasing, for sufficiently large n, this ratio is less than $1/2$ (or any other constant between 0 and 1). Thus eventually each term in the sequence is less than $1/2$ the previous term, so the sequence of errors approaches zero. Therefore, the Taylor series $1 - x^2/2! + x^4/4! - \cdots$ does converge to $\cos x$.

Problems 21 and 22 ask you to show that the Taylor series for $\sin x$ and e^x converge to the original function for all x. In each case, you again need the following limit:

$$\lim_{n \to \infty} \frac{x^n}{n!} = 0.$$

Deriving the Lagrange Error Bound

Recall that we constructed $P_n(x)$, the Taylor polynomial of f about 0, so that its first n derivatives equal the corresponding derivatives of $f(x)$. Therefore, $E_n(0) = 0$, $E_n'(0) = 0$, $E_n''(0) = 0$, $\cdots$, $E_n^{(n)}(0) = 0$. Since $P_n(x)$ is an nth-degree polynomial, its $(n+1)^{\text{st}}$ derivative is 0, so $E_n^{(n+1)}(x) = f^{(n+1)}(x)$. In addition, suppose that $\left|f^{(n+1)}(x)\right|$ is bounded by a positive constant M, for all positive values of x near 0, say for $0 \le x \le d$, so that

$$-M \le f^{(n+1)}(x) \le M \quad \text{for } 0 \le x \le d.$$

This means that

$$-M \le E_n^{(n+1)}(x) \le M \quad \text{for } 0 \le x \le d.$$

Writing t for the variable, we integrate this inequality from 0 to x, giving

$$-\int_0^x M \, dt \le \int_0^x E_n^{(n+1)}(t) \, dt \le \int_0^x M \, dt \quad \text{for } 0 \le x \le d,$$

so

$$-Mx \le E_n^{(n)}(x) \le Mx \quad \text{for } 0 \le x \le d.$$

We integrate this inequality again from 0 to x, giving

$$-\int_0^x Mt \, dt \le \int_0^x E_n^{(n)}(t) \, dt \le \int_0^x Mt \, dt \quad \text{for } 0 \le x \le d,$$

so

$$-\frac{1}{2}Mx^2 \le E_n^{(n-1)}(x) \le \frac{1}{2}Mx^2 \quad \text{for } 0 \le x \le d.$$

By repeated integration, we obtain the following bound:

$$-\frac{1}{(n+1)!}Mx^{n+1} \le E_n(x) \le \frac{1}{(n+1)!}Mx^{n+1} \quad \text{for } 0 \le x \le d,$$

which means that

$$|E_n(x)| = |f(x) - P_n(x)| \le \frac{1}{(n+1)!}Mx^{n+1} \quad \text{for } 0 \le x \le d.$$

When x is to the left of 0, so $-d \le x \le 0$, and when the Taylor series is centered at $a \ne 0$, similar calculations lead to Theorem 10.1.

Exercises and Problems for Section 10.4

Exercises

In Exercises 1–8, use Theorem 10.1 to find a bound for the error in approximating the quantity with a third-degree Taylor polynomial for the given function $f(x)$ about $x = 0$. Compare the bound with the actual error.

1. $e^{0.1}$, $f(x) = e^x$

2. $\sin(0.2)$, $f(x) = \sin x$

3. $\cos(-0.3)$, $f(x) = \cos x$

4. $\sqrt{0.9}$, $f(x) = \sqrt{1+x}$

5. $\ln(1.5)$, $f(x) = \ln(1+x)$

6. $1/\sqrt{3}$, $f(x) = (1+x)^{-1/2}$

7. $\tan 1$, $f(x) = \tan x$

8. $0.5^{1/3}$, $f(x) = (1-x)^{1/3}$

Problems

9. (a) Using a calculator, make a table of values to four decimal places of $\sin x$ for

$$x = -0.5, -0.4, \ldots, -0.1, 0, 0.1, \ldots, 0.4, 0.5.$$

(b) Add to your table the values of the error $E_1 = \sin x - x$ for these x-values.

(c) Using a calculator or computer, draw a graph of the quantity $E_1 = \sin x - x$ showing that

$$|E_1| < 0.03 \quad \text{for} \quad -0.5 \leq x \leq 0.5.$$

10. Find a bound on the magnitude of the error if we approximate $\sqrt{2}$ using the Taylor approximation of degree three for $\sqrt{1+x}$ about $x = 0$.

11. (a) Let $f(x) = e^x$. Find a bound on the magnitude of the error when $f(x)$ is approximated using $P_3(x)$, its Taylor approximation of degree 3 around 0 over the interval $[-2, 2]$.

(b) What is the actual maximum error in approximating $f(x)$ by $P_3(x)$ over the interval $[-2, 2]$?

12. Let $f(x) = \cos x$ and let $P_n(x)$ be the Taylor approximation of degree n for $f(x)$ around 0. Explain why, for any x, we can choose an n such that

$$|f(x) - P_n(x)| < 10^{-9}.$$

13. Consider the error in using the approximation $\sin \theta \approx \theta$ on the interval $[-1, 1]$.

(a) Reasoning informally, say where the approximation is an overestimate and where it is an underestimate.

(b) Use Theorem 10.1 to bound the error. Check your answer graphically on a computer or calculator.

14. Repeat Problem 13 for the approximation $\sin \theta \approx \theta - \theta^3/3!$.

15. You approximate $f(t) = e^t$ by a Taylor polynomial of degree 0 about $t = 0$ on the interval $[0, 0.5]$.

(a) Reasoning informally, say whether the approximation is an overestimate or an underestimate.

(b) Use Theorem 10.1 to bound the error. Check your answer graphically on a computer or calculator.

16. Repeat Problem 15 using the second-degree Taylor approximation to e^t.

17. (a) Use the graphs of $y = \cos x$ and its Taylor polynomials, $P_{10}(x)$ and $P_{20}(x)$, in Figure 10.18 to bound:

(i) The error in approximating $\cos 6$ by $P_{10}(6)$ and by $P_{20}(6)$.

(ii) The error in approximating $\cos x$ by $P_{20}(x)$ for $|x| \leq 9$.

(b) If we want to approximate $\cos x$ by $P_{10}(x)$ to an accuracy of within 0.1, what is the largest interval of x-values on which we can work? Give your answer to the nearest integer.

Figure 10.18

18. Give a bound for the error for the nth-degree Taylor polynomial about $x = 0$ approximating $\cos x$ on the interval $[0, 1]$. What is the bound for $\sin x$?

19. What degree Taylor polynomial about $x = 0$ do you need to calculate $\cos 1$ to four decimal places? To six decimal places? Justify your answer using the results of Problem 18.

20. For $|x| \leq 0.1$, graph the error

$$E_0 = \cos x - P_0(x) = \cos x - 1.$$

Explain the shape of the graph, using the Taylor expansion of $\cos x$. Find a bound for $|E_0|$ for $|x| \leq 0.1$.

21. Show that the Taylor series about 0 for e^x converges to e^x for every x. Do this by showing that the error $E_n(x) \to 0$ as $n \to \infty$.

22. Show that the Taylor series about 0 for $\sin x$ converges to $\sin x$ for every x.

23. To approximate π using a Taylor polynomial, we could use the series for the arctangent or the series for the arcsine. In this problem, we compare the two methods.

(a) Using the fact that $d(\arctan x)/dx = 1/(1 + x^2)$ and $\arctan 1 = \pi/4$, approximate the value of π using the third-degree Taylor polynomial of $4 \arctan x$ about $x = 0$.

(b) Using the fact that $d(\arcsin x)/dx = 1/\sqrt{1 - x^2}$ and $\arcsin 1 = \pi/2$, approximate the value of π using the third-degree Taylor polynomial of $2 \arcsin x$ about $x = 0$.

(c) Estimate the maximum error of the approximation you found in part (a).

(d) Explain the problem in estimating the error in the arcsine approximation.

Strengthen Your Understanding

In Problems 24–25, explain what is wrong with the statement.

24. Let $P_n(x)$ be a Taylor approximation of degree n for a function $f(x)$ about a, where a is a constant. Then $|f(a) - P_n(a)| > 0$ for any n.

25. Let $f(x)$ be a function whose Taylor series about $x = 0$ converges to $f(x)$ for all x. Then there exists a positive integer n such that the nth-degree Taylor polynomial $P_n(x)$ for $f(x)$ about $x = 0$ satisfies the inequality

$$|f(x) - P_n(x)| < 1 \quad \text{for all values of } x.$$

In Problems 26–28, give an example of:

26. A function $f(x)$ whose Taylor series converges to $f(x)$ for all values of x.

27. A polynomial $P(x)$ such that $|1/x - P(x)| < 0.1$ for all x in the interval $[1, 1.5]$.

28. A function $f(x)$ and an interval $[-c, c]$ such that the value of M in the error of the second-degree Taylor polynomial of $f(x)$ centered at 0 on the interval could be 4.

Decide if the statements in Problems 29–33 are true or false. Assume that the Taylor series for a function converges to that function. Give an explanation for your answer.

29. Let $P_n(x)$ be the nth Taylor polynomial for a function f near $x = a$. Although $P_n(x)$ is a good approximation to f near $x = a$, it is not possible to have $P_n(x) = f(x)$ for all x.

30. If $|f^{(n)}(x)| < 10$ for all $n > 0$ and all x, then the Taylor series for f about $x = 0$ converges to $f(x)$ for all x.

31. If $f^{(n)}(0) \geq n!$ for all n, then the Taylor series for f near $x = 0$ diverges at $x = 0$.

32. If $f^{(n)}(0) \geq n!$ for all n, then the Taylor series for f near $x = 0$ diverges at $x = 1$.

33. If $f^{(n)}(0) \geq n!$ for all n, then the Taylor series for f near $x = 0$ diverges at $x = 1/2$.

10.5 FOURIER SERIES

We have seen how to approximate a function by a Taylor polynomial of fixed degree. Such a polynomial is usually very close to the true value of the function near one point (the point at which the Taylor polynomial is centered), but not necessarily at all close anywhere else. In other words, Taylor polynomials are good approximations of a function *locally*, but not necessarily *globally*. In this section, we take another approach: we approximate the function by trigonometric functions, called *Fourier approximations*. The resulting approximation may not be as close to the original function at some points as the Taylor polynomial. However, the Fourier approximation is, in general, close over a larger interval. In other words, a Fourier approximation can be a better approximation globally. In addition, Fourier approximations are useful even for functions that are not continuous. Unlike Taylor approximations, Fourier approximations are periodic, so they are particularly useful for approximating periodic functions.

Many processes in nature are periodic or repeating, so it makes sense to approximate them by periodic functions. For example, sound waves are made up of periodic oscillations of air molecules. Heartbeats, the movement of the lungs, and the electrical current that powers our homes are all periodic phenomena. Two of the simplest periodic functions are the square wave in Figure 10.19 and the triangular wave in Figure 10.20. Electrical engineers use the square wave as the model for the flow of electricity when a switch is repeatedly flicked on and off.

Figure 10.19: Square wave

Figure 10.20: Triangular wave

Fourier Polynomials

We can express the square wave and the triangular wave by the formulas

$$f(x) = \begin{cases} \vdots & \vdots \\ 0 & -1 \le x < 0 \\ 1 & 0 \le x < 1 \\ 0 & 1 \le x < 2 \\ 1 & 2 \le x < 3 \\ 0 & 3 \le x < 4 \\ \vdots & \vdots \end{cases} \qquad g(x) = \begin{cases} \vdots & \vdots \\ -x & -1 \le x < 0 \\ x & 0 \le x < 1 \\ 2 - x & 1 \le x < 2 \\ x - 2 & 2 \le x < 3 \\ 4 - x & 3 \le x < 4 \\ \vdots & \vdots \end{cases}$$

However, these formulas are not particularly easy to work with. Worse, the functions are not differentiable at various points. Here we show how to approximate such functions by differentiable, periodic functions.

Since sine and cosine are the simplest periodic functions, they are the building blocks we use. Because they repeat every 2π, we assume that the function f we want to approximate repeats every 2π. (Later, we deal with the case where f has some other period.) We start by considering the square wave in Figure 10.21. Because of the periodicity of all the functions concerned, we only have to consider what happens in the course of a single period; the same behavior repeats in any other period.

$$f(x) = \begin{cases} 0 & -\pi \le x < 0 \\ 1 & 0 \le x < \pi \end{cases}$$

Figure 10.21: Square wave on $[-\pi, \pi]$

We will attempt to approximate f with a sum of trigonometric functions of the form

$$f(x) \approx F_n(x)$$
$$= a_0 + a_1 \cos x + a_2 \cos(2x) + a_3 \cos(3x) + \cdots + a_n \cos(nx)$$
$$+ b_1 \sin x + b_2 \sin(2x) + b_3 \sin(3x) + \cdots + b_n \sin(nx)$$
$$= a_0 + \sum_{k=1}^{n} a_k \cos(kx) + \sum_{k=1}^{n} b_k \sin(kx).$$

$F_n(x)$ is known as a *Fourier polynomial of degree n*, named after the French mathematician Joseph Fourier (1768–1830), who was one of the first to investigate it.[5] The coefficients a_k and b_k are called *Fourier coefficients*. Since each of the component functions $\cos(kx)$ and $\sin(kx)$, $k = 1, 2, \ldots, n$, repeats every 2π, $F_n(x)$ must repeat every 2π and so is a potentially good match for $f(x)$, which also repeats every 2π. The problem is to determine values for the Fourier coefficients that achieve a close match between $f(x)$ and $F_n(x)$. We choose the following values:

The Fourier Coefficients for a Periodic Function f of Period 2π

$$a_0 = \frac{1}{2\pi} \int_{-\pi}^{\pi} f(x)\,dx,$$

$$a_k = \frac{1}{\pi} \int_{-\pi}^{\pi} f(x) \cos(kx)\,dx \quad \text{for } k > 0,$$

$$b_k = \frac{1}{\pi} \int_{-\pi}^{\pi} f(x) \sin(kx)\,dx \quad \text{for } k > 0.$$

Notice that a_0 is just the average value of f over the interval $[-\pi, \pi]$.

---

[5] The Fourier polynomials are not polynomials in the usual sense of the word.

For an informal justification for the use of these values, see page 573. In addition, the integrals over $[-\pi, \pi]$ for a_k and b_k can be replaced by integrals over any interval of length 2π.

Example 1   Construct successive Fourier polynomials for the square wave function f, with period 2π, given by

$$f(x) = \begin{cases} 0 & -\pi \leq x < 0 \\ 1 & 0 \leq x < \pi. \end{cases}$$

Solution   Since a_0 is the average value of f on $[-\pi, \pi]$, we suspect from the graph of f that $a_0 = \frac{1}{2}$. We can verify this analytically:

$$a_0 = \frac{1}{2\pi} \int_{-\pi}^{\pi} f(x)\, dx = \frac{1}{2\pi} \int_{-\pi}^{0} 0\, dx + \frac{1}{2\pi} \int_{0}^{\pi} 1\, dx = 0 + \frac{1}{2\pi}(\pi) = \frac{1}{2}.$$

Furthermore,

$$a_1 = \frac{1}{\pi} \int_{-\pi}^{\pi} f(x) \cos x\, dx = \frac{1}{\pi} \int_{0}^{\pi} 1 \cos x\, dx = 0$$

and

$$b_1 = \frac{1}{\pi} \int_{-\pi}^{\pi} f(x) \sin x\, dx = \frac{1}{\pi} \int_{0}^{\pi} 1 \sin x\, dx = \frac{2}{\pi}.$$

Therefore, the Fourier polynomial of degree 1 is given by

$$f(x) \approx F_1(x) = \frac{1}{2} + \frac{2}{\pi} \sin x,$$

and the graphs of the function and the first Fourier approximation are shown in Figure 10.22.

We next construct the Fourier polynomial of degree 2. The coefficients a_0, a_1, b_1 are the same as before. In addition,

$$a_2 = \frac{1}{\pi} \int_{-\pi}^{\pi} f(x) \cos(2x)\, dx = \frac{1}{\pi} \int_{0}^{\pi} 1 \cos(2x)\, dx = 0$$

and

$$b_2 = \frac{1}{\pi} \int_{-\pi}^{\pi} f(x) \sin(2x)\, dx = \frac{1}{\pi} \int_{0}^{\pi} 1 \sin(2x)\, dx = 0.$$

Since $a_2 = b_2 = 0$, the Fourier polynomial of degree 2 is identical to the Fourier polynomial of degree 1. Let's look at the Fourier polynomial of degree 3:

$$a_3 = \frac{1}{\pi} \int_{-\pi}^{\pi} f(x) \cos(3x)\, dx = \frac{1}{\pi} \int_{0}^{\pi} 1 \cos(3x)\, dx = 0$$

and

$$b_3 = \frac{1}{\pi} \int_{-\pi}^{\pi} f(x) \sin(3x)\, dx = \frac{1}{\pi} \int_{0}^{\pi} 1 \sin(3x)\, dx = \frac{2}{3\pi}.$$

So the approximation is given by

$$f(x) \approx F_3(x) = \frac{1}{2} + \frac{2}{\pi} \sin x + \frac{2}{3\pi} \sin(3x).$$

Figure 10.22: First Fourier approximation to the square wave

Figure 10.23: Third Fourier approximation to the square wave

Figure 10.24: Fifth and seventh Fourier approximations to the square wave

The graph of F_3 is shown in Figure 10.23. This approximation is better than $F_1(x) = \frac{1}{2} + \frac{2}{\pi}\sin x$, as comparing Figure 10.23 to Figure 10.22 shows.

Without going through the details, we calculate the coefficients for higher-degree Fourier approximations:

$$F_5(x) = \frac{1}{2} + \frac{2}{\pi}\sin x + \frac{2}{3\pi}\sin(3x) + \frac{2}{5\pi}\sin(5x)$$

$$F_7(x) = \frac{1}{2} + \frac{2}{\pi}\sin x + \frac{2}{3\pi}\sin(3x) + \frac{2}{5\pi}\sin(5x) + \frac{2}{7\pi}\sin(7x).$$

Figure 10.24 shows that higher-degree approximations match the step-like nature of the square wave function more and more closely.

We could have used a Taylor series to approximate the square wave, provided we did not center the series at a point of discontinuity. Since the square wave is a constant function on each interval, all its derivatives are zero, and so its Taylor series approximations are the constant functions: 0 or 1, depending on where the Taylor series is centered. They approximate the square wave perfectly on each piece, but they do not do a good job over the whole interval of length 2π. That is what Fourier polynomials succeed in doing: they approximate a curve fairly well everywhere, rather than just near a particular point. The Fourier approximations above look a lot like square waves, so they approximate well *globally*. However, they may not give good values near points of discontinuity. (For example, near $x = 0$, they all give values near $1/2$, which are incorrect.) Thus Fourier polynomials may not be good *local* approximations.

> Taylor polynomials give good *local* approximations to a function;
> Fourier polynomials give good *global* approximations to a function.

Fourier Series

As with Taylor polynomials, the higher the degree of the Fourier approximation, generally the more accurate it is. Therefore, we carry this procedure on indefinitely by letting $n \to \infty$, and we call the resulting infinite series a *Fourier series*.

> **The Fourier Series for f on $[-\pi, \pi]$**
>
> $$f(x) = a_0 + a_1 \cos x + a_2 \cos 2x + a_3 \cos 3x + \cdots$$
> $$+ \, b_1 \sin x + b_2 \sin 2x + b_3 \sin 3x + \cdots$$
>
> where a_k and b_k are the Fourier coefficients.

Thus, the Fourier series for the square wave is

$$f(x) = \frac{1}{2} + \frac{2}{\pi}\sin x + \frac{2}{3\pi}\sin 3x + \frac{2}{5\pi}\sin 5x + \frac{2}{7\pi}\sin 7x + \cdots.$$

Harmonics

Let us start with a function $f(x)$ that is periodic with period 2π, expanded in a Fourier series:

$$f(x) = a_0 + a_1 \cos x + a_2 \cos 2x + a_3 \cos 3x + \cdots$$
$$+ b_1 \sin x + b_2 \sin 2x + b_3 \sin 3x + \cdots$$

The function

$$a_k \cos kx + b_k \sin kx$$

is referred to as the kth *harmonic* of f, and it is customary to say that the Fourier series expresses f in terms of its harmonics. The first harmonic, $a_1 \cos x + b_1 \sin x$, is sometimes called the *fundamental harmonic* of f.

Example 2   Find a_0 and the first four harmonics of a *pulse train* function f of period 2π shown in Figure 10.25:

$$f(x) = \begin{cases} 1 & 0 \le x < \pi/2 \\ 0 & \pi/2 \le x < 2\pi \end{cases}$$

Figure 10.25: A train of pulses with period 2π

Solution   First, a_0 is the average value of the function, so

$$a_0 = \frac{1}{2\pi} \int_{-\pi}^{\pi} f(x)\, dx = \frac{1}{2\pi} \int_0^{\pi/2} 1\, dx = \frac{1}{4}.$$

Next, we compute a_k and b_k, $k = 1, 2, 3,$ and 4. The formulas

$$a_k = \frac{1}{\pi} \int_{-\pi}^{\pi} f(x) \cos(kx)\, dx = \frac{1}{\pi} \int_0^{\pi/2} \cos(kx)\, dx$$

$$b_k = \frac{1}{\pi} \int_{-\pi}^{\pi} f(x) \sin(kx)\, dx = \frac{1}{\pi} \int_0^{\pi/2} \sin(kx)\, dx$$

lead to the harmonics

$$a_1 \cos x + b_1 \sin x = \frac{1}{\pi} \cos x + \frac{1}{\pi} \sin x$$

$$a_2 \cos(2x) + b_2 \sin(2x) = \frac{1}{\pi} \sin(2x)$$

$$a_3 \cos(3x) + b_3 \sin(3x) = -\frac{1}{3\pi} \cos(3x) + \frac{1}{3\pi} \sin(3x)$$

$$a_4 \cos(4x) + b_4 \sin(4x) = 0.$$

Figure 10.26 shows the graph of the sum of a_0 and these harmonics, which is the fourth Fourier approximation of f.

Figure 10.26: Fourth Fourier approximation to pulse train f equals the sum of a_0 and the first four harmonics

Energy and the Energy Theorem

The quantity $A_k = \sqrt{a_k^2 + b_k^2}$ is called the amplitude of the kth harmonic. The square of the amplitude has a useful interpretation. Adopting terminology from the study of periodic waves, we define the *energy E* of a periodic function f of period 2π to be the number

$$E = \frac{1}{\pi} \int_{-\pi}^{\pi} (f(x))^2 \, dx.$$

Problem 19 on page 576 asks you to check that for all positive integers k,

$$\frac{1}{\pi} \int_{-\pi}^{\pi} (a_k \cos(kx) + b_k \sin(kx))^2 \, dx = a_k^2 + b_k^2 = A_k^2.$$

This shows that the kth harmonic of f has energy A_k^2. The energy of the constant term a_0 of the Fourier series is $\frac{1}{\pi} \int_{-\pi}^{\pi} a_0^2 \, dx = 2a_0^2$, so we make the definition

$$A_0 = \sqrt{2} a_0.$$

It turns out that for all reasonable periodic functions f, the energy of f equals the sum of the energies of its harmonics:

The Energy Theorem for a Periodic Function f of Period 2π

$$E = \frac{1}{\pi} \int_{-\pi}^{\pi} (f(x))^2 \, dx = A_0^2 + A_1^2 + A_2^2 + \cdots$$

where $A_0 = \sqrt{2} a_0$ and $A_k = \sqrt{a_k^2 + b_k^2}$ (for all integers $k \geq 1$).

The graph of A_k^2 against k is called the *energy spectrum* of f. It shows how the energy of f is distributed among its harmonics.

Example 3   (a) Graph the energy spectrum of the square wave of Example 1.
(b) What fraction of the energy of the square wave is contained in the constant term and first three harmonics of its Fourier series?

Solution   (a) We know from Example 1 that $a_0 = 1/2$, $a_k = 0$ for $k \geq 1$, $b_k = 0$ for k even, and $b_k = 2/(k\pi)$ for k odd. Thus

$$A_0^2 = 2a_0^2 = \frac{1}{2}$$

$$A_k^2 = 0 \quad \text{if } k \text{ is even}, \quad k \geq 1,$$

$$A_k^2 = \left(\frac{2}{k\pi}\right)^2 = \frac{4}{k^2\pi^2} \quad \text{if } k \text{ is odd}, \quad k \geq 1.$$

The energy spectrum is graphed in Figure 10.27. Notice that it is customary to represent the energy A_k^2 of the kth harmonic by a vertical line of length A_k^2. The graph shows that the constant term and first harmonic carry most of the energy of f.

Figure 10.27: The energy spectrum of a square wave

(b) The energy of the square wave $f(x)$ is

$$E = \frac{1}{\pi} \int_{-\pi}^{\pi} (f(x))^2 \, dx = \frac{1}{\pi} \int_0^{\pi} 1 \, dx = 1.$$

The energy in the constant term and the first three harmonics of the Fourier series is

$$A_0^2 + A_1^2 + A_2^2 + A_3^2 = \frac{1}{2} + \frac{4}{\pi^2} + 0 + \frac{4}{9\pi^2} = 0.950.$$

The fraction of energy carried by the constant term and the first three harmonics is

$$0.95/1 = 0.95, \text{ or } 95\%.$$

Musical Instruments

You may have wondered why different musical instruments sound different, even when playing the same note. A first step might be to graph the periodic deviations from the average air pressure that form the sound waves they produce. This has been done for clarinet and trumpet in Figure 10.28.[6] However, it is more revealing to graph the energy spectra of these functions, as in Figure 10.29. The most striking difference is the relative weakness of the second and fourth harmonics for the clarinet, with the second harmonic completely absent. The trumpet sounds the second harmonic with as much energy as it does the fundamental.

Figure 10.28: Sound waves of a clarinet and trumpet

Figure 10.29: Energy spectra of a clarinet and trumpet

[6] Adapted from C.A. Culver, *Musical Acoustics* (New York: McGraw-Hill, 1956) pp. 204, 220.

What Do We Do If Our Function Does Not Have Period 2π?

We can adapt our previous work to find the Fourier series for a function of period b. Suppose $f(x)$ is given on the interval $[-b/2, b/2]$. In Problem 31, we see how to use a change of variable to get the following result:

The Fourier Series for f on $[-b/2, b/2]$

$$f(x) = a_0 + \sum_{k=1}^{\infty} \left(a_k \cos\left(\frac{2\pi kx}{b}\right) + b_k \sin\left(\frac{2\pi kx}{b}\right) \right)$$

where $a_0 = \dfrac{1}{b} \displaystyle\int_{-b/2}^{b/2} f(x)\, dx$ and, for $k \geq 1$,

$$a_k = \frac{2}{b} \int_{-b/2}^{b/2} f(x) \cos\left(\frac{2\pi kx}{b}\right)\, dx \text{ and } b_k = \frac{2}{b} \int_{-b/2}^{b/2} f(x) \sin\left(\frac{2\pi kx}{b}\right)\, dx.$$

The constant $2\pi k/b$ is called the angular frequency of the kth harmonic; b is the period of f.

Note that the integrals over $[-b/2, b/2]$ can be replaced by integrals over any interval of length b.

Example 4 Find the fifth-degree Fourier polynomial of the square wave $f(x)$ graphed in Figure 10.30.

Figure 10.30: Square wave f and its fifth Fourier approximation F_5

Solution Since $f(x)$ repeats outside the interval $[-1, 1]$, we have $b = 2$. As an example of how the coefficients are computed, we find b_1. Since $f(x) = 0$ for $-1 < x < 0$,

$$b_1 = \frac{2}{2} \int_{-1}^{1} f(x) \sin\left(\frac{2\pi x}{2}\right) dx = \int_{0}^{1} \sin(\pi x) dx = -\frac{1}{\pi} \cos(\pi x) \Big|_{0}^{1} = \frac{2}{\pi}.$$

Finding the other coefficients by a similar method, we have

$$f(x) \approx \frac{1}{2} + \frac{2}{\pi} \sin(\pi x) + \frac{2}{3\pi} \sin(3\pi x) + \frac{2}{5\pi} \sin(5\pi x).$$

Notice that the coefficients in this series are the same as those in Example 1. This is because the graphs in Figures 10.24 and 10.30 are the same except with different scales on the x-axes.

Seasonal Variation in the Incidence of Measles

Example 5   Fourier approximations have been used to analyze the seasonal variation in the incidence of diseases. One study[7] done in Baltimore, Maryland, for the years 1901–1931, studied $I(t)$, the average number of cases of measles per 10,000 susceptible children in the tth month of the year. The data points in Figure 10.31 show $f(t) = \log I(t)$. The curve in Figure 10.31 shows the second Fourier approximation of $f(t)$. Figure 10.32 contains the graphs of the first and second harmonics of $f(t)$, plotted separately as deviations about a_0, the average logarithmic incidence rate. Describe what these two harmonics tell you about incidence of measles.

Figure 10.31: Logarithm of incidence of measles per month (dots) and second Fourier approximation (curve)

Figure 10.32: First and second harmonics of $f(t)$ plotted as deviations from average log incidence rate, a_0

Solution   Taking the log of $I(t)$ has the effect of reducing the amplitude of the oscillations. However, since the log of a function increases when the function increases and decreases when it decreases, oscillations in $f(t)$ correspond to oscillations in $I(t)$.

Figure 10.32 shows that the first harmonic in the Fourier series has a period of one year (the same period as the original function); the second harmonic has a period of six months. The graph in Figure 10.32 shows that the first harmonic is approximately a sine function with amplitude about 0.7; the second harmonic is approximately the negative of a sine function with amplitude about 0.2. Thus, for t in months ($t = 0$ in January),

$$\log I(t) = f(t) \approx a_0 + 0.7 \sin\left(\frac{\pi}{6}t\right) - 0.2 \sin\left(\frac{\pi}{3}t\right),$$

where $\pi/6$ and $\pi/3$ are introduced to make the periods 12 and 6 months, respectively. We can estimate a_0 from the original graph of f: it is the average value of f, approximately 1.5. Thus

$$f(t) \approx 1.5 + 0.7 \sin\left(\frac{\pi}{6}t\right) - 0.2 \sin\left(\frac{\pi}{3}t\right).$$

Figure 10.31 shows that the second Fourier approximation of $f(t)$ is quite good. The harmonics of $f(t)$ beyond the second must be rather insignificant. This suggests that the variation in incidence in measles comes from two sources, one with a yearly cycle that is reflected in the first harmonic and one with a half-yearly cycle reflected in the second harmonic. At this point the mathematics can tell us no more; we must turn to the epidemiologists for further explanation.

Informal Justification of the Formulas for the Fourier Coefficients

Recall that the coefficients in a Taylor series (which is a good approximation locally) are found by differentiation. In contrast, the coefficients in a Fourier series (which is a good approximation globally) are found by integration.

---

[7]From C. I. Bliss and D. L. Blevins, *The Analysis of Seasonal Variation in Measles* (Am. J. Hyg. 70, 1959), reported by Edward Batschelet, *Introduction to Mathematics for the Life Sciences* (Springer-Verlag, Berlin, 1979).

We want to find the constants $a_0, a_1, a_2, \ldots$ and $b_1, b_2, \ldots$ in the expression

$$f(x) = a_0 + \sum_{k=1}^{\infty} a_k \cos(kx) + \sum_{k=1}^{\infty} b_k \sin(kx).$$

Consider the integral

$$\int_{-\pi}^{\pi} f(x)\, dx = \int_{-\pi}^{\pi} \left(a_0 + \sum_{k=1}^{\infty} a_k \cos(kx) + \sum_{k=1}^{\infty} b_k \sin(kx) \right) dx.$$

Splitting the integral into separate terms, and assuming we can interchange integration and summation, we get

$$\int_{-\pi}^{\pi} f(x)\, dx = \int_{-\pi}^{\pi} a_0\, dx + \int_{-\pi}^{\pi} \sum_{k=1}^{\infty} a_k \cos(kx)\, dx + \int_{-\pi}^{\pi} \sum_{k=1}^{\infty} b_k \sin(kx)\, dx$$

$$= \int_{-\pi}^{\pi} a_0\, dx + \sum_{k=1}^{\infty} \int_{-\pi}^{\pi} a_k \cos(kx)\, dx + \sum_{k=1}^{\infty} \int_{-\pi}^{\pi} b_k \sin(kx)\, dx.$$

But for $k \geq 1$, thinking of the integral as an area shows that

$$\int_{-\pi}^{\pi} \sin(kx)\, dx = 0 \quad \text{and} \quad \int_{-\pi}^{\pi} \cos(kx)\, dx = 0,$$

so all terms drop out except the first, giving

$$\int_{-\pi}^{\pi} f(x)\, dx = \int_{-\pi}^{\pi} a_0\, dx = a_0 x \Big|_{-\pi}^{\pi} = 2\pi a_0.$$

Thus, we get the following result:

$$\boxed{a_0 = \frac{1}{2\pi} \int_{-\pi}^{\pi} f(x)\, dx.}$$

Thus a_0 is the average value of f on the interval $[-\pi, \pi]$.

To determine the values of any of the other a_k or b_k (for positive k), we use a rather clever method that depends on the following facts. For all integers k and m,

$$\int_{-\pi}^{\pi} \sin(kx) \cos(mx)\, dx = 0,$$

and, provided $k \neq m$,

$$\int_{-\pi}^{\pi} \cos(kx) \cos(mx)\, dx = 0 \quad \text{and} \quad \int_{-\pi}^{\pi} \sin(kx) \sin(mx)\, dx = 0.$$

(See Problems 26–30 on page 577.) In addition, provided $m \neq 0$, we have

$$\int_{-\pi}^{\pi} \cos^2(mx)\, dx = \pi \quad \text{and} \quad \int_{-\pi}^{\pi} \sin^2(mx)\, dx = \pi.$$

To determine a_k, we multiply the Fourier series by $\cos(mx)$, where m is any positive integer:

$$f(x) \cos(mx) = a_0 \cos(mx) + \sum_{k=1}^{\infty} a_k \cos(kx) \cos(mx) + \sum_{k=1}^{\infty} b_k \sin(kx) \cos(mx).$$

We integrate this between $-\pi$ and π, term by term:

$$\int_{-\pi}^{\pi} f(x) \cos(mx)\, dx = \int_{-\pi}^{\pi} \left(a_0 \cos(mx) + \sum_{k=1}^{\infty} a_k \cos(kx) \cos(mx) + \sum_{k=1}^{\infty} b_k \sin(kx) \cos(mx) \right) dx$$

$$= a_0 \int_{-\pi}^{\pi} \cos(mx)\, dx + \sum_{k=1}^{\infty} \left(a_k \int_{-\pi}^{\pi} \cos(kx) \cos(mx)\, dx \right)$$

$$+ \sum_{k=1}^{\infty} \left(b_k \int_{-\pi}^{\pi} \sin(kx) \cos(mx)\, dx \right).$$

Provided $m \neq 0$, we have $\int_{-\pi}^{\pi} \cos(mx)\, dx = 0$. Since the integral $\int_{-\pi}^{\pi} \sin(kx) \cos(mx)\, dx = 0$, all the terms in the second sum are zero. Since $\int_{-\pi}^{\pi} \cos(kx) \cos(mx)\, dx = 0$ provided $k \neq m$, all the terms in the first sum are zero except where $k = m$. Thus the right-hand side reduces to one term:

$$\int_{-\pi}^{\pi} f(x) \cos(mx)\, dx = a_m \int_{-\pi}^{\pi} \cos(mx) \cos(mx)\, dx = \pi a_m.$$

This leads, for each value of $m = 1, 2, 3 \ldots$, to the following formula:

$$a_m = \frac{1}{\pi} \int_{-\pi}^{\pi} f(x) \cos(mx)\, dx.$$

To determine b_k, we multiply through by $\sin(mx)$ instead of $\cos(mx)$ and eventually obtain, for each value of $m = 1, 2, 3 \ldots$, the following result:

$$b_m = \frac{1}{\pi} \int_{-\pi}^{\pi} f(x) \sin(mx)\, dx.$$

Exercises and Problems for Section 10.5

Exercises

Which of the series in Exercises 1–4 are Fourier series?

1. $1 + \cos x + \cos^2 x + \cos^3 x + \cos^4 x + \cdots$

2. $\sin x + \sin(x+1) + \sin(x+2) + \cdots$

3. $\dfrac{\cos x}{2} + \sin x - \dfrac{\cos(2x)}{4} - \dfrac{\sin(2x)}{2} + \dfrac{\cos(3x)}{8} + \dfrac{\sin(3x)}{3} - \cdots$

4. $\dfrac{1}{2} - \dfrac{1}{3} \sin x + \dfrac{1}{4} \sin(2x) - \dfrac{1}{5} \sin(3x) + \cdots$

5. Construct the first three Fourier approximations to the square wave function

$$f(x) = \begin{cases} -1 & -\pi \leq x < 0 \\ 1 & 0 \leq x < \pi. \end{cases}$$

Use a calculator or computer to draw the graph of each approximation.

6. Repeat Problem 5 with the function

$$f(x) = \begin{cases} -x & -\pi \leq x < 0 \\ x & 0 \leq x < \pi. \end{cases}$$

7. What fraction of the energy of the function in Problem 6 is contained in the constant term and first three harmonics of its Fourier series?

For Exercises 8–10, find the nth Fourier polynomial for the given functions, assuming them to be periodic with period 2π. Graph the first three approximations with the original function.

8. $f(x) = x^2$, $-\pi < x \leq \pi$.

9. $h(x) = \begin{cases} 0 & -\pi < x \leq 0 \\ x & 0 < x \leq \pi. \end{cases}$

10. $g(x) = x$, $-\pi < x \leq \pi$.

Problems

11. Find the constant term of the Fourier series of the triangular wave function defined by $f(x) = |x|$ for $-1 \leq x \leq 1$ and $f(x + 2) = f(x)$ for all x.

12. Using your result from Problem 10, write the Fourier series of $g(x) = x$. Assume that your series converges to $g(x)$ for $-\pi < x < \pi$. Substituting an appropriate value of x into the series, show that

$$\sum_{k=1}^{\infty} (-1)^{k+1} \frac{1}{2k-1} = \frac{\pi}{4}.$$

13. (a) For $-2\pi \leq x \leq 2\pi$, use a calculator to sketch:
   i) $y = \sin x + \frac{1}{3} \sin 3x$
   ii) $y = \sin x + \frac{1}{3} \sin 3x + \frac{1}{5} \sin 5x$
   (b) Each of the functions in part (a) is a Fourier approximation to a function whose graph is a square wave. What term would you add to the right-hand side of the second function in part (a) to get a better approximation to the square wave?
   (c) What is the equation of the square wave function? Is this function continuous?

14. (a) Find and graph the third Fourier approximation of the square wave $g(x)$ of period 2π:

$$g(x) = \begin{cases} 0 & -\pi \leq x < -\pi/2 \\ 1 & -\pi/2 \leq x < \pi/2 \\ 0 & \pi/2 \leq x < \pi. \end{cases}$$

   (b) How does the result of part (a) differ from that of the square wave in Example 1?

15. Suppose we have a periodic function f with period 1 defined by $f(x) = x$ for $0 \leq x < 1$. Find the fourth-degree Fourier polynomial for f and graph it on the interval $0 \leq x < 1$. [Hint: Remember that since the period is not 2π, you will have to start by doing a substitution. Notice that the terms in the sum are not $\sin(nx)$ and $\cos(nx)$, but instead turn out to be $\sin(2\pi n x)$ and $\cos(2\pi n x)$.]

16. Suppose f has period 2 and $f(x) = x$ for $0 \leq x < 2$. Find the fourth-degree Fourier polynomial and graph it on $0 \leq x < 2$. [Hint: See Problem 15.]

17. Suppose that a spacecraft near Neptune has measured a quantity A and sent it to earth in the form of a periodic signal $A \cos t$ of amplitude A. On its way to earth, the signal picks up periodic noise, containing only second and higher harmonics. Suppose that the signal $h(t)$ actually received on earth is graphed in Figure 10.33. Determine the signal that the spacecraft originally sent and hence the value A of the measurement.

Figure 10.33

18. Figures 10.34 and 10.35 show the waveforms and energy spectra for notes produced by flute and bassoon.[8] Describe the principal differences between the two spectra.

Figure 10.34

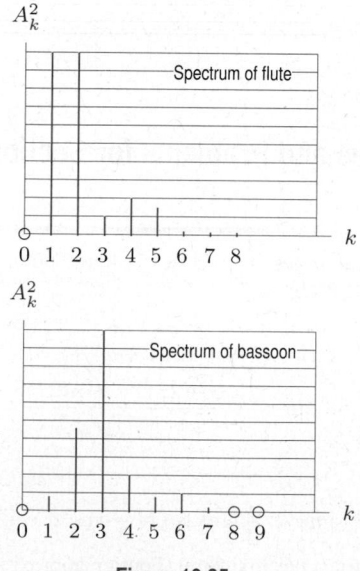

Figure 10.35

19. Show that for positive integers k, the periodic function $f(x) = a_k \cos kx + b_k \sin kx$ of period 2π has energy $a_k^2 + b_k^2$.

---

[8]Adapted from C.A. Culver, *Musical Acoustics* (New York: McGraw-Hill, 1956), pp. 200, 213.

20. Given the graph of f in Figure 10.36, find the first two Fourier approximations numerically.

Figure 10.36

21. Justify the formula $b_k = \frac{1}{\pi} \int_{-\pi}^{\pi} f(x) \sin(kx)\, dx$ for the Fourier coefficients, b_k, of a periodic function of period 2π. The argument is similar to that in the text for a_k.

In Problems 22–25, the pulse train of width c is the periodic function f of period 2π given by

$$f(x) = \begin{cases} 0 & -\pi \leq x < -c/2 \\ 1 & -c/2 \leq x < c/2 \\ 0 & c/2 \leq x < \pi. \end{cases}$$

22. Suppose that f is the pulse train of width 1.

  (a) What fraction of the energy of f is contained in the constant term of its Fourier series? In the constant term and the first harmonic together?

  (b) Find a formula for the energy of the kth harmonic of f. Use it to sketch the energy spectrum of f.

  (c) How many terms of the Fourier series of f are needed to capture 90% of the energy of f?

  (d) Graph f and its fifth Fourier approximation on the interval $[-3\pi, 3\pi]$.

23. Suppose that f is the pulse train of width 0.4.

  (a) What fraction of the energy of f is contained in the constant term of its Fourier series? In the constant term and the first harmonic together?

  (b) Find a formula for the energy of the kth harmonic of f. Use it to sketch the energy spectrum of f.

  (c) What fraction of the energy of f is contained in the constant term and the first five harmonics of f? (The constant term and the first thirteen harmonics are needed to capture 90% of the energy of f.)

  (d) Graph f and its fifth Fourier approximation on the interval $[-3\pi, 3\pi]$.

24. Suppose that f is the pulse train of width 2.

  (a) What fraction of the energy of f is contained in the constant term of its Fourier series? In the constant term and the first harmonic together?

  (b) How many terms of the Fourier series of f are needed to capture 90% of the energy of f?

  (c) Graph f and its third Fourier approximation on the interval $[-3\pi, 3\pi]$.

25. After working Problems 22–24, write a paragraph about the approximation of pulse trains by Fourier polynomials. Explain how the energy spectrum of a pulse train of width c changes as c gets closer and closer to 0 and how this affects the number of terms required for an accurate approximation.

For Problems 26–30, use the table of integrals inside the back cover to show that the following statements are true for positive integers k and m.

26. $\displaystyle\int_{-\pi}^{\pi} \cos(kx)\cos(mx)\, dx = 0, \quad \text{if } k \neq m.$

27. $\displaystyle\int_{-\pi}^{\pi} \cos^2(mx)\, dx = \pi.$

28. $\displaystyle\int_{-\pi}^{\pi} \sin^2(mx)\, dx = \pi.$

29. $\displaystyle\int_{-\pi}^{\pi} \sin(kx)\cos(mx)\, dx = 0.$

30. $\displaystyle\int_{-\pi}^{\pi} \sin(kx)\sin(mx)\, dx = 0, \quad \text{if } k \neq m.$

31. Suppose that $f(x)$ is a periodic function with period b. Show that

  (a) $g(t) = f(bt/2\pi)$ is periodic with period 2π and $f(x) = g(2\pi x/b)$.

  (b) The Fourier series for g is given by

  $$g(t) = a_0 + \sum_{k=1}^{\infty} \Big(a_k \cos(kt) + b_k \sin(kt)\Big)$$

  where the coefficients a_0, a_k, b_k are given in the box on page 572.

  (c) The Fourier series for f is given by

  $$f(x) = a_0 + \sum_{k=1}^{\infty} \left(a_k \cos\left(\frac{2\pi kx}{b}\right) + b_k \sin\left(\frac{2\pi kx}{b}\right)\right)$$

  where the coefficients are the same as in part (b).

Strengthen Your Understanding

In Problems 32–33, explain what is wrong with the statement.

32. $\int_{-\pi}^{\pi} \sin(kx)\cos(mx)\, dx = \pi$, where k, m are both positive integers.

33. In the Fourier series for $f(x)$ given by

$$a_0 + \sum_{k=1}^{\infty} a_k \cos(kx) + \sum_{k=1}^{\infty} b_k \sin(kx), \text{ we have } a_0 = f(0).$$

In Problems 34–35, give an example of:

34. A function, $f(x)$, with period 2π whose Fourier series has no sine terms.

35. A function, $f(x)$, with period 2π whose Fourier series has no cosine terms.

36. True or false? If f is an even function, then the Fourier series for f on $[-\pi, \pi]$ has only cosines. Explain your answer.

37. The graph in Figure 10.37 is the graph of the first three terms of the Fourier series of which of the following functions?

    (a) $f(x) = 3(x/\pi)^3$ on $-\pi < x < \pi$ and $f(x + 2\pi) = f(x)$

    (b) $f(t) = |x|$ on $-\pi < x < \pi$ and $f(x + 2\pi) = f(x)$

    (c) $f(x) = \begin{cases} -3 & , & -\pi < x < 0 \\ 3 & , & 0 < x < \pi \end{cases}$ and

$$f(x + 2\pi) = f(x)$$

    (d) $f(x) = \begin{cases} \pi + x & , & -\pi < x < 0 \\ \pi - x & , & 0 < x < \pi \end{cases}$ and

$$f(x + 2\pi) = f(x)$$

Figure 10.37

CHAPTER SUMMARY (see also Ready Reference at the end of the book)

- **Taylor series and polynomials**
  General expansion about $x = 0$ or $x = a$; specific series for $e^x, \sin x, \cos x, (1 + x)^p$; using known Taylor series to find others by substitution, multiplication, integration, and differentiation; interval of convergence; error in Taylor polynomial expansion

- **Fourier series**
  Formula for coefficients on $[-\pi, \pi], [-b, b]$; Energy theorem

REVIEW EXERCISES AND PROBLEMS FOR CHAPTER TEN

Exercises

For Exercises 1–4, find the second-degree Taylor polynomial about the given point.

1. e^x, $x = 1$

2. $\ln x$, $x = 2$

3. $\sin x$, $x = -\pi/4$

4. $\tan \theta$, $\theta = \pi/4$

5. Find the third-degree Taylor polynomial for $f(x) = x^3 + 7x^2 - 5x + 1$ at $x = 1$.

For Exercises 6–8, find the Taylor polynomial of degree n for x near the given point a.

6. $\dfrac{1}{1-x}$, $a = 2$, $n = 4$

7. $\sqrt{1+x}$, $a = 1$, $n = 3$

8. $\ln x$, $a = 2$, $n = 4$

9. Write out P_7, the Taylor polynomial of degree $n = 7$ approximating g near $x = 0$, given that

$$g(x) = \sum_{i=1}^{\infty} \frac{(-1)^{i+1} 3^i}{(i-1)!} x^{2i-1}.$$

10. Find the first four nonzero terms of the Taylor series around $x = 0$ for $f(x) = \cos^2 x$. [Hint: $\cos^2 x = 0.5 (1 + \cos 2x)$.]

In Exercises 11–18, find the first four nonzero terms of the Taylor series about the origin of the given functions.

11. $t^2 e^t$

12. $\cos(3y)$

13. $\theta^2 \cos \theta^2$

14. $\sin t^2$

15. $\dfrac{t}{1+t}$

16. $\dfrac{1}{1 - 4z^2}$

17. $\dfrac{1}{\sqrt{4-x}}$

18. $\dfrac{z^2}{\sqrt{1-z^2}}$

For Exercises 19–22, expand the quantity in a Taylor series around 0 in terms of the variable given. Give four nonzero terms.

19. $\dfrac{a}{a+b}$ in terms of $\dfrac{b}{a}$

20. $\dfrac{1}{(a+r)^{3/2}}$ in terms of $\dfrac{r}{a}$

21. $(B^2 + y^2)^{3/2}$ in terms of $\dfrac{y}{B}$, where $B > 0$

22. $\sqrt{R-r}$ in terms of $\dfrac{r}{R}$

Problems

23. A function f has $f(3) = 1$, $f'(3) = 5$ and $f''(3) = -10$. Find the best estimate you can for $f(3.1)$.

Find the exact value of the sums in Problems 24–28.

24. $3 + 3 + \dfrac{3}{2!} + \dfrac{3}{3!} + \dfrac{3}{4!} + \dfrac{3}{5!} + \cdots$

25. $1 - \dfrac{1}{3} + \dfrac{1}{9} - \dfrac{1}{27} + \dfrac{1}{81} - \cdots$

26. $1 - 2 + \dfrac{4}{2!} - \dfrac{8}{3!} + \dfrac{16}{4!} - \cdots$

27. $2 - \dfrac{8}{3!} + \dfrac{32}{5!} - \dfrac{128}{7!} + \cdots$

28. $(0.1)^2 - \dfrac{(0.1)^4}{3!} + \dfrac{(0.1)^6}{5!} - \dfrac{(0.1)^8}{7!} + \cdots$

29. Find an exact value for each of the following sums.

(a) $7(1.02)^3 + 7(1.02)^2 + 7(1.02) + 7 + \dfrac{7}{(1.02)} + \dfrac{7}{(1.02)^2} + \cdots + \dfrac{7}{(1.02)^{100}}.$

(b) $7 + 7(0.1)^2 + \dfrac{7(0.1)^4}{2!} + \dfrac{7(0.1)^6}{3!} + \cdots.$

30. Suppose all the derivatives of some function f exist at 0, and the Taylor series for f about $x = 0$ is

$$x + \frac{x^2}{2} + \frac{x^3}{3} + \frac{x^4}{4} + \cdots + \frac{x^n}{n} + \cdots.$$

Find $f'(0)$, $f''(0)$, $f'''(0)$, and $f^{(10)}(0)$.

31. Suppose x is positive but very small. Arrange the following expressions in increasing order:

$$x, \quad \sin x, \quad \ln(1+x), \quad 1 - \cos x,$$
$$e^x - 1, \quad \arctan x, \quad x\sqrt{1-x}.$$

32. By plotting several of its Taylor polynomials and the function $f(x) = 1/(1+x)$, estimate graphically the interval of convergence of the series expansion for this function about $x = 0$. Compute the radius of convergence analytically.

33. Find the radius of convergence of the Taylor series around $x = 0$ for $\dfrac{1}{1-2x}$.

34. Use Taylor series to evaluate $\displaystyle\lim_{x \to 0} \dfrac{\ln(1+x+x^2) - x}{\sin^2 x}$.

35. Referring to the table, use a fourth-degree Taylor polynomial to estimate the integral $\displaystyle\int_0^{0.6} f(x)\,dx.$

$f(0)$	$f'(0)$	$f''(0)$	$f'''(0)$	$f^{(4)}(0)$
0	1	−3	7	−15

36. Let $f(x) = e^{-x^3}$.

(a) Write the first five nonzero terms of the Taylor series for $f(x)$ centered at $x = 0$.

(b) Write the first four nonzero terms of the Taylor series for $f''(x)$ centered at $x = 0$.

37. Use a Taylor polynomial of degree $n = 8$ to estimate $\displaystyle\int_0^1 \cos\left(x^2\right)\,dx.$

38. (a) Find $\displaystyle\lim_{\theta \to 0} \dfrac{\sin(2\theta)}{\theta}$. Explain your reasoning.

(b) Use series to explain why $f(\theta) = \dfrac{\sin(2\theta)}{\theta}$ looks like a parabola near $\theta = 0$. What is the equation of the parabola?

39. (a) Find the Taylor series expansion of $\arcsin x$.

(b) Use Taylor series to find the limit as $x \to 0$ of

$$\frac{\arctan x}{\arcsin x}.$$

40. Let $f(0) = 1$ and $f^{(n)}(0) = \dfrac{(n+1)!}{2^n}$ for $n > 0$.

(a) Write the Taylor series for f at $x = 0$ using sigma sum notation. Simplify the general term. [Hint: Write out the first few terms of the Taylor series.]

(b) Does the series you found in part (a) converge for $x = 3$? Briefly explain your reasoning.

(c) Use the series you found in part (a) to evaluate $\displaystyle\int_0^1 f(x)\,dx.$ You may assume that

$$\int_0^1 \left(\sum_{n=1}^{\infty} a_n x^n\right) dx = \sum_{n=1}^{\infty} \left(\int_0^1 a_n x^n\,dx\right).$$

41. In this problem, you will investigate the error in the nth-degree Taylor approximation to e^x about 0 for various values of n.

(a) Let $E_1 = e^x - P_1(x) = e^x - (1+x)$. Using a calculator or computer, graph E_1 for $-0.1 \leq x \leq 0.1$. What shape is the graph of E_1? Use the graph to confirm that

$$|E_1| \leq x^2 \quad \text{for} \quad -0.1 \leq x \leq 0.1.$$

(b) Let $E_2 = e^x - P_2(x) = e^x - (1+x+x^2/2)$. Choose a suitable range and graph E_2 for $-0.1 \leq x \leq 0.1$. What shape is the graph of E_2? Use the graph to confirm that

$$|E_2| \leq x^3 \quad \text{for} \quad -0.1 \leq x \leq 0.1.$$

(c) Explain why the graphs of E_1 and E_2 have the shapes they do.

42. The table gives values of $f^{(n)}(0)$ where f is the *inverse hyperbolic tangent* function. Note that $f(0) = 0$.

n	1	2	3	4	5	6	7
$f^{(n)}(0)$	1	0	2!	0	4!	0	6!

(a) Find the Taylor polynomial of degree 7 for f about $x = 0$.

(b) Assuming the pattern in the table continues, write the Taylor series for this function.

43. A particle moving along the x-axis has potential energy at the point x given by $V(x)$. The potential energy has a minimum at $x = 0$.

(a) Write the Taylor polynomial of degree 2 for V about $x = 0$. What can you say about the signs of the coefficients of each of the terms of the Taylor polynomial?

(b) The force on the particle at the point x is given by $-V'(x)$. For small x, show that the force on the particle is approximately proportional to its distance from the origin. What is the sign of the proportionality constant? Describe the direction in which the force points.

44. Consider the functions $y = e^{-x^2}$ and $y = 1/(1 + x^2)$.

(a) Write the Taylor expansions for the two functions about $x = 0$. What is similar about the two series? What is different?

(b) Looking at the series, which function do you predict will be greater over the interval $(-1, 1)$? Graph both and see.

(c) Are these functions even or odd? How might you see this by looking at the series expansions?

(d) By looking at the coefficients, explain why it is reasonable that the series for $y = e^{-x^2}$ converges for all values of x, but the series for $y = 1/(1 + x^2)$ converges only on $(-1, 1)$.

---
[9]http://en.wikipedia.org/wiki/Exponential_integral.

45. The Lambert W function has the following Taylor series about $x = 0$:

$$W(x) = \sum_{n=1}^{\infty} \frac{(-n)^{n-1}}{n!} x^n.$$

Find P_4, the fourth-degree Taylor polynomial for $W(x)$ about $x = 0$.

46. Using the table, estimate the value of $\displaystyle\int_0^2 f(x)\,dx$.

$f(0)$	$f'(0)$	$f''(0)$	$f'''(0)$	$f^{(4)}(0)$	$f^{(5)}(0)$
2	0	-1	0	-3	6

47. Let $f(t)$ be the so called *exponential integral*, a special function with applications to heat transfer and water flow,[9] which has the property that

$$f'(t) = t^{-1} e^t.$$

Use the series for e^t about $t = 0$ to show that

$$f(t) \approx \ln t + P_3(t) + C,$$

where P_3 is a third-degree polynomial. Find P_3. You need not find the constant C.

48. The electric potential, V, at a distance R along the axis perpendicular to the center of a charged disc with radius a and constant charge density σ, is given by

$$V = 2\pi\sigma(\sqrt{R^2 + a^2} - R).$$

Show that, for large R,

$$V \approx \frac{\pi a^2 \sigma}{R}.$$

49. The *gravitational field* at a point in space is the gravitational force that would be exerted on a unit mass placed there. We will assume that the gravitational field strength at a distance d away from a mass M is

$$\frac{GM}{d^2}$$

where G is constant. In this problem you will investigate the gravitational field strength, F, exerted by a system consisting of a large mass M and a small mass m, with a distance r between them. (See Figure 10.38.)

Figure 10.38

(a) Write an expression for the gravitational field strength, F, at the point P.

(b) Assuming r is small in comparison to R, expand F in a series in r/R.

(c) By discarding terms in $(r/R)^2$ and higher powers, explain why you can view the field as resulting from a single particle of mass $M + m$, plus a correction term. What is the position of the particle of mass $M + m$? Explain the sign of the correction term.

50. A thin disk of radius a and mass M lies horizontally; a particle of mass m is at a height h directly above the center of the disk. The gravitational force, F, exerted by the disk on the mass m is given by

$$F = \frac{2GMmh}{a^2}\left(\frac{1}{h} - \frac{1}{(a^2 + h^2)^{1/2}}\right),$$

where G is a constant. Assume $a < h$ and think of F as a function of a, with the other quantities constant.

(a) Expand F as a series in a/h. Give the first two nonzero terms.

(b) Show that the approximation for F obtained by using only the first nonzero term in the series is independent of the radius, a.

(c) If $a = 0.02h$, by what percentage does the approximation in part (a) differ from the approximation in part (b)?

51. When a body is near the surface of the earth, we usually assume that the force due to gravity on it is a constant mg, where m is the mass of the body and g is the acceleration due to gravity at sea level. For a body at a distance h above the surface of the earth, a more accurate expression for the force F is

$$F = \frac{mgR^2}{(R + h)^2}$$

where R is the radius of the earth. We will consider the situation in which the body is close to the surface of the earth so that h is much smaller than R.

(a) Show that $F \approx mg$.

(b) Express F as mg multiplied by a series in h/R.

(c) The first-order correction to the approximation $F \approx mg$ is obtained by taking the linear term in the series but no higher terms. How far above the surface of the earth can you go before the first-order correction changes the estimate $F \approx mg$ by more than 10%? (Assume $R = 6400$ km.)

52. Expand $f(x + h)$ and $g(x + h)$ in Taylor series and take a limit to confirm the product rule:

$$\frac{d}{dx}(f(x)g(x)) = f'(x)g(x) + f(x)g'(x).$$

53. Use Taylor expansions for $f(y + k)$ and $g(x + h)$ to confirm the chain rule:

$$\frac{d}{dx}(f(g(x))) = f'(g(x)) \cdot g'(x).$$

54. All the derivatives of g exist at $x = 0$ and g has a critical point at $x = 0$.

(a) Write the nth Taylor polynomial for g at $x = 0$.

(b) What does the Second Derivative test for local maxima and minima say?

(c) Use the Taylor polynomial to explain why the Second Derivative test works.

55. (Continuation of Problem 54) You may remember that the Second Derivative test tells us nothing when the second derivative is zero at the critical point. In this problem you will investigate that special case.

Assume g has the same properties as in Problem 54, and that, in addition, $g''(0) = 0$. What does the Taylor polynomial tell you about whether g has a local maximum or minimum at $x = 0$?

56. Use the Fourier series for the square wave

$$f(x) = \begin{cases} -1 & -\pi < x \leq 0 \\ 1 & 0 < x \leq \pi \end{cases}$$

to explain why the following sum must approach $\pi/4$ as $n \to \infty$:

$$1 - \frac{1}{3} + \frac{1}{5} - \frac{1}{7} + \cdots + (-1)^n\frac{1}{2n + 1}.$$

You may assume that the Fourier series converges to $f(x)$ at $x = \pi/2$.

57. Suppose that $f(x)$ is a differentiable periodic function of period 2π. Assume the Fourier series of f is differentiable term by term.

(a) If the Fourier coefficients of f are a_k and b_k, show that the Fourier coefficients of its derivative f' are kb_k and $-ka_k$.

(b) How are the amplitudes of the harmonics of f and f' related?

(c) How are the energy spectra of f and f' related?

58. If the Fourier coefficients of f are a_k and b_k, and the Fourier coefficients of g are c_k and d_k, and if A and B are real, show that the Fourier coefficients of $Af + Bg$ are $Aa_k + Bc_k$ and $Ab_k + Bd_k$.

59. Suppose that f is a periodic function of period 2π and that g is a horizontal shift of f, say $g(x) = f(x + c)$. Show that f and g have the same energy.

CAS Challenge Problems

60. (a) Use a computer algebra system to find $P_{10}(x)$ and $Q_{10}(x)$, the Taylor polynomials of degree 10 about $x = 0$ for $\sin^2 x$ and $\cos^2 x$.

(b) What similarities do you observe between the two polynomials? Explain your observation in terms of properties of sine and cosine.

61. (a) Use your computer algebra system to find $P_7(x)$ and $Q_7(x)$, the Taylor polynomials of degree 7 about $x = 0$ for $f(x) = \sin x$ and $g(x) = \sin x \cos x$.

(b) Find the ratio between the coefficient of x^3 in the two polynomials. Do the same for the coefficients of x^5 and x^7.

(c) Describe the pattern in the ratios that you computed in part (b). Explain it using the identity $\sin(2x) = 2\sin x \cos x$.

62. (a) Calculate the equation of the tangent line to the function $f(x) = x^2$ at $x = 2$. Do the same calculation for $g(x) = x^3 - 4x^2 + 8x - 7$ at $x = 1$ and for $h(x) = 2x^3 + 4x^2 - 3x + 7$ at $x = -1$.

(b) Use a computer algebra system to divide $f(x)$ by $(x - 2)^2$, giving your result in the form

$$\frac{f(x)}{(x - 2)^2} = q(x) + \frac{r(x)}{(x - 2)^2},$$

where $q(x)$ is the quotient and $r(x)$ is the remainder. In addition, divide $g(x)$ by $(x - 1)^2$ and $h(x)$ by $(x + 1)^2$.

(c) For each of the functions, f, g, h, compare your answers to part (a) with the remainder, $r(x)$. What do you notice? Make a conjecture about the tangent line to a polynomial $p(x)$ at the point $x = a$ and the remainder, $r(x)$, obtained from dividing $p(x)$ by $(x - a)^2$.

(d) Use the Taylor expansion of $p(x)$ about $x = a$ to prove your conjecture.[10]

63. Let $f(x) = \dfrac{x}{e^x - 1} + \dfrac{x}{2}$. Although the formula for f is not defined at $x = 0$, we can make f continuous by setting $f(0) = 1$. If we do this, f has a Taylor series about $x = 0$.

(a) Use a computer algebra system to find $P_{10}(x)$, the Taylor polynomial of degree 10 about $x = 0$ for f.

(b) What do you notice about the degrees of the terms in the polynomial? What property of f does this suggest?

(c) Prove that f has the property suggested by part (b).

64. Let $S(x) = \int_0^x \sin(t^2) \, dt$.

(a) Use a computer algebra system to find $P_{11}(x)$, the Taylor polynomial of degree 11 about $x = 0$, for $S(x)$.

(b) What is the percentage error in the approximation of $S(1)$ by $P_{11}(1)$? What about the approximation of $S(2)$ by $P_{11}(2)$?

PROJECTS FOR CHAPTER TEN

1. Shape of Planets

Rotation causes planets to bulge at the equator. Let α be the angle between the direction downward perpendicular to the surface and the direction toward the center of the planet. At a point on the surface with latitude θ, we have

$$\cos \alpha = \frac{1 - A\cos^2 \theta}{(1 - 2A\cos^2 \theta + A^2 \cos^2 \theta)^{1/2}},$$

where A is a small positive constant that depends on the particular planet. (For earth, $A = 0.0034$.)

(a) Expand $\cos \alpha$ in powers of A to show that $\cos \alpha \approx 1 - \frac{1}{2}A^2 \cos^2 \theta \sin^2 \theta$.

(b) Show that $\alpha \approx \frac{1}{2}A\sin(2\theta)$.

(c) By what percentage is the approximation in part (b) in error for the earth at latitudes $\theta = 0°$, $20°$, $40°$, $60°$, $80°$?

---

[10]See "Tangents Without Calculus" by Jorge Aarao, *The College Mathematics Journal* Vol. 31, No. 5, Nov. 2000 (Mathematical Association of America).

2. Machin's Formula and the Value of π

(a) In the 17th century, Machin obtained the formula: $\pi/4 = 4\arctan(1/5) - \arctan(1/239)$. Use a calculator to check this formula.

(b) Use the Taylor polynomial approximation of degree 5 to the arctangent function to approximate the value of π. (Note: In 1873 William Shanks used this approach to calculate π to 707 decimal places. Unfortunately, in 1946 it was found that he made an error in the 528th place. Currently, several billion decimal places are known.)

(c) Why do the two series for arctangent converge so rapidly here while the series used in Example 6 on page 555 converges so slowly?

(d) Now we prove Machin's formula using the tangent addition formula

$$\tan(A+B) = \frac{\tan A + \tan B}{1 - \tan A \tan B}.$$

(i) Let $A = \arctan(120/119)$ and $B = -\arctan(1/239)$ and show that

$$\arctan\left(\frac{120}{119}\right) - \arctan\left(\frac{1}{239}\right) = \arctan 1.$$

(ii) Let $A = B = \arctan(1/5)$ and show that

$$2\arctan\left(\frac{1}{5}\right) = \arctan\left(\frac{5}{12}\right).$$

Use a similar method to show that

$$4\arctan\left(\frac{1}{5}\right) = \arctan\left(\frac{120}{119}\right).$$

(iii) Derive Machin's formula.

3. Approximating the Derivative

In applications, the values of a function $f(x)$ are frequently known only at discrete values $x_0,\ x_0 \pm h,\ x_0 \pm 2h, \ldots$. Suppose we are interested in approximating the derivative $f'(x_0)$. The definition

$$f'(x_0) = \lim_{h \to 0} \frac{f(x_0 + h) - f(x_0)}{h}$$

suggests that for small h we can approximate $f'(x)$ as follows:

$$f'(x_0) \approx \frac{f(x_0 + h) - f(x_0)}{h}.$$

Such *finite-difference approximations* are used frequently in programming a computer to solve differential equations.[11]

Taylor series can be used to analyze the error in this approximation. Substituting

$$f(x_0 + h) = f(x_0) + f'(x_0)h + \frac{f''(x_0)}{2}h^2 + \cdots$$

into the approximation for $f'(x_0)$, we find

$$\frac{f(x_0 + h) - f(x_0)}{h} = f'(x_0) + \frac{f''(x_0)}{2}h + \cdots.$$

This suggests (and it can be proved) that the error in the approximation is bounded as follows:

$$\left| \frac{f(x_0 + h) - f(x_0)}{h} - f'(x_0) \right| \le \frac{Mh}{2},$$

---

[11]From Mark Kunka.

where

$$|f''(x)| \le M \qquad \text{for} \qquad |x - x_0| \le |h|.$$

Notice that as $h \to 0$, the error also goes to zero, provided M is bounded.

As an example, we take $f(x) = e^x$ and $x_0 = 0$, so $f'(x_0) = 1$. The error for various values of h are given in Table 10.2. We see that decreasing h by a factor of 10 decreases the error by a factor of about 10, as predicted by the error bound $Mh/2$.

Table 10.2

h	$(f(x_0 + h) - f(x_0))/h$	Error
10^{-1}	1.05171	5.171×10^{-2}
10^{-2}	1.00502	5.02×10^{-3}
10^{-3}	1.00050	5.0×10^{-4}
10^{-4}	1.00005	5.0×10^{-5}

(a) Using Taylor series, suggest an error bound for each of the following finite-difference approximations.

(i) $f'(x_0) \approx \dfrac{f(x_0) - f(x_0 - h)}{h}$

(ii) $f'(x_0) \approx \dfrac{f(x_0 + h) - f(x_0 - h)}{2h}$

(iii) $f'(x_0) \approx \dfrac{-f(x_0 + 2h) + 8f(x_0 + h) - 8f(x_0 - h) + f(x_0 - 2h)}{12h}$

(b) Use each of the formulas in part (a) to approximate the first derivative of e^x at $x = 0$ for $h = 10^{-1}, 10^{-2}, 10^{-3}, 10^{-4}$. As h is decreased by a factor of 10, how does the error decrease? Does this agree with the error bounds found in part (a)? Which is the most accurate formula?

(c) Repeat part (b) using $f(x) = 1/x$ and $x_0 = 10^{-5}$. Why are these formulas not good approximations anymore? Continue to decrease h by factors of 10. How small does h have to be before formula (iii) is the best approximation? At these smaller values of h, what changed to make the formulas accurate again?

Chapter Eleven

DIFFERENTIAL EQUATIONS

Contents

11.1 WHAT IS A DIFFERENTIAL EQUATION?

How Fast Does a Person Learn?

Suppose we are interested in how fast an employee learns a new task. One theory claims that the more the employee already knows of the task, the slower he or she learns. In other words, if $y\%$ is the percentage of the task that has already been mastered and dy/dt the rate at which the employee learns, then dy/dt decreases as y increases.

What can we say about y as a function of time, t? Figure 11.1 shows three graphs whose slope, dy/dt, decreases as y increases. Figure 11.1(a) represents an employee who starts learning at $t = 0$ and who eventually masters 100% of the task. Figure 11.1(b) represents an employee who starts later but eventually masters 100% of the task. Figure 11.1(c) represents an employee who starts learning at $t = 0$ but who does not master the whole task (since y levels off below 100%).

Figure 11.1: Possible graphs showing percentage of task learned, y, as a function of time, t

Setting up a Differential Equation to Model How a Person Learns

To describe more precisely how a person learns, we need more exact information about how dy/dt depends on y. Suppose, if time is measured in weeks, that

$$\text{Rate a person learns} \quad = \quad \text{Percentage of task not yet learned.}$$

Since y is the percentage learned by time t (in weeks), the percentage not yet learned by that time is $100 - y$. So we have

$$\frac{dy}{dt} = 100 - y.$$

Such an equation, which gives information about the rate of change of an unknown function, is called a *differential equation*.

Solving the Differential Equation Numerically

Suppose that the person starts learning at time zero, so $y = 0$ when $t = 0$. Then initially the person is learning at a rate

$$\frac{dy}{dt} = 100 - 0 = 100\% \text{ per week.}$$

In other words, if the person were to continue learning at this rate, the task would be mastered in a week. In fact, however, the rate at which the person learns decreases, so it takes more than a week to get close to mastering the task. Let's assume a five-day work week and that the 100% per week learning rate holds for the whole first day. (It does not, but we assume this for now.) One day is 1/5 of a week, so during the first day the person learns $100(1/5) = 20\%$ of the task. By the end of the first day, the rate at which the person learns has therefore been reduced to

$$\frac{dy}{dt} = 100 - 20 = 80\% \text{ per week.}$$

Thus, during the second day the person learns $80(1/5) = 16\%$, so by the end of the second day, the person knows $20 + 16 = 36\%$ of the task. Continuing in this fashion, we compute the approximate y-values[1] in Table 11.1.

---
[1] The values of y after 6, 7, 8, 9, ..., 19 days were computed by the same method, but omitted from the table.

Table 11.1   *Approximate percentage of task learned as a function of time*

Time (working days)	0	1	2	3	4	5	10	20
Percentage learned	0	20	36	48.8	59.0	67.2	89.3	98.8

A Formula for the Solution to the Differential Equation

A function $y = f(t)$ that satisfies the differential equation is called a *solution*. Figure 11.1(a) shows a possible solution, and Table 11.1 shows approximate numerical values of a solution to the equation

$$\frac{dy}{dt} = 100 - y.$$

Later in this chapter, we see how to obtain a formula for the solution:

$$y = 100 + Ce^{-t},$$

where C is a constant. To check that this formula is correct, we substitute into the differential equation, giving:

$$\text{Left side} = \frac{dy}{dt} = \frac{d}{dt}(100 + Ce^{-t}) = -Ce^{-t}$$
$$\text{Right side} = 100 - y = 100 - (100 + Ce^{-t}) = -Ce^{-t}.$$

Since we get the same result on both sides, $y = 100 + Ce^{-t}$ is a solution of this differential equation.

Finding the Arbitrary Constant: Initial Conditions

To find a value for the arbitrary constant C, we need an additional piece of information—usually the initial value of y. If, for example, we are told that $y = 0$ when $t = 0$, then substituting into

$$y = 100 + Ce^{-t}$$

shows us that

$$0 = 100 + Ce^{0}, \quad \text{so} \quad C = -100.$$

So the function $y = 100 - 100e^{-t}$ satisfies the differential equation *and* the condition that $y = 0$ when $t = 0$.

The Family of Solutions

Any solution to this differential equation is of the form $y = 100 + Ce^{-t}$ for some constant C. Like a family of antiderivatives, this family contains an arbitrary constant, C. We say that the *general solution* to the differential equation $dy/dt = 100 - y$ is the family of functions $y = 100 + Ce^{-t}$. The solution $y = 100 - 100e^{-t}$ that satisfies the differential equation together with the *initial condition* that $y = 0$ when $t = 0$ is called a *particular solution*. The differential equation and the initial condition together are called an *initial value problem*. Several members of the family of solutions are graphed in Figure 11.2. The horizontal solution curve when $C = 0$ is called an *equilibrium solution*.

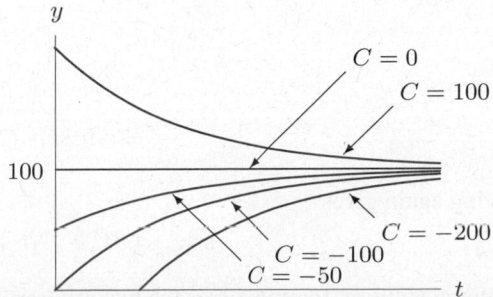

Figure 11.2: Solution curves for $dy/dt = 100 - y$:
Members of the family $y = 100 + Ce^{-t}$

First- and Second-Order Differential Equations

First, some more definitions. We often write y' to represent the derivative of y. The differential equation

$$y' = 100 - y$$

is called *first-order* because it involves the first derivative, but no higher derivatives. By contrast, if s is the height (in meters) of a body moving under the force of gravity and t is time (in seconds), then

$$\frac{d^2 s}{dt^2} = -9.8.$$

This is a *second-order* differential equation because it involves the second derivative of the unknown function, $s = f(t)$, but no higher derivatives.

Example 1   Show that $y = e^{2t}$ is not a solution to the second-order differential equation

$$\frac{d^2 y}{dt^2} + 4y = 0.$$

Solution   To decide whether the function $y = e^{2t}$ is a solution, substitute it into the differential equation:

$$\frac{d^2 y}{dt^2} + 4y = 2(2e^{2t}) + 4e^{2t} = 8e^{2t}.$$

Since $8e^{2t}$ is not identically zero, $y = e^{2t}$ is not a solution.

How Many Arbitrary Constants Should We Expect in the Family of Solutions?

Since a differential equation involves the derivative of an unknown function, solving it usually involves antidifferentiation, which introduces arbitrary constants. The solution to a first-order differential equation usually involves one antidifferentiation and one arbitrary constant (for example, the C in $y = 100 + Ce^{-t}$). Picking out one particular solution involves knowing one additional piece of information, such as an initial condition. Solving a second-order differential equation generally involves two antidifferentiations and so two arbitrary constants. Consequently, finding a particular solution usually involves two initial conditions.

For example, if s is the height (in meters) of a body above the surface of the earth at time t (in seconds), then

$$\frac{d^2 s}{dt^2} = -9.8.$$

Integrating gives

$$\frac{ds}{dt} = -9.8t + C_1,$$

and integrating again gives

$$s = -4.9t^2 + C_1 t + C_2.$$

Thus the general solution for s involves the two arbitrary constants C_1 and C_2. We can find C_1 and C_2 if we are told, for example, that the initial velocity is 30 meters per second upward and that the initial position is 5 meters above the ground. In this case, $C_1 = 30$ and $C_2 = 5$.

Exercises and Problems for Section 11.1

Exercises

1. Is $y = x^3$ a solution to the differential equation

$$xy' - 3y = 0?$$

2. Determine whether each function is a solution to the differential equation and justify your answer:

$$x\frac{dy}{dx} = 4y.$$

   (a) $y = x^4$ (b) $y = x^4 + 3$
   (c) $y = x^3$ (d) $y = 7x^4$

3. Determine whether each function is a solution to the differential equation and justify your answer:

$$y\frac{dy}{dx} = 6x^2.$$

   (a) $y = 4x^3$ (b) $y = 2x^{3/2}$ (c) $y = 6x^{3/2}$

4. Show that $y(x) = Ae^{\lambda x}$ is a solution to the equation $y' = \lambda y$ for any value of A.

5. Show that $y = \sin 2t$ satisfies

$$\frac{d^2y}{dt^2} + 4y = 0.$$

6. Show that, for any constant P_0, the function $P = P_0 e^t$ satisfies the equation

$$\frac{dP}{dt} = P.$$

7. Use implicit differentiation to show that $x^2 + y^2 = r^2$ is a solution to the differential equation $dy/dx = -x/y$.

8. A quantity Q satisfies the differential equation

$$\frac{dQ}{dt} = \frac{t}{Q} - 0.5.$$

   (a) If $Q = 8$ when $t = 2$, use dQ/dt to determine whether Q is increasing or decreasing at $t = 2$.
   (b) Use your work in part (a) to estimate the value of Q when $t = 3$. Assume the rate of change stays approximately constant over the interval from $t = 2$ to $t = 3$.

9. Fill in the missing values in the table given if you know that $dy/dt = 0.5y$. Assume the rate of growth given by dy/dt is approximately constant over each unit time interval and that the initial value of y is 8.

t	0	1	2	3	4
y	8				

10. Use the method that generated the data in Table 11.1 on page 587 to fill in the missing y-values for $t = 6, 7, \ldots, 19$ days.

In Exercises 11–14, find the particular solution to the differential equation, given the general solution and an initial condition. (C is the constant of integration.)

11. $x(t) = Ce^{3t}; x(0) = 5$

12. $P = C/t; P = 5$ when $t = 3$

13. $y = \sqrt{2t + C}$; the solution curve passes through $(1, 3)$

14. $Q = 1/(Ct + C); Q = 4$ when $t = 2$

Problems

15. Show that $y = A + Ce^{kt}$ is a solution to the equation

$$\frac{dy}{dt} = k(y - A).$$

16. Find the value(s) of ω for which $y = \cos \omega t$ satisfies

$$\frac{d^2y}{dt^2} + 9y = 0.$$

17. Show that any function of the form

$$x = C_1 \cosh \omega t + C_2 \sinh \omega t$$

   satisfies the differential equation

$$x'' - \omega^2 x = 0.$$

18. Suppose $Q = Ce^{kt}$ satisfies the differential equation

$$\frac{dQ}{dt} = -0.03Q.$$

   What (if anything) does this tell you about the values of C and k?

19. Find the values of k for which $y = x^2 + k$ is a solution to the differential equation

$$2y - xy' = 10.$$

20. For what values of k (if any) does $y = 5 + 3e^{kx}$ satisfy the differential equation

$$\frac{dy}{dx} = 10 - 2y?$$

21. (a) For what values of C and n (if any) is $y = Cx^n$ a solution to the differential equation

$$x\frac{dy}{dx} - 3y = 0?$$

(b) If the solution satisfies $y = 40$ when $x = 2$, what more (if anything) can you say about C and n?

22. (a) Find the value of A so that the equation $y' - xy - x = 0$ has a solution of the form $y(x) = A + Be^{x^2/2}$ for any constant B.

(b) If $y(0) = 1$, find B.

23. In Figure 11.3, the height, y, of the hanging cable above the horizontal line satisfies

$$\frac{d^2y}{dx^2} = k\sqrt{1 + \left(\frac{dy}{dx}\right)^2}.$$

(a) Show that $y = \dfrac{e^x + e^{-x}}{2}$ satisfies this differential equation if $k = 1$.

(b) For general k, one solution to this differential equation is of the form

$$y = \frac{e^{Ax} + e^{-Ax}}{2A}.$$

Substitute this expression for y into the differential equation to find A in terms of k.

Figure 11.3

24. Match solutions and differential equations. (Note: Each equation may have more than one solution.)

(a) $y'' - y = 0$ (I) $y = e^x$

(b) $x^2y'' + 2xy' - 2y = 0$ (II) $y = x^3$

(c) $x^2y'' - 6y = 0$ (III) $y = e^{-x}$

                           (IV) $y = x^{-2}$

25. Pick out which functions are solutions to which differential equations. (Note: Functions may be solutions to more than one equation or to none; an equation may have more than one solution.)

(a) $\dfrac{dy}{dx} = -2y$ (I) $y = 2\sin x$

(b) $\dfrac{dy}{dx} = 2y$ (II) $y = \sin 2x$

(c) $\dfrac{d^2y}{dx^2} = 4y$ (III) $y = e^{2x}$

(d) $\dfrac{d^2y}{dx^2} = -4y$ (IV) $y = e^{-2x}$

26. Families of curves often arise as solutions of differential equations. Match the families of curves with the differential equations of which they are solutions.

(a) $\dfrac{dy}{dx} = \dfrac{y}{x}$ (I) $y = xe^{kx}$

(b) $\dfrac{dy}{dx} = ky$ (II) $y = x^k$

(c) $\dfrac{dy}{dx} = ky + \dfrac{y}{x}$ (III) $y = e^{kx}$

(d) $\dfrac{dy}{dx} = \dfrac{ky}{x}$ (IV) $y = kx$

27. Is $y(x) = e^{3x}$ the general solution of $y' = 3y$?

28. (a) Let $y = A + Be^{-2t}$. For what values of A and B, if any, is y a solution to the differential equation

$$\frac{dy}{dt} = 100 - 2y?$$

Give the general solution to the differential equation.

(b) If the solution satisfies $y = 85$ when $t = 0$, what more (if anything) can you say about A and B? Give the particular solution to the differential equation with this initial condition.

Strengthen Your Understanding

In Problems 29–30, explain what is wrong with the statement.

29. $Q = 6e^{4t}$ is the general solution to the differential equation $dQ/dt = 4Q$.

30. If $dx/dt = 1/x$ and $x = 3$ when $t = 0$, then x is a decreasing function of t.

In Problems 31–37, give an example of:

31. A differential equation with an initial condition.

32. A second-order differential equation.

33. A differential equation and two different solutions to the differential equation.

34. A differential equation that has a trigonometric function as a solution.

35. A differential equation that has a logarithmic function as a solution.

36. A differential equation all of whose solutions are increasing and concave up.

37. A differential equation all of whose solutions have their critical points on the parabola $y = x^2$.

Are the statements in Problems 38–39 true or false? Give an explanation for your answer.

38. If $y = f(t)$ is a particular solution to a first-order differential equation, then the general solution is $y = f(t) + C$, where C is an arbitrary constant.

39. Polynomials are never solutions to differential equations.

In Problems 40–47, is the statement true or false? Assume that $y = f(x)$ is a solution to the equation $dy/dx = g(x)$. If the statement is true, explain how you know. If the statement is false, give a counterexample.

40. If $g(x)$ is increasing for all x, then the graph of f is concave up for all x.

41. If $g(x)$ is increasing for $x > 0$, then so is $f(x)$.

42. If $g(0) = 1$ and $g(x)$ is increasing for $x \geq 0$, then $f(x)$ is also increasing for $x \geq 0$.

43. If $g(x)$ is periodic, then $f(x)$ is also periodic.

44. If $\lim_{x \to \infty} g(x) = 0$, then $\lim_{x \to \infty} f(x) = 0$.

45. If $\lim_{x \to \infty} g(x) = \infty$, then $\lim_{x \to \infty} f(x) = \infty$.

46. If $g(x)$ is even, then so is $f(x)$.

47. If $g(x)$ is even, then $f(x)$ is odd.

11.2 SLOPE FIELDS

In this section, we see how to visualize a first-order differential equation. We start with the equation

$$\frac{dy}{dx} = y.$$

Any solution to this differential equation has the property that the slope at any point is equal to the y-coordinate at that point. (That's what the equation $dy/dx = y$ is telling us!) If the solution goes through the point $(0, 0.5)$, its slope there is 0.5; if it goes through a point with $y = 1.5$, its slope there is 1.5. See Figure 11.4.

In Figure 11.4 a small line segment is drawn at each of the marked points showing the slope of the curve there. Imagine drawing many of these line segments, but leaving out the curves; this gives the *slope field* for the equation $dy/dx = y$ in Figure 11.5. From this picture, we can see that above the x-axis, the slopes are all positive (because y is positive there), and they increase as we move upward (as y increases). Below the x-axis, the slopes are all negative and get more so as we move downward. On any horizontal line (where y is constant) the slopes are constant.

Figure 11.4: Solutions to $dy/dx = y$

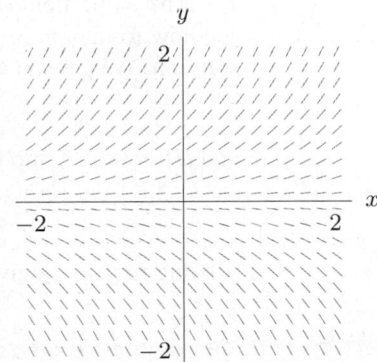

Figure 11.5: Slope field for $dy/dx = y$

In the slope field we can see the ghost of the solution curve lurking. Start anywhere on the plane and move so that the slope lines are tangent to our path; we trace out one of the solution curves. We think of the slope field as a set of signposts pointing in the direction we should go at each point. In this case, the slope field should trace out exponential curves of the form $y = Ce^x$, the solutions to the differential equation $dy/dx = y$.

Example 1   Figure 11.6 shows the slope field of the differential equation $dy/dx = 2x$.

(a) How does the slope field vary as we move around the xy-plane?

(b) Compare the solution curves sketched on the slope field with the formula for the solutions.

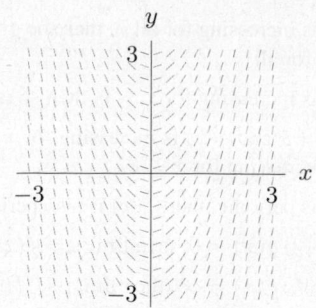

Figure 11.6: Slope field for $dy/dx = 2x$

Figure 11.7: Some solutions to $dy/dx = 2x$

Solution

(a) In Figure 11.6 we notice that on a vertical line (where x is constant) the slopes are constant. This is because in this differential equation dy/dx depends on x only. (In the previous example, $dy/dx = y$, the slopes depended on y only.)

(b) The solution curves in Figure 11.7 look like parabolas. By antidifferentiation, we see that the solution to the differential equation $dy/dx = 2x$ is

$$y = \int 2x\, dx = x^2 + C,$$

so the solution curves really are parabolas.

Example 2   Using the slope field, guess the form of the solution curves of the differential equation

$$\frac{dy}{dx} = -\frac{x}{y}.$$

Solution   The slope field is shown in Figure 11.8. On the y-axis, where x is 0, the slope is 0. On the x-axis, where y is 0, the line segments are vertical and the slope is infinite. At the origin the slope is undefined, and there is no line segment.

The slope field suggests that the solution curves are circles centered at the origin. Later we see how to obtain the solution analytically, but even without this, we can check that the circle is a solution. We take the circle of radius r,

$$x^2 + y^2 = r^2,$$

and differentiate implicitly, thinking of y as a function of x. Using the chain rule, we get

$$2x + 2y \cdot \frac{dy}{dx} = 0.$$

Solving for dy/dx gives our differential equation,

$$\frac{dy}{dx} = -\frac{x}{y}.$$

This tells us that $x^2 + y^2 = r^2$ is a solution to the differential equation.

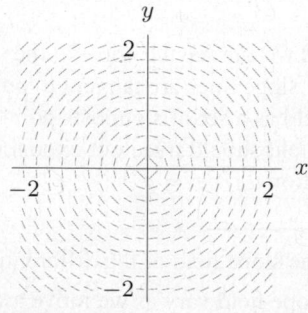

Figure 11.8: Slope field for $dy/dx = -x/y$

The previous example shows that the solution to a differential equation may be an implicit function.

Example 3   The slope fields of $dy/dt = 2 - y$ and $dy/dt = t/y$ are in Figures 11.9 and 11.10.

(a) On each slope field, sketch solution curves with initial conditions
      (i) $y = 1$ when $t = 0$ (ii) $y = 0$ when $t = 1$ (iii) $y = 3$ when $t = 0$

(b) For each solution curve, what can you say about the long-run behavior of y? For example, does $\lim_{t \to \infty} y$ exist? If so, what is its value?

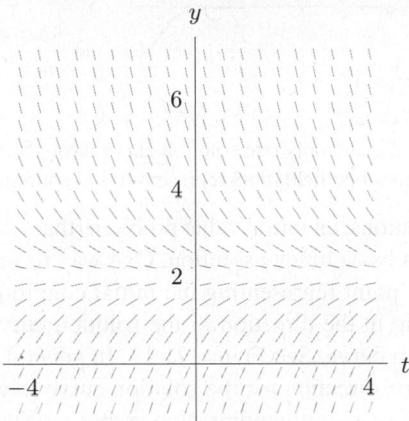

Figure 11.9: Slope field for $dy/dt = 2 - y$

Figure 11.10: Slope field for $dy/dt = t/y$

Solution   (a) See Figures 11.11 and 11.12.

(b) For $dy/dt = 2 - y$, all solution curves have $y = 2$ as a horizontal asymptote, so $\lim_{t \to \infty} y = 2$.

For $dy/dt = t/y$, as $t \to \infty$, it appears that either $y \to t$ or $y \to -t$.

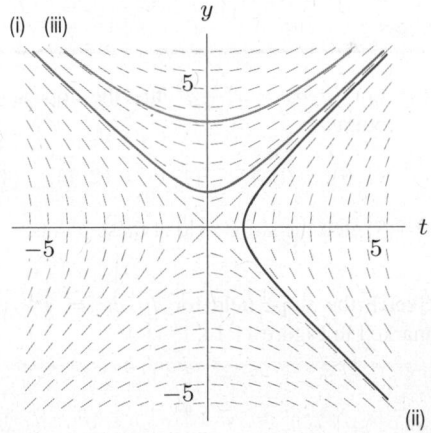

Figure 11.11: Solution curves for $dy/dt = 2 - y$

Figure 11.12: Solution curves for $dy/dt = t/y$

Existence and Uniqueness of Solutions

Since differential equations are used to model many real situations, the question of whether a solution is unique can have great practical importance. If we know how the velocity of a satellite is changing, can we know its velocity at any future time? If we know the initial population of a city and we know how the population is changing, can we predict the population in the future? Common sense says yes: if we know the initial value of some quantity and we know exactly how it is changing, we should be able to figure out its future value.

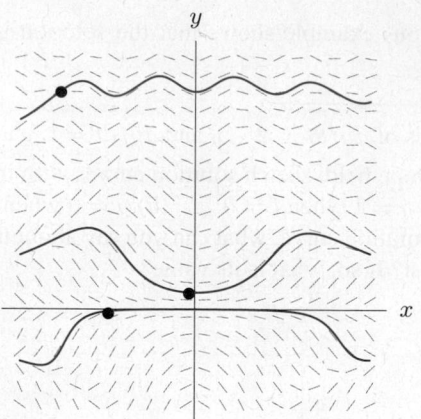

Figure 11.13: There's one and only one solution curve through each
point in the plane for this slope field (dots represent initial conditions).

In the language of differential equations, an initial value problem (that is, a differential equation and an initial condition) almost always has a unique solution. One way to see this is by looking at the slope field. Imagine starting at the point representing the initial condition. Through that point there is usually a line segment pointing in the direction of the solution curve. By following these line segments, we trace out the solution curve. See Figure 11.13. In general, at each point there is one line segment and therefore only one direction for the solution curve to go. The solution curve *exists* and is *unique* provided we are given an initial point. Notice that even though we can draw the solution curves, we may have no simple formula for them.

It can be shown that if the slope field is continuous as we move from point to point in the plane, we can be sure that a solution curve exists everywhere. Ensuring that each point has only one solution curve through it requires a slightly stronger condition.

Exercises and Problems for Section 11.2

Exercises

1. (a) For $dy/dx = x^2 - y^2$, find the slope at the following points:

$$(1,0), \quad (0,1), \quad (1,1), \quad (2,1), \quad (1,2), \quad (2,2)$$

(b) Sketch the slope field at these points.

2. Sketch the slope field for $dy/dx = x/y$ at the points marked in Figure 11.14.

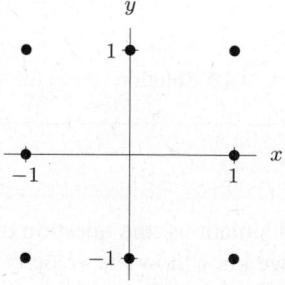

Figure 11.14

3. Sketch the slope field for $dy/dx = y^2$ at the points marked in Figure 11.15.

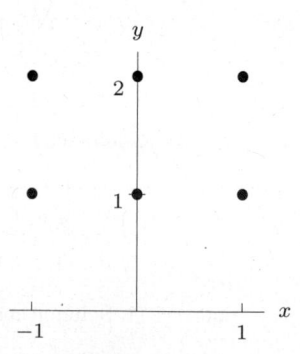

Figure 11.15

4. Match each of the slope field segments in (I)–(VI) with one or more of the differential equations in (a)–(f).

(a) $y' = e^{-x^2}$

(b) $y' = \cos y$

(c) $y' = \cos(4 - y)$

(d) $y' = y(4 - y)$

(e) $y' = y(3 - y)$

(f) $y' = x(3 - x)$

(I)

(II)

(III)

(IV)

(V)

(VI)

5. Sketch three solution curves for each of the slope fields in Figures 11.16 and 11.17.

Figure 11.16

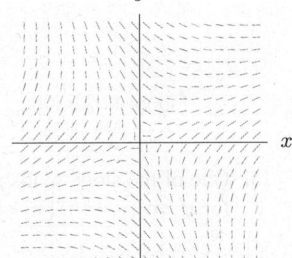

Figure 11.17

6. Sketch three solution curves for each of the slope fields in Figure 11.18.

Figure 11.18

7. One of the slope fields in Figure 11.18 is the slope field for $y' = x^2 - y^2$. Which one? On this field, where is the point $(0, 1)$? The point $(1, 0)$? (Assume that the x and y scales are the same.) Sketch the line $x = 1$ and the solution curve passing through $(0, 1)$ until it crosses $x = 1$.

8. The slope field for the equation $y' = x(y - 1)$ is shown in Figure 11.19.

(a) Sketch the solutions that pass through the points

  (i) $(0, 1)$ (ii) $(0, -1)$ (iii) $(0, 0)$

(b) From your sketch, write down the equation of the solution with $y(0) = 1$.

(c) Check your solution to part (b) by substituting it into the differential equation.

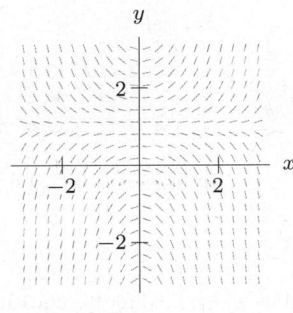

Figure 11.19

9. The slope field for the equation $y' = x + y$ is shown in Figure 11.20.

(a) Sketch the solutions that pass through the points

  (i) $(0, 0)$ (ii) $(-3, 1)$ (iii) $(-1, 0)$

(b) From your sketch, write the equation of the solution passing through $(-1, 0)$.

(c) Check your solution to part (b) by substituting it into the differential equation.

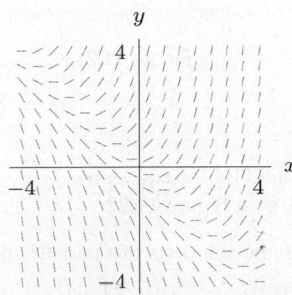

Figure 11.20: Slope field for $y' = x + y$

Problems

10. Sketch a slope field with the following properties. (Draw at least ten line segments, including some with $x < 0$, with $x > 0$, and with $x = 0$.)

$$\frac{dy}{dx} > 0 \text{ for } x < 0,$$

$$\frac{dy}{dx} < 0 \text{ for } x > 0,$$

$$\frac{dy}{dx} = 0 \text{ for } x = 0.$$

11. Sketch a slope field with the following properties. (Draw at least ten line segments, including some with $P < 2$, with $2 < P < 5$, and with $P > 5$.)

$$\frac{dP}{dt} > 0 \text{ for } 2 < P < 5,$$

$$\frac{dP}{dt} < 0 \text{ for } P < 2 \text{ or } P > 5,$$

$$\frac{dP}{dt} = 0 \text{ for } P = 2 \text{ and } P = 5.$$

12. (a) Sketch the slope field for the equation $y' = x - y$ in Figure 11.21 at the points indicated.
(b) Find the equation for the solution that passes through the point $(1, 0)$.

Figure 11.21

13. The slope field for the equation $dP/dt = 0.1P(10 - P)$, for $P \geq 0$, is in Figure 11.22.

(a) Sketch the solutions that pass through the points

   (i) $(0,0)$ (ii) $(1,4)$ (iii) $(4,1)$
   (iv) $(-5,1)$ (v) $(-2,12)$ (vi) $(-2,10)$

(b) For which positive values of P are the solutions increasing? Decreasing? If $P(0) = 5$, what is the limiting value of P as t gets large?

Figure 11.22

14. The slope field for $y' = 0.5(1 + y)(2 - y)$ is shown in Figure 11.23.

(a) Plot the following points on the slope field:
   (i)   the origin   (ii) $(0, 1)$ (iii) $(1, 0)$
   (iv) $(0, -1)$ (v) $(0, -5/2)$ (vi) $(0, 5/2)$

(b) Plot solution curves through the points in part (a).
(c) For which regions are all solution curves increasing? For which regions are all solution curves decreasing? When can the solution curves have horizontal tangents? Explain why, using both the slope field and the differential equation.

Figure 11.23: Note: x and y scales are equal

15. One of the slope fields in Figure 11.24 is the slope field for $y' = (x + y)/(x - y)$. Which one?

Figure 11.24

16. The slope field for $y' = (\sin x)(\sin y)$ is in Figure 11.25.

   (a) Sketch the solutions that pass through the points

      (i) $(0, -2)$ (ii) $(0, \pi)$

   (b) What is the equation of the solution that passes through $(0, n\pi)$, where n is any integer?

Figure 11.25

17. Match the slope fields in Figure 11.26 with their differential equations. Explain your reasoning.

   (a) $y' = -y$ **(b)** $y' = y$ **(c)** $y' = x$

   (d) $y' = 1/y$ **(e)** $y' = y^2$

18. Match the slope fields in Figure 11.27 to the corresponding differential equations:

   (a) $y' = xe^{-x}$ **(b)** $y' = \sin x$ **(c)** $y' = \cos x$

   (d) $y' = x^2 e^{-x}$ **(e)** $y' = e^{-x^2}$ **(f)** $y' = e^{-x}$

(I)

(II)

(III)

(IV)
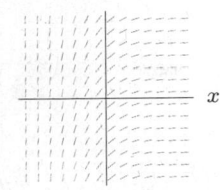

(V)
(VI)

Figure 11.27

(I)

(II)

(III)

(IV)

(V)

Figure 11.26: Each slope field is graphed for $-5 \le x \le 5, -5 \le y \le 5$

In Problems 19–22, match an equation with the slope field.

   (a) $y' = 0.05y(10 - y)$ **(b)** $y' = 0.05x(10 - x)$

   (c) $y' = 0.05y(5 - y)$ **(d)** $y' = 0.05x(5 - x)$

   (e) $y' = 0.05y(y - 10)$ **(f)** $y' = 0.05x(x - 10)$

   (g) $y' = 0.05y(y - 5)$ **(h)** $y' = 0.05x(x - 5)$

   (i) $y' = 0.05x(y - 5)$

19.

20.

21.

22.

23. Match the following differential equations with the slope fields shown in Figure 11.28. Explain your reasoning.

(a) $\dfrac{dy}{dx} = e^{x^2}$ **(b)** $\dfrac{dy}{dx} = e^{-2x^2}$

(c) $\dfrac{dy}{dx} = e^{-x^2/2}$ **(d)** $\dfrac{dy}{dx} = e^{-0.5x}\cos x$

(e) $\dfrac{dy}{dx} = \dfrac{1}{(1 + 0.5\cos x)^2}$

(f) $\dfrac{dy}{dx} = -e^{-x^2}$

(I)

(II)

(III)

(IV)

(V)

(VI)

Figure 11.28: Each slope field is graphed for $-3 \le x \le 3$, $-3 \le y \le 3$

24. The Gompertz equation, which models growth of animal tumors, is $y' = -ay\ln(y/b)$, where a and b are positive constants. Use Figures 11.29 and 11.30 to write a paragraph describing the similarities and/or differences between solutions to the Gompertz equation with $a = 1$ and $b = 2$ and solutions to the equation $y' = y(2 - y)$.

Figure 11.29: Slope field for $y' = -y\ln(y/2)$

Figure 11.30: Slope field for $y' = y(2 - y)$

Strengthen Your Understanding

In Problems 25–26, explain what is wrong with the statement.

25. There is a differential equation that has $y = x$ as one of its solutions and a slope field with a slope of 0 at the point $(1, 1)$.

26. Figure 11.31 shows the slope field of $y' = y$.

Figure 11.31

In Problems 27–30, give an example of:

27. A differential equation whose slope field has all the slopes positive.

28. A differential equation that has a slope field with all the slopes above the x-axis positive and all the slopes below the x-axis negative.

29. A slope field for a differential equation where the formula for dy/dx depends on x but not y.

30. A slope field for a differential equation where the formula for dy/dx depends on y but not x.

Are the statements in Problems 31–35 true or false? Give an explanation for your answer.

31. All solutions to the differential equation whose slope field is in Figure 11.32 have $\lim_{x \to \infty} y = \infty$.

Figure 11.32

32. All solutions to the differential equation whose slope field is in Figure 11.33 have $\lim_{x \to \infty} y = 0$.

Figure 11.33

33. All solutions to the differential equation whose slope field is in Figure 11.34 have the same limiting value as $x \to \infty$.

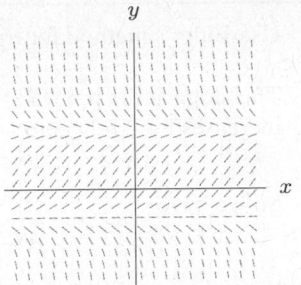

Figure 11.34

34. The solutions of the differential equation $dy/dx = x^2 + y^2 + 1$ are increasing at every point.

35. The solutions of the differential equation $dy/dx = x^2 + y^2 + 1$ are concave up at every point.

In Problems 36–44, decide whether the statement is true or false. Assume that $y = f(x)$ is a solution to the equation $dy/dx = 2x - y$. Justify your answer.

36. If $f(a) = b$, the slope of the graph of f at (a, b) is $2a - b$.

37. $f'(x) = 2x - f(x)$.

38. There could be more than one value of x such that $f'(x) = 1$ and $f(x) = 5$.

39. If $y = f(x)$, then $d^2y/dx^2 = 2 - (2x - y)$.

40. If $f(1) = 5$, then $(1, 5)$ could be a critical point of f.

41. The graph of f is decreasing whenever it lies above the line $y = 2x$ and is increasing whenever it lies below the line $y = 2x$.

42. All the inflection points of f lie on the line $y = 2x - 2$.

43. If $g(x)$ is another solution to the differential equation $dy/dx = 2x - y$, then $g(x) = f(x) + C$.

44. If $g(x)$ is a different solution to the differential equation $dy/dx = 2x - y$, then $\lim_{x \to \infty}(g(x) - f(x)) = 0$. [Hint: Show that $w = g(x) - f(x)$ satisfies the differential equation $dw/dx = -w$.]

11.3 EULER'S METHOD

In the preceding section we saw how to sketch a solution curve to a differential equation using its slope field. In this section we compute points on a solution curve numerically using *Euler's method*. (Leonhard Euler was an eighteenth-century Swiss mathematician.) In Section 11.4 we find formulas for some solution curves.

Here's the concept behind Euler's method. Think of the slope field as a set of signposts directing you across the plane. Pick a starting point (corresponding to the initial value), and calculate the slope at that point using the differential equation. This slope is a signpost telling you the direction to take. Head off a small distance in that direction. Stop and look at the new signpost. Recalculate the slope from the differential equation, using the coordinates of the new point. Change direction to correspond to the new slope, and move another small distance, and so on.

Example 1   Use Euler's method for $dy/dx = y$. Start at the point $P_0 = (0, 1)$ and take $\Delta x = 0.1$.

Solution   The slope at the point $P_0 = (0, 1)$ is $dy/dx = 1$. (See Figure 11.35.) As we move from P_0 to P_1, y increases by Δy, where

$$\Delta y = (\text{slope at } P_0)\Delta x = 1(0.1) = 0.1.$$

So we have

$$y\text{-value at } P_1 = (y \text{ value at } P_0) + \Delta y = 1 + 0.1 = 1.1.$$

Table 11.2   *Euler's method for $dy/dx = y$, starting at $(0, 1)$*

	x	y	$\Delta y = (\text{Slope})\Delta x$
P_0	0	1	$0.1 = (1)(0.1)$
P_1	0.1	1.1	$0.11 = (1.1)(0.1)$
P_2	0.2	1.21	$0.121 = (1.21)(0.1)$
P_3	0.3	1.331	$0.1331 = (1.331)(0.1)$
P_4	0.4	1.4641	$0.14641 = (1.4641)(0.1)$
P_5	0.5	1.61051	$0.161051 = (1.61051)(0.1)$

Figure 11.35: Euler's approximate solution to $dy/dx = y$

Thus the point P_1 is $(0.1, 1.1)$. Now, using the differential equation again, we see that

$$\text{slope at } P_1 = 1.1,$$

so if we move to P_2, then y changes by

$$\Delta y = (\text{slope at } P_1)\Delta x = (1.1)(0.1) = 0.11.$$

This means

$$y\text{-value at } P_2 = (y \text{ value at } P_1) + \Delta y = 1.1 + 0.11 = 1.21.$$

Thus P_2 is $(0.2, 1.21)$. Continuing gives the results in Table 11.2.

Since the solution curves of $dy/dx = y$ are exponentials, they are concave up and bend upward away from the line segments of the slope field. Therefore, in this case, Euler's method produces y-values which are too small.

Notice that Euler's method calculates approximate y-values for points on a solution curve; it does not give a formula for y in terms of x.

Example 2   Show that Euler's method for $dy/dx = y$ starting at $(0, 1)$ and using two steps with $\Delta x = 0.05$ gives $y \approx 1.1025$ when $x = 0.1$.

Solution   At $(0, 1)$, the slope is 1 and $\Delta y = (1)(0.05) = 0.05$, so new $y = 1 + 0.05 = 1.05$. At $(0.05, 1.05)$, the slope is 1.05 and $\Delta y = (1.05)(0.05) = 0.0525$, so new $y = 1.05 + 0.0525 = 1.1025$ at $x = 0.1$.

In general, dy/dx may be a function of both x and y. Euler's method still works, as the next example shows.

Example 3   Approximate four points on the solution curve to $dy/dx = -x/y$ starting at $(0, 1)$; use $\Delta x = 0.1$. Are the approximate values overestimates or underestimates?

Solution   The results from Euler's method are in Table 11.3, along with the y-values (to two decimals) calculated from the equation of the circle $x^2 + y^2 = 1$, which is the solution curve through $(0, 1)$. Since the curve is concave down, the approximate y-values are above the exact ones. (See Figure 11.36.)

Table 11.3   *Euler's method for $dy/dx = -x/y$, starting at $(0, 1)$*

x	Approx. y-value	$\Delta y = (Slope)\Delta x$	True y-value
0	1	$0 = (0)(0.1)$	1
0.1	1	$-0.01 = (-0.1/1)(0.1)$	0.99
0.2	0.99	$-0.02 = (-0.2/0.99)(0.1)$	0.98
0.3	0.97		0.95

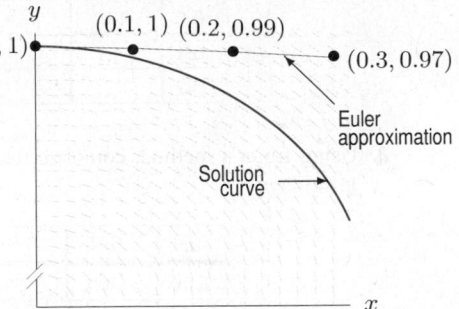

Figure 11.36: Euler's approximate solution to $dy/dx = -x/y$

The Accuracy of Euler's Method

To improve the accuracy of Euler's method, we choose a smaller step size, Δx. Let's go back to the differential equation $dy/dx = y$ and compare the exact and approximate values for different Δx's. The exact solution going through the point $(0, 1)$ is $y = e^x$, so the exact values are calculated using this function. (See Figure 11.37.) Where $x = 0.1$,

$$\text{Exact } y\text{-value } = e^{0.1} \approx 1.1051709.$$

In Example 1 we had $\Delta x = 0.1$, and where $x = 0.1$,

$$\text{Approximate } y\text{-value} = 1.1, \quad \text{so the error} \approx 0.005.$$

In Example 2 we decreased Δx to 0.05. After two steps, $x = 0.1$, and we had

$$\text{Approximate } y\text{-value} = 1.1025, \quad \text{so error} \approx 0.00267.$$

Thus, it appears that halving the step size has approximately halved the error.

Figure 11.37: Euler's approximate solution to $dy/dx = y$

The *error* in using Euler's method over a fixed interval is Exact value $-$ Approximate value. If the number of steps used is n, the error is approximately proportional to $1/n$.

Just as there are more accurate numerical integration methods than left and right Riemann sums, there are more accurate methods than Euler's for approximating solution curves. However, Euler's method is all we need.

Exercises and Problems for Section 11.3

Exercises

1. Using Euler's method, complete the following table for $y' = (x - 2)(y - 3)$.

x	y	y'
0.0	4.0	
0.1		
0.2		

2. Using Euler's method, complete the following table for $y' = 4xy$.

x	y	y'
1.00	−3.0	
1.01		
1.02		

3. A population, P, in millions, is 1500 at time $t = 0$ and its growth is governed by

$$\frac{dP}{dt} = 0.00008P(1900 - P).$$

Use Euler's method with $\Delta t = 1$ to estimate P at time $t = 1, 2, 3$.

4. (a) Use Euler's method to approximate the value of y at $x = 1$ on the solution curve to the differential equation $dy/dx = 3$ that passes through $(0, 2)$. Use $\Delta x = 0.2$.

   (b) What is the solution to the differential equation $dy/dx = 3$ with initial condition $y = 2$ when $x = 0$?

   (c) What is the error for the Euler's method approximation at $x = 1$?

   (d) Explain why Euler's method is exact in this case.

5. (a) Use five steps of Euler's method to determine an approximate solution for the differential equation $dy/dx = y - x$ with initial condition $y(0) = 10$, using step size $\Delta x = 0.2$. What is the estimated value of y at $x = 1$?

   (b) Does the solution to the differential equation appear to be concave up or concave down?

   (c) Are the approximate values overestimates or underestimates?

6. (a) Use ten steps of Euler's method to determine an approximate solution for the differential equation $y' = x^3$, $y(0) = 0$, using a step size $\Delta x = 0.1$.

   (b) What is the exact solution? Compare it to the computed approximation.

   (c) Use a sketch of the slope field for this equation to explain the results of part (b).

7. Consider the differential equation $y' = x + y$ whose slope field is in Figure 11.20 on page 595. Use Euler's method with $\Delta x = 0.1$ to estimate y when $x = 0.4$ for the solution curves satisfying

   (a) $y(0) = 1$ (b) $y(-1) = 0$.

8. (a) Using Figure 11.38, sketch the solution curve that passes through $(0, 0)$ for the differential equation

   $$\frac{dy}{dx} = x^3 - y^3.$$

   (b) Compute the points on the solution curve generated by Euler's method with 5 steps of $\Delta x = 0.2$.

   (c) Is your answer to part (b) an overestimate or an underestimate?

Figure 11.38: Slope field for $dy/dx = x^3 - y^3$

9. Consider the solution of the differential equation $y' = y$ passing through $y(0) = 1$.

   (a) Sketch the slope field for this differential equation, and sketch the solution passing through the point $(0, 1)$.

   (b) Use Euler's method with step size $\Delta x = 0.1$ to estimate the solution at $x = 0.1, 0.2, \ldots, 1$.

   (c) Plot the estimated solution on the slope field; compare the solution and the slope field.

   (d) Check that $y = e^x$ is the solution of $y' = y$ with $y(0) = 1$.

Problems

10. Consider the differential equation $y' = (\sin x)(\sin y)$.

    (a) Calculate approximate y-values using Euler's method with three steps and $\Delta x = 0.1$, starting at each of the following points:

        (i) $(0, 2)$ (ii) $(0, \pi)$

    (b) Use the slope field in Figure 11.25 on page 597 to explain your solution to part (a)(ii).

11. **(a)** Use Euler's method with five subintervals to approximate the solution curve to the differential equation $dy/dx = x^2 - y^2$ passing through the point $(0, 1)$ and ending at $x = 1$. (Keep the approximate function values to three decimal places.)

    (b) Repeat this computation using ten subintervals, again ending with $x = 1$.

12. Why are the approximate results you obtained in Problem 11 smaller than the true values? (Note: The slope field for this differential equation is one of those in Figure 11.18 on page 595.)

13. How do the errors of the five-step calculation and the ten-step calculation in Problem 11 compare? Estimate the true value of y on the solution through the point $(0, 1)$ when $x = 1$.

14. **(a)** Use ten steps of Euler's method to approximate y-values for $dy/dt = 1/t$, starting at $(1, 0)$ and using $\Delta t = 0.1$.

    (b) Using integration, solve the differential equation to find the exact value of y at the end of these ten steps.

    (c) Is your approximate value of y at the end of ten steps bigger or smaller than the exact value? Use a slope field to explain your answer.

15. Consider the differential equation

$$\frac{dy}{dx} = 2x, \quad \text{with initial condition } y(0) = 1.$$

    (a) Use Euler's method with two steps to estimate y when $x = 1$. Now use four steps.

    (b) What is the formula for the exact value of y?

    (c) Does the error in Euler's approximation behave as predicted in the box on page 601?

16. Consider the differential equation

$$\frac{dy}{dx} = \sin(xy), \quad \text{with initial condition } y(1) = 1.$$

Estimate $y(2)$, using Euler's method with step sizes $\Delta x = 0.2, 0.1, 0.05$. Plot the computed approximations for $y(2)$ against Δx. What do you conclude? Use your observations to estimate the exact value of $y(2)$.

17. Use Euler's method to estimate $B(1)$, given that

$$\frac{dB}{dt} = 0.05B$$

and $B = 1000$ when $t = 0$. Take:

    (a) $\Delta t = 1$ and 1 step   **(b)** $\Delta t = 0.5$ and 2 steps

    (c) $\Delta t = 0.25$ and 4 steps

    (d) Suppose B is the balance in a bank account earning interest. Explain why the result of your calculation in part (a) is equivalent to compounding the interest once a year instead of continuously.

    (e) Interpret the result of your calculations in parts (b) and (c) in terms of compound interest.

18. Consider the differential equation $dy/dx = f(x)$ with initial value $y(0) = 0$. Explain why using Euler's method to approximate the solution curve gives the same results as using left Riemann sums to approximate $\int_0^x f(t)\,dt$.

Strengthen Your Understanding

In Problems 19–20, explain what is wrong with the statement.

19. Euler's method never produces an exact solution to a differential equation at a point. There is always some error.

20. If we use Euler's method on the interval $[0, 1]$ to estimate the value of $x(1)$ where $dx/dt = x$, then we get an underestimate.

In Problems 21–22, give an example of:

21. A differential equation for which the approximate values found using Euler's method lie on a straight line.

22. A differential equation and initial condition such that for any step size, the approximate y-value found after one step of Euler's method is an underestimate of the solution value.

Are the statements in Problems 23–24 true or false? Give an explanation for your answer.

23. Euler's method gives the arc length of a solution curve.

24. Using Euler's method with five steps and $\Delta x = 0.2$ to approximate $y(1)$ when $dy/dx = f(x)$ and $y(0) = 0$ gives the same answer as the left Riemann sum approximation to $\int_0^1 f(x)\,dx$.

11.4 SEPARATION OF VARIABLES

We have seen how to sketch solution curves of a differential equation using a slope field and how to calculate approximate numerical solutions. Now we see how to solve certain differential equations analytically, finding an equation for the solution curve.

First, we look at a familiar example, the differential equation

$$\frac{dy}{dx} = -\frac{x}{y},$$

whose solution curves are the circles

$$x^2 + y^2 = C.$$

We can check that these circles are solutions by differentiation; the question now is how they were obtained. The method of *separation of variables* works by putting all the x-values on one side of the equation and all the y-values on the other, giving

$$y \, dy = -x \, dx.$$

We then integrate each side separately:

$$\int y \, dy = -\int x \, dx,$$

$$\frac{y^2}{2} = -\frac{x^2}{2} + k.$$

This gives the circles we were expecting:

$$x^2 + y^2 = C \qquad \text{where } C = 2k.$$

You might worry about whether it is legitimate to separate the dx and the dy. The reason it can be done is explained at the end of this section.

Example 1   Using separation of variables, solve the differential equation:

$$\frac{dy}{dx} = ky.$$

Solution   Separating variables,

$$\frac{1}{y} dy = k \, dx,$$

and integrating,

$$\int \frac{1}{y} \, dy = \int k \, dx,$$

gives

$$\ln |y| = kx + C \quad \text{for some constant } C.$$

Solving for $|y|$ leads to

$$|y| = e^{kx+C} = e^{kx} e^C = A e^{kx}$$

where $A = e^C$, so A is positive. Thus

$$y = (\pm A) e^{kx} = B e^{kx}$$

where $B = \pm A$, so B is any nonzero constant. Even though there's no C leading to $B = 0$, we can have $B = 0$ because $y = 0$ is a solution to the differential equation. We lost this solution when we divided through by y at the first step. Thus, the general solution is $y = B e^{kx}$ for any B.

The differential equation $dy/dx = ky$ always leads to exponential growth (if $k > 0$) or exponential decay (if $k < 0$). Graphs of solution curves for some fixed $k > 0$ are in Figure 11.39. For $k < 0$, the graphs are reflected in the y-axis.

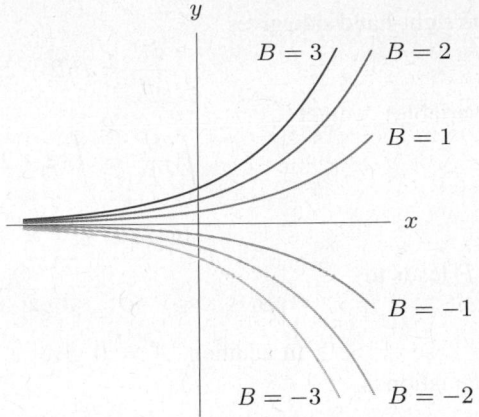

Figure 11.39: Graphs of $y = Be^{kx}$, which are solutions to $dy/dx = ky$, for some fixed $k > 0$

Example 2   For $k > 0$, find and graph solutions of

$$\frac{dH}{dt} = -k(H - 20).$$

Solution   The slope field in Figure 11.40 shows the qualitative behavior of the solutions. To find the equation of the solution curves, we separate variables and integrate:

$$\int \frac{1}{H - 20}\, dH = -\int k\, dt.$$

This gives

$$\ln|H - 20| = -kt + C.$$

Solving for H leads to:

$$|H - 20| = e^{-kt + C} = e^{-kt}e^{C} = Ae^{-kt}$$

or

$$H - 20 = (\pm A)e^{-kt} = Be^{-kt}$$
$$H = 20 + Be^{-kt}.$$

Again, $B = 0$ also gives a solution. Graphs for $k = 1$ and $B = -10, 0, 10$, with $t \geq 0$, are in Figure 11.40.

Figure 11.40: Slope field and some solution curves for $dH/dt = -k(H - 20)$, with $k = 1$

This differential equation can be used to represent the temperature, $H(t)$, in °C at time t of a cup of water standing in a room at 20°C. As Figure 11.40 shows, if the initial temperature is 10°C, the water warms up; if the initial temperature is 30°C, the water cools down. If the initial temperature is 20°C, the water remains 20°C.

Example 3   Find and sketch the solution to

$$\frac{dP}{dt} = 2P - 2Pt \qquad \text{satisfying } P = 5 \text{ when } t = 0.$$

Solution   Factoring the right-hand side gives

$$\frac{dP}{dt} = P(2 - 2t).$$

Separating variables, we get

$$\int \frac{dP}{P} = \int (2 - 2t)\,dt,$$

so

$$\ln|P| = 2t - t^2 + C.$$

Solving for P leads to

$$|P| = e^{2t-t^2+C} = e^C e^{2t-t^2} = A e^{2t-t^2}$$

with $A = e^C$, so $A > 0$. In addition, $A = 0$ gives a solution. Thus the general solution to the differential equation is

$$P = B e^{2t-t^2} \quad \text{for any } B.$$

To find the value of B, substitute $P = 5$ and $t = 0$ into the general solution, giving

$$5 = B e^{2\cdot 0 - 0^2} = B,$$

so

$$P = 5 e^{2t-t^2}.$$

The graph of this function is in Figure 11.41. Since the solution can be rewritten as

$$P = 5 e^{1-1+2t-t^2} = 5 e^1 e^{-1+2t-t^2} = (5e) e^{-(t-1)^2},$$

the graph has the same shape as the graph of $y = e^{-t^2}$, the bell-shaped curve of statistics. Here the maximum, normally at $t = 0$, is shifted one unit to the right to $t = 1$.

Figure 11.41: Bell-shaped solution curve

Justification for Separation of Variables

Suppose a differential equation can be written in the form

$$\frac{dy}{dx} = g(x)f(y).$$

Provided $f(y) \neq 0$, we write $f(y) = 1/h(y)$, so the right-hand side can be thought of as a fraction,

$$\frac{dy}{dx} = \frac{g(x)}{h(y)}.$$

If we multiply through by $h(y)$, we get

$$h(y)\frac{dy}{dx} = g(x).$$

Thinking of y as a function of x, so $y = y(x)$, and $dy/dx = y'(x)$, we can rewrite the equation as

$$h(y(x)) \cdot y'(x) = g(x).$$

Now integrate both sides with respect to x:

$$\int h(y(x)) \cdot y'(x)\,dx = \int g(x)\,dx.$$

The form of the integral on the left suggests that we use the substitution $y = y(x)$. Since $dy = y'(x)\, dx$, we get

$$\int h(y)\, dy = \int g(x)\, dx.$$

If we can find antiderivatives of h and g, then this gives the equation of the solution curve.

Note that transforming the original differential equation,

$$\frac{dy}{dx} = \frac{g(x)}{h(y)},$$

into

$$\int h(y)\, dy = \int g(x)\, dx$$

looks as though we have treated dy/dx as a fraction, cross-multiplied, and then integrated. Although that's not exactly what we have done, you may find this a helpful way of remembering the method. In fact, the dy/dx notation was introduced by Leibniz to allow shortcuts like this (more specifically, to make the chain rule look like cancellation).

Exercises and Problems for Section 11.4

Exercises

1. Determine which of the following differential equations are separable. Do not solve the equations.

   (a) $y' = y$ **(b)** $y' = x + y$

   (c) $y' = xy$ **(d)** $y' = \sin(x + y)$

   (e) $y' - xy = 0$ **(f)** $y' = y/x$

   (g) $y' = \ln(xy)$ **(h)** $y' = (\sin x)(\cos y)$

   (i) $y' = (\sin x)(\cos xy)$ **(j)** $y' = x/y$

   (k) $y' = 2x$ **(l)** $y' = (x + y)/(x + 2y)$

In Exercises 2–28, use separation of variables to find the solutions to the differential equations subject to the given initial conditions.

2. $\dfrac{dP}{dt} = -2P,\ \ P(0) = 1$

3. $\dfrac{dP}{dt} = 0.02P,\ \ P(0) = 20$

4. $\dfrac{dL}{dp} = \dfrac{L}{2},\ \ L(0) = 100$

5. $\dfrac{dQ}{dt} = \dfrac{Q}{5},\ \ Q = 50$ when $t = 0$

6. $P\dfrac{dP}{dt} = 1,\ \ P(0) = 1$

7. $\dfrac{dm}{dt} = 3m,\ \ m = 5$ when $t = 1$

8. $\dfrac{dI}{dx} = 0.2I,\ \ I = 6$ where $x = -1$

9. $\dfrac{1}{z}\dfrac{dz}{dt} = 5,\ \ z(1) = 5$

10. $\dfrac{dm}{ds} = m,\ \ m(1) = 2$

11. $2\dfrac{du}{dt} = u^2,\ \ u(0) = 1$

12. $\dfrac{dz}{dy} = zy,\ \ z = 1$ when $y = 0$

13. $\dfrac{dy}{dx} + \dfrac{y}{3} = 0,\ \ y(0) = 10$

14. $\dfrac{dy}{dt} = 0.5(y - 200),\ \ y = 50$ when $t = 0$

15. $\dfrac{dP}{dt} = P + 4,\ \ P = 100$ when $t = 0$

16. $\dfrac{dy}{dx} = 2y - 4,\ \ $ through $(2, 5)$

17. $\dfrac{dQ}{dt} = 0.3Q - 120,\ \ Q = 50$ when $t = 0$

18. $\dfrac{dm}{dt} = 0.1m + 200,\ \ m(0) = 1000$

19. $\dfrac{dR}{dy} + R = 1,\ \ R(1) = 0.1$

20. $\dfrac{dB}{dt} + 2B = 50,\ \ B(1) = 100$

21. $\dfrac{dy}{dt} = \dfrac{y}{3 + t},\ \ y(0) = 1$

22. $\dfrac{dz}{dt} = te^z,\ \ $ through the origin

23. $\dfrac{dy}{dx} = \dfrac{5y}{x},\ \ y = 3$ where $x = 1$

24. $\dfrac{dy}{dt} = y^2(1 + t),\ \ y = 2$ when $t = 1$

25. $\dfrac{dz}{dt} = z + zt^2,\ \ z = 5$ when $t = 0$

26. $\dfrac{dw}{d\theta} = \theta w^2 \sin \theta^2,\ \ w(0) = 1$

27. $\dfrac{dw}{d\psi} = -w^2 \tan \psi,\ \ w(0) = 2$

28. $x(x + 1)\dfrac{du}{dx} = u^2,\ \ u(1) = 1$

Problems

29. (a) Solve the differential equation

$$\frac{dy}{dx} = \frac{4x}{y^2}.$$

Write the solution y as an explicit function of x.
(b) Find the particular solution for each initial condition below and graph the three solutions on the same coordinate plane.

$$y(0) = 1, \qquad y(0) = 2, \qquad y(0) = 3.$$

Figure 11.42

30. (a) Solve the differential equation

$$\frac{dP}{dt} = 0.2P - 10.$$

Write the solution P as an explicit function of t.
(b) Find the particular solution for each initial condition below and graph the three solutions on the same coordinate plane.

$$P(0) = 40, \qquad P(0) = 50, \qquad P(0) = 60.$$

31. (a) Find the general solution to the differential equation modeling how a person learns:

$$\frac{dy}{dt} = 100 - y.$$

(b) Plot the slope field of this differential equation and sketch solutions with $y(0) = 25$ and $y(0) = 110$.
(c) For each of the initial conditions in part (b), find the particular solution and add to your sketch.
(d) Which of these two particular solutions could represent how a person learns?

32. A circular oil spill grows at a rate given by the differential equation $dr/dt = k/r$, where r represents the radius of the spill in feet, and time is measured in hours. If the radius of the spill is 400 feet 16 hours after the spill begins, what is the value of k? Include units in your answer.

33. Figure 11.42 shows the slope field for $dy/dx = y^2$.

(a) Sketch the solutions that pass through the points

(i) $(0, 1)$ (ii) $(0, -1)$ (iii) $(0, 0)$

(b) In words, describe the end behavior of the solution curves in part (a).
(c) Find a formula for the general solution.
(d) Show that all solution curves except for $y = 0$ have both a horizontal and a vertical asymptote.

Solve the differential equations in Problems 34–43. Assume a, b, and k are nonzero constants.

34. $\dfrac{dR}{dt} = kR$

35. $\dfrac{dQ}{dt} - \dfrac{Q}{k} = 0$

36. $\dfrac{dP}{dt} = P - a$

37. $\dfrac{dQ}{dt} = b - Q$

38. $\dfrac{dP}{dt} = k(P - a)$

39. $\dfrac{dR}{dt} = aR + b$

40. $\dfrac{dP}{dt} - aP = b$

41. $\dfrac{dy}{dt} = ky^2(1 + t^2)$

42. $\dfrac{dR}{dx} = a(R^2 + 1)$

43. $\dfrac{dL}{dx} = k(x + a)(L - b)$

Solve the differential equations in Problems 44–47. Assume $x, y, t > 0$.

44. $\dfrac{dy}{dt} = y(2 - y), \quad y(0) = 1$

45. $\dfrac{dx}{dt} = \dfrac{x \ln x}{t}$

46. $t\dfrac{dx}{dt} = (1 + 2\ln t) \tan x$

47. $\dfrac{dy}{dt} = -y \ln\left(\dfrac{y}{2}\right), \quad y(0) = 1$

48. Figure 11.43 shows the slope field for the equation

$$\frac{dy}{dx} = \begin{cases} y^2 & \text{if } |y| \geq 1 \\ 1 & \text{if } -1 \leq y \leq 1. \end{cases}$$

(a) Sketch the solutions that pass through $(0, 0)$.
(b) What can you say about the end behavior of the solution curve in part (a)?
(c) For each of the following regions, find a formula for the general solution

(i) $-1 \leq y \leq 1$ (ii) $y \leq -1$
(iii) $y \geq 1$

(d) Show that each solution curve has two vertical asymptotes.

(e) How far apart are the two asymptotes of a solution curve?

Figure 11.43

49. (a) Sketch the slope field for $y' = x/y$.
(b) Sketch several solution curves.
(c) Solve the differential equation analytically.

50. (a) Sketch the slope field for $y' = -y/x$.
(b) Sketch several solution curves.
(c) Solve the differential equation analytically.

51. Compare the slope field for $y' = x/y$, Problem 49, with that for $y' = -y/x$, Problem 50. Show that the solution curves of Problem 49 intersect the solution curves of Problem 50 at right angles.

Strengthen Your Understanding

In Problems 52–54, explain what is wrong with the statement.

52. Separating variables in $dy/dx = x + y$ gives $-y\,dy = x\,dx$.

53. The solution to $dP/dt = 0.2t$ is $P = Be^{0.2t}$.

54. Separating variables in $dy/dx = e^{x+y}$ gives $-e^y\,dy = e^x\,dx$.

In Problems 55–58, give an example of:

55. A differential equation that is not separable.

56. An expression for $f(x)$ such that the differential equation $dy/dx = f(x) + xy - \cos x$ is separable.

57. A differential equation all of whose solutions form the family of functions $f(x) = x^2 + C$.

58. A differential equation all of whose solutions form the family of hyperbolas $x^2 - y^2 = C$.

Are the statements in Problems 59–62 true or false? Give an explanation for your answer.

59. For all constants k, the equation $y' + ky = 0$ has exponential functions as solutions.

60. The differential equation $dy/dx = x + y$ can be solved by separation of variables.

61. The differential equation $dy/dx - xy = x$ can be solved by separation of variables.

62. The only solution to the differential equation $dy/dx = 3y^{2/3}$ passing through the point $(0, 0)$ is $y = x^3$.

11.5 GROWTH AND DECAY

In this section we look at exponential growth and decay equations. Consider the population of a region. If there is no immigration or emigration, the rate at which the population is changing is often proportional to the population. In other words, the larger the population, the faster it is growing because there are more people to have babies. If the population at time t is P and its continuous growth rate is 2% per unit time, then we know

$$\text{Rate of growth of population} = 2\%(\text{Current population}),$$

and we can write this as

$$\frac{dP}{dt} = 0.02P.$$

The 2% growth rate is called the *relative growth rate* to distinguish it from the *absolute growth rate*, dP/dt. Notice they measure different quantities. Since

$$\text{Relative growth rate} = 2\% = \frac{1}{P}\frac{dP}{dt},$$

the relative growth rate is a percent change per unit time, while

$$\text{Absolute growth rate} = \text{Rate of change of population} = \frac{dP}{dt}.$$

is a change in population per unit time.

We showed in Section 11.4 that since the equation $dP/dt = 0.02P$ is of the form $dP/dt = kP$ for $k = 0.02$, it has solution

$$P = P_0 e^{0.02t}.$$

Other processes are described by differential equations similar to that for population growth, but with negative values for k. In summary, we have the following result from the preceding section:

Every solution to the equation

$$\frac{dP}{dt} = kP$$

can be written in the form

$$P = P_0 e^{kt},$$

where P_0 is the value of P at $t = 0$, and $k > 0$ represents growth, whereas $k < 0$ represents decay.

Recall that the *doubling time* of an exponentially growing quantity is the time required for it to double. The *half-life* of an exponentially decaying quantity is the time required for half of it to decay.

Continuously Compounded Interest

At a bank, continuous compounding means that interest is accrued at a rate that is a fixed percentage of the balance at that moment. Thus, the larger the balance, the faster interest is earned and the faster the balance grows.

Example 1 A bank account earns interest continuously at a rate of 5% of the current balance per year. Assume that the initial deposit is $1000 and that no other deposits or withdrawals are made.

(a) Write the differential equation satisfied by the balance in the account.
(b) Solve the differential equation and graph the solution.

Solution (a) We are looking for B, the balance in the account in dollars, as a function of t, time in years. Interest is being added to the account continuously at a rate of 5% of the balance at that moment. Since no deposits or withdrawals are made, at any instant,

Rate balance increasing = Rate interest earned = 5%(Current balance),

which we write as

$$\frac{dB}{dt} = 0.05B.$$

This is the differential equation that describes the process. It does not involve the initial condition $1000 because the initial deposit does not affect the process by which interest is earned.

(b) Solving the differential equation by separation of variables gives

$$B = B_0 e^{0.05t},$$

where B_0 is the value of B at $t = 0$, so $B_0 = 1000$. Thus

$$B = 1000 e^{0.05t}$$

and this function is graphed in Figure 11.44.

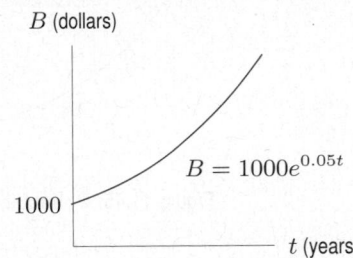

Figure 11.44: Bank balance against time

The Difference Between Continuous and Annual Percentage Growth Rates

If $P = P_0(1 + r)^t$ with t in years, we say that r is the *annual* growth rate, while if $P = P_0e^{kt}$, we say that k is the *continuous* growth rate.

The constant k in the differential equation $dP/dt = kP$ is not the annual growth rate, but the continuous growth rate. In Example 1, with a continuous interest rate of 5%, we obtain a balance of $B = B_0e^{0.05t}$, where time, t, is in years. At the end of one year the balance is $B_0e^{0.05}$. In that one year, our balance has changed from B_0 to $B_0e^{0.05}$, that is, by a factor of $e^{0.05} = 1.0513$. Thus the annual growth rate is 5.13%. This is what the bank means when it says "5% compounded continuously for an effective annual yield of 5.13%." Since $P_0e^{0.05t} = P_0(1.0513)^t$, we have two different ways to represent the same function.

Since most growth is measured over discrete time intervals, a continuous growth rate is an idealized concept. A demographer who says a population is growing at the rate of 2% per year usually means that after t years the population is $P = P_0(1.02)^t$. To find the continuous growth rate, k, we express the population as $P = P_0e^{kt}$. At the end of one year $P = P_0e^k$, so $e^k = 1.02$. Thus $k = \ln 1.02 \approx 0.0198$. The continuous growth rate, $k = 1.98\%$, is close to the annual growth rate of 2%, but it is not the same. Again, we have two different representations of the same function since $P_0(1.02)^t = P_0e^{0.0198t}$.

Pollution in the Great Lakes

In the 1960s pollution in the Great Lakes became an issue of public concern. We set up a model for how long it would take for the lakes to flush themselves clean, assuming no further pollutants are being dumped in the lakes.

Suppose Q is the total quantity of pollutant in a lake of volume V at time t. Suppose that clean water is flowing into the lake at a constant rate r and that water flows out at the same rate. Assume that the pollutant is evenly spread throughout the lake and that the clean water coming into the lake immediately mixes with the rest of the water.

We investigate how Q varies with time. Since pollutants are being taken out of the lake but not added, Q decreases, and the water leaving the lake becomes less polluted, so the rate at which the pollutants leave decreases. This tells us that Q is decreasing and concave up. In addition, the pollutants are never completely removed from the lake though the quantity remaining becomes arbitrarily small: in other words, Q is asymptotic to the t-axis. (See Figure 11.45.)

Setting Up a Differential Equation for the Pollution

To model exactly how Q changes with time, we write an equation for the rate at which Q changes. We know that

$$\begin{pmatrix} \text{Rate } Q \\ \text{changes} \end{pmatrix} = -\begin{pmatrix} \text{Rate pollutants} \\ \text{leave in outflow} \end{pmatrix}$$

Q (quantity of pollutant)

t (time)

Figure 11.45: Pollutant in lake versus time

where the negative sign represents the fact that Q is decreasing. At time t, the concentration of pollutants is Q/V, and water containing this concentration is leaving at rate r. Thus

$$\begin{matrix} \text{Rate pollutants} \\ \text{leave in outflow} \end{matrix} = \begin{matrix} \text{Rate of} \\ \text{outflow} \end{matrix} \times \text{Concentration} = r \cdot \frac{Q}{V}.$$

So the differential equation is

$$\frac{dQ}{dt} = -\frac{r}{V}Q,$$

and its solution is

$$Q = Q_0 e^{-rt/V}.$$

Table 11.4 contains values of r and V for four of the Great Lakes.[2] We use this data to calculate how long it would take for certain fractions of the pollution to be removed.

Table 11.4   *Volume and outflow in Great Lakes*[3]

	V (thousands of km^3)	r (km^3/year)
Superior	12.2	65.2
Michigan	4.9	158
Erie	0.46	175
Ontario	1.6	209

Example 2   According to this model, how long will it take for 90% of the pollution to be removed from Lake Erie? For 99% to be removed?

Solution   Substituting r and V for Lake Erie into the differential equation for Q gives

$$\frac{dQ}{dt} = -\frac{r}{V}Q = \frac{-175}{0.46 \times 10^3}Q = -0.38Q$$

where t is measured in years. Thus Q is given by

$$Q = Q_0 e^{-0.38t}.$$

When 90% of the pollution has been removed, 10% remains, so $Q = 0.1Q_0$. Substituting gives

$$0.1Q_0 = Q_0 e^{-0.38t}.$$

---

[2]Data from William E. Boyce and Richard C. DiPrima, *Elementary Differential Equations*, 9th Edition (New York: Wiley, 2009), pp. 63–64.

[3]www.epa.gov/greatlakes/

Canceling Q_0 and solving for t, we get

$$t = \frac{-\ln(0.1)}{0.38} \approx 6 \text{ years.}$$

When 99% of the pollution has been removed, $Q = 0.01Q_0$, so t satisfies

$$0.01Q_0 = Q_0 e^{-0.38t}.$$

Solving for t gives

$$t = \frac{-\ln(0.01)}{0.38} \approx 12 \text{ years.}$$

Newton's Law of Heating and Cooling

Newton proposed that the temperature of a hot object decreases at a rate proportional to the difference between its temperature and that of its surroundings. Similarly, a cold object heats up at a rate proportional to the temperature difference between the object and its surroundings.

For example, a hot cup of coffee standing on the kitchen table cools at a rate proportional to the temperature difference between the coffee and the surrounding air. As the coffee cools, the rate at which it cools decreases because the temperature difference between the coffee and the air decreases. In the long run, the rate of cooling tends to zero, and the temperature of the coffee approaches room temperature. See Figure 11.46.

Figure 11.46: Temperature of two cups of coffee with different initial temperatures

Example 3 When a murder is committed, the body, originally at $37°C$, cools according to Newton's Law of Cooling. Suppose that after two hours the temperature is $35°C$ and that the temperature of the surrounding air is a constant $20°C$.

(a) Find the temperature, H, of the body as a function of t, the time in hours since the murder was committed.
(b) Sketch a graph of temperature against time.
(c) What happens to the temperature in the long run? Show this on the graph and algebraically.
(d) If the body is found at 4 pm at a temperature of $30°C$, when was the murder committed?

Solution (a) We first find a differential equation for the temperature of the body as a function of time. Newton's Law of Cooling says that for some constant α,

$$\text{Rate of change of temperature} = \alpha(\text{Temperature difference}).$$

If H is the temperature of the body, then

$$\text{Temperature difference} = H - 20,$$

so

$$\frac{dH}{dt} = \alpha(H - 20).$$

What about the sign of α? If the temperature difference is positive (i.e., $H > 20$), then H is falling, so the rate of change must be negative. Thus α should be negative, so we write:

$$\frac{dH}{dt} = -k(H - 20), \qquad \text{for some } k > 0.$$

Separating variables and solving, as in Example 2 on page 605, gives:

$$H - 20 = Be^{-kt}.$$

To find B, substitute the initial condition that $H = 37$ when $t = 0$:

$$37 - 20 = Be^{-k(0)} = B,$$

so $B = 17$. Thus,

$$H - 20 = 17e^{-kt}.$$

To find k, we use the fact that after 2 hours, the temperature is $35°C$, so

$$35 - 20 = 17e^{-k(2)}.$$

Dividing by 17 and taking natural logs, we get:

$$\ln\left(\frac{15}{17}\right) = \ln(e^{-2k})$$
$$-0.125 = -2k$$
$$k \approx 0.063.$$

Therefore, the temperature is given by

$$H - 20 = 17e^{-0.063t}$$

or

$$H = 20 + 17e^{-0.063t}.$$

(b) The graph of $H = 20 + 17e^{-0.063t}$ has a vertical intercept of $H = 37$ because the temperature of the body starts at $37°C$. The temperature decays exponentially with $H = 20$ as the horizontal asymptote. (See Figure 11.47.)

Figure 11.47: Temperature of dead body

(c) "In the long run" means as $t \to \infty$. The graph shows that as $t \to \infty$, $H \to 20$. Algebraically, since $e^{-0.063t} \to 0$ as $t \to \infty$, we have

$$H = 20 + \underbrace{17e^{-0.063t}}_{\text{goes to 0 as } t \to \infty} \longrightarrow 20 \quad \text{as } t \to \infty.$$

(d) We want to know when the temperature reaches $30°C$. Substitute $H = 30$ and solve for t:

$$30 = 20 + 17e^{-0.063t}$$
$$\frac{10}{17} = e^{-0.063t}.$$

Taking natural logs:

$$-0.531 = -0.063t,$$

which gives

$$t \approx 8.4 \, \text{hours}.$$

Thus the murder must have been committed about 8.4 hours before 4 pm. Since 8.4 hours = 8 hours 24 minutes, the murder was committed at about 7:30 am.

Equilibrium Solutions

Figure 11.48 shows the temperature of several objects in a 20°C room. One is initially hotter than 20°C and cools down toward 20°C; another is initially cooler and warms up toward 20°C. All these curves are solutions to the differential equation

$$\frac{dH}{dt} = -k(H - 20)$$

for some fixed $k > 0$, and all the solutions have the form

$$H = 20 + Ae^{-kt}$$

for some A. Notice that $H \to 20$ as $t \to \infty$ because $e^{-kt} \to 0$ as $t \to \infty$. In other words, in the long run, the temperature of the object always tends toward 20°C, the temperature of the room. This means that what happens in the long run is independent of the initial condition.

In the special case when $A = 0$, we have the *equilibrium solution*

$$H = 20$$

for all t. This means that if the object starts at 20°C, it remains at 20°C for all time. Notice that such a solution can be found directly from the differential equation by solving $dH/dt = 0$:

$$\frac{dH}{dt} = -k(H - 20) = 0$$

giving

$$H = 20.$$

Regardless of the initial temperature, H always gets closer and closer to 20 as $t \to \infty$. As a result, $H = 20$ is called a *stable* equilibrium[4] for H.

Figure 11.48: $H = 20$ is stable equilibrium ($k > 0$)

Figure 11.49: $B = 10$ is unstable equilibrium ($k > 0$)

A different situation is displayed in Figure 11.49, which shows solutions to the differential equation

$$\frac{dB}{dt} = k(B - 10)$$

for some fixed $k > 0$. Solving $dB/dt = 0$ gives the equilibrium $B = 10$, which is *unstable* because if B starts near 10, it moves away as $t \to \infty$.

In general, we have the following definitions.

---

[4]In more advanced work, this behavior is described as asymptotic stability.

- An **equilibrium solution** is constant for all values of the independent variable. The graph is a horizontal line.
- An equilibrium is **stable** if a small change in the initial conditions gives a solution that tends toward the equilibrium as the independent variable tends to positive infinity.
- An equilibrium is **unstable** if a small change in the initial conditions gives a solution curve that veers away from the equilibrium as the independent variable tends to positive infinity.

Solutions that do not veer away from an equilibrium solution are also called stable. If the differential equation is of the form $y' = f(y)$, equilibrium solutions can be found by setting y' to zero.

Example 4   Find the equilibrium solution to the differential equation $dP/dt = -50 + 4P$ and determine whether the equilibrium is stable or unstable.

Solution   In order to find the equilibrium solution, we solve $dP/dt = -50 + 4P = 0$. Thus, we have one equilibrium solution at $P = 50/4 = 12.5$. We can determine whether the equilibrium is stable or unstable by analyzing the behavior of solutions with initial conditions near $P = 12.5$. For example, the solution with initial value $P = 13$ has initial slope $dP/dt = -50 + 4(13) = 2 > 0$. Thus, solutions above the equilibrium $P = 12.5$ will increase and move away from the equilibrium.

A solution with an initial value $P = 12$ has initial slope $dP/dt = -50 + 4(12) = -2 < 0$. Thus, solutions that have an initial value less than $P = 12.5$ will decrease and veer away from the equilibrium. Since a small change in the initial condition gives solutions that move away from the equilibrium, $P = 12.5$ is an unstable equilibrium. Notice it is possible to find equilibrium and study their stability without finding a formula for the general solution to the differential equation.

Exercises and Problems for Section 11.5

Exercises

1. Match the graphs in Figure 11.50 with the following descriptions.

   (a) The temperature of a glass of ice water left on the kitchen table.
   (b) The amount of money in an interest-bearing bank account into which $50 is deposited.
   (c) The speed of a constantly decelerating car.
   (d) The temperature of a piece of steel heated in a furnace and left outside to cool.

2. Each curve in Figure 11.51 represents the balance in a bank account into which a single deposit was made at time zero. Assuming continuously compounded interest, find:

   (a) The curve representing the largest initial deposit.
   (b) The curve representing the largest interest rate.
   (c) Two curves representing the same initial deposit.
   (d) Two curves representing the same interest rate.

Figure 11.51

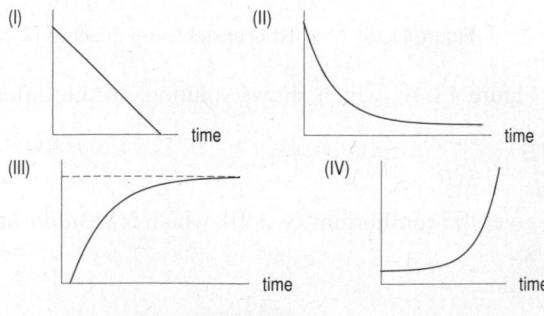

Figure 11.50

3. The slope field for $y' = 0.5(1 + y)(2 - y)$ is given in Figure 11.52.

  (a) List equilibrium solutions and state whether each is stable or unstable.

  (b) Draw solution curves on the slope field through each of the three marked points.

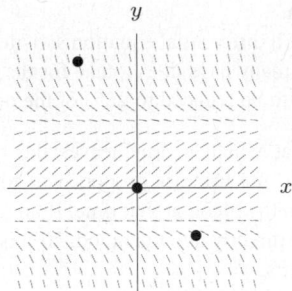

Figure 11.52

4. The slope field for a differential equation is given in Figure 11.53. Estimate all equilibrium solutions for this differential equation, and indicate whether each is stable or unstable.

Figure 11.53

For Exercises 5–6, sketch solution curves with a variety of initial values for the differential equations. You do not need to find an equation for the solution.

5. $\dfrac{dy}{dt} = \alpha - y$,

  where α is a positive constant.

6. $\dfrac{dw}{dt} = (w - 3)(w - 7)$

7. A yam is put in a $200°C$ oven and heats up according to the differential equation

$$\frac{dH}{dt} = -k(H - 200), \quad \text{for } k \text{ a positive constant.}$$

  (a) If the yam is at $20°C$ when it is put in the oven, solve the differential equation.

  (b) Find k using the fact that after 30 minutes the temperature of the yam is $120°C$.

8. (a) Find the equilibrium solution to the differential equation

$$\frac{dy}{dt} = 0.5y - 250.$$

  (b) Find the general solution to this differential equation.

  (c) Sketch the graphs of several solutions to this differential equation, using different initial values for y.

  (d) Is the equilibrium solution stable or unstable?

9. (a) Find all equilibrium solutions for the differential equation

$$\frac{dy}{dx} = 0.5y(y - 4)(2 + y).$$

  (b) Draw a slope field and use it to determine whether each equilibrium solution is stable or unstable.

10. (a) A cup of coffee is made with boiling water and stands in a room where the temperature is $20°$ C. If $H(t)$ is the temperature of the coffee at time t, in minutes, explain what the differential equation

$$\frac{dH}{dt} = -k(H - 20)$$

  says in everyday terms. What is the sign of k?

  (b) Solve this differential equation. If the coffee cools to $90°C$ in 2 minutes, how long will it take to cool to $60°C$ degrees?

11. In Example 2 on page 612, we saw that it would take about 6 years for 90% of the pollution in Lake Erie to be removed and about 12 years for 99% to be removed. Explain why one time is double the other.

12. Using the model in the text and the data in Table 11.4 on page 612, find how long it would take for 90% of the pollution to be removed from Lake Michigan and from Lake Ontario, assuming no new pollutants are added. Explain how you can tell which lake will take longer to be purified just by looking at the data in the table.

13. Use the model in the text and the data in Table 11.4 on page 612 to determine which of the Great Lakes would require the longest time and which would require the shortest time for 80% of the pollution to be removed, assuming no new pollutants are being added. Find the ratio of these two times.

Problems

In Problems 14–17,

(a) Define the variables.

(b) Write a differential equation to describe the relationship.

(c) Solve the differential equation.

14. In 2010, the population of India was 1.15 billion people and increasing at a rate proportional to its population. If the population is measured in billions of people and time is measured in years, the constant of proportionality is 0.0135.

15. Nicotine leaves the body at a rate proportional to the amount present, with constant of proportionality 0.347 if the amount of nicotine is in mg and time is in hours. The amount of nicotine in the body immediately after smoking a cigarette is 0.4 mg.

16. In 2007, world solar photovoltaic (PV) market installations were 2826 megawatts and were growing exponentially at a continuous rate of 48% per year.[5]

17. In 2007, Grinnell Glacier in Glacier National Park covered 142 acres and was estimated to be shrinking exponentially at a continuous rate of 4.3% per year.[6]

18. Since 1980, textbook prices have increased at 6.7% per year while inflation has been 3.3% per year.[7] Assume both rates are continuous growth rates and let time, t, be in years since the start of 1980.

(a) Write a differential equation satisfied by $B(t)$, the price of a textbook at time t.

(b) Write a differential equation satisfied by $P(t)$, the price at time t of an item growing at the inflation rate.

(c) Solve both differential equations.

(d) What is the doubling time of the price of a textbook?

(e) What is the doubling time of the price of an item growing according to the inflation rate?

(f) How is the ratio of the doubling times related to the ratio of the growth rates? Justify your answer.

19. Write a differential equation whose solution is the temperature as a function of time of a bottle of orange juice taken out of a $40°$F refrigerator and left in a $65°$F room. Solve the equation and graph the solution.

20. A roast is taken from the refrigerator, where the temperature is $40°$F, and put in a $350°$F oven. One hour later, the meat thermometer shows a temperature of $90°$F. If the roast is done when its temperature reaches $140°$F, what is the total time the roast should be in the oven?

21. Warfarin is a drug used as an anticoagulant. After administration of the drug is stopped, the quantity remaining in a patient's body decreases at a rate proportional to the

quantity remaining. The half-life of warfarin in the body is 37 hours.

(a) Sketch the quantity, Q, of warfarin in a patient's body as a function of the time, t, since stopping administration of the drug. Mark the 37 hours on your graph.

(b) Write a differential equation satisfied by Q.

(c) How many days does it take for the drug level in the body to be reduced to 25% of the original level?

22. The rate at which a drug leaves the bloodstream and passes into the urine is proportional to the quantity of the drug in the blood at that time. If an initial dose of Q_0 is injected directly into the blood, 20% is left in the blood after 3 hours.

(a) Write and solve a differential equation for the quantity, Q, of the drug in the blood after t hours.

(b) How much of this drug is in a patient's body after 6 hours if the patient is given 100 mg initially?

23. Oil is pumped continuously from a well at a rate proportional to the amount of oil left in the well. Initially there were 1 million barrels of oil in the well; six years later 500,000 barrels remain.

(a) At what rate was the amount of oil in the well decreasing when there were 600,000 barrels remaining?

(b) When will there be 50,000 barrels remaining?

24. The radioactive isotope carbon-14 is present in small quantities in all life forms, and it is constantly replenished until the organism dies, after which it decays to stable carbon-12 at a rate proportional to the amount of carbon-14 present, with a half-life of 5730 years. Suppose $C(t)$ is the amount of carbon-14 present at time t.

(a) Find the value of the constant k in the differential equation $C' = -kC$.

(b) In 1988 three teams of scientists found that the Shroud of Turin, which was reputed to be the burial cloth of Jesus, contained 91% of the amount of carbon-14 contained in freshly made cloth of the same material.[8] How old is the Shroud of Turin, according to these data?

25. The amount of radioactive carbon-14 in a sample is measured using a Geiger counter, which records each disintegration of an atom. Living tissue disintegrates at a rate of about 13.5 atoms per minute per gram of carbon. In 1977 a charcoal fragment found at Stonehenge, England, recorded 8.2 disintegrations per minute per gram of carbon. Assuming that the half-life of carbon-14 is 5730

[5]www.solarbuzz.com/marketbuzz2008. Accessed February 2010.
[6]"Warming climate shrinking Glacier Park's glaciers", www.usatoday.com, October 15, 2007.
[7]Data from "Textbooks headed for ash heap of history", http://educationtechnews.com, Vol. 5, 2010.
[8]*The New York Times*, October 18, 1988.

years and that the charcoal was formed during the building of the site, estimate the date at which Stonehenge was built.

26. A detective finds a murder victim at 9 am. The temperature of the body is measured at 90.3°F. One hour later, the temperature of the body is 89.0°F. The temperature of the room has been maintained at a constant 68°F.

    (a) Assuming the temperature, T, of the body obeys Newton's Law of Cooling, write a differential equation for T.

    (b) Solve the differential equation to estimate the time the murder occurred.

27. At 1:00 pm one winter afternoon, there is a power failure at your house in Wisconsin, and your heat does not work without electricity. When the power goes out, it is 68°F in your house. At 10:00 pm, it is 57°F in the house, and you notice that it is 10°F outside.

    (a) Assuming that the temperature, T, in your home obeys Newton's Law of Cooling, write the differential equation satisfied by T.

    (b) Solve the differential equation to estimate the temperature in the house when you get up at 7:00 am the next morning. Should you worry about your water pipes freezing?

    (c) What assumption did you make in part (a) about the temperature outside? Given this (probably incorrect) assumption, would you revise your estimate up or down? Why?

28. Before Galileo discovered that the speed of a falling body with no air resistance is proportional to the time since it was dropped, he mistakenly conjectured that the speed was proportional to the distance it had fallen.

    (a) Assume the mistaken conjecture to be true and write an equation relating the distance fallen, $D(t)$, at time t, and its derivative.

    (b) Using your answer to part (a) and the correct initial conditions, show that D would have to be equal to 0 for all t, and therefore the conjecture must be wrong.

29. (a) An object is placed in a 68°F room. Write a differential equation for H, the temperature of the object at time t.

    (b) Find the equilibrium solution to the differential equation. Determine from the differential equation whether the equilibrium is stable or unstable.

    (c) Give the general solution for the differential equation.

    (d) The temperature of the object is 40°F initially and 48°F one hour later. Find the temperature of the object after 3 hours.

30. Hydrocodone bitartrate is used as a cough suppressant. After the drug is fully absorbed, the quantity of drug in the body decreases at a rate proportional to the amount left in the body. The half-life of hydrocodone bitartrate in the body is 3.8 hours, and the usual oral dose is 10 mg.

    (a) Write a differential equation for the quantity, Q, of hydrocodone bitartrate in the body at time t, in hours since the drug was fully absorbed.

    (b) Find the equilibrium solution of the differential equation. Based on the context, do you expect the equilibrium to be stable or unstable?

    (c) Solve the differential equation given in part (a).

    (d) Use the half-life to find the constant of proportionality, k.

    (e) How much of the 10 mg dose is still in the body after 12 hours?

31. (a) Let B be the balance at time t of a bank account that earns interest at a rate of $r\%$, compounded continuously. What is the differential equation describing the rate at which the balance changes? What is the constant of proportionality, in terms of r?

    (b) Find the equilibrium solution to the differential equation. Determine whether the equilibrium is stable or unstable and explain what this means about the bank account.

    (c) What is the solution to this differential equation?

    (d) Sketch the graph of B as function of t for an account that starts with $1000 and earns interest at the following rates:

        (i) 4%   (ii) 10%   (iii) 15%

Strengthen Your Understanding

In Problems 32–34, explain what is wrong with the statement.

32. The line $y = 2$ is an equilibrium solution to the differential equation $dy/dx = y^3 - 4xy$.

33. The function $y = x^2$ is an equilibrium solution to the differential equation $dy/dx = y - x^2$.

34. At time $t = 0$, a roast is taken out of a 40°F refrigerator and put in a 350°F oven. If H represents the temperature of the roast at time t minutes after it is put in the oven, we have $dH/dt = k(H - 40)$.

In Problems 35–37, give an example of:

35. A differential equation for a quantity that is decaying exponentially at a continuous rate per unit time.

36. A differential equation with an equilibrium solution of $Q = 500$.

37. A graph of three possible solutions, with initial P-values of 20, 25, and 30, respectively, to a differential equation that has an unstable equilibrium solution at $P = 25$.

11.6 APPLICATIONS AND MODELING

Much of this book involves functions that represent real processes, such as how the temperature of a yam or the population of the US is changing with time. You may wonder where such functions come from. In some cases, we fit functions to experimental data by trial and error. In other cases, we take a more theoretical approach, leading to a differential equation whose solution is the function we want. In this section we give examples of the more theoretical approach.

How a Layer of Ice Forms

When ice forms on a lake, the water on the surface freezes first. As heat from the water travels up through the ice and is lost to the air, more ice is formed. The question we will consider is: How thick is the layer of ice as a function of time? Since the thickness of the ice increases with time, the thickness function is increasing. In addition, as the ice gets thicker, it insulates better. Therefore, we expect the layer of ice to form more slowly as time goes on. Hence, the thickness function is increasing at a decreasing rate, so its graph is concave down.

A Differential Equation for the Thickness of the Ice

To get more detailed information about the thickness function, we have to make some assumptions. Suppose y represents the thickness of the ice as a function of time, t. Since the thicker the ice, the longer it takes the heat to get through it, we will assume that the rate at which ice is formed is inversely proportional to the thickness. In other words, we assume that for some constant k,

$$\text{Rate thickness is increasing} = \frac{k}{\text{Thickness}},$$

so

$$\frac{dy}{dt} = \frac{k}{y} \quad \text{where} \quad k > 0.$$

This differential equation enables us to find a formula for y. Using separation of variables:

$$\int y\,dy = \int k\,dt$$

$$\frac{y^2}{2} = kt + C.$$

If we measure time so that $y = 0$ when $t = 0$, then $C = 0$. Since y must be non-negative, we have

$$y = \sqrt{2kt}.$$

Graphs of y against t are in Figure 11.54. Notice that the larger y is, the more slowly y increases. In addition, this model suggests that y increases indefinitely as time passes. (Of course, the value of y cannot increase beyond the depth of the lake.)

Figure 11.54: Thickness of ice as a function of time

The Net Worth of a Company

In the preceding section, we saw an example in which money in a bank account was earning interest (Example 1, page 610). Consider a company whose revenues are proportional to its net worth (like interest on a bank account) but that must also make payroll payments. The question is: under what circumstances does the company make money, and under what circumstances does it go bankrupt?

Common sense says that if the payroll exceeds the rate at which revenue is earned, the company will eventually be in trouble, whereas if revenue exceeds payroll, the company should do well. We assume that revenue is earned continuously and that payments are made continuously. (For a large company, this is a good approximation.) We also assume that the only factors affecting net worth are revenue and payroll.

Example 1   A company's revenue is earned at a continuous annual rate of 5% of its net worth. At the same time, the company's payroll obligations amount to $200 million a year, paid out continuously.

(a) Write a differential equation that governs the net worth of the company, W million dollars.
(b) Solve the differential equation, assuming an initial net worth of W_0 million dollars.
(c) Sketch the solution for $W_0 = 3000, 4000$, and 5000.

Solution   First, let's see what we can learn without writing a differential equation. For example, we can ask if there is any initial net worth W_0 that will exactly keep the net worth constant. If there's such an equilibrium, the rate at which revenue is earned must exactly balance the payments made, so

$$\text{Rate revenue is earned} \quad = \quad \text{Rate payments are made.}$$

If net worth is a constant W_0, revenue is earned at a constant rate of $0.05W_0$ per year, so we have

$$0.05W_0 = 200 \quad \text{giving} \quad W_0 = 4000.$$

Therefore, if the net worth starts at $4000 million, the revenue and payments are equal, and the net worth remains constant. Therefore, $4000 million is an equilibrium solution.

Suppose, however, the initial net worth is above $4000 million. Then, the revenue earned is more than the payroll expenses, and the net worth of the company increases, thereby increasing the revenue still further. Thus the net worth increases more and more quickly. On the other hand, if the initial net worth is below $4000 million, the revenue is not enough to meet the payments, and the net worth of the company declines. This decreases the revenue, making the net worth decrease still more quickly. The net worth will eventually go to zero, and the company goes bankrupt. See Figure 11.55.

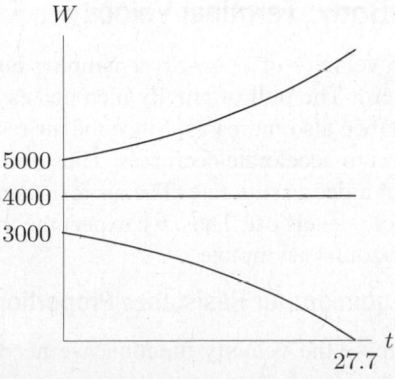

Figure 11.55: Net worth as a function of time: Solutions to $dW/dt = 0.05W - 200$

(a) Now we set up a differential equation for the net worth, using the fact that

$$\begin{array}{ccc} \text{Rate net worth} \\ \text{is increasing} \end{array} = \begin{array}{c} \text{Rate revenue} \\ \text{is earned} \end{array} - \begin{array}{c} \text{Rate payroll payments} \\ \text{are made} \end{array}.$$

In millions of dollars per year, revenue is earned at a rate of $0.05W$, and payments are made at a rate of 200 per year, so for t in years,

$$\frac{dW}{dt} = 0.05W - 200.$$

The equilibrium solution, $W = 4000$, is obtained by setting $dW/dt = 0$.

(b) We solve this equation by separation of variables. It is helpful to factor out 0.05 before separating, so that the W moves over to the left-hand side without a coefficient:

$$\frac{dW}{dt} = 0.05(W - 4000).$$

Separating and integrating gives

$$\int \frac{dW}{W - 4000} = \int 0.05 \, dt,$$

so

$$\ln|W - 4000| = 0.05t + C,$$

or

$$|W - 4000| = e^{0.05t + C} = e^C e^{0.05t}.$$

This means

$$W - 4000 = Ae^{0.05t} \qquad \text{where } A = \pm e^C.$$

To find A, we use the initial condition that $W = W_0$ when $t = 0$:

$$W_0 - 4000 = Ae^0 = A.$$

Substituting this value for A into $W = 4000 + Ae^{0.05t}$ gives

$$W = 4000 + (W_0 - 4000)e^{0.05t}.$$

(c) If $W_0 = 4000$, then $W = 4000$, the equilibrium solution.

If $W_0 = 5000$, then $W = 4000 + 1000e^{0.05t}$.

If $W_0 = 3000$, then $W = 4000 - 1000e^{0.05t}$. Substituting $t \approx 27.7$ gives $W = 0$, so the company goes bankrupt in its twenty-eighth year. These solutions are shown in Figure 11.55. Notice that if the net worth starts with W_0 near, but not equal to, \$4000 million, then W moves further away. Thus, $W = 4000$ is an unstable equilibrium.

The Velocity of a Falling Body: Terminal Velocity

Think about the velocity of a sky-diver jumping out of a plane. When the sky-diver first jumps, his velocity is zero. The pull of gravity then makes his velocity increase. As the sky-diver speeds up, the air resistance also increases. Since the air resistance partly balances the pull of gravity, the force causing him to accelerate decreases. Thus, the velocity is an increasing function of time, but it is increasing at a decreasing rate. The air resistance increases until it balances gravity, when the sky-diver's velocity levels off. Thus, we expect the the graph of velocity against time to be concave down with a horizontal asymptote.

A Differential Equation: Air Resistance Proportional to Velocity

In order to compute the velocity function, we need to know exactly how air resistance depends on velocity. To decide whether air resistance is, say, proportional to the velocity, or is some other function of velocity, requires either lab experiments or a theoretical idea of how the air resistance is created. We consider a very small object, such as a dust particle settling on a computer component during manufacturing,[9] and assume that air resistance is proportional to velocity. Thus, the net force on the object is $F = mg - kv$, where mg is the gravitational force, which acts downward, and kv is the air resistance, which acts upward, so $k > 0$. (See Figure 11.56.) Then, by Newton's Second Law of Motion,

$$\text{Force} = \text{Mass} \cdot \text{Acceleration},$$

we have

$$mg - kv = m\frac{dv}{dt}.$$

This differential equation can be solved by separation of variables. It is easier if we factor out $-k/m$ before separating, giving

$$\frac{dv}{dt} = -\frac{k}{m}\left(v - \frac{mg}{k}\right).$$

Separating and integrating gives

$$\int \frac{dv}{v - mg/k} = -\frac{k}{m}\int dt$$

$$\ln\left|v - \frac{mg}{k}\right| = -\frac{k}{m}t + C.$$

Solving for v, we have

$$\left|v - \frac{mg}{k}\right| = e^{-kt/m+C} = e^C e^{-kt/m}$$

$$v - \frac{mg}{k} = Ae^{-kt/m},$$

where A is an arbitrary constant. We find A from the initial condition that the object starts from rest, so $v = 0$ when $t = 0$. Substituting

$$0 - \frac{mg}{k} = Ae^0$$

gives

$$A = -\frac{mg}{k}.$$

Air resistance, kv

Force due to gravity, mg

Figure 11.56: Forces acting on a falling object

v (velocity)

$\frac{mg}{k}$

Terminal velocity

$$v = \frac{mg}{k}\left(1 - e^{-kt/m}\right)$$

t (time)

Figure 11.57: Velocity of falling dust particle assuming that air resistance is kv

Thus

$$v = \frac{mg}{k} - \frac{mg}{k}e^{-kt/m} = \frac{mg}{k}\left(1 - e^{-kt/m}\right).$$

The graph of this function is in Figure 11.57. The horizontal asymptote represents the *terminal velocity*, mg/k.

Notice that the terminal velocity can also be obtained from the differential equation by setting $dv/dt = 0$ and solving for v:

$$m\frac{dv}{dt} = mg - kv = 0, \quad \text{so} \quad v = \frac{mg}{k}.$$

---

[9]Example suggested by Howard Stone.

Compartmental Analysis: A Reservoir

Many processes can be modeled as a container with various solutions flowing in and out—for example, drugs given intravenously or the discharge of pollutants into a lake. We consider a city's water reservoir, fed partly by clean water from a spring and partly by run-off from the surrounding land. In New England and many other areas with much snow in the winter, the run-off contains salt that has been put on the roads to make them safe for driving. We consider the concentration of salt in the reservoir. If there is no salt in the reservoir initially, the concentration builds up until the rate at which the salt is entering into the reservoir balances the rate at which salt flows out. If, on the other hand, the reservoir starts with a great deal of salt in it, then initially, the rate at which the salt is entering is less than the rate at which it is flowing out, and the quantity of salt in the reservoir decreases. In either case, the salt concentration levels off at an equilibrium value.

A Differential Equation for Salt Concentration

A water reservoir holds 100 million gallons of water and supplies a city with 1 million gallons a day. The reservoir is partly refilled by a spring that provides 0.9 million gallons a day, and the rest of the water, 0.1 million gallons a day, comes from run-off from the surrounding land. The spring is clean, but the run-off contains salt with a concentration of 0.0001 pound per gallon. There was no salt in the reservoir initially, and the water is well mixed (that is, the outflow contains the concentration of salt in the tank at that instant). We find the concentration of salt in the reservoir as a function of time.

It is important to distinguish between the total quantity, Q, of salt in pounds and the concentration, C, of salt in pounds/gallon where

$$\text{Concentration} = C = \frac{\text{Quantity of salt}}{\text{Volume of water}} = \frac{Q}{100 \text{ million}} \left(\frac{\text{lb}}{\text{gal}} \right).$$

(The volume of the reservoir is 100 million gallons.) We will find Q first, and then C. We know that

$$\begin{matrix} \text{Rate of change of} \\ \text{quantity of salt} \end{matrix} = \text{Rate salt entering} - \text{Rate salt leaving}.$$

Salt is entering through the run-off of 0.1 million gallons per day, with each gallon containing 0.0001 pound of salt. Therefore,

$$\text{Rate salt entering} = \text{Concentration} \cdot \text{Volume per day}$$
$$= 0.0001 \left(\frac{\text{lb}}{\text{gal}} \right) \cdot 0.1 \left(\frac{\text{million gal}}{\text{day}} \right)$$
$$= 0.00001 \left(\frac{\text{million lb}}{\text{day}} \right) = 10 \text{ lb/day}.$$

Salt is leaving in the million gallons of water used by the city each day . Thus

$$\text{Rate salt leaving} = \text{Concentration} \cdot \text{Volume per day}$$
$$= \frac{Q}{100 \text{ million}} \left(\frac{\text{lb}}{\text{gal}} \right) \cdot 1 \left(\frac{\text{million gal}}{\text{day}} \right) = \frac{Q}{100} \text{ lb/day}.$$

Therefore, Q satisfies the differential equation

$$\frac{dQ}{dt} = 10 - \frac{Q}{100}.$$

We factor out $-1/100 = -0.01$ and separate variables, giving

$$\frac{dQ}{dt} = -0.01(Q - 1000)$$

$$\int \frac{dQ}{Q-1000} = -\int 0.01\, dt$$
$$\ln|Q-1000| = -0.01t + k$$
$$Q - 1000 = Ae^{-0.01t}.$$

There is no salt initially, so we substitute $Q = 0$ when $t = 0$:

$$0 - 1000 = Ae^0 \quad \text{giving} \quad A = -1000.$$

Thus

$$Q - 1000 = -1000e^{-0.01t},$$

so

$$Q = 1000(1 - e^{-0.01t}) \quad \text{pounds.}$$

Therefore

$$\text{Concentration} = C = \frac{Q}{100 \text{ million}} = \frac{1000}{10^8}(1 - e^{-0.01t}) = 10^{-5}(1 - e^{-0.01t}) \text{ lb/gal.}$$

A sketch of concentration against time is in Figure 11.58.

Figure 11.58: Concentration of salt in reservoir

Exercises and Problems for Section 11.6

Exercises

1. Match the graphs in Figure 11.59 with the following descriptions.

   (a) The population of a new species introduced onto a tropical island.
   (b) The temperature of a metal ingot placed in a furnace and then removed.
   (c) The speed of a car traveling at uniform speed and then braking uniformly.
   (d) The mass of carbon-14 in a historical specimen.
   (e) The concentration of tree pollen in the air over the course of a year.

Figure 11.59

In Exercises 2–5, write a differential equation for the balance B in an investment fund with time, t, measured in years.

2. The balance is earning interest at a continuous rate of 5% per year, and payments are being made out of the fund at a continuous rate of \$12,000 per year.

3. The balance is earning interest at a continuous rate of 3.7% per year, and money is being added to the fund at a continuous rate of \$5000 per year.

4. The balance is losing value at a continuous rate of 8% per year, and money is being added to the fund at a continuous rate of \$2000 per year.

5. The balance is losing value at a continuous rate of 6.5% per year, and payments are being made out of the fund at a continuous rate of \$50,000 per year.

6. A bank account that earns 10% interest compounded continuously has an initial balance of zero. Money is deposited into the account at a constant rate of \$1000 per year.

   (a) Write a differential equation that describes the rate of change of the balance $B = f(t)$.
   (b) Solve the differential equation to find the balance as a function of time.

7. At time $t = 0$, a bottle of juice at $90°F$ is stood in a mountain stream whose temperature is $50°F$. After 5 minutes, its temperature is $80°F$. Let $H(t)$ denote the temperature of the juice at time t, in minutes.

   (a) Write a differential equation for $H(t)$ using Newton's Law of Cooling.
   (b) Solve the differential equation.
   (c) When will the temperature of the juice have dropped to $60°F$?

8. The velocity, v, of a dust particle of mass m and acceleration a satisfies the equation

$$ma = m\frac{dv}{dt} = mg - kv, \quad \text{where } g, k \text{ are constant.}$$

By differentiating this equation, find a differential equation satisfied by a. (Your answer may contain m, g, k, but not v.) Solve for a, given that $a(0) = g$.

Problems

9. A deposit is made to a bank account paying 8% interest compounded continuously. Payments totaling $2000 per year are made from this account.

   (a) Write a differential equation for the balance, B, in the account after t years.
   (b) Find the equilibrium solution of the differential equation. Is the equilibrium stable or unstable? Explain what happens to an account that begins with slightly more money or slightly less money than the equilibrium value.
   (c) Write the solution to the differential equation.
   (d) How much is in the account after 5 years if the initial deposit is   (i) $20,000?   (ii) $30,000?

10. Dead leaves accumulate on the ground in a forest at a rate of 3 grams per square centimeter per year. At the same time, these leaves decompose at a continuous rate of 75% per year. Write a differential equation for the total quantity of dead leaves (per square centimeter) at time t. Sketch a solution showing that the quantity of dead leaves tends toward an equilibrium level. What is that equilibrium level?

11. A stream flowing into a lake brings with it a pollutant at a rate of 8 metric tons per year. The river leaving the lake removes the pollutant at a rate proportional to the quantity in the lake, with constant of proportionality -0.16 if time is measured in years.

   (a) Is the quantity of pollutant in the lake increasing or decreasing at a moment at which the quantity is 45 metric tons? At which the quantity is 55 metric tons?
   (b) What is the quantity of pollutant in the lake after a long time?

12. Caffeine is metabolized and excreted at a continuous rate of about 17% per hour. A person with no caffeine in the body starts drinking coffee, containing 130 mg of caffeine per cup, at 7 am. The person drinks coffee continuously all day at the rate of one cup an hour. Write a differential equation for A, the amount of caffeine in the body t hours after 7 am and give the particular solution to this differential equation. How much caffeine is in the person's body at 5 pm?

13. The rate (per foot) at which light is absorbed as it passes through water is proportional to the intensity, or brightness, at that point.

   (a) Find the intensity as a function of the distance the light has traveled through the water.
   (b) If 50% of the light is absorbed in 10 feet, how much is absorbed in 20 feet? 25 feet?

14. In 2010, the world population was 6.9 billion. The birth rate had stabilized to 140 million per year and is projected to remain constant. The death rate is projected to increase from 57 million per year in 2010 to 80 million per year in 2040 and to continue increasing at the same rate.

   (a) Assuming the death rate increases linearly, write a differential equation for $P(t)$, the world population in billions t years from 2010.
   (b) Solve the differential equation.
   (c) Find the population predicted for 2050.

15. The rate at which barometric pressure decreases with altitude is proportional to the barometric pressure at that altitude. If the barometric pressure is measured in inches of mercury, and the altitude in feet, then the constant of proportionality is $3.7 \cdot 10^{-5}$. The barometric pressure at sea level is 29.92 inches of mercury.

   (a) Calculate the barometric pressure at the top of Mount Whitney, 14,500 feet (the highest mountain in the US outside Alaska), and at the top of Mount Everest, 29,000 feet (the highest mountain in the world).
   (b) People cannot easily survive at a pressure below 15 inches of mercury. What is the highest altitude to which people can safely go?

16. According to a simple physiological model, an athletic adult male needs 20 calories per day per pound of body weight to maintain his weight. If he consumes more or fewer calories than those required to maintain his weight, his weight changes at a rate proportional to the difference between the number of calories consumed and the number needed to maintain his current weight; the constant of proportionality is $1/3500$ pounds per calorie. Suppose that a particular person has a constant caloric intake of I calories per day. Let $W(t)$ be the person's weight in pounds at time t (measured in days).

   (a) What differential equation has solution $W(t)$?

(b) Find the equilibrium solution of the differential equation. Based on the context, do you expect the equilibrium to be stable or unstable?

(c) Solve this differential equation.

(d) Graph $W(t)$ if the person starts out weighing 160 pounds and consumes 3000 calories a day.

17. Morphine is often used as a pain-relieving drug. The half-life of morphine in the body is 2 hours. Suppose morphine is administered to a patient intravenously at a rate of 2.5 mg per hour, and the rate at which the morphine is eliminated is proportional to the amount present.

(a) Use the half-life to show that, to three decimal places, the constant of proportionality for the rate at which morphine leaves the body (in mg/hour) is $k = -0.347$.

(b) Write a differential equation for the quantity, Q, of morphine in the blood after t hours.

(c) Use the differential equation to find the equilibrium solution. (This is the long-term amount of morphine in the body, once the system has stabilized.)

18. Water leaks out of a barrel at a rate proportional to the square root of the depth of the water at that time. If the water level starts at 36 inches and drops to 35 inches in 1 hour, how long will it take for all of the water to leak out of the barrel?

19. When a gas expands without gain or loss of heat, the rate of change of pressure with respect to volume is proportional to pressure divided by volume. Find a law connecting pressure and volume in this case.

20. A spherical snowball melts at a rate proportional to its surface area.

(a) Write a differential equation for its volume, V.

(b) If the initial volume is V_0, solve the differential equation and graph the solution.

(c) When does the snowball disappear?

21. Water leaks from a vertical cylindrical tank through a small hole in its base at a rate proportional to the square root of the volume of water remaining. If the tank initially contains 200 liters and 20 liters leak out during the first day, when will the tank be half empty? How much water will there be after 4 days?

22. As you know, when a course ends, students start to forget the material they have learned. One model (called the Ebbinghaus model) assumes that the rate at which a student forgets material is proportional to the difference between the material currently remembered and some positive constant, a.

(a) Let $y = f(t)$ be the fraction of the original material remembered t weeks after the course has ended. Set up a differential equation for y. Your equation will contain two constants; the constant a is less than y for all t.

(b) Solve the differential equation.

(c) Describe the practical meaning (in terms of the amount remembered) of the constants in the solution $y = f(t)$.

23. An item is initially sold at a price of $\$p$ per unit. Over time, market forces push the price toward the equilibrium price, $\$p^*$, at which supply balances demand. The Evans Price Adjustment model says that the rate of change in the market price, $\$p$, is proportional to the difference between the market price and the equilibrium price.

(a) Write a differential equation for p as a function of t.

(b) Solve for p.

(c) Sketch solutions for various different initial prices, both above and below the equilibrium price.

(d) What happens to p as $t \to \infty$?

24. Let L, a constant, be the number of people who would like to see a newly released movie, and let $N(t)$ be the number of people who have seen it during the first t days since its release. The rate that people first go see the movie, dN/dt (in people/day), is proportional to the number of people who would like to see it but haven't yet. Write and solve a differential equation describing dN/dt where t is the number of days since the movie's release. Your solution will involve L and a constant of proportionality, k.

25. A drug is administered intravenously at a constant rate of r mg/hour and is excreted at a rate proportional to the quantity present, with constant of proportionality $\alpha > 0$.

(a) Solve a differential equation for the quantity, Q, in milligrams, of the drug in the body at time t hours. Assume there is no drug in the body initially. Your answer will contain r and α. Graph Q against t. What is Q_∞, the limiting long-run value of Q?

(b) What effect does doubling r have on Q_∞? What effect does doubling r have on the time to reach half the limiting value, $\frac{1}{2}Q_\infty$?

(c) What effect does doubling α have on Q_∞? On the time to reach $\frac{1}{2}Q_\infty$?

26. When people smoke, carbon monoxide is released into the air. In a room of volume 60 m^3, air containing 5% carbon monoxide is introduced at a rate of 0.002 m^3/min. (This means that 5% of the volume of the incoming air is carbon monoxide.) The carbon monoxide mixes immediately with the rest of the air, and the mixture leaves the room at the same rate as it enters.

(a) Write a differential equation for $c(t)$, the concentration of carbon monoxide at time t, in minutes.

(b) Solve the differential equation, assuming there is no carbon monoxide in the room initially.

(c) What happens to the value of $c(t)$ in the long run?

27. (Continuation of Problem 26.) Government agencies warn that exposure to air containing 0.02% carbon monoxide can lead to headaches and dizziness.[10] How

---

[10]www.lni.wa.gov/Safety/Topics/AtoZ/CarbonMonoxide/, accessed on June 14, 2007.

long does it take for the concentration of carbon monoxide in the room in Problem 26 to reach this level?

28. An aquarium pool has volume $2 \cdot 10^6$ liters. The pool initially contains pure fresh water. At $t = 0$ minutes, water containing 10 grams/liter of salt is poured into the pool at a rate of 60 liters/minute. The salt water instantly mixes with the fresh water, and the excess mixture is drained out of the pool at the same rate (60 liters/minute).

   (a) Write a differential equation for $S(t)$, the mass of salt in the pool at time t.
   (b) Solve the differential equation to find $S(t)$.
   (c) What happens to $S(t)$ as $t \to \infty$?

29. In 1692, Johann Bernoulli was teaching the Marquis de l'Hopital calculus in Paris. Solve the following problem, which is similar to the one that they did. What is the equation of the curve which has subtangent (distance BC in Figure 11.60) equal to twice its abscissa (distance OC)?

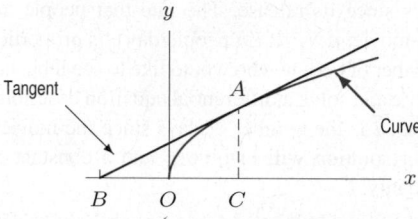

Figure 11.60

30. An object of mass m is thrown vertically upward from the surface of the earth with initial velocity v_0. We will calculate the value of v_0, called the escape velocity, with which the object can escape the pull of the gravity and never return to earth. Since the object is moving far from the surface of the earth, we must take into account the variation of gravity with altitude. If the acceleration due to gravity at sea level is g, and R is the radius of the earth, the gravitational force, F, on the object of mass m at an altitude h above the surface of the earth is given by

$$F = \frac{mgR^2}{(R+h)^2}.$$

(a) The velocity of the object (measured upward) is v at time t. Use Newton's Second Law of Motion to show that

$$\frac{dv}{dt} = -\frac{gR^2}{(R+h)^2}.$$

(b) Rewrite this equation with h instead of t as the independent variable using the chain rule $\frac{dv}{dt} = \frac{dv}{dh} \cdot \frac{dh}{dt}$. Hence, show that

$$v\frac{dv}{dh} = -\frac{gR^2}{(R+h)^2}.$$

(c) Solve the differential equation in part (b).
(d) Find the escape velocity, the smallest value of v_0 such that v is never zero.

31. A bank account earns 5% annual interest, compounded continuously. Money is deposited in a continuous cash flow at a rate of $1200 per year into the account.

(a) Write a differential equation that describes the rate at which the balance $B = f(t)$ is changing.
(b) Solve the differential equation given an initial balance $B_0 = 0$.
(c) Find the balance after 5 years.

32. (Continuation of Problem 31.) Now suppose the money is deposited once a month (instead of continuously) but still at a rate of $1200 per year.

(a) Write down the sum that gives the balance after 5 years, assuming the first deposit is made one month from today, and today is $t = 0$.
(b) The sum you wrote in part (a) is a Riemann sum approximation to the integral

$$\int_0^5 1200 e^{0.1t}\, dt.$$

Determine whether it is a left sum or right sum, and determine what Δt and n are. Then use your calculator to evaluate the sum.
(c) Compare your answer in part (b) to your answer to Problem 31(c).

Strengthen Your Understanding

In Problems 33–34, explain what is wrong with the statement.

33. At a time when a bank balance $\$B$, which satisfies $dB/dt = 0.08B - 250$, is $5000, the balance is going down.

34. The differential equation $dQ/dt = -0.15Q + 25$ represents the quantity of a drug in the body if the drug is metabolized at a continuous rate of 15% per day and an IV line is delivering the drug at a constant rate of 25 mg per hour.

In Problems 35–37, give an example of:

35. A differential equation for the quantity of a drug in a patient's body if the patient is receiving the drug at a constant rate through an IV line and is metabolizing the drug at a rate proportional to the quantity present.

36. A differential equation for any quantity which grows in two ways simultaneously: on its own at a rate proportional to the cube root of the amount present and from an external contribution at a constant rate.

37. A differential equation for a quantity that is increasing and grows fastest when the quantity is small and grows more slowly as the quantity gets larger.

11.7 THE LOGISTIC MODEL

Oil prices have a significant impact on the world's economies. In the eighteen months preceding July 2008, the price of oil more than doubled from about $60 a barrel to about $140 a barrel.[11] The impact of the increase was significant, from the auto industry, to family budgets, to how people commute. Even the threat of a price hike can send stock markets tumbling.

Many reasons are suggested for the increase, but one fact is inescapable: there is a finite supply of oil in the world. To fuel its expanding economy, the world consumes more oil each succeeding year. This cannot go on indefinitely. Economists and geologists are interested in estimating the remaining oil reserves and the date at which annual oil production is expected to peak (that is, reach a maximum).

US oil production has already peaked—and the date was predicted in advance. In 1956, geologist M. King Hubbert predicted that annual US oil production would peak some time in the period 1965–1970. Although many did not take his prediction seriously, US oil production did in fact peak in 1970. The economic impact was blunted by the US's increasing reliance on foreign oil.

In this section we introduce the *logistic differential equation* and use it, as Hubbert did, to predict the peak of US oil production.[12] Problems 29–32 investigate the peak of world oil production.

The Logistic Model

The logistic differential equation describes growth subject to a limit. For oil, the limit is the total oil reserves; for a population, the limit is the largest population that the environment can support; for the spread of information or a disease, the limit is the number of people that could be affected. The solution to this differential equation is the family of logistic functions introduced in Section 4.4.

Suppose P is growing logistically toward a limiting value of L, and the relative growth rate, $(1/P)dP/dt$, is k when $P = 0$. In the exponential model, the relative growth rate remains constant at k. But in the logistic model, the relative growth rate decreases linearly to 0 as P approaches L; see Figure 11.61.

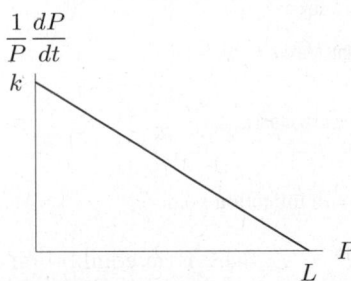

Figure 11.61: Logistic model: Relative growth rate is a linear function of P

So we have

$$\frac{1}{P}\frac{dP}{dt} = k - \frac{k}{L}P = k\left(1 - \frac{P}{L}\right).$$

The logistic differential equation can also be written

$$\frac{dP}{dt} = kP\left(1 - \frac{P}{L}\right).$$

This equation was first proposed as a model for population growth by the Belgian mathematician P. F. Verhulst in the 1830s. In Verhulst's model, L represents the *carrying capacity* of the environment, which is determined by the supply of food and arable land along with the available technology.

---

[11]http://www.nyse.tv/crude-oil-price-history.htm. Accessed February 2012.
[12]Based on an undergraduate project by Brad Ernst, Colgate University.

Qualitative Solution to the Logistic Equation

Figure 11.62 shows the slope field and characteristic *sigmoid*, or *S*-shaped, solution curve for the logistic model. Notice that for each fixed value of P, that is, along each horizontal line, the slopes are constant because dP/dt depends only on P and not on t. The slopes are small near $P = 0$ and near $P = L$; they are steepest around $P = L/2$. For $P > L$, the slopes are negative, so if the population is above the carrying capacity, the population decreases.

Figure 11.62: Slope field for
$dP/dt = kP(1 - P/L)$

Figure 11.63: $dP/dt = kP(1 - P/L)$

We can locate the inflection point where the slope is greatest using Figure 11.63. This graph is a parabola because dP/dt is a quadratic function of P. The horizontal intercepts are at $P = 0$ and $P = L$, so the maximum, where the slope is greatest, is at $P = L/2$. Figure 11.63 also tells us that for $0 < P < L/2$, the slope dP/dt is positive and increasing, so the graph of P against t is concave up. (See Figure 11.64.) For $L/2 < P < L$, the slope dP/dt is positive and decreasing, so the graph of P is concave down. For $P > L$, the slope dP/dt is negative, so P is decreasing.

Figure 11.64: Logistic growth with inflection point

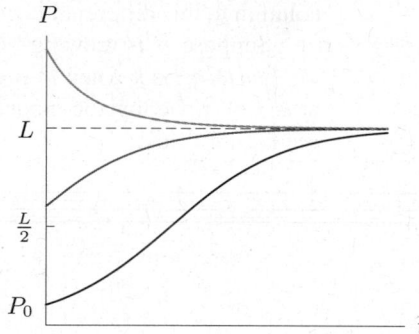

Figure 11.65: Solutions to the logistic equation

If $P = 0$ or $P = L$, there is an equilibrium solution. Figure 11.65 shows that $P = 0$ is an unstable equilibrium because solutions which start near 0 move away. However, $P = L$ is a stable equilibrium.

The Analytic Solution to the Logistic Equation

We have already obtained a lot of information about logistic growth without finding a formula for the solution. However, the equation can be solved analytically by separating variables:

$$\frac{dP}{dt} = kP\left(1 - \frac{P}{L}\right) = kP\left(\frac{L - P}{L}\right)$$

giving

$$\int \frac{dP}{P(L - P)} = \int \frac{k}{L}\, dt.$$

We can integrate the left side using the integral tables (Formula V 26) or by partial fractions:

$$\int \frac{1}{L}\left(\frac{1}{P} + \frac{1}{L - P}\right) dP = \int \frac{k}{L}\, dt.$$

Canceling the constant L, we integrate to get

$$\ln|P| - \ln|L - P| = kt + C.$$

Multiplying through by (-1) and using properties of logarithms, we have

$$\ln\left|\frac{L - P}{P}\right| = -kt - C.$$

Exponentiating both sides gives

$$\left|\frac{L - P}{P}\right| = e^{-kt-C} = e^{-C}e^{-kt}, \qquad \text{so} \qquad \frac{L - P}{P} = \pm e^{-C}e^{-kt}.$$

Then, writing $A = \pm e^{-C}$, we have

$$\frac{L - P}{P} = Ae^{-kt}.$$

We find A by substituting $P = P_0$ when $t = 0$, which gives

$$\frac{L - P_0}{P_0} = Ae^0 = A.$$

Since $(L - P)/P = (L/P) - 1$, we have

$$\frac{L}{P} = 1 + Ae^{-kt},$$

which gives the following result:

The solution to the logistic differential equation:

$$\frac{dP}{dt} = kP\left(1 - \frac{P}{L}\right) \qquad \text{with initial condition } P_0 \text{ when } t = 0$$

is the logistic function

$$P = \frac{L}{1 + Ae^{-kt}} \qquad \text{with} \quad A = \frac{L - P_0}{P_0}.$$

The parameter L represents the limiting value. The parameter k represents the relative growth rate when P is small relative to L. The parameter A depends on the initial condition P_0.

Peak Oil: US Production

We apply the logistic model to US oil production as Hubbert did in 1956. To make predictions, we need the values of k and L. We calculate these values from the oil production data Hubbert had available to him in the 1950s; see Table 11.5.

We define P to be the *total* amount of oil, in billions of barrels, produced in the US since 1859, the year the first oil well was built. See Table 11.5. With time, t, in years, dP/dt approximates the *annual* oil production in billions of barrels per year. Peak oil production occurs when dP/dt is a maximum.

Table 11.5 *US oil production[13] for 1931–1950 (billions of barrels)*

Year	dP/dt	P	Year	dP/dt	P	Year	dP/dt	P
1931	0.851	13.8	1938	1.21	21.0	1945	1.71	31.5
1932	0.785	14.6	1939	1.26	22.3	1946	1.73	33.2
1933	0.906	15.5	1940	1.50	23.8	1947	1.86	35.1
1934	0.908	16.4	1941	1.40	25.2	1948	2.02	37.1
1935	0.994	17.4	1942	1.39	26.6	1949	1.84	38.9
1936	1.10	18.5	1943	1.51	28.1	1950	1.97	40.9
1937	1.28	19.8	1944	1.68	29.8			

Figure 11.66 shows a scatterplot of the relative growth rate $(dP/dt)/P$ versus P. If the data follow a logistic differential equation, we see a linear relationship with intercept k and slope $-k/L$:

$$\frac{1}{P}\frac{dP}{dt} = k\left(1 - \frac{P}{L}\right) = k - \frac{k}{L}P.$$

Figure 11.66 shows a line fitted to the data.[14] The vertical intercept gives the value $k = 0.0649$.

The slope of the line is $-k/L = -0.00036$, so we have $L = 0.0649/0.00036 = 180$ billion barrels of oil. Thus, the model predicts that the total oil reserves in the US (the total amount in the ground before drilling started in 1859) were 180 billion barrels of oil.[15]

Figure 11.66: US oil production 1931–1950: Scatterplot and line for $1/P(dP/dt)$ versus P

If we let $t = 0$ be 1950, then $P_0 = 40.9$ billion barrels and $A = (180 - 40.9)/40.9 = 3.401$. The logistic function representing US oil production is

$$P = \frac{180}{1 + 3.401e^{-0.0649t}}.$$

Predicting Peak Oil Production

To predict, as Hubbert did, the year when annual US oil production would peak, we use the fact that the maximum value for dP/dt occurs when $P = L/2$. We derive a formula for the peak year (used again in Problems 29–32 to find peak production in world oil). The crucial observation is that, at the peak, the denominator of the expression for P must equal 2. Since

$$P = \frac{L}{2} = \frac{L}{1 + Ae^{-kt}}, \qquad \text{we have} \quad Ae^{-kt} = 1.$$

Using logarithms to solve the equation $Ae^{-kt} = 1$, we get $t = (1/k)\ln A$. Since $A = (L - P_0)/P_0$, we see that the time to peak oil production is an example of the following result:

---

[13]Data from http://www.eia.gov/dnav/pet/hist/LeafHandler.ashx?n=PET&s=MCRFPUS1&f=A. Accessed Feb, 2012.

[14]The line is a least-squares regression line.

[15]If the same analysis is repeated for other time periods, for example 1900–1950 or 1900–2000, the value for L varies between 120 and 220 billion barrels, while the value of k varies between 0.060 and 0.075.

> For a logistic function, the maximum value of dP/dt occurs when $P = L/2$, and
>
> $$\text{Time to the maximum rate of change} = \frac{1}{k} \ln A = \frac{1}{k} \ln \frac{L - P_0}{P_0}.$$

Thus, for the US,

$$\text{Time to peak oil production} = \frac{1}{0.0649} \ln \frac{180 - 40.9}{40.9} \approx 19 \text{ years};$$

that is, oil production was predicted to peak in the year $1950 + 19 = 1969$. That year, $P = L/2$ and annual production was expected to be

$$\frac{dP}{dt} = kP\left(1 - \frac{P}{L}\right) = 0.0649 \cdot \frac{180}{2}\left(1 - \frac{1}{2}\right) \approx 3 \text{ billion barrels.}$$

The actual peak in US oil production was 3.5 billion barrels in 1970. Repeating the analysis using other time periods gives peak oil years in the range 1965-1970, as Hubbert predicted.

Figure 11.67 shows annual US production data and the parabola predicting its peak around 1970. Figure 11.68 shows P as a logistic function of t, with the limiting value of $P = 180$ and maximum production at $P = 90$. In fact, the first major oil crisis hit the US in the 1970s, with spiraling gas prices and long lines at service stations. The decline in US oil production since 1970 was partly mitigated by the opening of the Alaskan oil fields, which led to a second but lower peak in 1985. However, the US has increasingly depended on foreign oil.

Although Hubbert's predictions of the peak year proved to be accurate, extrapolation into the future is risky. Figure 11.67 and Figure 11.68 show that since 1970, oil production has slowed, though not as much as predicted.

Figure 11.67: US oil production: dP/dt versus P, predicted (parabola) and actual

Figure 11.68: US oil production: P versus t, predicted (logistic) and actual

Interestingly, Hubbert used the logistic model only to estimate k; for L, he relied on geological studies. It is remarkable that using only annual oil production for 1930-1950, we get an estimate for L that is in such close agreement with the geological estimates.

US Population Growth

The logistic equation is often used to model population growth. Table 11.6 gives the annual census figures in millions for the US population from 1790 to 2010.[16] Since we have the population, $P(t)$, of the US at ten-year intervals, we compute the relative growth rate using averages of estimates of the form:

$$\frac{1}{P}\frac{dP}{dt} \quad \text{in } 1860 = \frac{1}{P(1860)} \cdot \frac{P(1870) - P(1860)}{10}.$$

(See Problem 19 for details.) If we focus on the period 1790–1940, a line fitted to the scatterplot of $(1/P)dP/dt$ versus P has intercept $k = 0.0317$ and slope $-k/L = -0.000165$, so $L \approx 192$. Thus the differential equation modeling the US population during this period is

---

[16]www.census.gov. Accessed February 12, 2012.

$$\frac{dP}{dt} = 0.0317P\left(1 - \frac{P}{192}\right).$$

Using 1790 as $t = 0$, we get

$$A = \frac{L - P_0}{P_0} = \frac{192 - 3.9}{3.9} \approx 48.$$

Thus the solution to the logistic differential equation is

$$P = \frac{192}{1 + 48e^{-0.0317t}}.$$

Table 11.6 shows the actual census data for 1790–1940 with projected values from a logistic model; the largest deviations are 4% in 1840 and 1870 (the Civil War accounts for the second one).[17]

Table 11.6 *US population, in millions, for 1790–2010, actual data and logistic predictions*

Year	Actual	Logistic	Year	Actual	Logistic	Year	Actual	Logistic	Year	Actual	Logistic
1790	3.9	3.9	1850	23.2	23.6	1910	92.2	92.9	1970	203.2	165.7
1800	5.3	5.4	1860	31.4	30.9	1920	106.0	108.0	1980	226.5	172.2
1810	7.2	7.3	1870	38.6	40.1	1930	123.2	122.6	1990	248.7	177.2
1820	9.6	9.8	1880	50.2	51.0	1940	132.2	136.0	2000	281.4	181.0
1830	12.9	13.3	1890	63.0	63.7	1950	151.3	147.7	2010	308.7	183.9
1840	17.1	17.8	1900	76.2	77.9	1960	179.3	157.6			

After 1940, the actual figures leave the logistic model in the dust. The model predicts an increase of 9.9 million from 1950 to 1960 versus the actual change of 28 million. By 1970 the actual population of 203.2 million exceeded the predicted limiting population of $L = 192$ million. The unprecedented surge in US population between 1945 and 1965 is referred to as the baby boom.

Exercises and Problems for Section 11.7

Exercises

1. (a) Show that $P = 1/(1 + e^{-t})$ satisfies the logistic equation

$$\frac{dP}{dt} = P(1 - P).$$

(b) What is the limiting value of P as $t \to \infty$?

2. A quantity P satisfies the differential equation

$$\frac{dP}{dt} = kP\left(1 - \frac{P}{100}\right).$$

Sketch approximate solutions satisfying each of the following initial conditions:

(a) $P_0 = 8$ **(b)** $P_0 = 70$ **(c)** $P_0 = 125$

3. A quantity Q satisfies the differential equation

$$\frac{dQ}{dt} = kQ(1 - 0.0004Q).$$

Sketch approximate solutions satisfying each of the following initial conditions:

(a) $Q_0 = 300$ **(b)** $Q_0 = 1500$ **(c)** $Q_0 = 3500$

4. A quantity P satisfies the differential equation

$$\frac{dP}{dt} = kP\left(1 - \frac{P}{250}\right), \quad \text{with } k > 0.$$

Sketch a graph of dP/dt as a function of P.

5. A quantity A satisfies the differential equation

$$\frac{dA}{dt} = kA(1 - 0.0002A), \quad \text{with } k > 0.$$

Sketch a graph of dA/dt as a function of A.

---

[17]Calculations were done with more precise values of the population data and the constants k, L, and A than those shown.

6. Figure 11.69 shows a graph of dP/dt against P for a logistic differential equation. Sketch several solutions of P against t, using different initial conditions. Include a scale on your vertical axis.

Figure 11.69

7. Figure 11.70 shows a slope field of a differential equation for a quantity Q growing logistically. Sketch a graph of dQ/dt against Q. Include a scale on the horizontal axis.

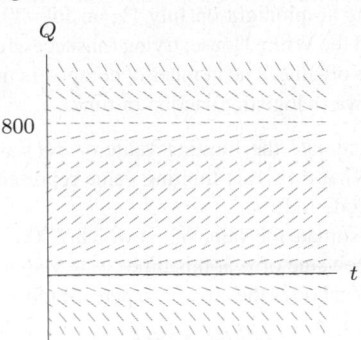

Figure 11.70

8. **(a)** On the slope field for $dP/dt = 3P - 3P^2$ in Figure 11.71, sketch three solution curves showing different types of behavior for the population, P.
   (b) Is there a stable value of the population? If so, what is it?
   (c) Describe the meaning of the shape of the solution curves for the population: Where is P increasing? Decreasing? What happens in the long run? Are there any inflection points? Where? What do they mean for the population?
   (d) Sketch a graph of dP/dt against P. Where is dP/dt positive? Negative? Zero? Maximum? How do your observations about dP/dt explain the shapes of your solution curves?

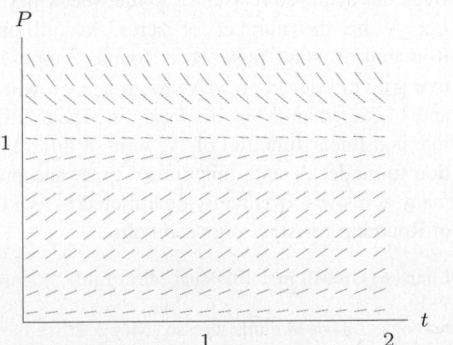

Figure 11.71

Exercises 9–10 give a graph of dP/dt against P.

(a) What are the equilibrium values of P?
(b) If $P = 500$, is dP/dt positive or negative? Is P increasing or decreasing?

9. dP/dt

10. dP/dt

For the logistic differential equations in Exercises 11–12,

(a) Give values for k and for L and interpret the meaning of each in terms of the growth of the quantity P.
(b) Give the value of P when the rate of change is at its peak.

11. $\dfrac{dP}{dt} = 0.035P \left(1 - \dfrac{P}{6000}\right)$

12. $\dfrac{dP}{dt} = 0.1P - 0.00008P^2$

In Exercises 13–16, give the general solution to the logistic differential equation.

13. $\dfrac{dP}{dt} = 0.05P \left(1 - \dfrac{P}{2800}\right)$

14. $\dfrac{dP}{dt} = 0.012P \left(1 - \dfrac{P}{5700}\right)$

15. $\dfrac{dP}{dt} = 0.68P(1 - 0.00025P)$

16. $\dfrac{dP}{dt} = 0.2P - 0.0008P^2$

In Exercises 17–20, give k, L, A, a formula for P as a function of time t, and the time to the peak value of dP/dt.

17. $\dfrac{dP}{dt} = 10P - 5P^2, \quad P_0 = L/4$

18. $\dfrac{dP}{dt} = 0.02P - 0.0025P^2, \quad P_0 = 1$

19. $\dfrac{1}{P}\dfrac{dP}{dt} = 0.3 \left(1 - \dfrac{P}{100}\right), \quad P_0 = 75$

20. $\dfrac{1}{10P}\dfrac{dP}{dt} = 0.012 - 0.002P, \quad P_0 = 2$

In Exercises 21–22, give the solution to the logistic differential equation with initial condition.

21. $\dfrac{dP}{dt} = 0.8P \left(1 - \dfrac{P}{8500}\right)$ with $P_0 = 500$

22. $\dfrac{dP}{dt} = 0.04P(1 - 0.0001P)$ with $P_0 = 200$

Problems

23. A rumor spreads among a group of 400 people. The number of people, $N(t)$, who have heard the rumor by time t in hours since the rumor started is approximated by

$$N(t) = \frac{400}{1 + 399e^{-0.4t}}.$$

   (a) Find $N(0)$ and interpret it.
   (b) How many people will have heard the rumor after 2 hours? After 10 hours?
   (c) Graph $N(t)$.
   (d) Approximately how long will it take until half the people have heard the rumor? 399 people?
   (e) When is the rumor spreading fastest?

24. The Tojolobal Mayan Indian community in southern Mexico has available a fixed amount of land. The proportion, P, of land in use for farming t years after 1935 is modeled with the logistic function in Figure 11.72:[18]

$$P = \frac{1}{1 + 2.968e^{-0.0275t}}.$$

   (a) What proportion of the land was in use for farming in 1935?
   (b) What is the long-run prediction of this model?
   (c) When was half the land in use for farming?
   (d) When is the proportion of land used for farming increasing most rapidly?

Figure 11.72

25. A model for the population, P, of carp in a landlocked lake at time t is given by the differential equation

$$\frac{dP}{dt} = 0.25P(1 - 0.0004P).$$

   (a) What is the long-term equilibrium population of carp in the lake?
   (b) A census taken ten years ago found there were 1000 carp in the lake. Estimate the current population.
   (c) Under a plan to join the lake to a nearby river, the fish will be able to leave the lake. A net loss of 10% of the carp each year is predicted, but the patterns of birth and death are not expected to change. Revise the differential equation to take this into account. Use the revised differential equation to predict the future development of the carp population.

26. Table 11.7 gives values for a logistic function $P = f(t)$.

   (a) Estimate the maximum rate of change of P and estimate the value of t when it occurs.
   (b) If P represents the growth of a population, estimate the carrying capacity of the population.

Table 11.7

t	0	10	20	30	40	50	60	70
P	120	125	135	155	195	270	345	385

27. Figure 11.73 shows the spread of the Code-red computer virus during July 2001. Most of the growth took place starting at midnight on July 19; on July 20, the virus attacked the White House, trying (unsuccessfully) to knock its site off-line. The number of computers infected by the virus was a logistic function of time.

   (a) Estimate the limiting value of $f(t)$ as t increased. What does this limiting value represent in terms of Code-red?
   (b) Estimate the value of t at which $f''(t) = 0$. Estimate the value of n at this time.
   (c) What does the answer to part (b) tell us about Code-red?
   (d) How are the answers to parts (a) and (b) related?

Figure 11.73

28. According to an article in *The New York Times*,[19] pigweed has acquired resistance to the weedkiller Roundup. Let N be the number of acres, in millions, where Roundup-resistant pigweed is found. Suppose the relative growth rate, $(1/N)dN/dt$, was 15% when $N = 5$ and 14.5% when $N = 10$. Assuming the relative growth rate is a linear function of N, write a differential equation to model N as a function of time, and predict how many acres will eventually be afflicted before the spread of Roundup-resistant pigweed halts.

---

[18] Adapted from J. S. Thomas and M. C. Robbins, "The Limits to Growth in a Tojolobal Maya Ejido," *Geoscience and Man 26* (Baton Rouge: Geoscience Publications, 1988), pp. 9–16.

[19] http://www.nytimes.com/2010/05/04/business/energy-environment/04weed.html, accessed May 3, 2010.

In Problems 29–33, we analyze world oil production.[20] When annual world oil production peaks and starts to decline, major economic restructuring will be needed. We investigate when this slowdown is projected to occur.

29. We define P to be the total oil production worldwide since 1859 in billions of barrels. In 1993, annual world oil production was 22.0 billion barrels and the total production was $P = 724$ billion barrels. In 2008, annual production was 26.9 billion barrels and the total production was $P = 1100$ billion barrels. Let t be time in years since 1993.

  (a) Estimate the rate of production, dP/dt, for 1993 and 2008.
  (b) Estimate the relative growth rate, $(1/P)(dP/dt)$, for 1993 and 2008.
  (c) Find an equation for the relative growth rate, $(1/P)(dP/dt)$, as a function of P, assuming that the function is linear.
  (d) Assuming that P increases logistically and that all oil in the ground will ultimately be extracted, estimate the world oil reserves in 1859 to the nearest billion barrels.
  (e) Write and solve the logistic differential equation modeling P.

30. In Problem 29 we used a logistic function to model P, total world oil production since 1859, as a function of time, t, in years since 1993. Use this function to answer the following questions:

  (a) When does peak annual world oil production occur?
  (b) Geologists have estimated world oil reserves to be as high as 3500 billion barrels.[21] When does peak world oil production occur with this assumption? (Assume k and P_0 are unchanged.)

31. As in Problem 29, let P be total world oil production since 1859. In 1998, annual world production was 24.4 billion barrels and total production was $P = 841$ billion barrels. In 2003, annual production was 25.3 billion barrels and total production was $P = 964$ billion barrels.

  (a) Graph dP/dt versus P from Problem 29 and show the data for 1998 and 2003. How well does the model fit the data?
  (b) Graph the logistic function modeling worldwide oil production (P versus t) from Problem 29 and show the data for 1998 and 2003. How well does the model fit the data?

32. Use the logistic function obtained in Problem 29 to model the growth of P, the total oil produced worldwide in billions of barrels since 1859:

  (a) Find the projected value of P for 2010.
  (b) Estimate the annual world oil production during 2010.

  (c) How much oil is projected to remain in the ground in 2010?
  (d) Compare the projected production in part (b) with the actual figure of 26.9 billion barrels.

33. With P, the total oil produced worldwide since 1859, in billions of barrels, modeled as a function of time t in years since 1993 as in Problem 29:

  (a) Predict the total quantity of oil produced by 2020.
  (b) In what year does the model predict that only 300 billion barrels remain?

34. The total number of people infected with a virus often grows like a logistic curve. Suppose that time, t, is in weeks and that 10 people originally have the virus. In the early stages, the number of people infected is increasing exponentially with $k = 1.78$. In the long run, 5000 people are infected.

  (a) Find a logistic function to model the number of people infected.
  (b) Sketch a graph of your answer to part (a).
  (c) Use your graph to estimate the length of time until the rate at which people are becoming infected starts to decrease. What is the vertical coordinate at this point?

35. Policy makers are interested in modeling the spread of information through a population. For example, agricultural ministries use models to understand the spread of technical innovations or new seed types through their countries. Two models, based on how the information is spread, follow. Assume the population is of a constant size M.

  (a) If the information is spread by mass media (TV, radio, newspapers), the rate at which information is spread is believed to be proportional to the number of people not having the information at that time. Write a differential equation for the number of people having the information by time t. Sketch a solution assuming that no one (except the mass media) has the information initially.
  (b) If the information is spread by word of mouth, the rate of spread of information is believed to be proportional to the product of the number of people who know and the number who don't. Write a differential equation for the number of people having the information by time t. Sketch the solution for the cases in which

  (i) No one   (ii) 5% of the population
  (iii) 75% of the population

  knows initially. In each case, when is the information spreading fastest?

36. In the 1930s, the Soviet ecologist G. F. Gause[22] studied the population growth of yeast. Fit a logistic curve, $dP/dt = kP(1 - P/L)$, to his data below using the method outlined below.

Time (hours)	0	10	18	23	34	42	47
Yeast pop	0.37	8.87	10.66	12.50	13.27	12.87	12.70

(a) Plot the data and use it to estimate (by eye) the carrying capacity, L.

(b) Use the first two pieces of data in the table and your value for L to estimate k.

(c) On the same axes as the data points, use your values for k and L to sketch the solution curve

$$P = \frac{L}{1 + Ae^{-kt}} \quad \text{where} \quad A = \frac{L - P_0}{P_0}.$$

37. The population data from another experiment on yeast by the ecologist G. F. Gause is given.

Time (hours)	0	13	32	56	77	101	125
Yeast pop	1.00	1.70	2.73	4.87	5.67	5.80	5.83

(a) Do you think the population is growing exponentially or logistically? Give reasons for your answer.

(b) Estimate the value of k (for either model) from the first two pieces of data. If you chose a logistic model in part (a), estimate the carrying capacity, L, from the data.

(c) Sketch the data and the approximate growth curve given by the parameters you estimated.

38. The spread of a non-fatal disease through a population of fixed size M can be modeled as follows. The rate that healthy people are infected, in people per day, is proportional to the product of the numbers of healthy and infected people. The constant of proportionality is $0.01/M$. The rate of recovery, in people per day, is 0.009 times the number of people infected. Construct a differential equation that models the spread of the disease. Assuming that initially only a small number of people are infected, plot a graph of the number of infected people against time. What fraction of the population is infected in the long run?

39. Many organ pipes in old European churches are made of tin. In cold climates such pipes can be affected with *tin pest*, when the tin becomes brittle and crumbles into a gray powder. This transformation can appear to take place very suddenly because the presence of the gray powder encourages the reaction to proceed. The rate of the reaction is proportional to the product of the amount of tin left and the quantity of gray powder, p, present at time t. Assume that when metallic tin is converted to gray powder, its mass does not change.

(a) Write a differential equation for p. Let the total quantity of metallic tin present originally be B.

(b) Sketch a graph of the solution $p = f(t)$ if there is a small quantity of powder initially. How much metallic tin has crumbled when it is crumbling fastest?

(c) Suppose there is no gray powder initially. (For example, suppose the tin is completely new.) What does this model predict will happen? How do you reconcile this with the fact that many organ pipes do get tin pest?

40. The logistic model can be applied to a renewable resource that is harvested, like fish. If a fraction c of the population is harvested each year, we have

$$\frac{dP}{dt} = kP\left(1 - \frac{P}{L}\right) - cP.$$

Figure 11.74 assumes $c < k$ and shows two graphs of dP/dt versus P: the parabola $dP/dt = kP(1 - P/L)$ and the line $dP/dt = cP$.

(a) Show that there is an equilibrium at $P = (k-c)L/k$ and that the annual harvest is then $H = c(k-c)L/k$.

(b) If k and L are constant and the population is at the equilibrium in part (a), show that the maximum possible annual harvest is $kL/4$ and occurs when $c = k/2$.

(c) How can the population and the annual harvest at equilibrium be identified on the graph? Explain what happens as c increases beyond $k/2$ toward k. (Assume k and L are constant.)

Figure 11.74

41. Federal or state agencies control hunting and fishing by setting a quota on how many animals can be harvested each season. Determining the appropriate quota means achieving a balance between environmental concerns and the interests of hunters and fishers. For example, when a June 8, 2007 decision by the Delaware Superior Court invalidated a two-year moratorium on catching horseshoe crabs, the Delaware Department of Natural Resources and Environmental Control imposed instead an annual quota of 100,000 on male horseshoe crabs. Environmentalists argued this would exacerbate a decrease in the protected Red Knot bird population that depends on the crab for food. For a population P that satisfies the logistic model with harvesting,

$$\frac{dP}{dt} = kP\left(1 - \frac{P}{L}\right) - H,$$

show that the quota, H, must satisfy $H \le kL/4$, or else the population P may die out. (In fact, H should be kept much less than $kL/4$ to be safe.)

---

[22]Data adapted from G. F. Gause, *The Struggle for Existence* (New York: Hafner Publishing Company, 1969).

Strengthen Your Understanding

In Problems 42–44, explain what is wrong with the statement.

42. The differential equation $dP/dt = 0.08P - 0.0032P^2$ has one equilibrium solution, at $P = 25$.

43. The maximum rate of change occurs at $t = 25$ for a quantity Q growing according to the logistic equation

$$\frac{dQ}{dt} = 0.13Q(1 - 0.02Q).$$

44. Figure 11.75 shows a quantity growing logistically.

Figure 11.75

In Problems 45–48, give an example of:

45. A quantity that increases logistically.

46. A logistic differential equation for a quantity P such that the maximum rate of change of P occurs when $P = 75$.

47. A graph of dQ/dt against Q if Q is growing logistically and has an equilibrium value at $Q = 500$.

48. A graph of dP/dt against P if P is a logistic function which increases when $0 < P < 20$ and which decreases when $P < 0$ or $P > 20$.

Are the statements in Problems 49–50 true or false? Give an explanation for your answer.

49. There is a solution curve for the logistic differential equation $dP/dt = P(2 - P)$ that goes through the points $(0, 1)$ and $(1, 3)$.

50. For any positive values of the constant k and any positive values of the initial value $P(0)$, the solution to the differential equation $dP/dt = kP(L - P)$ has limiting value L as $t \to \infty$.

11.8 SYSTEMS OF DIFFERENTIAL EQUATIONS

In Section 11.7 we modeled the growth of a single population over time. We now consider the growth of two populations that interact, such as a population of sick people infecting the healthy people around them. This involves not just one differential equation, but a system of two.

Diseases and Epidemics

Differential equations can be used to predict when an outbreak of a disease will become so severe that it is called an *epidemic*[23] and to decide what level of vaccination is necessary to prevent an epidemic. Let's consider a specific example.

Flu in a British Boarding School

In January 1978, 763 students returned to a boys' boarding school after their winter vacation. A week later, one boy developed the flu, followed by two others the next day. By the end of the month, nearly half the boys were sick. Most of the school had been affected by the time the epidemic was over in mid-February.[24]

Being able to predict how many people will get sick, and when, is an important step toward controlling an epidemic. This is one of the responsibilities of Britain's Communicable Disease Surveillance Centre and the US's Center for Disease Control and Prevention.

---

[23]Exactly when a disease should be called an epidemic is not always clear. The medical profession generally classifies a disease an epidemic when the frequency is higher than usually expected—leaving open the question of what is usually expected. See, for example, *Epidemiology in Medicine* by C. H. Hennekens and J. Buring (Boston: Little, Brown, 1987).

[24]Data from the Communicable Disease Surveillance Centre (UK); reported in "Influenza in a Boarding School," *British Medical Journal*, March 4, 1978, and by J. D. Murray in *Mathematical Biology* (New York: Springer Verlag, 1990).

The S-I-R Model

We apply one of the most commonly used models for an epidemic, called the S-I-R model, to the boarding school flu example. The population of the school is divided into three groups:

$S = $ the number of *susceptibles*, the people who are not yet sick
but who could become sick

$I = $ the number of *infecteds*, the people who are currently sick

$R = $ the number of *recovered*, or *removed*, the people who have
been sick and can no longer infect others or be reinfected.

The number of susceptibles decreases with time as people become infected. We assume that the rate at which people become infected is proportional to the number of contacts between susceptible and infected people. We expect the number of contacts between the two groups to be proportional to both S and I. (If S doubles, we expect the number of contacts to double; similarly, if I doubles, we expect the number of contacts to double.) Thus we assume that the number of contacts is proportional to the product, SI. In other words, we assume that for some constant $a > 0$,

$$\frac{dS}{dt} = -\left(\begin{array}{c} \text{Rate susceptibles} \\ \text{get sick} \end{array} \right) = -aSI.$$

(The negative sign is used because S is decreasing.)

The number of infecteds is changing in two ways: newly sick people are added to the infected group, and others are removed. The newly sick people are exactly those people leaving the susceptible group and so accrue at a rate of aSI (with a positive sign this time). People leave the infected group either because they recover (or die), or because they are physically removed from the rest of the group and can no longer infect others. We assume that people are removed at a rate proportional to the number of sick, or bI, where b is a positive constant. Thus,

$$\frac{dI}{dt} = \begin{array}{c} \text{Rate susceptibles} \\ \text{get sick} \end{array} - \begin{array}{c} \text{Rate infecteds} \\ \text{get removed} \end{array} = aSI - bI.$$

Assuming that those who have recovered from the disease are no longer susceptible, the recovered group increases at the rate of bI, so

$$\frac{dR}{dt} = bI.$$

We are assuming that having the flu confers immunity on a person, that is, that the person cannot get the flu again. (This is true for a given strain of flu, at least in the short run.)

In analyzing the flu, we can use the fact that the total population $S + I + R$ is not changing. (The total population, the total number of boys in the school, did not change during the epidemic.) Thus, once we know S and I, we can calculate R. So we restrict our attention to the two equations

$$\frac{dS}{dt} = -aSI$$

$$\frac{dI}{dt} = aSI - bI.$$

The Constants a and b

The constant a measures how infectious the disease is—that is, how quickly it is transmitted from the infecteds to the susceptibles. In the case of the flu, we know from medical accounts that the epidemic started with one sick boy, with two more becoming sick a day later. Thus, when $I = 1$ and

$S = 762$, we have $dS/dt \approx -2$, enabling us to roughly[25] approximate a:

$$a = -\frac{dS/dt}{SI} = \frac{2}{(762)(1)} = 0.0026.$$

The constant b represents the rate at which infected people are removed from the infected population. In this case of the flu, boys were generally taken to the infirmary within one or two days of becoming sick. About half the infected population was removed each day, so we take $b \approx 0.5$. Thus, our equations are:

$$\frac{dS}{dt} = -0.0026SI$$
$$\frac{dI}{dt} = 0.0026SI - 0.5I.$$

The Phase Plane

We can get a good idea of the progress of the disease from graphs. You might expect that we would look for graphs of S and I against t, and eventually we will. However, we first look at a graph of I against S. If we plot a point (S, I) representing the number of susceptibles and the number of infecteds at any moment in time, then, as the numbers of susceptibles and infecteds change, the point moves. The SI-plane on which the point moves is called the *phase plane*. The path along which the point moves is called the *phase trajectory*, or *orbit*, of the point.

To find the phase trajectory, we need a differential equation relating S and I directly. Thinking of I as a function of S, and S as a function of t, we use the chain rule to get

$$\frac{dI}{dt} = \frac{dI}{dS} \cdot \frac{dS}{dt},$$

giving

$$\frac{dI}{dS} = \frac{dI/dt}{dS/dt}.$$

Substituting for dI/dt and dS/dt, we get

$$\frac{dI}{dS} = \frac{0.0026SI - 0.5I}{-0.0026SI}.$$

Assuming I is not zero, this equation simplifies to approximately

$$\frac{dI}{dS} = -1 + \frac{192}{S}.$$

The slope field of this differential equation is shown in Figure 11.76. The trajectory with initial condition $S_0 = 762$, $I_0 = 1$ is shown in Figure 11.77. Time is represented by the arrow showing the direction that a point moves on the trajectory. The disease starts at the point $S_0 = 762$, $I_0 = 1$. At first, more people become infected and fewer are susceptible. In other words, S decreases and I increases. Later, I decreases as S continues to decrease.

Figure 11.76: Slope field for $dI/dS = -1 + 192/S$

Figure 11.77: Trajectory for $S_0 = 762$, $I_0 = 1$

[25]The values of a and b are close to those obtained by J. D. Murray in *Mathematical Biology* (New York: Springer Verlag, 1990).

What Does the SI-Phase Plane Tell Us?

To learn how the disease progresses, look at the shape of the curve in Figure 11.77. The value of I increases to about 300 (the maximum number infected and infectious at any one time); then I decreases to zero. This peak value of I occurs when $S \approx 200$. We can determine exactly when the peak value occurs by solving

$$\frac{dI}{dS} = -1 + \frac{192}{S} = 0,$$

which gives

$$S = 192.$$

Notice that the peak value for I always occurs at the same value of S, namely $S = 192$. The graph shows that if a trajectory starts with $S_0 > 192$, then I first increases and then decreases to zero. On the other hand, if $S_0 < 192$, there is no peak as I decreases right away.

For this example, the value $S_0 = 192$ is called a *threshold value*. If S_0 is around or below 192, there is no epidemic. If S_0 is significantly greater than 192, an epidemic occurs.[26]

The phase diagram makes clear that the maximum value of I is about 300. Another question answered by the phase plane diagram is the total number of students who are expected to get sick during the epidemic. (This is not the maximum value reached by I, which gives the maximum number infected at any one time.) The point at which the trajectory crosses the S-axis represents the time when the epidemic has passed (since $I = 0$). The S-intercept shows how many boys never get the flu and thus, how many do get it.

How Many People Should Be Vaccinated?

An epidemic can sometimes be avoided by vaccination. How many boys would have had to be vaccinated to prevent the flu epidemic? To answer this, think of vaccination as removing people from the S category (without increasing I), which amounts to moving the initial point on the trajectory to the left, parallel to the S-axis. To avoid an epidemic, the initial value of S_0 should be at or below the threshold value. Therefore, all but 192 boys would need to be vaccinated.

Graphs of S and I Against t

To find out exactly when I reaches its maximum, we need numerical methods. A modification of Euler's method was used to generate the solution curves of S and I against t in Figure 11.78. Notice that the number of susceptibles drops throughout the disease as healthy people get sick. The number of infecteds peaks after about 6 days and then drops. The epidemic has run its course in 20 days.

Analytical Solution for the SI-Phase Trajectory

The differential equation

$$\frac{dI}{dS} = -1 + \frac{192}{S}$$

can be integrated, giving

$$I = -S + 192 \ln S + C.$$

Using $S_0 = 762$ and $I_0 = 1$ gives $1 = -762 + 192 \ln 762 + C$, so we get $C = 763 - 192 \ln 762$. Substituting this value for C, we get:

$$I = -S + 192 \ln S - 192 \ln 762 + 763$$

$$I = -S + 192 \ln \left(\frac{S}{762} \right) + 763.$$

This is the equation of the solution curve in Figure 11.77.

---

[26]Here we are using J. D. Murray's definition of an epidemic as an outbreak in which the number of infecteds increases from the initial value, I_0. See *Mathematical Biology* (New York: Springer Verlag, 1990).

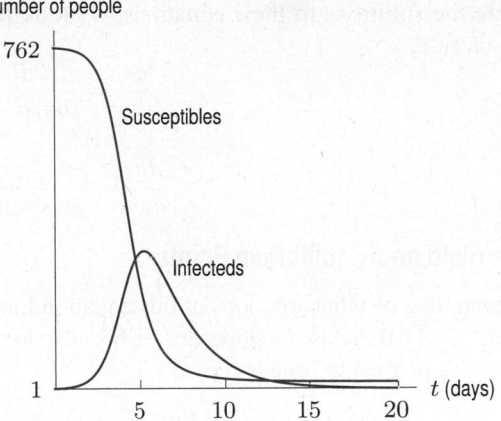

Figure 11.78: Progress of the flu over time

Two Interacting Populations: Predator-Prey

We now consider two populations which interact. They may compete for food, one may prey on the other, or they may enjoy a symbiotic relationship in which each helps the other. We model a predator-prey system using the *Lotka-Volterra equations*.

Robins and Worms

Let's look at an idealized case[27] in which robins are the predators and worms are the prey. There are r thousand robins and w million worms. If there were no robins, the worms would increase exponentially according to the equation

$$\frac{dw}{dt} = aw \quad \text{where } a \text{ is a constant and } a > 0.$$

If there were no worms, the robins would have no food and their population would decrease according to the equation[28]

$$\frac{dr}{dt} = -br \quad \text{where } b \text{ is a constant and } b > 0.$$

Now we account for the effect of the two populations on one another. Clearly, the presence of the robins is bad for the worms, so

$$\frac{dw}{dt} = aw - \text{Effect of robins on worms.}$$

On the other hand, the robins do better with the worms around, so

$$\frac{dr}{dt} = -br + \text{Effect of worms on robins.}$$

How exactly do the two populations interact? Let's assume the effect of one population on the other is proportional to the number of "encounters." (An encounter is when a robin eats a worm.) The number of encounters is likely to be proportional to the product of the populations because the more there are of either population, the more encounters there will be. So we assume

$$\frac{dw}{dt} = aw - cwr \quad \text{and} \quad \frac{dr}{dt} = -br + kwr,$$

where c and k are positive constants.

To analyze this system of equations, let's look at the specific example with $a = b = c = k = 1$:

$$\frac{dw}{dt} = w - wr \quad \text{and} \quad \frac{dr}{dt} = -r + wr.$$

---

[27]Based on ideas from Thomas A. McMahon.

[28]You might criticize this assumption because it predicts that the number of robins will decay exponentially, rather than die out in finite time.

To visualize the solutions to these equations, we look for trajectories in the phase plane. First we use the chain rule,

$$\frac{dr}{dw} = \frac{dr/dt}{dw/dt},$$

to obtain

$$\frac{dr}{dw} = \frac{-r + wr}{w - wr}.$$

The Slope Field and Equilibrium Points

We can get an idea of what solutions of this equation look like from the slope field in Figure 11.79. At the point $(1, 1)$ there is no slope drawn because at this point the rate of change of the worm population with respect to time is zero:

$$\frac{dw}{dt} = 1 - (1)(1) = 0.$$

The rate of change of the robin population with respect to time is also zero:

$$\frac{dr}{dt} = -1 + (1)(1) = 0.$$

Thus dr/dw is undefined. In terms of worms and robins, this means that if at some moment $w = 1$ and $r = 1$ (that is, there are 1 million worms and 1 thousand robins), then w and r remain constant forever. The point $w = 1$, $r = 1$ is therefore an equilibrium solution. The slope field suggests that there are no other equilibrium points except the origin.

At an **equilibrium point**, both w and r are constant, so

$$\frac{dw}{dt} = 0 \qquad \text{and} \qquad \frac{dr}{dt} = 0.$$

Therefore, we look for equilibrium points by solving

$$\frac{dw}{dt} = w - wr = 0 \quad \text{and} \quad \frac{dr}{dt} = -r + rw = 0,$$

which has $w = 0$, $r = 0$ and $w = 1$, $r = 1$ as the only solutions.

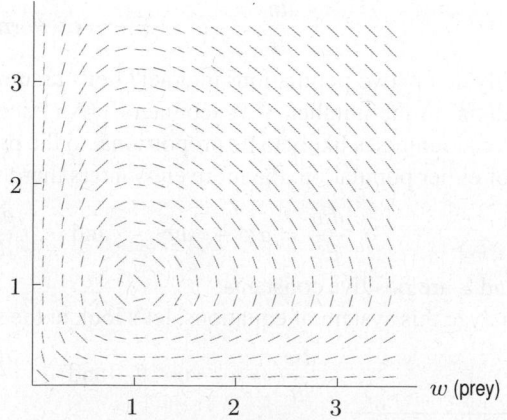

Figure 11.79: Slope field for $\dfrac{dr}{dw} = \dfrac{-r + wr}{w - wr}$

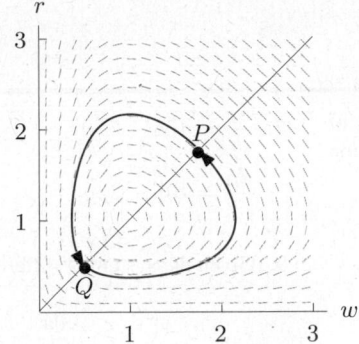

Figure 11.80: Solution curve is closed

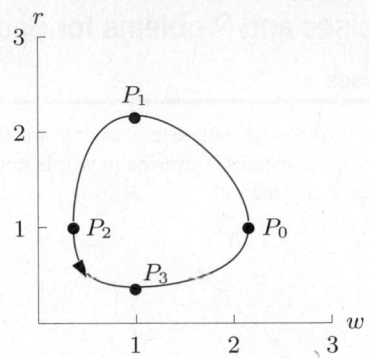

Figure 11.81: Trajectory in the phase plane

Trajectories in the wr-Phase Plane

Let's look at the trajectories in the phase plane. Remember that a point on a curve represents a pair of populations (w, r) existing at the same time t (though t is not shown on the graph). A short time later, the pair of populations is represented by a nearby point. As time passes, the point traces out a trajectory. The direction is marked on the curve by an arrow. (See Figure 11.80.)

How do we figure out which way to move on the trajectory? Approximating the solution numerically shows that the trajectory is traversed counterclockwise. Alternatively, look at the original pair of differential equations. At the point P_0 in Figure 11.81, where $w > 1$ and $r = 1$,

$$\frac{dr}{dt} = -r + wr = -1 + w > 0.$$

Therefore, r is increasing, so the point is moving counterclockwise around the closed curve.

Now let's think about why the solution curves are closed curves (that is, why they come back and meet themselves). Notice that the slope field is symmetric about the line $w = r$. We can confirm this by observing that interchanging w and r does not alter the differential equation for dr/dw. This means that if we start at point P on the line $w = r$ and travel once around the point $(1, 1)$, we arrive back at the same point P. The reason is that the second half of the path, from Q to P, is the reflection of the first half, from P to Q, in the line $w = r$. (See Figure 11.80.) If we did not end up at P again, the second half of our path would have a different shape from the first half.

The Populations as Functions of Time

The shape of the trajectories tells us how the populations vary with time. We start at $t = 0$ at the point P_0 in Figure 11.81. Then we move to P_1 at time t_1, to P_2 at time t_2, to P_3 at time t_3, and so on. At time t_4 we are back at P_0, and the whole cycle repeats. Since the trajectory is a closed curve, both populations oscillate periodically with the same period. The worms (the prey) are at their maximum a quarter of a cycle before the robins. (See Figure 11.82.)

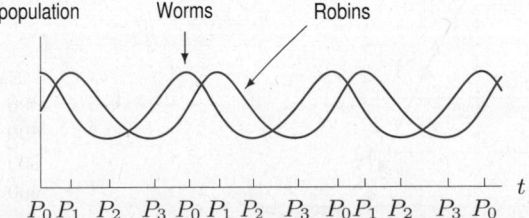

Figure 11.82: Populations of robins (in thousands) and worms (in millions) over time

Exercises and Problems for Section 11.8

Exercises

For Exercises 1–4, suppose x and y are the populations of two different species. Describe in words how each population changes with time.

1. y

2. y

3. y

4. y

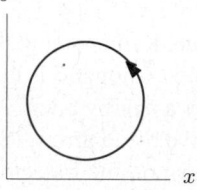

In Exercises 5–8, find all equilibrium points. Give answers as ordered pairs (x, y).

5. $\dfrac{dx}{dt} = -3x + xy$

$\dfrac{dy}{dt} = 5y - xy$

6. $\dfrac{dx}{dt} = -2x + 4xy$

$\dfrac{dy}{dt} = -8y + 2xy$

7. $\dfrac{dx}{dt} = 15x - 5xy$

$\dfrac{dy}{dt} = 10y + 2xy$

8. $\dfrac{dx}{dt} = x^2 - xy$

$\dfrac{dy}{dt} = 15y - 3y^2$

9. Given the system of differential equations

$$\frac{dx}{dt} = 5x - 3xy$$
$$\frac{dy}{dt} = -8y + xy$$

determine whether x and y are increasing or decreasing at the point

(a) $x = 3, y = 2$ (b) $x = 5, y = 1$

10. Given the system of differential equations

$$\frac{dP}{dt} = 2P - 10$$
$$\frac{dQ}{dt} = Q - 0.2PQ$$

determine whether P and Q are increasing or decreasing at the point

(a) $P = 2, Q = 3$ (b) $P = 6, Q = 5$

Problems

11. Figure 11.83 shows the trajectory through the SI phase plane of a 50-day epidemic.

(a) Make an approximate table of values for the number of susceptibles and infecteds on the days marked on the trajectory.

(b) When is the epidemic at its peak? How many people are infected then?

(c) During the course of the epidemic, how many catch the disease and how many are spared?

Figure 11.83: Days 8 through 44 of an epidemic

12. Figure 11.84 shows the number of susceptibles and infecteds in a population of 4000 through the course of a 60-day epidemic.

(a) How many are infected on day 20?

(b) How many have had the disease by day 20?

(c) How many have had the disease by the time the epidemic is over?

Figure 11.84

13. Humans vs Zombies[29] is a game in which one player starts as a zombie and turns human players into zombies by tagging them. Zombies have to "eat" on a regular basis by tagging human players, or they die of starvation and are out of the game. The game is usually played over a period of about five days. If we let H represent the size of the human population and Z represent the size of the zombie population in the game, then, for constant parameters a, b, and c, we have:

$$\frac{dH}{dt} = aHZ$$

$$\frac{dZ}{dt} = bZ + cHZ$$

  (a) Decide whether each of the parameters a, b, c is positive or negative.
  (b) What is the relationship, if any, between a and c?

14. Four pairs of species are given, with descriptions of how they interact.

  I. Bees/flowers: each needs the other to survive
  II. Owls/trees: owls need trees but trees are indifferent
  III. Elk/buffalo: in competition and would do fine alone
  IV. Fox/hare: fox eats the hare and needs it to survive

Match each system of differential equations with a species pair, and indicate which species is x and which is y.

  (a) $\dfrac{dx}{dt} = -0.2x + 0.03xy$

   $\dfrac{dy}{dt} = 0.4y - 0.08xy$

  (b) $\dfrac{dx}{dt} = 0.18x$

   $\dfrac{dy}{dt} = -0.4y + 0.3xy$

  (c) $\dfrac{dx}{dt} = -0.6x + 0.18xy$

   $\dfrac{dy}{dt} = -0.1y + 0.09xy$

  (d) Write a possible system of differential equations for the species pair that does not have a match.

15. Show that if S, I, and R satisfy the differential equations on page 640, the total population, $S + I + R$, is constant.

For Problems 16–24, let w be the number of worms (in millions) and r the number of robins (in thousands) living on an island. Suppose w and r satisfy the following differential equations, which correspond to the slope field in Figure 11.85.

$$\frac{dw}{dt} = w - wr, \qquad \frac{dr}{dt} = -r + wr.$$

Figure 11.85: $\dfrac{dr}{dw} = \dfrac{r(w-1)}{w(1-r)}$

16. Explain why these differential equations are a reasonable model for interaction between the two populations. Why have the signs been chosen this way?

17. Solve these differential equations in the two special cases when there are no robins and when there are no worms living on the island.

18. Describe and explain the symmetry you observe in the slope field. What consequences does this symmetry have for the solution curves?

19. Assume $w = 2$ and $r = 2$ when $t = 0$. Do the numbers of robins and worms increase or decrease at first? What happens in the long run?

20. For the case discussed in Problem 19, estimate the maximum and the minimum values of the robin population. How many worms are there at the time when the robin population reaches its maximum?

21. On the same axes, graph w and r (the worm and the robin populations) against time. Use initial values of 1.5 for w and 1 for r. You may do this without units for t.

22. People on the island like robins so much that they decide to import 200 robins all the way from England, to increase the initial population from $r = 2$ to $r = 2.2$ when $t = 0$. Does this make sense? Why or why not?

23. Assume that $w = 3$ and $r = 1$ when $t = 0$. Do the numbers of robins and worms increase or decrease initially? What happens in the long run?

24. For the case discussed in Problem 23, estimate the maximum and minimum values of the robin population. Estimate the number of worms when the robin population reaches its minimum.

The systems of differential equations in Problems 25–27 model the interaction of two populations x and y. In each case, answer the following two questions:

  (a) What kinds of interaction (symbiosis,[30] competition, predator-prey) do the equations describe?

---

[29] http://humansvszombies.org
[30] Symbiosis takes place when the interaction of two species benefits both. An example is the pollination of plants by insects.

(b) What happens in the long run? (For one of the systems, your answer will depend on the initial populations.) Use a calculator or computer to draw slope fields.

25. $\dfrac{1}{x}\dfrac{dx}{dt} = y - 1$

$\dfrac{1}{y}\dfrac{dy}{dt} = x - 1$

26. $\dfrac{1}{x}\dfrac{dx}{dt} = 1 - \dfrac{x}{2} - \dfrac{y}{2}$

$\dfrac{1}{y}\dfrac{dy}{dt} = 1 - x - y$

27. $\dfrac{1}{x}\dfrac{dx}{dt} = y - 1 - 0.05x$

$\dfrac{1}{y}\dfrac{dy}{dt} = 1 - x - 0.05y$

For Problems 28–31, consider a conflict between two armies of x and y soldiers, respectively. During World War I, F. W. Lanchester assumed that if both armies are fighting a conventional battle within sight of one another, the rate at which soldiers in one army are put out of action (killed or wounded) is proportional to the amount of fire the other army can concentrate on them, which is in turn proportional to the number of soldiers in the opposing army. Thus Lanchester assumed that if there are no reinforcements and t represents time since the start of the battle, then x and y obey the differential equations

$$\frac{dx}{dt} = -ay$$
$$\frac{dy}{dt} = -bx \quad a, b > 0.$$

28. Near the end of World War II a fierce battle took place between US and Japanese troops over the island of Iwo Jima, off the coast of Japan. Applying Lanchester's analysis to this battle, with x representing the number of US troops and y the number of Japanese troops, it has been estimated[31] that $a = 0.05$ and $b = 0.01$.

(a) Using these values for a and b and ignoring reinforcements, write a differential equation involving dy/dx and sketch its slope field.

(b) Assuming that the initial strength of the US forces was 54,000 and that of the Japanese was 21,500, draw the trajectory which describes the battle. What outcome is predicted? (That is, which side do the differential equations predict will win?)

(c) Would knowing that the US in fact had 19,000 reinforcements, while the Japanese had none, alter the outcome predicted?

29. (a) For two armies of strengths x and y fighting a conventional battle governed by Lanchester's differential equations, write a differential equation involving dy/dx and the constants of attrition a and b.

(b) Solve the differential equation and hence show that the equation of the phase trajectory is

$$ay^2 - bx^2 = C$$

for some constant C. This equation is called *Lanchester's square law*. The value of C depends on the initial sizes of the two armies.

30. Consider the battle of Iwo Jima, described in Problem 28. Take $a = 0.05$, $b = 0.01$ and assume the initial strength of the US troops to be 54,000 and that of the Japanese troops to be 21,500. (Again, ignore reinforcements.)

(a) Using Lanchester's square law derived in Problem 29, find the equation of the trajectory describing the battle.

(b) Assuming that the Japanese fought without surrendering until they had all been killed, as was the case, how many US troops does this model predict would be left when the battle ended?

31. In this problem we adapt Lanchester's model for a conventional battle to the case in which one or both of the armies is a guerrilla force. We assume that the rate at which a guerrilla force is put out of action is proportional to the product of the strengths of the two armies.

(a) Give a justification for the assumption that the rate at which a guerrilla force is put out of action is proportional to the product of the strengths of the two armies.

(b) Write the differential equations which describe a conflict between a guerrilla army of strength x and a conventional army of strength y, assuming all the constants of proportionality are 1.

(c) Find a differential equation involving dy/dx and solve it to find equations of phase trajectories.

(d) Describe which side wins in terms of the constant of integration. What happens if the constant is zero?

(e) Use your solution to part (d) to divide the phase plane into regions according to which side wins.

32. To model a conflict between two guerrilla armies, we assume that the rate that each one is put out of action is proportional to the product of the strengths of the two armies.

(a) Write the differential equations which describe a conflict between two guerrilla armies of strengths x and y, respectively.

(b) Find a differential equation involving dy/dx and solve to find equations of phase trajectories.

(c) Describe which side wins in terms of the constant of integration. What happens if the constant is zero?

(d) Use your solution to part (c) to divide the phase plane into regions according to which side wins.

33. The predator-prey model on page 643 for the number of robins, r, in thousands, and the number of worms, w, in millions, was for some positive constants a, b, c, k:

$$\frac{dw}{dt} = aw - cwr \quad \text{and} \quad \frac{dr}{dt} = -br + kwr.$$

(a) Find the equilibrium points of this system of equations.

---

[31] See Martin Braun, *Differential Equations and Their Applications*, 2nd ed. (New York: Springer Verlag, 1975).

(b) An insecticide is applied to the ground, causing a decline in the number of worms proportional to their population. What effect does this have on the equi-librium point? Interpret this in terms of the equilib-rium population of worms and robins.

Strengthen Your Understanding

In Problems 34–35, explain what is wrong with the statement.

34. If $dx/dt = 3x - 0.4xy$ and $dy/dt = 4y - 0.5xy$, then an increase in x corresponds to a decrease in y.

35. For a system of differential equations for x and y, at the point $(2, 3)$, we have $dx/dt < 0$ and $dy/dt > 0$ and $dy/dx > 0$.

In Problems 36–38, give an example of:

36. A system of differential equations for two populations X and Y such that Y needs X to survive and X is indif-ferent to Y and thrives on its own. Let x represent the size of the X population and y represent the size of the Y population.

37. A system of differential equations for the profits of two companies if each would thrive on its own but the two companies compete for business. Let x and y represent the profits of the two companies.

38. Two diseases D_1 and D_2 such that the parameter a in the S-I-R model on page 640 is larger for disease D_1 than it is for disease D_2. Explain your reasoning.

Are the statements in Problems 39–40 true or false? Give an explanation for your answer.

39. The system of differential equations $dx/dt = -x + xy^2$ and $dy/dt = y - x^2y$ requires initial conditions for both $x(0)$ and $y(0)$ to determine a unique solution.

40. Populations modeled by a system of differential equa-tions never die out.

11.9 ANALYZING THE PHASE PLANE

In the previous section we analyzed a system of differential equations using a slope field. In this section we analyze a system of differential equations using *nullclines*. We consider two species having similar *niches*, or ways of living, and that are in competition for food and space. In such cases, one species often becomes extinct. This phenomenon is called the *Principle of Competitive Exclusion*. We see how differential equations predict this in a particular case.

Competitive Exclusion: Citrus Tree Parasites

The citrus farmers of Southern California are interested in controlling the insects that live on their trees. Some of these insects can be controlled by parasites that live on the trees too. Scientists are, therefore, interested in understanding under what circumstances these parasites flourish or die out. One such parasite was introduced accidentally from the Mediterranean; later, other parasites were introduced from China and India; in each case the previous parasite became extinct over part of its habitat. In 1963 a lab experiment was carried out to determine which one of a pair of species became extinct when they were in competition with each other. The data on one pair of species, called A. *fisheri* and A. *melinus*, with populations P_1 and P_2 respectively, is given in Table 11.8 and shows that A. *melinus* (P_2) became extinct after 8 generations.[32]

Table 11.8 *Population (in thousands) of two species of parasite as a function of time*

Generation number	1	2	3	4	5	6	7	8
Population P_1 (thousands)	0.193	1.093	1.834	5.819	13.705	16.965	18.381	16.234
Population P_2 (thousands)	0.083	0.229	0.282	0.378	0.737	0.507	0.13	0

Data from the same experimenters indicates that, when alone, each population grows logisti-cally. In fact, their data suggests that, when alone, the population of P_1 might grow according to the

---

[32]Data adapted from Paul DeBach and Ragnhild Sundby, "Competitive Displacement Between Ecological Homologues," *Hilgardia 34*:17 (1963).

equation

$$\frac{dP_1}{dt} = 0.05 P_1 \left(1 - \frac{P_1}{20} \right),$$

and when alone, the population of P_2 might grow according to the equation

$$\frac{dP_2}{dt} = 0.09 P_2 \left(1 - \frac{P_2}{15} \right).$$

Now suppose both parasites are present. Each tends to reduce the growth rate of the other, so each differential equation is modified by subtracting a term on the right. The experimental data shows that together P_1 and P_2 can be well described by the equations

$$\frac{dP_1}{dt} = 0.05 P_1 \left(1 - \frac{P_1}{20} \right) - 0.002 P_1 P_2$$

$$\frac{dP_2}{dt} = 0.09 P_2 \left(1 - \frac{P_2}{15} \right) - 0.15 P_1 P_2.$$

The fact that P_2 dies out with time is reflected in these equations: the coefficient of $P_1 P_2$ is much larger in the equation for P_2 than in the equation for P_1. This indicates that the interaction has a much more devastating effect upon the growth of P_2 than on the growth of P_1.

The Phase Plane and Nullclines

We consider the phase plane with the P_1 axis horizontal and the P_2 axis vertical. To find the trajectories in the $P_1 P_2$ phase plane, we could draw a slope field as in the previous section. Instead, we use a method that gives a good qualitative picture of the behavior of the trajectories even without a calculator or computer. We find the *nullclines* or curves along which $dP_1/dt = 0$ or $dP_2/dt = 0$. At points where $dP_2/dt = 0$, the population P_2 is momentarily constant, so only population P_1 is changing with time. Therefore, at this point the trajectory is horizontal. (See Figure 11.86.) Similarly, at points where $dP_1/dt = 0$, the population P_1 is momentarily constant and population P_2 is the only one changing, so the trajectory is vertical there. A point where both $dP_1/dt = 0$ and $dP_2/dt = 0$ is called an *equilibrium point* because P_1 and P_2 both remain constant if they reach these values.

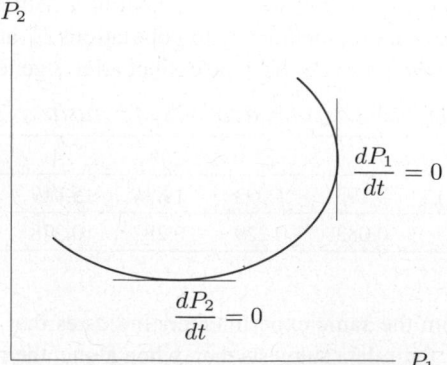

Figure 11.86: Points on a trajectory where
$dP_1/dt = 0$ or $dP_2/dt = 0$

> On the P_1P_2 phase plane:
> - If $\dfrac{dP_1}{dt} = 0$, the trajectory is vertical.
> - If $\dfrac{dP_2}{dt} = 0$, the trajectory is horizontal.
> - If $\dfrac{dP_1}{dt} = \dfrac{dP_2}{dt} = 0$, there is an equilibrium point.

Using Nullclines to Analyze the Parasite Populations

In order to see where $dP_1/dt = 0$ or $dP_2/dt = 0$, we factor the right side of our differential equations:

$$\frac{dP_1}{dt} = 0.05P_1\left(1 - \frac{P_1}{20}\right) - 0.002P_1P_2 = 0.001P_1(50 - 2.5P_1 - 2P_2)$$

$$\frac{dP_2}{dt} = 0.09P_2\left(1 - \frac{P_2}{15}\right) - 0.15P_1P_2 = 0.001P_2(90 - 150P_1 - 6P_2).$$

Thus $dP_1/dt = 0$ where $P_1 = 0$ or where $50 - 2.5P_1 - 2P_2 = 0$. Graphing these equations in the phase plane gives two lines, which are nullclines. Since the trajectory is vertical where $dP_1/dt = 0$, in Figure 11.87 we draw small vertical line segments on these nullclines to represent the direction of the trajectories as they cross the nullcline. Similarly $dP_2/dt = 0$ where $P_2 = 0$ or where $90 - 150P_1 - 6P_2 = 0$. These equations are graphed in Figure 11.87 with small horizontal line segments on them.

The equilibrium points are where both $dP_1/dt = 0$ and $dP_2/dt = 0$, namely the points $P_1 = 0, P_2 = 0$ (meaning that both species die out); $P_1 = 0, P_2 = 15$ (where P_1 is extinct); and $P_1 = 20, P_2 = 0$ (where P_2 is extinct).

What Happens in the Regions Between the Nullclines?

Nullclines are useful because they divide the plane into regions in which the signs of dP_1/dt and dP_2/dt are constant. In each region, the direction of every trajectory remains roughly the same.

In Region I, for example, we might try the point $P_1 = 20, P_2 = 25$. Then

$$\frac{dP_1}{dt} = 0.001(20)(50 - 2.5(20) - 2(25)) < 0$$

$$\frac{dP_2}{dt} = 0.001(25)(90 - 150(20) - 6(25)) < 0.$$

Figure 11.87: Analyzing three regions in the phase plane using nullclines (axes distorted) with equilibrium points represented by dots

Now $dP_1/dt < 0$, so P_1 is decreasing, which can be represented by an arrow in the direction $\leftarrow$. Also, $dP_2/dt < 0$, so P_2 is decreasing, as represented by the arrow $\downarrow$. Combining these directions, we know that the trajectories in this region go approximately in the diagonal direction $\nwarrow$ (See Region I in Figure 11.87.)

In Region II, try, for example, $P_1 = 1, P_2 = 1$. Then we have

$$\frac{dP_1}{dt} = 0.001(1)(50 - 2.5 - 2) > 0$$

$$\frac{dP_2}{dt} = 0.001(1)(90 - 150 - 6) < 0.$$

So here, P_1 is increasing while P_2 is decreasing. (See Region II in Figure 11.87.)

In Region III, try $P_1 = 0.1, P_2 = 0.1$:

$$\frac{dP_1}{dt} = 0.001(0.1)(50 - 2.5(0.1) - 2(0.1)) > 0$$

$$\frac{dP_2}{dt} = 0.001(0.1)(90 - 150(0.1) - 6(0.1)) > 0.$$

So here, both P_1 and P_2 are increasing. (See Region III in Figure 11.87.)

Notice that the behavior of the populations in each region makes biological sense. In region I both populations are so large that overpopulation is a problem, so both populations decrease. In Region III both populations are so small that they are effectively not in competition, so both grow. In Region II competition between the species comes into play. The fact that P_1 increases while P_2 decreases in Region II means that P_1 wins.

Solution Trajectories

Suppose the system starts with some of each population. This means that the initial point of the trajectory is not on one of the axes, and so it is in Region I, II, or III. Then the point moves on a trajectory like one of those computed numerically and shown in Figure 11.88. Notice that *all* these trajectories tend toward the point $P_1 = 20, P_2 = 0$, corresponding to a population of 20,000 for P_1 and extinction for P_2. Consequently, this model predicts that no matter what the initial populations are, provided $P_1 \neq 0$, the population of P_2 is excluded by P_1, and P_1 tends to a constant value. This makes biological sense: in the absence of P_2, we would expect P_1 to settle down to the carrying capacity of the niche, which is 20,000.

Figure 11.88: Trajectories showing exclusion of population P_2 (not to scale)

Exercises and Problems for Section 11.9

Exercises

In Exercises 1–5, use Figure 11.89.

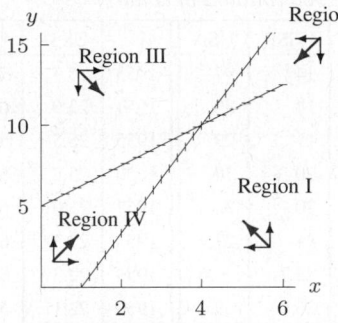

Figure 11.89: Nullclines in the phase plane of a system of differential equations

1. Give the coordinates for each equilibrium point.
2. At each point, give the signs of dx/dt and dy/dt.
   (a) $(4, 7)$ **(b)** $(4, 10)$ **(c)** $(6, 15)$
3. Draw a possible trajectory that starts at the point $(2, 5)$.
4. Draw a possible trajectory that starts at the point $(2, 10)$.
5. What is the long-run behavior of a trajectory that starts at any point in the first quadrant?

In Exercises 6–10, use Figure 11.90.

Figure 11.90: Nullclines in the phase plane of a system of differential equations

6. Give the approximate coordinates for each equilibrium point.
7. At each point, give the signs of dx/dt and dy/dt.
   (a) $(5, 2)$ **(b)** $(10, 2)$ **(c)** $(10, 1)$
8. Draw a possible trajectory that starts at the point $(2, 5)$.
9. Draw a possible trajectory that starts at the point $(10, 4)$.
10. What is the long-run behavior of a trajectory that starts at any point in the first quadrant?
11. Figure 11.91 shows a phase plane for a system of differential equations. Draw the nullclines.

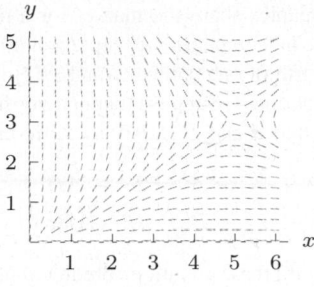

Figure 11.91

12. **(a)** Find the equilibrium points for the following system of equations

$$\frac{dx}{dt} = 20x - 10xy$$

$$\frac{dy}{dt} = 25y - 5xy.$$

   (b) Explain why $x = 2$, $y = 4$ is not an equilibrium point for this system.

Problems

For Problems 13–18, analyze the phase plane of the differential equations for x, $y \geq 0$. Show the nullclines and equilibrium points, and sketch the direction of the trajectories in each region.

13. $\dfrac{dx}{dt} = x(2 - x - y)$
    $\dfrac{dy}{dt} = y(1 - x - y)$

14. $\dfrac{dx}{dt} = x(2 - x - 3y)$
    $\dfrac{dy}{dt} = y(1 - 2x)$

15. $\dfrac{dx}{dt} = x(2 - x - 2y)$
    $\dfrac{dy}{dt} = y(1 - 2x - y)$

16. $\dfrac{dx}{dt} = x(1 - y - \frac{x}{3})$
    $\dfrac{dy}{dt} = y(1 - \frac{y}{2} - x)$

17. $\dfrac{dx}{dt} = x\left(1 - x - \frac{y}{3}\right)$
    $\dfrac{dy}{dt} = y\left(1 - y - \frac{x}{2}\right)$

18. $\dfrac{dx}{dt} = x\left(1 - \frac{x}{2} - y\right)$
    $\dfrac{dy}{dt} = y\left(1 - \frac{y}{3} - x\right)$

19. The equations describing the flu epidemic in a boarding school are

$$\frac{dS}{dt} = -0.0026SI$$

$$\frac{dI}{dt} = 0.0026SI - 0.5I.$$

(a) Find the nullclines and equilibrium points in the SI phase plane.

(b) Find the direction of the trajectories in each region.

(c) Sketch some typical trajectories and describe their behavior in words.

20. Use the idea of nullclines dividing the plane into sectors to analyze the equations describing the interactions of robins and worms:

$$\frac{dw}{dt} = w - wr$$

$$\frac{dr}{dt} = -r + rw.$$

21. Two companies share the market for a new technology. They have no competition except each other. Let $A(t)$ be the net worth of one company and $B(t)$ the net worth of the other at time t. Suppose that net worth cannot be negative and that A and B satisfy the differential equations

$$A' = 2A - AB$$

$$B' = B - AB.$$

(a) What do these equations predict about the net worth of each company if the other were not present? What effect do the companies have on each other?

(b) Are there any equilibrium points? If so, what are they?

(c) Sketch a slope field for these equations (using a computer or calculator), and hence describe the different possible long-run behaviors.

22. In the 1930s L. F. Richardson proposed that an arms race between two countries could be modeled by a system of differential equations. One arms race that can be reasonably well described by differential equations is the US-Soviet Union arms race between 1945 and 1960. If \$$x$ represents the annual Soviet expenditures on armaments (in billions of dollars) and \$$y$ represents the corresponding US expenditures, it has been suggested[33] that x and y obey the following differential equations:

$$\frac{dx}{dt} = -0.45x + 10.5$$

$$\frac{dy}{dt} = 8.2x - 0.8y - 142.$$

(a) Find the nullclines and equilibrium points for these differential equations. Which direction do the trajectories go in each region?

(b) Sketch some typical trajectories in the phase plane.

(c) What do these differential equations predict will be the long-term outcome of the US-Soviet arms race?

(d) Discuss these predictions in the light of the actual expenditures in Table 11.9.

Table 11.9 *Arms budgets of the United States and the Soviet Union for the years 1945–1960 (billions of dollars)*

	USSR	USA		USSR	USA
1945	14	97	1953	25.7	71.4
1946	14	80	1954	23.9	61.6
1947	15	29	1955	25.5	58.3
1948	20	20	1956	23.2	59.4
1949	20	22	1957	23.0	61.4
1950	21	23	1958	22.3	61.4
1951	22.7	49.6	1959	22.3	61.7
1952	26.0	69.6	1960	22.1	59.6

23. In the 1930s, the Soviet ecologist G. F. Gause performed a series of experiments on competition among two yeasts with populations P_1 and P_2, respectively. By performing population studies at low density in large volumes, he determined what he called the *coefficients of geometric increase* (and we would call continuous exponential growth rates). These coefficients described the growth of each yeast alone:

$$\frac{1}{P_1}\frac{dP_1}{dt} = 0.2$$

$$\frac{1}{P_2}\frac{dP_2}{dt} = 0.06$$

where P_1 and P_2 are measured in units that Gause established.

He also determined that, in his units, the carrying capacity of P_1 was 13 and the carrying capacity of P_2 was 6. He then observed that one P_2 occupies the niche space of 3 P_1 and that one P_1 occupied the niche space of 0.4 P_2. This led him to the following differential equations to describe the interaction of P_1 and P_2:

$$\frac{dP_1}{dt} = 0.2P_1\left(\frac{13 - (P_1 + 3P_2)}{13}\right)$$

$$\frac{dP_2}{dt} = 0.06P_2\left(\frac{6 - (P_2 + 0.4P_1)}{6}\right).$$

When both yeasts were growing together, Gause recorded the data in Table 11.10.

Table 11.10 *Gause's yeast populations*

Time (hours)	6	16	24	29	48	53
P_1	0.375	3.99	4.69	6.15	7.27	8.30
P_2	0.29	0.98	1.47	1.46	1.71	1.84

(a) Carry out a phase plane analysis of Gause's equations.

(b) Mark the data points on the phase plane and describe what would have happened had Gause continued the experiment.

---

[33]R. Taagepera, G. M. Schiffler, R. T. Perkins and D. L. Wagner, *Soviet-American and Israeli-Arab Arms Races and the Richardson Model* (General Systems, XX, 1975).

Strengthen Your Understanding

In Problems 24–25, explain what is wrong with the statement.

24. A solution trajectory and nullclines for a system of differential equations are shown in Figure 11.92.

Figure 11.92

25. The nullclines for a system of differential equations are shown in Figure 11.93. The system has an equilibrium at the point $(6, 6)$.

Figure 11.93

In Problems 26–28, give an example of:

26. A graph of the nullclines of a system of differential equations with exactly two equilibrium points in the first quadrant. Label the nullclines to show whether trajectories pass through the nullcline vertically or horizontally.

27. The nullclines of a system of differential equations with the trajectory shown in Figure 11.94.

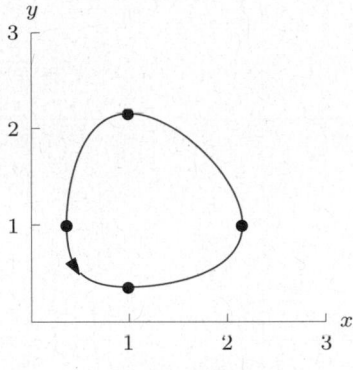

Figure 11.94

28. A trajectory for a system of differential equations with nullclines in Figure 11.95 and initial conditions $x = 1$ and $y = 2$.

Figure 11.95

CHAPTER SUMMARY (see also Ready Reference at the end of the book)

- **Differential equations terminology**
  Order, initial conditions, families of solutions, stable/unstable equilibrium solutions.

- **Solving first-order differential equations**
  Slope fields (graphical), Euler's method (numerical), separation of variables (analytical).

- **Modeling with differential equations**
  Growth and decay, Newton's Law of Heating and Cooling, compartment models, logistic model.

- **Systems of differential equations**
  S-I-R model, predator-prey model, phase plane.

REVIEW EXERCISES AND PROBLEMS FOR CHAPTER ELEVEN

Exercises

1. Which of the differential equations are satisfied by the functions on the right?

   (a) $y'' + 2y = 0$

   (b) $y'' - 2y = 0$

   (c) $y'' + 2y' + y = 0$

   (d) $y'' - 2y' + y = 0$

   (I) $y = xe^{x}$

   (II) $y = xe^{-x}$

2. Match the slope fields in Figure 11.96 with their differential equations:

(a) $y' = 1 + y^2$ (b) $y' = x$ (c) $y' = \sin x$

(d) $y' = y$ (e) $y' = x - y$ (f) $y' = 4 - y$

Figure 11.96: Each slope field is graphed for
$-5 \le x \le 5, -5 \le y \le 5$

3. The graphs in Figure 11.97 represent the temperature, $H(^\circ C)$, of four eggs as a function of time, t, in minutes. Match three of the graphs with the descriptions (a)–(c). Write a similar description for the fourth graph, including an interpretation of any intercepts and asymptotes.

(a) An egg is taken out of the refrigerator (just above 0°C) and put into boiling water.

(b) Twenty minutes after the egg in part (a) is taken out of the fridge and put into boiling water, the same thing is done with another egg.

(c) An egg is taken out of the refrigerator at the same time as the egg in part (a) and left to sit on the kitchen table.

Figure 11.97

Find a general solution to the differential equations in Exercises 4–9.

4. $\dfrac{dP}{dt} = t$

5. $\dfrac{dy}{dx} = 0.2y - 8$

6. $\dfrac{dP}{dt} = 10 - 2P$

7. $\dfrac{dH}{dt} = 0.5H + 10$

8. $\dfrac{dR}{dt} = 2R - 6R^2$

9. $\dfrac{dP}{dt} = 0.4P(1 - 0.01P)$

For the differential equations in Exercises 10–25, find a solution which passes through the given point.

10. $\dfrac{dy}{dx} + xy^2 = 0$, $y(1) = 1$

11. $\dfrac{dP}{dt} = 0.03P + 400$, $P(0) = 0$

12. $1 + y^2 - \dfrac{dy}{dx} = 0$, $y(0) = 0$

13. $2\sin x - y^2 \dfrac{dy}{dx} = 0$, $y(0) = 3$

14. $\dfrac{dk}{dt} = (1 + \ln t)k$, $k(1) = 1$

15. $\dfrac{dy}{dx} = \dfrac{y(3 - x)}{x(0.5y - 4)}$, $y(1) = 5$

16. $\dfrac{dy}{dx} = \dfrac{0.2y(18 + 0.1x)}{x(100 + 0.5y)}$, $(10, 10)$

17. $\dfrac{dz}{dt} = z(z - 1)$, $z(0) = 10$

18. $\dfrac{dy}{dt} = y(10 - y)$, $y(0) = 1$

19. $\dfrac{dy}{dx} = \dfrac{y(100 - x)}{x(20 - y)}$, $(1, 20)$

20. $\dfrac{df}{dx} = \sqrt{xf(x)}$, $f(1) = 1$

21. $\dfrac{dy}{dx} = e^{x-y}$, $y(0) = 1$

22. $\dfrac{dy}{dx} = e^{x+y}$, $y = 0$ where $x = 1$

23. $e^{-\cos\theta}\dfrac{dz}{d\theta} = \sqrt{1 - z^2}\sin\theta$, $z(0) = \frac{1}{2}$

24. $(1 + t^2)y\dfrac{dy}{dt} = 1 - y$, $y(1) = 0$

25. $\dfrac{dy}{dt} = 2^y \sin^3 t$, $y(0) = 0$

Problems

26. A population satisfies $dP/dt = 0.025P - 0.00005P^2$.

   (a) What are the equilibrium values for P?

   (b) For each of the following initial conditions, will P increase, decrease, or stay the same? Will the population increase or decrease without bound or to a limiting value? If to a limiting value, what is it?

     (a) $P_0 = 100$ **(b)** $P_0 = 400$

     (c) $P_0 = 500$ **(d)** $P_0 = 800$

27. (a) What are the equilibrium solutions for the differential equation

$$\frac{dy}{dt} = 0.2(y - 3)(y + 2)?$$

   (b) Use a slope field to determine whether each equilibrium solution is stable or unstable.

In Problems 28–29, is the function a solution to

$$y' = xy - y,$$

given that $y = f(x)$ satisfies this equation?

28. $y = 2f(x)$ **29.** $y = 2 + f(x)$

30. Find y when $x = 1/2$ on the solution passing through $(0, 0)$ of the differential equation

$$\frac{dy}{dx} = \frac{1}{(\cos x)(\cos y)}.$$

   (a) Use Euler's method with

     (i) $\Delta x = 1/2$ (1 step)   **(ii)** $\Delta x = 1/4$ (2 steps)
     (iii) $\Delta x = 1/8$ (4 steps)

   (b) Use separation of variables. Compare with your results in part (a).

31. Consider the initial value problem

$$y' = 5 - y, \quad y(0) = 1.$$

   (a) Use Euler's method with five steps to estimate $y(1)$.

   (b) Sketch the slope field for this differential equation in the first quadrant, and use it to decide if your estimate is an over- or underestimate.

   (c) Find the exact solution to the differential equation and hence find $y(1)$ exactly.

   (d) Without doing the calculation, roughly what would you expect the approximation for $y(1)$ to be with ten steps?

32. In 2007, the population of Switzerland was 7.5 million and was growing at a continuous rate of 0.38% per year.[34] Write an expression for the population as a function of time, t, in years since 2007.

33. The amount of land in use for growing crops increases as the world's population increases. Suppose $A(t)$ represents the total number of hectares of land in use in year t. (A hectare is about $2\frac{1}{2}$ acres.)

   (a) Explain why it is plausible that $A(t)$ satisfies the equation $A'(t) = kA(t)$. What assumptions are you making about the world's population and its relation to the amount of land used?

   (b) In 1966 about 4.55 billion hectares of land were in use; in 1996 the figure was 4.93 billion hectares.[35] If the total amount of land available for growing crops is thought to be 6 billion hectares, when does this model predict it will be exhausted? (Let $t = 0$ in 1966.)

34. The rate of growth of a tumor is proportional to the size of the tumor.

   (a) Write a differential equation satisfied by S, the size of the tumor, in mm, as a function of time, t.

   (b) Find the general solution to the differential equation.

   (c) If the tumor is 5 mm across at time $t = 0$, what does that tell you about the solution?

   (d) If, in addition, the tumor is 8 mm across at time $t = 3$, what does that tell you about the solution?

35. Money in a bank account grows continuously at an annual rate of r (when the interest rate is 5%, $r = 0.05$, and so on). Suppose $2000 is put into the account in 2010.

   (a) Write a differential equation satisfied by M, the amount of money in the account at time t, measured in years since 2010.

   (b) Solve the differential equation.

   (c) Sketch the solution until the year 2040 for interest rates of 5% and 10%.

36. Radioactive carbon (carbon-14) decays at a rate of approximately 1 part in 10,000 a year. For an initial quantity Q_0, write and solve a differential equation for the quantity of carbon-14 as a function of time. Sketch a graph of the solution.

37. Suppose $1000 is put into a bank account and earns interest continuously at a rate of i per year, and in addition, continuous payments are made out of the account at a rate of $100 a year. Find a formula and sketch the amount of money in the account as a function of time if the interest rate is

   (a) 5%   **(b)** 10%   **(c)** 15%

---

[34]http://www.un.org/esa/population/publications/wpp2006/WPP2006_Highlights_rev.pdf, accessed April 24, 2012.
[35]http://www.farmingsolutions.org/facts/factscontent_det.asp, accessed June 6, 2011.

38. A cell contains a chemical (the solute) dissolved in it at a concentration $c(t)$, and the concentration of the same substance outside the cell is a constant k. By Fick's law, if $c(t)$ and k are unequal, solute moves across the cell wall at a rate proportional to the difference between $c(t)$ and k, toward the region of lower concentration.

(a) Write a differential equation satisfied by $c(t)$.
(b) Solve the differential equation with the initial condition $c(0) = c_0$.
(c) Sketch the solution for $c_0 = 0$.

39. A bank account earns 5% annual interest compounded continuously. Continuous payments are made out of the account at a rate of $12,000 per year for 20 years.

(a) Write a differential equation describing the balance $B = f(t)$, where t is in years.
(b) Solve the differential equation given an initial balance of B_0.
(c) What should the initial balance be such that the account has zero balance after precisely 20 years?

40. In some chemical reactions, the rate at which the amount of a substance changes with time is proportional to the amount present. For example, this is the case as δ-glucono-lactone changes into gluconic acid.

(a) Write a differential equation satisfied by y, the quantity of δ-glucono-lactone present at time t.
(b) If 100 grams of δ-glucono-lactone is reduced to 54.9 grams in one hour, how many grams will remain after 10 hours?

41. When the electromotive force (emf) is removed from a circuit containing inductance and resistance but no capacitors, the rate of decrease of current is proportional to the current. If the initial current is 30 amps but decays to 11 amps after 0.01 seconds, find an expression for the current as a function of time.

42. A mothball is in the shape of a sphere and starts with radius 1 cm. The material in the mothball evaporates at a rate proportional to the surface area. After one month, the radius is 0.5 cm. How many months (from the start) is it before the radius is 0.2 cm?

43. Let P be the number of animals in a colony at time t. The growth of the population satisfies

$$\frac{1000}{P}\frac{dP}{dt} = 100 - P.$$

The initial population is 200 individuals. Sketch a graph of P against t. Will there ever be more than 200 individuals in the colony? Will there ever be fewer than 100 individuals? Explain.

44. Table 11.11 gives the percentage, P, of households with a DVD player as a function of year.

(a) Explain why a logistic model is a reasonable one to fit to this data.

(b) Use the data to estimate the point of inflection of P. What limiting value L does this point of inflection predict?
(c) The best logistic equation for this data, using t as years since 1997, turns out to be

$$P = \frac{86.395}{1 + 72.884.75e^{-0.786t}}.$$

What limiting value does this model predict?

Table 11.11 *Percentage of households with a DVD player*

Year	1998	1999	2000	2001	2002
$P(\%)$	1	5	13	21	35
Year	2003	2004	2005	2006	
$P(\%)$	50	70	75	81	

45. A chemical reaction involves one molecule of a substance A combining with one molecule of substance B to form one molecule of substance C, written $A + B \to C$. The Law of Mass Action states that the rate at which C is formed is proportional to the product of the quantities of A and B present. Assume a and b are the initial quantities of A and B and x is the quantity of C present at time t.

(a) Write a differential equation for x.
(b) Solve the equation with $x(0) = 0$.

46. If the initial quantities, a and b, in Problem 45 are the same, write and solve a differential equation for x, with $x(0) = 0$.

The differential equations in Problems 47–49 describe the rates of growth of two populations x and y (both measured in thousands) of species A and B, respectively. For each set:

(a) Describe in words what happens to the population of each species in the absence of the other.

(b) Describe in words how the species interact with one another. Give reasons why the populations might behave as described by the equations. Suggest species that might interact as described by the equations.

47. $\dfrac{dx}{dt} = 0.01x - 0.05xy$

$\dfrac{dy}{dt} = -0.2y + 0.08xy$

48. $\dfrac{dx}{dt} = 0.01x - 0.05xy$

$\dfrac{dy}{dt} = 0.2y - 0.08xy$

49. $\dfrac{dx}{dt} = 0.2x$

$\dfrac{dy}{dt} = 0.4xy - 0.1y$

50. A shrimp population P in a bay grows according to the logistic equation

$$\frac{dP}{dt} = 0.8P(1 - 0.01P),$$

with P in tons of shrimp and t in years.

(a) Sketch a graph of dP/dt against P.

(b) What is the predicted long-term population of shrimp in the bay, given any positive initial condition?

(c) If shrimp are harvested out of the bay by fishermen at a rate of 10 tons per year, what is the new differential equation showing both the natural logistic growth and the constant harvesting?

(d) Sketch a graph of dP/dt against P for the differential equation given in part (c).

(e) What are the equilibrium values for the differential equation given in part (c)?

(f) Use the graph in part (d) to determine whether the shrimp population increases or decreases from each of the following populations:

$$P = 12; \qquad P = 25; \qquad P = 75.$$

51. The concentrations of two chemicals A and B as functions of time are denoted by x and y respectively. Each alone decays at a rate proportional to its concentration. Put together, they also interact to form a third substance, at a rate proportional to the product of their concentrations. All this is expressed in the equations:

$$\frac{dx}{dt} = -2x - xy, \qquad \frac{dy}{dt} = -3y - xy.$$

(a) Find a differential equation describing the relationship between x and y, and solve it.

(b) Show that the only equilibrium state is $x = y = 0$. (Note that the concentrations are nonnegative.)

(c) Show that when x and y are positive and very small, y^2/x^3 is roughly constant. [Hint: When x is small, x is negligible compared to $\ln x$.]

If now the initial concentrations are $x(0) = 4$, $y(0) = 8$:

(d) Find the equation of the phase trajectory.

(e) What would be the concentrations of each substance if they become equal?

(f) If $x = e^{-10}$, find an approximate value for y.

52. We apply Lanchester's model to the Battle of Trafalgar (1805), when a fleet of 40 British ships expected to face a combined French and Spanish fleet of 46 ships. Suppose that there were x British ships and y opposing ships at time t. We assume that all the ships are identical so that constants in the differential equations in Lanchester's model are equal:

$$\frac{dx}{dt} = -ay$$

$$\frac{dy}{dt} = -ax.$$

(a) Write a differential equation involving dy/dx, and solve it using the initial sizes of the two fleets.

(b) If the battle were fought until all the British ships were put out of action, how many French/Spanish ships does this model predict would be left at the end of the battle?

Admiral Nelson, who was in command of the British fleet, did not in fact send his 40 ships against the 46 French and Spanish ships. Instead he split the battle into two parts, sending 32 of his ships against 23 of the French/Spanish ships and his other 8 ships against their other 23.

(c) Analyze each of these two sub-battles using Lanchester's model. Find the solution trajectory for each sub-battle. Which side is predicted to win each one? How many ships from each fleet are expected to be left at the end?

(d) Suppose, as in fact happened, that the remaining ships from each sub-battle then fought each other. Which side is predicted to win, and with how many ships remaining?

53. The following equations describe the rates of growth of an insect and bird population in a particular region, where x is the insect population in millions at time t and y is the bird population in thousands:

$$\frac{dx}{dt} = 3x - 0.02xy$$

$$\frac{dy}{dt} = -10y + 0.001xy.$$

(a) Describe in words the growth of each population in the absence of the other, and describe in words their interaction.

(b) Find the two points (x, y) at which the populations are in equilibrium.

(c) When the populations are at the nonzero equilibrium, 10 thousand additional birds are suddenly introduced. Let A be the point in the phase plane representing these populations. Find a differential equation in terms of just x and y (i.e., eliminate t), and find an equation for the particular solution passing through the point A.

(d) Show that the following points lie on the trajectory in the phase plane that passes through point A:

(i) $B\,(9646.91,\ 150)$ (ii) $C\,(10{,}000,\ 140.43)$
(iii) $D\,(10{,}361.60,\ 150)$

(e) Sketch this trajectory in the phase plane, with x on the horizontal axis, y on the vertical. Show the equilibrium point.

(f) In what order are the points A, B, C, D traversed? [Hint: Find dy/dt, dx/dt at each point.]

(g) On another graph, sketch x and y versus time, t. Use the same initial value as in part (c). You do not need to indicate actual numerical values on the t-axis.

(h) Find dy/dx at points A and C. Find dx/dy at points B and D. [Hint: $dx/dy = 1/(dy/dx)$. Notice that the points A and C are the maximum and minimum values of y, respectively, and B and D are the maximum and minimum values of x, respectively.]

54. When two countries are in an arms race, the rate at which each one spends money on arms is determined by its own current level of spending and by its opponent's level of spending. We expect that the more a country is already spending on armaments, the less willing it will be to increase its military expenditures. On the other hand, the more a country's opponent spends on armaments, the more rapidly the country will arm. If \$$x$ billion is the country's yearly expenditure on arms, and \$$y$ billion is its opponent's, then the *Richardson arms race model* proposes that x and y are determined by differential equations. Suppose that for some particular arms race the equations are

$$\frac{dx}{dt} = -0.2x + 0.15y + 20$$

$$\frac{dy}{dt} = 0.1x - 0.2y + 40.$$

(a) Explain the signs of the three terms on the right side of the equations for dx/dt.

(b) Find the equilibrium points for this system.
(c) Analyze the direction of the trajectories in each region.
(d) Are the equilibrium points stable or unstable?
(e) What does this model predict will happen if both countries disarm?
(f) What does this model predict will happen in the case of unilateral disarmament (one country disarms, and the other country does not)?
(g) What does the model predict will happen in the long run?

In Problems 55–57, a population $P(t)$ of animals satisfies

$$\frac{dP}{dt} = -kP\left(1 - \frac{P}{L}\right)\left(1 - \frac{P}{2L}\right), \quad \text{with } k, L > 0.$$

For the given initial condition, what happens to the animal population over time? [Hint: The equation has equilibrium solutions at $P = 0, L, 2L$.]

55. Initially, there are fewer than L animals.

56. Initially, there are between L and $2L$ animals.

57. Initially, there are more than $2L$ animals.

CAS Challenge Problems

58. Consider the differential equation

$$\frac{dP}{dt} = P(P - 1)(2 - P).$$

(a) Find all the equilibrium solutions.
(b) Show that the following two functions are solutions:

$$P_1(t) = 1 - \frac{e^t}{\sqrt{3 + e^{2t}}} \quad \text{and} \quad P_2(t) = 1 + \frac{e^t}{\sqrt{3 + e^{2t}}}.$$

[Hint: Use a computer algebra system to simplify the difference between the right and left-hand sides.]
(c) Find $P_1(0)$, $P_2(0)$, $\lim_{t \to \infty} P_1(t)$, and $\lim_{t \to \infty} P_2(t)$. Explain how you could have predicted the limits as $t \to \infty$ from the values at $t = 0$ without knowing the solutions explicitly.

59. In this problem we investigate *Picard's method* for approximating the solutions of differential equations. Consider the differential equation

$$y'(t) = y(t)^2 + t^2, \quad y(a) = b.$$

Integrating both sides with respect to t gives

$$y(s) - y(a) = \int_a^s y'(t)\, dt = \int_a^s \left(y(t)^2 + t^2\right) dt.$$

Since $y(a) = b$, we have

$$y(s) = b + \int_a^s \left(y(t)^2 + t^2\right) dt.$$

We have put the differential equation into the form of an *integral equation*. If we have an approximate solution $y_0(s)$, we can use the integral form to make a new approximation

$$y_1(s) = b + \int_a^s \left(y_0(t)^2 + t^2\right) dt.$$

Continuing this process, we get a sequence of approximations $y_0(s), y_1(s), \ldots, y_n(s), \ldots$ where each term in the sequence is defined in terms of the previous one by the equation

$$y_{n+1}(s) = b + \int_a^s \left(y_n(t)^2 + t^2\right) dt.$$

(a) Show that y_n satisfies the initial condition $y_n(a) = b$ for all n.
(b) Using the initial condition $y(1) = 0$, start with the approximation $y_0(s) = 0$ and use a computer algebra system to find the next three approximations y_1, y_2, and y_3.
(c) Use a computer algebra system to find the solution y satisfying $y(1) = 0$, and sketch y, y_1, y_2, y_3 on the same axes. On what domain do the approximations appear to be accurate? [The solution y cannot be expressed in terms of elementary functions. If your computer algebra system cannot solve the equation exactly, use a numerical method such as Euler's method.]

60. Figure 11.98 shows the slope field for the differential equation[36]

$$\frac{dy}{dx} = \sqrt{1 - y^2}.$$

(a) Sketch the solution with $y(0) = 0$ for $-3 \le x \le 3$.

(b) Use a computer algebra system to find the solution in part (a).

(c) Compare the computer algebra system's solution with your sketch. Do they agree? If not, which one is right?

Figure 11.98

PROJECTS FOR CHAPTER ELEVEN

1. Medical Case Study: Anaphylaxis[37]

During surgery, a patient's blood pressure was observed to be dangerously low. One possible cause is a severe allergic reaction called *anaphylaxis*. A diagnosis of anaphylaxis is based in part on a blood test showing the elevation of the serum *tryptase*, a molecule released by allergic cells. In anaphylaxis, the concentration of tryptase in the blood rises rapidly and then decays back to baseline in a few hours.

However, low blood pressure from an entirely different cause (say from a heart problem) can also lead to an elevation in tryptase. Before diagnosing anaphylaxis, the medical team needs to make sure that the observed tryptase elevation is the result of an allergy problem, not a heart problem. To do this, they need to know the peak level reached by the serum tryptase. The normal range for the serum tryptase is 0–15 ng/ml (nanograms per milliliter). Mild to moderate elevations from low blood pressure are common, but if the peak were three times the normal maximum (that is, above 45 ng/ml), then a diagnosis of anaphylaxis would be made.

The surgeons who resuscitated this patient ran two blood tests to measure T_r, the serum tryptase concentration; the results are in Table 11.12. Use the test results to estimate the peak serum tryptase level at the time of surgery by making an assumption of *first-order kinetics*: the rate of tryptase decay, dT_r/dt, is proportional to the concentration of tryptase, T_r. Did this patient experience anaphylaxis?

Table 11.12 *Serum tryptase levels*

t, hours since surgery	4	19.5
T_r, concentration in ng/ml	37	13

The Spread of SARS

In the spring of 2003, SARS (Severe Acute Respiratory Syndrome) spread rapidly in several Asian countries and Canada. Predicting the course of the disease—how many people would be infected, how long it would last—was important to officials trying to minimize the impact of the disease.

2. SARS Predictions for Hong Kong

This project compares three predictions about the spread of SARS in Hong Kong. We measure time, t, in days since March 17, 2003, the date the World Health Organization (WHO) started to publish daily SARS reports.[38] Let P be the total number of cases reported in Hong Kong by day t. On March 17, Hong Kong reported 95 cases.

---

[36] Adapted from David Lomen and David Lovelock, *Differential Equations* (New York: John Wiley & Sons, Inc., 1999).

[37] From David E. Sloane, M.D., drawing from an actual episode in his clinic.

[38] www.who.int/csr/country/en, accessed July 13, 2003.

The constants in the three differential equations whose predictions are analyzed in this project were determined using WHO data available in March 2003. We compare predictions from the three models for June 12, 2003, the last day a new case was reported in Hong Kong.

(a) (i) *A Linear Model.* Suppose P satisfies

$$\frac{dP}{dt} = 30.2, \quad \text{with } P(0) = 95.$$

Solve the differential equation and use your solution to predict the number of cases of SARS in Hong Kong by June 12 ($t = 87$).

(ii) *An Exponential Model.* Suppose P satisfies

$$\frac{1}{P}\frac{dP}{dt} = 0.12, \quad \text{with } P(0) = 95.$$

Solve the differential equation and use your solution to predict the number of cases of SARS in Hong Kong by June 12 ($t = 87$).

(iii) *A Logistic Model.* Suppose P satisfies

$$\frac{1}{P}\frac{dP}{dt} = 0.19 - 0.0002P, \quad \text{with } P(0) = 95.$$

Solve the differential equation and use your solution to predict the number of cases of SARS in Hong Kong by June 12 ($t = 87$).

(b) (i) Comment on the June 12 predictions from the three models.

(ii) What do each of the three models in part (a) predict about the trend in the number of new cases each day?

(iii) In May 2003, *The Lancet* published[39] a graph like Figure 11.99. What trend do you see in the data? What does this trend suggest about which model fits the data best?

(c) Assume that the data follow a logistic model, which is the only one in part (a) to predict that the total number of cases will level off:

(i) Use your answer to part (a) (iii) to predict the maximum number of SARS cases.

(ii) Assume that the data follow a logistic model, but not necessarily with the parameters given in part (a) (iii). Use Figure 11.99 and the fact that there had been a total of 998 cases of SARS by April 10 to predict the maximum number of SARS cases.

(d) To see how well the three models worked in practice, plot the data in Table 11.13 and each of the three solution curves from part (a).

Table 11.13 *Total number of SARS cases reported in Hong Kong by day t (where $t = 0$ is March 17, 2003)*

t	P	t	P	t	P	t	P
0	95	26	1108	54	1674	75	1739
5	222	33	1358	61	1710	81	1750
12	470	40	1527	68	1724	87	1755
19	800	47	1621				

Figure 11.99: Daily increase in Hong Kong SARS cases

---

[39]"SARS, Lay Epidemiology and Fear," by O. Razum, H. Beecher, A. Kapuan, T. Junghauss, *The Lancet,* May 2, 2003.

3. An S-I-R Model for SARS

This project analyzes the spread of SARS through interaction between infected and susceptible people.

The variables are S, the number of susceptibles, I, the number of infecteds who can infect others, and R, the number removed (this group includes those in quarantine and those who die, as well as those who have recovered and acquired immunity). Time, t, is in days since March 17, 2003, the date the World Health Organization (WHO) started to publish daily SARS reports. On March 17, Hong Kong reported 95 cases. In this model

$$\frac{dS}{dt} = -aSI$$

$$\frac{dI}{dt} = aSI - bI,$$

and $S + I + R = 6.8$ million, the population of Hong Kong in 2003.[40] Estimates based on WHO data give $a = 1.25 \cdot 10^{-8}$.

(a) What are S_0 and I_0, the initial values of S and I?

(b) During March 2003, the value of b was about 0.06. Using a calculator or computer, sketch the slope field for this system of differential equations and the solution trajectory corresponding to the initial conditions. (Use $0 \leq S \leq 7 \cdot 10^6, 0 \leq I \leq 0.4 \cdot 10^6$.)

(c) What does your graph tell you about the total number of people infected over the course of the disease if $b = 0.06$? What is the threshold value? What does this value tell you?

(d) During April, as public health officials worked to get the disease under control, people who had been in contact with the disease were quarantined. Explain why quarantining has the effect of raising the value of b.

(e) Using the April value, $b = 0.24$, sketch the slope field. (Use the same value of a and the same window.)

(f) What is the threshold value for $b = 0.24$? What does this tell you? Comment on the quarantine policy.

(g) Comment on the effectiveness of each of the following policies intended to prevent an epidemic and protect a city from an outbreak of SARS in a nearby region.

   I Close off the city from contact with the infected region. Shut down roads, airports, trains, and other forms of direct contact.

   II Install a quarantine policy. Isolate anyone who has been in contact with a SARS patient or anyone who shows symptoms of SARS.

---

[40]www.census.gov, International Data Base (IDB), accessed June 8, 2004.

4. Pareto's Law

In analyzing a society, sociologists are often interested in how incomes are distributed through the society. Pareto's law asserts that each society has a constant k such that the average income of all people wealthier than you is k times your income $(k > 1)$. If $p(x)$ is the number of people in the society with an income of x or above, we define $\Delta p = p(x + \Delta x) - p(x)$, for small Δx.

(a) Explain why the number of people with incomes between x and $x + \Delta x$ is represented by $-\Delta p$. Then show that the total amount of money earned by people with incomes between x and $x + \Delta x$ is approximated by $-x\Delta p$.

(b) Use Pareto's law to show that the total amount of money earned by people with incomes of x or above is $kxp(x)$. Then show that the total amount of money earned by people with incomes between x and $x + \Delta x$ is approximated by $-kp\Delta x - kx\Delta p$.

(c) Using your answers to parts (a) and (b), show that p satisfies the differential equation

$$(1 - k)xp' = kp.$$

(d) Solve this differential equation for $p(x)$.

(e) Sketch a graph of $p(x)$ for various values of k, some large and some near 1. How does the value of k alter the shape of the graph?

5. Vibrations in a Molecule

Suppose the force, F, between two atoms a distance r apart in a molecule is given by

$$F(r) = b\left(\frac{a^2}{r^3} - \frac{a}{r^2}\right)$$

where a and b are positive constants.

(a) Find the equilibrium distance, r, at which $F = 0$.

(b) Expand F in a series about the equilibrium position. Give the first two nonzero terms.

(c) Suppose one atom is fixed. Let x be the displacement of the other atom from the equilibrium position. Give the first two nonzero terms of the series for F in terms of x.

(d) Using Newton's Second Law of Motion, show that if x is small, the second atom oscillates about the equilibrium position. Find the period of the oscillation.

Chapter Twelve

FUNCTIONS OF SEVERAL VARIABLES

Contents

12.1 FUNCTIONS OF TWO VARIABLES

Function Notation

Suppose you want to calculate your monthly payment on a five-year car loan; this depends on both the amount of money you borrow and the interest rate. These quantities can vary separately: the loan amount can change while the interest rate remains the same, or the interest rate can change while the loan amount remains the same. To calculate your monthly payment you need to know both. If the monthly payment is m, the loan amount is L, and the interest rate is $r\%$, then we express the fact that m is a function of L and r by writing:

$$m = f(L, r).$$

This is just like the function notation of one-variable calculus. The variable m is called the dependent variable, and the variables L and r are called the independent variables. The letter f stands for the *function* or rule that gives the value of m corresponding to given values of L and r.

A function of two variables can be represented graphically, numerically by a table of values, or algebraically by a formula. In this section, we give examples of each.

Graphical Example: A Weather Map

Figure 12.1 shows a weather map from a newspaper. What information does it convey? It displays the predicted high temperature, T, in degrees Fahrenheit (°F), throughout the US on that day. The curves on the map, called *isotherms*, separate the country into zones, according to whether T is in the 60s, 70s, 80s, 90s, or 100s. (*Iso* means same and *therm* means heat.) Notice that the isotherm separating the 80s and 90s zones connects all the points where the temperature is exactly 90°F.

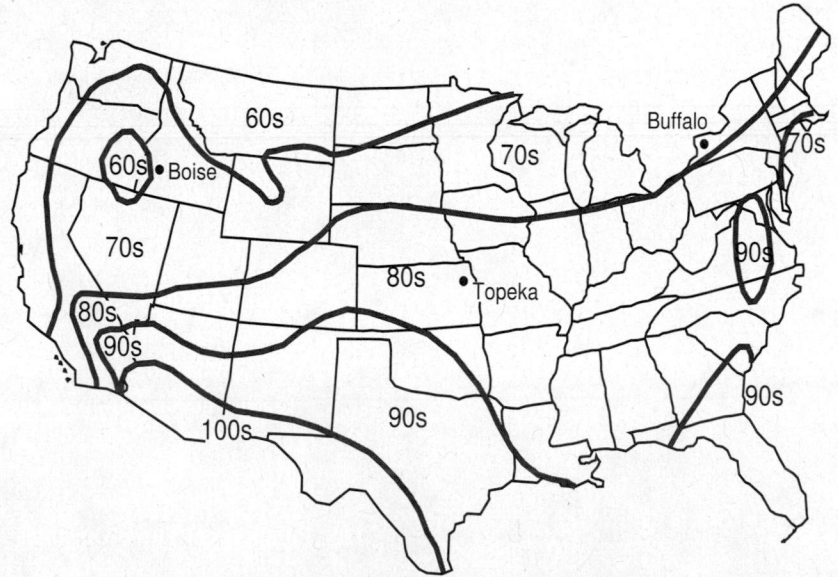

Figure 12.1: Weather map showing predicted high temperatures, T, on a summer day

---

Example 1   Estimate the predicted value of T in Boise, Idaho; Topeka, Kansas; and Buffalo, New York.

Solution   Boise and Buffalo are in the 70s region, and Topeka is in the 80s region. Thus, the predicted temperature in Boise and Buffalo is between 70 and 80 while the predicted temperature in Topeka is between 80 and 90. In fact, we can say more. Although both Boise and Buffalo are in the 70s, Boise is quite close to the $T = 70$ isotherm, whereas Buffalo is quite close to the $T = 80$ isotherm. So we estimate the temperature to be in the low 70s in Boise and in the high 70s in Buffalo. Topeka is about halfway between the $T = 80$ isotherm and the $T = 90$ isotherm. Thus, we guess the temperature in Topeka to be in the mid-80s. In fact, the actual high temperatures for that day were $71°F$ for Boise, $79°F$ for Buffalo, and $86°F$ for Topeka.

The predicted high temperature, T, illustrated by the weather map is a function of (that is, depends on) two variables, often longitude and latitude, or miles east-west and miles north-south of a fixed point, say, Topeka. The weather map in Figure 12.1 is called a *contour map* or *contour diagram* of that function. Section 12.2 shows another way of visualizing functions of two variables using surfaces; Section 12.3 looks at contour maps in detail.

Numerical Example: Beef Consumption

Suppose you are a beef producer and you want to know how much beef people will buy. This depends on how much money people have and on the price of beef. The consumption of beef, C (in pounds per week per household) is a function of household income, I (in thousands of dollars per year), and the price of beef, p (in dollars per pound). In function notation, we write:

$$C = f(I, p).$$

Table 12.1 contains values of this function. Values of p are shown across the top, values of I are down the left side, and corresponding values of $f(I, p)$ are given in the table.[1] For example, to find the value of $f(40, 3.50)$, we look in the row corresponding to $I = 40$ under $p = 3.50$, where we find the number 4.05. Thus,

$$f(40, 3.50) = 4.05.$$

This means that, on average, if a household's income is \$40,000 a year and the price of beef is \$3.50/lb, the family will buy 4.05 lbs of beef per week.

Table 12.1   *Quantity of beef bought (pounds/household/week)*

		Price of beef (\$/lb)			
		3.00	3.50	4.00	4.50
Household income per year, I (\$1000)	20	2.65	2.59	2.51	2.43
	40	4.14	4.05	3.94	3.88
	60	5.11	5.00	4.97	4.84
	80	5.35	5.29	5.19	5.07
	100	5.79	5.77	5.60	5.53

Notice how this differs from the table of values of a one-variable function, where one row or one column is enough to list the values of the function. Here many rows and columns are needed because the function has a value for every *pair* of values of the independent variables.

Algebraic Examples: Formulas

In both the weather map and beef consumption examples, there is no formula for the underlying function. That is usually the case for functions representing real-life data. On the other hand, for many idealized models in physics, engineering, or economics, there are exact formulas.

---

[1]Adapted from Richard G. Lipsey, *An Introduction to Positive Economics*, 3rd ed, (London: Weidenfeld and Nicolson, 1971).

Example 2   Give a formula for the function $M = f(B, t)$ where M is the amount of money in a bank account t years after an initial investment of B dollars, if interest is accrued at a rate of 1.2% per year compounded annually.

Solution   Annual compounding means that M increases by a factor of 1.012 every year, so

$$M = f(B, t) = B(1.012)^t.$$

Example 3   A cylinder with closed ends has radius r and height h. If its volume is V and its surface area is A, find formulas for the functions $V = f(r, h)$ and $A = g(r, h)$.

Solution   Since the area of the circular base is πr^2, we have

$$V = f(r, h) = \text{Area of base} \cdot \text{Height} = \pi r^2 h.$$

The surface area of the side is the circumference of the bottom, $2\pi r$, times the height h, giving $2\pi r h$. Thus,

$$A = g(r, h) = 2 \cdot \text{Area of base} + \text{Area of side} = 2\pi r^2 + 2\pi r h.$$

A Tour of 3-Space

In Section 12.2 we see how to visualize a function of two variables as a surface in space. Now we see how to locate points in three-dimensional space (3-space).

Imagine three coordinate axes meeting at the *origin*: a vertical axis, and two horizontal axes at right angles to each other. (See Figure 12.2.) Think of the xy-plane as being horizontal, while the z-axis extends vertically above and below the plane. The labels x, y, and z show which part of each axis is positive; the other side is negative. We generally use *right-handed axes* in which looking down the positive z-axis gives the usual view of the xy-plane. We specify a point in 3-space by giving its coordinates (x, y, z) with respect to these axes. Think of the coordinates as instructions telling you how to get to the point: start at the origin, go x units along the x-axis, then y units in the direction parallel to the y-axis, and finally z units in the direction parallel to the z-axis. The coordinates can be positive, zero or negative; a zero coordinate means "don't move in this direction," and a negative coordinate means "go in the negative direction parallel to this axis." For example, the origin has coordinates $(0, 0, 0)$, since we get there from the origin by doing nothing at all.

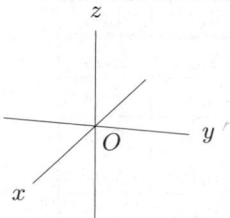

Figure 12.2: Coordinate axes in three-dimensional space

Figure 12.3: The point $(1, 2, 3)$ in 3-space

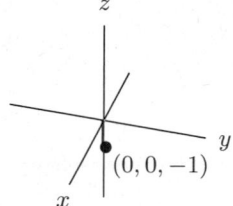

Figure 12.4: The point $(0, 0, -1)$ in 3-space

Example 4   Describe the position of the points with coordinates $(1, 2, 3)$ and $(0, 0, -1)$.

Solution   We get to the point $(1, 2, 3)$ by starting at the origin, going 1 unit along the x-axis, 2 units in the direction parallel to the y-axis, and 3 units up in the direction parallel to the z-axis. (See Figure 12.3.)

To get to $(0, 0, -1)$, we don't move at all in the x- and the y-direction, but move 1 unit in the negative z-direction. So the point is on the negative z-axis. (See Figure 12.4.) You can check that the position of the point is independent of the order of the x, y, and z displacements.

Example 5   You start at the origin, go along the y-axis a distance of 2 units in the positive direction, and then move vertically upward a distance of 1 unit. What are the coordinates of your final position?

Solution   You started at the point $(0, 0, 0)$. When you went along the y-axis, your y-coordinate increased to 2. Moving vertically increased your z-coordinate to 1; your x-coordinate did not change because you did not move in the x-direction. So your final coordinates are $(0, 2, 1)$. (See Figure 12.5.)

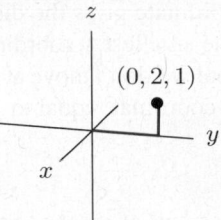

Figure 12.5: The point $(0, 2, 1)$ is reached by moving 2 along the y-axis and 1 upward

It is often helpful to picture a three-dimensional coordinate system in terms of a room. The origin is a corner at floor level where two walls meet the floor. The z-axis is the vertical intersection of the two walls; the x- and the y-axis are the intersections of each wall with the floor. Points with negative coordinates lie behind a wall in the next room or below the floor.

Graphing Equations in 3-Space

We can graph an equation involving the variables x, y, and z in 3-space; such a graph is a picture of all points (x, y, z) that satisfy the equation.

Example 6   What do the graphs of the equations $z = 0$, $z = 3$, and $z = -1$ look like?

Solution   To graph $z = 0$, we visualize the set of points whose z-coordinate is zero. If the z-coordinate is 0, then we must be at the same vertical level as the origin, that is, we are in the horizontal plane containing the origin. So the graph of $z = 0$ is the middle plane in Figure 12.6. The graph of $z = 3$ is a plane parallel to the graph of $z = 0$, but three units above it. The graph of $z = -1$ is a plane parallel to the graph of $z = 0$, but one unit below it.

Figure 12.6: The planes $z = -1$, $z = 0$, and $z = 3$

The plane $z = 0$ contains the x- and the y-coordinate axis, and is called the xy-plane. There are two other coordinate planes. The yz-plane contains both the y- and the z-axis, and the xz-plane contains the x- and the z-axis. (See Figure 12.7.)

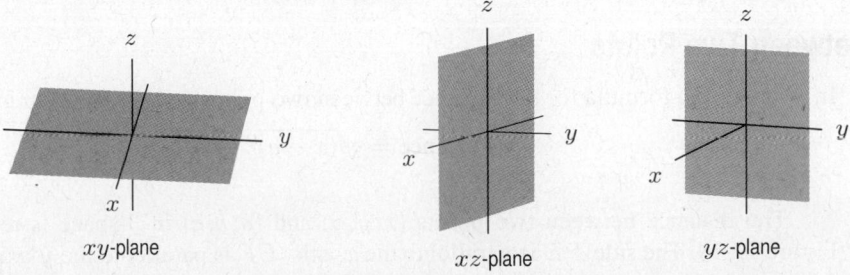

xy-plane xz-plane yz-plane

Figure 12.7: The three coordinate planes

Example 7   Which of the points $A = (1, -1, 0)$, $B = (0, 3, 4)$, $C = (2, 2, 1)$, and $D = (0, -4, 0)$ lies closest to the xz-plane? Which point lies on the y-axis?

Solution   The magnitude of the y-coordinate gives the distance to the xz-plane. The point A lies closest to that plane, because it has the smallest y-coordinate in magnitude. To get to a point on the y-axis, we move along the y-axis, but we don't move at all in the x- or the z-direction. Thus, a point on the y-axis has both its x- and z-coordinate equal to zero. The only point of the four that satisfies this is D. (See Figure 12.8.)

In general, if a point has one of its coordinates equal to zero, it lies in one of the coordinate planes. If a point has two of its coordinates equal to zero, it lies on one of the coordinate axes.

Figure 12.8: Which point lies closest to the xz-plane?
Which point lies on the y-axis?

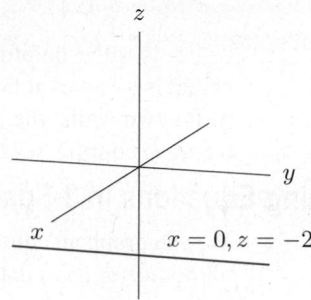

Figure 12.9: The line $x = 0$, $z = -2$

Example 8   You are 2 units below the xy-plane and in the yz-plane. What are your coordinates?

Solution   Since you are 2 units below the xy-plane, your z-coordinate is -2. Since you are in the yz-plane, your x-coordinate is 0; your y-coordinate can be anything. Thus, you are at the point $(0, y, -2)$. The set of all such points forms a line parallel to the y-axis, 2 units below the xy-plane, and in the yz-plane. (See Figure 12.9.)

Example 9   You are standing at the point $(4, 5, 2)$, looking at the point $(0.5, 0, 3)$. Are you looking up or down?

Solution   The point you are standing at has z-coordinate 2, whereas the point you are looking at has z-coordinate 3; hence you are looking up.

Example 10   Imagine that the yz-plane in Figure 12.7 is a page of this book. Describe the region behind the page algebraically.

Solution   The positive part of the x-axis pokes out of the page; moving in the positive x-direction brings you out in front of the page. The region behind the page corresponds to negative values of x, so it is the set of all points in 3-space satisfying the inequality $x < 0$.

Distance Between Two Points

In 2-space, the formula for the distance between two points (x, y) and (a, b) is given by

$$\text{Distance} = \sqrt{(x - a)^2 + (y - b)^2}.$$

The distance between two points (x, y, z) and (a, b, c) in 3-space is represented by PG in Figure 12.10. The side PE is parallel to the x-axis, EF is parallel to the y-axis, and FG is parallel to the z-axis.

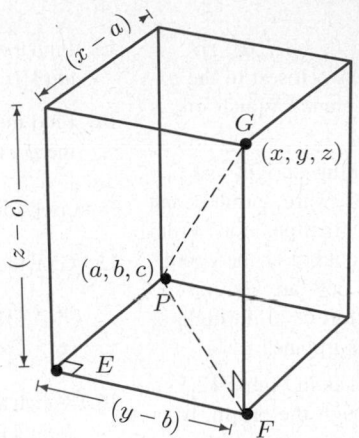

Figure 12.10: The diagonal PG gives the distance between the points (x, y, z) and (a, b, c)

Using Pythagoras' theorem twice gives

$$(PG)^2 = (PF)^2 + (FG)^2 = (PE)^2 + (EF)^2 + (FG)^2 = (x - a)^2 + (y - b)^2 + (z - c)^2.$$

Thus, a formula for the distance between the points (x, y, z) and (a, b, c) in 3-space is

$$\text{Distance} = \sqrt{(x - a)^2 + (y - b)^2 + (z - c)^2}.$$

Example 11   Find the distance between $(1, 2, 1)$ and $(-3, 1, 2)$.

Solution   Distance $= \sqrt{(-3 - 1)^2 + (1 - 2)^2 + (2 - 1)^2} = \sqrt{18} = 4.24$.

Example 12   Find an expression for the distance from the origin to the point (x, y, z).

Solution   The origin has coordinates $(0, 0, 0)$, so the distance from the origin to (x, y, z) is given by

$$\text{Distance} = \sqrt{(x - 0)^2 + (y - 0)^2 + (z - 0)^2} = \sqrt{x^2 + y^2 + z^2}.$$

Example 13   Find an equation for a sphere of radius 1 with center at the origin.

Solution   The sphere consists of all points (x, y, z) whose distance from the origin is 1, that is, which satisfy the equation

$$\sqrt{x^2 + y^2 + z^2} = 1.$$

This is an equation for the sphere. If we square both sides we get the equation in the form

$$x^2 + y^2 + z^2 = 1.$$

Note that this equation represents the *surface* of the sphere. The solid ball enclosed by the sphere is represented by the inequality $x^2 + y^2 + z^2 \leq 1$.

Exercises and Problems for Section 12.1

Exercises

1. Which of the points $P = (1, 2, 1)$ and $Q = (2, 0, 0)$ is closest to the origin?

2. Which two of the three points $P_1 = (1, 2, 3)$, $P_2 = (3, 2, 1)$ and $P_3 = (1, 1, 0)$ are closest to each other?

3. Which of the points $A = (1.3, -2.7, 0)$, $B = (0.9, 0, 3.2)$, $C = (2.5, 0.1, -0.3)$ is closest to the yz-plane? Which one lies on the xz-plane? Which one is farthest from the xy-plane?

4. You are at the point $(3, 1, 1)$, standing upright and facing the yz-plane. You walk 2 units forward, turn left, and walk another 2 units. What is your final position? From the point of view of an observer looking at the coordinate system in Figure 12.2 on page 668, are you in front of or behind the yz-plane? To the left or to the right of the xz-plane? Above or below the xy-plane?

5. On a set of x, y and z axes oriented as in Figure 12.5 on page 669, draw a straight line through the origin, lying in the yz-plane and such that if you move along the line with your y-coordinate increasing, your z-coordinate is increasing.

6. What is the midpoint of the line segment joining the points $(-1, 3, 9)$ and $(5, 6, -3)$?

In Exercises 7–10 sketch graphs of the equations in 3-space.

7. $z = 4$

8. $x = -3$

9. $y = 1$

10. $z = 2$ and $y = 4$

11. With the z-axis vertical, a sphere has center $(2, 3, 7)$ and lowest point $(2, 3, -1)$. What is the highest point on the sphere?

12. Find an equation of the sphere with radius 5 centered at the origin.

13. Find the equation of the sphere with radius 2 and centered at $(1, 0, 0)$.

14. Find the equation of the vertical plane perpendicular to the y-axis and through the point $(2, 3, 4)$.

Exercises 15–17 refer to the map in Figure 12.1 on page 666.

15. Give the range of daily high temperatures for:

(a) Pennsylvania   **(b)** North Dakota

(c) California

16. Sketch a possible graph of the predicted high temperature T on a line north-south through Topeka.

17. Sketch possible graphs of the predicted high temperature on a north-south line and an east-west line through Boise.

For Exercises 18–20, refer to Table 12.1 on page 667, where p is the price of beef and I is annual household income.

18. Give tables for beef consumption as a function of p, with I fixed at $I = 20$ and $I = 100$. Give tables for beef consumption as a function of I, with p fixed at $p = 3.00$ and $p = 4.00$. Comment on what you see in the tables.

19. Make a table of the proportion, P, of household income spent on beef per week as a function of price and income. (Note that P is the fraction of income spent on beef.)

20. How does beef consumption vary as a function of household income if the price of beef is held constant?

Problems

21. The temperature adjusted for wind chill is a temperature which tells you how cold it feels, as a result of the combination of wind and temperature.[2] See Table 12.2.

Table 12.2 *Temperature adjusted for wind chill (°F) as a function of wind speed and temperature*

		Temperature (°F)							
		35	30	25	20	15	10	5	0
Wind Speed (mph)	5	31	25	19	13	7	1	−5	−11
	10	27	21	15	9	3	−4	−10	−16
	15	25	19	13	6	0	−7	−13	−19
	20	24	17	11	4	−2	−9	−15	−22
	25	23	16	9	3	−4	−11	−17	−24

(a) If the temperature is 0°F and the wind speed is 15 mph, how cold does it feel?

(b) If the temperature is 35°F, what wind speed makes it feel like 24°F?

(c) If the temperature is 25°F, what wind speed makes it feel like 12°F?

(d) If the wind is blowing at 20 mph, what temperature feels like 0°F?

In Problems 22–23, use Table 12.2 to make tables with the given properties.

22. The temperature adjusted for wind chill as a function of wind speed for temperatures of 20°F and 0°F.

23. The temperature adjusted for wind chill as a function of temperature for wind speeds of 5 mph and 20 mph.

24. A car rental company charges $40 a day and 15 cents a mile for its cars.

(a) Write a formula for the cost, C, of renting a car as a function, f, of the number of days, d, and the number of miles driven, m.

(b) If $C = f(d, m)$, find $f(5, 300)$ and interpret it.

25. The gravitational force, F newtons, exerted on an object by the earth depends on the object's mass, m kilograms, and its distance, r meters, from the center of the earth, so $F = f(m, r)$. Interpret the following statement in terms of gravitation: $f(100, 7000000) \approx 820$.

---

[2]Data from www.nws.noaa.gov/om/windchill, accessed on May 30, 2004.

26. Consider the acceleration due to gravity, g, at a distance h from the center of a planet of mass m.

    (a) If m is held constant, is g an increasing or decreasing function of h? Why?
    (b) If h is held constant, is g an increasing or decreasing function of m? Why?

27. A cube is located such that its top four corners have the coordinates $(-1, -2, 2)$, $(-1, 3, 2)$, $(4, -2, 2)$ and $(4, 3, 2)$. Give the coordinates of the center of the cube.

28. Describe the set of points whose distance from the x-axis is 2.

29. Describe the set of points whose distance from the x-axis equals the distance from the yz-plane.

30. Find a formula for the shortest distance between a point (a, b, c) and the y-axis.

31. Find the equations of planes that just touch the sphere $(x - 2)^2 + (y - 3)^2 + (z - 3)^2 = 16$ and are parallel to

    (a) The xy-plane   (b) The yz-plane
    (c) The xz-plane

32. Find an equation of the largest sphere contained in the cube determined by the planes $x = 2$, $x = 6$; $y = 5$, $y = 9$; and $z = -1$, $z = 3$.

33. A cube has edges parallel to the axes. One corner is at $A = (5, 1, 2)$ and the corner at the other end of the longest diagonal through A is $B = (12, 7, 4)$.

    (a) What are the coordinates of the other three vertices on the bottom face?
    (b) What are the coordinates of the other three vertices on the top face?

34. Which of the points $P_1 = (-3, 2, 15)$, $P_2 = (0, -10, 0)$, $P_3 = (-6, 5, 3)$ and $P_4 = (-4, 2, 7)$ is closest to $P = (6, 0, 4)$?

35. (a) Find the equations of the circles (if any) where the sphere $(x - 1)^2 + (y + 3)^2 + (z - 2)^2 = 4$ intersects each coordinate plane.
    (b) Find the points (if any) where this sphere intersects each coordinate axis.

36. A rectangular solid lies with its length parallel to the y-axis, and its top and bottom faces parallel to the plane $z = 0$. If the center of the object is at $(1, 1, -2)$ and it has a length of 13, a height of 5 and a width of 6, give the coordinates of all eight corners and draw the figure labeling the eight corners.

37. An equilateral triangle is standing vertically with a vertex above the xy-plane and its two other vertices at $(7, 0, 0)$ and $(9, 0, 0)$. What is its highest point?

38. (a) Find the midpoint of the line segment joining $A = (1, 5, 7)$ to $B = (5, 13, 19)$.
    (b) Find the point one quarter of the way along the line segment from A to B.
    (c) Find the point one quarter of the way along the line segment from B to A.

Strengthen Your Understanding

In Problems 39–41, explain what is wrong with the statement.

39. In 3-space, $y = 1$ is a line parallel to the x-axis.

40. The xy-plane has equation $xy = 0$.

41. The distance from $(2, 3, 4)$ to the x-axis is 2.

In Problems 42–43, give an example of:

42. A formula for a function $f(x, y)$ that is increasing in x and decreasing in y.

43. A point in 3-space with all its coordinates negative and farther from the xz-plane than from the plane $z = -5$.

Are the statements in Problems 44–57 true or false? Give reasons for your answer.

44. If $f(x, y)$ is a function of two variables defined for all x and y, then $f(10, y)$ is a function of one variable.

45. The volume V of a box of height h and square base of side length s is a function of h and s.

46. If $H = f(t, d)$ is the function giving the water temperature $H°C$ of a lake at time t hours after midnight and depth d meters, then t is a function of d and H.

47. A table for a function $f(x, y)$ cannot have any values of f appearing twice.

48. If $f(x)$ and $g(y)$ are both functions of a single variable, then the product $f(x) \cdot g(y)$ is a function of two variables.

49. The point $(1, 2, 3)$ lies above the plane $z = 2$.

50. The graph of the equation $z = 2$ is a plane parallel to the xz-plane.

51. The points $(1, 0, 1)$ and $(0, -1, 1)$ are the same distance from the origin.

52. The point $(2, -1, 3)$ lies on the graph of the sphere $(x - 2)^2 + (y + 1)^2 + (z - 3)^2 = 25$.

53. There is only one point in the yz-plane that is a distance 3 from the point $(3, 0, 0)$.

54. There is only one point in the yz-plane that is distance 5 from the point $(3, 0, 0)$.

55. If the point $(0, b, 0)$ has distance 4 from the plane $y = 0$, then b must be 4.

56. A line parallel to the z-axis can intersect the graph of $f(x, y)$ at most once.

57. A line parallel to the y-axis can intersect the graph of $f(x, y)$ at most once.

12.2 GRAPHS AND SURFACES

The weather map on page 666 is one way of visualizing a function of two variables. In this section we see how to visualize a function of two variables in another way, using a surface in 3-space.

Visualizing a Function of Two Variables Using a Graph

For a function of one variable, $y = f(x)$, the graph of f is the set of all points (x, y) in 2-space such that $y = f(x)$. In general, these points lie on a curve in the plane. When a computer or calculator graphs f, it approximates by plotting points in the xy-plane and joining consecutive points by line segments. The more points, the better the approximation.

Now consider a function of two variables.

The **graph** of a function of two variables, f, is the set of all points (x, y, z) such that $z = f(x, y)$. In general, the graph of a function of two variables is a surface in 3-space.

Plotting the Graph of the Function $f(x, y) = x^2 + y^2$

To sketch the graph of f we connect points as for a function of one variable. We first make a table of values of f, such as in Table 12.3.

Table 12.3 *Table of values of $f(x, y) = x^2 + y^2$*

		-3	-2	-1	0	1	2	3
	-3	18	13	10	9	10	13	18
	-2	13	8	5	4	5	8	13
	-1	10	5	2	1	2	5	10
x	0	9	4	1	0	1	4	9
	1	10	5	2	1	2	5	10
	2	13	8	5	4	5	8	13
	3	18	13	10	9	10	13	18

The header row above the table reads y.

Now we plot points. For example, we plot $(1, 2, 5)$ because $f(1, 2) = 5$ and we plot $(0, 2, 4)$ because $f(0, 2) = 4$. Then, we connect the points corresponding to the rows and columns in the table. The result is called a *wire-frame* picture of the graph. Filling in between the wires gives a surface. That is the way a computer drew the graphs in Figure 12.11 and 12.12. As more points are plotted, we get the surface in Figure 12.13, called a *paraboloid*.

You should check to see if the sketches make sense. Notice that the graph goes through the origin since $(x, y, z) = (0, 0, 0)$ satisfies $z = x^2 + y^2$. Observe that if x is held fixed and y is allowed to vary, the graph dips down and then goes back up, just like the entries in the rows of Table 12.3. Similarly, if y is held fixed and x is allowed to vary, the graph dips down and then goes back up, just like the columns of Table 12.3.

Figure 12.11: Wire frame picture of $f(x, y) = x^2 + y^2$ for $-3 \leq x \leq 3, -3 \leq y \leq 3$

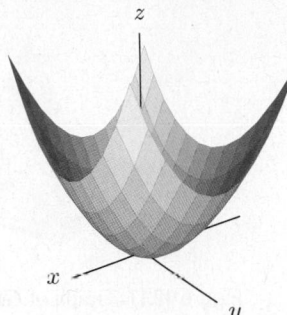

Figure 12.12: Wire frame picture of $f(x, y) = x^2 + y^2$ with more points plotted

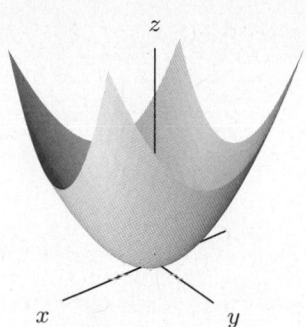

Figure 12.13: Graph of $f(x, y) = x^2 + y^2$ for $-3 \leq x \leq 3, -3 \leq y \leq 3$

New Graphs from Old

We can use the graph of a function to visualize the graphs of related functions.

Example 1 Let $f(x, y) = x^2 + y^2$. Describe in words the graphs of the following functions:

(a) $g(x, y) = x^2 + y^2 + 3$,   (b) $h(x, y) = 5 - x^2 - y^2$,   (c) $k(x, y) = x^2 + (y - 1)^2$.

Solution We know from Figure 12.13 that the graph of f is a paraboloid, or bowl with its vertex at the origin. From this we can work out what the graphs of g, h, and k will look like.

(a) The function $g(x, y) = x^2 + y^2 + 3 = f(x, y) + 3$, so the graph of g is the graph of f, but raised by 3 units. See Figure 12.14.

(b) Since $-x^2 - y^2$ is the negative of $x^2 + y^2$, the graph of $-x^2 - y^2$ is a paraboloid opening downward. Thus, the graph of $h(x, y) = 5 - x^2 - y^2 = 5 - f(x, y)$ looks like a downward-opening paraboloid with vertex at $(0, 0, 5)$, as in Figure 12.15.

(c) The graph of $k(x, y) = x^2 + (y - 1)^2 = f(x, y - 1)$ is a paraboloid with vertex at $x = 0, y = 1$, since that is where $k(x, y) = 0$, as in Figure 12.16.

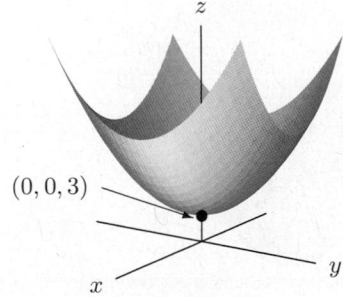

Figure 12.14: Graph of $g(x, y) = x^2 + y^2 + 3$

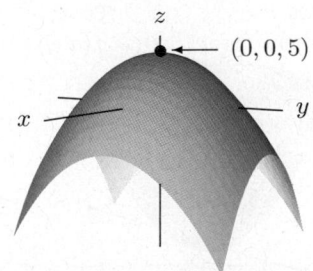

Figure 12.15: Graph of $h(x, y) = 5 - x^2 - y^2$

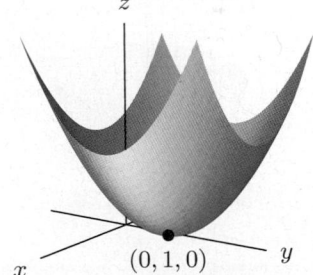

Figure 12.16: Graph of $k(x, y) = x^2 + (y - 1)^2$

Example 2 Describe the graph of $G(x, y) = e^{-(x^2 + y^2)}$. What symmetry does it have?

Solution Since the exponential function is always positive, the graph lies entirely above the xy-plane. From the graph of $x^2 + y^2$ we see that $x^2 + y^2$ is zero at the origin and gets larger as we move farther from the origin in any direction. Thus, $e^{-(x^2 + y^2)}$ is 1 at the origin, and gets smaller as we move away from the origin in any direction. It can't go below the xy-plane; instead it flattens out, getting closer and closer to the plane. We say the surface is *asymptotic* to the xy-plane. (See Figure 12.17.)

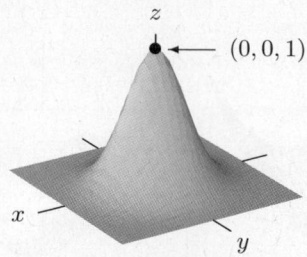

Figure 12.17: Graph of $G(x, y) = e^{-(x^2+y^2)}$

Now consider a point (x, y) on the circle $x^2 + y^2 = r^2$. Since

$$G(x, y) = e^{-(x^2+y^2)} = e^{-r^2},$$

the value of the function G is the same at all points on this circle. Thus, we say the graph of G has *circular symmetry*.

Cross-Sections and the Graph of a Function

We have seen that a good way to analyze a function of two variables is to let one variable vary while the other is kept fixed.

> For a function $f(x, y)$, the function we get by holding x fixed and letting y vary is called a **cross-section** of f with x fixed. The graph of the cross-section of $f(x, y)$ with $x = c$ is the curve, or cross-section, we get by intersecting the graph of f with the plane $x = c$. We define a cross-section of f with y fixed similarly.

For example, the cross-section of $f(x, y) = x^2 + y^2$ with $x = 2$ is $f(2, y) = 4 + y^2$. The graph of this cross-section is the curve we get by intersecting the graph of f with the plane perpendicular to the x-axis at $x = 2$. (See Figure 12.18.)

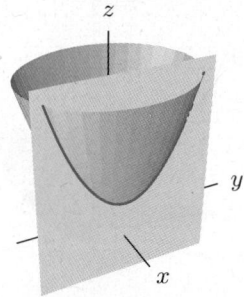

Figure 12.18: Cross-section of the surface $z = f(x, y)$ by the plane $x = 2$

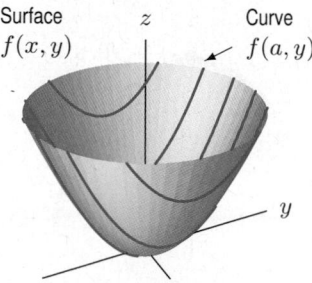

Figure 12.19: The curves $z = f(a, y)$ with a constant: cross-sections with x fixed

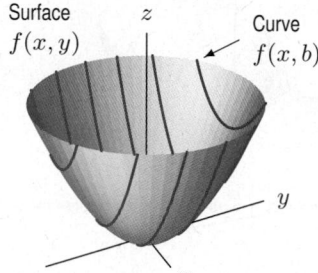

Figure 12.20: The curves $z = f(x, b)$ with b constant: cross-sections with y fixed

Figure 12.19 shows graphs of other cross-sections of f with x fixed; Figure 12.20 shows graphs of cross-sections with y fixed.

Example 3   Describe the cross-sections of the function $g(x, y) = x^2 - y^2$ with y fixed and then with x fixed. Use these cross-sections to describe the shape of the graph of g.

Solution   The cross-sections with y fixed at $y = b$ are given by

$$z = g(x, b) = x^2 - b^2.$$

Thus, each cross-section with y fixed gives a parabola opening upward, with minimum $z = -b^2$. The cross-sections with x fixed are of the form

$$z = g(a, y) = a^2 - y^2,$$

which are parabolas opening downward with a maximum of $z = a^2$. (See Figures 12.21 and 12.22.) The graph of g is shown in Figure 12.23. Notice the upward-opening parabolas in the x-direction and the downward-opening parabolas in the y-direction. We say that the surface is *saddle-shaped*.

Figure 12.21: Cross-sections of $g(x, y) = x^2 - y^2$ with y fixed

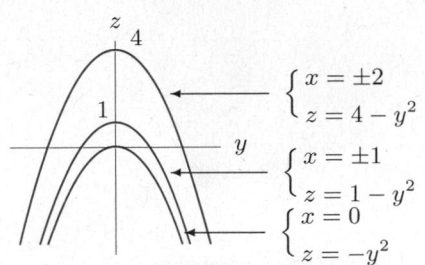

Figure 12.22: Cross-sections of $g(x, y) = x^2 - y^2$ with x fixed

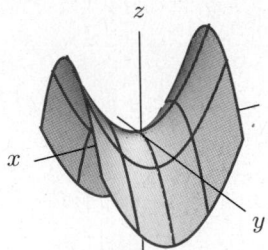

Figure 12.23: Graph of $g(x, y) = x^2 - y^2$ showing cross sections

Linear Functions

Linear functions are central to single-variable calculus; they are equally important in multivariable calculus. You may be able to guess the shape of the graph of a linear function of two variables. (It's a plane.) Let's look at an example.

Example 4   Describe the graph of $f(x, y) = 1 + x - y$.

Solution   The plane $x = a$ is vertical and parallel to the yz-plane. Thus, the cross-section with $x = a$ is the line $z = 1 + a - y$ which slopes downward in the y-direction. Similarly, the plane $y = b$ is parallel to the xz-plane. Thus, the cross-section with $y = b$ is the line $z = 1 + x - b$ which slopes upward in the x-direction. Since all the cross-sections are lines, you might expect the graph to be a flat plane, sloping down in the y-direction and up in the x-direction. This is indeed the case. (See Figure 12.24.)

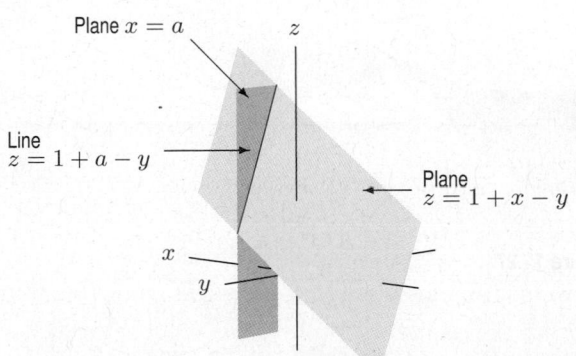

Figure 12.24: Graph of the plane $z = 1 + x - y$ showing cross-section with $x = a$

When One Variable is Missing: Cylinders

Suppose we graph an equation like $z = x^2$ which has one variable missing. What does the surface look like? Since y is missing from the equation, the cross-sections with y fixed are all the same parabola, $z = x^2$. Letting y vary up and down the y-axis, this parabola sweeps out the trough-shaped surface shown in Figure 12.25. The cross-sections with x fixed are horizontal lines obtained by cutting the surface by a plane perpendicular to the x-axis. This surface is called a *parabolic cylinder*, because it is formed from a parabola in the same way that an ordinary cylinder is formed from a circle; it has a parabolic cross-section instead of a circular one.

Figure 12.25: A parabolic cylinder $z = x^2$

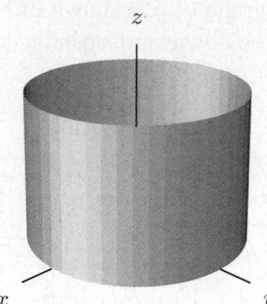

Figure 12.26: Circular cylinder $x^2 + y^2 = 1$

Example 5   Graph the equation $x^2 + y^2 = 1$ in 3-space.

Solution   Although the equation $x^2 + y^2 = 1$ does not represent a function, the surface representing it can be graphed by the method used for $z = x^2$. The graph of $x^2 + y^2 = 1$ in the xy-plane is a circle. Since z does not appear in the equation, the intersection of the surface with any horizontal plane will be the same circle $x^2 + y^2 = 1$. Thus, the surface is the cylinder shown in Figure 12.26.

Exercises and Problems for Section 12.2

Exercises

1. Figure 12.27 shows the graph of $z = f(x, y)$.

(a) Suppose y is fixed and positive. Does z increase or decrease as x increases? Graph z against x.

(b) Suppose x is fixed and positive. Does z increase or decrease as y increases? Graph z against y.

Figure 12.27

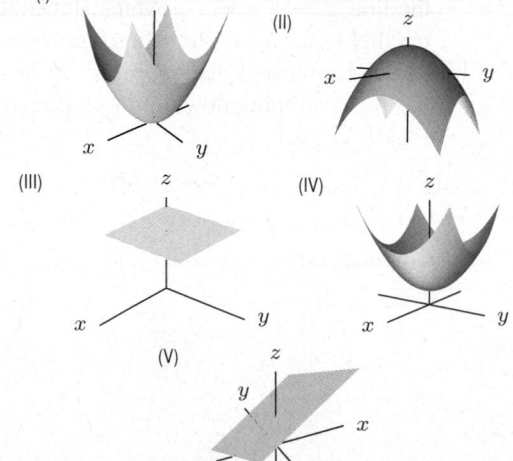

Figure 12.28

2. Without a calculator or computer, match the functions with their graphs in Figure 12.28.

(a) $z = 2 + x^2 + y^2$ (b) $z = 2 - x^2 - y^2$

(c) $z = 2(x^2 + y^2)$ (d) $z = 2 + 2x - y$

(e) $z = 2$

3. Without a calculator or computer, match the functions with their graphs in Figure 12.29.

(a) $z = \dfrac{1}{x^2 + y^2}$ (b) $z = -e^{-x^2 - y^2}$

(c) $z = x + 2y + 3$ (d) $z = -y^2$

(e) $z = x^3 - \sin y.$

(I)   (II)

(III)   (IV)

(V)

Figure 12.29

In Exercises 4–11, sketch a graph of the surface and briefly describe it in words.

4. $z = 3$ **5.** $x^2 + y^2 + z^2 = 9$

6. $z = x^2 + y^2 + 4$ **7.** $z = 5 - x^2 - y^2$

8. $z = y^2$ **9.** $2x + 4y + 3z = 12$

10. $x^2 + y^2 = 4$ **11.** $x^2 + z^2 = 4$

In Exercises 12–14, find the equation of the surface.

12. A cylinder of radius $\sqrt{7}$ with its axis along the y-axis.

13. A sphere of radius 3 centered at $(0, \sqrt{7}, 0)$.

14. The paraboloid obtained by moving the surface $z = x^2 + y^2$ so that its vertex is at $(1, 3, 5)$, its axis is parallel to the x-axis, and the surface opens towards negative x values.

Problems

15. Consider the function f given by $f(x, y) = y^3 + xy$. Draw graphs of cross-sections with:

    (a) x fixed at $x = -1$, $x = 0$, and $x = 1$.
    (b) y fixed at $y = -1$, $y = 0$, and $y = 1$.

Problems 16–18 concern the concentration, C, in mg per liter, of a drug in the blood as a function of x, the amount, in mg, of the drug given and t, the time in hours since the injection. For $0 \leq x \leq 4$ and $t \geq 0$, we have $C = f(x, t) = te^{-t(5-x)}$.

16. Find $f(3, 2)$. Give units and interpret in terms of drug concentration.

17. Graph the following single-variable functions and explain their significance in terms of drug concentration.

    (a) $f(4, t)$ **(b)** $f(x, 1)$

18. Graph $f(a, t)$ for $a = 1, 2, 3, 4$ on the same axes. Describe how the graph changes as a increases and explain what this means in terms of drug concentration.

19. Without a computer or calculator, match the equations (a)–(i) with the graphs (I)–(IX).

    (a) $z = xye^{-(x^2+y^2)}$ **(b)** $z = \cos(\sqrt{x^2+y^2})$

    (c) $z = \sin y$ **(d)** $z = -\dfrac{1}{x^2+y^2}$

    (e) $z = \cos^2 x \cos^2 y$ **(f)** $z = \dfrac{\sin(x^2+y^2)}{x^2+y^2}$

    (g) $z = \cos(xy)$ **(h)** $z = |x||y|$

    (i) $z = (2x^2+y^2)e^{1-x^2-y^2}$

(I)   (II)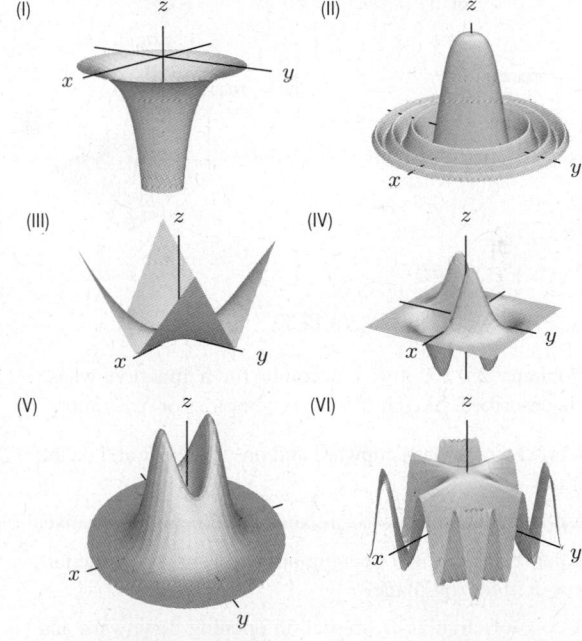

(III)   (IV)

(V)   (VI)

(VII)   (VIII)

(IX)

20. Decide whether the graph of each of the following equations is the shape of a bowl, a plate, or neither. Consider a plate to be any flat surface and a bowl to be anything that could hold water, assuming the positive z-axis is up.

(a) $z = x^2 + y^2$ **(b)** $z = 1 - x^2 - y^2$
(c) $x + y + z = 1$ **(d)** $z = -\sqrt{5 - x^2 - y^2}$
(e) $z = 3$

21. Sketch cross-sections for each function in Problem 20.

22. You like pizza and you like cola. Which of the graphs in Figure 12.30 represents your happiness as a function of how many pizzas and how much cola you have if

(a) There is no such thing as too many pizzas and too much cola?

(b) There is such a thing as too many pizzas or too much cola?

(c) There is such a thing as too much cola but no such thing as too many pizzas?

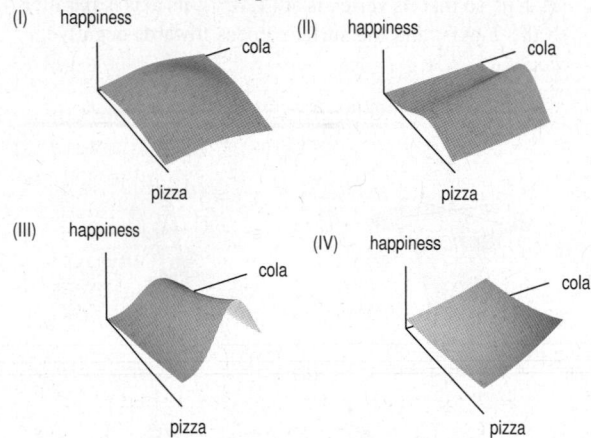

Figure 12.30

For Problems 23–26, give a formula for a function whose graph is described. Sketch it using a computer or calculator.

23. A bowl which opens upward and has its vertex at 5 on the z-axis.

24. A plane which has its x-, y-, and z-intercepts all positive.

25. A parabolic cylinder opening upward from along the line $y = x$ in the xy-plane.

26. A cone of circular cross-section opening downward and with its vertex at the origin.

27. Sketch cross-sections of $f(r, h) = \pi r^2 h$, first keeping h fixed, then keeping r fixed.

28. By setting one variable constant, find a plane that intersects the graph of $z = 4x^2 - y^2 + 1$ in a:

(a) Parabola opening upward
(b) Parabola opening downward
(c) Pair of intersecting straight lines

29. For each of the graphs I-IV in Problem 22 draw:

(a) Two cross-sections with pizza fixed
(b) Two cross-sections with cola fixed.

30. A wave travels along a canal. Let x be the distance along the canal, t be the time, and z be the height of the water above the equilibrium level. The graph of z as a function of x and t is in Figure 12.31.

(a) Draw the profile of the wave for $t = -1, 0, 1, 2$. (Put the x-axis to the right and the z-axis vertical.)

(b) Is the wave traveling in the direction of increasing or decreasing x?

(c) Sketch a surface representing a wave traveling in the opposite direction.

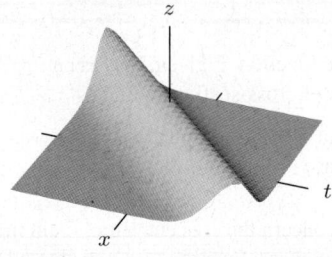

Figure 12.31

31. At time t, the displacement of a point on a vibrating guitar string stretched between $x = 0$ and $x = \pi$ is given by

$$f(x, t) = \cos t \sin x, \quad 0 \le x \le \pi, \quad 0 \le t \le 2\pi.$$

(a) Sketch the cross-sections of this function with t fixed at $t = 0, \pi/4$ and the cross-sections with x fixed at $x = \pi/4, \pi/2$.

(b) What is the value of f if $x = 0$ or $x = \pi$? Explain why this is to be expected.

(c) Explain the relation of the cross-sections to the surface representing f.

Strengthen Your Understanding

In Problems 32–33, explain what is wrong with the statement.

32. The graph of the function $f(x, y) = x^2 + y^2$ is a circle.

33. Cross-sections of the function $f(x, y) = x^2$ with x fixed are parabolas.

In Problems 34–36, give an example of:

34. A function whose graph lies above the xy-plane and intersects the plane $z = 2$ in a single point.

35. A function which intersects the xz-plane in a parabola and the yz-plane in a line.

36. A function which intersects the xy-plane in a circle.

Are the statements in Problems 37–50 true or false? Give reasons for your answer.

37. The function given by the formula $f(v, w) = e^v/w$ is an increasing function of v when w is a nonzero constant.

38. A function $f(x, y)$ can be an increasing function of x with y held fixed, and be a decreasing function of y with x held fixed.

39. A function $f(x, y)$ can have the property that $g(x) = f(x, 5)$ is increasing, whereas $h(x) = f(x, 10)$ is decreasing.

40. The plane $x + 2y - 3z = 1$ passes through the origin.

41. The plane $x + y + z = 3$ intersects the x-axis when $x = 3$.

42. The sphere $x^2 + y^2 + z^2 = 10$ intersects the plane $x = 10$.

43. The cross-section of the function $f(x, y) = x + y^2$ with $y = 1$ is a line.

44. The function $g(x, y) = 1 - y^2$ has identical parabolas for all cross-sections with x constant.

45. The function $g(x, y) = 1 - y^2$ has lines for all cross-sections with y constant.

46. The graphs of $f(x, y) = \sin(xy)$ and $g(x, y) = \sin(xy) + 2$ never intersect.

47. The graphs of $f(x, y) = x^2 + y^2$ and $g(x, y) = 1 - x^2 - y^2$ intersect in a circle.

48. If all the cross-sections of the graph of $f(x, y)$ with x constant are lines, then the graph of f is a plane.

49. The only point of intersection of the graphs of $f(x, y)$ and $-f(x, y)$ is the origin.

50. The point $(0, 0, 10)$ is the highest point on the graph of the function $f(x, y) = 10 - x^2 - y^2$.

51. The object in 3-space described by $x = 2$ is

  (a) A point   **(b)** A line

  (c) A plane   **(d)** Undefined.

12.3 CONTOUR DIAGRAMS

The surface which represents a function of two variables often gives a good idea of the function's general behavior—for example, whether it is increasing or decreasing as one of the variables increases. However it is difficult to read numerical values off a surface and it can be hard to see all of the function's behavior from a surface. Thus, functions of two variables are often represented by contour diagrams like the weather map on page 666. Contour diagrams have the additional advantage that they can be extended to functions of three variables.

Topographical Maps

One of the most common examples of a contour diagram is a topographical map like that shown in Figure 12.32. It gives the elevation in the region and is a good way of getting an overall picture of the terrain: where the mountains are, where the flat areas are. Such topographical maps are frequently colored green at the lower elevations and brown, red, or white at the higher elevations.

Figure 12.32: A topographical map showing the region around South Hamilton, NY

The curves on a topographical map that separate lower elevations from higher elevations are called *contour lines* because they outline the contour or shape of the land.[3] Because every point along the same contour has the same elevation, contour lines are also called *level curves* or *level sets*. The more closely spaced the contours, the steeper the terrain; the more widely spaced the contours, the flatter the terrain (provided, of course, that the elevation between contours varies by a constant amount). Certain features have distinctive characteristics. A mountain peak is typically surrounded by contour lines like those in Figure 12.33. A pass in a range of mountains may have contours that look like Figure 12.34. A long valley has parallel contour lines indicating the rising elevations on both sides of the valley (see Figure 12.35); a long ridge of mountains has the same type of contour lines, only the elevations decrease on both sides of the ridge. Notice that the elevation numbers on the contour lines are as important as the curves themselves. We usually draw contours for equally spaced values of z.

Figure 12.33: Mountain peak

Figure 12.34: Pass between two mountains

Figure 12.35: Long valley

Figure 12.36: Impossible contour lines

Notice that two contours corresponding to different elevations cannot cross each other as shown in Figure 12.36. If they did, the point of intersection of the two curves would have two different elevations, which is impossible (assuming the terrain has no overhangs).

Corn Production

Contour maps can display information about a function of two variables without reference to a surface. Consider the effect of weather conditions on US corn production. Figure 12.37 gives corn production $C = f(R, T)$ as a function of the total rainfall, R, in inches, and average temperature, T, in degrees Fahrenheit, during the growing season.[4] At the present time, $R = 15$ inches and $T = 76°$F. Production is measured as a percentage of the present production; thus, the contour through $R = 15, T = 76$, has value 100, that is, $C = f(15, 76) = 100$.

Example 1   Use Figure 12.37 to estimate $f(18, 78)$ and $f(12, 76)$ and interpret in terms of corn production.

Figure 12.37: Corn production, C, as a function of rainfall and temperature

---

[3] In fact they are usually not straight lines, but curves. They may also be in disconnected pieces.
[4] Adapted from S. Beaty and R. Healy, "The Future of American Agriculture," *Scientific American* 248, No. 2, February 1983.

Solution   The point with R-coordinate 18 and T-coordinate 78 is on the contour $C = 100$, so $f(18, 78) = 100$. This means that if the annual rainfall were 18 inches and the temperature were 78°F, the country would produce about the same amount of corn as at present, although it would be wetter and warmer than it is now.

The point with R-coordinate 12 and T-coordinate 76 is about halfway between the $C = 80$ and the $C = 90$ contours, so $f(12, 76) \approx 85$. This means that if the rainfall fell to 12 inches and the temperature stayed at 76°, then corn production would drop to about 85% of what it is now.

Example 2   Use Figure 12.37 to describe in words the cross-sections with T and R constant through the point representing present conditions. Give a common-sense explanation of your answer.

Solution   To see what happens to corn production if the temperature stays fixed at 76°F but the rainfall changes, look along the horizontal line $T = 76$. Starting from the present and moving left along the line $T = 76$, the values on the contours decrease. In other words, if there is a drought, corn production decreases. Conversely, as rainfall increases, that is, as we move from the present to the right along the line $T = 76$, corn production increases, reaching a maximum of more than 110% when $R = 21$, and then decreases (too much rainfall floods the fields).

If, instead, rainfall remains at the present value and temperature increases, we move up the vertical line $R = 15$. Under these circumstances corn production decreases; a 2° increase causes a 10% drop in production. This makes sense since hotter temperatures lead to greater evaporation and hence drier conditions, even with rainfall constant at 15 inches. Similarly, a decrease in temperature leads to a very slight increase in production, reaching a maximum of around 102% when $T = 74$, followed by a decrease (the corn won't grow if it is too cold).

Contour Diagrams and Graphs

Contour diagrams and graphs are two different ways of representing a function of two variables. How do we go from one to the other? In the case of the topographical map, the contour diagram was created by joining all the points at the same height on the surface and dropping the curve into the xy-plane.

How do we go the other way? Suppose we wanted to plot the surface representing the corn production function $C = f(R, T)$ given by the contour diagram in Figure 12.37. Along each contour the function has a constant value; if we take each contour and lift it above the plane to a height equal to this value, we get the surface in Figure 12.38.

Figure 12.38: Getting the graph of the corn yield function from the contour diagram

Notice that the raised contours are the curves we get by slicing the surface horizontally. In general, we have the following result:

> Contour lines, or level curves, are obtained from a surface by slicing it with horizontal planes. A contour diagram is a collection of level curves labeled with function values.

Finding Contours Algebraically

Algebraic equations for the contours of a function f are easy to find if we have a formula for $f(x, y)$. Suppose the surface has equation

$$z = f(x, y).$$

A contour is obtained by slicing the surface with a horizontal plane with equation $z = c$. Thus, the equation for the contour at height c is given by:

$$f(x, y) = c.$$

Example 3   Find equations for the contours of $f(x, y) = x^2 + y^2$ and draw a contour diagram for f. Relate the contour diagram to the graph of f.

Solution   The contour at height c is given by

$$f(x, y) = x^2 + y^2 = c.$$

This is a contour only for $c \geq 0$, For $c > 0$ it is a circle of radius $\sqrt{c}$. For $c = 0$, it is a single point (the origin). Thus, the contours at an elevation of $c = 1, 2, 3, 4, \ldots$ are all circles centered at the origin of radius $1, \sqrt{2}, \sqrt{3}, 2, \ldots$. The contour diagram is shown in Figure 12.39. The bowl–shaped graph of f is shown in Figure 12.40. Notice that the graph of f gets steeper as we move further away from the origin. This is reflected in the fact that the contours become more closely packed as we move further from the origin; for example, the contours for $c = 6$ and $c = 8$ are closer together than the contours for $c = 2$ and $c = 4$.

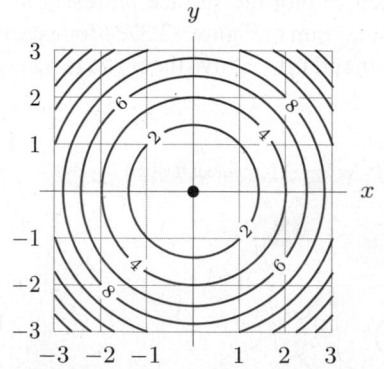

Figure 12.39: Contour diagram for $f(x, y) = x^2 + y^2$ (even values of c only)

Figure 12.40: The graph of $f(x, y) = x^2 + y^2$

Example 4   Draw a contour diagram for $f(x, y) = \sqrt{x^2 + y^2}$ and relate it to the graph of f.

Solution   The contour at level c is given by

$$f(x, y) = \sqrt{x^2 + y^2} = c.$$

For $c > 0$ this is a circle, just as in the previous example, but here the radius is c instead of $\sqrt{c}$. For $c = 0$, it is the origin. Thus, if the level c increases by 1, the radius of the contour increases by 1. This means the contours are equally spaced concentric circles (see Figure 12.41) which do not become more closely packed further from the origin. Thus, the graph of f has the same constant slope as we move away from the origin (see Figure 12.42), making it a cone rather than a bowl.

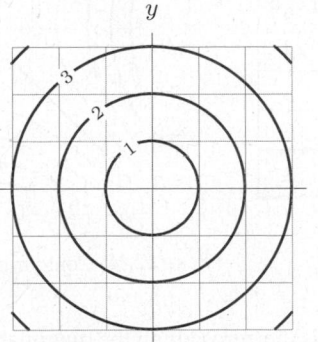

Figure 12.41: A contour diagram for
$f(x, y) = \sqrt{x^2 + y^2}$

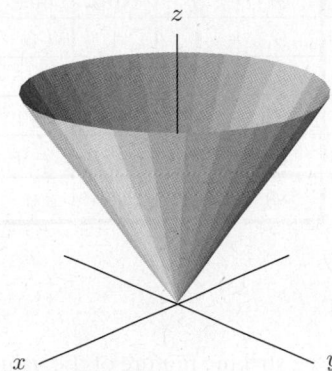

Figure 12.42: The graph of
$f(x, y) = \sqrt{x^2 + y^2}$

In both of the previous examples the level curves are concentric circles because the surfaces have circular symmetry. Any function of two variables which depends only on the quantity $(x^2 + y^2)$ has such symmetry: for example, $G(x, y) = e^{-(x^2+y^2)}$ or $H(x, y) = \sin(\sqrt{x^2 + y^2})$.

Example 5   Draw a contour diagram for $f(x, y) = 2x + 3y + 1$.

Solution   The contour at level c has equation $2x + 3y + 1 = c$. Rewriting this as $y = -(2/3)x + (c - 1)/3$, we see that the contours are parallel lines with slope $-2/3$. The y-intercept for the contour at level c is $(c - 1)/3$; each time c increases by 3, the y-intercept moves up by 1. The contour diagram is shown in Figure 12.43.

Figure 12.43: A contour diagram for $f(x, y) = 2x + 3y + 1$

Contour Diagrams and Tables

Sometimes we can get an idea of what the contour diagram of a function looks like from its table.

Example 6 Relate the values of $f(x, y) = x^2 - y^2$ in Table 12.4 to its contour diagram in Figure 12.44.

Table 12.4 *Table of values of $f(x, y) = x^2 - y^2$*

y							
3	0	−5	−8	−9	−8	−5	0
2	5	0	−3	−4	−3	0	5
1	8	3	0	−1	0	3	8
0	9	4	1	0	1	4	9
−1	8	3	0	−1	0	3	8
−2	5	0	−3	−4	−3	0	5
−3	0	−5	−8	−9	−8	−5	0
	−3	−2	−1	0	1	2	3

x

Figure 12.44: Contour map of $f(x, y) = x^2 - y^2$

Solution One striking feature of the values in Table 12.4 is the zeros along the diagonals. This occurs because $x^2 - y^2 = 0$ along the lines $y = x$ and $y = -x$. So the $z = 0$ contour consists of these two lines. In the triangular region of the table that lies to the right of both diagonals, the entries are positive. To the left of both diagonals, the entries are also positive. Thus, in the contour diagram, the positive contours lie in the triangular regions to the right and left of the lines $y = x$ and $y = -x$. Further, the table shows that the numbers on the left are the same as the numbers on the right; thus, each contour has two pieces, one on the left and one on the right. See Figure 12.44. As we move away from the origin along the x-axis, we cross contours corresponding to successively larger values. On the saddle-shaped graph of $f(x, y) = x^2 - y^2$ shown in Figure 12.45, this corresponds to climbing out of the saddle along one of the ridges. Similarly, the negative contours occur in pairs in the top and bottom triangular regions; the values get more and more negative as we go out along the y-axis. This corresponds to descending from the saddle along the valleys that are submerged below the xy-plane in Figure 12.45. Notice that we could also get the contour diagram by graphing the family of hyperbolas $x^2 - y^2 = 0, \pm 2, \pm 4, \ldots$.

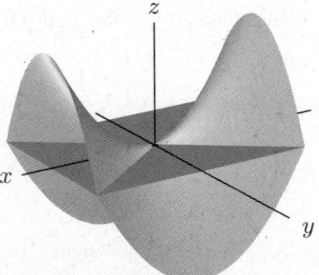

Figure 12.45: Graph of $f(x, y) = x^2 - y^2$ showing plane $z = 0$

Using Contour Diagrams: The Cobb-Douglas Production Function

Suppose you decide to expand your small printing business. Should you start a night shift and hire more workers? Should you buy more expensive but faster computers which will enable the current staff to keep up with the work? Or should you do some combination of the two?

Obviously, the way such a decision is made in practice involves many other considerations—such as whether you could get a suitably trained night shift, or whether there are any faster computers available. Nevertheless, you might model the quantity, P, of work produced by your business as a function of two variables: your total number, N, of workers, and the total value, V, of your equipment. What might the contour diagram of the production function look like?

Example 7   Explain why the contour diagram in Figure 12.46 does not model the behavior expected of the production function, whereas the contour diagram in Figure 12.47 does.

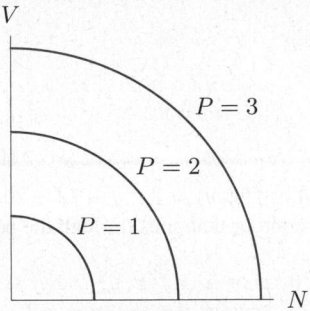

Figure 12.46: Incorrect contours
for printing production

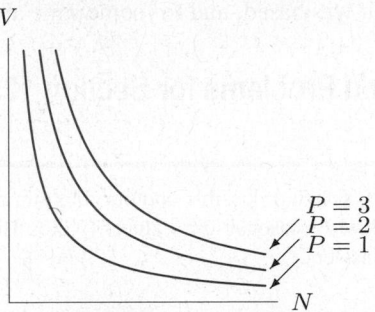

Figure 12.47: Correct contours for
printing production

Solution   Look at Figure 12.46. Notice that the contour $P = 1$ intersects the N- and the V- axis, suggesting that it is possible to produce work with no workers or with no equipment; this is unreasonable. However, no contours in Figure 12.47 intersect either the N- or the V-axis.

In Figure 12.47, fixing V and letting N increase corresponds to moving to the right, crossing contours less and less frequently. Production increases more and more slowly because hiring additional workers does little to boost production if the machines are already used to capacity.

Similarly, if we fix N and let V increase, Figure 12.47 shows production increasing, but at a decreasing rate. Buying machines without enough people to use them does not increase production much. Thus Figure 12.47 fits the expected behavior of the production function best.

Formula for a Production Function

Production functions are often approximated by formulas of the form

$$P = f(N, V) = cN^\alpha V^\beta$$

where P is the quantity produced and c, α, and β are positive constants, $0 < \alpha < 1$ and $0 < \beta < 1$.

Example 8   Show that the contours of the function $P = cN^\alpha V^\beta$ have approximately the shape of the contours in Figure 12.47.

Solution   The contours are the curves where P is equal to a constant value, say P_0, that is, where

$$cN^\alpha V^\beta = P_0.$$

Solving for V we get

$$V = \left(\frac{P_0}{c}\right)^{1/\beta} N^{-\alpha/\beta}.$$

Thus, V is a power function of N with a negative exponent, so its graph has the shape shown in Figure 12.47.

The Cobb-Douglas Production Model

In 1928, Cobb and Douglas used a similar function to model the production of the entire US economy in the first quarter of this century. Using government estimates of P, the total yearly production between 1899 and 1922, of K, the total capital investment over the same period, and of L, the total labor force, they found that P was well approximated by the *Cobb-Douglas production function*

$$P = 1.01 L^{0.75} K^{0.25}.$$

This function turned out to model the US economy surprisingly well, both for the period on which it was based, and for some time afterward.

Exercises and Problems for Section 12.3

Exercises

In Exercises 1–4, sketch a possible contour diagram for each surface, marked with reasonable z-values. (Note: There are many possible answers.)

1.

2.

3.

4.

In Exercises 5–13, sketch a contour diagram for the function with at least four labeled contours. Describe in words the contours and how they are spaced.

5. $f(x, y) = x + y$

6. $f(x, y) = 3x + 3y$

7. $f(x, y) = x^2 + y^2$

8. $f(x, y) = -x^2 - y^2 + 1$

9. $f(x, y) = xy$

10. $f(x, y) = y - x^2$

11. $f(x, y) = x^2 + 2y^2$

12. $f(x, y) = \sqrt{x^2 + 2y^2}$

13. $f(x, y) = \cos \sqrt{x^2 + y^2}$

14. Let $f(x, y) = 3x^2 y + 7x + 20$. Find an equation for the contour that goes through the point $(5, 10)$.

15. **(a)** For $z = f(x, y) = xy$, sketch and label the level curves $z = \pm 1$, $z = \pm 2$.
  (b) Sketch and label cross-sections of f with $x = \pm 1$, $x = \pm 2$.
  (c) The surface $z = xy$ is cut by a vertical plane containing the line $y = x$. Sketch the cross-section.

16. Match the surfaces (a)–(e) in Figure 12.48 with the contour diagrams (I)–(V) in Figure 12.49.

Figure 12.48

Figure 12.49

17. Match Tables 12.5–12.8 with contour diagrams (I)–(IV) in Figure 12.50.

Table 12.5

$y \backslash x$	-1	0	1
-1	2	1	2
0	1	0	1
1	2	1	2

Table 12.6

$y \backslash x$	-1	0	1
-1	0	1	0
0	1	2	1
1	0	1	0

Table 12.7

$y \backslash x$	-1	0	1
-1	2	0	2
0	2	0	2
1	2	0	2

Table 12.8

$y \backslash x$	-1	0	1
-1	2	2	2
0	0	0	0
1	2	2	2

Figure 12.50

18. Figure 12.51 shows a graph of $f(x, y) = (\sin x)(\cos y)$ for $-2\pi \leq x \leq 2\pi$, $-2\pi \leq y \leq 2\pi$. Use the surface $z = 1/2$ to sketch the contour $f(x, y) = 1/2$.

Figure 12.51

Problems

19. Total sales, Q, of a product are a function of its price and the amount spent on advertising. Figure 12.52 shows a contour diagram for total sales. Which axis corresponds to the price of the product and which to the amount spent on advertising? Explain.

Figure 12.52

20. Figure 12.53 shows contours of $f(x, y) = 100e^x - 50y^2$. Find the values of f on the contours. They are equally spaced multiples of 10.

Figure 12.53

21. Match the functions (a)–(f) with the level curves (I)–(VI):

(a) $f(x,y) = x^2 - y^2 - 2x + 4y - 3$
(b) $g(x,y) = x^2 + y^2 - 2x - 4y + 15$
(c) $h(x,y) = -x^2 - y^2 + 2x + 4y - 8$
(d) $j(x,y) = -x^2 + y^2 + 2x - 4y + 3$
(e) $k(x,y) = \sqrt{(x-1)^2 + (y-2)^2}$
(f) $l(x,y) = -\sqrt{(x-1)^2 + (y-2)^2}$

Figure 12.54

23. Figure 12.55 shows contour diagrams of $f(x,y)$ and $g(x,y)$. Sketch the smooth curve with equation $f(x,y) = g(x,y)$.

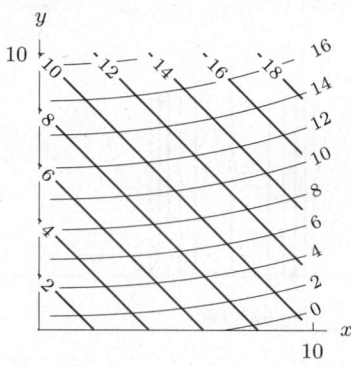

Figure 12.55: Black: $f(x,y)$. Blue: $g(x,y)$

24. Figure 12.56 shows the level curves of the temperature H in a room near a recently opened window. Label the three level curves with reasonable values of H if the house is in the following locations.

(a) Minnesota in winter (where winters are harsh).
(b) San Francisco in winter (where winters are mild).
(c) Houston in summer (where summers are hot).
(d) Oregon in summer (where summers are mild).

Figure 12.56

22. The wind chill tells you how cold it feels as a function of the air temperature and wind speed. Figure 12.54 is a contour diagram of wind chill (°F).

(a) If the wind speed is 15 mph, what temperature feels like −20°F?
(b) Estimate the wind chill if the temperature is 0°F and the wind speed is 10 mph.
(c) Humans are at extreme risk when the wind chill is below −50°F. If the temperature is −20°F, estimate the wind speed at which extreme risk begins.
(d) If the wind speed is 15 mph and the temperature drops by 20°F, approximately how much colder do you feel?

25. You are in a room 30 feet long with a heater at one end. In the morning the room is 65°F. You turn on the heater, which quickly warms up to 85°F. Let $H(x,t)$ be the temperature x feet from the heater, t minutes after the heater is turned on. Figure 12.57 shows the contour diagram for H. How warm is it 10 feet from the heater 5 minutes after it was turned on? 10 minutes after it was turned on?

Figure 12.57

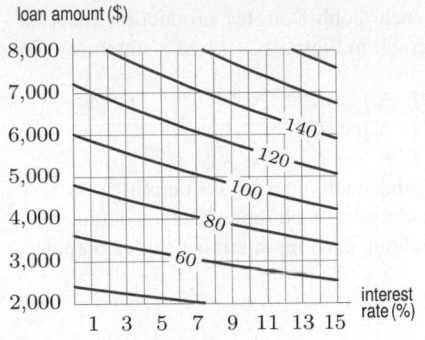

Figure 12.59

26. Using the contour diagram in Figure 12.57, sketch the graphs of the one-variable functions $H(x, 5)$ and $H(x, 20)$. Interpret the two graphs in practical terms, and explain the difference between them.

27. Figure 12.58 shows a contour map of a hill with two paths, A and B.

   (a) On which path, A or B, will you have to climb more steeply?

   (b) On which path, A or B, will you probably have a better view of the surrounding countryside? (Assume trees do not block your view.)

   (c) Alongside which path is there more likely to be a stream?

Figure 12.58

28. Figure 12.59 is a contour diagram of the monthly payment on a 5-year car loan as a function of the interest rate and the amount you borrow. The interest rate is 13% and you borrow $6000 for a used car.

   (a) What is your monthly payment?

   (b) If interest rates drop to 11%, how much more can you borrow without increasing your monthly payment?

   (c) Make a table of how much you can borrow, without increasing your monthly payment, as a function of the interest rate.

29. Hiking on a level trail going due east, you decide to leave the trail and climb toward the mountain on your left. The farther you go along the trail before turning off, the gentler the climb. Sketch a possible topographical map showing the elevation contours.

30. Match the functions (a)–(d) with the shapes of their level curves (I)–(IV). Sketch each contour diagram.

   (a) $f(x, y) = x^2$ **(b)** $f(x, y) = x^2 + 2y^2$
   (c) $f(x, y) = y - x^2$ **(d)** $f(x, y) = x^2 - y^2$

   I. Lines   II. Parabolas
   III. Hyperbolas   IV. Ellipses

31. Figure 12.60 shows the density of the fox population P (in foxes per square kilometer) for southern England. Draw two different cross-sections along a north-south line and two different cross-sections along an east-west line of the population density P.

Figure 12.60

32. A manufacturer sells two goods, one at a price of $3000 a unit and the other at a price of $12,000 a unit. A quantity q_1 of the first good and q_2 of the second good are sold at a total cost of $4000 to the manufacturer.

   (a) Express the manufacturer's profit, π, as a function of q_1 and q_2.

   (b) Sketch curves of constant profit in the q_1q_2-plane for $\pi = 10,000$, $\pi = 20,000$, and $\pi = 30,000$ and the break-even curve $\pi = 0$.

33. Match each Cobb-Douglas production function (a)–(c) with a graph in Figure 12.61 and a statement (D)–(G).

   (a) $F(L, K) = L^{0.25} K^{0.25}$
   (b) $F(L, K) = L^{0.5} K^{0.5}$
   (c) $F(L, K) = L^{0.75} K^{0.75}$
   (D) Tripling each input triples output.
   (E) Quadrupling each input doubles output.
   (G) Doubling each input almost triples output.

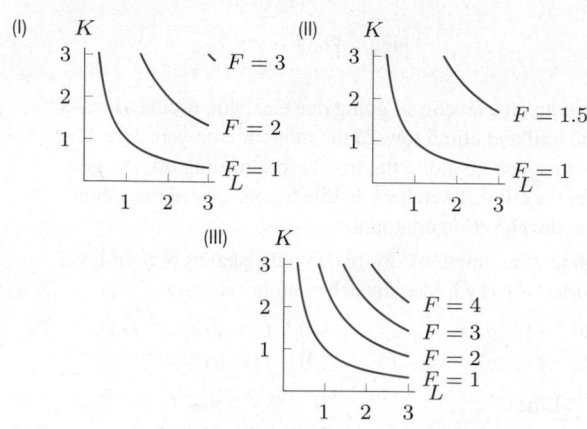

Figure 12.61

34. A Cobb-Douglas production function has the form

$$P = cL^{\alpha} K^{\beta} \quad \text{with } \alpha, \beta > 0.$$

What happens to production if labor and capital are both scaled up? For example, does production double if both labor and capital are doubled? Economists talk about

- *increasing returns to scale* if doubling L and K more than doubles P,
- *constant returns to scale* if doubling L and K exactly doubles P,
- *decreasing returns to scale* if doubling L and K less than doubles P.

What conditions on α and β lead to increasing, constant, or decreasing returns to scale?

35. (a) Match $f(x, y) = x^{0.2} y^{0.8}$ and $g(x, y) = x^{0.8} y^{0.2}$ with the level curves in Figures (I) and (II). All scales on the axes are the same.
   (b) Figure (III) shows the level curves of $h(x, y) = x^{\alpha} y^{1-\alpha}$ for $0 < \alpha < 1$. Find the range of possible values for α. Again, the scales are the same on both axes.

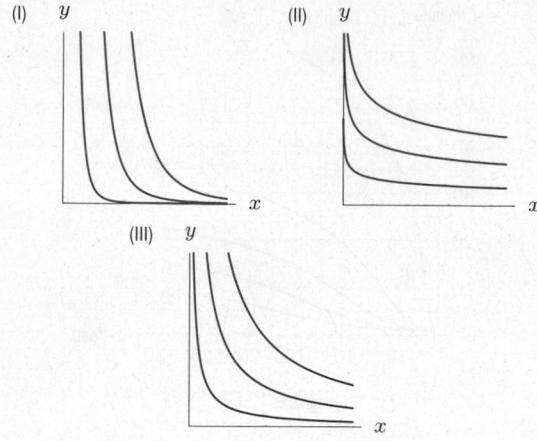

36. Match the functions (a)–(d) with the contour diagrams in Figures I–IV.

   (a) $f(x, y) = 0.7 \ln x + 0.3 \ln y$
   (b) $g(x, y) = 0.3 \ln x + 0.7 \ln y$
   (c) $h(x, y) = 0.3x^2 + 0.7y^2$
   (d) $j(x, y) = 0.7x^2 + 0.3y^2$

37. Figure 12.62 is the contour diagram of $f(x, y)$. Sketch the contour diagram of each of the following functions.

   (a) $3f(x, y)$ **(b)** $f(x, y) - 10$
   (c) $f(x - 2, y - 2)$ **(d)** $f(-x, y)$

Figure 12.62

38. Figure 12.63 shows part of the contour diagram of $f(x, y)$. Complete the diagram for $x < 0$ if

   (a) $f(-x, y) = f(x, y)$ **(b)** $f(-x, y) = -f(x, y)$

Figure 12.63

39. Let $f(x, y) = x^2 - y^2 = (x-y)(x+y)$. Use the factored form to sketch the contour $f(x, y) = 0$ and to find the regions in the xy-plane where $f(x, y) > 0$ and the regions where $f(x, y) < 0$. Explain how this sketch shows that the graph of $f(x, y)$ is saddle-shaped at the origin.

40. Use Problem 39 to find a formula for a "monkey saddle" surface $z = g(x, y)$ which has three regions with $g(x, y) > 0$ and three with $g(x, y) < 0$.

41. Use the contour diagram for $f(x, t) = \cos t \sin x$ in Figure 12.64 to describe in words the cross-sections of f with t fixed and the cross-sections of f with x fixed. Explain what you see in terms of the behavior of the string.

Figure 12.64

42. The power P produced by a windmill is proportional to the square of the diameter d of the windmill and to the cube of the speed v of the wind.[5]

   (a) Write a formula for P as a function of d and v.
   (b) A windmill generates 100 kW of power at a certain wind speed. If a second windmill is built having twice the diameter of the original, what fraction of the original wind speed is needed by the second windmill to produce 100 kW?
   (c) Sketch a contour diagram for P.

Strengthen Your Understanding

In Problems 43–44, explain what is wrong with the statement.

43. A contour diagram for $z = f(x, y)$ is a surface in xyz-space.

44. The functions $f(x, y) = \sqrt{x^2 + y^2}$ and $g(x, y) = x^2 + y^2$ have the same contour diagram.

In Problems 45–46, give an example of:

45. A function $f(x, y)$ whose $z = 10$ contour consists of two or more parallel lines.

46. A function whose contours are all parabolas.

Decide if the statements in Problems 47–51 must be true, might be true, or could not be true. The function $z = f(x, y)$ is defined everywhere.

47. The level curves corresponding to $z = 1$ and $z = -1$ cross at the origin.

48. The level curve $z = 1$ consists of the circle $x^2 + y^2 = 2$ and the circle $x^2 + y^2 = 3$, but no other points.

49. The level curve $z = 1$ consists of two lines which intersect at the origin.

50. If $z = e^{-(x^2+y^2)}$, there is a level curve for every value of z.

51. If $z = e^{-(x^2+y^2)}$, there is a level curve through every point (x, y).

Are the statements in Problems 52–59 true or false? Give reasons for your answer.

52. Two isotherms representing distinct temperatures on a weather map cannot intersect.

53. A weather map can have two isotherms representing the same temperature that do not intersect.

54. The contours of the function $f(x, y) = y^2 + (x-2)^2$ are either circles or a single point.

55. If the contours of $g(x, y)$ are concentric circles, then the graph of g is a cone.

56. If the contours for $f(x, y)$ get closer together in a certain direction, then f is increasing in that direction.

57. If all of the contours of $f(x, y)$ are parallel lines, then the graph of f is a plane.

58. If the $f = 10$ contour of the function $f(x, y)$ is identical to the $g = 10$ contour of the function $g(x, y)$, then $f(x, y) = g(x, y)$ for all (x, y).

59. The $f = 5$ contour of the function $f(x, y)$ is identical to the $g = 0$ contour of the function $g(x, y) = f(x, y) - 5$.

---

[5]From www.ecolo.org/documents/documents_in_english/WindmillFormula.htm, accessed on October 9, 2011.

12.4 LINEAR FUNCTIONS

What is a Linear Function of Two Variables?

Linear functions played a central role in one-variable calculus because many one-variable functions have graphs that look like a line when we zoom in. In two-variable calculus, a *linear function* is one whose graph is a plane. In Chapter 14, we see that many two-variable functions have graphs which look like planes when we zoom in.

What Makes a Plane Flat?

What makes the graph of the function $z = f(x, y)$ a plane? Linear functions of *one* variable have straight line graphs because they have constant slope. On a plane, the situation is a bit more complicated. If we walk around on a tilted plane, the slope is not always the same: it depends on the direction in which we walk. However, at every point on the plane, the slope is the same as long as we choose the same direction. If we walk parallel to the x-axis, we always find ourselves walking up or down with the same slope;[6] the same is true if we walk parallel to the y-axis. In other words, the slope ratios $\Delta z/\Delta x$ (with y fixed) and $\Delta z/\Delta y$ (with x fixed) are each constant.

Example 1   A plane cuts the z-axis at $z = 5$ and has slope 2 in the x-direction and slope -1 in the y-direction. What is the equation of the plane?

Solution   Finding the equation of the plane means constructing a formula for the z-coordinate of the point on the plane directly above the point (x, y) in the xy-plane. To get to that point start from the point above the origin, where $z = 5$. Then walk x units in the x-direction. Since the slope in the x-direction is 2, the height increases by $2x$. Then walk y units in the y-direction; since the slope in the y-direction is -1, the height decreases by y units. Since the height has changed by $2x - y$ units, the z-coordinate is $5 + 2x - y$. Thus, the equation for the plane is

$$z = 5 + 2x - y.$$

For any linear function, if we know its value at a point (x_0, y_0), its slope in the x-direction, and its slope in the y-direction, then we can write the equation of the function. This is just like the equation of a line in the one-variable case, except that there are two slopes instead of one.

If a **plane** has slope m in the x-direction, has slope n in the y-direction, and passes through the point (x_0, y_0, z_0), then its equation is

$$z = z_0 + m(x - x_0) + n(y - y_0).$$

This plane is the graph of the **linear function**

$$f(x, y) = z_0 + m(x - x_0) + n(y - y_0).$$

If we write $c = z_0 - mx_0 - ny_0$, then we can write $f(x, y)$ in the equivalent form

$$f(x, y) = c + mx + ny.$$

Just as in 2-space a line is determined by two points, so in 3-space a plane is determined by three points, provided they do not lie on a line.

---

[6]To be precise, walking in a vertical plane parallel to the x-axis while rising or falling with the plane you are on.

Example 2   Find the equation of the plane passing through the points $(1, 0, 1)$, $(1, -1, 3)$, and $(3, 0, -1)$.

Solution   The first two points have the same x-coordinate, so we use them to find the slope of the plane in the y-direction. As the y-coordinate changes from 0 to -1, the z-coordinate changes from 1 to 3, so the slope in the y-direction is $n = \Delta z/\Delta y = (3 - 1)/(-1 - 0) = -2$. The first and third points have the same y-coordinate, so we use them to find the slope in the x-direction; it is $m = \Delta z/\Delta x = (-1 - 1)/(3 - 1) = -1$. Because the plane passes through $(1, 0, 1)$, its equation is

$$z = 1 - (x - 1) - 2(y - 0) \quad \text{or} \quad z = 2 - x - 2y.$$

You should check that this equation is also satisfied by the points $(1, -1, 3)$ and $(3, 0, -1)$.

Example 2 was made easier by the fact that two of the points had the same x-coordinate and two had the same y-coordinate. An alternative method, which works for any three points, is to substitute the x, y, and z-values of each of the three points into the equation $z = c + mx + ny$. The resulting three equations in c, m, n are then solved simultaneously.

Linear Functions from a Numerical Point of View

To avoid flying planes with empty seats, airlines sell some tickets at full price and some at a discount. Table 12.9 shows an airline's revenue in dollars from tickets sold on a particular route, as a function of the number of full-price tickets sold, f, and the number of discount tickets sold, d.

Table 12.9   *Revenue from ticket sales (dollars)*

		Full-price tickets (f)			
		100	200	300	400
	200	39,700	63,600	87,500	111,400
	400	55,500	79,400	103,300	127,200
Discount tickets (d)	600	71,300	95,200	119,100	143,000
	800	87,100	111,000	134,900	158,800
	1000	102,900	126,800	150,700	174,600

In every column, the revenue jumps by \$15,800 for each extra 200 discount tickets. Thus, each column is a linear function of the number of discount tickets sold. In addition, every column has the same slope, $15,800/200 = 79$ dollars/ticket. This is the price of a discount ticket. Similarly, each row is a linear function and all the rows have the same slope, 239, which is the price in dollars of a full-fare ticket. Thus, R is a linear function of f and d, given by:

$$R = 239f + 79d.$$

We have the following general result:

A **linear function** can be recognized from its table by the following features:
- Each row and each column is linear.
- All the rows have the same slope.
- All the columns have the same slope (although the slope of the rows and the slope of the columns are generally different).

Example 3   The table contains values of a linear function. Fill in the blank and give a formula for the function.

$x \backslash y$	1.5	2.0
2	0.5	1.5
3	−0.5	?

Solution   In the first column the function decreases by 1 (from 0.5 to −0.5) as x goes from 2 to 3. Since the function is linear, it must decrease by the same amount in the second column. So the missing entry must be $1.5 - 1 = 0.5$. The slope of the function in the x-direction is −1. The slope in the y-direction is 2, since in each row the function increases by 1 when y increases by 0.5. From the table we get $f(2, 1.5) = 0.5$. Therefore, the formula is

$$f(x, y) = 0.5 - (x - 2) + 2(y - 1.5) = -0.5 - x + 2y.$$

What Does the Contour Diagram of a Linear Function Look Like?

The formula for the airline revenue function in Table 12.9 is $R = 239f + 79d$, where f is the number of full-fares and d is the number of discount fares sold.

Notice that the contours of this function in Figure 12.65 are parallel straight lines. What is the practical significance of the slope of these contour lines? Consider the contour $R = 100,000$; that means we are looking at combinations of ticket sales that yield \$100,000 in revenue. If we move down and to the right on the contour, the f-coordinate increases and the d-coordinate decreases, so we sell more full-fares and fewer discount fares. This is because to receive a fixed revenue of \$100,000, we must sell more full-fares if we sell fewer discount fares. The exact trade-off depends on the slope of the contour; the diagram shows that each contour has a slope of about −3. This means that for a fixed revenue, we must sell three discount fares to replace one full-fare. This can also be seen by comparing prices. Each full fare brings in \$239; to earn the same amount in discount fares we need to sell $239/79 \approx 3.03 \approx 3$ fares. Since the price ratio is independent of how many of each type of fare we sell, this slope remains constant over the whole contour map; thus, the contours are all parallel straight lines.

Notice also that the contours are evenly spaced. Thus, no matter which contour we are on, a fixed increase in one of the variables causes the same increase in the value of the function. In terms of revenue, no matter how many fares we have sold, an extra fare, whether full or discount, brings the same revenue as before.

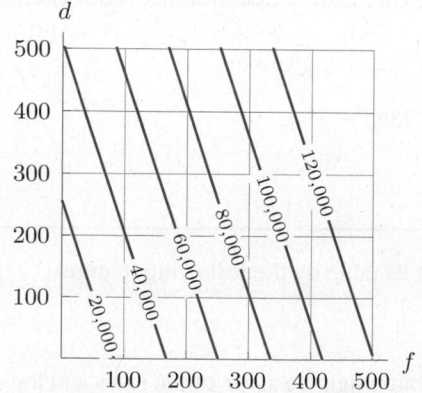

Figure 12.65: Revenue as a function of full and discount fares, $R = 239f + 79d$

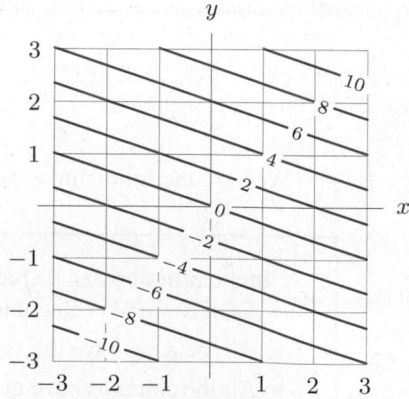

Figure 12.66: Contour map of linear function $f(x, y)$

Example 4   Find the equation of the linear function whose contour diagram is in Figure 12.66.

Solution   Suppose we start at the origin on the $z = 0$ contour. Moving 2 units in the y-direction takes us to the $z = 6$ contour; so the slope in the y-direction is $\Delta z/\Delta y = 6/2 = 3$. Similarly, a move of 2 in the x-direction from the origin takes us to the $z = 2$ contour, so the slope in the x-direction is $\Delta z/\Delta x = 2/2 = 1$. Since $f(0,0) = 0$, we have $f(x,y) = x + 3y$.

Exercises and Problems for Section 12.4

Exercises

Exercises 1–2 each contain a partial table of values for a linear function. Fill in the blanks.

1.

$x \backslash y$	0.0	1.0
0.0		1.0
2.0	3.0	5.0

2.

$x \backslash y$	−1.0	0.0	1.0
2.0	4.0		
3.0		3.0	5.0

In Exercises 3–6, could the tables of values represent a linear function?

3.

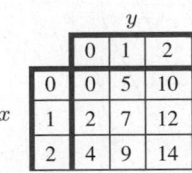

		y	
	0	1	2
0	0	1	4
x 1	1	0	1
2	4	1	0

4.

		y	
	0	1	2
0	10	13	16
x 1	6	9	12
2	2	5	8

5.

		y	
	0	1	2
0	0	5	10
x 1	2	7	12
2	4	9	14

6.

		y	
	0	1	2
0	5	7	9
x 1	6	9	12
2	7	11	15

In Exercises 7–8, could the contour diagram represent a linear function?

7.

8.

9. Find the equation of the linear function $z = c + mx + ny$ whose graph contains the points $(0, 0, 0)$, $(0, 2, -1)$, and $(-3, 0, -4)$.

10. Find the linear function whose graph is the plane through the points $(4, 0, 0)$, $(0, 3, 0)$ and $(0, 0, 2)$.

11. Find an equation for the plane containing the line in the xy-plane where $y = 1$, and the line in the xz-plane where $z = 2$.

12. Find the equation of the linear function $z = c + mx + ny$ whose graph intersects the xz-plane in the line $z = 3x + 4$ and intersects the yz-plane in the line $z = y + 4$.

13. Suppose that z is a linear function of x and y with slope 2 in the x-direction and slope 3 in the y-direction.

(a) A change of 0.5 in x and -0.2 in y produces what change in z?

(b) If $z = 2$ when $x = 5$ and $y = 7$, what is the value of z when $x = 4.9$ and $y = 7.2$?

14. (a) Find a formula for the linear function whose graph is a plane passing through point $(4, 3, -2)$ with slope 5 in the x-direction and slope -3 in the y-direction.

(b) Sketch the contour diagram for this function.

Problems

15. A store sells CDs at one price and DVDs at another price. Figure 12.67 shows the revenue (in dollars) of the music store as a function of the number, c, of CDs and the number, d, of DVDs that it sells. What is the price of a CD? What is the price of a DVD?

Figure 12.67

16. The charge, C, in dollars, to use an Internet service is a function of m, the number of months of use, and t, the total number of minutes on-line:

$$C = f(m, t) = 35 + 15m + 0.05t.$$

(a) Is f a linear function?
(b) Give units for the coefficients of m and t, and interpret them as charges.
(c) Interpret the intercept 35 as a charge.
(d) Find $f(3, 800)$ and interpret your answer.

17. A manufacturer makes two products out of two raw materials. Let q_1, q_2 be the quantities sold of the two products, p_1, p_2 their prices, and m_1, m_2 the quantities purchased of the two raw materials. Which of the following functions do you expect to be linear, and why? In each case, assume that all variables except the ones mentioned are held fixed.

(a) Expenditure on raw materials as a function of m_1 and m_2.
(b) Revenue as a function of q_1 and q_2.
(c) Revenue as a function of p_1 and q_1.

Problems 18–20 concern Table 12.10, which gives the number of calories burned per minute for someone roller-blading, as a function of the person's weight and speed.[7]

Table 12.10

	Calories burned per minute			
Weight	8 mph	9 mph	10 mph	11 mph
120 lbs	4.2	5.8	7.4	8.9
140 lbs	5.1	6.7	8.3	9.9
160 lbs	6.1	7.7	9.2	10.8
180 lbs	7.0	8.6	10.2	11.7
200 lbs	7.9	9.5	11.1	12.6

18. Does the data in Table 12.10 look approximately linear? Give a formula for B, the number of calories burned per minute in terms of the weight, w, and the speed, s. Does the formula make sense for all weights or speeds?

19. Who burns more total calories to go 10 miles: A 120 lb person going 10 mph or a 180 lb person going 8 mph? Which of these two people burns more calories per pound for the 10-mile trip?

20. Use Problem 18 to give a formula for P, the number of calories burned per pound, in terms of w and s, for a person weighing w lbs roller-blading 10 miles at s mph.

For Problems 21–22, find possible equations for linear functions with the given contour diagrams.

21.

22.

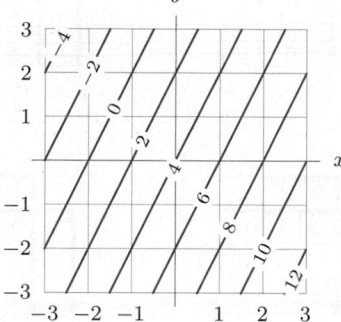

For Problems 23–24, find an equation for the linear function with the given values.

23.

$x\backslash y$	−1	0	1	2
0	1.5	1	0.5	0
1	3.5	3	2.5	2
2	5.5	5	4.5	4
3	7.5	7	6.5	6

24.

$x\backslash y$	10	20	30	40
100	3	6	9	12
200	2	5	8	11
300	1	4	7	10
400	0	3	6	9

[7]From the August 28, 1994, issue of *Parade Magazine*.

It is difficult to graph a linear function by hand. One method that works if the x, y, and z-intercepts are positive is to plot the intercepts and join them by a triangle as shown in Figure 12.68; this shows the part of the plane in the octant where $x \geq 0$, $y \geq 0$, $z \geq 0$. If the intercepts are not all positive, the same method works if the x, y, and z-axes are drawn from a different perspective. Use this method to graph the linear functions in Problems 25–28.

Figure 12.68

25. $z = 2 - 2x + y$

26. $z = 2 - x - 2y$

27. $z = 4 + x - 2y$

28. $z = 6 - 2x - 3y$

29. Let f be the linear function $f(x, y) = c + mx + ny$, where c, m, n are constants and $n \neq 0$.

    (a) Show that all the contours of f are lines of slope $-m/n$.

    (b) For all x and y, show $f(x + n, y - m) = f(x, y)$.

    (c) Explain the relation between parts (a) and (b).

Problems 30–31 refer to the linear function $z = f(x, y)$ whose values are in Table 12.11.

Table 12.11

		y				
		4	6	8	10	12
	5	3	6	9	12	15
	10	7	10	13	16	19
x	15	11	14	17	20	23
	20	15	18	21	24	27
	25	19	22	25	28	31

30. Each column of Table 12.11 is linear with the same slope, $m = \Delta z / \Delta x = 4/5$. Each row is linear with the same slope, $n = \Delta z / \Delta y = 3/2$. We now investigate the slope obtained by moving through the table along lines that are neither rows nor columns.

    (a) Move down the diagonal of the table from the upper left corner ($z = 3$) to the lower right corner ($z = 31$). What do you notice about the changes in z? Now move diagonally from $z = 6$ to $z = 27$. What do you notice about the changes in z now?

    (b) Move in the table along a line right one step, up two steps from $z = 19$ to $z = 9$. Then move in the same direction from $z = 22$ to $z = 12$. What do you notice about the changes in z?

    (c) Show that $\Delta z = m \Delta x + n \Delta y$. Use this to explain what you observed in parts (a) and (b).

31. If we hold y fixed, that is we keep $\Delta y = 0$, and step in the positive x-direction, we get the x-slope, m. If instead we keep $\Delta x = 0$ and step in the positive y-direction, we get the y-slope, n. Fix a step in which neither $\Delta x = 0$ nor $\Delta y = 0$. The slope in the Δx, Δy direction is

$$\text{Slope} = \frac{\text{Rise}}{\text{Run}} = \frac{\Delta z}{\text{Length of step}}$$

$$= \frac{\Delta z}{\sqrt{(\Delta x)^2 + (\Delta y)^2}}.$$

    (a) Compute the slopes for the linear function in Table 12.11 in the direction of $\Delta x = 5$, $\Delta y = 2$.

    (b) Compute the slopes for the linear function in Table 12.11 in the direction of $\Delta x = -10$, $\Delta y = 2$.

32. For the contour diagrams (I)–(IV) on $-2 \leq x, y \leq 2$, pick the corresponding function.

$f(x, y) = 2x + 3y + 10$ $k(x, y) = -2x + 3y + 12$

$g(x, y) = 2x + 3y + 60$ $m(x, y) = -2x + 3y + 60$

$h(x, y) = 2x - 3y + 12$ $n(x, y) = -2x - 3y + 14$

$j(x, y) = 2x - 3y + 60$ $p(x, y) = -2x - 3y + 60$

Strengthen Your Understanding

In Problems 33–34, explain what is wrong with the statement.

33. If the contours of f are all parallel lines, then f is linear.

34. A function $f(x, y)$ with linear cross-sections for x fixed and linear cross-sections for y fixed is a linear function.

In Problems 35–36, give an example of:

35. A table of values, with three rows and three columns, for a nonlinear function that is linear in each row and in each column.

36. A linear function whose contours are lines with slope 2.

Are the statements in Problems 37–48 true or false? Give reasons for your answer.

37. The planes $z = 3 + 2x + 4y$ and $z = 5 + 2x + 4y$ intersect.

38. The function represented in Table 12.12 is linear.

Table 12.12

$u\backslash v$	1.1	1.2	1.3	1.4
3.2	11.06	12.06	13.06	14.06
3.4	11.75	12.82	13.89	14.96
3.6	12.44	13.58	14.72	15.86
3.8	13.13	14.34	15.55	16.76
4.0	13.82	15.10	16.38	17.66

39. Contours of $f(x, y) = 3x + 2y$ are lines with slope 3.

40. If f is linear, then the contours of f are parallel lines.

41. If $f(0, 0) = 1, f(0, 1) = 4, f(0, 3) = 5$, then f cannot be linear.

42. The graph of a linear function is always a plane.

43. The cross-section $x = c$ of a linear function $f(x, y)$ is always a line.

44. There is no linear function $f(x, y)$ with a graph parallel to the xy-plane.

45. There is no linear function $f(x, y)$ with a graph parallel to the xz-plane.

46. A linear function $f(x, y) = 2x + 3y - 5$, has exactly one point (a, b) satisfying $f(a, b) = 0$.

47. In a table of values of a linear function, the columns have the same slope as the rows.

48. There is exactly one linear function $f(x, y)$ whose $f = 0$ contour is $y = 2x + 1$.

12.5 FUNCTIONS OF THREE VARIABLES

In applications of calculus, functions of any number of variables can arise. The density of matter in the universe is a function of three variables, since it takes three numbers to specify a point in space. Models of the US economy often use functions of ten or more variables. We need to be able to apply calculus to functions of arbitrarily many variables.

One difficulty with functions of more than two variables is that it is hard to visualize them. The graph of a function of one variable is a curve in 2-space, the graph of a function of two variables is a surface in 3-space, so the graph of a function of three variables would be a solid in 4-space. Since we can't easily visualize 4-space, we won't use the graphs of functions of three variables. On the other hand, it is possible to draw contour diagrams for functions of three variables, only now the contours are surfaces in 3-space.

Representing a Function of Three Variables Using a Family of Level Surfaces

A function of two variables, $f(x, y)$, can be represented by a family of level curves of the form $f(x, y) = c$ for various values of the constant, c.

> A **level surface**, or **level set** of a function of three variables, $f(x, y, z)$, is a surface of the form $f(x, y, z) = c$, where c is a constant. The function f can be represented by the family of level surfaces obtained by allowing c to vary.

The value of the function, f, is constant on each level surface.

Example 1 The temperature, in °C, at a point (x, y, z) is given by $T = f(x, y, z) = x^2 + y^2 + z^2$. What do the level surfaces of the function f look like and what do they mean in terms of temperature?

Solution The level surface corresponding to $T = 100$ is the set of all points where the temperature is 100°C. That is, where $f(x, y, z) = 100$, so

$$x^2 + y^2 + z^2 = 100.$$

This is the equation of a sphere of radius 10, with center at the origin. Similarly, the level surface corresponding to $T = 200$ is the sphere with radius $\sqrt{200}$. The other level surfaces are concentric spheres. The temperature is constant on each sphere. We may view the temperature distribution as a set of nested spheres, like concentric layers of an onion, each one labeled with a different temperature, starting from low temperatures in the middle and getting hotter as we go out from the center. (See Figure 12.69.) The level surfaces become more closely spaced as we move farther from the origin because the temperature increases more rapidly the farther we get from the origin.

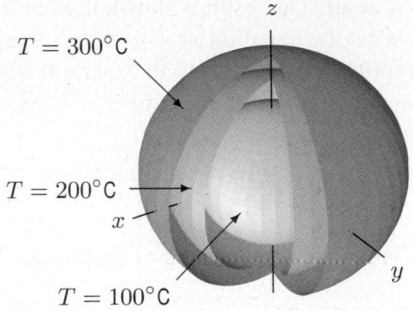

Figure 12.69: Level surfaces of $T = f(x, y, z) = x^2 + y^2 + z^2$, each one having a constant temperature

Example 2   What do the level surfaces of $f(x, y, z) = x^2 + y^2$ and $g(x, y, z) = z - y$ look like?

Solution   The level surface of f corresponding to the constant c is the surface consisting of all points satisfying the equation

$$x^2 + y^2 = c.$$

Since there is no z-coordinate in the equation, z can take any value. For $c > 0$, this is a circular cylinder of radius $\sqrt{c}$ around the z-axis. The level surfaces are concentric cylinders; on the narrow ones near the z-axis, f has small values; on the wider ones, f has larger values. See Figure 12.70.

The level surface of g corresponding to the constant c is the plane

$$z - y = c.$$

Since there is no x variable in the equation, these plane are parallel to the x-axis and cut the yz-plane in the line $z - y = c$. See Figure 12.71.

Figure 12.70: Level surfaces of $f(x, y, z) = x^2 + y^2$

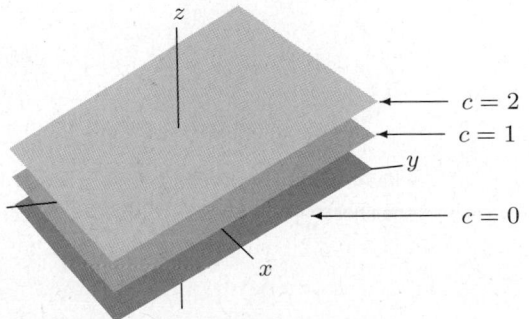

Figure 12.71: Level surfaces of $g(x, y, z) = z - y$

Example 3   What do the level surfaces of $f(x, y, z) = x^2 + y^2 - z^2$ look like?

Solution   In Section 12.3, we saw that the two-variable quadratic function $g(x, y) = x^2 - y^2$ has a saddle-shaped graph and three types of contours. The contour equation $x^2 - y^2 = c$ gives a hyperbola opening right-left when $c > 0$, a hyperbola opening up-down when $c < 0$, and a pair of intersecting lines when $c = 0$. Similarly, the three-variable quadratic function $f(x, y, z) = x^2 + y^2 - z^2$ has three types of level surfaces depending on the value of c in the equation $x^2 + y^2 - z^2 = c$.

Suppose that $c > 0$, say $c = 1$. Rewrite the equation as $x^2 + y^2 = z^2 + 1$ and think of what happens as we cut the surface perpendicular to the z-axis by holding z fixed. The result is a circle, $x^2 + y^2 = $ constant, of radius at least 1 (since the constant $z^2 + 1 \geq 1$). The circles get larger as z gets larger. If we take the $x = 0$ cross-section instead, we get the hyperbola $y^2 - z^2 = 1$. The result is shown in Figure 12.75, with $a = b = c = 1$.

Suppose instead $c < 0$, say $c = -1$. Then the horizontal cross-sections of $x^2 + y^2 = z^2 - 1$ are again circles except that the radii shrink to 0 at $z = \pm 1$ and between $z = -1$ and $z = 1$ there are no cross-sections at all. The result is shown in Figure 12.76 with $a = b = c = 1$.

When $c = 0$, we get the equation $x^2 + y^2 = z^2$. Again the horizontal cross-sections are circles, this time with the radius shrinking down to exactly 0 when $z = 0$. The resulting surface, shown in Figure 12.77 with $a = b = c = 1$, is the cone $z = \sqrt{x^2 + y^2}$ studied in Section 12.3, together with the lower cone $z = -\sqrt{x^2 + y^2}$.

A Catalog of Surfaces

For later reference, here is a small catalog of the surfaces we have encountered.

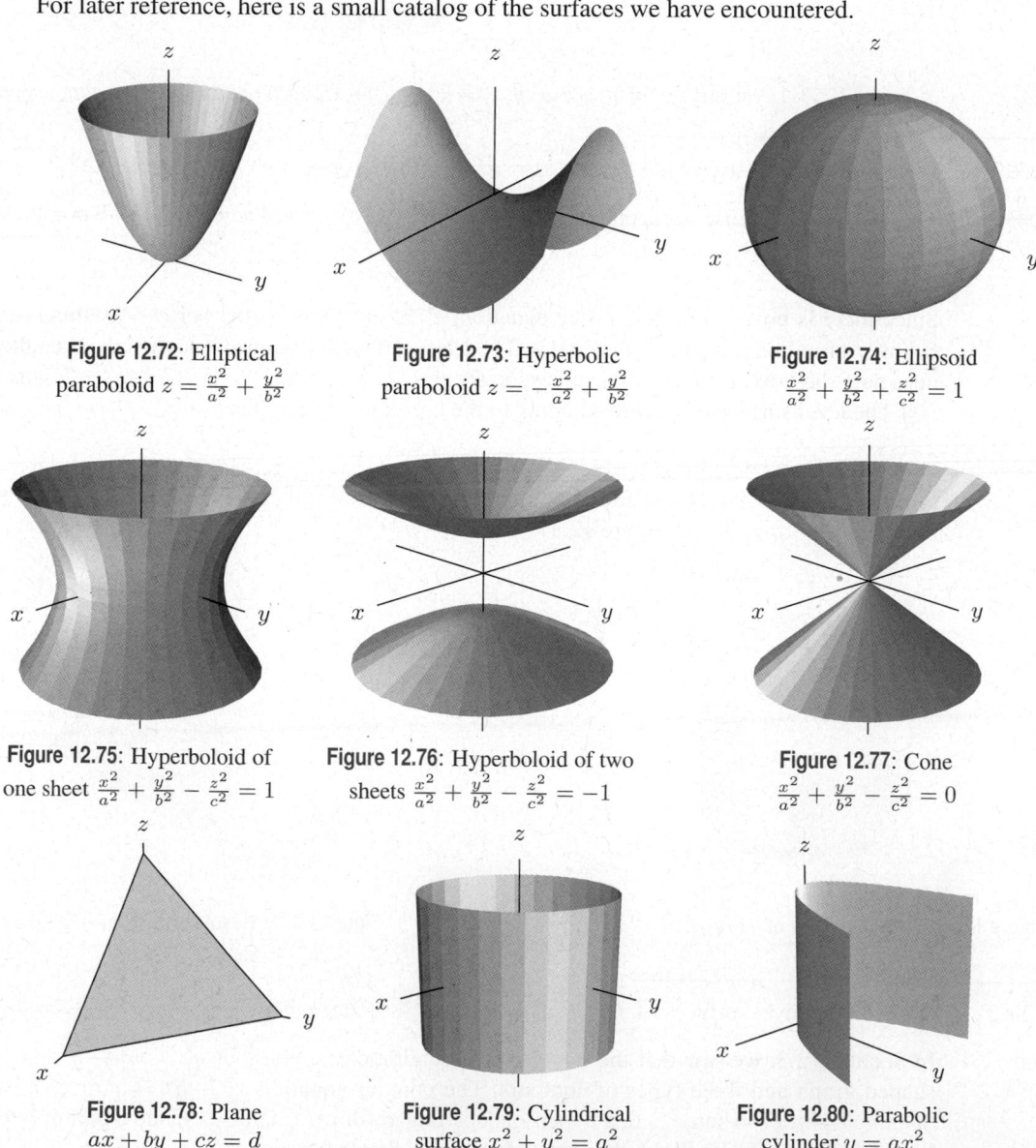

Figure 12.72: Elliptical paraboloid $z = \frac{x^2}{a^2} + \frac{y^2}{b^2}$

Figure 12.73: Hyperbolic paraboloid $z = -\frac{x^2}{a^2} + \frac{y^2}{b^2}$

Figure 12.74: Ellipsoid $\frac{x^2}{a^2} + \frac{y^2}{b^2} + \frac{z^2}{c^2} = 1$

Figure 12.75: Hyperboloid of one sheet $\frac{x^2}{a^2} + \frac{y^2}{b^2} - \frac{z^2}{c^2} = 1$

Figure 12.76: Hyperboloid of two sheets $\frac{x^2}{a^2} + \frac{y^2}{b^2} - \frac{z^2}{c^2} = -1$

Figure 12.77: Cone $\frac{x^2}{a^2} + \frac{y^2}{b^2} - \frac{z^2}{c^2} = 0$

Figure 12.78: Plane $ax + by + cz = d$

Figure 12.79: Cylindrical surface $x^2 + y^2 = a^2$

Figure 12.80: Parabolic cylinder $y = ax^2$

(These are viewed as equations in three variables $x, y,$ and z)

How Surfaces Can Represent Functions of Two Variables and Functions of Three Variables

You may have noticed that we have used surfaces to represent functions in two different ways. First, we used a *single* surface to represent a two-variable function $f(x, y)$. Second, we used a *family* of level surfaces to represent a three-variable function $g(x, y, z)$. These level surfaces have equation $g(x, y, z) = c$.

What is the relation between these two uses of surfaces? For example, consider the function

$$f(x, y) = x^2 + y^2 + 3.$$

Define

$$g(x, y, z) = x^2 + y^2 + 3 - z$$

The points on the graph of f satisfy $z = x^2 + y^2 + 3$, so they also satisfy $x^2 + y^2 + 3 - z = 0$. Thus the graph of f is the same as the level surface

$$g(x, y, z) = x^2 + y^2 + 3 - z = 0.$$

In general, we have the following result:

A single surface that is the graph of a two-variable function $f(x, y)$ can be thought of as one member of the family of level surfaces representing the three-variable function

$$g(x, y, z) = f(x, y) - z.$$

The graph of f is the level surface $g = 0$.

Conversely, a single level surface $g(x, y, z) = c$ can be regarded as the graph of a function $f(x, y)$ if it is possible to solve for z. Sometimes the level surface is pieced together from the graphs of two or more two-variable functions. For example, if $g(x, y, z) = x^2 + y^2 + z^2$, then one member of the family of level surfaces is the sphere

$$x^2 + y^2 + z^2 = 1.$$

This equation defines z implicitly as a function of x and y. Solving it gives two functions

$$z = \sqrt{1 - x^2 - y^2} \qquad \text{and} \qquad z = -\sqrt{1 - x^2 - y^2}.$$

The graph of the first function is the top half of the sphere and the graph of the second function is the bottom half.

Exercises and Problems for Section 12.5

Exercises

1. Match the following functions with the level surfaces in Figure 12.81.

   (a) $f(x, y, z) = y^2 + z^2$ **(b)** $h(x, y, z) = x^2 + z^2$.

Figure 12.81

2. Match the functions with the level surfaces in Figure 12.82.

   (a) $f(x, y, z) = x^2 + y^2 + z^2$
   (b) $g(x, y, z) = x^2 + z^2$.

Figure 12.82

3. Write the level surface $x + 2y + 3z = 5$ as the graph of a function $f(x, y)$.

4. Find a formula for a function $f(x, y, z)$ whose level surface $f = 4$ is a sphere of radius 2, centered at the origin.

5. Write the level surface $x^2 + y + \sqrt{z} = 1$ as the graph of a function $f(x, y)$.

6. Find a formula for a function $f(x, y, z)$ whose level surfaces are spheres centered at the point (a, b, c).

7. Which of the graphs in the catalog of surfaces on page 702 is the graph of a function of x and y?

Use the catalog on page 702 to identify the surfaces in Exercises 8–11.

8. $x^2 + y^2 - z = 0$

9. $-x^2 - y^2 + z^2 = 1$

10. $x + y = 1$

11. $x^2 + y^2/4 + z^2 = 1$

In Exercises 12–15, decide if the given level surface can be expressed as the graph of a function, $f(x, y)$.

12. $z - x^2 - 3y^2 = 0$

13. $2x + 3y - 5z - 10 = 0$

14. $x^2 + y^2 + z^2 - 1 = 0$

15. $z^2 = x^2 + 3y^2$

Problems

In Problems 16–18, represent the surface whose equation is given as the graph of a two-variable function, $f(x, y)$, and as the level surface of a three-variable function, $g(x, y, z) = c$. There are many possible answers.

16. The plane $4x - y - 2z = 6$

17. The top half of the sphere $x^2 + y^2 + z^2 - 10 = 0$

18. The bottom half of the ellipsoid $x^2 + y^2 + z^2/2 = 1$

19. Suppose the function $f(x, y, z) = 2x - 3y + z - 20$ gives the temperature, in degrees Fahrenheit, at a point (x, y, z).

   (a) Describe the isothermal surfaces of f.
   (b) Calculate and interpret $f_z(0, 0, 0)$.
   (c) If you are standing at the point $(0, 0, 0)$, in what direction should you move to increase your temperature the fastest?
   (d) Is $f(x, y) = -2x + 3y + 17$ an isothermal surface of f? If so, what is the temperature on this isotherm?

20. The balance, B, in dollars, in a bank account depends on the amount deposited, A dollars, the annual interest rate, $r\%$, and the time, t, in months since the deposit, so $B = f(A, r, t)$.

   (a) Is f an increasing or decreasing function of A? Of r? Of t?
   (b) Interpret the statement $f(1250, 1, 25) \approx 1276$. Give units.

21. The monthly payments, P dollars, on a mortgage in which A dollars were borrowed at an annual interest rate of $r\%$ for t years is given by $P = f(A, r, t)$. Is f an increasing or decreasing function of A? Of r? Of t?

22. Find a function $f(x, y, z)$ whose level surface $f = 1$ is the graph of the function $g(x, y) = x + 2y$.

23. Find two functions $f(x, y)$ and $g(x, y)$ so that the graphs of both together form the ellipsoid $x^2 + y^2/4 + z^2/9 = 1$.

24. Find a formula for a function $g(x, y, z)$ whose level surfaces are planes parallel to the plane $z = 2x + 3y - 5$.

25. The surface S is the graph of $f(x, y) = \sqrt{1 - x^2 - y^2}$.

   (a) Explain why S is the upper hemisphere of radius 1, with equator in the xy-plane, centered at the origin.

   (b) Find a level surface $g(x, y, z) = c$ representing S.

26. The surface S is the graph of $f(x, y) = \sqrt{1 - y^2}$.

   (a) Explain why S is the upper half of a circular cylinder of radius 1, centered along the x-axis.
   (b) Find a level surface $g(x, y, z) = c$ representing S.

27. A cone C, with height 1 and radius 1, has its base in the xz-plane and its vertex on the positive y-axis. Find a function $g(x, y, z)$ such that C is part of the level surface $g(x, y, z) = 0$. [Hint: The graph of $f(x, y) = \sqrt{x^2 + y^2}$ is a cone which opens up and has vertex at the origin.]

28. Describe the level surface $f(x, y, z) = x^2/4 + z^2 = 1$ in words.

29. Describe the level surface $g(x, y, z) = x^2 + y^2/4 + z^2 = 1$ in words. [Hint: Look at cross-sections with constant x, y, and z values.]

30. Describe in words the level surfaces of the function $g(x, y, z) = x + y + z$.

31. Describe in words the level surfaces of $f(x, y, z) = \sin(x + y + z)$.

32. Describe the surface $x^2 + y^2 = (2 + \sin z)^2$. In general, if $f(z) \geq 0$ for all z, describe the surface $x^2 + y^2 = (f(z))^2$.

33. What do the level surfaces of $f(x, y, z) = x^2 - y^2 + z^2$ look like? [Hint: Use cross-sections with y constant instead of cross-sections with z constant.]

34. Describe in words the level surfaces of $g(x, y, z) = e^{-(x^2 + y^2 + z^2)}$.

35. Sketch and label level surfaces of $h(x, y, z) = e^{z-y}$ for $h = 1, e, e^2$.

36. Sketch and label level surfaces of $f(x, y, z) = 4 - x^2 - y^2 - z^2$ for $f = 0, 1, 2$.

37. Sketch and label level surfaces of $g(x, y, z) = 1 - x^2 - y^2$ for $g = 0, -1, -2$.

Strengthen Your Understanding

In Problems 38–40, explain what is wrong with the statement.

38. The graph of a function $f(x, y, z)$ is a surface in 3-space.

39. The level surfaces of $f(x, y, z) = x^2 - y^2$ are all saddle-shaped.

40. The level surfaces of $f(x, y, z) = x^2 + y^2$ are paraboloids.

In Problems 41–44, give an example of:

41. A function $f(x, y, z)$ whose level surfaces are equally spaced planes perpendicular to the yz-plane.

42. A function $f(x, y, z)$ whose level sets are concentric cylinders centered on the y-axis.

43. A nonlinear function $f(x, y, z)$ whose level sets are parallel planes.

44. A function $f(x, y, z)$ whose level sets are paraboloids.

Are the statements in Problems 45–54 true or false? Give reasons for your answer.

45. The graph of the function $f(x, y) = x^2 + y^2$ is the same as the level surface $g(x, y, z) = x^2 + y^2 - z = 0$.

46. The graph of $f(x, y) = \sqrt{1 - x^2 - y^2}$ is the same as the level surface $g(x, y, z) = x^2 + y^2 + z^2 = 1$.

47. Any surface which is the graph of a two-variable function $f(x, y)$ can also be represented as the level surface of a three-variable function $g(x, y, z)$.

48. Any surface which is the level surface of a three-variable function $g(x, y, z)$ can also be represented as the graph of a two-variable function $f(x, y)$.

49. The level surfaces of the function $g(x, y, z) = x + 2y + z$ are parallel planes.

50. The level surfaces of $g(x, y, z) = x^2 + y + z^2$ are cylinders with axis along the y-axis.

51. A level surface of a function $g(x, y, z)$ cannot be a single point.

52. If $g(x, y, z) = ax + by + cz + d$, where a, b, c, d are nonzero constants, then the level surfaces of g are planes.

53. If the level surfaces of g are planes, then $g(x, y, z) = ax + by + cz + d$, where a, b, c, d are constants.

54. If the level surfaces $g(x, y, z) = k_1$ and $g(x, y, z) = k_2$ are the same surface, then $k_1 = k_2$.

12.6 LIMITS AND CONTINUITY

The sheer face of Half Dome, in Yosemite National Park in California, was caused by glacial activity during the Ice Age. (See Figure 12.83.) As we scale the rock from the west, the height of the terrain rises abruptly by nearly 5000 feet from the valley floor, 2000 feet of it vertical.

If we consider the function h giving the height of the terrain above sea level in terms of longitude and latitude, then h has a *discontinuity* along the path at the base of the cliff of Half Dome. Looking at the contour map of the region in Figure 12.84, we see that in most places a small change in position results in a small change in height, except near the cliff. There, no matter how small a step we take, we get a large change in height. (You can see how crowded the contours get near the cliff; some end abruptly along the discontinuity.)

This geological feature illustrates the ideas of continuity and discontinuity. Roughly speaking, a function is said to be *continuous* at a point if its values at places near the point are close to the value at the point. If this is not the case, the function is said to be *discontinuous*.

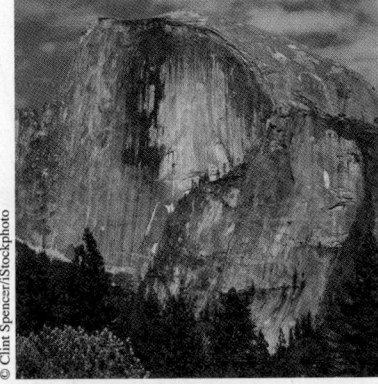

Figure 12.83: Half Dome in Yosemite National Park

Figure 12.84: A contour map of Half Dome

The property of continuity is one that, practically speaking, we usually assume of the functions we are studying. Informally, we expect (except under special circumstances) that values of a function do not change drastically when making small changes to the input variables. Whenever we model a one-variable function by an unbroken curve, we are making this assumption. Even when functions come to us as tables of data, we usually make the assumption that the missing function values between data points are close to the measured ones.

In this section we study limits and continuity a bit more formally in the context of functions of several variables. For simplicity we study these concepts for functions of two variables, but our discussion can be adapted to functions of three or more variables.

One can show that sums, products, and compositions of continuous functions are continuous, while the quotient of two continuous functions is continuous everywhere the denominator function is nonzero. Thus, each of the functions

$$\cos(x^2 y), \qquad \ln(x^2 + y^2), \qquad \frac{e^{x+y}}{x+y}, \qquad \ln(\sin(x^2 + y^2))$$

is continuous at all points (x, y) where it is defined. As for functions of one variable, the graph of a continuous function over an unbroken domain is unbroken—that is, the surface has no holes or rips in it.

Example 1   From Figures 12.85–12.88, which of the following functions appear to be continuous at $(0, 0)$?

(a) $f(x, y) = \begin{cases} \dfrac{x^2 y}{x^2 + y^2}, & (x, y) \neq (0, 0), \\ 0, & (x, y) = (0, 0). \end{cases}$

(b) $g(x, y) = \begin{cases} \dfrac{x^2}{x^2 + y^2}, & (x, y) \neq (0, 0), \\ 0, & (x, y) = (0, 0). \end{cases}$

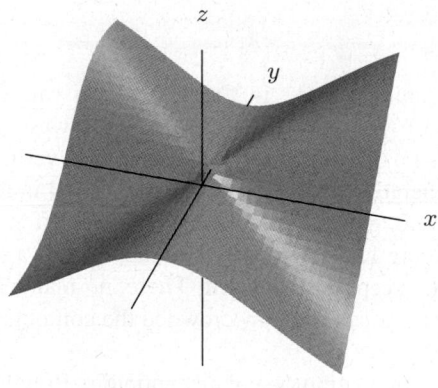

Figure 12.85: Graph of $z = x^2 y/(x^2 + y^2)$

Figure 12.86: Contour diagram of $z = x^2 y/(x^2 + y^2)$

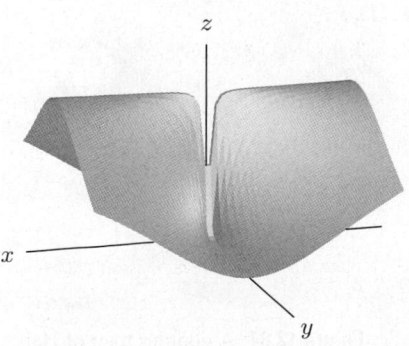

Figure 12.87: Graph of $z = x^2/(x^2 + y^2)$

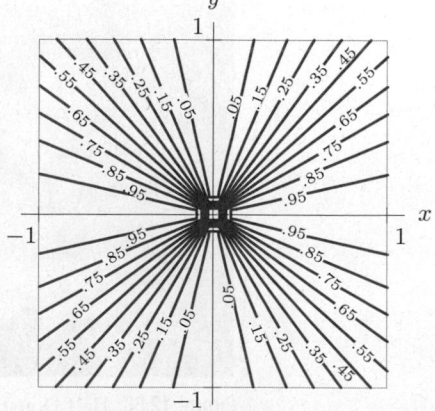

Figure 12.88: Contour diagram of $z = x^2/(x^2 + y^2)$

Solution   (a) The graph and contour diagram of f in Figures 12.85 and 12.86 suggest that f is close to 0 when (x, y) is close to $(0, 0)$. That is, the figures suggest that f is continuous at the point $(0, 0)$; the graph appears to have no rips or holes there.

However, the figures cannot tell us for sure whether f is continuous. To be certain we must investigate the limit analytically, as is done in Example 2(a) on page 707.

(b) The graph of g and its contours near $(0, 0)$ in Figure 12.87 and 12.88 suggest that g behaves differently from f: The contours of g seem to "crash" at the origin and the graph rises rapidly from 0 to 1 near $(0, 0)$. Small changes in (x, y) near $(0, 0)$ can yield large changes in g, so we expect that g is not continuous at the point $(0, 0)$. Again, a more precise analysis is given in Example 2(b) on page 707.

The previous example suggests that continuity *at* a point depends on a function's behavior *near* the point. To study behavior near a point more carefully we need the idea of a limit of a function of two variables. Suppose that $f(x, y)$ is a function defined on a set in 2-space, not necessarily containing the point (a, b), but containing points (x, y) arbitrarily close to (a, b); suppose that L is a number.

> The function f has a **limit** L at the point (a, b), written
> $$\lim_{(x,y)\to(a,b)} f(x, y) = L,$$
> if $f(x, y)$ is as close to L as we please whenever the distance from the point (x, y) to the point (a, b) is sufficiently small, but not zero.

We define continuity for functions of two variables in the same way as for functions of one variable:

> A function f is **continuous at the point** (a, b) if
> $$\lim_{(x,y)\to(a,b)} f(x, y) = f(a, b).$$
> A function is **continuous on a region** R in the xy-plane if it is continuous at each point in R.

Thus, if f is continuous at the point (a, b), then f must be defined at (a, b) and the limit, $\lim_{(x,y)\to(a,b)} f(x, y)$, must exist and be equal to the value $f(a, b)$. If a function is defined at a point (a, b) but is not continuous there, then we say that f is *discontinuous* at (a, b).

We now apply the definition of continuity to the functions in Example 1, showing that f is continuous at $(0, 0)$ and that g is discontinuous at $(0, 0)$.

Example 2   Let f and g be the functions in Example 1. Use the definition of the limit to show that:

(a) $\lim\limits_{(x,y)\to(0,0)} f(x, y) = 0$ (b) $\lim\limits_{(x,y)\to(0,0)} g(x, y)$ does not exist.

Solution   To investigate these limits of f and g, we consider values of these functions near, but not at, the origin, where they are given by the formulas

$$f(x, y) = \frac{x^2 y}{x^2 + y^2} \qquad g(x, y) = \frac{x^2}{x^2 + y^2}.$$

(a) The graph and contour diagram of f both suggest that $\lim_{(x,y)\to(0,0)} f(x, y) = 0$. To use the definition of the limit, we estimate $|f(x, y) - L|$ with $L = 0$:

$$|f(x, y) - L| = \left| \frac{x^2 y}{x^2 + y^2} - 0 \right| = \left| \frac{x^2}{x^2 + y^2} \right| |y| \le |y| \le \sqrt{x^2 + y^2}.$$

Now $\sqrt{x^2 + y^2}$ is the distance from (x, y) to $(0, 0)$. Thus, to make $|f(x, y) - 0| < 0.001$, for example, we need only require (x, y) be within 0.001 of $(0, 0)$. More generally, for any positive number u, no matter how small, we are sure that $|f(x, y) - 0| < u$ whenever (x, y) is no farther than u from $(0, 0)$. This is what we mean by saying that the difference $|f(x, y) - 0|$ can be made as small as we wish by choosing the distance to be sufficiently small. Thus, we conclude that

$$\lim_{(x,y)\to(0,0)} f(x, y) = \lim_{(x,y)\to(0,0)} \frac{x^2 y}{x^2 + y^2} = 0.$$

Notice that since this limit equals $f(0, 0)$, the function f is continuous at $(0, 0)$.

(b) Although the formula defining the function g looks similar to that of f, we saw in Example 1 that g's behavior near the origin is quite different. If we consider points $(x, 0)$ lying along the x-axis near $(0, 0)$, then the values $g(x, 0)$ are equal to 1, while if we consider points $(0, y)$ lying along the y-axis near $(0, 0)$, then the values $g(0, y)$ are equal to 0. Thus, within any distance (no matter how small) from the origin, there are points where $g = 0$ and points where $g = 1$. Therefore the limit $\lim_{(x,y)\to(0,0)} g(x, y)$ does not exist, and thus g is not continuous at $(0, 0)$.

While the notions of limit and continuity look formally the same for one- and two-variable functions, they are somewhat more subtle in the multivariable case. The reason for this is that on the line (1-space), we can approach a point from just two directions (left or right) but in 2-space there are an infinite number of ways to approach a given point.

Exercises and Problems for Section 12.6

Exercises

In Exercises 1–6, is the function continuous at all points in the given region?

1. $\dfrac{1}{x^2 + y^2}$ on the square $-1 \le x \le 1, -1 \le y \le 1$

2. $\dfrac{1}{x^2 + y^2}$ on the square $1 \le x \le 2, 1 \le y \le 2$

3. $\dfrac{y}{x^2 + 2}$ on the disk $x^2 + y^2 \le 1$

4. $\dfrac{e^{\sin x}}{\cos y}$ on the rectangle $-\frac{\pi}{2} \le x \le \frac{\pi}{2}, 0 \le y \le \frac{\pi}{4}$

5. $\tan(xy)$ on the square $-2 \le x \le 2, -2 \le y \le 2$

6. $\sqrt{2x - y}$ on the disk $x^2 + y^2 \le 4$

In Exercises 7–11, find the limit as $(x, y) \to (0, 0)$ of $f(x, y)$. Assume that polynomials, exponentials, logarithmic, and trigonometric functions are continuous.

7. $f(x, y) = e^{-x-y}$

8. $f(x, y) = x^2 + y^2$

9. $f(x, y) = \dfrac{x}{x^2 + 1}$

10. $f(x, y) = \dfrac{x + y}{(\sin y) + 2}$

11. $f(x, y) = \dfrac{\sin(x^2 + y^2)}{x^2 + y^2}$ [Hint: $\lim\limits_{t\to 0} \dfrac{\sin t}{t} = 1$.]

Problems

In Problems 12–13, show that the function $f(x, y)$ does not have a limit as $(x, y) \to (0, 0)$. [Hint: Use the line $y = mx$.]

12. $f(x, y) = \dfrac{x + y}{x - y}$, $x \ne y$

13. $f(x, y) = \dfrac{x^2 - y^2}{x^2 + y^2}$

14. By approaching the origin along the positive x-axis and the positive y-axis, show that the following limit does not exist:

$$\lim_{(x,y)\to(0,0)} \frac{2x - y^2}{2x + y^2}.$$

15. Show that $f(x, y)$ has no limit as $(x, y) \to (0, 0)$ if

$$f(x, y) = \frac{xy}{|xy|}, \qquad x \ne 0 \text{ and } y \ne 0.$$

16. Show that the function f does not have a limit at $(0, 0)$ by examining the limits of f as $(x, y) \to (0, 0)$ along the curve $y = kx^2$ for different values of k:

$$f(x, y) = \frac{x^2}{x^2 + y}, \qquad x^2 + y \ne 0.$$

17. Let $f(x, y) = \begin{cases} \dfrac{|x|}{x} y & \text{for } x \neq 0 \\ 0 & \text{for } x = 0. \end{cases}$

Is $f(x, y)$ continuous

(a) On the x-axis? **(b)** On the y-axis?

(c) At $(0, 0)$?

In Problems 18–19, determine whether there is a value for c making the function continuous everywhere. If so, find it. If not, explain why not.

18. $f(x, y) = \begin{cases} c + y, & x \leq 3, \\ 5 - x, & x > 3. \end{cases}$

19. $f(x, y) = \begin{cases} c + y, & x \leq 3, \\ 5 - y, & x > 3. \end{cases}$

20. Is the following function continuous at $(0, 0)$?

$$f(x, y) = \begin{cases} x^2 + y^2 & \text{if } (x, y) \neq (0, 0) \\ 2 & \text{if } (x, y) = (0, 0) \end{cases}$$

21. What value of c makes the following function continuous at $(0, 0)$?

$$f(x, y) = \begin{cases} x^2 + y^2 + 1 & \text{if } (x, y) \neq (0, 0) \\ c & \text{if } (x, y) = (0, 0) \end{cases}$$

22. (a) Use a computer to draw the graph and the contour diagram of the following function:

$$f(x, y) = \begin{cases} \dfrac{xy(x^2 - y^2)}{x^2 + y^2}, & (x, y) \neq (0, 0), \\ 0, & (x, y) = (0, 0). \end{cases}$$

(b) Do your answers to part (a) suggest that f is continuous at $(0, 0)$? Explain your answer.

Strengthen Your Understanding

In Problems 24–25, explain what is wrong with the statement.

24. If a function $f(x, y)$ has a limit as (x, y) approaches (a, b), then it is continuous at (a, b).

25. If both f and g are continuous at (a, b), then so are $f + g, fg$ and f/g.

In Problems 26–27, give an example of:

26. A function $f(x, y)$ which is continuous everywhere except at $(0, 0)$ and $(1, 2)$.

27. A function $f(x, y)$ that approaches 1 as (x, y) approaches $(0, 0)$ along the x-axis and approaches 2 as

23. The function f, whose graph and contour diagram are in Figures 12.89 and 12.90, is given by

$$f(x, y) = \begin{cases} \dfrac{xy}{x^2 + y^2}, & (x, y) \neq (0, 0), \\ 0, & (x, y) = (0, 0). \end{cases}$$

(a) Show that $f(0, y)$ and $f(x, 0)$ are each continuous functions of one variable.

(b) Show that rays emanating from the origin are contained in contours of f.

(c) Is f continuous at $(0, 0)$?

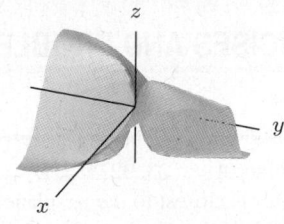

Figure 12.89: Graph of $z = xy/(x^2 + y^2)$

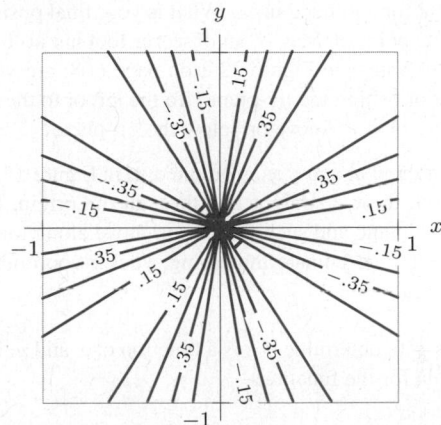

Figure 12.90: Contour diagram of $z = xy/(x^2 + y^2)$

(x, y) approaches $(0, 0)$ along the y-axis.

In Problems 28–30, construct a function $f(x, y)$ with the given property.

28. Not continuous along the line $x = 2$; continuous everywhere else.

29. Not continuous at the point $(2, 0)$; continuous everywhere else.

30. Not continuous along the curve $x^2 + y^2 = 1$; continuous everywhere else.

CHAPTER SUMMARY (see also Ready Reference at the end of the book)

- **3-Space**
  Cartesian coordinates, x-, y- and z-axes, xy-, xz- and yz-planes, distance formula.

- **Functions of Two Variables**
  Represented by: tables, graphs, formulas, cross-sections (one variable fixed), contours (function value fixed); cylinders (one variable missing).

- **Linear Functions**

- Recognizing linear functions from tables, graphs, contour diagrams, formulas. Converting from one representation to another.

- **Functions of Three Variables**
  Sketching level surfaces (function value fixed) in 3-space; graph of $z = f(x, y)$ is same as level surface $g(x, y, z) = f(x, y) - z = 0$.

- **Continuity**

REVIEW EXERCISES AND PROBLEMS FOR CHAPTER TWELVE

Exercises

1. Which of the points $A = (23, 92, 48)$, $B = (-60, 0, 0)$, $C = (60, 1, -92)$ is closest to the yz-plane? Which lies on the xz-plane? Which is farthest from the xy-plane?

2. You are at the point $(-1, -3, -3)$, standing upright and facing the yz-plane. You walk 2 units forward, turn left, and walk for another 2 units. What is your final position? From the point of view of an observer looking at the co-ordinate system in Figure 12.2 on page 668, are you in front of or behind the yz-plane? To the left or to the right of the xz-plane? Above or below the xy-plane?

3. On a set of x, y, and z axes oriented as in Figure 12.5 on page 669, draw a straight line through the origin, lying in the xz-plane and such that if you move along the line with your x-coordinate increasing, your z-coordinate is decreasing.

In Exercises 4–6, determine if z is a function of x and y. If so, find a formula for the function.

4. $6x - 4y + 2z = 10$

5. $x^2 + y^2 + z^2 = 100$

6. $3x^2 - 5y^2 + 5z = 10 + x + y$

7. Figure 12.91 shows the parabolas $z = f(x, b)$ for $b = -2, -1, 0, 1, 2$. Which of the graphs of $z = f(x, y)$ in Figure 12.92 best fits this information?

Figure 12.91

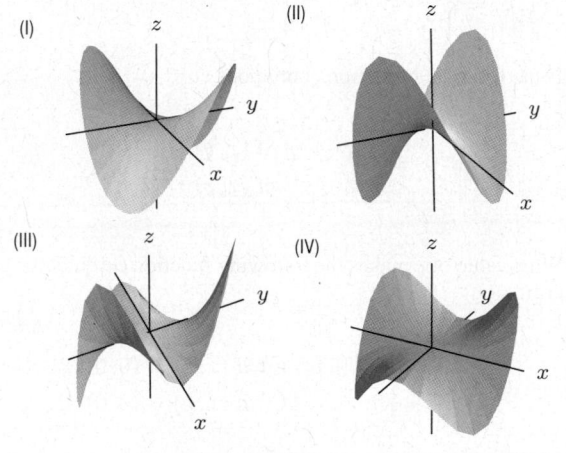

Figure 12.92

8. Match the pairs of functions (a)–(d) with the contour diagrams (I)–(IV). In each case, which contours represent f and which represent g? (The x- and y-scales are equal.)

(a) $f(x, y) = x + y$, $g(x, y) = x - y$
(b) $f(x, y) = 2x + 3y$, $g(x, y) = 2x - 3y$
(c) $f(x, y) = x^2 - y$, $g(x, y) = 2y + \ln |x|$
(d) $f(x, y) = x^2 - y^2$, $g(x, y) = xy$

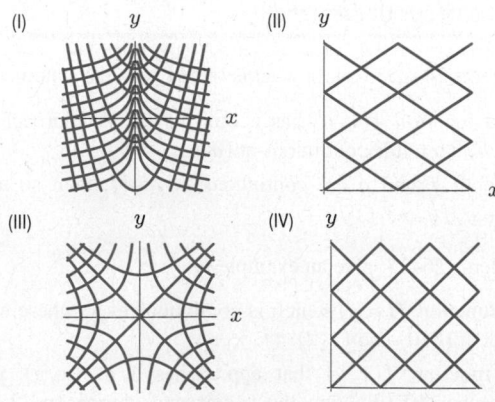

9. Match the contour diagrams (a)–(d) with the surfaces (I)–(IV). Give reasons for your choice.

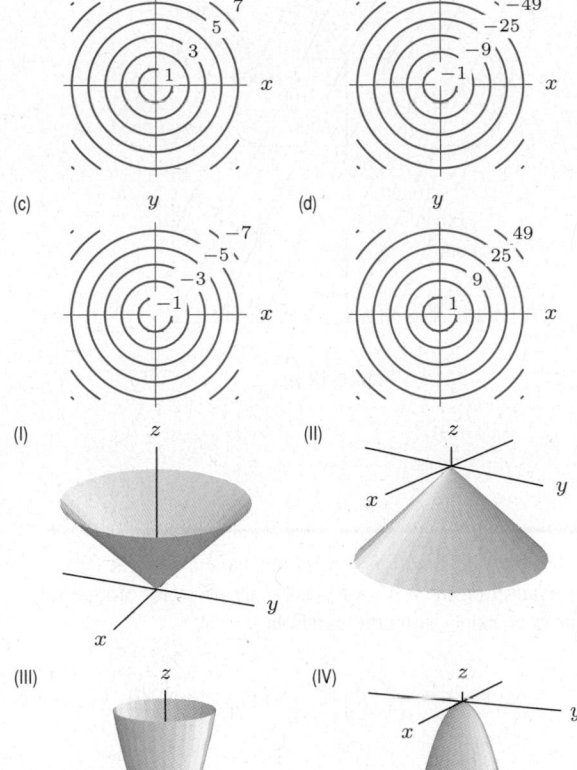

(a)

(b)

(c)

(d)

(I)

(II)

(III)

(IV)

In Exercises 10–13, make a contour plot for the function in the region $-2 < x < 2$ and $-2 < y < 2$. What is the equation and the shape of the contours?

10. $z = 3x - 5y + 1$

11. $z = \sin y$

12. $z = 2x^2 + y^2$

13. $z = e^{-2x^2 - y^2}$

14. Describe the set of points whose x coordinate is 2 and whose y coordinate is 1.

15. Find the equation of the sphere of radius 5 centered at $(1, 2, 3)$.

16. Find the equation of the plane through the points $(0, 0, 2), (0, 3, 0), (5, 0, 0)$.

17. Find the center and radius of the sphere with equation $x^2 + 4x + y^2 - 6y + z^2 + 12z = 0$.

Which of the contour diagrams in Exercises 18–19 could represent linear functions?

18.

19.

20. (a) Complete the table with values of a linear function $f(x, y)$.
　(b) Find a formula for $f(x, y)$.

		y	
	2.5	3.0	3.50
x	-1	6		8
	1		1	2
	3	-6		

21. Find a formula for a function $f(x, y, z)$ whose level surfaces look like those in Figure 12.93.

Figure 12.93

In Exercises 22–25, represent the surface as the graph of a function, $f(x, y)$, and by level surfaces of the form $g(x, y, z) = c$. (There are many possible answers.)

22. Paraboloid obtained by shifting $z = x^2 + y^2$ vertically 5 units

23. Plane with intercepts $x = 2$, $y = 3$, $z = 4$.

24. Upper half of unit sphere centered at the origin.

25. Lower half of sphere of radius 2 centered at $(3, 0, 0)$.

26. Describe in words the level surfaces of the function $g(x, y, z) = \cos(x + y + z)$.

Use the catalog on page 702 to identify the surfaces in Exercises 27–28.

27. $x^2 + z^2 = 1$ **28.** $-x^2 + y^2 - z^2 = 0$

29. (a) What features of the contour diagram of $g(x, y)$ in Figure 12.94 suggest that g is linear?

(b) Assuming g is linear, find a formula for $g(x, y)$.

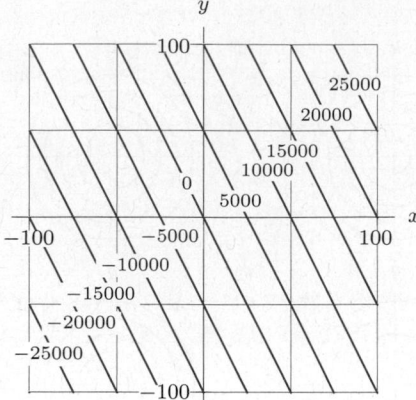

Figure 12.94

Problems

30. Use a computer or calculator to draw the graph of the vibrating guitar string function:

$$g(x, t) = \cos t \sin 2x, \quad 0 \le x \le \pi, \quad 0 \le t \le 2\pi.$$

Relate the shape of the graph to the cross-sections with t fixed and those with x fixed.

31. Consider the Cobb-Douglas production function $P = f(L, K) = 1.01 L^{0.75} K^{0.25}$. What is the effect on production of doubling both labor and capital?

32. (a) Sketch level curves of $f(x, y) = \sqrt{x^2 + y^2} + x$ for $f = 1, 2, 3$.
  (b) For what values of c can level curves $f = c$ be drawn?

33. Values of $f(x, y) = \frac{1}{2}(x + y - 2)(x + y - 1) + y$ are in Table 12.13.

  (a) Find a pattern in the table. Make a conjecture and use it to complete Table 12.13 without computation. Check by using the formula for f.
  (b) Using the formula, check that the pattern holds for all $x \ge 1$ and $y \ge 1$.

Table 12.13

		1	2	3	4	5	6
	1	1	3	6	10	15	21
	2	2	5	9	14	20	
x	3	4	8	13	19		
	4	7	12	18			
	5	11	17				
	6	16					

(column header label y above the table)

34. Show that the function f does not have a limit at $(0, 0)$ by examining the limits of f as $(x, y) \to (0, 0)$ along the line $y = x$ and along the parabola $y = x^2$:

$$f(x, y) = \frac{x^2 y}{x^4 + y^2}, \quad (x, y) \ne (0, 0).$$

35. By approaching the origin along the positive x-axis and the positive y-axis, show that the following limit does not exist:

$$\lim_{(x,y) \to (0,0)} \frac{x + y^2}{2x + y}.$$

36. Explain why the following function is not continuous along the line $y = 0$:

$$f(x, y) = \begin{cases} 1 - x, & y \ge 0, \\ -2, & y < 0. \end{cases}$$

37. A college admissions office uses the following equation to predict the grade point average of an incoming student:

$$z = 0.003x + 0.8y - 4,$$

where z is the predicted college GPA on a scale of 0 to 4.3, and x is the sum of the student's SAT Math and SAT Verbal on a scale of 400 to 1600, and y is the student's high school GPA on a scale of 0 to 4.3. The college admits students whose predicted GPA is at least 2.3.

  (a) Will a student with SATs of 1050 and high school GPA of 3.0 be admitted?

(b) Will every student with SATs of 1600 be admitted?

(c) Will every student with a high school GPA of 4.3 be admitted?

(d) Draw a contour diagram for the predicted GPA z with $400 \leq x \leq 1600$ and $0 \leq y \leq 4.3$. Shade the points corresponding to students who will be admitted.

(e) Which is more important, an extra 100 points on the SAT or an extra 0.5 of high school GPA?

38. By setting one variable constant, find a plane that intersects the graph of $z = (x^2 + 1)\sin y + xy^2$ in a:

(a) Parabola

(b) Straight line

(c) Sine curve

39. The temperature T (in °C) at any point in the region $-10 \leq x \leq 10$, $-10 \leq y \leq 10$ is given by the function

$$T(x, y) = 100 - x^2 - y^2.$$

(a) Sketch isothermal curves (curves of constant temperature) for $T = 100°C$, $T = 75°C$, $T = 50°C$, $T = 25°C$, and $T = 0°C$.

(b) A heat-seeking bug is put down at a point on the xy-plane. In which direction should it move to increase its temperature fastest? How is that direction related to the level curve through that point?

40. Find a linear function whose graph is the plane that intersects the xy-plane along the line $y = 2x+2$ and contains the point $(1, 2, 2)$.

41. **(a)** Sketch the level curves of $z = \cos\sqrt{x^2 + y^2}$.

(b) Sketch a cross-section through the surface $z = \cos\sqrt{x^2 + y^2}$ in the plane containing the x- and z-axes. Put units on your axes.

(c) Sketch the cross-section through the surface $z = \cos\sqrt{x^2 + y^2}$ in the plane containing the z-axis and the line $y = x$ in the xy-plane.

Problems 42–45 concern a vibrating guitar string. Snapshots of the guitar string at millisecond intervals are in Figure 12.95.

Figure 12.95: A vibrating guitar string: $f(x, t) = \cos t \sin x$ for four t values.

The guitar string is stretched tight along the x-axis from $x = 0$ to $x = \pi$. Each point on the string has an x-value, $0 \leq x \leq \pi$. As the string vibrates, each point on the string moves back and forth on either side of the x-axis. Let $y = f(x, t)$ be the displacement at time t of the point on the string located x units from the left end. A possible formula is

$$y = f(x, t) = \cos t \sin x, \quad 0 \leq x \leq \pi, \quad t \text{ in milliseconds.}$$

42. Explain what the functions $f(x, 0)$ and $f(x, 1)$ represent in terms of the vibrating string.

43. Explain what the functions $f(0, t)$ and $f(1, t)$ represent in terms of the vibrating string.

44. **(a)** Sketch graphs of y versus x for fixed t values, $t = 0$, $\pi/4$, $\pi/2$, $3\pi/4$, π.

(b) Use your graphs to explain why this function could represent a vibrating guitar string.

45. Describe the motion of the guitar strings whose displacements are given by the following:

(a) $y = g(x, t) = \cos 2t \sin x$

(b) $y = h(x, t) = \cos t \sin 2x$

CAS Challenge Problems

46. Let $A = (0, 0, 0)$ and $B = (2, 0, 0)$.

(a) Find a point C in the xy-plane that is a distance 2 from both A and B.

(b) Find a point D in 3-space that is a distance 2 from each of A, B, and C.

(c) Describe the figure obtained by joining A, B, C, and D with straight lines.

47. Let $f(x, y) = 3 + x + 2y$.

(a) Find formulas for $f(x, f(x, y)), f(x, f(x, f(x, y)))$ by hand.

(b) Consider $f(x, f(x, f(x, f(x, f(x, f(x, y))))))$. Conjecture a formula for this function and check your answer with a computer algebra system.

48. A function $f(x, y, z)$ has the property that $f(1, 0, 1) = 20$, $f(1, 1, 1) = 16$, and $f(1, 1, 2) = 21$.

(a) Estimate $f(1, 1, 3)$ and $f(1, 2, 1)$, assuming f is a linear function of each variable with the other variables held fixed.

(b) Suppose in fact that $f(x, y, z) = ax^2 + byz + czx^3 + d2^{x-y}$, for constants a, b, c and d. Which of your estimates in part (a) do you expect to be exact?

(c) Suppose in addition that $f(0, 0, 1) = 6$. Find an exact formula for f by solving for a, b, c, and d.

(d) Use the formula in part (c) to evaluate $f(1, 1, 3)$ and $f(1, 2, 1)$ exactly. Do the values confirm your answer to part (b)?

PROJECTS FOR CHAPTER TWELVE

1. Noise Levels at London's Heathrow Airport

The measure used by the UK government to monitor aircraft noise is called the Loudness Equivalent or Leq.[8] This takes the sound energy from each aircraft in decibels or dB and averages it over a 16-hour day for several months. Based on the official noise output of each aircraft type and historical data on aircraft movements and flight paths, the Leq is calculated for a wide area around Heathrow Airport, London. The results are shown as noise contour maps such as Figure 12.96, where contours are labeled in dB. The 57 dB contour is significant since a major study indicated that community annoyance generally becomes significant at this noise level.

(a) Identify the position of the main runways at Heathrow and estimate the noise level in dB on the runways.

(b) Planes prefer to take off and land facing into the wind. Using the fact that the wind is generally from the west, explain the shape of the contours at the western and eastern ends of the runways.

(c) In which direction does the sound level fall most rapidly? Explain.

(d) A sound can be measured by the physical intensity of the sound, L. The decibel measure of the sound, B, is obtained from the ratio of the sound intensity, L, to a base intensity, L_0:

$$B = 10 \log_{10}\left(\frac{L}{L_0}\right).$$

The contour levels are show at 3 dB intervals. How do sound intensity levels (L) compare on adjacent contours?

(e) If the noise level of the next generation of aircraft is 50% of current values, how will the contour map change?

Figure 12.96: Contours, in decibels (dB), showing noise levels around Heathrow Airport, London

2. A Heater in a Room

Figure 12.97 shows the contours of the temperature along one wall of a heated room through one winter day, with time indicated as on a 24-hour clock. The room has a heater located at the leftmost corner of the wall and one window in the wall. The heater is controlled by a thermostat about 2 feet from the window.

(a) Where is the window?

---

[8] ERCD Report 1001, Environmental Research and Consultancy Department, CAA report March 2010.

(b) When is the window open?

(c) When is the heat on?

(d) Draw graphs of the temperature along the wall of the room at 6 am, at 11 am, at 3 pm (15 hours) and at 5 pm (17 hours).

(e) Draw a graph of the temperature as a function of time at the heater, at the window and midway between them.

(f) The temperature at the window at 5 pm (17 hours) is less than at 11 am. Why do you think this might be?

(g) To what temperature do you think the thermostat is set? How do you know?

(h) Where is the thermostat?

Figure 12.97:

3. Light in a Wave-guide

Figure 12.98 shows the contours of light intensity as a function of location and time in a microscopic wave-guide.

time (nanoseconds)

distance from center
of wave-guide (microns)

Figure 12.98

(a) Draw graphs showing intensity as a function of location at times 0, 2, 4, 6, 8, and 10 nanoseconds.

(b) If you could create an animation showing how the graph of intensity as a function of location varies as time passes, what would it look like?

(c) Draw a graph of intensity as a function of time at locations −5, 0, and 5 microns from center of wave-guide.

(d) Describe what the light beams are doing in this wave-guide.

Chapter Thirteen

A FUNDAMENTAL TOOL: VECTORS

Contents

13.1 DISPLACEMENT VECTORS

Suppose you are a pilot planning a flight from Dallas to Pittsburgh. There are two things you must know: the distance to be traveled (so you have enough fuel to make it) and in what direction to go (so you don't miss Pittsburgh). Both these quantities together specify the displacement or *displacement vector* between the two cities.

> The **displacement vector** from one point to another is an arrow with its tail at the first point and its tip at the second. The **magnitude** (or length) of the displacement vector is the distance between the points and is represented by the length of the arrow. The **direction** of the displacement vector is the direction of the arrow.

Figure 13.1 shows a map with the displacement vectors from Dallas to Pittsburgh, from Albuquerque to Oshkosh, and from Los Angeles to Buffalo, SD. These displacement vectors have the same length and the same direction. We say that the displacement vectors between the corresponding cities are the same, even though they do not coincide. In other words

> Displacement vectors which point in the same direction and have the same magnitude are considered to be the same, even if they do not coincide.

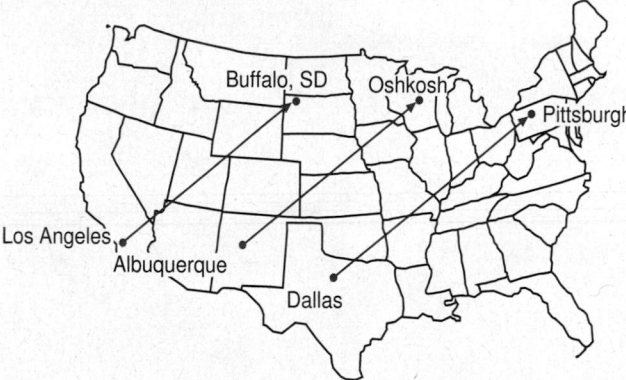

Figure 13.1: Displacement vectors between cities

Notation and Terminology

The displacement vector is our first example of a vector. Vectors have both magnitude and direction; in comparison, a quantity specified only by a number, but no direction, is called a *scalar*.[1] For instance, the time taken by the flight from Dallas to Pittsburgh is a scalar quantity. Displacement is a vector since it requires both distance and direction to specify it.

In this book, vectors are written with an arrow over them, $\vec{v}$, to distinguish them from scalars. Other books use a bold **v** to denote a vector. We use the notation $\overrightarrow{PQ}$ to denote the displacement vector from a point P to a point Q. The magnitude, or length, of a vector $\vec{v}$ is written $\|\vec{v}\|$.

Addition and Subtraction of Displacement Vectors

Suppose NASA commands a robot on Mars to move 75 meters in one direction and then 50 meters in another direction. (See Figure 13.2.) Where does the robot end up? Suppose the displacements are represented by the vectors $\vec{v}$ and $\vec{w}$, respectively. Then the sum $\vec{v} + \vec{w}$ gives the final position.

---

[1] So named by W. R. Hamilton because they are merely numbers on the *scale* from $-\infty$ to ∞.

The **sum**, $\vec{v} + \vec{w}$, of two vectors $\vec{v}$ and $\vec{w}$ is the combined displacement resulting from first applying $\vec{v}$ and then $\vec{w}$. (See Figure 13.3.) The sum $\vec{w} + \vec{v}$ gives the same displacement.

Figure 13.2: Sum of displacements of robots on Mars   **Figure 13.3**: The sum $\vec{v} + \vec{w} = \vec{w} + \vec{v}$

Suppose two different robots start from the same location. One moves along a displacement vector $\vec{v}$ and the second along a displacement vector $\vec{w}$. What is the displacement vector, $\vec{x}$, from the first robot to the second? (See Figure 13.4.) Since $\vec{v} + \vec{x} = \vec{w}$, we define $\vec{x}$ to be the difference $\vec{x} = \vec{w} - \vec{v}$. In other words, $\vec{w} - \vec{v}$ gets you from the first robot to the second.

The **difference**, $\vec{w} - \vec{v}$, is the displacement vector that, when added to $\vec{v}$, gives $\vec{w}$. That is, $\vec{w} = \vec{v} + (\vec{w} - \vec{v})$. (See Figure 13.4.)

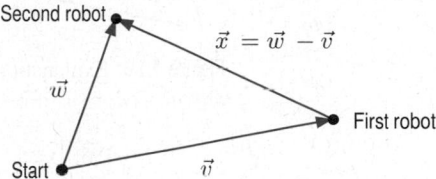

Figure 13.4: The difference $\vec{w} - \vec{v}$

If the robot ends up where it started, then its total displacement vector is the *zero vector*, $\vec{0}$. The zero vector has no direction.

The **zero vector**, $\vec{0}$, is a displacement vector with zero length.

Scalar Multiplication of Displacement Vectors

If $\vec{v}$ represents a displacement vector, the vector $2\vec{v}$ represents a displacement of twice the magnitude in the same direction as $\vec{v}$. Similarly, $-2\vec{v}$ represents a displacement of twice the magnitude in the opposite direction. (See Figure 13.5.)

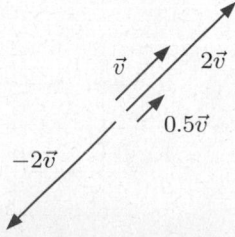

Figure 13.5: Scalar multiples of the vector $\vec{v}$

> If λ is a scalar and $\vec{v}$ is a displacement vector, the **scalar multiple of $\vec{v}$ by** λ, written $\lambda\vec{v}$, is the displacement vector with the following properties:
> - The displacement vector $\lambda\vec{v}$ is parallel to $\vec{v}$, pointing in the same direction if $\lambda > 0$ and in the opposite direction if $\lambda < 0$.
> - The magnitude of $\lambda\vec{v}$ is $|\lambda|$ times the magnitude of $\vec{v}$, that is, $\|\lambda\vec{v}\| = |\lambda|\,\|\vec{v}\|$.

Note that $|\lambda|$ represents the absolute value of the scalar λ while $\|\lambda\vec{v}\|$ represents the magnitude of the vector $\lambda\vec{v}$.

Example 1   Explain why $\vec{w} - \vec{v} = \vec{w} + (-1)\vec{v}$.

Solution   The vector $(-1)\vec{v}$ has the same magnitude as $\vec{v}$, but points in the opposite direction. Figure 13.6 shows that the combined displacement $\vec{w} + (-1)\vec{v}$ is the same as the displacement $\vec{w} - \vec{v}$.

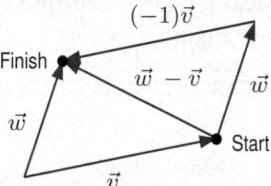

Figure 13.6: Explanation for why $\vec{w} - \vec{v} = \vec{w} + (-1)\vec{v}$

Parallel Vectors

Two vectors $\vec{v}$ and $\vec{w}$ are *parallel* if one is a scalar multiple of the other, that is, if $\vec{w} = \lambda\vec{v}$, for some scalar λ.

Components of Displacement Vectors: The Vectors $\vec{i}$, $\vec{j}$, and $\vec{k}$

Suppose that you live in a city with equally spaced streets running east-west and north-south and that you want to tell someone how to get from one place to another. You'd be likely to tell them how many blocks east-west and how many blocks north-south to go. For example, to get from P to Q in Figure 13.7, we go 4 blocks east and 1 block south. If $\vec{i}$ and $\vec{j}$ are as shown in Figure 13.7, then the displacement vector from P to Q is $4\vec{i} - \vec{j}$.

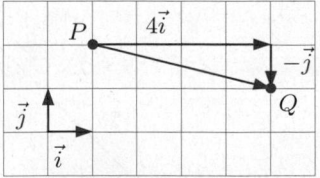

Figure 13.7: The displacement vector from P to Q is $4\vec{i} - \vec{j}$

We extend the same idea to 3 dimensions. First we choose a Cartesian system of coordinate axes. The three vectors of length 1 shown in Figure 13.8 are the vector $\vec{i}$, which points along the positive x-axis, the vector $\vec{j}$, along the positive y-axis, and the vector $\vec{k}$, along the positive z-axis.

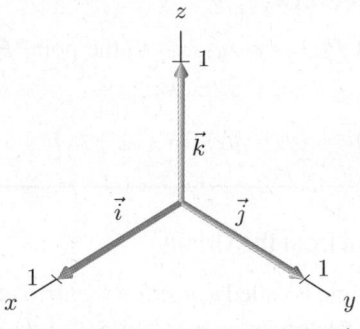

Figure 13.8: The vectors $\vec{i}$, $\vec{j}$ and $\vec{k}$ in 3-space

Figure 13.9: We resolve $\vec{v}$ into components by writing $\vec{v} = 3\vec{i} + 2\vec{j}$

Writing Displacement Vectors Using $\vec{i}$, $\vec{j}$, $\vec{k}$

Any displacement in 3-space or the plane can be expressed as a combination of displacements in the coordinate directions. For example, Figure 13.9 shows that the displacement vector $\vec{v}$ from the origin to the point $(3, 2)$ can be written as a sum of displacement vectors along the x- and y-axes:

$$\vec{v} = 3\vec{i} + 2\vec{j}.$$

This is called *resolving $\vec{v}$ into components*. In general:

> We **resolve** $\vec{v}$ into components by writing $\vec{v}$ in the form
>
> $$\vec{v} = v_1\vec{i} + v_2\vec{j} + v_3\vec{k},$$
>
> where v_1, v_2, v_3 are scalars. We call $v_1\vec{i}$, $v_2\vec{j}$, and $v_3\vec{k}$ the **components** of $\vec{v}$.

An Alternative Notation for Vectors

Many people write a vector in three dimensions as a string of three numbers, that is, as

$$\vec{v} = (v_1, v_2, v_3) \quad \text{instead of} \quad \vec{v} = v_1\vec{i} + v_2\vec{j} + v_3\vec{k}.$$

Since the first notation can be confused with a point and the second cannot, we usually use the second form.

Example 2   Resolve the displacement vector, $\vec{v}$, from the point $P_1 = (2, 4, 10)$ to the point $P_2 = (3, 7, 6)$ into components.

Solution   To get from P_1 to P_2, we move 1 unit in the positive x-direction, 3 units in the positive y-direction, and 4 units in the negative z-direction. Hence $\vec{v} = \vec{i} + 3\vec{j} - 4\vec{k}$.

Example 3   Decide whether the vector $\vec{v} = 2\vec{i} + 3\vec{j} + 5\vec{k}$ is parallel to each of the following vectors:

$$\vec{w} = 4\vec{i} + 6\vec{j} + 10\vec{k}, \quad \vec{a} = -\vec{i} - 1.5\vec{j} - 2.5\vec{k}, \quad \vec{b} = 4\vec{i} + 6\vec{j} + 9\vec{k}.$$

Solution   Since $\vec{w} = 2\vec{v}$ and $\vec{a} = -0.5\vec{v}$, the vectors $\vec{v}$, $\vec{w}$, and $\vec{a}$ are parallel. However, $\vec{b}$ is not a multiple of $\vec{v}$ (since, for example, $4/2 \neq 9/5$), so $\vec{v}$ and $\vec{b}$ are not parallel.

In general, Figure 13.10 shows us how to express the displacement vector between two points in components:

Components of Displacement Vectors

The displacement vector from the point $P_1 = (x_1, y_1, z_1)$ to the point $P_2 = (x_2, y_2, z_2)$ is given in components by

$$\overrightarrow{P_1P_2} = (x_2 - x_1)\vec{i} + (y_2 - y_1)\vec{j} + (z_2 - z_1)\vec{k}.$$

Position Vectors: Displacement of a Point from the Origin

A displacement vector whose tail is at the origin is called a *position vector*. Thus, any point (x_0, y_0, z_0) in space has associated with it the position vector $\vec{r}_0 = x_0\vec{i} + y_0\vec{j} + z_0\vec{k}$. (See Figure 13.11.) In general, a position vector gives the displacement of a point from the origin.

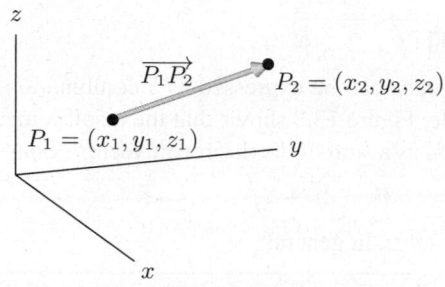

Figure 13.10: The displacement vector
$\overrightarrow{P_1P_2} = (x_2 - x_1)\vec{i} + (y_2 - y_1)\vec{j} + (z_2 - z_1)\vec{k}$

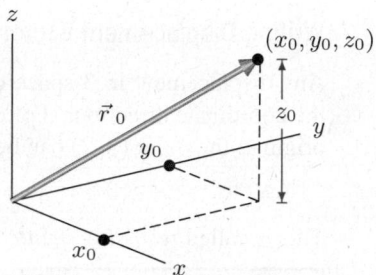

Figure 13.11: The position vector
$\vec{r}_0 = x_0\vec{i} + y_0\vec{j} + z_0\vec{k}$

The Components of the Zero Vector

The zero displacement vector has magnitude equal to zero and is written $\vec{0}$. So $\vec{0} = 0\vec{i} + 0\vec{j} + 0\vec{k}$.

The Magnitude of a Vector in Components

For a vector, $\vec{v} = v_1\vec{i} + v_2\vec{j}$, the Pythagorean theorem is used to find its magnitude, $\|\vec{v}\|$. (See Figure 13.12.) The angle θ gives the direction of $\vec{v}$.

Figure 13.12: Magnitude, $\|\vec{v}\|$, of a 2-dimensional vector, $\vec{v}$

In three dimensions, for a vector $\vec{v} = v_1\vec{i} + v_2\vec{j} + v_3\vec{k}$, we have

---

Magnitude of $\vec{v}$ $= \|\vec{v}\| = $ Length of the arrow $= \sqrt{v_1^2 + v_2^2 + v_3^2}$.

For instance, if $\vec{v} = 3\vec{i} - 4\vec{j} + 5\vec{k}$, then $\|\vec{v}\| = \sqrt{3^2 + (-4)^2 + 5^2} = \sqrt{50}$.

Addition and Scalar Multiplication of Vectors in Components

Suppose the vectors $\vec{v}$ and $\vec{w}$ are given in components:

$$\vec{v} = v_1\vec{i} + v_2\vec{j} + v_3\vec{k} \quad \text{and} \quad \vec{w} = w_1\vec{i} + w_2\vec{j} + w_3\vec{k}.$$

Then

$$\vec{v} + \vec{w} = (v_1 + w_1)\vec{i} + (v_2 + w_2)\vec{j} + (v_3 + w_3)\vec{k},$$

and

$$\lambda\vec{v} = \lambda v_1\vec{i} + \lambda v_2\vec{j} + \lambda v_3\vec{k}.$$

Figures 13.13 and 13.14 illustrate these properties in two dimensions. Finally, $\vec{v} - \vec{w} = \vec{v} + (-1)\vec{w}$, so we can write $\vec{v} - \vec{w} = (v_1 - w_1)\vec{i} + (v_2 - w_2)\vec{j} + (v_3 - w_3)\vec{k}$.

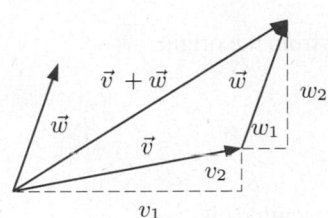

Figure 13.13: Sum $\vec{v} + \vec{w}$ in components

Figure 13.14: Scalar multiples of vectors showing $\vec{v}$, $2\vec{v}$, and $-3\vec{v}$

How to Resolve a Vector into Components

You may wonder how we find the components of a 2-dimensional vector, given its length and direction. Suppose the vector $\vec{v}$ has length v and makes an angle of θ with the x-axis, measured counterclockwise, as in Figure 13.15. If $\vec{v} = v_1\vec{i} + v_2\vec{j}$, Figure 13.15 shows that

$$v_1 = v\cos\theta \quad \text{and} \quad v_2 = v\sin\theta.$$

Thus, we resolve $\vec{v}$ into components by writing

$$\vec{v} = (v\cos\theta)\vec{i} + (v\sin\theta)\vec{j}.$$

Vectors in 3-space are resolved using direction cosines; see Problem 58 on page 754.

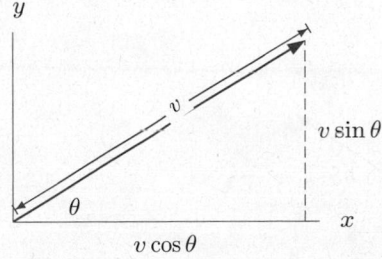

Figure 13.15: Resolving a vector: $\vec{v} = (v\cos\theta)\vec{i} + (v\sin\theta)\vec{j}$

Example 4   Resolve $\vec{v}$ into components if $\|\vec{v}\| = 2$ and $\theta = \pi/6$.

Solution   We have $\vec{v} = 2\cos(\pi/6)\vec{i} + 2\sin(\pi/6)\vec{j} = 2(\sqrt{3}/2)\vec{i} + 2(1/2)\vec{j} = \sqrt{3}\vec{i} + \vec{j}$.

Unit Vectors

A *unit vector* is a vector whose magnitude is 1. The vectors $\vec{i}$, $\vec{j}$, and $\vec{k}$ are unit vectors in the directions of the coordinate axes. It is often helpful to find a unit vector in the same direction as a given vector $\vec{v}$. Suppose that $\|\vec{v}\| = 10$; a unit vector in the same direction as $\vec{v}$ is $\vec{v}/10$. In general, a unit vector in the direction of any nonzero vector $\vec{v}$ is

$$\vec{u} = \frac{\vec{v}}{\|\vec{v}\|}.$$

Example 5   Find a unit vector, $\vec{u}$, in the direction of the vector $\vec{v} = \vec{i} + 3\vec{j}$.

Solution   If $\vec{v} = \vec{i} + 3\vec{j}$, then $\|\vec{v}\| = \sqrt{1^2 + 3^2} = \sqrt{10}$. Thus, a unit vector in the same direction is given by

$$\vec{u} = \frac{\vec{v}}{\sqrt{10}} = \frac{1}{\sqrt{10}}(\vec{i} + 3\vec{j}) = \frac{1}{\sqrt{10}}\vec{i} + \frac{3}{\sqrt{10}}\vec{j} \approx 0.32\vec{i} + 0.95\vec{j}.$$

Example 6   Find a unit vector at the point (x, y, z) that points radially outward away from the origin.

Solution   The vector from the origin to (x, y, z) is the position vector

$$\vec{r} = x\vec{i} + y\vec{j} + z\vec{k}.$$

Thus, if we put its tail at (x, y, z) it will point away from the origin. Its magnitude is

$$\|\vec{r}\| = \sqrt{x^2 + y^2 + z^2},$$

so a unit vector pointing in the same direction is

$$\frac{\vec{r}}{\|\vec{r}\|} = \frac{x\vec{i} + y\vec{j} + z\vec{k}}{\sqrt{x^2 + y^2 + z^2}} = \frac{x}{\sqrt{x^2 + y^2 + z^2}}\vec{i} + \frac{y}{\sqrt{x^2 + y^2 + z^2}}\vec{j} + \frac{z}{\sqrt{x^2 + y^2 + z^2}}\vec{k}.$$

Exercises and Problems for Section 13.1

Exercises

In Exercises 1–6, resolve the vectors into components.

1.

2.

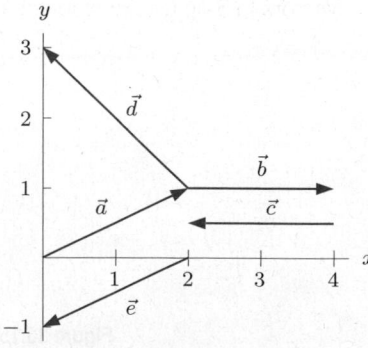

3. A vector starting at the point $Q = (4, 6)$ and ending at the point $P = (1, 2)$.

4. A vector starting at the point $P = (1, 2)$ and ending at the point $Q = (4, 6)$.

5.

6.

17. $\vec{v} = \vec{i} - \vec{j} + 3\vec{k}$

18. $\vec{v} = 7.2\vec{i} - 1.5\vec{j} + 2.1\vec{k}$

19. $\vec{v} = 1.2\vec{i} - 3.6\vec{j} + 4.1\vec{k}$

For Exercises 20–25, perform the indicated operations on the following vectors:

$$\vec{a} = 2\vec{j} + \vec{k}, \quad \vec{b} = -3\vec{i} + 5\vec{j} + 4\vec{k}, \quad \vec{c} = \vec{i} + 6\vec{j},$$

$$\vec{x} = -2\vec{i} + 9\vec{j}, \quad \vec{y} = 4\vec{i} - 7\vec{j}, \quad \vec{z} = \vec{i} - 3\vec{j} - \vec{k}.$$

For Exercises 7–14, perform the indicated computation.

7. $(4\vec{i} + 2\vec{j}) - (3\vec{i} - \vec{j})$

8. $(\vec{i} + 2\vec{j}) + (-3)(2\vec{i} + \vec{j})$

9. $-4(\vec{i} - 2\vec{j}) - 0.5(\vec{i} - \vec{k})$

10. $2(0.45\vec{i} - 0.9\vec{j} - 0.01\vec{k}) - 0.5(1.2\vec{i} - 0.1\vec{k})$

11. $(3\vec{i} - 4\vec{j} + 2\vec{k}) - (6\vec{i} + 8\vec{j} - \vec{k})$

12. $(4\vec{i} - 3\vec{j} + 7\vec{k}) - 2(5\vec{i} + \vec{j} - 2\vec{k})$

13. $(0.6\vec{i} + 0.2\vec{j} - \vec{k}) + (0.3\vec{i} + 0.3\vec{k})$

14. $\frac{1}{2}(2\vec{i} - \vec{j} + 3\vec{k}) + 3(\vec{i} - \frac{1}{6}\vec{j} + \frac{1}{2}\vec{k})$

In Exercises 15–19, find the length of the vectors.

15. $\vec{v} = \vec{i} - \vec{j} + 2\vec{k}$ **16.** $\vec{z} = \vec{i} - 3\vec{j} - \vec{k}$

20. $4\vec{z}$ **21.** $5\vec{a} + 2\vec{b}$ **22.** $\vec{a} + \vec{z}$

23. $2\vec{c} + \vec{x}$ **24.** $2\vec{a} + 7\vec{b} - 5\vec{z}$ **25.** $\|\vec{y} - \vec{x}\|$

26. (a) Draw the position vector for $\vec{v} = 5\vec{i} - 7\vec{j}$.
   (b) What is $\|\vec{v}\|$?
   (c) Find the angle between $\vec{v}$ and the positive x-axis.

27. Find the unit vector in the direction of $0.06\vec{i} - 0.08\vec{k}$.

28. Find the unit vector in the opposite direction to $\vec{i} - \vec{j} + \vec{k}$.

29. Find a unit vector in the opposite direction to $2\vec{i} - \vec{j} - \sqrt{11}\vec{k}$.

30. Find a vector with length 2 that points in the same direction as $\vec{i} - \vec{j} + 2\vec{k}$.

Problems

31. Find the value(s) of a making $\vec{v} = 5a\vec{i} - 3\vec{j}$ parallel to $\vec{w} = a^2\vec{i} + 6\vec{j}$.

32. (a) Find a unit vector from the point $P = (1, 2)$ and toward the point $Q = (4, 6)$.
   (b) Find a vector of length 10 pointing in the same direction.

33. If north is the direction of the positive y-axis and east is the direction of the positive x-axis, give the unit vector pointing northwest.

34. Resolve the following vectors into components:

   (a) The vector in 2-space of length 2 pointing up and to the right at an angle of $\pi/4$ with the x-axis.
   (b) The vector in 3-space of length 1 lying in the xz-plane pointing upward at an angle of $\pi/6$ with the positive x-axis.

35. (a) From Figure 13.16, read off the coordinates of the five points, A, B, C, D, E, and thus resolve into components the following two vectors:
   $\vec{u} = (2.5)\overrightarrow{AB} + (-0.8)\overrightarrow{CD}, \quad \vec{v} = (2.5)\overrightarrow{BA} - (-0.8)\overrightarrow{CD}$
   (b) What is the relation between $\vec{u}$ and $\vec{v}$? Why was this to be expected?

Figure 13.16

36. Find the components of a vector $\vec{p}$ that has the same direction as $\overrightarrow{EA}$ in Figure 13.16 and whose length equals two units.

37. For each of the four statements below, answer the following questions: Does the statement make sense? If yes, is it true for all possible choices of $\vec{a}$ and $\vec{b}$? If no, why not?

   (a) $\vec{a} + \vec{b} = \vec{b} + \vec{a}$
   (b) $\vec{a} + \|\vec{b}\| = \|\vec{a} + \vec{b}\|$
   (c) $\|\vec{b} + \vec{a}\| = \|\vec{a} + \vec{b}\|$
   (d) $\|\vec{a} + \vec{b}\| = \|\vec{a}\| + \|\vec{b}\|$.

38. Two adjacent sides of a regular hexagon are given as the vectors $\vec{u}$ and $\vec{v}$ in Figure 13.17. Label the remaining sides in terms of $\vec{u}$ and $\vec{v}$.

Figure 13.17

39. For what values of t are the following pairs of vectors parallel?

(a) $2\vec{i} + (t^2 + \frac{2}{3}t + 1)\vec{j} + t\vec{k}, \qquad 6\vec{i} + 8\vec{j} + 3\vec{k}$

(b) $t\vec{i} + \vec{j} + (t-1)\vec{k}, \qquad 2\vec{i} - 4\vec{j} + \vec{k}$

(c) $2t\vec{i} + t\vec{j} + t\vec{k}, \qquad 6\vec{i} + 3\vec{j} + 3\vec{k}.$

40. Find all vectors $\vec{v}$ in 2 dimensions having $\|\vec{v}\| = 5$ such that the $\vec{i}$-component of $\vec{v}$ is $3\vec{i}$.

41. Find all vectors $\vec{v}$ in the plane such that $\|\vec{v}\| = 1$ and $\|\vec{v} + \vec{i}\| = 1$.

42. Figure 13.18 shows a molecule with four atoms at O, A, B and C. Check that every atom in the molecule is 2 units away from every other atom.

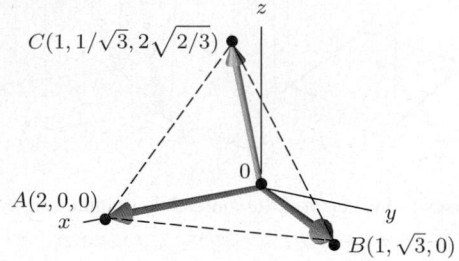

Figure 13.18

43. Show that the medians of a triangle intersect at a point $\frac{1}{3}$ of the way along each median from the side it bisects.

Strengthen Your Understanding

In Problems 44–47, explain what is wrong with the statement.

44. If $\|\vec{u}\| = 1$ and $\|\vec{v}\| > 0$, then $\|\vec{u} + \vec{v}\| \geq 1$.

45. The vector $c\vec{u}$ has the same direction as $\vec{u}$.

46. $\|\vec{v} - \vec{u}\|$ is the length of the shorter of the two diagonals of the parallelogram determined by $\vec{u}$ and $\vec{v}$.

47. Given three vectors $\vec{u}, \vec{v},$ and $\vec{w}$, if $\vec{u} + \vec{w} = \vec{u}$ then it is possible for $\vec{v} + \vec{w} \neq \vec{v}$.

In Problems 48–50, give an example of:

48. A vector $\vec{v}$ of length 2 with a positive $\vec{k}$-component and lying on a plane parallel to the yz-plane.

49. Two unit vectors $\vec{u}$ and $\vec{v}$ for which $\vec{v} - \vec{u}$ is also a unit vector.

50. Two vectors $\vec{u}$ and $\vec{v}$ that have difference vector $\vec{w} = 2\vec{i} + 3\vec{j}$.

Are the statements in Problems 51–60 true or false? Give reasons for your answer.

51. There is exactly one unit vector parallel to a given nonzero vector $\vec{v}$.

52. The vector $\frac{1}{\sqrt{3}}\vec{i} + \frac{-1}{\sqrt{3}}\vec{j} + \frac{2}{\sqrt{3}}\vec{k}$ is a unit vector.

53. The length of the vector $2\vec{v}$ is twice the length of the vector $\vec{v}$.

54. If $\vec{v}$ and $\vec{w}$ are any two vectors, then $\|\vec{v} + \vec{w}\| = \|\vec{v}\| + \|\vec{w}\|$.

55. If $\vec{v}$ and $\vec{w}$ are any two vectors, then $\|\vec{v} - \vec{w}\| = \|\vec{v}\| - \|\vec{w}\|$.

56. The vectors $2\vec{i} - \vec{j} + \vec{k}$ and $\vec{i} - 2\vec{j} + \vec{k}$ are parallel.

57. The vector $\vec{u} + \vec{v}$ is always larger in magnitude than both $\vec{u}$ and $\vec{v}$.

58. For any scalar c and vector $\vec{v}$ we have $\|c\vec{v}\| = c\|\vec{v}\|$.

59. The displacement vector from $(1, 1, 1)$ to $(1, 2, 3)$ is $-\vec{j} - 2\vec{k}$.

60. The displacement vector from (a, b) to (c, d) is the same as the displacement vector from (c, d) to (a, b).

13.2   VECTORS IN GENERAL

Besides displacement, there are many quantities that have both magnitude and direction and are added and multiplied by scalars in the same way as displacements. Any such quantity is called a *vector* and is represented by an arrow in the same manner we represent displacements. The length of the arrow is the *magnitude* of the vector, and the direction of the arrow is the direction of the vector.

Velocity Versus Speed

The speed of a moving body tells us how fast it is moving, say 80 km/hr. The speed is just a number; it is therefore a scalar. The velocity, on the other hand, tells us both how fast the body is moving and the direction of motion; it is a vector. For instance, if a car is heading northeast at 80 km/hr, then its velocity is a vector of length 80 pointing northeast.

> The **velocity vector** of a moving object is a vector whose magnitude is the speed of the object and whose direction is the direction of its motion.

The velocity vector is the displacement vector if the object moves at constant velocity for one unit of time.

Example 1   A car is traveling north at a speed of 100 km/hr, while a plane above is flying horizontally southwest at a speed of 500 km/hr. Draw the velocity vectors of the car and the plane.

Solution   Figure 13.19 shows the velocity vectors. The plane's velocity vector is five times as long as the car's, because its speed is five times as great.

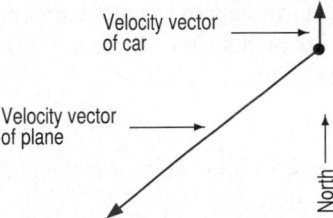

Figure 13.19: Velocity vector of the car is 100 km/hr north and of the plane is 500 km/hr southwest

The next example illustrates that the velocity vectors for two motions add to give the velocity vector for the combined motion, just as displacements do.

Example 2   A riverboat is moving with velocity $\vec{v}$ and a speed of 8 km/hr relative to the water. In addition, the river has a current $\vec{c}$ and a speed of 1 km/hr. (See Figure 13.20.) What is the physical significance of the vector $\vec{v} + \vec{c}$?

Figure 13.20: Boat's velocity relative to the river bed is the sum, $\vec{v} + \vec{c}$

Solution   The vector $\vec{v}$ shows how the boat is moving relative to the water, while $\vec{c}$ shows how the water is moving relative to the riverbed. During an hour, imagine that the boat first moves 8 km relative to the water, which remains still; this displacement is represented by $\vec{v}$. Then imagine the water moving 1 km while the boat remains stationary relative to the water; this displacement is represented by $\vec{c}$. The combined displacement is represented by $\vec{v} + \vec{c}$. Thus, the vector $\vec{v} + \vec{c}$ is the velocity of the boat relative to the riverbed.

Note that the effective speed of the boat is not necessarily 9 km/hr unless the boat is moving in the direction of the current. Although we add the velocity vectors, we do not necessarily add their lengths.

Scalar multiplication also makes sense for velocity vectors. For example, if $\vec{v}$ is a velocity vector, then $-2\vec{v}$ represents a velocity of twice the magnitude in the opposite direction.

Example 3   A ball is moving with velocity $\vec{v}$ when it hits a wall at a right angle and bounces straight back, with its speed reduced by 20%. Express its new velocity in terms of the old one.

Solution   The new velocity is $-0.8\vec{v}$, where the negative sign expresses the fact that the new velocity is in the direction opposite to the old.

We can represent velocity vectors in components in the same way we did on page 723.

Example 4   Represent the velocity vectors of the car and the plane in Example 1 using components. Take north to be the positive y-axis, east to be the positive x-axis, and upward to be the positive z-axis.

Solution   The car is traveling north at 100 km/hr, so the y-component of its velocity is $100\vec{j}$ and the x-component is $0\vec{i}$. Since it is traveling horizontally, the z-component is $0\vec{k}$. So we have

$$\text{Velocity of car} = 0\vec{i} + 100\vec{j} + 0\vec{k} = 100\vec{j}.$$

The plane's velocity vector also has $\vec{k}$ component equal to zero. Since it is traveling southwest, its $\vec{i}$ and $\vec{j}$ components have negative coefficients (north and east are positive). Since the plane is traveling at 500 km/hr, in one hour it is displaced $500/\sqrt{2} \approx 354$ km to the west and 354 km to the south. (See Figure 13.21.) Thus,

$$\text{Velocity of plane} = -(500\cos 45°)\vec{i} - (500\sin 45°)\vec{j} \approx -354\vec{i} - 354\vec{j}.$$

Of course, if the car were climbing a hill or if the plane were descending for a landing, then the $\vec{k}$ component would not be zero.

Figure 13.21: Distance traveled by the plane and car in one hour

Acceleration

Another example of a vector quantity is acceleration. Acceleration, like velocity, is specified by both a magnitude and a direction — for example, the acceleration due to gravity is 9.81 m/sec^2 vertically downward.

Force

Force is another example of a vector quantity. Suppose you push on an open door. The result depends both on how hard you push and in what direction. Thus, to specify a force we must give its magnitude (or strength) and the direction in which it is acting. For example, the gravitational force exerted on an object by the earth is a vector pointing from the object toward the center of the earth; its magnitude is the strength of the gravitational force.

Example 5   The earth travels around the sun in an ellipse. The gravitational force on the earth and the velocity of the earth are governed by the following laws:
Newton's Law of Gravitation: The gravitational attraction, $\vec{F}$, of a mass m_1 on a mass m_2 at a

distance r has magnitude $||\vec{F}|| = Gm_1m_2/r^2$, where G is a constant, and is directed from m_2 toward m_1.

Kepler's Second Law: The line joining a planet to the sun sweeps out equal areas in equal times.

(a) Sketch vectors representing the gravitational force of the sun on the earth at two different positions in the earth's orbit.

(b) Sketch the velocity vector of the earth at two points in its orbit.

Solution

(a) Figure 13.22 shows the earth orbiting the sun. Note that the gravitational force vector always points toward the sun and is larger when the earth is closer to the sun because of the r^2 term in the denominator. (In fact, the real orbit looks much more like a circle than we have shown here.)

(b) The velocity vector points in the direction of motion of the earth. Thus, the velocity vector is tangent to the ellipse. See Figure 13.23. Furthermore, the velocity vector is longer at points of the orbit where the planet is moving quickly, because the magnitude of the velocity vector is the speed. Kepler's Second Law enables us to determine when the earth is moving quickly and when it is moving slowly. Over a fixed period of time, say one month, the line joining the earth to the sun sweeps out a sector having a certain area. Figure 13.23 shows two sectors swept out in two different one-month time-intervals. Kepler's law says that the areas of the two sectors are the same. Thus, the earth must move farther in a month when it is close to the sun than when it is far from the sun. Therefore, the earth moves faster when it is closer to the sun and slower when it is farther away.

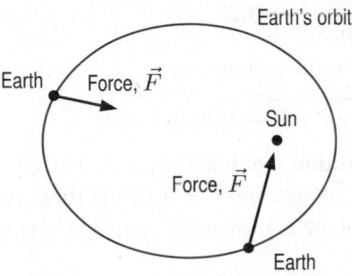

Figure 13.22: Gravitational force, $\vec{F}$, exerted by the sun on the earth: Greater magnitude closer to sun

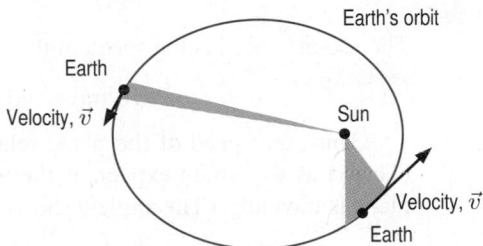

Figure 13.23: The velocity vector, $\vec{v}$, of the earth: Greater magnitude closer to the sun

Properties of Addition and Scalar Multiplication

In general, vectors add, subtract, and are multiplied by scalars in the same way as displacement vectors. Thus, for any vectors $\vec{u}$, $\vec{v}$, and $\vec{w}$ and any scalars α and β, we have the following properties:

Commutativity
1. $\vec{v} + \vec{w} = \vec{w} + \vec{v}$

Associativity
2. $(\vec{u} + \vec{v}) + \vec{w} = \vec{u} + (\vec{v} + \vec{w})$
3. $\alpha(\beta\vec{v}) = (\alpha\beta)\vec{v}$

Distributivity
4. $(\alpha + \beta)\vec{v} = \alpha\vec{v} + \beta\vec{v}$
5. $\alpha(\vec{v} + \vec{w}) = \alpha\vec{v} + \alpha\vec{w}$

Identity
6. $1\vec{v} = \vec{v}$
7. $0\vec{v} = \vec{0}$
8. $\vec{v} + \vec{0} = \vec{v}$
9. $\vec{w} + (-1)\vec{v} = \vec{w} - \vec{v}$

Problems 30–37 at the end of this section ask for a justification of these results in terms of displacement vectors.

Using Components

Example 6   A plane, heading due east at an airspeed of 600 km/hr, experiences a wind of 50 km/hr blowing toward the northeast. Find the plane's direction and ground speed.

Solution   We choose a coordinate system with the x-axis pointing east and the y-axis pointing north. See Figure 13.24.

The airspeed tells us the speed of the plane relative to still air. Thus, the plane is moving due east with velocity $\vec{v} = 600\vec{i}$ relative to still air. In addition, the air is moving with a velocity $\vec{w}$. Writing $\vec{w}$ in components, we have

$$\vec{w} = (50\cos 45°)\vec{i} + (50\sin 45°)\vec{j} = 35.4\vec{i} + 35.4\vec{j}.$$

The vector $\vec{v} + \vec{w}$ represents the displacement of the plane in one hour relative to the ground. Therefore, $\vec{v} + \vec{w}$ is the velocity of the plane relative to the ground. In components, we have

$$\vec{v} + \vec{w} = 600\vec{i} + \left(35.4\vec{i} + 35.4\vec{j}\right) = 635.4\vec{i} + 35.4\vec{j}.$$

The direction of the plane's motion relative to the ground is given by the angle θ in Figure 13.24, where

$$\tan \theta = \frac{35.4}{635.4}$$

so

$$\theta = \arctan\left(\frac{35.4}{635.4}\right) = 3.2°.$$

The ground speed is the speed of the plane relative to the ground, so

$$\text{Groundspeed} = \sqrt{635.4^2 + 35.4^2} = 636.4 \text{ km/hr}.$$

Thus, the speed of the plane relative to the ground has been increased slightly by the wind. (This is as we would expect, as the wind has a positive component in the direction in which the plane is traveling.) The angle θ shows how far the plane is blown off course by the wind.

Figure 13.24: Plane's velocity relative to the ground is the sum $\vec{v} + \vec{w}$

Vectors in n Dimensions

Using the alternative notation $\vec{v} = (v_1, v_2, v_3)$ for a vector in 3-space, we can define a vector in n dimensions as a string of n numbers. Thus, a vector in n dimensions can be written as

$$\vec{c} = (c_1, c_2, \ldots, c_n).$$

Addition and scalar multiplication are defined by the formulas

$$\vec{v} + \vec{w} = (v_1, v_2, \ldots, v_n) + (w_1, w_2, \ldots, w_n) = (v_1 + w_1, v_2 + w_2, \ldots, v_n + w_n)$$

and

$$\lambda\vec{v} = \lambda(v_1, v_2, \ldots, v_n) = (\lambda v_1, \lambda v_2, \ldots, \lambda v_n).$$

Why Do We Want Vectors in n Dimensions?

Vectors in two and three dimensions can be used to model displacement, velocities, or forces. But what about vectors in n dimensions? There is another interpretation of 3-dimensional vectors (or 3-vectors) that is useful: they can be thought of as listing three different quantities — for example, the displacements parallel to the x-, y-, and z-axes. Similarly, the n-vector

$$\vec{c} = (c_1, c_2, \ldots, c_n)$$

can be thought of as a way of keeping n different quantities organized. For example, a *population* vector $\vec{N}$ shows the number of children and adults in a population:

$$\vec{N} = (\text{Number of children}, \text{ Number of adults}),$$

or, if we are interested in a more detailed breakdown of ages, we might give the number in each ten-year age bracket in the population (up to age 110) in the form

$$\vec{N} = (N_1, N_2, N_3, N_4, \ldots, N_{10}, N_{11}),$$

where N_1 is the population aged 0–9, and N_2 is the population aged 10–19, and so on.

A *consumption* vector,

$$\vec{q} = (q_1, q_2, \ldots, q_n)$$

shows the quantities $q_1, q_2, \ldots, q_n$ consumed of each of n different goods. A *price* vector

$$\vec{p} = (p_1, p_2, \ldots, p_n)$$

contains the prices of n different items.

In 1907, Hermann Minkowski used vectors with four components when he introduced *space-time coordinates*, whereby each event is assigned a vector position $\vec{v}$ with four coordinates, three for its position in space and one for time:

$$\vec{v} = (x, y, z, t).$$

Example 7   Suppose the vector $\vec{I}$ represents the number of copies, in thousands, made by each of four copy centers in the month of December and $\vec{J}$ represents the number of copies made at the same four copy centers during the previous eleven months (the "year-to-date"). If $\vec{I} = (25, 211, 818, 642)$, and $\vec{J} = (331, 3227, 1377, 2570)$, compute $\vec{I} + \vec{J}$. What does this sum represent?

Solution   The sum is

$$\vec{I} + \vec{J} = (25 + 331, 211 + 3227, 818 + 1377, 642 + 2570) = (356, 3438, 2195, 3212).$$

Each term in $\vec{I} + \vec{J}$ represents the sum of the number of copies made in December plus those in the previous eleven months, that is, the total number of copies made during the entire year at that particular copy center.

Example 8   The price vector $\vec{p} = (p_1, p_2, p_3)$ represents the prices in dollars of three goods. Write a vector that gives the prices of the same goods in cents.

Solution   The prices in cents are $100p_1$, $100p_2$, and $100p_3$ respectively, so the new price vector is

$$(100p_1, 100p_2, 100p_3) = 100\vec{p}.$$

Exercises and Problems for Section 13.2

Exercises

In Exercises 1–5, say whether the given quantity is a vector or a scalar.

1. The population of the US.

2. The distance from Seattle to St. Louis.

3. The temperature at a point on the earth's surface.

4. The magnetic field at a point on the earth's surface.

5. The populations of each of the 50 states.

6. Give the components of the velocity vector for wind blowing at 10 km/hr toward the southeast. (Assume north is in the positive y-direction.)

7. Give the components of the velocity vector of a boat that is moving at 40 km/hr in a direction $20°$ south of west. (Assume north is in the positive y-direction.)

8. A car is traveling at a speed of 50 km/hr. The positive y-axis is north and the positive x-axis is east. Resolve the car's velocity vector (in 2-space) into components if the car is traveling in each of the following directions:

   (a) East   (b) South
   (c) Southeast   (d) Northwest.

9. Which is traveling faster, a car whose velocity vector is $21\vec{i} + 35\vec{j}$, or a car whose velocity vector is $40\vec{i}$, assuming that the units are the same for both directions?

10. What angle does a force of $\vec{F} = 15\vec{i} + 18\vec{j}$ make with the x-axis?

Problems

11. The velocity of the current in a river is $\vec{c} = 0.6\vec{i} + 0.8\vec{j}$ km/hr. A boat moves relative to the water with velocity $\vec{v} = 8\vec{i}$ km/hr.

    (a) What is the speed of the boat relative to the riverbed?
    (b) What angle does the velocity of the boat relative to the riverbed make with the vector $\vec{v}$? What does this angle tell us in practical terms?

12. Suppose the current in Problem 11 is twice as fast and in the opposite direction. What is the speed of the boat with respect to the riverbed?

13. A boat is heading due east at 25 km/hr (relative to the water). The current is moving toward the southwest at 10 km/hr.

    (a) Give the vector representing the actual movement of the boat.
    (b) How fast is the boat going, relative to the ground?
    (c) By what angle does the current push the boat off of its due east course?

14. A truck is traveling due north at 30 km/hr approaching a crossroad. On a perpendicular road a police car is traveling west toward the intersection at 40 km/hr. Both vehicles will reach the crossroad in exactly one hour. Find the vector currently representing the displacement of the truck with respect to the police car.

15. An airplane heads northeast at an airspeed of 700 km/hr, but there is a wind blowing from the west at 60 km/hr. In what direction does the plane end up flying? What is its speed relative to the ground?

16. Two forces, represented by the vectors $\vec{F}_1 = 8\vec{i} - 6\vec{j}$ and $\vec{F}_2 = 3\vec{i} + 2\vec{j}$, are acting on an object. Give a vector representing the force that must be applied to the object if it is to remain stationary.

17. An airplane is flying at an airspeed of 500 km/hr in a wind blowing at 60 km/hr toward the southeast. In what direction should the plane head to end up going due east? What is the airplane's speed relative to the ground?

18. An airplane is flying at an airspeed of 600 km/hr in a cross-wind that is blowing from the northeast at a speed of 50 km/hr. In what direction should the plane head to end up going due east?

19. The current in a river is pushing a boat in direction $25°$ north of east with a speed of 12 km/hr. The wind is pushing the same boat in a direction $80°$ south of east with a speed of 7 km/hr. Find the velocity vector of the boat's engine (relative to the water) if the boat actually moves due east at a speed of 40 km/hr relative to the ground.

20. A man wishes to row the shortest possible distance from north to south across a river that is flowing at 4 km/hr from the east. He can row at 5 km/hr.

    (a) In which direction should he steer?
    (b) If there is a wind of 10 km/hr from the southwest, in which direction should he steer to try and go directly across the river? What happens?

21. A large ship is being towed by two tugs. The larger tug exerts a force which is 25% greater than the smaller tug and at an angle of 30 degrees north of east. Which direction must the smaller tug pull to ensure that the ship travels due east?

22. An object P is pulled by a force $\vec{F}_1$ of magnitude 15 lb at an angle of 20 degrees north of east. In what direction must a force $\vec{F}_2$ of magnitude 20 lb pull to ensure that P moves due east?

23. An object is to be moved vertically upward by a crane. As the crane cannot get directly above the object, three ropes are attached to guide the object. One rope is pulled parallel to the ground with a force of 100 newtons in a direction $30°$ north of east. The second rope is pulled parallel to the ground with a force of 70 newtons in a direction $80°$ south of east. If the crane is attached to the

third rope and can pull with a total force of 3000 newtons, find the force vector for the crane. What is the resulting (total) force on the object? (Assume vector $\vec{i}$ points east, vector $\vec{j}$ points north, and vector $\vec{k}$ points vertically up.)

24. The earth is at the origin, the moon is at the point $(384, 0)$, and a spaceship is at $(280, 90)$, where distance is in thousands of kilometers.

   (a) What is the displacement vector of the moon relative to the earth? Of the spaceship relative to the earth? Of the spaceship relative to the moon?
   (b) How far is the spaceship from the earth? From the moon?
   (c) The gravitational force on the spaceship from the earth is 461 newtons and from the moon is 26 newtons. What is the resulting force?

25. A particle moving with speed v hits a barrier at an angle of $60°$ and bounces off at an angle of $60°$ in the opposite direction with speed reduced by 20 percent. See Figure 13.25. Find the velocity vector of the object after impact.

Figure 13.25

26. There are five students in a class. Their scores on the midterm (out of 100) are given by the vector $\vec{v} = (73, 80, 91, 65, 84)$. Their scores on the final (out of 100) are given by $\vec{w} = (82, 79, 88, 70, 92)$. If the final counts twice as much as the midterm, find a vector giving the total scores (as a percentage) of the students.

27. The price vector of beans, rice, and tofu is $(0.30, 0.20, 0.50)$ in dollars per pound. Express it in dollars per ounce.

28. An object is moving counterclockwise at a constant speed around the circle $x^2 + y^2 = 1$, where x and y are measured in meters. It completes one revolution every minute.

   (a) What is its speed?
   (b) What is its velocity vector 30 seconds after it passes the point $(1, 0)$? Does your answer change if the object is moving clockwise? Explain.

29. An object is attached by a string to a fixed point and rotates 30 times per minute in a horizontal plane. Show that the speed of the object is constant but the velocity is not. What does this imply about the acceleration?

In Problems 30–37, use the geometric definition of addition and scalar multiplication to explain each of the properties.

30. $\vec{w} + \vec{v} = \vec{v} + \vec{w}$

31. $(\alpha + \beta)\vec{v} = \alpha\vec{v} + \beta\vec{v}$

32. $\alpha(\vec{v} + \vec{w}) = \alpha\vec{v} + \alpha\vec{w}$

33. $\alpha(\beta\vec{v}) = (\alpha\beta)\vec{v}$

34. $\vec{v} + \vec{0} = \vec{v}$

35. $1\vec{v} = \vec{v}$

36. $\vec{v} + (-1)\vec{w} = \vec{v} - \vec{w}$

37. $(\vec{u} + \vec{v}) + \vec{w} = \vec{u} + (\vec{v} + \vec{w})$

38. In the game of laser tag, you shoot a harmless laser gun and try to hit a target worn at the waist by other players. Suppose you are standing at the origin of a three-dimensional coordinate system and that the xy-plane is the floor. Suppose that waist-high is 3 feet above floor level and that eye level is 5 feet above the floor. Three of your friends are your opponents. One is standing so that his target is 30 feet along the x-axis, another lying down so that his target is at the point $x = 20$, $y = 15$, and the third lying in ambush so that his target is at a point 8 feet above the point $x = 12$, $y = 30$.

   (a) If you aim with your gun at eye level, find the vector from your gun to each of the three targets.
   (b) If you shoot from waist height, with your gun one foot to the right of the center of your body as you face along the x-axis, find the vector from your gun to each of the three targets.

Strengthen Your Understanding

In Problems 39–40, explain what is wrong with the statement.

39. Two vectors in 3-space that have equal $\vec{k}$-components and the same magnitude must be the same vector.

40. A vector $\vec{v}$ in the plane whose $\vec{i}$-component is 0.5 has smaller magnitude than the vector $\vec{w} = 2\vec{i}$.

In Problems 41–42, give an example of:

41. A non-zero vector $\vec{F}$ on the plane that when combined with the force vector $\vec{G} = \vec{i} + \vec{j}$ results in a combined force vector $\vec{R}$ with a positive $\vec{i}$-component and a negative $\vec{j}$-component.

42. Non-zero vectors $\vec{u}$ and $\vec{v}$ such that $\|\vec{u} + \vec{v}\| = \|\vec{u}\| + \|\vec{v}\|$.

In Problems 43–48, is the quantity a vector? Give a reason for your answer.

43. Velocity   44. Speed   45. Force

46. Area   47. Acceleration   48. Volume

13.3 THE DOT PRODUCT

We have seen how to add vectors; can we multiply two vectors together? In the next two sections we will see two different ways of doing so: the *scalar product* (or *dot product*), which produces a scalar, and the *vector product* (or *cross product*), which produces a vector.

Definition of the Dot Product

The dot product links geometry and algebra. We already know how to calculate the length of a vector from its components; the dot product gives us a way of computing the angle between two vectors. For any two vectors $\vec{v} = v_1\vec{i} + v_2\vec{j} + v_3\vec{k}$ and $\vec{w} = w_1\vec{i} + w_2\vec{j} + w_3\vec{k}$, shown in Figure 13.26, we define a scalar as follows:

> The following two definitions of the **dot product**, or **scalar product**, $\vec{v} \cdot \vec{w}$, are equivalent:
> - **Geometric definition**
> $$\vec{v} \cdot \vec{w} = \|\vec{v}\|\|\vec{w}\| \cos\theta \qquad \text{where } \theta \text{ is the angle between } \vec{v} \text{ and } \vec{w} \text{ and } 0 \le \theta \le \pi.$$
> - **Algebraic definition**
> $$\vec{v} \cdot \vec{w} = v_1 w_1 + v_2 w_2 + v_3 w_3.$$
> Notice that the dot product of two vectors is a *number*, not a vector.

Why don't we give just one definition of $\vec{v} \cdot \vec{w}$? The reason is that both definitions are equally important; the geometric definition gives us a picture of what the dot product means and the algebraic definition gives us a way of calculating it.

How do we know the two definitions are equivalent—that is, they really do define the same thing? First, we observe that the two definitions give the same result in a particular example. Then we show why they are equivalent in general.

Figure 13.26: The vectors $\vec{v}$ and $\vec{w}$

Figure 13.27: Calculating the dot product of the vectors $v = \vec{i}$ and $\vec{w} = 2\vec{i} + 2\vec{j}$ geometrically and algebraically gives the same result

Example 1   Suppose $\vec{v} = \vec{i}$ and $\vec{w} = 2\vec{i} + 2\vec{j}$. Compute $\vec{v} \cdot \vec{w}$ both geometrically and algebraically.

Solution   To use the geometric definition, see Figure 13.27. The angle between the vectors is $\pi/4$, or $45°$, and the lengths of the vectors are given by

$$\|\vec{v}\| = 1 \quad \text{and} \quad \|\vec{w}\| = 2\sqrt{2}.$$

Thus,

$$\vec{v} \cdot \vec{w} = \|\vec{v}\|\|\vec{w}\| \cos\theta = 1 \cdot 2\sqrt{2} \cos\left(\frac{\pi}{4}\right) = 2.$$

Using the algebraic definition, we get the same result:

$$\vec{v} \cdot \vec{w} = 1 \cdot 2 + 0 \cdot 2 = 2.$$

Why the Two Definitions of the Dot Product Give the Same Result

In the previous example, the two definitions give the same value for the dot product. To show that the geometric and algebraic definitions of the dot product always give the same result, we must show that, for any vectors $\vec{v} = v_1\vec{i} + v_2\vec{j} + v_3\vec{k}$ and $\vec{w} = w_1\vec{i} + w_2\vec{j} + w_3\vec{k}$ with an angle θ between them:

$$\|\vec{v}\|\|\vec{w}\|\cos\theta = v_1w_1 + v_2w_2 + v_3w_3.$$

One method follows; a method that does not use trigonometry is given in Problem 69 on page 743.

Using the Law of Cosines. Suppose that $0 < \theta < \pi$, so that the vectors $\vec{v}$ and $\vec{w}$ form a triangle. (See Figure 13.28.) By the Law of Cosines, we have

$$\|\vec{v} - \vec{w}\|^2 = \|\vec{v}\|^2 + \|\vec{w}\|^2 - 2\|\vec{v}\|\|\vec{w}\|\cos\theta.$$

This result is also true for $\theta = 0$ and $\theta = \pi$. We calculate the lengths using components:

$$\|\vec{v}\|^2 = v_1^2 + v_2^2 + v_3^2$$
$$\|\vec{w}\|^2 = w_1^2 + w_2^2 + w_3^2$$
$$\|\vec{v} - \vec{w}\|^2 = (v_1 - w_1)^2 + (v_2 - w_2)^2 + (v_3 - w_3)^2$$
$$= v_1^2 - 2v_1w_1 + w_1^2 + v_2^2 - 2v_2w_2 + w_2^2 + v_3^2 - 2v_3w_3 + w_3^2.$$

Substituting into the Law of Cosines and canceling, we see that

$$-2v_1w_1 - 2v_2w_2 - 2v_3w_3 = -2\|\vec{v}\|\|\vec{w}\|\cos\theta.$$

Therefore we have the result we wanted, namely that:

$$v_1w_1 + v_2w_2 + v_3w_3 = \|\vec{v}\|\|\vec{w}\|\cos\theta.$$

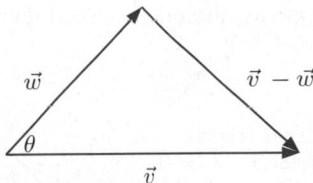

Figure 13.28: Triangle used in the justification of $\|\vec{v}\|\|\vec{w}\|\cos\theta = v_1w_1 + v_2w_2 + v_3w_3$

Properties of the Dot Product

The following properties of the dot product can be justified using the algebraic definition; see Problem 63 on page 742. For a geometric interpretation of Property 3, see Problem 66.

Properties of the Dot Product. For any vectors $\vec{u}$, $\vec{v}$, and $\vec{w}$ and any scalar λ,

1. $\vec{v} \cdot \vec{w} = \vec{w} \cdot \vec{v}$
2. $\vec{v} \cdot (\lambda\vec{w}) = \lambda(\vec{v} \cdot \vec{w}) = (\lambda\vec{v}) \cdot \vec{w}$
3. $(\vec{v} + \vec{w}) \cdot \vec{u} = \vec{v} \cdot \vec{u} + \vec{w} \cdot \vec{u}$

Perpendicularity, Magnitude, and Dot Products

Two vectors are perpendicular if the angle between them is $\pi/2$ or $90°$. Since $\cos(\pi/2) = 0$, if $\vec{v}$ and $\vec{w}$ are perpendicular, then $\vec{v} \cdot \vec{w} = 0$. Conversely, provided that $\vec{v} \cdot \vec{w} = 0$, then $\cos\theta = 0$, so $\theta = \pi/2$ and the vectors are perpendicular. Thus, we have the following result:

> Two non-zero vectors $\vec{v}$ and $\vec{w}$ are **perpendicular**, or **orthogonal**, if and only if
>
> $$\vec{v} \cdot \vec{w} = 0.$$

For example: $\vec{i} \cdot \vec{j} = 0, \vec{j} \cdot \vec{k} = 0, \vec{i} \cdot \vec{k} = 0.$

If we take the dot product of a vector with itself, then $\theta = 0$ and $\cos \theta = 1$. For any vector $\vec{v}$:

> Magnitude and dot product are related as follows:
>
> $$\vec{v} \cdot \vec{v} = \|\vec{v}\|^2.$$

For example: $\vec{i} \cdot \vec{i} = 1, \vec{j} \cdot \vec{j} = 1, \vec{k} \cdot \vec{k} = 1.$

Using the Dot Product

Depending on the situation, one definition of the dot product may be more convenient to use than the other. In Example 2, the geometric definition is the only one that can be used because we are not given components. In Example 3, the algebraic definition is used.

Example 2   Suppose the vector $\vec{b}$ is fixed and has length 2; the vector $\vec{a}$ is free to rotate and has length 3. What are the maximum and minimum values of the dot product $\vec{a} \cdot \vec{b}$ as the vector $\vec{a}$ rotates through all possible positions? What positions of $\vec{a}$ and $\vec{b}$ lead to these values?

Solution   The geometric definition gives $\vec{a} \cdot \vec{b} = \|\vec{a}\|\|\vec{b}\| \cos \theta = 3 \cdot 2 \cos \theta = 6 \cos \theta$. Thus, the maximum value of $\vec{a} \cdot \vec{b}$ is 6, and it occurs when $\cos \theta = 1$ so $\theta = 0$, that is, when $\vec{a}$ and $\vec{b}$ point in the same direction. The minimum value of $\vec{a} \cdot \vec{b}$ is -6, and it occurs when $\cos \theta = -1$ so $\theta = \pi$, that is, when $\vec{a}$ and $\vec{b}$ point in opposite directions. (See Figure 13.29.)

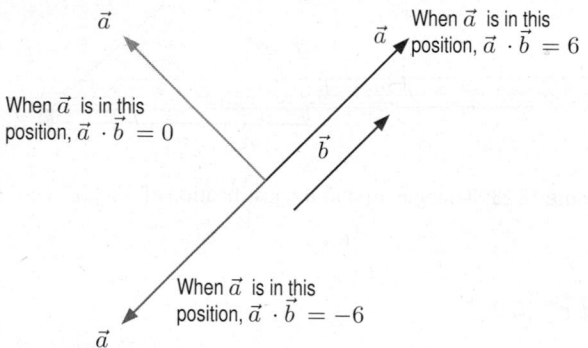

When $\vec{a}$ is in this position, $\vec{a} \cdot \vec{b} = 0$

When $\vec{a}$ is in this position, $\vec{a} \cdot \vec{b} = 6$

When $\vec{a}$ is in this position, $\vec{a} \cdot \vec{b} = -6$

Figure 13.29: Maximum and minimum values of $\vec{a} \cdot \vec{b}$ obtained from a fixed vector $\vec{b}$ of length 2 and rotating vector $\vec{a}$ of length 3

Example 3   Which pairs from the following list of 3-dimensional vectors are perpendicular to one another?

$$\vec{u} = \vec{i} + \sqrt{3}\,\vec{k}, \quad \vec{v} = \vec{i} + \sqrt{3}\,\vec{j}, \quad \vec{w} = \sqrt{3}\,\vec{i} + \vec{j} - \vec{k}.$$

Solution   The geometric definition tells us that two vectors are perpendicular if and only if their dot product is zero. Since the vectors are given in components, we calculate dot products using the algebraic definition:

$$\vec{v} \cdot \vec{u} = (\vec{i} + \sqrt{3}\,\vec{j} + 0\vec{k}) \cdot (\vec{i} + 0\vec{j} + \sqrt{3}\,\vec{k}) = 1 \cdot 1 + \sqrt{3} \cdot 0 + 0 \cdot \sqrt{3} = 1,$$
$$\vec{v} \cdot \vec{w} = (\vec{i} + \sqrt{3}\,\vec{j} + 0\vec{k}) \cdot (\sqrt{3}\,\vec{i} + \vec{j} - \vec{k}) = 1 \cdot \sqrt{3} + \sqrt{3} \cdot 1 + 0(-1) = 2\sqrt{3},$$
$$\vec{w} \cdot \vec{u} = (\sqrt{3}\,\vec{i} + \vec{j} - \vec{k}) \cdot (\vec{i} + 0\vec{j} + \sqrt{3}\,\vec{k}) = \sqrt{3} \cdot 1 + 1 \cdot 0 + (-1) \cdot \sqrt{3} = 0.$$

So the only two vectors that are perpendicular are $\vec{w}$ and $\vec{u}$.

Example 4   Compute the angle between the vectors $\vec{v}$ and $\vec{w}$ from Example 3.

Solution   We know that $\vec{v} \cdot \vec{w} = \|\vec{v}\| \|\vec{w}\| \cos\theta$, so $\cos\theta = \dfrac{\vec{v} \cdot \vec{w}}{\|\vec{v}\| \|\vec{w}\|}$. From Example 3, we know that $\vec{v} \cdot \vec{w} = 2\sqrt{3}$. This gives:

$$\cos\theta = \frac{2\sqrt{3}}{\|\vec{v}\| \|\vec{w}\|} = \frac{2\sqrt{3}}{\sqrt{1^2 + \left(\sqrt{3}\right)^2 + 0^2}\sqrt{\left(\sqrt{3}\right)^2 + 1^2 + (-1)^2}} = \frac{\sqrt{3}}{\sqrt{5}}$$

so $\theta = \arccos\left(\dfrac{\sqrt{3}}{\sqrt{5}}\right) = 39.2315°.$

Normal Vectors and the Equation of a Plane

In Section 12.4 we wrote the equation of a plane given its x-slope, y-slope and z-intercept. Now we write the equation of a plane using a vector $\vec{n}$ and a point P_0. The key idea is that all the displacement vectors from P_0 that are perpendicular to $\vec{n}$ form a plane. To picture this, imagine a pencil balanced on a table, with other pencils fanned out on the table in different directions. The upright pencil is $\vec{n}$, its base is P_0, the other pencils are perpendicular displacement vectors, and the table is the plane.

More formally, a *normal vector* to a plane is a vector that is perpendicular to the plane, that is, it is perpendicular to every displacement vector between any two points in the plane. Let $\vec{n} = a\vec{i} + b\vec{j} + c\vec{k}$ be a normal vector to the plane, let $P_0 = (x_0, y_0, z_0)$ be a fixed point in the plane, and let $P = (x, y, z)$ be any other point in the plane. Then $\overrightarrow{P_0P} = (x - x_0)\vec{i} + (y - y_0)\vec{j} + (z - z_0)\vec{k}$ is a vector whose head and tail both lie in the plane. (See Figure 13.30.) Thus, the vectors $\vec{n}$ and $\overrightarrow{P_0P}$ are perpendicular, so $\vec{n} \cdot \overrightarrow{P_0P} = 0$. The algebraic definition of the dot product gives $\vec{n} \cdot \overrightarrow{P_0P} = a(x - x_0) + b(y - y_0) + c(z - z_0)$, so we obtain the following result:

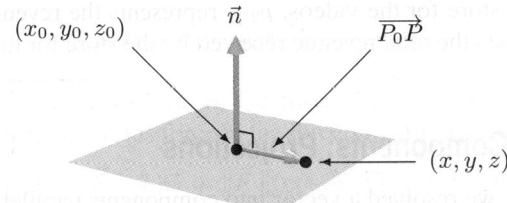

Figure 13.30: Plane with normal $\vec{n}$ and containing a fixed point (x_0, y_0, z_0)

The **equation of the plane** with normal vector $\vec{n} = a\vec{i} + b\vec{j} + c\vec{k}$ and containing the point $P_0 = (x_0, y_0, z_0)$ is

$$a(x - x_0) + b(y - y_0) + c(z - z_0) = 0.$$

Letting $d = ax_0 + by_0 + cz_0$ (a constant), we can write the equation of the plane in the form

$$ax + by + cz = d.$$

Example 5   (a) Find the equation of the plane perpendicular to $\vec{n} = -\vec{i} + 3\vec{j} + 2\vec{k}$ and passing through the point $(1, 0, 4)$.

(b) Find a vector parallel to the plane.

Solution   (a) The equation of the plane is

$$-(x - 1) + 3(y - 0) + 2(z - 4) = 0,$$

which can be written as

$$-x + 3y + 2z = 7.$$

Then the work done by $\vec{F}$ is defined to be

$$W = \|\vec{F}_{\text{parallel}}\| \, \|\vec{d}\|.$$

We see from Figure 13.33 that $\vec{F}_{\text{parallel}}$ has magnitude $\|\vec{F}\| \cos \theta$. So the work is given by the dot product:

$$W = (\|\vec{F}\| \cos \theta)\|\vec{d}\| = \|\vec{F}\| \|\vec{d}\| \cos \theta = \vec{F} \cdot \vec{d}.$$

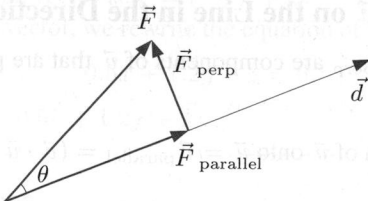

Figure 13.33: Resolving the force $\vec{F}$ into two forces, one parallel to $\vec{d}$, one perpendicular to $\vec{d}$

The formula $W = \vec{F} \cdot \vec{d}$ holds when $\pi/2 < \theta \le \pi$ also. In that case, the work done by the force is negative and the object is moving against the force. Thus, we have the following definition:

The **work**, W, done by a force $\vec{F}$ acting on an object through a displacement $\vec{d}$ is given by

$$W = \vec{F} \cdot \vec{d}.$$

Example 9   How much work does the wind do on the sailboat from Example 8 if the boat moves 20 m and the wind's force is 120 newtons?

Solution   From Example 8, we know that the force of the wind $\vec{F}$ makes a 30°angle with the boat's displacement $\vec{d}$. Since $\|\vec{F}\| = 120$ and $\|\vec{d}\| = 20$, the work done by the wind on the boat is

$$W = \vec{F} \cdot \vec{d} = \|\vec{F}\| \|\vec{d}\| \cos 30° = 2078.461 \text{ joules.}$$

Notice that if the vectors $\vec{F}$ and $\vec{d}$ are parallel and in the same direction, with magnitudes F and d, then $\cos \theta = \cos 0 = 1$, so $W = \|\vec{F}\| \|\vec{d}\| = Fd$, which is the original definition. When the vectors are perpendicular, $\cos \theta = \cos(\pi/2) = 0$, so $W = 0$ and no work is done in the technical definition of the word. For example, if you carry a heavy box across the room at the same horizontal height, no work is done by gravity because the force of gravity is vertical but the motion is horizontal.

Exercises and Problems for Section 13.3

Exercises

For Exercises 1–9, perform the following operations on the given 3-dimensional vectors.

$$\vec{a} = 2\vec{j} + \vec{k} \qquad \vec{b} = -3\vec{i} + 5\vec{j} + 4\vec{k} \qquad \vec{c} = \vec{i} + 6\vec{j}$$

$$\vec{y} = 4\vec{i} - 7\vec{j} \qquad \vec{z} = \vec{i} - 3\vec{j} - \vec{k}$$

1. $\vec{a} \cdot \vec{y}$

2. $\vec{c} \cdot \vec{y}$

3. $\vec{a} \cdot \vec{b}$

4. $\vec{a} \cdot \vec{z}$

5. $\vec{c} \cdot \vec{a} + \vec{a} \cdot \vec{y}$

6. $\vec{a} \cdot (\vec{c} + \vec{y})$

7. $(\vec{a} \cdot \vec{b})\vec{a}$

8. $(\vec{a} \cdot \vec{y})(\vec{c} \cdot \vec{z})$

9. $((\vec{c} \cdot \vec{c})\vec{a}) \cdot \vec{a}$

In Exercises 10–14, find a normal vector to the plane.

10. $2x + y - z = 5$

11. $2(x - z) = 3(x + y)$

12. $1.5x + 3.2y + z = 0$

13. $z = 3x + 4y - 7$

14. $\pi(x - 1) = (1 - \pi)(y - z) + \pi$

In Exercises 15–21, find an equation of a plane that satisfies the given conditions.

15. Through $(1, 5, 2)$ perpendicular to $3\vec{i} - \vec{j} + 4\vec{k}$

16. Through $(2, -1, 3)$ perpendicular to $5\vec{i} + 4\vec{j} - \vec{k}$.

17. Through $(1, 3, 5)$ and normal to $\vec{i} - \vec{j} + \vec{k}$.

18. Perpendicular to $5\vec{i} + \vec{j} - 2\vec{k}$ and passing through $(0, 1, -1)$.

19. Parallel to $2x + 4y - 3z = 1$ and through $(1, 0, -1)$.

20. Through $(-2, 3, 2)$ and parallel to $3x + y + z = 4$.

21. Perpendicular to $\vec{v} = 2\vec{i} - 3\vec{j} + 5\vec{k}$ and through $(4, 5, -2)$.

In Exercises 22–26, compute the angle between the vectors.

22. $\vec{i} + \vec{j} + \vec{k}$ and $\vec{i} - \vec{j} - \vec{k}$.

23. $\vec{i} + \vec{k}$ and $\vec{j} - \vec{k}$.

24. $\vec{i} + \vec{j} - \vec{k}$ and $2\vec{i} + 3\vec{j} + \vec{k}$.

25. $\vec{i} + \vec{j}$ and $\vec{i} + 2\vec{j} - \vec{k}$.

26. $\vec{i}$ and $2\vec{i} + 3\vec{j} - \vec{k}$.

Problems

27. Give a unit vector

  (a) In the same direction as $\vec{v} = 2\vec{i} + 3\vec{j}$.
  (b) Perpendicular to $\vec{v}$.

28. A plane has equation $z = 5x - 2y + 7$.

  (a) Find a value of λ making the vector $\lambda\vec{i} + \vec{j} + 0.5\vec{k}$ normal to the plane.
  (b) Find a value of a so that the point $(a + 1, a, a - 1)$ lies on the plane.

29. Consider the plane $5x - y + 7z = 21$.

  (a) Find a point on the x-axis on this plane.
  (b) Find two other points on the plane.
  (c) Find a vector perpendicular to the plane.
  (d) Find a vector parallel to the plane.

30. **(a)** Find a vector perpendicular to the plane $z = 2 + 3x - y$.
  (b) Find a vector parallel to the plane.

31. **(a)** Find a vector perpendicular to the plane $z = 2x + 3y$.
  (b) Find a vector parallel to the plane.

32. Match the planes in (a)–(d) with one or more of the descriptions in (I)–(IV). No reasons needed.

  (a) $3x - y + z = 0$ **(b)** $4x + y + 2z - 5 = 0$
  (c) $x + y = 5$ **(d)** $x = 5$

  I Goes through the origin.
  II Has a normal vector parallel to the xy-plane.
  III Goes through the point $(0, 5, 0)$.
  IV Has a normal vector whose dot products with $\vec{i}, \vec{j}, \vec{k}$ are all positive.

33. Which pairs (if any) of vectors from the following list

  (a) Are perpendicular?
  (b) Are parallel?
  (c) Have an angle less than $\pi/2$ between them?

  (d) Have an angle of more than $\pi/2$ between them?

$$\vec{a} = \vec{i} - 3\vec{j} - \vec{k}, \qquad \vec{b} = \vec{i} + \vec{j} + 2\vec{k},$$

$$\vec{c} = -2\vec{i} - \vec{j} + \vec{k}, \qquad \vec{d} = -\vec{i} - \vec{j} + \vec{k}.$$

34. List any vectors that are parallel to each other and any vectors that are perpendicular to each other:

$$\vec{v}_1 = \vec{i} - 2\vec{j} \qquad\qquad \vec{v}_2 = 2\vec{i} + 4\vec{j}$$
$$\vec{v}_3 = 3\vec{i} + 1.5\vec{j} \qquad\quad \vec{v}_4 = -1.2\vec{i} + 2.4\vec{j}$$
$$\vec{v}_5 = -5\vec{i} - 2.5\vec{j} \qquad \vec{v}_6 = 12\vec{i} - 12\vec{j}$$
$$\vec{v}_7 = 4\vec{i} + 2\vec{j} \qquad\qquad \vec{v}_8 = 3\vec{i} - 6\vec{j}$$
$$\vec{v}_9 = 0.70\vec{i} - 0.35\vec{j}$$

35. **(a)** Give a vector that is parallel to, but not equal to, $\vec{v} = 4\vec{i} + 3\vec{j}$.
  (b) Give a vector that is perpendicular to $\vec{v}$.

36. For what values of t are $\vec{u} = t\vec{i} - \vec{j} + \vec{k}$ and $\vec{v} = t\vec{i} + t\vec{j} - 2\vec{k}$ perpendicular? Are there values of t for which $\vec{u}$ and $\vec{v}$ are parallel?

37. Let θ be the angle between $\vec{v}$ and $\vec{w}$, with $0 < \theta < \pi/2$. What is the effect on $\vec{v} \cdot \vec{w}$ of increasing each of the following quantities? Does $\vec{v} \cdot \vec{w}$ increase or decrease?

  (a) $\|\vec{v}\|$ **(b)** θ

38. Write $\vec{a} = 3\vec{i} + 2\vec{j} - 6\vec{k}$ as the sum of two vectors, one parallel, and one perpendicular, to $\vec{d} = 2\vec{i} - 4\vec{j} + \vec{k}$.

39. Find angle BAC if $A = (2, 2, 2)$, $B = (4, 2, 1)$, and $C = (2, 3, 1)$.

40. The points $(5, 0, 0)$, $(0, -3, 0)$, and $(0, 0, 2)$ form a triangle. Find the lengths of the sides of the triangle and each of its angles.

41. Let S be the triangle with vertices $A = (2, 2, 2)$, $B = (4, 2, 1)$, and $C = (2, 3, 1)$.

  (a) Find the length of the shortest side of S.
  (b) Find the cosine of the angle BAC at vertex A.

In Problems 42–47, given $\vec{v} = 3\vec{i} + 4\vec{j}$ and force vector $\vec{F}$, find:

  (a) The component of $\vec{F}$ parallel to $\vec{v}$.
  (b) The component of $\vec{F}$ perpendicular to $\vec{v}$.
  (c) The work, W, done by force $\vec{F}$ through displacement $\vec{v}$.

42. $\vec{F} = 4\vec{i} + \vec{j}$ **43.** $\vec{F} = 0.2\vec{i} - 0.5\vec{j}$

44. $\vec{F} = 9\vec{i} + 12\vec{j}$ **45.** $\vec{F} = -0.4\vec{i} + 0.3\vec{j}$

46. $\vec{F} = -3\vec{i} - 5\vec{j}$ **47.** $\vec{F} = -6\vec{i} - 8\vec{j}$

In Problems 48–51, the force on an object is $\vec{F} = -20\vec{j}$. For vector $\vec{v}$, find:

  (a) The component of $\vec{F}$ parallel to $\vec{v}$.
  (b) The component of $\vec{F}$ perpendicular to $\vec{v}$.
  (c) The work, W, done by force $\vec{F}$ through displacement $\vec{v}$.

48. $\vec{v} = 2\vec{i} + 3\vec{j}$ **49.** $\vec{v} = 5\vec{i} - \vec{j}$

50. $\vec{v} = 3\vec{j}$ **51.** $\vec{v} = 5\vec{i}$

52. A basketball gymnasium is 25 meters high, 80 meters wide and 200 meters long. For a half-time stunt, the cheerleaders want to run two strings, one from each of the two corners above one basket to the diagonally opposite corners of the gym floor. What is the cosine of the angle made by the strings as they cross?

53. A 100-meter dash is run on a track in the direction of the vector $\vec{v} = 2\vec{i} + 6\vec{j}$. The wind velocity $\vec{w}$ is $5\vec{i} + \vec{j}$ km/hr. The rules say that a legal wind speed measured in the direction of the dash must not exceed 5 km/hr. Will the race results be disqualified due to an illegal wind? Justify your answer.

54. An airplane is flying toward the southeast. Which of the following wind velocity vectors increases the plane's speed the most? Which slows down the plane the most?

$$\vec{w}_1 = -4\vec{i} - \vec{j} \qquad \vec{w}_2 = \vec{i} - 2\vec{j} \qquad \vec{w}_3 = -\vec{i} + 8\vec{j}$$

$$\vec{w}_4 = 10\vec{i} + 2\vec{j} \qquad \vec{w}_5 = 5\vec{i} - 2\vec{j}$$

55. A canoe is moving with velocity $\vec{v} = 5\vec{i} + 3\vec{j}$ m/sec relative to the water. The velocity of the current in the water is $\vec{c} = \vec{i} + 2\vec{j}$ m/sec.

  (a) What is the speed of the current?
  (b) What is the speed of the current in the direction of the canoe's motion?

56. Find a vector that bisects the smaller of the two angles formed by $3\vec{i} + 4\vec{j}$ and $5\vec{i} - 12\vec{j}$.

57. Find the shortest distance between the planes $2x - 5y + z = 10$ and $z = 5y - 2x$.

58. A street vendor sells six items, with prices p_1 dollars per unit, p_2 dollars per unit, and so on. The vendor's price vector is $\vec{p} = (p_1, p_2, p_3, p_4, p_5, p_6) = (1.00, 3.50, 4.00, 2.75, 5.00, 3.00)$. The vendor sells q_1 units of the first item, q_2 units of the second item, and so on. The vendor's quantity vector is $\vec{q} = (q_1, q_2, q_3, q_4, q_5, q_6) = (43, 57, 12, 78, 20, 35)$. Find $\vec{p} \cdot \vec{q}$, give its units, and explain its significance to the vendor.

59. A course has four exams, weighted 10%, 15%, 25%, 50%, respectively. The class average on each of these exams is 75%, 91%, 84%, 87%, respectively. What do the vectors $\vec{a} = (0.75, 0.91, 0.84, 0.87)$ and $\vec{w} = (0.1, 0.15, 0.25, 0.5)$ represent, in terms of the course? Calculate the dot product $\vec{w} \cdot \vec{a}$. What does it represent, in terms of the course?

60. A consumption vector of three goods is defined by $\vec{x} = (x_1, x_2, x_3)$, where x_1, x_2 and x_3 are the quantities consumed of the three goods. A budget constraint is represented by the equation $\vec{p} \cdot \vec{x} = k$, where $\vec{p}$ is the price vector of the three goods and k is a constant. Show that the difference between two consumption vectors corresponding to points satisfying the same budget constraint is perpendicular to the price vector $\vec{p}$.

61. What does Property 2 of the dot product in the box on page 735 say geometrically?

62. Show that the vectors $(\vec{b} \cdot \vec{c})\vec{a} - (\vec{a} \cdot \vec{c})\vec{b}$ and $\vec{c}$ are perpendicular.

63. Show why each of the properties of the dot product in the box on page 735 follows from the algebraic definition of the dot product:

$$\vec{v} \cdot \vec{w} = v_1 w_1 + v_2 w_2 + v_3 w_3.$$

64. Show that if $\vec{u}$ and $\vec{v}$ are two vectors such that

$$\vec{u} \cdot \vec{w} = \vec{v} \cdot \vec{w}$$

for every vector $\vec{w}$, then

$$\vec{u} = \vec{v}.$$

65. Show that

$$\frac{\vec{u}}{\|\vec{u}\|^2} - \frac{\vec{v}}{\|\vec{v}\|^2} \quad \text{and} \quad \frac{\vec{u}}{\|\vec{u}\|\|\vec{v}\|} - \frac{\vec{v}}{\|\vec{u}\|\|\vec{v}\|}$$

have the same magnitude where $\vec{u}$ and $\vec{v}$ are nonzero vectors.

66. Figure 13.34 shows that, given three vectors $\vec{u}$, $\vec{v}$, and $\vec{w}$, the sum of the components of $\vec{v}$ and $\vec{w}$ in the direction of $\vec{u}$ is the component of $\vec{v} + \vec{w}$ in the direction of $\vec{u}$. (Although the figure is drawn in two dimensions, this result is also true in three dimensions.) Use this figure to explain why the geometric definition of the dot product satisfies $(\vec{v} + \vec{w}) \cdot \vec{u} = \vec{v} \cdot \vec{u} + \vec{w} \cdot \vec{u}$.

Figure 13.34: Component of $\vec{v} + \vec{w}$ in the direction of $\vec{u}$ is the sum of the components of $\vec{v}$ and $\vec{w}$ in that direction

67. (a) Using the geometric definition of the dot product, show that

$$\vec{u} \cdot (-\vec{v}) = -(\vec{u} \cdot \vec{v}).$$

[Hint: What happens to the angle when you multiply $\vec{v}$ by -1?]

(b) Using the geometric definition of the dot product, show that for any negative scalar λ

$$\vec{u} \cdot (\lambda \vec{v}) = \lambda(\vec{u} \cdot \vec{v})$$
$$(\lambda \vec{u}) \cdot \vec{v} = \lambda(\vec{u} \cdot \vec{v}).$$

68. The Law of Cosines for a triangle with side lengths a, b, and c, and with angle C opposite side c, says

$$c^2 = a^2 + b^2 - 2ab \cos C.$$

On page 735, we used the Law of Cosines to show that the two definitions of the dot product are equivalent. In this problem, use the geometric definition of the dot product and its properties in the box on page 735 to prove the Law of Cosines. [Hint: Let $\vec{u}$ and $\vec{v}$ be the displacement vectors from C to the other two vertices, and express c^2 in terms of $\vec{u}$ and $\vec{v}$.]

69. Use Problems 66 and 67 and the following steps to show (without trigonometry) that the geometric and algebraic definitions of the dot product are equivalent. Let $\vec{u} = u_1\vec{i} + u_2\vec{j} + u_3\vec{k}$ and $\vec{v} = v_1\vec{i} + v_2\vec{j} + v_3\vec{k}$ be any vectors. Write $(\vec{u} \cdot \vec{v})_{\text{geom}}$ for the result of the dot product computed geometrically. Substitute $\vec{u} = u_1\vec{i} + u_2\vec{j} + u_3\vec{k}$ and use Problems 66–67 to expand $(\vec{u} \cdot \vec{v})_{\text{geom}}$. Substitute for $\vec{v}$ and expand. Then calculate the dot products $\vec{i} \cdot \vec{i}$, $\vec{i} \cdot \vec{j}$, etc. geometrically.

70. For any vectors $\vec{v}$ and $\vec{w}$, consider the following function of t:

$$q(t) = (\vec{v} + t\vec{w}) \cdot (\vec{v} + t\vec{w}).$$

(a) Explain why $q(t) \geq 0$ for all real t.
(b) Expand $q(t)$ as a quadratic polynomial in t using the properties on page 735.
(c) Using the discriminant of the quadratic, show that

$$|\vec{v} \cdot \vec{w}| \leq \|\vec{v}\| \|\vec{w}\|.$$

Strengthen Your Understanding

In Problems 71–73, explain what is wrong with the statement.

71. For any 3-dimensional vectors $\vec{u}$, $\vec{v}$, $\vec{w}$, we have $(\vec{u} \cdot \vec{v}) \cdot \vec{w} = \vec{u} \cdot (\vec{v} \cdot \vec{w})$.

72. If $\vec{u} = \vec{i} + \vec{j}$ and $\vec{v} = 2\vec{i} + \vec{j}$, then the component of $\vec{v}$ parallel to $\vec{u}$ is $\vec{v}_{\text{parallel}} = (\vec{v} \cdot \vec{u})\vec{u} = 3\vec{i} + 3\vec{j}$.

73. A normal vector for the plane $z = 2x + 3y$ is $2\vec{i} + 3\vec{j}$.

In Problems 74–75, give an example of:

74. A point (a, b) such that the displacement vector from $(1, 1)$ to (a, b) is perpendicular to $\vec{i} + 2\vec{j}$.

75. A linear function $f(x, y) = mx + ny + c$ whose graph is perpendicular to $\vec{i} + 2\vec{j} + 3\vec{k}$.

Are the statements in Problems 76–85 true or false? Give reasons for your answer.

76. The quantity $\vec{u} \cdot \vec{v}$ is a vector.

77. The plane $x + 2y - 3z = 5$ has normal vector $\vec{i} + 2\vec{j} - 3\vec{k}$.

78. If $\vec{u} \cdot \vec{v} < 0$ then the angle between $\vec{u}$ and $\vec{v}$ is greater than $\pi/2$.

79. An equation of the plane with normal vector $\vec{i} + \vec{j} + \vec{k}$ containing the point $(1, 2, 3)$ is $z = x + y$.

80. The triangle in 3-space with vertices $(1, 1, 0), (0, 1, 0)$ and $(0, 1, 1)$ has a right angle.

81. The dot product $\vec{v} \cdot \vec{v}$ is never negative.

82. If $\vec{u} \cdot \vec{v} = 0$ then either $\vec{u} = 0$ or $\vec{v} = 0$.

83. If $\vec{u}$, $\vec{v}$ and $\vec{w}$ are all nonzero, and $\vec{u} \cdot \vec{v} = \vec{u} \cdot \vec{w}$, then $\vec{v} = \vec{w}$.

84. For any vectors $\vec{u}$ and $\vec{v}$: $(\vec{u} + \vec{v}) \cdot (\vec{u} - \vec{v}) = \|\vec{u}\|^2 - \|\vec{v}\|^2$.

85. If $\|\vec{u}\| = 1$, then the vector $\vec{v} - (\vec{v} \cdot \vec{u})\vec{u}$ is perpendicular to $\vec{u}$.

13.4   THE CROSS PRODUCT

In the previous section we combined two vectors to get a number, the dot product. In this section we see another way of combining two vectors, this time to get a vector, the *cross product*. Any two vectors in 3-space form a parallelogram. We define the cross product using this parallelogram.

The Area of a Parallelogram

Consider the parallelogram formed by the vectors $\vec{v}$ and $\vec{w}$ with an angle of θ between them. Then Figure 13.35 shows

$$\text{Area of parallelogram} = \text{Base} \cdot \text{Height} = \|\vec{v}\|\|\vec{w}\| \sin\theta.$$

How would we compute the area of the parallelogram if we were given $\vec{v}$ and $\vec{w}$ in components, $\vec{v} = v_1\vec{i} + v_2\vec{j} + v_3\vec{k}$ and $\vec{w} = w_1\vec{i} + w_2\vec{j} + w_3\vec{k}$? Project 1 on page 755 shows that if $\vec{v}$ and $\vec{w}$ are in the xy-plane so that $v_3 = w_3 = 0$, then

$$\text{Area of parallelogram} = |v_1 w_2 - v_2 w_1|.$$

What if $\vec{v}$ and $\vec{w}$ do not lie in the xy-plane? The cross product will enable us to compute the area of the parallelogram formed by any two vectors.

Figure 13.35: Parallelogram formed by $\vec{v}$ and $\vec{w}$ has
Area $= \|\vec{v}\|\|\vec{w}\| \sin\theta$

Definition of the Cross Product

We define the cross product of the vectors $\vec{v}$ and $\vec{w}$, written $\vec{v} \times \vec{w}$, to be a vector perpendicular to both $\vec{v}$ and $\vec{w}$. The magnitude of this vector is the area of the parallelogram formed by the two vectors. The direction of $\vec{v} \times \vec{w}$ is given by the normal vector, $\vec{n}$, to the plane defined by $\vec{v}$ and $\vec{w}$. If we require that $\vec{n}$ be a unit vector, there are two choices for $\vec{n}$, pointing out of the plane in opposite directions. We pick one by the following rule (see Figure 13.36):

> **The right-hand rule:** Place $\vec{v}$ and $\vec{w}$ so that their tails coincide and curl the fingers of your right hand through the smaller of the two angles from $\vec{v}$ to $\vec{w}$; your thumb points in the direction of the normal vector, $\vec{n}$.

Like the dot product, there are two equivalent definitions of the cross product:

The following two definitions of the **cross product** or **vector product** $\vec{v} \times \vec{w}$ are equivalent:

- **Geometric definition**

  If $\vec{v}$ and $\vec{w}$ are not parallel, then

  $$\vec{v} \times \vec{w} = \left(\begin{array}{c}\text{Area of parallelogram}\\ \text{with edges } \vec{v} \text{ and } \vec{w}\end{array}\right) \vec{n} = (\|\vec{v}\|\|\vec{w}\|\sin\theta)\vec{n},$$

  where $0 \leq \theta \leq \pi$ is the angle between $\vec{v}$ and $\vec{w}$ and $\vec{n}$ is the unit vector perpendicular to $\vec{v}$ and $\vec{w}$ pointing in the direction given by the right-hand rule. If $\vec{v}$ and $\vec{w}$ are parallel, then $\vec{v} \times \vec{w} = \vec{0}$.

- **Algebraic definition**

  $$\vec{v} \times \vec{w} = (v_2 w_3 - v_3 w_2)\vec{i} + (v_3 w_1 - v_1 w_3)\vec{j} + (v_1 w_2 - v_2 w_1)\vec{k}$$

  where $\vec{v} = v_1\vec{i} + v_2\vec{j} + v_3\vec{k}$ and $\vec{w} = w_1\vec{i} + w_2\vec{j} + w_3\vec{k}$.

Problems 45 and 48 at the end of this section show that the geometric and algebraic definitions of the cross product give the same result.

$\|\vec{v} \times \vec{w}\| = $ Area of parallelogram

Unit normal determined by right-hand rule

$\vec{w}$

$\vec{v}$

Figure 13.36: Area of parallelogram $= \|\vec{v} \times \vec{w}\|$

$\vec{v} \times \vec{w}$

$\vec{w}$

θ

$\vec{v}$

Figure 13.37: The cross product $\vec{v} \times \vec{w}$

The geometric definition shows us that the cross product is *rotation invariant*. Imagine the two vectors $\vec{v}$ and $\vec{w}$ as two metal rods welded together. Attach a third rod whose direction and length correspond to $\vec{v} \times \vec{w}$. (See Figure 13.37.) Then, no matter how we turn this set of rods, the third will still be the cross product of the first two.

The algebraic definition is more easily remembered by writing it as a 3×3 determinant. (See Appendix E.)

$$\vec{v} \times \vec{w} = \begin{vmatrix} \vec{i} & \vec{j} & \vec{k} \\ v_1 & v_2 & v_3 \\ w_1 & w_2 & w_3 \end{vmatrix} = (v_2 w_3 - v_3 w_2)\vec{i} + (v_3 w_1 - v_1 w_3)\vec{j} + (v_1 w_2 - v_2 w_1)\vec{k}.$$

Example 1   Find $\vec{i} \times \vec{j}$ and $\vec{j} \times \vec{i}$.

Solution   The vectors $\vec{i}$ and $\vec{j}$ both have magnitude 1 and the angle between them is $\pi/2$. By the right-hand rule, the vector $\vec{i} \times \vec{j}$ is in the direction of $\vec{k}$, so $\vec{n} = \vec{k}$ and we have

$$\vec{i} \times \vec{j} = \left(\|\vec{i}\|\|\vec{j}\|\sin\frac{\pi}{2}\right)\vec{k} = \vec{k}.$$

Similarly, the right-hand rule says that the direction of $\vec{j} \times \vec{i}$ is $-\vec{k}$, so

$$\vec{j} \times \vec{i} = (\|\vec{j}\|\|\vec{i}\|\sin\frac{\pi}{2})(-\vec{k}) = -\vec{k}.$$

Similar calculations show that $\vec{j} \times \vec{k} = \vec{i}$ and $\vec{k} \times \vec{i} = \vec{j}$.

Example 2   For any vector $\vec{v}$, find $\vec{v} \times \vec{v}$.

Solution   Since $\vec{v}$ is parallel to itself, $\vec{v} \times \vec{v} = \vec{0}$.

Example 3   Find the cross product of $\vec{v} = 2\vec{i} + \vec{j} - 2\vec{k}$ and $\vec{w} = 3\vec{i} + \vec{k}$ and check that the cross product is perpendicular to both $\vec{v}$ and $\vec{w}$.

Solution   Writing $\vec{v} \times \vec{w}$ as a determinant and expanding it into three two-by-two determinants, we have

$$\vec{v} \times \vec{w} = \begin{vmatrix} \vec{i} & \vec{j} & \vec{k} \\ 2 & 1 & -2 \\ 3 & 0 & 1 \end{vmatrix} = \vec{i} \begin{vmatrix} 1 & -2 \\ 0 & 1 \end{vmatrix} - \vec{j} \begin{vmatrix} 2 & -2 \\ 3 & 1 \end{vmatrix} + \vec{k} \begin{vmatrix} 2 & 1 \\ 3 & 0 \end{vmatrix}$$

$$= \vec{i} \, (1(1) - 0(-2)) - \vec{j} \, (2(1) - 3(-2)) + \vec{k} \, (2(0) - 3(1))$$
$$= \vec{i} - 8\vec{j} - 3\vec{k}.$$

To check that $\vec{v} \times \vec{w}$ is perpendicular to $\vec{v}$, we compute the dot product:

$$\vec{v} \cdot (\vec{v} \times \vec{w}) = (2\vec{i} + \vec{j} - 2\vec{k}) \cdot (\vec{i} - 8\vec{j} - 3\vec{k}) = 2 - 8 + 6 = 0.$$

Similarly,

$$\vec{w} \cdot (\vec{v} \times \vec{w}) = (3\vec{i} + 0\vec{j} + \vec{k}) \cdot (\vec{i} - 8\vec{j} - 3\vec{k}) = 3 + 0 - 3 = 0.$$

Thus, $\vec{v} \times \vec{w}$ is perpendicular to both $\vec{v}$ and $\vec{w}$.

Properties of the Cross Product

The right-hand rule tells us that $\vec{v} \times \vec{w}$ and $\vec{w} \times \vec{v}$ point in opposite directions. The magnitudes of $\vec{v} \times \vec{w}$ and $\vec{w} \times \vec{v}$ are the same, so $\vec{w} \times \vec{v} = -(\vec{v} \times \vec{w})$. (See Figure 13.38.)

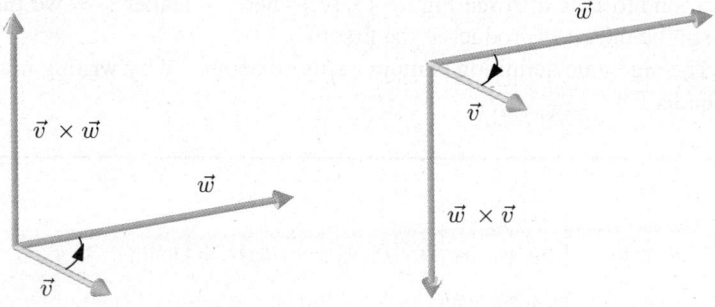

Figure 13.38: Diagram showing $\vec{v} \times \vec{w} = -(\vec{w} \times \vec{v})$

This explains the first of the following properties. The other two are derived in Problems 39, 40, and 48 at the end of this section.

Properties of the Cross Product

For vectors $\vec{u}, \vec{v}, \vec{w}$ and scalar λ

1. $\vec{w} \times \vec{v} = -(\vec{v} \times \vec{w})$
2. $(\lambda\vec{v}) \times \vec{w} = \lambda(\vec{v} \times \vec{w}) = \vec{v} \times (\lambda\vec{w})$
3. $\vec{u} \times (\vec{v} + \vec{w}) = \vec{u} \times \vec{v} + \vec{u} \times \vec{w}$.

The Equation of a Plane Through Three Points

As we saw on page 737, the equation of a plane is determined by a point $P_0 = (x_0, y_0, z_0)$ on the plane, and a normal vector, $\vec{n} = a\vec{i} + b\vec{j} + c\vec{k}$:

$$a(x - x_0) + b(y - y_0) + c(z - z_0) = 0.$$

However, a plane can also be determined by three points on it (provided they do not lie on the same line). In that case we can find an equation of the plane by first determining two vectors in the plane and then finding a normal vector using the cross product, as in the following example.

Example 4   Find an equation of the plane containing the points $P = (1, 3, 0), Q = (3, 4, -3)$, and $R = (3, 6, 2)$.

Solution   Since the points P and Q are in the plane, the displacement vector between them, $\overrightarrow{PQ}$, is in the plane, where

$$\overrightarrow{PQ} = (3 - 1)\vec{i} + (4 - 3)\vec{j} + (-3 - 0)\vec{k} = 2\vec{i} + \vec{j} - 3\vec{k}.$$

The displacement vector $\overrightarrow{PR}$ is also in the plane, where

$$\overrightarrow{PR} = (3 - 1)\vec{i} + (6 - 3)\vec{j} + (2 - 0)\vec{k} = 2\vec{i} + 3\vec{j} + 2\vec{k}.$$

Thus, a normal vector, $\vec{n}$, to the plane is given by

$$\vec{n} = \overrightarrow{PQ} \times \overrightarrow{PR} = \begin{vmatrix} \vec{i} & \vec{j} & \vec{k} \\ 2 & 1 & -3 \\ 2 & 3 & 2 \end{vmatrix} = 11\vec{i} - 10\vec{j} + 4\vec{k}.$$

Since the point $(1, 3, 0)$ is on the plane, the equation of the plane is

$$11(x - 1) - 10(y - 3) + 4(z - 0) = 0,$$

which simplifies to

$$11x - 10y + 4z = -19.$$

You should check that P, Q, and R satisfy this equation, since they lie on the plane.

Areas and Volumes Using the Cross Product and Determinants

We can use the cross product to calculate the area of the parallelogram with sides $\vec{v}$ and $\vec{w}$. We say that $\vec{v} \times \vec{w}$ is the *area vector* of the parallelogram. The geometric definition of the cross product tells us that $\vec{v} \times \vec{w}$ is normal to the parallelogram and gives us the following result:

Area of a parallelogram with edges $\vec{v} = v_1\vec{i} + v_2\vec{j} + v_3\vec{k}$ and $\vec{w} = w_1\vec{i} + w_2\vec{j} + w_3\vec{k}$ is given by

$$\text{Area} = \|\vec{v} \times \vec{w}\|, \qquad \text{where} \quad \vec{v} \times \vec{w} = \begin{vmatrix} \vec{i} & \vec{j} & \vec{k} \\ v_1 & v_2 & v_3 \\ w_1 & w_2 & w_3 \end{vmatrix}.$$

Example 5   Find the area of the parallelogram with edges $\vec{v} = 2\vec{i} + \vec{j} - 3\vec{k}$ and $\vec{w} = \vec{i} + 3\vec{j} + 2\vec{k}$.

Solution   We calculate the cross product:

$$\vec{v} \times \vec{w} = \begin{vmatrix} \vec{i} & \vec{j} & \vec{k} \\ 2 & 1 & -3 \\ 1 & 3 & 2 \end{vmatrix} = (2+9)\vec{i} - (4+3)\vec{j} + (6-1)\vec{k} = 11\vec{i} - 7\vec{j} + 5\vec{k}.$$

The area of the parallelogram with edges $\vec{v}$ and $\vec{w}$ is the magnitude of the vector $\vec{v} \times \vec{w}$:

$$\text{Area} = \|\vec{v} \times \vec{w}\| = \sqrt{11^2 + (-7)^2 + 5^2} = \sqrt{195}.$$

Volume of a Parallelepiped

Consider the parallelepiped with sides formed by $\vec{a}, \vec{b}$, and $\vec{c}$. (See Figure 13.39.) Since the base is formed by the vectors $\vec{b}$ and $\vec{c}$, we have

$$\text{Area of base of parallelepiped} = \|\vec{b} \times \vec{c}\|.$$

Figure 13.39: Volume of a parallelepiped

Figure 13.40: The vectors $\vec{a}, \vec{b}, \vec{c}$ are called a right-handed set

Figure 13.41: The vectors $\vec{a}, \vec{b}, \vec{c}$ are called a left-handed set

The vectors $\vec{a}, \vec{b}$, and $\vec{c}$ can be arranged either as in Figure 13.40 or as in Figure 13.41. In either case,

$$\text{Height of parallelepiped} = \|\vec{a}\| \cos \theta,$$

where θ is the angle shown in the figures. In Figure 13.40 the angle θ is less than $\pi/2$, so the product, $(\vec{b} \times \vec{c}) \cdot \vec{a}$, called the *triple product*, is positive. Thus, in this case

$$\text{Volume of parallelepiped} = \text{Base} \cdot \text{Height} = \|\vec{b} \times \vec{c}\| \cdot \|\vec{a}\| \cos \theta = (\vec{b} \times \vec{c}) \cdot \vec{a}.$$

In Figure 13.41, the angle, $\pi - \theta$, between $\vec{a}$ and $\vec{b} \times \vec{c}$ is more than $\pi/2$, so the product $(\vec{b} \times \vec{c}) \cdot \vec{a}$ is negative. Thus, in this case we have

$$\text{Volume} = \text{Base} \cdot \text{Height} = \|\vec{b} \times \vec{c}\| \cdot \|\vec{a}\| \cos \theta = -\|\vec{b} \times \vec{c}\| \cdot \|\vec{a}\| \cos(\pi - \theta)$$
$$= -(\vec{b} \times \vec{c}) \cdot \vec{a} = \left| (\vec{b} \times \vec{c}) \cdot \vec{a} \right|.$$

Therefore, in both cases the volume is given by $\left| (\vec{b} \times \vec{c}) \cdot \vec{a} \right|$. Using determinants, we can write

---

Volume of a parallelepiped with edges $\vec{a}, \vec{b}, \vec{c}$ is given by

$$\text{Volume} = \left| (\vec{b} \times \vec{c}) \cdot \vec{a} \right| = \text{Absolute value of the determinant} \begin{vmatrix} a_1 & a_2 & a_3 \\ b_1 & b_2 & b_3 \\ c_1 & c_2 & c_3 \end{vmatrix}.$$

Exercises and Problems for Section 13.4

Exercises

In Exercises 1–7, use the algebraic definition to find $\vec{v} \times \vec{w}$.

1. $\vec{v} = \vec{k}, \vec{w} = \vec{j}$
2. $\vec{v} = -\vec{i}, \vec{w} = \vec{j} + \vec{k}$
3. $\vec{v} = \vec{i} + \vec{k}, \vec{w} = \vec{i} + \vec{j}$
4. $\vec{v} = \vec{i} + \vec{j} + \vec{k}, \vec{w} = \vec{i} + \vec{j} + -\vec{k}$
5. $\vec{v} = 2\vec{i} - 3\vec{j} + \vec{k}, \vec{w} = \vec{i} + 2\vec{j} - \vec{k}$
6. $\vec{v} = 2\vec{i} - \vec{j} - \vec{k}, \vec{w} = -6\vec{i} + 3\vec{j} + 3\vec{k}$
7. $\vec{v} = -3\vec{i} + 5\vec{j} + 4\vec{k}, \vec{w} = \vec{i} - 3\vec{j} - \vec{k}$

Use the geometric definition in Exercises 8–9 to find:

8. $2\vec{i} \times (\vec{i} + \vec{j})$

9. $(\vec{i} + \vec{j}) \times (\vec{i} - \vec{j})$

In Exercises 10–11, use the properties on page 746 to find:

10. $\left((\vec{i} + \vec{j}) \times \vec{i}\right) \times \vec{j}$

11. $(\vec{i} + \vec{j}) \times (\vec{i} \times \vec{j})$

12. For $\vec{a} = 3\vec{i} + \vec{j} - \vec{k}$ and $\vec{b} = \vec{i} - 4\vec{j} + 2\vec{k}$, find $\vec{a} \times \vec{b}$ and check that it is perpendicular to both $\vec{a}$ and $\vec{b}$.

13. If $\vec{v} = 3\vec{i} - 2\vec{j} + 4\vec{k}$ and $\vec{w} = \vec{i} + 2\vec{j} - \vec{k}$, find $\vec{v} \times \vec{w}$ and $\vec{w} \times \vec{v}$. What is the relation between the two answers?

In Exercises 14–15, find an equation for the plane through the points.

14. $(1, 0, 0), (0, 1, 0), (0, 0, 1)$.

15. $(3, 4, 2), (-2, 1, 0), (0, 2, 1)$.

In Exercises 16–19, find the volume of the parallelogram with edges $\vec{a}, \vec{b}, \vec{c}$.

16. $\vec{a} = 3\vec{i} + 4\vec{j} + 5\vec{k}, \vec{b} = 5\vec{i} + 4\vec{j} + 3\vec{k}, \vec{c} = \vec{i} + \vec{j} + \vec{k}$.

17. $\vec{a} = -\vec{i} + \vec{j} + \vec{k}, \vec{b} = \vec{i} - \vec{j} + \vec{k}, \vec{c} = \vec{i} + \vec{j} - \vec{k}$.

18. $\vec{a} = -\vec{i} + 8\vec{j} + 7\vec{k}, \vec{b} = 2\vec{j} + 9\vec{k}, \vec{c} = 3\vec{k}$.

19. $\vec{a} = \vec{i} + \vec{j} + 2\vec{k}, \vec{b} = \vec{i} + \vec{k}, \vec{c} = \vec{j} + \vec{k}$.

Problems

20. Find a vector parallel to the line of intersection of the planes given by the equations $2x - 3y + 5z = 2$ and $4x + y - 3z = 7$.

21. Find the equation of the plane through the origin that is perpendicular to the line of intersection of the planes in Problem 20.

22. Find the equation of the plane through the point $(4, 5, 6)$ and perpendicular to the line of intersection of the planes in Problem 20.

23. Find an equation for the plane through the origin containing the points $(1, 3, 0)$ and $(2, 4, 1)$.

24. Find a vector parallel to the line of intersection of the two planes $4x - 3y + 2z = 12$ and $x + 5y - z = 25$.

25. Find a vector parallel to the intersection of the planes $2x - 3y + 5z = 2$ and $4x + y - 3z = 7$.

26. Find the equation of the plane through the origin that is perpendicular to the line of intersection of the planes in Problem 25.

27. Find the equation of the plane through the point $(4, 5, 6)$ that is perpendicular to the line of intersection of the planes in Problem 25.

28. Find the equation of a plane through the origin and perpendicular to $x - y + z = 5$ and $2x + y - 2z = 7$.

29. Given the points $P = (1, 2, 3)$, $Q = (3, 5, 7)$, and $R = (2, 5, 3)$, find:

(a) A unit vector perpendicular to a plane containing P, Q, R.
(b) The angle between PQ and PR.
(c) The area of the triangle PQR.
(d) The distance from R to the line through P and Q.

30. Let $A = (-1, 3, 0)$, $B = (3, 2, 4)$, and $C = (1, -1, 5)$.

(a) Find an equation for the plane that passes through these three points.
(b) Find the area of the triangle determined by these three points.

31. If $\vec{v}$ and $\vec{w}$ are both parallel to the xy-plane, what can you conclude about $\vec{v} \times \vec{w}$? Explain.

32. Suppose $\vec{v} \cdot \vec{w} = 5$ and $\|\vec{v} \times \vec{w}\| = 3$, and the angle between $\vec{v}$ and $\vec{w}$ is θ. Find

(a) $\tan \theta$ (b) θ.

33. If $\vec{v} \times \vec{w} = 2\vec{i} - 3\vec{j} + 5\vec{k}$, and $\vec{v} \cdot \vec{w} = 3$, find $\tan \theta$ where θ is the angle between $\vec{v}$ and $\vec{w}$.

34. Suppose $\vec{v} \cdot \vec{w} = 8$ and $\vec{v} \times \vec{w} = 12\vec{i} - 3\vec{j} + 4\vec{k}$ and that the angle between $\vec{v}$ and $\vec{w}$ is θ. Find

(a) $\tan \theta$ (b) θ

35. Why does a baseball curve? The baseball in Figure 13.42 has velocity $\vec{v}$ meters/sec and is spinning at ω radians per second about an axis in the direction of the unit vector $\vec{n}$. The ball experiences a force, called the Magnus force,[2] $\vec{F}_M$, that is proportional to $\omega\vec{n} \times \vec{v}$.

[2]Named after German physicist Heinrich Magnus, who first described it in 1853.

(a) What is the effect on $\vec{F}_M$ of increasing ω?

(b) The ball in Figure 13.42 is moving away from you. What is the direction of the Magnus force?

Figure 13.42: Spinning baseball

36. The point P in Figure 13.43 has position vector $\vec{v}$ obtained by rotating the position vector $\vec{r}$ of the point (x, y) by $90°$ counterclockwise about the origin.

(a) Use the geometric definition of the cross product to explain why $\vec{v} = \vec{k} \times \vec{r}$.

(b) Find the coordinates of P.

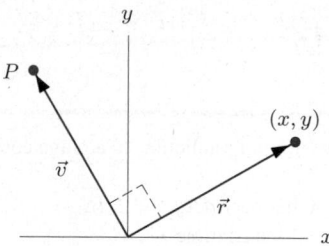

Figure 13.43

37. The points $P_1 = (0, 0, 0)$, $P_2 = (2, 4, 2)$, $P_3 = (3, 0, 0)$, and $P_4 = (5, 4, 2)$ are vertices of a parallelogram.

(a) Find the displacement vectors along each of the four sides. Check that these are equal in pairs.

(b) Find the area of the parallelogram.

38. Using the parallelogram in Problem 37 as a base, create a parallelopiped with side $\overrightarrow{P_1 P_5}$ where $P_5 = (1, 0, 4)$. Find the volume of this parallelepiped.

39. Use the algebraic definition to check that

$$\vec{a} \times (\vec{b} + \vec{c}) = (\vec{a} \times \vec{b}) + (\vec{a} \times \vec{c}).$$

40. If $\vec{v}$ and $\vec{w}$ are non-zero vectors, use the geometric definition of the cross product to explain why

$$(\lambda \vec{v}) \times \vec{w} = \lambda(\vec{v} \times \vec{w}) = \vec{v} \times (\lambda \vec{w}).$$

Consider the cases $\lambda > 0$, and $\lambda = 0$, and $\lambda < 0$ separately.

41. Use a parallelepiped to show that $\vec{a} \cdot (\vec{b} \times \vec{c}) = (\vec{a} \times \vec{b}) \cdot \vec{c}$ for any vectors $\vec{a}$, $\vec{b}$, and $\vec{c}$.

42. Show that $\|\vec{a} \times \vec{b}\|^2 = \|\vec{a}\|^2 \|\vec{b}\|^2 - (\vec{a} \cdot \vec{b})^2$.

43. If $\vec{a} + \vec{b} + \vec{c} = \vec{0}$, show that

$$\vec{a} \times \vec{b} = \vec{b} \times \vec{c} = \vec{c} \times \vec{a}.$$

Geometrically, what does this imply about $\vec{a}$, $\vec{b}$, and $\vec{c}$?

44. If $\vec{a} = a_1 \vec{i} + a_2 \vec{j} + a_3 \vec{k}$, $\vec{b} = b_1 \vec{i} + b_2 \vec{j} + b_3 \vec{k}$ and $\vec{c} = c_1 \vec{i} + c_2 \vec{j} + c_3 \vec{k}$ are any three vectors in space, show that

$$\vec{a} \cdot (\vec{b} \times \vec{c}) = \begin{vmatrix} a_1 & a_2 & a_3 \\ b_1 & b_2 & b_3 \\ c_1 & c_2 & c_3 \end{vmatrix}.$$

45. Use the fact that $\vec{i} \times \vec{i} = \vec{0}$, $\vec{i} \times \vec{j} = \vec{k}$, $\vec{i} \times \vec{k} = -\vec{j}$, and so on, together with the properties on page 746 to derive the algebraic definition for the cross product.

46. In this problem, we arrive at the algebraic definition for the cross product by a different route. Let $\vec{a} = a_1 \vec{i} + a_2 \vec{j} + a_3 \vec{k}$ and $\vec{b} = b_1 \vec{i} + b_2 \vec{j} + b_3 \vec{k}$. We seek a vector $\vec{v} = x \vec{i} + y \vec{j} + z \vec{k}$ that is perpendicular to both $\vec{a}$ and $\vec{b}$. Use this requirement to construct two equations for x, y, and z. Eliminate x and solve for y in terms of z. Then eliminate y and solve for x in terms of z. Since z can be any value whatsoever (the direction of $\vec{v}$ is unaffected), select the value for z which eliminates the denominator in the equation you obtained. How does the resulting expression for $\vec{v}$ compare to the formula we derived on page 745?

47. For vectors $\vec{a}$ and $\vec{b}$, let $\vec{c} = \vec{a} \times (\vec{b} \times \vec{a})$.

(a) Show that $\vec{c}$ lies in the plane containing $\vec{a}$ and $\vec{b}$.

(b) Use Problems 41 and 42 to show that $\vec{a} \cdot \vec{c} = 0$ and $\vec{b} \cdot \vec{c} = \|\vec{a}\|^2 \|\vec{b}\|^2 - (\vec{a} \cdot \vec{b})^2$.

(c) Show that

$$\vec{a} \times (\vec{b} \times \vec{a}) = \|\vec{a}\|^2 \vec{b} - (\vec{a} \cdot \vec{b}) \vec{a}.$$

48. Use the result of Problem 41 to show that the cross product distributes over addition. First, use distributivity for the dot product to show that for any vector $\vec{d}$,

$$[(\vec{a} + \vec{b}) \times \vec{c}] \cdot \vec{d} = [(\vec{a} \times \vec{c}) + (\vec{b} \times \vec{c})] \cdot \vec{d}.$$

Next, show that for any vector $\vec{d}$,

$$[((\vec{a} + \vec{b}) \times \vec{c}) - (\vec{a} \times \vec{c}) - (\vec{b} \times \vec{c})] \cdot \vec{d} = 0.$$

Finally, explain why you can conclude that

$$(\vec{a} + \vec{b}) \times \vec{c} = (\vec{a} \times \vec{c}) + (\vec{b} \times \vec{c}).$$

49. Figure 13.44 shows the tetrahedron determined by three vectors $\vec{a}$, $\vec{b}$, $\vec{c}$. The *area vector* of a face is a vector perpendicular to the face, pointing outward, whose magnitude is the area of the face. Show that the sum of the four outward pointing area vectors of the faces equals the zero vector.

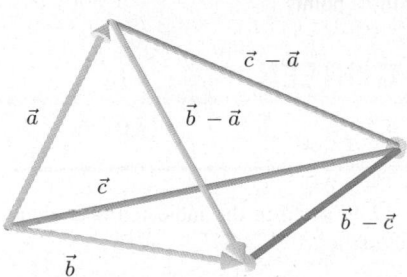

Figure 13.44

In Problems 50–52, find the vector representing the area of a surface. The magnitude of the vector equals the magnitude of the area; the direction is perpendicular to the surface. Since there are two perpendicular directions, we pick one by giving an orientation for the surface.

50. The rectangle with vertices $(0, 0, 0)$, $(0, 1, 0)$, $(2, 1, 0)$, and $(2, 0, 0)$, oriented so that it faces downward.

51. The circle of radius 2 in the yz-plane, facing in the direction of the positive x-axis.

52. The triangle ABC, oriented upward, where $A = (1, 2, 3)$, $B = (3, 1, 2)$, and $C = (2, 1, 3)$.

53. This problem relates the area of a parallelogram S lying in the plane $z = mx + ny + c$ to the area of its projection

R in the xy-plane. Let S be determined by the vectors $\vec{u} = u_1\vec{i} + u_2\vec{j} + u_3\vec{k}$ and $\vec{v} = v_1\vec{i} + v_2\vec{j} + v_3\vec{k}$. See Figure 13.45.

(a) Find the area of S.
(b) Find the area of R.
(c) Find m and n in terms of the components of $\vec{u}$ and $\vec{v}$.
(d) Show that

$$\text{Area of } S = \sqrt{1 + m^2 + n^2} \cdot \text{Area of } R.$$

Figure 13.45

Strengthen Your Understanding

In Problems 54–55, explain what is wrong with the statement.

54. There is only one unit vector perpendicular to two non-parallel vectors in 3-space.

55. $\vec{u} \times \vec{v} = \vec{0}$ when $\vec{u}$ and $\vec{v}$ are perpendicular.

In Problems 56–57, give an example of:

56. A vector $\vec{u}$ whose cross product with $\vec{v} = \vec{i} + \vec{j}$ is parallel to $\vec{k}$.

57. A vector $\vec{v}$ such that $\|\vec{u} \times \vec{v}\| = 10$, where $\vec{u} = 3\vec{i} + 4\vec{j}$.

Are the statements in Problems 58–67 true or false? Give reasons for your answer.

58. $\vec{u} \times \vec{v}$ is a vector.

59. $\vec{u} \times \vec{v}$ has direction parallel to both $\vec{u}$ and $\vec{v}$.

60. $\|\vec{u} \times \vec{v}\| = \|\vec{u}\| \|\vec{v}\|$.

61. $(\vec{i} \times \vec{j}) \cdot \vec{k} = \vec{i} \cdot (\vec{j} \times \vec{k})$.

62. If $\vec{v}$ is a non-zero vector and $\vec{v} \times \vec{u} = \vec{v} \times \vec{w}$, then $\vec{u} = \vec{w}$.

63. The value of $\vec{v} \cdot (\vec{v} \times \vec{w})$ is always 0.

64. The value of $\vec{v} \times \vec{w}$ is never the same as $\vec{v} \cdot \vec{w}$.

65. The area of the triangle with two sides given by $\vec{i} + \vec{j}$ and $\vec{j} + 2\vec{k}$ is $3/2$.

66. Given a non-zero vector $\vec{v}$ in 3-space, there is a non-zero vector $\vec{w}$ such that $\vec{v} \times \vec{w} = \vec{0}$.

67. It is never true that $\vec{v} \times \vec{w} = \vec{w} \times \vec{v}$.

CHAPTER SUMMARY (see also Ready Reference at the end of the book)

- **Vectors**
  Geometric definition of vector addition, subtraction and scalar multiplication, resolving into $\vec{i}$, $\vec{j}$, and $\vec{k}$ components, magnitude of a vector, algebraic properties of addition and scalar multiplication.

- **Dot Product**
  Geometric and algebraic definition, algebraic properties, using dot products to find angles and determine perpen-

dicularity, the equation of a plane with given normal vector passing through a given point, projection of a vector in a direction given by a unit vector.

- **Cross Product**
  Geometric and algebraic definition, algebraic properties, cross product and volume, finding the equation of a plane through three points.

REVIEW EXERCISES AND PROBLEMS FOR CHAPTER THIRTEEN

Exercises

In Exercises 1–2, is the quantity a vector or a scalar? Compute it.

1. $\vec{u} \cdot \vec{v}$, where $\vec{u} = 2\vec{i} - 3\vec{j} - 4\vec{k}$ and $\vec{v} = \vec{k} - \vec{j}$
2. $\vec{u} \times \vec{v}$, where $\vec{u} = 2\vec{i} - 3\vec{j} - 4\vec{k}$ and $\vec{v} = 3\vec{i} - \vec{j} + \vec{k}$.

In Exercises 3–4, calculate the quantity.

3. $(2\vec{i} - 3\vec{j} + 4\vec{k}) \cdot (2\vec{i} + 3\vec{j} + \vec{k})$
4. $\vec{i} \cdot (\vec{k} \times \vec{j})$
5. Resolve the vectors in Figure 13.46 into components.

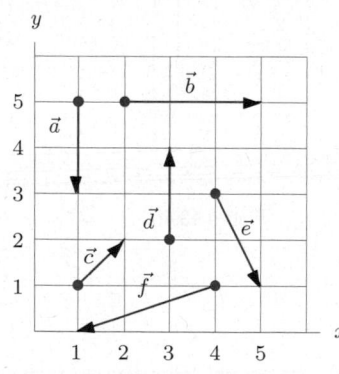

Figure 13.46

6. Resolve vector $\vec{v}$ into components if $\|\vec{v}\| = 8$ and the direction of $\vec{v}$ is shown in Figure 13.47.

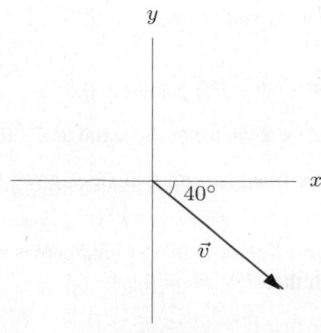

Figure 13.47

For Exercises 7–9, perform the indicated operations on the following vectors:

$$\vec{c} = \vec{i} + 6\vec{j}, \quad \vec{x} = -2\vec{i} + 9\vec{j}, \quad \vec{y} = 4\vec{i} - 7\vec{j}.$$

7. $5\vec{c}$ 8. $\vec{c} + \vec{x} + \vec{y}$ 9. $\|\vec{x} - \vec{c}\|$

In Exercises 10–19, use $\vec{v} = 2\vec{i} + 3\vec{j} - \vec{k}$ and $\vec{w} = \vec{i} - \vec{j} + 2\vec{k}$ to calculate the given quantities.

10. $\vec{v} + 2\vec{w}$ 11. $3\vec{v} - \vec{w} - \vec{v}$

12. $\|\vec{v} + \vec{w}\|$ 13. $\vec{v} \cdot \vec{w}$

14. $\vec{v} \times \vec{w}$ 15. $\vec{v} \times \vec{v}$

16. $(\vec{v} \cdot \vec{w})\vec{v}$ 17. $(\vec{v} \times \vec{w}) \cdot \vec{w}$

18. $(\vec{v} \times \vec{w}) \times \vec{w}$ 19. $(\vec{v} \times \vec{w}) \times (\vec{v} \times \vec{w})$

In Exercises 20–21, find a normal vector to the plane.

20. $2x + y - z = 23$
21. $z - 5(x - 2) = 3(5 - y)$
22. Find the equation of the plane through the origin which is parallel to $z = 4x - 3y + 8$.
23. Let $\vec{v} = 3\vec{i} + 2\vec{j} - 2\vec{k}$ and $\vec{w} = 4\vec{i} - 3\vec{j} + \vec{k}$. Find each of the following:

    (a) $\vec{v} \cdot \vec{w}$
    (b) $\vec{v} \times \vec{w}$
    (c) A vector of length 5 parallel to vector $\vec{v}$
    (d) The angle between vectors $\vec{v}$ and $\vec{w}$
    (e) The component of $\vec{v}$ in the direction of $\vec{w}$
    (f) A vector perpendicular to vector $\vec{v}$
    (g) A vector perpendicular to both vectors $\vec{v}$ and $\vec{w}$

In Exercises 24–30, find a vector with the given property.

24. Length 10, parallel to $2\vec{i} + 3\vec{j} - \vec{k}$.

25. Unit vector perpendicular to $\vec{i} + \vec{j}$ and $\vec{i} - \vec{j} - \vec{k}$

26. Unit vector in the xy-plane perpendicular to $3\vec{i} - 2\vec{j}$.

27. Normal to $4(x - 1) + 6(z + 3) = 12$.

28. Perpendicular to $x - y = 1 + z$.

29. The vector obtained from $4\vec{i} + 3\vec{j}$ by rotating it $90°$ counterclockwise.

30. A non-zero vector perpendicular to $\vec{v} = 3\vec{i} - \vec{j} + \vec{k}$ and $\vec{w} = \vec{i} - 2\vec{j} + \vec{k}$.

31. Which of the following vectors are parallel?

$$\vec{u} = 2\vec{i} + 4\vec{j} - 2\vec{k}, \quad \vec{p} = \vec{i} + \vec{j} + \vec{k},$$
$$\vec{v} = \vec{i} - \vec{j} + 3\vec{k}, \quad \vec{q} = 4\vec{i} - 4\vec{j} + 12\vec{k},$$
$$\vec{w} = -\vec{i} - 2\vec{j} + \vec{k}, \quad \vec{r} = \vec{i} - \vec{j} + \vec{k}.$$

In Exercises 32–37, find the parallel and perpendicular components of the force vector $\vec{F}$ in the direction of the displacement vector $\vec{d}$. Then find the work W done by $\vec{F}$ though the displacement $\vec{d}$.

32. $\vec{F} = 2\vec{i} + 4\vec{j}, \quad \vec{d} = \vec{i} + 2\vec{j}$

33. $\vec{F} = -2\vec{i} - 4\vec{j}, \quad \vec{d} = \vec{i} + 2\vec{j}$

34. $\vec{F} = 2\vec{i} + 4\vec{j}, \quad \vec{d} = 2\vec{i} - 1\vec{j}$

35. $\vec{F} = 2\vec{i} + 4\vec{j}, \quad \vec{d} = 3\vec{i} - 4\vec{j}$

36. $\vec{F} = 2\vec{i}, \quad \vec{d} = \vec{i} + \vec{j}$

37. $\vec{F} = 5\vec{i} + 2\vec{j}, \quad \vec{d} = 3\vec{j}$

38. Find the area of the triangle with vectors $\vec{a} = \vec{i} + 2\vec{j} - \vec{k}$ and $\vec{b} = 4\vec{i} - 2\vec{j} + \vec{k}$ as sides.

Problems

39. Figure 13.48 shows a rectangular box containing several vectors. Are the following statements true or false? Explain.

   (a) $\vec{c} = \vec{f}$ **(b)** $\vec{a} = \vec{d}$ **(c)** $\vec{a} = -\vec{b}$

   (d) $\vec{g} = \vec{f} + \vec{a}$ **(e)** $\vec{e} = \vec{a} - \vec{b}$ **(f)** $\vec{d} = \vec{g} - \vec{c}$

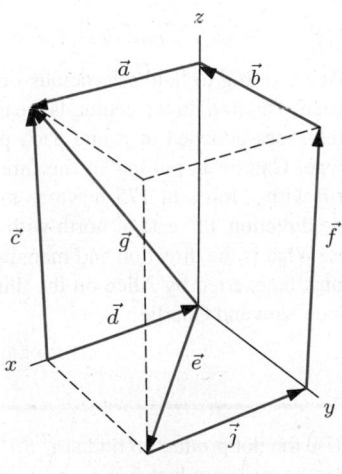

Figure 13.48

40. Shortly after takeoff, a plane is climbing northwest through still air at an airspeed of 200 km/hr, and rising at a rate of 300 m/min. Resolve its velocity vector into components. The x-axis points east, the y-axis points north, and the z-axis points up.

41. A plane is heading due east and climbing at the rate of 80 km/hr. If its airspeed is 480 km/hr and there is a wind blowing 100 km/hr to the northeast, what is the ground speed of the plane?

42. A model rocket is shot into the air at an angle with the earth of about $60°$. The rocket is going fast initially but slows down as it reaches its highest point. It picks up speed again as it falls to earth.

   (a) Sketch a graph showing the path of the rocket. Draw several velocity vectors on your graph.

   (b) A second rocket has a parachute that deploys as it begins its descent. How do the velocity vectors from part (a) change for this rocket?

43. A car drives clockwise around the track in Figure 13.49, slowing down at the curves and speeding up along the straight portions. Sketch velocity vectors at the points P, Q, and R.

Figure 13.49

44. A racing car drives clockwise around the track shown in Figure 13.49 at a constant speed. At what point on the track does the car have the longest acceleration vector, and in roughly what direction is it pointing? (Recall that acceleration is the rate of change of velocity.)

45. Which pairs of the vectors $\sqrt{3}\vec{i} + \vec{j}, 3\vec{i} + \sqrt{3}\vec{j}, \vec{i} - \sqrt{3}\vec{j}$ are parallel and which are perpendicular?

46. One force is pushing an object in a direction $50°$ south of east with a force of 25 newtons. A second force is simultaneously pushing the object in a direction $70°$ north of west with a force of 60 newtons. If the object is to remain stationary, give the direction and magnitude of the third force that must be applied to the object to counterbalance the first two.

47. What values of a make $\vec{v} = 2a\vec{i} - a\vec{j} + 16\vec{k}$ perpendicular to $\vec{w} = 5\vec{i} + a\vec{j} - \vec{k}$?

In Problems 48–49, find an equation of a plane that satisfies the given conditions.

48. Perpendicular to the vector $-\vec{i} + 2\vec{j} + \vec{k}$ and passing through the point $(1, 0, 2)$.

49. Perpendicular to the vector $2\vec{i} - 3\vec{j} + 7\vec{k}$ and passing through the point $(1, -1, 2)$.

50. Let $A = (0, 4)$, $B = (-1, -3)$, and $C = (-5, 1)$. Draw triangle ABC and find each of its interior angles.

51. Find the area of the triangle with vertices $P = (-2, 2, 0)$, $Q = (1, 3, -1)$, and $R = (-4, 2, 1)$.

52. A plane is drawn through the points $A = (2, 1, 0)$, $B = (0, 1, 3)$ and $C = (1, 0, 1)$. Find

(a) Two vectors lying in the plane.
(b) A vector perpendicular to the plane.
(c) The equation of the plane.

53. Let $P = (0, 1, 0)$, $Q = (-1, 1, 2)$, $R = (2, 1, -1)$. Find

(a) The area of the triangle PQR.
(b) The equation for a plane that contains P, Q, and R.

54. Find the distance from the point $P = (2, -1, 3)$ to the plane $2x + 4y - z = -1$.

55. Find an equation of the plane passing through the three points $(1, 1, 1)$, $(1, 4, 5)$, $(-3, -2, 0)$. Find the distance from the origin to the plane.

56. An airport is at the point $(200, 10, 0)$ and an approaching plane is at the point $(550, 60, 4)$. Assume that the xy-plane is horizontal, with the x-axis pointing eastward and the y-axis pointing northward. Also assume that the z-axis is upward and that all distances are measured in kilometers. The plane flies due west at a constant altitude at a speed of 500 km/hr for half an hour. It then descends at 200 km/hr, heading straight for the airport.

(a) Find the velocity vector of the plane while it is flying at constant altitude.
(b) Find the coordinates of the point at which the plane starts to descend.
(c) Find a vector representing the velocity of the plane when it is descending.

57. Find the vector $\vec{v}$ with all of the following properties:

- Magnitude 10
- Angle of $45°$ with positive x-axis
- Angle of $75°$ with positive y-axis
- Positive $\vec{k}$-component.

58. **(a)** A vector $\vec{v}$ of magnitude v makes an angle α with the positive x-axis, angle β with the positive y-axis, and angle γ with the positive z-axis. Show that

$$\vec{v} = v \cos \alpha \vec{i} + v \cos \beta \vec{j} + v \cos \gamma \vec{k}.$$

(b) Cos α, cos β, and cos γ are called *direction cosines*. Show that

$$\cos^2 \alpha + \cos^2 \beta + \cos^2 \gamma = 1.$$

59. Three people are trying to hold a ferocious lion still for the veterinarian. The lion, in the center, is wearing a collar with three ropes attached to it and each person has hold of a rope. Charlie is pulling in the direction $62°$ west of north with a force of 175 newtons and Sam is pulling in the direction $43°$ east of north with a force of 200 newtons. What is the direction and magnitude of the force that must be exerted by Alice on the third rope to counterbalance Sam and Charlie?

CAS Challenge Problems

60. Let $\vec{a} = x\vec{i} + y\vec{j} + z\vec{k}$, $\vec{b} = u\vec{i} + v\vec{j} + w\vec{k}$, and $\vec{c} = m\vec{a} + n\vec{b}$. Compute $(\vec{a} \times \vec{b}) \cdot \vec{c}$ and $(\vec{a} \times \vec{b}) \times (\vec{a} \times \vec{c})$, and explain the geometric meaning of your answers.

61. Let $\vec{a} = x\vec{i} + y\vec{j} + z\vec{k}$, $\vec{b} = u\vec{i} + v\vec{j} + w\vec{k}$ and $\vec{c} = r\vec{i} + s\vec{j} + t\vec{k}$. Show that the parallelepiped with edges $\vec{a}, \vec{b}, \vec{c}$ has the same volume as the parallelepiped with edges $\vec{a}, \vec{b}, 2\vec{a} - \vec{b} + \vec{c}$. Explain this result geometrically.

62. Let $\vec{a} = \vec{i} + 2\vec{j} + 3\vec{k}$ and $\vec{b} = 2\vec{i} + \vec{j} + 2\vec{k}$, and let θ be the angle between $\vec{a}$ and $\vec{b}$.

(a) For $\vec{c} = x\vec{i} + y\vec{j} + z\vec{k}$, write the following conditions as equations in x, y, z and solve them:

$$\vec{a} \cdot \vec{c} = 0, \quad \vec{b} \cdot \vec{c} = 0, \quad \|\vec{c}\|^2 = \|\vec{a}\|^2 \|\vec{b}\|^2 \sin^2 \theta.$$

[Hint: Use the dot product to find $\sin^2 \theta$.]

(b) Compute the cross product $\vec{a} \times \vec{b}$ and compare with your answer in part (a). What do you notice? Explain.

63. Let $A = (0, 0, 0)$, $B = (2, 0, 0)$, $C = (1, \sqrt{3}, 0)$ and $D = (1, 1/\sqrt{3}, 2\sqrt{2/3})$.

(a) Show that A, B, C, D are all the same distance from each other.

(b) Find the point $P = (x, y, z)$ that is equidistant from A, B, C and D by setting up and solving three equations in $x, y,$ and z.

(c) Use the dot product to find the angle APB. (In chemistry, this angle is often approximated by

109.5°. A methane molecule can be represented by four hydrogen atoms at points A, B, C and D, and a carbon atom at P.)

64. Let $P = (x, y, z)$, $Q = (u, v, w)$ and $R = (r, s, t)$ be points on the plane $ax + by + cz = d$.

(a) What is the relation between $\overrightarrow{PQ} \times \overrightarrow{PR}$ and the nor-

mal vector to the plane, $a\vec{i} + b\vec{j} + c\vec{k}$?

(b) Express $\overrightarrow{PQ} \times \overrightarrow{PR}$ in terms of $x, y, z, u, v, w, r, s, t$.

(c) Use the equation for the plane to eliminate z, w, and t from the expression you obtained in part (b), and simplify. Does your answer agree with what you said in part (a)?

PROJECTS FOR CHAPTER THIRTEEN

1. Cross Product of Vectors in the Plane

Let $\vec{a} = a_1\vec{i} + a_2\vec{j}$ and $\vec{b} = b_1\vec{i} + b_2\vec{j}$ be two nonparallel vectors in 2-space, as in Figure 13.50.

$$\vec{b} = b_1\vec{i} + b_2\vec{j} = (s\cos\beta)\vec{i} + (s\sin\beta)\vec{j}$$

$$\vec{a} = a_1\vec{i} + a_2\vec{j} = (r\cos\alpha)\vec{i} + (r\sin\alpha)\vec{j}$$

Figure 13.50

(a) Use the identity $\sin(\beta - \alpha) = (\sin\beta\cos\alpha - \cos\beta\sin\alpha)$ to derive the formula for the area of the parallelogram formed by $\vec{a}$ and $\vec{b}$:

$$\text{Area of parallelogram} = |a_1 b_2 - a_2 b_1|.$$

(b) Show that $a_1 b_2 - a_2 b_1$ is positive when the rotation from $\vec{a}$ to $\vec{b}$ is counterclockwise, and negative when it is clockwise.

(c) Use parts (a) and (b) to show that the geometric and algebraic definitions of $\vec{a} \times \vec{b}$ give the same result.

2. The Dot Product in Genetics[3]

We define[4] the angle between two n-dimensional vectors, $\vec{v}$ and $\vec{w}$, using the dot product:

$$\cos\theta = \frac{\vec{v} \cdot \vec{w}}{\|\vec{v}\|\|\vec{w}\|} = \frac{v_1 w_1 + v_2 w_2 + \cdots + v_n w_n}{\|\vec{v}\|\|\vec{w}\|}, \qquad \text{provided } \|\vec{v}\|, \|\vec{w}\| \neq 0.$$

We use this idea of angle to measure how close two populations are to one another genetically. The table shows the relative frequencies of four alleles (variants of a gene) in four populations.

Allele	Eskimo	Bantu	English	Korean
A_1	0.29	0.10	0.21	0.22
A_2	0.00	0.09	0.07	0.00
B	0.03	0.12	0.06	0.21
O	0.68	0.69	0.66	0.57

---

[3] Adapted from L. L. Cavalli-Sforza and A. W. F. Edwards, "Models and Estimation Procedures," Am. J. Hum. Genet., Vol. 19 (1967), pp. 223-57.

[4] The result of Problem 70 on page 743 shows that the quantity on the right-hand side of this equation is between -1 and 1, so this definition makes sense.

Let $\vec{a}_1$ be the 4-vector showing the square roots of the relative frequencies of the alleles in the Eskimo population. Let $\vec{a}_2, \vec{a}_3, \vec{a}_4$ be the corresponding vectors for the Bantu, English, and Korean populations, respectively. The genetic distance between two populations is defined as the angle between the corresponding vectors.

(a) Using this definition, is the English population closer genetically to the Bantus or to the Koreans? Explain.

(b) Is the English population closer to a half Eskimo, half Bantu population than to the Bantu population alone?

(c) Among all possible populations that are a mix of Eskimo and Bantu, find the mix that is closest to the English population.

3. A Warren Truss

A Warren truss is a structure for bearing a weight such as a roof or a bridge with two supports at either end of a gap. The truss in Figure 13.51 is loaded by weights at points D and E and is supported by vertical forces at points A and C. The horizontal bars in the truss are 10 ft long and the diagonal bars are 12 ft. Angles A and C are 65.38°.

Each bar exerts a force at the two joints at its ends. The two force vectors are parallel to the bar, equal in magnitude, and opposite in direction. If the bar pushes on the joints at its ends, then the bar is under compression, and if it pulls it is under tension, and the magnitude of the force is called the magnitude of the tension or compression.

Engineers need to know the magnitude of the compression or tension in each of the bars of the truss to prevent them from bending or breaking. To determine these magnitudes, we use the fact that at each joint the sum of the external forces from the weights and supports and the pushing and pulling forces exerted by the bars is zero. Find the magnitudes for all seven bars in this order:

(a) Joint A; Bars AB, AE

(b) Joint C; Bars BC, CD

(c) Joint D; Bars BD, DE

(d) Joint E; Bar BE

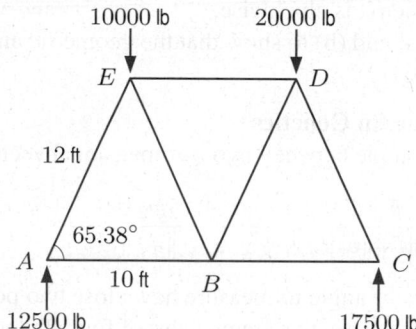

Figure 13.51

Chapter Fourteen

DIFFERENTIATING FUNCTIONS OF SEVERAL VARIABLES

Contents

14.1 THE PARTIAL DERIVATIVE

The derivative of a one-variable function measures its rate of change. In this section we see how a two-variable function has two rates of change: one as x changes (with y held constant) and one as y changes (with x held constant).

Rate of Change of Temperature in a Metal Rod: a One-Variable Problem

Imagine an unevenly heated metal rod lying along the x-axis, with its left end at the origin and x measured in meters. (See Figure 14.1.) Let $u(x)$ be the temperature (in °C) of the rod at the point x. Table 14.1 gives values of $u(x)$. We see that the temperature increases as we move along the rod, reaching its maximum at $x = 4$, after which it starts to decrease.

x (m)

0 1 2 3 4 5

Figure 14.1: Unevenly heated metal rod

Table 14.1   *Temperature $u(x)$ of the rod*

x (m)	0	1	2	3	4	5
$u(x)$ (°C)	125	128	135	160	175	160

Example 1   Estimate the derivative $u'(2)$ using Table 14.1 and explain what the answer means in terms of temperature.

Solution   The derivative $u'(2)$ is defined as a limit of difference quotients:

$$u'(2) = \lim_{h \to 0} \frac{u(2+h) - u(2)}{h}.$$

Choosing $h = 1$ so that we can use the data in Table 14.1, we get

$$u'(2) \approx \frac{u(2+1) - u(2)}{1} = \frac{160 - 135}{1} = 25.$$

This means that the temperature increases at a rate of approximately 25°C per meter as we go from left to right, past $x = 2$.

Rate of Change of Temperature in a Metal Plate

Imagine an unevenly heated thin rectangular metal plate lying in the xy-plane with its lower left corner at the origin and x and y measured in meters. The temperature (in °C) at the point (x, y) is $T(x, y)$. See Figure 14.2 and Table 14.2. How does T vary near the point $(2, 1)$? We consider the horizontal line $y = 1$ containing the point $(2, 1)$. The temperature along this line is the cross section, $T(x, 1)$, of the function $T(x, y)$ with $y = 1$. Suppose we write $u(x) = T(x, 1)$.

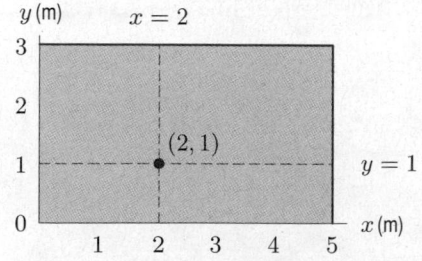

Figure 14.2: Unevenly heated metal plate

Table 14.2   *Temperature (°C) of a metal plate*

y (m)						
3	85	90	**110**	135	155	180
2	100	110	**120**	145	190	170
1	**125**	**128**	**135**	**160**	**175**	**160**
0	120	135	**155**	160	160	150
	0	1	2	3	4	5

x (m)

What is the meaning of the derivative $u'(2)$? It is the rate of change of temperature T *in the x-direction* at the point $(2, 1)$, keeping y fixed. Denote this rate of change by $T_x(2, 1)$, so that

$$T_x(2, 1) = u'(2) = \lim_{h \to 0} \frac{u(2+h) - u(2)}{h} = \lim_{h \to 0} \frac{T(2+h, 1) - T(2, 1)}{h}$$

We call $T_x(2, 1)$ the *partial derivative of T with respect to x at the point* $(2, 1)$. Taking $h = 1$, we can read values of T from the row with $y = 1$ in Table 14.2, giving

$$T_x(2, 1) \approx \frac{T(3, 1) - T(2, 1)}{1} = \frac{160 - 135}{1} = 25°\text{C/m}.$$

The fact that $T_x(2, 1)$ is positive means that the temperature of the plate is increasing as we move past the point $(2, 1)$ in the direction of increasing x (that is, horizontally from left to right in Figure 14.2).

Example 2   Estimate the rate of change of T in the y-direction at the point $(2, 1)$.

Solution   The temperature along the line $x = 2$ is the cross-section of T with $x = 2$, that is, the function $v(y) = T(2, y)$. If we denote the rate of change of T in the y-direction at $(2, 1)$ by $T_y(2, 1)$, then

$$T_y(2, 1) = v'(1) = \lim_{h \to 0} \frac{v(1 + h) - v(1)}{h} = \lim_{h \to 0} \frac{T(2, 1 + h) - T(2, 1)}{h}.$$

We call $T_y(2, 1)$ the *partial derivative of T with respect to y at the point* $(2, 1)$. Taking $h = 1$ so that we can use the column with $x = 2$ in Table 14.2, we get

$$T_y(2, 1) \approx \frac{T(2, 1 + 1) - T(2, 1)}{1} = \frac{120 - 135}{1} = -15°\text{C/m}.$$

The fact that $T_y(2, 1)$ is negative means that the temperature decreases as y increases.

Definition of the Partial Derivative

We study the influence of x and y separately on the value of the function $f(x, y)$ by holding one fixed and letting the other vary. This leads to the following definitions.

Partial Derivatives of f With Respect to x and y

For all points at which the limits exist, we define the **partial derivatives at the point** (a, b) by

$$f_x(a, b) = \begin{array}{c} \text{Rate of change of } f \text{ with respect to } x \\ \text{at the point } (a, b) \end{array} = \lim_{h \to 0} \frac{f(a + h, b) - f(a, b)}{h},$$

$$f_y(a, b) = \begin{array}{c} \text{Rate of change of } f \text{ with respect to } y \\ \text{at the point } (a, b) \end{array} = \lim_{h \to 0} \frac{f(a, b + h) - f(a, b)}{h}.$$

If we let a and b vary, we have the **partial derivative functions** $f_x(x, y)$ and $f_y(x, y)$.

Just as with ordinary derivatives, there is an alternative notation:

Alternative Notation for Partial Derivatives

If $z = f(x, y)$, we can write

$$f_x(x, y) = \frac{\partial z}{\partial x} \quad \text{and} \quad f_y(x, y) = \frac{\partial z}{\partial y},$$

$$f_x(a, b) = \frac{\partial z}{\partial x}\bigg|_{(a,b)} \quad \text{and} \quad f_y(a, b) = \frac{\partial z}{\partial y}\bigg|_{(a,b)}.$$

We use the symbol ∂ to distinguish partial derivatives from ordinary derivatives. In cases where the independent variables have names different from x and y, we adjust the notation accordingly. For example, the partial derivatives of $f(u, v)$ are denoted by f_u and f_v.

Visualizing Partial Derivatives on a Graph

The ordinary derivative of a one-variable function is the slope of its graph. How do we visualize the partial derivative $f_x(a, b)$? The graph of the one-variable function $f(x, b)$ is the curve where the vertical plane $y = b$ cuts the graph of $f(x, y)$. (See Figure 14.3.) Thus, $f_x(a, b)$ is the slope of the tangent line to this curve at $x = a$.

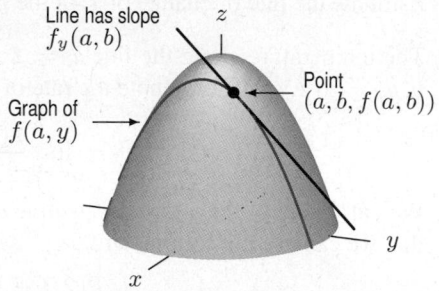

Figure 14.3: The curve $z = f(x, b)$ on the graph of f has slope $f_x(a, b)$ at $x = a$

Figure 14.4: The curve $z = f(a, y)$ on the graph of f has slope $f_y(a, b)$ at $y = b$

Similarly, the graph of the function $f(a, y)$ is the curve where the vertical plane $x = a$ cuts the graph of f, and the partial derivative $f_y(a, b)$ is the slope of this curve at $y = b$. (See Figure 14.4.)

Example 3   At each point labeled on the graph of the surface $z = f(x, y)$ in Figure 14.5, say whether each partial derivative is positive or negative.

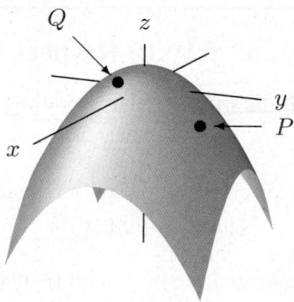

Figure 14.5: Decide the signs of f_x and f_y at P and Q

Solution   The positive x-axis points out of the page. Imagine heading off in this direction from the point marked P; we descend steeply. So the partial derivative with respect to x is negative at P, with quite a large absolute value. The same is true for the partial derivative with respect to y at P, since there is also a steep descent in the positive y-direction.

At the point marked Q, heading in the positive x-direction results in a gentle descent, whereas heading in the positive y-direction results in a gentle ascent. Thus, the partial derivative f_x at Q is negative but small (that is, near zero), and the partial derivative f_y is positive but small.

Estimating Partial Derivatives from a Contour Diagram

The graph of a function $f(x, y)$ often makes clear the sign of the partial derivatives. However, numerical estimates of these derivatives are more easily made from a contour diagram than a surface graph. If we move parallel to one of the axes on a contour diagram, the partial derivative is the rate of change of the value of the function on the contours. For example, if the values on the contours are increasing as we move in the positive direction, then the partial derivative must be positive.

Example 4   Figure 14.6 shows the contour diagram for the temperature $H(x, t)$ (in °C) in a room as a function of distance x (in meters) from a heater and time t (in minutes) after the heater has been turned on. What are the signs of $H_x(10, 20)$ and $H_t(10, 20)$? Estimate these partial derivatives and explain the answers in practical terms.

Figure 14.6: Temperature in a heated room: Heater at $x = 0$ is turned on at $t = 0$

Solution   The point $(10, 20)$ is nearly on the $H = 25$ contour. As x increases, we move toward the $H = 20$ contour, so H is decreasing and $H_x(10, 20)$ is negative. This makes sense because the $H = 30$ contour is to the left: As we move further from the heater, the temperature drops. On the other hand, as t increases, we move toward the $H = 30$ contour, so H is increasing; as t decreases H decreases. Thus, $H_t(10, 20)$ is positive. This says that as time passes, the room warms up.

To estimate the partial derivatives, use a difference quotient. Looking at the contour diagram, we see there is a point on the $H = 20$ contour about 14 units to the right of the point $(10, 20)$. Hence, H decreases by 5 when x increases by 14, so we find

$$\text{Rate of change of } H \text{ with respect to } x = H_x(10, 20) \approx \frac{-5}{14} \approx -0.36°\text{C/meter}.$$

This means that near the point 10 m from the heater, after 20 minutes the temperature drops about 0.36, or one third, of a degree, for each meter we move away from the heater.

To estimate $H_t(10, 20)$, we notice that the $H = 30$ contour is about 32 units directly above the point $(10, 20)$. So H increases by 5 when t increases by 32. Hence,

$$\text{Rate of change of } H \text{ with respect to } t = H_t(10, 20) \approx \frac{5}{32} = 0.16°\text{C/minute}.$$

This means that after 20 minutes the temperature is going up about 0.16, or 1/6, of a degree each minute at the point 10 m from the heater.

Using Units to Interpret Partial Derivatives

The meaning of a partial derivative can often be explained using units.

Example 5   Suppose that your weight w in pounds is a function $f(c, n)$ of the number c of calories you consume daily and the number n of minutes you exercise daily. Using the units for w, c and n, interpret in everyday terms the statements

$$\frac{\partial w}{\partial c}(2000, 15) = 0.02 \quad \text{and} \quad \frac{\partial w}{\partial n}(2000, 15) = -0.025.$$

Solution   The units of $\partial w / \partial c$ are pounds per calorie. The statement

$$\frac{\partial w}{\partial c}(2000, 15) = 0.02$$

means that if you are presently consuming 2000 calories daily and exercising 15 minutes daily, you will weigh 0.02 pounds more for each extra calorie you consume daily, or about 2 pounds for each extra 100 calories per day. The units of $\partial w/\partial n$ are pounds per minute. The statement

$$\frac{\partial w}{\partial n}(2000, 15) = -0.025$$

means that for the same calorie consumption and number of minutes of exercise, you will weigh 0.025 pounds less for each extra minute you exercise daily, or about 1 pound less for each extra 40 minutes per day. So if you eat an extra 100 calories each day and exercise about 80 minutes more each day, your weight should remain roughly steady.

Exercises and Problems for Section 14.1

Exercises

1. Given the following table of values for $z = f(x, y)$, estimate $f_x(3, 2)$ and $f_y(3, 2)$. Assume that f is differentiable.

$x \setminus y$	0	2	5
1	1	2	4
3	−1	1	2
6	−3	0	0

2. Using difference quotients, estimate $f_x(3, 2)$ and $f_y(3, 2)$ for the function given by

$$f(x, y) = \frac{x^2}{y + 1}.$$

[Recall: A difference quotient is an expression of the form $(f(a + h, b) − f(a, b))/h$.]

3. Use difference quotients with $\Delta x = 0.1$ and $\Delta y = 0.1$ to estimate $f_x(1, 3)$ and $f_y(1, 3)$ where

$$f(x, y) = e^{-x} \sin y.$$

Then give better estimates by using $\Delta x = 0.01$ and $\Delta y = 0.01$.

4. The price P in dollars to purchase a used car is a function of its original cost, C, in dollars, and its age, A, in years.

   (a) What are the units of $\partial P/\partial A$?
   (b) What is the sign of $\partial P/\partial A$ and why?
   (c) What are the units of $\partial P/\partial C$?
   (d) What is the sign of $\partial P/\partial C$ and why?

5. Your monthly car payment in dollars is $P = f(P_0, t, r)$, where $\$P_0$ is the amount you borrowed, t is the number of months it takes to pay off the loan, and $r\%$ is the interest rate. What are the units, the financial meaning, and the signs of $\partial P/\partial t$ and $\partial P/\partial r$?

6. A drug is injected into a patient's blood vessel. The function $c = f(x, t)$ represents the concentration of the drug at a distance x mm in the direction of the blood flow measured from the point of injection and at time t seconds since the injection. What are the units of the following partial derivatives? What are their practical interpretations? What do you expect their signs to be?

   (a) $\partial c/\partial x$ (b) $\partial c/\partial t$

7. You borrow $\$A$ at an interest rate of $r\%$ (per month) and pay it off over t months by making monthly payments of $P = g(A, r, t)$ dollars. In financial terms, what do the following statements tell you?

   (a) $g(8000, 1, 24) = 376.59$
   (b) $\left.\dfrac{\partial g}{\partial A}\right|_{(8000,1,24)} = 0.047$
   (c) $\left.\dfrac{\partial g}{\partial r}\right|_{(8000,1,24)} = 44.83$

8. The sales of a product, $S = f(p, a)$, are a function of the price, p, of the product (in dollars per unit) and the amount, a, spent on advertising (in thousands of dollars).

   (a) Do you expect f_p to be positive or negative? Why?
   (b) Explain the meaning of the statement $f_a(8, 12) = 150$ in terms of sales.

9. The quantity, Q, of beef purchased at a store, in kilograms per week, is a function of the price of beef, b, and the price of chicken, c, both in dollars per kilogram.

   (a) Do you expect $\partial Q/\partial b$ to be positive or negative? Explain.
   (b) Do you expect $\partial Q/\partial c$ to be positive or negative? Explain.
   (c) Interpret the statement $\partial Q/\partial b = -213$ in terms of quantity of beef purchased.

In Exercises 10–13, determine the sign of f_x and f_y at the point using the contour diagram of f in Figure 14.7.

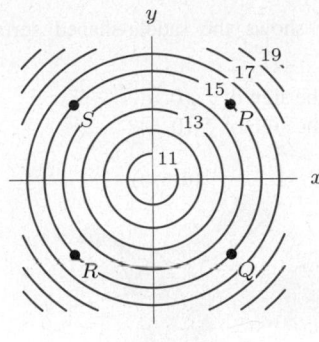

Figure 14.7

10. P **11.** Q **12.** R **13.** S

For Exercises 14–16, refer to Table 12.2 on page 672 giving the temperature adjusted for wind chill, C, in $^\circ$F, as a function $f(w, T)$ of the wind speed, w, in mph, and the temperature, T, in $^\circ$F. The temperature adjusted for wind chill tells you how cold it feels, as a result of the combination of wind and temperature.

14. Estimate $f_w(10, 25)$. What does your answer mean in practical terms?

15. Estimate $f_T(5, 20)$. What does your answer mean in practical terms?

16. From Table 12.2 you can see that when the temperature is 20°F, the temperature adjusted for wind-chill drops by an average of about 0.8°F with every 1 mph increase in wind speed from 5 mph to 10 mph. Which partial derivative is this telling you about?

Problems

17. Figure 14.8 is a contour diagram for $z = f(x, y)$. Is f_x positive or negative? Is f_y positive or negative? Estimate $f(2, 1)$, $f_x(2, 1)$, and $f_y(2, 1)$.

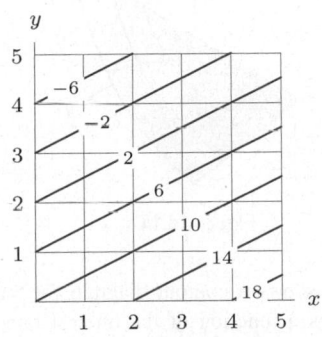

Figure 14.8

18. Approximate $f_x(3, 5)$ using the contour diagram of $f(x, y)$ in Figure 14.9.

Figure 14.9

19. The quantity Q (in pounds) of beef that a certain community buys during a week is a function $Q = f(b, c)$ of the prices of beef, b, and chicken, c, during the week. Do you expect $\partial Q/\partial b$ to be positive or negative? What about $\partial Q/\partial c$?

20. The average price of large cars getting low gas mileage ("gas guzzlers") is x and the average price of a gallon of gasoline is y. The number, q_1, of gas guzzlers bought in a year, depends on both x and y, so $q_1 = f(x, y)$. Similarly, if q_2 is the number of gallons of gas bought to fill gas guzzlers in a year, then $q_2 = g(x, y)$.

  (a) What do you expect the signs of $\partial q_1/\partial x$ and $\partial q_2/\partial y$ to be? Explain.

  (b) What do you expect the signs of $\partial q_1/\partial y$ and $\partial q_2/\partial x$ to be? Explain.

21. An experiment to measure the toxicity of formaldehyde yielded the data in Table 14.3. The values show the percent, $P = f(t, c)$, of rats surviving an exposure to formaldehyde at a concentration of c (in parts per million, ppm) after t months. Estimate $f_t(18, 6)$ and $f_c(18, 6)$. Interpret your answers in terms of formaldehyde toxicity.

Table 14.3

		Time t (months)					
		14	16	18	20	22	24
	0	100	100	100	99	97	95
Conc. c	2	100	99	98	97	95	92
(ppm)	6	96	95	93	90	86	80
	15	96	93	82	70	58	36

22. Figure 14.10 shows contours of $f(x, y)$ with values of f on the contours omitted. If $f_x(P) > 0$, find the sign of

(a) $f_y(P)$ **(b)** $f_y(Q)$ **(c)** $f_x(Q)$

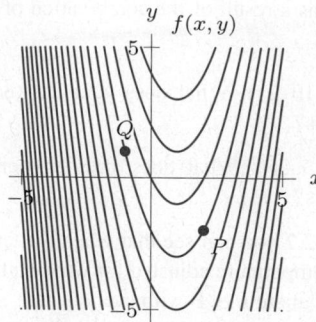

Figure 14.10

23. Figure 14.11 shows the contour diagram of $g(x, y)$. Mark the points on the contours where

(a) $g_x = 0$ **(b)** $g_y = 0$

Figure 14.11

24. The surface $z = f(x, y)$ is shown in Figure 14.12. The points A and B are in the xy-plane.

(a) What is the sign of
   (i) $f_x(A)$?   (ii) $f_y(A)$?

(b) The point P in the xy-plane moves along a straight line from A to B. How does the sign of $f_x(P)$ change? How does the sign of $f_y(P)$ change?

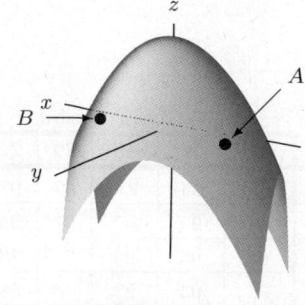

Figure 14.12

25. Figure 14.13 shows the saddle-shaped surface $z = f(x, y)$.

(a) What is the sign of $f_x(0, 5)$?

(b) What is the sign of $f_y(0, 5)$?

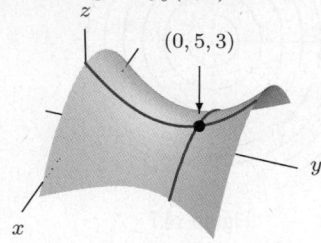

Figure 14.13

26. Figure 14.14 shows the graph of the function $f(x, y)$ on the domain $0 \leq x \leq 4$ and $0 \leq y \leq 4$. Use the graph to rank the following quantities in order from smallest to largest: $f_x(3, 2)$, $f_x(1, 2)$, $f_y(3, 2)$, $f_y(1, 2)$, 0.

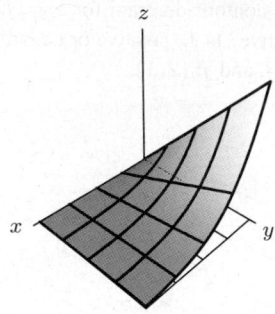

Figure 14.14

27. Figure 14.15 shows a contour diagram for the monthly payment P as a function of the interest rate, $r\%$, and the amount, L, of a 5-year loan. Estimate $\partial P/\partial r$ and $\partial P/\partial L$ at the following points. In each case, give the units and the everyday meaning of your answer.

(a) $r = 8, L = 4000$ **(b)** $r = 8, L = 6000$

(c) $r = 13, L = 7000$

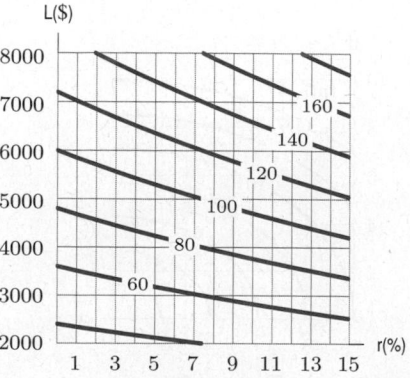

Figure 14.15

28. People commuting to a city can choose to go either by bus or by train. The number of people who choose either method depends in part upon the price of each. Let $f(P_1, P_2)$ be the number of people who take the bus when P_1 is the price of a bus ride and P_2 is the price of a train ride. What can you say about the signs of $\partial f/\partial P_1$ and $\partial f/\partial P_2$? Explain your answers.

29. When riding your bike in winter, the windchill temperature is a measure of how cold you feel as a result of the induced breeze caused by your travel. If W represents windchill temperature (in °F) that you experience, then $W = f(T, v)$, where T is the actual air temperature (in °F) and v is your speed, in meters per second. Match each of the practical interpretations below with a mathematical statement that most accurately describes it below. For the remaining mathematical statement, give a practical interpretation.

  (i) "The faster you ride, the colder you'll feel."
  (ii) "The warmer the day, the warmer you'll feel."

  (a) $f_T(T, v) > 0$
  (b) $f(0, v) \leq 0$
  (c) $f_v(T, v) < 0$

30. Figure 14.16 shows a contour diagram for the temperature T (in °C) along a wall in a heated room as a function of distance x along the wall and time t in minutes. Estimate $\partial T/\partial x$ and $\partial T/\partial t$ at the given points. Give units and interpret your answers.

  (a) $x = 15, t = 20$ (b) $x = 5, t = 12$

t (minutes)

Figure 14.16

An airport can be cleared of fog by heating the air. The amount of heat required depends on the air temperature and the wetness of the fog. Problems 31–33 involve Figure 14.17, which shows the heat $H(T, w)$ required (in calories per cubic meter of fog) as a function of the temperature T (in degrees Celsius) and the water content w (in grams per cubic meter of fog). Note that Figure 14.17 is not a contour diagram, but shows cross-sections of H with w fixed at 0.1, 0.2, 0.3, and 0.4.

H (calories/m^3)

Figure 14.17

31. Use Figure 14.17 to estimate $H_T(10, 0.1)$. Interpret the partial derivative in practical terms.

32. Make a table of values for $H(T, w)$ from Figure 14.17, and use it to estimate $H_T(T, w)$ for $T = 10, 20$, and 30 and $w = 0.1, 0.2$, and 0.3.

33. Repeat Problem 32 for $H_w(T, w)$ at $T = 10, 20$, and 30 and $w = 0.1, 0.2$, and 0.3. What is the practical meaning of these partial derivatives?

34. The cardiac output, represented by c, is the volume of blood flowing through a person's heart per unit time. The systemic vascular resistance (SVR), represented by s, is the resistance to blood flowing through veins and arteries. Let p be a person's blood pressure. Then p is a function of c and s, so $p = f(c, s)$.

  (a) What does $\partial p/\partial c$ represent?

  Suppose now that $p = kcs$, where k is a constant.

  (b) Sketch the level curves of p. What do they represent? Label your axes.
  (c) For a person with a weak heart, it is desirable to have the heart pumping against less resistance, while maintaining the same blood pressure. Such a person may be given the drug nitroglycerine to decrease the SVR and the drug Dopamine to increase the cardiac output. Represent this on a graph showing level curves. Put a point A on the graph representing the person's state before drugs are given and a point B for after.
  (d) Right after a heart attack, a patient's cardiac output drops, thereby causing the blood pressure to drop. A common mistake made by medical residents is to get the patient's blood pressure back to normal by using drugs to increase the SVR, rather than by increasing the cardiac output. On a graph of the level curves of p, put a point D representing the patient before the heart attack, a point E representing the patient right

after the heart attack, and a third point F representing the patient after the resident has given the drugs to increase the SVR.

35. In each case, give a possible contour diagram for the

function $f(x, y)$ if

(a) $f_x > 0$ and $f_y > 0$ (b) $f_x > 0$ and $f_y < 0$

(c) $f_x < 0$ and $f_y > 0$ (d) $f_x < 0$ and $f_y < 0$

Strengthen Your Understanding

In Problems 36–37, explain what is wrong with the statement.

36. For $f(x, y)$, $\partial f/\partial x$ has the same units as $\partial f/\partial y$.

37. The partial derivative with respect to y is not defined for functions such as $f(x, y) = x^2 + 5$ that have a formula that does not contain y explicitly.

In Problems 38–39, give an example of:

38. A table of values with three rows and three columns of a linear function $f(x, y)$ with $f_x < 0$ and $f_y > 0$.

39. A function $f(x, y)$ with $f_x > 0$ and $f_y < 0$ everywhere.

Are the statements in Problems 40–49 true or false? Give reasons for your answer.

40. If $f(x, y)$ is a function of two variables and $f_x(10, 20)$ is defined, then $f_x(10, 20)$ is a scalar.

41. If $f(x, y) = x^2 + y^2$, then $f_y(1, 1) < 0$.

42. If the graph of $f(x, y)$ is a hemisphere centered at the origin, then $f_x(0, 0) = f_y(0, 0) = 0$.

43. If $P = f(T, V)$ is a function expressing the pressure P (in grams/cm^3) of gas in a piston in terms of the temperature T (in degrees °C) and volume V (in cm^3), then $\partial P/\partial V$ has units of grams.

44. If $f_x(a, b) > 0$, then the values of f decrease as we move in the negative x-direction near (a, b).

45. If $g(r, s) = r^2 + s$, then for fixed s, the partial derivative g_r increases as r increases.

46. If $g(u, v) = (u + v)^u$, then $2.3 \le g_u(1, 1) \le 2.4$.

47. Let $P = f(m, d)$ be the purchase price (in dollars) of a used car that has m miles on its engine and originally cost d dollars when new. Then $\partial P/\partial m$ and $\partial P/\partial d$ have the same sign.

48. If $f(x, y)$ is a function with the property that $f_x(x, y)$ and $f_y(x, y)$ are both constant, then f is linear.

49. If $f(x, y)$ has $f_x(a, b) = f_y(a, b) = 0$ at the point (a, b), then f is constant everywhere.

14.2 COMPUTING PARTIAL DERIVATIVES ALGEBRAICALLY

Since the partial derivative $f_x(x, y)$ is the ordinary derivative of the function $f(x, y)$ with y held constant and $f_y(x, y)$ is the ordinary derivative of $f(x, y)$ with x held constant, we can use all the differentiation formulas from one-variable calculus to find partial derivatives.

Example 1   Let $f(x, y) = \dfrac{x^2}{y + 1}$. Find $f_x(3, 2)$ algebraically.

Solution   We use the fact that $f_x(3, 2)$ equals the derivative of $f(x, 2)$ at $x = 3$. Since

$$f(x, 2) = \frac{x^2}{2 + 1} = \frac{x^2}{3},$$

differentiating with respect to x, we have

$$f_x(x, 2) = \frac{\partial}{\partial x}\left(\frac{x^2}{3}\right) = \frac{2x}{3}, \qquad \text{and so} \qquad f_x(3, 2) = 2.$$

Example 2   Compute the partial derivatives with respect to x and with respect to y for the following functions.

(a) $f(x, y) = y^2 e^{3x}$ (b) $z = (3xy + 2x)^5$ (c) $g(x, y) = e^{x+3y} \sin(xy)$

Solution   (a) This is the product of a function of x (namely e^{3x}) and a function of y (namely y^2). When we differentiate with respect to x, we think of the function of y as a constant, and vice versa. Thus,

$$f_x(x, y) = y^2 \frac{\partial}{\partial x}\left(e^{3x}\right) = 3y^2 e^{3x},$$

$$f_y(x, y) = e^{3x} \frac{\partial}{\partial y}(y^2) = 2y e^{3x}.$$

(b) Here we use the chain rule:

$$\frac{\partial z}{\partial x} = 5(3xy + 2x)^4 \frac{\partial}{\partial x}(3xy + 2x) = 5(3xy + 2x)^4(3y + 2),$$

$$\frac{\partial z}{\partial y} = 5(3xy + 2x)^4 \frac{\partial}{\partial y}(3xy + 2x) = 5(3xy + 2x)^4 3x = 15x(3xy + 2x)^4.$$

(c) Since each function in the product is a function of both x and y, we need to use the product rule for each partial derivative:

$$g_x(x, y) = \left(\frac{\partial}{\partial x}(e^{x+3y})\right)\sin(xy) + e^{x+3y}\frac{\partial}{\partial x}(\sin(xy)) = e^{x+3y}\sin(xy) + e^{x+3y}y\cos(xy),$$

$$g_y(x, y) = \left(\frac{\partial}{\partial y}(e^{x+3y})\right)\sin(xy) + e^{x+3y}\frac{\partial}{\partial y}(\sin(xy)) = 3e^{x+3y}\sin(xy) + e^{x+3y}x\cos(xy).$$

For functions of three or more variables, we find partial derivatives by the same method: Differentiate with respect to one variable, regarding the other variables as constants. For a function $f(x, y, z)$, the partial derivative $f_x(a, b, c)$ gives the rate of change of f with respect to x along the line $y = b$, $z = c$.

Example 3 Find all the partial derivatives of $f(x, y, z) = \dfrac{x^2 y^3}{z}$.

Solution To find $f_x(x, y, z)$, for example, we consider y and z as fixed, giving

$$f_x(x, y, z) = \frac{2xy^3}{z}, \quad \text{and} \quad f_y(x, y, z) = \frac{3x^2 y^2}{z}, \quad \text{and} \quad f_z(x, y, z) = -\frac{x^2 y^3}{z^2}.$$

Interpretation of Partial Derivatives

Example 4 A vibrating guitar string, originally at rest along the x-axis, is shown in Figure 14.18. Let x be the distance in meters from the left end of the string. At time t seconds the point x has been displaced $y = f(x, t)$ meters vertically from its rest position, where

$$y = f(x, t) = 0.003\sin(\pi x)\sin(2765t).$$

Evaluate $f_x(0.3, 1)$ and $f_t(0.3, 1)$ and explain what each means in practical terms.

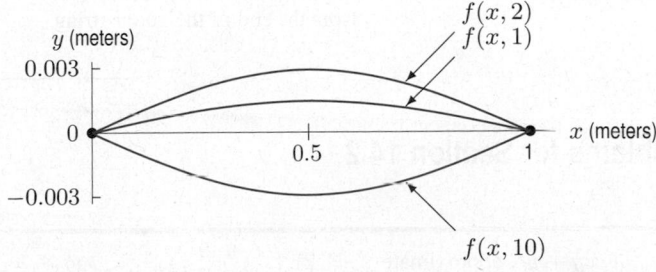

Figure 14.18: The position of a vibrating guitar string at several different times: Graph of $f(x, t)$ for $t = 1, 2, 10$.

Solution Differentiating $f(x, t) = 0.003\sin(\pi x)\sin(2765t)$ with respect to x, we have

$$f_x(x, t) = 0.003\pi\cos(\pi x)\sin(2765t).$$

In particular, substituting $x = 0.3$ and $t = 1$ gives

$$f_x(0.3, 1) = 0.003\pi\cos(\pi(0.3))\sin(2765) \approx 0.002.$$

To see what $f_x(0.3, 1)$ means, think about the function $f(x, 1)$. The graph of $f(x, 1)$ in Figure 14.19 is a snapshot of the string at the time $t = 1$. Thus, the derivative $f_x(0.3, 1)$ is the slope of the string at the point $x = 0.3$ at the instant when $t = 1$.

Similarly, taking the derivative of $f(x, t) = 0.003 \sin(\pi x) \sin(2765t)$ with respect to t, we get

$$f_t(x, t) = (0.003)(2765) \sin(\pi x) \cos(2765t) = 8.3 \sin(\pi x) \cos(2765t).$$

Since $f(x, t)$ is in meters and t is in seconds, the derivative $f_t(0.3, 1)$ is in m/sec. Thus, substituting $x = 0.3$ and $t = 1$,

$$f_t(0.3, 1) = 8.3 \sin(\pi(0.3)) \cos(2765(1)) \approx 6 \text{ m/sec}.$$

Figure 14.19: Graph of $f(x, 1)$: Snapshot of the shape of the string at $t = 1$ sec

To see what $f_t(0.3, 1)$ means, think about the function $f(0.3, t)$. The graph of $f(0.3, t)$ is a position versus time graph that tracks the up-and-down movement of the point on the string where $x = 0.3$. (See Figure 14.20.) The derivative $f_t(0.3, 1) = 6$ m/sec is the velocity of that point on the string at time $t = 1$. The fact that $f_t(0.3, 1)$ is positive indicates that the point is moving upward when $t = 1$.

Figure 14.20: Graph of $f(0.3, t)$: Position versus time graph of the point $x = 0.3$ m from the end of the guitar string

Exercises and Problems for Section 14.2

Exercises

1. (a) If $f(x, y) = 2x^2 + xy + y^2$, approximate $f_y(3, 2)$ using $\Delta y = 0.01$.
   (b) Find the exact value of $f_y(3, 2)$.

Find the partial derivatives in Exercises 2–40. Assume the variables are restricted to a domain on which the function is defined.

2. f_x and f_y if $f(x, y) = 5x^2y^3 + 8xy^2 - 3x^2$

3. $f_x(1, 2)$ and $f_y(1, 2)$ if $f(x, y) = x^3 + 3x^2y - 2y^2$

4. $\dfrac{\partial}{\partial y}(3x^5y^7 - 32x^4y^3 + 5xy)$

5. $\dfrac{\partial z}{\partial x}$ and $\dfrac{\partial z}{\partial y}$ if $z = (x^2 + x - y)^7$

6. f_x and f_y if $f(x, y) = A^\alpha x^{\alpha+\beta} y^{1-\alpha-\beta}$

7. f_x and f_y if $f(x, y) = \ln(x^{0.6} y^{0.4})$

8. z_x if $z = \dfrac{1}{2x^2ay} + \dfrac{3x^5abc}{y}$

9. z_x if $z = x^2 y + 2x^5 y$

10. V_r if $V = \frac{1}{3}\pi r^2 h$

11. $\dfrac{\partial}{\partial T}\left(\dfrac{2\pi r}{T}\right)$

12. $\dfrac{\partial}{\partial x}(a\sqrt{x})$

13. $\dfrac{\partial}{\partial x}(xe^{\sqrt{xy}})$

14. $\dfrac{\partial}{\partial t}e^{\sin(x+ct)}$

15. F_m if $F = mg$

16. a_v if $a = \dfrac{v^2}{r}$

17. $\dfrac{\partial A}{\partial h}$ if $A = \frac{1}{2}(a+b)h$

18. $\dfrac{\partial}{\partial m}\left(\frac{1}{2}mv^2\right)$

19. $\dfrac{\partial}{\partial B}\left(\dfrac{1}{u_0}B^2\right)$

20. $\dfrac{\partial}{\partial r}\left(\dfrac{2\pi r}{v}\right)$

21. F_v if $F = \dfrac{mv^2}{r}$

22. $\dfrac{\partial}{\partial v_0}(v_0 + at)$

23. $\dfrac{\partial F}{\partial m_2}$ if $F = \dfrac{Gm_1 m_2}{r^2}$

24. $\dfrac{\partial}{\partial x}\left(\dfrac{1}{a}e^{-x^2/a^2}\right)$

25. $\dfrac{\partial}{\partial a}\left(\dfrac{1}{a}e^{-x^2/a^2}\right)$

26. f_x if $f(x,y) = e^{xy}(\ln y)$

27. $\dfrac{\partial}{\partial t}\left(v_0 t + \dfrac{1}{2}at^2\right)$

28. $\dfrac{\partial}{\partial\theta}\left(\sin(\pi\theta\phi) + \ln(\theta^2 + \phi)\right)$

29. $\dfrac{\partial}{\partial M}\left(\dfrac{2\pi r^{3/2}}{\sqrt{GM}}\right)$

30. f_a if $f(a,b) = e^a\sin(a+b)$

31. z_x if $z = \sin(5x^3 y - 3xy^2)$

32. g_x if $g(x,y) = \ln(ye^{xy})$

33. F_L if $F(L,K) = 3\sqrt{LK}$

34. $\dfrac{\partial V}{\partial r}$ and $\dfrac{\partial V}{\partial h}$ if $V = \frac{4}{3}\pi r^2 h$

35. u_E if $u = \dfrac{1}{2}\epsilon_0 E^2 + \dfrac{1}{2\mu_0}B^2$

36. $\dfrac{\partial}{\partial x}\left(\dfrac{1}{\sqrt{2\pi}\sigma}e^{-(x-\mu)^2/(2\sigma^2)}\right)$

37. $\dfrac{\partial Q}{\partial K}$ if $Q = c(a_1 K^{b_1} + a_2 L^{b_2})^\gamma$

38. z_x and z_y for $z = x^7 + 2^y + x^y$

39. $\dfrac{\partial z}{\partial y}\bigg|_{(1,0.5)}$ if $z = e^{x+2y}\sin y$

40. $\dfrac{\partial f}{\partial x}\bigg|_{(\pi/3,1)}$ if $f(x,y) = x\ln(y\cos x)$

Problems

41. (a) Let $f(x,y) = x^2 + y^2$. Estimate $f_x(2,1)$ and $f_y(2,1)$ using the contour diagram for f in Figure 14.21.
  (b) Estimate $f_x(2,1)$ and $f_y(2,1)$ from a table of values for f with $x = 1.9, 2, 2.1$ and $y = 0.9, 1, 1.1$.
  (c) Compare your estimates in parts (a) and (b) with the exact values of $f_x(2,1)$ and $f_y(2,1)$ found algebraically.

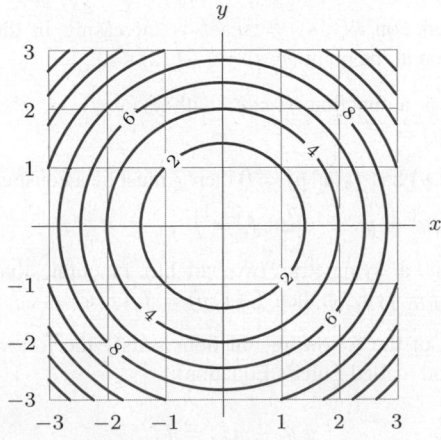

Figure 14.21

42. (a) Let $f(w,z) = e^{w\ln z}$. Use difference quotients with $h = 0.01$ to approximate $f_w(2,2)$ and $f_z(2,2)$.

(b) Now evaluate $f_w(2,2)$ and $f_z(2,2)$ exactly.

43. (a) The surface S is given, for some constant a, by

$$z = 3x^2 + 4y^2 - axy$$

Find the values of a which ensure that S is sloping upward when we move in the positive x-direction from the point $(1,2)$.

(b) With the values of a from part (a), if you move in the positive y-direction from the point $(1,2)$, does the surface slope up or down? Explain.

44. Money in a bank account earns interest at a continuous rate, r. The amount of money, $\$B$, in the account depends on the amount deposited, $\$P$, and the time, t, it has been in the bank according to the formula

$$B = Pe^{rt}.$$

Find $\partial B/\partial t$ and $\partial B/\partial P$ and interpret each in financial terms.

45. The acceleration g due to gravity, at a distance r from the center of a planet of mass m, is given by

$$g = \frac{Gm}{r^2},$$

where G is the universal gravitational constant.

(a) Find $\partial g/\partial m$ and $\partial g/\partial r$.

(b) Interpret each of the partial derivatives you found in part (a) as the slope of a graph in the plane and sketch the graph.

46. The Dubois formula relates a person's surface area, s, in m^2, to weight, w, in kg, and height, h, in cm, by

$$s = f(w, h) = 0.01 w^{0.25} h^{0.75}.$$

Find $f(65, 160)$, $f_w(65, 160)$, and $f_h(65, 160)$. Interpret your answers in terms of surface area, height, and weight.

47. The energy, E, of a body of mass m moving with speed v is given by the formula

$$E = mc^2 \left(\frac{1}{\sqrt{1 - v^2/c^2}} - 1 \right).$$

The speed, v, is nonnegative and less than the speed of light, c, which is a constant.

(a) Find $\partial E/\partial m$. What would you expect the sign of $\partial E/\partial m$ to be? Explain.

(b) Find $\partial E/\partial v$. Explain what you would expect the sign of $\partial E/\partial v$ to be and why.

48. Let $h(x, t) = 5 + \cos(0.5x - t)$ describe a wave. The value of $h(x, t)$ gives the depth of the water in cm at a distance x meters from a fixed point and at time t seconds. Evaluate $h_x(2, 5)$ and $h_t(2, 5)$ and interpret each in terms of the wave.

49. A one-meter long bar is heated unevenly, with temperature in °C at a distance x meters from one end at time t given by

$$H(x, t) = 100e^{-0.1t} \sin(\pi x) \qquad 0 \le x \le 1.$$

(a) Sketch a graph of H against x for $t = 0$ and $t = 1$.

(b) Calculate $H_x(0.2, t)$ and $H_x(0.8, t)$. What is the practical interpretation (in terms of temperature) of these two partial derivatives? Explain why each one has the sign it does.

(c) Calculate $H_t(x, t)$. What is its sign? What is its interpretation in terms of temperature?

50. Show that the Cobb-Douglas function

$$Q = bK^{\alpha} L^{1-\alpha} \quad \text{where} \quad 0 < \alpha < 1$$

satisfies the equation

$$K \frac{\partial Q}{\partial K} + L \frac{\partial Q}{\partial L} = Q.$$

51. Is there a function f which has the following partial derivatives? If so what is it? Are there any others?

$$f_x(x, y) = 4x^3 y^2 - 3y^4,$$
$$f_y(x, y) = 2x^4 y - 12xy^3.$$

Strengthen Your Understanding

In Problems 52–53, explain what is wrong with the statement.

52. The partial derivative of $f(x, y) = x^2 y^3$ is $2xy^3 + 3y^2 x^2$.

53. For $f(x, y)$, if $\dfrac{f(0.01, 0) - f(0, 0)}{0.01} > 0$, then $f_x(0, 0) > 0$.

In Problems 54–56, give an example of:

54. A nonlinear function $f(x, y)$ such that $f_x(0, 0) = 2$ and $f_y(0, 0) = 3$.

55. Functions $f(x, y)$ and $g(x, y)$ such that $f_x = g_x$ but $f_y \ne g_y$.

56. A non-constant function $f(x, y)$ such that $f_x = 0$ everywhere.

Are the statements in Problems 57–64 true or false? Give reasons for your answer.

57. There is a function $f(x, y)$ with $f_x(x, y) = y$ and $f_y(x, y) = x$.

58. The function $z(u, v) = u \cos v$ satisfies the equation

$$\cos v \frac{\partial z}{\partial u} - \frac{\sin v}{u} \frac{\partial z}{\partial v} = 1.$$

59. If $f(x, y)$ is a function of two variables and $g(x)$ is a function of a single variable, then

$$\frac{\partial}{\partial y} (g(x)f(x, y)) = g(x)f_y(x, y).$$

60. The function $k(r, s) = rse^s$ is increasing in the s-direction at the point $(r, s) = (-1, 2)$.

61. There is a function $f(x, y)$ with $f_x(x, y) = y^2$ and $f_y(x, y) = x^2$.

62. If $f(x, y)$ has $f_y(x, y) = 0$ then f must be a constant.

63. If $f(x, y) = ye^{g(x)}$ then $f_x = f$.

64. If f is a symmetric two-variable function, that is $f(x, y) = f(y, x)$, then $f_x(x, y) = f_y(x, y)$.

65. Which of the following functions satisfy the following equation (called Euler's Equation):

$$xf_x + yf_y = f?$$

(a) $x^2 y^3$ (b) $x+y+1$ (c) $x^2 + y^2$ (d) $x^{0.4} y^{0.6}$

14.3 LOCAL LINEARITY AND THE DIFFERENTIAL

In Sections 14.1 and 14.2 we studied a function of two variables by allowing one variable at a time to change. We now let both variables change at once to develop a linear approximation for functions of two variables.

Zooming In to See Local Linearity

For a function of one variable, local linearity means that as we zoom in on the graph, it looks like a straight line. As we zoom in on the graph of a two-variable function, the graph usually looks like a plane, which is the graph of a linear function of two variables. (See Figure 14.22.)

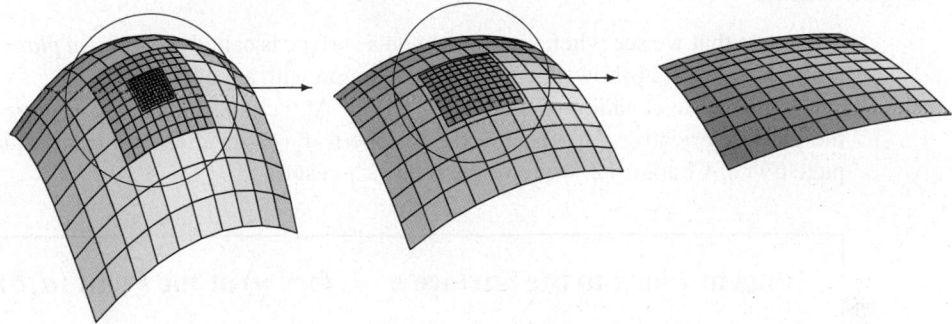

Figure 14.22: Zooming in on the graph of a function of two variables until the graph looks like a plane

Similarly, Figure 14.23 shows three successive views of the contours near a point. As we zoom in, the contours look more like equally spaced parallel lines, which are the contours of a linear function. (As we zoom in, we have to add more contours.)

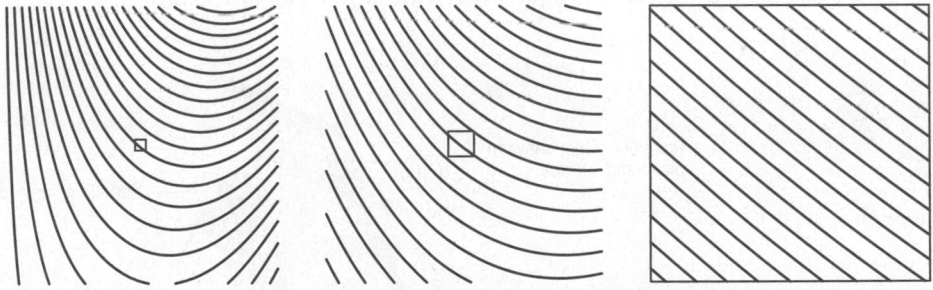

Figure 14.23: Zooming in on a contour diagram until the lines look parallel and equally spaced

This effect can also be seen numerically by zooming in with tables of values. Table 14.4 shows three tables of values for $f(x, y) = x^2 + y^3$ near $x = 2$, $y = 1$, each one a closer view than the previous one. Notice how each table looks more like the table of a linear function.

Table 14.4   *Zooming in on values of $f(x, y) = x^2 + y^3$ near $(2, 1)$ until the table looks linear*

		y	
		0	1	2
x	1	1	2	9
	2	4	5	12
	3	9	10	17

		y	
		0.9	1.0	1.1
x	1.9	4.34	4.61	4.94
	2.0	4.73	5.00	5.33
	2.1	5.14	5.41	5.74

		y	
		0.99	1.00	1.01
x	1.99	4.93	4.96	4.99
	2.00	4.97	5.00	5.03
	2.01	5.01	5.04	5.07

Zooming in Algebraically: Differentiability

Seeing a plane when we zoom in at a point tells us (provided the plane is not vertical) that $f(x, y)$ is closely approximated near that point by a linear function, $L(x, y)$:

$$f(x, y) \approx L(x, y).$$

The graph of the function $z = L(x, y)$ is the tangent plane at that point. Provided the approximation is sufficiently good, we say that $f(x, y)$ is *differentiable* at the point. Section 14.8 on page 815 defines precisely what is meant by the approximation being sufficiently good. The functions we encounter are differentiable at most points in their domain.

The Tangent Plane

The plane that we see when we zoom in on a surface is called the *tangent plane* to the surface at the point. Figure 14.24 shows the graph of a function with a tangent plane.

What is the equation of the tangent plane? At the point (a, b), the x-slope of the graph of f is the partial derivative $f_x(a, b)$ and the y-slope is $f_y(a, b)$. Thus, using the equation for a plane on page 694 of Chapter 12, we have the following result:

Tangent Plane to the Surface $z = f(x, y)$ at the Point (a, b)

Assuming f is differentiable at (a, b), the equation of the tangent plane is

$$z = f(a, b) + f_x(a, b)(x - a) + f_y(a, b)(y - b).$$

Here we are thinking of a and b as fixed, so $f(a, b)$, and $f_x(a, b)$, and $f_y(a, b)$ are constants. Thus, the right side of the equation is a linear function of x and y.

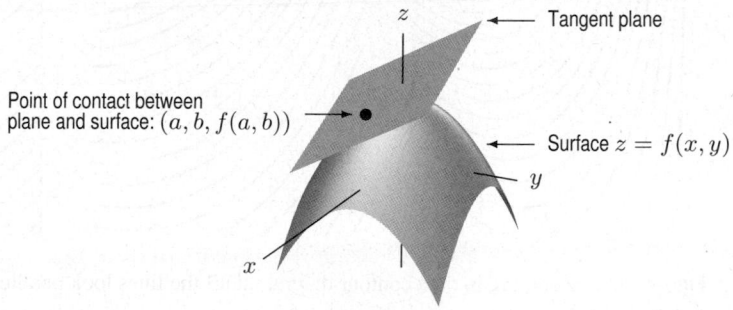

Figure 14.24: The tangent plane to the surface $z = f(x, y)$ at the point (a, b)

Example 1   Find the equation for the tangent plane to the surface $z = x^2 + y^2$ at the point $(3, 4)$.

Solution   We have $f_x(x, y) = 2x$, so $f_x(3, 4) = 6$, and $f_y(x, y) = 2y$, so $f_y(3, 4) = 8$. Also, $f(3, 4) = 3^2 + 4^2 = 25$. Thus, the equation for the tangent plane at $(3, 4)$ is

$$z = 25 + 6(x - 3) + 8(y - 4).$$

Local Linearization

Since the tangent plane lies close to the surface near the point at which they meet, z-values on the tangent plane are close to values of $f(x, y)$ for points near (a, b). Thus, replacing z by $f(x, y)$ in the equation of the tangent plane, we get the following approximation:

Tangent Plane Approximation to $f(x, y)$ for (x, y) Near the Point (a, b)

Provided f is differentiable at (a, b), we can approximate $f(x, y)$:

$$f(x, y) \approx f(a, b) + f_x(a, b)(x - a) + f_y(a, b)(y - b).$$

We are thinking of a and b as fixed, so the expression on the right side is linear in x and y. The right side of this approximation gives the **local linearization** of f near $x = a$, $y = b$.

Figure 14.25 shows the tangent plane approximation graphically.

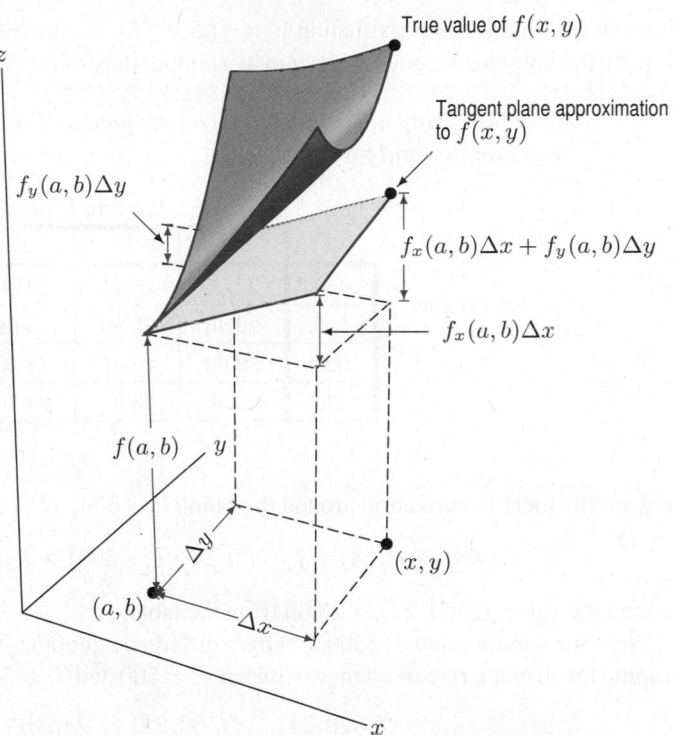

Figure 14.25: Local linearization: Approximating $f(x, y)$ by the z-value from the tangent plane

---

Example 2   Find the local linearization of $f(x, y) = x^2 + y^2$ at the point $(3, 4)$. Estimate $f(2.9, 4.2)$ and $f(2, 2)$ using the linearization and compare your answers to the true values.

Solution   Let $z = f(x, y) = x^2 + y^2$. In Example 1 on page 772, we found the equation of the tangent plane at $(3, 4)$ to be

$$z = 25 + 6(x - 3) + 8(y - 4).$$

Therefore, for (x, y) near $(3, 4)$, we have the local linearization

$$f(x, y) \approx 25 + 6(x - 3) + 8(y - 4).$$

Substituting $x = 2.9, y = 4.2$ gives

$$f(2.9, 4.2) \approx 25 + 6(-0.1) + 8(0.2) = 26.$$

This compares favorably with the true value $f(2.9, 4.2) = (2.9)^2 + (4.2)^2 = 26.05$.

However, the local linearization does not give a good approximation at points far away from $(3, 4)$. For example, if $x = 2$, $y = 2$, the local linearization gives

$$f(2, 2) \approx 25 + 6(-1) + 8(-2) = 3,$$

whereas the true value of the function is $f(2, 2) = 2^2 + 2^2 = 8$.

Example 3   Designing safe boilers depends on knowing how steam behaves under changes in temperature and pressure. Steam tables, such as Table 14.5, are published giving values of the function $V = f(T, P)$ where V is the volume (in ft^3) of one pound of steam at a temperature T (in °F) and pressure P (in lb/in^2).

(a) Give a linear function approximating $V = f(T, P)$ for T near 500°F and P near 24 lb/in^2.
(b) Estimate the volume of a pound of steam at a temperature of 505°F and a pressure of 24.3 lb/in^2.

Table 14.5   *Volume (in cubic feet) of one pound of steam at various temperatures and pressures*

		Pressure P (lb/in^2)			
		20	22	24	26
	480	27.85	25.31	23.19	21.39
Temperature	500	28.46	25.86	23.69	21.86
T	520	29.06	26.41	24.20	22.33
(°F)	540	29.66	26.95	24.70	22.79

Solution   (a) We want the local linearization around the point $T = 500$, $P = 24$, which is

$$f(T, P) \approx f(500, 24) + f_T(500, 24)(T - 500) + f_P(500, 24)(P - 24).$$

We read the value $f(500, 24) = 23.69$ from the table.

Next we approximate $f_T(500, 24)$ by a difference quotient. From the $P = 24$ column, we compute the average rate of change between $T = 500$ and $T = 520$:

$$f_T(500, 24) \approx \frac{f(520, 24) - f(500, 24)}{520 - 500} = \frac{24.20 - 23.69}{20} = 0.0255.$$

Note that $f_T(500, 24)$ is positive, because steam expands when heated.

Next we approximate $f_P(500, 24)$ by looking at the $T = 500$ row and computing the average rate of change between $P = 24$ and $P = 26$:

$$f_P(500, 24) \approx \frac{f(500, 26) - f(500, 24)}{26 - 24} = \frac{21.86 - 23.69}{2} = -0.915.$$

Note that $f_P(500, 24)$ is negative, because increasing the pressure on steam decreases its volume. Using these approximations for the partial derivatives, we obtain the local linearization:

$$V = f(T, P) \approx 23.69 + 0.0255(T - 500) - 0.915(P - 24) \text{ ft}^3 \quad \begin{array}{l} \text{for } T \text{ near } 500 \text{ °F} \\ \text{and } P \text{ near } 24 \text{ lb/in}^2. \end{array}$$

(b) We are interested in the volume at $T = 505°$F and $P = 24.3$ lb/in^2. Since these values are close to $T = 500°$F and $P = 24$ lb/in^2, we use the linear relation obtained in part (a).

$$V \approx 23.69 + 0.0255(505 - 500) - 0.915(24.3 - 24) = 23.54 \text{ ft}^3.$$

Local Linearity with Three or More Variables

Local linear approximations for functions of three or more variables follow the same pattern as for functions of two variables. The local linearization of $f(x, y, z)$ at (a, b, c) is given by

$$f(x, y, z) \approx f(a, b, c) + f_x(a, b, c)(x - a) + f_y(a, b, c)(y - b) + f_z(a, b, c)(z - c).$$

The Differential

We are often interested in the change in the value of the function as we move from the point (a, b) to a nearby point (x, y). Then we use the notation

$$\Delta f = f(x, y) - f(a, b) \quad \text{and} \quad \Delta x = x - a \quad \text{and} \quad \Delta y = y - b$$

to rewrite the tangent plane approximation

$$f(x, y) \approx f(a, b) + f_x(a, b)(x - a) + f_y(a, b)(y - b)$$

in the form

$$\Delta f \approx f_x(a, b)\Delta x + f_y(a, b)\Delta y.$$

For fixed a and b, the right side of this is a linear function of Δx and Δy that can be used to estimate Δf. We call this linear function the *differential*. To define the differential in general, we introduce new variables dx and dy to represent changes in x and y.

The Differential of a Function $z = f(x, y)$

The **differential**, df (or dz), at a point (a, b) is the linear function of dx and dy given by the formula

$$df = f_x(a, b)\, dx + f_y(a, b)\, dy.$$

The differential at a general point is often written $df = f_x\, dx + f_y\, dy$.

Note that the differential, df, is a function of four variables a, b, and dx, dy.

Example 4   Compute the differentials of the following functions.

(a) $f(x, y) = x^2 e^{5y}$ (b) $z = x \sin(xy)$ (c) $f(x, y) = x \cos(2x)$

Solution

(a) Since $f_x(x, y) = 2xe^{5y}$ and $f_y(x, y) = 5x^2 e^{5y}$, we have

$$df = 2xe^{5y}\, dx + 5x^2 e^{5y}\, dy.$$

(b) Since $\partial z/\partial x = \sin(xy) + xy\cos(xy)$ and $\partial z/\partial y = x^2 \cos(xy)$, we have

$$dz = (\sin(xy) + xy\cos(xy))\, dx + x^2 \cos(xy)\, dy.$$

(c) Since $f_x(x, y) = \cos(2x) - 2x\sin(2x)$ and $f_y(x, y) = 0$, we have

$$df = (\cos(2x) - 2x\sin(2x))\, dx + 0\, dy = (\cos(2x) - 2x\sin(2x))\, dx.$$

Example 5   The density ρ (in g/cm^3) of carbon dioxide gas CO_2 depends upon its temperature T (in °C) and pressure P (in atmospheres). The ideal gas model for CO_2 gives what is called the state equation:

$$\rho = \frac{0.5363P}{T + 273.15}.$$

Compute the differential $d\rho$. Explain the signs of the coefficients of dT and dP.

Solution   The differential for $\rho = f(T, P)$ is

$$d\rho = f_T(T, P)\, dT + f_P(T, P)dP = \frac{-0.5363P}{(T + 273.15)^2}\, dT + \frac{0.5363}{T + 273.15}\, dP.$$

The coefficient of dT is negative because increasing the temperature expands the gas (if the pressure is kept constant) and therefore decreases its density. The coefficient of dP is positive because increasing the pressure compresses the gas (if the temperature is kept constant) and therefore increases its density.

Where Does the Notation for the Differential Come From?

We write the differential as a linear function of the new variables dx and dy. You may wonder why we chose these names for our variables. The reason is historical: The people who invented calculus thought of dx and dy as "infinitesimal" changes in x and y. The equation

$$df = f_x dx + f_y dy$$

was regarded as an infinitesimal version of the local linear approximation

$$\Delta f \approx f_x \Delta x + f_y \Delta y.$$

In spite of the problems with defining exactly what "infinitesimal" means, some mathematicians, scientists, and engineers think of the differential in terms of infinitesimals.

Figure 14.26 illustrates a way of thinking about differentials that combines the definition with this informal point of view. It shows the graph of f along with a view of the graph around the point $(a, b, f(a, b))$ under a microscope. Since f is locally linear at the point, the magnified view looks like the tangent plane. Under the microscope, we use a magnified coordinate system with its origin at the point $(a, b, f(a, b))$ and with coordinates dx, dy, and dz along the three axes. The graph of the differential df is the tangent plane, which has equation $dz = f_x(a, b)\, dx + f_y(a, b)\, dy$ in the magnified coordinates.

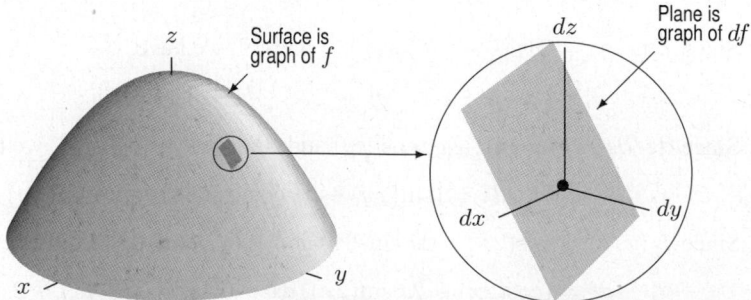

Figure 14.26: The graph of f, with a view through a microscope showing the tangent plane in the magnified coordinate system

Exercises and Problems for Section 14.3

Exercises

In Exercises 1–8, find the equation of the tangent plane at the given point.

1. $z = ye^{x/y}$ at the point $(1, 1, e)$

2. $z = \sin(xy)$ at $x = 2$, $y = 3\pi/4$

3. $z = \ln(x^2 + 1) + y^2$ at the point $(0, 3, 9)$

4. $z = e^y + x + x^2 + 6$ at the point $(1, 0, 9)$

5. $z = \frac{1}{2}(x^2 + 4y^2)$ at the point $(2, 1, 4)$

6. $x^2 + y^2 - z = 1$ at the point $(1, 3, 9)$

7. $x^2y^2 + z - 40 = 0$ at $x = 2$, $y = 3$

8. $x^2y + \ln(xy) + z = 6$ at the point $(4, 0.25, 2)$

In Exercises 9–12, find the differential of the function.

9. $f(x, y) = \sin(xy)$

10. $g(u, v) = u^2 + uv$

11. $z = e^{-x} \cos y$

12. $h(x, t) = e^{-3t} \sin(x + 5t)$

In Exercises 13–16, find the differential of the function at the given point.

13. $g(x, t) = x^2 \sin(2t)$ at $(2, \pi/4)$

14. $f(x, y) = xe^{-y}$ at $(1, 0)$

15. $P(L, K) = 1.01L^{0.25}K^{0.75}$ at $(100, 1)$

16. $F(m, r) = Gm/r^2$ at $(100, 10)$

Problems

17. At a distance of x feet from the beach, the price in dollars of a plot of land of area a square feet is $f(a, x)$.

(a) What are the units of $f_a(a, x)$?

(b) What does $f_a(1000, 300) = 3$ mean in practical terms?

(c) What are the units of $f_x(a, x)$?

(d) What does $f_x(1000, 300) = -2$ mean in practical terms?

(e) Which is cheaper: 1005 square feet that are 305 feet from the beach or 998 square feet that are 295 feet from the beach? Justify your answer.

18. A student was asked to find the equation of the tangent plane to the surface $z = x^3 - y^2$ at the point $(x, y) = (2, 3)$. The student's answer was

$$z = 3x^2(x - 2) - 2y(y - 3) - 1.$$

(a) At a glance, how do you know this is wrong?

(b) What mistake did the student make?

(c) Answer the question correctly.

19. (a) Check the local linearity of $f(x, y) = e^{-x} \sin y$ near $x = 1$, $y = 2$ by making a table of values of f for $x = 0.9$, 1.0, 1.1 and $y = 1.9$, 2.0, 2.1. Express values of f with 4 digits after the decimal point. Then make a table of values for $x = 0.99$, 1.00, 1.01 and $y = 1.99$, 2.00. 2.01, again showing 4 digits after the decimal point. Do both tables look nearly linear? Does the second table look more linear than the first?

(b) Give the local linearization of $f(x, y) = e^{-x} \sin y$ at $(1, 2)$, first using your tables, and second using the fact that $f_x(x, y) = -e^{-x} \sin y$ and $f_y(x, y) = e^{-x} \cos y$.

20. Find the local linearization of the function $f(x, y) = x^2y$ at the point $(3, 1)$.

21. For the differentiable function $h(x, y)$, we are told that $h(600, 100) = 300$ and $h_x(600, 100) = 12$ and $h_y(600, 100) = -8$. Estimate $h(605, 98)$.

22. (a) Find the equation of the plane tangent to the graph of $f(x, y) = x^2 e^{xy}$ at $(1, 0)$.

(b) Find the linear approximation of $f(x, y)$ for (x, y) near $(1, 0)$.

(c) Find the differential of f at the point $(1, 0)$.

23. Find the differential of $f(x, y) = \sqrt{x^2 + y^3}$ at the point $(1, 2)$. Use it to estimate $f(1.04, 1.98)$.

24. (a) Find the differential of $g(u, v) = u^2 + uv$.

(b) Use your answer to part (a) to estimate the change in g as you move from $(1, 2)$ to $(1.2, 2.1)$.

25. An unevenly heated plate has temperature $T(x, y)$ in °C at the point (x, y). If $T(2, 1) = 135$, and $T_x(2, 1) = 16$, and $T_y(2, 1) = -15$, estimate the temperature at the point $(2.04, 0.97)$.

26. A right circular cylinder has a radius of 50 cm and a height of 100 cm. Use differentials to estimate the change in volume of the cylinder if its height and radius are both increased by 1 cm.

27. Give the local linearization for the monthly car-loan payment function at each of the points investigated in Problem 27 on page 764.

28. In Example 3 on page 774 we found a linear approximation for $V = f(T, P)$ near $(500, 24)$. Now find a linear approximation near $(480, 20)$.

29. In Example 3 on page 774 we found a linear approximation for $V = f(T, p)$ near $(500, 24)$.

(a) Test the accuracy of this approximation by comparing its predicted value with the four neighboring values in the table. What do you notice? Which predicted values are accurate? Which are not? Explain your answer.

(b) Suggest a linear approximation for $f(T, p)$ near $(500, 24)$ that does not have the property you noticed in part (a). [Hint: Estimate the partial derivatives in a different way.]

30. In a room, the temperature is given by $T = f(x, t)$ degrees Celsius, where x is the distance from a heater (in meters) and t is the elapsed time (in minutes) since the heat has been turned on. A person standing 3 meters from the heater 5 minutes after it has been turned on observes the following: (1) The temperature is increasing by $1.2°C$ per minute, and (2) Walking away from the heater, the temperature decreases by $2°C$ per meter as time is held constant. Estimate how much cooler or warmer it would be 2.5 meters from the heater after 6 minutes.

31. Van der Waal's equation relates the pressure, P, and the volume, V, of a fixed quantity of a gas at constant temperature T. For a, b, n, R constants, the equation is

$$\left(P + \frac{n^2 a}{V^2}\right)(V - nb) = nRT.$$

(a) Express P as a function of T and V.
(b) Write a linear approximation for the change in pressure, $\Delta P = P - P_0$, resulting from a change in temperature $\Delta T = T - T_0$ and a change in pressure $\Delta V = V - V_0$.

32. The gas equation for one mole of oxygen relates its pressure, P (in atmospheres), its temperature, T (in K), and its volume, V (in cubic decimeters, dm^3):

$$T = 16.574 \frac{1}{V} - 0.52754 \frac{1}{V^2} - 0.3879 P + 12.187 V P.$$

(a) Find the temperature T and differential dT if the volume is $25\ dm^3$ and the pressure is 1 atmosphere.
(b) Use your answer to part (a) to estimate how much the volume would have to change if the pressure increased by 0.1 atmosphere and the temperature remained constant.

33. The coefficient, β, of thermal expansion of a liquid relates the change in the volume V (in m^3) of a fixed quantity of a liquid to an increase in its temperature T (in $°C$):

$$dV = \beta V\, dT.$$

(a) Let ρ be the density (in kg/m^3) of water as a function of temperature. (For a mass m of liquid, we have $\rho = m/V$.) Write an expression for $d\rho$ in terms of ρ and dT.

(b) The graph in Figure 14.27 shows density of water as a function of temperature. Use it to estimate β when $T = 20°C$ and when $T = 80°C$.

Figure 14.27

34. A fluid moves through a tube of length 1 meter and radius $r = 0.005 \pm 0.00025$ meters under a pressure $p = 10^5 \pm 1000$ pascals, at a rate $v = 0.625 \cdot 10^{-9}\ m^3$ per unit time. Use differentials to estimate the maximum error in the viscosity η given by

$$\eta = \frac{\pi}{8} \frac{p r^4}{v}.$$

35. The period, T, of oscillation in seconds of a pendulum clock is given by $T = 2\pi \sqrt{l/g}$, where g is the acceleration due to gravity. The length of the pendulum, l, depends on the temperature, t, according to the formula $l = l_0(1 + \alpha(t - t_0))$ where l_0 is the length of the pendulum at temperature t_0 and α is a constant which characterizes the clock. The clock is set to the correct period at the temperature t_0. How many seconds a day does the clock gain or lose when the temperature is $t_0 + \Delta t$? Show that this gain or loss is independent of l_0.

36. Two functions that have the same local linearization at a point have contours that are tangent at this point.

(a) If $f_x(a, b)$ or $f_y(a, b)$ is nonzero, use the local linearization to show that an equation of the line tangent at (a, b) to the contour of f through (a, b) is $f_x(a, b)(x - a) + f_y(a, b)(y - b) = 0$.
(b) Find the slope of the tangent line if $f_y(a, b) \neq 0$.
(c) Find an equation for the line tangent to the contour of $f(x, y) = x^2 + xy$ at $(3, 4)$.

Strengthen Your Understanding

In Problems 37–39, explain what is wrong with the statement.

37. An equation for the tangent plane to the surface $z = f(x, y)$ at the point $(3, 4)$ is

$$z = f(3, 4) + f_x(3, 4)x + f_y(3, 4)y.$$

38. If $f_x(0, 0) = g_x(0, 0)$ and $f_y(0, 0) = g_y(0, 0)$, then the surfaces $z = f(x, y)$ and $z = g(x, y)$ have the same tangent planes at the point $(0, 0)$.

39. The tangent plane to the surface $z = x^2 y$ at the point $(1, 2)$ has equation

$$z = 2 + 2xy(x - 1) + x^2(y - 2).$$

In Problems 40–41, give an example of:

40. Two different functions with the same differential.

41. A surface in three space whose tangent plane at $(0, 0, 3)$ is the plane $z = 3$.

Are the statements in Problems 42–49 true or false? Give reasons for your answer.

42. The tangent plane approximation of $f(x, y) = ye^{x^2}$ at the point $(0, 1)$ is $f(x, y) \approx y$.

43. If f is a function with differential $df = 2y\,dx + \sin(xy)\,dy$, then f changes by about -0.4 between the points $(1, 2)$ and $(0.9, 2.0002)$.

44. The local linearization of $f(x, y) = x^2 + y^2$ at $(1,1)$ gives an overestimate of the value of $f(x, y)$ at the point $(1.04, 0.95)$.

45. If two functions f and g have the same differential at the point $(1, 1)$, then $f = g$.

46. If two functions f and g have the same tangent plane at a point $(1, 1)$, then $f = g$.

47. If $f(x, y)$ is a constant function, then $df = 0$.

48. If $f(x, y)$ is a linear function, then df is a linear function of dx and dy.

49. If you zoom close enough near a point (a, b) on the contour diagram of any differentiable function, the contours will be *precisely* parallel and *exactly* equally spaced.

14.4 GRADIENTS AND DIRECTIONAL DERIVATIVES IN THE PLANE

The Rate of Change in an Arbitrary Direction: The Directional Derivative

The partial derivatives of a function f tell us the rate of change of f in the directions parallel to the coordinate axes. In this section we see how to compute the rate of change of f in an arbitrary direction.

Example 1 Figure 14.28 shows the temperature, in °C, at the point (x, y). Estimate the average rate of change of temperature as we walk from point A to point B.

Figure 14.28: Estimating rate of change on a temperature map

Solution At the point A we are on the $H = 45$°C contour. At B we are on the $H = 50$°C contour. The displacement vector from A to B has x component approximately $-100\vec{i}$ and y component approximately $25\vec{j}$, so its length is $\sqrt{(-100)^2 + 25^2} \approx 103$. Thus, the temperature rises by 5°C as we move 103 meters, so the average rate of change of the temperature in that direction is about $5/103 \approx 0.05$°C/m.

Suppose we want to compute the rate of change of a function $f(x, y)$ at the point $P = (a, b)$ in the direction of the unit vector $\vec{u} = u_1\vec{i} + u_2\vec{j}$. For $h > 0$, consider the point $Q = (a + hu_1, b + hu_2)$ whose displacement from P is $h\vec{u}$. (See Figure 14.29.) Since $\|\vec{u}\| = 1$, the distance from P to Q is h. Thus,

$$\frac{\text{Average rate of change}}{\text{in } f \text{ from } P \text{ to } Q} = \frac{\text{Change in } f}{\text{Distance from } P \text{ to } Q} = \frac{f(a + hu_1, b + hu_2) - f(a, b)}{h}.$$

Figure 14.29: Displacement of $h\vec{u}$ from the point (a, b)

Taking the limit as $h \to 0$ gives the instantaneous rate of change and the following definition:

Directional Derivative of f at (a, b) in the Direction of a Unit Vector $\vec{u}$

If $\vec{u} = u_1\vec{i} + u_2\vec{j}$ is a unit vector, we define the directional derivative, $f_{\vec{u}}$, by

$$f_{\vec{u}}(a, b) = \begin{matrix} \text{Rate of change} \\ \text{of } f \text{ in direction} \\ \text{of } \vec{u} \text{ at } (a, b) \end{matrix} = \lim_{h \to 0} \frac{f(a + hu_1, b + hu_2) - f(a, b)}{h},$$

provided the limit exists.

Notice that if $\vec{u} = \vec{i}$, so $u_1 = 1, u_2 = 0$, then the directional derivative is f_x, since

$$f_{\vec{i}}(a, b) = \lim_{h \to 0} \frac{f(a + h, b) - f(a, b)}{h} = f_x(a, b).$$

Similarly, if $\vec{u} = \vec{j}$ then the directional derivative $f_{\vec{j}} = f_y$.

What If We Do Not Have a Unit Vector?

We defined $f_{\vec{u}}$ for $\vec{u}$ a unit vector. If $\vec{v}$ is not a unit vector, $\vec{v} \neq \vec{0}$, we construct a unit vector $\vec{u} = \vec{v}/\|\vec{v}\|$ in the same direction as $\vec{v}$ and define the rate of change of f in the direction of $\vec{v}$ as $f_{\vec{u}}$.

Example 2   For each of the functions f, g, and h in Figure 14.30, decide whether the directional derivative at the indicated point is positive, negative, or zero, in the direction of the vector $\vec{v} = \vec{i} + 2\vec{j}$, and in the direction of the vector $\vec{w} = 2\vec{i} + \vec{j}$.

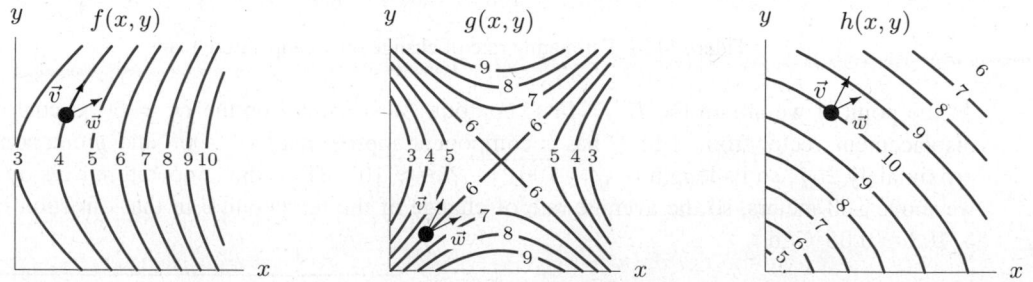

Figure 14.30: Contour diagrams of three functions with direction vectors $\vec{v} = \vec{i} + 2\vec{j}$ and $\vec{w} = 2\vec{i} + \vec{j}$ marked on each

Solution   On the contour diagram for f, the vector $\vec{v} = \vec{i} + 2\vec{j}$ appears to be tangent to the contour. Thus, in this direction, the value of the function is not changing, so the directional derivative in the direction of $\vec{v}$ is zero. The vector $\vec{w} = 2\vec{i} + \vec{j}$ points from the contour marked 4 toward the contour marked 5. Thus, the values of the function are increasing and the directional derivative in the direction of $\vec{w}$ is positive.

On the contour diagram for g, the vector $\vec{v} = \vec{i} + 2\vec{j}$ points from the contour marked 6 toward the contour marked 5, so the function is decreasing in that direction. Thus, the rate of change is negative. On the other hand, the vector $\vec{w} = 2\vec{i} + \vec{j}$ points from the contour marked 6 toward the contour marked 7, and hence the directional derivative in the direction of $\vec{w}$ is positive.

Finally, on the contour diagram for h, both vectors point from the $h = 10$ contour to the $h = 9$ contour, so both directional derivatives are negative.

Example 3   Calculate the directional derivative of $f(x, y) = x^2 + y^2$ at $(1, 0)$ in the direction of the vector $\vec{i} + \vec{j}$.

Solution   First we have to find the unit vector in the same direction as the vector $\vec{i} + \vec{j}$. Since this vector has magnitude $\sqrt{2}$, the unit vector is

$$\vec{u} = \frac{1}{\sqrt{2}}(\vec{i} + \vec{j}) = \frac{1}{\sqrt{2}}\vec{i} + \frac{1}{\sqrt{2}}\vec{j}.$$

Thus,

$$f_{\vec{u}}(1, 0) = \lim_{h \to 0} \frac{f(1 + h/\sqrt{2}, h/\sqrt{2}) - f(1, 0)}{h} = \lim_{h \to 0} \frac{(1 + h/\sqrt{2})^2 + (h/\sqrt{2})^2 - 1}{h}$$

$$= \lim_{h \to 0} \frac{\sqrt{2}h + h^2}{h} = \lim_{h \to 0} (\sqrt{2} + h) = \sqrt{2}.$$

Computing Directional Derivatives from Partial Derivatives

If f is differentiable, we will now see how to use local linearity to find a formula for the directional derivative which does not involve a limit. If $\vec{u}$ is a unit vector, the definition of $f_{\vec{u}}$ says

$$f_{\vec{u}}(a, b) = \lim_{h \to 0} \frac{f(a + hu_1, b + hu_2) - f(a, b)}{h} = \lim_{h \to 0} \frac{\Delta f}{h},$$

where $\Delta f = f(a + hu_1, b + hu_2) - f(a, b)$ is the change in f. We write Δx for the change in x, so $\Delta x = (a + hu_1) - a = hu_1$; similarly $\Delta y = hu_2$. Using local linearity, we have

$$\Delta f \approx f_x(a, b)\Delta x + f_y(a, b)\Delta y = f_x(a, b)hu_1 + f_y(a, b)hu_2.$$

Thus, dividing by h gives

$$\frac{\Delta f}{h} \approx \frac{f_x(a, b)hu_1 + f_y(a, b)hu_2}{h} = f_x(a, b)u_1 + f_y(a, b)u_2.$$

This approximation becomes exact as $h \to 0$, so we have the following formula:

$$f_{\vec{u}}(a, b) = f_x(a, b)u_1 + f_y(a, b)u_2.$$

Example 4   Use the preceding formula to compute the directional derivative in Example 3. Check that we get the same answer as before.

Solution   We calculate $f_{\vec{u}}(1, 0)$, where $f(x, y) = x^2 + y^2$ and $\vec{u} = \frac{1}{\sqrt{2}}\vec{i} + \frac{1}{\sqrt{2}}\vec{j}$.

The partial derivatives are $f_x(x, y) = 2x$ and $f_y(x, y) = 2y$. So, as before,

$$f_{\vec{u}}(1, 0) = f_x(1, 0)u_1 + f_y(1, 0)u_2 = (2)\left(\frac{1}{\sqrt{2}}\right) + (0)\left(\frac{1}{\sqrt{2}}\right) = \sqrt{2}.$$

The Gradient Vector

Notice that the expression for $f_{\vec{u}}(a, b)$ can be written as a dot product of $\vec{u}$ and a new vector:

$$f_{\vec{u}}(a, b) = f_x(a, b)u_1 + f_y(a, b)u_2 = (f_x(a, b)\vec{i} + f_y(a, b)\vec{j}) \cdot (u_1\vec{i} + u_2\vec{j}).$$

The new vector, $f_x(a,b)\vec{i} + f_y(a,b)\vec{j}$, turns out to be important. Thus, we make the following definition:

> **The Gradient Vector** of a differentiable function f at the point (a,b) is
>
> $$\operatorname{grad} f(a,b) = f_x(a,b)\vec{i} + f_y(a,b)\vec{j}$$

The formula for the directional derivative can be written in terms of the gradient as follows:

> ## The Directional Derivative and the Gradient
>
> If f is differentiable at (a,b) and $\vec{u} = u_1\vec{i} + u_2\vec{j}$ is a unit vector, then
>
> $$f_{\vec{u}}(a,b) = f_x(a,b)u_1 + f_y(a,b)u_2 = \operatorname{grad} f(a,b) \cdot \vec{u}.$$

Example 5   Find the gradient vector of $f(x,y) = x + e^y$ at the point $(1,1)$.

Solution   Using the definition, we have

$$\operatorname{grad} f = f_x\vec{i} + f_y\vec{j} = \vec{i} + e^y\vec{j},$$

so at the point $(1,1)$

$$\operatorname{grad} f(1,1) = \vec{i} + e\vec{j}.$$

Alternative Notation for the Gradient

You can think of $\dfrac{\partial f}{\partial x}\vec{i} + \dfrac{\partial f}{\partial y}\vec{j}$ as the result of applying the vector operator (pronounced "del")

$$\nabla = \frac{\partial}{\partial x}\vec{i} + \frac{\partial}{\partial y}\vec{j}$$

to the function f. Thus, we get the alternative notation

$$\operatorname{grad} f = \nabla f.$$

If $z = f(x,y)$, we can write $\operatorname{grad} z$ or ∇z for $\operatorname{grad} f$ or for ∇f.

What Does the Gradient Tell Us?

The fact that $f_{\vec{u}} = \operatorname{grad} f \cdot \vec{u}$ enables us to see what the gradient vector represents. Suppose θ is the angle between the vectors $\operatorname{grad} f$ and $\vec{u}$. At the point (a,b), we have

$$f_{\vec{u}} = \operatorname{grad} f \cdot \vec{u} = \|\operatorname{grad} f\| \underbrace{\|\vec{u}\|}_{1} \cos\theta = \|\operatorname{grad} f\| \cos\theta.$$

Figure 14.31: Values of the directional derivative at different angles to the gradient

Imagine that $\operatorname{grad} f$ is fixed and that $\vec{u}$ can rotate. (See Figure 14.31.) The maximum value of $f_{\vec{u}}$ occurs when $\cos\theta = 1$, so $\theta = 0$ and $\vec{u}$ is pointing in the direction of $\operatorname{grad} f$. Then

$$\text{Maximum } f_{\vec{u}} = \| \operatorname{grad} f \| \cos 0 = \| \operatorname{grad} f \|.$$

The minimum value of $f_{\vec{u}}$ occurs when $\cos\theta = -1$, so $\theta = \pi$ and $\vec{u}$ is pointing in the direction opposite to $\operatorname{grad} f$. Then

$$\text{Minimum } f_{\vec{u}} = \| \operatorname{grad} f \| \cos \pi = -\| \operatorname{grad} f \|.$$

When $\theta = \pi/2$ or $3\pi/2$, so $\cos\theta = 0$, the directional derivative is zero.

Properties of the Gradient Vector

We have seen that the gradient vector points in the direction of the greatest rate of change at a point and the magnitude of the gradient vector is that rate of change.

Figure 14.32 shows that the gradient vector at a point is perpendicular to the contour through that point. If the contours represent equally spaced f-values and f is differentiable, local linearity tells us that the contours of f around a point appear straight, parallel, and equally spaced. The greatest rate of change is obtained by moving in the direction that takes us to the next contour in the shortest possible distance; that is, perpendicular to the contour. Thus, we have the following:

Geometric Properties of the Gradient Vector in the Plane

If f is a differentiable function at the point (a, b) and $\operatorname{grad} f(a, b) \neq \vec{0}$, then:
- The direction of $\operatorname{grad} f(a, b)$ is
  - Perpendicular[1] to the contour of f through (a, b);
  - In the direction of the maximum rate of increase of f.
- The magnitude of the gradient vector, $\| \operatorname{grad} f \|$, is
  - The maximum rate of change of f at that point;
  - Large when the contours are close together and small when they are far apart.

Figure 14.32: Close-up view of the contours around (a, b), showing the gradient is perpendicular to the contours

Figure 14.33: A temperature map showing directions and relative magnitudes of two gradient vectors

---

[1]This assumes that the same scale is used on both axes.

Examples of Directional Derivatives and Gradient Vectors

Example 6   Explain why the gradient vectors at points A and C in Figure 14.33 have the direction and the relative magnitudes they do.

Solution   The gradient vector points in the direction of greatest increase of the function. This means that in Figure 14.33, the gradient points directly toward warmer temperatures. The magnitude of the gradient vector measures the rate of change. The gradient vector at A is longer than the gradient vector at C because the contours are closer together at A, so the rate of change is larger.

Example 2 on page 780 shows how the contour diagram can tell us the sign of the directional derivative. In the next example we compute the directional derivative in three directions, two that are close to that of the gradient vector and one that is not.

Example 7   Use the gradient to find the directional derivative of $f(x, y) = x + e^y$ at the point $(1, 1)$ in the direction of the vectors $\vec{i} - \vec{j}, \vec{i} + 2\vec{j}, \vec{i} + 3\vec{j}$.

Solution   In Example 5 we found

$$\operatorname{grad} f(1, 1) = \vec{i} + e\vec{j}.$$

A unit vector in the direction of $\vec{i} - \vec{j}$ is $\vec{s} = (\vec{i} - \vec{j})/\sqrt{2}$, so

$$f_{\vec{s}}(1, 1) = \operatorname{grad} f(1, 1) \cdot \vec{s} = (\vec{i} + e\vec{j}) \cdot \left(\frac{\vec{i} - \vec{j}}{\sqrt{2}}\right) = \frac{1 - e}{\sqrt{2}} \approx -1.215.$$

A unit vector in the direction of $\vec{i} + 2\vec{j}$ is $\vec{v} = (\vec{i} + 2\vec{j})/\sqrt{5}$, so

$$f_{\vec{v}}(1, 1) = \operatorname{grad} f(1, 1) \cdot \vec{v} = (\vec{i} + e\vec{j}) \cdot \left(\frac{\vec{i} + 2\vec{j}}{\sqrt{5}}\right) = \frac{1 + 2e}{\sqrt{5}} \approx 2.879.$$

A unit vector in the direction of $\vec{i} + 3\vec{j}$ is $\vec{w} = (\vec{i} + 3\vec{j})/\sqrt{10}$, so

$$f_{\vec{w}}(1, 1) = \operatorname{grad} f(1, 1) \cdot \vec{w} = (\vec{i} + e\vec{j}) \cdot \left(\frac{\vec{i} + 3\vec{j}}{\sqrt{10}}\right) = \frac{1 + 3e}{\sqrt{10}} \approx 2.895.$$

Now look back at the answers and compare with the value of $\| \operatorname{grad} f \| = \sqrt{1 + e^2} \approx 2.896$. One answer is not close to this value; the other two, $f_{\vec{v}} = 2.879$ and $f_{\vec{w}} = 2.895$, are close but slightly smaller than $\| \operatorname{grad} f \|$. Since $\| \operatorname{grad} f \|$ is the maximum rate of change of f at the point, we have for *any* unit vector $\vec{u}$:

$$f_{\vec{u}}(1, 1) \leq \| \operatorname{grad} f \|.$$

with equality when $\vec{u}$ is in the direction of $\operatorname{grad} f$. Since $e \approx 2.718$, the vectors $\vec{i} + 2\vec{j}$ and $\vec{i} + 3\vec{j}$ both point roughly, but not exactly, in the direction of the gradient vector $\operatorname{grad} f(1, 1) = \vec{i} + e\vec{j}$. Thus, the values of $f_{\vec{v}}$ and $f_{\vec{w}}$ are both close to the value of $\| \operatorname{grad} f \|$. The direction of the vector $\vec{i} - \vec{j}$ is not close to the direction of $\operatorname{grad} f$ and the value of $f_{\vec{s}}$ is not close to the value of $\| \operatorname{grad} f \|$.

Exercises and Problems for Section 14.4

Exercises

In Exercises 1–14, find the gradient of the function. Assume the variables are restricted to a domain on which the function is defined.

1. $f(x,y) = \frac{3}{2}x^5 - \frac{4}{7}y^6$ **2.** $Q = 50K + 100L$

3. $f(m,n) = m^2 + n^2$ **4.** $z = xe^y$

5. $f(\alpha, \beta) = \sqrt{5\alpha^2 + \beta}$ **6.** $f(r,h) = \pi r^2 h$

7. $z = (x+y)e^y$ **8.** $f(K,L) = K^{0.3}L^{0.7}$

9. $f(r, \theta) = r\sin\theta$ **10.** $f(x,y) = \ln(x^2 + y^2)$

11. $z = \sin(x/y)$ **12.** $z = \tan^{-1}(x/y)$

13. $f(\alpha, \beta) = \dfrac{2\alpha + 3\beta}{2\alpha - 3\beta}$ **14.** $z = x\dfrac{e^y}{x+y}$

In Exercises 15–22, find the gradient at the point.

15. $f(x,y) = x^2 y + 7xy^3$, at $(1,2)$

16. $f(m,n) = 5m^2 + 3n^4$, at $(5,2)$

17. $f(r,h) = 2\pi rh + \pi r^2$, at $(2,3)$

18. $f(x,y) = e^{\sin y}$, at $(0, \pi)$

19. $f(x,y) = \sin(x^2) + \cos y$, at $(\frac{\sqrt{\pi}}{2}, 0)$

20. $f(x,y) = \ln(x^2 + xy)$, at $(4,1)$

21. $f(x,y) = 1/(x^2 + y^2)$, at $(-1,3)$

22. $f(x,y) = \sqrt{\tan x + y}$, at $(0,1)$

In Exercises 23–26, find the directional derivative $f_{\vec{u}}(1,2)$ for the function f with $\vec{u} = (3\vec{i} - 4\vec{j})/5$.

23. $f(x,y) = xy + y^3$ **24.** $f(x,y) = 3x - 4y$

25. $f(x,y) = x^2 - y^2$ **26.** $f(x,y) = \sin(2x - y)$

27. If $f(x,y) = x^2 y$ and $\vec{v} = 4\vec{i} - 3\vec{j}$, find the directional derivative at the point $(2,6)$ in the direction of $\vec{v}$.

In Exercises 28–29, find the differential df from the gradient.

28. $\operatorname{grad} f = y\vec{i} + x\vec{j}$

29. $\operatorname{grad} f = (2x + 3e^y)\vec{i} + 3xe^y\vec{j}$

In Exercises 30–31, find $\operatorname{grad} f$ from the differential.

30. $df = 2x\,dx + 10y\,dy$

31. $df = (x+1)ye^x\,dx + xe^x\,dy$

In Exercises 32–37, use the contour diagram of f in Figure 14.34 to decide if the specified directional derivative is positive, negative, or approximately zero.

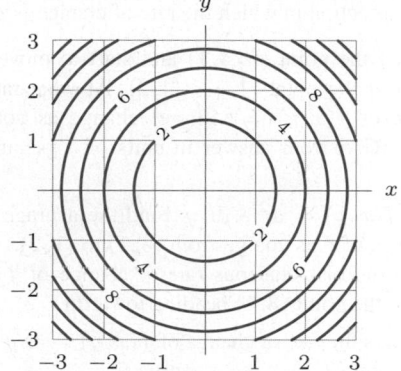

Figure 14.34

32. At point $(-2, 2)$, in direction $\vec{i}$.

33. At point $(0, -2)$, in direction $\vec{j}$.

34. At point $(0, -2)$, in direction $\vec{i} + 2\vec{j}$.

35. At point $(0, -2)$, in direction $\vec{i} - 2\vec{j}$.

36. At point $(-1, 1)$, in direction $\vec{i} + \vec{j}$.

37. At point $(-1, 1)$, in direction $-\vec{i} + \vec{j}$.

In Exercises 38–45, use the contour diagram of f in Figure 14.34 to find the approximate direction of the gradient vector at the given point.

38. $(-2, 0)$ **39.** $(0, -2)$ **40.** $(2, 0)$ **41.** $(0, 2)$

42. $(-2, 2)$ **43.** $(-2, -2)$ **44.** $(2, 2)$ **45.** $(2, -2)$

Problems

46. Let $f(P) = 15$ and $f(Q) = 20$ where $P = (3, 4)$ and $Q = (3.03, 3.96)$. Approximate the directional derivative of f at P in the direction of Q.

47. **(a)** Give Q, the point at a distance of 0.1 from $P = (4, 5)$ in the direction of $\vec{v} = -\vec{i} + 3\vec{j}$. Give five decimal places in your answer.

(b) Use P and Q to approximate the directional derivative of $f(x, y) = \sqrt{x + y}$ in the direction of $\vec{v}$.

(c) Give the exact value for the directional derivative you estimated in part (b).

48. Find the directional derivative of $f(x, y) = e^x \tan(y) + 2x^2 y$ at the point $(0, \pi/4)$ in the following directions

    (a) $\vec{i} - \vec{j}$ **(b)** $\vec{i} + \sqrt{3}\vec{j}$

49. Find the rate of change of $f(x, y) = x^2 + y^2$ at the point $(1, 2)$ in the direction of the vector $\vec{u} = 0.6\vec{i} + 0.8\vec{j}$.

50. **(a)** Let $f(x, y) = (x+y)/(1+x^2)$. Find the directional derivative of f at $P = (1, -2)$ in the direction of:

      (i) $\vec{v} = 3\vec{i} - 2\vec{j}$ (ii) $\vec{v} = -\vec{i} + 4\vec{j}$

    (b) What is the direction of greatest increase of f at P ?

51. Let $f(x, y) = x^2 y^3$. At the point $(-1, 2)$, find a vector

    (a) In the direction of maximum rate of change.
    (b) In the direction of minimum rate of change.
    (c) In a direction in which the rate of change is zero.

52. You are at the point $(\pi/4, 1)$ and start to move in the direction of the point $(1 + \pi/4, 2)$. At what rate does the value of $f(x, y) = \sin(xy)$ change as you leave $(\pi/4, 1)$? Give your answer in units of f per unit distance.

53. **(a)** Let $f(x, y) = x^2 + \ln y$. Find the average rate of change of f as you go from $(3, 1)$ to $(1, 2)$.
    (b) Find the instantaneous rate of change of f as you leave the point $(3, 1)$ heading toward $(1, 2)$.

54. **(a)** What is the rate of change of $f(x, y) = 3xy + y^2$ at the point $(2, 3)$ in the direction $\vec{v} = 3\vec{i} - \vec{j}$?
    (b) What is the direction of maximum rate of change of f at $(2, 3)$?
    (c) What is the maximum rate of change?

55. A student was asked to find the directional derivative of $f(x, y) = x^2 e^y$ at the point $(1, 0)$ in the direction of $\vec{v} = 4\vec{i} + 3\vec{j}$. The student's answer was

$$f_{\vec{u}}(1, 0) = \text{grad } f(1, 0) \cdot \vec{u} = \frac{8}{5}\vec{i} + \frac{3}{5}\vec{j}.$$

    (a) At a glance, how do you know this is wrong?
    (b) What is the correct answer?

For Problems 56–60 use Figure 14.35, showing level curves of $f(x, y)$, to estimate the directional derivatives.

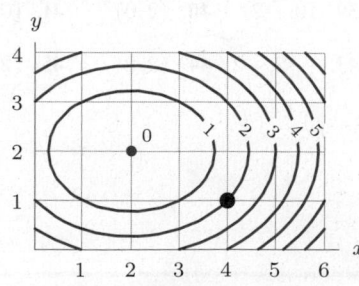

Figure 14.35

56. $f_{\vec{i}}(4, 1)$ **57.** $f_{\vec{j}}(4, 1)$

58. $f_{\vec{u}}(4, 1)$ where $\vec{u} = (\vec{i} - \vec{j})/\sqrt{2}$
59. $f_{\vec{u}}(4, 1)$ where $\vec{u} = (-\vec{i} + \vec{j})/\sqrt{2}$
60. $f_{\vec{u}}(4, 1)$ with $\vec{u} = (-2\vec{i} + \vec{j})/\sqrt{5}$

In Problems 61–64, check that the point $(2, 3)$ lies on the curve. Then, viewing the curve as a contour of $f(x, y)$, use grad $f(2, 3)$ to find a vector normal to the curve at $(2, 3)$ and an equation for the tangent line to the curve at $(2, 3)$.

61. $x^2 + y^2 = 13$ **62.** $xy = 6$

63. $y = x^2 - 1$ **64.** $(y - x)^2 + 2 = xy - 3$

65. The surface $z = g(x, y)$ is in Figure 14.36. What is the sign of each of the following directional derivatives?

    (a) $g_{\vec{u}}(2, 5)$ where $\vec{u} = (\vec{i} - \vec{j})/\sqrt{2}$.
    (b) $g_{\vec{u}}(2, 5)$ where $\vec{u} = (\vec{i} + \vec{j})/\sqrt{2}$.

Figure 14.36

66. The table gives values of a differentiable function $f(x, y)$. At the point $(1.2, 0)$, into which quadrant does the gradient vector of f point? Justify your answer.

		y	
	-1	0	1
1.0	0.7	0.1	-0.5
1.2	4.8	4.2	3.6
1.4	8.9	8.3	7.7

67. Figure 14.37 represents the level curves $f(x, y) = c$; the values of f on each curve are marked. In each of the following parts, decide whether the given quantity is positive, negative or zero. Explain your answer.

    (a) The value of $\nabla f \cdot \vec{i}$ at P.
    (b) The value of $\nabla f \cdot \vec{j}$ at P.
    (c) $\partial f/\partial x$ at Q.
    (d) $\partial f/\partial y$ at Q.

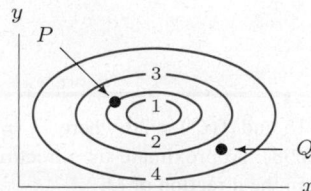

Figure 14.37

68. In Figure 14.37, which is larger: $\|\nabla f\|$ at P or $\|\nabla f\|$ at Q? Explain how you know.

In Problems 69–72, do the level curves of $f(x, y)$ cross the level curves of $g(x, y)$ at right angles? Sketch contour diagrams.

69. $f(x, y) = x + y, g(x, y) = x - y$

70. $f(x, y) = 2x + 3y, g(x, y) = 2x - 3y$

71. $f(x, y) = x^2 - y, g(x, y) = 2y + \ln|x|$

72. $f(x, y) = x^2 - y^2, g(x, y) = xy$

73. (a) Sketch the surface $z = f(x, y) = y^2$ in three dimensions.
    (b) Sketch the level curves of f in the xy-plane.
    (c) If you are standing on the surface $z = y^2$ at the point $(2, 3, 9)$, in which direction should you move to climb the fastest? (Give your answer as a 2-vector.)

74. You are standing above the point $(1, 3)$ on the surface $z = 20 - (2x^2 + y^2)$.

    (a) In which direction should you walk to descend fastest? (Give your answer as a 2-vector.)
    (b) If you start to move in this direction, what is the slope of your path?

75. Let P be a fixed point in the plane and let $f(x, y)$ be the distance from P to (x, y). Answer the following questions using geometric interpretations, not formulas.

    (a) What are the level curves of f?
    (b) In what direction does grad $f(x, y)$ point?
    (c) What is the magnitude $\| \text{grad } f(x, y) \|$?

76. The directional derivative of $z = f(x, y)$ at $(2, 1)$ in the direction toward the point $(1, 3)$ is $-2/\sqrt{5}$, and the directional derivative in the direction toward the point $(5, 5)$ is 1. Compute $\partial z/\partial x$ and $\partial z/\partial y$ at $(2, 1)$.

77. Consider the function $f(x, y)$. If you start at the point $(4, 5)$ and move toward the point $(5, 6)$, the directional derivative is 2. Starting at the point $(4, 5)$ and moving toward the point $(6, 6)$ gives a directional derivative of 3. Find ∇f at the point $(4, 5)$.

78. (a) For $g(x, y) = \sqrt{x^2 + 3y + 3}$, find grad $g(1, 4)$.
    (b) Find the best linear approximation of $g(x, y)$ for (x, y) near $(1, 4)$.
    (c) Use the approximation in part (b) to estimate $g(1.01, 3.98)$.

79. Find the directional derivative of $z = x^2 - y^2$ at the point $(3, -1)$ in the direction making an angle $\theta = \pi/4$ with the x-axis. In which direction is the directional derivative the largest?

80. The temperature H in °Fahrenheit y miles north of the Canadian border t hours after midnight is given by $H = 30 - 0.05y - 5t$. A moose runs north at a speed of 20 mph. At what rate does the moose perceive the temperature to be changing?

81. At a certain point on a heated plate, the greatest rate of temperature increase, $5°$ C per meter, is toward the northeast. If an object at this point moves directly north, at what rate is the temperature increasing?

82. You are climbing a mountain by the steepest route at a slope of $20°$ when you come upon a trail branching off at a $30°$ angle from yours. What is the angle of ascent of the branch trail?

83. Figure 14.39 is a graph of the directional derivative, $f_{\vec{u}}$, at the point (a, b) versus θ, the angle in Figure 14.38.

    (a) Which points on the graph in Figure 14.39 correspond to the greatest rate of increase of f? The greatest rate of decrease?
    (b) Mark points on the circle in Figure 14.38 corresponding to the points P, Q, R, S.
    (c) What is the amplitude of the function graphed in Figure 14.39? What is its formula?

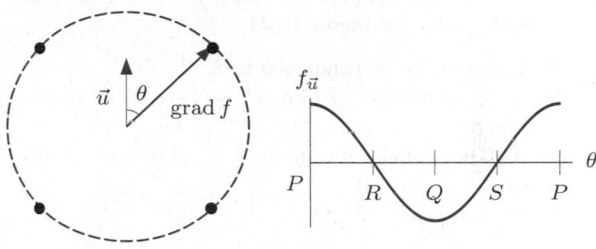

Figure 14.38   Figure 14.39

84. You are standing at the point $(1, 1, 3)$ on the hill whose equation is given by $z = 5y - x^2 - y^2$.

    (a) If you choose to climb in the direction of steepest ascent, what is your initial rate of ascent relative to the horizontal distance?
    (b) If you decide to go straight northwest, will you be ascending or descending? At what rate?
    (c) If you decide to maintain your altitude, in what directions can you go?

85. In this problem we see another way of obtaining the formula $f_{\vec{u}}(a, b) = \text{grad } f(a, b) \cdot \vec{u}$. Imagine zooming in on a function $f(x, y)$ at a point (a, b). By local linearity, the contours around (a, b) look like the contours of a linear function. See Figure 14.40. Suppose you want to find the directional derivative $f_{\vec{u}}(a, b)$ in the direction of a unit vector $\vec{u}$. If you move from P to Q, a small distance h in the direction of $\vec{u}$, then the directional derivative is approximated by the difference quotient

$$\frac{\text{Change in } f \text{ between } P \text{ and } Q}{h}.$$

    (a) Use the gradient to show that

$$\text{Change in } f \approx \| \text{grad } f \| (h \cos \theta).$$

    (b) Use part (a) to obtain $f_{\vec{u}}(a, b) = \text{grad } f(a, b) \cdot \vec{u}$.

Figure 14.40

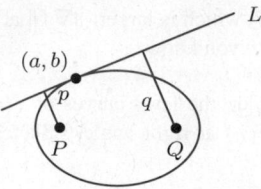

Figure 14.41

86. Let L be a line tangent to the ellipse $x^2/2 + y^2 = 1$ at the point (a, b). See Figure 14.41.

   (a) Find a vector perpendicular to L.

   (b) Find the distance p from $P = (-1, 0)$ to L as a function of a.

   (c) Find the distance q from $Q = (1, 0)$ to L as a function of a.

   (d) Show that $pq = 1$.

87. Let C be the contour C of $f(x, y)$ through (a, b) and grad $f(a, b) \neq \vec{0}$. Show that

   (a) The vector $-f_y(a, b)\vec{i} + f_x(a, b)\vec{j}$ is tangent to C at (a, b).

   (b) The slope of the line tangent to C at the point (a, b) is $-f_x(a, b)/f_y(a, b)$ if the tangent line is not vertical.

88. Let $\| \text{grad } f(x, y) \| = \| \text{grad } g(x, y) \|$ at a point P where these gradients are not the zero vector. Show that at P, the direction of the most rapid increase of $f + g$

   (a) Increases f and g at equal rates.

   (b) Bisects the angle between the contours of f and g that pass through P.

Strengthen Your Understanding

In Problems 89–91, explain what is wrong with the statement.

89. A function f has a directional derivative given by $f_{\vec{u}}(0, 0) = 3\vec{i} + 4\vec{j}$.

90. A function f has gradient grad $f(0, 0) = 7$.

91. The gradient vector grad $f(x, y)$ is perpendicular to the contours of f, and the closer together the contours for equally spaced values of f, the shorter the gradient vector.

In Problems 92–93, give an example of:

92. A unit vector $\vec{u}$ such that $f_{\vec{u}}(0, 0) < 0$, given that $f_x(0, 0) = 2$ and $f_y(0, 0) = 3$.

93. A contour diagram of a function with two points in the domain where the gradients are parallel but different lengths.

94. For the gradient $\nabla f(P)$ of f at a point P, describe the geometric interpretation of its

   (a) Direction

   (b) Magnitude

   (c) Dot product with a unit vector $\vec{u}$

Are the statements in Problems 95–106 true or false? Give reasons for your answer.

95. If the point (a, b) is on the contour $f(x, y) = k$, then the slope of the line tangent to this contour at (a, b) is $f_y(a, b)/f_x(a, b)$.

96. The gradient vector grad $f(a, b)$ is a vector in 3-space.

97. $\text{grad}(fg) = (\text{grad } f) \cdot (\text{grad } g)$

98. The gradient vector grad $f(a, b)$ is tangent to the contour of f at (a, b).

99. If you know the gradient vector of f at (a, b) then you can find the directional derivative $f_{\vec{u}}(a, b)$ for any unit vector $\vec{u}$.

100. If you know the directional derivative $f_{\vec{u}}(a, b)$ for all unit vectors $\vec{u}$ then you can find the gradient vector of f at (a, b).

101. The directional derivative $f_{\vec{u}}(a, b)$ is parallel to $\vec{u}$.

102. The gradient grad $f(3, 4)$ is perpendicular to the vector $3\vec{i} + 4\vec{j}$.

103. If grad $f(1, 2) = \vec{i}$, then f decreases in the $-\vec{i}$ direction at $(1, 2)$.

104. If grad $f(1, 2) = \vec{i}$, then $f(10, 2) > f(1, 2)$.

105. At the point $(3, 0)$, the function $g(x, y) = x^2 + y^2$ has the same maximal rate of increase as that of the function $h(x, y) = 2xy$.

106. If $f(x, y) = e^{x+y}$, then the directional derivative in any direction $\vec{u}$ (with $\|\vec{u}\| = 1$) at the point $(0, 0)$ is always less than or equal to $\sqrt{2}$.

Assume that $f(x, y)$ is a differentiable function. Are the statements in Problems 107–111 true or false? Explain your answer.

107. $f_{\vec{u}}(x_0, y_0)$ is a scalar.

108. $f_{\vec{u}}(a, b) = \|\nabla f(a, b)\|$

109. If $\vec{u}$ is tangent to the level curve of f at some point, then $\operatorname{grad} f \cdot \vec{u} = 0$ there.

110. There is always a direction in which the rate of change of f at (a, b) is 0.

111. There is a function with a point in its domain where $\|\operatorname{grad} f\| = 0$ and where there is a nonzero directional derivative.

14.5 GRADIENTS AND DIRECTIONAL DERIVATIVES IN SPACE

Directional Derivatives of Functions of Three Variables

We calculate directional derivatives of a function of three variables in the same way as for a function of two variables. If the function f is differentiable at the point (a, b, c), then the rate of change of $f(x, y, z)$ at the point (a, b, c) in the direction of a unit vector $\vec{u} = u_1\vec{i} + u_2\vec{j} + u_3\vec{k}$ is

$$f_{\vec{u}}(a, b, c) = f_x(a, b, c)u_1 + f_y(a, b, c)u_2 + f_z(a, b, c)u_3.$$

This can be justified using local linearity in the same way as for functions of two variables.

Example 1   Find the directional derivative of $f(x, y, z) = xy + z$ at the point $(-1, 0, 1)$ in the direction of the vector $\vec{v} = 2\vec{i} + \vec{k}$.

Solution   The magnitude of $\vec{v}$ is $\|\vec{v}\| = \sqrt{2^2 + 1} = \sqrt{5}$, so a unit vector in the same direction as $\vec{v}$ is

$$\vec{u} = \frac{\vec{v}}{\|\vec{v}\|} = \frac{2}{\sqrt{5}}\vec{i} + 0\vec{j} + \frac{1}{\sqrt{5}}\vec{k}.$$

The partial derivatives of f are $f_x(x, y, z) = y$ and $f_y(x, y, z) = x$ and $f_z(x, y, z) = 1$. Thus,

$$f_{\vec{u}}(-1, 0, 1) = f_x(-1, 0, 1)u_1 + f_y(-1, 0, 1)u_2 + f_z(-1, 0, 1)u_3$$

$$= (0)\left(\frac{2}{\sqrt{5}}\right) + (-1)(0) + (1)\left(\frac{1}{\sqrt{5}}\right) = \frac{1}{\sqrt{5}}.$$

The Gradient Vector of a Function of Three Variables

The gradient of a function of three variables is defined in the same way as for two variables:

$$\operatorname{grad} f(a, b, c) = f_x(a, b, c)\vec{i} + f_y(a, b, c)\vec{j} + f_z(a, b, c)\vec{k}.$$

Directional derivatives are related to gradients in the same way as for functions of two variables:

$$f_{\vec{u}}(a, b, c) = f_x(a, b, c)u_1 + f_y(a, b, c)u_2 + f_z(a, b, c)u_3 = \operatorname{grad} f(a, b, c) \cdot \vec{u}.$$

Since $\operatorname{grad} f(a, b, c) \cdot \vec{u} = \|\operatorname{grad} f(a, b, c)\|\cos\theta$, where θ is the angle between $\operatorname{grad} f(a, b, c)$ and $\vec{u}$, the value of $f_{\vec{u}}(a, b, c)$ is largest when $\theta = 0$, that is, when $\vec{u}$ is in the same direction as $\operatorname{grad} f(a, b, c)$. In addition, $f_{\vec{u}}(a, b, c) = 0$ when $\theta = \pi/2$, so $\operatorname{grad} f(a, b, c)$ is perpendicular to the level surface of f. The properties of gradients in space are similar to those in the plane:

Properties of the Gradient Vector in Space

If f is differentiable at (a, b, c) and $\vec{u}$ is a unit vector, then

$$f_{\vec{u}}(a, b, c) = \operatorname{grad} f(a, b, c) \cdot \vec{u}.$$

If, in addition, $\operatorname{grad} f(a, b, c) \neq \vec{0}$, then
- $\operatorname{grad} f(a, b, c)$ is in the direction of the greatest rate of increase of f
- $\operatorname{grad} f(a, b, c)$ is perpendicular to the level surface of f at (a, b, c)
- $\| \operatorname{grad} f(a, b, c)\|$ is the maximum rate of change of f at (a, b, c).

Example 2   Let $f(x, y, z) = x^2 + y^2$ and $g(x, y, z) = -x^2 - y^2 - z^2$. What can we say about the direction of the following vectors?

(a) $\operatorname{grad} f(0, 1, 1)$ (b) $\operatorname{grad} f(1, 0, 1)$ (c) $\operatorname{grad} g(0, 1, 1)$ (d) $\operatorname{grad} g(1, 0, 1)$.

Solution   The cylinder $x^2 + y^2 = 1$ in Figure 14.42 is a level surface of f and contains both the points $(0, 1, 1)$ and $(1, 0, 1)$. Since the value of f does not change at all in the z-direction, all the gradient vectors are horizontal. They are perpendicular to the cylinder and point outward because the value of f increases as we move out.

Similarly, the points $(0, 1, 1)$ and $(1, 0, 1)$ also lie on the same level surface of g, namely $g(x, y, z) = -x^2 - y^2 - z^2 = -2$, which is the sphere $x^2 + y^2 + z^2 = 2$. Part of this level surface is shown in Figure 14.43. This time the gradient vectors point inward, since the negative signs mean that the function increases (from large negative values to small negative values) as we move inward.

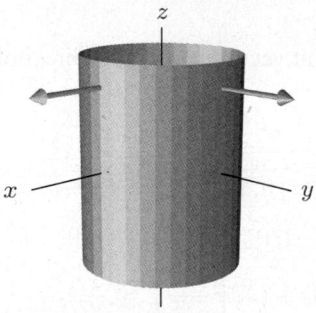

Figure 14.42: The level surface
$f(x, y, z) = x^2 + y^2 = 1$ with two gradient vectors

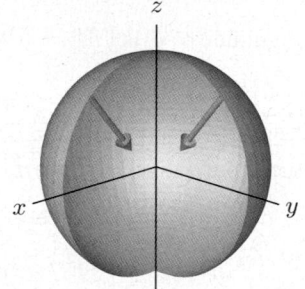

Figure 14.43: The level surface
$g(x, y, z) = -x^2 - y^2 - z^2 = -2$ with two gradient vectors

Example 3   Consider the functions $f(x, y) = 4 - x^2 - 2y^2$ and $g(x, y) = 4 - x^2$. Calculate a vector perpendicular to each of the following:

(a) The level curve of f at the point $(1, 1)$ (b) The surface $z = f(x, y)$ at the point $(1, 1, 1)$
(c) The level curve of g at the point $(1, 1)$ (d) The surface $z = g(x, y)$ at the point $(1, 1, 3)$

Solution   (a) The vector we want is a 2-vector in the plane. Since $\operatorname{grad} f = -2x\vec{i} - 4y\vec{j}$, we have

$$\operatorname{grad} f(1, 1) = -2\vec{i} - 4\vec{j}.$$

Any nonzero multiple of this vector is perpendicular to the level curve at the point $(1, 1)$.

(b) In this case we want a 3-vector in space. To find it we rewrite $z = 4 - x^2 - 2y^2$ as the level surface of the function F, where

$$F(x, y, z) = 4 - x^2 - 2y^2 - z = 0.$$

Then

$$\operatorname{grad} F = -2x\vec{i} - 4y\vec{j} - \vec{k},$$

so

$$\text{grad}\, F(1, 1, 1) = -2\vec{i} - 4\vec{j} - \vec{k},$$

and $\text{grad}\, F(1, 1, 1)$ is perpendicular to the surface $z = 4 - x^2 - 2y^2$ at the point $(1, 1, 1)$. Notice that $-2\vec{i} - 4\vec{j} - \vec{k}$ is not the only possible answer: any multiple of this vector will do.

(c) We are looking for a 2-vector. Since $\text{grad}\, g = -2x\vec{i} + 0\vec{j}$, we have

$$\text{grad}\, g(1, 1) = -2\vec{i}.$$

Any multiple of this vector is perpendicular to the level curve also.

(d) We are looking for a 3-vector. We rewrite $z = 4 - x^2$ as the level surface of the function G, where

$$G(x, y, z) = 4 - x^2 - z = 0.$$

Then

$$\text{grad}\, G = -2x\vec{i} - \vec{k}$$

So

$$\text{grad}\, G(1, 1, 3) = -2\vec{i} - \vec{k},$$

and any multiple of $\text{grad}\, G(1, 1, 3)$ is perpendicular to the surface $z = 4 - x^2$ at this point.

Example 4   (a) A hiker on the surface $f(x, y) = 4 - x^2 - 2y^2$ at the point $(1, -1, 1)$ starts to climb along the path of steepest ascent. What is the relation between the vector $\text{grad}\, f(1, -1)$ and a vector tangent to the path at the point $(1, -1, 1)$ and pointing uphill?

(b) At the point $(1, -1, 1)$ on the surface $f(x, y) = 4 - x^2 - 2y^2$, calculate a vector, $\vec{n}$, perpendicular to the surface and a vector, $\vec{T}$, tangent to the curve of steepest ascent.

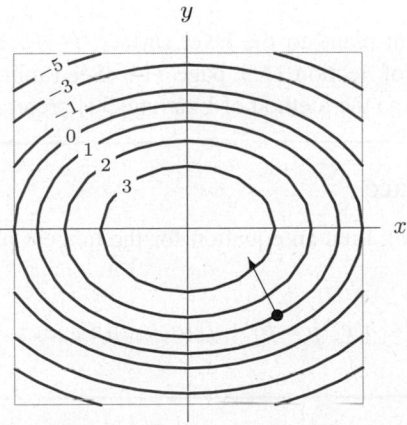

Figure 14.44: Contour diagram for $z = f(x, y) = 4 - x^2 - 2y^2$ showing direction of $\text{grad}\, f(1, -1)$

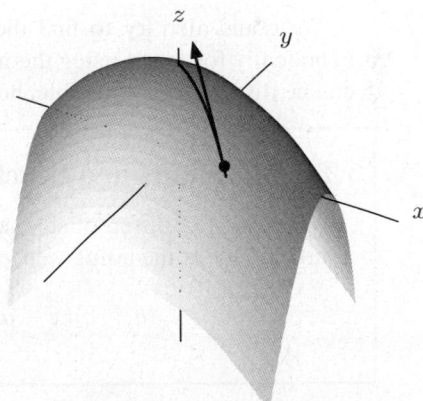

Figure 14.45: Graph of $f(x, y) = 4 - x^2 - 2y^2$ showing path of steepest ascent from the point $(1, -1, 1)$

Solution   (a) The hiker at the point $(1, -1, 1)$ lies directly above the point $(1, -1)$ in the xy-plane. The vector $\text{grad}\, f(1, -1)$ lies in 2-space, pointing like a compass in the direction in which f increases most rapidly. Therefore, $\text{grad}\, f(1, -1)$ lies directly under a vector tangent to the hiker's path at $(1, -1, 1)$ and pointing uphill. (See Figures 14.44 and 14.45.)

(b) The surface is represented by $F(x, y, z) = 4 - x^2 - 2y^2 - z = 0$. Since $\text{grad } F = -2x\vec{i} - 4y\vec{j} - \vec{k}$, the normal, $\vec{n}$, to the surface is given by

$$\vec{n} = \text{grad } F(1, -1, 1) = -2(1)\vec{i} - 4(-1)\vec{j} - \vec{k} = -2\vec{i} + 4\vec{j} - \vec{k}.$$

We take the $\vec{i}$ and $\vec{j}$ components of $\vec{T}$ to be the vector $\text{grad } f(1, -1) = -2\vec{i} + 4\vec{j}$. Thus, we have that, for some $a > 0$,

$$\vec{T} = -2\vec{i} + 4\vec{j} + a\vec{k}$$

We want $\vec{n} \cdot \vec{T} = 0$, so

$$\vec{n} \cdot \vec{T} = (-2\vec{i} + 4\vec{j} - \vec{k}) \cdot (-2\vec{i} + 4\vec{j} + a\vec{k}) = 4 + 16 - a = 0$$

So $a = 20$ and hence

$$\vec{T} = -2\vec{i} + 4\vec{j} + 20\vec{k}.$$

Example 5 Find the equation of the tangent plane to the sphere $x^2 + y^2 + z^2 = 14$ at the point $(1, 2, 3)$.

Solution We write the sphere as a level surface as follows:

$$f(x, y, z) = x^2 + y^2 + z^2 = 14.$$

We have

$$\text{grad } f = 2x\vec{i} + 2y\vec{j} + 2z\vec{k},$$

so the vector

$$\text{grad } f(1, 2, 3) = 2\vec{i} + 4\vec{j} + 6\vec{k}$$

is perpendicular to the sphere at the point $(1, 2, 3)$. Since the vector $\text{grad } f(1, 2, 3)$ is normal to the tangent plane, the equation of the plane is

$$2x + 4y + 6z = 2 \cdot 1 + 4 \cdot 2 + 6 \cdot 3 = 28 \quad \text{or} \quad x + 2y + 3z = 14.$$

We could also try to find the tangent plane to the level surface $f(x, y, z) = k$ by solving algebraically for z and using the method of Section 14.3, page 773. (See Problem 46.) Solving for z can be difficult or impossible, however, so the method of Example 5 is preferable.

Tangent Plane to a Level Surface

If $f(x, y, z)$ is differentiable at (a, b, c), then an equation for the tangent plane to the level surface of f at the point (a, b, c) is

$$f_x(a, b, c)(x - a) + f_y(a, b, c)(y - b) + f_z(a, b, c)(z - c) = 0.$$

Caution: Scale on the Axis and the Geometric Interpretation of the Gradient

When we interpreted the gradient of a function geometrically (page 783), we tacitly assumed that the units and scales along the x and y axes were the same. If the scales are not the same, the gradient vector may not look perpendicular to the contours. Consider the function $f(x, y) = x^2 + y$ with gradient vector $\text{grad } f = 2x\vec{i} + \vec{j}$. Figure 14.46 shows the gradient vector at $(1, 1)$ using the same scales in the x and y directions. As expected, the gradient vector is perpendicular to the contour line. Figure 14.47 shows contours of the same function with unequal scales on the two axes. Notice that the gradient vector no longer appears perpendicular to the contour lines. Thus, we see that the geometric interpretation of the gradient vector requires that the same scale be used on both axes.

Figure 14.46: The gradient vector with x and y scales equal

Figure 14.47: The gradient vector with x and y scales unequal

Exercises and Problems for Section 14.5

Exercises

In Exercises 1–12, find the gradient of the function.

1. $f(x, y, z) = x^2$

2. $f(x, y, z) = x^2 + y^3 - z^4$

3. $f(x, y, z) = e^{x+y+z}$

4. $f(x, y, z) = \cos(x + y) + \sin(y + z)$

5. $f(x, y, z) = yz^2/(1 + x^2)$

6. $f(x, y, z) = 1/(x^2 + y^2 + z^2)$

7. $f(x, y, z) = \sqrt{x^2 + y^2 + z^2}$

8. $f(x, y, z) = xe^y \sin z$

9. $f(x, y, z) = xy + \sin(e^z)$

10. $f(x_1, x_2, x_3) = x_1^2 x_2^3 x_3^4$

11. $f(p, q, r) = e^p + \ln q + e^{r^2}$

12. $f(x, y, z) = e^{z^2} + y \ln(x^2 + 5)$

In Exercises 13–18, find the gradient at the point.

13. $f(x, y, z) = zy^2$, at $(1, 0, 1)$

14. $f(x, y, z) = 2x + 3y + 4z$, at $(1, 1, 1)$

15. $f(x, y, z) = x^2 + y^2 - z^4$, at $(3, 2, 1)$

16. $f(x, y, z) = xyz$, at $(1, 2, 3)$

17. $f(x, y, z) = \sin(xy) + \sin(yz)$, at $(1, \pi, -1)$

18. $f(x, y, z) = x \ln(yz)$, at $(2, 1, e)$

In Exercises 19–24, find the directional derivative using $f(x, y, z) = xy + z^2$.

19. At $(1, 2, 3)$ in the direction of $\vec{i} + \vec{j} + \vec{k}$.

20. At $(1, 1, 1)$ in the direction of $\vec{i} + 2\vec{j} + 3\vec{k}$.

21. As you leave the point $(1, 1, 0)$ heading in the direction of the point $(0, 1, 1)$.

22. As you arrive at $(0, 1, 1)$ from the direction of $(1, 1, 0)$.

23. At the point $(2, 3, 4)$ in the direction of a vector making an angle of $3\pi/4$ with grad $f(2, 3, 4)$.

24. At the point $(2, 3, 4)$ in the direction of the maximum rate of change of f.

In Exercises 25–30, check that the point $(-1, 1, 2)$ lies on the given surface. Then, viewing the surface as a level surface for a function $f(x, y, z)$, find a vector normal to the surface and an equation for the tangent plane to the surface at $(-1, 1, 2)$.

25. $x^2 - y^2 + z^2 = 4$ 26. $z = x^2 + y^2$

27. $y^2 = z^2 - 3$ 28. $x^2 - xyz = 3$

29. $\cos(x + y) = e^{xz+2}$ 30. $y = 4/(2x + 3z)$

31. For $f(x, y, z) = 3x^2y^2 + 2yz$, find the directional derivative at the point $(-1, 0, 4)$ in the direction of
   (a) $\vec{i} - \vec{k}$ (b) $-\vec{i} + 3\vec{j} + 3\vec{k}$

32. If $f(x, y, z) = x^2 + 3xy + 2z$, find the directional derivative at the point $(2, 0, -1)$ in the direction of $2\vec{i} + \vec{j} - 2\vec{k}$.

33. (a) Let $f(x, y, z) = x^2 + y^2 - xyz$. Find grad f.
    (b) Find the equation for the tangent plane to the surface $f(x, y, z) = 7$ at the point $(2, 3, 1)$.

34. Find the equation of the tangent plane at the point $(3, 2, 2)$ to $z = \sqrt{17 - x^2 - y^2}$.

35. Find the equation of the tangent plane to $z = 8/(xy)$ at the point $(1, 2, 4)$.

36. Find an equation of the tangent plane and of a normal vector to the surface $x = y^3 z^7$ at the point $(1, -1, -1)$.

In Exercises 37–38, the gradient of f and a point P on the level surface $f(x, y, z) = 0$ are given. Find an equation for the tangent plane to the surface at the point P.

37. grad $f = yz\vec{i} + xz\vec{j} + xy\vec{k}$, $P = (1, 2, 3)$

38. grad $f = 2x\vec{i} + z^2\vec{j} + 2yz\vec{k}$, $P = (10, -10, 30)$

In Exercises 39–43, find an equation of the tangent plane to the surface at the given point.

39. $x^2 + y^2 + z^2 = 17$ at the point $(2, 3, 2)$

40. $x^2 + y^2 = 1$ at the point $(1, 0, 0)$

41. $z = 2x + y + 3$ at the point $(0, 0, 3)$

42. $3x^2 - 4xy + z^2 = 0$ at the point (a, a, a), where $a \neq 0$

43. $z = 9/(x + 4y)$ at the point where $x = 1$ and $y = 2$

Problems

44. Consider the surface $g(x, y) = 4 - x^2$. What is the relation between grad $g(-1, -1)$ and a vector tangent to the path of steepest ascent at $(-1, -1, 3)$? Illustrate your answer with a sketch.

45. Match the functions $f(x, y, z)$ in (a)–(d) with the descriptions of their gradients in (I)–(IV). No reasons needed.

    (a) $x^2 + y^2 + z^2$ **(b)** $x^2 + y^2$

    (c) $\dfrac{1}{x^2 + y^2 + z^2}$ **(d)** $\dfrac{1}{x^2 + y^2}$

    I   Points radially outward from the z-axis.
    II Points radially inward toward the z-axis.
    III Points radially outward from the origin.
    IV Points radially inward toward the origin.

46. Find the equation of the tangent plane at $(2, 3, 1)$ to the surface $x^2 + y^2 - xyz = 7$. Do this in two ways:

    (a) Viewing the surface as the level set of a function of three variables, $F(x, y, z)$.
    (b) Viewing the surface as the graph of a function of two variables $z = f(x, y)$.

47. Let $f(x, y, z) = x^2 + y^2 + z^2$. At the point $(1, 2, 1)$, find the rate of change of f in the direction perpendicular to the plane $x + 2y + 3z = 8$ and moving away from the origin.

48. Let $f(x, y) = \cos x \sin y$ and let S be the surface $z = f(x, y)$.

    (a) Find a normal vector to the surface S at the point $(0, \pi/2, 1)$.
    (b) What is the equation of the tangent plane to the surface S at the point $(0, \pi/2, 1)$?

49. Let $f(x, y, z) = \sin(x^2 + y^2 + z^2)$.

    (a) Describe in words the shape of the level surfaces of f.
    (b) Find grad f.
    (c) Consider the two vectors $\vec{r} = x\vec{i} + y\vec{j} + z\vec{k}$ and grad f at a point (x, y, z) where $\sin(x^2 + y^2 + z^2) \neq 0$. What is (are) the possible values(s) of the angle between these vectors?

50. Each diagram (I) – (IV) in Figure 14.48 represents the level curves of a function $f(x, y)$. For each function f, consider the point above P on the surface $z = f(x, y)$ and choose from the lists which follow:

    (a) A vector which could be the normal to the surface at that point;
    (b) An equation which could be the equation of the tangent plane to the surface at that point.

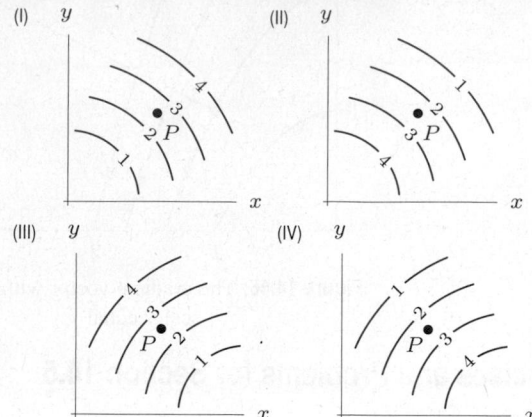

Figure 14.48

Vectors	Equations
(E) $2\vec{i} + 2\vec{j} - 2\vec{k}$	(J) $x + y + z = 4$
(F) $2\vec{i} + 2\vec{j} + 2\vec{k}$	(K) $2x - 2y - 2z = 2$
(G) $2\vec{i} - 2\vec{j} + 2\vec{k}$	(L) $-3x - 3y + 3z = 6$
(H) $-2\vec{i} + 2\vec{j} + 2\vec{k}$	(M) $-\dfrac{x}{2} + \dfrac{y}{2} - \dfrac{z}{2} = -7$

51. The surface S is represented by the equation $F = 0$ where $F(x, y, z) = x^2 - (y/z^2)$.

    (a) Find the unit vectors $\vec{u}_1$ and $\vec{u}_2$ pointing in the direction of maximum increase of F at the points $(0, 0, 1)$ and $(1, 1, 1)$ respectively.
    (b) Find the tangent plane to S at the points $(0, 0, 1)$ and $(1, 1, 1)$.
    (c) Find all points on S where a normal vector is parallel to the xy-plane.

52. Consider the function $f(x, y) = (e^x - x) \cos y$. Suppose S is the surface $z = f(x, y)$.

    (a) Find a vector which is perpendicular to the level curve of f through the point $(2, 3)$ in the direction in which f decreases most rapidly.
    (b) Suppose $\vec{v} = 5\vec{i} + 4\vec{j} + a\vec{k}$ is a vector in 3-space which is tangent to the surface S at the point P lying on the surface above $(2, 3)$. What is a?

53. **(a)** Find the tangent plane to the surface $x^2 + y^2 + 3z^2 = 4$ at the point $(0.6, 0.8, 1)$.
    (b) Is there a point on the surface $x^2 + y^2 + 3z^2 = 4$ at which the tangent plane is parallel to the plane $8x + 6y + 30z = 1$? If so, find it. If not, explain why not.

54. Your house lies on the surface $z = f(x, y) = 2x^2 - y^2$ directly above the point $(4, 3)$ in the xy-plane.

    (a) How high above the xy-plane do you live?
    (b) What is the slope of your lawn as you look from your house directly toward the z-axis (that is, along the vector $-4\vec{i} - 3\vec{j}$)?

(c) When you wash your car in the driveway, on this surface above the point $(4, 3)$, which way does the water run off? (Give your answer as a two-dimensional vector.)

(d) What is the equation of the tangent plane to this surface at your house?

55. (a) Sketch the contours of $z = y - \sin x$ for $z = -1, 0, 1, 2$.

(b) A bug starts on the surface at the point $(\pi/2, 1, 0)$ and walks on the surface $z = y - \sin x$ in the direction parallel to the y-axis, in the direction of increasing y. Is the bug walking in a valley or on top of a ridge? Explain.

(c) On the contour $z = 0$ in your sketch for part (a), draw the gradients of z at $x = 0$, $x = \pi/2$, and $x = \pi$.

56. At what point on the surface $z = 1 + x^2 + y^2$ is its tangent plane parallel to the following planes?

(a) $z = 5$ **(b)** $z = 5 + 6x - 10y$.

57. The concentration of salt in a fluid at (x, y, z) is given by $F(x, y, z) = x^2 + y^4 + x^2z^2$ mg/cm^3. You are at the point $(-1, 1, 1)$.

(a) In which direction should you move if you want the concentration to increase the fastest?

(b) You start to move in the direction you found in part (a) at a speed of 4 cm/sec. How fast is the concentration changing?

58. Let $g_x(2, 1, 7) = 3$, $g_y(2, 1, 7) = 10$, $g_z(2, 1, 7) = -5$. Find the equation of the tangent plane to $g(x, y, z) = 0$ at the point $(2, 1, 7)$.

59. The vector ∇f at point P and four unit vectors $\vec{u}_1, \vec{u}_2, \vec{u}_3, \vec{u}_4$ are shown in Figure 14.49. Arrange the following quantities in ascending order

$$f_{\vec{u}_1}, \quad f_{\vec{u}_2}, \quad f_{\vec{u}_3}, \quad f_{\vec{u}_4}, \quad \text{the number } 0.$$

The directional derivatives are all evaluated at the point P and the function $f(x, y)$ is differentiable at P.

Figure 14.49

60. The temperature of a gas at the point (x, y, z) is given by $G(x, y, z) = x^2 - 5xy + y^2z$.

(a) What is the rate of change in the temperature at the point $(1, 2, 3)$ in the direction $\vec{v} = 2\vec{i} + \vec{j} - 4\vec{k}$?

(b) What is the direction of maximum rate of change of temperature at the point $(1, 2, 3)$?

(c) What is the maximum rate of change at the point $(1, 2, 3)$?

61. The temperature at the point (x, y, z) in 3-space is given, in degrees Celsius, by $T(x, y, z) = e^{-(x^2+y^2+z^2)}$.

(a) Describe in words the shape of surfaces on which the temperature is constant.

(b) Find grad T.

(c) You travel from the point $(1, 0, 0)$ to the point $(2, 1, 0)$ at a speed of 3 units per second. Find the instantaneous rate of change of the temperature as you leave the point $(1, 0, 0)$. Give units.

62. A spaceship is plunging into the atmosphere of a planet. With coordinates in miles and the origin at the center of the planet, the pressure of the atmosphere at (x, y, z) is

$$P = 5e^{-0.1\sqrt{x^2+y^2+z^2}} \text{ atmospheres.}$$

The velocity, in miles/sec, of the spaceship at $(0, 0, 1)$ is $\vec{v} = \vec{i} - 2.5\vec{k}$. At $(0, 0, 1)$, what is the rate of change with respect to time of the pressure on the spaceship?

63. Let $\vec{r} = x\vec{i} + y\vec{j} + z\vec{k}$ and $\vec{a}$ be a constant vector. For each of the quantities in (a)–(c), choose the statement in (I)–(V) that describes it. No reasons needed.

(a) grad$(\vec{r} + \vec{a})$ **(b)** grad$(\vec{r} \cdot \vec{a})$ **(c)** grad$(\vec{r} \times \vec{a})$

  I   Scalar, independent of $\vec{a}$.
  II   Scalar, depends on $\vec{a}$.
  III   Vector, independent of $\vec{a}$.
  IV   Vector, depends on $\vec{a}$.
  V   Not defined.

64. The earth has mass M and is located at the origin in 3-space, while the moon has mass m. Newton's Law of Gravitation states that if the moon is located at the point (x, y, z) then the attractive force exerted by the earth on the moon is given by the vector

$$\vec{F} = -GMm\frac{\vec{r}}{\|\vec{r}\|^3},$$

where $\vec{r} = x\vec{i} + y\vec{j} + z\vec{k}$. Show that $\vec{F} = \text{grad}\,\varphi$, where φ is the function given by

$$\varphi(x, y, z) = \frac{GMm}{\|\vec{r}\|}.$$

65. Two surfaces are said to be *tangential* at a point P if they have the same tangent plane at P. Show that the surfaces $z = \sqrt{2x^2 + 2y^2 - 25}$ and $z = \frac{1}{5}(x^2 + y^2)$ are tangential at the point $(4, 3, 5)$.

66. Two surfaces are said to be *orthogonal* to each other at a point P if the normals to their tangent planes are perpendicular at P. Show that the surfaces $z = \frac{1}{2}(x^2 + y^2 - 1)$ and $z = \frac{1}{2}(1 - x^2 - y^2)$ are orthogonal at all points of intersection.

67. Let $\vec{r}$ be the position vector of the point (x, y, z). If $\vec{\mu} = \mu_1 \vec{i} + \mu_2 \vec{j} + \mu_3 \vec{k}$ is a constant vector, show that

$$\text{grad}(\vec{\mu} \cdot \vec{r}) = \vec{\mu}.$$

68. Let $\vec{r}$ be the position vector of the point (x, y, z). Show

that, if a is a constant,

$$\text{grad}(\|\vec{r}\|^a) = a\|\vec{r}\|^{a-2}\vec{r}, \qquad \vec{r} \neq \vec{0}.$$

69. Let f and g be functions on 3-space. Suppose f is differentiable and that

$$\text{grad } f(x, y, z) = (x\vec{i} + y\vec{j} + z\vec{k})g(x, y, z).$$

Explain why f must be constant on any sphere centered at the origin.

Strengthen Your Understanding

In Problems 70–71, explain what is wrong with the statement.

70. The gradient vector grad $f(x, y)$ points in the direction perpendicular to the surface $z = f(x, y)$.

71. The tangent plane at the origin to a surface $f(x, y, z) = 1$ that contains the point $(0, 0, 0)$ has equation

$$f_x(0, 0, 0)x + f_y(0, 0, 0)y + f_z(0, 0, 0)z + 1 = 0.$$

In Problems 72–74, give an example of:

72. A surface $z = f(x, y)$ such that the vector $\vec{i} - 2\vec{j} - \vec{k}$ is normal to the tangent plane at the point where $(x, y) = (0, 0)$.

73. A function $f(x, y, z)$ such that grad $f = 2\vec{i} + 3\vec{j} + 4\vec{k}$.

74. Two nonparallel unit vectors $\vec{u}$ and $\vec{v}$ such that $f_{\vec{u}}(0, 0, 0) = f_{\vec{v}}(0, 0, 0) = 0$, where $f(x, y, z) = 2x - 3y$.

Are the statements in Problems 75–78 true or false? Give reasons for your answer.

75. An equation for the tangent plane to the surface $z = x^2 + y^3$ at $(1, 1)$ is $z = 2 + 2x(x - 1) + 3y^2(y - 1)$.

76. There is a function $f(x, y)$ which has a tangent plane with equation $z = 0$ at a point (a, b).

77. There is a function with $\| \text{grad } f \| = 4$ and $f_{\vec{k}} = 5$ at some point.

78. There is a function with $\| \text{grad } f \| = 5$ and $f_{\vec{k}} = -3$ at some point.

79. Let $f(x, y, z)$ represent the temperature in °C at the point (x, y, z) with x, y, z in meters. Let $\vec{v}$ be your velocity in meters per second. Give units and an interpretation of each of the following quantities.

   (a) $\| \text{grad } f \|$ (b) $\text{grad } f \cdot \vec{v}$ (c) $\| \text{grad } f \| \cdot \| \vec{v} \|$

14.6 THE CHAIN RULE

Composition of Functions of Many Variables and Rates of Change

The chain rule enables us to differentiate *composite functions*. If we have a function of two variables $z = f(x, y)$ and we substitute $x = g(t), y = h(t)$ into $z = f(x, y)$, then we have a composite function in which z is a function of t:

$$z = f(g(t), h(t)).$$

If, on the other hand, we substitute $x = g(u, v), y = h(u, v)$, then we have a different composite function in which z is a function of u and v:

$$z = f(g(u, v), h(u, v)).$$

The next example shows how to calculate the rate of change of a composite function.

Example 1   Corn production, C, depends on annual rainfall, R, and average temperature, T, so $C = f(R, T)$. Global warming predicts that both rainfall and temperature depend on time. Suppose that according to a particular model of global warming, rainfall is decreasing at 0.2 cm per year and temperature is increasing at 0.1°C per year. Use the fact that at current levels of production, $f_R = 3.3$ and $f_T = -5$ to estimate the current rate of change, dC/dt.

Solution   By local linearity, we know that changes ΔR and ΔT generate a change, ΔC, in C given approximately by

$$\Delta C \approx f_R \Delta R + f_T \Delta T = 3.3 \Delta R - 5 \Delta T.$$

We want to know how ΔC depends on the time increment, Δt. A change Δt causes changes ΔR and ΔT, which in turn cause a change ΔC. The model of global warming tells us that

$$\frac{dR}{dt} = -0.2 \quad \text{and} \quad \frac{dT}{dt} = 0.1.$$

Thus, a time increment, Δt, generates changes of ΔR and ΔT given by

$$\Delta R \approx -0.2 \Delta t \quad \text{and} \quad \Delta T \approx 0.1 \Delta t.$$

Substituting for ΔR and ΔT in the expression for ΔC gives us

$$\Delta C \approx 3.3(-0.2 \Delta t) - 5(0.1 \Delta t) = -1.16 \Delta t.$$

Thus,

$$\frac{\Delta C}{\Delta t} \approx -1.16 \quad \text{and, therefore,} \quad \frac{dC}{dt} \approx -1.16.$$

The relationship between ΔC and Δt, which gives the value of dC/dt, is an example of the *chain rule*. The argument in Example 1 leads to more general versions of the chain rule.

The Chain Rule for $z = f(x, y)$, $x = g(t)$, $y = h(t)$

Since $z = f(g(t), h(t))$ is a function of t, we can consider the derivative dz/dt. The chain rule gives dz/dt in terms of the derivatives of f, g, and h. Since dz/dt represents the rate of change of z with t, we look at the change Δz generated by a small change, Δt.

We substitute the local linearizations

$$\Delta x \approx \frac{dx}{dt} \Delta t \quad \text{and} \quad \Delta y \approx \frac{dy}{dt} \Delta t$$

into the local linearization

$$\Delta z \approx \frac{\partial z}{\partial x} \Delta x + \frac{\partial z}{\partial y} \Delta y,$$

yielding

$$\Delta z \approx \frac{\partial z}{\partial x} \frac{dx}{dt} \Delta t + \frac{\partial z}{\partial y} \frac{dy}{dt} \Delta t$$
$$= \left(\frac{\partial z}{\partial x} \frac{dx}{dt} + \frac{\partial z}{\partial y} \frac{dy}{dt} \right) \Delta t.$$

Thus,

$$\frac{\Delta z}{\Delta t} \approx \frac{\partial z}{\partial x} \frac{dx}{dt} + \frac{\partial z}{\partial y} \frac{dy}{dt}.$$

Taking the limit as $\Delta t \to 0$, we get the following result.

If f, g, and h are differentiable and if $z = f(x, y)$, and $x = g(t)$, and $y = h(t)$, then

$$\frac{dz}{dt} = \frac{\partial z}{\partial x} \frac{dx}{dt} + \frac{\partial z}{\partial y} \frac{dy}{dt}.$$

Visualizing the Chain Rule with a Diagram

The diagram in Figure 14.50 provides a way of remembering the chain rule. It shows the chain of dependence: z depends on x and y, which in turn depend on t. Each line in the diagram is labeled with a derivative relating the variables at its ends.

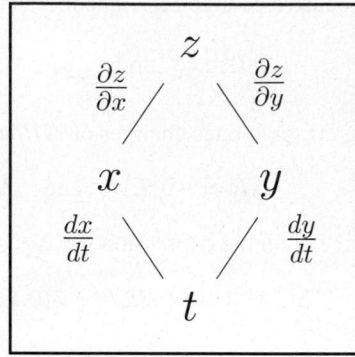

Figure 14.50: Diagram for $z = f(x, y)$, $x = g(t)$, $y = h(t)$. Lines represent dependence of z on x and y, and of x and y on t

The diagram keeps track of how a change in t propagates through the chain of composed functions. There are two paths from t to z, one through x and one through y. For each path, we multiply together the derivatives along the path. Then, to calculate dz/dt, we add the contributions from the two paths.

Example 2   Suppose that $z = f(x, y) = x \sin y$, where $x = t^2$ and $y = 2t + 1$. Let $z = g(t)$. Compute $g'(t)$ directly and using the chain rule.

Solution   Since $z = g(t) = f(t^2, 2t + 1) = t^2 \sin(2t + 1)$, it is possible to compute $g'(t)$ directly by one-variable methods:

$$g'(t) = t^2 \frac{d}{dt}(\sin(2t + 1)) + \left(\frac{d}{dt}(t^2)\right) \sin(2t + 1) = 2t^2 \cos(2t + 1) + 2t \sin(2t + 1).$$

The chain rule provides an alternative route to the same answer. We have

$$\frac{dz}{dt} = \frac{\partial z}{\partial x}\frac{dx}{dt} + \frac{\partial z}{\partial y}\frac{dy}{dt} = (\sin y)(2t) + (x \cos y)(2) = 2t \sin(2t + 1) + 2t^2 \cos(2t + 1).$$

Example 3   The capacity, C, of a communication channel, such as a telephone line, to carry information depends on the ratio of the signal strength, S, to the noise, N. For some positive constant k,

$$C = k \ln\left(1 + \frac{S}{N}\right).$$

Suppose that the signal and noise are given as a function of time, t in seconds, by

$$S(t) = 4 + \cos(4\pi t) \qquad N(t) = 2 + \sin(2\pi t).$$

What is dC/dt one second after transmission started? Is the capacity increasing or decreasing at that instant?

Solution   By the chain rule

$$\frac{dC}{dt} = \frac{\partial C}{\partial S}\frac{dS}{dt} + \frac{\partial C}{\partial N}\frac{dN}{dt}$$

$$= \frac{k}{1 + S/N} \cdot \frac{1}{N}(-4\pi \sin 4\pi t) + \frac{k}{1 + S/N}\left(-\frac{S}{N^2}\right)(2\pi \cos 2\pi t).$$

When $t = 1$, the first term is zero, $S(1) = 5$, and $N(1) = 2$, so

$$\frac{dC}{dt} = \frac{k}{1 + S(1)/N(1)} \left(-\frac{S(1)}{(N(1))^2} \right) \cdot 2\pi = \frac{k}{1 + \frac{5}{2}} \left(-\frac{5}{4} \right) \cdot 2\pi.$$

Since dC/dt is negative, the capacity is decreasing at time $t = 1$ second.

How to Formulate a General Chain Rule

A diagram can be used to write the chain rule for general compositions.

> To find the rate of change of one variable with respect to another in a chain of composed differentiable functions:
> - Draw a diagram expressing the relationship between the variables, and label each link in the diagram with the derivative relating the variables at its ends.
> - For each path between the two variables, multiply together the derivatives from each step along the path.
> - Add the contributions from each path.

The diagram keeps track of all the ways in which a change in one variable can cause a change in another; the diagram generates all the terms we would get from the appropriate substitutions into the local linearizations.

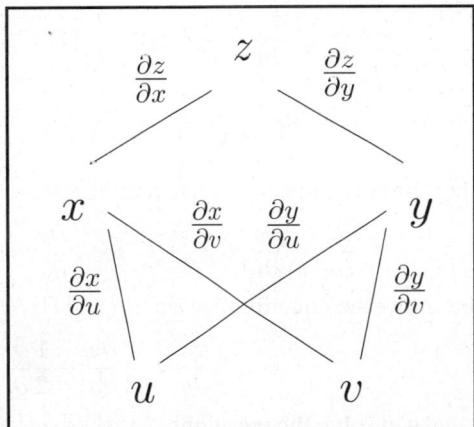

Figure 14.51: Diagram for $z = f(x, y)$, $x = g(u, v)$, $y = h(u, v)$. Lines represent dependence of z on x and y, and of x and y on u and v

For example, we can use Figure 14.51 to find formulas for $\partial z / \partial u$ and $\partial z / \partial v$. Adding the contributions for the two paths from z to u, we get the following results:

> If f, g, h are differentiable and if $z = f(x, y)$, with $x = g(u, v)$ and $y = h(u, v)$, then
>
> $$\frac{\partial z}{\partial u} = \frac{\partial z}{\partial x} \frac{\partial x}{\partial u} + \frac{\partial z}{\partial y} \frac{\partial y}{\partial u},$$
>
> $$\frac{\partial z}{\partial v} = \frac{\partial z}{\partial x} \frac{\partial x}{\partial v} + \frac{\partial z}{\partial y} \frac{\partial y}{\partial v}.$$

Example 4   Let $w = x^2 e^y$, $x = 4u$, and $y = 3u^2 - 2v$. Compute $\partial w / \partial u$ and $\partial w / \partial v$ using the chain rule.

Solution   Using the previous result, we have

$$\frac{\partial w}{\partial u} = \frac{\partial w}{\partial x}\frac{\partial x}{\partial u} + \frac{\partial w}{\partial y}\frac{\partial y}{\partial u} = 2xe^y(4) + x^2 e^y(6u) = (8x + 6x^2 u)e^y$$

$$= (32u + 96u^3)e^{3u^2 - 2v}.$$

Similarly,

$$\frac{\partial w}{\partial v} = \frac{\partial w}{\partial x}\frac{\partial x}{\partial v} + \frac{\partial w}{\partial y}\frac{\partial y}{\partial v} = 2xe^y(0) + x^2 e^y(-2) = -2x^2 e^y$$

$$= -32u^2 e^{3u^2 - 2v}.$$

Example 5   A quantity z can be expressed either as a function of x and y, so that $z = f(x, y)$, or as a function of u and v, so that $z = g(u, v)$. The two coordinate systems are related by

$$x = u + v, \quad y = u - v.$$

(a) Use the chain rule to express $\partial z / \partial u$ and $\partial z / \partial v$ in terms of $\partial z / \partial x$ and $\partial z / \partial y$.
(b) Solve the equations in part (a) for $\partial z / \partial x$ and $\partial z / \partial y$.
(c) Show that the expressions we get in part (b) are the same as we get by expressing u and v in terms of x and y and using the chain rule.

Solution   (a) We have $\partial x / \partial u = 1$ and $\partial x / \partial v = 1$, and also $\partial y / \partial u = 1$ and $\partial y / \partial v = -1$. Thus,

$$\frac{\partial z}{\partial u} = \frac{\partial z}{\partial x}(1) + \frac{\partial z}{\partial y}(1) = \frac{\partial z}{\partial x} + \frac{\partial z}{\partial y}$$

and

$$\frac{\partial z}{\partial v} = \frac{\partial z}{\partial x}(1) + \frac{\partial z}{\partial y}(-1) = \frac{\partial z}{\partial x} - \frac{\partial z}{\partial y}.$$

(b) Adding together the equations for $\partial z / \partial u$ and $\partial z / \partial v$, we get

$$\frac{\partial z}{\partial u} + \frac{\partial z}{\partial v} = 2\frac{\partial z}{\partial x}, \quad \text{so} \quad \frac{\partial z}{\partial x} = \frac{1}{2}\frac{\partial z}{\partial u} + \frac{1}{2}\frac{\partial z}{\partial v}.$$

Similarly, subtracting the equations for $\partial z / \partial u$ and $\partial z / \partial v$ yields

$$\frac{\partial z}{\partial y} = \frac{1}{2}\frac{\partial z}{\partial u} - \frac{1}{2}\frac{\partial z}{\partial v}.$$

(c) Alternatively, we can solve the equations

$$x = u + v, \quad y = u - v$$

for u and v, which yields

$$u = \frac{1}{2}x + \frac{1}{2}y, \quad v = \frac{1}{2}x - \frac{1}{2}y.$$

Now we can think of z as a function of u and v, and u and v as functions of x and y, and apply the chain rule again. This gives us

$$\frac{\partial z}{\partial x} = \frac{\partial z}{\partial u}\frac{\partial u}{\partial x} + \frac{\partial z}{\partial v}\frac{\partial v}{\partial x} = \frac{1}{2}\frac{\partial z}{\partial u} + \frac{1}{2}\frac{\partial z}{\partial v}$$

and

$$\frac{\partial z}{\partial y} = \frac{\partial z}{\partial u}\frac{\partial u}{\partial y} + \frac{\partial z}{\partial v}\frac{\partial v}{\partial y} = \frac{1}{2}\frac{\partial z}{\partial u} - \frac{1}{2}\frac{\partial z}{\partial v}.$$

These are the same expressions we got in part (b).

An Application to Physical Chemistry

A chemist investigating the properties of a gas such as carbon dioxide may want to know how the internal energy U of a given quantity of the gas depends on its temperature, T, pressure, P, and volume, V. The three quantities T, P, and V are not independent, however. For instance, according to the ideal gas law, they satisfy the equation

$$PV = kT$$

where k is a constant which depends only upon the quantity of the gas. The internal energy can then be thought of as a function of any two of the three quantities T, P, and V:

$$U = U_1(T, P) = U_2(T, V) = U_3(P, V).$$

The chemist writes, for example, $\left(\frac{\partial U}{\partial T}\right)_P$ to indicate the partial derivative of U with respect to T *holding P constant*, signifying that for this computation U is viewed as a function of T and P. Thus, we interpret $\left(\frac{\partial U}{\partial T}\right)_P$ as

$$\left(\frac{\partial U}{\partial T}\right)_P = \frac{\partial U_1(T, P)}{\partial T}.$$

If U is to be viewed as a function of T and V, the chemist writes $\left(\frac{\partial U}{\partial T}\right)_V$ for the partial derivative of U with respect to T holding V constant: thus, $\left(\frac{\partial U}{\partial T}\right)_V = \frac{\partial U_2(T,V)}{\partial T}$.

Each of the functions U_1, U_2, U_3 gives rise to one of the following formulas for the differential dU:

$$dU = \left(\frac{\partial U}{\partial T}\right)_P dT + \left(\frac{\partial U}{\partial P}\right)_T dP \qquad \text{corresponds to } U_1,$$

$$dU = \left(\frac{\partial U}{\partial T}\right)_V dT + \left(\frac{\partial U}{\partial V}\right)_T dV \qquad \text{corresponds to } U_2,$$

$$dU = \left(\frac{\partial U}{\partial P}\right)_V dP + \left(\frac{\partial U}{\partial V}\right)_P dV \qquad \text{corresponds to } U_3.$$

All the six partial derivatives appearing in formulas for dU have physical meaning, but they are not all equally easy to measure experimentally. A relationship among the partial derivatives, usually derived from the chain rule, may make it possible to evaluate one of the partials in terms of others that are more easily measured.

Example 6   Suppose a gas satisfies the equation $PV = 2T$ and $P = 3$ when $V = 4$. If $\left(\frac{\partial U}{\partial P}\right)_V = 7$ and $\left(\frac{\partial U}{\partial V}\right)_P = 8$, find the values of $\left(\frac{\partial U}{\partial P}\right)_T$ and $\left(\frac{\partial U}{\partial T}\right)_P$.

Solution   Since we know the values of $\left(\frac{\partial U}{\partial P}\right)_V$ and $\left(\frac{\partial U}{\partial V}\right)_P$, we think of U as a function of P and V and use the function U_3 to write

$$dU = \left(\frac{\partial U}{\partial P}\right)_V dP + \left(\frac{\partial U}{\partial V}\right)_P dV$$
$$dU = 7dP + 8dV.$$

To calculate $\left(\frac{\partial U}{\partial P}\right)_T$ and $\left(\frac{\partial U}{\partial T}\right)_P$, we think of U as a function of T and P. Thus, we want to substitute for dV in terms of dT and dP. Since $PV = 2T$, we have

$$PdV + VdP = 2dT,$$
$$3dV + 4dP = 2dT.$$

Solving gives $dV = (2dT - 4dP)/3$, so

$$dU = 7dP + 8\left(\frac{2dT - 4dP}{3}\right)$$

$$dU = -\frac{11}{3}dP + \frac{16}{3}dT.$$

Comparing with the formula for dU obtained from U_1,

$$dU = \left(\frac{\partial U}{\partial T}\right)_P dT + \left(\frac{\partial U}{\partial P}\right)_T dP,$$

we have

$$\left(\frac{\partial U}{\partial T}\right)_P = \frac{16}{3} \quad \text{and} \quad \left(\frac{\partial U}{\partial P}\right)_T = -\frac{11}{3}.$$

In Example 6, we could have substituted for dP instead of dV, leading to values of $\left(\frac{\partial U}{\partial T}\right)_V$ and $\left(\frac{\partial U}{\partial V}\right)_T$. See Problem 41.

In general, if for some particular P, V, and T, we can measure two of the six quantities $\left(\frac{\partial U}{\partial P}\right)_V$, $\left(\frac{\partial U}{\partial V}\right)_P$, $\left(\frac{\partial U}{\partial P}\right)_T$, $\left(\frac{\partial U}{\partial T}\right)_P$, $\left(\frac{\partial U}{\partial T}\right)_V$, $\left(\frac{\partial U}{\partial V}\right)_V$, then we can compute the other four using the relationship between dP, dV, and dT given by the gas law. General formulas for each partial derivative in terms of others can be obtained in the same way. See the following example and Problem 41.

Example 7   Express $\left(\frac{\partial U}{\partial T}\right)_P$ in terms of $\left(\frac{\partial U}{\partial T}\right)_V$ and $\left(\frac{\partial U}{\partial V}\right)_T$ and $\left(\frac{\partial V}{\partial T}\right)_P$.

Solution   Since we are interested in the derivatives $\left(\frac{\partial U}{\partial T}\right)_V$ and $\left(\frac{\partial U}{\partial V}\right)_T$, we think of U as a function of T and V and use the formula

$$dU = \left(\frac{\partial U}{\partial T}\right)_V dT + \left(\frac{\partial U}{\partial V}\right)_T dV \qquad \text{corresponding to } U_2.$$

We want to find a formula for $\left(\frac{\partial U}{\partial T}\right)_P$, which means thinking of U as a function of T and P. Thus, we want to substitute for dV. Since V is a function of T and P, we have

$$dV = \left(\frac{\partial V}{\partial T}\right)_P dT + \left(\frac{\partial V}{\partial P}\right)_T dP.$$

Substituting for dV into the formula for dU corresponding to U_2 gives

$$dU = \left(\frac{\partial U}{\partial T}\right)_V dT + \left(\frac{\partial U}{\partial V}\right)_T \left(\left(\frac{\partial V}{\partial T}\right)_P dT + \left(\frac{\partial V}{\partial P}\right)_T dP\right).$$

Collecting the terms containing dT and the terms containing dP gives

$$dU = \left(\left(\frac{\partial U}{\partial T}\right)_V + \left(\frac{\partial U}{\partial V}\right)_T \left(\frac{\partial V}{\partial T}\right)_P\right) dT + \left(\frac{\partial U}{\partial V}\right)_T \left(\frac{\partial V}{\partial P}\right)_T dP.$$

But we also have the formula

$$dU = \left(\frac{\partial U}{\partial T}\right)_P dT + \left(\frac{\partial U}{\partial P}\right)_T dP \qquad \text{corresponding to } U_1.$$

We now have two formulas for dU in terms of dT and dP. The coefficients of dT must be identical, so we conclude

$$\left(\frac{\partial U}{\partial T}\right)_P = \left(\frac{\partial U}{\partial T}\right)_V + \left(\frac{\partial U}{\partial V}\right)_T \left(\frac{\partial V}{\partial T}\right)_P.$$

Example 7 expresses $\left(\frac{\partial U}{\partial T}\right)_P$ in terms of three other partial derivatives. Two of them, namely $\left(\frac{\partial U}{\partial T}\right)_V$, the constant-volume heat capacity, and $\left(\frac{\partial V}{\partial T}\right)_P$, the expansion coefficient, can be easily measured experimentally. The third, the internal pressure, $\left(\frac{\partial U}{\partial V}\right)_T$, cannot be measured directly but can be related to $\left(\frac{\partial P}{\partial T}\right)_V$, which is measurable. Thus, $\left(\frac{\partial U}{\partial T}\right)_P$ can be determined indirectly using this identity.

Exercises and Problems for Section 14.6

Exercises

For Exercises 1–6, find dz/dt using the chain rule. Assume the variables are restricted to domains on which the functions are defined.

1. $z = xy^2$, $x = e^{-t}$, $y = \sin t$
2. $z = x \sin y + y \sin x$, $x = t^2$, $y = \ln t$
3. $z = \sin(x/y)$, $x = 2t$, $y = 1 - t^2$
4. $z = \ln(x^2 + y^2)$, $x = 1/t$, $y = \sqrt{t}$
5. $z = xe^y$, $x = 2t$, $y = 1 - t^2$
6. $z = (x + y)e^y$, $x = 2t$, $y = 1 - t^2$

For Exercises 7–15, find $\partial z/\partial u$ and $\partial z/\partial v$. The variables are restricted to domains on which the functions are defined.

7. $z = \sin(x/y)$, $x = \ln u$, $y = v$
8. $z = \ln(xy)$, $x = (u^2 + v^2)^2$, $y = (u^3 + v^3)^2$
9. $z = xe^y$, $x = \ln u$, $y = v$
10. $z = (x + y)e^y$, $x = \ln u$, $y = v$
11. $z = xe^y$, $x = u^2 + v^2$, $y = u^2 - v^2$
12. $z = (x + y)e^y$, $x = u^2 + v^2$, $y = u^2 - v^2$
13. $z = xe^{-y} + ye^{-x}$, $x = u \sin v$, $y = v \cos u$
14. $z = \cos(x^2 + y^2)$, $x = u \cos v$, $y = u \sin v$
15. $z = \tan^{-1}(x/y)$, $x = u^2 + v^2$, $y = u^2 - v^2$

Problems

16. Use the chain rule to find dz/dt, and check the result by expressing z as a function of t and differentiating directly.
$$z = x^3 y^2, \quad x = t^3, \quad y = t^2$$

17. Use the chain rule to find $\partial w/\partial \rho$ and $\partial w/\partial \theta$, given that
$$w = x^2 + y^2 - z^2,$$
and
$$x = \rho \sin \phi \cos \theta, \quad y = \rho \sin \phi \sin \theta, \quad z = \rho \cos \phi.$$

18. A bison is charging across the plain one morning. His path takes him to location (x, y) at time t where x and y are functions of t and north is in the direction of increasing y. The temperature is always colder farther north. As time passes, the sun rises in the sky, sending out more heat, and a cold front blows in from the east. At time t the air temperature H near the bison is given by $H = f(x, y, t)$. The chain rule expresses the derivative dH/dt as a sum of three terms:
$$\frac{dH}{dt} = \frac{\partial f}{\partial x}\frac{dx}{dt} + \frac{\partial f}{\partial y}\frac{dy}{dt} + \frac{\partial f}{\partial t}.$$
Identify the term that gives the contribution to the change in temperature experienced by the bison that is due to

(a) The rising sun.
(b) The coming cold front.
(c) The bison's change in latitude.

19. Let $z = f(x, y)$ where $x = g(t)$, $y = h(t)$ and f, g, h are all differentiable functions. Given the information in the table, find $\left.\dfrac{\partial z}{\partial t}\right|_{t=1}$.

$f(3, 10) = 7$	$f(4, 11) = -20$
$f_x(3, 10) = 100$	$f_y(3, 10) = 0.1$
$f_x(4, 11) = 200$	$f_y(4, 11) = 0.2$
$f(3, 4) = -10$	$f(10, 11) = -1$
$g(1) = 3$	$h(1) = 10$
$g'(1) = 4$	$h'(1) = 11$

20. The voltage, V, (in volts) across a circuit is given by Ohm's law: $V = IR$, where I is the current (in amps) flowing through the circuit and R is the resistance (in ohms). If we place two circuits, with resistance R_1 and R_2, in parallel, then their combined resistance, R, is given by
$$\frac{1}{R} = \frac{1}{R_1} + \frac{1}{R_2}.$$
Suppose the current is 2 amps and increasing at 10^{-2} amp/sec and R_1 is 3 ohms and increasing at 0.5 ohm/sec, while R_2 is 5 ohms and decreasing at 0.1 ohm/sec. Calculate the rate at which the voltage is changing.

21. The air pressure is decreasing at a rate of 2 pascals per kilometer in the eastward direction. In addition, the air pressure is dropping at a constant rate with respect to time everywhere. A ship sailing eastward at 10 km/hour past an island takes barometer readings and records a pressure drop of 50 pascals in 2 hours. Estimate the time rate of change of air pressure on the island. (A pascal is a unit of air pressure.)

22. A steel bar with square cross sections 5 cm by 5 cm and length 3 meters is being heated. For each dimension, the bar expands $13 \cdot 10^{-6}$ meters for each 1°C rise in temperature.[2] What is the rate of change in the volume of the steel bar?

23. Corn production, C, is a function of rainfall, R, and temperature, T. (See Example 1 on page 796.) Figures 14.52 and 14.53 show how rainfall and temperature are predicted to vary with time because of global warming. Suppose we know that $\Delta C \approx 3.3\Delta R - 5\Delta T$. Use this to estimate the change in corn production between the year 2020 and the year 2021. Hence, estimate dC/dt when $t = 2020$.

Figure 14.52: Rainfall as a function of time

Figure 14.53: Temperature as a function of time

24. The function $g(\rho)$ is graphed in Figure 14.54. Let $\rho = \sqrt{x^2 + y^2 + z^2}$. Define f, a function of x, y, z by $f(x, y, z) = g\left(\sqrt{x^2 + y^2 + z^2}\right)$. Let $\vec{F} = \text{grad } f$.

(a) Describe precisely in words the level surfaces of f.

---
[2]http://www.engineeringtoolbox.com/

(b) Give a unit vector in the direction of $\vec{F}$ at the point $(1, 2, 2)$.

(c) Estimate $\|\vec{F}\|$ at the point $(1, 2, 2)$.

(d) Estimate $\vec{F}$ at the point $(1, 2, 2)$.

(e) The points $(1, 2, 2)$ and $(3, 0, 0)$ are both on the sphere $x^2 + y^2 + z^2 = 9$. Estimate $\vec{F}$ at $(3, 0, 0)$.

(f) If P and Q are any two points on the sphere $x^2 + y^2 + z^2 = k^2$:

(i) Compare the magnitudes of $\vec{F}$ at P and at Q.

(ii) Describe the directions of $\vec{F}$ at P and at Q.

Figure 14.54

25. Let $z = g(u, v, w)$ and $u = u(s, t), v = v(s, t), w = w(s, t)$. How many terms are there in the expression for $\partial z / \partial t$?

26. Suppose $w = f(x, y, z)$ and that x, y, z are functions of u and v. Use a tree diagram to write down the chain rule formula for $\partial w / \partial u$ and $\partial w / \partial v$.

27. Suppose $w = f(x, y, z)$ and that x, y, z are all functions of t. Use a tree diagram to write down the chain rule for dw/dt.

28. Let $F(u, v)$ be a function of two variables. Find $f'(x)$ if

(a) $f(x) = F(x, 3)$ **(b)** $f(x) = F(3, x)$

(c) $f(x) = F(x, x)$ **(d)** $f(x) = F(5x, x^2)$

In Problems 29–30, let $z = f(x, y)$, $x = x(u, v)$, $y = y(u, v)$ and $x(1, 2) = 5$, $y(1, 2) = 3$, calculate the partial derivative in terms of some of the numbers a, b, c, d, e, k, p, q:

$$f_x(1, 2) = a \quad f_y(1, 2) = c \quad x_u(1, 2) = e \quad y_u(1, 2) = p$$
$$f_x(5, 3) = b \quad f_y(5, 3) = d \quad x_v(1, 2) = k \quad y_v(1, 2) = q$$

29. $z_u(1, 2)$ **30.** $z_v(1, 2)$

31. The equation $f(x, y) = f(a, b)$ defines a level curve through a point (a, b) where $\text{grad } f(a, b) \neq \vec{0}$. Use implicit differentiation and the chain rule to show that the slope of the line tangent to this curve at the point (a, b) is $-f_x(a, b)/f_y(a, b)$ if $f_y(a, b) \neq 0$.

32. Let $z = f(t)g(t)$. Use the chain rule applied to $h(x, y) = f(x)g(y)$ to show that $dz/dt = f'(t)g(t) + f(t)g'(t)$. The one-variable product rule for differentiation is a special case of the two-variable chain rule.

33. A function $f(x, y)$ is *homogeneous of degree p* if $f(tx, ty) = t^p f(x, y)$ for all t. Show that any differentiable, homogeneous function of degree p satisfies Euler's Theorem:

$$x f_x(x, y) + y f_y(x, y) = p f(x, y).$$

[Hint: Define $g(t) = f(tx, ty)$ and compute $g'(1)$.]

34. Let $F(x, y, z)$ be a function and define a function $z = f(x, y)$ implicitly by letting $F(x, y, f(x, y)) = 0$. Use the chain rule to show that

$$\frac{\partial z}{\partial x} = -\frac{\partial F/\partial x}{\partial F/\partial z} \quad \text{and} \quad \frac{\partial z}{\partial y} = -\frac{\partial F/\partial y}{\partial F/\partial z}.$$

In Problems 35–36, let $z = f(x, y)$, $x = x(u, v)$, $y = y(u, v)$ and $x(4, 5) = 2$, $y(4, 5) = 3$. Calculate the partial derivative in terms of $a, b, c, d, e, k, p, q, r, s, t, w$:

$$
\begin{array}{llll}
f_x(4,5) = a & f_y(4,5) = c & x_u(4,5) = e & y_u(4,5) = p \\
f_x(2,3) = b & f_y(2,3) = d & x_v(4,5) = k & y_v(4,5) = q \\
x_u(2,3) = r & y_u(2,3) = s & x_v(2,3) = t & y_v(2,3) = w
\end{array}
$$

35. $z_u(4, 5)$ **36.** $z_v(4, 5)$

For Problems 37–38, suppose that $x > 0, y > 0$ and that z can be expressed either as a function of Cartesian coordinates (x, y) or as a function of polar coordinates (r, θ), so that $z = f(x, y) = g(r, \theta)$. [Recall that $x = r \cos \theta, y = r \sin \theta, r = \sqrt{x^2 + y^2}$, and, for $x > 0, y > 0, \theta = \arctan(y/x)$]

37. (a) Use the chain rule to find $\partial z/\partial r$ and $\partial z/\partial \theta$ in terms of $\partial z/\partial x$ and $\partial z/\partial y$.

    (b) Solve the equations you have just written down for $\partial z/\partial x$ and $\partial z/\partial y$ in terms of $\partial z/\partial r$ and $\partial z/\partial \theta$.

    (c) Show that the expressions you get in part (b) are the same as you would get by using the chain rule to find $\partial z/\partial x$ and $\partial z/\partial y$ in terms of $\partial z/\partial r$ and $\partial z/\partial \theta$.

38. Show that

$$\left(\frac{\partial z}{\partial x}\right)^2 + \left(\frac{\partial z}{\partial y}\right)^2 = \left(\frac{\partial z}{\partial r}\right)^2 + \frac{1}{r^2}\left(\frac{\partial z}{\partial \theta}\right)^2.$$

Problems 39–44 are continuations of the physical chemistry example on page 802.

39. Write $\left(\frac{\partial U}{\partial P}\right)_V$ as a partial derivative of one of the functions U_1, U_2, or U_3.

40. Write $\left(\frac{\partial U}{\partial P}\right)_T$ as a partial derivative of one of the functions U_1, U_2, U_3.

41. For the gas in Example 6, find $\left(\frac{\partial U}{\partial T}\right)_V$ and $\left(\frac{\partial U}{\partial V}\right)_T$. [Hint: Use the same method as the example, but substitute for dP instead of dV.]

42. Show that $\left(\frac{\partial T}{\partial V}\right)_P = 1 / \left(\frac{\partial V}{\partial T}\right)_P$.

43. Use Example 7 and Problem 42 to show that

$$\left(\frac{\partial U}{\partial V}\right)_P = \left(\frac{\partial U}{\partial V}\right)_T + \frac{\left(\frac{\partial U}{\partial T}\right)_V}{\left(\frac{\partial V}{\partial T}\right)_P}.$$

44. In Example 6, we calculated values of $(\partial U/\partial T)_P$ and $(\partial U/\partial P)_T$ using the relationship $PV = 2T$ for a specific gas. In this problem, you will derive general relationships for these two partial derivatives.

    (a) Think of V as a function of P and T and write an expression for dV.

    (b) Substitute for dV into the following formula for dU (thinking of U as a function of P and V):

$$dU = \left(\frac{\partial U}{\partial P}\right)_V dP + \left(\frac{\partial U}{\partial V}\right)_P dV.$$

    (c) Thinking of U as a function of P and T, write an expression for dU.

    (d) By comparing coefficients of dP and dT in your answers to parts (b) and (c), show that

$$\left(\frac{\partial U}{\partial T}\right)_P = \left(\frac{\partial U}{\partial V}\right)_P \cdot \left(\frac{\partial V}{\partial T}\right)_P$$

$$\left(\frac{\partial U}{\partial P}\right)_T = \left(\frac{\partial U}{\partial P}\right)_V + \left(\frac{\partial U}{\partial V}\right)_P \cdot \left(\frac{\partial V}{\partial P}\right)_T.$$

Problems 45–47 concern differentiating an integral in one variable, y, which also involves another variable x, either in the integrand, or in the limits, or both:

$$\int_0^5 (x^2 y + 4)\, dy \quad \text{or} \quad \int_0^x (y + 4)\, dy \quad \text{or} \quad \int_0^x (xy + 4)\, dy.$$

To differentiate the first integral with respect to x, it can be shown that in most cases we can differentiate with respect to x inside the integral:

$$\frac{d}{dx}\left(\int_0^5 (x^2 y + 4)\, dy\right) = \int_0^5 2xy\, dy.$$

Differentiating the second integral with respect to x uses the Fundamental Theorem of Calculus:

$$\frac{d}{dx}\int_0^x (y + 4)\, dy = x + 4.$$

Differentiating the third integral involves the chain rule, as shown in Problem 47. Assume that the function F is continuously differentiable and b is constant throughout.

45. Let $f(x) = \int_0^b F(x, y)\, dy$. Find $f'(x)$.

46. Let $f(x) = \int_0^x F(b, y)\, dy$. Find $f'(x)$.

47. Let $f(x) = \int_0^x F(x, y)\, dy$. Use Problem 45 and Problem 46 to find $f'(x)$ by the following steps:

    (a) Let $G(u, w) = \int_0^w F(u, y)\, dy$. Find $G_u(u, w)$ and $G_w(u, w)$.

    (b) Use part (a) and the chain rule applied to $G(x, x) = f(x)$ to show:

$$f'(x) = \int_0^x F_x(x, y)\, dy + F(x, x).$$

Strengthen Your Understanding

In Problems 48–50, explain what is wrong with the statement.

48. If $z = f(g(t), h(t))$, then $dz/dt = f(g'(t), h(t)) + f(g(t), h'(t))$.

49. If $C = C(R, T), R = R(x, y), T = T(x, y)$ and $R(0, 2) = 5, T(0, 2) = 1$, then $C_x(0, 2) = C_R(0, 2)R_x(0, 2) + C_T(0, 2)T_x(0, 2)$.

50. If $z = f(x, y)$ and $x = g(t), y = h(t)$ with $g(0) = 2$ and $h(0) = 3$, then

$$\left. \frac{dz}{dt} \right|_{t=0} = f_x(0, 0)g'(0) + f_y(0, 0)h'(0).$$

In Problems 51–55, give an example of:

51. Functions $x = g(t)$ and $y = h(t)$ such that $(dz/dt)|_{t=0} = 9$, given that $z = x^2 y$.

52. A function $z = f(x, y)$ such that $dz/dt|_{t=0} = 10$, given that $x = e^{2t}$ and $y = \sin t$.

53. Functions z, x and y where you need to follow the diagram in order to answer questions about the derivative of z with respect to the other variables.

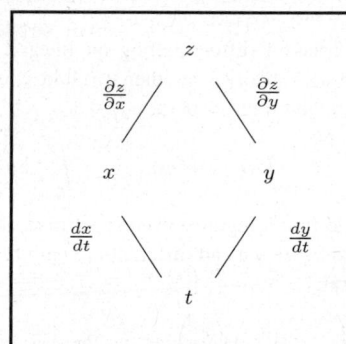

54. Functions w, u and v where you need to follow the diagram in order to answer questions about the derivative of w with respect to the other variables.

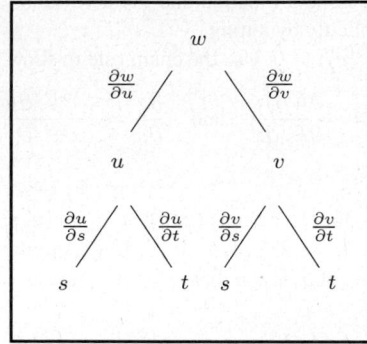

55. Function $z = f(x, y)$ where x and y are functions of one variable, t, for which $\dfrac{\partial z}{\partial t} = 2$.

56. Let $z = g(u, v)$ and $u = u(x, y, t), v = v(x, y, t)$ and $x = x(t), y = y(t)$. Then the expression for dz/dt has

(a) Three terms	**(b)** Four terms
(c) Six terms	**(d)** Seven terms
(e) Nine terms	**(f)** None of the above

14.7 SECOND-ORDER PARTIAL DERIVATIVES

Since the partial derivatives of a function are themselves functions, we can differentiate them, giving *second-order partial derivatives*. A function $z = f(x, y)$ has two first-order partial derivatives, f_x and f_y, and four second-order partial derivatives.

The Second-Order Partial Derivatives of $z = f(x, y)$

$$\frac{\partial^2 z}{\partial x^2} = f_{xx} = (f_x)_x, \qquad \frac{\partial^2 z}{\partial x \partial y} = f_{yx} = (f_y)_x,$$

$$\frac{\partial^2 z}{\partial y \partial x} = f_{xy} = (f_x)_y, \qquad \frac{\partial^2 z}{\partial y^2} = f_{yy} = (f_y)_y.$$

It is usual to omit the parentheses, writing f_{xy} instead of $(f_x)_y$ and $\dfrac{\partial^2 z}{\partial y\, \partial x}$ instead of $\dfrac{\partial}{\partial y}\left(\dfrac{\partial z}{\partial x} \right)$.

Example 1   Compute the four second-order partial derivatives of $f(x, y) = xy^2 + 3x^2 e^y$.

Solution   From $f_x(x, y) = y^2 + 6xe^y$ we get

$$f_{xx}(x, y) = \frac{\partial}{\partial x}(y^2 + 6xe^y) = 6e^y \quad \text{and} \quad f_{xy}(x, y) = \frac{\partial}{\partial y}(y^2 + 6xe^y) = 2y + 6xe^y.$$

From $f_y(x, y) = 2xy + 3x^2 e^y$ we get

$$f_{yx}(x, y) = \frac{\partial}{\partial x}(2xy + 3x^2 e^y) = 2y + 6xe^y \quad \text{and} \quad f_{yy}(x, y) = \frac{\partial}{\partial y}(2xy + 3x^2 e^y) = 2x + 3x^2 e^y.$$

Observe that $f_{xy} = f_{yx}$ in this example.

Example 2   Use the values of the function $f(x, y)$ in Table 14.6 to estimate $f_{xy}(1, 2)$ and $f_{yx}(1, 2)$.

Table 14.6   *Values of $f(x, y)$*

$y \backslash x$	0.9	1.0	1.1
1.8	4.72	5.83	7.06
2.0	6.48	8.00	9.60
2.2	8.62	10.65	12.88

Solution   Since $f_{xy} = (f_x)_y$, we first estimate f_x

$$f_x(1, 2) \approx \frac{f(1.1, 2) - f(1, 2)}{0.1} = \frac{9.60 - 8.00}{0.1} = 16.0,$$

$$f_x(1, 2.2) \approx \frac{f(1.1, 2.2) - f(1, 2.2)}{0.1} = \frac{12.88 - 10.65}{0.1} = 22.3.$$

Thus,

$$f_{xy}(1, 2) \approx \frac{f_x(1, 2.2) - f_x(1, 2)}{0.2} = \frac{22.3 - 16.0}{0.2} = 31.5.$$

Similarly,

$$f_{yx}(1, 2) \approx \frac{f_y(1.1, 2) - f_y(1, 2)}{0.1} \approx \frac{1}{0.1}\left(\frac{f(1.1, 2.2) - f(1.1, 2)}{0.2} - \frac{f(1, 2.2) - f(1, 2)}{0.2}\right)$$

$$= \frac{1}{0.1}\left(\frac{12.88 - 9.60}{0.2} - \frac{10.65 - 8.00}{0.2}\right) = 31.5.$$

Observe that in this example also, $f_{xy} = f_{yx}$.

The Mixed Partial Derivatives Are Equal

It is not an accident that the estimates for $f_{xy}(1, 2)$ and $f_{yx}(1, 2)$ are equal in Example 2, because the same values of the function are used to calculate each one. The fact that $f_{xy} = f_{yx}$ in Examples 1 and 2 corroborates the following general result; Problem 54 suggests why you might expect it to be true.[3]

Theorem 14.1: Equality of Mixed Partial Derivatives

If f_{xy} and f_{yx} are continuous at (a, b), an interior point of their domain, then

$$f_{xy}(a, b) = f_{yx}(a, b).$$

---

[3]For a proof, see M. Spivak, *Calculus on Manifolds*, p. 26 (New York: Benjamin, 1965).

For most functions f we encounter and most points (a, b) in their domains, not only are f_{xy} and f_{yx} continuous at (a, b), but all their higher-order partial derivatives (such as f_{xxy} or f_{xyyy}) exist and are continuous at (a, b). In that case we say f is *smooth* at (a, b). We say f is smooth on a region R if it is smooth at every point of R.

What Do the Second-Order Partial Derivatives Tell Us?

Example 3   Let us return to the guitar string of Example 4, page 767. The string is 1 meter long and at time t seconds, the point x meters from one end is displaced $f(x, t)$ meters from its rest position, where

$$f(x, t) = 0.003 \sin(\pi x) \sin(2765t).$$

Compute the four second-order partial derivatives of f at the point $(x, t) = (0.3, 1)$ and describe the meaning of their signs in practical terms.

Solution   First we compute $f_x(x, t) = 0.003\pi \cos(\pi x) \sin(2765t)$, from which we get

$$f_{xx}(x, t) = \frac{\partial}{\partial x}(f_x(x, t)) = -0.003\pi^2 \sin(\pi x) \sin(2765t), \qquad \text{so} \qquad f_{xx}(0.3, 1) \approx -0.01;$$

and

$$f_{xt}(x, t) = \frac{\partial}{\partial t}(f_x(x, t)) = (0.003)(2765)\pi \cos(\pi x) \cos(2765t), \qquad \text{so} \qquad f_{xt}(0.3, 1) \approx 14.$$

On page 767 we saw that $f_x(x, t)$ gives the slope of the string at any point and time. Therefore, $f_{xx}(x, t)$ measures the concavity of the string. The fact that $f_{xx}(0.3, 1) < 0$ means the string is concave down at the point $x = 0.3$ when $t = 1$. (See Figure 14.55.)

On the other hand, $f_{xt}(x, t)$ is the rate of change of the slope of the string with respect to time. Thus, $f_{xt}(0.3, 1) > 0$ means that at time $t = 1$ the slope at the point $x = 0.3$ is increasing. (See Figure 14.56.)

Figure 14.55: Interpretation of $f_{xx}(0.3, 1) < 0$: The concavity of the string at $t = 1$

Figure 14.56: Interpretation of $f_{xt}(0.3, 1) > 0$: The slope of one point on the string at two different times

Now we compute $f_t(x, t) = (0.003)(2765) \sin(\pi x) \cos(2765t)$, from which we get

$$f_{tx}(x, t) = \frac{\partial}{\partial x}(f_t(x, t)) = (0.003)(2765)\pi \cos(\pi x) \cos(2765t), \quad \text{so} \quad f_{tx}(0.3, 1) \approx 14$$

and

$$f_{tt}(x, t) = \frac{\partial}{\partial t}(f_t(x, t)) = -(0.003)(2765)^2 \sin(\pi x) \sin(2765t), \quad \text{so} \quad f_{tt}(0.3, 1) \approx -7200.$$

On page 767 we saw that $f_t(x, t)$ gives the velocity of the string at any point and time. Therefore, $f_{tx}(x, t)$ and $f_{tt}(x, t)$ will both be rates of change of velocity. That $f_{tx}(0.3, 1) > 0$ means that at time $t = 1$ the velocities of points just to the right of $x = 0.3$ are greater than the velocity at $x = 0.3$. (See Figure 14.57.) That $f_{tt}(0.3, 1) < 0$ means that the velocity of the point $x = 0.3$ is decreasing at time $t = 1$. Thus, $f_{tt}(0.3, 1) = -7200$ m/sec^2 is the acceleration of this point. (See Figure 14.58.)

Figure 14.57: Interpretation of $f_{tx}(0.3, 1) > 0$: The velocity of different points on the string at $t = 1$

Figure 14.58: Interpretation of $f_{tt}(0.3, 1) < 0$: Negative acceleration. The velocity of one point on the string at two different times

Taylor Approximations

We use second derivatives to construct quadratic Taylor approximations. In Section 14.3, we saw how to approximate $f(x, y)$ by a linear function (its local linearization). We now see how to improve this approximation of $f(x, y)$ using a quadratic function.

Linear and Quadratic Approximations Near (0,0)

For a function of one variable, local linearity tells us that the best *linear* approximation is the degree-1 Taylor polynomial

$$f(x) \approx f(a) + f'(a)(x - a) \quad \text{for } x \text{ near } a.$$

A better approximation to $f(x)$ is given by the degree-2 Taylor polynomial:

$$f(x) \approx f(a) + f'(a)(x - a) + \frac{f''(a)}{2}(x - a)^2 \quad \text{for } x \text{ near } a.$$

For a function of two variables the local linearization for (x, y) near (a, b) is

$$f(x, y) \approx L(x, y) = f(a, b) + f_x(a, b)(x - a) + f_y(a, b)(y - b).$$

In the case $(a, b) = (0, 0)$, we have:

Taylor Polynomial of Degree 1 Approximating $f(x, y)$ for (x, y) near (0,0)
If f has continuous first-order partial derivatives, then

$$f(x, y) \approx L(x, y) = f(0, 0) + f_x(0, 0)x + f_y(0, 0)y.$$

We get a better approximation to f by using a quadratic polynomial. We choose a quadratic polynomial $Q(x, y)$, with the same partial derivatives as the original function f. You can check that the following Taylor polynomial of degree 2 has this property.

Taylor Polynomial of Degree 2 Approximating $f(x, y)$ for (x, y) near (0,0)
If f has continuous second-order partial derivatives, then

$$f(x, y) \approx Q(x, y)$$
$$= f(0, 0) + f_x(0, 0)x + f_y(0, 0)y + \frac{f_{xx}(0, 0)}{2}x^2 + f_{xy}(0, 0)xy + \frac{f_{yy}(0, 0)}{2}y^2.$$

Example 4   Let $f(x, y) = \cos(2x + y) + 3\sin(x + y)$

(a) Compute the linear and quadratic Taylor polynomials, L and Q, approximating f near $(0, 0)$.

(b) Explain why the contour plots of L and Q for $-1 \leq x \leq 1$, $-1 \leq y \leq 1$ look the way they do.

Solution   (a) We have $f(0, 0) = 1$. The derivatives we need are as follows:

$$f_x(x, y) = -2\sin(2x + y) + 3\cos(x + y) \quad \text{so} \quad f_x(0, 0) = 3,$$
$$f_y(x, y) = -\sin(2x + y) + 3\cos(x + y) \quad \text{so} \quad f_y(0, 0) = 3,$$
$$f_{xx}(x, y) = -4\cos(2x + y) - 3\sin(x + y) \quad \text{so} \quad f_{xx}(0, 0) = -4,$$
$$f_{xy}(x, y) = -2\cos(2x + y) - 3\sin(x + y) \quad \text{so} \quad f_{xy}(0, 0) = -2,$$
$$f_{yy}(x, y) = -\cos(2x + y) - 3\sin(x + y) \quad \text{so} \quad f_{yy}(0, 0) = -1.$$

Thus, the linear approximation, $L(x, y)$, to $f(x, y)$ at $(0, 0)$ is given by

$$f(x, y) \approx L(x, y) = f(0, 0) + f_x(0, 0)x + f_y(0, 0)y = 1 + 3x + 3y.$$

The quadratic approximation, $Q(x, y)$, to $f(x, y)$ near $(0, 0)$ is given by

$$f(x, y) \approx Q(x, y)$$
$$= f(0, 0) + f_x(0, 0)x + f_y(0, 0)y + \frac{f_{xx}(0, 0)}{2}x^2 + f_{xy}(0, 0)xy + \frac{f_{yy}(0, 0)}{2}y^2$$
$$= 1 + 3x + 3y - 2x^2 - 2xy - \frac{1}{2}y^2.$$

Notice that the linear terms in $Q(x, y)$ are the same as the linear terms in $L(x, y)$. The quadratic terms in $Q(x, y)$ can be thought of as "correction terms" to the linear approximation.

(b) The contour plots of $f(x, y)$, $L(x, y)$, and $Q(x, y)$ are in Figures 14.59–14.61.

Figure 14.59: Original function, $f(x, y)$

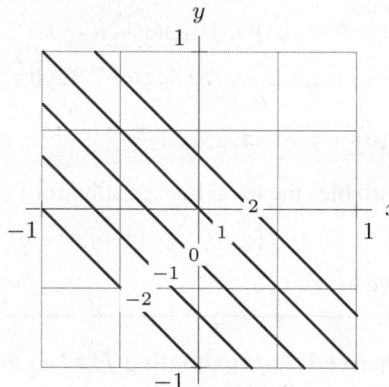

Figure 14.60: Linear approximation, $L(x, y)$

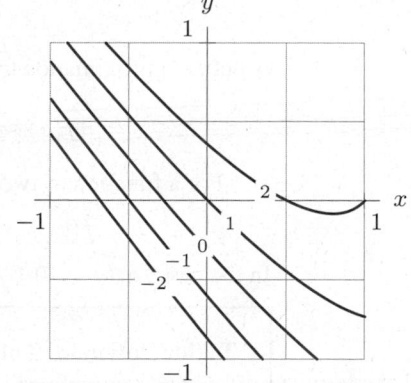

Figure 14.61: Quadratic approximation, $Q(x, y)$

Notice that the contour plot of Q is more similar to the contour plot of f than is the contour plot of L. Since L is linear, the contour plot of L consists of parallel, equally spaced lines.

An alternative, and much quicker, way to find the Taylor polynomial in the previous example is to use the single-variable approximations. For example, since

$$\cos u = 1 - \frac{u^2}{2!} + \frac{u^4}{4!} + \cdots \quad \text{and} \quad \sin v = v - \frac{v^3}{3!} + \cdots,$$

we can substitute $u = 2x + y$ and $v = x + y$ and expand. We discard terms beyond the second (since we want the quadratic polynomial), getting

$$\cos(2x + y) = 1 - \frac{(2x + y)^2}{2!} + \frac{(2x + y)^4}{4!} + \cdots \approx 1 - \frac{1}{2}(4x^2 + 4xy + y^2) = 1 - 2x^2 - 2xy - \frac{1}{2}y^2$$

and

$$\sin(x+y) = (x+y) - \frac{(x+y)^3}{3!} + \cdots \approx x+y.$$

Combining these results, we get

$$\cos(2x+y) + 3\sin(x+y) \approx 1 - 2x^2 - 2xy - \frac{1}{2}y^2 + 3(x+y) = 1 + 3x + 3y - 2x^2 - 2xy - \frac{1}{2}y^2.$$

Linear and Quadratic Approximations near (a, b)

The local linearization for a function $f(x, y)$ at a point (a, b) is

> **Taylor Polynomial of Degree** 1 **Approximating** $f(x, y)$ **for** (x, y) **near** (a, b)
>
> If f has continuous first-order partial derivatives, then
>
> $$f(x, y) \approx L(x, y) = f(a, b) + f_x(a, b)(x - a) + f_y(a, b)(y - b).$$

This suggests that a quadratic polynomial approximation $Q(x, y)$ for $f(x, y)$ near a point (a, b) should be written in terms of $(x - a)$ and $(y - b)$ instead of x and y. If we require that $Q(a, b) = f(a, b)$ and that the first- and second-order partial derivatives of Q and f at (a, b) be equal, then we get the following polynomial:

> **Taylor Polynomial of Degree** 2 **Approximating** $f(x, y)$ **for** (x, y) **near** (a, b)
>
> If f has continuous second-order partial derivatives, then
>
> $$f(x, y) \approx Q(x, y)$$
> $$= f(a, b) + f_x(a, b)(x - a) + f_y(a, b)(y - b)$$
> $$+ \frac{f_{xx}(a, b)}{2}(x - a)^2 + f_{xy}(a, b)(x - a)(y - b) + \frac{f_{yy}(a, b)}{2}(y - b)^2.$$

These coefficients are derived in exactly the same way as for $(a, b) = (0, 0)$.

Example 5 Find the Taylor polynomial of degree 2 at the point $(1, 2)$ for the function $f(x, y) = \dfrac{1}{xy}$.

Solution Table 14.7 contains the partial derivatives and their values at the point $(1, 2)$.

Table 14.7 *Partial derivatives of $f(x, y) = 1/(xy)$*

Derivative	Formula	Value at $(1, 2)$	Derivative	Formula	Value at $(1, 2)$
$f(x, y)$	$1/(xy)$	$1/2$	$f_{xx}(x, y)$	$2/(x^3y)$	1
$f_x(x, y)$	$-1/(x^2y)$	$-1/2$	$f_{xy}(x, y)$	$1/(x^2y^2)$	$1/4$
$f_y(x, y)$	$-1/(xy^2)$	$-1/4$	$f_{yy}(x, y)$	$2/(xy^3)$	$1/4$

So, the quadratic Taylor polynomial for f near $(1, 2)$ is

$$\frac{1}{xy} \approx Q(x, y)$$

$$= \frac{1}{2} - \frac{1}{2}(x - 1) - \frac{1}{4}(y - 2) + \frac{1}{2}(1)(x - 1)^2 + \frac{1}{4}(x - 1)(y - 2) + \left(\frac{1}{2}\right)\left(\frac{1}{4}\right)(y - 2)^2$$

$$= \frac{1}{2} - \frac{x - 1}{2} - \frac{y - 2}{4} + \frac{(x - 1)^2}{2} + \frac{(x - 1)(y - 2)}{4} + \frac{(y - 2)^2}{8}.$$

Exercises and Problems for Section 14.7

Exercises

In Exercises 1–11, calculate all four second-order partial derivatives and check that $f_{xy} = f_{yx}$. Assume the variables are restricted to a domain on which the function is defined.

1. $f(x, y) = (x + y)^2$ **2.** $f(x, y) = (x + y)^3$

3. $f(x, y) = 3x^2y + 5xy^3$ **4.** $f(x, y) = e^{2xy}$

5. $f(x, y) = (x + y)e^y$ **6.** $f(x, y) = xe^y$

7. $f(x, y) = \sin(x/y)$ **8.** $f(x, y) = \sqrt{x^2 + y^2}$

9. $f(x, y) = 5x^3y^2 - 7xy^3 + 9x^2 + 11$

10. $f(x, y) = \sin(x^2 + y^2)$

11. $f(x, y) = 3\sin 2x \cos 5y$

In Exercises 12–19, find the quadratic Taylor polynomials about $(0, 0)$ for the function.

12. $(y - 1)(x + 1)^2$ **13.** $(x - y + 1)^2$

14. $e^{-2x^2 - y^2}$ **15.** $e^x \cos y$

16. $1/(1 + 2x - y)$ **17.** $\cos(x + 3y)$

18. $\sin 2x + \cos y$ **19.** $\ln(1 + x^2 - y)$

In Exercises 20–21, find the best quadratic approximation for $f(x, y)$ for (x, y) near $(0, 0)$.

20. $f(x, y) = \ln(1 + x - 2y)$

21. $f(x, y) = \sqrt{1 + 2x - y}$

In Exercises 22–31, use the level curves of the function $z = f(x, y)$ to decide the sign (positive, negative, or zero) of each of the following partial derivatives at the point P. Assume the x- and y-axes are in the usual positions.

(a) $f_x(P)$ **(b)** $f_y(P)$ **(c)** $f_{xx}(P)$
(d) $f_{yy}(P)$ **(e)** $f_{xy}(P)$

22.

23.

24.

25.

26.

27.

28.

29.

30.

31.

Problems

In Problems 32–36, find the linear, $L(x,y)$, and quadratic, $Q(x,y)$, Taylor polynomials valid near $(1,0)$. Compare the values of the approximations $L(0.9, 0.2)$ and $Q(0.9, 0.2)$ with the exact value of the function $f(0.9, 0.2)$.

32. $f(x,y) = \sqrt{x + 2y}$ **33.** $f(x,y) = x^2 y$

34. $f(x,y) = xe^{-y}$

35. $F(x,y) = e^x \sin y + e^y \sin x$

36. $f(x,y) = \sin(x-1)\cos y$

In Problems 37–38, show that the function satisfies Laplace's equation, $F_{xx} + F_{yy} = 0$.

37. $F(x,y) = e^{-x}\sin y$

38. $F(x,y) = \arctan(y/x)$

39. If $u(x,t) = e^{at}\sin(bx)$ satisfies the heat equation $u_t = u_{xx}$, find the relationship between a and b.

40. (a) Check that $u(x,t)$ satisfies the heat equation $u_t = u_{xx}$ for $t > 0$ and all x, where

$$u(x,t) = \frac{1}{2\sqrt{\pi t}}e^{-x^2/(4t)}$$

(b) Graph $u(x,t)$ against x for $t = 0.01, 0.1, 1, 10$. These graphs represent the temperature in an infinitely long insulated rod that at $t = 0$ is $0°C$ everywhere except at the origin $x = 0$, and that is infinitely hot at $t = 0$ at the origin.

41. Figure 14.62 shows a graph of $z = f(x,y)$. Is $f_{xx}(0,0)$ positive or negative? Is $f_{yy}(0,0)$ positive or negative? Give reasons for your answers.

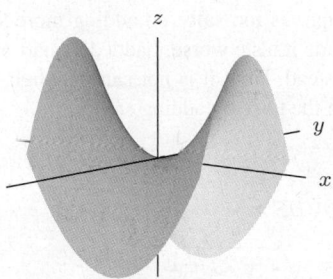

Figure 14.62

42. If $z = f(x) + yg(x)$, what can you say about z_{yy}? Explain your answer.

43. If $z_{xy} = 4y$, what can you say about the value of
(a) z_{yx}?   **(b)** z_{xyx}?   **(c)** z_{xyy}?

44. A contour diagram for the smooth function $z = f(x,y)$ is in Figure 14.63.

(a) Is z an increasing or decreasing function of x? Of y?
(b) Is f_x positive or negative? How about f_y?
(c) Is f_{xx} positive or negative? How about f_{yy}?
(d) Sketch the direction of grad f at points P and Q.
(e) Is grad f longer at P or at Q? How do you know?

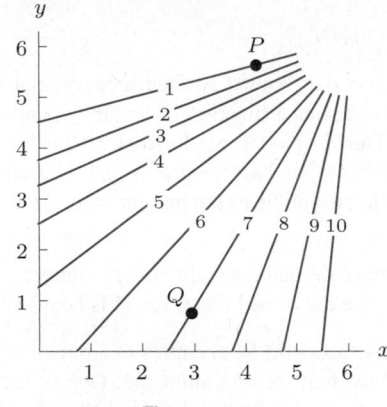

Figure 14.63

Problems 45–48 give tables of values of quadratic polynomials $P(x,y) = a + bx + cy + dx^2 + exy + fy^2$. Determine whether each of the coefficients d, e and f of the quadratic terms is positive, negative, or zero.

45.

		10	12	14
	10	35	37	39
y	15	45	47	49
	20	55	57	59

x

46.

		10	12	14
	10	26	36	54
y	15	31	41	59
	20	36	46	64

x

47.

		10	12	14
	10	90	82	74
y	15	75	87	99
	20	10	42	74

x

48.

		10	12	14
	10	13	33	61
y	15	28	28	36
	20	93	73	61

x

49. You are hiking on a level trail going due east and planning to strike off cross country up the mountain to your left. The slope up to the left is too steep now and seems to be gentler the further you go along the trail, so you decide to wait before turning off.

(a) Sketch a topographical contour map that illustrates this story.
(b) What information does the story give about partial derivatives? Define all variables and functions that you use.
(c) What partial derivative influenced your decision to wait before turning?

50. The weekly production, Y, in factories that manufacture a certain item is modeled as a function of the quantity of capital, K, and quantity of labor, L, at the factory. Data shows that hiring a few extra workers increases production. Moreover, for two factories with the same number of workers, hiring a few extra workers increases production more for the factory with more capital. (With more equipment, additional labor can be used more effectively.) What does this tell you about the sign of

(a) $\partial Y/\partial L$?

(b) $\partial^2 Y/(\partial K \partial L)$?

51. Data suggests that human surface area, S, can reasonably be modeled as a function of height, h, and weight, w. In the Dubois model, we have $\partial^2 S/\partial w^2 < 0$ and $\partial^2 S/(\partial h \partial w) > 0$. Two people A and B each gain 1 pound. Which experiences the greater increase in surface area if

(a) They have the same weight but A is taller?

(b) They have the same height, but A is heavier?

52. Figure 14.64 shows the level curves of a function $f(x,y)$ around a maximum or minimum, M. One of the points P and Q has coordinates (x_1, y_1) and the other has coordinates (x_2, y_2). Suppose $b > 0$ and $c > 0$. Consider the two linear approximations to f given by

$$f(x,y) \approx a + b(x - x_1) + c(y - y_1)$$
$$f(x,y) \approx k + m(x - x_2) + n(y - y_2).$$

(a) What is the relationship between the values of a and k?

(b) What are the coordinates of P?

(c) Is M a maximum or a minimum?

(d) What can you say about the sign of the constants m and n?

Figure 14.64

53. Consider the function $f(x,y) = (\sin x)(\sin y)$.

(a) Find the Taylor polynomials of degree 2 for f about the points $(0,0)$ and $(\pi/2, \pi/2)$.

(b) Use the Taylor polynomials to sketch the contours of f close to each of the points $(0,0)$ and $(\pi/2, \pi/2)$.

54. Give an explanation of why you might expect $f_{xy}(a,b) = f_{yx}(a,b)$ using the following steps.

(a) Write the definition of $f_x(a,b)$.

(b) Write a definition of $f_{xy}(a,b)$ as $(f_x)_y$.

(c) Substitute for f_x in the definition of f_{xy}.

(d) Write an expression for f_{yx} similar to the one for f_{xy} you obtained in part (c).

(e) Compare your answers to parts (c) and (d). What do you have to assume to conclude that f_{xy} and f_{yx} are equal?

55. You plan to buy a used car. You are debating between a 5-year old car and a 10-year old car and thinking about the price. Experts report that the original price matters more when buying a 5-year old car than a 10-year old car. This suggests that we model the average market price, P, in dollars as a function of two variables: the original price, C, in dollars, and the age of the car, A, in years.

(a) Give units for the following partial derivatives and say whether you think they are positive or negative. Explain your reasoning.

(a) $\partial P/\partial A$ (b) $\partial P/\partial C$

(b) Express the experts' report in terms of partial derivatives.

(c) Using a quadratic polynomial to model P, we have

$$P = a + bC + cA + dC^2 + eCA + fA^2.$$

Which term in this polynomial is most relevant to the experts' report?

56. The tastiness, T, of a soup depends on the volume, V, of the soup in the pot and the quantity, S, of salt in the soup. If you have more soup, you need more salt to make it taste good. Match the three stories (a)–(c) to the three statements (I)–(III) about partial derivatives.

(a) I started adding salt to the soup in the pot. At first the taste improved, but eventually the soup became too salty and continuing to add more salt made it worse.

(b) The soup was too salty, so I started adding unsalted soup. This improved the taste at first, but eventually there was too much soup for the salt, and continuing to add unsalted soup just made it worse.

(c) The soup was too salty, so adding more salt would have made it taste worse. I added a quart of unsalted soup instead. Now it is not salty enough, but I can improve the taste by adding salt.

(I) $\partial^2 T/\partial V^2 < 0$

(II) $\partial^2 T/\partial S^2 < 0$

(III) $\partial^2 T/\partial V \partial S > 0$

57. Let $f(x,y) = \sqrt{x + 2y + 1}$.

(a) Compute the local linearization of f at $(0,0)$.

(b) Compute the quadratic Taylor polynomial for f at $(0,0)$.

(c) Compare the values of the linear and quadratic approximations in part (a) and part (b) with the true values for $f(x,y)$ at the points $(0.1, 0.1)$, $(-0.1, 0.1)$, $(0.1, -0.1)$, $(-0.1, -0.1)$. Which approximation gives the closest values?

58. Using a computer and your answer to Problem 57, draw the six contour diagrams of $f(x, y) = \sqrt{x + 2y + 1}$ and its linear and quadratic approximations, $L(x, y)$ and $Q(x, y)$, in the two windows $[-0.6, 0.6] \times [-0.6, 0.6]$ and $[-2, 2] \times [-2, 2]$. Explain the shape of the contours, their spacing, and the relationship between the contours of f, L, and Q.

59. Suppose that $f(x, y)$ has continuous partial derivatives f_x and f_y. Using the Fundamental Theorem of Calculus to evaluate the integrals, show that

$$f(a, b) = f(0, 0) + \int_{t=0}^{a} f_x(t, 0) dt + \int_{t=0}^{b} f_y(a, t) dt.$$

60. Suppose that $f(x, y)$ has continuous partial derivatives and that $f(0, 0) = 0$ and $|f_x(x, y)| \leq A$ and $|f_y(x, y)| \leq B$ for all points (x, y) in the plane. Use Problem 59 to show that $|f(x, y)| \leq A|x| + B|y|$.

This inequality shows how bounds on the partial derivatives of f limit the growth of f.

Strengthen Your Understanding

In Problems 61–62, explain what is wrong with the statement.

61. If $f(x, y) \neq 0$, then the Taylor polynomial of degree 2 approximating $f(x, y)$ near $(0, 0)$ is also nonzero.

62. There is a function $f(x, y)$ with partial derivatives $f_x = xy$ and $f_y = y^2$.

In Problems 63–65, give an example of:

63. A function $f(x, y)$ such that $f_{xx} \neq 0$, $f_{yy} \neq 0$, and $f_{xy} = 0$.

64. Formulas for two different functions $f(x, y)$ and $g(x, y)$ with the same quadratic approximation near $(0, 0)$.

65. Contour diagrams for two different functions $f(x, y)$ and $g(x, y)$ that have the same quadratic approximations near $(0, 0)$.

14.8 DIFFERENTIABILITY

In Section 14.3 we gave an informal introduction to the concept of differentiability. We called a function $f(x, y)$ *differentiable* at a point (a, b) if it is well approximated by a linear function near (a, b). This section focuses on the precise meaning of the phrase "well approximated." By looking at examples, we shall see that local linearity requires the existence of partial derivatives, but they do not tell the whole story. In particular, existence of partial derivatives at a point is not sufficient to guarantee local linearity at that point.

We begin by discussing the relation between continuity and differentiability. As an illustration, take a sheet of paper, crumple it into a ball and smooth it out again. Wherever there is a crease it would be difficult to approximate the surface by a plane—these are points of nondifferentiability of the function giving the height of the paper above the floor. Yet the sheet of paper models a graph which is continuous—there are no breaks. As in the case of one-variable calculus, continuity does not imply differentiability. But differentiability does *require* continuity: there cannot be linear approximations to a surface at points where there are abrupt changes in height.

Differentiability for Functions of Two Variables

For a function of two variables, as for a function of one variable, we define differentiability at a point in terms of the error and the distance from the point. If the point is (a, b) and a nearby point is $(a + h, b + k)$, the distance between them is $\sqrt{h^2 + k^2}$. (See Figure 14.65.)

A function $f(x, y)$ is **differentiable at the point** (a, b) if there is a linear function $L(x, y) = f(a, b) + m(x - a) + n(y - b)$ such that if the *error* $E(x, y)$ is defined by

$$f(x, y) = L(x, y) + E(x, y),$$

and if $h = x - a$, $k = y - b$, then the *relative error* $E(a + h, b + k)/\sqrt{h^2 + k^2}$ satisfies

$$\lim_{\substack{h \to 0 \\ k \to 0}} \frac{E(a + h, b + k)}{\sqrt{h^2 + k^2}} = 0.$$

The function f is **differentiable on a region** R if it is differentiable at each point of R. The function $L(x, y)$ is called the *local linearization* of $f(x, y)$ near (a, b).

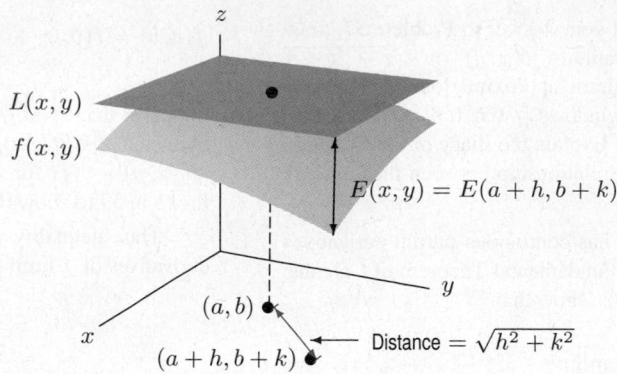

Figure 14.65: Graph of function $z = f(x, y)$ and its local linearization $z = L(x, y)$ near the point (a, b)

Partial Derivatives and Differentiability

In the next example, we show that this definition of differentiability is consistent with our previous notion — that is, that $m = f_x$ and $n = f_y$ and that the graph of $L(x, y)$ is the tangent plane.

Example 1   Show that if f is a differentiable function with local linearization $L(x, y) = f(a, b) + m(x - a) + n(y - b)$, then $m = f_x(a, b)$ and $n = f_y(a, b)$.

Solution   Since f is differentiable, we know that the relative error in $L(x, y)$ tends to 0 as we get close to (a, b). Suppose $h > 0$ and $k = 0$. Then we know that

$$0 = \lim_{h \to 0} \frac{E(a + h, b + k)}{\sqrt{h^2 + k^2}} = \lim_{h \to 0} \frac{E(a + h, b)}{h} = \lim_{h \to 0} \frac{f(a + h, b) - L(a + h, b)}{h}$$

$$= \lim_{h \to 0} \frac{f(a + h, b) - f(a, b) - mh}{h}$$

$$= \lim_{h \to 0} \left(\frac{f(a + h, b) - f(a, b)}{h} \right) - m = f_x(a, b) - m.$$

A similar result holds if $h < 0$, so we have $m = f_x(a, b)$. The result $n = f_y(a, b)$ is found in a similar manner.

The previous example shows that if a function is differentiable at a point, it has partial derivatives there. Therefore, if any of the partial derivatives fail to exist, then the function cannot be differentiable. This is what happens in the following example of a cone.

Example 2   Consider the function $f(x, y) = \sqrt{x^2 + y^2}$. Is f differentiable at the origin?

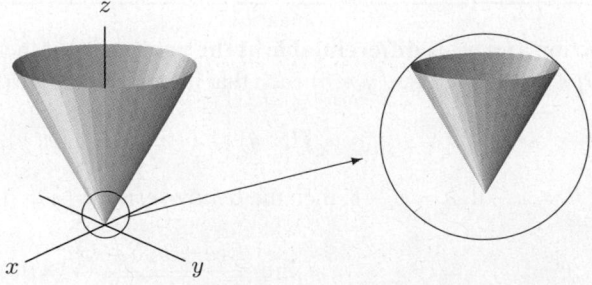

Figure 14.66: The function $f(x, y) = \sqrt{x^2 + y^2}$ is not locally linear at $(0, 0)$: Zooming in around $(0, 0)$ does not make the graph look like a plane

Solution

If we zoom in on the graph of the function $f(x, y) = \sqrt{x^2 + y^2}$ at the origin, as shown in Figure 14.66, the sharp point remains; the graph never flattens out to look like a plane. Near its vertex, the graph does not look as if is well approximated (in any reasonable sense) by any plane.

Judging from the graph of f, we would not expect f to be differentiable at $(0, 0)$. Let us check this by trying to compute the partial derivatives of f at $(0, 0)$:

$$f_x(0, 0) = \lim_{h \to 0} \frac{f(h, 0) - f(0, 0)}{h} = \lim_{h \to 0} \frac{\sqrt{h^2 + 0} - 0}{h} = \lim_{h \to 0} \frac{|h|}{h}.$$

Since $|h|/h = \pm 1$, depending on whether h approaches 0 from the left or right, this limit does not exist and so neither does the partial derivative $f_x(0, 0)$. Thus, f cannot be differentiable at the origin. If it were, both of the partial derivatives, $f_x(0, 0)$ and $f_y(0, 0)$, would exist.

Alternatively, we could show directly that there is no linear approximation near $(0, 0)$ that satisfies the small relative error criterion for differentiability. Any plane passing through the point $(0, 0, 0)$ has the form $L(x, y) = mx + ny$ for some constants m and n. If $E(x, y) = f(x, y) - L(x, y)$, then

$$E(x, y) = \sqrt{x^2 + y^2} - mx - ny.$$

Then for f to be differentiable at the origin, we would need to show that

$$\lim_{\substack{h \to 0 \\ k \to 0}} \frac{\sqrt{h^2 + k^2} - mh - nk}{\sqrt{h^2 + k^2}} = 0.$$

Taking $k = 0$ gives

$$\lim_{h \to 0} \frac{|h| - mh}{|h|} = 1 - m \lim_{h \to 0} \frac{h}{|h|}.$$

This limit exists only if $m = 0$ for the same reason as before. But then the value of the limit is 1 and not 0 as required. Thus, we again conclude f is not differentiable.

In Example 2 the partial derivatives f_x and f_y did not exist at the origin and this was sufficient to establish nondifferentiability there. We might expect that if both partial derivatives do exist, then f *is* differentiable. But the next example shows that this not necessarily true: the existence of both partial derivatives at a point is *not* sufficient to guarantee differentiability.

Example 3 Consider the function $f(x, y) = x^{1/3}y^{1/3}$. Show that the partial derivatives $f_x(0, 0)$ and $f_y(0, 0)$ exist, but that f is not differentiable at $(0, 0)$.

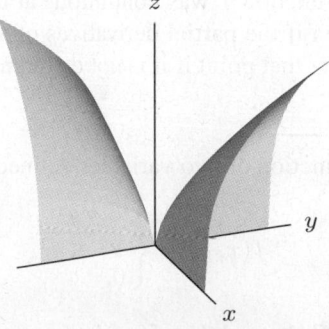

Figure 14.67: Graph of $z = x^{1/3}y^{1/3}$ for $z \geq 0$

Solution   See Figure 14.67 for the part of the graph of $z = x^{1/3}y^{1/3}$ when $z \geq 0$. We have $f(0,0) = 0$ and we compute the partial derivatives using the definition:

$$f_x(0,0) = \lim_{h \to 0} \frac{f(h,0) - f(0,0)}{h} = \lim_{h \to 0} \frac{0-0}{h} = 0,$$

and similarly

$$f_y(0,0) = 0.$$

So, if there did exist a linear approximation near the origin, it would have to be $L(x,y) = 0$. But we can show that this choice of $L(x,y)$ does not result in the small relative error that is required for differentiability. In fact, since $E(x,y) = f(x,y) - L(x,y) = f(x,y)$, we need to look at the limit

$$\lim_{\substack{h \to 0 \\ k \to 0}} \frac{h^{1/3}k^{1/3}}{\sqrt{h^2 + k^2}}.$$

If this limit exists, we get the same value no matter how h and k approach 0. Suppose we take $k = h > 0$. Then the limit becomes

$$\lim_{h \to 0} \frac{h^{1/3}h^{1/3}}{\sqrt{h^2 + h^2}} = \lim_{h \to 0} \frac{h^{2/3}}{h\sqrt{2}} = \lim_{h \to 0} \frac{1}{h^{1/3}\sqrt{2}}.$$

But this limit does not exist, since small values for h will make the fraction arbitrarily large. So the only possible candidate for a linear approximation at the origin does not have a sufficiently small relative error. Thus, this function is *not* differentiable at the origin, even though the partial derivatives $f_x(0,0)$ and $f_y(0,0)$ exist. Figure 14.67 confirms that near the origin the graph of $z = f(x,y)$ is not well approximated by any plane.

In summary,

- If a function is differentiable at a point, then both partial derivatives exist there.
- Having both partial derivatives at a point does not guarantee that a function is differentiable there.

Continuity and Differentiability

We know that differentiable functions of one variable are continuous. Similarly, it can be shown that if a function of two variables is differentiable at a point, then the function is continuous there.

In Example 3 the function f was continuous at the point where it was not differentiable. Example 4 shows that even if the partial derivatives of a function exist at a point, the function is not necessarily continuous at that point if it is not differentiable there.

Example 4   Suppose that f is the function of two variables defined by

$$f(x,y) = \begin{cases} \dfrac{xy}{x^2 + y^2}, & (x,y) \neq (0,0), \\ 0, & (x,y) = (0,0). \end{cases}$$

Problem 23 on page 709 showed that $f(x,y)$ is not continuous at the origin. Show that the partial derivatives $f_x(0,0)$ and $f_y(0,0)$ exist. Could f be differentiable at $(0,0)$?

Solution   From the definition of the partial derivative we see that

$$f_x(0,0) = \lim_{h \to 0} \frac{f(h,0) - f(0,0)}{h} = \lim_{h \to 0} \left(\frac{1}{h} \cdot \frac{0}{h^2 + 0^2} \right) = \lim_{h \to 0} \frac{0}{h} = 0,$$

and similarly

$$f_y(0,0) = 0.$$

So, the partial derivatives $f_x(0,0)$ and $f_y(0,0)$ exist. However, f cannot be differentiable at the origin since it is not continuous there.

In summary,

- If a function is differentiable at a point, then it is continuous there.
- Having both partial derivatives at a point does not guarantee that a function is continuous there.

How Do We Know If a Function Is Differentiable?

Can we use partial derivatives to tell us if a function is differentiable? As we see from Examples 3 and 4, it is not enough that the partial derivatives exist. However, the following theorem gives conditions that *do* guarantee differentiability[4]:

Theorem 14.2: Continuity of Partial Derivatives Implies Differentiability

If the partial derivatives, f_x and f_y, of a function f exist and are continuous on a small disk centered at the point (a, b), then f is differentiable at (a, b).

We will not prove this theorem, although it provides a criterion for differentiability which is often simpler to use than the definition. It turns out that the requirement of continuous partial derivatives is more stringent than that of differentiability, so there exist differentiable functions which do not have continuous partial derivatives. However, most functions we encounter will have continuous partial derivatives. The class of functions with continuous partial derivatives is given the name C^1.

Example 5   Show that the function $f(x, y) = \ln(x^2 + y^2)$ is differentiable everywhere in its domain.

Solution   The domain of f is all of 2-space except for the origin. We shall show that f has continuous partial derivatives everywhere in its domain (that is, the function f is in C^1). The partial derivatives are

$$f_x = \frac{2x}{x^2 + y^2} \quad \text{and} \quad f_y = \frac{2y}{x^2 + y^2}.$$

Since each of f_x and f_y is the quotient of continuous functions, the partial derivatives are continuous everywhere except the origin (where the denominators are zero). Thus, f is differentiable everywhere in its domain.

Most functions built up from elementary functions have continuous partial derivatives, except perhaps at a few obvious points. Thus, in practice, we can often identify functions as being C^1 without explicitly computing the partial derivatives.

---

[4]For a proof, see M. Spivak, *Calculus on Manifolds*, p. 31 (New York: Benjamin, 1965).

Exercises and Problems for Section 14.8

Exercises

In Exercises 1–10, list the points in the xy-plane, if any, at which the function $z = f(x, y)$ is not differentiable.

1. $z = -\sqrt{x^2 + y^2}$ **2.** $z = \sqrt{(x + 1)^2 + y^2}$

3. $z = |x| + |y|$ **4.** $z = |x + 2| - |y - 3|$

5. $z = e^{-(x^2 + y^2)}$ **6.** $z = x^{1/3} + y^2$

7. $z = |x - 3|^2 + y^3$ **8.** $z = (\sin x)(\cos |y|)$

9. $z = 4 + \sqrt{(x - 1)^2 + (y - 2)^2}$

10. $z = 1 + \left((x - 1)^2 + (y - 2)^2\right)^2$

Problems

In Problems 11–14, a functions f is given.

(a) Use a computer to draw a contour diagram for f.

(b) Is f differentiable at all points $(x, y) \neq (0, 0)$?

(c) Do the partial derivatives f_x and f_y exist and are they continuous at all points $(x, y) \neq (0, 0)$?

(d) Is f differentiable at $(0, 0)$?

(e) Do the partial derivatives f_x and f_y exist and are they continuous at $(0, 0)$?

11. $f(x, y) = \begin{cases} \dfrac{x}{y} + \dfrac{y}{x}, & x \neq 0 \text{ and } y \neq 0, \\ 0, & x = 0 \text{ or } y = 0. \end{cases}$

12. $f(x, y) = \begin{cases} \dfrac{2xy}{(x^2 + y^2)^2}, & (x, y) \neq (0, 0), \\ 0, & (x, y) = (0, 0). \end{cases}$

13. $f(x, y) = \begin{cases} \dfrac{x^2 y}{x^4 + y^2}, & (x, y) \neq (0, 0), \\ 0, & (x, y) = (0, 0). \end{cases}$

14. $f(x, y) = \begin{cases} \dfrac{xy}{\sqrt{x^2 + y^2}}, & (x, y) \neq (0, 0), \\ 0, & (x, y) = (0, 0). \end{cases}$

15. Consider the function

$$f(x, y) = \begin{cases} \dfrac{xy^2}{x^2 + y^2}, & (x, y) \neq (0, 0), \\ 0, & (x, y) = (0, 0). \end{cases}$$

(a) Use a computer to draw the contour diagram for f.

(b) Is f differentiable for $(x, y) \neq (0, 0)$?

(c) Show that $f_x(0, 0)$ and $f_y(0, 0)$ exist.

(d) Is f differentiable at $(0, 0)$?

(e) Suppose $x(t) = at$ and $y(t) = bt$, where a and b are constants, not both zero. If $g(t) = f(x(t), y(t))$, show that

$$g'(0) = \frac{ab^2}{a^2 + b^2}.$$

(f) Show that

$$f_x(0, 0)x'(0) + f_y(0, 0)y'(0) = 0.$$

Does the chain rule hold for the composite function $g(t)$ at $t = 0$? Explain.

(g) Show that the directional derivative $f_{\vec{u}}(0, 0)$ exists for each unit vector $\vec{u}$. Does this imply that f is differentiable at $(0, 0)$?

16. Consider the function $f(x, y) = \sqrt{|xy|}$.

(a) Use a computer to draw the contour diagram for f. Does the contour diagram look like that of a plane when we zoom in on the origin?

(b) Use a computer to draw the graph of f. Does the graph look like a plane when we zoom in on the origin?

(c) Is f differentiable for $(x, y) \neq (0, 0)$?

(d) Show that $f_x(0, 0)$ and $f_y(0, 0)$ exist.

(e) Is f differentiable at $(0, 0)$? [Hint: Consider the directional derivative $f_{\vec{u}}(0, 0)$ for $\vec{u} = (\vec{i} + \vec{j})/\sqrt{2}$.]

17. Consider the function

$$f(x, y) = \begin{cases} \dfrac{xy^2}{x^2 + y^4}, & (x, y) \neq (0, 0), \\ 0, & (x, y) = (0, 0). \end{cases}$$

(a) Use a computer to draw the contour diagram for f.

(b) Show that the directional derivative $f_{\vec{u}}(0, 0)$ exists for each unit vector $\vec{u}$.

(c) Is f continuous at $(0, 0)$? Is f differentiable at $(0, 0)$? Explain.

18. Suppose $f(x, y)$ is a function such that $f_x(0, 0) = 0$ and $f_y(0, 0) = 0$, and $f_{\vec{u}}(0, 0) = 3$ for $\vec{u} = (\vec{i} + \vec{j})/\sqrt{2}$.

(a) Is f differentiable at $(0, 0)$? Explain.

(b) Give an example of a function f defined on 2-space which satisfies these conditions. [Hint: The function f does not have to be defined by a single formula valid over all of 2-space.]

19. Consider the following function:

$$f(x, y) = \begin{cases} \dfrac{xy(x^2 - y^2)}{x^2 + y^2}, & (x, y) \neq (0, 0), \\ 0, & (x, y) = (0, 0). \end{cases}$$

The graph of f is shown in Figure 14.68, and the contour diagram of f is shown in Figure 14.69.

(a) Find $f_x(x, y)$ and $f_y(x, y)$ for $(x, y) \neq (0, 0)$.

(b) Show that $f_x(0, 0) = 0$ and $f_y(0, 0) = 0$.

(c) Are the functions f_x and f_y continuous at $(0, 0)$?

(d) Is f differentiable at $(0, 0)$?

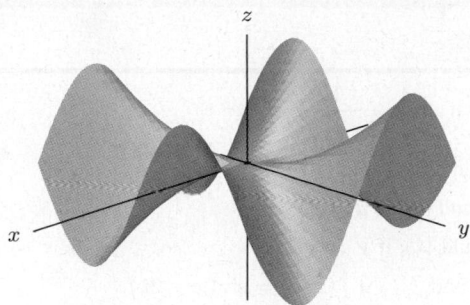

Figure 14.68: Graph of $\dfrac{xy(x^2 - y^2)}{x^2 + y^2}$

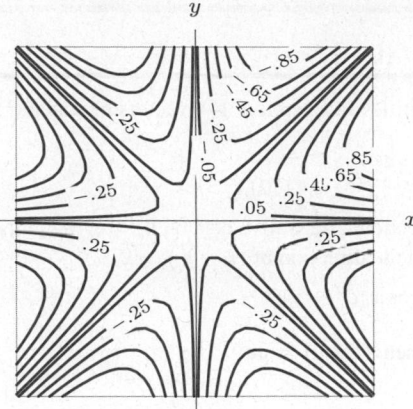

Figure 14.69: Contour diagram of
$$\dfrac{xy(x^2 - y^2)}{x^2 + y^2}$$

20. Suppose a function f is differentiable at the point (a, b). Show that f is continuous at (a, b).

Strengthen Your Understanding

In Problems 21–22, explain what is wrong with the statement.

21. If $f(x, y)$ is continuous at the origin, then it is differentiable at the origin.

22. If the partial derivatives $f_x(0, 0)$ and $f_y(0, 0)$ both exist, then $f(x, y)$ is differentiable at the origin.

In Problems 23–24, give an example of:

23. A continuous function $f(x, y)$ that is not differentiable at the origin.

24. A continuous function $f(x, y)$ that is not differentiable on the line $x = 1$.

25. Which of the following functions $f(x, y)$ is differentiable at the given point?

(a) $\sqrt{1 - x^2 - y^2}$ at $(0, 0)$ (b) $\sqrt{4 - x^2 - y^2}$ at $(2, 0)$

(c) $-\sqrt{x^2 + 2y^2}$ at $(0, 0)$ (d) $-\sqrt{x^2 + 2y^2}$ at $(2, 0)$

CHAPTER SUMMARY (see also Ready Reference at the end of the book)

- **Partial Derivatives**
  Definition as a difference quotient, visualizing on a graph, estimating from a contour diagram, computing from a formula, interpreting units, alternative notation.

- **Local Linearity**
  Zooming on a surface, contour diagram, or table to see local linearity, the idea of tangent plane, formula for a tangent plane in terms of partials, the differential.

- **Directional Derivatives**
  Definition as a difference quotient, interpretation as a rate of change, computation using partial derivatives.

- **Gradient Vector**

  Definition in terms of partial derivatives, geometric properties of gradient's length and direction, relation to directional derivative, relation to contours and level surfaces.

- **Chain Rule**
  Local linearity and differentials for composition of functions, tree diagrams, chain rule in general, application to physical chemistry.

- **Second- and Higher-Order Partial Derivatives**
  Interpretations, mixed partials are equal.

- **Taylor Approximations**
  Linear and quadratic polynomial approximations to functions near a point.

REVIEW EXERCISES AND PROBLEMS FOR CHAPTER FOURTEEN

Exercises

Are the quantities in Exercises 1–4 vectors or scalars? Calculate them.

1. $\operatorname{grad}(x^3 e^{-y/2})$ at $(1, 2)$

2. The directional derivative of $f(x, y) = x^2 y^3$ at the point $(1, 1)$ in the direction of $(\vec{i} + \vec{j})/\sqrt{2}$.

3. $\operatorname{grad}((\cos x)e^y + z)$

4. $\dfrac{\partial^2 f}{\partial x^2}$ when $f(x, y) = ye^{x^2 y}$

For Exercises 5–28, find the partial derivatives. Assume the variables are restricted to a domain on which the function is defined.

5. f_x and f_y if $f(x, y) = x^2 y + x^3 - 7xy^6$

6. $\dfrac{\partial w}{\partial h}$ if $w = 320\pi g h^2 (20 - h)$

7. $\dfrac{\partial T}{\partial l}$ if $T = 2\pi \sqrt{\dfrac{l}{g}}$

8. $\dfrac{\partial B}{\partial t}$ and $\dfrac{\partial B}{\partial r}$ when $B = P(1 + r)^t$.

9. f_x and f_y if $f(x, y) = \dfrac{x^2 y}{x^2 + y^2}$

10. $\dfrac{\partial F}{\partial r}$ and $\dfrac{\partial F}{\partial r}$ if $F = \dfrac{G\mu m y}{(r^2 + y^2)^{3/2}}$

11. f_p and f_q if $f(p, q) = e^{p/q}$

12. $z_x(2, 3)$ if $z = (\cos x) + y$

13. f_N if $f(N, V) = cN^\alpha V^\beta$

14. f_x and f_y if $f(x, y) = \sqrt{(x - a)^2 + (y - b)^2}$

15. $\dfrac{\partial}{\partial \omega}\left(\tan \sqrt{\omega x}\right)$

16. $\dfrac{\partial y}{\partial t}$ if $y = \sin(ct - 5x)$

17. z_y if $z = \dfrac{3x^2 y^7 - y^2}{15xy - 8}$

18. $\dfrac{\partial \alpha}{\partial \beta}$ if $\alpha = \dfrac{e^{x\beta - 3}}{2y\beta + 5}$

19. $\dfrac{\partial}{\partial w}\left(\sqrt{2\pi xyw - 13x^7 y^3 v}\right)$

20. $\dfrac{\partial}{\partial \lambda}\left(\dfrac{x^2 y\lambda - 3\lambda^5}{\sqrt{\lambda^2 - 3\lambda + 5}}\right)$

21. $\dfrac{\partial}{\partial w}\left(\dfrac{x^2 yw - xy^3 w^7}{w - 1}\right)^{-7/2}$

22. $\dfrac{\partial}{\partial x}(e^x \cos(xy) + ay^2)$, $\dfrac{\partial}{\partial y}(e^x \cos(xy) + ay^2)$,
$\dfrac{\partial}{\partial a}(e^x \cos(xy) + ay^2)$

23. $\dfrac{\partial f_0}{\partial L}$ if $f_0 = \dfrac{1}{2\pi\sqrt{LC}}$

24. f_{xx} and f_{xy} if $f(x, y) = 1/\sqrt{x^2 + y^2}$

25. u_{xx} and u_{yy} if $u = e^x \sin y$

26. V_{rr} and V_{rh} if $V = \pi r^2 h$

27. f_{xxy} and f_{yxx} if $f(x, y) = \sin(x - 2y)$

28. $\dfrac{\partial^2}{\partial x^2}(e^{ax-bt}) + \dfrac{\partial^2}{\partial t^2}(e^{ax-bt})$

In Exercises 29–39, find the gradient of the function.

29. $f(x, y, z) = x^2 + y^2 + y^3$

30. $f(x, y, z) = x^3 + z^3 - xyz$

31. $f(x, y, z) = 1/(xyz)$

32. $f(x, y) = \sin(y^2 - xy)$

33. $z = \sin(x^2 + y^2)$

34. $f(x, y, z) = xe^y + \ln(xz)$

35. $f(x, y, z) = \sin(x^2 + y^2 + z^2)$

36. $f(\rho, \phi, \theta) = \rho \sin \phi \cos \theta$

37. $f(s, t) = \dfrac{1}{\sqrt{s}}(t^2 - 2t + 4)$

38. $f(x, y) = \sqrt{x^2 + y^2}$

39. $f(x, y) = \sin(xy) + \cos(xy)$

In Exercises 40–41, find the gradient of f at the point.

40. $f(x, y, z) = x^2$ at $(0, 0, 0)$

41. $f(x, y, z) = x^2 z$, at $(1, 1, 1)$

In Exercises 42–47, find the directional derivative of the function.

42. $f(x, y) = x^3 - y^3$ at $(2, -1)$ in the direction of $\vec{i} - \vec{j}$

43. $f(x, y) = xe^y$ at $(3, 0)$ in the direction of $4\vec{i} - 3\vec{j}$

44. $f(x, y, z) = x^2 + y^2 - z^2$ at $(2, 3, 4)$ in the direction of $2\vec{i} - 2\vec{j} + \vec{k}$

45. $f(x, y, z) = 3x^2 y^2 + 2yz$ at $(-1, 0, 4)$ in the direction of $\vec{i} - \vec{k}$

46. $f(x, y, z) = 3x^2 y^2 + 2yz$ at $(-1, 0, 4)$ in the direction of $-\vec{i} + 3\vec{j} + 3\vec{k}$

47. $f(x, y, z) = e^{x+z} \cos y$ at $(1, 0, -1)$ in the direction of $\vec{i} + \vec{j} + \vec{k}$

In Exercises 48–50, find a vector normal to the curve or surface at the point.

48. $x^2 - y^2 = 3$ at $(2, 1)$

49. $xy + xz + yz = 11$ at $(1, 2, 3)$

50. $z^2 - 2xyz = x^2 + y^2$ at $(1, 2, -1)$

51. Find an equation of the tangent plane to the surface $z^2 - 4x^2 - 3y^2 = 9$ at the point $(1, 1, 4)$.

52. Find an equation of the tangent plane to the surface $x^3 = 2y^2 - z$ at the point $(1, 0, -1)$.

53. Find an equation of the tangent plane to the surface $z - 1/(xy) = 0$ at the point $(1, 1, 1)$.

54. Compute all four second-order partial derivatives of $f(x, y) = x^2 y^2 - 5xy^3$.

In Exercises 55–60, find dz/dt using the chain rule. Assume the variables are restricted to domains on which the functions are defined.

55. $z = x \sin y, x = \sin t, y = \cos t$

56. $z = \sin(x^2 + y^2), x = 2t, y = t^2$

57. $z = (x^2 + y)^2, x = 2t, y = t^2$

58. $z = (x + y)e^x, x = t^2, y = 1 - t^2$

59. $z = \ln y + \ln x, x = t^3, y = t^2 + 1$

60. $z = \sin(pq), p = \sin t, q = \cos t^2$

In Exercises 61–63, find the quadratic Taylor polynomial for the function.

61. $f(x, y) = (x + 1)^3 (y + 2)$ about $(0, 0)$

62. $f(x, y) = \cos x \cos 3y$ about $(0, 0)$

63. $f(x, y) = \sqrt{2x - y}$ about $(3, 5)$

Problems

64. Match each function $f(x, y, z)$ in (a)–(d) with the description of its gradient in (I)–(VI).

 (a) $x^2 + y^2 + z^2$ (b) $\sqrt{x^2 + y^2 + z^2}$
 (c) $3x + 4y$ (d) $3x + 4z$

  I   Constant, parallel to xy-plane.
  II Constant, parallel to xz-plane.
  III Constant, parallel to yz-plane.
  IV Radial, increasing in magnitude away from the origin.
  V   Radial, constant magnitude.
  VI Radial, decreasing in magnitude away from the origin.

65. (a) Find an equation of the tangent plane to the surface $2x^2 - 2xy^2 + az = a$ at the point $(1, 1, 1)$.
 (b) For which value of a does the tangent plane pass through the origin?

66. The monthly mortgage payment in dollars, P, for a house is a function of three variables:

$$P = f(A, r, N),$$

where A is the amount borrowed in dollars, r is the interest rate, and N is the number of years before the mortgage is paid off.

 (a) $f(92000, 14, 30) = 1090.08$. What does this tell you, in financial terms?
 (b) $\left. \dfrac{\partial P}{\partial r} \right|_{(92000, 14, 30)} = 72.82$. What is the financial significance of the number 72.82?
 (c) Would you expect $\partial P / \partial A$ to be positive or negative? Why?
 (d) Would you expect $\partial P / \partial N$ to be positive or negative? Why?

67. Figure 14.70 is a contour diagram of $f(x, y)$. In each of the following cases, list the marked points in the diagram (there may be none or more than one) at which

 (a) $f_x < 0$ (b) $f_y > 0$
 (c) $f_{xx} > 0$ (d) $f_{yy} < 0$

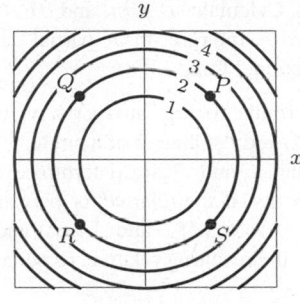

Figure 14.70

68. Figure 14.71 gives a contour diagram for the number n of foxes per square kilometer in southwestern England. Estimate $\partial n / \partial x$ and $\partial n / \partial y$ at the points A, B, and C, where x is kilometers east and y is kilometers north.

Figure 14.71

69. The cost of producing one unit of a product is given by

$$c = a + bx + ky,$$

where x is the amount of labor used (in man hours) and y is the amount of raw material used (by weight) and a and b and k are constants. What does $\partial c/\partial x = b$ mean? What is the practical interpretation of b?

70. (a) Let $f(u, v) = u(u^2 + v^2)^{3/2}$. Use a difference quotient to approximate $f_u(1, 3)$ with $h = 0.001$.
   (b) Now evaluate $f_u(1, 3)$ exactly. Was the approximation in part (a) reasonable?

71. The gravitational force, F newtons, exerted on a mass of m kg at a distance of r meters from the center of the earth is given by

$$F = \frac{GMm}{r^2}$$

where the mass of the earth $M = 6 \cdot 10^{24}$ kilograms, and $G = 6.67 \cdot 10^{-11}$. Find the gravitational force on a person with mass 70 kg at the surface of the earth $(r = 6.4 \cdot 10^6)$. Calculate $\partial F/\partial m$ and $\partial F/\partial r$ for these values of m and r. Interpret these partial derivatives in terms of gravitational force.

72. (a) Write a formula for the number π using only the perimeter L and the area A of a circle.
   (b) Suppose that L and A are determined experimentally. Show that if the relative, or percent, errors in the measured values of L and A are λ and μ, respectively, then the resulting relative, or percent, error in π is $2\lambda - \mu$.

73. A company uses x hours of unskilled labor and y hours of skilled labor to produce $F(x, y) = 60x^{2/3}y^{1/3}$ units of output. It currently employs 400 hours of unskilled labor and 50 hours of skilled labor. The company is planning to hire an additional 5 hours of skilled labor.

   (a) Use a linear approximation to decide by about how much the company can reduce its use of unskilled labor and keep its output at current level.
   (b) Calculate the exact value of the reduction.

74. One mole of ammonia gas is contained in a vessel which is capable of changing its volume (a compartment sealed by a piston, for example). The total energy U (in joules) of the ammonia is a function of the volume V (in m^3) of the container, and the temperature T (in K) of the gas. The differential dU is given by

$$dU = 840\, dV + 27.32\, dT.$$

   (a) How does the energy change if the volume is held constant and the temperature is increased slightly?
   (b) How does the energy change if the temperature is held constant and the volume is increased slightly?
   (c) Find the approximate change in energy if the gas is compressed by 100 cm^3 and heated by 2 K.

75. Figure 14.72 shows grad $f(x, y)$. In each of the following cases, list the marked points (if any) at which

   (a) $f_x > 0$ (b) $f_y < 0$
   (c) $f_{xx} > 0$ (d) $f_{yy} < 0$

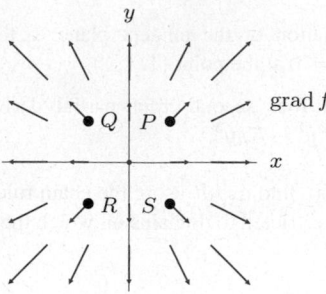

Figure 14.72

In Problems 76–81, use the contour diagram for $f(x, y)$ in Figure 14.73 to estimate the directional derivative of $f(x, y)$ in the direction $\vec{v}$ at the point given.

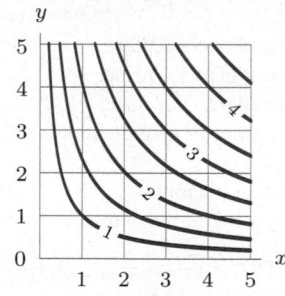

Figure 14.73

76. $\vec{v} = \vec{i}$ at $(1, 1)$ **77.** $\vec{v} = \vec{j}$ at $(1, 1)$
78. $\vec{v} = \vec{i} + \vec{j}$ at $(1, 1)$ **79.** $\vec{v} = \vec{i} + \vec{j}$ at $(4, 1)$
80. $\vec{v} = -2\vec{i} + \vec{j}$ at $(3, 3)$ **81.** $\vec{v} = -2\vec{i} + \vec{j}$ at $(4, 1)$

82. Figure 14.73 shows the level curves of $f(x, y)$. At the points $(1, 1)$ and $(1, 4)$, draw a vector representing grad f. Explain how you know the direction and length of each vector.

83. Find the directional derivative of $z = x^2y$ at $(1, 2)$ in the direction making an angle of $5\pi/4$ with the x-axis. In which direction is the directional derivative the largest?

84. An ant is crawling across a heated plate with velocity $\vec{v}$ cm/sec, and the temperature of the plate at position (x, y) is $H(x, y)$ degrees, where x and y are in centimeters. Which of the following (if any) is correct? The rate of change in deg/sec of the temperature felt by the ant is:

   (a) $\| \operatorname{grad} H \| \| \vec{v} \|$, because it is the product of the ant's speed and the rate of change of H with respect to distance.

(b) grad $H \cdot \vec{v}$, because it is the product of the ant's speed and the directional derivative of H in the direction of $\vec{v}$.

(c) $H_{\vec{u}}$, where $\vec{u} = \vec{v}/\|\vec{v}\|$, because it is the rate of change of H in the direction of $\vec{v}$.

85. The depth, in feet, of a lake at a point x miles east and y miles north of a buoy is given by

$$h(x, y) = 150 - 30x^2 - 20y^2.$$

(a) A rowboat is 1 mile east and 2 miles south of the buoy. At what rate is the depth changing with respect to distance in the direction of the buoy?

(b) The boat starts moving toward the buoy at a rate of 3 mph. At what rate is the depth of the lake beneath the boat changing with respect to time?

86. A differentiable function $f(x, y)$ has the property that $f(1, 3) = 7$ and grad $f(1, 3) = 2\vec{i} - 5\vec{j}$.

(a) Find the equation of the tangent line to the level curve of f through the point $(1, 3)$.

(b) Find the equation of the tangent plane to the surface $z = f(x, y)$ at the point $(1, 3, 7)$.

87. Let x, y, z be in meters. At the point (x, y, z) in space, the temperature, H, in $°C$, is given by

$$H = e^{-(x^2 + 2y^2 + 3z^2)}.$$

(a) A particle at the point $(2, 1, 5)$ starts to move in the direction of increasing x. How fast is the temperature changing with respect to distance? Give units.

(b) If the particle in part (a) moves at 10 meters/sec, how fast is the temperature changing with respect to time? Give units.

(c) What is the maximum rate of change of temperature with respect to distance at the point $(2, 1, 5)$?

88. A differentiable function $f(x, y)$ has the property that $f(4, 1) = 3$ and $f_x(4, 1) = 2$ and $f_y(4, 1) = -1$. Find the equation of the tangent plane at the point on the surface $z = f(x, y)$ where $x = 4$, $y = 1$.

89. The temperature at (x, y) is $T(x, y) = 100 - x^2 - y^2$. In which direction should a heat-seeking bug move from the point (x, y) to increase its temperature fastest?

90. A car is driving northwest at v mph across a sloping plain whose height, in feet above sea level, at a point N miles north and E miles east of a city is given by

$$h(N, E) = 2500 + 100N + 50E.$$

(a) At what rate is the height above sea level changing with respect to distance in the direction the car is driving?

(b) Express the rate of change of the height of the car with respect to time in terms of v.

91. Do the level curves of $f(x, y) = \sqrt{x^2 + y^2} + x$ and $g(x, y) = \sqrt{x^2 + y^2} - x$ cross at right angles?

92. At any point (x, y, z) outside a spherically symmetric mass m located at the point (x_0, y_0, z_0), the gravitational potential, V, is defined by $V = -Gm/r$, where r is the distance from (x, y, z) to (x_0, y_0, z_0) and G is a constant. Show that, for all points outside the mass, V satisfies Laplace's equation:

$$\frac{\partial^2 V}{\partial x^2} + \frac{\partial^2 V}{\partial y^2} + \frac{\partial^2 V}{\partial z^2} = 0.$$

93. Suppose that f is any differentiable function of one variable. Define V, a function of two variables, by

$$V(x, t) = f(x + ct).$$

Show that V satisfies the equation

$$\frac{\partial V}{\partial t} = c\frac{\partial V}{\partial x}.$$

94. Given $z = u^2 - ue^v$, $u = x + 2y$, $v = 2x - y$, use the chain rule to find:

(a) $\partial z/\partial x|_{(x,y)=(1,2)}$ **(b)** $\partial z/\partial y|_{(x,y)=(1,2)}$

95. Let $F(u, v, w)$ be a function of three variables. Find $G_x(x, y)$ if

(a) $G(x, y) = F(x, y, 3)$ **(b)** $G(x, y) = F(3, y, x)$

(c) $G(x, y) = F(x, y, x)$ **(d)** $G(x, y) = F(x, y, xy)$

96. In analyzing a factory and deciding whether or not to hire more workers, it is useful to know under what circumstances productivity increases. Suppose $P = f(x_1, x_2, x_3)$ is the total quantity produced as a function of x_1, the number of workers, and any other variables x_2, x_3. We define the average productivity of a worker as P/x_1. Show that the average productivity increases as x_1 increases when marginal production, $\partial P/\partial x_1$, is greater than the average productivity, P/x_1.

97. For the Cobb-Douglas function $P = 40L^{0.25}K^{0.75}$, find the differential dP when $L = 2$ and $K = 16$.

98. The period, T, of a pendulum is $T = 2\pi\sqrt{l/g}$. If the approximate length is $l = 2$ meters, find the approximate error in T if the true length is $l = 1.99$ and we take $g = 9.8$ as an approximation for $g = 9.81$ m/s^2.

99. Figure 14.74 shows the monthly payment, m, on a 5-year car loan if you borrow P dollars at r percent interest. Find a formula for a linear function which approximates m. What is the practical significance of the constants in your formula?

Figure 14.74

(d) Write an equation for the level curve through the point $(2, 3)$.

(e) Find a vector tangent to the level curve of f through the point $(2, 3)$.

(f) Find the differential of f at the point $(2, 3)$. If $dx = 0.03$ and $dy = 0.04$, find df. What does df represent in this case?

Table 14.8

		x	
		2.00	2.01
y	3.00	7.56	7.42
	3.02	7.61	7.47

In Problems 100–107, the function f is differentiable and $f_x(2, 1) = -3$, $f_y(2, 1) = 4$, and $f(2, 1) = 7$.

100. (a) Give an equation for the tangent plane to the graph of f at $x = 2, y = 1$.

(b) Give an equation for the tangent line to the contour for f at $x = 2, y = 1$.

101. (a) Find a vector perpendicular to the tangent plane to the graph of f at $x = 2, y = 1$.

(b) Find a vector perpendicular to the tangent line to the contour for f at $x = 2, y = 1$.

102. Near $x = 2$ and $y = 1$, how far apart are the contours $f(x, y) = 7$ and $f(x, y) = 7.3$?

103. Give an approximate table of values of f for $x = 1.8, 2.0, 2.2$ and $y = 0.9, 1.0, 1, 1$.

104. Give an approximate contour diagram for f for $1 \leq x \leq 3, 0 \leq y \leq 2$, using contour values $\ldots 5, 6, 7, 8, 9 \ldots$.

105. The function f gives temperature in °C and x and y are in centimeters. A bug leaves $(2, 1)$ at 3 cm/min so that it cools off as fast as possible. In which direction does the bug head? At what rate does it cool off, in °C/min?

106. Find $f_r(2, 1)$ and $f_\theta(2, 1)$, where r and θ are polar coordinates, $x = r \cos \theta$ and $y = r \sin \theta$. If $\vec{u}$ is the unit vector in the direction $2\vec{i} + \vec{j}$, show that $f_{\vec{u}}(2, 1) = f_r(2, 1)$ and explain why this should be the case.

107. Find approximately the largest value of f on or inside the circle of radius 0.1 about the point $(2, 1)$. At what point does f achieve this value?

108. Values of the function $f(x, y)$ near the point $x = 2$, $y = 3$ are given in Table 14.8. Estimate the following.

(a) $\left. \dfrac{\partial f}{\partial x} \right|_{(2,3)}$ and $\left. \dfrac{\partial f}{\partial y} \right|_{(2,3)}$.

(b) The rate of change of f at $(2, 3)$ in the direction of the vector $\vec{i} + 3\vec{j}$.

(c) The maximum possible rate of change of f as you move away from the point $(2, 3)$. In which direction should you move to obtain this rate of change?

109. Find the quadratic Taylor polynomial about $(0, 0)$ for $f(x, y) = \cos(x + 2y) \sin(x - y)$.

110. Suppose $f(x, y) = e^{(x-1)^2 + (y-3)^2}$.

(a) Find the first-order Taylor polynomial about $(0, 0)$.

(b) Find the second-order (quadratic) Taylor polynomial about the point $(1, 3)$.

(c) Find a 2-vector perpendicular to the level curve through $(0, 0)$.

(d) Find a 3-vector perpendicular to the surface $z = f(x, y)$ at the point $(0, 0)$.

111. Figure 14.75 shows a contour diagram for a vibrating string function, $f(x, t)$.

(a) Is $f_t(\pi/2, \pi/2)$ positive or negative? How about $f_t(\pi/2, \pi)$? What does the sign of $f_t(\pi/2, b)$ tell you about the motion of the point on the string at $x = \pi/2$ when $t = b$?

(b) Find all t for which f_t is positive, for $0 \leq t \leq 5\pi/2$.

(c) Find all x and t such that f_x is positive.

Figure 14.75

CAS Challenge Problems

112. (a) Find the quadratic Taylor polynomial about $(0,0)$ of
$$f(x,y) = \frac{e^x(1+\sin(3y))^2}{5+e^{2x}}.$$
(b) Find the quadratic Taylor polynomial about 0 of the one-variable functions $g(x) = e^x/(5+e^{2x})$ and $h(y) = (1+\sin(3y))^2$. Multiply these polynomials together and compare with your answer to part (a).
(c) Show that if $f(x,y) = g(x)h(y)$, then the quadratic Taylor polynomial of f about $(0,0)$ is the product of the quadratic Taylor polynomials of $g(x)$ and $h(y)$ about 0. [If you use a computer algebra system, make sure that f, g and h do not have any previously assigned formula.]

113. Let
$$f(x,y) = A_0 + A_1x + A_2y + A_3x^2 + A_4xy + A_5y^2,$$
$$g(t) = 1 + B_1t + B_2t^2,$$
$$h(t) = 2 + C_1t + C_2t^2.$$

(a) Find $L(x,y)$, the linear approximation to $f(x,y)$ at the point $(1,2)$. Also find $m(t)$ and $n(t)$, the linear

approximations to $g(t)$ and $h(t)$ at $t = 0$.
(b) Calculate $(d/dt)f(g(t),h(t))|_{t=0}$ and $(d/dt)L(m(t),n(t))|_{t=0}$. Describe what you notice and explain it in terms of the chain rule.

114. Let $f(x,y) = A_0 + A_1x + A_2y + A_3x^2 + A_4xy + A_5y^2$.

(a) Find the quadratic Taylor approximation for $f(x,y)$ near the point $(1,2)$, and expand the result in powers of x and y.
(b) Explain what you notice in part (a) and formulate a generalization to points other than $(1,2)$.
(c) Repeat part (a) for the linear approximation. How does it differ from the quadratic?

115. Suppose that $w = f(x,y,z)$, that x and y are functions of u and v, and that $z, u,$ and v are functions of t. Use a computer algebra system to find the derivative
$$\frac{d}{dt}f(x(u(t),v(t)), y(u(t),v(t)), z(t))$$
and explain the answer using a tree diagram.

PROJECTS FOR CHAPTER FOURTEEN

1. Heat Equation

The function $T(x,y,z,t)$ is a solution to the *heat equation*
$$T_t = K(T_{xx} + T_{yy} + T_{zz})$$
and gives the temperature at the point (x,y,z) in 3-space and time t. The constant K is the *thermal conductivity* of the medium through which the heat is flowing.

(a) Show that the function
$$T(x,y,z,t) = \frac{1}{(4\pi Kt)^{3/2}}e^{-(x^2+y^2+z^2)/4Kt}$$
is a solution to the heat equation for all (x,y,z) in 3-space and $t > 0$.
(b) For each fixed time t, what are the level surfaces of the function $T(x,y,z,t)$ in 3-space?
(c) Regard t as fixed and compute $\operatorname{grad} T(x,y,z,t)$. What does $\operatorname{grad} T(x,y,z,t)$ tell us about the direction and magnitude of the heat flow?

2. Matching Birthdays

Consider a class of m students and a year with n days. Let $q(m,n)$ denote the probability, expressed as a number between 0 and 1, that at least two students have the same birthday. Surprisingly, $q(23, 365) \approx 0.5073$. (This means that there is slightly better than an even chance that at least two students in a class of 23 have the same birthday.) A general formula for q is complicated, but it can be shown that
$$\frac{\partial q}{\partial m} \approx +\frac{m}{n}(1-q) \qquad \text{and} \qquad \frac{\partial q}{\partial n} \approx -\frac{m^2}{2n^2}(1-q).$$

(These approximations hold when n is a good deal larger than m, and m is a good deal larger than 1.)

(a) Explain why the $+$ and $-$ signs in the approximations for $\partial q/\partial m$ and $\partial q/\partial n$ are to be expected.

(b) Suppose there are 21 students in a class. What is the approximate probability that at least two students in the class have the same birthday? (Assume that a year always has 365 days.)

(c) Suppose there is a class of 24 students and you know that no one was born in the first week of the year. (This has the effect of making $n = 358$.) What is the approximate value of q for this class?

(d) If you want to bet that a certain class of 23 students has at least two matching birthdays, would you prefer to have two more students added to the class or to be told that no one in the class was born in December?

(e) (Optional) Find the actual formula for q. [Hint: It's easier to find $1 - q$. There are $n \cdot n \cdot n \cdots n = n^m$ different choices for the students' birthdays. How many such choices have no matching birthdays?]

Chapter Fifteen

OPTIMIZATION: LOCAL AND GLOBAL EXTREMA

Contents

15.1 CRITICAL POINTS: LOCAL EXTREMA AND SADDLE POINTS

Functions of several variables, like functions of one variable, can have *local* and *global* extrema. (That is, local and global maxima and minima.) A function has a local extremum at a point where it takes on the largest or smallest value in a small region around the point. Global extrema are the largest or smallest values anywhere on the domain under consideration. (See Figures 15.1 and 15.2.)

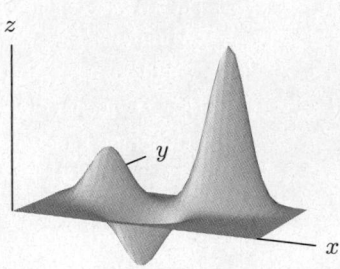

Figure 15.1: Local and global extrema for a function of two variables on $0 \leq x \leq a$, $0 \leq y \leq b$

Figure 15.2: Contour map of the function in Figure 15.1

More precisely, considering only points at which f is defined, we say:

- f has a **local maximum** at the point P_0 if $f(P_0) \geq f(P)$ for all points P near P_0.
- f has a **local minimum** at the point P_0 if $f(P_0) \leq f(P)$ for all points P near P_0.

How Do We Detect a Local Maximum or Minimum?

Recall that if the gradient vector of a function is defined and nonzero, then it points in a direction in which the function increases. Suppose that a function f has a local maximum at a point P_0 which is not on the boundary of the domain. If the vector $\operatorname{grad} f(P_0)$ were defined and nonzero, then we could increase f by moving in the direction of $\operatorname{grad} f(P_0)$. Since f has a local maximum at P_0, there is no direction in which f is increasing. Thus, if $\operatorname{grad} f(P_0)$ is defined, we must have

$$\operatorname{grad} f(P_0) = \vec{0}.$$

Similarly, suppose f has a local minimum at the point P_0. If $\operatorname{grad} f(P_0)$ were defined and nonzero, then we could decrease f by moving in the direction opposite to $\operatorname{grad} f(P_0)$, and so we must again have $\operatorname{grad} f(P_0) = \vec{0}$. Therefore, we make the following definition:

Points where the gradient is either $\vec{0}$ or undefined are called **critical points** of the function.

If a function has a local maximum or minimum at a point P_0, not on the boundary of its domain, then P_0 is a critical point. For a function of two variables, we can also see that the gradient vector must be zero or undefined at a local maximum by looking at its contour diagram and a plot of its gradient vectors. (See Figures 15.3 and 15.4.) Around the maximum the vectors are all pointing inward, perpendicularly to the contours. At the maximum the gradient vector must be zero or undefined. A similar argument shows that the gradient must be zero or undefined at a local minimum.

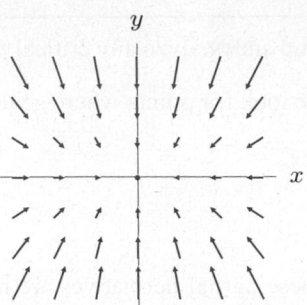

Figure 15.3: Contour diagram around a local maximum of a function

Figure 15.4: Gradients pointing toward the local maximum of the function in Figure 15.3

Finding and Analyzing Critical Points

To find critical points of f we set grad $f = f_x\vec{i} + f_y\vec{j} + f_z\vec{k} = \vec{0}$, which means setting all the partial derivatives of f equal to zero. We must also look for the points where one or more of the partial derivatives is undefined.

Example 1   Find and analyze the critical points of $f(x, y) = x^2 - 2x + y^2 - 4y + 5$.

Solution   To find the critical points, we set both partial derivatives equal to zero:

$$f_x(x, y) = 2x - 2 = 0$$
$$f_y(x, y) = 2y - 4 = 0.$$

Solving these equations gives $x = 1$, $y = 2$. Hence, f has only one critical point, namely $(1, 2)$. To see the behavior of f near $(1, 2)$, look at the values of the function in Table 15.1.

Table 15.1   *Values of $f(x, y)$ near the point $(1, 2)$*

		x			
		0.8	0.9	1.0	1.1	1.2
	1.8	0.08	0.05	0.04	0.05	0.08
	1.9	0.05	0.02	0.01	0.02	0.05
y	2.0	0.04	0.01	0.00	0.01	0.04
	2.1	0.05	0.02	0.01	0.02	0.05
	2.2	0.08	0.05	0.04	0.05	0.08

The table suggests that the function has a local minimum value of 0 at $(1, 2)$. We can confirm this by completing the square:

$$f(x, y) = x^2 - 2x + y^2 - 4y + 5 = (x - 1)^2 + (y - 2)^2.$$

Figure 15.5 shows that the graph of f is a paraboloid with vertex at the point $(1, 2, 0)$. It is the same shape as the graph of $z = x^2 + y^2$ (see Figure 12.12 on page 675), except that the vertex has been shifted to $(1, 2)$. So the point $(1, 2)$ is a local minimum of f (as well as a global minimum).

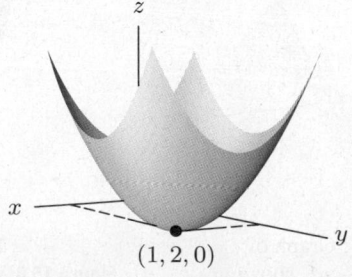

$(1, 2, 0)$

Figure 15.5: The graph of $f(x, y) = x^2 - 2x + y^2 - 4y + 5$ with a local minimum at the point $(1, 2)$

Example 2   Find and analyze any critical points of $f(x, y) = -\sqrt{x^2 + y^2}$.

Solution   We look for points where grad $f = \vec{0}$ or is undefined. The partial derivatives are given by

$$f_x(x, y) = -\frac{x}{\sqrt{x^2 + y^2}},$$

$$f_y(x, y) = -\frac{y}{\sqrt{x^2 + y^2}}.$$

These partial derivatives are never simultaneously zero, but they are undefined at $x = 0$, $y = 0$. Thus, $(0, 0)$ is a critical point and a possible extreme point. The graph of f (see Figure 15.6) is a cone, with vertex at $(0, 0)$. So f has a local and global maximum at $(0, 0)$.

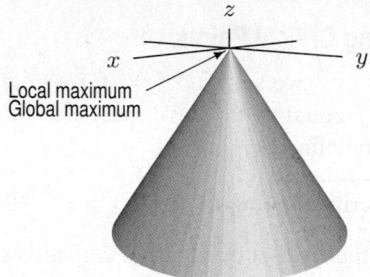

Figure 15.6: Graph of $f(x, y) = -\sqrt{x^2 + y^2}$

Example 3   Find and analyze any critical points of $g(x, y) = x^2 - y^2$.

Solution   To find the critical points, we look for points where both partial derivatives are zero:

$$g_x(x, y) = 2x = 0$$

$$g_y(x, y) = -2y = 0.$$

Solving gives $x = 0$, $y = 0$, so the origin is the only critical point.

Figure 15.7 shows that near the origin g takes on both positive and negative values. Since $g(0, 0) = 0$, the origin is a critical point which is neither a local maximum nor a local minimum. The graph of g looks like a saddle.

The previous examples show that critical points can occur at local maxima or minima, or at points which are neither: The functions g and h in Figures 15.7 and 15.8 both have critical points at the origin. Figure 15.9 shows level curves of g. They are hyperbolas showing both positive and negative values of g near $(0, 0)$. Contrast this with the level curves of h near the local minimum in Figure 15.10.

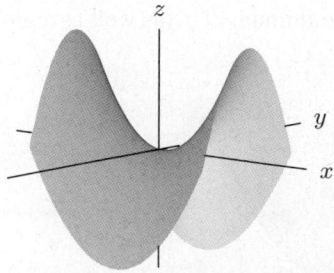

Figure 15.7: Graph of $g(x, y) = x^2 - y^2$, showing saddle shape at the origin

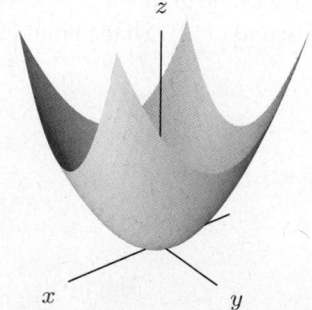

Figure 15.8: Graph of $h(x, y) = x^2 + y^2$, showing minimum at the origin

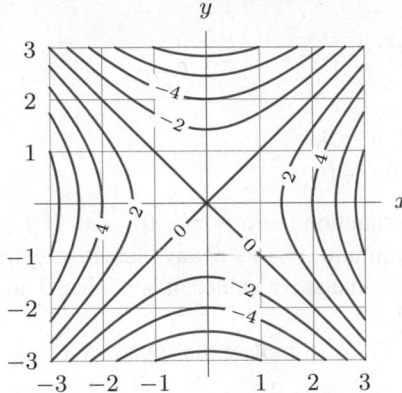

Figure 15.9: Contours of $g(x, y) = x^2 - y^2$, showing a saddle shape at the origin

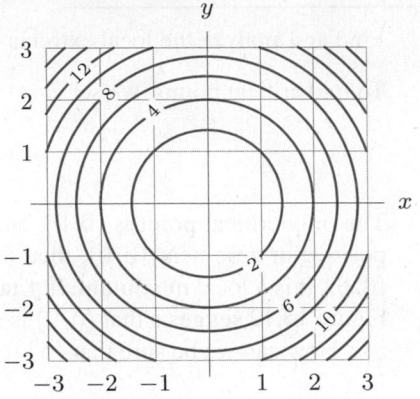

Figure 15.10: Contours of $h(x, y) = x^2 + y^2$, showing a local minimum at the origin

Example 4   Find the local extrema of the function $f(x, y) = 8y^3 + 12x^2 - 24xy$.

Solution   We begin by looking for critical points:

$$f_x(x, y) = 24x - 24y,$$
$$f_y(x, y) = 24y^2 - 24x.$$

Setting these expressions equal to zero gives the system of equations

$$x = y, \qquad x = y^2,$$

which has two solutions, $(0, 0)$ and $(1, 1)$. Are these local maxima, local minima or neither? Figure 15.11 shows contours of f near the points. Notice that $f(1, 1) = -4$ and that there is no other -4 contour. The contours near $(1, 1)$ suggest that f has a local minimum at the point $(1, 1)$.

We have $f(0, 0) = 0$ and the contours near $(0, 0)$ show that f takes both positive and negative values nearby. This suggests that $(0, 0)$ is a critical point which is neither a local maximum nor a local minimum.

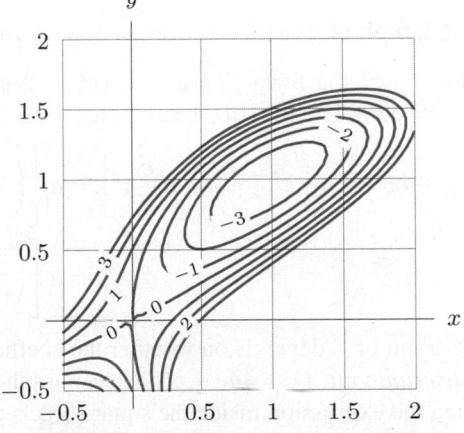

Figure 15.11: Contour diagram of $f(x, y) = 8y^3 + 12x^2 - 24xy$ showing critical points at $(0, 0)$ and $(1, 1)$

Classifying Critical Points

We can see whether a critical point of a function, f, is a local maximum, local minimum, or neither by looking at the contour diagram. There is also an analytic method for making this distinction.

Quadratic Functions of the Form $f(x, y) = ax^2 + bxy + cy^2$

Near most critical points, a function has the same behavior as its quadratic Taylor approximation about that point. Thus, we start by investigating critical points of quadratic functions of the form $f(x, y) = ax^2 + bxy + cy^2$, where a, b and c are constants.

Example 5   Find and analyze the local extrema of the function $f(x, y) = x^2 + xy + y^2$.

Solution   To find critical points, we set

$$f_x(x, y) = 2x + y = 0,$$
$$f_y(x, y) = x + 2y = 0.$$

The only critical point is $(0, 0)$, and the value of the function there is $f(0, 0) = 0$. If f is always positive or zero near $(0, 0)$, then $(0, 0)$ is a local minimum; if f is always negative or zero near $(0, 0)$, it is a local maximum; if f takes both positive and negative values, it is neither. The graph in Figure 15.12 suggests that $(0, 0)$ is a local minimum.

How can we be sure that $(0, 0)$ is a local minimum? We complete the square. Writing

$$f(x, y) = x^2 + xy + y^2 = \left(x + \frac{1}{2}y\right)^2 + \frac{3}{4}y^2,$$

shows that $f(x, y)$ is a sum of two nonnegative terms, so it is always greater than or equal to zero. Thus, the critical point is both a local and a global minimum.

Local minimum

Figure 15.12: Graph of $f(x, y) = x^2 + xy + y^2 = (x + \frac{1}{2}y)^2 + \frac{3}{4}y^2$
showing local minimum at the origin

The Shape of the Graph of $f(x, y) = ax^2 + bxy + cy^2$

In general, a function of the form $f(x, y) = ax^2 + bxy + cy^2$ has one critical point at $(0, 0)$. Assuming $a \neq 0$, we complete the square and write

$$ax^2 + bxy + cy^2 = a\left[x^2 + \frac{b}{a}xy + \frac{c}{a}y^2\right] = a\left[\left(x + \frac{b}{2a}y\right)^2 + \left(\frac{c}{a} - \frac{b^2}{4a^2}\right)y^2\right]$$

$$= a\left[\left(x + \frac{b}{2a}y\right)^2 + \left(\frac{4ac - b^2}{4a^2}\right)y^2\right].$$

The shape of the graph of f depends on whether the coefficient of y^2 is positive, negative, or zero. The sign of the *discriminant*, $D = 4ac - b^2$, determines the sign of the coefficient of y^2.

- If $D > 0$, then the expression inside the square brackets is positive or zero, so the function has a local maximum or a local minimum.
  - If $a > 0$, the function has a local minimum, since the graph is a right-side-up paraboloid, like $z = x^2 + y^2$. (See Figure 15.13.)
  - If $a < 0$, the function has a local maximum, since the graph is an upside-down paraboloid, like $z = -x^2 - y^2$. (See Figure 15.14.)
- If $D < 0$, then the function goes up in some directions and goes down in others, like $z = x^2 - y^2$. We say the function has a *saddle point*. (See Figure 15.15.)
- If $D = 0$, then the quadratic function is $a(x + by/2a)^2$, whose graph is a parabolic cylinder. (See Figure 15.16.)

Figure 15.13: Local minimum: $D > 0$ and $a > 0$ **Figure 15.14:** Local maximum: $D > 0$ and $a < 0$ **Figure 15.15:** Saddle point: $D < 0$ **Figure 15.16:** Parabolic cylinder: $D = 0$

More generally, the graph of $g(x, y) = a(x - x_0)^2 + b(x - x_0)(y - y_0) + c(y - y_0)^2$ has the same shape as the graph of $f(x, y) = ax^2 + bxy + cy^2$, except that the critical point is at (x_0, y_0) rather than $(0, 0)$.[1]

Classifying the Critical Points of a Function

Suppose that f is any function with grad $f(0, 0) = \vec{0}$. Its quadratic Taylor polynomial near $(0, 0)$,

$$f(x, y) \approx f(0, 0) + f_x(0, 0)x + f_y(0, 0)y$$
$$+ \frac{1}{2}f_{xx}(0, 0)x^2 + f_{xy}(0, 0)xy + \frac{1}{2}f_{yy}(0, 0)y^2,$$

can be simplified using $f_x(0, 0) = f_y(0, 0) = 0$, which gives

$$f(x, y) - f(0, 0) \approx \frac{1}{2}f_{xx}(0, 0)x^2 + f_{xy}(0, 0)xy + \frac{1}{2}f_{yy}(0, 0)y^2.$$

The discriminant of this quadratic polynomial is

$$D = 4ac - b^2 = 4\left(\frac{1}{2}f_{xx}(0, 0)\right)\left(\frac{1}{2}f_{yy}(0, 0)\right) - (f_{xy}(0, 0))^2,$$

which simplifies to

$$D = f_{xx}(0, 0)f_{yy}(0, 0) - (f_{xy}(0, 0))^2.$$

There is a similar formula for D if the critical point is at (x_0, y_0). An analogy with quadratic functions suggests the following test for classifying a critical point of a function of two variables:

Second-Derivative Test for Functions of Two Variables

Suppose (x_0, y_0) is a point where grad $f(x_0, y_0) = \vec{0}$. Let

$$D = f_{xx}(x_0, y_0)f_{yy}(x_0, y_0) - (f_{xy}(x_0, y_0))^2.$$

- If $D > 0$ and $f_{xx}(x_0, y_0) > 0$, then f has a local minimum at (x_0, y_0).
- If $D > 0$ and $f_{xx}(x_0, y_0) < 0$, then f has a local maximum at (x_0, y_0).
- If $D < 0$, then f has a saddle point at (x_0, y_0).
- If $D = 0$, anything can happen: f can have a local maximum, or a local minimum, or a saddle point, or none of these, at (x_0, y_0).

Example 6   Find the local maxima, minima, and saddle points of $f(x, y) = \frac{1}{2}x^2 + 3y^3 + 9y^2 - 3xy + 9y - 9x$.

Solution   Setting the partial derivatives of f to zero gives

$$f_x(x, y) = x - 3y - 9 = 0,$$
$$f_y(x, y) = 9y^2 + 18y + 9 - 3x = 0.$$

---

[1] We assumed that $a \neq 0$. If $a = 0$ and $c \neq 0$, the same argument works. If both $a = 0$ and $c = 0$, then $f(x, y) = bxy$, which has a saddle point.

Eliminating x gives $9y^2 + 9y - 18 = 0$, with solutions $y = -2$ and $y = 1$. The corresponding values of x are $x = 3$ and $x = 12$, so the critical points of f are $(3, -2)$ and $(12, 1)$. The discriminant is

$$D(x, y) = f_{xx}f_{yy} - f_{xy}^2 = (1)(18y + 18) - (-3)^2 = 18y + 9.$$

Since $D(3, -2) = -36 + 9 < 0$, we know that $(3, -2)$ is a saddle point of f. Since $D(12, 1) = 18 + 9 > 0$ and $f_{xx}(12, 1) = 1 > 0$, we know that $(12, 1)$ is a local minimum of f.

The second-derivative test does not give any information if $D = 0$. However, as the following example illustrates, we may still be able to classify the critical points.

Example 7   Classify the critical points of $f(x, y) = x^4 + y^4$, and $g(x, y) = -x^4 - y^4$, and $h(x, y) = x^4 - y^4$.

Solution   Each of these functions has a critical point at $(0, 0)$. Since all the second partial derivatives are 0 there, each function has $D = 0$. Near the origin, the graphs of f, g and h look like the surfaces in Figures 15.13–15.15, respectively, so f has a local minimum at $(0, 0)$, and g has a local maximum at $(0, 0)$, and h is saddle-shaped at $(0, 0)$.

We can get the same results algebraically. Since $f(0, 0) = 0$ and $f(x, y) > 0$ elsewhere, f has a local minimum at the origin. Since $g(0, 0) = 0$ and $g(x, y) < 0$ elsewhere, g has a local maximum at the origin. Lastly, h is saddle-shaped at the origin since $h(0, 0) = 0$ and, away from the origin, $h(x, y) > 0$ on the x-axis and $h(x, y) < 0$ on the y-axis.

Exercises and Problems for Section 15.1

Exercises

1. Figures (I)–(VI) show level curves of six functions around a critical point P. Does each function have a local maximum, a local minimum, or a saddle point at P?

2. Which of the points A, B, C in Figure 15.17 appear to be critical points? Classify those that are critical points.

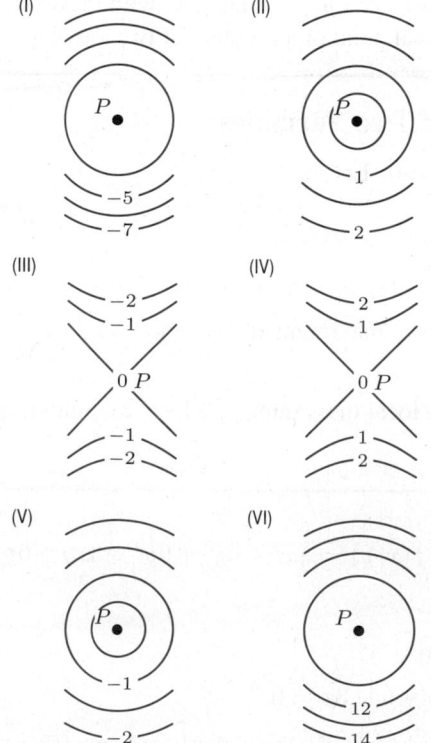

3. Which of the points D–G in Figure 15.17 appear to be

(a) Local maxima?
(b) Local minima?
(c) Saddle points?

Figure 15.17

Each function in Exercises 4–7 has a critical point at $(0,0)$. What sort of critical point is it?

4. $g(x,y) = x^4 + y^3$ **5.** $f(x,y) = x^6 + y^6$

6. $k(x,y) = \sin x \sin y$ **7.** $h(x,y) = \cos x \cos y$

For Exercises 8–20, find the critical points and classify them as local maxima, local minima, saddle points, or none of these.

8. $f(x,y) = x^2 - 2xy + 3y^2 - 8y$

9. $f(x,y) = 5 + 6x - x^2 + xy - y^2$

10. $f(x,y) = x^2 - y^2 + 4x + 2y$

11. $f(x,y) = 400 - 3x^2 - 4x + 2xy - 5y^2 + 48y$

12. $f(x,y) = 15 - x^2 + 2y^2 + 6x - 8y$

13. $f(x,y) = x^2y + 2y^2 - 2xy + 6$

14. $f(x,y) = 2x^3 - 3x^2y + 6x^2 - 6y^2$

15. $f(x,y) = x^3 - 3x + y^3 - 3y$

16. $f(x,y) = x^3 + y^3 - 3x^2 - 3y + 10$

17. $f(x,y) = x^3 + y^3 - 6y^2 - 3x + 9$

18. $f(x,y) = (x+y)(xy+1)$

19. $f(x,y) = 8xy - \frac{1}{4}(x+y)^4$

20. $f(x,y) = e^{2x^2+y^2}$

Problems

21. Find A and B so that $f(x,y) = x^2 + Ax + y^2 + B$ has a local minimum value of 20 at $(1,0)$.

22. For $f(x,y) = x^2 + xy + y^2 + ax + by + c$, find values of $a, b,$ and c giving a local minimum at $(2,5)$ and so that $f(2,5) = 11$.

23. **(a)** Find critical points for $f(x,y) = e^{-(x-a)^2-(y-b)^2}$.
  (b) Find a and b such that the critical point is at $(-1,5)$.
  (c) For the values of a and b in part (b), is $(-1,5)$ a local maximum, local minimum, or a saddle point?

24. Let $f(x,y) = kx^2 + y^2 - 4xy$. Determine the values of k (if any) for which the critical point at $(0,0)$ is:

  (a) A saddle point
  (b) A local maximum
  (c) A local minimum

For Problems 25–27, use the contours of f in Figure 15.18.

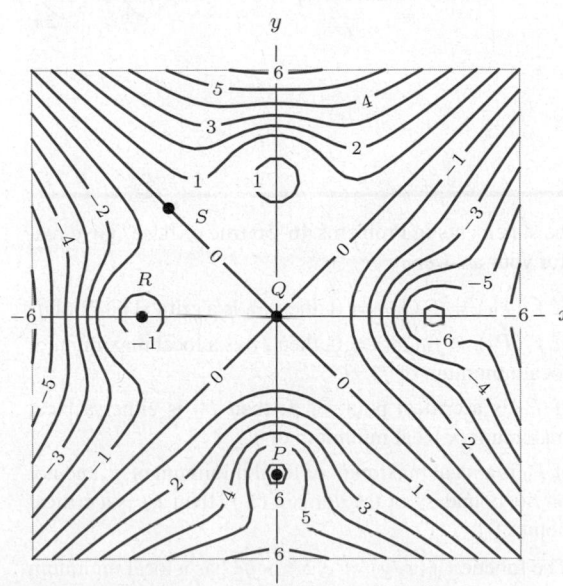

Figure 15.18

25. Decide whether you think each point is a local maximum, local minimum, saddle point, or none of these.

  (a) P **(b)** Q **(c)** R **(d)** S

26. Sketch the direction of ∇f at several points around each of $P, Q,$ and R.

27. At the points where $\|\nabla f\|$ is largest, put arrows showing the direction of ∇f.

For Problems 28–31, find critical points and classify them as local maxima, local minima, saddle points, or none of these.

28. $f(x,y) = x^3 + e^{-y^2}$

29. $f(x,y) = \sin x \sin y$

30. $f(x,y) = 1 - \cos x + y^2/2$

31. $f(x,y) = e^x(1 - \cos y)$

32. At the point $(1,3)$, suppose that $f_x = f_y = 0$ and $f_{xx} > 0, f_{yy} > 0, f_{xy} = 0$.

  (a) What can you conclude about the behavior of the function near the point $(1,3)$?
  (b) Sketch a possible contour diagram.

33. At the point (a,b), suppose that $f_x = f_y = 0, f_{xx} > 0, f_{yy} = 0, f_{xy} > 0$.

  (a) What can you conclude about the shape of the graph of f near the point (a,b)?
  (b) Sketch a possible contour diagram.

34. Draw a possible contour diagram of f such that $f_x(-1,0) = 0, f_y(-1,0) < 0, f_x(3,3) > 0, f_y(3,3) > 0,$ and f has a local maximum at $(3,-3)$.

35. Draw a possible contour diagram of a function with a saddle point at $(2,1)$, a local minimum at $(2,4)$, and no other critical points. Label the contours.

36. For constants a and b with $ab \neq 0$ and $ab \neq 1$, let

$$f(x,y) = ax^2 + by^2 - 2xy - 4x - 6y.$$

(a) Find the x- and y-coordinates of the critical point. Your answer will be in terms of a and b.

(b) If $a = b = 2$, is the critical point a local maximum, a local minimum, or neither? Give a reason for your answer.

(c) Classify the critical point for all values of a and b with $ab \neq 0$ and $ab \neq 1$.

37. (a) Find the critical point of $f(x,y) = (x^2-y)(x^2+y)$.

(b) Show that at the critical point, the discriminant $D = 0$, so the second-derivative test gives no information about the nature of the critical point.

(c) Sketch contours near the critical point to determine whether it is a local maximum, a local minimum, a saddle point, or none of these.

38. On a computer, draw contour diagrams for functions

$$f(x,y) = k(x^2 + y^2) - 2xy$$

for $k = -2, -1, 0, 1, 2$. Use these figures to classify the critical point at $(0,0)$ for each value of k. Explain your observations using the discriminant, D.

39. The behavior of a function can be complicated near a critical point where $D = 0$. Suppose that

$$f(x,y) = x^3 - 3xy^2.$$

Show that there is one critical point at $(0,0)$ and that $D = 0$ there. Show that the contour for $f(x,y) = 0$ consists of three lines intersecting at the origin and that these lines divide the plane into six regions around the origin where f alternates from positive to negative. Sketch a contour diagram for f near $(0,0)$. The graph of this function is called a *monkey saddle*.

40. The contour diagrams for four functions $z = f(x,y)$ are in (a)–(d). Each function has a critical point with $z = 0$ at the origin. Graphs (I)–(IV) show the value of z for these four functions on a small circle around the origin, expressed as function of θ, the angle between the positive x-axis and a line through the origin. Match the contour diagrams (a)–(d) with the graphs (I)–(IV). Classify the critical points as local maxima, local minima or saddle points.

Strengthen Your Understanding

In Problems 41–43, explain what is wrong with the statement.

41. If $f_x = f_y = 0$ at $(1,3)$, then f has a local maximum or local minimum at $(1,3)$.

42. For $f(x,y)$, if $D = f_{xx}f_{yy} - (f_{xy})^2 = 0$ at (a,b), then (a,b) is a saddle point.

43. A critical point (a,b) for the function f must be a local minimum if both cross-sections for $x = a$ and $y = b$ are concave up.

In Problems 44–45, give an example of:

44. A nonlinear function having no critical points

45. A function $f(x,y)$ with a local maximum at $(2,-3,4)$.

Are the statements in Problems 46–56 true or false? Give reasons for your answer.

46. If $f_x(P_0) = f_y(P_0) = 0$, then P_0 is a critical point of f.

47. If $f_x(P_0) = f_y(P_0) = 0$, then P_0 is a local maximum or local minimum of f.

48. If P_0 is a critical point of f, then P_0 is either a local maximum or local minimum of f.

49. If P_0 is a local maximum or local minimum of f, and not on the boundary of the domain of f, then P_0 is a critical point of f.

50. The function $f(x,y) = \sqrt{x^2 + y^2}$ has a local minimum at the origin.

51. The function $f(x,y) = x^2 - y^2$ has a local minimum at the origin.

52. If f has a local minimum at P_0 then so does the function $g(x, y) = f(x, y) + 5$.

53. If f has a local minimum at P_0 then the function $g(x, y) = -f(x, y)$ has a local maximum at P_0.

54. Every function has at least one local maximum.

55. If P_0 is a local maximum of f, then $f(a, b) \leq f(P_0)$ for all points (a, b) in 2-space.

56. If P_0 is a local maximum of f, then P_0 is also a global maximum of f.

15.2 OPTIMIZATION

Suppose we want to find the highest and the lowest points in Colorado. A contour map is shown in Figure 15.19. The highest point is the top of a mountain peak (point A on the map, Mt. Elbert, 14,440 feet high). What about the lowest point? Colorado does not have large pits without drainage, like Death Valley in California. A drop of rain falling at any point in Colorado will eventually flow out of the state. If there is no local minimum inside the state, where is the lowest point? It must be on the state boundary at a point where a river is flowing out of the state (point B where the Arikaree River leaves the state, 3,315 feet high). The highest point in Colorado is a global maximum for the elevation function in Colorado and the lowest point is the global minimum.

Figure 15.19: The highest and lowest points in the state of Colorado

In general, if we are given a function f defined on a region R, we say:

- f has a **global maximum on** R at the point P_0 if $f(P_0) \geq f(P)$ for all points P in R.
- f has a **global minimum on** R at the point P_0 if $f(P_0) \leq f(P)$ for all points P in R.

The process of finding a global maximum or minimum for a function f on a region R is called *optimization*. If the region R is not stated explicitly, we take it to be the whole xy-plane unless the context of the problem suggests otherwise.

How Do We Find Global Maxima and Minima?

As the Colorado example illustrates, a global extremum can occur either at a critical point inside the region or at a point on the boundary of the region. This is analogous to single-variable calculus, where a function achieves its global extrema on an interval either at a critical point inside the interval or at an endpoint of the interval.

To locate **global maxima and minima**:

- Find the critical points.
- Investigate whether the critical points give global maxima or minima.

Not all functions have a global maximum or minimum: it depends on the function and the region. First, we consider applications in which global extrema are expected from practical considerations. At the end of this section, we examine the conditions that lead to global extrema. In general, the fact that a function has a single local maximum or minimum does not guarantee that the point is the global maximum or minimum. (See Problem 26.) An exception is if the function is quadratic, in which case the local maximum or minimum is the global maximum or minimum. (See Example 1 on page 831 and Example 5 on page 834.)

Maximizing Profit and Minimizing Cost

In planning production of an item, a company often chooses the combination of price and quantity that maximizes its profit. We use

$$\text{Profit} = \text{Revenue} - \text{Cost},$$

and, provided the price is constant,

$$\text{Revenue} = \text{Price} \cdot \text{Quantity} = pq.$$

In addition, we need to know how the cost and price depend on quantity.

Example 1   A company manufactures two items which are sold in two separate markets where it has a monopoly. The quantities, q_1 and q_2, demanded by consumers, and the prices, p_1 and p_2 (in dollars), of each item are related by

$$p_1 = 600 - 0.3q_1 \quad \text{and} \quad p_2 = 500 - 0.2q_2.$$

Thus, if the price for either item increases, the demand for it decreases. The company's total production cost is given by

$$C = 16 + 1.2q_1 + 1.5q_2 + 0.2q_1q_2.$$

To maximize its total profit, how much of each product should be produced? What is the maximum profit? [2]

Solution   The total revenue, R, is the sum of the revenues, p_1q_1 and p_2q_2, from each market. Substituting for p_1 and p_2, we get

$$R = p_1q_1 + p_2q_2 = (600 - 0.3q_1)q_1 + (500 - 0.2q_2)q_2$$
$$= 600q_1 - 0.3q_1^2 + 500q_2 - 0.2q_2^2.$$

Thus, the total profit P is given by

$$P = R - C = 600q_1 - 0.3q_1^2 + 500q_2 - 0.2q_2^2 - (16 + 1.2q_1 + 1.5q_2 + 0.2q_1q_2)$$
$$= -16 + 598.8q_1 - 0.3q_1^2 + 498.5q_2 - 0.2q_2^2 - 0.2q_1q_2.$$

Since q_1 and q_2 cannot be negative,[3] the region we consider is the first quadrant with boundary $q_1 = 0$ and $q_2 = 0$.

To maximize P, we look for critical points by setting the partial derivatives equal to 0:

$$\frac{\partial P}{\partial q_1} = 598.8 - 0.6q_1 - 0.2q_2 = 0,$$

$$\frac{\partial P}{\partial q_2} = 498.5 - 0.4q_2 - 0.2q_1 = 0.$$

---

[2] Adapted from M. Rosser, *Basic Mathematics for Economists*, p. 316 (New York: Routledge, 1993).
[3] Restricting prices to be nonnegative further restricts the region but does not alter the solution.

Since grad P is defined everywhere, the only critical points of P are those where grad $P = \vec{0}$. Thus, solving for q_1, and q_2, we find that

$$q_1 = 699.1 \quad \text{and} \quad q_2 = 896.7.$$

The corresponding prices are

$$p_1 = 390.27 \quad \text{and} \quad p_2 = 320.66.$$

To see whether or not we have found a local maximum, we compute second partial derivatives:

$$\frac{\partial^2 P}{\partial q_1^2} = -0.6, \quad \frac{\partial^2 P}{\partial q_2^2} = -0.4, \quad \frac{\partial^2 P}{\partial q_1 \partial q_2} = -0.2,$$

so,

$$D = \frac{\partial^2 P}{\partial q_1^2}\frac{\partial^2 P}{\partial q_2^2} - \left(\frac{\partial^2 P}{\partial q_1 \partial q_2}\right)^2 = (-0.6)(-0.4) - (-0.2)^2 = 0.2.$$

Therefore we have found a local maximum. The graph of P is an upside-down paraboloid, so $(699.1, 896.7)$ is a global maximum. This point is within the region, so points on the boundary give smaller values of P.

The company should produce 699.1 units of the first item priced at \$390.27 per unit, and 896.7 units of the second item priced at \$320.66 per unit. The maximum profit $P(699.1, 896.7) \approx$ \$433,000.

Example 2   A delivery of 480 cubic meters of gravel is to be made to a landfill. The trucker plans to purchase an open-top box in which to transport the gravel in numerous trips. The total cost to the trucker is the cost of the box plus \$80 per trip. The box must have height 2 meters, but the trucker can choose the length and width. The cost of the box is \$100/m² for the ends, \$50/m² for the sides and \$200/m² for the bottom. Notice the tradeoff: A smaller box is cheaper to buy but requires more trips. What size box should the trucker buy to minimize the total cost? [4]

Solution   We first get an algebraic expression for the trucker's cost. Let the length of the box be x meters and the width be y meters; the height is 2 meters. (See Figure 15.20.)

Table 15.2   *Trucker's itemized cost*

Expense	Cost in dollars
Travel: $480/(2xy)$ at \$80/trip	$(240 \cdot 80)/(xy)$
Ends: 2 at \$100/m² $\cdot$ $2y$ m²	$400y$
Sides: 2 at \$50/m² $\cdot$ $2x$ m²	$200x$
Bottom: 1 at \$200/m² $\cdot$ xy m²	$200xy$

Figure 15.20: The box for transporting gravel

The volume of the box is $2xy$ m³, so delivery of 480 m³ of gravel requires $480/(2xy)$ trips. The number of trips is a whole number; however, we treat it as continuous so that we can optimize using derivatives. The trucker's cost is itemized in Table 15.2. The problem is to minimize

$$\text{Total cost} = \frac{240 \cdot 80}{xy} + 400y + 200x + 200xy = 200\left(\frac{96}{xy} + 2y + x + xy\right).$$

---

[4] Adapted from Claude McMillan, Jr., *Mathematical Programming*, 2nd ed., p. 156-157 (New York: Wiley, 1978).

The length and width of the box must be positive. Thus, the region is the first quadrant but it does not contain the boundary, $x = 0$ and $y = 0$.

Our problem is to minimize

$$f(x, y) = \frac{96}{xy} + 2y + x + xy.$$

The critical points of this function occur where

$$f_x(x, y) = -\frac{96}{x^2 y} + 1 + y = 0$$

$$f_y(x, y) = -\frac{96}{xy^2} + 2 + x = 0.$$

We put the $96/(x^2 y)$ and $96/(xy^2)$ terms on the other side of the the equation, divide, and simplify:

$$\frac{96/(x^2 y)}{96/(xy^2)} = \frac{1+y}{2+x} \quad \text{so} \quad \frac{y}{x} = \frac{1+y}{2+x} \quad \text{giving} \quad 2y = x.$$

Substituting $x = 2y$ in the equation $f_y(x, y) = 0$ gives

$$-\frac{96}{2y \cdot y^2} + 2 + 2y = 0$$

$$y^4 + y^3 - 24 = 0.$$

The only positive solution to this equation is $y = 2$, so the only critical point in the region is $(4, 2)$.

To check that the critical point is a local minimum, we use the second-derivative test. Since

$$D(4, 2) = f_{xx} f_{yy} - (f_{xy})^2 = \frac{192}{4^3 \cdot 2} \cdot \frac{192}{4 \cdot 2^3} - \left(\frac{96}{4^2 \cdot 2^2} + 1 \right)^2 = 9 - \frac{25}{4} > 0$$

and $f_{xx}(4, 2) > 0$, the point $(4, 2)$ is a local minimum. Since the value of f increases without bound as x or y increases without bound and as $x \to 0^+$ and $y \to 0^+$, it can be shown that $(4, 2)$ is a global minimum. (See Problem 29.) Thus, the optimal box is 4 meters long and 2 meters wide.

Fitting a Line to Data: Least Squares

Suppose we want to fit the "best" line to some data in the plane. We measure the distance from a line to the data points by adding the squares of the vertical distances from each point to the line. The smaller this sum of squares is, the better the line fits the data. The line with the minimum sum of square distances is called the *least squares line*, or the *regression line*. If the data is nearly linear, the least squares line is a good fit; otherwise it may not be. (See Figure 15.21.)

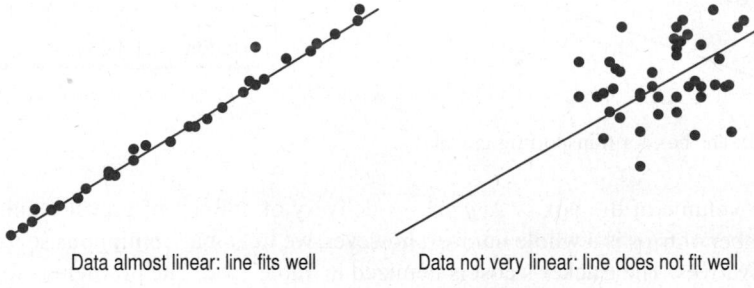

Data almost linear: line fits well   Data not very linear: line does not fit well

Figure 15.21: Fitting lines to data points

Example 3   Find a least squares line for the following data points: $(1, 1)$, $(2, 1)$, and $(3, 3)$.

Solution   Suppose the line has equation $y = b + mx$. If we find b and m then we have found the line. So, for this problem, b and m are the two variables. Any values of m and b are possible, so this is an unconstrained problem. We want to minimize the function $f(b, m)$ that gives the sum of the three squared vertical distances from the points to the line in Figure 15.22.

Figure 15.22: The least squares line minimizes the sum of the squares of these vertical distances

The vertical distance from the point $(1, 1)$ to the line is the difference in the y-coordinates $1 - (b + m)$; similarly for the other points. Thus, the sum of squares is

$$f(b, m) = (1 - (b + m))^2 + (1 - (b + 2m))^2 + (3 - (b + 3m))^2.$$

To minimize f we look for critical points. First we differentiate f with respect to b:

$$\frac{\partial f}{\partial b} = -2(1 - (b + m)) - 2(1 - (b + 2m)) - 2(3 - (b + 3m))$$
$$= -2 + 2b + 2m - 2 + 2b + 4m - 6 + 2b + 6m$$
$$= -10 + 6b + 12m.$$

Now we differentiate with respect to m:

$$\frac{\partial f}{\partial m} = 2(1 - (b + m))(-1) + 2(1 - (b + 2m))(-2) + 2(3 - (b + 3m))(-3)$$
$$= -2 + 2b + 2m - 4 + 4b + 8m - 18 + 6b + 18m$$
$$= -24 + 12b + 28m.$$

The equations $\dfrac{\partial f}{\partial b} = 0$ and $\dfrac{\partial f}{\partial m} = 0$ give a system of two linear equations in two unknowns:

$$-10 + 6b + 12m = 0,$$
$$-24 + 12b + 28m = 0.$$

The solution to this pair of equations is the critical point $b = -1/3$ and $m = 1$. Since

$$D = f_{bb}f_{mm} - (f_{mb})^2 = (6)(28) - 12^2 = 24 \quad \text{and} \quad f_{bb} = 6 > 0,$$

we have found a local minimum. The graph of $f(b, m)$ is a parabolic bowl, so the local minimum is the global minimum of f. Thus, the least squares line is

$$y = x - \frac{1}{3}.$$

As a check, notice that the line $y = x$ passes through the points $(1, 1)$ and $(3, 3)$. It is reasonable that introducing the point $(2, 1)$ moves the y-intercept down from 0 to $-1/3$.

The general formulas for the slope and y-intercept of a least squares line are in Project 2 on page 865. Many calculators have built-in formulas for b and m, as well as for the *correlation coefficient*, which measures how well the data points fit the least squares line.

How Do We Know Whether a Function Has a Global Maximum or Minimum?

Under what circumstances does a function of two variables have a global maximum or minimum? The next example shows that a function may have both a global maximum and a global minimum on a region, or just one, or neither.

Example 4   Investigate the global maxima and minima of the following functions:

(a) $h(x, y) = 1 + x^2 + y^2$ on the disk $x^2 + y^2 \leq 1$.
(b) $f(x, y) = x^2 - 2x + y^2 - 4y + 5$ on the xy-plane.
(c) $g(x, y) = x^2 - y^2$ on the xy-plane.

Solution

(a) The graph of $h(x, y) = 1 + x^2 + y^2$ is a bowl-shaped paraboloid with a global minimum of 1 at $(0, 0)$, and a global maximum of 2 on the edge of the region, $x^2 + y^2 = 1$.

(b) The graph of f in Figure 15.5 on page 831 shows that f has a global minimum at the point $(1, 2)$ and no global maximum (because the value of f increases without bound as $x \to \infty$, $y \to \infty$).

(c) The graph of g in Figure 15.7 on page 832 shows that g has no global maximum because $g(x, y) \to \infty$ as $x \to \infty$ if y is constant. Similarly, g has no global minimum because $g(x, y) \to -\infty$ as $y \to \infty$ if x is constant.

Sometimes a function is guaranteed to have a global maximum and minimum. For example, a continuous function, $h(x)$, of one variable has a global maximum and minimum on every closed interval $a \leq x \leq b$. On a non-closed interval, such as $a \leq x < b$ or $a < x < b$, or on an unbounded interval, such as $a < x < \infty$, then h may not have a maximum or minimum value.

What is the situation for functions of two variables? As it turns out, a similar result is true for continuous functions defined on regions which are closed and bounded, analogous to the closed and bounded interval $a \leq x \leq b$. In everyday language we say

- A **closed** region is one which contains its boundary;
- A **bounded** region is one which does not stretch to infinity in any direction.

More precise definitions follow. Suppose R is a region in 2-space. A point (x_0, y_0) is a *boundary point* of R if, for every $r > 0$, the disk $(x - x_0)^2 + (y - y_0)^2 < r^2$ with center (x_0, y_0) and radius r contains both points which are in R and points which are not in R. See Figure 15.23. A point (x_0, y_0) can be a boundary point of the region R without belonging to R. A point (x_0, y_0) in R is an *interior point* if it is not a boundary point; thus, for small enough $r > 0$, the disk of radius r centered at (x_0, y_0) lies entirely in the region R. See Figure 15.24. The collection of all the boundary points is the *boundary* of R and the collection of all the interior points is the *interior* of R. The region R is *closed* if it contains its boundary; it is *open* if every point in R is an interior point.

A region R in 2-space is *bounded* if the distance between every point (x, y) in R and the origin is less than some constant K. Closed and bounded regions in 3-space are defined in the same way.

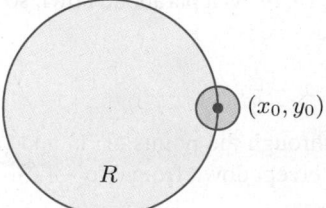

Figure 15.23: Boundary point (x_0, y_0) of R

Figure 15.24: Interior point (x_0, y_0) of R

Example 5   (a) The square $-1 \leq x \leq 1$, $-1 \leq y \leq 1$ is closed and bounded.
(b) The first quadrant $x \geq 0$, $y \geq 0$ is closed but is not bounded.

(c) The disk $x^2 + y^2 < 1$ is open and bounded, but is not closed.

(d) The half-plane $y > 0$ is open, but is neither closed nor bounded.

The reason that closed and bounded regions are useful is the following theorem, which is also true for functions of three or more variables:[5]

Theorem 15.1: Extreme Value Theorem for Multivariable Functions

If f is a continuous function on a closed and bounded region R, then f has a global maximum at some point (x_0, y_0) in R and a global minimum at some point (x_1, y_1) in R.

If f is not continuous or the region R is not closed and bounded, there is no guarantee that f achieves a global maximum or global minimum on R. In Example 4, the function g is continuous but does not achieve a global maximum or minimum in 2-space, a region which is closed but not bounded. Example 6 illustrates what can go wrong when the region is bounded but not closed.

Example 6   Does the function f have a global maximum or minimum on the region R given by $0 < x^2 + y^2 \le 1$?

$$f(x, y) = \frac{1}{x^2 + y^2}$$

Solution   The region R is bounded, but it is not closed since it does not contain the boundary point $(0, 0)$. We see from the graph of $z = f(x, y)$ in Figure 15.25 that f has a global minimum on the circle $x^2 + y^2 = 1$. However, $f(x, y) \to \infty$ as $(x, y) \to (0, 0)$, so f has no global maximum.

Figure 15.25: Graph showing $f(x, y) = \frac{1}{x^2+y^2}$ has no global maximum on $0 < x^2 + y^2 \le 1$

Exercises and Problems for Section 15.2

Exercises

1. By looking at the weather map in Figure 12.1 on page 666, find the maximum and minimum daily high temperatures in the states of Mississippi, Alabama, Pennsylvania, New York, California, Arizona, and Massachusetts.

In Exercises 2–4, estimate the position and approximate value of the global maxima and minima on the region shown.

2.

3.

4.

---

[5]For a proof, see W. Rudin, *Principles of Mathematical Analysis*, 2nd ed., p. 89 (New York: McGraw-Hill, 1976).

In Exercises 5–7, find the global maximum and minimum of the function on $-1 \le x \le 1$, $-1 \le y \le 1$, and say whether it occurs on the boundary of the square. [Hint: Use graphs.]

5. $z = x^2 + y^2$ **6.** $z = -x^2 - y^2$ **7.** $z = x^2 - y^2$

In Exercises 8–12, do the functions have global maxima and minima in the xy-plane?

8. $f(x, y) = x^2 - 2y^2$ **9.** $g(x, y) = x^2 y^2$

10. $h(x, y) = x^3 + y^3$ **11.** $f(x, y) = -2x^2 - 7y^2$

12. $f(x, y) = x^2/2 + 3y^3 + 9y^2 - 3x$

Problems

13. **(a)** Compute and classify the critical points of $f(x, y) = 2x^2 - 3xy + 8y^2 + x - y$.
   (b) By completing the square, plot the contour diagram of f and show that the local extremum found in part (a) is a global one.

14. A missile has a guidance device which is sensitive to both temperature, $t°C$, and humidity, h. The range in km over which the missile can be controlled is given by

   Range $= 27,800 - 5t^2 - 6ht - 3h^2 + 400t + 300h$.

   What are the optimal atmospheric conditions for controlling the missile?

15. A closed rectangular box has volume 32 cm^3. What are the lengths of the edges giving the minimum surface area?

16. A closed rectangular box with faces parallel to the co-ordinate planes has one bottom corner at the origin and the opposite top corner in the first octant on the plane $3x + 2y + z = 1$. What is the maximum volume of such a box?

17. An international airline has a regulation that each passenger can carry a suitcase having the sum of its width, length and height less than or equal to 135 cm. Find the dimensions of the suitcase of maximum volume that a passenger may carry under this regulation.

18. Design a rectangular milk carton box of width w, length l, and height h which holds 512 cm^3 of milk. The sides of the box cost 1 cent/cm^2 and the top and bottom cost 2 cent/cm^2. Find the dimensions of the box that minimize the total cost of materials used.

19. Find the point on the plane $3x + 2y + z = 1$ that is closest to the origin by minimizing the square of the distance.

20. What is the shortest distance from the surface $xy + 3x + z^2 = 9$ to the origin?

21. For constants a, b, and c, let $f(x, y) = ax + by + c$ be a linear function, and let R be a region in the xy-plane.

   (a) If R is any disk, show that the maximum and minimum values of f on R occur on the boundary of the disk.
   (b) If R is any rectangle, show that the maximum and minimum values of f on R occur at the corners of the rectangle. They may occur at other points of the rectangle as well.

(c) Use a graph of the plane $z = f(x, y)$ to explain your answers in parts (a) and (b).

22. Two products are manufactured in quantities q_1 and q_2 and sold at prices of p_1 and p_2, respectively. The cost of producing them is given by

$$C = 2q_1^2 + 2q_2^2 + 10.$$

   (a) Find the maximum profit that can be made, assuming the prices are fixed.
   (b) Find the rate of change of that maximum profit as p_1 increases.

23. A company operates two plants which manufacture the same item and whose total cost functions are

$$C_1 = 8.5 + 0.03q_1^2 \quad \text{and} \quad C_2 = 5.2 + 0.04q_2^2,$$

where q_1 and q_2 are the quantities produced by each plant. The company is a monopoly. The total quantity demanded, $q = q_1 + q_2$, is related to the price, p, by

$$p = 60 - 0.04q.$$

How much should each plant produce in order to maximize the company's profit?[6]

24. The quantity of a product demanded by consumers is a function of its price. The quantity of one product demanded may also depend on the price of other products. For example, the demand for tea is affected by the price of coffee; the demand for cars is affected by the price of gas. The quantities demanded, q_1 and q_2, of two products depend on their prices, p_1 and p_2, as follows:

$$q_1 = 150 - 2p_1 - p_2$$

$$q_2 = 200 - p_1 - 3p_2.$$

   (a) What does the fact that the coefficients of p_1 and p_2 are negative tell you? Give an example of two products that might be related this way.
   (b) If one manufacturer sells both products, how should the prices be set to generate the maximum possible revenue? What is that maximum possible revenue?

[6]Adapted from M. Rosser, *Basic Mathematics for Economists*, p. 318 (New York: Routledge, 1993).

25. A company manufactures a product which requires capital and labor to produce. The quantity, Q, of the product manufactured is given by the Cobb-Douglas function

$$Q = AK^a L^b,$$

where K is the quantity of capital; L is the quantity of labor used; and A, a, and b are positive constants with $0 < a < 1$ and $0 < b < 1$. One unit of capital costs $\$k$ and one unit of labor costs $\$\ell$. The price of the product is fixed at $\$p$ per unit.

   (a) If $a + b < 1$, how much capital and labor should the company use to maximize its profit?
   (b) Is there a maximum profit in the case $a + b = 1$? What about $a + b \geq 1$? Explain.

26. Let $f(x,y) = x^2(y+1)^3 + y^2$. Show that f has only one critical point, namely $(0,0)$, and that point is a local minimum but not a global minimum. Contrast this with the case of a function with a single local minimum in one-variable calculus.

27. Find the parabola of the form $y = ax^2 + b$ which best fits the points $(1,0)$, $(2,2)$, $(3,4)$ by minimizing the sum of squares, S, given by

$$S = (a+b)^2 + (4a+b-2)^2 + (9a+b-4)^2.$$

28. Find the least squares line for the data points $(0,4)$, $(1,3)$, $(2,1)$.

29. Let $f(x,y) = 80/(xy) + 20y + 10x + 10xy$ in the region R where $x, y > 0$.

   (a) Explain why $f(x,y) > f(2,1)$ at every point in R where
   (i) $x > 20$ (ii) $y > 20$
   (iii) $x < 0.01$ and $y \leq 20$
   (iv) $y < 0.01$ and $x \leq 20$
   (b) Explain why f must have a global minimum at a critical point in R.
   (c) Explain why f must have a global minimum in R at the point $(2,1)$.

30. Let $f(x,y) = 2/x + 3/y + 4x + 5y$ in the region R where $x, y > 0$.

   (a) Explain why f must have a global minimum at some point in R.
   (b) Find the global minimum.

31. (a) The energy, E, required to compress a gas from a fixed initial pressure P_0 to a fixed final pressure P_F through an intermediate pressure p is[7]

$$E = \left(\frac{p}{P_0}\right)^2 + \left(\frac{P_F}{p}\right)^2 - 1.$$

   How should p be chosen to minimize the energy?
   (b) Now suppose the compression takes place in two stages with two intermediate pressures, p_1 and p_2. What choices of p_1 and p_2 minimize the energy if

$$E = \left(\frac{p_1}{P_0}\right)^2 + \left(\frac{p_2}{p_1}\right)^2 + \left(\frac{P_F}{p_2}\right)^2 - 2?$$

32. The Dorfman-Steiner rule shows how a company which has a monopoly should set the price, p, of its product and how much advertising, a, it should buy. The price of advertising is p_a per unit. The quantity, q, of the product sold is given by $q = Kp^{-E}a^\theta$, where $K > 0$, $E > 1$, and $0 < \theta < 1$ are constants. The cost to the company to make each item is c.

   (a) How does the quantity sold, q, change if the price, p, increases? If the quantity of advertising, a, increases?
   (b) Show that the partial derivatives can be written in the form $\partial q/\partial p = -Eq/p$ and $\partial q/\partial a = \theta q/a$.
   (c) Explain why profit, π, is given by $\pi = pq - cq - p_a a$.
   (d) If the company wants to maximize profit, what must be true of the partial derivatives, $\partial\pi/\partial p$ and $\partial\pi/\partial a$?
   (e) Find $\partial\pi/\partial p$ and $\partial\pi/\partial a$.
   (f) Use your answers to parts (d) and (e) to show that at maximum profit,

$$\frac{p-c}{p} = \frac{1}{E} \quad \text{and} \quad \frac{p-c}{p_a} = \frac{a}{\theta q}.$$

   (g) By dividing your answers in part (f), show that at maximum profit,

$$\frac{p_a a}{pq} = \frac{\theta}{E}.$$

   This is the Dorfman-Steiner rule, that the ratio of the advertising budget to revenue does not depend on the price of advertising.

Strengthen Your Understanding

In Problems 33–35, explain what is wrong with the statement.

33. A function having no critical points in a region R cannot have a global maximum in the region.

34. No continuous function has a global minimum on an unbounded region R.

35. If $f(x,y)$ has a local maximum value of 1 at the origin, then the global maximum is 1.

In Problems 36–37, give an example of:

36. A continuous function $f(x,y)$ that has no global maximum and no global minimum on the xy-plane.

37. A function $f(x,y)$ and a region R such that the maximum value of f on R is on the boundary of R.

---

[7]Adapted from Aris Rutherford, *Discrete Dynamic Programming*, p. 35 (New York: Blaisdell, 1964).

Are the statements in Problems 38–46 true or false? Give reasons for your answer.

38. If P_0 is a global maximum of f, where f is defined on all of 2-space, then P_0 is also a local maximum of f.

39. Every function has a global maximum.

40. The region consisting of all points (x, y) satisfying $x^2 + y^2 < 1$ is bounded.

41. The region consisting of all points (x, y) satisfying $x^2 + y^2 < 1$ is closed.

42. The function $f(x, y) = x^2 + y^2$ has a global minimum on the region $x^2 + y^2 < 1$.

43. The function $f(x, y) = x^2 + y^2$ has a global maximum on the region $x^2 + y^2 < 1$.

44. If P and Q are two distinct points in 2-space, and f has a global maximum at P, then f cannot have a global maximum at Q.

45. The function $f(x, y) = \sin(1 + e^{xy})$ must have a global minimum in the square region $0 \leq x \leq 1, 0 \leq y \leq 1$.

46. If P_0 is a global minimum of f on a closed and bounded region, then P_0 need not be a critical point of f.

15.3 CONSTRAINED OPTIMIZATION: LAGRANGE MULTIPLIERS

Many, perhaps most, real optimization problems are constrained by external circumstances. For example, a city wanting to build a public transportation system has only a limited number of tax dollars it can spend on the project. In this section, we see how to find an optimum value under such constraints.

In Section 15.2, we saw how to optimize a function $f(x, y)$ on a region R. If the region R is the entire xy-plane, we have *unconstrained optimization*; if the region R is not the entire xy-plane, that is, if x or y is restricted in some way, then we have *constrained optimization*.

Graphical Approach: Maximizing Production Subject to a Budget Constraint

Suppose we want to maximize the production under a budget constraint. Suppose production, f, is a function of two variables, x and y, which are quantities of two raw materials, and that

$$f(x, y) = x^{2/3} y^{1/3}.$$

If x and y are purchased at prices of p_1 and p_2 thousands of dollars per unit, what is the maximum production f that can be obtained with a budget of c thousand dollars?

To maximize f without regard to the budget, we simply increase x and y. However, the budget constraint prevents us from increasing x and y beyond a certain point. Exactly how does the budget constrain us? With prices of p_1 and p_2, the amount spent on x is $p_1 x$ and the amount spent on y is $p_2 y$, so we must have

$$g(x, y) = p_1 x + p_2 y \leq c,$$

where $g(x, y)$ is the total cost of the raw materials and c is the budget in thousands of dollars.

Let's look at the case when $p_1 = p_2 = 1$ and $c = 3.78$. Then

$$x + y \leq 3.78.$$

Figure 15.26 shows some contours of f and the budget constraint represented by the line $x + y = 3.78$. Any point on or below the line represents a pair of values of x and y that we can afford. A point on the line completely exhausts the budget, while a point below the line represents values of x and y which can be bought without using up the budget. Any point above the line represents a pair of values that we cannot afford.

To maximize f, we find the point which lies on the level curve with the largest possible value of f *and* which lies within the budget. The point must lie on the budget constraint because we should spend all the available money. Unless we are at the point where the budget constraint is tangent to the contour $f = 2$, we can increase f by moving along the line representing the budget constraint in Figure 15.26. For example, if we are on the line to the left of the point of tangency, moving right on the constraint will increase f; if we are on the line to the right of the point of tangency, moving left will increase f. Thus, the maximum value of f on the budget constraint occurs at the point where the budget constraint is tangent to the contour $f = 2$.

Figure 15.26: Optimal point, P, where budget constraint
is tangent to a level of production function

Analytical Solution: Lagrange Multipliers

Figure 15.26 suggests that maximum production is achieved at the point where the budget constraint is tangent to a level curve of the production function. The method of Lagrange multipliers uses this fact in algebraic form. Figure 15.27 shows that at the optimum point, P, the gradient of f and the normal to the budget line $g(x, y) = 3.78$ are parallel. Thus, at P, grad f and grad g are parallel, so for some scalar λ, called the *Lagrange multiplier,*

$$\text{grad } f = \lambda \, \text{grad } g.$$

Since grad $f = \left(\frac{2}{3}x^{-1/3}y^{1/3}\right)\vec{i} + \left(\frac{1}{3}x^{2/3}y^{-2/3}\right)\vec{j}$ and grad $g = \vec{i} + \vec{j}$, equating components gives

$$\frac{2}{3}x^{-1/3}y^{1/3} = \lambda \quad \text{and} \quad \frac{1}{3}x^{2/3}y^{-2/3} = \lambda.$$

Eliminating λ gives

$$\frac{2}{3}x^{-1/3}y^{1/3} = \frac{1}{3}x^{2/3}y^{-2/3}, \quad \text{which leads to} \quad 2y = x.$$

Since the constraint $x + y = 3.78$ must be satisfied, we have $x = 2.52$ and $y = 1.26$. Then

$$f(2.52, 1.26) = (2.52)^{2/3}(1.26)^{1/3} \approx 2.$$

As before, we see that the maximum value of f is approximately 2. Thus, to maximize production on a budget of \$3780, we should use 2.52 units of one raw material and 1.26 units of the other.

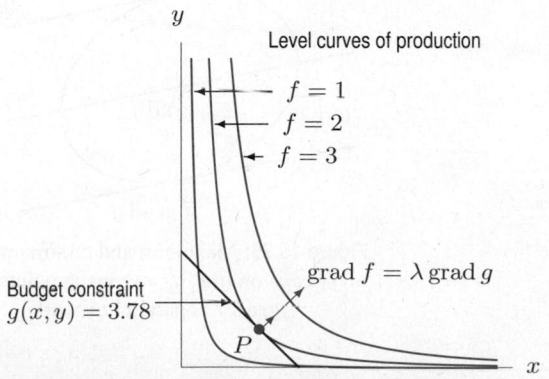

Figure 15.27: At the point, P, of maximum production,
the vectors grad f and grad g are parallel

Lagrange Multipliers in General

Suppose we want to optimize an *objective function* $f(x, y)$ subject to a *constraint* $g(x, y) = c$. We look for extrema among the points which satisfy the constraint. We make the following definition.

Suppose P_0 is a point satisfying the constraint $g(x, y) = c$.
- f has a **local maximum** at P_0 **subject to the constraint** if $f(P_0) \geq f(P)$ for all points P near P_0 satisfying the constraint.
- f has a **global maximum** at P_0 **subject to the constraint** if $f(P_0) \geq f(P)$ for all points P satisfying the constraint.

Local and global minima are defined similarly.

As we saw in the production example, constrained extrema occur at points of tangency of contours of f and g; they can also occur at endpoints of constraints. At a point of tangency, grad f is perpendicular to the constraint and so parallel to grad g. At interior points on the constraint where grad f is not perpendicular to the constraint, the value of f can be increased or decreased by moving along the constraint. Therefore constrained extrema occur only at points where grad f and grad g are parallel or at endpoints of the constraint. (See Figure 15.28.) At points where the gradients are parallel, provided grad $g \neq \vec{0}$, there is a constant λ such that grad $f = \lambda$ grad g.

Optimizing f Subject to the Constraint $g = c$:
If a smooth function, f, has a maximum or minimum subject to a smooth constraint $g = c$ at a point P_0, then either P_0 satisfies the equations

$$\text{grad } f = \lambda \text{ grad } g \quad \text{and} \quad g = c,$$

or P_0 is an endpoint of the constraint, or grad $g(P_0) = \vec{0}$. To find P_0, compare values of f at the points satisfying these three conditions. The number λ is called the **Lagrange multiplier**.

If the set of points satisfying the constraint is closed and bounded, such as a circle or line segment, then there must be a global maximum and minimum of f subject to the constraint. If the constraint is not closed and bounded, such as a line or hyperbola, then there may or may not be a global maximum and minimum.

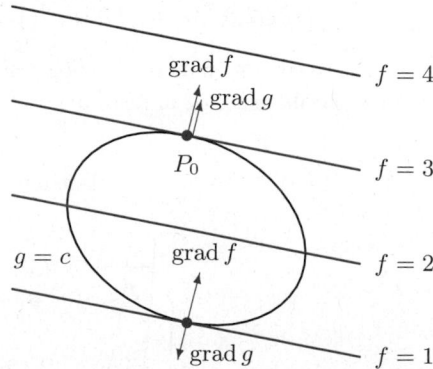

Figure 15.28: Maximum and minimum values of $f(x, y)$ on $g(x, y) = c$ are at points where grad f is parallel to grad g

Example 1   Find the maximum and minimum values of $x + y$ on the circle $x^2 + y^2 = 4$.

Solution   The objective function is

$$f(x, y) = x + y,$$

and the constraint is

$$g(x, y) = x^2 + y^2 = 4.$$

Since $\operatorname{grad} f = f_x \vec{i} + f_y \vec{j} = \vec{i} + \vec{j}$ and $\operatorname{grad} g = g_x \vec{i} + g_y \vec{j} = 2x\vec{i} + 2y\vec{j}$, the condition $\operatorname{grad} f = \lambda \operatorname{grad} g$ gives

$$1 = 2\lambda x \quad \text{and} \quad 1 = 2\lambda y,$$

so

$$x = y.$$

We also know that

$$x^2 + y^2 = 4,$$

giving $x = y = \sqrt{2}$ or $x = y = -\sqrt{2}$. The constraint has no endpoints (it's a circle) and $\operatorname{grad} g \neq \vec{0}$ on the circle, so we compare values of f at $(\sqrt{2}, \sqrt{2})$ and $(-\sqrt{2}, -\sqrt{2})$. Since $f(x, y) = x + y$, the maximum value of f is $f(\sqrt{2}, \sqrt{2}) = 2\sqrt{2}$; the minimum value is $f(-\sqrt{2}, -\sqrt{2}) = -2\sqrt{2}$. (See Figure 15.29.)

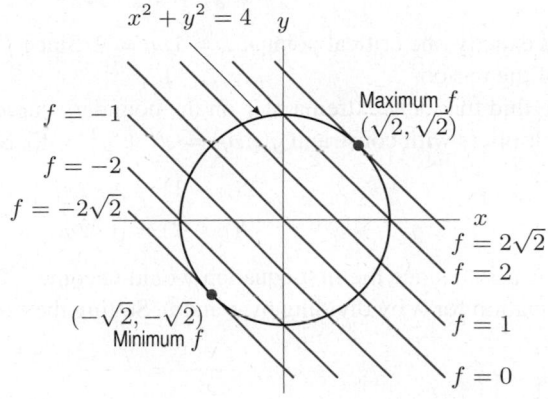

Figure 15.29: Maximum and minimum values of $f(x, y) = x + y$ on the circle $x^2 + y^2 = 4$ are at points where contours of f are tangent to the circle

How to Distinguish Maxima from Minima

There is a second-derivative test[8] for classifying the critical points of constrained optimization problems, but it is more complicated than the test in Section 15.1. However, a graph of the constraint and some contours usually shows which points are maxima, which points are minima, and which are neither.

Optimization with Inequality Constraints

The production problem that we looked at first was to maximize production $f(x, y)$ subject to a budget constraint

$$g(x, y) = p_1 x + p_2 y \leq c.$$

Since the inputs are nonnegative, $x \geq 0$ and $y \geq 0$, we have three inequality constraints, which restrict (x, y) to a region of the plane rather than to a curve in the plane. In principle, we should first check to see whether or not $f(x, y)$ has any critical points in the interior:

$$p_1 x + p_2 y < c, \qquad x > 0 \quad y > 0.$$

However, in the case of a budget constraint, we can see that the maximum of f must occur when the budget is exhausted, so we look for the maximum value of f on the boundary line:

$$p_1 x + p_2 y = c, \qquad x \geq 0 \quad y \geq 0.$$

[8]See J. E. Marsden and A. J. Tromba, *Vector Calculus*, 4th ed., p. 218 (New York: W.H. Freeman, 1996).

> **Strategy for Optimizing** $f(x, y)$ **Subject to the Constraint** $g(x, y) \leq c$
> - Find all points in the region $g(x, y) < c$ where grad f is zero or undefined.
> - Use Lagrange multipliers to find the local extrema of f on the boundary $g(x, y) = c$.
> - Evaluate f at the points found in the previous two steps and compare the values.

From Section 15.2 we know that if f is continuous on a closed and bounded region, R, then f is guaranteed to attain its global maximum and minimum values on R.

Example 2   Find the maximum and minimum values of $f(x, y) = (x - 1)^2 + (y - 2)^2$ subject to the constraint $x^2 + y^2 \leq 45$.

Solution   First, we look for all critical points of f in the interior of the region. Setting

$$f_x(x, y) = 2(x - 1) = 0$$
$$f_y(x, y) = 2(y - 2) = 0.$$

we find f has exactly one critical point at $x = 1$, $y = 2$. Since $1^2 + 2^2 < 45$, that critical point is in the interior of the region.

Next, we find the local extrema of f on the boundary curve $x^2 + y^2 = 45$. To do this, we use Lagrange multipliers with constraint $g(x, y) = x^2 + y^2 = 45$. Setting grad $f = \lambda$ grad g, we get

$$2(x - 1) = \lambda \cdot 2x,$$
$$2(y - 2) = \lambda \cdot 2y.$$

We can't have $x = 0$ since the first equation would become $-2 = 0$. Similarly, $y \neq 0$. So we can solve each equation for λ by dividing by x and y. Setting the expressions for λ equal gives

$$\frac{x - 1}{x} = \frac{y - 2}{y},$$

so

$$y = 2x.$$

Combining this with the constraint $x^2 + y^2 = 45$, we get

$$5x^2 = 45$$

so

$$x = \pm 3.$$

Since $y = 2x$, we have possible local extrema at $x = 3$, $y = 6$ and $x = -3$, $y = -6$.

We conclude that the only candidates for the maximum and minimum values of f in the region occur at $(1, 2)$, $(3, 6)$, and $(-3, -6)$. Evaluating f at these three points, we find

$$f(1, 2) = 0, \qquad f(3, 6) = 20, \qquad f(-3, -6) = 80.$$

Therefore, the minimum value of f is 0 at $(1, 2)$ and the maximum value is 80 at $(-3, -6)$.

The Meaning of λ

In the uses of Lagrange multipliers so far, we never found (or needed) the value of λ. However, λ does have a practical interpretation. In the production example, we wanted to maximize

$$f(x, y) = x^{2/3} y^{1/3}$$

subject to the constraint

$$g(x, y) = x + y = 3.78.$$

We solved the equations

$$\frac{2}{3}x^{-1/3}y^{1/3} = \lambda,$$

$$\frac{1}{3}x^{2/3}y^{-2/3} = \lambda,$$

$$x + y = 3.78,$$

to get $x = 2.52, y = 1.26$ and $f(2.52, 1.26) \approx 2$. Continuing to find λ gives us

$$\lambda \approx 0.53.$$

Now we do another, apparently unrelated, calculation. Suppose our budget is increased slightly, from 3.78 to 4.78, giving a new budget constraint of $x + y = 4.78$. Then the corresponding solution is at $x = 3.19$ and $y = 1.59$ and the new maximum value (instead of $f = 2$) is

$$f = (3.19)^{2/3}(1.59)^{1/3} \approx 2.53.$$

Notice that the amount by which f has increased is 0.53, the value of λ. Thus, in this example, the value of λ represents the extra production achieved by increasing the budget by one—in other words, the extra "bang" you get for an extra "buck" of budget. In fact, this is true in general:

- The value of λ is approximately the increase in the optimum value of f when the budget is increased by 1 unit.

More precisely:

- The value of λ represents the rate of change of the optimum value of f as the budget increases.

An Expression for λ

To interpret λ, we look at how the optimum value of the objective function f changes as the value c of the constraint function g is varied. In general, the optimum point (x_0, y_0) depends on the constraint value c. So, provided x_0 and y_0 are differentiable functions of c, we can use the chain rule to differentiate the optimum value $f(x_0(c), y_0(c))$ with respect to c:

$$\frac{df}{dc} = \frac{\partial f}{\partial x}\frac{dx_0}{dc} + \frac{\partial f}{\partial y}\frac{dy_0}{dc}.$$

At the optimum point (x_0, y_0), we have $f_x = \lambda g_x$ and $f_y = \lambda g_y$, and therefore

$$\frac{df}{dc} = \lambda\left(\frac{\partial g}{\partial x}\frac{dx_0}{dc} + \frac{\partial g}{\partial y}\frac{dy_0}{dc}\right) = \lambda\frac{dg}{dc}.$$

But, as $g(x_0(c), y_0(c)) = c$, we see that $dg/dc = 1$, so $df/dc = \lambda$. Thus, we have the following interpretation of the Lagrange multiplier λ:

The value of λ is the rate of change of the optimum value of f as c increases (where $g(x, y) = c$). If the optimum value of f is written as $f(x_0(c), y_0(c))$, then

$$\frac{d}{dc}f(x_0(c), y_0(c)) = \lambda.$$

Example 3   The quantity of goods produced according to the function $f(x, y) = x^{2/3}y^{1/3}$ is maximized subject to the budget constraint $x + y \leq 3.78$. The budget is increased to allow for a small increase in production. What is the price of the product if the sale of the additional goods covers the budget increase?

Solution   We know that $\lambda = 0.53$, which tells us that $df/dc = 0.53$. The constraint corresponds to a budget of $3.78 thousand. Therefore increasing the budget by $1000 increases production by about 0.53 units. In order to make the increase in budget profitable, the extra goods produced must sell for more than $1000. Thus, if p is the price of each unit of the good, then $0.53p$ is the revenue from the extra 0.53 units sold. Thus, we need $0.53p \geq 1000$ so $p \geq 1000/0.53 = \$1890$.

The Lagrangian Function

Constrained optimization problems are frequently solved using a *Lagrangian function*, $\mathcal{L}$. For example, to optimize $f(x, y)$ subject to the constraint $g(x, y) = c$, we use the Lagrangian function

$$\mathcal{L}(x, y, \lambda) = f(x, y) - \lambda(g(x, y) - c).$$

To see how the function $\mathcal{L}$ is used, compute the partial derivatives of $\mathcal{L}$:

$$\frac{\partial \mathcal{L}}{\partial x} = \frac{\partial f}{\partial x} - \lambda \frac{\partial g}{\partial x},$$

$$\frac{\partial \mathcal{L}}{\partial y} = \frac{\partial f}{\partial y} - \lambda \frac{\partial g}{\partial y},$$

$$\frac{\partial \mathcal{L}}{\partial \lambda} = -(g(x, y) - c).$$

Notice that if (x_0, y_0) is an extreme point of $f(x, y)$ subject to the constraint $g(x, y) = c$ and λ_0 is the corresponding Lagrange multiplier, then at the point (x_0, y_0, λ_0) we have

$$\frac{\partial \mathcal{L}}{\partial x} = 0 \quad \text{and} \quad \frac{\partial \mathcal{L}}{\partial y} = 0 \quad \text{and} \quad \frac{\partial \mathcal{L}}{\partial \lambda} = 0.$$

In other words, (x_0, y_0, λ_0) is a critical point for the unconstrained Lagrangian function, $\mathcal{L}(x, y, \lambda)$. Thus, the Lagrangian converts a constrained optimization problem to an unconstrained problem.

Example 4   A company has a production function with three inputs x, y, and z given by

$$f(x, y, z) = 50x^{2/5}y^{1/5}z^{1/5}.$$

The total budget is $24,000 and the company can buy x, y, and z at $80, $12, and $10 per unit, respectively. What combination of inputs will maximize production? [9]

Solution   We need to maximize the objective function

$$f(x, y, z) = 50x^{2/5}y^{1/5}z^{1/5},$$

subject to the constraint

$$g(x, y, z) = 80x + 12y + 10z = 24,000.$$

The method for functions of two variables works for functions of three variables, so we construct the Lagrangian function

$$\mathcal{L}(x, y, z, \lambda) = 50x^{2/5}y^{1/5}z^{1/5} - \lambda(80x + 12y + 10z - 24,000),$$

[9] Adapted from M. Rosser, *Basic Mathematics for Economists*, p. 363 (New York: Routledge, 1993).

and solve the system of equations we get from $\text{grad}\,\mathcal{L} = \vec{0}$:

$$\frac{\partial \mathcal{L}}{\partial x} = 20x^{-3/5}y^{1/5}z^{1/5} - 80\lambda = 0,$$

$$\frac{\partial \mathcal{L}}{\partial y} = 10x^{2/5}y^{-4/5}z^{1/5} - 12\lambda = 0,$$

$$\frac{\partial \mathcal{L}}{\partial z} = 10x^{2/5}y^{1/5}z^{-4/5} - 10\lambda = 0,$$

$$\frac{\partial \mathcal{L}}{\partial \lambda} = -(80x + 12y + 10z - 24{,}000) = 0.$$

Simplifying this system gives

$$\lambda = \frac{1}{4}x^{-3/5}y^{1/5}z^{1/5},$$

$$\lambda = \frac{5}{6}x^{2/5}y^{-4/5}z^{1/5},$$

$$\lambda = x^{2/5}y^{1/5}z^{-4/5},$$

$$80x + 12y + 10z = 24{,}000.$$

Eliminating z from the first two equations gives $x = 0.3y$. Eliminating x from the second and third equations gives $z = 1.2y$. Substituting for x and z into $80x + 12y + 10z = 24{,}000$ gives

$$80(0.3y) + 12y + 10(1.2y) = 24{,}000,$$

so $y = 500$. Then $x = 150$ and $z = 600$, and $f(150, 500, 600) = 4{,}622$ units.

The graph of the constraint, $80x + 12y + 10z = 24{,}000$, is a plane. Since the inputs x, y, z must be nonnegative, the graph is a triangle in the first octant, with edges on the coordinate planes. On the boundary of the triangle, one (or more) of the variables x, y, z is zero, so the function f is zero. Thus production is maximized within the budget using $x = 150$, $y = 500$, and $z = 600$.

Exercises and Problems for Section 15.3

Exercises

In Exercises 1–17, use Lagrange multipliers to find the maximum and minimum values of f subject to the given constraint, if such values exist.

1. $f(x, y) = x + y, \quad x^2 + y^2 = 1$

2. $f(x, y) = x + 3y + 2, \quad x^2 + y^2 = 10$

3. $f(x, y) = (x - 1)^2 + (y + 2)^2, \quad x^2 + y^2 = 5$

4. $f(x, y) = x^3 + y, \quad 3x^2 + y^2 = 4$

5. $f(x, y) = 3x - 2y, \quad x^2 + 2y^2 = 44$

6. $f(x, y) = 2xy, \quad 5x + 4y = 100$

7. $f(x_1, x_2) = x_1^2 + x_2^2, \quad x_1 + x_2 = 1$

8. $f(x, y) = x^2 + y, \quad x^2 - y^2 = 1$

9. $f(x, y, z) = x + 3y + 5z, \quad x^2 + y^2 + z^2 = 1$

10. $f(x, y, z) = x^2 - y^2 - 2z, \quad x^2 + y^2 = z$

11. $f(x, y, z) = xyz, \quad x^2 + y^2 + 4z^2 = 12$

12. $f(x, y) = x^2 + 2y^2, \quad x^2 + y^2 \leq 4$

13. $f(x, y) = x + 3y, \quad x^2 + y^2 \leq 2$

14. $f(x, y) = xy, \quad x^2 + 2y^2 \leq 1$

15. $f(x, y) = x^3 + y, \quad x + y \geq 1$

16. $f(x, y) = (x + 3)^2 + (y - 3)^2, \quad x^2 + y^2 \leq 2$

17. $f(x, y) = x^2 y + 3y^2 - y, \quad x^2 + y^2 \leq 10$

18. Decide whether each point appears to be a maximum, minimum, or neither for the function f constrained by the loop in Figure 15.30.

   (a) P **(b)** Q **(c)** R **(d)** S

Figure 15.30

Problems

19. Find the maximum value of $f(x, y) = x + y - (x - y)^2$ on the triangular region $x \geq 0, y \geq 0, x + y \leq 1$.

20. (a) Draw contours of $f(x, y) = 2x + y$ for $z = -7, -5, -3, -1, 1, 3, 5, 7$.
(b) On the same axes, graph the constraint $x^2 + y^2 = 5$.
(c) Use the graph to approximate the points at which f has a maximum or a minimum value subject to the constraint $x^2 + y^2 = 5$.
(d) Use Lagrange multipliers to find the maximum and minimum values of $f(x, y) = 2x + y$ subject to $x^2 + y^2 = 5$.

21. Let $f(x, y) = x^\alpha y^{1-\alpha}$ for $0 < \alpha < 1$. Find the value of α such that the maximum value of f on the line $2x + 3y = 6$ occurs at $(1.5, 1)$.

22. Figure 15.31 shows contours of f. Does f have a maximum value subject to the constraint $g(x, y) = c$ for $x \geq 0, y \geq 0$? If so, approximately where is it and what is its value? Does f have a minimum value subject to the constraint? If so, approximately where and what?

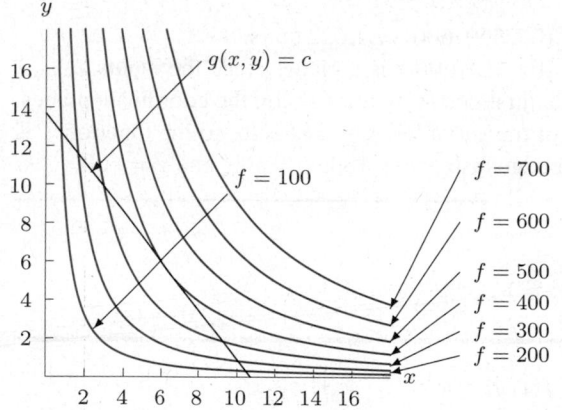

Figure 15.31

23. Each person tries to balance his or her time between leisure and work. The tradeoff is that as you work less your income falls. Therefore each person has *indifference curves* which connect the number of hours of leisure, l, and income, s. If, for example, you are indifferent between 0 hours of leisure and an income of $1125 a week on the one hand, and 10 hours of leisure and an income of $750 a week on the other hand, then the points $l = 0$, $s = 1125$, and $l = 10$, $s = 750$ both lie on the same indifference curve. Table 15.3 gives information on three indifference curves, I, II, and III.

Table 15.3

Weekly income			Weekly leisure hours		
I	II	III	I	II	III
1125	1250	1375	0	20	40
750	875	1000	10	30	50
500	625	750	20	40	60
375	500	625	30	50	70
250	375	500	50	70	90

(a) Graph the three indifference curves.
(b) You have 100 hours a week available for work and leisure combined, and you earn $10/hour. Write an equation in terms of l and s which represents this constraint.
(c) On the same axes, graph this constraint.
(d) Estimate from the graph what combination of leisure hours and income you would choose under these circumstances. Give the corresponding number of hours per week you would work.

24. Figure 15.32 shows ∇f for a function $f(x, y)$ and two curves $g(x, y) = 1$ and $g(x, y) = 2$. Mark the following:

(a) The point(s) A where f has a local maximum.
(b) The point(s) B where f has a saddle point.
(c) The point C where f has a maximum on $g = 1$.
(d) The point D where f has a minimum on $g = 1$.
(e) If you used Lagrange multipliers to find C, what would the sign of λ be? Why?

Figure 15.32

25. The point P is a maximum or minimum of the function f subject to the constraint $g(x, y) = x + y = c$, with $x, y \geq 0$. For the graphs (a) and (b), does P give a maximum or a minimum of f? What is the sign of λ? If P gives a maximum, where does the minimum of f occur? If P gives a minimum, where does the maximum of f occur?

26. Figure 15.33 shows the optimal point (marked with a dot) in three optimization problems with the same constraint. Arrange the corresponding values of λ in increasing order. (Assume λ is positive.)

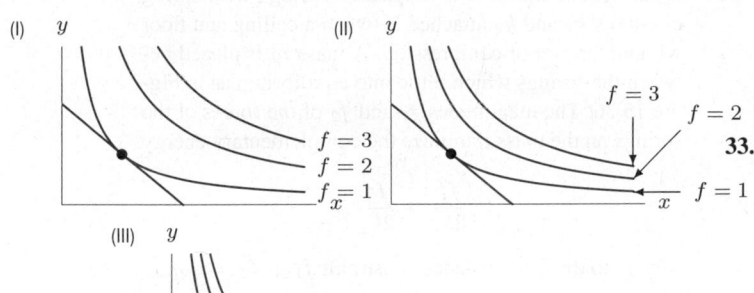

Figure 15.33

27. If the right side of the constraint in Exercise 5 is changed by the small amount Δc, by approximately how much do the maximum and minimum values change?

28. If the right side of the constraint in Exercise 16 is changed by the small amount Δc, by approximately how much do the maximum and minimum values change?

29. The function $P(x, y)$ gives the number of units produced and $C(x, y)$ gives the cost of production.

    (a) A company wishes to maximize production at a fixed cost of \$50,000. What is the objective function f? What is the constraint equation? What is the meaning of λ in this situation?

    (b) A company wishes to minimize costs at a fixed production level of 2000 units. What is the objective function f? What is the constraint equation? What is the meaning of λ in this situation?

30. Design a closed cylindrical container which holds 100 cm^3 and has the minimal possible surface area. What should its dimensions be?

31. A company manufactures x units of one item and y units of another. The total cost in dollars, C, of producing these two items is approximated by the function

$$C = 5x^2 + 2xy + 3y^2 + 800.$$

    (a) If the production quota for the total number of items (both types combined) is 39, find the minimum production cost.

    (b) Estimate the additional production cost or savings if the production quota is raised to 40 or lowered to 38.

32. An international organization must decide how to spend the \$2000 they have been allotted for famine relief in a remote area. They expect to divide the money between buying rice at \$5/sack and beans at \$10/sack. The number, P, of people who would be fed if they buy x sacks of rice and y sacks of beans is given by

$$P = x + 2y + \frac{x^2 y^2}{2 \cdot 10^8}.$$

What is the maximum number of people that can be fed, and how should the organization allocate its money?

33. The quantity, q, of a product manufactured depends on the number of workers, W, and the amount of capital invested, K, and is given by

$$q = 6W^{3/4} K^{1/4}.$$

Labor costs are \$10 per worker and capital costs are \$20 per unit, and the budget is \$3000.

    (a) What are the optimum number of workers and the optimum number of units of capital?

    (b) Show that at the optimum values of W and K, the ratio of the marginal productivity of labor $(\partial q/\partial W)$ to the marginal productivity of capital $(\partial q/\partial K)$ is the same as the ratio of the cost of a unit of labor to the cost of a unit of capital.

    (c) Recompute the optimum values of W and K when the budget is increased by one dollar. Check that increasing the budget by \$1 allows the production of λ extra units of the good, where λ is the Lagrange multiplier.

34. A neighborhood health clinic has a budget of \$600,000 per quarter. The director of the clinic wants to allocate the budget to maximize the number of patient visits, V, which is given as a function of the number of doctors, D, and the number of nurses, N, by

$$V = 1000 D^{0.6} N^{0.3}.$$

A doctor gets \$40,000 per quarter; nurses get \$10,000 per quarter.

    (a) Set up the director's constrained optimization problem.

    (b) Describe, in words, the conditions which must be satisfied by $\partial V/\partial D$ and $\partial V/\partial N$ for V to have an optimum value.

    (c) Solve the problem formulated in part (a).

    (d) Find the value of the Lagrange multiplier and interpret its meaning in this problem.

    (e) At the optimum point, what is the marginal cost of a patient visit (that is, the cost of an additional visit)? Will that marginal cost rise or fall with the number of visits? Why?

35. (a) In Problem 33, does the value of λ change if the budget changes from \$3000 to \$4000?

    (b) In Problem 34, does the value of λ change if the budget changes from \$600,000 to \$700,000?

    (c) What condition must a Cobb-Douglas production function, $Q = cK^a L^b$, satisfy to ensure that the marginal increase of production (that is, the rate of increase of production with budget) is not affected by the size of the budget?

36. The production function $P(K, L)$ gives the number of pairs of skis produced per week at a factory operating with K units of capital and L units of labor. The contour diagram for P is in Figure 15.34; the parallel lines are budget constraints for budgets, B, in dollars.

(a) On each budget constraint, mark the point that gives the maximum production.

(b) Complete the table, where the budget, B, is in dollars and the maximum production is the number of pairs of skis to be produced each week.

B	2000	4000	6000	8000	10000
M					

(c) Estimate the Lagrange multiplier $\lambda = dM/dB$ at a budget of $6000. Give units for the multiplier.

Figure 15.34

37. A doctor wants to schedule visits for two patients who have been operated on for tumors so as to minimize the expected delay in detecting a new tumor. Visits for patients 1 and 2 are scheduled at intervals of x_1 and x_2 weeks, respectively. A total of m visits per week is available for both patients combined.

The recurrence rates for tumors for patients 1 and 2 are judged to be v_1 and v_2 tumors per week, respectively. Thus, $v_1/(v_1 + v_2)$ and $v_2/(v_1 + v_2)$ are the probabilities that patient 1 and patient 2, respectively, will have the next tumor. It is known that the expected delay in detecting a tumor for a patient checked every x weeks is $x/2$. Hence, the expected detection delay for both patients combined is given by[10]

$$f(x_1, x_2) = \frac{v_1}{v_1 + v_2} \cdot \frac{x_1}{2} + \frac{v_2}{v_1 + v_2} \cdot \frac{x_2}{2}.$$

Find the values of x_1 and x_2 in terms of v_1 and v_2 that minimize $f(x_1, x_2)$ subject to the fact that m, the number of visits per week, is fixed.

38. What is the value of the Lagrange multiplier in Problem 37? What are the units of λ? What is its practical significance to the doctor?

39. Figure 15.35 shows two weightless springs with spring constants k_1 and k_2 attached between a ceiling and floor without tension or compression. A mass m is placed between the springs which settle into equilibrium as in Figure 15.36. The magnitudes f_1 and f_2 of the forces of the springs on the mass minimize the complementary energy

$$\frac{f_1^2}{2k_1} + \frac{f_2^2}{2k_2}$$

subject to the force balance constraint $f_1 + f_2 = mg$.

(a) Determine f_1 and f_2 by the method of Lagrange multipliers.

(b) If you are familiar with Hooke's law, find the meaning of λ.

Figure 15.35   **Figure 15.36**

40. (a) If $\sum_{i=1}^{3} x_i = 1$, find the values of x_1, x_2, x_3 making $\sum_{i=1}^{3} x_i^2$ minimum.

(b) Generalize the result of part (a) to find the minimum value of $\sum_{i=1}^{n} x_i^2$ subject to $\sum_{i=1}^{n} x_i = 1$.

41. Let $f(x, y) = ax^2 + bxy + cy^2$. Show that the maximum value of $f(x, y)$ subject to the constraint $x^2 + y^2 = 1$ is equal to λ, the Lagrange multiplier.

42. Find the minimum distance from the point $(1, 2, 10)$ to the paraboloid given by the equation $z = x^2 + y^2$. Give a geometric justification for your answer.

43. A company produces one product from two inputs (for example, capital and labor). Its production function $g(x, y)$ gives the quantity of the product that can be produced with x units of the first input and y units of the second. The *cost function* (or *expenditure function*) is the three-variable function $C(p, q, u)$ where p and q are the unit prices of the two inputs. For fixed p, q, and u, the value $C(p, q, u)$ is the minimum of $f(x, y) = px + qy$ subject to the constraint $g(x, y) = u$.

(a) What is the practical meaning of $C(p, q, u)$?

(b) Find a formula for $C(p, q, u)$ if $g(x, y) = xy$.

---

[10]Adapted from Daniel Kent, Ross Shachter, *et al.*, Efficient Scheduling of Cystoscopies in Monitoring for Recurrent Bladder Cancer in *Medical Decision Making* (Philadelphia: Hanley and Belfus, 1989).

44. A *utility function* $U(x, y)$ for two items gives the utility (benefit) to a consumer of x units of item 1 and y units of item 2. The *indirect utility function* is the three-variable function $V(p, q, I)$ where p and q are the unit prices of the two items. For fixed p, q, and I, the value $V(p, q, I)$ is the maximum of $U(x, y)$ subject to the constraint $px + qy = I$.

   (a) What is the practical meaning of $V(p, q, I)$?

   (b) The Lagrange multiplier λ that arises in the maximization defining V is called the *marginal utility of money*. What is its practical meaning?

   (c) Find formulas for $V(p, q, I)$ and λ if $U(x, y) = xy$.

45. The function $h(x, y) = x^2 + y^2 - \lambda(2x + 4y - 15)$ has a minimum value $m(\lambda)$ for each value of λ.

   (a) Find $m(\lambda)$.

   (b) For which value of λ is $m(\lambda)$ the largest and what is that maximum value?

   (c) Find the minimum value of $f(x, y) = x^2 + y^2$ subject to the constraint $2x + 4y = 15$ using the method of Lagrange multipliers and evaluate λ.

   (d) Compare your answers to parts (b) and (c).

46. Let f be differentiable and grad $f(2, 1) = -3\vec{i} + 4\vec{j}$. You want to see if $(2, 1)$ is a candidate for the maximum and minimum values of f subject to a constraint satisfied by the point $(2, 1)$.

   (a) Show $(2, 1)$ is not a candidate if the constraint is $x^2 + y^2 = 5$.

   (b) Show $(2, 1)$ is a candidate if the constraint is $(x - 5)^2 + (y + 3)^2 = 25$. From a sketch of the contours for f near $(2, 1)$ and the constraint, decide whether $(2, 1)$ is a candidate for a maximum or minimum.

   (c) Do the same as part (b), but using the constraint $(x + 1)^2 + (y - 5)^2 = 25$.

47. A person's satisfaction from consuming a quantity x_1 of one item and a quantity x_2 of another item is given by

$$S = u(x_1, x_2) = a \ln x_1 + (1 - a) \ln x_2,$$

where a is a constant, $0 < a < 1$. The prices of the two items are p_1 and p_2 respectively, and the budget is b.

   (a) Express the maximum satisfaction that can be achieved as a function of p_1, p_2, and b.

   (b) Find the amount of money that must be spent to achieve a particular level of satisfaction, c, as a function of p_1, p_2, and c.

48. This problem illustrates the Envelope Theorem, which relates the maxima of $z = f(x, y)$ subject to the constraint $x = c$ to the contour diagram in Figure 15.37 and the cross-sections in Figure 15.38.

   (a) For each value c, there is a maximum value of $f(x, y)$ with $x = c$. On Figure 15.37, sketch the curve that goes through the points where the maxima are achieved.

   (b) On Figure 15.38, sketch the curve going through the points corresponding to the same maximum values in part (a). This curve is called the envelope of the cross-sections.

   (c) Show that the Lagrange multiplier λ for this constrained optimization problem is the slope of the envelope curve in part (b).

Figure 15.37: Contour diagram of f

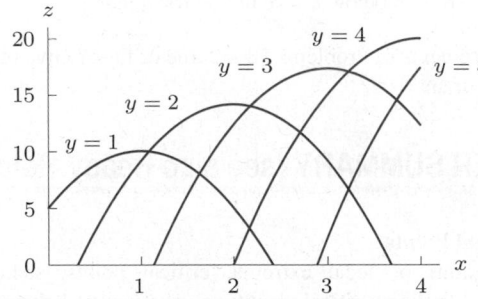

Figure 15.38: Cross-sections of f

Strengthen Your Understanding

In Problems 49–50, explain what is wrong with the statement.

49. The function $f(x, y) = xy$ has a maximum of 2 on the constraint $x + y = 2$.

50. If the level curves of $f(x, y)$ and the level curves of $g(x, y)$ are not tangent at any point on the constraint $g(x, y) = c$, $x \geq 0$, $y \geq 0$, then f has no maximum on the constraint.

In Problems 51–55, give an example of:

51. A function $f(x, y)$ whose maximum subject to the constraint $x^2 + y^2 = 5$ is at $(3, 4)$.

52. A function $f(x, y)$ to be optimized with constraint $x^2 + 2y^2 \leq 1$ such that the minimum value does not change when the constraint is changed to $x^2 + y^2 \leq 1 + c$ for $c > 0$.

53. A function $f(x, y)$ with a minimum at $(1, 1)$ on the constraint $x + y = 2$.

54. A function $f(x, y)$ that has a maximum but no minimum on the constraint $x + y = 4$.

55. A contour diagram of a function f whose maximum value on the constraint $x + 2y = 6$, $x \geq 0$, $y \geq 0$ occurs at one of the endpoints.

For Problems 56–57, use Figure 15.39. The grid lines are one unit apart.

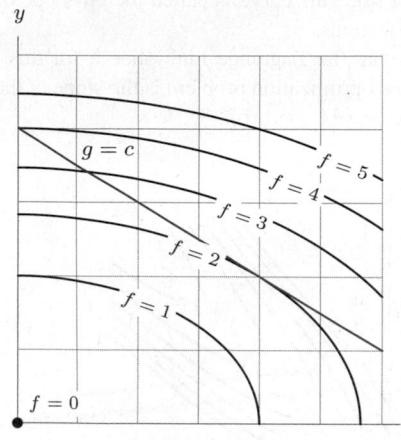

Figure 15.39

56. Find the maximum and minimum values of f on $g = c$. At which points do they occur?

57. Find the maximum and minimum values of f on the triangular region below $g = c$ in the first quadrant.

Are the statements in Problems 58–62 true or false? Give reasons for your answer.

58. If $f(x, y)$ has a local maximum at (a, b) subject to the constraint $g(x, y) = c$, then $g(a, b) = c$.

59. If $f(x, y)$ has a local maximum at (a, b) subject to the constraint $g(x, y) = c$, then $\mathrm{grad}\, f(a, b) = \vec{0}$.

60. The function $f(x, y) = x + y$ has no global maximum subject to the constraint $x - y = 0$.

61. The point $(2, -1)$ is a local minimum of $f(x, y) = x^2 + y^2$ subject to the constraint $x + 2y = 0$.

62. If $\mathrm{grad}\, f(a, b)$ and $\mathrm{grad}\, g(a, b)$ point in opposite directions, then (a, b) is a local minimum of $f(x, y)$ constrained by $g(x, y) = c$.

In Problems 63–70, suppose that M and m are the maximum and minimum values of $f(x, y)$ subject to the constraint $g(x, y) = c$ and that (a, b) satisfies $g(a, b) = c$. Decide whether the statements are true or false. Give an explanation for your answer.

63. If $f(a, b) = M$, then $f_x(a, b) = f_y(a, b) = 0$.

64. If $f(a, b) = M$, then $f(a, b) = \lambda g(a, b)$ for some value of λ.

65. If $\mathrm{grad}\, f(a, b) = \lambda \, \mathrm{grad}\, g(a, b)$, then $f(a, b) = M$ or $f(a, b) = m$.

66. If $f(a, b) = M$ and $f_x(a, b)/f_y(a, b) = 5$, then $g_x(a, b)/g_y(a, b) = 5$.

67. If $f(a, b) = m$ and $g_x(a, b) = 0$, then $f_x(a, b) = 0$.

68. Increasing the value of c increases the value of M.

69. Suppose that $f(a, b) = M$ and that $\mathrm{grad}\, f(a, b) = 3 \, \mathrm{grad}\, g(a, b)$. Then increasing the value of c by 0.02 increases the value of M by about 0.06.

70. Suppose that $f(a, b) = m$ and that $\mathrm{grad}\, f(a, b) = 3 \, \mathrm{grad}\, g(a, b)$. Then increasing the value of c by 0.02 decreases the value of m by about 0.06.

CHAPTER SUMMARY (see also Ready Reference at the end of the book)

- **Critical Points**
  Definitions of local extrema, critical points, saddle points, finding critical points algebraically, behavior of contours near critical points, discriminant, second-derivative test to classify critical points.

- **Unconstrained Optimization**
  Definitions of global extrema, method of least squares,

closed and bounded regions, existence of global extrema.

- **Constrained Optimization**
  Objective function and constraint, definitions of extrema subject to a constraint, geometric interpretation of Lagrange multiplier method, solving Lagrange multiplier problems algebraically, inequality constraints, meaning of the Lagrange multiplier λ, the Lagrangian function.

REVIEW EXERCISES AND PROBLEMS FOR CHAPTER FIFTEEN

Exercises

For Exercises 1–6, find the critical points of the given function and classify them as local maxima, local minima, saddle points, or none of these.

1. $f(x, y) = x^2 + 2xy - y^2 - 4x - 8y + 9$

2. $f(x, y) = 2xy^2 - x^2 - 2y^2 + 1$

3. $f(x, y) = x^3 + y^2 - 3x^2 + 10y + 6$

4. $f(x, y) = x^2y + 2y^2 - 2xy + 6$

5. $f(x, y) = \dfrac{80}{xy} + 10x + 10xy + 20y$

6. $f(x, y) = \sin x + \sin y + \sin(x + y), \quad 0 < x < \pi,$
$0 < y < \pi.$

For Exercises 7–10, find the local maxima, local minima, and saddle points of the function. Decide if the local maxima or minima are global maxima or minima. Explain.

7. $f(x, y) = 10 + 12x + 6y - 3x^2 - y^2$

8. $f(x, y) = x^2 + y^3 - 3xy$

9. $f(x, y) = x + y + \dfrac{1}{x} + \dfrac{4}{y}$

10. $f(x, y) = xy + \ln x + y^2 - 10, \qquad x > 0$

For Exercises 11–22, use Lagrange multipliers to find the maximum and minimum values of f subject to the constraint.

11. $f(x, y) = 3x - 4y, \quad x^2 + y^2 = 5$

12. $f(x, y) = x^2 + y^2, \quad x^4 + y^4 = 2$

13. $f(x, y) = x^2 + y^2, \quad 4x - 2y = 15$

14. $f(x, y) = x^2 - xy + y^2, \quad x^2 - y^2 = 1$

15. $f(x, y) = x^2 + 2y^2, \quad 3x + 5y = 200$

16. $f(x, y) = xy, \quad 4x^2 + y^2 = 8$

17. $f(x, y) = -3x^2 - 2y^2 + 20xy, \quad x + y = 100$

18. $f(x, y, z) = x^2 - 2y + 2z^2, \quad x^2 + y^2 + z^2 = 1$

19. $f(x, y, z) = 2x + y + 4z, \quad x^2 + y + z^2 = 16$

20. $z = 4x^2 - xy + 4y^2, \quad x^2 + y^2 \le 2$

21. $f(x, y) = x^2 - y^2, \quad x^2 \ge y$

22. $f(x, y) = x^3 - y^2, \quad x^2 + y^2 \le 1$

In Exercises 23–26, does $f(x, y) = x^2 - y^2$ have a maximum, a minimum, neither, or both when subject to the constraint?

23. $x = 10$

24. $y = 10$

25. $x^2 + y^2 = 10$

26. $xy = 10$

Problems

27. Maximize $0.3 \ln x + 0.7 \ln y$ on $2x + 3y = 6$.

28. (a) Write an expression for the distance between the points $(3, 4)$ and (x, y).
(b) Minimize this distance if (x, y) lies on the unit circle centered at the origin. At what point does the minimum occur?
(c) What is the maximum distance? At what point does it occur?

29. If the right side of the constraint in Exercise 12 is changed by the small amount Δc, by approximately how much do the maximum and minimum values change?

30. Compute the regression line for the points $(-1, 2)$, $(0, -1)$, $(1, 1)$ using least squares.

31. At the point $(1, 3)$, suppose $f_x = f_y = 0$ and $f_{xx} < 0$, $f_{yy} < 0$, $f_{xy} = 0$. Draw a possible contour diagram.

32. For $f(x, y) = A - (x^2 + Bx + y^2 + Cy)$, what values of A, B, and C give f a local maximum value of 15 at the point $(-2, 1)$?

33. A biological rule of thumb states that as the area A of an island increases tenfold, the number of animal species, N, living on it doubles. The table contains data for islands in the West Indies. Assume that N is a power function of A.

(a) Use the biological rule of thumb to find
(i) N as a function of A
(ii) $\ln N$ as a function of $\ln A$
(b) Using the data given, tabulate $\ln N$ against $\ln A$ and find the line of best fit. Does your answer agree with the biological rule of thumb?

Island	Area (sq km)	Number of species
Redonda	3	5
Saba	20	9
Montserrat	192	15
Puerto Rico	8858	75
Jamaica	10854	70
Hispaniola	75571	130
Cuba	113715	125

34. A firm manufactures a commodity at two different factories. The total cost of manufacturing depends on the quantities, q_1 and q_2, supplied by each factory, and is expressed by the *joint cost function*,

$$C = f(q_1, q_2) = 2q_1^2 + q_1q_2 + q_2^2 + 500.$$

The company's objective is to produce 200 units, while minimizing production costs. How many units should be supplied by each factory?

35. (a) Let $f(x, y) = x^2 + 2y^2$. Find the minimum value $m(c)$ of f on the line $x + y = c$ as a function of c.
(b) Give the value of the Lagrange multiplier λ at this minimum.
(c) What is the relation between your answers in parts (a) and (b)?

36. The maximum value of $f(x, y)$ subject to the constraint $g(x, y) = 240$ is 6300. The method of Lagrange multipliers gives $\lambda = 20$. Find an approximate value for the maximum of $f(x, y)$ subject to the constraint $g(x, y) = 242$.

37. An industry manufactures a product from two raw materials. The quantity produced, Q, can be given by the Cobb-Douglas function:

$$Q = cx^a y^b,$$

where x and y are quantities of each of the two raw materials used and a, b, and c are positive constants. The first raw material costs $\$P_1$ per unit and the second costs $\$P_2$ per unit. Find the maximum production possible if no more than $\$K$ can be spent on raw materials.

38. The quantity, Q, of a product manufactured by a company is given by

$$Q = aK^{0.6}L^{0.4},$$

where a is a positive constant, K is the quantity of capital and L is the quantity of labor used. Capital costs are \$20 per unit, labor costs are \$10 per unit, and the company wants costs for capital and labor combined to be no higher than \$150. Suppose you are asked to consult for the company, and learn that 5 units each of capital and labor are being used.

   (a) What do you advise? Should the company use more or less labor? More or less capital? If so, by how much?
   (b) Write a one-sentence summary that could be used to sell your advice to the board of directors.

39. Figure 15.40 shows contours labeled with values of $f(x, y)$ and a constraint $g(x, y) = c$. Mark the approximate points at which:

   (a) $\text{grad } f = \lambda \text{ grad } g$
   (b) f has a maximum
   (c) f has a maximum on the constraint $g = c$.

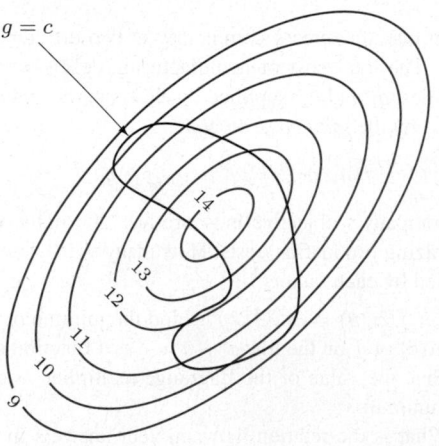

$g = c$

14

13

12

11

10

9

Figure 15.40

40. A mountain climber at the summit of a mountain wants to descend to a lower altitude as fast as possible. The altitude of the mountain is given approximately by

$$h(x, y) = 3000 - \frac{1}{10,000}(5x^2 + 4xy + 2y^2) \text{ meters},$$

where x, y are horizontal coordinates on the earth (in meters), with the mountain summit located above the origin. In thirty minutes, the climber can reach any point (x, y) on a circle of radius 1000 m. In which direction should she travel in order to descend as far as possible?

41. Let $f(x, y, z) = \sqrt{(x-a)^2 + (y-b)^2 + (z-c)^2}$. Minimize f subject to $Ax + By + Cz + D = 0$. What is the geometric meaning of your solution?

42. A company sells two products which are partial substitutes for each other, such as coffee and tea. If the price of one product rises, then the demand for the other product rises. The quantities demanded, q_1 and q_2, are given as a function of the prices, p_1 and p_2, by

$$q_1 = 517 - 3.5p_1 + 0.8p_2, \quad q_2 = 770 - 4.4p_2 + 1.4p_1.$$

What prices should the company charge in order to maximize the total sales revenue? [11]

43. The quantity, Q, of a certain product manufactured depends on the quantity of labor, L, and of capital, K, used according to the function

$$Q = 900L^{1/2}K^{2/3}.$$

Labor costs \$100 per unit and capital costs \$200 per unit. What combination of labor and capital should be used to produce 36,000 units of the goods at minimum cost? What is that minimum cost?

44. A company manufactures a product using inputs x, y, and z according to the production function

$$Q(x, y, z) = 20x^{1/2}y^{1/4}z^{2/5}.$$

The prices per unit are \$20 for x, and \$10 for y, and \$5 for z. What quantity of each input should be used in order to manufacture 1,200 units at minimum cost? [12]

45. The Cobb-Douglas function models the quantity, q, of a commodity produced as a function of the number of workers, W, and the amount of capital invested, K:

$$q = cW^{1-a}K^a,$$

where a and c are positive constants. Labor costs are $\$p_1$ per worker, capital costs are $\$p_2$ per unit, and there is a fixed budget of $\$b$. Show that when W and K are at their optimal levels, the ratio of marginal productivity of labor to marginal productivity of capital equals the ratio of the cost of one unit of labor to one unit of capital.

[11] Adapted from M. Rosser, *Basic Mathematics for Economists*, p. 318 (New York: Routledge, 1993).
[12] Adapted from M. Rosser, *Basic Mathematics for Economists*, p. 363 (New York: Routledge, 1993).

46. An electrical current I flows through a circuit containing the resistors R_1 and R_2 in Figure 15.41. The currents i_1 and i_2 through the individual resistors minimize energy loss $i_1^2 R_1 + i_2^2 R_2$ subject to the constraint $i_1 + i_2 = I$ given by Kirchoff's current law.

  (a) Find the currents i_1 and i_2 by the method of Lagrange multipliers.

  (b) If you are familiar with Ohm's law, find the meaning of λ.

Figure 15.41

47. An open rectangular box has volume $32\,\text{cm}^3$. What are the lengths of the edges giving the minimum surface area?

48. The function $f(x,y)$ is defined for all x, y and the origin does not lie on the surface representing $z = f(x,y)$. There is a unique point $P = (a, b, c)$ on the surface which is closest to the origin. Explain why the position vector from the origin to P must be perpendicular to the surface at that point.

49. In a curious game, you and your opponent will choose three real numbers. The rules say that you must first choose a value λ, then your opponent is free to choose any values for x and y. Your goal is to make the value of $\mathcal{L}(x, y, \lambda) = 10 - x^2 - y^2 - 2x - \lambda(2x + 2y)$ as small as you can, and your opponent's goal is to make it as large as possible. What value of λ should you choose (assuming you have a brilliant opponent who never makes mistakes)?

50. An irrigation canal has a trapezoidal cross-section of area $50\,\text{m}^2$, as in Figure 15.42. The average flow rate in the canal is inversely proportional to the wetted perimeter, p, of the canal, that is, to the perimeter of the trapezoid in Figure 15.42, excluding the top. Thus, to maximize the flow rate we must minimize p. Find the depth d, base width w, and angle θ that give the maximum flow rate.[13]

Figure 15.42

CAS Challenge Problems

51. Let $f(x,y) = \dfrac{\sqrt{a + x + y}}{1 + y + \sqrt{a + x}}$, for $x, y > 0$, where a is a positive constant.

  (a) Find the critical points of f and classify them as local maxima, local minima, saddle points, or none of these.

  (b) Describe how the position and type of the critical points changes with respect to a, and explain this in terms of the graph of f.

52. Students are asked to find the global maximum of $f(x, y) = x^2 + y$ subject to the constraint $g(x, y) = x^2 + 2xy + y^2 - 9 = 0$. Student A uses the method of Lagrange multipliers with the help of a computer algebra system, and says that the global maximum is 11/4. Student B looks at a contour diagram of f and a graph of $g = 0$ and says there is no global maximum. Which student is correct and what mistake is the other one making?

53. Let $f(x, y) = 3x + 2y + 5$, $g(x, y) = 2x^2 - 4xy + 5y^2$.

  (a) Find the maximum of f subject to the constraint $g = 20$.

  (b) Using the value of λ in part (a), estimate the maximum of f subject to each of the constraints $g = 20.5$ and $g = 20.2$.

  (c) Use Lagrange multipliers to find the two maxima in part (b) exactly. Compare them with the estimates.

---

[13]Adapted from Robert M. Stark and Robert L. Nichols, *Mathematical Foundations of Design: Civil Engineering Systems* (New York: McGraw-Hill, 1972).

PROJECTS FOR CHAPTER FIFTEEN

1. **Optimization in Manufacturing**

   A recycling company makes paper from a combination of two raw materials A and B where A is wood pulp from a timber company and B is waste paper from a recycling depot. The production function is $Q = f(x, y)$ where Q is the quantity of paper the company can make using x units of A and y units of B. The cost of acquiring these materials is given by the cost function $C = g(x, y) = px + qy$, where p is the unit price of A and q is the unit price of B.

   (a) If the company decides to reduce the amount of A that it buys, then it can use the money saved to buy additional B. The *economic rate of substitution*, or *ERS*, of B for A tells how much additional B can be bought for the cost of a unit of A. Show that the *ERS* is $g_x/g_y = p/q$.

   (b) If the company decides to reduce slightly the amount of A that it buys, then it must buy additional B in order to maintain a constant level of production. The *technical rate of substitution*, or *TRS*, of B for A tells how much additional B to buy per unit reduction in A. Show that the *TRS* is f_x/f_y. [Hint: The *TRS* is the rate at which y increases with respect to x as a point (x, y) slides in the direction of decreasing x along a fixed contour $f(x, y) = Q$ of the production function.]

   (c) Show that to maximize the quantity of paper produced with a fixed budget the company should use raw materials A and B in quantities such that *ERS = TRS*.

   (d) Show that to minimize the cost of producing a fixed quantity of paper the company should use raw materials A and B in quantities such that *ERS = TRS*.

2. **Fitting a Line to Data Using Least Squares**

   In this problem you will derive the general formulas for the slope and y-intercept of a least squares line. Assume that you have n data points $(x_1, y_1), (x_2, y_2), \ldots, (x_n, y_n)$. Let the equation of the least squares line be $y = b + mx$.

   (a) For each data point (x_i, y_i), show that the corresponding point directly above or below it on the least squares line has y-coordinate $b + mx_i$.

   (b) For each data point (x_i, y_i), show that the square of the vertical distance from it to the point found in part (a) is $(y_i - (b + mx_i))^2$.

   (c) Form the function $f(b, m)$ which is the sum of all of the n squared distances found in part (b). That is,

   $$f(b, m) = \sum_{i=1}^{n} (y_i - (b + mx_i))^2.$$

   Show that the partial derivatives $\dfrac{\partial f}{\partial b}$ and $\dfrac{\partial f}{\partial m}$ are given by

   $$\frac{\partial f}{\partial b} = -2 \sum_{i=1}^{n} (y_i - (b + mx_i))$$

   and

   $$\frac{\partial f}{\partial m} = -2 \sum_{i=1}^{n} (y_i - (b + mx_i)) \cdot x_i.$$

   (d) Show that the critical point equations $\dfrac{\partial f}{\partial b} = 0$ and $\dfrac{\partial f}{\partial m} = 0$ lead to a pair of simultaneous linear equations in b and m:

   $$nb + \left(\sum x_i \right) m = \sum y_i$$

   $$\left(\sum x_i \right) b + \left(\sum x_i^2 \right) m = \sum x_i y_i$$

(e) Solve the equations in part (d) for b and m, getting

$$b = \left(\sum_{i=1}^{n} x_i^2 \sum_{i=1}^{n} y_i - \sum_{i=1}^{n} x_i \sum_{i=1}^{n} x_i y_i\right) \Bigg/ \left(n \sum_{i=1}^{n} x_i^2 - \left(\sum_{i=1}^{n} x_i\right)^2\right)$$

$$m = \left(n \sum_{i=1}^{n} x_i y_i - \sum_{i=1}^{n} x_i \sum_{i=1}^{n} y_i\right) \Bigg/ \left(n \sum_{i=1}^{n} x_i^2 - \left(\sum_{i=1}^{n} x_i\right)^2\right)$$

(f) Apply the formulas of part (e) to the data points $(1,1), (2,1), (3,3)$ to check that you get the same result as in Example 3 on page 842.

3. **Hockey and Entropy**

Thirty teams compete for the Stanley Cup in the National Hockey League (after expansion in 2000). At the beginning of the season an experienced fan estimates that the probability that team i will win is some number p_i, where $0 \leq p_i \leq 1$ and

$$\sum_{i=1}^{30} p_i = 1.$$

Exactly one team will actually win, so the probabilities have to add to 1. If one of the teams, say team i, is certain to win then p_i is equal to 1 and all the other p_j are zero. Another extreme case occurs if all the teams are equally likely to win, so all the p_i are equal to $1/30$, and the outcome of the hockey season is completely unpredictable. Thus, the *uncertainty* in the outcome of the hockey season depends on the probabilities $p_1, \ldots, p_{30}$. In this problem we measure this uncertainty quantitatively using the following function:

$$S(p_1, \ldots, p_{30}) = -\sum_{i=1}^{30} p_i \frac{\ln p_i}{\ln 2}.$$

Note that as $p_i \leq 1$, we have $-\ln p_i \geq 0$ and hence $S \geq 0$.

(a) Show that $\lim_{p \to 0} p \ln p = 0$. (This means that S is a continuous function of the p_i, where $0 \leq p_i \leq 1$ and $1 \leq i \leq 30$, if we set $p \ln p|_{p=0}$ equal to zero. Since S is then a continuous function on a closed and bounded region, it attains a maximum and a minimum value on this region.)

(b) Find the maximum value of $S(p_1, \ldots, p_{30})$ subject to the constraint $p_1 + \cdots + p_{30} = 1$. What are the values of p_i in this case? What does your answer mean in terms of the uncertainty in the outcome of the hockey season?

(c) Find the minimum value of $S(p_1, \ldots, p_{30})$, subject to the constraint $p_1 + \cdots + p_{30} = 1$. What are the values of p_i in this case? What does your answer mean in terms of the uncertainty in the outcome of the hockey season?

[Note: The function S is an example of an *entropy* function; the concept of entropy is used in information theory, statistical mechanics, and thermodynamics when measuring the uncertainty in an experiment (the hockey season in this problem) or physical system.]

Chapter Sixteen

INTEGRATING FUNCTIONS OF SEVERAL VARIABLES

Contents

16.1 THE DEFINITE INTEGRAL OF A FUNCTION OF TWO VARIABLES

The definite integral of a continuous one-variable function, f, is a limit of Riemann sums:

$$\int_a^b f(x)\,dx = \lim_{\Delta x \to 0} \sum_i f(x_i)\,\Delta x,$$

where x_i is a point in the ith subdivision of the interval $[a, b]$. In this section we extend this definition to functions of two variables. We start by considering how to estimate total population from a two-variable population density.

Population Density of Foxes in England

The fox population in parts of England is important to public health officials concerned about the disease rabies, which is spread by animals. Biologists use a contour diagram to display the fox population density, D; see Figure 16.1, where D is in foxes per square kilometer.[1] The bold contour is the coastline, which may be thought of as the $D = 0$ contour; clearly the density is zero outside it. We can think of D as a function of position, $D = f(x, y)$ where x and y are in kilometers from the southwest corner of the map.

Figure 16.1: Population density of foxes in southwestern England

---

Example 1   Estimate the total fox population in the region represented by the map in Figure 16.1.

Solution   We subdivide the map into the rectangles shown in Figure 16.1 and estimate the population in each rectangle. For simplicity, we use the population density at the northeast corner of each rectangle. For example, in the bottom left rectangle, the density is 0 at the northeast corner, in the next rectangle to the east (right), the density in the northeast corner is 1. Continuing in this way, we get the estimates in Table 16.1. To estimate the population in a rectangle, we multiply the density by the area of the rectangle, $30 \cdot 25 = 750$ km^2. Adding the results, we obtain

$$\begin{aligned}
\text{Estimate of population} &= (0.2 + 0.7 + 1.2 + 1.2 + 0.1 + 1.6 + 0.5 + 1.4 \\
&\quad + 1.1 + 1.6 + 1.5 + 1.8 + 1.5 + 1.3 + 1.1 + 2.0 \\
&\quad + 1.4 + 1.0 + 1.0 + 0.6 + 1.2)750 = 18{,}000 \text{ foxes.}
\end{aligned}$$

Taking the upper and lower bounds for the population density on each rectangle enables us to find upper and lower estimates for the population. Using the same rectangles, the upper estimate is approximately 35,000 and the lower estimate is 4,000. There is a wide discrepancy between the upper and lower estimates; we could make them closer by taking finer subdivisions.

---

[1] Adapted from J. D. Murray, *Mathematical Biology*, Springer-Verlag, 1989.

Table 16.1 *Estimates of population density (northeast corner)*

0.0	0.0	0.2	0.7	1.2	1.2
0.0	0.0	0.0	0.0	0.1	1.6
0.0	0.0	0.5	1.4	1.1	1.6
0.0	0.0	1.5	1.8	1.5	1.3
0.0	1.1	2.0	1.4	1.0	0.0
0.0	1.0	0.6	1.2	0.0	0.0

Definition of the Definite Integral

The sums used to approximate the fox population are Riemann sums. We now define the definite integral for a function f of two variables on a rectangular region. Given a continuous function $f(x, y)$ defined on a region $a \leq x \leq b$ and $c \leq y \leq d$, we subdivide each of the intervals $a \leq x \leq b$ and $c \leq y \leq d$ into n and m equal subintervals respectively, giving nm subrectangles. (See Figure 16.2.)

Figure 16.2: Subdivision of a rectangle into nm subrectangles

The area of each subrectangle is $\Delta A = \Delta x \, \Delta y$, where $\Delta x = (b - a)/n$ is the width of each subdivision on the x-axis, and $\Delta y = (d - c)/m$ is the width of each subdivision on the y-axis. To compute the Riemann sum, we multiply the area of each subrectangle by the value of the function at a point in the rectangle and add the resulting numbers. Choosing the point which gives the maximum value, M_{ij}, of the function on each rectangle, we get the *upper sum*, $\sum_{i,j} M_{ij} \Delta x \Delta y$.

The *lower sum*, $\sum_{i,j} L_{ij} \Delta x \Delta y$, is obtained by taking the minimum value on each rectangle. If (u_{ij}, v_{ij}) is any point in the ij-th subrectangle, any other Riemann sum satisfies

$$\sum_{i,j} L_{ij} \Delta x \Delta y \leq \sum_{i,j} f(u_{ij}, v_{ij}) \, \Delta x \, \Delta y \leq \sum_{i,j} M_{ij} \Delta x \Delta y.$$

We define the definite integral by taking the limit as the numbers of subdivisions, n and m, tend to infinity. By comparing upper and lower sums, as we did for the fox population, it can be shown that the limit exists when the function, f, is continuous. We get the same limit by letting Δx and Δy tend to 0. Thus, we have the following definition:

Suppose the function f is continuous on R, the rectangle $a \leq x \leq b$, $c \leq y \leq d$. If (u_{ij}, v_{ij}) is any point in the ij-th subrectangle, we define the **definite integral** of f over R

$$\int_R f \, dA = \lim_{\Delta x, \Delta y \to 0} \sum_{i,j} f(u_{ij}, v_{ij}) \Delta x \Delta y.$$

Such an integral is called a **double integral**.

The case when R is not rectangular is considered on page 872. Sometimes we think of dA as being the area of an infinitesimal rectangle of length dx and height dy, so that $dA = dx\,dy$. Then we use the notation[2]

$$\int_R f\,dA = \int_R f(x,y)\,dx\,dy.$$

For this definition, we used a particular type of Riemann sum with equal-sized rectangular subdivisions. In a general Riemann sum, the subdivisions do not all have to be the same size.

Interpretation of the Double Integral as Volume

Just as the definite integral of a positive one-variable function can be interpreted as an area, so the double integral of a positive two-variable function can be interpreted as a volume. In the one-variable case we visualize the Riemann sums as the total area of rectangles above the subdivisions. In the two-variable case we get solid bars instead of rectangles. As the number of subdivisions grows, the tops of the bars approximate the surface better, and the volume of the bars gets closer to the volume under the graph of the function. (See Figure 16.3.)

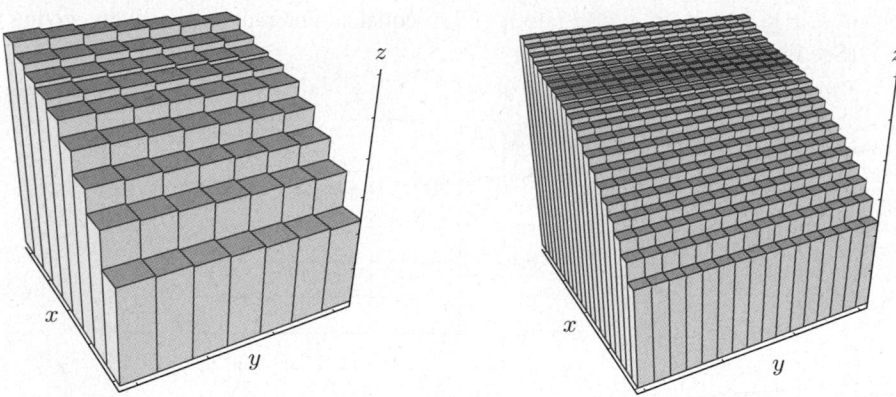

Figure 16.3: Approximating volume under a graph with finer and finer Riemann sums

Thus, we have the following result:

> If x, y, z represent length and f is positive, then
>
> $$\text{Volume under graph of } f \text{ above region } R = \int_R f\,dA.$$

Example 2   Let R be the rectangle $0 \le x \le 1$ and $0 \le y \le 1$. Use Riemann sums to make upper and lower estimates of the volume of the region above R and under the graph of $z = e^{-(x^2+y^2)}$.

Solution   If R is the rectangle $0 \le x \le 1$, $0 \le y \le 1$, the volume we want is given by

$$\text{Volume} = \int_R e^{-(x^2+y^2)}\,dA.$$

We divide R into 16 subrectangles by dividing each edge into four parts. Figure 16.4 shows that $f(x,y) = e^{-(x^2+y^2)}$ decreases as we move away from the origin. Thus, to get an upper sum we evaluate f on each subrectangle at the corner nearest the origin. For example, in the rectangle $0 \le x \le 0.25$, $0 \le y \le 0.25$, we evaluate f at $(0,0)$. Using Table 16.2, we find that

---

[2]Another common notation for the double integral is $\int \int_R f\,dA$.

Figure 16.4: Graph of $e^{-(x^2+y^2)}$ above the rectangle R

$$\text{Upper sum} = (\ 1 + 0.9394 + 0.7788 + 0.5698$$
$$+ 0.9394 + 0.8825 + 0.7316 + 0.5353$$
$$+ 0.7788 + 0.7316 + 0.6065 + 0.4437$$
$$+ 0.5698 + 0.5353 + 0.4437 + 0.3247)(0.0625) = 0.68.$$

To get a lower sum, we evaluate f at the opposite corner of each rectangle because the surface slopes down in both the x and y directions. This yields a lower sum of 0.44. Thus,

$$0.44 \leq \int_R e^{-(x^2+y^2)}\, dA \leq 0.68.$$

To get a better approximation, we use more subdivisions. See Table 16.3.

Table 16.2   *Values of $f(x,y) = e^{-(x^2+y^2)}$ on the rectangle R*

			y		
		0.0	0.25	0.50	0.75	1.00
	0.0	1	0.9394	0.7788	0.5698	0.3679
	0.25	0.9394	0.8825	0.7316	0.5353	0.3456
x	0.50	0.7788	0.7316	0.6065	0.4437	0.2865
	0.75	0.5698	0.5353	0.4437	0.3247	0.2096
	1.00	0.3679	0.3456	0.2865	0.2096	0.1353

Table 16.3   *Riemann sum approximations to $\int_R e^{-(x^2+y^2)}\, dA$*

	Number of subdivisions in x and y directions			
	8	16	32	64
Upper	0.6168	0.5873	0.5725	0.5651
Lower	0.4989	0.5283	0.5430	0.5504

The true value of the double integral, $0.5577\ldots$, is trapped between the lower and upper sums. Notice that the lower sum increases and the upper sum decreases as the number of subdivisions increases. However, even with 64 subdivisions, the lower and upper sums agree with the true value of the integral only in the first decimal place.

Interpretation of the Double Integral as Area

In the special case that $f(x,y) = 1$ for all points (x,y) in the region R, each term in the Riemann sum is of the form $1 \cdot \Delta A = \Delta A$ and the double integral gives the area of the region R:

$$\text{Area}(R) = \int_R 1\, dA = \int_R dA.$$

Interpretation of the Double Integral as Average Value

As in the one-variable case, the definite integral can be used to compute the average value of a function:

$$\frac{\text{Average value of } f}{\text{on the region } R} = \frac{1}{\text{Area of } R} \int_R f\, dA$$

We can rewrite this as

$$\text{Average value} \times \text{Area of } R = \int_R f\, dA.$$

If we interpret the integral as the volume under the graph of f, then we can think of the average value of f as the height of the box with the same volume that is on the same base. (See Figure 16.5.) Imagine that the volume under the graph is made out of wax. If the wax melted within the perimeter of R, then it would end up box-shaped with height equal to the average value of f.

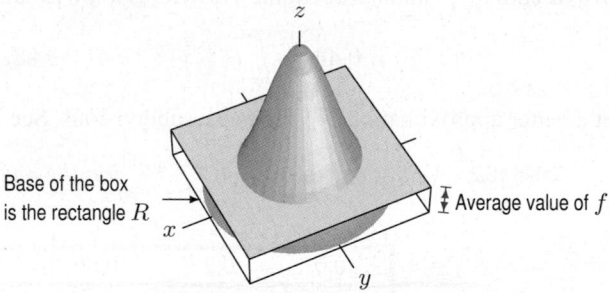

Figure 16.5: Volume and average value

Integral over Regions that Are Not Rectangles

We defined the definite integral $\int_R f(x, y)\, dA$, for a rectangular region R. Now we extend the definition to regions of other shapes, including triangles, circles, and regions bounded by the graphs of piecewise continuous functions.

To approximate the definite integral over a region, R, which is not rectangular, we use a grid of rectangles approximating the region. We obtain this grid by enclosing R in a large rectangle and subdividing that rectangle; we consider just the subrectangles which are inside R.

As before, we pick a point (u_{ij}, v_{ij}) in each subrectangle and form a Riemann sum

$$\sum_{i,j} f(u_{ij}, v_{ij}) \Delta x \Delta y.$$

This time, however, the sum is over only those subrectangles within R. For example, in the case of the fox population we can use the rectangles which are entirely on land. As the subdivisions become finer, the grid approximates the region R more closely. For a function, f, which is continuous on R, we define the definite integral as follows:

$$\int_R f\, dA = \lim_{\Delta x, \Delta y \to 0} \sum_{i,j} f(u_{ij}, v_{ij}) \Delta x \Delta y$$

where the Riemann sum is taken over the subrectangles inside R.

You may wonder why we can leave out the rectangles which cover the edge of R—if we included them, might we get a different value for the integral? The answer is that for any region that we are likely to meet, the area of the subrectangles covering the edge tends to 0 as the grid becomes finer. Therefore, omitting these rectangles does not affect the limit.

Convergence of Upper and Lower Sums to Same Limit

We have said that if f is continuous on the rectangle R, then the difference between upper and lower sums for f converges to 0 as Δx and Δy approach 0. In the following example, we show this in a particular case. The ideas in this example can be used in a general proof.

Example 3   Let $f(x,y) = x^2 y$ and let R be the rectangle $0 \le x \le 1, 0 \le y \le 1$. Show that the difference between upper and lower Riemann sums for f on R converges to 0, as Δx and Δy approach 0.

Solution   The difference between the sums is

$$\sum M_{ij}\Delta x \Delta y - \sum L_{ij}\Delta x \Delta y = \sum (M_{ij} - L_{ij})\Delta x \Delta y,$$

where M_{ij} and L_{ij} are the maximum and minimum of f on the ij-th subrectangle. Since f increases in both the x and y directions, M_{ij} occurs at the corner of the subrectangle farthest from the origin and L_{ij} at the closest. Moreover, since the slopes in the x and y directions don't decrease as x and y increase, the difference $M_{ij} - L_{ij}$ is largest in the subrectangle R_{nm} which is farthest from the origin. Thus,

$$\sum (M_{ij} - L_{ij})\Delta x \Delta y \le (M_{nm} - L_{nm})\sum \Delta x \Delta y = (M_{nm} - L_{nm})\text{Area}(R).$$

Thus, the difference converges to 0 as long as $(M_{nm} - L_{nm})$ does. The maximum M_{nm} of f on the nm-th subrectangle occurs at $(1, 1)$, the subrectangle's top right corner, and the minimum L_{nm} occurs at the opposite corner, $(1 - 1/n, 1 - 1/m)$. Substituting into $f(x,y) = x^2 y$ gives

$$M_{nm} - L_{nm} = (1)^2(1) - \left(1 - \frac{1}{n}\right)^2\left(1 - \frac{1}{m}\right) = \frac{2}{n} - \frac{1}{n^2} + \frac{1}{m} - \frac{2}{nm} + \frac{1}{n^2 m}.$$

The right-hand side converges to 0 as $n, m \to \infty$, that is, as $\Delta x, \Delta y \to 0$.

Exercises and Problems for Section 16.1

Exercises

1. Table 16.4 gives values of the function $f(x,y)$, which is increasing in x and decreasing in y on the region $R : 0 \le x \le 6, 0 \le y \le 1$. Make the best possible upper and lower estimates of $\int_R f(x,y)\,dA$.

Table 16.4

		\(x\)		
		0	3	6
	0	5	7	10
y	0.5	4	5	7
	1	3	4	6

2. Values of $f(x,y)$ are in Table 16.5. Let R be the rectangle $1 \le x \le 1.2, 2 \le y \le 2.4$. Find Riemann sums which are reasonable over and underestimates for $\int_R f(x,y)\,dA$ with $\Delta x = 0.1$ and $\Delta y = 0.2$.

Table 16.5

		\(x\)		
		1.0	1.1	1.2
	2.0	5	7	10
y	2.2	4	6	8
	2.4	3	5	4

3. Figure 16.6 shows contours of $g(x,y)$ on the region R, with $5 \le x \le 11$ and $4 \le y \le 10$. Using $\Delta x = \Delta y = 2$, find an overestimate and an underestimate for $\int_R g(x,y)dA$.

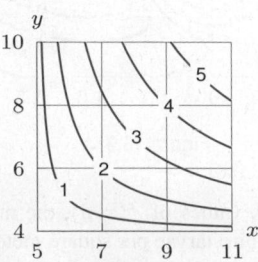

Figure 16.6

4. Figure 16.7 shows contours of $f(x, y)$ on the rectangle R with $0 \leq x \leq 30$ and $0 \leq y \leq 15$. Using $\Delta x = 10$ and $\Delta y = 5$, find an overestimate and an underestimate for $\int_R f(x, y) dA$.

Figure 16.7

5. Figure 16.8 shows a contour plot of population density, people per square kilometer, in a rectangle of land 3 km by 2 km. Estimate the population in the region represented by Figure 16.8.

Figure 16.8

Problems

In Problems 6–12, decide (without calculation) whether the integrals are positive, negative, or zero. Let D be the region inside the unit circle centered at the origin, let R be the right half of D and let B be the bottom half of D.

6. $\int_D dA$

7. $\int_R 5x \, dA$

8. $\int_B 5x \, dA$

9. $\int_D (y^3 + y^5) \, dA$

10. $\int_B (y^3 + y^5) \, dA$

11. $\int_D (y - y^3) \, dA$

12. $\int_B (y - y^3) \, dA$

13. Figure 16.9 shows contours of $f(x, y)$. Let R be the square $-0.5 \leq x \leq 1$, $-0.5 \leq y \leq 1$. Is the integral $\int_R f \, dA$ positive or negative? Explain your reasoning.

Figure 16.9

14. Table 16.6 gives values of $f(x, y)$, the number of milligrams of mosquito larvae per square meter in a swamp.

If x and y are in meters and R is the rectangle $0 \leq x \leq 8$, $0 \leq y \leq 6$, estimate $\int_R f(x, y) dA$. Give units and interpret your answer.

Table 16.6

		x	
		0	4	8
	0	1	3	6
y	3	2	5	9
	6	4	9	15

15. Figure 16.10 shows the temperature, in °C, in a 5 meter by 5 meter heated room. Using Riemann sums, estimate the average temperature in the room.

Figure 16.10

16. Use four subrectangles to approximate the volume of the object whose base is the region $0 \leq x \leq 4$ and $0 \leq y \leq 6$, and whose height is given by $f(x, y) = x + y$. Find an overestimate and an underestimate and average the two.

Strengthen Your Understanding

In Problems 17–18, explain what is wrong with the statement.

17. For all f, the integral $\int_R f(x, y) \, dA$ gives the volume of the solid under the graph of f over the region R.

18. If R is a region in the third quadrant where $x < 0, y < 0$, then $\int_R f(x, y) \, dA$ is negative.

In Problems 19–20, give an example of:

19. A function $f(x, y)$ and rectangle R such that the Riemann sums obtained using the lower left-hand corner of each subrectangle are an overestimate.

20. A function $f(x, y)$ whose average value over the square $0 \leq x \leq 1, 0 \leq y \leq 1$ is negative.

Are the statements in Problems 21–30 true or false? Give reasons for your answer.

21. The double integral $\int_R f \, dA$ is always positive.

22. If $f(x, y) = k$ for all points (x, y) in a region R then $\int_R f \, dA = k \cdot \text{Area}(R)$.

23. If R is the rectangle $0 \leq x \leq 1, 0 \leq y \leq 1$ then $\int_R e^{xy} \, dA > 3$.

24. If R is the rectangle $0 \leq x \leq 2, 0 \leq y \leq 3$ and S is the rectangle $-2 \leq x \leq 0, -3 \leq y \leq 0$ then $\int_R f \, dA = -\int_S f \, dA$.

25. Let $\rho(x, y)$ be the population density of a city, in people per km². If R is a region in the city, then $\int_R \rho \, dA$ gives the total number of people in the region R.

26. If $\int_R f \, dA = 0$ then $f(x, y) = 0$ at all points of R.

27. If $g(x, y) = kf(x, y)$, where k is constant, then $\int_R g \, dA = k \int_R f \, dA$.

28. If f and g are two functions continuous on a region R, then $\int_R f \cdot g \, dA = \int_R f \, dA \cdot \int_R g \, dA$.

29. If R is the rectangle $0 \leq x \leq 1, 0 \leq y \leq 2$ and S is the square $0 \leq x \leq 1, 0 \leq y \leq 1$, then $\int_R f \, dA = 2 \int_S f \, dA$.

30. If R is the rectangle $2 \leq x \leq 4, 5 \leq y \leq 9$, $f(x, y) = 2x$ and $g(x, y) = x + y$, then the average value of f on R is less than the average value of g on R.

16.2 ITERATED INTEGRALS

In Section 16.1 we approximated double integrals using Riemann sums. In this section we see how to compute double integrals exactly using one-variable integrals.

The Fox Population Again: Expressing a Double Integral as an Iterated Integral

To estimate the fox population, we computed a sum of the form

$$\text{Total population} \approx \sum_{i,j} f(u_{ij}, v_{ij}) \Delta x \, \Delta y,$$

where $1 \leq i \leq n$ and $1 \leq j \leq m$ and the values $f(u_{ij}, v_{ij})$ can be arranged as in Table 16.7.

Table 16.7   *Estimates for fox population densities for $n = m = 6$*

0.0	0.0	0.2	0.7	1.2	1.2
0.0	0.0	0.0	0.0	0.1	1.6
0.0	0.0	0.5	1.4	1.1	1.6
0.0	0.0	1.5	1.8	1.5	1.3
0.0	1.1	2.0	1.4	1.0	0.0
0.0	1.0	0.6	1.2	0.0	0.0

For any values of n and m, we can either add across the rows first or add down the columns first. If we add rows first, we can write the sum in the form

$$\text{Total population} \approx \sum_{j=1}^{m} \left(\sum_{i=1}^{n} f(u_{ij}, v_{ij}) \Delta x \right) \Delta y.$$

The inner sum, $\sum_{i=1}^{n} f(u_{ij}, v_{ij}) \Delta x$, approximates the integral $\int_0^{180} f(x, v_{ij}) \, dx$. Thus, we have

$$\text{Total population} \approx \sum_{j=1}^{m} \left(\int_0^{180} f(x, v_{ij}) \, dx \right) \Delta y.$$

The outer Riemann sum approximates another integral, this time with integrand $\int_0^{180} f(x, y) \, dx$, which is a function of y. Thus, we can write the total population in terms of nested, or *iterated*, one-variable integrals:

$$\text{Total population} = \int_0^{150} \left(\int_0^{180} f(x, y) \, dx \right) \, dy.$$

Since the total population is represented by $\int_R f \, dA$, this suggests the method of computing double integrals in the following theorem:[3]

Theorem 16.1: Writing a Double Integral as an Iterated Integral

If R is the rectangle $a \leq x \leq b$, $c \leq y \leq d$ and f is a continuous function on R, then the integral of f over R exists and is equal to the **iterated integral**

$$\int_R f \, dA = \int_{y=c}^{y=d} \left(\int_{x=a}^{x=b} f(x, y) \, dx \right) \, dy.$$

The expression $\int_{y=c}^{y=d} \left(\int_{x=a}^{x=b} f(x, y) \, dx \right) \, dy$ can be written $\int_c^d \int_a^b f(x, y) \, dx \, dy$.

To evaluate the iterated integral, first perform the inside integral with respect to x, holding y constant; then integrate the result with respect to y.

Example 1   A building is 8 meters wide and 16 meters long. It has a flat roof that is 12 meters high at one corner, and 10 meters high at each of the adjacent corners. What is the volume of the building?

Solution   If we put the high corner on the z-axis, the long side along the y-axis, and the short side along the x-axis, as in Figure 16.11, then the roof is a plane with z-intercept 12, and x slope $(-2)/8 = -1/4$, and y slope $(-2)/16 = -1/8$. Hence, the equation of the roof is

$$z = 12 - \tfrac{1}{4}x - \tfrac{1}{8}y.$$

The volume is given by the double integral

$$\text{Volume} = \int_R (12 - \tfrac{1}{4}x - \tfrac{1}{8}y) \, dA,$$

where R is the rectangle $0 \leq x \leq 8, 0 \leq y \leq 16$. Setting up an iterated integral, we get

$$\text{Volume} = \int_0^{16} \int_0^8 (12 - \tfrac{1}{4}x - \tfrac{1}{8}y) \, dx \, dy.$$

The inside integral is

$$\int_0^8 (12 - \tfrac{1}{4}x - \tfrac{1}{8}y) \, dx = \left(12x - \tfrac{1}{8}x^2 - \tfrac{1}{8}xy \right) \Big|_{x=0}^{x=8} = 88 - y.$$

---

[3] For a proof, see M. Spivak, *Calculus on Manifolds*, pp. 53 and 58 (New York: Benjamin, 1965).

Then the outside integral gives

$$\text{Volume} = \int_0^{16} (88 - y)\, dy = \left. \left(88y - \tfrac{1}{2}y^2\right) \right|_0^{16} = 1280.$$

The volume of the building is 1280 cubic meters.

Figure 16.11: A slant-roofed building

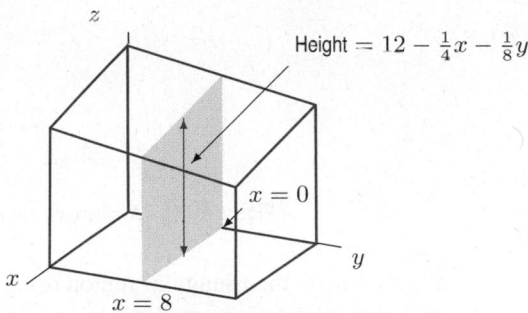

Figure 16.12: Cross-section of a building

Notice that the inner integral $\int_0^8 (12 - \tfrac{1}{4}x - \tfrac{1}{8}y)\, dx$ in Example 1 gives the area of the cross section of the building perpendicular to the y-axis in Figure 16.12.

The iterated integral $\int_0^{16} \int_0^8 (12 - \tfrac{1}{4}x - \tfrac{1}{8}y)\, dx\, dy$ thus calculates the volume by adding the volumes of thin cross-sectional slabs.

The Order of Integration

In computing the fox population, we could have chosen to add columns (fixed x) first, instead of the rows. This leads to an iterated integral where x is constant in the inner integral instead of y. Thus,

$$\int_R f(x, y)\, dA = \int_a^b \left(\int_c^d f(x, y)\, dy \right) dx$$

where R is the rectangle $a \leq x \leq b$ and $c \leq y \leq d$.

For any function we are likely to meet, it does not matter in which order we integrate over a rectangular region R; we get the same value for the double integral either way.

$$\int_R f\, dA = \int_c^d \left(\int_a^b f(x, y)\, dx \right) dy = \int_a^b \left(\int_c^d f(x, y)\, dy \right) dx$$

Example 2   Compute the volume of Example 1 as an iterated integral by integrating with respect to y first.

Solution   Rewriting the integral, we have

$$\text{Volume} = \int_0^8 \left(\int_0^{16} (12 - \tfrac{1}{4}x - \tfrac{1}{8}y)\, dy \right) dx = \int_0^8 \left(\left. \left(12y - \tfrac{1}{4}xy - \tfrac{1}{16}y^2\right) \right|_{y=0}^{y=16} \right) dx$$

$$= \int_0^8 (176 - 4x)\, dx = \left. (176x - 2x^2) \right|_0^8 = 1280 \text{ meter}^3.$$

Iterated Integrals Over Non-Rectangular Regions

Example 3   The density at the point (x, y) of a triangular metal plate, as shown in Figure 16.13, is $\delta(x, y)$. Express its mass as an iterated integral.

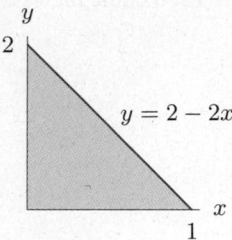

Figure 16.13: A triangular metal plate with density $\delta(x, y)$ at the point (x, y)

Solution   Approximate the triangular region using a grid of small rectangles of sides Δx and Δy. The mass of one rectangle is given by

$$\text{Mass of rectangle} \approx \text{Density} \cdot \text{Area} \approx \delta(x, y) \Delta x \Delta y.$$

Summing over all rectangles gives a Riemann sum which approximates the double integral:

$$\text{Mass} = \int_R \delta(x, y)\, dA,$$

where R is the triangle. We want to compute this integral using an iterated integral.

Think about how the iterated integral over the rectangle $a \leq x \leq b$, $c \leq y \leq d$ works:

$$\int_a^b \int_c^d f(x, y)\, dy\, dx.$$

The inside integral with respect to y is along vertical strips which begin at the horizontal line $y = c$ and end at the line $y = d$. There is one such strip for each x between $x = a$ and $x = b$. (See Figure 16.14.)

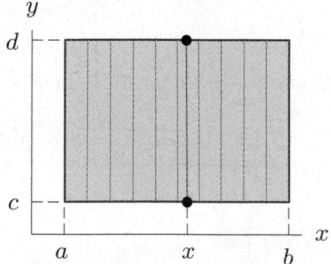

Figure 16.14: Integrating over a rectangle using vertical strips

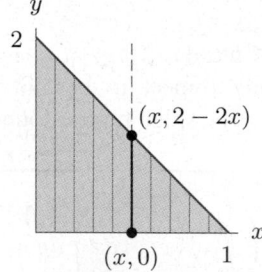

Figure 16.15: Integrating over a triangle using vertical strips

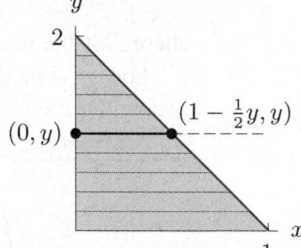

Figure 16.16: Integrating over a triangle using horizontal strips

For the triangular region in Figure 16.13, the idea is the same. The only difference is that the individual vertical strips no longer all go from $y = c$ to $y = d$. The vertical strip that starts at the point $(x, 0)$ ends at the point $(x, 2 - 2x)$, because the top edge of the triangle is the line $y = 2 - 2x$. See Figure 16.15. On this vertical strip, y goes from 0 to $2 - 2x$. Hence, the inside integral is

$$\int_0^{2-2x} \delta(x, y)\, dy.$$

Finally, since there is a vertical strip for each x between 0 and 1, the outside integral goes from $x = 0$ to $x = 1$. Thus, the iterated integral we want is

$$\text{Mass} = \int_0^1 \int_0^{2-2x} \delta(x, y)\, dy\, dx.$$

We could have chosen to integrate in the opposite order, keeping y fixed in the inner integral instead of x. The limits are formed by looking at horizontal strips instead of vertical ones, and expressing the x-values at the end points in terms of y. To find the right endpoint of the strip, we use the equation of the top edge of the triangle in the form $x = 1 - \frac{1}{2}y$. Thus, a horizontal strip goes from $x = 0$ to $x = 1 - \frac{1}{2}y$. Since there is a strip for every y from 0 to 2, the iterated integral is

$$\text{Mass} = \int_0^2 \int_0^{1-\frac{1}{2}y} \delta(x, y) \, dx \, dy.$$

Limits on Iterated Integrals

- The limits on the outer integral must be constants.
- The limits on the inner integral can involve only the variable in the outer integral. For example, if the inner integral is with respect to x, its limits can be functions of y.

Example 4   Find the mass M of a metal plate R bounded by $y = x$ and $y = x^2$, with density given by $\delta(x, y) = 1 + xy$ kg/meter^2. (See Figure 16.17.)

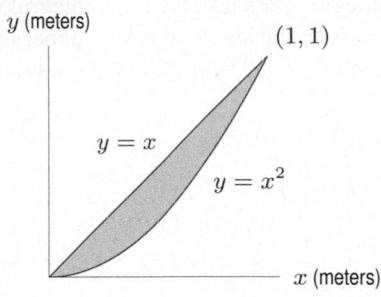

Figure 16.17: A metal plate with density $\delta(x, y)$

Solution   The mass is given by

$$M = \int_R \delta(x, y) \, dA.$$

We integrate along vertical strips first; this means we do the y integral first, which goes from the bottom boundary $y = x^2$ to the top boundary $y = x$. The left edge of the region is at $x = 0$ and the right edge is at the intersection point of $y = x$ and $y = x^2$, which is $(1, 1)$. Thus, the x-coordinate of the vertical strips can vary from $x = 0$ to $x = 1$, and so the mass is given by

$$M = \int_0^1 \int_{x^2}^x \delta(x, y) \, dy \, dx = \int_0^1 \int_{x^2}^x (1 + xy) \, dy \, dx.$$

Calculating the inner integral first gives

$$M = \int_0^1 \int_{x^2}^x (1 + xy) \, dy \, dx = \int_0^1 \left(y + x\frac{y^2}{2} \right) \Big|_{y=x^2}^{y=x} dx$$

$$= \int_0^1 \left(x - x^2 + \frac{x^3}{2} - \frac{x^5}{2} \right) dx = \left(\frac{x^2}{2} - \frac{x^3}{3} + \frac{x^4}{8} - \frac{x^6}{12} \right) \Big|_0^1 = \frac{5}{24} = 0.208 \text{ kg}.$$

Example 5   A city occupies a semicircular region of radius 3 km bordering on the ocean. Find the average distance from points in the city to the ocean.

Solution   Think of the ocean as everything below the x-axis in the xy-plane and think of the city as the upper half of the circular disk of radius 3 bounded by $x^2 + y^2 = 9$. (See Figure 16.18.)

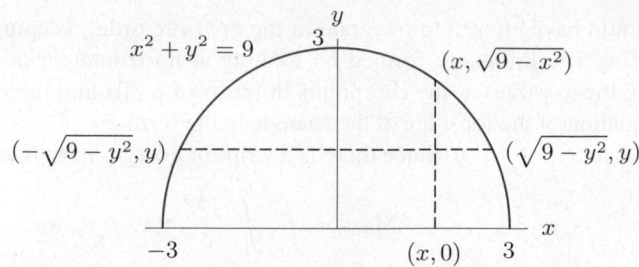

Figure 16.18: The city by the ocean showing a typical vertical strip and a typical horizontal strip

The distance from any point (x, y) in the city to the ocean is the vertical distance to the x-axis, namely y. Thus, we want to compute

$$\text{Average distance} = \frac{1}{\text{Area}(R)} \int_R y \, dA,$$

where R is the region between the upper half of the circle $x^2 + y^2 = 9$ and the x-axis. The area of R is $\pi 3^2/2 = 9\pi/2$.

To compute the integral, let's take the inner integral with respect to y. A vertical strip goes from the x-axis, namely $y = 0$, to the semicircle. The upper limit must be expressed in terms of x, so we solve $x^2 + y^2 = 9$ to get $y = \sqrt{9 - x^2}$. Since there is a strip for every x from -3 to 3, the integral is:

$$\int_R y \, dA = \int_{-3}^{3} \left(\int_0^{\sqrt{9-x^2}} y \, dy \right) dx = \int_{-3}^{3} \left(\frac{y^2}{2} \Big|_{y=0}^{y=\sqrt{9-x^2}} \right) dx$$

$$= \int_{-3}^{3} \frac{1}{2}(9 - x^2) \, dx = \frac{1}{2} \left(9x - \frac{x^3}{3} \right) \Big|_{-3}^{3} = \frac{1}{2}(18 - (-18)) = 18.$$

Therefore, the average distance is $18/(9\pi/2) = 4/\pi = 1.273$ km.

What if we choose the inner integral with respect to x? Then we get the limits by looking at horizontal strips, not vertical, and we solve $x^2 + y^2 = 9$ for x in terms of y. We get $x = -\sqrt{9 - y^2}$ at the left end of the strip and $x = \sqrt{9 - y^2}$ at the right. There is a strip for every y from 0 to 3, so

$$\int_R y \, dA = \int_0^3 \left(\int_{-\sqrt{9-y^2}}^{\sqrt{9-y^2}} y \, dx \right) dy = \int_0^3 \left(yx \Big|_{x=-\sqrt{9-y^2}}^{x=\sqrt{9-y^2}} \right) dy = \int_0^3 2y\sqrt{9 - y^2} \, dy$$

$$= -\frac{2}{3}(9 - y^2)^{3/2} \Big|_0^3 = -\frac{2}{3}(0 - 27) = 18.$$

We get the same result as before. The average distance to the ocean is $(2/(9\pi))18 = 4/\pi = 1.273$ km.

In the examples so far, a region was given and the problem was to determine the limits for an iterated integral. Sometimes the limits are known and we want to determine the region.

Example 6   Sketch the region of integration for the iterated integral $\int_0^6 \int_{x/3}^2 x\sqrt{y^3 + 1} \, dy \, dx$.

Solution   The inner integral is with respect to y, so we imagine the region built of vertical strips. The bottom of each strip is on the line $y = x/3$, and the top is on the horizontal line $y = 2$. Since the limits of the outer integral are 0 and 6, the whole region is contained between the vertical lines $x = 0$ and $x = 6$. Notice that the lines $y = 2$ and $y = x/3$ meet where $x = 6$. See Figure 16.19.

Figure 16.19: The region of integration for Example 6, showing the vertical strip

Reversing the Order of Integration

It is sometimes helpful to reverse the order of integration in an iterated integral. An integral which is difficult or impossible with the integration in one order can be quite straightforward in the other. The next example is such a case.

Example 7   Evaluate $\displaystyle\int_0^6 \int_{x/3}^2 x\sqrt{y^3+1}\; dy\, dx$ using the region sketched in Figure 16.19.

Solution   Since $\sqrt{y^3+1}$ has no elementary antiderivative, we cannot calculate the inner integral symbolically. We try reversing the order of integration. From Figure 16.19, we see that horizontal strips go from $x=0$ to $x=3y$ and that there is a strip for every y from 0 to 2. Thus, when we change the order of integration we get

$$\int_0^6 \int_{x/3}^2 x\sqrt{y^3+1}\, dy\, dx = \int_0^2 \int_0^{3y} x\sqrt{y^3+1}\, dx\, dy.$$

Now we can at least do the inner integral because we know the antiderivative of x. What about the outer integral?

$$\int_0^2 \int_0^{3y} x\sqrt{y^3+1}\, dx\, dy = \int_0^2 \left(\frac{x^2}{2}\sqrt{y^3+1}\right)\Bigg|_{x=0}^{x=3y} dy = \int_0^2 \frac{9y^2}{2}(y^3+1)^{1/2}\, dy$$

$$= (y^3+1)^{3/2}\Big|_0^2 = 27 - 1 = 26.$$

Thus, reversing the order of integration made the integral in the previous problem much easier. Notice that to reverse the order it is essential first to sketch the region over which the integration is being performed.

Exercises and Problems for Section 16.2

Exercises

In Exercises 1–4, sketch the region of integration.

1. $\displaystyle\int_0^\pi \int_0^x y\sin x\, dy\, dx$

2. $\displaystyle\int_0^1 \int_{y^2}^y xy\, dx\, dy$

3. $\displaystyle\int_0^2 \int_0^{y^2} y^2 x\, dx\, dy$

4. $\displaystyle\int_0^1 \int_{x-2}^{\cos \pi x} y\, dy\, dx$

For Exercises 5–12, evaluate the integral.

5. $\displaystyle\int_0^3 \int_0^4 (4x+3y)\, dx\, dy$

6. $\displaystyle\int_0^2 \int_0^3 (x^2+y^2)\, dy\, dx$

7. $\displaystyle\int_0^3 \int_0^2 6xy\, dy\, dx$

8. $\displaystyle\int_0^1 \int_0^2 x^2 y\, dy\, dx$

9. $\displaystyle\int_0^1 \int_0^1 ye^{xy}\, dx\, dy$

10. $\displaystyle\int_0^2 \int_0^y y\, dx\, dy$

11. $\displaystyle\int_0^3 \int_0^y \sin x\, dx\, dy$

12. $\displaystyle\int_0^{\pi/2} \int_0^{\sin x} x\, dy\, dx$

For Exercises 13–16, sketch the region of integration and evaluate the integral.

13. $\displaystyle\int_1^3 \int_0^4 e^{x+y}\, dy\, dx$

14. $\displaystyle\int_0^2 \int_0^x e^{x^2}\, dy\, dx$

15. $\displaystyle\int_1^5 \int_x^{2x} \sin x\, dy\, dx$

16. $\displaystyle\int_1^4 \int_{\sqrt{y}}^y x^2 y^3\, dx\, dy$

In Exercises 17–22, write $\int_R f \, dA$ as an iterated integral for the shaded region R.

17.

18.

19.

20.

21.

22.

For Exercises 23–27, evaluate the integral.

23. $\int_R \sqrt{x+y} \, dA$, where R is the rectangle $0 \leq x \leq 1$, $0 \leq y \leq 2$.

24. Calculate the integral in Exercise 23 using the other order of integration.

25. $\int_R (5x^2 + 1) \sin 3y \, dA$, where R is the rectangle $-1 \leq x \leq 1$, $0 \leq y \leq \pi/3$.

26. $\int_R xy \, dA$, where R is the triangle $x + y \leq 1$, $x \geq 0$, $y \geq 0$.

27. $\int_R (2x + 3y)^2 \, dA$, where R is the triangle with vertices at $(-1, 0)$, $(0, 1)$, and $(1, 0)$.

Problems

In Problems 28–31, integrate $f(x, y) = xy$ over the region R.

28.

29.

30.

31.

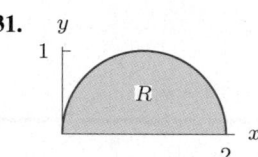

32. (a) Use four subrectangles to approximate the volume of the object whose base is the region $0 \leq x \leq 4$ and $0 \leq y \leq 6$, and whose height is given by $f(x, y) = xy$. Find an overestimate and an underestimate and average the two.

(b) Integrate to find the exact volume of the three-dimensional object described in part (a).

In Problems 33–37, evaluate the integral by reversing the order of integration.

33. $\int_0^1 \int_y^1 e^{x^2} \, dx \, dy$

34. $\int_0^1 \int_y^1 \sin(x^2) \, dx \, dy$

35. $\int_0^1 \int_{\sqrt{y}}^1 \sqrt{2 + x^3} \, dx \, dy$

36. $\int_0^3 \int_{y^2}^9 y \sin(x^2) \, dx \, dy$

37. $\int_0^1 \int_{e^y}^e \frac{x}{\ln x} \, dx \, dy$

38. Find the volume under the graph of the function $f(x, y) = 6x^2 y$ over the region shown in Figure 16.20.

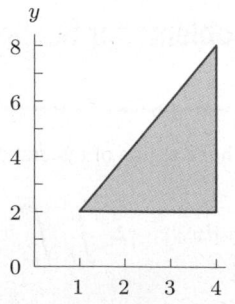

Figure 16.20

39. (a) Find the volume below the surface $z = x^2 + y^2$ and above the xy-plane for $-1 \leq x \leq 1, -1 \leq y \leq 1$.

(b) Find the volume above the surface $z = x^2 + y^2$ and below the plane $z = 2$ for $-1 \leq x \leq 1$, $-1 \leq y \leq 1$.

40. Compute the integral

$$\int\int_R (2x^2 + y)\, dA,$$

where R is the triangular region with vertices at $(0, 1)$, $(-2, 3)$ and $(2, 3)$.

41. (a) Sketch the region in the xy-plane bounded by the x-axis, $y = x$, and $x + y = 1$.
   (b) Express the integral of $f(x, y)$ over this region in terms of iterated integrals in two ways. (In one, use $dx\, dy$; in the other, use $dy\, dx$.)
   (c) Using one of your answers to part (b), evaluate the integral exactly with $f(x, y) = x$.

42. Let $f(x, y) = x^2 e^{x^2}$ and let R be the triangle bounded by the lines $x = 3$, $x = y/2$, and $y = x$ in the xy-plane.

   (a) Express $\int_R f\, dA$ as a double integral in two different ways.
   (b) Evaluate one of them.

43. Find the average value of $f(x, y) = x^2 + 4y$ on the rectangle $0 \le x \le 3$ and $0 \le y \le 6$.

44. Find the average value of $f(x, y) = xy^2$ on the rectangle $0 \le x \le 4, 0 \le y \le 3$.

In Problems 45–47 set up, but do not evaluate, an iterated integral for the volume of the solid.

45. Under the graph of $f(x, y) = 25 - x^2 - y^2$ and above the xy-plane.

46. Below the graph of $f(x, y) = 25 - x^2 - y^2$ and above the plane $z = 16$.

47. The three-sided pyramid whose base is on the xy-plane and whose three sides are the vertical planes $y = 0$ and $y - x = 4$, and the slanted plane $2x + y + z = 4$.

In Problems 48–53, find the volume of the solid region.

48. Under the graph of $f(x, y) = xy$ and above the square $0 \le x \le 2, 0 \le y \le 2$ in the xy-plane.

49. Under the graph of $f(x, y) = x^2 + y^2$ and above the triangle $0 \le y \le x, 0 \le x \le 1$.

50. Under the graph of $f(x, y) = x + y$ and above the region $y^2 \le x, 0 \le x \le 9, y \ge 0$.

51. Under the graph of $2x + y + z = 4$ in the first octant.

52. The solid between the planes $z = 3x + 2y + 1$ and $z = x + y$, and above the triangle with vertices $(1, 0, 0)$, $(2, 2, 0)$, and $(0, 1, 0)$ in the xy-plane. See Figure 16.21.

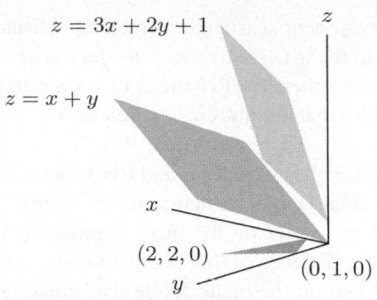

$z = 3x + 2y + 1$

$z = x + y$

$(2, 2, 0)$

$(0, 1, 0)$

Figure 16.21

53. The solid region R bounded by the coordinate planes and the graph of $ax + by + cz = 1$. Assume a, b, and $c > 0$.

54. If R is the region $x + y \ge a, x^2 + y^2 \le a^2$, with $a > 0$, evaluate the integral

$$\int_R xy\, dA.$$

55. The region W lies below the surface $f(x, y) = 2e^{-(x-1)^2 - y^2}$ and above the disk $x^2 + y^2 \le 4$ in the xy-plane.

   (a) Describe in words the contours of f, using $f(x, y) = 1$ as an example.
   (b) Write an integral giving the area of the cross-section of W in the plane $x = 1$.
   (c) Write an iterated double integral giving the volume of W.

56. Find the average distance to the x-axis for points in the region bounded by the x-axis and the graph of $y = x - x^2$.

57. Give the contour diagram of a function f whose average value on the square $0 \le x \le 1, 0 \le y \le 1$ is

   (a) Greater than the average of the values of f at the four corners of the square.
   (b) Less than the average of the values of f at the four corners of the square.

58. The function $f(x, y) = ax + by$ has an average value of 20 on the rectangle $0 \le x \le 2, 0 \le y \le 3$.

   (a) What can you say about the constants a and b?
   (b) Find two different choices for f that have average value 20 on the rectangle, and give their contour diagrams on the rectangle.

59. The function $f(x, y) = ax^2 + bxy + cy^2$ has an average value of 20 on the square $0 \le x \le 2, 0 \le y \le 2$.

   (a) What can you say about the constants a, b, and c?
   (b) Find two different choices for f that have average value 20 on the square, and give their contour diagrams on the square.

60. Show that for a right triangle the average distance from any point in the triangle to one of the legs is one-third the length of the other leg. (The legs of a right triangle are the two sides that are not the hypotenuse.)

61. A rectangular plate of sides a and b is subjected to a normal force (that is, perpendicular to the plate). The pressure, p, at any point on the plate is proportional to the square of the distance of that point from one corner. Find the total force on the plate. [Note that pressure is force per unit area.]

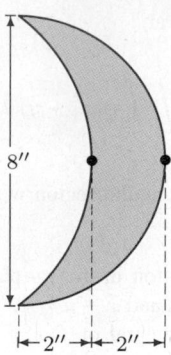

Figure 16.22

62. Find the area of the crescent-moon shape with circular arcs as edges and the dimensions shown in Figure 16.22.

Strengthen Your Understanding

In Problems 63–64, explain what is wrong with the statement.

63. $\int_0^1 \int_0^x f(x,y)\, dy\, dx = \int_0^1 \int_0^y f(x,y)\, dx\, dy$

64. $\int_0^1 \int_0^y xy\, dx\, dy = \int_0^y \int_0^1 xy\, dy\, dx$

In Problems 65–67, give an example of:

65. An iterated double integral, with limits of integration, giving the volume of a cylinder standing vertically with a circular base in the xy-plane.

66. A nonconstant function, f, whose integral is 4 over the triangular region with vertices $(0,0)$, $(1,0)$, $(1,1)$.

67. A double integral representing the volume of a triangular prism of base area 6.

Are the statements in Problems 68–75 true or false? Give reasons for your answer.

68. The iterated integral $\int_0^1 \int_5^{12} f\, dx\, dy$ is computed over the rectangle $0 \le x \le 1, 5 \le y \le 12$.

69. If R is the region inside the triangle with vertices $(0,0), (1,1)$ and $(0,2)$, then the double integral $\int_R f\, dA$ can be evaluated by an iterated integral of the form $\int_0^2 \int_0^1 f\, dx\, dy$.

70. The region of integration of the iterated integral $\int_1^2 \int_{x^2}^{x^3} f\, dy\, dx$ lies completely in the first quadrant (that is, $x \ge 0, y \ge 0$).

71. If the limits a, b, c and d in the iterated integral $\int_a^b \int_c^d f\, dy\, dx$ are all positive, then the value of $\int_a^b \int_c^d f\, dy\, dx$ is also positive.

72. If $f(x,y)$ is a function of y only, then $\int_a^b \int_0^1 f\, dx\, dy = \int_a^b f\, dy$.

73. If R is the region inside a circle of radius a, centered at the origin, then $\int_R f\, dA = \int_{-a}^a \int_0^{\sqrt{a^2-x^2}} f\, dy\, dx$.

74. If $f(x,y) = g(x) \cdot h(y)$, where g and h are single-variable functions, then

$$\int_a^b \int_c^d f\, dy\, dx = \left(\int_a^b g(x)\, dx \right) \cdot \left(\int_c^d h(y)\, dy \right).$$

75. If $f(x,y) = g(x) + h(y)$, where g and h are single-variable functions, then

$$\int_a^b \int_c^d f\, dx\, dy = \left(\int_a^b g(x)\, dx \right) + \left(\int_c^d h(y)\, dy \right).$$

16.3 TRIPLE INTEGRALS

A continuous function of three variables can be integrated over a solid region W in 3-space in the same way as a function of two variables is integrated over a flat region in 2-space. Again, we start with a Riemann sum. First we subdivide W into smaller regions, then we multiply the volume of each region by a value of the function in that region, and then we add the results. For example, if W is the box $a \le x \le b, c \le y \le d, p \le z \le q$, then we subdivide each side into n, m, and l pieces, thereby chopping W into nml smaller boxes, as shown in Figure 16.23.

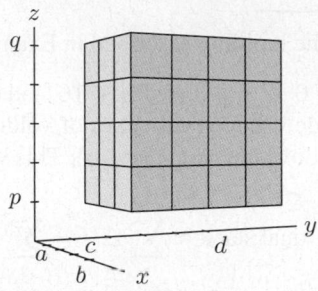

Figure 16.23: Subdividing a three-dimensional box

The volume of each smaller box is

$$\Delta V = \Delta x \Delta y \Delta z,$$

where $\Delta x = (b-a)/n$, and $\Delta y = (d-c)/m$, and $\Delta z = (q-p)/l$. Using this subdivision, we pick a point $(u_{ijk}, v_{ijk}, w_{ijk})$ in the ijk-th small box and construct a Riemann sum

$$\sum_{i,j,k} f(u_{ijk}, v_{ijk}, w_{ijk}) \, \Delta V.$$

If f is continuous, as Δx, Δy, and Δz approach 0, this Riemann sum approaches the definite integral, $\int_W f \, dV$, called a *triple integral*, which is defined as

$$\int_W f \, dV = \lim_{\Delta x, \Delta y, \Delta z \to 0} \sum_{i,j,k} f(u_{ijk}, v_{ijk}, w_{ijk}) \, \Delta x \, \Delta y \, \Delta z.$$

As in the case of a double integral, we can evaluate this integral as an iterated integral:

Triple integral as an iterated integral

$$\int_W f \, dV = \int_p^q \left(\int_c^d \left(\int_a^b f(x,y,z) \, dx \right) dy \right) dz,$$

where y and z are treated as constants in the innermost (dx) integral, and z is treated as a constant in the middle (dy) integral. Other orders of integration are possible.

Example 1 A cube C has sides of length 4 cm and is made of a material of variable density. If one corner is at the origin and the adjacent corners are on the positive x, y, and z axes, then the density at the point (x,y,z) is $\delta(x,y,z) = 1 + xyz$ gm/cm^3. Find the mass of the cube.

Solution Consider a small piece ΔV of the cube, small enough so that the density remains close to constant over the piece. Then

$$\text{Mass of small piece} = \text{Density} \cdot \text{Volume} \approx \delta(x,y,z) \, \Delta V.$$

To get the total mass, we add the masses of the small pieces and take the limit as $\Delta V \to 0$. Thus, the mass is the triple integral

$$M = \int_C \delta \, dV = \int_0^4 \int_0^4 \int_0^4 (1 + xyz) \, dx \, dy \, dz = \int_0^4 \int_0^4 \left(x + \frac{1}{2}x^2 yz \right) \Big|_{x=0}^{x=4} dy \, dz$$

$$= \int_0^4 \int_0^4 (4 + 8yz) \, dy \, dz = \int_0^4 \left(4y + 4y^2 z \right) \Big|_{y=0}^{y=4} dz = \int_0^4 (16 + 64z) \, dz = 576 \, \text{gm}.$$

Example 2   Express the volume of the building described in Example 1 on page 876 as a triple integral.

Solution   The building is given by $0 \le x \le 8$, $0 \le y \le 16$, and $0 \le z \le 12 - x/4 - y/8$. (See Figure 16.24.) To find its volume, divide it into small cubes of volume $\Delta V = \Delta x \, \Delta y \, \Delta z$ and add. First, make a vertical stack of cubes above the point $(x, y, 0)$. This stack goes from $z = 0$ to $z = 12 - x/4 - y/8$, so

$$\text{Volume of vertical stack} \approx \sum_z \Delta V = \sum_z \Delta x \, \Delta y \, \Delta z = \left(\sum_z \Delta z \right) \Delta x \, \Delta y.$$

Next, line up these stacks parallel to the y-axis to form a slice from $y = 0$ to $y = 16$. So

$$\text{Volume of slice} \approx \left(\sum_y \sum_z \Delta z \, \Delta y \right) \Delta x.$$

Finally, line up the slices along the x-axis from $x = 0$ to $x = 8$ and add up their volumes, to get

$$\text{Volume of building} \approx \sum_x \sum_y \sum_z \Delta z \, \Delta y \, \Delta x.$$

Thus, in the limit,

$$\text{Volume of building} = \int_0^8 \int_0^{16} \int_0^{12-x/4-y/8} 1 \, dz \, dy \, dx.$$

Figure 16.24: Volume of building (shown to left) divided into blocks and slabs for a triple integral

Example 3   Set up an iterated integral to compute the mass of the solid cone bounded by $z = \sqrt{x^2 + y^2}$ and $z = 3$, if the density is given by $\delta(x, y, z) = z$.

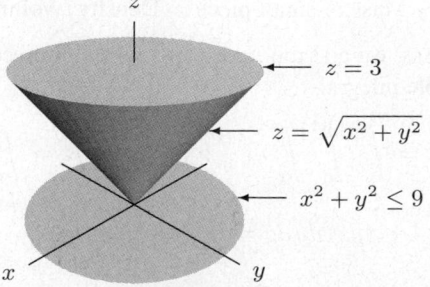

Figure 16.25

Solution   We break the cone in Figure 16.25 into small cubes of volume $\Delta V = \Delta x \, \Delta y \, \Delta z$, on which the density is approximately constant, and approximate the mass of each cube by $\delta(x, y, z) \, \Delta x \, \Delta y \, \Delta z$. Stacking the cubes vertically above the point $(x, y, 0)$, starting on the cone at height $z = \sqrt{x^2 + y^2}$ and going up to $z = 3$, tells us that the inner integral is

$$\int_{\sqrt{x^2+y^2}}^{3} \delta(x, y, z) \, dz = \int_{\sqrt{x^2+y^2}}^{3} z \, dz.$$

There is a stack for every point in the xy-plane in the shadow of the cone. The cone $z = \sqrt{x^2 + y^2}$ intersects the horizontal plane $z = 3$ in the circle $x^2 + y^2 = 9$, so there is a stack for all (x, y) in the region $x^2 + y^2 \leq 9$. Lining up the stacks parallel to the y-axis gives a slice from $y = -\sqrt{9 - x^2}$ to $y = \sqrt{9 - x^2}$, for each fixed value of x. Thus, the limits on the middle integral are

$$\int_{-\sqrt{9-x^2}}^{\sqrt{9-x^2}} \int_{\sqrt{x^2+y^2}}^{3} z \, dz \, dy.$$

Finally, there is a slice for each x between -3 and 3, so the integral we want is

$$\text{Mass} = \int_{-3}^{3} \int_{-\sqrt{9-x^2}}^{\sqrt{9-x^2}} \int_{\sqrt{x^2+y^2}}^{3} z \, dz \, dy \, dx.$$

Notice that setting up the limits on the two outer integrals was just like setting up the limits for a double integral over the region $x^2 + y^2 \leq 9$.

As the previous example illustrates, for a region W contained between two surfaces, the innermost limits correspond to these surfaces. The middle and outer limits ensure that we integrate over the "shadow" of W in the xy-plane.

Limits on Triple Integrals

- The limits for the outer integral are constants.
- The limits for the middle integral can involve only one variable (that in the outer integral).
- The limits for the inner integral can involve two variables (those on the two outer integrals).

Exercises and Problems for Section 16.3

Exercises

In Exercises 1–4, find the triple integrals of the function over the region W.

1. $f(x, y, z) = x^2 + 5y^2 - z$, W is the rectangular box $0 \leq x \leq 2, -1 \leq y \leq 1, 2 \leq z \leq 3$.

2. $h(x, y, z) = ax + by + cz$, W is the rectangular box $0 \leq x \leq 1, 0 \leq y \leq 1, 0 \leq z \leq 2$.

3. $f(x, y, z) = \sin x \cos(y + z)$, W is the cube $0 \leq x \leq \pi$, $0 \leq y \leq \pi, 0 \leq z \leq \pi$.

4. $f(x, y, z) = e^{-x-y-z}$, W is the rectangular box with corners at $(0, 0, 0), (a, 0, 0), (0, b, 0),$ and $(0, 0, c)$.

Sketch the region of integration in Exercises 5–13.

5. $\displaystyle\int_{0}^{1} \int_{-1}^{1} \int_{0}^{\sqrt{1-x^2}} f(x, y, z) \, dz \, dx \, dy$

6. $\displaystyle\int_{0}^{1} \int_{-1}^{1} \int_{0}^{\sqrt{1-z^2}} f(x, y, z) \, dy \, dz \, dx$

7. $\displaystyle\int_{0}^{1} \int_{-1}^{1} \int_{-\sqrt{1-x^2}}^{\sqrt{1-x^2}} f(x, y, z) \, dz \, dx \, dy$

8. $\int_{-1}^{1}\int_{0}^{1}\int_{-\sqrt{1-z^2}}^{\sqrt{1-z^2}} f(x,y,z)\,dy\,dz\,dx$

9. $\int_{-1}^{1}\int_{-\sqrt{1-x^2}}^{\sqrt{1-x^2}}\int_{0}^{\sqrt{1-x^2-z^2}} f(x,y,z)\,dy\,dz\,dx$

10. $\int_{0}^{1}\int_{-\sqrt{1-z^2}}^{\sqrt{1-z^2}}\int_{0}^{\sqrt{1-x^2-z^2}} f(x,y,z)\,dy\,dx\,dz$

11. $\int_{0}^{1}\int_{0}^{\sqrt{1-y^2}}\int_{-\sqrt{1-x^2-y^2}}^{\sqrt{1-x^2-y^2}} f(x,y,z)\,dz\,dx\,dy$

12. $\int_{0}^{1}\int_{-\sqrt{1-z^2}}^{\sqrt{1-z^2}}\int_{-\sqrt{1-y^2-z^2}}^{\sqrt{1-y^2-z^2}} f(x,y,z)\,dx\,dy\,dz$

13. $\int_{0}^{1}\int_{0}^{\sqrt{1-z^2}}\int_{-\sqrt{1-x^2-z^2}}^{\sqrt{1-x^2-z^2}} f(x,y,z)\,dy\,dx\,dz$

Problems

In Problems 14–18, decide whether the integrals are positive, negative, or zero. Let S be the solid sphere $x^2 + y^2 + z^2 \leq 1$, and T be the top half of this sphere (with $z \geq 0$), and B be the bottom half (with $z \leq 0$), and R be the right half of the sphere (with $x \geq 0$), and L be the left half (with $x \leq 0$).

14. $\int_{T} e^z\,dV$ **15.** $\int_{B} e^z\,dV$ **16.** $\int_{S} \sin z\,dV$

17. $\int_{T} \sin z\,dV$ **18.** $\int_{R} \sin z\,dV$

Let W be the solid cone bounded by $z = \sqrt{x^2 + y^2}$ and $z = 2$. For Problems 19–27, decide (without calculating its value) whether the integral is positive, negative, or zero.

19. $\int_{W} y\,dV$ **20.** $\int_{W} x\,dV$

21. $\int_{W} z\,dV$ **22.** $\int_{W} xy\,dV$

23. $\int_{W} xyz\,dV$ **24.** $\int_{W} (z-2)\,dV$

25. $\int_{W} \sqrt{x^2+y^2}\,dV$ **26.** $\int_{W} e^{-xyz}\,dV$

27. $\int_{W} (z-\sqrt{x^2+y^2})\,dV$

28. Find the volume of the region bounded by the planes $z = 3y$, $z = y$, $y = 1$, $x = 1$, and $x = 2$.

29. Find the volume of the region bounded by $z = x^2$, $0 \leq x \leq 5$, and the planes $y = 0$, $y = 3$, and $z = 0$.

30. Find the volume of the region in the first octant bounded by the coordinate planes and the surface $x + y + z = 2$.

31. A trough with triangular cross-section lies along the x-axis for $0 \leq x \leq 10$. The slanted sides are given by $z = y$ and $z = -y$ for $0 \leq z \leq 1$ and the ends by $x = 0$ and $x = 10$, where x, y, z are in meters. The trough contains a sludge whose density at the point (x, y, z) is $\delta = e^{-3x}$ kg per m^3.

   (a) Express the total mass of sludge in the trough in terms of triple integrals.

   (b) Find the mass.

32. Find the volume of the region bounded by $z = x+y$, $z = 10$, and the planes $x = 0$, $y = 0$.

In Problems 33–38, write a triple integral, including limits of integration, that gives the specified volume.

33. Between $z = x + y$ and $z = 1 + 2x + 2y$ and above $0 \leq x \leq 1$, $0 \leq y \leq 2$.

34. Between the paraboloid $z = x^2 + y^2$ and the sphere $x^2 + y^2 + z^2 = 4$ and above the disk $x^2 + y^2 \leq 1$.

35. Between $2x + 2y + z = 6$ and $3x + 4y + z = 6$ and above $x + y \leq 1$, $x \geq 0$, $y \geq 0$.

36. Under the sphere $x^2 + y^2 + z^2 = 9$ and above the region between $y = x$ and $y = 2x - 2$ in the xy-plane in the first quadrant.

37. Between the top portion of the sphere $x^2 + y^2 + z^2 = 9$ and the plane $z = 2$.

38. Under the sphere $x^2 + y^2 + z^2 = 4$ and above the region $x^2 + y^2 \leq 4$, $0 \leq x \leq 1$, $0 \leq y \leq 2$ in the xy-plane.

In Problems 39–42, write limits of integration for the integral $\int_{W} f(x, y, z)\,dV$ where W is the quarter or half sphere or cylinder shown.

39.

40.

41.

42.

43. Find the volume of the region between the plane $z = x$ and the surface $z = x^2$, and the planes $y = 0$, and $y = 3$.

44. Find the volume of the region bounded by $z = x + y$, $0 \le x \le 5$, $0 \le y \le 5$, and the planes $x = 0$, $y = 0$, and $z = 0$.

45. Find the volume of the pyramid with base in the plane $z = -6$ and sides formed by the three planes $y = 0$ and $y - x = 4$ and $2x + y + z = 4$.

46. Find the volume between the planes $z = 1 + x + y$ and $x + y + z = 1$ and above the triangle $x + y \le 1$, $x \ge 0$, $y \ge 0$ in the xy-plane.

47. Find the volume between the plane $x + y + z = 1$ and the xy-plane, for $x + y \le 2$, $x \ge 0$, $y \ge 0$.

48. A solid shaped like a wedge of cheese has as its base the xy-plane, bounded by the x-axis, the line $y = x$ and the line $x + y = 1$. Its sides are vertical, and its top is the plane $x + y + z = 2$. At any point, the density of the solid is four times the distance from the xy-plane.

   (a) Express the mass of the region in terms of triple integrals.
   (b) Find the mass.

49. Find the mass of a triangular-shaped solid bounded by the planes $z = 1 + x$, $z = 1 - x$, $z = 0$, and with $0 \le y \le 3$. The density is $\delta = 10 - z$ gm/(cm)^3, and x, y, z are in cm.

50. Find the mass of the solid bounded by the xy-plane, yz-plane, xz-plane, and the plane $(x/3) + (y/2) + (z/6) = 1$, if the density of the solid is given by $\delta(x, y, z) = x + y$.

51. Find the mass of the pyramid with base in the plane $z = -6$ and sides formed by the three planes $y = 0$ and $y - x = 4$ and $2x + y + z = 4$, if the density of the solid is given by $\delta(x, y, z) = y$.

52. Let E be the solid pyramid bounded by the planes $x + z = 6$, $x - z = 0$, $y + z = 6$, $y - z = 0$, and above the plane $z = 0$ (see Figure 16.26). The density at any point in the pyramid is given by $\delta(x, y, z) = z$ grams per cm^3, where x, y, and z are measured in cm.

   (a) Explain in practical terms what the triple integral $\int_E z \, dV$ represents.
   (b) In evaluating the integral from part (a), how many separate triple integrals would be required if we chose to integrate in the z-direction first?
   (c) Evaluate the triple integral from part (a) by integrating in a well-chosen order.

Figure 16.26

53. (a) What is the equation of the plane passing through the points $(1, 0, 0)$, $(0, 1, 0)$, and $(0, 0, 1)$?
   (b) Find the volume of the region bounded by this plane and the planes $x = 0$, $y = 0$, and $z = 0$.

Problems 54–56 refer to Figure 16.27, which shows triangular portions of the planes $2x + 4y + z = 4$, $3x - 2y = 0$, $z = 2$, and the three coordinate planes $x = 0$, $y = 0$, and $z = 0$. For each solid region E, write down an iterated integral for the triple integral $\int_E f(x, y, z) \, dV$.

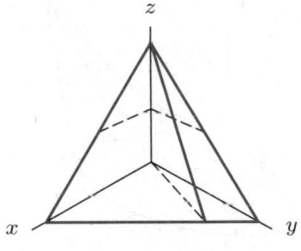

Figure 16.27

54. E is the region bounded by $y = 0$, $z = 0$, $3x - 2y = 0$, and $2x + 4y + z = 4$.

55. E is the region bounded by $x = 0$, $y = 0$, $z = 0$, $z = 2$, and $2x + 4y + z = 4$.

56. E is the region bounded by $x = 0$, $z = 0$, $3x - 2y = 0$, and $2x + 4y + z = 4$.

57. Figure 16.28 shows part of a spherical ball of radius 5 cm. Write an iterated triple integral which represents the volume of this region.

2 cm

Figure 16.28

58. A solid region D is a half cylinder of radius 1 lying horizontally with its rectangular base in the xy-plane and its axis along the y-axis from $y = 0$ to $y = 10$. (The region is above the xy-plane.)

   (a) What is the equation of the curved surface of this half cylinder?

   (b) Write the limits of integration of the integral $\int_D f(x, y, z)\, dV$ in Cartesian coordinates.

59. Set up, but do not evaluate, an iterated integral for the volume of the solid formed by the intersections of the cylinders $x^2 + z^2 = 1$ and $y^2 + z^2 = 1$.

Problems 60–62 refer to Figure 16.29, which shows E, the region in the first octant bounded by the parabolic cylinder $z = 6y^2$ and the elliptical cylinder $x^2 + 3y^2 = 12$. For the given order of integration, write an iterated integral equivalent to the triple integral $\int_E f(x, y, z)\, dV$.

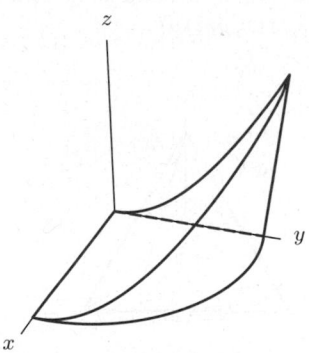

Figure 16.29

60. $dz\, dx\, dy$ **61.** $dx\, dz\, dy$ **62.** $dy\, dz\, dx$

63. Find the average value of the sum of the squares of three numbers x, y, z, where each number is between 0 and 2.

64. Let E be the region in the first octant bounded between the plane $x + 2y + z = 4$, the parabolic cylinder $x = 2y^2$, and the coordinate planes (see Figure 16.30). For each of the following orders of integration, write down an iterated integral equivalent to the triple integral $\int_E f(x, y, z)\, dV$.

   (a) $dz\, dy\, dx$

   (b) $dy\, dz\, dx$

Figure 16.30

Problems 65–66 concern the *center of mass*, the point at which the mass of a solid body in motion can be considered to be concentrated. If the object has density $\rho(x, y, z)$ at the point (x, y, z) and occupies a region W, then the coordinates $(\bar{x}, \bar{y}, \bar{z})$ of the center of mass are given by

$$\bar{x} = \frac{1}{m} \int_W x\rho\, dV \quad \bar{y} = \frac{1}{m} \int_W y\rho\, dV \quad \bar{z} = \frac{1}{m} \int_W z\rho\, dV$$

where $m = \int_W \rho\, dV$ is the total mass of the body.

65. A solid is bounded below by the square $z = 0, 0 \le x \le 1, 0 \le y \le 1$ and above by the surface $z = x + y + 1$. Find the total mass and the coordinates of the center of mass if the density is 1 gm/cm^3 and x, y, z are measured in centimeters.

66. Find the center of mass of the tetrahedron that is bounded by the xy, yz, xz planes and the plane $x + 2y + 3z = 1$. Assume the density is 1 gm/cm^3 and x, y, z are in centimeters.

Problems 67–69 concern a rotating solid body and its *moment of inertia* about an axis; this moment relates angular acceleration to torque (an analogue of force). For a body of constant density and mass m occupying a region W of volume V, the moments of inertia about the coordinate axes are

$$I_x = \frac{m}{V} \int_W (y^2 + z^2)\, dV \qquad I_y = \frac{m}{V} \int_W (x^2 + z^2)\, dV$$

$$I_z = \frac{m}{V} \int_W (x^2 + y^2)\, dV.$$

67. Find the moment of inertia about the z-axis of the rectangular solid of mass m given by $0 \le x \le 1, 0 \le y \le 2, 0 \le z \le 3$.

68. Find the moment of inertia about the x-axis of the rectangular solid $-a \le x \le a, -b \le y \le b$ and $-c \le z \le c$ of mass m.

69. Let a, b, and c denote the moments of inertia of a homogeneous solid object about the x, y and z-axes respectively. Explain why $a + b > c$.

Strengthen Your Understanding

In Problems 70–71, explain what is wrong with the statement.

70. Let S be the solid sphere $x^2 + y^2 + z^2 \leq 1$ and let U be the upper half of S where $z \geq 0$. Then $\int_S f(x, y, z)\, dV = 2 \int_U f(x, y, z)\, dV$.

71. $\int_0^1 \int_0^x \int_0^y f(x, y, z)\, dz\, dy\, dx = \int_0^1 \int_y^1 \int_0^x f(x, y, z)\, dz\, dx\, dy$

In Problems 72–73, give an example of:

72. A function f such that $\int_R f\, dV = 7$, where R is the cylinder $x^2 + y^2 \leq 4, 0 \leq z \leq 3$.

73. A nonconstant function $f(x, y, z)$ such that if B is the region enclosed by the sphere of radius 1 centered at the origin, the integral $\int_B f(x, y, z)\, dx\, dy\, dz$ is zero.

Are the statements in Problems 74–83 true or false? Give reasons for your answer.

74. If $\rho(x, y, z)$ is mass density of a material in 3-space, then $\int_W \rho(x, y, z)\, dV$ gives the volume of the solid region W.

75. The region of integration of the triple iterated integral $\int_0^1 \int_0^1 \int_0^x f\, dz\, dy\, dx$ lies above a square in the xy-plane and below a plane.

76. If W is the entire unit ball $x^2 + y^2 + z^2 \leq 1$ then an iterated integral over W has limits $\int_0^1 \int_0^{\sqrt{1-x^2}} \int_0^{\sqrt{1-x^2-y^2}} f\, dz\, dy\, dx$.

77. The iterated integrals $\int_0^1 \int_0^{1-x} \int_0^{1-x-y} f\, dz\, dy\, dx$ and $\int_0^1 \int_0^{1-z} \int_0^{1-y-z} f\, dx\, dy\, dz$ are equal.

78. The iterated integrals $\int_{-1}^1 \int_0^1 \int_0^{1-x^2} f\, dz\, dy\, dx$ and $\int_0^1 \int_0^1 \int_{-\sqrt{1-z}}^{\sqrt{1-z}} f\, dx\, dy\, dz$ are equal.

79. If W is a rectangular solid in 3-space, then $\int_W f\, dV = \int_a^b \int_c^d \int_e^k f\, dz\, dy\, dx$, where a, b, c, d, e, and k are constants.

80. If W is the unit cube $0 \leq x \leq 1, 0 \leq y \leq 1, 0 \leq z \leq 1$ and $\int_W f\, dV = 0$, then $f = 0$ everywhere in the unit cube.

81. If $f > g$ at all points in the solid region W, then $\int_W f\, dV > \int_W g\, dV$.

82. If W_1 and W_2 are solid regions with volume(W_1) > volume(W_2) then $\int_{W_1} f\, dV > \int_{W_2} f\, dV$.

83. Both double and triple integrals can be used to compute volume.

16.4 DOUBLE INTEGRALS IN POLAR COORDINATES

Integration in Polar Coordinates

We started this chapter by putting a rectangular grid on the fox population density map, to estimate the total population using a Riemann sum. However, sometimes a polar grid is more appropriate.

Example 1 A biologist studying insect populations around a circular lake divides the area into the polar sectors in Figure 16.31. The approximate population density in each sector is shown in millions per square km. Estimate the total insect population around the lake.

Shore of the lake

Figure 16.31: An insect-infested lake showing the insect population density by sector

Solution   To get the estimate, we multiply the population density in each sector by the area of that sector. Unlike the rectangles in a rectangular grid, the sectors in this grid do not all have the same area. The inner sectors have area

$$\frac{1}{4}(\pi 3^2 - \pi 2^2) = \frac{5\pi}{4} \approx 3.93 \text{ km}^2,$$

and the outer sectors have area

$$\frac{1}{4}(\pi 4^2 - \pi 3^2) = \frac{7\pi}{4} \approx 5.50 \text{ km}^2,$$

so we estimate

$$\text{Population} \approx (20)(3.93) + (17)(3.93) + (14)(3.93) + (17)(3.93) +$$
$$(13)(5.50) + (10)(5.50) + (8)(5.50) + (10)(5.50)$$
$$= 492.74 \text{ million insects.}$$

What Is dA in Polar Coordinates?

The previous example used a polar grid rather than a rectangular grid. A rectangular grid is constructed from vertical and horizontal lines of the form $x = k$ (a constant) and $y = l$ (another constant). In polar coordinates, $r = k$ gives a circle of radius k centered at the origin and $\theta = l$ gives a ray emanating from the origin (at angle l with the x-axis). A polar grid is built out of these circles and rays. Suppose we want to integrate $f(r, \theta)$ over the region R in Figure 16.32.

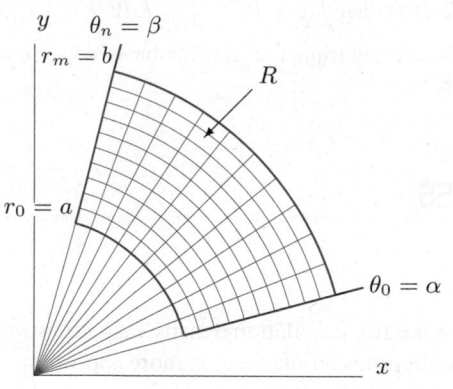

Figure 16.32: Dividing up a region using a polar grid

Figure 16.33: Calculating area ΔA in polar coordinates

Choosing (r_{ij}, θ_{ij}) in the ij-th bent rectangle in Figure 16.32 gives a Riemann sum:

$$\sum_{i,j} f(r_{ij}, \theta_{ij}) \Delta A.$$

To calculate the area ΔA, look at Figure 16.33. If Δr and $\Delta \theta$ are small, the shaded region is approximately a rectangle with sides $r \Delta \theta$ and Δr, so

$$\Delta A \approx r \Delta \theta \Delta r.$$

Thus, the Riemann sum is approximately

$$\sum_{i,j} f(r_{ij}, \theta_{ij}) r_{ij} \Delta \theta \Delta r.$$

If we take the limit as Δr and $\Delta \theta$ approach 0, we obtain

$$\int_R f \, dA = \int_\alpha^\beta \int_a^b f(r, \theta) \, r \, dr \, d\theta.$$

When computing integrals in polar coordinates, use $x = r \cos \theta, y = r \sin \theta, x^2 + y^2 = r^2$. Put $dA = r \, dr \, d\theta$ or $dA = r \, d\theta \, dr$.

Example 2   Compute the integral of $f(x, y) = 1/(x^2 + y^2)^{3/2}$ over the region R shown in Figure 16.34.

Figure 16.34: Integrate f over the polar region

Solution   The region R is described by the inequalities $1 \leq r \leq 2$, $0 \leq \theta \leq \pi/4$. In polar coordinates, $r = \sqrt{x^2 + y^2}$, so we can write f as

$$f(x, y) = \frac{1}{(x^2 + y^2)^{3/2}} = \frac{1}{(r^2)^{3/2}} = \frac{1}{r^3}.$$

Then

$$\int_R f \, dA = \int_0^{\pi/4} \int_1^2 \frac{1}{r^3} r \, dr \, d\theta = \int_0^{\pi/4} \left(\int_1^2 r^{-2} \, dr \right) d\theta$$

$$= \int_0^{\pi/4} \left. -\frac{1}{r} \right|_{r=1}^{r=2} d\theta = \int_0^{\pi/4} \frac{1}{2} \, d\theta = \frac{\pi}{8}.$$

Example 3   For each region in Figure 16.35, decide whether to integrate using polar or Cartesian coordinates. On the basis of its shape, write an iterated integral of an arbitrary function $f(x, y)$ over the region.

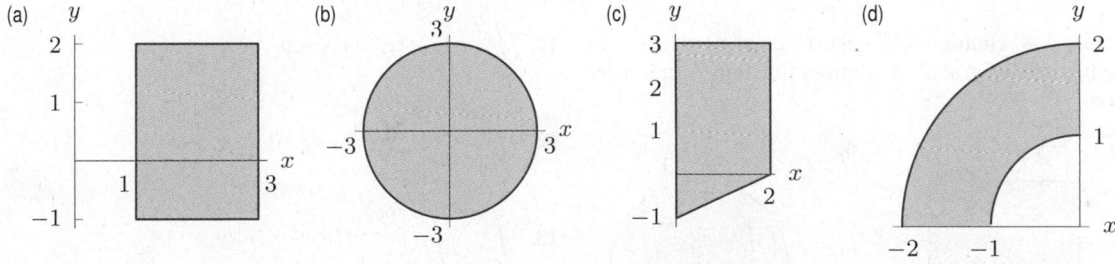

Figure 16.35

Solution   (a) Since this is a rectangular region, Cartesian coordinates are likely to be a better choice. The rectangle is described by the inequalities $1 \leq x \leq 3$ and $-1 \leq y \leq 2$, so the integral is

$$\int_{-1}^2 \int_1^3 f(x, y) \, dx \, dy.$$

(b) A circle is best described in polar coordinates. The radius is 3, so r goes from 0 to 3, and to describe the whole circle, θ goes from 0 to 2π. The integral is

$$\int_0^{2\pi} \int_0^3 f(r \cos \theta, r \sin \theta) \, r \, dr \, d\theta.$$

(c) The bottom boundary of this trapezoid is the line $y = (x/2) - 1$ and the top is the line $y = 3$, so we use Cartesian coordinates. If we integrate with respect to y first, the lower limit of the integral is $(x/2) - 1$ and the upper limit is 3. The x limits are $x = 0$ to $x = 2$. So the integral is

$$\int_0^2 \int_{(x/2)-1}^3 f(x, y) \, dy \, dx.$$

(d) This is another polar region: it is a piece of a ring in which r goes from 1 to 2. Since it is in the second quadrant, θ goes from $\pi/2$ to π. The integral is

$$\int_{\pi/2}^{\pi} \int_1^2 f(r\cos\theta, r\sin\theta)\, r\, dr\, d\theta.$$

Exercises and Problems for Section 16.4

Exercises

For the regions R in Exercises 1–4, write $\int_R f\, dA$ as an iterated integral in polar coordinates.

1.

2.

3.

4.

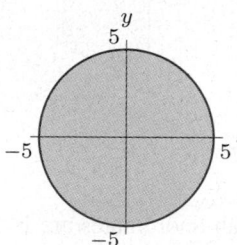

In Exercises 5–8, choose rectangular or polar coordinates to set up an iterated integral of an arbitrary function $f(x, y)$ over the region.

5.

6.

7.

8.

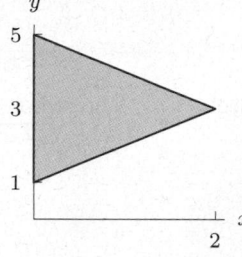

Sketch the region of integration in Exercises 9–15.

9. $\displaystyle\int_0^4 \int_{-\pi/2}^{\pi/2} f(r,\theta)\, r\, d\theta\, dr$

10. $\displaystyle\int_{\pi/2}^{\pi} \int_0^1 f(r,\theta)\, r\, dr\, d\theta$

11. $\displaystyle\int_0^{2\pi} \int_1^2 f(r,\theta)\, r\, dr\, d\theta$

12. $\displaystyle\int_{\pi/6}^{\pi/3} \int_0^1 f(r,\theta)\, r\, dr\, d\theta$

13. $\displaystyle\int_0^{\pi/4} \int_0^{1/\cos\theta} f(r,\theta)\, r\, dr\, d\theta$

14. $\displaystyle\int_3^4 \int_{3\pi/4}^{3\pi/2} f(r,\theta)\, r\, d\theta\, dr$

15. $\displaystyle\int_{\pi/4}^{\pi/2} \int_0^{2/\sin\theta} f(r,\theta)\, r\, dr\, d\theta$

Problems

In Exercises 16–18, evaluate the integral.

16. $\int_R \sqrt{x^2+y^2}\, dx\, dy$ where R is $4 \le x^2+y^2 \le 9$.

17. $\int_R \sin(x^2+y^2)\, dA$, where R is the disk of radius 2 centered at the origin.

18. $\int_R (x^2-y^2)\, dA$, where R is the first quadrant region between the circles of radius 1 and radius 2.

Convert the integrals in Problems 19–21 to polar coordinates and evaluate.

19. $\displaystyle\int_{-1}^0 \int_{-\sqrt{1-x^2}}^{\sqrt{1-x^2}} x\, dy\, dx$

20. $\displaystyle\int_0^{\sqrt6} \int_{-x}^x dy\, dx$

21. $\displaystyle\int_0^{\sqrt2} \int_y^{\sqrt{4-y^2}} xy\, dx\, dy$

22. Consider the integral $\int_0^3 \int_{x/3}^1 f(x, y)\, dy\, dx$.

(a) Sketch the region R over which the integration is being performed.

(b) Rewrite the integral with the order of integration reversed.

(c) Rewrite the integral in polar coordinates.

23. (a) Use integration in the following coordinates to find the volume of a solid orange wedge with $x \geq 0$ and cut out by the planes $y = 0$, $y = x/\sqrt{3}$, and a sphere of radius 5 centered at the origin. Which coordinates are the most efficient?

(i) Spherical coordinates

(ii) Cylindrical coordinates, in two different ways

(b) Calculate the volume without integration

24. Evaluate the integral by converting it into Cartesian coordinates:

$$\int_0^{\pi/6} \int_0^{2/\cos\theta} r\, dr\, d\theta.$$

25. (a) Sketch the region of integration of

$$\int_0^1 \int_{\sqrt{1-x^2}}^{\sqrt{4-x^2}} x\, dy\, dx + \int_1^2 \int_0^{\sqrt{4-x^2}} x\, dy\, dx$$

(b) Evaluate the quantity in part (a).

26. Find the volume of the region between the graph of $f(x, y) = 25 - x^2 - y^2$ and the xy plane.

27. Find the volume of an ice cream cone bounded by the hemisphere $z = \sqrt{8 - x^2 - y^2}$ and the cone $z = \sqrt{x^2 + y^2}$.

28. (a) For $a > 0$, find the volume under the graph of $z = e^{-(x^2+y^2)}$ above the disk $x^2 + y^2 \leq a^2$.

(b) What happens to the volume as $a \to \infty$?

29. A circular metal disk of radius 3 lies in the xy-plane with its center at the origin. At a distance r from the origin, the density of the metal per unit area is $\delta = \dfrac{1}{r^2 + 1}$.

(a) Write a double integral giving the total mass of the disk. Include limits of integration.

(b) Evaluate the integral.

30. A city surrounds a bay as shown in Figure 16.36. The population density of the city (in thousands of people per square km) is $\delta(r, \theta)$, where r and θ are polar coordinates and distances are in km.

(a) Set up an iterated integral in polar coordinates giving the total population of the city.

(b) The population density decreases the farther you live from the shoreline of the bay; it also decreases the farther you live from the ocean. Which of the following functions best describes this situation?

(i) $\delta(r, \theta) = (4 - r)(2 + \cos\theta)$

(ii) $\delta(r, \theta) = (4 - r)(2 + \sin\theta)$

(iii) $\delta(r, \theta) = (r + 4)(2 + \cos\theta)$

(c) Estimate the population using your answers to parts (a) and (b).

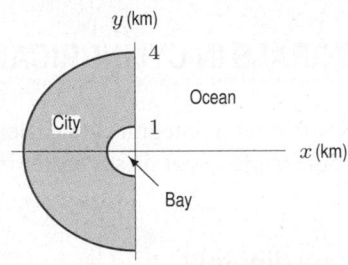

Figure 16.36

31. A disk of radius 5 cm has density 10 gm/cm^2 at its center and density 0 at its edge, and its density is a linear function of the distance from the center. Find the mass of the disk.

32. Electric charge is distributed over the xy-plane, with density inversely proportional to the distance from the origin. Show that the total charge inside a circle of radius R centered at the origin is proportional to R. What is the constant of proportionality?

33. (a) Graph $r = 1/(2\cos\theta)$ for $-\pi/2 \leq \theta \leq \pi/2$ and $r = 1$.

(b) Write an iterated integral representing the area inside the curve $r = 1$ and to the right of $r = 1/(2\cos\theta)$. Evaluate the integral.

34. (a) Sketch the circles $r = 2\cos\theta$ for $-\pi/2 \leq \theta \leq \pi/2$ and $r = 1$.

(b) Write an iterated integral representing the area inside the circle $r = 2\cos\theta$ and outside the circle $r = 1$. Evaluate the integral.

35. Two circular disks, each of radius 1, have centers which are 1 unit apart. Write, but do not evaluate, a double integral, including limits of integration, giving the area of overlap of the disks in

(a) Cartesian coordinates (b) Polar coordinates

36. Find the area inside the curve $r = 2 + 3\cos\theta$ and outside the circle $r = 2$.

Strengthen Your Understanding

In Problems 37–38, explain what is wrong with the statement.

37. If R is the region bounded by $x = 1$, $y = 0$, $y = x$, then in polar coordinates $\int_R x\, dA = \int_0^{\pi/4} \int_0^1 r^2 \cos\theta\, dr\, d\theta$.

38. If R is the region $x^2 + y^2 \leq 4$, then $\int_R (x^2 + y^2)\, dA = \int_0^{2\pi} \int_0^2 r^2\, dr\, d\theta$.

In Problems 39–40, give an example of:

39. A region R of integration in the first quadrant which suggests the use of polar coordinates.

40. An integrand $f(x, y)$ that suggests the use of polar coordinates.

41. Which of the following integrals give the area of the unit circle?

(a) $\displaystyle\int_{-1}^{1} \int_{-\sqrt{1-x^2}}^{\sqrt{1-x^2}} dy\, dx$ (b) $\displaystyle\int_{-1}^{1} \int_{-\sqrt{1-x^2}}^{\sqrt{1-x^2}} x\, dy\, dx$

(c) $\displaystyle\int_{0}^{2\pi} \int_{0}^{1} r\, dr\, d\theta$ (d) $\displaystyle\int_{0}^{2\pi} \int_{0}^{1} dr\, d\theta$

(e) $\displaystyle\int_{0}^{1} \int_{0}^{2\pi} r\, d\theta\, dr$ (f) $\displaystyle\int_{0}^{1} \int_{0}^{2\pi} d\theta\, dr$

42. Describe the region of integration for $\int_{\pi/4}^{\pi/2} \int_{1/\sin\theta}^{4/\sin\theta} f(r, \theta) r\, dr\, d\theta$.

16.5   INTEGRALS IN CYLINDRICAL AND SPHERICAL COORDINATES

Some double integrals are easier to evaluate in polar, rather than Cartesian, coordinates. Similarly, some triple integrals are easier in non-Cartesian coordinates.

Cylindrical Coordinates

The cylindrical coordinates of a point (x, y, z) in 3-space are obtained by representing the x and y coordinates in polar coordinates and letting the z-coordinate be the z-coordinate of the Cartesian coordinate system. (See Figure 16.37.)

Relation Between Cartesian and Cylindrical Coordinates

Each point in 3-space is represented using $0 \leq r < \infty, 0 \leq \theta \leq 2\pi, -\infty < z < \infty$.

$$x = r \cos \theta,$$
$$y = r \sin \theta,$$
$$z = z.$$

As with polar coordinates in the plane, note that $x^2 + y^2 = r^2$.

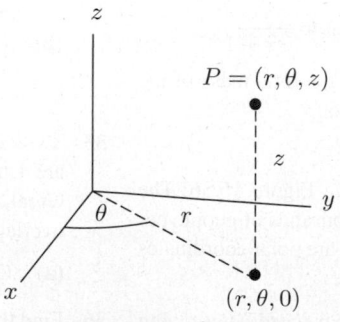

Figure 16.37: Cylindrical coordinates: (r, θ, z)

A useful way to visualize cylindrical coordinates is to sketch the surfaces obtained by setting one of the coordinates equal to a constant. See Figures 16.38–16.40.

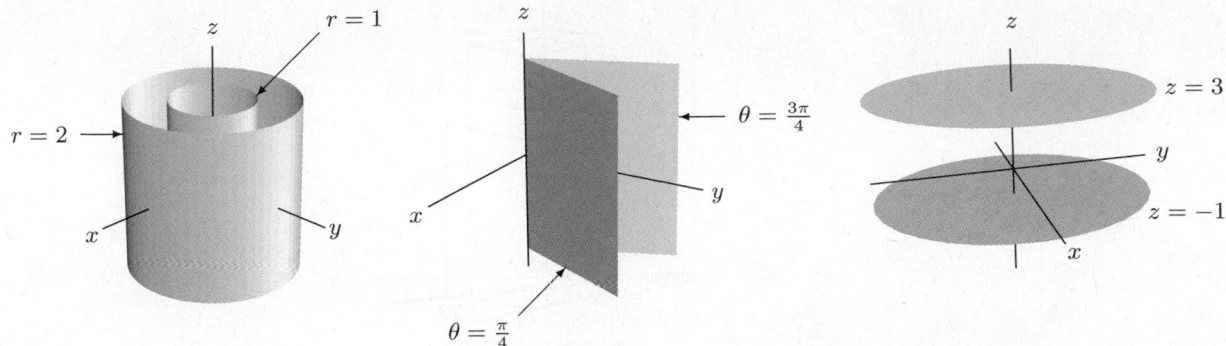

Figure 16.38: The surfaces $r = 1$ and $r = 2$

Figure 16.39: The surfaces $\theta = \pi/4$ and $\theta = 3\pi/4$

Figure 16.40: The surfaces $z = -1$ and $z = 3$

Setting $r = c$ (where c is constant) gives a cylinder around the z-axis whose radius is c. Setting $\theta = c$ gives a half-plane perpendicular to the xy plane, with one edge along the z-axis, making an angle c with the x-axis. Setting $z = c$ gives a horizontal plane $|c|$ units from the xy-plane. We call these *fundamental surfaces*.

The regions that can most easily be described in cylindrical coordinates are those regions whose boundaries are such fundamental surfaces. (For example, vertical cylinders, or wedge-shaped parts of vertical cylinders.)

Example 1   Describe in cylindrical coordinates a wedge of cheese cut from a cylinder 4 cm high and 6 cm in radius; this wedge subtends an angle of $\pi/6$ at the center. (See Figure 16.41.)

Solution   The wedge is described by the inequalities $0 \leq r \leq 6$, and $0 \leq z \leq 4$, and $0 \leq \theta \leq \pi/6$.

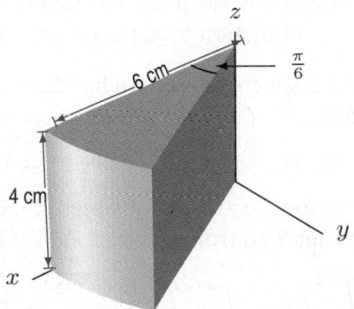

Figure 16.41: A wedge of cheese

Integration in Cylindrical Coordinates

To integrate in polar coordinates, we had to express the area element dA in terms of polar coordinates: $dA = r \, dr \, d\theta$. To evaluate a triple integral $\int_W f \, dV$ in cylindrical coordinates, we need to express the volume element dV in cylindrical coordinates.

In Figure 16.42, consider the volume element ΔV bounded by fundamental surfaces. The area of the base is $\Delta A \approx r \Delta r \Delta \theta$. Since the height is Δz, the volume element is given approximately by $\Delta V \approx r \, \Delta r \, \Delta \theta \, \Delta z$.

When computing integrals in cylindrical coordinates, put $dV = r \, dr \, d\theta \, dz$. Other orders of integration are also possible.

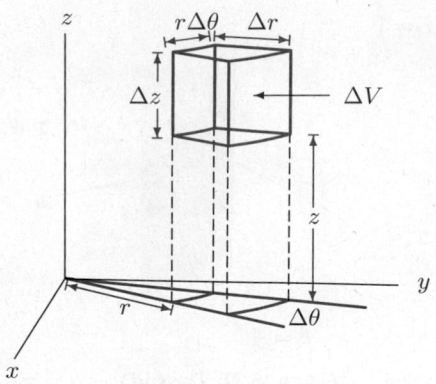

Figure 16.42: Volume element in cylindrical coordinates

Example 2   Find the mass of the wedge of cheese in Example 1, if its density is 1.2 grams/cm^3.

Solution   If the wedge is W, its mass is

$$\int_W 1.2 \, dV.$$

In cylindrical coordinates this integral is

$$\int_0^4 \int_0^{\pi/6} \int_0^6 1.2 \, r \, dr \, d\theta \, dz = \int_0^4 \int_0^{\pi/6} 0.6r^2 \Big|_0^6 \, d\theta \, dz = 21.6 \int_0^4 \int_0^{\pi/6} d\theta \, dz$$

$$= 21.6 \left(\frac{\pi}{6}\right) 4 = 45.239 \text{ grams.}$$

Example 3   A water tank in the shape of a hemisphere has radius a; its base is its plane face. Find the volume, V, of water in the tank as a function of h, the depth of the water.

Solution   In Cartesian coordinates, a sphere of radius a has the equation $x^2 + y^2 + z^2 = a^2$. (See Figure 16.43.) In cylindrical coordinates, $r^2 = x^2 + y^2$, so this becomes

$$r^2 + z^2 = a^2.$$

Thus, if we want to describe the amount of water in the tank in cylindrical coordinates, we let r go from 0 to $\sqrt{a^2 - z^2}$, we let θ go from 0 to 2π, and we let z go from 0 to h, giving

$$\begin{aligned}
\text{Volume} \atop \text{of water} \quad &= \int_W dV = \int_0^{2\pi} \int_0^h \int_0^{\sqrt{a^2-z^2}} r \, dr \, dz \, d\theta = \int_0^{2\pi} \int_0^h \frac{r^2}{2}\bigg|_{r=0}^{r=\sqrt{a^2-z^2}} dz \, d\theta \\
&= \int_0^{2\pi} \int_0^h \frac{1}{2}(a^2 - z^2) \, dz \, d\theta = \int_0^{2\pi} \frac{1}{2}\left(a^2 z - \frac{z^3}{3}\right)\bigg|_{z=0}^{z=h} d\theta \\
&= \int_0^{2\pi} \frac{1}{2}\left(a^2 h - \frac{h^3}{3}\right) d\theta = \pi\left(a^2 h - \frac{h^3}{3}\right).
\end{aligned}$$

Figure 16.43: Hemispherical water tank with radius a and water of depth h

Spherical Coordinates

In Figure 16.44, the point P has coordinates (x, y, z) in the Cartesian coordinate system. We define spherical coordinates ρ, ϕ, and θ for P as follows: $\rho = \sqrt{x^2 + y^2 + z^2}$ is the distance of P from the origin; ϕ is the angle between the positive z-axis and the line through the origin and the point P; and θ is the same as in cylindrical coordinates.

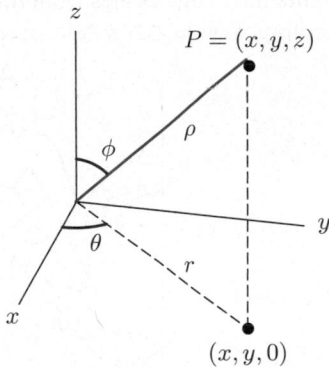

Figure 16.44: Spherical coordinates: (ρ, ϕ, θ)

In cylindrical coordinates,

$$x = r\cos\theta, \quad \text{and} \quad y = r\sin\theta, \quad \text{and} \quad z = z.$$

From Figure 16.44 we have $z = \rho\cos\phi$ and $r = \rho\sin\phi$, giving the following relationship:

Relation Between Cartesian and Spherical Coordinates

Each point in 3-space is represented using $0 \le \rho < \infty$, $0 \le \phi \le \pi$, and $0 \le \theta \le 2\pi$.

$$x = \rho\sin\phi\cos\theta$$
$$y = \rho\sin\phi\sin\theta$$
$$z = \rho\cos\phi.$$

Also, $\rho^2 = x^2 + y^2 + z^2$.

This system of coordinates is useful when there is spherical symmetry with respect to the origin, either in the region of integration or in the integrand. The fundamental surfaces in spherical coordinates are $\rho = k$ (a constant), which is a sphere of radius k centered at the origin, $\theta = k$ (a constant), which is the half-plane with its edge along the z-axis, and $\phi = k$ (a constant), which is a cone if $k \ne \pi/2$ and the xy-plane if $k = \pi/2$. (See Figures 16.45–16.47.)

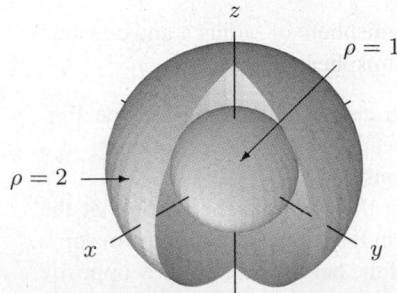

Figure 16.45: The surfaces $\rho = 1$ and $\rho = 2$

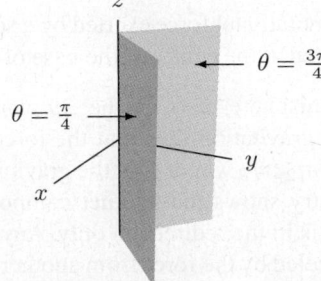

Figure 16.46: The surfaces $\theta = \pi/4$ and $\theta = 3\pi/4$

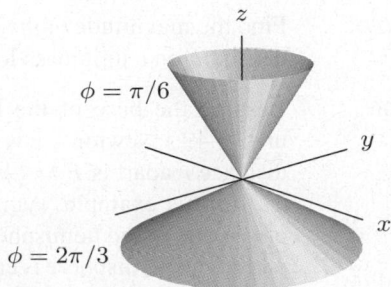

Figure 16.47: The surfaces $\phi = \pi/6$ and $\phi = 2\pi/3$

Integration in Spherical Coordinates

To use spherical coordinates in triple integrals we need to express the volume element, dV, in spherical coordinates. From Figure 16.48, we see that the volume element can be approximated by a box with curved edges. One edge has length $\Delta\rho$. The edge parallel to the xy-plane is an arc of a circle made from rotating the cylindrical radius r ($=\rho\sin\phi$) through an angle $\Delta\theta$, and so has length $\rho\sin\phi\,\Delta\theta$. The remaining edge comes from rotating the radius ρ through an angle $\Delta\phi$, and so has length $\rho\,\Delta\phi$. Therefore, $\Delta V \approx \Delta\rho(\rho\,\Delta\phi)(\rho\sin\phi\,\Delta\theta) = \rho^2\sin\phi\,\Delta\rho\,\Delta\phi\,\Delta\theta$.

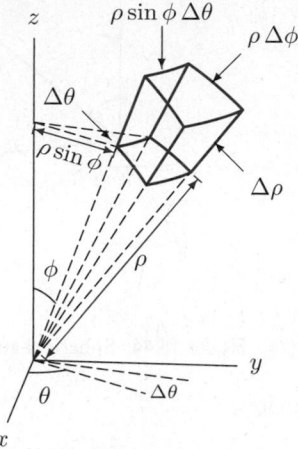

Figure 16.48: Volume element in spherical coordinates

Thus,

When computing integrals in spherical coordinates, put $dV = \rho^2\sin\phi\,d\rho\,d\phi\,d\theta$. Other orders of integration are also possible.

Example 4   Use spherical coordinates to derive the formula for the volume of a ball of radius a.

Solution   In spherical coordinates, a ball of radius a is described by the inequalities $0 \le \rho \le a$, $0 \le \theta \le 2\pi$, and $0 \le \phi \le \pi$. Note that θ goes from 0 to 2π, whereas ϕ goes from 0 to π. We find the volume by integrating the constant density function 1 over the ball:

$$\text{Volume} = \int_R 1\,dV = \int_0^{2\pi}\int_0^{\pi}\int_0^a \rho^2\sin\phi\,d\rho\,d\phi\,d\theta = \int_0^{2\pi}\int_0^{\pi}\frac{1}{3}a^3\sin\phi\,d\phi\,d\theta$$

$$= \frac{1}{3}a^3\int_0^{2\pi} -\cos\phi\Big|_0^{\pi}\,d\theta = \frac{2}{3}a^3\int_0^{2\pi}d\theta = \frac{4\pi a^3}{3}.$$

Example 5   Find the magnitude of the gravitational force exerted by a solid hemisphere of radius a and constant density δ on a unit mass located at the center of the base of the hemisphere.

Solution   Assume the base of the hemisphere rests on the xy-plane with center at the origin. (See Figure 16.49.) Newton's law of gravitation says that the force between two masses m_1 and m_2 at a distance r apart is $F = Gm_1m_2/r^2$, where G is the gravitation constant.

In this example, symmetry shows that the net component of the force on the particle at the origin due to the hemisphere is in the z direction only. Any force in the x or y direction from some part of the hemisphere is canceled by the force from another part of the hemisphere directly opposite the first.

To compute the net z-component of the gravitational force, we imagine a small piece of the hemisphere with volume ΔV, located at spherical coordinates (ρ, θ, ϕ). This piece has mass $\delta\Delta V$, and exerts a force of magnitude F on the unit mass at the origin. The z-component of this force is given by its projection onto the z-axis, which can be seen from the figure to be $F \cos \phi$. The distance from the mass $\delta \Delta V$ to the unit mass at the origin is the spherical coordinate ρ. Therefore, the z-component of the force due to the small piece ΔV is

$$\begin{array}{c} z\text{-component} \\ \text{of force} \end{array} = \frac{G(\delta \Delta V)(1)}{\rho^2} \cos \phi.$$

Adding the contributions of the small pieces, we get a vertical force with magnitude

$$F = \int_0^{2\pi} \int_0^{\pi/2} \int_0^a \left(\frac{G\delta}{\rho^2} \right) (\cos \phi) \rho^2 \sin \phi \, d\rho \, d\phi \, d\theta = \int_0^{2\pi} \int_0^{\pi/2} G\delta(\cos \phi \sin \phi) \rho \Big|_{\rho=0}^{\rho=a} d\phi \, d\theta$$

$$= \int_0^{2\pi} \int_0^{\pi/2} G\delta a \cos \phi \sin \phi \, d\phi \, d\theta = \int_0^{2\pi} G\delta a \left(-\frac{(\cos \phi)^2}{2} \right) \Big|_{\phi=0}^{\phi=\pi/2} d\theta$$

$$= \int_0^{2\pi} G\delta a \left(\frac{1}{2} \right) d\theta = G\delta a\pi.$$

The integral in this example is improper because the region of integration contains the origin, where the force is undefined. However, it can be shown that the result is nevertheless correct.

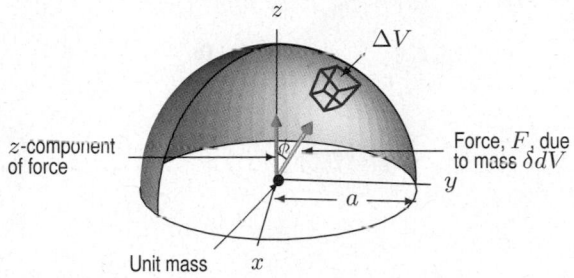

Figure 16.49: Gravitational force of hemisphere on mass at origin

Exercises and Problems for Section 16.5

Exercises

1. Match the equations in (a)–(f) with one of the surfaces in (I)–(VII).

(a) $x = 5$ (b) $x^2 + z^2 = 7$ (c) $\rho = 5$
(d) $z = 1$ (e) $r = 3$ (f) $\theta = 2\pi$

  (I) Cylinder, centered on x-axis.
 (II) Cylinder, centered on y-axis.
(III) Cylinder, centered on z-axis.
(IV) Plane, perpendicular to the x-axis.
 (V) Plane, perpendicular to the y-axis.
(VI) Plane, perpendicular to the z-axis.
(VII) Sphere.

In Exercises 2–7, find an equation for the surface.

2. The vertical plane $y = x$ in cylindrical coordinates.

3. The top half of the sphere $x^2 + y^2 + z^2 = 1$ in cylindrical coordinates.

4. The cone $z = \sqrt{x^2 + y^2}$ in cylindrical coordinates.

5. The cone $z = \sqrt{x^2 + y^2}$ in spherical coordinates.

6. The plane $z = 10$ in spherical coordinates.

7. The plane $z = 4$ in spherical coordinates.

In Exercises 8–9, evaluate the triple integrals in cylindrical coordinates over the region W.

8. $f(x, y, z) = \sin(x^2 + y^2)$, W is the solid cylinder with height 4 and with base of radius 1 centered on the z axis at $z = -1$.

9. $f(x, y, z) = x^2 + y^2 + z^2$, W is the region $0 \le r \le 4$, $\pi/4 \le \theta \le 3\pi/4$, $-1 \le z \le 1$.

In Exercises 10–11, evaluate the triple integrals in spherical coordinates.

10. $f(\rho, \theta, \phi) = \sin \phi$, over the region $0 \leq \theta \leq 2\pi$, $0 \leq \phi \leq \pi/4$, $1 \leq \rho \leq 2$.

11. $f(x, y, z) = 1/(x^2 + y^2 + z^2)^{1/2}$ over the bottom half of the sphere of radius 5 centered at the origin.

For Exercises 12–18, choose coordinates and set up a triple integral, including limits of integration, for a density function f over the region.

12.

13.

14.

15.
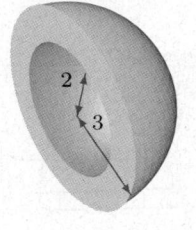

16. A piece of a sphere; angle at the center is $\pi/3$.

17.

18.
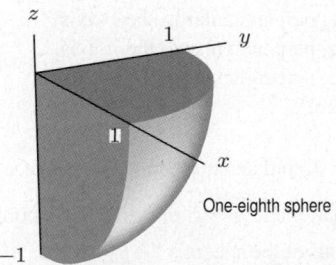

Problems

19. Write a triple integral in cylindrical coordinates giving the volume of a sphere of radius K centered at the origin. Use the order $dz\, dr\, d\theta$.

20. Write a triple integral in spherical coordinates giving the volume of a sphere of radius K centered at the origin. Use the order $d\theta\, d\rho\, d\phi$.

If W is the region in Figure 16.50, what are the limits of integration in Exercises 21–23?

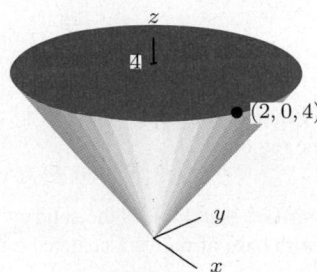

Figure 16.50: Cone with flat top, symmetric about z-axis

21. $\displaystyle\int_{?}^{?} \int_{?}^{?} \int_{?}^{?} f(r, \theta, z)\, r\, dz\, dr\, d\theta$

22. $\displaystyle\int_{?}^{?} \int_{?}^{?} \int_{?}^{?} g(\rho, \phi, \theta)\rho^2 \sin\phi\, d\rho\, d\phi\, d\theta$

23. $\displaystyle\int_{?}^{?} \int_{?}^{?} \int_{?}^{?} h(x, y, z)\, dz\, dy\, dx$

For the regions W shown in Problems 24–26, write the limits of integration for $\int_W dV$ in the following coordinates:

(a) Cartesian   **(b)** Cylindrical   **(c)** Spherical

24.

25.

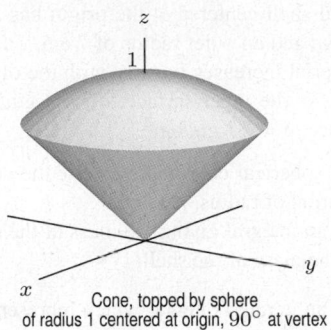

Cone, topped by sphere
of radius 1 centered at origin, $90°$ at vertex

26.

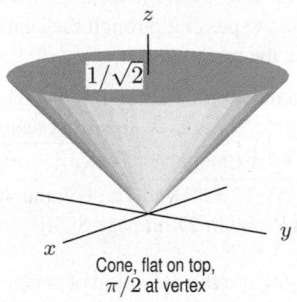

Cone, flat on top,
$\pi/2$ at vertex

27. Write a triple integral representing the volume above the cone $z = \sqrt{x^2 + y^2}$ and below the sphere of radius 2 centered at the origin. Include limits of integration but do not evaluate. Use:

  (a) Cylindrical coordinates
  (b) Spherical coordinates

28. Write a triple integral representing the volume of the region between spheres of radius 1 and 2, both centered at the origin. Include limits of integration but do not evaluate. Use:

  (a) Spherical coordinates.
  (b) Cylindrical coordinates. Write your answer as the difference of two integrals.

In Problems 29–34, write a triple integral including limits of integration that gives the specified volume.

29. Under $\rho = 3$ and above $\phi = \pi/3$.

30. Under $\rho = 3$ and above $z = r$.

31. The region between $z = 5$ and $z = 10$, with $2 \leq x^2 + y^2 \leq 3$ and $0 \leq \theta \leq \pi$.

32. Between the cone $z = \sqrt{x^2 + y^2}$ and the first quadrant of the xy-plane, with $x^2 + y^2 \leq 7$.

33. The cap of the solid sphere $x^2 + y^2 + z^2 \leq 10$ cut off by the plane $z = 1$.

34. Below the cone $z = r$, above the xy-plane, and inside the sphere $x^2 + y^2 + z^2 = 8$.

35. **(a)** Write an integral (including limits of integration) representing the volume of the region inside the cone $z = \sqrt{3(x^2 + y^2)}$ and below the plane $z = 1$.
  (b) Evaluate the integral.

36. Find the volume between the cone $z = \sqrt{x^2 + y^2}$ and the plane $z = 10 + x$ above the disk $x^2 + y^2 \leq 1$.

37. Find the volume between the cone $x = \sqrt{y^2 + z^2}$ and the sphere $x^2 + y^2 + z^2 = 4$.

38. The sphere of radius 2 centered at the origin is sliced horizontally at $z = 1$. What is the volume of the cap above the plane $z = 1$?

39. Suppose W is the region outside the cylinder $x^2 + y^2 = 1$ and inside the sphere $x^2 + y^2 + z^2 = 2$. Calculate

$$\int_W (x^2 + y^2)\, dV.$$

40. Write a triple integral representing the volume of a slice of the cylindrical cake of height 2 and radius 5 between the planes $\theta = \pi/6$ and $\theta = \pi/3$. Evaluate this integral.

41. Write a triple integral representing the volume of the cone in Figure 16.51 and evaluate it.

$5/\sqrt{2}$ cm

Figure 16.51

Without performing the integration, decide whether each of the integrals in Problems 42–43 is positive, negative, or zero. Give reasons for your decision.

42. W_1 is the unit ball, $x^2 + y^2 + z^2 \leq 1$.

  (a) $\int_{W_1} \sin\phi\, dV$ **(b)** $\int_{W_1} \cos\phi\, dV$

43. W_2 is $0 \leq z \leq \sqrt{1 - x^2 - y^2}$, the top half of the unit ball.

  (a) $\int_{W_2} (z^2 - z)\, dV$ **(b)** $\int_{W_2} (-xz)\, dV$

44. The insulation surrounding a pipe of length l is the region between two cylinders with the same axis. The inner cylinder has radius a, the outer radius of the pipe, and the insulation has thickness h. Write a triple integral, including limits of integration, giving the volume of the insulation. Evaluate the integral.

45. Assume p, q, r are positive constants. Find the volume contained between the coordinate planes and the plane

$$\frac{x}{p} + \frac{y}{q} + \frac{z}{r} = 1.$$

46. A cone stands with its flat base on a table. The cone's circular base has radius a; the vertex (tip) is at a height of h above the center of the base. Write a triple integral, including limits of integration, representing the volume of the cone. Evaluate the integral.

47. A half-melon is approximated by the region between two concentric spheres, one of radius a and the other of radius b, with $0 < a < b$. Write a triple integral, including limits of integration, giving the volume of the half-melon. Evaluate the integral.

48. A bead is made by drilling a cylindrical hole of radius 1 mm through a sphere of radius 5 mm. See Figure 16.52.

    (a) Set up a triple integral in cylindrical coordinates representing the volume of the bead.

    (b) Evaluate the integral.

1 mm

5 mm

Figure 16.52

49. A pile of hay is approximately in the shape of $0 \leq z \leq 2 - x^2 - y^2$, where x, y, z are in meters. At height z, the density of the hay is $\delta = (2 - z)$ kg/m^3.

    (a) Write an integral representing the mass of hay in the pile.

    (b) Evaluate the integral.

50. Find the mass M of the solid region W given in spherical coordinates by $0 \leq \rho \leq 3, 0 \leq \theta < 2\pi, 0 \leq \phi \leq \pi/4$. The density, $\delta(P)$, at any point P is given by the distance of P from the origin.

51. Write an integral representing the mass of a sphere of radius 3 if the density of the sphere at any point is twice the distance of that point from the center of the sphere.

52. A sphere is made of material whose density at each point is proportional to the square of the distance of the point from the z-axis. The density is 2 gm/cm^3 at a distance of 2 cm from the axis. What is the mass of the sphere if it is centered at the origin and has radius 3 cm?

53. The density of a solid sphere at any point is proportional to the square of the distance of the point to the center of the sphere. What is the ratio of the mass of a sphere of radius 1 to a sphere of radius 2?

54. A spherical shell centered at the origin has an inner radius of 6 cm and an outer radius of 7 cm. The density, δ, of the material increases linearly with the distance from the center. At the inner surface, $\delta = 9$ gm/cm^3; at the outer surface, $\delta = 11$ gm/cm^3.

    (a) Using spherical coordinates, write the density, δ, as a function of radius, ρ.

    (b) Write an integral giving the mass of the shell.

    (c) Find the mass of the shell.

55. **(a)** Write an iterated integral which represents the mass of a solid ball of radius a. The density at each point in the ball is k times the distance from that point to a fixed plane passing through the center of the ball.

    (b) Evaluate the integral.

56. Use appropriate coordinates to find the average distance to the origin for points in the ice cream cone region bounded by the hemisphere $z = \sqrt{8 - x^2 - y^2}$ and the cone $z = \sqrt{x^2 + y^2}$. [Hint: The volume of this region is computed in Problem 27 on page 895.]

For Problems 57–60, use the definition of center of mass given on page 890. Assume x, y, z are in cm.

57. Let C be a solid cone with both height and radius 1 and contained between the surfaces $z = \sqrt{x^2 + y^2}$ and $z = 1$. If C has constant mass density of 1 gm/cm^3, find the z-coordinate of C's center of mass.

58. The density of the cone C in Problem 57 is given by $\delta(z) = z^2$ gm/cm^3. Find

    (a) The mass of C.

    (b) The z-coordinate of C's center of mass.

59. For $a > 0$, consider the family of solids bounded below by the paraboloid $z = a(x^2 + y^2)$ and above by the plane $z = 1$. If the solids all have constant mass density 1 gm/cm^3, show that the z-coordinate of the center of mass is $2/3$ and so independent of the parameter a.

60. Find the location of the center of mass of a hemisphere of radius a and density b gm/cm^3.

For Problems 61–62, use the definition of moment of inertia given on page 890.

61. The moment of inertia of a solid homogeneous ball B of mass 1 and radius a centered at the origin is the same about any of the coordinate axes (due to the symmetry of the ball). It is easier to evaluate the sum of the three integrals involved in computing the moment of inertia about each of the axes than to compute them individually. Find the sum of the moments of inertia about the x, y and z-axes and thus find the individual moments of inertia.

62. Find the moment of inertia about the z-axis of the solid "fat ice cream cone" given in spherical coordinates by $0 \leq \rho \leq a, 0 \leq \phi \leq \frac{\pi}{3}$ and $0 \leq \theta \leq 2\pi$. Assume that the solid is homogeneous with mass m.

Problems 63–64 deal with the energy stored in an electric field. If a region of space W contains an electric field whose magnitude at a point (x, y, z) is $E(x, y, z)$, then

$$\text{Energy stored by field} = \frac{1}{2} \int_W \epsilon E^2 \, dV,$$

where ϵ is a property of the material called the *permittivity*.

63. The region between two concentric spheres, with radii $a < b$, contains an electric field with magnitude $E = q/(4\pi\epsilon\rho^2)$, where ρ is the distance from the center of the spheres and q is the charge on the inner sphere. Assuming the permittivity, ϵ, is constant, find the total energy stored in the region between the two spheres.

64. Figure 16.53 shows a coaxial cable consisting of two cylindrical conductors centered on the same axis, of radii $a < b$. The electric field between the conductors has magnitude $E = q/(2\pi\epsilon r)$, where r is the distance from the axis and q is the charge per unit length on the cable. The permittivity of the material between the conductors is constant.[4] Show that the stored energy per unit length is proportional to $\ln(b/a)$.

Figure 16.53

65. The density, δ, of a gas in the region under $z = 4 - x^2 - y^2$ and above the xy-plane is $\delta = e^{-x-y}\text{gm/cm}^3$, where x, y, z are in cm. Write an integral, with limits of integration, representing the mass of gas.

66. The density, δ, of the cylinder $x^2 + y^2 \le 4, 0 \le z \le 3$ varies with the distance, r, from the z-axis:

$$\delta = 1 + r \text{ gm/cm}^3.$$

Find the mass of the cylinder, assuming x, y, z are in cm.

67. The density of material at a point in a solid cylinder is proportional to the distance of the point from the z-axis. What is the ratio of the mass of the cylinder $x^2 + y^2 \le 1$, $0 \le z \le 2$ to the mass of the cylinder $x^2 + y^2 \le 9$, $0 \le z \le 2$?

68. A region W consists of the points above the xy-plane and outside the sphere of radius 1 centered at the origin and within the sphere of radius 3 centered at $(0, 0, -1)$. Write an expression for the volume of W. Use cylindrical coordinates and include limits of integration.

69. Compute the force of gravity exerted by a solid cylinder of radius R, height H, and constant density δ on a unit mass at the center of the base of the cylinder.

70. Electric charge is distributed throughout 3-space, with density proportional to the distance from the xy-plane. Show that the total charge inside a cylinder of radius R and height h, sitting on the xy-plane and centered along the z-axis, is proportional to $R^2 h^2$.

71. Electric charge is distributed throughout 3-space with density inversely proportional to the distance from the origin. Show that the total charge inside a sphere of radius R is proportional to R^2.

72. Figure 16.54 shows an alternative notation for spherical coordinates, used often in electrical engineering. Write the volume element dV in this coordinate system.

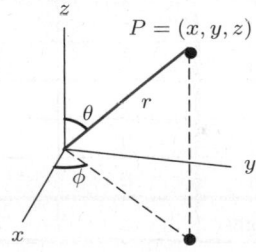

Figure 16.54

Strengthen Your Understanding

73. Which of the following integrals give the volume of the unit sphere?

(a) $\displaystyle\int_0^{2\pi} \int_0^{2\pi} \int_0^1 d\rho \, d\theta \, d\phi$

(b) $\displaystyle\int_0^{\pi} \int_0^{2\pi} \int_0^1 d\rho \, d\theta \, d\phi$

(c) $\displaystyle\int_0^{\pi} \int_0^{2\pi} \int_0^1 \rho^2 \sin\phi \, d\rho \, d\theta \, d\phi$

(d) $\displaystyle\int_0^{\pi} \int_0^{2\pi} \int_0^1 \rho^2 \sin\phi \, d\rho \, d\phi \, d\theta$

(e) $\displaystyle\int_0^{\pi} \int_0^{2\pi} \int_0^1 \rho \, d\rho \, d\phi \, d\theta$

In Problems 74–75, explain what is wrong with the statement.

74. The integral $\displaystyle\int_0^{2\pi} \int_0^{\pi} \int_0^1 1 \, d\rho \, d\phi \, d\theta$ gives the volume inside the sphere of radius 1.

[4] See C. R. Paul and S. A. Nasar, *Introduction to Electromagnetic Fields*, 2nd ed. (New York: McGraw-Hill, 1987).

75. Changing the order of integration gives

$$\int_0^{2\pi} \int_0^{\pi/4} \int_0^{2/\cos\phi} \rho^2 \sin\phi \, d\rho \, d\phi \, d\theta$$

$$= \int_0^{2/\cos\phi} \int_0^{\pi/4} \int_0^{2\pi} \rho^2 \sin\phi \, d\theta \, d\phi \, d\rho.$$

In Problems 76–77, give an example of:

76. An integral in spherical coordinates that gives the volume of a hemisphere.

77. An integral for which it is more convenient to use spherical coordinates than to use Cartesian coordinates.

16.6 APPLICATIONS OF INTEGRATION TO PROBABILITY

To represent how a quantity such as height or weight is distributed throughout a population, we use a density function. To study two or more quantities at the same time and see how they are related, we use a multivariable density function.

Density Functions

Distribution of Weight and Height in Expectant Mothers

Table 16.8 shows the distribution of weight and height in a survey of expectant mothers. The histogram in Figure 16.55 is constructed so that the volume of each bar represents the percentage in the corresponding weight and height range. For example, the bar representing the mothers who weighed 60–70 kg and were 160–165 cm tall has base of area 10 kg · 5 cm = 50 kg cm. The volume of this bar is 12%, so its height is 12%/50 kg cm = 0.24%/ kg cm. Notice that the units on the vertical axis are % per kg cm, so the volume of a bar is a %. The total volume is 100% = 1.

Table 16.8 *Distribution of weight and height in a survey of expectant mothers, in %*

	45-50 kg	50-60 kg	60-70 kg	70-80 kg	80-105 kg	Totals by height
150-155 cm	2	4	4	2	1	13
155-160 cm	0	12	8	2	1	23
160-165 cm	1	7	12	4	3	27
165-170 cm	0	8	12	6	2	28
170-180 cm	0	1	3	4	1	9
Totals by weight	3	32	39	18	8	100

Figure 16.55: Histogram representing the data in Table 16.8

Example 1   Find the percentage of mothers in the survey with height between 170 and 180 cm.

Solution   We add the percentages across the row corresponding to the 170–180 cm height range; this is equivalent to adding the volumes of the corresponding rectangular solids in the histogram.

$$\text{Percentage of mothers} = 0 + 1 + 3 + 4 + 1 = 9\%.$$

Smoothing the Histogram

If we group the data using narrower weight and height groups (and a larger sample), we can draw a smoother histogram and get finer estimates. In the limit, we replace the histogram with a smooth surface, in such a way that the volume under the surface above a rectangle is the percentage of mothers in that rectangle. We define a *density function*, $p(w, h)$, to be the function whose graph is the smooth surface. It has the property that

$$\begin{array}{c}\text{Fraction of sample with} \\ \text{weight between } a \text{ and } b \text{ and} \\ \text{height between } c \text{ and } d\end{array} = \begin{array}{c}\text{Volume under graph of } p \\ \text{over the rectangle} \\ a \leq w \leq b, c \leq h \leq d\end{array} = \int_a^b \int_c^d p(w, h)\, dh\, dw.$$

This density also gives the probability that a mother is in these height and weight groups.

Joint Probability Density Functions

We generalize this idea to represent any two characteristics, x and y, distributed throughout a population.

A function $p(x, y)$ is called a **joint probability density function**, or **pdf**, for x and y if

$$\begin{array}{c}\text{Probability that member of} \\ \text{population has } x \text{ between } a \text{ and } b \\ \text{and } y \text{ between } c \text{ and } d\end{array} = \begin{array}{c}\text{Volume under graph of } p \\ \text{above the rectangle} \\ a \leq x \leq b, c \leq y \leq d\end{array} = \int_a^b \int_c^d p(x, y)\, dy\, dx$$

where

$$\int_{-\infty}^{\infty} \int_{-\infty}^{\infty} p(x, y)\, dy\, dx = 1 \quad \text{and} \quad p(x, y) \geq 0 \text{ for all } x \text{ and } y.$$

The probability that x falls in an interval of width Δx around x_0 and y falls in an interval of width Δy around y_0 is approximately $p(x_0, y_0)\Delta x \Delta y$.

A joint density function need not be continuous, as in Example 2. In addition, as in Example 4, the integrals involved may be improper and must be computed by methods similar to those used for improper one-variable integrals.

Example 2   Let $p(x, y)$ be defined on the square $0 \leq x \leq 1, 0 \leq y \leq 1$ by $p(x, y) = x + y$; let $p(x, y) = 0$ if (x, y) is outside this square. Check that p is a joint density function. In terms of the distribution of x and y in the population, what does it mean that $p(x, y) = 0$ outside the square?

Solution   First, we have $p(x, y) \geq 0$ for all x and y. To check that p is a joint density function, we show that the total volume under the graph is 1:

$$\int_{-\infty}^{\infty} \int_{-\infty}^{\infty} p(x, y) \, dy \, dx = \int_0^1 \int_0^1 (x + y) \, dy \, dx$$

$$= \int_0^1 \left(xy + \frac{y^2}{2} \right) \Big|_0^1 dx = \int_0^1 \left(x + \frac{1}{2} \right) dx = \left(\frac{x^2}{2} + \frac{x}{2} \right) \Big|_0^1 = 1.$$

The fact that $p(x, y) = 0$ outside the square means that the variables x and y never take values outside the interval $[0, 1]$; that is, the value of x and y for any individual in the population is always between 0 and 1.

Example 3   Two variables x and y are distributed in a population according to the density function of Example 2. Find the fraction of the population with $x \leq 1/2$, the fraction with $y \leq 1/2$, and the fraction with both $x \leq 1/2$ and $y \leq 1/2$.

Solution   The fraction with $x \leq 1/2$ is the volume under the graph to the left of the line $x = 1/2$:

$$\int_0^{1/2} \int_0^1 (x + y) \, dy \, dx = \int_0^{1/2} \left(xy + \frac{y^2}{2} \right) \Big|_0^1 dx = \int_0^{1/2} \left(x + \frac{1}{2} \right) dx$$

$$= \left(\frac{x^2}{2} + \frac{x}{2} \right) \Big|_0^{1/2} = \frac{1}{8} + \frac{1}{4} = \frac{3}{8}.$$

Since the function and the regions of integration are symmetric in x and y, the fraction with $y \leq 1/2$ is also 3/8. Finally, the fraction with both $x \leq 1/2$ and $y \leq 1/2$ is

$$\int_0^{1/2} \int_0^{1/2} (x + y) \, dy \, dx = \int_0^{1/2} \left(xy + \frac{y^2}{2} \right) \Big|_0^{1/2} dx = \int_0^{1/2} \left(\frac{1}{2} x + \frac{1}{8} \right) dx$$

$$= \left(\frac{1}{4} x^2 + \frac{1}{8} x \right) \Big|_0^{1/2} = \frac{1}{16} + \frac{1}{16} = \frac{1}{8}.$$

Recall that a one-variable density function $p(x)$ is a function such that $p(x) \geq 0$ for all x, and $\int_{-\infty}^{\infty} p(x) \, dx = 1$.

Example 4   Let p_1 and p_2 be one-variable density functions for x and y, respectively. Check that $p(x, y) = p_1(x) p_2(y)$ is a joint density function.

Solution   Since both p_1 and p_2 are density functions, they are nonnegative everywhere. Thus, their product $p_1(x) p_2(x) = p(x, y)$ is nonnegative everywhere. Now we must check that the volume under the graph of p is 1. Since $\int_{-\infty}^{\infty} p_2(y) \, dy = 1$ and $\int_{-\infty}^{\infty} p_1(x) \, dx = 1$, we have

$$\int_{-\infty}^{\infty} \int_{-\infty}^{\infty} p(x, y) \, dy \, dx = \int_{-\infty}^{\infty} \int_{-\infty}^{\infty} p_1(x) p_2(y) \, dy \, dx = \int_{-\infty}^{\infty} p_1(x) \left(\int_{-\infty}^{\infty} p_2(y) \, dy \right) dx$$

$$= \int_{-\infty}^{\infty} p_1(x)(1) \, dx = \int_{-\infty}^{\infty} p_1(x) \, dx = 1.$$

Example 5   A machine in a factory is set to produce components 10 cm long and 5 cm in diameter. In fact, there is a slight variation from one component to the next. A component is usable if its length and diameter deviate from the correct values by less than 0.1 cm. With the length, x, in cm and the diameter, y, in cm, the probability density function is

$$p(x, y) = \frac{50\sqrt{2}}{\pi} e^{-100(x-10)^2} e^{-50(y-5)^2}.$$

What is the probability that a component is usable? (See Figure 16.56.)

Figure 16.56: The density function $p(x, y) = \frac{50\sqrt{2}}{\pi} e^{-100(x-10)^2} e^{-50(y-5)^2}$

Solution   We know that

$$
\begin{array}{l}
\text{Probability that } x \text{ and } y \text{ satisfy} \\
x_0 - \Delta x \le x \le x_0 + \Delta x \\
y_0 - \Delta y \le y \le y_0 + \Delta y
\end{array}
= \frac{50\sqrt{2}}{\pi} \int_{y_0 - \Delta y}^{y_0 + \Delta y} \int_{x_0 - \Delta x}^{x_0 + \Delta x} e^{-100(x-10)^2} e^{-50(y-5)^2} \, dx \, dy.
$$

Thus,

$$
\begin{array}{l}
\text{Probability that} \\
\text{component is usable}
\end{array}
= \frac{50\sqrt{2}}{\pi} \int_{4.9}^{5.1} \int_{9.9}^{10.1} e^{-100(x-10)^2} e^{-50(y-5)^2} \, dx \, dy.
$$

The double integral must be evaluated numerically. This yields

$$
\begin{array}{l}
\text{Probability that} \\
\text{component is usable}
\end{array}
= \frac{50\sqrt{2}}{\pi} (0.02556) = 0.57530.
$$

Thus, there is a 57.530% chance that the component is usable.

Exercises and Problems for Section 16.6

Exercises

In Exercises 1–6, check whether p is a joint density function. Assume $p(x, y) = 0$ outside the region R.

1. $p(x, y) = 1/2$, where R is $4 \le x \le 5, -2 \le y \le 0$
2. $p(x, y) = 1$, where R is $0 \le x \le 1, 0 \le y \le 2$
3. $p(x, y) = x + y$, where R is $-1 \le x \le 1, 0 \le y \le 1$
4. $p(x, y) = 6(y - x)$, where R is $0 \le x \le y \le 2$
5. $p(x, y) = (2/\pi)(1 - x^2 - y^2)$, where R is $x^2 + y^2 \le 1$
6. $p(x, y) = xye^{-x-y}$, where R is $x \ge 0, y \ge 0$

In Exercises 7–14, let p be the joint density function such that $p(x, y) = xy$ in R, the rectangle $0 \le x \le 2, 0 \le y \le 1$, and

$p(x, y) = 0$ outside R. Find the fraction of the population satisfying the given constraints.

7. $x \ge 3$ 8. $x = 1$

9. $x + y \le 3$ 10. $-1 \le x \le 1$

11. $x \ge y$ 12. $x + y \le 1$

13. $0 \le x \le 1, 0 \le y \le 1/2$

14. Within a distance 1 from the origin

Problems

15. Let x and y have joint density function

$$p(x,y) = \begin{cases} \frac{2}{3}(x+2y) & \text{for } 0 \le x \le 1, 0 \le y \le 1, \\ 0 & \text{otherwise.} \end{cases}$$

Find the probability that

(a) $x > 1/3$. **(b)** $x < (1/3) + y$.

16. The joint density function for x, y is given by

$$f(x,y) = \begin{cases} kxy & \text{for } 0 \le x \le y \le 1, \\ 0 & \text{otherwise.} \end{cases}$$

(a) Determine the value of k.
(b) Find the probability that (x, y) lies in the shaded region in Figure 16.57.

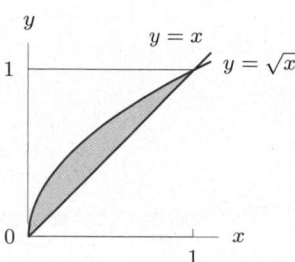

Figure 16.57

17. A joint density function is given by

$$f(x,y) = \begin{cases} kx^2 & \text{for } 0 \le x \le 2 \text{ and } 0 \le y \le 1, \\ 0 & \text{otherwise.} \end{cases}$$

(a) Find the value of the constant k.
(b) Find the probability that (x, y) satisfies $x + y \le 2$.
(c) Find the probability that (x, y) satisfies $x \le 1$ and $y \le 1/2$.

18. A point is chosen at random from the region S in the xy-plane containing all points (x, y) such that $-1 \le x \le 1, -2 \le y \le 2$ and $x - y \ge 0$ ("at random" means that the density function is constant on S).

(a) Determine the joint density function for x and y.
(b) If T is a subset of S with area α, then find the probability that a point (x, y) is in T.

19. A health insurance company wants to know what proportion of its policies are going to cost the company a lot of money because the insured people are over 65 and sick. In order to compute this proportion, the company defines a *disability index*, x, with $0 \le x \le 1$, where $x = 0$ represents perfect health and $x = 1$ represents total disability. In addition, the company uses a density function, $f(x, y)$, defined in such a way that the quantity

$$f(x,y)\,\Delta x\,\Delta y$$

approximates the fraction of the population with disability index between x and $x + \Delta x$, and aged between y and $y + \Delta y$. The company knows from experience that a policy no longer covers its costs if the insured person is over 65 and has a disability index exceeding 0.8. Write an expression for the fraction of the company's policies held by people meeting these criteria.

20. The probability that a radioactive substance will decay at time t is modeled by the density function

$$p(t) = \lambda e^{-\lambda t}$$

for $t \ge 0$, and $p(t) = 0$ for $t < 0$. The positive constant λ depends on the material, and is called the decay rate.

(a) Check that p is a density function.
(b) Two materials with decay rates λ and μ decay independently of each other; their joint density function is the product of the individual density functions. Write the joint density function for the probability that the first material decays at time t and the second at time s.
(c) Find the probability that the first substance decays before the second.

21. Figure 16.58 represents a baseball field, with the bases at $(1, 0)$, $(1, 1)$, $(0, 1)$, and home plate at $(0, 0)$. The outer bound of the outfield is a piece of a circle about the origin with radius 4. When a ball is hit by a batter we record the spot on the field where the ball is caught. Let $p(r, \theta)$ be a function in the plane that gives the density of the distribution of such spots. Write an expression that represents the probability that a hit is caught in

(a) The right field (region R).
(b) The center field (region C).

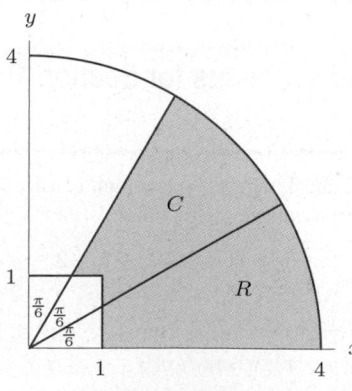

Figure 16.58

22. Two independent random numbers x and y between 0 and 1 have joint density function

$$p(x, y) = \begin{cases} 1 & \text{if } 0 \leq x, y \leq 1 \\ 0 & \text{otherwise.} \end{cases}$$

This problem concerns the average $z = (x+y)/2$, which has a one-variable probability density function of its own.

(a) Find $F(t)$, the probability that $z \leq t$. Treat separately the cases $t \leq 0, 0 < t \leq 1/2, 1/2 < t \leq 1$, $1 < t$. Note that $F(t)$ is the cumulative distribution function of z.

(b) Find and graph the probability density function of z.

(c) Are x and y more likely to be near 0, 1/2, or 1? What about z?

Strengthen Your Understanding

In Problems 23–24, explain what is wrong with the statement.

23. If $p_1(x, y)$ and $p_2(x, y)$ are joint density functions, then $p_1(x, y) + p_2(x, y)$ is a joint density function.

24. If $p(w, h)$ is the probability density function of the weight and height of mothers discussed in Section 16.6, then the probability that a mother weighs 60 kg and has a height of 170 cm is $p(60, 170)$.

In Problems 25–26, give an example of:

25. Values for a, b, c and d such that f is a joint density function:

$$f(x, y) = \begin{cases} 1 \text{ for } a \leq x \leq b \text{ and } c \leq y \leq d, \\ 0 \text{ otherwise} \end{cases}$$

26. A one-variable function $g(y)$ such that f is a joint density function:

$$f(x, y) = \begin{cases} g(y) \text{ for } 0 \leq x \leq 2 \text{ and } 0 \leq y \leq 1, \\ 0 \qquad \text{otherwise} \end{cases}$$

For Problems 27–30, let $p(x, y)$ be a joint density function for x and y. Are the following statements true or false?

27. $\displaystyle\int_a^b \int_{-\infty}^{\infty} p(x, y) \, dy \, dx$ is the probability that $a \leq x \leq b$.

28. $0 \leq p(x, y) \leq 1$ for all x.

29. $\displaystyle\int_a^b p(x, y) \, dx$ is the probability that $a \leq x \leq b$.

30. $\displaystyle\int_{-\infty}^{\infty} \int_{-\infty}^{\infty} p(x, y) \, dy \, dx = 1$.

CHAPTER SUMMARY (see also Ready Reference at the end of the book)

- **Double Integral**
  Definition as a limit of Riemann sum; interpretation as volume under graph, as area, as average value, or as total mass from density; estimating from contour diagrams or tables; evaluating using iterated integrals; setting up in polar coordinates.

- **Triple Integral**

  Definition as a limit of Riemann sum; interpretation as volume of solid, as total mass, or as average value; evaluating using iterated integrals; setting up in cylindrical or spherical coordinates.

- **Probability**
  Joint density functions, using integrals to calculate probability.

REVIEW EXERCISES AND PROBLEMS FOR CHAPTER SIXTEEN

Exercises

For Exercises 1–3, sketch the region of integration and evaluate the integral.

1. $\displaystyle\int_0^3 \int_0^{2x} (x^2 + y^2) \, dy \, dx$

2. $\displaystyle\int_0^\pi \int_0^x \sin x \, dy \, dx$

3. $\displaystyle\int_{-2}^0 \int_{-\sqrt{9-x^2}}^0 2xy \, dy \, dx$

In Exercises 4–9, sketch the region of integration.

4. $\displaystyle\int_{-1}^1 \int_{-\sqrt{1-x^2}}^{\sqrt{1-x^2}} f(x, y) \, dy \, dx$

5. $\displaystyle\int_0^2 \int_{-\sqrt{4-y^2}}^0 f(x, y) \, dx \, dy$

6. $\displaystyle\int_1^4 \int_{-\sqrt{y}}^{\sqrt{y}} f(x, y) \, dx \, dy$

7. $\displaystyle\int_0^1 \int_0^{\sin^{-1} y} f(x, y)\, dx\, dy$

8. $\displaystyle\int_{-1}^1 \int_{-1}^1 \int_0^{\sqrt{1-z^2}} f(x, y, z)\, dy\, dz\, dx$

9. $\displaystyle\int_0^1 \int_0^y \int_0^x f(x, y, z)\, dz\, dx\, dy$

In Exercises 10–13, choose coordinates and write a triple integral for a function over the region. Include limits of integration.

10.

11.

12.

13.

14. Write $\int_R f(x, y)\, dA$ as an iterated integral if R is the region in Figure 16.59.

Figure 16.59

15. Consider the integral $\int_0^4 \int_0^{-(y-4)/2} g(x, y)\, dx\, dy$.

   (a) Sketch the region over which the integration is being performed.

   (b) Write the integral with the order of the integration reversed.

16. Evaluate $\int_R \sqrt{x^2 + y^2}\, dA$ where R is the region in Figure 16.60.

Figure 16.60

In Exercises 17–23, calculate the integral exactly.

17. $\displaystyle\int_0^{10} \int_0^{0.1} x e^{xy}\, dy\, dx$

18. $\displaystyle\int_0^1 \int_3^4 (\sin(2-y)) \cos(3x-7)\, dx\, dy$

19. $\displaystyle\int_0^1 \int_0^y (\sin^3 x)(\cos x)(\cos y)\, dx\, dy$

20. $\displaystyle\int_3^4 \int_0^1 x^2 y \cos(xy)\, dy\, dx$

21. $\displaystyle\int_0^1 \int_{-\sqrt{1-x^2}}^{\sqrt{1-x^2}} e^{-(x^2+y^2)}\, dy\, dx$

22. $\displaystyle\int_0^1 \int_0^z \int_0^2 (y+z)^7\, dx\, dy\, dz$

23. $\displaystyle\int_0^1 \int_0^z \int_0^y xyz\, dx\, dy\, dz$

24. Using Cartesian, cylindrical, or spherical coordinates, write an equation for the following surfaces. Each equation should be of the form "Coordinate = Constant."

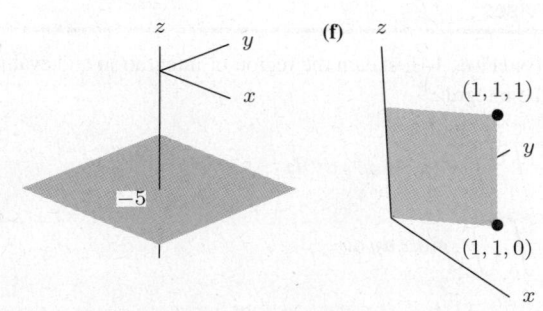

If W is the region in Figure 16.61, what are the limits of integration in Problems 25–27?

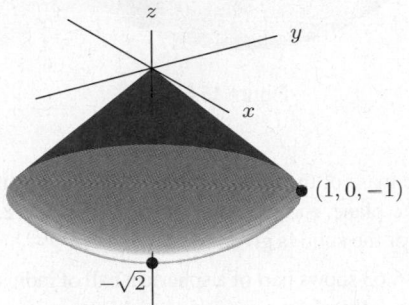

Figure 16.61: Cone with spherical cap

25. $\int_?^? \int_?^? \int_?^? f(\rho, \phi, \theta) \rho^2 \sin \phi \, d\rho \, d\phi \, d\theta$

26. $\int_?^? \int_?^? \int_?^? g(r, \theta, z) r \, dz \, dr \, d\theta$

27. $\int_?^? \int_?^? \int_?^? h(x, y, z) \, dz \, dy \, dx$

28. Set up $\int_R f \, dV$ as an iterated integral in all six possible orders of integration, where R is the hemisphere bounded by the upper half of $x^2 + y^2 + z^2 = 1$ and the xy-plane.

Problems

In Problems 29–37, decide (without calculating its value) whether the integral is positive, negative, or zero. Let W be the solid half-cone bounded by $z = \sqrt{x^2 + y^2}$, $z = 2$ and the yz-plane with $x \geq 0$.

29. $\int_W x \, dV$

30. $\int_W z \, dV$

31. $\int_W (z - \sqrt{x^2 + y^2}) \, dV$

32. $\int_W \sqrt{x^2 + y^2} \, dV$

33. $\int_W (z - 2) \, dV$

34. $\int_W y \, dV$

35. $\int_W xy \, dV$

36. $\int_W xyz \, dV$

37. $\int_W e^{-xyz} \, dV$

38. (a) Set up a triple integral giving the volume of the tetrahedron bounded by the three coordinate planes and the plane $z - x + y = 2$.
 (b) Evaluate the integral.

39. Let B be the solid sphere of radius 1 centered at the origin; let T be the top half of the sphere ($z \geq 0$); let R be the right half of the sphere ($x \geq 0$).

 (a) Without calculation, decide which of the following integrals are zero. What are the signs of the others?
   (i) $\int_B dV$ (ii) $\int_T z \, dV$ (iii) $\int_R z \, dV$
 (b) Evaluate, numerically where necessary, any of the three integrals that is not zero.

40. Sketch the region R over which the integration is being performed:

$$\int_0^{\pi/2} \int_{\pi/2}^{\pi} \int_0^1 f(\rho, \phi, \theta) \rho^2 \sin \phi \, d\rho \, d\phi \, d\theta.$$

41. (a) Convert the following triple integral to spherical coordinates:

$$\int_0^{2\pi} \int_0^3 \int_0^r r \, dz \, dr \, d\theta.$$

(b) Evaluate either the original integral or your answer to part (a).

In Problems 42–45, sketch the region of integration and write a triple integral, including limits, over the region.

42. Region: $0 \leq z \leq 1 + x$, $0 \leq x \leq 2$, $0 \leq y \leq 1$.

43. Region: $2 \leq z \leq 3$, $5 \leq x^2 + y^2 \leq 6$.

44. Region: $3 \leq x^2 + y^2 + z^2 \leq 4$, $0 \leq \theta \leq \pi$.

45. Region: $x^2 + y^2 + z^2 \leq 9$, $x^2 + y^2 \leq 1$, $z \geq 0$.

In Problems 46–50, is the double integral positive or negative, or is it impossible to tell? The finite regions T, B, R, L are in the xy-plane.

T lies in the region where $y > 0$,
R lies in the region where $x > 0$,
B lies in the region where $y < 0$,
L lies in the region where $x < 0$.

46. $\int_T e^{-x} \, dA$

47. $\int_B y^3 \, dA$

48. $\int_R (x + y^2) \, dA$

49. $\int_L y^3 \, dA$

50. $\int_L (x + y^2) \, dA$

In Problems 51–58, decide (without calculating its value) whether the integral is positive, negative, or zero. Let W be the solid sphere bounded by $x^2 + y^2 + z^2 = 1$.

51. $\int_W z \, dV$

52. $\int_W x \, dV$

53. $\int_W xy \, dV$

54. $\int_W \sin(\frac{\pi}{2} xy) \, dV$

55. $\int_W xyz \, dV$

56. $\int_W e^{-xyz} \, dV$

57. $\int_W (z^2 - 1) \, dV$

58. $\int_W \sqrt{x^2 + y^2 + z^2} \, dV$

In Problems 59–62, evaluate the integral by changing it to cylindrical or spherical coordinates.

59. $\int_{-\sqrt{3}}^{\sqrt{3}} \int_{-\sqrt{3-x^2}}^{\sqrt{3-x^2}} \int_{1}^{4-x^2-y^2} \frac{1}{z^2} \, dz \, dy \, dx$

60. $\int_{0}^{1} \int_{0}^{\sqrt{1-x^2}} \int_{0}^{\sqrt{x^2+y^2}} (z + \sqrt{x^2+y^2}) \, dz \, dy \, dx$

61. $\int_{0}^{3} \int_{-\sqrt{9-z^2}}^{\sqrt{9-z^2}} \int_{-\sqrt{9-y^2-z^2}}^{\sqrt{9-y^2-z^2}} x^2 \, dx \, dy \, dz$

62. $\int_{W} \frac{z}{(x^2+y^2)^{3/2}} \, dV$, if W is $1 \le x^2 + y^2 \le 4$,
$$0 \le z \le 4$$

63. (a) Sketch the region of integration of
$$\int_{2}^{\sqrt{8}} \int_{0}^{\sqrt{8-y^2}} e^{-x^2-y^2} \, dx \, dy + \int_{0}^{2} \int_{0}^{y} e^{-x^2-y^2} \, dx \, dy$$

(b) Evaluate the quantity in part (a).

64. A circular lake 10 km in diameter has a circular island 2 km in diameter at its center. At t kilometers from the island the depth of the lake is $100t(4-t)$ meters, where $0 \le t \le 4$. What is the volume of water in the lake?

65. A solid region D is a half cylinder with radius 1 lying horizontally with its rectangular base in the xy-plane and its axis along the line $y = 1$ from $x = 0$ to $x = 10$. (The region is above the xy-plane.)

(a) What is the equation of the curved surface of this half cylinder?

(b) Write the limits of integration of the integral $\int_{D} f(x, y, z) \, dV$ in Cartesian coordinates.

66. Find the volume of the region bounded by $z = x + y$, $0 \le x \le 5$, $0 \le y \le 5$, and the planes $x = 0$, $y = 0$, and $z = 0$.

67. (a) Sketch the region of integration, or describe it precisely in words, for the following integral:
$$\int_{-1}^{1} \int_{-1}^{1} \int_{0}^{\sqrt{1-z^2}} f(x, y, z) \, dy \, dz \, dx.$$

(b) Evaluate the integral with $f(x, y, z) = (y^2 + z^2)^{3/2}$.

68. A thin circular disk of radius 12 cm has density which increases linearly from 1 gm/cm^2 at the center to 25 gm/cm^2 at the rim.

(a) Write an iterated integral representing the mass of the disk.

(b) Evaluate the integral.

69. Figure 16.62 shows part of a spherical ball of radius 5 cm. Write an integral in cylindrical coordinates representing the volume of this region and evaluate it.

Figure 16.62

70. Find the mass of the solid bounded by the xy-plane, yz-plane, xz-plane, and the plane $4x + 3y + z = 12$, if the density of the solid is given by $\delta(x, y, z) = x^2$.

71. Figure 16.63 shows part of a spherical ball of radius 5 cm. Write an integral in spherical coordinates representing the volume of this region and evaluate it.

Figure 16.63

72. A forest next to a road has the shape in Figure 16.64. The population density of rabbits is proportional to the distance from the road. It is 0 at the road, and 10 rabbits per square mile at the opposite edge of the forest. Find the total rabbit population in the forest.

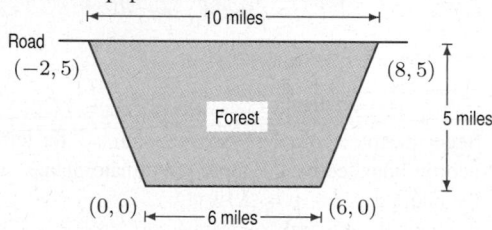

Figure 16.64

73. A solid hemisphere of radius 2 cm has density, in gm/cm^3, at each point equal to the distance in centimeters from the point to the center of the base. Write a triple integral representing the total mass of the hemisphere. Evaluate the integral.

74. Find the volume that remains after a cylindrical hole of radius R is bored through a sphere of radius a, where $0 < R < a$, passing through the center of the sphere along the pole.

75. Two spheres, one of radius 1, one of radius $\sqrt{2}$, have centers that are 1 unit apart. Write a triple integral, including limits of integration, giving the volume of the smaller region that is outside one sphere and inside the other. Evaluate the integral.

For Problems 76–77, use the definition of moment of inertia on page 890.

76. Consider a rectangular brick with length 5, width 3, and height 1, and of uniform density 1. Compute the moment of inertia about each of the three axes passing through the center of the brick, perpendicular to one of the sides.

77. Compute the moment of inertia of a ball of radius R about an axis passing through its center. Assume that the ball has a constant density of 1.

78. A particle of mass m is placed at the center of one base of a circular cylindrical shell of inner radius r_1, outer ra-dius r_2, height h, and constant density δ. Find the force of gravity exerted by the cylinder on the particle.

79. **(a)** Find the constant k such that $f(x,y) = k(x+y)$ is a probability density function the quarter disk $x^2 + y^2 \leq 100$, $x \geq 0$, $y \geq 0$. [Hint: Use polar coordinates.]
  (b) Find the probability that a point chosen in the quarter disk according to the probability density in part (a) is less than 7 units from the origin.

CAS Challenge Problems

80. Let D be the region inside the triangle with vertices $(0,0)$, $(1,1)$ and $(0,1)$. Express the double integral $\int_D e^{y^2} \, dA$ as an iterated integral in two different ways. Calculate whichever of the two you can do by hand, and calculate the other with a computer algebra system if possible. Compare the answers.

81. Let D be the region inside the circle $x^2 + y^2 = 1$. Express the integral $\int_D \sqrt[3]{x^2 + y^2} \, dA$ as an iterated integral in both Cartesian and polar coordinates. Calculate whichever of the two you can do by hand, and calculate the other with a computer algebra system if possible. Compare the answers.

82. Compute the iterated integrals $\int_0^1 \int_{-1}^0 \frac{x+y}{(x-y)^3} \, dy dx$

and $\int_{-1}^0 \int_0^1 \frac{x+y}{(x-y)^3} \, dx dy$. Explain why your answers do not contradict Theorem 16.1 on page 876.

83. For each of the following functions, find its average value over the square $-h \leq x \leq h$, $-h \leq y \leq h$, calculate the limit of your answer as $h \to 0$, and compare with the value of the function at $(0,0)$. Assume a, b, c, d, e, and k are constants.

$$F(x,y) = a + bx^4 + cy^4 + dx^2y^2 + ex^3y^3$$
$$G(x,y) = a\sin(kx) + b\cos(ky) + c$$
$$H(x,y) = ax^2e^{x+y} + by^2e^{x-y}$$

Formulate a conjecture from your results and explain why it makes sense.

PROJECTS FOR CHAPTER SIXTEEN

1. A Connection Between e and π

In this problem you will derive one of the remarkable formulas of mathematics, namely that

$$\int_{-\infty}^{\infty} e^{-x^2} \, dx = \sqrt{\pi}.$$

(a) Change the following double integral into polar coordinates and evaluate it:

$$\int_{-\infty}^{\infty} \int_{-\infty}^{\infty} e^{-(x^2+y^2)} \, dx dy.$$

(b) Explain why

$$\int_{-\infty}^{\infty} \int_{-\infty}^{\infty} e^{-(x^2+y^2)} \, dx dy = \left(\int_{-\infty}^{\infty} e^{-x^2} \, dx \right)^2.$$

(c) Explain why the answers to parts (a) and (b) give the formula we want.

2. Average Distance Walked to an Airport Gate

At airports, departure gates are often lined up in a terminal like points along a line. If you arrive at one gate and proceed to another gate for a connecting flight, what proportion of the length of the terminal will you have to walk, on average?

(a) One way to model this situation is to randomly choose two numbers, $0 \leq x \leq 1$ and $0 \leq y \leq 1$, and calculate the average value of $|x - y|$. Use a double integral to show that, on average, you have to walk $1/3$ the length of the terminal.

(b) The terminal gates are not actually located continuously from 0 to 1, as we assumed in part (a). There are only a finite number of gates and they are likely to be equally spaced. Suppose there are $n + 1$ gates located $1/n$ units apart from one end of the terminal $(x_0 = 0)$ to the other $(x_n = 1)$. Assuming that all pairs (i, j) of arrival and departure gates are equally likely, show that

$$\text{Average distance between gates} = \frac{1}{(n+1)^2} \cdot \sum_{i=0}^{n} \sum_{j=0}^{n} \left| \frac{i}{n} - \frac{j}{n} \right|.$$

Identify this sum as approximately (but not exactly) a Riemann sum with n subdivisions for the integrand used in part (a). Compute this sum for $n = 5$ and $n = 10$ and compare to the answer of $1/3$ obtained in part (a).

Chapter Seventeen

PARAMETERIZATION AND VECTOR FIELDS

Contents

17.1 PARAMETERIZED CURVES

A curve in the plane may be parameterized by a pair of equations of the form $x = f(t)$, $y = g(t)$. As the parameter t changes, the point (x, y) traces out the curve. In this section we find parametric equations for curves in three dimensions, and we see how to write parametric equations using position vectors.

Parametric Equations in Three Dimensions

We describe motion in the plane by giving parametric equations for x and y in terms of t. To describe a motion in 3-space parametrically, we need a third equation giving z in terms of t.

Example 1   Find parametric equations for the curve $y = x^2$ in the xy-plane.

Solution   A possible parameterization in two dimensions is $x = t$, $y = t^2$. Since the curve is in the xy-plane, the z-coordinate is zero, so a parameterization in three dimensions is

$$x = t, \quad y = t^2, \quad z = 0.$$

Example 2   Find parametric equations for a particle that starts at $(0, 3, 0)$ and moves around a circle as shown in Figure 17.1.

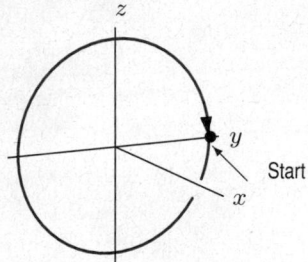

Figure 17.1: Circle of radius 3 in the yz-plane, centered at origin

Solution   Since the motion is in the yz-plane, we have $x = 0$ at all times t. Looking at the yz-plane from the positive x-direction we see motion around a circle of radius 3 in the clockwise direction. Thus,

$$x = 0, \quad y = 3\cos t, \quad z = -3\sin t.$$

Example 3   Describe in words the motion given parametrically by

$$x = \cos t, \quad y = \sin t, \quad z = t.$$

Solution   The particle's x- and y-coordinates give circular motion in the xy-plane, while the z-coordinate increases steadily. Thus, the particle traces out a rising spiral, like a coiled spring. (See Figure 17.2.) This curve is called a *helix*.

Figure 17.2: The helix $x = \cos t, y = \sin t, z = t$

Example 4   Find parametric equations for the line parallel to the vector $2\vec{i} + 3\vec{j} + 4\vec{k}$ and through the point $(1, 5, 7)$.

Solution   Let's imagine a particle at the point $(1, 5, 7)$ at time $t = 0$ and moving through a displacement of $2\vec{i} + 3\vec{j} + 4\vec{k}$ for each unit of time, t. When $t = 0$, $x = 1$ and x increases by 2 units for every unit of time. Thus, at time t, the x-coordinate of the particle is given by

$$x = 1 + 2t.$$

Similarly, the y-coordinate starts at $y = 5$ and increases at a rate of 3 units for every unit of time. The z-coordinate starts at $y = 7$ and increases by 4 units for every unit of time. Thus, the parametric equations of the line are

$$x = 1 + 2t, \quad y = 5 + 3t, \quad z = 7 + 4t.$$

We can generalize the previous example as follows:

Parametric Equations of a Line through the point (x_0, y_0, z_0) and parallel to the vector $a\vec{i} + b\vec{j} + c\vec{k}$ are
$$x = x_0 + at, \quad y = y_0 + bt, \quad z = z_0 + ct.$$

Notice that the coordinates x, y, and z are linear functions of the parameter t.

Example 5   (a) Describe in words the curve given by the parametric equations $x = 3 + t$, $y = 2t$, $z = 1 - t$.
(b) Find parametric equations for the line through the points $(1, 2, -1)$ and $(3, 3, 4)$.

Solution   (a) The curve is a line through the point $(3, 0, 1)$ and parallel to the vector $\vec{i} + 2\vec{j} - \vec{k}$.
(b) The line is parallel to the vector between the points $P = (1, 2, -1)$ and $Q = (3, 3, 4)$.

$$\overrightarrow{PQ} = (3 - 1)\vec{i} + (3 - 2)\vec{j} + (4 - (-1))\vec{k} = 2\vec{i} + \vec{j} + 5\vec{k}.$$

Thus, using the point P, the parametric equations are

$$x = 1 + 2t, \quad y = 2 + t, \quad z = -1 + 5t.$$

Using the point Q gives the equations $x = 3 + 2t$, $y = 3 + t$, $z = 4 + 5t$, which represent the same line.

Using Position Vectors to Write Parameterized Curves as Vector-Valued Functions

A point in the plane with coordinates (x, y) can be represented by the position vector $\vec{r} = x\vec{i} + y\vec{j}$ in Figure 17.3. Similarly, in 3-space we write $\vec{r} = x\vec{i} + y\vec{j} + z\vec{k}$. (See Figure 17.4.)

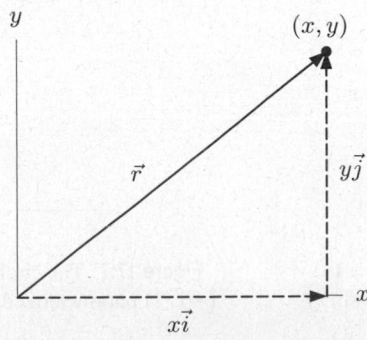

Figure 17.3: Position vector $\vec{r}$ for the point (x, y)

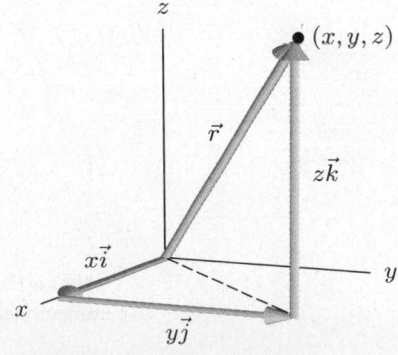

Figure 17.4: Position vector $\vec{r}$ for the point (x, y, z)

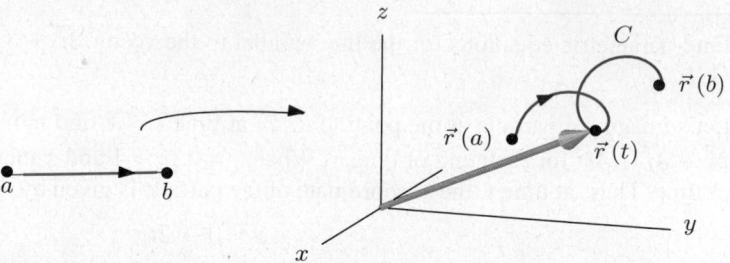

Figure 17.5: The parameterization sends the interval, $a \leq t \leq b$, to the curve, C, in 3-space

We can write the parametric equations $x = f(t)$, $y = g(t)$, $z = h(t)$ as a single vector equation

$$\vec{r}(t) = f(t)\vec{i} + g(t)\vec{j} + h(t)\vec{k}$$

called a *parameterization*. As the parameter t varies, the point with position vector $\vec{r}(t)$ traces out a curve in 3-space. For example, the circular motion in the plane

$$x = \cos t, y = \sin t \quad \text{can be written as} \quad \vec{r} = (\cos t)\vec{i} + (\sin t)\vec{j}$$

and the helix in 3-space

$$x = \cos t, y = \sin t, z = t \quad \text{can be written as} \quad \vec{r} = (\cos t)\vec{i} + (\sin t)\vec{j} + t\vec{k}.$$

See Figure 17.5.

Example 6 Use vectors to give a parameterization for the circle of radius $\frac{1}{2}$ centered at the point $(-1, 2)$.

Solution The circle of radius 1 centered at the origin is parameterized by the vector-valued function

$$\vec{r}_1(t) = \cos t\vec{i} + \sin t\vec{j}, \quad 0 \leq t \leq 2\pi.$$

The point $(-1, 2)$ has position vector $\vec{r}_0 = -\vec{i} + 2\vec{j}$. The position vector, $\vec{r}(t)$, of a point on the circle of radius $\frac{1}{2}$ centered at $(-1, 2)$ is found by adding $\frac{1}{2}\vec{r}_1$ to $\vec{r}_0$. (See Figures 17.6 and 17.7.) Thus,

$$\vec{r}(t) = \vec{r}_0 + \frac{1}{2}\vec{r}_1(t) = -\vec{i} + 2\vec{j} + \frac{1}{2}(\cos t\vec{i} + \sin t\vec{j}) = (-1 + \frac{1}{2}\cos t)\vec{i} + (2 + \frac{1}{2}\sin t)\vec{j},$$

or, equivalently,

$$x = -1 + \frac{1}{2}\cos t, \quad y = 2 + \frac{1}{2}\sin t, \quad 0 \leq t \leq 2\pi.$$

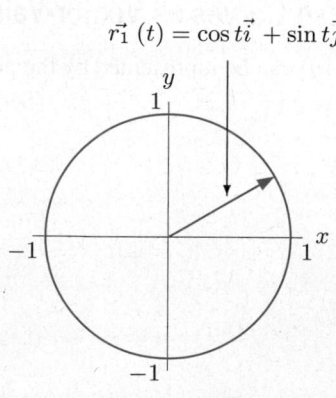

Figure 17.6: The circle $x^2 + y^2 = 1$ parameterized by $\vec{r}_1(t) = \cos t\vec{i} + \sin t\vec{j}$

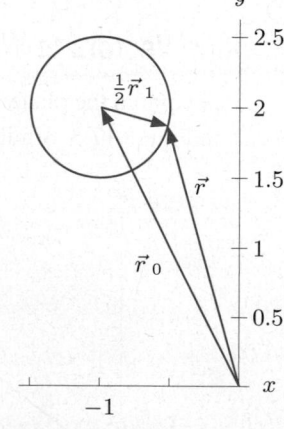

Figure 17.7: The circle of radius $\frac{1}{2}$ and center $(-1, 2)$ parameterized by $\vec{r}(t) = \vec{r}_0 + \frac{1}{2}\vec{r}_1(t)$

Parametric Equation of a Line

Consider a straight line in the direction of a vector $\vec{v}$ passing through the point (x_0, y_0, z_0) with position vector $\vec{r}_0$. We start at $\vec{r}_0$ and move up and down the line, adding different multiples of $\vec{v}$ to $\vec{r}_0$. (See Figure 17.8.)

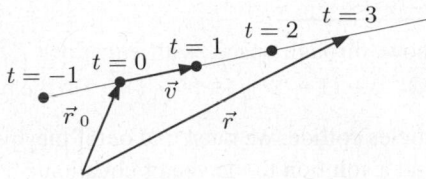

Figure 17.8: The line $\vec{r}(t) = \vec{r}_0 + t\vec{v}$

In this way, every point on the line can be written as $\vec{r}_0 + t\vec{v}$, which yields the following:

Parametric Equation of a Line in Vector Form

The line through the point with position vector $\vec{r_0} = x_0\vec{i} + y_0\vec{j} + z_0\vec{k}$ in the direction of the vector $\vec{v} = a\vec{i} + b\vec{j} + c\vec{k}$ has parametric equation

$$\vec{r}(t) = \vec{r}_0 + t\vec{v}.$$

Example 7   (a) Find parametric equations for the line passing through the points $(2, -1, 3)$ and $(-1, 5, 4)$.
                (b) Represent the line segment from $(2, -1, 3)$ to $(-1, 5, 4)$ parametrically.

Solution   (a) The line passes through $(2, -1, 3)$ and is parallel to the displacement vector $\vec{v} = -3\vec{i} + 6\vec{j} + \vec{k}$ from $(2, -1, 3)$ to $(-1, 5, 4)$. Thus, the parametric equation is

$$\vec{r}(t) = 2\vec{i} - \vec{j} + 3\vec{k} + t(-3\vec{i} + 6\vec{j} + \vec{k}).$$

(b) In the parameterization in part (a), $t = 0$ corresponds to the point $(2, -1, 3)$ and $t = 1$ corresponds to the point $(-1, 5, 4)$. So the parameterization of the segment is

$$\vec{r}(t) = 2\vec{i} - \vec{j} + 3\vec{k} + t(-3\vec{i} + 6\vec{j} + \vec{k}), \qquad 0 \le t \le 1.$$

Intersection of Curves and Surfaces

Parametric equations for a curve enable us to find where a curve intersects a surface.

Example 8   Find the points at which the line $x = t$, $y = 2t$, $z = 1 + t$ pierces the sphere of radius 10 centered at the origin.

Solution   The equation for the sphere of radius 10 and centered at the origin is

$$x^2 + y^2 + z^2 = 100.$$

To find the intersection points of the line and the sphere, substitute the parametric equations of the line into the equation of the sphere, giving

$$t^2 + 4t^2 + (1 + t)^2 = 100,$$

so

$$6t^2 + 2t - 99 = 0,$$

which has the two solutions at approximately $t = -4.23$ and $t = 3.90$. Using the parametric equation for the line, $(x, y, z) = (t, 2t, 1 + t)$, we see that the line cuts the sphere at the two points

$$(x, y, z) = (-4.23, 2(-4.23), 1 + (-4.23)) = (-4.23, -8.46, -3.23),$$

and

$$(x, y, z) = (3.90, 2(3.90), 1 + 3.90) = (3.90, 7.80, 4.90).$$

We can also use parametric equations to find the intersection of two curves.

Example 9   Two particles move through space, with equations $\vec{r}_1(t) = t\vec{i} + (1 + 2t)\vec{j} + (3 - 2t)\vec{k}$ and $\vec{r}_2(t) = (-2 - 2t)\vec{i} + (1 - 2t)\vec{j} + (1 + t)\vec{k}$. Do the particles ever collide? Do their paths cross?

Solution   To see if the particles collide, we must find out if they pass through the same point at the same time t. So we must find a solution to the vector equation $\vec{r}_1(t) = \vec{r}_2(t)$, which is the same as finding a common solution to the three scalar equations

$$t = -2 - 2t, \qquad 1 + 2t = 1 - 2t, \qquad 3 - 2t = 1 + t.$$

Separately, the solutions are $t = -2/3$, $t = 0$, and $t = 2/3$, so there is no common solution, and the particles don't collide. To see if their paths cross, we find out if they pass through the same point at two possibly different times, t_1 and t_2. So we solve the equations

$$t_1 = -2 - 2t_2, \qquad 1 + 2t_1 = 1 - 2t_2, \qquad 3 - 2t_1 = 1 + t_2.$$

We solve the first two equations simultaneously and get $t_1 = 2$, $t_2 = -2$. Since these values also satisfy the third equation, the paths cross. The position of the first particle at time $t = 2$ is the same as the position of the second particle at time $t = -2$, namely the point $(2, 5, -1)$.

Example 10   Are the lines $x = -1 + t, y = 1 + 2t, z = 5 - t$ and $x = 2 + 2t, y = 4 + t, z = 3 + t$ parallel? Do they intersect?

Solution   In vector form the lines are parameterized by

$$\vec{r} = -\vec{i} + \vec{j} + 5\vec{k} + t(\vec{i} + 2\vec{j} - \vec{k})$$
$$\vec{r} = 2\vec{i} + 4\vec{j} + 3\vec{k} + t(2\vec{i} + \vec{j} + \vec{k})$$

Their direction vectors $\vec{i} + 2\vec{j} - \vec{k}$ and $2\vec{i} + \vec{j} + \vec{k}$ are not multiples of each other, so the lines are not parallel. To find out if they intersect, we see if they pass through the same point at two possibly different times, t_1 and t_2:

$$-1 + t_1 = 2 + 2t_2, \qquad 1 + 2t_1 = 4 + t_2, \qquad 5 - t_1 = 3 + t_2.$$

The first two equations give $t_1 = 1$, $t_2 = -1$. Since these values do not satisfy the third equation, the paths do not cross, and so the lines do not intersect.

The next example shows how to tell if two different parameterizations give the same line.

Example 11   Show that the following two lines are the same:

$$\vec{r} = -\vec{i} - \vec{j} + \vec{k} + t(3\vec{i} + 6\vec{j} - 3\vec{k})$$
$$\vec{r} = \vec{i} + 3\vec{j} - \vec{k} + t(-\vec{i} - 2\vec{j} + \vec{k})$$

Solution   The direction vectors of the two lines, $3\vec{i} + 6\vec{j} - 3\vec{k}$ and $-\vec{i} - 2\vec{j} + \vec{k}$, are multiples of each other, so the lines are parallel. To see if they are the same, we pick a point on the first line and see if it is on the second line. For example, the point on the first line with $t = 0$ has position vector $-\vec{i} - \vec{j} + \vec{k}$. Solving

$$\vec{i} + 3\vec{j} - \vec{k} + t(-\vec{i} - 2\vec{j} + \vec{k}) = -\vec{i} - \vec{j} + \vec{k}$$

we get $t = 2$, so the two lines have a point in common. Thus, they are the same line, parameterized in two different ways.

Exercises and Problems for Section 17.1

Exercises

In Exercises 1–6, find a parameterization for the curve shown.

1.

2.

3.

4.

5.

6.

In Exercises 7–17, find parametric equations for the line.

7. The line in the direction of the vector $\vec{i} - \vec{k}$ and through the point $(0, 1, 0)$.

8. The line in the direction of the vector $\vec{i} + 2\vec{j} - \vec{k}$ and through the point $(3, 0, -4)$.

9. The line parallel to the z-axis passing through the point $(1, 0, 0)$.

10. The line in the direction of the vector $5\vec{j} + 2\vec{k}$ and through the point $(5, -1, 1)$.

11. The line in the direction of the vector $3\vec{i} - 3\vec{j} + \vec{k}$ and through the point $(1, 2, 3)$.

12. The line in the direction of the vector $2\vec{i} + 2\vec{j} - 3\vec{k}$ and through the point $(-3, 4, -2)$.

13. The line through $(-3, -2, 1)$ and $(-1, -3, -1)$.

14. The line through the points $(1, 5, 2)$ and $(5, 0, -1)$.

15. The line through the points $(2, 3, -1)$ and $(5, 2, 0)$.

16. The line through $(3, -2, 2)$ and intersecting the y-axis at $y = 2$.

17. The line intersecting the x-axis at $x = 3$ and the z-axis at $z = -5$.

In Exercises 18–34, find a parameterization for the curve.

18. A line segment between $(2, 1, 3)$ and $(4, 3, 2)$.

19. A circle of radius 3 centered on the z-axis and lying in the plane $z = 5$.

20. A line perpendicular to the plane $z = 2x - 3y + 7$ and through the point $(1, 1, 6)$.

21. The circle of radius 2 in the xy-plane, centered at the origin, clockwise.

22. The circle of radius 2 parallel to the xy-plane, centered at the point $(0, 0, 1)$, and traversed counterclockwise when viewed from below.

23. The circle of radius 2 in the xz-plane, centered at the origin.

24. The circle of radius 3 parallel to the xy-plane, centered at the point $(0, 0, 2)$.

25. The circle of radius 3 in the yz-plane, centered at the point $(0, 0, 2)$.

26. The circle of radius 5 parallel to the yz-plane, centered at the point $(-1, 0, -2)$.

27. The curve $x = y^2$ in the xy-plane.

28. The curve $y = x^3$ in the xy-plane.

29. The curve $x = -3z^2$ in the xz-plane.

30. The curve in which the plane $z = 2$ cuts the surface $z = \sqrt{x^2 + y^2}$.

31. The curve $y = 4 - 5x^4$ through the point $(0, 4, 4)$, parallel to the xy-plane.

32. The ellipse of major diameter 5 parallel to the y-axis and minor diameter 2 parallel to the z-axis, centered at $(0, 1, -2)$.

33. The ellipse of major diameter 6 along the x-axis and minor diameter 4 along the y-axis, centered at the origin.

34. The ellipse of major diameter 3 parallel to the x-axis and minor diameter 2 parallel to the z-axis, centered at $(0, 1, -2)$.

In Exercises 35–42, find a parametric equation for the curve segment. (There are many possible answers.)

35. Line from $(-1, 2, -3)$ to $(2, 2, 2)$.

36. Line from $P_0 = (-1, -3)$ to $P_1 = (5, 2)$.

37. Line from $P_0 = (1, -3, 2)$ to $P_1 = (4, 1, -3)$.

38. Semicircle from $(0, 0, 5)$ to $(0, 0, -5)$ in the yz-plane with $y \geq 0$.

39. Semicircle from $(1, 0, 0)$ to $(-1, 0, 0)$ in the xy-plane with $y \geq 0$.

40. Graph of $y = \sqrt{x}$ from $(1, 1)$ to $(16, 4)$.

41. Arc of a circle of radius 5 from $P = (0, 0)$ to $Q = (10, 0)$.

42. Quarter-ellipse from $(4, 0, 3)$ to $(0, -3, 3)$ in the plane $z = 3$.

Problems

In Problems 43–47, parameterize the line through $P = (2, 5)$ and $Q = (12, 9)$ so that the points P and Q correspond to the given parameter values.

43. $t = 0$ and 1

44. $t = 0$ and 5

45. $t = 20$ and 30

46. $t = 10$ and 11

47. $t = 0$ and -1

48. At the point where $t = -1$, find an equation for the plane perpendicular to the line

$$x = 5 - 3t, \quad y = 5t - 7, \quad \frac{z}{t} = 6.$$

49. Determine whether the following line is parallel to the plane $2x - 3y + 5z = 5$:

$$x = 5 + 7t, \quad y = 4 + 3t, \quad z = -3 - 2t.$$

50. Show that the equations $x = 3 + t, y = 2t, z = 1 - t$ satisfy the equations $x + y + 3z = 6$ and $x - y - z = 2$. What does this tell you about the curve parameterized by these equations?

51. **(a)** Explain why the line of intersection of two planes must be parallel to the cross product of a normal vector to the first plane and a normal vector to the second.
(b) Find a vector parallel to the line of intersection of the two planes $x + 2y - 3z = 7$ and $3x - y + z = 0$.
(c) Find parametric equations for the line in part (b).

52. Find an equation for the plane containing the point $(2, 3, 4)$ and the line $x = 1 + 2t, y = 3 - t, z = 4 + t$.

53. **(a)** Find an equation for the line perpendicular to the plane $2x - 3y = z$ and through the point $(1, 3, 7)$.
(b) Where does the line cut the plane?
(c) What is the distance between the point $(1, 3, 7)$ and the plane?

54. Consider two points P_0 and P_1 in 3-space.

(a) Show that the line segment from P_0 to P_1 can be parametrized by

$$\vec{r}(t) = (1 - t)\overrightarrow{OP_0} + t\overrightarrow{OP_1}, \quad 0 \le t \le 1.$$

(b) What is represented by the parametric equation

$$\vec{r}(t) = t\overrightarrow{OP_0} + (1 - t)\overrightarrow{OP_1}, \quad 0 \le t \le 1?$$

55. **(a)** Find a vector parallel to the line of intersection of the planes $2x - y - 3z = 0$ and $x + y + z = 1$.
(b) Show that the point $(1, -1, 1)$ lies on both planes.
(c) Find parametric equations for the line of intersection.

56. Find the intersection of the line $x = 5 + 7t, y = 4 + 3t$, $z = -3 - 2t$ and the plane $2x - 3y + 5z = -7$.

In Problems 57–59 two parameterized lines are given. Are they the same line?

57. $\vec{r}_1(t) = (5 - 3t)\vec{i} + 2t\vec{j} + (7 + t)\vec{k}$
$\vec{r}_2(t) = (5 - 6t)\vec{i} + 4t\vec{j} + (7 + 3t)\vec{k}$

58. $\vec{r}_1(t) = (5 - 3t)\vec{i} + (1 + t)\vec{j} + 2t\vec{k}$
$\vec{r}_2(t) = (2 + 6t)\vec{i} + (2 - 2t)\vec{j} + (2 - 4t)\vec{k}$

59. $\vec{r}_1(t) = (5 - 3t)\vec{i} + (1 + t)\vec{j} + 2t\vec{k}$
$\vec{r}_2(t) = (2 + 6t)\vec{i} + (2 - 2t)\vec{j} + (3 - 4t)\vec{k}$

60. If it exists, find the value of c for which the lines $l(t) = (c + t, 1 + t, 5 + t)$ and $m(s) = (s, 1 - s, 3 + s)$ intersect.

61. **(a)** Where does the line $\vec{r} = 2\vec{i} + 5\vec{j} + t(3\vec{i} + \vec{j} + 2\vec{k})$ cut the plane $x + y + z = 1$?
(b) Find a vector perpendicular to the line and lying in the plane.
(c) Find an equation for the line that passes through the point of intersection of the line and plane, is perpendicular to the line, and lies in the plane.

In Problems 62–65, find parametric equations for the line.

62. The line of intersection of the planes $x - y + z = 3$ and $2x + y - z = 5$.

63. The line of intersection of the planes $x + y + z = 3$ and $x - y + 2z = 2$.

64. The line perpendicular to the surface $z = x^2 + y^2$ at the point $(1, 2, 5)$.

65. The line through the point $(-4, 2, 3)$ and parallel to a line in the yz-plane which makes a $45°$ angle with the positive y-axis and the positive z-axis.

66. Is the point $(-3, -4, 2)$ visible from the point $(4, 5, 0)$ if there is an opaque ball of radius 1 centered at the origin?

67. Two particles are traveling through space. At time t the first particle is at the point $(-1 + t, 4 - t, -1 + 2t)$ and the second particle is at $(-7 + 2t, -6 + 2t, -1 + t)$.

(a) Describe the two paths in words.
(b) Do the two particles collide? If so, when and where?
(c) Do the paths of the two particles cross? If so, where?

68. For $t > 0$, a particle moves along the curve $x = a + b\sin kt, y = a + b\cos kt$, where a, b, k are positive constants.

(a) Describe the motion in words.
(b) What is the effect on the curve of the following changes?
  (i) Increasing b
  (ii) Increasing a
  (iii) Increasing k
  (iv) Setting a and b equal

69. In the Atlantic Ocean off the coast of Newfoundland, Canada, the temperature and salinity (saltiness) vary throughout the year. Figure 17.9 shows a parametric curve giving the average temperature, T (in °C) and salinity (in grams of salt per kg of water) for t in months, with $t = 1$ corresponding to mid-January.[1]

(a) Why does the parameterized curve form a loop?
(b) When is the water temperature highest?
(c) When is the water saltiest?
(d) Estimate dT/dt at $t = 6$, and give the units. What is the meaning of your answer for seawater?

Figure 17.9

70. The concentration (in micrograms/m³) of a pollutant at the point (x, y, z) is given, for x, y, z in meters, by

$$c(x, y, z) = e^{-\left(x^2 + y^2 + z^2\right)}.$$

(a) A particle at point $(0, 1, 0)$ moves in the direction of the point $(-2, 2, -2)$. What is the rate at which the concentration is changing with respect to distance at the moment the particle leaves the point $(0, 1, 0)$?
(b) Now suppose the particle is moving along the path, with time, t, in seconds, given by

$$x = 1 - t^2, \quad y = t, \quad z = 1 - t^2 \quad \text{for } -\infty < t < \infty.$$

When is the concentration a maximum?

71. A light shines on the helix of Example 3 on page 918 from far down each axis. Sketch the shadow the helix casts on each of the coordinate planes: xy, xz, and yz.

72. For a positive constant a and $t \geq 0$, the parametric equations I-V represent the curves described in (a)-(e). Match each description (a)-(e) with its parametric equations and write an equation involving only x and y for the curve.

(a) Line through the origin.
(b) Line not through the origin.
(c) Hyperbola opening along x-axis.
(d) Circle traversed clockwise.
(e) Circle traversed counterclockwise.

I. $x = a \sin t, y = a \cos t$ II. $x = a \sin t, y = a \sin t$
III. $x = a \cos t, y = a \sin t$ IV. $x = a \cos^2 t, y = a \sin^2 t$
V. $x = a / \cos t, y = a \tan t$

73. (a) Find a parametric equation for the line through the point $(2, 1, 3)$ and in the direction of $a\vec{i} + b\vec{j} + c\vec{k}$.
(b) Find conditions on a, b, c so that the line you found in part (a) goes through the origin. Give a reason for your answer.

74. Consider the line $x = 5 - 2t, y = 3 + 7t, z = 4t$ and the plane $ax + by + cz = d$. All the following questions have many possible answers. Find values of a, b, c, d such that:

(a) The plane is perpendicular to the line.
(b) The plane is perpendicular to the line and through the point $(5, 3, 0)$.
(c) The line lies in the plane.

75. Explain the significance of the constants $\alpha > 0$ and $\beta > 0$ in the family of helices given by $\vec{r} = \alpha \cos t\vec{i} + \alpha \sin t\vec{j} + \beta t\vec{k}$.

76. Find parametric equations of the line passing through the points $(1, 2, 3)$, $(3, 5, 7)$ and calculate the shortest distance from the line to the origin.

77. A line has equation $\vec{r} = \vec{a} + t\vec{b}$ where $\vec{r} = x\vec{i} + y\vec{j} + z\vec{k}$ and $\vec{a}$ and $\vec{b}$ are constant vectors such that $\vec{a} \neq \vec{0}, \vec{b} \neq \vec{0}, \vec{b}$ not parallel or perpendicular to $\vec{a}$. For each of the planes (a)-(c), pick the equation (i)-(ix) which represents it. Explain your choice.

(a) A plane perpendicular to the line and through the origin.
(b) A plane perpendicular to the line and not through the origin.
(c) A plane containing the line.

(i) $\vec{a} \cdot \vec{r} = \|\vec{b}\|$ (ii) $\vec{b} \cdot \vec{r} = \|\vec{a}\|$
(iii) $\vec{a} \cdot \vec{r} = \vec{b} \cdot \vec{r}$ (iv) $(\vec{a} \times \vec{b}) \cdot (\vec{r} - \vec{a}) = 0$
(v) $\vec{r} - \vec{a} = \vec{b}$ (vi) $\vec{a} \cdot \vec{r} = 0$
(vii) $\vec{b} \cdot \vec{r} = 0$ (viii) $\vec{a} + \vec{r} = \vec{b}$
(ix) $(\vec{a} \times \vec{b}) \cdot (\vec{r} - \vec{b}) = \|\vec{a}\|$

78. (a) Find a parametric equation for the line through the point $(1, 5, 2)$ and in the direction of the vector $2\vec{i} + 3\vec{j} - \vec{k}$.
(b) By minimizing the square of the distance from a point on the line to the origin, find the exact point on the line which is closest to the origin.

79. A plane from Denver, Colorado, (altitude 1650 meters) flies to Bismark, North Dakota (altitude 550 meters). It travels at 650 km/hour along a horizontal line at 8,000 meters above the line joining Denver and Bismark. Bismark is about 850 km in the direction 60° north of east from Denver. Find parametric equations describing the plane's motion. Assume the origin is at sea level beneath Denver, that the x-axis points east and the y-axis points north, and that the earth is flat. Measure distances in kilometers and time in hours.

---

[1] Based on http://www.vub.ac.be. Accessed Nov 2011.

80. The plane $x + 3y - 2z = 6$ is colored blue and the plane $2x + y + z = 3$ is colored yellow. The planes intersect in a line, which is colored green. You are at the point $P = (1, -2, -1)$.

  (a) You look in the direction $\vec{v} = \vec{i} + 2\vec{j} + \vec{k}$. Do you see the blue plane or the yellow plane?
  (b) In what direction(s) are you looking directly at the green line?
  (c) In what direction(s) should you look to see the yellow plane? The blue plane?

81. The vector $\vec{n}$ is perpendicular to the plane P_1. The vector $\vec{v}$ is parallel to the line L.

  (a) If $\vec{n} \cdot \vec{v} = 0$, what does this tell you about the directions of P_1 and L? (Are they parallel? Perpendicular? Or is it impossible to tell?)
  (b) Suppose $\vec{n} \times \vec{v} \neq \vec{0}$. The plane P_2 has normal $\vec{n} \times \vec{v}$. What can you say about the directions of

  (i) P_1 and P_2?   (ii) L and P_2?

82. Figure 17.10 shows the parametric curve $x = x(t), y = y(t)$ for $a \leq t \leq b$.

Figure 17.10

  (a) Match a graph to each of the parametric curves given, for the same t values, by

  (i) $(-x(t), -y(t))$ (ii) $(-x(t), y(t))$
  (iii) $(x(t) + 1, y(t))$ (iv) $(x(t) + 1, y(t) + 1)$

  (b) Which of the following could be the formulas for the functions $x(t), y(t)$?

  (i) $x = 10\cos t \quad y = 10\sin t$
  (ii) $x = (10 + 8t)\cos t \quad y = (10 + 8t)\sin t$
  (iii) $x = e^{t^2/200}\cos t \quad y = e^{t^2/200}\sin t$
  (iv) $x = (10 - 8t)\cos t \quad y = (10 - 8t)\sin t$
  (v) $x = 10\cos(t^2 + t) \quad y = 10\sin(t^2 + t)$

Strengthen Your Understanding

In Problems 83–84, explain what is wrong with the statement.

83. The curve parameterized by $\vec{r}_1(t) = \vec{r}(t - 2)$, defined for all t, is a shift in the $\vec{i}$-direction of the curve parameterized by $\vec{r}(t)$.

84. All points of the curve $\vec{r}(t) = R\cos t\vec{i} + R\sin t\vec{j} + t\vec{k}$ are the same distance, R, from the origin.

In Problems 85–87, give an example of:

85. Parameterizations of two different circles that have the same center and equal radii.

86. Parameterizations of two different lines that intersect at the point $(1, 2, 3)$.

87. A parameterization of the line $x = t, y = 2t, z = 3 + 4t$ that is not given by linear functions.

Are the statements in Problems 88–99 true or false? Give reasons for your answer.

88. The parametric curve $x = 3t + 2, y = -2t$ for $0 \leq t \leq 5$ passes through the origin.

89. The parametric curve $x = t^2, y = t^4$ for $0 \leq t \leq 1$ is a parabola.

90. A parametric curve $x = g(t), y = h(t)$ for $a \leq t \leq b$ is always the graph of a function $y = f(x)$.

91. The parametric curve $x = (3t + 2)^2, y = (3t + 2)^2 - 1$ for $0 \leq t \leq 3$ is a line.

92. The parametric curve $x = -\sin t$, $y = -\cos t$ for $0 \le t \le 2\pi$ traces out a unit circle counterclockwise as t increases.

93. A parameterization of the graph of $y = \ln x$ for $x > 0$ is given by $x = e^t$, $y = t$ for $-\infty < t < \infty$.

94. Both $x = -t + 1$, $y = 2t$ and $x = 2s$, $y = -4s + 2$ describe the same line.

95. The line of intersection of the two planes $z = x + y$ and $z = 1 - x - y$ can be parameterized by $x = t$, $y = \frac{1}{2} - t$, $z = \frac{1}{2}$.

96. The two lines given by $x = t$, $y = 2 + t$, $z = 3 + t$ and $x = 2s$, $y = 1 - s$, $z = s$ do not intersect.

97. The line parameterized by $x = 1$, $y = 2t$, $z = 3 + t$ is parallel to the x-axis.

98. The equation $\vec{r}(t) = 3t\vec{i} + (6t + 1)\vec{j}$ parameterizes a line.

99. The lines parameterized by $\vec{r}_1(t) = t\vec{i} + (-2t + 1)\vec{j}$ and $\vec{r}_2(t) = (2t + 5)\vec{i} + (-t)\vec{j}$ are parallel.

17.2 MOTION, VELOCITY, AND ACCELERATION

In this section we see how to find the vector quantities of velocity and acceleration from a parametric equation for the motion of an object.

The Velocity Vector

The velocity of a moving particle can be represented by a vector with the following properties:

The **velocity vector** of a moving object is a vector $\vec{v}$ such that:
- The magnitude of $\vec{v}$ is the speed of the object.
- The direction of $\vec{v}$ is the direction of motion.

Thus, the speed of the object is $\|\vec{v}\|$ and the velocity vector is tangent to the object's path.

Example 1   A child is sitting on a Ferris wheel of diameter 10 meters, making one revolution every 2 minutes. Find the speed of the child and draw velocity vectors at two different times.

Solution   The child moves at a constant speed around a circle of radius 5 meters, completing one revolution every 2 minutes. One revolution around a circle of radius 5 is a distance of 10π, so the child's speed is $10\pi/2 = 5\pi \approx 15.7$ m/min. Hence, the magnitude of the velocity vector is 15.7 m/min. The direction of motion is tangent to the circle, and hence perpendicular to the radius at that point. Figure 17.11 shows the direction of the vector at two different times.

Velocity
15.7 m/min

5 m

5 m

Velocity
15.7 m/min

Figure 17.11: Velocity vectors of a child on a Ferris wheel (Note that vectors would be in opposite direction if viewed from the other side)

Computing the Velocity

We find the velocity, as in one-variable calculus, by taking a limit. If the position vector of the particle is $\vec{r}(t)$ at time t, then the displacement vector between its positions at times t and $t + \Delta t$ is $\Delta \vec{r} = \vec{r}(t + \Delta t) - \vec{r}(t)$. (See Figure 17.12.) Over this interval,

$$\text{Average velocity} = \frac{\Delta \vec{r}}{\Delta t}.$$

In the limit as Δt goes to zero we have the instantaneous velocity at time t:

> The **velocity vector**, $\vec{v}(t)$, of a moving object with position vector $\vec{r}(t)$ at time t is
>
> $$\vec{v}(t) = \lim_{\Delta t \to 0} \frac{\Delta \vec{r}}{\Delta t} = \lim_{\Delta t \to 0} \frac{\vec{r}(t + \Delta t) - \vec{r}(t)}{\Delta t},$$
>
> whenever the limit exists. We use the notation $\vec{v} = \dfrac{d\vec{r}}{dt} = \vec{r}'(t)$.

Notice that the direction of the velocity vector $\vec{r}'(t)$ in Figure 17.12 is approximated by the direction of the vector $\Delta \vec{r}$ and that the approximation gets better as $\Delta t \to 0$.

Figure 17.12: The change, $\Delta \vec{r}$, in the position vector for a particle moving on a curve and the velocity vector $\vec{v} = \vec{r}'(t)$

The Components of the Velocity Vector

If we represent a curve parametrically by $x = f(t), y = g(t), z = h(t)$, then we can write its position vector as: $\vec{r}(t) = f(t)\vec{i} + g(t)\vec{j} + h(t)\vec{k}$. Now we can compute the velocity vector:

$$
\begin{aligned}
\vec{v}(t) &= \lim_{\Delta t \to 0} \frac{\vec{r}(t + \Delta t) - \vec{r}(t)}{\Delta t} \\
&= \lim_{\Delta t \to 0} \frac{(f(t + \Delta t)\vec{i} + g(t + \Delta t)\vec{j} + h(t + \Delta t)\vec{k}) - (f(t)\vec{i} + g(t)\vec{j} + h(t)\vec{k})}{\Delta t} \\
&= \lim_{\Delta t \to 0} \left(\frac{f(t + \Delta t) - f(t)}{\Delta t}\vec{i} + \frac{g(t + \Delta t) - g(t)}{\Delta t}\vec{j} + \frac{h(t + \Delta t) - h(t)}{\Delta t}\vec{k} \right) \\
&= f'(t)\vec{i} + g'(t)\vec{j} + h'(t)\vec{k} \\
&= \frac{dx}{dt}\vec{i} + \frac{dy}{dt}\vec{j} + \frac{dz}{dt}\vec{k}.
\end{aligned}
$$

Thus, we have the following result:

> The **components of the velocity vector** of a particle moving in space with position vector $\vec{r}(t) = f(t)\vec{i} + g(t)\vec{j} + h(t)\vec{k}$ at time t are given by
>
> $$\vec{v}(t) = f'(t)\vec{i} + g'(t)\vec{j} + h'(t)\vec{k} = \frac{dx}{dt}\vec{i} + \frac{dy}{dt}\vec{j} + \frac{dz}{dt}\vec{k}.$$

Example 2   Find the components of the velocity vector for the child on the Ferris wheel in Example 1 using a coordinate system which has its origin at the center of the Ferris wheel and which makes the rotation counterclockwise.

Solution   The Ferris wheel has radius 5 meters and completes 1 revolution counterclockwise every 2 minutes. The motion is parameterized by an equation of the form

$$\vec{r}(t) = 5\cos(\omega t)\vec{i} + 5\sin(\omega t)\vec{j},$$

where ω is chosen to make the period 2 minutes. Since the period of $\cos(\omega t)$ and $\sin(\omega t)$ is $2\pi/\omega$, we must have

$$\frac{2\pi}{\omega} = 2, \quad \text{so} \quad \omega = \pi.$$

Thus, the motion is described by the equation

$$\vec{r}(t) = 5\cos(\pi t)\vec{i} + 5\sin(\pi t)\vec{j},$$

where t is in minutes. The velocity is given by

$$\vec{v} = \frac{dx}{dt}\vec{i} + \frac{dy}{dt}\vec{j} = -5\pi\sin(\pi t)\vec{i} + 5\pi\cos(\pi t)\vec{j}.$$

To check, we calculate the magnitude of $\vec{v}$,

$$\|\vec{v}\| = \sqrt{(-5\pi)^2\sin^2(\pi t) + (5\pi)^2\cos^2(\pi t)} = 5\pi\sqrt{\sin^2(\pi t) + \cos^2(\pi t)} = 5\pi \approx 15.7,$$

which agrees with the speed we calculated in Example 1. To see that the direction is correct, we must show that the vector $\vec{v}$ at any time t is perpendicular to the position vector of the particle at time t. To do this, we compute the dot product of $\vec{v}$ and $\vec{r}$:

$$\vec{v} \cdot \vec{r} = (-5\pi\sin(\pi t)\vec{i} + 5\pi\cos(\pi t)\vec{j}) \cdot (5\cos(\pi t)\vec{i} + 5\sin(\pi t)\vec{j})$$
$$= -25\pi\,\sin(\pi t)\,\cos(\pi t) + 25\pi\cos(\pi t)\,\sin(\pi t) = 0.$$

So the velocity vector, $\vec{v}$, is perpendicular to $\vec{r}$ and hence tangent to the circle. (See Figure 17.13.)

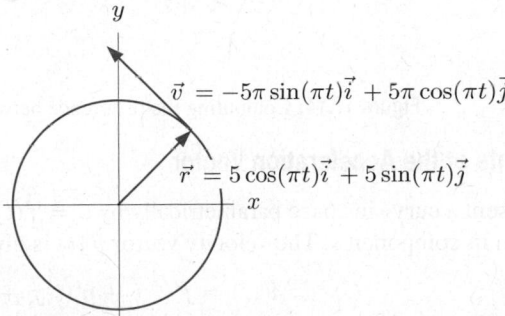

Figure 17.13: Velocity and radius vector of motion around a circle

Velocity Vectors and Tangent Lines

Since the velocity vector is tangent to the path of motion, it can be used to find parametric equations for the tangent line, if there is one.

Example 3　Find the tangent line at the point $(1, 1, 2)$ to the curve defined by the parametric equation

$$\vec{r}(t) = t^2\vec{i} + t^3\vec{j} + 2t\vec{k}.$$

Solution　At time $t = 1$ the particle is at the point $(1, 1, 2)$ with position vector $\vec{r}_0 = \vec{i} + \vec{j} + 2\vec{k}$. The velocity vector at time t is $\vec{r}'(t) = 2t\vec{i} + 3t^2\vec{j} + 2\vec{k}$, so at time $t = 1$ the velocity is $\vec{v} = \vec{r}'(1) = 2\vec{i} + 3\vec{j} + 2\vec{k}$. The tangent line passes through $(1, 1, 2)$ in the direction of $\vec{v}$, so it has the parametric equation

$$\vec{r}(t) = \vec{r}_0 + t\vec{v} = (\vec{i} + \vec{j} + 2\vec{k}) + t(2\vec{i} + 3\vec{j} + 2\vec{k}).$$

The Acceleration Vector

Just as the velocity of a particle moving in 2-space or 3-space is a vector quantity, so is the rate of change of the velocity of the particle, namely its acceleration. Figure 17.14 shows a particle at time t with velocity vector $\vec{v}(t)$ and then a little later at time $t + \Delta t$. The vector $\Delta \vec{v} = \vec{v}(t + \Delta t) - \vec{v}(t)$ is the change in velocity and points approximately in the direction of the acceleration. So,

$$\text{Average acceleration} = \frac{\Delta \vec{v}}{\Delta t}.$$

In the limit as $\Delta t \to 0$, we have the instantaneous acceleration at time t:

> The **acceleration vector** of an object moving with velocity $\vec{v}(t)$ at time t is
>
> $$\vec{a}(t) = \lim_{\Delta t \to 0} \frac{\Delta \vec{v}}{\Delta t} = \lim_{\Delta t \to 0} \frac{\vec{v}(t + \Delta t) - \vec{v}(t)}{\Delta t},$$
>
> if the limit exists. We use the notation $\vec{a} = \dfrac{d\vec{v}}{dt} = \dfrac{d^2 \vec{r}}{dt^2} = \vec{r}\,''(t)$.

Figure 17.14: Computing the difference between two velocity vectors

Components of the Acceleration Vector

If we represent a curve in space parametrically by $x = f(t)$, $y = g(t)$, $z = h(t)$, we can express the acceleration in components. The velocity vector $\vec{v}(t)$ is given by

$$\vec{v}(t) = f'(t)\vec{i} + g'(t)\vec{j} + h'(t)\vec{k}.$$

From the definition of the acceleration vector, we have

$$\vec{a}(t) = \lim_{\Delta t \to 0} \frac{\vec{v}(t + \Delta t) - \vec{v}(t)}{\Delta t} = \frac{d\vec{v}}{dt}.$$

Using the same method to compute $d\vec{v}/dt$ as we used to compute $d\vec{r}/dt$ on page 928, we obtain

> The **components of the acceleration vector**, $\vec{a}(t)$, at time t of a particle moving in space with position vector $\vec{r}(t) = f(t)\vec{i} + g(t)\vec{j} + h(t)\vec{k}$ at time t are given by
>
> $$\vec{a}(t) = f''(t)\vec{i} + g''(t)\vec{j} + h''(t)\vec{k} = \frac{d^2 x}{dt^2}\vec{i} + \frac{d^2 y}{dt^2}\vec{j} + \frac{d^2 z}{dt^2}\vec{k}.$$

Motion in a Circle and Along a Line

We now consider the velocity and acceleration vectors for two basic motions: uniform motion around a circle, and motion along a straight line.

Example 4   Find the acceleration vector for the child on the Ferris wheel in Examples 1 and 2.

Solution   The child's position vector is given by $\vec{r}(t) = 5\cos(\pi t)\vec{i} + 5\sin(\pi t)\vec{j}$. In Example 2 we saw that the velocity vector is

$$\vec{v}(t) = \frac{dx}{dt}\vec{i} + \frac{dy}{dt}\vec{j} = -5\pi\sin(\pi t)\vec{i} + 5\pi\cos(\pi t)\vec{j}.$$

Thus, the acceleration vector is

$$\vec{a}(t) = \frac{d^2x}{dt^2}\vec{i} + \frac{d^2y}{dt^2}\vec{j} = -(5\pi) \cdot \pi \cos(\pi t)\vec{i} - (5\pi) \cdot \pi \sin(\pi t)\vec{j}$$
$$= -5\pi^2 \cos(\pi t)\vec{i} - 5\pi^2 \sin(\pi t)\vec{j}.$$

Notice that $\vec{a}(t) = -\pi^2 \vec{r}(t)$. Thus, the acceleration vector is a multiple of $\vec{r}(t)$ and points toward the origin.

The motion of the child on the Ferris wheel is an example of uniform circular motion, whose properties follow. (See Problem 44.)

Uniform Circular Motion: For a particle whose motion is described by

$$\vec{r}(t) = R\cos(\omega t)\vec{i} + R\sin(\omega t)\vec{j}$$

- Motion is in a circle of radius R with period $2\pi/|\omega|$.
- Velocity, $\vec{v}$, is tangent to the circle and speed is constant $\|\vec{v}\| = |\omega|R$.
- Acceleration, $\vec{a}$, points toward the center of the circle with $\|\vec{a}\| = \|\vec{v}\|^2/R$.

In uniform circular motion, the acceleration vector is perpendicular to the velocity vector, $\vec{v}$, because $\vec{v}$ does not change in magnitude, only in direction. There is no acceleration in the direction of $\vec{v}$.

We now look at straight-line motion in which the velocity vector always has the same direction but its magnitude changes. In straight-line motion, the acceleration vector points in the same direction as the velocity vector if the speed is increasing and in the opposite direction to the velocity vector if the speed is decreasing.

Example 5   Consider the motion given by the vector equation

$$\vec{r}(t) = 2\vec{i} + 6\vec{j} + (t^3 + t)(4\vec{i} + 3\vec{j} + \vec{k}).$$

Show that this is straight-line motion in the direction of the vector $4\vec{i} + 3\vec{j} + \vec{k}$ and relate the acceleration vector to the velocity vector.

Solution   The velocity vector is
$$\vec{v} = (3t^2 + 1)(4\vec{i} + 3\vec{j} + \vec{k}).$$

Since $(3t^2 + 1)$ is a positive scalar, the velocity vector $\vec{v}$ always points in the direction of the vector $4\vec{i} + 3\vec{j} + \vec{k}$. In addition,

$$\text{Speed} = \|\vec{v}\| = (3t^2 + 1)\sqrt{4^2 + 3^2 + 1^2} = \sqrt{26}(3t^2 + 1).$$

Notice that the speed is decreasing until $t = 0$, then starts increasing. The acceleration vector is

$$\vec{a} = 6t(4\vec{i} + 3\vec{j} + \vec{k}).$$

For $t > 0$, the acceleration vector points in the same direction as $4\vec{i} + 3\vec{j} + \vec{k}$, which is the same direction as $\vec{v}$. This makes sense because the object is speeding up. For $t < 0$, the acceleration vector $6t(4\vec{i} + 3\vec{j} + \vec{k})$ points in the opposite direction to $\vec{v}$ because the object is slowing down.

Motion in a Straight Line: For a particle whose motion is described by

$$\vec{r}(t) = \vec{r}_0 + f(t)\vec{v}$$

- Motion is along a straight line through the point with position vector $\vec{r}_0$ parallel to $\vec{v}$.
- Velocity, $\vec{v}$, and acceleration, $\vec{a}$, are parallel to the line.

If $f(t) = t$, then we have $\vec{r}(t) = \vec{r}_0 + t\vec{v}$, the equation of a line obtained on page 921.

The Length of a Curve

The speed of a particle is the magnitude of its velocity vector:

$$\text{Speed} = \|\vec{v}\| = \sqrt{\left(\frac{dx}{dt}\right)^2 + \left(\frac{dy}{dt}\right)^2 + \left(\frac{dz}{dt}\right)^2}.$$

As in one dimension, we can find the distance traveled by a particle along a curve by integrating its speed. Thus,

$$\text{Distance traveled} = \int_a^b \|\vec{v}(t)\|\, dt.$$

If the particle never stops or reverses its direction as it moves along the curve, the distance it travels will be the same as the length of the curve. This suggests the following formula, which is justified in Problem 53:

If the curve C is given parametrically for $a \leq t \leq b$ by smooth functions and if the velocity vector $\vec{v}$ is not $\vec{0}$ for $a < t < b$, then

$$\text{Length of } C = \int_a^b \|\vec{v}\|\, dt.$$

Example 6   Find the circumference of the ellipse given by the parametric equations

$$x = 2\cos t, \quad y = \sin t, \quad 0 \leq t \leq 2\pi.$$

Solution   The circumference of this curve is given by an integral which must be calculated numerically:

$$\text{Circumference} = \int_0^{2\pi} \sqrt{\left(\frac{dx}{dt}\right)^2 + \left(\frac{dy}{dt}\right)^2}\, dt = \int_0^{2\pi} \sqrt{(-2\sin t)^2 + (\cos t)^2}\, dt$$

$$= \int_0^{2\pi} \sqrt{4\sin^2 t + \cos^2 t}\, dt = 9.69.$$

Since the ellipse is inscribed in a circle of radius 2 and circumscribes a circle of radius 1, we would expect the length of the ellipse to be between $2\pi(2) \approx 12.57$ and $2\pi(1) \approx 6.28$, so the value of 9.69 is reasonable.

Exercises and Problems for Section 17.2

Exercises

In Exercises 1–6, find the velocity and acceleration vectors.

1. $x = 2 + 3t, y = 4 + t, z = 1 - t$

2. $x = 2 + 3t^2, y = 4 + t^2, z = 1 - t^2$

3. $x = t, y = t^2, z = t^3$

4. $x = t, y = t^3 - t$

5. $x = 3\cos t, y = 4\sin t$

6. $x = 3\cos(t^2), y = 3\sin(t^2), z = t^2$

In Exercises 7–12, find the velocity $\vec{v}(t)$ and speed $\|\vec{v}(t)\|$. Find any times at which the particle stops.

7. $x = t, y = t^2, z = t^3$

8. $x = \cos 3t, y = \sin 5t$

9. $x = 3t^2, y = t^3 + 1$

10. $x = (t - 1)^2, y = 2, z = 2t^3 - 3t^2$

11. $x = 3\sin(t^2) - 1, y = 3\cos(t^2)$

12. $x = 3\sin^2 t, y = \cos t - 1, \quad z = t^2$

In Exercises 13–16, find the length of the curve.

13. $x = 3 + 5t, y = 1 + 4t, z = 3 - t$ for $1 \le t \le 2$. Check by calculating the length by another method.

14. $x = \cos 3t, y = \sin 5t$ for $0 \le t \le 2\pi$.

15. $x = \cos(e^t), y = \sin(e^t)$ for $0 \le t \le 1$. Check by calculating the length by another method.

16. $\vec{r}(t) = 2t\vec{i} + \ln t\vec{j} + t^2\vec{k}$ for $1 \le t \le 2$.

In Exercises 17–18, find the velocity and acceleration vectors of the uniform circular motion and check that they are perpendicular. Check that the speed and magnitude of the acceleration are constant.

17. $x = 3\cos(2\pi t), y = 3\sin(2\pi t), z = 0$

18. $x = 2\pi, y = 2\sin(3t), z = 2\cos(3t)$

In Exercises 19–20, find the velocity and acceleration vectors of the straight-line motion. Check that the acceleration vector points in the same direction as the velocity vector if the speed is increasing and in the opposite direction if the speed is decreasing.

19. $x = 2 + t^2, y = 3 - 2t^2, z = 5 - t^2$

20. $x = -2t^3 - 3t + 1, y = 4t^3 + 6t - 5, z = 6t^3 + 9t - 2$

21. Find parametric equations for the tangent line at $t = 2$ for Exercise 10.

Problems

22. A particle passes through the point $P = (5, 4, -2)$ at time $t = 4$, moving with constant velocity $\vec{v} = 2\vec{i} - 3\vec{j} + \vec{k}$. Find a parametric equation for its motion.

In Problems 23–24, find all values of t for which the particle is moving parallel to the x-axis and to the y-axis. Determine the end behavior and graph the particle's path.

23. $x = t^2 - 6t, \quad y = t^3 - 3t$

24. $x = t^3 - 12t, \quad y = t^2 + 10t$

25. The table gives x and y coordinates of a particle in the plane at time t. Assuming that the particle moves smoothly and that the points given show all the major features of the motion, estimate the following quantities:

(a) The velocity vector and speed at time $t = 2$.
(b) Any times when the particle is moving parallel to the y-axis.
(c) Any times when the particle has come to a stop.

t	0	0.5	1.0	1.5	2.0	2.5	3.0	3.5	4.0
x	1	4	6	7	6	3	2	3	5
y	3	2	3	5	8	10	11	10	9

26. A particle starts at the point $P = (3, 2, -5)$ and moves along a straight line toward $Q = (5, 7, -2)$ at a speed of 5 cm/sec. Let x, y, z be measured in centimeters.

(a) Find the particle's velocity vector.
(b) Find parametric equations for the particle's motion.

27. A particle moves at a constant speed along a line from the point $P = (2, -1, 5)$ at time $t = 0$ to the point $Q = (5, 3, -1)$. Find parametric equations for the particle's motion if:

(a) The particle takes 5 seconds to move from P to Q.
(b) The speed of the particle is 5 units per second.

28. A particle travels along the line $x = 1 + t, y = 5 + 2t, z = -7 + t$, where t is in seconds and x, y, z are in meters.

(a) When and where does the particle hit the plane $x + y + z = 1$?
(b) How fast is the particle going when it hits the plane? Give units.

29. A stone is thrown from a rooftop at time $t = 0$ seconds. Its position at time t is given by

$$\vec{r}(t) = 10t\vec{i} - 5t\vec{j} + (6.4 - 4.9t^2)\vec{k}.$$

The origin is at the base of the building, which is standing on flat ground. Distance is measured in meters. The vector $\vec{i}$ points east, $\vec{j}$ points north, and $\vec{k}$ points up.

(a) How high is the rooftop above the ground?
(b) At what time does the stone hit the ground?
(c) How fast is the stone moving when it hits the ground?
(d) Where does the stone hit the ground?
(e) What is the stone's acceleration when it hits the ground?

30. A child wanders slowly down a circular staircase from the top of a tower. With x, y, z in feet and the origin at the base of the tower, her position t minutes from the start is given by

$$x = 10\cos t, \quad y = 10\sin t, \quad z = 90 - 5t.$$

(a) How tall is the tower?
(b) When does the child reach the bottom?
(c) What is her speed at time t?
(d) What is her acceleration at time t?

31. The origin is on flat ground and the z-axis points upward. For time $0 \le t \le 10$ in seconds and distance in centimeters, a particle moves along a path given by

$$\vec{r} = 2t\vec{i} + 3t\vec{j} + (100 - (t-5)^2)\vec{k}.$$

(a) When is the particle at the highest point? What is that point?
(b) When in the interval $0 \le t \le 10$ is the particle moving fastest? What is its speed at that moment?
(c) When in the interval $0 \le t \le 10$ is the particle moving slowest? What is its speed at that moment?

32. The function $w = f(x, y, z)$ has grad $f(7, 2, 5) = 4\vec{i} - 3\vec{j} + \vec{k}$. A particle moves along the curve $\vec{r}(t)$ arriving at the point $(7, 2, 5)$ with velocity $2\vec{i} + 3\vec{j} + 6\vec{k}$ when $t = 0$. Find the rate of change of w with respect to time at $t = 0$.

33. Suppose x measures horizontal distance in meters, and y measures distance above the ground in meters. At time $t = 0$ in seconds, a projectile starts from a point h meters above the origin with speed v meters/sec at an angle θ to the horizontal. Its path is given by

$$x = (v\cos\theta)t, \quad y = h + (v\sin\theta)t - \frac{1}{2}gt^2.$$

Using this information about a general projectile, analyze the motion of a ball which travels along the path

$$x = 20t, \quad y = 2 + 25t - 4.9t^2.$$

(a) When does the ball hit the ground?
(b) Where does the ball hit the ground?
(c) At what height above the ground does the ball start?
(d) What is the value of g, the acceleration due to gravity?
(e) What are the values of v and θ?

34. A particle is moving on a path in the xz-plane given by $x = 20t$, $z = 5t - 0.5t^2$, where z is the height of the particle above the ground in meters, x is the horizontal distance in meters, and t is time in seconds.

(a) What is the equation of the path in terms of x and z only?
(b) When is the particle at ground level?
(c) What is the velocity of the particle at time t?
(d) What is the speed of the particle at time t?
(e) Is the speed ever 0?
(f) When is the particle at the highest point?

35. The base of a 20-meter tower is at the origin; the base of a 20-meter tree is at $(0, 20, 0)$. The ground is flat and the z-axis points upward. The following parametric equations describe the motion of six projectiles each launched at time $t = 0$ in seconds.

(I) $\vec{r}(t) = (20 + t^2)\vec{k}$
(II) $\vec{r}(t) = 2t^2\vec{j} + 2t^2\vec{k}$
(III) $\vec{r}(t) = 20\vec{i} + 20\vec{j} + (20 - t^2)\vec{k}$
(IV) $\vec{r}(t) = 2t\vec{j} + (20 - t^2)\vec{k}$
(V) $\vec{r}(t) = (20 - 2t)\vec{i} + 2t\vec{j} + (20 - t)\vec{k}$
(VI) $\vec{r}(t) = t\vec{i} + t\vec{j} + t\vec{k}$

(a) Which projectile is launched from the top of the tower and goes downward? When and where does it hit the ground?
(b) Which projectile hits the top of the tree? When? From where is it launched?
(c) Which projectile is not launched from somewhere on the tower and hits the tree? Where and when does it hit the tree?

36. A particle moves on a circle of radius 5 cm, centered at the origin, in the xy-plane (x and y measured in centimeters). It starts at the point $(0, 5)$ and moves counterclockwise, going once around the circle in 8 seconds.

(a) Write a parameterization for the particle's motion.
(b) What is the particle's speed? Give units.

37. Determine the position vector $\vec{r}(t)$ for a rocket which is launched from the origin at time $t = 0$ seconds, reaches its highest point of $(x, y, z) = (1000, 3000, 10,000)$, where x, y, z are in meters, and after the launch is subject only to the acceleration due to gravity, 9.8 m/sec^2.

38. Emily is standing on the outer edge of a merry-go-round, 10 meters from the center. The merry-go-round completes one full revolution every 20 seconds. As Emily passes over a point P on the ground, she drops a ball from 3 meters above the ground.

(a) How fast is Emily going?
(b) How far from P does the ball hit the ground? (The acceleration due to gravity is 9.8 m/sec^2.)
(c) How far from Emily does the ball hit the ground?

39. A point P moves in a circle of radius a. Show that $\vec{r}(t)$, the position vector of P, and its velocity vector $\vec{r}\,'(t)$ are perpendicular.

40. A wheel of radius 1 meter rests on the x-axis with its center on the y-axis. There is a spot on the rim at the point $(1, 1)$. See Figure 17.15. At time $t = 0$ the wheel starts rolling on the x-axis in the direction shown at a rate of 1 radian per second.

   (a) Find parametric equations describing the motion of the center of the wheel.

   (b) Find parametric equations describing the motion of the spot on the rim. Plot its path.

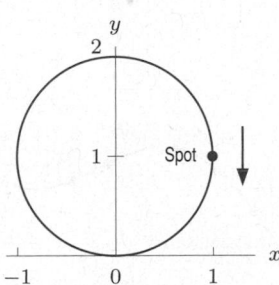

Figure 17.15

41. Suppose $\vec{r}(t) = \cos t\, \vec{i} + \sin t\, \vec{j} + 2t\, \vec{k}$ represents the position of a particle on a helix, where z is the height of the particle above the ground.

   (a) Is the particle ever moving downward? When?

   (b) When does the particle reach a point 10 units above the ground?

   (c) What is the velocity of the particle when it is 10 units above the ground?

   (d) When it is 10 units above the ground, the particle leaves the helix and moves along the tangent. Find parametric equations for this tangent line.

42. Show that the helix $\vec{r} = \alpha \cos t\, \vec{i} + \alpha \sin t\, \vec{j} + \beta t\, \vec{k}$ is parameterized with constant speed.

43. An ant crawls along the radius from the center to the edge of a circular disk of radius 1 meter, moving at a constant rate of 1 cm/sec. Meanwhile, the disk is turning counterclockwise about its center at 1 revolution per second.

   (a) Parameterize the motion of the ant.

   (b) Find the velocity and speed of the ant.

   (c) Determine the acceleration and magnitude of the acceleration of the ant.

44. The motion of a particle is given by $\vec{r}(t) = R\cos(\omega t)\vec{i} + R\sin(\omega t)\vec{j}$, with $R > 0$, $\omega > 0$.

   (a) Show that the particle moves on a circle and find the radius, direction, and period.

   (b) Determine the velocity vector of the particle and its direction and speed.

   (c) What are the direction and magnitude of the acceleration vector of the particle?

45. You bicycle along a straight flat road with a safety light attached to one foot. Your bike moves at a speed of 25 km/hr and your foot moves in a circle of radius 20 cm centered 30 cm above the ground, making one revolution per second.

   (a) Find parametric equations for x and y which describe the path traced out by the light, where y is distance (in cm) above the ground.

   (b) Sketch the light's path.

   (c) How fast (in revolutions/sec) would your foot have to be rotating if an observer standing at the side of the road sees the light moving backward?

46. How do the motions of objects A and B differ, if A has position vector $\vec{r}_A(t)$ and B has position vector $\vec{r}_B(t) = \vec{r}_A(2t)$ for $t \geq 0$. Illustrate your answer with $\vec{r}_A(t) = t\vec{i} + t^2\vec{j}$.

47. At time $t = 0$ an object is moving with velocity vector $\vec{v} = 2\vec{i} + \vec{j}$ and acceleration vector $\vec{a} = \vec{i} + \vec{j}$. Can it be in uniform circular motion about some point in the plane?

48. Figure 17.16 shows the velocity and acceleration vectors of an object in uniform circular motion about a point in the plane at a particular moment. Is it moving round the circle in the clockwise or counterclockwise direction?

Figure 17.16

49. The position of a particle at time t is given by $\vec{r}(t)$. Let $r = \|\vec{r}\|$ and $\vec{a}$ be a constant vector. Differentiate:

   (a) $\vec{r} \cdot \vec{r}$ **(b)** $\vec{a} \times \vec{r}$ **(c)** $r^3 \vec{r}$

50. The function $f(x, y, z)$ is defined and smooth at every point in 3-space and $\operatorname{grad} f(1, 7, 2) = \vec{i} - (\sqrt{6})\vec{j} + \vec{k}$. The curve C is $\vec{r} = (t+1)^2\vec{i} + 7\cos t\vec{j} + 2e^t\vec{k}$.

   (a) Find an equation of the tangent plane to the level surface of f at the point $(1, 7, 2)$.

   (b) Find the angle between the normal to the level surface of f and the tangent to the curve C at $(1, 7, 2)$. (Note: There are two possible angles; give the smaller one. Your answer should be in radians.)

   (c) With x, y, z in centimeters, let f be the concentration of a pollutant in parts per million (ppm) at the point (x, y, z). A particle moves along the curve C with the given parameterization and t in seconds. Find how fast the concentration is changing at the time $t = 0$. Give units with your answer.

51. Let $\vec{v}(t)$ be the velocity of a particle moving in the plane. Let $s(t)$ be the magnitude of $\vec{v}$ and let $\theta(t)$ be the angle of $\vec{v}(t)$ with the positive x-axis at time t, so that $\vec{v} = s\cos\theta\,\vec{i} + s\sin\theta\,\vec{j}$.

Let $\vec{T}$ be the unit vector in the direction of $\vec{v}$, and let $\vec{N}$ be the unit vector in the direction of $\vec{k} \times \vec{v}$, perpendicular to $\vec{v}$. Show that the acceleration $\vec{a}(t)$ is given by

$$\vec{a} = \frac{ds}{dt}\vec{T} + s\frac{d\theta}{dt}\vec{N}.$$

This shows how to separate the acceleration into the sum of one component, $\dfrac{ds}{dt}\vec{T}$, due to changing speed and a perpendicular component, $s\dfrac{d\theta}{dt}\vec{N}$, due to changing direction of the motion.

52. A point particle P is acted on by a force, $\vec{F}$, which is directed toward a fixed point O; this is called a central force. Let $\vec{r}(t)$ be the position of the particle with respect to O and let $\vec{v}(t)$ be its velocity. Use Newton's second law $\vec{F} = m\vec{a}$, where m is mass and $\vec{a}$ is acceleration, to show that $\vec{r}(t) \times \vec{v}(t) = \vec{c}$, a constant vector. Explain why this tells us that the particle always moves in the same plane.

53. In this problem we justify the formula for the length of a curve given on page 932. Suppose the curve C is given by smooth parametric equations $x = x(t)$, $y = y(t)$, $z = z(t)$ for $a \le t \le b$. By dividing the parameter interval $a \le t \le b$ at points $t_1, \ldots, t_{n-1}$ into small segments of length $\Delta t = t_{i+1} - t_i$, we get a corresponding division of the curve C into small pieces. See Figure 17.17, where the points $P_i = (x(t_i), y(t_i), z(t_i))$ on the curve C correspond to parameter values $t = t_i$. Let C_i be the portion of the curve C between P_i and P_{i+1}.

(a) Use local linearity to show that

$$\text{Length of } C_i \approx \sqrt{x'(t_i)^2 + y'(t_i)^2 + z'(t_i)^2}\,\Delta t.$$

(b) Use part (a) and a Riemann sum to explain why

$$\text{Length of } C = \int_a^b \sqrt{x'(t)^2 + y'(t)^2 + z'(t)^2}\,dt.$$

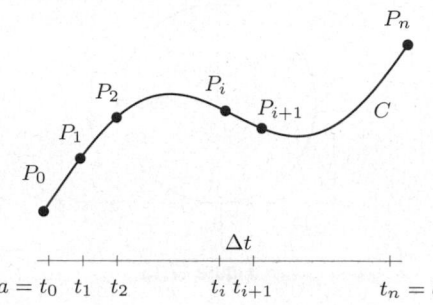

Figure 17.17: A subdivision of the parameter interval and the corresponding subdivision of the curve C

Strengthen Your Understanding

In Problems 54–56, explain what is wrong with the statement.

54. When a particle moves around a circle its velocity and acceleration are always orthogonal.

55. A particle with position $\vec{r}(t)$ at time t has acceleration equal to 3 m/sec^2 at time $t = 0$.

56. A parameterized curve $\vec{r}(t)$, $A \le t \le B$, has length $B - A$.

In Problems 57–58, give an example of:

57. A function $\vec{r}(t)$ such that the particle with position $\vec{r}(t)$ at time t has velocity $\vec{v} = \vec{i} + 2\vec{j}$ and acceleration $\vec{a} = 4\vec{i} + 6\vec{k}$ at $t = 0$.

58. An interval $a \le t \le b$ corresponding to a piece of the helix $\vec{r}(t) = \cos t\,\vec{i} + \sin t\,\vec{j} + t\,\vec{k}$ of length 10.

Are the statements in Problems 59–66 true or false? Give reasons for your answer.

59. A particle whose motion in the plane is given by $\vec{r}(t) = t^2\vec{i} + (1-t)\vec{j}$ has the same velocity at $t = 1$ and $t = -1$.

60. A particle whose motion in the plane is given by $\vec{r}(t) = t^2\vec{i} + (1-t)\vec{j}$ has the same speed at $t = 1$ and $t = -1$.

61. If a particle is moving along a parameterized curve $\vec{r}(t)$ then the acceleration vector at any point is always perpendicular to the velocity vector at that point.

62. If a particle is moving along a parameterized curve $\vec{r}(t)$ then the acceleration vector at a point cannot be parallel to the velocity vector at that point.

63. If $\vec{r}(t)$ for $a \le t \le b$ is a parameterized curve, then $\vec{r}(-t)$ for $a \le t \le b$ is the same curve traced backward.

64. If $\vec{r}(t)$ for $a \le t \le b$ is a parameterized curve C and the speed $\|\vec{v}(t)\| = 1$, then the length of C is $b - a$.

65. If a particle moves with motion $\vec{r}(t) = 3t\vec{i} + 2t\vec{j} + t\vec{k}$, then the particle stops at the origin.

66. If a particle moves with constant speed, the path of the particle must be a line.

For Problems 67–70, decide if the statement is true or false for all smooth parameterized curves $\vec{r}(t)$ and all values of t for which $\vec{r}'(t) \ne \vec{0}$.

67. The vector $\vec{r}'(t)$ is tangent to the curve at the point with position vector $\vec{r}(t)$.

68. $\vec{r}'(t) \times \vec{r}(t) = \vec{0}$

69. $\vec{r}'(t) \cdot \vec{r}(t) = 0$

70. $\vec{r}''(t) = -\omega^2 \vec{r}(t)$

17.3 VECTOR FIELDS

Introduction to Vector Fields

A *vector field* is a function that assigns a vector to each point in the plane or in 3-space. One example of a vector field is the gradient of a function $f(x, y)$; at each point (x, y) the vector grad $f(x, y)$ points in the direction of maximum rate of increase of f. In this section we look at other vector fields representing velocities and forces.

Velocity Vector Fields

Figure 17.18 shows the flow of a part of the Gulf Stream, a current in the Atlantic Ocean.[2] It is an example of a *velocity vector field*: each vector shows the velocity of the current at that point. The current is fastest where the velocity vectors are longest in the middle of the stream. Beside the stream are eddies where the water flows round and round in circles.

Force Fields

Another physical quantity represented by a vector is force. When we experience a force, sometimes it results from direct contact with the object that supplies the force (for example, a push). Many forces, however, can be felt at all points in space. For example, the earth exerts a gravitational pull on all other masses. Such forces can be represented by vector fields.

Figure 17.19 shows the gravitational force exerted by the earth on a mass of one kilogram at different points in space. This is a sketch of the vector field in 3-space. You can see that the vectors all point toward the earth (which is not shown in the diagram) and that the vectors farther from the earth are smaller in magnitude.

Figure 17.18: The velocity vector field of the Gulf Stream

[2]Based on data supplied by Avijit Gangopadhyay of the Jet Propulsion Laboratory.

Figure 17.19: The gravitational field of the earth

Definition of a Vector Field

Now that you have seen some examples of vector fields, we give a more formal definition.

A **vector field** in 2-space is a function $\vec{F}(x, y)$ whose value at a point (x, y) is a 2-dimensional vector. Similarly, a vector field in 3-space is a function $\vec{F}(x, y, z)$ whose values are 3-dimensional vectors.

Notice the arrow over the function, $\vec{F}$, indicating that its value is a vector, not a scalar. We often represent the point (x, y) or (x, y, z) by its position vector $\vec{r}$ and write the vector field as $\vec{F}(\vec{r})$.

Visualizing a Vector Field Given by a Formula

Since a vector field is a function that assigns a vector to each point, a vector field can often be given by a formula.

Example 1   Sketch the vector field in 2-space given by $\vec{F}(x, y) = -y\vec{i} + x\vec{j}$.

Solution   Table 17.1 shows the value of the vector field at a few points. Notice that each value is a vector. To plot the vector field, we plot $\vec{F}(x, y)$ with its tail at (x, y). (See Figure 17.20.)

Table 17.1   *Values of $\vec{F}(x, y) = -y\vec{i} + x\vec{j}$*

		y	
	-1	0	1
-1	$\vec{i} - \vec{j}$	$-\vec{j}$	$-\vec{i} - \vec{j}$
x 0	$\vec{i}$	$\vec{0}$	$-\vec{i}$
1	$\vec{i} + \vec{j}$	$\vec{j}$	$-\vec{i} + \vec{j}$

Now we look at the formula. The magnitude of the vector at (x, y) is the distance from (x, y) to the origin since

$$\|\vec{F}(x, y)\| = \| -y\vec{i} + x\vec{j} \| = \sqrt{x^2 + y^2}.$$

Therefore, all the vectors at a fixed distance from the origin (that is, on a circle centered at the origin) have the same magnitude. The magnitude gets larger as we move farther from the origin.

What about the direction? Figure 17.20 suggests that at each point (x, y) the vector $\vec{F}(x, y)$ is perpendicular to the position vector $\vec{r} = x\vec{i} + y\vec{j}$. We confirm this using the dot product:

$$\vec{r} \cdot \vec{F}(x, y) = (x\vec{i} + y\vec{j}) \cdot (-y\vec{i} + x\vec{j}) = 0.$$

Thus, the vectors are tangent to circles centered at the origin and get longer as we go out. In Figure 17.21, the vectors have been scaled so that they do not obscure each other.

Figure 17.20: The value $\vec{F}(x, y)$ is placed at the point (x, y)

Figure 17.21: The vector field $\vec{F}(x, y) = -y\vec{i} + x\vec{j}$, vectors scaled smaller to fit in diagram

---

Example 2 Sketch the vector fields in 2-space given by (a) $\vec{F}(x, y) = x\vec{j}$ (b) $\vec{G}(x, y) = x\vec{i}$.

Solution (a) The vector $x\vec{j}$ is parallel to the y-direction, pointing up when x is positive and down when x is negative. Also, the larger $|x|$ is, the longer the vector. The vectors in the field are constant along vertical lines since the vector field does not depend on y. (See Figure 17.22.)

Figure 17.22: The vector field $\vec{F}(x, y) = x\vec{j}$

Figure 17.23: The vector field $\vec{F}(x, y) = x\vec{i}$

(b) This is similar to the previous example, except that the vector $x\vec{i}$ is parallel to the x-direction, pointing to the right when x is positive and to the left when x is negative. Again, the larger $|x|$ is the longer the vector, and the vectors are constant along vertical lines, since the vector field does not depend on y. (See Figure 17.23.)

Example 3 Describe the vector field in 3-space given by $\vec{F}(\vec{r}) = \vec{r}$, where $\vec{r} = x\vec{i} + y\vec{j} + z\vec{k}$.

Solution The notation $\vec{F}(\vec{r}) = \vec{r}$ means that the value of $\vec{F}$ at the point (x, y, z) with position vector $\vec{r}$ is the vector $\vec{r}$ with its tail at (x, y, z). Thus, the vector field points outward. See Figure 17.24. Note that the lengths of the vectors have been scaled down so as to fit into the diagram.

Figure 17.24: The vector field $\vec{F}(\vec{r}) = \vec{r}$

Figure 17.25: Force exerted on mass m by mass M

Finding a Formula for a Vector Field

Example 4   Newton's Law of Gravitation states that the magnitude of the gravitational force exerted by an object of mass M on an object of mass m is proportional to M and m and inversely proportional to the square of the distance between them. The direction of the force is from m to M along the line connecting them. (See Figure 17.25.) Find a formula for the vector field $\vec{F}(\vec{r})$ that represents the gravitational force, assuming M is located at the origin and m is located at the point with position vector $\vec{r}$.

Solution   Since the mass m is located at $\vec{r}$, Newton's law says that the magnitude of the force is given by

$$\|\vec{F}(\vec{r})\| = \frac{GMm}{\|\vec{r}\|^2},$$

where G is the universal gravitational constant. A unit vector in the direction of the force is $-\vec{r}/\|\vec{r}\|$, where the negative sign indicates that the direction of force is toward the origin (gravity is attractive). By taking the product of the magnitude of the force and a unit vector in the direction of the force, we obtain an expression for the force vector field:

$$\vec{F}(\vec{r}) = \frac{GMm}{\|\vec{r}\|^2}\left(-\frac{\vec{r}}{\|\vec{r}\|}\right) = \frac{-GMm\vec{r}}{\|\vec{r}\|^3}.$$

We have already seen a picture of this vector field in Figure 17.19.

Gradient Vector Fields

The gradient of a scalar function f is a function that assigns a vector to each point, and is therefore a vector field. It is called the *gradient field* of f. Many vector fields in physics are gradient fields.

Example 5   Sketch the gradient field of the functions in Figures 17.26–17.28.

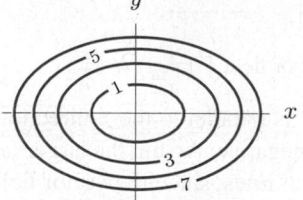

Figure 17.26: The contour map of $f(x, y) = x^2 + 2y^2$

Figure 17.27: The contour map of $g(x, y) = 5 - x^2 - 2y^2$

Figure 17.28: The contour map of $h(x, y) = x + 2y + 3$

Solution   See Figures 17.29–17.31. For a function $f(x, y)$, the gradient vector of f at a point is perpendicular to the contours in the direction of increasing f and its magnitude is the rate of change in that direction. The rate of change is large when the contours are close together and small when they are far apart. Notice that in Figure 17.29 the vectors all point outward, away from the local minimum of f, and in Figure 17.30 the vectors of grad g all point inward, toward the local maximum of g. Since h is a linear function, its gradient is constant, so grad h in Figure 17.31 is a constant vector field.

Figure 17.29: grad f

Figure 17.30: grad g

Figure 17.31: grad h

Exercises and Problems for Section 17.3

Exercises

For Exercises 1–6, find formulas for the vector fields. (There are many possible answers.)

1.

2.

3.

4.

5.

6.

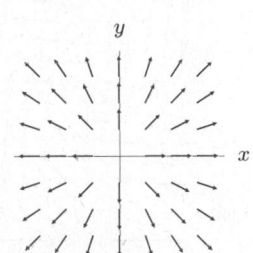

In Exercises 7–10, assume $x, y > 0$ and decide if

(a) The vector field is parallel to the x-axis, parallel to the y-axis, or neither.

(b) As x increases, the length increases, decreases, or neither.

(c) As y increases, the length increases, decreases, or neither.

Assume $x, y > 0$.

7. $\vec{F} = x\vec{j}$

8. $\vec{F} = y\vec{i} + \vec{j}$

9. $\vec{F} = (x + e^{1-y})\vec{i}$

10. $\mathrm{grad}(x^4 + e^{3y})$

Sketch the vector fields in Exercises 11–19 in the xy-plane.

11. $\vec{F}(x, y) = 2\vec{i} + 3\vec{j}$

12. $\vec{F}(x, y) = y\vec{i}$

13. $\vec{F}(x, y) = -y\vec{j}$

14. $\vec{F}(\vec{r}) = 2\vec{r}$

15. $\vec{F}(\vec{r}) = \vec{r}/\|\vec{r}\|$

16. $\vec{F}(\vec{r}) = -\vec{r}/\|\vec{r}\|^3$

17. $\vec{F} = y\vec{i} - x\vec{j}$

18. $\vec{F}(x, y) = 2x\vec{i} + x\vec{j}$

19. $\vec{F}(x, y) = (x + y)\vec{i} + (x - y)\vec{j}$

20. For each description of a vector field in (a)-(d), choose one or more of the vector fields I-IX.

(a) Pointing radially outward, increasing in length away from the origin.

(b) Pointing in a circular direction around the origin, remaining the same length.

(c) Pointing towards the origin, increasing in length farther from the origin.

(d) Pointing clockwise around the origin.

I. $\dfrac{x\vec{i} + y\vec{j}}{\sqrt{x^2 + y^2}}$ II. $\dfrac{-y\vec{i} + x\vec{j}}{\sqrt{x^2 + y^2}}$ III. $\vec{r}$

IV. $-\vec{r}$ V. $-y\vec{i} + x\vec{j}$ VI. $y\vec{i} - x\vec{j}$

VII. $y\vec{i} + x\vec{j}$ VIII. $\dfrac{\vec{r}}{\|\vec{r}\|^3}$ IX. $-\dfrac{\vec{r}}{\|\vec{r}\|^3}$

21. Each vector field in Figures (I)–(IV) represents the force on a particle at different points in space as a result of another particle at the origin. Match up the vector fields with the descriptions below.

(a) A repulsive force whose magnitude decreases as distance increases, such as between electric charges of the same sign.

(b) A repulsive force whose magnitude increases as distance increases.

(c) An attractive force whose magnitude decreases as distance increases, such as gravity.

(d) An attractive force whose magnitude increases as distance increases.

(I)

(II)

(III)

(IV)

Problems

In Problems 22–26, give an example of a vector field $\vec{F}(x, y)$ in 2-space with the stated properties.

22. $\vec{F}$ is constant

23. $\vec{F}$ has a constant direction but $\|\vec{F}\|$ is not constant

24. $\|\vec{F}\|$ is constant but $\vec{F}$ is not constant

25. Neither $\|\vec{F}\|$ nor the direction of $\vec{F}$ is constant

26. $\vec{F}$ is perpendicular to $\vec{G} = (x + y)\vec{i} + (1 + y^2)\vec{j}$ at every point

27. Match the level curves in (I)–(IV) with the gradient fields in (A)–(D). All figures use the same square window.

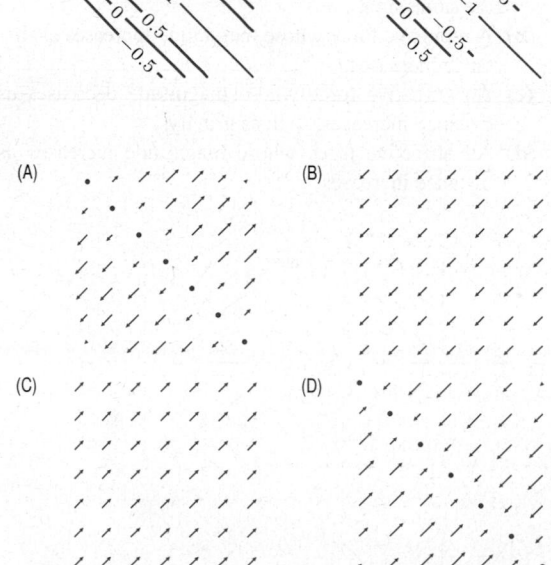

Problems 28–29 concern the vector fields $\vec{F} = x\vec{i} + y\vec{j}$, $\vec{G} = -y\vec{i} + x\vec{j}$, and $\vec{H} = x\vec{i} - y\vec{j}$.

28. Match $\vec{F}$, $\vec{G}$, $\vec{H}$ with their sketches in (I)–(III).

29. Match the vector fields with their sketches, (I)–(IV).

  (a) $\vec{F} + \vec{G}$ (b) $\vec{F} + \vec{H}$ (c) $\vec{G} + \vec{H}$ (d) $-\vec{F} + \vec{G}$

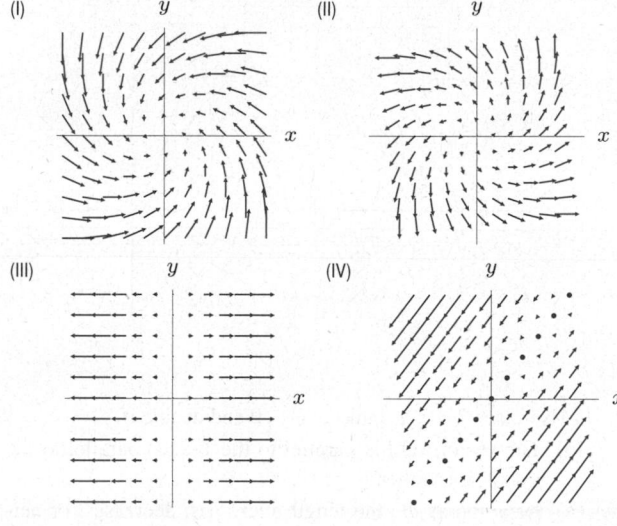

In Problems 30–32, write formulas for vector fields with the given properties.

30. All vectors are parallel to the x-axis; all vectors on a vertical line have the same magnitude.

31. All vectors point toward the origin and have constant length.

32. All vectors are of unit length and perpendicular to the position vector at that point.

33. (a) Let $\vec{F} = x\vec{i} + (x + y)\vec{j} + (x - y + z)\vec{k}$. Find a point at which $\vec{F}$ is parallel to l, the line $x = 5 + t$, $y = 6 - 2t$, $z = 7 - 3t$.

(b) Find a point at which $\vec{F}$ and l are perpendicular.

(c) Give an equation for and describe in words the set of all points at which $\vec{F}$ and l are perpendicular.

In Problems 34–35, let $\vec{F} = x\vec{i} + y\vec{j}$ and $\vec{G} = -y\vec{i} + x\vec{j}$.

34. Sketch the vector field $\vec{L} = a\vec{F} + \vec{G}$ if:

    (a) $a = 0$ **(b)** $a > 0$ **(c)** $a < 0$

35. Sketch the vector field $\vec{L} = \vec{F} + b\vec{G}$ if:

    (a) $b = 0$ **(b)** $b > 0$ **(c)** $b < 0$

36. In the middle of a wide, steadily flowing river there is a fountain that spouts water horizontally in all directions. The river flows in the $\vec{i}$-direction in the xy-plane and the fountain is at the origin.

    (a) If $A > 0$, $K > 0$, explain why the following expression could represent the velocity field for the combined flow of the river and the fountain:

$$\vec{v} = A\vec{i} + K(x^2 + y^2)^{-1}(x\vec{i} + y\vec{j}).$$

    (b) What is the significance of the constants A and K?

    (c) Using a computer, sketch the vector field $\vec{v}$ for $K = 1$ and $A = 1$ and $A = 2$, and for $A = 0.2$, $K = 2$.

37. Figures 17.32 and 17.33 show the gradient of the functions $z = f(x, y)$ and $z = g(x, y)$.

    (a) For each function, draw a rough sketch of the level curves, showing possible z-values.

    (b) The xz-plane cuts each of the surfaces $z = f(x, y)$ and $z = g(x, y)$ in a curve. Sketch each of these curves, making clear how they are similar and how they are different from one another.

Figure 17.32: Gradient of $z = f(x, y)$ **Figure 17.33**: Gradient of $z = g(x, y)$

38. Let $\vec{F} = u\vec{i} + v\vec{j}$ be a vector field in 2-space with magnitude $F = \|\vec{F}\|$.

    (a) Let $\vec{T} = (1/F)\vec{F}$. Show that $\vec{T}$ is the unit vector in the direction of $\vec{F}$. See Figure 17.34.

    (b) Let $\vec{N} = (1/F)(\vec{k} \times \vec{F}) = (1/F)(-v\vec{i} + u\vec{j})$. Show that $\vec{N}$ is the unit vector pointing to the left of and at right angles to $\vec{F}$. See Figure 17.34.

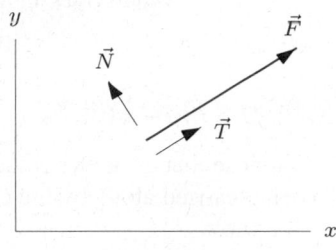

Figure 17.34

Strengthen Your Understanding

In Problems 39–40, explain what is wrong with the statement.

39. A plot of the vector field $\vec{G}(x, y, z) = \vec{F}(2x, 2y, 2z)$ can be obtained from a plot of the vector field $\vec{F}(x, y, z)$ by doubling the lengths of all the arrows.

40. A vector field $\vec{F}$ is defined by the formula $\vec{F}(x, y, z) = x^2 - yz$.

In Problems 41–42, give an example of:

41. A nonconstant vector field that is parallel to $\vec{i} + \vec{j} + \vec{k}$ at every point.

42. A nonconstant vector field with magnitude 1 at every point.

17.4 THE FLOW OF A VECTOR FIELD

When an iceberg is spotted in the North Atlantic, it is important to be able to predict where the iceberg is likely to be a day or a week later. To do this, one needs to know the velocity vector field of the ocean currents, that is, how fast and in what direction the water is moving at each point.

In this section we use differential equations to find the path of an object in a fluid flow. This path is called a flow line. Figure 17.35 shows several flow lines for the Gulf Stream velocity vector field in Figure 17.18 on page 937. The arrows on each flow line indicate the direction of flow.

Figure 17.35: Flow lines for objects in the Gulf Stream with different starting points

How Do We Find a Flow Line?

Suppose that $\vec{F}$ is the velocity vector field of water on the surface of a creek and imagine a seed being carried along by the current. We want to know the position vector $\vec{r}(t)$ of the seed at time t. We know

$$\text{Velocity of seed at time } t = \text{Velocity of current at seed's position at time } t$$

that is,

$$\vec{r}'(t) = \vec{F}(\vec{r}(t)).$$

We make the following definition:

A **flow line** of a vector field $\vec{v} = \vec{F}(\vec{r})$ is a path $\vec{r}(t)$ whose velocity vector equals $\vec{v}$. Thus,

$$\vec{r}'(t) = \vec{v} = \vec{F}(\vec{r}(t)).$$

The **flow** of a vector field is the family of all of its flow lines.

A flow line is also called an *integral curve* or a *streamline*. We define flow lines for any vector field, as it turns out to be useful to study the flow of fields (for example, electric and magnetic) that are not velocity fields.

Resolving $\vec{F}$ and $\vec{r}$ into components, $\vec{F} = F_1\vec{i} + F_2\vec{j}$ and $\vec{r}(t) = x(t)\vec{i} + y(t)\vec{j}$, the definition of a flow line tells us that $x(t)$ and $y(t)$ satisfy the system of differential equations

$$x'(t) = F_1(x(t), y(t)) \quad \text{and} \quad y'(t) = F_2(x(t), y(t)).$$

Solving these differential equations gives a parameterization of the flow line.

Example 1   Find the flow line of the constant velocity field $\vec{v} = 3\vec{i} + 4\vec{j}$ cm/sec that passes through the point $(1, 2)$ at time $t = 0$.

Solution   Let $\vec{r}(t) = x(t)\vec{i} + y(t)\vec{j}$ be the position in cm of a particle at time t, where t is in seconds. We have

$$x'(t) = 3 \quad \text{and} \quad y'(t) = 4.$$

Thus,

$$x(t) = 3t + x_0 \quad \text{and} \quad y(t) = 4t + y_0.$$

Since the path passes the point $(1, 2)$ at $t = 0$, we have $x_0 = 1$ and $y_0 = 2$ and so

$$x(t) = 3t + 1 \qquad \text{and} \qquad y(t) = 4t + 2.$$

Thus, the path is the line given parametrically by

$$\vec{r}(t) = (3t + 1)\vec{i} + (4t + 2)\vec{j}.$$

(See Figure 17.36.) To find an explicit equation for the path, eliminate t between these expressions to get

$$\frac{x - 1}{3} = \frac{y - 2}{4} \qquad \text{or} \qquad y = \frac{4}{3}x + \frac{2}{3}.$$

Figure 17.36: Vector field $\vec{F} = 3\vec{i} + 4\vec{j}$ with the flow line through $(1, 2)$

Example 2   The velocity of a flow at the point (x, y) is $\vec{F}(x, y) = \vec{i} + x\vec{j}$. Find the path of motion of an object in the flow that is at the point $(-2, 2)$ at time $t = 0$.

Solution   Figure 17.37 shows this field. Since $\vec{r}'(t) = \vec{F}(\vec{r}(t))$, we are looking for the flow line that satisfies the system of differential equations

$$x'(t) = 1, \quad y'(t) = x(t) \qquad \text{satisfying } x(0) = -2 \text{ and } y(0) = 2.$$

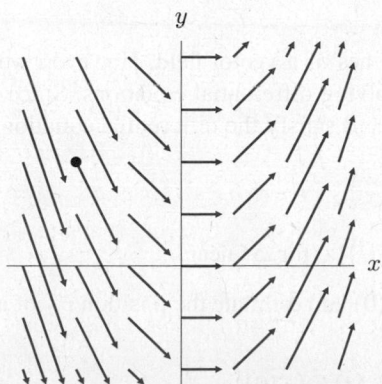

Figure 17.37: The velocity field $\vec{v} = \vec{i} + x\vec{j}$

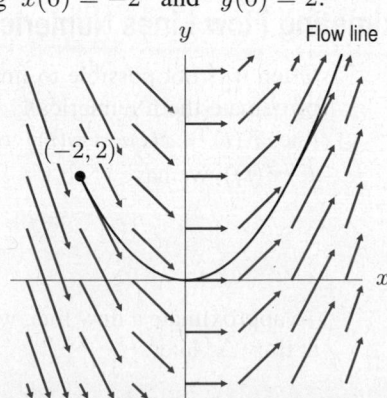

Figure 17.38: A flow line of the velocity field $\vec{v} = \vec{i} + x\vec{j}$

Solving for $x(t)$ first, we get $x(t) = t + x_0$, where x_0 is a constant of integration. Thus, $y'(t) = t + x_0$, so $y(t) = \frac{1}{2}t^2 + x_0 t + y_0$, where y_0 is also a constant of integration. Since $x(0) = x_0 = -2$ and $y(0) = y_0 = 2$, the path of motion is given by

$$x(t) = t - 2, \quad y(t) = \tfrac{1}{2}t^2 - 2t + 2,$$

or, equivalently,

$$\vec{r}(t) = (t - 2)\vec{i} + (\tfrac{1}{2}t^2 - 2t + 2)\vec{j}.$$

The graph of this flow line in Figure 17.38 looks like a parabola. We check this by seeing that an explicit equation for the path is $y = \frac{1}{2}x^2$.

Example 3   Determine the flow of the vector field $\vec{v} = -y\vec{i} + x\vec{j}$.

Solution   Figure 17.39 suggests that the flow consists of concentric counterclockwise circles, centered at the origin. The system of differential equations for the flow is

$$x'(t) = -y(t) \qquad y'(t) = x(t).$$

The equations $(x(t), y(t)) = (a\cos t, a\sin t)$ parameterize a family of counterclockwise circles of radius a, centered at the origin. We check that this family satisfies the system of differential equations:

$$x'(t) = -a\sin t = -y(t) \quad \text{and} \quad y'(t) = a\cos t = x(t).$$

Figure 17.39: The flow of the
vector field $\vec{v} = -y\vec{i} + x\vec{j}$

Approximating Flow Lines Numerically

Often it is not possible to find formulas for the flow lines of a vector field. However, we can approximate them numerically by Euler's method for solving differential equations. Since the flow lines $\vec{r}(t) = x(t)\vec{i} + y(t)\vec{j}$ of a vector field $\vec{v} = \vec{F}(x, y)$ satisfy the differential equation $\vec{r}'(t) = \vec{F}(\vec{r}(t))$, we have

$$\vec{r}(t + \Delta t) \approx \vec{r}(t) + (\Delta t)\vec{r}'(t)$$
$$= \vec{r}(t) + (\Delta t)\vec{F}(\vec{r}(t)) \quad \text{for } \Delta t \text{ near } 0.$$

To approximate a flow line, we start at a point $\vec{r}_0 = \vec{r}(0)$ and estimate the position $\vec{r}_1$ of a particle at time Δt later:

$$\vec{r}_1 = \vec{r}(\Delta t) \approx \vec{r}(0) + (\Delta t)\vec{F}(\vec{r}(0))$$
$$= \vec{r}_0 + (\Delta t)\vec{F}(\vec{r}_0).$$

We then repeat the same procedure starting at $\vec{r}_1$, and so on. The general formula for getting from one point to the next is

$$\vec{r}_{n+1} = \vec{r}_n + (\Delta t)\vec{F}(\vec{r}_n).$$

The points with position vectors $\vec{r}_0, \vec{r}_1, \ldots$ trace out the path, as shown in the next example.

Example 4   Use Euler's method to approximate the flow line through $(1, 2)$ for the vector field $\vec{v} = y^2\vec{i} + 2x^2\vec{j}$.

Solution   The flow is determined by the differential equations $\vec{r}'(t) = \vec{v}$, or equivalently

$$x'(t) = y^2, \qquad y'(t) = 2x^2.$$

We use Euler's method with $\Delta t = 0.02$, giving

$$\vec{r}_{n+1} = \vec{r}_n + 0.02\,\vec{v}(x_n, y_n)$$
$$= x_n\vec{i} + y_n\vec{j} + 0.02(y_n^2\vec{i} + 2x_n^2\vec{j}),$$

or equivalently,

$$x_{n+1} = x_n + 0.02y_n{}^2, \qquad y_{n+1} = y_n + 0.02 \cdot 2x_n{}^2.$$

When $t = 0$, we have $(x_0, y_0) = (1, 2)$. Then

$$x_1 = x_0 + 0.02 \cdot y_0{}^2 = 1 + 0.02 \cdot 2^2 = 1.08,$$
$$y_1 = y_0 + 0.02 \cdot 2x_0^2 = 2 + 0.02 \cdot 2 \cdot 1^2 = 2.04.$$

So after one step $x(0.02) \approx 1.08$ and $y(0.02) \approx 2.04$. Similarly, $x(0.04) = x(2\Delta t) \approx 1.16$, $y(0.04) = y(2\Delta t) \approx 2.08$ and so on. Farther values along the flow line are given in Table 17.2 and plotted in Figure 17.40.

Table 17.2   *Approximated flow line starting at $(1, 2)$ for the vector field $\vec{v} = y^2\vec{i} + 2x^2\vec{j}$*

t	0	0.02	0.04	0.06	0.08	0.1	0.12	0.14	0.16	0.18
x	1	1.08	1.16	1.25	1.34	1.44	1.54	1.65	1.77	1.90
y	2	2.04	2.08	2.14	2.20	2.28	2.36	2.45	2.56	2.69

Figure 17.40: Euler's method solution to $x' = y^2$, $y' = 2x^2$

Exercises and Problems for Section 17.4

Exercises

In Exercises 1–3, sketch the vector field and its flow.

1. $\vec{v} = 2\vec{j}$ **2.** $\vec{v} = 3\vec{i}$ **3.** $\vec{v} = 3\vec{i} - 2\vec{j}$

In Exercises 4–9, sketch the vector field and the flow. Then find the system of differential equations associated with the vector field and check that the flow satisfies the system.

4. $\vec{v} = x\vec{i}$; $x(t) = ae^t, y(t) = b$

5. $\vec{v} = x\vec{j}$; $x(t) = a, y(t) = at + b$

6. $\vec{v} = x\vec{i} + y\vec{j}$; $x(t) = ae^t, y(t) = be^t$

7. $\vec{v} = x\vec{i} - y\vec{j}$; $x(t) = ae^t, y(t) = be^{-t}$

8. $\vec{v} = y\vec{i} - x\vec{j}$; $x(t) = a\sin t, y(t) = a\cos t$

9. $\vec{v} = y\vec{i} + x\vec{j}$; $x(t) = a(e^t + e^{-t}), y(t) = a(e^t - e^{-t})$

10. Use a computer or calculator with Euler's method to approximate the flow line through $(1, 2)$ for the vector field $\vec{v} = y^2\vec{i} + 2x^2\vec{j}$ using 5 steps with $\Delta t = 0.1$.

Problems

For Problems 11–14, find the region of the Gulf Stream velocity field in Figure 17.18 on page 937 represented by the given table of velocity vectors (in cm/sec).

11.

$35\vec{i} + 131\vec{j}$	$48\vec{i} + 92\vec{j}$	$47\vec{i} + \vec{j}$
$-32\vec{i} + 132\vec{j}$	$-44\vec{i} + 92\vec{j}$	$-42\vec{i} + \vec{j}$
$-51\vec{i} + 73\vec{j}$	$-119\vec{i} + 84\vec{j}$	$-128\vec{i} + 6\vec{j}$

12.

$10\vec{i} - 3\vec{j}$	$11\vec{i} + 16\vec{j}$	$20\vec{i} + 75\vec{j}$
$53\vec{i} - 7\vec{j}$	$58\vec{i} + 23\vec{j}$	$64\vec{i} + 80\vec{j}$
$119\vec{i} - 8\vec{j}$	$121\vec{i} + 31\vec{j}$	$114\vec{i} + 66\vec{j}$

13.

$97\vec{i} - 41\vec{j}$	$72\vec{i} - 24\vec{j}$	$54\vec{i} - 10\vec{j}$
$134\vec{i} - 49\vec{j}$	$131\vec{i} - 44\vec{j}$	$129\vec{i} - 18\vec{j}$
$103\vec{i} - 36\vec{j}$	$122\vec{i} - 30\vec{j}$	$131\vec{i} - 17\vec{j}$

14.

$-95\vec{i} - 60\vec{j}$	$18\vec{i} - 48\vec{j}$	$82\vec{i} - 22\vec{j}$
$-29\vec{i} + 48\vec{j}$	$76\vec{i} + 63\vec{j}$	$128\vec{i} - 16\vec{j}$
$26\vec{i} + 105\vec{j}$	$49\vec{i} + 119\vec{j}$	$88\vec{i} + 13\vec{j}$

15. $\vec{F}(x, y)$ and $\vec{G}(x, y) = 2\vec{F}(x, y)$ are two vector fields. Illustrating your answer with $\vec{F}(x, y) = -y\vec{i} + x\vec{j}$, describe the graphical difference between:

    (a) The vector fields   **(b)** Their flows

16. Match the vector fields (a)–(f) with their flow lines (I)–(VI). Put arrows on the flow lines indicating the direction of flow.

(a) $y\vec{i} + x\vec{j}$ **(b)** $-y\vec{i} + x\vec{j}$

(c) $x\vec{i} + y\vec{j}$ **(d)** $-y\vec{i} + (x + y/10)\vec{j}$

(e) $-y\vec{i} + (x - y/10)\vec{j}$ **(f)** $(x - y)\vec{i} + (x - y)\vec{j}$

(I)

(II)

(III)

(IV)

(V)

(VI)

17. Show that the acceleration $\vec{a}$ of an object flowing in a velocity field $\vec{F}(x, y) = u(x, y)\vec{i} + v(x, y)\vec{j}$ is given by $\vec{a} = (u_x u + u_y v)\vec{i} + (v_x u + v_y v)\vec{j}$.

18. A velocity vector field $\vec{v} = -H_y\vec{i} + H_x\vec{j}$ is based on the partial derivatives of a smooth function $H(x, y)$. Explain why

(a) $\vec{v}$ is perpendicular to grad H.
(b) the flow lines of $\vec{v}$ are along the level curves of H.

In Problems 19–21, show that every flow line of the vector field $\vec{v}$ lies on a level curve for the function $f(x, y)$.

19. $\vec{v} = x\vec{i} - y\vec{j}$, $f(x, y) = xy$

20. $\vec{v} = y\vec{i} + x\vec{j}$, $f(x, y) = x^2 - y^2$

21. $\vec{v} = ay\vec{i} + bx\vec{j}$, $f(x, y) = bx^2 - ay^2$

22. A solid metal ball has its center at the origin of a fixed set of axes. The ball rotates once every 24 hours around

the z-axis. The direction of rotation is counterclockwise when viewed from above. Let $\vec{v}(x, y, z)$ be the velocity vector of the particle of metal at the point (x, y, z) inside the ball. Time is in hours and x, y, z are in meters.

(a) Find a formula for the vector field $\vec{v}$. Give units for your answer.
(b) Describe in words the flow lines of $\vec{v}$.

23. **(a)** Show that $h(t) = e^{-2at}(x^2 + y^2)$ is constant along any flow line of $\vec{v} = (ax - y)\vec{i} + (x + ay)\vec{j}$.
(b) Show that points moving with the flow that are on the unit circle centered at the origin at time 0 are on the circle of radius e^{at} centered at the origin at time t.

Strengthen Your Understanding

In Problems 24–25, explain what is wrong with the statement.

24. The flow lines of a vector field whose components are linear functions are all straight lines.

25. If the flow lines of a vector field are all straight lines with the same slope pointing in the same direction, then the vector field is constant.

In Problems 26–27, give an example of:

26. A vector field $\vec{F}(x, y, z)$ such that the path $\vec{r}(t) = t\vec{i} + t^2\vec{j} + t^3\vec{k}$ is a flow line.

27. A vector field whose flow lines are rays from the origin.

Are the statements in Problems 28–37 true or false? Give reasons for your answer.

28. The flow lines for $\vec{F}(x, y) = x\vec{j}$ are parallel to the y-axis.

29. The flow lines of $\vec{F}(x, y) = y\vec{i} - x\vec{j}$ are hyperbolas.

30. The flow lines of $\vec{F}(x, y) = x\vec{i}$ are parabolas.

31. The vector field in Figure 17.41 has a flow line which lies in the first and third quadrants.

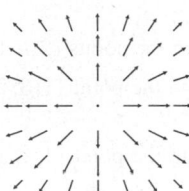

Figure 17.41

32. The vector field in Figure 17.41 has a flow line on which both x and y tend to infinity.

33. If $\vec{F}$ is a gradient vector field, $\vec{F}(x, y) = \nabla f(x, y)$, then the flow lines for $\vec{F}$ are the contours for f.

34. If the flow lines for the vector field $\vec{F}(\vec{r})$ are all concentric circles centered at the origin, then $\vec{F}(\vec{r}) \cdot \vec{r} = 0$ for all $\vec{r}$.

35. If the flow lines for the vector field $\vec{F}(x, y)$ are all straight lines parallel to the constant vector $\vec{v} = 3\vec{i} + 5\vec{j}$, then $\vec{F}(x, y) = \vec{v}$.

36. No flow line for the vector field $\vec{F}(x, y) = x\vec{i} + 2\vec{j}$ has a point where the y-coordinate reaches a relative maximum.

37. The vector field $\vec{F}(x, y) = e^x\vec{i} + y\vec{j}$ has a flow line that crosses the x-axis.

CHAPTER SUMMARY (see also Ready Reference at the end of the book)

- **Parameterized Curves**
  Parameterizations representing motion in 2- and 3-space, change of parameter, vector form of parametric equations, parametric equation of a line.

- **Velocity and Acceleration Vectors**
  Computing velocity and acceleration, uniform circular motion, the length of a parametric curve.

- **Vector Fields**
  Definition of vector field, visualizing fields, gradient fields.

- **Flow Lines**
  Parametric equations of flow lines, approximating flow lines numerically.

REVIEW EXERCISES AND PROBLEMS FOR CHAPTER SEVENTEEN

Exercises

Write a parameterization for the curves in Exercises 1–13.

1. The equation of the line through $(2, -1, 3)$ and parallel to $5\vec{i} + 4\vec{j} - \vec{k}$.

2. The line passing through the points $(1, 2, 3)$ and $(3, 5, 7)$.

3. The horizontal line through the point $(0, 5)$.

4. The circle of radius 2 centered at the origin starting at the point $(0, 2)$ when $t = 0$.

5. The circle of radius 4 centered at the point $(4, 4)$ starting on the x-axis when $t = 0$.

6. The circle of radius 1 in the xy-plane centered at the origin, traversed counterclockwise when viewed from above.

7. The line through the points $(2, -1, 4)$ and $(1, 2, 5)$.

8. The line through the point $(1, 3, 2)$ perpendicular to the xz-plane.

9. The line through the point $(1, 1, 1)$ perpendicular to the plane $2x - 3y + 5z = 4$.

10. The circle of radius 3 in the xy-plane, centered at the origin, counterclockwise.

11. The circle of radius 3 parallel to the xz-plane, centered at the point $(0, 5, 0)$, and traversed counterclockwise when viewed from $(0, 10, 0)$.

12. The line of intersection of the planes $z = 4 + 2x + 5y$ and $z = 3 + x + 3y$.

13. The circle of radius 10 centered at the point $(0, 0, 7)$, lying horizontally, and traversed in a clockwise direction viewed from the point $(0, 0, 11)$. The parameterization should have period 30.

In Exercises 14–18, find the velocity vector.

14. $x = 3\cos t, y = 4\sin t$

15. $x = t, y = t^3 - t$

16. $x = 2 + 3t, y = 4 + t, z = 1 - t$

17. $x = 2 + 3t^2, y = 4 + t^2, z = 1 - t^2$

18. $x = t, y = t^2, z = t^3$

In Exercises 19–22, are the following quantities vectors or scalars? Find them.

19. The velocity of a particle moving, for $t \geq 0$, along the curve $x = 2 + 3\sin\sqrt{2t + 1}$, $y = 4 + 3\cos\sqrt{2t + 1}$, $z = 10 + \sqrt{2t + 1}$.

20. The speed of a particle moving along the curve $x = t^2$, $y = e^t$.

21. The velocity of a particle moving along the curve $x = 5 - \sqrt{3 + \sin t}, y = \sqrt{3 + \cos t}$.

22. The acceleration of a particle moving along the curve $x = te^t, y = e^{2t}$.

23. Are the lines $x = 3 + 2t, y = 5 - t, z = 7 + 3t$ and $x = 3 + t, y = 5 + 2t, z = 7 + 2t$ parallel?

24. Are the lines $x = 3 + 2t, y = 5 - t, z = 7 + 3t$ and $x = 5 + 4t, y = 3 - 2t, z = 1 + 6t$ parallel?

25. Explain how you know the following equations parameterize the same line:

$$\vec{r} = (3 - t)\vec{i} + (3 + 4t)\vec{j} - (1 + 2t)\vec{k}$$
$$\vec{r} = (1 + 2t)\vec{i} + (11 - 8t)\vec{j} + (4t - 5)\vec{k}$$

26. A line is parameterized by $\vec{r} = 10\vec{k} + t(\vec{i} + 2\vec{j} + 3\vec{k})$.

(a) Suppose we restrict ourselves to $t < 0$. What part of the line do we get?

(b) Suppose we restrict ourselves to $0 \leq t \leq 1$. What part of the line do we get?

Sketch the vector fields in Exercises 27–29.

27. $\vec{F}(x, y) = -y\vec{i} + x\vec{j}$

28. $\vec{F} = \dfrac{y}{x^2 + y^2}\vec{i} - \dfrac{x}{x^2 + y^2}\vec{j}$

29. $\vec{F} = \dfrac{y}{\sqrt{x^2 + y^2}}\vec{i} - \dfrac{x}{\sqrt{x^2 + y^2}}\vec{j}$

Problems

30. Where does the line $x = 2t + 1, y = 3t - 2, z = -t + 3$ intersect the sphere $(x - 1)^2 + (y + 1)^2 + (z - 2)^2 = 2$?

31. A particle travels along a line, with position at time t given by $\vec{r}(t) = (2 + 5t)\vec{i} + (3 + t)\vec{j} + 2t\vec{k}$.

(a) Where is the particle when $t = 0$?

(b) When does the particle reach the point $(12, 5, 4)$?

(c) Does the particle ever reach $(12, 4, 4)$? Explain.

32. Consider the parametric equations for $0 \leq t \leq \pi$:

(I) $\vec{r} = \cos(2t)\vec{i} + \sin(2t)\vec{j}$

(II) $\vec{r} = 2\cos t\vec{i} + 2\sin t\vec{j}$

(III) $\vec{r} = \cos(t/2)\vec{i} + \sin(t/2)\vec{j}$

(IV) $\vec{r} = 2\cos t\vec{i} - 2\sin t\vec{j}$

(a) Match the equations above with four of the curves C_1, C_2, C_3, C_4, C_5 and C_6 in Figure 17.42. (Each curve is part of a circle.)

(b) Give parametric equations for the curves which have not been matched, again assuming $0 \leq t \leq \pi$.

Figure 17.42

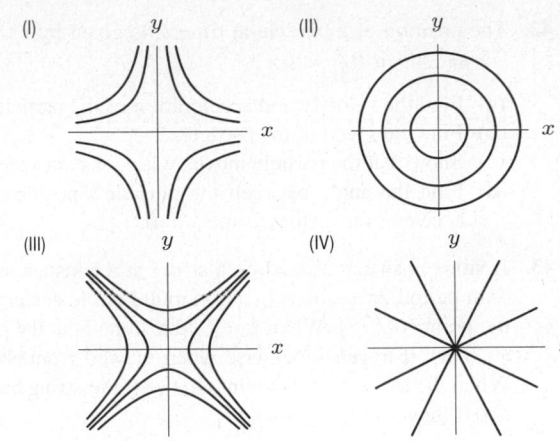

33. (a) What is meant by a vector field?
  (b) Suppose $\vec{a} = a_1\vec{i} + a_2\vec{j} + a_3\vec{k}$ is a constant vector. Which of the following are vector fields? Explain.

  (i) $\vec{r} + \vec{a}$ (ii) $\vec{r} \cdot \vec{a}$
  (iii) $x^2\vec{i} + y^2\vec{j} + z^2\vec{k}$ (iv) $x^2 + y^2 + z^2$

34. Match the level curves in (I)–(IV) with the gradient fields in (A)–(D). All figures have $-2 \le x \le 2, -2 \le y \le 2$.

35. Each of the vector fields $\vec{E}, \vec{F}, \vec{G}, \vec{H}$ is tangent to one of the families of curves (I)–(IV). Match them.

$$\vec{E} = x\vec{i} + y\vec{j} \quad \vec{F} = x\vec{i} - y\vec{j}$$
$$\vec{G} = y\vec{i} - x\vec{j} \quad \vec{H} = y\vec{i} + x\vec{j}$$

36. A particle passes through the point $P = (5, 4, 3)$ at time $t = 7$, moving with constant velocity $\vec{v} = 3\vec{i} + \vec{j} + 2\vec{k}$. Find equations for its position at time t.

37. An object moving with constant velocity in 3-space, with coordinates in meters, passes through the point $(1, 1, 1)$, then through $(2, -1, 3)$ five seconds later. What is its velocity vector? What is its acceleration vector?

38. Find parametric equations for a particle moving along the line $y = -2x + 5$ with speed 3.

39. The temperature in °C at (x, y) in the plane is $H = f(x, y)$, where x, y are in centimeters. A particle moves along the curve $x = g(t)$, $y = k(t)$, with t in seconds.

  (a) What does the quantity $\| \operatorname{grad} f \|$ represent in this context? What is its units?
  (b) Write an expression for the speed of the particle. What is its units?
  (c) Write an expression for the rate of change of the particle's temperature with time. What is its units?

40. Find parametric equations for motion along the line $y = 3x + 7$ such that the x-coordinate decreases by 2 units for each unit of time.

41. The y-axis is vertical and the x-axis is horizontal; t represents time. The motion of a particle is given by

$$x = t^3 - 3t, \quad y = t^2 - 2t.$$

  (a) Does the particle ever come to a stop? If so, when and where?
  (b) Is the particle ever moving straight up or down? If so, when and where?
  (c) Is the particle ever moving straight horizontally right or left? If so, when and where?

42. The position of a particle at time t, is given by $\vec{r}(t) = \cos 4t\vec{i} + \sin 4t\vec{j} + 3t\vec{k}$.

  (a) Find the velocity and acceleration of the particle.
  (b) Find the speed of the particle.
  (c) Show that the particle moves with constant speed.
  (d) Find the angle between the particle's position and acceleration vector at time $t = 0$.

43. A stone is swung around on a string at a constant speed with period 2π seconds in a horizontal circle centered at the point $(0, 0, 8)$. When $t = 0$, the stone is at the point $(0, 5, 8)$; it travels clockwise when viewed from above. When the stone is at the point $(5, 0, 8)$, the string breaks and it moves under gravity.

  (a) Parameterize the stone's circular trajectory.
  (b) Find the velocity and acceleration of the stone at the moment before the string breaks.
  (c) Write, but do not solve, the differential equations (with initial conditions) satisfied by the coordinates x, y, z giving the position of the stone after it has left the circle.

44. The origin is on the surface of the earth, and the z-axis points upward. For $t \geq 0$, a particle moves according to

$$x(t) = 5t, \quad y(t) = 3t, \quad z(t) = 15 - t^2 + 2t.$$

  (a) What is the position, velocity, and acceleration at time $t = 0$?
  (b) When and where does the particle hit the ground? How fast is it moving then?

45. Let $f(x, y) = \dfrac{x^2 - y^2}{x^2 + y^2}$.

  (a) In which direction should you move from the point $(1, 1)$ to obtain the maximum rate of increase of f?
  (b) Find a direction in which the directional derivative at the point $(1, 1)$ is equal to zero.
  (c) Suppose you move along the curve $x = e^{2t}, y = 2t^3 + 6t + 1$. What is df/dt at $t = 0$?

46. An ant, starting at the origin, moves at 2 units/sec along the x-axis to the point $(1, 0)$. The ant then moves counterclockwise along the unit circle to $(0, 1)$ at a speed of $3\pi/2$ units/sec, then straight down to the origin at a speed of 2 units/sec along the y-axis.

  (a) Express the ant's coordinates as a function of time, t, in secs.
  (b) Express the reverse path as a function of time.

47. The temperature at the point (x, y) in the plane is given by $F(x, y) = 1/(x^2 + y^2)$. A ladybug moves along a parabola according to the parametric equations

$$x = t, \ y = t^2.$$

Assuming that the ladybug's temperature is the same as the plane at her current location, find the rate of change in the temperature of the ladybug at time t. Use the chain rule to show that for any temperature function $F(x, y)$ and any path of the ladybug $\vec{r} = x(t)\vec{i} + y(t)\vec{j}$, then writing $\vec{v}(t) = d\vec{r}/dt$ gives:

$$\text{Rate of change of temperature } = \nabla F(x, y) \cdot \vec{v}.$$

48. The motion of the particle is given by the parametric equations

$$x = t^3 - 3t, \ y = t^2 - 2t.$$

Give parametric equations for the tangent line to the path of the particle at time $t = -2$.

49. At time $t = 0$ a particle in uniform circular motion in the plane has velocity $\vec{v} = 6\vec{i} - 4\vec{j}$ and acceleration $\vec{a} = 2\vec{i} + 3\vec{j}$. Find the radius and center of its orbit if at time $t = 0$ it is at the point

  (a) $P = (0, 0)$ **(b)** $P = (10, 50)$

50. Find parametric equations of the line passing through the points $(1, 2, 3)$, $(3, 5, 7)$ and calculate the shortest distance from the line to the origin.

51. On a calculator or a computer, plot $x = 2t/(t^2 + 1)$, $y = (t^2 - 1)/(t^2 + 1)$, first for $-50 \leq t \leq 50$ then for $-5 \leq t \leq 5$. Explain what you see. Is the curve really a circle?

52. A cheerleader has a 0.4 m long baton with a light on one end. She throws the baton in such a way that it moves entirely in a vertical plane. The origin is on the ground and the y-axis is vertical. The center of the baton moves along a parabola and the baton rotates counterclockwise around the center with a constant angular velocity. The baton is initially horizontal and 1.5 m above the ground; its initial velocity is 8 m/sec horizontally and 10 m/sec vertically, and its angular velocity is 2 revolutions per second. Find parametric equations describing the following motions:

  (a) The center of the baton relative to the ground.
  (b) The end of the baton relative to its center.
  (c) The path traced out by the end of the baton relative to the ground.
  (d) Sketch a graph of the motion of the end of the baton.

53. For a and ω positive constants and $t \geq 0$, the position vector of a particle moving in a spiral counterclockwise outward from the origin is given by

$$\vec{r}(t) = at \cos(\omega t)\vec{i} + at \sin(\omega t)\vec{j}.$$

What is the significance of the parameters ω and a?

54. An object is moving on a straight-line path. Can you conclude at all times that:

  (a) Its velocity vector is parallel to the line? Justify your answer.
  (b) Its acceleration vector is parallel to the line? Justify your answer.

55. If $\vec{F} = \vec{r}/\|\vec{r}\|^3$, find the following quantities in terms of x, y, z, or t.

(a) $\|\vec{F}\|$

(b) $\vec{F} \cdot \vec{r}$

(c) A unit vector parallel to $\vec{F}$ and pointing in the same direction

(d) A unit vector parallel to $\vec{F}$ and pointing in the opposite direction

(e) $\vec{F}$ if $\vec{r} = \cos t\vec{i} + \sin t\vec{j} + \vec{k}$

(f) $\vec{F} \cdot \vec{r}$ if $\vec{r} = \cos t\vec{i} + \sin t\vec{j} + \vec{k}$

56. Each of the following vector fields represents an ocean current. Sketch the vector field, and sketch the path of an iceberg in this current. Determine the location of an iceberg at time $t = 7$ if it is at the point $(1, 3)$ at time $t = 0$.

(a) The current everywhere is $\vec{i}$.

(b) The current at (x, y) is $2x\vec{i} + y\vec{j}$.

(c) The current at (x, y) is $-y\vec{i} + x\vec{j}$.

57. Wire is stretched taught from the point $P = (7, 12, -10)$ to the point $Q = (-2, -3, 2)$ and from the point $R = (-20, 17, 1)$ to the point $S = (37, 2, 25)$. Spherical beads of radius 8 cm slide along each wire through holes along an axis through their centers. Can the beads pass each other without touching, regardless of their position?

58. A particle moves with displacement vector $\vec{r}$ and constant speed. Show that the vector representing the velocity is perpendicular to the vector representing the acceleration.

CAS Challenge Problems

59. Let $\vec{r}_0 = x_0\vec{i} + y_0\vec{j} + z_0\vec{k}$, and let $\vec{e}_1$ and $\vec{e}_2$ be perpendicular unit vectors. A circle of radius R, centered at (x_0, y_0, z_0), and lying in the plane parallel to $\vec{e}_1$ and $\vec{e}_2$, is parameterized by $\vec{r}(t) = \vec{r}_0 + R\cos t\vec{e}_1 + R\sin t\vec{e}_2$. We want to parameterize a circle in 3-space with radius 5, centered at $(1, 2, 3)$, and lying in the plane $x + y + z = 6$.

(a) Let $\vec{e}_1 = a\vec{i} + b\vec{j}$ and $\vec{e}_2 = c\vec{i} + d\vec{j} + e\vec{k}$. Write down conditions on $\vec{e}_1$ and $\vec{e}_2$ that make them unit vectors, perpendicular to each other, and lying in the given plane.

(b) Solve the equations in part (a) for a, b, c, d, and e and write a parameterization of the circle.

60. Let $\vec{F}(x, y) = -y(1 - y^2)\vec{i} + x(1 - y^2)\vec{j}$.

(a) Show that $\vec{r} \cdot \vec{F} = 0$. What does this tell you about the shape of the flow lines?

(b) Show that $\vec{r}(t) = \cos t\vec{i} + \sin t\vec{j}$ has velocity vector parallel to $\vec{F}$ at every point, but is not a flow line.

(c) Show $\vec{r}(t) = (1/(\sqrt{1 + t^2}))\vec{i} + (t/(\sqrt{1 + t^2}))\vec{j}$

is a flow line for $\vec{F}$. What is the difference between this curve and the one in part (b)?

61. Let $\vec{F}(x, y) = (x + y)\vec{i} + (4x + y)\vec{j}$.

(a) Show that $\vec{r}(t) = (ae^{3t} + be^{-t})\vec{i} + (2ae^{3t} - 2be^{-t})\vec{j}$, for constant a, b, is a flow line for $\vec{F}$.

(b) Find the flow line passing through $(1, -2)$ at $t = 0$ and describe its behavior as $t \to \infty$. Do the same for the points $(1, -1.99)$ and $(1, -2.01)$. Compare the behavior of the three flow lines.

62. Two surfaces generally intersect in a curve. For each of the following pair of surfaces $f(x, y, z) = 0$ and $g(x, y, z) = 0$, find a parameterization for the curve of intersection by solving for two of the variables in terms of the third.

(a) $3x - 5y + z = 5, 2x + y + z = 3$,

(b) $3x^2 - 5y + z = 5, 2x + y + z = 3$,

(c) $x^2 + y^2 = 2, 3x - y + z = 5$.

PROJECTS FOR CHAPTER SEVENTEEN

1. Shooting a Basketball

A basketball player shoots the ball from 6 feet above the ground toward a basket that is 10 feet above the ground and 15 feet away horizontally.

(a) Suppose she shoots the ball at an angle of A degrees above the horizontal $(0 < A < \pi/2)$ with an initial speed V. Give the x- and y-coordinates of the position of the basketball at time t. Assume the x-coordinate of the basket is 0 and that the x-coordinate of the shooter is -15. [Hint: There is an acceleration of -32 ft/sec^2 in the y-direction; there is no acceleration in the x-direction. Ignore air resistance.]

(b) Using the parametric equations you obtained in part (a), experiment with different values for V and A, plotting the path of the ball on a graphing calculator or computer to see how close the ball comes to the basket. (The tick marks on the y-axis can be used to locate the basket.) Find some values of V and A for which the shot goes in.

(c) Find the angle A that minimizes the velocity needed for the ball to reach the basket. (This is a lengthy computation. First find an equation in V and A that holds if the path of the ball passes through the point 15 feet from the shooter and 10 feet above the ground. Then minimize V.)

2. Kepler's Second Law

The planets do not orbit in circles with the sun at the center, nor does the moon orbit in a circle with the earth at the center. In fact, the moon's distance from the earth varies from 220,000 to 260,000 miles. In the last half of the 16th century the Danish astronomer Tycho Brahe (1546–1601) made measurements of the positions of the planets. Johann Kepler (1571–1630) studied this data and arrived at three laws now known as *Kepler's Laws*:

I. The orbit of each planet is an ellipse with the sun at one focus. In particular, the orbit lies in a plane containing the sun.

II. As a planet orbits around the sun, the line segment from the sun to the planet sweeps out equal areas in equal times. See Figure 17.43.

III. The ratio p^2/d^3 is the same for every planet orbiting around the sun, where p is the period of the orbit (time to complete one revolution) and d is the mean distance of the orbit (average of the shortest and farthest distances from the sun).

Kepler's Laws, impressive as they are, were purely descriptive; Newton's great achievement was to find an underlying cause for them. In this project, you will derive Kepler's Second Law from Newton's Law of Gravity.

Consider a coordinate system centered at the sun.[3] Let $\vec{r}$ be the position vector of a planet and let $\vec{v}$ and $\vec{a}$ be the planet's velocity and acceleration, respectively. Define $\vec{L} = \vec{r} \times \vec{v}$. (This is a multiple of the planet's angular momentum.)

(a) Show that $\dfrac{d\vec{L}}{dt} = \vec{r} \times \vec{a}$.

(b) Consider the planet moving from $\vec{r}$ to $\vec{r} + \Delta\vec{r}$. Explain why the area ΔA about the origin swept out by the planet is approximately $\frac{1}{2}\|\Delta\vec{r} \times \vec{r}\|$.

(c) Using part (b), explain why $\dfrac{dA}{dt} = \dfrac{1}{2}\|\vec{L}\|$.

(d) Newton's Laws imply that the planet's gravitational acceleration, $\vec{a}$, is directed toward the sun. Using this fact and part (a), explain why $\vec{L}$ is constant.

(e) Use parts (c) and (d) to explain Kepler's Second Law.

(f) Using Kepler's Second Law, determine whether a planet is moving most quickly when it is closest to, or farthest from, the sun.

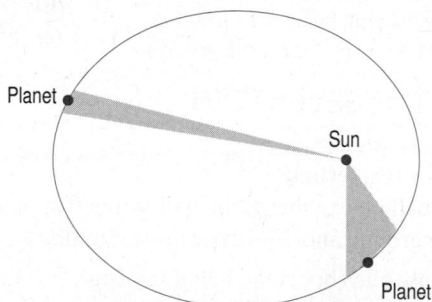

Figure 17.43: The line segment joining a planet to the sun sweeps out equal areas in equal times

---

[3]We are assuming the center of the sun is the same as the center of mass of the planet/sun system. This is only approximately true.

3. Flux Diagrams

A *flux diagram* uses flow lines to represent a vector field. The arrows drawn on a flow line indicate the direction of the vector field. The flow lines are drawn in such a way that their density is proportional to the magnitude of the vector field at each point. (The density is the number of flow lines per unit length along a curve perpendicular to the vector field.)

Figure 17.44 is a flux diagram for the vector field in 2-space $\vec{F} = \vec{r}/\|\vec{r}\|^2$. Since the field points radially away from the origin, the flow lines are straight lines radiating from the origin. The number of flow lines passing through any circle centered at the origin is a constant k. Therefore, the flow lines passing through a small circle are more densely packed than those passing through a large circle, indicating that the magnitude of the vector field decreases as we move away from the origin. In fact,

$$\text{Density of lines} = \frac{\text{Number of lines passing through circle}}{\text{Circumference of circle}} = \frac{k}{2\pi r} = \frac{k}{2\pi} 1/r,$$

so that the density is proportional to $1/r$, the magnitude of the field.

Sometimes we have to start new lines to make the density proportional to the magnitude. For example, the flow lines of $\vec{v} = x\vec{i}$ are horizontal straight lines directed away from the y-axis. However, since the magnitude of $\vec{v}$ increases linearly with x, we have to make the density of lines increase linearly with x. We achieve this by starting new lines at regular intervals. (See Figure 17.45.)

Draw flux diagrams for the following vector fields:

(a) $\vec{v} = \vec{i}$ **(b)** $\vec{v} = -y\vec{i} + x\vec{j}$ **(c)** $\vec{v} = y\vec{i}$ **(d)** $\vec{v} = y\vec{j}$

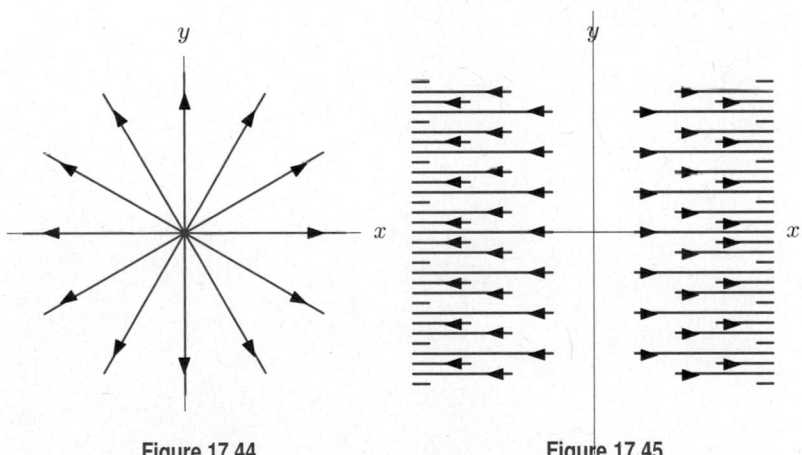

Figure 17.44   Figure 17.45

Chapter Eighteen

LINE INTEGRALS

Contents

18.1 THE IDEA OF A LINE INTEGRAL

Imagine that you are rowing on a river with a noticeable current. At times you may be working against the current and at other times you may be moving with it. At the end you have a sense of whether, overall, you were helped or hindered by the current. The line integral, defined in this section, measures the extent to which a curve in a vector field is, overall, going with the vector field or against it.

Orientation of a Curve

A curve can be traced out in two directions, as shown in Figure 18.1. We need to choose one direction before we can define a line integral.

> A curve is said to be **oriented** if we have chosen a direction of travel on it.

Figure 18.1: A curve with two different orientations represented by arrowheads

Definition of the Line Integral

Consider a vector field $\vec{F}$ and an oriented curve C. We begin by dividing C into n small, almost straight pieces along which $\vec{F}$ is approximately constant. Each piece can be represented by a displacement vector $\Delta\vec{r}_i = \vec{r}_{i+1} - \vec{r}_i$ and the value of $\vec{F}$ at each point of this small piece of C is approximately $\vec{F}(\vec{r}_i)$. See Figures 18.2 and 18.3.

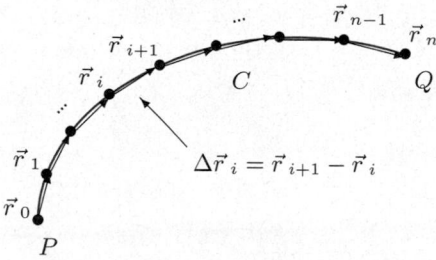

Figure 18.2: The curve C, oriented from P to Q, approximated by straight line segments represented by displacement vectors $\Delta\vec{r}_i = \vec{r}_{i+1} - \vec{r}_i$

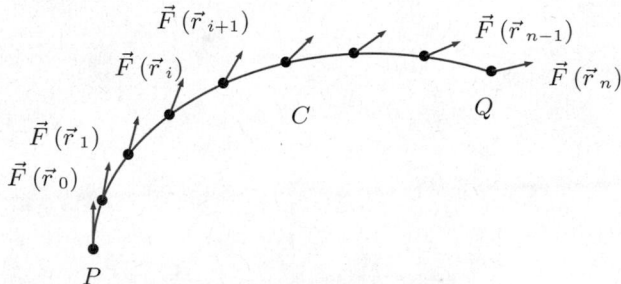

Figure 18.3: The vector field $\vec{F}$ evaluated at the points with position vector $\vec{r}_i$ on the curve C oriented from P to Q

Returning to our initial example, the vector field $\vec{F}$ represents the current and the oriented curve C is the path of the person rowing the boat. We wish to determine to what extent the vector field $\vec{F}$ helps or hinders motion along C. Since the dot product can be used to measure to what extent two vectors point in the same or opposing directions, we form the dot product $\vec{F}(\vec{r}_i) \cdot \Delta\vec{r}_i$ for each point with position vector $\vec{r}_i$ on C. Summing over all such pieces, we get a Riemann sum:

$$\sum_{i=0}^{n-1} \vec{F}(\vec{r}_i) \cdot \Delta\vec{r}_i.$$

We define the line integral, written $\int_C \vec{F} \cdot d\vec{r}$, by taking the limit as $\|\Delta\vec{r}_i\| \to 0$. Provided the limit exists, we make the following definition:

> The **line integral** of a vector field $\vec{F}$ along an oriented curve C is
>
> $$\int_C \vec{F} \cdot d\vec{r} = \lim_{\|\Delta \vec{r}_i\| \to 0} \sum_{i=0}^{n-1} \vec{F}(\vec{r}_i) \cdot \Delta \vec{r}_i.$$

How Does the Limit Defining a Line Integral Work?

The limit in the definition of a line integral exists if $\vec{F}$ is continuous on the curve C and if C is made by joining end to end a finite number of smooth curves. (A vector field $\vec{F} = F_1\vec{i} + F_2\vec{j} + F_3\vec{k}$ is *continuous* if F_1, F_2, and F_3 are continuous, and a *smooth curve* is one that can be parameterized by smooth functions.) We subdivide the curve using a parameterization which goes from one end of the curve to the other, in the forward direction, without retracing any portion of the curve. A subdivision of the parameter interval gives a subdivision of the curve. All the curves we consider in this book are *piecewise smooth* in this sense. Section 18.2 shows how to use a parameterization to compute a line integral.

Example 1   Find the line integral of the constant vector field $\vec{F} = \vec{i} + 2\vec{j}$ along the path from $(1, 1)$ to $(10, 10)$ shown in Figure 18.4.

Figure 18.4: The constant vector field $\vec{F} = \vec{i} + 2\vec{j}$ and the path from $(1, 1)$ to $(10, 10)$

Solution   Let C_1 be the horizontal segment of the path going from $(1, 1)$ to $(10, 1)$. When we break this path into pieces, each piece $\Delta\vec{r}$ is horizontal, so $\Delta\vec{r} = \Delta x\vec{i}$ and $\vec{F} \cdot \Delta\vec{r} = (\vec{i} + 2\vec{j}) \cdot \Delta x\vec{i} = \Delta x$. Hence,

$$\int_{C_1} \vec{F} \cdot d\vec{r} = \int_{x=1}^{x=10} dx = 9.$$

Similarly, along the vertical segment C_2, we have $\Delta\vec{r} = \Delta y\vec{j}$ and $\vec{F} \cdot \Delta\vec{r} = (\vec{i} + 2\vec{j}) \cdot \Delta y\vec{j} = 2\Delta y$, so

$$\int_{C_2} \vec{F} \cdot d\vec{r} = \int_{y=1}^{y=10} 2 \, dy = 18.$$

Thus,

$$\int_C \vec{F} \cdot d\vec{r} = \int_{C_1} \vec{F} \cdot d\vec{r} + \int_{C_2} \vec{F} \cdot d\vec{r} = 9 + 18 = 27.$$

What Does the Line Integral Tell Us?

Remember that for any two vectors $\vec{u}$ and $\vec{v}$, the dot product $\vec{u} \cdot \vec{v}$ is positive if $\vec{u}$ and $\vec{v}$ point roughly in the same direction (that is, if the angle between them is less than $\pi/2$). The dot product is zero if $\vec{u}$ is perpendicular to $\vec{v}$ and is negative if they point roughly in opposite directions (that is, if the angle between them is greater than $\pi/2$).

The line integral of $\vec{F}$ adds the dot products of $\vec{F}$ and $\Delta \vec{r}$ along the path. If $\|\vec{F}\|$ is constant, the line integral gives a positive number if $\vec{F}$ is mostly pointing in the same direction as C, and a negative number if $\vec{F}$ is mostly pointing in the opposite direction to C. The line integral is zero if $\vec{F}$ is perpendicular to the path at all points or if the positive and negative contributions cancel out. In general, the line integral of a vector field $\vec{F}$ along a curve C measures the extent to which C is going with $\vec{F}$ or against it.

Example 2   The vector field $\vec{F}$ and the oriented curves C_1, C_2, C_3, C_4 are shown in Figure 18.5. The curves C_1 and C_3 are the same length. Which of the line integrals $\int_{C_i} \vec{F} \cdot d\vec{r}$, for $i = 1, 2, 3, 4$, are positive? Which are negative? Arrange these line integrals in ascending order.

Figure 18.5: Vector field and paths C_1, C_2, C_3, C_4

Solution   The vector field $\vec{F}$ and the line segments $\Delta \vec{r}$ are approximately parallel and in the same direction for the curves C_1, C_2, and C_3. So the contributions of each term $\vec{F} \cdot \Delta \vec{r}$ are positive for these curves. Thus, $\int_{C_1} \vec{F} \cdot d\vec{r}$, $\int_{C_2} \vec{F} \cdot d\vec{r}$, and $\int_{C_3} \vec{F} \cdot d\vec{r}$ are each positive. For the curve C_4, the vector field and the line segments are in opposite directions, so each term $\vec{F} \cdot \Delta \vec{r}$ is negative, and therefore the integral $\int_{C_4} \vec{F} \cdot d\vec{r}$ is negative.

Since the magnitude of the vector field is smaller along C_1 than along C_3, and these two curves are the same length, we have

$$\int_{C_1} \vec{F} \cdot d\vec{r} < \int_{C_3} \vec{F} \cdot d\vec{r}.$$

In addition, the magnitude of the vector field is the same along C_2 and C_3, but the curve C_2 is longer than the curve C_3. Thus,

$$\int_{C_3} \vec{F} \cdot d\vec{r} < \int_{C_2} \vec{F} \cdot d\vec{r}.$$

Putting these results together with the fact that $\int_{C_4} \vec{F} \cdot d\vec{r}$ is negative, we have

$$\int_{C_4} \vec{F} \cdot d\vec{r} < \int_{C_1} \vec{F} \cdot d\vec{r} < \int_{C_3} \vec{F} \cdot d\vec{r} < \int_{C_2} \vec{F} \cdot d\vec{r}.$$

Interpretations of the Line Integral

Work

Recall from Section 13.3 that if a constant force $\vec{F}$ acts on an object while it moves along a straight line through a displacement $\vec{d}$, the work done by the force on the object is

$$\text{Work done} = \vec{F} \cdot \vec{d}.$$

Now suppose we want to find the work done by gravity on an object moving far above the surface of the earth. Since the force of gravity varies with distance from the earth and the path may not be straight, we can't use the formula $\vec{F} \cdot \vec{d}$. We approximate the path by line segments which are small enough that the force is approximately constant on each one. Suppose the force at a point with position vector $\vec{r}$ is $\vec{F}(\vec{r})$, as in Figures 18.2 and 18.3. Then

$$\text{Work done by force } \vec{F}(\vec{r}_i) \text{ over small displacement } \Delta \vec{r}_i \approx \vec{F}(\vec{r}_i) \cdot \Delta \vec{r}_i,$$

and so,

$$\text{Total work done by force along oriented curve } C \approx \sum_i \vec{F}(\vec{r}_i) \cdot \Delta \vec{r}_i.$$

Taking the limit as $\|\Delta \vec{r}_i\| \to 0$, we get

$$\text{Work done by force } \vec{F}(\vec{r}) \text{ along curve } C = \lim_{\|\Delta \vec{r}_i\| \to 0} \sum_i \vec{F}(\vec{r}_i) \cdot \Delta \vec{r}_i = \int_C \vec{F} \cdot d\vec{r}.$$

Example 3 A mass lying on a flat table is attached to a spring whose other end is fastened to the wall. (See Figure 18.6.) The spring is extended 20 cm beyond its rest position and released. If the axes are as shown in Figure 18.6, when the spring is extended by a distance of x, the force exerted by the spring on the mass is given by

$$\vec{F}(x) = -kx\vec{i},$$

where k is a positive constant that depends on the strength of the spring.

Suppose the mass moves back to the rest position. How much work is done by the force exerted by the spring?

Figure 18.6: Force on mass due to an extended spring

Figure 18.7: Dividing up the interval $0 \le x \le 20$ in order to calculate the work done

Solution The path from $x = 20$ to $x = 0$ is divided as shown in Figure 18.7, with a typical segment represented by

$$\Delta \vec{r} = \Delta x \vec{i}.$$

Since we are moving from $x = 20$ to $x = 0$, the quantity Δx will be negative. The work done by the force as the mass moves through this segment is approximated by

$$\text{Work done} \approx \vec{F} \cdot \Delta \vec{r} = (-kx\vec{i}) \cdot (\Delta x \vec{i}) = -kx\, \Delta x.$$

Thus, we have

$$\text{Total work done} \approx \sum -kx\, \Delta x.$$

In the limit, as $\|\Delta x\| \to 0$, this sum becomes an ordinary definite integral. Since the path starts at $x = 20$, this is the lower limit of integration; $x = 0$ is the upper limit. Thus, we get

$$\text{Total work done} = \int_{x=20}^{x=0} -kx\, dx = -\frac{kx^2}{2}\Big|_{20}^{0} = \frac{k(20)^2}{2} = 200k.$$

Note that the work done is positive, since the force acts in the direction of motion.

Example 3 shows how a line integral over a path parallel to the x-axis reduces to a one-variable integral. Section 18.2 shows how to convert *any* line integral into a one-variable integral.

Example 4   A particle with position vector $\vec{r}$ is subject to a force, $\vec{F}$, due to gravity. What is the *sign* of the work done by $\vec{F}$ as the particle moves along the path C_1, a radial line through the center of the earth, starting 8000 km from the center and ending 10,000 km from the center? (See Figure 18.8.)

Solution   We divide the path into small radial segments, $\Delta\vec{r}$, pointing away from the center of the earth and parallel to the gravitational force. The vectors $\vec{F}$ and $\Delta\vec{r}$ point in opposite directions, so each term $\vec{F}\cdot\Delta\vec{r}$ is negative. Adding all these negative quantities and taking the limit results in a negative value for the total work. Thus, the work done by gravity is negative. The negative sign indicates that we would have to do work *against* gravity to move the particle along the path C_1.

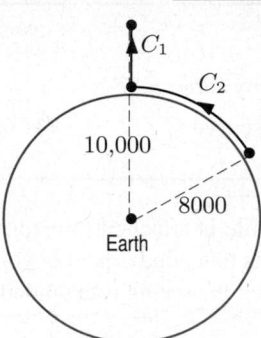

Figure 18.8: The earth

Example 5   Find the sign of the work done by gravity along the curve C_1 in Example 4, but with the opposite orientation.

Solution   Tracing a curve in the opposite direction changes the sign of the line integral because all the segments $\Delta\vec{r}$ change direction, and so every term $\vec{F}\cdot\Delta\vec{r}$ changes sign. Thus, the result will be the negative of the answer found in Example 4. Therefore, the work done by gravity as a particle moves along C_1 toward the center of the earth is positive.

Example 6   Find the work done by gravity as a particle moves along C_2, an arc of a circle 8000 km long at a distance of 8000 km from the center of the earth. (See Figure 18.8.)

Solution   Since C_2 is everywhere perpendicular to the gravitational force, $\vec{F}\cdot\Delta\vec{r}=0$ for all $\Delta\vec{r}$ along C_2. Thus,

$$\text{Work done}=\int_{C_2}\vec{F}\cdot d\vec{r}=0,$$

so the work done is zero. This is why satellites can remain in orbit without expending any fuel, once they have attained the correct altitude and velocity.

Circulation

The velocity vector field for the Gulf Stream on page 937 shows distinct eddies or regions where the water circulates. We can measure this circulation using a *closed curve*, that is, one that starts and ends at the same point.

If C is an oriented closed curve, the line integral of a vector field $\vec{F}$ around C is called the **circulation** of $\vec{F}$ around C.

Circulation is a measure of the net tendency of the vector field to point around the curve C. To emphasize that C is closed, the circulation is sometimes denoted $\oint_C \vec{F} \cdot d\vec{r}$, with a small circle on the integral sign.

Example 7   Describe the rotation of the vector fields in Figures 18.9 and 18.10. Find the sign of the circulation of the vector fields around the indicated paths.

Figure 18.9: A circulating flow

Figure 18.10: A flow with zero circulation

Solution   Consider the vector field in Figure 18.9. If you think of this as representing the velocity of water flowing in a pond, you see that the water is circulating. The line integral around C_1, measuring the circulation around C_1, is positive, because the vectors of the field are all pointing in the direction of the path. By way of contrast, look at the vector field in Figure 18.10. Here the line integral around C_2 is zero because the vertical portions of the path are perpendicular to the field and the contributions from the two horizontal portions cancel out. This means that there is no net tendency for the water to circulate around C_2.

It turns out that the vector field in Figure 18.10 has the property that its circulation around *any* closed path is zero. Water moving according to this vector field has no tendency to circulate around any point, and a leaf dropped into the water will not spin. We'll look at such special fields again later when we introduce the notion of the *curl* of a vector field.

Properties of Line Integrals

Line integrals share some basic properties with ordinary one-variable integrals:

For a scalar constant λ, vector fields $\vec{F}$ and $\vec{G}$, and oriented curves C, C_1, and C_2,

1. $\displaystyle\int_C \lambda\vec{F} \cdot d\vec{r} = \lambda\int_C \vec{F} \cdot d\vec{r}.$ 2. $\displaystyle\int_C (\vec{F} + \vec{G}) \cdot d\vec{r} = \int_C \vec{F} \cdot d\vec{r} + \int_C \vec{G} \cdot d\vec{r}.$

3. $\displaystyle\int_{-C} \vec{F} \cdot d\vec{r} = -\int_C \vec{F} \cdot d\vec{r}.$ 4. $\displaystyle\int_{C_1+C_2} \vec{F} \cdot d\vec{r} = \int_{C_1} \vec{F} \cdot d\vec{r} + \int_{C_2} \vec{F} \cdot d\vec{r}.$

Properties 3 and 4 are concerned with the curve C over which the line integral is taken. If C is an oriented curve, then $-C$ is the same curve traversed in the opposite direction, that is, with the opposite orientation. (See Figure 18.11 on page 964.) Property 3 holds because if we integrate along $-C$, the vectors $\Delta\vec{r}$ point in the opposite direction and the dot products $\vec{F} \cdot \Delta\vec{r}$ are the negatives of what they were along C.

If C_1 and C_2 are oriented curves with C_1 ending where C_2 begins, we construct a new oriented curve, called $C_1 + C_2$, by joining them together. (See Figure 18.12.) Property 4 is the analogue for line integrals of the property for definite integrals which says that

$$\int_a^b f(x)\,dx = \int_a^c f(x)\,dx + \int_c^b f(x)\,dx.$$

Figure 18.11: A curve, C, and its opposite, $-C$

Figure 18.12: Joining two curves, C_1, and C_2, to make a new one, $C_1 + C_2$

Exercises and Problems for Section 18.1

Exercises

In Exercises 1–6, say whether you expect the line integral of the pictured vector field over the given curve to be positive, negative, or zero.

1.

2.

3.

4.

5.

6.

In Exercises 7–15, calculate the line integral of the vector field along the line between the given points.

7. $\vec{F} = x\vec{j}$,   from $(1, 0)$ to $(3, 0)$

8. $\vec{F} = x\vec{j}$,   from $(2, 0)$ to $(2, 5)$

9. $\vec{F} = 6\vec{i} - 7\vec{j}$,   from $(0, 0)$ to $(7, 6)$

10. $\vec{F} = 6\vec{i} + y^2\vec{j}$,   from $(3, 0)$ to $(7, 0)$

11. $\vec{F} = 3\vec{i} + 4\vec{j}$,   from $(0, 6)$ to $(0, 13)$

12. $\vec{F} = x\vec{i}$,   from $(2, 0)$ to $(6, 0)$

13. $\vec{F} = x\vec{i} + y\vec{j}$,   from $(2, 0)$ to $(6, 0)$

14. $\vec{F} = \vec{r} = x\vec{i} + y\vec{j}$,   from $(2, 2)$ to $(6, 6)$

15. $\vec{F} = x\vec{i} + 6\vec{j} - \vec{k}$,   from $(0, -2, 0)$ to $(0, -10, 0)$

In Exercises 16–18, find $\int_C \vec{F} \cdot d\vec{r}$ for the given $\vec{F}$ and C.

16. $\vec{F} = 5\vec{i} + 7\vec{j}$, and C is the x-axis from $(-1, 0)$ to $(-9, 0)$.

17. $\vec{F} = x^2\vec{i} + y^2\vec{j}$, and C is the x-axis from $(2, 0)$ to $(3, 0)$.

18. $\vec{F} = 6x\vec{i} + (x + y^2)\vec{j}$; C is the y-axis from $(0, 3)$ to $(0, 5)$.

In Exercises 19–22, calculate the line integral.

19. $\int_C (2\vec{j} + 3\vec{k}) \cdot d\vec{r}$ where C is the y-axis from the origin to the point $(0, 10, 0)$.

20. $\int_C (2x\vec{i} + 3y\vec{j}) \cdot d\vec{r}$, where C is the line from $(1, 0, 0)$ to $(1, 0, 5)$.

21. $\int_C ((2y + 7)\vec{i} + 3x\vec{j}) \cdot d\vec{r}$, where C is the line from $(1, 0, 0)$ to $(5, 0, 0)$.

22. $\int_C (x\vec{i} + y\vec{j} + z\vec{k}) \cdot d\vec{r}$ where C is the unit circle in the xy-plane, oriented counterclockwise.

Problems

In Problems 23–26, let C_1 be the line from $(0, 0)$ to $(0, 1)$; let C_2 be the line from $(1, 0)$ to $(0, 1)$; let C_3 be the semicircle in the upper half plane from $(-1, 0)$ to $(1, 0)$. Do the line integrals of the vector field along each of the paths C_1, C_2, and C_3 appear to be positive, negative, or zero?

23.

24.

25.

26.

27. Consider the vector field $\vec{F}$ shown in Figure 18.13, together with the paths C_1, C_2, and C_3. Arrange the line integrals $\int_{C_1} \vec{F} \cdot d\vec{r}$, $\int_{C_2} \vec{F} \cdot d\vec{r}$ and $\int_{C_3} \vec{F} \cdot d\vec{r}$ in ascending order.

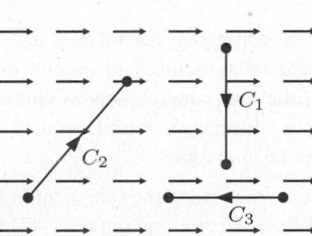

Figure 18.13

28. Compute $\int_C \vec{F} \cdot d\vec{r}$, where C is the oriented curve in Figure 18.14 and $\vec{F}$ is a vector field constant on each of the three straight segments of C:

$$\vec{F} = \begin{cases} \vec{i} & \text{on } PQ \\ 2\vec{i} - \vec{j} & \text{on } QR \\ 3\vec{i} + \vec{j} & \text{on } RS. \end{cases}$$

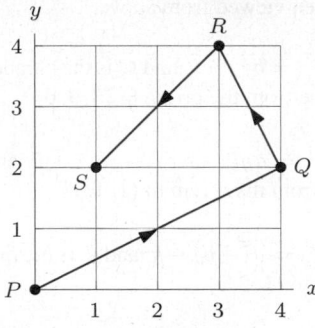

Figure 18.14

29. An object moves along the curve C in Figure 18.15 while being acted on by the force field $\vec{F}(x, y) = y\vec{i} + x^2\vec{j}$.

(a) Evaluate $\vec{F}$ at the points $(0, -1)$, $(1, -1)$, $(2, -1)$, $(3, -1)$, $(4, -1)$, $(4, 0)$, $(4, 1)$, $(4, 2)$, $(4, 3)$.
(b) Make a sketch showing the force field along C.
(c) Find the work done by $\vec{F}$ on the object.

Figure 18.15

30. Let $\vec{F}$ be the constant force field $\vec{j}$ in Figure 18.16. On which of the paths C_1, C_2, C_3 is zero work done by $\vec{F}$? Explain.

Figure 18.16

In Problems 31–35, give conditions on one or more of the constants a, b, c to ensure that the line integral $\int_C \vec{F} \cdot d\vec{r}$ has the given sign.

31. Positive for $\vec{F} = a\vec{i} + b\vec{j} + c\vec{k}$ and C is the line from the origin to $(10, 0, 0)$.

32. Positive for $\vec{F} = ay\vec{i} + c\vec{k}$ and C is the unit circle in the xy-plane, centered at the origin and oriented counterclockwise when viewed from above.

33. Negative for $\vec{F} = b\vec{j} + c\vec{k}$ and C is the parabola $y = x^2$ in the xy-plane from the origin to $(3, 9, 0)$.

34. Positive for $\vec{F} = ay\vec{i} - ax\vec{j} + (c - 1)\vec{k}$ and C is the line segment from the origin to $(1, 1, 1)$.

35. Negative for $\vec{F} = a\vec{i} + b\vec{j} - \vec{k}$ and C is the line segment from $(1, 2, 3)$ to $(1, 2, c)$.

36. (a) For each of the vector fields, $\vec{F}$, shown in Figure 18.17, sketch a curve for which the integral $\int_C \vec{F} \cdot d\vec{r}$ is positive.
   (b) For which of the vector fields is it possible to make your answer to part (a) a closed curve?

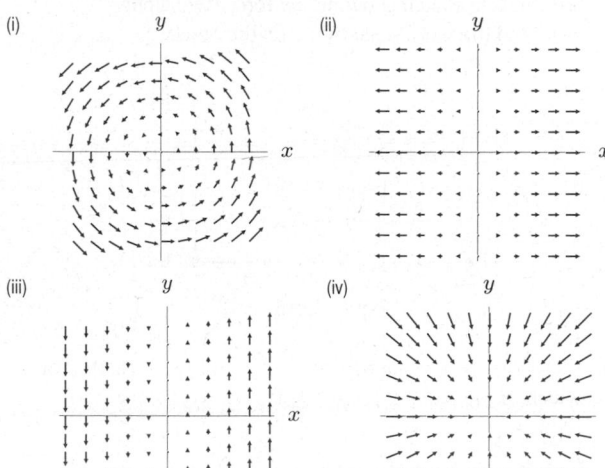

Figure 18.17

For Problems 37–41, say whether you expect the given vector field to have positive, negative, or zero circulation around the closed curve $C = C_1 + C_2 + C_3 + C_4$ in Figure 18.18. The segments C_1 and C_3 are circular arcs centered at the origin; C_2 and C_4 are radial line segments. You may find it helpful to sketch the vector field.

Figure 18.18

37. $\vec{F}(x, y) = x\vec{i} + y\vec{j}$ **38.** $\vec{F}(x, y) = -y\vec{i} + x\vec{j}$

39. $\vec{F}(x, y) = y\vec{i} - x\vec{j}$ **40.** $\vec{F}(x, y) = x^2\vec{i}$

41. $\vec{F}(x, y) = -\dfrac{y}{x^2 + y^2}\vec{i} + \dfrac{x}{x^2 + y^2}\vec{j}$

42. A horizontal square has sides of 1000 km running north-south and east-west. A wind blows from the east and decreases in magnitude toward the north at a rate of 6 meter/sec for every 500 km. Compute the circulation of the wind counterclockwise around the square.

43. Let $\vec{F} = x\vec{i} + y\vec{j}$ and let C_1 be the line joining $(1, 0)$ to $(0, 2)$ and let C_2 be the line joining $(0, 2)$ to $(-1, 0)$. Is $\int_{C_1} \vec{F} \cdot d\vec{r} = -\int_{C_2} \vec{F} \cdot d\vec{r}$? Explain.

44. The vector field $\vec{F}$ has $\|\vec{F}\| \leq 7$ everywhere and C is the circle of radius 1 centered at the origin. What is the largest possible value of $\int_C \vec{F} \cdot d\vec{r}$? The smallest possible value? What conditions lead to these values?

45. Along a curve C, a vector field $\vec{F}$ is everywhere tangent to C in the direction of orientation and has constant magnitude $\|\vec{F}\| = m$. Use the definition of the line integral to explain why

$$\int_C \vec{F} \cdot d\vec{r} = m \cdot \text{Length of } C.$$

46. Explain why the following statement is true: Whenever the line integral of a vector field around every closed curve is zero, the line integral along a curve with fixed endpoints has a constant value independent of the path taken between the endpoints.

47. Explain why the converse to the statement in Problem 46 is also true: Whenever the line integral of a vector field depends only on endpoints and not on paths, the circulation around every closed curve is zero.

In Problems 48–49, use the fact that the force of gravity on a particle of mass m at the point with position vector $\vec{r}$ is

$$\vec{F} = -\frac{GMm\vec{r}}{\|\vec{r}\|^3}$$

where and G is a constant and M is the mass of the earth.

48. Calculate the work done by the force of gravity on a particle of mass m as it moves radially from 8000 km to 10,000 km from the center of the earth.

49. Calculate the work done by the force of gravity on a particle of mass m as it moves radially from 8000 km from the center of the earth to infinitely far away.

In Problems 50–53 we explore the notion of the electric potential of an electric field $\vec{E}$. We chose a point P_0 to be the ground, that is, the potential at P_0 is zero. Then the potential $\phi(P)$ at a point P is defined to be the work done moving a particle of charge 1 coulomb from P_0 to P. (The potential does not depend on the path chosen.) Q, E are constants.

50. Write a line integral for $\phi(P)$, using the fact that the electric field acts on a particle with force $\vec{E}$.

51. Let $\vec{E} = \left(\dfrac{Q}{4\pi\epsilon}\right)\dfrac{\vec{r}}{\|\vec{r}\,\|^3}$, and let P_0 be a point a units from the origin. Describe the set of points with zero potential.

52. An equipotential surface is a surface on which the potential is constant. Describe the equipotential surfaces of $\vec{E} = \dfrac{Q}{4\pi\epsilon}\dfrac{\vec{r}}{\|\vec{r}\,\|^3}$, where the ground P_0 is chosen to be at distance a from the origin.

53. Let $\vec{E} = \dfrac{Q}{4\pi\epsilon}\dfrac{\vec{r}}{\|\vec{r}\,\|^3}$ and let the ground P_0 be chosen to be a units from the origin.

   (a) Find a formula for ϕ.
   (b) Engineers often choose the ground point to be "at infinity." Why?

Strengthen Your Understanding

In Problems 54–55, explain what is wrong with the statement.

54. If $\vec{F}$ is a vector field and C is an oriented curve, then $\int_{-C}\vec{F}\cdot d\vec{r}$ must be less than zero.

55. It is possible that for a certain vector field $\vec{F}$ and oriented path C, we have $\int_C\vec{F}\cdot d\vec{r} = 2\vec{i} - 3\vec{j}$.

In Problems 56–57, give an example of:

56. A nonzero vector field $\vec{F}$ such that $\int_C\vec{F}\cdot d\vec{r} = 0$, where C is the straight line curve from $(0,0)$ to $(1,1)$.

57. Two oriented curves C_1 and C_2 in the plane such that, for $\vec{F}(x,y) = x\vec{j}$, we have $\int_{C_1}\vec{F}\cdot d\vec{r} > 0$ and $\int_{C_2}\vec{F}\cdot d\vec{r} < 0$.

Are the statements in Problems 58–60 true or false? Explain why or give a counterexample.

58. $\int_C\vec{F}\cdot d\vec{r}$ is a vector.

59. Suppose C_1 is the unit square joining the points $(0,0)$, $(1,0)$, $(1,1)$, $(0,1)$ oriented clockwise and C_2 is the same square but traversed twice in the opposite direction. If $\int_{C_1}\vec{F}\cdot d\vec{r} = 3$, then $\int_{C_2}\vec{F}\cdot d\vec{r} = -6$.

60. The line integral of $\vec{F} = x\vec{i} + y\vec{j} = \vec{r}$ along the semicircle $x^2 + y^2 = 1, y \geq 0$, oriented counterclockwise, is zero.

Are the statements in Problems 61–67 true or false? Give reasons for your answer.

61. The line integral $\int_C\vec{F}\cdot d\vec{r}$ is a scalar.

62. If C_1 and C_2 are oriented curves, and the length of C_1 is greater than the length of C_2, then $\int_{C_1}\vec{F}\cdot d\vec{r} > \int_{C_2}\vec{F}\cdot d\vec{r}$.

63. If C is an oriented curve and $\int_C\vec{F}\cdot d\vec{r} = 0$, then $\vec{F} = \vec{0}$.

64. If $\vec{F} - \vec{i}$ is a vector field in 2-space, then $\int_C\vec{F}\cdot d\vec{r} > 0$, where C is the oriented line from $(0,0)$ to $(1,0)$.

65. If $\vec{F} = \vec{i}$ is a vector field in 2-space, then $\int_C\vec{F}\cdot d\vec{r} > 0$, where C is the oriented line from $(0,0)$ to $(0,1)$.

66. If C_1 is the upper semicircle $x^2 + y^2 = 1, y \geq 0$ and C_2 is the lower semicircle $x^2 + y^2 = 1, y \leq 0$, both oriented counterclockwise, then for any vector field $\vec{F}$, we have $\int_{C_1}\vec{F}\cdot d\vec{r} = -\int_{C_2}\vec{F}\cdot d\vec{r}$.

67. The work done by the force $\vec{F} = -y\vec{i} + x\vec{j}$ on a particle moving clockwise around the boundary of the square $-1 \leq x \leq 1, -1 \leq y \leq 1$ is positive.

18.2 COMPUTING LINE INTEGRALS OVER PARAMETERIZED CURVES

The goal of this section is to show how to use a parameterization of a curve to convert a line integral into an ordinary one-variable integral.

Using a Parameterization to Evaluate a Line Integral

Recall the definition of the line integral,

$$\int_C\vec{F}\cdot d\vec{r} = \lim_{\|\Delta\vec{r}_i\|\to 0}\sum\vec{F}(\vec{r}_i)\cdot\Delta\vec{r}_i,$$

where the $\vec{r}_i$ are the position vectors of points subdividing the curve into short pieces. Now suppose we have a smooth parameterization, $\vec{r}(t)$, of C for $a \leq t \leq b$, so that $\vec{r}(a)$ is the position vector of the starting point of the curve and $\vec{r}(b)$ is the position vector of the end. Then we can divide C into n pieces by dividing the interval $a \leq t \leq b$ into n pieces, each of size $\Delta t = (b - a)/n$. See Figures 18.19 and 18.20.

At each point $\vec{r}_i = \vec{r}(t_i)$ we want to compute

$$\vec{F}(\vec{r}_i) \cdot \Delta \vec{r}_i.$$

Figure 18.20: Corresponding subdivision of the parameterized path C

Figure 18.19: Subdivision of the interval $a \leq t \leq b$

Since $t_{i+1} = t_i + \Delta t$, the displacement vectors $\Delta \vec{r}_i$ are given by

$$\begin{aligned}
\Delta \vec{r}_i &= \vec{r}(t_{i+1}) - \vec{r}(t_i) \\
&= \vec{r}(t_i + \Delta t) - \vec{r}(t_i) \\
&= \frac{\vec{r}(t_i + \Delta t) - \vec{r}(t_i)}{\Delta t} \cdot \Delta t \\
&\approx \vec{r}\,'(t_i) \Delta t,
\end{aligned}$$

where we use the facts that Δt is small and that $\vec{r}(t)$ is differentiable to obtain the last approximation.

Therefore,

$$\int_C \vec{F} \cdot d\vec{r} \approx \sum \vec{F}(\vec{r}_i) \cdot \Delta \vec{r}_i \approx \sum \vec{F}(\vec{r}(t_i)) \cdot \vec{r}\,'(t_i) \, \Delta t.$$

Notice that $\vec{F}(\vec{r}(t_i)) \cdot \vec{r}\,'(t_i)$ is the value at t_i of a one-variable function of t, so this last sum is really a one-variable Riemann sum. In the limit as $\Delta t \to 0$, we get a definite integral:

$$\lim_{\Delta t \to 0} \sum \vec{F}(\vec{r}(t_i)) \cdot \vec{r}\,'(t_i) \, \Delta t = \int_a^b \vec{F}(\vec{r}(t)) \cdot \vec{r}\,'(t) \, dt.$$

Thus, we have the following result:

If $\vec{r}(t)$, for $a \leq t \leq b$, is a smooth parameterization of an oriented curve C and $\vec{F}$ is a vector field which is continuous on C, then

$$\int_C \vec{F} \cdot d\vec{r} = \int_a^b \vec{F}(\vec{r}(t)) \cdot \vec{r}\,'(t) \, dt.$$

In words: To compute the line integral of $\vec{F}$ over C, take the dot product of $\vec{F}$ evaluated on C with the velocity vector, $\vec{r}\,'(t)$, of the parameterization of C, then integrate along the curve.

Even though we assumed that C is smooth, we can use the same formula to compute line integrals over curves which are *piecewise smooth*, such as the boundary of a rectangle. If C is piecewise smooth, we apply the formula to each one of the smooth pieces and add the results by applying property 4 on page 963.

Example 1   Compute $\int_C \vec{F} \cdot d\vec{r}$ where $\vec{F} = (x+y)\vec{i} + y\vec{j}$ and C is the quarter unit circle, oriented counterclockwise as shown in Figure 18.21.

Figure 18.21: The vector field $\vec{F} = (x+y)\vec{i} + y\vec{j}$ and the quarter circle C

Solution   Since most of the vectors in $\vec{F}$ along C point generally in a direction opposite to the orientation of C, we expect our answer to be negative. The first step is to parameterize C by

$$\vec{r}(t) = x(t)\vec{i} + y(t)\vec{j} = \cos t\,\vec{i} + \sin t\,\vec{j}, \quad 0 \le t \le \frac{\pi}{2}.$$

Substituting the parameterization into $\vec{F}$, we get $\vec{F}(x(t), y(t)) = (\cos t + \sin t)\vec{i} + \sin t\,\vec{j}$. The vector $\vec{r}'(t) = x'(t)\vec{i} + y'(t)\vec{j} = -\sin t\,\vec{i} + \cos t\,\vec{j}$. Then

$$\int_C \vec{F} \cdot d\vec{r} = \int_0^{\pi/2} ((\cos t + \sin t)\vec{i} + \sin t\,\vec{j}) \cdot (-\sin t\,\vec{i} + \cos t\,\vec{j})\,dt$$

$$= \int_0^{\pi/2} (-\cos t \sin t - \sin^2 t + \sin t \cos t)\,dt$$

$$= \int_0^{\pi/2} -\sin^2 t\, dt = -\frac{\pi}{4} \approx -0.7854.$$

So the answer is negative, as expected.

Example 2   Consider the vector field $\vec{F} = x\vec{i} + y\vec{j}$.

(a) Suppose C_1 is the line segment joining $(1,0)$ to $(0,2)$ and C_2 is a part of a parabola with its vertex at $(0,2)$, joining the same points in the same order. (See Figure 18.22.) Verify that

$$\int_{C_1} \vec{F} \cdot d\vec{r} = \int_{C_2} \vec{F} \cdot d\vec{r}.$$

(b) If C is the triangle shown in Figure 18.23, show that $\int_C \vec{F} \cdot d\vec{r} = 0$.

Figure 18.22

Figure 18.23

Solution   (a) We parameterize C_1 by $\vec{r}(t) = (1-t)\vec{i} + 2t\vec{j}$ with $0 \le t \le 1$. Then $\vec{r}'(t) = -\vec{i} + 2\vec{j}$, so

$$\int_{C_1} \vec{F} \cdot d\vec{r} = \int_0^1 \vec{F}(1-t, 2t) \cdot (-\vec{i} + 2\vec{j})\,dt = \int_0^1 ((1-t)\vec{i} + 2t\vec{j}) \cdot (-\vec{i} + 2\vec{j})\,dt$$

$$= \int_0^1 (5t - 1)\,dt = \frac{3}{2}.$$

To parameterize C_2, we use the fact that it is part of a parabola with vertex at $(0, 2)$, so its equation is of the form $y = -kx^2 + 2$ for some k. Since the parabola crosses the x-axis at $(1, 0)$, we find that $k = 2$ and $y = -2x^2 + 2$. Therefore, we use the parameterization $\vec{r}(t) = t\vec{i} + (-2t^2 + 2)\vec{j}$ with $0 \le t \le 1$, which has $\vec{r}' = \vec{i} - 4t\vec{j}$. This traces out C_2 in reverse, since $t = 0$ gives $(0, 2)$, and $t = 1$ gives $(1, 0)$. Thus, we make $t = 0$ the upper limit of integration and $t = 1$ the lower limit:

$$\int_{C_2} \vec{F} \cdot d\vec{r} = \int_1^0 \vec{F}(t, -2t^2 + 2) \cdot (\vec{i} - 4t\vec{j}) \, dt = -\int_0^1 (t\vec{i} + (-2t^2 + 2)\vec{j}) \cdot (\vec{i} - 4t\vec{j}) \, dt$$

$$= -\int_0^1 (8t^3 - 7t) \, dt = \frac{3}{2}.$$

So the line integrals of $\vec{F}$ along C_1 and C_2 have the same value.

(b) We break $\int_C \vec{F} \cdot d\vec{r}$ into three pieces, one of which we have already computed (namely, the piece connecting $(1, 0)$ to $(0, 2)$, where the line integral has value $3/2$). The piece running from $(0, 2)$ to $(0, 0)$ can be parameterized by $\vec{r}(t) = (2 - t)\vec{j}$ with $0 \le t \le 2$. The piece running from $(0, 0)$ to $(1, 0)$ can be parameterized by $\vec{r}(t) = t\vec{i}$ with $0 \le t \le 1$. Then

$$\int_C \vec{F} \cdot d\vec{r} = \frac{3}{2} + \int_0^2 \vec{F}(0, 2 - t) \cdot (-\vec{j}) \, dt + \int_0^1 \vec{F}(t, 0) \cdot \vec{i} \, dt$$

$$= \frac{3}{2} + \int_0^2 (2 - t)\vec{j} \cdot (-\vec{j}) \, dt + \int_0^1 t\vec{i} \cdot \vec{i} \, dt$$

$$= \frac{3}{2} + \int_0^2 (t - 2) \, dt + \int_0^1 t \, dt = \frac{3}{2} + (-2) + \frac{1}{2} = 0.$$

Example 3   Let C be the closed curve consisting of the upper half-circle of radius 1 and the line forming its diameter along the x-axis, oriented counterclockwise. (See Figure 18.24.) Find $\int_C \vec{F} \cdot d\vec{r}$ where $\vec{F}(x, y) = -y\vec{i} + x\vec{j}$.

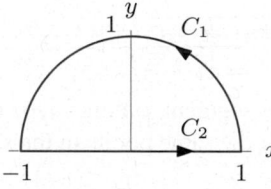

Figure 18.24: The curve $C = C_1 + C_2$ for Example 3

Solution   We write $C = C_1 + C_2$ where C_1 is the half-circle and C_2 is the line, and compute $\int_{C_1} \vec{F} \cdot d\vec{r}$ and $\int_{C_2} \vec{F} \cdot d\vec{r}$ separately. We parameterize C_1 by $\vec{r}(t) = \cos t\, \vec{i} + \sin t\, \vec{j}$, with $0 \le t \le \pi$. Then

$$\int_{C_1} \vec{F} \cdot d\vec{r} = \int_0^\pi (-\sin t\, \vec{i} + \cos t\, \vec{j}) \cdot (-\sin t\, \vec{i} + \cos t\, \vec{j}) \, dt$$

$$= \int_0^\pi (\sin^2 t + \cos^2 t) \, dt = \int_0^\pi 1 \, dt = \pi.$$

For C_2, we have $\int_{C_2} \vec{F} \cdot d\vec{r} = 0$, since the vector field $\vec{F}$ has no $\vec{i}$ component along the x-axis (where $y = 0$) and is therefore perpendicular to C_2 at all points.

Finally, we can write

$$\int_C \vec{F} \cdot d\vec{r} = \int_{C_1} \vec{F} \cdot d\vec{r} + \int_{C_2} \vec{F} \cdot d\vec{r} = \pi + 0 = \pi.$$

It is no accident that the result for $\int_{C_1} \vec{F} \cdot d\vec{r}$ is the same as the length of the curve C_1. See Problem 45 on page 966 and Problem 35 on page 973.

The next example illustrates the computation of a line integral over a path in 3-space.

Example 4   A particle travels along the helix C given by $\vec{r}(t) = \cos t\vec{i} + \sin t\vec{j} + 2t\vec{k}$ and is subject to a force $\vec{F} = x\vec{i} + z\vec{j} - xy\vec{k}$. Find the total work done on the particle by the force for $0 \le t \le 3\pi$.

Solution   The work done is given by a line integral, which we evaluate using the given parameterization:

$$\text{Work done} = \int_C \vec{F} \cdot d\vec{r} = \int_0^{3\pi} \vec{F}(\vec{r}(t)) \cdot \vec{r}'(t)\, dt$$

$$= \int_0^{3\pi} (\cos t\vec{i} + 2t\vec{j} - \cos t \sin t\vec{k}) \cdot (-\sin t\vec{i} + \cos t\vec{j} + 2\vec{k})\, dt$$

$$= \int_0^{3\pi} (-\cos t \sin t + 2t \cos t - 2\cos t \sin t)\, dt$$

$$= \int_0^{3\pi} (-3\cos t \sin t + 2t \cos t)\, dt = -4.$$

The Differential Notation $\int_C P\, dx + Q\, dy + R dz$

There is an alternative notation for line integrals that is often useful. For the vector field $\vec{F} = P(x, y, z)\vec{i} + Q(x, y, z)\vec{j} + R(x, y, z)\vec{k}$ and an oriented curve C, if we write $d\vec{r} = dx\vec{i} + dy\vec{j} + dz\vec{k}$ we have

$$\int_C \vec{F} \cdot d\vec{r} = \int_C P(x, y, z)dx + Q(x, y, z)dy + R(x, y, z)dz.$$

Example 5   Evaluate $\int_C xy\, dx - y^2\, dy$ where C is the line segment from $(0, 0)$ to $(2, 6)$.

Solution   We parameterize C by $x = t, y = 3t$, $0 \le t \le 2$. Thus, $dx = dt, dy = 3dt$, so

$$\int_C xy\, dx - y^2\, dy = \int_0^2 t(3t)dt - (3t)^2(3dt) = \int_0^2 (-24t^2)\, dt = -64.$$

Line integrals can be expressed either using vectors or using differentials. If the independent variables are distances, then visualizing a line integral in terms of dot products can be useful. However, if the independent variables are, for example, temperature and volume, then the dot product does not have physical meaning, so differentials are more natural.

Independence of Parameterization

Since there are many different ways of parameterizing a given oriented curve, you may be wondering what happens to the value of a given line integral if you choose another parameterization. The answer is that the choice of parameterization makes no difference. Since we initially defined the line integral without reference to any particular parameterization, this is exactly as we would expect.

Example 6   Consider the oriented path which is a straight-line segment L running from $(0, 0)$ to $(1, 1)$. Calculate the line integral of the vector field $\vec{F} = (3x - y)\vec{i} + x\vec{j}$ along L using each of the parameterizations

(a) $A(t) = (t, t), \quad 0 \le t \le 1,$ (b) $D(t) = (e^t - 1, e^t - 1), \quad 0 \le t \le \ln 2.$

Solution   The line L has equation $y = x$. Both $A(t)$ and $D(t)$ give a parameterization of L: each has both coordinates equal and each begins at (0,0) and ends at (1,1). Now let's calculate the line integral of the vector field $\vec{F} = (3x - y)\vec{i} + x\vec{j}$ using each parameterization.

(a) Using $A(t)$, we get

$$\int_L \vec{F} \cdot d\vec{r} = \int_0^1 ((3t - t)\vec{i} + t\vec{j}) \cdot (\vec{i} + \vec{j})\, dt = \int_0^1 3t\, dt = \frac{3t^2}{2}\Big|_0^1 = \frac{3}{2}.$$

(b) Using $D(t)$, we get

$$\int_L \vec{F} \cdot d\vec{r} = \int_0^{\ln 2} \Big(\big(3(e^t - 1) - (e^t - 1) \big) \vec{i} + (e^t - 1)\vec{j} \Big) \cdot (e^t \vec{i} + e^t \vec{j}) \, dt$$

$$= \int_0^{\ln 2} 3(e^{2t} - e^t) \, dt = 3 \left(\frac{e^{2t}}{2} - e^t \right) \Bigg|_0^{\ln 2} = \frac{3}{2}.$$

The fact that both answers are the same illustrates that the value of a line integral is independent of the parameterization of the path. Problems 38–40 at the end of this section give another way of seeing this.

Exercises and Problems for Section 18.2

Exercises

In Exercises 1–3, write $\int_C \vec{F} \cdot d\vec{r}$ in the form $\int_a^b g(t) dt$. (Give a formula for g and numbers for a and b. You do not need to evaluate the integral.)

1. $\vec{F} = y\vec{i} + x\vec{j}$ and C is the semicircle from $(0, 1)$ to $(0, -1)$ with $x > 0$.

2. $\vec{F} = x\vec{i} + z^2\vec{k}$ and C is the line from $(0, 1, 0)$ to $(2, 3, 2)$.

3. $\vec{F} = (\cos x)\vec{i} + (\cos y)\vec{j} + (\cos z)\vec{k}$ and C is the unit circle in the plane $z = 10$, centered on the z-axis and oriented counterclockwise when viewed from above.

In Exercises 4–8, find the line integral.

4. $\displaystyle\int_C (3\vec{i} + (y + 5)\vec{j}) \cdot d\vec{r}$ where C is the line from $(0, 0)$ to $(0, 3)$.

5. $\displaystyle\int_C (2x\vec{i} + 3y\vec{j}) \cdot d\vec{r}$ where C is the line from $(1, 0, 0)$ to $(5, 0, 0)$.

6. $\int_C (2y^2\vec{i} + x\vec{j}) \cdot d\vec{r}$ where C is the line segment from $(3, 1)$ to $(0, 0)$.

7. $\int_C (x\vec{i} + y\vec{j}) \cdot d\vec{r}$ where C is the semicircle with center at $(2, 0)$ and going from $(3, 0)$ to $(1, 0)$ in the region $y > 0$.

8. Find $\int_C ((x^2 + y)\vec{i} + y^3\vec{j}) \cdot d\vec{r}$ where C consists of the three line segments from $(4, 0, 0)$ to $(4, 3, 0)$ to $(0, 3, 0)$ to $(0, 3, 5)$.

In Exercises 9–23, find $\int_C \vec{F} \cdot d\vec{r}$ for the given $\vec{F}$ and C.

9. $\vec{F} = 2\vec{i} + \vec{j}$; C is the x-axis from $x = 10$ to $x = 7$.

10. $\vec{F} = 3\vec{j} - \vec{i}$; C is the line $y = x$ from $(1, 1)$ to $(5, 5)$.

11. $\vec{F} = x\vec{i} + y\vec{j}$ and C is the line from $(0, 0)$ to $(3, 3)$.

12. $\vec{F} = y\vec{i} - x\vec{j}$ and C is the right-hand side of the unit circle, starting at $(0, 1)$.

13. $\vec{F} = x^2\vec{i} + y^2\vec{j}$ and C is the line from the point $(1, 2)$ to the point $(3, 4)$.

14. $\vec{F} = -y \sin x\vec{i} + \cos x\vec{j}$ and C is the parabola $y = x^2$ between $(0, 0)$ and $(2, 4)$.

15. $\vec{F} = y^3\vec{i} + x^2\vec{j}$ and C is the line from $(0, 0)$ to $(3, 2)$.

16. $\vec{F} = 2y\vec{i} - (\sin y)\vec{j}$ counterclockwise around the unit circle C starting at the point $(1, 0)$.

17. $\vec{F} = \ln y\vec{i} + \ln x\vec{j}$ and C is the curve given parametrically by $(2t, t^3)$, for $2 \le t \le 4$.

18. $\vec{F} = x\vec{i} + 6\vec{j} - \vec{k}$, and C is the line $x = y = z$ from $(0, 0, 0)$ to $(2, 2, 2)$.

19. $\vec{F} = (2x - y + 4)\vec{i} + (5y + 3x - 6)\vec{j}$ and C is the triangle with vertices $(0, 0), (3, 0), (3, 2)$ traversed counterclockwise.

20. $\vec{F} = x\vec{i} + 2zy\vec{j} + x\vec{k}$ and C is $\vec{r} = t\vec{i} + t^2\vec{j} + t^3\vec{k}$ for $1 \le t \le 2$.

21. $\vec{F} = x^3\vec{i} + y^2\vec{j} + z\vec{k}$ and C is the line from the origin to the point $(2, 3, 4)$.

22. $\vec{F} = -y\vec{i} + x\vec{j} + 5\vec{k}$ and C is the helix $x = \cos t, y = \sin t, z = t$, for $0 \le t \le 4\pi$.

23. $\vec{F} = e^y\vec{i} + \ln(x^2 + 1)\vec{j} + \vec{k}$ and C is the circle of radius 2 centered at the origin in the yz-plane in Figure 18.25.

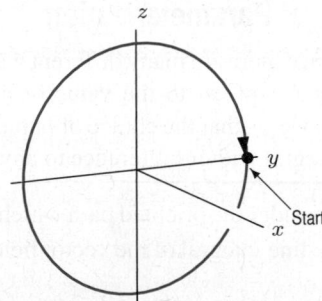

Figure 18.25

In Exercises 24–25, express the line integral $\int_C \vec{F} \cdot d\vec{r}$ in differential notation.

24. $\vec{F} = 3x\vec{i} - y \sin x\vec{j}$

25. $\vec{F} = y^2\vec{i} + z^2\vec{j} + (x^2 - 5)\vec{k}$

In Exercises 26–27, find $\vec{F}$ so that the line integral equals $\int_C \vec{F} \cdot d\vec{r}$.

26. $\int_C (x + 2y)dx + x^2 y \, dy$

27. $\int_C e^{-3y} dx - yz(\sin x)dy + (y + z)dy$

Evaluate the line integrals in Exercises 28–29.

28. $\int_C y \, dx + x \, dy$ where C is the parameterized path $x = t^2$, $y = t^3$, $1 \le t \le 5$.

29. $\int_C dx + y \, dy + z \, dz$ where C is one turn of the helix $x = \cos t$, $y = \sin t$, $z = 3t$, $0 \le t \le 2\pi$.

Evaluate the line integrals in Exercises 30–31.

30. $\int_C 3y \, dx + 4x \, dy$ where C is the straight-line path from $(1, 3)$ to $(5, 9)$.

31. $\int_C x \, dx + z \, dy - y \, dz$ where C is the circle of radius 3 in the yz plane centered at the origin, oriented counterclockwise when viewed from the positive y-axis.

Problems

32. In Example 6 on page 971 we integrated $\vec{F} = (3x - y)\vec{i} + x\vec{j}$ over two parameterizations of the line from $(0, 0)$ to $(1, 1)$, getting $3/2$ each time. Now compute the line integral along two different paths with the same endpoints, and show that the answers are different.

(a) The path (t, t^2), with $0 \le t \le 1$
(b) The path (t^2, t), with $0 \le t \le 1$

33. Curves C_1 and C_2 are parametrized as follows:

C_1 is $(x(t), y(t)) = (0, t)$ for $-1 \le t \le 1$

C_2 is $(x(t), y(t)) = (\cos t, \sin t)$ for $\frac{\pi}{2} \le t \le \frac{3\pi}{2}$.

(a) Sketch C_1 and C_2 with arrows showing their orientation.
(b) Suppose $\vec{F} = (x + 3y)\vec{i} + y\vec{j}$. Calculate $\int_C \vec{F} \cdot d\vec{r}$, where C is the curve given by $C = C_1 + C_2$.

34. Calculate the line integral of $\vec{F} = (3x - y)\vec{i} + x\vec{j}$ along the line segment L from $(0, 0)$ to $(1, 1)$ using each of the parameterizations

(a) $B(t) = (2t, 2t)$, $0 \le t \le 1/2$
(b) $C(t) = \left(\dfrac{t^2 - 1}{3}, \dfrac{t^2 - 1}{3} \right)$, $1 \le t \le 2$

35. Let $\vec{F} = -y\vec{i} + x\vec{j}$ and let C be the unit circle oriented counterclockwise.

(a) Show that $\vec{F}$ has a constant magnitude of 1 on C.
(b) Show that $\vec{F}$ is always tangent to the circle C.
(c) Show that $\int_C \vec{F} \cdot d\vec{r} = $ Length of C.

36. A spiral staircase in a building is in the shape of a helix of radius 5 meters. Between two floors of the building, the stairs make one full revolution and climb by 4 meters. A person carries a bag of groceries up two floors. The combined mass of the person and the groceries is 70 kg and the gravitational force is $70g$ downward, where g is the acceleration due to gravity. Calculate the work done by the person against gravity.

37. If C is $\vec{r} = (t + 1)\vec{i} + 2t\vec{j} + 3t\vec{k}$ for $0 \le t \le 1$, we know $\int_C \vec{F}(\vec{r}) \cdot d\vec{r} = 5$. Find the value of the integrals:

(a) $\int_1^0 \vec{F}((t + 1)\vec{i} + 2t\vec{j} + 3t\vec{k}) \cdot (\vec{i} + 2\vec{j} + 3\vec{k})dt$
(b) $\int_0^1 \vec{F}((t^2+1)\vec{i} +2t^2\vec{j} +3t^2\vec{k}) \cdot (2t\vec{i} +4t\vec{j} +6t\vec{k})dt$

(c) $\int_{-1}^1 \vec{F}((t^2 + 1)\vec{i} + 2t^2\vec{j} + 3t^2\vec{k}) \cdot (2t\vec{i} + 4t\vec{j} + 6t\vec{k})dt$

In Example 6 on page 971 two parameterizations, $A(t)$, and $D(t)$, are used to convert a line integral into a definite integral. In Problem 34, two other parameterizations, $B(t)$ and $C(t)$, are used on the same line integral. In Problems 38–40 show that two definite integrals corresponding to two of the given parameterizations are equal by finding a substitution which converts one integral to the other. This gives us another way of seeing why changing the parameterization of the curve does not change the value of the line integral.

38. $A(t)$ and $B(t)$ **39.** $A(t)$ and $C(t)$

40. $A(t)$ and $D(t)$

41. Suppose C is the line segment from the point $(0, 0)$ to the point $(4, 12)$ and $\vec{F} = xy\vec{i} + x\vec{j}$.

(a) Is $\int_C \vec{F} \cdot d\vec{r}$ greater than, less than, or equal to zero? Give a geometric explanation.
(b) A parameterization of C is $(x(t), y(t)) = (t, 3t)$ for $0 \le t \le 4$. Use this to compute $\int_C \vec{F} \cdot d\vec{r}$.
(c) Suppose a particle leaves the point $(0, 0)$, moves along the line toward the point $(4, 12)$, stops before reaching it and backs up, stops again and reverses direction, then completes its journey to the endpoint. All travel takes place along the line segment joining the point $(0, 0)$ to the point $(4, 12)$. If we call this path C', explain why $\int_{C'} \vec{F} \cdot d\vec{r} = \int_C \vec{F} \cdot d\vec{r}$.
(d) A parameterization for a path like C' is given, for $0 \le t \le 4$, by

$$(x(t), y(t)) = \left(\frac{t^3 - 6t^2 + 11t}{3}, (t^3 - 6t^2 + 11t) \right).$$

Check that this parameterization begins at the point $(0, 0)$ and ends at the point $(4, 12)$. Check also that all points of C' lie on the line segment connecting the point $(0, 0)$ to the point $(4, 12)$. What are the values of t at which the particle changes direction?
(e) Find $\int_{C'} \vec{F} \cdot d\vec{r}$ using the parameterization in part (d). Do you get the same answer as in part (b)?

Strengthen Your Understanding

In Problems 42–43, explain what is wrong with the statement.

42. For the vector field $\vec{F} = x\vec{i} - y\vec{j}$ and oriented path C parameterized by $x = \cos t$, $y = \sin t$, $0 \leq t \leq \pi/2$, we have

$$\int_C \vec{F} \cdot d\vec{r} = \int_0^{\pi/2} (\cos t\vec{i} - \sin t\vec{j}) \cdot (\cos t\vec{i} + \sin t\vec{j}) \, dt.$$

43. $\int_C 3 \, dx + 4 \, dy > 0$

In Problems 44–45, give an example of:

44. A vector field $\vec{F}$ such that, for the parameterized path $\vec{r}(t) = 3\cos t\vec{i} + 3\sin t\vec{j}$, $-\pi/2 \leq t \leq \pi/2$, the integral $\int_C \vec{F} \cdot d\vec{r}$ can be computed geometrically, without using the parameterization.

45. A parameterized path C such that, for the vector field $\vec{F}(x, y) = \sin y\vec{i}$, the integral $\int_C \vec{F} \cdot d\vec{r}$ is nonzero and can be computed geometrically, without using the parameterization.

Are the statements in Problems 46–54 true or false? Give reasons for your answer.

46. If C_1 and C_2 are oriented curves with C_2 beginning where C_1 ends, then $\int_{C_1 + C_2} \vec{F} \cdot d\vec{r} > \int_{C_1} \vec{F} \cdot d\vec{r}$.

47. The line integral $\int_C 4\vec{i} \cdot d\vec{r}$ over the curve C parameterized by $\vec{r}(t) = t\vec{i} + t^2\vec{j}$, for $0 \leq t \leq 2$, is positive.

48. If C_1 is the curve parameterized by $\vec{r}_1(t) = \cos t\vec{i} + \sin t\vec{j}$, with $0 \leq t \leq \pi$, and C_2 is the curve parameterized by $\vec{r}_2(t) = \cos t\vec{i} - \sin t\vec{j}$, $0 \leq t \leq \pi$, then for any vector field $\vec{F}$ we have $\int_{C_1} \vec{F} \cdot d\vec{r} = \int_{C_2} \vec{F} \cdot d\vec{r}$.

49. If C_1 is the curve parameterized by $\vec{r}_1(t) = \cos t\vec{i} + \sin t\vec{j}$, with $0 \leq t \leq \pi$, and C_2 is the curve parameterized by $\vec{r}_2(t) = \cos(2t)\vec{i} + \sin(2t)\vec{j}$, $0 \leq t \leq \frac{\pi}{2}$,

then for any vector field $\vec{F}$ we have $\int_{C_1} \vec{F} \cdot d\vec{r} = \int_{C_2} \vec{F} \cdot d\vec{r}$.

50. If C is the curve parameterized by $\vec{r}(t)$, for $a \leq t \leq b$ with $\vec{r}(a) = \vec{r}(b)$, then $\int_C \vec{F} \cdot d\vec{r} = 0$ for any vector field $\vec{F}$. (Note that C starts and ends at the same place.)

51. If C_1 is the line segment from $(0, 0)$ to $(1, 0)$ and C_2 is the line segment from $(0, 0)$ to $(2, 0)$, then for any vector field $\vec{F}$, we have $\int_{C_2} \vec{F} \cdot d\vec{r} = 2 \int_{C_1} \vec{F} \cdot d\vec{r}$.

52. If C is a circle of radius a, centered at the origin and oriented counterclockwise, then $\int_C 2x\vec{i} + y\vec{j} \cdot d\vec{r} = 0$.

53. If C is a circle of radius a, centered at the origin and oriented counterclockwise, then $\int_C 2y\vec{i} + x\vec{j} \cdot d\vec{r} = 0$.

54. If C_1 is the curve parameterized by $\vec{r}_1(t) = t\vec{i} + t^2\vec{j}$, with $0 \leq t \leq 2$, and C_2 is the curve parameterized by $\vec{r}_2(t) = (2 - t)\vec{i} + (2 - t)^2\vec{j}$, $0 \leq t \leq 2$, then for any vector field $\vec{F}$ we have $\int_{C_1} \vec{F} \cdot d\vec{r} = -\int_{C_2} \vec{F} \cdot d\vec{r}$.

55. If C_1 is the path parameterized by $\vec{r}_1(t) = (t, t)$, $0 \leq t \leq 1$, and if C_2 is the path parameterized by $\vec{r}_2(t) = (1 - t, 1 - t)$, $0 \leq t \leq 1$, and if $\vec{F} = x\vec{i} + y\vec{j}$, which of the following is true?

(a) $\int_{C_1} \vec{F} \cdot d\vec{r} > \int_{C_2} \vec{F} \cdot d\vec{r}$

(b) $\int_{C_1} \vec{F} \cdot d\vec{r} < \int_{C_2} \vec{F} \cdot d\vec{r}$

(c) $\int_{C_1} \vec{F} \cdot d\vec{r} = \int_{C_2} \vec{F} \cdot d\vec{r}$

56. If C_1 is the path parameterized by $\vec{r}_1(t) = (t, t)$, for $0 \leq t \leq 1$, and if C_2 is the path parameterized by $\vec{r}_2(t) = (\sin t, \sin t)$, for $0 \leq t \leq 1$, and if $\vec{F} = x\vec{i} + y\vec{j}$, which of the following is true?

(a) $\int_{C_1} \vec{F} \cdot d\vec{r} > \int_{C_2} \vec{F} \cdot d\vec{r}$

(b) $\int_{C_1} \vec{F} \cdot d\vec{r} < \int_{C_2} \vec{F} \cdot d\vec{r}$

(c) $\int_{C_1} \vec{F} \cdot d\vec{r} = \int_{C_2} \vec{F} \cdot d\vec{r}$

18.3   GRADIENT FIELDS AND PATH-INDEPENDENT FIELDS

For a function, f, of one variable, the Fundamental Theorem of Calculus tells us that the definite integral of a rate of change, f', gives the total change in f:

$$\int_a^b f'(t) \, dt = f(b) - f(a).$$

What about functions of two or more variables? The quantity that describes the rate of change is the gradient vector field. If we know the gradient of a function f, can we compute the total change in f between two points? The answer is yes, using a line integral.

Finding the Total Change in f from grad f: The Fundamental Theorem

To find the change in f between two points P and Q, we choose a smooth path C from P to Q, then divide the path into many small pieces. See Figure 18.26.

First we estimate the change in f as we move through a displacement $\Delta \vec{r}_i$ from $\vec{r}_i$ to $\vec{r}_{i+1}$. Suppose $\vec{u}$ is a unit vector in the direction of $\Delta \vec{r}_i$. Then the change in f is given by

$$f(\vec{r}_{i+1}) - f(\vec{r}_i) \approx \text{Rate of change of } f \times \text{Distance moved in direction of } \vec{u}$$

$$= f_{\vec{u}}(\vec{r}_i)\|\Delta \vec{r}_i\|$$

$$= \text{grad} f \cdot \vec{u}\,\|\Delta \vec{r}_i\|$$

$$= \text{grad} f \cdot \Delta \vec{r}_i. \qquad \text{since } \Delta \vec{r}_i = \|\Delta \vec{r}_i\|\vec{u}$$

Therefore, summing over all pieces of the path, the total change in f is given by

$$\text{Total change} = f(Q) - f(P) \approx \sum_{i=0}^{n-1} \text{grad} f(\vec{r}_i) \cdot \Delta \vec{r}_i.$$

In the limit as $\|\Delta \vec{r}_i\|$ approaches zero, this suggests the following result:

Theorem 18.1: The Fundamental Theorem of Calculus for Line Integrals

Suppose C is a piecewise smooth oriented path with starting point P and ending point Q. If f is a function whose gradient is continuous on the path C, then

$$\int_C \text{grad} f \cdot d\vec{r} = f(Q) - f(P).$$

Notice that there are many different paths from P to Q. (See Figure 18.27.) However, the value of the line integral $\int_C \text{grad} f \cdot d\vec{r}$ depends only on the endpoints of C; it does not depend on where C goes in between. Problem 61 on page 984 shows how the Fundamental Theorem for Line Integrals can be derived from the one-variable Fundamental Theorem of Calculus.

Figure 18.26: Subdivision of the path from P to Q. We estimate the change in f along $\Delta \vec{r}_i$

Figure 18.27: There are many different paths from P to Q: all give the same value of $\int_C \text{grad} f \cdot d\vec{r}$

Example 1 Suppose that grad f is everywhere perpendicular to the curve joining P and Q shown in Figure 18.28.

(a) Explain why you expect the path joining P and Q to be a contour.

(b) Using a line integral, show that $f(P) = f(Q)$.

Figure 18.28: The gradient vector field of the function f

Solution   (a) The gradient of f is everywhere perpendicular to the path from P to Q, as you expect along a contour.

(b) Consider the path from P to Q shown in Figure 18.28 and evaluate the line integral

$$\int_C \text{grad}\, f \cdot d\vec{r} = f(Q) - f(P).$$

Since grad f is everywhere perpendicular to the path, the line integral is 0. Thus, $f(Q) = f(P)$.

Example 2   Consider the vector field $\vec{F} = x\vec{i} + y\vec{j}$. In Example 2 on page 969 we calculated $\int_{C_1} \vec{F} \cdot d\vec{r}$ and $\int_{C_2} \vec{F} \cdot d\vec{r}$ over the oriented curves shown in Figure 18.29 and found they were the same. Find a scalar function f with grad $f = \vec{F}$. Hence, find an easy way to calculate the line integrals, and explain how we could have expected them to be the same.

Figure 18.29: Find the line integral of $\vec{F} = x\vec{i} + y\vec{j}$ over the curves C_1 and C_2

Solution   One possibility for f is

$$f(x, y) = \frac{x^2}{2} + \frac{y^2}{2}.$$

You can check that grad $f = x\vec{i} + y\vec{j}$. Now we can use the Fundamental Theorem to compute the line integral. Since $\vec{F} = \text{grad}\, f$ we have

$$\int_{C_1} \vec{F} \cdot d\vec{r} = \int_{C_1} \text{grad}\, f \cdot d\vec{r} = f(0, 2) - f(1, 0) = \frac{3}{2}.$$

Notice that the calculation looks exactly the same for C_2. Since the value of the integral depends only on the values of f at the endpoints, it is the same no matter what path we choose.

Path-Independent, or Conservative, Vector Fields

In the previous example, the line integral was independent of the path taken between the two (fixed) endpoints. We give vector fields whose line integrals have this property a special name.

> A vector field $\vec{F}$ is said to be **path-independent**, or **conservative**, if for any two points P and Q, the line integral $\int_C \vec{F} \cdot d\vec{r}$ has the same value along any piecewise smooth path C from P to Q lying in the domain of $\vec{F}$.

If, on the other hand, the line integral $\int_C \vec{F} \cdot d\vec{r}$ does depend on the path C joining P to Q, then $\vec{F}$ is said to be a *path-dependent* vector field.

Now suppose that $\vec{F}$ is any continuous gradient field, so $\vec{F} = \operatorname{grad} f$. If C is a path from P to Q, the Fundamental Theorem for Line Integrals tells us that

$$\int_C \vec{F} \cdot d\vec{r} = f(Q) - f(P).$$

Since the right-hand side of this equation does not depend on the path, but only on the endpoints of the path, the vector field $\vec{F}$ is path-independent. Thus, we have the following important result:

> If $\vec{F}$ is a continuous gradient vector field, then $\vec{F}$ is path-independent.

Why Do We Care About Path-Independent, or Conservative, Vector Fields?

Many of the fundamental vector fields of nature are path-independent—for example, the gravitational field and the electric field of particles at rest. The fact that the gravitational field is path-independent means that the work done by gravity when an object moves depends only on the starting and ending points and not on the path taken. For example, the work done by gravity (computed by the line integral) on a bicycle being carried to a sixth floor apartment is the same whether it is carried up the stairs in a zig-zag path or taken straight up in an elevator.

When a vector field is path-independent, we can define the *potential energy* of a body. When the body moves to another position, the potential energy changes by an amount equal to the work done by the vector field, which depends only on the starting and ending positions. If the work done had not been path-independent, the potential energy would depend both on the body's current position *and* on how it got there, making it impossible to define a useful potential energy.

Project 1 on page 1002 explains why path-independent force vector fields are also called *conservative* vector fields: When a particle moves under the influence of a conservative vector field, the *total energy* of the particle is *conserved*. It turns out that the force field is obtained from the gradient of the potential energy function.

Path-Independent Fields and Gradient Fields

We have seen that every gradient field is path-independent. What about the converse? That is, given a path-independent vector field $\vec{F}$, can we find a function f such that $\vec{F} = \operatorname{grad} f$? The answer is yes, provided that $\vec{F}$ is continuous.

How to Construct f from $\vec{F}$

First, notice that there are many different choices for f, since we can add a constant to f without changing $\operatorname{grad} f$. If we pick a fixed starting point P, then by adding or subtracting a constant to f, we can ensure that $f(P) = 0$. For any other point Q, we define $f(Q)$ by the formula

$$f(Q) = \int_C \vec{F} \cdot d\vec{r}, \quad \text{where } C \text{ is any path from } P \text{ to } Q.$$

Since $\vec{F}$ is path-independent, it does not matter which path we choose from P to Q. On the other hand, if $\vec{F}$ is not path-independent, then different choices might give different values for $f(Q)$, so f would not be a function (a function has to have a single value at each point).

We still have to show that the gradient of the function f really is $\vec{F}$; we do this on page 979. However, by constructing a function f in this manner, we have the following result:

Theorem 18.2: Path-independent Fields Are Gradient Fields

If $\vec{F}$ is a continuous path-independent vector field on an open region R, then $\vec{F} = \operatorname{grad} f$ for some f defined on R.

Combining Theorems 18.1 and 18.2, we have

A continuous vector field $\vec{F}$ defined on an open region is path-independent if and only if $\vec{F}$ is a gradient vector field.

The function f is sufficiently important that it is given a special name:

If a vector field $\vec{F}$ is of the form $\vec{F} = \operatorname{grad} f$ for some scalar function f, then f is called a **potential function** for the vector field $\vec{F}$.

Warning

Physicists use the convention that a function ϕ is a potential function for a vector field $\vec{F}$ if $\vec{F} = -\operatorname{grad} \phi$. See Problem 62 on page 984.

Example 3   Show that the vector field $\vec{F}(x, y) = y \cos x \vec{i} + (\sin x + y)\vec{j}$ is path-independent.

Solution   Let's suppose $\vec{F}$ does have a potential function f, so that $\vec{F} = \operatorname{grad} f$. This means

$$\frac{\partial f}{\partial x} = y \cos x \qquad \text{and} \qquad \frac{\partial f}{\partial y} = \sin x + y.$$

Integrating the expression for $\partial f/\partial x$ with respect to x shows that

$$f(x, y) = y \sin x + C(y) \qquad \text{where } C(y) \text{ is a function of } y \text{ only.}$$

The constant of integration here is an arbitrary function $C(y)$ of y, since $\partial(C(y))/\partial x = 0$. Differentiating this expression for $f(x, y)$ with respect to y and using $\partial f/\partial y = \sin x + y$ gives

$$\frac{\partial f}{\partial y} = \sin x + C'(y) = \sin x + y.$$

Thus, we must have $C'(y) = y$, so $g(y) = y^2/2 + A$, where A is some constant. Thus,

$$f(x, y) = y \sin x + \frac{y^2}{2} + A$$

is a potential function for $\vec{F}$. Therefore, $\vec{F}$ is path-independent.

Example 4   The gravitational field, $\vec{F}$, of an object of mass M is given by

$$\vec{F} = -\frac{GM}{r^3}\vec{r}.$$

Show that $\vec{F}$ is a gradient field by finding a potential function for $\vec{F}$.

Solution   The vector $\vec{F}$ points directly in toward the origin. If $\vec{F} = \operatorname{grad} f$, then $\vec{F}$ must be perpendicular to the level surfaces of f, so the level surfaces of f must be spheres. Also, if $\operatorname{grad} f = \vec{F}$, then

$\| \operatorname{grad} f \| = \| \vec{F} \| = GM/r^2$ is the rate of change of f in the direction toward the origin. Now, differentiating with respect to r gives the rate of change in a radially outward direction. Thus, if $w = f(x, y, z)$ we have

$$\frac{dw}{dr} = -\frac{GM}{r^2} = GM \left(-\frac{1}{r^2} \right) = GM \frac{d}{dr} \left(\frac{1}{r} \right).$$

So let's try

$$w = \frac{GM}{r} \quad \text{or} \quad f(x, y, z) = \frac{GM}{\sqrt{x^2 + y^2 + z^2}}.$$

We calculate

$$f_x = \frac{\partial}{\partial x} \frac{GM}{\sqrt{x^2 + y^2 + z^2}} = \frac{-GMx}{(x^2 + y^2 + z^2)^{3/2}},$$

$$f_y = \frac{\partial}{\partial y} \frac{GM}{\sqrt{x^2 + y^2 + z^2}} = \frac{-GMy}{(x^2 + y^2 + z^2)^{3/2}},$$

$$f_z = \frac{\partial}{\partial z} \frac{GM}{\sqrt{x^2 + y^2 + z^2}} = \frac{-GMz}{(x^2 + y^2 + z^2)^{3/2}}.$$

So

$$\operatorname{grad} f = f_x \vec{i} + f_y \vec{j} + f_z \vec{k} = \frac{-GM}{(x^2 + y^2 + z^2)^{3/2}} (x\vec{i} + y\vec{j} + z\vec{k}) = \frac{-GM}{r^3} \vec{r} = \vec{F}.$$

Our computations show that $\vec{F}$ is a gradient field and that $f = GM/r$ is a potential function for $\vec{F}$.

Path-independent vector fields are rare, but often important. Section 18.4 gives a method for determining whether a vector field has the property.

Why Path-Independent Vector Fields Are Gradient Fields: Showing grad $f = \vec{F}$

Suppose $\vec{F}$ is a path-independent vector field. On page 977 we defined the function f, which we hope will satisfy $\operatorname{grad} f = \vec{F}$, as follows:

$$f(x_0, y_0) = \int_C \vec{F} \cdot d\vec{r},$$

where C is a path from a fixed starting point P to a point $Q = (x_0, y_0)$. This integral has the same value for any path from P to Q because $\vec{F}$ is path-independent. Now we show why $\operatorname{grad} f = \vec{F}$. We consider vector fields in 2-space; the argument in 3-space is essentially the same.

First, we write the line integral in terms of the components $\vec{F}(x, y) = F_1(x, y)\vec{i} + F_2(x, y)\vec{j}$ and the components $d\vec{r} = dx\vec{i} + dy\vec{j}$:

$$f(x_0, y_0) = \int_C F_1(x, y)dx + F_2(x, y)dy.$$

We want to compute the partial derivatives of f, that is, the rate of change of f at (x_0, y_0) parallel to the axes. To do this easily, we choose a path which reaches the point (x_0, y_0) on a horizontal or vertical line segment. Let C' be a path from P which stops short of Q at a fixed point (a, b) and let L_x and L_y be the paths shown in Figure 18.30. Then we can split the line integral into three pieces. Since $d\vec{r} = \vec{j}\, dy$ on L_y and $d\vec{r} = \vec{i}\, dx$ on L_x, we have:

$$f(x_0, y_0) = \int_{C'} \vec{F} \cdot d\vec{r} + \int_{L_y} \vec{F} \cdot d\vec{r} + \int_{L_x} \vec{F} \cdot d\vec{r} = \int_{C'} \vec{F} \cdot d\vec{r} + \int_b^{y_0} F_2(a, y)dy + \int_a^{x_0} F_1(x, y_0)dx.$$

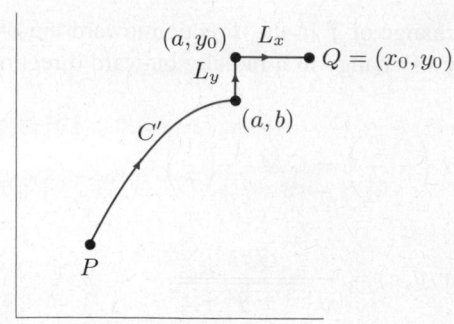

Figure 18.30: The path $C' + L_y + L_x$ is used to show $f_x = F_1$

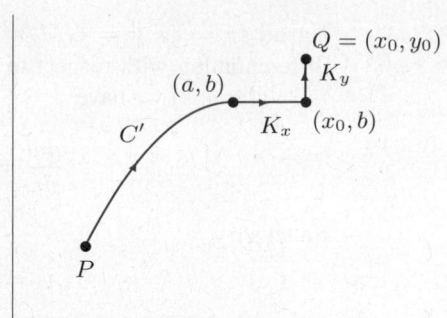

Figure 18.31: The path $C' + K_x + K_y$ is used to show $f_y = F_2$

The first two integrals do not involve x_0. Thinking of x_0 as a variable and differentiating with respect to it gives

$$f_{x_0}(x_0, y_0) = \frac{\partial}{\partial x_0} \int_{C'} \vec{F} \cdot d\vec{r} + \frac{\partial}{\partial x_0} \int_b^{y_0} F_2(a, y)dy + \frac{\partial}{\partial x_0} \int_a^{x_0} F_1(x, y_0)dx$$
$$= 0 + 0 + F_1(x_0, y_0) = F_1(x_0, y_0),$$

and thus

$$f_x(x, y) = F_1(x, y).$$

A similar calculation for y using the path from P to Q shown in Figure 18.31 gives

$$f_{y_0}(x_0, y_0) = F_2(x_0, y_0).$$

Therefore, as we claimed,

$$\text{grad } f = f_x \vec{i} + f_y \vec{j} = F_1 \vec{i} + F_2 \vec{j} = \vec{F}.$$

Exercises and Problems for Section 18.3

Exercises

1. If $\vec{F} = \text{grad}(x^2 + y^4)$, find $\int_C \vec{F} \cdot d\vec{r}$ where C is the quarter of the circle $x^2 + y^2 = 4$ in the first quadrant, oriented counterclockwise.

2. If $\vec{F} = \text{grad}(\sin(xy) + e^z)$, find $\int_C \vec{F} \cdot d\vec{r}$ where C consists of a line from $(0, 0, 0)$ to $(0, 0, 1)$ followed by a line to $(0, \sqrt{2}, 3)$, followed by a line to $(\sqrt{2}, \sqrt{5}, 2)$.

In Exercises 3–6, let C be the curve consisting of a square of side 2, centered at the origin with sides on the lines $x = \pm 1$, $y = \pm 1$ and traversed counterclockwise. What is the sign of the line integrals of the vector fields around the curve C? Indicate whether each vector field is path-independent.

5.

6.

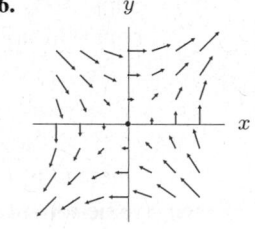

In Exercises 7–12, does the vector field appear to be path-independent (conservative)?

3.

4.

7. **8.**

9.   **10.**

11.   **12.**

13. Find f if grad $f = 2xy\vec{i} + x^2\vec{j}$.

14. Find f if grad $f = 2xy\vec{i} + (x^2 + 8y^3)\vec{j}$.

15. Find f if grad $f = (yze^{xyz} + z^2\cos(xz^2))\vec{i} + xze^{xyz}\vec{j} + (xye^{xyz} + 2xz\cos(xz^2))\vec{k}$.

16. Let $f(x, y, z) = x^2 + 2y^3 + 3z^4$ and $\vec{F} = $ grad f. Find $\int_C \vec{F} \cdot d\vec{r}$ where C consists of four line segments from $(4, 0, 0)$ to $(4, 3, 0)$ to $(0, 3, 0)$ to $(0, 3, 5)$ to $(0, 0, 5)$.

In Exercises 17–25, use the Fundamental Theorem of Line Integrals to calculate $\int_C \vec{F} \cdot d\vec{r}$ exactly.

17. $\vec{F} = 3x^2\vec{i} + 4y^3\vec{j}$ around the top of the unit circle from $(1, 0)$ to $(-1, 0)$.

18. $\vec{F} = (x + 2)\vec{i} + (2y + 3)\vec{j}$ and C is the line from $(1, 0)$ to $(3, 1)$.

19. $\vec{F} = 2\sin(2x + y)\vec{i} + \sin(2x + y)\vec{j}$ along the path consisting of a line from $(\pi, 0)$ to $(2, 5)$ followed by a line to $(5\pi, 0)$ followed by a quarter circle to $(0, 5\pi)$.

20. $\vec{F} = 2x\vec{i} - 4y\vec{j} + (2z - 3)\vec{k}$ and C is the line from $(1, 1, 1)$ to $(2, 3, -1)$.

21. $\vec{F} = x^{2/3}\vec{i} + e^{7y}\vec{j}$, and C is the unit circle oriented clockwise.

22. $\vec{F} = x^{2/3}\vec{i} + e^{7y}\vec{j}$, and C is the quarter of the unit circle in the first quadrant, traced counterclockwise from $(1, 0)$ to $(0, 1)$.

23. $\vec{F} = ye^{xy}\vec{i} + xe^{xy}\vec{j} + (\cos z)\vec{k}$ along the curve consisting of a line from $(0, 0, \pi)$ to $(1, 1, \pi)$ followed by the parabola $z = \pi x^2$ in the plane $y = 1$ to the point $(3, 1, 9\pi)$.

24. $\vec{F} = y\sin(xy)\vec{i} + x\sin(xy)\vec{j}$ and C is the parabola $y = 2x^2$ from $(1, 2)$ to $(3, 18)$.

25. $\vec{F} = 2xy^2ze^{x^2y^2z}\vec{i} + 2x^2yze^{x^2y^2z}\vec{j} + x^2y^2e^{x^2y^2z}\vec{k}$ and C is the circle of radius 1 in the plane $z = 1$, centered on the z-axis, starting at $(1, 0, 1)$ and oriented counterclockwise viewed from above.

Problems

26. Let $\vec{v} = $ grad$(x^2 + y^2)$. Consider the path C which is a line between any two of the following points: $(0, 0)$; $(5, 0)$; $(-5, 0)$; $(0, 6)$; $(0, -6)$; $(5, 4)$; $(-3, -5)$. Suppose you want to choose the path C in order to maximize $\int_C \vec{v} \cdot d\vec{r}$. What point should be the start of C? What point should be the end of C? Explain your answer.

27. Let $\vec{F} = $ grad$(2x^2 + 3y^2)$. Which one of the three paths PQ, QR, and RS in Figure 18.32 should you choose as C in order to maximize $\int_C \vec{F} \cdot d\vec{r}$?

28. Compute $\int_C \left(\cos(xy)e^{\sin(xy)}(y\vec{i} + x\vec{j}) + \vec{k} \right) \cdot d\vec{r}$ where C is the line from $(\pi, 2, 5)$ to $(0.5, \pi, 7)$.

29. The vector field $\vec{F}(x, y) = x\vec{i} + y\vec{j}$ is path-independent. Compute geometrically the line integrals over the three paths A, B, and C shown in Figure 18.33 from $(1, 0)$ to $(0, 1)$ and check that they are equal. Here A is a portion of a circle, B is a line, and C consists of two line segments meeting at a right angle.

Figure 18.32

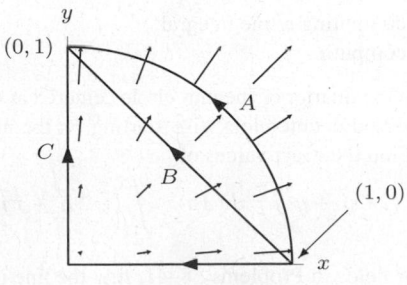

Figure 18.33

30. The vector field $\vec{F}(x,y) = x\vec{i} + y\vec{j}$ is path-independent. Compute algebraically the line integrals over the three paths A, B, and C shown in Figure 18.34 from $(0,0)$ to $(1,1)$ and check that they are equal. Here A is a line segment, B is part of the graph of $f(x) = x^2$, and C consists of two line segments meeting at a right angle.

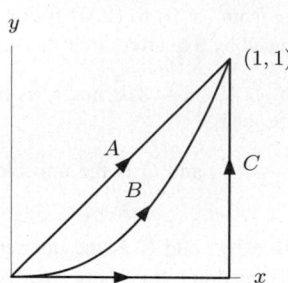

Figure 18.34

In Problems 31–34, decide whether the vector field could be a gradient vector field. Justify your answer.

31. $\vec{F}(x,y) = x\vec{i}$

32. $\vec{G}(x,y) = (x^2 - y^2)\vec{i} - 2xy\vec{j}$

33. $\vec{F}(\vec{r}) = \vec{r}/\|\vec{r}\|^3$,   where $\vec{r} = x\vec{i} + y\vec{j} + z\vec{k}$

34. $\vec{F}(x,y,z) = \dfrac{-z}{\sqrt{x^2+z^2}}\vec{i} + \dfrac{y}{\sqrt{x^2+z^2}}\vec{j} + \dfrac{x}{\sqrt{x^2+z^2}}\vec{k}$

35. If $\vec{F}(x,y,z) = 2xe^{x^2+yz}\vec{i} + ze^{x^2+yz}\vec{j} + ye^{x^2+yz}\vec{k}$, find exactly the line integral of $\vec{F}$ along the curve consisting of the two half circles in the plane $z = 0$ in Figure 18.35.

Figure 18.35

36. Let $\operatorname{grad} f = 2xe^{x^2}\sin y\vec{i} + e^{x^2}\cos y\vec{j}$. Find the change in f between $(0,0)$ and $(1, \pi/2)$:

(a) By computing a line integral.
(b) By computing f.

37. Let C be the quarter of the unit circle centered at the origin, traversed counterclockwise starting on the negative x-axis. Find the exact values of

(a) $\displaystyle\int_C (2\pi x\vec{i} + y^2\vec{j}) \cdot d\vec{r}$ **(b)** $\displaystyle\int_C (-2y\vec{i} + x\vec{j}) \cdot d\vec{r}$

For the vector fields in Problems 38–41, find the line integral along the curve C from the origin along the x-axis to the point $(3, 0)$ and then counterclockwise around the circumference of the circle $x^2 + y^2 = 9$ to the point $(3/\sqrt{2}, 3/\sqrt{2})$.

38. $\vec{F} = x\vec{i} + y\vec{j}$

39. $\vec{H} = -y\vec{i} + x\vec{j}$

40. $\vec{F} = y(x+1)^{-1}\vec{i} + \ln(x+1)\vec{j}$

41. $\vec{G} = (ye^{xy} + \cos(x+y))\vec{i} + (xe^{xy} + \cos(x+y))\vec{j}$

42. Let C be the helix $x = \cos t$, $y = \sin t$, $z = t$ for $0 \le t \le 1.25\pi$. Find $\int_C \vec{F} \cdot d\vec{r}$ exactly for

$$\vec{F} = yz^2 e^{xyz^2}\vec{i} + xz^2 e^{xyz^2}\vec{j} + 2xyz e^{xyz^2}\vec{k}.$$

43. Let $\vec{F} = 2x\vec{i} + 2y\vec{j} + 2z\vec{k}$ and $\vec{G} = (2x + y)\vec{i} + 2y\vec{j} + 2z\vec{k}$. Let C be the line from the origin to the point $(1, 5, 9)$. Find $\int_C \vec{F} \cdot d\vec{r}$ and use the result to find $\int_C \vec{G} \cdot d\vec{r}$.

44. (a) If $\vec{F} = ye^x\vec{i} + e^x\vec{j}$, explain how the Fundamental Theorem of Line Integrals enables you to calculate $\int_C \vec{F} \cdot d\vec{r}$ where C is any curve going from the point $(1, 2)$ to the point $(3, 7)$. Explain why it does not matter how the curve goes.

(b) If C is the line from the point $(1, 2)$ to the point $(3, 7)$, calculate the line integral in part (a) without using the Fundamental Theorem.

45. Calculate the line integral $\int_C \vec{F} \cdot d\vec{r}$ exactly, where C is the curve from P to Q in Figure 18.36 and

$$\vec{F} = \sin\left(\frac{x}{2}\right)\sin\left(\frac{y}{2}\right)\vec{i} - \cos\left(\frac{x}{2}\right)\cos\left(\frac{y}{2}\right)\vec{j}.$$

The curves PR, RS and SQ are trigonometric functions of period 2π and amplitude 1.

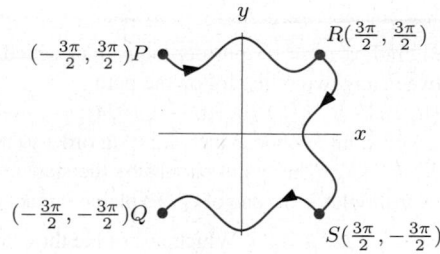

Figure 18.36

46. The domain of $f(x,y)$ is the xy-plane; values of f are in Table 18.1. Find $\int_C \operatorname{grad} f \cdot d\vec{r}$, where C is

(a) A line from $(0, 2)$ to $(3, 4)$.
(b) A circle of radius 1 centered at $(1, 2)$ traversed counterclockwise.

Table 18.1

$y \backslash x$	0	1	2	3	4
0	53	57	59	58	56
1	56	58	59	59	57
2	57	58	59	60	59
3	59	60	61	62	61
4	62	63	65	66	69

47. Figure 18.37 shows the vector field $\vec{F}(x, y) = x\vec{j}$.

(a) Find paths C_1, C_2, and C_3 from P to Q such that

$$\int_{C_1} \vec{F} \cdot d\vec{r} = 0, \quad \int_{C_2} \vec{F} \cdot d\vec{r} > 0, \quad \int_{C_3} \vec{F} \cdot d\vec{r} < 0.$$

(b) Is $\vec{F}$ a gradient field? Explain.

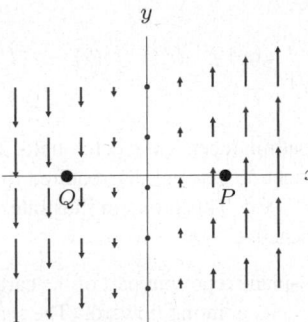

Figure 18.37

48. (a) Figure 18.38 shows level curves of $f(x, y)$. Sketch a vector at P in the direction of grad f.

(b) Is the length of grad f at P longer, shorter, or the same length as the length of grad f at Q?

(c) If C is a curve going from P to Q, evaluate $\int_C \text{grad } f \cdot d\vec{r}$.

Figure 18.38

49. Consider the line integrals, $\int_{C_i} \vec{F} \cdot d\vec{r}$, for $i = 1, 2, 3, 4$, where C_i is the path from P_i to Q_i shown in Figure 18.39 and $\vec{F} = \text{grad } f$. Level curves of f are also shown in Figure 18.39.

(a) Which of the line integral(s) is (are) zero?

(b) Arrange the four line integrals in ascending order (from least to greatest).

(c) Two of the nonzero line integrals have equal and opposite values. Which are they? Which is negative and which is positive?

Figure 18.39

50. Consider the vector field $\vec{F}$ shown in Figure 18.40.

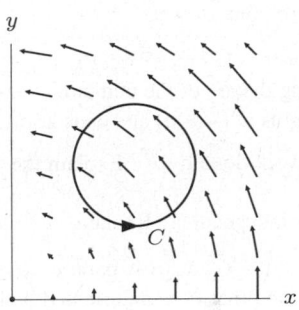

Figure 18.40

(a) Is $\int_C \vec{F} \cdot d\vec{r}$ positive, negative, or zero?

(b) From your answer to part (a), can you determine whether or not $\vec{F} = \text{grad } f$ for some function f?

(c) Which of the following formulas best fits $\vec{F}$?

$$\vec{F}_1 = \frac{x}{x^2 + y^2}\vec{i} + \frac{y}{x^2 + y^2}\vec{j},$$

$$\vec{F}_2 = -y\vec{i} + x\vec{j},$$

$$\vec{F}_3 = \frac{-y}{(x^2 + y^2)^2}\vec{i} + \frac{x}{(x^2 + y^2)^2}\vec{j}.$$

51. If $\vec{F}$ is a path-independent vector field, with $\int_{(0,0)}^{(1,0)} \vec{F} \cdot d\vec{r} = 5.1$ and $\int_{(1,0)}^{(1,1)} \vec{F} \cdot d\vec{r} = 3.2$ and $\int_{(0,1)}^{(1,1)} \vec{F} \cdot d\vec{r} = 4.7$, find

$$\int_{(0,1)}^{(0,0)} \vec{F} \cdot d\vec{r}.$$

52. The path C is a line segment of length 10 in the plane starting at $(2, 1)$. For $f(x, y) = 3x + 4y$, consider

$$\int_C \text{grad } f \cdot d\vec{r}.$$

(a) Where should the other end of the line segment C be placed to maximize the value of the integral?

(b) What is the maximum value of the integral?

53. Let $\vec{r} = x\vec{i} + y\vec{j} + z\vec{k}$ and $\vec{a} = a_1\vec{i} + a_2\vec{j} + a_3\vec{k}$, a constant vector.

   (a) Find $\text{grad}(\vec{r} \cdot \vec{a})$
   (b) Let C be a path from the origin to the point with position vector $\vec{r}_0$. Find $\int_C \text{grad}(\vec{r} \cdot \vec{a}) \cdot d\vec{r}$.
   (c) If $\|\vec{r}_0\| = 10$, what is the maximum possible value of $\int_C \text{grad}(\vec{r} \cdot \vec{a}) \cdot d\vec{r}$? Explain.

54. The force exerted by gravity on a refrigerator of mass m is $\vec{F} = -mg\vec{k}$.

   (a) Find the work done against this force in moving from the point $(1, 0, 0)$ to the point $(1, 0, 2\pi)$ along the curve $x = \cos t, y = \sin t, z = t$ by calculating a line integral.
   (b) Is $\vec{F}$ conservative (that is, path independent)? Give a reason for your answer.

55. A particle subject to a force $\vec{F}(x, y) = y\vec{i} - x\vec{j}$ moves clockwise along the arc of the unit circle, centered at the origin, that begins at $(-1, 0)$ and ends at $(0, 1)$.

   (a) Find the work done by $\vec{F}$. Explain the sign of your answer.
   (b) Is $\vec{F}$ path-independent? Explain.

56. Suppose $\vec{F}(x, y) - \vec{G}(x, y)$ is parallel to $\text{grad}\, h(x, y)$ at every point, and that C is an oriented path from P to Q lying entirely on a contour of h.

   (a) Show that $\int_C \vec{F} \cdot d\vec{r} = \int_C \vec{G} \cdot d\vec{r}$.
   (b) If $\vec{G} = \text{grad}\, \phi$, show that $\int_C \vec{F} \cdot d\vec{r} = \phi(Q) - \phi(P)$. This result can be useful when $\vec{F}$ is not a gradient field.

In Problems 57–60, let $\vec{F} = y\vec{i} + 2x\vec{j}$.
   (a) Show that $\vec{F} - \text{grad}\, \phi$ is parallel to $\text{grad}\, h$.
   (b) Use ϕ and the Fundamental Theorem of Calculus for Line Integrals to evaluate $\int_C \vec{F} \cdot d\vec{r}$, where C is the oriented path on a contour of h from P to Q.

57. $\phi = xy$, $h = y$, $P = (3, 10)$, $Q = (8, 10)$

58. $\phi = 2xy$, $h = x$, $P = (3, 5)$, $Q = (3, 10)$

59. $\phi = 2x^3/3 + xy$, $h = y - x^2$, $P = (0, 4)$, $Q = (6, 40)$

60. $\phi = x^2/2 + 3xy + y^2$, $h = x + y$, $P = (10, 30)$, $Q = (20, 20)$

61. In this problem, we see how the Fundamental Theorem for Line Integrals can be derived from the Fundamental Theorem for ordinary definite integrals. Suppose that $(x(t), y(t))$, for $a \leq t \leq b$, is a parameterization of C, with endpoints $P = (x(a), y(a))$ and $Q = (x(b), y(b))$. The values of f along C are given by the single variable function $h(t) = f(x(t), y(t))$.

   (a) Use the chain rule to show that
   $$h'(t) = f_x(x(t), y(t))x'(t) + f_y(x(t), y(t))y'(t).$$
   (b) Use the Fundamental Theorem of Calculus applied to $h(t)$ to show

   $$\int_C \text{grad}\, f \cdot d\vec{r} = f(Q) - f(P).$$

62. Let $\vec{F}$ be a path-independent vector field. In physics, the potential function ϕ is usually required to satisfy the equation $\vec{F} = -\nabla\phi$. This problem illustrates the significance of the negative sign.[1]

   (a) Let the xy-plane represent part of the earth's surface with the z-axis pointing upward. (The scale is small enough that a flat plane is a good approximation to the earth's surface.) Let $\vec{r} = x\vec{i} + y\vec{j} + z\vec{k}$, with $z \geq 0$ and x, y, z in meters, be the position vector of a rock of unit mass. The gravitational potential energy function for the rock is $\phi(x, y, z) = gz$, where $g \approx 9.8$ m/sec^2. Describe in words the level surfaces of ϕ. Does the potential energy increase or decrease with height above the earth?
   (b) What is the relation between the gravitational vector, $\vec{F}$, and the vector $\nabla\phi$? Explain the significance of the negative sign in the equation $\vec{F} = -\nabla\phi$.

63. An *ideal electric dipole* consists of two equal and opposite charges separated by a small distance and is represented by a dipole moment vector $\vec{p}$. The electric field $\vec{D}$, at the point with position vector $\vec{r}$, due to an ideal electric dipole located at the origin is given by

   $$\vec{D}(\vec{r}) = 3\frac{(\vec{r} \cdot \vec{p})\vec{r}}{\|\vec{r}\|^5} - \frac{\vec{p}}{\|\vec{r}\|^3}.$$

   (a) Check that φ is a potential function for $\vec{D}$, in the sense that $\vec{D} = -\text{grad}\, \varphi$, where

   $$\varphi(\vec{r}) = \frac{\vec{p} \cdot \vec{r}}{\|\vec{r}\|^3}.$$

   (b) Is $\vec{D}$ a path-independent vector field?

Strengthen Your Understanding

In Problems 64–66, explain what is wrong with the statement.

64. If $\vec{F}$ is a gradient field and C is an oriented path from point P to point Q, then $\int_C \vec{F} \cdot d\vec{r} = \vec{F}(Q) - \vec{F}(P)$.

65. Given any vector field $\vec{F}$ and a point P, the function $f(Q) = \int_C \vec{F} \cdot d\vec{r}$, where C is a path from P to Q, is a potential function for $\vec{F}$.

---

[1] Adapted from V.I. Arnold, *Mathematical Methods of Classical Mechanics*, 2nd edition, Graduate Texts in Mathematics, Springer, 1989. Potential energy is also discussed in Project 1 on page 1002.

66. If a vector field $\vec{F}$ is not a gradient vector field, then $\int_C \vec{F} \cdot d\vec{r}$ can't be evaluated.

In Problems 67–68, give an example of:

67. A vector field $\vec{F}$ such that $\int_C \vec{F} \cdot d\vec{r} = 100$, for every oriented path C from $(0, 0)$ to $(1, 2)$.

68. A path-independent vector field.

In Problems 69–72, each of the statements is *false*. Explain why or give a counterexample.

69. If $\int_C \vec{F} \cdot d\vec{r} = 0$ for one particular closed path C, then $\vec{F}$ is path-independent.

70. $\int_C \vec{F} \cdot d\vec{r}$ is the total change in $\vec{F}$ along C.

71. If the vector fields $\vec{F}$ and $\vec{G}$ have $\int_C \vec{F} \cdot d\vec{r} = \int_C \vec{G} \cdot d\vec{r}$ for a particular path C, then $\vec{F} = \vec{G}$.

72. If the total change of a function f along a curve C is zero, then C must be a contour of f.

Are the statements in Problems 73–74 true or false? Explain why or give a counterexample.

73. The fact that the line integral of a vector field $\vec{F}$ is zero around the unit circle $x^2 + y^2 = 1$ means that $\vec{F}$ must be a gradient vector field.

74. If C is the line segment that starts at $(0, 0)$ and ends at (a, b) then $\int_C (x\vec{i} + y\vec{j}) \cdot d\vec{r} = \frac{1}{2}(a^2 + b^2)$.

Are the statements in Problems 75–83 true or false? Give reasons for your answer.

75. The circulation of any vector field $\vec{F}$ around any closed curve C is zero.

76. If $\vec{F} = \operatorname{grad} f$, then $\vec{F}$ is path-independent.

77. If $\vec{F}$ is path-independent, then $\int_{C_1} \vec{F} \cdot d\vec{r} = \int_{C_2} \vec{F} \cdot d\vec{r}$, where C_1 and C_2 are any paths.

78. The line integral $\int_C \vec{F} \cdot d\vec{r}$ is the total change of $\vec{F}$ along C.

79. If $\vec{F}$ is path-independent, then there is a potential function for $\vec{F}$.

80. If $f(x, y) = e^{\cos(xy)}$, and C_1 is the upper semicircle $x^2 + y^2 = 1$ from $(-1, 0)$ to $(1, 0)$, and C_2 is the line from $(-1, 0)$ to $(1, 0)$, then $\int_{C_1} \operatorname{grad} f \cdot d\vec{r} = \int_{C_2} \operatorname{grad} f \cdot d\vec{r}$.

81. If $\vec{F}$ is path-independent, and C is any closed curve, then $\int_C \vec{F} \cdot d\vec{r} = 0$.

82. The vector field $\vec{F}(x, y) = y^2\vec{i} + k\vec{j}$, where k is constant, is a gradient field.

83. If $\int_C \vec{F} \cdot d\vec{r} = 0$, where C is any circle of the form $x^2 + y^2 = a^2$, then $\vec{F}$ is path-independent.

18.4 PATH-DEPENDENT VECTOR FIELDS AND GREEN'S THEOREM

Suppose we are given a vector field but are not told whether it is path-independent. How can we tell if it has a potential function, that is, if it is a gradient field?

How to Tell If a Vector Field Is Path-Dependent Using Line Integrals

One way to decide if a vector field is path-dependent is to find two paths with the same endpoints such that the line integrals of the vector field along the two paths have different values.

Example 1 Is the vector field $\vec{G}$ shown in Figure 18.41 path-independent? At any point $\vec{G}$ has magnitude equal to the distance from the origin and direction perpendicular to the line joining the point to the origin.

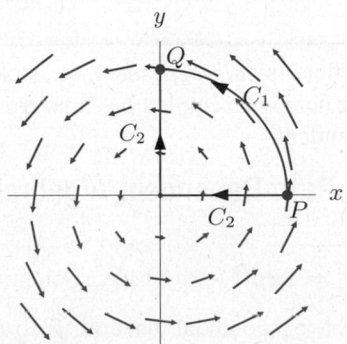

Figure 18.41: Is this vector field path-independent?

Solution   We choose $P = (1, 0)$ and $Q = (0, 1)$ and two paths between them: C_1, a quarter circle of radius 1, and C_2, formed by parts of the x- and y-axes. (See Figure 18.41.)

Along C_1, the line integral $\int_{C_1} \vec{G} \cdot d\vec{r} > 0$, since $\vec{G}$ points in the direction of the curve. Along C_2, however, we have $\int_{C_2} \vec{G} \cdot d\vec{r} = 0$, since $\vec{G}$ is perpendicular to C_2 everywhere. Thus, $\vec{G}$ is not path-independent.

Path-Dependent Fields and Circulation

Notice that the vector field in the previous example has nonzero circulation around the origin. What can we say about the circulation of a general path-independent vector field $\vec{F}$ around a closed curve, C? Suppose C is a *simple* closed curve, that is, a closed curve that does not cross itself. If P and Q are any two points on the path, then we can think of C (oriented as shown in Figure 18.42) as made up of the path C_1 followed by $-C_2$. Since $\vec{F}$ is path-independent, we know that

$$\int_{C_1} \vec{F} \cdot d\vec{r} = \int_{C_2} \vec{F} \cdot d\vec{r}.$$

Thus, we see that the circulation around C is zero:

$$\int_C \vec{F} \cdot d\vec{r} = \int_{C_1} \vec{F} \cdot d\vec{r} + \int_{-C_2} \vec{F} \cdot d\vec{r} = \int_{C_1} \vec{F} \cdot d\vec{r} - \int_{C_2} \vec{F} \cdot d\vec{r} = 0.$$

If the closed curve C does cross itself, we break it into simple closed curves as shown in Figure 18.43 and apply the same argument to each one.

Now suppose we know that the line integral around any closed curve is zero. For any two points, P and Q, with two paths, C_1 and C_2, between them, create a closed curve, C, as in Figure 18.42. Since the circulation around this closed curve, C, is zero, the line integrals along the two paths, C_1 and C_2, are equal.[2] Thus, $\vec{F}$ is path-independent.

Figure 18.42: A simple closed curve C broken into two pieces, C_1 and C_2

Figure 18.43: A curve C which crosses itself can be broken into simple closed curves

Thus, we have the following result:

A vector field is path-independent if and only if $\displaystyle\int_C \vec{F} \cdot d\vec{r} = 0$ for every closed curve C.

Hence, to see if a field is *path-dependent*, we look for a closed path with nonzero circulation. For instance, the vector field in Example 1 has nonzero circulation around a circle around the origin, showing it is path-dependent.

How to Tell If a Vector Field Is Path-Dependent Algebraically: The Curl

Example 2   Does the vector field $\vec{F} = 2xy\vec{i} + xy\vec{j}$ have a potential function? If so, find it.

Solution   Let's suppose $\vec{F}$ does have a potential function, f, so $\vec{F} = \text{grad } f$. This means that

$$\frac{\partial f}{\partial x} = 2xy \quad \text{and} \quad \frac{\partial f}{\partial y} = xy.$$

---

[2]A similar argument is used in Problems 46 and 47 on page 966.

Integrating the expression for $\partial f / \partial x$ shows that we must have

$$f(x, y) = x^2 y + C(y) \qquad \text{where } C(y) \text{ is a function of } y.$$

Differentiating this expression for $f(x, y)$ with respect to y and using the fact that $\partial f / \partial y = xy$, we get

$$\frac{\partial f}{\partial y} = x^2 + C'(y) = xy.$$

Thus, we must have

$$C'(y) = xy - x^2.$$

But this expression for $C'(y)$ is impossible because $C'(y)$ is a function of y alone. This argument shows that there is no potential function for the vector field $\vec{F}$.

Is there an easier way to see that a vector field has no potential function, other than by trying to find the potential function and failing? The answer is yes. First we look at a 2-dimensional vector field $\vec{F} = F_1 \vec{i} + F_2 \vec{j}$. If $\vec{F}$ is a gradient field, then there is a potential function f such that

$$\vec{F} = F_1 \vec{i} + F_2 \vec{j} = \frac{\partial f}{\partial x} \vec{i} + \frac{\partial f}{\partial y} \vec{j}.$$

Thus,

$$F_1 = \frac{\partial f}{\partial x} \quad \text{and} \quad F_2 = \frac{\partial f}{\partial y}.$$

Let us assume that f has continuous second partial derivatives. Then, by the equality of mixed partial derivatives,

$$\frac{\partial F_1}{\partial y} = \frac{\partial^2 f}{\partial y \partial x} = \frac{\partial^2 f}{\partial x \partial y} = \frac{\partial F_2}{\partial x}.$$

Thus, we have the following result:

If $\vec{F}(x, y) = F_1 \vec{i} + F_2 \vec{j}$ is a gradient vector field with continuous partial derivatives, then

$$\frac{\partial F_2}{\partial x} - \frac{\partial F_1}{\partial y} = 0.$$

If $\vec{F}(x, y) = F_1 \vec{i} + F_2 \vec{j}$ is an arbitrary vector field, then we define the 2-dimensional or scalar **curl** of the vector field $\vec{F}$ to be

$$\frac{\partial F_2}{\partial x} - \frac{\partial F_1}{\partial y}.$$

Notice that we now know that if $\vec{F}$ is a gradient field, then its curl is 0. We do not (yet) know whether the converse is true. (That is: If the curl is 0, does $\vec{F}$ have to be a gradient field?) However, the curl already enables us to show that a vector field is *not* a gradient field.

Example 3   Show that $\vec{F} = 2xy \vec{i} + xy \vec{j}$ cannot be a gradient vector field.

Solution   We have $F_1 = 2xy$ and $F_2 = xy$. Since $\partial F_1 / \partial y = 2x$ and $\partial F_2 / \partial x = y$, in this case

$$\partial F_2 / \partial x - \partial F_1 / \partial y \neq 0$$

so $\vec{F}$ cannot be a gradient field.

Green's Theorem

We now have two ways of seeing that a vector field $\vec{F}$ in the plane is path-dependent. We can evaluate $\int_C \vec{F} \cdot d\vec{r}$ for some closed curve and find it is not zero, or we can show that $\partial F_2/\partial x - \partial F_1/\partial y \neq 0$. It's natural to think that

$$\int_C \vec{F} \cdot d\vec{r} \quad \text{and} \quad \frac{\partial F_2}{\partial x} - \frac{\partial F_1}{\partial y}$$

might be related. The relation is called Green's Theorem.

Theorem 18.3: Green's Theorem

Suppose C is a piecewise smooth simple closed curve that is the boundary of a region R in the plane and oriented so that the region is on the left as we move around the curve. See Figure 18.44. Suppose $\vec{F} = F_1 \vec{i} + F_2 \vec{j}$ is a smooth vector field on an open region containing R and C. Then

$$\int_C \vec{F} \cdot d\vec{r} = \int_R \left(\frac{\partial F_2}{\partial x} - \frac{\partial F_1}{\partial y} \right) dx\, dy.$$

The online supplement at www.wiley.com/college/hughes-hallett contains a proof of Green's Theorem with different, but equivalent, conditions on the region R.

We first prove Green's Theorem in the case where the region R is the rectangle $a \leq x \leq b, c \leq y \leq d$. Figure 18.45 shows the boundary of R divided into four curves.

On C_1, where $y = c$ and $dy = 0$, we have $d\vec{r} = dx\vec{i}$ and thus

$$\int_{C_1} \vec{F} \cdot d\vec{r} = \int_a^b F_1(x, c)\, dx.$$

Similarly, on C_3 where $y = d$ we have

$$\int_{C_3} \vec{F} \cdot d\vec{r} = \int_b^a F_1(x, d)\, dx = -\int_a^b F_1(x, d)\, dx.$$

Hence

$$\int_{C_1+C_3} \vec{F} \cdot d\vec{r} = \int_a^b F_1(x, c)\, dx - \int_a^b F_1(x, d)\, dx = -\int_a^b \left(F_1(x, d) - F_1(x, c) \right) dx.$$

By the Fundamental Theorem of Calculus,

$$F_1(x, d) - F_1(x, c) = \int_c^d \frac{\partial F_1}{\partial y}\, dy$$

and therefore

$$\int_{C_1+C_3} \vec{F} \cdot d\vec{r} = -\int_a^b \int_c^d \frac{\partial F_1}{\partial y}\, dy\, dx = -\int_c^d \int_a^b \frac{\partial F_1}{\partial y}\, dx\, dy.$$

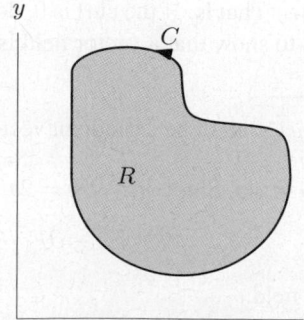

Figure 18.44: Boundary C oriented with R on the left

Along the curve C_2, where $x = b$, and the curve C_4, where $x = a$, we get, by a similar argument,

$$\int_{C_2+C_4} \vec{F} \cdot d\vec{r} = \int_c^d (F_2(b, y) - F_2(a, y))\, dy = \int_c^d \int_a^b \frac{\partial F_2}{\partial x}\, dx\, dy.$$

Adding the line integrals over $C_1 + C_3$ and $C_2 + C_4$, we get

$$\int_C \vec{F} \cdot d\vec{r} = \int_R \left(\frac{\partial F_2}{\partial x} - \frac{\partial F_1}{\partial y} \right) dx\, dy.$$

If R is not a rectangle, we subdivide it into small rectangular pieces as shown in Figure 18.46. The contribution to the integral of the non-rectangular pieces can be made as small as we like by making the subdivision fine enough. The double integrals over each piece add up to the double integral over the whole region R. Figure 18.47 shows how the circulations around adjacent pieces cancel along the common edge, so the circulations around all the pieces add up to the circulation around the boundary C. Since Green's Theorem holds for the rectangular pieces, it holds for the whole region R.

Figure 18.45: The boundary of a rectangle broken into C_1, C_2, C_3, C_4

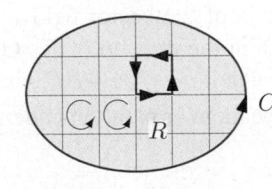

Figure 18.46: Region R bounded by a closed curve C and split into many small regions, ΔR

Figure 18.47: Two adjacent small closed curves

Example 4   Use Green's Theorem to evaluate $\int_C \left(y^2 \vec{i} + x \vec{j} \right) \cdot d\vec{r}$ where C is the counterclockwise path around the perimeter of the rectangle $0 \le x \le 2$, $0 \le y \le 3$.

Solution   We have $F_1 = y^2$ and $F_2 = x$. By Green's Theorem

$$\int_C \left(y^2 \vec{i} + x \vec{j} \right) \cdot d\vec{r} = \int_R \left(\frac{\partial F_2}{\partial x} - \frac{\partial F_1}{\partial y} \right) dx\, dy = \int_0^3 \int_0^2 (1 - 2y)\, dx\, dy = -12.$$

The Curl Test for Vector Fields in the Plane

We already know that if $\vec{F} = F_1 \vec{i} + F_2 \vec{j}$ is a gradient field with continuous partial derivatives, then

$$\frac{\partial F_2}{\partial x} - \frac{\partial F_1}{\partial y} = 0.$$

Now we show that the converse is true if the domain of $\vec{F}$ has no holes in it. This means that we assume that

$$\frac{\partial F_2}{\partial x} - \frac{\partial F_1}{\partial y} = 0$$

and show that $\vec{F}$ is path-independent. If C is any oriented simple closed curve in the domain of $\vec{F}$ and R is the region inside C, then

$$\int_R \left(\frac{\partial F_2}{\partial x} - \frac{\partial F_1}{\partial y} \right) dx\, dy = 0$$

since the integrand is identically 0. Therefore, by Green's Theorem,

$$\int_C \vec{F} \cdot d\vec{r} = \int_R \left(\frac{\partial F_2}{\partial x} - \frac{\partial F_1}{\partial y} \right) dx\, dy = 0.$$

Thus, $\vec{F}$ is path-independent and therefore a gradient field. This argument is valid for every closed curve, C, provided the region R is entirely in the domain of $\vec{F}$. Thus, we have the following result:

The Curl Test for Vector Fields in 2-Space

Suppose $\vec{F} = F_1\vec{i} + F_2\vec{j}$ is a vector field with continuous partial derivatives such that
- The domain of $\vec{F}$ has the property that every closed curve in it encircles a region that lies entirely within the domain. In particular, the domain of $\vec{F}$ has no holes.
- $\dfrac{\partial F_2}{\partial x} - \dfrac{\partial F_1}{\partial y} = 0$.

Then $\vec{F}$ is path-independent, so $\vec{F}$ is a gradient field and has a potential function.

Why Are Holes in the Domain of the Vector Field Important?

The reason for assuming that the domain of the vector field $\vec{F}$ has no holes is to ensure that the region R inside C is actually contained in the domain of $\vec{F}$. Otherwise, we cannot apply Green's Theorem. The next two examples show that if $\partial F_2/\partial x - \partial F_1/\partial y = 0$ but the domain of $\vec{F}$ contains a hole, then $\vec{F}$ can either be path-independent or path-dependent.

Example 5   Let $\vec{F}$ be the vector field given by $\vec{F}(x, y) = \dfrac{-y\vec{i} + x\vec{j}}{x^2 + y^2}$.

(a) Calculate $\dfrac{\partial F_2}{\partial x} - \dfrac{\partial F_1}{\partial y}$. Does the curl test imply that $\vec{F}$ is path-independent?

(b) Calculate $\displaystyle\int_C \vec{F} \cdot d\vec{r}$, where C is the unit circle centered at the origin and oriented counterclockwise. Is $\vec{F}$ a path-independent vector field?

(c) Explain why the answers to parts (a) and (b) do not contradict Green's Theorem.

Solution   (a) Taking partial derivatives, we have

$$\frac{\partial F_2}{\partial x} = \frac{\partial}{\partial x}\left(\frac{x}{x^2 + y^2}\right) = \frac{1}{x^2 + y^2} - \frac{x \cdot 2x}{(x^2 + y^2)^2} = \frac{y^2 - x^2}{(x^2 + y^2)^2}.$$

Similarly,

$$\frac{\partial F_1}{\partial y} = \frac{\partial}{\partial y}\left(\frac{-y}{x^2 + y^2}\right) = \frac{-1}{x^2 + y^2} + \frac{y \cdot 2y}{(x^2 + y^2)^2} = \frac{y^2 - x^2}{(x^2 + y^2)^2}.$$

Thus,

$$\frac{\partial F_2}{\partial x} - \frac{\partial F_1}{\partial y} = 0.$$

Since $\vec{F}$ is undefined at the origin, the domain of $\vec{F}$ contains a hole. Therefore, the curl test does not apply.

(b) On the unit circle, $\vec{F}$ is tangent to the circle and $||\vec{F}|| = 1$. Thus,[3]

$$\int_C \vec{F} \cdot d\vec{r} = ||\vec{F}|| \cdot \text{Length of curve} = 1 \cdot 2\pi = 2\pi.$$

Since the line integral around the closed curve C is nonzero, $\vec{F}$ is not path-independent. We observe that $\vec{F} = \text{grad}(\arctan(y/x))$ and $\arctan(y/x)$ is θ from polar coordinates, for $-\pi/2 < \theta < \pi/2$. The fact that θ increases by 2π each time we wind once around the origin counterclockwise explains why $\vec{F}$ is not path-independent.

---

[3]See Problem 45 on page 966.

(c) The domain of $\vec{F}$ is the "punctured plane," as shown in Figure 18.48. Since $\vec{F}$ is not defined at the origin, which is inside C, Green's Theorem does not apply. In this case

$$2\pi = \int_C \vec{F} \cdot d\vec{r} \neq \int_R \left(\frac{\partial F_2}{\partial x} - \frac{\partial F_1}{\partial y} \right) dxdy = 0.$$

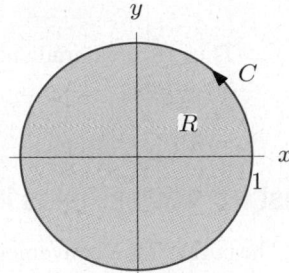

Figure 18.48: The domain of $\vec{F}(x, y) = \frac{-y\vec{i}+x\vec{j}}{x^2+y^2}$ is the plane minus the origin

Figure 18.49: The region R is *not* contained in the domain of $\vec{F}(x, y) = \frac{-y\vec{i}+x\vec{j}}{x^2+y^2}$

Although the vector field $\vec{F}$ in the last example was not defined at the origin, this by itself does not prevent the vector field from being path-independent, as we see in the following example.

Example 6 Consider the vector field $\vec{F}$ given by $\vec{F}(x, y) = \dfrac{x\vec{i} + y\vec{j}}{x^2 + y^2}$.

(a) Calculate $\dfrac{\partial F_2}{\partial x} - \dfrac{\partial F_1}{\partial y}$. Does the curl test imply that $\vec{F}$ is path-independent?

(b) Explain how we know that $\displaystyle\int_C \vec{F} \cdot d\vec{r} = 0$, where C is the unit circle centered at the origin and oriented counterclockwise. Does this imply that $\vec{F}$ is path-independent?

(c) Check that $f(x, y) = \frac{1}{2}\ln(x^2 + y^2)$ is a potential function for $\vec{F}$. Does this imply that $\vec{F}$ is path-independent?

Solution (a) Taking partial derivatives, we have

$$\frac{\partial F_2}{\partial x} = \frac{\partial}{\partial x}\left(\frac{y}{x^2+y^2} \right) = \frac{-2xy}{(x^2+y^2)^2}, \quad \text{and} \quad \frac{\partial F_1}{\partial y} = \frac{\partial}{\partial y}\left(\frac{x}{x^2+y^2} \right) = \frac{-2xy}{(x^2+y^2)^2}.$$

Therefore,

$$\frac{\partial F_2}{\partial x} - \frac{\partial F_1}{\partial y} = 0.$$

This does *not* imply that $\vec{F}$ is path-independent: The domain of $\vec{F}$ contains a hole since $\vec{F}$ is undefined at the origin. Thus, the curl test does not apply.

(b) Since $\vec{F}(x, y) = x\vec{i} + y\vec{j} = \vec{r}$ on the unit circle C, the field $\vec{F}$ is everywhere perpendicular to C. Thus

$$\int_C \vec{F} \cdot d\vec{r} = 0.$$

The fact that $\int_C \vec{F} \cdot d\vec{r} = 0$ when C is the unit circle does *not* imply that $\vec{F}$ is path-independent. To be sure that $\vec{F}$ is path-independent, we would have to show that $\int_C \vec{F} \cdot d\vec{r} = 0$ for *every* closed curve C in the domain of $\vec{F}$, not just the unit circle.

(c) To check that grad $f = \vec{F}$, we differentiate f:

$$f_x = \frac{1}{2}\frac{\partial}{\partial x}\ln(x^2 + y^2) = \frac{1}{2}\frac{2x}{x^2 + y^2} = \frac{x}{x^2 + y^2},$$

and

$$f_y = \frac{1}{2}\frac{\partial}{\partial y}\ln(x^2 + y^2) = \frac{1}{2}\frac{2y}{x^2 + y^2} = \frac{y}{x^2 + y^2},$$

so that

$$\operatorname{grad} f = \frac{x\vec{i} + y\vec{j}}{x^2 + y^2} = \vec{F}.$$

Thus, $\vec{F}$ is a gradient field and therefore is path-independent—even though $\vec{F}$ is undefined at the origin.

The Curl Test for Vector Fields in 3-Space

The curl test is a convenient way of deciding whether a 2-dimensional vector field is path-independent. Fortunately, there is an analogous test for 3-dimensional vector fields, although we cannot justify it until Chapter 20.

If $\vec{F}(x, y, z) = F_1\vec{i} + F_2\vec{j} + F_3\vec{k}$ is a vector field on 3-space we define a new vector field, $\operatorname{curl} \vec{F}$, on 3-space by

$$\operatorname{curl} \vec{F} = \left(\frac{\partial F_3}{\partial y} - \frac{\partial F_2}{\partial z}\right)\vec{i} + \left(\frac{\partial F_1}{\partial z} - \frac{\partial F_3}{\partial x}\right)\vec{j} + \left(\frac{\partial F_2}{\partial x} - \frac{\partial F_1}{\partial y}\right)\vec{k}.$$

The vector field $\operatorname{curl} \vec{F}$ can be used to determine whether the vector field $\vec{F}$ is path-independent.

The Curl Test for Vector Fields in 3-Space

Suppose $\vec{F}$ is a vector field on 3-space with continuous partial derivatives such that
- The domain of $\vec{F}$ has the property that every closed curve in it can be contracted to a point in a smooth way, staying at all times within the domain.
- $\operatorname{curl} \vec{F} = \vec{0}$.

Then $\vec{F}$ is path-independent, so $\vec{F}$ is a gradient field and has a potential function.

For the 2-dimensional curl test, the domain of $\vec{F}$ must have no holes. This meant that if $\vec{F}$ was defined on a simple closed curve C, then it was also defined at all points inside C. One way to test for holes is to try to "lasso" them with a closed curve. If every closed curve in the domain can be pulled to a point without hitting a hole, that is, without straying outside the domain, then the domain has no holes. In 3-space, we need the same condition to be satisfied: we must be able to pull every closed curve to a point, like a lasso, without straying outside the domain.

Example 7　Decide if the following vector fields are path-independent and whether or not the curl test applies.

(a)　$\vec{F} = \dfrac{x\vec{i} + y\vec{j} + z\vec{k}}{(x^2 + y^2 + z^2)^{3/2}}$　　　　　　(b)　$\vec{G} = \dfrac{-y\vec{i} + x\vec{j}}{x^2 + y^2} + z^2\vec{k}$

Solution　(a) Suppose $f = -(x^2 + y^2 + z^2)^{-1/2}$. Then $f_x = x(x^2 + y^2 + z^2)^{-3/2}$ and f_y and f_z are similar, so $\operatorname{grad} f = \vec{F}$. Thus, $\vec{F}$ is a gradient field and therefore path-independent. Calculations show $\operatorname{curl} \vec{F} = \vec{0}$. The domain of $\vec{F}$ is all of 3-space minus the origin, and any closed curve in the domain can be pulled to a point without leaving the domain. Thus, the curl test applies.

(b) Let C be the circle $x^2 + y^2 = 1, z = 0$ traversed counterclockwise when viewed from the positive z-axis. Since $z = 0$ on the curve C, the vector field $\vec{G}$ reduces to the vector field in Example 5 and is everywhere tangent to C and of magnitude 1, so

$$\int_C \vec{G} \cdot d\vec{r} = \|\vec{G}\| \cdot \text{Length of curve} = 1 \cdot 2\pi = 2\pi.$$

Since the line integral around this closed curve is nonzero, $\vec{G}$ is path-dependent. Computations show $\text{curl}\,\vec{G} = \vec{0}$. However, the domain of $\vec{G}$ is all of 3-space minus the z-axis, and it does not satisfy the curl test domain criterion. For example, the circle, C, is lassoed around the z-axis, and cannot be pulled to a point without hitting the z-axis. Thus, the curl test does not apply.

Exercises and Problems for Section 18.4

Exercises

In Exercises 1–10, decide if the given vector field is the gradient of a function f. If so, find f. If not, explain why not.

1. $y\vec{i} - x\vec{j}$

2. $2xy\vec{i} + x^2\vec{j}$

3. $y\vec{i} + y\vec{j}$

4. $2xy\vec{i} + 2xy\vec{j}$

5. $(x^2 + y^2)\vec{i} + 2xy\vec{j}$

6. $(2xy^3 + y)\vec{i} + (3x^2y^2 + x)\vec{j}$

7. $\dfrac{\vec{i}}{x} + \dfrac{\vec{j}}{y} + \dfrac{\vec{k}}{z}$

8. $\dfrac{\vec{i}}{x} + \dfrac{\vec{j}}{y} + \dfrac{\vec{k}}{xy}$

9. $2x\cos(x^2 + z^2)\vec{i} + \sin(x^2 + z^2)\vec{j} + 2z\cos(x^2 + z^2)\vec{k}$

10. $\dfrac{y}{x^2 + y^2}\vec{i} - \dfrac{x}{x^2 + y^2}\vec{j}$

11. Use Green's Theorem to evaluate $\int_C \left(y^2\vec{i} + x\vec{j}\right) \cdot d\vec{r}$ where C is the counterclockwise path around the perimeter of the rectangle $0 \le x \le 2$, $0 \le y \le 3$.

In Exercises 12–15, use Green's Theorem to calculate the circulation of $\vec{F}$ around the curve, oriented counterclockwise.

12. $\vec{F} = y\vec{i} - x\vec{j}$ around the unit circle.

13. $\vec{F} = xy\vec{j}$ around the square $0 \le x \le 1$, $0 \le y \le 1$.

14. $\vec{F} = (2x^2 + 3y)\vec{i} + (2x + 3y^2)\vec{j}$ around the triangle with vertices $(2, 0)$, $(0, 3)$, $(-2, 0)$.

15. $\vec{F} = 3y\vec{i} + xy\vec{j}$ around the unit circle.

16. Calculate $\int_C((3x + 5y)\vec{i} + (2x + 7y)\vec{j}) \cdot d\vec{r}$ where C is the circular path with center (a, b) and radius m, oriented counterclockwise. Use Green's Theorem.

17. (a) Sketch $\vec{F} = y\vec{i}$ and determine the sign of the circulation of $\vec{F}$ around the unit circle centered at the origin and traversed counterclockwise.
    (b) Use Green's Theorem to compute the circulation in part (a) exactly.

Problems

18. Let $\vec{F} = (\sin x)\vec{i} + (x + y)\vec{j}$. Find the line integral of $\vec{F}$ around the perimeter of the rectangle with corners $(3, 0)$, $(3, 5)$, $(-1, 5)$, $(-1, 0)$, traversed in that order.

19. Find $\displaystyle\int_C (\sin(x^2)\cos y)\vec{i} + (\sin(y^2) + e^x)\vec{j} \cdot d\vec{r}$ where C is the square of side 1 in the first quadrant of the xy-plane, with one vertex at the origin and sides along the axes, and oriented counterclockwise when viewed from above.

20. Find the line integral of $\vec{F} = (x - y)\vec{i} + x\vec{j}$ around the closed curve in Figure 18.50. (The arc is part of a circle.)

21. Find the line integral of $\vec{F} = (x + y)\vec{i} + \sin y\vec{j}$ around the closed curve in Figure 18.50. (The arc is part of a circle.)

22. Let $\vec{F} = 2xe^y\vec{i} + x^2e^y\vec{j}$ and $\vec{G} = (x - y)\vec{i} + (x + y)\vec{j}$. Let C be the line from $(0, 0)$ to $(2, 4)$. Find exactly:
    (a) $\displaystyle\int_C \vec{F} \cdot d\vec{r}$ (b) $\displaystyle\int_C \vec{G} \cdot d\vec{r}$

23. Let $\vec{F} = y\vec{i} + x\vec{j}$ and $\vec{G} = 3y\vec{i} - 3x\vec{j}$. In Figure 18.51, the curve C_2 is the semicircle centered at the origin from $(-1, 1)$ to $(1, -1)$ and C_1 is the line segment from $(-1, 1)$ to $(1, -1)$, and $C = C_2 - C_1$. Find the following line integrals:
    (a) $\displaystyle\int_{C_1} \vec{F} \cdot d\vec{r}$ (b) $\displaystyle\int_C \vec{F} \cdot d\vec{r}$
    (c) $\displaystyle\int_{C_2} \vec{F} \cdot d\vec{r}$ (d) $\displaystyle\int_{C_2} \vec{G} \cdot d\vec{r}$
    (e) $\displaystyle\int_C \vec{G} \cdot d\vec{r}$ (f) $\displaystyle\int_{C_1} \vec{G} \cdot d\vec{r}$
    (g) $\displaystyle\int_C (\vec{F} + \vec{G}) \cdot d\vec{r}$

Figure 18.50

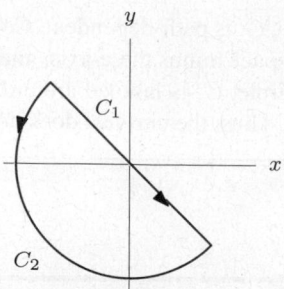

Figure 18.51

24. Calculate $\int_C \left((x^2 - y)\vec{i} + (y^2 + x)\vec{j} \right) \cdot d\vec{r}$ if:

(a) C is the circle $(x - 5)^2 + (y - 4)^2 = 9$ oriented counterclockwise.

(b) C is the circle $(x - a)^2 + (y - b)^2 = R^2$ in the xy-plane oriented counterclockwise.

25. Consider the following parametric equations:

$$C_1 : \vec{r}(t) = t\cos(2\pi t)\,\vec{i} + t\sin(2\pi t)\,\vec{k}\,, 0 \le t \le 2$$
$$C_2 : \vec{r}(t) = t\cos(2\pi t)\,\vec{i} + t\vec{j} + t\sin(2\pi t)\,\vec{k}\,, 0 \le t \le 2$$

(a) Describe, in words, the motion of a particle moving through each of the paths.

(b) Evaluate $\int_{C_2} \vec{F} \cdot d\vec{r}$, for the vector field $\vec{F} = yz\,\vec{i} + z(x + 1)\,\vec{j} + (xy + y + 1)\,\vec{k}$.

(c) Find a non-zero vector field $\vec{G}$ such that:

$$\int_{C_1} \vec{G} \cdot d\vec{r} = \int_{C_2} \vec{G} \cdot d\vec{r}.$$

Explain how you reasoned to find $\vec{G}$.

(d) Find two different, non-zero vector fields $\vec{H}_1$, $\vec{H}_2$ such that:

$$\int_{C_1} \vec{H}_1 \cdot d\vec{r} = \int_{C_1} \vec{H}_2 \cdot d\vec{r}.$$

Explain how you reasoned to find the two fields.

26. Show that the line integral of $\vec{F} = x\vec{j}$ around a closed curve in the xy-plane, oriented as in Green's Theorem, measures the area of the region enclosed by the curve.

In Problems 27–29, use the result of Problem 26 to calculate the area of the region within the parameterized curves. In each case, sketch the curve.

27. The ellipse $x^2/a^2 + y^2/b^2 = 1$ parameterized by $x = a\cos t$, $y = b\sin t$, for $0 \le t \le 2\pi$.

28. The hypocycloid $x^{2/3} + y^{2/3} = a^{2/3}$ parameterized by $x = a\cos^3 t$, $y = a\sin^3 t$, $0 \le t \le 2\pi$.

29. The folium of Descartes, $x^3 + y^3 = 3xy$, parameterized by $x = \dfrac{3t}{1 + t^3}$, $y = \dfrac{3t^2}{1 + t^3}$, for $0 \le t < \infty$.

30. The vector field $\vec{F}$ is defined on the disk D of radius 5 centered at the origin in the plane:

$$\vec{F} = (-y^3 + y\sin(xy))\vec{i} + (4x(1 - y^2) + x\sin(xy))\vec{j}.$$

Consider the line integral $\int_C \vec{F} \cdot d\vec{r}$, where C is some closed curve contained in D. For which C is the value of this integral the largest? [Hint: Assume C is a closed curve, made up of smooth pieces and never crossing itself, and oriented counterclockwise.]

31. Example 1 on page 985 showed that the vector field in Figure 18.52 could not be a gradient field by showing that it is not path-independent. Here is another way to see the same thing. Suppose that the vector field were the gradient of a function f. Draw and label a diagram showing what the contours of f would have to look like, and explain why it would not be possible for f to have a single value at any given point.

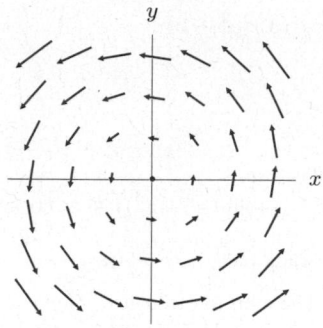

Figure 18.52

32. Repeat Problem 31 for the vector field in Problem 47 on page 983.

33. (a) By finding potential functions, show that each of the vector fields $\vec{F}, \vec{G}, \vec{H}$ is a gradient field on some domain (not necessarily the whole plane).

(b) Find the line integrals of $\vec{F}, \vec{G}, \vec{H}$ around the unit circle in the xy-plane, centered at the origin, and traversed counterclockwise.

(c) For which of the three vector fields can Green's Theorem be used to calculate the line integral in part (b)? Why or why not?

$$\vec{F} = y\vec{i} + x\vec{j}, \quad \vec{G} = \frac{y\vec{i} - x\vec{j}}{x^2 + y^2}, \quad \vec{H} = \frac{x\vec{i} + y\vec{j}}{(x^2 + y^2)^{1/2}}$$

34. (a) For which of the following can you use Green's Theorem to evaluate the integral? Explain.

I $\displaystyle\int_C (x^2 + y^2)\,dx + (x^2 + y^2)\,dy$ where C is the curve defined by $y = x$, $y = x^2, 0 \le x \le 1$ with counterclockwise orientation.

II $\displaystyle\int_C \frac{1}{\sqrt{x^2 + y^2}}\,dx - \frac{1}{\sqrt{x^2 + y^2}}\,dy$ where C is the unit circle centered at the origin, oriented counterclockwise.

III $\int_C \vec{F} \cdot d\vec{r}$ where $\vec{F} = x\vec{i} + y\vec{j}$ and C is the line segment from the origin to $(1, 1)$.

(b) Use Green's Theorem to evaluate the integrals in part (a) that can be done that way.

35. Arrange the line integrals L_1, L_2, L_3 in ascending order, where

$$L_i = \int_{C_i} (-x^2 y\vec{i} + (xy^2 - x)\vec{j}) \cdot d\vec{r}.$$

The points A, B, D lie on the unit circle and C_i is one of the curves shown in Figure 18.53.

C_1: Line segment A to B

C_2: Line segment A to D followed by line segment D to B

C_3: Semicircle ADB

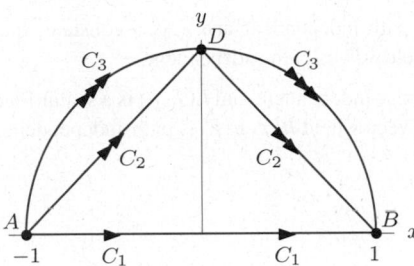

Figure 18.53

36. For all x, y, let $\vec{F} = F_1(x, y)\vec{i} + F_2(x, y)\vec{j}$ satisfy

$$\frac{\partial F_2}{\partial x} - \frac{\partial F_1}{\partial y} = 3.$$

(a) Calculate $\int_{C_1} \vec{F} \cdot d\vec{r}$ where C_1 is the unit circle in the xy-plane centered at the origin, oriented counterclockwise.

(b) Calculate $\int_{C_2} \vec{F} \cdot d\vec{r}$ where C_2 is the boundary of the rectangle of $4 \leq x \leq 7, 5 \leq y \leq 7$, oriented counterclockwise.

(c) Let C_3 be the circle of radius 7 centered at the point $(10, 2)$; let C_4 be the circle of radius 8 centered at the origin; let C_5 be the square of side 14 centered at $(7, 7)$ with sides parallel to the axes; C_3, C_4, C_5 are all oriented counterclockwise. Arrange the integrals $\int_{C_3} \vec{F} \cdot d\vec{r}, \int_{C_4} \vec{F} \cdot d\vec{r}, \int_{C_5} \vec{F} \cdot d\vec{r}$ in increasing order.

37. Let $\vec{F} = (3x^2 y + y^3 + e^x)\vec{i} + (e^{y^2} + 12x)\vec{j}$. Consider the line integral of $\vec{F}$ around the circle of radius a, centered at the origin and traversed counterclockwise.

(a) Find the line integral for $a = 1$.

(b) For which value of a is the line integral a maximum? Explain.

38. Let

$$\vec{F}(x, y) = \frac{-y\vec{i} + x\vec{j}}{x^2 + y^2}$$

and let oriented curves C_1 and C_2 be as in Figure 18.54. The curve C_2 is an arc of the unit circle centered at the origin. Show that

(a) The curl of $\vec{F}$ is zero.

(b) $\int_{C_1} \vec{F} \cdot d\vec{r} = \int_{C_2} \vec{F} \cdot d\vec{r}$.

(c) $\int_{C_1} \vec{F} \cdot d\vec{r} = \theta$, the angle at the origin subtended by the oriented curve C_1.

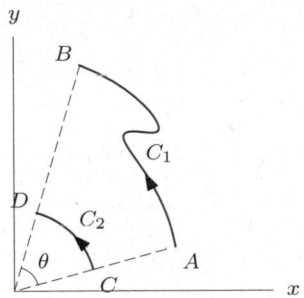

Figure 18.54

39. The electric field $\vec{E}$, at the point with position vector $\vec{r}$ in 3-space, due to a charge q at the origin is given by

$$\vec{E}(\vec{r}) = q\frac{\vec{r}}{\|\vec{r}\|^3}.$$

(a) Compute curl $\vec{E}$. Is $\vec{E}$ a path-independent vector field? Explain.

(b) Find a potential function φ for $\vec{E}$, if possible.

Strengthen Your Understanding

In Problems 40–41, explain what is wrong with the statement.

40. If $\int_C \vec{F} \cdot d\vec{r} = 0$ for a specific closed path C, then $\vec{F}$ must be path-independent.

41. Let $\vec{F} = F_1(x, y)\vec{i} + F_2(x, y)\vec{j}$ with

$$\frac{\partial F_2}{\partial x} - \frac{\partial F_1}{\partial y} = 3$$

and let C be the path consisting of line segments from $(0, 0)$ to $(1, 1)$ to $(2, 0)$. Then

$$\int_C \vec{F} \cdot d\vec{r} = 3.$$

In Problems 42–44, give an example of:

42. A function $Q(x, y)$ such that $\vec{F} = xy\vec{i} + Q(x, y)\vec{j}$ is a gradient field.

43. Two oriented curves, C_1 and C_2, from $(1, 0)$ to $(0, 1)$ such that if

$$\vec{F}(x, y) = \frac{-y\vec{i} + x\vec{j}}{x^2 + y^2},$$

then

$$\int_{C_1} \vec{F} \cdot d\vec{r} \neq \int_{C_2} \vec{F} \cdot d\vec{r}.$$

[Note that the scalar curl of $\vec{F}$ is 0 where $\vec{F}$ is defined.]

44. A vector field that is not a gradient field.

Are the statements in Problems 45–52 true or false? Give reasons for your answer.

45. If $f(x)$ and $g(y)$ are continuous one-variable functions, then the vector field $\vec{F} = f(x)\vec{i} + g(y)\vec{j}$ is path-independent.

46. If $\vec{F} = \operatorname{grad} f$, and C is the perimeter of a square of side length a oriented counterclockwise and surrounding the region R, then

$$\int_C \vec{F} \cdot d\vec{r} = \int_R f \, dA.$$

47. If $\vec{F}$ and $\vec{G}$ are both path-independent vector fields, then $\vec{F} + \vec{G}$ is path-independent.

48. If $\vec{F}$ and $\vec{G}$ are both path-dependent vector fields, then $\vec{F} + \vec{G}$ is path-dependent.

49. The vector field $\vec{F}(\vec{r}) = \vec{r}$ in 3-space is path-independent.

50. A constant vector field $\vec{F} = a\vec{i} + b\vec{j}$ is path-independent.

51. If $\vec{F}$ is path-independent and k is a constant, then the vector field $k\vec{F}$ is path-independent.

52. If $\vec{F}$ is path-independent and $h(x, y)$ is a scalar function, then the vector field $h(x, y)\vec{F}$ is path-independent.

CHAPTER SUMMARY (see also Ready Reference at the end of the book)

- **Line Integrals**
  Oriented curves, definition as a limit of a Riemann sum, work interpretation, circulation, algebraic properties, computing line integrals over parameterized curves, independence of parameterization, differential notation.

- **Gradient Fields**

Fundamental Theorem for line integrals, path-independent (conservative) fields and their relation to gradient fields, potential functions.

- **Green's Theorem**
  Statement of the theorem, curl test for path-independence, holes in the domain.

REVIEW EXERCISES AND PROBLEMS FOR CHAPTER EIGHTEEN

Exercises

The figures in Exercises 1–2 show a vector field $\vec{F}$ and a curve C. Decide if $\int_C \vec{F} \cdot d\vec{r}$ is positive, zero, or negative.

1.

2.

For the vector fields in Exercises 3–4, is the line integral positive, negative, or zero along

(a) A? **(b)** C_1, C_2, C_3, C_4?
(c) C, the closed curve consisting of all the Cs together?

3.

4.

5. Is $\int_C (3\vec{i} + 4\vec{j}) \cdot d\vec{r}$, where C is the line from $(5, 2)$ to $(1, 8)$, a vector or a scalar? Calculate it.

6. Is $\int_C (x\vec{i} + y\vec{j}) \cdot d\vec{r}$, where C is the line from $(0, 2)$ to $(0, 6)$, a vector or a scalar? Calculate it.

In Exercises 7–12, find $\int_C \vec{F} \cdot d\vec{r}$ for the given $\vec{F}$ and C.

7. $\vec{F} = 6\vec{i} - 7\vec{j}$, and C is an oriented curve from $(2, -6)$ to $(4, 4)$.

8. $\vec{F} = x\vec{i} + y\vec{j}$ and C is the unit circle in xy-plane oriented counterclockwise.

9. $\vec{F} = x\vec{i} + y\vec{j}$ and C is the y-axis from the origin to $(0, 10)$.

10. $\vec{F} = (x^2 - y)\vec{i} + (y^2 + x)\vec{j}$ and C is the parabola $y = x^2 + 1$ traversed from $(0, 1)$ to $(1, 2)$.

11. $\vec{F} = x\vec{i} + y\vec{j} + z\vec{k}$ and C is the path consisting of a line from $(2, 3, 0)$ to $(4, 5, 0)$, followed by a line from $(4, 5, 0)$ to $(0, 0, 7)$.

12. $\vec{F} = xy\vec{i} + (x-y)\vec{j}$ and C is the triangle joining $(1, 0)$, $(0, 1)$ and $(-1, 0)$ in the clockwise direction.

In Exercises 13–14, evaluate the line integrals.

13. $\int_C 3x^2 dx + 4y dy$ where C is the path $y = x^2$ from $(1, 1)$ to $(5, 25)$.

14. $\int_C y dx + x dy$ where C is the path $y = \sin x$ from $(0, 0)$ to $(\pi/2, 1)$.

In Exercises 15–21, which of the vector fields are path-independent on all of 3-space?

15. $y\vec{i}$ **16.** $y\vec{j}$ **17.** $z\vec{k}$

18. $z\vec{j} + z\vec{k}$ **19.** $y\vec{i} + x\vec{j}$ **20.** $(x + y)\vec{i}$

21. $yz\vec{i} + zx\vec{j} + xy\vec{k}$

In Exercises 22–27, find the line integral of $\vec{F} = 5x\vec{i} + 3x\vec{j}$ along the path C.

22. C is the line from $(2, 3)$ to $(2, 8)$.

23. C is the line from $(2, 3)$ to $(12, 3)$.

24. C is the curve $y = x^2$ from $(1, 1)$ to $(2, 4)$.

25. C is the semicircle of radius 3 from $(3, 0)$ to $(-3, 0)$ in the upper half plane.

26. C is the path in Figure 18.55.

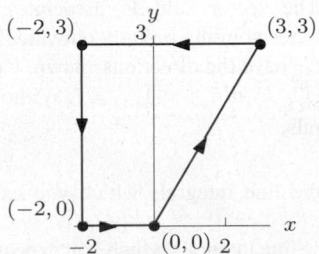

Figure 18.55

27. C is the path in Figure 18.56.

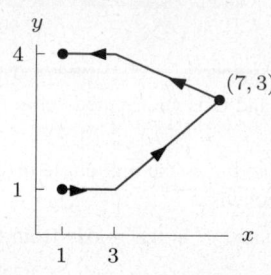

Figure 18.56

In Exercises 28–30, find the line integral of $\vec{F}$ around C_1 and C_2, where C_1 is the circle of radius 3, centered at $(5, 4)$ and oriented clockwise and C_2 is the semicircle starting at $(3, 4)$ and ending at $(7, 4)$, passing above the line $y = 4$.

28. $\vec{F} = 5\vec{i} + 4\vec{j}$

29. $\vec{F} = 5x\vec{i} + 4y\vec{j}$

30. $\vec{F} = 5y\vec{i} + 4x\vec{j}$

Problems

31. Which two of the vector fields (i)-(iv) could represent gradient vector fields on the whole plane? Give reasons for your answer.

(i)

(ii)

(iii)

(iv)

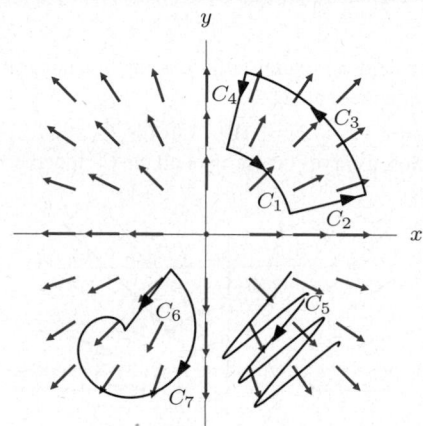

Figure 18.57

32. Let $\vec{F}(x, y)$ be the path-independent vector field in Figure 18.57. The vector field $\vec{F}$ associates with each point a unit vector pointing radially outward. The curves $C_1, C_2, \ldots, C_7$ have the directions shown. Consider the line integrals $\int_{C_i} \vec{F} \cdot d\vec{r}, i = 1, \ldots, 7$. Without computing any integrals,

(a) List all the line integrals which you expect to be zero.

(b) List all the line integrals which you expect to be negative.

(c) Arrange the positive line integrals in ascending order.

33. If C is $\vec{r} = (\cos t)\vec{i} + (\sin t)\vec{j}$ for $0 \le t \le 2\pi$, we know $\int_C \vec{F}(\vec{r}) \cdot d\vec{r} = 12$. Find the value of the integrals:

(a) $\int_0^{4\pi} \vec{F}((\cos t)\vec{i} + (\sin t)\vec{j}) \cdot ((-\sin t)\vec{i} + (\cos t)\vec{j})dt$

(b) $\int_{2\pi}^0 \vec{F}((\cos t)\vec{i} + (\sin t)\vec{j}) \cdot ((\sin t)\vec{i} - (\cos t)\vec{j})dt$

(c) $\int_0^{2\pi} \vec{F}((\sin t)\vec{i} + (\cos t)\vec{j}) \cdot ((-\cos t)\vec{i} - (\sin t)\vec{j})dt$

34. Let C be the straight path from $(0, 0)$ to $(5, 5)$ and let $\vec{F} = (y - x + 2)\vec{i} + (\sin(y - x) + 2)\vec{j}$.

(a) At each point of C, what angle does $\vec{F}$ make with a tangent vector to C?

(b) Find the magnitude $\|\vec{F}\|$ at each point of C.

(c) Evaluate $\int_C \vec{F} \cdot d\vec{r}$.

35. The line integral of $\vec{F} = (x + y)\vec{i} + x\vec{j}$ along each of the following paths is $3/2$:

(i) The path (t, t^2), with $0 \le t \le 1$

(ii) The path (t^2, t), with $0 \le t \le 1$

(iii) The path (t, t^n), with $n > 0$ and $0 \le t \le 1$

Show this

(a) Using the given parameterization to compute the line integral.

(b) Using the Fundamental Theorem of Calculus for Line Integrals.

Problems 36–39 refer to the star-shaped region R in Figure 18.58.

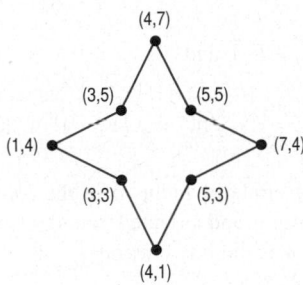

Figure 18.58

36. Let C be the path from $(5, 5)$ to $(4, 7)$. Find

$$\int_C (2\vec{i} + 13\vec{j}) \cdot d\vec{r}.$$

37. Let C be the path from $(5, 5)$ to $(4, 7)$. Find

$$\int_C (4x\vec{i} + 3y\vec{j}) \cdot d\vec{r}.$$

38. Let C be the path from $(5, 5)$ to $(4, 7)$. Find

$$\int_C ((4x + 5y)\vec{i} + (2x + 3y)\vec{j}) \cdot d\vec{r}.$$

39. Let C be the path around the outside of the star, traced counterclockwise. Find $\int_C ((4x + 5y)\vec{i} + (2x + 3y)\vec{j}) \cdot d\vec{r}$.

40. Let $\vec{F} = 2y\vec{i} + 5x\vec{j}$. Let C be the M-shaped closed curve consisting of line segments starting at $(-5, 1)$, going along the line $y = 1$ to $(15, 1)$, then to $(10, 9)$, then to $(5, 1)$, then to $(0, 9)$, and then back to $(-5, 1)$. Let C_1 be the part of C along the line $y = 1$; let C_2 be the rest of C and $C = C_1 + C_2$.

(a) Find $\int_C \vec{F} \cdot d\vec{r}$.

(b) Find $\int_{C_1} \vec{F} \cdot d\vec{r}$.

(c) Find $\int_{C_2} \vec{F} \cdot d\vec{r}$.

41. Let $\vec{F} = 2xe^y\vec{i} + x^2 e^y\vec{j}$ and $\vec{G} = (x-y)\vec{i} + (x+y)\vec{j}$. Let C be the path consisting of lines from $(0, 0)$ to $(3, 0)$ to $(3, 8)$ to $(0, 0)$. Find exactly:

(a) $\int_C \vec{F} \cdot d\vec{r}$ **(b)** $\int_C \vec{G} \cdot d\vec{r}$

42. Let $\vec{F} = (x^2 + 3x^2 y^4)\vec{i} + 4x^3 y^3\vec{j}$ and $\vec{G} = (x^4 + x^3 y^2)\vec{i} + x^2 y^3\vec{j}$. Let C_1 be the path along the x-axis from $(2, 0)$ to $(-2, 0)$; let C_2 be the semi-circle in the upper half plane from $(2, 0)$ to $(-2, 0)$. Find exactly:

(a) $\int_{C_1} \vec{F} \cdot d\vec{r}$ **(b)** $\int_{C_2} \vec{F} \cdot d\vec{r}$

(c) $\int_{C_1} \vec{G} \cdot d\vec{r}$ **(d)** $\int_{C_2} \vec{G} \cdot d\vec{r}$

43. Calculate the line integral of $\vec{F} = -y\vec{i} + x\vec{j}$ along the following paths in the xy-plane.

(a) Line from the origin to the point $(2, 3)$.

(b) Line from $(2, 3)$ to $(0, 3)$.

(c) Counterclockwise around a circle of radius 5 centered at the origin, starting from $(5, 0)$ to $(0, -5)$.

(d) Counterclockwise around the perimeter of a triangle of area 7.

44. Let C_1 and C_2 be the curves in Figure 18.59. Let $\vec{F} = (6x + y^2)\vec{i} + 2xy\vec{j}$ and $\vec{G} = (x - y)\vec{i} + (x + y)\vec{j}$. [Note C_1 is made up of line segments and C_2 is part of a circle.] Compute the following line integrals.

(a) $\displaystyle\int_{C_1} \vec{F} \cdot d\vec{r}$ **(b)** $\displaystyle\int_{C_1} \vec{G} \cdot d\vec{r}$

(c) $\displaystyle\int_{C_2} \vec{F} \cdot d\vec{r}$ **(d)** $\displaystyle\int_{C_2} \vec{G} \cdot d\vec{r}$

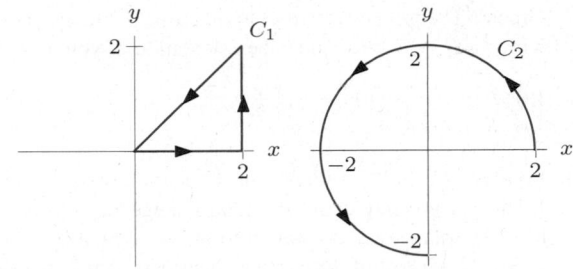

Figure 18.59

45. Let $\vec{F} = x\vec{i} + y\vec{j}$. Find the line integral of $\vec{F}$:

(a) Along the x-axis from the origin to the point $(3, 0)$.

(b) Around the path from A to B to O in Figure 18.60. (The curve is part of a circle centered at the origin.)

Figure 18.60

46. (a) Sketch the curves C_1 and C_2:

C_1 is $(x, y) = (0, t)$ for $-1 \leq t \leq 1$

C_2 is $(x, y) = (\cos t, \sin t)$ for $\pi/2 \leq t \leq 3/\pi/2$.

(b) Find $\int_C ((x+3y)\vec{i} + y\vec{j} \cdot)d\vec{r}$, where $C = C_1 + C_2$.

47. Draw an oriented curve C and a vector field $\vec{F}$ along C that is not always perpendicular to C, but for which $\int_C \vec{F} \cdot d\vec{r} = 0$.

48. (a) Sketch the curve, C, consisting of three parts, $C = C_1 + C_2 + C_3$, where C_1 is $\vec{r} = t\vec{i}$ for $0 \leq t \leq 1$, and C_2 is $x = 1 - t, y = t$ for $0 \leq t \leq 1$, and C_3 is $\vec{r} = (1 - t)\vec{j}$ for $0 \leq t \leq 1$. Label the coordinates of the points where C_1, C_2, C_3 meet. Each curve is oriented in the direction of increasing t.

(b) Sketch the vector field $\vec{F} = -\vec{i} + \vec{j}$

(c) Find

(i) $\int_{C_1} \vec{F} \cdot d\vec{r}$ (ii) $\int_{C_2} \vec{F} \cdot d\vec{r}$

(iii) $\int_{C_3} \vec{F} \cdot d\vec{r}$ (iv) $\int_C \vec{F} \cdot d\vec{r}$

49. For each of the following vector fields in the plane, use Green's Theorem to sketch a closed curve, C, in the plane with $\int_C \vec{F} \cdot d\vec{r} > 0$. Show the orientation of your curve.

(a) $\vec{F} = (x^3 - y)\vec{i} + (y^5 + x)\vec{j}$
(b) $\vec{F} = x^3\vec{i} + (y^5 - xy)\vec{j}$

50. Suppose P and Q both lie on the same contour of f. What can you say about the total change in f from P to Q? Explain your answer in terms of $\int_C \text{grad} f \cdot d\vec{r}$ where C is a part of the contour that goes from P to Q.

51. Figure 18.61 shows level curves of the function $f(x, y)$.

(a) Sketch ∇f at P.
(b) Is the vector ∇f at P longer than, shorter than, or the same length as, ∇f at Q?
(c) If C is a curve from P to Q, evaluate $\int_C \nabla f \cdot d\vec{r}$.

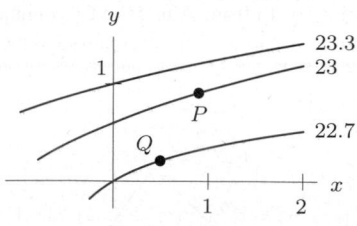

Figure 18.61

52. (a) Compute $\int_C \vec{v} \cdot d\vec{r}$ where $\vec{v} = y\vec{i} + 2x\vec{j}$ and C is

(i) The line joining $(0, 1)$ to $(1, 0)$

(ii) The arc of the unit circle joining $(0, 1)$ to $(1, 0)$

(b) What can you conclude about $\vec{v}$?

53. Let C be the straight path from $(0,0)$ to $(5,5)$ and let $\vec{F} = (y - x + 2)\vec{i} + (\sin(y - x) - 2)\vec{j}$.

(a) At each point of C, what angle does $\vec{F}$ make with a tangent vector to C?
(b) Evaluate $\int_C \vec{F} \cdot d\vec{r}$.

54. Let $\vec{F} = F_1\vec{i} + F_2\vec{j}$ and

$$\frac{\partial F_2}{\partial x} - \frac{\partial F_1}{\partial y} = 3(x^2 + y^2) - (x^2 + y^2)^{3/2}.$$

Let C_a be the circle of radius a in the xy-plane, centered at the origin and oriented counterclockwise. For what value of a is the line integral $\int_{C_a} \vec{F} \cdot d\vec{r}$ largest? What is the largest value?

55. The fact that an electric current gives rise to a magnetic field is the basis for some electric motors. Ampère's Law relates the magnetic field $\vec{B}$ to a steady current I. It says

$$\int_C \vec{B} \cdot d\vec{r} = kI$$

where I is the current[4] flowing through a closed curve C and k is a constant. Figure 18.62 shows a rod carrying a current and the magnetic field induced around the rod. If the rod is very long and thin, experiments show that the magnetic field $\vec{B}$ is tangent to every circle that is perpendicular to the rod and has center on the axis of the rod (like C in Figure 18.62). The magnitude of $\vec{B}$ is constant along every such circle. Use Ampère's Law to show that around a circle of radius r, the magnetic field due to a current I has magnitude given by

$$\|\vec{B}\| = \frac{kI}{2\pi r}.$$

(In other words, the strength of the field is inversely proportional to the radial distance from the rod.)

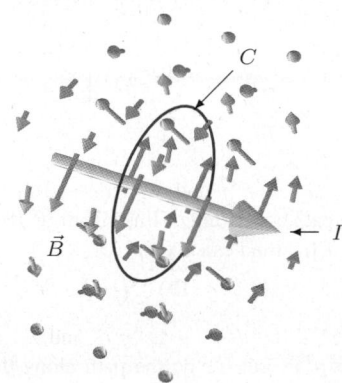

Figure 18.62

---

[4]More precisely, I is the net current through any surface that has C as its boundary.

56. A *central vector field* is a vector field whose direction is always toward (or away from) a fixed point O (the center) and whose magnitude at a point P is a function only of the distance from P to O. In two dimensions this means that the vector field has constant magnitude on circles centered at O. The gravitational and electrical fields of spherically symmetric sources are both central fields.

(a) Sketch an example of a central vector field.

(b) Suppose that the central field $\vec{F}$ is a gradient field, that is, $\vec{F} = \text{grad } f$. What must be the shape of the contours of f? Sketch some contours for this case.

(c) Is every gradient field a central vector field? Explain.

(d) In Figure 18.63, two paths are shown between the points Q and P. Assuming that the three circles C_1, C_2, and C_3 are centered at O, explain why the work done by a central vector field $\vec{F}$ is the same for either path.

(e) It is in fact true that every central vector field is a gradient field. Use an argument suggested by Figure 18.63 to explain why any central vector field must be path-independent.

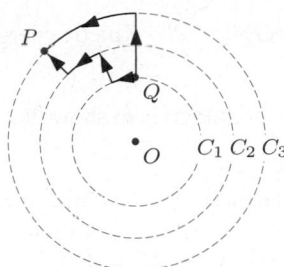

Figure 18.63

57. A *free vortex* circulating about the origin in the xy-plane (or about the z-axis in 3-space) has vector field $\vec{v} = K(x^2 + y^2)^{-1}(-y\vec{i} + x\vec{j})$ where K is a constant. The Rankine model of a tornado hypothesizes an inner core that rotates at constant angular velocity, surrounded by a free vortex. Suppose that the inner core has radius 100 meters and that $\|\vec{v}\| = 3 \cdot 10^5$ meters/hr at a distance of 100 meters from the center.

(a) Assuming that the tornado rotates counterclockwise (viewed from above the xy-plane) and that $\vec{v}$ is continuous, determine ω and K such that

$$\vec{v} = \begin{cases} \omega(-y\vec{i} + x\vec{j}) & \text{if } \sqrt{x^2 + y^2} < 100 \\ K(x^2 + y^2)^{-1}(-y\vec{i} + x\vec{j}) \\ \qquad \text{if } \sqrt{x^2 + y^2} \geq 100. \end{cases}$$

(b) Sketch the vector field $\vec{v}$.

(c) Find the circulation of $\vec{v}$ around the circle of radius r centered at the origin, traversed counterclockwise.

58. Figure 18.64 shows the tangential velocity as a function of radius for the tornado that hit Dallas on April 2, 1957. Use it and Problem 57 to estimate K and ω for the Rankine model of this tornado.[5]

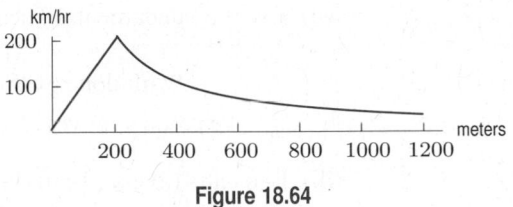

Figure 18.64

CAS Challenge Problems

59. Let C_a be the circle of radius a, centered at the origin, oriented in the counterclockwise direction, and let

$$\vec{F} = \left(-y + \frac{2}{3}y^3\right)\vec{i} + \left(2x - \frac{x^3}{3} + xy^2\right)\vec{j}.$$

(a) Evaluate $\int_{C_a} \vec{F} \cdot d\vec{r}$. For what positive value of a does the integral take its maximum value?

(b) Use Green's Theorem to convert the integral to a double integral. Without evaluating the double integral, give a geometric explanation of the value of a you found in part (a).

60. If f is a potential function for the two-dimensional vector field $\vec{F}$ then the Fundamental Theorem of Calculus for Line Integrals says that $\int_C \vec{F} \cdot d\vec{r} = f(x, y) - f(0, 0)$

where C is any path from $(0, 0)$ to (x, y). Using this fact and choosing C to be a straight line, find potential functions for the following conservative fields (where a, b, c are constants):

(a) $\vec{F} = ay\vec{i} + ax\vec{j}$

(b) $\vec{F} = abye^{bxy}\vec{i} + (c + abxe^{bxy})\vec{j}$

61. Let $\vec{F} = (ax + by)\vec{i} + (cx + dy)\vec{j}$. Evaluate the line integral of $\vec{F}$ along the paths

$$C_1 : \vec{r}(t) = 2t\vec{i} + t^2\vec{j}, \quad 0 \leq t \leq 3$$
$$C_2 : \vec{r}(t) = 2(3 - t)\vec{i} + (3 - t)^2\vec{j}, \quad 0 \leq t \leq 3$$

Describe and explain the relationship between the two integrals.

---

[5]Adapted from *Encyclopædia Britannica, Macropædia*, Vol. 16, page 477, "Climate and the Weather," Tornados and Waterspouts, 1991.

PROJECTS FOR CHAPTER EIGHTEEN

1. **Conservation of Energy**

   (a) A particle moves with position vector $\vec{r}(t) = x(t)\vec{i} + y(t)\vec{j} + z(t)\vec{k}$. Let $\vec{v}(t)$ and $\vec{a}(t)$ be its velocity and acceleration vectors. Show that

   $$\frac{1}{2}\frac{d}{dt}\|\vec{v}(t)\|^2 = \vec{a}(t) \cdot \vec{v}(t).$$

   (b) We now derive the principle of Conservation of Energy. The kinetic energy of a particle of mass m moving with speed v is $(1/2)mv^2$. Suppose the particle has potential energy $f(\vec{r})$ at the position $\vec{r}$ due to a force field $\vec{F} = -\nabla f$. If the particle moves with position vector $\vec{r}(t)$ and velocity $\vec{v}(t)$, then the Conservation of Energy principle says that

   $$\text{Total energy} = \text{Kinetic energy} + \text{Potential energy} = \frac{1}{2}m\|\vec{v}(t)\|^2 + f(\vec{r}(t)) = \text{Constant}.$$

   Let P and Q be two points in space and let C be a path from P to Q parameterized by $\vec{r}(t)$ for $t_0 \leq t \leq t_1$, where $\vec{r}(t_0) = P$ and $\vec{r}(t_1) = Q$.

   (i) Using part (a) and Newton's law $\vec{F} = m\vec{a}$, show

   $$\begin{array}{l} \text{Work done by } \vec{F} \\ \text{as particle moves along } C \end{array} = \text{Kinetic energy at } Q - \text{Kinetic energy at } P.$$

   (ii) Use the Fundamental Theorem of Calculus for Line Integrals to show that

   $$\begin{array}{l} \text{Work done by } \vec{F} \\ \text{as particle moves along } C \end{array} = \text{Potential energy at } P - \text{Potential energy at } Q.$$

   (iii) Use parts (a) and (b) to show that the total energy at P is the same as at Q.

   This problem explains why force vector fields which are *path-independent* are usually called *conservative* (force) vector fields.

2. **Planimeters**

   A planimeter is a mechanical device that exploits Green's Theorem to find the area of a planar region by tracing out its boundary.

   A *linear planimeter* is a rod with one end, the foot, that moves along a straight track as a wheel at the other end rolls and slides along a curve being traced. The rod acts as an axle for the wheel so that the wheel rolls without sliding for motion perpendicular to the rod, and slides without rolling for motion parallel to the rod. The wheel vector is defined by rotating the displacement vector from wheel to foot clockwise 90°. For motion in a direction making an angle θ with the wheel vector, the ratio of roll to distance traveled is $\cos\theta$. (This counts rolling as positive for one direction of rotation and negative for the other.) A meter on the planimeter measures the amount the wheel rolls. When the user has finished tracing out a closed curve, the total roll of the wheel determines the area of the enclosed region. In Figure 18.65 the foot of a planimeter of length L slides up and down the x-axis as the wheel moves along C from P to Q.

   The key fact that makes this work is that the planimeter computes the line integral of the vector field of unit vectors $\vec{F}$ in the direction of the wheel vector along the oriented curve C:

   $$\int_C \vec{F} \cdot d\vec{r} = \text{Total roll of wheel}.$$

   To see this, divide C into n small, almost straight pieces along which $\vec{F}$ has approximately constant direction. Each piece can be represented by a displacement vector $\Delta\vec{r}_i = \vec{r}_{i+1} - \vec{r}_i$, and $\vec{F}(\vec{r}_i)$ is the unit vector in the direction of the wheel vector at the point of C with position vector $\vec{r}_i$. We have

$$\vec{F}(\vec{r}_i) \cdot \Delta\vec{r}_i = \|\vec{F}(\vec{r}_i)\|\|\Delta\vec{r}_i\| \cos\theta_i \approx 1 \cdot (\text{Length of } i\text{th piece of } C) \cdot \cos\theta_i \approx \text{Roll on } i\text{th piece of } C.$$

Summing over all the pieces and taking the limit as $\|\Delta\vec{r}_i\| \to 0$ gives the result.

In the problems, we find a formula for $\vec{F}$ and use it to show how area is computed.

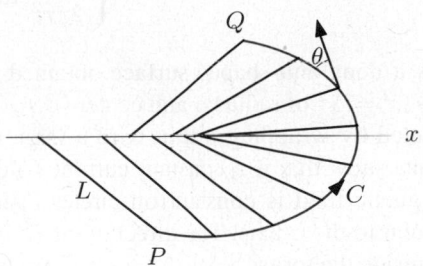

Figure 18.65

(a) Let $L > 0$, and define $\vec{F}(x, y)$ in the horizontal strip $-L < y < L$ as follows. Let $\vec{m}$ be the displacement vector of magnitude L from a point $(a, 0)$ on the x-axis to the point (x, y) in the strip, where $a < x$. Let $\vec{F}(x, y)$ be the unit vector in the direction of $\vec{k} \times \vec{m}$, perpendicular to $\vec{m}$. The flow lines of $\vec{F}$ are arcs of circles of radius L with center on the x-axis, oriented counterclockwise. See Figure 18.66. Show that

$$\vec{F}(x, y) = \frac{-y}{L}\vec{i} + \frac{1}{L}\sqrt{L^2 - y^2}\,\vec{j}.$$

Figure 18.66

(b) Show that curl $\vec{F} = 1/L$, for $\vec{F}$ as in part (a).
(c) Let C be a simple closed curve oriented counterclockwise in the strip $-L < y < L$, and let R be the enclosed region. Use Green's Theorem to show that

$$\text{Area of } R = L \int_C \vec{F} \cdot d\vec{r} = L \cdot (\text{Total roll of planimeter wheel}).$$

3. Ampère's Law

Ampère's Law, introduced in Problem 55 on page 1000, relates the net current, I, flowing through a surface to the magnetic field around the boundary, C, of the surface. The law says that

$$\int_C \vec{B} \cdot d\vec{r} = kI, \quad \text{for some constant } k.$$

The orientation of C is given by the right-hand rule: if the fingers of your right hand lie against the surface and curl in the direction of the oriented curve C, then your thumb points in the direction of positive current.

(a) We consider an infinitely long cylindrical wire having a radius r_0, where $r_0 > 0$. Suppose the wire is centered on the z-axis and carries a constant current, I, uniformly distributed across a cross-section of the wire. The magnitude of $\vec{B}$ is constant along any circle which is centered on and perpendicular to the z-axis. The direction of $\vec{B}$ is tangent to such circles. Show that the magnitude of $\vec{B}$, at a distance r from the z-axis, is given by

$$
\|\vec{B}\| = \begin{cases} \dfrac{aI}{2\pi r} & \text{for } r \geq r_0 \\[2mm] \dfrac{aIr}{2\pi r_0^2} & \text{for } r < r_0. \end{cases}
$$

(b) A *torus* is a doughnut-shaped surface obtained by rotating around the z-axis the circle $(x - \beta)^2 + z^2 = \alpha^2$ of radius α and center $(\beta, 0, 0)$, where $0 < \alpha < \beta$. A *toroidal solenoid* is constructed by wrapping a thin wire a large number, say N, times around the torus. Experiments show that if a constant current I flows though the wire, then the magnitude of the magnetic field is constant on circles inside the torus which are centered on and perpendicular to the z-axis. The direction of $\vec{B}$ is tangent to such circles. Explain why, at all points inside the torus,

$$
\|\vec{B}\| = \frac{aNI}{2\pi r},
$$

and $\|\vec{B}\| = 0$ otherwise. [Hint: Apply Ampère's Law to a suitably chosen surface S with boundary curve C. What is the net current passing through S?]

4. Conservative Forces, Friction, and Gravity

The work done by a conservative force on an object does not depend on the path taken but only on the endpoints—in other words, the vector field representing the force is path-independent. Only for a conservative force is the work done stored as energy; for a non-conservative force, the work may be dissipated.

(a) The frictional drag force $\vec{F}$ on an airplane flying through the air with velocity $\vec{v}$ is given by

$$
\vec{F} = -c\|\vec{v}\|\vec{v}.
$$

The constant c is positive and depends on the shape of the airplane. One airplane takes off from an airport located at the point $(2, 0, 0)$ and follows the path

$$
\vec{r}(t) = (2\cos t)\vec{\imath} + (2\sin t)\vec{\jmath} + 3t\vec{k}, \quad \text{from } t = 0 \text{ to } t = \pi.
$$

An identical airplane takes off from the same point and follows the path

$$
\vec{r}(t) = \frac{2 - 4t}{\pi}t\vec{\imath} + 3t\vec{k} \quad \text{also from } t = 0 \text{ to } t = \pi.
$$

(i) Compute the total work done by the drag force $\vec{F}$ on each airplane.

(ii) Is the drag force conservative? Explain.

(b) Suppose the two airplanes of the preceding problem each have mass m, while the earth has mass M. The gravitational force $\vec{F}$ acting on either airplane at a point with position vector $\vec{r}$ is given by

$$
\vec{F}(\vec{r}) = -GMm\frac{\vec{r}}{\|\vec{r}\|^3}, \quad \text{where } G \text{ is the gravitational constant.}
$$

(i) Compute the total work done by the gravitational force $\vec{F}$ on each airplane as it moves from the point $(2, 0, 0)$ to the point $(-2, 0, 3\pi)$.

(ii) Is the gravitational force conservative? Explain.

Chapter Nineteen

FLUX INTEGRALS AND DIVERGENCE

Contents

19.1 THE IDEA OF A FLUX INTEGRAL

Flow Through a Surface

Imagine water flowing through a fishing net stretched across a stream. Suppose we want to measure the flow rate of water through the net, that is, the volume of fluid that passes through the surface per unit time.

Example 1   A flat square surface of area A, in m^2, is immersed in a fluid. The fluid flows with constant velocity $\vec{v}$, in m/sec, perpendicular to the square. Write an expression for the rate of flow in m^3/sec.

Figure 19.1: Fluid flowing perpendicular
to a surface

Solution   In one second a given particle of water moves a distance of $\|\vec{v}\|$ in the direction perpendicular to the square. Thus, the entire body of water moving through the square in one second is a box of length $\|\vec{v}\|$ and cross-sectional area A. So the box has volume $\|\vec{v}\|A$ m^3, and

$$\text{Flow rate} = \|\vec{v}\|A \text{ m}^3/\text{sec}.$$

This flow rate is called the *flux* of the fluid through the surface. We can also compute the flux of vector fields, such as electric and magnetic fields, where no flow is actually taking place. If the vector field is constant and perpendicular to the surface, and if the surface is flat, as in Example 1, the flux is obtained by multiplying the speed by the area.

Next we find the flux of a constant vector field through a flat surface that is not perpendicular to the vector field, using a dot product. In general, we break a surface into small pieces which are approximately flat and where the vector field is approximately constant, leading to a flux integral.

Orientation of a Surface

Before computing the flux of a vector field through a surface, we need to decide which direction of flow through the surface is the positive direction; this is described as choosing an orientation.[1]

> At each point on a smooth surface there are two unit normals, one in each direction. **Choosing an orientation** means picking one of these normals at every point of the surface in a continuous way. The unit normal vector in the direction of the orientation is denoted by $\vec{n}$. For a closed surface (that is, the boundary of a solid region), we choose the **outward orientation** unless otherwise specified.

We say the flux through a piece of surface is positive if the flow is in the direction of the orientation and negative if it is in the opposite direction. (See Figure 19.2.)

---

[1]Although we will not study them, there are a few surfaces for which this cannot be done. See page 1012.

Figure 19.2: An oriented surface showing directions of positive and negative flow

Figure 19.3: Area vector $\vec{A} = \vec{n}\,A$ of flat surface with area A and orientation $\vec{n}$

The Area Vector

The flux through a flat surface depends both on the area of the surface and its orientation. Thus, it is useful to represent its area by a vector as shown in Figure 19.3.

> The **area vector** of a flat, oriented surface is a vector $\vec{A}$ such that
> - The magnitude of $\vec{A}$ is the area of the surface.
> - The direction of $\vec{A}$ is the direction of the orientation vector $\vec{n}$.

The Flux of a Constant Vector Field Through a Flat Surface

Suppose the velocity vector field, $\vec{v}$, of a fluid is constant and $\vec{A}$ is the area vector of a flat surface. The flux through this surface is the volume of fluid that flows through in one unit of time. The skewed box in Figure 19.4 has cross-sectional area $\|\vec{A}\|$ and height $\|\vec{v}\|\cos\theta$, so its volume is $(\|\vec{v}\|\cos\theta)\,\|\vec{A}\| = \vec{v}\cdot\vec{A}$. Thus, we have the following result:

> If $\vec{v}$ is constant and $\vec{A}$ is the area vector of a flat surface, then
>
> $$\text{Flux through surface} = \vec{v}\cdot\vec{A}.$$

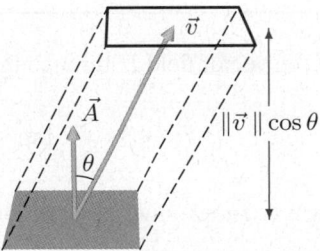

Figure 19.4: Flux of $\vec{v}$ through a surface with area vector $\vec{A}$ is the volume of this skewed box

---

Example 2   Water is flowing down a cylindrical pipe 2 cm in radius with a velocity of 3 cm/sec. Find the flux of the velocity vector field through the ellipse-shaped region shown in Figure 19.5. The normal to the ellipse makes an angle of θ with the direction of flow and the area of the ellipse is $4\pi/(\cos\theta)$ cm^2.

Figure 19.5: Flux through ellipse-shaped region across a cylindrical pipe

Solution   There are two ways to approach this problem. One is to use the formula we just derived, which gives

$$\text{Flux through ellipse} = \vec{v} \cdot \vec{A} = \|\vec{v}\|\|\vec{A}\| \cos\theta = 3(\text{Area of ellipse}) \cos\theta$$

$$= 3\left(\frac{4\pi}{\cos\theta}\right)\cos\theta = 12\pi \ \text{cm}^3/\text{sec}.$$

The second way is to notice that the flux through the ellipse is equal to the flux through the circle perpendicular to the pipe in Figure 19.5. Since the flux is the rate at which water is flowing down the pipe, we have

$$\text{Flux through circle} = \frac{\text{Velocity}}{\text{of water}} \times \frac{\text{Area of}}{\text{circle}} = \left(3\,\frac{\text{cm}}{\text{sec}}\right)(\pi 2^2 \ \text{cm}^2) = 12\pi \ \text{cm}^3/\text{sec}.$$

The Flux Integral

If the vector field, $\vec{F}$, is not constant or the surface, S, is not flat, we divide the surface into a patchwork of small, almost flat pieces. (See Figure 19.6.) For a particular patch with area ΔA, we pick a unit orientation vector $\vec{n}$ at a point on the patch and define the area vector of the patch, $\Delta\vec{A}$, as

$$\Delta\vec{A} = \vec{n}\,\Delta A.$$

(See Figure 19.7.) If the patches are small enough, we can assume that $\vec{F}$ is approximately constant on each piece. Then we know that

$$\text{Flux through patch} \approx \vec{F} \cdot \Delta\vec{A},$$

so, adding the fluxes through all the small pieces, we have

$$\text{Flux through whole surface} \approx \sum \vec{F} \cdot \Delta\vec{A},$$

As each patch becomes smaller and $\|\Delta\vec{A}\| \to 0$, the approximation gets better and we get

$$\text{Flux through } S = \lim_{\|\Delta\vec{A}\| \to 0} \sum \vec{F} \cdot \Delta\vec{A}.$$

Thus, provided the limit exists, we make the following definition:

The **flux integral** of the vector field $\vec{F}$ through the oriented surface S is

$$\int_S \vec{F} \cdot d\vec{A} = \lim_{\|\Delta\vec{A}\| \to 0} \sum \vec{F} \cdot \Delta\vec{A}.$$

If S is a closed surface oriented outward, we describe the flux through S as the flux out of S.

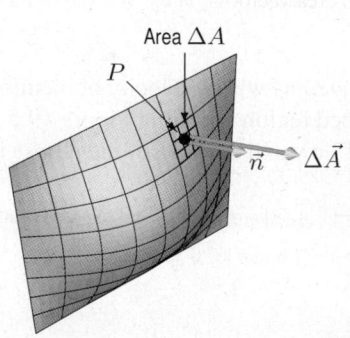

Figure 19.6: Surface S divided into small, almost flat pieces, showing a typical orientation vector $\vec{n}$ and area vector $\Delta\vec{A}$

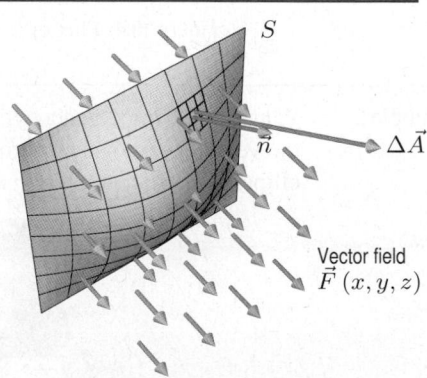

Figure 19.7: Flux of a vector field through a curved surface S

In computing a flux integral, we have to divide the surface up in a reasonable way, or the limit might not exist. In practice this problem seldom arises; however, one way to avoid it is to define flux integrals by the method used to compute them shown in Section 21.3.

Flux and Fluid Flow

If $\vec{v}$ is the velocity vector field of a fluid, we have

$$\begin{array}{ccccc} \text{Rate fluid flows} & = & \text{Flux of } \vec{v} & = & \int_S \vec{v} \cdot d\vec{A} \\ \text{through surface } S & & \text{through } S & & \end{array}$$

The rate of fluid flow is measured in units of volume per unit time.

Example 3   Find the flux of the vector field $\vec{B}(x, y, z)$ shown in Figure 19.8 through the square S of side 2 shown in Figure 19.9, oriented in the $\vec{j}$ direction, where

$$\vec{B}(x, y, z) = \frac{-y\vec{i} + x\vec{j}}{x^2 + y^2}.$$

Figure 19.8: The vector field $\vec{B}(x, y, z) = \frac{-y\vec{i}+x\vec{j}}{x^2+y^2}$

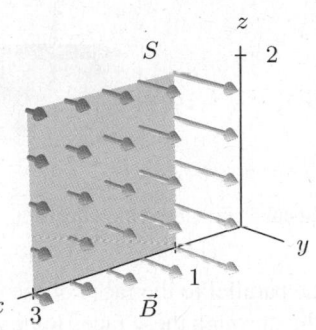

Figure 19.9: Flux of $\vec{B}$ through the square S of side 2 in xy-plane and oriented in $\vec{j}$ direction

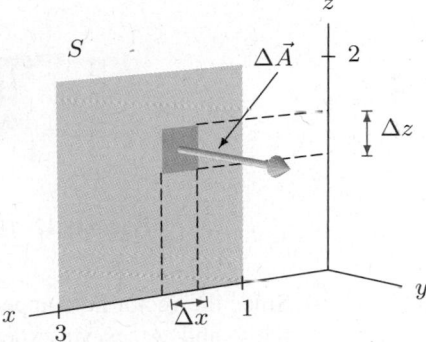

Figure 19.10: A small patch of surface with area $\|\Delta \vec{A}\| = \Delta x \Delta z$

Solution   Consider a small rectangular patch with area vector $\Delta \vec{A}$ in S, with sides Δx and Δz so that $\|\Delta \vec{A}\| = \Delta x \Delta z$. Since $\Delta \vec{A}$ points in the $\vec{j}$ direction, we have $\Delta \vec{A} = \vec{j} \Delta x \Delta z$. (See Figure 19.10.)

At the point $(x, 0, z)$ in S, substituting $y = 0$ into $\vec{B}$ gives $\vec{B}(x, 0, z) = (1/x)\vec{j}$. Thus, we have

$$\text{Flux through small patch} \approx \vec{B} \cdot \Delta \vec{A} = \left(\frac{1}{x}\vec{j}\right) \cdot (\vec{j} \, \Delta x \Delta z) = \frac{1}{x} \Delta x \, \Delta z.$$

Therefore,

$$\text{Flux through surface} = \int_S \vec{B} \cdot d\vec{A} = \lim_{\|\Delta \vec{A}\| \to 0} \sum \vec{B} \cdot \Delta \vec{A} = \lim_{\substack{\Delta x \to 0 \\ \Delta z \to 0}} \sum \frac{1}{x} \Delta x \, \Delta z.$$

This last expression is a Riemann sum for the double integral $\int_R \frac{1}{x} \, dA$, where R is the square $1 \le x \le 3$, $0 \le z \le 2$. Thus,

$$\text{Flux through surface} = \int_S \vec{B} \cdot d\vec{A} = \int_R \frac{1}{x} \, dA = \int_0^2 \int_1^3 \frac{1}{x} \, dx \, dz = 2 \ln 3.$$

The result is positive since the vector field is passing through the surface in the positive direction.

Example 4   Each of the vector fields in Figure 19.11 consists entirely of vectors parallel to the xy-plane, and is constant in the z direction (that is, the vector field looks the same in any plane parallel to the xy-plane). For each one, say whether you expect the flux through a closed surface surrounding the origin to be positive, negative, or zero. In part (a) the surface is a closed cube with faces perpendicular to the axes; in parts (b) and (c) the surface is a closed cylinder. In each case we choose the outward orientation. (See Figure 19.12.)

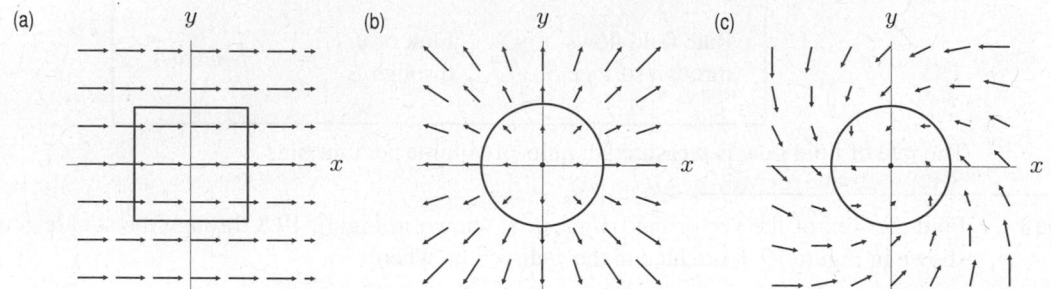

Figure 19.11: Flux of a vector field through the closed surfaces whose cross-sections are shown in the xy-plane

Figure 19.12: The closed cube and closed cylinder, both oriented outward

Solution   (a) Since the vector field appears to be parallel to the faces of the cube which are perpendicular to the y- and z-axes, we expect the flux through these faces to be zero. The fluxes through the two faces perpendicular to the x-axis appear to be equal in magnitude and opposite in sign, so we expect the net flux to be zero.

(b) Since the top and bottom of the cylinder are parallel to the flow, the flux through them is zero. On the curved surface of the cylinder, $\vec{v}$ and $\Delta\vec{A}$ appear to be everywhere parallel and in the same direction, so we expect each term $\vec{v} \cdot \Delta\vec{A}$ to be positive, and therefore the flux integral $\int_S \vec{v} \cdot d\vec{A}$ to be positive.

(c) As in part (b), the flux through the top and bottom of the cylinder is zero. In this case $\vec{v}$ and $\Delta\vec{A}$ are not parallel on the round surface of the cylinder, but since the fluid appears to be flowing inward as well as swirling, we expect each term $\vec{v} \cdot \Delta\vec{A}$ to be negative, and therefore the flux integral to be negative.

Calculating Flux Integrals Using $d\vec{A} = \vec{n}\, d\, A$

For a small patch of surface ΔS with unit normal $\vec{n}$ and area ΔA, the area vector is $\Delta\vec{A} = \vec{n}\, \Delta A$. The next example shows how we can use this relationship to compute a flux integral.

Example 5   An electric charge q is placed at the origin in 3-space. The resulting electric field $\vec{E}(\vec{r})$ at the point with position vector $\vec{r}$ is given by

$$\vec{E}(\vec{r}) = q\frac{\vec{r}}{\|\vec{r}\|^3}, \qquad \vec{r} \neq \vec{0}.$$

Find the flux of $\vec{E}$ out of the sphere of radius R centered at the origin. (See Figure 19.13.)

Figure 19.13: Flux of $\vec{E} = q\vec{r}/\|\vec{r}\|^3$ through the surface of a sphere of radius R centered at the origin

Solution   This vector field points radially outward from the origin in the same direction as $\vec{n}$. Thus, since $\vec{n}$ is a unit vector,

$$\vec{E} \cdot \Delta\vec{A} = \vec{E} \cdot \vec{n}\, \Delta A = \|\vec{E}\|\, \Delta A.$$

On the sphere, $\|\vec{E}\| = q/R^2$, so

$$\int_S \vec{E} \cdot d\vec{A} = \lim_{\|\Delta\vec{A}\| \to 0} \sum \vec{E} \cdot \Delta\vec{A} = \lim_{\Delta A \to 0} \sum \frac{q}{R^2} \Delta A = \frac{q}{R^2} \lim_{\Delta A \to 0} \sum \Delta A.$$

The last sum approximates the surface area of the sphere. In the limit as the subdivisions get finer we have

$$\lim_{\Delta A \to 0} \sum \Delta A = \text{Surface area of sphere.}$$

Thus, the flux is given by

$$\int_S \vec{E} \cdot d\vec{A} = \frac{q}{R^2} \lim_{\Delta A \to 0} \sum \Delta A = \frac{q}{R^2} \cdot (\text{Surface area of sphere}) = \frac{q}{R^2}(4\pi R^2) = 4\pi q.$$

This result is known as Gauss's law.

To compute a flux with an integral instead of Riemann sums, we often write $d\vec{A} = \vec{n}\, dA$, as in the next example.

Example 6   Suppose S is the surface of the cube bounded by the six planes $x = \pm 1$, $y = \pm 1$, and $z = \pm 1$. Compute the flux of the electric field $\vec{E}$ of the previous example outward through S.

Solution   It is enough to compute the flux of $\vec{E}$ through a single face, say the top face S_1 defined by $z = 1$, where $-1 \leq x \leq 1$ and $-1 \leq y \leq 1$. By symmetry, the flux of $\vec{E}$ through the other five faces of S must be the same.

On the top face, S_1, we have $d\vec{A} = \vec{n}\, dA = \vec{k}\, dx\, dy$ and

$$\vec{E}(x, y, 1) = q\frac{x\vec{i} + y\vec{j} + \vec{k}}{(x^2 + y^2 + 1)^{3/2}}.$$

The corresponding flux integral is given by

$$\int_{S_1} \vec{E} \cdot d\vec{A} = q \int_{-1}^{1}\int_{-1}^{1} \frac{x\vec{i} + y\vec{j} + \vec{k}}{(x^2 + y^2 + 1)^{3/2}} \cdot \vec{k}\, dx\, dy = q \int_{-1}^{1}\int_{-1}^{1} \frac{1}{(x^2 + y^2 + 1)^{3/2}}\, dx\, dy.$$

Computing this integral numerically shows that

$$\text{Flux through top face} = \int_{S_1} \vec{E} \cdot d\vec{A} \approx 2.0944q.$$

Thus,

$$\text{Total flux of } \vec{E} \text{ out of cube} = \int_S \vec{E} \cdot d\vec{A} \approx 6(2.0944q) = 12.5664q.$$

Example 5 on page 1010 showed that the flux of $\vec{E}$ through a sphere of radius R centered at the origin is $4\pi q$. Since $4\pi \approx 12.5664$, Example 6 suggests that

$$\text{Total flux of } \vec{E} \text{ out of cube} = 4\pi q.$$

By computing the flux integral in Example 6 exactly, it is possible to verify that the flux of $\vec{E}$ through the cube and the sphere are exactly equal. When we encounter the Divergence Theorem in Chapter 20 we will see why this is so.

Notes on Orientation

Two difficulties can occur in choosing an orientation. The first is that if the surface is not smooth, it may not have a normal vector at every point. For example, a cube does not have a normal vector along its edges. When we have a surface, such as a cube, which is made of a finite number of smooth pieces, we choose an orientation for each piece separately. The best way to do this is usually clear. For example, on the cube we choose the outward orientation on each face. (See Figure 19.14.)

Figure 19.14: The orientation vector field $\vec{n}$ on the cube surface determined by the choice of unit normal vector at the point P

Figure 19.15: The Möbius strip is an example of a non-orientable surface

The second difficulty is that there are some surfaces which cannot be oriented at all, such as the *Möbius strip* in Figure 19.15.

Exercises and Problems for Section 19.1

Exercises

In Exercises 1–4, find the area vector of the oriented flat surface.

1. The triangle with vertices $(0, 0, 0)$, $(0, 2, 0)$, $(0, 0, 3)$ oriented in the negative x direction.

2. Circular disc of radius 5 in the xy-plane, oriented upward.

3. $y = 10$, $0 \leq x \leq 5$, $0 \leq z \leq 3$, oriented away from the xz-plane.

4. $y = -10$, $0 \leq x \leq 5$, $0 \leq z \leq 3$, oriented away from the xz-plane.

5. Find an oriented flat surface with area vector $150\vec{j}$.

6. Let S be the disk of radius 3 perpendicular the the y-axis, centered at $(0, 6, 0)$ and oriented away from the origin. Is

$$\int_S (x\vec{i} + y\vec{j}) \cdot d\vec{A}$$

a vector or a scalar?

7. Compute $\int_S (4\vec{i} + 5\vec{k}) \cdot d\vec{A}$, where S is the square of side length 3 perpendicular to the z-axis, centered at $(0, 0, -2)$ and oriented

   (a) Toward the origin.   (b) Away from the origin.

8. Compute $\int_S (2\vec{i} + 3\vec{k}) \cdot d\vec{A}$, where S is the disk of radius 4 perpendicular to the x-axis, centered at $(5, 0, 0)$ and oriented

   (a) Toward the origin.   (b) Away from the origin.

9. Let $\vec{F}(x, y, z) = z\vec{i}$. For each of the surfaces in (a)–(e), say whether the flux of $\vec{F}$ through the surface is positive, negative, or zero. The orientation of the surface is indicated by a normal vector.

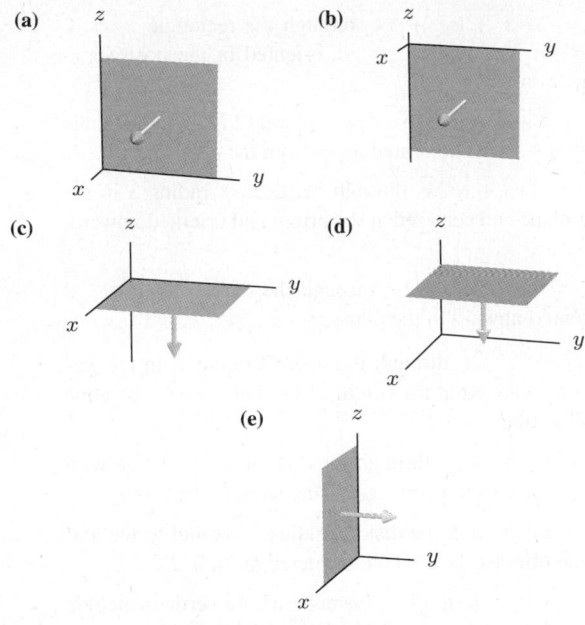

(a)

(b)

(c)

(d)

(e)

10. Repeat Exercise 9 with $\vec{F}(x, y, z) = -z\vec{i} + x\vec{k}$.

11. Repeat Exercise 9 with the vector field $\vec{F}(\vec{r}) = \vec{r}$.

In Exercises 12–15, compute the flux of $\vec{v} = \vec{i} + 2\vec{j} - 3\vec{k}$ through the rectangular region with the orientation shown.

12.

$(0, 0, 2)$ $(0, 2, 2)$ $(2, 2, 2)$ $(2, 0, 2)$

13. $(3, 2, 4)$ $(3, 0, 4)$ $(3, 2, 0)$ $(3, 0, 0)$

14.

$(2, 0, 4)$ $(0, 0, 4)$ $(2, 2, 0)$ $(0, 2, 0)$

15. $(0, 0, 3)$ $(0, 2, 3)$ $(2, 2, 0)$ $(2, 0, 0)$

For Exercises 16–19 find the flux of the constant vector field $\vec{v} = \vec{i} - \vec{j} + 3\vec{k}$ through the given surface.

16. A disk of radius 2 in the xy-plane oriented upward.

17. A triangular plate of area 4 in the yz-plane oriented in the positive x-direction.

18. A square plate of area 4 in the yz-plane oriented in the positive x-direction.

19. The triangular plate with vertices $(1, 0, 0)$, $(0, 1, 0)$, $(0, 0, 1)$, oriented away from the origin.

In Exercises 20–22, find the flux of $\vec{H} = 2\vec{i} + 3\vec{j} + 5\vec{k}$ through the surface S.

20. S is the cylinder $x^2 + y^2 = 1$, closed at the ends by the planes $z = 0$ and $z = 1$ and oriented outward.

21. S is the disk of radius 1 in the plane $x = 2$ oriented in the positive x-direction.

22. S is the disk of radius 1 in the plane $x + y + z = 1$ oriented in upward.

Find the flux of the vector fields in Exercises 23–25 out of the closed box $0 \le x \le 1, 0 \le y \le 2, 0 \le z \le 3$.

23. $\vec{F} = 3\vec{i} + 2\vec{j} + \vec{k}$ **24.** $\vec{G} = x\vec{i}$

25. $\vec{H} = zx\vec{k}$

In Exercises 26–29, calculate the flux integral.

26. $\int_S (x\vec{i} + 4\vec{j}) \cdot d\vec{A}$ where S is the disk of radius 5 perpendicular to the x-axis, centered at $(3, 0, 0)$ and oriented toward the origin.

27. $\int_S \vec{r} \cdot d\vec{A}$ where S is the sphere of radius 3 centered at the origin.

28. $\int_S (\sin x\, \vec{i} + (y^2 + z^2)\vec{j} + y^2\vec{k}) \cdot d\vec{A}$ where S is a disk of radius π in the plane $x = 3\pi/2$, oriented in the positive x-direction.

29. $\int_S (5\vec{i} + 5\vec{j} + 5\vec{k}) \cdot d\vec{A}$ where S is a disk of radius 3 in the plane $x + y + z = 1$, oriented upward.

In Exercises 30–52, calculate the flux of the vector field through the surface.

30. $\vec{F} = 2\vec{i} + 3\vec{j}$ through the square of side π in the xy-plane, oriented upward.

31. $\vec{F} = 2\vec{i} + 3\vec{j}$ through the unit disk in the yz-plane, centered at the origin and oriented in the positive x-direction.

32. $\vec{F} = x\vec{i} + y\vec{j} + z\vec{k}$ through the square of side 1.6 centered at $(2, 5, 8)$, parallel to the xz-plane and oriented away from the origin.

33. $\vec{F} = z\vec{k}$ through a square of side $\sqrt{14}$ in a horizontal plane 2 units below the xy-plane and oriented downward.

34. $\vec{F} = -y\vec{i} + x\vec{j}$ and S is the square plate in the yz-plane with corners at $(0, 1, 1)$, $(0, -1, 1)$, $(0, 1, -1)$, and $(0, -1, -1)$, oriented in the positive x-direction.

35. $\vec{F} = 7\vec{i} + 6\vec{j} + 5\vec{k}$ and S is a disk of radius 2 in the yz-plane, centered at the origin and oriented in the positive x-direction.

36. $\vec{F} = x\vec{i} + 2y\vec{j} + 3z\vec{k}$ and S is a square of side 2 in the plane $y = 3$, oriented in the positive y-direction.

37. $\vec{F} = 7\vec{i} + 6\vec{j} + 5\vec{k}$ and S is a sphere of radius π centered at the origin.

38. $\vec{F} = -5\vec{r}$ through the sphere of radius 2 centered at the origin.

39. $\vec{F} = x\vec{i} + y\vec{j} + (z^2 + 3)\vec{k}$ and S is the rectangle $z = 4$, $0 \leq x \leq 2$, $0 \leq y \leq 3$, oriented in the positive z-direction.

40. $\vec{F} = 6\vec{i} + 7\vec{j}$ through triangle of area 10 in the plane $x + y = 5$, oriented in the positive x-direction.

41. $\vec{F} = 6\vec{i} + x^2\vec{j} - \vec{k}$, through the square of side 4 in the plane $y = 3$, centered on the y-axis, with sides parallel to the x and z axes, and oriented in the positive y-direction.

42. $\vec{F} = (x + 3)\vec{i} + (y + 5)\vec{j} + (z + 7)\vec{k}$ through the rectangle $x = 4$, $0 \leq y \leq 2$, $0 \leq z \leq 3$, oriented in the positive x-direction.

43. $\vec{F} = 7\vec{r}$ through the sphere of radius 3 centered at the origin.

44. $\vec{F} = -3\vec{r}$ through the sphere of radius 2 centered at the origin.

45. $\vec{F} = 2z\vec{i} + x\vec{j} + x\vec{k}$ through the rectangle $x = 4$, $0 \leq y \leq 2$, $0 \leq z \leq 3$, oriented in the positive x-direction.

46. $\vec{F} = \vec{i} + 2\vec{j}$ through a square of side 2 lying in the plane $x + y + z = 1$, oriented away from the origin.

47. $\vec{F} = (x^2 + y^2)\vec{k}$ through the disk of radius 3 in the xy-plane and centered at the origin and oriented upward.

48. $\vec{F} = \cos(x^2 + y^2)\vec{k}$ through the disk $x^2 + y^2 \leq 9$ oriented upward in the plane $z = 1$.

49. $\vec{F} = e^{y^2 + z^2}\vec{i}$ through the disk of radius 2 in the yz-plane, centered at the origin and oriented in the positive x-direction.

50. $\vec{F} = -y\vec{i} + x\vec{j}$ through the disk in the xy-plane with radius 2, oriented upward and centered at the origin.

51. $\vec{F} = \vec{r}$ through the disk of radius 2 parallel to the xy-plane oriented upward and centered at $(0, 0, 2)$.

52. $\vec{F} = (2 - x)\vec{i}$ through the cube whose vertices include the points $(0, 0, 0)$, $(3, 0, 0)$, $(0, 3, 0)$, $(0, 0, 3)$, and oriented outward.

Problems

53. Let B be the surface of a box centered at the origin, with edges parallel to the axes and in the planes $x = \pm 1$, $y = \pm 1$, $z = \pm 1$, and let S be the sphere of radius 1 centered at origin.

    (a) Indicate whether the following flux integrals are positive, negative, or zero. No reasons needed.

      (a) $\int_B x\vec{i} \cdot d\vec{A}$ **(b)** $\int_B y\vec{i} \cdot d\vec{A}$

      (c) $\int_S |x|\vec{i} \cdot d\vec{A}$ **(d)** $\int_S (y - x)\vec{i} \cdot d\vec{A}$

    (b) Explain with reasons how you know which flux integral is greater:

$$\int_S x\vec{i} \cdot d\vec{A} \quad \text{or} \quad \int_B x\vec{i} \cdot d\vec{A} \,?$$

54. Suppose that $\vec{E}$ is a uniform electric field on 3-space, so $\vec{E}(x, y, z) = a\vec{i} + b\vec{j} + c\vec{k}$, for all points (x, y, z), where a, b, c are constants. Show, with the aid of symmetry, that the flux of $\vec{E}$ through each of the following closed surfaces S is zero:

    (a) S is the cube bounded by the planes $x = \pm 1$, $y = \pm 1$, and $z = \pm 1$.

    (b) S is the sphere $x^2 + y^2 + z^2 = 1$.

    (c) S is the cylinder bounded by $x^2 + y^2 = 1$, $z = 0$, and $z = 2$.

55. Water is flowing down a cylindrical pipe of radius 2 cm; its speed is $(3 - (3/4)r^2)$ cm/sec at a distance r cm from the center of the pipe. Find the flux through the circular cross-section of the pipe, oriented so that the flux is positive.

56. (a) What do you think will be the electric flux through the cylindrical surface that is placed as shown in the constant electric field in Figure 19.16? Why?

    (b) What if the cylinder is placed upright, as shown in Figure 19.17? Explain.

Figure 19.16

Figure 19.17

57. Let S be part of a cylinder centered on the y-axis. Explain why the three vectors fields $\vec{F}$, $\vec{G}$, and $\vec{H}$ have the same flux through S. Do not compute the flux.

$$\vec{F} = x\vec{i} + 2yz\vec{k}$$
$$\vec{G} = x\vec{i} + y\sin x\vec{j} + 2yz\vec{k}$$
$$\vec{H} = x\vec{i} + \cos(x^2 + z)\vec{j} + 2yz\vec{k}$$

58. Find the flux of $\vec{F} = \vec{r}/\|\vec{r}\|^3$ out of the sphere of radius R centered at the origin.

59. Find the flux of $\vec{F} = \vec{r}/\|r\|^2$ out of the sphere of radius R centered at the origin.

60. Consider the flux of the vector field $\vec{F} = \vec{r}/\|\vec{r}\|^p$ for $p \geq 0$ out of the sphere of radius 2 centered at the origin.

(a) For what value of p is the flux a maximum?

(b) What is that maximum value?

61. Let S be the cube with side length 2, faces parallel to the coordinate planes, and centered at the origin.

(a) Calculate the total flux of the constant vector field $\vec{v} = -\vec{i} + 2\vec{j} + \vec{k}$ out of S by computing the flux through each face separately.

(b) Calculate the flux out of S for any constant vector field $\vec{v} = a\vec{i} + b\vec{j} + c\vec{k}$.

(c) Explain why the answers to parts (a) and (b) make sense.

62. Let S be the tetrahedron with vertices at the origin and at $(1, 0, 0)$, $(0, 1, 0)$ and $(0, 0, 1)$.

(a) Calculate the total flux of the constant vector field $\vec{v} = -\vec{i} + 2\vec{j} + \vec{k}$ out of S by computing the flux through each face separately.

(b) Calculate the flux out of S in part (a) for any constant vector field $\vec{v}$.

(c) Explain why the answers to parts (a) and (b) make sense.

63. Let $P(x, y, z)$ be the pressure at the point (x, y, z) in a fluid. Let $\vec{F}(x, y, z) = P(x, y, z)\vec{k}$. Let S be the surface of a body submerged in the fluid. If S is oriented inward, show that $\int_S \vec{F} \cdot d\vec{A}$ is the buoyant force on the body, that is, the force upward on the body due to the pressure of the fluid surrounding it. [Hint: $\vec{F} \cdot d\vec{A} = P(x, y, z)\vec{k} \cdot d\vec{A} = (P(x, y, z)\,d\vec{A}) \cdot \vec{k}$.]

64. A region of 3-space has a temperature which varies from point to point. Let $T(x, y, z)$ be the temperature at a point (x, y, z). Newton's law of cooling says that $\operatorname{grad} T$ is proportional to the heat flow vector field, $\vec{F}$, where $\vec{F}$ points in the direction in which heat is flowing and has magnitude equal to the rate of flow of heat.

(a) Suppose $\vec{F} = k\operatorname{grad} T$ for some constant k. What is the sign of k?

(b) Explain why this form of Newton's law of cooling makes sense.

(c) Let W be a region of space bounded by the surface S. Explain why

$$\begin{array}{l}\text{Rate of heat} \\ \text{loss from } W\end{array} = k\int_S (\operatorname{grad} T) \cdot d\vec{A}.$$

65. The z-axis carries a constant electric charge density of λ units of charge per unit length, with $\lambda > 0$. The resulting electric field is $\vec{E}$.

(a) Sketch the electric field, $\vec{E}$, in the xy-plane, given

$$\vec{E}(x, y, z) = 2\lambda\frac{x\vec{i} + y\vec{j}}{x^2 + y^2}.$$

(b) Compute the flux of $\vec{E}$ outward through the cylinder $x^2 + y^2 = R^2$, for $0 \leq z \leq h$.

66. An infinitely long straight wire lying along the z-axis carries an electric current I flowing in the $\vec{k}$ direction. Ampère's Law in magnetostatics says that the current gives rise to a magnetic field $\vec{B}$ given by

$$\vec{B}(x, y, z) = \frac{I}{2\pi}\frac{-y\vec{i} + x\vec{j}}{x^2 + y^2}.$$

(a) Sketch the field $\vec{B}$ in the xy-plane.

(b) Suppose S_1 is a disk with center at $(0, 0, h)$, radius a, and parallel to the xy-plane, oriented in the $\vec{k}$ direction. What is the flux of $\vec{B}$ through S_1? Is your answer reasonable?

(c) Suppose S_2 is the rectangle given by $x = 0$, $a \leq y \leq b$, $0 \leq z \leq h$, and oriented in the $-\vec{i}$ direction. What is the flux of $\vec{B}$ through S_2? Does your answer seem reasonable?

67. An ideal electric dipole in electrostatics is characterized by its position in 3-space and its dipole moment vector $\vec{p}$. The electric field $\vec{D}$, at the point with position vector $\vec{r}$, of an ideal electric dipole located at the origin with dipole moment $\vec{p}$ is given by

$$\vec{D}(\vec{r}) = 3\frac{(\vec{r} \cdot \vec{p})\vec{r}}{\|\vec{r}\|^5} - \frac{\vec{p}}{\|\vec{r}\|^3}.$$

Assume $\vec{p} = p\vec{k}$, so the dipole points in the $\vec{k}$ direction and has magnitude p.

(a) What is the flux of $\vec{D}$ through a sphere S with center at the origin and radius $a > 0$?

(b) The field $\vec{D}$ is a useful approximation to the electric field $\vec{E}$ produced by two "equal and opposite" charges, q at $\vec{r}_2$ and $-q$ at $\vec{r}_1$, where the distance $\|\vec{r}_2 - \vec{r}_1\|$ is small. The dipole moment of this configuration of charges is defined to be $q(\vec{r}_2 - \vec{r}_1)$. Gauss's Law in electrostatics says that the flux of $\vec{E}$ through S is equal to 4π times the total charge enclosed by S. What is the flux of $\vec{E}$ through S if the charges at $\vec{r}_1$ and $\vec{r}_2$ are enclosed by S? How does this compare with your answer for the flux of $\vec{D}$ through S if $\vec{p} = q(\vec{r}_2 - \vec{r}_1)$?

Strengthen Your Understanding

In Problems 68–69, explain what is wrong with the statement.

68. For a certain vector field $\vec{F}$ and oriented surface S, we have $\int_S \vec{F} \cdot d\vec{A} = 2\vec{i} - 3\vec{j} + \vec{k}$.

69. If S is a region in the xy-plane oriented upwards then $\int_S \vec{F} \cdot d\vec{A} > 0$.

In Problems 70–71, give an example of:

70. A nonzero vector field $\vec{F}$ such that $\int_S \vec{F} \cdot d\vec{A} = 0$, where S is the triangular surface with corners $(1,0,0)$, $(0,1,0)$, $(0,0,1)$, oriented away from the origin.

71. A nonconstant vector field $\vec{F}(x,y,z)$ and an oriented surface S such that $\int_S \vec{F} \cdot d\vec{A} = 1$.

Are the statements in Problems 72–81 true or false? Give reasons for your answer.

72. The value of a flux integral is a scalar.

73. The area vector $\vec{A}$ of a flat, oriented surface is parallel to the surface.

74. If S is the unit sphere centered at the origin, oriented outward and the flux integral $\int_S \vec{F} \cdot d\vec{A}$ is zero, then $\vec{F} = \vec{0}$.

75. The flux of the vector field $\vec{F} = \vec{i}$ through the plane $x = 0$, with $0 \le y \le 1, 0 \le z \le 1$, oriented in the $\vec{i}$ direction is positive.

76. If S is the unit sphere centered at the origin, oriented outward and $\vec{F} = x\vec{i} + y\vec{j} + z\vec{k} = \vec{r}$, then the flux integral $\int_S \vec{F} \cdot d\vec{A}$ is positive.

77. If S is the cube bounded by the six planes $x = \pm 1, y = \pm 1, z = \pm 1$, oriented outward, and $\vec{F} = \vec{k}$, then $\int_S \vec{F} \cdot d\vec{A} = 0$.

78. If S is an oriented surface in 3-space, and $-S$ is the same surface, but with the opposite orientation, then $\int_S \vec{F} \cdot d\vec{A} = -\int_{-S} \vec{F} \cdot d\vec{A}$.

79. If S_1 is a rectangle with area 1 and S_2 is a rectangle with area 2, then $2\int_{S_1} \vec{F} \cdot d\vec{A} = \int_{S_2} \vec{F} \cdot d\vec{A}$.

80. If $\vec{F} = 2\vec{G}$, then $\int_S \vec{F} \cdot d\vec{A} = 2\int_S \vec{G} \cdot d\vec{A}$.

81. If $\int_S \vec{F} \cdot d\vec{A} > \int_S \vec{G} \cdot d\vec{A}$ then $||\vec{F}|| > ||\vec{G}||$ at all points on the surface S.

82. For each of the surfaces in (a)–(e), pick the vector field $\vec{F}_1, \vec{F}_2, \vec{F}_3, \vec{F}_4, \vec{F}_5$, with the largest flux through the surface. The surfaces are all squares of the same size. Note that the orientation is shown.

$$\vec{F}_1 = 2\vec{i} - 3\vec{j} - 4\vec{k}$$
$$\vec{F}_2 = \vec{i} - 2\vec{j} + 7\vec{k}$$
$$\vec{F}_3 = -7\vec{i} + 5\vec{j} + 6\vec{k}$$
$$\vec{F}_4 = -11\vec{i} + 4\vec{j} - 5\vec{k}$$
$$\vec{F}_5 = -5\vec{i} + 3\vec{j} + 5\vec{k}$$

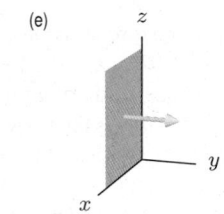

19.2 FLUX INTEGRALS FOR GRAPHS, CYLINDERS, AND SPHERES

In Section 19.1 we computed flux integrals in certain simple cases. In this section we see how to compute flux through surfaces that are graphs of functions, through cylinders, and through spheres.

Flux of a Vector Field Through the Graph of $z = f(x, y)$

Suppose S is the graph of the differentiable function $z = f(x, y)$, oriented upward, and that $\vec{F}$ is a smooth vector field. In Section 19.1 we subdivided the surface into small pieces with area vector $\Delta\vec{A}$ and defined the flux of $\vec{F}$ through S as follows:

$$\int_S \vec{F} \cdot d\vec{A} = \lim_{||\Delta\vec{A}|| \to 0} \sum \vec{F} \cdot \Delta\vec{A}.$$

How do we divide S into small pieces? One way is to use the cross-sections of f with x or y constant and take the patches in a wire frame representation of the surface. So we must calculate the area vector of one of these patches, which is approximately a parallelogram.

The Area Vector of a Coordinate Patch

According to the geometric definition of the cross product on page 745, the vector $\vec{v} \times \vec{w}$ has magnitude equal to the area of the parallelogram formed by $\vec{v}$ and $\vec{w}$ and direction perpendicular to this parallelogram and determined by the right-hand rule. Thus, we have

$$\text{Area vector of parallelogram} = \vec{A} = \vec{v} \times \vec{w}.$$

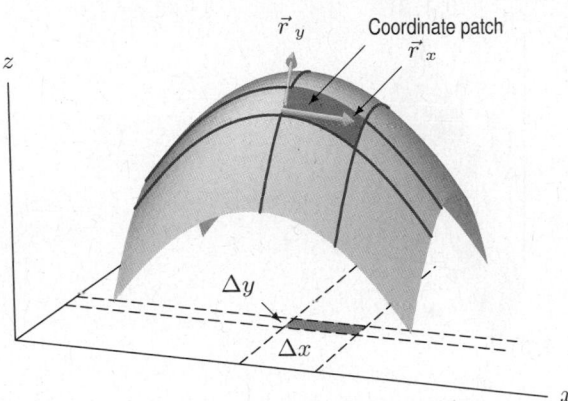

Figure 19.18: Surface showing coordinate patch and tangent vectors $\vec{r}_x$ and $\vec{r}_y$

Figure 19.19: Parallelogram-shaped patch in the tangent plane to the surface

Consider the patch of surface above the rectangular region with sides Δx and Δy in the xy-plane shown in Figure 19.18. We approximate the area vector, $\Delta \vec{A}$, of this patch by the area vector of the corresponding patch on the tangent plane to the surface. See Figure 19.19. This patch is the parallelogram determined by the vectors $\vec{v}_x$ and $\vec{v}_y$, so its area vector is given by

$$\Delta \vec{A} \approx \vec{v}_x \times \vec{v}_y.$$

To find $\vec{v}_x$ and $\vec{v}_y$, notice that a point on the surface has position vector $\vec{r} = x\vec{i} + y\vec{j} + f(x,y)\vec{k}$. Thus, a cross-section of S with y constant has tangent vector

$$\vec{r}_x = \frac{\partial \vec{r}}{\partial x} = \vec{i} + f_x\vec{k},$$

and a cross-section with x constant has tangent vector

$$\vec{r}_y = \frac{\partial \vec{r}}{\partial y} = \vec{j} + f_y\vec{k}.$$

The vectors $\vec{r}_x$ and $\vec{v}_x$ are parallel because they are both tangent to the surface and parallel to the xz-plane. Since the x-component of $\vec{r}_x$ is $\vec{i}$ and the x-component of $\vec{v}_x$ is $(\Delta x)\vec{i}$, we have $\vec{v}_x = (\Delta x)\vec{r}_x$. Similarly, we have $\vec{v}_y = (\Delta y)\vec{r}_y$. So the upward-pointing area vector of the parallelogram is

$$\Delta \vec{A} \approx \vec{v}_x \times \vec{v}_y = (\vec{r}_x \times \vec{r}_y)\,\Delta x\,\Delta y = \left(-f_x\vec{i} - f_y\vec{j} + \vec{k}\right)\Delta x\,\Delta y.$$

This is our approximation for the area vector $\Delta \vec{A}$ on the surface. Replacing $\Delta \vec{A}$, Δx, and Δy by $d\vec{A}$, dx and dy, we write

$$d\vec{A} = \left(-f_x\vec{i} - f_y\vec{j} + \vec{k}\right)dx\,dy.$$

> ### The Flux of $\vec{F}$ Through a Surface Given by a Graph of $z = f(x, y)$
>
> Suppose the surface S is the part of the graph of $z = f(x, y)$ above a region R in the xy-plane, and suppose S is oriented upward. The flux of $\vec{F}$ through S is
>
> $$\int_S \vec{F} \cdot d\vec{A} = \int_R \vec{F}(x, y, f(x, y)) \cdot \left(-f_x\vec{i} - f_y\vec{j} + \vec{k} \right) \, dx \, dy.$$

Example 1   Compute $\int_S \vec{F} \cdot d\vec{A}$ where $\vec{F}(x, y, z) = z\vec{k}$ and S is the rectangular plate with corners $(0, 0, 0)$, $(1, 0, 0)$, $(0, 1, 3)$, $(1, 1, 3)$, oriented upward. See Figure 19.20.

Figure 19.20: The vector field $\vec{F} = z\vec{k}$ on the rectangular surface S

Solution   We find the equation for the plane S in the form $z = f(x, y)$. Since f is linear, with x-slope equal to 0 and y-slope equal to 3, and $f(0, 0) = 0$, we have

$$z = f(x, y) = 0 + 0x + 3y = 3y.$$

Thus, we have

$$d\vec{A} = (-f_x\vec{i} - f_y\vec{j} + \vec{k}) \, dx \, dy = (0\vec{i} - 3\vec{j} + \vec{k}) \, dx \, dy = (-3\vec{j} + \vec{k}) \, dx \, dy.$$

The flux integral is therefore

$$\int_S \vec{F} \cdot d\vec{A} = \int_0^1 \int_0^1 3y\vec{k} \cdot (-3\vec{j} + \vec{k}) \, dx \, dy = \int_0^1 \int_0^1 3y \, dx \, dy = 1.5.$$

Flux of a Vector Field Through a Cylindrical Surface

Consider the cylinder of radius R centered on the z-axis illustrated in Figure 19.21 and oriented away from the z-axis. The coordinate patch in Figure 19.22 has surface area given by

$$\Delta A \approx R \, \Delta\theta \, \Delta z.$$

The outward unit normal $\vec{n}$ points in the direction of $x\vec{i} + y\vec{j}$, so

$$\vec{n} = \frac{x\vec{i} + y\vec{j}}{\|x\vec{i} + y\vec{j}\|} = \frac{R\cos\theta\vec{i} + R\sin\theta\vec{j}}{R} = \cos\theta\vec{i} + \sin\theta\vec{j}.$$

Therefore, the area vector of the coordinate patch is approximated by

$$\Delta\vec{A} = \vec{n} \, \Delta A \approx \left(\cos\theta\vec{i} + \sin\theta\vec{j} \right) R \, \Delta z \, \Delta\theta.$$

Figure 19.21: Outward-oriented cylinder

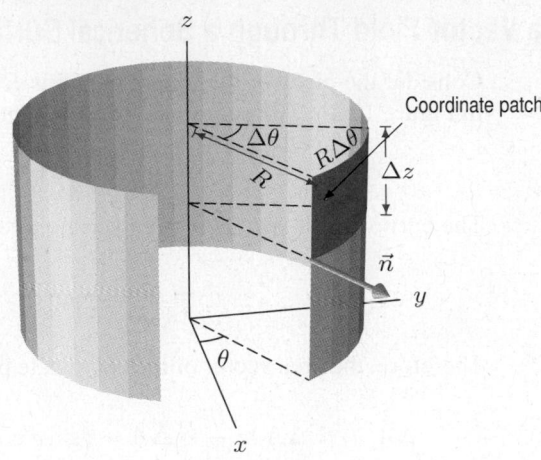

Figure 19.22: Coordinate patch with area $\Delta\vec{A}$ on surface of a cylinder

Replacing $\Delta\vec{A}$, Δz, and $\Delta\theta$ by $d\vec{A}$, dz, and $d\theta$, we write

$$d\vec{A} = \left(\cos\theta\vec{i} + \sin\theta\vec{j}\right) R\,dz\,d\theta.$$

This gives the following result:

The Flux of a Vector Field Through a Cylinder

The flux of $\vec{F}$ through the cylindrical surface S, of radius R and oriented away from the z-axis, is given by

$$\int_S \vec{F}\cdot d\vec{A} = \int_T \vec{F}(R,\theta,z)\cdot\left(\cos\theta\vec{i} + \sin\theta\vec{j}\right) R\,dz\,d\theta,$$

where T is the θz-region corresponding to S.

Example 2   Compute $\int_S \vec{F}\cdot d\vec{A}$ where $\vec{F}(x,y,z) = y\vec{j}$ and S is the part of the cylinder of radius 2 centered on the z-axis with $x \geq 0$, $y \geq 0$, and $0 \leq z \leq 3$. The surface is oriented toward the z-axis.

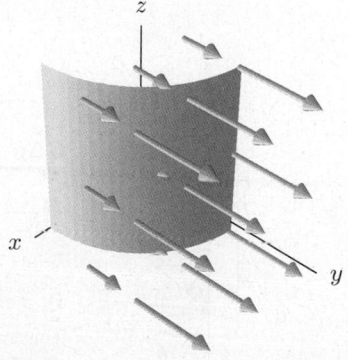

Figure 19.23: The vector field $\vec{F} = y\vec{j}$ on the surface S

Solution   In cylindrical coordinates, we have $R = 2$ and $\vec{F} = y\vec{j} = 2\sin\theta\vec{j}$. Since the orientation of S is toward the z-axis, the flux through S is given by

$$\int_S \vec{F}\cdot d\vec{A} = -\int_T 2\sin\theta\vec{j}\cdot(\cos\theta\vec{i} + \sin\theta\vec{j})2\,dz\,d\theta = -4\int_0^{\pi/2}\int_0^3 \sin^2\theta\,dz\,d\theta = -3\pi.$$

Flux of a Vector Field Through a Spherical Surface

Consider the piece of the sphere of radius R centered at the origin, oriented outward, as illustrated in Figure 19.24. The coordinate patch in Figure 19.24 has surface area given by

$$\Delta A \approx R^2 \sin \phi \, \Delta \phi \, \Delta \theta.$$

The outward unit normal $\vec{n}$ points in the direction of $\vec{r} = x\vec{i} + y\vec{j} + z\vec{k}$, so

$$\vec{n} = \frac{\vec{r}}{\|\vec{r}\|} = \sin \phi \cos \theta \vec{i} + \sin \phi \sin \theta \vec{j} + \cos \phi \vec{k}.$$

Therefore, the area vector of the coordinate patch is approximated by

$$\Delta \vec{A} \approx \vec{n} \, \Delta A = \frac{\vec{r}}{\|\vec{r}\|} \Delta A = \left(\sin \phi \cos \theta \vec{i} + \sin \phi \sin \theta \vec{j} + \cos \phi \vec{k} \right) R^2 \sin \phi \, \Delta \phi \, \Delta \theta.$$

Replacing $\Delta \vec{A}$, $\Delta \phi$, and $\Delta \theta$ by $d\vec{A}$, $d\phi$, and $d\theta$, we write

$$d\vec{A} = \frac{\vec{r}}{\|\vec{r}\|} dA = \left(\sin \phi \cos \theta \vec{i} + \sin \phi \sin \theta \vec{j} + \cos \phi \vec{k} \right) R^2 \sin \phi \, d\phi \, d\theta.$$

Thus, we obtain the following result:

The Flux of a Vector Field Through a Sphere

The flux of $\vec{F}$ through the spherical surface S, with radius R and oriented away from the origin, is given by

$$\int_S \vec{F} \cdot d\vec{A} = \int_S \vec{F} \cdot \frac{\vec{r}}{\|\vec{r}\|} dA$$

$$= \int_T \vec{F}(R, \theta, \phi) \cdot \left(\sin \phi \cos \theta \vec{i} + \sin \phi \sin \theta \vec{j} + \cos \phi \vec{k} \right) R^2 \sin \phi \, d\phi \, d\theta,$$

where T is the $\theta\phi$-region corresponding to S.

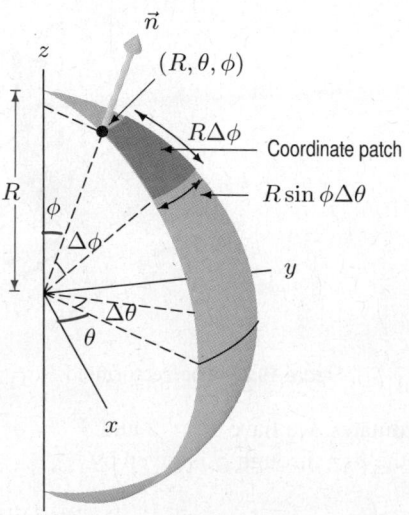

Figure 19.24: Coordinate patch with area $\Delta \vec{A}$ on surface of a sphere

Example 3   Find the flux of $\vec{F} = z\vec{k}$ through S, the upper hemisphere of radius 2 centered at the origin, oriented outward.

Solution   The hemisphere S is parameterized by spherical coordinates θ and ϕ, with $0 \leq \theta \leq 2\pi$ and $0 \leq \phi \leq \pi/2$. Since $R = 2$ and $\vec{F} = z\vec{k} = 2\cos\phi\vec{k}$, the flux is

$$\int_S \vec{F} \cdot d\vec{A} = \int_S 2\cos\phi\vec{k} \cdot (\sin\phi\cos\theta\vec{i} + \sin\phi\sin\theta\vec{j} + \cos\phi\vec{k})4\sin\phi\,d\phi\,d\theta$$

$$= \int_0^{2\pi} \int_0^{\pi/2} 8\sin\phi\cos^2\phi\,d\phi\,d\theta = 2\pi\left(8\left(\frac{-\cos^3\phi}{3}\right)\Big|_{\phi=0}^{\pi/2}\right) = \frac{16\pi}{3}.$$

Example 4   The magnetic field $\vec{B}$ due to an *ideal magnetic dipole*, $\vec{\mu}$, located at the origin is defined to be

$$\vec{B}(\vec{r}) = -\frac{\vec{\mu}}{\|\vec{r}\|^3} + \frac{3(\vec{\mu} \cdot \vec{r})\vec{r}}{\|\vec{r}\|^5}.$$

Figure 19.25 shows a sketch of $\vec{B}$ in the plane $z = 0$ for the dipole $\vec{\mu} = \vec{i}$. Notice that $\vec{B}$ is similar to the magnetic field of a bar magnet with its north pole at the tip of the vector $\vec{i}$ and its south pole at the tail of the vector $\vec{i}$.

Compute the flux of $\vec{B}$ outward through the sphere S with center at the origin and radius R.

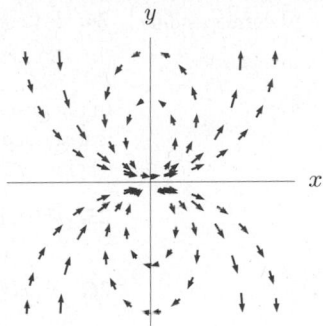

Figure 19.25: The magnetic field of a dipole, $\vec{i}$, at the origin: $\vec{B} = \dfrac{-\vec{i}}{\|\vec{r}\|^3} + \dfrac{3(\vec{i} \cdot \vec{r})\vec{r}}{\|\vec{r}\|^5}$

Solution   Since $\vec{i} \cdot \vec{r} = x$ and $\|\vec{r}\| = R$ on the sphere of radius R, we have

$$\int_S \vec{B} \cdot d\vec{A} = \int_S \left(-\frac{\vec{i}}{\|\vec{r}\|^3} + \frac{3(\vec{i} \cdot \vec{r})\vec{r}}{\|\vec{r}\|^5}\right) \cdot \frac{\vec{r}}{\|\vec{r}\|}\,dA = \int_S \left(-\frac{\vec{i} \cdot \vec{r}}{\|\vec{r}\|^4} + \frac{3(\vec{i} \cdot \vec{r})\|\vec{r}\|^2}{\|\vec{r}\|^6}\right) dA$$

$$= \int_S \frac{2\vec{i} \cdot \vec{r}}{\|\vec{r}\|^4}\,dA = \int_S \frac{2x}{\|\vec{r}\|^4}\,dA = \frac{2}{R^4}\int_S x\,dA.$$

But the sphere S is centered at the origin. Thus, the contribution to the integral from each positive x-value is canceled by the contribution from the corresponding negative x-value; so $\int_S x\,dA = 0$. Therefore,

$$\int_S \vec{B} \cdot d\vec{A} = \frac{2}{R^4}\int_S x\,dA = 0.$$

Exercises and Problems for Section 19.2

Exercises

In Exercises 1–4, find the area vector $d\vec{A}$ for the surface $z = f(x, y)$, oriented upward.

1. $f(x, y) = 3x - 5y$ **2.** $f(x, y) = 8x + 7y$

3. $f(x, y) = 2x^2 - 3y^2$ **4.** $f(x, y) = xy + y^2$

In Exercises 5–8, write an iterated integral for the flux of $\vec{F}$ through the surface S, which is the part of the graph of $z = f(x, y)$ corresponding to the region R, oriented upward. Do not evaluate the integral.

5. $\vec{F}(x, y, z) = 10\vec{i} + 20\vec{j} + 30\vec{k}$
    $f(x, y) = 2x - 3y$
    $R: -2 \leq x \leq 3, 0 \leq y \leq 5$

6. $\vec{F}(x, y, z) = z\vec{i} + x\vec{j} + y\vec{k}$
    $f(x, y) = 50 - 4x + 10y$
    $R: 0 \leq x \leq 4, 0 \leq y \leq 8$

7. $\vec{F}(x, y, z) = yz\vec{i} + xy\vec{j} + xy\vec{k}$
    $f(x, y) = \cos x + \sin 2y$
    $R:$ Triangle with vertices $(0, 0), (0, 5), (5, 0)$

8. $\vec{F}(x, y, z) = \cos(x + 2y)\vec{j}$
    $f(x, y) = xe^{3y}$
    $R:$ Quarter disk of radius 5 centered at the origin, in quadrant I

In Exercises 9–12, compute the flux of $\vec{F}$ through the surface S, which is the part of the graph of $z = f(x, y)$ corresponding to region R, oriented upward.

9. $\vec{F}(x, y, z) = 3\vec{i} - 2\vec{j} + 6\vec{k}$
    $f(x, y) = 4x - 2y$
    $R: 0 \leq x \leq 5, 0 \leq y \leq 10$

10. $\vec{F}(x, y, z) = \vec{i} - 2\vec{j} + z\vec{k}$
    $f(x, y) = xy$
    $R: 0 \leq x \leq 10, 0 \leq y \leq 10$

11. $\vec{F}(x, y, z) = \cos y\vec{i} + z\vec{j} + \vec{k}$
    $f(x, y) = x^2 + 2y$
    $R: 0 \leq x \leq 1, 0 \leq y \leq 1$

12. $\vec{F}(x, y, z) = x\vec{i} + z\vec{k}$
    $f(x, y) = x + y + 2$
    $R:$ Triangle with vertices $(-1, 0), (1, 0), (0, 1)$

In Exercises 13–16, write an iterated integral for the flux of $\vec{F}$ through the cylindrical surface S centered on the z-axis, oriented away from the z-axis. Do not evaluate the integral.

13. $\vec{F}(x, y, z) = \vec{i} + 2\vec{j} + 3\vec{k}$
    $S:$ radius 10, $x \geq 0, y \geq 0, 0 \leq z \leq 5$

14. $\vec{F}(x, y, z) = x\vec{i} + 2y\vec{j} + 3z\vec{k}$
    $S:$ radius 10, $0 \leq z \leq 5$

15. $\vec{F}(x, y, z) = z^2\vec{i} + e^x\vec{j} + \vec{k}$
    $S:$ radius 6, inside sphere of radius 10

16. $\vec{F}(x, y, z) = x^2yz\vec{j} + z^3\vec{k}$
    $S:$ radius 2, between the xy-plane and the paraboloid $z = x^2 + y^2$

In Exercises 17–20, compute the flux of $\vec{F}$ through the cylindrical surface S centered on the z-axis, oriented away from the z-axis.

17. $\vec{F}(x, y, z) = z\vec{j} + 6x\vec{k}$
    $S:$ radius 5, $y \geq 0, 0 \leq z \leq 20$

18. $\vec{F}(x, y, z) = y\vec{i} + xz\vec{k}$
    $S:$ radius 10, $x \geq 0, y \geq 0, 0 \leq z \leq 3$

19. $\vec{F}(x, y, z) = xyz\vec{j} + xe^z\vec{k}$
    $S:$ radius 2, $0 \leq y \leq x, 0 \leq z \leq 10$

20. $\vec{F}(x, y, z) = xy\vec{i} + 2z\vec{j}$
    $S:$ radius 1, $x \geq 0, 0 \leq y \leq 1/2, 0 \leq z \leq 2$

In Exercises 21–24, write an iterated integral for the flux of $\vec{F}$ through the spherical surface S centered at the origin, oriented away from the origin. Do not evaluate the integral.

21. $\vec{F}(x, y, z) = \vec{i} + 2\vec{j} + 3\vec{k}$
    $S:$ radius 10, $z \geq 0$

22. $\vec{F}(x, y, z) = x\vec{i} + 2y\vec{j} + 3z\vec{k}$
    $S:$ radius 5, entire sphere

23. $\vec{F}(x, y, z) = z^2\vec{i}$
    $S:$ radius 2, $x \geq 0$

24. $\vec{F}(x, y, z) = e^x\vec{k}$
    $S:$ radius 3, $y \geq 0, z \leq 0$

In Exercises 25–27, compute the flux of $\vec{F}$ through the spherical surface S centered at the origin, oriented away from the origin.

25. $\vec{F}(x, y, z) = z\vec{i}$
    $S:$ radius 20, $x \geq 0, y \geq 0, z \geq 0$

26. $\vec{F}(x, y, z) = y\vec{i} - x\vec{j} + z\vec{k}$
    $S:$ radius 4, entire sphere

27. $\vec{F}(x, y, z) = x\vec{i} + y\vec{j}$
    $S:$ radius 1, above the cone $\phi = \pi/4$.

In Exercises 28–29, compute the flux of $\vec{v} = z\vec{k}$ through the rectangular region with the orientation shown.

28.

29.

Problems

In Problems 30–45 compute the flux of the vector field $\vec{F}$ through the surface S.

30. $\vec{F} = z\vec{k}$ and S is the portion of the plane $x + y + z = 1$ that lies in the first octant, oriented upward.

31. $\vec{F} = (x-y)\vec{i} + z\vec{j} + 3x\vec{k}$ and S is the part of the plane $z = x + y$ above the rectangle $0 \le x \le 2, 0 \le y \le 3$, oriented upward.

32. $\vec{F} = 2x\vec{j} + y\vec{k}$ and S is the part of the surface $z = -y + 1$ above the square $0 \le x \le 1, 0 \le y \le 1$, oriented upward.

33. $\vec{F} = -y\vec{j} + z\vec{k}$ and S is the part of the surface $z = y^2 + 5$ over the rectangle $-2 \le x \le 1, 0 \le y \le 1$, oriented upward.

34. $\vec{F} = \ln(x^2)\vec{i} + e^x\vec{j} + \cos(1-z)\vec{k}$ and S is the part of the surface $z = -y + 1$ above the square $0 \le x \le 1$, $0 \le y \le 1$, oriented upward.

35. $\vec{F} = 5\vec{i} + 7\vec{j} + z\vec{k}$ and S is a closed cylinder of radius 3 centered on the z-axis, with $-2 \le z \le 2$, and oriented outward.

36. $\vec{F} = x\vec{i} + y\vec{j} + z\vec{k}$ and S is a closed cylinder of radius 2 centered on the y-axis, with $-3 \le y \le 3$, and oriented outward.

37. $\vec{F} = 3x\vec{i} + y\vec{j} + z\vec{k}$ and S is the part of the surface $z = -2x - 4y + 1$, oriented upward, with (x, y) in the triangle R with vertices $(0,0), (0,2), (1,0)$.

38. $\vec{F} = x\vec{i} + y\vec{j}$ and S is the part of the surface $z = 25 - (x^2 + y^2)$ above the disk of radius 5 centered at the origin, oriented upward.

39. $\vec{F} = \cos(x^2 + y^2)\vec{k}$ and S is as in Exercise 38.

40. $\vec{F} = \vec{r}$ and S is the part of the plane $x + y + z = 1$ above the rectangle $0 \le x \le 2, 0 \le y \le 3$, oriented downward.

41. $\vec{F} = \vec{r}$ and S is the part of the surface $z = x^2 + y^2$ above the disk $x^2 + y^2 \le 1$, oriented downward.

42. $\vec{F} = xz\vec{i} + y\vec{k}$ and S is the hemisphere $x^2 + y^2 + z^2 = 9, z \ge 0$, oriented upward.

43. $\vec{F} = -xz\vec{i} - yz\vec{j} + z^2\vec{k}$ and S is the cone $z = \sqrt{x^2 + y^2}$ for $0 \le z \le 6$, oriented upward.

44. $\vec{F} = y\vec{i} + \vec{j} - xz\vec{k}$ and S is the surface $y = x^2 + z^2$, with $x^2 + z^2 \le 1$, oriented in the positive y-direction.

45. $\vec{F} = x^2\vec{i} + y^2\vec{j} + z^2\vec{k}$ and S is the oriented triangular surface shown in Figure 19.26.

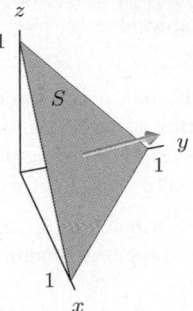

Figure 19.26

In Problems 46–47, compute the flux of $\vec{F}$ through the cylindrical surface in Figure 19.27, oriented away from the z-axis.

Figure 19.27

46. $\vec{F} = x\vec{i} + y\vec{j}$

47. $\vec{F} = xz\vec{i} + yz\vec{j} + z^3\vec{k}$

In Problems 48–51, compute the flux of $\vec{F}$ through the spherical surface, S.

48. $\vec{F} = z\vec{k}$ and S is the upper hemisphere of radius 2 centered at the origin, oriented outward.

49. $\vec{F} = y\vec{i} - x\vec{j} + z\vec{k}$ and S is the spherical cap given by $x^2 + y^2 + z^2 = 1, z \ge 0$, oriented upward.

50. $\vec{F} = z^2\vec{k}$ and S is the upper hemisphere of the sphere $x^2 + y^2 + z^2 = 25$, oriented away from the origin.

51. $\vec{F} = x\vec{i} + y\vec{j} + z\vec{k}$ and S is the surface of the sphere $x^2 + y^2 + z^2 = a^2$, oriented outward.

52. Compute the flux of $\vec{F} = x\vec{i} + y\vec{j} + z\vec{k}$ over the quarter cylinder S given by $x^2 + y^2 = 1, 0 \le x \le 1, 0 \le y \le 1$, $0 \le z \le 1$, oriented outward.

53. Compute the flux of $\vec{F} = x\vec{i} + \vec{j} + \vec{k}$ through the surface S given by $x = \sin y \sin z$, with $0 \le y \le \pi/2$, $0 \le z \le \pi/2$, oriented in the direction of increasing x.

54. Compute the flux of $\vec{F} = (x + z)\vec{i} + \vec{j} + z\vec{k}$ through the surface S given by $y = x^2 + z^2$, with $0 \le y \le 1$, $x \ge 0, z \ge 0$, oriented toward the xz-plane.

55. Let $\vec{F} = (xze^{yz})\vec{i} + xz\vec{j} + (5 + x^2 + y^2)\vec{k}$. Calculate the flux of $\vec{F}$ through the disk $x^2 + y^2 \leq 1$ in the xy-plane, oriented upward.

56. Let $\vec{H} = (e^{xy} + 3z + 5)\vec{i} + (e^{xy} + 5z + 3)\vec{j} + (3z + e^{xy})\vec{k}$. Calculate the flux of $\vec{H}$ through the square of side 2 with one vertex at the origin, one edge along the positive y-axis, one edge in the xz-plane with $x > 0$, $z > 0$, and the normal $\vec{n} = \vec{i} - \vec{k}$.

57. Electric charge is distributed in space with density (in coulomb/m^3) given in spherical coordinates by

$$\delta(\rho, \phi, \theta) = \begin{cases} \delta_0 \text{ (a constant)} & \rho \leq a \\ 0 & \rho > a. \end{cases}$$

(a) Describe the charge distribution in words.
(b) Find the electric field $\vec{E}$ due to δ. Assume that $\vec{E}$ can be written in spherical coordinates as $\vec{E} = E(\rho)\vec{e}_\rho$, where $\vec{e}_\rho$ is the unit outward normal to the

sphere of radius ρ. In addition, $\vec{E}$ satisfies Gauss's Law for any simple closed surface S enclosing a volume W:

$$\int_S \vec{E} \cdot d\vec{A} = k \int_W \delta \, dV, \quad k \text{ a constant.}$$

58. Electric charge is distributed in space with density (in coulomb/m^3) given in cylindrical coordinates by

$$\delta(r, \theta, z) = \begin{cases} \delta_0 \text{ (a constant)} & \text{if } r \leq a \\ 0 & \text{if } r > a \end{cases}$$

(a) Describe the charge distribution in words.
(b) Find the electric field $\vec{E}$ due to δ. Assume that $\vec{E}$ can be written in cylindrical coordinates as $\vec{E} = E(r)\vec{e}_r$, where $\vec{e}_r$ is the unit outward vector to the cylinder of radius r, and that $\vec{E}$ satisfies Gauss's Law (see Problem 57).

Strengthen Your Understanding

In Problems 59–60, explain what is wrong with the statement.

59. Flux outward through the cone, given in cylindrical coordinates by $z = r$, can be computed using the formula $d\vec{A} = \left(\cos\theta\vec{i} + \sin\theta\vec{j}\right) R \, dz \, d\theta$.

60. For the surface $z = f(x, y)$ oriented upward, the formula

$$d\vec{A} = \vec{n} \, dA = \left(-f_x\vec{i} - f_y\vec{j} + \vec{k}\right) dx \, dy$$

gives $\vec{n} = -f_x\vec{i} - f_y\vec{j} + \vec{k}$ and $dA = dx \, dy$.

In Problems 61–62, give an example of:

61. A function $f(x, y)$ such that, for the surface $z = f(x, y)$ oriented upwards, we have $d\vec{A} = (\vec{i} + \vec{j} + \vec{k}) \, dx \, dy$.

62. An oriented surface S on the cylinder of radius 10 centered on the z-axis such that $\int_S \vec{F} \cdot d\vec{A} = 600$, where $\vec{F} = x\vec{i} + y\vec{j}$.

Are the statements in Problems 63–65 true or false? Give reasons for your answer.

63. If S is the part of the graph of f lying above $a \leq x \leq b, c \leq y \leq d$, then S has surface area $\int_a^b \int_c^d \sqrt{f_x^2 + f_y^2 + 1} \, dx \, dy$.

64. If $\vec{A}(x, y)$ is the area vector for $z = f(x, y)$ oriented upward and $\vec{B}(x, y)$ is the area vector for $z = -f(x, y)$ oriented upward, then $\vec{A}(x, y) = -\vec{B}(x, y)$.

65. If S is the sphere $x^2 + y^2 + z^2 = 1$ oriented outward and $\int_S \vec{F} \cdot d\vec{A} = 0$, then $\vec{F}(x, y, z)$ is perpendicular to $x\vec{i} + y\vec{j} + z\vec{k}$ at every point of S.

66. The vector field, $\vec{F}$, in Figure 19.28 depends only on z; that is, it is of the form $g(z)\vec{k}$, where g is an increasing function. The integral $\int_S \vec{F} \cdot d\vec{A}$ represents the flux of $\vec{F}$ through this rectangle, S, oriented upward. In each of the following cases, how does the flux change?

(a) The rectangle is twice as wide in the x-direction, with new corners at the origin, $(2, 0, 0)$, $(2, 1, 3)$, $(0, 1, 3)$.
(b) The rectangle is moved so that its corners are at $(1, 0, 0)$, $(2, 0, 0)$, $(2, 1, 3)$, $(1, 1, 3)$.
(c) The orientation is changed to downward.
(d) The rectangle is tripled in size, so that its new corners are at the origin, $(3, 0, 0)$, $(3, 3, 9)$, $(0, 3, 9)$.

Figure 19.28

19.3 THE DIVERGENCE OF A VECTOR FIELD

Imagine that the vector fields in Figures 19.29 and 19.30 are velocity vector fields describing the flow of a fluid.[2] Figure 19.29 suggests outflow from the origin; for example, it could represent the expanding cloud of matter in the big-bang theory of the origin of the universe. We say that the origin is a *source*. Figure 19.30 suggests flow into the origin; in this case we say that the origin is a *sink*.

In this section we use the flux out of a closed surface surrounding a point to measure the outflow per unit volume there, also called the *divergence*, or *flux density*.

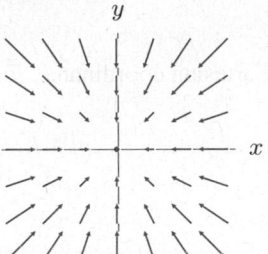

Figure 19.29: Vector field showing a source

Figure 19.30: Vector field showing a sink

Definition of Divergence

To measure the outflow per unit volume of a vector field at a point, we calculate the flux out of a small sphere centered at the point, divide by the volume enclosed by the sphere, then take the limit of this flux-to-volume ratio as the sphere contracts around the point.

> ### Geometric Definition of Divergence
>
> The **divergence**, or **flux density**, of a smooth vector field $\vec{F}$, written **div** $\vec{F}$, is a scalar-valued function defined by
>
> $$\operatorname{div} \vec{F}(x, y, z) = \lim_{\text{Volume} \to 0} \frac{\int_S \vec{F} \cdot d\vec{A}}{\text{Volume of } S}.$$
>
> Here S is a sphere centered at (x, y, z), oriented outward, that contracts down to (x, y, z) in the limit.

The limit can be computed using other shapes as well, such as the cubes in Example 2.

> ### Cartesian Coordinate Definition of Divergence
>
> If $\vec{F} = F_1 \vec{i} + F_2 \vec{j} + F_3 \vec{k}$, then
>
> $$\operatorname{div} \vec{F} = \frac{\partial F_1}{\partial x} + \frac{\partial F_2}{\partial y} + \frac{\partial F_3}{\partial z}.$$

The dot product formula gives an easy way to remember the Cartesian coordinate definition, and suggests another common notation for div $\vec{F}$, namely $\nabla \cdot \vec{F}$. Using $\nabla = \frac{\partial}{\partial x}\vec{i} + \frac{\partial}{\partial y}\vec{j} + \frac{\partial}{\partial z}\vec{k}$, we can write

$$\operatorname{div} \vec{F} = \nabla \cdot \vec{F} = \left(\frac{\partial}{\partial x}\vec{i} + \frac{\partial}{\partial y}\vec{j} + \frac{\partial}{\partial z}\vec{k} \right) \cdot (F_1 \vec{i} + F_2 \vec{j} + F_3 \vec{k}) = \frac{\partial F_1}{\partial x} + \frac{\partial F_2}{\partial y} + \frac{\partial F_3}{\partial z}.$$

---

[2] Although not all vector fields represent physically realistic fluid flows, it is useful to think of them in this way.

Example 1   Calculate the divergence of $\vec{F}(\vec{r}) = \vec{r}$ at the origin

     (a) Using the geometric definition.

     (b) Using the Cartesian coordinate definition.

Solution   (a) Using the method of Example 5 on page 1010, you can calculate the flux of $\vec{F}$ out of the sphere of radius a, centered at the origin; it is $4\pi a^3$. So we have

$$\text{div}\,\vec{F}(0,0,0) = \lim_{a \to 0} \frac{\text{Flux}}{\text{Volume}} = \lim_{a \to 0} \frac{4\pi a^3}{\frac{4}{3}\pi a^3} = \lim_{a \to 0} 3 = 3.$$

     (b) In Cartesian coordinates, $\vec{F}(x,y,z) = x\vec{i} + y\vec{j} + z\vec{k}$, so

$$\text{div}\,\vec{F} = \frac{\partial}{\partial x}(x) + \frac{\partial}{\partial y}(y) + \frac{\partial}{\partial z}(z) = 1 + 1 + 1 = 3.$$

The next example shows that the divergence can be negative if there is net inflow to a point.

Example 2   (a) Using the geometric definition, find the divergence of $\vec{v} = -x\vec{i}$ at: (i) $(0,0,0)$ (ii) $(2,2,0)$.

     (b) Confirm that the coordinate definition gives the same results.

Solution   (a) (i) The vector field $\vec{v} = -x\vec{i}$ is parallel to the x-axis and is shown in the xy-plane in Figure 19.31. To compute the flux density at $(0,0,0)$, we use a cube S_1, centered at the origin with edges parallel to the axes, of length $2c$. Then the flux through the faces perpendicular to the y- and z-axes is zero (because the vector field is parallel to these faces). On the faces perpendicular to the x-axis, the vector field and the outward normal are parallel but point in opposite directions. On the face at $x = c$, where $\vec{v} = -c\vec{i}$ and $\Delta\vec{A} = \|\vec{A}\|\vec{i}$, we have

$$\vec{v} \cdot \Delta\vec{A} = -c\,\|\Delta\vec{A}\|.$$

On the face at $x = -c$, where $\vec{v} = c\vec{i}$ and $\Delta\vec{A} = -\|\vec{A}\|\vec{i}$, the dot product is still negative:

$$\vec{v} \cdot \Delta\vec{A} = -c\,\|\Delta\vec{A}\|.$$

Therefore, the flux through the cube is given by

$$\int_{S_1} \vec{v} \cdot d\vec{A} = \int_{\text{Face } x=-c} \vec{v} \cdot d\vec{A} + \int_{\text{Face } x=c} \vec{v} \cdot d\vec{A}$$

$$= -c \cdot \text{Area of one face} + (-c) \cdot \text{Area of other face} = -2c(2c)^2 = -8c^3.$$

Thus,

$$\text{div}\,\vec{v}(0,0,0) = \lim_{\text{Volume} \to 0} \frac{\int_S \vec{v} \cdot d\vec{A}}{\text{Volume of cube}} = \lim_{c \to 0} \left(\frac{-8c^3}{(2c)^3} \right) = -1.$$

Since the vector field points inward toward the yz-plane, it makes sense that the divergence is negative at the origin.

     (ii) Take S_2 to be a cube as before, but centered this time at the point $(2,2,0)$. See Figure 19.31. As before, the flux through the faces perpendicular to the y- and z-axes is zero. On the face at $x = 2 + c$,

$$\vec{v} \cdot \Delta\vec{A} = -(2+c)\,\|\Delta\vec{A}\|.$$

On the face at $x = 2 - c$ with outward normal, the dot product is positive, and

$$\vec{v} \cdot \Delta\vec{A} = (2-c)\,\|\Delta\vec{A}\|.$$

Therefore, the flux through the cube is given by

$$\int_{S_2} \vec{v} \cdot d\vec{A} = \int_{\text{Face } x=2-c} \vec{v} \cdot d\vec{A} + \int_{\text{Face } x=2+c} \vec{v} \cdot d\vec{A}$$

$$= (2-c) \cdot \text{Area of one face} - (2+c) \cdot \text{Area of other face} = -2c(2c)^2 = -8c^3.$$

Then, as before,

$$\text{div } \vec{v}\,(2,2,0) = \lim_{\text{Volume} \to 0} \frac{\int_S \vec{v} \cdot d\vec{A}}{\text{Volume of cube}} = \lim_{c \to 0} \left(\frac{-8c^3}{(2c)^3} \right) = -1.$$

Although the vector field is flowing away from the point $(2, 2, 0)$ on the left, this outflow is smaller in magnitude than the inflow on the right, so the net outflow is negative.

(b) Since $\vec{v} = -x\vec{i} + 0\vec{j} + 0\vec{k}$, the formula gives

$$\text{div } \vec{v} = \frac{\partial}{\partial x}(-x) + \frac{\partial}{\partial y}(0) + \frac{\partial}{\partial z}(0) = -1 + 0 + 0 = -1.$$

Figure 19.31: Vector field $\vec{v} = -x\vec{i}$ in the xy-plane

Why Do the Two Definitions of Divergence Give the Same Result?

The geometric definition defines div $\vec{F}$ as the flux density of $\vec{F}$. To see why the coordinate definition is also the flux density, imagine computing the flux out of a small box-shaped surface S at (x_0, y_0, z_0), with sides of length Δx, Δy, and Δz parallel to the axes. On S_1 (the back face of the box shown in Figure 19.32, where $x = x_0$), the outward normal is in the negative x-direction, so $d\vec{A} = -dy\,dz\,\vec{i}$. Assuming $\vec{F}$ is approximately constant on S_1, we have

$$\int_{S_1} \vec{F} \cdot d\vec{A} = \int_{S_1} \vec{F} \cdot (-\vec{i})\,dy\,dz \approx -F_1(x_0, y_0, z_0) \int_{S_1} dy\,dz$$

$$= -F_1(x_0, y_0, z_0) \cdot \text{Area of } S_1 = -F_1(x_0, y_0, z_0)\,\Delta y\,\Delta z.$$

On S_2, the face where $x = x_0 + \Delta x$, the outward normal points in the positive x-direction, so $d\vec{A} = dy\,dz\,\vec{i}$. Therefore,

$$\int_{S_2} \vec{F} \cdot d\vec{A} = \int_{S_2} \vec{F} \cdot \vec{i}\,dy\,dz \approx F_1(x_0 + \Delta x, y_0, z_0) \int_{S_2} dy\,dz$$

$$= F_1(x_0 + \Delta x, y_0, z_0) \cdot \text{Area of } S_2 = F_1(x_0 + \Delta x, y_0, z_0)\,\Delta y\,\Delta z.$$

Figure 19.32: Box used to find div $\vec{F}$ at (x_0, y_0, z_0)

Thus,

$$\int_{S_1} \vec{F} \cdot d\vec{A} + \int_{S_2} \vec{F} \cdot d\vec{A} \approx F_1(x_0 + \Delta x, y_0, z_0)\Delta y \Delta z - F_1(x_0, y_0, z_0)\Delta y \Delta z$$

$$= \frac{F_1(x_0 + \Delta x, y_0, z_0) - F_1(x_0, y_0, z_0)}{\Delta x}\Delta x \Delta y \Delta z$$

$$\approx \frac{\partial F_1}{\partial x}\Delta x \Delta y \Delta z.$$

By an analogous argument, the contribution to the flux from S_3 and S_4 (the surfaces perpendicular to the y-axis) is approximately

$$\frac{\partial F_2}{\partial y}\Delta x \, \Delta y \, \Delta z,$$

and the contribution to the flux from S_5 and S_6 is approximately

$$\frac{\partial F_3}{\partial z}\Delta x \, \Delta y \, \Delta z.$$

Thus, adding these contributions, we have

$$\text{Total flux through } S \approx \frac{\partial F_1}{\partial x}\Delta x \, \Delta y \, \Delta z + \frac{\partial F_2}{\partial y}\Delta x \, \Delta y \, \Delta z + \frac{\partial F_3}{\partial z}\Delta x \, \Delta y \, \Delta z.$$

Since the volume of the box is $\Delta x \, \Delta y \, \Delta z$, the flux density is

$$\frac{\text{Total flux through } S}{\text{Volume of box}} \approx \frac{\frac{\partial F_1}{\partial x}\Delta x \Delta y \Delta z + \frac{\partial F_2}{\partial y}\Delta x \Delta y \Delta z + \frac{\partial F_3}{\partial z}\Delta x \Delta y \Delta z}{\Delta x \Delta y \Delta z}$$

$$= \frac{\partial F_1}{\partial x} + \frac{\partial F_2}{\partial y} + \frac{\partial F_3}{\partial z}.$$

Divergence-Free Vector Fields

A vector field $\vec{F}$ is said to be *divergence free* or *solenoidal* if $\text{div}\vec{F} = 0$ everywhere that $\vec{F}$ is defined.

Example 3   Figure 19.33 shows, for three values of the constant p, the vector field

$$\vec{E} = \frac{\vec{r}}{\|\vec{r}\|^p} \qquad \vec{r} = x\vec{i} + y\vec{j} + z\vec{k}, \ \vec{r} \neq \vec{0}.$$

(a) Find a formula for $\text{div}\,\vec{E}$.

(b) Is there a value of p for which $\vec{E}$ is divergence-free? If so, find it.

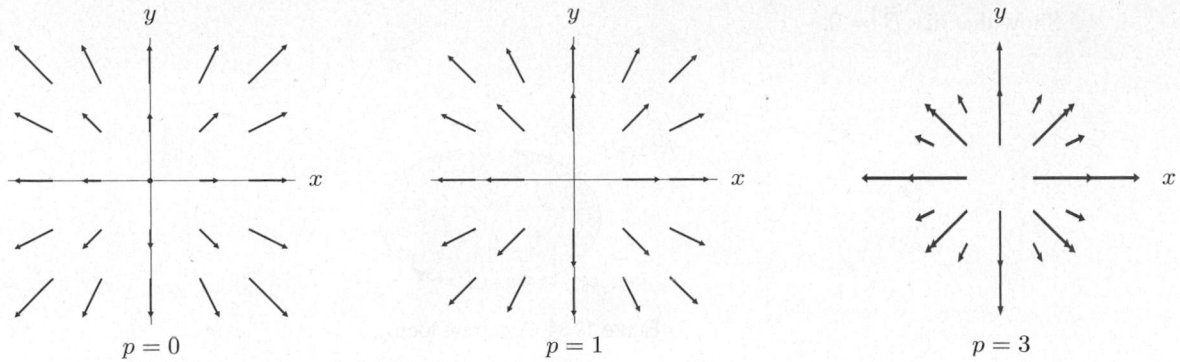

Figure 19.33: The vector field $\vec{E}\,(\vec{r}) = \vec{r}\,/\|\vec{r}\,\|^p$ for $p = 0$, 1, and 3 in the xy-plane

Solution

(a) The components of $\vec{E}$ are

$$\vec{E} = \frac{x}{(x^2 + y^2 + z^2)^{p/2}}\vec{i} + \frac{y}{(x^2 + y^2 + z^2)^{p/2}}\vec{j} + \frac{z}{(x^2 + y^2 + z^2)^{p/2}}\vec{k}\,.$$

We compute the partial derivatives

$$\frac{\partial}{\partial x}\left(\frac{x}{(x^2 + y^2 + z^2)^{p/2}}\right) = \frac{1}{(x^2 + y^2 + z^2)^{p/2}} - \frac{px^2}{(x^2 + y^2 + z^2)^{(p/2)+1}}$$

$$\frac{\partial}{\partial y}\left(\frac{y}{(x^2 + y^2 + z^2)^{p/2}}\right) = \frac{1}{(x^2 + y^2 + z^2)^{p/2}} - \frac{py^2}{(x^2 + y^2 + z^2)^{(p/2)+1}}$$

$$\frac{\partial}{\partial z}\left(\frac{z}{(x^2 + y^2 + z^2)^{p/2}}\right) = \frac{1}{(x^2 + y^2 + z^2)^{p/2}} - \frac{pz^2}{(x^2 + y^2 + z^2)^{(p/2)+1}}.$$

So

$$\begin{aligned}
\operatorname{div}\vec{E} &= \frac{3}{(x^2 + y^2 + z^2)^{p/2}} - \frac{p(x^2 + y^2 + z^2)}{(x^2 + y^2 + z^2)^{(p/2)+1}} \\
&= \frac{3-p}{(x^2 + y^2 + z^2)^{p/2}} = \frac{3-p}{\|\vec{r}\,\|^p}.
\end{aligned}$$

(b) The divergence is zero when $p = 3$, so $\vec{F}\,(\vec{r}) = \vec{r}\,/\|\vec{r}\,\|^3$ is a divergence-free vector field. Notice that the divergence is zero even though the vectors point outward from the origin.

Magnetic Fields

An important class of divergence-free vector fields is the magnetic fields. One of Maxwell's Laws of Electromagnetism is that the magnetic field $\vec{B}$ satisfies

$$\operatorname{div}\vec{B} = 0.$$

Example 4   An infinitesimal current loop, similar to that shown in Figure 19.34, is called a *magnetic dipole*. Its magnitude is described by a constant vector μ, called the dipole moment. The magnetic field due to a magnetic dipole with moment $\vec{\mu}$ is

$$\vec{B} = -\frac{\vec{\mu}}{\|\vec{r}\,\|^3} + \frac{3(\vec{\mu}\cdot\vec{r}\,)\vec{r}}{\|\vec{r}\,\|^5}, \qquad \vec{r} \neq \vec{0}\,.$$

Show that $\operatorname{div} \vec{B} = 0$.

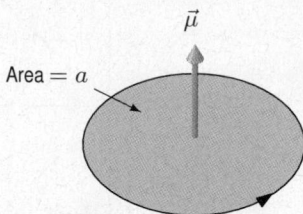

Area $= a$

$\vec{\mu}$

Figure 19.34: A current loop

Solution

To show that $\operatorname{div} \vec{B} = 0$ we can use the following version of the product rule for the divergence: if g is a scalar function and $\vec{F}$ is a vector field, then

$$\operatorname{div}(g\vec{F}) = (\operatorname{grad} g) \cdot \vec{F} + g \operatorname{div} \vec{F}.$$

(See Problem 36 on page 1032.) Thus, since $\operatorname{div} \vec{\mu} = 0$, we have

$$\operatorname{div}\left(\frac{\vec{\mu}}{\|\vec{r}\|^3}\right) = \operatorname{div}\left(\frac{1}{\|\vec{r}\|^3}\vec{\mu}\right) = \operatorname{grad}\left(\frac{1}{\|\vec{r}\|^3}\right) \cdot \vec{\mu} + \left(\frac{1}{\|\vec{r}\|^3}\right) 0$$

and

$$\operatorname{div}\left(\frac{(\vec{\mu}\cdot\vec{r})\vec{r}}{\|\vec{r}\|^5}\right) = \operatorname{div}\left(\vec{\mu}\cdot\vec{r}\,\frac{\vec{r}}{\|\vec{r}\|^5}\right) = \operatorname{grad}(\vec{\mu}\cdot\vec{r}) \cdot \frac{\vec{r}}{\|\vec{r}\|^5} + (\vec{\mu}\cdot\vec{r})\operatorname{div}\left(\frac{\vec{r}}{\|\vec{r}\|^5}\right).$$

From Problems 67 and 68 on page 796 and Example 3 on page 1028, we have

$$\operatorname{grad}\left(\frac{1}{\|\vec{r}\|^3}\right) = \frac{-3\vec{r}}{\|\vec{r}\|^5}, \qquad \operatorname{grad}(\vec{\mu}\cdot\vec{r}) = \vec{\mu}, \qquad \operatorname{div}\left(\frac{\vec{r}}{\|\vec{r}\|^5}\right) = \frac{-2}{\|\vec{r}\|^5}.$$

Putting these results together gives

$$\operatorname{div} \vec{B} = -\operatorname{grad}\left(\frac{1}{\|\vec{r}\|^3}\right) \cdot \vec{\mu} + 3\operatorname{grad}(\vec{\mu}\cdot\vec{r}) \cdot \frac{\vec{r}}{\|\vec{r}\|^5} + 3(\vec{\mu}\cdot\vec{r})\operatorname{div}\left(\frac{\vec{r}}{\|\vec{r}\|^5}\right)$$

$$= \frac{3\vec{r}\cdot\vec{\mu}}{\|\vec{r}\|^5} + \frac{3\vec{\mu}\cdot\vec{r}}{\|\vec{r}\|^5} - \frac{6\vec{\mu}\cdot\vec{r}}{\|\vec{r}\|^5}$$

$$= 0.$$

Exercises and Problems for Section 19.3

Exercises

Are the quantities in Exercises 1–2 vectors or scalars? Calculate them.

1. $\operatorname{div}\left((x^2+y)\vec{i} + (xye^z)\vec{j} - \ln(x^2+y^2)\vec{k}\right)$

2. $\operatorname{div}\left((2\sin(xy)+\tan z)\vec{i} + (\tan y)\vec{j} + (e^{x^2+y^2})\vec{k}\right)$

3. Which of the following two vector fields, sketched in the xy-plane, appears to have the greater divergence at the origin? The scales are the same on each.

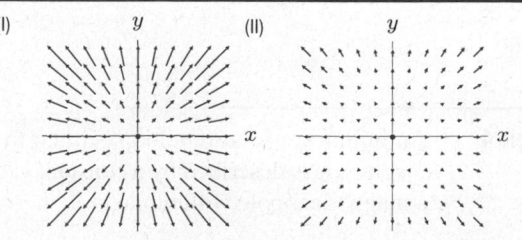

4. For each of the following vector fields, sketched in the xy-plane, decide if the divergence is positive, zero, or negative at the indicated point.

(a)

(b)

(c)

In Exercises 5–13, find the divergence of the vector field. (Note: $\vec{r} = x\vec{i} + y\vec{j} + z\vec{k}$.)

5. $\vec{F}(x, y) = -y\vec{i} + x\vec{j}$

6. $\vec{F}(x, y) = -x\vec{i} + y\vec{j}$

7. $\vec{F}(x, y, z) = (-x + y)\vec{i} + (y + z)\vec{j} + (-z + x)\vec{k}$

8. $\vec{F}(x, y) = (x^2 - y^2)\vec{i} + 2xy\vec{j}$

9. $\vec{F}(x, y, z) = 3x^2\vec{i} - \sin(xz)(\vec{i} + \vec{k})$

10. $\vec{F} = \left(\ln\left(x^2 + 1\right)\vec{i} + (\cos y)\vec{j} + (xye^z)\vec{k}\right)$

11. $\vec{F}(\vec{r}) = \vec{a} \times \vec{r}$

12. $\vec{F}(x, y) = \dfrac{-y\vec{i} + x\vec{j}}{x^2 + y^2}$

13. $\vec{F}(\vec{r}) = \dfrac{\vec{r} - \vec{r}_0}{\|\vec{r} - \vec{r}_0\|}, \quad \vec{r} \neq \vec{r}_0$

Problems

14. Draw two vector fields that have positive divergence everywhere.

15. Draw two vector fields that have negative divergence everywhere.

16. Draw two vector fields that have zero divergence everywhere.

17. A small sphere of radius 0.1 surrounds the point $(2, 3, -1)$. The flux of a vector field $\vec{G}$ into this sphere is 0.00004π. Estimate $\operatorname{div} \vec{G}$ at the point $(2, 3, -1)$.

18. A smooth vector field $\vec{F}$ has $\operatorname{div} \vec{F}(1, 2, 3) = 5$. Estimate the flux of $\vec{F}$ out of a small sphere of radius 0.01 centered at the point $(1, 2, 3)$.

19. Let $\vec{F}$ be a vector field with $\operatorname{div} \vec{F} = x^2 + y^2 - z$. Estimate $\int_S \vec{F} \cdot d\vec{A}$ where S is

  (a) (i) A sphere of radius 0.1 centered at $(2, 0, 0)$.

     (ii) A box of side 0.2 with edges parallel to the axes and centered at $(0, 0, 10)$.

  (b) The point $(2, 0, 0)$ is called a *source* for the vector field $\vec{F}$; the point $(0, 0, 10)$ is called a *sink*. Explain the reason for these names using your answer to part (a).

20. The flux of $\vec{F}$ out of a small sphere of radius 0.1 centered at $(4, 5, 2)$, is 0.0125. Estimate:

  (a) $\operatorname{div} \vec{F}$ at $(4, 5, 2)$

  (b) The flux of $\vec{F}$ out of a sphere of radius 0.2 centered at $(4, 5, 2)$.

21. (a) Find the flux of $\vec{F} = 2x\vec{i} - 3y\vec{j} + 5z\vec{k}$ through a box with four of its corners at the points $(a, b, c), (a + w, b, c), (a, b + w, c), (a, b, c + w)$ and edge length w. See Figure 19.35.

  (b) Use the geometric definition and part (a) to find $\operatorname{div} \vec{F}$ at the point (a, b, c).

  (c) Find $\operatorname{div} \vec{F}$ using partial derivatives.

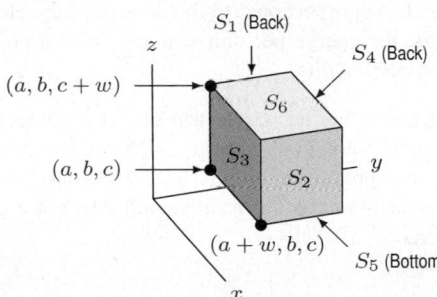

Figure 19.35

22. Suppose $\vec{F} = (3x + 2)\vec{i} + 4x\vec{j} + (5x + 1)\vec{k}$. Use the method of Exercise 21 to find $\operatorname{div} \vec{F}$ at the point (a, b, c) by two different methods.

23. Use the geometric definition of divergence to find $\operatorname{div} \vec{v}$ at the origin, where $\vec{v} = -2\vec{r}$. Check that you get the same result using the definition in Cartesian coordinates.

24. (a) Let $f(x, y) = axy + ax^2y + y^3$. Find $\operatorname{div} \operatorname{grad} f$.

  (b) If possible, choose a so that $\operatorname{div} \operatorname{grad} f = 0$ for all x, y.

25. Let

$$\vec{F} = (9a^2x + 10ay^2)\vec{i} + (10z^3 - 6ay)\vec{j} - (3z + 10x^2 + 10y^2)\vec{k}.$$

Find the value(s) of a making $\operatorname{div} \vec{F}$

(a) 0   **(b)** A minimum

26. The vector field $\vec{F}(\vec{r}) = \vec{r}/\|\vec{r}\|^3$ is not defined at the origin. Nevertheless, we can attempt to use the flux definition to compute div $\vec{F}$ at the origin. What is the result?

27. The divergence of a magnetic vector field $\vec{B}$ must be zero everywhere. Which of the following vector fields cannot be a magnetic vector field?

   (a) $\vec{B}(x, y, z) = -y\vec{i} + x\vec{j} + (x + y)\vec{k}$
   (b) $\vec{B}(x, y, z) = -z\vec{i} + y\vec{j} + x\vec{k}$
   (c) $\vec{B}(x, y, z) = (x^2 - y^2 - x)\vec{i} + (y - 2xy)\vec{j}$

28. Let $\vec{F}(x, y, z) = z\vec{k}$.

   (a) Calculate div $\vec{F}$.
   (b) Sketch $\vec{F}$. Does it appear to be diverging? Does this agree with your answer to part (a)?

29. Let $\vec{F}(\vec{r}) = \vec{r}/\|\vec{r}\|^3$ (in 3-space), $\vec{r} \neq \vec{0}$.

   (a) Calculate div $\vec{F}$.
   (b) Sketch $\vec{F}$. Does it appear to be diverging? Does this agree with your answer to part (a)?

Problems 30–31 involve electric fields. Electric charge produces a vector field $\vec{E}$, called the electric field, which represents the force on a unit positive charge placed at the point. Two positive or two negative charges repel one another, whereas two charges of opposite sign attract one another. The divergence of $\vec{E}$ is proportional to the density of the electric charge (that is, the charge per unit volume), with a positive constant of proportionality.

30. A certain distribution of electric charge produces the electric field shown in Figure 19.36. Where are the charges that produced this electric field concentrated? Which concentrations are positive and which are negative?

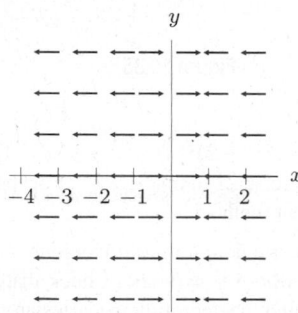

y

x

$-4 \; -3 \; -2 \; -1 \qquad 1 \quad 2$

Figure 19.36

31. The electric field at the point $\vec{r}$ as a result of a point charge at the origin is $\vec{E}(\vec{r}) = k\vec{r}/\|\vec{r}\|^3$.

   (a) Calculate div $\vec{E}$ for $\vec{r} \neq \vec{0}$.
   (b) Calculate the limit suggested by the geometric definition of div $\vec{E}$ at the point $(0, 0, 0)$.
   (c) Explain what your answers mean in terms of charge density.

32. Due to roadwork ahead, the traffic on a highway slows linearly from 55 miles/hour to 15 miles/hour over a 2000-foot stretch of road, then crawls along at 15 miles/hour for 5000 feet, then speeds back up linearly to 55 miles/hour in the next 1000 feet, after which it moves steadily at 55 miles/hour.

   (a) Sketch a velocity vector field for the traffic flow.
   (b) Write a formula for the velocity vector field $\vec{v}$ (miles/hour) as a function of the distance x feet from the initial point of slowdown. (Take the direction of motion to be $\vec{i}$ and consider the various sections of the road separately.)
   (c) Compute div $\vec{v}$ at $x = 1000, 5000, 7500, 10,000$. Be sure to include the proper units.

33. The velocity field $\vec{v}$ in Problem 32 does not give a complete description of the traffic flow, for it takes no account of the spacing between vehicles. Let ρ be the density (cars/mile) of highway, where we assume that ρ depends only on x.

   (a) Using your highway experience, arrange in ascending order: $\rho(0), \rho(1000), \rho(5000)$.
   (b) What are the units and interpretation of the vector field $\rho\vec{v}$?
   (c) Would you expect $\rho\vec{v}$ to be constant? Why? What does this mean for div$(\rho\vec{v})$?
   (d) Determine $\rho(x)$ if $\rho(0) = 75$ cars/mile and $\rho\vec{v}$ is constant.
   (e) If the highway has two lanes, find the approximate number of feet between cars at $x = 0, 1000$, and 5000.

34. Let $\vec{r} = x\vec{i} + y\vec{j} + z\vec{k}$ and $\vec{c} = c_1\vec{i} + c_2\vec{j} + c_3\vec{k}$, a constant vector; let S be a sphere of radius R centered at the origin. Find

   (a) div$(\vec{r} \times \vec{c})$ **(b)** $\int_S (\vec{r} \times \vec{c}) \cdot d\vec{A}$

35. Show that if $\vec{a}$ is a constant vector and $f(x, y, z)$ is a function, then div$(f\vec{a}) = (\text{grad } f) \cdot \vec{a}$.

36. Show that if $g(x, y, z)$ is a scalar-valued function and $\vec{F}(x, y, z)$ is a vector field, then

$$\text{div}(g\vec{F}) = (\text{grad } g) \cdot \vec{F} + g \, \text{div } \vec{F}.$$

37. If $f(x, y, z)$ and $g(x, y, z)$ are functions with continuous second partial derivatives, show that

$$\text{div}(\text{grad } f \times \text{grad } g) = 0.$$

In Problems 38–40, use Problems 36 and 37 to find the divergence of the vector field. The vectors $\vec{a}$ and $\vec{b}$ are constant.

38. $\vec{F} = \dfrac{1}{\|\vec{r}\|^p}\vec{a} \times \vec{r}$ **39.** $\vec{B} = \dfrac{1}{x^a}\vec{r}$

40. $\vec{G} = (\vec{b} \cdot \vec{r})\vec{a} \times \vec{r}$

41. Let $\vec{F}(x,y) = u(x,y)\vec{i} + v(x,y)\vec{j}$ be a 2-dimensional vector field. Let $F(x,y)$ be the magnitude of $\vec{F}$ and let $\theta(x,y)$ be the angle of $\vec{F}$ with the positive x-axis at the point (x,y), so that $u = F\cos\theta$ and $v = F\sin\theta$. Let $\vec{T}$ be the unit vector in the direction of $\vec{F}$, and let $\vec{N}$ be the unit vector in the direction of $\vec{k} \times \vec{F}$, perpendicular to $\vec{F}$. Show that

$$\operatorname{div}\vec{F} = F\theta_{\vec{N}} + F_{\vec{T}}.$$

This problem shows that the divergence of the vector field $\vec{F}$ is the sum of two terms. The first term, $F\theta_{\vec{N}}$, is due to changes in the direction of $\vec{F}$ perpendicular to the flow lines, so it reflects the extent to which flow lines of $\vec{F}$ fail to be parallel. The second term, $F_{\vec{T}}$, is due to changes in the magnitude of $\vec{F}$ along flow lines of $\vec{F}$.

42. In Problem 64 on page 1015 it was shown that the rate of heat loss from a volume V in a region of non-uniform temperature equals $k\int_S (\operatorname{grad} T)\cdot d\vec{A}$, where k is a constant, S is the surface bounding V, and $T(x,y,z)$ is the temperature at the point (x,y,z) in space. By taking the limit as V contracts to a point, show that, at that point,

$$\frac{\partial T}{\partial t} = B\operatorname{div}\operatorname{grad} T$$

where B is a constant with respect to x, y, z, but may depend on time, t.

43. A vector field, $\vec{v}$, in the plane is a *point source* at the origin if its direction is away from the origin at every point, its magnitude depends only on the distance from the origin, and its divergence is zero away from the origin.

(a) Explain why a point source at the origin must be of the form $\vec{v} = \left[f(x^2 + y^2)\right](x\vec{i} + y\vec{j})$ for some positive function f.

(b) Show that $\vec{v} = K(x^2 + y^2)^{-1}(x\vec{i} + y\vec{j})$ is a point source at the origin if $K > 0$.

(c) What is the magnitude $\|\vec{v}\|$ of the source in part (b) as a function of the distance from its center?

(d) Sketch the vector field $\vec{v} = (x^2 + y^2)^{-1}(x\vec{i} + y\vec{j})$.

(e) Show that $\phi = \frac{K}{2}\log(x^2 + y^2)$ is a potential function for the source in part (b).

44. A vector field, $\vec{v}$, in the plane is a *point sink* at the origin if its direction is toward the origin at every point, its magnitude depends only on the distance from the origin, and its divergence is zero away from the origin.

(a) Explain why a point sink at the origin must be of the form $\vec{v} = \left[f(x^2 + y^2)\right](x\vec{i} + y\vec{j})$ for some negative function f.

(b) Show that $\vec{v} = K(x^2 + y^2)^{-1}(x\vec{i} + y\vec{j})$ is a point sink at the origin if $K < 0$.

(c) Determine the magnitude $\|\vec{v}\|$ of the sink in part (b) as a function of the distance from its center.

(d) Sketch $\vec{v} = -(x^2 + y^2)^{-1}(x\vec{i} + y\vec{j})$.

(e) Show that $\phi = \frac{K}{2}\log(x^2 + y^2)$ is a potential function for the sink in part (b).

Strengthen Your Understanding

In Problems 45–47, explain what is wrong with the statement.

45. $\operatorname{div}(2x\vec{i}) = 2\vec{i}$.

46. For $\vec{F}(x,y,z) = (x^2+y)\vec{i} + (2y+z)\vec{j} - z^2\vec{k}$ we have $\operatorname{div}\vec{F} = 2x\vec{i} + 2\vec{j} - 2z\vec{k}$.

47. The divergence of $f(x,y,z) = x^2 + yz$ is given by $\operatorname{div} f(x,y,z) = 2x + z + y$.

In Problems 48–50, give an example of:

48. A vector field $\vec{F}(x,y,z)$ whose divergence is a nonzero constant.

49. A nonzero vector field $\vec{F}(x,y,z)$ whose divergence is zero.

50. A vector field that is not divergence free.

Are the statements in Problems 51–63 true or false? Give reasons for your answer.

51. $\operatorname{div}(\vec{F} + \vec{G}) = \operatorname{div}\vec{F} + \operatorname{div}\vec{G}$

52. $\operatorname{grad}(\vec{F}\cdot\vec{G}) = \vec{F}(\operatorname{div}\vec{G}) + (\operatorname{div}\vec{F})\vec{G}$

53. $\operatorname{div}\vec{F}$ is a scalar whose value can vary from point to point.

54. If $\vec{F}$ is a vector field in 3-space, then $\operatorname{div}\vec{F}$ is also a vector field.

55. A constant vector field $\vec{F} = a\vec{i} + b\vec{j} + c\vec{k}$ has zero divergence.

56. If a vector field $\vec{F}$ in 3-space has zero divergence then $\vec{F} = a\vec{i} + b\vec{j} + c\vec{k}$ where a, b and c are constants.

57. If $\vec{F}$ is a vector field in 3-space, and f is a scalar function, then $\operatorname{div}(f\vec{F}) = f\operatorname{div}\vec{F}$.

58. If $\vec{F}$ is a vector field in 3-space, and $\vec{F} = \operatorname{grad} f$, then $\operatorname{div}\vec{F} = 0$.

59. If $\vec{F}$ is a vector field in 3-space, then $\operatorname{grad}(\operatorname{div}\vec{F}) = \vec{0}$.

60. The field $\vec{F}(\vec{r}) = \vec{r}$ is divergence free.

61. If $f(x,y,z)$ is any given continuous scalar function, then there is at least one vector field $\vec{F}$ such that $\operatorname{div}\vec{F} = f$.

62. If $\vec{F}$ and $\vec{G}$ are vector fields satisfying $\operatorname{div}\vec{F} = \operatorname{div}\vec{G}$ then $\vec{F} = \vec{G}$.

63. There exist a scalar function f and a vector field $\vec{F}$ satisfying $\operatorname{div}(\operatorname{grad} f) = \operatorname{grad}(\operatorname{div}\vec{F})$.

64. For $\vec{r} = x\vec{i} + y\vec{j} + z\vec{k}$, an arbitrary function $f(x, y, z)$ and an arbitrary vector field, $\vec{F}(x, y, z)$, which of the following is a vector field, and which is a constant vector field?

    (a)   grad f **(b)** $(\text{div}\,\vec{F})\vec{i}$ **(c)** $(\text{div}\,\vec{r})\vec{i}$

    (d) $(\text{div}\,\vec{i})\vec{F}$ **(e)**   grad$(\text{div}\,\vec{F})$

19.4 THE DIVERGENCE THEOREM

The Divergence Theorem is a multivariable analogue of the Fundamental Theorem of Calculus; it says that the integral of the flux density over a solid region equals the flux integral through the boundary of the region.

The Boundary of a Solid Region

A solid region is an open region in 3-space. The boundary of a solid region may be thought of as the skin between the interior of the region and the space around it. For example, the boundary of a solid ball is a spherical surface, the boundary of a solid cube is its six faces, and the boundary of a solid cylinder is a tube sealed at both ends by disks. (See Figure 19.37). A surface which is the boundary of a solid region is called a *closed surface*.

Figure 19.37: Several solid regions and their boundaries

Calculating the Flux from the Flux Density

Consider a solid region W in 3-space whose boundary is the closed surface S. There are two ways to find the total flux of a vector field $\vec{F}$ out of W. One is to calculate the flux of $\vec{F}$ through S:

$$\text{Flux out of } W = \int_S \vec{F} \cdot d\vec{A}.$$

Another way is to use div $\vec{F}$, which gives the flux density at any point in W. We subdivide W into small boxes, as shown in Figure 19.38. Then, for a small box of volume ΔV,

$$\text{Flux out of box} \approx \text{Flux density} \cdot \text{Volume} = \text{div}\,\vec{F}\,\Delta V.$$

What happens when we add the fluxes out of all the boxes? Consider two adjacent boxes, as shown in Figure 19.39. The flux through the shared wall is counted twice, once out of the box on each side. When we add the fluxes, these two contributions cancel, so we get the flux out of the solid region formed by joining the two boxes. Continuing in this way, we find that

Figure 19.38: Subdivision of region into small boxes

Fluxes through inner wall cancel

Figure 19.39: Adding the flux out of adjacent boxes

$$\text{Flux out of } W = \sum \text{Flux out of small boxes} \approx \sum \text{div}\,\vec{F}\,\Delta V.$$

We have approximated the flux by a Riemann sum. As the subdivision gets finer, the sum approaches an integral, so

$$\text{Flux out of } W = \int_W \text{div}\,\vec{F}\,dV.$$

We have calculated the flux in two ways, as a flux integral and as a volume integral. Therefore, these two integrals must be equal. This result holds even if W is not a rectangular solid. Thus, we have the following result.[3]

Theorem 19.1: The Divergence Theorem

If W is a solid region whose boundary S is a piecewise smooth surface, and if $\vec{F}$ is a smooth vector field on an open region containing W and S, then

$$\int_S \vec{F} \cdot d\vec{A} = \int_W \text{div}\,\vec{F}\,dV,$$

where S is given the outward orientation.

Example 1 Use the Divergence Theorem to calculate the flux of the vector field $\vec{F}(\vec{r}) = \vec{r}$ through the sphere of radius a centered at the origin.

Solution In Example 5 on page 1010 we computed the flux using the definition of a flux integral, giving

$$\int_S \vec{r} \cdot d\vec{A} = 4\pi a^3.$$

Now we use $\text{div}\,\vec{F} = \text{div}(x\vec{i} + y\vec{j} + z\vec{k}) = 3$ and the Divergence Theorem:

$$\int_S \vec{r} \cdot d\vec{A} = \int_W \text{div}\,\vec{F}\,dV = \int_W 3\,dV = 3 \cdot \frac{4}{3}\pi a^3 = 4\pi a^3.$$

Example 2 Use the Divergence Theorem to calculate the flux of the vector field

$$\vec{F}(x, y, z) = (x^2 + y^2)\vec{i} + (y^2 + z^2)\vec{j} + (x^2 + z^2)\vec{k}$$

through the cube in Figure 19.40.

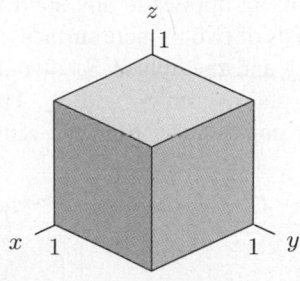

Figure 19.40

Solution The divergence of $\vec{F}$ is $\text{div}\,\vec{F} = 2x + 2y + 2z$. Since $\text{div}\,\vec{F}$ is positive everywhere in the first quadrant, the flux through S is positive. By the Divergence Theorem,

---

[3]A proof of the Divergence Theorem using the coordinate definition of the divergence can be found in the online supplement at www.wiley.com/college/hughes-hallett.

$$\int_S \vec{F} \cdot d\vec{A} = \int_0^1 \int_0^1 \int_0^1 2(x+y+z)\, dx\, dy\, dz = \int_0^1 \int_0^1 (x^2 + 2x(y+z))\Big|_0^1 dy\, dz$$

$$= \int_0^1 \int_0^1 1 + 2(y+z)\, dy\, dz = \int_0^1 (y + y^2 + 2yz)\Big|_0^1 dz$$

$$= \int_0^1 (2+2z)\, dz = (2z + z^2)\Big|_0^1 = 3.$$

The Divergence Theorem and Divergence-Free Vector Fields

An important application of the Divergence Theorem is the study of divergence-free vector fields.

Example 3   In Example 3 on page 1028 we saw that the following vector field is divergence free:

$$\vec{F}(\vec{r}) = \frac{\vec{r}}{\|\vec{r}\|^3}, \qquad \vec{r} \neq \vec{0}.$$

Calculate $\int_S \vec{F} \cdot d\vec{A}$, using the Divergence Theorem if possible, for the following surfaces:

(a) S_1 is the sphere of radius a centered at the origin.
(b) S_2 is the sphere of radius a centered at the point $(2a, 0, 0)$.

Solution   (a) We cannot use the Divergence Theorem directly because $\vec{F}$ is not defined everywhere inside the sphere (it is not defined at the origin). Since $\vec{F}$ points outward everywhere on S_1, the flux out of S_1 is positive. On S_1,

$$\vec{F} \cdot d\vec{A} = \|\vec{F}\| dA = \frac{a}{a^3} dA,$$

so

$$\int_{S_1} \vec{F} \cdot d\vec{A} = \frac{1}{a^2} \int_{S_1} dA = \frac{1}{a^2}(\text{Area of } S_1) = \frac{1}{a^2} 4\pi a^2 = 4\pi.$$

Notice that the flux is not zero, although div $\vec{F}$ is zero everywhere it is defined.

(b) Suppose W is the solid region enclosed by S_2. Since div $\vec{F} = 0$ everywhere in W, we can use the Divergence Theorem in this case, giving

$$\int_{S_2} \vec{F} \cdot d\vec{A} = \int_W \text{div } \vec{F} \, dV = \int_W 0 \, dV = 0.$$

The Divergence Theorem applies to any solid region W and its boundary S, even in cases where the boundary consists of two or more surfaces. For example, if W is the solid region between the sphere S_1 of radius 1 and the sphere S_2 of radius 2, both centered at the same point, then the boundary of W consists of both S_1 and S_2. The Divergence Theorem requires the outward orientation, which on S_2 points away from the center and on S_1 points toward the center. (See Figure 19.41.)

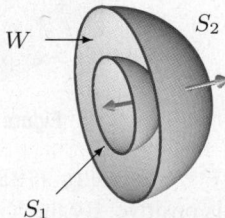

Figure 19.41: Cut-away view of the region W between two spheres, showing orientation vectors

Example 4   Let S_1 be the sphere of radius 1 centered at the origin and let S_2 be the ellipsoid $x^2 + y^2 + 4z^2 = 16$, both oriented outward. For

$$\vec{F}(\vec{r}) = \frac{\vec{r}}{\|\vec{r}\|^3}, \qquad \vec{r} \neq \vec{0},$$

show that

$$\int_{S_1} \vec{F} \cdot d\vec{A} = \int_{S_2} \vec{F} \cdot d\vec{A}.$$

Solution   The ellipsoid contains the sphere; let W be the solid region between them. Since W does not contain the origin, div $\vec{F}$ is defined and equal to zero everywhere in W. Thus, if S is the boundary of W, then

$$\int_S \vec{F} \cdot d\vec{A} = \int_W \operatorname{div} \vec{F} \, dV = 0.$$

But S consists of S_2 oriented outward and S_1 oriented inward, so

$$0 = \int_S \vec{F} \cdot d\vec{A} = \int_{S_2} \vec{F} \cdot d\vec{A} - \int_{S_1} \vec{F} \cdot d\vec{A},$$

and thus

$$\int_{S_2} \vec{F} \cdot d\vec{A} = \int_{S_1} \vec{F} \cdot d\vec{A}.$$

In Example 3 we showed that $\int_{S_1} \vec{F} \cdot d\vec{A} = 4\pi$, so $\int_{S_2} \vec{F} \cdot d\vec{A} = 4\pi$ also. Note that it would have been more difficult to compute the integral over the ellipsoid directly.

Electric Fields

The electric field produced by a positive point charge q placed at the origin is

$$\vec{E} = q \frac{\vec{r}}{\|\vec{r}\|^3}.$$

Using Example 3, we see that the flux of the electric field through any sphere centered at the origin is $4\pi q$. In fact, using the idea of Example 4, we can show that the flux of $\vec{E}$ through any closed surface containing the origin is $4\pi q$. See Problems 36 and 37 on page 1039. This is a special case of Gauss's Law, which states that the flux of an electric field through any closed surface is proportional to the total charge enclosed by the surface. Carl Friedrich Gauss (1777–1855) also discovered the Divergence Theorem, which is sometimes called Gauss's Theorem.

Exercises and Problems for Section 19.4

Exercises

For Exercises 1–5, compute the flux integral $\int_S \vec{F} \cdot d\vec{A}$ in two ways, if possible, directly and using the Divergence Theorem. In each case, S is closed and oriented outward.

1. $\vec{F}(\vec{r}) = \vec{r}$ and S is the cube enclosing the volume $0 \leq x \leq 2, 0 \leq y \leq 2$, and $0 \leq z \leq 2$.

2. $\vec{F} = y\vec{j}$ and S is a closed vertical cylinder of height 2, with its base a circle of radius 1 on the xy-plane, centered at the origin.

3. $\vec{F} = x^2\vec{i} + 2y^2\vec{j} + 3z^2\vec{k}$ and S is the surface of the box with faces $x = 1, x = 2, y = 0, y = 1, z = 0, z = 1$.

4. $\vec{F} = (z^2 + x)\vec{i} + (x^2 + y)\vec{j} + (y^2 + z)\vec{k}$ and S is the closed cylinder $x^2 + z^2 = 1$, with $0 \leq y \leq 1$, oriented outward.

5. $\vec{F} = -z\vec{i} + x\vec{k}$ and S is a square pyramid with height 3 and base on the xy-plane of side length 1.

Find the flux of the vector fields in Exercises 6–12 out of the closed box $0 \leq x \leq 2, 0 \leq y \leq 3, 0 \leq z \leq 4$.

6. $\vec{F} = 4\vec{i} + 7\vec{j} - \vec{k}$

7. $\vec{G} = y\vec{i} + z\vec{k}$

8. $\vec{H} = xy\vec{i} + z\vec{j} + y\vec{k}$

9. $\vec{J} = xy^2\vec{j} + x\vec{k}$

10. $\vec{N} = e^z\vec{i} + \sin(xy)\vec{k}$

11. $\vec{M} = ((3x + 4y)\vec{i} + (4y + 5z)\vec{j} + (5z + 3x)\vec{k}$

12. $\vec{M}$ where div $\vec{M} = xy + 5$

Problems

13. Find the flux of $\vec{F} = z\vec{i} + y\vec{j} + x\vec{k}$ out of a sphere of radius 3 centered at the origin.

14. Find the flux of $\vec{F} = xy\vec{i} + yz\vec{j} + zx\vec{k}$ out of a sphere of radius 1 centered at the origin.

15. Find the flux of $\vec{F} = x^3\vec{i} + y^3\vec{j} + z^3\vec{k}$ through the closed surface bounding the solid region $x^2 + y^2 \leq 4$, $0 \leq z \leq 5$, oriented outward.

16. The region W lies between the spheres $x^2 + y^2 + z^2 = 4$ and $x^2 + y^2 + z^2 = 9$ and within the cone $z = \sqrt{x^2 + y^2}$ with $z \geq 0$; its boundary is the closed surface, S, oriented outward. Find the flux of $\vec{F} = x^3\vec{i} + y^3\vec{j} + z^3\vec{k}$ out of S.

17. Find the flux of $\vec{F}$ through the closed cylinder of radius 2, centered on the z-axis, with $3 \leq z \leq 7$, if $\vec{F} = (x + 3e^{yz})\vec{i} + (\ln(x^2z^2 + 1) + y)\vec{j} + z\vec{k}$.

18. Find the flux of $\vec{F} = e^{y^2z^2}\vec{i} + (\tan(0.001x^2z^2) + y^2)\vec{j} + (\ln(1 + x^2y^2) + z^2)\vec{k}$ out of the closed box $0 \leq x \leq 5, 0 \leq y \leq 4, 0 \leq z \leq 3$.

19. Find the flux of $\vec{F} = x^2\vec{i} + z\vec{j} + y\vec{k}$ out of the closed cone $x = \sqrt{y^2 + z^2}$, with $0 \leq x \leq 1$.

20. Suppose $\vec{F}$ is a vector field with div $\vec{F} = 10$. Find the flux of $\vec{F}$ out of a cylinder of height a and radius a, centered on the z-axis and with base in the xy-plane.

21. A cone has its tip at the point $(0, 0, 5)$ and its base the disk D, $x^2 + y^2 \leq 1$, in the xy-plane. The surface of the cone is the curved and slanted face, S, oriented upward, and the flat base, D, oriented downward. The flux of the constant vector field $\vec{F} = a\vec{i} + b\vec{j} + c\vec{k}$ through S is given by
$$\int_S \vec{F} \cdot d\vec{A} = 3.22.$$
Is it possible to calculate $\int_D \vec{F} \cdot d\vec{A}$? If so, give the answer. If not, explain what additional information you would need to be able to make this calculation.

22. If V is a volume surrounded by a closed surface S, show that $\frac{1}{3} \int_S \vec{r} \cdot d\vec{A} = V$.

23. A vector field $\vec{F}$ satisfies div$\vec{F} = 0$ everywhere. Show that $\int_S \vec{F} \cdot d\vec{A} = 0$ for every closed surface S.

24. Let $\vec{r} = x\vec{i} + y\vec{j} + z\vec{k}$ and let $\vec{F}$ be the vector field given by
$$\vec{F} = \frac{\vec{r}}{\|\vec{r}\|^3}.$$

(a) Calculate the flux of $\vec{F}$ out of the unit sphere $x^2 + y^2 + z^2 = 1$ oriented outward.

(b) Calculate div $\vec{F}$. Show your work and simplify your answer completely.

(c) Use your answers to parts (a) and (b) to calculate the flux out of a box of side 10 centered at the origin and with sides parallel to the coordinate planes. (The box is also oriented outward.)

25. (a) Find div$(\vec{r}/\|\vec{r}\|^2)$ where $\vec{r} = x\vec{i} + y\vec{j}$ for $\vec{r} \neq \vec{0}$.

(b) Can you use the Divergence Theorem to compute the flux of $\vec{r}/\|\vec{r}\|^2$ out of a closed cylinder of radius 1, length 2, centered at the origin, and with its axis along the z-axis?

(c) Compute the flux of $\vec{r}/\|\vec{r}\|^2$ out of the cylinder in part (b).

(d) Find the flux of $\vec{r}/\|\vec{r}\|^2$ out of a closed cylinder of radius 2, length 2, centered at the origin, and with its axis along the z-axis.

26. Let S be the cube in the first quadrant with side 2, one corner at the origin and edges parallel to the axes. Let
$$\vec{F}_1 = (xy^2 + 3xz^2)\vec{i} + (3x^2y + 2yz^2)\vec{j} + 3zy^2\vec{k}$$
$$\vec{F}_2 = (xy^2 + 5e^{yz})\vec{i} + (yz^2 + 7\sin(xz))\vec{j} + (x^2z + \cos(xy))\vec{k}$$
$$\vec{F}_3 = \left(xz^2 + \frac{x^3}{3}\right)\vec{i} + \left(yz^2 + \frac{y^3}{3}\right)\vec{j} + \left(zy^2 + \frac{z^3}{3}\right)\vec{k}.$$

Arrange the flux integrals of $\vec{F}_1$, $\vec{F}_2$, $\vec{F}_3$ out of S in increasing order.

27. Let div $\vec{F} = 2(6 - x)$ and $0 \leq a, b, c \leq 10$.

(a) Find the flux of $\vec{F}$ out of the rectangular solid $0 \leq x \leq a, 0 \leq y \leq b, 0 \leq z \leq c$.

(b) For what values of a, b, c is the flux largest? What is that largest flux?

28. Assume $\vec{r} \neq \vec{0}$. Let $\vec{F} = \vec{r}/\|\vec{r}\|^3$.

(a) Calculate the flux of $\vec{F}$ out of the unit sphere $x^2 + y^2 + z^2 = 1$ oriented outward.

(b) Calculate div $\vec{F}$. Simplify your answer completely.

(c) Use your answer to parts (a) and (b) to calculate the flux out of a box of side 10 centered at the origin and with sides parallel to the coordinate planes. (The box is also oriented outward.)

In Problems 29–30, find the flux of $\vec{F} = \vec{r}/\|\vec{r}\|^3$ through the surface. [Hint: Use the method of Problem 28.]

29. S is the ellipsoid $x^2 + 2y^2 + 3z^2 = 6$.

30. S is the closed cylinder $y^2 + z^2 = 4$, $-2 \leq x \leq 2$.

31. (a) Let div $\vec{F} = x^2+y^2+z^2+3$. Calculate $\int_{S_1} \vec{F} \cdot d\vec{A}$ where S_1 is the sphere of radius 1 centered at the origin.

(b) Let S_2 be the sphere of radius 2 centered at the origin; let S_3 be the sphere of radius 3 centered at the origin; let S_4 be the box of side 6 centered at the origin with edges parallel to the axes. Without calculating them, arrange the following integrals in increasing order:

$$\int_{S_2} \vec{F} \cdot d\vec{A}, \quad \int_{S_3} \vec{F} \cdot d\vec{A}, \quad \int_{S_4} \vec{F} \cdot d\vec{A}.$$

32. Suppose div $\vec{F} = xyz^2$.

(a) Find div $\vec{F}$ at the point $(1, 2, 1)$. [Note: You are given div $\vec{F}$, not $\vec{F}$.]

(b) Using your answer to part (a), but no other information about the vector field $\vec{F}$, estimate the flux out of a small box of side 0.2 centered at the point $(1, 2, 1)$ and with edges parallel to the axes.

(c) Without computing the vector field $\vec{F}$, calculate the exact flux out of the box.

33. Suppose div $\vec{F} = x^2+y^2+3$. Find a surface S such that $\int_S \vec{F} \cdot d\vec{A}$ is negative, or explain why no such surface exists.

34. As a result of radioactive decay, heat is generated uniformly throughout the interior of the earth at a rate of 30 watts per cubic kilometer. (A watt is a rate of heat production.) The heat then flows to the earth's surface where it is lost to space. Let $\vec{F}(x, y, z)$ denote the rate of flow of heat measured in watts per square kilometer. By definition, the flux of $\vec{F}$ across a surface is the quantity of heat flowing through the surface per unit of time.

(a) What is the value of div $\vec{F}$? Include units.

(b) Assume the heat flows outward symmetrically. Verify that $\vec{F} = \alpha\vec{r}$, where $\vec{r} = x\vec{i} + y\vec{j} + z\vec{k}$ and α is a suitable constant, satisfies the given conditions. Find α.

(c) Let $T(x, y, z)$ denote the temperature inside the earth. Heat flows according to the equation $\vec{F} = -k\,\text{grad}\,T$, where k is a constant. Explain why this makes sense physically.

(d) If T is in °C, then $k = 30{,}000$ watts/km°C. Assuming the earth is a sphere with radius 6400 km and surface temperature 20°C, what is the temperature at the center?

35. If a surface S is submerged in an incompressible fluid, a force $\vec{F}$ is exerted on one side of the surface by the pressure in the fluid. If the z-axis is vertical, with the positive direction upward and the fluid level at $z = 0$, then the component of force in the direction of a unit vector $\vec{u}$ is given by the following:

$$\vec{F} \cdot \vec{u} = -\int_S z\delta g\vec{u} \cdot d\vec{A},$$

where δ is the density of the fluid (mass/volume), g is the acceleration due to gravity, and the surface is oriented away from the side on which the force is exerted. In this problem we consider a totally submerged closed surface enclosing a volume V. We are interested in the force of the liquid on the external surface, so S is oriented inward. Use the Divergence Theorem to show that:

(a) The force in the $\vec{i}$ and $\vec{j}$ directions is zero.

(b) The force in the $\vec{k}$ direction is δgV, the weight of the volume of fluid with the same volume as V. This is *Archimedes' Principle*.

36. According to Coulomb's Law, the electrostatic field $\vec{E}$ at the point $\vec{r}$ due to a charge q at the origin is given by

$$\vec{E}(\vec{r}) = q\frac{\vec{r}}{\|\vec{r}\|^3}.$$

(a) Compute div $\vec{E}$.

(b) Let S_a be the sphere of radius a centered at the origin and oriented outward. Show that the flux of $\vec{E}$ through S_a is $4\pi q$.

(c) Could you have used the Divergence Theorem in part (b)? Explain why or why not.

(d) Let S be an arbitrary, closed, outward-oriented surface surrounding the origin. Show that the flux of $\vec{E}$ through S is again $4\pi q$. [Hint: Apply the Divergence Theorem to the solid region lying between a small sphere S_a and the surface S.]

37. According to Coulomb's Law, the electric field $\vec{E}$ at the point $\vec{r}$ due to a charge q at the point $\vec{r}_0$ is given by

$$\vec{E}(\vec{r}) = q\frac{(\vec{r} - \vec{r}_0)}{\|\vec{r} - \vec{r}_0\|^3}.$$

Suppose S is a closed, outward-oriented surface and that $\vec{r}_0$ does not lie on S. Use Problem 36 to show that

$$\int_S \vec{E} \cdot d\vec{A} = \begin{cases} 4\pi q & \text{if } q \text{ lies inside } S, \\ 0 & \text{if } q \text{ lies outside } S. \end{cases}$$

Strengthen Your Understanding

In Problems 38–39, explain what is wrong with the statement.

38. The flux integral $\int_S \vec{F} \cdot d\vec{A}$ can be evaluated using the Divergence Theorem, where $\vec{F} = 2x\vec{i} - 3\vec{j}$ and S is the triangular surface with corners $(1, 0, 0)$, $(0, 1, 0)$, $(0, 0, 1)$ oriented away from the origin.

39. If S is the boundary of a solid region W, where S is oriented outward, and $\vec{F}$ is a vector field, then

$$\int_S \text{div}\,\vec{F}\,d\vec{A} = \int_W \vec{F}\,dV.$$

In Problems 40–41, give an example of:

40. A surface S that is the boundary of a solid region such that $\int_S \vec{F} \cdot d\vec{A} = 0$ if $\vec{F}(x, y, z) = y\vec{i} + xz\vec{j} + y^2\vec{k}$.

41. A vector field $\vec{F}$ such that the flux of $\vec{F}$ out of a sphere of radius 1 centered at the origin is 3.

Are the statements in Problems 42–46 true or false? The smooth vector field $\vec{F}$ is defined everywhere in 3-space and has constant divergence equal to 4.

42. The field $\vec{F}$ has a net inflow per unit volume at the point $(-3, 4, 0)$.

43. The vector field $\vec{F}$ could be the field $\vec{F} = x\vec{i} + (3y)\vec{j} + (y - 5x)\vec{k}$.

44. The vector field $\vec{F}$ could be a constant field.

45. The flux of $\vec{F}$ through a circle of radius 5 lying anywhere on the xy-plane and oriented upward is $4(\pi 5^2)$.

46. The flux of $\vec{F}$ through a closed cylinder of radius 1 centered along the y-axis, $0 \le y \le 3$ and oriented outward is $4(3\pi)$.

Are the statements in Problems 47–55 true or false? Give reasons for your answer.

47. $\int_S \vec{F} \cdot d\vec{A} = \operatorname{div} \vec{F}$.

48. If $\vec{F}$ is a vector field in 3-space, and W is a solid region with boundary surface S, then $\int_S \operatorname{div} \vec{F} \cdot d\vec{A} = \int_W \vec{F} \, dV$.

49. If $\vec{F}$ is a divergence-free vector field in 3-space, and S is a closed surface oriented inward, then $\int_S \vec{F} \cdot d\vec{A} = 0$.

50. If $\vec{F}$ is a vector field in 3-space satisfying $\operatorname{div} \vec{F} = 1$, and S is a closed surface oriented outward, then $\int_S \vec{F} \cdot d\vec{A}$ is equal to the volume enclosed by S.

51. Let W be the solid region between the sphere S_1 of radius 1 and S_2 of radius 2, both centered at the origin. If $\vec{F}$ is a vector field in 3-space, then $\int_W \operatorname{div} \vec{F} \, dV = \int_{S_2} \vec{F} \cdot d\vec{A} - \int_{S_1} \vec{F} \cdot d\vec{A}$, where both S_1 and S_2 are oriented outward.

52. Let S_1 be the square $0 \le x \le 1, 0 \le y \le 1, z = 0$ oriented downward and let S_2 be the square $0 \le x \le 1, 0 \le y \le 1, z = 1$ oriented upward. If $\vec{F}$ is a vector field, then $\int_W \operatorname{div} \vec{F} \, dV = \int_{S_2} \vec{F} \cdot d\vec{A} + \int_{S_1} \vec{F} \cdot d\vec{A}$, where W is the solid cube $0 \le x \le 1, 0 \le y \le 1, 0 \le z \le 1$.

53. Let S_1 be the square $0 \le x \le 1, 0 \le y \le 1, z = 0$ oriented downward and let S_2 be the square $0 \le x \le 1, 0 \le y \le 1, z = 1$ oriented upward. If $\vec{F} = \cos(xyz)\vec{k}$, then $\int_W \operatorname{div} \vec{F} \, dV = \int_{S_2} \vec{F} \cdot d\vec{A} + \int_{S_1} \vec{F} \cdot d\vec{A}$, where W is the solid cube $0 \le x \le 1, 0 \le y \le 1, 0 \le z \le 1$.

54. If S is a sphere of radius 1, centered at the origin, oriented outward, and $\vec{F}$ is a vector field satisfying $\int_S \vec{F} \cdot d\vec{A} = 0$, then $\operatorname{div} \vec{F} = 0$ at all points inside S.

55. Let S_h be the surface consisting of a cylinder of height h, closed at the top. The curved sides are $x^2 + y^2 = 1$, for $0 \le z \le h$, and the top $x^2 + y^2 \le 1$, for $z = h$, oriented outward. If $\vec{F}$ is divergence free, then $\int_{S_h} \vec{F} \cdot d\vec{A}$ is independent of the height h.

56. Let $\vec{F} = (5x + 7y)\vec{i} + (7y + 9z)\vec{j} + (9z + 11x)\vec{k}$, and let Q_i be the flux of $\vec{F}$ through the surfaces S_i for $i = 1$–4. Arrange Q_i in ascending order, where

(a) S_1 is the sphere of radius 2 centered at the origin
(b) S_2 is the cube of side 2 centered at the origin and with sides parallel to the axes
(c) S_3 is the sphere of radius 1 centered at the origin
(d) S_4 is a pyramid with all four corners lying on S_3

CHAPTER SUMMARY (see also Ready Reference at the end of the book)

- **Flux Integrals**
  Oriented surfaces, definition of flux through a surface, definition of flux integral as a limit of a Riemann sum

- **Calculating flux integrals** over surfaces
  Graphs: $d\vec{A} = (-f_x\vec{i} - f_y\vec{j} + \vec{k}) \, dx \, dy$
  Cylinders: $d\vec{A} = (\cos\theta\vec{i} + \sin\theta\vec{j})R \, dz \, d\theta$
  Spheres:
  $d\vec{A} = (\sin\phi\cos\theta\vec{i} + \sin\phi\sin\theta\vec{j} + \cos\phi\vec{k})R^2 \, d\phi \, d\theta$

- **Divergence**
  Geometric and coordinate definition of divergence, calculating divergence, interpretation in terms of outflow per unit volume.

- **The Divergence Theorem**
  Statement of the theorem, divergence-free fields, harmonic functions.

REVIEW EXERCISES AND PROBLEMS FOR CHAPTER NINETEEN

Exercises

1. Let S be the disk of radius 5 perpendicular to the y-axis, centered at $(0, 7, 0)$ and oriented toward the origin. Is
$$\int_S (3\vec{i} + 4\vec{j}) \cdot d\vec{A}$$
a vector or a scalar? Calculate it.

2. Is $\operatorname{div}\left(\dfrac{y\vec{i} - x\vec{j}}{x^2 + y^2}\right)$ a vector or a scalar? Calculate it.

3. Let $\vec{F}(x, y, z) = \vec{i} + 2\vec{j} + \vec{k}$. Each of the surfaces in (a)–(e) are squares of side length 4, with orientation given by the normal vector shown. Compute the flux of $\vec{F}$ through these surfaces.

(a)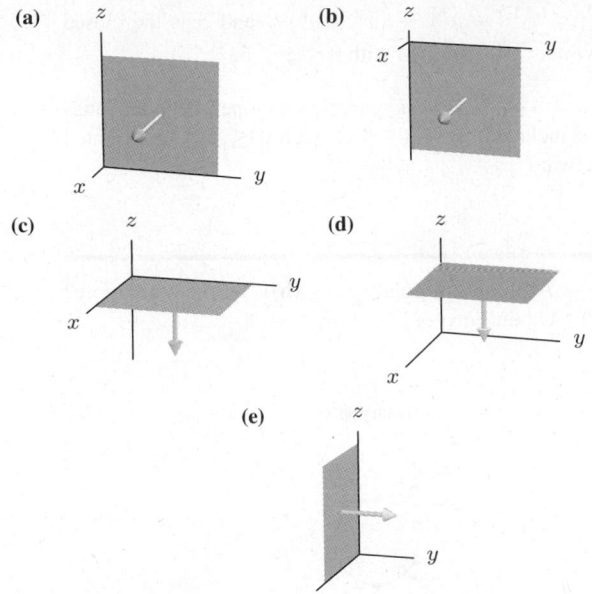

(b)

(c)

(d)

(e)

In Exercises 4–7, are the flux integrals positive, negative, or zero? Let S be a disk of radius 3 in the plane $x = 7$, centered on the x-axis and oriented toward the origin.

4. $\displaystyle\int_S (x\vec{j} + y\vec{k}) \cdot d\vec{A}$ **5.** $\displaystyle\int_S (x\vec{i} + y\vec{k}) \cdot d\vec{A}$

6. $\displaystyle\int_S (y\vec{i} + x\vec{k}) \cdot d\vec{A}$

7. $\displaystyle\int_S ((x - 10)\vec{i} + (x + 10)\vec{j}) \cdot d\vec{A}$

In Exercises 8–23, find the flux of the vector field through the surface S.

8. $\vec{F} = 2\vec{i} + 3\vec{j}$ through a disk of radius 5 in the plane $y = 2$ oriented in the direction of increasing y.

9. $\vec{F} = \vec{i} + 2\vec{j}$ through a sphere of radius 3 at the origin.

10. $\vec{F} = y\vec{j}$ through the square of side 4 in the plane $y = 5$. The square is centered on the y-axis, has sides parallel to the axes, and is oriented in the positive y-direction.

11. $\vec{F} = x\vec{i}$ through a square of side 3 in the plane $x = -5$. The square is centered on the x-axis, has sides parallel to the axes, and is oriented in the positive x-direction.

12. $\vec{F} = (y+3)\vec{j}$ through a square of side 2 in the xz-plane, oriented in the negative y-direction.

13. $\vec{F} = x\vec{k}$ through the square $0 \le x \le 3, 0 \le y \le 3$ in the xy-plane, with sides parallel to the axes, and oriented upward.

14. $\vec{F} = \vec{i} - \vec{j} - \vec{k}$ through a cube of side 2 with sides parallel to the axes.

15. $\vec{F} = 6\vec{i} + x^2\vec{j} - \vec{k}$, through a square of side 2 in the plane $z = 3$, oriented upward.

16. $\vec{F} = (x^2 + y^2)\vec{i} + xy\vec{j}$ and S is the square in the xy-plane with corners at $(1, 1, 0)$, $(-1, 1, 0)$, $(1, -1, 0)$, $(-1, -1, 0)$, and oriented upward.

17. $\vec{F} = z\vec{i} + y\vec{j} + 2x\vec{k}$ and S is the rectangle $z = 4$, $0 \le x \le 2$, $0 \le y \le 3$, oriented in the positive z-direction.

18. $\vec{F} = (x + \cos z)\vec{i} + y\vec{j} + 2x\vec{k}$ and S is the rectangle $x = 2$, $0 \le y \le 3$, $0 \le z \le 4$, oriented in the positive x-direction.

19. $\vec{F} = x^2\vec{i} + (x + e^y)\vec{j} - \vec{k}$, and S is the rectangle $y = -1$, $0 \le x \le 2$, $0 \le z \le 4$, oriented in the negative y-direction.

20. $\vec{F} = (5 + xy)\vec{i} + z\vec{j} + yz\vec{k}$ and S is the 2×2 square plate in the yz-plane centered at the origin, oriented in the positive x-direction.

21. $\vec{F} = x\vec{i} + y\vec{j}$ and S is the surface of a closed cylinder of radius 2 and height 3 centered on the z-axis with its base in the xy-plane.

22. $\vec{F} = -y\vec{i} + x\vec{j} + z\vec{k}$ and S is the surface of a closed cylinder of radius 1 centered on the z-axis with base in the plane $z = -1$ and top in the plane $z = 1$.

23. $\vec{F} = x^2\vec{i} + y^2\vec{j} + z\vec{k}$ and S is the cone $z = \sqrt{x^2 + y^2}$, oriented upward with $x^2 + y^2 \le 1$, $x \ge 0$, $y \ge 0$.

In Problems 24–27, give conditions on one or more of the constants a, b, c to ensure that the flux integral $\int_S \vec{F} \cdot d\vec{A}$ has the given sign.

24. Positive for $\vec{F} = a\vec{i} + b\vec{j} + c\vec{k}$ and S is a disk perpendicular to the y-axis, through $(0, 5, 0)$ and oriented away from the origin.

25. Negative for $\vec{F} = a\vec{i} + b\vec{j} + c\vec{k}$ and S is the upper half of the unit sphere centered at the origin and oriented downward.

26. Positive for $\vec{F} = ax\vec{i} + ay\vec{j} + az\vec{k}$ and S is a sphere centered at the origin.

27. Positive for $\vec{F} = a\vec{i} + b\vec{j} + c\vec{k}$ and S is the triangle cut off by $x + y + z = 1$ in the first quadrant, oriented upward.

28. Calculate the flux of $\vec{F} = xy\vec{i} + yz\vec{j} + zx\vec{k}$ out of the closed box $0 \le x \le 1, 0 \le y \le 1, 0 \le z \le 1$
   (a) Directly **(b)** Using the Divergence Theorem.

29. Compute the flux integral $\int_S (x^3\vec{i} + 2y\vec{j} + 3\vec{k}) \cdot d\vec{A}$, where S is the $2 \times 2 \times 2$ rectangular surface centered at the origin, oriented outward. Do this in two ways:
   (a) Directly **(b)** Using the Divergence Theorem

In Exercises 30–35, use the Divergence Theorem to calculate the flux of the vector field out of the surface.

30. $\vec{F} = -x\vec{i} + 2y\vec{j} + (3+2z)\vec{k}$ out of the sphere of radius 2 centered at $(1, 2, 3)$.

31. $\vec{F} = (2x+y)\vec{i} + (3y+z)\vec{j} + (4z+x)\vec{k}$ and S is the sphere of radius 5 centered at the origin.

32. $\vec{F} = x^2\vec{i} + y^2\vec{j} + e^{xy}\vec{k}$ and S is the cube of side 3 in the first octant with one corner at the origin, and sides parallel to the axes.

33. $\vec{F} = (e^z + x)\,\vec{i} + (2y + \sin x)\vec{j} + \left(e^{x^2} - z\right)\vec{k}$ and S is the sphere of radius 1 centered at $(2, 1, 0)$.

34. $\vec{F} = x^3\vec{i} + y^3\vec{j} + \left(x^2 + y^2\right)\vec{k}$ and S is the closed cylinder $x^2 + y^2 = 4$ with $0 \le z \le 5$.

35. $\vec{F} = x\vec{i} + y\vec{j} + z\vec{k}$ and S is the open cylinder (ends not included) $x^2 + y^2 \le 1$, with $0 \le z \le 1$, oriented outward.

Problems

36. Arrange the following flux integrals, $\int_{S_i} \vec{F} \cdot d\vec{A}$, with $i = 1, 2, 3, 4$, in ascending order if $\vec{F} = -\vec{i} - \vec{j} + \vec{k}$ and if the S_i are the following surfaces:

- S_1 is a horizontal square of side 1 with one corner at $(0, 0, 2)$, above the first quadrant of the xy-plane, oriented upward.
- S_2 is a horizontal square of side 1 with one corner at $(0, 0, 3)$, above the third quadrant of the xy-plane, oriented upward.
- S_3 is a square of side $\sqrt{2}$ in the xz-plane with one corner at the origin, one edge along the positive x-axis, one along the negative z-axis, oriented in the negative y-direction.
- S_4 is a square of side $\sqrt{2}$ with one corner at the origin, one edge along the positive y-axis, one corner at $(1, 0, 1)$, oriented upward.

37. Let $f(x, y, z) = xy + e^{xyz}$. Find

 (a) grad f
 (b) $\int_C$ grad $f \cdot d\vec{r}$, where C is the line from the point $(1, 1, 1)$ to $(2, 3, 4)$.
 (c) $\int_S$ grad $f \cdot d\vec{A}$, where S is the quarter disk in the xy-plane $x^2 + y^2 \le 4$, $x \ge 0$, $y \ge 0$, oriented upward.

38. The flux of the constant vector field $a\vec{i} + b\vec{j} + c\vec{k}$ through the square of side 2 in the plane $x = 5$, oriented in the positive x-direction, is 24. Which of the constants a, b, c can be determined from the information given? Give the value(s).

39. (a) Let $\vec{F} = (x^2 + 4)\vec{i} + y\vec{j}$. Which of the following flux integrals is the largest? Explain.

 $\int_{S_1} \vec{F} \cdot d\vec{A}$, where S_1 is the disk of radius 1 in the plane $x = 2$ centered on the x-axis and oriented away from the origin.

 $\int_{S_2} \vec{F} \cdot d\vec{A}$, where S_2 is the disk of radius 1 in the plane $y = 4$ centered on the y-axis and oriented away from the origin.

 $\int_{S_3} \vec{F} \cdot d\vec{A}$, where S_3 is the disk of radius 1 in the plane $x = -3$ centered on the x-axis and oriented toward the origin.

 (b) Calculate the integral you chose in part (a).

40. Figure 19.42 shows a cross-section of the earth's magnetic field. Assume that the earth's magnetic and geographic poles coincide. Is the magnetic flux through a horizontal plate, oriented skyward, positive, negative, or zero if the plate is

 (a) At the north pole? **(b)** At the south pole?
 (c) On the equator?

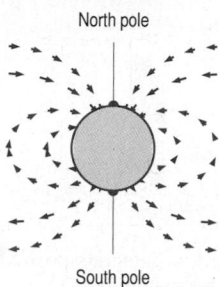

North pole

South pole

Figure 19.42

41. (a) Let $\operatorname{div}(\vec{F}) = x^2 + y^2 - z^2$. Estimate the flux out of a small sphere of radius 0.1 centered at each of the following points

 (i) $(2, 1, 1)$ **(ii)** $(0, 0, 1)$

 (b) What do the signs of your answers to part (a) tell you about the vector field near each of these two points?

For Problems 42–44,

(a) Find the flux of the given vector field out of a cube in the first octant with edge length c, one corner at the origin and edges along the axes.

(b) Use your answer to part (a) to find div $\vec{F}$ at the origin using the geometric definition.

(c) Compute div $\vec{F}$ at the origin using partial derivatives.

42. $\vec{F} = x\vec{i}$

43. $\vec{F} = 2\vec{i} + y\vec{j} + 3\vec{k}$

44. $\vec{F} = x\vec{i} + y\vec{j}$

In Problems 45–49, calculate the flux of $\vec{F}$ through the cylinder $x^2 + y^2 = 2$, $-3 \le z \le 3$ and its base, oriented outward. The cylinder is open at the top.

45. $\vec{F} = z^2\vec{i} + x^2\vec{j} + 5\vec{k}$

46. $\vec{F} = y^2\vec{i} + z^2\vec{j} + (x^2 + y^2)\vec{k}$

47. $\vec{F} = z\vec{i} + x\vec{j} + y\vec{k}$

48. $\vec{F} = y^2\vec{i} + x^2\vec{j} + 7z\vec{k}$

49. $\vec{F} = x^3\vec{i} + y^3\vec{j} + \vec{k}$

50. Find the constant vector field $\vec{F}$ parallel to $\vec{i} + \vec{k}$ and giving a flux of -7 through S, the cone $z = r$, with $0 \le z \le 4$, oriented upward.

51. (a) Find $\operatorname{div}(\vec{r}/\|\vec{r}\|^2)$ where $\vec{r} = x\vec{i} + y\vec{j}$ for $\vec{r} \ne \vec{0}$.

(b) Where in 3-space is $\operatorname{div}(\vec{r}/\|\vec{r}\|^2)$ undefined?

(c) Find the flux of $\vec{r}/\|\vec{r}\|^2$ through the closed cylinder of radius 2, length 3, centered at $(5, 0, 0)$, with its axis parallel to the z-axis.

(d) Find the flux of $\vec{r}/\|\vec{r}\|^2$ through the curved sides of the open cylinder in part (c).

52. (a) Let $\vec{F}$ be a smooth vector field defined throughout 3-space. What must be true of $\vec{F}$ if the flux of $\vec{F}$ through any closed surface is zero?

(b) What value of a ensures that the flux of $\vec{F} = a(e^x + y^2 - x)\vec{i} + 12y(1 - e^x)\vec{j}$ through any closed surface is zero?

53. Let $\vec{a} = a_1\vec{i} + a_2\vec{j} + a_3\vec{k}$ be a constant vector and let $\vec{r} = x\vec{i} + y\vec{j} + z\vec{k}$.

(a) Calculate $\operatorname{div}(\vec{r} \times \vec{a})$.

(b) Calculate the flux of $\vec{r} \times \vec{a}$ out of a cube of side 5 centered at the origin with edges parallel to the axes.

54. Find the flux of $\vec{F}$ out of the closed surface S given by $x^2 + y^2 + z^2 = 100$. You are given that $\vec{F}$ is continuous, with $\operatorname{div}\vec{F} = 3$ inside the cube $-2 \le x \le 2$, $-2 \le y \le 2$, $-2 \le z \le 2$ and $\operatorname{div}\vec{F} = 5$ outside the cube.

55. The closed surface S consists of S_1, the cone $x = \sqrt{y^2 + z^2}$ for $0 \le x \le 2$, and a disk S_2. Let $\vec{F} = 3x\vec{i} + 4y\vec{j} + 5z\vec{k}$.

(a) In what plane does the disk S_2 lie? How is it oriented?

(b) Find the flux of $\vec{F}$ through

(i) S_2 (ii) S_1

56. Find the flux integral, using $\vec{r} = x\vec{i} + y\vec{j} + z\vec{k}$.

(a) $\displaystyle\int_{S_1} \vec{r} \cdot d\vec{A}$, where S_1 is the disk $x = 5$, $y^2 + z^2 \le 7$, oriented away from the origin.

(b) $\displaystyle\int_{S_2} \vec{r} \cdot d\vec{A}$, where S_2 is the closed cylinder $y^2 + z^2 = 7$, $0 \le x \le 5$.

(c) $\displaystyle\int_{S_3} \vec{r} \cdot d\vec{A}$, where S_3 is the curved side of the open cylinder $y^2 + z^2 = 7$, $0 \le x \le 5$, oriented away from the x-axis.

57. Let $\vec{F}(x, y, z) = f_1(x, y, z)\vec{i} + f_2(x, y, z)\vec{j} + \vec{k}$ be a vector field with the property that $\operatorname{div}\vec{F} = 5$ everywhere. Let S be the hemisphere $z = -\sqrt{9 - x^2 - y^2}$, with its boundary in the xy-plane and oriented downward. Find $\displaystyle\int_S \vec{F} \cdot d\vec{A}$.

58. Let $\vec{F} = \vec{r}/\|\vec{r}\|^3$.

(a) Calculate $\operatorname{div}\vec{F}$. Where is $\operatorname{div}\vec{F}$ undefined?

(b) Find $\displaystyle\int_S \vec{F} \cdot d\vec{A}$ where S is a sphere of radius 10 centered at the origin.

(c) Find $\displaystyle\int_{B_1} \vec{F} \cdot d\vec{A}$ where B_1 is a box of side 1 centered at the point $(3, 0, 0)$ with sides parallel to the axes.

(d) Find $\displaystyle\int_{B_2} \vec{F} \cdot d\vec{A}$ where B_2 is a box of side 1 centered at the origin with sides parallel to the axes.

(e) Using your results to parts (c) and (d), explain how, with no further calculation, you can find the flux of this vector field through any closed surface, provided the origin does not lie on the surface.

59. The gravitational field, $\vec{F}$, of a planet of mass m at the origin is given by

$$\vec{F} = -Gm\frac{\vec{r}}{\|\vec{r}\|^3}.$$

Use the Divergence Theorem to show that the flux of the gravitational field through the sphere of radius a is independent of a. [Hint: Consider the region bounded by two concentric spheres.]

60. A basic property of the electric field $\vec{E}$ is that its divergence is zero at points where there is no charge. Suppose that the only charge is along the z-axis, and that the electric field $\vec{E}$ points radially out from the z-axis and its magnitude depends only on the distance r from the z-axis. Use the Divergence Theorem to show that the magnitude of the field is proportional to $1/r$. [Hint: Consider a solid region consisting of a cylinder of finite length whose axis is the z-axis, and with a smaller concentric cylinder removed.]

61. A fluid is flowing along a cylindrical pipe of radius a in the $\vec{i}$ direction. The velocity of the fluid at a radial distance r from the center of the pipe is $\vec{v} = u(1 - r^2/a^2)\vec{i}$.

(a) What is the significance of the constant u?

(b) What is the velocity of the fluid at the wall of the pipe?

(c) Find the flux through a circular cross-section of the pipe.

62. A closed surface S encloses a volume W. The function $\rho(x, y, z)$ gives the electrical charge density at points in space. The vector field $\vec{J}(x, y, z)$ gives the electric current density at any point in space and is defined so that the current through a small area $d\vec{A}$ is given by

Current through small area $\approx \vec{J} \cdot d\vec{A}$.

(a) What do the following integrals represent, in terms of electricity?

(i) $\displaystyle\int_W \rho\, dV$ (ii) $\displaystyle\int_S \vec{J} \cdot d\vec{A}$

(b) Using the fact that an electric current through a surface is the rate at which electric charge passes through the surface per unit time, explain why

$$\int_S \vec{J} \cdot d\vec{A} = -\frac{\partial}{\partial t}\left(\int_W \rho\, dV\right).$$

63. **(a)** A river flows across the xy-plane in the positive x-direction and around a circular rock of radius 1 centered at the origin. The velocity of the river can be modeled using the potential function $\phi = x + (x/(x^2 + y^2))$. Compute the velocity vector field, $\vec{v} = \operatorname{grad} \phi$.
    (b) Show that $\operatorname{div} \vec{v} = 0$.
    (c) Show that the flow of $\vec{v}$ is tangent to the circle $x^2 + y^2 = 1$. This means that no water crosses the circle. The water on the outside must therefore all flow around the circle.
    (d) Use a computer to sketch the vector field $\vec{v}$ in the region outside the unit circle.

64. A vector field is a *point source* at the origin in 3-space if its direction is away from the origin at every point, its magnitude depends only on the distance from the origin, and its divergence is zero except at the origin. (Such a vector field might be used to model the photon flow out of a star or the neutrino flow out of a supernova.)
    (a) Show that $\vec{v} = K(x^2 + y^2 + z^2)^{-3/2}(x\vec{i} + y\vec{j} + z\vec{k})$ is a point source at the origin if $K > 0$.
    (b) Determine the magnitude $\|\vec{v}\|$ of the source in part (a) as a function of the distance from its center.
    (c) Compute the flux of $\vec{v}$ through a sphere of radius r centered at the origin.
    (d) Compute the flux of $\vec{v}$ through a closed surface that does not contain the origin.

CAS Challenge Problems

65. Let S be the part of the ellipsoid $x^2 + y^2 + 2z^2 = 1$ lying above the rectangle $-1/2 \le x \le 1/2$, $-1/2 \le y \le 1/2$, oriented upward. For each vector field (a)–(c), say whether you expect $\int_S \vec{F} \cdot d\vec{A}$ to be positive, negative, or zero. Then evaluate the integral exactly using a computer algebra system and find numerical approximations for your answers. Describe and explain what you notice.

    (a) $\vec{F} = x\vec{i}$
    (b) $\vec{F} = (x + 1)\vec{i}$
    (c) $\vec{F} = y\vec{j}$

66. Let $\vec{F} = (z + 4)\vec{k}$, and let S be the surface with normal pointing in the direction of the negative y-axis parameterized, for $0 \le s \le 2, 0 \le t \le 2\pi$, by

$$\vec{r}(s, t) = s^2 \cos t\vec{i} + s\vec{j} + s^2 \sin t\vec{k}.$$

    (a) Sketch S and, without evaluating the integral, say whether $\int_S \vec{F} \cdot d\vec{A}$ is positive, negative, or zero. Give a geometric explanation for your answer.
    (b) Evaluate the flux integral. Does it agree with your answer to part (a)?

PROJECTS FOR CHAPTER NINETEEN

1. **Solid Angle**

    Let

$$\vec{F}(x, y) = \frac{x\vec{i} + y\vec{j} + z\vec{k}}{(x^2 + y^2 + z^2)^{3/2}}$$

    and let oriented surfaces S_1 and S_2 be as in Figure 19.43. The surface S_2 is on the unit sphere centered at the origin. Lines from the origin to the boundary of S_1 intersect the unit sphere at the boundary of S_2. Both surfaces are oriented away from the origin. Show that

    (a) The divergence of $\vec{F}$ is zero.
    (b) $\int_{S_1} \vec{F} \cdot d\vec{A} = \int_{S_2} \vec{F} \cdot d\vec{A}$
    (c) $\int_{S_1} \vec{F} \cdot d\vec{r} = \Omega$, the area of S_2. The value Ω is called the *solid angle* subtended by S_1 at the origin.

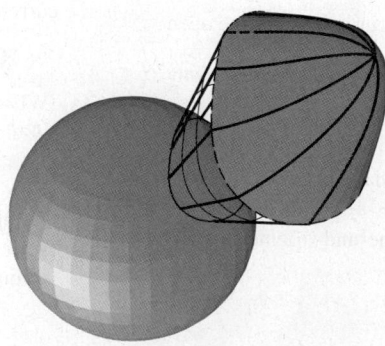

Figure 19.43

2. **Divergence of Spherically Symmetric Vector Fields**

A vector field is spherically symmetric about the origin if, on every sphere centered at the origin, it has constant magnitude and points either away from or toward the origin. A vector field that is spherically symmetric about the origin can be written in terms of the spherical coordinate $\rho = \|\vec{r}\|$ as $\vec{F} = f(\rho)\vec{e}_\rho$ where f is a function of the distance ρ from the origin, $f(0) = 0$, and $\vec{e}_\rho$ is a unit vector pointing away from the origin.

(a) Show that

$$\operatorname{div} \vec{F} = \frac{1}{\rho^2} \frac{d}{d\rho} \left(\rho^2 f(\rho) \right), \quad \rho \neq 0.$$

(b) Use part (a) to show that if $\vec{F}$ is a spherically symmetric vector field such that $\operatorname{div} \vec{F} = 0$ away from the origin then, for some constant k,

$$\vec{F} = k\frac{1}{\rho^2}\vec{e}_\rho, \quad \rho \neq 0.$$

(c) Use part (a) to confirm the Divergence Theorem for the flux of a spherically symmetric vector field through a sphere centered at the origin.

(d) A form of Gauss's Law for an electric field $\vec{E}$ states that $\operatorname{div} \vec{E}(\vec{r}) = \delta(\vec{r})$, where δ is a scalar-valued function giving the density of electric charge at every point. Use Gauss's Law and part (a) to find the electric field when the charge density is

$$\delta(\vec{r}) = \begin{cases} \delta_0 & \|\vec{r}\| \leq a \\ 0 & \|\vec{r}\| > a, \end{cases}$$

for some nonnegative a. Assume that $\vec{E}$ is spherically symmetric and continuous everywhere.

3. **Gauss's Law Applied to a Charged Wire and a Charged Sheet**

Gauss's Law states that the flux of an electric field through a closed surface, S, is proportional to the quantity of charge, q, enclosed within S. That is,

$$\int_S \vec{E} \cdot d\vec{A} = kq.$$

In this project we use Gauss's Law to calculate the electric field of a uniformly charged wire in part (a) and a flat sheet of charge in part (b).

(a) Consider the electric field due to an infinitely long, straight, uniformly charged wire. (There is no current running through the wire—all charges are fixed.) Assuming that the wire is infinitely long means that we can assume that the electric field is perpendicular to any cylinder that has the wire as an axis and that the magnitude of the field is constant on any such cylinder. Denote by E_r the magnitude of the electric field due to the wire on a cylinder of radius r. (See Figure 19.44.)

Imagine a closed surface S made up of two cylinders, one of radius a and one of larger radius b, both coaxial with the wire, and the two washers that cap the ends. (See Figure 19.45.) The outward orientation of S means that a normal on the outer cylinder points away from the wire and a normal on the inner cylinder points toward the wire.

(i) Explain why the flux of $\vec{E}$, the electric field, through the washers is 0.

(ii) Explain why Gauss's Law implies that the flux through the inner cylinder is the same as the flux through the outer cylinder. [Hint: The charge on the wire is not inside the surface S].

(iii) Use part (ii) to show that $E_b/E_a = a/b$.

(iv) Explain why part (iii) shows that the strength of the field due to an infinitely long uniformly charged wire is proportional to $1/r$.

Figure 19.44   Figure 19.45   Figure 19.46

(b) Now consider an infinite flat sheet uniformly covered with charge. As in part (a), symmetry shows that the electric field $\vec{E}$ is perpendicular to the sheet and has the same magnitude at all points that are the same distance from the sheet. Use Gauss's Law to explain why, on any one side of the sheet, the electric field is the same at all points in space off the sheet. [Hint: Consider the flux through the box with sides parallel to the sheet shown in Figure 19.46.]

4. **Flux Across a Cylinder: Obtaining Gauss's Law from Coulomb's Law**

An electric charge q is placed at the origin in 3-space. The induced electric field $\vec{E}(\vec{r})$ at the point with position vector $\vec{r}$ is given by Coulomb's Law, which says

$$\vec{E}(\vec{r}) = q\frac{\vec{r}}{\|\vec{r}\|^3}, \qquad \vec{r} \neq \vec{0}.$$

In this project, Gauss's Law is obtained for a cylinder enclosing a point charge by direct calculation from Coulomb's Law.

(a) Let S be the open cylinder of height $2H$ and radius R given by $x^2 + y^2 = R^2$, $-H \leq z \leq H$, oriented outward.

   (i) Show that the flux of $\vec{E}$, the electric field, through S is given by

$$\int_S \vec{E} \cdot d\vec{A} = 4\pi q\frac{H}{\sqrt{H^2 + R^2}}.$$

   (ii) What are the limits of the flux $\int_S \vec{E} \cdot d\vec{A}$ if
   - $H \to 0$ or $H \to \infty$ when R is fixed?
   - $R \to 0$ or $R \to \infty$ when H is fixed?

(b) Let T be the outward-oriented, closed cylinder of height $2H$ and radius R whose curved side is given by $x^2 + y^2 = R^2$, $-H \leq z \leq H$, whose top is given by $z = H$, $x^2 + y^2 \leq R^2$, and bottom by $z = -H$, $x^2 + y^2 \leq R^2$. Use part (a) to show that the flux of the electric field, $\vec{E}$, through T is given by

$$\int_T \vec{E} \cdot d\vec{A} = 4\pi q.$$

Notice that this is Gauss's Law. In particular, the flux is independent of both the height, H, and radius, R, of the cylinder.

Chapter Twenty

THE CURL AND STOKES' THEOREM

Contents

20.1 THE CURL OF A VECTOR FIELD

The divergence is a scalar derivative which measures the outflow of a vector field per unit volume. Now we introduce a vector derivative, the curl, which measures the circulation of a vector field.

Imagine holding the paddle-wheel in Figure 20.1 in the flow shown by Figure 20.2. The speed at which the paddle-wheel spins measures the strength of circulation. Notice that the angular velocity depends on the direction in which the stick is pointing. If the stick is pointing horizontally the paddle-wheel does not spin; if the stick is vertical, the paddle wheel spins.

Figure 20.1: A device for measuring circulation

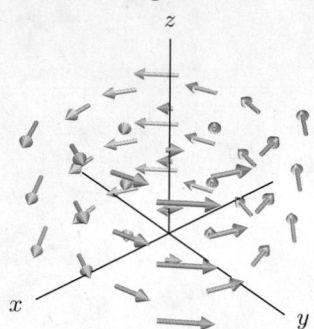

Figure 20.2: A vector field with circulation about the z-axis

Circulation Density

We measure the strength of the circulation using a closed curve. Suppose C is a circle with center $P = (x, y, z)$ in the plane perpendicular to $\vec{n}$, traversed in the direction determined from $\vec{n}$ by the right-hand rule. (See Figures 20.3 and 20.4.)

Figure 20.3: Direction of C relates to direction of $\vec{n}$ by the right-hand rule

Figure 20.4: When the thumb points in the direction of $\vec{n}$, the fingers curl in the forward direction around C

We make the following definition:

> The **circulation density** of a smooth vector field $\vec{F}$ at (x, y, z) around the direction of the unit vector $\vec{n}$ is defined, provided the limit exists, to be
>
> $$\text{circ}_{\vec{n}}\, \vec{F}(x, y, z) = \lim_{\text{Area} \to 0} \frac{\text{Circulation around } C}{\text{Area inside } C} = \cdot \lim_{\text{Area} \to 0} \frac{\int_C \vec{F} \cdot d\vec{r}}{\text{Area inside } C},$$
>
> The circle C is in the plane perpendicular to $\vec{n}$ and oriented by the right-hand rule.

We can use other closed curves for C, such as rectangles, that lie in a plane perpendicular to $\vec{n}$ and include (x, y, z).

The circulation density determines the angular velocity of the paddle-wheel in Figure 20.1 provided you could make one sufficiently small and light and insert it without disturbing the flow.

Example 1

Consider the vector field $\vec{F}$ in Figure 20.2. Suppose that $\vec{F}$ is parallel to the xy-plane and that at a distance r from the z-axis it has magnitude $2r$. Calculate $\text{circ}_{\vec{n}}\ \vec{F}$ at the origin for

(a) $\vec{n} = \vec{k}$ (b) $\vec{n} = -\vec{k}$ (c) $\vec{n} = \vec{i}$.

Solution

(a) Take a circle C of radius a in the xy-plane, centered at the origin, traversed in a direction determined from $\vec{k}$ by the right hand rule. Then, since $\vec{F}$ is tangent to C everywhere and points in the forward direction around C, we have

$$\text{Circulation around } C = \int_C \vec{F} \cdot d\vec{r} = \|\vec{F}\| \cdot \text{Circumference of } C = 2a(2\pi a) = 4\pi a^2.$$

Thus, the circulation density is

$$\text{circ}_{\vec{k}}\ \vec{F} = \lim_{a \to 0} \frac{\text{Circulation around } C}{\text{Area inside } C} = \lim_{a \to 0} \frac{4\pi a^2}{\pi a^2} = 4.$$

(b) If $\vec{n} = -\vec{k}$ the circle is traversed in the opposite direction, so the line integral changes sign. Thus,

$$\text{circ}_{-\vec{k}}\ \vec{F} = -4.$$

(c) The circulation around $\vec{i}$ is calculated using circles in the yz-plane. Since $\vec{F}$ is everywhere perpendicular to such a circle C,

$$\int_C \vec{F} \cdot d\vec{r} = 0.$$

Thus, we have

$$\text{circ}_{\vec{i}}\ \vec{F} = \lim_{a \to 0} \frac{\int_C \vec{F} \cdot d\vec{r}}{\pi a^2} = \lim_{a \to 0} \frac{0}{\pi a^2} = 0.$$

Definition of the Curl

Example 1 shows that the circulation density of a vector field can be positive, negative, or zero, depending on the direction. We assume that there is one direction in which the circulation density is greatest and define a single vector quantity that incorporates all these different circulation densities. We give two definitions, one geometric and one algebraic, which turn out to lead to the same result.

Geometric Definition of Curl

The curl of a smooth vector field $\vec{F}$, written $\text{curl}\ \vec{F}$, is the vector field with the following properties
- The direction of $\text{curl}\ \vec{F}\ (x, y, z)$ is the direction $\vec{n}$ for which $\text{circ}_{\vec{n}}\ \vec{F}\ (x, y, z)$ is the greatest.
- The magnitude of $\text{curl}\ \vec{F}\ (x, y, z)$ is the circulation density of $\vec{F}$ around that direction.

If the circulation density is zero around every direction, then we define the curl to be $\vec{0}$.

Cartesian Coordinate Definition of Curl

If $\vec{F} = F_1\vec{i} + F_2\vec{j} + F_3\vec{k}$, then

$$\text{curl}\ \vec{F} = \left(\frac{\partial F_3}{\partial y} - \frac{\partial F_2}{\partial z}\right)\vec{i} + \left(\frac{\partial F_1}{\partial z} - \frac{\partial F_3}{\partial x}\right)\vec{j} + \left(\frac{\partial F_2}{\partial x} - \frac{\partial F_1}{\partial y}\right)\vec{k}.$$

The cross-product formula gives an easy way to remember the Cartesian coordinate definition, and suggests another common notation for curl $\vec{F}$, namely $\nabla \times \vec{F}$. Using $\nabla = \dfrac{\partial}{\partial x}\vec{i} + \dfrac{\partial}{\partial y}\vec{j} + \dfrac{\partial}{\partial z}\vec{k}$, we can write

$$\operatorname{curl}\vec{F} = \nabla \times \vec{F} = \begin{vmatrix} \vec{i} & \vec{j} & \vec{k} \\ \dfrac{\partial}{\partial x} & \dfrac{\partial}{\partial y} & \dfrac{\partial}{\partial z} \\ F_1 & F_2 & F_3 \end{vmatrix}.$$

Example 2   For each field in Figure 20.5, use the sketch and the geometric definition to decide whether the curl at the origin appears to point up, down, or to be the zero vector. Then check your answer using the coordinate definition of curl. Note that the vector fields have no z-components and are independent of z.

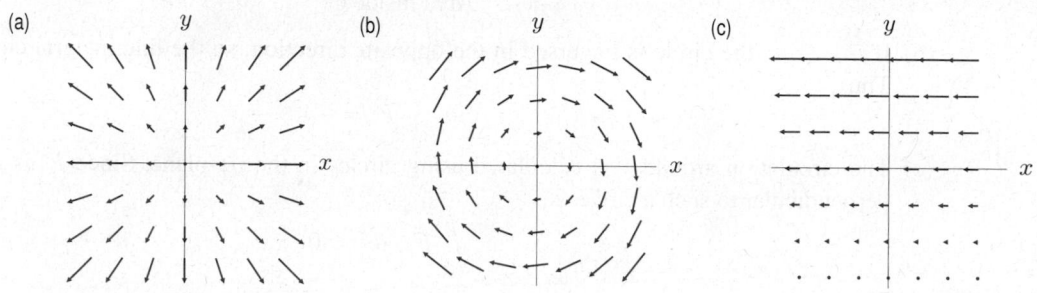

Figure 20.5: Sketches in the xy-plane of (a) $\vec{F} = x\vec{i} + y\vec{j}$ (b) $\vec{F} = y\vec{i} - x\vec{j}$ (c) $\vec{F} = -(y+1)\vec{i}$

Solution

(a) This vector field shows no rotation, and the circulation around any circle in the xy-plane centered at the origin appears to be zero, so we suspect that the circulation density around $\vec{k}$ is zero. The coordinate definition of curl gives

$$\operatorname{curl}\vec{F} = \left(\frac{\partial(0)}{\partial y} - \frac{\partial y}{\partial z}\right)\vec{i} + \left(\frac{\partial x}{\partial z} - \frac{\partial(0)}{\partial x}\right)\vec{j} + \left(\frac{\partial y}{\partial x} - \frac{\partial x}{\partial y}\right)\vec{k} = \vec{0}.$$

(b) This vector field appears to be rotating around the z-axis. By the right-hand rule, the circulation density around $\vec{k}$ is negative, so we expect the z-component of the curl points down. The coordinate definition gives

$$\operatorname{curl}\vec{F} = \left(\frac{\partial(0)}{\partial y} - \frac{\partial(-x)}{\partial z}\right)\vec{i} + \left(\frac{\partial y}{\partial z} - \frac{\partial(0)}{\partial x}\right)\vec{j} + \left(\frac{\partial(-x)}{\partial x} - \frac{\partial y}{\partial y}\right)\vec{k} = -2\vec{k}.$$

(c) At first glance, you might expect this vector field to have zero curl, as all the vectors are parallel to the x-axis. However, if you find the circulation around the curve C in Figure 20.6, the sides contribute nothing (they are perpendicular to the vector field), the bottom contributes a negative quantity (the curve is in the opposite direction to the vector field), and the top contributes a larger positive quantity (the curve is in the same direction as the vector field and the magnitude of the vector field is larger at the top than at the bottom). Thus, the circulation around C is positive and hence we expect the curl to be nonzero and point up. The coordinate definition gives

$$\operatorname{curl}\vec{F} = \left(\frac{\partial(0)}{\partial y} - \frac{\partial(0)}{\partial z}\right)\vec{i} + \left(\frac{\partial(-(y+1))}{\partial z} - \frac{\partial(0)}{\partial x}\right)\vec{j} + \left(\frac{\partial(0)}{\partial x} - \frac{\partial(-(y+1))}{\partial y}\right)\vec{k} = \vec{k}.$$

Another way to see that the curl is nonzero in this case is to imagine the vector field representing the velocity of moving water. A boat sitting in the water tends to rotate, as the water moves faster on one side than the other.

Figure 20.6: Rectangular curve in xy-plane

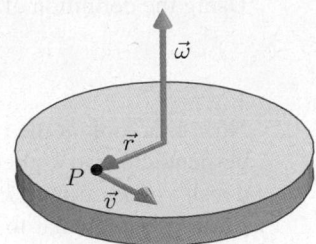

Figure 20.7: Rotating flywheel

Example 3

A flywheel is rotating with angular velocity $\vec{\omega}$ and the velocity of a point P with position vector $\vec{r}$ is given by $\vec{v} = \vec{\omega} \times \vec{r}$. (See Figure 20.7.) Calculate $\text{curl}\,\vec{v}$.

Solution

If $\vec{\omega} = \omega_1 \vec{i} + \omega_2 \vec{j} + \omega_3 \vec{k}$, using the determinant notation introduced in Section 13.4, we have

$$\vec{v} = \vec{\omega} \times \vec{r} = \begin{vmatrix} \vec{i} & \vec{j} & \vec{k} \\ \omega_1 & \omega_2 & \omega_3 \\ x & y & z \end{vmatrix} = (\omega_2 z - \omega_3 y)\vec{i} + (\omega_3 x - \omega_1 z)\vec{j} + (\omega_1 y - \omega_2 x)\vec{k}.$$

The curl formula can also be written using a determinant:

$$\text{curl}\,\vec{v} = \begin{vmatrix} \vec{i} & \vec{j} & \vec{k} \\ \frac{\partial}{\partial x} & \frac{\partial}{\partial y} & \frac{\partial}{\partial z} \\ \omega_2 z - \omega_3 y & \omega_3 x - \omega_1 z & \omega_1 y - \omega_2 x \end{vmatrix}$$

$$- \left(\frac{\partial}{\partial y}(\omega_1 y - \omega_2 x) - \frac{\partial}{\partial z}(\omega_3 x - \omega_1 z) \right)\vec{i} + \left(\frac{\partial}{\partial z}(\omega_2 z - \omega_3 y) - \frac{\partial}{\partial x}(\omega_1 y - \omega_2 x) \right)\vec{j}$$

$$+ \left(\frac{\partial}{\partial x}(\omega_3 x - \omega_1 z) - \frac{\partial}{\partial y}(\omega_2 z - \omega_3 y) \right)\vec{k}$$

$$= 2\omega_1 \vec{i} + 2\omega_2 \vec{j} + 2\omega_3 \vec{k} = 2\vec{\omega}.$$

Thus, as we would expect, $\text{curl}\,\vec{v}$ is parallel to the axis of rotation of the flywheel (namely, the direction of $\vec{\omega}$) and the magnitude of $\text{curl}\,\vec{v}$ is larger the faster the flywheel is rotating (that is, the larger the magnitude of $\vec{\omega}$).

Why Do the Two Definitions of Curl Give the Same Result?

Using Green's Theorem in Cartesian coordinates, we can show that for $\text{curl}\,\vec{F}$ defined in Cartesian coordinates

$$\boxed{\text{curl}\,\vec{F} \cdot \vec{n} = \text{circ}_{\vec{n}}\,\vec{F}.}$$

This shows that $\text{curl}\,\vec{F}$ defined in Cartesian coordinates satisfies the geometric definition, since the left-hand side takes its maximum value when $\vec{n}$ points in the same direction as $\text{curl}\,\vec{F}$, and in that case its value is $\|\text{curl}\,\vec{F}\|$.

The following example justifies this formula in a specific case.

Example 4

Use the definition of curl in Cartesian coordinates and Green's Theorem to show that

$$\left(\text{curl}\,\vec{F} \right) \cdot \vec{k} = \text{circ}_{\vec{k}}\,\vec{F}.$$

Solution   Using the definition of curl in Cartesian coordinates, the left-hand side of the formula is

$$\left(\text{curl}\,\vec{F}\right) \cdot \vec{k} = \frac{\partial F_2}{\partial x} - \frac{\partial F_1}{\partial y}.$$

Now let's look at the right hand side. The circulation density around $\vec{k}$ is calculated using circles perpendicular to $\vec{k}$; hence, the $\vec{k}$-component of $\vec{F}$ does not contribute to it; that is, the circulation density of $\vec{F}$ around $\vec{k}$ is the same as the circulation density of $F_1\vec{i} + F_2\vec{j}$ around $\vec{k}$. But in any plane perpendicular to $\vec{k}$, z is constant, so in that plane F_1 and F_2 are functions of x and y alone. Thus, $F_1\vec{i} + F_2\vec{j}$ can be thought of as a two-dimensional vector field on the horizontal plane through the point (x, y, z) where the circulation density is being calculated. Let C be a circle in this plane, with radius a and centered at (x, y, z), and let R be the region enclosed by C. Green's Theorem says that

$$\int_C (F_1\vec{i} + F_2\vec{j}) \cdot d\vec{r} = \int_R \left(\frac{\partial F_2}{\partial x} - \frac{\partial F_1}{\partial y}\right) dA.$$

When the circle is small, $\partial F_2/\partial x - \partial F_1/\partial y$ is approximately constant on R, so

$$\int_R \left(\frac{\partial F_2}{\partial x} - \frac{\partial F_1}{\partial y}\right) dA \approx \left(\frac{\partial F_2}{\partial x} - \frac{\partial F_1}{\partial y}\right) \cdot \text{Area of } R = \left(\frac{\partial F_2}{\partial x} - \frac{\partial F_1}{\partial y}\right) \pi a^2.$$

Thus, taking a limit as the radius of the circle goes to zero, we have

$$\text{circ}_{\vec{k}}\,\vec{F}(x, y, z) = \lim_{a \to 0} \frac{\int_C (F_1\vec{i} + F_2\vec{j}) \cdot d\vec{r}}{\pi a^2} = \lim_{a \to 0} \frac{\int_R \left(\frac{\partial F_2}{\partial x} - \frac{\partial F_1}{\partial y}\right) dA}{\pi a^2} = \frac{\partial F_2}{\partial x} - \frac{\partial F_1}{\partial y}.$$

Curl-Free Vector Fields

A vector field is said to be *curl free* or *irrotational* if curl $\vec{F} = \vec{0}$ everywhere that $\vec{F}$ is defined.

Example 5   Figure 20.8 shows the vector field $\vec{B}$ for three values of the constant p, where $\vec{B}$ is defined on 3-space by

$$\vec{B} = \frac{-y\vec{i} + x\vec{j}}{(x^2 + y^2)^{p/2}}.$$

(a) Find a formula for curl $\vec{B}$.
(b) Is there a value of p for which $\vec{B}$ is curl free? If so, find it.

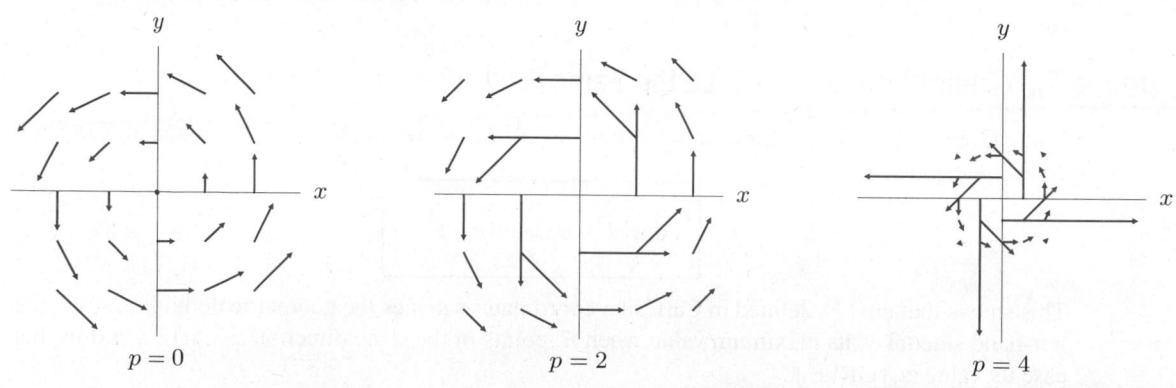

$p = 0$ $p = 2$ $p = 4$

Figure 20.8: The vector field $\vec{B}(\vec{r}) = (-y\vec{i} + x\vec{j})/(x^2 + y^2)^{p/2}$ for $p = 0, 2,$ and 4

Solution   (a) We can use the following version of the product rule for curl. If ϕ is a scalar function and $\vec{F}$ is a vector field, then

$$\text{curl}(\phi\vec{F}) = \phi\,\text{curl}\,\vec{F} + (\text{grad}\,\phi) \times \vec{F}.$$

(See Problem 29 on page 1054.) We write $\vec{B} = \phi\vec{F} = \dfrac{1}{(x^2 + y^2)^{p/2}}(-y\vec{i} + x\vec{j})$. Then

$$\operatorname{curl}\vec{F} = \operatorname{curl}(-y\vec{i} + x\vec{j}) = 2\vec{k}$$

$$\operatorname{grad}\phi = \operatorname{grad}\left(\frac{1}{(x^2 + y^2)^{p/2}}\right) = \frac{-p}{(x^2 + y^2)^{(p/2)+1}}(x\vec{i} + y\vec{j}).$$

Thus, we have

$$\begin{aligned}
\operatorname{curl}\vec{B} &= \frac{1}{(x^2 + y^2)^{p/2}}\operatorname{curl}(-y\vec{i} + x\vec{j}) + \operatorname{grad}\left(\frac{1}{(x^2 + y^2)^{p/2}}\right) \times (-y\vec{i} + x\vec{j}) \\
&= \frac{1}{(x^2 + y^2)^{p/2}}2\vec{k} + \frac{-p}{(x^2 + y^2)^{(p/2)+1}}(x\vec{i} + y\vec{j}) \times (-y\vec{i} + x\vec{j}) \\
&= \frac{1}{(x^2 + y^2)^{p/2}}2\vec{k} + \frac{-p}{(x^2 + y^2)^{(p/2)+1}}(x^2 + y^2)\vec{k} \\
&= \frac{2 - p}{(x^2 + y^2)^{p/2}}\vec{k}.
\end{aligned}$$

(b) The curl is zero when $p = 2$. Thus, when $p = 2$ the vector field is curl free:

$$\vec{B} = \frac{-y\vec{i} + x\vec{j}}{x^2 + y^2}.$$

Exercises and Problems for Section 20.1

Exercises

1. Is $\operatorname{curl}(z\vec{i} - x\vec{j} + y\vec{k})$ a vector or a scalar? Calculate it.

2. Is $\operatorname{curl}(-2z\vec{i} - z\vec{j} + xy\vec{k})$ a vector or scalar? Calculate it.

In Exercises 3–10, compute the curl of the vector field.

3. $\vec{F} = 3x\vec{i} - 5z\vec{j} + y\vec{k}$

4. $\vec{F} = (x^2 - y^2)\vec{i} + 2xy\vec{j}$

5. $\vec{F} = (-x + y)\vec{i} + (y + z)\vec{j} + (-z + x)\vec{k}$

6. $\vec{F} = 2yz\vec{i} + 3xz\vec{j} + 7xy\vec{k}$

7. $\vec{F} = x^2\vec{i} + y^3\vec{j} + z^4\vec{k}$

8. $\vec{F} = e^x\vec{i} + \cos y\vec{j} + e^{z^2}\vec{k}$

9. $\vec{F} = (x + yz)\vec{i} + (y^2 + xzy)\vec{j} + (zx^3y^2 + x^7y^6)\vec{k}$

10. $\vec{F}(\vec{r}) = \vec{r}/\|\vec{r}\|$

In Exercises 11–14, decide whether the vector field appears to have nonzero curl at the origin. The vector field is shown in the xy-plane; it has no z-component and is independent of z.

11.

12.

13.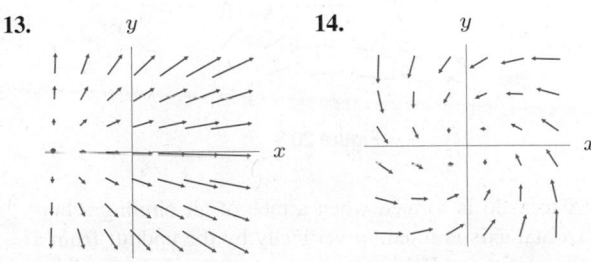

14.

Problems

15. Let $\vec{F}$ be the vector field in Figure 20.2 on page 1048. It is rotating counterclockwise around the z-axis when viewed from above. At a distance r from the z-axis, $\vec{F}$ has magnitude $2r$.

    (a) Find a formula for $\vec{F}$.

    (b) Find $\operatorname{curl}\vec{F}$ using the coordinate definition and relate your answer to circulation density.

16. Use the geometric definition to find the curl of the vector field $\vec{F}(\vec{r}) = \vec{r}$. Check your answer using the coordinate definition.

17. A smooth vector field $\vec{G}$ has curl $\vec{G}(0,0,0) = 2\vec{i} - 3\vec{j} + 5\vec{k}$. Estimate the circulation around a circle of radius 0.01 centered at the origin in each of the following planes:

   (a) xy-plane, oriented counterclockwise when viewed from the positive z-axis.

   (b) yz-plane, oriented counterclockwise when viewed from the positive x-axis.

   (c) xz-plane, oriented counterclockwise when viewed from the positive y-axis.

18. Three small circles, C_1, C_2, and C_3, each with radius 0.1 and centered at the origin are in the xy-, yz-, and xz-planes, respectively. The circles are oriented counterclockwise when viewed from the positive z-, x-, and y-axes, respectively. A vector field, $\vec{F}$, has circulation around C_1 of 0.02π, around C_2 of 0.5π, and around C_3 of 3π. Estimate curl $\vec{F}$ at the origin.

19. Using your answers to Exercises 7–8, make a conjecture about a particular form of the vector field $\vec{F} \neq \vec{0}$ that has curl $\vec{F} = \vec{0}$. What form? Show why your conjecture is true.

20. **(a)** Find curl $\vec{G}$ if $\vec{G} = (ay^3 + be^z)\vec{i} + (cz + dx^2)\vec{j} + (e\sin x + fy)\vec{k}$ and a, b, c, d, e, f are constants.

   (b) If curl $\vec{G}$ is everywhere parallel to the yz-plane, what can you say about the constants a–f?

   (c) If curl $\vec{G}$ is everywhere parallel to the z-axis, what can you say about the constants a–f?

21. Figure 20.9 gives a sketch of the velocity vector field $\vec{F} = y\vec{i} + x\vec{j}$ in the xy-plane.

   (a) What is the direction of rotation of a thin twig placed at the origin along the x-axis?

   (b) What is the direction of rotation of a thin twig placed at the origin along the y-axis?

   (c) Compute curl $\vec{F}$.

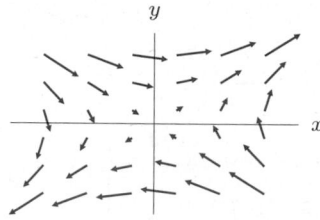

Figure 20.9

22. A tornado is formed when a tube of air circling a horizontal axis is tilted up vertically by the updraft from a thunderstorm. If t is time, this process can be modeled by the wind velocity field

$$\vec{F}(t, x, y, z) = (\cos t\vec{j} + \sin t\vec{k}) \times \vec{r} \quad \text{and} \quad 0 \le t \le \frac{\pi}{2}.$$

Determine the direction of curl $\vec{F}$:

   (a) At $t = 0$ **(b)** At $t = \pi/2$

   (c) For $0 < t < \pi/2$

23. A large fire becomes a fire-storm when the nearby air acquires a circulatory motion. The associated updraft has the effect of bringing more air to the fire, causing it to burn faster. Records show that a fire-storm developed during the Chicago Fire of 1871 and during the Second World War bombing of Hamburg, Germany, but there was no fire-storm during the Great Fire of London in 1666. Explain how a fire-storm could be identified using the curl of a vector field.

24. A vortex that rotates at constant angular velocity ω about the z-axis has velocity vector field $\vec{v} = \omega(-y\vec{i} + x\vec{j})$.

   (a) Sketch the vector field with $\omega = 1$ and the vector field with $\omega = -1$.

   (b) Determine the speed $\|\vec{v}\|$ of the vortex as a function of the distance from its center.

   (c) Compute div $\vec{v}$ and curl $\vec{v}$.

   (d) Compute the circulation of $\vec{v}$ counterclockwise about the circle of radius R in the xy-plane, centered at the origin.

25. A central vector field is one of the form $\vec{F} = f(r)\vec{r}$ where f is any function of $r = \|\vec{r}\|$. Show that any central vector field is irrotational.

26. Show that curl $(\vec{F} + \vec{C}) = $ curl $\vec{F}$ for a constant vector field $\vec{C}$.

27. If $\vec{F}$ is any vector field whose components have continuous second partial derivatives, show div curl $\vec{F} = 0$.

28. We have seen that the Fundamental Theorem of Calculus for Line Integrals implies $\int_C \text{grad } f \cdot d\vec{r} = 0$ for any smooth closed path C and any smooth function f.

   (a) Use the geometric definition of curl to deduce that curl grad $f = \vec{0}$.

   (b) Show that curl grad $f = \vec{0}$ using the coordinate definition.

29. Show that curl $(\phi\vec{F}) = \phi$ curl $\vec{F} + (\text{grad } \phi) \times \vec{F}$ for a scalar function ϕ and a vector field $\vec{F}$.

30. Show that if $\vec{F} = f \text{ grad } g$ for some scalar functions f and g, then curl $\vec{F}$ is everywhere perpendicular to $\vec{F}$.

31. Let $\vec{F}$ be a smooth vector field and let $\vec{u}$ and $\vec{v}$ be constant vectors. Using the definition of curl $\vec{F}$ in Cartesian coordinates, show that

$$\text{grad}(\vec{F} \cdot \vec{v}) \cdot \vec{u} - \text{grad}(\vec{F} \cdot \vec{u}) \cdot \vec{v} = (\text{curl } \vec{F}) \cdot \vec{u} \times \vec{v}.$$

32. Let $\vec{T} = a\vec{i} + b\vec{j}$ be a fixed unit vector, and let $\vec{F} = F(x, y)\vec{T}$ be a vector field everywhere parallel to $\vec{T}$, but of varying magnitude F. Show that curl $\vec{F}$ equals $\vec{k}$ times the directional derivative of F in the direction of $\vec{F} \times \vec{k}$. Do this in two ways:

   (a) Graphically, using line integrals

(b) Algebraically

(Note: The direction of $\vec{F} \times \vec{k}$ is obtained by rotating $\vec{F}$ through $90°$ clockwise as viewed from above the xy-plane.)

33. Let $r = (x^2 + y^2)^{1/2}$. Figure 20.10 shows the vector field $r^A(-y\vec{i} + x\vec{j})$ for $r \neq 0$ and $A = -1, -2,$ and -3. The vector fields are shown in the xy-plane; they have no z-component and are independent of z.

   (a) Show that $\text{curl}(r^A(-y\vec{i} + x\vec{j})) = (2 + A)r^A\vec{k}$ for any constant A.

   (b) Using your answer to part (a), find the direction of the curl of the three vector fields for $A = -1, -2, -3$.

   (c) For each value of A, what (if anything) does your answer to part (b) tell you about the sign of the circulation around a small circle oriented counterclockwise when viewed from above, and centered at $(1, 1, 1)$? Centered at $(0, 0, 0)$?

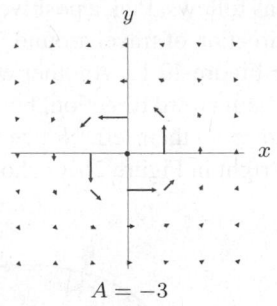

$A = -3$

Figure 20.10: The vector field $r^A(-y\vec{i} + x\vec{j})$ for three values of A

Strengthen Your Understanding

In Problems 34–35, explain what is wrong with the statement.

34. A vector field $\vec{F}$ has curl given by $\text{curl}\,\vec{F} = 2x - 3y$.

35. If all the vectors of a vector field $\vec{F}$ are parallel, then $\text{curl}\,\vec{F} = \vec{0}$.

In Problems 36–37, give an example of:

36. A vector field $\vec{F}(x, y, z)$ such that $\text{curl}\,\vec{F} = \vec{0}$.

37. A vector field $\vec{F}(x, y, z)$ such that $\text{curl}\,\vec{F} = \vec{j}$.

In Problems 38–46, is the statement true or false? Assume $\vec{F}$ and $\vec{G}$ are smooth vector fields and f is a smooth function on 3-space. Explain.

38. The circulation density, $\text{circ}_{\vec{n}}\,\vec{F}(x, y, z)$, is a scalar.

39. $\text{curl}\,\text{grad}\,f = 0$

40. If $\vec{F}$ is a vector field with $\text{div}\,\vec{F} = 0$ and $\text{curl}\,\vec{F} = \vec{0}$, then $\vec{F} = \vec{0}$.

41. If $\vec{F}$ and $\vec{G}$ are vector fields, then $\text{curl}(\vec{F} + \vec{G}) = \text{curl}\,\vec{F} + \text{curl}\,\vec{G}$.

42. If $\vec{F}$ and $\vec{G}$ are vector fields, then $\text{curl}(\vec{F} \cdot \vec{G}) = \text{curl}\,\vec{F} \cdot \text{curl}\,\vec{G}$.

43. If $\vec{F}$ and $\vec{G}$ are vector fields, then $\text{curl}(\vec{F} \times \vec{G}) = (\text{curl}\,\vec{F}) \times (\text{curl}\,\vec{G})$.

44. $\text{curl}(f\vec{G}) = (\text{grad}\,f) \times \vec{G} + f(\text{curl}\,\vec{G})$

45. For any vector field $\vec{F}$, the curl of $\vec{F}$ is perpendicular at every point to $\vec{F}$.

46. If $\vec{F}$ is as shown in Figure 20.11, then $\text{curl}\,\vec{F} \cdot \vec{j} > 0$.

Figure 20.11

47. Of the following vector fields, which ones have a curl which is parallel to one of the axes? Which axis?

   (a) $y\vec{i} - x\vec{j} + z\vec{k}$ **(b)** $y\vec{i} + z\vec{j} + x\vec{k}$ **(c)** $-z\vec{i} + y\vec{j} + x\vec{k}$
   (d) $x\vec{i} + z\vec{j} - y\vec{k}$ **(e)** $z\vec{i} + x\vec{j} + y\vec{k}$

20.2   STOKES' THEOREM

The Divergence Theorem says that the integral of the flux density over a solid region is equal to the flux through the surface bounding the region. Similarly, Stokes' Theorem says that the integral of the circulation density over a surface is equal to the circulation around the boundary of the surface.

The Boundary of a Surface

The *boundary* of a surface S is the curve or curves running around the edge of S (like the hem around the edge of a piece of cloth). An orientation of S determines an orientation for its boundary, C, as follows. Pick a positive normal vector $\vec{n}$ on S, near C, and use the right-hand rule to determine a direction of travel around $\vec{n}$. This in turn determines a direction of travel around the boundary C. See Figure 20.12. Another way of describing the orientation on C is that someone walking along C in the forward direction, body upright in the direction of the positive normal on S, would have the surface on their left. Notice that the boundary can consist of two or more curves, as the surface on the right in Figure 20.12 shows.

Figure 20.12: Two oriented surfaces and their boundaries

Calculating the Circulation from the Circulation Density

Consider a closed, oriented curve C in 3-space. We can find the circulation of a vector field $\vec{F}$ around C by calculating the line integral:

$$\text{Circulation around } C = \int_C \vec{F} \cdot d\vec{r}.$$

If C is the boundary of an oriented surface S, there is another way to calculate the circulation using $\text{curl} \, \vec{F}$. We subdivide S into pieces as shown on the surface on the left in Figure 20.12. If $\vec{n}$ is a positive unit normal vector to a piece of surface with area ΔA, then $\Delta \vec{A} = \vec{n} \, \Delta A$. In addition, $\text{circ}_{\vec{n}} \, \vec{F}$ is the circulation density of $\vec{F}$ around $\vec{n}$, so

$$\text{Circulation of } \vec{F} \text{ around boundary of the piece} \approx \left(\text{circ}_{\vec{n}} \, \vec{F} \right) \Delta A = ((\text{curl} \, \vec{F}) \cdot \vec{n}) \Delta A = (\text{curl} \vec{F}) \cdot \Delta \vec{A}.$$

Next we add up the circulations around all the small pieces. The line integral along the common edge of a pair of adjacent pieces appears with opposite sign in each piece, so it cancels out. (See Figure 20.13.) When we add up all the pieces the internal edges cancel and we are left with the circulation around C, the boundary of the entire surface. Thus,

$$\text{Circulation around } C = \sum \text{Circulation around boundary of pieces} \approx \sum \text{curl} \, \vec{F} \cdot \Delta \vec{A}.$$

Taking the limit as $\Delta A \to 0$, we get

$$\text{Circulation around } C = \int_S \text{curl} \, \vec{F} \cdot d\vec{A}.$$

Figure 20.13: Two adjacent pieces of the surface

We have expressed the circulation as a line integral around C and as a flux integral over S; thus, the two integrals must be equal. Hence we have[1]

Theorem 20.1: Stokes' Theorem

If S is a smooth oriented surface with piecewise smooth, oriented boundary C, and if $\vec{F}$ is a smooth vector field on an open region containing S and C, then

$$\int_C \vec{F} \cdot d\vec{r} = \int_S \operatorname{curl} \vec{F} \cdot d\vec{A}.$$

The orientation of C is determined from the orientation of S according to the right-hand rule.

Example 1   Let $\vec{F}(x, y, z) = -2y\vec{i} + 2x\vec{j}$. Use Stokes' Theorem to find $\int_C \vec{F} \cdot d\vec{r}$, where C is a circle

(a) Parallel to the yz-plane, of radius a, centered at a point on the x-axis, with either orientation.
(b) Parallel to the xy-plane, of radius a, centered at a point on the z-axis, oriented counterclockwise as viewed from a point on the z-axis above the circle.

Solution   We have $\operatorname{curl} \vec{F} = 4\vec{k}$. Figure 20.14 shows sketches of $\vec{F}$ and $\operatorname{curl} \vec{F}$.

(a) Let S be the disk enclosed by C. Since S lies in a vertical plane and $\operatorname{curl} \vec{F}$ points vertically everywhere, the flux of $\operatorname{curl} \vec{F}$ through S is zero. Hence, by Stokes' Theorem,

$$\int_C \vec{F} \cdot d\vec{r} = \int_S \operatorname{curl} \vec{F} \cdot d\vec{A} = 0.$$

It makes sense that the line integral is zero. If C is parallel to the yz-plane (even if it is not lying in the plane), the symmetry of the vector field means that the line integral of $\vec{F}$ over the top half of the circle cancels the line integral over the bottom half.

(b) Let S be the horizontal disk enclosed by C. Since $\operatorname{curl} \vec{F}$ is a constant vector field pointing in the direction of $\vec{k}$, we have, by Stokes' Theorem,

$$\int_C \vec{F} \cdot d\vec{r} = \int_S \operatorname{curl} \vec{F} \cdot d\vec{A} = \| \operatorname{curl} \vec{F} \| \cdot \text{Area of } S = 4\pi a^2.$$

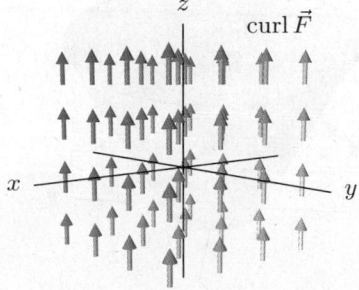

Figure 20.14: The vector fields $\vec{F}$ and $\operatorname{curl} \vec{F}$

---

[1]A proof of Stokes' Theorem using the coordinate definition of curl can be found in the online supplement at www.wiley.com/college/hughes-hallett.

Since $\vec{F}$ is circling around the z-axis in the same direction as C, we expect the line integral to be positive. In fact, in Example 1 on page 1049, we computed this line integral directly.

Curl Free Vector Fields

Stokes' Theorem applies to any oriented surface S and its boundary C, even in cases where the boundary consists of two or more curves. This is useful in studying curl-free vector fields.

Example 2   A current I flows along the z-axis in the $\vec{k}$ direction. The induced magnetic field $\vec{B}(x, y, z)$ is

$$\vec{B}(x, y, z) = \frac{2I}{c}\left(\frac{-y\vec{i} + x\vec{j}}{x^2 + y^2}\right),$$

where c is the speed of light. In Example 5 on page 1052 we showed that $\operatorname{curl}\vec{B} = \vec{0}$.

(a) Compute the circulation of $\vec{B}$ around the circle C_1 in the xy-plane of radius a, centered at the origin, and oriented counterclockwise when viewed from above.

(b) Use part (a) and Stokes' Theorem to compute $\int_{C_2}\vec{B}\cdot d\vec{r}$, where C_2 is the ellipse $x^2 + 9y^2 = 9$ in the plane $z = 2$, oriented counterclockwise when viewed from above.

Solution   (a) On the circle C_1, we have $\|\vec{B}\| = 2I/(ca)$. Since $\vec{B}$ is tangent to C_1 everywhere and points in the forward direction around C_1,

$$\int_{C_1}\vec{B}\cdot d\vec{r} = \|\vec{B}\| \cdot \text{Length of } C_1 = \frac{2I}{ca}\cdot 2\pi a = \frac{4\pi I}{c}.$$

(b) Let S be the conical surface extending from C_1 to C_2 in Figure 20.15. The boundary of this surface has two pieces, $-C_2$ and C_1. The orientation of C_1 leads to the outward normal on S, which forces us to choose the clockwise orientation on C_2. By Stokes' Theorem,

$$\int_{S}\operatorname{curl}\vec{B}\cdot d\vec{A} = \int_{-C_2}\vec{B}\cdot d\vec{r} + \int_{C_1}\vec{B}\cdot d\vec{r} = -\int_{C_2}\vec{B}\cdot d\vec{r} + \int_{C_1}\vec{B}\cdot d\vec{r}.$$

Since $\operatorname{curl}\vec{B} = \vec{0}$, we have $\displaystyle\int_{S}\operatorname{curl}\vec{B}\cdot d\vec{A} = 0$, so the two line integrals must be equal:

$$\int_{C_2}\vec{B}\cdot d\vec{r} = \int_{C_1}\vec{B}\cdot d\vec{r} = \frac{4\pi I}{c}.$$

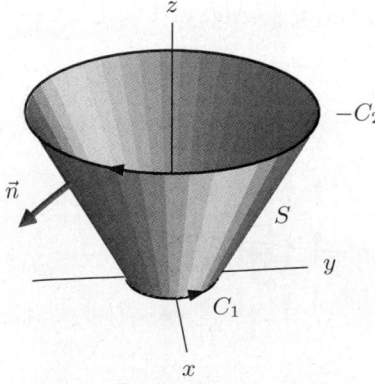

Figure 20.15: Surface joining C_1 to C_2, oriented to satisfy the conditions of Stokes' Theorem

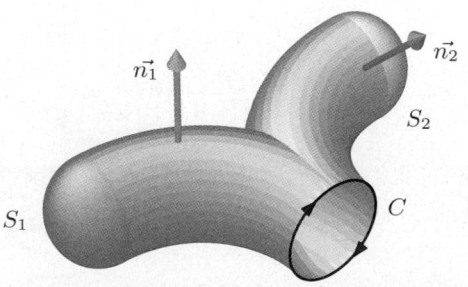

Figure 20.16: The flux of a curl is the same through the two surfaces S_1 and S_2 if they determine the same orientation on the boundary, C

Curl Fields

A vector field $\vec{F}$ is called a *curl field* if $\vec{F} = \text{curl}\,\vec{G}$ for some vector field $\vec{G}$. Recall that if $\vec{F} = \text{grad}f$, then f is called a potential function. By analogy, if a vector field $\vec{F} = \text{curl}\,\vec{G}$, then $\vec{G}$ is called a *vector potential* for $\vec{F}$. The following example shows that the flux of a curl field through a surface depends only on the boundary of the surface. This is analogous to the fact that the line integral of a gradient field depends only on the endpoints of the path.

Example 3   Suppose $\vec{F} = \text{curl}\,\vec{G}$. Suppose that S_1 and S_2 are two oriented surfaces with the same boundary C. Show that, if S_1 and S_2 determine the same orientation on C (as in Figure 20.16), then

$$\int_{S_1} \vec{F} \cdot d\vec{A} = \int_{S_2} \vec{F} \cdot d\vec{A}.$$

If S_1 and S_2 determine opposite orientations on C, then

$$\int_{S_1} \vec{F} \cdot d\vec{A} = -\int_{S_2} \vec{F} \cdot d\vec{A}.$$

Solution   Since $\vec{F} = \text{curl}\,\vec{G}$, by Stokes' Theorem we have

$$\int_{S_1} \vec{F} \cdot d\vec{A} = \int_{S_1} \text{curl}\,\vec{G} \cdot d\vec{A} = \int_C \vec{G} \cdot d\vec{r}$$

and

$$\int_{S_2} \vec{F} \cdot d\vec{A} = \int_{S_2} \text{curl}\,\vec{G} \cdot d\vec{A} = \int_C \vec{G} \cdot d\vec{r}.$$

In each case the line integral on the right must be computed using the orientation determined by the surface. Thus, the two flux integrals of $\vec{F}$ are the same if the orientations are the same and they are opposite if the orientations are opposite.

Exercises and Problems for Section 20.2

Exercises

In Exercises 1–5, calculate the circulation, $\int_C \vec{F} \cdot d\vec{r}$, in two ways, directly and using Stokes' Theorem.

1. $\vec{F} = (x + z)\vec{i} + x\vec{j} + y\vec{k}$ and C is the upper half of the circle $x^2 + z^2 = 9$ in the plane $y = 0$, together with the x-axis from $(3, 0, 0)$ to $(-3, 0, 0)$, traversed counterclockwise when viewed from the positive y-axis.

2. $\vec{F} = y\vec{i} - x\vec{j}$ and C is the boundary of S, the part of the surface $z = 4 - x^2 - y^2$ above the xy-plane, oriented upward.

3. $\vec{F} = (x - y + z)(\vec{i} + \vec{j})$ and C is the triangle with vertices $(0, 0, 0)$, $(5, 0, 0)$, $(5, 5, 0)$, traversed in that order.

4. $\vec{F} = xy\vec{i} + yz\vec{j} + xz\vec{k}$ and C is the boundary of S, the surface $z = 1 - x^2$ for $0 \le x \le 1$ and $-2 \le y \le 2$, oriented upward. Sketch S and C.

5. $\vec{F} = y\vec{i} + z\vec{j} + x\vec{k}$ and C is the boundary of S, the paraboloid $z = 1 - (x^2 + y^2)$, $z \ge 0$ oriented upward. [Hint: Use polar coordinates.]

In Exercises 6–9, use Stokes' Theorem to calculate the integral.

6. $\int_C \vec{F} \cdot d\vec{r}$ where $\vec{F} = x^2\vec{i} + y^2\vec{j} + z^2\vec{k}$ and C is the unit circle in the xz-plane, oriented counterclockwise when viewed from the positive y-axis.

7. $\int_C \vec{F} \cdot d\vec{r}$ where $\vec{F} = (y - x)\vec{i} + (z - y)\vec{j} + (x - z)\vec{k}$ and C is the circle $x^2 + y^2 = 5$ in the xy-plane, oriented counterclockwise when viewed from above.

8. $\int_S \text{curl}\,\vec{F} \cdot d\vec{A}$ where $\vec{F} = -y\vec{i} + x\vec{j} + (xy + \cos z)\vec{k}$ and S is the disk $x^2 + y^2 \le 9$, oriented upward in the xy-plane.

9. $\int_S \text{curl}\,\vec{F} \cdot d\vec{A}$ where $\vec{F} = (x + 7)\vec{j} + e^{x+y+z}\vec{k}$ and S is the rectangle $0 \le x \le 3$, $0 \le y \le 2$, $z = 0$, oriented counterclockwise when viewed from above.

10. Let $\vec{F} = y\vec{i} - x\vec{j}$ and let C be the unit circle in the xy-plane centered at the origin and oriented counterclockwise when viewed from above.

    (a) Calculate $\int_C \vec{F} \cdot d\vec{r}$ by parameterizing the circle.

(b) Calculate curl $\vec{F}$.

(c) Calculate $\int_C \vec{F} \cdot d\vec{r}$ using your result from part (b).

(d) What theorem did you use in part (c)?

11. (a) If $\vec{F} = (\cos x)\vec{i} + e^y\vec{j} + (x - y - z)\vec{k}$, find curl $\vec{F}$.

(b) Find $\int_C \vec{F} \cdot d\vec{r}$ where C is the circle of radius 3 in

Problems

13. At all points in 3-space curl $\vec{F}$ points in the direction of $\vec{i} - \vec{j} - \vec{k}$. Let C be a circle in the yz-plane, oriented clockwise when viewed from the positive x-axis. Is the circulation of $\vec{F}$ around C positive, zero, or negative?

14. If curl $\vec{F} = (x^2 + z^2)\vec{j} + 5\vec{k}$, find $\int_C \vec{F} \cdot d\vec{r}$, where C is a circle of radius 3, centered at the origin, with

(a) C in the xy-plane, oriented counterclockwise when viewed from above.

(b) C in the xz-plane, oriented counterclockwise, when viewed from the positive y-axis.

15. (a) Find curl$(y\vec{i} + z\vec{j} + x\vec{k})$.

(b) Find $\int_C (y\vec{i} + z\vec{j} + x\vec{k}) \cdot d\vec{r}$ where C is the boundary of the triangle with vertices $(2, 0, 0)$, $(0, 3, 0)$, $(-2, 0, 0)$, traversed in that order.

16. (a) Let $\vec{F} = y\vec{i} + z\vec{j} + x\vec{k}$. Find curl $\vec{F}$.

(b) Calculate $\int_C \vec{F} \cdot d\vec{r}$ where C is

(i) A circle of radius 2 centered at $(1, 1, 3)$ in the plane $z = 3$, oriented counterclockwise when viewed from above.

(ii) The triangle obtained by tracing out the path $(2, 0, 0)$ to $(2, 0, 5)$ to $(2, 3, 5)$ to $(2, 0, 0)$.

17. (a) Find curl$(z\vec{i} + x\vec{j} + y\vec{k})$.

(b) Find $\int_C (z\vec{i} + x\vec{j} + y\vec{k}) \cdot d\vec{r}$ where C is a square of side 2 lying in the plane $x + y + z = 5$, oriented counterclockwise when viewed from the origin.

In Problems 18–23, find $\int_C \vec{F} \cdot d\vec{r}$ where C is a circle of radius 2 in the plane $x + y + z = 3$, centered at $(1, 1, 1)$ and oriented clockwise when viewed from the origin.

18. $\vec{F} = \vec{i} + \vec{j} + 3\vec{k}$

19. $\vec{F} = -y\vec{i} + x\vec{j} + z\vec{k}$

20. $\vec{F} = y\vec{i} - x\vec{j} + (y - x)\vec{k}$

21. $\vec{F} = (2y + e^x)\vec{i} + ((\sin y) - x)\vec{j} + (2y - x + \cos z^2)\vec{k}$

22. $\vec{F} = -z\vec{j} + y\vec{k}$

23. $\vec{F} = (z - y)\vec{i} + (x - z)\vec{j} + (y - x)\vec{k}$

24. For positive constants a, b, and c, let

$$f(x, y, z) = \ln(1 + ax^2 + by^2 + cz^2).$$

(a) What is the domain of f?

(b) Find grad$f$.

(c) Find curl(grad$f$).

the plane $x + y + z = 1$, centered at $(1, 0, 0)$ oriented counterclockwise when viewed from above.

12. Can you use Stokes' Theorem to compute the line integral $\int_C (2x\vec{i} + 2y\vec{j} + 2z\vec{k}) \cdot d\vec{r}$ where C is the straight line from the point $(1, 2, 3)$ to the point $(4, 5, 6)$? Why or why not?

(d) Find $\int_C \vec{F} \cdot d\vec{r}$ where C is the helix $x = \cos t$, $y = \sin t$, $z = t$ for $0 \le t \le 13\pi/2$ and

$$\vec{F} = \frac{2x\vec{i} + 4y\vec{j} + 6z\vec{k}}{1 + x^2 + 2y^2 + 3z^2}.$$

25. Figure 20.17 shows an open cylindrical can, S, standing on the xy-plane. (S has a bottom and sides, but no top.)

(a) Give equation(s) for the rim, C.

(b) If S is oriented outward and downward, find $\int_S \text{curl}(-y\vec{i} + x\vec{j} + z\vec{k}) \cdot d\vec{A}$.

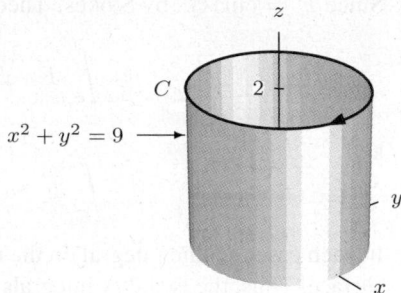

Figure 20.17

26. Evaluate $\int_C (-z\vec{i} + y\vec{j} + x\vec{k}) \cdot d\vec{r}$, where C is a circle of radius 2, parallel to the xz-plane and around the y-axis with the orientation shown in Figure 20.18.

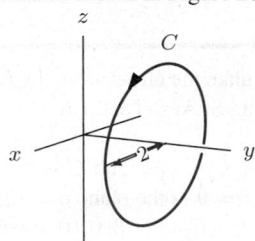

Figure 20.18

27. Evaluate the circulation of $\vec{G} = xy\vec{i} + z\vec{j} + 3y\vec{k}$ around a square of side 6, centered at the origin, lying in the yz-plane, and oriented counterclockwise viewed from the positive x-axis.

28. Find the flux of $\vec{F} = \text{curl}((x^3 + \cos(z^2))\vec{i} + (x + \sin(y^2))\vec{j} + (y^2 \sin(x^2))\vec{k})$ through the upper half of the sphere of radius 2, with center at the origin and oriented upward.

29. Suppose that C is a closed curve in the xy-plane, oriented counterclockwise when viewed from above. Show that $\frac{1}{2} \int_C (-y\vec{i} + x\vec{j}) \cdot d\vec{r}$ equals the area of the region R in the xy-plane enclosed by C.

30. In the region between the circles $C_1 : x^2 + y^2 = 4$ and $C_2 : x^2 + y^2 = 25$ in the xy-plane, the vector field $\vec{F}$ has curl $\vec{F} = 3\vec{k}$. If C_1 and C_2 are both oriented counterclockwise when viewed from above, find the value of

$$\int_{C_2} \vec{F} \cdot d\vec{r} - \int_{C_1} \vec{F} \cdot d\vec{r}.$$

31. Let curl $\vec{F} = 3x\vec{i} + 3y\vec{j} - 6z\vec{k}$ and let C_1 and C_2 be the closed curves in the planes $z = 0$ and $z = 5$ in Figure 20.19. Find

$$\int_{C_1} \vec{F} \cdot d\vec{r} + \int_{C_2} \vec{F} \cdot d\vec{r}.$$

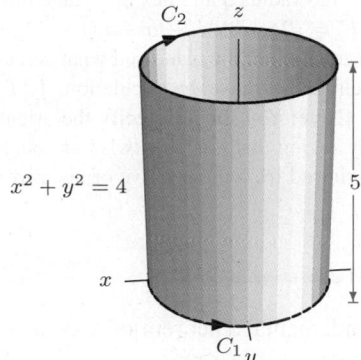

Figure 20.19

32. **(a)** Find curl$(x^3\vec{i} + \sin(y^3)\vec{j} + e^{z^3}\vec{k})$.
   (b) What does your answer to part (a) tell you about $\int_C (x^3\vec{i} + \sin(y^3)\vec{j} + e^{z^3}\vec{k}) \cdot d\vec{r}$ where C is the circle $(x - 10)^2 + (y - 20)^2 = 1$ in the xy-plane, oriented clockwise?
   (c) If C is any closed curve, what can you say about $\int_C (x^3\vec{i} + \sin(y^3)\vec{j} + e^{z^3}\vec{k}) \cdot d\vec{r}$?

33. Let $\vec{F}(x, y, z) = F_1(x, y)\vec{i} + F_2(x, y)\vec{j}$, where F_1 and F_2 are continuously differentiable for all x, y.

   (a) Describe in words how $\vec{F}$ varies through space.

   (b) Find an expression for curl $\vec{F}$ in terms of F_1 and F_2.
   (c) Let C be a closed curve in the xy-plane, oriented counterclockwise when viewed from above, and let S be the region enclosed by C. Use your answer to part (b) to simplify the statement of Stokes' Theorem for this $\vec{F}$ and C.
   (d) The result in part (c) is usually known by another name. What is it?

34. Water in a bathtub has velocity vector field near the drain given, for x, y, z in cm, by

$$\vec{F} = -\frac{y + xz}{(z^2 + 1)^2}\vec{i} - \frac{yz - x}{(z^2 + 1)^2}\vec{j} - \frac{1}{z^2 + 1}\vec{k} \text{ cm/sec}.$$

   (a) Rewriting $\vec{F}$ as follows, describe in words how the water is moving:

$$\vec{F} = \frac{-y\vec{i} + x\vec{j}}{(z^2 + 1)^2} + \frac{-z(x\vec{i} + y\vec{j})}{(z^2 + 1)^2} - \frac{\vec{k}}{z^2 + 1}.$$

   (b) The drain in the bathtub is a disk in the xy-plane with center at the origin and radius 1 cm. Find the rate at which the water is leaving the bathtub. (That is, find the rate at which water is flowing through the disk.) Give units for your answer.
   (c) Find the divergence of $\vec{F}$.
   (d) Find the flux of the water through the hemisphere of radius 1, centered at the origin, lying below the xy-plane and oriented downward.
   (e) Find $\int_C \vec{G} \cdot d\vec{r}$ where C is the edge of the drain, oriented clockwise when viewed from above, and where

$$\vec{G} = \frac{1}{2}\left(\frac{y}{z^2 + 1}\vec{i} - \frac{x}{z^2 + 1}\vec{j} - \frac{x^2 + y^2}{(z^2 + 1)^2}\vec{k}\right).$$

   (f) Calculate curl $\vec{G}$.
   (g) Explain why your answers to parts (d) and (e) are equal.

Strengthen Your Understanding

In Problems 35–36, explain what is wrong with the statement.

35. The line integral $\int_C \vec{F} \cdot d\vec{r}$ can be evaluated using Stokes' Theorem, where $\vec{F} = 2x\vec{i} - 3\vec{j} + \vec{k}$ and C is an oriented curve from $(0, 0, 0)$ to $(3, 4, 5)$.

36. If S is the unit circular disc $x^2 + y^2 \leq 1$, $z = 0$, in the xy-plane, oriented downward, and C is the unit circle in the xy-plane oriented counterclockwise, and $\vec{F}$ is a vector field, then

$$\int_C \vec{F} \cdot d\vec{r} = \int_S \text{curl } \vec{F} \cdot d\vec{A}.$$

In Problems 37–38, give an example of:

37. An oriented closed curve C such that $\int_C \vec{F} \cdot d\vec{r} = 0$, where $\vec{F}(x, y, z) = x\vec{i} + y^2\vec{j} + z^3\vec{k}$.

38. A surface S, oriented appropriately to use Stokes' Theorem, which has as its boundary the circle C of radius 1 centered at the origin, lying in the xy-plane, and oriented counterclockwise, when viewed from above.

In Problems 39–47, is the statement true or false? Give a reason for your answer.

39. If curl $\vec{F}$ everywhere perpendicular to the z-axis, and if C is a circle in the xy-plane, then the circulation of $\vec{F}$ around C is zero.

40. If S is the upper unit hemisphere $x^2+y^2+z^2 = 1$, $z \geq 0$, oriented upward, then the boundary of S used in Stokes' Theorem is the circle $x^2 + y^2 = 1$, $z = 0$, with orientation counterclockwise when viewed from the positive z-axis.

41. Let S be the cylinder $x^2 + z^2 = 1$, $0 \leq y \leq 2$, oriented with inward pointing normal. Then the boundary of S consists of two circles C_1 $(x^2 + z^2 = 1, y = 0)$ and C_2 $(x^2 + z^2 = 1, y = 2)$, both oriented clockwise when viewed from the positive y-axis.

42. If C is the boundary of an oriented surface S, oriented by the right-hand rule, then $\int_C \text{curl}\,\vec{F} \cdot d\vec{r} = \int_S \vec{F} \cdot d\vec{A}$.

43. Let S_1 be the disk $x^2 + y^2 \leq 1$, $z = 0$ and let S_2 be the upper unit hemisphere $x^2 + y^2 + z^2 = 1$, $z \geq 0$, both oriented upward. If $\vec{F}$ is a vector field then $\int_{S_1} \text{curl}\vec{F} \cdot d\vec{A} = \int_{S_2} \text{curl}\vec{F} \cdot d\vec{A}$.

44. Let S be the closed unit sphere $x^2+y^2+z^2 = 1$, oriented outward. If $\vec{F}$ is a vector field, then $\int_S \text{curl}\vec{F} \cdot d\vec{A} = 0$.

45. If $\vec{F}$ and $\vec{G}$ are vector fields satisfying $\text{curl}\vec{F} = \text{curl}\vec{G}$, then $\int_C \vec{F} \cdot d\vec{r} = \int_C \vec{G} \cdot d\vec{r}$, where C is any oriented circle in 3-space.

46. If $\vec{F}$ is a vector field satisfying $\text{curl}\vec{F} = \vec{0}$, then $\int_C \vec{F} \cdot d\vec{r} = 0$, where C is any oriented path around a rectangle in 3-space.

47. Let S be an oriented surface, with oriented boundary C, and suppose that $\vec{F}$ is a vector field such that $\int_C \vec{F} \cdot d\vec{r} = 0$. Then $\text{curl}\,\vec{F} = \vec{0}$ everywhere on S.

48. The circle C has radius 3 and lies in a plane through the origin. Let $\vec{F} = (2z + 3y)\vec{i} + (x - z)\vec{j} + (6y - 7x)\vec{k}$. What is the equation of the plane and what is the orientation of the circle that make the circulation, $\int_C \vec{F} \cdot d\vec{r}$, a maximum? [Note: You should specify the orientation of the circle by saying that it is clockwise or counterclockwise when viewed from the positive or negative x- or y- or z-axis.]

20.3 THE THREE FUNDAMENTAL THEOREMS

We have now seen three multivariable versions of the Fundamental Theorem of Calculus. In this section we will examine some consequences of these theorems.

Fundamental Theorem of Calculus for Line Integrals

$$\int_C \text{grad} f \cdot d\vec{r} = f(Q) - f(P).$$

Stokes' Theorem

$$\int_S \text{curl}\,\vec{F} \cdot d\vec{A} = \int_C \vec{F} \cdot d\vec{r}.$$

Divergence Theorem

$$\int_W \text{div}\vec{F}\, dV = \int_S \vec{F} \cdot d\vec{A}.$$

Notice that, in each case, the region of integration on the right is the boundary of the region on the left (except that for the first theorem we simply evaluate f at the boundary points); the integrand on the left is a sort of derivative of the integrand on the right; see Figure 20.20.

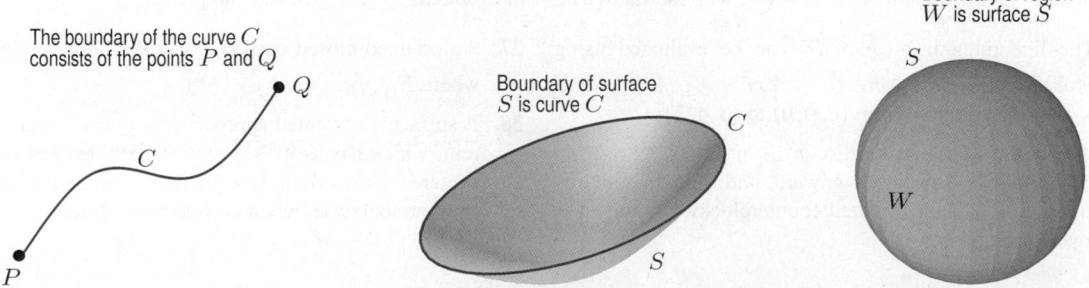

Figure 20.20: Regions and their boundaries for the three fundamental theorems

The Gradient and the Curl

Suppose that $\vec{F}$ is a smooth gradient field, so $\vec{F} = \operatorname{grad} f$ for some function f. Using the Fundamental Theorem for Line Integrals, we saw in Chapter 18 that

$$\int_C \vec{F} \cdot d\vec{r} = 0$$

for any closed curve C. Thus, for any unit vector $\vec{n}$

$$\operatorname{circ}_{\vec{n}} \vec{F} = \lim_{\text{Area} \to 0} \frac{\displaystyle\int_C \vec{F} \cdot d\vec{r}}{\text{Area of } C} = \lim_{\text{Area} \to 0} \frac{0}{\text{Area}} = 0,$$

where the limit is taken over circles C in a plane perpendicular to $\vec{n}$, and oriented by the right-hand rule. Thus, the circulation density of $\vec{F}$ is zero in every direction, so $\operatorname{curl} \vec{F} = \vec{0}$, that is,

$$\boxed{\operatorname{curl} \operatorname{grad} f = \vec{0}.}$$

(This formula can also be verified using the coordinate definition of curl. See Problem 28 on page 1054.)

Is the converse true? Is any vector field whose curl is zero a gradient field? Suppose that $\operatorname{curl} \vec{F} = \vec{0}$ and let us consider the line integral $\int_C \vec{F} \cdot d\vec{r}$ for a closed curve C contained in the domain of $\vec{F}$. If C is the boundary curve of an oriented surface S that lies wholly in the domain of $\operatorname{curl} \vec{F}$, then Stokes' Theorem asserts that

$$\int_C \vec{F} \cdot d\vec{r} = \int_S \operatorname{curl} \vec{F} \cdot d\vec{A} = \int_S \vec{0} \cdot d\vec{A} = 0.$$

If we knew that $\int_C \vec{F} \cdot d\vec{r} = 0$ for every closed curve C, then $\vec{F}$ would be path-independent, and hence a gradient field. Thus, we need to know whether every closed curve in the domain of $\vec{F}$ is the boundary of an oriented surface contained in the domain. It can be quite difficult to determine if a given curve is the boundary of a surface (suppose, for example, that the curve is knotted in a complicated way). However, if the curve can be contracted smoothly to a point, remaining all the time in the domain of $\vec{F}$, then it is the boundary of a surface, namely, the surface it sweeps through as it contracts. Thus, we have proved the test for a gradient field that we stated in Chapter 18.

The Curl Test for Vector Fields in 3-Space

Suppose $\vec{F}$ is a smooth vector field on 3-space such that
- The domain of $\vec{F}$ has the property that every closed curve in it can be contracted to a point in a smooth way, staying at all times within the domain.
- $\operatorname{curl} \vec{F} = \vec{0}$.

Then $\vec{F}$ is path-independent, and thus is a gradient field.

Example 7 on page 992 shows how the curl test is applied.

The Curl and the Divergence

In this section we will use the second two fundamental theorems to get a test for a vector field to be a curl field, that is, a field of the form $\vec{F} = \operatorname{curl} \vec{G}$ for some $\vec{G}$.

Example 1   Suppose that $\vec{F}$ is a smooth curl field. Use Stokes' Theorem to show that for any closed surface, S, contained in the domain of $\vec{F}$

$$\int_S \vec{F} \cdot d\vec{A} = 0.$$

Solution   Suppose $\vec{F} = \text{curl}\,\vec{G}$. Draw a closed curve C on the surface S, thus dividing S into two surfaces S_1 and S_2 as shown in Figure 20.21. Pick the orientation for C corresponding to S_1; then the orientation of C corresponding to S_2 is the opposite. Thus, using Stokes' Theorem,

$$\int_{S_1} \vec{F} \cdot d\vec{A} = \int_{S_1} \text{curl}\,\vec{G} \cdot d\vec{A} = \int_C \vec{G} \cdot d\vec{r} = -\int_{S_2} \text{curl}\,\vec{G} \cdot d\vec{A} = -\int_{S_2} \vec{F} \cdot d\vec{A}.$$

Thus, for any closed surface S, we have

$$\int_S \vec{F} \cdot d\vec{A} = \int_{S_1} \vec{F} \cdot d\vec{A} + \int_{S_2} \vec{F} \cdot d\vec{A} = 0.$$

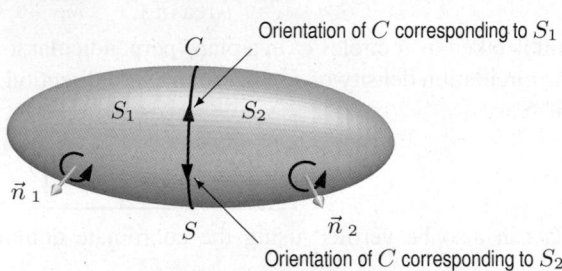

Figure 20.21: The closed surface S divided into two surfaces S_1 and S_2

Thus, if $\vec{F} = \text{curl}\,\vec{G}$, we use the result of Example 1 to see that

$$\text{div}\,\vec{F} = \lim_{\text{Volume}\to 0} \frac{\displaystyle\int_S \vec{F} \cdot d\vec{A}}{\text{Volume enclosed by } S} = \lim_{\text{Volume}\to 0} \frac{0}{\text{Volume}} = 0,$$

where the limit is taken over spheres S contracting down to a point. So we conclude that:

$$\boxed{\text{div}\,\text{curl}\,\vec{G} = 0.}$$

(This formula can also be verified using coordinates. See Problem 27 on page 1054.)

Is every vector field whose divergence is zero a curl field? It turns out that we have the following analogue of the curl test, though we will not prove it.

The Divergence Test for Vector Fields in 3-Space

Suppose $\vec{F}$ is a smooth vector field on 3-space such that
- The domain of $\vec{F}$ has the property that every closed surface in it is the boundary of a solid region completely contained in the domain.
- $\text{div}\,\vec{F} = 0$.

Then $\vec{F}$ is a curl field.

Example 2   Consider the vector fields $\vec{E} = q\dfrac{\vec{r}}{\|\vec{r}\|^3}$ and $\vec{B} = \dfrac{2I}{c}\left(\dfrac{-y\vec{i} + x\vec{j}}{x^2 + y^2}\right)$.

(a) Calculate $\text{div}\,\vec{E}$ and $\text{div}\,\vec{B}$.
(b) Do $\vec{E}$ and $\vec{B}$ satisfy the divergence test?
(c) Is either $\vec{E}$ or $\vec{B}$ a curl field?

Solution   (a) Example 3 on page 1028 shows that div $\vec{E} = 0$. The following calculation shows div $\vec{B} = 0$ also:

$$\text{div } \vec{B} = \frac{2I}{c}\left(\frac{\partial}{\partial x}\left(\frac{-y}{x^2 + y^2}\right) + \frac{\partial}{\partial y}\left(\frac{x}{x^2 + y^2}\right) + \frac{\partial}{\partial z}(0)\right)$$
$$= \frac{2I}{c}\left(\frac{2xy}{(x^2 + y^2)^2} + \frac{-2yx}{(x^2 + y^2)^2}\right) = 0.$$

(b) The domain of $\vec{E}$ is 3-space minus the origin, so a region is contained in the domain if it misses the origin. Thus, the surface of a sphere centered at the origin is contained in the domain of E, but the solid ball inside is not. Hence, $\vec{E}$ does not satisfy the divergence test.

   The domain of $\vec{B}$ is 3-space minus the z-axis, so a region is contained in the domain if it avoids the z-axis. If S is a surface bounding a solid region W, then the z-axis cannot pierce W without piercing S as well. Hence, if S avoids the z-axis, so does W. Thus, $\vec{B}$ satisfies the divergence test.

(c) In Example 3 on page 1036 we computed the flux of $\vec{r}/\|\vec{r}\|^3$ through a sphere centered at the origin, and found it was 4π, so the flux of $\vec{E}$ through this sphere is $4\pi q$. Thus, $\vec{E}$ cannot be a curl field, because by Example 1, the flux of a curl field through a closed surface is zero.

   On the other hand, $\vec{B}$ satisfies the divergence test, so it must be a curl field. In fact, Problem 24 shows that

$$\vec{B} = \text{curl}\left(\frac{-I}{c}\ln(x^2 + y^2)\vec{k}\right).$$

Exercises and Problems for Section 20.3

Exercises

In Exercises 1–6, is the vector field a gradient field?

1. $\vec{F} = 2x\vec{i} + z\vec{j} + y\vec{k}$

2. $\vec{F} = y\vec{i} + z\vec{j} + x\vec{k}$

3. $\vec{F} = (y + 2z)\vec{i} + (x + z)\vec{j} + (2x + y)\vec{k}$

4. $\vec{F} = (y - 2z)\vec{i} + (x - z)\vec{j} + (2x - y)\vec{k}$

5. $\vec{G} = -y\vec{i} + x\vec{j}$

6. $\vec{F} = yz\vec{i} + (xz + z^2)\vec{j} + (xy + 2yz)\vec{k}$

In Exercises 7–12, is the vector field a curl field?

7. $\vec{F} = z\vec{i} + x\vec{j} + y\vec{k}$

8. $\vec{F} = z\vec{i} + y\vec{j} + x\vec{k}$

9. $\vec{F} = 2x\vec{i} - y\vec{j} - z\vec{k}$

10. $\vec{F} = (x + y)\vec{i} + (y + z)\vec{j} + (x + z)\vec{k}$

11. $\vec{F} = (-xy)\vec{i} + (2yz)\vec{j} + (yz - z^2))\vec{k}$

12. $\vec{F} = (xy)\vec{i} + (xy)\vec{j} + (xy)\vec{k}$

In Exercises 13–16, can the curl test and the divergence test be applied to a vector field whose domain is the given region?

13. All points (x, y, z) such that $z > 0$.

14. All points (x, y, z) not on the y-axis.

15. All points (x, y, z) not on the positive z-axis.

16. All points (x, y, z) except the x-axis with $0 \leq x \leq 1$.

Problems

17. Let $\vec{B} = b\vec{k}$, for some constant b. Show that the following are all possible vector potentials for $\vec{B}$:

   (a) $\vec{A} = -by\vec{i}$ (b) $\vec{A} = bx\vec{j}$
   (c) $\vec{A} = \frac{1}{2}\vec{B} \times \vec{r}$.

18. Find a vector field $\vec{F}$ such that curl $\vec{F} = 2\vec{i} - 3\vec{j} + 4\vec{k}$. [Hint: Try $\vec{F} = \vec{v} \times \vec{r}$ for some vector $\vec{v}$.]

19. Find a vector potential for the constant vector field $\vec{B}$ whose value at every point is $\vec{b}$.

20. Express $(3x + 2y)\vec{i} + (4x + 9y)\vec{j}$ as the sum of a curl-free vector field and a divergence-free vector field.

In Problems 21–22, does a vector potential exist for the vector field given? If so, find one.

21. $\vec{G} = x^2\vec{i} + y^2\vec{j} + z^2\vec{k}$

22. $\vec{F} = 2x\vec{i} + (3y - z^2)\vec{j} + (x - 5z)\vec{k}$

23. An electric charge q at the origin produces an electric field $\vec{E} = q\vec{r}/\|\vec{r}\|^3$.

    (a) Does curl $\vec{E} = \vec{0}$?
    (b) Does $\vec{E}$ satisfy the curl test?
    (c) Is $\vec{E}$ a gradient field?

24. Show that $\vec{A} = \dfrac{-I}{c} \ln(x^2 + y^2)\vec{k}$ is a vector potential for

$$\vec{B} = \frac{2I}{c}\left(\frac{-y\vec{i} + x\vec{j}}{x^2 + y^2}\right).$$

25. Suppose c is the speed of light. A thin wire along the z-axis carrying a current I produces a magnetic field

$$\vec{B} = \frac{2I}{c}\left(\frac{-y\vec{i} + x\vec{j}}{x^2 + y^2}\right).$$

    (a) Does curl $\vec{B} = \vec{0}$?
    (b) Does $\vec{B}$ satisfy the curl test?
    (c) Is $\vec{B}$ a gradient field?

26. For constant p, consider the vector field $\vec{E} = \dfrac{\vec{r}}{\|\vec{r}\|^p}$.

    (a) Find curl $\vec{E}$.
    (b) Find the domain of $\vec{E}$.
    (c) For which values of p does $\vec{E}$ satisfy the curl test? For those values of p, find a potential function for $\vec{E}$.

27. Use Stokes' Theorem to show that if $u(x,y)$ and $v(x,y)$ are two functions of x and y and C is a closed curve in the xy-plane oriented counterclockwise, then

$$\int_C (u\vec{i} + v\vec{j}) \cdot d\vec{r} = \int_R \left(\frac{\partial v}{\partial x} - \frac{\partial u}{\partial y}\right) dx\,dy$$

where R is the region in the xy-plane enclosed by C. This is Green's Theorem.

28. The magnetic field, $\vec{B}$, due to a magnetic dipole with moment $\vec{\mu}$ satisfies div $\vec{B} = 0$ and is given by

$$\vec{B} = -\frac{\vec{\mu}}{\|\vec{r}\|^3} + \frac{3(\vec{\mu} \cdot \vec{r})\vec{r}}{\|\vec{r}\|^5}, \qquad \vec{r} \neq \vec{0}.$$

    (a) Does $\vec{B}$ satisfy the divergence test?
    (b) Show that $\vec{A} = \dfrac{\vec{\mu} \times \vec{r}}{\|\vec{r}\|^3}$ is a vector potential for $\vec{B}$. [Hint: Use Problem 29 on page 1054. The identities in Example 3 on page 1051, Problem 68 on page 796, and Problem 47 on page 750 may also be useful.]
    (c) Does your answer to part (a) contradict your answer to part (b)? Explain.

29. Suppose that $\vec{A}$ is a vector potential for $\vec{B}$.

    (a) Show that $\vec{A} + \text{grad }\psi$ is also a vector potential for $\vec{B}$, for any function ψ with continuous second-order partial derivatives. (The vector potentials $\vec{A}$ and $\vec{A} + \text{grad }\psi$ are called *gauge equivalent* and the transformation, for any ψ, from $\vec{A}$ to $\vec{A} + \text{grad }\psi$ is called a *gauge transformation*.)
    (b) What is the divergence of $\vec{A} + \text{grad }\psi$? How should ψ be chosen such that $\vec{A} + \text{grad }\psi$ has zero divergence? (If div $\vec{A} = 0$, the magnetic vector potential $\vec{A}$ is said to be in *Coulomb gauge*.)

Strengthen Your Understanding

In Problems 30–31, explain what is wrong with the statement.

30. The curl of a vector field $\vec{F}$ is given by curl $\vec{F} = x\vec{i}$.

31. For a certain vector field $\vec{F}$, we have curl div $\vec{F} = y\vec{i}$.

In Problems 32–33, give an example of:

32. A vector field $\vec{F}$ that is not the curl of another vector field.

33. A function f such that div grad $f \neq 0$.

In Problems 34–37, is the statement true or false? Give a reason for your answer.

34. There exists a vector field $\vec{F}$ with curl $\vec{F} = \vec{i}$.

35. There exists a vector field $\vec{F}$ (whose components have continuous second partial derivatives) satisfying curl $\vec{F} = x\vec{i}$.

36. Let S be an oriented surface, with oriented boundary C, and suppose that $\vec{F}$ is a vector field such that $\int_S \text{curl}\vec{F} \cdot d\vec{A} = 0$. Then $\vec{F}$ is a gradient field.

37. If $\vec{F}$ is a gradient field, then $\int_S \text{curl }\vec{F} \cdot d\vec{A} = 0$, for any smooth oriented surface, S, in 3-space.

38. Let $f(x,y,z)$ be a scalar function with continuous second partial derivatives. Let $\vec{F}(x,y,z)$ be a vector field with continuous second partial derivatives. Which of the following quantities are identically zero?

    (a) curl grad f **(b)** $\vec{F} \times \text{curl }\vec{F}$
    (c) grad div $\vec{F}$ **(d)** div curl $\vec{F}$
    (e) div grad f

CHAPTER SUMMARY (see also Ready Reference at the end of the book)

- **Curl**
  Geometric and coordinate definition of curl, calculating curl, interpretation in terms of circulation per unit area.

- **Stokes' Theorem**
  Statement of the theorem, curl-free and curl fields.

- **Three Fundamental Theorems**
  Combining the fundamental theorem of line integrals, Stokes' theorem and the Divergence theorem to show $\operatorname{curl}\operatorname{grad} f = \vec{0}$ and $\operatorname{div}\operatorname{curl}\vec{G} = 0$.
  Curl test for gradient field in 3-space.
  Divergence test for curl field in 3-space.

REVIEW EXERCISES AND PROBLEMS FOR CHAPTER TWENTY

Exercises

1. Find $\operatorname{curl}((x + y)\vec{i} - (y + z)\vec{j} + (x + z)\vec{k})$

2. Find $(\operatorname{curl}\vec{n}) \cdot \vec{j}$
  where $\vec{n} = (2x + 3y)\vec{i} + (4y + 5z)\vec{j} + (6z + 7x)\vec{k}$

Exercises 3–5 concern the vector fields in Figure 20.22. In each case, assume that the cross-section is the same in all other planes parallel to the given cross-section.

Figure 20.22

3. Three of the vector fields have zero curl at each point shown. Which are they? How do you know?

4. Three of the vector fields have zero divergence at each point shown. Which are they? How do you know?

5. Four of the line integrals $\int_{C_i} \vec{F} \cdot d\vec{r}$ are zero. Which are they? How do you know?

In Exercises 6–9, are the quantities defined? For those that are, is the quantity a vector or scalar? Let $f(x, y, z)$ be a smooth function and let $\vec{F}(\vec{r})$ and $\vec{G}(\vec{r})$ be smooth vector fields.

6. $\displaystyle\int_C (\operatorname{grad}\vec{F}) \cdot d\vec{r}$

7. $\displaystyle\int_S (\vec{F}(\vec{r}) \times \vec{G}(\vec{r})) \cdot d\vec{A}$

8. $\operatorname{div}((\operatorname{grad} f) \times \vec{r})$

9. $(\operatorname{curl}\vec{F}) \times \vec{F}$

In Exercises 10–11 decide whether the vector fields appear to have nonzero curl at the point marked. The vector field is shown in the xy-plane; it has no z-component and is independent of z.

10.

11.

In Exercises 12–15, calculate $\operatorname{div}\vec{F}$ and $\operatorname{curl}\vec{F}$. Is $\vec{F}$ solenoidal or irrotational?

12. $\vec{F} = x^2\vec{i} + y^3\vec{j} + z^4\vec{k}$

13. $\vec{F} = xy\vec{i} + yz\vec{j} + zx\vec{k}$

14. $\vec{F} = (\cos x)\vec{i} + e^y\vec{j} + (x + y + z)\vec{k}$

15. $\vec{F} = e^{y+z}\vec{i} + \sin(x + z)\vec{j} + (x^2 + y^2)\vec{k}$

16. Let S be the curved side of the cylinder $y^2 + z^2 = 5$, for $0 \le x \le 3$, oriented outward. Let $\vec{F} = xz\vec{j} - xy\vec{k}$. Find $\int_S \operatorname{curl}\vec{F} \cdot d\vec{A}$

  (a) Directly   **(b)** Using Stokes' Theorem

17. Compute $\int_C ((yz^2 - y)\vec{i} + (xz^2 + x)\vec{j} + 2xyz\vec{k}) \cdot d\vec{r}$, where the line integral is around C, the circle of radius 3 in the xy-plane, centered at the origin, oriented counterclockwise as viewed from the positive z-axis. Do this in two ways:

  (a) Directly   **(b)** Using Stokes' Theorem

18. Find the flux of $\text{curl}(e^{x^2}\vec{i} + (x+y)\vec{k})$ through the disk $y^2 + z^2 \leq 1$, $x = 0$, oriented toward the positive x-axis using:

(a) Stokes' Theorem   (b) Direct calculation

In Exercises 19–22, use Stokes' Theorem to find the circulation of the vector field around the given paths.

19. $\vec{F} = (z - 2y)\vec{i} + (3x - 4y)\vec{j} + (z + 3y)\vec{k}$ and C is the circle $x^2 + y^2 = 4$, $z = 1$, oriented counterclockwise when viewed from above.

20. $\vec{F} = (2x - y)\vec{i} + (x + 4y)\vec{j}$ and C is a circle of radius 10, centered at the origin.

(a) In the xy-plane, oriented clockwise as viewed from the positive z-axis.

(b) In the yz-plane, oriented clockwise as viewed from the positive x-axis.

21. $\vec{F} = \vec{r}/\|\vec{r}\|^3$ and C is the path consisting of line segments from $(1, 0, 1)$ to $(1, 0, 0)$ to $(0, 0, 1)$ to $(1, 0, 1)$.

22. $\vec{F} = xz\vec{i} + (x + yz)\vec{j} + x^2\vec{k}$ and C is the circle $x^2 + y^2 = 1$, $z = 2$, oriented counterclockwise when viewed from above.

Problems

23. Let $\vec{r} = x\vec{i} + y\vec{j} + z\vec{k}$ and $\vec{a}$ be a constant vector. For each of the quantities in (a)–(f), choose one of the statements in (I)–(V).

(a) $\text{div}(\vec{r} + \vec{a})$ (b) $\text{div}(\vec{r} \times \vec{a})$ (c) $\text{div}(\vec{r} \cdot \vec{a})$
(d) $\text{curl}(\vec{r} + \vec{a})$ (e) $\text{curl}(\vec{r} \times \vec{a})$ (f) $\text{curl}(\vec{r} \cdot \vec{a})$

(I) Scalar, independent of $\vec{a}$.
(II) Scalar, depends on $\vec{a}$.
(III) Vector, independent of $\vec{a}$.
(IV) Vector, depends on $\vec{a}$.
(V) Not defined.

24. Calculate the following quantities or say why it is impossible. Let $\vec{r} = x\vec{i} + y\vec{j} + z\vec{k}$ and let $\vec{a} = a_1\vec{i} + a_2\vec{j} + a_3\vec{k}$ be a constant vector.

(a) $\text{grad}(\vec{r} \cdot \vec{a})$ (b) $\text{div}(\vec{r} \cdot \vec{a})$
(c) $\text{curl}(\vec{r} \cdot \vec{a})$ (d) $\text{grad}(\vec{r} \times \vec{a})$
(e) $\text{div}(\vec{r} \times \vec{a})$ (f) $\text{curl}(\vec{r} \times \vec{a})$

25. Calculate each of the following integrals or say why it cannot be done with the methods and theorems in this book. Let $\vec{F} = x^3\vec{i} + y^3\vec{j} + z^3\vec{k}$.

(a) $\int_S \vec{F} \cdot d\vec{A}$ where S is the disk of radius 3 in the plane $y = 5$, oriented toward the origin.
(b) $\int_W \vec{F} \, dV$ where W is the solid sphere of radius 2 centered at the origin.
(c) $\int_S \text{curl}\vec{F} \cdot d\vec{A}$ where S is the disk of radius 3 in the plane $y = 5$, oriented toward the origin.
(d) $\int_C \text{grad}\vec{F} \cdot d\vec{r}$ where C is the line from the origin to $(2, 3, 4)$.
(e) $\int_W \text{div}\vec{F} \, dV$ where W is the solid sphere of radius 2 centered at the origin.
(f) $\int_C \vec{F} \cdot d\vec{r}$ where C is the line from the origin to $(2, 3, 4)$.
(g) $\int_W \text{curl}\vec{F} \, dV$ where W is the box $0 \leq x \leq 1, 0 \leq y \leq 2, 0 \leq z \leq 3$.
(h) $\int_W \vec{F} \cdot (\vec{i} + \vec{j} + \vec{k}) \, dV$ where W is the box $0 \leq x \leq 1, 0 \leq y \leq 2, 0 \leq z \leq 3$.

26. Let $\vec{F}$ be a vector field with continuous partial derivatives at all points in 3-space. Let S_1 be the upper half of the sphere of radius 1 centered at the origin, oriented upward. Let S_2 be the disk of radius 1 in the xy-plane centered at the origin and oriented upward. Let C be the unit circle in the xy-plane, oriented counterclockwise when viewed from above. For each of the following integrals, say whether or not it is defined. If it is defined, list which of the other integrals it must equal (if any) and name the theorem.

(a) $\int_C \vec{F} \cdot d\vec{r}$ (b) $\int_C \vec{F} \cdot d\vec{A}$

(c) $\int_{S_1} \vec{F} \cdot d\vec{r}$ (d) $\int_{S_2} \vec{F} \cdot d\vec{A}$

(e) $\int_{S_1} \text{curl}\vec{F} \cdot d\vec{A}$ (f) $\int_{S_2} \text{curl}\vec{F} \cdot d\vec{A}$

(g) $\int_C \text{curl}\vec{F} \cdot d\vec{r}$

27. Let $\text{curl}\,\vec{F} = 2x\vec{i} + 5\vec{j} - 2z\vec{k}$, let $P = (3, 2, 4)$, and let C be the circle of radius 0.01 centered at P in the plane $x + y + z = 9$, oriented clockwise when viewed from the origin.

(a) Find $\text{curl}\,\vec{F} \cdot (\vec{i} + \vec{j} + \vec{k})$ at P.
(b) What does your answer to part (a) tell you about $\int_C \vec{F} \cdot d\vec{r}$?

28. Three small squares, S_1, S_2, and S_3, each with side 0.1 and centered at the point $(4, 5, 7)$, lie parallel to the xy-, yz- and xz-planes, respectively. The squares are oriented counterclockwise when viewed from the positive z-, x-, and y-axes, respectively. A vector field $\vec{G}$ has circulation around S_1 of -0.02, around S_2 of 6, and around S_3 of -5. Estimate $\text{curl}\,\vec{G}$ at the point $(4, 5, 7)$.

29. Figures 20.23 and 20.24 show the vector fields $\vec{F}$ and $\vec{G}$. Each vector field has no z-component and is independent of z. All the axes have the same scales.

(a) What can you say about $\text{div}\,\vec{F}$ and $\text{div}\,\vec{G}$ at the origin?
(b) What can you say about $\text{curl}\,\vec{F}$ and $\text{curl}\,\vec{G}$ at the origin?
(c) Is there a closed surface around the origin such that $\vec{F}$ has a nonzero flux through it?

(d) Repeat part (c) for $\vec{G}$.

(e) Is there a closed curve around the origin such that $\vec{F}$ has a nonzero circulation around it?

(f) Repeat part (e) for $\vec{G}$.

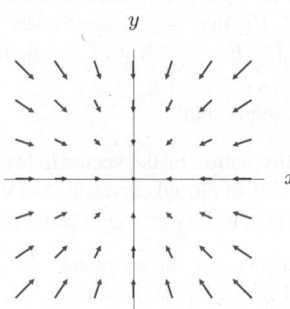

Figure 20.23: Cross-section of $\vec{F}$

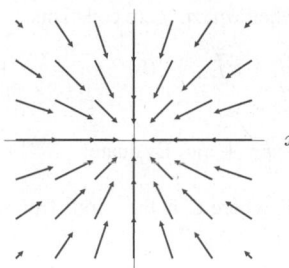

Figure 20.24: Cross-section of $\vec{G}$

30. Let $\vec{F} = y\vec{i} + \pi x\vec{j} + z\vec{k}$. Find the following integrals:

(a) $\displaystyle\int_S \vec{F} \cdot d\vec{A}$, where S is the disk $x^2 + y^2 \leq 10$, $z = \sqrt{5}$, oriented downward.

(b) $\displaystyle\int_C \vec{F} \cdot d\vec{r}$, where C is the line from $(0, \sqrt{3}, 0)$ to $(2, \sqrt{3}, 0)$.

(c) $\displaystyle\int_S \operatorname{curl} \vec{F} \cdot d\vec{A}$, where S is the rectangle with corners at $(0,0,0)$, $(0, \sqrt{3}, 0)$, $(2, \sqrt{3}, 0)$, $(2, 0, 0)$, oriented upward.

In Problems 31–42, calculate the integral.

31. $\int_C \left(x^2\vec{i} + y^2\vec{j} + (x+y+z)\vec{k}\right) \cdot d\vec{r}$ where C is the circle $(x-1)^2 + (y-2)^2 = 4$ in the xy-plane, oriented counterclockwise when viewed from the positive z-axis.

32. $\int_C (-y^3\vec{i} + x^3\vec{j} + e^z\vec{k}) \cdot d\vec{r}$ where C is $x^2 + y^2 = 3$, $z = 4$, oriented counterclockwise when viewed from above.

33. $\int_C \left(\sin\left(x^2\right)\vec{i} + \cos\left(y^2\right)\vec{j} + (x+y)\vec{k}\right) \cdot d\vec{r}$ where C is the circle $(y-1)^2 + (z-2)^2 = 4$ in the yz-plane, oriented counterclockwise when viewed from the positive x-axis.

34. $\int_S \operatorname{curl}\vec{F} \cdot d\vec{A}$ where $\vec{F} = (z+y)\vec{i} - (z+x)\vec{j} + (y+x)\vec{k}$. and S is the disk $y^2 + z^2 \leq 3, x = 0$, oriented in the positive x-direction.

35. $\int_S \vec{F} \cdot d\vec{A}$, where $\vec{F} = 3x\vec{i} + 4y\vec{j} + xy\vec{k}$ and S is the closed rectangular box whose top face has corners $(0, 0, 0)$, $(3, 0, 0)$, $(3, 5, 0)$, $(0, 5, 0)$, and whose bottom face contains the corner $(0, 0, -2)$.

36. $\int_S \vec{F} \cdot d\vec{A}$ where $\vec{F} = \left(y^2 + 3x\right)\vec{i} + \left(x^2 - y\right)\vec{j} + 2z\vec{k}$ and S is the unit sphere centered at the origin.

37. $\int_S \vec{F} \cdot d\vec{A}$ where $\vec{F} = x^3\vec{i} + y^3\vec{j} + z^3\vec{k}$ and S is the sphere of radius 1 centered at the origin.

38. $\int_C \vec{F} \cdot d\vec{r}$ where $\vec{F} = (x+y)\vec{i} + (y+2z)\vec{j} + (z+3x)\vec{k}$ and C is a square of side 7 in the xz-plane, oriented counterclockwise when viewed from the positive y-axis.

39. $\int_C \vec{F} \cdot d\vec{r}$ where $\vec{F} = (x - y^3 + z)\vec{i} + (x^3 + y + z)\vec{j} + (x + y + z^3)\vec{k}$ and C is the circle $x^2 + y^2 = 10$, oriented counterclockwise when viewed from above.

40. $\int_S \vec{F} \cdot d\vec{A}$ where $\vec{F} = (y^3z^3)\vec{i} + y^3\vec{j} + z^3\vec{k}$ and S is the cylinder $y^2 + z^2 = 16, -1 \leq x \leq 1$.

41. $\int_S \operatorname{curl} \vec{F} \cdot d\vec{A}$ where $\vec{F} = -xe^y\vec{i} + ye^x\vec{j} + x^2y^2z\vec{k}$ and S is the top and sides of the cube $0 \leq x \leq 1$, $0 \leq y \leq 1$, $0 \leq z \leq 1$, oriented outward.

42. $\int_C \vec{F} \cdot d\vec{r}$ if $\operatorname{curl} \vec{F} = 4\vec{k}$ and C is a unit circle in the xy-plane, oriented counterclockwise when viewed from above.

43. A box of side 1 in the first octant has faces in the planes $x = 0$, $x = 3$, $y = 0$, $y = 3$, $z = 0$, $z = 3$. Remove the face in the yz-plane to have an open surface, S, with a square boundary C. Let $\vec{F} = (x+y)\vec{i} - z\vec{j} + y\vec{k}$.

(a) Calculate $\int_C \vec{F} \cdot d\vec{r}$, where C is oriented counterclockwise when viewed from the positive x-axis.

(b) Calculate $\int_S \vec{F} \cdot d\vec{A}$, when S is oriented in the direction of the positive x-axis.

44. Suppose $\operatorname{div} \vec{F}(x, y, z) = 4$ everywhere. Which of the following quantities can be computed from this information? Give the value of those that can be computed.

(a) $\int_S \vec{F} \cdot d\vec{A}$, where S is a sphere of radius 2 centered at the origin and oriented outward.

(b) $\int_C \vec{F} \cdot d\vec{r}$, where C is the unit circle in the xy-plane, oriented counterclockwise viewed from above.

(c) $\int_S \operatorname{curl} \vec{F} \cdot d\vec{A}$, where S is a sphere of radius 2 centered at the origin and oriented outward.

45. Are the following vector fields conservative?

(a) $\vec{F}(x, y, z) = y^2z\vec{i} + 2xyz\vec{j} + xy\vec{k}$

(b) The vector field in Figure 20.25.

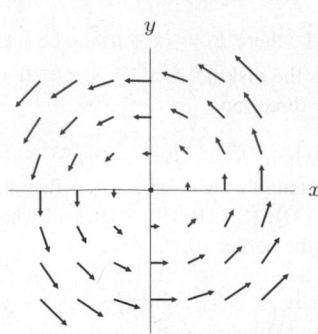

Figure 20.25

46. Let $\vec{F} = \dfrac{-y\vec{i} + x\vec{j}}{x^2 + y^2}$.

(a) Calculate curl $\vec{F}$. What is the domain of curl $\vec{F}$?

(b) Find the circulation of $\vec{F}$ around the unit circle C_1 in the xy-plane, oriented counterclockwise when viewed from above.

(c) Find the circulation of $\vec{F}$ around the circle C_2 in the plane $z = 4$ and with equation $(x - 3)^2 + y^2 = 1$, oriented counterclockwise when viewed from above.

(d) Find the circulation of $\vec{F}$ around the square S with corners $(2, 2, 0)$, $(-2, 2, 0)$, $(-2, -2, 0)$, $(2, -2, 0)$, oriented counterclockwise when viewed from above.

(e) Using your results to parts (b)–(d) explain how, with no additional calculation, you can find the circulation of $\vec{F}$ around any simple closed curve in the xy-plane, provided it does not intersect the z-axis. (A simple closed curve does not cross itself.)

47. Let C_1 be the circle of radius 3 in the xy-plane oriented counterclockwise and centered at the origin. Let

$$\vec{F} = \frac{-y\vec{i} + x\vec{j}}{x^2 + y^2}.$$

(a) Find $\int_{C_1} \vec{F} \cdot d\vec{r}$ by direct computation.

(b) Calculate curl $\vec{F}$.

(c) If possible, use Stokes' Theorem to calculate $\int_{C_1} \vec{F} \cdot d\vec{r}$? If it cannot be used, explain why not.

(d) Let C_2 be the circle of radius 3 in the xy-plane centered at $(5, 0)$. If possible, use Stokes' Theorem to calculate $\int_{C_2} \vec{F} \cdot d\vec{r}$? If it cannot be used, explain why not.

(e) Is $\vec{F}$ a gradient field?

48. Consider the circulation of the vector fields in parts (a)–(c) around the sets of closed curves in (I)–(V). For which of the sets, (I)–(V), is the circulation zero on every curve?

(I) All closed curves in the xy-plane.

(II) All closed curves in the yz-plane.

(III) All closed curves in the xz-plane.

(IV) All closed curves in the plane $x + y + z = 0$.

(V) All closed curves in all planes of the form $mx + ny = d$, where m, n, d are constants.

(a) $\vec{F} = -y\vec{i} + x\vec{j}$ (b) $\vec{G} = y\vec{i} + x\vec{j}$

(c) $\vec{H} = z\vec{j}$

49. Let $\vec{F} = y\vec{i} - x\vec{j} + z\vec{k}$. Evaluate:

(a) $\displaystyle\int_C \vec{F} \cdot d\vec{r}$ where C is the z-axis from the origin to $(0, 0, 10)$.

(b) $\displaystyle\int_S \vec{F} \cdot d\vec{A}$ where S is the disk $x^2 + y^2 \le 3$, $z = 10$.

(c) $\displaystyle\int_S \vec{F} \cdot d\vec{A}$ where S is the closed box with edges of length 2 in the first octant, with one corner at the origin and edges along the axes.

(d) $\displaystyle\int_C \vec{F} \cdot d\vec{r}$ where C is the circle of radius 3, centered on the z-axis in the plane $z = 4$, and oriented counterclockwise when viewed from above.

CAS Challenge Problems

50. (a) Let $\vec{F} = x^3 y\vec{i} + 2xz^3\vec{j} + (z^3 + 4x^2)\vec{k}$. Compute curl $\vec{F}(1, 2, 1)$.

(b) Consider the family of curves C_a given, for $0 \le t \le 2\pi$, by

$$\vec{r}(t) = \vec{i} + (2 + a\cos t)\vec{j} + (1 + a\sin t)\vec{k}.$$

Evaluate the line integral $\int_{C_a} \vec{F} \cdot d\vec{r}$ and compute the limit

$$\lim_{a \to 0} \frac{\int_{C_a} \vec{F} \cdot d\vec{r}}{\pi a^2}.$$

(c) Repeat part (b) for the family D_a given, for $0 \le t \le 2\pi$, by

$$\vec{r}(t) = (1 + a\sin t)\vec{i} + 2\vec{j} + (1 + a\cos t)\vec{k}.$$

(d) Repeat part (b) for the family E_a given, for $0 \le t \le 2\pi$, by

$$\vec{r}(t) = (1 + a\cos t)\vec{i} + (2 + a\sin t)\vec{j} + \vec{k}.$$

(e) Compare your answers to parts (b)-(d) with part (a) and explain using the geometric definition of curl.

51. Let S be the sphere of radius R centered at the origin with outward orientation and let

$$\vec{F} = (ax^2 + bxz)\vec{i} + (cy^2 + py)\vec{j} + (qz + rx^3)\vec{k}.$$

(a) Use the Divergence Theorem to express the flux integral $\int_S \vec{F} \cdot d\vec{A}$ as a triple integral. Then use symmetry and the volume formula for a sphere to evaluate the triple integral.

(b) Check your answer in part (a) by computing the flux integral directly.

52. Let $\vec{F}(x,y,z) = x^2 y\vec{i} + 2xz\vec{j} + (z^3 + 4x^2)\vec{k}$ and let S_a be the sphere of radius a centered at $(1,1,1)$, oriented outward, parameterized by $\vec{r}(\phi,\theta) = (1 + a\sin\phi\cos\theta)\vec{i} + (1 + a\sin\phi\sin\theta)\vec{j} + (1 + a\cos\phi)\vec{k}$, $0 \le \phi \le \pi, 0 \le \theta \le 2\pi$.

  (a) Compute div $\vec{F}(1,1,1)$.

  (b) Use the geometric definition of divergence to estimate $\int_{S_a} \vec{F} \cdot d\vec{A}$ for $a = 0.1$.

  (c) Evaluate the flux integral $\int_{S_a} \vec{F} \cdot d\vec{A}$. Compare its

value for $a = 0.1$ with your answer to part (b). Then compute the limit

$$\lim_{a \to 0} \frac{\int_{S_a} \vec{F} \cdot d\vec{A}}{\text{Volume inside } S_a}$$

and compare your result with part (a). Explain your answer in terms of the geometric definition of the divergence.

PROJECTS FOR CHAPTER TWENTY

1. Magnetic Field Generated by a Current in a Wire

Under steady-state conditions, a magnetic field $\vec{B}$ has curl $\vec{B} = \vec{0}$ in a region where there is no current. We study the steady-state magnetic field $\vec{B}$ due to a constant current in an infinitely long straight thin wire. The magnitude of the magnetic field at a point depends only on the distance from the wire and its direction is tangent to the circle around the wire and determined by the right-hand rule. Suppose the current is flowing upward along the z-axis. Then $\vec{B}$ is parallel to the xy-plane and, by the right-hand rule, points counterclockwise around a circle centered on the z-axis. (See Figure 20.26.)

  (a) Find the flux of curl $\vec{B}$ through the surface S between two concentric circles in the xy-plane of radius R_1 and R_2 centered on the wire.

  (b) Calculate the circulation of $\vec{B}$ around each of the two boundary pieces of S, where their orientations are determined by the upward orientation of S.

  (c) Use Stokes' Theorem to deduce that the magnitude of the magnetic field $\vec{B}$ is proportional to the reciprocal of the distance from the wire.

  (d) Compare the magnitude $\|\vec{B}\|$ at two points P and Q if Q is twice as far from the wire as P.

  (e) To decrease the magnitude of $\vec{B}$ by 20%, by what factor does the distance from the wire have to increase?

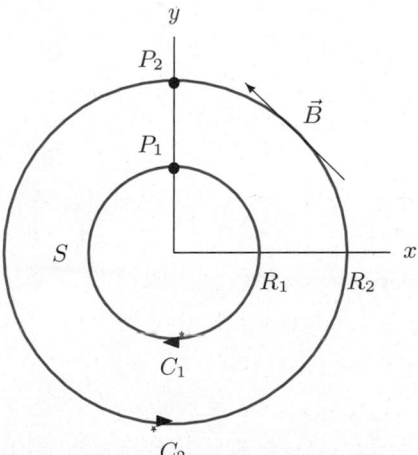

Figure 20.26: Current along positive z-axis
(out of page)

2. Curl in Natural Coordinates

Let $\vec{F}(x,y) = u(x,y)\vec{i} + v(x,y)\vec{j}$ be a 2-dimensional vector field. Let $F(x,y)$ be the magnitude of $\vec{F}$ and let $\theta(x,y)$ be the angle of $\vec{F}$ with the positive x-axis at the point (x,y), so that $u = F \cos \theta$ and $v = F \sin \theta$. Let $\vec{T}$ be the unit vector in the direction of $\vec{F}$, and let $\vec{N}$ be the unit vector in the direction of $\vec{k} \times \vec{F}$, perpendicular to $\vec{F}$. Show that

$$\text{curl}\, \vec{F} = c\vec{k} \qquad \text{where} \qquad c = F\theta_{\vec{T}} - F_{\vec{N}}.$$

The scalar c is called the *scalar curl* or the *vorticity* of the vector field $\vec{F}$. This problem shows that the vorticity is the difference of two terms, the *curvature vorticity*, $F\theta_{\vec{T}}$, due to turning of the flow lines of $\vec{F}$, and the *shear vorticity*, $F_{\vec{N}}$, due to changes in the magnitude of $\vec{F}$ in a direction normal to $\vec{F}$.

Chapter Twenty-One

PARAMETERS, COORDINATES, AND INTEGRALS

Contents

21.1 COORDINATES AND PARAMETERIZED SURFACES

In Chapter 17 we parameterized curves in 2- and 3-space, and in Chapter 16 we used polar, cylindrical, and spherical coordinates to simplify iterated integrals. We now take a second look at parameterizations and coordinate systems, and see that they are the same thing in different disguises: functions from one space to another.

We have already seen this with parameterized curves, which we view as a function from an interval $a \leq t \leq b$ to a curve in xyz-space. See Figure 21.1.

Figure 21.1: The parameterization is a function from the interval, $a \leq t \leq b$, to 3-space, whose image is the curve, C

Polar, Cylindrical, and Spherical Coordinates Revisited

The equations for polar coordinates,

$$x = r \cos \theta$$
$$y = r \sin \theta,$$

can also be viewed as defining a function from the $r\theta$-plane into the xy-plane. This function transforms the rectangle on the left of Figure 21.2 into the quarter disk on the right. We need two parameters to describe this disk because it is a two-dimensional object.

Polar Coordinates as Families of Parameterized Curves

Polar coordinates give two families of parameterized curves, which form the polar coordinate grid. The lines $r = $ Constant in the $r\theta$-plane correspond to circles in the xy-plane, each circle parameterized by θ; the lines $\theta = $ Constant correspond to rays in the xy-plane, each ray parameterized by r.

Cylindrical and Spherical Coordinates

Similarly, cylindrical and spherical coordinates may be viewed as functions from 3-space to 3-space. Cylindrical coordinates take rectangular boxes in $r\theta z$-space and map them to cylindrical regions in xyz-space; spherical coordinates take rectangular boxes in $\rho\theta\phi$-space and map them to spherical regions in xyz-space.

Figure 21.2: A grid in the $r\theta$-plane and the corresponding curved grid in the xy-plane

General Parameterizations

In general, a parameterization or coordinate system provides a way of representing a curved object by means of a simple region in the *parameter space* (an interval, rectangle, or rectangular box), along with a function mapping that region into the curved object. In the next section, we use this idea to parameterize curved surfaces in 3-space.

How Do We Parameterize a Surface?

In Section 17.1 we parameterized a circle in 2-space using the equations

$$x = \cos t, \quad y = \sin t.$$

In 3-space, the same circle in the xy-plane has parametric equations

$$x = \cos t, \quad y = \sin t, \quad z = 0.$$

We add the equation $z = 0$ to specify that the circle is in the xy-plane. If we wanted a circle in the plane $z = 3$, we would use the equations

$$x = \cos t, \quad y = \sin t, \quad z = 3.$$

Suppose now we let z vary freely, as well as t. We get circles in every horizontal plane, forming a cylinder as in the left of Figure 21.3. Thus, we need two parameters, t and z, to parameterize the cylinder.

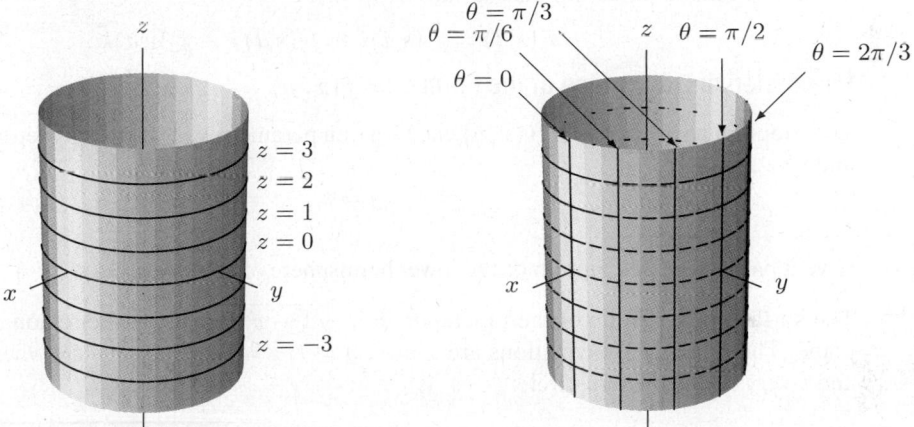

Figure 21.3: The cylinder $x = \cos t$, $y = \sin t$, $z = z$

We can contrast curves and surfaces. A curve, though it may live in two or three dimensions, is itself one-dimensional; if we move along it we can only move backward and forward in one direction. Thus, it only requires one parameter to trace out a curve.

A surface is 2-dimensional; at any given point there are two independent directions we can move. For example, on the cylinder we can move vertically, or we can circle around the z-axis horizontally. So we need *two* parameters to describe it. We can think of the parameters as map coordinates, like longitude and latitude on the surface of the earth. Just as polar coordinates give a polar grid on a circular region, so the parameters for a surface give a grid on the surface. See Figure 21.3 on the right.

In the case of the cylinder our parameters are t and z, so

$$x = \cos t, \quad y = \sin t, \quad z = z, \qquad 0 \le t < 2\pi, \quad -\infty < z < \infty.$$

The last equation, $z = z$, looks strange, but it reminds us that we are in three dimensions, not two, and that the z-coordinate on our surface is allowed to vary freely.

In general, we express the coordinates, (x, y, z), of a point on a surface S in terms of two parameters, s and t:

$$x = f_1(s, t), \quad y = f_2(s, t), \quad z = f_3(s, t).$$

As the values of s and t vary, the corresponding point (x, y, z) sweeps out the surface, S. (See Figure 21.4.) The function which sends the point (s, t) to the point (x, y, z) is called the *parameterization of the surface*.

Figure 21.4: The parameterization sends each point (s, t) in the parameter region, R, to a point $(x, y, z) = (f_1(s, t), f_2(s, t), f_3(s, t))$ in the surface, S

Using Position Vectors

We can use the position vector $\vec{r} = x\vec{i} + y\vec{j} + z\vec{k}$ to combine the three parametric equations for a surface into a single vector equation. For example, the parameterization of the cylinder $x = \cos t, y = \sin t, z = z$ can be written as

$$\vec{r}(t, z) = \cos t\vec{i} + \sin t\vec{j} + z\vec{k} \qquad 0 \le t < 2\pi, \quad -\infty < z < \infty.$$

For a general parameterized surface S, we write

$$\vec{r}(s, t) = f_1(s, t)\vec{i} + f_2(s, t)\vec{j} + f_3(s, t)\vec{k}.$$

Parameterizing a Surface of the Form $z = f(x, y)$

The graph of a function $z = f(x, y)$ can be given parametrically simply by letting the parameters s and t be x and y:

$$x = s, \quad y = t, \quad z = f(s, t).$$

Example 1   Give a parametric description of the lower hemisphere of the sphere $x^2 + y^2 + z^2 = 1$.

Solution   The surface is the graph of the function $z = -\sqrt{1 - x^2 - y^2}$ over the region $x^2 + y^2 \le 1$ in the plane. Then parametric equations are $x = s, y = t, z = -\sqrt{1 - s^2 - t^2}$, where the parameters s and t vary inside the unit circle.

In practice we often think of x and y as parameters rather than introduce new parameters s and t. Thus, we may write $x = x, y = y, z = f(x, y)$.

Parameterizing Planes

Consider a plane containing two nonparallel vectors $\vec{v}_1$ and $\vec{v}_2$ and a point P_0 with position vector $\vec{r}_0$. We can get to any point on the plane by starting at P_0 and moving parallel to $\vec{v}_1$ or $\vec{v}_2$, adding multiples of them to $\vec{r}_0$. (See Figure 21.5.)

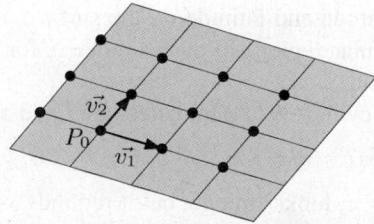

Figure 21.5: The plane $\vec{r}(s, t) = \vec{r}_0 + s\vec{v}_1 + t\vec{v}_2$ and some points corresponding to various choices of s and t

Since $s\vec{v}_1$ is parallel to $\vec{v}_1$ and $t\vec{v}_2$ is parallel to $\vec{v}_2$, we have the following result:

Parameterizing a Plane

The plane through the point with position vector $\vec{r}_0$ and containing the two nonparallel vectors $\vec{v}_1$ and $\vec{v}_2$ has parameterization

$$\vec{r}(s,t) = \vec{r}_0 + s\vec{v}_1 + t\vec{v}_2.$$

If $\vec{r}_0 = x_0\vec{i} + y_0\vec{j} + z_0\vec{k}$, and $\vec{v}_1 = a_1\vec{i} + a_2\vec{j} + a_3\vec{k}$, and $\vec{v}_2 = b_1\vec{i} + b_2\vec{j} + b_3\vec{k}$, then the parameterization of the plane can be expressed with the parametric equations

$$x = x_0 + sa_1 + tb_1, \quad y = y_0 + sa_2 + tb_2, \quad z = z_0 + sa_3 + tb_3.$$

Notice that the parameterization of the plane expresses the coordinates x, y, and z as linear functions of the parameters s and t.

Example 2   Write a parameterization for the plane through the point $(2, -1, 3)$ and containing the vectors $\vec{v}_1 = 2\vec{i} + 3\vec{j} - \vec{k}$ and $\vec{v}_2 = \vec{i} - 4\vec{j} + 5\vec{k}$.

Solution   A possible parameterization is

$$\vec{r}(s,t) = \vec{r}_0 + s\vec{v}_1 + t\vec{v}_2 = 2\vec{i} - \vec{j} + 3\vec{k} + s(2\vec{i} + 3\vec{j} - \vec{k}) + t(\vec{i} - 4\vec{j} + 5\vec{k})$$
$$= (2 + 2s + t)\vec{i} + (-1 + 3s - 4t)\vec{j} + (3 - s + 5t)\vec{k},$$

or equivalently,

$$x = 2 + 2s + t, \quad y = -1 + 3s - 4t, \quad z = 3 - s + 5t.$$

Parameterizations Using Spherical Coordinates

Recall the spherical coordinates ρ, ϕ, and θ introduced on page 899 of Chapter 16. On a sphere of radius $\rho = a$ we can use ϕ and θ as coordinates, similar to latitude and longitude on the surface of the earth. (See Figure 21.6.) The latitude, however, is measured from the equator, whereas ϕ is measured from the north pole. If the positive x-axis passes through the Greenwich meridian, the longitude and θ are equal for $0 \leq \theta \leq \pi$.

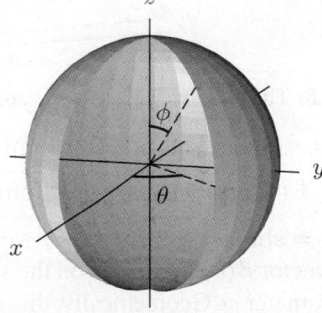

Figure 21.6: Parameterizing the sphere by ϕ and θ

Example 3   You are at a point on a sphere with $\phi = 3\pi/4$. Are you in the northern or southern hemisphere? If ϕ decreases, do you move closer to or farther from the equator?

Solution   The equator has $\phi = \pi/2$. Since $3\pi/4 > \pi/2$, you are in the southern hemisphere. If ϕ decreases, you move closer to the equator.

Example 4   On a sphere, you are standing at a point with coordinates θ_0 and ϕ_0. Your *antipodal* point is the point on the other side of the sphere on a line through you and the center. What are the θ, ϕ coordinates of your antipodal point?

Solution   Figure 21.7 shows that the coordinates are $\theta = \theta_0 + \pi$ if $\theta_0 < \pi$ or $\theta = \theta_0 - \pi$ if $\pi \leq \theta_0 \leq 2\pi$, and $\phi = \pi - \phi_0$. Notice that if you are on the equator, then so is your antipodal point.

Figure 21.7: Two views of the xyz-coordinate system showing coordinates of antipodal points

Parameterizing a Sphere Using Spherical Coordinates

The sphere with radius 1 centered at the origin is parameterized by

$$x = \sin \phi \cos \theta, \qquad y = \sin \phi \sin \theta, \qquad z = \cos \phi,$$

where $0 \leq \theta \leq 2\pi$ and $0 \leq \phi \leq \pi$. (See Figure 21.8.)

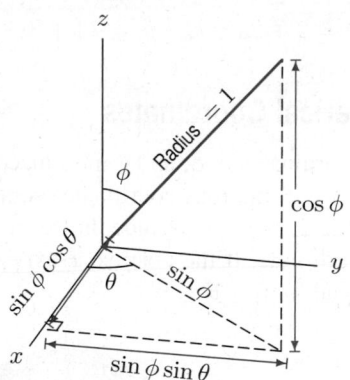

Figure 21.8: The relationship between x, y, z and ϕ, θ on a sphere of radius 1

We can also write these equations in vector form:

$$\vec{r}(\theta, \phi) = \sin \phi \cos \theta \, \vec{i} + \sin \phi \sin \theta \, \vec{j} + \cos \phi \, \vec{k}.$$

Since $x^2 + y^2 + z^2 = \sin^2 \phi (\cos^2 \theta + \sin^2 \theta) + \cos^2 \phi = \sin^2 \phi + \cos^2 \phi = 1$, this verifies that the point with position vector $\vec{r}(\theta, \phi)$ does lie on the sphere of radius 1. Notice that the z-coordinate depends only on the parameter ϕ. Geometrically, this means that all points on the same latitude have the same z-coordinate.

Example 5   Find parametric equations for the following spheres:

(a) Center at the origin and radius 2.
(b) Center at the point $(2, -1, 3)$ and radius 2.

Solution   (a) We must scale the distance from the origin by 2. Thus, we have

$$x = 2 \sin \phi \cos \theta, \qquad y = 2 \sin \phi \sin \theta, \qquad z = 2 \cos \phi,$$

where $0 \leq \theta \leq 2\pi$ and $0 \leq \phi \leq \pi$. In vector form, this is written

$$\vec{r}(\theta, \phi) = 2 \sin \phi \cos \theta \vec{i} + 2 \sin \phi \sin \theta \vec{j} + 2 \cos \phi \vec{k}.$$

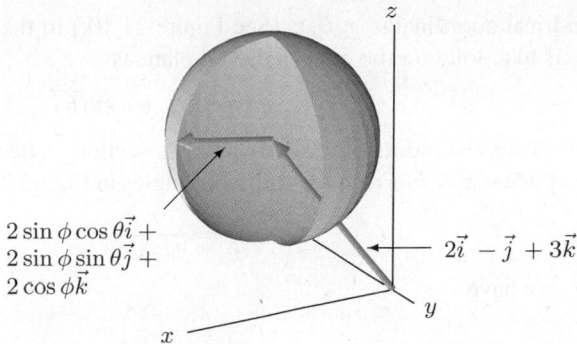

$2\sin\phi\cos\theta\vec{i}\,+$
$2\sin\phi\sin\theta\vec{j}\,+$
$2\cos\phi\vec{k}$

$2\vec{i}\,-\vec{j}\,+3\vec{k}$

Figure 21.9: Sphere with center at the point $(2,-1,3)$ and radius 2

(b) To shift the center of the sphere from the origin to the point $(2,-1,3)$, we add the vector parameterization we found in part (a) to the position vector of $(2,-1,3)$. (See Figure 21.9.) This gives

$$\vec{r}\,(\theta,\phi)=2\vec{i}\,-\vec{j}\,+3\vec{k}\,+(2\sin\phi\cos\theta\vec{i}\,+2\sin\phi\sin\theta\vec{j}\,+2\cos\phi\vec{k}\,)$$
$$=(2+2\sin\phi\cos\theta)\vec{i}\,+(-1+2\sin\phi\sin\theta)\vec{j}\,+(3+2\cos\phi)\vec{k}\,,$$

where $0\le\theta\le2\pi$ and $0\le\phi\le\pi$. Alternatively,

$$x=2+2\sin\phi\cos\theta,\qquad y=-1+2\sin\phi\sin\theta,\qquad z=3+2\cos\phi.$$

Note that the same point can have more than one value for θ or ϕ. For example, points with $\theta=0$ also have $\theta=2\pi$, unless we restrict θ to the range $0\le\theta<2\pi$. Also, the north pole, at $\phi=0$, and the south pole, at $\phi=\pi$, can have any value of θ.

Parameterizing Surfaces of Revolution

Many surfaces have an axis of rotational symmetry and circular cross-sections perpendicular to that axis. These surfaces are referred to as *surfaces of revolution*.

Example 6   Find a parameterization of the cone whose base is the circle $x^2+y^2=a^2$ in the xy-plane and whose vertex is at height h above the xy-plane. (See Figure 21.10.)

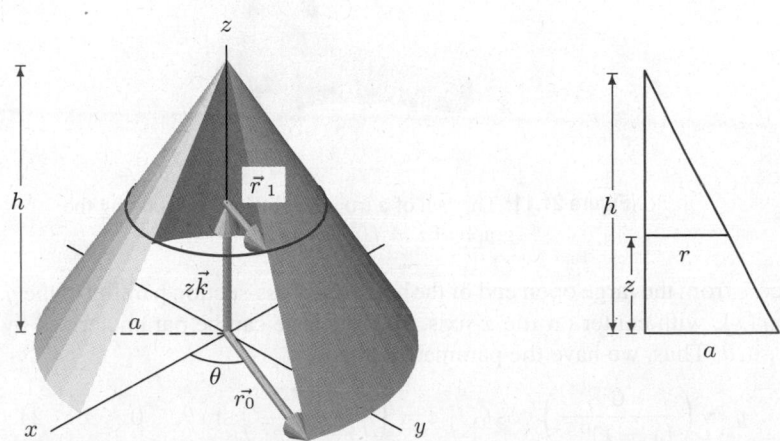

Figure 21.10: The cone whose base is the circle $x^2+y^2=a^2$ in the xy-plane and whose vertex is at the point $(0,0,h)$ and the vertical cross-section through the cone

Solution   We use cylindrical coordinates, r, θ, z. (See Figure 21.10.) In the xy-plane, the radius vector, $\vec{r}_0$, from the z-axis to a point on the cone in the xy-plane is

$$\vec{r}_0 = a\cos\theta\vec{i} + a\sin\theta\vec{j}.$$

Above the xy-plane, the radius of the circular cross-section, r, decreases linearly from $r = a$ when $z = 0$ to $r = 0$ when $z = h$. From the similar triangles in Figure 21.10,

$$\frac{a}{h} = \frac{r}{h - z}.$$

Solving for r, we have

$$r = \left(1 - \frac{z}{h}\right)a.$$

The horizontal radius vector, $\vec{r}_1$, at height z has components similar to $\vec{r}_0$, but with a replaced by r:

$$\vec{r}_1 = r\cos\theta\vec{i} + r\sin\theta\vec{j} = \left(1 - \frac{z}{h}\right)a\cos\theta\vec{i} + \left(1 - \frac{z}{h}\right)a\sin\theta\vec{j}.$$

As θ goes from 0 to 2π, the vector $\vec{r}_1$ traces out the horizontal circle in Figure 21.10. We get the position vector, $\vec{r}$, of a point on the cone by adding the vector $z\vec{k}$, so

$$\vec{r} = \vec{r}_1 + z\vec{k} = a\left(1 - \frac{z}{h}\right)\cos\theta\vec{i} + a\left(1 - \frac{z}{h}\right)\sin\theta\vec{j} + z\vec{k}, \quad \text{for } 0 \le z \le h \text{ and } 0 \le \theta \le 2\pi.$$

These equations can be written as

$$x = \left(1 - \frac{z}{h}\right)a\cos\theta, \quad y = \left(1 - \frac{z}{h}\right)a\sin\theta, \quad z = z.$$

The parameters are θ and z.

Example 7   Consider the bell of a trumpet. A model for the radius $z = f(x)$ of the horn (in cm) at a distance x cm from the large open end is given by the function

$$f(x) = \frac{6}{(x + 1)^{0.7}}.$$

The bell is obtained by rotating the graph of f about the x-axis. Find a parameterization for the first 24 cm of the bell. (See Figure 21.11.)

Figure 21.11: The bell of a trumpet obtained by rotating the
graph of $z = f(x)$ about the x-axis

Solution   At distance x from the large open end of the horn, the cross-section parallel to the yz-plane is a circle of radius $f(x)$, with center on the x-axis. Such a circle can be parameterized by $y = f(x)\cos\theta$, $z = f(x)\sin\theta$. Thus, we have the parameterization

$$x = x, \quad y = \left(\frac{6}{(x + 1)^{0.7}}\right)\cos\theta, \quad z = \left(\frac{6}{(x + 1)^{0.7}}\right)\sin\theta, \quad 0 \le x \le 24, \quad 0 \le \theta \le 2\pi.$$

The parameters are x and θ.

Parameter Curves

On a parameterized surface, the curve obtained by setting one of the parameters equal to a constant and letting the other vary is called a *parameter curve*. If the surface is parameterized by

$$\vec{r}(s,t) = f_1(s,t)\vec{i} + f_2(s,t)\vec{j} + f_3(s,t)\vec{k},$$

there are two families of parameter curves on the surface, one family with t constant and the other with s constant.

Example 8   Consider the vertical cylinder

$$x = \cos t, \quad y = \sin t, \quad z = z.$$

(a) Describe the two parameter curves through the point $(0, 1, 1)$.
(b) Describe the family of parameter curves with t constant and the family with z constant.

Solution   (a) Since the point $(0, 1, 1)$ corresponds to the parameter values $t = \pi/2$ and $z = 1$, there are two parameter curves, one with $t = \pi/2$ and the other with $z = 1$. The parameter curve with $t = \pi/2$ has the parametric equations

$$x = \cos\left(\frac{\pi}{2}\right) = 0, \quad y = \sin\left(\frac{\pi}{2}\right) = 1, \quad z = z,$$

with parameter z. This is a line through the point $(0, 1, 1)$ parallel to the z-axis.
 The parameter curve with $z = 1$ has the parametric equations

$$x = \cos t, \quad y = \sin t, \quad z = 1,$$

with parameter t. This is a unit circle parallel to and one unit above the xy-plane centered on the z-axis.
(b) First, fix $t = t_0$ for t and let z vary. The curves parameterized by z have equations

$$x = \cos t_0, \quad y = \sin t_0, \quad z = z.$$

These are vertical lines on the cylinder parallel to the z-axis. (See Figure 21.12.)
 The other family is obtained by fixing $z = z_0$ and varying t. Curves in this family are parameterized by t and have equations

$$x = \cos t, \quad y = \sin t, \quad z = z_0.$$

They are circles of radius 1 parallel to the xy-plane centered on the z-axis. (See Figure 21.13.)

Figure 21.12: The family of parameter curves with $t = t_0$ for the cylinder $x = \cos t, y = \sin t, z = z$

Figure 21.13: The family of parameter curves with $z = z_0$ for the cylinder $x = \cos t, y = \sin t, z = z$

Example 9   Describe the families of parameter curves with $\theta = \theta_0$ and $\phi = \phi_0$ for the sphere

$$x = \sin\phi\cos\theta, \quad y = \sin\phi\sin\theta, \quad z = \cos\phi,$$

where $0 \leq \theta \leq 2\pi, 0 \leq \phi \leq \pi$.

Solution   Since ϕ measures latitude, the family with ϕ constant consists of the circles of constant latitude. (See Figure 21.14.) Similarly, the family with θ constant consists of the meridians (semicircles) running between the north and south poles. (See Figure 21.15.)

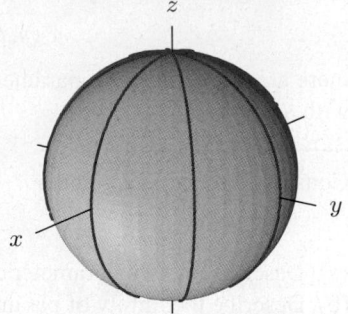

Figure 21.14: The family of parameter curves with $\phi = \phi_0$ for the sphere parameterized by (θ, ϕ)

Figure 21.15: The family of parameter curves with $\theta = \theta_0$ for the sphere parameterized by (θ, ϕ)

We have seen parameter curves before on pages 675-676 of Section 12.2: The cross-sections with $x = a$ or $y = b$ on a surface $z = f(x, y)$ are examples of parameter curves. So are the grid lines on a computer sketch of a surface. The small regions shaped like parallelograms surrounded by nearby pairs of parameter curves are called *parameter rectangles*. See Figure 21.16.

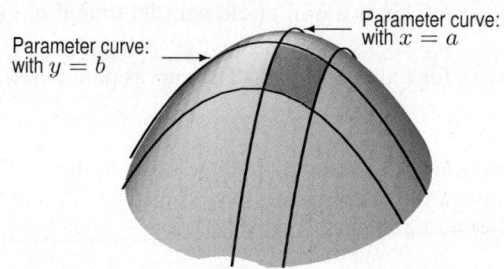

Parameter curve: with $y = b$

Parameter curve: with $x = a$

Figure 21.16: Parameter curves $x = a$ or $y = b$ on a surface $z = f(x, y)$; the darker region is a parameter rectangle

Exercises and Problems for Section 21.1

Exercises

In Exercises 1–4 decide if the parameterization describes a curve or a surface.

1. $\vec{r}(s) = s\vec{i} + (3 - s)\vec{j} + s^2\vec{k}$

2. $\vec{r}(s, t) = (s + t)\vec{i} + (3 - s)\vec{j}$

3. $\vec{r}(s, t) = \cos s\,\vec{i} + \sin s\,\vec{j} + t^2\vec{k}$

4. $\vec{r}(s) = \cos s\,\vec{i} + \sin s\,\vec{j} + s^2\vec{k}$

Describe in words the objects parameterized by the equations in Exercises 5–8. (Note: r and θ are cylindrical coordinates.)

5. $x = r\cos\theta \qquad y = r\sin\theta \qquad z = 7$
$\quad 0 \leq r \leq 5 \qquad 0 \leq \theta \leq 2\pi$

6. $x = 5\cos\theta \qquad y = 5\sin\theta \qquad z = z$
$\quad 0 \leq \theta \leq 2\pi \qquad 0 \leq z \leq 7$

7. $x = 5\cos\theta \qquad y = 5\sin\theta \qquad z = 5\theta$
$\quad 0 \leq \theta \leq 2\pi$

8. $x = r\cos\theta \qquad y = r\sin\theta \qquad z = r$
$\quad 0 \leq r \leq 5 \qquad 0 \leq \theta \leq 2\pi$

In Exercises 9–12, for a sphere parameterized using the spherical coordinates θ and ϕ, describe in words the part of the sphere given by the restrictions.

9. $0 \leq \theta < 2\pi, \quad 0 \leq \phi \leq \pi/2$

10. $\pi \leq \theta < 2\pi, \quad 0 \leq \phi \leq \pi$

11. $\pi/4 \leq \theta < \pi/3, \quad 0 \leq \phi \leq \pi$

12. $0 \leq \theta \leq \pi, \quad \pi/4 \leq \phi < \pi/3$

Problems

In Problems 13–14, parameterize the plane that contains the three points.

13. $(0,0,0), (1,2,3), (2,1,0)$

14. $(1,2,3), (2,5,8), (5,2,0)$

In Problems 15–16, parameterize the plane through the point with the given normal vector.

15. $(3,5,7), \vec{i} + \vec{j} + \vec{k}$

16. $(5,1,4), \vec{i} + 2\vec{j} + 3\vec{k}$

17. Does the plane $\vec{r}(s,t) = (2+s)\vec{i} + (3+s+t)\vec{j} + 4t\vec{k}$ contain the following points?
  (a) $(4,8,12)$ (b) $(1,2,3)$

18. Are the following two planes parallel?

$$x = 2+s+t, \quad y = 4+s-t, \quad z = 1+2s, \quad \text{and}$$

$$x = 2+s+2t, \quad y = t, \quad z = s-t.$$

In Problems 19–22, describe the families of parameter curves with $s = s_0$ and $t = t_0$ for the parameterized surface.

19. $x = s, \quad y = t, \quad z = 1$ for $-\infty < s < \infty$, $-\infty < t < \infty$

20. $x = s, \quad y = \cos t, \quad z = \sin t$ for $-\infty < s < \infty$, $0 \le t \le 2\pi$

21. $x = s \quad y = t, \quad z = s^2 + t^2$ for $-\infty < s < \infty$, $-\infty < t < \infty$

22. $x = \cos s \sin t \quad y = \sin s \sin t, \quad z = \cos t$ for $0 \le s \le 2\pi, 0 \le t \le \pi$

23. A city is described parametrically by the equation

$$\vec{r} = (x_0\vec{i} + y_0\vec{j} + z_0\vec{k}) + s\vec{v_1} + t\vec{v_2}$$

where $\vec{v}_1 = 2\vec{i} - 3\vec{j} + 2\vec{k}$ and $\vec{v}_2 = \vec{i} + 4\vec{j} + 5\vec{k}$. A city block is a rectangle determined by $\vec{v}_1$ and $\vec{v}_2$. East is in the direction of $\vec{v}_1$ and north is in the direction of $\vec{v}_2$. Starting at the point (x_0, y_0, z_0), you walk 5 blocks east, 4 blocks north, 1 block west and 2 blocks south. What are the parameters of the point where you end up? What are your x, y and z coordinates at that point?

24. You are at a point on the earth with longitude 80° West of Greenwich, England, and latitude 40° North of the equator.

  (a) If your latitude decreases, have you moved nearer to or farther from the equator?
  (b) If your latitude decreases, have you moved nearer to or farther from the north pole?
  (c) If your longitude increases (say, to 90° West), have you moved nearer to or farther from Greenwich?

25. Describe in words the curve $\phi = \pi/4$ on the surface of the globe.

26. Describe in words the curve $\theta = \pi/4$ on the surface of the globe.

27. A decorative oak post is $48''$ long and is turned on a lathe so that its profile is sinusoidal, as shown in Figure 21.17.

  (a) Describe the surface of the post parametrically using cylindrical coordinates.
  (b) Find the volume of the post.

Figure 21.17

28. Find parametric equations for the sphere $(x-a)^2 + (y-b)^2 + (z-c)^2 = d^2$.

29. Suppose you are standing at a point on the equator of a sphere, parameterized by spherical coordinates θ_0 and ϕ_0. If you go halfway around the equator and halfway up toward the north pole along a longitude, what are your new θ and ϕ coordinates?

30. Find parametric equations for the cone $x^2 + y^2 = z^2$.

31. Parameterize the cone in Example 6 on page 1079 in terms of r and θ.

32. Give a parameterization of the circle of radius a centered at the point (x_0, y_0, z_0) and in the plane parallel to two given unit vectors $\vec{u}$ and $\vec{v}$ such that $\vec{u} \cdot \vec{v} = 0$.

For Problems 33–35,
 (a) Write an equation in x, y, z and identify the parametric surface.
 (b) Draw a picture of the surface.

33. $x = 2s \quad y = s+t \quad z = 1+s-t$
    $0 \le s \le 1 \quad\quad 0 \le t \le 1$

34. $x = s \quad y = t \quad z = \sqrt{1 - s^2 - t^2}$
    $s^2 + t^2 \le 1 \quad\quad s, t \ge 0$

35. $x = s+t \quad y = s-t \quad z = s^2 + t^2$
    $0 \le s \le 1 \quad\quad 0 \le t \le 1$

Strengthen Your Understanding

In Problems 36–37, explain what is wrong with the statement.

36. The parameter curves of a parameterized surface intersect at right angles.

37. The parameter curves for constant ϕ on the sphere $\vec{r}(\theta, \phi) = R \sin \phi \cos \theta \vec{i} + R \sin \phi \sin \theta \vec{j} + R \cos \phi \vec{k}$ are circles of radius R.

In Problems 38–40, give an example of:

38. A parameterization $\vec{r}(s, t)$ of the plane tangent to the unit sphere at the point where $\theta = \pi/4$ and $\phi = \pi/4$.

39. An equation of the form $f(x, y, z) = 0$ for the plane

$$\vec{r}(s, t) = (s + 1)\vec{i} + (t + 2)\vec{j} + (s + t)\vec{k}.$$

40. A parameterized curve on the sphere $\vec{r}(\theta, \phi) = \sin \phi \cos \theta \vec{i} + \sin \phi \sin \theta \vec{j} + \cos \phi \vec{k}$ that is not a parameter curve.

Are the statements in Problems 41–47 true or false? Give reasons for your answer.

41. The equations $x = s + 1$, $y = t - 2$, $z = 3$ parameterize a plane.

42. The equations $x = 2s - 1$, $y = -s + 3$, $z = 4 + s$ parameterize a plane.

43. If $\vec{r} = \vec{r}(s, t)$ parameterizes the upper hemisphere $x^2 + y^2 + z^2 = 1$, $z \geq 0$, then $\vec{r} = -\vec{r}(s, t)$ parameterizes the lower hemisphere $x^2 + y^2 + z^2 = 1$, $z \leq 0$.

44. If $\vec{r} = \vec{r}(s, t)$ parameterizes the upper hemisphere $x^2 + y^2 + z^2 = 1$, $z \geq 0$, then $\vec{r} = \vec{r}(-s, -t)$ parameterizes the lower hemisphere $x^2 + y^2 + z^2 = 1$, $z \leq 0$.

45. If $\vec{r_1}(s, t)$ parameterizes a plane then $\vec{r_2}(s, t) = \vec{r}_1(s, t) + 2\vec{i} - 3\vec{j} + \vec{k}$ parameterizes a parallel plane.

46. Every point on a parameterized surface has a parameter curve passing through it.

47. If $s_0 \neq s_1$, then the parameter curves $\vec{r}(s_0, t)$ and $\vec{r}(s_1, t)$ do not intersect.

48. Match the parameterizations (I)–(IV) with the surfaces (a)–(d). In all cases $0 \leq s \leq \pi/2$, $0 \leq t \leq \pi/2$. Note that only part of the surface may be described by the given parameterization.

(a) Cylinder
(b) Plane
(c) Sphere
(d) Cone

I. $x = \cos s$, $\quad y = \sin t$, $\quad z = \cos s + \sin t$
II. $x = \cos s$, $\quad y = \sin s$, $\quad z = \cos t$
III. $x = \sin s \cos t$, $\quad y = \sin s \sin t$, $\quad z = \cos s$
IV. $x = \cos s$, $\quad y = \sin t$, $\quad z = \sqrt{\cos^2 s + \sin^2 t}$

21.2 CHANGE OF COORDINATES IN A MULTIPLE INTEGRAL

In Chapter 16 we used polar, cylindrical, and spherical coordinates to simplify iterated integrals. In this section, we discuss more general changes of coordinate. In the process, we see where the factors r and $\rho^2 \sin \phi$ come from when we convert to polar, cylindrical, or spherical coordinates (see pages 892, 897, and 900).

Polar Change of Coordinates Revisited

Consider the integral $\int_R (x + y) \, dA$ where R is the region in the first quadrant bounded by the circle $x^2 + y^2 = 16$ and the x and y-axes. Writing the integral in Cartesian and polar coordinates, we have

$$\int_R (x + y) \, dA = \int_0^4 \int_0^{\sqrt{16 - x^2}} (x + y) \, dy \, dx = \int_0^{\pi/2} \int_0^4 (r \cos \theta + r \sin \theta) r \, dr d\theta.$$

The integral on the right is over the rectangle in the $r\theta$-plane given by $0 \leq r \leq 4$, $0 \leq \theta \leq \pi/2$. The conversion from polar to Cartesian coordinates changes this rectangle into a quarter-disk. Figure 21.18 shows how a typical rectangle (shaded) in the $r\theta$-plane with sides of length Δr and $\Delta \theta$ corresponds to a curved rectangle in the xy-plane with sides of length Δr and $r\Delta \theta$. The extra r is needed because the correspondence between r, θ and x, y not only curves the lines $r = 1, 2, 3 \ldots$ into circles, it also stretches those lines around larger and larger circles.

Figure 21.18: A grid in the $r\theta$-plane and the corresponding curved grid in the xy-plane

General Change of Coordinates

We now consider a general change of coordinates, where x, y coordinates are related to s, t coordinates by the differentiable functions

$$x = x(s, t) \quad y = y(s, t).$$

Just as a rectangular region in the $r\theta$-plane corresponds to a region in the xy-plane, a rectangular region, T, in the st-plane corresponds to a region, R, in the xy-plane. We assume that the change of coordinates is one-to-one, that is, that each point in R corresponds to only one point in T.

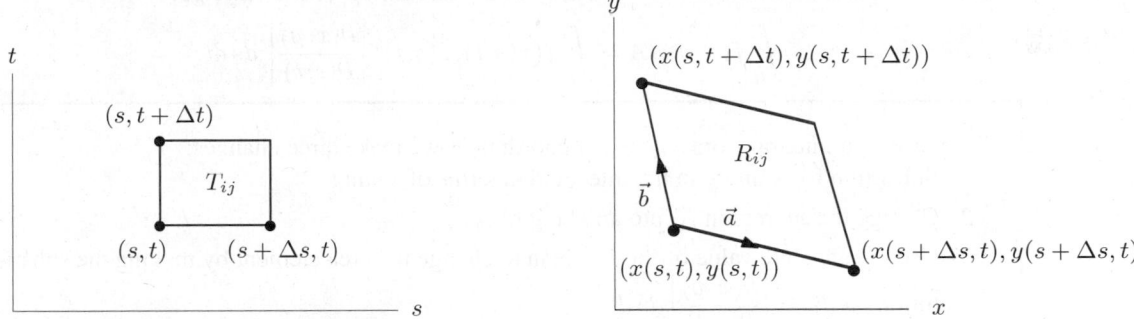

Figure 21.19: A small rectangle T_{ij} in the st-plane and the corresponding region R_{ij} of the xy-plane

We divide T into small rectangles T_{ij} with sides of length Δs and Δt. (See Figure 21.19.) The corresponding piece R_{ij} of the xy-plane is a quadrilateral with curved sides. If we choose Δs and Δt small, then by local linearity of $x(s, t)$ and $y(s, t)$, we know R_{ij} is approximately a parallelogram.

Recall from Chapter 13 that the area of the parallelogram with sides $\vec{a}$ and $\vec{b}$ is $\|\vec{a} \times \vec{b}\|$. Thus, we need to find the sides of R_{ij} as vectors. The side of R_{ij} corresponding to the bottom side of T_{ij} has endpoints $(x(s, t), y(s, t))$ and $(x(s + \Delta s, t), y(s + \Delta s, t))$, so in vector form that side is

$$\vec{a} = (x(s + \Delta s, t) - x(s, t))\vec{i} + (y(s + \Delta s, t) - y(s, t))\vec{j} \approx \left(\frac{\partial x}{\partial s}\Delta s\right)\vec{i} + \left(\frac{\partial y}{\partial s}\Delta s\right)\vec{j}.$$

Similarly, the side of R_{ij} corresponding to the left edge of T_{ij} is given by

$$\vec{b} \approx \left(\frac{\partial x}{\partial t}\Delta t\right)\vec{i} + \left(\frac{\partial y}{\partial t}\Delta t\right)\vec{j}.$$

Computing the cross product, we get

$$\text{Area } R_{ij} \approx \|\vec{a} \times \vec{b}\| \approx \left| \left(\frac{\partial x}{\partial s}\Delta s\right)\left(\frac{\partial y}{\partial t}\Delta t\right) - \left(\frac{\partial x}{\partial t}\Delta t\right)\left(\frac{\partial y}{\partial s}\Delta s\right) \right|$$

$$= \left| \frac{\partial x}{\partial s} \cdot \frac{\partial y}{\partial t} - \frac{\partial x}{\partial t} \cdot \frac{\partial y}{\partial s} \right| \Delta s \Delta t.$$

Using determinant notation,[1] we define the *Jacobian*, $\dfrac{\partial(x, y)}{\partial(s, t)}$, as follows:

$$\frac{\partial(x, y)}{\partial(s, t)} = \frac{\partial x}{\partial s} \cdot \frac{\partial y}{\partial t} - \frac{\partial x}{\partial t} \cdot \frac{\partial y}{\partial s} = \begin{vmatrix} \frac{\partial x}{\partial s} & \frac{\partial x}{\partial t} \\ \\ \frac{\partial y}{\partial s} & \frac{\partial y}{\partial t} \end{vmatrix}.$$

Thus, we can write

$$\text{Area } R_{ij} \approx \left| \frac{\partial(x, y)}{\partial(s, t)} \right| \Delta s \, \Delta t.$$

To compute $\int_R f(x, y)\, dA$, where f is a continuous function, we look at the Riemann sum obtained by dividing the region R into the small curved regions R_{ij}, giving

$$\int_R f(x, y)\, dA \approx \sum_{i,j} f(u_{ij}, v_{ij}) \cdot \text{Area of } R_{ij} \approx \sum_{i,j} f(u_{ij}, v_{ij}) \left| \frac{\partial(x, y)}{\partial(s, t)} \right| \Delta s \, \Delta t.$$

Each point (u_{ij}, v_{ij}) in R_{ij} corresponds to a point (s_{ij}, t_{ij}) in T_{ij}, so the sum can be written in terms of s and t:

$$\sum_{i,j} f(x(s_{ij}, t_{ij}), y(s_{ij}, t_{ij})) \left| \frac{\partial(x, y)}{\partial(s, t)} \right| \Delta s \, \Delta t.$$

This is a Riemann sum in terms of s and t, so as Δs and Δt approach 0, we get

$$\int_R f(x, y)\, dA = \int_T f(x(s, t), y(s, t)) \left| \frac{\partial(x, y)}{\partial(s, t)} \right| ds \, dt.$$

To convert an integral from x, y to s, t coordinates we make three changes:

1. Substitute for x and y in the integrand in terms of s and t.

2. Change the xy region R into an st region T.

3. Use the absolute value of the Jacobian to change the area element by making the substitution $dx \, dy = \left| \dfrac{\partial(x, y)}{\partial(s, t)} \right| ds \, dt$.

Example 1   Check that the Jacobian $\dfrac{\partial(x, y)}{\partial(r, \theta)} = r$ for polar coordinates $x = r\cos\theta$, $y = r\sin\theta$.

Solution   We have $\dfrac{\partial(x, y)}{\partial(r, \theta)} = \begin{vmatrix} \frac{\partial x}{\partial r} & \frac{\partial x}{\partial \theta} \\ \\ \frac{\partial y}{\partial r} & \frac{\partial y}{\partial \theta} \end{vmatrix} = \begin{vmatrix} \cos\theta & -r\sin\theta \\ \sin\theta & r\cos\theta \end{vmatrix} = r\cos^2\theta + r\sin^2\theta = r.$

Example 2   Find the area of the ellipse $\dfrac{x^2}{a^2} + \dfrac{y^2}{b^2} = 1$.

Solution   Let $x = as$, $y = bt$. Then the ellipse $x^2/a^2 + y^2/b^2 = 1$ in the xy-plane corresponds to the circle $s^2 + t^2 = 1$ in the st-plane. The Jacobian is $\begin{vmatrix} a & 0 \\ 0 & b \end{vmatrix} = ab$. Thus, if R is the ellipse in the xy-plane and T is the unit circle in the st-plane, we get

$$\text{Area of } xy\text{-ellipse} = \int_R 1 \, dA = \int_T 1 \cdot ab \, ds \, dt = ab \int_T ds \, dt = ab \cdot \text{Area of } st\text{-circle} = \pi ab.$$

---

[1]See Appendix E.

Change of Coordinates in Triple Integrals

For triple integrals, there is a similar formula. Suppose the differentiable functions

$$x = x(s, t, u), \quad y = y(s, t, u), \quad z = z(s, t, u)$$

define a one-to-one change of coordinates from a region S in stu-space to a region W in xyz-space. Then, the Jacobian of this change of coordinates is given by the determinant[2]

$$\frac{\partial(x, y, z)}{\partial(s, t, u)} = \begin{vmatrix} \frac{\partial x}{\partial s} & \frac{\partial x}{\partial t} & \frac{\partial x}{\partial u} \\ \frac{\partial y}{\partial s} & \frac{\partial y}{\partial t} & \frac{\partial y}{\partial u} \\ \frac{\partial z}{\partial s} & \frac{\partial z}{\partial t} & \frac{\partial z}{\partial u} \end{vmatrix}.$$

Just as the Jacobian in two dimensions gives us the change in the area element, the Jacobian in three dimensions represents the change in the volume element. Thus, we have

$$\int_W f(x, y, z)\, dx\, dy\, dz = \int_S f(x(s,t,u), y(s,t,u), z(s,t,u)) \left| \frac{\partial(x, y, z)}{\partial(s, t, u)} \right| ds\, dt\, du.$$

Problem 11 at the end of this section asks you to check that the Jacobian for the change of coordinates to spherical coordinates is $\rho^2 \sin\phi$. The next example generalizes Example 2 to ellipsoids.

Example 3   Find the volume of the ellipsoid $\dfrac{x^2}{a^2} + \dfrac{y^2}{b^2} + \dfrac{z^2}{c^2} = 1$.

Solution   Let $x = as$, $y = bt$, $z = cu$. The Jacobian is computed to be abc. The xyz-ellipsoid corresponds to the stu-sphere $s^2 + t^2 + u^2 = 1$. Thus, as in Example 2,

$$\text{Volume of } xyz\text{-ellipsoid} = abc \cdot \text{Volume of } stu\text{-sphere} = abc\frac{4}{3}\pi = \frac{4}{3}\pi abc.$$

Exercises and Problems for Section 21.2

Exercises

In Exercises 1–4, find the absolute value of the Jacobian, $\left| \frac{\partial(x,y)}{\partial(s,t)} \right|$, for the given change of coordinates.

1. $x = 5s + 2t, y = 3s + t$

2. $x = s^2 - t^2, y = 2st$

3. $x = e^s \cos t, y = e^s \sin t$

4. $x = s^3 - 3st^2, y = 3s^2t - t^3$

In Exercises 5–7, find positive numbers a and b so that the change of coordinates $s = ax, t = by$ transforms the integral $\int \int_R dx\, dy$ into

$$\int \int_T \left| \frac{\partial(x, y)}{\partial(s, t)} \right| ds\, dt$$

for the given regions R and T.

5. R is the rectangle $0 \le x \le 10$, $0 \le y \le 1$ and T is the square $0 \le s, t \le 1$.

6. R is the rectangle $0 \le x \le 1$, $0 \le y \le 1/4$ and T is the square $0 \le s, t \le 1$.

7. R is the rectangle $0 \le x \le 50$, $0 \le y \le 10$ and T is the square $0 \le s, t \le 1$.

In Exercises 8–9, find a number a so that the change of coordinates $s = x + ay, t = y$ transforms the integral $\int \int_R dx\, dy$ over the parallelogram R in the xy-plane into an integral

$$\int \int_T \left| \frac{\partial(x, y)}{\partial(s, t)} \right| ds\, dt$$

over a rectangle T in the st-plane.

8. R has vertices $(0, 0)$, $(10, 0)$, $(12, 3)$, $(22, 3)$

9. R has vertices $(0, 0)$, $(10, 0)$, $(-15, 5)$, $(-5, 5)$

---

[2]See Appendix E.

Problems

10. Find the region R in the xy-plane corresponding to the region $T = \{(s,t) \mid 0 \leq s \leq 3,\ 0 \leq t \leq 2\}$ under the change of coordinates $x = 2s - 3t,\ y = s - 2t$. Check that

$$\int_R dx\,dy = \int_T \left| \frac{\partial(x,y)}{\partial(s,t)} \right| ds\,dt.$$

11. Compute the Jacobian for the change of coordinates into spherical coordinates:

$$x = \rho \sin\phi \cos\theta, \quad y = \rho \sin\phi \sin\theta, \quad z = \rho \cos\phi.$$

12. For the change of coordinates $x = 3s - 4t,\ y = 5s + 2t$, show that

$$\frac{\partial(x,y)}{\partial(s,t)} \cdot \frac{\partial(s,t)}{\partial(x,y)} = 1$$

13. Use the change of coordinates $x = 2s + t,\ y = s - t$ to compute the integral $\int_R (x+y)\,dA$, where R is the parallelogram formed by $(0,0)$, $(3,-3)$, $(5,-2)$, and $(2,1)$.

14. Use the change of coordinates $s = x + y,\ t = y$ to find the area of the ellipse $x^2 + 2xy + 2y^2 \leq 1$.

15. Use the change of coordinates $s = y,\ t = y - x^2$ to evaluate $\int \int_R x\,dx\,dy$ over the region R in the first quadrant bounded by $y = 0$, $y = 16$, $y = x^2$, and $y = x^2 - 9$.

16. If R is the triangle bounded by $x + y = 1$, $x = 0$, and $y = 0$, evaluate the integral $\int_R \cos\left(\frac{x-y}{x+y}\right)\,dx\,dy$.

17. Two independent random numbers x and y from a normal distribution with mean 0 and standard deviation σ have joint density function $p(x,y) = (1/(2\pi\sigma^2))e^{-(x^2+y^2)/(2\sigma^2)}$. The average $z = (x+y)/2$ has a one-variable probability density function of its own.

(a) Give a double integral expression for $F(t)$, the probability that $z \leq t$.

(b) Give a single integral expression for $F(t)$. To do this, make the change of coordinates: $u = (x+y)/2$, $v = (x-y)/2$ and then do the integral on dv. Use the fact that $\int_{-\infty}^{\infty} e^{-x^2/a^2}\,dx = a\sqrt{\pi}$.

(c) Find the probability density function $F'(t)$ of z.

(d) What is the name of the distribution of z?

18. A river follows the path $y = f(x)$ where x, y are in kilometers. Near the sea, it widens into a lagoon, then narrows again at its mouth. See Figure 21.20. At the point (x,y), the depth, $d(x,y)$, of the lagoon is given by

$$d(x,y) = 40 - 160(y - f(x))^2 - 40x^2 \text{ meters.}$$

The lagoon itself is described by $d(x,y) \geq 0$. What is the volume of the lagoon in cubic meters? [Hint: Use new coordinates $u = x/2$, $v = y - f(x)$ and Jacobians.]

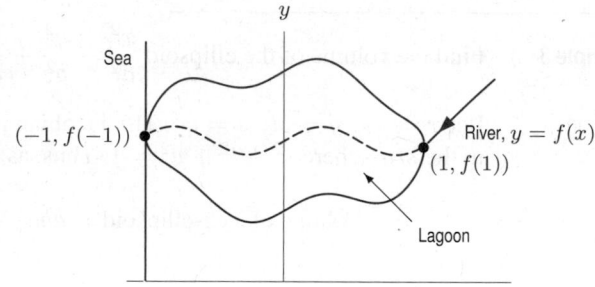

Figure 21.20

Strengthen Your Understanding

In Problems 19–20, explain what is wrong with the statement.

19. If R is the region $0 \leq x \leq 1$, $0 \leq y \leq 4$ and T is the region $0 \leq s \leq 1$, $-2 \leq t \leq 2$, using the formulas $x = s$, $y = t^2$, we have

$$\int_R f(x,y)\,dx\,dy = \int_T f(s,t^2)\left|\frac{\partial(x,y)}{\partial(s,t)}\right| ds\,dt.$$

20. If R and T are corresponding regions of the xy- and st-planes, the change of coordinates $x = t^3$, $y = s$ leads to the formula

$$\int_R (x + 2y)\,dx\,dy = \int_T \left(t^3 + 2s\right)\left(-3t^2\right) ds\,dt.$$

In Problems 21–22, give an example of:

21. A change of coordinates $x = x(s,t)$, $y = y(s,t)$ where the rectangle $0 \leq s \leq 1$, $0 \leq t \leq 1$ in the st-plane corresponds to a different rectangle in the xy-plane.

22. A change of coordinates $x = x(s,t)$, $y = y(s,t)$ where every region in the st-plane corresponds to a region in the xy-plane with twice the area.

In Problems 23–24, consider a change of variable in the integral $\int_R f(x,y)\,dA$ from x,y to s,t. Are the following statements true or false?

23. If the Jacobian $\left|\dfrac{\partial(x,y)}{\partial(s,t)}\right| > 1$, the value of the s,t-integral is greater than the original x,y-integral.

24. The Jacobian cannot be negative.

21.3 FLUX INTEGRALS OVER PARAMETERIZED SURFACES

Most of the flux integrals we are likely to encounter can be computed using the methods of Sections 19.1 and 19.2. In this section, we briefly consider the general case: how to compute the flux of a smooth vector field $\vec{F}$ through a smooth oriented surface, S, parameterized by

$$\vec{r} = \vec{r}(s, t),$$

for (s, t) in some region R of the parameter space. The method is similar to the one used for graphs in Section 19.2. We consider a parameter rectangle on the surface S corresponding to a rectangular region with sides Δs and Δt in the parameter space. (See Figure 21.21.)

Figure 21.21: Parameter rectangle on the surface S corresponding to a small rectangular region in the parameter space, R

If Δs and Δt are small, the area vector, $\Delta \vec{A}$, of the patch is approximately the area vector of the parallelogram defined by the vectors

$$\vec{r}(s + \Delta s, t) - \vec{r}(s, t) \approx \frac{\partial \vec{r}}{\partial s} \Delta s, \quad \text{and} \quad \vec{r}(s, t + \Delta t) - \vec{r}(s, t) \approx \frac{\partial \vec{r}}{\partial t} \Delta t.$$

Thus,

$$\Delta \vec{A} \approx \frac{\partial \vec{r}}{\partial s} \times \frac{\partial \vec{r}}{\partial t} \Delta s \, \Delta t.$$

We assume that the vector $\partial \vec{r}/\partial s \times \partial \vec{r}/\partial t$ is never zero and points in the direction of the unit normal orientation vector $\vec{n}$. If the vector $\partial \vec{r}/\partial s \times \partial \vec{r}/\partial t$ points in the opposite direction to $\vec{n}$, we reverse the order of the cross product. Replacing $\Delta \vec{A}$, Δs, and Δt by $d\vec{A}$, ds, and dt, we write

$$d\vec{A} = \left(\frac{\partial \vec{r}}{\partial s} \times \frac{\partial \vec{r}}{\partial t} \right) ds \, dt.$$

The Flux of a Vector Field Through a Parameterized Surface

The flux of a smooth vector field $\vec{F}$ through a smooth oriented surface S parameterized by $\vec{r} = \vec{r}(s, t)$, where (s, t) varies in a parameter region R, is given by

$$\int_S \vec{F} \cdot d\vec{A} = \int_R \vec{F}(\vec{r}(s, t)) \cdot \left(\frac{\partial \vec{r}}{\partial s} \times \frac{\partial \vec{r}}{\partial t} \right) ds \, dt.$$

We choose the parameterization so that $\partial \vec{r}/\partial s \times \partial \vec{r}/\partial t$ is never zero and points in the direction of $\vec{n}$ everywhere.

Example 1   Find the flux of the vector field $\vec{F} = x\vec{i} + y\vec{j}$ through the surface S, oriented downward and given by

$$x = 2s, \quad y = s + t, \quad z = 1 + s - t, \qquad \text{where } 0 \le s \le 1, \quad 0 \le t \le 1.$$

Solution   Since S is parameterized by

$$\vec{r}(s,t) = 2s\vec{i} + (s+t)\vec{j} + (1+s-t)\vec{k},$$

we have

$$\frac{\partial \vec{r}}{\partial s} = 2\vec{i} + \vec{j} + \vec{k} \quad \text{and} \quad \frac{\partial r}{\partial t} = \vec{j} - \vec{k},$$

so

$$\frac{\partial \vec{r}}{\partial s} \times \frac{\partial \vec{r}}{\partial t} = \begin{vmatrix} \vec{i} & \vec{j} & \vec{k} \\ 2 & 1 & 1 \\ 0 & 1 & -1 \end{vmatrix} = -2\vec{i} + 2\vec{j} + 2\vec{k}.$$

Since the vector $-2\vec{i} + 2\vec{j} + 2\vec{k}$ points upward, we use $2\vec{i} - 2\vec{j} - 2\vec{k}$ for downward orientation. Thus, the flux integral is given by

$$\int_S \vec{F} \cdot d\vec{A} = \int_0^1 \int_0^1 (2s\vec{i} + (s+t)\vec{j}) \cdot (2\vec{i} - 2\vec{j} - 2\vec{k}) \, ds \, dt$$

$$= \int_0^1 \int_0^1 (4s - 2s - 2t) \, ds\,dt = \int_0^1 \int_0^1 (2s - 2t) \, ds \, dt$$

$$= \int_0^1 \left(s^2 - 2st \Big|_{s=0}^{s=1} \right) dt = \int_0^1 (1 - 2t) \, dt = t - t^2 \Big|_0^1 = 0.$$

Area of a Parameterized Surface

The area ΔA of a small parameter rectangle is the magnitude of its area vector $\Delta \vec{A}$. Therefore,

$$\text{Area of } S = \sum \Delta A = \sum \|\Delta \vec{A}\| \approx \sum \left\| \frac{\partial \vec{r}}{\partial s} \times \frac{\partial \vec{r}}{\partial t} \right\| \Delta s \, \Delta t.$$

Taking the limit as the area of the parameter rectangles tends to zero, we are led to the following expression for the area of S.

> ### The Area of a Parameterized Surface
>
> The area of a surface S which is parameterized by $\vec{r} = \vec{r}(s,t)$, where (s,t) varies in a parameter region R, is given by
>
> $$\int_S dA = \int_R \left\| \frac{\partial \vec{r}}{\partial s} \times \frac{\partial \vec{r}}{\partial t} \right\| ds \, dt.$$

Example 2   Compute the surface area of a sphere of radius a.

Solution   We take the sphere S of radius a centered at the origin and parameterize it with the spherical coordinates ϕ and θ. The parameterization is

$$x = a \sin \phi \cos \theta, \quad y = a \sin \phi \sin \theta, \quad z = a \cos \phi, \qquad \text{for } 0 \le \theta \le 2\pi, \quad 0 \le \phi \le \pi.$$

We compute

$$\frac{\partial \vec{r}}{\partial \phi} \times \frac{\partial \vec{r}}{\partial \theta} = (a \cos \phi \cos \theta \vec{i} + a \cos \phi \sin \theta \vec{j} - a \sin \phi \vec{k}) \times (-a \sin \phi \sin \theta \vec{i} + a \sin \phi \cos \theta \vec{j})$$

$$= a^2 (\sin^2 \phi \cos \theta \vec{i} + \sin^2 \phi \sin \theta \vec{j} + \sin \phi \cos \phi \vec{k})$$

and so

$$\left\| \frac{\partial \vec{r}}{\partial \phi} \times \frac{\partial \vec{r}}{\partial \theta} \right\| = a^2 \sin \phi.$$

Thus, we see that the surface area of the sphere S is given by

$$\text{Surface area} = \int_S dA = \int_R \left\| \frac{\partial \vec{r}}{\partial \phi} \times \frac{\partial \vec{r}}{\partial \theta} \right\| d\phi d\theta = \int_{\phi=0}^{\pi} \int_{\theta=0}^{2\pi} a^2 \sin \phi \, d\theta \, d\phi = 4\pi a^2.$$

Exercises and Problems for Section 21.3

Exercises

In Exercises 1–4 compute $d\vec{A}$ for the given parameterization for one of the two orientations.

1. $x = s + t, \quad y = s - t, \quad z = st$

2. $x = \sin t, \quad y = \cos t, \quad z = s + t$

3. $x = e^s, \quad y = \cos t, \quad z = \sin t$

4. $x = 0, \quad y = u + v, \quad z = u - v$

In Exercises 5–9 compute the flux of the vector field $\vec{F}$ through the parameterized surface S.

5. $\vec{F} = z\vec{k}$ and S is oriented upward and given, for $0 \leq s \leq 1, \ 0 \leq t \leq 1$, by

$$x = s + t, \quad y = s - t, \quad z = s^2 + t^2.$$

6. $\vec{F} = x\vec{i} + y\vec{j}$ and S is oriented downward and given, for $0 \leq s \leq 1, 0 \leq t \leq 1$, by

$$x = 2s, \quad y = s + t, \quad z = 1 + s - t.$$

7. $\vec{F} = x\vec{i}$ through the surface S oriented downward and parameterized for $0 \leq s \leq 4, 0 \leq t \leq \pi/6$ by

$$x = e^s, \quad y = \cos(3t), z = 6s.$$

8. $\vec{F} = y\vec{i} + x\vec{j}$ and S is oriented away from the z-axis and given, for $0 \leq s \leq \pi, \ 0 \leq t \leq 1$, by

$$x = 3 \sin s, \quad y = 3 \cos s, \quad z = t + 1.$$

9. $\vec{F} = x^2 y^2 z\vec{k}$ and S is the cone $\sqrt{x^2 + y^2} = z$, with $0 \leq z \leq R$, oriented downward. Parameterize the cone using cylindrical coordinates. (See Figure 21.22.)

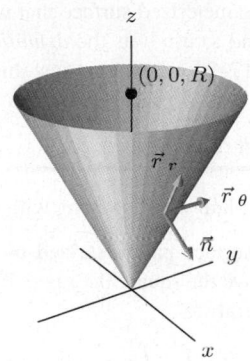

Figure 21.22

In Exercises 10–11, find the surface area.

10. A cylinder of radius a and length L.

11. The region S in the plane $z = 3x + 2y$ such that $0 \leq x \leq 10$ and $0 \leq y \leq 20$.

Problems

12. Compute the flux of the vector field $\vec{F} = (x + z)\vec{i} + \vec{j} + z\vec{k}$ through the surface S given by $y = x^2 + z^2$, $1/4 \leq x^2 + z^2 \leq 1$ oriented away from the y-axis.

13. Find the area of the ellipse S on the plane $2x + y + z = 2$ cut out by the circular cylinder $x^2 + y^2 = 2x$. (See Figure 21.23.)

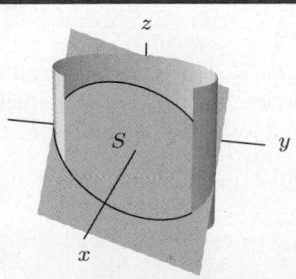

Figure 21.23

14. Consider the surface S formed by rotating the graph of $y = f(x)$ around the x-axis between $x = a$ and $x = b$. Assume that $f(x) \geq 0$ for $a \leq x \leq b$. Show that the surface area of S is $2\pi \int_a^b f(x)\sqrt{1 + f'(x)^2}\, dx$.

15. A rectangular channel of width w and depth h meters lies in the $\vec{j}$ direction. At a point d_1 meters from one side and d_2 meters from the other side, the velocity vector of fluid in the channel is $\vec{v} = kd_1 d_2 \vec{j}$ meters/sec. Find the flux through a rectangle stretching the full width and depth of the channel, and perpendicular to the flow.

16. The base of a cone is the unit circle centered at the origin in the xy-plane and vertex $P = (a, b, c)$, where $c > 0$.

   (a) Parameterize the cone.
   (b) Express the surface area of the cone as an integral.
   (c) Use a numerical method to find the surface area of the cone with vertex $P = (2, 0, 1)$.

As we remarked in Section 19.1, the limit defining a flux integral might not exist if we subdivide the surface in the wrong way. One way to get around this is to take the formula for a flux integral over a parameterized surface that we have developed in this section and to use it as the *definition* of the flux integral. In Problems 17–20 we explore how this works.

17. Use a parameterization to verify the formula for a flux integral over a surface graph on page 1018.

18. Use a parameterization to verify the formula for a flux integral over a cylindrical surface on page 1019.

19. Use a parameterization to verify the formula for a flux integral over a spherical surface on page 1020.

20. One problem with defining the flux integral using a parameterization is that the integral appears to depend on the choice of parameterization. However, the flux through a surface ought not to depend on how the surface is parameterized. Suppose that the surface S has two parameterizations, $\vec{r} = \vec{r}(s, t)$ for (s, t) in the region R of st-space, and also $\vec{r} = r(u, v)$ for (u, v) in the region T in uv-space, and suppose that the two parameterizations are related by the change of coordinates

$$u = u(s, t) \quad v = v(s, t).$$

Suppose that the Jacobian determinant $\partial(u, v)/\partial(s, t)$ is positive at every point (s, t) in R. Use the change of coordinates formula for double integrals on page 1086 to show that computing the flux integral using either parameterization gives the same result.

Strengthen Your Understanding

In Problems 21–22, explain what is wrong with the statement.

21. The area of the surface parameterized by $x = s, y = t, z = f(s, t)$ above the square $0 \leq x \leq 1, 0 \leq y \leq 1$ is given by the integral

$$\text{Area} = \int_0^1 \int_0^1 f(s, t)\, ds\, dt.$$

22. The surface S parameterized by $x = f(s, t), y = g(s, t), z = h(s, t)$, where $0 \leq s \leq 2, 0 \leq t \leq 3$, has area 6.

In Problems 23–24, give an example of:

23. A parameterization $\vec{r} = \vec{r}(s, t)$ of the xy-plane such that $dA = 2\, ds\, dt$.

24. A vector field $\vec{F}$ such that $\int_S \vec{F} \cdot d\vec{A} > 0$, where S is the surface $\vec{r} = (s - t)\vec{i} + t^2 \vec{j} + (s + t)\vec{k}, 0 \leq s \leq 1, 0 \leq t \leq 1$, oriented in the direction of $\dfrac{\partial \vec{r}}{\partial s} \times \dfrac{\partial \vec{r}}{\partial t}$.

Are the statements in Problems 25–27 true or false? Give reasons for your answer.

25. If $\vec{r}(s, t), 0 \leq s \leq 1, 0 \leq t \leq 1$ is an oriented parameterized surface S, and $\vec{F}$ is a vector field that is everywhere tangent to S, then the flux of $\vec{F}$ through S is zero.

26. For any parameterization of the surface $x^2 - y^2 + z^2 = 6$, $d\vec{A}$ at $(1, 2, 3)$ is a multiple of $(2\vec{i} - 4\vec{j} + 6\vec{k})dx\, dy$.

27. If you parameterize the plane $3x + 4y + 5z = 7$, then there is a constant c such that, at any point (x, y, z), $d\vec{A} = c(3\vec{i} + 4\vec{j} + 5\vec{k})dx\, dy$.

28. Let S be the hemisphere $x^2 + y^2 + z^2 = 1$ with $x \leq 0$, oriented away from the origin. Which of the following integrals represents the flux of $\vec{F}(x, y, z)$ through S?

  (a) $\displaystyle\int_R \vec{F}(x, y, z(x, y)) \cdot \frac{\partial \vec{r}}{\partial x} \times \frac{\partial \vec{r}}{\partial y}\, dx\, dy$

  (b) $\displaystyle\int_R \vec{F}(x, y, z(x, y)) \cdot \frac{\partial \vec{r}}{\partial y} \times \frac{\partial \vec{r}}{\partial x}\, dy\, dx$

  (c) $\displaystyle\int_R \vec{F}(x, y(x, z), z) \cdot \frac{\partial \vec{r}}{\partial x} \times \frac{\partial \vec{r}}{\partial z}\, dx\, dz$

  (d) $\displaystyle\int_R \vec{F}(x, y(x, z), z) \cdot \frac{\partial \vec{r}}{\partial z} \times \frac{\partial \vec{r}}{\partial x}\, dz\, dx$

  (e) $\displaystyle\int_R \vec{F}(x(y, z), y, z) \cdot \frac{\partial \vec{r}}{\partial y} \times \frac{\partial \vec{r}}{\partial z}\, dy\, dz$

  (f) $\displaystyle\int_R \vec{F}(x(y, z), y, z) \cdot \frac{\partial \vec{r}}{\partial z} \times \frac{\partial \vec{r}}{\partial y}\, dz\, dy$

CHAPTER SUMMARY (see also Ready Reference at the end of the book)

- **Parameterized Curves and Surfaces**
  Parametric equations for curves in 2- and 3-space, planes, graphs of functions, spheres, and cylinders; parameter curves.

- **Change of Variable**
  Polar coordinates, spherical and cylindrical coordinates, general change of variables and Jacobians.

- **Calculating flux integrals over parameterized surfaces**
  Surfaces parameterized by $\vec{r}\,(s,t)$:
  $d\vec{A} = (\partial \vec{r}\,/\partial s) \times (\partial \vec{r}\,/\partial t)\, ds\, dt$

- **Area of parameterized surface**
  $dA = \|(\partial \vec{r}\,/\partial s) \times (\partial \vec{r}\,/\partial t)\|\, ds\, dt$

REVIEW EXERCISES AND PROBLEMS FOR CHAPTER TWENTY-ONE

Exercises

Describe in words the objects parameterized by the equations in Exercises 1–2.

1. $x = 2z\cos\theta \qquad y = 2z\sin\theta \qquad z = z$
   $0 \le z \le 7 \qquad 0 \le \theta \le 2\pi$

2. $x = x \qquad y = x^2 \qquad z = z$
   $-5 \le x \le 5 \qquad 0 \le z \le 7$

In Exercises 3–4, find positive numbers a and b so that the change of coordinates $s = ax, t = by$ transforms the integral $\int \int_R dx\, dy$ into

$$\int \int_T \left|\frac{\partial(x,y)}{\partial(s,t)}\right| ds\, dt$$

for the given regions R and T.

3. R is the circular disc of radius 15 centered at the origin and T is the circular disc $s^2 + t^2 \le 1$.

4. R is the elliptical region $x^2/4 + y^2/9 \le 1$ and T is the circular disc $s^2 + t^2 \le 1$.

5. Find a number a so that the change of coordinates $s = x + ay, t = y$ transforms the integral $\int \int_R dx\, dy$ over the parallelogram R with vertices $(10, 15)$, $(30, 15)$,

$(20, 35)$, $(40, 35)$ in the xy-plane into an integral

$$\int \int_T \left|\frac{\partial(x,y)}{\partial(s,t)}\right| ds\, dt$$

over a rectangle T in the st-plane.

In Exercises 6–7 compute the flux of the vector field $\vec{F}$ through the parameterized surface S.

6. $\vec{F} = z\vec{i} + x\vec{j}$ and S is oriented upward and given, for $0 \le s \le 1, \ 1 \le t \le 3$, by

$$x = s^2, \quad y = 2s + t^2, \quad z = 5t.$$

7. $\vec{F} = -\dfrac{2}{x}\vec{i} + \dfrac{2}{y}\vec{j}$ and S is oriented upward and parameterized by a and θ, where, for $1 \le a \le 3, \ 0 \le \theta \le \pi$,

$$x = a\cos\theta, \quad y = a\sin\theta, \quad z = \sin a^2.$$

8. Parameterize the plane containing the three points $(5, 5, 5)$, $(10, -10, 10)$, $(0, 20, 40)$.

9. Find parametric equations for the sphere centered at the point $(2, -1, 3)$ and with radius 5.

Problems

10. Parameterize a cone of height h and maximum radius a with vertex at the origin and opening upward. Do this in two ways, giving the range of values for each parameter in each case: **(a)** Use r and θ. **(b)** Use z and θ.

11. **(a)** Describe the surface given parametrically by the equations

    $$x = \cos(s - t), \quad y = \sin(s - t), \quad z = s + t.$$

    (b) Describe the two families of parameter curves on the surface.

12. Find a parameterization for the plane through $(1, 3, 4)$ and orthogonal to $\vec{n} = 2\vec{i} + \vec{j} - \vec{k}$.

13. Adapt the parameterization for the sphere to find a parameterization for the ellipsoid

    $$\frac{x^2}{a^2} + \frac{y^2}{b^2} + \frac{z^2}{c^2} = 1.$$

14. Parameterize a vase formed by rotating the curve $z = 10\sqrt{x-1}, 1 \le x \le 2$, around the z-axis. Sketch the vase.

15. For the surface given parametrically by

    $$x = 3\sin s \quad y = 3\cos s \quad z = t + 1,$$

    where $0 \le s \le \pi$ and $0 \le t \le 1$

(a) Write an equation in x, y, z and identify the parametric surface.

(b) Draw a picture of the surface.

16. Find the region R in the xy-plane corresponding to the region $T = \{(s, t) \mid 0 \leq s \leq 2, \, s \leq t \leq 2\}$ under the change of coordinates $x = s^2$, $y = t$. Check that

$$\int_R dx\, dy = \int_T \left| \frac{\partial(x, y)}{\partial(s, t)} \right| ds\, dt.$$

17. Use the change of coordinates $s = x - y$, $t = x + y$ to evaluate $\int \int_R \sin(x + y)\, dx\, dy$ over the disc $x^2 + y^2 \leq 1$.

18. Use the change of coordinates $s = xy$, $t = xy^2$ to compute $\int_R xy^2\, dA$, where R is the region bounded by $xy = 1$, $xy = 4$, $xy^2 = 1$, $xy^2 = 4$.

19. Evaluate $\int_S \vec{F} \cdot d\vec{A}$, where $\vec{F} = (bx/a)\vec{i} + (ay/b)\vec{j}$ and S is the elliptic cylinder oriented away from the z-axis, and given by $x^2/a^2 + y^2/b^2 = 1$, $|z| \leq c$, where a, b, c are positive constants.

20. Find $\int_S (x^2 \vec{i} + y^2 \vec{j} + z^2 \vec{k}) \cdot d\vec{A}$ where S is the surface of the sphere $(x - a)^2 + (y - b)^2 + (z - c)^2 = d^2$, oriented outward.

PROJECTS FOR CHAPTER TWENTY-ONE

1. Stereographic Projection

We parameterize the sphere $x^2 + y^2 + z^2 = 1$ by a famous method called stereographic projection. Draw a line from a point (x, y) in the xy-plane to the north pole $(0, 0, 1)$. This line intersects the sphere in a point (x, y, z). This gives a parameterization of the sphere by points in the plane.

(a) Which point corresponds to the south pole?

(b) Which points correspond to the equator?

(c) Do we get all the points of the sphere by this parameterization?

(d) Which points correspond to the upper hemisphere?

(e) Which points correspond to the lower hemisphere?

2. Parameterizing a Torus

A torus (doughnut) is constructed by rotating a small circle of radius a in a large circle of radius b about the origin. The small circle is in a (rotating) vertical plane through the z-axis and the large circle is in the xy-plane. See Figure 21.24. Parameterize the torus as follows.

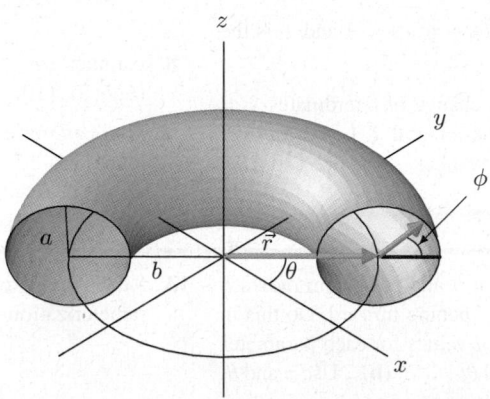

Figure 21.24

(a) Parameterize the large circle.

(b) For a typical point on the large circle, find two unit vectors which are perpendicular to one another and in the plane of the small circle at that point. Use these vectors to parameterize the small circle relative to its center.

(c) Combine your answers to parts (b) and (c) to parameterize the torus.

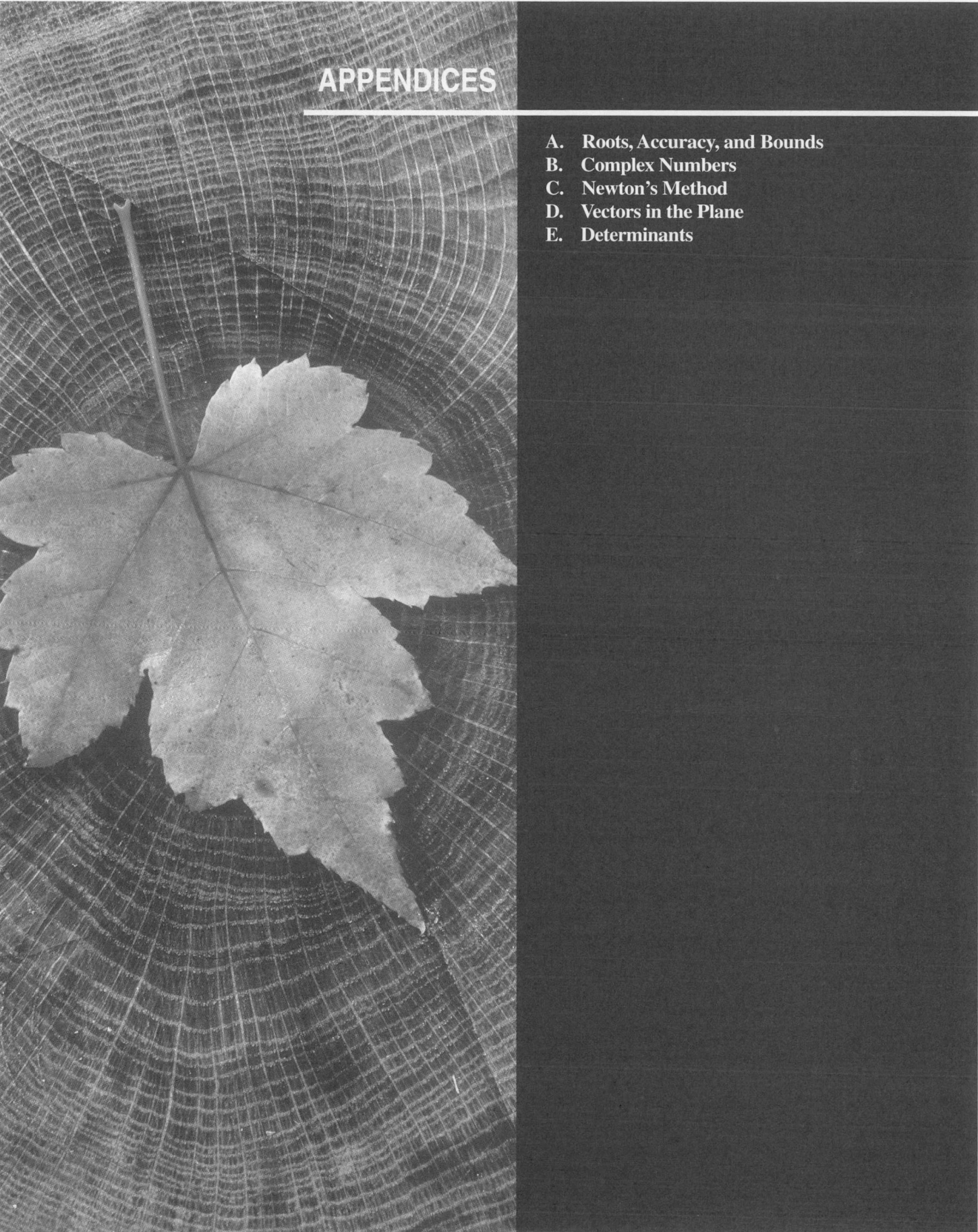

APPENDICES

A   ROOTS, ACCURACY, AND BOUNDS

It is often necessary to find the zeros of a polynomial or the points of intersection of two curves. So far, you have probably used algebraic methods, such as the quadratic formula, to solve such problems. Unfortunately, however, mathematicians' search for similar solutions to more complicated equations has not been all that successful. The formulas for the solutions to third- and fourth-degree equations are so complicated that you'd never want to use them. Early in the nineteenth century, it was proved that there is no algebraic formula for the solutions to equations of degree 5 and higher. Most non-polynomial equations cannot be solved using a formula either.

However, we can still find roots of equations, provided we use approximation methods, not formulas. In this section we will discuss three ways to find roots: algebraic, graphical, and numerical. Of these, only the algebraic method gives exact solutions.

First, let's get some terminology straight. Given the equation $x^2 = 4$, we call $x = -2$ and $x = 2$ the *roots*, or *solutions of the equation*. If we are given the function $f(x) = x^2 - 4$, then -2 and 2 are called the *zeros of the function*; that is, the zeros of the function f are the roots of the equation $f(x) = 0$.

The Algebraic Viewpoint: Roots by Factoring

If the product of two numbers is zero, then one or the other or both must be zero, that is, if $AB = 0$, then $A = 0$ or $B = 0$. This observation lies behind finding roots by factoring. You may have spent a lot of time factoring polynomials. Here you will also factor expressions involving trigonometric and exponential functions.

Example 1   Find the roots of $x^2 - 7x = 8$.

Solution   Rewrite the equation as $x^2 - 7x - 8 = 0$. Then factor the left side: $(x + 1)(x - 8) = 0$. By our observation about products, either $x + 1 = 0$ or $x - 8 = 0$, so the roots are $x = -1$ and $x = 8$.

Example 2   Find the roots of $\dfrac{1}{x} - \dfrac{x}{(x+2)} = 0$.

Solution   Rewrite the left side with a common denominator:

$$\frac{x + 2 - x^2}{x(x+2)} = 0.$$

Whenever a fraction is zero, the numerator must be zero. Therefore we must have

$$x + 2 - x^2 = (-1)(x^2 - x - 2) = (-1)(x - 2)(x + 1) = 0.$$

We conclude that $x - 2 = 0$ or $x + 1 = 0$, so 2 and -1 are the roots. They can be checked by substitution.

Example 3   Find the roots of $e^{-x} \sin x - e^{-x} \cos x = 0$.

Solution   Factor the left side: $e^{-x}(\sin x - \cos x) = 0$. The factor e^{-x} is never zero; it is impossible to raise e to a power and get zero. Therefore, the only possibility is that $\sin x - \cos x = 0$. This equation is equivalent to $\sin x = \cos x$. If we divide both sides by $\cos x$, we get

$$\frac{\sin x}{\cos x} = \frac{\cos x}{\cos x} \quad \text{so} \quad \tan x = 1.$$

The roots of this equation are

$$\ldots, \frac{-7\pi}{4}, \frac{-3\pi}{4}, \frac{\pi}{4}, \frac{5\pi}{4}, \frac{9\pi}{4}, \frac{13\pi}{4}, \ldots.$$

Warning: Using factoring to solve an equation only works when one side of the equation is 0. It is not true that if, say, $AB = 7$ then $A = 7$ or $B = 7$. For example, you *cannot* solve $x^2 - 4x = 2$ by factoring $x(x - 4) = 2$ and then assuming that either x or $x - 4$ equals 2.

The problem with factoring is that factors are not easy to find. For example, the left side of the quadratic equation $x^2 - 4x - 2 = 0$ does not factor, at least not into "nice" factors with integer coefficients. For the general quadratic equation

$$ax^2 + bx + c = 0,$$

there is the quadratic formula for the roots:

$$x = \frac{-b \pm \sqrt{b^2 - 4ac}}{2a}.$$

Thus the roots of $x^2 - 4x - 2 = 0$ are $(4 \pm \sqrt{24})/2$, or $2 + \sqrt{6}$ and $2 - \sqrt{6}$.

Notice that in each of these examples, we have found the roots exactly.

The Graphical Viewpoint: Roots by Zooming

To find the roots of an equation $f(x) = 0$, it helps to draw the graph of f. The roots of the equation, that is the zeros of f, are *the values of x where the graph of f crosses the x-axis*. Even a very rough sketch of the graph can be useful in determining how many zeros there are and their approximate values. If you have a computer or graphing calculator, then finding solutions by graphing is the easiest method, especially if you use the zoom feature. However, a graph can never tell you the exact value of a root, only an approximate one.

Example 4   Find the roots of $x^3 - 4x - 2 = 0$.

Solution   Attempting to factor the left side with integer coefficients will convince you it cannot be done, so we cannot easily find the roots by algebra. We know the graph of $f(x) = x^3 - 4x - 2$ will have the usual cubic shape; see Figure A.1.

There are clearly three roots: one between $x = -2$ and $x = -1$, another between $x = -1$ and $x = 0$, and a third between $x = 2$ and $x = 3$. Zooming in on the largest root with a graphing calculator or computer shows that it lies in the following interval:

$$2.213 < x < 2.215.$$

Thus, the root is $x = 2.21$, accurate to two decimal places. Zooming in on the other two roots shows them to be $x = -1.68$ and $x = -0.54$, accurate to two decimal places.

Useful trick: Suppose you want to solve the equation $\sin x - \cos x = 0$ graphically. Instead of graphing $f(x) = \sin x - \cos x$ and looking for zeros, you may find it easier to rewrite the equation as $\sin x = \cos x$ and graph $g(x) = \sin x$ and $h(x) = \cos x$. (After all, you already know what these two graphs look like. See Figure A.2.) The roots of the original equation are then precisely the x coordinates of the points of intersection of the graphs of $g(x)$ and $h(x)$.

Figure A.1: The cubic
$f(x) = x^3 - 4x - 2$

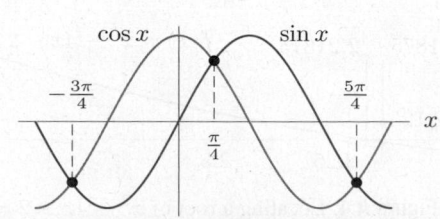

Figure A.2: Finding roots of
$\sin x - \cos x = 0$

Example 5   Find the roots of $2\sin x - x = 0$.

Solution   Rewrite the equation as $2\sin x = x$, and graph both sides. Since $g(x) = 2\sin x$ is always between -2 and 2, there are no roots of $2\sin x = x$ for $x > 2$ or for $x < -2$. We need only consider the graphs between -2 and 2 (or between $-\pi$ and π, which makes graphing the sine function easier). Figure A.3 shows the graphs. There are three points of intersection: one appears to be at $x = 0$, one between $x = \pi/2$ and $x = \pi$, and one between $x = -\pi/2$ and $x = -\pi$. You can tell that $x = 0$ is the exact value of one root because it satisfies the original equation exactly. Zooming in shows that there is a second root $x \approx 1.9$, and the third root is $x \approx -1.9$ by symmetry.

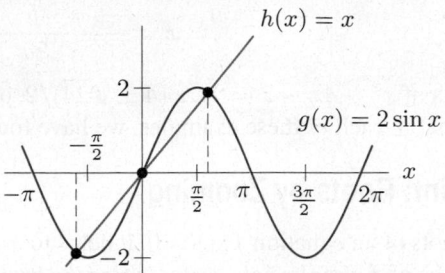

Figure A.3: Finding roots of $2\sin x - x = 0$

The Numerical Viewpoint: Roots by Bisection

We now look at a numerical method of approximating the solutions to an equation. This method depends on the idea that if the value of a function $f(x)$ changes sign in an interval, and if we believe there is no break in the graph of the function there, then there is a root of the equation $f(x) = 0$ in that interval.

Let's go back to the problem of finding the root of $f(x) = x^3 - 4x - 2 = 0$ between 2 and 3. To locate the root, we close in on it by evaluating the function at the midpoint of the interval, $x = 2.5$. Since $f(2) = -2$, $f(2.5) = 3.625$, and $f(3) = 13$, the function changes sign between $x = 2$ and $x = 2.5$, so the root is between these points. Now we look at $x = 2.25$.

Since $f(2.25) = 0.39$, the function is negative at $x = 2$ and positive at $x = 2.25$, so there is a root between 2 and 2.25. Now we look at 2.125. We find $f(2.125) = -0.90$, so there is a root between 2.125 and 2.25, ... and so on. (You may want to round the decimals as you work.) See Figure A.4. The intervals containing the root are listed in Table A.1 and show that the root is $x = 2.21$ to two decimal places.

Figure A.4: Locating a root of $x^3 - 4x - 2 = 0$

Table A.1   *Intervals containing root of* $x^3 - 4x - 2 = 0$ *(Note:* $[2,3]$ *means* $2 \le x \le 3$)

$[2, 3]$
$[2, 2.5]$
$[2, 2.25]$
$[2.125, 2.25]$
$[2.1875, 2.25]$ So $x = 2.2$ rounded to one decimal place
$[2.1875, 2.21875]$
$[2.203125, 2.21875]$
$[2.2109375, 2.21875]$
$[2.2109375, 2.2148438]$ So $x = 2.21$ rounded to two decimal places

This method of estimating roots is called the **Bisection Method**:

- To solve an equation $f(x) = 0$ using the bisection method, we need two starting values for x, say, $x = a$ and $x = b$, such that $f(a)$ and $f(b)$ have opposite signs and f is continuous on $[a, b]$.

- Evaluate f at the midpoint of the interval $[a, b]$, and decide in which half-interval the root lies.

- Repeat, using the new half-interval instead of $[a, b]$.

There are some problems with the bisection method:

- The function may not change signs near the root. For example, $f(x) = x^2 - 2x + 1 = 0$ has a root at $x = 1$, but $f(x)$ is never negative because $f(x) = (x - 1)^2$, and a square cannot be negative. (See Figure A.5.)

- The function f must be continuous between the starting values $x = a$ and $x = b$.

- If there is more than one root between the starting values $x = a$ and $x = b$, the method will find only one of the roots. For example, if we had tried to solve $x^3 - 4x - 2 = 0$ starting at $x = -12$ and $x = 10$, the bisection method would zero in on the root between $x = -2$ and $x = -1$, not the root between $x = 2$ and $x = 3$ that we found earlier. (Try it! Then see what happens if you use $x = -10$ instead of $x = -12$.)

- The bisection method is slow and not very efficient. Applying bisection three times in a row only traps the root in an interval $\left(\frac{1}{2}\right)^3 = \frac{1}{8}$ as large as the starting interval. Thus, if we initially know that a root is between, say, 2 and 3, then we would need to apply the bisection method at least four times to know the first digit after the decimal point.

There are much more powerful methods available for finding roots, such as Newton's method, which are more complicated but which avoid some of these difficulties.

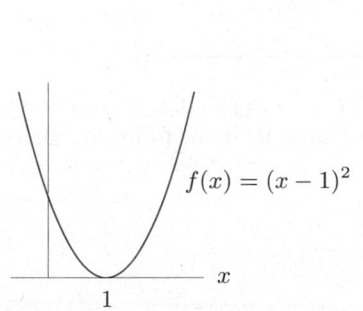

Figure A.5: f does not change sign at the root

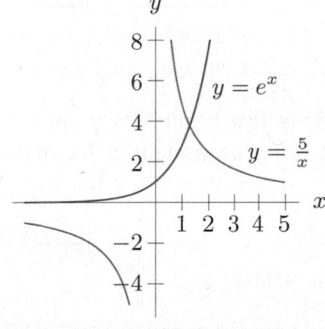

Figure A.6: Intersection of $y = e^x$ and $y = 5/x$

Table A.2   *Bisection method for*
$f(x) = xe^x - 5 = 0$ *(Note that*
$[1, 2]$ *means the interval* $1 \leq x \leq 2$)

Interval Containing Root
$[1, 2]$
$[1, 1.5]$
$[1.25, 1.5]$
$[1.25, 1.375]$
$[1.3125, 1.375]$
$[1.3125, 1.34375]$

Example 6   Find all the roots of $xe^x = 5$ to at least one decimal place.

Solution   If we rewrite the equation as $e^x = 5/x$ and graph both sides, as in Figure A.6, it is clear that there is exactly one root, and it is somewhere between 1 and 2. Table A.2 shows the intervals obtained by the bisection method. After five iterations, we have the root trapped between 1.3125 and 1.34375, so we can say the root is $x = 1.3$ to one decimal place.

Iteration

Both zooming in and bisection as discussed here are examples of *iterative* methods, in which a sequence of steps is repeated over and over again, using the results of one step as the input for the next. We can use such methods to locate a root to any degree of accuracy. In bisection, each iteration traps the root in an interval that is half the length of the previous one. Each time you zoom in on a calculator, you trap the root in a smaller interval; how much smaller depends on the settings on the calculator.

Accuracy and Error

In the previous discussion, we used the phrase "accurate to 2 decimal places." For an iterative process where we get closer and closer estimates of some quantity, we take a common-sense approach to accuracy: we watch the numbers carefully, and when a digit stays the same for several iterations, we assume it has stabilized and is correct, especially if the digits to the right of that digit also stay the same. For example, suppose 2.21429 and 2.21431 are two successive estimates for a zero of $f(x) = x^3 - 4x - 2$. Since these two estimates agree to the third digit after the decimal point, we probably have at least 3 decimal places correct.

There is a problem with this, however. Suppose we are estimating a root whose true value is 1, and the estimates are converging to the value from below—say, 0.985, 0.991, 0.997 and so on. In this case, not even the first decimal place is "correct," even though the difference between the estimates and the actual answer is very small—much less than 0.1. To avoid this difficulty, we say that an estimate a for some quantity r is *accurate to p decimal places* if the error, which is the absolute value of the difference between a and r, or $|r - a|$, is as follows:

Accuracy to p decimal places	means	Error less than
$p = 1$		0.05
2		0.005
3		0.0005
$\vdots$		$\vdots$
n		$0.\underbrace{000\ldots0}_{n}5$

This is the same as saying that r must lie in an interval of length twice the maximum error, centered on a. For example, if a is accurate to 1 decimal place, r must lie in the following interval:

$$a - 0.05 \qquad a \qquad a + 0.05$$

Since both the graphing calculator and the bisection method give us an interval in which the root is trapped, this definition of decimal accuracy is a natural one for these processes.

Example 7   Suppose the numbers $\sqrt{10}$, 22/7, and 3.14 are given as approximations to $\pi = 3.1415\ldots$. To how many decimal places is each approximation accurate?

Solution   Using $\sqrt{10} = 3.1622\ldots$,

$$|\sqrt{10} - \pi| = |3.1622\ldots - 3.1415\ldots| = 0.0206\ldots < 0.05,$$

so $\sqrt{10}$ is accurate to one decimal place. Similarly, using $22/7 = 3.1428\ldots$,

$$\left|\frac{22}{7} - \pi\right| = |3.1428\ldots - 3.1415\ldots| = 0.0013\ldots < 0.005,$$

so 22/7 is accurate to two decimal places. Finally,

$$|3.14 - 3.1415\ldots| = 0.0015\ldots < 0.005,$$

so 3.14 is accurate to two decimal places.

Warning:

- Saying that an approximation is accurate to, say, 2 decimal places does *not* guarantee that its first two decimal places are "correct," that is, that the two digits of the approximation are the same as the corresponding two digits in the true value. For example, an approximate value of 5.997 is accurate to 2 decimal places if the true value is 6.001, but neither of the 9s in the approximation agrees with the 0s in the true value (nor does the digit 5 agree with the digit 6).

- When finding a root r of an equation, the number of decimal places of accuracy refers to the number of digits that have stabilized in the root. It does *not* refer to the number of digits of $f(r)$ that are zero. For example, Table A.1 on page 1098 shows that $x = 2.2$ is a root of $f(x) = x^3 - 4x - 2 = 0$, accurate to one decimal place. Yet, $f(2.2) = -0.152$, so $f(2.2)$ does not have one zero after the decimal point. Similarly, $x = 2.21$ is the root accurate to two decimal places, but $f(2.21) = -0.046$ does not have two zeros after the decimal point.

Example 8   Is $x = 2.2143$ a zero of $f(x) = x^3 - 4x - 2$ accurate to four decimal places?

Solution   We want to know whether r, the exact value of the zero, lies in the interval

$$2.2143 - 0.00005 < r < 2.2143 + 0.00005$$

which is the same as

$$2.21425 < r < 2.21435.$$

Since $f(2.21425) < 0$ and $f(2.21435) > 0$, the zero does lie in this interval, and so $r = 2.2143$ is accurate to four decimal places.

How to Write a Decimal Answer

The graphing calculator and bisection method naturally give an interval for a root or a zero. However, other numerical techniques do not give a pair of numbers bounding the true value, but rather a single number near the true value. What should you do if you want a single number, rather than an interval, for an answer? In general, averaging the endpoint of the interval is the best solution.

When giving a single number as an answer and interpreting it, be careful about giving rounded answers. For example, suppose you know a root lies in the interval between 0.81 and 0.87. Averaging gives 0.84 as a single number estimating the root. But it would be wrong to round 0.84 to 0.8 and say that the answer is 0.8 accurate to one decimal place; the true value could be 0.86, which is not within 0.05 of 0.8. The right thing to say is that the answer is 0.84 accurate to one decimal place. Similarly, to give an answer accurate to, say, 2 decimal places, you may have to show 3 decimal places in your answer.

Bounds of a Function

Knowing how big or how small a function gets can sometimes be useful, especially when you can't easily find exact values of the function. You can say, for example, that $\sin x$ always stays between -1 and 1 and that $2\sin x + 10$ always stays between 8 and 12. But 2^x is not confined between any two numbers, because 2^x will exceed any number you can name if x is large enough. We say that $\sin x$ and $2\sin x + 10$ are *bounded* functions, and that 2^x is an *unbounded* function.

> A function f is **bounded** on an interval if there are numbers L and U such that
>
> $$L \leq f(x) \leq U$$
>
> for all x in the interval. Otherwise, f is **unbounded** on the interval.
>
> We say that L is a **lower bound** for f on the interval, and that U is an **upper bound** for f on the interval.

Example 9   Use Figures A.7 and A.8 to decide which of the following functions are bounded.

(a) x^3 on $-\infty < x < \infty$; on $0 \leq x \leq 100$.

(b) $2/x$ on $0 < x < \infty$; on $1 \leq x < \infty$.

Figure A.7: Is x^3 bounded?   Figure A.8: Is $2/x$ bounded?

Solution

(a) The graph of x^3 in Figure A.7 shows that x^3 will exceed any number, no matter how large, if x is big enough, so x^3 does not have an upper bound on $-\infty < x < \infty$. Therefore, x^3 is unbounded on $-\infty < x < \infty$. But on the interval $0 \leq x \leq 100$, x^3 stays between 0 (a lower bound) and $100^3 = 1{,}000{,}000$ (an upper bound). Therefore, x^3 is bounded on the interval $0 \leq x \leq 100$. Notice that upper and lower bounds, when they exist, are not unique. For example, -100 is another lower bound and $2{,}000{,}000$ another upper bound for x^3 on $0 \leq x \leq 100$.

(b) $2/x$ is unbounded on $0 < x < \infty$, since it has no upper bound on that interval. But $0 \leq 2/x \leq 2$ for $1 \leq x < \infty$, so $2/x$ is bounded, with lower bound 0 and upper bound 2, on $1 \leq x < \infty$. (See Figure A.8.)

Best Possible Bounds

Consider a group of people whose height in feet, h, ranges from 5 feet to 6 feet. Then 5 feet is a lower bound for the people in the group and 6 feet is an upper bound:

$$5 \leq h \leq 6.$$

But the people in this group are also all between 4 feet and 7 feet, so it is also true that

$$4 \leq h \leq 7.$$

So, there are many lower bounds and many upper bounds. However, the 5 and the 6 are considered the best bounds because they are the closest together of all the possible pairs of bounds.

> The **best possible bounds** for a function, f, over an interval are numbers A and B such that, for all x in the interval,
>
> $$A \leq f(x) \leq B$$
>
> and where A and B are as close together as possible. A is called the **greatest lower bound** and B is the **least upper bound**.

What Do Bounds Mean Graphically?

Upper and lower bounds can be represented on a graph by horizontal lines. See Figure A.9.

Figure A.9: Upper and lower bounds for the function f

Exercises for Appendix A

1. Use a calculator or computer graph of $f(x) = 13 - 20x - x^2 - 3x^4$ to determine:

   (a) The range of this function;
   (b) The number of zeros of this function.

For Problems 2–12, determine the roots or points of intersection to an accuracy of one decimal place.

2. (a) The root of $x^3 - 3x + 1 = 0$ between 0 and 1
   (b) The root of $x^3 - 3x + 1 = 0$ between 1 and 2
   (c) The smallest root of $x^3 - 3x + 1 = 0$

3. The root of $x^4 - 5x^3 + 2x - 5 = 0$ between -2 and -1

4. The root of $x^5 + x^2 - 9x - 3 = 0$ between -2 and -1

5. The largest real root of $2x^3 - 4x^2 - 3x + 1 = 0$

6. All real roots of $x^4 - x - 2 = 0$

7. All real roots of $x^5 - 2x^2 + 4 = 0$

8. The smallest positive root of $x \sin x - \cos x = 0$

9. The left-most point of intersection between $y = 2x$ and $y = \cos x$

10. The left-most point of intersection between $y = 1/2^x$ and $y = \sin x$

11. The point of intersection between $y = e^{-x}$ and $y = \ln x$

12. All roots of $\cos t = t^2$

13. Estimate all real zeros of the following polynomials, accurate to 2 decimal places:

    (a) $f(x) = x^3 - 2x^2 - x + 3$
    (b) $f(x) = x^3 - x^2 - 2x + 2$

14. Find the largest zero of

$$f(x) = 10xe^{-x} - 1$$

to two decimal places, using the bisection method. Make sure to demonstrate that your approximation is as good as you claim.

15. (a) Find the smallest positive value of x where the graphs of $f(x) = \sin x$ and $g(x) = 2^{-x}$ intersect.
    (b) Repeat with $f(x) = \sin 2x$ and $g(x) = 2^{-x}$.

16. Use a graphing calculator to sketch $y = 2\cos x$ and $y = x^3 + x^2 + 1$ on the same set of axes. Find the positive zero of $f(x) = 2\cos x - x^3 - x^2 - 1$. A friend claims there is one more real zero. Is your friend correct? Explain.

17. Use the table below to investigate the zeros of the function

$$f(\theta) = (\sin 3\theta)(\cos 4\theta) + 0.8$$

in the interval $0 \leq \theta \leq 1.8$.

θ	0	0.2	0.4	0.6	0.8	1.0	1.2	1.4	1.6	1.8
$f(\theta)$	0.80	1.19	0.77	0.08	0.13	0.71	0.76	0.12	-0.19	0.33

(a) Decide how many zeros the function has in the interval $0 \leq \theta \leq 1.8$.
(b) Locate each zero, or a small interval containing each zero.
(c) Are you sure you have found all the zeros in the interval $0 \leq \theta \leq 1.8$? Graph the function on a calculator or computer to decide.

18. **(a)** Use Table A.3 to locate approximate solution(s) to

$$(\sin 3x)(\cos 4x) = \frac{x^3}{\pi^3}$$

in the interval $1.07 \leq x \leq 1.15$. Give an interval of length 0.01 in which each solution lies.

Table A.3

x	x^3/π^3	$(\sin 3x)(\cos 4x)$
1.07	0.0395	0.0286
1.08	0.0406	0.0376
1.09	0.0418	0.0442
1.10	0.0429	0.0485
1.11	0.0441	0.0504
1.12	0.0453	0.0499
1.13	0.0465	0.0470
1.14	0.0478	0.0417
1.15	0.0491	0.0340

(b) Make an estimate for each solution accurate to two decimal places.

19. **(a)** With your calculator in radian mode, take the arctangent of 1 and multiply that number by 4. Now, take the arctangent of the result and multiply it by 4. Continue this process 10 times or so and record each result as in the accompanying table. At each step, you get 4 times the arctangent of the result of the previous step.

$$1$$
$$3.14159\ldots$$
$$5.05050\ldots$$
$$5.50129\ldots$$
$$\vdots$$

(b) Your table allows you to find a solution of the equation

$$4 \arctan x = x.$$

Why? What is that solution?

(c) What does your table in part (a) have to do with Figure A.10?
[Hint: The coordinates of P_0 are $(1, 1)$. Find the coordinates of P_1, P_2, P_3,...]

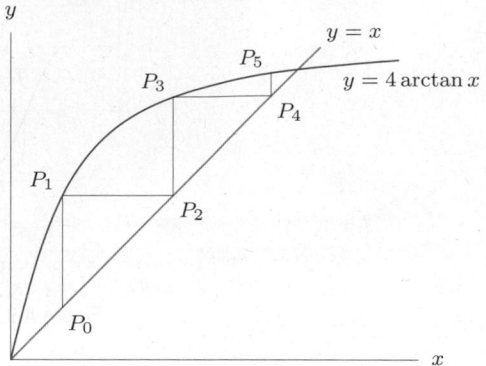

Figure A.10

(d) In part (a), what happens if you start with an initial guess of 10? Of -10? What types of behavior do you observe? (That is, for which initial guesses is the sequence increasing, and for which is it decreasing; does the sequence approach a limit?) Explain your answers graphically, as in part (c).

20. Using radians, apply the iteration method of Problem 19 to the equation

$$\cos x = x.$$

Represent your results graphically, as in Figure A.10.

For Problems 21–23, draw a graph to decide if the function is bounded on the interval given. Give the best possible upper and lower bounds for any function which is bounded.

21. $f(x) = 4x - x^2$ on $[-1, 4]$

22. $h(\theta) = 5 + 3\sin\theta$ on $[-2\pi, 2\pi]$

23. $f(t) = \dfrac{\sin t}{t^2}$ on $[-10, 10]$

B   COMPLEX NUMBERS

The quadratic equation

$$x^2 - 2x + 2 = 0$$

is not satisfied by any real number x. If you try applying the quadratic formula, you get

$$x = \frac{2 \pm \sqrt{4 - 8}}{2} = 1 \pm \frac{\sqrt{-4}}{2}.$$

Apparently, you need to take a square root of -4. But -4 does not have a square root, at least, not one which is a real number. Let's give it a square root.

We define the imaginary number i to be a number such that

$$i^2 = -1.$$

Using this i, we see that $(2i)^2 = -4$, so

$$x = 1 \pm \frac{\sqrt{-4}}{2} = 1 \pm \frac{2i}{2} = 1 \pm i.$$

This solves our quadratic equation. The numbers $1 + i$ and $1 - i$ are examples of complex numbers.

A **complex number** is defined as any number that can be written in the form

$$z = a + bi,$$

where a and b are real numbers and $i^2 = -1$, so we say $i = \sqrt{-1}$.
The *real part* of z is the number a; the *imaginary part* is the number b.

Calling the number i imaginary makes it sound as if i does not exist in the same way that real numbers exist. In some cases, it is useful to make such a distinction between real and imaginary numbers. For example, if we measure mass or position, we want our answers to be real numbers. But the imaginary numbers are just as legitimate mathematically as the real numbers are.

As an analogy, consider the distinction between positive and negative numbers. Originally, people thought of numbers only as tools to count with; their concept of "five" or "ten" was not far removed from "five arrows" or "ten stones." They were unaware that negative numbers existed at all. When negative numbers were introduced, they were viewed only as a device for solving equations like $x + 2 = 1$. They were considered "false numbers," or, in Latin, "negative numbers." Thus, even though people started to use negative numbers, they did not view them as existing in the same way that positive numbers did. An early mathematician might have reasoned: "The number 5 exists because I can have 5 dollars in my hand. But how can I have -5 dollars in my hand?" Today we have an answer: "I have -5 dollars" means I owe somebody 5 dollars. We have realized that negative numbers are just as useful as positive ones, and it turns out that complex numbers are useful too. For example, they are used in studying wave motion in electric circuits.

Algebra of Complex Numbers

Numbers such as 0, 1, $\frac{1}{2}$, π, and $\sqrt{2}$ are called *purely real* because they contain no imaginary components. Numbers such as i, $2i$, and $\sqrt{2}i$ are called *purely imaginary* because they contain only the number i multiplied by a nonzero real coefficient.

Two complex numbers are called *conjugates* if their real parts are equal and if their imaginary parts are opposites. The complex conjugate of the complex number $z = a + bi$ is denoted $\overline{z}$, so we have

$$\overline{z} = a - bi.$$

(Note that z is real if and only if $z = \overline{z}$.) Complex conjugates have the following remarkable property: if $f(x)$ is any polynomial with real coefficients ($x^3 + 1$, say) and $f(z) = 0$, then $f(\overline{z}) = 0$. This means that if z is the solution to a polynomial equation with real coefficients, then so is $\overline{z}$.

- Two complex numbers are equal if and only if their real parts are equal and their imaginary parts are equal. Consequently, if $a + bi = c + di$, then $a = c$ and $b = d$.

- Adding two complex numbers is done by adding real and imaginary parts separately:

$$(a + bi) + (c + di) = (a + c) + (b + d)i.$$

- Subtracting is similar:

$$(a + bi) - (c + di) = (a - c) + (b - d)i.$$

- Multiplication works just as for polynomials, using $i^2 = -1$:

$$
\begin{aligned}
(a + bi)(c + di) &= a(c + di) + bi(c + di) \\
&= ac + adi + bci + bdi^2 \\
&= ac + adi + bci - bd = (ac - bd) + (ad + bc)i.
\end{aligned}
$$

- Powers of i: We know that $i^2 = -1$; then $i^3 = i \cdot i^2 = -i$, and $i^4 = (i^2)^2 = (-1)^2 = 1$. Then $i^5 = i \cdot i^4 = i$, and so on. Thus we have

$$i^n = \begin{cases} i & \text{for } n = 1, 5, 9, 13, \dots \\ -1 & \text{for } n = 2, 6, 10, 14, \dots \\ -i & \text{for } n = 3, 7, 11, 15, \dots \\ 1 & \text{for } n = 0, 4, 8, 12, 16, \dots \end{cases}$$

- The product of a number and its conjugate is always real and nonnegative:

$$z \cdot \overline{z} = (a + bi)(a - bi) = a^2 - abi + abi - b^2 i^2 = a^2 + b^2.$$

- Dividing by a nonzero complex number is done by multiplying the denominator by its conjugate, thereby making the denominator real:

$$\frac{a + bi}{c + di} = \frac{a + bi}{c + di} \cdot \frac{c - di}{c - di} = \frac{ac - adi + bci - bdi^2}{c^2 + d^2} = \frac{ac + bd}{c^2 + d^2} + \frac{bc - ad}{c^2 + d^2} i.$$

Example 1   Compute $(2 + 7i)(4 - 6i) - i$.

Solution $(2 + 7i)(4 - 6i) - i = 8 + 28i - 12i - 42i^2 - i = 8 + 15i + 42 = 50 + 15i.$

Example 2   Compute $\dfrac{2 + 7i}{4 - 6i}$.

Solution

$$\frac{2 + 7i}{4 - 6i} = \frac{2 + 7i}{4 - 6i} \cdot \frac{4 + 6i}{4 + 6i} = \frac{8 + 12i + 28i + 42i^2}{4^2 + 6^2} = \frac{-34 + 40i}{52} = \frac{-17}{26} + \frac{10}{13} i.$$

You can check by multiplying out that $(-17/26 + 10i/13)(4 - 6i) = 2 + 7i$.

The Complex Plane and Polar Coordinates

It is often useful to picture a complex number $z = x + iy$ in the plane, with x along the horizontal axis and y along the vertical. The xy-plane is then called the *complex plane*. Figure B.11 shows the complex numbers $-2i$, $1 + i$, and $-2 + 3i$.

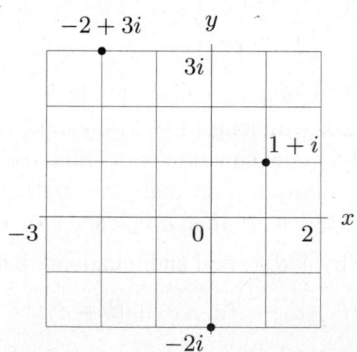

Figure B.11: Points in the complex plane

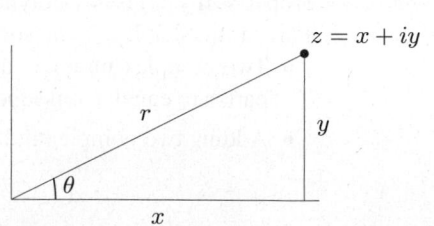

Figure B.12: The point $z = x + iy$ in the complex plane, showing polar coordinates

The triangle in Figure B.12 shows that a complex number can be written using polar coordinates as follows:

$$z = x + iy = r \cos \theta + ir \sin \theta.$$

Example 3 Express $z = -2i$ and $z = -2 + 3i$ using polar coordinates. (See Figure B.11.)

Solution For $z = -2i$, the distance of z from the origin is 2, so $r = 2$. Also, one value for θ is $\theta = 3\pi/2$. Using polar coordinates, $-2i = 2\cos(3\pi/2) + i\,2(\sin 3\pi/2)$.

For $z = -2 + 3i$, we have $x = -2$, $y = 3$. So $r = \sqrt{(-2)^2 + 3^2} \approx 3.61$, and one solution of $\tan\theta = 3/(-2)$ with θ in quadrant II is $\theta \approx 2.16$. So $-2 + 3i \approx 3.61\cos(2.16) + i\,3.61\sin(2.16)$.

Example 4 Consider the point with polar coordinates $r = 5$ and $\theta = 3\pi/4$. What complex number does this point represent?

Solution Since $x = r\cos\theta$ and $y = r\sin\theta$ we see that $x = 5\cos 3\pi/4 = -5/\sqrt{2}$, and $y = 5\sin 3\pi/4 = 5/\sqrt{2}$, so $z = -5/\sqrt{2} + i\,5/\sqrt{2}$.

Derivatives and Integrals of Complex-Valued Functions

Suppose $z(t) = x(t) + iy(t)$, where t is real, then we define $z'(t)$ and $\int z(t)\,dt$ by treating i like any other constant:

$$z'(t) = x'(t) + iy'(t)$$

$$\int z(t)\,dt = \int x(t)\,dt + i\int y(t)\,dt.$$

With these definitions, all the usual properties of differentiation and integration hold, such as

$$\int z'(t)\,dt = z(t) + C, \qquad \text{for } C \text{ is a complex constant.}$$

Euler's Formula

Consider the complex number z lying on the unit circle in Figure B.13. Writing z in polar coordinates, and using the fact that $r = 1$, we have

$$z = f(\theta) = \cos\theta + i\sin\theta.$$

It turns out that there is a particularly beautiful and compact way of rewriting $f(\theta)$ using complex exponentials. We take the derivative of f using the fact that $i^2 = -1$:

$$f'(\theta) = -\sin\theta + i\cos\theta = i\cos\theta + i^2\sin\theta.$$

Factoring out an i gives

$$f'(\theta) = i(\cos\theta + i\sin\theta) = i \cdot f(\theta).$$

As you know from Chapter 11, page 610, the only real-valued function whose derivative is proportional to the function itself is the exponential function. In other words, we know that if

$$g'(x) = k \cdot g(x), \quad \text{then} \quad g(x) = Ce^{kx}$$

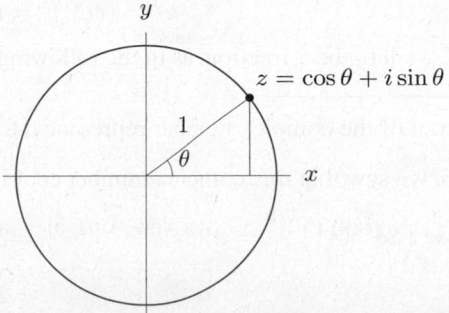

Figure B.13: Complex number represented by a point on the unit circle for some constant C. If we assume that a similar result holds for complex-valued functions, then we have

$$f'(\theta) = i \cdot f(\theta), \quad \text{so} \quad f(\theta) = Ce^{i\theta}$$

for some constant C. To find C we substitute $\theta = 0$. Now $f(0) = Ce^{i\cdot 0} = C$, and since $f(0) = \cos 0 + i \sin 0 = 1$, we must have $C = 1$. Therefore $f(\theta) = e^{i\theta}$. Thus we have

---

Euler's formula

$$e^{i\theta} = \cos\theta + i\sin\theta.$$

This elegant and surprising relationship was discovered by the Swiss mathematician Leonhard Euler in the eighteenth century, and it is particularly useful in solving second-order differential equations. Another way of obtaining Euler's formula (using Taylor series) is given in Problem 46 on page 551. It allows us to write the complex number represented by the point with polar coordinates (r, θ) in the following form:

$$z = r(\cos\theta + i\sin\theta) = re^{i\theta}.$$

Similarly, since $\cos(-\theta) = \cos\theta$ and $\sin(-\theta) = -\sin\theta$, we have

$$re^{-i\theta} = r\left(\cos(-\theta) + i\sin(-\theta)\right) = r(\cos\theta - i\sin\theta).$$

Example 5   Evaluate $e^{i\pi}$.

Solution   Using Euler's formula, $e^{i\pi} = \cos\pi + i\sin\pi = -1$.

Example 6   Express the complex number represented by the point $r = 8$, $\theta = 3\pi/4$ in Cartesian form and polar form, $z = re^{i\theta}$.

Solution   Using Cartesian coordinates, the complex number is

$$z = 8\left(\cos\left(\frac{3\pi}{4}\right) + i\sin\left(\frac{3\pi}{4}\right)\right) = \frac{-8}{\sqrt{2}} + i\frac{8}{\sqrt{2}}.$$

Using polar coordinates, we have

$$z = 8e^{i\,3\pi/4}.$$

The polar form of complex numbers makes finding powers and roots of complex numbers much easier. Writing $z = re^{i\theta}$, we find any power of z as follows:

$$z^p = (re^{i\theta})^p = r^p e^{ip\theta}.$$

To find roots, we let p be a fraction, as in the following example.

Example 7   Find a cube root of the complex number represented by the point with polar coordinates $(8, 3\pi/4)$.

Solution   In Example 6, we saw that this complex number could be written as $z = 8e^{i3\pi/4}$. So,

$$\sqrt[3]{z} = \left(8e^{i\,3\pi/4}\right)^{1/3} = 8^{1/3}e^{i(3\pi/4)\cdot(1/3)} = 2e^{\pi i/4} = 2\left(\cos(\pi/4) + i\sin(\pi/4)\right)$$

$$= 2\left(1/\sqrt{2} + i/\sqrt{2}\right) = \sqrt{2}(1+i).$$

You can check by multiplying out that $(\sqrt{2}(1+i))^3 = -(8/\sqrt{2}) + i(8/\sqrt{2}) = z$.

Using Complex Exponentials

Euler's formula, together with the fact that exponential functions are simple to manipulate, allows us to obtain many results about trigonometric functions easily.

The following example uses the fact that for complex z, the function e^z has all the usual algebraic properties of exponents.

Example 8   Use Euler's formula to obtain the double-angle identities

$$\cos 2\theta = \cos^2 \theta - \sin^2 \theta \qquad \text{and} \qquad \sin 2\theta = 2 \cos \theta \sin \theta.$$

Solution   We use the fact that $e^{2i\theta} = e^{i\theta} \cdot e^{i\theta}$. This can be rewritten as

$$\cos 2\theta + i \sin 2\theta = (\cos \theta + i \sin \theta)^2.$$

Multiplying out $(\cos \theta + i \sin \theta)^2$, using the fact that $i^2 = -1$ gives

$$\cos 2\theta + i \sin 2\theta = \cos^2 \theta - \sin^2 \theta + i(2 \cos \theta \sin \theta).$$

Since two complex numbers are equal only if the real and imaginary parts are equal, we must have

$$\cos 2\theta = \cos^2 \theta - \sin^2 \theta \qquad \text{and} \qquad \sin 2\theta = 2 \cos \theta \sin \theta.$$

If we solve $e^{i\theta} = \cos \theta + i \sin \theta$ and $e^{-i\theta} = \cos \theta - i \sin \theta$ for $\sin \theta$ and $\cos \theta$, we obtain

$$\sin \theta = \frac{e^{i\theta} - e^{-i\theta}}{2i} \qquad \text{and} \qquad \cos \theta = \frac{e^{i\theta} + e^{-i\theta}}{2}.$$

By differentiating the formula $e^{ik\theta} = \cos(k\theta) + i \sin(k\theta)$, for θ real and k a real constant, it can be shown that

$$\frac{d}{d\theta}\left(e^{ik\theta}\right) = ik e^{ik\theta} \qquad \text{and} \qquad \int e^{ik\theta}\, d\theta = \frac{1}{ik} e^{ik\theta} + C.$$

Thus complex exponentials are differentiated and integrated just like real exponentials.

Example 9   Use $\cos \theta = \left(e^{i\theta} + e^{-i\theta}\right)/2$ to obtain the derivative formula for $\cos \theta$.

Solution   Differentiating gives

$$\frac{d}{d\theta}(\cos \theta) = \frac{d}{d\theta}\left(\frac{e^{i\theta} + e^{-i\theta}}{2}\right) = \frac{i e^{i\theta} - i e^{-i\theta}}{2} = \frac{i(e^{i\theta} - e^{-i\theta})}{2}$$

$$= -\frac{e^{i\theta} - e^{-i\theta}}{2i} = -\sin \theta.$$

The facts that e^z has all the usual properties when z is complex leads to

$$\frac{d}{d\theta}(e^{(a+ib)\theta}) = (a+ib)e^{(a+ib)\theta} \qquad \text{and} \qquad \int e^{(a+ib)\theta}\, d\theta = \frac{1}{a+ib} e^{(a+ib)\theta} + C.$$

Example 10   Use the formula for $\int e^{(a+ib)\theta}\, d\theta$ to obtain formulas for $\int e^{ax}\cos bx\, dx$ and $\int e^{ax}\sin bx\, dx$.

Solution   The formula for $\int e^{(a+ib)\theta}\, d\theta$ allows us to write

$$\int e^{ax}e^{ibx}\, dx = \int e^{(a+ib)x}\, dx = \frac{1}{a+ib}e^{(a+ib)x} + C = \frac{a-ib}{a^2+b^2}e^{ax}e^{ibx} + C.$$

The left-hand side of this equation can be rewritten as

$$\int e^{ax}e^{ibx}\, dx = \int e^{ax}\cos bx\, dx + i\int e^{ax}\sin bx\, dx.$$

The right-hand side can be rewritten as

$$\frac{a-ib}{a^2+b^2}e^{ax}e^{ibx} = \frac{e^{ax}}{a^2+b^2}(a-ib)(\cos bx + i\sin bx),$$

$$= \frac{e^{ax}}{a^2+b^2}(a\cos bx + b\sin bx + i(a\sin bx - b\cos bx)).$$

Equating real parts gives

$$\int e^{ax}\cos bx\, dx = \frac{e^{ax}}{a^2+b^2}(a\cos bx + b\sin bx) + C,$$

and equating imaginary parts gives

$$\int e^{ax}\sin bx\, dx = \frac{e^{ax}}{a^2+b^2}(a\sin bx - b\cos bx) + C.$$

These two formulas are usually obtained by integrating by parts twice.

Example 11   Using complex exponentials, find a formula for $\int \sin 2x \sin 3x\, dx$.

Solution   Replacing $\sin 2x$ and $\sin 3x$ by their exponential form, we have

$$\int \sin 2x \sin 3x\, dx = \int \frac{\left(e^{2ix} - e^{-2ix}\right)}{2i}\frac{\left(e^{3ix} - e^{-3ix}\right)}{2i}\, dx$$

$$= \frac{1}{(2i)^2}\int \left(e^{5ix} - e^{-ix} - e^{ix} + e^{-5ix}\right)\, dx$$

$$= -\frac{1}{4}\left(\frac{1}{5i}e^{5ix} + \frac{1}{i}e^{-ix} - \frac{1}{i}e^{ix} - \frac{1}{5i}e^{-5ix}\right) + C$$

$$= -\frac{1}{4}\left(\frac{e^{5ix} - e^{-5ix}}{5i} - \frac{e^{ix} - e^{-ix}}{i}\right) + C$$

$$= -\frac{1}{4}\left(\frac{2}{5}\sin 5x - 2\sin x\right) + C$$

$$= -\frac{1}{10}\sin 5x + \frac{1}{2}\sin x + C.$$

This result is usually obtained by using a trigonometric identity.

Exercises for Appendix B

For Problems 1–8, express the given complex number in polar form, $z = re^{i\theta}$.

For Problems 9–18, perform the indicated calculations. Give your answer in Cartesian form, $z = x + iy$.

1. $2i$

2. -5

3. $1+i$

4. $-3-4i$

9. $(2+3i) + (-5-7i)$

10. $(2+3i)(5+7i)$

5. 0

6. $-i$

7. $-1+3i$

8. $5-12i$

11. $(2+3i)^2$

12. $(1+i)^2 + (1+i)$

13. $(0.5 - i)(1 - i/4)$

14. $(2i)^3 - (2i)^2 + 2i - 1$

15. $(e^{i\pi/3})^2$

16. $\sqrt{e^{i\pi/3}}$

17. $(5e^{i7\pi/6})^3$

18. $\sqrt[4]{10e^{i\pi/2}}$

By writing the complex numbers in polar form, $z = re^{i\theta}$, find a value for the quantities in Problems 19–28. Give your answer in Cartesian form, $z = x + iy$.

19. $\sqrt{i}$ **20.** $\sqrt{-i}$ **21.** $\sqrt[3]{i}$

22. $\sqrt{7i}$ **23.** $(1 + i)^{100}$ **24.** $(1 + i)^{2/3}$

25. $(-4 + 4i)^{2/3}$ **26.** $(\sqrt{3} + i)^{1/2}$ **27.** $(\sqrt{3} + i)^{-1/2}$

28. $(\sqrt{5} + 2i)^{\sqrt{2}}$

29. Calculate i^n for $n = -1, -2, -3, -4$. What pattern do you observe? What is the value of i^{-36}? Of i^{-41}?

Solve the simultaneous equations in Problems 30–31 for A_1 and A_2.

30. $A_1 + A_2 = 2$
$(1 - i)A_1 + (1 + i)A_2 = 3$

31. $A_1 + A_2 = 2$
$(i - 1)A_1 + (1 + i)A_2 = 0$

32. **(a)** Calculate a and b if $\dfrac{3 - 4i}{1 + 2i} = a + bi$.
    (b) Check your answer by calculating $(1 + 2i)(a + bi)$.

33. Check that $z = \dfrac{ac + bd}{c^2 + d^2} + \dfrac{bc - ad}{c^2 + d^2}i$ is the quotient $\dfrac{a + bi}{c + di}$ by showing that the product $z \cdot (c + di)$ is $a + bi$.

34. Let $z_1 = -3 - i\sqrt{3}$ and $z_2 = -1 + i\sqrt{3}$.
    (a) Find $z_1 z_2$ and z_1/z_2. Give your answer in Cartesian form, $z = x + iy$.
    (b) Put z_1 and z_2 into polar form, $z = re^{i\theta}$. Find $z_1 z_2$ and z_1/z_2 using the polar form, and verify that you get the same answer as in part (a).

35. Let $z_1 = a_1 + b_1 i$ and $z_2 = a_2 + b_2 i$. Show that $\overline{z_1 z_2} = \bar{z}_1 \bar{z}_2$.

36. If the roots of the equation $x^2 + 2bx + c = 0$ are the complex numbers $p \pm iq$, find expressions for p and q in terms of b and c.

Are the statements in Problems 37–42 true or false? Explain your answer.

37. Every nonnegative real number has a real square root.

38. For any complex number z, the product $z \cdot \bar{z}$ is a real number.

39. The square of any complex number is a real number.

40. If f is a polynomial, and $f(z) = i$, then $f(\bar{z}) = i$.

41. Every nonzero complex number z can be written in the form $z = e^w$, where w is another complex number.

42. If $z = x + iy$, where x and y are positive, then $z^2 = a + ib$ has a and b positive.

For Problems 43–47, use Euler's formula to derive the following relationships. (Note that if a, b, c, d are real numbers, $a + bi = c + di$ means that $a = c$ and $b = d$.)

43. $\sin^2 \theta + \cos^2 \theta = 1$ **44.** $\sin 2\theta = 2\sin\theta\cos\theta$

45. $\cos 2\theta = \cos^2\theta - \sin^2\theta$ **46.** $\dfrac{d}{d\theta}\sin\theta = \cos\theta$

47. $\dfrac{d^2}{d\theta^2}\cos\theta = -\cos\theta$

48. Use complex exponentials to show that
$$\sin(-x) = -\sin x.$$

49. Use complex exponentials to show that
$$\sin(x + y) = \sin x \cos y + \cos x \sin y.$$

50. For real t, show that if $z_1(t) = x_1(t) + iy_1(t)$ and $z_2(t) = x_2(t) + iy_2(t)$ then
$$(z_1 + z_2)' = z_1' + z_2' \quad \text{and} \quad (z_1 z_2)' = z_1' z_2 + z_1 z_2'.$$

C   NEWTON'S METHOD

Many problems in mathematics involve finding the root of an equation. For example, we might have to locate the zeros of a polynomial, or determine the point of intersection of two curves. Here we will see a numerical method for approximating solutions which cannot be calculated exactly.

One such method, bisection, is described in Appendix A. Although it is very simple, the bisection method has two major drawbacks. First, it cannot locate a root where the curve is tangent to, but does not cross, the x-axis. Second, it is relatively slow in the sense that it requires a considerable number of iterations to achieve a desired level of accuracy. Although speed may not be important in solving a single equation, a practical problem may involve solving thousands of equations as a parameter changes. In such a case, any reduction in the number of steps can be important.

Using Newton's Method

We now consider a powerful root-finding method developed by Newton. Suppose we have a function $y = f(x)$. The equation $f(x) = 0$ has a root at $x = r$, as shown in Figure C.14. We begin with an initial estimate, x_0, for this root. (This can be a guess.) We will now obtain a better estimate x_1. To do this, construct the tangent line to the graph of f at the point $x = x_0$, and extend it until it crosses the x-axis, as shown in Figure C.14. The point where it crosses the axis is usually much closer to r, and we use that point as the next estimate, x_1. Having found x_1, we now repeat the process starting with x_1 instead of x_0. We construct a tangent line to the curve at $x = x_1$, extend it until it crosses the x-axis, use that x-intercept as the next approximation, x_2, and so on. The resulting sequence of x-intercepts usually converges rapidly to the root r.

Let's see how this looks algebraically. We know that the slope of the tangent line at the initial estimate x_0 is $f'(x_0)$, and so the equation of the tangent line is

$$y - f(x_0) = f'(x_0)(x - x_0).$$

At the point where this tangent line crosses the x-axis, we have $y = 0$ and $x = x_1$, so that

$$0 - f(x_0) = f'(x_0)(x_1 - x_0).$$

Solving for x_1, we obtain

$$x_1 = x_0 - \frac{f(x_0)}{f'(x_0)}$$

provided that $f'(x_0)$ is not zero. We now repeat this argument and find that the next approximation is

$$x_2 = x_1 - \frac{f(x_1)}{f'(x_1)}.$$

Summarizing, for any $n = 0, 1, 2, \ldots$, we obtain the following result.

Newton's Method to Solve the Equation $f(x) = 0$

Choose x_0 near a solution and compute the sequence $x_1, x_2, x_3 \ldots$ using the rule

$$x_{n+1} = x_n - \frac{f(x_n)}{f'(x_n)}$$

provided that $f'(x_n)$ is not zero. For large n, the solution is well approximated by x_n.

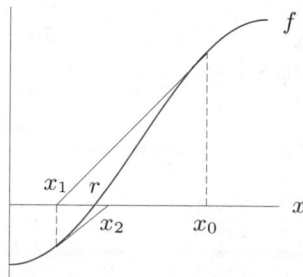

Figure C.14: Newton's method: successive approximations $x_0, x_1, x_2, \ldots$ to the root, r

---

Example 1   Use Newton's method to find the fifth root of 23. (By calculator, this is 1.872171231, correct to nine decimal places.)

Solution   To use Newton's method, we need an equation of the form $f(x) = 0$ having $23^{1/5}$ as a root. Since $23^{1/5}$ is a root of $x^5 = 23$ or $x^5 - 23 = 0$, we take $f(x) = x^5 - 23$. The root of this equation is between 1 and 2 (since $1^5 = 1$ and $2^5 = 32$), so we will choose $x_0 = 2$ as our initial estimate. Now $f'(x) = 5x^4$, so we can set up Newton's method as

$$x_{n+1} = x_n - \frac{x_n^5 - 23}{5x_n^4}.$$

In this case, we can simplify using a common denominator, to obtain

$$x_{n+1} = \frac{4x_n^5 + 23}{5x_n^4}.$$

Therefore, starting with $x_0 = 2$, we find that $x_1 = 1.8875$. This leads to $x_2 = 1.872418193$ and $x_3 = 1.872171296$. These values are in Table C.4. Since we have $f(1.872171231) > 0$ and $f(1.872171230) < 0$, the root lies between 1.872171230 and 1.872171231. Therefore, in just four iterations of Newton's method, we have achieved eight-decimal accuracy.

Table C.4   *Newton's method: $x_0 = 2$*

n	x_n	$f(x_n)$
0	2	9
1	1.8875	0.957130661
2	1.872418193	0.015173919
3	1.872171296	0.000004020
4	1.872171231	0.000000027

Table C.5   *Newton's method: $x_0 = 10$*

n	x_n	n	x_n
0	10	6	2.679422313
1	8.000460000	7	2.232784753
2	6.401419079	8	1.971312452
3	5.123931891	9	1.881654220
4	4.105818871	10	1.872266333
5	3.300841811	11	1.872171240

As a general guideline for Newton's method, once the first correct decimal place is found, each successive iteration approximately doubles the number of correct digits.

What happens if we select a very poor initial estimate? In the preceding example, suppose x_0 were 10 instead of 2. The results are in Table C.5. Notice that even with $x_0 = 10$, the sequence of values moves reasonably quickly toward the solution: We achieve six-decimal place accuracy by the eleventh iteration.

Example 2   Find the first point of intersection of the curves given by $f(x) = \sin x$ and $g(x) = e^{-x}$.

Solution   The graphs in Figure C.15 make it clear that there are an infinite number of points of intersection, all with $x > 0$. In order to find the first one numerically, we consider the function

$$F(x) = f(x) - g(x) = \sin x - e^{-x}$$

whose derivative is $F'(x) = \cos x + e^{-x}$. From the graph, we see that the point we want is fairly close to $x = 0$, so we start with $x_0 = 0$. The values in Table C.6 are approximations to the root. Since $F(0.588532744) > 0$ and $F(0.588532743) < 0$, the root lies between 0.588532743 and 0.588532744. (Remember, your calculator must be set in radians.)

Table C.6   *Successive approximations to root of $\sin x = e^{-x}$*

n	x_n
0	0
1	0.5
2	0.585643817
3	0.588529413
4	0.588532744
5	0.588532744

Figure C.15: Root of $\sin x = e^{-x}$

When Does Newton's Method Fail?

In most practical situations, Newton's method works well. Occasionally, however, the sequence x_0, x_1, x_2, ... fails to converge or fails to converge to the root you want. Sometimes, for example, the sequence can jump from one root to another. This is particularly likely to happen if the magnitude of the derivative $f'(x_n)$ is small for some x_n. In this case, the tangent line is nearly horizontal and so x_{n+1} will be far from x_n. (See Figure C.16.)

If the equation $f(x) = 0$ has *no* root, then the sequence will not converge. In fact, the sequence obtained by applying Newton's method to $f(x) = 1 + x^2$ is one of the best known examples of *chaotic behavior* and has attracted considerable research interest recently. (See Figure C.17.)

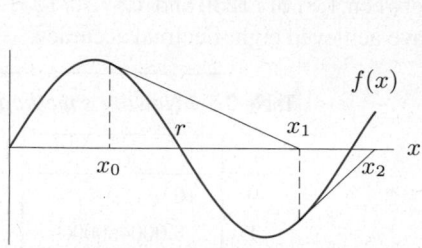

Figure C.16: Problems with Newton's method: Converges to wrong root

Figure C.17: Problems with Newton's method: Chaotic behavior

Exercises for Appendix C

1. Suppose you want to find a solution of the equation

$$x^3 + 3x^2 + 3x - 6 = 0.$$

   Consider $f(x) = x^3 + 3x^2 + 3x - 6$.

   (a) Find $f'(x)$, and use it to show that $f(x)$ increases everywhere.
   (b) How many roots does the original equation have?
   (c) For each root, find an interval which contains it.
   (d) Find each root to two decimal places, using Newton's method.

For Problems 2–4, use Newton's method to find the given quantities to two decimal places:

2. $\sqrt[3]{50}$ 3. $\sqrt[4]{100}$ 4. $10^{-1/3}$

For Problems 5–8, solve each equation and give each answer to two decimal places:

5. $\sin x = 1 - x$ 6. $\cos x = x$

7. $e^{-x} = \ln x$

8. $e^x \cos x = 1$, for $0 < x < \pi$

9. Find, to two decimal places, all solutions of $\ln x = 1/x$.

10. How many zeros do the following functions have? For each zero, find an upper and a lower bound which differ by no more than 0.1.
    (a) $f(x) = x^3 + x - 1$ (b) $f(x) = \sin x - \frac{2}{3}x$
    (c) $f(x) = 10xe^{-x} - 1$

11. Find the largest zero of

$$f(x) = x^3 + x - 1$$

    to six decimal places, using Newton's method. How do you know your approximation is as good as you claim?

12. For any positive number, a, the problem of calculating the square root, $\sqrt{a}$, is often done by applying Newton's method to the function $f(x) = x^2 - a$. Apply the method to obtain an expression for x_{n+1} in terms of x_n. Use this to approximate $\sqrt{a}$ for $a = 2, 10, 1000$, and π, correct to four decimal places, starting at $x_0 = a/2$ in each case.

D   VECTORS IN THE PLANE

Position Vectors

Consider a point (a, b) lying on a curve C in the plane (see Figure D.18). The arrow from the origin to the point (a, b) is called the *position vector* of the point, written $\vec{r}$. As the point moves

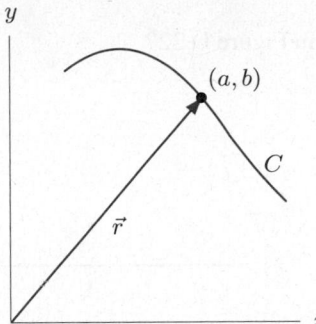

Figure D.18: A position vector $\vec{r}$

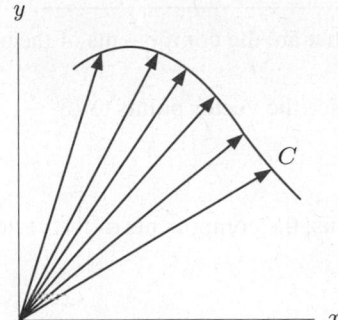

Figure D.19: Position vectors of points on curve C

along the curve, the position vector sweeps across the plane, the arrowhead touching the curve (see Figure D.19).

A position vector is defined by its magnitude (or length) and its direction. Figure D.20 shows two position vectors with the same magnitude but different directions. Figure D.21 shows two position vectors with the same direction but different magnitudes. An object that possesses both magnitude and direction is called a *vector*, and a position vector is one example. Other physical quantities (such as force, electric and magnetic fields, velocity and acceleration) that have both magnitude and direction can be represented by vectors. To distinguish them from vectors, real numbers (which have magnitude but no direction) are sometimes called *scalars*.

Vectors can be written in several ways. One is to write $\langle a, b \rangle$ for the position vector with tip at (a, b)— the use of the angle brackets signifies that we're talking about a vector, not a point. Another notation uses the special vectors $\vec{i}$ and $\vec{j}$ along the axes. The position vector $\vec{i}$ points to $(1, 0)$ and $\vec{j}$ points to $(0, 1)$; both have magnitude 1. The position vector $\vec{r}$ pointing to (a, b) can be written

$$\vec{r} = a\vec{i} + b\vec{j}.$$

The terms $a\vec{i}$ and $b\vec{j}$ are called the *components* of the vector.

Other special vectors include the zero vector, $\vec{0} = 0\vec{i} + 0\vec{j}$. Any vector with magnitude 1 is called a *unit vector*.

Figure D.20: Position vectors with same magnitude, different direction

Figure D.21: Position vectors with same direction, different magnitude

Example 1   What are the components of the position vector in Figure D.22?

Solution   Since the vector points to $(3, -\sqrt{3})$, we have

$$\vec{r} = 3\vec{i} - \sqrt{3}\,\vec{j}.$$

Thus, the components of the vector are $3\vec{i}$ and $-\sqrt{3}\,\vec{j}$.

Figure D.22: Find the components
of this position vector

Magnitude and Direction

If $\vec{r}$ is the position vector $a\vec{i} + b\vec{j}$, then the Pythagorean Theorem gives the magnitude of $\vec{r}$, written $\|\vec{r}\|$. From Figure D.23, we see

$$\|\vec{r}\| = \|a\vec{i} + b\vec{j}\| = \sqrt{a^2 + b^2}.$$

The direction of a position vector $\vec{r} = a\vec{i} + b\vec{j}$ is given by the angle θ between the vector and the positive x-axis, measured counterclockwise. This angle satisfies

$$\tan\theta = \left(\frac{b}{a}\right).$$

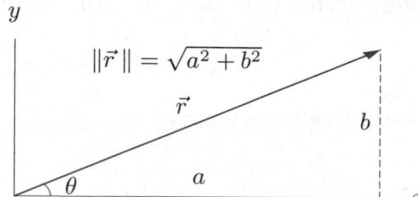

Figure D.23: Magnitude $\|\vec{r}\|$ and
direction of the position vector $\vec{r}$

Figure D.24: Magnitude and direction of
the vector $3\vec{i} - \sqrt{3}\vec{j}$

Example 2   Find the magnitude and direction of the position vector $\vec{r} = 3\vec{i} - \sqrt{3}\vec{j}$ in Figure D.22.

Solution   The magnitude is $\|\vec{r}\| = \sqrt{3^2 + (-\sqrt{3})^2} = \sqrt{12} = 2\sqrt{3}$. For the direction, we find $\arctan(-\sqrt{3}/3) = -\pi/6$. Thus, the angle with the positive x-axis is $\theta = 2\pi - \pi/6 = 11\pi/6$. See Figure D.24.

Describing Motion with Position Vectors

The motion given by the parametric equations

$$x = f(t), y = g(t)$$

can be represented by a changing position vector

$$\vec{r}(t) = f(t)\vec{i} + g(t)\vec{j}.$$

For example, $\vec{r}(t) = \cos t\vec{i} + \sin t\vec{j}$ represents the motion $x = \cos t, y = \sin t$ around the unit circle.

Displacement Vectors

Position vectors are vectors that begin at the origin. More general vectors can start at any point in the plane. We view such an arrow as an instruction to move from one point to another and call it a displacement vector. Figure D.25 shows the same displacement vector starting at two different points; we say they are the same vector since they have the same direction and magnitude. Thus, a position vector $\vec{r}$ is a displacement vector beginning at the origin. The zero vector $\vec{0} = 0\vec{i} + 0\vec{j}$ represents no displacement at all.

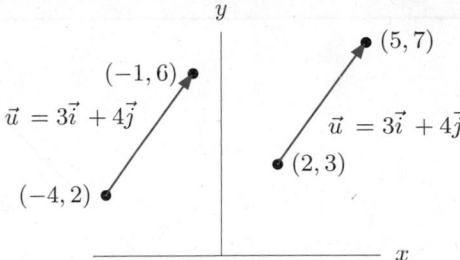

Figure D.25: Two equal displacement vectors:
Same magnitude and direction

Vector Operations

The sum $\vec{u}_1 + \vec{u}_2$ of two displacement vectors is the result of displacing an object first by $\vec{u}_1$ and then by $\vec{u}_2$; see Figure D.26. In terms of components:

If $\vec{u}_1 = a_1\vec{i} + b_1\vec{j}$ and $\vec{u}_2 = a_2\vec{i} + b_2\vec{j}$, then the sum is

$$\vec{u}_1 + \vec{u}_2 = (a_1 + a_2)\vec{i} + (b_1 + b_2)\vec{j}.$$

In other words, to add vectors, add their components separately.

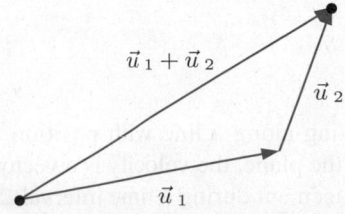

Figure D.26: Vector addition

Example 3   Find the sum of the following pairs of vectors:

(a) $3\vec{i} + 2\vec{j}$ and $-\vec{i} + \vec{j}$ (b) $\vec{i}$ and $3\vec{i} + \vec{j}$ (c) $\vec{i}$ and $\vec{j}$.

Solution   (a) $(3\vec{i} + 2\vec{j}) + (-\vec{i} + \vec{j}) = 2\vec{i} + 3\vec{j}$
(b) $(\vec{i} + 0\vec{j}) + (3\vec{i} + \vec{j}) = 4\vec{i} + \vec{j}$
(c) $(\vec{i} + 0\vec{j}) + (0\vec{i} + \vec{j}) = \vec{i} + \vec{j}$.

Vectors can be multiplied by a number. This operation is called scalar multiplication because it represents changing ("scaling") the magnitude of a vector while keeping its direction the same or reversing it. See Figure D.27.

If c is a real number and $\vec{u} = a\vec{i} + b\vec{j}$, then the *scalar multiple of $\vec{u}$ by c, $c\vec{u}$*, is

$$c\vec{u} = ca\vec{i} + cb\vec{j}.$$

In other words, to multiply a vector by a scalar c, multiply each component by c.

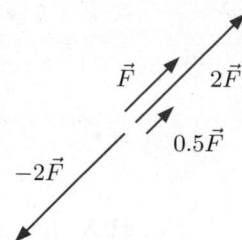

Figure D.27: Scalar multiplication

Example 4   If $\vec{u}_1 = 2\vec{i}$ and $\vec{u}_2 = \vec{i} + 3\vec{j}$, evaluate $6\vec{u}_2$, $(-2)\vec{u}_1$, and $2\vec{u}_1 + 5\vec{u}_2$.

Solution   We have

$$6\vec{u}_2 = 6\vec{i} + 18\vec{j},$$
$$(-2)\vec{u}_1 = -4\vec{i},$$
$$2\vec{u}_1 + 5\vec{u}_2 = (4\vec{i}) + (5\vec{i} + 15\vec{j}) = 9\vec{i} + 15\vec{j}.$$

Velocity Vectors

For a particle moving along a line with position $s(t)$, the instantaneous velocity is ds/dt. For a particle moving in the plane, the velocity is a vector. If the position vector is $\vec{r}(t) = x(t)\vec{i} + y(t)\vec{j}$, the particle's displacement during a time interval Δt is

$$\Delta\vec{r}(t) = \Delta x\vec{i} + \Delta y\vec{j}.$$

Dividing by Δt and letting $\Delta t \to 0$, we get the following result:

> For motion in the plane with position vector $\vec{r}(t) = x(t)\vec{i} + y(t)\vec{j}$, the **velocity vector** is
> $$\vec{v}(t) = \frac{dx}{dt}\vec{i} + \frac{dy}{dt}\vec{j}.$$
> The direction of $\vec{v}(t)$ is tangent to the curve. The magnitude $\|\vec{v}(t)\|$ is the **speed**.

Notice the vector viewpoint agrees with the formulas for speed, v_x and v_y, given in Section 4.8, so we write

$$\vec{v}(t) = v_x\vec{i} + v_y\vec{j}.$$

Recall that for motion on a line, the acceleration is $a = dv/dt = d^2s/dt^2$. For motion in the plane, we have the following:

> If the position vector is $\vec{r}(t) = x(t)\vec{i} + y(t)\vec{j}$, the **acceleration vector** is
> $$\vec{a}(t) = \frac{d^2x}{dt^2}\vec{i} + \frac{d^2y}{dt^2}\vec{j}.$$
> The acceleration measures both change in speed and change in direction of the velocity vector.

Example 5   Let $\vec{r}(t) = \cos(2t)\vec{i} + \sin(2t)\vec{j}$. Find the

    (a) Velocity   (b) Speed   (c) Acceleration

Solution   (a) Differentiating $\vec{r}(t)$ gives the velocity vector

$$\text{Velocity} = \vec{v}(t) = -2\sin(2t)\vec{i} + 2\cos(2t)\vec{j}.$$

(b) Finding the magnitude of $\vec{v}(t)$, we have

$$\text{Speed} = \|\vec{v}(t)\| = \sqrt{(-2\sin(2t))^2 + (2\cos(2t))^2} = 2.$$

Notice that the speed is constant.

(c) Differentiating $\vec{v}(t)$ gives the acceleration vector

$$\text{Acceleration} = \vec{a}(t) = -4\cos(2t)\vec{i} - 4\sin(2t)\vec{j}.$$

Notice that even though the speed is constant, the acceleration vector is not $\vec{0}$, since the velocity vector is changing direction.

Exercises for Appendix D

Exercises

In Exercises 1–3, find the magnitude of the vector and the angle between the vector and the positive x-axis.

1. $3\vec{i}$ **2.** $2\vec{i} + \vec{j}$

3. $-\sqrt{2}\,\vec{i} + \sqrt{2}\,\vec{j}$

In Exercises 4–6, perform the indicated operations on the following vectors

$$\vec{u} = 2\vec{j} \qquad \vec{v} = \vec{i} + 2\vec{j} \qquad \vec{w} = -2\vec{i} + 3\vec{j}.$$

4. $\vec{v} + \vec{w}$ **5.** $2\vec{v} + \vec{w}$ **6.** $\vec{w} + (-2)\vec{u}$

Exercises 7–9 concern the following vectors:

$$3\vec{i} + 4\vec{j}, \quad \vec{i} + \vec{j}, \quad -5\vec{i}, \quad 5\vec{j}, \quad \sqrt{2}\vec{j}, \quad 2\vec{i} + 2\vec{j}, \quad -6\vec{j}$$

7. Which vectors have the same magnitude?

8. Which vectors have the same direction?

9. Which vectors have opposite direction?

10. If k is any real number and $\vec{r} = a\vec{i} + b\vec{j}$ is any vector, show that $\|k\vec{r}\| = |k|\|\vec{r}\|$.

11. Find a unit vector (that is, with magnitude 1) that is

   (a) In the same direction as the vector $-3\vec{i} + 4\vec{j}$.
   (b) In the direction opposite to the vector $-3\vec{i} + 4\vec{j}$.

In Exercises 12–15, express the vector in components.

12. The vector of magnitude 5 making an angle of $90°$ with the positive x-axis.

13. The vector in the same direction as $4\vec{i} - 3\vec{j}$ but with twice the magnitude.

14. The vector with the same magnitude as $4\vec{i} - 3\vec{j}$ and in the opposite direction.

15. The vector from $(3, 2)$ to $(4, 4)$.

In Exercises 16–19, determine whether the vectors are equal.

16. $6\vec{i} - 6\vec{j}$ and the vector from $(6, 6)$ to $(-6, -6)$.

17. The vector from $(7, 9)$ to $(9, 11)$ and the vector from $(8, 10)$ to $(10, 12)$.

18. $-\vec{i} + \vec{j}$ and the vector of length $\sqrt{2}$ making an angle of $\pi/4$ with the positive x-axis.

19. $5\vec{i} - 2\vec{j}$ and the vector from $(1, 12)$ to $(6, 10)$.

In Exercises 20–22, find the velocity vector and the speed, and acceleration.

20. $\vec{r}(t) = t\vec{i} + t^2\vec{j}, \quad t = 1$

21. $\vec{r}(t) = e^t\vec{i} + \ln(1 + t)\vec{j}, \quad t = 0$

22. $\vec{r}(t) = 5\cos t\,\vec{i} + 5\sin t\,\vec{j}, \quad t = \pi/2$

23. A particle is moving along the curve $\vec{r}(t) = \cos t\,\vec{i} + \sin t\,\vec{j}$. Find the particle's position and velocity vectors and its speed when $t = \pi/4$.

E   DETERMINANTS

We introduce the determinant of an array of numbers. Each 2 by 2 array of numbers has another number associated with it, called its determinant, which is given by

$$\begin{vmatrix} a_1 & a_2 \\ b_1 & b_2 \end{vmatrix} = a_1 b_2 - a_2 b_1.$$

For example

$$\begin{vmatrix} 2 & 5 \\ -4 & -6 \end{vmatrix} = 2(-6) - 5(-4) = 8.$$

Each 3 by 3 array of numbers also has a number associated with it, also called a determinant, which is defined in terms of 2 by 2 determinants as follows:

$$\begin{vmatrix} a_1 & a_2 & a_3 \\ b_1 & b_2 & b_3 \\ c_1 & c_2 & c_3 \end{vmatrix} = a_1 \begin{vmatrix} b_2 & b_3 \\ c_2 & c_3 \end{vmatrix} - a_2 \begin{vmatrix} b_1 & b_3 \\ c_1 & c_3 \end{vmatrix} + a_3 \begin{vmatrix} b_1 & b_2 \\ c_1 & c_2 \end{vmatrix}.$$

Notice that the determinant of the 2 by 2 array multiplied by a_i is the determinant of the array found by removing the row and column containing a_i. Also, note the minus sign in the second term. An example is given by

$$\begin{vmatrix} 2 & 1 & -3 \\ 0 & 3 & -1 \\ 4 & 0 & 5 \end{vmatrix} = 2 \begin{vmatrix} 3 & -1 \\ 0 & 5 \end{vmatrix} - 1 \begin{vmatrix} 0 & -1 \\ 4 & 5 \end{vmatrix} + (-3) \begin{vmatrix} 0 & 3 \\ 4 & 0 \end{vmatrix} = 2(15 + 0) - 1(0 - (-4)) + (-3)(0 - 12) = 62.$$

Suppose the vectors $\vec{a}$ and $\vec{b}$ have components $\vec{a} = a_1\vec{i} + a_2\vec{j} + a_3\vec{k}$ and $\vec{b} = b_1\vec{i} + b_2\vec{j} + b_3\vec{k}$. Recall that the cross product $\vec{a} \times \vec{b}$ is given by the expression

$$\vec{a} \times \vec{b} = (a_2b_3 - a_3b_2)\vec{i} + (a_3b_1 - a_1b_3)\vec{j} + (a_1b_2 - a_2b_1)\vec{k}.$$

Notice that if we expand the following determinant, we get the cross product:

$$\begin{vmatrix} \vec{i} & \vec{j} & \vec{k} \\ a_1 & a_2 & a_3 \\ b_1 & b_2 & b_3 \end{vmatrix} = \vec{i}\,(a_2b_3 - a_3b_2) - \vec{j}\,(a_1b_3 - a_3b_1) + \vec{k}\,(a_1b_2 - a_2b_1) = \vec{a} \times \vec{b}.$$

Determinants give a useful way of computing cross products.

READY REFERENCE

This section contains a concise summary of the main definitions, theorems, and ideas presented throughout the book.

READY REFERENCE

A Library of Functions

Linear functions (p. 4) have the form $y = f(x) = b + mx$, where m is the **slope**, or rate of change of y with respect to x (p. 5) and b is the **vertical intercept**, or value of y when x is zero (p. 5). The slope is

$$m = \frac{\text{Rise}}{\text{Run}} = \frac{\Delta y}{\Delta x} = \frac{f(x_2) - f(x_1)}{x_2 - x_1} \quad \text{(p. 5)}.$$

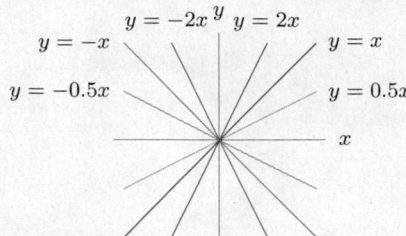

Figure R.1: The family $y = mx$
(with $b = 0$) (p. 6)

Figure R.2: The family $y = b + x$
(with $m = 1$) (p. 6)

Exponential functions have the form $P = P_0 a^t$ (p. 13) or $P = P_0 e^{kt}$ (p. 16), where P_0 is the initial quantity (p. 13), a is the growth (decay) factor per unit time (p. 13), $|k|$ is the continuous growth (decay) rate (pp. 16, 610), and $r = |a - 1|$ is the growth (decay) rate per unit time (p. 14).

Suppose $P_0 > 0$. If $a > 1$ or $k > 0$, we have **exponential growth**; if $0 < a < 1$ or $k < 0$, we have **exponential decay** (p. 15). The **doubling time** (for growth) is the time required for P to double (p. 14). The **half-life** (for decay) is the time required for P to be reduced by a factor of one half (p. 14). The continuous growth rate $k = \ln(1 + r)$ is slightly less than, but very close to, r, provided r is small (p. 611).

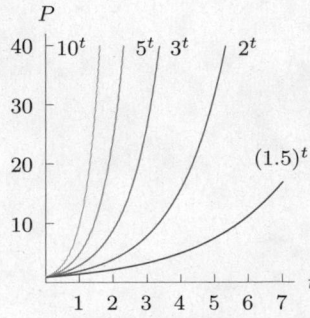

Figure R.3: Exponential growth:
$P = a^t$, for $a > 1$ (p. 15)

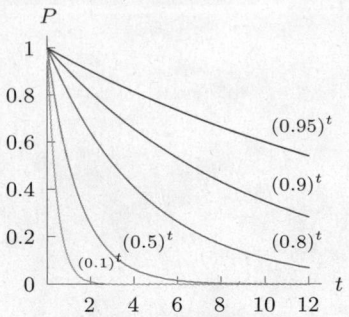

Figure R.4: Exponential decay:
$P = a^t$, for $0 < a < 1$ (p. 15)

Common Logarithm and Natural Logarithm

$\log_{10} x = \log x = $ power of 10 that gives x (p. 29)
$\log_{10} x = c$ means $10^c = x$ (p. 29)
$\ln x = $ power of e that gives x (p. 29)
$\ln x = c$ means $e^c = x$ (p. 29)
$\log x$ and $\ln x$ are not defined if x is negative or 0 (p. 30).

Properties of Logarithms (p. 30)

1. $\log(AB) = \log A + \log B$ 4. $\log(10^x) = x$

2. $\log\left(\frac{A}{B}\right) = \log A - \log B$ 5. $10^{\log x} = x$

3. $\log(A^p) = p \log A$ 6. $\log 1 = 0$

The natural logarithm satisfies properties 1, 2, and 3, and $\ln e^x = x$, $e^{\ln x} = x$, $\ln 1 = 0$ (p. 30).

Trigonometric Functions The sine and cosine are defined in Figure R.5 (see also p. 37). The tangent is $\tan t = \frac{\sin t}{\cos t} = $ slope of the line through the origin $(0, 0)$ and P if $\cos t \neq 0$ (p. 40). The period of sin and cos is 2π (p. 37), the period of tan is π (p. 40).

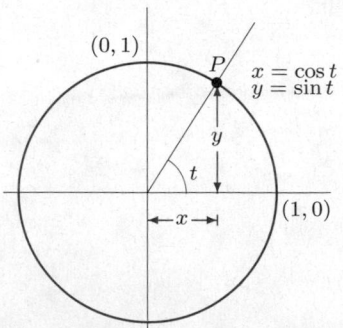

Figure R.5: The definitions of $\sin t$
and $\cos t$ (p. 37)

A **sinusoidal function** (p. 38) has the form
$y = C + A\sin(B(t + h))$ or $y = C + A\cos(B(t + h))$.

The **amplitude** is $|A|$, (p. 38), and the **period** is $2\pi/|B|$ (p. 38).

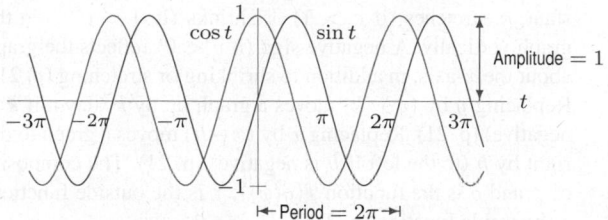

Figure R.6: Graphs of $\cos t$ and $\sin t$ (p. 37)

Trigonometric Identities

$$\sin^2 x + \cos^2 x = 1$$
$$\sin(2x) = 2\sin x \cos x$$
$$\cos(2x) = \cos^2 x - \sin^2 x = 2\cos^2 x - 1 = 1 - 2\sin^2 x$$
$$\cos(a+b) = \cos a \cos b - \sin a \sin b$$
$$\sin(a+b) = \sin a \cos b + \cos a \sin b$$

Inverse Trigonometric Functions: $\arcsin y = x$ means $\sin x = y$ with $-(\pi/2) \le x \le (\pi/2)$ (p. 41), $\arccos y = x$ means $\cos x = y$ with $0 \le x \le \pi$ (Problem 55, p. 44), $\arctan y = x$ means $\tan x = y$ with $-(\pi/2) < x < (\pi/2)$ (p. 41). The domain of arcsin and arccos is $[-1, 1]$ (p. 41), the domain of arctan is all numbers (p. 41). **Power Functions** have the form $f(x) = kx^p$ (p. 45). Graphs for positive powers:

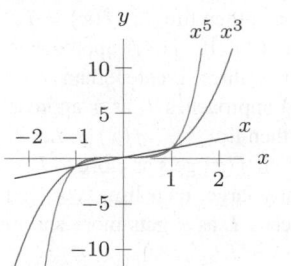

Figure R.7: Odd integer powers of x: "Seat" shaped for $k > 1$ (p. 46)

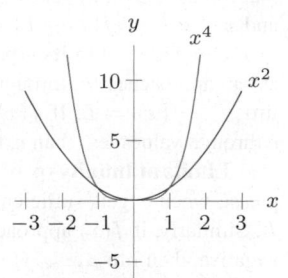

Figure R.8: Even integer powers of x: $\bigcup$-shaped (p. 46)

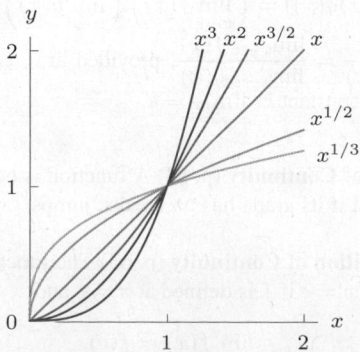

Figure R.9: Comparison of some fractional powers of x

Graphs for zero and negative powers:

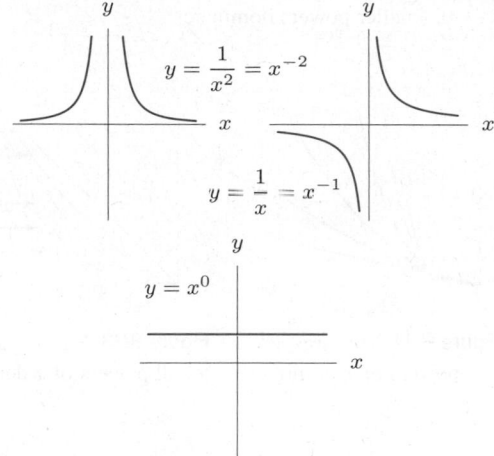

Figure R.10: Comparison of zero and negative powers of x

Polynomials have the form

$$f(x) = a_n x^n + a_{n-1}x^{n-1} + \cdots + a_1 x + a_0, \ a_n \ne 0 \ (\text{p. 46}).$$

The **degree** is n (p. 47) and the **leading coefficient** is a_n (p. 47).

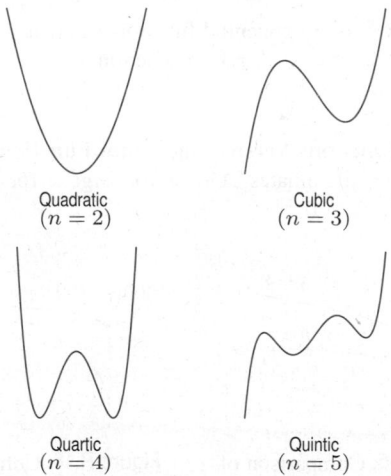

Figure R.11: Graphs of typical polynomials of degree n (p. 47)

Rational Functions have the form $f(x) = \dfrac{p(x)}{q(x)}$, where p and q are polynomials (p. 49). There is usually a vertical asymptote at $x = a$ if $q(a) = 0$ and a horizontal asymptote at $y = L$ if $\lim_{x\to\infty} f(x) = L$ or $\lim_{x\to-\infty} f(x) = L$ (p. 49).

Hyperbolic Functions:

$$\cosh x = \frac{e^x + e^{-x}}{2} \quad \sinh x = \frac{e^x - e^{-x}}{2} \quad (\text{p. 165}).$$

Relative Growth Rates of Functions

Power Functions As $x \to \infty$, higher powers of x dominate, as $x \to 0$, smaller powers dominate.

Figure R.12: For large x:
Large powers of x dominate

Figure R.13: For $0 \leq x \leq 1$:
Small powers of x dominate

Power Functions Versus Exponential Functions Every exponential growth function eventually dominates every power function (p. 46).

Figure R.14: Exponential function eventually dominates power function

Power Functions Versus Logarithm Functions The power function x^p dominates $A \log x$ for large x for all values of $p > 0$ and $A > 0$.

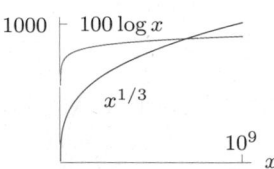

Figure R.15: Comparison of $x^{1/3}$ and $\log x$

Figure R.16: Comparison of $x^{1/3}$ and $100 \log x$

Numerical comparisons of growth rates:

Table R.1 *Comparison of* $x^{0.001}$ *and* $1000 \log x$

x	$x^{0.001}$	$1000 \log x$
10^{5000}	10^5	$5 \cdot 10^6$
10^{6000}	10^6	$6 \cdot 10^6$
10^{7000}	10^7	$7 \cdot 10^6$

Table R.2 *Comparison of* x^{100} *and* 1.01^x

x	x^{100}	1.01^x
10^4	10^{400}	$1.6 \cdot 10^{43}$
10^5	10^{500}	$1.4 \cdot 10^{432}$
10^6	10^{600}	$2.4 \cdot 10^{4321}$

Operations on Functions

Shifts, Stretches, and Composition Multiplying by a constant, c, stretches (if $c > 1$) or shrinks (if $0 < c < 1$) the graph vertically. A negative sign (if $c < 0$) reflects the graph about the x-axis, in addition to shrinking or stretching (p. 21). Replacing y by $(y - k)$ moves a graph up by k (down if k is negative) (p. 21). Replacing x by $(x - h)$ moves a graph to the right by h (to the left if h is negative) (p. 21). The composite of f and g is the function $f(g(x))$; f is the outside function, g the inside function (p. 21).

Symmetry We say f is an **even** function if $f(-x) = f(x)$ (p. 22) and f is an **odd** function if $f(-x) = -f(x)$ (p. 22).

Inverse Functions A function f has an inverse if (and only if) its graph intersects any horizontal line at most once (p. 24). If f has an inverse, it is written f^{-1}, and $f^{-1}(x) = y$ means $f(y) = x$ (p. 24). Provided the x and y scales are equal, the graph of f^{-1} is the reflection of the graph of f about the line $y = x$ (p. 25).

Proportionality We say y is proportional to x if $y = kx$ for k a nonzero constant. We say y is inversely proportional to x if $y = k(1/x)$ (p. 6).

Limits and Continuity

Idea of Limit (p. 58) If there is a number L such that $f(x)$ is as close to L as we please whenever x is sufficiently close to c (but $x \neq c$), then $\lim_{x \to c} f(x) = L$.

Definition of Limit (p. 59) If there is a number L such that for any $\epsilon > 0$, there exists a $\delta > 0$ such that if $|x - c| < \delta$ and $x \neq c$, then $|f(x) - L| < \epsilon$, then $\lim_{x \to c} f(x) = L$.

One-sided Limits (p. 61) If $f(x)$ approaches L as x approaches c through values greater than c, then $\lim_{x \to c^+} f(x) = L$. If $f(x)$ approaches L as x approaches c through values less than c, then $\lim_{x \to c^-} f(x) = L$.

Limits at Infinity (p. 63) If $f(x)$ gets as close to L as we please when x gets sufficiently large, then $\lim_{x \to \infty} f(x) = L$. Similarly, if $f(x)$ approaches L as x gets more and more negative, then $\lim_{x \to -\infty} f(x) = L$.

Theorem: Properties of Limits (p. 60) Assuming all the limits on the right-hand side exist:

1. If b is a constant, then $\lim\limits_{x \to c} (bf(x)) = b \left(\lim\limits_{x \to c} f(x) \right)$.
2. $\lim\limits_{x \to c} (f(x) + g(x)) = \lim\limits_{x \to c} f(x) + \lim\limits_{x \to c} g(x)$.
3. $\lim\limits_{x \to c} (f(x)g(x)) = \left(\lim\limits_{x \to c} f(x) \right) \left(\lim\limits_{x \to c} g(x) \right)$.
4. $\lim\limits_{x \to c} \dfrac{f(x)}{g(x)} = \dfrac{\lim_{x \to c} f(x)}{\lim_{x \to c} g(x)}$, provided $\lim_{x \to c} g(x) \neq 0$.
5. For any constant k, $\lim\limits_{x \to c} k = k$.
6. $\lim\limits_{x \to c} x = c$.

Idea of Continuity (p. 53) A function is **continuous on an interval** if its graph has no breaks, jumps, or holes in that interval.

Definition of Continuity (p. 63) The function f is **continuous** at $x = c$ if f is defined at $x = c$ and

$$\lim_{x \to c} f(x) = f(c).$$

The function is **continuous on an interval** if it is continuous at every point in the interval.

Theorem: Continuity of Sums, Products, Quotients (p. 64) Suppose that f and g are continuous on an interval and that b is a constant. Then, on that same interval, the following functions are also continuous: $bf(x)$, $f(x) + g(x)$, $f(x)g(x)$. Further, $f(x)/g(x)$ is continuous provided $g(x) \neq 0$ on the interval.

Theorem: Continuity of Composite Functions (p. 64) Suppose f and g are continuous and $f(g(x))$ is defined on an interval. Then on that interval $f(g(x))$ is continuous.

Intermediate Value Theorem (p. 55) Suppose f is continuous on a closed interval $[a, b]$. If k is any number between $f(a)$ and $f(b)$, then there is at least one number c in $[a, b]$ such that $f(c) = k$.

The Extreme Value Theorem (p. 196) If f is continuous on the interval $[a, b]$, then f has a global maximum and a global minimum on that interval.

The Derivative

The slope of the secant line of $f(x)$ over an interval $[a, b]$ gives:

$$\text{\textbf{Average rate of change}} \atop \text{\textbf{of} } f \text{ \textbf{over} } [a, b] = \frac{f(b) - f(a)}{b - a} \quad \text{(p. 83)}.$$

Figure R.17: Visualizing the average rate of change of f (p. 84)

The **derivative** of f at a is the slope of the line tangent to the graph of f at the point $(a, f(a))$:

$$f'(a) = \lim_{h \to 0} \frac{f(a + h) - f(a)}{h},$$

and gives the **instantaneous rate of change** of f at a (p. 83). The function f is **differentiable** at a if this limit exists (p. 83). The **second derivative** of f, denoted f'', is the derivative of f' (p. 104).

Figure R.18: Visualizing the instantaneous rate of change of f (p. 84)

The **units** of $f'(x)$ are: $\dfrac{\text{Units of } f(x)}{\text{Units of } x}$ (p. 99). If $f' > 0$ on an interval, then f is **increasing** over that interval (p. 92). If $f' < 0$ on an interval, then f is **decreasing** over that interval (p. 92). If $f'' > 0$ on an interval, then f is **concave up** over that interval (p. 104). If $f'' < 0$ on an interval, then f is **concave down** over that interval (p. 104).

The **tangent line** at $(a, f(a))$ is the graph of $y = f(a) + f'(a)(x - a)$ (p. 169). The **tangent line approximation** says that for values of x near a, $f(x) \approx f(a) + f'(a)(x - a)$. The expression $f(a) + f'(a)(x - a)$ is called the **local linearization** of f near $x = a$ (p. 169).

Derivatives of elementary functions

$$\frac{d}{dx}(x^n) = nx^{n-1} \quad \text{(p. 126)} \qquad \frac{d}{dx}(e^x) = e^x \quad \text{(p. 133)}$$

$$\frac{d}{dx}(a^x) = (\ln a)a^x \quad \text{(p. 134)} \qquad \frac{d}{dx}(\ln x) = \frac{1}{x} \quad \text{(p. 156)}$$

$$\frac{d}{dx}(\sin x) = \cos x \qquad \frac{d}{dx}(\cos x) = -\sin x \quad \text{(p. 151)}$$

$$\frac{d}{dx}(\arctan x) = \frac{1}{1 + x^2} \quad \text{(p. 157)}$$

$$\frac{d}{dx}(\arcsin x) = \frac{1}{\sqrt{1 - x^2}} \quad \text{(p. 158)}$$

Derivatives of sums, differences, and constant multiples

$$\frac{d}{dx}[f(x) \pm g(x)] = f'(x) \pm g'(x) \quad \text{(p. 125)}$$

$$\frac{d}{dx}[cf(x)] = cf'(x) \quad \text{(p. 124)}$$

Product and quotient rules

$$(fg)' = f'g + fg' \quad \text{(p. 137)}$$

$$\left(\frac{f}{g}\right)' = \frac{f'g - fg'}{g^2} \quad \text{(p. 138)}$$

Chain rule

$$\frac{d}{dx}f(g(x)) = f'(g(x)) \cdot g'(x) \quad \text{(p. 143)}$$

Derivative of an inverse function (p. 158). If f has a differentiable inverse, f^{-1}, then

$$\frac{d}{dx}(f^{-1}(x)) = \frac{1}{f'(f^{-1}(x))}.$$

Implicit differentiation (p. 162) If y is implicitly defined as a function of x by an equation, then, to find dy/dx, differentiate the equation (remembering to apply the chain rule).

Applications of the Derivative

A function f has a **local maximum** at p if $f(p)$ is greater than or equal to the values of f at points near p, and a **local minimum** at p if $f(p)$ is less than or equal to the values of f at points near p (p. 187). It has a **global maximum** at p if $f(p)$ is greater than or equal to the value of f at any point in the interval, and a **global minimum** at p if $f(p)$ is less than or equal to the value of f at any point in the interval (p. 196).

A **critical point** of a function $f(x)$ is a point p in the domain of f where $f'(p) = 0$ or $f'(p)$ is undefined (p. 187).

Theorem: Local maxima and minima which do not occur at endpoints of the domain occur at critical points (pp. 188, 192).

The First-Derivative Test for Local Maxima and Minima (p. 188):

- If f' changes from negative to positive at p, then f has a local minimum at p.

- If f' changes from positive to negative at p, then f has a local maximum at p.

The Second-Derivative Test for Local Maxima and Minima (p. 189):

- If $f'(p) = 0$ and $f''(p) > 0$ then f has a local minimum at p.

- If $f'(p) = 0$ and $f''(p) < 0$ then f has a local maximum at p.

- If $f'(p) = 0$ and $f''(p) = 0$ then   the test tells us nothing.

To find the **global maximum and minimum** of a function on an interval we compare values of f at all critical points in the interval and at the endpoints of the interval (or $\lim_{x \to \pm\infty} f(x)$ if the interval is unbounded) (p. 197).

An **inflection point** of f is a point at which the graph of f changes concavity (p. 190); f'' is zero or undefined at an inflection point (p. 190).

L'Hopital's rule (p. 243) If f and g are continuous, $f(a) = g(a) = 0$, and $g'(a) \neq 0$, then

$$\lim_{x \to a} \frac{f(x)}{g(x)} = \frac{f'(a)}{g'(a)}.$$

Parametric equations (p. 249) If a curve is given by the parametric equations $x = f(t)$, $y = g(t)$, the slope of the curve as a function of t is $dy/dx = (dy/dt)/(dx/dt)$.

Theorems About Derivatives

Theorem: Local Extrema and Critical Points (pp. 188, 192) Suppose f is defined on an interval and has a local maximum or minimum at the point $x = a$, which is not an endpoint of the interval. If f is differentiable at $x = a$, then $f'(a) = 0$.

The Mean Value Theorem (p. 175) If f is continuous on $[a, b]$ and differentiable on (a, b), then there exists a number c, with $a < c < b$, such that

$$f'(c) = \frac{f(b) - f(a)}{b - a}.$$

The Increasing Function Theorem (p. 176) Suppose that f is continuous on $[a, b]$ and differentiable on (a, b).

- If $f'(x) > 0$ on (a, b), then f is increasing on $[a, b]$.

- If $f'(x) \geq 0$ on (a, b), then f is nondecreasing on $[a, b]$.

The Constant Function Theorem (p. 177) Suppose that f is continuous on $[a, b]$ and differentiable on (a, b). If $f'(x) = 0$ on (a, b), then f is constant on $[a, b]$.

The Racetrack Principle (p. 177) Suppose that g and h are continuous on $[a, b]$ and differentiable on (a, b), and that $g'(x) \leq h'(x)$ for $a < x < b$.

- If $g(a) = h(a)$, then $g(x) \leq h(x)$ for $a \leq x \leq b$.

- If $g(b) = h(b)$, then $g(x) \geq h(x)$ for $a \leq x \leq b$.

Theorem: Differentiability and Local Linearity (p. 170) Suppose f is differentiable at $x = a$ and $E(x)$ is the error in the tangent line approximation, that is: $E(x) = f(x) - f(a) - f'(a)(x - a)$. Then $\lim_{x \to a} \dfrac{E(x)}{x - a} = 0$.

Theorem: A Differentiable Function Is Continuous (p. 113) If $f(x)$ is differentiable at a point $x = a$, then $f(x)$ is continuous at $x = a$.

The Definite Integral

The **definite integral of f from** a **to** b (p. 282), denoted $\int_a^b f(x)\, dx$, is the limit of the left and the right sums as the width of the rectangles is shrunk to 0, where

Left-hand sum $= \displaystyle\sum_{i=0}^{n-1} f(x_i)\Delta x$ (p. 276)

$$= f(x_0)\Delta x + f(x_1)\Delta x + \cdots + f(x_{n-1})\Delta x$$

Right-hand sum $= \displaystyle\sum_{i=1}^{n} f(x_i)\Delta x$ (p. 281)

$$= f(x_1)\Delta x + f(x_2)\Delta x + \cdots + f(x_n)\Delta x$$

Figure R.19: Left-hand sum (p. 276)

Figure R.20: Right-hand sum (p. 276)

If f is nonnegative, $\int_a^b f(x)\,dx$ represents the area under the curve between $x = a$ and $x = b$ (p. 283). If f has any sign, $\int_a^b f(x)\,dx$ is the sum of the areas above the x-axis, counted positively, and the areas below the x-axis, counted negatively (p. 284). If $F'(t)$ is the rate of change of some quantity $F(t)$, then $\int_a^b F'(t)\,dt$ is the **total change** in $F(t)$ between $t = a$ and $t = b$ (p. 291). The **average value** of f on the interval $[a, b]$ is given by $\dfrac{1}{b-a}\displaystyle\int_a^b f(x)\,dx$ (p. 304).

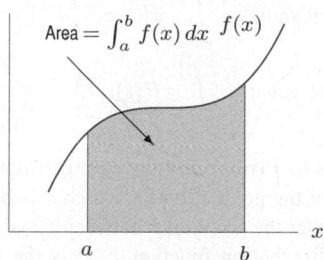

Figure R.21: The definite integral $\int_a^b f(x)\,dx$ (p. 283)

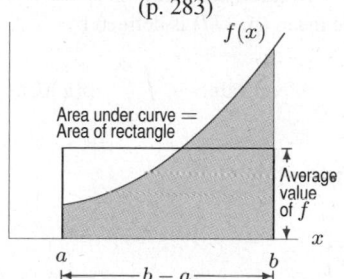

Figure R.22: Area and average value (p. 305)

The **units** of $\int_a^b f(x)\,dx$ are Units of $f(x)$ × Units of x (p. 289).

The Fundamental Theorem of Calculus If f is continuous on $[a, b]$ and $f(x) = F'(x)$, then

$$\int_a^b f(x)\,dx = F(b) - F(a) \quad \text{(p. 290)}.$$

Properties of Definite Integrals (pp. 298, 300)
If a, b, and c are any numbers and f, g are continuous functions, then

$$\int_b^a f(x)\,dx = -\int_a^b f(x)\,dx$$

$$\int_a^b (f(x) \pm g(x))\,dx = \int_a^b f(x)\,dx \pm \int_a^b g(x)\,dx$$

$$\int_a^c f(x)\,dx + \int_c^b f(x)\,dx = \int_a^b f(x)\,dx$$

$$\int_a^b cf(x)\,dx = c\int_a^b f(x)\,dx$$

Antiderivatives

An **antiderivative** of a function $f(x)$ is a function $F(x)$ such that $F'(x) = f(x)$ (p. 320). There are infinitely many antiderivatives of f since $F(x) + C$ is an antiderivative of f for any constant C, provided $F'(x) = f(x)$ (p. 320). The **indefinite integral** of f is the family of antiderivatives $\int f(x)\,dx = F(x) + C$ (p. 326).

Construction Theorem (Second Fundamental Theorem of Calculus) If f is a continuous function on an interval and a is any number in that interval, then $F(x) = \int_a^x f(t)\,dt$ is an antiderivative of f (p. 340).

Properties of Indefinite Integrals (p. 329)

$$\int (f(x) \pm g(x))\,dx = \int f(x)\,dx \pm \int g(x)\,dx$$

$$\int cf(x)\,dx = c\int f(x)\,dx$$

Some antiderivatives:

$$\int k\,dx = kx + C \quad \text{(p. 327)}$$

$$\int x^n\,dx = \frac{x^{n+1}}{n+1} + C, \quad n \neq -1 \quad \text{(p. 327)}$$

$$\int \frac{1}{x}\,dx = \ln|x| + C \quad \text{(p. 328)}$$

$$\int e^x\,dx = e^x + C \quad \text{(p. 328)}$$

$$\int \cos x\,dx = \sin x + C \quad \text{(p. 328)}$$

$$\int \sin x\,dx = -\cos x + C \quad \text{(p. 328)}$$

$$\int \frac{dx}{1+x^2} = \arctan x + C \quad \text{(p. 382)}$$

$$\int \frac{dx}{\sqrt{1-x^2}} = \arcsin x + C \quad \text{(p. 380)}$$

Substitution (p. 354) For integrals of the form $\int f(g(x))g'(x)\,dx$, let $w = g(x)$. Choose w, find dw/dx and substitute for x and dx. Convert limits of integration for definite integrals.

Integration by Parts (p. 364) Used mainly for products; also for integrating $\ln x$, $\arctan x$, $\arcsin x$.

$$\int uv'\,dx = uv - \int u'v\,dx$$

Partial Fractions (p. 376) To integrate a rational function, $P(x)/Q(x)$, express as a sum of a polynomial and terms of the form $A/(x-c)^n$ and $(Ax+B)/q(x)$, where $q(x)$ is an unfactorable quadratic.

Trigonometric Substitutions (p. 380) To simplify $\sqrt{x^2-a^2}$, try $x = a\sin\theta$ (p. 380). To simplify a^2+x^2 or $\sqrt{a^2+x^2}$, try $x = a\tan\theta$ (p. 382).

Numerical Approximations for Definite Integrals (p. 387)
Riemann sums (left, right, midpoint) (p. 387), trapezoid rule (p. 388), Simpson's rule (p. 391)

Approximation Errors (p. 389)
f concave up: midpoint underestimates, trapezoid overestimates (p. 389)
f concave down: trapezoid underestimates, midpoint overestimates (p. 389)

Evaluating Improper Integrals (p. 395)

- Infinite limit of integration: $\int_a^\infty f(x)\,dx = \lim_{b\to\infty}\int_a^b f(x)\,dx$ (p. 395)

- For $a < b$, if integrand is unbounded at $x = b$, then: $\int_a^b f(x)\,dx = \lim_{c\to b^-}\int_a^c f(x)\,dx$ (p. 398)

Testing Improper Integrals for Convergence by Comparison (p. 404):

- If $0 \le f(x) \le g(x)$ and $\int_a^\infty g(x)\,dx$ converges, then $\int_a^\infty f(x)\,dx$ converges

- If $0 \le g(x) \le f(x)$ and $\int_a^\infty g(x)\,dx$ diverges, then $\int_a^\infty f(x)\,dx$ diverges

Applications of Integration

Total quantities can be approximated by slicing them into small pieces and summing the pieces. The limit of this sum is a definite integral which gives the exact total quantity.

Applications to Geometry
To calculate the volume of a solid, slice the volume into pieces whose volumes you can estimate (pp. 414, 422). Use this method to calculate volumes of revolution (p. 422) and volumes of solids with known cross sectional area (p. 425). Curve $f(x)$ from $x = a$ to $x = b$ has

$$\text{Arc length} = \int_a^b \sqrt{1 + (f'(x))^2}\,dx \quad \text{(p. 426).}$$

Mass and Center of Mass from Density, δ

$$\text{Total mass} = \int_a^b \delta(x)\,dx \quad \text{(p. 440)}$$

$$\text{Center of mass} = \frac{\int_a^b x\delta(x)\,dx}{\int_a^b \delta(x)\,dx} \quad \text{(p. 444)}$$

To find the center of mass of two- and three-dimensional objects, use the formula separately on each coordinate (p. 445).

Applications to Physics

$$\text{Work done} = \text{Force} \times \text{Distance} \quad \text{(p. 449)}$$

$$\text{Pressure} = \text{Density} \times g \times \text{Depth} \quad \text{(p. 454)}$$

$$\text{Force} = \text{Pressure} \times \text{Area} \quad \text{(p. 454)}$$

Applications to Economics
Present and future value of income stream, $P(t)$ (p. 459); consumer and producer surplus (p. 462).

$$\text{Present value} = \int_0^M P(t)e^{-rt}\,dt \quad \text{(p. 459)}$$

$$\text{Future value} = \int_0^M P(t)e^{r(M-t)}\,dt \quad \text{(p. 459)}$$

Applications to Probability
Given a density function $p(x)$, the fraction of the population for which x is between a and b is the area under the graph of p between a and b (p. 469). The cumulative distribution function $P(t)$ is the fraction having values of x below t (p. 469). The median is the value T such that half the population has values of x less than or equal to T (p. 475). The mean (p. 477) is defined by

$$\text{Mean value} = \int_{-\infty}^\infty x p(x)\,dx.$$

Polar Coordinates

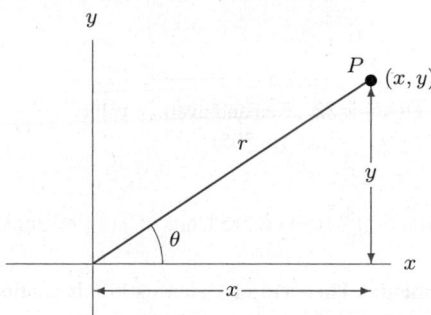

Figure R.23: Cartesian and polar coordinates for the point P

The **polar coordinates** (p. 432) of a point are related to its Cartesian coordinates by

- $x = r\cos\theta$ and $y = r\sin\theta$
- $r = \sqrt{x^2+y^2}$ and $\tan\theta = \dfrac{y}{x}$, $x \ne 0$

For a constant a, the equation $r = a$ gives a circle of radius a, and the equation $\theta = a$ gives a ray from the origin making an angle of θ with the positive x-axis. The equation $r = \theta$ gives an **Archimedean spiral** (p. 433).

Area in Polar Coordinates (p. 436)
For a curve $r = f(\theta)$, with $\alpha \le \theta \le \beta$, which does not cross itself,

$$\text{Area of region enclosed} = \frac{1}{2}\int_\alpha^\beta f(\theta)^2\,d\theta.$$

Slope and Arclength in Polar Coordinates (p. 437)

For a curve $r = f(\theta)$, we can express x and y in terms of θ as a parameter, giving

$$x = r\cos\theta = f(\theta)\cos\theta \quad \text{and} \quad y = r\sin\theta = f(\theta)\sin\theta.$$

Then

$$\text{Slope} = \frac{dy}{dx} = \frac{dy/d\theta}{dx/d\theta}$$

and

$$\text{Arc length} = \int_\alpha^\beta \sqrt{\left(\frac{dx}{d\theta}\right)^2 + \left(\frac{dy}{d\theta}\right)^2}\, d\theta.$$

Alternatively (p. 439),

$$\text{Arc length} = \int_\alpha^\beta \sqrt{(f'(\theta))^2 + (f(\theta))^2}\, d\theta.$$

Sequences and Series

A **sequence** $s_1, s_2, s_3, \ldots, s_n, \ldots$ has a **limit** L, written $\lim_{n\to\infty} s_n = L$, if we can make s_n as close to L as we please by choosing a sufficiently large n. The sequence **converges** if a limit exists, **diverges** if no limit exists (see p. 494). Limits of sequences satisfy the same properties as limits of functions stated in Theorem 1.2 (p. 60) and

$$\lim_{n\to\infty} x^n = 0 \quad \text{if } |x| < 1 \qquad \lim_{n\to\infty} 1/n = 0 \quad \text{(p. 494)}$$

A sequence s_n is **bounded** if there are constants K and M such that $K \leq s_n \leq M$ for all n (p. 494). A convergent sequence is bounded. A sequence is monotone if it is either increasing, that is $s_n < s_{n+1}$ for all n, or decreasing, that is $s_n > s_{n+1}$ for all n (p. 495).

Theorem: Convergence of a Monotone, Bounded Sequence (p. 495): If a sequence s_n is bounded and monotone, it converges.

A **series** is an infinite sum $\sum a_n = a_1 + a_2 + \cdots$. The nth **partial sum** is $S_n = a_1 + a_2 + \cdots + a_n$ (p. 505). If $S = \lim_{n\to\infty} S_n$ exists, then the series $\sum a_n$ **converges**, and its sum is S (p. 505). If a series does not converge, we say that it **diverges** (p. 505). The sum of a **finite geometric series** is (p. 500):

$$a + ax + ax^2 + \cdots + ax^{n-1} = \frac{a(1-x^n)}{1-x}, \qquad x \neq 1.$$

The sum of an **infinite geometric series** is (p. 501):

$$a + ax + ax^2 + \cdots + ax^n + \cdots = \frac{a}{1-x}, \qquad |x| < 1.$$

The p-**series** $\sum 1/n^p$ converges if $p > 1$ and diverges if $p \leq 1$ (p. 509). The **harmonic series** $\sum 1/n$ diverges (p. 507), the **alternating harmonic series** $\sum (-1)^{n-1}(1/n)$ converges (p. 517). An **alternating series** can be absolutely or conditionally convergent (p. 518).

Convergence Tests

Theorem: Convergence Properties of Series (p. 507)

1. If $\sum a_n$ and $\sum b_n$ converge and if k is a constant, then
   - $\sum(a_n + b_n)$ converges to $\sum a_n + \sum b_n$.
   - $\sum ka_n$ converges to $k\sum a_n$.

2. Changing a finite number of terms in a series does not change whether or not it converges, although it may change the value of its sum if it does converge.

3. If $\lim_{n\to\infty} a_n \neq 0$ or $\lim_{n\to\infty} a_n$ does not exist, then $\sum a_n$ diverges.

4. If $\sum a_n$ diverges, then $\sum ka_n$ diverges if $k \neq 0$.

Theorem: Integral Test (p. 509) Suppose $c \geq 0$ and $f(x)$ is a decreasing positive function, defined for all $x \geq c$, with $a_n = f(n)$ for all n.

- If $\displaystyle\int_c^\infty f(x)\, dx$ converges, then $\sum a_n$ converges.

- If $\displaystyle\int_c^\infty f(x)\, dx$ diverges, then $\sum a_n$ diverges.

Theorem: Comparison Test (p. 512) Suppose $0 \leq a_n \leq b_n$ for all n.

- If $\sum b_n$ converges, then $\sum a_n$ converges.
- If $\sum a_n$ diverges, then $\sum b_n$ diverges.

Theorem: Limit Comparison Test (p. 514) Suppose $a_n > 0$ and $b_n > 0$ for all n. If

$$\lim_{n\to\infty} \frac{a_n}{b_n} = c \qquad \text{where } c > 0,$$

then the two series $\sum a_n$ and $\sum b_n$ either both converge or both diverge.

Theorem: Convergence of Absolute Values Implies Convergence (p. 515): If $\sum |a_n|$ converges, then so does $\sum a_n$.

We say $\sum a_n$ is **absolutely convergent** if $\sum a_n$ and $\sum |a_n|$ both converge and **conditionally convergent** if $\sum a_n$ converges but $\sum |a_n|$ diverges (p. 518).

Theorem: The Ratio Test (p. 515) For a series $\sum a_n$, suppose the sequence of ratios $|a_{n+1}|/|a_n|$ has a limit:

$$\lim_{n\to\infty} \frac{|a_{n+1}|}{|a_n|} = L.$$

- If $L < 1$, then $\sum a_n$ converges.
- If $L > 1$, or if L is infinite, then $\sum a_n$ diverges.
- If $L = 1$, the test does not tell us anything about the convergence of $\sum a_n$.

Theorem: Alternating Series Test (p. 517) A series of the form

$$\sum_{n=1}^\infty (-1)^{n-1} a_n = a_1 - a_2 + a_3 - a_4 + \cdots + (-1)^{n-1} a_n + \cdots$$

converges if $0 < a_{n+1} < a_n$ for all n and $\lim_{n\to\infty} a_n = 0$.

Theorem: Error Bounds for Alternating Series (p. 518) Let $S_n = \sum_{i=1}^{n} (-1)^{i-1} a_i$ be the nth partial sum of an alternating series and let $S = \lim_{n \to \infty} S_n$. Suppose that $0 < a_{n+1} < a_n$ for all n and $\lim_{n \to \infty} a_n = 0$. Then $|S - S_n| < a_{n+1}$.

Power Series

$$P(x) = C_0 + C_1(x-a) + C_2(x-a)^2 + \cdots$$
$$+ C_n(x-a)^n + \cdots$$
$$= \sum_{n=0}^{\infty} C_n(x-a)^n \quad \text{(p. 521)}.$$

The **radius of convergence** is 0 if the series converges only for $x = a$, ∞ if it converges for all x, and the positive number R if it converges for $|x-a| < R$ and diverges for $|x-a| > R$ (p. 523). The **interval of convergence** is the interval between $a - R$ and $a + R$, including any endpoint where the series converges (p. 523).

Theorem: Method for Computing Radius of Convergence (p. 524) To calculate the radius of convergence, R, for the power series $\sum_{n=0}^{\infty} C_n(x-a)^n$, use the ratio test with $a_n = C_n(x-a)^n$.

- If $\lim_{n \to \infty} |a_{n+1}|/|a_n|$ is infinite, then $R = 0$.
- If $\lim_{n \to \infty} |a_{n+1}|/|a_n| = 0$, then $R = \infty$.
- If $\lim_{n \to \infty} |a_{n+1}|/|a_n| = K|x-a|$, where K is finite and nonzero, then $R = 1/K$.

Approximations

The **Taylor polynomial of degree** n approximating $f(x)$ for x near a is:

$$P_n(x) = f(a) + f'(a)(x-a) + \frac{f''(a)}{2!}(x-a)^2 + \cdots\cdots$$
$$+ \frac{f^{(n)}(a)}{n!}(x-a)^n \quad \text{(p. 541)}$$

The **Taylor series** approximating $f(x)$ for x near a is:

$$f(x) = f(a) + f'(a)(x-a) + \frac{f''(a)}{2!}(x-a)^2 + \cdots$$
$$+ \frac{f^{(n)}(a)}{n!}(x-a)^n + \cdots \quad \text{(p. 547)}$$

Theorem: The Lagrange Error Bound for $P_n(x)$ (p. 560) Suppose f and all its derivatives are continuous. If $P_n(x)$ is the nth Taylor polynomial for to $f(x)$ about a, then

$$|E_n(x)| = |f(x) - P_n(x)| \le \frac{M}{(n+1)!}|x-a|^{n+1},$$

where $\max \left| f^{(n+1)} \right| \le M$ on the interval between a and x.

Taylor Series for $\sin x$, $\cos x$, e^x (p. 547):

$$\sin x = x - \frac{x^3}{3!} + \frac{x^5}{5!} - \frac{x^7}{7!} + \frac{x^9}{9!} - \cdots$$

$$\cos x = 1 - \frac{x^2}{2!} + \frac{x^4}{4!} - \frac{x^6}{6!} + \frac{x^8}{8!} - \cdots$$

$$e^x = 1 + x + \frac{x^2}{2!} + \frac{x^3}{3!} + \frac{x^4}{4!} + \cdots$$

Taylor Series for $\ln x$ about $x = 1$ converges for $0 < x \le 2$ (p. 548):

$$(x-1) - \frac{(x-1)^2}{2} + \frac{(x-1)^3}{3} - \frac{(x-1)^4}{4} + \cdots$$

The **Binomial Series** for $(1+x)^p$ converges for $-1 < x < 1$ (p. 549):

$$1 + px + \frac{p(p-1)}{2!}x^2 + \frac{p(p-1)(p-2)}{3!}x^3 + \cdots$$

The **Fourier Series** of $f(x)$ is (p. 568)

$$f(x) = a_0 + a_1 \cos x + a_2 \cos 2x + a_3 \cos 3x + \cdots$$
$$+ b_1 \sin x + b_2 \sin 2x + b_3 \sin 3x + \cdots,$$

where

$$a_0 = \frac{1}{2\pi} \int_{-\pi}^{\pi} f(x)\, dx,$$

$$a_k = \frac{1}{\pi} \int_{-\pi}^{\pi} f(x) \cos(kx)\, dx \quad \text{for } k \text{ a positive integer,}$$

$$b_k = \frac{1}{\pi} \int_{-\pi}^{\pi} f(x) \sin(kx)\, dx \quad \text{for } k \text{ a positive integer.}$$

Differential Equations

A **differential equation** for the function $y(x)$ is an equation involving x, y and the derivatives of y (p. 586). The **order** of a differential equation is the order of the highest-order derivative appearing in the equation (p. 588). A **solution** to a differential equation is any function y that satisfies the equation (p. 587). The **general solution** to a differential equation is the **family of functions** that satisfies the equation (p. 587). An **initial value problem** is a differential equation together with an **initial condition**; a solution to an initial value problem is called a **particular solution** (p. 587). An **equilibrium solution** to a differential equation is a particular solution where y is constant and $dy/dx = 0$ (p. 615).

First-order equations: methods of solution. A **slope field** corresponding to a differential equation is a plot in the xy-plane of small line segments with slope given by the differential equation (p. 591). **Euler's method** approximates the solution of an initial value problem with a string of small line segments (p. 599). Differential equations of the form $dy/dx = g(x)f(y)$ can be solved analytically by **separation of variables** (p. 604).

First-order equations: applications. The differential equation for **exponential growth and decay** is of the form

$$\frac{dP}{dt} = kP.$$

The **solution** is of the form $P = P_0 e^{kt}$, where P_0 is the initial value of P, and positive k represents growth while negative k represents decay (p. 610). Applications of growth and decay include **continuously compounded interest (p. 610), population growth (p. 629)**, and **Newton's law of heating and cooling (p. 613)**. The **logistic equation** for population growth is of the form

$$\frac{dP}{dt} = kP\left(1 - \frac{P}{L}\right),$$

where L is the **carrying capacity** of the population (p. 629). The **solution to the logistic equation** is of the form $P = \dfrac{L}{1 + Ae^{-kt}}$, where $A = \dfrac{L - P_0}{P_0}$ (p. 630).

Systems of differential equations. Two interacting populations, w and r, can be modeled by two equations

$$\frac{dw}{dt} = aw - cwr \quad \text{and} \quad \frac{dr}{dt} = -br + kwr \quad \text{(p. 643)}.$$

Solutions can be visualized as **trajectories** in the wr-**phase plane** (p. 644). An **equilibrium point** is one at which $dw/dt = 0$ and $dr/dt = 0$ (p. 644). A **nullcline** is a curve along which $dw/dt = 0$ or $dr/dt = 0$ (p. 650).

Multivariable Functions

Points in 3-space are represented by a system of **Cartesian coordinates** (p. 668). The **distance** between (x, y, z) and (a, b, c) is $\sqrt{(x-a)^2 + (y-b)^2 + (z-c)^2}$ (p. 671).

Functions of two variables can be represented by **graphs** (p. 674), **contour diagrams** (p. 681), **cross-sections** (p. 676), and **tables** (p. 667).

Functions of three variables can be represented by the family of **level surfaces** $f(x, y, z) = c$ for various values of the constant c (p. 700).

A **linear function** $f(x, y)$ has equation

$$f(x, y) = z_0 + m(x - x_0) + n(y - y_0) \text{ (p. 694)}$$
$$= c + mx + ny, \text{ where } c = z_0 - mx_0 - ny_0.$$

Its **graph** is a plane with slope m in the x-direction, slope n in the y-direction, through (x_0, y_0, z_0) (p. 694). Its **table of values** has linear rows (of same slope) and linear columns (of same slope) (p. 695). Its **contour diagram** is equally spaced parallel straight lines (p. 696).

The **limit** of f at the point (a, b), written $\lim_{(x,y)\to(a,b)} f(x, y)$, is the number L, if one exists, such that $f(x, y)$ is as close to L as we please whenever the distance from the point (x, y) to the point (a, b) is sufficiently small, but not zero. (p. 707).

A function f is **continuous at the point** (a, b) if $\lim_{(x,y)\to(a,b)} f(x, y) = f(a, b)$. A function is **continuous on a region** R if it is continuous at each point of R (p. 707).

Vectors

A **vector** $\vec{v}$ has **magnitude** (denoted $\|\vec{v}\|$) and **direction**. Examples are **displacement vectors** (p. 718), **velocity and acceleration vectors** (pp. 727, 728). and **force** (p. 728). We can add vectors, and multiply a vector by a scalar (p. 719). Two non-zero vectors, $\vec{v}$ and $\vec{w}$, are **parallel** if one is a scalar multiple of the other (p. 720).

A **unit vector** has magnitude 1. The vectors $\vec{i}$, $\vec{j}$, and $\vec{k}$ are unit vectors in the directions of the coordinate axes. A unit vector in the direction of any nonzero vector $\vec{v}$ is $\vec{u} = \vec{v}/\|\vec{v}\|$ (p. 724). We **resolve** $\vec{v}$ **into components** by writing $\vec{v} = v_1\vec{i} + v_2\vec{j} + v_3\vec{k}$ (p. 721).

If $\vec{v} = v_1\vec{i} + v_2\vec{j} + v_3\vec{k}$ and $\vec{w} = w_1\vec{i} + w_2\vec{j} + w_3\vec{k}$ then

$$\|\vec{v}\| = \sqrt{v_1^2 + v_2^2 + v_3^2} \text{ (p. 722)}$$
$$\vec{v} + \vec{w} = (v_1 + w_1)\vec{i} + (v_2 + w_2)\vec{j} + (v_3 + w_3)\vec{k} \text{ (p. 723)},$$
$$\lambda\vec{v} = \lambda v_1\vec{i} + \lambda v_2\vec{j} + \lambda v_3\vec{k} \text{ (p. 723)}.$$

The **displacement vector** from $P_1 = (x_1, y_1, z_1)$ to $P_2 = (x_2, y_2, z_2)$ is

$$\overrightarrow{P_1P_2} = (x_2 - x_1)\vec{i} + (y_2 - y_1)\vec{j} + (z_2 - z_1)\vec{k} \quad \text{(p. 722)}.$$

The **position vector** of $P = (x, y, z)$ is $\overrightarrow{OP}$ (p. 722). A **vector in** n **dimensions** is a string of numbers $\vec{v} = (v_1, v_2, \ldots, v_n)$ (p. 730).

Dot Product (Scalar Product) (p. 734).
Geometric definition: $\vec{v} \cdot \vec{w} = \|\vec{v}\|\|\vec{w}\|\cos\theta$ where θ is the angle between $\vec{v}$ and $\vec{w}$ and $0 \leq \theta \leq \pi$.
Algebraic definition: $\vec{v} \cdot \vec{w} = v_1w_1 + v_2w_2 + v_3w_3$.

Two nonzero vectors $\vec{v}$ and $\vec{w}$ are **perpendicular** if and only if $\vec{v} \cdot \vec{w} = 0$ (p. 736). Magnitude and dot product are related by $\vec{v} \cdot \vec{v} = \|\vec{v}\|^2$ (p. 736). If $\vec{u} = (u_1, \ldots, u_n)$ and $\vec{v} = (v_1, \ldots, v_n)$ then the dot product of $\vec{u}$ and $\vec{v}$ is $\vec{u} \cdot \vec{v} = u_1v_1 + \ldots + u_nv_n$ (p. 738).

The **equation of the plane** with **normal vector** $\vec{n} = a\vec{i} + b\vec{j} + c\vec{k}$ and containing the point $P_0 = (x_0, y_0, z_0)$ is $\vec{n} \cdot (\vec{r} - \vec{r}_0) = a(x - x_0) + b(y - y_0) + c(z - z_0) = 0$ or $ax + by + cz = d$, where $d = ax_0 + by_0 + cz_0$ (p. 737).

If $\vec{v}_{\text{parallel}}$ and $\vec{v}_{\text{perp}}$ are components of $\vec{v}$ which are parallel and perpendicular, respectively, to a unit vector $\vec{u}$, then $\vec{v}_{\text{parallel}} = (\vec{v} \cdot \vec{u})\vec{u}$ and $\vec{v}_{\text{perp}} = \vec{v} - \vec{v}_{\text{parallel}}$ (p. 738).

The **work**, W, done by a force $\vec{F}$ acting on an object through a displacement $\vec{d}$ is $W = \vec{F} \cdot \vec{d}$ (p. 740).

Cross Product (Vector Product) (p. 744, 745)
Geometric definition

$$\vec{v} \times \vec{w} = \begin{pmatrix} \text{Area of parallelogram} \\ \text{with edges } \vec{v} \text{ and } \vec{w} \end{pmatrix} \vec{n}$$

$$= (\|\vec{v}\| \|\vec{w}\| \sin\theta)\vec{n},$$

where $0 \le \theta \le \pi$ is the angle between $\vec{v}$ and $\vec{w}$ and $\vec{n}$ is the unit vector perpendicular to $\vec{v}$ and $\vec{w}$ pointing in the direction given by the **right-hand rule**.

Algebraic definition

$$\vec{v} \times \vec{w} = (v_2 w_3 - v_3 w_2)\vec{i} + (v_3 w_1 - v_1 w_3)\vec{j}$$
$$+ (v_1 w_2 - v_2 w_1)\vec{k}$$

$$\vec{v} = v_1\vec{i} + v_2\vec{j} + v_3\vec{k}, \vec{w} = w_1\vec{i} + w_2\vec{j} + w_3\vec{k}.$$

To find the **equation of a plane through three points** that do not lie on a line, determine two vectors in the plane and then find a normal vector using the cross product (p. 747). The **area of a parallelogram** with edges $\vec{v}$ and $\vec{w}$ is $\|\vec{v} \times \vec{w}\|$. The **volume of a parallelepiped** with edges $\vec{a}$, $\vec{b}$, $\vec{c}$ is $|(\vec{b} \times \vec{c}) \cdot \vec{a}|$ (p. 748).

Differentiation of Multivariable Functions

Partial derivatives of f (p. 759).

$$f_x(a,b) = \begin{array}{c} \text{Rate of change of } f \text{ with respect to } x \\ \text{at the point } (a,b) \end{array}$$

$$= \lim_{h \to 0} \frac{f(a+h, b) - f(a,b)}{h},$$

$$f_y(a,b) = \begin{array}{c} \text{Rate of change of } f \text{ with respect to } y \\ \text{at the point } (a,b) \end{array}$$

$$= \lim_{h \to 0} \frac{f(a, b+h) - f(a,b)}{h}.$$

On the graph of f, the partial derivatives $f_x(a,b)$ and $f_y(a,b)$ give the slope in the x and y directions, respectively (p. 760). The **tangent plane** to $z = f(x,y)$ at (a,b) is

$$z = f(a,b) + f_x(a,b)(x-a) + f_y(a,b)(y-b) \quad \text{(p. 772)}.$$

Partial derivatives can be estimated from a contour diagram or table of values using difference quotients (p. 760), and can be computed algebraically using the same rules of differentiation as for one-variable calculus (p. 766). Partial derivatives for functions of three or more variables are defined and computed in the same way (p 767).

The gradient vector grad f of f is grad $f(a,b) = f_x(a,b)\vec{i} + f_y(a,b)\vec{j}$ (2 variables) (p. 782) or grad $f(a,b,c) = f_x(a,b,c)\vec{i} + f_y(a,b,c)\vec{j} + f_z(a,b,c)\vec{k}$ (3 variables) (p. 789). The gradient vector at P: Points in the direction of increasing f; is perpendicular to the level curve or level surface of f through P; and has magnitude $\|$ grad $f\|$

equal to the maximum rate of change of f at P (pp. 783, 790). The magnitude is large when the level curves or surfaces are close together and small when they are far apart.

The **directional derivative** of f at P in the direction of a unit vector $\vec{u}$ is (pp. 780, 782)

$$f_{\vec{u}}(P) = \begin{array}{c} \text{Rate of change} \\ \text{of } f \text{ in direction} \\ \text{of } \vec{u} \text{ at } P \end{array} = \text{grad } f(P) \cdot \vec{u}$$

The **tangent plane approximation** to $f(x,y)$ for (x,y) near the point (a,b) is

$$f(x,y) \approx f(a,b) + f_x(a,b)(x-a) + f_y(a,b)(y-b).$$

The right-hand side is the **local linearization** (p. 773). The **differential of** $z = f(x,y)$ at (a,b) is the linear function of dx and dy

$$df = f_x(a,b)\,dx + f_y(a,b)\,dy \quad \text{(p. 775)}.$$

Local linearity with three or more variables follows the same pattern as for functions of two variables (p. 775).

The **tangent plane to a level surface** of a function of three-variables f at (a,b,c) is (p. 792)

$$f_x(a,b,c)(x-a) + f_y(a,b,c)(y-b) + f_z(a,b,c)(z-c) = 0.$$

The Chain Rule for the partial derivative of one variable with respect to another in a chain of composed functions (p. 799):

- Draw a diagram expressing the relationship between the variables, and label each link in the diagram with the derivative relating the variables at its ends.

- For each path between the two variables, multiply together the derivatives from each step along the path.

- Add the contributions from each path.

If $z = f(x,y)$, and $x = g(t)$, and $y = h(t)$, then

$$\frac{dz}{dt} = \frac{\partial z}{\partial x}\frac{dx}{dt} + \frac{\partial z}{\partial y}\frac{dy}{dt} \quad \text{(p. 797)}.$$

If $z = f(x,y)$, with $x = g(u,v)$ and $y = h(u,v)$, then

$$\frac{\partial z}{\partial u} = \frac{\partial z}{\partial x}\frac{\partial x}{\partial u} + \frac{\partial z}{\partial y}\frac{\partial y}{\partial u},$$

$$\frac{\partial z}{\partial v} = \frac{\partial z}{\partial x}\frac{\partial x}{\partial v} + \frac{\partial z}{\partial y}\frac{\partial y}{\partial v} \quad \text{(p. 799)}.$$

Second-order partial derivatives (p. 806)

$$\frac{\partial^2 z}{\partial x^2} = f_{xx} = (f_x)_x, \qquad \frac{\partial^2 z}{\partial x \partial y} = f_{yx} = (f_y)_x,$$

$$\frac{\partial^2 z}{\partial y \partial x} = f_{xy} = (f_x)_y, \qquad \frac{\partial^2 z}{\partial y^2} = f_{yy} = (f_y)_y.$$

Theorem: Equality of Mixed Partial Derivatives. If f_{xy} and f_{yx} are continuous at (a,b), an interior point of their domain, then $f_{xy}(a,b) = f_{yx}(a,b)$ (p. 807).

Taylor Polynomial of Degree 1 **Approximating** $f(x, y)$ **for** (x, y) **near** (a, b) **(p. 811)**

$$f(x, y) \approx L(x, y) = f(a, b) + f_x(a, b)(x-a) + f_y(a, b)(y-b).$$

Taylor Polynomial of Degree 2 **(p. 811)**

$$f(x, y) \approx Q(x, y)$$
$$= f(a, b) + f_x(a, b)(x - a) + f_y(a, b)(y - b)$$
$$+ \frac{f_{xx}(a, b)}{2}(x - a)^2 + f_{xy}(a, b)(x - a)(y - b)$$
$$+ \frac{f_{yy}(a, b)}{2}(y - b)^2.$$

Definition of Differentiability (p. 815). A function $f(x, y)$ is **differentiable at the point** (a, b) if there is a linear function $L(x, y) = f(a, b) + m(x - a) + n(y - b)$ such that if the **error** $E(x, y)$ is defined by

$$f(x, y) = L(x, y) + E(x, y),$$

and if $h = x - a, k = y - b$, then the **relative error** $E(a + h, b + k)/\sqrt{h^2 + k^2}$ satisfies

$$\lim_{\substack{h \to 0 \\ k \to 0}} \frac{E(a + h, b + k)}{\sqrt{h^2 + k^2}} = 0.$$

Theorem: Continuity of Partial Derivatives Implies Differentiability (p. 819). If the partial derivatives, f_x and f_y, of a function f exist and are continuous on a small disk centered at the point (a, b), then f is differentiable at (a, b).

Optimization

A function f has a **local maximum** at the point P_0 if $f(P_0) \geq f(P)$ for all points P near P_0, and a **local minimum** at the point P_0 if $f(P_0) \leq f(P)$ for all points P near P_0 (p. 830). A **critical point** of a function f is a point where grad f is either $\vec{0}$ or undefined. If f has a local maximum or minimum at a point P_0, not on the boundary of its domain, then P_0 is a critical point (p. 830). A **quadratic function** $f(x, y) = ax^2 + bxy + cz^2$ generally has one critical point, which can be a local maximum, a local minimum, or a **saddle point** (p. 833).

Second derivative test for functions of two variables (p. 835). Suppose grad $f(x_0, y_0) = \vec{0}$. Let $D = f_{xx}(x_0, y_0)f_{yy}(x_0, y_0) - (f_{xy}(x_0, y_0))^2$.

- If $D > 0$ and $f_{xx}(x_0, y_0) > 0$, then f has a local minimum at (x_0, y_0).

- If $D > 0$ and $f_{xx}(x_0, y_0) < 0$, then f has a local maximum at (x_0, y_0).

- If $D < 0$, then f has a saddle point at (x_0, y_0).

- If $D = 0$, anything can happen.

Unconstrained optimization
A function f defined on a region R has a **global maximum on** R at the point P_0 if $f(P_0) \geq f(P)$ for all points P in R, and a **global minimum on** R at the point P_0 if $f(P_0) \leq f(P)$ for

all points P in R (p. 839). For an **unconstrained optimization problem**, find the critical points and investigate whether the critical points give global maxima or minima (p. 839).

A **closed** region is one which contains its boundary; a **bounded** region is one which does not stretch to infinity in any direction (p. 844).

Extreme Value Theorem for Multivariable Functions. If f is a continuous function on a closed and bounded region R, then f has a global maximum at some point (x_0, y_0) in R and a global minimum at some point (x_1, y_1) in R (p. 845).

Constrained optimization
Suppose P_0 is a point satisfying the constraint $g(x, y) = c$. A function f has a **local maximum** at P_0 **subject to the constraint** if $f(P_0) \geq f(P)$ for all points P near P_0 satisfying the constraint (p. 850). It has a **global maximum** at P_0 **subject to the constraint** if $f(P_0) \geq f(P)$ for all points P satisfying the constraint (p. 850). Local and global minima are defined similarly (p. 850). A local maximum or minimum of $f(x, y)$ subject to a constraint $g(x, y) = c$ occurs at a point where the constraint is tangent to a level curve of f, and thus where grad g is parallel to grad f (p. 850).

To optimize f **subject to the constraint** $g = c$ **(p. 850)**, find the points satisfying the equations

$$\text{grad } f = \lambda \text{ grad } g \quad \text{and} \quad g = c.$$

Then compare values of f at these points, at points on the constraint where grad $g = \vec{0}$, and at the endpoints of the constraint. The number λ is called the **Lagrange multiplier**.

To optimize f **subject to the constraint** $g \leq c$ **(p. 852)**, find all points in the interior $g(x, y) < c$ where grad f is zero or undefined; then use Lagrange multipliers to find the local extrema of f on the boundary $g(x, y) = c$. Evaluate f at the points found and compare the values.

The value of λ is the rate of change of the optimum value of f as c increases (where $g(x, y) = c$) (p. 853). The **Lagrangian function** $\mathcal{L}(x, y, \lambda) = f(x, y) - \lambda(g(x, y) - c)$ can be used to convert a constrained optimization problem for f subject the constraint $g = c$ into an unconstrained problem for $\mathcal{L}$ (p. 854).

Multivariable Integration

The **definite integral** of f, a continuous function of two variables, over R, the rectangle $a \leq x \leq b$, $c \leq y \leq d$, is called a **double integral**, and is a limit of **Riemann sums**

$$\int_R f \, dA = \lim_{\Delta x, \Delta y \to 0} \sum_{i,j} f(u_{ij}, v_{ij}) \Delta x \Delta y \quad \text{(p. 869)}.$$

The Riemann sum is constructed by subdividing R into subrectangles of width Δx and height Δy, and choosing a point (u_{ij}, v_{ij}) in the ij-th rectangle.

A **triple integral** of f, a continuous function of three variables, over W, the box $a \leq x \leq b, c \leq y \leq d, p \leq z \leq q$ in 3-space, is defined in a similar way using three-variable Riemann sums (p. 885).

Interpretations

If $f(x, y)$ is positive, $\int_R f \, dA$ is the **volume** under graph of f above the region R (p. 870). If $f(x, y) = 1$ for all x and y, then the area of R is $\int_R 1 \, dA = \int_R dA$ (p. 871). If $f(x, y)$ is a **density**, then $\int_R f \, dA$ is the **total quantity** in the region R (p. 868). The **average value** of $f(x, y)$ on the region R is $\frac{1}{\text{Area of } R} \int_R f \, dA$ (p. 872). In probability, if $p(x, y)$ is a **joint density function** then $\int_a^b \int_c^d p(x, y) \, dy \, dx$ is the fraction of population with $a \le x \le b$ and $c \le y \le d$ (p. 907).

Iterated integrals

Double and triple integrals can be written as **iterated integrals**

$$\int_R f \, dA = \int_c^d \int_a^b f(x, y) \, dx \, dy \text{ (p. 876)}$$

$$\int_W f \, dV = \int_p^q \int_c^d \int_a^b f(x, y, z) \, dx \, dy \, dz \text{ (p. 885)}$$

Other orders of integration are possible. For iterated integrals over **non-rectangular regions** (p. 878), limits on outer integral are constants and limits on inner integrals involve only the variables in the integrals further out (pp. 879, 887).

Integrals in other coordinate systems

When computing double integrals in polar coordinates, put $dA = r \, dr \, d\theta$ or $dA = r \, d\theta \, dr$ (p. 891). Cylindrical coordinates are given by $x = r \cos \theta$, $y = r \sin \theta$, $z = z$, for $0 \le r < \infty$, $0 \le \theta \le 2\pi$, $-\infty < z < \infty$ (p. 896). Spherical coordinates are given by $x = \rho \sin \phi \cos \theta$, $y = \rho \sin \phi \sin \theta$, $z = \rho \cos \phi$, for $0 \le \rho < \infty$, $0 \le \phi \le \pi$, $0 \le \theta \le 2\pi$ (p. 899). When computing triple integrals in cylindrical or spherical coordinates, put $dV = r \, dr \, d\theta \, dz$ for cylindrical coordinates (p. 897), $dV = \rho^2 \sin \phi \, d\rho \, d\phi \, d\theta$ for spherical coordinates (p. 900). Other orders of integration are also possible.

For a **change of variables** $x = x(s, t)$, $y = y(s, t)$, the **Jacobian** is

$$\frac{\partial(x, y)}{\partial(s, t)} = \frac{\partial x}{\partial s} \cdot \frac{\partial y}{\partial t} - \frac{\partial x}{\partial t} \cdot \frac{\partial y}{\partial s} = \begin{vmatrix} \frac{\partial x}{\partial s} & \frac{\partial x}{\partial t} \\ \frac{\partial y}{\partial s} & \frac{\partial y}{\partial t} \end{vmatrix} \text{ (p. 1086)}.$$

To convert an integral from x, y to s, t coordinates (p. 1086): Substitute for x and y in terms of s and t, change the xy region R into an st region T, and change the area element by making the substitution $dx \, dy = \left| \frac{\partial(x,y)}{\partial(s,t)} \right| ds \, dt$. For triple integrals, there is a similar formula (p. 1087).

Parameterizations and Vector Fields

Parameterized curves

The motion of a particle is described by **parametric equations** $x = f(t), y = g(t)$ (2-space) or $x = f(t), y = g(t), z = h(t)$ (3-space). The path of the particle is a **parameterized curve** (p. 918). Parameterizations are also written in **vector form** $\vec{r}(t) = f(t)\vec{i} + g(t)\vec{j} + h(t)\vec{k}$ (p. 919). For a

curve segment we restrict the parameter to to a closed interval $a \le t \le b$ (p. 921). **Parametric equations for the graph** of $y = f(x)$ are $x = t$, $y = f(t)$.

Parametric equations for a line through (x_0, y_0) in the direction of $\vec{v} = a\vec{i} + b\vec{j}$ are $x = x_0 + at$, $y = y_0 + bt$. In 3-space, the line through (x_0, y_0, z_0) in the direction of $\vec{v} = a\vec{i} + b\vec{j} + c\vec{k}$ is $x = x_0 + at$, $y = y_0 + bt$, $z = z_0 + ct$ (p. 919). In vector form, the equation for a line is $\vec{r}(t) = \vec{r}_0 + t\vec{v}$, where $\vec{r}_0 = x_0\vec{i} + y_0\vec{j} + z_0\vec{k}$ (p. 921).

Parametric equations for a circle of radius R in the plane, centered at the origin are $x = R \cos t$, $y = R \sin t$ (counterclockwise), $x = R \cos t$, $y = -R \sin t$ (clockwise).

To find the **intersection points** of a curve $\vec{r}(t) = f(t)\vec{i} + g(t)\vec{j} + h(t)\vec{k}$ with a surface $F(x, y, z) = c$, solve $F(f(t), g(t), h(t)) = c$ for t (p. 921). To find the intersection points of two curves $\vec{r}_1(t)$ and $\vec{r}_2(t)$, solve $\vec{r}_1(t_1) = \vec{r}_2(t_2)$ for t_1 and t_2 (p. 921).

The **length of a curve segment** C given parametrically for $a \le t \le b$ with velocity vector $\vec{v}$ is $\int_a^b \|\vec{v}\| dt$ if $\vec{v} \ne \vec{0}$ for $a < t < b$ (p. 932).

The **velocity** and **acceleration** of a moving object with position vector $\vec{r}(t)$ at time t are

$$\vec{v}(t) = \lim_{\Delta t \to 0} \frac{\Delta \vec{r}}{\Delta t} \quad \text{(p. 928)}$$

$$\vec{a}(t) = \lim_{\Delta t \to 0} \frac{\Delta \vec{v}}{\Delta t} \quad \text{(p. 930)}$$

We write $\vec{v} = \frac{d\vec{r}}{dt} = \vec{r}'(t)$ and $\vec{a} = \frac{d\vec{v}}{dt} = \frac{d^2\vec{r}}{dt^2} = \vec{r}''(t)$.

The **components of the velocity and acceleration vectors** are

$$\vec{v}(t) = \frac{dx}{dt}\vec{i} + \frac{dy}{dt}\vec{j} + \frac{dz}{dt}\vec{k} \quad \text{(p. 928)}$$

$$\vec{a}(t) = \frac{d^2x}{dt^2}\vec{i} + \frac{d^2y}{dt^2}\vec{j} + \frac{d^2z}{dt^2}\vec{k} \quad \text{(p. 930)}$$

The **speed** is $\|\vec{v}\| = \sqrt{(dx/dt)^2 + (dy/dt)^2 + (dz/dt)^2}$ (p. 932). Analogous formulas for velocity, speed, and acceleration hold in 2-space.

Uniform Circular Motion (p. 931) For a particle $\vec{r}(t) = R \cos(\omega t)\vec{i} + R \sin(\omega t)\vec{j}$: motion is in a circle of radius R with period $2\pi/\omega$; velocity, $\vec{v}$, is tangent to the circle and speed is constant $\|\vec{v}\| = \omega R$; acceleration, $\vec{a}$, points toward the center of the circle with $\|\vec{a}\| = \|\vec{v}\|^2/R$.

Motion in a Straight Line (p. 932) For a particle $\vec{r}(t) = \vec{r}_0 + f(t)\vec{v}_0$: Motion is along a straight line through the point with position vector $\vec{r}_0$ parallel to $\vec{v}_0$; velocity, $\vec{v}$, and acceleration, $\vec{a}$, are parallel to the line.

Vector fields

A **vector field** in 2-space is a function $\vec{F}(x, y)$ whose value at a point (x, y) is a 2-dimensional vector (p. 937). Similarly, a vector field in 3-space is a function $\vec{F}(x, y, z)$ whose values are 3-dimensional vectors (p. 937). Examples are the **gradient** of a differentiable function f, the **velocity field** of a fluid flow, and **force fields** (p. 937). A **flow line** of a vector field $\vec{v} = \vec{F}(\vec{r})$ is a path $\vec{r}(t)$ whose velocity vector equals $\vec{v}$, thus $\vec{r}'(t) = \vec{v} = \vec{F}(\vec{r}(t))$ (p. 944). The **flow** of a vector field is the family of all of its flow line (p. 944). Flow lines can be approximated numerically using Euler's method (p. 946).

Parameterized surfaces

We **parameterize a surface** with two parameters, $x = f_1(s,t)$, $y = f_2(s,t)$, $z = f_3(s,t)$ (p. 1076). We also use the vector form $\vec{r}(s,t) = f_1(s,t)\vec{i} + f_2(s,t)\vec{j} + f_3(s,t)\vec{k}$ (p. 1076). **Parametric equations for the graph** of $z = f(x,y)$ are $x = s$, $y = t$, and $z = f(s,t)$ (p. 1076). **Parametric equation for a plane** through the point with position vector $\vec{r}_0$ and containing the two nonparallel vectors $\vec{v}_1$ and $\vec{v}_2$ is $\vec{r}(s,t) = \vec{r}_0 + s\vec{v}_1 + t\vec{v}_2$ (p. 1077). **Parametric equation for a sphere** of radius R centered at the origin is $\vec{r}(\theta, \phi) = R\sin\phi\cos\theta\,\vec{i} + R\sin\phi\sin\theta\,\vec{j} + \cos\phi\,\vec{k}$, $0 \le \theta \le 2\pi, 0 \le \phi \le \pi$ (p. 1077). **Parametric equation for a cylinder** of radius R along the z-axis is $\vec{r}(\theta, z) = R\cos\theta\vec{i} + R\sin\theta\vec{j} + z\vec{k}$, $0 \le \theta \le 2\pi, -\infty < z < \infty$ (p. 1075). A **parameter curve** is the curve obtained by holding one of the parameters constant and letting the other vary (p. 1081).

Line Integrals

The **line integral** of a vector field $\vec{F}$ along an **oriented curve** C (p. 958) is

$$\int_C \vec{F} \cdot d\vec{r} = \lim_{\|\Delta\vec{r}_i\| \to 0} \sum_{i=0}^{n-1} \vec{F}(\vec{r}_i) \cdot \Delta\vec{r}_i,$$

where the direction of $\Delta\vec{r}_i$ is the direction of the orientation (p. 959).

The line integral measures the extent to which C is going with $\vec{F}$ or against it (p. 959). For oriented curves C, C_1, and C_2, $\int_{-C} \vec{F} \cdot d\vec{r} = -\int_C \vec{F} \cdot d\vec{r}$, where $-C$ is the curve C parameterized in the opposite direction, and $\int_{C_1+C_2} \vec{F} \cdot d\vec{r} = \int_{C_1} \vec{F} \cdot d\vec{r} + \int_{C_2} \vec{F} \cdot d\vec{r}$, where $C_1 + C_2$ is the curve obtained by joining the endpoint of C_1 to the starting point of C_2 (p. 963).

The **work done by a force** $\vec{F}$ along a curve C is $\int_C \vec{F} \cdot d\vec{r}$ (p. 960). The **circulation** of $\vec{F}$ around an oriented closed curve is $\int_C \vec{F} \cdot d\vec{r}$ (p. 962).

Given a **parameterization of** C, $\vec{r}(t)$, for $a \le t \le b$, the line integral can be calculated as

$$\int_C \vec{F} \cdot d\vec{r} = \int_a^b \vec{F}(\vec{r}(t)) \cdot \vec{r}'(t)\,dt \quad \text{(p. 968)}.$$

Fundamental Theorem for Line Integrals (p. 975):

Suppose C is a piecewise smooth oriented path with starting point P and endpoint Q. If f is a function whose gradient is continuous on the path C, then

$$\int_C \operatorname{grad} f \cdot d\vec{r} = f(Q) - f(P).$$

Path-independent fields and gradient fields

A vector field $\vec{F}$ is said to be **path-independent**, or **conservative**, if for any two points P and Q, the line integral

$\int_C \vec{F} \cdot d\vec{r}$ has the same value along any piecewise smooth path C from P to Q lying in the domain of $\vec{F}$ (p. 976). A **gradient field** is a vector field of the form $\vec{F} = \operatorname{grad} f$ for some scalar function f, and f is called a **potential function** for the vector field $\vec{F}$ (p. 978). A vector field $\vec{F}$ is path-independent if and only if $\vec{F}$ is a gradient vector field (p. 978). A vector field $\vec{F}$ is path-independent if and only if $\int_C \vec{F} \cdot d\vec{r} = 0$ for every closed curve C (p. 986). If $\vec{F}$ is a gradient field, then $\frac{\partial F_2}{\partial x} - \frac{\partial F_1}{\partial y} = 0$ (p. 987). The quantity $\frac{\partial F_2}{\partial x} - \frac{\partial F_1}{\partial y}$ is called the 2-dimensional or scalar **curl** of $\vec{F}$.

Green's Theorem (p. 988):

Suppose C is a piecewise smooth simple closed curve that is the boundary of an open region R in the plane and oriented so that the region is on the left as we move around the curve. Suppose $\vec{F} = F_1\vec{i} + F_2\vec{j}$ is a smooth vector field defined at every point of the region R and boundary C. Then

$$\int_C \vec{F} \cdot d\vec{r} = \int_R \left(\frac{\partial F_2}{\partial x} - \frac{\partial F_1}{\partial y} \right) dx\,dy.$$

Curl test for vector fields in 2-space: If $\frac{\partial F_2}{\partial x} - \frac{\partial F_1}{\partial y} = 0$ and the domain of $\vec{F}$ has no holes, then $\vec{F}$ is path-independent, and hence a gradient field (p. 990). The condition that the domain have no holes is important. It is not always true that if the scalar curl of $\vec{F}$ is zero then $\vec{F}$ is a gradient field (p. 990).

Surface Integrals

A surface is **oriented** if a unit normal vector $\vec{n}$ has been chosen at every point on it in a continuous way (p. 1006). For a closed surface, we usually choose the outward orientation (p. 1006). The **area vector** of a flat, oriented surface is a vector $\vec{A}$ whose magnitude is the area of the surface, and whose direction is the direction of the orientation vector $\vec{n}$ (p. 1007). If $\vec{v}$ is the velocity vector of a constant fluid flow and $\vec{A}$ is the area vector of a flat surface, then the total flow through the surface in units of volume per unit time is called the **flux** of $\vec{v}$ through the surface and is given by $\vec{v} \cdot \vec{A}$ (p. 1007).

The **surface integral** or **flux integral** of the vector field $\vec{F}$ through the oriented surface S is

$$\int_S \vec{F} \cdot d\vec{A} = \lim_{\|\Delta\vec{A}\| \to 0} \sum \vec{F} \cdot \Delta\vec{A},$$

where the direction of $\Delta\vec{A}$ is the direction of the orientation (p. 1008). If $\vec{v}$ is a variable vector field and then $\int_S \vec{v} \cdot d\vec{A}$ is the flux through the surface S (p. 1009).

Simple flux integrals can be calculated by putting $d\vec{A} = \vec{n}\,dA$ and using geometry or converting to a double integral (p. 1010).

The **flux through a graph** of $z = f(x,y)$ above a region R in the xy-plane, oriented upward, is

$$\int_R \vec{F}(x, y, f(x,y)) \cdot \left(-f_x\vec{i} - f_y\vec{j} + \vec{k} \right) dx\,dy \quad \text{(p. 1018)}.$$

The **flux through a cylindrical surface** S of radius R and oriented away from the z-axis is

$$\int_T \vec{F}(R, \theta, z) \cdot \left(\cos\theta\vec{i} + \sin\theta\vec{j}\right) R\, dz\, d\theta \quad \text{(p. 1019)},$$

where T is the θz-region corresponding to S.

The **flux through a spherical surface** S of radius R and oriented away from the origin is

$$\int_T \vec{F}(R, \theta, \phi) \cdot \left(\sin\phi\cos\theta\vec{i} + \sin\phi\sin\theta\vec{j} + \cos\phi\vec{k}\right)$$
$$R^2\sin\phi\, d\phi\, d\theta, \quad \text{(p. 1020)}$$

where T is the $\theta\phi$-region corresponding to S.

The **flux through a parameterized surface** S, parameterized by $\vec{r} = \vec{r}(s, t)$, where (s, t) varies in a parameter region R, is

$$\int_R \vec{F}(\vec{r}(s, t)) \cdot \left(\frac{\partial\vec{r}}{\partial s} \times \frac{\partial\vec{r}}{\partial t}\right) ds\, dt \quad \text{(p. 1089)}.$$

We choose the parameterization so that $\partial\vec{r}/\partial s \times \partial\vec{r}/\partial t$ is never zero and points in the direction of $\vec{n}$ everywhere.

The **area of a parameterized surface** S, parameterized by $\vec{r} = \vec{r}(s, t)$, where (s, t) varies in a parameter region R, is

$$\int_S dA = \int_R \left\|\frac{\partial\vec{r}}{\partial s} \times \frac{\partial\vec{r}}{\partial t}\right\| ds\, dt \quad \text{(p. 1090)}.$$

Divergence and Curl

Divergence

Definition of Divergence (p. 1025).
Geometric definition: The **divergence** of $\vec{F}$ is

$$\text{div }\vec{F}(x, y, z) = \lim_{\text{Volume}\to 0} \frac{\int_S \vec{F} \cdot d\vec{A}}{\text{Volume of } S}.$$

Here S is a sphere centered at (x, y, z), oriented outwards, that contracts down to (x, y, z) in the limit.

Cartesian coordinate definition: If $\vec{F} = F_1\vec{i} + F_2\vec{j} + F_3\vec{k}$, then

$$\text{div }\vec{F} = \frac{\partial F_1}{\partial x} + \frac{\partial F_2}{\partial y} + \frac{\partial F_3}{\partial z}.$$

The divergence can be thought of as the outflow per unit volume of the vector field. A vector field $\vec{F}$ is said to be **divergence free** or **solenoidal** if $\text{div }\vec{F} = 0$ everywhere that $\vec{F}$ is defined. Magnetic fields are divergence free (p. 1028).

The Divergence Theorem (p. 1035). If W is a solid region whose boundary S is a piecewise smooth surface, and if $\vec{F}$ is a smooth vector field which is defined everywhere in W and on S, then

$$\int_S \vec{F} \cdot d\vec{A} = \int_W \text{div }\vec{F}\, dV,$$

where S is given the outward orientation. In words, the Divergence Theorem says that the total flux out of a closed surface is the integral of the flux density over the volume it encloses.

Curl

The **circulation density** of a smooth vector field $\vec{F}$ at (x, y, z) around the direction of the unit vector $\vec{n}$ is defined to be

$$\text{circ}_{\vec{n}}\,\vec{F}(x, y, z) = \lim_{\text{Area}\to 0} \frac{\text{Circulation around } C}{\text{Area inside } C}$$
$$= \lim_{\text{Area}\to 0} \frac{\int_C \vec{F} \cdot d\vec{r}}{\text{Area inside } C} \quad \text{(p. 1048)}.$$

Circulation density is calculated using the **right-hand rule** (p. 1048).

Definition of curl (p. 1049).
Geometric definition The curl of $\vec{F}$, written $\text{curl }\vec{F}$, is the vector field with the following properties

- The direction of $\text{curl }\vec{F}(x, y, z)$ is the direction $\vec{n}$ for which $\text{circ}_{\vec{n}}(x, y, z)$ is greatest.

- The magnitude of $\text{curl }\vec{F}(x, y, z)$ is the circulation density of $\vec{F}$ around that direction.

Cartesian coordinate definition If $\vec{F} = F_1\vec{i} + F_2\vec{j} + F_3\vec{k}$, then

$$\text{curl }\vec{F} = \left(\frac{\partial F_3}{\partial y} - \frac{\partial F_2}{\partial z}\right)\vec{i} + \left(\frac{\partial F_1}{\partial z} - \frac{\partial F_3}{\partial x}\right)\vec{j}$$
$$+ \left(\frac{\partial F_2}{\partial x} - \frac{\partial F_1}{\partial y}\right)\vec{k}.$$

Curl and circulation density are related by $\text{circ}_{\vec{n}}\,\vec{F} = \text{curl }\vec{F} \cdot \vec{n}$ (p. 1051). A vector field is said to be **curl free** or **irrotational** if $\text{curl }\vec{F} = \vec{0}$ everywhere that $\vec{F}$ is defined (p. 1052).

Given an oriented surface S with a boundary curve C we use the right-hand rule to determine the orientation of C (p. 1056).

Stokes' Theorem (p. 1057). If S is a smooth oriented surface with piecewise smooth, oriented boundary C, and if $\vec{F}$ is a smooth vector field which is defined on S and C, then

$$\int_C \vec{F} \cdot d\vec{r} = \int_S \text{curl }\vec{F} \cdot d\vec{A}.$$

Stokes' Theorem says that the total circulation around C is the integral over S of the circulation density. A **curl field** is a vector field $\vec{F}$ that can be written as $\vec{F} = \text{curl }\vec{G}$ for some vector field $\vec{G}$, called a **vector potential** for $\vec{F}$ (p. 1059).

Relation between divergence, gradient, and curl

The curl and gradient are related by $\operatorname{curl} \operatorname{grad} f = 0$ (p. 1063). Divergence and curl are related by $\operatorname{div} \operatorname{curl} \vec{F} = 0$ (p. 1064).

The curl test for vector fields in 3-space (p. 1063) Suppose that $\operatorname{curl} \vec{F} = \vec{0}$, and that the domain of $\vec{F}$ has the property that every closed curve in it can be contracted to a point in a smooth way, staying at all times within the domain.

Then $\vec{F}$ is path-independent, so $\vec{F}$ is a gradient field and has a potential function.

The divergence test for vector fields in 3-space (p. 1064) Suppose that $\operatorname{div} \vec{F} = 0$, and that the domain of $\vec{F}$ has the property that every closed surface in it is the boundary of a solid region completely contained in the domain. Then $\vec{F}$ is a curl field.

ANSWERS TO ODD NUMBERED PROBLEMS

Section 1.1

1 Pop 12 million in 2005

5 $y = (1/2)x + 2$

7 $y = 2x + 2$

9 Slope: $-12/7$
   Vertical intercept: $2/7$

11 Slope: 2
    Vertical intercept: $-2/3$

13 (a) (V)
    (b) (VI)
    (c) (I)
    (d) (IV)
    (e) (III)
    (f) (II)

15 $y - c = m(x - a)$

17 $y = -\frac{1}{5}x + \frac{7}{5}$

19 Parallel: $y = m(x - a) + b$
    Perpendicular:
    $y = (-1/m)(x - a) + b$

21 Domain: $1 \le x \le 5$
    Range: $1 \le y \le 6$

23 Domain: $0 \le x \le 5$
    Range: $0 \le y \le 4$

25 Domain: all x
    Range: $0 < y \le 1/2$

27 $V = kr^3$

29 $S = kh^2$

31 $N = k/l^2$

33 $f(0)$ meters

35 $f(0) = f(1) + 0.001$

37 V (thousand dollars)

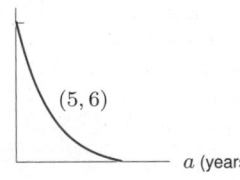

$(5, 6)$

a (years)

41 (a) $C = 4.16 + 0.12w$
    (b) 0.12 $/gal
    (c) $4.16

43 (a) $C_1 = 40 + 0.15m$
       $C_2 = 50 + 0.10m$
    (b) C (cost in dollars)

$C_1(m) = 40 + 0.15m$

$C_2(m) = 50 + 0.10m$

m (miles)

    (c) For distances less than 200 miles, C_1 is cheaper.
       For distances more than 200 miles, C_2 is cheaper.

45 driving speed

time

47 distance from exit

time

49 (a) (i) $f(1985) = 13$
       (ii) $f(1990) = 99$
    (b) $(f(1990) - f(1985))/(1990 - 1985) = 17.2$ billionaires/yr
    (c) $f(t) = 17.2t - 34{,}129$

51 (a) 2005–2007
    (b) 2004–2007

53 (a) 7.094 meters
    (b) 1958, 1883

55 (a) $\Delta w/\Delta h$ constant
    (b) $w = 5h - 174$; 5 lbs/in
    (c) $h = 0.2w + 34.8$; 0.2 in/lb

57 (a) $C = 10 + 0.2x$
    (c) Vertical intercept
       Slope of line

59 (a) $(-2, 4)$
    (b) $(-b, b^2)$

61 $y = 0.5 - 3x$ is decreasing

63 $y = 2x + 3$

65 False

67 False; $y = x + 1$ at points $(1, 2)$ and $(2, 3)$

69 (b), (c)

Section 1.2

1 Concave up

3 Neither

5 5; 7%

7 3.2; 3% (continuous)

9 $P = 15(1.2840)^t$; growth

11 $P = P_0(1.2214)^t$; growth

13 (a) 1.5
    (b) 50%

15 (a) $P = 1000 + 50t$
    (b) $P = 1000(1.05)^t$

17 (a) D to E, H to I
    (b) A to B, E to F
    (c) C to D, G to H
    (d) B to C, F to G

19 (a) $h(x) = 31 - 3x$
    (b) $g(x) = 36(1.5)^x$

21 Table D

23 (a) $P = 10^6(e^{0.02t})$
    (b)

P

1,000,000

t

25 (a) 125%
    (b) 9 times

27 (a) revenue

advertising

(b) temperature

time

29 (a) $g(x)$
    (b) $h(x)$
    (c) $f(x)$

31 $y = 3(2^x)$

33 $y = 2(3^x)$

35 $f(1) = 15, f(3) = 25, f(4) = 30$
    $g(1) = 10\sqrt{2}, g(3) = 20\sqrt{2}, g(4) = 40$

37 (a) 2.3 years

39 (a) $H, 2H, 3H$
    (b) $t/H; A = 325(1/2)^{t/H}$

41 30.268%

43 (a) 261 million gallons, 358 million gallons
    (b) consumption of biodiesel (mn gal)

400

200

2006   2008   year

45 (a) 16 trillion BTUs, 32 trillion BTUs
    (b) consumption of hydro. power (trillion BTU)

35
25
15
5

2005   2007   2009   year

    (c) 2007, 13 trillion BTUs

47 (a) Increased: 2006, 2008; decreased: none
    (b) Yes

49 $y = 2x$ not concave up

51 $f(x) = 2(1.1)^x$

53 False

55 False

57 True; $f(x) = (0.5)^x$

59 True

Section 1.3

1 (a)

y

4

-2 2 x

-4

(b)

(c)

(d)

(e)

(f)

3 (a)

5

7

(b)

(c)

(d)

(e)

(f)

9 (a) $\sqrt{5}$
(b) 5
(c) $\sqrt{x^2 + 4}$
(d) $x + 4$
(e) $t^2\sqrt{t + 4}$

11 (a) $\dfrac{1}{7}$

(b) 7

(c) $\dfrac{1}{3x + 4}$

(d) $\dfrac{3}{x} + 4$

(e) $3 + \dfrac{4}{t}$

13 (a) $t^2 + 2t + 2$
(b) $t^4 + 2t^2 + 2$
(c) 5
(d) $2t^2 + 2$
(e) $t^4 + 2t^2 + 2$

15 $2zh + h^2$

17 $4hz$

21 (a) $y = 2x^2 + 1$

(b) $y = 2(x^2 + 1)$
(c) No

23 Not invertible

25 not invertible

27 Invertible

29 Neither

31 Neither

33 Even

35 Neither

37 $f(x) = x + 1$
$g(x) = x^3$

39 $f(x) = e^x$
$g(x) = 2x$

41 $y = (x - 2)^3 - 1$

43 $\{3, -7, 19, 4, 178, 2, 1\}$

45 Not invertible

47 Not invertible

49 $g(2r)$ ft^3

51 $f^{-1}(g^{-1}(10,000))$ min

53 18

55 Cannot be done

57 0.4

59 -0.9

61

63 (a) $f(15) \approx 48$
   (b) Yes
   (c) $f^{-1}(120) \approx 35$
       Rock is 35 millions yrs old at depth
       of 120 meters

65 $4000\pi/3$ cm^3

67 Reflected about t-axis,
   shifted up S

69 Shift left

71 $f^{-1}(x) = x$

73 $f(x) = x^2 + 2$

75 $f(x) = 1.5x, g(x) = 1.5x + 3$

77 True

79 False

81 True

83 True; $f(x) = 0$

85 Impossible

87 Impossible

Section 1.4

1 1/2

3 $5A^2$

5 $-1 + \ln A + \ln B$

7 $(\log 11)/(\log 3) = 2.2$

9 $(\log(2/5))/(\log 1.04) = -23.4$

11 1.68

13 6.212

15 0.26

17 1

19 $(\log a)/(\log b)$

21 $(\log Q - \log Q_0)/(n \log a)$

23 $\ln(a/b)$

25 $P = 15e^{0.4055t}$

27 $P = 174e^{-0.1054t}$

29 $p^{-1}(t) \approx 58.708 \log t$

31 $f^{-1}(t) = e^{t-1}$

33 16 kg

35 (a) 2023
   (b) 338.65 million people

37 (a) $Q_0(1.0033)^x$
   (b) 210.391 microgm/cu m

39 (a) 10 mg
   (b) 18%
   (c) 3.04 mg
   (d) 11.60 hours

41 $C = 2, \alpha = -\ln 2 = -0.693, y(2) = 1/2$

43 (a) $B(t) = B_0 e^{0.067t}$
   (b) $P(t) = P_0 e^{0.033t}$
   (c) $t = 20.387$; in 2000

45 2023

47 (a) 0.00664
   (b) $t = 2.167$; March 2, 2013

49 6,301 yrs; 385,081 yrs

51 (a) 47.6%
   (b) 23.7%

53 2054

55 Yes

57 To the left

59 No effect

61 Function even

63 $f(x) = -x$

65 True

67 False

Section 1.5

1 Negative
  0
  Undefined

3 Positive
  Positive
  Positive

5 Positive
  Positive
  Positive

7 Positive
  Negative
  Negative

9 Negative
  Positive
  Negative

11 $8\pi; 3$

13 2; 0.1

15 $f(x) = 5\cos(x/3)$

17 $f(x) = -8\cos(x/10)$

19 $f(x) = 2\cos(5x)$

21 $f(x) = 3\sin(\pi x/9)$

23 $f(x) = 3 + 3\sin((\pi/4)x)$

25 0.588

27 $(\sin^{-1}(2/5))/3 \approx 0.1372$

29 $(\tan^{-1} 2)/5 = 0.221$

31 No solution

33 If $f(x) = \sin x$ and
   $g(x) = x^2$ then
   $\sin x^2 = f(g(x))$
   $\sin^2 x = g(f(x))$
   $\sin(\sin x) = f(f(x))$

35 (a)
   (b) $P = 800 - 100\cos(\pi t/6)$

37 (a) $f(t) = -0.5 + \sin t$
       $g(t) = 1.5 + \sin t$
       $h(t) = -1.5 + \sin t$
       $k(t) = 0.5 + \sin t$
   (b) $g(t) = 1 + k(t)$

39 (a) $\frac{1}{60}$ second
   (b) V_0 represents the amplitude of oscillation.
   (c)

41 $\theta = \pi/4; R = v_0^2/g$

$R = \frac{v_0^2}{g}\sin 2\theta$

43 (a) Average depth of water
   (b) $A = 7.5$
   (c) $B = 0.507$
   (d) The time of a high tide

45 0.3 seconds

47 27.3 days $\approx$ one month

49 $f(t)$ is C; $g(t)$ is B; $h(t)$ is A; $r(t)$ is D

51 (a) 2π

53 (a) 0.4 and 2.7
    (b) $\arcsin(0.4) \approx 0.4$
        $\pi - \arcsin(0.4) \approx 2.7$
    (c) -0.4 and -2.7.
    (d) $-0.4 \approx -\arcsin(0.4)$
        $-2.7 \approx \arcsin(0.4) - \pi$

55 (b)

    (c) The domain of arccos and arcsin are the same because their inverses (sine and cosine) have the same range
    (d) $[0, \pi]$
    (e) On $[-\pi/2, \pi/2]$ sine is invertible but cosine is not

57 Max $y = A + C$

59 $400(\cos x) + 1600$.

61 False

63 False

65 False

67 True

69 True

71 True

Section 1.6

1 As $x \to \infty, y \to \infty$
  As $x \to -\infty, y \to -\infty$

3 $f(x) \to -\infty$ as $x \to +\infty$
  $f(x) \to -\infty$ as $x \to -\infty$

5 $f(x) \to +\infty$ as $x \to +\infty$
  $f(x) \to +\infty$ as $x \to -\infty$

7 $f(x) \to 3$ as $x \to +\infty$
  $f(x) \to 3$ as $x \to -\infty$

9 $f(x) \to 0$ as $x \to +\infty$
  $f(x) \to 0$ as $x \to -\infty$

11 $0.2x^5$

13 1.05^x

15 $25 - 40x^2 + x^3 + 3x^5$

17 (I) (a) 3 (b) Negative
  (II) (a) 4 (b) Positive
  (III) (a) 4 (b) Negative
  (IV) (a) 5 (b) Negative
  (V) (a) 5 (b) Positive

19 $y = -\frac{1}{2}(x+2)^2(x-2)$

21 $f(x) = kx(x+3)(x-4)$
  $(k < 0)$

23 $f(x) =$
  $k(x+2)(x-2)^2(x-5)$
  $(k < 0)$

25 r

27 1, 2, 3, 4, or 5 roots

  (a) 5 roots

  (b) 4 roots

  (c) 3 roots

  (d) 2 roots

  (e) 1 root

29 $-10^5 \leq x \leq 10^5, \; -10^{15} \leq y \leq 10^{15}$

31 (a) $1.3 \, \text{m}^2$
  (b) $86.8 \, \text{kg}$
  (c) $h = 112.6 s^{4/3}$

33 (a) $R = kr^4$
    (k is a constant)
  (b) $R = 4.938 r^4$
  (c) $3086.42 \, \text{cm}^3/\text{sec}$

35 (a) $S = 2\pi r^2 + 2V/r$
  (b) $S \to \infty$ as $r \to \infty$
  (c)

37 Horizontal: $y = 1$;
  Vertical: $x = -2, x = 2$

39 (a) 0
  (b) $t = 2v_0/g$
  (c) $t = v_0/g$
  (d) $(v_0)^2/(2g)$

41 (a) (i) $1 = a + b + c$
    (ii) $b = -2a$ and $c = 1 + a$
    (iii) $c = 6$
  (b) $y = 5x^2 - 10x + 6$

43 $(3/x) + 6/(x - 2)$
  Horizontal asymptote: x-axis
  Vertical asymptote: $x = 0$ and $x = 2$

45 $h(t) = ab^t$
  $g(t) = kt^3$
  $f(t) = ct^2$

47 (a) $R(P) = kP(L - P)$
    $(k > 0)$
  (b)

49 (a) $v = 3 \cdot 10^8$
  (b) $v < 1.5 \cdot 10^8$

51 $f(x) = (x^3 + 1)/x$ has no horizontal asymptote

53 $f(x) = 3x/(x - 10)$

55 $f(x) = 1/(x + 7\pi)$

57 $f(x) = (x - 1)/(x - 2)$

59 True

Section 1.7

1 Yes

3 Yes

5 Yes

7 No

9 No

15 (a) Continuous
  (b) Not continuous

17 Velocity: Not continuous
  Distance: Continuous

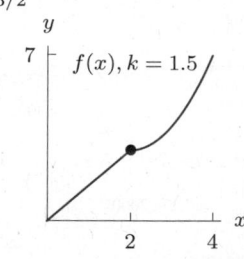

19 $k = 5/3$

21 $k = 5/4$

23 (a)

  (b) $3/2$
  (c)

25 $k = -3$

27 $k = (\ln 3)/2$

29 $k = (e^6 - 1)/2$

31 No

33 $Q = \begin{cases} 1.2t & 0 \leq t \leq 0.5 \\ 0.6e^{0.001}e^{-.002t} & 0.5 < t \end{cases}$

35 Three zeros: one between 5 and 10, one between 10 and 12, the third either less than 5 or greater than 12

37 (a)

(b) No

39 Only for continuous function

41 $f(x) = \begin{cases} 1 & x \geq 15 \\ -1 & x < 15 \end{cases}$

43 $f(x) = \begin{cases} 1 & x \leq 2 \\ x & x > 2 \end{cases}$

45 False, $f(x) = \begin{cases} 1 & x \leq 3 \\ 2 & x > 3 \end{cases}$

47 False

Section 1.8

1 (a) 3
  (b) 7
  (c) Does not exist
  (d) 8

3 (a) 8
  (b) 6
  (c) 15
  (d) 4

5 Other answers are possible

7 Other answers are possible

9 Other answers are possible

11 $\lim_{x \to -\infty} f(x) = +\infty$;
   $\lim_{x \to +\infty} f(x) = -\infty$

13 $\lim_{x \to -\infty} f(x) = 3/5$;
   $\lim_{x \to +\infty} f(x) = 3/5$

15 $\lim_{x \to -\infty} f(x) = 0$;
   $\lim_{x \to +\infty} f(x) = +\infty$

17 0

19 2

21 0.01745...

23 1

25 0.693

27 0

29 $\lim_{x \to 4+} f(x) = 1$, $\lim_{x \to 4-} f(x) = -1$, $\lim_{x \to 4} f(x)$ does not exist

31 $\lim_{x \to 3+} f(x) = \lim_{x \to 3-} f(x) = \lim_{x \to 3} f(x) = 7$

35 No. Limit does not exist at 0

37 No. $f(0) \neq$ limit at 0

39 2.71828...

47 (b) −1
   (c)

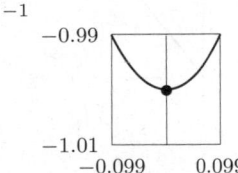

   (d) $-0.099 < x < 0.099$,
       $-1.01 < y < -0.99$

49 (b) 0
   (c)

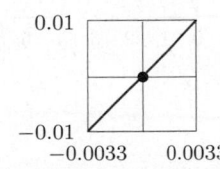

   (d) $-0.0033 < x < 0.0033$,
       $-0.01 < y < 0.01$

51 (b) 3
   (c)

2.99 < y < 3.01

   (d) $-0.047 < x < 0.047$,
       $2.99 < y < 3.01$

53 (b) 2
   (c)

   (d) $-0.0049 < x < 0.0049$,
       $1.99 < y < 2.01$

55 $3/\pi$

57 1/3

59 2/3

61 3/2

63 3/2

65 5

67 $k \geq 2$

69 $k \geq 3$

71 $k \geq 0$

73 0.46, 0.21, 0.09

75 (a) $x = 1/(n\pi)$,
       $n = 1, 2, 3, \ldots$
   (b) $x = 2/(n\pi)$,
       $n = 1, 5, 9, \ldots$
   (c) $x = 2/(n\pi)$,
       $n = 3, 7, 11, \ldots$

77 (b) 0
   (c)

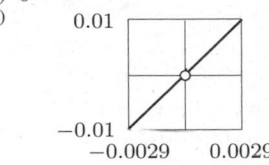

   (d) $-0.0029 < x < 0.0029$,
       $-0.01 < y < 0.01$

85 Limit does not exist

87 $f(x) = (x + 3)(x - 1)/(x - 1)$

89 True

91 True

93 False

95 True

97 False

99 False

101 (a) Follows
    (b) Does not follow (although true)
    (c) Follows
    (d) Does not follow

Chapter 1 Review

1 $y = 2x - 10$

3 $y = -3x^2 + 3$

5 $y = 2 + \sqrt{9 - (x + 1)^2}$

7 $y = -5x/(x - 2)$

9

administration
of drug

11 (a) $[0, 7]$
   (b) $[-2, 5]$
   (c) 5
   (d) $(1, 7)$
   (e) Concave up
   (f) 1
   (g) No

13 (a) Min gross income for $100,000 loan
   (b) Size of loan for income of $75,000

15 $t \approx 35.003$

17 $t = \log(12.01/5.02)/\log(1.04/1.03) = 90.283$

19 $P = 5.23e^{-1.6904t}$

21 $f(x) = x^3$
   $g(x) = \ln x$

23 Amplitude: 2
   Period: $2\pi/5$

25 (a) $f(x) \to \infty$
     as $x \to \infty$;
     $f(x) \to -\infty$
     as as $x \to -\infty$
   (b) $f(x) \to -\infty$
     as as $x \to \pm\infty$
   (c) $f(x) \to 0$ as $x \to \pm\infty$
   (d) $f(x) \to 6$ as $x \to \pm\infty$

27 $0.25\sqrt{x}$

29 $y = e^{0.4621x}$ or $y = (1.5874)^x$

31 $y = -k(x^2 + 5x)$
   $(k > 0)$

33 $z = 1 - \cos\theta$

35 $x = k(y^2 - 4y)$
   $(k > 0)$

37 $y = -(x + 5)(x + 1)(x - 3)^2$

39 Simplest is $y = 1 - e^{-x}$

41 $f(x) = \sin(2(\pi/5)x)$

43 Not continuous

45 $\lim_{x \to 3^+} f(x) = 54$, $\lim_{x \to 3^-} f(x) = -54$, $\lim_{x \to 3} f(x)$ does not exist

47 (b) 200 bushels
   (c) 80 lbs
   (d) $0 \le Y \le 550$
   (e) Decreasing
   (f) Concave down

49 (a) (i) $q = 320 - (2/5)p$
     (ii) $p = 800 - (5/2)q$
   (b)

51 (a) (i) Attractive force, pulling atoms together

     (ii) Repulsive force, pushing atoms apart
   (b) Yes

53 2011

55 (a) Increased: 2009; decreased: 2006, 2007
   (b) False
   (c) True

57 Parabola opening downward

59 10 hours

61 About 14.21 years

63 (a) 81%
   (b) 32.9 hours
   (c)

65 One hour

67 US: 156 volts max, 60 cycles/sec
   Eur: 339 volts max, 50 cycles/sec

69 (a) (i) $V = 3\pi r^2$
     (ii) $V = \pi r^2 h$
   (b) (i)

     (ii)

71 (a)

73 (a) III
   (b) IV
   (c) I
   (d) II

75 $0.1, 0.05, 0.00007$

77 20

79 (a) $f(x) = (x - a)(x + a)(x + b)(x - c)$
   (b)

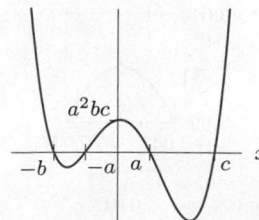

81 (a) $f(x) \to \infty$ as $x \to \infty$
     $f(x) \to 16$ as $x \to -\infty$
   (b) $(e^x + 1)(e^{2x} - 2)(e^x - 2)(e^{2x} + 2e^x + 4)$
     Two zeros
   (c) $(\ln 2)/2, \ln 2$
     One twice other

83 (a) $p(x) = x^2 + 3x + 9$
     $r(x) = -3, q(x) = x - 3$
   (b) $f(x) \approx -3/(x - 3)$ for x near 3
   (c) $f(x) \approx x^2 + 3x + 9$ as $x \to \pm\infty$

85 (a) $1 - 8\cos^2 x + 8\cos^4 x$
   (b) $1 - 8\sin^2 x + 8\sin^4 x$

Section 2.1

1 $265/3$ km/hr

3 -3 angstroms/sec

5 2 meters/sec

7 0 cm/sec

9 (a) (i) 0.04 m/sec
     (ii) 0.0004 m/sec
     (iii) 0.000004 m/sec
   (b) 0 m/sec

11

13

15 0

17 2.7

19 Positive: A and D
   Negative: C and F
   Most positive: A
   Most negative: F

21 $F < B < E < 0 < D < A < C$

23

25 4

27 12

29 $|\text{velocity}| = \text{speed}$

33 $s(t) = t^2$

35 False

37 True

39 False

Section 2.2

1 12

3 (a) 70 \$/kg; 50 \$/kg
 (b) About 60 \$/kg

5 (b) 0.24
 (c) 0.22

7 negative

9 $f'(2) \approx 9.89$

11 $f'(d) = 0$, $f'(b) = 0.5$, $f'(c) = 2$, $f'(a) = -0.5$, $f'(e) = -2$

13 About 41

15 (a) $f(4)$
 (b) $f(2) - f(1)$
 (c) $(f(2) - f(1))/(2-1)$
 (d) $f'(1)$

17 $(4, 25)$; $(4.2, 25.3)$; $(3.9, 24.85)$

19

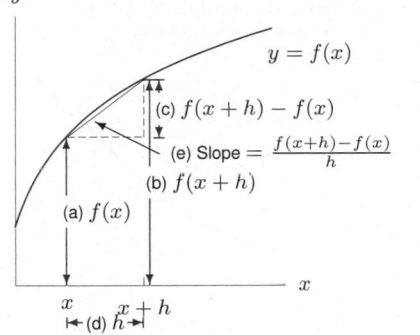

21 (a) $(f(b) - f(a))/(b - a)$
 (b) Slopes same
 (c) Yes

23 $g'(-4) = 5$

25 $y = 7x - 9$

27 $f'(2) \approx 6.77$

29 $f'(1) \approx -1.558$
  $f'(\frac{\pi}{4}) \approx -1$

31 8.84 million people/year
  9.28 million people/year

35 -6

37 -1

39 $1/4$

41 100

43 -1

45 $-1/4$

47 $y = 100x - 500$

49 $y = x$

51 $f'(0.5) > 0$

53 $f(x) = e^x$

55 True

57 True

Section 2.3

1 (a) 3
 (b) Positive: $0 < x < 4$
  Negative: $4 < x < 12$

3

5

7

9

11

13

15

17

19 $-1/x^2$

21 $4x$

23

(a)

(b)

(c)

(d)

25 $f'(1) = 1$
  $f'(2) = 0.5$
  $f'(5) = 0.2$
  $f'(10) = 0.1$
  $f'(x) = \frac{1}{x}$

27 5.2

1148

29

31

33

35

37

39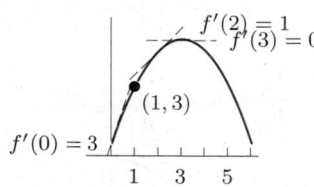

41 (a) $t = 3$
  (b) $t = 9$
  (c) $t = 14$
  (d)

43 (a) $x_1 < x < x_3$
  (b) $0 < x < x_1$; $x_3 < x < x_5$

45 (a) Periodic: period 1 year

(b) Max of 4500 on July 1st
  Min of 3500 on Jan 1st
  (c) Growing fastest:
    around April 1st
    Decreasing fastest:
    around Oct 1st
  (d) ≈ 0

47

49 0

53 Counterexample: e^{-x}

55 $f(t) = t(1 - t)$

57 True

59 False

Section 2.4

1 (a) Costs $1300 for 200 gallons
  (b) Costs about $6 for 201st gallon

3 (a) Positive
  (b) $^{\circ}$F/min

5 (a) Quarts; dollars.
  (b) Quarts; dollars/quart

7 Dollars/percent; positive

9 Dollars/year; negative

11 (a) Investing the $1000 at 5%
    would yield about $1649 after 10 years
  (b) Extra percentage point would yield an increase of about $165; dollars/%

13 (b) Pounds/(Calories/day)

15

or

19 (a) 1986: pop. Mexico inc. 2 m. people/yr
  (b) Pop. 95.5 m. in 1996
  (c) 95.5 m.: about 0.46 yrs for pop. inc. of 1 m

21 (a) Depth 3 ft at $t = 5$ hrs
  (b) Depth increases 0.7 ft/hr
  (c) Time 7 hrs when depth 5 ft
  (d) Depth at 5 ft increases 1 ft in 1.2 hrs

23 Inches/year
  $g'(10) > 0$
  $g'(30) = 0$

25 Barrels/year; negative

27 (a) Gal/minute
  (b) (i) 0
    (ii) Negative
    (iii) 0

29 (a) 0.0851 people/sec
  (b) 12 seconds

31 Number of people 65.5–66.5 inches
  Units: People per inch
  $P'(66)$ between 17 and 34 million people/in
  $P'(x)$ is never negative

33 (a) $2.6 \cdot 10^{12}$; not compressible
  (b) $1.5 \cdot 10^{17}$; even less compressible

35 $r(t)$ is decreasing

39 True

41 False

43 (b), (d)

Section 2.5

1 (a) Increasing, concave up
  (b) Decreasing, concave down

3 B

5 (a)

(b)

(c)

(d)

7

9 $f'(x) < 0$
   $f''(x) = 0$

11 $f'(x) < 0$
    $f''(x) > 0$

13 $f'(x) < 0$
    $f''(x) < 0$

15 (a) Positive; negative
   (b) Neither; positive
   (c) Number of cars increasing at
        600,000 million cars per year in 2005

17   (a)

   (b)

   (c)

19
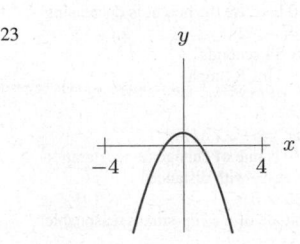

21

23

25 (a) utility

   (b) Derivative of utility is positive
        2nd derivative of utility is negative

29 (a) t_3, t_4, t_5
   (b) t_2, t_3
   (c) t_1, t_2, t_5
   (d) t_1, t_4, t_5
   (e) t_3, t_4

31 22 only possible value

33 It could be neither

35 $f(x) = b + ax, a \neq 0$

37 True

39 True

41 False

Section 2.6

1 (a) $x = 1$
  (b) $x = 1, 2, 3$

3 No

5 Yes

7 Yes

9 Yes

11 (a) Yes
   (b) Not at $t = 0$

13 (a) Yes
   (b) No

15 (a) Yes
   (b) No

17 Other cases are possible

19 $f(x) = |x - 2|$

21 $f(x) = (x^2 - 1)/(x^2 - 4)$

23 True; $f(x) = x^2$

25 True; $f(x) = \begin{cases} 1 & x \geq 0 \\ -1 & x < 0 \end{cases}$

27 (a) Not a counterexample
   (b) Counterexample
   (c) Not a counterexample
   (d) Not a counterexample

Chapter 2 Review

1 $72/7 = 10.286$ cm/sec

3 $(\ln 3)/2 = 0.549$ mm/sec

5 0 mm/sec

7 0 mm/sec

9   distance

    time

11 (a)

$y = x \sin x$

   (b) Seven

(c) Increasing at $x = 1$
     Decreasing at $x = 4$
(d) $6 \leq x \leq 8$
(e) $x = -9$

13

15

17

19

21

23 $-1/x^2$

25 (a) (i) C and D
        (ii) B and C
   (b) A and B,
        C and D

27 $10x$

29 $6x$

31 $2a$

33 $-2/a^3$

35 $-1/(2(\sqrt{a})^3)$

37 From smallest to largest:
    0, Vel at C, Vel at B, Av vel between A and B,
    1, Vel at A

39 (a) $A, C, F,$ and H.
   (b) Acceleration 0

41 (a) $f'(t) > 0$: depth increasing
        $f'(t) < 0$: depth decreasing
   (b) Depth increasing 20 cm/min
   (c) 12 meters/hr

43 (a) Thousand \$ per \$ per gallon
    Rate change revenue with price/gal
  (b) \$ per gal/thousand \$
    Rate change price/gal with revenue

47 Concave up

49 (a)

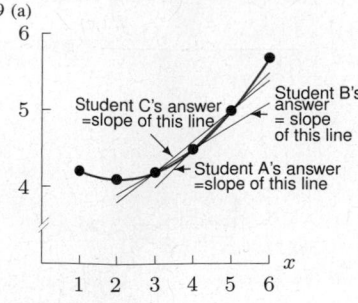

  (b) Student C's
  (c) $f'(x) = \dfrac{f(x+h) - f(x-h)}{2h}$

51 $x_1 = 0.9, x_2 = 1, x_3 = 1.1$
   $y_1 = 2.8, y_2 = 3, y_3 = 3.2$

53 (a) Negative
  (b) $dw/dt = 0$
  (c) $|dw/dt|$ increases; dw/dt decreases

55 (a) Dose for 140 lbs is 120 mg
    Dose increases by 3mg/lb
  (b) About 135 mg

57 $P'(t) = 0.008P(t)$

59 (a) $f'(0.6) \approx 0.5$
    $f'(0.5) \approx 2$
  (b) $f''(0.6) \approx -15$
  (c) Maximum: near $x = 0.8$
    minimum: near $x = 0.3$

61 (a) At $(0, \sqrt{19})$: slope $= 0$
    At $(\sqrt{19}, 0)$: slope is undefined
  (b) slope $\approx 1/2$
  (c) At $(-2, \sqrt{15})$: slope $\approx 1/2$
    At $(-2, -\sqrt{15})$: slope $\approx -1/2$
    At $(2, \sqrt{15})$: slope $\approx -1/2$

63 (a) Period 12 months

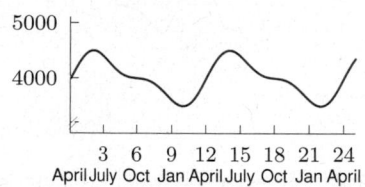

  (b) Max of 4500 on June 1st
  (c) Min of 3500 on Feb 1st
  (d) Growing fastest:
    April 1st
    Decreasing fastest:
    July 15 and Dec 15
  (e) About 400 deer/month

65 (a) Concave down

(b) $120° < T < 140°$
(c) $135° < T < 140°$
(d) $45 < t < 50$

67 (a) $f'(0) = 1.00000$
    $f'(0.3) = 1.04534$
    $f'(0.7) = 1.25521$
    $f'(1) = 1.54314$
  (b) They are about the same

69 0, because $f(x)$ constant

71 (a) $-2a/e^{ax^2} + 4a^2x^2/e^{ax^2}$
  (b)

$a = 1$

$a = 2$

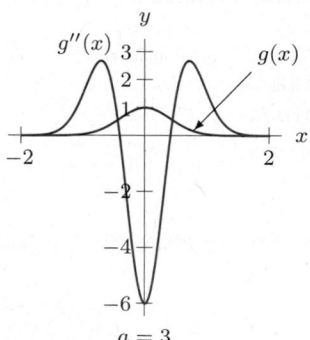

$a = 3$

73 (a) $4x(x^2+1), 6x(x^2+1)^2, 8x(x^2+1)^3$
  (b) $2nx(x^2+1)^{n-1}$

Section 3.1

3 Do not apply

5 $y' = \pi x^{\pi-1}$ (power rule)

7 $11x^{10}$

9 $-12x^{-13}$

11 $-3x^{-7/4}/4$

13 $3x^{-1/4}/4$

15 $3t^2 - 6t + 8$

17 $-5t^{-6}$

19 $-(7/2)r^{-9/2}$

21 $x^{-3/4}/4$

23 $-(3/2)x^{-5/2}$

25 $6x^{1/2} - \frac{5}{2}x^{-1/2}$

27 $17 + 12x^{-1/2}$

29 $20x^3 - 2/x^3$

31 $-12x^3 - 12x^2 - 6$

33 $6t - 6/t^{3/2} + 2/t^3$

35 $3t^{1/2} + 2t$

37 $(1/2)\theta^{-1/2} + \theta^{-2}$

39 $(z^2 - 1)/3z^2$

41 $1/(2\sqrt{\theta}) + 1/(2\theta^{3/2})$

43 $3x^2/a + 2ax/b - c$

45 a/c

47 $3ab^2$

49 $b/(2\sqrt{t})$

51 Rules of this section do not apply

53 $6x$
  (power rule and sum rule)

55 $-2/3z^3$
  (power rule and sum rule)

57 $y = 2x - 1$

59 $y = 7x - 9$

61 $y = 2x$ and $y = -6x$

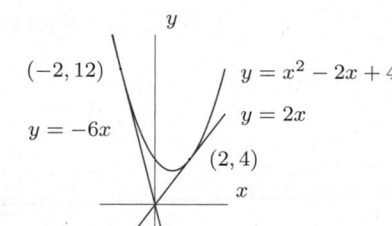

63 $x > 1$

65 $f'(x) = 12x + 1$ and
  $f''(x) = 12$

67 Proportional to r^2

69 (a) $v(t) = -32t$
    $v \le 0$ because the height is decreasing
  (b) $a(t) = -32$
  (c) $t = 8.84$ seconds
    $v = -192.84$ mph

71 56 cm/sec^2

73 (a) $dg/dr = -2GM/r^3$
  (b) dg/dr is rate of change of acceleration
    g decreases with distance
  (c) -3.05×10^{-6}
  (d) Magnitude of dg/dr small; reasonable

75 (a) $dA/dr = 2\pi r$
  (b) Circumference of a circle

79 $n = 1/13$

81 (a) $a = 4$
  (b) No

83 $x^2 + a$

85 $f(x) = x^2, g(x) = 3x$

87 $f(x) = 3x^2$

89 False

91 True

Section 3.2

1 $2e^x + 2x$

3 $5\ln(a)a^{5x}$

5 $10x + (\ln 2)2^x$

7 $4(\ln 10)10^x - 3x^2$

9 $((\ln 3)3^x)/3 - (33x^{-3/2})/2$

11 $(\ln 4)^2 4^x$

13 $5 \cdot 5^t \ln 5 + 6 \cdot 6^t \ln 6$

15 ex^{e-1}

17 $(\ln \pi)\pi^x$

19 $(\ln k)k^x$

21 e^{t+2}

23 $a^x \ln a + ax^{a-1}$

25 $2 + 1/(3x^{4/3}) + 3^x \ln 3$

27 $2x + (\ln 2)2^x$

29 Rules do not apply

31 e^{x+5}

33 Rules do not apply

35 Rules do not apply

37 Rules do not apply

39 ≈ 7.95 cents/year

41 US, since $dU/dt > dM/dt$ at $t = 0$

43 (a) $f'(0) = -1$
   (b) $y = -x$
   (c) $y = x$

45 $g(x) = x^2/2 + x + 1$

47 e

49 $f'(x) = (\ln 2)2^x$

51 $f(x) = 0.5^x$

53 False; $f(x) = \ln x$

55 False; $f(x) = |x|$

Section 3.3

1 $5x^4 + 10x$

3 $e^x(x + 1)$

5 $2^x/(2\sqrt{x}) + \sqrt{x}(\ln 2)2^x$

7 $3^x[(\ln 3)(x^2 - x^{\frac{1}{2}}) + (2x - 1/(2\sqrt{x}))]$

9 $(1 - x)/e^x$

11 $(1 - (t + 1)\ln 2)/2^t$

13 $6/(5r + 2)^2$

15 $1/(5t + 2)^2$

17 $2e^t + 2te^t + 1/(2t^{3/2})$

19 $2y - 6,\ y \neq 0$

21 $\sqrt{z}(3 - z^{-2})/2$

23 $2r(r + 1)/(2r + 1)^2$

25 $17e^x(1 - \ln 2)/2^x$

27 $1, x \neq -1$

29 $6x(x^2 + 5)^2(3x^3 - 2)(6x^3 + 15x - 2)$

31 (a) 4

(b) Does not exist

(c) -4

33 (a) -2
   (b) Does not exist
   (c) 0

35 Approx 0.4

37 Approx 0.7

39 Approx -21.2

41 $f'(x) = 2e^{2x}$

43 $x > -2$

45 $y = 7x - 5$

47 (a) $\dfrac{d}{dx}\left(\dfrac{e^x}{x}\right) = \dfrac{e^x}{x} - \dfrac{e^x}{x^2}$

$\dfrac{d}{dx}\left(\dfrac{e^x}{x^2}\right) = \dfrac{e^x}{x^2} - \dfrac{2e^x}{x^3}$

$\dfrac{d}{dx}\left(\dfrac{e^x}{x^3}\right) = \dfrac{e^x}{x^3} - \dfrac{3e^x}{x^4}$

(b) $\dfrac{d}{dx}\left(\dfrac{e^x}{x^n}\right) = \dfrac{e^x}{x^n} - \dfrac{ne^x}{x^{n+1}}$

49 $4^x(\ln 4 \cdot f(x) + \ln 4 \cdot g(x) + f'(x) + g'(x))$

51 $(f'(x)g(x)h(x) + f(x)g'(x)h(x) - f(x)g(x)h'(x))/(h(x))^2$

53 (a) 19
   (b) -11

55 $f(x) = x^{10}e^x$

57 $r_2^2/(r_1 + r_2)^2$

59 (a) $g(v) = 1/f(v)$
       $g(80) = 20$ km/liter
       $g'(80) = -(1/5)$ km/liter for each
       1 km/hr increase in speed
   (b) $h(v) = v \cdot f(v)$
       $h(80) = 4$ liters/hr
       $h'(80) = 0.09$ liters/hr for
       each 1 km/hr inc. in speed

61 (a) $f'(x) = (x - 2) + (x - 1)$
   (b) $f'(x) = (x - 2)(x - 3) + (x - 1)(x - 3) + (x - 1)(x - 2)$
   (c) $f'(x) = (x - 2)(x - 3)(x - 4) + (x - 1)(x - 3)(x - 4) + (x - 1)(x - 2)(x - 4) + (x - 1)(x - 2)(x - 3)$

63 (a) $(FGH)' = F'GH + FG'H + FGH'$
   (c) $f_1'f_2 f_3 \cdots f_n + f_1 f_2' f_3 \cdots f_n + \cdots + f_1 \cdots f_{n-1} f_n'$

65 $f''(x)g(x) + 2f'(x)g'(x) + f(x)g''(x)$

67 Signs in numerator reversed

69 $f(x) = e^x \sin x$

71 False

73 False; $f(x) = x^2, g(x) = x^2 - 1$

Section 3.4

1 $99(x + 1)^{98}$

3 $56x(4x^2 + 1)^6$

5 $e^x/(2\sqrt{e^x + 1})$

7 $5(w^4 - 2w)^4(4w^3 - 2)$

9 $2r^3/\sqrt{r^4 + 1}$

11 $e^{2x}\left[2x^2 + 2x + (\ln 5 + 2)5^x\right]$

13 $\pi e^{\pi x}$

15 $-200xe^{-x^2}$

17 $(\ln \pi)\pi^{(x+2)}$

19 $e^{5-2t}(1 - 2t)$

21 $(2t - ct^2)e^{-ct}$

23 $(e^{\sqrt{s}})/(2\sqrt{s})$

25 $3s^2/(2\sqrt{s^3 + 1})$

27 $(e^{-z})/(2\sqrt{z}) - \sqrt{z}e^{-z}$

29 $5 \cdot \ln 2 \cdot 2^{5t-3}$

31 $-(\ln 10)(10^{\frac{5}{2} - \frac{y}{2}})/2$

33 $(1 - 2z \ln 2)/(2^{z+1}\sqrt{z})$

35 $\dfrac{\sqrt{x + 3}(x^2 + 6x - 9)}{2\sqrt{x^2 + 9}(x + 3)^2}$

37 $-(3e^{3x} + 2x)/(e^{3x} + x^2)^2$

39 $-1.5x^2(x^3 + 1)^{-1.5}$

41 $(2t + 3)(1 - e^{-2t}) + (t^2 + 3t)(2e^{-2t})$

43 $30e^{5x} - 2xe^{-x^2}$

45 $2we^{w^2}(5w^2 + 8)$

47 $-3te^{-3t^2}/\sqrt{e^{-3t^2} + 5}$

49 $2ye^{[e^{(y^2)} + y^2]}$

51 $6ax(ax^2 + b)^2$

53 $ae^{-bx} - abxe^{-bx}$

55 $abce^{-cx}e^{-be^{-cx}}$

57 (a) 2
   (b) Chain rule does not apply
   (c) -2

59 (a) Chain rule does not apply
   (b) Chain rule does not apply
   (c) Chain rule does not apply

61 1/2

63 -1

65 $y = 3x - 5$

67 $y = -16.464t + 87.810$

69 $x < 2$

71 (a) 13,394 fish
   (b) 8037 fish/month

73 (a) 4
   (b) 2
   (c) 1/2

75 $e^{(x^6)}/6$

77 (a) $g'(1) = 3/4$
   (b) $h'(1) = 3/2$

79 $d; 0$

81 Decreasing

83 Value of $h(x)$ decreases from d to $-d$

85 $P = 308.75e^{0.00923t}$

87 $f(5) = 6.3$ billion dollars;
    $f'(5) = 0.272$ billion dollars per year

89 (a) $P(1 + r/100)^t \ln(1 + r/100)$
   (b) $Pt(1 + r/100)^{t-1}/100$

91 (a) $dm/dv = m_0 v/\left(c^2\sqrt{(1 - v^2/c^2)^3}\right)$
   (b) Rate of change of mass with respect to speed v

95 $f''(x)(g(x))^{-1} - 2f'(x)(g(x))^{-2}g'(x) + 2f(x)(g(x))^{-3}(g'(x))^2 - f(x)(g(x))^{-2}g''(x)$

97 $w'(x) = 2xe^{x^2}$

99 $f(x) = (x^2 + 1)^2$

101 False; $f(x) = 5x + 7$, $g(x) = x + 2$

Section 3.5

3 $\cos^2\theta - \sin^2\theta = \cos 2\theta$

5 $3\cos(3x)$

7 $-8\sin(2t)$

9 $3\pi\sin(\pi x)$

11 $3\pi\cos(\pi t)(2 + \sin(\pi t))^2$

13 $e^t\cos(e^t)$

15 $(\cos y)e^{\sin y}$

17 $3\cos(3\theta)e^{\sin(3\theta)}$

19 $2x/\cos^2(x^2)$

21 $4\cos(8x)(3 + \sin(8x))^{-0.5}$

23 $\cos x/\cos^2(\sin x)$

25 $2\sin(3x) + 6x\cos(3x)$

27 $e^{-2x}[\cos x - 2\sin x]$

29 $5\sin^4\theta\cos\theta$

31 $-3e^{-3\theta}/\cos^2(e^{-3\theta})$

33 $-2e^{2x}\sin(e^{2x})$

35 $-\sin\alpha + 3\cos\alpha$

37 $3\theta^2\cos\theta - \theta^3\sin\theta$

39 $\cos(\cos x + \sin x) \cdot$
    $(\cos x - \sin x)$

41 $(-t\sin t - 3\cos t)/t^4$

43 $\dfrac{\sqrt{1 - \cos x}(1 - \cos x - \sin x)}{2\sqrt{1 - \sin x}(1 - \cos x)^2}$

45 $(6\sin x\cos x)/(\cos^2 x + 1)^2$

47 $-ab\sin(bt + c)$

49 $y = 6t - 13.850$

51 $(\sin x + x\cos x)x\sin x$

53 $F(x) = -(1/4)\cos(4x)$

55 $2\sin(x^4) + 8x^4\cos(x^4)$

57 (a) $v(t) = 2\pi\cos(2\pi t)$
    (b)

$y = 15 + \sin 2\pi t$

$v = 2\pi\cos 2\pi t$

59 (a) $t = (\pi/2)(m/k)^{1/2}$;
        $t = 0$;
        $t = (3\pi/2)(m/k)^{1/2}$
    (b) $T = 2\pi(m/k)^{1/2}$
    (c) $dT/dm = \pi/\sqrt{km}$;
        Positive sign means an increase in
        mass causes the period to increase

61 (a) $0 \le t \le 2$
    (b) No, not at $t = 2$

63 At $x = 0$:
    $y = x$, $\sin(\pi/6) \approx 0.524$
    At $x = \pi/3$:
    $y = x/2 + (3\sqrt{3} - \pi)/6$,
    $\sin(\pi/6) \approx 0.604$

69 Cannot use product rule

71 $\sin x$

73 True

Section 3.6

1 $2t/(t^2 + 1)$

3 $10x/(5x^2 + 3)$

5 $1/\sqrt{1 - (x + 1)^2}$

7 $(6x + 15)/(x^2 + 5x + 3)$

9 2

11 $e^{-x}/(1 - e^{-x})$

13 $e^x/(e^x + 1)$

15 $ae^{ax}/(e^{ax} + b)$

17 $3w^2\ln(10w) + w^2$

19 e

21 $1/t$

23 $-1/(1 + (2 - x)^2)$

25 $e^{\arctan(3t^2)}(6t)/(1 + 9t^4)$

27 $(\ln 2)z^{(\ln 2 - 1)}$

29 k

31 $-x/\sqrt{1 - x^2}$

33 $-1/z(\ln z)^2$

35 $3w^{-1/2} - 2w^{-3} + 5/w$

37 $(\cos x - \sin x)/(\sin x + \cos x)$

39 $1/(1 + 2u + 2u^2)$

41 $-(x + 1)/(\sqrt{1 - (x + 1)^2})$

43 $-1 < x < 1$

45 $\dfrac{d}{dx}(\log x) = \dfrac{1}{(\ln 10)x}$

47 $g(5000) = 32.189$ years
    $g'(5000) = 0.004$ years per dollar

49 (a) $y = x - 1$
    (b) 0.1; 1
    (c) Yes

51 (a) $f'(x) = 0$
    (b) f is a constant function

53 Any x with $25 < x < 50$

55 Any x with $75 < x < 100$

57 2.8

59 1.4

61 -0.12

63 (a) 12
    (b) $f^{-1}(x) = \sqrt[3]{x}$
    (c) $1/12$

65 $1/5$

67 (a) Pop is 296 m in 2005
    (b) 2005
    (c) Pop incr by 2.65 m/yr
    (d) 0.377 yr/million

69 $1/3$

71 (a) 1
    (b) 1
    (c) 1

73 (a) 1
    (c) e

75 $f'(x) = 1/(x\ln x)$

77 $f(x) = 2^x$

79 $y = \ln x$

81 False

Section 3.7

1 $dy/dx = -x/y$

3 $dy/dx = (y^2 - y - 2x)/(x - 3y^2 - 2xy)$

5 $-(1 + y)/(1 + x)$

7 $dy/dx = (y - 2xy^3)/(3x^2y^2 - x)$

9 $dy/dx = -\sqrt{y/x}$

11 $-3x/2y$

13 $-y/(2x)$

15 $dy/dx = (2 - y\cos(xy))/(x\cos(xy))$

17 $(y^2 + x^4y^4 - 2xy)/(x^2 - 2xy - 2x^5y^3)$

19 $(a - x)/y$

21 $(y + b\sin(bx))/$
    $(a\cos(ay) - x)$

23 Slope is infinite

25 $-23/9$

27 $y = e^2 x$

29 $y = x/a$

31 (a) $(4 - 2x)/(2y + 7)$
    (b) Horizontal if $x = 2$,
        Vertical if $y = -7/2$

33 $y = 2$, $y = -2$

35 (a) $dy/dx = (y^2 - 3x^2)/(3y^2 - 2xy)$
    (c) $y \approx 1.9945$
    (d) Horizontal:
        $(1.1609, 2.0107)$
        and
        $(-0.8857, 1.5341)$
        Vertical:
        $(1.8039, 1.2026)$
        and
        $(\sqrt[3]{5}, 0)$

37 (a) $-(1/2P)f(1 - f^2)$

41 $(nb - V)/(P - n^2a/V^2 + 2n^3ab/V^3)$

43 Formula applies if point is on circle

45 $-x^2 + y^2 = 1$

Section 3.8

1 $3\cosh(3z + 5)$

3 $2\cosh t \cdot \sinh t$

5 $3t^2\sinh t + t^3\cosh t$

7 $\cosh x/(\cosh^2(3 + \sinh x))$

9 $\tanh(1 + \theta)$

11 0

15 $(t^2 + 1)/2t$

19 $\sinh(2x) = 2\sinh x\cosh x$

23 0

25 1

27 $|k| \le 3$

29 (a) $0.54\,T/w$

31 (a)

$y = 2e^x + 5e^{-x}$

$(0.5, 6.3)$

(b) $A = 6.325$
    (stretch factor)
    $c = 0.458$
    (horizontal shift)

33 (a) 0
   (b) Positive for $x > 0$
       Negative for $x < 0$
       Zero for $x = 0$
   (c) Increasing everywhere
   (d) $1, -1$

   (e) Yes; derivative positive everywhere

35 $f'(x) = \sinh x$

37 $\tanh x \to 1$ as $x \to \infty$

39 $k = 0$

41 True

43 True

45 False

Section 3.9

1 $\sqrt{1+x} \approx 1 + x/2$

3 $1/x \approx 2 - x$

5 $e^{x^2} \approx 2ex - e$

9 $|\text{Error}| < 0.2$
   Overestimate, $x > 0$
   Underestimate, $x < 0$

11 (a) $L(x) = 1 + x$
   (b) Positive for $x \neq 0$
   (c) 0.718

   (d) $E(1)$ larger
   (e) 0.005

13 (a) and (c)

   (b) $y = 3x - 3$

15 $a = 1; f(a) = 1$
   Underestimate
   $f(1.2) \approx 1.4$

17 0.1

19 (b) 0.1

21 (a)

   (b) $y = (-9.69 \times 10^{-4})h + 30$
   (c) $P = 30 - 0.001h$
   (d) Both have P intercepts of 30, and slopes are almost the same
   (e) Too small because it has a slightly smaller slope

23 (b) 1% increase

25 $f(1 + \Delta x) \geq f(1) + f'(1)\Delta x$

27 (a) 16,398 m
   (b) $16,398 + 682(\theta - 20)$ m
   (c) True: 17,070 m
       Approx: 17,080 m

29 (a) 1492 m
   (b) $1492 + 143(\theta - 20)$ m
   (c) True: 1638 m
       Approx: 1635 m

31 $f(x) \approx 1 + kx$
   $e^{0.3} \approx 1.3$

33 $E(x) = x^4 - (1 + 4(x - 1))$
   $k = 6; f''(1) = 12$
   $E(x) \approx 6(x - 1)^2$

35 $E(x) = e^x - (1 + x)$
   $k = 1/2; f''(0) = 1$
   $E(x) \approx (1/2)x^2$

37 $E(x) = \ln x - (x - 1)$
   $k = -1/2; f''(1) = -1$
   $E(x) \approx -(1/2)(x - 1)^2$

39 (c) 0

45 Only near $x = 0$

47 $f(x) = x^3 + 1, g(x) = x^4 + 1$

49 $f(x) = |x + 1|$

Section 3.10

1 False

3 False

5 True

7 No; no

9 No; no

11 $f'(c) = -0.5, f'(x_1) > -0.5$,
   $f'(x_2) < -0.5$

13 6 distinct zeros

19 Racetrack

21 Constant Function

23 $21 \leq f(2) \leq 25$

31 Not continuous

33 $1 \leq x \leq 2$

35 Possible answer: $f(x) = |x|$

37 Possible answer
   $f(x) = \begin{cases} x^2 & \text{if } 0 \leq x < 1 \\ 1/2 & \text{if } x = 1 \end{cases}$

39 False

41 False

Chapter 3 Review

1 $200t(t^2 + 1)^{99}$

3 $(t^2 + 2t + 2)/(t + 1)^2$

5 $-8/(4 + t)^2$

7 $x^2 \ln x$

9 $(\cos \theta)e^{\sin \theta}$

11 $-\tan(w - 1)$

13 $kx^{k-1} + k^x \ln k$

15 $3 \sin^2 \theta \cos \theta$

17 $6 \tan(2 + 3\alpha) \cos^{-2}(2 + 3\alpha)$

19 $(-e^{-t} - 1)/(e^{-t} - t)$

21 $1/\sin^2 \theta - 2\theta \cos \theta / \sin^3 \theta$

23 $-(2^w \ln 2 + e^w)/(2^w + e^w)^2$

25 $1/(\sqrt{\sin(2z)}\sqrt{\cos^3(2z)})$

27 $2^{-4z}[-4\ln(2)\sin(\pi z) + \pi \cos(\pi z)]$

29 $e^{(e^\theta + e^{-\theta})}(e^\theta - e^{-\theta})$

31 $e^{\tan(\sin \alpha)}\cos \alpha / \cos^2(\sin \alpha)$

33 $e(\tan 2 + \tan r)^{e-1}/\cos^2 r$

35 $2e^{2x}\sin(3x)$
   $(\sin(3x) + 3\cos(3x))$

37 $2^{\sin x}\left((\ln 2)\cos^2 x - \sin x\right)$

39 $e^{\theta - 1}$

41 $(-cat^2 + 2at - bc)e^{-ct}$

43 $(\ln 5)5^x$

45 $(2abr - ar^4)/(b + r^3)^2$

47 $-2/(x^2 + 4)$

49 $20w/(a^2 - w^2)^3$

51 $ae^{au}/(a^2 + b^2)$

53 $\ln x/(1 + \ln x)^2$

55 $e^t \cos \sqrt{e^t + 1}/(2\sqrt{e^t + 1})$

57 $18x^2 + 8x - 2$

59 $(2 \ln 3)z + (\ln 4)e^z$

61 $3x^2 + 3^x \ln 3$

63 $-\frac{5}{2}\frac{\sin(5\theta)}{\sqrt{\cos(5\theta)}} + 12\sin(6\theta)\cos(6\theta)$

65 $4s^3 - 1$

67 $ke^{kt}(\sin at + \cos bt) +$
   $e^{kt}(a \cos at - b \sin bt)$

69 $f'(t) = 4(\sin(2t) - \cos(3t))^3$
   $(2\cos(2t) + 3\sin(3t))$

71 $-16 - 12x + 48x^2 - 32x^3 +$
   $28x^6 - 9x^8 + 20x^9$

73 $f'(z) = \frac{5}{2}(5z)^{-1/2} + \frac{5}{2}z^{-1/2} - \frac{5}{2}z^{-3/2} +$
   $\frac{\sqrt{5}}{2}z^{-3/2}$

75 $dy/dx = 0$

77 $dy/dx = -3$

79 $f'(t) = 6t^2 - 8t + 3$
   $f''(t) = 12t - 8$

81 $x = -1$ and $x = 5$

83 (a) -6
   (b) 0
   (c) -2

85 (a) 0
   (b) 4

87 (a) −10
   (b) 4

89 Approx 0.8

91 Approx −0.4

93 (a) $h(4) = 1$
   (b) $h'(4) = 2$
   (c) $h(4) = 3$
   (d) $h'(4) = 3$
   (e) $h'(4) = -5/16$
   (f) $h'(4) = 13$

95 (a) $f'(2) = 20$
   (b) $f'(2) = 11/9$
   (c) $f'(2) = -4$
   (d) $f'(2) = -24$
   (e) $f'(2) = \sin 3 - 8\cos 3$
   (f) $f'(2) = 4\ln 3 - 16/3$

97 These functions look like the line $y = 0$:
$$\sin x - \tan x, \quad \frac{x^2}{x^2 + 1}$$
$$x - \sin x, \quad \frac{1 - \cos x}{\cos x}$$
These functions look like the line $y = x$:
$$\arcsin x, \quad \frac{\sin x}{1 + \sin x}$$
$$\arctan x, \quad \frac{e^x - 1}{x}$$
$$\frac{x}{x + 1}, \frac{x}{x^2 + 1}$$
These functions are undefined at the origin:
$$\frac{\sin x}{x} - 1, -x\ln x$$
Defined at the origin but with a vertical tangent:
$$x^{10} + \sqrt[10]{x}$$

99 Perpendicular; $x = 0$ and $x = 1$

101 $y = x - e^b$

103 −2

105 (a) $y = 2 + (x - 4)/4$
    (b) $2.02485\ldots, 2.025$
    (c) True = 4, Approx = 5

107 (a) $f(t)$: linear
       $g(t)$: quadratic polynomial
       $h(t)$: exponential
    (b) $0.006°$C/yr; $0.0139°$C/yr; $0.00574°$C/yr
    (c) $0.78°$C; $1.807°$C; $0.746°$C
    (d) $0.78°$C; $0.793°$C; $0.728°$C
    (e) Linear
    (f) Quadratic

109 $-2GMm/r^3$

111 (a) $P'(t) = kP(t)$

113 (a) 1,000,000 people
    (b) No. Max number of people to fall sick in a
         day is 25,000

115 (c) −0.135%

117 $(f^{-1})'(5) \neq 1/f'(10)$

119 (b)

123 (a) $x(x + 1)^{x-1} + (x + 1)^x \ln(x + 1)$
         $x\cos x(\sin x)^{x-1} + (\sin x)^x \ln(\sin x)$
    (b) $xf'(x)(f(x))^{x-1} + (f(x))^x \ln(f(x))$
    (c) $(\ln x)^{x-1} + (\ln x)^x \ln(\ln x)$

125 (a) 0
    (b) 0
    (c) $2^{-2r}4^r = 1$

Section 4.1

1

3

5 Critical points: $x = 0$, $x = -\sqrt{6}$, $x = \sqrt{6}$
   Inflection points: $x = 0$, $x = -\sqrt{3}$, $x = \sqrt{3}$

7 Critical point: $x = 3/5$
   No inflection points

9 Critical points:
   $x = 0$ and $x = 1$
   Extrema:
   $f(1)$ local minimum
   $f(0)$ not a local extremum

11 Critical points:
    $x = 0$ and $x = 2$
    Extrema:
    $f(2)$ local minimum
    $f(0)$ not a local extremum.

13 Critical point: $x = 1/3$, local maximum

15 (a) Critical point $x \approx 0$;
        Inflection points between -1 and 0
        and between 0 and 1
   (b) Critical point at $x = 0$,
        Inflection points at $x = \pm 1/\sqrt{2}$

17 (a) Increasing for all x
   (b) No maxima or minima

19 (a) Incr: $-1 < x < 0$ and $x > 1$
        Decr: $x < -1$ and $0 < x < 1$
   (b) Local max: $f(0)$
        Local min: $f(-1)$ and $f(1)$

21 (a) $x = b$
   (b) Local minimum

23 $t = 0.5\ln(V/U)$

25

27

29

31 (a) $x \approx 2.5$ (or any $2 < x < 3$)
        $x \approx 6.5$ (or any $6 < x < 7$)
        $x \approx 9.5$ (or any $9 < x < 10$)
   (b) $x \approx 2.5$: local max;
        $x \approx 6.5$: local min;
        $x \approx 9.5$: local max

33

35 $x = 0$: not max/min
    $x = 3/7$: local max
    $x = 1$: local min

37 (a) Yes, at 2000 rabbits

    population of rabbits

    (b) 1787
         1000 rabbits

39 $a = -1/3$

41 Most: $x = 0, \pm 2\pi, \pm 4\pi, \pm 6\pi \ldots$
    Least: $x = \pm \pi, \pm 3\pi, \pm 5\pi \ldots$

43 $C = f, B = f', A = f''$

45 I, III even; II odd
    I is f'', II is f', III is f

47 Incr: $-105 < x < 5$
    Decr: $x < -105$ and $x > 5$

49 (a) $x = \pm 2$
   (b) $x = 0, \pm\sqrt{5}$

51 (a) No critical points
   (b) Decreasing everywhere

53 Consider $f(x) = x^3$

55 $f(x) = x$

57 $f(x) = \cos x$ or $f(x) = \sin x$

59 True

61 False

63 True

65 False

67 $f(x) = x^2 + 1$

69 $f(x) = -x^2 - 1$

71 Impossible

73 (a), (c)

Section 4.2

1

Global and local max
Local min
Global and local min

3 (a)

y
57
50

4

(b) $x = 4, y = 57$

5 Max: 9 at $x = -3$;
Min: -16 at $x = -2$

7 Max: 2 at $x = 1$;
Min: -2 at $x = -1, 8$

9 Max: 8 at $x = 4$;
Min: -1 at $x = -1, 1$

11 (a) $f(1)$ local minimum;
$f(0), f(2)$ local maxima
(b) $f(1)$ global minimum
$f(2)$ global maximum

13 (a) $f(2\pi/3)$ local maximum
$f(0)$ and $f(\pi)$ local minima
(b) $f(2\pi/3)$ global maximum
$f(0)$ global minimum

15 Global min $= 2$ at $x = 1$
No global max

17 Global min $= 1$ at $x = 1$
No global max

19 Global max $= 2$ at $t = 0, \pm 2\pi, \dots$
Global min $= -2$ at $t = \pm\pi, \pm 3\pi, \dots$

21 $0.91 < y \leq 1.00$

23 $0 \leq y \leq 2\pi$

25 $0 \leq y < 1.61$

27 $x = -b/2a$,
Max if $a < 0$, min if $a > 0$

29 $t = 2/b$

31 (a) Ordering: a/q
Storage: bq
(b) $\sqrt{a/b}$

33 (a) $0 \leq y \leq a$

rate (gm/sec)
Max rate
$a/2$ a y (gm)

(b) $y = a/2$

35 $r = 3B/(2A)$

37 (a) $k(\ln k - \ln S_0) - k + S_0 + I_0$
(b) Both

39
$(3, 3)$
$y = t(x)$

41

$(-1, 2)$ $h(x)$
-2 -1 1 x

43 $x = \left(\sum_{i=1}^{n} a_i\right)/n$

47 On $1 \leq x \leq 2$, global minimum at $x = 1$

49 $f(x) = 1 - x$

51 $\sqrt{2} \leq x \leq \sqrt{5}$

53 True

55 True

57 True

59 False

61 True

63 True

Section 4.3

1 2500

3 1536

5 1250 square feet

7 $x = 16^{1/3}$ cm, $h = 16^{1/3}/2$ cm

9 $r = h = (8/\pi)^{1/3}$ cm

11 0

13 Max: 0.552; Min: 0.358

15 $2000 - (1200/\sqrt{5})$

17 $w = 34.64$ cm, $h = 48.99$ cm

19 $1/\sqrt{2}$

21 (a) $xy + \pi y^2/4$
(b) $2x + \pi y$
(c) $x = 0, y = 100/\pi$

23 (a) Min at $x = \pi L/(4 + \pi)$
Max at $x = L$
(c) Yes

25 $5, \sqrt{125}$

27 $5\sqrt{5}, 25$

29 (a) $(9/4, \pm\sqrt{7}/4)$
(b) $(3, 0)$

31 Radius $= \sqrt{2/3}$
Height $= \sqrt{1/3}$

33 13.13 mi from first smokestack

35 Minimum: $x = -r_0/\sqrt{2}$
Maximum: $x = r_0/\sqrt{2}$

37 (a) $T^{2/3}/2^{1/3}$
(b) Increases by $\approx 58.74\%$

39 15 miles/hour

41 (a)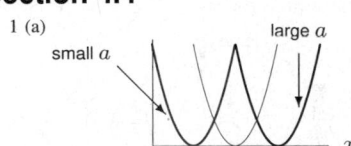
load
(number of worms)
8
4
Number of worms
time
P O

(b) 7 worms
(c) increases

43 (a) $E = 500e\left(\dfrac{2 - \cos\theta}{\sin\theta}\right) + 2000e$
$\left(\arctan\left(\dfrac{500}{2000}\right) \leq \theta \leq \pi/2\right)$
(b) $\theta = \pi/3$
(c) Independent of e, but dependent on $\overline{AB}/\overline{AL}$

45 (a) $x = 1, P = (1, 1)$

47 (a) The arithmetic mean unless $a = b$,
in which case the two means are equal
(b) The arithmetic mean unless $a = b = c$,
in which case the two means are equal

49 (b) 2 hours
(c) Equal

51 (b) $f(v) = v \cdot a(v)$
(c) When $a(v) = f'(v)$
(d) $a(v)$

53 (a) $g(v) = f(v)/v$
(b) 220 mph
(c) 300 mph

55 Max V on $0 \leq h \leq 10$

57 9 cm by 1 cm

Section 4.4

1 (a)
large a
small a
x

(b) Critical point moves right
(c) $x = a$

3 (a)
large a
small a
x

(b) 2 critical points move closer to origin
(c) $x = \pm\sqrt{1/(3a)}$

5 (a)
small a
large a
x

(b) Nonzero critical point moves down to the left
(c) $x = 0, 2/a$

7 (a) Larger $|A|$, steeper
(b) Shifted horizontally by B
Left for $B > 0$; right for $B < 0$
Vertical asymptote $x = -B$
(c)

$A = 2, B = 5$
$A = 20, B = 0$
$A = 2, B = 0$

9 A has $a = 1$, B has $a = 2$, C has $a = 5$

11 (a)

small a
large a

(b)

large b

small b

(c) a moves critical point right;
b moves critical point up
(d) $x = a$

13 (a)

large a
small a

(b)

large b

small b

(c) a moves one critical point up, does not move the other;
b moves one critical point up to right, moves the other right
(d) $x = b/3, b$

15 (a)

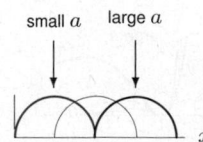

small a large a

(b)

small b
large b

(c) a moves critical points to the right;
b moves one critical point left, one up, one right
(d) $x = a, a \pm \sqrt{b}$

17 C has $a = 1$, B has $a = 2$, A has $a = 3$

19 (a)

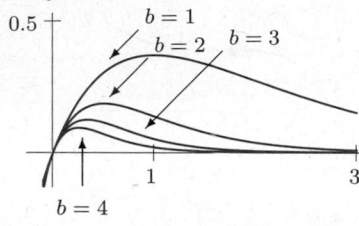

0.5
$b = 1$
$b = 2$ $b = 3$
1   3
$b = 4$

(b) $(1/b, 1/be)$

21 $Ax^3 + Cx$, Two

23 (a)

$a = 0.5$
10    $a = 3$
-10 10
-10

(b) $-1 \leq a \leq 1$

25 Flatten out, raises min

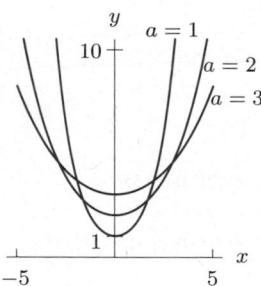

y
$a = 1$
10    $a = 2$
$a = 3$
1
-5 5

29 (a) $x = -1/b$
(b) Local minimum

31 $k > 0$

33 $y = 3x^{-x^2/2}$

35 $y = 12/(1 + 2e^{-1.386x})$

37 $y = x^3 - 3x^2 + 6$

39 $y = (3/(2\pi)) \sin(\pi t^2/2)$

41 $y = e^{1-x} + x$

43 $y = 2t + 18/t$

45 (a) $x = e^a$
(b) $a = -1$:

1
1   2   3
-1

(b)

$a = 1$:

1
1   2   3
-1

(c) Max at (e^{a-1}, e^{a-1}) for any a

49 (a) $x = 0$ and $x = \pm\sqrt{-a/2}$
(b) For any a or b, $x = 0$ is crit pt.
Only crit pt if $a \geq 0$
Local minimum
(c) If a is negative:
$x = 0$ is local max,
$x = \pm\sqrt{-a/2}$ are local min
(d) No

51 (a) $b = 20°C, a = 180°C$
(b) $k = (1/90)\text{min}^{-1}$

53

U F
a $2a$ $3a$ x
$(2a, -b/4)$
$(3a, -b/(27a))$

55 (a) Zero: $r = B/A$
Vertical asymptote:
$r = 0$
Horizontal asymptote:
$f(r) = 0$
(b) Minimum:
$\left(3B/(2A), -4A^3/(27B^2)\right)$
Point of inflection:
$\left(2B/A, -A^3/(8B^2)\right)$
(c)

$f(r)$
r
$\dfrac{B}{A}$
$\left(\dfrac{3B}{2A}, \dfrac{-4A^3}{27B^2}\right)$ $\left(\dfrac{2B}{A}, \dfrac{-A^3}{8B^2}\right)$

57 $f(x) = x^2 + 1$ has no zeros

59 $f(x) = kx(x - b)$

61 One possibility:
$f(x) = ax^2, a \neq 0$

63 (a), (c)

Section 4.5

1 $5.5 < q < 12.5$ positive;
$0 < q < 5.5$ and $q > 12.5$ negative;
Maximum at $q \approx 9.5$

3 $5000, $2.40, $4

5 $C(q) = 35,000 + 10q, R(q) = 15q,$
   $\pi(q) = 5q - 35,000.$

7 $C(q) = 0.20q, R(q) = 0.25q,$
   $\pi(q) = 0.05q$

9 Global maximum of $6875 at $q = 75$

11 (a) $q = 2500$
   (b) $3 per unit
   (c) $3000

13 (a) Fixed costs
   (b) Decreases slowly, then increases

15 Increased

17 (a) No
   (b) Yes

19 $L = [\beta pcK^\alpha/w]^{1/(1-\beta)}$

21 (a) and (b)

Line through origin
is tangent here

$R(x)$

Optimal point on $r(x)$

$r(x)$

x

23 (a) $C(q) = 0.01q^3 - 0.6q^2 + 13q$
   (b) $1
   (c) $q = 30, a(30) = 4$
   (d) Marginal cost is 4

25 (a)

$x^2 + y^2 = 9$
$x^2 + y^2 = 4$
$x^2 + y^2 = 1$

y

4

$x + y = 4$

x

4

(c) 8

27 (a)

y

4

$C = 4$

$C = 3$

2

$C = 2$

$Q = x^{1/2}y^{1/2}$

x

2   4

(c) $2\sqrt{2}$

29 Maximum profit $\approx 13,000$ units

31

y

C

R

x

Section 4.6

1 $-0.32°C/min$; $-0.262°C/min$

3 $-81/R^2$

5 $-1°C$ minute

7 -4 newtons/sec

9 0.9 cm^2/min

11 (a) $-a/q^2$ dollars/cell phone
   (b) $-100a/q^2$ dollars/week; decreasing

13 24 meters^3/yr

15 (a) 1.19 meter^2
   (b) 0.0024 meter^2/year

17 1.8 cm/min

19 $1/16$ cm/min

21 (a) $CD - D^2$
   (b) $D < C$

23 (a) $2A/r^3 - 3B/r^4$; units of force/units of distance
   (b) $k(2A/r^3 - 3B/r^4)$; units of force/units of time

25 (a) 0.218 m/sec
   (b) 0.667 m/sec

27 0.038 meter/min

29 2513.3 cm^3/sec

31 (a) $-92.8V^{-2.4}$ atm/cm^3
   (b) Decreasing at 0.0529 atm/min

33 (a) 94.248 m^2/min
   (b) 0.0000267 m/min

35 (a) $80\pi = 251.327$ sec
   (b) $V = 3\pi h^3/25$ cm^3
   (c) 0.0207 cm/sec

37 $8/\pi$ meters/min

39 0.253 meters/second

41 (a) 0.04 gal/mile; 0.06 gal/mile
   (b) 25 mpg; 16.67 mpg
   (d) 1.4 gallons
   (e) 2.8 gal/hour; 1.8 gal/hour

43 (a) $k \approx 0.067$
   (b) $t \approx 10.3$ hours
   (c) Formula:
        $T(24) \approx 74.1°$F,
        rule of thumb: $73.6°$F

45 $2/\cos^2\theta$

47 $(1/V)dV/dt$

49 No

51 (b) (i) Brian's affection decreases
        (ii) Brian's affection increases
   (c) (i) Angela's affection increases
        (ii) Angela's affection decreases
   (d) Brian

53 $dD/dt = 2 \cdot dR/dt$

55 $y = f(x) = 2x + 1$ and $x = g(t) = 5t$

57 True

59 (c)

Section 4.7

1 $1/4$

3 1.5

5 0

7 0

9 0

11 $(1/3)a^{-2/3}$

13 $0.01x^3$

15 $e^{0.1x}$

17 Negative

19 Negative

21 0

23 0

25 ∞/∞, yes

27 none, no

29 none, no

31 $1/2$

33 1

35 2

37 Does not exist

39 ∞

41 e^3

43 ∞

45 0.909297

47 Does not exist

49 e^2

53 3

55 $\sqrt{15}$

57 0

59 $-1/6$

61 1

63 e^x dominates x^n for all positive integers n

65 $\lim_{x \to 0} \frac{x+1}{x+2}$

67 False

Section 4.8

1 The particle moves on straight lines from $(0, 1)$ to $(1, 0)$ to $(0, -1)$ to $(-1, 0)$ and back to $(0, 1)$

3 Two diamonds meeting at $(1, 0)$

5 $x = 3\cos t, y = -3\sin t, 0 \le t \le 2\pi$

7 $x = 2 + 5\cos t, y = 1 + 5\sin t,$
   $0 \le t \le 2\pi$

9 $x = t, y = -4t + 7$

11 $x = -3\cos t, y = -7\sin t,$
   $0 \le t \le 2\pi$

13 Clockwise for all t

15 Clockwise: $-\sqrt{1/3} < t < \sqrt{1/3}$
    Counterclockwise: $t < -\sqrt{1/3}$ or $t > \sqrt{1/3}$

17 Clockwise: $2k\pi < t < (2k + 1)\pi$
    Counterclockwise: $(2k - 1)\pi < t < 2k\pi$

19 Line segment:
    $y + x = 4, 1 \le x \le 3$

21 Line $y = (x - 13)/3$, left to right

23 Parabola $y = x^2 - 8x + 13$, left to right

25 Circle $x^2 + y^2 = 9$, counterclockwise

27 $(y - 4) = (4/11)(x - 6)$

29 $y = -(4/3)x$

31 Speed $= 2|t|$, stops at $t = 0$

33 Speed $= ((2t - 4)^2 + (3t^2 - 12)^2)^{1/2}$,
    Stops at $t = 2$

35

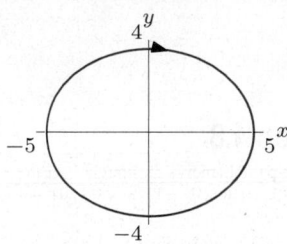

37 (a) The part of the line with
$x < 10$ and $y < 0$
(b) The line segment between
$(10, 0)$ and $(11, 2)$

39 (a) Both parameterize line
$y = 3x - 2$
(b) Slope $= 3$
y-intercept $= -2$

41 (a) $a = b = 0, k = 5$ or -5
(b) $a = 0, b = 5, k = 5$ or -5
(c) $a = 10, b = -10, k = \sqrt{200}$ or $-\sqrt{200}$

43 A straight line through the point $(3, 5)$

45 (a) $dy/dx = 4e^t$
(b) $y = 2x^2$
(c) $dy/dx = 4x$

47 (a) (i) $t = -0.25 \ln 3 = -0.275$
(ii) No vertical tangent
(b) $(3e^{2t} - e^{-2t})/(e^{2t} + e^{-2t})$
(c) 3

49 (a)

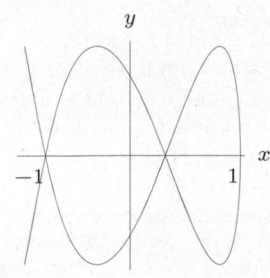

(b) $x(\pi/4) = 5$ and $y(\pi/4) = 0$;
$x'(\pi/4) = 0$ and $y'(\pi/4) = -8$
(c) Twice
(d) Parallel to y-axis, negative y direction
(e) 10

51 (a) No
(b) $k = 1$
(c) Particle B

53 (a) $y + \frac{1}{2} = -\frac{\sqrt{3}}{3}(x - \pi)$
(b) $t = \pi$
(c) 0.291, concave up

55 (a) $t = \pi/4$; at that time, speed $= \sqrt{9/2}$
(b) Yes, when $t = \pi/2$ or $t = 3\pi/2$
(c) Concave down everywhere

57

59

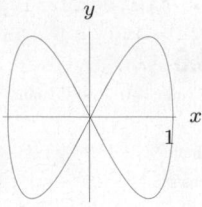

61 (b) For example:
$R = 12, t = \pi$
(c)

63 Gives circle centered at $(0, 0)$
65 $x = t, y = 2t, 0 \le t \le 1$
67 False

Chapter 4 Review

1

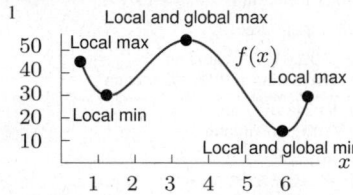

3 (a) $f'(x) = 3x(x - 2)$
$f''(x) = 6(x - 1)$
(b) $x = 0$
$x = 2$
(c) Inflection point: $x = 1$
(d) Endpoints:
$f(-1) = -4$ and $f(3) = 0$
Critical points:
$f(0) = 0$ and $f(2) = -4$
Global max:
$f(0) = 0$ and $f(3) = 0$
Global min:
$f(-1) = -4$ and $f(2) = -4$
(e) f increasing:
for $x < 0$ and $x > 2$
f decreasing:
for $0 < x < 2$
f concave up:
for $x > 1$
f concave down:
for $x < 1$

5 (a) $f'(x) =$
$-e^{-x} \sin x + e^{-x} \cos x$
$f''(x) = -2e^{-x} \cos x$

(b) Critical points:
$x = \pi/4$ and $5\pi/4$
(c) Inflection points:
$x = \pi/2$ and $3\pi/2$
(d) Endpoints:
$f(0) = 0$ and $f(2\pi) = 0$
Global max:
$f(\pi/4) = e^{-\pi/4}(\sqrt{2}/2)$
Global min:
$f(5\pi/4) = -e^{-5\pi/4}(\sqrt{2}/2)$
(e) f increasing:
$0 < x < \pi/4$ and
$5\pi/4 < x < 2\pi$
f decreasing:
$\pi/4 < x < 5\pi/4$
f concave down:
for $0 \le x < \pi/2$
and $3\pi/2 < x \le 2\pi$
f concave up:
for $\pi/2 < x < 3\pi/2$

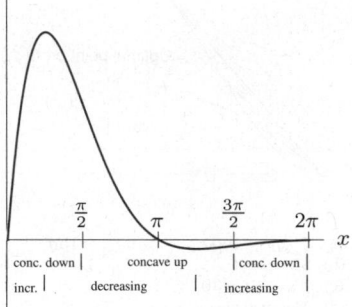

7 $\lim_{x \to \infty} f(x) = \infty$
$\lim_{x \to -\infty} f(x) = -\infty$
(a) $f'(x) = 6(x - 2)(x - 1)$
$f''(x) = 6(2x - 3)$
(b) $x = 1$ and $x = 2$
(c) $x = 3/2$
(d) Critical points:
$f(1) = 6, f(2) = 5$
Local max: $f(1) = 6$
Local min: $f(2) = 5$
Global max and min: none
(e) f increasing: $x < 1$ and $x > 2$
Decreasing: $1 < x < 2$
f concave up: $x > 3/2$
f concave down: $x < 3/2$

9 $\lim_{x \to -\infty} f(x) = -\infty$
   $\lim_{x \to \infty} f(x) = 0$

   (a) $f'(x) = (1-x)e^{-x}$
       $f''(x) = (x-2)e^{-x}$
   (b) Only critical point is at $x = 1$
   (c) Inflection point: $f(2) = 2/e^2$
   (d) Global max: $f(1) = 1/e$
       Local and global min: none
   (e) f increasing: $x < 1$
       f decreasing: $x > 1$
       f concave up: $x > 2$
       f concave down: $x < 2$

11 Max: 22.141 at $x = \pi$;
    Min: 2 at $x = 0$

13 Max: 1 at $x = 0$;
    Min: Approx 0 at $x = 10$

15 Global max $= 1$ at $t = 0$
    No global min

17 Local max: $f(-3) = 12$
    Local min: $f(1) = -20$
    Inflection pt: $x = -1$
    Global max and min: none

19 Global and local min: $x = 2$
    Global and local max: none
    Inflection pts: none

21 Local max: $f(-2/5)$
    Global and local min: $f(0)$
    Inflection pts: $x = (-2 \pm \sqrt{2})/5$
    Global max: none

23 Max: $r = \frac{2}{3}a$; Min: $r = 0, a$

25 A has $a = 1$, B has $a = 2$, C has $a = 3$

27 (a) Critical points: $x = 0$, $x = \sqrt{a}$,
        $x = -\sqrt{a}$
        Inflection points: $x = \sqrt{a/3}$,
        $x = -\sqrt{a/3}$
    (b) $a = 4, b = 21$
    (c) $x = \sqrt{4/3}$, $x = -\sqrt{4/3}$

29 Domain: All real numbers except $x = b$;
    Critical points: $x = 0$, $x = 2b$

31 18

33 (a) $C(q) = 3 + 0.4q$ m
    (b) $R(q) = 0.5q$ m
    (c) $\pi(q) = 0.1q - 3$ m

35 2.5 gm/hr

37 Line $y = -2x + 9$, right to left

39 (a) x_3
    (b) x_1, x_5
    (c) x_2
    (d) 0

41

43 $y = x^3 - 6x^2 + 9x + 5$

45 $y = 3x^{-1/2} \ln x$

47 $y = 2xe^{(1-x^2)/2}$

49 $x = \sqrt{8/3}$ cm, $h = \sqrt{2/3}$ cm

51 $r = h = \sqrt{8/3\pi}$ cm

53 $-4.81 \leq f(x) \leq 1.82$

55 Max: $m = -5k/(12j)$

57 (a) $t = 0$ and $t = 2/b$
    (b) $b = 0.4$; $a = 3.547$
    (c) Local min: $t = 0$; Local max: $t = 5$

59

61 1.688 mm/sec away from lens

63 Minimum: -2 amps
    Maximum: 2 amps

65 Max area $= 1$
    $\left(\pm\frac{1}{\sqrt{2}}, 0\right)$; $\left(\pm\frac{1}{\sqrt{2}}, \frac{1}{\sqrt{2}}\right)$

67 (0.59, 0.35)

69 $r = \sqrt{2A/(4+\pi)}$;
    $h = \frac{A}{2} \cdot \frac{\sqrt{4+\pi}}{\sqrt{2A}} - \frac{\pi}{4} \cdot \frac{\sqrt{2A}}{\sqrt{4+\pi}}$

71 40 feet by 80 feet

73 (a) $\pi(q)$ max when
        $R(q) > C(q)$ and R and Q are farthest
        apart

   (b) $C'(q_0) = R'(q_0) = p$
   (c) $

75 About 331 meters, Maintain course

77 (a) $g(e)$ is a global maximum;
        there is no minimum
    (b) There are exactly two solutions
    (c) $x = 5$ and $x \approx 1.75$

79 (a) depth of water

    (b) depth of water

81 -0.0545 m^3/min

83 0/0, yes

85 $-1/2$

87 $-1/6$

89 $1/\pi \approx 0.32 \mu$m/day

91 (a) Angular velocity
    (b) $v = a(d\theta/dt)$

93 $dM/dt = K(1 - 1/(1 + r))dr/dt$

95 Height: $0.3/(\pi h^2)$ meters/hour
    Radius: $(0.3/\sqrt{3})/(\pi h^2)$ meters/hour

97 (a) Increasing
    (b) Not changing
    (c) Decreasing

99 398.103 mph

101 (a) Decreases
    (b) -0.25 cm^3/min

103 (a)

$a = 0.5$

$a = 1$

$a = 2$

(b) Same graph all a

(c) dy/dx simplifies to $\sqrt{x}/(2x(1+x))$

105 (a) $1/\sqrt{x^2 - 1}$

107 (a) $dy/dx = \dfrac{\tan(x/2)}{2\sqrt{(1-\cos x)/(1+\cos x)}}$

(b) $dy/dx = 1/2$ on $0 < x < \pi$
$dy/dx = -1/2$ on $\pi < x < 2\pi$

Section 5.1

1 (a) Left sum
(b) Upper estimate

(c) 6
(d) $\Delta t = 2$
(e) Upper estimate ≈ 24.4

3 (a) 408
(b) 390

5 Between 140 and 150 meters

7 (a) Always same direction; speeding up, then slowing down
(b) Overestimate = 15 cm; Underestimate = 6 cm

9 0 cm, no change in position

11 15 cm to the left

13 (a) 2; 15, 17, 19, 21, 23; 10, 13, 18, 20, 30
(b) 122; 162
(c) 4; 15, 19, 23; 10, 18, 30
(d) 112; 192

15 (a) Lower estimate = 5.25 mi
Upper estimate = 5.75 mi
(b) Lower estimate = 11.5 mi
Upper estimate = 14.5 mi
(c) Every 30 seconds

17 1/5

19 0.0157

21 (a)

(b) 3 sec, 144 feet
(c) 80 feet

23 (a) 14.73 minutes
15.93 minutes
(b) 0.60 minutes

25 (a) A: 8 hrs
B: 4 hrs
(b) 100 km/hr
(c) A: 400 km
B: 100 km

27 (a)

(b) 125 feet
(c) 4 times as far

29 $v(t) = 32t$ ft/sec
For $\Delta t = 1$:
Right sum = 320 feet
Left sum = 192 feet
Precise dist = 256 feet

31 About 335 feet

33 If the acceleration is large the difference between the estimates can be large.

35 $f(x) = 10x$, $[a, b] = [0, 1]$

37 True

39 (a) $3 \le t \le 5, 9 \le t \le 10$
(b) 3600 ft east
(c) At $t = 8$ minutes
(d) 30 seconds longer

Section 5.2

1 (a) Right
(b) Upper
(c) 3
(d) 2

3 (a) Left; smaller

(b) $0, 2, 6, 1/3$

5 28.5

7 1.4936

9 0.3103

11 17,000, $n = 4$, $\Delta x = 10$

13 543

15 60

17 −40

19 (a) 13
(b) 1

21 (a) 16.25
(b) 15.75
(c) No

23 1

25 1.977

27 24.694

29 (a) 13
(b) −2
(c) 11
(d) 15

31 (a) −2
(b) $-A/2$

33 (a)

(b) 3.084
(c) 2.250

35 Positive

37 (a) $(\ln 1.5)0.5$

(b) $(\ln 1.5)0.5 + (ln 2)0.5$

(c) Right: overestimate
left: underestimate

39 (a) 78

(b) 46; underestimate

(c) 118; overestimate

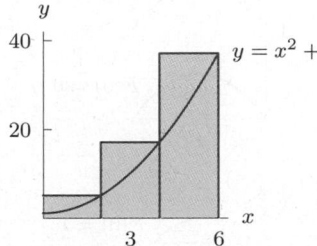

41 Left-hand sum $= 1.96875$
Right-hand sum $= 2.71875$
The most the estimate could be off is 0.375

43

45 (c) $n \geq 10^5$

47 Too many terms in sum

49 $f(x) = 2 - x$

51 False

53 False

55 False

57

Section 5.3

1 Dollars

3 Foot-pounds

5 Change in velocity; km/hr

7 Change in salinity; gm/liter

9 $\int_1^3 2t \, dt = 8$

11 $\int_1^5 1/t \, dt = \ln 5$

13 $\int_2^3 7 \ln(4) \cdot 4^t \, dt = 336$

15 (a) $3x^2 + 1$

(b) 10

17 (a) $\sin t \cos t$
(b) (i) ≈ 0.056
(ii) $\frac{1}{2}(\sin^2(0.4) - \sin^2(0.2))$

19 (a) Removal rate 500 kg/day on day 12
(b) Days, days, kilograms
(c) 4000 kg removed between day 5 and day 15

21 (a) $\int_0^2 R(t) \, dt$
(b)

(c) lower estimate: 2.81
upper estimate: 3.38

23 (a) $\int_0^5 f(t) \, dt$
(b) 177.270 billion barrels
(c) Lower estimate of year's oil consumption

25 (a) Upper estimate: 340 liters
Lower estimate: 240 liters
(b)

27 $2392.87

29 About $13,800

31 $45.8°C$.

33 $f(1) < f(0)$

35 12 newton · meters

37 (iii) < (ii) < (i) < (iv)

39 0.732 gals, 1.032 gals;
Better estimates possible

41 $\int_{2t_0}^{3t_0} r(t) \, dt$ $<$ $\int_{t_0}^{2t_0} r(t) \, dt$ $<$
$\int_0^{2t_0} r(t) \, dt$

43 0.14

45 1.53

47 0.5; cost of preparing is $0.5 million

49 $\int_2^4 r(t) \, dt > \int_0^2 r(t) \, dt$

51 $\int_0^8 r(t) \, dt < 64$ million

53 $\frac{d}{dx}(\sqrt{x}) \neq \sqrt{x}$

55 velocity
(miles/hour)

Section 5.4

1 10

3 9

5 $2c_1 + 12c_2^2$

7 2

9 2

11 (a) 8.5
(b) 1.7

13 4.389

15 0.083

17 7.799

19 0.172

21 (a) 2
(b) 12, 2
(c) 0, 0

23 (a) $\int_a^b 1 \, dx = b - a$
(b) (i) $\int_2^5 1 \, dx = 3$
(ii) $\int_{-3}^8 1 \, dx = 11$
(iii) $\int_1^3 23 \, dx = 46$

25 $6080

27 30

29 0

31 14/3

33 (a) -4
(b) (ii)

35 (a) 140.508 million
(b) 142.743 million
(c) Graph below secant line

39

41

43 (viii) < (ii) < (iii) < (vi) < (i) <
(v) < (iv) < (vii)

45 (b) 0.64

47 Not enough information

49 5

51 25

53 (a)

(b) Largest to smallest:
$n = 1, n = 3,$
$n = 4,$ and $n = 2$

55

59 $\int_a^b (5 + 3f(x))\,dx = 5(b - a) + 3\int_a^b f(x)\,dx$

61 $f(x) = -1$

63 $(1/5)\int_0^5 v(t)\,dt$, where $v(t)$ miles/hr at t hours

65 False

67 True

69 True

71 False

73 True

75 False

77 True

79 (a) Does not follow
(b) Follows
(c) Follows

Chapter 5 Review

1 (a) Lower estimate = 122 ft
Upper estimate = 298 ft

(b)

3 20

5 396

7 (a) Upper estimate = 34.16 m/sec
Lower estimate = 27.96 m/sec
(b) 31.06 m/sec;
It is too high

9 $\int_{-2}^1 (12t^3 - 15t^2 + 5)\,dt = -75$

11 36

13 1.142

15 13.457

17 $\int_{-1}^1 |x|\,dx = 1$

19 (a) 260 ft
(b) Every 0.5 sec

21 0.399 miles

23 (a) Emissions 1970–2000, m. metric tons
(b) 772.8 million metric tons

25 (a) Overestimate = 7 tons
Underestimate = 5 tons
(b) Overestimate = 74 tons
Underestimate = 59 tons
(c) Every 2 days

27 (a) $(1/5)\int_0^5 f(x)\,dx$
(b) $(1/5)(\int_0^2 f(x)\,dx - \int_2^5 f(x)\,dx)$

29 (a) $f(1), f(2)$
(b) $2, 2.31, 2.80, 2.77$

31 (a) $F(0) = 0$
(b) F increases
(c) $F(1) \approx 0.7468$
$F(2) \approx 0.8821$
$F(3) \approx 0.8862$

33 4

35 3

37 3

39 (a) Odd integrand; areas cancel
(b) 0.4045
(c) −0.4049
(d) No. Different sized rectangles

41 (a) 21,000 megawatts; 189,525.284 megawatts
(b) 22%
(c) 76,602.402 megawatts

43 $\int_0^{0.5T} r(t)\,dt > \int_{0.5T}^T r(t)\,dt$

45 $\int_0^{T_h} r(t)\,dt < \int_0^{0.5T} r(t)\,dt$

47 30/7

49 V < IV < II < III < I
I, II, III positive
IV, V negative

51 2.5; ice 2.5 in thick at 4 am

53 (a) $2\int_0^2 f(x)\,dx$
(b) $\int_0^5 f(x)\,dx - \int_2^5 f(x)\,dx$
(c) $\int_{-2}^5 f(x)\,dx - \frac{1}{2}\int_{-2}^2 f(x)\,dx$

55 (a) At $t = 17, 23, 27$ seconds
(b) Right: $t = 10$ seconds
Left: $t = 40$ seconds
(c) Right: $t = 17$ seconds
Left: $t = 40$ seconds
(d) $t = 10$ to 17 seconds,
20 to 23 seconds, and
24 to 27 seconds
(e) At $t = 0$ and $t = 35$

57 About 48 feet

59 (a) 300 m³/sec
(b) 250 m³/sec
(c) 1996: 1250 m³/sec
1957: 3500 m³/sec
(d) 1996: 10 days
1957: 4 months
(e) 10^9 meter³
(f) $2 \cdot 10^{10}$ meter³

61 Overestimate

63 Overestimate

65 (a) $\int_0^T (f(t) - H_{\min})\,dt$
(b) $T \approx 11$ days

67 (a) $\sum_{i=1}^n i^4/n^5$
(b) $(6n^4 + 15n^3 + 10n^2 - 1)/30n^4$
(c) 1/5

69 (a) $\sum_{i=0}^{n-1} (n + i)/n^2$
(b) $3/2 - 1/(2n)$
(c) 3/2
(d) 3/2

71 (a) $\sum_{i=1}^n \sin(i\pi/n)\pi/n$
(b) $\pi\cos(\pi/2n)/n\sin(\pi/2n)$
(c) 2
(d) 2

73 (a) $-\ln(1 + a^2 b)/2b + \ln(1 + c^2 b)/2b$
(b) $\ln(1 + bx^2)/2b$

Section 6.1

1 (a) Increasing
(b) Concave up

3 $1, 0, -1/2, 0, 1$

5

7

9

11

13 128, 169, 217

15 Oscillates between $x = 5$ and $x = 15$

17

19 Critical points: $(0, 5), (2, 21), (4, 13), (5, 15)$

21

21 Max at $x = \sqrt{\pi}$;
$F(\sqrt{\pi}) = 0.895$

23 500

25 (a) 0

(b)

(c) $F(x) \geq 0$ everywhere
$F(x) = 0$ only at integer multiples of π

27 (a) $R(0) = 0$, R is an odd function.
(b) Increasing everywhere
(c) Concave up for $x > 0$, concave down for $x < 0$.
(d)

(e) 1/2

29 2.747

31 1.99, overestimate; or 1.85, underestimate

33 $w'(0.4) = 3.9$; exact

35 $2x \ln(1 + x^4)$

37 $-2\sin(\sqrt{2t})$

39 $\text{erf}(x) + (2/\sqrt{\pi})xe^{-x^2}$

41 $3x^2 e^{-x^6}$

43 $\frac{d}{dx}\int_0^5 t^2\,dt = 0$

45 Local min at $x = -1$ and $x = 3$

47 $G(x) = \int_7^x e^t\,dt$

49 True

51 False

53 True

Chapter 6 Review

3

5 (a) -19
(b) 6

7 $x^4/4 + C$

9 $x^4/4 - 2x + C$

11 $-4/t + C$

13 $8w^{3/2}/3 + C$

15 $\sin\theta + C$

17 $x^2/2 + 2x^{1/2} + C$

19 $3\sin t + 2t^{3/2} + C$

21 $\tan x + C$

23 $(1/2)x^2 + x + \ln|x| + C$

25 $2^x/\ln 2 + C$

27 $2e^x - 8\sin x + C$

29 4

31 $x^4/4 + +2x^3 - 4x + 4.$

33 $e^x + 3$

35 $\sin x + 4$

39 $x^4/4 + 5x + C$

41 $8t^{3/2}/3 + C$

43 $2x^3 + 2x^2 - 14$

45 $-16t^2 + 100t + 50$

47 $-\cos(t^3)$

49 $(0, 1); (2, 3); (6, -4); (8, 0)$

51 (a) $x = 1, x = 3$
(b) Local min at $x = 1$, local max at $x = 3$
(c)

53 (a) $f(x)$ is greatest at x_1
(b) $f(x)$ is least at x_5
(c) $f'(x)$ is greatest at x_3
(d) $f'(x)$ is least at x_5
(e) $f''(x)$ is greatest at x_1
(f) $f''(x)$ is least at x_5

55 21

57 1/20

59 1/3

61 $4\sqrt{2}$

63 $2\sinh 1$

65 $c = 3$

67 $c = 6$

69 0.4

71 16/3

73 $3x^2\sin(x^6)$

75 $2e^{-x^4}$

77 (a) $f(t) = Q - \frac{Q}{A}t$
(b) $Q/2$

79 (a) $t = 2, t = 5$
(b) $f(2) \approx 55, f(5) \approx 40$
(c) -10

81 (a) 14,000 revs/min²
(b) 180 revolutions

83 19.55 ft/sec²

85 (b) Highest pt: $t = 2.5$ sec
Hits ground: $t = 5$ sec
(c) Left sum:
136 ft (an overest.)
Right sum:
56 ft (an underest.)
(d) 100 ft

87 $V(r) = (4/3)\pi r^3$

89 (b) $t = 6$ hours
(c) $t = 11$ hrs

bacteria

time (hours)
5 10 15 20

bacteria

time (hours)
5   ≈ 11 15   20

91 Increasing; concave down

93 (a) Zeros: $x = 0, 5$; Critical points: $x = 3$
(b) Zeros: $x = 1$; Critical points: $x = 0, 5$

95 (a) $\Delta x = (b - a)/n$
$x_i = a + i(b - a)/n$
(b) $(b^4 - a^4)/4$

97 (a) $-(1/3)\cos(3x), -(1/4)\cos(4x),$
$-(1/3)\cos(3x + 5)$
(b) $-(1/a)\cos(ax + b)$

99 (a) $(1/2)(\ln|x - 3| - \ln|x - 1|),$
$(1/3)(\ln|x - 4| - \ln|x - 1|),$
$(1/4)(\ln|x + 3| - \ln|x - 1|)$
(b) $(1/(b - a))(\ln|x - b| - \ln|x - a|)$

Section 7.1

1 (a) $(\ln 2)/2$
(b) $(\ln 2)/2$

3 $(1/3)e^{3x} + C$

5 $-e^{-x} + C$

7 $-0.5\cos(2x) + C$

9 $\cos(3 - t) + C$

11 $(r + 1)^4/4 + C$

13 $(1/18)(1 + 2x^3)^3 + C$

15 $(1/6)(x^2 + 3)^3 + C$

17 $(1/5)y^5 + (1/2)y^4 + (1/3)y^3 + C$

19 $(1/3)e^{x^3 + 1} + C$

21 $-2\sqrt{4 - x} + C$

23 $-(1/8)(\cos\theta + 5)^8 + C$

25 $(1/7)\sin^7\theta + C$

27 $(1/35)\sin^7 5\theta + C$

29 $(1/3)(\ln z)^3 + C$

31 $t + 2\ln|t| - 1/t + C$

33 $(1/\sqrt{2})\arctan(\sqrt{2}x) + C$

35 $2\sin\sqrt{x} + C$

37 $2\sqrt{x + e^x} + C$

39 $(1/2)\ln(x^2 + 2x + 19) + C$

41 $\ln(e^x + e^{-x}) + C$

43 $(1/3)\cosh 3t + C$

45 $(1/2)\sinh(2w + 1) + C$

47 $\frac{1}{3}\cosh^3 x + C$

49 $(\pi/4)t^4 + 2t^2 + C$

51 $\sin x^2 + C$

53 $(1/5)\cos(2 - 5x) + C$

55 $(1/2)\ln(x^2 + 1) + C$

57 0

59 $1 - (1/e)$

61 $2e(e-1)$

63 $2(\sin 2 - \sin 1)$

65 40

67 $\ln 3$

69 14/3

71 $(2/5)(y+1)^{5/2} - (2/3)(y+1)^{3/2} + C$

73 $(2/5)(t+1)^{5/2} - (2/3)(t+1)^{3/2} + C$

75 $(2/7)(x-2)^{7/2} + (8/5)(x-2)^{5/2} + (8/3)(x-2)^{3/2} + C$

77 $(2/3)(t+1)^{3/2} - 2(t+1)^{1/2} + C$

79 $y = 3x$

81 $w = e^z$

83 $1/(2\sqrt{w})$

85 Substitute $w = \sin x$

87 Substitute $w = \sin x, w = \arcsin x$

89 Substitute $w = x+1, w = 1 + \sqrt{x}$

91 $e^{11} - e^7$

93 3

95 218/3

97 $(g(x))^5/5$

99 $-\cos g(x) + C$

101 $w = 1 - 4x^3, k = -1/12, n = 1/2$

103 $w = x^2 - 3, k = 1, n = -2$

105 $k = 1/\ln 2, n = -1, w_0 = 4, w_1 = 35$

107 $w = -x^2, k = -1/2$

109 $w = 0.5r, k = 2$

111 $w = 5t, k = 1/(5e^4)$

113 $a = 1, b = -1, A = -1/\pi, w = \cos(\pi t)$

115 (a) Yes; $-0.5\cos(x^2) + C$
    (b) No
    (c) No
    (d) Yes; $-1/(2(1+x^2)) + C$
    (e) No
    (f) Yes; $-\ln|2 + \cos x| + C$

117 $\ln 3$

119 $e^3(e^6 - 1)/3$

121 $3\ln 3 - 2$

123 $(1/2)\ln 3$

$f(x) = \dfrac{1}{1+x}$
0.54931

125 (a) 10
    (b) 5

127 (a) 0
    (b) 2/3

129 (a) $(\sin^2\theta)/2 + C$
    (b) $-(\cos^2\theta)/2 + C$
    (c) $-(\cos 2\theta)/4 + C$
    (d) Functions differ by a constant

131 $k = 1/2, w = \ln(x^2 + 1), a = \ln 5, b = \ln 26$

135 (a) I $C(t) = 1.3t + 311$
      II $C(t) = 0.5t + 0.015t^2 + 311$
      III $C(t) = 25e^{0.02t} + 286$

(b) I 402 ppm
     II 419.5 ppm
     III 387.380 ppm

137 (a) 6.9 billion, 7.8 billion
    (b) 6.5 billion

139 (a) $E(t) = 1.4e^{0.07t}$
    (b) $0.2(e^7 - 1) \approx 219$ million megawatt-hours
    (c) 1972
    (d) Graph $E(t)$ and estimate t such that $E(t) = 219$

141 $(mg/k)t - (m^2g/k^2)(1 - e^{-kt/m}) + h_0$

143 (a) First case: 19,923
      Second case: 1.99 billion
    (b) In both cases, 6.47 yrs
    (c) 3.5 yrs

145 Integrand needs extra factor of $f'(x)$

147 Change limits of integration for substitution in definite integral

149 $\int \sin(x^3 - 3x)(x^2 - 1)\,dx$

151 False

Section 7.2

1 (a) $x^3 e^x/3 - (1/3)\int x^3 e^x\,dx$
    (b) $x^2 e^x - 2\int x e^x\,dx$

3 $-t\cos t + \sin t + C$

5 $\frac{1}{5}te^{5t} - \frac{1}{25}e^{5t} + C$

7 $-10pe^{(-0.1)p} - 100e^{(-0.1)p} + C$

9 $(1/2)x^2\ln x - (1/4)x^2 + C$

11 $(1/6)q^6\ln 5q - (1/36)q^6 + C$

13 $-(1/2)\sin\theta\cos\theta + \theta/2 + C$

15 $t(\ln t)^2 - 2t\ln t + 2t + C$

17 $(2/3)y(y+3)^{3/2} - (4/15)(y+3)^{5/2} + C$

19 $-(\theta+1)\cos(\theta+1) + \sin(\theta+1) + C$

21 $-x^{-1}\ln x - x^{-1} + C$

23 $-2t(5-t)^{1/2} - (4/3)(5-t)^{3/2} - 14(5-t)^{1/2} + C$

25 $r^2[(\ln r)^2 - \ln r + (1/2)]/2 + C$

27 $z\arctan 7z - \frac{1}{14}\ln(1 + 49z^2) + C$

29 $(1/2)x^2 e^{x^2} - (1/2)e^{x^2} + C$

31 $x\cosh x - \sinh x + C$

33 $5\ln 5 - 4 \approx 4.047$

35 $-11e^{-10} + 1 \approx 0.9995$

37 $\pi/4 - (1/2)\ln 2 \approx 0.439$

39 $\pi/2 - 1 \approx 0.571$

41 (a) Parts
    (b) Substitution
    (c) Substitution
    (d) Substitution
    (e) Substitution
    (f) Parts
    (g) Parts

43 $w = 5 - 3x, k = -2/3$

45 $w = \ln x, k = 3$

47 $2\arctan 2 - (\ln 5)/2$

49 $2\ln 2 - 1$

51 π

53 Integration by parts gives:
    $(1/2)\sin\theta\cos\theta + (1/2)\theta + C$
    The identity for $\cos^2\theta$ gives:
    $(1/2)\theta + (1/4)\sin 2\theta + C$

55 $(1/2)e^\theta(\sin\theta + \cos\theta) + C$

57 $(1/2)\theta e^\theta(\sin\theta + \cos\theta) - (1/2)e^\theta\sin\theta + C$

59 $xf'(x) - f(x) + C$

61 Integrate by parts choosing $u = x^n, v' = e^x$

63 Integrate by parts, choosing $u = x^n, v' = \sin ax$

65 (a) $A = a/(a^2 + b^2)$, $B = -b/(a^2 + b^2)$
    (b) $e^{ax}(b\sin bx + a\cos bx)/(a^2 + b^2) + C$

67 3

69 -5

71 45.71 (ng/ml)-hours

73 (a) $-(1/a)Te^{-aT} + (1/a^2)(1 - e^{-aT})$
    (b) $\lim_{T\to\infty} E = 1/a^2$

75 (a) $v = x, u' = (2/\sqrt{\pi})e^{-x^2}1, v' = 1$
    (b) $w = -x^2, dw = -2x\,dx$
    (c) $x\operatorname{erf}(x) + (1/\sqrt{\pi})e^{-x^2} + C$

77 $u = \ln t, v' = t$

79 $\int f(x)\,dx = xf(x) - \int xf'(x)\,dx$

81 $\int x^3 e^x\,dx$

83 True

85 False

Section 7.3

1 $(1/6)x^6\ln x - (1/36)x^6 + C$

3 $-(1/5)x^3\cos 5x + (3/25)x^2\sin 5x + (6/125)x\cos 5x - (6/625)\sin 5x + C$

5 $(1/7)x^7 + (5/2)x^4 + 25x + C$

7 $-(1/4)\sin^3 x\cos x - (3/8)\sin x\cos x + (3/8)x + C$

9 $((1/3)x^2 - (2/9)x + 2/27)e^{3x} + C$

11 $((1/3)x^4 - (4/9)x^3 + (4/9)x^2 - (8/27)x + (8/81))e^{3x} + C$

13 $(1/\sqrt{3})\arctan(y/\sqrt{3}) + C$

15 $(1/4)\arcsin(4x/5) + C$

17 $(5/16)\sin 3\theta\sin 5\theta + (3/16)\cos 3\theta\cos 5\theta + C$

19 $\frac{1}{2}\frac{\sin x}{\cos^2 x} + \frac{1}{4}\ln\left|\frac{\sin x+1}{\sin x-1}\right| + C$

21 $(1/34)e^{5x}(5\sin 3x - 3\cos 3x) + C$

23 $-(1/2)y^2\cos 2y + (1/2)y\sin 2y + (1/4)\cos 2y + C$

25 $\frac{1}{21}(\tan 7x/\cos^2 7x) + \frac{2}{21}\tan 7x + C$

27 $-\frac{1}{2\tan 2\theta} + C$

29 $\frac{1}{2}(\ln|x+1| - \ln|x+3|) + C$

31 $-(1/3)(\ln|z| - \ln|z-3|) + C$

33 $\arctan(z+2) + C$

35 $-\cos x + (1/3)\cos^3 x + C$

37 $\frac{1}{5}\cosh^5 x - \frac{1}{3}\cosh^3 x + C$

39 $-(1/9)(\cos^3 3\theta) + (1/15)(\cos^5 3\theta) + C$

41 $\frac{1}{3}(1 - \frac{\sqrt{2}}{2})$

43 $9/8 - 6\ln 2 = -3.034$

45 1/2

47 $\pi/12$

49 0.5398

51 $k = 0.5, w = 2x + 1, n = 3$

53 Form (i) with $a = -1/6, b = -1/4, c = 5$

55 Form (iii) with $a = 1, b = -5, c = 6, n = 7$

57 $a = 5, b = 4, \lambda = 2$

61 (a) 0

    (b) $V_0/\sqrt{2}$

    (c) 156 volts

63 Use V-26

65 $\frac{1}{4}e^{2x+1}(\sin(2x+1) - \cos(2x+1)) + C$

67 Table only has formulas for $\int p(x)\sin x\,dx$ where $p(x)$ polynomial

69 $\int 1/\sin^4 x\,dx$

71 False

73 True

Section 7.4

1 $(1/6)/(x) + (5/6)/(6+x)$

3 $1/(w-1) - 1/w - 1/w^2 - 1/w^3$

5 $-2/y + 1/(y-2) + 1/(y+2)$

7 $1/(2(s-1)) - 1/(2(s+1)) - 1/(s^2+1)$

9 $-2\ln|5-x| + 2\ln|5+x| + C$

11 $\ln|y-1| + \arctan y - \frac{1}{2}\ln\left|y^2+1\right| + C$

13 $\ln|s| - \ln|s+2| + C$

15 $\ln|x-2| + \ln|x+1| + \ln|x-3| + K$

17 $2\ln|x-5| - \ln\left|x^2+1\right| + K$

19 $x^3/3 + \ln|x+1| - \ln|x+2| + C$

21 $\arcsin(x-2) + C$

23 (a) Yes; $x = 3\sin\theta$

    (b) No

25 $w = 3x^2 - x - 2, k = 2$

27 $a = -5/3, b = 4/5, c = -2/15, d = -3/5$

29 $A = 3.5, B = -1.5, w = e^x, dw = e^x dx, r = 1, s = 7$

31 $x = (\tan\theta) - 1$

33 $y = (\tan\theta) - 3/2$

35 $z = (\sin\theta) + 1$

37 $w = (t+2)^2 + 3$

39 $(\ln|x-5| - \ln|x-3|)/2 + C$

41 $(-\ln|x+7| + \ln|x-2|)/9 + C$

43 $\ln|z| - \ln|z+1| + C$

45 $(1/3)\ln|P/(1-P)| + C$

47 $(3/2)\ln|2y+1| - \ln|y+1| + C$

49 $\ln|x| + (2/x) - (1/2)\ln\left|1+x^2\right| + 2\arctan x + K$

51 $z/(4\sqrt{4-z^2}) + C$

53 $\arctan((x+2)/3)/3 + C$

55 $-(\sqrt{1+x^2})/x + C$

57 $-\sqrt{1-4x^2}/x - 2\arcsin(2x) + C$

59 $(1/6)\ln|(\sqrt{9-4x^2} - 3)/(\sqrt{9-4x^2} + 3)| + C$

61 $-(1/4)\sqrt{4-x^2}/x + C$

63 $(1/16)(x/\sqrt{16-x^2}) + C$

65 $5\ln 2$

67 $\pi/12 - \sqrt{3}/8$

69 $\ln(1 + \sqrt{2})$

71 $(\ln|1+x| - \ln|1-x|)/2 + C$

73 $\ln|x| + \ln\left|x^2+1\right| + K$

75 (a) $(\ln|x-a| - \ln|x-b|)/(a-b) + C$

    (b) $-1/(x-a) + C$

77 (a) $(\ln\left|x - \sqrt{a}\right| - \ln\left|x + \sqrt{a}\right|)/(2\sqrt{a}) + C$

    (b) $-1/x + C$

    (c) $(1/\sqrt{-a})\arctan(x/\sqrt{-a}) + C$

79 (a) $(k/(b-a))\ln|(2b-a)/b|$

    (b) $T \to \infty$

81 $1/(x-1)$ term missing

83 $f(x) = 1/(1+x^2)$

85 $P(x) = x, Q(x) = x^2 + 1$

87 False

89 (e)

Section 7.5

1 (a) Underestimate

    (b) Overestimate

    (c) Overestimate

    (d) Underestimate

3 (a) Underestimate

    (b) Overestimate

    (c) Underestimate

    (d) Overestimate

5 (a) Underestimate

    (b) Overestimate

(c) Overestimate

(d) Underestimate

7 (a) 27
  (b) 135
  (c) 81
  (d) 67.5
9 (a) MID(2)= 24;
     TRAP(2)= 28
  (b) MID(2) underestimate;
     TRAP(2) overestimate

$f(x) = x^2 + 1$

Area shaded = MID(2)

$f(x) = x^2 + 1$

Area shaded = TRAP(2)

11 -2.2
13 0.1703
15 (a) (i) 0.8160
        (ii) 0.7535
        (iii) 0.7847
17 RIGHT $<$ TRAP $<$ Exact $<$ MID $<$ LEFT
19 RIGHT: over; LEFT: under
21 LEFT, TRAP: over; RIGHT, MID: under
23 (a) 16.392
  (b) $2(4^{3/2}) = 16$
  (c) -0.392
  (d) -0.00392
  (e) 16.00392

25 (a) TRAP(4); 1027.5
  (b) Underestimate
27 Large $|f'|$ gives large error
29 (a)

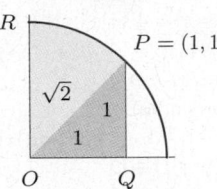

R $P = (1,1)$
$\sqrt{2}$ 1
1
O Q

  (b) LEFT(5) ≈ 1.32350
      error ≈ -0.03810
      RIGHT(5) ≈ 1.24066
      error ≈ 0.04474
      TRAP(5) ≈ 1.28208
      error ≈ 0.00332
      MID(5) ≈ 1.28705
      error ≈ -0.001656

35 RIGHT(10) = 5.556
    TRAP(10) = 4.356
    LEFT(20) = 3.199
    RIGHT(20) = 4.399
    TRAP(20) = 3.799
39 TRAP(n) approaches value of definite integral, not 0
41 Total time grows exponentially with number of digits
43 $f(x) = e^x$
45 False
47 True
49 False
51 True
53 False
55 False

Section 7.6

1 (a)

y

1

  (b)

y

1

3 (a) 0.9596, 0.9995, 0.99999996
  (b) 1.0
5 Diverges
7 -1
9 Converges to 1/2
11 1
13 ln 2
15 4
17 Does not converge
19 $\pi/4$
21 Does not converge

23 Does not converge
25 0.01317
27 $1/\ln 3$
29 1/3
31 Does not converge
33 Does not converge
35 (a) 0.421
  (b) 0.500
37 The area is infinite
39 1/2
41 2/27
43 (b) $t = 2$
  (c) 4000 people
45 $\sqrt{b\pi}$
47 $\pi^4/120$
49 $f(x) = g(x) = 1/x$
51 $f(x) = 1/x$
53 True
55 False
57 True
59 True
61 True

Section 7.7

1 Converges; behaves like $1/x^2$
3 Diverges; behaves like $1/x$
5 Diverges; behaves like $1/x$
7 Converges; behaves like $5/x^3$
9 Converges; behaves like $1/x^2$
11 Does not converge
13 Converges
15 Does not converge
17 Converges
19 Converges
21 Converges
23 Converges
25 Does not converge
27 Converge
29 Converges for $p < 1$
    Diverges for $p \geq 1$
31 (a) e^t is concave up for all t
33 Converges
35 $f(x) = 1/x^2$
37 $f(x) = 3/(7x + 2)$
39 True

Chapter 7 Review

1 $(t + 1)^3/3$
3 $5^x/\ln 5$
5 $3w^2/2 + 7w + C$
7 $-\cos t + C$
9 $(1/5)e^{5z} + C$
11 $(-1/2)\cos 2\theta + C$
13 $2x^{5/2}/5 + 3x^{5/3}/5 + C$
15 $-e^{-z} + C$
17 $x^2/2 + \ln|x| - x^{-1} + C$
19 $(1/2)e^{t^2} + C$
21 $((1/2)x^2 - (1/2)x + 1/4)e^{2x} + C$

23 $(1/2)y^2 \ln y - (1/4)y^2 + C$

25 $x(\ln x)^2 - 2x \ln x$
    $+ 2x + C$

27 $(1/3)\sin^3 \theta + C$

29 $(1/2)u^2 + 3u + 3\ln|u| - 1/u + C$

31 $\tan z + C$

33 $(1/12)t^{12} - (10/11)t^{11} + C$

35 $(1/3)(\ln x)^3 + C$

37 $(1/3)x^3 + x^2 + \ln|x| + C$

39 $(1/2)e^{t^2+1} + C$

41 $(1/10)\sin^2(5\theta) + C$ (other forms of answer
    are possible)

43 $\arctan z + C$

45 $-(1/8)\cos^4 2\theta + C$

47 $(-1/4)\cos^4 z +$
    $(1/6)\cos^6 z + C$

49 $(2/3)(1 + \sin\theta)^{3/2} + C$

51 $t^3 e^t - 3t^2 e^t + 6te^t - 6e^t + C$

53 $(3z + 5)^4/12 + C$

55 $\arctan(\sin w) + C$

57 $-\cos(\ln x) + C$

59 $y - (1/2)e^{-2y} + C$

61 $\ln|\ln x| + C$

63 $\sin\sqrt{x^2 + 1} + C$

65 $ue^{ku}/k - e^{ku}/k^2 + C$

67 $(1/\sqrt{2})e^{\sqrt{2}+3} + C$

69 $(u^3 \ln u)/3 - u^3/9 + C$

71 $-\cos(2x)/(4\sin^2(2x))$
    $+ \frac{1}{8}\ln\left|\frac{(\cos(2x)-1)}{(\cos(2x)+1)}\right| + C$

73 $-y^2\cos(cy)/c + 2y\sin(cy)/c^2$
    $+ 2\cos(cy)/c^3 + C$

75 $\frac{1}{34}e^{5x}(5\cos(3x) + 3\sin(3x)) + C$

77 $(\sqrt{3}/4)(2x\sqrt{1 + 4x^2}$
    $+ \ln|2x + \sqrt{1 + 4x^2}|) + C$

79 $x^2/2 - 3x - \ln|x + 1|$
    $+ 8\ln|x + 2| + C$

81 $(1/b)(\ln|x| - \ln|x + b/a|) + C$

83 $(x^3/27) + 2x - (9/x) + C$

85 $-(1/\ln 10)10^{1-x} + C$

87 $\left((1/2)v^2 - 1/4\right)\arcsin v +$
    $(1/4)v\sqrt{1 - v^2} + K$

89 $z^3/3 + 5z^2/2 + 25z$
    $+ 125\ln|z - 5| + C$

91 $(1/3)\ln|\sin(3\theta)| + C$

93 $(2/3)x^{3/2} + 2\sqrt{x} + C$

95 $(4/3)(\sqrt{x} + 1)^{3/2} + C$

97 $-1/(4(z^2 - 5)^2) + C$

99 $(1 + \tan x)^4/4 + C$

101 $e^{x^2+x} + C$

103 $-(2/9)(2 + 3\cos x)^{3/2} + C$

105 $\sin^3(2\theta)/6 - \sin^5(2\theta)/10 + C$

107 $(x + \sin x)^4/4 + C$

109 $\frac{1}{3}\sinh^3 x + C$

111 $49932\frac{1}{6}$

113 $201,760$

115 $3/2 + \ln 2$

117 $e - 2 \approx 0.71828$

119 $-11e^{-10} + 1$

121 $3(e^2 - e)$

123 0

125 $\frac{1}{2}\ln|x - 1| - \frac{1}{2}\ln|x + 1| + C$

127 $(\ln|x| - \ln|L - x|)/L + C$

129 $\arcsin(x/5) + C$

131 $(1/3)\arcsin(3x) + C$

133 $2\ln|x - 1| - \ln|x + 1| - \ln|x| + K$

135 $\arctan(x + 1) + C$

137 $(1/b)\arcsin(bx/a) + C$

139 $(1/2)(\ln|e^x - 1| - \ln|e^x + 1|) + C$

141 Does not converge

143 6

145 Does not converge

147 Does not converge

149 Converges to $\pi/8$

151 Converges to $2\sqrt{15}$

153 Does not converge

155 Converges to value between 0 and $\pi/2$

157 Does not converge

159 $e^9/3 - e^6/2 + 1/6$

161 Area $= 2\sqrt{2}$

163 $w = 3x^5 + 2, p = 1/2, k = 1/5$

165 $A = 2/5, B = -3/5$

167 $\int 0.5ue^u \, du;$
    $k = 0.5, u = -x^2$

169 Substitute $w = x^2$ into second integral

171 Substitute $w = 1 - x^2$, $w = \ln x$

173 $w = 2x$

175 5/6

177 (a) 3.5
     (b) 35

179 11/9

181 Wrong; improper integral treated as
     proper integral, integral diverges

183 $RT(5) < RT(10) < TR(10) < $ Exact $< MID(10)$
     $< LF(10) < LF(5)$

185 (a) 4 places: 2 seconds
          8 places: $\approx$ 6 hours
          12 places: $\approx$ 6 years
          20 places: $\approx$ 600 million years
     (b) 4 places: 2 seconds
          8 places: $\approx$ 3 minutes
          12 places: $\approx$ 6 hours
          20 places: $\approx$ 6 years

187 (a) $(k/L)\ln 3$
     (b) $T \to \infty$

189 (a) 0.5 ml
     (b) 99.95%

191 (a) 360 degree-days
     (b)

     (c) $T_2 = 36$

193 (a) $(\ln x)^2/2, (\ln x)^3/3, (\ln x)^4/4$
     (b) $(\ln x)^{n+1}/(n + 1)$

195 (a) $(-9\cos x + \cos(3x))/12$
     (b) $(3\sin x - \sin(3x))/4$

197 (a) $x + x/(2(1 + x^2)) - (3/2)\arctan x$
     (b) $1 - (x^2/(1 + x^2)^2) - 1/(1 + x^2)$

Section 8.1

1 (a) $\sum 2x \, \Delta x$
   (b) 9

3 (a) $\sum (3 - y/2) \, \Delta y$
   (b) 9

5 15

7 15/2

9 $(5/2)\pi$

11 1/6

13 $\int_0^9 4\pi \, dx = 36\pi$ cm^3

15 $\int_0^5 (4\pi/25)y^2 \, dy = 20\pi/3$ cm^3

17 $\int_0^5 \pi(5^2 - y^2) \, dy = 250\pi/3$ mm^3

19 Triangle; $b, h = 1, 3$

21 Quarter circle $r = \sqrt{15}$

23

25 (a) $\int_0^4 ((12 - x) - 2x) \, dx = 24$
    (b) $\int_0^8 (y/2) \, dy + \int_8^{12} (12 - y) \, dy = 16 +$
         $8 = 24$

27 (a) $\int_0^3 2x \, dx + \int_3^5 6 \, dx = 9 + 12 = 21$
    (b) $\int_0^6 (5 - (y/2)) \, dy = 21$

29 Cone, $h = 12, r = 4$

31 Hemisphere $r = 2$

33 $36\pi = 113.097$ m^3

35 (a) $3\Delta x$;
         $\int_0^4 3 \, dx = 12$ cm^3

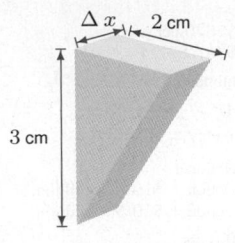

(b) $8(1 - h/3)\Delta h$;
$\int_0^3 8(1 - h/3)\, dh = 12 \text{ cm}^3$

37 $\int_0^{150} 1400(160 - h)\, dh = 1.785 \cdot 10^7 \text{ m}^3$

39 Change to $\int_{-10}^{10} \pi \left(10^2 - x^2\right) dx$

41 Region between positive x-axis, positive y-axis, and $y = 1 - x$

43 False

45 True

Section 8.2

1 (a) $4\pi \int_0^3 x^2\, dx$
 (b) 36π

3 (a) $(\pi/4) \int_0^6 (36 - y^2)\, dy$
 (b) 36π

5 $\pi/5$

7 $256\pi/15$

9 $\pi(e^2 - e^{-2})/2$

11 $\pi/2$

13 $2\pi/15$

15 2.958

17 2.302

19 π

21 $\sqrt{42}$

23 ≈ 24.6

25 $V = \int_0^2 [\pi(9 - y^3)^2 - \pi(9 - 4y)^2]\, dy$

27 $V = \int_0^9 [\pi(2 + \frac{1}{3}x)^2 - \pi 2^2]\, dx$

29 $V = \int_0^5 \pi((5x)^2 - (x^2)^2)\, dx$

31 $V = \int_0^5 \pi((4 + 5x)^2 - (4 + x^2)^2)\, dx$

33 3.820

35 (a) $16\pi/3$
 (b) 1.48

37 $V = (16/7)\pi \approx 7.18$

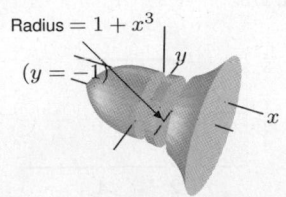

Radius $= 1 + x^3$
$(y = -1)$

39 $V = (\pi^2/2) \approx 4.935$

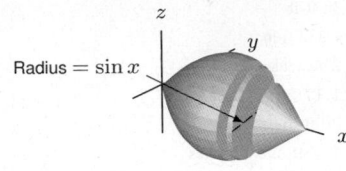

Radius $= \sin x$

41 $4\pi/5$

43 8/15

45 $\sqrt{3}/8$

47 $V \approx 42.42$

49 $V = (e^2 - 1)/2$

51 $g(x) = 2\sin x, -2\sin x$

53 2267.32 cubic feet

55 (a) Volume $\approx 152 \text{ in}^3$
 (b) About 15 apples

57 $40,000LH^{3/2}/(3\sqrt{a})$

59 (a) $dh/dt = -6/\pi$
 (b) $t = \pi/6$

61 (a) $4 \int_0^r \sqrt{1 + (-x/y)^2}\, dx$
 (b) $2\pi r$

63 $\int_0^4 \sqrt{1 + (4 - 2x)^2}\, dx$

65 $\int_{-\sqrt{1/2}}^{\sqrt{1/2}} \sqrt{1 + 4x^2 e^{-2x^2}}\, dx$

67 4.624 meters

69 (c) $f(x) = \sqrt{3}x$

71 Change to $\int_0^5 \left(\pi(3x)^2 - \pi(2x)^2\right) dx$

73 Greater than 32

75 Region bounded by $y = 2x$, x-axis, $0 \le x \le 1$

77 $f(x) = x^2$

79 False

81 False

Section 8.3

1 $(-1/2, \sqrt{3}/2)$

3 $(3, -\sqrt{3})$

5 $(\sqrt{2}, \pi/4)$

7 $(2\sqrt{2}, -\pi/6)$

9 (b)

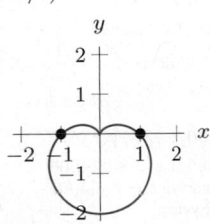

(c) Cartesian:
 $(\sqrt{3}/4, 1/4)$;
 $(-\sqrt{3}/4, 1/4)$ or polar:
 $r = 1/2, \theta = \pi/6$ or $5\pi/6$
(d)

11 Looks the same

13 Rotated by $90°$ clockwise

15 $\pi/4 \le \theta \le 5\pi/4$;
 $0 \le \theta \le \pi/4$ and $5\pi/4 \le \theta \le 2\pi$

17 $\sqrt{8} \le r \le \sqrt{18}$ and $\pi/4 \le \theta \le \pi/2$

19 $0 \le \theta \le \pi/2$ and $1 \le r \le 2/\cos\theta$

21 -1

23 $\sqrt{2}(e^\pi - e^{\pi/2})$

25

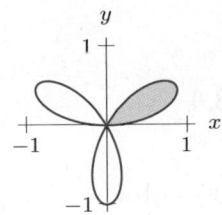

27 $4\pi^3$

29 (a) $r = 1/\cos\theta; r = 2$
 (b) $\frac{1}{2} \int_{-\pi/3}^{\pi/3} (2^2 - (1/\cos\theta)^2)\, d\theta$
 (c) $(4\pi/3) - \sqrt{3}$

31 $2\pi a$

33 $(5\pi/6) + 7\sqrt{3}/8$

35 (a)

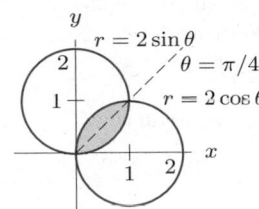

$r = 2\sin\theta$
$\theta = \pi/4$
$r = 2\cos\theta$

(b) $(\pi/2) - 1$

37 (a)

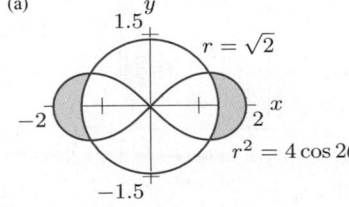

$r = \sqrt{2}$
$r^2 = 4\cos 2\theta$

(b) $2\sqrt{3} - 2\pi/3$

39 Horiz: $(\pm 1.633, \pm 2.309)$; $(0, 0)$
 Vert: $(\pm 2.309, \pm 1.633)$; $(0, 0)$

41 (a) $y = (2/\pi)x + (2/\pi)$
 (b) $y = 1$

43 21.256

47 2.828

49 Points are in quadrant IV

51
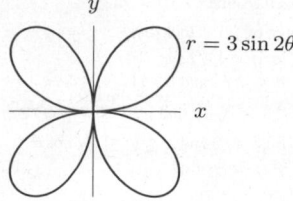
$r = 3\sin 2\theta$

53 $r = 100$

55 $r = 1 + \cos\theta$

Section 8.4

1 $1 - e^{-10}$ gm

3 (a) $\displaystyle\sum_{i=1}^{N}(2 + 6x_i)\Delta x$
  (b) 16 grams

5 (b) $\displaystyle\sum_{i=1}^{N}[600 + 300\sin(4\sqrt{x_i + 0.15})](20/N)$
  (c) ≈ 11513

7 2 cm to right of origin

9 45

11 186,925

13 1 gm

15 (a) 3 miles
  (b) 282,743

17 (a) $\displaystyle\int_0^5 2\pi r(0.115e^{-2r})\,dr$
  (b) 181 cubic meters

19 (a) $\pi r^2 l/2$
  (b) $2klr^3/3$

21 $\displaystyle\int_0^{60}(1/144)g(t)\,dt\ \text{ft}^3$

23 $x = 2$

25 $\pi/2$

27 (a) Right
  (b) $2/(1 + 6e - e^2) \approx 0.2$

29 (a) 2/3 gm
  (b) Greater than 1/2

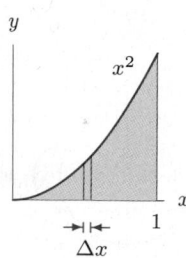

  (c) $\overline{x} = 3/4$ cm

33 $\overline{x} = (1 - 3e^{-2})/(2 - 2e^{-2}) \approx 0.343$;
  $\overline{y} = 0$

35 Density cannot be negative

37 $\delta(x) = x^2$, for $-1 \leq x \leq 1$

39 $\delta(x) = \begin{cases} 5, & 0 \leq x \leq 1 \\ 1, & 1 < x < 5 \\ 4, & 5 \leq x \leq 10 \end{cases}$

41 $\delta(x) = 1$

43 False

45 True

47 True

Section 8.5

1 30 ft-lb

3 1.333 ft-lb

5 27/2 joules

7 $1.176 \cdot 10^7$ lb

9 20 ft-lb

11 $1.489 \cdot 10^{10}$ joules

13 3437.5 ft-lbs

15 6860 joules

17 784.14 ft-lb

19 1,058,591.1 ft-lbs

21 (a) 156,828 ft-lbs
  (b) 313,656 ft-lbs
  (c) 150,555 ft-lbs

23 27,788 ft-lbs

25 $0.366(k + 1.077)g\pi$ joules

27 (a) Force on dam
  $\approx \displaystyle\sum_{i=0}^{N-1}1000(62.4h_i)\Delta h$
  (b) $\displaystyle\int_0^{50} = 1000(62.4h)\,dh = 78,000,000$ pounds

29 4,992,000 lbs

31 (a) $1.76 \cdot 10^6$ nt/m^2
  (b) $1.96 \cdot 10^7 \displaystyle\int_0^{180} h\,dh = 3.2 \cdot 10^{11}$ nt

33 (a) 780,000 lb/ft^2
  About 5400 lb/in^2
  (b) $124.8\displaystyle\int_{-3}^3(12,500 - h)\sqrt{9 - h^2}\,dh$
  $= 2.2 \cdot 10^7$ lb

35 Potential
  $= 2\pi\sigma(\sqrt{R^2 + a^2} - R)$

37 15231 ergs

39 $\dfrac{GM_1M_2}{l_1l_2}\ln\left(\dfrac{(a + l_1)(a + l_2)}{a(a + l_1 + l_2)}\right)$

41 $(2GMmy/a^2)\left(y^{-1} - (a^2 + y^2)^{-1/2}\right)$

43 Less than twice as much

45 Book raised given vertical distance

47 False

49 False

51 False

Section 8.6

1 $C(1 + 0.03)^{25}$ dollars

3 $C/e^{0.03(5)}$ dollars

5 $\displaystyle\int_0^{15}C\,e^{0.02(15-t)}\,dt$ dollars

7 $\ln(25,000/C)/30$ per year

9 (a) Future value = $6389.06
  Present value = $864.66
  (b) 17.92 years

11 (a) $43,645.71
  (b) $20,000.00
  (c) $23,645.71

13 4.621%/ yr

15 $4000/ yr; $21,034.18

17 $1000/ yr; $24,591.23

19 $/year

t (years from present)

21 (a) $5820 per year
  (b) $36,787.94

23 Installments

25 3.641%/ yr

27 9.519%/ yr

29 (a) Option 1
  (b) Option 1: $10.929 million;
  Option 2: $10.530 million

31 In 10 years

33 (a) $\displaystyle\sum_{i=0}^{n-1}(2000 - 100t_i)e^{-0.1t_i}\Delta t$
  (b) $\displaystyle\int_0^M e^{-0.10t}(2000 - 100t)\,dt$
  (c) After 20 years
  $11,353.35

35 $85,750,000

39 (a) Less
  (b) Can't tell
  (c) Less

41 Future value more than $20,000

43 PV requires integral

47 5%, $4761.90

Section 8.7

1 (a)-(II), (b)-(I), (c)-(III)

3 % of population
  per dollar of income

  income

  % of population having
  at least this income

  income

5 pdf; 1/4

7 cdf; 1

9 cdf; 1/3

11 For small Δx around 70, fraction of families with incomes in that interval about $0.05\Delta x$

13 A is 300 kelvins; B is 500 kelvins

15 (a) 0.9 m–1.1 m

19 (a) Cumulative distribution increasing
   (b) Vertical 0.2, horizontal 2

21 (a) 22.1%
   (b) 33.0%
   (c) 30.1%
   (d) $C(h) = 1 - e^{-0.4h}$

23 (b) About 3/4

25 Prob $0.02\Delta x$ in interval around 1

27 $\int_{-\infty}^{\infty} p(t)\, dt \neq 1$

29 $P(x)$ grows without bound as $x \to \infty$, instead of approaching 1

31 Cumulative distribution increasing

33 $P(t) = \begin{cases} 0, & t < 0 \\ t, & 0 \leq t \leq 1 \\ 1, & t > 1 \end{cases}$

35 $P(x) = (x-3)/4, 3 \leq x \leq 7$

37 False

Section 8.8

5 Mean 2/3; Median $2 - \sqrt{2} = 0.586$

7 (a) 0.684 : 1
   (b) 1.6 hours
   (c) 1.682 hours

9 (a) $P(t)$ = Fraction of population who survive up to t years after treatment
   (b) $S(t) = e^{Ct}$
   (c) 0.178

11 (a) $p(x) = \frac{1}{15\sqrt{2\pi}} e^{-\frac{1}{2}\left(\frac{x-100}{15}\right)^2}$
   (b) 6.7% of the population

13 (c) μ represents the mean of the distribution, while σ is the standard deviation

15 (b)

17 (a) $p(r) = 4r^2 e^{-2r}$

(b) Mean: 1.5 Bohr radii
   Median: 1.33 Bohr radii
   Most likely:
   1 Bohr radius

19 Median cannot be 1 since all of the area is to the left of $x = 1$

21 $p(x) = \begin{cases} 0 & \text{for} & x < 0 \\ 1 & \text{for} & 0 \leq x \leq 1 \\ 0 & \text{for} & x > 1 \end{cases}$

23 True

25 False

Chapter 8 Review

1

3 $2\int_{-r}^{r} \sqrt{r^2 - x^2}\, dx = \pi r^2$

5 $3772\pi/15 = 790.006$

7 $\pi(1 - e^{-4})/4 = 0.771$

9 $27\pi = 84.823$

11 $V = \int_0^2 \pi(y^3)^2\, dy$

13 $V = \int_0^2 \left[\pi(10 - 4y)^2 - \pi(2)^2\right] dy$

15 $V = \int_0^2 \left[\pi(4y + 3)^2 - \pi(y^3 + 3)^2\right] dx$

17 $V = \pi$

19 $36\pi = 113.097$ m^3

21 $2\int_{-a}^{a} \sqrt{1 + b^2 x^2/(a^2(a^2 - x^2))}\, dx$

23 45.230

25 4.785

27 15.865

29 $\int_0^1 f(x)\, dx < 1/2$

31 $\int_0^1 f^{-1}(x)\, dx > 1/2$

33 $\int_0^1 \sqrt{1 + (f'(x))^2}\, dx > \sqrt{2}$

35

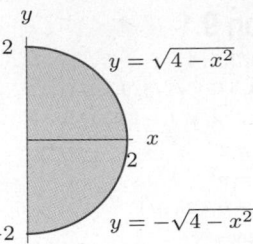

37 $V = \int_0^{25} \pi((8 - y/5)^2 - (8 - \sqrt{y})^2)\, dy$

39 (a) $V = 5\pi/6$
   (b) $V = 4\pi/5$

41 (a) $(1 - e^{-b})/b$
   (b) $\pi(1 - e^{-2b})/(2b)$

43 $736\pi/3 = 770.737$

45 $2\pi/3$

47 $\pi^2/2 - 2\pi/3 = 2.840$

49 $\pi/24$

51 Area under graph of f from $x = 0$ to $x = 3$

53 $e - e^{-1}$

55 (a) $a = b/l$
   (b) $(1/3)\pi b^2 l$

57 Volume = $6\pi^2$

59 5π cubic inches/second

61 πa^2

63 (a) $(\sin^2\theta - \cos^2\theta)/(2\cos\theta\sin\theta)$
   (b) $\pi/4$

65 $\int_{-2}^{1} \pi\left((x-1)^2(x+2)\right)^2 dx$

67 (a) 2/3 gm
   (b) Less than 1/2

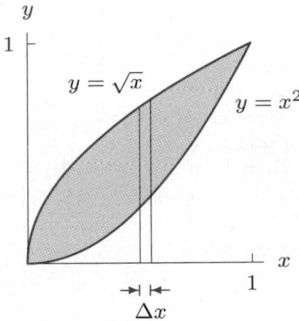

(c) $\overline{x} = \overline{y} = 9/20$ cm

69 100 ft-lbs

71 1,404,000 ft-lbs

73 20,617 ft-lbs

75 21,600 ft-lbs

77 49 kg

79 $y = x^4$

81 B

83 \$6.2828 billion

85 1.25 gallons

87 (a) $y = h + (2 - 2h)x^2$
   (b) Both events happen simultaneously

89 The hoop rotating about the cylindrical axis

91 (a) $\frac{1}{2}t\sqrt{1 + 4t^2} + \frac{1}{4}\text{arcsinh}\,(2t)$
   (b) t^2

93 (b) $(4\pi/3)(r^2 - a^2)^{3/2}$

Section 9.1

1 $0, 3, 2, 5, 4$

3 $2/3, 4/5, 6/7, 8/9, 10/11$

5 $1, -1/2, 1/4, -1/8, 1/16$

7 $s_n = 2^{n+1}$

9 $s_n = n^2 + 1$

11 $s_n = n/(2n+1)$

13 Diverges

15 Converges to 3

17 Diverges

19 Converges to 2

21 Diverges

23 Converges to 0

25 (a) (IV)
   (b) (III)
   (c) (II)
   (d) (I)

27 (a) (II)
   (b) (III)
   (c) (IV)
   (d) (I)
   (e) (V)

29 $1, 3, 6, 10, 15, 21$

31 $1, 5, 7, 17, 31, 65$

33 $13, 27, 50, 85$

35 $0.25, 0.00, 0.25, 1.00, 2.25, 4.00$

37 $0.841, 0.455, 0.047, -0.189, -0.192, -0.047$

39 $0, 0, 6, 6, 6, 0, 0 \ldots$ and
   $0, 2, 4, 6, 4, 2, \ldots$

41 $s_n = s_{n-1} + 2, s_1 = 1$

43 $s_n = 2s_{n-1} - 1, s_1 = 3$

45 $s_n = s_{n-1} + n, s_1 = 1$

51 Converges to 0.5671

53 Converges to 1

55 (a) $2, 4, 2^n$
   (b) 33 generations; overlap

57 (a) k rows; $a_n = n$
   (b) $T_n = T_{n-1} + n, n > 1; T_1 = 1$

61 For all $\epsilon > 0$, there is an N such
   that $|s_n - L| < \epsilon$ for all $n \geq N$

63 Converges to $3/7$

65 $s_n = -1/n$

67 False

69 True

71 False

73 True

75 (b)

Section 9.2

1 Sequence

3 Sequence

5 Series

7 Series

9 No

11 Yes, $a = 1$, ratio $= -1/2$

13 Yes, $a = 1$, ratio $= 2z$

15 Yes, $a = 1$, ratio $= -x$

17 Yes, $a = y^2$, ratio $= y$

19 26 terms; 2.222

21 9 terms; 0.0000222

23 54

25 $80\sqrt{2}/(\sqrt{2} - 1) = 273.137.$

27 $1/(1 - 3x), -1/3 < x < 1/3$

29 $2/(1 + 2z), -1/2 < z < 1/2$

31 $4 + y/(1 - y/3), -3 < z < 3$

33 (a) $P_n =$
       $250(0.04) + 250(0.04)^2$
       $+ 250(0.04)^3 + \cdots$
       $+ 250(0.04)^{n-1}$
   (b) $P_n =$
       $250 \cdot 0.04(1 - (0.04)^{n-1})/(1 - 0.04)$
   (c) $\lim_{n \to \infty} P_n \approx 10.42$
       Difference between them is 250 mg

35

37 (a) 14.916 years
   (b) 6.25 % annual reduction in consumption

39 (a) (i)   \$16.43 million
       (ii) \$24.01 million
   (b) \$16.87 million

41 \$65,742.60

43 \$400 million

45 \$900 million

49 $|x| \geq 1$

51 $1 + (-1) + 1 + (-1) + \ldots$

53 $\sum_{n=0}^{\infty} 5(1/2)^n$

Section 9.3

1 $1, 3, 6, 10, 15$

3 $1/2, 2/3, 3/4, 4/5, 5/6$

5 Diverges

7 Converges

11 $f(x) = (-1)^x/x$ undefined

13 Diverges

15 Diverges

17 Converges

19 Converges

21 Converges

23 Diverges

25 Converges

27 Diverges

29 Diverges

31 Converges

35 (a) $\ln(n+1)$
   (b) Diverges

37 (b) $S_3 = 1 - 1/4; S_{10} = 1 - 1/11; S_n =$
       $1 - 1/(n+1)$

49 (a) 1.596
   (b) 3.09
   (c) 1.635; 3.13
   (d) 0.05; 0.01

53 Terms approaching zero does not guarantee convergence

55 $\sum_{n=1}^{\infty} 1/n$

57 True

59 False

61 True

63 False

65 (d)

Section 9.4

5 Behaves like $\sum_{n=1}^{\infty} 1/n^2$; Converges

7 Behaves like $\sum_{n=1}^{\infty} 1/n^{1/2}$; Diverges

9 Converges

11 Converges

13 Diverges

15 Converges

17 Converges

19 Converges

21 Alternating

23 Not alternating

25 Converges

27 Converges

29 Absolutely convergent

31 Divergent

33 Conditionally convergent

35 Conditionally convergent

37 Absolutely convergent

39 Converges

41 Converges

43 Diverges

45 Diverges

47 Converges

49 Terms not positive

51 Limit of ratios is 1

53 $a_{n+1} > a_n$ or $\lim_{n \to \infty} a_n \neq 0$

55 $\lim_{n \to \infty} a_n \neq 0$

57 Does not converge

59 Converges to approximately 0.3679

61 Converges

63 Diverges

65 Diverges

67 Converges

69 Diverges

71 Diverges

73 Converges

75 Diverges

77 Converges

79 Converges if $a > 1$ and diverges if $a \leq 1$

81 Converges for $1/e < a < e$; diverges for
   $a \geq e$ and $0 < a \leq 1/e$

83 Converges

85 12 or more terms

87 $\sum c_n$ converges, $\sum a_n$ diverges

95 Converges

97 Limit of ratios is 1, so ratio test inconclusive

99 $\sum_{n=1}^{\infty} (-1)^n/n$

101 $a_n = 3^n$

103 False

105 True

107 False

109 False

111 True

113 True

115 True

117 True

Section 9.5

1 Yes

3 No

5 $1 \cdot 3 \cdot 5 \cdots (2n-1)x^n/(2^n \cdot n!); n \geq 1$

7 $(-1)^k(x-1)^{2k}/(2k)!; k \geq 0$

9 $(x-a)^n/(2^{n-1} \cdot n!); n \geq 1$

11 1

13 1

15 2

17 2

19 1

21 1/4

23 1

25 (a) $R = 1$
 (b) $-1 < x \leq 1$

27 $-3 < x < 3$

29 $-2 < x < 2$

31 $-\infty < x < \infty$

33 $-1/5 \leq x < 1/5$

35 $\sum_{n=0}^{\infty}(-2z)^n, -1/2 < z < 1/2$

37 $\sum_{n=0}^{\infty}3(z/2)^n, -2 < z < 2$

39 1

41 $5 \leq R \leq 7$

43 (a) False
 (b) True
 (c) False
 (d) Cannot determine

45 (a) All real numbers
 (b) $J(0) = 1$
 (c) $S_4(x) = 1 - \frac{x^2}{4} + \frac{x^4}{64} - \frac{x^6}{2304} + \frac{x^8}{147,456}$
 (d) 0.765
 (e) 0.765

47 (a) Odd; $g(0) = 0$
 (c) $\sin x$

49 Radius ∞, not 0

51 $\sum_{n=0}^{\infty}(x-2)^n/n$

53 $\sum x^n/n^2$

55 True

57 True

59 False

61 True

63 False

65 False

67 (d)

Chapter 9 Review

1 $3(2^{11}-1)/2^{10}$

3 619.235

5 $b^5(1-b^6)/(1-b)$ when $b \neq 1$;
 6 when $b = 1$

7 $(3^{17}-1)/(2 \cdot 3^{20})$

9 36, 48, 52, 53.333;
 $S_n = 36(1-(1/3)^n)/(1-1/3); S = 54$

11 $-810, -270, -630, -390$;
 $S_n = -810(1-(-2/3)^n)/(1+2/3)$;

$S = -486$

13 Converges 4/7

15 Diverges

17 Converges

19 Converges

21 Converges

23 Diverges

25 Converges

27 Divergent

29 Divergent

33 Converges

35 Converges

37 Converges

39 Converges

41 Diverges

43 Diverges

45 Convergent

47 Converges

49 Converges

51 Diverges

53 Converges

55 Diverges

57 Diverges

59 ∞

61 1

63 $-3 < x < 7$

65 $-\infty < x < \infty$

67 $s_n = 2n + 3$

69 9, 15, 23

71 Converges if $r > 1$, diverges if $0 < r \leq 1$

73 (a) All real numbers
 (b) Even

75 240 million tons

77 $926.40

79 (a) $124.50
 (b) $125

81 £250

83 (a) (i) $B_0 4^n$
 (ii) $B_0 2^{n/10}$
 (iii) $(2^{1.9})^n$
 (b) 10.490 hours

85 5/6

87 $\sum(3/2)^n, \sum(1/2)^n$, other answers possible

89 Converges

91 Not enough information

93 Converges

95 (a) C_0 ———————
 C_1 ————   ————
 C_2 — —   — —
 C_3 -- --   -- --

 (b) $1/3 + 2/9 + 4/27 + \cdots + (1/3)(2/3)^{n-1}$
 (c) 1

97 12

Section 10.1

1 $P_3(x) = 1 + x + x^2 + x^3$
 $P_5(x) = 1 + x + x^2 + x^3$

$+ x^4 + x^5$
$P_7(x) = 1 + x + x^2 + x^3$
$+ x^4 + x^5 + x^6 + x^7$

3 $P_2(x) = 1 + (1/2)x - (1/8)x^2$
 $P_3(x) = 1 + (1/2)x - (1/8)x^2 + (1/16)x^3$
 $P_4(x) = 1 + (1/2)x - (1/8)x^2$
 $+ (1/16)x^3 - (5/128)x^4$

5 $P_2(x) = 1 - x^2/2!$
 $P_4(x) = 1 - x^2/2! + x^4/4!$
 $P_6(x) = 1 - x^2/2! + x^4/4! - x^6/6!$

7 $P_3(x) = P_4(x) = x - (1/3)x^3$

9 $P_2(x) = 1 - (1/2)x + (3/8)x^2$
 $P_3(x) = 1 - (1/2)x + (3/8)x^2$
 $- (5/16)x^3$
 $P_4(x) = 1 - (1/2)x + (3/8)x^2$
 $- (5/16)x^3 + (35/128)x^4$

11 $P_3(x) = 1 - \frac{x}{2} - \frac{x^2}{8} - \frac{x^3}{16}$

13 $P_4(x) = \frac{1}{3}[1 - \frac{x-2}{3}$
 $+ \frac{(x-2)^2}{3^2} - \frac{(x-2)^3}{3^3}$
 $+ \frac{(x-2)^4}{3^4}]$

15 $P_3(x) = \frac{\sqrt{2}}{2}[-1 + \left(x + \frac{\pi}{4}\right)$
 $+ \frac{1}{2}\left(x + \frac{\pi}{4}\right)^2 - \frac{1}{6}\left(x + \frac{\pi}{4}\right)^3]$

17 $1 - x/3 + 5x^2/7 + 8x^3$

19 $P_2(x) = 4x^2 - 7x + 2$
 $f(x) = P_2(x)$

21 (a) If $f(x)$ is a polynomial of degree n, then $P_n(x)$, the nth degree Taylor polynomial for $f(x)$ about $x = 0$, is $f(x)$ itself

23 $-3 + 5x - x^2 - x^4/24 + x^5/30$

25 $c < 0, b > 0, a > 0$

27 $a < 0, b > 0, c > 0$

31 (a) 1/2
 (b) 1/6

33 (a) fs are Figure 10.9
 gs are Figure 10.8
 (b) $A = (0,1)$
 $B = (0,2)$
 (c) $f_1 = $ III, $f_2 = $ I, $f_3 = $ II
 $g_1 = $ III, $g_2 = $ II, $g_3 = $ I

35 (a) $1 + 3x + 2x^2$
 (b) $1 + 3x + 7x^2$
 (c) No

37 (a) $P_4(x) = 1 + x^2 + (1/2)x^4$
 (b) If we substitute x^2 for x in the Taylor polynomial for e^x of degree 2, we will get $P_4(x)$, the Taylor polynomial for e^{x^2} of degree 4
 (c) $P_{20}(x) = 1 + x^2/1! + x^4/2!$
 $+ \cdots + x^{20}/10!$
 (d) $e^{-2x} \approx 1 - 2x + 2x^2$
 $- (4/3)x^3 + (2/3)x^4 - (4/15)x^5$

39 (a) Infinitely many; 3
 (h) That near $x = 0$
 Taylor poly only accurate near 0

41 (b) 0, 0.2

43 $f'(0) = 1$

45 $p(x) = 1 + 3(x-1) + (x-1)^3$

47 False

49 False

51 False

53 True

Section 10.2

1 $f(x) = 1 + 3x/2 + 3x^2/8 - x^3/16 + \cdots$

3 $f(x) = -x + x^3/3! - x^5/5! + x^7/7! + \cdots$

5 $f(x) = 1 + x + x^2$
$\quad + x^3 + \cdots$

7 $f(y) = 1 - y/3 - y^2/9$
$\quad - 5y^3/81 - \cdots$

9 $\cos\theta = \sqrt{2}/2 - (\sqrt{2}/2)(\theta - \pi/4)$
$\quad - (\sqrt{2}/4)(\theta - \pi/4)^2$
$\quad (\sqrt{2}/12)(\theta - \pi/4)^3$
$\quad - \cdots$

11 $\sin\theta = -\sqrt{2}/2 + (\sqrt{2}/2)(\theta + \pi/4)$
$\quad + (\sqrt{2}/4)(\theta + \pi/4)^2$
$\quad - (\sqrt{2}/12)(\theta + \pi/4)^3 + \cdots$

13 $1/x = 1 - (x-1) +$
$\quad (x-1)^2 - (x-1)^3 + \cdots$

15 $\frac{1}{x} = -1 - (x+1)$
$\quad - (x+1)^2 - (x+1)^3$
$\quad - \cdots$

17 $(-1)^n x^n; n \geq 0$

19 $(-1)^{n-1} x^n/n; n \geq 1$

21 $(-1)^k x^{2k+1}/(2k+1); k \geq 0$

23 $(-1)^k x^{4k+2}/(2k)!; k \geq 0$

25 $-1 < x < 1$

27 (a) $-1 < x < 1$
(b) 1

29 1

31 1

33 $\frac{d}{dx}(x^2 e^{x^2})|_{x=0} = 0$
$\quad \frac{d^6}{dx^6}(x^2 e^{x^2})|_{x=0} = \frac{6!}{2} = 360$

35 e^2

37 4/3

39 $\ln(3/2)$

41 e^3

43 $e^{-0.1}$

45 $e^{0.2} - 1$

47 Only converges for $-1 < x < 1$

49 $f(x) = \cos x$

51 False

53 True

55 True

Section 10.3

1 $e^{-x} = 1 - x + x^2/2!$
$\quad - x^3/3! + \cdots$

3 $\cos(\theta^2) = 1 - \theta^4/2! + \theta^8/4!$
$\quad - \theta^{12}/6! + \cdots$

5 $\arcsin x = x + (1/6)x^3$
$\quad + (3/40)x^5 + (5/112)x^7 + \cdots$

7 $1/\sqrt{1-z^2} = 1 + (1/2)z^2 + (3/8)z^4$
$\quad + (5/16)z^6 + \cdots$

9 $\phi^3 \cos(\phi^2) = \phi^3 - \phi^7/2!$
$\quad + \phi^{11}/4! - \phi^{15}/6! + \cdots$

11 $1 + 3x + 3x^2 + x^3$
$\quad 0 \cdot x^n$ for $n \geq 4$

13 $1 + (1/2)y^2 + (3/8)y^4 + \cdots +$
$\quad ((1/2)(3/2)\cdots(1/2 + n - 1)y^{2n})/n! +$
$\quad \cdots;$
$\quad n \geq 1$

15 $\sqrt{T+h} = \sqrt{T}(1 + (1/2)(h/T)$
$\quad - (1/8)(h/T)^2 + (1/16)(h/T)^3 + \cdots)$

17 $1/(a+r)^2 = (1/a^2)(1 - 2(r/a)$
$\quad + 3(r/a)^2 - 4(r/a)^3 + \cdots)$

19 $a/\sqrt{a^2 + x^2} = 1 - (1/2)(x/a)^2 +$

$(3/8)(x/a)^4$
$\quad - (5/16)(x/a)^6 + \cdots$

21 $e^t \cos t = 1 + t - t^3/3$
$\quad - t^4/6 + \cdots$

23 $1 + t + t^2/2 + t^3/3$

25 (a) $2x + x^3/3 + x^5/60 + \cdots$
(b) $P_3(x) = 2x + x^3/3$

27 $1/(1-x)^2$

29 $1 + \sin\theta \leq e^\theta \leq 1/\sqrt{1-2\theta}$

31 (a) I
(b) IV
(c) III
(d) II

33 $f(x) = (1/3)x^3 - (1/42)x^7 + (1/1320)x^{11} - (1/75,600)x^{15} + \cdots$

35 1

37 $\sinh 2x = \sum_{m=0}^{\infty} (2x)^{2m+1}/(2m+1)!$
$\quad \cosh 2x = \sum_{m=0}^{\infty} (2x)^{2m}/(2m)!$

39 (a) $f(x) = 1 + (a-b)x$
$\quad + (b^2 - ab)x^2 + \cdots$
(b) $a = 1/2, b = -1/2$

41 (a) If $M >> m$, then
$\quad \mu \approx mM/M = m$
(b) $\mu = m[1 - m/M + (m/M)^2$
$\quad - (m/M)^3 + \cdots]$
(c) -0.0545%

43 (a) $((l_1 + l_2)/c) \cdot$
$\quad (v^2/c^2 + (5/4)v^4/c^4)$
(b) $v^2, (l_1 + l_2)/c^3$

45 (a) Set $dV/dr = 0$, solve for r. Check for max or min.
(b) $V(r) = -V_0$
$\quad + 72V_0 r_0^{-2} \cdot (r - r_0)^2(1/2)$
$\quad + \cdots$
(d) $F = 0$ when $r - r_0$

47 Right hand missing a factor of $1/2$

49 $\ln x$

51 True

53 False

55 False

57 (c)

Section 10.4

1 $|E_3| \leq 0.00000460, E_3 = 0.00000425$

3 $|E_3| \leq 0.000338, E_3 = 0.000336$

5 $|E_4| \leq 0.0156, E_3 = -0.0112$

7 $|E_3| \leq 16.5, E_3 = 0.224$

9 (c)

11 (a) 5
(b) 1.06

13 (a) Overestimate:
$\quad 0 < \theta \leq 1$
$\quad$ Underestimate:
$\quad -1 \leq \theta < 0$
(b) $|E_2| \leq 0.17$

15 (a) Underestimate
(b) 1

17 (a) (i) $4, 0.2$
$\quad$ (ii) 1
(b) $-4 \leq x \leq 4$

---

19 Four decimal places: $n = 7$
$\quad$ Six decimal places: $n = 9$

23 (a) $\pi \approx 2.67$
(b) $\pi \approx 2.33$
(c) $|E_n| \leq 0.78$
(d) Derivatives unbounded near $x = 1$

25 Cannot make $|f(x) - P_n(x)| < 1$ for all x simultaneously

27 $1 - (x-1) + (x-1)^2 - (x-1)^3$

29 False

31 False

33 False

Section 10.5

1 Not a Fourier series

3 Fourier series

5 $F_1(x) = F_2(x) = (4/\pi)\sin x$
$\quad F_3(x) = (4/\pi)\sin x + (4/3\pi)\sin 3x$

$F_1(x) = F_2(x) = \frac{4}{\pi}\sin x$

$F_3(x) = \frac{4}{\pi}\sin x + \frac{4}{3\pi}\sin 3x$

7 99.942% of the total energy

9 $H_n(x) =$
$\quad \pi/4 + \sum_{i=1}^{n} ((-1)^{i+1}\sin(ix))/i +$
$\quad \sum_{i=1}^{[n/2]} (-2/((2i-1)^2\pi))\cos((2i-1)x),$
$\quad$ where $[n/2]$ denotes the biggest integer smaller than or equal to $n/2$

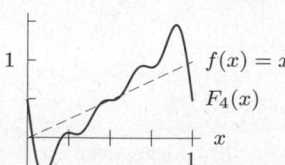

11 $a_0 = 1/2$

13 (b) $(1/7)\sin 7x$
(c) $f(x) = 1$ for $2\pi \leq x < -\pi$
$\quad f(x) = -1$ for $-\pi \leq x < 0$
$\quad f(x) = 1$ for $0 \leq x < \pi$
$\quad f(x) = -1$ for $\pi \leq x < 2\pi\ldots$
$\quad$ Not continuous

15 $F_4(x) = 1/2 - (2/\pi)\sin(2\pi x)$
$\quad - (1/\pi)\sin(4\pi x) - (2/3\pi)\sin(6\pi x)$
$\quad - (1/2\pi)\sin(8\pi x)$

17 52.93

23 (a) 6.3662%, 18.929%
   (b) $(4\sin^2(k/5))/(k^2\pi^2)$
   (c) 61.5255%
   (d) $F_5(x) =$
        $1/(5\pi) + (2\sin(1/5)/\pi)\cos x$
        $+ (\sin(2/5)/\pi)\cos 2x +$
        $(2\sin(3/5)/(3\pi))\cos 3x$
        $+ (\sin(4/5)/(2\pi))\cos 4x +$
        $(2\sin 1/(5\pi))\cos 5x$

25 The energy of the pulse train is spread out over more harmonics as c gets closer to 0

33 a_0 is average of $f(x)$ on interval of approximation

35 Any odd function with period 2π

37 (b)

Chapter 10 Review

1 $e^x \approx 1 + e(x-1) + (e/2)(x-1)^2$

3 $\sin x \approx -1/\sqrt{2} + (1/\sqrt{2})(x + \pi/4)$
   $+ (1/2\sqrt{2})(x + \pi/4)^2$

5 $P_3(x) = 4 + 12(x-1)$
   $+ 10(x-1)^2 + (x-1)^3$

7 $P_3(x) = \sqrt{2}[1 + (x-1)/4$
   $- (x-1)^2/32 + (x-1)^3/128]$

9 $P_7 = 3x - 9x^3 + (27/2)x^5 - (27/2)x^7$

11 $t^2 + t^3 + (1/2)t^4 + (1/6)t^5 + \cdots$

13 $\theta^2 \cos\theta^2 =$
   $\theta^2 - \theta^6/2! + \theta^{10}/4! - \theta^{14}/6! + \cdots$

15 $t/(1+t) = t - t^2 + t^3$
   $- t^4 + \cdots$

17 $1/\sqrt{4-x} =$
   $1/2 + (1/8)x + (3/64)x^2 + (5/256)x^3 + \cdots$

19 $a/(a+b) = 1 - b/a + (b/a)^2 - (b/a)^3 \cdots$

21 $(B^2 + y^2)^{3/2} = B^3(1 + (3/2)(y/B)^2$
   $+ (3/8)(y/B)^4 - (1/16)(y/B)^6 + \cdots)$

23 1.45

25 3/4

27 $\sin 2$

29 (a) $7(1.02^{104} - 1)/$
        $(0.02(1.02)^{100})$
   (b) $7e^{0.01}$

31 Smallest to largest:
   $1 - \cos x, \; x\sqrt{1-x},$
   $\ln(1+x), \arctan x, \sin x,$
   $x, \; e^x - 1$

33 1/2

35 0.10008

37 0.9046

39 (a) $\arcsin x = x + (1/6)x^3 + (3/40)x^5 +$
        $(5/112)x^7 + (35/1152)x^9 + \cdots$
   (b) 1

41 (a)

(b)

43 (a) $V(x) \approx V(0) + V''(0)x^2/2$
        $V''(0) > 0$
   (b) Force $\approx -V''(0)x$
        $V''(0) > 0$
        Toward origin

45 $x - x^2 + (3/2)x^3 - (8/3)x^4$

47 $P_3(t) = t + t^2/4 + (1/18)t^3$

49 (a) $F = GM/R^2 + Gm/(R+r)^2$
   (b) $F = GM/R^2$
        $+ (Gm/R^2)(1 - 2(r/R)$
        $+ 3(r/R)^2 - \cdots)$

51 (b) $F = mg(1 - 2h/R + 3h^2/R^2$
        $- 4h^3/R^3 + \cdots)$
   (c) 300 km

57 (b) If the amplitude of the kth harmonic of f is A_k, then the amplitude of the kth harmonic of f' is kA_k
   (c) The energy of the kth harmonic of f' is k^2 times the energy of the kth harmonic of f

61 (a) $P_7(x) = x - x^3/6 + x^5/120 - x^7/5040$
        $Q_7(x) = x - 2x^3/3 + 2x^5/15 - 4x^7/315$
   (b) For n odd, ratio of coefficients of x^n is 2^{n-1}

63 (a) $P_{10}(x) = 1 + x^2/12 - x^4/720 + x^6/30240 - x^8/1209600 + x^{10}/47900160$
   (b) All even powers
   (c) f even

Section 11.1

1 Yes

3 (a) Not a solution
   (b) Solution
   (c) Not a solution

9 12, 18, 27, 40.5

11 $x(t) = 5e^{3t}$

13 $y = \sqrt{2t + 7}$

19 $k = 5$

21 (a) $C = 0$ and any n; $C \neq 0$ and $n = 3$
   (b) $C = 5$ and $n = 3$

23 (b) $A = k$

25 (a) (IV)
   (b) (III)
   (c) (III), (IV)
   (d) (II)

27 No

29 $Q = 6e^{4t}$ is particular solution, not general

31 $dy/dx = x/y$ and $y = 100$ when $x = 0$

33 $dy/dx = 2x$ with solutions $y = x^2$ and $y = x^2 + 5$

35 $dy/dx = 1/x$

37 $dy/dx = y - x^2$

39 False

41 False

43 False

45 True

47 False

Section 11.2

1 (a) $1; -1; 0; 3; -3; 0$
   (b)

3

5 Possible curves:

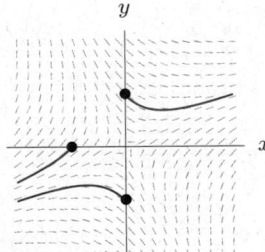

7 First graph

9 (a)

(b) $y = -x - 1$

11

13 (a)

(-2, 12)
(-2, 10)
(1, 4)
(-5, 1)
(4, 1)
(0, 0)

(b) Incr: $0 < P < 10$; decr: $P > 10$; P tends to 10

15 Slope field (b)

17 (a) (II)
(b) (I)
(c) (V)
(d) (III)
(e) (IV)

19 (e) $y' = 0.05y(y - 10)$

21 (b)

23 (a) IV
(b) I
(c) III
(d) V
(e) II
(f) VI

25 Graph of $y = x$ not tangent to slope field at $(1, 1)$

27 $dy/dx = x^2 + 1$

29

31 False

33 False

35 False

37 True

39 True

41 True

43 False

Section 11.3

3 1548, 1591.5917, 1630.860

5 (a) 24.39
(b) Concave up
(c) Underestimates

7 (a) $y(0.4) \approx 1.5282$
(b) $y(0.4) = -1.4$

9 (a)

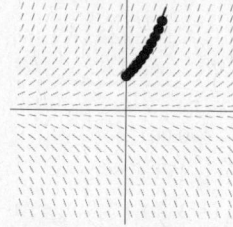

11 (a) $y = 0.667$
(b) $y = 0.710$

13 Error in ten-step is half error ins five-step; $y = 0.753$

15 (a) $\Delta x = 0.5, y(1) \approx 1.5$
$\Delta x = 0.25, y \approx 1.75$
(b) $y = x^2 + 1$, so $y(1) = 2$
(c) Yes

17 (a) $B \approx 1050$
(b) $B \approx 1050.63$
(c) $B \approx 1050.94$

19 For $dy/dx = k$, Euler's method gives exact solutions.

21 $dy/dx = 5$

23 False

Section 11.4

1 (a) Yes (b) No (c) Yes
(d) No (e) Yes (f) Yes
(g) No (h) Yes (i) No
(j) Yes (k) Yes (l) No

3 $P = 20e^{0.02t}$

5 $Q = 50e^{(1/5)t}$

7 $m = 5e^{3t-3}$

9 $z = 5e^{5t-5}$

11 $u = 1/(1 - (1/2)t)$

13 $y = 10e^{-x/3}$

15 $P = 104e^t - 4$

17 $Q = 400 - 350e^{0.3t}$

19 $R = 1 - 0.9e^{1-y}$

21 $y = (1/3)(3 + t)$

23 $y = 3x^5$

25 $z = 5e^{t+t^3/3}$

27 $w = -1/(\ln|\cos\psi| - 1/2)$

29 (a) $y = \sqrt[3]{6x^2 + B}$
(b) $y = \sqrt[3]{6x^2 + 1}$; $y = \sqrt[3]{6x^2 + 8}$; $y = \sqrt[3]{6x^2 + 27}$

31 (a) $y(t) = 100 - Ae^{-t}$
(b)

(c) $y(t) = 100 - 75e^{-t}$
$y(t) = 100 + 10e^{-t}$
(d) $y(t) = 100 - 75e^{-t}$

33 (a)

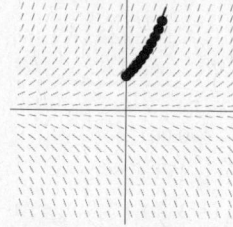
(0, 1)
(0, 0)
(0, -1)

(b) One end asymptotic to $y = 0$, other end unbounded
(c) $y = -1/(x + C), x \neq -C$

35 $Q = Ae^{t/k}$

37 $Q = b - Ae^{-t}$

39 $R = -(b/a) + Ae^{at}$

41 $y = -1/\left(k(t + t^3/3) + C\right)$

43 $L = b + Ae^{k((1/2)x^2 + ax)}$

45 $x = e^{At}$

47 $y = 2(2^{-e^{-t}})$

49 (a) and (b)

(c) $y^2 - x^2 = 2C$

53 Solution to $dP/dt = 0.2t$ is $P = 0.1t^2 + C$

55 $dy/dx = x + y$

57 $dy/dx = 2x$

59 True

61 True

Section 11.5

1 (a) (III)
(b) (IV)
(c) (I)
(d) (II)

3 (a) $y = 2$: stable; $y = -1$: unstable
(b)

5

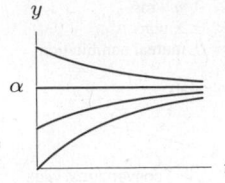

7 (a) $H = 200 - 180e^{-kt}$
 (b) $k \approx 0.027$ (if t is in minutes)

9 (a) $y = 0, y = 4, y = -2$
 (b) $y = 0$ stable, $y = 4$ and $y = -2$ unstable

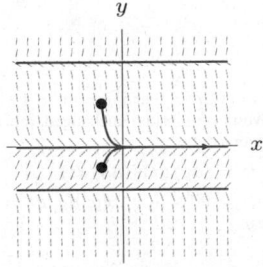

13 Longest: Lake Superior
 Shortest: Lake Erie
 The ratio is about 75

15 (a) N = amount of nicotine in mg at time t;
 t = number of hours since smoking a cigarette
 (b) $dN/dt = -0.347N$
 (c) $N = 0.4e^{0.347t}$

17 (a) G = size in acres of Grinnell Glacier in year t;
 t = number of years since 2007
 (b) $dG/dt = -0.043G$
 (c) $G = 142e^{-0.043t}$

19 $dS/dt = -k(S - 65), k > 0$
 $S = 65 - 25e^{-kt}$

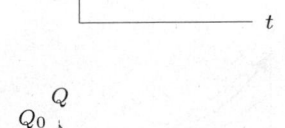

21 (a)

 (b) $dQ/dt = -0.0187Q$
 (c) 3 days

23 (a) 69,300 barrels/year
 (b) 25.9 years

25 About 2150 B.C.

27 (a) $dT/dt = -k(T - 10)$
 (b) $48°F$
 The pipes won't freeze

29 (a) $dH/dt = k(68 - H)$
 (b) $H = 68$, stable
 (c) $H = 68 - Ae^{-kt}$

(d) $57.8°F$

31 (a) $dB/dt = (r/100)B$
 Constant = $r/100$
 (b) $B = 0$, unstable
 (c) $B = Ae^{(r/100)t}$
 (d)

33 $y = x^2$ is not a constant solution

35 $dy/dt = -2y$

37

Section 11.6

1 (a) (III)
 (b) (V)
 (c) (I)
 (d) (II)
 (e) (IV)

3 $dB/dt = 0.037B + 5000$

5 $dB/dt = -0.065D - 50,000$

7 (a) $H' = k(H - 50); H(0) = 90$
 (b) $H(t) = 50 + 40e^{-0.05754t}$
 (c) 24 minutes

9 (a) $dB/dt = 0.08B - 2000$
 (b) $B = 25000$, unstable
 (c) $B = 25,000 + Ae^{0.08t}$
 (d) (i) $17,540.88
 (ii) $32,459.12

11 (a) Increasing; decreasing
 (b) Approach 50 metric tons

13 (a) $I = Ae^{-kl}$
 (b) 20 feet: 75%
 25 feet: 82.3%

15 (a) Mt. Whitney:
 17.50 inches
 Mt. Everest:
 10.23 inches
 (b) 18,661.5 feet

17 (b) $dQ/dt = -0.347Q + 2.5$
 (c) $Q = 7.2$ mg

19 $P = AV^k$

21 5.7 days, 126.32 liters

23 (a) $dp/dt = -k(p - p^*)$
 (b) $p = p^* + (p_0 - p^*)e^{-kt}$
 (c)

 (d) As $t \to \infty, p \to p^*$

25 (a) $Q = (r/\alpha)(1 - e^{-\alpha t})$
 $Q_\infty = r/\alpha$

 (b) Doubling r doubles Q_∞;
 Altering r does not alter the time it takes to reach $(1/2)Q_\infty$
 (c) Both Q_∞ and the time to reach $(1/2)Q_0$ are halved by doubling α

27 $t = 133.601$ min

29 $y = A\sqrt{x}$

31 (a) $dB/dt = 0.05B + 1200$
 (b) $B = 24,000(e^{0.05t} - 1)$
 (c) $6816.61

33 $dB/bt > 0$ when $B = 5000$

35 $dQ/dt = 50 - 0.08Q$

37 $dQ/dt = 0.5(1/Q)$

Section 11.7

1 (b) 1

3

5

7

9 (a) $P = 0, P = 2000$
 (b) dP/dt positive; P increasing

11 (a) $k = 0.035$; gives relative growth rate when P is small
 $L = 6000$; gives limiting value on the size of P
 (b) $P = 3000$

13 $P = 2800/(1 + Ae^{-0.05t})$

15 $P = 4000/(1 + Ae^{-0.68t})$

17 $k = 10, L = 2, A = 3, P = 2/(1 + 3e^{-10t}), t = \ln(3)/10$

19 $k = 0.3, L = 100, A = 1/3, P = 100/(1 + e^{-0.3t}/3), t = -\ln(3)/0.3$

21 $P = 8500/(1 + 16e^{-0.8t})$

23 (a) 1
 (b) 2 people; 48 people

1178

(c)

(d) About 15 hours; 30 hours
(e) When 200 people have heard the rumor

25 (a) 2500 fish
   (b) 2230 fish
   (c) 1500 fish

27 (a) 36 thousand; total number infected
   (b) $t \approx 16$, $n \approx 18$ thousand
   (c) Virus spreading fastest
   (d) Number infected half total

29 (a) 22.0 bn barrels/yr, 26.9 bn barrels/yr
   (b) 3.04% per year, 2.45% per year
   (c) $(1/P)(dP/dt) = 0.0418 - 0.0000157P$
   (d) 2662 billion barrels
   (e) $dP/dt = 0.0418P(1 - P/2662)$
       $P = 2662/(1 + 2.677e^{-0.0418t})$

31 (a)

(b)

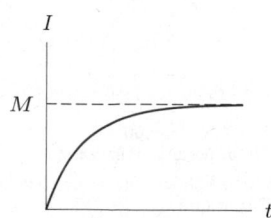

33 (a) 1426.603 bn barrels
   (b) 2066

35 (a) $dI/dt = k(M - I)$
       $(k > 0)$

(b) $dI/dt = kI(M - I)$
    $(k > 0)$

37 (a) logistically
   (b) $k \approx 0.045$
       $L \approx 5.8$

39 (a) $dp/dt = kp(B - p)$
       $(k > 0)$
   (b) Half of the tin

43 Occurs at $Q = 25$ not $t = 25$

45 Sales of a new product

47

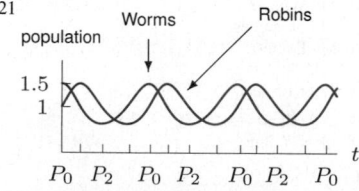

49 False

Section 11.8

1 x and y increase, about same rate

3 x decreases quickly while y increases more slowly

5 $(0, 0)$ and $(5, 3)$

7 $(0, 0)$ and $(-5, 3)$

9 (a) Both x and y are decreasing
   (b) x is increasing; y is decreasing

11 (a) Susceptibles: 1950,1850, 1550, 1000, 750, 550, 350, 250, 200, 200, 200
       Infecteds: 20, 80, 240, 460, 500, 460, 320, 180, 100, 40, 20
   (b) Day 22, 500
   (c) 1800, 200

13 (a) a is negative; b is negative; c is positive
   (b) $a = -c$

17 $r = r_0 e^{-t}$, $w = w_0 e^t$

19 Worms decrease, robins increase. Long run: populations oscillate

21

23 Robins increase;
   Worms constant, then decrease;
   Both oscillate in long run

25 (a) Symbiosis
   (b) Both $\to \infty$ or both $\to 0$

27 (a) Predator-prey
   (b) x, y tend to ≈ 1

29 (a) $dy/dx = bx/ay$

31 (b) $dx/dt = -xy$, $dy/dt = -x$
   (c) $dy/dx = 1/y$
       soln: $y^2/2 = x + C$

(d) If $C > 0$, y wins
    If $C < 0$, x wins
    If $C = 0$, mutual annihilation

(e)

33 (a) $w = 0$, $r = 0$ and $w = b/k$, $r = a/c$
   (b) Worm equilibrium unchanged, robin equilibrium reduced

35 $dy/dx = (dy/dt)/(dx/dt)$

37 $dx/dt = 0.5x - 0.2xy$; $dy/dt = 0.1y - 0.3xy$

39 True

Section 11.9

1 $(4, 10)$

3

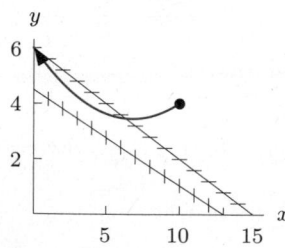

5 Tends towards point $(4, 10)$

7 (a) $dx/dt > 0$ and $dy/dt > 0$
   (b) $dx/dt < 0$ and $dy/dt = 0$
   (c) $dx/dt = 0$ and $dy/dt > 0$

9

11

13 Vertical nullclines:
$x = 0, x + y = 2$
Horizontal nullclines:
$y = 0, x + y = 1$
Equilibrium points:
$(0, 0), (0, 1), (2, 0)$

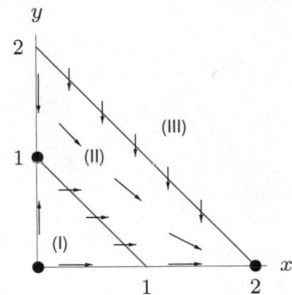

15 Horizontal nullclines;
$y = 0, y = 1 - 2x$
Vertical nullclines;
$x = 0, y = (1/2)(2 - x)$
Equilibrium points;
$(0, 0), (0, 1), (2, 0)$

17 $dx/dt = 0$ when
$x = 0$ or $x + y/3 = 1$
$dy/dt = 0$ when
$y = 0$ or $y + x/2 = 1$
Equilibrium points:
$(0, 0), (0, 1), (1, 0), (4/5, 3/5)$

19 (a) $dS/dt = 0$ where $S = 0$ or $I = 0$
$dI/dt = 0$ where $I = 0$ or $S = 192$
  (b) Where $S > 192$,
       $dS/dt < 0$ and $dI/dt > 0$
       Where $S < 192$,
       $dS/dt < 0$ and $dI/dt < 0$
  (c)

21 (a) In the absence of the other, each company
         grows exponentially
         The two companies restrain each other's
         growth if they are both present
   (b) $(0, 0)$ and $(1, 2)$
   (c) In the long run, one of the companies will go
         out of business

23 (a) $dP_1/dt = 0$ where $P = 0$ or
         $P_1 + 3P_2 = 13$
         $dP_2/dt = 0$ where $P = 0$ or
         $P_2 + 0.4P_1 = 6$

25 $dx/dt \neq 0$

27

Chapter 11 Review

1 (I) satisfies equation (d)
   (II) satisfies equation (c)

3 (a) (I)
  (b) (IV)
  (c) (III)

5 $y(x) = 40 + Ae^{0.2x}$

7 $H = Ae^{0.5t} - 20$

9 $P = 100Ae^{0.4t}/(1 + Ae^{0.4t})$

11 $P = (40000/3)(e^{0.03t} - 1)$

13 $y = \sqrt[3]{33 - 6\cos x}$

15 $\frac{1}{2}y - 4\ln|y| = 3\ln|x| - x + \frac{7}{2} - 4\ln 5$

17 $z(t) = 1/(1 - 0.9e^t)$

19 $20\ln|y| - y = 100\ln|x| - x + 20\ln 20 - 19$

21 $y = \ln(e^x + e - 1)$

23 $z = \sin(-e^{\cos\theta} + \pi/6 + e)$

25 $y = -\ln(\frac{\ln 2}{3}\sin^2 t\cos t + \frac{2\ln 2}{3}\cos t - \frac{2\ln 2}{3} + 1)/\ln 2$

27 (a) $y = 3$ and $y = -2$
   (b) $y = 3$ unstable;
        $y = -2$ stable

29 No

31 (a) $y(1) \approx 3.689$
   (b) Overestimate

   (c) $y = 5 - 4e^{-x}$
        $y(1) = 5 - 4e^{-1} \approx 3.528$
   (d) ≈ 3.61

33 (b) 2070

35 (a) $dM/dt = rM$
   (b) $M = 2000e^{rt}$
   (c)

37

B

1000

$i = 0.15$

$i = 0.1$

$i = 0.05$
years
$t \approx 13.86$

39 (a) $dB/dt = 0.05B - 12{,}000$
(b) $B = (B_0 - 240{,}000)e^{0.05t}$
$+ 240{,}000$
(c) $\$151{,}708.93$

41 $C(t) = 30e^{-100.33t}$

43 No, no

P

200

100

t

45 (a) $dx/dt = k(a-x)(b-x)$
(b) $x = ab(e^{bkt} - e^{akt})/(be^{bkt} - ae^{akt})$

47 (a) $x \to \infty$ exponentially
$y \to 0$ exponentially
(b) Predator-prey

49 (a) $x \to \infty$ exponentially
$y \to 0$ exponentially

(b) y is helped by the presence of x

51 (a) $dy/dx = y(x+3)/(x(y+2))$
$y^2 e^y = Ax^3 e^x$
(d) $y^2 e^y = x^3 e^{x+4}$
(e) $y = x = e^{-4} \approx 0.0183$
(f) $y \approx e^{-13}$

53 (a) $x \to \infty$ if $y = 0$
$y \to 0$ if $x = 0$
(b) $(0, 0)$ and $(10{,}000, 150)$
(c) $dy/dx = y(-10 + 0.001x)/(x(3 - 0.02y))$
$3\ln y - 0.02y =$
$-10\ln x + 0.001x + 94.1$
(f) $A \to B \to C \to D$
(h) At points A and C:
$dy/dx = 0$
At points B and D:
$dx/dy = 0$

55 P decreases to 0

57 P decreases towards $2L$

59 (c)

y

$y_3(s)$
$y(s)$
$y_2(s)$
$y_1(s)$

3

2

1

-0.5
1
2
x

Section 12.1

1 Q

3 B, B, B

5

z

x

y

7

z

x

y

9

z

$y = 1$

y

1

x

11 $(2, 3, 15)$

13 $(x-1)^2 + y^2 + z^2 = 4$

15 (a) $80\text{-}90°\text{F}$
(b) $60\text{-}72°\text{F}$
(c) $60\text{-}100°\text{F}$

17

Boise

100
80
60

North ———————— South

Boise

100
80
60

West ———————— East

21 (a) $-19°\text{F}$
(b) 20 mph
(c) About 17.5 mph
(d) About $16.7°\text{F}$

27 $(1.5, 0.5, -0.5)$

29 Cone, tip at origin, along x-axis with slope of 1

31 (a) $z = 7, z = -1$
(b) $x = 6, x = -2$
(c) $y = 7, y = -1$

33 (a) $(12, 7, 2); (5, 7, 2); (12, 1, 2)$
(b) $(5, 1, 4); (5, 7, 4); (12, 1, 4)$

35 (a) yz-plane: circle $(y+3)^2 + (z-2)^2 = 3$
xz-plane: none
xy-plane: point $(1, -3, 0)$

(b) Does not intersect

37 $(8, 0, \sqrt{3})$

39 $y = 1$ is a plane, not a line

41 Distance is 5

43 $(-2, -1, -5)$

45 True

47 False

49 True

51 True

53 True

55 False

57 False

Section 12.2

1 (a) Decreases

z

x

(b) Increases

z

y

3 (a) I
(b) V
(c) IV
(d) II
(e) III

5 Sphere, radius 3

z

3

x 3 3 y

7 Upside-down bowl, vertex $(0, 0, 5)$

z

5

x y

9 Plane, x-intercept 6, y-intercept 3, z-intercept 4

11 Circular cylinder extended in the y direction

13 $x^2 + (y - \sqrt{7})^2 + z^2 = 9$

15 (a)

(b)

17 (a) C (mg per liter)

(b) C (mg per liter)

19 (a) is (IV)
(b) is (IX)
(c) is (VII)
(d) is (I)
(e) is (VIII)
(f) is (II)
(g) is (VI)
(h) is (III)
(i) is (V)

21 (a) (i)

(ii)

(b) (i)

(ii)

(c) (i)

(ii)

(d) (i)

(ii)

(e) (i)

(ii)

23

25

27

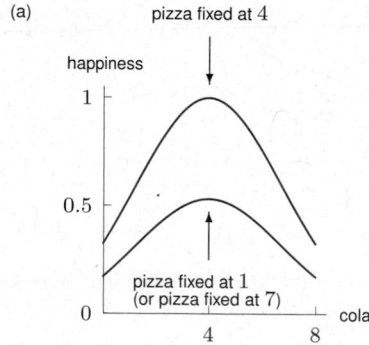

29 Cross-sections graph I:

(a)

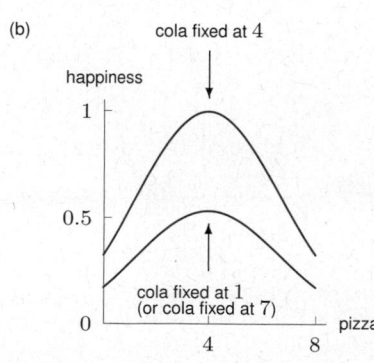

(b)

Cross-sections graph II:

(a)

(b)

Cross-sections graph III:

(a)

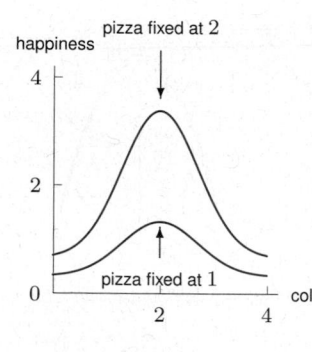

(b)

Cross-sections graph IV:

(a)

(b)

31 (a)

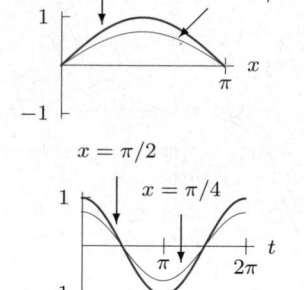

(b) $f = 0$; ends of string don't move

33 Cross-sections are lines parallel to y-axis

35 $f(x, y) = x^2 - 1$

37 False

39 True

41 True

43 True

45 True

47 True

49 False

51 (c)

Section 12.3

1

3

5 Contours evenly spaced

7

9

11

15 (a)

(b)

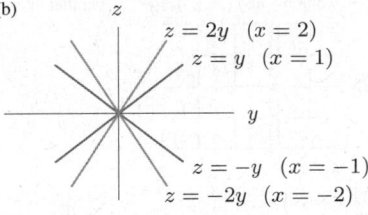

$z = 2y \quad (x = 2)$
$z = y \quad (x = 1)$
$z = -y \quad (x = -1)$
$z = -2y \quad (x = -2)$

(c)

Curve $z = x^2$

Line $x = y$

17 Table 12.5 matches (II)
Table 12.6 matches (III)
Table 12.7 matches (IV)
Table 12.8 matches (I)

19 Price: x; Advertising: y

21 (a) is III
(b) is VI
(c) is I
(d) is IV
(e) is II
(f) is V

23

25 72°F; 76°F

27 (a) A
(b) B
(c) A

29 Elevation in meters

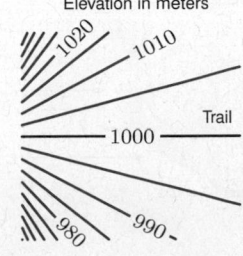

Trail

31 E-W, $N = 50$:

E-W, $N = 100$:

N-S, $E = 60$:

N-S, $E = 120$:

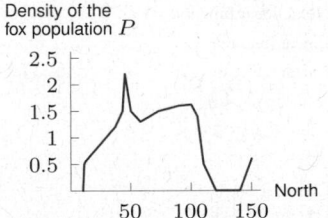

33 (a) (II) (E)
(b) (I) (D)
(c) (III) (G)

35 (a) (I) g
(II) f
(b) $0.2 < \alpha < 0.8$

37 (a)

(b)

(c)

(d)

43 Contour diagram is curves in xy-plane
45 $f(x, y) = x^2$
47 Could not be true
49 Might be true
51 True
53 True
55 False
57 False
59 True

Section 12.4

1 -1.0
3 Not a linear function
5 Linear function
7 Linear
9 $z = \frac{4}{3}x - \frac{1}{2}y$
11 $z = -2y + 2$
13 $\Delta z = 0.4; \quad z = 2.4$
15 CDs cost $8
    DVDs cost $12
17 (a) Linear
   (b) Linear
   (c) Not linear
19 180 lb person at 8 mph
    120 lb person at 10 mph
21 $g(x, y) = 3x + y$
23 $f(x, y) = 2x - 0.5y + 1$
25

27

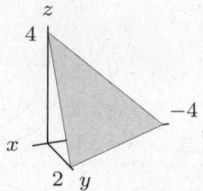

31 (a) $7/\sqrt{29}$
   (b) $-5/\sqrt{104}$
33 Contours of $f(x, y) = e^{x+y}$ parallel lines

35

$x \backslash y$	1	2	3
1	1	2	3
2	2	4	6
3	3	6	9

37 False
39 False
41 True
43 True
45 True
47 False

Section 12.5

1 (a) I
  (b) II
3 $f(x, y) = \frac{1}{3}(5 - x - 2y)$
5 $f(x, y) = (1 - x^2 - y)^2$
7 Elliptical and hyperbolic paraboloid, plane
9 Hyperboloid of two sheets
11 Ellipsoid
13 Yes, $f(x, y) = (2x + 3y - 10)/5$
15 No
17 $f(x, y) = \sqrt{10 - x^2 - y^2}$
    $g(x, y, z) = x^2 + y^2 + z^2 = 10$
19 (a) Parallel planes: $2x - 3y + z = c + 20$
   (b) $f_z(0, 0, 0) = 1$
   (c) $\vec{n} = 2\vec{i} - 3\vec{j} + \vec{k}$
   (d) Yes; $-3°F$
21 Incr of A and r
    Decr of t
23 $f(x, y) = 3\sqrt{1 - x^2 - y^2/4};$
    $g(x, y) = -3\sqrt{1 - x^2 - y^2/4}$
25 (a) Graph of f is graph of
    $x^2 + y^2 + z^2 = 1, z \geq 0$
   (b) $\sqrt{1 - x^2 - y^2} - z = 0$
27 $g(x, y, z) = 1 - \sqrt{x^2 + z^2} - y = 0$
29 Ellipsoid
31 Parallel planes
35

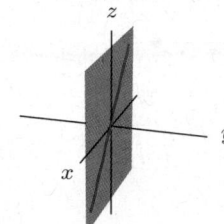

37

37 False
39 Level surfaces hyperbolic cylinders
41 $f(x, y, z) = y + z$
43 $f(x, y, z) = (x + y + z)^2$
45 True
47 True
49 True
51 False
53 False

Section 12.6

1 Not continuous
3 Continuous
5 Not continuous
7 1
9 0
11 1
19 No
21 $c = 1$
23 (c) No
25 For quotient, need $g(a, b) \neq 0$
27 $f(x, y) = (x^2 + 2y^2)/(x^2 + y^2)$
29 $f(x, y) = 1/((x - 2)^2 + y^2)$

Chapter 12 Review

1 A, B, C
3

5 Not a function
7 IV
9 (a) is (I)
  (b) is (IV)
  (c) is (II)
  (d) is (III)
11 $y = k$

13 $2x^2 + y^2 = k$

15 $(x - 1)^2 + (y - 2)^2 + (z - 3)^2 = 25$

17 $(-2, 3, -6); 7$

19 Linear

21 $f(x, y, z) = x^2 + y^2$

23 $z = f(x, y) = 4 - 2x - 4y/3$
$g(x, y, z) = (x/2) + (y/3) + (z/4) = 1$

25 $z = f(x, y) = -\sqrt{4 - (x - 3)^2 - y^2}$
$g(x, y, z) = (x - 3)^2 + y^2 + z^2 = 4$

27 Cylinder

29 $g(x, y) = 200x + 100y$

31 Doubles production

37 (a) No
(b) No
(c) No
(e) 0.5 of GPA

39 (a)

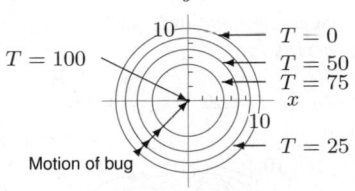

Motion of bug

(b) Toward origin

41 (a)

(b)

(c)

47 (a) $9 + 3x + 4y, 21 + 7x + 8y$
(b) $189 + 63x + 64y$

Section 13.1

1 $\vec{a} = \vec{i} + 3\vec{j}$
$\vec{b} = 3\vec{i} + 2\vec{j}$
$\vec{v} = -2\vec{i} - 2\vec{j}$
$\vec{w} = -\vec{i} + 2\vec{j}$

3 $-3\vec{i} - 4\vec{j}$

5 $\vec{a} = \vec{b} = \vec{c} = 3\vec{k}$
$\vec{d} = 2\vec{i} + 3\vec{k}$
$\vec{e} = \vec{j}$
$\vec{f} = -2\vec{i}$

7 $\vec{i} + 3\vec{j}$

9 $-4.5\vec{i} + 8\vec{j} + 0.5\vec{k}$

11 $-3\vec{i} - 12\vec{j} + 3\vec{k}$

13 $0.9\vec{i} + 0.2\vec{j} - 0.7\vec{k}$

15 $\sqrt{6}$

17 $\sqrt{11}$

19 5.6

21 $-6\vec{i} + 20\vec{j} + 13\vec{k}$

23 $21\vec{j}$

25 $2\sqrt{73}$

27 $0.6\vec{i} - 0.8\vec{k}$

29 $-\vec{i}/2 + \vec{j}/4 + \sqrt{11}\vec{k}/4$

31 $0, -10$

33 $-\frac{1}{\sqrt{2}}\vec{i} + \frac{1}{\sqrt{2}}\vec{j}$.

35 (a) $\vec{u} = 8.2\vec{i} + 1.8\vec{j}$,
$\vec{v} = -8.2\vec{i} - 1.8\vec{j}$
(b) $\vec{v} = -\vec{u}$

37 (a) True
(b) Does not makes sense
(c) True
(d) False

39 (a) $t = 1$
(b) No t values
(c) Any t values

41 $-\vec{i}/2 + \sqrt{3}\vec{j}/2$
$-\vec{i}/2 - \sqrt{3}\vec{j}/2$

45 Opposite direction if $c < 0$, no direction if $c = 0$

47 $\vec{w} = \vec{0}$ so $\vec{v} + \vec{w} = \vec{v}$

49 $\vec{u} = \vec{i}, \vec{v} = (1/2)\vec{i} + (\sqrt{3}/2)\vec{j}$

51 False

53 True

55 False

57 False

59 False

Section 13.2

1 Scalar

3 Scalar

5 Vector

7 $-37.59\vec{i}, -13.68\vec{j}$

9 $21\vec{i} + 35\vec{j}$

11 (a) 8.64 km/hr
(b) 0.093 radian or about 5° off course

13 (a) $17.93\vec{i} - 7.07\vec{j}$
(b) 19.27 km/hr
(c) 21.52° south of east

15 48.3° east of north
744 km/hr

17 4.87° north of east
540.63 km/hr

19 $\vec{E} = 27.908\vec{i} + 1.823\vec{j}$
Speed 27.97 km/hr in direction 3.74° north of east

21 38.7° south of east

23 $-98.76\vec{i} + 18.94\vec{j} + 2998.31\vec{k}$
2998.31 newtons directly up

25 $0.4v\vec{i} + 0.7v\vec{j}$

27 $0.01875\vec{i} + .0125\vec{j} + .03125\vec{k}$

39 $\vec{i}$ or $\vec{j}$ components could be different

41 $\vec{F} = \vec{i} - 2\vec{j}$

43 Yes

45 Yes

47 Yes

Section 13.3

1 -14

3 14

5 -2

7 $28\vec{j} + 14\vec{k}$

9 185

11 $\vec{i} + 3\vec{j} + 2\vec{k}$ (multiples of)

13 $3\vec{i} + 4\vec{j} - \vec{k}$ (multiples of)

15 $3x - y + 4z = 6$

17 $x - y + z = 3$

19 $2x + 4y - 3z = 5$

21 $2x - 3y + 5z = -17$

23 $2\pi/3$ radians (120°)

25 $\pi/6$ radians (30°)

27 (a) $(2/\sqrt{13})\vec{i} + (3/\sqrt{13})\vec{j}$
(b) Multiples of $3\vec{i} - 2\vec{j}$

29 (a) $(21/5, 0, 0)$
(b) $(0, -21, 0); (0, 0, 3)$ (for example)
(c) $\vec{n} = 5\vec{i} - \vec{j} + 7\vec{k}$ (for example)
(d) $21\vec{j} + 3\vec{k}$ (for example)

31 Possible answers:
(a) $2\vec{i} + 3\vec{j} - \vec{k}$
(b) $3\vec{i} - 2\vec{j}$

33 (a) $(\vec{a}, \vec{c})$ and $(\vec{b}, \vec{d})$
(b) None
(c) $(\vec{a}, \vec{d})$ and $(\vec{c}, \vec{d})$
(d) $(\vec{a}, \vec{b})$ and $(\vec{b}, \vec{c})$

35 Many answers possible
(a) $8\vec{i} + 6\vec{j}$
(b) $-3\vec{i} + 4\vec{j}$

37 (a) Increases
(b) Decreases

39 71.57°

41 (a) $\sqrt{2}$
(b) 0.32

43 (a) $\vec{F}$ parallel $= -0.168\vec{i} - 0.224\vec{j}$
(b) $\vec{F}$ perp $= 0.368\vec{i} - 0.276\vec{j}$
(c) $W = -1.4$

45 (a) $\vec{F}$ parallel $= \vec{0}$
(b) $\vec{F}$ perp $= \vec{F}$
(c) $W = 0$

47 (a) $\vec{F}$ parallel $= \vec{F}$

(b) $\vec{F}_{\text{perp}} = \vec{0}$
(c) $W = -50$

49 (a) $\vec{F}_{\text{parallel}} = 3.846\vec{i} - 0.769\vec{j}$
(b) $\vec{F}_{\text{perp}} = -3.846\vec{i} - 19.231\vec{j}$
(c) $W = 20$

51 (a) $\vec{F}_{\text{parallel}} = \vec{0}$
(b) $\vec{F}_{\text{perp}} = \vec{F}$
(c) $W = 0$

53 No

55 (a) 2.24 m/sec
(b) 1.89 m/sec

57 $10/\sqrt{30}$

59 Averages; weightings
85.65%; class average

71 Can't take dot product of a scalar and a vector

73 Normal vector is $2\vec{i} + 3\vec{j} - \vec{k}$

75 $f(x, y) = (-1/3)x + (-2/3)y$

77 True

79 False

81 True

83 False

85 True

Section 13.4

1 $-\vec{i}$

3 $-\vec{i} + \vec{j} + \vec{k}$

5 $\vec{i} + 3\vec{j} + 7\vec{k}$

7 $7\vec{i} + \vec{j} + 4\vec{k}$

9 $-2\vec{k}$

11 $\vec{i} - \vec{j}$

13 $\vec{v} \times \vec{w} = -6\vec{i} + 7\vec{j} + 8\vec{k}$
$\vec{w} \times \vec{v} = 6\vec{i} - 7\vec{j} - 8\vec{k}$
$\vec{v} \times \vec{w} = -(\vec{w} \times \vec{v})$

15 $x - y - z = -3$

17 4

19 0

21 $4x + 26y + 14z = 0$

23 $3x - y - 2z = 0$

25 $4\vec{i} + 26\vec{j} + 14\vec{k}$

27 $4(x - 4) + 26(y - 5) + 14(z - 6) = 0$

29 (a) $\vec{u}$ and $-\vec{u}$ where
$\vec{u} = \frac{12}{13}\vec{i} - \frac{4}{13}\vec{j} - \frac{3}{13}\vec{k}$
(b) $\theta \approx 49.76°$
(c) $13/2$
(d) $13/\sqrt{29}$

31 Parallel to the z-axis

33 $\sqrt{38}/3$

35 (a) Increases force
(b) Ball moves down and to the left

37 (a) $\overrightarrow{P_1 P_2} = \overrightarrow{P_3 P_4} = 2\vec{i} + 4\vec{j} + 2\vec{k}$;
$\overrightarrow{P_1 P_3} = \overrightarrow{P_2 P_4} = 3\vec{i}$
(b) $\sqrt{180}$

51 $4\pi\vec{i}$

53 (a) $((u_2 v_3 - u_3 v_2)^2 + (u_3 v_1 - u_1 v_3)^2 + (u_1 v_2 - u_2 v_1)^2)^{1/2}$
(b) $|u_1 v_2 - u_2 v_1|$
(c) $m = (u_2 v_3 - u_3 v_2)/(u_2 v_1 - u_1 v_2)$,
$n = (u_3 v_1 - u_1 v_3)/(u_2 v_1 - u_1 v_2)$

55 Parallel, not perpendicular

57 $\vec{v} = (8\vec{i} - 6\vec{j})/5$

59 False

61 True

63 True

65 True

67 False

Chapter 13 Review

1 Scalar; -1

3 -1

5 $\vec{a} = -2\vec{j}, \vec{b} = 3\vec{i}, \vec{c} = \vec{i} + \vec{j}$,
$\vec{d} = 2\vec{j}, \vec{e} = \vec{i} - 2\vec{j}, \vec{f} = -3\vec{i} - \vec{j}$

7 $5\vec{i} + 30\vec{j}$

9 $3\sqrt{2}$

11 $3\vec{i} + 7\vec{j} - 4\vec{k}$

13 -3

15 $\vec{0}$

17 0

19 $\vec{0}$

21 $-5\vec{i} + 3\vec{j} + \vec{k}$ (multiples of)

23 (a) 4
(b) $-4\vec{i} - 11\vec{j} - 17\vec{k}$
(c) $3.64\vec{i} + 2.43\vec{j} - 2.43\vec{k}$
(d) $79.0°$
(e) 0.784.
(f) $2\vec{i} - 2\vec{j} + \vec{k}$ (many answers possible)
(g) $-4\vec{i} - 11\vec{j} - 17\vec{k}$.

25 $\pm(-\vec{i} + \vec{j} - 2\vec{k})/\sqrt{6}$

27 $\vec{n} = 4\vec{i} + 6\vec{k}$

29 $-3\vec{i} + 4\vec{j}$

31 $\vec{u}$ and $\vec{w}$; $\vec{v}$ and $\vec{q}$.

33 $\vec{F}_{\text{parallel}} = \vec{F}$
$\vec{F}_{\text{perp}} = \vec{0}$
$W = -10$

35 $\vec{F}_{\text{parallel}} = -(6/5)\vec{i} + (8/5)\vec{j}$
$\vec{F}_{\text{perp}} = (16/5)\vec{i} + (12/5)\vec{j}$
$W = -10$

37 $\vec{F}_{\text{parallel}} = 2\vec{j}$
$\vec{F}_{\text{perp}} = 5\vec{i}$
$W = 6$

39 (a) True
(b) False
(c) False
(d) True
(e) True
(f) False

41 548.6 km/hr

43

45 Parallel:
$3\vec{i} + \sqrt{3}\vec{j}$ and $\sqrt{3}\vec{i} + \vec{j}$
Perpendicular:
$\sqrt{3}\vec{i} + \vec{j}$ and $\vec{i} - \sqrt{3}\vec{j}$
$3\vec{i} + \sqrt{3}\vec{j}$ and $\vec{i} - \sqrt{3}\vec{j}$

47 2, 8

49 $2x - 3y + 7z = 19$

51 $\sqrt{6}/2$

53 (a) 1.5

(b) $y = 1$

55 $9x - 16y + 12z = 5$
0.23

57 $7.0710\vec{i} + 2.5882\vec{j} + 6.580\vec{k}$

59 228.43 newtons
85.5° south of east

61 $|ywr - vzr + zus - xws + xvt - yut|$

63 (b) $(1, 1/\sqrt{3}, \sqrt{6}/6)$
(c) $109.471°$

Section 14.1

1 $f_x(3, 2) \approx -2/5$; $f_y(3, 2) \approx 3/5$

3 $-0.0493, -0.3660$
$-0.0501, -0.3629$

5 $\partial P/\partial t$:
dollars/month
Rate of change in payments with time
negative
$\partial P/\partial r$:
dollars/percentage point
Rate of change in payments with interest rate
positive

7 (a) Payment $376.59/mo at 1% for 24 mos
(b) 4.7¢ extra/mo for $1 increase
(c) Approx $44.83 increase for 1% interest increase

9 (a) Negative
(b) Positive

11 $f_x > 0, f_y < 0$

13 $f_x < 0, f_y > 0$

15 $f_T(5, 20) \approx 1.2°\text{F}/°\text{F}$

17 Positive, Negative, 10, 2, -4

19 $\partial Q/\partial b < 0$
$\partial Q/\partial c > 0$

21 -1.5 and -1.22

23 (a)

(b)

25 (a) Negative
(b) Positive

27 (a) 2.5, 0.02
(b) 3.33, 0.02
(c) 3.33, 0.02

29 (i)(c); (ii)(a)

31 -2.5

33

	w (gm/m^3)		
T (°C)		0.1	0.2	0.3
10	1300	900	1200
20	800	800	900
30	800	700	800

35 (a)

(b)

(c)

(d)

37 $f_y = 0$

39 $f(x, y) = 4x - y$

41 False

43 False

45 True

47 False

49 False

Section 14.2

1 (a) 7.01

  (b) 7

3 $f_x(1, 2) = 15,$
  $f_y(1, 2) = -5$

5 $\partial z/\partial x = \frac{14x+7}{(x^2+x-y)^{-6}}$
  $\partial z/\partial y = -7(x^2 + x - y)^6$

7 $f_x = 0.6/x$
  $f_y = 0.4/y$

9 $2xy + 10x^4y$

11 $-2\pi r/T^2$

13 $e^{\sqrt{xy}}(1 + \sqrt{xy}/2)$

15 g

17 $(a + b)/2$

19 $2B/u_0$

21 $2mv/r$

23 Gm_1/r^2

25 $-e^{-x^2/a^2}(a^2 - 2x^2)/a^4$

27 $v_0 + at$

29 $-\pi r^{3/2}/(M\sqrt{GM})$

31 $(15x^2y - 3y^2)\cos(5x^3y - 3xy^2)$

33 $\partial F/\partial L = \frac{3}{2}\sqrt{K/L}$

35 $\epsilon_0 E$

37 $c\gamma a_1 b_1 K^{b_1-1}(a_1 K^{b_1} + a_2 L^{b_2})^{\gamma-1}$

39 13.6

41 (a) 3.3, 2.5
   (b) 4.1, 2.1
   (c) 4, 2

43 (a) $a < 3$
   (b) Up

45 (a) $\partial g/\partial m = G/r^2$
      $\partial g/\partial r = -2Gm/r^3$
   (b)

47 (a) $c^2((1 - v^2/c^2)^{-1/2} - 1)$; positive
   (b) $mv(1 - v^2/c^2)^{-3/2}$; positive

49 (a)

$H(x, 0) = 100\sin(\pi x)$

$H(x, 1) = 100e^{-0.1}\sin(\pi x)$
$= 90.5\sin(\pi x)$

   (b) $254.2e^{-0.1t}$ °C/m

(c) $-254.2e^{-0.1t}$ °C/m

(d) $-10e^{-0.1t}\sin(\pi x)$ °C/sec

51 $f(x, y) = x^4y^2 - 3xy^4 + C$

53 Derivative is limit, not a difference quotient
   Counterexample: $f(x, y) = x^2 + y^2$

55 $f(x, y) = xy, g(x, y) = xy + y^2$

57 True

59 True

61 False

63 False

65 (d)

Section 14.3

1 $z = ex$

3 $z = 6y - 9$

5 $z = -4 + 2x + 4y$

7 $z = -36x - 24y + 148$

9 $df = y\cos(xy)\, dx + x\cos(xy)\, dy$

11 $dz = -e^{-x}\cos(y)dx - e^{-x}\sin(y)dy$

13 $dg = 4\, dx$

15 $dP \approx 2.395\, dK + 0.008\, dL$

17 (a) Dollars/Square foot
   (b) Larger plots at same distance $3/ft^2 more
   (c) Dollars/Foot
   (d) Farther from beach but same area $2/ft less
   (e) 998 ft^2

19 (b) $f(x, y) \approx$
      $0.3345 - 0.33(x - 1) - 0.15(y - 2)$
   (c) $f(x, y) \approx 0.3345 -$
      $0.3345(x - 1) - 0.1531(y - 2)$

21 376

23 $df = \frac{1}{3}dx + 2dy$
   $f(1.04, 1.98) \approx 2.973$

25 136.09°C

27 $P(r, L) \approx$
   $80 + 2.5(r - 8) + 0.02(L - 4000)$
   $P(r, L) \approx$
   $120 + 3.33(r - 8) + 0.02(L - 6000)$
   $P(r, L) \approx$
   $160 + 3.33(r - 13) + 0.02(L - 7000)$

31 (a) $nRT/(V - nb) - n^2a/V^2$
   (b) $\Delta P \approx (nR/(V_0 - nb))\Delta T + (2n^2a/V_0^3 - nRT_0/((V_0 - nb)^2))\Delta V$

33 (a) $d\rho = -\beta\rho\, dT$
   (b) $0.00015, \beta \approx 0.0005$

35 $-43200\Delta t$
   Slow if $\Delta t > 0$; fast if $\Delta t < 0$

37 $z = f(3, 4) + f_x(3, 4)(x - 3) + f_y(3, 4)(y - 4)$

39 Equation not linear

41 sphere of radius 3 centered at the origin

43 True

45 False

47 True

49 False

Section 14.4

1 $(\frac{15}{2}x^4)\vec{i} - (\frac{24}{7}y^5)\vec{j}$

3 $2m\vec{i} + 2n\vec{j}$

5 $\left(\frac{5\alpha}{\sqrt{5\alpha^2+\beta}}\right)\vec{i} + \left(\frac{1}{2\sqrt{5\alpha^2+\beta}}\right)\vec{j}$

7 $\nabla z = e^y\vec{i} + e^y(1 + x + y)\vec{j}$

9 $\sin\theta\vec{i} + r\cos\theta\vec{j}$

11 $\nabla z = \frac{1}{y}\cos\left(\frac{x}{y}\right)\vec{i} - \frac{x}{y^2}\cos\left(\frac{x}{y}\right)\vec{j}$

13 $\left(\frac{-12\beta}{(2\alpha - 3\beta)^2}\right)\vec{i} + \left(\frac{12\alpha}{(2\alpha - 3\beta)^2}\right)\vec{j}$

15 $60\vec{i} + 85\vec{j}$

17 $10\pi\vec{i} + 4\pi\vec{j}$

19 $(\pi/2)^{1/2}\vec{i}$

21 $\frac{1}{100}(2\vec{i} - 6\vec{j})$

23 $-46/5$

25 $22/5$

27 $84/5$

29 $(2x + 3e^y)dx + 3xe^y dy$

31 $(x + 1)ye^x\vec{i} + xe^x\vec{j}$

33 Negative

35 Positive

37 Positive

39 $-\vec{j}$

41 $\vec{j}$

43 $-\vec{i} - \vec{j}$

45 $\vec{i} - \vec{j}$

47 (a) $(3.96838, 5.09487)$
    (b) 0.1052
    (c) $1/(3\sqrt{10})$

49 4.4

51 (a) $-16\vec{i} + 12\vec{j}$
    (b) $16\vec{i} - 12\vec{j}$
    (c) $12\vec{i} + 16\vec{j}$; answers may vary

53 (a) -3.268
    (b) -4.919

55 (a) Should be number
    (b) $11/5$

57 -0.5; better estimate is -1.35

59 -1.1; better estimate is -1.8

61 $4\vec{i} + 6\vec{j}$; $4(x - 2) + 6(y - 3) = 0$

63 $-4\vec{i} + \vec{j}$; $-4(x - 2) + (y - 3) = 0$

65 (a) Negative
    (b) Negative

67 (a) Negative
    (b) Positive
    (c) Positive
    (d) Negative

69 Yes

71 Yes

73 (a)

(b)

(c) $\vec{j}$

75 (a) Circles centered at P
    (b) away from P
    (c) 1

77 $(3\sqrt{5} - 2\sqrt{2})\vec{i} + (4\sqrt{2} - 3\sqrt{5})\vec{j}$

79 $4\sqrt{2}$,
    $6\vec{i} + 2\vec{j}$

81 $5/\sqrt{2}$

83 (a) P, Q
    (b)

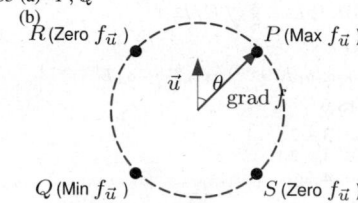

    (c) $\|\text{grad } f\|$
         $f_{\vec{u}} = \|\text{grad } f\|\cos\theta$

89 $f_{\vec{u}}(0, 0)$ is scalar, not vector

91 Closer contours give longer gradients

93

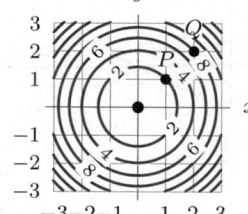

95 False

97 False

99 True

101 False

103 True

105 True

107 True

109 True

111 False

Section 14.5

1 $2x\vec{i}$

3 $e^x e^y e^z(\vec{i} + \vec{j} + \vec{k})$

5 $\frac{-2xyz^2}{(1 + x^2)^2}\vec{i} + \frac{z^2}{1 + x^2}\vec{j} + \frac{2yz}{1 + x^2}\vec{k}$

7 $(x\vec{i} + y\vec{j} + z\vec{k})/\sqrt{x^2 + y^2 + z^2}$

9 $y\vec{i} + x\vec{j} + e^z\cos(e^z)\vec{k}$

11 $e^p\vec{i} + (1/q)\vec{j} + 2re^{r^2}\vec{k}$

13 $\vec{0}$

15 $6\vec{i} + 4\vec{j} - 4\vec{k}$

17 $-\pi\vec{i} - \pi\vec{k}$

19 $9/\sqrt{3}$

21 $-1/\sqrt{2}$

23 $-\sqrt{77/2}$

25 $-2\vec{i} - 2\vec{j} + 4\vec{k}$;
    $-2(x + 1) - 2(y - 1) + 4(z - 2) = 0$

27 $2\vec{j} - 4\vec{k}$; $2(y - 1) - 4(z - 2) = 0$

29 $-2\vec{i} + \vec{k}$; $-2(x + 1) + (z - 2) = 0$

31 (a) 0
    (b) $24/\sqrt{19}$

33 (a) $(2x - yz)\vec{i} + (2y - xz)\vec{j} - xy\vec{k}$
    (b) $x + 4y + 6z = 20$

35 $z = 12 - 4x - 2y$

37 $6(x - 1) + 3(y - 2) + 2(z - 1) = 0$

39 $2x + 3y + 2z = 17$

41 $z = 2x + y + 3$

43 $x + 4y + 10z = 18$

45 (a) is (III); (b) is (I); (c) is (IV); (d) is (II)

47 $22/\sqrt{14}$

49 (a) Spheres centered at the origin
    (b) $2x\sin(x^2 + y^2 + z^2)\vec{i} + 2y\sin(x^2 + y^2 + z^2)\vec{j} + 2z\sin(x^2 + y^2 + z^2)\vec{k}$
    (c) $0, 180°$

51 (a) $-\vec{j}$,
         $\frac{2}{3}\vec{i} - \frac{1}{3}\vec{j} + \frac{2}{3}\vec{k}$
    (b) $y = 0$; $2x - y + 2z = 3$
    (c) $x = y = 0$ and $z \neq 0$

53 (a) $1.2x + 1.6y + 6z = 8$
    (b) Yes; $\pm(0.8, 0.6, 1)$

55 (a)

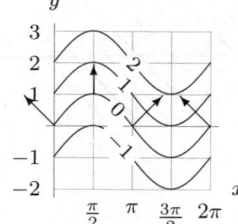

    (b) Valley

57 (a) $-4\vec{i} + 4\vec{j} + 2\vec{k}$
    (b) 24 mg/cm^3/sec

59 $f_{\vec{u}_3} < f_{\vec{u}_2} < 0 < f_{\vec{u}_4} < f_{\vec{u}_1}$

61 (a) Spheres centered at origin
    (b) $(-2x\vec{i} - 2y\vec{j} - 2z\vec{k})e^{-(x^2 + y^2 + z^2)}$
    (c) $-3\sqrt{2}e^{-1}$ degrees/sec

63 (a) is (V); (b) is (IV); (c) is (V)

71 $f_x(0, 0, 0)x + f_y(0, 0, 0)y + f_z(0, 0, 0)z = 0$

73 $f(x, y, z) = 2x + 3y + 4z + 100$

75 False

77 False

79 (a) °C per meter
    (b) °C per second
    (c) °C per second

Section 14.6

1 $\dfrac{dz}{dt} = e^{-t}\sin(t)(2\cos t - \sin t)$

3 $2\cos\left(\dfrac{2t}{1-t^2}\right)\dfrac{1+t^2}{(1-t^2)^2}$

5 $2e^{1+t^2}(1-2t^2)$

7 $\dfrac{\partial z}{\partial u} = \dfrac{1}{vu}\cos\left(\dfrac{\ln u}{v}\right)$
$\dfrac{\partial z}{\partial v} = -\dfrac{\ln u}{v^2}\cos\left(\dfrac{\ln u}{v}\right)$

9 $\dfrac{\partial z}{\partial u} = \dfrac{e^v}{u}$
$\dfrac{\partial z}{\partial v} = e^v\ln u$

11 $\dfrac{\partial z}{\partial u} = 2ue^{(u^2-v^2)}(1+u^2+v^2)$
$\dfrac{\partial z}{\partial v} = 2ve^{(u^2-v^2)}(1-u^2-v^2)$

13 $\dfrac{\partial z}{\partial u} =$
$(e^{-v\cos u} - v(\cos u)e^{-u\sin v})\sin v$
$- (-u(\sin v)e^{-v\cos u} + e^{-u\sin v})v\sin u$
$\dfrac{\partial z}{\partial v} =$
$(e^{-v\cos u} - v(\cos u)e^{-u\sin v})u\cos v$
$+ (-u(\sin v)e^{-v\cos u} + e^{-u\sin v})\cos u$

15 $\dfrac{\partial z}{\partial u} = \dfrac{-2uv^2}{u^4+v^4}$
$\dfrac{\partial z}{\partial v} = \dfrac{2vu^2}{u^4+v^4}$

17 $-2\rho\cos 2\phi,\ 0$

19 401.1

21 -5 pascal/hour

23 -0.6

25 Three

27 $\dfrac{dw}{dt} = \dfrac{\partial w}{\partial x}\dfrac{dx}{dt} + \dfrac{\partial w}{\partial y}\dfrac{dy}{dt} + \dfrac{\partial w}{\partial z}\dfrac{dz}{dt}$

29 $b\cdot e + d\cdot p$

35 $b\cdot e + d\cdot p$

37 (a) $\dfrac{\partial z}{\partial r} = \cos\theta\dfrac{\partial z}{\partial x} + \sin\theta\dfrac{\partial z}{\partial y}$
$\dfrac{\partial z}{\partial\theta} = r(\cos\theta\dfrac{\partial z}{\partial y} - \sin\theta\dfrac{\partial z}{\partial x})$

(b) $\dfrac{\partial z}{\partial y} = \sin\theta\dfrac{\partial z}{\partial r} + \dfrac{\cos\theta}{r}\dfrac{\partial z}{\partial\theta}$
$\dfrac{\partial z}{\partial x} = \cos\theta\dfrac{\partial z}{\partial r} - \dfrac{\sin\theta}{r}\dfrac{\partial z}{\partial\theta}$

39 $\left(\dfrac{\partial U_3}{\partial P}\right)_V$

41 $\left(\dfrac{\partial U}{\partial T}\right)_V = 7/2$
$\left(\dfrac{\partial U}{\partial V}\right)_T = 11/4$

45 $\displaystyle\int_0^b F_u(x,y)\,dy$

49 C_R and C_T must be evaluated at $(5,1)$

51 $g(t) = 3+t,\ h(t) = t$

53 $z = x+y,\ x = e^t$ and $y = t^2$, many other answers are possible

55 $z = x+y,\ x = t$ and $y = t$

Section 14.7

1 $f_{xx} = 2$
$f_{yy} = 2$
$f_{yx} = 2$
$f_{xy} = 2$

3 $f_{xx} = 6y$
$f_{xy} = 6x + 15y^2$
$f_{yx} = 6x + 15y^2$
$f_{yy} = 30xy$

5 $f_{xx} = 0$
$f_{yx} = e^y = f_{xy}$
$f_{yy} = e^y(x+2+y)$

7 $f_{xx} = -\left(\sin\left(\dfrac{x}{y}\right)\right)\left(\dfrac{1}{y^2}\right)$
$f_{xy} = -\left(\sin\left(\dfrac{x}{y}\right)\right)\left(\dfrac{-x}{y^2}\right)\left(\dfrac{1}{y}\right)$
$+ \left(\cos\left(\dfrac{x}{y}\right)\right)\left(\dfrac{-1}{y^2}\right) = f_{yx}$
$f_{yy} = -\left(\sin\left(\dfrac{x}{y}\right)\right)\left(\dfrac{-x}{y^2}\right)^2$
$+ \left(\cos\left(\dfrac{x}{y}\right)\right)\left(\dfrac{2x}{y^3}\right)$

9 $f_{xx} = 30xy^2 + 18$
$f_{xy} = 30x^2y - 21y^2$
$f_{yx} = 30x^2y - 21y^2$
$f_{yy} = 10x^3 - 42xy$

11 $f_{xx} = -12\sin 2x\cos 5y$
$f_{xy} = -30\cos 2x\sin 5y$
$f_{yx} = -30\cos 2x\sin 5y$
$f_{yy} = -75\sin 2x\cos 5y$

13 $Q(x,y) = 1 + 2x - 2y + x^2 - 2xy + y^2$

15 $Q(x,y) = 1 + x + x^2/2 - y^2/2$

17 $Q(x,y) = 1 - x^2/2 - 3xy - (9/2)y^2$

19 $Q(x,y) = -y + x^2 - y^2/2$

21 $1 + x - y/2 - x^2/2 + xy/2 - y^2/8$

23 (a) Negative
(b) Zero
(c) Negative
(d) Zero
(e) Zero

25 (a) Positive
(b) Zero
(c) Positive
(d) Zero
(e) Zero

27 (a) Zero
(b) Negative
(c) Zero
(d) Negative
(e) Zero

29 (a) Positive
(b) Positive
(c) Zero
(d) Zero
(e) Zero

31 (a) Positive
(b) Negative
(c) Negative
(d) Negative
(e) Positive

33 $L(x,y) = y$
$Q(x,y) = y + 2(x-1)y$
$L(0.9, 0.2) = 0.2$
$Q(0.9, 0.2) = 0.16$
$f(0.9, 0.2) = 0.162$

39 $a = -b^2$

41 Positive, negative

43 (a) $z_{yx} = 4y$
(b) $z_{xyx} = 0$
(c) $z_{xyy} = 4$

45 $d = e = f = 0$

47 $d = 0, e > 0, f < 0$

49 (a)

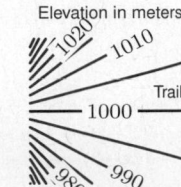

Elevation in meters
Trail
1020 1010 1000 990 980

(b) $\partial h/\partial x = 0,\ \partial h/\partial y > 0,$
$(\partial^2 h)/(\partial x\partial y) < 0$
(c) $(\partial^2 h)/(\partial x\partial y)$

51 (a) A
(b) B

53 (a) xy
$1 - \frac{1}{2}(x - \frac{\pi}{2})^2 - \frac{1}{2}(y - \frac{\pi}{2})^2$
(b)

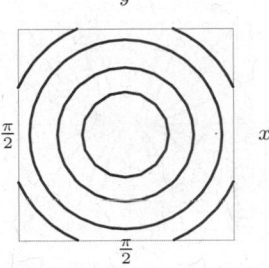

55 (a) (i) Dollars/Year, negative, (ii) Dollars/Dollar, positive
(b) $\partial^2 P/(\partial A\partial C) < 0$
(c) eCA

57 (a) $1 + x/2 + y$
(b) $1 + x/2 + y - x^2/8 - xy/2 - y^2/2$

61 Counterexample: $f(x,y) = x^3 + y^4$

63 $f(x,y) = x^2 + y^2$

65

Section 14.8

1 $(0,0)$

3 x-axis and y-axis

5 None

7 None

9 $(1, 2)$

11 (a)

(b) No
(c) No
(d) No
(e) Exist, not continuous

13 (a)

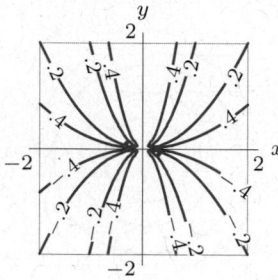

(b) Yes
(c) Yes
(d) No
(e) Exist, not continuous

15 (a)

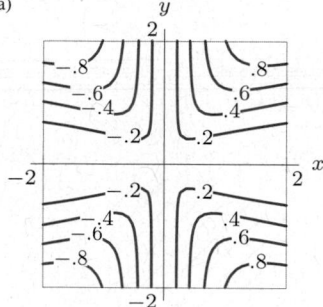

(b) Yes
(d) No
(f) No

17 (a)

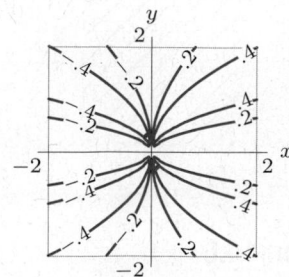

(c) No, no

---

19 (a) $f_x(x, y) =$
$(x^4 y + 4x^2 y^3 - y^5)/(x^2 + y^2)^2$
$f_y(x, y) =$
$(x^5 - 4x^3 y^2 - xy^4)/(x^2 + y^2)^2$
(c) Yes
(d) Yes

21 Counterexample: $\sqrt{x^2 + y^2}$

23 $f(x, y) = \sqrt{x^2 + y^2}$

25 (a) Differentiable
(b) Not differentiable
(c) Not differentiable
(d) Differentiable

Chapter 14 Review

1 Vector; $3e^{-1}\vec{i} - \frac{1}{2}e^{-1}\vec{j}$

3 Vector; $-(\sin x)e^y \vec{i} + (\cos x)e^y \vec{j} + \vec{k}$

5 $f_x = 2xy + 3x^2 - 7y^6$
$f_y = x^2 - 42xy^5$

7 $\pi / \sqrt{lg}$

9 $f_x = \frac{2xy^3}{(x^2+y^2)^2}$, $f_y = \frac{x^4 - x^2 y^2}{(x^2+y^2)^2}$

11 $\partial f / \partial p = (1/q)e^{p/q}$
$\partial f / \partial q = -(p/q^2)e^{p/q}$

13 $f_N = c\alpha N^{\alpha-1} V^\beta$

15 $x / \left(2\sqrt{\omega x}\cos^2\left(\sqrt{\omega x}\right)\right)$

17 $\dfrac{270x^3 y^7 - 168x^2 y^6 - 15xy^2 + 16y}{(15xy - 8)^2}$

19 $\pi xy / \sqrt{2\pi xyw - 13x^7 y^3 v}$

21 $\frac{7}{2}\left(\frac{w-1}{x^2 yw - xy^3 w^7}\right)^{-9/2}$
$\left(\frac{x^2 y + 6xy^3 w^7 - 7xy^3 w^6}{(w-1)^2}\right)$

23 $-1/(4\pi L\sqrt{LC})$

25 $u_{xx} = e^x \sin y$, $u_{yy} = -e^x \sin y$

27 $f_{xxy} = f_{yxx} = 2\cos(x - 2y)$

29 $2x\vec{i} + (2y + 3y^2)\vec{j}$

31 $-((1/x)\vec{i} + (1/y)\vec{j} + (1/z)\vec{k})/(xyz)$

33 $\nabla z = 2x\cos(x^2 + y^2)\vec{i}$
$\quad + 2y\cos(x^2 + y^2)\vec{j}$

35 $\cos(x^2 + y^2 + z^2)\left(2x\vec{i} + 2y\vec{j} + 2z\vec{k}\right)$

37 $-\frac{(t^2 - 2t + 4)}{(2s\sqrt{s})}\vec{i} + \frac{(2t-2)}{\sqrt{s}}\vec{j}$

39 $y[\cos(xy) - \sin(xy)]\vec{i}$
$\quad + x[\cos(xy) - \sin(xy)]\vec{j}$

41 $2\vec{i} + \vec{k}$

43 -1

45 0

47 $2/\sqrt{3}$

49 $5\vec{i} + 4\vec{j} + 3\vec{k}$

51 $-4x - 3y + 4z = 9$

53 $x + y + z = 3$

55 $\cos t \sin(\cos t) - \sin^2 t \cos(\cos t)$

57 $100t^3$

59 $3/t + 2t/(t^2 + 1)$

61 $Q(x, y) = 2 + 6x + y + 6x^2 + 3xy$

63 $Q(x, y) = 1 + (x - 3) - \frac{1}{2}(y - 5)$
$\quad - \frac{1}{2}(x-3)^2 + \frac{1}{2}(x-3)(y-5) - \frac{1}{8}(y-5)^2$

65 (a) $2x - 4y + az = a - 2$

(b) $a = 2$

67 (a) Q, R
(b) Q, P
(c) P, Q, R, S
(d) None

71 $F = 684$ newtons,
$\partial F / \partial m = 9.77$ newtons/kg,
$\partial F / \partial r = -0.000214$ newtons/meter

73 (a) 20 hours per day
(b) 18.615 hours per day

75 (a) P, S
(b) R, S
(c) P, Q, R, S
(d) None

77 0.3

79 0.8

81 0

83 (a) $-5\sqrt{2}/2$
(b) $4\vec{i} + \vec{j}$

85 (a) 98.387 ft/mile
(b) 295.161 ft/hour

87 (a) $-4e^{-81}$ °C/meter
(b) $-40e^{-81}$ °C/sec
(c) $\sqrt{932}e^{-81}$ °C/meter

89 $-2x\vec{i} - 2y\vec{j}$

91 Yes

95 (a) $F_u(x, y, 3)$
(b) $F_w(3, y, x)$
(c) $F_u(x, y, x) + F_w(x, y, x)$
(d) $F_u(x, y, xy) + yF_w(x, y, xy)$

97 $dP \approx 47.6\,dL + 17.8\,dK$

101 (a) $-3\vec{i} + 4\vec{j} - \vec{k}$
(b) $-3\vec{i} + 4\vec{j}$

105 15°C/minute

107 Approx 7.5 at $(1.94, 1.08)$

109 $x - y$

111 (a) Negative, positive,
Up if positive, down if negative
(b) $\pi < t < 2\pi$
(c) $0 < x < 3\pi/2$ and
$0 < t < \pi/2$ or $3\pi/2 < t < 5\pi/2$

113 (a) $A_0 + A_1 + 2A_2 + A_3 + 2A_4 + 4A_5 +$
$(A_1 + 2A_3 + 2A_4)(x - 1) + (A_2 + A_4 +$
$4A_5)(y - 2), 1 + B_1 t, 2 + C_1 t$
(b) $A_1 B_1 + 2A_3 B_1 + 2A_4 B_1 + A_2 C_1 +$
$A_4 C_1 + 4A_5 C_1$

115 $\frac{\partial w}{\partial x}\frac{\partial x}{\partial u}\frac{du}{dt} + \frac{\partial w}{\partial y}\frac{\partial y}{\partial u}\frac{du}{dt} + \frac{\partial w}{\partial x}\frac{\partial x}{\partial v}\frac{dv}{dt} +$
$\frac{\partial w}{\partial y}\frac{\partial y}{\partial v}\frac{dv}{dt} + \frac{\partial w}{\partial z}\frac{dz}{dt}$

Section 15.1

1 (I) and (V) Local maximum, (II) and (VI) Local minimum, (III) and (IV) Saddle point

3 (a) None
(b) E, G
(c) D, F

5 Local minimum

7 Local maximum

9 Local max: $(4, 2)$

11 Local max: $(1, 5)$

13 Saddle point: $(0, 0)$
Saddle point: $(2, 0)$
Local min: $(1, 0.25)$

15 Saddle pts: $(1, -1), (-1, 1)$
Local max: $(-1, -1)$
Local min: $(1, 1)$

17 Local max: $(-1, 0)$

Saddle pts: $(1, 0), (-1, 4)$
Local min: $(1, 4)$

19 Saddle point: $(0, 0)$
Local max: $(1, 1), (-1, -1)$

21 $A = -2, B = 21$

23 (a) (a, b)
(b) $a = -1, b = 5$
(c) Local maximum

25 (a) Local maximum
(b) Saddle point
(c) Local minimum
(d) None of these

27

29 $(k\pi, l\pi)$,
for $k = 0, \pm 1, \pm 2, \cdots$,
$l = 0, \pm 1, \pm 2, \cdots$
$(k\pi + \frac{\pi}{2}, l\pi + \frac{\pi}{2})$,
for $k = 0, \pm 1, \pm 2, \cdots$,
$l = 0, \pm 1, \pm 2, \cdots$
$(k\pi, l\pi), k = 0, \pm 1, \pm 2, \cdots$,
$l = 0, \pm 1, \pm 2, \cdots$ are saddle points
If k and l are both even or k and l are both odd,
then $(k\pi + \frac{\pi}{2}, l\pi + \frac{\pi}{2})$ are local max
If k is even but l is odd or k is odd but l is even,
then $(k\pi + \frac{\pi}{2}, l\pi + \frac{\pi}{2})$ are local min

31 $y = 0, \pm 2\pi, \pm 4\pi, \ldots$ Local minima

33 (a) (a, b) is a saddle point.
(b)

35

37 (a) $(0, 0)$
(b) $D = -24x^2$
(c) Saddle point

39

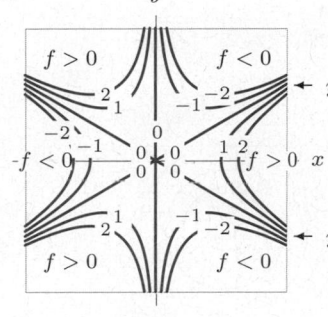

41 $(1, 3)$ could be saddle point

43 Can be saddle if f_{xy} large

45 $f(x, y) = 4 - (x - 2)^2 - (y + 3)^2$

47 False

49 True

51 False

53 True

55 False

Section 15.2

1 Mississippi:
$87 - 88$ (max), $83 - 87$ (min)
Alabama:
$88 - 89$ (max), $83 - 87$ (min)
Pennsylvania:
$89 - 90$ (max), 80 (min)
New York:
$81 - 84$ (max), $74 - 76$ (min)
California:
$100 - 101$ (max), $65 - 68$ (min)
Arizona:
$102 - 107$ (max), $85 - 87$ (min)
Massachusetts:
$81 - 84$ (max), 70 (min)

3 Max: 30.5 at $(0, 0)$
Min: 20.5 at $(2.5, 5)$

5 Min $= 0$ at $(0, 0)$
(not on boundary)
Max $= 2$ at $(1, 1), (1, -1)$,
$(-1, -1)$ and $(-1, 1)$
(on boundary)

7 max$= 1$ at $(1, 0)$ and $(-1, 0)$
(on boundary)
min$= -1$ at $(0, 1), (0, -1)$
(on boundary)

9 Global min

11 Global max $= 0$
No global min

13 (a) Local min: $(-13/55, 1/55)$
(b) 0.5

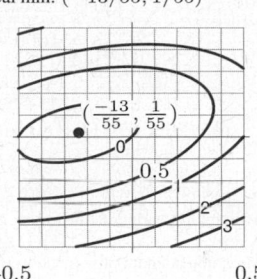

15 All edges $(32)^{1/3}$ cm

17 $l = w = h = 45$ cm

19 $(3/14, 1/7, 1/14)$

23 $q_1 = 300, q_2 = 225$.

25 (a) $L = \left[pA \left(\frac{a}{k} \right)^a \left(\frac{l}{b} \right)^{(a-1)} \right]^{1/(1-a-b)}$
$K = \frac{la}{kb} L$
(b) No

27 $y = 24x^2/49 - 2/7$

31 (a) $p = \sqrt{P_0 P_F}$
(b) $p_1 = \sqrt[3]{P_0^2 P_F}, p_2 = \sqrt[3]{P_0 P_F^2}$

33 Must have global maximum if continuous and R closed, bounded

35 Local max not necessarily global max

37 $f(x, y) = x^2 + y^2$, R is $0 \le x, y \le 1$

39 False

41 False

43 False

45 True

Section 15.3

1 Min $= -\sqrt{2}$, max $= \sqrt{2}$

3 Max: 20 at $(-1, 2)$;
Min: 0 at $(1, -2)$

5 Min $= -22$, max $= 22$

7 Global min: $1/2$
No global max

9 Min $= -\sqrt{35}$, max $= \sqrt{35}$

11 Max: 4 at $(2, 2, 1), (2, -2, -1)$,
$(-2, 2, -1), (-2, -2, 1)$;
Min: -4 at $(-2, -2, -1), (-2, 2, 1)$,
$(2, -2, 1), (2, 2, -1)$

13 Max $= f\left(\frac{1}{\sqrt{5}}, \frac{3}{\sqrt{5}} \right) = 2\sqrt{5}$
Min $= f\left(-\frac{1}{\sqrt{5}}, -\frac{3}{\sqrt{5}} \right) = -2\sqrt{5}$

15 No global extrema

17 Max: $30 + \sqrt{10}$ at $(0, -\sqrt{10})$;
Min: -5 at $(\pm 3, -1)$

19 1 at $(1/2, 1/2)$

21 0.5

23 (a)

(b) $s = 1000 - 10l$

25 (a) Min; max at endpt of constraint
λ neg
(b) Max; min at endpt of constraint
λ pos

27 $\Delta c/4; -\Delta c/4$

31 (a) $C = \$4349$
(b) $\$182$

33 (a) $W = 225$
$K = 37.5$
(c) $W = 225$
$K = 37.5$
$\lambda = 0.29$

35 (a) No
(b) Yes
(c) $a + b = 1$

37 $x_1 = ((v_1)^{1/2} + (v_2)^{1/2})/(m(v_1)^{1/2})$
$x_2 = ((v_1)^{1/2} + (v_2)^{1/2})/(m(v_2)^{1/2})$

39 (a) $f_1 = \frac{k_1}{k_1+k_2} mg, f_2 = \frac{k_2}{k_1+k_2} mg$
(b) Distance the mass stretches the top spring and compresses the lower spring

43 (a) Cost of producing quantity u when prices are p, q
(b) $2\sqrt{pqu}$

45 (a) $-5\lambda^2 + 15\lambda$
(b) $1.5, 11.25$
(c) $11.25, 1.5$
(d) same

47 (a) $S = \ln(a^a(1-a)^{(1-a)}) + \ln b - a\ln p_1 - (1-a)\ln p_2$
(b) $b = e^c p_1^a p_2^{(1-a)}/(a^a(1-a)^{(1-a)})$

49 Maximum value is 1

51 $f(x, y) = 3x + 4y$

53 $f(x, y) = x^2 + y^2$

55

59 False

61 False

63 False

65 False

67 True

69 True

Chapter 15 Review

1 $(3, -1)$, Saddle point

3 Saddle pt: $(0, -5)$
Local min: $(2, -5)$

5 $(2, 1)$; local min

7 $(2, 3)$: Local and global max

9 Local minimum: $(1, 2)$
Local maximum: $(-1, -2)$
Saddle points: $(1, -2)$ and $(-1, 2)$
No global maximum or minimum

11 Minimum $f(-3/\sqrt{5}, 4/\sqrt{5}) = -5\sqrt{5}$,
Maximum $f(3/\sqrt{5}, -4/\sqrt{5}) = 5\sqrt{5}$

13 Min $= 11.25$; no max

15 Minimum $f(27.907, 23.256) = 1860.484$;
No maximum

17 Maximum $= f(48, 52) = 37,600$
No minimum

19 Max $= 21$, no min

21 No global extrema.

23 Maximum

25 Both

27 0.204

29 $\Delta c/2; \Delta c/(2\sqrt{2})$

31

33 (a) (i) Power function
(ii) Linear function
(b) $\ln N = 1.20 + 0.32 \ln A$
Agrees with biological rule

35 (a) $2c^2/3$
(b) $4c/3$
(c) $\lambda = m'(c)$

37 $c \left(\frac{aK}{(a+b)P_1} \right)^a \left(\frac{bK}{(a+b)P_2} \right)^b$

39 (a) Points A, B, C, D, E
(b) Point F
(c) Point D

41 $f(x, y, z) = \frac{|Aa+Bb+Cc+D|}{\sqrt{A^2+B^2+C^2}}$

43 $K = 20$
$L = 30$
$C = \$7,000$

47 Base: 4 cm by 4 cm
Height: 2 cm

49 $-1/2$

51 (a) $x = 1/4 - a, y = 1$, saddle point

53 (a) 21.0208
(b) $g = 20.5, 21.2211; g = 20.2, 21.1008$
(c) $g = 20.5, 21.2198; g = 20.2, 21.1007$

Section 16.1

1 $24; 43.5$

3 Over: Approx 137
Under: Approx 60

5 about 2300

7 Positive

9 Zero

11 Zero

13 Positive

15 $25.2°C$

17 Need f nonnegative everywhere

19 $f(x, y) = 5 - x - y$; R is square with vertices $(\pm 1, \pm 1)$

21 False

23 False

25 True

27 True

29 False

Section 16.2

1 $\int_0^\pi \int_0^x y \sin x \, dy \, dx$

3 $\int_0^2 \int_0^{y^2} y^2 x \, dx \, dy$

5 150

7 54

9 $e - 2$

11 $3 - \sin 3$

13 $(e^4 - 1)(e^2 - 1)e$

15 -2.678

17 $\int_1^4 \int_1^2 f \, dy \, dx$ or $\int_1^2 \int_1^4 f \, dx \, dy$

19 $\int_{-1}^3 \int_{-2}^{(1-3x)/4} f \, dy \, dx$
or $\int_{-2}^1 \int_{-1}^{(1-4y)/3} f \, dx \, dy$

21 $\int_1^3 \int_{\frac{1}{2}(y-1)}^{-\frac{1}{2}(y-5)} f \, dx \, dy$

23 $\frac{4}{15}(9\sqrt{3} - 4\sqrt{2} - 1) = 2.38176$

25 32/9

27 13/6

29 0

31 2/3

33 $(e-1)/2$

35 $\frac{2}{9}(3\sqrt{3} - 2\sqrt{2})$

37 $\frac{1}{2}(e^2 - 1)$

39 (a) 8/3
   (b) 16/3

41 (a) $\int_0^{1/2} \int_y^{1-y} f(x,y) \, dx \, dy$

   $\int_0^{1/2} \int_0^x f(x,y) \, dy \, dx$

   $\int_{1/2}^1 \int_0^{1-x} f(x,y) \, dy \, dx$

   (b) 1/8

43 15

45 $\int_{-5}^5 \int_{-\sqrt{25-y^2}}^{\sqrt{25-y^2}} (25 - x^2 - y^2) \, dx \, dy$

47 $\int_0^4 \int_{y-4}^{(4-y)/2} (4 - 2x - y) \, dx \, dy$

49 1/3

51 16/3

53 Volume = $1/(6abc)$

55 (a) Circles centered at $(1, 0)$

   (b) $\int_{-\sqrt{3}}^{\sqrt{3}} e^{-y^2} \, dy$

   (c) $\int_{-2}^2 \int_{-\sqrt{4-x^2}}^{\sqrt{4-x^2}} e^{-(x-1)^2 - y^2} \, dy \, dx$

57 (a)

(b)

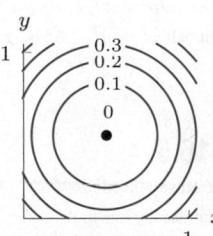

59 (a) $(4/3)a + b + (4/3)c = 20$
   (b) $f(x,y) = x^2 + \frac{44}{3}xy + 3y^2$:

$f(x,y) = -3x^2 + 24xy$:

61 $k(a^3 b + ab^3)/3$

63 Integrals not over same region

65 $\int_{-1}^1 \int_{-\sqrt{1-x^2}}^{\sqrt{1-x^2}} 2 \, dx \, dy$

+ 67 $\int_0^2 \int_0^{6-3y} 1 \, dx \, dy$

69 False

71 False

73 False

75 False

Section 16.3

1 2

3 −8

5

7

9

11

13

15 Positive

17 Positive

19 Zero

21 Positive

23 Zero

25 Positive

27 Positive

29 125

31 (a) $2\int_0^{10} \int_0^1 \int_y^1 e^{-3x} \, dz \, dy \, dx$
   Other answers are possible
   (b) $(1 - e^{-30})/3$

33 $V = \int_0^1 \int_0^2 \int_{x+y}^{1+2x+2y} 1 \, dz \, dy \, dx$
   Can reverse order x, y

35 $V = \int_0^1 \int_0^{1-x} \int_{6-3x-4y}^{6-2x-2y} 1 \, dz \, dy \, dx$
   Can reverse order x, y

37 $V = \int_{-\sqrt{5}}^{\sqrt{5}} \int_{-\sqrt{5-x^2}}^{\sqrt{5-x^2}} \int_2^{\sqrt{9-x^2-y^2}} 1 \, dz \, dy \, dx$
   Can reverse order x, y

39 $\int_0^1 \int_{-r}^r \int_0^{\sqrt{r^2-x^2}} f(x,y,z) \, dz \, dx \, dy$

41 $\int_{-r}^r \int_{-\sqrt{r^2-x^2}}^{\sqrt{r^2-x^2}} \int_0^{\sqrt{r^2-x^2-z^2}} f(x,y,z) \, dy \, dz \, dx$

43 1/2

45 162

47 1

49 29 gm

51 243

53 (a) $x + y + z = 1$
   (b) 1/6

55 $\int_0^2 \int_0^{1-\frac{z}{4}} \int_0^{2-2y-\frac{z}{2}} f(x,y,z) \, dx \, dy \, dz$

57 $\int_{-4}^4 \int_{-\sqrt{16-x^2}}^{\sqrt{16-x^2}} \int_3^{\sqrt{25-x^2-y^2}} dz \, dy \, dx$

59 $\int_{-1}^1 \int_{-\sqrt{1-x^2}}^{\sqrt{1-x^2}} \int_{-\sqrt{1-z^2}}^{\sqrt{1-z^2}} dy \, dz \, dx$

61 $\int_0^2 \int_0^{6y^2} \int_0^{\sqrt{12-3y^2}} f(x,y,z) \, dx \, dz \, dy$

63 4

65 $m = 2$;
   $(\bar{x}, \bar{y}, \bar{z}) = (13/24, 13/24, 25/24)$

67 $5m/3$

71 Need same limits on innermost integral

73 $f(x,y,z) = z$

75 True

77 True

79 False

81 True

83 True

Section 16.4

1 $\int_0^{\pi/2} \int_0^{1/2} f \, r \, dr \, d\theta$

3 $\int_{\pi/4}^{3\pi/4} \int_0^2 f \, r \, dr \, d\theta$

5 $\int_1^5 \int_2^4 f(x, y)\, dy\, dx$

7 $\int_\pi^{2\pi} \int_2^4 f(r\cos\theta, r\sin\theta)\, r\, dr\, d\theta$

9

11

13

15

17 $\pi(1 - \cos 4)$

19 $-2/3$

21 1.

23 (a) (i) $\int_0^{\pi/6} \int_0^\pi \int_0^5 \rho^2 \sin\phi\, d\rho\, d\phi\, d\theta$; $125\pi/9$

(ii) $\int_0^{\pi/6} \int_0^5 \int_{-\sqrt{25-r^2}}^{\sqrt{25-r^2}} r\, dz\, dr\, d\theta$; $2\int_0^{\pi/6} \int_0^5 \int_0^{\sqrt{25-z^2}} r\, dr\, dz\, d\theta$; $125\pi/9$

(b) $1/12(4/3\pi 5^3)$

25 (a)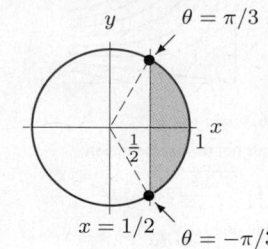

(b) 7/3

27 $32\pi(\sqrt{2} - 1)/3$

29 (a) $\int_0^\pi \int_0^3 r/(r^2 + 1)\, dr\, d\theta$

(b) $\pi \ln 10$

31 $250\pi/3$ grams

33 (a)

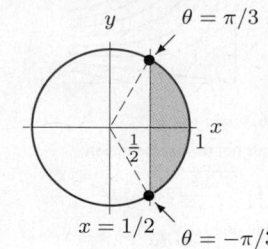

(b) $(4\pi - 3\sqrt{3})/12$

35 (a) $\int_{-\sqrt{3}/2}^{\sqrt{3}/2} \int_{1-\sqrt{1-y^2}}^{\sqrt{1-y^2}} dx\, dy$

(b) $\int_0^1 \int_{-\arccos(r/2)}^{\arccos(r/2)} r\, d\theta\, dr$

37 Upper limit for inner integral $1/\cos\theta$

39 Quarter disk $0 \le x \le 1, 0 \le y \le \sqrt{1 - x^2}$

41 (a), (c), (e)

Section 16.5

1 (a) is (IV); (b) is (II); (c) is (VII); (d) is (VI); (e) is (III); (f) is (V)

3 $z = \sqrt{1 - r^2}$

5 $\phi = \pi/4$

7 $\rho = 4/\cos\phi$

9 $200\pi/3$

11 25π

13 $\int_0^1 \int_0^{2\pi} \int_0^4 f \cdot r\, dr\, d\theta\, dz$

15 $\int_0^\pi \int_0^\pi \int_2^3 f \cdot \rho^2 \sin\phi\, d\rho\, d\phi\, d\theta$

17 $\int_0^5 \int_0^2 \int_0^{x/5} f\, dz\, dy\, dx$

19 $\int_0^{2\pi} \int_0^K \int_{-\sqrt{K^2-r^2}}^{\sqrt{K^2-r^2}} r\, dz\, dr\, d\theta$

21 $\int_0^{2\pi} \int_0^2 \int_{2r}^4 f(r, \theta, z) r\, dz\, dr\, d\theta$

23 $\int_{-2}^2 \int_{-\sqrt{4-x^2}}^{\sqrt{4-x^2}} \int_{2\sqrt{x^2+y^2}}^4 h(x, y, z)\, dz\, dy\, dx$

25 (a) $\int_{-1/\sqrt{2}}^{1/\sqrt{2}} \int_{-\sqrt{(1/2)-x^2}}^{\sqrt{(1/2)-x^2}} \int_{\sqrt{x^2+y^2}}^{\sqrt{1-x^2-y^2}} dz\, dy\, dx$

(b) $\int_0^{2\pi} \int_0^{1/\sqrt{2}} \int_r^{\sqrt{1-r^2}} r\, dz\, dr\, d\theta$

(c) $\int_0^{2\pi} \int_0^{\pi/4} \int_0^1 \rho^2 \sin\phi\, d\rho\, d\phi\, d\theta$

27 (a) $\int_0^{2\pi} \int_0^{\sqrt{2}} \int_r^{\sqrt{4-r^2}} r\, dz\, dr\, d\theta$

(b) $\int_0^{2\pi} \int_0^{\pi/4} \int_0^2 \rho^2 \sin\phi\, d\rho\, d\phi\, d\theta$

29 $V = \int_0^{2\pi} \int_0^{\pi/3} \int_0^3 \rho^2 \sin\phi\, d\rho\, d\phi\, d\theta$ Order of integration can be altered; other coordinates can be used

31 $V = \int_0^\pi \int_{\sqrt{2}}^{\sqrt{3}} \int_5^{10} r\, dz\, dr\, d\theta$; Order of integration can be altered; other coordinates can be used

33 $V = \int_0^{2\pi} \int_0^3 \int_1^{\sqrt{10-r^2}} r\, dz\, dr\, d\theta$ or $V = \int_0^{2\pi} \int_1^{\sqrt{10}} \int_0^{\sqrt{10-z^2}} r\, dr\, dz\, d\theta$ Order of integration can be altered; other coordinates can be used

35 (a) $\int_0^{2\pi} \int_0^{1/\sqrt{3}} \int_{\sqrt{3}r}^1 r\, dz\, dr\, d\theta$

(b) $\pi/9$

37 $16\pi(\sqrt{2} - 1)/(3\sqrt{2})$

39 $28\pi/15$

41 $\int_0^{2\pi} \int_0^{5/\sqrt{2}} \int_r^{5/\sqrt{2}} r\, dz\, dr\, d\theta = 125\pi/(6\sqrt{2}) = 46.28$ cm^3

43 (a) Negative

(b) Zero

45 $pqr/6$

47 $\int_0^{2\pi} \int_0^{\pi/2} \int_a^b \rho^2 \sin\phi\, d\rho\, d\phi\, d\theta = 2\pi(b^3 - a^3)/3$

49 (a) $\int_0^{2\pi} \int_0^{\sqrt{2}} \int_0^{2-r^2} (2 - z)r\, dz\, dr\, d\theta$

(b) $\left(\frac{16\sqrt{2}}{3} - \frac{4}{3}\right) \pi$

51 $\int_0^{2\pi} \int_0^\pi \int_0^3 2\rho^3 \sin\phi\, d\rho\, d\phi\, d\theta$

53 $1/32$

55 (a) Mass = $\int_0^{2\pi} \int_0^a \int_{-\sqrt{a^2-r^2}}^{\sqrt{a^2-r^2}} k|z|r\, dz\, dr\, d\theta$

(b) $\pi k a^4/2$

57 $3/4$

61 $3I = \frac{6}{5}a^2; I = \frac{2}{5}a^2$

63 $(q^2/8\pi\epsilon)((1/a) - (1/b))$

65 Mass = $\int_{-2}^2 \int_{-\sqrt{4-x^2}}^{\sqrt{4-x^2}} \int_0^{4-x^2-y^2} e^{-x-y}\, dz\, dy\, dx$ gm

67 $1/27$

69 $2\pi G\delta(H + R - \sqrt{R^2 + H^2})$

71 Total charge = $2\pi k R^2$

73 (c)

75 Limits of outer integral not constant

77 $\int_W \sqrt{x^2 + y^2 + z^2}\, dx\, dy\, dz$; W is unit ball $x^2 + y^2 + z^2 \le 1$

Section 16.6

1 Is a joint density function

3 Not a joint density function

5 Is joint density function

7 0

9 1

11 7/8

13 1/16

15 (a) 20/27

(b) 199/243

17 (a) $k = 3/8$

(b) 15/32

(c) 1/16

19 $\int_{65}^{100} \int_{0.8}^1 f(x, y)\, dx\, dy$

23 $\int_{-\infty}^\infty \int_{-\infty}^\infty (p_1(x, y) + p_2(x, y))\, dx\, dy = 2$

25 $a = 0, b = 1, c = 0, d = 1$

27 True

29 False

Chapter 16 Review

1 94.5

3 14

5

$x^2 + y^2 = 4$

7

$y = \sin x$ or $x = \sin^{-1} y$

11 $\int_0^{2\pi} \int_0^2 \int_0^3 fr\, dr\, dz\, d\theta$

13 $\int_0^{\pi/2} \int_0^{\pi} \int_0^5 f\rho^2 \sin\phi\, d\rho\, d\phi\, d\theta$

15 (a) y

$x = -(y-4)/2$ or $y = -2x + 4$

(b) $\int_0^2 \int_0^{-2x+4} g(x,y)\, dy\, dx$

17 $10(e-2)$

19 $(1/20)\sin^5 1$

21 $(\pi/2)(1 - e^{-1})$

23 1/48

25 $\int_0^{2\pi} \int_{3\pi/4}^{\pi} \int_0^{\sqrt2} f(\rho, \phi, \theta)\rho^2 \sin\phi\, d\rho\, d\phi\, d\theta$

27 $\int_{-1}^1 \int_{-\sqrt{1-x^2}}^{\sqrt{1-x^2}} \int_{-\sqrt{2-x^2-y^2}}^{-\sqrt{x^2+y^2}} h(x,y,z)\, dz\, dy\, dx$

29 Positive

31 Positive

33 Negative

35 Zero

37 Positive

39 1.571

41 (a) $\int_0^{2\pi} \int_{\pi/4}^{\pi/2} \int_0^{3/\sin\theta} \rho^2 \sin\phi\, d\rho\, d\phi\, d\theta$

(b) 18π

43

$z = 3$

$z = 2$

$\int_0^{2\pi} \int_2^3 \int_{\sqrt5}^{\sqrt6} r\, dr\, dz\, d\theta$
Order of integration can be changed

45

Sphere: $x^2 + y^2 + z^2 = 9$

Cylinder: $x^2 + y^2 = 1$

$\int_0^{2\pi} \int_0^1 \int_0^{\sqrt{9-r^2}} r\, dz\, dr\, d\theta$

47 Negative

49 Can't tell

51 Zero

53 Zero

55 Zero

57 Negative

59 $\pi(3 - 2\ln 2)$

61 $162\pi/5$

63 (a) y

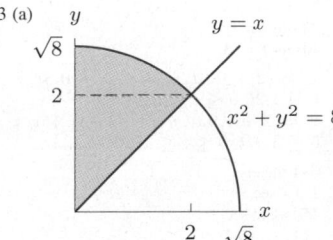

$y = x$

$\sqrt8$

$x^2 + y^2 = 8$

(b) $\pi(1 - e^{-8})/8$

65 (a) $z = \sqrt{1 - (y-1)^2}$, $0 \le y \le 2$, $0 \le x \le 10$

(b) $\int_0^{10} \int_0^2 \int_0^{\sqrt{1-(y-1)^2}} f(x,y,z)\, dz\, dy\, dx$

67 (a) Half cylinder, radius 1, along x-axis, $y \ge 0, -1 \le x \le 1$

(b) $2\pi/5$

69 $\int_0^{2\pi} \int_0^4 \int_3^{\sqrt{25-r^2}} r\, dz\, dr\, d\theta$
$= 52\pi/3 = 54.45$ cm³

71 $\int_0^{2\pi} \int_{3/\cos\phi}^{\arccos(3/5)} \int_{3/\cos\phi}^5 \rho^2 \sin\phi\, d\rho\, d\phi\, d\theta$
$= 52\pi/3 = 54.45$ cm³

73 8π gm

75 $\int_{-1}^1 \int_{-\sqrt{1-x^2}}^{\sqrt{1-x^2}} \int_{-1+\sqrt{2-x^2-y^2}}^{\sqrt{1-x^2-y^2}} dz\, dy\, dx$
$= 2\pi((7/6) - 2\sqrt2/3)$

77 $8\pi R^5/15$

79 (a) 3/2000
(b) 343/1000

81 $6\pi/7$

83 $a, b+c, 0$

Section 17.1

1 $x = 0, y = t, -2 \le t \le 1$

3 $x = t, \quad y = 3 - 3t, \quad 0 \le t \le 1$

5 $x = 1 + 2t, \quad y = 1 + t, \quad 0 \le t < 1$

7 $x = t, y = 1, z = -t$

9 $x = 1, \quad y = 0, \quad z = t$

11 $x = 1 + 3t, \quad y = 2 - 3t, \quad z = 3 + t$

13 $x = -3 + 2t, y = -2 - t, z = 1 - 2t$

15 $x = 2 + 3t, \quad y = 3 - t, \quad z = -1 + t$

17 $x = 3 - 3t, y = 0, z = -5t$

19 $x = 3\cos t, y = 3\sin t, z = 5, 0 \le t < 2\pi$

21 $x = 2\cos t, y = -2\sin t, z = 0$

23 $x = 2\cos t, y = 0, z = 2\sin t$

25 $x = 0, y = 3\cos t, z = 2 + 3\sin t$

27 $x = t^2, y = t, z = 0$

29 $x = -3t^2, y = 0, z = t$

31 $x = t, y = 4 - 5t^4, z = 4$

33 $x = 3\cos t, y = 2\sin t, z = 0$

35 $x = -1 + 3t, y = 2, z = -3 + 5t$

37 $\vec{r}(t) = \vec{i} - 3\vec{j} + 2\vec{k} + t(3\vec{i} + 4\vec{j} - 5\vec{k})$,
$0 \le t \le 1$, $x = 1 + 3t, y = -3 + 4t$,
$z = 2 - 5t, 0 \le t \le 1$

39 $x = \cos t, y = \sin t, z = 0, 0 \le t \le \pi$

41 Two arcs:
$\vec{r}(t) = 5\vec{i} + 5(-\cos t\vec{i} + \sin t\vec{j})$,
$0 \le t \le \pi$ or
$\vec{r}(t) = 5\vec{i} + 5(\cos t\vec{i} + \sin t\vec{j})$,
$\pi \le t \le 2\pi$

43 $\vec{r}(t) = (2 + 10t)\vec{i} + (5 + 4t)\vec{j}$

45 $\vec{r}(t) = (2 + ((t - 20)/10)10)\vec{i}$
$+ (5 + ((t - 20)/10)4)\vec{j}$

47 $\vec{r}(t) = (2 - 10t)\vec{i} + (5 - 4t)\vec{j}$

49 No

51 (b) $-\vec{i} - 10\vec{j} - 7\vec{k}$
(c) $\vec{r} = (1 - t)\vec{i} + (3 - 10t)\vec{j} - 7t\vec{k}$

53 (a) $\vec{r} = (\vec{i} + 3\vec{j} + 7\vec{k}) + t(2\vec{i} - 3\vec{j} - \vec{k})$
(b) $(3, 0, 6)$
(c) $\sqrt{14}$

55 (a) $2\vec{i} - 5\vec{j} + 3\vec{k}$
(c) $x = 1 + 2t, y = -1 - 5t, z = 1 + 3t$

57 Different lines

59 Different lines

61 (a) $(-1, 4, -2)$
(b) $-\vec{i} - \vec{j} + 2\vec{k}$; other answers possible
(c) $\vec{r} = -\vec{i} + 4\vec{j} - 2\vec{k} + t(-\vec{i} - \vec{j} + 2\vec{k})$

63 $x = -\frac{3}{2}t + \frac{5}{2}, y = \frac{1}{2}t + \frac{1}{2}, z = t.$

65 $x = -4, y = 2 + t, z = 3 + t$

67 (a) Straight lines
(b) No
(c) $(1, 2, 3)$

69 (a) Repeats every year
(b) Mid-August
(c) Mid-April
(d) 2°C per month

71 Circle, cosine, sine

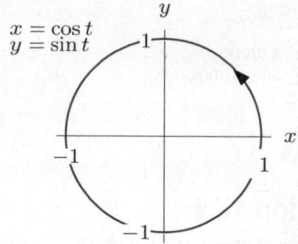

$x = \cos t$
$y = \sin t$

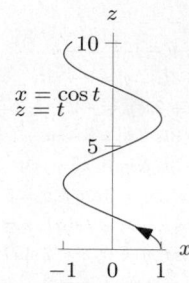

$x = \cos t$
$z = t$

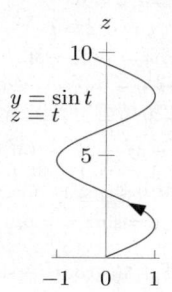

$y = \sin t$
$z = t$

73 (a) $x = 2 + at, y = 1 + bt, z = 3 + ct$
   (b) $a/2 = b/1 = c/3$

75 α is radius of cylinder
   β determines vertical distance moved

77 (a) (vii)
   (b) (ii)
   (c) (iv)

79 $\vec{r} = 9.65\vec{k} + t(325\vec{i} + 563\vec{j} - 0.84\vec{k})$

81 (a) Parallel
   (b)   (i) Perpendicular
        (ii) Parallel

83 Different parameterization of same curve

85 $x = \cos t, y = \sin t, z = 0$
    $x = 0, y = \cos t, z = \sin t$

87 $x = t^3, y = 2t^3, z = 3 + 4t^3$

89 True

91 True

93 True

95 True

97 False

99 False

Section 17.2

1 $\vec{v} = 3\vec{i} + \vec{j} - \vec{k}, \quad \vec{a} = \vec{0}$

3 $\vec{v} = \vec{i} + 2t\vec{j} + 3t^2\vec{k}, \quad \vec{a} = 2\vec{j} + 6t\vec{k}$

5 $\vec{v} = -3\sin t\vec{i} + 4\cos t\vec{j},$
   $\vec{a} = -3\cos t\vec{i} - 4\sin t\vec{j}$

7 $\vec{v} = \vec{i} + 2t\vec{j} + 3t^2\vec{k},$
   Speed $= \sqrt{1 + 4t^2 + 9t^4}$,
   Particle never stops

9 $\vec{v} = 6t\vec{i} + 3t^2\vec{j},$
   $\|\vec{v}\| = 3|t| \cdot \sqrt{4 + t^2}$,
   Stops when $t = 0$

11 $\vec{v} = 6t\cos(t^2)\vec{i} - 6t\sin(t^2)\vec{j}$,
   $\|\vec{v}\| = 6|t|$,
   Stops when $t = 0$

13 Length $= \sqrt{42}$

15 Length $= e - 1$

17 $\vec{v} = -6\pi\sin(2\pi t)\vec{i} + 6\pi\cos(2\pi t)\vec{j}$,
   $\vec{a} = -12\pi^2\cos(2\pi t)\vec{i} - 12\pi^2\sin(2\pi t)\vec{j}$,
   $\vec{v} \cdot \vec{a} = 0, \|\vec{v}\| = 6\pi, \|\vec{a}\| = 12\pi^2$

19 Line through $(2, 3, 5)$ in direction of
   $\vec{i} - 2\vec{j} - \vec{k}$,
   $\vec{v} = 2t(\vec{i} - 2\vec{j} - \vec{k}), \vec{a} = 2(\vec{i} - 2\vec{j} - \vec{k})$

21 $x = 1 + 2(t - 2), y = 2, z = 4 + 12(t - 2)$

23 Vertical: $t = 3$
   Horizontal: $t = \pm 1$
   As $t \to \infty, x \to \infty, y \to \infty$
   As $t \to -\infty, x \to \infty, y \to -\infty$

25 (a) $\vec{v}(2) \approx -4\vec{i} + 5\vec{j}$,
      Speed $\approx \sqrt{41}$
   (b) About $t = 1.5$
   (c) About $t = 3$

27 (a) $x = 2 + 0.6t, y = -1 + 0.8t, z = 5 - 1.2t, 0 \le t \le 5$
   (b) $x = 2 + 1.92t, y = -1 + 2.56t, z = 5 - 3.84t, 0 \le t \le 1.56$

29 (a) 6.4 meters
   (b) 1.14 sec
   (c) 15.81 m/sec
   (d) $(11.4, -5.7, 0)$
   (e) -9.8 m/sec^2

31 (a) 5 secs; $(10, 15, 100)$
   (b) $t = 0, 10$ secs, $\sqrt{113}$ cm/sec
   (c) 5 secs, $\sqrt{13}$ cm/sec

33 (a) $t = 5.181$ sec
   (b) $x = 103.616$ meters
   (c) 2 meters
   (d) 9.8 meters/sec^2
   (e) $\theta = 0.896; v = 32.016$ meters/sec

35 (a) (IV); 4.5 sec; $(0, 8.9$ m, $0)$
   (b) (II); 3.2 sec; base of tower
   (c) (V); 10 sec; halfway up

37 $\vec{r}(t) = 22.1t\vec{i} + 66.4t\vec{j} + (442.7t - 4.9t^2)\vec{k}$

41 (a) No
   (b) $t = 5$
   (c) $\vec{v}(5) \approx 0.959\vec{i} + 0.284\vec{j} + 2\vec{k}$
   (d) $\vec{r} \approx 0.284\vec{i} - 0.959\vec{j} + 10\vec{k} + (t - 5)(0.959\vec{i} + 0.284\vec{j} + 2\vec{k})$.

43 (a) $\vec{r}(t) = t\cos(2\pi t)\vec{i} + t\sin(2\pi t)\vec{j}$,
      $0 \le t \le 100$

(b) $\vec{v} = \vec{r}'(t) = (\cos(2\pi t) - 2\pi t\sin(2\pi t))\vec{i} + (\sin(2\pi t) + 2\pi t\cos(2\pi t))\vec{j}$
   $\|\vec{v}\| = (1 + 4\pi^2 t^2)^{1/2}$ cm/sec

(c) $\vec{a} = \vec{v}'(t) = (-4\pi\sin(2\pi t) - 4\pi^2 t\cos(2\pi t))\vec{i} + (4\pi\cos(2\pi t) - 4\pi^2 t\sin(2\pi t))\vec{j}$
   $\|\vec{a}\| = 4\pi(1 + \pi^2 t^2)^{1/2}$ cm/sec^2

45 (a) $x \approx 694.444t + 20\cos(2\pi t)$cm
      $y = 30 + 20\sin(2\pi t)$ cm
   (c) At least 5.526 revs/sec

47 No

49 (a) $2\vec{r} \cdot d\vec{r}/dt$
   (b) $\vec{a} \times d\vec{r}/dt$
   (c) $r^3 d\vec{r}/dt + 3r^2\vec{r}$

55 Acceleration is a vector, not a scalar

57 $\vec{r}(t) = \left(t + 2t^2\right)\vec{i} + 2t\vec{j} + 3t^2\vec{k}$

59 False

61 False

63 False

65 False

67 True

69 False

Section 17.3

1 $\vec{V} = x\vec{i}$

3 $\vec{V} = x\vec{i} + y\vec{j} = \vec{r}$

5 $\vec{V} = -x\vec{i} - y\vec{j} = -\vec{r}$

7 (a) y-axis
   (b) Increasing
   (c) Neither

9 (a) x-axis
   (b) Increases
   (c) Decreases

11

13

Section 17.4

15

17

19

(b) Spirals outward counterclockwise around origin

(c) Spirals outward clockwise around origin

37 (a) $z = f(x, y)$:

$z = g(x, y)$:

(b)

39 To plot $\vec{G}(x, y, z)$ move arrows of $\vec{F}(2x, 2y, 2z)$ halfway to origin

41 $(x^2 + 1)\left(\vec{i} + \vec{j} + \vec{k}\right)$

1 Field:

Flow, $x = $ constant:

3 Field:

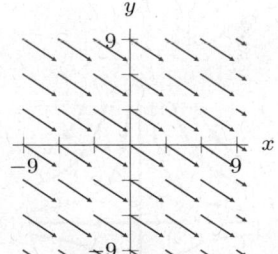

Flow, $y = -(2/3)x + c$:

21 (a) IV
  (b) III
  (c) I
  (d) II

23 $(1 + x^2)(3\vec{i} + 2\vec{j})$, other answers possible

25 $x\vec{i} + y\vec{j}$, other answers possible

27 (A) = (IV); (B) = (II); (C) = (I); (D) = (III)

29 (a) II
  (b) III
  (c) IV
  (d) I

31 $\vec{F}(x, y) = \frac{-x\vec{i} - y\vec{j}}{\sqrt{x^2 + y^2}}$ (for example)

33 (a) $(1, -3, -7)$; other answers possible
  (b) $(0, 0, 0)$; other answers possible
  (c) $-4x + y - 3z = 0$; plane through origin

35 (a) Radiates out from origin

5 Field:

Flow:

7 Field:

Flow:

9 Field:

Flow:

15 (a) Same directions, different magnitudes
   (b) Same curves, different parameterizations
23 (a) $h'(t) = 0$
25 Counterexample: $\vec{F}(x, y, z) = (x^2 + 1)\vec{i}$
27 $\vec{F}(x, y, z) = x\vec{i} + y\vec{j} + z\vec{k}$
29 False
31 False.
33 False
35 False
37 False

Chapter 17 Review

1 $\vec{r} = 2\vec{i} - \vec{j} + 3\vec{k} + t(5\vec{i} + 4\vec{j} - \vec{k})$
3 $x = t, y = 5$
5 $x = 4 + 4\sin t, y = 4 - 4\cos t$
7 $x = 2 - t, y = -1 + 3t, z = 4 + t$.
9 $x = 1 + 2t, y = 1 - 3t, z = 1 + 5t$.
11 $x = 3\cos t$
   $y = 5$
   $z = -3\sin t$
13 $\vec{r} = 10\cos(2\pi t/30)\vec{i} - 10\sin(2\pi t/30)\vec{j} + 7\vec{k}$
15 $\vec{v} = \vec{i} + (3t^2 - 1)\vec{j}$
17 $\vec{v} = 6t\vec{i} + 2t\vec{j} - 2t\vec{k}$
19 Vector; $\left((3\cos\sqrt{2t+1})\vec{i} - (3\sin\sqrt{2t+1})\vec{j} + \vec{k} \right)/\sqrt{2t+1}$
21 Vector; $-(\cos t/(2\sqrt{3+\sin t}))\vec{i} - (\sin t/(2\sqrt{3+\cos t}))\vec{j}$
23 No
25 Same direction $-\vec{i} + 4\vec{j} - 2\vec{k}$, point $(3, 3, -1)$ in common
27

29

31 (a) $(2, 3, 0)$
   (b) 2
   (c) No; not on line
33 (b) (i) Yes
      (ii) No
      (iii) Yes
      (iv) No
35 $\vec{E}$: (IV); $\vec{F}$: (I);
   $\vec{G}$: (II); $\vec{H}$: (III)
37 $\vec{v} = 0.2\vec{i} - 0.4\vec{j} + 0.4\vec{k}$ m/sec
   $\vec{a} = \vec{0}$
39 (a) Max rate change temp with distance; $^\circ$C/cm
   (b) $\sqrt{(g'(t))^2 + (k'(t))^2}$; cm/sec
   (c) $f_x \cdot g'(t) + f_y \cdot k'(t)$; $^\circ$C/sec
41 (a) Yes, $t = 1, (x, y) = (-2, -1)$
   (b) Yes, $t = -1, (x, y) = (2, 3)$
   (c) No
43 (a) $x(t) = 5\sin t, y(t) = 5\cos t, z(t) = 8$
   (b) $\vec{v} = -5\vec{j}, \vec{a} = -5\vec{i}$
   (c) $x_{tt}(t) = y_{tt}(t) = 0$,
      $z_{tt}(t) = -g$,
      $x_t(0) = z_t(0) = 0$,
      $y_t(0) = -5, x_t(0) = 5, y_t(0) = 0$,
      $z_t(0) = 8$
45 (a) In the direction given by the vector: $\vec{i} - \vec{j}$
   (b) Directions given by unit vectors:
      $\frac{1}{\sqrt{2}}\vec{i} + \frac{1}{\sqrt{2}}\vec{j}$
      $-\frac{1}{\sqrt{2}}\vec{i} - \frac{1}{\sqrt{2}}\vec{j}$
   (c) -4
47 $-(2 + 4t^2)/(t^3(1 + t^2)^2)$
49 (a) $52/\sqrt{13}, (8, 12)$
   (b) $52/\sqrt{13}, (18, 62)$
51 No, since the point $(0, 1)$ is not on the curve
53 ω: Rate of change of polar angle θ of particle,
   a: Rate of change of particle's distance from origin
55 (a) $\frac{1}{x^2+y^2+z^2}$
   (b) $\frac{1}{\sqrt{x^2+y^2+z^2}}$
   (c) $\frac{x}{\sqrt{x^2+y^2+z^2}}\vec{i} + \frac{y}{\sqrt{x^2+y^2+z^2}}\vec{j} + \frac{z}{\sqrt{x^2+y^y+z^2}}\vec{k}$
   (d) $\frac{-x}{\sqrt{x^+y^2+z^2}}\vec{i} + \frac{-y}{\sqrt{x^2+y^2+z^2}}\vec{j} + \frac{-z}{\sqrt{x^2+y^y+z^2}}\vec{k}$
   (e) $\frac{\cos t}{2\sqrt{2}}\vec{i} + \frac{\sin t}{2\sqrt{2}}\vec{j} + \frac{1}{2\sqrt{2}}\vec{k}$
   (f) $\frac{1}{\sqrt{2}}$
57 No
59 (b) $\vec{i} + 2\vec{j} + 3\vec{k} + 5\cos t((1/\sqrt{2})\vec{i} - (1/\sqrt{2})\vec{j}) + 5\sin t((1/\sqrt{6})\vec{i} + (1/\sqrt{6})\vec{j} - (\sqrt{2}/\sqrt{3})\vec{k})$
61 (b) $e^{-t}\vec{i} - 2e^{-t}\vec{j}$,
      $(0.0025e^{3t} + 0.9975e^{-t})\vec{i} + (0.005e^{3t} - 1.995e^{-t})\vec{j}$,

$(-0.0025e^{3t} + 1.0025e^{-t})\vec{i}$
$+(-0.005e^{3t} + 2.005e^{-t})\vec{j}$

Section 18.1

1 Negative

3 Zero

5 Zero

7 0

9 0

11 28

13 16

15 −48

17 19/3

19 20

21 28

23 C_1 is pos; C_2, C_3 are zero

25 C_1 is neg; C_2 is neg; C_3 is zero

27 $\int_{C_3} \vec{F} \cdot d\vec{r} < \int_{C_1} \vec{F} \cdot d\vec{r} < \int_{C_2} \vec{F} \cdot d\vec{r}$

29 (b)

  (c) 60

31 $a > 0$

33 $b < 0$

35 $c > 3$

37 0

39 Negative

41 0

43 Yes

49 $-GMm/8000$

51 Sphere of radius a centered at the origin

53 (a) $\phi(\vec{r}) = -\dfrac{Q}{4\pi\epsilon}\dfrac{1}{a} + \dfrac{Q}{4\pi\epsilon}\dfrac{1}{||\vec{r}||}$

  (b) Because then $\phi(\vec{r}) = \dfrac{Q}{4\pi\epsilon}\dfrac{1}{||\vec{r}||}$

55 Value of a line integral is not a vector

57

59 True

61 True

63 False

65 False

67 False

Section 18.2

1 $\int_0^\pi (\cos^2 t - \sin^2 t)\, dt$
  Other answers are possible

3 $\int_0^{2\pi} (-\sin t \cos(\cos t)$
  $\cos t \cos(\sin t))dt$

5 24

7 −4

9 −6

11 9

13 82/3

15 12

17 116.28

19 12

21 21

23 0

25 $\int_C y^2\, dx + z^2\, dy + (x^2 - 5)dz$

27 $e^{-3y}\vec{i} - yz(\sin x)\vec{j} + (y + z)\vec{k}$

29 $18\pi^2$

31 -18π

33 (a)

  (b) $0; -3\pi/2$

37 (a) −5

  (b) 5

  (c) 0

41 (a) Greater than zero

  (b) 88

  (d) $t = 2 \pm 1/\sqrt{3}$

  (e) 88; yes

43 Sign depends on C

45 $y = \pi/2, x = t, 0 \le t \le 3, \int_C \vec{F} \cdot d\vec{r} = 3$

47 True

49 True

51 False

53 False

Section 18.3

1 12

3 Negative, not path-independent

5 Negative, not path-independent

7 Path-independent

9 Path-independent

11 Path-independent

13 $f(x, y) = x^2 y + K$

15 $f(x, y, z) = e^{xyz} + \sin(xz^2) + C$
  $C = $ constant

17 −2

19 2

21 0

23 $e^3 - 1$

25 0

27 PQ

31 Yes

33 Yes.

35 $e^9 - 1$

37 (a) $-(1/3) - \pi$

  (b) $3\pi/4$

39 $9\pi/4$

41 $e^{9/2} + \sin(3\sqrt{2}) - 1$

43 107; 109.5

45 −2

47 (b) No

49 (a) $\int_{C_2} \vec{F} \cdot d\vec{r}$

  (b) $\int_{C_3} \vec{F} \cdot d\vec{r} < \int_{C_2} \vec{F} \cdot d\vec{r}$
    $< \int_{C_4} \vec{F} \cdot d\vec{r} < \int_{C_1} \vec{F} \cdot d\vec{r}$

  (c) $\int_{C_3} \vec{F} \cdot d\vec{r} = -\int_{C_4} \vec{F} \cdot d\vec{r} < 0$

51 −3.6

53 (a) $\vec{a}$

  (b) $\vec{r}_0 \cdot \vec{a}$

  (c) $10||\vec{a}||$

55 (a) $\pi/2$

  (b) No

57 (a) $\vec{F} - \operatorname{grad}\psi = x\operatorname{grad} h$

  (b) 50

59 (a) $\vec{F} - \operatorname{grad}\phi = x\operatorname{grad} h$

  (b) 384

63 (b) Yes

65 Only if $\vec{F}$ is path-independent

67 $\vec{F} = \operatorname{grad} f, f(x, y) = 50xy$

73 False

75 False

77 False

79 True

81 True

83 False

Section 18.4

1 No

3 No

5 $f(x, y) = x^3/3 + xy^2 + C$

7 Yes, $f = \ln A|xyz|$ where $A > 0$

9 No

11 −12

13 1/2

15 -3π

17 (a)

  (b) $-\pi$

19 $e - \cos 1$

21 $-9\pi/8$

23 (a) 0

  (b) 0

  (c) 0

  (d) -6π

  (e) -6π

  (f) 0

  (g) -6π

25 (b) 0
   (c) $\vec{G} = \nabla(xyz + zy + z)$
   (d) $\vec{H_1} = \nabla(yx^2)$, $\vec{H_2} = \nabla(y(x+z))$

27 πab

29 3/2

31

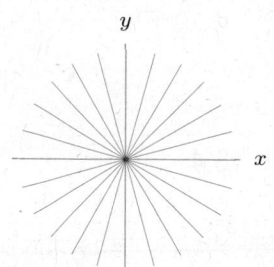

33 (a) Possible answers are:
     $\vec{F} = \text{grad}(xy)$
     $\vec{G} = \text{grad}(\arctan(x/y))$, $y \neq 0$
     $\vec{H} = \text{grad}\left((x^2 + y^2)^{1/2}\right)$, $(x,y) \neq$
     $(0,0)$
   (b) $0, -2\pi, 0$
   (c) Does not apply to $\vec{G}$, $\vec{H}$; holes in domain

35 $L_1 < L_2 < L_3$

37 (a) $21\pi/2$
   (b) 2

39 (a) $\vec{0}$
   (b) $q/||\vec{r}||$

41 Green's Theorem does not apply;
    Line integral depends on $\vec{F}$

43

45 True

47 True

49 True

51 True

Chapter 18 Review

1 Positive

3 (a) Zero
   (b) C_1, C_3: Zero
      C_2: Negative
      C_4: Positive
   (c) Zero

5 Scalar; 12

7 -58

9 50

11 18

13 1372

15 Not path-independent

17 Path-independent

19 Path-independent

21 Path-independent

23 350

25 $27\pi/2$

27 45

29 0, 100

31 (ii), (iv)

33 (a) 24
   (b) 12
   (c) -12

37 18

39 -36

41 (a) 0
   (b) 24

43 (a) 0
   (b) 6
   (c) $75\pi/2$
   (d) 14

45 (a) 9/2
   (b) $-9/2$

47

49 (a) Closed curve oriented counterclockwise
   (b) Closed curve oriented clockwise
     with $y > 0$ or
     Closed curve oriented counterclockwise
     if $y < 0$
       (Other answers are possible)

51 (a)

   (b) Longer

(c) -0.3

53 (a) $\pi/2$
   (b) 0

57 (a) $\omega = 3000$ rad/hr
     $K = 3 \cdot 10^7$ m$^2 \cdot$rad/hr
   (b) Inside tornado:

View from great distance:

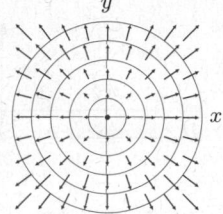

   (c) $r < 100$ m, circulation is $2\omega\pi r^2$
     $r \geq 100$ m, circulation is $2K\pi$

59 (a) $-(\pi/2)(-6a^2 + a^4)$, $a = \sqrt{3}$
   (b) Integrand $3 - x^2 - y^2$ positive inside disk
     of radius $\sqrt{3}$, negative outside

61 $18a + 18b + 36c + (81d/2)$,
    $-18a - 18b - 36c - (81d/2)$,
    curves go in opposite directions

Section 19.1

1 $-3\vec{i}$

3 $15\vec{j}$

5 Rectangle in xz plane with area 150, oriented
   pos y direction

7 (a) 45
   (b) -45

9 (a) Positive
   (b) Negative
   (c) Zero
   (d) Zero
   (e) Zero

11 (a) Zero
   (b) Zero
   (c) Zero
   (d) Negative
   (e) Zero

13 8

15 -6

17 4

19 3/2

21 2π

23 0

25 3

27 108π

29 $9\pi\sqrt{75}$

31 2π

33 28

35 28π

37 0

39 114

41 $64/3$

43 756π

45 18

47 $81\pi/2$

49 $\pi(e^4 - 1)$

51 8π

53 (a)   (i) Positive
      (ii) Zero
      (iii) Zero
      (iv) Negative
  (b) Integral over B

55 $6\pi \text{ cm}^3/\text{sec}$

57 $\vec{j}$ components parallel to S, other components same

59 $4\pi R$

61 (a) Zero
  (b) Zero

65 (a)

  (b) $4\pi\lambda h$

67 (a) 0
  (b) 0

69 Sign of $\int_S \vec{F} \cdot d\vec{A}$ depends on both $\vec{F}$ and S

71 $\vec{F} = z\vec{k}$
    $S: 0 \le x \le 1, 0 \le y \le 1, z = 1,$ oriented upwards

73 False

75 True

77 True

79 False

81 False

Section 19.2

1 $\left(-3\vec{i} + 5\vec{j} + \vec{k}\right) dx\, dy$

3 $\left(-4x\vec{i} + 6y\vec{j} + \vec{k}\right) dx\, dy$

5 $\int_{-2}^{3} \int_0^5 70\, dy\, dx$

7 $\int_0^5 \int_0^{5-x} (yz \sin x \; - \; 2xy \cos 2y \; + \; xy)\, dy\, dx$

9 -500

11 $-5/3 - \sin 1 = -2.508$

13 $\int_0^{\pi/2} \int_0^5 10 \left(\cos\theta + 2\sin\theta\right) dz\, d\theta$

15 $\int_0^{2\pi} \int_{-8}^{8} \left(6z^2 \cos\theta + 6\sin\theta e^{6\cos\theta}\right) dz\, d\theta$

17 2000

19 $100\sqrt{2}/3$

21 $\int_0^{2\pi} \int_0^{\pi/2} 100 \left(\sin\phi\cos\theta + 2\sin\phi\sin\theta + 3\cos\phi\right) \sin\phi\, d\phi\, d\theta$

23 $\int_{-\pi/2}^{\pi/2} \int_0^{\pi} 16\cos^2\phi \sin^2\phi \cos\theta\, d\phi\, d\theta$

25 $8000/3$

27 $(8 - 5\sqrt{2})\pi/6 = 0.486$

29 6

31 6

33 18

35 36π

37 $7/3$

39 $\pi \sin 25$

41 $\pi/2$

43 1296π

45 $1/4$

47 36π

49 $2\pi/3$

51 $4\pi a^3$

53 -1

55 $11\pi/2$

57 (a) Constant inside sphere of radius a
  (b) $\vec{E} = \begin{cases} k\dfrac{\delta_0}{3}\rho\vec{e}_\rho & \rho \le a \\[2mm] k\dfrac{\delta_0 a^3}{3r^3}\vec{e}_\rho & \rho > a \end{cases}$

59 Cone not on a cylinder

61 $f(x, y) = -x - y$

63 True

65 False

Section 19.3

1 $2x + xe^z$

3 (I)

5 0

7 -1

9 $6x - (x + z)\cos(xz)$

11 0

13 $2/\|\vec{r} - \vec{r}_0\|$

15

17 -0.030

19 (a) (i) $0.016\pi/3$

    (ii) -0.08

  (b) Flux positive at $(2, 0, 0)$ and negative at $(0, 0, 10)$

21 (a) 48
  (b) 4
  (c) 4

23 $\text{div}\,\vec{v} = -6$

25 (a) $-1/3, 1$
  (b) $1/3$

27 (b)

29 (a) 0
  (b)

31 (a) 0
  (b) Undefined

33 (a) $\rho(0) < \rho(1000) < \rho(5000)$
  (b) cars/hour
  (d) $\rho(x) = 4125/(55 - x/50)$
     if $0 \le x < 2000$
    $\rho(x) = 4125/15 = 275$
     if $2000 \le x < 7000$
    $\rho(x) = \dfrac{4125}{(15 + (x - 7000)/25)}$
     if $7000 \le x < 8000$
    $\rho(x) = 4125/55 = 75$
     if $x \ge 8000$
  (e) 139 ft. at $x = 0$
    89 ft. at $x = 1000$
    38 ft. at $x = 5000$

39 $(3 - a)x^{-a}$

43 (d)

45 $\text{div}(2x\vec{i}) = 2$

47 Only vector fields have divergence

49 $\vec{F}(x, y, z) = y^2\vec{i} + xz\vec{j} + x\vec{k}$

51 True

53 True

55 True

57 False

59 False

61 True

63 False

Section 19.4

1 24

3 8

5 Zero

7 24

9 72

11 288

13 36π

15 620π

17 48π

19 1.571

21 Yes; -3.22

23 $\int_S \vec{F} \cdot d\vec{A} = \int_W \text{div}\,\vec{F}\,dV = 0$

25 (a) 0
   (b) No
   (c) 4π
   (d) 4π

27 (a) $cb(12a - a^2)$
   (b) 6, 10, 10; 3600

29 4π

31 (a) $24\pi/5$
   (b) $\int_{S_2} \vec{F} \cdot d\vec{A} < \int_{S_3} \vec{F} \cdot d\vec{A} < \int_{S_4} \vec{F} \cdot d\vec{A}$

33 S closed, oriented inward

39 $\int_S \vec{F} \cdot d\vec{A} = \int_W \text{div}\,\vec{F}\,dV$

41 $\vec{F} = (9x/4\pi)\vec{i}$

43 True.

45 False.

47 False.

49 True

51 True

53 True

55 True

Chapter 19 Review

1 Scalar; -100π

3 (a) 16
   (b) 16
   (c) -16
   (d) -16
   (e) 32

5 Negative

7 Positive

9 0

11 -45

13 27/2

15 -4

17 12

19 $-8(1 + e^{-1})$

21 24π

23 $(\pi/6) - 1/3$

25 $c > 0$

27 $a + b + c > 0$

29 (a) 24
   (b) 24

31 1500π

33 $8\pi/3$

35 2π

37 (a) $(y + yze^{xyz})\vec{i} + (x + xze^{xyz})\vec{j} + xye^{xyz}\vec{k}$
   (b) $5 + e^{24} - e^1$
   (c) 2

39 (a) Flux through S_3

   (b) 13π

41 (a)   (i) 0.0168
      (ii) -0.004
      (i) Pointing outward
      (ii) Pointing inward

43 (a) Flux = c^3
   (b) 1
   (c) 1

45 -10π

47 0

49 34π

51 (a) 0
   (b) z-axis
   (c) 0
   (d) 0

53 (a) 0
   (b) 0

55 (a) $x = 2, \vec{i}$ direction
   (b) (i) 24π
      (ii) 8π

57 81π

61 (a) Maximum speed
   (b) 0
   (c) $\pi u a^2/2$

63 (a) $\left(1 + \dfrac{y^2 - x^2}{(x^2 + y^2)^2}\right)\vec{i} + \dfrac{-2xy}{(x^2 + y^2)^2}\vec{j}$
   (d)

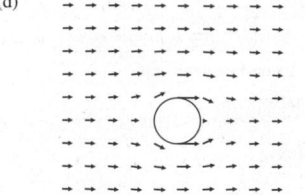

65 (a) 0.0958
   (b) 0.0958
   (c) 0.0958

Section 20.1

1 Vector: $\vec{i} + \vec{j} - \vec{k}$

3 $6\vec{i}$

5 $-\vec{i} - \vec{j} - \vec{k}$

7 $\vec{0}$

9 $(2x^3yz + 6x^7y^5 - xy)\vec{i}$
   $+ (-3x^2y^2z - 7x^6y^6 + y)\vec{j}$
   $+ (yz - z)\vec{k}$

11 Nonzero curl

13 Zero curl

15 (a) $-2y\vec{i} + 2x\vec{j}$
   (b) $4\vec{k}$

17 (a) 0.0005π
   (b) 0.0002π
   (c) -0.0003π

19 $\text{curl}(F_1(x)\vec{i} + F_2(y)\vec{j} + F_3(z)\vec{k}) = \vec{0}$

21 (a) Counterclockwise
   (b) Clockwise
   (c) $\vec{0}$

33 (b) Direction of $\vec{k}$ for $A = -1$
   Zero vector for $A = -2$
   Direction of $-\vec{k}$ for $A = -3$
   (c) At $(1, 1, 1)$: Positive for $A = -1$
   Zero for $A = -2$

   Negative for $A = -3$
   At $(0, 0, 0)$: Can't say anything

35 Counterexample: $\vec{F} = y\vec{i}$

37 $\vec{F} = z\vec{i}$

39 True.

41 True

43 False

45 False

Section 20.2

1 $9\pi/2$

3 25

5 $-\pi$

7 -5π

9 6

11 $-6\sqrt{3}\pi$

13 Negative

15 (a) $-\vec{i} - \vec{j} - \vec{k}$
   (b) -6

17 (a) $\vec{i} + \vec{j} + \vec{k}$
   (b) $-4\sqrt{3}$

19 $8\pi/\sqrt{3}$

21 0

23 $8\sqrt{3}\pi$

25 (a) $x^2 + y^2 = 9, z = 2$
   (b) -18π

27 72

31 120π

33 (a) Parallel to xy-plane; same in all horizontal planes
   (b) $(\partial F_2/\partial x - \partial F_1/\partial y)\vec{k}$
   (d) Green's Theorem

35 C not the boundary of a surface

37 Any oriented circle

39 True

41 False

43 True

45 True

47 False

Section 20.3

1 Yes

3 Yes

5 No

7 Yes

9 Yes

11 Yes

13 Curl yes; Divergence yes

15 Curl yes; Divergence yes

19 $(1/2)\vec{b} \times \vec{r}$

21 No

23 (a) Yes
   (b) Yes
   (c) Yes

25 (a) Yes
   (b) No
   (c) No

29 (b) $\nabla^2 \psi = -\text{div}\,\vec{A}$

31 Curl of scalar function not defined

33 $f(x, y, z) = x^2$

35 False

37 True

Chapter 20 Review

1 $\vec{i} - \vec{j} - \vec{k}$

3 $(c), (d), (f)$

5 C_2, C_3, C_4, C_6

7 Defined; scalar

9 Defined; vector

11 Nonzero curl

13 div $\vec{F} = y + z + x$
curl $\vec{F} = -y\vec{i} - z\vec{j} - x\vec{k}$
$\vec{F}$ not solenoidal; not irrotational

15 div $\vec{F} = 0$
curl $\vec{F} = (2y - \cos(x+z))\vec{i} -$
$\left(2x - e^{y+z}\right)\vec{j} + \left(\cos(x+z) - e^{y+z}\right)\vec{k}$
$\vec{F}$ is solenoidal; not irrotational

17 (a) 18π
(b) 18π

19 20π

21 0

23 (a) is (I); (b) is (I); (c) is (V); (d) is (III); (e) is (IV); (f) is (V)

25 (a) -1125π
(b) Not defined
(c) 0
(d) Not defined
(e) $384\pi/5$
(f) $353/4$
(g) Not defined
(h) 54

27 (a) 23
(b) Approx $0.0003\pi/\sqrt{3}$

29 (a) div $\vec{F} < 0$, div $\vec{G} < 0$
(b) curl $\vec{F} = 0$, curl $\vec{G} = 0$
(c) Yes
(d) Yes
(e) No
(f) No

31 0

33 4π

35 210

37 $12\pi/5$

39 150π

41 $e - 1$

43 (a) 18
(b) $81/2$

45 (a) No
(b) No

47 (a) 2π
(b) $\vec{0}$ except on z-axis
(c) No
(d) Yes; 0
(e) No

49 (a) 50
(b) 30π
(c) 8
(d) -18π

51 (a) $(4(p+q)\pi R^3/3)$
(b) $(4(p+q)\pi R^3/3)$

Section 21.1

1 Curve

3 Surface

5 Horizontal disk of radius 5 in plane $z = 7$

7 Helix radius 5 about z-axis

9 Top hemisphere

11 Vertical segment

13 $\vec{r}(s, t) = (s + 2t)\vec{i} + (2s + t)\vec{j} + 3s\vec{k}$, other answers possible

15 $\vec{r}(s, t) = (3+s+t)\vec{i} + (5-s)\vec{j} + (7-t)\vec{k}$, other answers possible

17 (a) Yes
(b) No

19 $s = s_0$: lines parallel to y-axis with $z = 1$
$t = t_0$: lines parallel to x-axis with $z = 1$

21 $s = s_0$: parabolas in planes parallel to yz-plane
$t = t_0$: parabolas in planes parallel to xz-plane

23 $s = 4, t = 2$
$(x, y, z) = (x_0 + 10, y_0 - 4, z_0 + 18)$

25 Horizontal circle

27 (a) $x = \left(\cos\left(\frac{\pi}{3}t\right) + 3\right)\cos\theta$
$y = \left(\cos\left(\frac{\pi}{3}t\right) + 3\right)\sin\theta$
$z = t \qquad 0 \le \theta \le 2\pi, \, 0 \le t \le 48$
(b) 456π in.^{3}

29 If $\theta < \pi$, then $(\theta + \pi, \pi/4)$
If $\theta \ge \pi$, then $(\theta - \pi, \pi/4)$

31 $x = r\cos\theta, \qquad 0 \le r \le a$
$y = r\sin\theta, \qquad 0 \le \theta \le 2\pi$
$z = (1 - r/a)h$

33 (a) $-x + y + z = 1$,
$0 \le x \le 2$,
$-1 \le y - z \le 1$
(b)

35 (a) $z = (x^2/2) + (y^2/2)$
$0 \le x + y \le 2$
$0 \le x - y \le 2$
(b)

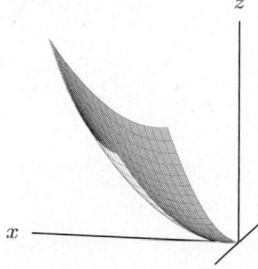

37 Radius: $R\sin\phi$

39 $x + y - z - 3 = 0$

41 True

43 True

45 True

47 False

Section 21.2

1 1

3 e^{2s}

5 $a = 1/10, b = 1$

7 $a = 1/50, b = 1/10$

9 3

11 $\rho^2 \sin\phi$

13 13.5

15 72

17 (a) $(1/(2\pi\sigma^2)) \int_{-\infty}^{\infty} \int_{-\infty}^{2t-x} e^{-(x^2+y^2)/(2\sigma^2)} \, dy \, dx$
(b) $(1/(\sqrt{\pi}\sigma)) \int_{-\infty}^{t} e^{-u^2/\sigma^2} \, du$
(c) $(1/(\sqrt{\pi}\sigma))e^{-t^2/\sigma^2}$
(d) Normal, mean 0, standard deviation $\sigma/\sqrt{2}$

19 R does not correspond to T

21 $x = 2s, y = 3t$

23 False

Section 21.3

1 $((s+t)\vec{i} - (s-t)\vec{j} - 2\vec{k}) \, ds \, dt$

3 $-e^s(\cos t\, \vec{j} + \sin t\, \vec{k}) \, ds \, dt$

5 4/3

7 $6(e^4 - 1)$

9 $-\pi R^7/28$

11 $200\sqrt{14}$

13 $\sqrt{6}\pi$

15 $khw^3/6$ meter^3/sec.

21 Integral gives volume

23 $\vec{r}(s, t) = 2s\vec{i} + t\vec{j}$

25 True

27 False

Chapter 21 Review

1 Cone, height 7 and radius 14

3 $a = 1/15, b = 1/15$

5 $-1/2$

7 0

9 $x = 2 + 5\sin\phi\cos\theta$
$y = -1 + 5\sin\phi\sin\theta$
$z = 3 + 5\cos\phi$

11 (a) Cylinder
(b) Helices

13 $x = a\sin\phi\cos\theta \quad 0 \le \phi \le \pi$
$y = b\sin\phi\sin\theta \quad 0 \le \theta \le 2\pi$
$z = c\cos\phi$

15 (a) $x^2 + y^2 = 9, x \ge 0, 1 \le z \le 2$.
(b)

17 0

19 $2\pi c(a^2 + b^2)$

Appendix A

1 (a) $y \le 30$
(b) two zeros

3 -1.05

5 2.5

7 $x = -1.1$

9 0.45

11 1.3

13 (a) $x = -1.15$
   (b) $x = 1$, $x = 1.41$,
        and $x = -1.41$

15 (a) $x \approx 0.7$
   (b) $x \approx 0.4$

17 (a) 4 zeros
   (b) $[0.65, 0.66]$, $[0.72, 0.73]$,
        $[1.43, 1.44]$, $[1.7, 1.71]$

19 (b) $x \approx 5.573$

21 Bounded $-5 \leq f(x) \leq 4$

23 Not bounded

Appendix B

1 $2e^{i\pi/2}$

3 $\sqrt{2}e^{i\pi/4}$

5 $0e^{i\theta}$, for any θ.

7 $\sqrt{10}e^{i(\arctan(-3)+\pi)}$

9 $-3 - 4i$

11 $-5 + 12i$

13 $1/4 - 9i/8$

15 $-1/2 + i\sqrt{3}/2$

17 $-125i$

19 $\sqrt{2}/2 + i\sqrt{2}/2$

21 $\sqrt{3}/2 + i/2$

23 -2^{50}

25 $2i\sqrt[3]{4}$

27 $(1/\sqrt{2})\cos(-\pi/12) + (i/\sqrt{2})\sin(-\pi/12)$

29 $-i, -1, i, 1$
    $i^{-36} = 1$, $i^{-41} = -i$

31 $A_1 = 1 + i$
    $A_2 = 1 - i$

37 True

39 False

41 True

Appendix C

1 (a) $f'(x) = 3x^2 + 6x + 3$
  (b) At most one
  (c) $[0, 1]$
  (d) $x \approx 0.913$

3 $\sqrt[4]{100} \approx 3.162$

5 $x \approx 0.511$

7 $x \approx 1.310$

9 $x \approx 1.763$

11 $x \approx 0.682328$

Appendix D

1 3, 0 radians

3 2, $3\pi/4$ radians

5 $7\vec{j}$

7 $\|3\vec{i} + 4\vec{j}\| = \|-5\vec{i}\| = \|5\vec{j}\|$, $\|\vec{i} + \vec{j}\| = \|\sqrt{2}\vec{j}\|$

9 $5\vec{j}$ and $-6\vec{j}$; $\sqrt{2}\vec{j}$ and $-6\vec{j}$

11 (a) $(-3/5)\vec{i} + (4/5)\vec{j}$
   (b) $(3/5)\vec{i} + (-4/5)\vec{j}$

13 $8\vec{i} - 6\vec{j}$

15 $\vec{i} + 2\vec{j}$

17 Equal

19 Equal

21 $\vec{i} + \vec{j}$, $\sqrt{2}$, $\vec{i} - \vec{j}$

23 Pos: $(1/\sqrt{2})\vec{i} + (1/\sqrt{2})\vec{j}$
    Vel: $(-1/\sqrt{2})\vec{i} + (1/\sqrt{2})\vec{j}$
    Speed: 1

INDEX